ITALIAN WINES 2003

Gambero Rosso Editore

Slow Food Editore

ITALIAN WINES 2003
GAMBERO ROSSO® - SLOW FOOD EDITORE

EDITORIAL STAFF FOR THE ORIGINAL EDITION

CHIEF EDITORS
DANIELE CERNILLI AND GIGI PIUMATTI

SENIOR EDITORS
GIANNI FABRIZIO AND MARCO SABELLICO

TECHNICAL SUPERVISION
TIZIANO GAIA, ERNESTO GENTILI, VITTORIO MANGANELLI, FABIO RIZZARI

MEMBERS OF THE FINAL TASTING PANELS
DARIO CAPPELLONI, GIULIO COLOMBA, EGIDIO FEDELE DELL'OSTE, ROSANNA FERRARO,
NICOLA FRASSON, FABIO GIAVEDONI, GIACOMO MOJOLI, MARCO OREGGIA,
PIERO SARDO

CONTRIBUTORS
NINO AJELLO, GILBERTO ARRU, STEFANO ASARO, ANTONIO ATTORRE, PAOLO BATTIMELLI,
ENRICO BATTISTELLA, ALBERTO BETTINI, FRANCESCA BIDASIO DEGLI IMBERTI,
WALTER BORDO, MICHELE BRESSAN, DARIO CAPPELLONI, DIONISIO CASTELLO,
DANIELE CERNILLI, ROBERTO CHECCHETTO, VALERIO CHIARINI, ANTONIO CIMINELLI,
GIULIO COLOMBA, IAN DOMENICO D'AGATA, EGIDIO FEDELE DELL'OSTE, MASSIMO DI CINTIO,
GIANNI FABRIZIO, ROSANNA FERRARO, NICOLA FRASSON, LUCA FURLOTTI, TIZIANO GAIA,
FABIO GIAVEDONI, ERNESTO GENTILI, VITO LACERENZA, GIANCARLO LO SICCO,
MASSIMO LANZA, GIACOMO MOJOLI, MARCO OREGGIA, STEFANO PASTOR,
NEREO PEDERZOLLI, PIERPAOLO PENCO, FRANCESCO PENSOVECCHIO, ANGELO PERETTI,
NICOLA PICCININI, GUIDO PIRAZZOLI, GIGI PIUMATTI, MARIO PLAZIO, PIERPAOLO RASTELLI,
FABIO RIZZARI, LEONARDO ROMANELLI, FABRIZIO RUSSO, MARCO SABELLICO,
DIEGO SORACCO, HERBERT TASCHLER, MASSIMO TOFFOLO, ANDREA VANNELLI,
MASSIMO VOLPARI, PAOLO ZACCARIA, ALBERTO ZACCONE

MEMBERS OF THE PRELIMINARY TASTING PANELS
FRANCESCO BEGHI, PAOLA BERTINOTTI, SIMONE BROGI, PASQUALE BUFFA,
ALESSANDRO BULZONI, TEODOSIO BUONGIORNO, REMO CAMURANI, SERGIO CECCARELLI,
ANGELO DAL BON, MASSIMO DOGLIOLO, FAUSTO FERRONI, ELEONORA GUERINI,
DAVIDE GHIRARDI, DARIO LAURENZI, ALDO MANZONI, MIRCO MARCONI, MINO MARTUCCI,
ENZO MERZ, DANNY MURARO, VANNI MURARO, PENNY MURRAY, UGO ONGARETTO,
ROBERTO PALMIERI, LINA PAOLILLO, NICOLA PERULLO, LIANO PETROZZI,
CRISTIANA POLIMENO, RENZO PRIORI, SILVANO PROMPICAI, VALENTINO RAMELLI,
FRANCA RATTI, GABRIELE RICCI ALUNNI, HELMUT RIEBSCHLÄGER, RENATO TEDESCO,
BETTINA TORNUSCIOLO, PAOLO VALDASTRI, RICCARDO VISCARDI, VALERIO ZORZI

EDITING
DARIO CAPPELLONI, MARCO OREGGIA, UMBERTO TAMBURINI, PAOLO ZACCARIA

EDITORIAL CO-ORDINATOR
GIORGIO ACCASCINA

TRANSLATIONS CO-ORDINATED AND EDITED BY
GILES WATSON

TRANSLATORS
MAUREEN ASHLEY, KAREN CHRISTENFELD, HELEN DONALD, STEPHEN JACKSON,
ANDREW L. MILLER, GILES WATSON, AILSA WOOD

PUBLISHER
GAMBERO ROSSO, INC.
PRESIDENT STEFANO BONILLI
636 BROADWAY - SUITE 1111 - NEW YORK, NY 10012
TEL. 212- 253-5653 FAX 212- 253-8349 - E-MAIL: gamberousa@aol.com

DISTRIBUTION:
USA AND CANADA BY ANTIQUE COLLECTOR'S CLUB, MARKET STREET INDUSTRIAL PARK,
WAPPINGER FALLS, NY 12590, USA;
UK AND AUSTRALIA BY GRUB STREET, THE BASEMENT, 10 CHIVALRY ROAD,
LONDON SW11 1HT, UK.

COPYRIGHT© 2003 G.R.H. SPA - ROMA - ITALY
ALL RIGHTS RESERVED. NO PART OF THIS PUBLICATION MAY BE REPRODUCED, STORED IN A
RETRIEVAL SYSTEM OR TRANSMITTED IN ANY FORM OR BY ANY MEANS: ELECTRONIC,
ELECTROSTATIC, MAGNETIC TAPE, MECHANICAL, PHOTOCOPYING, RECORDING OR
OTHERWISE WITHOUT WRITTEN PERMISSION FROM THE PUBLISHER.
GAMBERO ROSSO IS A REGISTERED TRADE MARK

ITALIAN WINES 2003 WAS CLOSED ON 26 SEPTEMBER, 2002

PRINTED IN ITALY BY TIPOGRAFICA LA PIRAMIDE SRL
VIA ANTON MARIA VALSALVA, 34 - ROMA

CONTENTS

INTRODUCTION	6
THREE GLASS AWARDS 2003	8
THE STARS	12
GUIDE TO VINTAGES	13
HOW TO USE THE GUIDE	14

THE REGIONS

VALLE D'AOSTA	15
PIEDMONT	21
LIGURIA	161
LOMBARDY	177
TRENTINO	223
ALTO ADIGE	249
VENETO	281
FRIULI VENEZIA GIULIA	345
EMILIA ROMAGNA	421
TUSCANY	451
MARCHE	607
UMBRIA	639
LAZIO	661
ABRUZZO AND MOLISE	675
CAMPANIA	689
BASILICATA	707
PUGLIA	715
CALABRIA	735
SICILY	743
SARDINIA	765

INDEXES

WINES	781
PRODUCERS	829

INTRODUCTION

The 16th edition Gambero Rosso and Slow Food's Italian Wines hits the bookshops after a difficult vintage in 2002 and at a crucial moment for premium wines in Italy. A slump in exports was predictable enough, given the international economic crisis, but it is still creating problems and a lack of confidence among producers. It has to be said that the over-enthusiastic rush to raise prices in recent years has stirred up disaffection on the part of many consumers. Add to this the arrival on the scene, in grand style, of countries like Australia, Chile and South Africa, which are proving increasingly successful at wresting market share from Italian and French wines, then the general picture becomes even gloomier and less reassuring. However, we can make one or two tentative forecasts about where consumer preference will focus in the short term. For a start, the era of very high prices for premium bottles is over, with the exception of a few cult wines, such as Sassicaia. Those who fondly imagine they can continue to sell Barolos or Supertuscans at the cellar door for more than € 40.00 may be in for a nasty surprise. Space at the top of the pyramid is limited and reserved for a select group of producers who have earned it with years of hard work. In the midst of all this, the 2003 Guide emerges to celebrate, as we said, its 16th year of publication. Italian Wines has grown with winemaking in Italy and the initial print run of 5,000 copies in November 1987 has mushroomed to 80,000 copies printed this year. Factor in the German and English-language editions and the number rises to 150,000. The Guide is a joint effort by about 90 collaborators, including tasting panellists, the reviewers who actually draft the profiles and our editorial staff. Our contributors take part in about 30 tasting sessions up and down Italy. Each panel comprises a minimum of three and a maximum of six tasters and this year, their sensory receptors appraised roughly 25,000 wines. All the bottles are carefully masked – Guide panels are some of Italy's largest consumers of tinfoil – and in many cases, we involved protection consortia, chambers of commerce and regional wine cellars to provide the sample bottles and organize the tastings. We are not the only guide publishers to do so but we have always worked this way. In fact, we source at least 80 per cent of our wine through such bodies. They represent the producers and monitor our activities, checking that tastings are carried out fairly. We ask for, or request the consortia to ask for, samples from producers for two reasons. The first is that, by sending samples, the winery demonstrates its willingness to be assessed by us. The second reason is that if we were to purchase the wines in the shops, we would end up with a Guide that was out of date before it was published. About five months elapse between the first tastings and publication of the Italian-language edition. Wines on sale five months ago are not the ones you will find on the shelves now. So the Guide would be describing and evaluating wines that were no longer available, and would thus lose much of its validity. And – just between ourselves, of course – our way is precisely what wine guides all over the world do. Leading wine assessment publications round the globe will ask for sample from the producers themselves, or from their distributors or importers, whether they are in Italy, the USA, France or the UK. But let's get back to the tastings. In the first phase, we award points out of 100 and select the roughly 1,500 wines that will go on to the Three Glass taste-offs. After this herculean effort, the final awards committee meets. Made up of leading figures from local tasting panels, the committee examines all the wines sent to the final round. Again, all tastings are blind. The judgement this time is more drastic: a straight yes or no. Each decision is carefully reasoned out. Every quality of every wine is discussed, analysed and marked separately. For this Guide, the following panellists joined Daniele Cernilli, Gigi Piumatti, Gianni Fabrizio and Marco Sabellico for at least one of the three final taste-offs: Fabio Rizzari, Ernesto Gentili, Vittorio Manganelli, Tiziano Gaia, Dario Cappelloni, Giulio Colomba, Nicola Frasson, Giacomo Mojoli, Piero Sardo, Egidio Fedele dell'Oste, Fabio

Giavedoni, Rosanna Ferraro and Marco Oreggia. That's a total of 17 individuals who are jointly responsible for the assessments that awarded 250 wines from all over Italy our legendary Three Glasses. The panellists are a formidable tasting team that elaborates reasoned evaluations, not just numerical scores, in an attempt to offer valid indications to the wine-loving readers who are the Guide's main point of reference. Our method incorporates subsequent counterchecks and crosschecks, the only way – in our opinion – to compile a serious, credible Guide and not some pretentious "bible of wine". It's hard work. The final taste-offs took place in the months of July and August 2002, in Rome, at the Paris restaurant, at Verduno, in the Castello di Verduno hotel, and at Colloredo di Monte Albano, at the Là di Petros restaurant. Panellists used the same medium-sized, long-stemmed Spiegelau glasses for all three final taste-off sessions. In the end, the 250 Three Glass awards went to 63 wines from Tuscany, 60 from Piedmont, 25 from Friuli, 19 each from Alto Adige and the Veneto, 11 from Lombardy, nine from Sicily, eight from Marche, six from Campania, five each from Umbria and Trentino, four each from Puglia and Emilia Romagna, three from Basilicata, two each from Abruzzo, Sardinia and Lazio, and one each from Valle d'Aosta, Calabria and Molise. Sadly, there were no winners from Liguria. All the other finalists are indicated in the Guide by Two red Glasses to distinguish them from the Two Glass wines that failed to make the last stage. Are there too many? Or too few? There will now follow the usual protests. Some will say we were too generous, others that we were too harsh. Still others will claim we got it all wrong. We can only say that behind all the selections and awards lies a huge amount of work. It is a complex job that involves tasting, writing, inputting data and final proofreading. Inevitably, there will be the odd mistake for, sadly, we are not perfect. Having said that, let's move on to the latest Guide news. After 15 years, Carlo Petrini has handed his Slow Food Chief Editor's hat over to Gigi Piumatti, who has been co-ordinating activities since work on the Guide began back in the spring of '87. Gianni Fabrizio takes over as Senior Editor. On the Gambero Rosso side of the team, Daniele Cernilli and Marco Sabellico remain at their desks. We will conclude by expressing our appreciation to everyone who has helped to make the publication of this book possible. We would like to thank in particular the following consortia: Marchio Storico del Chianti Classico, Brunello di Montalcino, Rosso di Montalcino, Nobile di Montepulciano, Bolgheri, Vernaccia di San Gimignano, Franciacorta, Oltrepò Pavese, Valtellina, Soave, Valpolicella and Gavi, the Enoteca Regionale del Roero, the Enoteca Regionale di Dozza, the Enoteca Regionale di Gattinara, the Istituto Agronomico Mediterraneo at Valenzano, the Centro Agroalimentare Umbro at Foligno, the Bolzano Chamber of Commerce, the Caserta Chamber of Commerce, the Trento Chamber of Commerce, Assivip at Majolati Spontini, the Vineria della Signora in Rosso at Nizza Monferrato and Vinea at Offida. Our apologies, naturally, go to anyone we have left out. Thanks also go to all those who, often just for the sheer love of participating, have organized tastings, uncorked, tinfoiled and served wines, or visited cellars to pick up samples. We owe them much. This Guide is not written by a lone taster, sampling and assessing in solitude. Ours is a team effort and the Chief Editors are nothing more or less than the team's two captains.

Daniele Cernilli e Gigi Piumatti

THREE GLASS AWARDS 2003

VALLE D'AOSTA
Valle d'Aosta Chardonnay Cuvée Frissonnière Les Crêtes Cuvée Bois '00	Les Crêtes	17

PIEDMONT
Asti De Miranda M. Cl. '00	Contratto	55
Barbaresco Bricco Asili '99	Bricco Rocche - Bricco Asili	62
Barbaresco Camp Gros '98	Tenute Cisa Asinari dei Marchesi di Grésy	31
Barbaresco Cottà '99	Sottimano	122
Barbaresco Ovello '99	Cantina del Pino	30
Barbaresco Rombone '99	Fiorenzo Nada	143
Barbaresco Sorì Paitin Vecchie Vigne '99	Paitin	121
Barbaresco Vanotu '99	Pelissero	144
Barbaresco Vigneti in Rio Sordo Ris. '97	Produttori del Barbaresco	35
Barbaresco Vigneto Starderi '99	La Spinetta	58
Barbera d'Alba Asili '00	Cascina Luisin	33
Barbera d'Alba Ciabot du Re '00	F.lli Revello	95
Barbera d'Alba Giada '00	Andrea Oberto	93
Barbera d'Alba Scarrone Vigna Vecchia '00	Vietti	65
Barbera d'Alba Sup. '00	Armando Parusso	109
Barbera d'Alba Sup. '00	G. D. Vajra	43
Barbera d'Alba Vigna Gattere '00	Mauro Molino	92
Barbera d'Alba Vigneto della Chiesa '00	F.lli Seghesio	112
Barbera d'Alba Vigneto Pozzo dell'Annunziata Ris. '99	Roberto Voerzio	98
Barbera d'Asti La Crena '99	Vietti	65
Barbera d'Asti SanSì Sel. '99	Scagliola	49
Barbera d'Asti Sup. '00	La Spinetta	58
Barbera d'Asti Sup. Alfiera '00	Marchesi Alfieri	131
Barolo '98	Bartolo Mascarello	39
Barolo Brunate '98	Roberto Voerzio	98
Barolo Bussia '98	Prunotto	27
Barolo Cerequio '98	Michele Chiarlo	47
Barolo Cerretta '98	Ettore Germano	137
Barolo Falletto Ris. '96	Bruno Giacosa	120
Barolo Gavarini Vigna Chiniera '98	Elio Grasso	108
Barolo La Serra '98	Gianni Voerzio	97
Barolo nei Cannubi '98	Poderi Einaudi	75
Barolo Percristina '97	Domenico Clerico	104
Barolo Rocche dell'Annunziata Ris. '96	Paolo Scavino	64
Barolo S. Giovanni '98	Gianfranco Alessandria	104
Barolo Sorì Ginestra '98	Conterno Fantino	106
Barolo Vecchie Vigne '98	Giovanni Corino	90
Barolo Vigna La Rosa '98	Fontanafredda	136
Barolo Vigna Rionda '98	F.lli Oddero	94
Barolo Vigna Rionda Ris. '96	Vigna Rionda - Massolino	138
Barolo Vigne di Proprietà in Barolo '98	Marchesi di Barolo	39
Barolo Vigneto Arborina '98	Elio Altare - Cascina Nuova	88
Bricco Appiani '99	Flavio Roddolo	111
Dolcetto di Dogliani Sirì d'Jermu '01	F.lli Pecchenino	76
Fara Caramino '99	Dessilani	78
Harys '00	Giovanni Battista Gillardi	79
Langhe Dolcetto Barturot '01	Ca' Viola	74
Langhe Nebbiolo Sorì S. Lorenzo '98	Gaja	32
Langhe Nebbiolo Sorì Tildin '98	Gaja	32
Langhe Rosso Alta Bussia '00	Attilio Ghisolfi	107
Langhe Rosso Quatr Nas '99	Podere Rocche dei Manzoni	110
Monferrato Rosso Rivalta '00	Villa Sparina	85
Monferrato Rosso Sonvico '00	Cascina La Barbatella	123
Monferrato Rosso Sul Bric '00	Franco M. Martinetti	141
Nebbiolo d'Alba '00	Hilberg - Pasquero	127
Nebbiolo d'Alba Vigna di Lino '00	Cascina Val del Prete	128
Roero Bric Valdiana '00	Giovanni Almondo	113
Roero Ròche d'Ampsèj '99	Matteo Correggia	51
Roero Printi '99	Monchiero Carbone	54
Roero Sup. Trinità '99	Malvirà	53

LOMBARDY
Franciacorta Brut Cabochon '98	Monte Rossa	185
Franciacorta Cuvée Annamaria Clementi '95	Ca' del Bosco	193
Franciacorta Electo Brut '97	Majolini	203
Franciacorta Extra Brut '98	Villa	201
Franciacorta Gran Cuvée Brut '98	Bellavista	192

Franciacorta Satèn Magnificentia	Uberti	195
Garda Cabernet Le Zalte '00	Cascina La Pertica	204
TdF Chardonnay '00	Ca' del Bosco	193
Valtellina Sforzato '00	Triacca	211
Valtellina Sforzato Albareda '00	Mamete Prevostini	197
Valtellina Sforzato Canua '00	Conti Sertoli Salis	209

TRENTINO

Granato '00	Foradori	236
Olivar '01	Cesconi	231
Rosso Faye '00	Pojer & Sandri	228
San Leonardo '99	Tenuta San Leonardo	225
Trento Methius Ris. '95	F.lli Dorigati - Metius	234

ALTO ADIGE

A. A. Bianco Beyond the Clouds '00	Castel Ringberg & Kastelaz Elena Walch	275
A. A. Cabernet Sauvignon '99	Plattner - Waldgries	260
A. A. Cabernet St. Valentin '00	C. P. San Michele Appiano	254
A. A. Chardonnay Baron Salvadori '00	C. P. Nalles Niclara Magrè	272
A. A. Chardonnay Cornell '00	C. P. Colterenzio	251
A. A. Gewürztraminer Puntay '01	Prima & Nuova/Erste & Neue	265
A. A. Gewürztraminer Kolbenhof '01	Hofstätter	275
A. A. Gewürztraminer Nussbaumerhof '01	C. P. Termeno	276
A. A. Lagrein Praepositus Ris. '00	Abbazia di Novacella	277
A. A. Lagrein Scuro Abtei Ris. '99	Cantina Convento Muri-Gries	256
A. A. Lagrein Scuro Fohrhof '00	C. P. Cortaccia	268
A. A. Lagrein Scuro Grieser Prestige Line Ris. '99	Cantina Gries/Cantina di Bolzano	255
A. A. Lagrein Scuro Ris. '99	Josephus Mayr - Erbhof Unterganzner	258
A. A. Lagrein Scuro Taberhof Ris. '00	C. P. Santa Maddalena/ Cantina di Bolzano	260
A. A. Lagrein Scuro Tor di Lupo '00	C. P. Andriano	250
A. A. Moscato Giallo Passito Serenade '99	Cantina Viticoltori di Caldaro	264
A. A. Sauvignon St. Valentin '01	C. P. San Michele Appiano	254
A. A. Terlano '91	Cantina Terlano	274
Kaiton '01	Kuenhof - Peter Pliger	263

VENETO

Amarone della Valpolicella Campo dei Gigli '97	Tenuta Sant'Antonio	297
Amarone della Valpolicella Cl. '98	Allegrini	288
Amarone della Valpolicella Cl. '98	Brigaldara	314
Amarone della Valpolicella Cl. Ambrosan '98	Angelo Nicolis e Figli	315
Amarone della Valpolicella Cl. Capitel Monte Olmi '99	F.lli Tedeschi	317
Amarone della Valpolicella Cl. Casa dei Bepi '97	Viviani	307
Amarone della Valpolicella Cl. Vigneto Monte Sant'Urbano '97	F.lli Speri	316
Amarone della Valpolicella Vigneto di Monte Lodoletta '97	Romano Dal Forno	290
Breganze Cabernet Vigneto Due Santi '00	Vigneto Due Santi	284
Capitel Croce '00	Roberto Anselmi	300
Fratta '00	Maculan	285
Recioto della Valpolicella Cl. '00	Lorenzo Begali	314
Recioto della Valpolicella Cl. Acinatico '00	Stefano Accordini	313
Recioto della Valpolicella Cl. TB '99	Tommaso Bussola	304
Soave Cl. Sup. La Rocca '00	Leonildo Pieropan	323
Soave Cl. Sup. Le Rive '00	Suavia	323
Soave Cl. Sup. Monte Alto '00	Ca' Rugate	300
Soave Cl. Sup. Monte Pressoni '01	Cantina del Castello	321
Soave Cl. Sup. Vigneto Du Lot '00	Inama	310

FRIULI VENEZIA GIULIA

Braide Alte '00	Livon	410
COF Merlot '00	Le Due Terre	400
COF Merlot '99	Miani	350
COF Merlot Vigne Cinquant'Anni '99	Le Vigne di Zamò	387
COF Montsclapade '99	Girolamo Dorigo	349
COF Pinot Bianco Zuc di Volpe '01	Volpe Pasini	415
COF Refosco P. R. '99	Livio Felluga	363
COF Verduzzo Friulano Graticcio '99	Scubla	398
Collio Bianco Russiz Disôre '00	Russiz Superiore	353
Collio Chardonnay '00	Borgo del Tiglio	359
Collio Chardonnay Gräfin de La Tour '00	Villa Russiz	354
Collio Chardonnay Ris. '91	Josko Gravner	382
Collio Merlot Graf de La Tour '99	Villa Russiz	354
Collio Pinot Bianco '01	Castello di Spessa	351
Collio Pinot Bianco '01	Franco Toros	370
Collio Sauvignon Ronco delle Mele '01	Venica & Venica	377
Collio Tocai Friulano '01	Edi Keber	364
Collio Tocai Friulano '01	Dario Raccaro	367
Friuli Grave Pinot Bianco '01	Vigneti Le Monde	395

Friuli Isonzo Chardonnay Jurosa '00	Lis Neris - Pecorari	411
Friuli Isonzo Sauvignon Vieris '00	Vie di Romans	390
Friuli Isonzo Tocai Friulano '01	Ronco del Gelso	368
Ronc '00	Paolo Rodaro	358
Vespa Bianco '00	Bastianich	396
Vintage Tunina '01	Vinnaioli Jermann	380

EMILIA ROMAGNA

C. B. Merlot Giòtondo '00	Santarosa	435
Marzieno '00	Fattoria Zerbina	429
Sangiovese di Romagna Sup. Avi Ris. '99	San Patrignano	428
Sangiovese di Romagna Sup. Calisto '01	Stefano Berti	430

TUSCANY

Avvoltore '00	Moris Farms	498
Bolgheri Rosso Sup. Grattamacco '99	Colle Massari	461
Bolgheri Sassicaia '99	Tenuta San Guido	457
Bolgheri Sup. Ornellaia '99	Tenuta dell'Ornellaia	457
Brancaia Il Blu '00	La Brancaia	551
Brunello di Montalcino '97	Cerbaiona	505
Brunello di Montalcino '97	Fanti - San Filippo	508
Brunello di Montalcino '97	La Togata - Tenuta Carlina	512
Brunello di Montalcino '97	Mastrojanni	514
Brunello di Montalcino '97	Siro Pacenti	515
Brunello di Montalcino '97	Podere Salicutti	518
Brunello di Montalcino '97	Salvioni - La Cerbaiola	518
Brunello di Montalcino '97	Solaria - Cencioni	519
Brunello di Montalcino Manachiara '97	Tenute Silvio Nardi	514
Brunello di Montalcino Poggio Banale '97	La Poderina	512
Brunello di Montalcino Tenuta Nuova '97	Casanova di Neri	503
Camartina '99	Querciabella	488
Carmignano Ris. '99	Piaggia	548
Cerviolo Rosso '00	San Fabiano Calcinaia	467
Chianti Cl. Casasilia '99	Poggio al Sole	577
Chianti Cl. Castello di Ama '99	Castello di Ama	478
Chianti Cl. Castello di Brolio '99	Barone Ricasoli	479
Chianti Cl. Castello di Fonterutoli '99	Castello di Fonterutoli	463
Chianti Cl. Giorgio Primo '00	La Massa	542
Chianti Cl. Grosso Sanese '00	Podere Il Palazzino	481
Chianti Cl. Monna Lisa Ris. '99	Villa Vignamaggio	491
Chianti Cl. Ris. '99	Carobbio	540
Chianti Cl. Ris. '99	Riecine	483
Chianti Cl. Ris. '99	San Vincenti	485
Chianti Cl. Vigneto S. Marcellino Ris. '99	Rocca di Montegrossi	484
Corbaia '99	Castello di Bossi	468
D'Alceo '00	Castello dei Rampolla	540
Fontalloro '99	Fattoria di Felsina	470
Galatrona '00	Fattoria Petrolo	538
Giramonte '00	Fattoria Castiglioni e Montagnana	536
I Sodi di San Niccolò '98	Castellare di Castellina	463
Il Futuro '99	Il Colombaio di Cencio	480
Le Stanze '00	Poliziano	532
Lupicaia '00	Castello del Terriccio	467
Masseto '99	Tenuta dell'Ornellaia	457
Messorio '99	Le Macchiole	456
Morellino di Scansano CapaTosta '00	Poggio Argentiera	493
Nambrot '00	Tenuta di Ghizzano	545
Nardo '00	Montepeloso	574
Nobile di Montepulciano Asinone '99	Poliziano	532
Nobile di Montepulciano Vigna d'Alfiero '99	Tenuta Valdipiatta	534
Nobile di Montepulciano Vigneto Antica Chiusina '99	Fattoria del Cerro	528
Oreno '00	Tenuta Sette Ponti	577
Percarlo '99	San Giusto a Rentennano	484
Prunaio '99	Viticcio	492
Redigaffi '00	Tua Rita	575
Roccato '99	Rocca delle Macìe	466
Romitorio di Santedame '00	Tenimenti Ruffino	548
Saffredi '00	Fattoria Le Pupille	492
San Martino '99	Villa Cafaggio	544
Sant'Antimo Excelsus '99	Banfi	500
Saxa Calida '00	Il Paradiso	564
Siepi '00	Castello di Fonterutoli	463
Solaia '99	Marchesi Antinori	475
Syrah '99	Isole e Olena	454
Val di Cornia Rosso Barbicone '00	Russo	575
Varramista '00	Varramista	538
Vin Santo Occhio di Pernice '90	Avignonesi	526

MARCHE

Kurni '00		Oasi degli Angeli	615
Ludi '00		Ercole Velenosi	610
Rosso Conero Adeodato '00		Monteschiavo	619
Rosso Conero Traiano '00		Silvano Strologo	612
Rosso Piceno Sup. Vigna Monteprandone '00		Saladini Pilastri	634
Solo Sangiovese '00		Fattoria Dezi	633
Verdicchio dei Castelli di Jesi Cl. Serra Fiorese Ris. '99		Gioacchino Garofoli	618
Verdicchio dei Castelli di Jesi Cl. Villa Bucci Ris. '99		Bucci	627

UMBRIA

Armaleo '00		Palazzone	653
Campoleone '00		Lamborghini - La Fiorita	654
Cervaro della Sala '00		Castello della Sala	644
Montefalco Sagrantino '99		Colpetrone	646
Montefalco Sagrantino 25 Anni '99		Arnaldo Caprai - Val di Maggio	648

LAZIO

Montiano '00		Falesco	670
Vigna del Vassallo '00		Di Mauro - Colle Picchioni	668

ABRUZZO AND MOLISE

Montepulciano d'Abruzzo Villa Gemma '98		Gianni Masciarelli	684
Trebbiano d'Abruzzo '99		Edoardo Valentini	679
Molise Aglianico Contado '99		Di Majo Norante	676

CAMPANIA

Bue Apis '00		Cantina del Taburno	693
Montevetrano '00		Montevetrano	700
Pàtrimo '00		Feudi di San Gregorio	702
Serpico '00		Feudi di San Gregorio	702
Taurasi Vigna Macchia dei Goti '99		Antonio Caggiano	702
Casavecchia Rosso '01		Vestini - Campagnano	691

BASILICATA

Aglianico del Vulture La Firma '00		Cantine del Notaio	712
Aglianico del Vulture Re Manfredi '99		Terre degli Svevi	713
Aglianico del Vulture Rotondo '00		Paternoster	709

PUGLIA

Le Braci '00		Masseria Monaci	720
Masseria Maime '00		Tormaresca	729
Nero '00		Conti Zecca	725
Salento Primitivo Visellio '01		Tenute Rubino	717

CALABRIA

Scavigna Vigna Garrone '99		Odoardi	740

SICILY

Burdese '00		Planeta	752
Cometa '01		Planeta	752
Deliella '00		Feudo Principi di Butera	745
Don Antonio '00		Morgante	749
Faro Palari '00		Palari	753
Harmonium '00		Casa Vinicola Firriato	754
Litra '00		Abbazia Santa Anastasia	747
Sole di Sesta '00		Cottanera	748
Solinero '00		Tenute Rapitalà	746

SARDINIA

Carignano del Sulcis Sup. Terre Brune '98		C. S. Santadi	773
Turriga '98		Antonio Argiolas	775

WINERY OF THE YEAR
CA' DEL BOSCO

OENOLOGIST OF THE YEAR
MARCO PALLANTI

THE YEAR'S BEST WINES

THE SPARKLER
TRENTO METHIUS RIS. '95 — F.LLI DORIGATI - METIUS

THE WHITE
COLLIO CHARDONNAY GRÄFIN DE LA TOUR '00 — VILLA RUSSIZ

THE RED
PATRIMO '00 — FEUDI DI SAN GREGORIO

THE SWEET
ASTI DE MIRANDA M. CL. '00 — CONTRATTO

THE STARS

In 16 editions of Italian Wines, fully 45 wineries have won Three Glasses at least ten times. Twelve of the big hitters are from Tuscany, 12 from Piedmont, eight from Friuli, four are from the Veneto and there are two each from Lombardy, Alto Adige and Sicily. Trentino, Umbria and Abruzzo have one winery each. This time, Angelo Gaja adds a third star, having now won 31 Three Glass awards over the years. Runner up is Ca' del Bosco, whose Franciacortia wines have hit the jackpot 22 times. That's once more than Elio Altare and the Rivetti brothers' La Spinetta, two celebrated Piedmont cellars. There are 18 awards for the Veneto's Allegrini and 17 for Castello di Fonterutoli, the leading Tuscan contender. We should, however, point out that if we were to add together all the Three Glass awards earned by the Antinori group, the total would come to a record 33.

★ ★ ★
31
GAJA (Piedmont)

★ ★
22
CA' DEL BOSCO
(Lombardy)

21
ELIO ALTARE
(Piedmont)
LA SPINETTA (Piedmont)

★
18
ALLEGRINI (Veneto)

17
CASTELLO DI FONTERUTOLI
(Tuscany)

16
FATTORIA DI FELSINA
(Tuscany)
VINNAIOLI JERMANN
(Friuli Venezia Giulia)

14
MARCHESI ANTINORI
(Tuscany)
DOMENICO CLERICO
(Piedmont)
POLIZIANO (Tuscany)
PAOLO SCAVINO
(Piedmont)

13
BELLAVISTA (Lombardy)
CANTINA PRODUTTORI
SAN MICHELE APPIANO (Alto Adige)

CASTELLO DELLA SALA (Umbria)
MARIO SCHIOPETTO
(Friuli Venezia Giulia)
TENIMENTI RUFFINO (Tuscany)
VIE DI ROMANS (Friuli Venezia Giulia)
VILLA RUSSIZ (Friuli Venezia Giulia)

12
BANFI (Tuscany)
CASTELLO DI AMA (Tuscany)
FERRARI (Trentino)
GIROLAMO DORIGO
(Friuli Venezia Giulia)
ISOLE E OLENA (Tuscany)
CASCINA LA BARBATELLA
(Piedmont)
LIVIO FELLUGA
(Friuli Venezia Giulia)
MIANI (Friuli Venezia Giulia)
PODERI ALDO CONTERNO
(Piedmont)
ROBERTO VOERZIO (Piedmont)
TENUTA FONTODI (Tuscany)
TENUTA SAN GUIDO (Tuscany)
EDOARDO VALENTINI (Abruzzo)

11
GIACOMO CONTERNO (Piedmont)
MATTEO CORREGGIA (Piedmont)
ROMANO DAL FORNO (Veneto)
IOSKO GRAVNER
(Friuli Venezia Giulia)

10
CANTINA PRODUTTORI COLTERENZIO
(Alto Adige)
BRICCO ROCCHE - BRICCO ASILI
(Piedmont)
MACULAN (Veneto)
PIEROPAN (Veneto)
PLANETA (Sicily)
QUERCIABELLA (Tuscany)
TASCA D'ALMERITA (Sicily)
TENUTA DELL'ORNELLAIA (Tuscany)
CONTERNO FANTINO (Piedmont)

A GUIDE TO VINTAGES, 1971 - 1999

Year	BARBARESCO	BRUNELLO DI MONTALCINO	BAROLO	CHIANTI CLASSICO	NOBILE DI MONTEPULCIANO	AMARONE
1971	●●●●	●●●	●●●●●	●●●●●	●●●●	●●●●
1973	●●	●●●	●●	●●	●●●	●●
1974	●●●●	●●	●●●●	●●●	●●●	●●●●
1975	●●	●●●●●	●●	●●●●	●●●●	●●●
1976	●●	●	●●	●●	●●	●●●●
1977	●●	●●●●	●●	●●●●	●●●●	●●●
1978	●●●●●	●●●●	●●●●●	●●●●●	●●●●●	●●●
1979	●●●●	●●●●	●●●●	●●●●	●●●●	●●●●
1980	●●●●	●●●	●●●●	●●●●	●●●	●●●
1981	●●●	●●●	●●●	●●●	●●●	●●●
1982	●●●●●	●●●●●	●●●●	●●●●	●●●●	●
1983	●●●●	●●●●	●●●●	●●●●	●●●●	●●●●●
1984	●	●●	●●	●	●	●●
1985	●●●●●	●●●●●	●●●●●	●●●●●	●●●●●	●●●●
1986	●●●	●●●	●●●	●●●●	●●●●	●●●
1987	●●	●●	●●	●●	●●	●●
1988	●●●●●	●●●●●	●●●●●	●●●●●	●●●●●	●●●●●
1989	●●●●●	●●	●●●●●	●	●	●●
1990	●●●●●	●●●●●	●●●●●	●●●●●	●●●●●	●●●●●
1991	●●●	●●●	●●●	●●●	●●●	●●
1992	●●	●●	●●	●	●	●
1993	●●●	●●●●	●●●	●●●●	●●●●●	●●●●
1994	●●	●●●	●●	●●	●●	●●
1995	●●●●	●●●●●	●●●●	●●●●●	●●●●●	●●●●
1996	●●●●●	●●●●	●●●●●	●●●●	●●●	●●●
1997	●●●●●	●●●●●	●●●●●	●●●●●	●●●●●	●●●●●
1998	●●●●●	●●●●	●●●●●	●●●●	●●●	●●●
1999	●●●●	●●●●	●●●●	●●●●	●●●●	●●●

HOW TO USE THE GUIDE

KEY
○ WHITE WINES
● RED WINES
☉ ROSÉ WINES

RATINGS

LISTING WITHOUT A GLASS SYMBOL:
A WELL-MADE WINE OF AVERAGE QUALITY IN ITS CATEGORY

🍷
ABOVE AVERAGE TO GOOD IN ITS CATEGORY, EQUIVALENT TO 70-79/100

🍷🍷
VERY GOOD TO EXCELLENT IN ITS CATEGORY, EQUIVALENT TO 80-89/100

🍷
VERY GOOD TO EXCELLENT WINE SELECTED FOR FINAL TASTINGS

🍷🍷🍷
EXCELLENT WINE IN ITS CATEGORY, EQUIVALENT TO 90-99/100

(🍷, 🍷🍷, 🍷🍷🍷) WINES RATED IN PREVIOUS EDITIONS OF THE GUIDE ARE INDICATED BY WHITE GLASSES, PROVIDED THEY ARE STILL DRINKING AT THE LEVEL FOR WHICH THE ORIGINAL AWARD WAS MADE

STAR ★
EACH STAR INDICATES TEN THREE GLASS AWARDS

PRICE RANGES [1]
1 UP TO $ 8 AND UP TO £6
2 FROM $ 8 TO $ 12 AND FROM £ 6 TO £ 8
3 FROM $ 12 TO $ 18 AND FROM £ 8 TO £ 11
4 FROM $ 18 TO $ 27 AND FROM £ 11 TO £ 15
5 FROM $ 27 TO $ 40 AND FROM £ 15 TO £ 20
6 MORE THAN $ 40 AND MORE THAN £ 20

[1] Approx. retail prices in USA and UK

ASTERISK *
INDICATES ESPECIALLY GOOD VALUE FOR MONEY

NOTE
PRICES INDICATED REFER TO RETAIL AVERAGES. INDICATIONS OF PRICE NEXT TO WINES ASSIGNED WHITE GLASSES (AWARDS MADE IN PREVIOUS EDITIONS) TAKE INTO ACCOUNT APPRECIATION OVER TIME WHERE APPROPRIATE

ABBREVIATIONS

A. A.	Alto Adige
C.	Colli
Cl.	Classico
C.S.	Cantina Sociale (co-operative winery)
Cant.	Cantina (cellar or winery)
Cast.	Castello (castle)
C. B.	Colli Bolognesi
C. P.	Colli Piacentini
COF	Colli Orientali del Friuli
Cons.	Consorzio (consortium)
Coop.Agr.	Cooperativa Agricola (farming co-operative)
DOC	Denominazione di Origine Controllata (category of wines created in 1963)
DOCG	Denominazione di Origine Controllata e Garantita (superior category of wines created in 1963)
Et.	Etichetta (label)
IGT	Indicazione Geografica Tipica (category of wines created in 1992)
M.	Metodo
M.to	Monferrato
OP	Oltrepò Pavese
P.R.	Peduncolo Rosso (red bunchstem)
P.	Prosecco
Rif. Agr.	Riforma Agraria (agrarian reform)
Ris.	Riserva
Sel.	Selezione
Sup.	Superiore
TdF	Terre di Franciacorta
V.	Vigna (vine)
Vign.	Vigneto (vineyard)
V. T.	Vendemmia Tardiva (late harvest)

VALLE D'AOSTA

There have been no significant changes in the front rank of winemakers in Valle d'Aosta. The leading figure is still Costantino Charrère, who makes top quality wines at his family winery and at Les Crêtes. Costantino's Chardonnay Cuvée Boise has again won Three Glasses and his Coteau La Tour came very close, although all of Charrère's wines offer very impressive evidence of his competence as a producer. The valley's winemaking scene was once the exclusive territory of co-operatives but now privately owned wineries are sending out encouraging signals. For the time being, however, the private cellars are turning out comparatively small quantities. The Anselmet family came up with another excellent range and Giorgio, son of Renato, the grand old man of Valle d'Aosta wine, has joined the business this year. Upcoming youngster Marco Martin, of the Lo Triolet winery, also makes very good wines, and the Grosjean family continue to demonstrate the solid quality of their products. Making its debut this year is the winery owned by Elvira Stefania Rini and her husband Andrea Barmaz, chairman of Cervim and former regional oenologist. From this year, Andrea will be working full- time in his own winery. There is insufficient space in the Guide to mention all of the 24 small wineries in the Assocazione Viticulteurs Encaveurs that provide grapes for its less than 300,000 bottles per year. Compare this to Les Crêtes (150,000 bottles) or Grosjean (65,000) and you get a clear idea of how tiny these cellars are. In any case, we only have room to mention 16 of them this year: Carlo Celegato (Morgex, 1,300 bottles), Marziano Vevey (Morgex, 6,000), Piero Brunet (Morgex, 1,500), Ermes Pavese (Morgex, 4,000), Danilo Thomain (Arvier, 2,000), Bregy e Gillioz (Saint Pierre, 9,300), Graziano Teppex (Aymavilles, 3,200), Fernanda Saraillon (Aymavilles, 8,000), Elio Cassol (Sarre, 1,500), Vallet – Rivelli (Sarre, 7,000), Costantino Praz (Jovençan, 5,000), Diego Curtaz (Gressan, 4,800), Ildo Bianquin (Charvensod, 3,300), Vinirari di Giulio Moriondo (Quart, 3,400), Fabrizio Priod (Issogne, 1,700) and Dino Bonin (Arnad, 10,000). These core cellars have already become an important economic and agricultural resource for the region. Turning to the co-operatives, we note a slight setback this year for the Cave du Vin Blanc de Morgex. The wines aren't quite up to previous year's standards. In contrast, the regional authority-run Insititut Agricole at Aosta provided positive results, as did Crotta di Vegneron at Chambave, which remains a benchmark co-operative for the mid Valle d'Aosta area and a stimulus to the many small-scale growers in the municipalities of Nus and Chambave. Their memorable Chambave Moscato Passito is as good as any in Italy.

AOSTA

INSTITUT AGRICOLE RÉGIONAL
RÉGION LA ROCHERE, 1/A
11100 AOSTA
TEL. 0165215811
E-MAIL: agriruda@interbusiness.it

The regional agricultural institute maintains close contact with local growers and produces a good range of its own. Many of the experts who are now running or improving Valle d'Aosta's farms and wineries studied here, where the viticulture section is in the capable hands of Luciano Rigazio. With the help of his excellent staff, Luciano releases a series of good to excellent wines every year, in two distinct lines. Wines aged exclusively in stainless steel are produced in greater volume while the second range is for experimental barrique-aged products (no more than 1,000 units of each selection are bottled). The wines aged in steel include a very good Pinot Gris, which has become a cornerstone of the Institut's range. The golden yellow introduces super-ripe fruit aromas and a generous, almost honeyed, palate that reminds us how much extract there is in this wine, which also flaunts 14 per cent alcohol. The barrique-aged Chardonnay is the best of the oak-conditioned selections. Its vanilla mingles pleasantly with the hints of apples and pears, then the admirable structure on the palate is softened by toasty oak. The monovarietal sauvignon Comète reveals smoky notes in its generous, complex bouquet and a palate whose rich fruit is still slightly dominated by oak-derived vanilla. The Petite Arvine is flowery, full-flavoured and nicely balanced while the viognier-based Élite is drier and more predictable. The last of the whites is the acidulous and uncomplicated Müller Thurgau. The reds, both stainless steel-aged and cask-conditioned, gave a less impressive performance.

○ La Comète '00	♉♉	5
○ Valle d'Aosta Chardonnay Barrique '00	♉♉	5
○ Valle d'Aosta Petite Arvine '01	♉♉	4*
○ Valle d'Aosta Pinot Gris '01	♉♉	4*
○ Élite '00	♉	5
● Rouge du Prieur '00	♉	5
● Trésor du Caveau '00	♉	5
● Vin du Prévôt '00	♉	5
○ Valle d'Aosta Müller Thurgau '01		4
● Valle d'Aosta Pinot Noir '01		4
● Rouge du Prieur '99	♉♉	5
● Trésor du Caveau '99	♉♉	5
○ Valle d'Aosta Chardonnay Barrique '99	♉♉	5

AYMAVILLES (AO)

COSTANTINO CHARRÈRE
LES MOULINS, 28
11010 AYMAVILLES (AO)
TEL. 0165902135
E-MAIL: info@lescretesvins.it

Costantino Charrère has again shown that he is the driving force behind Valle d'Aosta winemaking, as well as a kind of icon for his colleagues in the region. This is due to a combination of factors. Costantino is a tireless detective who searches out native varieties on the brink of extinction. He also keeps the small association of local producers on its toes and his competence as a grower is beyond dispute. It is well known that Charrère divides his energies between the famous Les Crêtes winery and the "family" winery we are reviewing here, where he makes the best grenache-based wines in Valle d'Aosta, Les Fourches. The 2001 version is a deep, almost purple, red with complex aromas of ripe fruit, redcurrants and blackberries that meld deliciously with pencil lead and toasty oak. The palate has bags of personality. The sweet entry precedes a long, subtle finish with a bitterish twist and it all adds up to a thoroughly convincing wine. The Prëmetta is just as good and sings a paean of praise to this native variety, saved at the eleventh hour. The colour has a lovely hint of onionskin while the aromas mingle unripe berry fruit with spice. The palate has only moderate structure but is beautifully even and enjoyable. Charrère also makes another excellent wine, the Vin de la Sabla, from petit rouge, fumin and barbera. Its attractively intense, almost purplish, garnet colour precedes aromas of ripe fruit, especially blackberries, and a full, etheric palate with a hint of almonds in the finish. The Torrette is well typed and nicely balanced.

● Vin de La Sabla '01	♉♉	4
● Vin Les Fourches '01	♉♉	5
● Valle d'Aosta Prëmetta '01	♉	4
● Valle d'Aosta Torrette '01	♉	4
● Vin de La Sabla '00	♉♉	4
● Vin Les Fourches '99	♉♉	5

AYMAVILLES (AO)

Les Crêtes
Loc. Villetos, 50
11010 Aymavilles (AO)
Tel. 0165902274
E-mail: info@lescretesvins.it

We have already talked about Costantino Charrère when we were reviewing his family winery, so now we'll move on to the important news from Les Crêtes, the Aymavilles winery Charrère has run for years in partnership with other well-known figures in the region. From 2002, Charrère is the sole owner of this famous Valle d'Aosta "maison", the first to attract serious recognition for the region's wines. Quality is nothing new from Charrère. He keeps a constant and very keen eye on winemaking on the far side of the Alps, especially Burgundy, and this year he delighted the panel with two excellent reds, the 100 per cent syrah Coteau La Tour and the Fumin, both from 2000. The Coteau La Tour enjoys longer ageing and the toasty oak notes from the wood have mellowed. The colour is very intense, and the aromas include redcurrant and blackberries, but the palate is quite spectacular. Sweet, juicy and mouthfilling, it reveals lingering tannins that show no trace of rough edges. The stylish, intriguing Fumin is a reliable bottle with sweet, succulent fruit. However, it was the superbly impressive Chardonnay Cuvée Bois 2000 that won Three Glasses. It unveils delightful apple, pear and vanilla aromas, a generous, harmonious and beautifully balanced palate, then a long finish with mineral notes that are never swamped by the wood. An opulent wine of discreet power, it offers lashings of fruit and outstanding style. The Petite Arvine has interesting spring flower aromas, and the Chardonnay aged in steel has good structure and length.

○	Valle d'Aosta Chardonnay Cuvée Frissonnière Les Crêtes Cuvée Bois '00 ♀♀♀	5
●	Coteau La Tour '00 ♀♀	5
●	Valle d'Aosta Fumin Vigne La Tour '00 ♀♀	5
○	Valle d'Aosta Chardonnay Cuvée Frissonnière Les Crêtes '01 ♀♀	4*
○	Valle d'Aosta Petite Arvine Vigne Champorette '01 ♀♀	4*
●	Valle d'Aosta Pinot Noir Vigne La Tour '01 ♀	4
●	Valle d'Aosta Torrette Vigne Les Toules '01 ♀	4
○	Valle d'Aosta Chardonnay Cuvée Frissonnière Les Crêtes Cuvée Bois '99 ♀♀♀	5

CHAMBAVE (AO)

La Crotta di Vegneron
P.zza Roncas, 2
11023 Chambave (AO)
Tel. 016646670
E-mail: lacrotta@libero.it

Elio Cornaz is the new chairman of this co-operative in the lower part of Valle d'Aosta, which vinifies fruit from 130 member growers whose vineyards are in the municipalities of Nus and Chambave. The leading wine is, as usual, the Chambave Moscato Passito. The 2000 edition of this selection - the pride of Chambave – made it through to the final taste-offs. One of the best "passito" wines in Italy, it justly earns Two very full, red Glasses. This is a very impressive wine all round. The straw yellow is flecked with golden highlights, the nose is fascinating and intrigues with upfront varietal aromas layered over honeyed notes and ripe apple and pear fruit. In the mouth, it never cloys, its subtle elegance revealing very good structure and balance. All in all, this is an excellent performance from a wine that has now entered the front rank of Italy's dried-grape "passito" wines. The quality of the other wines has dropped a little compared to previous years but the dry Muscat, the Malvoisie Flétrì, a typical sweet wine from Nus, and the dry pinot grigio-based Malvoisie all acquitted themselves well, though the Müller Thurgau only just earned a mention. We weren't particularly impressed by the 2000 debut Chambave Rouge Quatre Vignobles which is the winery's newest release, while the Fumin, also from 2000 and aged in wood, has an enjoyable palate but aromas that are slightly below par.

○	Valle d'Aosta Chambave Moscato Passito '00 ♀♀	6
●	Valle d'Aosta Fumin '00 ♀	4
○	Valle d'Aosta Nus Malvoisie Flétrì '00 ♀	5
○	Valle d'Aosta Chambave Muscat '01 ♀	4
○	Valle d'Aosta Nus Malvoisie '01 ♀	4
○	Valle d'Aosta Müller Thurgau '01	4
●	Valle d'Aosta Nus Rouge '01	3
○	Valle d'Aosta Chambave Moscato Passito '99 ♀♀	6
●	Valle d'Aosta Fumin '99 ♀	4

INTROD (AO)

Lo Triolet - Marco Martin
Fraz. Junod, 7
11010 Introd (AO)
Tel. 016595437 - 016595067
E-mail: lotriolet@libero.it

This small winery in the upper part of the valley is also a delightful farm holiday centre with two flats that sleep four or five people. It is situated at the entrance to the Rhêmes and Valsavarenche valleys, on the edge of the Gran Paradiso national park. Marco Martin runs the winery with the help of his parents, Renato and Emilia. Annual production from the estate's own vineyards is currently 10,000 bottles at most. The property is planted mainly to pinot grigio and the vines are in the municipality of Introd, at altitudes of up to 850 metres above sea level. There are two selections, one aged in wood and the other in stainless steel. The first is interesting from every point of view and, although it was aged in barrique, it is not excessively marked by toastiness from the oak. Its straw yellow is flecked with greenish highlights and there is an acidulous varietal note of rennet apples in the delicate, stylish aromas. The palate is well structured and rich in extract, with nice vanilla tones. The stainless steel-aged Pinot Grigio is even more elegant, with ripe apple and pear fruit and Alpine flowers on the nose, then a balanced palate with a citrus note in the pleasant finish. The Coteau Barrage, from syrah and fumin grapes grown at Nus, is a very impressively juicy, headily alcohol-rich, red with upfront fruit and a long mouthfilling palate. The Gamay and Nus Rouge are simpler but well made.

● Coteau Barrage '01	♛♛	5
○ Valle d'Aosta Pinot Gris Élevé en Fût de Chêne '01	♛♛	5
○ Valle d'Aosta Pinot Gris Lo Triolet '01	♛♛	4*
● Valle d'Aosta Gamay '01	♛	3
● Valle d'Aosta Nus Rouge '01	♛	3
● Coteau Barrage '00	♛♛	5
○ Valle d'Aosta Pinot Gris Élevé en Fût de Chêne '00	♛♛	5

QUART (AO)

F.lli Grosjean
Fraz. Ollignan, 1
11020 Quart (AO)
Tel. 0165775791 - 0165765704

Not for the first time, the most interesting product from this lovely estate, owned by the Grosjean family, is the Pinot Noir. The winery is situated on low hills in the municipality of Quart, a few kilometres from the centre of Aosta and can now at last use its new, more spacious, premises. Delfino helps his sons, Piergiorgio, Eraldo, Marco and Fernando, who are led by Vincent, one of the most highly qualified oenologists in the region. Annual production is around 65,000 bottles from the seven hectares of estate-owned vineyards at Quart and Saint-Christophe and the wide range covers the main Aosta wine types. As we mentioned, the barrique-aged Pinot Noir 2000 is our favourite. Its bright ruby red ushers in berry fruit and spice on the nose, then the balanced palate, more stylish than powerful, reveals an marked vein of acidity. The Fumin 2000 also gave a good performance. It shows an orange hue at the rim and the nose is reminiscent of spice, then the clean palate is medium long, and the piquant aromas are echoed in the finish. The grape-derived citrus aromas of the Petite Arvine, a traditional local white, are followed by medium structure and a clean, forthright mouthfeel. The Torrette is balanced, the standard-label Pinot Noir enjoyable and the Gamay is a little too simple. All are from 2001.

● Valle d'Aosta Fumin '00	♛♛	5
● Valle d'Aosta Pinot Noir Élevé en Barrique '00	♛♛	4*
○ Valle d'Aosta Petite Arvine '01	♛	4
● Valle d'Aosta Pinot Noir '01	♛	4
● Valle d'Aosta Torrette '01	♛	4
● Valle d'Aosta Gamay '01		4
● Valle d'Aosta Fumin '99	♛♛	5
● Valle d'Aosta Pinot Noir Élevé en Barrique '99	♛♛	4

VILLENEUVE (AO)

Anselmet
Fraz. La Crete, 194
11018 Villeneuve (AO)
Tel. 016595217 - 016595419
E-mail: renato.anselmet@tiscalinet.it

There is news from this little family-run winery in Villeneuve, a winemaking village north of Aosta near Courmayeur. Renato, an emblematic figure in regional winemaking, has stepped aside to make way for his 38-year-old son Giorgio, who has plenty of winemaking experience from the Institut Agricole Régional at Aosta and the co-operatives in Chambave and Aymavilles. Renato will, however, continue to lend a hand in vineyard and cellar. The five hectares of Anselmet vineyards are mainly situated in the municipality of Saint-Pierre, though some are at Villeneuve. Their grapes make 20-25,000 bottles of wine a year. The winery classics include a new oak-aged Torrette Superiore from 2001 that was good enough to walk away with Two Glasses. It may not have huge structure but it is balanced and mouthfilling. The vanilla from the wood is still a little assertive. The wood-aged Chardonnay is also very good, its toasty oak blending with the fruit to give the wine elegance and finesse. The standard Chardonnay is simpler but pleasantly drinkable, and the appetizing Müller Thurgau is backed up by good acidity. We also recommend the Petit Rouge and the standard Torrette. The dried-grape Arline and Declivium made interesting debuts. The Arline - only two barriques were made - is obtained with pinot grigio from French and local cuttings while the Declivium is from pinot grigio and gewürztraminer raisined on the vine. Lastly, the experimental Henri, from syrah, and the Le Prissonier Vigne de Torrette both gave interesting performances.

VILLENEUVE (AO)

Di Barrò
Fraz. Veyne, 11
11018 Villeneuve (AO)
Tel. 016595260
E-mail: dibarro@mediavallee.it

Elvira Stefania Rini and Andrea Barmaz own Di Barrò, which stood out among the small Viticulteurs Encaveurs producers this year. In local dialect, the name Di Barrò means "of the barrels". The name is formed from the first syllables of the surnames Barmaz and Rossan, the former owners, as well as parents-in-law of the current owner, who grew wine in the family vineyards in Monte Torrette back in the 1960s. In the late 1980s, the Rossan winery was one of the first to use the Valle d'Aosta Torrette DOC and this, in fact, is the cellar's leading wine. Annual production is only 8,000 bottles and the vine stock is also modest. Only 13,000 square metres are in production and another 7,000 square metres of new vineyards will soon join them for a total of just two hectares. The wine itself is made from 90 per cent petit rouge with mayolet, vien de Nus, neblou, cornalin and fumin making up the remainder. All are grown with great respect for the environment in the municipality of Saint-Pierre, at a height of between 650 and 850 metres above sea level. The Torrette Superiore 2000 has well-focused aromas and palate. Ruby red, it has a nose of blackberries and pencil lead. The palate is not massive but nonetheless pleasant and well balanced, and the finish is lifted by mellow, lingering tannins. The pinot grigio-based sweet wine, Lo Bien Flapì, also impressed with notes of honey offset by marked toastiness. The standard Petit Rouge is simple but not banal.

○ Valle d'Aosta Chardonnay Élevé en Fût de Chêne '01	▼▼	5
● Valle d'Aosta Torrette Sup. Élevé en Fût de Chêne '01	▼▼	5
○ Arline Élevé en Fût de Chêne	▼▼	6
○ Declivium	▼▼	6
○ Valle d'Aosta Chardonnay '01	▼	4
○ Valle d'Aosta Müller Thurgau '01	▼	4
● Valle d'Aosta Pinot Noir Élevé en Fût de Chêne '01	▼	5
● Valle d'Aosta Petit Rouge '01		4
● Valle d'Aosta Torrette '01		4
○ Valle d'Aosta Chardonnay Élevé en Fût de Chêne '00	▼▼	5

● Valle d'Aosta Torrette Sup. '00	▼▼	5
● Valle d'Aosta Petit Rouge '01	▼	4
○ Lo Bien Flapì	▼	5

OTHER WINERIES

GABRIELLA MINUZZO
FRAZ. SIZAN, 6
11020 CHALLAND SAINT VICTOR (AO)
TEL. 0125967365 - 0125967514
E-MAIL: gabriella.minuzzo@migrazioni.net

We are again recommending Gabriella Minuzzo's small cellar, which makes no more than 4,000 bottles a year of Müller Thurgau and Pinot Nero. The Pinot Nero ages in both barrique and stainless steel while the Müller Thurgau is one of the best in the region.

○ Valle d'Aosta Müller Thurgau '01	▽	4

CAVES COOPERATIVES DE DONNAS
VIA ROMA, 97
11020 DONNAS (AO)
TEL. 0125807096
E-MAIL: essevi@tin.it

The vineyards of this co-operative, situated at the entry to the valley, yield two selections of Donnas, a dessert wine from 85 per cent nebbiolo, with freisa and neyret. The very good Donnas Napoleone '99 aged for eight months in barrique and a further eight in large barrels.

● Valle d'Aosta Donnas Napoleone '99	▽	5

CAVE DU VIN BLANC
FRAZ. LA RUINE
11017 MORGEX (AO)
TEL. 0165800331
E-MAIL: caveduvinblanc@hotmail.com

The two selections of Blanc de Morgex et de La Salle come from the highest vineyards in Europe. The Rayon is especially good, with its greenish hue and Alpine flower-led nose. The palate shows a vein of acidity through to the medium long finish. The traditional Blanc de Morgex is also quite good.

○ Valle d'Aosta Blanc de Morgex et de La Salle '01	▽	3
○ Valle d'Aosta Blanc de Morgex et de La Salle Rayon '01	▽	4

MAISON ALBERT VEVEY
S.DA DEL VILLAIR, 57
11017 MORGEX (AO)
TEL. 0165808930
E-MAIL: mariovevey@tiscalinet.it

Vevey is a respected name in the Blanc de Morgex DOC and their 6,000 bottles each year continue production of what is known as the "bianco dei ghiacciai", or "glacier white". The 2001 vintage is excellent. Fresh and fragrant on the nose, it has a clean palate with citrus in the finish.

○ Valle d'Aosta Blanc de Morgex et de La Salle '01	▽	4

PIEDMONT

Piedmont is one of the jewels in Italy's winemaking crown. With Tuscany, it continues to keep the flag of Italian wine flying high around the globe. The facts bear this out. Several positive factors have helped Piedmont's wine production to achieve yet another glorious year, proof that the region is bursting with health and vigour. Just take a look at the figures. We tasted approximately 3,500 wines from every corner of the region for this edition of the Guide. Two hundred made it to the final Three Glass tastings and 60 took home the coveted top award. It is important to note that, for the first time, these Three Glass winners come from the whole region, bringing kudos to areas that until now had remained on the fringe. This is further proof of Piedmont's overall good health. Our recent tastings were from excellent, in fact extraordinary, vintages and this no doubt gave the very accomplished Piedmontese winemakers a helping hand. Barolo has profited from the harvest of '98 and has absolutely nothing to envy the legendary vintages of '96 and '97. The same can be said of the Barbaresco, superb in '99, and for the other big categories. There were some magnificent '00 Barberas, as well as standard-label and 2001 vintage wines that have taken full advantage of the perfect weather conditions. For the sake of objectivity, however, we should point out that the overall improvement in quality has been matched by a general increase in prices. This has given – continues to give – cause for alarm, particularly in those areas that have suffered most from international competition. It might not be a bad idea for the producers to sit down and calmly review the situation.

In our review of the Piedmont panorama, the Langhe again confirmed its undisputed authority. Both of its signature types, Barolo and Barbaresco, produced Three Glass wines by the truckload. Roero, across the River Tanaro, also produced sterling results. This land of lightweight whites (Arneis) and reds has come into its own with the red appellation that takes its name from the territory. Some of the wines are very impressive. The vast Monferrato area continues to make progress, with Asti in particular finally finding a faithful warhorse, in the shape of its Barbera, and reinforcements in an ambitious new subzone, Nizza. Our notes would not be complete without a brief mention of this year's star performers. A special round of applause goes to the estates that took home two Three Glasses: Angelo Gaja, La Spinetta, Vietti and Roberto Voerzio. Northern Piedmont celebrates its first Three Glass success with a truly remarkable Fara from the Dessilani estate. Hats off, too, to the impressive return to top form of that grand master of Barolo, Bartolo Mascarello, to a brand new Fontanafredda Barolo and to the Asti De Miranda from the Canelli-based Contratto estate, voted Sweet Wine of the Year, which we hope may breathe new life into the Asti DOC zone, currently a bit under par.

AGLIANO TERME (AT)

DACAPO
STRADA ASTI MARE, 4
14041 AGLIANO TERME (AT)
TEL. 0141964921
E-MAIL: info@dacapo.it

Paolo Dania and Dino Riccomagno, who have been at the helm of the Dacapo estate since its inception in 1997, have gradually fitted out their brand new cellars in Agliano Terme to make them modern and functional. In addition to their two hectares of barbera in Agliano, which provide the base for their Barbera d'Asti Superiore Nizza Vigna Dacapo, Paolo and Dino have an extra three hectares at Castagnole Monferrato planted to barbera and a few rows of merlot and ruché that they rent from Dino's father-in-law. In anticipation of next year's release of the Monferrato Rosso 2001, Dacapo has added a few bottles (less than 1,000) of Ruché di Castagnole Monferrato to the estate's two Barberas, a number that will increase with the next harvest. The strength of this light red, which is not suitable for lengthy cellaring because of its low acidity, lies in its unusually refined aromas of faintly peppery roses. The two Barberas reflect their respective terroirs to perfection. The Castagnole is more immediate and easy-drinking whereas the Superiore di Agliano, released as a Nizza subzone product, is more full-bodied and cellarable. The first of the two, Sanbastiàn, is aged entirely in stainless steel and has a nose redolent of very ripe, predominantly cherry and plum, fruit and a balance that delivers to incredible softness. The other Barbera, Vigna Dacapo, is vinified in oak vats and ages for 12 months in barriques. It possesses greater length, a better defined structure that offsets intense aromas of plum jam against roasted coffee beans, and roundness that is almost overdone.

● Barbera d'Asti Sanbastiàn '00	∏	4*
● Barbera d'Asti Sup. Nizza Vigna Dacapo '00	∏	5
● Ruché di Castagnole Monferrato Bric Majoli '01	♀	4
● Barbera d'Asti Vigna Dacapo '98	∏	4
● Barbera d'Asti Vigna Dacapo '99	∏	4

AGLIANO TERME (AT)

ROBERTO FERRARIS
FRAZ. DOGLIANI, 33
14041 AGLIANO TERME (AT)
TEL. 0141954234
E-MAIL: az.ferraris@virgilio.it

The "new frontier" of Barbera d'Asti looks as if it runs through Agliano Terme, a small, active community in lower Monferrato, that over the last few years has added a passion for viticulture to the traditional tourism and related commercial activities linked to its curative spring waters. Today, the Agliano countryside is dominated barbera vineyards. A good 95 per cent of the land under vine in the municipality is planted with this variety. It is here that Roberto Ferraris, a skilled, enthusiastic grower-producer with a small family business at Dogliani, makes his wines. Roberto's six hectares surround the winery where his wife and brother assist him and Giuliano Noè acts as technical consultant. His annual production of 30,000 bottles of Barbera, which has gradually replaced the tradition of bulk wine started by his grandfather, comes in three versions. We very much liked the La Cricca selection. If it was good before, now it astonishes with the complexity of its aromas, red berry fruit, spices and geranium to the fore, and a richness of palate that make it an excellent wine. The Nobbio, the estate's other major Barbera, is hot on its heels: matured in stainless steel, it is opaque in appearance and very fragrant. Well-rounded on the palate, it promises even better things for the future. Finally, the standard Barbera is pleasant and refreshing, just the way it should be.

● Barbera d'Asti La Cricca '99	∏	5
● Barbera d'Asti '00	♀	3*
● Barbera d'Asti Sup. Nobbio '00	♀	4
● Barbera d'Asti Sup. Nobbio '99	∏	4
● Barbera d'Asti La Cricca '98	♀	5

AGLIANO TERME (AT)

Tenuta Garetto
Strada Asti Mare, 30
14041 Agliano Terme (AT)
tel. 0141954068
e-mail: tenutagaretto@garetto.it

The younger generation has been moving in at many Asti wineries recently. Cellars, once run by wine merchants, are converting into estates, or are at least cutting back on grapes bought in from other zones. Ranges have fewer labels, focusing more on Barbera, and wine is no longer being sold in demijohns. Alessandro Garetto took over from his father in 1997, when he was 27, taking charge of both production and marketing. Since then, the house of Garetto, too, has seen some quite radical changes. Alessandro has almost 20 hectares of vines in Agliano, 14 of which are currently in production. He makes three Barbera selections with the help of oenologist Lorenzo Quinterno. His basic version, the Barbera Tra Neuit e Dì, offers a discreetly refined bouquet of black cherry and rain-soaked earth and a no-nonsense palate where the alcohol makes its presence felt. The In Pectore '00, aged half in used barriques and half in big barrels of Slavonian oak, has a wider-ranging nose that reveals notes of liquorice and leather over and above the regular aromas of black cherry. The palate has a strong, austere character. Alcohol-rich and almost tannic, it recalls traditional Barberas. In contrast, the Barbera Favà '00, matured for 12 months in 50 per cent new barriques, has a more international style. The purplish, almost impenetrable, appearance is accompanied by a nose whose oaky aromas of vanilla and roasted coffee beans combine with grape aromas of cherry and ripe plum, and a juicy, leisurely palate with good balance. Last comes the Chardonnay '01, pleasant if oak-dominated.

• Barbera d'Asti Sup. Favà '00	♛♛	5
• Barbera d'Asti Sup. In Pectore '00	♛♛	4*
• Barbera d'Asti Tra Neuit e Dì '01	♛	3*
○ Piemonte Chardonnay Diversamente '01	♛	4
• Barbera d'Asti Sup. Favà '99	♛♛	5
• Barbera d'Asti Sup. Favà '97	♛♛	5
• Barbera d'Asti Sup. In Pectore '97	♛♛	4
• Barbera d'Asti Sup. Favà '98	♛♛	5
• Barbera d'Asti Sup. In Pectore '98	♛	4
• Barbera d'Asti Sup. In Pectore '99	♛	4

AGLIANO TERME (AT)

Agostino Pavia e Figli
Fraz. Bologna, 33
14041 Agliano Terme (AT)
tel. 0141954125
e-mail: mauro.pavia@crasti.it

Agostino Pavia is a point of reference for Monferrato wines. Firstly, his estate vinifies exclusively its own grapes from a vine stock of almost eight hectares, all in the municipality of Agliano, so the wines are terroir-driven. Secondly, the Pavia family of Agostino and sons Giuseppe and Mauro has devoted itself heart and soul to barbera, which accounts for over 80 per cent of their production. The range of wines offered by the estate comprises three Barbera d'Astis, obtained from single vineyards and vinified using various techniques, and 5,000 bottles of a classic Grignolino offering a white pepper bouquet and rugged tannins. Next year will see the addition of a new recruit to the ranks, the Monferrato Rosso – just 2,000 bottles –, a blend of 85 per cent barbera with merlot and cabernet sauvignon. Here's the rundown on the Pavias' Barberas: 10,000 bottles of Marescialla, obtained from a nearly 60-year-old vineyard, which ages for 13 months in half new barriques; just over 15,000 bottles of Moliss, matured for 11 months partly in 30-hectolitre barrels of Slavonian oak and partly in 900-litre Allier casks; and 18,000 bottles of Bricco Blina, aged entirely in stainless steel. The '00 vintage of the Marescialla is notable for a strong personality that comes through in the bouquet, full of minerally and fruity bottled cherry nuances, and on the palate, which has extraordinary force and a long, harmonious finish. Close behind we have the Moliss, more complex and intricate in its aromas, and the Bricco Blina, which is simpler but velvet-smooth.

• Barbera d'Asti La Marescialla '00	♛♛	5
• Barbera d'Asti Moliss '00	♛♛	4*
• Barbera d'Asti Bricco Blina '00	♛	4
• Grignolino d'Asti '01	♛	3
• Barbera d'Asti La Marescialla '96	♛♛	5
• Barbera d'Asti La Marescialla '98	♛♛	5
• Barbera d'Asti La Marescialla '99	♛♛	5
• Barbera d'Asti Moliss '99	♛♛	4
• Barbera d'Asti La Marescialla '97	♛	5
• Barbera d'Asti Bricco Blina '99	♛	4

AGLIÈ (TO)

Cieck
Fraz. San Grato
Strada Bardesono
10011 Agliè (TO)
tel. 0124330522
e-mail: info@cieck.it

The Cieck estate, one of the most prestigious in the whole Canavese, again presented the panel with a range of very high quality wines. The company that runs this lovely winery in the province of Turin – Remo Falconieri was replaced by daughter Lia in 2000 – offers wines that are made exclusively from the typical varieties of the territory. Erbaluce reigns supreme among the whites while the reds are obtained from barbera, nebbiolo, freisa and the indigenous neretto, a grape that Cieck has exploited with considerable success. The 15 hectares planted to vine, 12 belonging to the estate and three rented, produce approximately 80,000 bottles a year with various versions of Erbaluce di Caluso taking centre stage. Moving onto the tasting notes, we liked both the oak-conditioned Erbaluce di Caluso Calliope and the Misobolo, aged entirely in stainless steel. The first of is a lovely yellow gold and the initial flowery notes open to reveal more complex aromas, all softened by the vanilla tones of the oak. The palate displays lovely structure and good balance. The simpler but highly enjoyable Vigna Misobolo is vinified from start to finish in stainless steel. The Cieck partners - Lodovico Bardesono and Domenico Caretto are the other two – have also proved themselves as "spumante" makers. The "metodo tradizionale" Calliope, from a barrique-conditioned base wine, stands out. One Glass goes to the ever so slightly cloying passito and Two to the very solid Rosso Cieck.

○	Erbaluce di Caluso Vigna Misobolo '01	🍷🍷	3*
●	Canavese Rosso Cieck '00	🍷🍷	4
○	Erbaluce di Caluso Calliope '00	🍷🍷	4
○	Caluso Passito Alladium Vigneto Runc '97	🍷	5
○	Erbaluce di Caluso Spumante Brut Calliope '97	🍷	5
○	Erbaluce di Caluso Spumante Brut S. Giorgio '97	🍷	4

ALBA (CN)

Boroli
Loc. Madonna di Como, 34
12051 Alba (CN)
tel. 0173365477
e-mail: borolivini@borolivini.com

Newcomers Silvano and Elena Boroli have called in experienced oenologist Beppe Caviola to give them a kick-start. Their focus on quality is most clearly evident in the renovation of their vinification cellar and the replanting of the vineyards around the two "cascine", or farmhouses, on the estate, Bompè at Madonna di Como, Alba, and Brunella in Castiglione Falletto. The first has about 14 hectares planted to vine. Moscato, barbera and dolcetto are already in production and cabernet sauvignon and merlot will follow in 2003. The nine hectares at Brunella are largely given over to nebbiolo for Barolo, with some chardonnay. The Moscato Aureum '01 is very well made, flaunting varietal aromas of flowers and ripe grapes, enhanced by grassy notes of moss, sage and new-mown hay. The palate is big, with a good follow-through and a lingering finish. The bright garnet Barolo Villero '98 performs well. Its characterful nose suggests earthiness and wild berries while the progression on the palate is nicely buttressed by an austere, vigorous tannic weave. The basic Barolo is more approachable. Paler in appearance, it has a seductive nose that has yet to develop complexity. The palate is soft and the finish complex. Release of the Barbera Bricco dei Fagiani '00 has been delayed until 2003 so we consoled ourselves with the Bricco 4 Fratelli selection, another '00 vintage, which has a deep garnet hue, plum aromas and a pleasant, harmonious palate. The Dolcetto d'Alba Madonna di Como '01 is up to its usual high standards. A ripe blackberry nose precedes an exceptionally well-balanced palate.

○	Moscato d'Asti Aureum '01	🍷🍷	4*
●	Dolcetto d'Alba Madonna di Como '01	🍷🍷	4
●	Barolo Villero '98	🍷🍷	8
●	Barbera d'Alba Bricco 4 Fratelli '00	🍷	4
●	Barolo '98	🍷	7
●	Barolo La Brunella '96	🍷🍷	7
●	Barolo Bussia '97	🍷🍷	8
●	Barolo Villero '97	🍷🍷	8
●	Dolcetto d'Alba Madonna di Como '00	🍷🍷	4

ALBA (CN)

CERETTO
LOC. SAN CASSIANO, 34
12051 ALBA (CN)
TEL. 0173282582
E-MAIL: ceretto@ceretto.com

ALBA (CN)

GIANLUIGI LANO
FRAZ. SAN ROCCO SENO D'ELVIO
STRADA BASSO, 38
12051 ALBA (CN)
TEL. 0173286958

The tasting notes for Ceretto include the wines of La Bernardina, that magnificent structure in a sea of vines at the entrance to Alba from Barolo, as well as the wines that bear the name of the owners on the labels. The three La Bernardina offerings are obtained from international varieties but still manage to display the typical characteristics of the Langhe. The Langhe Rosso Monsordo, from cabernet sauvignon, pinot nero, merlot and a dash of nebbiolo, is superb. An intense, almost opaque, ruby ushers in faint yet well developed vegetal aromas. The palate is flavoursome and complex, with strong tannins that lend the wine an air of nobility. The Arbarei, a white from 100 per cent riesling, is also quite excellent, its brilliant gold colour already hinting at the wine's generosity. A word of advice here. To enjoy it at its best, don't over-chill it or you will risk losing the tropical fruit and roasted hazelnut aromas. Last in the Bernardina range we have a wonderful "spumante" made from 75 per cent chardonnay with pinot nero. This year, the Barbaresco Asij has excelled itself and captures all the generosity of the vintage. Rich in colour, it has a bouquet that mingles ripe fruit tones with more complex notes of tobacco and spice. The fabulous palate is warm and pervasive, with sweet, smooth tannins. The Barolo Zonchera '98 is austere and classic. The Dolcetto, Barbera and Nebbiolo d'Alba each take home a Glass.

Gianluigi Lano, a keen young winemaker from San Rocco Seno d'Elvio, presented us with a very respectable range of wines this year, despite a spell of very unpredictable weather that saw a vicious hailstorm assault his Barbera vineyards in July. Damage was, of course, considerable. A painstaking selection of the grapes allowed Gianluigi to produce a version of his Fondo Prà that deserves every point of its Two Glass score. The intense, bright ruby hue ushers in a bouquet of cherry and blackberry jam, with notes of vanilla from the barriques that weave perfectly into the rich tapestry of aromas. It is lively on the palate, showing its exuberant youth in a few rough edges that will smooth out over time. Still, the balance of the powerful structure, marked tannins and perceptible but not oppressive vein of acidity is admirable and leads into a clean, satisfying finish. The Barbera d'Alba is also very interesting. A ruby red offering of medium concentration aged in 25-quintal barrels, its nose resonates with cherry and raspberry and the velvet-soft palate shows impressive balance and good length. The garnet Barbaresco '99 is limpid in the glass and possesses varietal aromas of interesting complexity. It is warm and agreeable on the palate, with mature tannins and a long, well-defined finish. The Favorita is simple and fruity while the two Dolcettos are well made. The Ronchella is gutsier and more complex than the basic version, which is still decent.

● Langhe Rosso Monsordo La Bernardina '99	🍷	6
○ Langhe Arbarei La Bernardina '00	🍷🍷	5
○ Piemonte Brut La Bernardina '96	🍷🍷	5
● Barolo Zonchera '98	🍷🍷	7
● Barbaresco Asij '99	🍷🍷	7
● Barbera d'Alba Piana '00	🍷	5
● Nebbiolo d'Alba Lantasco '00	🍷	5
● Dolcetto d'Alba Rossana '01	🍷	4
● Langhe Rosso Monsordo La Bernardina '98	🍷🍷	6
● Barbaresco Asij '98	🍷🍷	7

● Barbera d'Alba '00	🍷🍷	4*
● Barbera d'Alba Fondo Prà '00	🍷🍷	5
● Barbaresco '99	🍷🍷	6*
● Dolcetto d'Alba '01	🍷	3
● Dolcetto d'Alba Ronchella '01	🍷	3
○ Langhe Favorita '01	🍷	3
● Barbaresco '97	🍷🍷	6
● Barbera d'Alba Fondo Prà '97	🍷🍷	5
● Barbaresco '98	🍷🍷	6
● Barbera d'Alba Fondo Prà '98	🍷🍷	5
● Barbera d'Alba Fondo Prà '99	🍷🍷	5

ALBA (CN)

Pio Cesare
Via Cesare Balbo, 6
12051 Alba (CN)
tel. 0173440386
e-mail: piocesare@piocesare.it

Established in 1881, this famous Alba winery is in the midst of renovating its cellars to create more space for the areas given over to vinification. The most impressive of the wines we sampled during our tasting was the Barolo Ornato '98, whose lovely deep garnet-ruby hue heralds a rich bouquet of red berry fruit, cocoa powder and liquorice. The palate, concentrated and potent, reveals just how big the wine's structure is, leading into a long, lingering, complex finish that is luxuriously velvety. The basic Barolo, if not quite up to the standards of its older brother, still boasts a rigorous, tidy nose, vibrant, well-extracted tannins and an austere finish. The Barbaresco Bricco '98 puts on a very youthful show, with a nose that still lacks the harmony and depth to do justice to its solid structure. The basic Barbaresco is very good indeed, with aromas of earth, mint and red berry fruit. There is good weight on the palate, which reveals mature, aristocratic tannins that lead into a sweetly elegant finish. The Chardonnay PiodiLei '00, fermented and aged in barriques, combines a wealth of extract with a stylish personality. The L'Altro '01, obtained from the same variety, offers fruity tones of citrus and banana, then consistent progression on a palate that is extremely agreeable. The Barbera Fides is very tasty and has firm character but is dominated by the oak.

● Barbaresco Bricco '98	♟♟	8
● Barolo Ornato '98	♟♟	8
○ Langhe Chardonnay PiodiLei '00	♟♟	6
● Barolo '98	♟♟	8
● Barbaresco '99	♟♟	8
● Barbera d'Alba Fides '99	♟♟	6
○ Gavi '01	♟	4
○ Langhe Arneis '01	♟	4
○ Piemonte Chardonnay L'Altro '01	♟	4
● Barolo Ornato '85	♟♟♟	6
● Barolo Ornato '89	♟♟♟	6
● Barbaresco Bricco '97	♟♟♟	6

ALBA (CN)

Poderi Colla
Fraz. San Rocco Seno d'Elvio, 82
12051 Alba (CN)
tel. 0173290148
e-mail: info@podericolla.it

The energetic Tino Colla and his niece Federica, with the invaluable support of Federica's father, Beppe, run a lovely estate with 27 hectares planted to vine split across Cascine Drago at San Rocco Seno d'Elvio, in the municipality of Alba, Tenuta Roncaglia in Barbaresco, and Dardi Le Rose in the municipality of Monforte d'Alba, bang in the centre of the Barolo zone. Annual production of 150,000 bottles includes most important wine types of the Alba area. We begin our tasting notes with the flavoursome Barolo Dardi Le Rose. Ruby with orange highlights, it releases lovely complex aromas of cherry and cocoa powder layered over balsam. Nice and fleshy on the palate, it has a generous, lively texture that takes you through to a lingering, consistent finish. The forceful Barbaresco Tenuta Roncaglia hints at traces of raspberry and crushed flowers, then offers a vibrant, full-bodied palate. The superb Bricco del Drago '99, a dolcetto and nebbiolo blend, is intense in colour and unveils notes of violet and tobacco with just a hint of toastiness. The dry palate opens out confidently, ending on a nice bitterish final note. The Barbera d'Alba suggests wild berries and mint against a smoky backdrop then the palate reveals the acidic backbone of the variety. The charming Sanrocco, made from pinot nero vinified without the skins, chardonnay and riesling renano, has lovely aromas of citrus fruit and fruit and a tangy palate of medium intensity. Last on the list is the Nebbiolo d'Alba, a decent wine with a slightly over-evolved, austere bouquet and a not overly challenging palate.

● Barolo Bussia Dardi Le Rose '98	♟♟	7
● Barbaresco Tenuta Roncaglia '99	♟♟	7
● Langhe Bricco del Drago '99	♟♟	5
● Barbera d'Alba '00	♟	4
● Nebbiolo d'Alba '00	♟	5
○ Langhe Sanrocco '01	♟	4
● Barolo Bussia Dardi Le Rose '96	♟♟	7
● Barbaresco Tenuta Roncaglia '97	♟♟	7
● Langhe Bricco del Drago '97	♟♟	5
● Barbaresco Tenuta Roncaglia '98	♟♟	7
○ Bonmé	♟♟	5

ALBA (CN)

PRUNOTTO
REG. SAN CASSIANO, 4/G
12051 ALBA (CN)
TEL. 0173280017
E-MAIL: prunotto@prunotto.it

This celebrated Piedmont estate, established in 1923 by Alfredo Prunotto, was bought by the historic Tuscan house of Antinori at the end of the 1980s. In the last 12 years, the Antinoris have continued to apply the estate's traditional methods. The already impressive quality of the wines has reached even greater heights. Albiera, daughter of Marchese Piero Antinori, is at the helm and has taken on a young oenologist from Alba, Gianluca Torrengo, himself the son of a winemaker. One winning move on the part of the Antinori family has been to invest in vine stock. They have acquired seven hectares in Bussia di Monforte for the production of Barolo, and 27 at Agliano Terme, one of the most important centres for the production of Barbera d'Asti. This year's wines are topped by the stellar Barolo Bussia, whose '98 vintage is an austere offering that fills the mouth and impresses with its character. It's a Barolo that is modern in style but keeps in touch with tradition. We awarded Three well-deserved Glasses to this wine, which weds all the power of a Barolo with the elegance of the Monforte terroir. The high-quality Barbera d'Asti Costamiòle '00 selection has ranked among the best in its category for quite a few years now. Then came the Barbaresco Bric Turot '99, as good as ever, the full-bodied, harmonious fruit of an exceptional harvest, and the Barbera Pian Romualdo '00, which no devotee of the DOC zone should leave untried. The Nebbiolo d'Alba Occhetti and the Dolcetto d'Alba Mosesco add the finishing touch to the magnificent range of Prunotto selections.

● Barolo Bussia '98	▼▼▼	8
● Barbera d'Asti Costamiòle '00	▼▼	7
● Barbera d'Alba Pian Romualdo '00	▼▼	6
● Dolcetto d'Alba Mosesco '00	▼▼	5
● Nebbiolo d'Alba Occhetti '00	▼▼	6
● Barolo '98	▼▼	7
● Barbaresco Bric Turot '99	▼▼	8
● Barbera d'Alba '00	▼	4
● Barbera d'Asti Fiulòt '01	▼	4
● Barbera d'Asti Costamiòle '96	▼▼▼	7
● Barolo Bussia '96	▼▼▼	8
● Barbera d'Asti Costamiòle '97	▼▼▼	7
● Barbera d'Asti Costamiòle '99	▼▼▼	7
● Barolo Bussia '97	▼▼	8
● Barbaresco Bric Turot '98	▼▼	8

ALBA (CN)

MAURO SEBASTE
FRAZ. GALLO
VIA GARIBALDI, 222/BIS
12051 ALBA (CN)
TEL. 0173262148
E-MAIL: maurosebaste@maurosebaste.it

Mauro Sebaste's passion for wine was born in the family winery. He set up his own cellar, which bears his name, in 1991. Mauro buys his grapes from a select group of growers and vinifies them in cellars equipped with state-of-the-art technology. The steady progress in quality is clear from this year's four Two Glass winners. The two Barolos are from the Monvigliero vineyard at Verduno and Prapò at Serralunga. The first offers a refined interpretation, with a seductive bouquet of complex rhubarb, violet and liquorice, then a palate that may not be muscular but is balanced, clean, consistent and long. The Prapò is notable for its bigger structure and a more marked – but not too obvious – note of oak. The Nebbiolo Parigi surprised us with its modern, clean style and nice typicity. The first-rate Dolcetto Santa Rosalia has distinct, lingering aromas of almond, plum, blueberry and violet. The generous, well-sustained palate has just the right note of tannin and a long finish that echoes the nose. The Arneis '01 is a fine example of its category. Elegant notes of apricot and peach, with faint minerally undertones, are followed by a dry mouthfeel that is surprisingly firm and full. The Centobricchi Bianco, a sauvignon-based non-DOC wine compensates for its high-spirited oak with quite remarkable weight and chewiness. The varietal notes, however, are rather muted. The Langhe Rosso Centobricchi, an 80-20 barbera and nebbiolo mix, offers warm, satisfying aromas of super-ripe fruit. Finally, the straightforward Barbera Santa Rosalia combines oak with fruit very well.

● Nebbiolo d'Alba Parigi '00	▼▼	5
● Dolcetto d'Alba S. Rosalia '01	▼▼	4*
● Barolo Monvigliero '98	▼▼	7
● Barolo Prapò '98	▼▼	7
● Barbera d'Alba S. Rosalia '00	▼	4
● Langhe Rosso Centobricchi '00	▼	5
○ Centobricchi '01	▼	5
○ Roero Arneis '01	▼	4
● Barolo Monvigliero '97	▼▼	7
● Barolo Prapò '97	▼▼	7

ALBA (CN)

PODERI SINAGLIO
FRAZ. SAN ROCCO CHERASCA
12051 ALBA (CN)
TEL. 0173612209
E-MAIL: poderi.sinaglio@tiscalinet.it

Bruno and Silvano Accomo, and their parents Amabile and Olga, are the force behind this estate, which has been bottling only since 1995. On the 13 hectares, in the municipalities of Alba and Diano, they grow dolcetto, nebbiolo, barbera, moscato, chardonnay and sauvignon. From this raw material, the Accomo family have, in just a few years, managed to make its mark with wines that score high for quality and value for money. Poderi Sinaglio turns out faultless products, made with scrupulous care, after combing the vineyards for ripe grapes to transform into first-class wines. This year, the array presented to us for tasting was particularly interesting and almost all of the selections romped home with Two Glasses. First on the list is one of the best Diano d'Albas of the year. Almost impenetrable in colour, it throws aromas of ripe fruit, with black cherry and blueberry to the fore, and has a full-bodied, long lingering palate. The Langhe Rosso Sinaij, from freisa, nebbiolo and barbera, is every bit as good, with cherry aromas and a caressing palate whose oak-derived tannins lend a mouthpuckering astringency to the finish. One step up from these is the Barbera Vigna Erta '00, a wine that again demonstrates the potential of the Ricca d'Alba terroir for this grape. Dark in hue, it offers redcurrant with faint traces of vanilla, then mouthfilling roundness on the palate, where the fruit is lifted by hints of spice. The Boccabarile excels among the whites. It's a Chardonnay that still needs to work out the assertiveness left by the oak but it will mellow over the next few months.

● Barbera d'Alba Vigna Erta '00	ȲȲ	4*
● Langhe Rosso Sinaij '00	ȲȲ	4*
● Diano d'Alba Sörì Bricco Maiolica '01	ȲȲ	3*
○ Langhe Chardonnay Boccabarile '00	Ȳ	4
○ Langhe Chardonnay '01	Ȳ	3
● Diano d'Alba Sörì Bricco Maiolica '00	ȲȲ	3
● Langhe Rosso Sinaij '99	ȲȲ	4
● Barbera d'Alba Vigna Erta '99	Ȳ	4
● Nebbiolo d'Alba Giachét '99	Ȳ	4

ALFIANO NATTA (AL)

TENUTA CASTELLO DI RAZZANO
FRAZ. CASARELLO
LOC. GESSI, 2
15021 ALFIANO NATTA (AL)
TEL. 0141922124 – 0141922426
E-MAIL: info@castellodirazzano.it

Thanks to the impressive performance of all the wines in the range, Castello di Razzano has reclaimed its place in the Guide, establishing itself as one of the leading wineries in the Alessandria area of Monferrato that borders on the province of Asti. Augusto Olearo deserves a standing ovation for his work, after taking on, 30 years ago, this panoramic, aristocratic seat built in the 1600s with a stunning view over the surrounding vineyards. Augusto has turned it, sensitively and respectfully, into the functional winery headquarters where all the key operations are carried out. Meanwhile, the estate continues to expand. It now totals 100 hectares, 40 of which are planted to vine, and the annual production capacity is 180,000 bottles, a number that is destined to grow. The Barberas were the best of the wines we tasted this year. The Vigna del Beneficio is fruitier and more complex than usual, with a robust palate that can only improve with cellaring. The Campasso selection is very decent. Produced in large barrels, it is particularly enjoyable for its spicy aromas and round, supple palate. We welcome the Barbera Vigna Valentino Caligaris to the ranks. It's a product that Olearo has earmarked as the future signature wine of the range. Fragrant and vigorous, it is blessed with wonderful, complex balance. Also very good is the Onero, from 100 per cent pinot nero. It is well-structured and has a fragrant fruit nose.

● Barbera d'Asti Sup. Vigna del Beneficio '00	ȲȲ	5
● Barbera d'Asti Sup. Vigna Valentino Caligaris '00	ȲȲ	6
● Barbera d'Asti Sup. Campasso '00	Ȳ	4
● Monferrato Rosso Onero '00	Ȳ	5
● Barbera d'Asti Sup. Campasso '99	Ȳ	4
● Barbera d'Asti Sup. Vigna del Beneficio '99	Ȳ	5
● Monferrato Rosso Onero '99	Ȳ	5

ALICE BEL COLLE (AL)

Ca' Bianca
Reg. Spagna, 58
15010 Alice Bel Colle (AL)
tel. 0144745420
e-mail: giv@giv.it

Ca' Bianca belongs to the Gruppo Italiano Vini. The estate nestles in a charming corner of the countryside among row after row of vine-covered slopes. Marco Galeazzo, the oenologist in charge of the estate, is happy to show off the latest cellar renovations and replantings. The estate's range includes all the major Piedmont wines but focuses on Barbera, which accounts for 50 per cent of the 900,000 bottles produced annually. The cream of the crop is the Chersì, a selection of barbera from the oldest and best vines on the estate. The impressively deep, inky black has a purple edge, then the nose is concentrated and very dense, the initial impression of tobacco and vanilla opening out into plum, cherry, and walnut. The palate bowled us over with its depth and structure. The evident quality of the fruit is more than a match for the rather spirited oak. The Gavi '01 is one of the best in the category. Its bouquet is alluring, with clear, lingering, very varietal aromas, and the palate is harmonious and sophisticated, with an intensity that comes from its sheer frankness. The Barolo '98 offers a refined, mature bouquet with a winning cornucopia of fragrances. The palate melds the fruity, silk-smooth sensations of its modern style with the austere nobility of a traditional Barolo. The Barbera d'Asti '00, correct and vaguely rustic, suggests red fruit, notably raspberry and cherry, vanilla and sweet spices, then displays typical freshness and a pervasive, soft fruitiness on the palate. The Dolcetto d'Acqui '01 has everything you could ask for from a wine for everyday dining.

ASTI

F.lli Rovero
Fraz. San Marzanotto
Loc. Val Donata
14100 Asti
tel. 0141592460
e-mail: grapparovero@inwind.it

The Rovero family get 80,000 bottles a year out of their 16 hectares of vineyards and since 1992, they have carried the AIAB mark, signifying that the wine is made organically. Brothers Claudio, Franco and Michele were joined in 2001 by Enrico, son of Michele, who holds a degree in nutrition and, in addition to the winery, the estate boasts an "agriturismo" farm holiday centre and a distillery. As in previous years, we were offered an array of well-made wines to taste, starting with the dense garnet Barbera Rouvé, which has a concentrated, compelling nose of black berry fruit and pepper. The palate is full-bodied and well sustained. Its somewhat austere character takes you through to a finish that mirrors the aromas on the nose. The cabernet-based Rosso Rocca Schiavino is rich and intense, as is immediately apparent from its deep colour. The aromas range from plum and cakes to green leaf. In the mouth, there is plenty of body, potent tannins and a lengthy finish shot through with liquorice. The Sauvignon Villa Guani has clear but skilfully judged overtones of oak that mingle with nice peach, banana and citrus fruit peel, as well as varietal vegetal aromas The full-bodied palate lingers. The Villa Drago has substantial body and alcohol. The aromas of tomato and country herbs reveal in no uncertain terms the elegant varietal character of this stainless steel-aged Sauvignon. We liked the pinot nero-based Lajetto and enjoyed the vivacious, spicy Grignolino d'Asti.

● Barbera d'Asti Chersì '00	6
○ Gavi '01	4*
● Barolo '98	6
● Barbera d'Asti '00	4
● Dolcetto d'Acqui '01	4
● Barbera d'Asti Chersì '99	6

● Barbera d'Asti Sup. Rouvé '99	5
○ Monferrato Bianco Villa Guani '00	5
○ Monferrato Bianco Villa Drago '01	4*
● Monferrato Rosso Rocca Schiavino '99	5
● Monferrato Rosso Lajetto '00	4
● Grignolino d'Asti Vigneto La Castellina '01	4
● Monferrato Rosso Cabernet '97	5
● Barbera d'Asti Sup. Rouvé '98	5
● Monferrato Rosso Cabernet '98	5

BARBARESCO (CN)

CA' ROMÈ - ROMANO MARENGO
VIA RABAJÀ, 36
12050 BARBARESCO (CN)
TEL. 0173635126
E-MAIL: info@carome.com

The estate run by Romano Marengo and his children Giuseppe and Paola has an annual production of 30,000 bottles, obtained from seven hectares of vines. They have taken the important step of expanding the cellars, which will give them one-third more space to play with than is currently available. The new section of the building, all of which lies below ground level, will connect the two existing structures, making all operations far more efficient. Among the wines we sampled this time around, the Barbaresco Sorì Rio Sordo made a very favourable impression. The '99 vintage is quite a deep garnet, with an orange edge, and has an invigorating bouquet of ginger and pepper with delicate hints of violet, cake and fruit. Harmonious balance and a generous character are in evidence on a palate rounded off by a long, very spirited finish. The Maria di Brun flaunts fabulous finesse and sophistication and a very impressive palate with breadth and a pervasive tannic weave. The standard Barbaresco is decent, with marked aromas of flowers and a pleasantly rugged palate. The Barolo Rapet has a seductive bouquet that ranges from black berry fruit and almond to autumn leaves, then a robust, dry palate. The Barolo Vigna Cerretta has a mineral vein on the nose and a reasonably substantial palate. The Barbera La Gamberaja is slightly etheric on the nose and has a juicy mouthfeel while the Langhe Da Pruvé '99, from nebbiolo and barbera, is pleasant if already a tad forward.

• Barolo Rapet '98	▼▼	7
• Barbaresco Maria di Brun '99	▼▼	8
• Barbaresco Sorì Rio Sordo '99	▼▼	7
• Barbera d'Alba La Gamberaja '00	▼	5
• Barolo Vigna Cerretta '98	▼	7
• Barbaresco '99	▼	6
• Langhe Rosso Da Pruvé '99	▼	5
• Barbaresco Maria di Brun '95	▽▽	8
• Barbaresco Maria di Brun '96	▽▽	8
• Barolo Rapet '96	▽▽	7
• Barbaresco Maria di Brun '97	▽▽	8
• Barolo Rapet '97	▽▽	7
• Barbaresco Maria di Brun '98	▽▽	8

BARBARESCO (CN)

CANTINA DEL PINO
VIA OVELLO, 15
12050 BARBARESCO (CN)
TEL. 0173635147
E-MAIL: cantinadelpino@libero.it

The wines from this estate are made with grapes grown on its six hectares of vineyards, all in the territory of the municipality of Barbaresco. Approximately half of the land is planted to nebbiolo and the rest is shared by dolcetto, barbera and freisa. The Freisa has undergone a transformation since the last vintage. No longer barrique-conditioned, it has perked up again, its medium ruby red ushering in aromas of raspberry, mulberry and delightful flowery tones. The palate, ever so slightly rustic, has decent good nose-palate consistency and the wine is quite well made. The Dolcetto performed better. Deep ruby with violet highlights, its alcohol-rich, red berry fruit nose is followed by a full, well-structured palate with close-knit tannins and a long, clean finish. The Barbera d'Alba, vinified in one and two-year-old barriques, is a medium dark garnet. The nose, redolent of discreetly assertive oak, reveals deep, pervasive sensations of fruit. The palate develops softly and consistently, leading into an enjoyable finish of considerable length. The Barbaresco Ovello, from a zone that produces markedly tannic nebbiolos, is a fairly intense garnet. The initial aromas of oak-derived vanilla are followed by rich notes of fruit and spices. The palate is warm and velvety, displaying a fabulous breadth of flavour, fine-grained tannins and a long, harmonious finish that fulfilled our highest expectations. It's a quite outstanding wine and, for the first time, earned Three Glasses.

• Barbaresco Ovello '99	▼▼▼	6*
• Barbera d'Alba '00	▼▼	4*
• Dolcetto d'Alba '01	▼	3
• Langhe Freisa '01	▼	3
• Barbaresco Ovello '97	▽▽	6
• Barbaresco Ovello '98	▽▽	6
• Barbera d'Alba '98	▽▽	4
• Barbera d'Alba '99	▽▽	4

BARBARESCO (CN)

Tenute Cisa Asinari
dei Marchesi di Grésy
Via Rabajà, 43
12050 Barbaresco (CN)
tel. 0173635221 - 0173635222
e-mail: wine@marchesidigresy.com

This beautiful Barbaresco estate lies in the amphitheatre-like setting of Martinenga. The magic of this enchanting countryside is slightly marred at the moment by restructuring and extension work, improvements that will add an extra 1,000 square metres to the cellar area and create a tasting room worthy of the professionals and winelovers that visit the estate. This year, the cellar only released two Barbarescos, the Camp Gros '98 and the Martinenga '99. The '99 vintages of the Camp Gros and the Gaiun will not be available until 2003, in line with a rational decision by the estate to allow them extra ageing time in the bottle. The Camp Gros '98 is a paragon of its kind and earns Three Glasses. Garnet ruby tinged with orange at the edge, it has a seductive, eloquent nose of liquorice, liqueur cherries and tobacco. The palate has backbone, assertive but aristocratic tannins and an austere finish that lingers endlessly. One for the cellar. The less concentrated Martinenga '99 has a refined, harmonious nose. The Virtus, a cabernet sauvignon and barbera blend, has a fruity, grassy nose and a palate of character and personality. The Dolcetto Monte Aribaldo, the Nebbiolo and the Villa Martis are all very presentable. The latest white, the Villa Giulia, is good and we also very much liked the well-typed Sauvignon, for its broad, lingering aromas, and the barrique-conditioned Chardonnay Grésy. The two Moscatos also performed well.

●	Barbaresco Camp Gros '98	▼▼▼	8
○	Langhe Chardonnay Grésy '00	▼▼	6
○	Langhe Sauvignon '01	▼▼	4*
○	Moscato d'Asti La Serra '01	▼▼	4*
●	Barbaresco Martinenga '99	▼▼	7
●	Langhe Rosso Virtus '99	▼▼	6
○	Piemonte Moscato Passito L'Altro Moscato	▼▼	5
●	Dolcetto d'Alba Monte Aribaldo '01	▼	4
○	Langhe Bianco Villa Giulia '01	▼	4
○	Langhe Chardonnay '01	▼	4
●	Langhe Nebbiolo Martinenga '01	▼	4
●	Langhe Rosso Villa Martis '98	▼	4
●	Barbaresco Gaiun '85	▼▼▼	8
●	Barbaresco Gaiun '97	▼▼▼	8

BARBARESCO (CN)

Giuseppe Cortese
Via Rabajà, 35
12050 Barbaresco (CN)
tel. 0173635131
e-mail: az.cortesegiuseppe@jumpy.it

Giuseppe and Piercarlo Cortese have just finished restructuring and expanding their cellar, which will make operations far more efficient. The style of this small winery, in Rabajà, one of the most beautiful vineyards in Barbaresco, owes much to Langhe tradition but the pair also offer wines of a more modern bent, such as their Chardonnay and Barbera Morassina, both aged in barriques. The Barbaresco Rabajà '99 is garnet with a very faint orange edge. Its slightly evolved nose has touches of jam and spice that lead into subtle nuances of leather. The tonic palate boasts solid structure rounded off by a long, tidy finish. The deep garnet-ruby Barbera d'Alba Morassina parades aromas of blackberry, hay, forest floor and cocoa powder that meld together very seductively, then the full-bodied palate vaunts good weight and character, as well as a finish that mirrors the nose. The Dolcetto Trifolera has a minerally, somewhat rustic, bouquet and an astringent palate. The garnet-flecked ruby of the Nebbiolo hints at red berry fruit and earthiness then the moderately intense palate shows admirable personality. Finally, the pale gold Chardonnay Scapulin has a lovely bouquet of ripe apples and pears but needs to work on balancing the oak.

●	Barbaresco Rabajà '99	▼▼	6
●	Barbera d'Alba Morassina '99	▼▼	4*
○	Langhe Chardonnay Scapulin '00	▼	4
●	Langhe Nebbiolo '00	▼	4
●	Dolcetto d'Alba Trifolera '01	▼	3
●	Barbaresco Rabajà '95	▼▼	6
●	Barbaresco Rabajà '96	▼▼	6
●	Barbaresco Rabajà '97	▼▼	6
●	Barbaresco Rabajà '98	▼▼	6
●	Langhe Nebbiolo '99	▼▼	4

BARBARESCO (CN)

★★★ Gaja
Via Torino, 36
12050 Barbaresco (CN)
tel. 0173635158

BARBARESCO (CN)

Carlo Giacosa
Via Ovello, 8
12050 Barbaresco (CN)
tel. 0173635116

This celebrated Langhe winery has added yet another jewel to crown – three Guide stars, signifying that it has attained the remarkable total of over 30 wines (31 to be precise) deemed worthy of Three Glasses over the 16 editions of the Guide. No other estate in Italy comes close. This year, we sampled seven wines and awarded each of them very high marks. Two took home the top prize, two made it through to the final taste-offs and three won Two Glasses apiece. The Langhe Nebbiolo Sorì San Lorenzo, like its twin Sorì Tildin, is an exercise in elegance. An extraordinary wine that flaunts its class right from the outset in an almost impenetrably deep ruby red. The bouquet is absolutely perfect, offering ringing tones of ripe fruit, blackcurrant and morello cherry layered over a toastiness that never dominates. The palate is rock solid, long and powerful, with fine-grained tannins that enhance the nebbiolo fruit. The Sorì Tildin, another '98, is very similar. A tad more austere in the finish, it will balance out as it ages. The Langhe Darmagi '99, a pure cabernet sauvignon that never fails to delight, has a complex fruity nose of redcurrant and morello cherry and a pronounced, spicy palate. On a par is the Barbaresco '99, which takes advantage of the excellent vintage to acquire extra austerity and elegance. Costa Russi, Sperss and Conteisa, all DOC Langhe Nebbiolo, are extremely well made, lacking just a whisker of the character displayed by the others.

Carlo Giacosa, flanked by daughter Maria Grazia, runs a winery of five hectares, all in the municipality of Barbaresco, except for just over a hectare at Mucin in the municipality of Neive from which Carlo produces a Barbera selection. Annual production totals 35,000 bottles, 18,000 of which are Barbaresco, released in two versions, Montefico and Narin. The former is rich in colour. The fragrant nose is a riot of fruit, ranging from raspberry to redcurrant, that blends well with the flowery tones. The palate is nice and weighty. Its vitality and intensity will grow as it matures. The Narin is not quite so complex, offering aromas of plum and spice and a full body with a faintly bitter finish. The Barbera Lina '00 starts out a little edgy but moves on to release aromas of blueberry and cherry. The palate displays its characteristic sinew and the progression is borne up by a typically acidulous vein right through to the finish, which echoes the nose. The Barbera Mucin '01 is an interesting wine, uncomplicated and carefree yet fleshy. It has a delicious almond and mint nose while the palate is supple and well-balanced. The Dolcetto Cuchet reveals mineral and earthy notes layered over wild berries and comes across ever so slightly aggressive on the palate because of its marked tanginess. The Maria Grazia, a monovarietal Nebbiolo, has a lovely fruity tone and impressive weight.

• Langhe Nebbiolo Sorì S. Lorenzo '98	♛♛♛	8
• Langhe Nebbiolo Sorì Tildin '98	♛♛♛	8
• Barbaresco '99	♛♛	8
• Langhe Darmagi '99	♛♛	8
• Langhe Nebbiolo Conteisa '98	♛♛	8
• Langhe Nebbiolo Costa Russi '98	♛♛	8
• Langhe Nebbiolo Sperss '98	♛♛	8
• Barbaresco Sorì Tildin '93	♛♛♛	8
• Barbaresco Costa Russi '95	♛♛♛	8
• Barbaresco Sorì S. Lorenzo '95	♛♛♛	8
• Langhe Darmagi '96	♛♛♛	8
• Langhe Nebbiolo Costa Russi '96	♛♛♛	8
• Langhe Nebbiolo Sperss '96	♛♛♛	8
• Langhe Nebbiolo Sorì Tildin '97	♛♛♛	8

• Barbera d'Alba Lina '00	♛♛	4*
• Barbaresco Montefico '99	♛♛	6
• Barbera d'Alba Mucin '01	♛	3
• Dolcetto d'Alba Cuchet '01	♛	3
• Maria Grazia '01	♛	4
• Barbaresco Narin '99	♛	6
• Barbaresco Montefico '97	♛♛	6
• Barbaresco Narin '97	♛♛	6
• Barbaresco Montefico '98	♛♛	6
• Barbaresco Narin '98	♛♛	6

BARBARESCO (CN)

Cascina Luisin
Loc. Rabajà, 23
12050 Barbaresco (CN)
Tel. 0173635154

Luigi and Roberto Minuto, owners of this well-known estate, employ modern vinification techniques and meticulous vineyard management to produce terroir-driven wines that age very well indeed. Again this year, we awarded them very high marks in our tasting. The purple-tinged ruby Dolcetto d'Alba Bric Trifüla presents youthful fruity aromas of ripe cherry and plum followed by a velvety, moderately lengthy palate. The dark ruby red Barbera Maggiur possesses the heady, red berry nose typical of a young wine. It is firmly structured on the palate, with noticeable alcohol and a very strong acidic element that lends it balance and zest. The finish is gratifying, moderately long and lively. The Nebbiolo is rather unusual, showing powerful, fascinating notes of raspberry, strawberry and wild red berry fruits in complex nose reminiscent of a Pinot Nero. The Barbaresco Rabajà '99's release on the market has been postponed until 2003. This is a wine that boasts an incredible mouthfeel, but its bouquet is as yet undeveloped and will doubtless benefit from a longer period of ageing in bottle. The dark, garnet Barbaresco Sorì Paolin releases sweet tones of liquorice and morello cherry that spill over onto the palate, which is lifted by rich tannins and a lovely lingering finish. The Barbera Asili '00 has nothing to envy the magnificent '99 vintage. It is exuberant, extraordinarily balanced and pervasive. A truly great wine, its triumphant marriage of power and elegance earns it a resounding Three Glasses.

●	Barbera d'Alba Asili '00	🍷🍷🍷	5
●	Barbera d'Alba Maggiur '01	🍷🍷	4*
●	Langhe Nebbiolo '01	🍷🍷	4
●	Barbaresco Sorì Paolin '99	🍷🍷	6*
●	Dolcetto d'Alba Bric Trifüla '01	🍷	3
●	Barbera d'Alba Asili Barrique '97	🍷🍷🍷	5
●	Barbera d'Alba Asili '99	🍷🍷🍷	5
●	Barbaresco Rabajà '98	🍷🍷	7
●	Barbaresco Sorì Paolin '98	🍷🍷	6
●	Barbaresco Rabajà '97	🍷🍷	7
●	Barbera d'Alba Asili '98	🍷🍷	5

BARBARESCO (CN)

Moccagatta
Via Rabajà, 24
12050 Barbaresco (CN)
Tel. 0173635228 - 0173635152

The estate of Sergio and Franco Minuto has long since passed into the annals of Barbaresco. It commenced activity in 1952 and started bottling its own selections about 30 years later. There are three estate Barbarescos, all superb. The Basarin, obtained from the vineyard with the same name in Neive, the Cole and the Bric Balin, products of the vineyards around the "cascina", or farmhouse, in Barbaresco. The garnet-ruby Basarin is notable for its clean aromas and its impressive execution. The Balin puts on its customary elegant, modern-style performance, with an eloquent, layered nose that discloses sophisticated notes of berry fruit and dried roses. The opulent palate is unbelievably velvety with oaky tones that reverberate throughout the full, satisfying follow-through. The Cole has metamorphosed over the last few years. It remains the most traditional and austere of the three, but since the '95 vintage has been vinified in the same way as the others. Gone are the big barrels and in their place has come skilled use of barriques. The bouquet is full of earthy, fruity sensations through which can be discerned notes of violets and liquorice. The palate is potent, structured and lingering, ending in a substantial, satisfying finish. We liked the Barbera d'Alba Basarin's generous, fruity swansong, for it wasn't released in 2001. The lively Freisa merits One Glass and the juicy Barbera is agreeable and easy to drink. For the Chardonnays, the Buschet is very decent and the simpler standard version is enjoyable.

●	Barbaresco Bric Balin '99	🍷🍷	7
●	Barbera d'Alba Basarin '00	🍷🍷	6
○	Langhe Chardonnay Buschet '00	🍷🍷	5
●	Barbaresco Basarin '99	🍷🍷	7
●	Barbaresco Cole '99	🍷🍷	8
●	Barbera d'Alba '01	🍷	4
○	Langhe Chardonnay '01	🍷	4
●	Langhe Freisa '01	🍷	4
●	Barbaresco Bric Balin '90	🍷🍷🍷	7
●	Barbaresco Cole '97	🍷🍷🍷	7
●	Barbaresco Bric Balin '98	🍷🍷	7

BARBARESCO (CN)

MONTARIBALDI
FRAZ. TRE STELLE
VIA RIO SORDO, 30/A
12050 BARBARESCO (CN)
TEL. 0173638220
E-MAIL: montaribaldi@tiscali.it

Luciano and Roberto Taliano, assisted by their respective wives Antonella and Franca, and by their parents, cultivate approximately 15 hectares of vines, from which they get an annual production of 38,000 bottles. New developments on the estate include the expansion of the cellars that, along with the new equipment they have acquired, will make their operations more efficient. Best of the wines offered for tasting was the Barbera dü Gir, with its dense garnet and seductive aromas of cake, hay and jam. Entry on the palate is full, then there is good balance and energy in mid palate, followed by a long finish. The Barbaresco Sörì Montaribaldi is a tad under par this year but is still very pleasant. Dark in hue, it has a fruity, rather evolved nose, with hints of fresh sea breezes. The palate is characteristically full-bodied. The Chardonnay Stissa d'le Favole is good, if somewhat overawed by the oak. Its rich colour ushers in a nose that ranges from cake to fruit. The palate is quite pervasive and the finish hints at caramel. We gave One Glass to the Arneis for its frank fruity tones and supple, very satisfying palate. The Nebbiolo Gambarin has a sweet, flowery nose and a no-nonsense, pleasantly rustic, flavour. Last but not least, the year 2000 produced 2,500 bottles of a new Barbaresco selection, Palazzina, which we will be coming back to in the next edition the Guide.

BARBARESCO (CN)

I PAGLIERI
LOC. PAJÉ
VIA RABAJÀ, 8
12050 BARBARESCO (CN)
TEL. 0173635109

"Looking to the future from tradition" would make a fitting motto for I Paglieri, whose cellars snuggle in the Pajé vineyard at Barbaresco. The Roagna family has run this winery for four generations, according to the same philosophy: make high quality wine and treat vines and land with the utmost respect. Sometimes, as this year, they delay the release of some of their wines. Consequently, we will not have the pleasure of tasting the Barbaresco Crichèt Pajé '98 or the Opera Prima XV until next year, as they are still ageing. The future lies in the hands of Luca, who has just graduated from the school of oenology in Alba and enrolled at the Faculty of Agrarian Science in Turin to hone his wine-making skills. He is determined to develop the family business, much to the joy of his parents, Alfredo and Luigina. Moving onto the wines, we sampled the chardonnay-based Langhe Bianco '01, the estate's sole concession to international varieties. Golden yellow, with a bouquet of aniseed, ripe fruit, and acacia blossom, it has a palate buttressed by rich fruitiness and acidity that is kept in check by the structure. The Barolo La Rocca e La Pira '98 is excellent. It comes from a vineyard at Castiglione Falletto known for austere nebbiolo. The Barbaresco Pajé '99 presents aromas of rhubarb and spice, a severe palate, big body and fine-grained tannins that linger through the unhurried finish. The golden yellow Solea '00, from chardonnay with a dash of nebbiolo vinified without the skins, looks tempting but the nose and the palate reveal over-evolved tones let the structure down.

● Barbera d'Alba dü Gir '00	▼	4*
○ Langhe Chardonnay Stissa d'le Favole '00	▼	4
● Langhe Nebbiolo Gambarin '00	▼	5
○ Roero Arneis '01	▼	4
● Barbaresco Sörì Montaribaldi '99	▼	6
● Barbera d'Alba dü Gir '99	▼▼	4
● Barbaresco Sörì Montaribaldi '97	▼▼	6
● Barbaresco Sörì Montaribaldi '98	▼▼	6
● Barbera d'Alba dü Gir '98	▼▼	4

○ Langhe Bianco '01	▼▼	4*
● Barolo La Rocca e La Pira '98	▼▼	8
● Barbaresco Pajé '99	▼▼	8
○ Langhe Solea '00	▼	5
● Barbaresco Crichèt Pajé '96	▼▼	8
● Barolo La Rocca e La Pira '96	▼▼	8
● Barbaresco Crichèt Pajé '97	▼▼	8
● Barolo La Rocca e La Pira '97	▼▼	8
● Opera Prima XIV	▼▼	8

BARBARESCO (CN)

PRODUTTORI DEL BARBARESCO
VIA TORINO, 52
12050 BARBARESCO (CN)
TEL. 0173635139
E-MAIL: produttori@barbaresco.com

Established in 1958, the Cantina dei Produttori del Barbaresco today numbers around 60 members who work a total of 100 hectares and produce 400,000 bottles annually. These are impressive statistics that, combined with the growing quality of their wines, put this winery at the forefront of the Barbaresco worldwide. There are several Riservas from the most prestigious vineyards in the DOC zone. Of these, the Rio Sordo earns Three Glasses and the Montestefano takes home two and a half. The former proffers alluring smoky tones over a strong fruity backdrop of blackberry and plum. The well-structured palate has all the typical rigour of a traditional Nebbiolo and signs off with a fantastically long finish that smacks of liquorice. The Rabajà releases aromas of balsam and cocoa powder and has a slightly meeker palate. The Moccagatta revels in an aromatic herb and fruit bouquet and a long, pleasant palate. The Pora offers hints of cake and a full, dry palate with reasonably long length. Mineral notes can be discerned in the bouquet of the Pajé, whose palate strongly echoes the fruit. The magnificent Montestefano boasts a spicy nose profile and a decisive, richly extracted palate. The Ovello is somewhat evolved, while the Asili has a sweet if not altogether harmonious bouquet. The Montefico is a tad severe, offering aromas of hay, mint and jam. Rounding off the range we have the staunchly reliable standard Barbaresco, a nice, well-managed wine.

- Barbaresco Vigneti in Rio Sordo Ris. '97   6*
- Barbaresco Vigneti in Montestefano Ris. '97   6*
- Barbaresco Vigneti in Moccagatta Ris. '97   6
- Barbaresco Vigneti in Ovello Ris. '97   6
- Barbaresco Vigneti in Pajé Ris. '97   6
- Barbaresco Vigneti in Pora Ris. '97   6
- Barbaresco Vigneti in Rabajà Ris. '97   6
- Barbaresco Vigneti in Asili Ris. '97   6
- Barbaresco '98   5

BARBARESCO (CN)

ALBINO ROCCA
VIA RABAJÀ, 15
12050 BARBARESCO (CN)
TEL. 0173635145
E-MAIL: roccaalbino@globwine.com

Angelo Rocca, an energetic and enthusiastic winemaker, is the owner of this beautiful winery in the municipality of Barbaresco. He has slightly increased his total area of vineyards this year with the acquisition of a new plot of nebbiolo straddling San Rocco and Treiso. This will permit him to extend the estate's range of wines and release a new label in 2004. We'll start our tasting notes with the most seductive of his offerings, the Brich Ronchi '99. It's a splendid, brilliant garnet-ruby Barbaresco with a full, complex nose ranging from berry fruit and liquorice to balsam and sweet hints of oak. The palate is round and mirrors the nose, unveiling mature, tightly-knit tannins and a harmonious, never-ending finish. The garnet Vigneto Loreto is less intense in appearance than the Ronchi and has a more austere character. Its bouquet, full and spicy, suggests plum and heralds a big body and dense, chewy mouthfeel. This thoroughbred Barbaresco has a very clean, lingering finish. Our advice is to stow it in the cellar for a few years. The Barbera Gepin, blessed with fascinating aromas and remarkable extract, is as yet very young and slightly untogether. The Dolcetto Vignalunga is fruity and extremely enjoyable. Of the whites on offer, we particularly enjoyed the Langhe La Rocca, obtained from barrique-conditioned cortese grapes. We are happy to welcome Paola to the winery's ranks. She has just graduated from the school of oenology in Alba and is willing and eager to work with her father, Angelo.

- Barbaresco Vigneto Brich Ronchi '99   7
- Barbaresco Vigneto Loreto '99   7
- Barbera d'Alba Gepin '00   5
- Dolcetto d'Alba Vignalunga '01   4*
- O Langhe Bianco La Rocca '01   5
- O Langhe Chardonnay da Bertü '00   4
- Barbaresco Vigneto Brich Ronchi '93   7
- Barbaresco Vigneto Brich Ronchi '96   7
- Barbaresco Vigneto Brich Ronchi '97   7
- Barbaresco Vigneto Loreto '98   7
- Barbera d'Alba Gepin '99   5

BARBARESCO (CN)

Bruno Rocca
Via Rabajà, 29
12050 Barbaresco (CN)
tel. 0173635112
e-mail: brunorocca@libero.it

A pioneer of quality in Barbaresco, Bruno Rocca steadfastly continues to pursue his goal of imbuing all his wines with the uniqueness of their territory. His results justify his enormous enthusiasm. Bruno's wines, which favour elegance over power, are again excellent this year. The Rabajà '99, from one of the most prestigious Barbaresco vineyards, captivates with an exhilarating performance, again affirming the extraordinary personality of this selection. Deep, dark garnet, it has a spicy, well-developed, complex nose that still has room to develop. Aromas range from hazelnut, berry fruit, tobacco and violets to cocoa powder. The palate is quite simply awe-inspiring, echoing the aromas of the bouquet to perfection in a wonderfully velvety, harmonious framework of verve and vigour. The Barbaresco Coparossa, from the same great vintage, is also very good. It is comes from grapes grown at Neive and presents a garnet-ruby colour, a seductive, extremely sophisticated nose with sweet aromas of ripe peach and traces of balsam that blend nicely with the oak, then a voluptuous, well-balanced palate. The Barbera '00 is superb, its profound ruby tinged with purple ushering in a deep, concentrated bouquet redolent of plum and blackberry jam, then impressive structure. The Rabajolo '99, a cabernet sauvignon, nebbiolo and barbera blend, the dense, fruity Dolcetto '01 and the barrique-conditioned Chardonnay '00 are all very enjoyable and irreproachably made.

● Barbera d'Alba '00	♟♟	6
● Barbaresco Rabajà '99	♟♟	8
○ Langhe Chardonnay Cadet '00	♟♟	5
● Dolcetto d'Alba Vigna Trifolé '01	♟♟	4
● Barbaresco Coparossa '99	♟♟	8
● Langhe Rosso Rabajolo '99	♟♟	7
● Barbaresco Rabajà '93	♟♟♟	8
● Barbaresco Rabajà '96	♟♟♟	8
● Barbaresco Coparossa '97	♟♟♟	8
● Barbaresco Rabajà '98	♟♟♟	8
● Barbera d'Alba '99	♟♟	6

BARBARESCO (CN)

Rino Varaldo
Via Secondine, 2
12050 Barbaresco (CN)
tel. 0173635160

Brothers Rino and Michele Veraldo, assisted by their father Pier, make a wide range of excellent wines that together bring total production to 45,000 bottles a year. Their Barolo Vigna di Aldo '98, obtained from a plot in the municipality of Barolo that lies in the Terlo vineyard, is garnet with a bouquet that on first impression comes across a bit minerally. Then it slowly opens to embrace notes of fruit, green leaf and spices. Liveliness and flavoursome flesh are evident on the palate and flow into a long, liquorice finish. The Bricco Libero is the better made of the two '99 vintage Barbarescos, revealing a rich garnet-ruby hue with a compact edge and lovely aromas of liquorice, wild berries, and thyme, all set against a complex mineral background. The palate has austerity and confidence, with alcoholic warmth in mid palate and lingering after-aromas that dwell on fruit. The Sorì Loreto has a slightly evolved nose but lovely weight in the mouth. The Barbera Vigna delle Fate '00, flanked this year by the simple standard Barbera, shows aromas of tobacco, dried flowers and truffle and a palate that progresses brightly and juicily, ending on a note of cocoa powder. The barbera, nebbiolo, cabernet and merlot-based Rosso Fantasia 4.20 (the four grape types are matured in barriques for 20 months) displays a balanced, clean fruitiness. The Dolcetto is pleasant and invigorating, while the Freisa is sturdy and the Nebbiolo simple.

● Barbaresco Bricco Libero '99	♟♟	7
● Barbera d'Alba Vigna delle Fate '00	♟♟	5
● Langhe Rosso Fantasia 4.20 '00	♟♟	5
● Barolo Vigna di Aldo '98	♟♟	7
● Barbaresco Sorì Loreto '99	♟♟	7
● Dolcetto d'Alba '01	♟	4
● Langhe Freisa '01	♟	4
● Langhe Nebbiolo '00		5
● Barbera d'Alba '01		4
● Barbaresco Bricco Libero '97	♟♟♟	8
● Barbaresco Bricco Libero '98	♟♟	8
● Barolo Vigna di Aldo '95	♟♟	8
● Barbaresco Bricco Libero '96	♟♟	8
● Barbaresco Sorì Loreto '98	♟♟	8

BAROLO (CN)

GIACOMO BORGOGNO & FIGLI
VIA GIOBERTI, 1
12060 BAROLO (CN)
TEL. 017356108
E-MAIL: borgogno-barolo@libero.it

Traditionally, Barolos, and in particular those from a great vintage like '97, require a prolonged period of bottle ageing to develop their full potential. This rule, scrupulously observed by many of the renowned Barolo producers, has been adopted by the Borgogno estate at Barolo, which can trace its winemaking origins all the way back to 1761. Every year, the cellar puts several thousand bottles of Barolo to one side, in its quest to observe tradition, and today can include several legendary vintages on its list, including the '47, the '58 and the '67. All are still absolutely sound and eminently drinkable. Of the wines we tasted for this year's edition of the Guide, the Barolo Liste stood out, distinguished by the estate label originally used in the 1800s and resurrected to adorn this major selection. Liste is a prestigious, quite small, vineyard on the borders of the municipal territories of Barolo and La Morra. The Borgongo cellar makes about 4,000 bottles a year from this selection. The '97 releases aromas of violets and liquorice that meld with etheric hints tones and notes of tar. Austere and balanced on the palate, it has a refined, elegant flavour and the finish is lifted by fine-grained tannins. The Barolo Classico, obtained from grapes grown in the Liste, San Pietro delle Viole, Cannubi, Cannubi Boschis and Brunate vineyards, all in the municipality of Barolo, also displays good character. The standard Barolo is a bit more predictable, the Barbera d'Alba fruity, and the second-label Dolcetto is youthful and alcohol-rich.

● Barolo Liste '97	♛♛	8
● Barolo Cl. '97	♛♛	7
● Barbera d'Alba '01	♛	4
● Dolcetto d'Alba '01	♛	4
● Barolo '97	♛	7
● Barolo Cl. '93	♛♛	8
● Barolo Cl. '96	♛♛	8
● Barolo Liste '96	♛♛	8

BAROLO (CN)

GIACOMO BREZZA & FIGLI
VIA LOMONDO, 4
12060 BAROLO (CN)
TEL. 0173560921
E-MAIL: brezza@brezza.it

The Brezza winery has become a must-see at Barolo for food and wine tourists, especially the German-speaking variety, who have peacefully invaded the Langhe region over the last few years. The Brezzas also have a restaurant serving traditional food attached to a comfortable hotel, a small welcoming "osteria"-style bar and cellars where visitors can buy a broad range of local wines, including several Barolos. Thanks to – or because of – the foreign tourists, this estate, which has an impressive total of almost 23 hectares under vine, has yet to win the recognition it deserves with Italian wine lovers. And yet the combined efforts of brothers Marco and Giacomo, who work some of the best vineyards in the municipality of Barolo, and their cousin Enzo in the cellars, produce fabulous wines that reflect the austerity of their production methods. Best of the three Barolos offered was the Sarmassa '98, which impressed the panel and came close to a third Glass. It has a well-developed, complex nose with distinct, mature notes of dried roses and strawberry jam, followed by a very vigorous, powerful palate and a long, zesty finish. We were less impressed with the Barolos from Cannubi. The '97 is decent and has an impressively wide-ranging bouquet but lacks the depth and balance of the Sarmassa, while the '98 combines a mature nose with a bit of a lean palate. The Dolcetto San Lorenzo and the Freisa Santa Rosalia '01 also take home Two Glasses this year. Both are well-structured and wonderfully drinkable, admirably exemplifying their respective grape types.

● Barolo Sarmassa '98	♛♛	7
● Dolcetto d'Alba S. Lorenzo '01	♛♛	4
● Langhe Freisa Santa Rosalia '01	♛♛	3*
● Barolo Cannubi '97	♛♛	7
● Barolo Cannubi '98	♛	7
● Barolo Cannubi '96	♛♛♛	7
● Barolo Bricco Sarmassa '97	♛♛	7
● Barolo Cannubi '90	♛♛	8
● Barolo Castellero Ris. '90	♛♛	8
● Barolo Sarmassa '96	♛♛	7
● Barolo Sarmassa '97	♛♛	7
● Barolo Cannubi '95	♛	7

BAROLO (CN)

DAMILANO
VICOLO SAN SEBASTIANO, 2
12060 BAROLO (CN)
TEL. 017356265 - 017356105
E-MAIL: damilanog@damilanog.com

The Damilano estate has taken on a youthful aspect over the last two years. Giovanni Damilano, who breathed new life into this well-known Barolo winery, has retired, having passed on his substantial winemaking skills to his sons Mario and Paolo and grandchildren Margherita and Guido. The new generations have brought a slew of innovations, from the revamping – largely from a cosmetic point of view – of the old but functional cellars to the quest for vineyards to enhance the four hectares they already own. Next on the list is the probable release of their Barolo Cannubi Boschis '01 and, a little further down the line, of a Barolo Meriondino. Their strategic objective for the next ten years is to expand the current production of 18,000 bottles, almost all of it Barolo, to about 60,000 bottles. In terms of numbers, they still have a long way to go but in terms of quality the Damilanos have already scaled the heights, scoring very high marks with both of their Barolo selections, the '98 Liste and Cannubi vintages. The first of these, half conditioned in new barriques, has a sophisticated, complex nose of Peruvian bark, tar and Eastern spices that blend with nuances of raspberry. The wonderfully harmonious palate is backed up by the caressing silkiness of the sweet tannins. The Cannubi '98, aged for 24 months in new barriques, is also a winner. It has a touch less force but all the balance of a thoroughbred. The fruity Barbera d'Alba '00 is drinking well now, while the simple Dolcetto '01 could stand a little more time in the cellar.

• Barolo Cannubi '98	🍷🍷	8
• Barolo Liste '98	🍷🍷	7
• Barbera d'Alba '00	🍷🍷	5
• Dolcetto d'Alba '01	🍷	4
• Barolo '97	🍷🍷	6
• Barolo Cannubi '97	🍷🍷	8
• Barbera d'Alba '99	🍷🍷	5

BAROLO (CN)

GIACOMO GRIMALDI
VIA LUIGI EINAUDI, 8
12060 BAROLO (CN)
TEL. 017335256

We welcome a newcomer to the Guide this year in the shape of the Giacomo Grimaldi estate, competently run by the entire family (mother, father and son). The energetic 36-year-old Ferruccio can take the credit for having pushed the winery to start bottling in 1996. The estate's almost eight hectares are not all in production yet but by the time it is up and running, around 2006, it should have a total capacity of over 40,000 bottles. Until the harvest of 1999, the grapes of their one and only Barolo came from Le Coste at Barolo but 2000 will see the release of a Sotto Castello selection from Novello and in 2001, there will also be a Terlo, from Barolo. In its third vintage, the Barolo Le Coste has adjusted its sights and a strong, personal style is emerging. The Le Coste '98, still rather closed but promising well for the future if it is left to age longer in the bottle, stunned us with its dense ruby colour. The firm fruit and spice bouquet has yet to realize its full potential while the palate shows fabulous body and good length. With time, it will become soft and velvety. Of the two Barberas, we favoured the Pistìn '01 for its distinctive, upfront cherry fruit, over the Fornaci '00, which spends 18 months in barrique and comes across as alcohol-rich and rather oaky. The oak from barrique and barrel is less persistent in the excellent Nebbiolo d'Alba, which has its origins at Valmaggiore, Vezza d'Alba, in Roero and gives full rein to the flowery aromas of its variety. The estate also has a fine, distinctively typical Dolcetto '01 with heady fruit aromas and silky tannins.

• Nebbiolo d'Alba '00	🍷🍷	4
• Barbera d'Alba Pistìn '01	🍷🍷	4
• Dolcetto d'Alba '01	🍷🍷	3*
• Barolo Le Coste '98	🍷🍷	7
• Barbera d'Alba Fornaci '00	🍷	5

BAROLO (CN)

MARCHESI DI BAROLO
VIA ALBA, 12
12060 BAROLO (CN)
TEL. 0173564400
E-MAIL: marchesi.barolo@marchesibarolo.com

Every year the range of wines released by the Marchesi di Barolo winery is more solid and quality is always extremely high. The roots of this success lie in the technical skills of oenologist Roberto Vezza and, above all, in the new entrepreneurial spirit that has infected the estate run by Ernesto Abbona and his wife Anna. This year is no exception and the wines of the Marchesi di Barolo enjoyed a great reception from our tasting panel, which particularly liked the '98 Barolos. We start with the Barolo Vigne di Proprietà in Barolo (formerly labelled Estate Vineyard), which represents the estate at its most innovative. Deep garnet, it has subtle, elegant aromas with undertones of toastiness never threaten to intrude. The palate is richly extracted, long and velvety, with an etheric note of alcohol that melds with tannins that have mellowed during cask-conditioning. This very sophisticated wine again wins Three Glasses. The other two Barolos, obtained from superb vineyard selections from Cannubi and Sarmassa, are a notch below. The Cannubi is refined and velvety while the Sarmassa is austere and well-rounded. We liked the Boschetti best of the Dolcettos. It's a very well-structured wine that foregrounds the great fruit of the dolcetto grape. The Barbera d'Alba Pajagal, from the famed Barolo vineyard of the same name, performed very well. Dark, opaque ruby red, it unveils ripe fruit aromas tinged with attractive oaky notes. Sweet on the palate, it is long and harmoniously fruity.

BAROLO (CN)

BARTOLO MASCARELLO
VIA ROMA, 15
12060 BAROLO (CN)
TEL. 017356125

Last year, we noted in the Guide that: "Vintage after vintage Bartolo Mascarello has been repeating the same winemaking rituals, defending them against the temptations of modernity he sees as incompatible with typicity and tradition". When we tasted his Barolo '98, obtained from grapes grown in Cannubi, San Lorenzo, Ruè and Rocche, we found that it bore out this sentiment. It is the most convincing edition we have tasted for a long time. The bottle enables Bartolo Mascarello, who was joined by his daughter Maria Teresa a few years ago, to restake his claim to our highest award. The Barolo '98 is a superb tribute to the fruit from the estate's plots, displaying balance, elegance and austerity. Its appearance, already showing orange at the edge, is the perfect embodiment of Barolo's typicity. Red berry fruit, tobacco and liquorice rise to tempt the nostrils in a bouquet of exceptional complexity and sheer delight. Triumphant and awesomely aristocratic, it will entrance all those who love oak and toastiness. The palate comes close to perfection with its earthy tones. Acidity and tannins are firmly braced by the noble structure. This is a wine to be savoured with the calm, reflective wisdom of the true connoisseur. The Dolcetto d'Alba '01 shows nice body and the Barbera San Lorenzo, which has had an extra year to mature, has managed to bring the variety's trademark acidity under control.

Wine	Glasses	Score
● Barolo Vigne di Proprietà in Barolo '98	ỲỲỲ	8
● Barbera d'Alba Pajagal '00	ỲỲ	5
● Langhe Rosso Pi Cit '00	ỲỲ	7
● Dolcetto d'Alba Boschetti '01	ỲỲ	4*
● Barolo Cannubi '98	ỲỲ	7
● Barolo Sarmassa '98	ỲỲ	7
● Barbera d'Alba Ruvei '00	Ỳ	4
● Dolcetto d'Alba Madonna di Como '01	Ỳ	4
● Barolo Ris. Grande Annata '95	Ỳ	7
● Barbaresco Ris. Grande Annata '97	Ỳ	6
● Barolo Estate Vineyard '90	ỲỲỲ	8
● Barolo Estate Vineyard '97	ỲỲỲ	8
● Barolo Sarmassa '97	ỲỲ	8

Wine	Glasses	Score
● Barolo '98	ỲỲỲ	8
● Dolcetto d'Alba Monrobiolo e Ruè '01	ỲỲ	4
● Barbera d'Alba Vigna S. Lorenzo '00	Ỳ	5
● Barolo '83	ỲỲỲ	8
● Barolo '84	ỲỲỲ	8
● Barolo '85	ỲỲỲ	8
● Barolo '89	ỲỲỲ	8
● Barolo '88	ỲỲ	8
● Barolo '90	ỲỲ	8
● Barolo '93	ỲỲ	8
● Barolo '96	ỲỲ	8
● Barolo '97	ỲỲ	8

BAROLO (CN)

E. Pira & Figli - Chiara Boschis
Via Vittorio Veneto, 1
12060 Barolo (CN)
Tel. 017356247
E-mail: piracb@libero.it

This small Barolo winery, which has only two and half hectares to its name in Cannubi and Via Nuova (the latter will make its debut with the '99 vintage), has made the transition from a fiercely traditional style, best embodied by old Gigi Pira, the last man in the Langhe to tread his grapes, to an extremely innovative approach. The person responsible is Chiara Boschis, one of the first to adopt malolactic fermentation and vinify her Barolo entirely in new barriques, starting with the harvest of '94. The Boschis family, who own Borgogno, bought the estate in 1981 and today it belongs to the dynamic Chiara. Long famed for Barolo (approximately 10,000 bottles a year), this time round there are also 2,000 bottles each of Dolcetto and Barbera. Both are oak-conditioned – used barriques for the Dolcetto and some new for the Barbera – to give the wine greater harmony. The Dolcetto '01 blends notes of tobacco with classic red berry fruit and on the palate has a tannic weave that is a tad austere but very alluring. The Barbera '00 is softer, with barely discernible fumé notes and sophisticated liqueur cherries. The mainstay of this prestigious estate is clearly its Barolo Cannubi, whose '98 vintage is just a whisker shy of the Three Glass mark. Dazzling garnet-ruby in colour, it shows powerful aromas of mainly raspberry and strawberry fruit, offset by refined touches of vanilla. In deference to the vintage and the selection, the palate foregrounds elegance and balance.

- Barolo Cannubi '98 🍷🍷 8
- Barbera d'Alba '00 🍷🍷 5
- Dolcetto d'Alba '01 🍷🍷 3*
- Barolo Ris. '90 🍷🍷🍷 8
- Barolo '94 🍷🍷🍷 8
- Barolo Cannubi '96 🍷🍷🍷 8
- Barolo Cannubi '97 🍷🍷🍷 8
- Barolo '93 🍷🍷 8
- Barolo Cannubi '95 🍷🍷 8

BAROLO (CN)

Giuseppe Rinaldi
Via Monforte, 3
12060 Barolo (CN)
Tel. 017356156

To discuss Beppe Rinaldi's winery is to evoke the history of Barolo in the 19th and 20th centuries. In 1870, the family bought a "cascina" that came with vineyards in Barolo from a Falletti estate manager. In the 1920s, Battista Rinaldi inherited from his father Giuseppe the approximately eight hectares planted to vine in the municipality's most prestigious vineyards as well as the main property, just outside Barolo. Today, they still make up the vineyards and cellars of the estate. Battista Rinaldi, who graduated with a degree in oenology in the early 1940s, pioneered Barolo vinification methods of long macerations on the skins, extended ageing in large barrels of Slavonian oak and prolonged cellaring in the bottle before release on the market with two other grand masters, Giulio Mascarello and Giacomo Conterno. When Battista passed away in 1992, his son Beppe gave up his career as a vet to follow in his father's footsteps. Currently, the estate has a total of ten hectares under vine and produces almost exclusively Barolo, plus a few bottles of Barbera, Dolcetto and an interesting Ruché called Rosae. This year's Brunate-Le Coste almost matched last year's version. It has the wonderful complexity of a classic Barolo, with pungent aromas of liqueur cherries, dried roses, liquorice and juniper berries. The palate is juicy with fabulous balance, rising in a crescendo in the finish. The Barolo Cannubi San Lorenzo-Ravera is satisfying, soft and leisurely, with just a shade less character than the Brunate-Le Coste.

- Barolo Brunate-Le Coste '98 🍷🍷 7
- Barolo Cannubi S. Lorenzo-Ravera '98 🍷🍷 7
- Barolo Brunate-Le Coste '97 🍷🍷🍷 7
- Barolo Brunate-Le Coste '95 🍷🍷 7
- Barolo Brunate-Le Coste '96 🍷🍷 7
- Barolo Cannubi S. Lorenzo-Ravera '95 🍷🍷 7
- Barolo Cannubi S. Lorenzo-Ravera '96 🍷🍷 7
- Barolo Cannubi S. Lorenzo-Ravera '97 🍷🍷 7

BAROLO (CN)

Luciano Sandrone
Via Pugnane, 4
12060 Barolo (CN)
Tel. 0173560023 - 0173560024
E-mail: info@sandroneluciano.com

Luciano Sandrone has completed work on his new cellars in the lower part of Barolo and while he has already vinified his last few harvests in this magnificent locale, winemaking will now be a much more relaxed affair for the family. The new structure can deal efficiently with the grapes produced on the estate's approximately 21 hectares of vineyards, partially their own and partially rented, that provide just under 100,000 bottles a year. With more refined vinification and conditioning in predominantly new 900-litre casks, the functional new space will allow Sandrone to give full rein to his style, which favours velvety wines bursting with fruity sensations. The Cannubi Boschis '98 is right at home in this line-up. Vibrant in colour, it flaunts a well-defined bouquet of raspberry-led fruit that melds with toastiness, spice and traces of juniper berry. The palate is potent and flavour-packed, filling the mouth with a wealth of smooth tannins. The Le Vigne has pretensions to greater things but lacks the class and the character of its stablemate. A blend of barbera and nebbiolo, the Langhe Rosso Pe Mol '00 is distinctive for the velvety lushness of its fruit. All this plus a range of basic wines that consistently rank among the best in the Langhe. The Barbera d'Alba '00, oak-aged and ripe with aromas of cherry and sweet spices, is borne aloft by a powerful fruity palate that signs off with a long, velvet-smooth finish. Last of the wines on offer are the soft, warm Dolcetto '01 and the well-balanced, flowery Nebbiolo d'Alba '00.

BAROLO (CN)

Giorgio Scarzello e Figli
Via Alba, 29
12060 Barolo (CN)
Tel. 017356170
E-mail: cantina-scarzello@libero.it

Giorgio Scarzello, assisted by his son Federico, runs an estate of five hectares under vine that produces approximately 20,000 bottles a year. The Scarzello production style is traditional and employs large barrels or, occasionally, 900-litre casks, and quite lengthy macerations on the skins. Of the wines on offer for this edition of the Guide, we found the Barbera Superiore to be particularly interesting. Its deep garnet-ruby ushers in striking mulberry and forest floor laced with a lovely note of toastiness. The palate reveals generous body and a soft personality rounded off by a long finish that echoes the nose. A bit simpler and rather rustic, the basic Barbera offers a nose dominated by moderately elegant fruitiness and a lively palate that displays a typical vein of acidity. Hints of wild berries and rhubarb layered over dried rose petals are evident in the characteristically bright garnet Barolo Vigna Merenda, which has a dry palate with good thrust. The basic Barolo flaunts aromas ranging from mineral tones and mature flowers to sweet hints of jam. The palate is tidy and very satisfying. Last up, the estate's Nebbiolo offers hints of fresh sea breezes in a not particularly refined nose and an uncomplicated palate.

Wine	Rating	Score
● Barolo Cannubi Boschis '98	♛♛	8
● Barbera d'Alba '00	♛♛	6
● Langhe Rosso Pe Mol '00	♛♛	6
● Nebbiolo d'Alba Valmaggiore '00	♛♛	6
● Dolcetto d'Alba '01	♛♛	4*
● Barolo Le Vigne '98	♛♛	8
● Barolo '83	♛♛♛	8
● Barolo '84	♛♛♛	8
● Barolo Cannubi Boschis '86	♛♛♛	8
● Barolo Cannubi Boschis '87	♛♛♛	8
● Barolo Cannubi Boschis '89	♛♛♛	8
● Barolo Cannubi Boschis '90	♛♛♛	8

Wine	Rating	Score
● Barolo Vigna Merenda '98	♛♛	6*
● Barbera d'Alba Sup. '99	♛♛	4*
● Barbera d'Alba '00	♛	3
● Barolo '98	♛	6
● Langhe Nebbiolo '00		4
● Barolo Vigna Merenda '90	♛♛	6
● Barolo '95	♛♛	6
● Barolo '96	♛♛	6
● Barbera d'Alba Sup. '97	♛♛	4
● Barolo '97	♛♛	6
● Barbera d'Alba Sup. '98	♛♛	4

BAROLO (CN)

TENUTA LA VOLTA - CABUTTO
VIA SAN PIETRO, 13
12060 BAROLO (CN)
TEL. 017356168

Little by little, Bruno and Osvaldo Cabutto are expanding Tenuta La Volta with new plots and new plantations. At present, they get 55,000 bottles a year out of their 15 hectares of vines but in the space of a few years, they hope to increase this figure substantially. Never, the brothers are quick to point out, will they abandon their quest for quality. This quality is evident in wines that once again were awarded enviable marks by our panel for this year's Guide. In the line-up this time, the Barolo Vigna La Volta is flanked by the Riserva del Fondatore '96, a selection of grapes grown in the estate's vineyards, vinified only in the very best of vintages. The last of these was 1990. Both of these wines present a traditional profile with rich mineral notes filtering through the aromas of red berry fruit and dried flowers. They are fairly austere on the palate and well supported by complex structure that is more evident in the Riserva. The opaque garnet Langhe Vendemmia, a blend of nebbiolo and barbera, is more modern in style. Its nose weds fruity tones of black cherry with toastiness and cake. On the palate, it is vibrant and assured, taking its leave with a delightfully dynamic finish. The Barbera Superiore suggests fruit, aromatic herbs and earth in an overall framework that is pleasantly rustic, then the palate reveals good body and some nice roughish edges.

•	Barolo Ris. del Fondatore '96	♟♟	8
•	Dolcetto d'Alba Vigna La Volta '01	♟♟	4*
•	Barolo Vigna La Volta '98	♟♟	7
•	Langhe Vendemmiaio '99	♟♟	6
•	Barbera d'Alba Sup. '00	♟	5
•	Barolo Vigna La Volta '97	♟♟	7
•	Barolo Ris. del Fondatore '90	♟♟	8
•	Barolo Vigna La Volta '96	♟♟	7
•	Barbera d'Alba Sup. Bricco delle Viole '99	♟♟	5

BAROLO (CN)

TERRE DA VINO
VIA BERGESIA, 6
12060 BAROLO (CN)
TEL. 0173564611
E-MAIL: info@terredavino.it

Opened in September 2000, the generous cellars of this winery extend over an area of 5,000 square metres and occupy a two and a half-hectare plot of estate-owned land. Terre da Vino needs every square centimetre to accommodate the 1,000,000 bottles produced at this co-operative, which brings together 14 wineries, and, crucially, to maintain the level of quality that the market demands. We start with a round of applause for the wines we tasted this year, every single one of which was high quality. The Barbera d'Asti La Luna e i Falò continues the positive trend it has set over recent years. It is flanked by other offerings of equal or – dare we say it – even better class, such as the Barbera d'Alba Croere, made from grapes grown in the municipality of Castagnito. This is a modern wine that is still recognizably a Barbera. Fruit, rotundity, maturity and just the right dose of acidity are all there. The Barolo Scarrone '98, from vineyards at Castiglione Falletto, performs very well and replaces the Barolo Poderi Parussi. Deep garnet, with the briefest of edges, it regales the nose with pronounced aromas that go from Peruvian bark to black berry fruit. Flavoursome and confident on the palate, its firm, invigorating progression reveals a note of liquorice in the finish. The La Malora selection, obtained entirely from nebbiolo grapes from Roero, also makes a triumphant debut. Monferrato Tra Donne Sole, a chardonnay and sauvignon blend, is head and shoulders above the rest of the whites, offering green, fruity sensations and a good weighty palate that ends in a tidy finish.

•	Barbera d'Alba Croere '00	♟♟	5
•	Barbera d'Asti Sup. La Luna e i Falò '00	♟♟	4*
•	Langhe Nebbiolo La Malora '00	♟♟	5
○	Monferrato Bianco Tra Donne Sole '01	♟♟	4*
•	Barolo Poderi Scarrone '98	♟♟	7
○	Piemonte Chardonnay Tenuta la Magnona '00	♟	4
•	Barbera d'Asti San Nicolao '01	♟	4
○	Gavi Ca' da Bosio '01	♟	4
○	Gavi Masseria dei Carmelitani '01	♟	4
•	Barolo Paesi Tuoi '98	♟	7
•	Barbera d'Asti La Luna e i Falò '99	♟♟	4

BAROLO (CN)

G. D. Vajra
Fraz. Vergne
Via delle Viole, 25
12060 Barolo (CN)
tel. 017356257
e-mail: gdvajra@tin.it

Aldo and Milena Vajra with children Giuseppe – already active in the cellar –, Francesca and Isidoro are a model Langhe family, dedicated to their land, respectful of the environment and serious about their work. This year, their magnificent winery wins Three resounding Glasses for a wine of quite exceptional quality, the Barbera d'Alba Superiore, from the harvest of 2000. It's not a new wine but simply the result of applying the rule that forbids giving the same subzone name to more than one category of wine. Indeed, the grapes that go into this wine are the very ones that have always yielded Barbera d'Alba Bricco delle Viole, an incomparable selection that from this year on will nominally be reserved for Barolo only. This Barbera bowled us over right from the start with its almost impenetrable ruby red and cornucopia of aromas mingling ripe fruit, spices and pepper into an elegant bouquet. The palate won our hearts with rich extract and a lingering, sweet fruitiness that builds to a climax in the finish. Every bit as good is the austere, tannic Barolo, a wine that puts nebbiolo centre stage. Another marvellous bottle is the Dolcetto Coste & Fossati '01, superb both on the nose and palate, where its vigorous alcohol is lifted by notes of almond. The complex riesling-based Langhe Bianco is quite delightful, its mineral tones and dry palate leading smoothly through to a delicate, wonderfully clean finish. We'll end our notes with the austere, very traditional, Freisa Kyè and two uncomplicated but attractive standard labels, the Barbera and the Dolcetto d'Alba.

● Barbera d'Alba Sup. '00	🍷🍷🍷	6
● Dolcetto d'Alba Coste & Fossati '01	🍷🍷	5
● Barolo Bricco delle Viole '97	🍷🍷	8
● Langhe Freisa Kyè '00	🍷🍷	7
○ Langhe Bianco '01	🍷🍷	5
● Barbera d'Alba '01	🍷	5
● Dolcetto d'Alba '01	🍷	4
● Dolcetto d'Alba Coste & Fossati '00	🍷🍷	5
● Barbera d'Alba Bricco delle Viole '99	🍷🍷	5
● Barolo Bricco delle Viole '95	🍷🍷	8
● Barolo Bricco delle Viole '96	🍷🍷	8

BASTIA MONDOVÌ (CN)

Bricco del Cucù
Fraz. Bricco, 21
12060 Bastia Mondovì (CN)
tel. 017460153
e-mail: briccocucu@libero.it

Dario Strolla has set out to produce wines of quality. So hard does he work on his estate that it has only taken him a few short years to completely revolutionize its outlook. He used to sell all his wine in bulk very profitably in the lively Genoa market but he now releases almost 50,000 bottles a year, to the delight of a more varied and demanding clientele. All this bodes well for the future. For the moment, we are happy to note that several of his wines have made significant progress, while others have suffered some minor setbacks from a run of extremely hot, dry years. One such is the Dogliani Superiore Bricco San Bernardo, whose '00 vintage is less than perfect. Notes of super-ripeness dominate the fruit. It has good flesh, though, and a reasonably dense palate that reveals the good quality of the original grapes. Moving on to the wines that fared better at our tastings, the standard-label Dolcetto di Dogliani did well with its opaque ruby red hue and its rather complex bouquet of blackberry, cocoa powder and spices. Its pervasive palate is borne up by a good dose of alcohol and the lengthy finish echoes the fruit sensations of the nose. The Langhe Dolcetto is also very well made, flaunting a warm, refreshing nose, soft palate and agreeable acidity.

● Dolcetto di Dogliani '01	🍷🍷	3*
● Langhe Dolcetto '01	🍷🍷	3*
● Dolcetto di Dogliani Sup. Bricco S. Bernardo '00	🍷	4
● Dolcetto di Dogliani '00	🍷🍷	3
● Langhe Dolcetto '00	🍷🍷	3
● Dolcetto di Dogliani Sup. Bricco S. Bernardo '99	🍷🍷	4

BERZANO DI TORTONA (AL)

TERRALBA
FRAZ. INSELMINA
15050 BERZANO DI TORTONA (AL)
TEL. 0131866791

The Terralba estate is here to stay. It followed up last year's spectacular performance with a new raft of very creditable wines. Making its debut on the market, the Colli Tortonesi Bianco Stato, from timorasso grapes harvested in 2000, swept up a fine Two Glasses. Its rich colour is the prelude to a confident, almost rugged, nose that is complex and well balanced. The palate is backed up by the robust alcohol typical of the grape and characteristic terroir-led aromas that hint at chalk before opening into subtle tones of fresh fruit. La Vetta, the other, cortese-based, white is also a wine to be reckoned with. It may lack the structure of its stablemate, but the length of its intense aromas and the sophistication and harmony of the palate are quite astonishing. Stefano Daffonchio has named his flagship bottle Barbera Terralba. This wine is allowed to mature in oak barrels for 14 months and comes into its own after a medium to long period of ageing in bottle. The '99 vintage that we tasted this year bowled us over with its nearly impenetrable appearance and a bouquet that releases aromas verging on the gamey. After aeration in the glass, the aromas develop to welcome spicy notes of cinnamon and coffee. The palate is vibrant and offers pleasant bitter chocolate and a raspberry finish. Monleale is another big red. Predominantly barbera, with a little croatina, it is softer than the Terralba but is still a sturdy, elegant glassful. The estate's two other reds, also worth trying, are the croatina-based Montegrande and Strà Loja, a dolcetto selection.

○	Colli Tortonesi Bianco Stato '00	ㅎㅎ	5
●	Colli Tortonesi Rosso Monleale '00	ㅎㅎ	5
○	Colli Tortonesi Bianco La Vetta '01	ㅎㅎ	4*
●	Colli Tortonesi Rosso Terralba '99	ㅎㅎ	6
●	Colli Tortonesi Rosso Montegrande '00	ㅎ	6
●	Colli Tortonesi Rosso Strà Loja '00	ㅎ	5
●	Piemonte Barbera Identità '01	ㅎ	4
○	Colli Tortonesi Bianco La Vetta '00	ㅎㅎ	4
●	Colli Tortonesi Rosso Terralba '98	ㅎㅎ	6

BORGONE SUSA (TO)

CARLOTTA
VIA CONDOVE, 61
10050 BORGONE SUSA (TO)
TEL. 0119646150
E-MAIL: rfrancesca@libero.it

Viticulture at Carlotta can be described without fear of exaggeration as legendary. Carla Cometto tends, with painstaking care and dedication, one and a half hectares of vines at an altitude of between 500 and 1,000 metres on slopes so steep that it is impossible to cultivate them mechanically. Frequently, fruit is lost to the ravages of wild boar and other creatures. The finest of the wines from the harvest of 2001 is the Costadoro, thanks to good structure and balance. This blend of neretta cuneese, ciliegiolo, barbera and other local varieties is ruby garnet with a purple rim and unveils cherry and raspberry fruit, enriched with peppery tones. It is nice and gutsy on the palate, where there is good acidic grip, lots of character and a dry, lingering finish that echoes the nose. The Vignacombe, predominantly barbera with proportions of neretta, freisa and gamay, is a shade less rounded. It has a bouquet of wild berries layered over a grassy backdrop and an assertive, full-bodied palate that signs off with vibrant notes of liquorice. The Rocca del Lupo, a mix of avanà and barbera from the estate's highest plot, is more subtle in character. Youthful in appearance, it has wild berry aromas and a no-nonsense, tangy palate. Finally, the Roceja is a barbera and nebbiolo-based table wine with a clean, fruity nose and quite a vigorous palate.

●	Valsusa Costadoro '01	ㅎㅎ	5
●	Valsusa Vignacombe '01	ㅎㅎ	5
●	Roceja '01	ㅎ	5
●	Valsusa Rocca del Lupo '01	ㅎ	5
●	Roceja '00	ㅎㅎ	5
●	Valsusa Rocca del Lupo '00	ㅎㅎ	5

BOSIO (AL)

DOMENICO GHIO E FIGLI
VIA CIRCONVALLAZIONE, 2
15060 BOSIO (AL)
TEL. 0143684117
E-MAIL: ghiovini@novi.it

There has been a renaissance in winemaking at Bosio and one of its results is this Guide profile for the small Ghio family winery. For generations, the Ghios have been involved in the wine trade and today, they turn out some very well-made selections. A proportion of their wine, made from grapes they buy in from trusted growers, is still sold in bulk but they are bottling more and more each year in response to growing appreciation for their flagship labels. Almost everyone in the family lends a hand in the winery. Grandfather Domenico, his sons Emilio and Giuseppe, and grandchildren Alessandro, Roberto, Marina and Laura form a tightly knit team that shares out the tasks involved in running the six and half estate-owned hectares (three each of cortese and dolcetto), in the cellars and on the business side. Turning now to the wines, we were most impressed by the two Dolcetto di Ovada Superiore selections. The Drac Rosso, made from lightly raisined grapes slowly aged in small barrels, boasts crisp, fruity aromas, a warm, velvety palate, as well as impressive length. The slightly less structured Arciprete is also very decent. We liked both of the Gavis we sampled. The Drac Bianco has the benefit of an extra year in the cellar that gives it a more concentrated nose, with spring flowers, acacia blossom, honey and citrus fruit to the fore, and good body. The standard version is simpler but refreshing and eminently enjoyable.

● Dolcetto di Ovada Sup. Drac Rosso '00	♟♟	5
○ Gavi Drac Bianco '00	♟♟	5
● Dolcetto di Ovada Sup. L'Arciprete '00	♟	4
○ Gavi Etichetta Nera '01	♟	3
● Dolcetto di Ovada Sup. Drac Rosso '99	♛♛	5
● Piemonte Barbera Bricco del Tempo '98	♟	4

BOSIO (AL)

LA SMILLA
VICO GARIBALDI, 7
15060 BOSIO (AL)
TEL. 0143684245
E-MAIL: info@lasmilla.it

What a delight it is – if, like the panel, you have the chance – to spend a day in the country in the company of the Guido family. First, because they are deeply committed to their work, and second because as we chatted, they shared with us all kinds of fascinating historical snippets about this "border" territory that straddles Liguria and Piedmont. Tucked between hills, mountains and, a stone's throw away, the sea in the shape of Genoa, a city that sends hordes of summer visitors and whose market sucks up almost every last drop of wine in the zone. Consequently, it gives us even greater pleasure to write that the Guidos' range of wines has made a quantum leap forward. Young Danilo has applied a firm hand to operations in the cellars, which are situated in the heart of Bosio's old town, ably assisted by oenologist Francesco Bergaglio and numerous family members who play a variety of roles both in the vineyards and on the selling side. The end result is 50,000 bottles a year of good quality wine obtained from grapes grown on the estate's own six hectares or bought in from selected growers. We really liked the Gavis and, while we wait to try the new version of I Bergi, which from now on will be aged for an extra year before release onto the market, we can recommend the very refreshing and fruity Gavi di Gavi, and the simpler but far from banal basic Gavi, both of which are pleasant. Of the reds, we preferred the fragrant, full-bodied Dolcetto di Ovada Nsè Pesa selection. The easy-drinking standard version is also well-executed.

● Dolcetto di Ovada Nsè Pesa '00	♟♟	4*
○ Gavi del Comune di Gavi '01	♟♟	4*
● Dolcetto di Ovada '01	♟	3
○ Gavi '01	♟	3
● Dolcetto di Ovada '00	♛♛	3
○ Gavi del Comune di Gavi '00	♛♛	4
○ Gavi I Bergi '00	♛♛	4

BRA (CN)

ASCHERI
VIA PIUMATI, 23
12042 BRA (CN)
TEL. 0172412394
E-MAIL: ascherivini@tin.it

The winery run by Matteo Ascheri with the support of oenologist Giuliano Bedino is experiencing a period of sea change that started back in 1994. That was when Ascheri began the daunting task of replanting his vineyards, rigorously selecting the clones. Today is payday, as one after another the new plantings go into production. Meanwhile, Matteo has embarked upon a radical restructuring of his cellar at Bra that will see a hotel appear where now stand the estate's headquarters and the Osteria Muri Vecchi restaurant, which also belongs to the family. Moving onto the wines, the estate's Barolo Sorano '98 made a big impression with its dried flower and mint aromas and solid weight on the palate, which is powerful and somewhat austere. Although less demanding, the Vigna dei Pola offers nuances of cake and barely discernible acidity. The two wines from the experimental plot at Montalupa in Bra are very successful. The Bianco '00, with a viognier base, has a nose of grass and apricot and a characterful palate. The Rosso '99 clearly reflects the characteristics of its variety, syrah. It shows a very concentrated palate with rather a rugged personality. This estate certainly knows how to imbue all its many wines with very high quality, as is obvious from the impressive list of stemware.

BRIGNANO FRASCATA (AL)

PAOLO POGGIO
VIA ROMA, 67
15050 BRIGNANO FRASCATA (AL)
TEL. 0131784929 - 0131784650

It is no mean feat to make wine at Brignano Frascata, where the vines are at an altitude of over 400 metres. Paolo Poggio has to call on all his experience, particularly when the vintages are not up to scratch. But when, as in 2000 and 2001, the weather decides to give him a helping hand, the results are spectacular. We start with the pick of the estate's crop, the Derio, whose '00 vintage is one of the best this winery has produced. Its well-defined ruby is the prelude to a full, complex nose redolent of spice and tobacco that shades into more delicate hints of sweet black cherry. It delights with its balance in the mouth of upfront varietal flavours and velvety, caressing mouthfeel. The steel-conditioned Barbera was equally surprising. This '01, a "younger brother" of the Derio, is distinctive for its generous, well-rounded palate of strawberry and wild berries. The line-up of reds includes a Freisa with a simpler palate that has delightful aromas of liquorice and wild strawberry. For some years now, Paolo Poggio has also been vinifying a monovarietal Timorasso that bears the local name, Timürasso. The '00 version, mentioned by mistake in last year's edition of the Guide, is a cut above the '99, flaunting mineral tones and complex, harmonious sensations of apricot jam and apple. Rounding off the range, we have a cortese-based bottle that is worth mentioning for its refreshing drinkability, and a lovely sweet Moscato that would make the perfect end to a meal.

● Barolo Sorano '98	🍷🍷	7
○ Langhe Bianco Montalupa '00	🍷🍷	6
● Montalupa Rosso '99	🍷🍷	6
● Nebbiolo d'Alba Bricco S. Giacomo '00	🍷	5
● Barbera d'Alba Vigna Fontanelle '01	🍷	4
● Dolcetto d'Alba Vigna Nirane '01	🍷	4
○ Roero Arneis Cristina Ascheri '01	🍷	4
● Barolo Vigna dei Pola '98	🍷	6
● Barolo Sorano '96	🍷🍷	7
● Barolo Sorano '97	🍷🍷	7
● Montalupa Rosso '98	🍷🍷	6
○ Montalupa Bianco '99	🍷🍷	6

● Colli Tortonesi Barbera Derio '00	🍷🍷	6
○ Colli Tortonesi Bianco Timürasso '00	🍷🍷	5
● Colli Tortonesi Barbera '01	🍷🍷	4*
○ Colli Tortonesi Cortese '01	🍷	4
● Colli Tortonesi Freisa '01	🍷	4
○ Muscatè '01	🍷	3
● Colli Tortonesi Barbera Derio '98	🍷🍷	6
● Colli Tortonesi Barbera Derio '99	🍷🍷	6

BRUSNENGO (BI)

BARNI
VIA FORTE, 63
13082 BRUSNENGO (BI)
TEL. 015985977

Filippo Barni, a talented, inquisitive experimenter, started his winemaking business in Gattinara before settling at Brusnengo in the Bramaterra area. The estate has about four hectares in the Mesola valley, which is perfect for growing grapes, and a small, picturesque plot in the town itself. Filippo respects nature in the vineyard, eschewing herbicides and insecticides. His excellent, varied range is produced under the supervision of Gianfranco Cordero and this year, the Coste della Sesia Torrearsa '00 fell just short of Three Glasses. A blend of cabernet and vespolina with a little croatina, its impenetrably dark, violet-tinged hue grabs your attention. The aromas are tight-knit, concentrated, lingering nuances of plum, mulberry and red pepper with aniseed and ginger spice emerge, then the structured palate exhibits a soft, generous fruitiness backed by a wealth of very elegant tannins. The Mesolone is obtained from vineyards that are over 60 years old, and traditionally planted to 80 per cent croatina with nebbiolo and uva rara. The pervasive nose flaunts mulberry, cherry, violet and coffee against a backdrop of roses, cocoa powder and spice. The dense palate has a silky fruit that swamps the tangy vein. The Albaciara, a blend of 70 per cent chardonnay with erbaluce, is balanced, tidy and bursting with aromas. In the mouth, there is good structure and freshness. The Bramaterra '99 shows off its fine quality fruit but is still overawed by the oak. A new recruit will be joining the ranks next year. It's an extremely rigorous white dried-grape white.

● Coste della Sesia Rosso Torrearsa '00	♟♟	5
○ Albaciara Bianco '01	♟♟	4*
● Coste della Sesia Rosso Mesolone '99	♟♟	5
● Bramaterra '99	♟	5
● Mesolone Rosso '98	♟♟	5
● Coste della Sesia Rosso Torrearsa '99	♟♟	5

CALAMANDRANA (AT)

MICHELE CHIARLO
STRADA NIZZA-CANELLI, 99
14042 CALAMANDRANA (AT)
TEL. 0141769030
E-MAIL: chiarlo@tin.it

Michele Chiarlo, the owner of this major Monferrato estate, has carved out a solid niche for his winery at the peak of Piedmont winemaking. Chiarlo's wide range of products is distinctive for its high quality but this year, its ranks are a bit thin. Michele has decided to stop producing his Barilot and Barbera Valle del Sole and to release only one version each of the Dolcetto and Grignolino. On top of this, there will be no '99 vintage of the Barbaresco Asili, which fell victim to hail. The Barolos on offer include the graceful Cerequio '98, which romped home to an easy Three Glasses. Deep garnet, it flaunts a wonderfully clean nose that brims over with well-typed aromas of ripe fruit and mint leaf, followed by a full-bodied palate. This modern, elegantly made Barolo authoritatively embodies the assertiveness and the grip of the nebbiolo grape. The Brunate '98, garnet shading into orange, has a subtle bouquet of medium intensity that preludes a firm, broad palate. The magnificent Barolo Cannubi '98 gives further proof of its elegant, complex personality in delightful notes of dried rose and blackberry, ripe, silky tannins and aristocratic length. The Barolo Riserva '96 Triumviratum performs splendidly, happily marrying the grapes of the three Barolo vineyards from which it is obtained. La Court '99 is excellent and with a little more flesh could have made it to a third Glass. The Countacc! '99 and the Barbera Cipressi della Court '00 are on top form, as are the very well-made whites. The Gavi Fornaci di Tassarolo '00 stands out for its clean nose and flavoursome palate.

● Barolo Cerequio '98	♟♟♟	8
● Barolo Cannubi '98	♟♟	8
● Barbera d'Asti Sup. La Court '99	♟♟	6
● Barbera d'Asti Sup. Cipressi della Court '00	♟♟	4*
○ Gavi Fornaci di Tassarolo '00	♟♟	6
● Barolo Triumviratum Ris. '96	♟♟	8
● Barolo Brunate '98	♟♟	8
● Monferrato Countacc! '99	♟♟	6
○ Piemonte Chardonnay Plenilunio '00	♟	5
○ Moscato d'Asti Smentiò '01	♟	5
● Barolo Cerequio '95	♟♟♟	8
● Barolo Cerequio '96	♟♟♟	8
● Barolo Cerequio '97	♟♟♟	8

CALAMANDRANA (AT)

Hastae
Fraz. Quartino, 6
14042 Calamandrana (AT)
tel. 0141769146

The Hastae project is in its fourth year. We can now draw our first conclusions about this ambitious plan to promote Barbera d'Asti, spearheaded by a group of famous Piedmont producers. All have vineyards, and a vested interest, in Asti and Monferrato, as well as other areas. The prestigious Barbera, Quorum, is the leading edge of the enterprise. This wine has made a name for itself both in Italy and abroad, and the forces assembled to create a top quality wine have done just that. Carefully selected vineyards, expert advice from Federico Curtaz in the vineyard and Riccardo Cotarella in the cellar and brilliant promotion have contributed but that's not all. The Hastae group also sponsors a slew of other activities, including conferences and round tables to discuss important oenological issues and a fund to finance wine research. Let's here a round of applause for those who emerged victorious from the fray: Braida, Coppo, Chiarlo, Prunotto, Vietti and Berta. The most important development is the new purpose-built cellar in Calamandrana, overseen by oenologist Paco Perletto and tailored to produce Quorum. The group has also bought a "collective" four-hectare vineyard in the municipalities of Nizza and Vinchio, to add to the one hectare each member contributes. Despite a slightly veiled nose, the '00 Quorum displays impressive structure. Its fruity tones are just starting to evolve into a more complex profile, then entry on the palate is sweet and richly extracted. The long finish is marked by the acidulous note typical of the variety.

- Barbera d'Asti Quorum '00 ▼▼ 8
- Barbera d'Asti Quorum '97 ▽▽ 8
- Barbera d'Asti Quorum '98 ▽▽ 8
- Barbera d'Asti Quorum '99 ▽▽ 8

CALAMANDRANA (AT)

La Giribaldina
Fraz. San Vito, 39
14042 Calamandrana (AT)
tel. 0141718043
e-mail: info@giribaldina.com

To reach the "cascina" that houses La Giribaldina, a rising star in this corner, near Asti, of Piedmont's winemaking panorama, you have to leave Calamandrana and wend your way up the twisting country lanes. Tucked away in this quiet spot, the Colombo family, originally from Varese but resident here since 1995, seems to have found its place in the world. Since they settled here, Maria Grazia Macchi, supported by her restlessly active son Emanuele, a nutrition graduate who runs a wine shop in Calamandrana, and her husband Francesco Colombo, has taken the full weight of the estate upon her shoulders. Agronomist Piero Roseo and oenologist Piergiorgio Berta also work with the family. The Colombo vineyards extend over eight hectares, all in excellent positions in the municipalities of Calamandrana and Vaglio Serra. La Giribaldina produces approximately 40,000 bottles a year and Barbera d'Asti, in three versions, naturally accounts for the lion's share. The Cala delle Mandrie selection, aged for 18 months in new and once-used barriques, impresses with the fragrance of its aromas and the fullness of its flesh. It has a formidable character and will only improve in the cellar. The Rossobaldo, matured in big barrels, is also good, as is the Monte del Mare '00, which is conditioned entirely in stainless steel. La Giribaldina also produces an excellent DOC Monferrato Bianco Sauvignon that is wonderfully tangy and extremely drinkable.

- Barbera d'Asti Sup.
  Cala delle Mandrie '00 ▼▼ 5
- ○ Monferrato Bianco
  Ferro di Cavallo '00 ▼▼ 4*
- Barbera d'Asti
  Monte del Mare '00 ▼ 3
- Barbera d'Asti Sup.
  Rossobaldo '00 ▼ 4

CALOSSO (AT)

SCAGLIOLA
FRAZ. SAN SIRO, 42
14052 CALOSSO (AT)
TEL. 0141853183

The wines released by this family-owned estate on the Langhe-Monferrato border keep on getting better. There are three different Scagliola Barbera labels and this year the two leading versions, both named SanSì, have surpassed themselves. In particular, the '99 vintage has incomparable body and elegance. This wine fully deserves its Three Glasses and pays tribute to the collective efforts of a family that is justifiably proud of its country roots. The Barbera SanSì Selezione, aged for 18 months in new barriques, has a ruby colour that shades into garnet, to ushers in concentrated, refined notes of red berry fruits and spices. These mingle seductively with barrique-derived oaky tones. The palate is full and fleshy, regaling the taste receptors with extremely enjoyable tannic astringency that leads through to a long, balanced, mouthfilling finish. The Barbera Sansì '00 is not far behind. Its profound, garnet-ruby appearance and alluring aromas of morello cherry and cocoa powder. Softness and strength combine on the palate with moderate supporting acidity that adds a generous note of delicious freshness. The Frem '01, aged in large barrels, is pleasant and well put together, albeit simpler than in previous vintages. The 100 per cent steel-conditioned Dolcetto Busiord '01 is opaque ruby with flecks of purple. Its bouquet opens on fruity tones of mulberry and cherry, then a chewy palate reveals good length and a typical hint of almonds in the finish. The Moscato d'Asti is alluring, thanks to well-judged, leisurely sweetness.

● Barbera d'Asti SanSì Sel. '99	🍷🍷🍷	6
● Barbera d'Asti SanSì '00	🍷🍷	5
○ Moscato d' Asti Volo di Farfalle '01	🍷🍷	4*
● Langhe Dolcetto Busiord '01	🍷🍷	3*
● Barbera d'Asti Frem '01	🍷	4
● Barbera d'Asti SanSì Sel. '98	🍷🍷	6
● Barbera d'Asti SanSì '96	🍷🍷	5
● Barbera d'Asti SanSì '97	🍷🍷	5
● Barbera d'Asti SanSì Sel. '97	🍷🍷	6
● Barbera d'Asti SanSì '98	🍷🍷	5

CALOSSO (AT)

TENUTA DEI FIORI
FRAZ. RODOTIGLIA
VIA VALCALOSSO, 3
14052 CALOSSO (AT)
TEL. 0141826938
E-MAIL: info@tenutadeifiori.com

Walter Bosticardo gave up his day job selling agricultural equipment this year to devote himself full-time to his winery. His Tenuta dei Fiori covers just over five hectares planted to vine and has an annual production of between 15,000 and 18,000 bottles. The wines he presented included a cabernet-based Monferrato Rosso that rises head and shoulders above the rest. The dense garnet-hued '99 vintage proffers notes of wild berries against a lovely backdrop of mineral tones and autumn leaves, then the full-bodied palate reveals velvet softness, with well-sustained texture and a long lingering finish that recalls fruit and liquorice. The Barbera Vigneto del Tulipano Nero has a sweet nose of cherry syrup and cake followed by a characterful palate. The finish echoes the aromas on the nose. Walter is a staunch believer in the cellar potential of his Gamba di Pernice, so much so that he has opted to release his '90 only in 2002. In fact, it is a rather captivating wine that discloses distinct notes of tar, with traces of raisined grapes and a palate that stays dry right through the very minerally finish. The Gamba di Pernice '98 possesses a pronounced aromatic vein suggesting biscuits, jam and flowers. The palate is a little sweetish but has good tannin support. The barbera and cabernet Cinque File makes its first appearance, presenting a fruity, vegetal nose and a palate of medium consistency. The Chardonnay il Vento has an apple and pear nose and a tidy palate. Lastly, the rustic Barbera Is is not overly challenging.

● Barbera d'Asti Vigneto del Tulipano Nero '00	🍷🍷	4*
● Monferrato Rosso '99	🍷🍷	4*
● Barbera d'Asti Is '00	🍷	4
● Monferrato Rosso Cinque File '00	🍷	5
○ Il Vento Chardonnay '01	🍷	4
● Gamba di Pernice '90	🍷	5
● Gamba di Pernice '98	🍷	4
● Barbera d'Asti Rodotiglia Castello di Calosso '99	🍷🍷	6

CAMINO (AL)

Tenuta Gaiano
Via Trino, 8
15020 Camino (AL)
tel. 0142469440
e-mail: tenutagaiano@tiscalinet.it

The earliest documentary evidence of viticulture around the Cistercian monastery of Gaiano dates from 943 AD. Today, this beautiful spot and these ancient walls are home to Tenuta Gaiano, founded in 1995 by Gigi Lavander and Pier Iviglia. The time-worn cellars are very simply equipped but the emphasis here is on the quality of the grapes, which is assured by the fabulous position and age of the vines, some of which are more than 60 years old. The estate's Barbera Vigna della Torretta '99, barrique-conditioned for one year, is up to its usual high standards. Its impenetrable inky black is the prelude to tight-knit aromas that marry mulberry and cherries with oak-derived vanilla. The superbly structured palate has velvet fruit and a fleshy mouthfeel. The basic Barbera '00 astounded us with its intense, clean fragrances that usher in a rich, silky palate of tremendous harmony. The Gallianum '00, a selection of barbera, vinified entirely without the use of oak, weds rock-solid structure with remarkable elegance and textbook typicity. The Birbarossa '01, an unusual blend of ruché, freisa and various lesser known varieties, has a vaguely aromatic nose suggesting blueberry, wild strawberry, violet and orange peel. The strong, velvety palate with lively fruit borne up by firm tannins. The Grignolino '01 is one of the best of its category, boasting deep colour, good weight in the mouth and intense, well-defined varietal aromas. The slightly fuzzy Grignolino Vigna del Convento '01 is full-bodied but lacks a little elegance.

CANALE (CN)

Cascina Ca' Rossa
Loc. Cascina Ca' Rossa, 56
12043 Canale (CN)
tel. 017398348

Angelo Ferrio's lovely winery has achieved a solid level of dependability. The cellars, which have been revamped and extended over the course of the last year, are to be found on the road leading out of Canale towards Asti. The area under vine now totals 15 hectares, with the two main plots lying in Vezza d'Alba, home of the steep Audinaggio vineyard, and in Canale's Mompissano vineyard. Until his son Stefano - who is responsible for the cheerful design of the Roero Mompissano label - joins him full-time, Angelo is relying on the support of his father Alfonso, who helps in the vineyard. The 60,000 bottles released each year make up a wide range of excellent wines and we like to think that Angelo learned a lot from his friend, the much-lamented Matteo Correggia. This year, the Roero Audinaggio is back on top form with a '00 vintage that shows a lovely ruby shading into garnet, rich, complex berry fruit jam aromas and a warm, enfolding palate swathed in soft tannins. It is strongly reminiscent of the famous '96 and came oh-so-close to a Three Glass score, missing out by the thinnest of whiskers. The second release of the Roero Mompissano is very good, showing distinct, but not overwhelming, oak. The Barbera d'Alba Mulassa is, as ever, a grand wine, boasting a clean, fruity nose and a dense, characterful palate, if just a shade less body than the '99. The '01 Barberas and Nebbiolos are decent. Completing the range, we have a nice, tangy Roero Arneis and a Birbet that is technically well made and most enjoyable.

• Barbera del M.to Vigna della Torretta '99	♆♆	5
• Barbera del M.to '00	♆♆	3*
• Barbera del M.to Gallianum '00	♆♆	4
• Birbarossa '01	♆♆	3*
• Grignolino del M.to Casalese '01	♆♆	3*
• Grignolino del M.to Casalese Vigna del Convento '01	♆	4
• Barbera del M.to Vigna della Torretta '98	♆♆	5

• Barbera d'Alba Mulassa '00	♆♆	6
• Roero Vigna Audinaggio '00	♆♆	6
• Roero Mompissano '00	♆♆	6
○ Roero Arneis Merica '01	♆♆	4
• Barbera d'Alba '01	♆	4
• Langhe Nebbiolo '01	♆	4
• Birbet	♆	3
• Roero Vigna Audinaggio '96	♆♆♆	6
• Barbera d'Alba Mulassa '99	♆♆♆	6
• Roero Vigna Audinaggio '98	♆♆	6
• Roero Mompissano '99	♆♆	6
• Roero Vigna Audinaggio '99	♆♆	6

CANALE (CN)

Cascina Chicco
Via Valentino, 144
12043 Canale (CN)
tel. 0173979069
e-mail: cascinachicco@cascinachicco.com

The Faccenda estate is one of the most important in Roero winemaking, above all in terms of sheer size. The property now extends over 20 hectares, principally in the municipalities of Canale, Vezza and Castellinaldo, where an ambitious project has led to the creation of a magnificent amphitheatre of vines. Annual production of approximately 140,000 bottles comes from the picturesque cellars just outside Canale. With this kind of backing, young Enrico and Marco, who have been skilfully introduced to winemaking by their father Federico, can go about their work with confidence as they pursue their ambitious goals. All of their reds are extremely good. We preferred the mouthfilling Valmaggiore '99 of the two Roeros. It takes advantage of an extra year's in the cellar to present a concentrated nose, with berry fruit and chocolate to the fore, and a velvet-smooth palate. The Montespinato '00 is simpler but still well made, while the Nebbiolo Mompissano is very good indeed, unveiling delicious spicy tones and a warm, fleshy palate. The Bric Loira selection, from Castellinaldo, is the pick of the two Barberas. The nose flaunts the customary complexity and charm, revealing strong hints of berry fruit, apples and pears. The palate opens out to fill the mouth and ends in a lingering finish. Putting the finishing touches to the estate's impressive range are two dry whites, a pleasant, fresh Arneis and a simple, fragrant Langhe Favorita, and the sweet, easy-drinking Birbet.

● Barbera d'Alba Bric Loira '00	🍷🍷	5
● Roero Valmaggiore '99	🍷🍷	5
● Nebbiolo d'Alba Mompissano '00	🍷🍷	5
● Roero Montespinato '00	🍷🍷	4*
● Barbera d'Alba Granera Alta '01	🍷🍷	4*
● Birbét	🍷	4
○ Langhe Favorita '01	🍷	4
○ Roero Arneis Anterisio '01	🍷	4
● Barbera d'Alba Bric Loira '97	🍷🍷🍷	5
● Barbera d'Alba Bric Loira '98	🍷🍷🍷	5
● Nebbiolo d'Alba Mompissano '99	🍷🍷🍷	5
● Roero Valmaggiore '98	🍷🍷	5
● Barbera d'Alba Bric Loira '99	🍷🍷	5

CANALE (CN)

★ Matteo Correggia
Case Sparse Garbinetto, 124
12043 Canale (CN)
tel. 0173978009
e-mail: matteo@matteocorreggia.com

More than a year after he passed away, the image, or rather the star you can see on this pages next to his name, of Matteo Correggia shines more brightly than ever on Roero. We're not just talking about the wines he left us – again, these bowled our tasting panel over – but a moral and cultural legacy. Over the last few months, that legacy has had a profound effect. After the initial shock of Matteo's death passed, many young producers have been stirred to follow the trail blazed by the modest, unassuming master winemaker. Rhetoric apart, we like to think that this shows how Matteo is still very much present in these hills and among these people. Meanwhile, as mentioned, we were privileged to taste some truly extraordinary wines this year. Praise must go to the people who have taken over at the helm of the winery, not least Matteo's determined widow, Ornella, and the very talented Luca Rostagno, a young Roero technician that Matteo insisted on taking on board. The Roero Ròche d'Ampsèj is now a cult wine, emblematic of Matteo's spirit. The elegant force of this wine never ceases to amaze and it notched up another Three Glass award. The estate's other two great reds, the Barbera Marun and the Nebbiolo La Val dei Preti, are up to their usual superb standards. Both are mouthfilling and characterful as they are refreshing and seductively drinkable. The second release of the monovarietal sauvignon Langhe Bianco Matteo Correggia confirms just how sumptuous it is. The other wines in the range are sound and dependable.

● Roero Ròche d'Ampsèj '99	🍷🍷🍷	8
● Barbera d'Alba Marun '00	🍷🍷	6
● Nebbiolo d'Alba La Val dei Preti '00	🍷🍷	6
○ Langhe Bianco Matteo Correggia '01	🍷🍷	6
● Barbera d'Alba '01	🍷🍷	4*
● Roero '01	🍷🍷	4*
○ Roero Arneis '01	🍷🍷	4*
● Roero Ròche d'Ampsèj '96	🍷🍷🍷	8
● Barbera d'Alba Marun '97	🍷🍷🍷	6
● Roero Ròche d'Ampsèj '97	🍷🍷🍷	8
● Roero Ròche d'Ampsèj '98	🍷🍷🍷	8
● Barbera d'Alba Marun '99	🍷🍷🍷	6

CANALE (CN)

DELTETTO
C.SO ALBA, 43
12043 CANALE (CN)
TEL. 0173979383
E-MAIL: deltetto@deltetto.com

"Great oaks from little acorns grow" might be a fitting motto for this estate. Under Antonio Deltetto, it is making a name for itself throughout Roero for the number and quality of its wines. Deltetto gets 120,000 bottles a year from his 15 hectares planted to vine in the municipalities of Canale, Castellinaldo and Santo Stefano Roero. He runs it all himself with the help of his wife Graziella, looking forward to the day when his son Carlo, currently studying at the school of oenology in Alba, is ready to join them full-time. We welcome to the Guide the second edition of a Barolo, the Bussia '98, which impressed us more for its technical excellence and character than for its complexity. Moving onto the array of "house" wines, the deep ruby Roero Braja performed very well, flaunting a rich, complex nose of fruit offset by a faint trace of spice. Progression on the palate is warm and caressing in a wonderfully harmonious overall framework. The two Barberas included the debuting Rocca delle Marasche from the Castellinaldo vineyard. It made quite an impression on us with its elegance and expertly gauged alcohol. In fact, we liked it better than the Bramè selection, which was still very successful particularly for its complex aromas. Moving on to the whites, we liked both of the Arneis but preferred the San Michele. Especially good is the Langhe Bianco Suasì, from 80 per cent sauvignon and 20 per cent chardonnay. It stands out for a fruit-led nose redolent of aromatic herbs and a big, seriously complex, palate. We end with the Langhe Nebbiolo, an uncomplicated crowd-pleaser.

● Roero Braja '00	🍷	5
● Barbera d'Alba Bramè '00	🍷🍷	5
● Barbera d'Alba Rocca delle Marasche '00	🍷🍷	6
● Barolo Bussia '98	🍷🍷	7
○ Langhe Bianco Suasì '01	🍷🍷	4*
○ Roero Arneis S. Michele '01	🍷🍷	4*
● Langhe Nebbiolo '00	🍷	5
○ Roero Arneis Daivej '01	🍷	4
● Roero Braja '98	🍷🍷	5
● Roero Braja '99	🍷🍷	5
● Roero Madonna dei Boschi '99	🍷🍷	5

CANALE (CN)

FUNTANIN
VIA TORINO, 191
12043 CANALE (CN)
TEL. 0173979488

Funtanin is one of a hard core of Canale producers who have played a role in the success of Roero winemaking these last few years. The winery, run by Bruno and Piercarlo Sperone, is a reliable indicator for the health of the territory's wines. The pair currently produce about 60,000 bottles a year but this figure will grow with the replantings planned and already started by the brothers. At present, the estate boasts a dozen hectares situated principally in Canale. Almost all of are in excellent positions. In the capable, experienced hands of the Sperones, the high quality grapes are turned into well-made wines with loads of personality. Moving onto the wines we tasted, we note that as usual the big reds – the Roero Bricco Barbisa and Barbera Ciabot Pierin '00 – put on a good show. The first has a lovely concentration of berry fruit, spice and faint toastiness. The powerful thrust on the palate ends in a lingering finish of characterful elegance. The second is dark ruby with a complex nose of red and black berry fruit taking you into a round, weighty palate. Staying with the reds, the basic Barbera '00 is good and the Langhe Rosso Ménico '00, a blend of 70 per cent nebbiolo and barbera with a little freisa, makes a good impression. We sampled two whites, the no-nonsense, well-made Arneis Pierin di Soc and the Langhe Chardonnay Papé Bianc '99, which is one of the best versions we've ever tried. Tasty and refreshing, it has a deliciously clean keynote of apples and pears.

● Barbera d'Alba Ciabot Pierin '00	🍷🍷	5
● Roero Sup. Bricco Barbisa '00	🍷🍷	5
○ Langhe Chardonnay Papé Bianc '99	🍷🍷	4
● Barbera d'Alba '00	🍷	4
● Langhe Rosso Ménico '00	🍷	4
○ Roero Arneis Pierin di Soc '01	🍷	4
● Barbera d'Alba Ciabot Pierin '99	🍷🍷	5
● Barbera d'Alba Ciabot Pierin '98	🍷🍷	5
● Roero Sup. Bricco Barbisa '98	🍷🍷	5
● Roero Sup. Bricco Barbisa '99	🍷🍷	5

CANALE (CN)

Filippo Gallino
Fraz. Valle del Pozzo, 63
12043 Canale (CN)
Tel. 017398112
E-mail: gallino.filippo@libero.it

Good results from the Gallinos, whose cellars are immersed in vineyards in the quiet district of Valle del Pozzo, two kilometres from Canale. First, we would like to announce that Laura has entered the business full-time, joining brother Gianni and their parents, Filippo and Maria. Second, two new hectares planted with nebbiolo, barbera and arneis are ready to go into production, making a grand total of 12 hectares, all in the municipality of Canale. The number of bottles produced has also grown over the last few years and now tops 60,000: fairly modest, admittedly, but quite impressive when compared to the average Roero output. We are less interested in figures, though, than quality and we must say that here the Gallinos don't put a foot wrong. The two big reds to come out of the 2000 harvest – a Roero and a Barbera, both Superiores – live up to expectations. The first boasts a deep, dark red hue and a potent nose lifted by grace notes of liqueur fruit and sweet spices. The palate is robust and balanced, with just the right dose of tannins. The Barbera Superiore distinguished itself for its flower and fruit aromas, and a markedly alcohol-rich palate that shows great balance and sophistication. Both of these wines made it through to the final tastings and came very close to Three Glasses, proof of the cellar's high quality standards. The basic '01 versions of the Roero and the Barbera are well typed, if less concentrated. The Arneis '01 is refreshing and the Birbet is nice.

●	Barbera d'Alba Sup. '00	▼▼	5
●	Roero Sup. '00	▼▼	6
●	Roero '01	▼▼	4*
●	Barbera d'Alba '01	▼	4
○	Roero Arneis '01	▼	4
●	Birbet	▼	4
●	Barbera d'Alba Sup. '97	▼▼▼	5
●	Roero Sup. '98	▼▼▼	6
●	Roero Sup. '99	▼▼▼	6
●	Barbera d'Alba Sup. '96	▼▼	5
●	Roero Sup. '97	▼▼	6
●	Barbera d'Alba Sup. '99	▼▼	5

CANALE (CN)

Malvirà
Loc. Canova
Case Sparse, 144
12043 Canale (CN)
Tel. 0173978145
E-mail: malvira@malvira.com

The range released by the Damonte brothers just keep getting better, proof that the estate has a length in a broad range of wine types. Massimo and Roberto, with wives Federica and Patrizia, have ambitions that go beyond the results achieved so far. They are emerging ever more strongly as one of Roero's flagship estates. Quality and numbers bear out this progress: the estate includes 36 hectares planted to vine and has an annual production of 200,000 bottles a year. On top of this, the Damontes are shortly due to open their beautiful country hotel, which is well placed to become one of the chief standard bearers for the image of the entire territory. There are new developments on the wine front too. Their famed Roero Superiore has been repackaged as two selections. The Trinità '99 impresses with the intensity of its aromas, a lusty, harmonious palate and fabulous overall balance. It's drinking well now but can only improve with cellaring, One of the very finest examples of its type, it's a champion that has won another Three Glasses for Malvirà. The quite exceptional Mombeltramo '99 is more subtle, its spicy nose anticipating a warm, enfolding palate. Staying with the reds, both the Barbera San Michele and the Langhe Nebbiolo '99 are pleasing. The Malvirà cellar performed superbly with all the whites. The three Arneis selections (last year's Saglietto was a '99, not a 2000) are, as usual, thoroughbreds. Rounding off the range in style, the Tre Uve '00, from sauvignon, chardonnay and arneis, is the best version we've ever tasted.

●	Roero Sup. Trinità '99	▼▼▼	6
●	Roero Sup. Mombeltramo '99	▼▼	6
○	Langhe Bianco Tre Uve '00	▼▼	5
○	Roero Arneis Saglietto '00	▼▼	4
○	Roero Arneis Renesio '01	▼▼	4
○	Roero Arneis Trinità '01	▼▼	4
○	Roero Arneis '01	▼	3
●	Barbera d'Alba S. Michele '99	▼	4
●	Langhe Nebbiolo '99	▼	4
●	Roero Sup. '90	▼▼▼	6
●	Roero Sup. '93	▼▼▼	6
●	Roero Sup. '97	▼▼▼	6
●	Roero Sup. '98	▼▼	6
●	Langhe Rosso S. Guglielmo '98	▼▼	5
○	Roero Arneis Saglietto '99	▼▼	4

CANALE (CN)

Monchiero Carbone
Via Santo Stefano Roero, 2
12043 Canale (CN)
tel. 017395568
e-mail: info@monchierocarbone.com

The time has come for young Francesco, born in 1975, to claim his place in the winery. The responsibilities that bear down on his father, who is not only mayor of Canale but also a successful oenologist who works all over Italy, have inevitably meant that Francesco has had to get involved sooner than he might have planned. Still, he can always rely on the help of his mother, Lucia. Marco, too, is still around, dispensing advice and strategic counsel from his experience and day-to-day dealings with other major producers. All this has borne fruit and the estate is growing. It now has an annual production of 80,000 bottles and around 10 hectares planted to vine. At our tastings this year, we resampled the classic labels while waiting for the release of two new wines, a Brut and a moscato-based Passito. Both Roero selections are excellent. The Srü seduces on both nose and, above all, on the palate, which shows character and rotundity in a setting of fabulous balance. The Printi, aged for a year longer, is a major bottle that releases clean notes of berry fruit and wild berries. The opulent bouquet has enormous personality, mellowed a little by oaky tones that never dominate, and good long length. This wonderful product brings the estate its very first Three Glass award. The Barbera MonBirone performs splendidly, flaunting a modern style that pays due tribute to its variety of origin. Complexity and elegance are again its strong suits. The whites are good: we preferred the Roero Arneis over the Langhe Tamardì, a 75-25 mix of arneis and chardonnay.

●	Roero Printi '99	▼▼▼	6
●	Barbera d'Alba MonBirone '00	▼▼	5
●	Roero Srü '00	▼▼	5
○	Roero Arneis Re Cit '01	▼▼	4
○	Langhe Bianco Tamardì '00	▼	4
●	Roero Printi '98	▼▼	6
●	Barbera d'Alba MonBirone '99	▼▼	5
●	Roero Printi '97	▼▼	6
●	Roero Srü '98	▼▼	5
●	Roero Srü '99	▼▼	5

CANALE (CN)

Porello
C.so Alba, 71
12043 Canale (CN)
tel. 0173979324
e-mail: marcoporello@virgilio.it

The Porello estate is back in the Guide with a good range of medium to excellent quality wines, staking its claim to prominent place in winemaking panorama of Roero. A quick update on the last 10 years is in order. First, young Marco Porello is the sole owner and is now assisted by his parents, Riccardo and Lorenzina, and wife Paola. The winery offices are still in Canale, as is the vinification cellar, but there have been big developments on the construction front. As we write, the finishing touches are being put to a magnificent ageing cellar right next to the castle. Finally, the Porellos have expanded the estate's vine stock to a total of 15 hectares in Canale and Vezza d'Alba. Currently, production is running at about 60,000 bottles. After this glimpse at the estate, let's move on to the wines. The two big reds, the Barbera and the Roero, are superb, both coming from Brich Torretta at Canale. The Barbera has a very well-defined, clean nose and a rounded palate that fades away in faintly sweet, oak-softened tones. The Roero is a wonderful example of what you can do with nebbiolo. Garnet-ruby in hue, it throws a complex nose of berry fruit and coffee, then a rich, caressing palate that unveils dry tannins to lend a note of austerity. The basic versions of both are a bit simpler but still agreeable and well made. The Roero Arneis is well typed and refreshing.

●	Barbera d'Alba Bric Torretta '00	▼▼	4*
●	Roero Bric Torretta '00	▼▼	4*
●	Barbera d'Alba '01	▼	4
●	Roero '01	▼	4
○	Roero Arneis Camestrì '01	▼	3
●	Roero Bric Torretta '99	▼▼	4
●	Barbera d'Alba Bric Torretta '99	▼	4

CANELLI (AT)

Cascina Barisél
Reg. San Giovanni, 2
14053 Canelli (AT)
tel. 0141824849
e-mail: barisel@inwind.it

Young Franco and Fiorenzo Penna, with the help and experience of their father Enrico, organically cultivate four hectares of vines around their Barisél "cascina". They obtain an average annual production of approximately 28,000 bottles of Barbera d'Asti and Moscato. The flagship wine of the estate is, of course, the Barbera La Cappelletta, of which a total of 3,000 bottles are produced from half an acre of their finest soil. This ruby red wine has purple highlights and a nose that hints at its conditioning in new barriques with nuances of vanilla and toastiness that accompany the cherry and plum fruit. The palate is succulent and velvety, borne up by acidity through to a fruit-rich, spicy and slightly dry finish. There were a further Two well-deserved Glasses this year for this admirable wine. The Moscato d'Asti dei Penna has reasonably concentrated aromas and moderate prickle, with citrus fruit and sage evident on the nose. The palate is full-flavoured and sweet but never cloying, making it a worthy match even for rich desserts. The Barbera d'Asti '00, erroneously listed in last year's Guide, is not up to the giddy heights of the Cappelletta but is a good interpretation of the variety in a fresh-tasting, easy-drinking wine with lots of fruit and average length.

CANELLI (AT)

Contratto
Via G. B. Giuliani, 56
14053 Canelli (AT)
tel. 0141823349
e-mail: info@contratto.it

A visit to Contratto is a glance at both past and future. The past lives on in the old cellars and "spumante" tradition, while the future can be seen in the ongoing quest to improve the already excellent wines. The driving force behind all this is the Bocchino family, who are taking Contratto into the front rank of Italy's great winemaking estates. Yet again, the wines they offered us came up to expectations. We'll start our notes with the Brut Riserva Giuseppe Contratto '98, which has lovely perlage, aromas of citrus fruit and butter, softness and restrained acidity. The Asti Metodo Classico De Miranda '00, obtained from partially raisined grapes, is stunning. A quite exceptional bottle, it took home not only Three Glasses but also the coveted Sweet Wine of the Year award. The colour shades into gold and the nose flaunts very subtle, sophisticated notes of ripe apples and pears. The creamy, unctuous palate unfurls astonishing length. The Barolo Cerequio '98 is another masterpiece, embodying to perfection a justifiably famous vineyard that combines power and elegance. Varietal notes of balsam and mint mingle with berry fruit and faint traces of liquorice on a fleshy palate of admirable length. The Barbera Solus Ad '00 comes from old vines and rigorous thinning, which lend it remarkable concentration. Vanilla and toasty notes overlay cherry, blackberry and delicious hints of spice. The simpler Barbera d'Asti Panta Rei '00 is enviably true to type. The golden Chardonnay La Sabauda '00 completes the range, its oak-derived notes already fused with the fruit.

● Barbera d'Asti Sup. La Cappelletta '00	♛♛	5
○ Moscato d'Asti '01	♛♛	3*
● Barbera d'Asti '00	♛	3
● Barbera d'Asti Sup. La Cappelletta '97	♛♛	5
● Barbera d'Asti Sup. La Cappelletta '98	♛♛	5
● Barbera d'Asti Sup. La Cappelletta '99	♛♛	5

○ Asti De Miranda M. Cl. '00	♛♛♛	6
● Barbera d'Asti Solus Ad '00	♛♛	6
● Barolo Cerequio Tenuta Secolo '98	♛♛	8
○ Spumante M. Cl. Brut Ris. Giuseppe Contratto '98	♛♛	6
○ Piemonte Chardonnay La Sabauda '00	♛♛	5
● Barbera d'Asti Panta Rei '00	♛	4
○ Spumante M. Cl. Brut Ris. Giuseppe Contratto '96	♛♛♛	6
○ Asti De Miranda M. Cl. '97	♛♛♛	6
● Barolo Cerequio Tenuta Secolo '97	♛♛♛	8

CANELLI (AT)

Luigi Coppo e Figli
Via Alba, 68
14053 Canelli (AT)
tel. 0141823146
e-mail: info@coppo.it

We have come to expect high quality from the Coppo family's wines. Their sparklers, whites and reds all bear witness to the serious, methodical approach that makes the Coppos a force to be reckoned with in the Asti area and in Piedmont as a whole. This year we welcome to the ranks two new recruits, the Barbera and the Chardonnay Riserva della Famiglia '98. Both are produced in limited quantities and matured for two years longer than the Barbera Pomorosso and the Chardonnay Monteriolo. The Monteriolo is a white that has proved ideal for tucking away in the cellar. The '00 vintage is very good indeed, aged to perfection in barriques, and with a tangy vein of acidity that supports the wine's nice fruit. The Riserva della Famiglia is every bit its equal and shows just how much cellar potential the best Piedmont Chardonnays can muster. The cream of the Coppos' Barbera crop is again the Pomorosso, a deep ruby wine with seductive hints of mulberry and cherry, layered over spice and balsam. The aromas spill over onto the palate, which displays power, balance, concentration and lingering length. The Barbera Riserva della Famiglia '98 is also superb, marrying subtle elegance with wonderful harmony. We also liked the Camp du Rouss '00, which is just a shade less concentrated than its brothers. Maintaining the high standard, the Freisa Mondaccione '00 shows clear strawberry aromas and a graceful, velvety body. The Alterego '00, a mix of cabernet sauvignon and barbera, is further proof of the extraordinary skills of Roberto Coppo, the estate's oenologist.

● Barbera d'Asti Pomorosso '00	♟♟	7
● Monferrato Alterego '00	♟♟	6
● Barbera d'Asti Riserva della Famiglia '98	♟♟	8
● Barbera d'Asti Camp du Rouss '00	♟♟	4*
● Langhe Rosso Mondaccione '00	♟♟	6
○ Piemonte Chardonnay Monteriolo '00	♟♟	6
○ Piemonte Chardonnay Riserva della Famiglia '98	♟♟	8
○ Moscato d'Asti Moncalvina '01	♟♟	4
● Barbera d'Asti Pomorosso '90	♟♟♟	7
● Barbera d'Asti Pomorosso '99	♟♟♟	7
● Monferrato Alterego '99	♟♟	6

CANELLI (AT)

Villa Giada
Reg. Ceirole, 4
14053 Canelli (AT)
tel. 0141831100
e-mail: villagiada@atlink.it

Villa Giada stands on the slopes of Ceirole, a few kilometres outside the town of Canelli. The winery has been in the business for years and today vinifies grapes grown in the vineyards near the cellars in Canelli, Calosso and Agliano Terme, all areas that are ideal for the production of Barbera and Moscato d'Asti. The entire Faccia family works in the vineyards and cellars to turn out a very sound range of wines. Again this year, their two best were the Barbera Bricco Dani and the Moscato Ceirole. The first is barrique-conditioned. Its deep, dense ruby red introduces rich, lingering aromas of berry fruit and spice. The palate requires a little more maturing to bring out the best in the acidity and structure but is already warm, the pervasive aromas hinting at morello cherry and liquorice. The Moscato offers more in terms of flesh and softness than effervescence, combining melon, orange peel and sage on the nose. In the mouth, it is moderately sweet and would complement a heavy dessert very nicely. The steel-conditioned Barbera Ajan and the Barbera La Quercia, aged in large barrels, are both decent examples of their respective wine types. Finally, the vibrant, green-flecked yellow of the Chardonnay Bricco Manè precedes pleasing notes of fruit and vanilla.

○ Moscato d'Asti Ceirole '01	♟♟	3*
● Barbera d'Asti Sup. Bricco Dani '00	♟♟	5
● Barbera d'Asti Sup. Ajan '00	♟	4
● Barbera d'Asti Sup. Vigneto La Quercia '00	♟	4
○ Piemonte Chardonnay Bricco Manè '01	♟	3
● Barbera d'Asti Sup. Bricco Dani '97	♟♟	5
● Barbera d'Asti Sup. Bricco Dani '98	♟♟	5
● Barbera d'Asti Sup. Bricco Dani '99	♟♟	5

CAREMA (TO)

Cantina dei Produttori Nebbiolo
di Carema
Via Nazionale, 32
10010 Carema (TO)
tel. 0125811160
e-mail: cantinacarema@libero.it

The Cantina dei Produttori Nebbiolo di Carema is a small, dynamic co-operative that brings together about 60 local growers, most of whom have very small vineyards (under a hectare in size) at altitudes of between 300 and 600 metres above sea level. Their collective production is also limited and currently amounts to around 50,000 bottles a year of Carema DOC, plus a few simpler wines sold almost exclusively at the winery itself. The Carema, however, is the territory's forte. Made from a base of nebbiolo, known locally as picotener, it is sturdy, austere and aristocratic. The Cantina gave us two versions to taste this year, a barrique-conditioned version and the Carema Carema, which has captured the hearts of devotees of the style. The oak-aged wine, a '97, has a colour of medium intensity and an orange rim, and proffers aromas of stewed fruit that need some time to breathe before they come through in a complex, wonderfully elegant nose. The alcohol-rich palate has good structure and austere tannins accompanied by notes of toastiness. The Carema Carema is a big wine, even if it gives an initial impression of over-evolution on the nose. Spice, liquorice, cocoa powder and tobacco tones are foregrounded in a wine that impresses more for its complexity than for its power.

CASSINASCO (AT)

Karin e Remo Hohler
Reg. Bricco Bosetti, 85
14050 Cassinasco (AT)
tel. 0141851209
e-mail: remohohler@hotmail.com

There is an interesting story behind this small winery in the vineyards and woods around Cassinasco, a few kilometres from Canelli. Husband and wife team Karin and Remo Hohler, originally from the German-speaking part of Switzerland, dreamed of buying a piece of land in Piedmont and leading a quiet life in the country. An announcement in a Basel newspaper gave them their chance and in 1990, they purchased an estate outside Cassinasco, complete with house, cellars and three hectares of well-aspected vines. This was the first step on their journey into wine. Soon, winemaking became the sole occupation of a family that also numbers four children, one of whom is currently studying at the school of oenology in Alba. Under the expert guidance of Giuliano Noè, the Hohlers have developed a style and a very clear philosophy over the years – make a limited number of labels (only three) that aim for the highest possible quality. And that's exactly what they've done, if the two selections of Barbera d'Asti we tasted are anything to go by. The standard Pian Bosco '00, the steel-conditioned version, is fragrant and very, very enjoyable. The fresh, fruity varietal aromas of blackberry and violets precede a lovely, heady palate with seriously good structure. The finish is long and caressing. The barrique-aged version stays for eight months in small casks. It, too, is excellent, with a barely discernible trace of charred oak on the nose lending the fruit softness and elegance. The palate is powerful and austere through to the long finish. The dry Moscato, Cenerentola, is well made.

• Carema Selezione '97	ŶŶ	5
• Carema Carema '97	Ŷ	4
• Carema Carema '95	ŶŶ	4
• Carema Selezione '96	ŶŶ	5
• Carema Carema '96	Ŷ	4

• Barbera d'Asti Pian Bosco '00	ŶŶ	5
• Barbera d'Asti Pian Bosco Barrique '00	ŶŶ	5
○ Cenerentola '01	Ŷ	4
• Barbera d'Asti Pian Bosco Barrique '98	ŶŶ	5
• Barbera d'Asti Pian Bosco '99	ŶŶ	5

CASTAGNOLE DELLE LANZE (AT)

★★ La Spinetta
Fraz. Annunziata, 17
14054 Castagnole delle Lanze (AT)
tel. 0141877396
e-mail: arivetti@libero.it

As we wait for the first Barolo from grapes grown on the estate acquired in 2000, work goes ahead on the new cellars in Grinzane Cavour. This will become the vinification centre for all the La Spinetta Langhe wines, from the Barbaresco and Barolo selections to the Barbera Gallina. The current base in Castagnole Lanze, also restructured, will continue to host Asti production and the winery's headquarters. The range of wines presented this year is one of the best in the area and there were two Three Glass awards to prove it. The Barbaresco, from Starderi at Neive, provided an encore of last year's winning performance. Readier to drink than the other two selections, it has a dense colour and distinct impressions of plum, balsam and liquorice. Entry on the palate is sweet and backed up by powerful fruit, then the finish finds a nice balance of acidity and tannins. The toasty tones of the oak used for ageing are barely perceptible. The Barbera d'Asti Superiore won a first Three Glass award. This year it's even better than the Barbera d'Alba Gallina. The rich extract is evident right from the start in its purple ruby appearance. The palate is very harmonious, disclosing delightful sweet fruit and superb length, enhanced by elegant tones of charred oak. The Barbaresco Valeirano, Pin and Barbera Gallina are all very good, while the Barbaresco Gallina is still a little oak-heavy. The Barbera d'Asti Ca' di Pian is youthfully vinous and eminently drinkable. The sauvignon-based Langhe Bianco, the Chardonnay, the Moscato and the dried-grape Oro complete this outstanding range.

● Barbera d'Asti Sup. '00	▼▼▼	7
● Barbaresco Vigneto Starderi '99	▼▼▼	8
● Monferrato Rosso Pin '00	▼▼	7
● Barbaresco Vigneto Gallina '99	▼▼	8
● Barbaresco Vigneto Valeirano '99	▼▼	8
● Barbera d'Alba Vigneto Gallina '00	▼▼	7
○ Langhe Bianco '00	▼▼	6
○ Piemonte Chardonnay Lidia '00	▼▼	6
○ Moscato d'Asti Bricco Quaglia '01	▼▼	4
● Barbera d'Asti Ca' di Pian '01	▼▼	5
○ La Spinetta Oro '98	▼▼	6
● Barbaresco Vigneto Starderi '98	▼▼▼	8
● Barbaresco Vigneto Valeirano '98	▼▼▼	8
● Barbera d'Alba Vigneto Gallina '99	▼▼▼	7

CASTEL BOGLIONE (AT)

Araldica - Il Cascinone
V.le Laudano, 2
14040 Castel Boglione (AT)
tel. 014176319
e-mail: claudio@araldicavini.com

Il Cascinone, the large Acqui estate and Araldica's latest venture, is almost ready. The cellars are nearly finished and 42 of the 70 hectares planted to vine have already gone into production. Il Cascinone is destined to be the most important selection of a company – Araldica – that numbers 290 members, a collective total of 800 hectares and turns out 4,000,000 bottles a year. Their deep garnet-ruby Barbera Rive has aromas of flowers and cocoa powder with balsamic undertones. On the palate, there is good structure, a well-sustained follow-through and a long finish that mirrors the nose. The Monferrato Rosso Luce Monaca, with a barbera, cabernet and merlot base, has dense colour and a bouquet of berry fruit and pepper layered over vaguely vegetal notes. The palate is full-bodied and balanced with quite a firm character and good length. The Monferrato Bianco Camillona has a clear, intense nose that proffers aromas ranging from fruit to sage to citrus fruit. The fairly well-sustained palate finishes on an aromatic sauvignon-themed note. The Chardonnay Roleto has a typical nose that opens out gradually and a refreshing, reasonably full-bodied, palate. The fruity, spicy Pinot Nero Renero shows good body and tannic weave on the palate, while the Arneis Sorilaria is alcohol-rich and shot through with notes of super-ripeness. The nicely textured Nebbiolo Castellero reveals just a hint of alcohol on the nose.

● Barbera d'Asti Sup. Rive '00	▼▼	4*
● Monferrato Rosso Luce Monaca '00	▼▼	4*
○ Monferrato Bianco Camillona '01	▼▼	4*
○ Piemonte Chardonnay Roleto '01	▼	4
○ Roero Arneis Sorilaria '01	▼	4
● Nebbiolo d'Alba Castellero '00	▼	5
● Monferrato Rosso Renero '00	▼	4
● Barbera d'Asti Sup. Rive '99	▼▼	4
● Monferrato Rosso Luce Monaca '99	▼▼	4

CASTEL BOGLIONE (AT)

Cascina Garitina
Via Gianola, 20
14040 Castel Boglione (AT)
tel. 0141762162
e-mail: info@cascinagaritina.it

Little by little, Gianluca Morino is taking over from his father, Pasquale, at the helm of this winery. In his young and enthusiastic hands, the estate is expanding and now boasts approximately 20 hectares of vines. Over the next three years, Gianluca aims to take his annual production to 150,000 bottles. But that's not all. he also wants to transform the cellars along the lines of the great Bordeaux châteaux, offering a limited range of high-quality wines instead of a mixed production. His goal is to release 100,000 bottles of Barbera and another 50,000 of Barbera Superiore and Monferrato Rosso. At present, Cascina Garitina offers just over 20,000 bottles of Barbera Neuvsent, which is aged for more than a year, 70 per cent in barrique and 30 per cent in tonneaux, half of which are new; 35,000 bottles of Barbera Bricco Garitta, only one third of which goes into oak; 16,000 bottles of Monferrato Amis, a blend of 40 per cent barbera, 35 per cent pinot nero and 25 per cent cabernet; and a few thousand bottles of Dolcetto Caranzana and Barbera Morinaccio. The Cabernet Estremis has gone out of production. The Barbera d'Asti Superiore Nizza Neuvsent '00 flaunts toasty aromas, mingling with cherry jam, and the powerful, balanced structure of the great Asti reds. The Monferrato Rosso Amis '00 has a fruit and balsam nose but the tannins are a little edgy. The Barbera Bricco Garitta was just below for its aromas of stewed fruit and acidulous hints in the finish. The Dolcetto Caranzana '01 is quite rich but a tad rustic.

CASTELLINALDO (CN)

Raffaele Gili
Reg. Pautasso, 7
12050 Castellinaldo (CN)
tel. 0173639011

The story of this small Castellinaldo winery is in many ways typical of the winemaking scene of Roero over the last few years. After his introduction to viticulture by his father Francesco, who still gives him an invaluable hand in the vineyards, young Raffaele Gili took the big step of setting up on his own to make high-quality wines. The upshot is a beautiful new cellar at the entrance to the town, five meticulously tended hectares planted to vine and an impressive collection of wines, all worthy of close attention. Before taking a look at the wines we sampled this time around, we would like to note that the estate has an annual production of 40,000 bottles and that Raffaele runs his winery with his wife Laura. We very much liked the Roero Bric Angelino. It's very concentrated on the nose with clear notes of berry fruit, wild berries and coffee. On the palate, progression is vigorous, round and velvety, in anticipation of a lingering, very harmonious finish. The Nebbiolo Sansivé also performed very well, displaying all the characteristics of the variety without allowing the oak to dominate. The Castellinaldo Barbera offers a very respectable interpretation of the grape. It's another example of Raffaele's skilful use of small casks to make a distinguished wine with an upfront nose of delightful cherry sensations and round, supple palate. Finally, the Roero Arneis is well-managed and agreeable.

● Barbera d'Asti Sup. Nizza Neuvsent '00	ŸŸ	5
● Monferrato Rosso Amis '00	ŸŸ	4
● Barbera d'Asti Bricco Garitta '01	Ÿ	3*
● Dolcetto d'Asti Caranzana '01	Ÿ	3
● Barbera d'Asti Sup. Neuvsent '96	ŸŸ	5
● Barbera d'Asti Sup. Neuvsent '98	ŸŸ	5
● Monferrato Rosso Amis '98	ŸŸ	4
● Barbera d'Asti Bricco Garitta '99	ŸŸ	3
● Barbera d'Asti Sup. Neuvsent '99	ŸŸ	5
● Monferrato Rosso Amis '99	ŸŸ	4
● Monferrato Rosso Estremis '99	Ÿ	5

● Castellinaldo Barbera d'Alba '00	ŸŸ	5
● Nebbiolo d'Alba Sansivé '00	ŸŸ	5
● Roero Bric Angelino '00	ŸŸ	5
○ Roero Arneis '01	Ÿ	3
● Castellinaldo Barbera d'Alba '99	ŸŸ	5
● Nebbiolo d'Alba Sansivé '99	Ÿ	5

CASTELLINALDO (CN)

Fabrizio Pinsoglio
Fraz. Madonna dei Cavalli, 8
12050 Castellinaldo (CN)
Tel. 0173213078

This year we tasted a magnificent Barbera, courtesy of Fabrizio Pinsoglio, a young man who has earned himself a place in the winemaking panorama of Roero for his determination and indisputable talent. That talent caught the eye of Matteo Correggia, Fabrizio's maestro in the vineyards and cellars, along with his own father, Oreste. Well-prepared by the invaluable lessons he learned at their sides, Fabrizio now runs this winery with the help of three women: his fiancée Andreina, sister Teresa and mother Maria. Work has recently been completed on the new cellars and the new plantings that have already gone into production takes the total number of hectares planted to vine to eight and a half. The estate produces 30,000 bottles a year under five labels. As we mentioned, the Barbera Bric La Rondolina is superlative. Dazzling garnet in hue, it offers sweet sensations of berry fruit, violets and morello cherry in the bouquet, a succulent palate and an austere, lingering, wonderfully balanced finish. The Roero is also on top form, boasting an intense ruby colour and complex aromas of autumn leaves and dried flowers. The palate packs plenty of energy and character in a lovely overall structure. The Nebbiolo d'Alba is pleasant and well put together. Of the whites on offer, the Arneis is tangy and pleasant but a special mention must go to the first edition of the Oreste, a white table wine named after Fabrizio's late father. This well-structured Chardonnay is young and has still to come to terms with the oak.

CASTELLINALDO (CN)

Vielmin
Via San Damiano, 16
12050 Castellinaldo (CN)
Tel. 0173213298 - 0173611248
E-mail: ivan.gili@tin.it

Vielmin is the name of the small estate run with zeal and skill by young Ivan Gili, brother of Raffaele, who also makes an appearance in this year's edition of the Guide. Ivan didn't set up his on own because of any problems on the family front (the brothers are the best of friends and their father Francesco helps both of them without favouritism). He wanted to prove to himself that he could make good wines even without the benefit of long experience and, above all, on his own. With the support of his wife, he set up a small cellar in the centre of Castellinaldo, bought some splendid plots in the Granera area, the town's best in terms of wine production, and produced his first wines. These immediately caught our attention. Today, after several years of experimentation, Ivan is on the brink of bigger things and we are right behind him. All the wines he offered us this year were good, particularly the two Barberas, which impressed with their fragrance and personality. Despite its extreme youth, the Srëi is already very sophisticated and has very well-defined fruit aromas. It obviously lacks depth on the palate but is notable for its amazing suppleness. The Castellinaldo Barbera, in contrast, is more mature, offering a complex bouquet and an austere palate buttressed by just the right dose of oak. The Roero La Rocca is also a great success, with a concentrated nose and very confident palate. The Arneis is tangy and satisfying.

● Barbera d'Alba Bric La Rondolina '00	🍷🍷	5
● Roero '00	🍷🍷	5
● Nebbiolo d'Alba '00	🍷	4
○ Roero Arneis Vigneto Malinot '01	🍷	3
○ Oreste	🍷	4
● Roero '98	🍷🍷	4
● Barbera d'Alba Bric La Rondolina '99	🍷🍷	4
● Roero '99	🍷🍷	4
● Barbera d'Alba '99	🍷	3

● Barbera d'Alba Srëi '01	🍷🍷	4*
● Roero La Rocca '01	🍷🍷	5
● Castellinaldo Barbera d'Alba '00	🍷🍷	5
○ Roero Arneis '01	🍷	3
● Castellinaldo Barbera d'Alba '99	🍷🍷	5
● Barbera d'Alba '99	🍷	4
● Nebbiolo d'Alba '99	🍷	5

CASTELNUOVO DON BOSCO (AT)

Cascina Gilli
Via Nevissano, 36
14022 Castelnuovo Don Bosco (AT)
tel. 0119876984
e-mail: cascinagilli@libero.it

Gianni Vergnano's estate comprises 20 or so hectares planted to vine around Cascina Gilli, where the well-designed cellars are to be found. The philosophy of this estate is to employ modern techniques and equipment to produce exceptional wines that are very traditional in style. We don't need to remind you that Freisa plays an important role in the traditions of these hills and Cascina Gilli releases many different versions of the wine. Their Vigna del Forno earns Two Glasses for the sweet timbre of a bouquet that releases lovely hints of almond, mint and berry fruit, and for the balanced fullness of its palate, which signs off with a gorgeous flourish of fruit. The Barbera Vigna delle More is always good and the '01 vintage has a rich garnet-ruby colour with a youthful rim, introducing nuances of black cherry, confectioner's cream and mint against a backdrop of autumn leaves. It is surefooted, well-sustained, full-bodied and complex on the palate, which is rounded off by a lovely finish redolent of fruit and liquorice. The better of the two other Freisas we tasted was the lively but full-bodied Luna di Maggio but the basic version is nevertheless agreeable. The varietal notes of rose released by the Malvasia are quite mature. Effervescence and understated tannins combine to produce a gutsy palate. The Bianco Rafé, with its base of chardonnay and cortese, is uncomplicated and faintly grassy, while the barbera-and-freisa Monferrato Rosso is correct and the Bonarda easy to drink.

● Barbera d'Asti Vigna delle More '01	ΨΨ	3*
● Freisa d'Asti Vigna del Forno '01	ΨΨ	3*
● Malvasia di Castelnuovo Don Bosco '01	ΨΨ	3*
● Freisa d'Asti Luna di Maggio '01	Ψ	3
● Freisa d'Asti Vivace '01	Ψ	3
● Monferrato Rosso '01	Ψ	3
○ Rafé Bianco '01	Ψ	3
● Piemonte Bonarda '01		3
● Barbera d'Asti Vigna delle More '00	ΨΨ	3

CASTIGLIONE FALLETTO (CN)

Azelia
Fraz. Garbelletto
Via Alba-Barolo, 53
12060 Castiglione Falletto (CN)
tel. 017362859

Luigi and Lorella Scavino get 55,000 bottles a year from the grapes grown on their ten hectare estate. The Barolo Azelia selections have always been at the top of their class, thanks in part to their prestigious vineyards of origin in the municipalities of Castiglione Falletto and Serralunga. The San Rocco '98 is an excellent wine. Already offering a wealth of seductive aromas, it has magnificent structure that will develop superbly as it ages. Ruby red with a garnet edge, it discloses delightful notes of spice and balsam mingling with hints of black berry fruit and wild rose. The palate reveals its force with soft tannins and a never-ending finish that ends on a touch of liquorice. The Bricco Fiasco '98, too, is no less than exquisite. Forty per cent aged in new casks, like the San Rocco, it opens with refined berry fruit and tobacco, then the velvety palate is buttressed by good acidity with captivating nuances of spice in the finish. Both these very interesting Barolos came very close to the Three Glass mark. The standard Barolo can hold its head up in the company of the two selections, offering a more direct, approachable interpretation of the providential harvest of 1998. The Barbera Vigneto Punta '00 is obtained from 50-year-old vines and discloses its sojourn in barriques in aromas of charred wood and vanilla. These merge with distinct fruit notes that carry over onto the palate, where they are well supported by classic, varietal acidity. The Dolcetto d'Alba Bricco dell'Oriolo '01 is potent and caressing. It can only benefit from a few years in the cellar.

● Barolo Bricco Fiasco '98	ΨΨ	8
● Barolo S. Rocco '98	ΨΨ	8
● Barbera d'Alba Vigneto Punta '00	ΨΨ	5
● Dolcetto d'Alba Bricco dell'Oriolo '01	ΨΨ	4*
● Barolo '98	ΨΨ	7
● Barolo '91	ΨΨΨ	8
● Barolo Bricco Fiasco '93	ΨΨΨ	8
● Barolo Bricco Fiasco '95	ΨΨΨ	8
● Barolo Bricco Fiasco '96	ΨΨΨ	8
● Barolo Bricco Fiasco '97	ΨΨ	8
● Barolo S. Rocco '97	ΨΨ	8
● Barbera d'Alba Vigneto Punta '99	ΨΨ	5

CASTIGLIONE FALLETTO (CN)

Cascina Bongiovanni
Via Alba-Barolo, 4
12060 Castiglione Falletto (CN)
tel. 0173262184

The high level of quality attained by Davide Mozzoni's wines has ceased to surprise us. The 30,000 bottles produced from his six hectares planted to vine are now divided into six categories, including two newcomers, the Dolcetto di Diano and the Barbera. The steel-conditioned Dolcetto d'Alba, from grapes grown in Castiglione Falletto and Monforte, is pleasant and well-balanced. The fruity, flowery Diano d'Alba is even better, with more concentrated colour and an abundance of flesh and tannins. The Barbera comes from Serralunga and its 45-day sojourn in barriques imbues it with lovely, yielding tones of vanilla that melt into fruity notes of black cherry and blackberry. The Langhe Faletto, a blend this year of cabernet sauvignon, barbera and merlot, is deep ruby and alluring on the nose with hints of redcurrant, raspberry and cocoa powder. The soft, harmonious palate shows fine-grained tannins and ends on a final note of coffee and tobacco. The Barolo '98 is most impressive and extremely satisfying for its cornucopia of vibrant, pervasive aromas of plum, rose, berry fruit and pepper. Assured yet soft tannins caress the palate and are sustained by a good level of acidity. But it is the Barolo Pernanno that towers over this year's range of offerings from Cascina Bongiovanni. A four-square wine with a deeply absorbing personality, it hovers on the brink of a third Glass. Ruby shading into garnet, it proffers a raspberry and cocoa powder nose then a palate that is balanced and full-bodied with traces of pepper and liquorice in the finish.

● Barolo Pernanno '98	🍷🍷	8
● Barbera d'Alba '01	🍷🍷	5
● Diano d'Alba '01	🍷🍷	4
● Dolcetto d'Alba '01	🍷🍷	3*
● Barolo '98	🍷🍷	7
● Langhe Rosso Faletto '00	🍷🍷	6
● Barolo Pernanno '95	🍷	8
● Barolo '96	🍷	7
● Barolo Pernanno '96	🍷	8
● Barolo '97	🍷	7
● Barolo Pernanno '97	🍷	8
● Langhe Rosso Faletto '97	🍷	6
● Langhe Rosso Faletto '98	🍷	6

CASTIGLIONE FALLETTO (CN)

★ Bricco Rocche - Bricco Asili
Via Monforte, 63
12060 Castiglione Falletto (CN)
tel. 0173282582
e-mail: ceretto@ceretto.com

From the futuristic cube that crowns the Bricco Rocche winery, all the great vineyards of Barolo stretch out before the eye. In front of the winery are the slopes of Brunate, to the left those of Cerequio and its tiny village, and further over we can even see Barolo, the castle and Cannubi. If we look up, again the left, Bussia and the best vineyards in Monforte come into view, while a 180-degree turn reveals Vigna Rionda, Prapò and the Gabutti vines of Serralunga d'Alba. The unique panorama is filled with the vineyards that long ago overran the Langhe hills and elbowed out every other kind of agriculture. Bricco Rocche is where Ceretto makes its great Barolos, which take their names from the estate's vineyard selections: Bricco Rocche at Castiglione Falletto, Prapò at Serralunga d'Alba and Brunate at La Morra. 1998 has given us three superlative Barolos, the more structured and powerful Prapò showing the vintage off to its best advantage. The captivating, velvety Bricco Rocche is every bit as good, whereas the Brunate is sophisticated and a little less structured than its stablemates. But this year, the greatest Ceretto triumph comes in the form of a Barbaresco from Bricco Asili, the '99. This is quite simply one of the best Barbarescos of its vintage with a superb taste profile. Its rich red colour with garnet highlights is the prelude to a well-defined, potent nose with berry fruit, tobacco and violet to the fore. Powerful and concentrated on the palate, it also has enviable balance and elegance. A resounding Three Glasses for this perfect, eminently cellarable wine.

● Barbaresco Bricco Asili '99	🍷🍷🍷	8
● Barolo Prapò Bricco Rocche '98	🍷🍷	8
● Barolo Bricco Rocche '98	🍷🍷	8
● Barolo Brunate Bricco Rocche '98	🍷🍷	8
● Barbaresco Bernardot Bricco Asili '99	🍷🍷	8
● Barbaresco Faset Bricco Asili '99	🍷	8
● Barolo Prapò Bricco Rocche '83	🍷🍷🍷	8
● Barbaresco Bricco Asili '88	🍷🍷🍷	8
● Barbaresco Bricco Asili '89	🍷🍷🍷	8
● Barolo Bricco Rocche '89	🍷🍷🍷	8
● Barolo Brunate Bricco Rocche '90	🍷🍷🍷	8
● Barbaresco Bricco Asili '96	🍷🍷🍷	8
● Barbaresco Bricco Asili '97	🍷🍷🍷	8

CASTIGLIONE FALLETTO (CN)

Brovia
Fraz. Garbelletto
Via Alba-Barolo, 54
12060 Castiglione Falletto (CN)
tel. 017362852
e-mail: gibrovia@tin.it

The Brovia team has grown: Raffaele, Giacinto, young Elena and Cristina have been joined by Alex, Elena's husband, who has moved to the Langhe from Catalonia. The Brovias' vineyards are in excellent locations and yield wines steeped in tradition, made with a skilled hand. The Dolcetto Solatìo, an unusual version of this wine, hails from Serralunga. Its slightly super-ripe fruit, high level of alcohol and powerful body bestow satisfying sensations of ripe fruit, notably cherry, enriched with touches of pepper and spice. The Barbera Brea is juicy and fruity, dense ruby in appearance, richly extracted with just the right amount of acidity. The Barolos are very successful. The standard version is obtained from young vines and offers a happy union of power and elegance. The selections are more serious. The sandy terrain that produced the Rocche dei Brovia can take credit for the wealth of aromas that greet the nose and usher in a full, succulent palate of gentle tannins with hints of cocoa powder and spice. The Ca' Mia displays the muscle typical of a Serralunga Barolo and will come into its own after a few years in the cellar. At the moment, its full potential is evident in the wonderful balance and generous, alluring aromas that will open out in time. The Barolo Villero possesses a berry fruit and dried rose bouquet, as well as robust tannins that meld in a remarkable structure on the palate. The finish is extraordinarily long and leaves a final sensation of liquorice and tobacco in the mouth.

• Barolo Ca' Mia '98	🍷🍷	8
• Barolo Rocche dei Brovia '98	🍷🍷	7
• Barbera d'Alba Brea '00	🍷🍷	5
• Dolcetto d'Alba Solatìo '00	🍷🍷	5
• Barolo Villero '98	🍷🍷	7
• Barolo '98	🍷	6
• Barolo Monprivato '90	🍷🍷🍷	8
• Barolo Ca' Mia '96	🍷🍷🍷	8
• Dolcetto d'Alba Solatìo '99	🍷🍷	5
• Barolo Ca' Mia '97	🍷🍷	8
• Barolo Rocche dei Brovia '97	🍷🍷	7
• Barolo Villero '97	🍷🍷	7

CASTIGLIONE FALLETTO (CN)

F.lli Cavallotto
Loc. Bricco Boschis
Via Alba-Monforte
12060 Castiglione Falletto (CN)
tel. 017362814
e-mail: info@cavallotto.com

Giuseppe and Alfio Cavallotto, both oenologists, are the chief wine makers at this winery, which started to produce and sell its own wines in 1948. The approximately 23 hectares under vine that make up the estate are mainly planted to nebbiolo destined for Barolo. They are located in the prestigious vineyards of Bricco Boschis and Vignolo. The Cavallotto vinification style is traditional, involving Slavonian oak barrels for the Barolo and Barbera and fairly long macerations to produce wines that are not massively powerful but quite elegant and long-lived. The pick of the bunch this year is the Barolo Vigna San Giuseppe, which is very youthful but which will open out given time. It is garnet with an orange rim and the nose gradually reveals notes of forest floor, dried rose and mint. On the palate, the no-nonsense tannins are nicely balanced by acidity and support a progression that finishes on nuances of liquorice and coffee. The more approachable, easier-to-like Barolo Bric Boschis has a slightly less challenging structure. At the time of our tasting, the nose of the Vignolo was going through a period of withdrawal but with time and ageing, the tertiary aromas will emerge, signalling another triumph for this selection. The Barbera d'Alba Vigna del Cuculo and the Dolcetto Vigna Scot take home a Glass apiece. The Barbera is tangy and easy-drinking, the Dolcetto fruit-rich and flowery.

• Barolo Vigna S. Giuseppe Ris. '97	🍷🍷	8
• Barolo Bricco Boschis '98	🍷🍷	7
• Dolcetto d'Alba Vigna Scot '01	🍷	4
• Barolo Vignolo Ris. '97	🍷	8
• Barbera d'Alba Vigna del Cuculo '99	🍷	4
• Barolo Vigna S. Giuseppe Ris. '89	🍷🍷🍷	8
• Barolo Vignolo Ris. '95	🍷🍷	8
• Barolo Bricco Boschis '96	🍷🍷	7
• Barolo Vigna S. Giuseppe Ris. '96	🍷🍷	8
• Barolo Vignolo Ris. '96	🍷🍷	8
• Barolo Bricco Boschis '97	🍷🍷	7

CASTIGLIONE FALLETTO (CN)

★ Paolo Scavino
Fraz. Garbelletto
Via Alba-Barolo, 59
12060 Castiglione Falletto (CN)
tel. 017362850
e-mail: e.scavino@libero.it

Careful vineyard management, a clean, well-organized cellar, vinification methods that respect the fruit and a skilled hand with the oak: these are the elements that year after year enable Enrico Scavino to produce the wines that have earned him recognition as the grand master of Langhe winemen. His distinctive Barolos embody the best of nebbiolo in a framework of supreme elegance, with discreet but never overwhelming oak. The Barolo Bric '98 stands out for its deep ruby hue, verging on garnet, its cornucopia of aromas featuring berry fruit, pepper, cocoa powder and mint, and a palate that is muscular but not unsophisticated. A good wine from a good vintage. The Rocche dell'Annunziata '96 is magnificent – the best ever – developing gradually to end in a long, long finish of leather, tobacco and cocoa powder. This is a triumphant return to Three Glass form for a wine that enchants right from the start with a rich colour, a complex nose lifted by well-integrated oak, and an imposing palate with long, silky tannins. The basic Barolo is also extremely good, captivating with its generous, fruit-led, pervasive nose. It is very enjoyable, revealing delightful, soft tannins and perfect acidity. Another success, the Cannubi, offers mint, eucalyptus and red fruit. The Carobric has alluring hints of fruit, flowers, pepper and spice. In the Corale, nebbiolo, barbera and cabernet combine happily in a blend that is now well established in the Langhe. The Barbera and Dolcetto perform well, while the attractive Sorriso, a white from chardonnay and sauvignon, is fruity and medium-bodied.

CASTIGLIONE FALLETTO (CN)

Terre del Barolo
Via Alba-Barolo, 5
12060 Castiglione Falletto (CN)
tel. 0173262749
e-mail: tdb@terredelbarolo.com

The 2001 vintage marked the beginning of Terre del Barolo's "Project Quality", in which 70 associate growers were selected and asked to focus on vineyard management, in close collaboration with the supervisors of this big Langhe co-operative winery. The approximately 400 members of Terre del Barolo have a collective output of well over 1,000,000 bottles a year and offer a vast range of well-typed DOC and DOCG wines. The cellar adopts traditional vinification methods that aspire to bring out the typical characteristics of the grapes and the individual vineyards. For this edition of the Guide, the winery presented the Barolo Riserva '96 crus. Best of these, in the panel's opinion, is the Monvigliero for its typical dried rose bouquet and a palate that finishes on toasty, liquorice notes. The other selections and the basic version are also very good indeed. All have a garnet hue with an orange edge and reveal still-beefy tannins and good acidity. There is a long string of Dolcetto di Dianos and Dolcetto d'Albas. The pick of these is the Montagrillo, a good ambassador for the Diano d'Alba terroir, a zone well suited to the production of Dolcettos. The Barbera Valdisera and the Pelaverga are also both worthy of note and embody the qualities of their respective varieties. The first is fruity, tangy and very drinkable while the second has the trademark Pelaverga pepper and spice nose.

● Barolo Rocche dell'Annunziata Ris. '96	ŸŸŸ	8
● Barolo Bric dël Fiasc '98	ŸŸ	8
● Dolcetto d'Alba '01	ŸŸ	4
● Barolo '98	ŸŸ	8
● Barolo Cannubi '98	ŸŸ	8
● Barolo Carobric '98	ŸŸ	8
● Barbera d'Alba Affinata in Carati '99	ŸŸ	6
● Langhe Rosso Corale '99	ŸŸ	7
○ Langhe Bianco Sorriso '00	Ÿ	5
● Barolo Rocche dell'Annunziata Ris. '90	ŸŸŸ	8
● Barolo Bric dël Fiasc '95	ŸŸŸ	8
● Barolo Bric dël Fiasc '96	ŸŸŸ	8

● Barolo Monvigliero Ris. '96	ŸŸ	6
● Diano d'Alba Montagrillo '00	ŸŸ	3*
● Barbera d'Alba Valdisera '00	Ÿ	3
● Diano d'Alba Cascinotto '00	Ÿ	3
● Dolcetto d'Alba Le Passere '01	Ÿ	3
● Barolo Castello Ris. '96	Ÿ	6
● Barolo di Castiglione Falletto Ris. '96	Ÿ	6
● Barolo Rocche Ris. '96	Ÿ	6
● Barolo '98	Ÿ	6
● Verduno Pelaverga '01	Ÿ	4
● Barolo Codana '95	ŸŸ	7
● Barbera d'Alba Sup. '99	ŸŸ	5

CASTIGLIONE FALLETTO (CN)

Vietti
P.zza Vittorio Veneto, 5
12060 Castiglione Falletto (CN)
Tel. 017362825
E-mail: info@vietti.com

Mario Cordero and Luca Currado gave us some very good wines at this year's tastings but two in particular, the Barbera d'Asti La Crena and the Barbera d'Alba Scarrone Vigna Vecchia, were outstanding and walked away with Three Glasses. These two intriguing selections marry a healthy respect for tradition with the use of modern technology in the cellars. As always, meticulous work in the vineyard is the magic ingredient in producing the highest-quality wines. The majestic Barbera d'Asti La Crena '99 is deep ruby, with faint purple highlights, and its nose is an explosion of fruit, spice and vanilla. The palate is succulent and aroma-rich, supported by good acidity and rounded off by a never-ending finish that won't let go. Every bit as good is the Barbera d'Alba Scarrone Vigna Vecchia, another DOCG champ. The sheer eloquence of the fruit is awesome and the overall balance remarkable. The other two Barberas, the Tre Vigne and the Scarrone, are a great deal simpler but very drinkable. Turning to the Barolos, we have four very traditional wines with a garnet appearance and confident tannins, combined with well-defined varietal characteristics of nebbiolo, good acidity and extraordinary length. The Villero Riserva '96 is the most austere in the line-up, with liquorice, tobacco and leather tones rounding off a very impressive profile. The other Barolos, all '98 vintages, include a very good Brunate and a nice Lazzarito. The first is powerful, fragrant and still shows rugged tannins, while the Lazzarito is softer and more open, with captivating spice and balsam.

● Barbera d'Alba Scarrone Vigna Vecchia '00	🍷🍷🍷	7
● Barbera d'Asti La Crena '99	🍷🍷🍷	6
● Barolo Villero Ris. '96	🍷🍷	8
● Barolo Brunate '98	🍷🍷	8
● Barolo Lazzarito '98	🍷🍷	8
● Barbera d'Alba Scarrone '00	🍷	6
● Barbera d'Asti Tre Vigne '00	🍷	4
● Barolo Castiglione '98	🍷	7
● Barolo Rocche di Castiglione '98	🍷	8
● Barolo Rocche di Castiglione '85	🍷🍷🍷	8
● Barolo Rocche di Castiglione '88	🍷🍷🍷	8
● Barbera d'Alba Scarrone Vigna Vecchia '99	🍷🍷🍷	7
● Barolo Brunate '96	🍷🍷	8

CASTIGLIONE TINELLA (CN)

Caudrina
Strada Brosia, 20
12053 Castiglione Tinella (CN)
Tel. 0141855126
E-mail: romano@caudrina.it

Work at Castiglione Tinella goes on apace to complete the enormous new Dogliotti cellars. Romano and his sons Alessandro, Sergio and Marco have taken an active role in the construction of the building, which stands a few dozen metres from the winery's former headquarters. When complete, the cellars will allow the Dogliottis to deal much more efficiently with the fruit that goes into their 170,000 bottles a year. Castiglione Tinella is in the Moscato production zone – Romano is also president of the producers' consortium – and Moscato accounts for the lion's share of the estate's range. For some years now, the Dogliottis have been working on their two Barbera selections and a white made from chardonnay. The new vintages – 2001 for the Piemonte Chardonnay Mej and the Barbera d'Asti La Solista, 2000 for the Barbera d'Asti Superiore Montevenere – will be released a few months from now, to allow them more ageing time in bottle, In consequence, we are unable to pronounce judgement upon them. We did, however, taste the three wines that have made this winery's name: the Moscato d'Asti La Galeisa, from the estate's best vineyard, is straw yellow with faint flecks of gold and vaunts a range of aromas from spring flowers and peach to the sweeter tones of candied fruit. The palate is very chewy, well-sustained and refined. La Caudrina, the other selection, is a bit more mature and offers a less complex palate than the Galeisa. The Asti La Selvatica '01, one of the few Astis to be produced by a small winery, is excellent, revealing lovely lemony notes both in the nose and on the palate.

○ Moscato d'Asti La Galeisa '01	🍷🍷	4*
○ Asti La Selvatica '01	🍷🍷	4
○ Moscato d'Asti Caudrina '01	🍷🍷	4
● Barbera d'Asti Sup. Monte Venere '99	🍷🍷	5
● Barbera d'Asti La Solista '00	🍷	4
○ Piemonte Chardonnay Mej '00	🍷	4

CASTIGLIONE TINELLA (CN)

ICARDI
FRAZ. SANTUARIO - LOC. SAN LAZZARO
VIA BALBI, 30
12053 CASTIGLIONE TINELLA (CN)
TEL. 0141855159
E-MAIL: icardivino@libero.it

Claudio Icardi runs an estate of 63 hectares in the Langhe and Asti Monferrato that gives him 350,000 bottles a year. The range of wines on offer is wide and quality is high. We'll start our notes with the excellent Monferrato Rosso Cascina Bricco del Sole, a barbera, nebbiolo and cabernet blend that again this year made it through to the Three Glass taste-offs. Its attractive appearance introduces a generous nose and a confident palate. The balsamic aromas meld with hints of ripe berry fruit and a note of toastiness its sojourn in oak. The palate is potent and fruity, the sweet nuances in the finish marrying perfectly with the flavour. If we move on to the Barberas, both the Nuj Suj, whose deep garnet 2000 version has a pervasive nose of delightful jam and rhubarb, and the Surì di Mù, with its soft, very gratifying palate, are very good indeed. The dark Nebbiolo Surìsjvan elegantly proffers alluring hints of blackberry and raspberry. The palate is robust but free of rough edges. The Langhe Rosso Pafoj has a lovely fruit and liquorice nose and a full, inviting palate that hints at fruit in the finish. The sauvignon and chardonnay-based Pafoj Bianco flaunts gorgeous notes of herbs, spring flowers and cakes, then a velvety, rather dense palate. The Moscato La Rosa Selvatica has rich varietal notes that mingle with aromas of fermentation- The confident vein of sweetness in the mouth is nicely offset by effervescence. Finally, the Barolo Parej suggests rose and spice. The palate is nice and pulpy and there is no trace of tannin-derived asperity.

CASTIGLIONE TINELLA (CN)

LA MORANDINA
LOC. MORANDINI, 11
12053 CASTIGLIONE TINELLA (CN)
TEL. 0141855261
E-MAIL: lamorandina@tin.it

The beautiful La Morandina estate comprises 20 hectares planted to vine that produce an average of 70,000 bottles per harvest. This year's collection from brothers Paolo and Giulio Morando featured an interesting new recruit, a red table wine called Costa Nera, obtained from international grape types that wins Two Glasses on its debut performance. Garnet with an orange rim, it flaunts a vibrant, seductive nose that marries ripe fruit with green notes and spice, then reveals a subtle texture in the mouth. But the Barbera Varmat '00 is the big hitter from this estate. It's an intense wine with no-nonsense aromas of black cherry and ripe raspberry, mingled with hints of charred oak. The palate is forceful, showing lots of alcohol and acidity that meld in the very full body. The simpler Barbera d'Asti Zucchetto is deep hued and has a nose where sweet tones dominate, with suggestions of marzipan, cherry, aromatic herbs and tobacco. The palate is full, discreetly powerful and finishes harmoniously with mouthwatering traces of liquorice. The Costa del Sole, a dried-grape wine from moscato and riesling italico, is gold shading into amber. The nose offers dried fruit and rhubarb layered over evolved tones of leather. In the mouth, a prominent sweet vein and a long after-aroma round off the rich mouthfeel. Pleasant sage and orange blossom aromas are the hallmark of the Moscato, which is tangy and full-bodied on the palate. The Chardonnay is consistent and agreeable, delivering notes of fermentation and a generous dose of alcohol.

● Monferrato Rosso Cascina Bricco del Sole '00	▼▼	6
● Barbera d'Alba Surì di Mù '00	▼▼	5
● Barbera d'Asti Nuj Suj '00	▼▼	5
● Langhe Nebbiolo Surìsjvan '00	▼▼	5
● Langhe Rosso Pafoj '01	▼▼	7
○ Moscato d'Asti La Rosa Selvatica '01	▼	4
● Barbera d'Asti Tabarin '01	▼	4
○ Monferrato Bianco Pafoj '01	▼	5
● Barolo Parej '98	▼	8
● Monferrato Rosso Cascina Bricco del Sole '99	▽▽	6
● Langhe Rosso Pafoj '00	▽▽	7
● Barolo Parej '97	▽▽	8

● Barbera d'Asti Varmat '00	▼▼	6
● Barbera d'Asti Zucchetto '00	▼▼	4*
● Costa Nera '00	▼▼	7
○ Moscato d'Asti '01	▼▼	4*
○ Costa del Sole '99	▼▼	5
○ Langhe Chardonnay '01	▼	4
● Barbera d'Asti Varmat '97	▽▽	6
● Barbera d'Asti Varmat '98	▽▽	6
● Barbera d'Asti Varmat '99	▽▽	6

CASTIGLIONE TINELLA (CN)

Elio Perrone
Strada San Martino, 3/bis
12053 Castiglione Tinella (CN)
tel. 0141855803
e-mail: elioperr@tin.it

Stefano Perrone has about 10 hectares planted to vine and an annual production of 80,000 bottles. The grapes come from estate-owned vineyards and – in the case of a few wines only – from other suppliers. Stefano's range was up to its customary standards, but it is the Barbera Mongovone, a newcomer, that made the biggest impact on its first release. This big Barbera comes from a vineyard in Mongovone, Isola d'Asti, which dates back to 1932 and was bought by Stefano in 2000. The wine comes in elegant, one-litre bottles and 2,800 bottles were produced. Dense in hue, with a youthful edge, it throws a nose that is at once seductive and complex, with gorgeous blackberry and cherry set against chocolate and autumn leaves. The palate immediately shows all the vigour of the great Barberas and the progression hangs tightly together through to a warm, lingering finish that echoes the aromas of the nose. The simpler Barbera Grivò is enjoyable for the sweetness of its fragrances and its good weight in the mouth. The Sourgal is the most rounded of the Moscatos on offer, with an enveloping, concentrated nose laced with sage and peach, then a refreshing prickle on the palate that balances to perfection the remarkably rich flavour. The Moscato Clarté has a subtler nose and a less challenging palate that is still jolly and very satisfying. Last but not least, the sweet Bigarò, obtained principally from brachetto grapes, is aromatic and fresh-tasting.

CASTIGLIONE TINELLA (CN)

Paolo Saracco
Via Circonvallazione, 6
12053 Castiglione Tinella (CN)
tel. 0141855113

Paolo Saracco works 30 hectares of vineyards, some of which he has planted over the last few years, to obtain a production that is heavily dominated by two Moscatos: a standard version and the first-rate Moscato d'Autunno. These celebrated bottles are flanked by an assortment of whites: the Chardonnay Bianch del Luv, which was not made in 2000; the Chardonnay Prasué, less challenging than its previous version; and the Bianco Graffagno from sauvignon and riesling renano. This last comes first in our tasting notes. It is a rich, vibrant, straw yellow and has a lovely nose in which the aromatic tones of the two varieties are layered over each other to enhance an unusual nose profile, with nuances of fresh grass, tomato leaf and salt-encrusted rock. On the palate, it is rounded, well-sustained, soft and full-flavoured, with a long finish that echoes the nose. The delightful, rich Moscato d'Autunno is limpid, yielding ripe, warm aromas of peach and orange blossom whose opulence spills over onto the palate. The strong sweet vein is nicely kept in check by the effervescence. The basic Moscato is subtler, offering harmonious varietal aromas and a zesty, no-nonsense palate. The Chardonnay Prasué is a rich, lustrous gold, regaling the nose with varietal flowers and hazelnuts, then a supple palate of moderate intensity.

● Barbera d'Asti Mongovone '00	🍷🍷	6
● Barbera d'Asti Grivò '00	🍷🍷	4*
○ Moscato d'Asti Sourgal '01	🍷🍷	4*
○ Moscato d'Asti Clarté '01	🍷	2
● Bigarò '01	🍷	4
● Barbera d'Asti Grivò '99	🍷🍷	4
● Barbera d'Asti Grivò '98	🍷	4

○ Piemonte Moscato d'Autunno '01	🍷🍷	4
○ Langhe Bianco Graffagno '00	🍷🍷	4
○ Moscato d'Asti '01	🍷🍷	4
○ Langhe Chardonnay Prasuè '01	🍷	4
○ Langhe Bianco Graffagno '98	🍷🍷	4
○ Langhe Chardonnay Bianch del Luv '98	🍷🍷	5
○ Langhe Bianco Graffagno '99	🍷🍷	4
○ Langhe Chardonnay Bianch del Luv '99	🍷🍷	5

CERRINA MONFERRATO (AL)

CA.VI.MON.
Fraz. Montaldo
Via Centrale, 27
15020 Cerrina Monferrato (AL)
tel. 0142943894 - 014294123
E-MAIL: cavimon@libero.it

An impressive performance by two wines earns Fabrizio Iuli's small, tenacious estate its first entry in the Guide. It lies in Montaldo di Cerrina, in a green and somewhat overlooked corner of the Alessandria part of Monferrato, well off the traditional paths of Piedmontese wine. The thick woods, the nearby river Po and the odd contours of the hills, which resemble small mountains with very steep slopes, combine to create an unusual environment where viticulture, once widespread in these parts, is no longer the main agricultural activity today. Nevertheless, there is a group of young winemakers who are determined to put Valle Cerrina back on the oenological map. One of these is Fabrizio, who attended the school for goldsmiths in Valenza only to find that his burning vocation was for a country life. His family run a well-known "osteria" in Montaldo. Once he realized this, there was no stopping him. He set up a company, Ca.Vi.Mon. (Cantina Viticoltori del Monferrato), with his sister and her husband, opened a cellar and started to produce excellent wines from his 15 estate-owned and rented hectares. To date, he has only put two of his labels on the market. One is the Barbera del Monferrato Barabba '00, notable for its bright ruby red and a nose of ripe fruit, tobacco and spice. Full in the mouth, it is pervasive and balanced, with a lingering liquorice finish. Displaying a little less body, the Rossore is a standard table wine obtained from the barbera grapes of an old vineyard. It delights with its tanginess and approachable, warm sensations.

| ● Barbera del M.to Barabba '00 | 🍷🍷 | 7 |
| ● Rossore '01 | 🍷🍷 | 6 |

COCCONATO (AT)

BAVA
Strada Monferrato, 2
14023 Cocconato (AT)
tel. 0141907083
E-MAIL: bava@bava.com

Roberto, Paolo and Giulio Bava – Giulio has recently been nominated president of the Piedmont association of oenologists – run this historic Asti winery with their father Piero. One of the estate's strong points is the sheer breadth of the range of wines it offers, all top quality, from their sparklers, whites, reds, and sweet wines to the Barolo Chinato. The Barberas we sampled this year include the dense garnet Libera, that offers up aromas of wild berries and dried leaves, then a palate showing good consistency and medium weight. The Piano Alto boasts a dry, gutsy palate and a nice finish that follows through well, while the Arbest reveals slightly etheric tones layered over notes of pepper and quite a closed palate. The "spumante" wines are all good but we particularly liked the Metodo Classico Anteprima for its hints of apricot jam and fresh-tasting, tidy palate. The Brut Giulio Cocchi is consistent and agreeable. The satisfying Alteserre, obtained from cortese and chardonnay, is reasonably dark in colour and has a fruit-rich nose with notes of fermentation and a well-rounded, harmonious palate. The Chardonnay Thou Blanc shows nice typicity. Finally, the two sweet wines, the Moscato d'Asti Bass-Tuba and the Malvasia di Castelnuovo Don Bosco, called Rosa Canina, are both enjoyable.

● Barbera d'Asti Sup.		
Nizza Piano Alto '00	🍷🍷	6
○ Monferrato Bianco Alteserre '00	🍷🍷	4
● Barbera d'Asti Libera '00	🍷	3
○ Moscato d'Asti Bass-Tuba '01	🍷	4
○ Piemonte Chardonnay Thou Bianc '01	🍷	3
○ Giulio Cocchi Brut '95	🍷	5
● Barbera d'Asti Sup. Arbest '98	🍷	4
○ Alta Langa M. Cl. Anteprima Giulio Cocchi	🍷	6
● Barbera d'Asti Sup. Piano Alto '98	🍷🍷	6

COSSOMBRATO (AT)

Carlo Quarello
Via Marconi, 3
14020 Cossombrato (AT)
tel. 0141905204

We take great pleasure every year in presenting this small family winery. Regardless of the pressure from clients, it has managed to retain its traditional style. Here time stands still and even the decision to modernize the cellars was taken with appropriate solemnity. The new structure, however, will finally go up at the beginning of next year and the range of wines will be determined, as far as labels and selections to be released are concerned. For the time being, we thoroughly enjoyed the excellent Grignolino del Monferrato Casalese Cré Marcaleone '01 for its rather rustic nose and palate. It is ruby red with orange highlights and proffers notes of ripe fruit that mingle with exciting peppery sensations and more complex nuances of autumn leaves and mushroom. Although not massively structured, the palate is very austere with tannins that lift the lingering finish. This wine, meticulously made and very reasonably priced by the Quarello family, harks back to another age. For this year's edition of the Guide, we only tasted the Grignolino as the nebbiolo, a variety "foreign" to these latitudes, and the barbera have been vinified separately and it has yet to be decided if, and how, they will go into a new vintage of Crebarné. Meanwhile, Carlo and his wife Bianca have been joined in the winery by their son Valerio and have decided to increase the total area under vine from five to the seven hectares that will soon be in production.

- Grignolino del M.to Casalese Cré Marcaleone '01 — 4*
- Monferrato Rosso Crebarné '98 — 5
- Monferrato Rosso Crebarné '99 — 5

COSTA VESCOVATO (AL)

Luigi Boveri
Fraz. Montale Celli
Via XX Settembre, 6
15050 Costa Vescovato (AL)
tel. 0131838165
e-mail: boveriluigimichele@virgilio.it

Luigi Boveri has gone about his work this year with renewed enthusiasm following the birth of his son, Francesco. His estate has re-affirmed its position at the peak of Colli Tortonesi winemaking with a series of terroir-driven wines. The only exception is the Leopoldo, which was named after Luigi's father and is obtained from an old vineyard of riesling renano. The cream of the white crop is the Filari di Timorasso and the 2000 vintage comes to us in a new guise, for Luigi decided to vinify it entirely without wood. It's a winning move that nets him Two brimming Glasses. The wine sports a rich hue and aromas that range from mineral tones to chalk before developing into more mature notes of peach and apricot. The Vigna del Prete, a cortese-based white, is simpler and has fresh grassy tones. It is with his Barbera, however, that Luigi has got the best results. The Vignalunga is in another class altogether. The appearance instantly gives you to understand that you are holding a glass of mightily structured wine. The nose runs the gamut of aromas from pepper to forest floor and the palate is warm, velvety and brimming with well-gauged tannins. The Poggio delle Amarene also surprised us. Even though it is not aged in oak, it is well structured and has clear notes of black cherry and berry fruit. Finally, the less pretentious Boccanera, another barbera-based offering, is excellent value for money, which can't be bad.

- Colli Tortonesi Barbera Vignalunga '00 — 5
- Colli Tortonesi Barbera Poggio delle Amarene '00 — 4
- ○ Colli Tortonesi Bianco Filari di Timorasso '00 — 5
- Colli Tortonesi Barbera Boccanera '01 — 3*
- ○ Colli Tortonesi Cortese Vigna del Prete '01 — 3*
- Colli Tortonesi Barbera Vignalunga '99 — 5
- Colli Tortonesi Barbera Vignalunga '98 — 5

COSTIGLIOLE D'ASTI (AT)

Carlo Benotto
Via San Carlo, 52
14055 Costigliole d'Asti (AT)
Tel. 0141966406 - 0141961671

The Benotto brothers' wines are distinctive for fullness, often combined with a charming nose that weds balanced fruit with sweet oaky tones. Their Barbera Balau '99 is very good, presenting a dense garnet and an alluringly complex nose that releases attractive hints of black cherry and tamarind layered over balsamic undertones. On the palate, it is soft, full-bodied, well-sustained and warm thanks to generous alcohol, right through to a lingering finish tinged with fruit and liquorice. The Rupestris '00 also performs well, offering a deep colour, warm sensations of fruit, herbs, pepper and peach, and an invigorating, leisurely palate that harks back to the fruit on the nose. The Gamba di Pernice is particularly good this year. It comes from a now rare indigenous variety of the same name, so called because of its reddish grape stalk that resembles a "partridge's leg". Ruby red with a faintly orange edge, it throws a nose full of pleasant violet, liquorice and mint tones. The palate is dry and vigorous with prominent tannins and good length. The well-made Barbera Vigneto Casot is simpler and less challenging than its two stablemates and the Dolcetto Plissé is blessed with a lovely rustic personality.

● Barbera d'Asti Sup. Rupestris '00 ♈♈	5
● Gamba di Pernice '00 ♈♈	4
● Barbera d'Asti Sup. Balau '99 ♈♈	4*
● Barbera d'Asti Sup. Vigneto Casot '00 ♈	4
● Monferrato Dolcetto Plissé '01 ♈	3
● Barbera d'Asti Sup. Rupestris '97 ♈♈	5
● Barbera d'Asti Sup. Balau '98 ♈♈	4
● Barbera d'Asti Sup. Rupestris '98 ♈♈	5
● Barbera d'Asti Sup. Rupestris '99 ♈♈	5

COSTIGLIOLE D'ASTI (AT)

Poderi Bertelli
Fraz. San Carlo, 38
14100 Costigliole d'Asti (AT)
Tel. 0141966137

Tasting wines in the cellar-cum-workshop of Alberto Bertelli is quite an experience. His numerous wines, always produced in limited quantities, have a personality that hits you like a train. Since the late 1970s, when he started to cultivate the family's few hectares of vines (which today total seven), Bertelli has experimented with the most unusual of grape types. He is fired by tremendous passion and has always held in high esteem those regions and winemakers that have never permitted modern winemaking techniques to overshadow the sheer magic of the great wines. This explains why his production features such diverse varieties as barbera, cabernet, chardonnay and a host of others. A long-standing believer in non-invasive techniques in vineyard and cellar, Alberto has lately become interested in the biodynamic philosophy preached by Rudolph Steiner and, more recently, by Nicolas Joly. Who knows, Alberto may well soon be one of the first to recover indigenous varieties to make whites, too. In this year's tastings, our preference was for the Montetusa and Sant'Antonio '99 Barberas, which have distinctive characters, and the classically opulent, minerally Chardonnay '00. The two Fossarettis, the sauvignon-based white and the cabernet sauvignon red, were both nice, with balsamic noses and harmonious palates. The near-sweet San Marsan Bianco '00 and the San Marsan Rosso '99 have rich, gamey aromas and are a bit more difficult, but still very seductive. The Barbera Giarone '99, however, lacks the complexity of its best vintages.

○ Monferrato Bianco I Fossaretti '00 ♈♈	6
○ Piemonte Chardonnay Giarone '00 ♈♈	6
○ San Marsan Bianco '00 ♈♈	6
● Barbera d'Asti Montetusa '99 ♈♈	6
● Barbera d'Asti S. Antonio Vieilles Vignes '99 ♈♈	6
● Monferrato Cabernet Fossaretti '99 ♈♈	6
● San Marsan Rosso '99 ♈♈	6
● Barbera d'Asti Giarone '99 ♈	6
● Barbera d'Asti Montetusa '98 ♈♈	6
● Barbera d'Asti S. Antonio Vieilles Vignes '98 ♈♈	6

COSTIGLIOLE D'ASTI (AT)

Cascina Castlèt
Strada Castelletto, 6
14055 Costigliole d'Asti (AT)
tel. 0141966651
e-mail: castlet@tin.it

Cascina Castlèt comprises 16 hectares planted to vine and has an annual production of about 130,000 bottles. Mariuccia Borio, owner and a dynamic Donna del Vino (member of the "woman of wine" association), runs this lovely property with enormous enthusiasm. She focuses almost exclusively on the indigenous barbera and moscato varieties, with only a small area given over to the cabernet sauvignon that goes into her Policalpo. The Barbera d'Asti Superiore Passum '00 stood head and shoulders above the other wines she offered the panel, who loved its black berry fruit, aromatic herbs and liquorice aromas. The nicely rounded palate progresses steadily to a finish that is slightly tarnished by a bitterish vein. The simple, rustic Barbera '01 flaunts typical cherry tones, while the Barbera del Monferrato Goj, the jolliest of the estate's Barberas, offers faintly earthy notes and a palate enlivened by discreet carbon dioxide. The clear straw-yellow Moscato '01 has a subtle nose of flowers and fruit. The pronounced prickle on the palate keeps the sweetness under control in an overall profile that is light and stylish. The Moscato Passito Avié '99 is gold with faint flecks of amber and throws an evolved nose, with fruit in syrup and leather to the fore. The palate reveals a pleasantly distinct, lingering sweet vein. We shall have to wait until the next edition of the Guide to pass judgement on the Policalpo '00 but our retasting of the '99 vintage served to confirm last year's favourable impression.

● Barbera d'Asti Sup. Passum '00	🍷🍷	5
○ Piemonte Moscato Passito Avié '99	🍷🍷	5
● Barbera d'Asti '01	🍷	3
● Barbera del M.to Goj '01	🍷	3
○ Moscato d'Asti '01	🍷	3
● Barbera d'Asti Sup. Passum '99	🍷🍷	5
● Monferrato Rosso Policalpo '97	🍷🍷	5
● Barbera d'Asti Sup. Passum '98	🍷🍷	5
● Monferrato Rosso Policalpo '98	🍷🍷	5
● Monferrato Rosso Policalpo '99	🍷🍷	5

COSTIGLIOLE D'ASTI (AT)

Cascina Roera
Fraz. Bionzo, 32
14055 Costigliole d'Asti (AT)
tel. 0141968437

Cascina Roera is run in tandem by two Costigliole d'Asti producers. Agronomist Piero Nebiolo takes overall responsibility for the estate's seven hectares of vines while Claudio Rosso focuses on activities in the cellars, although they could easily swap roles as both have considerable experience in all aspects of running a winery. Costigliole d'Asti is synonymous with good Barbera and Barbera d'Asti accounts for the lion's share of Cascina Roera's 15,000 to 20,000-bottle annual production. The Cardin '00, their most prestigious selection, is garnet in hue and has a concentrated, well-defined nose with notes of cherry, forest floor and confectioner's cream set against a backdrop of balsam. The palate is very vigorous and full-bodied with a warm, lingering finish that is slightly dried out by the light tannins. The basic Barbera d'Asti flaunts rich texture but puts the emphasis on freshness with an earlier than usual release on the market. When we sampled it, it hadn't been in the bottle quite long enough but impressed nevertheless with the fragrant fullness of its fruit and the pervasiveness of the palate. The excellent Cardin Riserva '00, of which on 600 bottles are currently produced, is impenetrable in hue. It has a deep, clean nose and delightfully generous structure. The San Martino '00 is a rustic, full-bodied Barbera and the Chardonnay Le Aie and the Ciapin Bianco '01, a blend of chardonnay and arneis with a dash of cortese, are both pleasant.

● Barbera d'Asti Sup. Cardin '00	🍷🍷	4*
● Barbera d'Asti Sup. Cardin Ris. '00	🍷🍷	5
● Barbera d'Asti '01	🍷🍷	4*
● Barbera d'Asti Sup. S. Martino '00	🍷	4
○ Ciapin Bianco '01	🍷	3*
○ Piemonte Chardonnay Le Aie '01	🍷	4
● Barbera d'Asti Sup. Cardin '99	🍷🍷	4

COSTIGLIOLE D'ASTI (AT)

Sciorio
Via Asti Nizza, 87
14055 Costigliole d'Asti (AT)
tel. 0141966610

Mauro and Giuseppe Gozzelino are expanding their estate one step at a time. At present, the family works four hectares planted to vine with a further hectare's worth of new vines soon to go into production. They are also in the process of restructuring their cellars which, once complete, will give them greater production capacity. The two Barberas, Sciorio (traditional in style and aged in big barrels) and Beneficio (conditioned in small casks), were deemed not yet ready for our tasting panel so we'll come back to them for next year's Guide. This time around, our detailed notes regard just two wines, but what wines they are. The Barbera Reginal is modern in style with a big personality and the Rosso Antico Vitigno is a muscular heavyweight of a Cabernet Sauvignon. The Reginal boasts a deep ruby colour and an intense, refined nose of alluring cherry, autumn leaf and menthol. The palate then progresses generously and surefootedly to climax in a warm, dynamic finish that lingers over fruity sensations. The equally impenetrably Antico Vitigno also offers refreshing balsamic tones and a dry, well-structured palate. The two reds are very good, but the Chardonnay Vigna Levi disappointed for its distinctly forward nose.

● Barbera d'Asti Sup. Reginal '99	♛♛	5
● Monferrato Rosso Antico Vitigno '99	♛♛	5
○ Piemonte Chardonnay Vigna Levi '00		5
● Barbera d'Asti Sup. Beneficio '97	♛♛	5
● Barbera d'Asti Sup. Sciorio '97	♛♛	5
● Monferrato Rosso Reginal '97	♛♛	5
● Barbera d'Asti Sup. Beneficio '98	♛♛	5
● Barbera d'Asti Sup. Sciorio '98	♛♛	5
● Monferrato Rosso Antico Vitigno '98	♛♛	5

COSTIGLIOLE D'ASTI (AT)

Valfieri
Strada Loreto, 5
14055 Costigliole d'Asti (AT)
tel. 0141966881
e-mail: ncler@tin.it

Valfieri had another good year, a tribute to the sound choices and effort made to date. Maria Chiara Clerici handles the administration and commercial sides of the business with aplomb but the real engineer of change is her brother Angelo. In a short time, he has revolutionized production, creating a unified team to whom the Valfieri name owes much of the success it enjoys today. Oenologist Luca Caramellino leads the team with Giampiero Romana in charge of things in the vineyards. Their first step was to overhaul the estate's plots at Agliano, an area of about six hectares, and the two hectares they rent at Costigliole. Next, they intensified technical collaboration with their growers. As is to be expected, they are focusing their efforts on Barbera and aim to imbue their three versions with as much character as possible. What they refuse to do is sacrifice the quality of the basic version, which in terms of sheer number (26,000 bottles) is their most important product. As fresh-tasting a young red as you will find, it flaunts its personality in a crisp, fruity nose and velvety roundness. The Barbera Superiore, and in particular the Filari Lunghi '00, possess more complex aromas, with ripe cherry and mineral tones to the fore, as well as a fullness that promises great things to come on the palate. Notes of mint and cocoa powder dominate the nose of the 100 per cent-merlot Matot '00, whose tight-knit tannins in the mouth give it authority. The two Chardonnays and the Cassabò, a barbera and nebbiolo blend, are not quite so appealing.

● Barbera d'Asti I Filari Lunghi '00	♛♛	5
● Barbera d'Asti Sup. '00	♛♛	4
● Monferrato Rosso Matot '00	♛♛	5
● Barbera d'Asti '01	♛♛	3*
● Cassabò Rosso '00	♛	5
○ Langhe Chardonnay '01	♛	3*
○ Langhe Chardonnay Barricello '01	♛	4
● Barbera d'Asti Sup. I Filari Lunghi '99	♛♛	5
● Monferrato Rosso Matot '99	♛♛	5
● Barbera d'Asti Sup. '99	♛	4
● Cassabò Rosso '99	♛	5

DIANO D'ALBA (CN)

Claudio Alario
Via Santa Croce, 23
12055 Diano d'Alba (CN)
tel. 0173231808

DIANO D'ALBA (CN)

Bricco Maiolica
Fraz. Ricca
Via Bolangino, 7
12055 Diano d'Alba (CN)
tel. 0173612049
e-mail: accomo@briccomaiolica.it

Claudio Alario, a talented grower-producer from Diano d'Alba, has a fine estate of eight hectares under vine. Two of these are planted to nebbiolo destined for Barolo: one in the municipality of Verduno gives him his Barolo Riva and the other in Serralunga's Sorano vineyard will go into production in 2004. This year, Claudio expanded his property with the acquisition of two more hectares in the subzone of Pra du Rent. The fruit will go into a new Dolcetto. All of the plots are in excellent positions and supply high quality grapes that Claudio's skilled hand turns into first-class wines. We'll open our notes with the seductive Barolo Riva, whose austere '98 vintage has a nose of liquorice and wild rose, then a powerful palate full of sweet, silky tannins. There is little to choose between the Diano Dolcettos, although the Montagrillo '01 (6,000 bottles) is readier and easier to drink. In contrast, the Costa Fiore '01 is still quite closed. It has a blueberry and raspberry nose and a full-bodied, explosive palate with a long almond finish. The Barbera Valletta '00, from a vineyard with southeasterly exposure overlooking Valle Talloria, also performed very well. Dark garnet in appearance, its clear fruit and vanilla aromas blend nicely while the potent palate is a tad marked by oak in the finish. Complex aromas of liquorice and graphite permeate the elegant, austere Nebbiolo d'Alba Cascinotto '00, an exceedingly seductive wine that embodies to perfection the qualities of nebbiolo grapes grown in zones that border the Barolo DOCG.

Bricco Maiolica, the estate that belongs to the Accomo family, consists of 20 hectares planted to vine on the slopes of Ricca d'Alba, in the municipality of Diano, and produces 100,000 bottles a year. Beppe heads up operations with the help of his father Angelo, a well-known cattle breeder who has carried off numerous prizes at the Fiera del Bue Grasso cattle fair in Carrù. Various other relatives contribute, helping Beppe in his decade-long search for quality. He tends his vines like a garden and applies meticulous standards in the cellars to produce wines that are notable not only for excellence but also for their fair prices. This year, it was the Dolcetto Sörì Bricco Maiolica '01 that won our hearts. Like the previous vintage, which is still very good, it scored points for approachability and roundness. The nose releases aromas of violet and hazelnut, nicely borne up by a rich alcoholic note that underscores its youth. Starting out powerful and soft, the palate displays good balance that is enriched by chewy fruitiness and rounded off by lovely sweet tannins. Two full Glasses go to the Barbera d'Alba Vigna Vigia '00 for its raspberry and ripe fruit nose and its warm, embracing palate, supported by a discreet oaky presence. The Langhe Bianco Rolando is a very successful wine, with a nose of tropical fruit and a forthright palate with delicious length. The nose of the Cumot '00, a pure nebbiolo that in this area is labelled Nebbiolo d'Alba DOC, is not particularly refined. The basic Dolcetto is pleasant and the pinot nero-based Langhe Lorié '99 rustic and spicy.

● Nebbiolo d'Alba Cascinotto '00	ŸŸ	5
● Barbera d'Alba Valletta '00	ŸŸ	5
● Diano d'Alba Costa Fiore '01	ŸŸ	4*
● Diano d'Alba Montagrillo '01	ŸŸ	4*
● Barolo Riva '98	ŸŸ	7
● Diano d'Alba Costa Fiore '00	ŸŸ	4
● Diano d'Alba Montagrillo '00	ŸŸ	4
● Barolo Riva '96	ŸŸ	7
● Barolo Riva '97	ŸŸ	7
● Barbera d'Alba Valletta '99	ŸŸ	5
● Nebbiolo d'Alba Cascinotto '99	ŸŸ	5

● Barbera d'Alba Vigna Vigia '00	ŸŸ	5
● Diano d'Alba Sörì Bricco Maiolica '01	ŸŸ	4*
○ Langhe Bianco Rolando '01	ŸŸ	4*
● Nebbiolo d'Alba Cumot '00	Ÿ	5
● Dolcetto di Diano d'Alba '01	Ÿ	3
● Langhe Rosso Lorié '99	Ÿ	5
● Barbera d'Alba Vigna Vigia '98	ŸŸŸ	5
● Diano d'Alba Sörì Bricco Maiolica '00	ŸŸ	4
● Barbera d'Alba Vigna Vigia '99	ŸŸ	5
● Nebbiolo d'Alba Cumot '99	ŸŸ	5

DOGLIANI (CN)

Marziano e Enrico Abbona
Via Torino, 242
12063 Dogliani (CN)
tel. 0173721317
e-mail: abbona.marziano@tiscalinet.it

The Three Glasses awarded last year to the Abbonas did not come out of the blue. This year, the range of wines presented to our tasting panel confirmed the winery, run by Marziano Abbona with his wife and three daughters, as a force to be reckoned with around Dogliani. It is much larger than most in the area and includes properties in Dogliani and the DOCG areas of Barolo and Barbaresco. We welcome to the market, and to the pages of the Guide, the Barolo Pressenda '98, which comes from one of the most important vineyards at Monforte and reflects all the classic features of its tradition in its powerful, pervasive palate. Its limpid ruby red releases notes of black berry fruit and cherries in alcohol, enhancing the sweet nose. The nose is bolstered by traces of toastiness from its sojourn in oak. The full structure and body in the mouth take you through to an austere finish veined with fine-grained tannins. Once again, the 2001 Papà Celso dominates the Dolcettos thanks to an intense, raspberry-led nose and a mature palate that lingers unhurriedly to round off the juicy progression. The less complex Vigneto Muntâ has a heady nose and a down-to-earth palate. Just as austere are the good Barolo Terlo Ravera '98 and the seductive Barbaresco Faset '99. The Barbera d'Alba Rinaldi '00 is as attractive as ever and the Langhe Rosso I Due Ricu from the same vintage, a blend of nebbiolo, barbera and cabernet, is very full-bodied and ethereal. Character and personality are the hallmarks of the Cinerino '01, a white with an already quite developed nose and a mature palate.

● Dolcetto di Dogliani Papà Celso '01	ππ	4*
● Barolo Pressenda '98	ππ	7
● Barbera d'Alba Rinaldi '00	ππ	4*
● Langhe Rosso I Due Ricu '00	ππ	5
● Barolo Vigneto Terlo Ravera '98	ππ	7
● Barbaresco Faset '99	ππ	6
○ Cinerino Bianco '01	π	4
● Dolcetto di Dogliani Vigneto Muntâ '01	π	4
● Dolcetto di Dogliani Papà Celso '00	πππ	4
● Barbaresco Faset '98	ππ	6
● Barolo Vigneto Terlo Ravera '97	ππ	7
● Langhe Rosso I Due Ricu '99	ππ	5

DOGLIANI (CN)

Ca' Viola
Fraz. S. Luigi, 11
12063 Dogliani (CN)
tel. 017370547
e-mail: caviola@caviola.com

Beppe Caviola has moved the nerve centre of his estate from Montelupo Albese, where he continues to produce 40,000 bottles a year from eight hectares of vines. Now, his base is at Dogliani, in the heart of the Dolcetto di Dogliani DOC zone. A small 19th-century palazzo and a "cascina", or farm, that dates back even further are home to Beppe's new headquarters on top of the San Luigi hill. We'll begin with the wines that have made the name of this gifted oenologist. First up is the Bric du Luv '00, a Langhe Rosso with a barbera and pinot nero base. Deep, dense garnet, it has a concentrated nose that releases notes of cherry and cocoa powder layered over an attractive minerally undertone. It develops steadily on the palate, showing good body and breadth, and the vigorous, sweet tannins sustain you through to a long, elegant finish. Fragrantly delicious notes of liquorice and mint lift the back palate. Although good, this version doesn't quite have the power that earned it Three Glasses in previous vintages. Instead, Three Glasses went to the lovely Langhe Dolcetto Barturot '01, which is actually a Dolcetto d'Alba denied DOC status this year by a technicality concerning the relocation of the winery. This dark ruby red monster has aromas of ripe raspberry and cherry fruit, which are nicely offset by the robust alcohol. The palate is a work of art. Full and forceful, it unveils lingering sweet fruit tones that exalt the finish, which is lifted by soft tannins. The rather simpler Langhe Dolcetto Vilot '01 and the velvety pinot nero Langhe Rosso Rangone '00 are very enjoyable.

● Langhe Dolcetto Barturot '01	πππ	5
● Langhe Rosso Bric du Luv '00	ππ	6
● Langhe Rosso Rangone '00	ππ	6
● Langhe Dolcetto Vilot '01	ππ	4*
● Langhe Rosso Bric du Luv '95	πππ	6
● Dolcetto d'Alba Barturot '96	πππ	5
● Langhe Rosso Bric du Luv '96	πππ	6
● Dolcetto d'Alba Barturot '98	πππ	5
● Langhe Rosso Bric du Luv '98	πππ	6
● Langhe Rosso Bric du Luv '99	πππ	6
● Dolcetto d'Alba Barturot '00	ππ	5
● Langhe Rosso Rangone '99	ππ	6

DOGLIANI (CN)

QUINTO CHIONETTI & FIGLIO
FRAZ. SAN LUIGI, 44
12063 DOGLIANI (CN)
TEL. 017371179
E-MAIL: chionettiquinto@chionettiquinto.com

If every wine-producing area has a spiritual leader, a sort of father figure who is credited with being the first to recognize the promise of a certain terrain, then the Dogliani region title rightfully belongs to Quinto Chionetti. His personal philosophy, his production style and his strong commitment impart a set of values that have set the wine world, today increasingly influenced by the dictates of the market and fashion, back on track towards more authentic and, in many ways more romantic, goals. "Modern" is a dirty word here. Quinto continues to produce his two historic Dolcettos from two prestigious Dogliani vineyards and we continue to pay homage to this grand master of Piedmont wine. Not for the first time, our favourite was his Briccolero selection. It is deep ruby red in colour and the nose opens to embrace clear notes of jam and berries in a very clean, pronounced nose profile. Entry on the palate is full-bodied, progressing powerfully and caressingly to the long finish that hints at almond. Every bit as appealing, the San Luigi only lacks a little of its stablemate's structure. Its deep, almost opaque, red ushers in nuances of black berry fruit and plum jam. The palate displays more elegance than power and the overall harmony is most enjoyable. As usual, it deserves its place on the quality podium.

● Dolcetto di Dogliani Briccolero '01	♉♉	4*
● Dolcetto di Dogliani S. Luigi '01	♉♉	4*
● Dolcetto di Dogliani Briccolero '00	♉♉	4
● Dolcetto di Dogliani S. Luigi '00	♉♉	4
● Dolcetto di Dogliani Briccolero '99	♉♉	4

DOGLIANI (CN)

PODERI EINAUDI
B.TA GOMBE, 31
12063 DOGLIANI (CN)
TEL. 017370191
E-MAIL: pleinaudi@libero.it

Poderi Einaudi is a major player at Dogliani. Its 110 hectares include 30 planted to vine that stretch across the hills of Santa Lucia, San Luigi and Gombe; almost eight planted to Barolo in the Terlo-Via Nuova and Cannubi vineyards; and five in Neive and Neviglie that have yet to go into production. The combined vine stock currently gives an annual production of around 160,000 bottles. First on our list are the three Barolos, one of which, the '98, is the best Cannubi ever to come out of this estate. It bowled us over with the elegance and sophistication of its raspberry, liquorice, vanilla and violet nose and sweet, tight-knit tannins. The Costa Grimaldi, a big wine from Terlo, and the basic Barolo, another '98, are also very good. The first is closed, austere and subtle, with cinnamon and cloves-led spice, while the second seduces with redcurrant fruit and an easy-drinking but firmly structured palate. The delightful nebbiolo, cabernet, merlot and barbera-based Luigi Einaudi '00 is potent and velvety. Like all true Langhe Bordeaux-style wines, it is only held back by its youth. Two full Glasses go to Dolcettos Vigna Tecc and I Filari '00, both deep purple with fruit jam aromas. The first is dense, succulent and smooth whereas I Filari is full, earthy and gutsy. The Barbera '00, from the same base as the Luigi Einaudi, shows character and elegance while the Nebbiolo and the Vigna Meira '00 are less complex. The latter is obtained from an Alsatian clone called Tokay Pinot Gris and offers grapefruit and vanilla aromas. The solid Dolcetto di Dogliani also did well.

● Barolo nei Cannubi '98	♉♉♉	8
● Langhe Rosso Luigi Einaudi '00	♉♉	6
● Dolcetto di Dogliani I Filari '00	♉♉	5
● Dolcetto di Dogliani Vigna Tecc '00	♉♉	4*
● Piemonte Barbera '00	♉♉	5
● Barolo '98	♉♉	7
● Barolo Costa Grimaldi '98	♉♉	7
● Dolcetto di Dogliani '00	♉	3*
● Langhe Nebbiolo '00	♉	4
○ Langhe Vigna Meira '00	♉	4
● Langhe Rosso Luigi Einaudi '97	♉♉♉	6
● Langhe Rosso Luigi Einaudi '98	♉♉♉	6
● Langhe Rosso Luigi Einaudi '99	♉♉♉	6
● Barolo nei Cannubi '97	♉♉	8

DOGLIANI (CN)

F.lli Pecchenino
B.ta Valdiberti, 59
12063 Dogliani (CN)
Tel. 017370686
E-mail: a.pecchenino@onw.net

In his new cellar, Orlando Pecchenino and his brother Attilio produce approximately 80,000 bottles a year from plots in the best Dolcetto di Dogliani areas. The capable Orlando concentrates all his efforts on this wine type. His ambition since he entered the profession in the mid 1980s has been to produce very rich, characterful Dolcettos. The results are very gratifying and have earned the Peccheninos top honours in no less than six editions of the Guide. This year is no exception. Their Dolcetto selections are superb, with Three Glasses going to the Sirì d'Jermu '01, but actually, the entire range is outstanding. Although the Dolcetto di Dogliani San Luigi '01, the estate's warhorse, is not up to its previous vintage, it is still one of the best in the zone. We have another champ in the Superiore Bricco Botti which, in contrast to the Sirì d'Jermu, is entirely oak-conditioned and aged for an extra year. It boasts intense colour and a complex nose of black berry fruits and rhubarb, then the pleasing palate shows harmonious oaky tones that have already integrated well into the structure. The Sirì d'Jermu is less spirited than the 2000 version but makes up with its poise and elegance. Richly extracted and almost purplish, it reveals an extremely lively, enjoyable palate with good length and texture. A barbera, nebbiolo and cabernet blend, the excellent Langhe La Castella '99 is the estate's sole concession to other red varieties. Finally, the Langhe Vigna Maestro '00, chardonnay with a small addition of arneis and sauvignon, is still very much in thrall to the oak.

DOGLIANI (CN)

Pira
B.ta Valdiberti, 69
12063 Dogliani (CN)
Tel. 017378538
E-mail: vini.pira@onw.net

Gianmatteo Pira runs his eight-hectare estate with passion and skill. Its location at the top of the municipality of Dogliani, rubbing shoulders with Monforte d'Alba, gives him two Dolcetto DOCs, Alba and Dogliani, and a Nebbiolo d'Alba, which is a new recruit to the ranks. Another newcomer comes in the shape of a Langhe DOC red, the monovarietal merlot-based Camerlot whose first release is a credit to the talents of this gifted winemaker. Its deep colour is the prelude to a nose of delicate, ripe fruit tones with just a hint of liqueur cherries to hint at the robust alcohol content. The powerful palate's sweet, lingering finish also hints at etheric notes. We enjoyed the debut performance of the Nebbiolo d'Alba Vigna Bricco dell'Asino '00, which displays a garnet colour of medium intensity, notes of rain-soaked earth and liquorice, then a caressing palate with a tannin-rich finish. Of the Dolcettos on offer, our preference was for the complex Vigna Bricco dei Botti '00, which benefits from an extra year in the cellar to present a potent palate with nicely integrated tannins. Still in Dogliani, the Dolcetto Vigna Landes also shows enormous roundness on the palate while its nose is dominated by black cherry and super-ripe fruit. Neither the Dolcetto d'Alba Vigna Fornaci '01 nor the Barbera d'Alba '00 had been bottled at the time of our tasting.

● Dolcetto di Dogliani Sirì d'Jermu '01	🍷🍷🍷	5
● Dolcetto di Dogliani Sup. Bricco Botti '00	🍷🍷	6
● Dolcetto di Dogliani S. Luigi '01	🍷🍷	4*
● Langhe La Castella '99	🍷🍷	6
○ Langhe Vigna Maestro '00	🍷	4
● Dolcetto di Dogliani S. Luigi '00	🍷🍷🍷	4
● Dolcetto di Dogliani Sirì d'Jermu '97	🍷🍷🍷	4
● Dolcetto di Dogliani Sirì d'Jermu '98	🍷🍷🍷	4
● Dolcetto di Dogliani Sirì d'Jermu '99	🍷🍷🍷	4

● Dolcetto di Dogliani Vigna Bricco dei Botti '00	🍷🍷	4*
● Langhe Rosso Camerlot '00	🍷🍷	5
● Dolcetto di Dogliani Vigna Landes '01	🍷🍷	4*
● Nebbiolo d'Alba Vigna Bricco dell'Asino '00	🍷	5
● Dolcetto d'Alba Vigna Fornaci '00	🍷🍷	4
● Dolcetto di Dogliani Vigna Landes '00	🍷🍷	4
● Dolcetto di Dogliani Vigna Bricco dei Botti '99	🍷🍷	4
● Piemonte Barbera Briccobotti '99	🍷🍷	5

DOGLIANI (CN)

SAN FEREOLO
B.TA VALDIBÀ, 59
12063 DOGLIANI (CN)
TEL. 0173742075

DOGLIANI (CN)

SAN ROMANO
B.TA GIACHELLI, 8
12063 DOGLIANI (CN)
TEL. 017376289
E-MAIL: bchionetti@sanromano.com

Dogliani continues to bask in the glory of San Fereolo, one of the estates that best represents the entire Dolcetto di Dogliano DOC zone. Nicoletta Bocca and Francesco Stralla remain in charge here. Nicoletta is a strong-minded Donna del Vino (member of the "woman of wine" association) who is very much involved in the complex issues of winemaking today and always happy to discuss her strategies and her products. Francesco is a talented grower-producer who gets the very best out of his seven hectares, all in the best parts of Dogliani, namely Valdiberti and San Luigi. San Fereolo now has a new vinification cellar that will streamline the whole production process. For this year's tastings, Nicoletta and Francesco presented us with just two wines, a Barbera aged in barriques and 900-litre casks called Langhe Rosso Brumaio, and the Dolcetto Valdibà. The San Fereolo 2001 vintage, which will carry the Superiore mark on its label, is not due for release until spring 2003. The Valdibà pleases at first glance with its deep, almost violet red. Notes of black cherry emerge in the sweet nose, then the juicy, fruit-rich palate is braced by a hint of almond in the finish. The Brumaio is a now familiar face and the 2000 vintage makes a big impact with its dark, nearly opaque, red. The ripe fruit and vanilla nose is followed by a peppery palate with a sweet, lingering fruitiness in the finish.

Eight and a half hectares on the slopes over the town of Dogliani, in the direction of Farigliano, and an output of 35,000 bottles a year tell you all about this small but already well-known winery, which belongs to Bruno Chionetti. Bruno's chief product is Dolcetto di Dogliani and he vinifies little else, just some pinot nero destined for his Martin Sec and a little chardonnay that will shortly produce a Spumante Metodo Classico. The estate has built its reputation on two flagship wines, the Vigna del Pilone and the Dolianum. The second is obtained from a Vigna del Pilone selection conditioned entirely in barriques and used 900-litre casks, then aged for more than a year in bottle. The 2000 vintage is very impressive indeed, surpassing previous editions in both quality and power. Profound garnet in hue, it shows complex aromas with hints of hazelnut, and a richly extracted palate that has already fused the oak-derived tannins beautifully. From grapes grown at an altitude of between 400 and 500 metres, the Vigna del Pilone selection is also very good. The basic Dolcetto di Dogliani was a nice surprise, thanks to a distinctive purple red hue and a fruit-led, exceptionally delicate nose. It is dense and structured on the palate but nonetheless very enjoyable. The Langhe Rosso Martin Sec '00 concludes the estate's array of wines. It's a monovarietal Pinot Nero that is starting to show positive results despite the fact it comes from a recently planted vineyard.

• Dolcetto di Dogliani Valdibà '01	🍷🍷	4*
• Langhe Rosso Brumaio '00	🍷🍷	5
• Dolcetto di Dogliani S. Fereolo '97	🍷🍷🍷	4
• Langhe Rosso Brumaio '97	🍷🍷🍷	5
• Dolcetto di Dogliani S. Fereolo '99	🍷🍷🍷	4
• Dolcetto di Dogliani S. Fereolo '00	🍷🍷	4
• Dolcetto di Dogliani Sup. 1593 '97	🍷🍷	4
• Langhe Rosso Brumaio '99	🍷🍷	5

• Dolcetto di Dogliani Sup. Dolianum '00	🍷🍷	5
• Langhe Rosso Martin Sec '00	🍷🍷	5
• Dolcetto di Dogliani '01	🍷🍷	4*
• Dolcetto di Dogliani Vigna del Pilone '01	🍷🍷	4*
• Dolcetto di Dogliani Vigna del Pilone '97	🍷🍷🍷	4
• Dolcetto di Dogliani Vigna del Pilone '98	🍷🍷🍷	4
• Dolcetto di Dogliani Vigna del Pilone '99	🍷🍷🍷	4
• Dolcetto di Dogliani Vigna del Pilone '00	🍷🍷	4

FARA NOVARESE (NO)

Dessilani
Via Cesare Battisti, 21
28073 Fara Novarese (NO)
tel. 0321829252
e-mail: dessilani@onw.net

This has been a big year for viticulture in northern Piedmont. For the first time, a wine from these parts takes home Three Glasses. The prize honours both an area that has made giant strides in quality and the talented Enzio Lucca, whose wines embody that improvement. The wine that earned our top award – and thoroughly deserved to – is an extraordinary Fara Caramino '99. Its exceptional elegance is immediately apparent in the intense, clean spice of the nose, where clear, lingering tones of cocoa powder, redcurrant, black pepper and mint leaf keep the oak in check. Despite its fabulous structure, the palate is not over-concentrated and the balance of alcohol and acidity is superb. The spice and coffee finish is long and lingers. The strong oaky tones of the Fara Lochera fail to detract from the refined notes of pomegranate, roses, violets and spices on the nose. The palate, although full and complex, is just a tad astringent. The excellent Nebbiolo '99 unleashes aromas of enormous personality, with redcurrant and blackberry to the fore. There are also hints of green pepper and ginger, all layered over minty, faintly grassy undertones, then the palate offers more in the way of balance and elegance than power. The Ghemme '98 has an upfront nose of raspberry and mixed spice that reveals cumin and white pepper. Its full, well-sustained palate shows refined tannins and an agreeable tanginess in the central phase. The finish echoes the nose but is not very concentrated. Collefino, a white from greco, an erbaluce clone, is lightweight but pleasantly refreshing and zesty.

● Fara Caramino '99	🍷🍷🍷	5
● Ghemme '98	🍷🍷	5
● Colline Novaresi Nebbiolo '99	🍷🍷	4*
● Fara Lochera '99	🍷🍷	5
○ Colline Novaresi Bianco Collefino '01	🍷	3*
● Fara Caramino '98	🍷🍷	5
● Fara Lochera '98	🍷🍷	5

FARIGLIANO (CN)

Anna Maria Abbona
Fraz. Moncucco, 21
12060 Farigliano (CN)
tel. 0173797228
e-mail: amabbona@amabbona.com

This Farigliano estate is small, comprising only eight hectares under vine for a production of 50,000 bottles a year, dedicated almost exclusively to the zone's flagship wine, Dolcetto di Dogliani. Nonetheless, Anna Maria Abbona has already made quite a name for itself. She is one of the many women who, over the last decade, have a carved out a solid niche for themselves in the wine world. Her philosophy is simple: produce top quality wines in the local tradition without resorting to international varieties or overcomplicated production processes. First on the list of wines we sampled is the youthful, heady Sorì dij But '01, a simple but well made Dolcetto with a pleasant palate that finishes on a faint note of almond. A step up in terms of concentration, and especially power, is the Maioli '01, from a selection of fruit from old estate vines. Its opaque violet red colour immediately reveals a structure that is quite extraordinary for a standard Dolcetto. Sweet notes of ripe fruit and a deep, substantial palate complete the profile. Better still is the Dolcetto di Dogliani Superiore Maioli '00. It enjoys an extra year's ageing, which takes place in barriques, 900-litre barrels, small casks of Slavonian oak and bottles. The wine is a veritable cornucopia of aromas, with nicely integrated notes of autumn leaf and liquorice introducing a full, austere palate that offers impeccable elegance. Excellent, too, is the Langhe Rosso Cadò '00, a barbera-based wine with a little dolcetto in the mix.

● Dolcetto di Dogliani Sup. Maioli '00	🍷🍷	5
● Langhe Rosso Cadò '00	🍷🍷	5
● Dolcetto di Dogliani Maioli '01	🍷🍷	4*
● Dolcetto di Dogliani Sorì dij But '01	🍷	4
● Dolcetto di Dogliani Maioli '00	🍷🍷	4
● Langhe Rosso Cadò '98	🍷🍷	5
● Dolcetto di Dogliani Sup. Maioli '99	🍷🍷	5
● Langhe Rosso Cadò '99	🍷🍷	5

FARIGLIANO (CN)

GIOVANNI BATTISTA GILLARDI
CASCINA CORSALETTO, 69
12060 FARIGLIANO (CN)
TEL. 017376306
E-MAIL: gillardi@gillardi.it

The solid level of quality attained by the wines of this estate is now a given. Giovanni Battista Gillardi and his wife Giuseppina, helped by their son Giacolino, lavish care and attention on the vines surrounding their small but elegant and well-equipped cellars in the small village of Corsaletto, near Farigliano. Once again, their Harys sent our tasting panel into raptures. Obtained from French grape types, it is a wine of enormous personality and won the Guide's highest accolade. Year after year, this wine continues to give further proof of its true greatness with a modern style and fruit that has the opportunity on these hills to achieve an extraordinary degree of ripeness. The Harys '00 has taken full advantage of the superb harvest to present a deep, almost impenetrable garnet red, a compact, complex nose suggesting refined touches of pepper-rich spice and ripe fruit. It follows up with a harmonious palate of marvellous length and elegance, whose finish is ennobled by silky tannins. The Dolcetto Cursalet, from an old vineyard owned by the Gillardis, is also worthy of close attention. It has an intense, almost purplish red hue and distinctive aromas with fruit very much to the fore. The richly extracted palate is well-balanced and the finish is slightly dried by the rather severe tannins. The Vigna Maestra, another Dolcetto di Dogliani, is less complex, showing a closed nose and a down-to-earth yet agreeable palate. We also liked the Langhe Rosso Yeta '00, a 90-10 mix of dolcetto with cabernet, for its pencil lead aromas and its austere, potent palate.

● Harys '00	🍷🍷🍷	7
● Dolcetto di Dogliani Cursalet '01	🍷🍷	4*
● Langhe Rosso Yeta '00	🍷🍷	5
● Dolcetto di Dogliani Vigneto Maestra '01	🍷	4
● Harys '98	🍷🍷🍷	7
● Harys '99	🍷🍷🍷	7
● Dolcetto di Dogliani Cursalet '00	🍷🍷	4
● Harys '96	🍷🍷	7
● Harys '97	🍷🍷	7
● Langhe Rosso Yeta '99	🍷🍷	5

GATTINARA (VC)

ANTONIOLO
C.SO VALSESIA, 277
13045 GATTINARA (VC)
TEL. 0163833612
E-MAIL: antoniolovini@gattinara.alpcom.it

Our best wishes and congratulations go to Rosanna Antoniolo, who with justifiable pride celebrated 50 years in viticulture in 2002. One of the first women to venture into the wine world, Rosanna's goal has always been quality and today her estate, where her children Alberto and Lorella are increasingly active, enjoys a very good reputation. Her Gattinara Osso San Grato '98 is a wine of great complexity and fascination that has little to envy any of the Langhe's other, more famous, wines. The nose revels in the warm, ripe floweriness shared by all great traditional-style nebbiolos and a faint mineral note from the terroir. The abundant aromas include roses, violets, liquorice and fresh fennel. The wonderfully balanced palate is aristocratic and austere. Next on the list was the San Francesco, which also impressed with its elegance and complexity. Notes of liquorice, rose, raspberry and a soft spiciness intermingle in a very pervasive aromatic profile. The refined and very varietal palate has good length. The Gattinara Castelle, the estate's only barrique-aged wine, releases tobacco and oak-derived hints of vanilla through which varietal aromas of raspberry and crushed rose emerge. The palate shows satisfying depth and body yet still maintains a traditional style. The clean, layered aromas of the basic Gattinara are redolent of its terroir then the palate is fresh, tangy and very round. The Bricco Lorella possesses remarkable structure for a rosé as well as distinct notes of wild roses and redcurrants. Lastly, we enjoyed the fresh-tasting, zesty Erbaluce di Caluso '01.

● Gattinara Vigneto Osso S. Grato '98	🍷🍷	7
● Gattinara '98	🍷🍷	5
● Gattinara Vigneto Castelle '98	🍷🍷	6
● Gattinara Vigneto S. Francesco '98	🍷🍷	6
● Coste della Sesia Nebbiolo Juvenia '01	🍷	3
○ Erbaluce di Caluso '01	🍷	3
● Gattinara Vigneto Castelle '97	🍷🍷	6
● Gattinara Vigneto Osso S. Grato '97	🍷🍷	6
● Gattinara Vigneto S. Francesco '97	🍷🍷	6

GATTINARA (VC)

ANZIVINO
C.so Valsesia, 162
13045 Gattinara (VC)
TEL. 0163827172
E-MAIL: anzivino@anzivino.net

Born of Emanuele's long-cherished dream that he would sooner or later live the country life (he started out in construction), the Anzivino winery makes its first appearance in the Guide this year. Determined to make his dream come true, Emanuele moved from Milan in 1999 and bought a 19th-century cloister that had previously housed a distillery in old part of Gattinara. These evocative surroundings, now expertly restored, contain his vinification cellars and a lovely, warm "agriturismo" holiday centre. The estate has five hectares planted to vine, including one at Sostegno in the zone of Bramaterra. The total will rise to 13-14 when the acquisitions and new plantings planned for the next few years are complete. Emanuele's Gattinara is macerated unhurriedly in wooden vats and aged for a year in barriques. Its elegant nose opens on an unusual chalky note before moving on to raspberry, violet and faint hints of pennyroyal. The palate displays sustained, very solid structure and an acidulous vein that never disturbs the balance. The Bramaterra, different by design, is vinified in a modern rotofermenter. It stays very briefly on the skins and matures in barrique. The cherry and blackberry nose has a strong note of cocoa powder and invigorating hints of aniseed and ginger. Although not over-endowed with structure, the palate shows good balance and gives a clean overall impression. The Tarlo, a 50-50 nebbiolo and croatina mix, offers lovely pomegranate and redcurrant berry fruit aromas laced with geranium, and a stylish, clean palate perked up by a hint of acidity.

- Gattinara '98   5
- Bramaterra '99   4
- Tarlo Rosso '99   3

GATTINARA (VC)

NERVI
C.so Vercelli, 117
13045 Gattinara (VC)
TEL. 0163833228
E-MAIL: avnervi@gattinara.alpcom.it

Founded in the 1900s by Luigi Nervi, this famous winery is today the property of the Bocciolone family. They have 30 hectares under vine, nine of which lie in the prestigious, top-quality Molsino area. The estate's guiding principles dictate total respect for typicity without falling into the trap of dull conservatism. In other words, it's a happy mix of tradition and openness to new ideas that is more than evident on a visit to the beautiful cellars. Giorgio Aliata, a friendly, dynamic viticulturist, is the estate's guiding spirit. The Gattinara Vigneto Molsino is one of the best in its category. It is fermented at controlled temperatures, partly in wooden vats and partly in stainless steel tanks, and aged in large wood for a period of at least three years. A deep, seamless garnet red introduces clean, complex, varietal aromas of raspberry, redcurrant and dried roses that mingle with the mint and spice that the local soil imparts to the nebbiolo grape. Entry on the palate is very full, with balanced tannins. Mid palate is well-sustained and full of fruit, with a bright, refreshing note, then the long finish highlights the superb nose-palate consistency with tanginess and a delightful citrus after-aroma. The basic Gattinara is simpler. Pale garnet in the glass, it offers flowery tones of roses and violets that mingle with raspberry fruit and pennyroyal. After a strong, fruit-driven entry, the palate falls away in the central phase but comes back in the pleasantly bitterish finish.

- Gattinara Vigneto Molsino '98   6
- Gattinara '98   5
- Gattinara '97   5
- Gattinara Vigneto Molsino '97   6

GATTINARA (VC)

GIANCARLO TRAVAGLINI
VIA DELLE VIGNE, 36
13045 GATTINARA (VC)
TEL. 0163833588
E-MAIL: travaglini.gattinara@libero.it

Giancarlo Travaglini has always been a staunch believer in Gattinara and continued to invest money and energy here while many others abandoned what they considered to be a sinking ship. Today, he has 39 hectares of nebbiolo in production and another ten newly planted at Valferana and Uccineglio. This is an impressive spread, especially in light of the fact that Gattinara only has a total of 105 hectares under vine. Roughly 90 per cent of Giancarlo's almost 250,000 bottles a year are sold abroad. The distinctive shape of the bottles, conceived in 1959 by Travaglini himself, inspired by the shapes of old hand-blown bottles, has become both a cellar tradition and a winery trademark. Giancarlo's Gattinara undergoes a modern vinification process in paddle-type rotofermenters at controlled temperatures, with micro-aeration, and is then matured for the most part in large oak barrels. Only part of the wine ages for ten months in barrique. Deep garnet ruby in colour, the '99 vintage's intense liquorice aromas introduce an austere, delicately nuanced, varietal nose of blackberry, rhubarb, tar and coffee, highlighted by touches of spice and mint. The complex, richly fruity palate has a refreshing acidulous vein and the clean, lingering finish presents powerful redcurrant sensations, then an elegant return of the coffee notes. This year, we were unable to taste the estate's two most important selections, the Riserva and the Tre Vigne, which will require further ageing to develop to their considerable potential.

GAVI (AL)

NICOLA BERGAGLIO
FRAZ. ROVERETO
LOC. PEDAGGERI, 59
15066 GAVI (AL)
TEL. 0143682195

Gianluigi Bergaglio's newly completed and very spacious cellars feature some cosy tasting rooms for visitors. We fully recommend a visit if you're in the area, as it will give you the chance to meet a talented producer. The reserved but hospitable Gianluigi has for more than 30 years lavished care on his beloved vines, which bask in the fresh, fragrant topoclimate of Rovereto. With the help of his dependable son Diego, Gianluigi obtains two first-rate Gavis from his approximately 15 hectares, four of which will only go into production next year. The Minaia is a classic vineyard selection, hovering somewhere between straw yellow and gold in colour. It releases delicate fragrances of pineapple and spring flowers, then the palate displays balance, body and harmonious length. The Bergaglios have produced no less than 35,000 bottles of this wine, which is obtained from the finest selection of fruit from their oldest vineyard, opposite the "cascina" building itself. In contrast, the basic Gavi di Gavi is bright and lively in character. Its gold-flecked green ushers in well-defined aromas of flowers and fruit, then the pleasantly tangy palate suggests white peach and ends on a lingering, typically acidulous note. It's an impressive version that pays tribute to the estate's solid style.

● Gattinara '99	♛♛	5
● Gattinara Ris. '97	♛♛	6
● Gattinara Ris. '96	♛♛	6
● Gattinara Tre Vigne '97	♛♛	6
● Gattinara Tre Vigne '98	♛♛	6

○ Gavi del Comune di Gavi Minaia '01	♛♛	4
○ Gavi del Comune di Gavi '01	♛	3*

GAVI (AL)

Gian Piero Broglia
Tenuta La Meirana
Loc. Lomellina, 14
15066 Gavi (AL)
tel. 0143642998
e-mail: broglia.azienda@tin.it

Having resigned as head of the Gavi protection consortium, Piero Broglia now has more time to dedicate to his own estate, which commands a view of breathtaking beauty. The undulating vine-covered panorama embraces most of the estate's 49 hectares that include several new plantations partly given over to red grape varieties. Broglia works closely with Federico Curtaz to produce an excellent range of very individual wines. Their classic Gavi La Meirana '01 offers proof of its reliable quality in its delicate array of flowery and fresh almond aromas. The palate is soft with a warm, seductive finish. The Gavi Bruno Broglia '00, on the other hand, is ten per cent barrique-conditioned. Its origins lie in a plot on the crest of the hill and the vines have reached the grand old age of 50 years. Its rich gold is a prelude to generous notes of peach and flowers of the field, then the palate reveals the vineyard's character with good weight and length. Rounding off the Gavis, we have the Villa Broglia '01, which displays aromatic freshness and remarkable nose-palate consistency. The Monferrato Rosso Bruno Broglia '99 is a very successful blend of 70 per cent indigenous barbera blended with merlot and cabernet and aged unhurriedly in barrique. The result is a dense wine, with blood red highlights, that is strongly redolent of raspberry. The palate, ennobled by vigorous notes of plum, tobacco and liquorice, reveals well-judged, lingering tannins.

GAVI (AL)

Castellari Bergaglio
Fraz. Rovereto, 136
15066 Gavi (AL)
tel. 0143644000
e-mail: gavi@castellaribergaglio.it

With the support of his parents and the help of his sister Barbara, young Marco Bergaglio this year embarked upon an admirable enterprise. Although his wines are already of very high quality, thanks to the stunning positions enjoyed by the family's vineyards, he is determined to improve them even further. He produces a total of four Gavis, each distinct and recognizable for its own special qualities. The Pilìn was again downgraded to a table wine in the '99 version because of a continuing oversight in Gavi DOCG regulations that did not permit ageing in oak. The issue has been resolved for 2000 and subsequent vintages. Nevertheless, Pilìn is one of the best wines in the area. Obtained from the estate's oldest vineyards, the fruit is partially dried for a period of 20 days and subjected to alcoholic and malolactic fermentation in four-fifths new barriques, where it remains for a year. The sojourn in oak leaves its mark in the vanilla, tea biscuit and hazelnut aromas. Happily, they do not mask the wine's lovely fleshy, weighty fruit, which returns on the palate with surprising force. The Gavi Rovereto Vignavecchia comes from the grapes of 80-year-old ungrafted vines that have been macerated for 72 hours to produce a complex wine. Despite its serious structure, it still manages to express youthful fruit notes of pink grapefruit and pineapple. The Gavi di Gavi Rolona is still a bit closed but already alluringly reminiscent of mineral and rennet apple. The Gavi Fornaci, the estate's basic wine, is also very satisfying, with an intense nose of hawthorn, banana and unripe melon.

○ Gavi del Comune di Gavi Bruno Broglia '00	♟♟	5
○ Gavi del Comune di Gavi La Meirana '01	♟♟	4
○ Gavi del Comune di Gavi Villa Broglia '01	♟♟	4
● Monferrato Rosso Bruno Broglia '99	♟♟	5
● Monferrato Rosso Bruno Broglia '98	♟♟	5
○ Gavi del Comune di Gavi Bruno Broglia '99	♟♟	5

○ Pilìn '99	♟♟	5
○ Gavi del Comune di Gavi Rolona '01	♟♟	4
○ Gavi Rovereto Vignavecchia '01	♟♟	4
○ Gavi Fornaci '01	♟	3*
○ Pilìn '98	♟♟	5
○ Gavi del Comune di Gavi Rolona '00	♟♟	4
○ Gavi Rovereto Vignavecchia '00	♟♟	4

GAVI (AL)

LA CHIARA
LOC. VALLEGGE, 24/2
15066 GAVI (AL)
TEL. 0143642293

Roberto Bergaglio comes from a family that has always been involved in winemaking. In the mid 1970s, Roberto started to make his own wine at La Chiara, the "cascina" passed down through his father's side of the family, which nestles among the vineyards opposite the foothills of the Apennines. Since then, he has gradually developed his skills as a cellarman, demonstrating aptitude and realistic optimism. Several years ago, a young, high-spirited Giacomo Bologna kitted out the small but impressive cellar with a stock of barriques. This move gave rise to an idea and an experiment that became Vigneto Groppella, a wine from a 30-year-old, south-facing vineyard. Roberto makes 6,000 bottles of this wine, which he obtains from carefully selected bunches of grapes gathered in cases then fermented in oak. A year's ageing produces a delicately golden wine, almost amber in hue, with an elegant, superbly concentrated nose of honey and medlar. The '01 has a pleasantly rounded, complex palate smoothed by oak ageing that gives it remarkable, fascinating length: definitely one for the cellar. The Gavi La Chiara performed handsomely, offering typical, heady aromas and subtle nuances of bitter apple. Its clean, refreshing palate has a classic, attractive almond finish. Roberto's ambition is to create a new selection that he will produce from only the best vintages but in the meantime, he is honing his skills by experimenting with new reds and "metodo classico" sparkling wines. What delights, we wonder, does he have in store for us?

○ Gavi del Comune di Gavi Vigneto Groppella '00	🍷🍷 4*
○ Gavi del Comune di Gavi La Chiara '01	🍷 3
○ Gavi del Comune di Gavi Vigneto Groppella '98	🍷🍷 4
○ Gavi del Comune di Gavi Vigneto Groppella '99	🍷🍷 4

GAVI (AL)

LA GIUSTINIANA
FRAZ. ROVERETO, 5
15066 GAVI (AL)
TEL. 0143682132
E-MAIL: lagiustiniana@libarnanet.it

History, culture and quality have combined to make this dynamic winery what it is today. It is named for the wealthy Giustiniani family, who obtained it from the Republic of Genoa around 1615. The Giustinianis built a fine residence and planted their vineyards in the favourable Rovereto topoclimate. The estate's finest Gavi is the dazzling straw-yellow Montessora, a round, mellow wine that the rich local earth imbues with a velvety finish of apple and fresh pineapple. The palate of the crisp, clean Lugarara brims with lovely flowery fragrances. From cortese grapes partially vinified in a casks of various sizes, the refined Just Bianco is concentrated and persuasive with its warm, golden straw yellow hue and a hint of vanilla that dominates the fruit. Moving on to the reds, we enjoyed the opaque ruby Monferrato Just, with its distinct jammy aromas and a long, tannin-led finish that echoes the palate. The varietal Dolcetto d'Acqui '01 is less characterful but a pleasant enough wine nonetheless. The distinctive characteristics of the Strevi subzone earned high marks for the Moscato d'Asti, the best of the aromatic wines. The standard-cork version, rich in sage and juniper aromas, astounds with its breadth and length. The concentrated, creamy Passito, released only in the best years, has a very different character. The Brachetto and the Dolcetto d'Acqui are more approachable. The estate obtains its 200,000-bottle annual production from 40 hectares of vines skilfully tended by Enrico Tomalino, the brains behind the Just brand, which hints at the Latin root of Giustiniani.

○ Just Bianco '00	🍷🍷 5
○ Moscato Passito di Strevi '00	🍷🍷 5
○ Gavi del Comune di Gavi Montessora '01	🍷🍷 4
○ Moscato d'Asti Contero '01	🍷🍷 4
● Monferrato Rosso Just '99	🍷🍷 5
● Brachetto d'Acqui Contero '01	🍷 4
● Dolcetto d'Acqui '01	🍷 4
○ Gavi del Comune di Gavi Lugarara '01	🍷 4
● Monferrato Rosso Just '98	🍷🍷 5
○ Just Bianco '99	🍷🍷 5

GAVI (AL)

PRODUTTORI DEL GAVI
VIA CAVALIERI DI VITTORIO VENETO, 45
15066 GAVI (AL)
TEL. 0143642786
E-MAIL: cantina.prodgavi@libero.it

Hats off to this Gavi co-operative, which manages to combine quality with quantity. That rare feat has been achieved by the deliberate change of policy adopted by members and oenologist Roberto Sarotto in 1999. Even the mass market wines, such as the basic Gavi di Gavi or the Gavi Il Forte, are quite decent: neither run of the mill nor, horror of horrors, industrial. Their most successful products, though, are the selections and of these we particularly liked the Gavi Cascine dell'Aureliana. The grapes are obtained from the best estate vineyards and 20 per cent ferments in oak casks. Its fruit-led aromas meld with notes of vanilla and almond but it really comes into its own on the palate, where it shows warmth, flavour, length and balance. Close on its heels is the Gavi di Gavi La Maddalena, which offers a tangy nose of lemon leaf, apple and Williams pear. On the palate, the residual sugar gives ageing potential and balance without affecting the dry character of the wine. The ripe pear, peach and apricot fruit aromas of the Gavi Primuva are attractive, if not excessively concentrated, and the wine is markedly more assertive on the palate. We were less impressed, however, by the Piemonte Cortese DiVino. Despite the care and attention lavished on it in the cellar, we found that the follow-through on the palate lacked balance, with the fruit and oak distinctly at odds. Finally, we tried the well-typed Gavi Brut. Drinking well now, it will only improve over time given that the wine, disgorged in autumn 2001, was oenologist Sarotto's first stab at it.

O Gavi Cascine dell'Aureliana '01	ΥΥ	3*
O Gavi di Gavi La Maddalena '01	ΥΥ	4
O Gavi Primuva '01	ΥΥ	3*
O Piemonte Cortese DiVino '00	Υ	3
O Gavi di Gavi '01	Υ	3
O Gavi Il Forte '01	Υ	3
O Gavi Brut M. Cl.	Υ	5

GAVI (AL)

SAN BARTOLOMEO
LOC. VALLEGGE
CASCINA SAN BARTOLOMEO, 26
15066 GAVI (AL)
TEL. 0143643180

The San Bartolomeo estate triumphs with a delightful range of Gavi labels that have been the focus of young Fulvio Bergaglio's undoubted skills. Recognizing that the territory of Gavi is particularly well suited to whites, Fulvio has opted to concentrate solely on wines of this type and, if this year's brilliant results are anything to go by, we fully support his decision. But first, a quick update on the estate itself is in order. Currently consisting of 13 hectares under vine, San Bartolomeo has bought a further six that are ready to go into production. Annual production amounts to 25,000 bottles plus a small amount of bulk wine that Fulvio and his father Quintino make in the spacious new cellars situated right next door to the vineyards. As for the wines, the most important selections are the two Gavis from the municipal territory of Gavi, Pelöia and Cappello del Diavolo. The first of these is steel-conditioned. It boasts a vivid straw-yellow colour and an intense nose of flowers and citrus fruit. The pleasant, tangy palate has no shortage of flesh and the finish lingers. The Cappello del Diavolo enjoys a brief spell in oak that renders it soft on nose and palate. The oaky tones do not overwhelm, however, and leave plenty of space for the powerful fruit to emerge. All in all, this is a first-rate wine. The Gavi di Gavi is also good, if simpler than the other two, while the basic Gavi is well-typed and easy-drinking, which is precisely what you would expect.

O Gavi del Comune di Gavi Cappello del Diavolo '01	ΥΥ	5
O Gavi del Comune di Gavi Pelöia '01	ΥΥ	4
O Gavi '01	Υ	3
O Gavi del Comune di Gavi '01	Υ	3
O Gavi del Comune di Gavi Pelöia '00	Υ	4

GAVI (AL)

Villa Sparina
Fraz. Monterotondo, 36
15066 Gavi (AL)
Tel. 0143633835
E-mail: villasparina@villasparina.it

The Moccagatta family – Mario was joined a couple of years ago by his sons Stefano and Massimo – has almost completed its ambitious project. In spring 2003, their country hotel on the crown of the Monterotondo hill will open, putting 28 bedrooms and a restaurant at visitors' disposal. In the interim, the Moccagattas have expanded their cellars and kitted out a warehouse for cellaring and ageing. Their technical partnership with Beppe Caviola is still going strong on the oenological front and two years ago, they brought in Tuscan Marco Pierucci to look after the vineyards. The estate's 50 hectares supply the grapes that go to make up a wide range of high quality wines. Top of our tasting notes comes an exceptional Monferrato Rosso Rivalta, a barbera-based wine with a very small proportion of cabernet sauvignon. It is a purplish red so dark that it is impenetrable to the eye. The well-defined nose offers crisp aromas of spice, pepper and ripe black berry fruit. The palate is very concentrated, with a sweet, lingering fruitiness and a finish enhanced by peppery tones that recall the nose. It's a sound wine with a great future ahead of it. The Monferrato Sampò, youthful and vinous in its '98 version, and the Dolcetto d'Acqui Bric Maioli complete the red line-up. The Monte Rotondo selection stands head and shoulders above the rest of the whites. In fact, it is a Gavi with fine structure and equal to a few years in the cellar. The Spumante Villa Sparina is very good, the standard Gavi is fruity and agreeable and the flowery, aromatic Müller Thurgau is a little simpler.

● Monferrato Rosso Rivalta '00	???	6
○ Gavi del Comune di Gavi Monte Rotondo '01	??	6
● Monferrato Rosso Sampò '98	??	4*
● Dolcetto d'Acqui Bric Maioli '01	??	3*
○ Villa Sparina Brut M. Cl.	??	5
○ Gavi del Comune di Gavi '01	?	4
○ Monferrato Bianco Müller Thurgau '01	?	3
● Monferrato Rosso Rivalta '99	???	6
● Barbera del M.to Rivalta '97	???	6
○ Gavi del Comune di Gavi Monte Rotondo '99	???	6
● Monferrato Rosso Rivalta '98	??	6

GHEMME (NO)

Antichi Vigneti di Cantalupo
Via Michelangelo Buonarroti, 5
28074 Ghemme (NO)
Tel. 0163840041
E-mail: cantalupovigneti@tiscalinet.it

Ghemme is one of the great, cellarable Piedmont red wine types, made from either 100 per cent nebbiolo or nebbiolo blended with small quantities of two local varieties, vespolina and uva rara. The changes currently being mooted to the regulations for this wine will, in the opinion of many, only serve to dilute the DOC. It is by no means clear that the introduction of international varieties would do anything to improve a wine of such daunting history and personality. The Arlunnos, whose estate is responsible for Ghemme's fame worldwide, are the unchallenged custodians of its history and their roots here go as far back as 1550. Their extensive list includes four Ghemmes and a series of more approachable labels that are perfect for everyday drinking. A brief round-up might mention the delicately satisfying rosé Il Mimo; the white Carolus, with a full, zesty palate and flowery fragrances; the Villa Horte and the Primigenia '01, both refreshingly drinkable; and the Agamium '00, a characterful nebbiolo. The basic Ghemme '98 is best appreciated for its fruit-rich, wonderfully harmonious palate and clear aromas. The Ghemme Collis Carellae, one of the estate's flagship products, was not available this year. The Two Glass Signore di Bayard '98, a modern-style Ghemme, shows off the superb quality of the fruit but remains a little in awe of the oak. The excellent, aristocratic Collis Breclemae '97 is a classic Ghemme that proffers slightly balsamic aromas of violets and berry fruit, then a generous, well-balanced palate with good length.

● Ghemme Collis Breclemae '97	??	6
● Ghemme '98	??	5
● Ghemme Signore di Bayard '98	??	6
● Colline Novaresi Agamium '00	?	3
○ Carolus '01	?	2*
⊙ Colline Novaresi Il Mimo '01	?	3
● Colline Novaresi Primigenia '01	?	3
● Colline Novaresi Vespolina Villa Horta '01	?	3
● Ghemme Collis Carellae '96	??	5
● Ghemme Collis Carellae '97	??	5
● Ghemme Signore di Bayard '97	??	5
● Ghemme Collis Breclemae '96	?	5

GHEMME (NO)

ROVELLOTTI
VIA PRIVATA TAMIOTTI, 3
28074 GHEMME (NO)
TEL. 0163840478
E-MAIL: info@rovellotti.it

INCISA SCAPACCINO (AT)

ERMANNO E ALESSANDRA BREMA
VIA POZZOMAGNA, 9
14045 INCISA SCAPACCINO (AT)
TEL. 014174019 - 014174617
E-MAIL: vinibrema@inwind.it

The winery of Antonello and Paolo Rovellotti is a rising star in northern Piedmont and well worth a visit. It is located in Ricetto di Ghemme, a fortified mediaeval centre, and its vinification and ageing rooms are in 12 small, tastefully restructured cellars that date from the 14th century. The 15 hectares under vine all lie together at Baraggiole. The very dense garnet Ghemme Riserva '98 came close to Three Glasses this year for its deep, intense aromas and modern, but not exaggerated, style. Hints of black berry fruit, tobacco and violet subtly laced with spice haunt the nose, then the extremely complex palate displays a wonderful intensity of taste throughout the its progression. The Ghemme '98 starts out oaky but soon gives way to notes of flowers, mainly rose and violet, and ripe berry fruit with refreshing aniseed tones. Entry on the palate is quite full, the nicely balanced tannins leading into a refreshing, well-sustained mid palate then a concentrated redcurrant and tobacco finish. The Valdenrico '99, a "passito" made from erbaluce grapes, has a warmer Mediterranean style than the refined '98 version. Its amber hue ushers in a nose of dried flowers, honey and hazelnut, and a generous, structured palate that is sweet but not cloying. The 100 per cent greco (another name for erbaluce) Colline Novaresi Bianco boasts a typical, elegant nose and medium structure with pronounced, invigorating tanginess. The standard-label Nebbiolo and Vespolina are well-typed, approachable reds perfect for everyday consumption.

Founded in 1887, this historic Incisa Scapaccino winery passed into the hands of the Brema family in 1950. First Carlo then Ermanno Brema turned their attention to Barbera d'Asti and as the estate developed, the family gradually stopped selling bulk wine. As far back as 1971, they were concentrating on bottling their own products while constantly seeking to improve their quality. Today, Ermanno and his wife Alessandra have 13 hectares under vine planted largely to barbera. It follows that the estate's flagship wine should be a Barbera, the Bricco della Volpettona. The '00 vintage is a rich garnet and possesses nice varietal notes of cherry with complex mineral undertones. It is well-sustained and dry on the palate, staying bright and lively right through to a warm, reasonably long finish that resoundingly echoes the nose with balanced fruit and mineral notes. The Bricconizza, the estate's other big Barbera, is also decent and comes from grapes grown in one of the most prestigious Nizza vineyards. Toasty, balsamic aromas pervade the nose then the palate displays good flesh and structure. The acidic vein is evident but well tempered by the superb body. The Barbera Cascina Croce has a ruby colour shading into garnet and a not very concentrated nose with earthy tones that emerge through the fruit. The palate could do with just a tad more structure and length: all told, it's only a moderately challenging wine. The Grignolino and the Brachetto are varietal and well-typed.

● Ghemme Ris. '98	♟♟	7
● Ghemme '98	♟♟	6
○ Valdenrico Passito '99	♟♟	6
○ Colline Novaresi Bianco '01	♟	4
● Colline Novaresi Nebbiolo '01	♟	4
● Colline Novaresi Vespolina '01	♟	4
● Ghemme '97	♟♟	6
● Ghemme Ris. '97	♟♟	7
○ Valdenrico Passito '98	♟♟	6

● Barbera d'Asti Sup. Bricco della Volpettona '00	♟♟	6
● Barbera d'Asti Sup. Bricconizza '00	♟♟	5
● Grignolino d'Asti Brich Le Roche '01	♟	3
● Piemonte Brachetto Carlotta '01	♟	4
● Barbera d'Asti Sup. Cascina Croce '00		4
● Barbera d'Asti Sup. Bricco della Volpettona '98	♟♟	6
● Barbera d'Asti Sup. Bricco della Volpettona '99	♟♟	6
● Barbera d'Asti Sup. Bricconizza '99	♟♟	5

INCISA SCAPACCINO (AT)

Tenuta Olim Bauda
Strada Prata, 22
14045 Incisa Scapaccino (AT)
tel. 014174266
e-mail: giannibertolino@yahoo.it

To reach this beautiful new Asti estate, head past Nizza Monferrato and, along the road to Incisa Scapaccino, take the turning for the magnificent 18th-century villa that dominates the surrounding countryside from its hilltop. This is the headquarters of the winery that belongs to the Bertolino siblings, Gianni, Dino and Diana, the rising young wine stars of lower Monferrato (their combined ages come to less than 100). We have kept an interested eye on them since they started four years ago and are now pleased to afford them a well-deserved entry in the Guide. The Bertolinos are serious wine makers. They have a modern cellar next to the villa, 25 hectares planted to vine, a new tasting room with an annex for visitors opening soon and – the ace up their sleeve – a friendly partnership with an oenologist who requires no introduction, Beppe Caviola. With a winning hand of this kind, it was only a matter of time before they hit the jackpot and this is exactly what they did in 2002. We tasted three Barbera d'Astis. The simplest, a product of the 2001 harvest, is notable for the clarity of its nose and a palate that is already harmonious despite its youth. The Superiore '99 impressed us, too, with an even richer array of aromas and a strong, generous personality. But it is the deep, dark Superiore Nizza '00 that gets our vote for its gorgeous nose of roses, plums and spice, followed by a characterful, elegantly rounded palate that ends in a caressing finish. The Bertolinos also produce an oak-conditioned Chardonnay that is fresh-tasting and pleasant.

●	Barbera d'Asti Sup. Nizza '00	♟♟	6
●	Barbera d'Asti '01	♟♟	4*
●	Barbera d'Asti Sup. '99	♟♟	5
○	Piemonte Chardonnay '01	♟	4
●	Barbera d'Asti Sup. '98	♟♟	5

IVREA (TO)

Ferrando
Via Torino, 599/a
10015 Ivrea (TO)
tel. 0125641176 - 0125633550
e-mail: info@ferrandovini.it

The Carema Etichetta Nera '97, reviewed erroneously in last year's edition of the Guide, has the distinction of being not only the best wine to come out of the Ferrando estate but also, beyond any doubt, the best wine to come out of the Canavese area. This year, Luigi Ferrando, who runs his estate with sons Roberto in the cellar and Andrea in charge of distribution, presented a Carema that takes us back to some of the glorious selections from the late 1980s and early 1990s. Its class is evident in the concentrated ruby red, whose finely nuanced hues are the prelude to a wide-ranging, complex nose worthy of the very best nebbiolos. The nose is a riot of spice, cinnamon and tobacco then the palate reveals a wealth of extract that renders the wine harmonious despite its extreme youth. The finish is tempered by a generous dose of sweet, silky tannins. The standard Carema is pleasant but nowhere near as good. The only visible difference from the selection is the label, which is white. The Cariola Etichetta Nera '00 is missing from the ranks of the Erbaluce whites and is replaced by the fruity, slightly fermentative Cariola '01. The basic Erbaluce offers good value for money. The new Spumante Ferrando, an Erbaluce di Caluso DOC wine, did well on its first release. The monovarietal erbaluce Canavese Bianco del Castello di Loranzé is agreeable and the Solativo is balanced but a little oaky.

●	Carema Etichetta Nera '97	♟♟	7
○	Erbaluce di Caluso		
	Ferrando Brut '98	♟♟	5
○	Solativo '00	♟	6
○	Canavese Bianco		
	Castello di Loranzé '01	♟	4
○	Erbaluce di Caluso		
	Cariola Etichetta Verde '01	♟	4
●	Carema Etichetta Bianca '98	♟	6
○	Erbaluce di Caluso '01		4
●	Carema Etichetta Nera '95	♟♟	7
●	Carema Etichetta Nera '96	♟♟	7
○	Caluso Passito		
	Vigneto Cariola '97	♟♟	8

LA MORRA (CN)

★★ Elio Altare - Cascina Nuova
Fraz. Annunziata, 51
12064 La Morra (CN)
tel. 017350835

The future of this winery looks secure and set to benefit from the feminine touch as Silvia Altare, Elio's eldest daughter, has almost finished university and is becoming more involved in the business. We tasted some magnificent wines here this summer, first and foremost a stellar, bright ruby and garnet Barolo Vigneto Arborina'98 that shows just how good its terroir is. Pervasive and almost minerally on the nose, it boasts a superb, extremely fruit-rich, palate of superb refinement. Equally seductive is the Barolo Brunate'98, obtained from a plot made available by Marc De Grazia. Destined for the overseas market, it scored high marks. The sweet spicy tones of this dark, dazzling ruby wine blend nicely with the fruit, and its fabulous texture sweetly caresses the palate right through to the lingering finish. We gave two full Glasses to the traditional Barolo '98. Judging the three Langhe '00 vintages was an arduous but very enjoyable task as they had only just been bottled. All showed rich colour, closed nose and an authoritative palate. The barbera-based Larigi has power, character and a soft, warm finish. The charming nebbiolo-based Arborina distinguishes itself with dense, compact tannins that leave the palate wonderfully opulent and velvety while the La Villa, a barbera and nebbiolo blend, was the most sinewy. Of the standard wines, the warm, fruit-sweet Dolcetto has the edge over the more approachable Barbera. The supremely elegant new version of the Insieme is also very good but was not reviewed as it is part of a charity project. We highly recommend it in any case.

● Barolo Vigneto Arborina '98	▼▼▼	8
● Langhe Arborina '00	▼▼	8
● Langhe La Villa '00	▼▼	8
● Langhe Larigi '00	▼▼	8
● Barolo Brunate '98	▼▼	8
● Dolcetto d'Alba '01	▼▼	4
● Barolo '98	▼▼	8
● Barbera d'Alba '01	▼	4
● Langhe Larigi '95	▼▼▼	8
● Langhe Arborina '96	▼▼▼	8
● Langhe Arborina '97	▼▼▼	8
● Langhe Larigi '97	▼▼▼	8
● Langhe La Villa '99	▼▼▼	8
● Langhe Larigi '99	▼▼▼	8
● Langhe Arborina '99	▼▼	8

LA MORRA (CN)

Batasiolo
Fraz. Annunziata, 87
12064 La Morra (CN)
tel. 017350130 - 017350131
e-mail: info@batasiolo.com

The Doglianis' large estate is in the heart of the Langhe on the road from Alba to Barolo. Its impressive dimensions make it one of the zone's major wineries in terms of area (currently 115 hectares) and of bottles released (about 2,000,000 every year). Wines are produced from both estate-grown grapes and fruit that is bought in. The technical side of operations is run by Giorgio Lavagna, an oenologist who learned his craft at Batasiolo and who knows the territory inside out. The area includes prestigious vineyards such as Cerequio at La Morra, Corda della Briccolina, Boscareto at Serralunga, and Bofani at Monforte. This year, the range has expanded to include Dolcetto d'Alba Arsigà and the Langhe Bianco Sunsì. The former comes from very ripe grapes from all over the estate. The fruit is aged in oak to produce a very well-typed wine. The Langhe Bianco is a Chardonnay vinified using micro-aeration that weds freshness to a solid structure. But the austere, tannic Barolo Corda della Briccolina impressed us most. It possesses all the best qualities of a Serralunga Barolo and discloses them one by one. The Cerequio is readier to drink and has a spice and ripe red fruit nose followed by a well-extracted, velvety palate. The pleasant Barbera Sovrana shows body while the youthful Dolcetto d'Alba Bricco di Vergne is driven by fruit and alcohol. We enjoyed the steel-conditioned Chardonnay Serbato but the Morino selection is still oak-dominated. Finally, the Moscato Bosc d'la Rei is aromatic and well-paced while the moscato-based Muscatel Tardì is one-dimensional.

● Barolo Corda della Briccolina '98	▼▼	8
● Barbera d'Alba Sovrana '00	▼▼	5
● Dolcetto d'Alba Arsigà '01	▼▼	4
● Barolo Cerequio '98	▼▼	8
● Dolcetto d'Alba Bricco di Vergne '01	▼	4
○ Langhe Chardonnay Morino '00	▼	6
○ Piemonte Muscatel Tardì '00	▼	7
○ Moscato d'Asti Bosc d'la Rei '01	▼	4
○ Langhe Bianco Sunsì '01	▼	4
○ Langhe Chardonnay Serbato '01	▼	4
● Barolo Corda della Briccolina '88	▼▼▼	8
● Barolo Corda della Briccolina '89	▼▼▼	8
● Barolo Corda della Briccolina '90	▼▼▼	8
● Barolo Corda della Briccolina '97	▼▼	8

LA MORRA (CN)

Enzo Boglietti
Via Roma, 37
12064 La Morra (CN)
tel. 017350330
e-mail: enzoboglietti@virgilio.it

In just ten years, the Boglietti brothers' estate has made quite a name for itself with its versions of classic Langhe wines. The 12 hectares, soon to become 17, give it 70,000 bottles a year that for the moment are vinified in awkward cellars where conditions are far from ideal and production processes difficult to carry out. The large wine list includes three very impressive '98 Barolos. The Fossati flaunts good flesh and power, as well as a nose of liquorice that mingles harmoniously with hints of berry fruit. The deep garnet Case Nere still suggests charred oak but displays character and big tannins on the palate. The palest of the three, the Brunate, has an impressively complex, broad nose of skilfully judged oak, tobacco, fruit in alcohol, earth and mint. The palate, too, offers complex, warm sensations. The fruit-led, big-hearted Dolcetto Tigli Neri '01 and the zesty, elegant Barbera Roscaleto '00, both barrique-conditioned, are very good wines. Two Glasses also went to the deliciously peppery Nebbiolo '01, which combines quaffability with the gravitas of the variety. Finally, we sampled the Buio '00, a nebbiolo and barbera mix that is still very oaky, and the well-managed Dolcetto and Barbera, both from 2001.

• Barolo Brunate '98	🍷🍷	8
• Barolo Fossati '98	🍷🍷	8
• Barbera d'Alba Roscaleto '00	🍷🍷	5
• Langhe Rosso Buio '00	🍷🍷	6
• Dolcetto d'Alba Tigli Neri '01	🍷🍷	4
• Langhe Nebbiolo '01	🍷🍷	5
• Barolo Case Nere '98	🍷🍷	8
• Barbera d'Alba '01	🍷	4
• Dolcetto d'Alba '01	🍷	3
• Barbera d'Alba Vigna dei Romani '94	🍷🍷🍷	6
• Barolo Fossati '96	🍷🍷🍷	8
• Barolo Brunate '97	🍷🍷🍷	8

LA MORRA (CN)

Gianfranco Bovio
Fraz. Annunziata
B.ta Ciotto, 63
12064 La Morra (CN)
tel. 017350667 - 017350190
e-mail: az.agr.boviogianfranco@areacom.it

We'll start our notes with the three jewels in the Bovio crown. The Barolo '98 Vigna Arborina presents as a dry, austere wine whose nose is still closed but suggests fruit and spice, with touches of violets and wild roses. The palate is well-structured and moderately acidic, showing nicely gauged tannins and a pleasantly flowery finish with liquorice tones. The nose of the Barolo Vigna Gattera '98 is more open, its fresh fragrances of medium intensity revealing its origins in a vineyard with less uniform exposure to sunlight and humus-rich soil. The palate displays ripe fruit, reasonably soft flesh and strong, lively aromas. The aristocratic Barolo '98 Rocchettevino soon abandons its etheric notes to show sweet nuances of ripe plum and redcurrant fruit, with strong mineral undertones. There were newcomers in the tangy Barbera Parussi '00, from a Castiglione Falletto vineyard that offers a wealth of varietal aromas and good acidity. Riper in its fruit, the succulent Barbera Regiaveja '00 has a soft, smooth, elegantly complex palate. The delicate, fragrant Nebbiolo '01 offers excellent value for money in a fairly lightweight wine that is perfect for everyday drinking. The dark ruby Dolcetto d'Alba Dabbene '01 has aromas of medium length and a tangy, agreeably fruity palate with quite a strong acid vein, while the Barbera Il Ciotto '01 offers youthful fruitiness. The estate also releases two Chardonnays. The oak-conditioned Alessandro '00 is well-structured with sweet, rich fruit, and the Vigna La Villa '01 has a flowery nose and a refreshing, sophisticated palate.

• Barbera d'Alba Parussi '00	🍷🍷	5
• Barbera d'Alba Regiaveja '00	🍷🍷	5
O Langhe Chardonnay Alessandro '00	🍷🍷	5
• Barolo Rocchettevino '98	🍷🍷	8
• Barolo Vigna Arborina '98	🍷🍷	8
• Barolo Vigna Gattera '98	🍷🍷	8
• Barbera d'Alba Il Ciotto '01	🍷	4
• Dolcetto d'Alba Dabbene '01	🍷	4
O Langhe Chardonnay Vigna La Villa '01	🍷	4
• Langhe Nebbiolo '01	🍷	4
• Barolo Vigna Arborina '90	🍷🍷🍷	8
• Barolo Rocchettevino '97	🍷🍷	8
• Barolo Vigna Arborina '97	🍷🍷	8

LA MORRA (CN)

CASCINA BALLARIN
FRAZ. ANNUNZIATA, 115
12064 LA MORRA (CN)
TEL. 017350365
E-MAIL: cascina@cascinaballarin.it

Brothers Giorgio and Gianni Viberti of Cascina Ballarin released an extremely elegant Barolo Bussia '98 this year. Intense ruby red with orange highlights, its refined, very varietal nose reveals concentrated fruit mingling with mineral notes and hints of forest floor. The palate has decent body enlivened by firm acidity and is full of sweet, well-integrated tannins. Its lingering aromas highlight plum and cherry while the finish hints at liquorice. The garnet red Barolo Bricco Rocca '98 has brick red nuances and is even more traditional in style. It flaunts a nose of violets, herbs and cherries, an austere, sophisticated, dry body and a concentrated, leisurely finish where acidity, tannins and aromatic length come through. Less imposing but still a fine example of a good Langhe wine is the nebbiolo-based Barolo '98. Its grassy tones are nuanced with spice and fruit, as well as the odd note of mint and truffle. The nose shows breadth but has not yet found its balance, although the wine has a fairly even structure, measured acidity and alluring fruit. The Barbera Giuli '00 is very impressive. Its generous, richly extracted nose smacks of wild berries and vanilla, while the sturdy palate reveals good acidity, mature flesh and reasonable length. The Dolcetto Bussia '01 presents a rich ruby and vinous, zesty young aromas. The vibrantly aromatic palate introduces a lean, elegant body. The Langhe Nebbiolo '01 is harmonious, agreeable and easy-drinking. The estate recently released two other wines to watch out for, the Langhe Rosso '00 and the Langhe Bianco '01.

●	Barbera d'Alba Giuli '00	🍷🍷	5
●	Barolo Bricco Rocca '98	🍷🍷	8
●	Barolo Bussia '98	🍷🍷	8
●	Langhe Rosso '00	🍷	5
●	Dolcetto d'Alba Bussia '01	🍷	4
○	Langhe Bianco '01	🍷	4
●	Langhe Nebbiolo '01	🍷	4
●	Barolo '98	🍷	7
●	Barolo Bricco Rocca '97	🍷🍷	8
●	Barolo Bussia '97	🍷🍷	8
●	Barbera d'Alba Giuli '99	🍷🍷	5

LA MORRA (CN)

GIOVANNI CORINO
FRAZ. ANNUNZIATA, 24
12064 LA MORRA (CN)
TEL. 017350219 - 0173509452

The first version of the Barolo Vecchie Vigne, a '97, was a big hit with our tasting panel. This year, Renato and Giuliano Corino came up trumps again with their '98, winning a resounding Three Glasses for a wine with a wonderful nose and a superb palate. The delicate vanilla entry gives way to complex, richly extracted fruit sensations and a liquorice finish, all framed in a dark, dazzling ruby. The palate displays ripe fruit and firm, concentrated pulp. There is extraordinary balance in the flavours and aromas, while marked acidity and tannins combine to create a wine whose classic soul belies its ultra-modern appearance. The Barolo Vigna Giachini '98 is another big wine, although its body and nose are no match for those of its elder brother. Its aromas range from grass to autumn leaves and the palate is warm and harmonious. The third selection, Vigneto Arborina '98, has come of age. Its nose of fairly pronounced, well-balanced liquorice and spice tones is a little more evolved than those of the previous two. The palate shows weighty fruit, a cornucopia of clean fragrances layered over balsam, sweet tannins and moderate acidity. Not quite as generous on the nose, the Vigneto Rocche '98 is still full and enjoyable on the palate, where plum and stewed cherry aromas are to the fore. This magnificent quartet of Barolo selections is a tribute to the skill of the Corino brothers. The standard Barolo '98 is also good, the dark Dolcetto d'Alba '01 has lots of fruit and an almond finish and the agreeable Barbera d'Alba '01 pleases with its measured acidity and delicate flavour.

●	Barolo Vecchie Vigne '98	🍷🍷🍷	8
●	Barbera d'Alba '01	🍷🍷	4*
●	Barolo Vigna Giachini '98	🍷🍷	8
●	Barolo Vigneto Arborina '98	🍷🍷	8
●	Barolo Vigneto Rocche '98	🍷🍷	8
●	Dolcetto d'Alba '01	🍷	4
●	Barolo '98	🍷	7
●	Barolo Vigna Giachini '89	🍷🍷🍷	8
●	Barolo Rocche '90	🍷🍷🍷	8
●	Barbera d'Alba Vigna Pozzo '96	🍷🍷🍷	8
●	Barbera d'Alba Vigna Pozzo '97	🍷🍷🍷	8
●	Barolo Vecchie Vigne '97	🍷🍷	8
●	Barolo Vigna Giachini '97	🍷🍷	8
●	Barolo Vigneto Rocche '97	🍷🍷	8

LA MORRA (CN)

Silvio Grasso
Fraz. Annunziata
Cascina Luciani, 112
12064 La Morra (CN)
tel. 017350322

This year, Paolo joined his father Federico full-time on the estate. We'll start our notes with the Barolo Ciabot Manzoni '98, from a south-facing vineyard in the eastern part of Annunziata. Its close-knit, vibrant aromas range from wild roses to full, rich blackberry and cherry. The fruit is sweet and chewy on the palate, where the palpable acidity lends a note of intense freshness and the tannins leave it dry and tidy, giving it a traditional style. This Barolo has immense character. The Barolo Bricco Luciani '98, obtained from plots adjacent to the winery, starts out on notes of aromatic mint and thyme that open out into fruit that although rich does not quite match the Manzoni. There is good balance on the palate, where the warmth of the alcohol and the lively acidity complement each other perfectly, and tannins usher in a finish redolent of blackberry and black cherry. Federico Grasso also offers a third Barolo, Pì Vigne, so-called because its grapes come from several vineyards. The first release, a '98, possesses subtle fragrances of wild berry fruit with undertones of liquorice and spice. It boasts abundant structure and pleasant, complex aromas. The Barbera d'Alba Fontanile '00 offers a refined nose and close-knit texture in a soft, fruity palate. The Barbera '01 is another full-bodied wine, while the Dolcetto weds fullness of taste with an alcohol-rich nose. Finally, the attractive new Langhe Nebbiolo Peirass '00 has ripe fruit and a sophisticated palate.

LA MORRA (CN)

Poderi Marcarini
P.zza Martiri, 2
12064 La Morra (CN)
tel. 017350222
e-mail: marcarini@marcarini.it

This historic winery at the gates of La Morra was founded in the second half of the 1800s. Expanded in the 1960s by the original Marcarini, a notary public, it was restructured again only recently by the current owners, Manuel Marchetti and his wife Luisa, who work with oenologist Armando Cordero. Prominent in the range of wines they offered us for tasting this year are the 2001 vintages, which the estate considers good enough to warrant postponing the release of the 2001 Barbera Ciabot Camerano. The 3,000 bottles of flawless 2001 Dolcetto Boschi di Berri were obtained from a venerable vineyard, part of which dates back to pre-phylloxera days. Deep ruby with purple highlights, it has a rich, well-developed nose that releases well-defined cherry and raspberry fruit mingled with spicy tones of tobacco and liquorice. The palate is potent, austere and flavoursome, with tightly-knit tannins and elegant length. This is a true thoroughbred. Obtained from a plot behind Brunate, the Dolcetto Fontanazza '01 merits Two Glasses for its deep colour, bramble and mint nose, and warm, impressive palate with vigorous, dry tannins. The Nebbiolo Lasarin '01 (the name means "little greenhouse" in the local dialect) has quite a different palate altogether. It's simple but classy and redolent of raspberries. The two Barolos are both dark in hue, but we prefer the fruity, coherent La Serra to the Brunate, which is still closed and edgy but sure to develop as it ages in the bottle.

Wine	Glasses	Score
● Barolo Ciabot Manzoni '98	ΨΨ	8
● Barolo Bricco Luciani '98	ΨΨ	8
● Barbera d'Alba Fontanile '00	ΨΨ	5
● Langhe Nebbiolo Peirass '00	ΨΨ	6
● Barolo Pì Vigne '98	ΨΨ	7
● Barbera d'Alba '01	Ψ	4
● Dolcetto d'Alba '01	Ψ	4
● Barolo Bricco Luciani '90	ΨΨΨ	8
● Barolo Bricco Luciani '95	ΨΨΨ	8
● Barolo Bricco Luciani '96	ΨΨΨ	8
● Barolo Bricco Luciani '97	ΨΨ	8
● Barolo Ciabot Manzoni '95	ΨΨ	8
● Barolo Ciabot Manzoni '96	ΨΨ	8
● Barolo Ciabot Manzoni '97	ΨΨ	8

Wine	Glasses	Score
● Dolcetto d'Alba Boschi di Berri '01	ΨΨ	4
● Dolcetto d'Alba Fontanazza '01	ΨΨ	4
● Barolo Brunate '98	ΨΨ	7
● Barolo La Serra '98	ΨΨ	7
● Langhe Nebbiolo Lasarin '01	Ψ	4
● Barolo Brunate Ris. '85	ΨΨΨ	8
● Dolcetto d'Alba Boschi di Berri '96	ΨΨΨ	5
● Barolo La Serra '95	ΨΨ	7
● Barolo Brunate '96	ΨΨ	7
● Barolo La Serra '96	ΨΨ	7

LA MORRA (CN)

Mario Marengo
Via XX Settembre, 36
12064 La Morra (CN)
Tel. 017350127 - 017350115

LA MORRA (CN)

Mauro Molino
Fraz. Annunziata
B.ta Gancia, 111
12064 La Morra (CN)
Tel. 017350814
E-mail: mauromolino@escom.it

This is the smallest La Morra estate in the Guide, but size this has no bearing whatsoever on its wines, which bear comparison with products from more famous estates. Marco Marengo has dedicated himself full-time to the winery started by his father, Mario, and his goals are few but clear. He aims to make first-class wines from his two hectares and offer them at reasonable prices. The simplest, most approachable wines are the best. In 2001, Marco produced only 1,500 bottles of a superb Dolcetto d'Alba. This deep purplish wine possesses a pronounced, clear nose of liquorice and tobacco, raspberry fruit and hints of mint and almond. The powerful but balanced palate also has good flesh and fruit. The Nebbiolo d'Alba '00 comes from a vineyard Marco rents in the Valmaggiore district of Vezza and offers varietal aromas that range from fruit in alcohol to citrus peel, cocoa powder and oak-derived liquorice. The palate is big and very warm with a fabulous finish. We'll end our notes with the two Barolos, one of which, the Bricco Viole '98, made quite an impression with its deep, vibrant hue. Although a bit closed, it still captivates with its berry fruit, leather and mint nose, then a palate that is quite well-balanced and offers dryish tannins. The Brunate '98 has a somewhat evolved appearance and a muddled nose with too much oak, but settles down on the palate, where it displays character and strength if no real elegance.

Lying among the vineyards of Annunziata in La Morra, and tastefully refurbished only recently, Mauro Molino's lovely estate has an annual production of about 45,000 bottles. Its three Barolos are stupendous. Simple but attractive, the basic version opens out on the palate with generous fruit and good balance. The deep, lustrous Vigna Conca reveals notes of fruit in alcohol and vanilla, silky tannins and superb structure that marks it as a selection of personality. The Vigna Gancia is different but just as good. It has a dense, dark garnet colour, a less mature nose of sweet cherry and cinnamon, and a palate that explodes with warmth and power. The Vigna Gattere selection never disappoints and again confidently added another Three Glasses to its trophy case, proving that it is a prince among Langhe Barberas. The still oak-dominated 2000 Vigna Gattere has strong blackcurrant and violet aromas while the palate is well-extracted and refined, with sweet, lingering tannins. It's a fabulous, fascinating wine that will reveal its full potential with cellar time. The basic Barbera '01 is also nice. It comes from a good year and careful vinification, making a real impact in the mouth with its big body and upfront, fluent style. The Acanzio '00, a barbera, nebbiolo and cabernet blend, is still young, with a toasty nose and rather unripe tannins. The golden Chardonnay Livrot '01 has yet to find balance but has sweet notes of chestnut and vanilla. The Dolcetto '01 is fresh and almondy and the new Langhe Nebbiolo is simple and pleasant to drink.

● Nebbiolo d'Alba Valmaggiore '00	♟♟	5
● Dolcetto d'Alba '01	♟♟	3*
● Barolo Bricco Viole '98	♟♟	8
● Barolo Brunate '98	♟	8
● Barolo Brunate '95	♟♟	8
● Barolo Brunate '96	♟♟	8
● Barolo Bricco Viole '97	♟♟	8
● Barolo Brunate '97	♟♟	8

● Barbera d'Alba Vigna Gattere '00	♟♟♟	6
● Barolo Vigna Conca '98	♟♟	8
● Barolo Vigna Gancia '98	♟♟	8
● Langhe Rosso Acanzio '00	♟♟	5
● Barolo '98	♟♟	7
● Barbera d'Alba '01	♟	4
● Dolcetto d'Alba '01	♟	4
○ Langhe Chardonnay Livrot '01	♟	5
● Langhe Nebbiolo '01	♟	4
● Barbera d'Alba Vigna Gattere '96	♟♟♟	5
● Barolo Vigna Conca '96	♟♟♟	8
● Barbera d'Alba Vigna Gattere '97	♟♟♟	6
● Barolo Vigna Conca '97	♟♟♟	8
● Barolo Vigna Gancia '96	♟♟	6

LA MORRA (CN)

Monfalletto
Cordero di Montezemolo
Fraz. Annunziata, 67
12064 La Morra (CN)
tel. 017350344
e-mail: monfalletto@corderodimontezemolo.com

With their excellent range of wines, Gianni and Enrico Cordero show theirs is an estate to be reckoned with. From the hill of Monfalletto, easily identifiable from the magnificent cedar of Lebanon that crowns it, they dispatch their elegant, austere wines to the world's markets. One of these is the Barolo Enrico VI '98, from plots at Castiglione Falletto. Its garnet hue introduces exquisitely fine, lingering notes of rose, spice and ripe black cherry, then the palate shows density and aristocratic tannins. The Gattera, from a prestigious Annunziata selection, has done a tidy job of integrating its oak and shows vibrant aromas of berry fruit then a vital, no-nonsense palate with a lovely balsamic finish. The classic Monfalletto, made with grapes from several vineyards aged in casks of varying sizes, offers a wealth of ripe nuances, strong acidity and varietal tannins in the elegant finish. The exhilarating Barbera Funtanì boasts a warm, complex nose of blackberry and fresh cocoa powder. Full and balanced on the palate, it reveals refined tobacco aromas and a harmonious tannic weave in the very long finish. Strawberry and raspberry fragrances dominate the nose of the well-made, eloquent basic Barbera. Rounding off the reds, the Dolcetto is compact and agreeable and the Langhe Nebbiolo delicately austere and restrained. Neither the Chardonnay nor the red Curdé was available so we were unable to pass judgement, but we did taste the tangy, flowery white Arneis. There were no Three Glass winners this year but the entire range performed splendidly.

• Barolo Enrico VI '98	🍷🍷	8
• Barbera d'Alba Sup. Funtanì '99	🍷🍷	6
• Barbera d'Alba '00	🍷🍷	5
• Barolo Monfalletto '98	🍷🍷	8
• Barolo Vigna Bricco Gattera '98	🍷🍷	8
• Dolcetto d'Alba '01	🍷	4
○ Langhe Arneis '01	🍷	4
• Langhe Nebbiolo '01	🍷	4
• Barolo Enrico VI '96	🍷🍷🍷	8
• Barolo Enrico VI '97	🍷🍷🍷	8
• Barolo Enrico VI '95	🍷🍷	8
• Barolo Monfalletto '96	🍷🍷	8
• Barolo Monfalletto '97	🍷🍷	8
• Barolo Vigna Bricco Gattera '97	🍷🍷	8

LA MORRA (CN)

Andrea Oberto
Borgata Simane, 11
Strada La Morra-Verduno
12064 La Morra (CN)
tel. 0173509262 - 017350104

Andrea Oberto has moved to spacious, well-equipped new cellars on the road to Verduno, a kilometre or so from La Morra. His '98 Barolos, from the estate's two selections, are superb, the Barbera d'Alba Giada is even better, and the whole range is first-class. The magnificent Giada selection romped home to Three Glasses with a profound purple-ruby hue, a concentrated nose of complex, harmoniously succulent fruit that recalls black currant and black cherry, balanced acidity and a powerful, flawless structure. The Albarella has a generously harmonious, intense nose with youthful aromas of aromatic herbs and cassis. The compact, solid flesh, confident, caressing fruit, marked acidity and vibrant tannic weave all impressed. Another big wine, the Barolo Vigneto Rocche unleashes mineral and liquorice that meld with notes of crushed black cherries. This is a wine with structure that brings together power and an attractively well-balanced range of flavours and aromas with sweet fruit, sharp acidity and dry, well-integrated tannins. Not to be outdone, the Barolo from the other estate plots is an excellent product. The two '01 Dolcetto d'Albas, San Francesco and Vantrino Albarella, are decent, the first a tad tart in its fruit, the second riper. The nebbiolo and barbera '00 Langhe Rosso Fabio is, as usual, well made. The potent, sweet fruit of the Barbera d'Alba '01 is slightly offset by acidity, while the Dolcetto d'Alba is rich in alcohol and raspberry aromas. The Nebbiolo is subtle and stylish.

• Barbera d'Alba Giada '00	🍷🍷🍷	6
• Barolo Vigneto Albarella '98	🍷🍷	8
• Barolo Vigneto Rocche '98	🍷🍷	8
• Langhe Rosso Fabio '00	🍷🍷	6
• Barbera d'Alba '01	🍷🍷	4*
• Dolcetto d'Alba Vigneto S. Francesco '01	🍷🍷	4*
• Dolcetto d'Alba Vigneto Vantrino Albarella '01	🍷🍷	4*
• Barolo '98	🍷🍷	7
• Dolcetto d'Alba '01	🍷	4
• Langhe Nebbiolo '01	🍷	4
• Barbera d'Alba Giada '96	🍷🍷🍷	6
• Barolo Vigneto Rocche '96	🍷🍷🍷	8
• Barbera d'Alba Giada '97	🍷🍷🍷	6

LA MORRA (CN)

F.lli Oddero
Fraz. Santa Maria, 28
12064 La Morra (CN)
tel. 017350618
e-mail: info@odderofratelli.it

Cristina Oddero shoulders the lion's share of responsibility for this winery, which has belonged to one of the great Barolo dynasties for over 100 years. She is not alone. Her uncle Luigi and father Giacomo keep a watchful eye on their 35-hectares of nebbiolo extending across the slopes of La Morra, Serralunga, Castiglione Falletto and Monforte. The estate produces several Barolo selections and three from the harvest of 1998 particularly impressed us. The Rocche dei Rivera di Castiglione is notable for its imposing nose and powerful body. The aromas mingle notes of earth and fruit, then the palate displays reasonably well-defined notes that combine the sweet, ripe flesh of cherry with the dryness of the tannins. The strong imprint of terroir in this Barolo is tempered by the oaky sensations imparted by ageing in small barrels. Even more strongly territory-driven, the Vigna Rionda has a nose of rich fruit, autumn leaves and hay. The palate, which is both gentle and potent at the same time, is enormously fruity and already hints at a fabulous moment in the near future when the liquorice tones will merge into the truffle. This giant of its category, which has yet to realize the full potential that further ageing will bring out, deserved its Three Glasses. The '97 vintage Mondoca was a Three Glass winner but the wine didn't quite make the grade with the '98. Austere in character and still quite closed, it has a traditional soul in a fairly well-balanced. The palate is well developed, the finish long and sincere.

LA MORRA (CN)

Renato Ratti
Fraz. Annunziata, 7
12064 La Morra (CN)
tel. 017350185

Work to renovate the Ratti estate started in July 2002 and is likely to last a year. We visited before it all began and can report that the outcome will be a magnificent building at one with its surroundings. Production has been moved nearby temporarily so that the building and restructuring of the new cellars can continue unhindered. As for the wines, they are better and more enjoyable than ever. We tasted three '98 Barolos and gave the thumbs up to the Rocche, of which 8,000 bottles are released. Deep garnet, its spice and vanilla aromas with a backdrop of fruit in alcohol follow through on the well-rounded, leisurely palate. This is a Barolo that stands out for its elegance and roundness, as well as its austere but sweet tannins. The Marcenasco (40,000 bottles) has a fuller colour, a fruit-led nose of morello cherry and raspberry, and a nice traditional, elegant palate. Back after a year's sabbatical, the Barolo Conca (4,000 bottles) is the most aggressive and forceful of the trio, thanks to its rugged tannins. The Dolcetto Colombè '01, still youthful and heady on the nose, although the palate is already well-balanced, earned Two comfortable Glasses. Charred oak tones derived the barrique dominate the primary aromas of the Barbera Torriglione '00 but it settles down well on the palate. A notch below, but decent just the same, the Ochetti '00 is a Nebbiolo d'Alba from the estate's Roero plots.

● Barolo Vigna Rionda '98	🍷🍷🍷	8
● Barolo Mondoca di Bussia Soprana '98	🍷🍷	8
● Barolo Rocche dei Rivera di Castiglione '98	🍷🍷	7
● Langhe Furesté '00	🍷	5
● Barolo Vigna Rionda '89	🍷🍷🍷	8
● Barolo Mondoca di Bussia Soprana '97	🍷🍷🍷	8
● Barolo Rocche dei Rivera di Castiglione '97	🍷🍷	7
● Barolo Rocche di Castiglione '97	🍷🍷	7
● Barolo Vigna Rionda '97	🍷🍷	8

● Barolo Rocche Marcenasco '98	🍷🍷	8
● Barbera d'Alba Torriglione '00	🍷🍷	4*
● Dolcetto d'Alba Colombè '01	🍷🍷	4*
● Barolo Conca Marcenasco '98	🍷🍷	8
● Barolo Marcenasco '98	🍷🍷	7
● Nebbiolo d'Alba Ochetti '00	🍷	5
● Barolo Rocche Marcenasco '83	🍷🍷🍷	8
● Barolo Rocche Marcenasco '84	🍷🍷🍷	8
● Barolo Rocche Marcenasco '97	🍷🍷	8
● Barolo Rocche Marcenasco '96	🍷🍷	8
● Barolo Marcenasco '97	🍷🍷	8
● Monferrato Villa Pattono '98	🍷🍷	5

LA MORRA (CN)

F.LLI REVELLO
FRAZ. ANNUNZIATA, 103
12064 LA MORRA (CN)
TEL. 017350276

LA MORRA (CN)

ROCCHE COSTAMAGNA
VIA VITTORIO EMANUELE, 8
12064 LA MORRA (CN)
TEL. 0173509225
E-MAIL: barolo@rocchecostamagna.it

Brothers Carlo and Enzo Revello work plots in three famous vineyards at Annunziata in La Morra. As ever, they show their class with a glance at the bottle. The Vigna Conca '98 is an imposing Barolo and a glorious tribute to its terrain. It possesses a concentrated nose of complex, compact aromas, robust structure and a full, generous palate with a lovely, lingering finish resonant with notes of blackcurrant, plum and bramble. Fresh fragrances and lively fruit permeate the Rocche dell'Annunziata '98, another very poised thoroughbred. The Vigna Giachini '98 offers a pleasant nose of aromatic herbs, with black cherry and fleshy blackberry on the palate that melt into the jammy sweetness of the finish. But the cream of the estate's crop is the Barbera d'Alba Ciabot du Re '00, a wine of such depth of colour that it is almost opaque. That appearance is a prelude to an extremely well-defined nose whose dominant ripe black cherry and redcurrant aromas meld with very harmonious tones of charred oak. The palate is a triumph, brimming with flesh and fruit, and an acid vein in the finish invigorates the elegant whole. The did well Insieme again this year. It's a wine whose personality shows off the all Revellos' skill in blending nebbiolo and barbera with Bordeaux varieties. The Barbera '01 is leaner in structure but has a tangy nose and measured acidity. We also recommend the flawless Dolcetto d'Alba, which has a broad nose, fragrant fruit and a dark colour.

Alessandro Locatelli mans the helm of this well-known Rocche Costamagna estate whose plots lie in Rocche dell'Annunziata, the vineyard responsible for both of the '98 Barolos we tasted. The Bricco Francesco's early grassy notes open to embrace a broader spectrum of aromas including roses, violets and ripe berry fruit with liquorice nuances in the finish. The austere palate displays persistent fruit, marked acidity and strong but not overwhelming tannins. The Barolo Rocche dell'Annunziata possesses a refined nose with mineral, mint and resin to the fore. The palate shows good balance of acidity, alcohol and tannins. All in all, it's a dry, eminently cellarable patrician of a Barolo. The Barbera d'Alba Annunziata '00 seduces with its gorgeous purple-flecked ruby and fresh rose fragrances. The palate is very fruity, complex, sweet and warm with lovely nuances of cherry, raspberry and bramble jam. There is harmony on the nose, round aromas and a well-made, reasonably firm mouthfeel. The deep purple Dolcetto d'Alba Rubis '01 offers a concentrated, open nose, complex palate, and potent, lingering aromas of fruit that all come together to produce an attractive, very powerful wine. The Langhe Nebbiolo Roccardo '00 has sweet fruit and quite a dense texture. Last but not least, the Langhe Chardonnay Flavo '01 has a pleasant nose, youthful structure and a clean finish.

●	Barbera d'Alba Ciabot du Re '00	♟♟♟	6
●	Barolo Rocche dell'Annunziata '98	♟♟	8
●	Barolo Vigna Conca '98	♟♟	8
●	Dolcetto d'Alba '01	♟♟	4*
●	Barolo Vigna Giachini '98	♟♟	8
●	Barbera d'Alba '01	♟	4
●	Barolo '98	♟	8
●	Barolo '93	♟♟♟	8
●	Barolo Rocche dell'Annunziata '97	♟♟♟	8
●	Barolo Vigna Conca '97	♟♟	8
●	Barolo Vigna Giachini '97	♟♟	8
●	Barbera d'Alba Ciabot du Re '99	♟♟	5

●	Barbera d'Alba Annunziata '00	♟♟	5
●	Dolcetto d'Alba Rubis '01	♟♟	4*
●	Barolo Bricco Francesco Rocche dell'Annunziata '98	♟♟	8
●	Barolo Rocche dell'Annunziata '98	♟♟	7
○	Langhe Chardonnay Flavo '01	♟	4
●	Langhe Nebbiolo Roccardo '00	♟	4
●	Barolo Bricco Francesco Rocche dell'Annunziata '97	♟♟	8
●	Barolo Rocche dell'Annunziata '97	♟♟	7
●	Barbera d'Alba Rocche delle Rocche '99	♟♟	5

LA MORRA (CN)

Mauro Veglio
Fraz. Annunziata
Cascina Nuova, 50
12064 La Morra (CN)
tel. 0173509212
e-mail: mauro.veglio@libero.it

Mauro Veglio and his wife Daniela are a go-getting couple who combine professional seriousness and competency with good taste. Almost ten years have passed since they embarked upon their winemaking careers. Today, they obtain their current annual production of around 55,000 bottles from 11 hectares of vineyards, most of which are at La Morra with some in the village of Perno at Monforte. This year, they offered us a number of excellent wines that show elegance and a hint of hay on the nose that sets the tone for the aromas. Just a whisker shy of Three Glasses, the Barbera Cascina Nuova '00 is one of the most interesting interpretations of its variety. It is dark, with aromas of ripe cherry and vanilla, and a palate with a warm, strong, sweet progression. We liked the lusty Castelletto best of the four '98 vintage Barolos we tried, a wonderful example of the power of Monforte's nebbiolo grapes. The nose is still closed but offers very faint cocoa powder, leather and raspberry aromas while the palate is well defined and long. The La Morra selections are altogether more refined. The hard, austere, minerally Arborina has the edge over the spicy, zest of the traditional-style Gattera and the Rocche which, although very concentrated and rich in character, is still a bit dried by the oak. The standard wines are very well managed. The Dolcetto is fresh and youthfully alcohol-rich with the odd tart note, and the elegant Barbera is clean and tangy. Both are very reasonably priced.

• Barbera d'Alba Cascina Nuova '00	🍷🍷	6
• Barolo Arborina '98	🍷🍷	7
• Barbera d'Alba '01	🍷🍷	4*
• Barolo Castelletto '98	🍷🍷	7
• Barolo Gattera '98	🍷🍷	7
• Barolo Vigneto Rocche '98	🍷🍷	8
• Dolcetto d'Alba '01	🍷	3*
• Barbera d'Alba Cascina Nuova '96	🍷🍷🍷	5
• Barolo Vigneto Rocche '96	🍷🍷🍷	8
• Barbera d'Alba Cascina Nuova '99	🍷🍷🍷	6
• Barolo Vigneto Rocche '97	🍷🍷	8
• Barolo Castelletto '97	🍷🍷	7
• Barolo Arborina '97	🍷🍷	7
• Barolo Gattera '97	🍷🍷	7

LA MORRA (CN)

Eraldo Viberti
Fraz. Santa Maria
B.ta Tetti dei Turchi, 53
12064 La Morra (CN)
tel. 017350308

Eraldo Viberti has just finished restructuring and expanding his cellars. The result is very gratifying both in terms of space and from the artistic point of view. A mural serves as a backdrop to the barriques. But there's more. Eraldo has just taken on a partner that brought with him a generous dowry of half a dozen hectares planted to nebbiolo and barbera at Diano d'Alba and Verduno. We are anxious to taste their new products, the Barolo di Verduno, the Nebbiolo Gilat '01 and the Barbera Nirane '00, but in the meantime had to content ourselves with sampling the estate's other wines. The Barolo '98 stood out for its refined fruit, elegantly expressed on the nose and powerfully present on the palate. Aromas of blackberry, cherry and raspberry follow through on the palate, where they lift the firm, sweet mouthfeel. The soft, velvety texture is enlivened by measured acidity and barely discernible tannins that nicely offset the warmth of the alcohol. We have come to expect this kind of personality from Eraldo's Barolos but we have never before tasted one with the sheer power of this vintage. The very dark, vibrant purple ruby Barbera d'Alba Vigna Clara '99 is another fine wine. Its clean, lingeringly pervasive aromas offer a riot of fruit fragrances. The palate, which starts out sweet and warm, becomes fresh and lively as its acid tones intensify before finishing on a note of ripe, generous fruit. The Dolcetto d'Alba '01 also boasts rich colour and fruit in the concentrated nose and full palate.

• Barolo '98	🍷🍷	8
• Barbera d'Alba Vigna Clara '99	🍷🍷	6
• Dolcetto d'Alba '01	🍷🍷	4*
• Barolo '93	🍷🍷🍷	8
• Barolo '97	🍷🍷	8
• Barbera d'Alba Vigna Clara '98	🍷🍷	6
• Gilat Rosso '99	🍷🍷	6

LA MORRA (CN)

OSVALDO VIBERTI
FRAZ. SANTA MARIA
B.TA SERRA DEI TURCHI, 95
12064 LA MORRA (CN)
TEL. 017350374

Osvaldo Viberti's small estate has seven hectares planted to vine on the slopes of Serra dei Turchi and neighbouring areas but he does not yet bottle all his wine. The current production of around 10,000 bottles will almost double over the next few years when Osvaldo releases the Barolo obtained from his new plantings. Meanwhile, the Barolo Serra dei Turchi '98 has a fine, elegant nose that releases intense, lingering aromas and a ripe, sweet fruit on a palate that evokes cherry and plum jam. It weds soft tannins with restrained acidity and the warmth of the alcohol to finish on a lingering note of liquorice. This is a seamless Barolo with an unambiguous, well-rounded personality. The Barbera d'Alba Mancine '00 is a quite distinct purplish ruby and has reasonably pronounced, tangy tones of strawberry, raspberry and redcurrant, with the odd note of acidity. The pulpy palate is a revelation, with the sweet, ripe fruit is enlivened by unobtrusive acidity that lends freshness. The Langhe Nebbiolo '01 has aromas of rose and delicate spice and a pleasantly bracing acidity that leaves the palate refreshing and supple. Its rather muted tannins support a structure of medium texture. The deep violet red Dolcetto d'Alba Galletto '01 has a heady and very faintly lemony nose that reveals still rather unripe fruit.

● Barbera d'Alba Mancine '00	🍷🍷	5
● Barolo Serra dei Turchi '98	🍷🍷	7
● Dolcetto d'Alba Galletto '01	🍷	4
● Langhe Nebbiolo '01	🍷	4
● Barolo Serra dei Turchi '97	🍷🍷	7
● Barbera d'Alba Mancine '99	🍷	4

LA MORRA (CN)

GIANNI VOERZIO
STRADA LORETO, 1
12064 LA MORRA (CN)
TEL. 0173509194

This year sees yet another elegant performance from Gianni Voerzio's wines. First, we have the estate's thoroughbred Barolo '98 La Serra, a brilliant ruby wine with a faint orange rim. Rose meets black cherry on a nose that immediately reveals very concentrated aromas. The palate has marvellous structure, the flavours that mingle deliciously and full, lingering ripe fruit aromas. Delicate notes of aromatic herbs put the finishing touches to the alluring nose. This Barolo earns Three Glasses for its sweet, soft, fruity tones and the perfect balance between the tannins and acids. Pervasive aromas and very balanced flavours and fragrances on the palate characterize the Langhe Rosso Serrapiù '00, a nebbiolo and barbera blend with a lovely ripe fruit finish. The Barbera Ciabot della Luna '00 is forthright, warm and full on the palate with pleasant hints of blackberry and raspberry. The Dolcetto d'Alba '01 is notable for its rich, refreshing fruit, its profound ruby colour with violet red lights, and its sweet almond finish. The Langhe Nebbiolo Ciabot della Luna '00 is another wine of character with an agreeable, weighty palate. We have come to expect a very rich, distinctive Arneis from Gianni's Bricco Cappellina and the '01 does not disappoint. Full of delightful flowery, honeyed aromas and sweet, caressing fruit, it mingles notes of citrus fruit, acacia blossom and chamomile.

● Barolo La Serra '98	🍷🍷🍷	8
● Barbera d'Alba Ciabot della Luna '00	🍷🍷	5
● Langhe Rosso Serrapiù '00	🍷🍷	6
● Dolcetto d'Alba Rocchettevino '01	🍷🍷	4
○ Roero Arneis Bricco Cappellina '01	🍷🍷	5
● Langhe Nebbiolo Ciabot della Luna '00	🍷	6
● Barolo La Serra '96	🍷🍷🍷	8
● Barolo La Serra '97	🍷🍷🍷	8
● Barolo La Serra '95	🍷🍷	8
● Langhe Rosso Serrapiù '99	🍷🍷	6

LA MORRA (CN)

★ Roberto Voerzio
Loc. Cerreto, 1
12064 La Morra (CN)
tel. 0173509196

Six big wines from six big La Morra vineyards are just part of the range that Roberto Voerzio and his wife Pinuccia offer their admiring clients. The six have a very distinctive style that has developed over the 20 successful years of the winery's history. The formula is simple but effective: extremely prestigious plots (at La Serra, Sarmassa, Cerequio, Brunate, Pozzo dell'Annunziata and Capalot), traditional varieties (barbera and nebbiolo), vines with advanced average age, very low yields obtained by severe pruning, and meticulous vinification that aims to bring out the superb quality of the grapes. The result is a range of enormous character whose new vintages have swept the boards. We'll open with the selections that took Three full Glasses. The Barolo Brunate '98 is simply majestic. It flaunts an intense garnet colour with a very narrow rim and a slightly evolved nose of ripe berry fruit, spices, eucalyptus, tobacco and, faintly, charred oak. The palate thrilled us with its structure and leisurely progression. The silky texture combines with austere tannins to usher in a long finish exalted by grace notes of liquorice and violet. The Barbera d'Alba Vigneto Pozzo, available in magnums only, is also very impressive. It excels in every department but nowhere more so than on the palate, where it is potent and sweet yet charming and sophisticated at the same time. Magnificent, too, is the word for the Barolo Sarmassa '98, on its first release, and the Barolo Vecchie Viti '97, both bottled in magnums, and also for the La Serra '98. The aroma-led Cerequio is not far behind.

● Barolo Brunate '98	♛♛♛	8
● Barbera d'Alba Vigneto Pozzo dell'Annunziata Ris. '99	♛♛♛	8
● Barolo Vecchie Viti dei Capalot e delle Brunate Ris. '97	♛♛	8
● Barolo La Serra '98	♛♛	8
● Barolo Sarmassa '98	♛♛	8
● Barolo Cerequio '98	♛♛	8
● Barolo Cerequio '90	♛♛♛	8
● Barolo Brunate '93	♛♛♛	8
● Barbera d'Alba Vigneto Pozzo dell'Annunziata Ris. '96	♛♛♛	8
● Barolo Brunate '96	♛♛♛	8
● Barolo Cerequio '96	♛♛♛	8
● Barolo Brunate '97	♛♛	8

LESSONA (BI)

Sella
Via IV Novembre, 110
13853 Lessona (BI)
tel. 01599455

Descended from banker Venanzio and statesman Quintino Sella, this old Piedmont family has had vineyards in Lessona since the late 1600s. With manager and agronomist Pietro Marocchino and consultant oenologist Giancarlo Scaglione, they are just about the only makers of the noble and hard-to-find nebbiolo-based Lessona. The San Sebastiano allo Zoppo '98, emblematic of both the estate and the category is, as usual, superb. The initial oaky notes open out into very compact, black berry fruit with soft but captivating hints of pepper and pennyroyal. The well-structured palate tells you how good the grapes are, its rich fruit buttressed by a tangy vein and a deluge of sweet tannins. The simpler Lessona '98 suggests raspberry and cocoa powder with flowery undertones of rose and violet layered over balsam and spice. The palate has fine, generous tannins, elegant, rounded fruit and good flavour. Berry fruit, forest floor and liquorice tones emerge from the Bramaterra, whose palate balances austerity with silky fruit. The Orbello '00, 75 per cent barbera with cabernet, has a clear, lingering nose that foregrounds the trademark aromas of the French grape. Entry on the palate is impressive, the mouthfeel velvety, and the finish a little less intense. Obtained from nebbiolo with other local varieties, the Piccone '00 offers delicious raspberry, black pepper and ginger, then a leisurely, pleasantly refreshing palate with medium structure and good balance. The La Doranda '01 is a clean, not too serious white from erbaluce.

● Lessona '98	♛♛	5
● Lessona S. Sebastiano allo Zoppo '98	♛♛	5
● Coste della Sesia Rosso Orbello '00	♛	3
● Coste della Sesia Rosso Piccone '00	♛	3
○ Coste della Sesia Bianco La Doranda '01	♛	3
● Bramaterra '98	♛	4
● Lessona '97	♛♛	5

LOAZZOLO (AT)

Borgo Maragliano
Reg. San Sebastiano, 2
14050 Loazzolo (AT)
tel. 014487132
e-mail: maragliano@inwind.it

The Galliano family's excellent range of wines owes much to the main variety in these parts, moscato. The Loazzolo Vendemmia Tardiva '99, obtained from moscato as regulations dictate, took home Two Glasses for the concentration of its aromas and the fullness of the palate. It colour is intense and the nose is a textbook example of what a moscato should be, with its alluring hints of peach and flowers with undertones of super-ripeness. The full-bodied and invigorating palate possesses a clean vein of sweetness and long length. Although not overly complex, it is well made and perhaps a little uncomplicated. Crisp notes of elderflower, sage and peach come to the fore in the nose of the rich straw-yellow Moscato La Caliera '01. The palate is smooth and confident with tangy acidity and well-gauged carbon dioxide that in no way compromises the tidy, consistent finish. El Calié is a simple, enjoyable, not very alcoholic wine made from partially fermented must, whose moscato base is clear from the nose. The palate shows a very elegant, sweet aromatic profile. The agreeable, fruity Chardonnay Crevoglio has a medium-weight palate, the Giuseppe Galliano Brut '98 is soft and fairly intense, while the less challenging Giuseppe Galliano Chardonnay Brut offers fruit and a palate that is almost sweet.

LOAZZOLO (AT)

Forteto della Luja
Reg. Bricco Casa Rosso, 4
14050 Loazzolo (AT)
tel. 0141831596
e-mail: fortetodellaluja@inwind.it

Immersed in the green depths of the hill that leads from Canelli to Loazzolo, this jewel of Monferrato winemaking jewel belongs to the Scaglione family. They have eight hectares planted to vine and an annual production of 40,000 bottles. Silvia and Gianni run the estate with the help of their father, a leading oenologist who is well-known far beyond the bounds of the region. Their plots all lie in the municipality of Loazzolo, except for two and a half hectares in Moscato Piasa San Maurizio at Santo Stefano Belbo. For years now, the Loazzolo Piasa Rischei has been one of the best Italian dried-grape wines. It expresses all the aromas of the grape type and the local Piedmont terroir with personality and extraordinary elegance. Above all, it has all the intensity of a south Italian "passito" combined with the complexity you expect from a truly great wine. The moscato grapes from which it is derived are dried partly on the vine, and are thus exposed to botrytis, and partly on rush mats. They are then barrique-fermented with local yeasts very, very slowly for up to two years until the density and the opulence of the fruit brings the process to a natural conclusion. This is the key to the enormous success of a wine that again impressed our tasting panel. The brachetto-based Pian dei Sogni '00 is less complex but still seductive, thanks to its cherry and ripe black cherry nose, while the Moscato San Maurizio '01 is well made. The red Le Grive '00, obtained from barbera and pinot nero, is distinctive and very satisfying on the palate. Serve it at cellar temperature.

○ Moscato d'Asti La Caliera '01	ΨΨ	3*
○ Loazzolo Borgo Maragliano V. T. '99	ΨΨ	6
○ El Calié '01	Ψ	3
○ Piemonte Chardonnay Crevoglio '01	Ψ	3
○ Giuseppe Galliano Brut M. Cl. '98	Ψ	5
○ Giuseppe Galliano Chardonnay Brut	Ψ	3
○ Giuseppe Galliano Brut M. Cl. '97	ΨΨ	5
○ Loazzolo Borgo Maragliano V. T. '98	ΨΨ	6

○ Loazzolo Piasa Rischei '99	ΨΨ	7
● Monferrato Rosso Le Grive '00	ΨΨ	6
● Piemonte Brachetto Forteto Pian dei Sogni '00	ΨΨ	6
○ Moscato d'Asti Piasa San Maurizio '01	ΨΨ	4
○ Loazzolo Piasa Rischei '93	ΨΨΨ	7
○ Loazzolo Piasa Rischei '94	ΨΨΨ	7
○ Loazzolo Piasa Rischei '95	ΨΨΨ	7
○ Loazzolo Piasa Rischei '96	ΨΨΨ	7
○ Loazzolo Piasa Rischei '97	ΨΨΨ	7
○ Loazzolo Piasa Rischei '98	ΨΨ	7
● Piemonte Brachetto Forteto Pian dei Sogni '99	ΨΨ	6

LU (AL)

CASALONE
VIA MARCONI, 92
15040 LU (AL)
TEL. 0131741280
E-MAIL: info@casalone.com

With the support of his parents Ernesto and Maria Luisa, Paolo Casalone works full-time on the family's ten-hectare estate, producing 40,000 bottles a year. The wines he offered us for tasting included the Rus '00, which we liked very much. Its base of barbera, merlot and pinot nero give a very concentrated, almost opaque hue and a dense, reasonably complex nose of black berry fruit, hay, autumn leaves and rosemary. Confident tannins make the palate rather austere but the finish is long and echoes the nose, adding the faintest of bitterish notes. The crushed cherry and forest floor aromas of the intense garnet Barbera Rubermillo are offset by a faint trace of dried flowers, while the palate shows firm structure, even firmer tannins, and a long, lingering finish. Simpler and agreeably rustic, the Barbera Bricco Morlantino reveals earthy tones and a marked but tidy aciduous vein. The Grignolino La Capletta '01 releases lovely notes of flowers, berry fruit and pepper before the uncomplicated palate shows its good weight and a varietal sensation of astringency that enhances the finish. The Freisa is fruit-rich and lively, the pinot nero Chiaretto pleasant and quite light and the Monemvasia is faintly aromatic. Finally, the Monferrato Munsret, a Chardonnay matured for six months in barrique, is bold and vibrant.

● Monferrato Rosso Rus '00		5
● Barbera d'Asti Rubermillo '00		4*
● Barbera del M.to Bricco Morlantino '00		4
○ Monemvasia '01		3
○ Monferrato Bianco Munsret '01		4
● Monferrato Freisa '01		2*
● Piemonte Grignolino La Capletta '01		3
◉ Monferrato Chiaretto La Rosella del Bric '01		2
● Barbera d'Asti Rubermillo '99		4
● Monferrato Rosso Rus '99		5

LU (AL)

TENUTA SAN SEBASTIANO
CASCINA SAN SEBASTIANO, 41
15040 LU (AL)
TEL. 0131741353
E-MAIL: dealessi@libero.it

Another fine assortment of wines from Roberto De Alessi confirms him as a major player in the territory's wine league. Headquartered at Lu, between Casale and Alessandria in Monferrato, he runs his estate with his wife Noemi. The winemaking tradition goes way back in these parts but it is only in recent years that the efforts of talented and ambitious producers such as Roberto have started to produce high quality wines. Roberto still has a long way to go but the professional style of his winery – hard work in the vineyards and healthy competition with other producers are his guiding principles – shows he is on the right road. We look forward to next year's tastings, when we will be able to sample the new Monferrato Rosso Soldò, a blend of cabernet sauvignon, cabernet franc and pinot nero. On the subject of innovation, work on the cellars is now complete and the new structure boasts a tasting room, an area for stainless steel vats, and a brand new space for small casks. Of the wines we did taste, the out and out winner was the Barbera Mepari '00. This rich ruby red offering has a nose of crisp blackberry, cherry and spice, then a well-sustained palate with good alcohol, backed up by structure and body. It signs off with a leisurely, tannic finish. The standard-label Barbera del Monferrato is simpler but shows plenty of character and good body on nose and palate. The Piemonte Grignolino '01 has a spicy nose and a very agreeable palate.

● Barbera del M.to Mepari '00		4*
● Barbera del M.to '01		3
● Piemonte Grignolino '01		3
● Barbera del M.to Mepari '97		4
● Barbera del M.to Mepari '98		4
● Barbera del M.to Mepari '99		4

MANGO (CN)

Cascina Fonda
Loc. Cascina Fonda, 45
12056 Mango (CN)
Tel. 0173677156
E-mail: cascinafonda@cascinafonda.com

Their newly finished cellars have given the Barbero family the beautiful setting and the production space they have always wanted. The range this year is enhanced by the addition of a few new products, including the superlative Moscato Passito '00. This fine wine is obtained from the barrique-conditioned fruit of an old vineyard and produced in the limited quantity of 2,000 half bottles. Golden, almost amber in colour, it has a complex, pervasive nose that releases dried fruit and brown sugar aromas over mineral nuances. The palate flaunts a sweet, but not too sweet, vein and dense, glycerine-rich texture with a long, invigorating finish that perfectly mirrors the nose. The rich-hued Moscato '01 boasts aromas ranging from elderflower and sage to the fruit tones of peach and pineapple. The sweet, flavoursome palate is perked up by a lovely acidulous vein. The Asti also has quite a deep colour and a nose that brims with invigorating citrus fruit set against a backdrop of fruit and flowers. The prickle on the palate is refreshingly stylish and alluring. The Bianco, a simple, slightly sparkling wine made from cortese and favorita, and the Langhe Rosso, a barbera, dolcetto and pinot nero blend with a somewhat rustic nose and a bracing, agreeable palate, are both newcomers. The Dolcetto d'Alba Brusalino hints at earth and forest floor and has rather an aggressive palate. Last on the list is the Brachetto, which has slightly forward aromas and a rather rugged palate.

MANGO (CN)

Sergio Degiorgis
Via Circonvallazione, 3
12056 Mango (CN)
Tel. 014189107
E-mail: degiorgis.sergio@tin.it

In an area with a strong vocation for Moscato, Sergio and Patrizia Degiorgis also manage to produce some very interesting reds, one example being their Barbera d'Alba. The 2000 vintage is deep ruby and boasts a luscious, complex nose with layered black berry fruit, smoke and autumn leaves. It is full and dense on the palate, which is buttressed by vibrant extract, and ends in a leisurely finish that echoes the fruit on the nose, underscoring them with refreshing touches of balsam. The nose of the extraordinarily dark Dolcetto Bricco Peso '01 brims a wealth of fragrances, in which warm notes of super-ripeness filter through blackberry and green leaf. The palate has a powerful, gutsy thrust to it with robust tannins and tangy acidity. We also awarded Two Glasses to the Moscato Sorì del Re for its bright, rich straw yellow and aromas of super-ripe fruit and elderflower, nuanced with faint grassy hints. The prickle keeps the sweetness under control on the big, round palate, which offers a lengthy finish laced with hints of peaches in syrup. The rich, straw-yellow chardonnay and pinot nero-based Bianco Accordo '01 has a reasonably delicate nose of fruit, flowers and hazelnut. Although full-bodied, the palate could do with just a touch more backbone. The Essenza, an almost amber "passito", has a nose of peach and wild fennel and a sweet, dense palate.

O	Piemonte Moscato Passito '00	ΨΨ	5
O	Asti '01	ΨΨ	4*
O	Moscato d'Asti '01	ΨΨ	4*
●	Langhe Rosso '00	Ψ	4
●	Dolcetto d'Alba Brusalino '01	Ψ	4
O	Bianco	Ψ	3
●	Piemonte Brachetto '01		4

O	Moscato d'Asti Sorì del Re '01	ΨΨ	4
●	Dolcetto d'Alba Bricco Peso '01	ΨΨ	4
●	Barbera d'Alba '00	ΨΨ	5
O	Accordo Bianco '01	Ψ	4
O	Essenza '00	Ψ	6
●	Dolcetto d'Alba Bricco Peso '00	ΨΨ	4
●	Langhe Rosso Riella '99	ΨΨ	5

MOASCA (AT)

La Ghersa
Via San Giuseppe, 19
14050 Moasca (AT)
tel. 0141856012
e-mail: info@laghersa.it

Since Massimo Pastura Barbero started working alongside his parents in 1990, he has set his sights on high quality. He works equally meticulously in both vineyard and cellar. Massimo draws his inspiration from the few brave souls who pioneered Barbera d'Asti on world markets and whom he holds in great esteem. The wine that best embodies La Ghersa is the Barbera d'Asti Superiore La Vignassa, from the subzone of Nizza. As its 2000 vintage has not yet been bottled, we could only taste it off the record. It is dark garnet, with a nose of fruit and minerals lifted by a lovely touch of almond. The very well-structured palate has lots of no-nonsense extract that underpins the progression right through to the long finish, which echoes the nose. The barbera, cabernet and merlot-based Monferrato La Ghersa has complex notes of leather and a tangy salinity that pleasantly enhance its fruit. It comes into its own on the palate, where the progression is dry and well-sustained through to the lovely finish, which mirrors the fruit tones and adds a hint of liquorice. Another very good wine, the cortese, chardonnay and sauvignon-based Sivoj, is a rich straw yellow and reveals an apricot and mimosa nose with faint traces of super-ripeness. The flavoursome, mouthfilling palate leads confidently into a long citrus finish. The well-sustained Barbera Camparò romped home with Two Glasses for its generous, harmonious palate. Finally, we would like to announce the release of the Moscato Giorgia '01, dedicated to Massimo's daughter, another new arrival in 2001.

● Barbera d'Asti Camparò '00	ҰҰ	4*
○ Monferrato Bianco Sivoj '01	ҰҰ	4*
● Monferrato Rosso La Ghersa '99	ҰҰ	6
● Monferrato Rosso Piagè '00	Ұ	3
○ Moscato d'Asti Giorgia '01	Ұ	4
● Barbera d'Asti Sup. La Vignassa '99	ҰҰ	6
● Barbera d'Asti Sup. La Vignassa '97	ҰҰ	6
● Barbera d'Asti Sup La Vignassa '98	ҰҰ	6
● Monferrato Rosso La Ghersa '98	ҰҰ	6

MOMBARUZZO (AT)

Malgrà
Loc. Bazzana
Via Nizza, 8
14046 Mombaruzzo (AT)
tel. 0141725055 - 0141726377
e-mail: wine@malgra.it

We wish a warm welcome to this very young, ambitious Mombaruzzo-based estate now making its debut among the "big" profiles. Malgrà is run by Nico Conta and Massimiliano Diotto, already well-known in wine circles as largely responsible for the recent success of the famous Bersano brand. They now work with Ezio and Giorgio Chiarle and since its founding two years ago, the partnership has produced an explosive cocktail of tradition and modernity. This is nowhere more evident than in their futuristic cellars on the edge of town. Malgrà, which means "village idiot" in the local dialect, has put immense effort into these early stages of growth. There are 104 hectares planted to vine, 64 of which belong to the estate, current annual production is 350,000 bottles and there is an impressive assortment of wines featuring all the major regional varieties. Need we say more? Add to this the quality of some of the wines we tasted for the cellar benefits from the magic touch of Giuliano Noè. The Mora di Sassi from the new subzone of Nizza is the best of the Barbera d'Astis. Gorgeous both in colour and on the nose, its clear notes of rose and wild berries are complemented by a richly textured palate and velvety softness. The Gaiana selection is a bit simpler. As for the blends, the cabernet sauvignon and barbera Monferrato Emmerosso has the edge over the pinot nero and barbera Malgrà, thanks to its greater complexity and crispness. The best of the whites is the fresh-tasting and highly enjoyable Gavi Poggio Basco.

● Barbera d'Asti Sup. Nizza Mora di Sassi '00	ҰҰ	6
● Monferrato Rosso Emmerosso '99	ҰҰ	4
● Barbera d'Asti Sup. Gaiana '00	Ұ	4
● Monferrato Rosso Malgrà '00	Ұ	5
○ Gavi del Comune di Gavi Poggio Basco '01	Ұ	4
● Barbera d'Asti Sup. Gaiana '98	ҰҰ	5
● Barbera d'Asti Sup. Mora di Sassi '99	Ұ	6

MONCHIERO (CN)

Giuseppe Mascarello e Figlio
Via Borgonuovo, 108
12060 Monchiero (CN)
Tel. 0173792126
E-mail: mauromascarello@mascarello1881.com

This historic winery started bottling in 1881. In 1919, the headquarters moved to an 18th-century building in Monchiero previously used for the production and storage of ice. Only 12 of Mauro Mascarello's 18 hectares planted to vine are in production, but they are all in top vineyards, such as Monprivato, Villero and Codana in Castiglione Falletto and Santo Stefano di Perno at Monforte. The Barolo Riserva Cà d'Morissio '95 is the cream of the crop. Fermented on the skins for a month, it spends six years in Slavonian oak barrels to emerge with a dazzling garnet and intense, youthful aromas of raspberry, citrus fruit peel, liquorice and mint. The palate is austere, imposing and wonderfully long. The '97 Barolo selections include a brace of Two Glass winners, the Bricco and the Monprivato. The first is very concentrated and fruity, with undertones of vanilla, and the well-rounded Monprivato offers notes of jam, cocoa powder and minty herbs. Neither the Villero, with its hay and tobacco aromas, nor the salty, rather fuzzy Santo Stefano di Perno, meets the lofty standards set by their stablemates. Both the Barbera Codana '99 and the Dolcetto Bricco '00 show enormous character. The full, fleshy, fruity Barbera has a sweet, unhurried palate, while the Dolcetto's nose is still alcohol-driven and earthy but will improve with age. The Nebbiolo San Rocco '99, an elegant, Burgundy-style wine, unveils strawberry and redcurrant with touches of eucalyptus and a refined, balanced palate. Only youth prevented the Barbera '99 and Dolcetto Santo Stefano di Perno '00 from scoring higher.

● Barolo Monprivato Cà d' Morissio Ris. '95	ŸŸ	8
● Barolo Bricco '97	ŸŸ	8
● Barolo Monprivato '97	ŸŸ	8
● Barbera d'Alba Codana '99	ŸŸ	7
● Barbera d'Alba S. Stefano di Perno '00	Ÿ	5
● Dolcetto d'Alba Bricco '00	Ÿ	4
● Dolcetto d'Alba S. Stefano di Perno '00	Ÿ	4
● Barolo S. Stefano di Perno '97	Ÿ	8
● Barolo Villero '97	Ÿ	8
● Nebbiolo d'Alba S. Rocco '99	Ÿ	5
● Barolo Monprivato '85	ŸŸŸ	8
● Barolo Villero '96	ŸŸŸ	8

MONDOVÌ (CN)

Il Colombo - Barone Riccati
Via dei Sent, 2
12084 Mondovì (CN)
Tel. 017441607

The Mondovì area of the Langhe, which for years has been a little excluded from the inner circle of Italian winemaking, has found a champion in the estate of Carlo Riccati and his wife Adriana Giusta. These talented producers have sounded a clarion call to the entire territory with a few simple but essential rules: care in the vineyards; careful choices in the cellar, under the watchful eye of Beppe Caviola; and a driving ambition to best the competition from Dogliani. Their approach has created a range of wines that for years now has impressed us with its consistently high quality. The three wines they produced this year all have a dolcetto base. The La Chiesetta selection is the simplest, obtained from the grapes of a ten-year-old vineyard facing west and northwest at an altitude of about 500 metres. Down-to-earth but exceedingly well made, it has a nose of medium intensity full of dried flower and hazelnut notes. It is agreeably harmonious on the palate and an aftertaste of almond enriches the finish. On another level altogether, the Colombo '01 is the real Riccati family "cru". It comes from a south and southwest-facing plot whose vines are over 30 years old and never yield more than 50 quintals per hectare. The fruit is matured in stainless steel and used 900-litre casks to produce a purplish wine full of caressing, and very alluring, ripe blackberry aromas. The palate is potent and fruity, with just the right dose of tannins in the long finish. The sturdy Monteregale '00 is also excellent, derived from 50-year-old vines whose grapes age slowly in 600-litre oak casks.

● Dolcetto delle Langhe Monregalesi Il Colombo '01	ŸŸ	4*
● Dolcetto delle Langhe Monregalesi Sup. Monteregale '00	ŸŸ	5
● Dolcetto delle Langhe Monregalesi Vigna della Chiesetta '01	ŸŸ	3*
● Dolcetto delle Langhe Monregalesi Il Colombo '97	ŸŸŸ	4
● Dolcetto delle Langhe Monregalesi Il Colombo '98	ŸŸŸ	4
● Dolcetto delle Langhe Monregalesi Sup. Monteregale '99	ŸŸ	5
● Dolcetto delle Langhe Monregalesi Il Colombo '00	ŸŸ	4

MONFORTE D'ALBA (CN)

GIANFRANCO ALESSANDRIA
LOC. MANZONI, 13
12065 MONFORTE D'ALBA (CN)
TEL. 017378576

Barely five years have passed since young Gianfranco Alessandria claimed his first Three Glasses, but he is already considered a veteran among the brilliant new generation of Barolo makers. After his triumph with the Barolo '93, he has come back year after year for another Three Glass title. He does not have a large area under vine to play with – his estate is only about four hectares – but he produces two true bluebloods, both nebbiolo and barbera blends, that take it in turns to dazzle our panel. This is the year of the Barolo San Giovanni, which hails from a plot bordering Monforte d'Alba and Barolo, successfully combining the best characteristics of both municipalities. Its deep, rich ruby alludes to freshness and youth, as do its initial aromas of intense, unadulterated raspberry. These move over to make room for hints of menthol and cinnamon spice. After a low-key entry, the palate progresses slowly to end in a soft, lingering finish of enormous class. The '98 Barolo is also up to scratch, although it lacks the structure and balance of the San Giovanni and consequently seems less complete. The estate's other champ, the opulent and exuberant Barbera Vittoria '00, has pronounced cherry tones but remains somewhat in thrall to the oak. The standard-label Dolcetto and Barbera do not disappoint.

• Barolo S. Giovanni '98	🍷🍷🍷	8
• Barbera d'Alba Vittoria '00	🍷🍷	6
• Barbera d'Alba '01	🍷🍷	4*
• Dolcetto d'Alba '01	🍷🍷	4*
• Barolo '98	🍷🍷	8
• Barolo '93	🍷🍷🍷	8
• Barbera d'Alba Vittoria '96	🍷🍷🍷	6
• Barbera d'Alba Vittoria '97	🍷🍷🍷	6
• Barolo S. Giovanni '97	🍷🍷🍷	8
• Barbera d'Alba Vittoria '98	🍷🍷🍷	6
• Barbera d'Alba Vittoria '99	🍷🍷	6
• Barolo S. Giovanni '96	🍷🍷	8

MONFORTE D'ALBA (CN)

★ DOMENICO CLERICO
LOC. MANZONI, 67
12065 MONFORTE D'ALBA (CN)
TEL. 017378171
E-MAIL: domenicoclerico@interfree.it

Domenico Clerico is a real comedian and always ready with a quip but don't be deceived. He is no stranger to hard work. With his family and Massimo Conterno to back him up, he and his cellar have scaled the heights of Italian wine and planted their flag firmly on the peak. The winery turns out around 85,000 bottles every year, just under a third of which go to make up the three Barolo labels. Two, the Ciabot Mentin Ginestra and Pajana, come from the Ginestra vineyard and the third, Percristina, hails from Mosconi. There is little to choose between them in terms of quality, but the Percristina '97's sweet, velvety tannins just give it the edge. An extra 12 months in the bottle account for both the extract and for the wine's elegant nose, which leans towards ripe berry fruit and sweet spice. Still very young, the Ciabot Mentin Ginestra and the Pajana, both '98s, have yet to realize their full, and considerable, potential. For the time being, we prefer the Ciabot Mentin Ginestra for its classic minty tones and forceful, austere personality. The Pajana is fabulously mouthfilling but a bit muddled, and tends to lurk behind a veil of oak. The Arte '00 (90 per cent nebbiolo with small quantities of barbera and cabernet sauvignon aged for 16 months in new barriques), the Barbera Trevigne '00 and the Langhe Dolcetto Visadì '01 are all up to their usual high standards.

• Barolo Percristina '97	🍷🍷🍷	8
• Barolo Ciabot Mentin Ginestra '98	🍷🍷	8
• Barbera d'Alba Trevigne '00	🍷🍷	5
• Langhe Rosso Arte '00	🍷🍷	6
• Langhe Dolcetto Visadì '01	🍷🍷	4
• Barolo Pajana '98	🍷🍷	8
• Barolo Ciabot Mentin Ginestra '85	🍷🍷🍷	8
• Barolo Ciabot Mentin Ginestra '89	🍷🍷🍷	8
• Arte '90	🍷🍷🍷	8
• Barolo Pajana '90	🍷🍷🍷	8
• Barolo Pajana '93	🍷🍷🍷	8
• Barolo Pajana '95	🍷🍷🍷	8
• Barolo Percristina '95	🍷🍷🍷	8
• Barolo Percristina '96	🍷🍷🍷	8

MONFORTE D'ALBA (CN)

★ Aldo Conterno
Loc. Bussia, 48
12065 Monforte d'Alba (CN)
Tel. 017378150

Supported by sons Franco, Giacomo and Stefano, Aldo Conterno and his estate have had an outstanding year, with two of their wines making it through to the final taste-offs. The first of these is the Barolo Gran Bussia '96, which matches its '95 performance with a combination of austerity, elegance, ageing potential and complexity. Notes of walnut and plain chocolate already reveal solid development in a wine that will reach its peak over the next few years. Every bit as good is the Barolo Vigna Cicala '98, which is better in that vintage than either the Colonnello or the basic Barolo. It is full of cherry and blackberry aromas with traces of autumn leaves, rain-soaked earth and coffee. People will either love or hate the Langhe Bianco Bussiador '99, but it's certain to make an impression. This rich-hued offering parades notes of medlar, minerals, flint and hay before opening out after a couple of hours to reveal notes of lavender blossom. A strong hint of oak does nothing to detract from its enormous quality. Another excellent wine, the Langhe Nebbiolo Il Favot, is the Conternos' very successful concession to modernity. Here, they have used barriques, which are firmly excluded from their Barolo vinification, to imbue the wine with perfectly gauged vanilla and sweet tannins. A blend of two blends – nebbiolo and barbera with cabernet and merlot – the Langhe Rosso Quartetto possesses nice black cherry nuances but the '99 has more in the way of tang than tannins and lacks the balance of previous editions.

● Barolo Gran Bussia Ris. '96	🍷🍷	8
● Barolo Cicala '98	🍷🍷	8
● Barolo Colonnello '98	🍷🍷	8
○ Langhe Bianco Bussiador '99	🍷🍷	6
● Langhe Nebbiolo Il Favot '99	🍷🍷	7
● Barolo '98	🍷	8
● Langhe Rosso Quartetto '99	🍷	6
● Barolo Gran Bussia Ris. '82	🍷🍷🍷	8
● Barolo Gran Bussia Ris. '88	🍷🍷🍷	8
● Barolo Gran Bussia Ris. '89	🍷🍷🍷	8
● Barolo Vigna del Colonnello '89	🍷🍷🍷	8
● Barolo Gran Bussia Ris. '90	🍷🍷🍷	8
● Barolo Vigna del Colonnello '90	🍷🍷🍷	8
● Barolo Gran Bussia Ris. '95	🍷🍷🍷	8
● Barolo Colonnello '97	🍷🍷	8

MONFORTE D'ALBA (CN)

★ Giacomo Conterno
Loc. Ornati, 2
12065 Monforte d'Alba (CN)
Tel. 017378221

Big changes are afoot at the famous Monforte d'Alba winery that used to belong to Giacomo Conterno. Giovanni Conterno, his wife and their son Roberto have taken the plunge and decided to focus exclusively on nebbiolo and barbera. Devotees of their superb Freisa and excellent Dolcetto will just have to grin and bear it. The Conternos have already ripped out the plots where they grew the varieties in the Francia vineyard at Serralunga d'Alba, where all of the family's 16 hectares are located in a single block. In place of the freisa and dolcetto, the Conternos have introduced nebbiolo and barbera cuttings. When the five newly planted hectares go into production, the estate will gradually increase the total number of bottles of Barolo and Barbera d'Alba released. At present, production is limited to about 25,000 bottles of Cascina Francia and Monfortino Barolo, and a similar quantity of Barbera d'Alba. For this edition of the Guide, we were only able to taste the two Barolos. We'll have to wait until next year to sample the Barbera 2001. Produced only in the very best years, and given prolonged ageing in barrels, the Monfortino has shaped the history of Barolo since the First World War. The brilliant garnet '95 releases complex aromas of raspberry jam, liquorice, dried roses and coffee. The powerful palate is already soft and harmonious, thanks to the sweetness of the tannins that come through in the finish. The Cascina Francia '98 is still very hard. Its fruit is less exuberant than that of the Monfortino.

● Barolo Monfortino Ris. '95	🍷🍷	8
● Barolo Cascina Francia '98	🍷🍷	8
● Barolo Monfortino Ris. '82	🍷🍷🍷	8
● Barolo Cascina Francia '85	🍷🍷🍷	8
● Barolo Monfortino Ris. '85	🍷🍷🍷	8
● Barolo Cascina Francia '87	🍷🍷🍷	8
● Barolo Monfortino Ris. '87	🍷🍷🍷	8
● Barolo Monfortino Ris. '88	🍷🍷🍷	8
● Barolo Cascina Francia '89	🍷🍷🍷	8
● Barolo Cascina Francia '90	🍷🍷🍷	8
● Barolo Monfortino Ris. '90	🍷🍷🍷	8
● Barolo Cascina Francia '97	🍷🍷🍷	8
● Barolo Monfortino Ris. '93	🍷🍷	8

MONFORTE D'ALBA (CN)

Paolo Conterno
Via Ginestra, 34
12065 Monforte d'Alba (CN)
Tel. 017378415
E-mail: ginestra@paoloconterno.com

This beautiful estate in Ginestra, one of the best vineyards in Monforte, has been in the Conterno family for four generations now. Giorgio Conterno runs the production side the enthusiastic support of his sister and young nephew enables him to release a total of more than 50,000 bottles every year. Giorgio's vineyards, which enjoy some of the very best positions, are tended with loving care to produce wines that remain absolutely typical yet manage to be the quintessence of body combined with elegance. They have Beppe Caviola to thank for an approach that is eloquently justified by the Conterno Dolcetto '01. Four thousand bottles of this excellent vintage contain attractive hints of violet and a balanced palate that is pleasantly fruit-rich and satisfying. The two Ginestra Barolos are, as usual, excellent. The Riserva is clearly superior, confidently showing that it knows how to exploit oak to develop and complement the complex, fragrant nose of jam and spice. The palate is mouthfilling and the finish seduces the palate with notes of morello cherry and liquorice that merge with the tannins Ginestra is famous for. The rich garnet of the Ginestra '98 precedes a typically austere, vibrant nose then the palate reveals vivid elegance and a long, warm, harmonious finish that follows through well. The Langhe Nebbiolo Brich is good, combining fullness and fragrance in a very enjoyable framework of fine-grained tannins. The fine array of wines from this estate ends with the Barbera and its well-defined raspberry aromas. The generous, consistent palate makes it very easy to drink.

Wine	Rating	Price
● Barolo Ginestra Ris. '97	♛♛	8
● Barbera d'Alba Ginestra '00	♛♛	5
● Langhe Nebbiolo Brich Ginestra '00	♛♛	6
● Dolcetto d'Alba Ginestra '01	♛♛	4*
● Barolo Ginestra '98	♛♛	8
● Barolo Ginestra Ris. '93	♛♛	8
● Barolo Ginestra '95	♛♛	8
● Barolo Ginestra '96	♛♛	8
● Barolo Ginestra Ris. '96	♛♛	8
● Barolo Ginestra '97	♛♛	8
● Langhe Brich Ginestra '98	♛♛	8
● Langhe Brich Ginestra '99	♛♛	8

MONFORTE D'ALBA (CN)

★ Conterno Fantino
Via Ginestra, 1
12065 Monforte d'Alba (CN)
Tel. 017378204
E-mail: info@conternofantino.it

From its panoramic perch on the edge of Ginestra, the estate of Guido Fantino and Claudio Conterno interprets the special nature of the fruit from its various plots in a series of modern, classy wines. One of these is the Vigna del Gris, which astounds with the complexity of its redcurrant, cherry and forest floor aromas. The elegant, captivating harmony in the mouth then offers lingering notes of cocoa powder and fine herbs. The Sorì Ginestra '98 is completely different in character and made a triumphant return to take Three full Glasses from our appreciative tasters. This dense, dazzling garnet Barolo flaunts potent, pervasive aromas of superior tobacco and black berry fruit and then explodes onto the palate, where its energy is overwhelming. Silky tannins and well-assimilated toastiness add even more complexity. The Parussi has a nice personality with ripe black cherry aromas and an alluring typicity. The Monprà, a blend of nebbiolo, barbera and cabernet sauvignon fermented separately in oak casks, teases the senses. Dark and intense, it then fills the palate with plum, liquorice and mint before opening out caressingly and elegantly over well-judged tannins. The Barbera Vignota has absorbed its oak conditioning and develops on the palate with impressive fruit and soft length. The classic violet red Dolcetto, the only wine on the estate vinified entirely in stainless steel, is more direct and very dynamic. Last, the Chardonnay Bastia '00, which is the golden colour of citrus fruit, has a clear, refined nose of sage and tropical fruit and a creamy, seamless palate.

Wine	Rating	Price
● Barolo Sorì Ginestra '98	♛♛♛	8
● Langhe Rosso Monprà '00	♛♛	6
● Barolo Vigna del Gris '98	♛♛	8
○ Langhe Chardonnay Bastia '00	♛♛	5
● Barbera d'Alba Vignota '01	♛♛	4*
● Barolo Parussi '98	♛♛	8
● Dolcetto d'Alba Bricco Bastia '01	♛	4
● Barolo Sorì Ginestra '90	♛♛♛	8
● Barolo Sorì Ginestra '91	♛♛♛	8
● Monprà '94	♛♛♛	6
● Langhe Rosso Monprà '95	♛♛♛	8
● Barolo Vigna del Gris '96	♛♛♛	8
● Barolo Vigna del Gris '97	♛♛♛	8
● Langhe Rosso Monprà '97	♛♛♛	6
● Langhe Rosso Monprà '98	♛♛♛	6

MONFORTE D'ALBA (CN)

ALESSANDRO E GIAN NATALE FANTINO
VIA G. SILVANO, 18
12065 MONFORTE D'ALBA (CN)
TEL. 017378253

The Fantino brothers run an artisan-style cellar that they have refurbished into a practical, welcoming winery. They get 40,000 bottles a year out of their eight hectares at Bussia, where for years now they have worked their vines with the utmost respect for the natural environment. They divide operations into two equal parts. Alessandro concentrates more on the vineyards while Gian Natale watches over the production side. Together, they produce a series of wines from the Vigna dei Dardi vineyard that weds tradition to a very distinctive personality. Their Barolo '98 is excellent and takes advantage of the great weather that year to present a refined nose, perked up by notes of mushroom and black berry fruit jam. The palate opens out generously on a cocoa powder theme to display powerful, aristocratic tannins in the finish. The purple hue of the Barbera '00 heralds a fresh nose of plum and a flavoursome entry on the palate that pleasantly recalls violet. The unusual, complex Nepas is obtained from selected nebbiolo grapes harvested early and set to dry on rush mats in well-ventilated rooms. After the three-month drying period, during which the fruit is slightly attacked by grey mould, it is crushed to produce a limited number of bottles of a dense garnet wine with ripe, caressing chocolate and dried fig on the nose. Its lingering, satisfying aromas are laced with fine-grained tannins.

● Barolo Vigna dei Dardi '98	ŸŸ	6
● Nepas Rosso '99	ŸŸ	6
● Barbera d'Alba Vigna dei Dardi '99	ŸŸ	4*
● Barolo Vigna dei Dardi '93	ŸŸ	6
● Barolo Vigna dei Dardi '95	ŸŸ	6
● Barolo Vigna dei Dardi '96	ŸŸ	6
● Barolo Vigna dei Dardi '97	ŸŸ	6
● Nepas Rosso '98	ŸŸ	6
● Barbera d'Alba Vigna dei Dardi '99	ŸŸ	4

MONFORTE D'ALBA (CN)

ATTILIO GHISOLFI
LOC. BUSSIA, 27
12065 MONFORTE D'ALBA (CN)
TEL. 017378345

We open with a wine that last year earned Attilio and Gian Marco Ghisolfi their first Three Glass prize, the Langhe Rosso Alta Bussia. The '00 is well up to standard and confirms the wine's class with the exemplary balance of the 80-20 mix of barbera and nebbiolo fruit and vanilla from its 12 months in barriques of various ages. The nose suggests blueberry and Peruvian bark, then the palate has extraordinary length, softness and roundness. Put all this together and you have another masterpiece, one of the best and most fascinating reds to come out of the Langhe this year and one that earned the judges' approval at the final tastings. The Langhe Rosso Carlin, the estate's other blend, this time of 60 per cent nebbiolo with freisa, is not quite as awesome. Nevertheless, the 3,000 bottles, almost all of which are sold overseas, contain a fine wine of enormous dignity, from its morello cherry nose to the rich plain chocolate aromas on the palate. The newcomer of the year at the Ghisolfi cellar is the Pinay '00, another Langhe Rosso from a pinot nero plot that is barely three years old but can already point to good fruit. The rose, violet and redcurrant nose is followed by an agreeable palate whose only, fairly predictable, weak spot is its rather light structure. It's a wine to watch out for, though. The Barbera d'Alba Vigna Lisi '00 marks a return to Langhe tradition with its enormous concentration and seductive coffee aromas. The minty tones of the rich garnet Barolo Bricco Visette '98 usher in notes of cinnamon and cloves and tannins that are nicely mature.

● Langhe Rosso Alta Bussia '00	ŸŸŸ	5
● Barbera d'Alba Vigna Lisi '00	ŸŸ	5
● Langhe Rosso Carlin '00	ŸŸ	5
● Langhe Rosso Pinay '00	ŸŸ	5
● Barolo Bricco Visette '98	ŸŸ	7
● Langhe Rosso Alta Bussia '99	ŸŸŸ	5
● Barolo Bricco Visette '96	ŸŸ	7
● Barolo Bricco Visette '97	ŸŸ	7
● Barbera d'Alba Vigna Lisi '98	ŸŸ	5
● Langhe Rosso Alta Bussia '98	ŸŸ	5

MONFORTE D'ALBA (CN)

Elio Grasso
Loc. Ginestra, 40
12065 Monforte d'Alba (CN)
tel. 017378491
e-mail: elio.grasso@isiline.it

With wife Marina and son Gianluca, Elio Grasso runs one of the most stunningly located estates in Monforte. It looks out over several of its own vineyards, including the deservedly famous Runcot. The nose of wild berry fruit, black cherry, wild rose, tobacco and liquorice of the Barolo Runcot '97 almost equals the '96. Its oak ageing gives it just the right dose of vanilla and sweet tannins, while the palate is complex and pervasive. These elements all combine, year after year, to give us a Barolo of superb quality. This year, however, it is the Gavarini Vigna Chiniera '98 that reigns supreme. Its youthful aromas suggest blackberry, spice and mint and the palate is no less than spectacular, with a well-sustained follow-through and sweet, silky tannins that just go on and on. An irresistible Three Glass winner. As with the '97, the Barolo Ginestra Vigna Casa Maté '98 is closed, and even edgy, at the moment but experience shows that it will mature well, even if it takes a few years in the cellar. The oak-heavy Langhe Chardonnay Educato '01 will appeal to some more than to others, but its balsamic tones and hints of sweetness are attractive. The Barbera d'Alba Vigna Martina '99 is very decent, with a nose of wild berry fruit, toastiness and tobacco. It comes into its own on the palate, where well-judged oak has lent pleasantly sweet tannins and low yields give good acidity. Finally, the well-managed Dolcetto d'Alba Gavarini Vigna dei Grassi '01 is obtained from a variety that has given ample proof of its potential for even more complex wines.

● Barolo Gavarini Vigna Chiniera '98 🍷🍷🍷	8
● Barolo Runcot '97 🍷🍷	8
○ Langhe Chardonnay Educato '01 🍷🍷	5
● Barolo Ginestra Vigna Casa Maté '98 🍷🍷	8
● Barbera d'Alba Vigna Martina '99 🍷🍷	5
● Dolcetto d'Alba Gavarini Vigna dei Grassi '01 🍷	4
● Barolo Gavarini Vigna Chiniera '89 🍷🍷🍷	8
● Barolo Ginestra Vigna Casa Maté '90 🍷🍷🍷	8
● Barolo Ginestra Vigna Casa Maté '93 🍷🍷🍷	8
● Barolo Runcot '96 🍷🍷🍷	8
● Barolo Runcot '95 🍷🍷	8

MONFORTE D'ALBA (CN)

Giovanni Manzone
Via Castelletto, 9
12065 Monforte d'Alba (CN)
tel. 017378114
e-mail: manzone.giovanni@tiscalinet.it

Smack in the middle of his seven-hectare property, Giovanni Manzone's "cascina" commands a 360-degree view of almost every municipality in the Barolo DOCG. Last year's performance was a hard act to follow but he should be proud of this year's list of Two Glass winners. We turn first to his Barolo Gramolere Riserva '97, whose extra year of ageing has smoothed out some of the excesses of that harvest. Today, the wine is full, round and very harmonious. We were also impressed by the Gramolere Bricat '98, from a plot in this famous vineyard owned exclusively by the Manzone family. Already, the wine is showing developed aromas of spice and leather. In contrast, the nose of the Gramolere '98 is more closed, and the palate is dominated by tannins. The two Langhes are very well made. The Nebbiolo Il Crutin has nice wild berry tones while the Tris, in particular, has a Piedmontese soul. Obtained from almost equal parts of Nebbiolo, Barbera and Dolcetto, its year in 700-litre casks has lent it oaky tones that in now way detract from the fruit or its plum and morello cherry aromas. Neither of the Barberas, the basic '00 and the '99 from the La Serra vineyard, were really up to scratch. Although hinting at dried roses, Peruvian bark and rhubarb, the latter fails to bring out its aromas with sufficient definition. It should be noted, however, that the wines we sampled, including the Dolcetto d'Alba '01, had only been bottled a couple of days prior to our tasting. This may account for our disappointment.

● Langhe Nebbiolo Il Crutin '01 🍷🍷	4*
● Barolo Gramolere Ris. '97 🍷🍷	8
● Barolo Gramolere Bricat '98 🍷🍷	7
● Langhe Rosso Tris '99 🍷🍷	5
● Barbera d'Alba '00 🍷	4
○ Rosserto Bianco '00 🍷	5
● Dolcetto d'Alba '01 🍷	4
● Barolo Gramolere '98 🍷	7
● Barbera d'Alba La Serra '99 🍷	5
● Barolo Gramolere Ris. '96 🍷🍷	8
● Barolo Gramolere Ris. '95 🍷🍷	8
● Barolo Gramolere Bricat '96 🍷🍷	7
● Barolo Gramolere '97 🍷🍷	7
● Barolo Gramolere Bricat '97 🍷🍷	7
● Langhe Rosso Tris '98 🍷🍷	5

MONFORTE D'ALBA (CN)

Monti
Fraz. Camia
Loc. San Sebastiano, 39
12065 Monforte d'Alba (CN)
Tel. 017378391
E-mail: wine@paolomonti.com

Pier Paolo Monti's young winery continues to grow by leaps and bounds, both in terms of quality and in size, with several new or replanted plots. The results of all this will include the release in 2003 of Pier Paolo's Barolo '99 Bussia and the first vinification of grapes from another celebrated Monforte vineyard, Le Coste, with the harvest of 2002. The range currently on offer is already very interesting and there is a good assortment of local and international varieties. Up first, we have approximately 6,000 bottles of the Langhe Bianco L'Aura '01, obtained from 70 percent chardonnay aged in new barriques and 30 per cent riesling, conditioned entirely in stainless steel. The charred oak tones of this elegant wine never mask the aromas of banana, pear and peach and there is also a nice, vaguely sweetish, hint in the finish. Then there is the Langhe Rosso Dossi Rossi '00, from 20 per cent Nebbiolo with equal parts Cabernet Sauvignon and Merlot. Separate vinification and ageing in barriques of various ages for differing lengths of time produce a wine that, just 20 days after bottling, offered a nose that was still rather closed but an already delightfully balanced palate. From more than 40-year-old vines at Bussia, and others at San Martino, the Barbera d'Alba '00 is very good indeed. The nose is full of lovely fleshy fruit, despite its 15-month period of oak-conditioning, and the rich structure on the palate mellows the acidity of the barbera.

MONFORTE D'ALBA (CN)

Armando Parusso
Loc. Bussia, 55
12065 Monforte d'Alba (CN)
Tel. 017378257

The efficient new cellars are finished so Marco and Tiziana Parusso have turned their attention to the vineyards scattered across Monforte, from Bussia to Mosconi. In 1995, they used barriques for all their wines but they still seek to give each selection a personality of its own, as the Barolos show. The deep garnet Vigna Fiurin flaunts warm, complex aromas of black cherry and redcurrant, with soft notes of vanilla and spice, and a cocoa powder and tobacco palate ending in a richly tannic finish. The wonderful Vigna Munie has a very refined, intense nose of cherry and ripe fig, with character, vigour and length lifting its austerity. The Vigna Rocche is typically full and pervasive, with a good tannic vein and a lovely finish, while the Mariondino has elegant, vigorous berry fruit and liquorice tones. The Piccole Vigne, from relatively new vine stock, is readier for uncorking and fresher-tasting. The five Barolo selections are all superb but the Three Glass crown goes go to the Barbera d'Alba Superiore. From an old vineyard, it reveals awesome complexity and breadth on the palate, where mushrooms and violets emerge. This marvellous Barbera of enormous character develops caressingly on the palate into a lingering finish. The Rosso Bricco Rovella, a nebbiolo, barbera and cabernet blend, has noble hints of pomegranate and cherries, with a discreet touch of oak. The golden-yellow Bricco Rovella Bianco is always good. The barrique-fermented sauvignon grapes offer a refined nose of white peach, chamomile and roses. The sweet palate does not detract from the fragrant finish.

● Barbera d'Alba '00	¶¶	5
● Langhe Rosso Dossi Rossi '00	¶¶	6
○ Langhe Bianco L'Aura '01	¶¶	5
○ Langhe Bianco L'Aura '00	¶¶	5
● Barbera d'Alba '97	¶¶	5
● Barbera d'Alba '99	¶¶	5
● Langhe Rosso Dossi Rossi '99	¶¶	6

● Barbera d'Alba Sup. '00	¶¶¶	6
● Barolo Bussia Vigna Munie '98	¶¶	8
● Barolo Bussia Vigna Rocche '98	¶¶	8
○ Langhe Bianco Bricco Rovella '00	¶¶	5
● Langhe Rosso Bricco Rovella '00	¶¶	6
● Barolo Bussia Vigna Fiurin '98	¶¶	8
● Barolo Mariondino '98	¶¶	8
● Barolo Piccole Vigne '98	¶¶	8
● Barolo Bussia Vigna Munie '96	¶¶¶	8
● Langhe Rosso Bricco Rovella '96	¶¶¶	6
● Barolo Bussia Vigna Munie '97	¶¶¶	8
● Barolo Bussia Vigna Rocche '97	¶¶	8
● Barolo Mariondino '97	¶¶	8
● Barolo Piccole Vigne '97	¶¶	8

MONFORTE D'ALBA (CN)

FERDINANDO PRINCIPIANO
VIA ALBA, 19
12065 MONFORTE D'ALBA (CN)
TEL. 0173787158

In 2003, Ferdinando Principiano will have been vinifying his own grapes for ten years and the results just keep on getting better. He is waiting for several new plots to come onstream but his present yearly production come to fewer than 30,000 bottles, a number that allows him to keep a watchful eye over every phase of production. Both of his '98 Barolos, the Le Coste from a noted Monforte vineyard and the Boscareto from an equally famous one at Serralunga, are magnificent. The first returns from a sabbatical that has lasted since 1997 to present us with a nose of still youthful fruit that ranges from morello cherry to plums, and an already soft, delightful palate that will no doubt thrill newcomers to wine. More complex and in many ways more austere, the Boscareto is a very rich garnet with already mature aromas of liquorice. The palate displays tannins that, although very sweet, are very much present. Honest and courageous as ever, Ferdinando has refused to release his Barbera d'Alba La Romualda '99, which had problems with several of its barrique lots. In its place, we have the 2000 vintage, the first wine from his collaboration with Beppe Caviola. Well-defined, clean violet aromas on the nose are followed by a the palate of extraordinary length and a spirited, but not over-zealous, tang. We would expect no less from its low-yielding vines, which are more than 70-year-old. Caviola's touch is also evident in the Dolcetto d'Alba Sant'Anna '01, which now adds body to its customary drinkability.

MONFORTE D'ALBA (CN)

PODERE ROCCHE DEI MANZONI
LOC. MANZONI SOPRANI, 3
12065 MONFORTE D'ALBA (CN)
TEL. 017378421
E-MAIL: rocchedeimanzoni@libero.it

Work on the new Migliorini cellar is progressing well. Valentino, Iolanda and their children's new winery features a Pantheon-like cupola that will turn the ageing rooms into a sort of secular temple to wine. Valentino is also set to launch his new Barolos, the Pianpolvere and the Castelletto. This year's Barolo Vigna Cappella di Santo Stefano and Langhe Quatr Nas are quite simply superb. The austere Barolo has notes of plum, blackberry, spice and leather, perfectly gauged tannins and big structure. Definitely one for the cellar. The Three Glass Quatr Nas is a skilful blend of 50 per cent nebbiolo with cabernet, merlot and pinot nero. The result is a wine of extraordinary elegance and nose-palate harmony, whose measured oak lets aromas of wild berries, grass and tobacco emerge. The rest of the range is almost as good. The Valentino Brut Zero Riserva '97 has kept us on tenterhooks but it was worth the wait. This is one of the best versions we have ever tasted. The perlage is generous and the aromas of butter and crusty bread delight. The other two Barolos are on a par with it. The Vigna d'la Roul weds traditional tar aromas with the vanilla of modern barrique ageing and the Big 'd Big, presently drinking sweeter more easily, is a little lighter in structure. The estate has high hopes for the Langhe Pinònero '99, which gets better every year. We recommend it for its typical Piedmont hue, redcurrant and cherry nose, and fabulous body. Up last, we have the Angelica '98 - we've tasted better - and the Bricco Manzoni '99, as ever a well-judged barbera and nebbiolo mix.

● Barolo Boscareto '98	🍷🍷	7
● Barbera d'Alba La Romualda '00	🍷🍷	6
● Barolo Le Coste '98	🍷🍷	7
● Dolcetto d'Alba S. Anna '01	🍷🍷	4
● Barolo Boscareto '93	🍷🍷🍷	7
● Barolo Boscareto '97	🍷🍷	7
● Barbera d'Alba La Romualda '98	🍷🍷	6
● Barolo Boscareto '95	🍷🍷	7
● Barolo Boscareto '96	🍷🍷	7
● Barolo Le Coste '96	🍷🍷	7

● Langhe Rosso Quatr Nas '99	🍷🍷🍷	7
○ Valentino Brut Zero Ris. '97	🍷🍷	6
● Barolo Vigna Cappella di S. Stefano '98	🍷🍷	8
● Barolo Vigna Big 'd Big '98	🍷🍷	8
● Barolo Vigna d'la Roul '98	🍷🍷	8
● Langhe Rosso Bricco Manzoni '99	🍷🍷	6
● Langhe Rosso Pinònero '99	🍷🍷	7
○ Langhe Chardonnay L'Angelica '98	🍷	6
● Barolo Vigna Big Ris. '89	🍷🍷🍷	8
● Barolo Vigna Big Ris. '90	🍷🍷🍷	8
● Barolo Vigna d'la Roul Ris. '90	🍷🍷🍷	8
● Barolo Vigna Cappella di S. Stefano '96	🍷🍷🍷	8
● Langhe Rosso Quatr Nas '96	🍷🍷🍷	8

MONFORTE D'ALBA (CN)

Flavio Roddolo
Fraz. Bricco Appiani
Loc. Sant'Anna, 5
12065 Monforte d'Alba (CN)
tel. 017378535

If you climb the slope up to Flavio Roddolo's "cascina", or farm, you'll find a true Langa artist. Flavio is a man who lives for his vineyards and makes wines that bring out both the personality of the grape and the nature of the soil on which they grow. Flavio's six hectares yield about 24,000 bottles a year. He's considering an extension to the cellar because he will soon have a new plot of nebbiolo to deal with. We'll begin with the stunning Nebbiolo d'Alba, a wine of amazing character and robustness. The nose is triumphantly pervasive, then notes of cocoa powder, redcurrants and morello cherry explode onto the palate. The finish is matchless. The elegant garnet of the Barolo Ravera is tinged with ochre, then delicate, austere aromas disclose characterful balsam and spice on the palate. Yet the Bricco Appiani '99 is the most deliciously cohesive wine in the Roddolo range. It is simply the finest Cabernet Sauvignon in Piedmont, and one of the best in Italy. Close-knit and massive on the faintly herbaceous nose, it releases superb notes of bramble, mushroom and black pepper. The opulent palate has a graciously gamey note and a quite delectable finish, backed by fine-grained tannins. The dark purple Dolcetto is equally well-made, hints of roses and spices emerging over a firm body with nicely gauged tannins. We'll conclude with the Barbera. Its warm, blood red hue is confirmed by excellent concentration, power and a firm, fruit-rich finish. All these are wines of immense quality and will require some cellar time to reach their inimitable best.

● Bricco Appiani '99	♟♟♟	6
● Nebbiolo d'Alba '99	♟♟	5
● Dolcetto d'Alba Sup. '00	♟♟	4*
● Barolo Ravera '98	♟♟	6
● Barbera d'Alba Sup. '99	♟♟	5
● Barolo Ravera '97	♟♟♟	6
● Bricco Appiani '98	♟♟	6
● Barolo '96	♟♟	6
● Bricco Appiani '97	♟♟	6
● Nebbiolo d'Alba '98	♟♟	4
● Dolcetto d'Alba Sup. '99	♟♟	3

MONFORTE D'ALBA (CN)

Ruggeri Corsini
Loc. Bussia Corsini, 106
12065 Monforte d'Alba (CN)
tel. 017378625
e-mail: podereruggericorsini@libero.it

Seven years ago, husband and wife Loredana Addari and Nicola Argamante bought an old "cascina", or farm, in a quiet spot away from the centre of town. They then built a new cellar near the original building and little by little bought the surrounding vineyards from the many smallholders who owned them. Property tends to get broken up when passing between generations round here. This is not a particularly celebrated area for vines but the positions are good and the plants are old. Excellent raw material is thus guaranteed. In the cellar, the skills of the two owners shine through – both are agronomists specialized in viticulture and oenology. They also have a valid helper in Loredana's brother, Lorenzo. We especially liked two of the wines, the Barolo Corsini '98 and the Barbera d'Alba Armujan 2000. The Barolo shows its class in its deep ruby red hue. On the nose, there is ripe berry fruit in a profile that gains in definition as the wine aerates. The soft, velvet-smooth palate is deliciously stylish and the oak-derived toastiness never threatens to intrude. The Barbera Armujan is perhaps the cellar's flagship bottle, particularly in terms of bottles produced. Intense on the nose, it flaunts spice over redcurrant and vanilla before the rich, lingering palate reveals its robust structure and luscious mouthfeel. The delightfully long finish rounds off with an attractive reprise of fruit. The rest of the range performed well, from the well-defined, tannic Nebbiolo 2000 to the straightforward, fresh-tasting basic Barbera and the well-typed Dolcetto d'Alba 2001.

● Barbera d'Alba Sup. Armujan '00	♟♟	5
● Barolo Corsini '98	♟♟	6
● Langhe Nebbiolo '00	♟	4
● Barbera d'Alba '01	♟	4
● Dolcetto d'Alba '01	♟	3

MONFORTE D'ALBA (CN)

F.lli Seghesio
Loc. Castelletto, 19
12065 Monforte d'Alba (CN)
tel. 017378108

It was yet another excellent vintage for brothers Aldo and Riccardo Seghesio. Their ten hectares lie in the enviably located Castelletto area, which gives superbly concentrated fruit that is ideal for making solidly structured wines that are also rich in fruit. For proof, try the Barbera Vigneto della Chiesa. Vineyard selection and ageing in new oak have lent it uncommon depth. Its dark ruby hue introduces fascinating hints of raspberry and cherry, which are followed by a broad, harmonious palate that goes on and on. This marvellous wine brought Three well-deserved Glasses to Castelletto, rewarding the efforts of a family that personifies the hardworking intelligence of the country folk in this corner of the Langhe. The Langhe Bouquet, a mix of nebbiolo, cabernet sauvignon and merlot, is also outstanding. The enticingly dense palate offers fine-grained tannins and pleasing notes of liquorice and spice that shrewdly gauged oak melds harmoniously. The Barolo La Villa has something extra to offer on the nose, with its warm, pervasive nuances of fine tobacco. The palate is soft, generous and attractively fresh, with convincing length. Only a notch or two below was the tangy, intensely fruity Dolcetto and the standard Barbera, which shows concentration and hints of ripe bramble. Soon to come is an extension to the cellar, which will further bolster a production that now hovers at around 50,000 bottles a year.

● Barbera d'Alba Vigneto della Chiesa '00	♀♀♀	5*
● Langhe Rosso Bouquet '00	♀♀	5
● Barbera d'Alba '01	♀♀	4
● Dolcetto d'Alba Vigneto della Chiesa '01	♀♀	3*
● Barolo Vigneto La Villa '98	♀♀	7
● Barolo Vigneto La Villa '91	♀♀♀	7
● Barbera d'Alba Vigneto della Chiesa '97	♀♀♀	5
● Barolo Vigneto La Villa '97	♀♀	7
● Barbera d'Alba Vigneto della Chiesa '99	♀♀	6

MONLEALE (AL)

Vigneti Massa
P.zza G. Capsoni, 10
15059 Monleale (AL)
tel. 013180302

It's not easy to talk about Walter Massa and his wines without letting the man himself influence your judgement. Walter is an eclectic type who has decided to produce premium wines. This year, he left his Bigolla to age and will release it only next year. Instead, the Cerreta has returned. This concentrated barbera-based blend is a superb mix of intensity and charm with a nose of plum, green tea and caramel. On the soft palate, bottled berry fruit joins warm sensations of chocolate. The Monleale has less muscle but more allure, hints of redcurrant and blueberry on the nose preceding a spice and cocoa powder palate. The Sentieri is another Barbera, this time stainless steel fermented, that wins your heart with its simplicity. The Colli Tortonesi Pertichetta, a monovarietal Croatina, deserves attention for its faintly balsamic notes and good structure in the mouth. No Walter Massa profile would be complete without a mention of timorasso. Walter has long believed in the potential of this native variety, whose worth he has amply demonstrated. It is thanks to him that timorasso is enjoying a renaissance. The 2000 Costa del Vento is already drinking superbly and will certainly improve in the cellar. Unlike most other whites, this is a wine to lay down. Also on the list are a nice Cortese, the Casareggio, and a slightly sparkling Freisa, the delicious Pietra del Gallo.

● Colli Tortonesi Cerreta '99	♀♀	7
○ Colli Tortonesi Timorasso Costa del Vento '00	♀♀	7
● Colli Tortonesi Croatina Pertichetta '00	♀♀	6
○ Muscaté '01	♀♀	4*
● Colli Tortonesi Monleale '99	♀♀	6
● Colli Tortonesi Freisa Pietra del Gallo '01	♀	4
● Piemonte Barbera Sentieri '01	♀	5
○ Piemonte Cortese Casareggio '01	♀	4
● Colli Tortonesi Bigolla '98	♀♀♀	7
● Colli Tortonesi Bigolla '99	♀♀	7
● Colli Tortonesi Cerreta '98	♀♀	7

MONTÀ (CN)

GIOVANNI ALMONDO
VIA SAN ROCCO, 26
12046 MONTÀ (CN)
TEL. 0173975256
E-MAIL: almondo@giovannialmondo.com

Domenico Almondo's range is always seriously good. He has no trouble combining winemaking with his day job as mayor of Montà. Domenico's cellar and vineyards – ten or so hectares in two main plots – are all at Montà, too, where his tireless parents, Giovanni and Teresina, and wife Antonella all lend a hand. Each year, the cellar turns out about 60,000 bottles, a figure that makes this relatively modest winery a major producer in an area where small properties are the rule. The style Domenico imparts to his limited number of scrupulously made wines is inspired by modernity – in moderation – and tempered by respect for Roero and its heritage. For the first time, the stellar Roero Bric Valdiana 2000 won Three Glasses, taking full advantage of a favourable vintage to outstrip the previous editions. A deep garnet ruby introduces a nose with crisp notes of berry fruit and spices. In the mouth, the superb texture is obvious yet never compromises the overall elegance and a balance that astounds. The other great red is the Barbera Valbianchera. The panel especially liked the fruit and the leisurely finish on the delicious palate. The name Almondo is also synonymous with classy whites, though. The Arneis Bricco delle Ciliegie, one of the finest in the DOC zone, continues to amaze and the Vigne Sparse is only slightly less complex. It's a very nice, fresh-tasting wine.

MONTÀ (CN)

MICHELE TALIANO
C.SO A. MANZONI, 24
12046 MONTÀ (CN)
TEL. 0173976512 - 0173976100
E-MAIL: taliano@libero.it

The panel was looking forward to tasting the new wines from this Montà-based winery, which earned its Guide profile last year thanks to a series of very persuasive bottles. Our expectations were fulfilled in spades so here goes with the new range fashioned by brothers Alberto and Ezio Taliano, with the assistance of their father, Michele. Only the 2000 Roero is missing from the list. The Talianos have decided to give this product another year in the cellar so they can release a more complete wine in 2003. We'll begin our review with the other major red, a Barbera Laboriosa that took the panel's collective breath away last year. Our notes this time report an impenetrably dark hue and a nose with crisp notes of berry fruit, juniper and spice. The seriously good palate is backed up by good alcohol. We also very much liked the Barbaresco Ad Altiora, from a lovely vineyard at San Rocco Seno d'Elvio (the other estate plots are all at Montà and Canale, for a total of about ten hectares). Although still a little young, the Ad Altiora can offer a frank nose of rich fruit and a well-rounded, nicely tannic palate. All the other wines are good, including an attractively refreshing second-label Barbera, a well-typed Arneis and an enticingly drinkable Dolcetto.

● Roero Bric Valdiana '00	🍷🍷🍷	6
● Barbera d'Alba Valbianchera '00	🍷🍷	5
○ Roero Arneis Bricco delle Ciliegie '01	🍷🍷	4
○ Roero Arneis Vigne Sparse '01	🍷	4
● Roero Bric Valdiana '99	🍷🍷	6
● Barbera d'Alba Valbianchera '97	🍷🍷	5
● Roero Bric Valdiana '97	🍷🍷	6
● Roero Sup. Giovanni Almondo '97	🍷🍷	7
● Barbera d'Alba Valbianchera '98	🍷🍷	5
● Roero Bric Valdiana '98	🍷🍷	6
● Barbera d'Alba Valbianchera '99	🍷🍷	5

● Barbera d'Alba Laboriosa '00	🍷🍷	4*
● Barbaresco Ad Altiora '99	🍷🍷	6
● Barbera d'Alba A Bon Rendre '01	🍷	3
● Dolcetto d'Alba Ciabot Vigna '01	🍷	3
○ Roero Arneis Sernì '01	🍷	3
● Barbaresco Ad Altiora '98	🍷🍷	6
● Barbera d'Alba Laboriosa '99	🍷🍷	4
● Roero Ròche dra Bòssora '99	🍷🍷	4

MONTEGROSSO D'ASTI (AT)

Tenuta La Meridiana
Fraz. Tana Bassa, 5
14048 Montegrosso d'Asti (AT)
Tel. 0141956250 - 0141956172
E-mail: meridiana@vininternet.com

Giampiero Bianco's Montegrosso d'Asti-based winery has is a consistent performer and is making a name for itself thanks to the overall quality of the range and for its Barbera d'Asti wines in particular. Giampiero owns about a dozen hectares in the municipality of Montegrosso, and rents other plots at Castelnuovo Calcea, Vinchio and Incisa Scapaccino. Annual production is around 60,000 bottles, with two Barbera selections – there's also a basic version – accounting for most of them. The cellar, where Giampiero's wife also lends a hand, can rely on the assistance of consultant Lorenzo Quinterno. Of the wines tasted, our panel preferred the Monferrato Rosso Rivaia '99, a 60-30-10 mix of nebbiolo, barbera and cabernet. A red in the modern idiom, entirely barrique-aged, it stands out for its pervasive aromas and a rich palate with elegant tannins and great length. The Barbera Tra Terra e Cielo has plenty of body. Old vines and new wood have lent the wine remarkable complexity, which comes out in the character and personality of the palate. Bricco Sereno '99 is more delicate and elegant, with notes of rain-soaked earth prominent on the nose. Less complex, but still well-executed, are the Grignolino Vignamaestra 2001 and the '99 Barbera d'Asti Le Gagie. Bringing up the rear is a dainty, approachable Monferrato Bianco Puntet 2001, from chardonnay, cortese and favorita grapes.

● Barbera d'Asti Sup. Bricco Sereno '99	🍷🍷	5
● Barbera d'Asti Sup. Tra Terra e Cielo '99	🍷🍷	5
● Monferrato Rosso Rivaia '99	🍷🍷	5
● Grignolino d'Asti Vignamaestra '01	🍷	3*
○ Monferrato Bianco Puntet '01	🍷	3*
● Barbera d'Asti Le Gagie '99	🍷	3*
● Barbera d'Asti Sup. Tra Terra e Cielo '98	🍷🍷	5
● Monferrato Rosso Rivaia '98	🍷🍷	5
● Barbera d'Asti Sup. Bricco Sereno '98	🍷	5

MONTELUPO ALBESE (CN)

Destefanis
Via Mortizzo, 8
12050 Montelupo Albese (CN)
Tel. 0173617189
E-mail: marcodestefanis@marcodestefanis.com

Montelupo Albese is one of the most interesting corners of the Dolcetto d'Alba DOC and Marco Destefanis is a producer who brings out the best in the wine type. His association with Beppe Caviola, the well-know oenologist who is himself from Montelupo, is proving a fruitful one, as this year's wines amply demonstrate. Marco gets his grapes from four estate-owned hectares near the cellar, in Montelupo and Diano d'Alba, and a further three rented at Ponte Pietro in the municipality of Alba. On his list, there are two Dolcettos, the Vigna Monia Bassa vineyard selection and a second-label wine, a Nebbiolo, a Barbera d'Alba – hail prevented Marco from releasing the barrique-aged version this year – and a chardonnay-based white. News from the winery includes rationalization of the facilities and extension of the winery. Marco's flagship wine is the Dolcetto d'Alba Monia Bassa 2001, from an old vineyard that now gives very modest yields. The Dolcetto obtained is outstandingly typed. Its vibrant ruby, almost purplish, red ushers in aromas of hazelnut, raspberry and ripe cherry. Firm and well-extracted on the palate, it signs off with a velvet-smooth finish. The Nebbiolo d'Alba 2000 is an exciting wine that combines lovely smoky notes with an austere palate and a finish lifted by elegantly smooth tannins. The flavoursome standard Dolcetto d'Alba and Barbera are well-executed, marrying quality to excellent value for money. The Chardonnay, entirely steel-fermented and aged in the 2001 edition, is straightforward and fresh-tasting.

● Dolcetto d'Alba Vigna Monia Bassa '01	🍷🍷	4
● Nebbiolo d'Alba '00	🍷🍷	4
● Dolcetto d'Alba '01	🍷🍷	3*
● Barbera d'Alba '01	🍷	3
○ Langhe Chardonnay '01		3
● Dolcetto d'Alba Vigna Monia Bassa '00	🍷🍷	4
● Nebbiolo d'Alba '99	🍷🍷	4

MONTEU ROERO (CN)

ANGELO NEGRO & FIGLI
FRAZ. SANT'ANNA, 1
12040 MONTEU ROERO (CN)
TEL. 017390252
E-MAIL: negro@negroangelo.it

Giovanni Negro has been mayor of Monteu Roero for many years and his winery deserves credit for having always believed firmly in the potential of the Roero area. Ever in the front line of the campaigns to promote first Arneis, then Roero, Angelo Negro & Figli is today one of the most dependable cellars in the DOC zone. Capacity has now reached 230,000 bottles a year and the vines covers 54 hectares in three properties in the municipalities of Monteu Roero, Canale and Barbaresco (a Negro Barbaresco will be released in a couple of years). Work continues on the lovely new cellar, where the family will soon be settling in. Winery staff includes Giovanni's wife Marisa and their children Gabriele, Angelo, Manuela and Giuseppe. The move has done no harm to the wines, which were well up to snuff this year. The two Roero selections are good. The Prachiosso put the emphasis on drinkability whereas the Sodisfà is a very serious wine, its spicy complex nose bolstered by a rich, austere palate with a fine finish. The two Barberas never disappoint. The Nicolon is slightly minerally on the nose and full in the mouth and the Bric Bertu releases notes of cherry and autumn leaves before revealing a warm, caressing palate. We liked the fuller, more concentrated Perdaudin better than the other Arneis selection, the Gianat. And a final tip of the hat for the Passito di Arneis. You won't find a better example of this type anywhere.

●	Roero Sup. Sodisfà '99	♀♀	6
●	Barbera d'Alba Bric Bertu '00	♀♀	5
●	Barbera d'Alba Nicolon '00	♀♀	4*
○	Perdaudin Passito '99	♀♀	6
●	Roero Prachiosso '00	♀	5
○	Roero Arneis Gianat '01	♀	5
○	Roero Arneis Perdaudin '01	♀	4
○	Perdaudin Passito '97	♀♀	6
●	Roero Sup. Sodisfà '98	♀♀	6
●	Barbera d'Alba Bric Bertu '99	♀♀	5

MONTEU ROERO (CN)

CASCINA PELLERINO
FRAZ. SANT'ANNA
12040 MONTEU ROERO (CN)
TEL. 0173979083 - 0173978171
E-MAIL: gythbo@tin.it

In the past, Cristian Bono has often been called one of Roero's most promising young growers. Today, he is fulfilling that promise. The years he spent under the watchful eye of Matteo Correggia, whose advice Cristian absorbed and digested intelligently, have enabled his small winery – currently, it releases 50,000 bottles a year – to become a prominent feature on the local winemaking scene. Cristian and his indefatigable father, Luciano, cultivate eight hectares of estate-owned vines in excellent locations around the municipalities of Monteu Roero, Santo Stefano Roero and Canale. Monteu is also the home of the lovely, newly renovated cellar, which is the heart of operations. This year's offerings included two major reds that impressed the panel. The Roero Vicot unveils a complex, crisply defined nose where berry fruit is well to the fore. Flavoursome on the palate, it has loads of character and a lingering finish. The vibrant ruby Barbera Gran Madre satisfies on the nose with clean berry fruit and spices, then the rich, robust palate is harmonious and well-balanced through to the finish. The two second-label reds are only a little less complex. Both are very enticing and impeccably executed. The Arneis di Bono is one of the best wines in its category, showing enviably freshness and cleanness. The dried grape, arneis-based Poch ma Bon also convinced the panel.

●	Roero Vicot '00	♀♀	5
●	Barbera d'Alba Sup. Gran Madre '00	♀♀	5
○	Roero Arneis Boneur '01	♀♀	3
●	Barbera d'Alba '01	♀	3
●	Roero '01	♀	4
○	Poch ma Bon Passito	♀	6
●	Roero Vicot '98	♀♀	5
●	Barbera d'Alba Sup. Gran Madre '99	♀♀	5
●	Roero Vicot '99	♀♀	5

MORSASCO (AL)

La Guardia
Reg. La Guardia
15010 Morsasco (AL)
tel. 014473076
e-mail: guardia@libero.it

This lovely Monferrato estate is run by the Priarone family. It can point to a wide range of wines, the best of which are obtained from the two traditional local vines, dolcetto and barbera. The wines we liked best on our visit were the Barbera Vigna di Dante and the Dolcetto Delfini. The Barbera has an intense hue with a youthful rim. On the nose, hints of mint, violets and cherry come through, lifted by nuances of cream. The palate has plenty of substance and the long finish reveals tempting notes of cocoa powder. The Villa Delfini is another youthful-looking wine. Complex and ripe on the jam and spice nose, it has a concentrated, warm palate that elects drinkability as its keynote. The decently long finish timidly allows the elegance of the tannins to peek through. One Glass went to the Dolcetto Il Gamondino for its fruit notes on the nose and good weight in the mouth. The Barbera Aspettando l'Ornovo flanks the fruit on the nose with earthier notes. The palate is fluent but hardly challenging. The nose of the Cortese La Vigna di Lena is a tad one-dimensional, with notes of fermentation, but the palate has decent weight and flavour. Finally, the fascinating Sacroeprofano blend of cabernet and barbera is more successful than the still very good Innominato, from dolcetto and cabernet.

- Monferrato Rosso Sacroeprofano '00 — 5
- Barbera del M.to Vigna di Dante '99 — 5
- Dolcetto di Ovada Sup. Villa Delfini '99 — 5
- Barbera del M.to Aspettando l'Ornovo '00 — 4
- Dolcetto di Ovada Sup. Il Gamondino '00 — 4
- O Cortese dell'Alto M.to La Vigna di Lena '01 — 4
- Monferrato Rosso Innominato '99 — 5
- Barbera del M.to Ornovo '98 — 4

MURISENGO (AL)

Isabella
Fraz. Corteranzo
Via Gianoli, 64
15020 Murisengo (AL)
tel. 0141693000
e-mail: calvo@isabellavini.com

Gabriele Calvo, owner of the Isabella cellar, may look quiet but he has an enterprising, inquisitive personality. The range of wines released bears witness to this. Gabriele's more approachable bottles line up with selections of Monferrato varieties unjustly considered to be secondary, as well as the classic barbera. The 2001 Freisa Bioc and, especially, the Grignolino Montecastello from the same vintage, are right at the top of their categories. The Freisa is inky black with intense aromas of ripe black berry fruit and roses over an enticing basso continuo of mint and spices. The fruit is deep and juicy, backed up by fine-grained tannins and lively acidity. The Grignolino offers a dense hue and crisp, subtly nuanced varietal aromas that range from flowers to fruit and spice. Well-structured and refreshing, it shows good fruit before the attractively tangy finish signs off on an elegant note of spice. The Barbera Truccone has an impenetrable hue that releases pervasive aromas of very ripe plum and bramble, with a grace note of cinnamon. The entry on the palate is broad and velvety, becoming soft and well-sustained in mid palate before the refreshing finish reprises black berry fruit. There basic Grignolino has well-defined varietal aromas and a tangy palate that is a little blurry on entry, then offers a lovely almond and spice finish. The barrique-fermented Chardonnay has soft, ripe fruit but lacks a touch of freshness. This year, the flagship Barbera selection , the Bric Stupui, was not released. Its huge structure demands further ageing before it goes to market.

- Barbera d'Asti Truccone '00 — 4
- Grignolino del M.to Casalese Montecastello '01 — 4
- Monferrato Freisa Bioc '01 — 4
- O Piemonte Chardonnay '00 — 4
- Grignolino del M.to Casalese '01 — 3*
- Barbera d'Asti Bric Stupui '98 — 5
- Barbera d'Asti Bric Stupui '99 — 5

MURISENGO (AL)

La Zucca
Fraz. Sorina
Via Sorina, 53/55
15020 Murisengo (AL)
tel. 0118193343 - 0141993154
e-mail: info@lazucca.com

Ester Accornero's winery is a reflection of its owner's enterprise and spirit. The new plantings are completed and the estate now has 20 hectares under vine. Quality is the watchword as yields are being cut back and some second-label wines are discontinued. The wines are made in the Monferrato style and the 2001 vintage saw the arrival of Mario Ronco as consultant. The apple of Ester's eye is the Barbera Martizza, obtained from a selection of the best grapes. The 2000 edition is as outstanding as ever, as you can see from its inky black colour. Close-knit aromas of blueberry and bramble berry fruit mingles beautifully with the oak, which adds hints of tobacco and vanilla. The nose is enhanced by intriguing nuances of mint and elegant geranium. The admirably structured, fruit-rich palate has substantial weight and is well backed up by the variety's hallmark vein of fresh acidity. The Barbera 'I Sulì 2001, vinified without recourse to wood, came close to a second Glass. Its rich, youthful colour heralds intense aromas where typical notes of bramble and black cherry meld with eucalyptus. The fresh-tasting palate has good presence and nice fruit. The Grignolino Marmanest 2001 is a deep cherry red, with varietal notes of strawberries, hints of flowers, especially elegant geraniums and roses, as well as green pepper and ginger spice. These are echoed on the substantial palate, which a deliciously astringent note and marked tanginess keep whistle-clean. The Freisa 2001 layers raspberry and violets over discreet vanilla, which the fresh-tasting palate picks up satisfyingly.

- Barbera d'Asti Martizza '00 — 5
- Barbera d'Asti 'I Sulì '01 — 4
- Freisa d'Asti '01 — 4
- Grignolino del M.to Casalese Marmanest '01 — 4
- Barbera d'Asti Martizza '99 — 5

NEIVE (CN)

Piero Busso
Via Albesani, 8
12057 Neive (CN)
tel. 017367156
e-mail: goxxpiero@libero.it

Piero Busso and his wife Lucia began to vinify their own wine in the latter half of the 1980s, at first releasing no more than a few thousand bottles. Then their children, Pierguido and Emanuela, became interested in the world of wine, so the business grew. Currently, Piero uses natural, low-input techniques to cultivate about seven estate-owned and rented hectares under vine in the Barbaresco DOCG zone. As the Bussos wait for the two new Gallina and Santo Stefanetto selections to come onstream, Vigna Borgese and Bricco Mondino continue to lead the range. The '99 vintage was favourable for the convincing Vigna Borgese, from the Albesani hill, has enough red berry fruit to withstand the balsamic aromas from the oak and sufficient extract to sustain the long, characterful finish. In contrast, the powerful Bricco Mondino is a tad fuzzy on the nose and there are still rough edges on the palate. The Barbera and Dolcetto are both good, perfectly exemplifying Piero's view that his wines should be approachable, easy to drink and not too challenging. The 2000 Barbera has a broad yet concentrated nose where black cherry is prominent. Long and well-structured on the palate, it is perked up by attractively refreshing acidity. The Dolcetto 2001 runs true to type. The notes of alcohol and bramble on the nose are followed by down-to-earth tannins on the palate. Bianco di Busso, a mix of chardonnay and sauvignon that this year is presented without DOC status, is less exciting than usual but this is probably due to the fact that it only recently went into the bottle.

- Barbaresco Vigna Borgese '99 — 7
- Barbera d'Alba Vigna Majano '00 — 4*
- Barbaresco Bricco Mondino '99 — 7
- Bianco di Busso '00 — 4
- Dolcetto d'Alba Vigna Majano '01 — 3*
- Barbaresco Vigna Borgese '97 — 7
- Barbaresco Bricco Mondino '98 — 7
- Barbaresco Vigna Borgese '95 — 7
- Barbaresco Vigna Borgese '96 — 7
- Barbaresco Bricco Mondino '97 — 7
- Barbaresco Vigna Borgese '98 — 7
- Barbaresco Bricco Mondino '96 — 7

NEIVE (CN)

CASCINA VANO
VIA RIVETTI, 9
12057 NEIVE (CN)
TEL. 017367263 - 0173677705
E-MAIL: cascina.vano@tiscalinet.it

Bruno Rivetti and his father Beppe look after five hectares of their vines, as well as nearly four more that they rent, which means they can turn out about 35,000 bottles of wine a year. There have been some significant changes in the range. Starting with the 1999 vintage, the Barbaresco bears the name of its subzone, Canova, on the label and there are plans to launch a second vineyard selection, the Rivetti. From 2000, the Rivettis are vinifying separately the barbera from a vineyard more than 50 years located on the Canova hill, on the border with the municipality of Coazzolo. The cellar's overall performance this year was very encouraging. There are three Two Glass wines and a fourth came close. In its first vintage, the 2000 Barbera Carulot made a good impression. Nearly 7,000 bottles are released of this wine, which ages for 16 months in part new barriques and tonneaux. Its impenetrable purple-red hue introduces a nose that harmoniously combines ripe cherry and plum fruit with toasty notes reminiscent of dried mushrooms. The fullness and elegant balance of flavours on the palate delight, as does the long finish. Close behind comes the fruit-rich, beautifully textured Barbaresco Canova '99, which aged in barrels that hold more than ten quintals, and the powerful, mouthfilling Langhe Duetto 2000, a 50-50 mix of nebbiolo and barbera. Finally, the Dolcetto d'Alba 2001 completes this range of constantly improving and very affordable wines.

• Barbera d'Alba Carulot '00	ΨΨ	5
• Langhe Rosso Duetto '00	ΨΨ	5
• Barbaresco Canova '99	ΨΨ	6*
• Dolcetto d'Alba '01	Ψ	3
• Barbaresco '96	ΨΨ	6
• Barbaresco '97	ΨΨ	6
• Barbaresco '98	ΨΨ	6
• Langhe Rosso Duetto '98	ΨΨ	5
• Barbera d'Alba '99	ΨΨ	4
• Langhe Rosso Duetto '99	ΨΨ	5

NEIVE (CN)

F.LLI CIGLIUTI
VIA SERRA BOELLA, 17
12057 NEIVE (CN)
TEL. 0173677185
E-MAIL: cigliutirenato@libero.it

Renato Cigliuti has been on a roll since the late 1970s so he can justly be considered one of the grand old men of Barbaresco. Even though he is looked up to by many younger producers, Renato is not about to sit back and take things easy. In fact, the assistance of his wife Dina, who has been working alongside Renato for years, and the increasing involvement of their daughters Claudia and Silvia, mean that the cellar is poised for even greater things. Output from the six hectares under vine never tops 30,000 bottles a year but the range has been extended with the first release of Barbera Campass. Obtained from grapes grown in the best part of the Serraboella vineyard, it ages for 15 months in half new barriques. As usual, the Barbaresco Serraboella '99 is an excellent wine and came close to earning a third Glass. This red of irresistibly muscular alcohol and tannins offers concentrated aromas of incense, resin and rain-soaked earth that mingle with more varietal notes of raspberry jam and bottled plums. To uncork it now is to deny your palate the sensations that will emerge with further ageing. Bricco Serra 2000 is a barrique-aged blend of barbera and nebbiolo that flaunts crisp, ripe fruit and cossets the palate with sweet alcohol. Of the two 2000 Barberas, we preferred the new Campass. It is slightly softer and reveals a masterly use of oak. In contrast, the Serraboella is a tad rougher and more austere on the back palate. As in previous years, the Cigliuti Dolcetto is moderately concentrated and offers simple, fresh, alcohol-led aromas that come together quite well.

• Barbaresco Serraboella '99	ΨΨ	8
• Barbera d'Alba Campass '00	ΨΨ	6
• Barbera d'Alba Serraboella '00	ΨΨ	5
• Langhe Rosso Bricco Serra '00	ΨΨ	7
• Dolcetto d'Alba Serraboella '01	Ψ	4
• Barbaresco Serraboella '90	ΨΨΨ	8
• Barbaresco Serraboella '96	ΨΨΨ	8
• Barbaresco Serraboella '97	ΨΨΨ	8
• Barbaresco Serraboella '98	ΨΨ	8
• Barbaresco Serraboella '93	ΨΨ	8
• Barbaresco Serraboella '95	ΨΨ	8
• Langhe Rosso Bricco Serra '99	ΨΨ	7

NEIVE (CN)

FONTANABIANCA
VIA BORDINI, 15
12057 NEIVE (CN)
TEL. 017367195
E-MAIL: fontanabianca@libero.it

The excellent results achieved this year by Aldo Pola and Bruno Ferro's Fontanabianca winery come as no surprise. The overall quality of the cellar's bottles is consistently high. Obviously, the flagship wines are the two Barbarescos and the Barbera Brunet but the so-called basic wines receive just as much care and attention. The estate's professionalism begins in the vineyard – there are ten hectares plus a further three rented – and continues in the cellar, where Aldo can call on Beppe Caviola's advice. Although it just missed out on a repeat of the previous vintage's exploit, the Sorì Burdin '99 is an outstanding red. The dense, bright ruby red introduces a nose of concentrated, complex aromas – we noted vanilla, cinnamon, very ripe berry fruit and a twist of orange peel – and a powerful, elegant palate with a sensuously velvety mouthfeel and impressive, almost sweet, tannic length. The standard version is only 20 per cent aged in new barriques and has less body. Actually, it is still a little in thrall to the oak. The Barbera Brunet 2000 is dedicated to Aldo's father-in-law, who owns the almost 60-year-old vineyard. It mingles fruity varietal notes of cherry and plum with toasty coffee from the oak then the palate shows remarkable weight and attractive freshness. Finally, we tasted the splendidly drinkable Dolcetto, a nice standard Barbera and an Arneis with more muscle than finesse, all from 2001.

• Barbaresco Sorì Burdin '99	🍷🍷	7
• Barbera d'Alba Brunet '00	🍷🍷	5
• Barbera d'Alba '01	🍷🍷	4*
• Dolcetto d'Alba Bordini '01	🍷🍷	4*
• Barbaresco '99	🍷🍷	6
○ Langhe Arneis '01	🍷	4
• Barbaresco Sorì Burdin '98	🍷🍷🍷	7
• Barbaresco '96	🍷🍷	6
• Barbaresco Sorì Burdin '97	🍷🍷	7
• Barbaresco '98	🍷🍷	6
• Barbera d'Alba '99	🍷🍷	4
• Barbera d'Alba Brunet '99	🍷🍷	5

NEIVE (CN)

GASTALDI
VIA ALBESANI, 20
12057 NEIVE (CN)
TEL. 0173677400

The Gastaldi estate has 15 hectares in some of the finest vineyards in the Langhe to work with. The cellar and the nebbiolo vines are in Albesani, at the foot of the hill that leads to the town of Neive once you cross the bridge over the Tanaro. At Neive, Dino Gastaldi has magnificent plots at Serra Boella and at Starderi for nebbiolo while grapes for his Dolcetto d'Alba and whites come from the municipality of Rodello. The Le Coste vineyard at Monforte provides the fruit for the Langhe Rosso Castlé and will soon also yield grapes for Barolo. Dino tends his estate with scrupulous care, obtaining superb fruit that he transforms into outstanding, rigorously executed wines. When we arrived for our tastings, the 2000 and 2001 whites, thoroughbred wines that demand slow ageing, had not yet been released. The line-up included only four reds, an approachable Dolcetto and the more challenging Rosso Gastaldi, Barbaresco and Rosso Castlé. The results were very good indeed, with the Rosso Gastaldi '98 back at its best, on a par with the still exquisite '88 and '89 selections. Its intense ruby red is impenetrably close-knit. On the nose, it opens with spices, tobacco and ripe fruit then the impressive palate shows great balance and silky tannins. The Rosso Castlé '97, from nebbiolo with a little merlot, is more austere, displaying to good effect the characteristics of nebbiolo from this part of Monforte, which lies higher up than the Barolo DOCG zone. The Barbaresco '97 has complex aromas and a pervasive mouthfeel. Finally, the Dolcetto Moriolo 2001 is very pleasant.

• Langhe Rosso Gastaldi '98	🍷🍷	8
• Barbaresco '97	🍷🍷	7
• Langhe Rosso Castlé '97	🍷🍷	7
• Dolcetto d'Alba Moriolo '01	🍷	4
• Gastaldi Rosso '88	🍷🍷🍷	8
• Gastaldi Rosso '89	🍷🍷🍷	8
• Dolcetto d'Alba Sup. Moriolo '90	🍷🍷🍷	6
• Langhe Rosso Castlé '96	🍷🍷	7
○ Langhe Bianco Gastaldi '99	🍷🍷	5
○ Langhe Chardonnay '99	🍷🍷	5

NEIVE (CN)

F.LLI GIACOSA
VIA XX SETTEMBRE, 64
12052 NEIVE (CN)
TEL. 017367013
E-MAIL: giacosa@giacosa.it

The Giacosa family is one of the longest-established on the Langhe winemaking scene. As long ago as the late 19th century, the Giacosas were wine merchants and that enthusiasm has been handed down unchanged to the present generation, brothers Valerio and Renzo and their respective heirs, Maurizio and Paolo. The main difference is that today's Giacosas aim exclusively for quality, a path that looks like the only way to success nowadays and the only effective response to an increasingly challenging market. For the past few years, we have been noting improvements in the traditional Giacosa range of wines, which features some very exciting labels. We'll begin with the excellent Barolo Vigna Mandorlo, a low-yielding plot at Castiglione Falletto that accounts for a modest 10,000 bottles a year or so. Its garnet hue is tinged with orange and the aromas of spices and liquorice are lifted by well-gauged toastiness. The palate is elegant, despite the lively tannins that have still to mellow. The Barbaresco Rio Sordo '99, a selection made with fruit bought in from one of the area's finest vineyards, is another excellent bottle. The Barolo Bussia is traditional and a tad evolved. With the '99 vintage, the Barbera d'Alba Maria Gioana is back on form. Its concentration and persistence are compromised only by a faint hint of bitterish astringency on the back palate. Also presented were a fresh, fruity Chardonnay Roera and the uncomplicated Dolcetto Madonna di Como.

NEIVE (CN)

BRUNO GIACOSA
VIA XX SETTEMBRE, 52
12057 NEIVE (CN)
TEL. 017367027
E-MAIL: brunogiacosa@brunogiacosa.it

Bruno Giacosa is one of the last surviving wise old men of the Langhe, a sage who knows the territory and its secrets like the back of his hand and whose more than 50 years of experience have given him an ability to vinify nebbiolo as few others can. Although he no longer makes the legendary Vigna Rionda, worthily replaced by the Falletto from Serralunga d'Alba, Bruno's Barolo and Barbaresco selections are still writing the history of Piedmontese winemaking. Like the Falletto '96 a couple of years ago, the Falletto Riserva '96 is one of Italy's finest wines. It has benefited from longer ageing than its predecessor and the four years or so it spent in French oak barrels of 50 and 100 hectolitres has enabled it bring out all the true class of the nebbiolo grape. The wide range of aromas on the nose embrace dried flowers, cloves, juniper berries and liquorice while the superbly rich palate evinces all the austere, full-bodied personality of a Barolo from Serralunga. For now, there is little to choose between the two youthful '98 Barolos, the Falletto and the Rocche di Falletto. The Falletto is fruitier whereas its stablemate is more rugged and minerally. The Barbaresco Asili '98 offers more finesse and delicacy while maintaining a firm varietal character. The other wines include a full-bodied, velvety Nebbiolo Valmaggiore 2000 from Roero, made with maceration on the skins almost halved with respect to the 18-20 days used for the Langhe wines, a fruit-driven Barbera Falletto 2000 and an easy-drinking 2001 Roero Arneis.

● Barolo Vigna Mandorlo '98	🍷🍷	7
● Barbaresco Rio Sordo '99	🍷🍷	6
● Barbera d'Alba Maria Gioana '99	🍷🍷	4
● Barolo Bussia '98	🍷	6
● Dolcetto d'Alba Madonna di Como '01		3
○ Langhe Chardonnay Roera '01		3
● Barolo Vigna Mandorlo '95	🍷🍷	7
● Barolo Vigna Mandorlo '96	🍷🍷	7
● Barbaresco Rio Sordo '97	🍷🍷	6
● Barolo Vigna Mandorlo '97	🍷🍷	7
● Barbaresco Rio Sordo '98	🍷🍷	6

● Barolo Falletto Ris. '96	🍷🍷🍷	8
● Barbaresco Asili '98	🍷🍷	8
● Barolo Falletto '98	🍷🍷	8
● Barolo Le Rocche del Falletto '98	🍷🍷	8
● Barbera d'Alba Falletto '00	🍷	6
● Nebbiolo d'Alba Valmaggiore '00	🍷	5
○ Roero Arneis '01		5
● Barolo Collina Rionda Ris. '82	🍷🍷🍷	8
● Barolo Rocche di Castiglione Falletto '85	🍷🍷🍷	8
● Barbaresco Asili Ris. '96	🍷🍷🍷	8
● Barolo Falletto '96	🍷🍷🍷	8
● Barbaresco Asili '97	🍷🍷	8
● Barolo Falletto '97	🍷🍷	8
● Barolo Le Rocche del Falletto '97	🍷🍷	8

NEIVE (CN)

Ugo Lequio
Via del Molino, 10
12057 Neive (CN)
tel. 0173677224
e-mail: ugolequio@libero.it

Ugo Lequio makes 28,000 bottles of wine with grapes he purchases from a limited number of trusted suppliers. The close relationship he has built up with his growers is the secret of the excellent quality and dependability that are the hallmarks of his wines. Ugo's style is traditional. He believes in longish maceration and ageing in large barrels, which he replaces every seven or eight years to guarantee they stay clean enough to make premium-quality wines. Only the Barbera is aged in barrels smaller than the 20-30 hectolitres that are the norm in the Langhe but Ugo never goes below containers with a capacity of 500 litres. We'll begin our round-up with the Barbera Gallina. The 2000 edition has a garnet ruby hue with an orange rim and pronounced aromas of cocoa powder and cherry layered over a faint note of minerals. The variety's lively trademark acidity lends the concentrated, well-structured palate good grip through to the admirably long finish. The Dolcetto 2001 is concentrated and well-defined, showing notes of almonds and dried herbs as well as a soft-textured palate. The Barbaresco Gallina '99 isn't quite up to the standards of recent years but still proffers nice fruit and balsam notes along with very respectable structure in the mouth. Finally, the Arneis is generous and approachable.

•	Barbera d'Alba Gallina '00	ƠƠ	4*
•	Dolcetto d'Alba '01	ƠƠ	4*
O	Langhe Arneis '01	Ơ	4
•	Barbaresco Gallina '99	Ơ	6
•	Barbaresco Gallina '96	ƠƠ	6
•	Barbaresco Gallina '97	ƠƠ	6
•	Barbaresco Gallina '98	ƠƠ	6
•	Barbera d'Alba Gallina '98	ƠƠ	4
•	Barbera d'Alba Gallina '99	Ơ	4

NEIVE (CN)

Paitin
Via Serra Boella, 20
12057 Neive (CN)
tel. 017367343
e-mail: info@paitin.com

Like many other winemaking families in the Langhe, the Pasquero-Elias have roots in Roero. Today, the estate owns 17 hectares scattered across the Langhe, at Neive and Alba, and Roero, in Vezza d'Alba. Secondo runs things, with the help of his sons Giovanni and Silvano. Careful cellar and vineyard management have enabled the family to produce excellent wines for some years. Standards are high across the range this time and even the second-label wines are up to snuff. This time round, the star performer is the Barbaresco Sorì Paitin Vecchie Vigne, which replaces the former Riserva version, last produced in the 1990 vintage. The new selection comes from vines that are about 40 years old and is half aged in new barriques. The nose is impressively complex, unveiling elegant notes of raspberries, dried flowers and spices, then an exceptionally good palate with silky tannins and aromas that linger for an astoundingly long time. The standard version, another '99, is harmonious and very pleasant but lacks the depth of the Vecchie Vigne. The Langhe Paitin 2000, a mix of nebbiolo, barbera and cabernet sauvignon (all 30 per cent) rounded off by ten per cent syrah, very nearly won a third Glass for its exuberant aromas and palate. Fruit explodes onto the nose and is backed up by a full-bodied palate with a fleshy mouthfeel. The best of the rest were the powerful Barbera Campolive 2000, the delicious Dolcetto Sorì Paitin 2001 and the Nebbiolo Ca Veja 2000 with its complex nose.

•	Barbaresco Sorì Paitin Vecchie Vigne '99	ƠƠƠ	8
•	Langhe Paitin '00	ƠƠ	6*
•	Barbera d'Alba Campolive '00	ƠƠ	5
•	Nebbiolo d'Alba Ca Veja '00	ƠƠ	5
•	Dolcetto d'Alba Sorì Paitin '01	ƠƠ	4
•	Barbaresco Sorì Paitin '99	ƠƠ	7
•	Barbera d'Alba Serra Boella '01	Ơ	4
O	Roero Arneis Vigna Elisa '01	Ơ	4
•	Barbaresco Sorì Paitin '95	ƠƠƠ	7
•	Barbaresco Sorì Paitin '97	ƠƠƠ	7
•	Langhe Paitin '97	ƠƠƠ	6
•	Barbaresco Sorì Paitin '98	ƠƠ	7
•	Langhe Paitin '99	ƠƠ	6

NEIVE (CN)

Sottimano
Fraz. Cottà, 21
12057 Neive (CN)
tel. 0173635186
e-mail: sottimano@libero.it

The entire Sottimano family lends a hand on the estate. Rino and his wife Anna, with their children Andrea, Elena and even young Claudia are all hard at work. The property will grow over the next few years to about 14 hectares as new plots, totalling five and a half hectares, come onstream. The new vines include two hectares at Cottà and three and a half at the new San Cristoforo vineyard, where the first wines will be from the 2001 vintage. Over three years, annual production will grow from the present 40,000 bottles to more than 70,000, two thirds of which will be Barbaresco. Nevertheless, the most significant changes have come in terms of quality. Ruthless cutting back of yields, and Rino and Andrea's experiments with fermentation techniques and wood, have kept the improvements coming since the '95 vintage. All four '99 Barbarescos are magnificently structured but reveal distinctive personalities. For the time being, the one that best combines finesse with power is the Cottà while the elegant aromas of the Currà still let the oak show through and the Pajoré reveals a certain austerity. The Fausoni, on the other hand, is a more docile, less demanding bottle. We were also impressed by the opulent, exotic Barbera Pairolero. Like all the Sottimano's top wines, it undergoes malolactic fermentation in barrique and subsequently ages in one third new oak containers. This year, the Dolcettos were also particularly good, from the meaty, fruit-rich Cottà to the more vinous Bric del Salto. Finally, the Sottimanos release a few bottles of a fragrant dry Brachetto called Maté.

● Barbaresco Cottà '99	🍷🍷🍷	7
● Barbaresco Currà '99	🍷🍷	7
● Barbaresco Fausoni '99	🍷🍷	7
● Barbaresco Pajoré '99	🍷🍷	7
● Barbera d'Alba Pairolero '00	🍷🍷	5
● Dolcetto d'Alba Bric del Salto '01	🍷🍷	4*
● Dolcetto d'Alba Cottà '01	🍷🍷	3*
● Maté Rosso '01	🍷	3
● Barbaresco Fausoni Vigna del Salto '96	🍷🍷🍷	7
● Barbaresco Cottà Vigna Brichet '97	🍷🍷🍷	7
● Barbaresco Cottà '98	🍷🍷🍷	7
● Barbaresco Pajoré '98	🍷🍷🍷	7

NEVIGLIE (CN)

F.lli Bera
Cascina Palazzo, 12
12050 Neviglie (CN)
tel. 0173630194
e-mail: info@bera.it

Brothers Walter and Attilio Bera, aided by their parents Sisto and Maria, devote most of their production to Moscato, which accounts for 90,000 bottles out of the annual total of 110,000 they obtain from nearly 19 hectares under vine. As well as Moscato, they release a few characterful, modern-style reds to complete their admirable range. First on the list was the Langhe Sassisto, from barbera, nebbiolo and merlot. The dense colour introduces a concentrated nose of plum, bramble and hay over tobacco leaf. On the palate, the firm extract is free of rough edges and signs off with a long, caramel-themed finish. The Barbera Superiore 2000 is equally concentrated in hue and offers notes of cherry over balsam on the nose. The firm, dry palate is well sustained through to a lively finish that echoes the aromas on the nose. The straw-yellow Moscato Su Reimond unveils complex flowery notes of hedgerow on the nose, then the moderately effervescent palate is very satisfying indeed. The Asti and standard Moscato are more straightforward. The Nebbiolo is a well-structured wine with rather ripe aromas and the Bera Brut Metodo Classico '94 is moderately full-flavoured and also slightly evolved. The standard Barbera shows reasonable finesse in a fairly full-bodied palate. Finally, the undemanding Dolcetto proffers an attractively rustic nose.

● Barbera d'Alba Sup. '00	🍷🍷	4
○ Moscato d'Asti Su Reimond '01	🍷🍷	4
● Langhe Sassisto '99	🍷🍷	5
● Barbera d'Alba '00	🍷	3
○ Asti Cascina Palazzo Sel. '01	🍷	3
○ Moscato d'Asti '01	🍷	3
○ Bera Brut M. Cl. '94	🍷	5
● Dolcetto d'Alba '01	🍷	3
● Langhe Nebbiolo '98	🍷	5
● Langhe Sassisto '98	🍷🍷	5
● Barbera d'Alba Sup. '99	🍷🍷	4

NIZZA MONFERRATO (AT)

Bersano & Riccadonna
P.zza Dante, 21
14049 Nizza Monferrato (AT)
tel. 0141720211
E-mail: wine@bersano.it

The lovely Castegaro vineyard provides grapes for a wine that, in the 2001 version, is probably the best Brachetto d'Acqui the Bersano cellar has ever released. It is a superior wine with an unexpectedly vibrant ruby red hue that shades into purple. The nose foregrounds ripe berry fruit, with strawberry and black cherry dominant. In the mouth, the character, fullness and ripe fruit are undeniable, then comes the long finish, deliciously lifted by acidity and tannins that temper the underlying sweetness. Bersano is also capable of turning out great dry wines, as the Barbera d'Asti Generala and the Monferrato Pomona amply demonstrate. The former is one of the best Barbera d'Astis around, and not for the first time, with great character and a tangy, mouthfilling palate, whereas the barbera and cabernet sauvignon Pomona stands out for its vegetal hints on the nose and elegance on the palate. There was a Glass for the Barbera d'Asti Cremosina, from the property that has always been the Bersano favourite. The 2000 selection is concentrated on both nose and palate. From this year, Bersano is taking advantage of the new Nizza subzone for its Barbera d'Asti Superiore. The 2000 edition is proof positive of the winemakers' expertise with the barbera grape. The Barolo Badarina '97 comes from a vineyard at Serralunga and is well up to the austere standards of wines from that part of the Langhe. The Gavi Marchese Raggio, Erbaluce di Caluso Albaluce and the Arturo Bersano Talento "spumante" are frank and enticing, confirming just how far this long-established winery has come.

Wine	Glasses
● Barbera d'Asti Sup. Generala '00	7
● Brachetto d'Acqui Castelgaro '01	4*
● Barbera d'Asti Sup. Nizza '00	5
● Monferrato Pomona '00	7
● Barolo Badarina '97	8
● Barbera d'Asti Cremosina '00	4
○ Erbaluce di Caluso Albaluce '00	6
○ Gavi del Comune di Gavi Marchese Raggio '01	4
○ Arturo Bersano Talento Ris. M. Cl.	5
● Barbera d'Asti Sup. Generala '97	7
● Barbera d'Asti Sup. Generala '99	7
● Monferrato Pomona '99	7

NIZZA MONFERRATO (AT)

★ Cascina La Barbatella
Strada Annunziata, 55
14049 Nizza Monferrato (AT)
tel. 0141701434

Angelo Sonvico settled in Monferrato after moving from Milan. He is a food and wine buff with a particular interest in the Asti area. His sincere love of this part of Italy has made La Barbatella one of the region's leading estates for more than two decades. Angelo has earned respect the hard way, winning our Three Glass award on 11 occasions. After a year on the sidelines – the very good '99 selections missed out on a third Glass by a hair's breadth – the Sonvico stable is once again in the front rank, thanks to the Monferrato Rosso Sonvico. The 2000 edition took full advantage of the superb vintage to acquire the breadth and harmony that distinguish a true thoroughbred. Concentrated in hue, it mingles aromas of morello cherry and ripe cherry with toastiness from the oak used for ageing. The palate is austere, fruit-driven and faintly vegetal while the finish is supported by an excellent balance of acidity and tannins. Cabernet sauvignon and barbera come together with poise and harmony to produce a distinctly superior wine. The Barbera Vigna dell'Angelo is also very good, revealing a fascinatingly elegant fullness and solidity of structure. Finally, the Barbera d'Asti La Barbatella 2001 is a winner, and indeed one of the best wines in its category. The innovative Mystère, from barbera, cabernet sauvignon and pinot nero, has a subtle nose and an agreeably juicy mouthfeel while the Non è white, from cortese and sauvignon, is citrus-like and rich in fruit.

Wine	Glasses
● Monferrato Rosso Sonvico '00	8
● Barbera d'Asti Sup. Nizza Vigna dell'Angelo '00	7
○ Monferrato Bianco Non è '00	5
● Barbera d'Asti La Barbatella '01	5
● Monferrato Rosso Mystère '00	7
○ Monferrato Bianco Noè '01	5
● La Vigna di Sonvico '95	8
● Barbera d'Asti Sup. Vigna dell'Angelo '96	7
● La Vigna di Sonvico '96	8
● Monferrato Rosso Sonvico '97	8
● Barbera d'Asti Sup. Vigna dell'Angelo '98	7
● Monferrato Rosso Sonvico '98	8

NIZZA MONFERRATO (AT)

SCARPA - ANTICA CASA VINICOLA
VIA MONTEGRAPPA, 6
14049 NIZZA MONFERRATO (AT)
TEL. 0141721331
E-MAIL: casascarpa@libero.it

"Timeless" is the only adjective for the story, and the attitude, of Mario Pesce. This shrewd patriarch of winemaking in Asti is the force behind the well-known Scarpa estate, whose base and cellars are in the centre of Nizza Monferrato. Scrutiny of the list of products on sale will give you an idea of the man. Next to recent vintages, which Mario is ever wary of releasing too early, you will see wines from long ago that Scarpa keeps in the cellar for the delight of his faithful clientele. The legendary Barolo Riserva Speciale '61 may recently have run out but you'll find the '62, or the Barbarescos from 1982, through to the celebrated Rouchet Bricco Rosa '90, which won Three Glasses when our panel came to taste it. Truth to tell, things are changing. About a year ago, there was an injection of Swiss capital and a new managing director, Annamaria Zola, arrived. Mario Pesce's nephews, Mario and Carlo Castino, are increasingly involved in sales and production respectively. The range remains traditional, with all the labels that have made Scarpa famous, but there is also a perceptible effort to cater for those who look for more approachable wines. This year, we tasted a very good Rouchet Bricco Rosa 2000, a wine with a spicy nose and an austere palate, backed up by excellent structure and alcohol. The Dolcetto La Selva di Moirano 2000 is complex and balanced while the Freisa from the same vineyard and vintage is fruit-driven, with the variety's dry finish. Last on our list was the traditional Nebbiolo d'Alba, an elegant wine with fine-grained tannins.

● Rouchet Bricco Rosa '00	🍷🍷	6
● Monferrato Freisa		
La Selva di Moirano '00	🍷🍷	4
● Nebbiolo d'Alba Bric du Nota '98	🍷🍷	6
● Dolcetto d'Acqui		
La Selva di Moirano '00	🍷	4
● Rouchet Bricco Rosa '90	🍷🍷🍷	8
● Barbera d'Asti Sup.		
La Bogliona '97	🍷🍷	8
● Barbera d'Asti Sup.		
La Bogliona '98	🍷	8

NIZZA MONFERRATO (AT)

FRANCO E MARIO SCRIMAGLIO
STRADA ALESSANDRIA, 67
14049 NIZZA MONFERRATO (AT)
TEL. 0141721385 - 0141727052
E-MAIL: info@scrimaglio.it

The Scrimaglio cellar has inaugurated the new Nizza subzone with an outstanding Barbera Superiore. Not for the first time, we note the extraordinary quality of Acsé, a fantastic selection from old vines in a single plot in the Nizza Monferrato hills overlooking the municipality of Vinchio. It didn't quite earn Three Glasses but it came very close. The dense, purplish hue ushers in aromas of ripe bramble and blackcurrant, well backed up by toasty oak from cask conditioning. The palate is massive and velvet-smooth, offering an earthy note of minerals that takes you through to the lingering, pervasive finish. Tantra also scored well. It's a Monferrato Rosso from barbera and cabernet that, in the 2000 version, gives ample proof of the reliability of the Scrimaglio range. Best of the Barberas was again the Croutin selection, which enjoys leisurely ageing in bottle. The ruby red '99 has an intriguing nose with dried fruit and spice aromas. The palate offers attractive texture and a finish that is a tad austere. There was a full Glass for the Barbera Bricco Sant'Ippolito, even and persuasive in the mouth, and for Sogno, a Barbera d'Asti made by a group of Asti and Langhe-based producers. The delightful Sauvignon Bricco Sant'Ippolito stood out from the other whites. It puts balance before body but oak-derived aromas still tend to overpower the fruit. To close this review, we'll mention the Futuro, an uncomplicated, approachable One Glass white from native Monferrato varieties.

● Barbera d'Asti Sup. Acsé '00	🍷🍷	6
● Monferrato Rosso Tantra '00	🍷🍷	6
● Barbera d'Asti Sup. Croutin '99	🍷🍷	5
● Barbera d'Asti Sup		
Bricco S. Ippolito '00	🍷	4
○ Monferrato Bianco		
Bricco S. Ippolito '00	🍷	4
○ Futuro '01	🍷	3
● Barbera d'Asti Sup. Il Sogno '99	🍷	4
● Barbera d'Asti Sup. Acsé '99	🍷🍷	6
● Barbera d'Asti Sup. Acsé '98	🍷🍷	6
● Barbera d'Asti Sup. Croutin '98	🍷🍷	5
● Monferrato Rosso Tantra '99	🍷🍷	6

NOVELLO (CN)

Elvio Cogno
Via Ravera, 2
12060 Novello (CN)
tel. 0173744006
e-mail: elviocogno@elviocogno.com

Of all the Barolo municipalities, Novello looks the most off the beaten track, perhaps because there are no big name producers to give it greater visibility. Well, that may have been the case in the past but we can now safely say that such a winery exists. It is located on the Ravera "bricco", or hill, and it is the Elvio Cogno cellar, run by Walter Fissore, Nadia Cogno and her ever-active father Elvio. After a decade's hard work, annual production is about 50,000 bottles from seven hectares under vine, four planted to nebbiolo for Barolo. The white Nas-Cetta 2001, from a long neglected local variety, is interesting. It has a bright gold hue and a complex nose that ranges from apricot blossom to honey, rosemary and pepper. The balanced, tangy palate has good structure. The two Barolos are outstanding. The Ravera '98 is irresistibly gutsy, its cherry fruit mingling with notes of tobacco, leather and dry earth. The Vigna Elena '98, from a superb plot in the Ravera vineyard, is a deep, subtle wine for Barolo connoisseurs. Its notes of raspberries, tobacco and mint bring to mind certain old Brunate selections that Elvio used to make when he was at Poderi Marcarini. The endless finish features austere yet unobtrusive tannins. Two Glasses also went to the juicy, balsamic Dolcetto Vigna del Mandorlo 2001, the stylish, tangy Barbera Bricco dei Merli 2000, which finds a fine balance of wood and fruit, and the fruity, muscular Barolo-style Langhe Montegrilli 2000.

NOVI LIGURE (AL)

Il Vignale
Loc. Lomellina
Via Gavi, 130
15067 Novi Ligure (AL)
tel. 014372715
e-mail: ilvignale@ilvignale.it

The lovely estate of Piero and Vilma Cappelletti – 23 hectares of which just over ten are planted to vine – yields wines that are as congenial as the couple that make them. Most of the production is Gavi, in two versions from around eight hectares of vines. The rest of the property, comprising cabernet and pinot nero, gives the fruit for the Monferrato Rosso di Malì. We should say straight away that the 2000 vintage of this Rosso has not been released. It was produced but proved not to be up to the Cappellettis' exacting standards. The panel did retaste the '99, reviewed last year, which has found better balance, and we also tasted vat samples of the 2001. It is already showing promising structure but won't be in the shops until late 2003. But now for two serious Gavis. The Vigne Alte is the second label but still gets the full benefit of oenologist Giuseppe Bassi's attention. The nose opens on a flowery note then shifts to butter and sage. In the mouth, there is attractive freshness. A greater proportion of the Vilma Cappelletti is aged for longer in barrique, adding hints of vanilla and balsam to the wine's mint-themed freshness. The palate is well-sustained and the varietal acidity of the cortese fruit melds nicely with the substantial body, taking you through to a remarkably long finish.

● Barolo Vigna Elena '98	🍷🍷	7
● Barbera d'Alba Bricco dei Merli '00	🍷🍷	5
● Langhe Rosso Montegrilli '00	🍷🍷	5
● Dolcetto d'Alba Vigna del Mandorlo '01	🍷🍷	4*
● Barolo Ravera '98	🍷🍷	7
○ Nas-Cetta '01	🍷	4
● Barolo Vigna Elena '97	🍷🍷	7
● Barolo Ravera '95	🍷🍷	7
● Barolo Ravera '96	🍷🍷	7
● Barolo Ravera '97	🍷🍷	7
● Langhe Rosso Montegrilli '99	🍷🍷	5
● Langhe Rosso Montegrilli '98	🍷	5

○ Gavi Vigne Alte '01	🍷🍷	4*
○ Gavi Vilma Cappelletti '01	🍷🍷	4*
● Monferrato Rosso di Malì '99	🍷	5

NOVI LIGURE (AL)

Vigne del Pareto
Via Gavi, 105
15067 Novi Ligure (AL)
tel. 0108398776
e-mail: ilpareto@iol.it

The Pareto estate dates from the late 17th century and has been restored to new splendour by Pietro Occhetti. After years of painstaking renovation and modernization, it was only in 1994 that the cellar began to release Gavis obtained from the estate's historic vineyards. In the meantime, there have been new acquisitions so vines now cover 13 of the estate's 28 hectares. Two reds will available from 2002, one a monovarietal barbera and the other a blend of barbera and pinot nero. Consultant winemaker Mario Ronco helps Pareto produce about 50,000 bottles of DOCG Gavi wines a year. The standard Vigne del Pareto has a youthful, green-flecked colour and equally young aromas of flowers and citrus, which meld with red peppers, sage and mint. Thanks to only partially complete malolactic fermentation, the palate is delightfully fresh-tasting and impressively long. The Ricella Alta selection is surprisingly different. It is obtained from the estate's best-positioned vineyard, with very low yields, brief maceration on the skins and barrique conditioning. There are notes of minerals, hay and fire-cured tobacco, then the palate finds a good balance between cortese's acid freshness and the roundness that comes from the intelligent use of oak. To sum up, it's a very interesting, well-typed Gavi that shows a way forward for the DOCG zone.

○ Gavi Ricella Alta '01	♟♟	4
○ Gavi Vigne del Pareto '01	♟♟	3*

PIOBESI D'ALBA (CN)

Tenuta Carretta
Loc. Carretta, 2
12040 Piobesi d'Alba (CN)
tel. 0173619119
e-mail: t.carretta@tenutacarretta.it

The panel was happy to confirm last year's very positive impression at this splendid winery, owned by the Miroglio Dracone family. All the promises have been kept and the cellar has made great progress. It is now ready to take its place in the front rank of Roero winemaking. In addition, work on the new conference centre and hospitality facilities is almost complete, giving the estate a further string to its very robust bow. Praise for all this must go to the Carretta staff, with a special mention for Gian Domenico Negro, the enthusiastic and highly competent oenologist at the Piobesi-based winery. With Marco Monchiero, Gian Domenico has created an outstanding range of wines in which the nebbiolo grape has pride of place. The Barbaresco is extremely well interpreted. Powerful and austere in the mouth, it has sweet oak that never masks the fruit, lending harmony and complexity to the whole. The Roero Bric Paradiso is equally impressive. The slightly minerally nose is spicy, foregrounding red berry fruit, then the warm, mouthfilling palate offers great balance and a long, long finish. Both wines came within an ace of Three Glasses and the Barolo is up there with them. The grapes in the Cannubi selection ensure a characterful wine, with well-gauged tannins and great length. The 85-15 barbera and nebbiolo Rosso Bric Quercia is well-executed, as are the Dolcetto and the Roero Arneis, while the Barbera d'Alba is delightfully substantial.

● Roero Sup. Bric Paradiso '00	♟♟	5
● Barbaresco Cascina Bordino '99	♟♟	8
● Barbera d'Alba Podium Serre '00	♟♟	5
● Barolo Vigneti in Cannubi '98	♟♟	8
● Langhe Rosso Bric Quercia '00	♟	5
● Dolcetto d'Alba Vigna del Pozzo '01	♟	4
○ Roero Arneis Vigna Canorei '01	♟	5
● Roero Sup. Bric Paradiso '99	♟♟	5
● Barolo Vigneti in Cannubi '97	♟♟	8
● Barbaresco Cascina Bordino '98	♟♟	8
● Langhe Bric Quercia '98	♟♟	5
● Roero Sup. Bric Paradiso '98	♟♟	5

PORTACOMARO (AT)

Castello del Poggio
Loc. Il Poggio, 9
14038 Portacomaro (AT)
Tel. 0141202543
E-mail: info@poggio.it

We are very pleased to record yet another success from the Zonin group. The Gambellara-based winery owns estates in six of Italy's finest winemaking regions and has made its mark in Piedmont, thanks to the results of the Castello del Poggio cellar, based at Portacomaro d'Asti. This spectacular property is well worth a visit. There's a 17th-century castle that once belonged to the Templars and was also a holiday retreat for the influential bishop of Asti. It looks out onto an amphitheatre of vines that cover 140 hectares of the enchanting Valle del Tempo. Shrewd replanting, the introduction of modern technology in the cellar at the foot of the castle and the intelligent estate management of Corrado Surano have enabled Castello del Poggio to express its full potential in a few short years. We would also like to mention Piedmont-born Franco Giacosa, general manager of the group, whose skill at piecing together the various parts of the Zonin empire is increasingly obvious. The panel particularly enjoyed three convincing Barberas. The standard version is fresh and well-typed. The two first-label selections, the Bunéis – which has ten per cent merlot – and the Masaréj, are both very fruity and have great body. We gave a slightly higher score to the Masaréj. Castello del Poggio also makes a very fine Grignolino d'Asti. The 2001 edition is an excellent example of this traditional local wine type. Finally, a word of praise for the very pleasant Dolcetto del Monferrato.

• Barbera d'Asti Masaréj Gianni Zonin Vineyards '00	ㅗㅗ	5
• Piemonte Barbera Bunéis Gianni Zonin Vineyards '00	ㅗㅗ	6
• Barbera d'Asti '00	ㅗ	4
• Grignolino d'Asti '01	ㅗ	4
• Monferrato Dolcetto '01	ㅗ	4

PRIOCCA (CN)

Hilberg - Pasquero
Via Bricco Gatti, 16
12040 Priocca (CN)
Tel. 0173616197 - 0173616369
E-mail: hilberg@libero.it

Michele Pasquero has no intention of changing strategy, despite the repeated success of his wines. He is adamant that his winery at Bricco Gatti, just outside Priocca, is going to stay small. The attractive little cellar is the same as it always was, despite the fact that very buoyant demand for Michele's wines might suggest expansion. "Miclo", as he is known, continues to release about 25,000 bottles, obtained from a vine stock that covers five hectares. Helping Michele to run the winery are his determined wife, Annette Hilberg, and his mother Clementina. This efficient family team has again produced the expected range of superb wines. Awesome, as ever, is the Nebbiolo d'Alba, which confirms the impression left by last year's edition. The vibrant garnet red ushers in a clean, complex nose of oak-derived spice and red berry fruit and roses. The muscular, characterful palate signs off with a beautifully balanced finish. It all adds up to Three Glasses, and no mistake. The cellar's other flagship red, the Barbera Superiore, is an equally serious wine. The complex, pervasive nose is followed by an enviable mouthfeel, then a sweet, lingering finish. The Langhe Pedrocha, which bears the ancient name of Priocca, is an enticingly successful 60-40 blend of nebbiolo and barbera. The unusual Vareij is an admirably successful mix of 35 per cent barbera with 65 per cent brachetto. And to round off the tasting, the panel sampled the fresh, well-made basic Barbera.

• Nebbiolo d'Alba '00	ㅗㅗㅗ	6
• Barbera d'Alba Sup. '00	ㅗㅗ	6
• Langhe Rosso Pedrocha '00	ㅗㅗ	5
• Vareij Rosso '01	ㅗㅗ	4
• Barbera d'Alba '01	ㅗ	4
• Barbera d'Alba Sup. '97	ㅗㅗㅗ	6
• Barbera d'Alba Sup. '98	ㅗㅗㅗ	6
• Nebbiolo d'Alba '99	ㅗㅗㅗ	6
• Barbera d'Alba Sup. '99	ㅗㅗ	6
• Nebbiolo d'Alba '97	ㅗㅗ	6
• Nebbiolo d'Alba '98	ㅗㅗ	6

PRIOCCA (CN)

Cascina Val del Prete
Strada Santuario, 2
12040 Priocca (CN)
Tel. 0173616534
E-mail: valdelprete@tiscalinet.it

Sadly, our review this year starts with news of the recent death of Bartolomeo Roagna, the founding father of this attractive Priocca-based family estate. The example, experience and insights of "Lino" have now passed into the safe hands of Mario, who is very much aware of the role that this small but dynamic estate is able to play in promoting Roero's winemaking image. We have no doubt that Mario and the rest of the family will be able to bring further lustre to Bartolomeo's heritage. That heritage has given these Roero hills a well-deserved Three Glass wine, the splendid Nebbiolo d'Alba Vigna di Lino, named after the great man. This stylish Nebbiolo has a near-perfect nose of redcurrant and raspberries, mingling with tobacco and spices. The austere, yet assertive, palate reveals shrewdly judged tannins and great length. The most important new wine is a Roero aged for three years, on which Mario is pinning many of his hopes. He wants to focus increasingly on this major local wine type, and in time achieve a precisely defined profile in a product that will embody the territory. For the time being, we can enjoy this intriguing experiment. It's a fragrant Roero with rich notes of berry fruit and spices, a characterful palate and a lingering finish. The Barbera Carolina performed well, showing spice and almonds on the nose, then a well-rounded, alcohol-rich palate. Finally, the basic Barbera and the Arneis Luet are both well-typed and agreeable.

ROCCA GRIMALDA (AL)

Cascina La Maddalena
Loc. Piani del Padrone, 258
15078 Rocca Grimalda (AL)
Tel. 0143876074
E-mail: info@cascina-maddalena.com

Anna Poggio, Cristina Bozzano and Marilena De Gasperi are the enthusiastic trio who run this small winery near Ovada. They obtain 20,000 bottles from their five hectares, which will soon become six. They have recently acquired a new plot, at Rocca Grimalda in San Giacomo, which they will soon be planting to vine. Historically, Rocca Grimalda is a dolcetto-growing area and La Maddalena releases two wines made with the grape, a standard wine and the Bricco del Bagatto selection. The selection is aged for longer using, for the first time in 2000, one-year-old barriques. This means that we will be reviewing it in the next edition of the Guide. The second-label Dolcetto is a fairly pale ruby red and its uncomplicated nose shows hints of dry earth and wild berries. The palate has moderate texture and gutsy tannins. The Monferrato Rosso Bricco Maddalena and Barbera Rossa d'Ocra are two very interesting barbera-based wines. The garnet-ruby Bricco Maddalena has a narrow rim and an enticing nose of cakes and fruit. Full and well-sustained on the palate, it finishes on a very attractive liquorice and mint-themed note. The youthful, concentrated Rossa d'Ocra tempts with notes of cocoa powder, cherry and rosemary. Warm and substantial on the flavoursome palate, it takes its leave with a delicious reprise of the initial fruit notes.

● Nebbiolo d'Alba Vigna di Lino '00	🍷🍷🍷	5
● Barbera d'Alba Sup. Carolina '00	🍷🍷	5
● Barbera d'Alba '01	🍷🍷	4*
● Roero '99	🍷🍷	6
○ Roero Arneis Luet '01	🍷	4
● Nebbiolo d'Alba Vigna di Lino '99	🍷🍷	5
● Barbera d'Alba Sup. Carolina '97	🍷🍷	5
● Barbera d'Alba Sup. Carolina '98	🍷🍷	5
● Nebbiolo d'Alba Vigna di Lino '98	🍷🍷	5
● Roero '98	🍷🍷	6
● Barbera d'Alba Sup. Carolina '99	🍷🍷	5

● Barbera del M.to Rossa d'Ocra '00	🍷🍷	4*
● Monferrato Rosso Bricco Maddalena '00	🍷🍷	5
● Dolcetto di Ovada '01	🍷	2
● Monferrato Rosso Bricco Maddalena '98	🍷🍷	5
● Barbera del M.to Rossa d'Ocra '99	🍷🍷	4
● Dolcetto di Ovada Bricco del Bagatto '99	🍷🍷	4
● Monferrato Rosso Bricco Maddalena '99	🍷🍷	5

ROCCHETTA TANARO (AT)

Braida
Via Roma, 94
14030 Rocchetta Tanaro (AT)
tel. 0141644113
e-mail: info@braida.it

Braida was the first cellar to raise the visibility of Barbera d'Asti, thanks to that extraordinary wineman, the late Giacomo Bologna. Its high-profile labels, which earned a place among the great international wines, opened the door for the subsequent success of the Piedmontese variety and continue along the road mapped out by the founder. The Bologna family's 2000 Barberas enjoyed an excellent vintage and confirmed their class at our tastings with some very good scores indeed. The vibrant garnet-red La Bricco dell'Uccellone has a delicious nose of bramble jam and chocolate over faint minerally nuances. The firm, full palate has plenty of thrust that takes you through to the pervasive texture of the very long finish. The Ai Suma is equally concentrated in colour, revealing notes of aromatic wood and orange peel as well as the trademark varietal hints of morello cherry. The vivacious, close-knit palate ends in a leisurely finish that has yet to fully assimilate the wood. The Barbera Bricco della Bigotta was only a shade less stylish and has plenty of intensity and fullness to offer. The Moscato Vigna Senza Nome 2001 has personality, ripe, clean aromas and a tight, full-bodied mouthfeel. Good, too, are the wines from the Serra dei Fiori property, owned by the Bologna, Giacosa and Macaluso families. They include the Chardonnay Asso di Fiori 2000, the chardonnay and riesling blend, Il Fiore, and a very nice 2001 Dolcetto d'Alba.

RODELLO (CN)

F.lli Mossio
Fraz. Cascina Caramelli
Via Montà, 12
12050 Rodello (CN)
tel. 0173617149
e-mail: mossio@mossio.com

The extraordinary success last year of the Dolcetto d'Alba Bricco Caramelli, which won Three Glasses in our Guide and enthusiastic plaudits from many other reviewers, has certainly not gone to the heads of the Mossios. The lovely Rodello winery continues determinedly along its chosen path and the range of wines presented for 2002 was well up to its previous high standards. The Mossio formula is simple. It involves the scrupulous, concerted effort of the entire family. Cousins Valerio and Remo work full-time at the winery but Mauro, Guido and Claudio also lend a hand. Consultant Beppe Caviola supervises work in the cellar. The eight estate hectares are all in Rodello and yield 50,000 bottles, released under a few, excellent labels. The rustic, alcohol-rich standard Dolcetto is a very good wine but the Piano delli Perdoni and Bricco Caramelli selections, from the 2001 vintage like the basic wine, are astonishingly powerful and harmonious. The Bricco Caramelli is dense garnet, with notes of fresh grass and ripe berry fruit on the nose. The irresistibly full palate reveals its youth in the prominent tannic weave. The surprising Piano delli Perdoni is equally purplish and impenetrable in hue, then offers an intense, fruit-rich nose and a palate with firm thrust and plenty of extract. It's an outstandingly successful wine that retains its balance and velvety smoothness despite lavish alcohol. The very enjoyable barbera and nebbiolo-based Langhe Rosso 2000 only lacks a little personality and flesh in the mouth to scale the heights.

● Barbera d'Asti Ai Suma '00	♛♛	8
● Barbera d'Asti Bricco dell'Uccellone '00	♛♛	7
● Barbera d'Asti Bricco della Bigotta '00	♛♛	7
○ Moscato d'Asti Vigna Senza Nome '01	♛♛	4
○ Langhe Bianco Asso di Fiori '00	♛	5
● Monferrato Rosso Il Baciale '00	♛	4
● Brachetto d'Acqui '01	♛	4
● Dolcetto d'Alba Serra dei Fiori '01	♛	5
● Grignolino d'Asti '01	♛	4
○ Langhe Bianco Il Fiore '01	♛	4
● Barbera d'Asti Bricco dell'Uccellone '98	♛♛♛	7

● Dolcetto d'Alba Bricco Caramelli '01	♛♛	4*
● Dolcetto d'Alba Piano delli Perdoni '01	♛♛	4*
● Langhe Rosso '00	♛♛	4*
● Dolcetto d'Alba '01	♛♛	3*
● Dolcetto d'Alba Bricco Caramelli '00	♛♛♛	4
● Dolcetto d'Alba Piano delli Perdoni '00	♛♛	4

ROSIGNANO MONFERRATO (AL)

Vicara
Cascina Madonna delle Grazie, 5
15030 Rosignano Monferrato (AL)
tel. 0142488054
e-mail: vicara@vicara.it

The Vicara winery, founded by Diego Visconti, Carlo Cassinis and Domenico Ravizza, brings together the estates of the three partners at Ozzano, Salabue and Rosignano Monferrato. Production comes from a total of 15 hectares under vine and for years, the cellar has released successful versions of the local wine types. This year's offerings included a particularly delicious Barbera Superiore and Barbera Cantico della Crosia selection, both from 2000. The first is ruby shading into garnet and unveils ripe notes of plum over liquorice on the nose. It has attractive texture in the mouth, with well-defined tannins and a finish that echoes the nose and palate. Cantico della Crosia is dense in hue and tempts the nose with hints of wild berries, mint and pepper over an unobtrusive grassy note. Progression on the palate is dynamic, taking you through to a very satisfying finish. The Monferrato Rubello also performed well. In the 2000 version, this mix of barbera, nebbiolo and cabernet sauvignon flaunts very well-defined fruit, vegetal and minerally notes. There is good balance and enough structure to bring it close to the very best wines in its category. The Sarnì 2000 is a barrique-aged chardonnay with a flowery nose and good weight. The Barbera Volpuva 2001 is a gutsy, no-nonsense wine while the Airales 2001, from cortese, chardonnay and sauvignon, has fresh aromas over fruit and a light, easy-drinking palate. The typically dry Grignolino 2001 offers flower and spice aromas. Closing this year's range is the well-made 2000 Monferrato L'Uccelletta, from grignolino and pinot nero.

●	Barbera del M.to Sup. '00	♀♀	4*
●	Barbera del M.to Sup. Cantico della Crosia '00	♀♀	5
●	Monferrato Rubello '00	♀♀	5
○	Monferrato Sarnì '00	♀	6
●	Barbera del M.to Volpuva '01	♀	3*
○	Monferrato Airales '01	♀	3*
●	Monferrato L'Uccelletta '00	♀	4
●	Grignolino del M.to Casalese '01		4
●	Monferrato Rosso Rubello '97	♀♀	5
●	Barbera del M.to Sup. Cantico della Crosia '98	♀♀	5
●	Barbera del M.to Sup. Cantico della Crosia '99	♀♀	5

SAN GIORGIO CANAVESE (TO)

Orsolani
Via Michele Chiesa, 12
10090 San Giorgio Canavese (TO)
tel. 012432386
e-mail: orsolani@tiscalinet.it

The Orsolani winery dates back to the late 19th century, when Gigi's great-grandfather Giovanni opened a hostelry in the Canavese area and began to make wine to sell at the bar. Today, the cellar is one of the leading producers in the province of Turin and beyond. Gigi Orsolani oversees winemaking with the assistance of consultant Donato Lanati. The products are the classics of the Canavese, with emphasis on the erbaluce grape. The range starts with two still Erbaluce selections, the Rustìa and the Sant'Antonio, and continues with the "spumante" sparklers and the dried-grape Caluso Passito. For the past two years, Gigi has been diversifying the range with a structured red, again from the Canavese DOC, the Carema. But let's talk about the wines. Excellent as ever, but this year with even more fullness, is the La Rustìa 2001. A classic Erbaluce, it regales the nose with ripe fruit, piquant notes and minerals that bring to mind sun-scorched grapeskins. The tangy, mouthfilling palate offers an elegant and very long finish. The Vignot Sant'Antonio, also excellent in its 2000 version, leaves more room for the oak to come through. Another successful wine is the Carema Le Tabbie '97, with persuasive spice on the nose and an austere palate with delicious tannins. The Passito Sulé keeps up these high standards, in fact it's the best in the DOC zone. Finally, there was a Glass for the Spumante Cuvée Storica Gran Riserva '97, which is more high-spirited than previous editions.

○	Caluso Bianco Vignot S. Antonio '00	♀♀	4*
○	Erbaluce di Caluso La Rustìa '01	♀♀	4*
○	Caluso Passito Sulé '97	♀♀	7
●	Carema Le Tabbie '97	♀♀	6
○	Cuvée Storica Spumante M. Cl. Gran Ris. '97	♀	5
○	Erbaluce di Caluso La Rustìa '00	♀♀	4
○	Caluso Passito Sulé '96	♀♀	7
●	Carema Le Tabbie '96	♀	6

SAN MARTINO ALFIERI (AT)

Marchesi Alfieri
P.zza Alfieri, 32
14010 San Martino Alfieri (AT)
tel. 0141976015
e-mail: latota@tin.it

The winery, owned by Giovanna, Antonella and Emanuela San Martino di San Germano, and competently run by oenologist Mario Olivero with the external consultancy of Giancarlo Scaglione, is currently expanding. Two new hectares of barbera are gradually coming onstream, bringing the total vine stock to 20 hectares. Barbera is the flagship wine and the Alfiera shows how good it can get. The 2000 is dense garnet, revealing warm notes that range from crushed wild berries to liquorice and balsam. There's plenty of fullness on the well-sustained palate and a note of tobacco emerges in the leisurely finish. This wine of breathtaking finesse again deservedly wins Three Glasses. The dense-hued Barbera La Tota is well-made, tempting the nose with hints of cakes and berry fruit. Its gutsy character emerges on a palate that also shows appreciable length. There are some very interesting results from the attention the estate is dedicating to Grignolino, vinified with an initial cold maceration that enables selective extraction, by reducing maceration times during fermentation, and yields more prominent aromas. The Sansoero 2001 has warm notes of pepper and flowers, then the close-knit full-bodied palate ends with a satisfying finish. The Pinot Nero San Germano, slightly austere on the palate, has a well-typed nose. Finally, the barbera and pinot nero Rosso dei Marchesi is a good wine, as is the riesling italico-based Bianco dei Marchesi.

●	Barbera d'Asti Sup. Alfiera '00	▼▼▼	6
●	Barbera d'Asti La Tota '00	▼▼	4*
●	Piemonte Grignolino Sansoero '01	▼▼	4*
●	Monferrato Rosso S. Germano '99	▼▼	5
●	Monferrato Rosso dei Marchesi '00	▼	3
○	Monferrato Bianco dei Marchesi '01	▼	3
●	Barbera d'Asti Sup. Alfiera '99	▼▼▼	6
●	Monferrato Rosso S. Germano '97	▼▼	5
●	Barbera d'Asti Sup. Alfiera '98	▼▼	6

SAN MARZANO OLIVETO (AT)

Alfiero Boffa
Via Leiso, 50
14050 San Marzano Oliveto (AT)
tel. 0141856115
e-mail: alfieroboffa@tin.it

Rossano Boffa and his father Alfiero have again turned out a very convincing series of delicious Barberas, each with a personality of its own. These are Barberas made with fruit from superbly positioned and, above all, very old vines that yield very little, but extremely concentrated, fruit. Some of the plots date from the 1950s and La Riva was planted as long ago as 1930. The intense garnet-ruby La Riva selection delivers a nose of cherry and dust over faint balsamic notes. Very convincing in the mouth, where the full body sustains the follow-through, it shows subtly understated tannins and a very long, warm finish. Only a whisper less concentrated in hue is the 2000 Cua Longa, with its aromas of almond paste, autumn leaves and very ripe fruit. The stylish palate is well-balanced, building up to a lingering finish that is veined with liquorice and fruit. The Vigna delle More is interesting for its citrus nuances over fruit and soft, full-bodied texture in the mouth, as well as a generous finish. The Collina della Vedova '99 has a close-knit hue and a nose where hints of cakes come through, together with green notes. The pleasing palate is a little lightweight but nonetheless satisfying. We conclude with the Muntrivé 2000, which reveals berry fruit aromas and decent weight on the palate, which is laced with a hint of tanginess.

●	Barbera d'Asti Sup. Vigna Cua Longa '00	▼▼	4*
●	Barbera d'Asti Sup. Vigna delle More '00	▼▼	4*
●	Barbera d'Asti Sup. Vigna La Riva '99	▼▼	5
●	Barbera d'Asti Sup. Collina della Vedova '99	▼	5
●	Barbera d'Asti Sup. Vigna Muntrivé '00	▼	4
●	Barbera d'Asti Sup. Collina della Vedova '98	▼▼	5
●	Velo di Maya '98	▼▼	5

SAN MARZANO OLIVETO (AT)

Tenuta dell'Arbiola
Loc. Arbiola
Reg. Saline, 56
14050 San Marzano Oliveto (AT)
tel. 0141856194 - 0115187122
e-mail: arbiola@tin.it

The Terzano family's winery is improving fast, thanks to the decision to go for quality. The wines are ever more crisply defined, for which much of the credit must go to the expert help of Beppe Caviola in the cellar and Federico Curtaz in the vineyard. There were two newcomers waiting for us in this year's range, the Arbiola Bianco and the Chardonnay Clelie VI. The sauvignon and chardonnay Arbiola Bianco is rich straw yellow, shading into gold. On the nose, it unveils attractive tomato leaf, pears and apples against a teasing backdrop of Mediterranean herbs. The generous alcohol emerges on the substantial palate and the finish is full. Although enjoyable and full-bodied, the chardonnay-based Monferrato Bianco Clelie has still to come to terms with the wood. From the 2000 vintage, the Monferrato Rosso has added Arbiola to its name. Its intense garnet introduces a nose of plum and autumn leaves over intriguing minerally nuances. On the palate, the full body and assertive tannins call the shots. The Barbera Romilda VI 2000 is the first version released under the new Nizza subzone. Another densely hued wine, it has a nose of toastiness and black berry fruit nuanced with balsamic notes and a concentrated, lingering palate. Less demanding is the straightforward Carlotta selection, with fruit and vanilla aromas and a roughish acidic edge on the palate. The Moscato d'Asti Ferlingot 2001 is a buttery, ripe interpretation of the variety. It's a wine to bank on and a must-have for lovers of this sweet, aroma-rich grape.

● Barbera d'Asti Sup. Nizza Romilda VI '00	ŶŶ	6
● Monferrato Rosso Arbiola '00	ŶŶ	5
○ Moscato d'Asti Ferlingot '01	ŶŶ	3*
○ Monferrato Bianco Arbiola '01	ŶŶ	5
● Barbera d'Asti Carlotta '00	Ŷ	4
○ Monferrato Bianco Clelie VI '01	Ŷ	4
● Barbera d'Asti Sup. La Romilda V '99	ŶŶ	6
● Monferrato Rosso Dom '99	ŶŶ	5

SANTO STEFANO BELBO (CN)

Ca' d'Gal
Fraz. Valdivilla
Satrada Vecchia, 108
12058 Santo Stefano Belbo (CN)
tel. 0141847103

Assisted by his parents, Rina and Riccardo, and by wife Carla, Alessandro Boido tends an estate of eight hectares, six under vine, and releases each year a total of 42,000 bottles. Most of Ca' d'Gal's production is vinified from moscato, which is very much at home in Santo Stefano Belbo. And there's is an exciting newcomer among the Moscatos this year, the Lumine. Serious crop thinning has given us a full-bodied, crisply defined wine. Fairly intense in hue, it shows great finesse on the nose, where pears and orange blossom emerge. The firm, fleshy palate has lovely balance, the prickle providing a perfect counterweight to the distinct vein of sweetness. In the cellar's strategy, Lumine will gradually replace the standard Moscato, Vigneti Ca' d'Gal. The leading label is still Moscato Vigna Vecchia, though. The 2001 edition displays a rich colour and a ripe nose of peach, elderflower, pears and apples. Its rich mouthfeel makes it one of the best Moscatos around. The standard Moscato offers less complexity and concentration. The line-up is completed by a juicy Dolcetto with a slightly rustic personality and two uncomplicated whites. Unfortunately, the Chardonnay Pian del Gaje was not yet ready at the time of our tasting.

○ Moscato d'Asti Lumine '01	ŶŶ	4*
○ Moscato d'Asti Vigna Vecchia '01	ŶŶ	4*
○ Moscato d'Asti Vigneti Ca' d'Gal '01	Ŷ	3
● Dolcetto d'Alba '01	Ŷ	3
○ Langhe Bianco '01	Ŷ	4
○ Langhe Chardonnay '01	Ŷ	3

SANTO STEFANO BELBO (CN)

Piero Gatti
Loc. Moncucco, 28
12058 Santo Stefano Belbo (CN)
tel. 0141840918

Rita Gatti looks after her small family winery very competently, producing just over 50,000 bottles every year. Technical consultancy is provided by oenologist Sergio Stella, who has been working at the cellar since 1988. Here on the hills of Santo Stefano Belbo the moscato grape is king and this year the Piemonte Moscato dei Gatti earned its Two Glasses for a clean, intense nose and the well-balanced fullness of its palate. The moderately intense straw yellow introduces a nose with attractive hints of ripe peach and elderflower, with faint nuances of banana adding sweetness. The bright prickle offsets the sweet residual sugar on the seamlessly well-sustained palate, which ends on a delightful note of fruit. The Verbeia 2000 is an 80-20 mix of barbera and freisa. The fairly close-knit garnet ruby introduces a nose that ranges from flowery notes through to sweet wild berries. The good weight on the palate is lifted by crisp acidity and nicely judged tannins that accompany the unhurried finish. The dense hue of the Freisa La Violetta precedes berry fruit, hay and autumn leaves on the nose, then the very drinkable palate is rendered slightly aggressive by the combination of acidity and varietal tannins. Last on the list is the Brachetto, which has a slightly evolved nose and decent body.

●	Verbeia '00	♛♛	4*
○	Piemonte Moscato '01	♛♛	4*
●	Langhe Freisa La Violetta '00	♛	4
●	Piemonte Brachetto '01	♛	4

SANTO STEFANO BELBO (CN)

Sergio Grimaldi - Ca' du Sindic
Loc. San Grato, 15
12058 Santo Stefano Belbo (CN)
tel. 0141840341
e-mail: grimaldi.sergio@virgilio.it

Sergio Grimaldi is ably assisted by his father, Ilario, and wife Angela. In fact, his elder son is also a wine enthusiast and currently studies at the wine school in Alba. Sergio is gradually extending his estate, which small purchases and new plantings have taken to a total area under vine of about ten hectares. Moscato d'Asti, the most important wine in these parts, demands excellent quality fruit and technology in the cellar, a point that Sergio has not overlooked. Each year, he acquires some new item of cellar equipment. The Moscato Ca' du Sindic Capsula Oro comes from an old vineyard in a marvellous position on the hill of San Maurizio. Its vibrant straw yellow is flecked with gold and there is breadth on the nose, with its intense tropical fruit and orange blossom. The attack is full-bodied and buttery, the attractive prickle perking up the palate and the long finish nicely reflecting the nose. Moscato Capsula Argento is a shade less challenging but very well-executed, elderflower aromas taking you into a tidy, well-balanced palate. Sergio's Barbera d'Asti is from a small plot in the municipality of San Marzano Oliveto. Sweet and fairly complex on the nose, it unveils raspberry and mint over crushed flowers, then a juicy palate with a softish mouthfeel. The 2001 Brachetto and Barbera Vivace are straightforward, well-made wines.

●	Barbera d'Asti '00	♛♛	4*
○	Moscato d'Asti Ca' du Sindic Capsula Oro '01	♛♛	4*
○	Moscato d'Asti Ca' du Sindic Capsula Argento '01	♛	3
●	Piemonte Barbera Vivace '01	♛	3
●	Piemonte Brachetto Ca' du Sindic '01	♛	4

SANTO STEFANO BELBO (CN)

I Vignaioli di S. Stefano
Fraz. Marini, 12
12058 Santo Stefano Belbo (CN)
Tel. 0141840419
E-mail: ivignaioli@virgilio.it

Santo Stefano Belbo is smack in the middle of the production zone for Asti and Moscato d'Asti, and the natural point of reference for all admirers of these wines. The hills around the town, where Cesare Pavesi set his celebrated novels and short stories, are covered with the moscato vines from which the I Vignaioli di Santo Stefano obtain the fruit for their premium wines. The cellar's admirable work produces about 180,000 bottles a year from about 40 hectares under vine. The range is not extensive – it covers only three types – but the average level of quality is more than satisfying. We'll begin with Piemonte Moscato Passito IL '99. A rich straw yellow with golden highlights ushers in delicious aromas of ripe fruit, sugar glazing and walnut. The sweet, soft mouthfeel never cloys, thanks to elegant structure, building up to long finish that mirrors the sugar of the nose. The Asti Spumante 2001 is equally impressive. The intense straw-yellow accompanies a fresh, attractively fruity nose. In the mouth, it is round, clean and even through to the long finish, which is backed up by refreshing effervescence. Finally, the panel sampled the Moscato d'Asti. The lively hue is complemented by crisp berry fruit mingling with peaches, apricot and citrus. The round, rich palate has just the right note of acidity and a sweet note that lingers through to the leisurely, soft finish. Fruit returns on the back palate.

○ Asti '01	🍷🍷	4
○ Piemonte Moscato Passito IL '99	🍷🍷	6
○ Moscato d'Asti '01	🍷	4

SAREZZANO (AL)

Mutti
Loc. San Ruffino, 49
15050 Sarezzano (AL)
Tel. 0131884119

The Mutti estate is a Guide regular that presents the panel with exciting, reliable wines every year. In recent vintages, Andrea Mutti has made some of the finest Colli Tortonesi Timorasso wines, from the local variety of the same name, as it was our pleasure to confirm when we tasted the Castagnoli selection. The difficulties faced by producers of Timorasso in vineyard and cellar only add to our admiration of those who tackle this very cellarable white. The 2000 edition released this year is lip-smackingly good. Intense on the nose, it shows mineral and chalk notes before apricot and melon emerge. Vigorous but unassertive, it warms the palate with its complex flavours and delightful fragrance. A wine that comes from profound knowledge of the territory, as well as Andrea's agronomic skills, is the Sauvignon Sull'Aia. It's unusual to find this wine in the Colli Tortonesi but here we have a version with ripe aromas of tropical fruit and figs, then a fresh-tasting palate with good depth and attractive length. There's also a barbera-based Colli Tortonesi named after the San Ruffino vineyard. Fruit from the low-yielding plot is aged in small oak barrels, lending the wine a magnificent ruby red hue. Tobacco and morello cherry on the nose are followed by a serious palate of ripe berry fruit. The wine from cabernet sauvignon is called Rivadestra. Vibrant and dark, it shows a plum jam and almond nose. Less structured but still worth investigating is the Dolcetto Zerba Soprana.

○ Colli Tortonesi Bianco Timorasso Castagnoli '00	🍷🍷	4*
● Colli Tortonesi Rosso S. Ruffino '00	🍷🍷	5
○ Colli Tortonesi Bianco Sull'Aia '01	🍷🍷	4*
● Colli Tortonesi Rosso Rivadestra '00	🍷	5
● Colli Tortonesi Dolcetto Zerba Soprana '01	🍷	3
● Colli Tortonesi Rosso Rivadestra '98	🍷🍷	5
● Colli Tortonesi Rosso Rivadestra '99	🍷🍷	5

SCURZOLENGO (AT)

Cantine Sant'Agata
Reg. Mezzena, 19
14030 Scurzolengo (AT)
tel. 0141203186
e-mail: info@santagata.com

With the help of their parents, Franco and Claudio Cavallero produce 130,000 bottles a year from 12 hectares under vine and some bought-in grapes. The rather extensive range is dominated by Barbera and Ruché, an aromatic local variety much-admired on the hills that look from Asti look towards Casale and, especially Castagnole Monferrato. Best of the Barberas is the Cavalé, which has a particularly well-defined nose and good weight in the mouth. Its intense garnet ruby introduces a nose of cherry, bramble and autumn leaves. On the well-sustained palate, the good weave carries through to a long, liquorice-themed finish. The Altea shows flowers and smoky notes on the nose, then acidic grip and a faintly bitterish finish in the mouth. The Piatin '99 is again very good and the Monferrato Genesi, from raisined barbera and ruché, is more than just interesting. Its close-knit hue offers tar, ripe cherry and dried flowers, then the palate reveals concentration, sinew and solid structure. The Ruché di Castagnole Monferrato 'Na Vota has a typical aromatic note of spices and roses, then a tidy, very drinkable palate. The 2001 vintage also sees the release of the Pro Nobis, from 20-year-old vines. The concentrated depth of the nose tempts with nuances of flowers, fruit and cakes. Characterful on the palate, it flaunts prominent tannins and admirable length. Finally, there was a well-earned Glass each for the Bianco Eliseo, from 60 per cent chardonnay and 40 per cent cortese, the well-typed Grignolino d'Asti and the pleasing Barbera Piatin.

●	Ruché di Castagnole M.to Pro Nobis '01	ŸŸ	5
●	Monferrato Rosso Genesi '98	ŸŸ	6
●	Barbera d'Asti Sup. Cavalé '99	ŸŸ	5
●	Barbera d'Asti Sup. Piatin '99	Ÿ	4
●	Grignolino d'Asti Miravalle '01	Ÿ	3*
○	Monferrato Bianco Eliseo '01	Ÿ	4
●	Ruché di Castagnole M.to 'Na Vota '01	Ÿ	4
●	Barbera d'Asti Sup. Altea '99	Ÿ	3*
●	Ruché di Castagnole M.to 'Na Vota '00	ŸŸ	4
●	Monferrato Rosso Genesi '97	ŸŸ	6
●	Barbera d'Asti Sup. Cavalé '98	ŸŸ	5

SERRALUNGA D'ALBA (CN)

Luigi Baudana
Fraz. Baudana, 43
12050 Serralunga d'Alba (CN)
tel. 0173613354
e-mail: luigibaudana@bdv-serralunga.com

In this delightful little cellar, where time seems to have stood still, Fiorina and Luigi Baudana produce more than 25,000 bottles a year. They tend their five or so hectares with what can only be described as passion. This year's reds are delicious while the two well-made whites earned just One Glass. Both the standard Dolcetto and the Sörì Baudana gained a second Glass. The first, drinking well already, has good ripe fruit and nice structure but the Sörì has more breadth to its slightly balsamic aromas and chewy fruit in the mouth. The Langhe Lorenso and Barbera Donatella, both from 2000, are distinctly international in style. The Lorenso, a blend of nebbiolo, barbera and merlot, delicately mingles vanilla and herbs on the nose, then the impressively concentrated palate shows sweet tannins. In contrast, the Barbera is a tad ruffled, its toastiness having yet to meld with the varietal fruit. Good balance and close-knit tannins, as well as generous body, make the palate more convincing. Pride of place, however, must go the Barolo Cerretta Piani. The '98 has a deep, dark hue and breadth on a nose reminiscent of raspberry, then fennel, then vanilla again. Depth of fruit and attractive length on the palate make this a stylish but characterful wine. A notch lower comes the well-typed Barolo '98, with hints of cocoa powder and rugged tannins.

●	Barolo Cerretta Piani '98	ŸŸ	7
●	Barbera d'Alba Donatella '00	ŸŸ	5
●	Dolcetto d'Alba '01	ŸŸ	3*
●	Dolcetto d'Alba Sörì Baudana '01	ŸŸ	4*
●	Barolo '98	ŸŸ	6
●	Langhe Rosso Lorenso '00	ŸŸ	5
○	Langhe Chardonnay '01	Ÿ	3
○	Langhe Bianco Lorenso '00	Ÿ	4
●	Langhe Rosso Lorenso '99	ŸŸ	5
●	Barolo Cerretta Piani '96	ŸŸ	7
●	Barolo Cerretta Piani '97	ŸŸ	7
●	Langhe Rosso Lorenso '98	ŸŸ	5
●	Barbera d'Alba Donatella '99	ŸŸ	5

SERRALUNGA D'ALBA (CN)

Cascina Cucco
Via Mazzini, 10
12050 Serralunga d'Alba (CN)
tel. 0173613003

As you go up to Serralunga, you will see on your left, just under the castle, the lovely Cascina Cucco, renovated not long ago and now equipped with the best in winemaking technology. It has belonged to the Stroppiana family for more than 30 years but it has only recently adopted a quality-first strategy, under the watchful eye of consultant Beppe Caviola. There are 11 hectares under vine, eight of which – still not in full production – are planted to nebbiolo for Barolo. Four are in the Cerrati vineyard, two in Cucco and two in Vughera. The remaining three hectares are planted to chardonnay, dolcetto and barbera. Cascina Cucco wines are improving fast and the next few years could bring us some very pleasant surprises. The lovely violet-flecked purple of the Dolcetto Vughera 2001 introduces a youthfully vinous nose. Hints of bramble are echoed in the mouth and supported by hard, slightly bitterish tannins. The Barbera d'Alba 2000 stays in barrique for a year longer. Its nose of bottled cherries is veiled by toasty oak and followed by warm, powerful body on the palate. Both Barolos did very well. The Cerrati '98 has a richer hue and a personality driven by the terroir of Serralunga. Rich fruit melds with liquorice, tobacco and spices, and dry tannins perk up the firm flavour. Paler in colour, the Cucco is subtle and intense, the complex nose of vanilla pepper, rosemary and incense ushering in a long palate, where the tannins are rather assertive.

SERRALUNGA D'ALBA (CN)

Fontanafredda
Via Alba, 15
12050 Serralunga d'Alba (CN)
tel. 0173613161
e-mail: fontanafredda@fontanafredda.it

Gian Minetti, the Fontanafredda manager, and Danilo Drocco, in charge of the technical side, continue to work tirelessly at this magnificent estate, which is owned by the Monte dei Paschi di Siena bank. The main offices at Serralunga, always ready to welcome visitors, send a range of good to very good wines all over the world. The vineyards have been replanted and the estate has a clear strategy, symbolized in the new label design and bottle style. In short, Fontanafredda aims for wines that can be enjoyed in the short term whereas in the past, the line imposed by the highly skilled former technical director, Livio Testa, produced bottles that required lengthy cellaring. Proof can be found in the exquisite Fontanafredda Barolos from 1978, 1982, 1985 and especially the fabulous 1958, which we were lucky enough to retaste recently. The Lazzarito is the only Barolo aged entirely in new wood, as toasty notes on nose and palate tell you. But the La Rosa wins Fontanafredda's first Three Glasses. Ruby red, with delicious aromas of roses and spices, it is as austere and mouthfilling as a truly great Barolo should be. Both other Le Vigne selections, the La Villa-Paiagallo and La Delizia, are excellent. The Barolo Serralunga is less demanding but very agreeable and great value for money. The Barbera d'Alba Papagena is a paragon. The Diano d'Alba La Lepre easily won the Two Glasses it has regularly obtained in recent years and the Barbaresco Coste Rubìn is a sophisticatedly satisfying red. Finally, we tasted the austere Nebbiolo d'Alba Marne Brune and the Brut Alta Langa.

● Barolo Vigna Cerrati '98	🍷🍷	7
● Barolo Vigna Cucco '98	🍷🍷	7
● Barbera d'Alba '00	🍷	5
● Dolcetto d'Alba Vughera '01	🍷	4
● Barolo Vigna Cucco '97	🍷🍷	7
● Barolo Vigna Cerrati '97	🍷	7

● Barolo Vigna La Rosa '98	🍷🍷🍷	8
● Barolo Vigna Lazzarito '98	🍷🍷	8
● Barolo Vigna La Delizia '98	🍷🍷	8
● Barbera d'Alba Sup. Papagena '00	🍷🍷	5
● Diano d'Alba Vigna La Lepre '01	🍷🍷	4*
○ Piemonte Alta Langa Talento Brut '96	🍷🍷	6
● Barolo Vigna La Villa-Paiagallo '98	🍷🍷	8
● Barbaresco Coste Rubìn '99	🍷🍷	6
● Nebbiolo d'Alba Marne Brune '00	🍷	4
● Barolo Serralunga d'Alba '98	🍷	6*
● Barolo Vigna La Rosa '97	🍷🍷	8
● Barolo Vigna La Delizia '97	🍷🍷	8
● Barolo Vigna Lazzarito '97	🍷🍷	8

SERRALUNGA D'ALBA (CN)

GABUTTI - FRANCO BOASSO
B.TA GABUTTI, 3/A
12050 SERRALUNGA D'ALBA (CN)
TEL. 0173613165
E-MAIL: gabutti.boasso@libero.it

Franco Boasso's winery is right in the centre of Serralunga, at the bottom of the road leading to the Gabutti vineyard, past the hamlet of Parafada. Currently, Boasso releases 30,000 bottles a year from six hectares under vine, all in the municipality of Serralunga, at Gabutti, Meriame, Gombe and Serra. The 2001 vintage is regarded as excellent and Franco is very pleased with the wines. He was quick to offer us a sample of Gabutti nebbiolo from the barrel. This promising, fruit-led wine has depth and complexity, and will be released as a Barolo in three years' time. The Dolcetto Meriame 2001 is another biggie. Dark, violet-flecked purple red in hue, it proffers clean, alcohol-rich notes of plum jam, balsamic herbs and violets. The fruit follows through onto the palate, which has enough juicy flesh to withstand the hard tannins that are characteristic in these parts. Less ready for drinking, at least when the panel tasted it, the Barbera 2001 has a superb dark purple red colour with bright, vibrant highlights. The nose is less fascinating as the oak still masks the fruit and the hard palate reveals distinct acidity that threatens the lovely fruit in the finish. Finally, there are two Barolos, the Gabutti '98 and the Serralunga '98. Tasting blind, of course, the panel preferred the depth of aroma and warm, intense drinkability of the Gabutti, with its raspberry, dried rose, leather and minty herb nuances, to the Serralunga, which is a tad one-dimensional and astringent.

● Dolcetto d'Alba Meriame '01	ŸŸ	4*
● Barolo Gabutti '98	ŸŸ	7
● Barbera d'Alba '01	Ÿ	4
● Barolo Serralunga '98	Ÿ	6
● Barolo Gabutti '90	ŸŸ	7
● Barolo Gabutti '96	ŸŸ	7
● Barolo '97	ŸŸ	6
● Barolo Gabutti '97	ŸŸ	7
● Barolo Gabutti '95	Ÿ	7

SERRALUNGA D'ALBA (CN)

ETTORE GERMANO
LOC. CERRETTA, 1
12050 SERRALUNGA D'ALBA (CN)
TEL. 0173613528
E-MAIL: germanoettore@germanoettore.it

Sergio Germano and his father, Ettore, one of the best vine grafters in the Langhe, now tend about seven hectares, mainly in Serralunga, and produce almost 50,000 bottles a year. There are three '98 Barolos but it is the magnificent, and unusually distinctive, Cerretta that takes Three Glasses. The close-knit garnet red is impenetrable, then the wine's depth and complexity come through in notes of leather, cocoa and ripe fruit. Muscle power and length are obvious on a palate that reveals a perfect marriage of fruit from this marvellous Serralunga vineyard with top-notch technique in cellar and vineyard. The stylish standard spice and mint-nuanced Barolo is very convincing. However, the balsamic notes and hard mouthfeel of the Prapò show that it still has to mellow out the rough edges typical of Barolos from Serralunga. When we moved on to the more approachable wines, we particularly liked the Binel 2000, an unusual mix of chardonnay and riesling that flaunts quite a personality. A golden wine with delicious notes of lime blossom on the nose, it holds up well in the mouth thanks to great structure and lovely balance. Good as ever were the Barbera Vigna della Madre and the Langhe Balàu, both 2000 vintages aged in small oak casks. The concentrated colour of the Barbera precedes stylish fruit peeking out from beneath the oak while the dark, vibrant-hued Balàu, a blend of 65 per cent dolcetto, 25 per cent barbera and merlot, shows punchy tannins and a finish that focuses on blueberry and liquorice. Lastly, we tasted the juicy Dolcetto Pra di Po' and the nice Chardonnay 2001.

● Barolo Cerretta '98	ŸŸŸ	7
● Barbera d'Alba Vigna della Madre '00	ŸŸ	5
○ Langhe Bianco Binel '00	ŸŸ	4*
● Langhe Rosso Balàu '00	ŸŸ	5
● Barolo '98	ŸŸ	6*
● Barolo Prapò '98	ŸŸ	7
● Dolcetto d'Alba Vigneto Pra di Pò '01	Ÿ	4
○ Langhe Chardonnay '01	Ÿ	4
● Barbera d'Alba Vigna della Madre '99	ŸŸ	5
● Barolo Cerretta '96	ŸŸ	7
● Barolo Cerretta '97	ŸŸ	7
● Barolo Prapò '97	ŸŸ	7

SERRALUNGA D'ALBA (CN)

Luigi Pira
Via XX Settembre, 9
12050 Serralunga d'Alba (CN)
Tel. 0173613106

In the centre of Serralunga, you will find the historic Luigi Pira cellar. It has only been bottling on-site since 1995, when it ceased to sell wine unbottled. Giampaolo is just over 30 years old. With the help of his brother Romolo and father Luigi, as well as consultancy from Beppe Caviola, he looks after seven hectares of vineyard to produce about 40,000 bottles, half of them Barolo. The standard version ages in large barrels, as does 70 per cent of the Margheria (the rest goes into barrique), the Marenca matures in barrique and tonneaux, and the 900 splendid bottles of Vigna Rionda age exclusively in new barriques. The '98s are exceptionally good. The standard version is typically Serralungaesque, with its cocoa powder, tobacco, spice and mint aromas. The palate is equally classic, revealing hard tannins that lead through to the long finish. The Vigneto Margheria is much darker. The boisterous nose throws serious fruit, lifted by spice and balsamic notes that pervade the palate. The finish is very long and even elegant. Finally, the Vigneto Marenca is markedly more powerful than the previous two. Its sombre hue ushers in notes of chocolate, vanilla and fruit jam, then the palate thrills to the warmth and power of the hard tannins. A further Two Glasses went to the very nice Dolcetto 2001. Vibrant purple, it has yet open but the nose shows earthy and balsamic aromas. Although still hard, the palate has enough pulp and alcohol already to be very enjoyable.

● Barolo Vigneto Marenca '98	🍷🍷	8
● Barolo Vigneto Margheria '98	🍷🍷	8
● Dolcetto d'Alba '01	🍷🍷	3*
● Barolo '98	🍷🍷	7
● Barolo Vigneto Marenca '97	🍷🍷🍷	8
● Barolo Vigneto Marenca '95	🍷🍷	8
● Barolo Vigneto Marenca '96	🍷🍷	8
● Barolo Vigneto Margheria '96	🍷🍷	8
● Barolo Vigneto Margheria '97	🍷🍷	8

SERRALUNGA D'ALBA (CN)

Vigna Rionda - Massolino
P.zza Cappellano, 8
12050 Serralunga d'Alba (CN)
Tel. 0173613138
E-mail: vignarionda@libero.it

The years pass and Massolino wines get better, perhaps because yields are now lower and much effort has been lavished on the vineyards. The two and a half hectares planted to nebbiolo at Vigna Rionda give the best grapes, which go into the Barolo Riserva. Released two years later than the other wines, the '96 this time persuaded the panel to part with Three Glasses. Vinified traditionally, it macerates on the skins for 20 days and then spends three and a half years in large barrels. Taste it and savour perfection. Broad jam and spice aromas usher in a palate that combines power and depth with elegant softness. Sweet, close-knit tannins carry the palate to the leisurely finish. The lingering Margheria was the panel's favourite from the three '98 Barolos. Raspberry aromas and concentration in the mouth put it ahead of the more modern vanilla and chocolate Parafada, a soft wine with a rather straightforward finish. There were two more Glasses for the berry fruit and mint of the balanced basic Barolo. A blend of 20 per cent cabernet with equal parts of nebbiolo and barbera produces the Langhe Piria, a soft, sweet wine in the '99 version. You'd hardly think it came from Serralunga. The Dolcetto Barilot 2001 is very good. Its vibrant, dark hue introduces cherry, liquorice and autumn leaves on the nose, then the palate reveals weight and personality. The uncomplicated Dolcetto and Barbera 2001 are good, as are the austere Nebbiolo '99, the Chardonnay 2000 and the rich Moscato 2001. The Barbera Gisep 2000 will be released next year.

● Barolo Vigna Rionda Ris. '96	🍷🍷🍷	8
● Barolo Margheria '98	🍷🍷	7
● Dolcetto d'Alba Barilot '01	🍷🍷	4
● Barolo '98	🍷🍷	6
● Barolo Parafada '98	🍷🍷	7
● Langhe Rosso Piria '99	🍷🍷	6
○ Langhe Chardonnay '00	🍷	4
○ Moscato d'Asti di Serralunga '01	🍷	4
● Barbera d'Alba '01	🍷	3
● Dolcetto d'Alba '01	🍷	3
● Langhe Nebbiolo '99	🍷	4
● Barolo Parafada Ris. '90	🍷🍷🍷	8
● Barolo Vigna Rionda Ris. '90	🍷🍷🍷	8
● Barolo Parafada '96	🍷🍷🍷	7

SERRALUNGA DI CREA (AL)

Tenuta La Tenaglia
Via Santuario di Crea, 6
15020 Serralunga di Crea (AL)
tel. 0142940252
e-mail: info@latenaglia.com

After 20 years of winemaking, and after having given this lovely Monferrato estate a well-defined personality of its own (it is currently one of Piedmont's most exciting producers), Delfina Quattrocolo has handed over the reins, and her holding in the property, to Alois Ehrmann from Germany. The handover comes at the peak of a career studded with success, and sealed by a memorable '99 version of the flagship La Tenaglia wine, Barbera d'Asti Emozioni. Luckily, the new owner intends to continue making premium-quality bottles. That's why he has decided to keep on the estate staff who have achieved such great things in the past. Attilio Pagli will still be looking after the cellar and agronomist Diego Curtaz will keep an eye on the vine stock while Delfina's daughter, Erika Nobbio, continues to run the administrative side of things. Sadly, there was no Barbera Emozioni 2000 waiting for the panel because at tasting time, it had yet to be bottled. Our first, unofficial assays indicate that it will bring out to the full the potential of barbera, a variety that is enjoying a new lease of life thanks to cellars such as La Tenaglia. Meanwhile, we can savour the excellent syrah-based Paradiso '99, with its berry fruit and pepper aromas laced with briny sensations. The palate has very nice weight and a bitterish hint in the finish. The Giorgio Tenaglia and 2000 Tenaglia are well-made Barberas and the 2001 Grignolino and Chardonnay both earned One full Glass.

- Barbera d'Asti Giorgio Tenaglia '00 🍷🍷 5
- Barbera del M.to Sup. Tenaglia '00 🍷🍷 5
- Paradiso Rosso '99 🍷🍷 6
- Grignolino del M.to Casalese '01 🍷 4
- ○ Piemonte Chardonnay '01 🍷 4
- Barbera d'Asti Emozioni '99 🍷🍷🍷 6
- Barbera d'Asti Emozioni '98 🍷🍷 6
- Barbera d'Asti Giorgio Tenaglia '99 🍷🍷 5

SPIGNO MONFERRATO (AL)

Traversa - Cascina Bertolotto
Via Pietro Porro, 70
15018 Spigno Monferrato (AL)
tel. 014491223 - 014491551

In recent years, the Traversa family has been steadily expanding its vine stock and now has a total area under vine of 22 hectares. Growth has been fuelled mainly by restructuring and replanting the Cascina Gergi estate, already owned by the family, so now production comes from the two Traversa-owned "cascine", or properties, Bertolotto and Gergi. These developments have made the winery's former name, Cascina Bertolotto, no longer appropriate and the estate is now Azienda Agricola Traversa. Currently looking after it are Giuseppe Traversa and his children, Fabio and Marida. Two of this year's wines that gained a very full One Glass are the house Dolcettos, La Muïette and La Cresta. The first comes from a fairly late harvest and offers evolved jammy notes and good density. It could do with a touch more freshness, though. La Cresta has more balanced notes of super-ripeness and combines attractive hints of green leaf with wild berries. Smooth and well-sustained in the mouth, it is an easy-drinking wine with very decent length. La Tia – it means "the lime" – is named after the venerable tree overlooking the vineyard its fruit comes from. The wine is an admirably made dry Brachetto, obtained from grapes part-raisined on the vine, with a full palate and crisp nose. The sweet Il Virginio Brachetto and the lively La Sbarazzina Barbera are well-made. Finally, we're going to have to wait until next year for the 2000 Barbera I Cheini.

- Rosso La Tia 🍷🍷 5
- Dolcetto d'Acqui La Muïette '00 🍷 4
- Dolcetto d'Acqui La Cresta '01 🍷 4
- Barbera del M.to La Sbarazzina '01 4
- Brachetto d'Acqui Il Virginio '01 4
- Dolcetto d'Acqui La Muïette '98 🍷🍷 4
- Barbera del M.to I Cheini '99 🍷🍷 4
- Dolcetto d'Acqui La Muïette '99 🍷🍷 4

STREVI (AL)

Marenco
P.zza Vittorio Emanuele II, 10
15019 Strevi (AL)
tel. 0144363133
e-mail: marencovini@libero.it

The Strevi-based winery run by sisters Michela, Patrizia and Doretto Marenco has an extensive vine stock, covering 65 of the estate's 80 hectares, and a well-equipped, modern cellar. The wide range of wines caters for all tastes and year by year gains character and personality, thanks in large part to the contribution oenologist Beppe Caviola has made to the technical side of the business. Our review starts with an excellent, cask-conditioned Barbera d'Asti Ciresa selection from the '99 vintage. Its intense garnet ruby introduces a nose that foregrounds sweet notes of oak, with sensations of almond paste backed up by fruit. Mouthfilling density, solid structure and good length with a faint bitterish hint all come out on the palate. The impressively rich Dolcetto Marchesa also performed well. Moving on to the whites, we tasted the Carialoso, from an almost extinct native variety. There are hints of hazelnut on the evolved nose, then a tidy well-rounded palate of juicy pulp. Hints of fermentation emerged from the Chardonnay Galet, an easy-drinking, undemanding tipple. Sweet wines have always been the forte of this territory and the Marencos propose an attractively rose-scented Brachetto Pineto, the ripe, full-bodied Moscato d'Asti Scrapona and a dense, sugar-rich Moscato Passito Passrì di Scrapona.

● Barbera d'Asti Ciresa '99	¶¶	5
○ Piemonte Moscato Passito Passrì di Scrapona '00	¶¶	6
● Dolcetto d'Acqui Marchesa '01	¶¶	4*
○ Moscato d'Asti Scrapona '01	¶	4
● Brachetto d'Acqui Pineto '01	¶	4
○ Carialoso '01	¶	3
○ Piemonte Chardonnay Galet '01	¶	4
● Barbera d'Asti Ciresa '98	¶¶	5
● Barbera d'Asti Bassina '99	¶¶	4

STREVI (AL)

Vigne Regali
Via Vittorio Veneto, 22
15019 Strevi (AL)
tel. 0144363485
e-mail: vglst@tin.it

After more than 20 years, Giuseppina Viglierchio – a "Donna del Vino" and chair of several consortia and associations, as well as manager of this lovely Banfi group estate at Strevi, has finally retired. The exodus was a general one for her husband, technical manager Attilio Viglierchio, and oenologist Silvano Marchetti left at the same time. The trio have been replaced by Attilio's nephew, Enrico, as chairman while Alberto Lazzarino is now in charge of production. There have been no great changes in cellar or vineyard; Vigne Regali continues along the road mapped out by the former management team. New developments will concern experimentation with a now-extinct variety, albarosa, in the framework of a project also backed by Chiarlo, Antinori and the viticulture institute at Asti. Another Vigne Regali priority is to exploit the full potential of the vineyards at Strevi and their two main varieties, moscato and brachetto. This year, the panel enjoyed an attractive Gavi Principessa Gavia 2001, which reveals notes of fermentation on the nose and a lightweight but nicely balanced palate. The 2001 L'Ardì offers a limpid purple red hue and youthful notes of morello cherry. In contrast, the '99 Argusto – also a Dolcetto d'Acqui – has more character and a well-knit freshness that you don't often find in this wine type. Vigne Regali always makes fine sparkling wines and this time, we liked the '98 Banfi Brut, from chardonnay and pinot nero with a touch of pinot bianco. The Moscato Strevi is mature and creamy, and the Brachetto d'Acqui 2001 reveals uncomplicated fragrances of roses.

● Dolcetto d'Acqui Argusto '99	¶¶	4*
○ Talento Banfi Brut M.Cl. '98	¶¶	5
○ Gavi Principessa Gavia '01	¶	4
○ Moscato d'Asti Strevi '01	¶	4
● Brachetto d'Acqui Rosa Regale '01	¶	4
● Dolcetto d'Acqui L'Ardì '01	¶	3
● Barbera d'Asti Vigneto Banin '99	¶¶	5
○ Alta Langa Brut M.Cl. '97	¶¶	5

TASSAROLO (AL)

CASTELLO DI TASSAROLO
CASCINA ALBORINA, 1
15060 TASSAROLO (AL)
TEL. 0143342248

Marchese Paolo Spinola looks to Bordeaux as the model for his whites. As a result, he seeks balance and elegance above all in his wines. That's why his bottles were especially enjoyable at a time, not so many years ago, when most of the Gavis around were hard on the palate. Too many producers were unable to tame the robust natural acidity of the cortese grape. Today, as Gavi production in general is expanding fast and adapting excellently to an increasingly demanding market, the Castello di Tassarolo wines are still some of the most exciting in the DOCG zone. Gavi Castello di Tassarolo 2001 is a lustrous straw yellow. Intriguing fruit on the nose is laced with notes of Mediterranean shrubland then the well-sustained palate is never in thrall to its discreet oak, from part-ageing in barrique. There is a very special note of mineral on the nose of the Vigneto Alborina, which is tidy and full-bodied in the mouth. The Tassarolo S may be more straightforward but its apple and sugared almond aromas and vigorous palate make it a very successful wine. There are fascinating smoky hints on the nose of the Ambrogio Spinola, from sémillon, sauvignon and cortese. Finally, the Rosso dei Marchesi is a very decent mix of cabernet and barbera.

O	Gavi Castello di Tassarolo '01	YY	4*
O	Gavi Vigneto Alborina '99	YY	5
O	Gavi Tassarolo S '01	Y	3
O	Monferrato Bianco Ambrogio Spinola '97	Y	4
●	Monferrato Rosso dei Marchesi '99	Y	4
O	Gavi Vigneto Alborina '98	YY	5

TORINO

FRANCO M. MARTINETTI
VIA SAN FRANCESCO DA PAOLO, 18
10123 TORINO
TEL. 0118395937
E-MAIL: gmartinetti@ciaoweb.it

Three Glasses again for Franco Martinetti, one of the most extraordinary characters in Italian winemaking. He continues to adhere to the strategy that so far has brought him great success. Franco organizes all his winemaking from his office in Turin, letting his products age in peace in various tried and trusted cellars scattered across southern Piedmont. Like the true wineman he is, Martinetti keeps a very close eye on every stage of production, from the vineyards that supply his fruit to the cellar, where he has a first-class staff of collaborators led by his very competent son, Guido. The result is a range of increasingly serious labels, with more than one thoroughbred. Head and shoulders above the rest this year is the Monferrato Sul Bric. It's a blend of the local barbera with the international cabernet grape and the wine they produce is impressively elegant on both nose and palate. This is a bottle that neatly sums up its maker's philosophy. Persuasive, mouthfilling fruit is lifted by the elegant finesse of the nose. Another Monferrato wine is the Barbera d'Asti Monruc while the austere Barolo Marasco comes from the heart of the Langhe. The Barbera has an irresistible nose of minerals nuanced with black cherries and pencil lead. The characterful Barolo hits the spot, showing great personality and roundness on the palate. The range ends with two whites, the monovarietal timorasso-based Martin, which pipped the elegant Gavi Minaia at the post. As we wait for the new Oltrepò Pavese "spumante", there is a nice, youthfully alcoholic Barbera Bric dei Banditi 2001 to enjoy.

●	Monferrato Rosso Sul Bric '00	YYY	6
●	Barbera d'Asti Sup. Montruc '00	YY	6
O	Colli Tortonesi Martin '00	YY	6
●	Barolo Marasco '98	YY	8
O	Gavi Minaia '00	YY	6
●	Barbera d'Asti Bric dei Banditi '01	YY	4*
●	Sul Bric '94	YYY	6
●	Sul Bric '95	YYY	6
●	Barbera d'Asti Sup. Montruc '96	YYY	6
●	Barbera d'Asti Sup. Montruc '97	YYY	6
O	Minaia '98	YYY	6
●	Barbera d'Asti Sup. Montruc '99	YY	6
●	Monferrato Rosso Sul Bric '99	YY	6

TORTONA (AL)

CLAUDIO MARIOTTO
LOC. VHO
STRADA PER SAREZZANO, 29
15057 TORTONA (AL)
TEL. 0131868500

A few years ago, Claudio Mariotto decided to make quality the first priority for his range. It was a brave move but it has brought him a lot of satisfaction, as well as quite a few problems to solve. Enthusiasm has carried him through and the results are there in his wines. Well-structured or light and nimble, they are never banal. Best of the whites is the timorasso-based Colli Tortonesi Derthona. Its flowery, pear and apple fruit nose introduces a rounded, well-orchestrated palate that handles its 13.5 per cent alcohol with nonchalance. The fragrant, cortese-based Profilo is lighter. The palate is reminiscent of spring flowers and closes on a faint note of sweet almonds. But Claudio Mariotto also knows how to tackle reds. As we wait for his special selection to age in wood, we can console ourselves with his monovarietal Barbera Vho. Barrique ageing lends the nose crisp, well-defined spice and vanilla, then the prominent but unassertive tannins mingle with morello cherry and chocolate in the mouth. The range includes a nice stainless steel-aged Barbera, the Territorio, whose lovely hue is followed by tobacco and strawberry aromas. Raspberry and sweet black cherries lift the admirable structure of the palate. A couple of more approachable wines round off the list, the Cortese Coccalina and the lively red Martirella, from bonarda, freisa and barbera.

○ Colli Tortonesi Bianco Derthona '00	ΥΥ	5
● Piemonte Barbera Vho '00	ΥΥ	5
● Piemonte Barbera Territorio '01	ΥΥ	4*
○ Colli Tortonesi Bianco Profilo '01	Υ	4
● Colli Tortonesi Rosso Martirella '01		3
○ Piemonte Cortese Coccalina '01		3
● Piemonte Barbera Vho '99	ΥΥ	4

TREISO (CN)

CA' DEL BAIO
VIA FERRERE, 33
12050 TREISO (CN)
TEL. 0173638219
E-MAIL: cadelbaio@cadelbaio.com

Under Giulio Grasso, Ca' del Baio has been steadily improving its quality standards. The 21 hectares under vine include 18 currently in production at premium vineyards such as Asili, in Barbaresco, and Marcarini and Valgrande (around the cellar) at Treiso. This year, we tasted his excellent Barbaresco selections. The Valgrande '99 ages in large barrels. Its deep, vibrant colour introduces crisp aromas of cherry, tobacco, tea and lemon peel. The sweetness of the tannins cossets the palate through to a delicious, albeit slightly one-dimensional, finish. The Asili '99 ages half in barrique and half in Slavonian oak and has a more sombre hue. Oak-derived spiciness, and balsamic, minty notes, dominate the raspberry fruit on the nose. The fleshy palate has class and character, and the serious tannins are backed up by rich fruit that carries through to the long finish. Two Glasses also went to the fragrant Nebbiolo 2000, a well-executed, versatile wine that can accompany a wide range of foods. It is a young, uncomplicated Barbaresco that shows, power, warmth and balance. The 2001 wines include a good, fresh Dolcetto Lodoli with slightly roughish, green tannins, a very warm, almost sweet Chardonnay that has rich notes of smoke and ripe pineapple, and a clean, thirst-quenching Moscato 2001 with a tangy palate that never cloys. We were unable to taste the Barberas before the Guide deadline closed so we'll be back for them next year.

● Langhe Nebbiolo Bric del Baio '00	ΥΥ	5
● Barbaresco Asili '99	ΥΥ	6
● Barbaresco Valgrande '99	ΥΥ	6
● Dolcetto d'Alba Lodoli '01	Υ	3
○ Langhe Chardonnay Sermine '01	Υ	5
○ Moscato d'Asti '01	Υ	4
● Barbaresco Asili '96	ΥΥ	6
● Barbaresco Asili Barrique '96	ΥΥ	6
● Barbaresco Asili '97	ΥΥ	6
● Barbaresco Asili Barrique '97	ΥΥ	6
● Barbaresco Asili Barrique '98	ΥΥ	6
● Barbaresco Valgrande '98	Υ	6

TREISO (CN)

ADA NADA
VIA AUSARIO, 12
12050 TREISO (CN)
TEL. 0173638127
E-MAIL: info@adanada.it

The Nada family bought their farm and land at Rombone as long ago as 1919. Currently, the estate belongs to architecture graduate Annalisa, who with husband Elvio and father Giancarlo, the cellar manager, looks after ten hectares that turn out 50,000 bottles every year. Since 1997, their commodious "agriturismo" holiday centre has had seven rooms available for visitors. For the past few years, two versions of the Barbaresco have been released, the Valeirano and the Cichin. Although both vineyards are on the same southwest-facing hillslope, only a few hundred metres apart, their wines have very different characteristics. The Valeirano '99 is an orange-flecked garnet wine with a nose of spices, herbs and hay. The palate is austere, with dry tannins. In contrast, the Cichin '99, a major wine from the Rombone vineyard, has a garnet-flecked ruby colour and is much more fruity and well-defined. On the mouth, it is equally powerful, showing fleshy pulp and sweetness. All in all, a delicious wine. Another Two Glass wine is the Langhe Rosso La Bisbetica '99, from nebbiolo and barbera aged in new barriques. Its deep garnet colour still reveals oak-derived notes but lovely raspberry and redcurrant fruit still emerges before the pervasive, warm palate shows its sweet, velvety tannins. Only a notch lower down come the more straightforward roughish Dolcetto Autinot 2001 with its notes of bitter cherry, the tangy, upfront Barbera Salgà '99 and the fuzzy, bitterish Barbera Vigna 'd Pierin 2000.

TREISO (CN)

FIORENZO NADA
LOC. ROMBONE
VIA AUSARIO, 12/C
12050 TREISO (CN)
TEL. 0173638254
E-MAIL: nadafiorenzo@nada.it

Bruno Nada is a reliable producer who releases near-perfect wines. The main features of his style are the increasingly marked fruit, elegance and character of his wines. The overall quality level of Bruno's wines this year is very, very good. At the top, we find his magnificent Barbaresco Rombone '99, one of the finest of its type. A lively, dark garnet red, it opens slowly after being allowed to breathe, with hints of vanilla, cocoa powder and marmalade. Dense, concentrated and powerful, it flaunts well-knit, sweet tannins. A masterpiece. The Barbaresco '99 is also deep garnet and releases aromas of raspberry, cocoa powder, leather, citrus peel and earth. Less weighty in the mouth, it shows juicy fruit and softness, despite its hefty tannins. The superb Seifile '99 came within an ace of a third Glass. Vanilla and oak mingle with bottled cherries on the nose then the almost perfect sweet palate is pervasive with a delightful hint of violets and liquorice. The recent maturing of a vineyard near the cellar has produced the new Barbera d'Alba, which in 2000 has good fruit and balance with a distinct hint of well-integrated oak on the palate. Finally, there is a marvellous Dolcetto 2001, one of the classic Langhe reds. The dark purple hue introduces a nose of cherry and almond with a juicy, tangy palate that is drinking marvellously already.

● Barbaresco Cichin '99	♟♟ 7
● Barbaresco Valeirano '99	♟♟ 7
● Langhe Rosso La Bisbetica '99	♟♟ 6
● Dolcetto d'Alba Autinot '01	♟ 4
● Barbera d'Alba Salgà '99	♟ 5
● Barbera d'Alba Vigna 'd Pierin '00	4
● Barbaresco Cichin '98	♟♟ 7
● Langhe Rosso La Bisbetica '98	♟♟ 6
● Barbaresco Valeirano '98	♟♟ 7

● Barbaresco Rombone '99	♟♟♟ 8
● Langhe Rosso Seifile '99	♟♟ 8
● Barbera d'Alba '00	♟♟ 5
● Dolcetto d'Alba '01	♟♟ 4*
● Barbaresco '99	♟♟ 7
● Seifile '93	♟♟♟ 8
● Langhe Rosso Seifile '95	♟♟♟ 8
● Langhe Rosso Seifile '96	♟♟♟ 8
● Barbaresco Rombone '97	♟♟♟ 8
● Barbaresco Rombone '98	♟♟ 8
● Langhe Rosso Seifile '98	♟♟ 8
● Barbaresco '97	♟♟ 7
● Langhe Rosso Seifile '97	♟♟ 8
● Barbaresco '98	♟♟ 7

TREISO (CN)

PELISSERO
VIA FERRERE, 10
12050 TREISO (CN)
TEL. 0173638430
E-MAIL: pelissero@pelissero.com

There's a new wine at Pelissero. It's the Langhe Long Now, which is also the name, borrowed from an American association founded by musician Brian Eno, of a special clock. Giorgio will forgive us if we refer interested readers to the relevant website, www.longnow.org. We'll move straight on to the wines, where there was a spectacular Three Glass Vanotu '99. It's deep ruby is dark but lustrous, then the broad nose tempts with raspberry, vanilla, leather, earth, mint and sage. The palate is a hymn to concentration, length, depth and softness. The Barbaresco Annata '99 drinks more like a selection than a base wine. The classic aromas are backed up by seriously firm tannins and rounded off by a long, fruity finish. The Dolcetto Augenta 2001 is another high scorer. The weave of jam and liquorice is a tad closed and stand-offish, but pervades the palate with a dense, juicy mouthfeel that lingers nicely. Another charmer is the Barbera Piani 2001, its shrewdly judged oak and cherry notes caressing the palate with softness and a hint of tanginess. The Long Now 2000 is a nebbiolo and barbera mix that ages for 20 months in 80 per cent new barriques. We were impressed by the sweet blackcurrant fruit and complex aromas, ranging from printer's ink to pencil lead and vanilla. Silky tannins provide the perfect counterpoint. The attractive golden-hued Favorita is unusual but well-structured, with tropical aromas of grapefruit and white peach. The traditional Nebbiolo, Dolcetto Munfrina and Grignolino, all from the 2001 vintage, are less demanding.

TREISO (CN)

VIGNAIOLI ELVIO PERTINACE
LOC. PERTINACE, 2
12050 TREISO (CN)
TEL. 0173442238
E-MAIL: c.vignaioli@areacom.it

Marketing director Cesare Barbero and oenologist Roberto Giacone are at the helm of this 200,000 bottle a year cellar, which also sells some of its wine unbottled. The make a range of typical Langhe wines from their roughly 80 hectares under vine, half planted to nebbiolo for Barbaresco. The Barbaresco Marcarini precisely mirrors the finesse that nebbiolo from Treiso has on the nose. Its intense ruby introduces ripe raspberry over flowers and a hint of mineral. Lively and characterful in the mouth, it powers through to an unhurried, liquorice-themed finish. The Barbaresco Nervo comes from one of the finest vineyards in Treiso. Elegance on the nose is followed by seamless power on the palate, which ends in a convincing, tannin-supported finish. The Castellizzano is a little forward. Leather and jam lead into a palate with rather marked acidity and a nice fruit-rich finish. Dried flowers and tempting, if less concentrated, drinkability are the hallmarks of the good standard Barbaresco. The nebbiolo, barbera and cabernet-based Langhe Pertinace is interesting, its almond and berry fruit aromas accompanying good texture on the palate, which has nice acidic grip. Best of the 2001 Dolcetti d'Albas is the Castellizzano, which has most finesse and the fullest flavour. Finally, the Chardonnay 2001 is well-made, if unchallenging.

● Barbaresco Vanotu '99	￸￸￸	8
● Langhe Rosso Long Now '00	￸￸	6
● Barbera d'Alba Piani '01	￸￸	4*
● Dolcetto d'Alba Augenta '01	￸￸	4*
○ Langhe Favorita '01	￸￸	3*
● Barbaresco Annata '99	￸￸	7
● Dolcetto d'Alba Munfrina '01	￸	3
● Langhe Nebbiolo '01	￸	6
● Piemonte Grignolino '01	￸	3
● Barbaresco Vanotu '95	￸￸￸	8
● Barbaresco Vanotu '97	￸￸￸	8
● Barbaresco Vanotu '98	￸￸	8
● Barbera d'Alba Piani '00	￸￸	4
● Barbaresco Vanotu '96	￸￸	8

● Dolcetto d'Alba Castellizzano '01	￸￸	4*
● Barbaresco Vigneto Marcarini '99	￸￸	6
● Barbaresco Vigneto Nervo '99	￸￸	6
● Langhe Pertinace '99	￸￸	5
● Dolcetto d'Alba '01	￸	3
● Dolcetto d'Alba Vigneto Nervo '01	￸	4
○ Langhe Chardonnay '01	￸	3
● Barbaresco '99	￸	5
● Barbaresco Vigneto Castellizzano '99	￸	6
● Barbaresco Vigneto Nervo '98	￸￸	6

VERDUNO (CN)

F.lli Alessandria
Via Beato Valfré, 59
12060 Verduno (CN)
tel. 0172470113

Gian Alessandria, his son Vittore and oenologist Franco Alessandria are getting exciting results with wines that are absolutely faithful to the territory where they are produced. The Barolos show finesse – a feature of the best vineyards at Verduno – married to great structure that comes from excellent work among the vines. The San Lorenzo '98 has a tight-knit hue and aromas of ripe berry fruit, laced with leather and notes of fresh-cut grass. Rich and powerful in the mouth, it unveils assertive tannins that dry out the long finish, where delicious fruit and cocoa powder emerge. The bouquet of the Barolo Monvigliero '98 is an extremely complex weave of mineral and animal nuances, then the palate builds up relentlessly to a long finish that mirrors the aromas of the nose. The second-label Barolo from the same vintage isn't quite such a big wine but drinks satisfyingly nonetheless. There is an interesting new vintage of Barbera, which from 2000 will be called La Priora. Its dark red, mineral and ripe fruit aromas and power on the palate lead up to a long, toastiness-veined finish that is still trying to find a point of equilibrium. The Langhe Rosso Luna 2000, from barrique-aged freisa, nebbiolo and barbera, is nicely made. Its ripe fruit and tobacco aromas usher in a lively, well-structured palate. Turning to the 2001 wines, we find tempting hints of almonds and roses offsetting the spice of the eminently drinkable Pelaverga. The uncomplicated, approachable Dolcetto offers fruit pastille aromas. Finally, the Favorita has good weight and crisp notes of fruit.

● Barolo S. Lorenzo '98	ŸŸ	7
● Barbera d'Alba La Priora '00	ŸŸ	4*
● Langhe Rosso Luna '00	ŸŸ	5
● Barolo '98	ŸŸ	6
● Barolo Monvigliero '98	ŸŸ	7
● Dolcetto d'Alba '01	Ÿ	3
○ Langhe Favorita '01	Ÿ	3
● Verduno Pelaverga '01	Ÿ	4
● Barolo Monvigliero '95	ŸŸŸ	7
● Barolo S. Lorenzo '97	ŸŸŸ	7
● Barolo Monvigliero '96	ŸŸ	7
● Barbera d'Alba '99	ŸŸ	4
● Langhe Rosso Luna '99	ŸŸ	5

VERDUNO (CN)

Bel Colle
Fraz. Castagni, 56
12060 Verduno (CN)
tel. 0172470196
e-mail: belcolle@tin.it

Paolo Torchio winery produces 150,000 bottles a year, obtained mainly from estate-owned vines – Bel Colle has about six hectares at Verduno – and in part with fruit purchased from trusted growers. In 2002, Paolo planted two more hectares to pelaverga and nebbiolo but the most significant news is that major restructuring is under way to extend the cellar and fit it out with more efficient, modern equipment. We'll start our review with the Barbaresco Roncaglie, a concentrated garnet wine with a faintly evolved nose where fruit dominates. The palate has good body and holds well through to the liquorice-laced finish. The orange-flecked ruby of the Barolo Monvigliero ushers in a nose that layers raspberry over leather and autumn leaves. The dry, substantial palate has a nice bitterish twist in the finish. The Dolcetto Borgo Castagni 2001 is well-executed. Its close-knit hue introduces attractive sensations of fruit, autumn leaves and mint, then a robust palate with attractive acidic grip. The Pelaverga has spicy and earthy hints on the nose, then a dry, pleasantly rustic mouthfeel. The Barbera Le Masche shows moderate finesse on the nose and juicy flesh. The Chardonnay Le Masche is predictable and undemanding. Finally, the Arneis and the Favorita are well made.

● Dolcetto d'Alba Borgo Castagni '01	ŸŸ	4*
● Barolo Monvigliero '98	ŸŸ	6
● Barbaresco Roncaglie '99	ŸŸ	6
● Barbera d'Alba Sup. Le Masche '99	Ÿ	4
○ Langhe Chardonnay Le Masche '01	Ÿ	4
○ Langhe Favorita '01	Ÿ	3
○ Roero Arneis '01	Ÿ	4
● Verduno Pelaverga '01	Ÿ	4
● Barolo Monvigliero '96	ŸŸ	6
● Barbaresco Roncaglie '97	ŸŸ	6
● Barbera d'Alba Sup. Le Masche '97	ŸŸ	4
● Barolo Monvigliero '97	ŸŸ	6

VERDUNO (CN)

G. B. BURLOTTO
VIA VITTORIO EMANUELE, 28
12060 VERDUNO (CN)
TEL. 0172470122
E-MAIL: burlotto@burlotto.it

The 11 hectares owned by Marina Burlotto, who is assisted by husband Giuseppe and their son Fabio, are in the municipal territory of Verduno. The sole exception is their plot in the legendary Cannubi vineyard at Barolo, from which the Burlottos obtain their vineyard selection. This year, the intense garnet Barolo Vigneto Cannubi '98 flaunts an attractive, fruit-dominated nose lifted by delightful hints of rhubarb. Dry and firm on the palate, it also shows nice pulp and a long finish that echoes the nose. The Barolo Monvigliero comes from Verduno's most important vineyard. Its intense colour leads into a distinctive nose of Peruvian bark and crushed flowers layered over leather and wild berries, then the juicy fruit of the attractively rugged palate lingers satisfyingly. The Mores, from nebbiolo and barbera, accompanies sweet notes with ripe plum and a full-bodied palate that is slightly austere but never stand-offish. The Dives comes from sauvignon grown on the hillslopes at Verduno. Scrupulously made, it brings out the varietal character of the grape with attractive warmth, following its golden hue with nice fruit and tomato leaf. A hint of alcohol peeks through in the finish of the full, tangy palate. The pleasant, even Barbera Aves has flowery aromas and the Pelaverga reveals a mineral, flowery, fairly spicy nose, then conviction and plenty of body in the mouth.

O	Langhe Bianco Dives '00		4*
●	Barolo Vigneto Cannubi '98		7
●	Barolo Vigneto Monvigliero '98		7
●	Langhe Mores '00		5
●	Barbera d'Alba Aves '00		5
●	Verduno Pelaverga '01		4
●	Barolo '96		7
●	Barolo Vigneto Cannubi '96		7
●	Barolo Vigneto Cannubi '97		7
●	Barbera d'Alba Vigneto Boscato '98		5

VERDUNO (CN)

CASTELLO DI VERDUNO
VIA UMBERTO I, 9
12060 VERDUNO (CN)
TEL. 0172470284 - 0172470125
E-MAIL: castellodiverduno@castellodiverduno.com

The superb castle that once belonged to the Savoy king, Carlo Alberto – and which today has been partly converted into an elegant hotel and restaurant – is the setting where Gabriella Burlotto and her husband Franco Bianco bottle, age and sell the wines from their vineyards at Verduno and Barbaresco. Ageing takes place in the well-equipped cellars owned by Franco's family. We particularly liked the '98 Barolo and Barbaresco Riserva wines this year, the Massara and Rabajà. The Barolo came within an ace of a third Glass, thanks to its rich ruby with an orange rim and aromas that open slowly to reveal distinctive, well-defined bottled fruit, chocolate and cakes laced with alcohol. The palate has juicy fruit and cocoa powder returns on the long finish. It's a Barolo that has taken full advantage of leisurely ageing, as has the Barbaresco Rabajà Riserva. The latter's bouquet ranges from ripe wild berries to leather and minerally nuances, then the austerity of the palate is mellowed by generous alcohol. The vigorous Barbaresco Faset '98 shows fresh green notes and well-expressed fruit. The Barbaresco Rabajà '99 is a little evolved and slightly dry. The Barolo Monvigliero '98 is well-made, showing complex aromas and a palate rendered slightly aggressive by its alcohol. There are notes of cinnamon and almond from the warm, full-bodied Barbera Bricco del Cuculo 2000. The very pleasant, charmingly distinctive Pelaverga di Verduno Basadone 2001 mingles roses, pepper and minerals on the nose. Finally, a gutsy Dolcetto Campot, again from 2001, brings this fine range to a close.

●	Barolo Massara Ris. '96		7
●	Barbera d'Alba Bricco del Cuculo '00		4*
●	Verduno Basadone '01		4*
●	Barbaresco Rabajà Ris. '96		7
●	Barbaresco Faset '98		6
●	Barolo Monvigliero '98		7
●	Dolcetto d'Alba Campot '01		4
●	Barbaresco Rabajà '99		7
●	Barbaresco Rabajà '96		7
●	Barolo Monvigliero '96		7
●	Barbaresco Rabajà '97		7
●	Barolo Massara '97		7
●	Barbaresco Rabajà '98		7

VIGNALE MONFERRATO (AL)

Giulio Accornero e Figli
Ca' Cima, 1
15049 Vignale Monferrato (AL)
tel. 0142933317
e-mail: azaccornero@tin.it

Ermanno and Massimo Accornero's winery lies between Vignale and Casorzo, in the heart of Monferrato wine country. Recently, it has hit the quality heights thanks to a Barbera, the Bricco Battista, that has earned Three Glasses on more than one occasion. This year, the wine pulled up just short of a third Glass but still managed to impress. The impenetrable inky hue is flecked with cyclamen then the close-knit bramble and black cherry aromas, delicately laced with tobacco and sweet spice, show depth and concentration. Outstanding structure tells you how good the grapes are as it unfolds seamlessly over a fresh note of typical barbera acidity. The Monferrato Centenario is a fine blend of cabernet and barbera, created in 1997 to celebrate the winery's centenary. The two varieties meld with French oak in an admirably complete aromatic profile, then the dense, well-structured palate is lifted by serious, yet gentle, tannins. The Grignolino Bricco del Bosco 2001 has raspberry, strawberry, roses and elegant geraniums over stimulating notes of spice, then a soft, rather full, mouthfeel. The '99 Pico is a dried gape "passito" from malvasia di Casorzo that unveils hints of roses, gooseberries and tea leaves laced with rhubarb. Roses come through again on the sweet palate, where they are offset nicely by the robust structure. The fragrant, uncomplicated Brigantino 2001 has a silky mousse and sweetness that never cloys. Fonsìna is a fresh-tasting 50-50 mix of chardonnay and cortese that has great balance. Closing the range is the pleasingly rustic Barbera Giulìn 2001.

- Barbera del M.to Sup. Bricco Battista '00 — 5
- Grignolino del M.to Casalese Bricco del Bosco '01 — 3*
- Monferrato Rosso Centenario '98 — 6
- Casorzo Malvasia Passito Pico '99 — 6
- Barbera del M.to Giulìn '01 — 4
- Casorzo Malvasia Brigantino '01 — 4
- O Monferrato Bianco Fonsìna '01 — 3
- Barbera del M.to Sup. Bricco Battista '99 — 5
- Barbera del M.to Sup. Bricco Battista '98 — 5

VIGNALE MONFERRATO (AL)

Bricco Mondalino
Reg. Mondalino, 5
15049 Vignale Monferrato (AL)
tel. 0142933204

Mauro Gaudio bottles about 90,000 units a year, all from 18 hectares under vine in the municipality of Vignale, with the exception of one and a half hectares planted to malvasia at Casorzo. The extensive range embraces all the wine types of the area, with barbera and grignolino accounting for the lion's share. This year, Mauro has taken the courageous decision to delay the release of his leading labels, secure in the knowledge that further ageing will give harmony and mellow roundness to fruit that is extremely extract-rich. That's why the Barbera Gaudium Magnum, the Zerolegno and the Grignolino Bricco Mondalino will feature in the next edition of the Guide. In the meantime, the Barbera Il Brigantino 2000 has the qualities required to fill, at least in part, the gap left by the flagship bottles. Its intense garnet and nose of ripe fruit with more complex notes of cocoa powder, mint and tar precede a vigorous palate, where assertive tannins are backed up by good structure. The finish shows good length. One Glass went to the Grignolino 2001 for its flower and spice nose and characteristically dry palate, rounded off by a faintly bitterish note. The uncomplicated Barbera Superiore 2000 offers violets and acid grip in the mouth. The nose of the Malvasia di Casorzo is slightly forward. It ushers in a refreshing, satisfying palate. Finally, the slightly sparkling Cortese has lots of fruit.

- Barbera d'Asti Il Bergantino '00 — 4*
- Barbera del M.to Sup. '00 — 3
- Grignolino del M.to Casalese '01 — 3
- Malvasia di Casorzo d'Asti Molignano '01 — 3
- O Monferrato Casalese Cortese '01 — 3
- Barbera d'Asti Sel. Gaudium Magnum '99 — 5
- Grignolino del M.to Casalese Bricco Mondalino '00 — 4
- Barbera d'Asti Sel. Gaudium Magnum '98 — 5
- Barbera d'Asti Il Bergantino '99 — 4

VIGNALE MONFERRATO (AL)

Marco Canato
Cascina Baldea, 18
15049 Vignale Monferrato (AL)
tel. 0142933653
e-mail: canatovini@yahoo.it

After their inclusion in the Guide for the first time last year, the Canatos have confirmed their high winemaking standards. Marco and Roberto Canato are the competent estate managers and can call on advice from skilled oenologist Enzo Bailo. They are at their best when vinifying the classic local variety in this part of Monferrato, barbera. Their two Barbera del Monferrato selections, Rapet and La Baldea, won Two Glasses for their distinctive, albeit very different, personalities. The Rapet is a charming modern-style wine with a concentrated garnet-ruby hue and a nose that focuses on sweet notes of morello cherry, peach and almond. The smooth, well-sustained palate ends on a high note with an after-aroma that again foregrounds fruit. The full ruby La Baldea proffers the nose berry fruit and sweet liquorice. The tidy palate has good texture and is rounded off nicely by a long finish laced with fruit. The Grignolino Celio has lovely bramble and pepper layered over faint hints of super-ripeness. The palate is lively and delicious, well-gauged tannins offering admirable support. The juicy, well-rounded Chardonnay Piasì has pear and apples on the nose and generous alcohol. There is a tad too much oak in the Chardonnay Bric di Bric while the Barbera Gambaloita is an undemanding, well-made standard wine.

● Barbera del M.to Sup. La Baldea '00	ΨΨ 4*
● Barbera del M.to Rapet '99	ΨΨ 5
● Grignolino del M.to Casalese Celio '01	Ψ 4
○ Piemonte Chardonnay Bric di Bric '01	Ψ 5
○ Piemonte Chardonnay Piasì '01	Ψ 4
● Barbera del M.to Gambaloita '01	5
● Barbera del M.to Rapet '98	ΨΨ 5
● Barbera del M.to Sup. La Baldea '98	ΨΨ 4

VIGNALE MONFERRATO (AL)

Colonna
Fraz. San Lorenzo
Ca' Accatino, 1
15049 Vignale Monferrato (AL)
tel. 0142933239
e-mail: vini.colonna@onw.net

When your subject is Alessandra Colonna, you run no risk of having nothing to write about. Her activities are manifold and we could start by mentioning that as well as being a highly successful winemaker, she also holds a chair of economics and management of tourism-related enterprises in Milan. Another important piece of news is the excellent Cabernet Amani, named after the Swahili word for peace. A limited number of magnums are released and the proceeds go towards an aid project for Africa. Meanwhile, the estate "agriturismo", or farm holiday centre, continues to grow and recently a lovely new tasting room was inaugurated. The panel really liked the excellent 2001 Monferrato Rosso Amani. Its impenetrable hue ushers in a bewitching nose of sweet notes and slightly evolved ripe berry fruit. After a few seconds, elegant mint emerges and the palate is laudably harmonious and tempting. It's a juicy, powerful Cabernet with great length and sweet fruit in the mouth. The Mondone '99 is from barbera, cabernet and pinot nero. The nose is balsamic and complex, then the robust palate takes you through to a liquorice-themed finish. The Barbera La Rossa 2001 is an uncomplicated but irresistible red. The oak-aged Chardonnay Passione 2000 is lovely and the upfront Chardonnay Armonia is very drinkable. "Typical" and "frank" sum up the Grignolino Sansìn 2001 while the pinot nero-based Monferrato Rosso Bigio 2000 is fruit-rich and spicy. Missing from the range is the Barbera Alessandra 2000, which will undergo longer ageing in bottle.

● Monferrato Rosso Amani '00	ΨΨ 8
○ Piemonte Chardonnay Passione '00	ΨΨ 4
● Barbera del M.to La Rossa '01	ΨΨ 4*
● Monferrato Rosso Mondone '99	ΨΨ 5
● Monferrato Rosso Bigio '00	Ψ 5
● Grignolino del M.to Casalese Sansìn '01	Ψ 4
○ Piemonte Chardonnay Armonia '01	Ψ 4
● Barbera del M.to Alessandra '98	ΨΨ 5
● Monferrato Rosso Mondone '98	ΨΨ 5
● Barbera del M.to Alessandra '99	ΨΨ 5
● Monferrato Rosso Amani '99	ΨΨ 8

VIGNALE MONFERRATO (AL)

La Scamuzza
Cascina Pomina, 17
15049 Vignale Monferrato (AL)
Tel. 0142926214
E-mail: lascamuzza@tiscalinet.it

After several years of tastings and retastings, we can at last report a significant improvement in quality at La Scamuzza, the cellar run with enthusiasm and drive by Laura Zavattaro with the assistance of husband Massimo Bertone and wine technician Mario Ronco. Today, the estate includes six hectares under vine, a mere drop in the property's 80-hectare ocean, most of which is planted to arable crops. Massimo Bertone runs a well-known seed company. Disastrous hailstorms last year destroyed up to 99 per cent of the crop in some plots. This jeopardized part of the cellar's production but our panels very much enjoyed the wines they were able to taste. We'll begin our round-up with the flagship Barbera Vigneto della Amorosa, which has an attractive dark ruby hue and a complex nose of berry fruit, wild berries and spices. The rounded, well-structured palate has loads of personality and is in no hurry to sign off. Baciamisubito ("kiss-me-quick"), the well-crafted 2001 Barbera, has the freshness and character you expect from a product in this price range. The Monferrato Bricco San Tomaso, a 50-50 mix of barbera and cabernet, is more than just interesting. It has breadth and good fruit on the nose, and plenty of muscle on the harmonious palate. Finally, the Grignolino is nicely made and very tasty.

• Barbera del M.to Vigneto della Amorosa '00	ΨΨ	5
• Monferrato Rosso Bricco San Tomaso '00	ΨΨ	5
• Barbera del M.to Baciamisubito '01	Ψ	4
• Grignolino del M.to Casalese Tumas '01	Ψ	4
• Barbera del M.to Vigneto della Amorosa Sup. '99	ΨΨ	5
• Monferrato Rosso Bricco San Tomaso '99	Ψ	5

VINCHIO (AT)

Cantina Sociale di Vinchio e Vaglio Serra
Strada Provinciale, 40
14040 Vinchio (AT)
Tel. 0141950903
E-mail: info@vinchio.com

The Cantina Sociale di Vinchio e Vaglio Serra co-operative winery was founded in 1959 by 19 members. Today, it has 224 of them, who cultivate 320 hectares under vine. The co-operative is located in an area – the hills of upper Monferrato – that may justly be considered one of the finest barbera zones there is. In fact, much of the winery's output is devoted to Barbera d'Asti. First, there is a well-made Vigne Vecchie, which, in the 2000 edition, has been labelled as a wine from the Nizza subzone. This is a part of the Asti hill country that embraces 18 municipalities around the town of Nizza Monferrato and the producers who have supported the subzone's creation intend to make it the home of a super-Barbera. The intense, garnet-ruby Vigne Vecchie has rich fruit on the nose where cherry dominates. Dry and robustly textured, it drives through to a lingering finish that echoes the nose. The Barbera d'Asti Superiore is slightly pale in hue and evolved on the nose, where there are lovely hints of fruit and liquorice. Fleshy and delicious in the mouth, it signs off with a moderately long finish. The youthful colour of the Barbera d'Asti 2001 ushers in an attractively rustic nose and a less than challenging palate that reveals a certain warmth in the finish. The balanced, delicate Grignolino has distinct aromas of almond and pepper.

• Barbera d'Asti Sup. Nizza Vigne Vecchie '00	ΨΨ	5
• Barbera d'Asti Sup. '00	Ψ	3
• Barbera d'Asti '01	Ψ	3
• Grignolino d'Asti '01	Ψ	3
• Barbera d'Asti Sup. Vigne Vecchie '96	ΨΨ	5
• Barbera d'Asti Sup. Vigne Vecchie '97	ΨΨ	5
• Barbera d'Asti Sup. Vigne Vecchie '98	ΨΨ	5
• Barbera d'Asti Sup. Vigne Vecchie '99	ΨΨ	5

OTHER WINERIES

Giovanni Silva
Cascine Rogge, 1/B
10011 Agliè (TO)
Tel. 012433356
E-mail: silvastefano@eurexnet.it

Emerging Canavese DOC zone producer Giovanni Silva earned a place in the Guide this year. His Erbaluce di Caluso Tre Ciochè 2001 is pleasantly fresh, with aniseed and hedgerow on the nose, and a full palate with a bitter twist in the finish. The Canavese Rosso Tre Ciochè 2000 is well-balanced.

● Canavese Rosso Tre Ciochè '00	▼▼	4*
○ Erbaluce di Caluso Tre Ciochè '01	▼	3

Eugenio Bocchino
Loc. Serre, 2
12051 Alba (CN)
Tel. 0173364226
E-mail: laperucca@libero.it

The barbera and nebbiolo-based Suo di Giacomo 2000 is one of Eugenio Bocchino's most interesting wines. It has a dense hue and a nose that mingles fruit with oak-derived hints of toastiness and cakes. The somewhat mouthdrying palate has good texture. The Nebbiolo La Perucca is nice.

● Langhe Rosso		
Suo di Giacomo '00	▼▼	6
● Nebbiolo d'Alba La Perucca '00	▼	6

Cascina Morassino
Loc. Ovello, 32
12050 Barbaresco (CN)
Tel. 0173635149

Encouraging results continue to arrive from this small winery in the heart of Barbaresco territory. The two '99 Barbaresco selections, the Morassino and the Ovello, have thoroughly convincing personalities. The Langhe Nebbiolo 2000 has good body and the pleasant Barbera is very drinkable.

● Barbaresco Ovello '99	▼▼	7
● Barbaresco Morassino '99	▼▼	6*
● Barbera d'Alba Vignot '00	▼	5
● Langhe Nebbiolo '00	▼	5

La Caplana
Via Circonvallazione, 4
15060 Bosio (AL)
Tel. 0143684182

Young Natalino Guido is the enthusiastic, competent manager of this small winery in the centre of Bosio, where work on the efficient new cellar is almost complete. We note with pleasure good results from the main 2000 labels, Gavi Porfirio, Dolcetto d'Ovada Barricco and Barbera d'Asti Rubis.

○ Gavi Porfirio '00	▼▼	4*
● Barbera d'Asti Rubis '00	▼	4
● Dolcetto d'Ovada Barricco '00	▼	4

CORNAREA
VIA VALENTINO, 105
12043 CANALE (CN)
TEL. 017365636 - 0173979091
E-MAIL: cornarea@tiscalinet.it

The Canale-based Cornarea winery turned out a good range. One of the first cellars to exploit the arneis grape, Cornarea has released a flavoursome 2001 Roero white with good texture and length. The Nebbiolo d'Alba '99 is elegant and the honey-sweet arneis Passito Tarasco '98 fills the mouth.

○ Roero Arneis '01	🍷🍷	4*
○ Tarasco Passito '98	🍷	5
● Nebbiolo d'Alba '99	🍷	4

L'ARMANGIA
REG. SAN GIOVANNI, 14/C
14053 CANELLI (AT)
TEL. 0141824947
E-MAIL: armangia@inwind.it

In an area that produces excellent Barbera, it is nice to see the odd outsider, like the Chardonnay Robi e Robi '99. Its rich colour and tropical fruit over vegetal notes lead into a juicy, balanced palate. The other wines include a good Moscato Il Giai and, of course, a well-made Barbera, Titon.

○ Piemonte Chardonnay Robi e Robi '99	🍷🍷	4*
● Barbera d'Asti Sup. Titon '99	🍷	4
○ Moscato d'Asti Il Giai '01	🍷	3

NE.NE.
REG. SERRA MASIO, 30
14053 CANELLI (AT)
TEL. 0141831152

There are three interesting wines from this Canelli winery. Two are Barberas and one is a white. The Martleina Barbera offers jam, Peruvian bark and flowers on the nose then a well-sustained, dry palate. The standard version is upfront and less demanding. The Bianco Valon is well-executed.

● Barbera d'Asti Martleina '00	🍷	5
● Barbera d'Asti '01	🍷	4
○ Valon	🍷	4

GIACOMO SCAGLIOLA E FIGLIO
REG. SANTA LIBERA, 20
14053 CANELLI (AT)
TEL. 0141831146
E-MAIL: aziendascagliola@libero.it

This family-run estate, founded in 1945, is in the hills at Canelli. The current owners tend 15 hectares under vine, producing the classic Monferrato wines, especially Barbera. In fact, the well-structured Barbera Vigna dei Mandorli '99 is this year's best wine but the Moscato d'Asti is good, too.

● Barbera d'Asti Vigna dei Mandorli '99	🍷🍷	4*
○ Moscato d'Asti '01	🍷	3

LUIGI TACCHINO
VIA MARTIRI DELLA BENEDICTA, 26
15060 CASTELLETTO D'ORBA (AL)
TEL. 0143830115
E-MAIL: luigitacchinovini@libero.it

The Tacchinos have been in wine for half a century. A few years ago, they started releasing premium wines from their own estate. There are three reds, the well-structured Monferrato Rosso Eresia 2000, from barbera, cabernet and dolcetto, the juicy Dolcetto d'Ovada 2000 and the fresh Barbera 2001.

● Monferrato Rosso Eresia '00	🍷🍷	4
● Dolcetto di Ovada Sup. Du Riva '00	🍷	4
● Barbera del M.to '01	🍷	2*

MARSAGLIA
VIA MUSSONE, 2
12050 CASTELLINALDO (CN)
TEL. 0173213048
E-MAIL: cantina@cantinamarsaglia.it

Marsaglia makes good Roero wines that have proved very reliable over the years. The Arneis 2001 has a nose of hedgerow with banana, and a palate perked up by a hint of acidity. The Barbera d'Alba San Cristoforo 2000 is forthright while the well-made Roero Brich d'America has nice balance.

● Barbera d'Alba San Cristoforo '00	🍷	4
● Roero Sup. Brich d'America '00	🍷	5
○ Roero Arneis San Servasio '01	🍷	4

Stefanino Morra
Via Castagnito, 22
12050 Castellinaldo (CN)
Tel. 0173213489

Stefanino Morra's cellar releases a comprehensive range of good Roero wines. This year, we liked the Barbera Castellinaldo '99 and the Roero Arneis San Pietro 2000, both well-made, easy-drinking bottles. But the best of the bunch is the Roero Superiore, a full-bodied wine with great fruit.

● Roero Sup. '00	ᵧᵧ 4*
○ Roero Arneis Vigneto San Pietro '00	ᵧ 5
● Castellinaldo Barbera d'Alba '99	ᵧ 5

Villa Fiorita
Via Case Sparse, 2
14034 Castello di Annone (AT)
Tel. 0141401231 - 0141401852
E-mail: villafiorita-wines@villafiorita-wines.com

The Rondolino family make a reliable Barbera d'Asti Superiore called Giorgione. The '99 has a dense hue, then aromas of fruit and tar, before the nice texture of the palate takes you through to a slightly dry, tannic finish. The spicy, frank Grignolino and the tidy Rosso Maniero are also nice.

● Barbera d'Asti Sup. Giorgione '99	ᵧᵧ 6
● Monferrato Rosso Maniero '99	ᵧ 5
● Grignolino d'Asti Pian delle Querce '01	ᵧ 3*

Ca' dei Mandorli
Via IV Novembre, 5 bis
14010 Castel Rocchero (AT)
Tel. 0141760131
E-mail: stefanoricagno@cadeimandorli.com

Stefano Ricagno and his father, Paolo, president of the Brachetto protection consortium, run an estate of more than 110 hectares on the hills in the provinces of Asti and Alessandria. The wines include two flagship labels, a fresh, sparkling Brachetto and the Barbera d'Asti La Bellalda d'Oro.

● Brachetto d'Acqui Le Donne dei Boschi '01	ᵧᵧ 4*
● Barbera d'Asti Sup. La Bellalda d'Oro '99	ᵧ 5

Renzo Beccaris
Fraz. Madonnina, 26
14055 Costigliole d'Asti (AT)
Tel. 0141966592

Renzo Beccaris has had major problems recently with flavescence dorée but his wines are very convincing. The mouthfilling Barbera San Lorenzo '99 has impressive structure while the elegant, fruit-rich Monferrato Bricco della Ghiandaia '98 is also good. The Barbera Bric d'Alì '99 is very pleasant.

● Barbera d'Asti Sup. S. Lorenzo '99	ᵧᵧ 4*
● Monferrato Bricco della Ghiandaia '98	ᵧᵧ 5
● Barbera d'Asti Sup. Bric d'Alì '99	ᵧ 4

Alfonso Boeri
Via Bionzo, 2
14055 Costigliole d'Asti (AT)
Tel. 0141968171
E-mail: boeri@boerivini.it

The Boeri family makes a remarkably flavoursome Barbera d'Asti, Porlapà. The '99 has a very dense colour and a nose that ranges from balsamic notes to hints of plum and spice. The close-knit and well-structured, if slightly mouthdrying, palate ends on an attractive note of flowers.

● Barbera d'Asti Sup. Porlapà '99	ᵧᵧ 5

Liedholm
Villa Boemia
15040 Cuccaro Monferrato (AL)
Tel. 0131771916
E-mail: c.liedholm@liedholm.com

Carlo Liedholm makes a fine Barbera whose personality comes through in mineral notes and varietal acidity. The flowers and spice Grignolino 2001 is also well-typed. For now, the cellar's flagship bottles are not available so we'll have to wait for the Rosso della Boemia and the Barbera Tonneau.

● Grignolino del M.to Casalese '01	ᵧ 3*
● Barbera d'Asti '00	ᵧ 3*

F.LLI ABRIGO
VIA MOGLIA, 1
12055 DIANO D'ALBA (CN)
TEL. 017369104

The Abrigos grow their grapes in the excellent Sörì dei Berfi vineyard and make two interesting Dolcetto di Diano d'Alba 2001 selections. They're a tad unsophisticated but very pleasant to drink. Vigna Pietrìn 2001 has impressive structure and the Sörì dei Berfi is distinctly agreeable.

- Diano d'Alba Sörì dei Berfi
  Vigna Pietrìn '01   ŸŸ 4*
- Diano d'Alba Sörì dei Berfi '01   Ÿ 3

CASAVECCHIA
VIA ROMA, 2
12055 DIANO D'ALBA (CN)
TEL. 017369205

The Casavecchia brothers – Carlo is an oenologist with Corvo – run this Diano cellar, releasing fine versions of the local classics. Sörì Richin has still to be bottled so we tasted the refreshing 2001 Sörì Bruni, a delicious Barbera San Quirico and the excellent Langhe Rosso Passo del Lupo '99.

- Langhe Rosso
  Passo del Lupo '99   ŸŸ 4*
- Diano d'Alba Sörì Bruni '01   Ÿ 3
- Barbera d'Alba San Quirico '99   Ÿ 4

PAOLO MONTE - CASCINA FLINO
VIA ABELLONI, 7
12055 DIANO D'ALBA (CN)
TEL. 017369231

The range of wines released by Paolo Monte is increasingly reliable. The Dolcetto Vigna Vecchia 2001 is well-structured and faithfully mirrors the fruit-rich characteristics of the wine type. In contrast, the Barbera d'Alba Flin 2000 is appreciably flavoursome and fills the mouth well.

- Diano d'Alba Vigna Vecchia '01   ŸŸ 3*
- Barbera d'Alba Flin '00   ŸŸ 4

MASSIMO ODDERO
VIA SAN SEBASTIANO, 1
12055 DIANO D'ALBA (CN)
TEL. 017369169
E-MAIL: massimo.oddero@isiline.it

There are two very good wines from the cellar run by Massimo Oddero, one of the longest-established winemakers at Diano. His Rosso del Notaio, a blend of barbera and nebbiolo, is a serious wine, with complex aromas and a rich, etheric palate. The Dolcetto Sorba 2001 is fresh and easy-drinking.

- Rosso del Notaio   ŸŸ 5
- Diano d'Alba Sorba '01   Ÿ 4

RICCHINO - TIZIANA MENEGALDO
CASCINA RICCHINO
12055 DIANO D'ALBA (CN)
TEL. 0142488884

This family-run estate makes only one wine, a Dolcetto di Diano d'Alba. The Rizieri vineyard yields a few, very convincing bottles – the 2000 is better now than it was last year – and is one of the DOC zone's finest selections. Purple red in hue, it has fruit on the nose and a full-bodied palate.

- Diano d'Alba Rizieri '01   ŸŸ 4

GIOVANNI VEGLIO E FIGLI
FRAZ. VALLE TALLORIA
VIA CANE, 7
12055 DIANO D'ALBA (CN)
TEL. 0173231752

The Veglios from Valle Talloria are back in the Guide after a couple of years' absence with an excellent Diano d'Alba Puncia d'l Bric 2001. It is short on finesse but very authentic, with aromas of plum and hazelnut introducing a warm, harmonious palate and a bitterish twist in the finish.

- Diano d'Alba Puncia d'l Bric '01   ŸŸ 3*

Osvaldo Barberis
B.ta Valdibà, 42
12063 Dogliani (CN)
tel. 017370054
e-mail: brekos@jumpy.it

Barberis has two nice, very well-typed 2001 Dolcetto di Dogliani wines, Puncin and San Lorenzo. Puncin offers a compact hue and creamy notes layered over fruit, then a palate with a vibrant tannic weave. The San Lorenzo is more straightforward while the Barbera Brichat 2001 is pleasingly soft.

- Dolcetto di Dogliani Puncin '01   4*
- Dolcetto di Dogliani
  San Lorenzo '01   3
- Piemonte Barbera Brichat '01   4

Boschis
Fraz. San Martino di Pianezzo, 57
12063 Dogliani (CN)
tel. 017370574
e-mail: m.boschis@tiscalinet.it

This year's range includes two good 2001 Dolcettos, Vigna Sorì San Martino and Pianezzo. We preferred the first, for its dense colour, a nose that opens with hints of crushed fruit, and its attractive structure. The Pianezzo is drier and less complex, revealing nice warmth in the finish.

- Dolcetto di Dogliani
  Vigna Sorì San Martino '01   4*
- Dolcetto di Dogliani Pianezzo '01   3

Ribote
Fraz. San Luigi
B.ta Valdiberti, 24
12063 Dogliani (CN)
tel. 017370371

Bruno Porro's wines continue to convince, in fact he seems to have given the cellar a new lease of life. We liked both Bruno's Dolcetto 2001 selections but the more elegant, cleaner Ribote came out ahead of the Monetti.

- Dolcetto di Dogliani Ribote '01   4*
- Dolcetto di Dogliani Monetti '01   3

Eraldo Revelli
Loc. Pianbosco, 29
12060 Farigliano (CN)
tel. 0173797154
e-mail: eraldorevelli@tin.it

The Revellis make excellent Dolcettos, starting with the San Matteo, a deep-hued wine with aromas of wild berries and hay over creamy notes. The palate has great breadth and depth, and the finish lingers. The Autin Lungh has notes of fruit pastilles and good acidic grip in the mouth.

- Dolcetto di Dogliani
  San Matteo '01   4*
- Dolcetto di Dogliani
  Autin Lungh '01   4

Castello di Lignano
Reg. Lignano
15035 Frassinello Monferrato (AL)
tel. 0142925326
e-mail: vinidoc@castellodilignano.it

The many 2000 wines presented by Giuseppe Gaiero included a fine Lhennius. This minerally blend of barbera, cabernet and freisa has a decently structured palate. There was also a well-typed Barbera Vigna Stramba with gutsy acidity and a bright, pleasant Freisa La Frassinella.

- Monferrato Freisa
  La Frassinella '00   4
- Monferrato Rosso Lhennius '00   5
- Barbera d'Asti Vigna Stramba '00   5

Il Rocchin
Loc. Vallemme, 39
15066 Gavi (AL)
tel. 0143642228

The Zerbos make Gavi and Dolcetto. Best of the Gavis is the Vigna del Bosco, a green-flecked, straw-yellow wine with aromas of apples and pears, and tidy balance in the mouth. The basic Gavi is uncompromising, with a marked vein of acidity and a slightly fuzzy nose. The Dolcetto packs a punch.

- ○ Gavi del Comune di Gavi
  Vigna del Bosco '01   4*
- ○ Gavi del Comune di Gavi '01   3
- Dolcetto di Ovada '01   3

La Scolca
Fraz. Rovereto, 170/r
15066 Gavi (AL)
Tel. 0143682176
E-mail: info@scolca.it

This historic Gavi winery presented a range that isn't quite up to previous standards. The Gavi Etichetta Nera is only satisfactory but the Brut Soldati La Scolca '96 is delicious, revealing yeasty aromas and a characterful palate. The non-vintage Soldati Brut La Scolca is also pleasant.

○ Soldati La Scolca Brut '96	🍷🍷	6
○ Gavi dei Gavi Etichetta Nera '01	🍷	6
○ Soldati La Scolca Brut	🍷	5

Santa Seraffa
Loc. Colombare
15066 Gavi (AL)
Tel. 0143643600
E-mail: santaseraffa@libarnanet.it

We are happy to record the continuing improvements at Santa Seraffa, tucked away in the woods just outside Gavi. As we await the new Gavi Ca' di Maggio, there are three wines of note, the Gavi Le Colombare, the Piemonte Cortese Tejolo and the red Dioniso, a blend of cabernet, merlot and barbera.

○ Gavi del Comune di Gavi Le Colombare '01	🍷🍷	4*
○ Piemonte Cortese Tejolo '01	🍷	3
● Dioniso	🍷	4

Torraccia del Piantavigna
Via Romagnano, 69/a
28074 Ghemme (NO)
Tel. 0163844711

Alessandro Francoli's cellar makes a fine range of wines from estate-grown grapes. The Ghemme '98 is well-made but lacks expressiveness. The Gattinara '98 is no more than well-made while the Nebbiolo Tre Confini is a great red to drink through the meal. It shows silky fruit and nice breadth.

● Ghemme '98	🍷	5
● Gattinara '98	🍷	5
● Colline Novaresi Nebbiolo Tre Confini '01	🍷	3

F.lli Ferrero
Fraz. Annunziata, 30
12064 La Morra (CN)
Tel. 017350691
E-mail: renato.ferrero@tiscalinet.it

The Ferrero family's wines get better every year. They are made with selected fruit from the best plots in Annunziata, at La Morra. The '98 Barolo Manzoni is a fine, austere wine with great length, as is the Gattere Bricco Luciani. The 2000 Barbera d'Alba Goretta is concentrated and balanced.

● Barolo Manzoni '98	🍷🍷	7
● Barolo Gattere Bricco Luciani '98	🍷🍷	7
● Barbera d'Alba Goretta '00	🍷	5

Gianni Gagliardo
Fraz. Santa Maria
12064 La Morra (CN)
Tel. 017350829
E-mail: gagliardo@gagliardo.it

There aren't many producers of Barolo Chinato but one of the best is Gianni Gagliardo. His version has notes of medicinal herbs and liquorice. The sweetness is kept under control and dry tannins lend tidy balance. The evolved Barolo '98 has good tertiary aromas and the Dolcetto 2001 is tannin-rich.

● Barolo Chinato	🍷🍷	7
● Barolo '98	🍷	8
● Dolcetto d'Alba Paulin '01	🍷	5

Aurelio Settimo
Fraz. Annunziata, 30
12064 La Morra (CN)
Tel. 017350803
E-mail: a.settimo@winecompany.net

This cellar's Rocche is one of the best traditional Barolos around. The Riserva '96 is well up to par with its dense hue and hints of leather and jam layered over a briny note. Well-structured on the palate, it ends on a hint of cocoa powder. The spicy, dryish standard Barolo is as good as ever.

● Barolo Rocche Ris. '96	🍷🍷	7
● Barolo '98	🍷	6

Luigi Spertino
Strada Lea, 505
14044 Mombercelli (AT)
tel. 0141959098

Mauro Spertino runs this winery with his father, Luigi. They are known in Italy for their Grignolino selections. The Spertinos use estate-grown and bought-in grapes to make traditional wines, like the Barbera d'Asti 2000, and more innovative bottles, like the pinot nero and cabernet '98 Rosso N. 1.

• Barbera d'Asti '00	🍷🍷	4*
• Rosso N. 1 '98	🍷🍷	6
• Grignolino d'Asti '01	🍷	4

Cascina Orsolina
Via Caminata, 28
14036 Moncalvo (AT)
tel. 0141917277
e-mail: cascinaorsolina@tin.it

Monferrato Rosso Sole '99 adds lustre to the De Negri family range. Intense in hue, it has a nose of fruit and green notes, lifted by oak. The palate has fleshy fruit, a bright personality and a long finish. The Grignolino 2001 and the Barbera Bricco dei Cappuccini '99 are both good.

• Monferrato Rosso Sole '99	🍷🍷	5
• Barbera d'Asti Sup. Bricco dei Cappuccini '99	🍷	5
• Grignolino d'Asti San Giacu '01	🍷	3

Bussia Soprana
Loc. Bussia, 81
12065 Monforte d'Alba (CN)
tel. 039305182

The Mosconi is the best of the '98 Barolos from Bussia Soprana. The crisp nose offers hints of violets, liquorice and jam, then the juicy palate shows nice balance. The Vigna Colonello has good structure and a nose laced with cream and balsam. The basic Barolo is less demanding and a tad austere.

• Barolo Mosconi '98	🍷🍷	7
• Barolo Vigna Colonnello '98	🍷	7
• Barolo '98	🍷	7

Renato Boveri
Via XXV Aprile, 1
15059 Monleale (AL)
tel. 013180560

Renato Boveri has an intriguing list of wines, ranging from Barbera and Dolcetto through to Croatina. The Colli Tortonesi Cortese '97 is very distinctive. After unhurried barrique ageing, it emerged to win Two Glasses. The full-bodied, pervasive Barbera Monleale '98 is also very good.

• Colli Tortonesi Barbera Monleale '98	🍷🍷	6
○ Colli Tortonesi Cortese Munprò '97	🍷🍷	6

Valerio Aloi
Via Milano, 45
12052 Montà (CN)
tel. 0173975604

Valerio Aloi's range is going places. His Roero Bricco Morinaldo 2000 is a fine example of its type, with lots of fruit and body. The Barbera Bricco Valpiana, another 2000, is a supple, moreish wine. Also good is the Roero Arneis Liffrei 2001, as enjoyably refreshing as an Arneis should be.

• Roero Bricco Morinaldo '00	🍷🍷	4*
• Barbera d'Alba Bricco Valpiana '00	🍷🍷	4*
○ Roero Arneis Liffrei '01	🍷	3

Cantina del Glicine
Via Giulio Cesare, 1
12057 Neive (CN)
tel. 017367215
e-mail: cantinaglicine@tiscalinet.it

The ancient cellars of this historic Neive winery are worth a visit. You will find past vintages of the Barbaresco that the cellar still makes to a very high standard. The '99 edition brought an elegant Curà with stylish notes of autumn leaves and leather, as well as a robust, tannic Marcorino.

• Barbaresco Curà '99	🍷🍷	7
• Barbaresco Marcorino '99	🍷	7

Castello di Neive
Via Castelborgo, 1
12057 Neive (CN)
Tel. 017367171
E-mail: neive-castello@tin.it

Castello di Neive is one of the leading wineries in the Barbaresco DOCG zone. This year, it released two selections, the Santo Stefano and the La Rocca di Santo Stefano, both '98s. The first is excellent, the second austere and elegant. Castello di Neive also makes a fine Dolcetto d'Alba.

- Barbaresco Santo Stefano '98 — 7
- Barbaresco La Rocca di Santo Stefano '98 — 8
- Dolcetto d'Alba Basarin '01 — 4

Ottavio Lequio - Prinsi
Via Gaia, 6
12057 Neive (CN)
Tel. 017367192

Ottavio Lequio made his name with two excellent Barbarescos. The Gallina is from one of the DOCG zone's finest vineyards. The '98 is ruby, shading into orange at the rim, with complex aromas and an austere palate. The basic '99 is already fresh and tempting but will improve with more cellar time.

- Barbaresco Gallina '98 — 6*
- Barbaresco '99 — 6*

Punset
Fraz. Moretta, 5
12057 Neive (CN)
Tel. 017367072
E-mail: punset@punset.com

This Neive winery makes a fine range of wines from organically grown grapes. Especially impressive at our tastings were the two 1999 Barbarescos. The Campo Quadro selection stood out for its aroma-rich nose and fine palate. The second-label version is less challenging but still well-made.

- Barbaresco Campo Quadro '99 — 7
- Barbaresco '99 — 6

Antonio Baldizzone
Cascina Lana
C.so Acqui, 187
14049 Nizza Monferrato (AT)
Tel. 0141726734

This year, the panel particularly liked Antonio Baldizzone's Moscato, a rich-hued wine with lovely notes of citrus peel, peach and honey. The tight weave of the palate, the discreet prickle and above all the long finish are very satisfying. The Barbera Vin ed Michen is proving ever more reliable.

- Moscato d'Asti 01 — 4*
- Barbera d'Asti Sup. Vin ed Michen '00 — 5

Cascina Giovinale
Strada San Nicolao, 102
14049 Nizza Monferrato (AT)
Tel. 0141793005

Cascina Giovenale is making headway on the Nizza Monferrato wine scene. The two much-praised Barbera d'Asti selections have been joined by the Nizza Anssèma. We retasted the attractive standard Barbera, the fruity Anssèma and the elegantly structured Anssèma Nizza, all from the 2000 vintage.

- Barbera d'Asti Sup. Anssèma '00 — 5
- Barbera d'Asti Sup. Nizza Anssèma '00 — 5
- Barbera d'Asti '00 — 4

Erede di Armando Chiappone
Strada San Michele, 51
14049 Nizza Monferrato (AT)
Tel. 0141721424
E-mail: info@eredechiappone.com

This cellar has ten hectares planted to vine at San Michele, on the hills overlooking Nizza Monferrato. The most impressive of the wines we tasted was the powerful 2000 Barbera d'Asti Superiore from the Nizza subzone. The Barbera Brentura is well-executed, albeit less full-bodied.

- Barbera d'Asti Sup. Nizza '00 — 5
- Barbera d'Asti Brentura '00 — 3

Cascina Ulivi
Strada Mazzola, 14
15067 Novi Ligure (AL)
Tel. 0143744598 - 01436756430
E-mail: cascinaulivi@libero.it

Cascina Ulivi always turns out an interesting range from its organically grown grapes. The panel liked the 2000 Barbera Mounbè best for its roundness and breadth. The Barbera Venta Quemada is as good as ever while the Gavi is frank and well-made.

● Piemonte Barbera Mounbè '00	🍷🍷	4*
● Piemonte Barbera Venta Quemada '01	🍷	3
○ Gavi Filagnotti '01	🍷	3

Valditerra
Strada Monterotondo, 75
15067 Novi Ligure (AL)
Tel. 0143321451

Good news from this lovely cellar at Novi Ligure. The Rosso FiorDesAri 2000, from barbera, merlot, cabernet and freisa, is very good and coasted to a second Glass, thanks to a palate with structure and plenty of thrust. The fruit aromas and robust palate of the Gavi 2001 are also worthy of note.

● FiorDesAri Rosso '00	🍷🍷	5
○ Gavi Sel. Valditerra '01	🍷	4

Favaro
Via Chiusure, 1/bis
10010 Piverone (TO)
Tel. 012572606
E-mail: favaro.chiusure@hotmail.com

This small Piverone cellar is as dependable as ever, turning out a limited number of bottles of excellent Erbaluce di Caluso from less than one hectare of vineyard. The Vigna delle Chiusure 2001 has an almost musky nose and good length on the palate, which closes on a varietal bitterish note.

○ Erbaluce di Caluso Vigna delle Chiusure '01	🍷🍷	4*

Verrina
Via San Rocco, 14
15010 Prasco (AL)
Tel. 0144375745

Dolcetto from this area is named after Ovada and it is the mainstay of this admirable eight-hectare estate. The fragrant, fruity Vigna Oriali 2001 is a very good selection. In contrast, the Semonina is more assertive, but nonetheless deliciously drinkable.

● Dolcetto di Ovada Vigna Oriali '01	🍷🍷	3*
● Dolcetto di Ovada Vigna Semonina '01	🍷	3

Viticoltori Associati di Rodello
Fraz. Vaj - Via Montà, 13
12050 Rodello (CN)
Tel. 0173617318
E-mail: assovini@assovini.it

Viticoltori Associati di Rodello make some nice Dolcetto d'Alba selections. Two of the best are the fragrant Vigna Deserto, which has a varietal twist of almond in the finish, and the more closed but tangy Vigna Campasso. The Langhe Rosso Vàj '99, an 80-20 blend of barbera and nebbiolo, is good.

● Langhe Rosso Vàj '99	🍷🍷	4
● Dolcetto d'Alba Vigna Campasso '01	🍷	3*
● Dolcetto d'Alba Vigna Deserto '01	🍷	3*

Saccoletto
S.S. Casale-Asti, 82
15020 San Giorgio Monferrato (AL)
Tel. 0142806509
E-mail: saccolettovini@libero.it

Daniele Saccoletto continues to make a large range of wines, encompassing all the main Monferrato types, from organically cultivated fruit. We liked the Barbera Aureum, a robust tipple not without a certain elegance, and the deliciously frank Brìna, from part-fermented moscato must.

● Barbera del M.to Aureum '00	🍷	4
○ Brìna	🍷	4

Guido Berta
Loc. Saline, 53
14050 San Marzano Oliveto (AT)
Tel. 0141856193
E-mail: bgpm@inwind.it

San Marzano Oliveto is in the heart of the Barbera d'Asti DOC zone and Guido Berta makes a couple of very good selections of this wine. His Barbera Superiore 2000 has good fruit and plenty of body. The well-extracted Canto di Luna has more complexity on the nose and a fruit-led palate.

● Barbera d'Asti Sup. Canto di Luna '00	▼▼ 4
● Barbera d'Asti Sup. '00	▼ 3

Carussin
Reg. Mariano, 22
14050 San Marzano Oliveto (AT)
Tel. 0141831358
E-mail: carussin@inwind.it

The Ferro family cultivate 13 hectares with the help of oenologist Vincenzo Munì. This year, they presented two very good Barbera d'Asti selections. The Ferro Carlo has intriguing fruit aromas and robust body. The convincing, well-typed Lia Vì is fresh-tasting and approachable.

● Barbera d'Asti Sup. Ferro Carlo '99	▼▼ 4*
● Barbera d'Asti Lia Vì '01	▼ 3

Franco Mondo
Reg. Mariano, 33
14050 San Marzano Oliveto (AT)
Tel. 0141834096
E-mail: francomondo@inwind.it

The '99 Barbera d'Asti Vigna delle Rose has a rich hue and a well-defined nose that reveals a persistent minerally note. The palate is mouthfilling, although not quite up to the previous vintage's standard. The easy-drinking, but not flabby, Dolcetto Trevigne satisfies, thanks to a good tannic weave.

● Barbera d'Asti Sup. Vigna delle Rose '99	▼ 4
● Monferrato Dolcetto Trevigne '01	▼ 3

Tenuta Il Falchetto
Fraz. Ciombi - Via Valle Tinella, 16
12058 Santo Stefano Belbo (CN)
Tel. 0141840344
E-mail: tenuta@ilfalchetto.com

The strong suit of the Forno family's range is Moscato. Tenuta del Fant is a moderately intense straw yellow. The subtle nose has good finesse, with flowers, apples and pears perceptible, then a palate enlivened by acidity and unobtrusive effervescence. The Barbera Lurèi 2000 is rustic and juicy.

○ Moscato d'Asti Tenuta del Fant '01	▼ 3
● Barbera d'Asti Sup. Lurèi '00	▼ 4

Giovanni Rosso
Via Foglio, 18
12050 Serralunga d'Alba (CN)
Tel. 0173613142
E-mail: wine@giovannirosso.com

There have been improvements in the range of the Serralunga-based Rossi family. Young Davide, an oenologist, has joined the team and is making his presence felt. Both Barolo '98 selections are good, although we preferred the more austere, full-bodied Ceretta. The Barbera d'Alba 2000 is also nice.

● Barolo Cerretta '98	▼▼ 7
● Barolo Serralunga '98	▼ 7
● Barbera d'Alba Donna Margherita '00	▼ 5

Bianchi
Via Roma, 37
28070 Sizzano (NO)
Tel. 0321810004
E-mail: e.bianchi@bianchibiowine.it

This historic cellar makes a range of wines using organic farming methods. The Eloise, from erbaluce and chardonnay, is an excellent blended white. The Primosole, a merlot, barbera and nebbiolo mix, is also interesting. Best of the DOCG wines was the typical, well-defined, standard Gattinara.

○ Eloise Bianco '00	▼▼ 3*
● Primosole Rosso '00	▼ 4
● Gattinara '97	▼ 4
● Gattinara Vigneto Valferana '97	▼ 5

La Zerba
Strada per Francavilla, 1
15060 Tassarolo (AL)
tel. 0143342259
e-mail: lazerba@novaonline.com

Luigi Lorenzi and his brother-in-law Andrea Mascherini run this small estate in Gavi country, on the slopes of Tassarolo. They make two wines, a basic Gavi and the Terrarossa selection. The Gavi is well-made and the Terrarossa reveals attractive hints of yeast and fruit, as well as a lively palate.

○ Gavi Terrarossa '01	🍷	3
○ Gavi '01	🍷	3

La Colombera
Fraz. Vho
15057 Tortona (AL)
tel. 0131867795
e-mail: la.semina@libero.it

Pier Carlo Semino and daughter Elisa Rosso are putting their plans to increase production and extend the cellar into effect. There are two new wines from La Colombera this year, the Timorasso Derthona and the Dolcetto Nibiò, both from the 2000 vintage. The Timorasso is particularly good.

● Colli Tortonesi Rosso Nibio '00	🍷🍷	6
○ Colli Tortonesi Bianco Derthona '00	🍷🍷	5

Orlando Abrigo
Via Cappelletto, 5
12050 Treiso (CN)
tel. 0173630232 - 017356120
e-mail: orlandoabrigo@libero.it

There are three fine wines in Abrigo's range, the Montersino and Rongallo Barbarescos and the merlot-based Livraie. The first has aromas of mineral and almonds, then a soft, decently structured palate. The Rongallo is sweet on the nose and has a slightly austere palate. The Livraie has good bite.

● Barbaresco Vigna Montersino '99	🍷🍷	6
● Barbaresco Vigna Rongallo '99	🍷	6

Pioiero
Loc. Pioiero, 1
12040 Vezza d'Alba (CN)
tel. 017365492
e-mail: info@pioiero.com

Antonio Rabino and his relations are doing a good job at this small Roero winery. We reds we liked were the full-bodied, stylish Roero Superiore 2000 and the young, very drinkable, Barbera d'Alba 2001. Equally convincing was the Arneis, which combines approachability with notes of sweetness.

● Barbera d'Alba '01	🍷	2*
● Roero Sup. '00	🍷	3
○ Roero Arneis Bric e Val '01	🍷	3

Cascina Montagnola
Strada Montagnola, 1
15058 Viguzzolo (AL)
tel. 0131898558
e-mail: cascina.montagnola@libero.it

Cascina Montagnola is a firmly established Colli Tortonesi estate. This year, the cellar did not release any barbera-based wines, having decided to allow them to improve with extended ageing. As usual, the Chardonnay Risveglio 2001 is impressive.

○ Risveglio Chardonnay '01	🍷🍷	5
○ Vergato Cortese '01	🍷	4

La Cella di San Michele
Via Cascine di Ponente, 21
13886 Viverone (BI)
tel. 016198245

The Enrietti family's winery has a lovely lakeside location at Viverone. Over the years, it has won a reputation for one of the finest Erbaluce di Caluso wines around. The 2001 is tangy, minerally and rich, with a good finish. The fragrant Brut, with its delicate perlage, is worth investigating.

○ Erbaluce di Caluso Cella Grande '01	🍷🍷	4*
○ Cella Grande di San Michele Brut	🍷	4

LIGURIA

Liguria's winemaking face is wearing a smile. There has been a significant burst of progress from Levante to Ponente, or from east to west, if you prefer. Slipshod winemaking is practically a thing of the past and several wineries have achieved excellence. Major estates are raising their sights higher with every vintage. The 2001 vintage goes down in the annals as a good one, despite a few problems with hail here and there. It is no coincidence that more pages in the Guide are dedicated to Liguria this year and the number of wineries with profiles or mentions in the Other Wineries section has gone up to 38. Although none has been awarded top honours, five seriously good wines have been rewarded with Two red Glasses. We have known for some time that Liguria has the potential for greatness, particularly since it became clear that the production philosophy of many wineries is driven by quality-oriented decisions. We can see evidence of this in investment, in research and experimentation, and in the collaboration of outside experts. Witness also the thoughtful, critical loyalty of growers to certain varieties, such as vermentino, pigato, bosco, rossese di Dolceacqua and ormeasco, which have forged Liguria's winemaking tradition and continue to symbolize it. However, this does not stop growers from obtaining modest quantities from international varieties. The winner of most Guide stemware this year is the Cascine delle Terre Rosse, a winery that has made great progress. Their Vermentino is outstanding and the Solitario is a very good red that is on its way to the top. Staying with reds, Tenuta Giuncheo has proved its worth with the Syrah Sirius and offers the best interpretation of rossese di Dolceacqua in its Pian del Vescovo selection. As for the other rossese wines, Mandino Cane's Vigneto Morghe and Terre Rosse's Bricco Arcagna have done well, and Terre Bianche also hit the spot with its Pigato. The same variety starred in Riccardo Bruna's range. Other fine Rosseses came from Vio, Alessandri, De Andreis, Calleri and Aschero, all of whom add a personal touch to their wines. Vermentino has become very popular and is grown throughout the region. It has proved to be very successful and Emanuele Trevia produced the top-scoring example. Trevia made a fine haul of Glasses and Lupi also charmed the panel with his standard version, the Le Serre selection and the seductive Vignamare. To the east, Lambruschi continues to show the way ahead with the Costa Marina and Sarticola crus while Pietra del Focolare deserves praise for the cellar's hard work and Santo Paterno selection. The tenacious 'R Mesueto and Il Torchio wineries have made tangible progress with excellent Vermentinos.

Walter De Battè has been as careful as ever in vineyard and cellar, where he enthusiastically continues his researches into Cinque Terre and Sciacchetrà, a wine type also nicely crafted by Buranco, one of this year's most exciting newcomers.

ALBENGA (SV)

CALLERI
REGIONE FRATTI, 2
17031 ALBENGA (SV)
TEL. 018220085

The Calleri range of wines is getting more interesting with every passing year. Meticulous selection of grapes purchased from trusted growers, plus the commitment and skill with which Marcello supervises the vinification process, have paved the way for some exciting new-generation whites that sink their roots firmly in tradition. The 2001 vintage includes two of the best selections from this winery in recent years. The first is the vigorous Vermentino I Muzazzi, named after a traditional vineyard in Pietra Ligure. Generous, well defined and nicely typed on the nose, it has subtle hints of wood resin, peaches, wild flowers and herbs, then the warm, rounded, flavoursome palate shows good balance and a long finish. The other outstanding selection, Pigato Saleasco, is proof of the huge potential of local varieties. The impressive, irresistibly fragrant nose of aromatic herbs, flowers and a touch of fruit ushers in a seamlessly substantial mouthfeel, sustained by good freshness, velvety flavour and almondy finish. The standard-label Pigato has generous aromas of ripe apricots and spring flowers that are mirrored on the dense, balanced palate. The base Vermentino was equally good. Grass and flower aromas, including broom and wistaria, precede a refreshingly drinkable palate with decent structure, good length and fresh acidity that is nicely offset by alcohol.

○ Riviera Ligure di Ponente
  Pigato Saleasco '01   4
○ Riviera Ligure di Ponente
  Vermentino I Muzazzi '01   4
○ Riviera Ligure di Ponente
  Pigato '01   4
○ Riviera Ligure di Ponente
  Vermentino '01   4

ALBENGA (SV)

CASCINA FEIPU DEI MASSARETTI
FRAZ. BASTIA
REG. MASSARETTI, 7
17031 ALBENGA (SV)
TEL. 018220131

The name Cascina Feipu is well known to lovers of fine wines. Enthusiasts and experts who make the pilgrimage have always enjoyed Pippo Parodi's sometimes caustic lectures on Ligurian winemaking as much as actually tasting his wines. A leading figure in the sector thanks to his professional ability and human qualities, Parodi is considered in Liguria as the precursor of the new approach to winemaking. Today, Pippo is a grand old gentleman who has stepped aside in order to make room for his daughter Ivana and son-in-law Mirko Mastroianni, although he has not given up dispensing good advice. The four and a half hectares are planted mainly to pigato – apparently the variety first reached the Albenga area in the early 17th century – and to a lesser extent rossese, barbera, dolcetto and brachetto. These provide the grapes for the two red wines made by Cascina Feipu. Mirko is in charge of the productive sector, leaving the marketing side to his wife, and devotes scrupulous care to the vineyards and cellars, which are equipped with all the most up to date technology. In the cellar, Mirko enjoys the technical assistance of Piedmontese winemaker Mino Moretti. Although sometimes the final product just fails to take off, quality is reliable, as is evident from the latest vintage. Straw yellow in colour, it releases subtle, delicate aromas that mingle hints of moss, undergrowth and honey with green apples and citrus fruit. The mouthfeel is pleasantly velvety, with slightly accentuated softness on the back palate, reasonable weight and enjoyable consistency of flavour.

○ Riviera Ligure di Ponente
  Pigato '01   4

ALBENGA (SV)

Fausto De Andreis
Fraz. Salea
Reg. Ruato, 4
17030 Albenga (SV)
tel. 018221175

First, here's a little information about the size of the estate, which also grows flowers. There's barely one hectare of vineyards here, yielding about 8,000 bottles per year, with the help of bought-in grapes. Still, there may be a significant expansion in the future with the arrival of new partners. Fausto himself is worth meeting. He's a versatile character, who has worked in electronics, sailing boats and furnishing, and a unique interpreter of pigato, which he vinifies with the skins. He uses six or seven-day floating cap macerations, scrupulously pumping the must over the cap and keeping the must temperature at about four degrees Celsius, though the cap itself can reach 20-22 degrees. This process gives the wine everything it needs to age unhurriedly in the cellar. The Spigàu 2001 gets your attention at once with its deep, gold-tinged straw yellow and an intriguingly complex nose that marries notes of minerals and balsam with almond blossom and peach fruit. It follows through well on the palate, where the clean, upfront flavour has good length and a pleasantly bitterish finish. The Crociata selection has the same intense nose as its stablemate, showing citron, iodine, wistaria, talcum powder and a marked aromatic note. Elegantly alcohol-rich on the very soft palate, it has reasonable structure and goodish balance.

ALBENGA (SV)

La Vecchia Cantina
Fraz. Salea
Via Corta, 3
17031 Albenga (SV)
tel. 0182559881

Umberto Calleri is above all serious. A man of few words, who knows his own mind, he has four hectares of vineyards, extending across Scuea, Cianboschi and Frati. The plots are planted to pigato, vermentino and rossese, and Umberto's wines are well-made, persuasive, drinkable and also worth laying down. Calleri does not like to delegate so he divides his time between the well cared-for vineyards and the small, but well-appointed cellar, which has all the appropriate technology. His interpretations of Ponente whites are inspired by a modern vinification style that leaves space for the benefits of tradition. Of the wines tasted this year, the Vermentino is especially successful, with its confident, subtly persistent, aromas of wild flowers, herbs, pine resin and almonds. The fresh-tasting palate echoes the nose with reasonable structure and a pleasantly bitterish aftertaste. The Pigato has an elegant, fragrant nose that shows quite good length but is not especially intense. Fruity and with hints of aromatic herbs and moss, it introduces an enjoyable but not particularly close-knit texture. A firm note of acidity adds freshness. Umberto's treasured new Passito – a small quantity of this wine type used to be made in this part of Albenga – is still ageing so we'll have to wait till next year to taste it.

○ Spigàu '01	🍷🍷	4*
○ Spigàu Crociata '01	🍷	4

○ Riviera Ligure di Ponente Pigato '01	🍷	4
○ Riviera Ligure di Ponente Vermentino '01	🍷	4

CAMPOROSSO (IM)

TENUTA GIUNCHEO
LOC. GIUNCHEO
18033 CAMPOROSSO (IM)
TEL. 0184288639
E-MAIL: info@tenutagiuncheo.it

Tenuta Giuncheo is strikingly beautiful. The geometric patterns of the vineyards – some on very steep slopes – alternate with large expanses of olives. But the winery is also impressive for the steps it is taking to improve quality. This year's range of wines is excellent. Particularly good are the two elegant, high profile reds which both show skilful use of oak, among other qualities. One of these is the Pian del Vescovo 2000, a Rossese di Dolceacqua selection, with rich, generous aromas of blackberry, strawberry, plum and white pepper as well as well-gauged oak. The long, velvety palate has a refreshing tang and room for further ageing. Sirius 2000 makes an even more attractive impact on the nose. A monovarietal syrah with an intense, complex bouquet that foregrounds mineral and spice, it has weight and a close-knit texture on the complex palate, where dense tannins emerge. The well-made base Rossese di Dolceacqua has a pleasantly fruity nose, then a tangy, drinkable palate with a reasonably long flavour. Moving on to the Vermentinos, the Le Palme selection is as persuasive as ever. The ripe aromas recall peaches, apples, almonds and honey, then the palate benefits from well-judged oak and good overall balance. The standard-label Vermentino is untypical but distinctive and immediately appealing. Pervasive, intense fruit is joined on the nose by hints of balsam, then a silky, warm, juicy entry on the palate.

● Sirius '00	▼▼	7
● Rossese di Dolceacqua Vigneto Pian del Vescovo '00	▼▼	5
○ Riviera Ligure di Ponente Vermentino '01	▼	4
○ Riviera Ligure di Ponente Vermentino Le Palme '01	▼	4
● Rossese di Dolceacqua '01	▼	4
● Rossese di Dolceacqua Vigneto Pian del Vescovo '99	▼▼	5
● Sirius '99	▼▼	7

CASTELNUOVO MAGRA (SP)

IL TORCHIO
VIA PROVINCIALE, 202
19030 CASTELNUOVO MAGRA (SP)
TEL. 0187674075

Giorgio Tendola continues the quest for quality he began a few years ago and the latest wines confirm this amiable grower's good work. It is not simply a question of technique. It's also Giorgio's astute interpretation of the raw materials at his disposal, and attempts to capture their best aspects in products of distinctive character. The most positive note comes from the Vermentino, the principal grape variety and wine in the Colle di Luni DOC. Thanks to a few hours of skin contact, it has a deep straw-yellow colour and confident character, with enjoyably upfront aromas that start with attractive vegetal hints, followed by honey, mimosa and damson and pear fruit. It opens out gradually and harmoniously on the silky, fresh-tasting, well-sustained palate that has fairly good structure and a clean, almondy finish. The Rosso, a blend of sangiovese and merlot with small proportions of other black grapes, ages in 25-hectolitre barrels. It shows interesting sweet aromas of ripe fruit, bottled cherries, and leather, which are mirrored well on the palate. The mouthfeel has good balance and weight, as well as laudable consistency and decent roundness, The alcohol is backed up by a vein of acidity. Il Torchio has about seven hectares of mostly south-facing vineyards, planted at a density of 4,000 vines per hectare for a yield about 70 quintals.

○ Colli di Luni Vermentino '01	▼▼	4*
● Colli di Luni Rosso '00	▼	4

CASTELNUOVO MAGRA (SP)

OTTAVIANO LAMBRUSCHI
VIA OLMARELLO, 28
19030 CASTELNUOVO MAGRA (SP)
TEL. 0187674261
E-MAIL: ottavianolambruschi@libero.it

The name Lambruschi has for some time been a sort of guarantee of quality for Ligurian Vermentino del Levante. Father and son Ottaviano and Fabio are united by a common passion and philosophy – the determined pursuit of quality. They are fully aware that quality can only come from good vineyard technique and vines planted to exploit the most favourable positions. The Lunigiana hills are hard to cultivate, and covered with the fragrant Mediterranean undergrowth that can often be distinguished in the aromas of Lambruschi Vermentinos. The wine from the latest vintage that impressed most at our blind tastings was the Costa Marina. A clear, lustrous straw yellow introduces a fresh, clean nose of aromatic herbs and Ligurian flowers that mingle well with soft floral, fruity and honeyed sensations. It has substance and balance in the mouth, with reasonable density, supple and consistency, then a long, delicious finish. The other selection, the Sarticola, is also good, as is the standard-label Vermentino. The Sarticola is subtle, stylish and fairly intense on the nose, where spring flowers, scrubland, citrus fruit, chestnut flower honey and light balsamic hints come through. Enjoyable tangy in the mouth, it has nice warmth and decent length. Despite its rather evanescent flavours, the base Vermentino has good aromas of myrtle, pine resin and wild flowers. The Rosso Maniero needs fine-tuning, as the wood still dominates the fruit and it lacks complexity.

○ Colli di Luni Vermentino Costa Marina '01	♛♛	4*
○ Colli di Luni Vermentino Sarticola '01	♛♛	4*
○ Colli di Luni Vermentino '01	♛	4
● Colli di Luni Rosso Maniero '01		4
○ Colli di Luni Vermentino Sarticola '00	♛♛	4
○ Colli di Luni Vermentino Costa Marina '00	♛	4

CHIAVARI (GE)

ENOTECA BISSON
C.SO GIANELLI, 28
16043 CHIAVARI (GE)
TEL. 0185314462
E-MAIL: bisson@bissonvini.it

Piero Lugano, an emblematic figure in the Golfo del Tigullio DOC, could not be said to lack enterprise. The work under way in his winery will allow him to break away from the mass of local growers and make wine exclusively from his own grapes. Progress has been reasonably quick, considering how much there was to be done. Piero now has ten hectares of vineyards available, and although these are mainly recent plantings, they promise well. The reduction in the number of wine types will nudge the winery towards results that reflect the effort Piero has put in. Best of the wines tasted this time is the Il Musaico Vigna dell'Intrigoso, from dolcetto and barbera. Clear ruby red with a pleasantly fruity nose, it reveals balanced freshness followed by subtle structure on the palate. Moving on to the whites, the Cinque Terre Marea has aromatic sea breeze aromas and good nose-palate consistency, backed up by light acidity. The Acini Rari, the winery's flagship "passito", is amber in colour with subtle hints of liquorice, almonds and walnuts on the nose, then balance and measured intensity in the mouth. Lastly ,the white U Pastine is a monovarietal Bianchetta made with grapes from a variety native to the province of Genoa. The pale, straw yellow has bright greenish hues, then the light nose of wild herbs and fennel precedes a dry flavour with well-controlled acidity.

○ Cinque Terre Marea '01	♛	4
○ Golfo del Tigullio Bianchetta Genovese U Pastine '01	♛	3
● Golfo del Tigullio Rosso Il Musaico Vigna dell'Intrigoso '01	♛	4
○ Acini Rari Passito '99	♛	6
○ Cinque Terre Marea Barrique '00		4
○ Golfo del Tigullio Vermentino Vigna Erta '01		4
○ Caratello Passito '99		5

CHIUSANICO (IM)

La Rocca di San Nicolao
Fraz. Gazzelli
Via Dante, 10
18023 Chiusanico (IM)
tel. 018352850 - 018352304
e-mail: info@roccasannicolao.it

The 2001 vintage confirms the status this young winery – its first wines were vinified only in 1994 – obtained in last year's Guide. The estate is named after the Benedictine monastery of San Nicolao, built around 1200 AD. Today, the Proxi vineyard, the winery's "cru", enjoys a dry climate and adequate ventilation. It is sheltered by a small chapel built from the rubble of the mediaeval monastery and also sits in a large natural amphitheatre. Six hectares of vineyards, with new vines planted at a density of around 8,500 plants per hectare, are supplemented with grapes bought in from other good local growers to guarantee enough fruit for about 80,000 bottles a year. The Pigato Vigna Proxi is nice. A lustrous colour introduces a varied, subtle, pervasive range of spring flower, pear and peach aromas. The palate needs time to mellow but is already balanced and lingering. The Vermentino Proxi is well-typed on the nose with Mediterranean scrubland and hints of wildflowers and herbs. However, it is still a little green on the palate, where there is reasonable texture and a long almondy finish. The appetizing standard-label Vermentino has light aromas of chamomile and pear, and the supple body is well-backed up with acidity. The base Pigato is a little disappointing. An enjoyably fresh nose, with hints of ferns, rosemary and citron, is followed by a rather uninspiring palate.

DIANO CASTELLO (IM)

Maria Donata Bianchi
Via delle Torri, 16
18010 Diano Castello (IM)
tel. 0183498233

The 2001 vintage was a good one for Emanuele Trevia's wines. One in particular stands out as one of the most successful and highest scoring whites in all our tastings. It is the cellar's base Vermentino, which combines the typical features of the variety – clearly defined aromas of Mediterranean scrubland, resin, Alpine herbs and aniseed – with complexity, elegance and considerable balance. The generous, complex progression on the palate has freshness and full structure. Year after year, the cellar proves its strength and dynamism – new plantings of grenache and syrah will soon yield a major red – and work in the cellar is guided by an astute balance of innovation and conservatism. The area's vocation for Vermentino (traditionally, Diano Castello has been synonymous with quality) is also confirmed in the highly successful Diana selection. Generous on the nose, with lavish aromas of citrus, apple, white damson and flowers, it has a harmonious, long palate and a pleasant almondy finish. The Pigatos come from the vineyards of Andora and Cisano sul Neva. The golden yellow base version has a stylish, nicely aromatic nose with fruity hints, all reflected on the full, generous palate. Artemide seemed a little more muted on the nose, with slightly sweet, fruit-rich aromas while velvety, fairly close-knit mouthfeel has a subtle twist of almond.

○	Riviera Ligure di Ponente Pigato Vigna Proxi '01	ΥΥ	4
○	Riviera Ligure di Ponente Vermentino '01	Υ	3
○	Riviera Ligure di Ponente Vermentino Vigna Proxi '01	Υ	4
○	Riviera Ligure di Ponente Pigato '01		3
●	Riviera Ligure di Ponente Rossese '01		3
○	Riviera Ligure di Ponente Pigato Vigna Proxi '00	ΥΥ	4

○	Riviera Ligure di Ponente Vermentino '01	ΥΥ	4
○	Riviera Ligure di Ponente Pigato '01	ΥΥ	4
○	Riviera Ligure di Ponente Vermentino Diana '01	ΥΥ	5
○	Riviera Ligure di Ponente Pigato Artemide '01	Υ	5
○	Riviera Ligure di Ponente Pigato Artemide '00	ΥΥ	5

DIANO MARINA (IM)

MONTALI E TEMESIO
FRAZ. GORLERI
STRADA SAVOIA
18013 DIANO MARINA (IM)
TEL. 0183495207
E-MAIL: info@montalitemesio.com

Notary Niccolò Temesio's winery has been in business since the 1970s. It is best known for its Vermentino, a serious and very dependable bottle. The cellar and three hectares of well-aspected hillslope vineyards with limy soil are in Diano Gorleri, a small inland town between Imperia and Diano Marina. Here, the breezes mingle country fragrances and seaside aromas that are also present in the wine. The best product this year is the Vermentino Costa dei Pini, which is more convincing this time thanks to well-expressed aromas and overall balance in the mouth. The clean, subtle nose has hints of dried herbs, spring flowers and peaches. The front and mid palate are good, with enjoyable freshness and reasonable weight. The Vigna Sorì – this is not the Piedmontese term for a hillslope vineyard but the name of the road running alongside the plot – is simpler. The nose has light aromatic notes of citron, herbs and wildflowers but the palate lacks complexity, even though it is tangy, balanced and fairly close-knit. Marco Temesio, who put his degree in political science back in the drawer to pursue his vocation, runs the winery with the enthusiasm and ability to innovate typical of the younger generation of winemakers. Ormeasco is his creation. It's a red made from dolcetto a raspo verde grapes grown in the small vineyard he rents at Pornassio in the upper Arroscia valley.

DOLCEACQUA (IM)

GIOBATTA MANDINO CANE
VIA ROMA, 21
18035 DOLCEACQUA (IM)
TEL. 0184206120

Dolceacqua is a pretty little town in the Nervia river valley. It has old stone houses, narrow alleyways, a splendid castle built by the Dorias and a charming arched bridge – as well as Rossese di Dolceacqua, otherwise known simply as Dolceacqua. This wine has ancient origins and bags of attitude. As appealing as a "vino novello", it also has the austerity of a mature wine. The virtues of the Dolceacqua hillslopes have long been famous and it is here you will find the property of Mandino Cane, a sprightly 70-year-old who was one of the first to commit to the recovery of Rossese. The range is limited to two Superiore wines, a standard label and a Vermentino. Best of the bunch is the Morghe, which again proved its worth in 2001. The name comes from a vineyard on the hill of the same name behind the old town centre. The wine is bright ruby red with pronounced red berry fruit, especially redcurrants and raspberries, and notes of minerals and spice. On the palate, the overall profile is stylish, with good extract showing skilful winemanship. The Arcagna is also quite interesting. This is the winery's classic label and it has a less ambitious flavour profile while still showing plenty of character. The balsamic and floral sensations, led by dried roses, are intense and the flavour is also satisfying. It's not madly complex but balanced and lingering. Lastly, the younger brother of these two selections, the standard-label Rossese, is fruity, fresh-tasting and balanced, but rather lean.

● Riviera Ligure di Ponente Ormeasco '01	♀	4
○ Riviera Ligure di Ponente Vermentino Costa dei Pini '01	♀	4
○ Riviera Ligure di Ponente Vermentino Vigna Sorì '01	♀	4

● Rossese di Dolceacqua Sup. Vigneto Morghe '01	♀♀	4
● Rossese di Dolceacqua Sup. Vigneto Arcagna '01	♀	4
● Rossese di Dolceacqua '01		3
● Rossese di Dolceacqua Sup. Vigneto Morghe '00	♀♀	4
● Rossese di Dolceacqua Sup. Vigneto Arcagna '00	♀	4

DOLCEACQUA (IM)

Terre Bianche
Loc. Arcagna
18035 Dolceacqua (IM)
Tel. 018431426 - 018431230
E-mail: terrebianche@terrebianche.com

Thanks to the excellent position of the estate, which faces southeast at 400 metres above sea level, the mild climate and the composition of the soil where vines flourish, Terre Bianche produces excellent grapes. If you add to these factors the commitment and technical skill of Paolo Rondelli's team, consisting of his nephew Filippo, Franco Laconi and Mario Ronco, it becomes clear why Terre Bianche wines score well every year. The selection presented for tasting this year was up to the usual standard, starting with the Bricco Arcagna, a monovarietal Rossese aged in small oak barrels. The 2000 is deep ruby red with pervasive, generous aromas that open on an oaky note and follow up with blackberry, blackcurrant and a hint of balsam. The entry on the palate is authoritative and there is good structure and decent tannin content. Two Glasses for the Pigato as well, which is well-defined, distinctive and well-typed. Intense, persistent aromas of wild herbs, citrus fruit, broom and almond blossom usher in a palate with balance and firm body. The delicious Vermentino has fresh flower aromas that are echoed on the balanced palate with its bitterish finish. The Arcana Rosso, from rossese and cabernet sauvignon, is good enough but lacks a little finesse. The fruity Rossese and the enjoyable Arcana Bianco, a blend of vermentino and pigato aged in barriques, are both worth uncorking.

FINALE LIGURE (SV)

Cascina delle Terre Rosse
Via Manie, 3
17024 Finale Ligure (SV)
Tel. 019698782

Vladimiro Galluzzo refused to rest on his laurels. He gambled on his own ideas and in just over ten years, brought the wines of Terre Rosse to levels of excellence, thanks to an interest in winemaking that soon became an all-consuming passion. It is no coincidence that his Solitario, a blend of grenache, barbera and rossese that ages slowly in barriques, has come on in leaps and bounds. A dense, ruby red colour that shades into garnet, it reveals mulberry and blueberry hints mingling with balsamic spice, notes that are reflected on the stylish palate, with its fine tannins, rich extract, good progression generous, lingering finish. The whites are just as good, though. The splendid Vermentino unveils a concentrated nose with hints of pear and banana, lifted by faintly aromatic notes of flowers. The firm, harmonious palate has refreshing acidity, consistency and good depth. The Pigatos behave like the aristocrats they are. The seductive golden yellow Apogeo has distinct white plum, apricot and tropical fruit aromas, with a hint of flowers. The close-knit texture has good balance and lots of juicy flesh. The base Pigato is similar. Generous, with well-focused aromas of peach, damson, aromatic herbs and resin, it reveals a tangy palate whose nicely balanced constituents unfold offer an interesting range of flavours and a long finish. The flavoursome Le Banche 2001, a blend of vermentino and pigato, is also satisfying.

● Rossese di Dolceacqua Bricco Arcagna '00	🍷🍷	4
○ Riviera Ligure di Ponente Pigato '01	🍷🍷	4
○ Arcana Bianco '00	🍷	5
● Arcana Rosso '00	🍷	6
○ Riviera Ligure di Ponente Vermentino '01	🍷	4
● Rossese di Dolceacqua '01	🍷	4
○ Riviera Ligure di Ponente Pigato '00	🍷🍷	4
● Rossese di Dolceacqua Bricco Arcagna '98	🍷🍷	6
● Rossese di Dolceacqua Bricco Arcagna '99	🍷	6

● Solitario '00	🍷🍷	7
○ Riviera Ligure di Ponente Vermentino '01	🍷🍷	4
○ Le Banche '01	🍷🍷	5
○ Riviera Ligure di Ponente Pigato '01	🍷🍷	4
○ Riviera Ligure di Ponente Pigato Apogeo '01	🍷🍷	5
○ Riviera Ligure di Ponente Pigato '99	🍷🍷🍷	4
○ Riviera Ligure di Ponente Pigato Apogeo '00	🍷🍷	5
○ Le Banche '00	🍷🍷	5
● Solitario '97	🍷🍷	7

IMPERIA

COLLE DEI BARDELLINI
LOC. BARDELLINI
VIA FONTANAROSA, 12
18100 IMPERIA
TEL. 0183291370 - 010594513

Pino Sola and wine is an alliance attested by long membership of the Italian Sommeliers' Association, by the wine shop in the centre of Genoa and, of course, by this winery, run with commitment and a practical approach. Four of the estate's six and a half hectares are given over to vineyards, in a sunny hillside position on a upland plain behind Oneglia. Gianni Briatore supervises the vineyards while the transformation of grapes into wine is entrusted to the experience of Giuliano Noè. The wines from the last vintage did not perform as well as we have come to expect in recent years, but both selections were awarded One Glass. The Vermentino Vigna U Munte has nice clear straw-yellow hue and low-key aromas that marry hints of Mediterranean scrubland harmoniously with wild flowers and musky sensations. It is rounded, fairly full and lingers on the palate, which is tangy and clean-tasting. The Pigato Vigna La Torretta fills the nostrils with soft aromas of apricot and peach. Entry on the palate is succulent and fresh-tasting, with considerable balance. The structure is noticeably fragile and the length rather limited. As well as the wines presented, Colle dei Bardellini makes standard-label Pigato and Vermentino, a Rossese Riviera Ligure di Ponente and extravirgin olive oil.

○ Riviera Ligure di Ponente Pigato Vigna La Torretta '01	♀	4
○ Riviera Ligure di Ponente Vermentino Vigna U Munte '01	♀	4
○ Riviera Ligure di Ponente Vermentino Vigna U Munte '00	♀♀	4

MONTEROSSO AL MARE (SP)

BURANCO
VIA BURANCO, 72
19016 MONTEROSSO AL MARE (SP)
TEL. 0187817677
E-MAIL: wachter@buranco.li

It's quite a way from Liechtenstein to the Cinque Terre, but its beauty convinced Kurt and Sonja Wachter that the Buranco river valley, from which the winery takes its name, was the ideal location to realize their life's dream: high-quality ecocompatible farming (the estate conforms to the regulations of AIAB – the Italian organic farming association). The adventure started in 1993 and work began in the vineyards the following year. The entire 27,000-square metre property is situated in Maggioa, on terraces at 40 to 90 metres above sea level. Vines cover about 10,000 square metres of the estate and olives and lemons grow on the rest. The splendid extract and aroma-rich grapes ripen on steep slopes that make cultivation difficult but enjoy excellent south-facing positions and in 2000, went into an excellent Sciacchetrà. This nectar-sweet wine has a lustrous amber colour and an intense, pervasive nose of dried figs, dried apricots, spices and balsam. Balance and softness – not opulence – are the keynotes on the palate, which has succulent fruit and good length. The dry Cinque Terre is made by fermenting 15 per cent of the must in barriques and the rest in stainless steel at a controlled temperature. The two parts are blended after a period on the yeasts with lees stirring, to make a wine with a clear, concentrated colour. The aromas range from charred oak to floral notes while the palate is delicate and noticeably tangy. These results are obtained with the help of Federico Curtaz, Giorgio Bacigalupi and Walter De Battè, a trusted workmate in the cellar.

○ Cinque Terre Sciacchetrà '00	♀♀	8
● Buranco '00	♀	6
○ Cinque Terre '01	♀	5

ORTONOVO (SP)

La Pietra del Focolare
Fraz. Isola di Ortonovo
Via Dogana, 209
19034 Ortonovo (SP)
Tel. 0187662129
E-mail: lapietradelfocolare@libero.it

A small, new winery and two young people with high hopes at the helm, husband and wife Stefano and Laura Salvetti. They only have a few vintages behind them so far and, although they are still flying by the seat of their pants to some extent, they know exactly where they want to land – with a wine that will bring out the very best of vermentino's unique features. This quest still involves the separate vinification of four selections. The Solarancio does not live up to the expectations we had formed from recent vintages and is only worth a mention. The estate's leading wine this year is the Santo Paterno, which stays in contact with the skins for 48 hours. Its deep straw yellow is flecked with gold, then interestingly complex aromas of ripe pears, pineapple, banana, chestnut honey, almonds and acacia blossom. The soft, warm palate is as good as the nose leads you to expect. There was a well-deserved One Glass for the Villa Linda, which has an attractive nose of Mediterranean scrubland, wildflowers and herbs but unravels a little in the mouth. The Augusto has rather forward aromas of ripe fruit, toasted bread, dried almonds and broom, and an enjoyable entry on the palate that is not, sadly, followed by sufficient weight. The finish has a distinctly bitterish note. This year, the red Re Carlo, from sangiovese, canaiolo and merlot, makes its debut. It is fresh and fairly astringent, but a little immature and lacking in weight.

○ Colli di Luni Vermentino Santo Paterno '01	🍷🍷	4*
○ Colli di Luni Vermentino Villa Linda '01	🍷	4
● Colli di Luni Rosso Re Carlo '00		4
○ Colli di Luni Vermentino Augusto '01		4
○ Colli di Luni Vermentino Solarancio '01		4

PIEVE DI TECO (IM)

Tommaso e Angelo Lupi
Via Mazzini, 9
18026 Pieve di Teco (IM)
Tel. 018336161 - 0183291610
E-mail: info@vinilupi.it

Adding up the numbers from this year's tastings, we can see that the results achieved by Tommaso and Angelo Lupi, with the help of their respective children, are far from insignificant. We have always admired the work of this major winery, which turns out 160,000 bottles a year and has a good reputation on foreign markets. Since it was founded in 1977, the cellar has unfailingly demonstrated it knows a thing or two about quality. The determined pursuit of a stylish white with plenty of finesse has borne fruit, in the shape of the Vignamare, a seductive blend of barrique-aged vermentino and pigato. The generous, tempting aromas interlace soft oak with notes of peach, apple and flowers. The palate mirrors the nose well, showing consistency, structure, length and silky texture. The Vermentino le Serre is very successful. Subtle aromas of pear, damson and pineapple tease the nose while on the palate there is rounded smoothness, a fruit-driven progression and good length. Another wine that plays the softness card – actually, they all do to some extent – is the standard Vermentino, with its delicate honey, apple, citron and spring flowers. The palate is warm, mouthfilling, balanced and weighty. Of the Pigatos, it was the Le Petraie selection that made the best impression. Delicately typical on the nose, it suggests moss, pine resin and aromatic herbs. Soothingly soft in the mouth, it also has decent thrust. The base Pigato, in contrast, is fairly one-dimensional.

○ Vignamare '00	🍷🍷	5
○ Riviera Ligure di Ponente Vermentino Le Serre '01	🍷🍷	5
○ Riviera Ligure di Ponente Pigato Le Petraie '01	🍷	5
○ Riviera Ligure di Ponente Vermentino '01	🍷	4
○ Riviera Ligure di Ponente Pigato '01		4
● Riviera Ligure di Ponente Ormeasco Sup. Le Braje '99	🏆	5
○ Vignamare '99	🏆	5

PONTEDASSIO (IM)

Laura Aschero
P.zza V. Emanuele, 7
18027 Pontedassio (IM)
tel. 0183293515

Let it never be said that Laura Aschero lacks energy or determination. Although nearly 80 years old, she has no intention of yielding control and continues to run the winery confidently, helped by her sons, Marco and Cesare. Laura frankly admits that her decision to plant vermentino and pigato vineyards in 1980, and later rossese, on the family lands was taken for investment reasons, and that her real passion only developed later, as recognition came. Today's production comes from three hectares in the Monti e Posai area of the municipality of Pontedassio, and grapes purchased around Diano from regular suppliers. The old winery in the centre of the little town has acquired more space and brought in modern, functional winemaking equipment ensure dependable quality, with a little help from oenologist Giampaolo Ramò. About 50,000 bottles of admirably typical monovarietal Vermentino and Pigato are produced each year. The excellent Vermentino is seductive, with intense aromas of wild flowers and broom, subtle woodland notes and a slightly fruity finish. The fresh flavour is supple, balanced and well sustained, echoing the nose well. The Pigato is a cut above, thanks to lingering aromas redolent of Mediterranean scrubland, forest herbs, moss and a hint of balsam. The palate echoes the nose with subtle warmth and a full, velvety flavour.

○ Riviera Ligure di Ponente Pigato '01	ŸŸ 4*
○ Riviera Ligure di Ponente Vermentino '01	ŸŸ 4*

RANZO (IM)

A Maccia
Fraz. Borgo
Via Umberto I, 54
18028 Ranzo (IM)
tel. 0183318003

Take three hectares of good land near Ranzo, one of the best areas for growing pigato, the prince of white Ligurian grapes. Expert Piedmontese winemaker Rossano Abbona is on hand. Add a cellar that has become increasingly well-organized over time and an olive grove of about seven hectares, including some orchards, which yields taggiasco olives, used to make excellent extravirgin olive oil. Put it all together and you have A Maccia, the estate that is Loredana Faraldi's pride and joy. Loredana uses grapes that ripen at 150-200 metres above sea level, vinifying them scrupulously with great attention to fermentation temperatures, which are controlled using the cold water circulation method, and giving the must a limited period of skin contact (about six hours). That's how Loredana obtains her 12,000 bottles per year of consistently good wine. The 2001 Pigato is clear straw yellow with subtle greenish highlights. The nose has stylish, whistle-clean nuances of fruit and woodland fragrances, with hints of freshness. The palate powers through determinedly. Although it could have been fuller, it has decent balance and length. A Maccia also makes a few bottles of Rossese in the Riviera Ligure di Ponente DOC zone, which is very different from the better-known Dolceacqua Rossese. The 2001 tempts the nose with pleasant fruity sensations that introduce a dry but warm palate with moderate structure but good nose-palate consistency and an absolutely typical bitterish finish.

○ Riviera Ligure di Ponente Pigato '01	Ÿ 4
● Riviera Ligure di Ponente Rossese '01	Ÿ 4

RANZO (IM)

ALESSANDRI
FRAZ. COSTA PARROCCHIA
18028 RANZO (IM)
TEL. 018253458

Like its owner, this winery is young but in just a handful of years, it has found a length and has taken its place among the emerging wineries of the Ligurian Ponente. We are in Ranzo, a small town in Valle Arroscia, surrounded by olive groves and vineyards. Massimo Alessandri's three and a half hectares of pigato, with small quantities of syrah and grenache, are in Bonfigliara, at 250 and 350 metres above sea level. The site climates and soil types here are especially well-suited to growing pigato grapes and the wines of this area are usually bursting with character. Since he began making wine – his first wines were on the market in 1997 – Massimo has put the emphasis on vineyard work, which is followed by vinification that shuns extremes of technology but instead adopts traditional practices, like leaving the must in contact with the skins for a couple of days. Technical advice comes from highly respected Piedmontese winemaker Walter Bonetti, who has made a valuable contribution to quality improvement. The Costa de Vigne 2001 stood out in the tasting – despite partial damage to the grapes by hail – for its very good typing. The deep colour is followed by a generous aroma with hints of citrus fruit, peaches and sage, and a touch of mineral. The flavour is complex and pleasantly almondy, echoing the aroma-rich nose, while the development is supported by good texture, tangy softness and balance, leading through to an enjoyable finish.

○ Riviera Ligure di Ponente Pigato Costa de Vigne '01	🍷🍷	4

RANZO (IM)

BRUNA
VIA UMBERTO I, 81
18028 RANZO (IM)
TEL. 0183318082
E-MAIL: aziendaagricolabruna@libero.it

Riccardo Bruna has worked in the wine sector for 30-odd years and can still astonish with his enterprise – he has been planting new vineyards and varieties – and the unwavering enthusiasm that has also infected his daughters. The soil and climate enjoyed by hillside plantations like Russeghine have earned themselves a fine reputation. This is also where most of the grapes used for the winery's leading Pigato, U Bacan, come from. The 2001 version, which shows definite growth potential, has pervasively warm, Mediterranean nuances and intense floral, and slightly fruity, aromas. The palate is a perfect balance of tanginess, freshness and alcohol; there is good nose-palate consistency, an enjoyable almondy vein and an unusually well-defined and stylish finish. To achieve his very typical wines year after year, Riccardo has decided to limit technical input in the vinification and ageing phases to the bare necessities. The resulting wines are dense and do not follow the same calendar as more immediately drinkable bottles. That is the case with this year's Pigato Villa Torrachetta. It has a good, complex nose with hints of peaches, apricots, aromatic herbs and undergrowth, along with sinew, consistency, good structure and complexity on the palate. The Pigato Le Russeghine is another interpretation of the same DOC. Its intense, strongly fruity nose is lifted by aromatic complexity and there's plenty of freshness on the palate.

○ Riviera Ligure di Ponente Pigato U Bacan '01	🍷🍷	5
○ Riviera Ligure di Ponente Pigato Villa Torrachetta '01	🍷🍷	4
○ Riviera Ligure di Ponente Pigato Le Russeghine '01	🍷🍷	4
○ Riviera Ligure di Ponente Pigato U Bacan '00	🍷🍷	5
○ Riviera Ligure di Ponente Pigato Le Russeghine '00	🍷🍷	4

RIOMAGGIORE (SP)

Walter De Batté
Via Trarcantu, 25
19017 Riomaggiore (SP)
tel. 0187920127

Few people still work this hard, ungenerous land, growing the grapes that go into the two jewels in the crown of Cinque Terre winemaking, Sciacchetrà and the dry local white. These two extraordinary wines are made from the ancient albarola and bosco grapes traditionally grown in this strip of land from Monterosso to Riomaggiore, which have gradually been replaced over the years by the more profitable vermentino. Walter De Battè is one of the emblematic winegrowers in this tiny wedge of Liguria. He's an uncompromising character who works his few metres of terraced vineyards with traditional methods and low yields. Walter is also a convinced supporter of the bosco variety and, in recent years, has worked hard to give it the attention it deserves. His passion is revealed in the wines he makes. Extremely rigorous selections aim to marry local tradition and the winemaking techniques adopted in the best areas for white and dried-grape wines. Walter's best result is the Cinque Terre 2001, whose lustrous yellow hue gives an early glimpse of its potential. On the nose, this wine is slow to express itself, opening with hints of Mediterranean scrubland and interesting mineral notes. It explodes onto the palate and the mineral notes make a strong comeback in a thoroughly decent body. The 2000 Sciacchetrà is also praiseworthy. Amber in colour, its aromas of baked and dried fruit, honey and vanilla introduce a richly extracted palate that is sweet but not cloying, contrasting well with the assertive toastiness of the oak.

O Cinque Terre Sciacchetrà '00	¶¶	8
O Cinque Terre '01	¶¶	6
O Cinque Terre Sciacchetrà Ris. '98	¶¶	8

VENDONE (SV)

Claudio Vio
Fraz. Crosa
17032 Vendone (SV)
tel. 018276338

Claudio Vio rejoins the Two Glass club with the 2001 vintage, thanks to his excellent Pigato and its intense, warm aromas of scrubland, broom and basil-led aromatic herbs. The colour is deep and the balanced palate dry and velvety, lingering unhurriedly as it mirrors the aromas on the nose. It's a wine with bags of personality and a good clean finish. The Vermentino is also good, and, as expected, rather like a Pigato in the Vio version. Clear, straw yellow, it has an interestingly long and rather generous nose, with aromas of Ligurian herbs, sage and conifers. The palate is fresh and stylish, with a pleasant almondy hint in the finish. This is a good performance from a young local winegrower who has followed in his father's footsteps. The south-facing hillside vineyards, at 300 metres above sea level, are surrounded by local flora and entirely owned by Vio's family. The vines are gobelet-trained on mainly sedimentary soil and the yield is 60-65 quintals per hectare. The equipment in the small winery has been slightly updated in the last year and work is being carried out there under the supervision of Walter Bonetti, the respected Piedmontese oenologist. This is Pigato country and the wine type accounts for 11,000 of the 14,000 bottles the winery produces each year.

O Riviera Ligure di Ponente Pigato '01	¶¶	4*
O Riviera Ligure di Ponente Vermentino '01	¶	4

OTHER WINERIES

Anfossi
Fraz. Bastia - Via Paccini, 39
17030 Albenga (SV)
tel. 018220024
e-mail: anfossi@aziendaagrariaanfossi.it

Mario Anfossi and Paolo Grossi produce about 70,000 bottles a year of Riviera Ligure di Ponente DOC wines. This year the best performance came from their Rossese, whose light fruity aromas are lifted by spicy notes. Attractively balanced in the mouth, it shows a typically almondy finish.

● Riviera Ligure di Ponente Rossese '01	▼ 4

Il Chioso
Loc. Baccano
19038 Arcola (SP)
tel. 0187986620 - 0187625147

Conte Nino Picedi Benettini is a historic figure in the winemaking world of eastern Liguria. His Vermentino Il Chioso is very good. Fresh, restrained hints of pears, rennet apples, spring flowers and herbs accompany a well-typed but not especially broad palate.

○ Colli di Luni Vermentino Il Chioso '01	▼ 3

'R Mesueto
Via Masignano, 61
19021 Arcola (SP)
tel. 0187987418
e-mail: maurobiassoli@interfree.it

Mauro Biassoli's Vermentino is a lovely wine with a deep, lustrous straw-yellow hued flecked with gold. The enthralling bouquet offers flowers and notes of plum, apricot and citron fruit while the rich, soft palate lingering silkily, braced up by well-judged acidity.

○ Colli di Luni Vermentino '01	▼▼ 4

Giacomelli
Via Palvotrisia, 134
19030 Castelnuovo Magra (SP)
tel. 0187674155
e-mail: giacomelli71@libero.it

Roberto Petacchi releases about 40,000 bottles a year from the grapes grown on his five hectares in Ortonovo and Castelnuovo Magra. The 2001 Vermentino has a superior nose of conifer, Mediterranean scrubland and wild flowers. The palate is soft, tangy, fresh and very drinkable.

○ Colli di Luni Vermentino '01	▼ 4

Enoteca Andrea Bruzzone
Via Bolzaneto, 94/96
16100 Genova
tel. 0107455157
e-mail: andreabruzz@libero.it

Andrea Bruzzone runs this thriving wine shop but for a few years now has also been indulging his real passion – buying in grapes from growers in Val Polcevera and making the traditional local varieties into wine. The enjoyably heady, fruit-driven Rosso has a fresh flavour and drinks deliciously.

• Val Polcevera Rosso Treipaexi '01	3

Nicola Guglierame
Via Castello, 10
18020 Pornassio (IM)
tel. 018333037

The typical features of the ormeasco grape are all present in this winery's Ormeasco Superiore 2000. Moderately deep ruby red, it is slow to release its rich youthful, morello cherry and pine resin aromas. The palate, which mirrors the nose, is quite well balanced.

• Riviera Ligure di Ponente Ormeasco Sup. '00	3

Giampaolo Ramò
Via S. Antonio, 9
18020 Pornassio (IM)
tel. 018333097

Professional oenologist Giampaolo Ramò is a skilled interpreter of the ormeasco grape. His rosé "Sciac-tra" is tangy and drinkable whereas the version fermented on the skins is ruby red, with a fruity nose, dry, slightly tannic palate and a pleasant almondy finish.

• Riviera Ligure di Ponente Ormeasco '01	4

Innocenzo Turco
Via Bertone, 7/a
17040 Quiliano (SV)
tel. 019887120

Lorenzo Turco has a few rows of granaccia, locally known as alicante, clinging to the hillslopes behind Savona. He turns the fruit into about 2,500 bottles of wine each year, some aged in barriques. The 2000 has a pleasant fruity, oak-enhanced nose that is echoed on the palate.

• Granaccia di Quiliano Vigneto Cappuccini Ris. '00	7

Forlini Cappellini
Loc. Manarola
Via Riccobaldi, 45
19010 Riomaggiore (SP)
tel. 0187920496

Helped by son Giacomo, Alberto and Germana produce a few thousand bottles of impeccably reliable dry Cinque Terre. The 2001 version is straw yellow flecked with gold and its nose is laced with herbal, floral and salty notes. Progression in the mouth is tangy and intriguing.

○ Cinque Terre '01	5

Cantina Cinqueterre
Loc. Groppo - Fraz. Manarola
19010 Riomaggiore (SP)
tel. 0187920435
e-mail: info5t@cantinacinqueterre.com

This co-operative is real local institution. Many winegrowers bring their grapes here to be vinified as vineyard selections. The standard Cinque Terre obtained most points, thanks to its upfront aromas and approachable palate. The amber-hued Sciacchetrà has marked fruity and honey sensations.

○ Cinque Terre Sciacchetrà '00	7
○ Cinque Terre '01	4

Il Monticello
Via Groppolo, 7
19038 Sarzana (SP)
tel. 0187621432
e-mail: sub@libero.it

Alessandro and Davide Neri make about 40,000 bottles of Vermentino and Rosso from five hectares on mainly clay and silt, south and southwest-facing terrain. The ruby red Rupestro has flower and ripe fruit aromas and still prominent tannins. It is worth investigating, as is the standard Vermentino.

● Colli di Luni Rosso Rupestro '01	♇	4
○ Colli di Luni Vermentino '01	♇	4

Santa Caterina
Via Santa Caterina, 6
19038 Sarzana (SP)
tel. 0187629429
e-mail: akih@libero.it

Andrea Kihlgren owns one of the emerging wineries in Colli di Luni. The Vermentino Poggi Alti stands out. It comes from a mixture of must macerated on the skins with some fermented at fairly high temperatures. The nose is subtle and captivating, the generous palate well sustained.

○ Colli di Luni Vermentino Poggi Alti '01	♇	4

Sancio
Via Laiolo, 73
17028 Spotorno (SV)
tel. 019747666
e-mail: archit@libero.it

The Sancio family boasts years of experience in the wine business. The six-hectare estate is run by Armando and Riccardo using ecocompatible farming methods and is situated on the Spotorno, Vezzi, Finale and Gorra hills. The Pigato 2001 has good impact on the nose and drinks very nicely.

○ Riviera Ligure di Ponente Pigato '01	♇	4

La Polenza
Fraz. Corniglia
19018 Vernazza (SP)
tel. 0187821214
e-mail: lapolenza@libero.it

Lorenzo Casté cultivates his own two hectares and rents another six. His consultant is the expert Giorgio Bacigalupi. Cinque Terre 2001, a happy marriage of oak and stainless steel, has clean, very varietal aromas. The soft mouthfeel has balance and lingers on the palate.

○ Cinque Terre '01	♇	5

LOMBARDY

As we write this introduction to Lombardy, the news reaching us from the harvest is unencouraging. Bad weather hit several areas during the summer of 2002. The rains and at times disastrous hailstorms in the Oltrepò, Franciacorta and across the Garda could have jeopardized the results of the vintage. In contrast, our tastings produced exciting results again this year. In addition to confirming that winemaking in Franciacorta is enjoying an excellent season, the panels reported that other zones had also caught "renewal fever", starting with Valtellina. The number of Three Glass awards this year fell by one unit and the Oltrepò Pavese again failed to make the cut. Monsupello contributed a good four wines to the final tastings, earning more than flattering reviews, and many other wineries in the province of Pavia made it to the final phases of our tastings. That tells you a lot of work is being done in this zone. "Metodo classico" sparklers, Pinot Nero, Cabernet Sauvignon, Barbera and Bonarda, Riesling and Pinot Grigio display increasingly better defined characteristics in this cradle of Lombard winemaking. Valtellina celebrates the Three Glasses won this year by three Sfursats, from Triacca, Prevostini and Sertoli Salis. Again, we would like to emphasize the work done by the Consorzio dei Vini della Valtellina, and the producers themselves in vineyard and cellar, to imbue the great reds from the area with such magnificent personality. Moving on to Franciacorta, we find seven top awards, making one more than last year. Franciacorta is one of the most dynamic winemaking zones on the Italian scene, and one that concentrates on a difficult wine type, "metodo classico" sparkling wines. The results are there in front of everyone's eyes – and noses. In ten years, great names such as Ca' del Bosco (our Winery of the Year, with two awards, one for the very elegant Chardonnay and the other for the superlative Franciacorta Cuvée Annamaria Clementi), and Bellavista, awarded the prize for their intense Franciacorta Gran Cuvée Brut '97, have been joined by at least a dozen other wineries that can compete on quality. Here are a few of them: Villa and Majolini, both of which finally join the Three Glass club; Uberti and Monte Rossa, confirming their elevated status; Cavalleri, a noble and historic winery; and Mosnel, which is on the verge of a breakthrough. There are many others. Over on Lake Garda, there is a second consecutive endorsement for Ruggero Brunori's Cascina La Pertica, a very competently managed boutique winery that unfortunately suffered disastrous hail damage in August. Not a single bunch of grapes survived from the 2002 vintage. Our best wishes go to Ruggero and all the other winemakers in Lombardy.

ADRO (BS)

CONTADI CASTALDI
LOC. FORNACE BIASCA
VIA COLZANO, 32
25030 ADRO (BS)
TEL. 0307450126
E-MAIL: contadicastaldi@contadicastaldi.it

Set up a few years ago as an offshoot of Bellavista, Contadi Castaldi now shines on its own as one of the most dynamic, best managed wineries in Franciacorta. Credit goes to Martino De Rosa, general manager of Terre Moretti, the holding company for the large group of estates belonging to the Vittorio Moretti family, and Mario Falcetti, an oenologist with a history as a researcher and now manager of Contadi Castaldi. This estate embraces about 60 hectares under vine and buys grapes from trusted growers whose progress is followed over the course of the year. The result is a range of high quality wines and Franciacortas whose crowning achievement is the vintage Satèn Selezione. The '97 we tasted this year just missed Three Glasses but is still one of the very best of its type. Its brilliant greenish straw yellow and dense, very fine, persistent bead introduce an intense nose that focuses on sweet notes of ripe fruit and fades out delicately on hints of vanilla and caramel. It has nice structure on the palate, the freshness supporting the juiciness of the fruit very well, and the finish is very persistent. Other wines that particularly impressed us are the Marco Nero '99, a monovarietal Cabernet Sauvignon aged in new oak, which displays body and rich blackberry and blueberry fruit on nose and palate, very fine tannins and remarkable balance; and the Manca Pane '00, an elegant thoroughbred Chardonnay with depth and beautifully sculpted fruit and oak-derived aromas. The other labels from Contadi Castaldi are also excellent.

○ Franciacorta Satèn Sel. '97	🍷🍷	5*
○ TdF Bianco Manca Pane '00	🍷🍷	5
○ TdF Bianco '01	🍷🍷	4*
● Marco Nero '99	🍷🍷	5
● TdF Rosso '00	🍷	4
○ Franciacorta Brut	🍷	5
◉ Franciacorta Rosé	🍷	5
○ Franciacorta Zéro	🍷	5
○ Franciacorta Magno Brut '94	🍷🍷	6
○ Franciacorta Magno Brut '95	🍷🍷	6
○ Franciacorta Satèn '95	🍷🍷	5
○ Franciacorta Satèn '97	🍷🍷	5
○ Pinodisé	🍷🍷	6

CALVIGNANO (PV)

TRAVAGLINO
LOC. TRAVAGLINO, 6
27025 CALVIGNANO (PV)
TEL. 0383872222

Oenologist Fabrizio Maria Marzi makes remarkable wines in the recently renovated cellar, with grapes from the 70 hectares of vineyard at this historic estate owned by the Corvi family in Calvignano. The whites are excellent, the Chardonnay Campo della Mojetta '00 taking pride of place among them. A bright gold, it shows tropical fruit, moss and bay leaf layered over well-gauged oak-derived vanilla. Full in the mouth, it is soft yet still fresh. The Riesling '00 Campo della Fojada More, from 70 per cent riesling italico and 30 per cent riesling renano, is just as well-mannered. Its green-gold ushers in mineral and grassy notes, then a fresh, confidently tangy palate with a persistent hint of almonds. The other Riesling, the late-harvest Vendemmia Tardiva Pajarolo '98, harvested in several selections beginning in late September, confirmed the Two Glass status it achieved in the last Guide. The Marc'Antonio '99, which ages for 12 months in small oak casks, is also very good. A brilliant garnet red, with a bouquet of fruit preserves, dried hay and spices, it has a warm, well-supported palate with almost a Cabernet-type finish, which is pleasant but out of place in an Oltrepò Pavese Rosso Riserva; DOC regulations do not allow the variety. The Pinot Nero '99 Poggio della Buttinera is clearly varietal, showing cassis, autumn leaves, leather and animal skin aromas, but further bottle-age should give it greater harmony of flavour. Finally, there was another endorsement for the Classese Brut '97, from 80 per cent pinot nero and 20 per cent chardonnay. It's mature but holding up well.

○ OP Chardonnay Campo della Mojetta '00	🍷🍷	4
○ OP Riesling Campo della Fojada '00	🍷🍷	3*
● OP Pinot Nero Poggio della Buttinera '99	🍷🍷	4
● OP Rosso Ris. Marc'Antonio '99	🍷🍷	4
○ OP Brut Class. Classese '97	🍷🍷	4
● OP Pinot Nero Poggio della Buttinera '98	🍷🍷	4
○ OP Riesling Vendemmia Tardiva Pajarolo '98	🍷🍷	4
● OP Rosso Ris. Marc'Antonio '98	🍷🍷	4
○ OP Pinot Nero Brut Class. Grand Cuvée	🍷	3

CANEVINO (PV)

Caseo
Fraz. Caseo, 9
27040 Canevino (PV)
tel. 038599937

The Caseo estate has existed since the 13th century at Canevino, on hills 350 to 450 metres high that are ideal for white grapes but create problems for late-harvest red fruit, which run greater risks of bad weather. The property is a single 70-hectare plot, with 54 hectares under vine. The very nice new cellar is under construction and will help improve these already interesting wines. Credit goes to the grapes, and the skill of Piedmont-born oenologist, Marco Goia, who gained his early experience with the Zonin group. Canabium is the first Riserva produced with 70 per cent croatina, 20 per cent barbera and 10 per cent pinot nero. Ruby with garnet tinges, it has a developed nose but is still a bit rugged in the mouth, thanks to tannins from the croatina. The Oltrepò Pavese Rosso, Canabium '98, is less rustic and more fruit-led, having aged only in steel. The Malleo, a blend of separately vinified cabernet sauvignon, barbera and pinot nero, is excellent. Dark ruby red, with notes of super-ripe berry fruit, it is warm and full in the mouth. The slightly sparkling Bonarda '00 Campo delle More is agreeable and mature. Unsurprisingly – the name means "blackberry field" – it has a note of blackberries. The whites were good. First, the Chardonnay '99 I Ronchi has a bit too much oak but excellent structure; then the well-developed Riesling Renano Le Segrete '99 shows crisp mineral notes; and the Sauvignon Blanc '00 I Crocioni has an intense aroma of sage. Our list ends, sweetly, with the honey-rich Moscato Passito Soleggia '99, which spends six months in small casks.

● Malleo '98	ŸŸ	4
○ OP Chardonnay I Ronchi '99	ŸŸ	4
○ OP Riesling Renano Le Segrete '99	ŸŸ	4
● OP Bonarda Campo delle More '00	Ÿ	3
○ OP Sauvignon Blanc I Crocioni '00	Ÿ	3
● OP Rosso Ris. Canabium '97	Ÿ	5
● OP Rosso Canabium '98	Ÿ	4
○ OP Moscato Passito Soleggia '99	Ÿ	4

CANNETO PAVESE (PV)

F.lli Giorgi
Fraz. Camponoce, 39/a
27044 Canneto Pavese (PV)
tel. 0385262151
e-mail: fgiorgi@tin.it

The Giorgi brothers (Gianfranco, the oenologist, and Antonio) produce a total of 1,600,000 bottles a year at Canneto Pavese. The range runs from simple, anytime wines, like the Pinot Nero in Bianco Premium, fermented without the skins, a clean, bright bottle with discreet residual sugar, to the slightly sparkling Bonarda Vivace La Brughera and the sweet, sparkling Malvasia, all the way through to several more important labels. The Buttafuoco Casa del Corno '00 hit the Two Glass mark this year. A blend of 45 per cent barbera, 45 per cent bonarda, 10 per cent uva rara and ughetta, it comes from the oldest vineyards on the property. Vinified with a long maceration, aged first a year in oak barrels and then in barrique, it acquires an intense garnet, a bouquet of spices and blackberry, and a dry, austere, properly tannic flavour. The sparkling Sangue di Giuda Frizzante '00 La Badalucca is completely different but just as sound. From equal parts of barbera and croatina, with 20 per cent uva rara, ughetta and pinot nero, it is purple with a red mousse, the fragrant aroma of berry jam and a sweet, fruity flavour. The Chardonnay Mesdì '00 is good, with nice body and a complex, slightly vanillaed bouquet of hawthorn and moss. The Sangue di Giuda '01 is fruity and charming, though not as good as La Badalucca. The Pinot Nero Monteroso '99 from the La Diana vineyard ferments on the skins. Worth Two Glasses last year, it is now reaching its peak. Drink it soon.

● OP Buttafuoco Casa del Corno '00	ŸŸ	4
● OP Sangue di Giuda Frizzante La Badalucca '00	ŸŸ	4
○ OP Chardonnay Mesdì '00	Ÿ	3
● OP Bonarda Vivace La Brughera '01	Ÿ	3
○ OP Malvasia Dolce '01	Ÿ	3
● OP Sangue di Giuda '01	Ÿ	3
○ OP Pinot Nero in Bianco Premium '01		4
● OP Buttafuoco Vivace La Manna '00	ŸŸ	3
● OP Pinot Nero Monteroso '99	ŸŸ	4

CANNETO PAVESE (PV)

FRANCESCO QUAQUARINI
LOC. MOTEVENEROSO
VIA CASA ZAMBIANCHI, 26
27044 CANNETO PAVESE (PV)
TEL. 038560152

The third generation of Quaquarinis, Maria Teresa (administrator) and Umberto (oenologist), is hard at work producing 600,000 bottles from grapes harvested on their 40 hectares of vineyards, under the supervision of their father, Francesco. This family winery lies in the first range of hills in the Oltrepò, traditionally red country. It is no coincidence that the flagship wine is the Sangue di Giuda '01, the best we have tasted this year. From 75 per cent croatina, barbera and ughetta di Canneto (vespolina), vinified with a light refermentation in a pressure tank, it has just six per cent acquired alcohol and seven per cent potential alcohol. In other words, it is sweet without being cloying. It is, however, fresh and fruity, with a full bouquet of violets and blackberries, deep purple colour and lively red fizz. Try it with chestnuts or a homemade tart. Another top product is the Magister Oltrepò Pavese, with a high proportion of pinot nero (40 per cent), mixed with 25 per cent croatina, 10 per cent barbera and five per cent ughetta. The oak-aged 1999 is a lucid garnet. It leads off with cassis and leather from the pinot nero, then offers a dry, elegant palate. Although already mature, it will cellar well. The still Buttafuoco Vigna Pregana '98, partially aged in barrique, is good but still evolving. The 50 per cent croatina gives it rather rugged tannins. It will improve in the bottle. The Sangue di Giuda '00 is also good. Finally, we enjoyed three sparkling reds: the dry Buttafuoco and Barbera, and the "amabile" medium-sweet Bonarda, all from the latest vintage.

CANNETO PAVESE (PV)

BRUNO VERDI
VIA VERGOMBERRA, 5
27044 CANNETO PAVESE (PV)
TEL. 038588023
E-MAIL: info@verdibruno.it

The Oltrepò Pavese Rosso Riserva Cavariola has established itself as the top of the range for Paolo, the seventh generation of Verdis to make wine at Vergomberra in Canneto. The wine ages 18 months in mid-toasted French barriques. The '99 vintage may not have the concentration of the previous edition but it is still elegant, full and supported by good acidity and tannins that are not too tough, despite the croatina that makes up 65 per cent of the blend. It will hold up for a long time and improve further. The Barbera Campo del Marrone from the '00 vintage is also a great red from ten "pertiche", or just over half a hectare, of low-yield vines on sandy soil near the village of Canneto. Dark ruby, it has aromas of violet, cloves, tobacco and leather, with a soft hint of pennyroyal. The palate is vigorous, solid and already nice but still developing positively. The Bonarda Possessione di Vergomberra '01 is also good, having gained a "vivace" prickle from light pressure tank refermentation. Deep crimson, with a broad bouquet of strawberry and blackberry aromas and a fruity, slightly tannic palate, it reveals a bitterish note of peaches softened by well-gauged residual sugar. The list of whites features the flower and mineral Riesling Renano '01 Vigna Costa. Its acidity is a bit too pronounced but that will soften over time. The Pinot Grigio '01 is clearly varietal and the Oltrepò Pavese Brut Classico Vergomberra '98 is very good. It's obtained from a cuvée of pinot nero, chardonnay, pinot grigio and pinot meunier and ages for around 30 months on the lees.

● OP Sangue di Giuda '01	▼▼	3*
● OP Buttafuoco Vigna Pregana '98	▼▼	4
● OP Rosso Magister '99	▼▼	4
● OP Sangue di Giuda '00	▼	3
● OP Bonarda '01	▼	3
● OP Buttafuoco '01	▼	3
● OP Barbera Frizzante '01	▼	3
● OP Buttafuoco Frizzante '00	▼▼	3
● OP Bonarda Vivace '00	▼	2*
○ OP Pinot Nero Brut Cl.	▼	3

● OP Rosso Cavariola Ris. '99	▼▼	5
● OP Barbera Campo del Marrone '00	▼▼	4
● OP Bonarda Vivace Possessione di Vergomberra '01	▼▼	3*
○ OP Riesling Renano Vigneto Costa '01	▼▼	4*
○ OP Pinot Grigio '01	▼	3
○ OP Brut Cl. Vergomberra '98	▼	4
● OP Rosso Cavariola Ris. '98	▼▼	5
● OP Bonarda Vivace Possessione di Vargomberra '00	▼▼	3
● OP Sangue di Giuda Dolce Paradiso '00	▼▼	3
● OP Barbera Campo del Marrone '97	▼▼	3

CAPRIOLO (BS)

LANTIERI DE PARATICO
VIA SIMEONE PARATICO, 50
25031 CAPRIOLO (BS)
TEL. 030736151
E-MAIL: lantierideparatico@numerica.it

Fabio Lantieri de Paratico guides his family's estate with a sure hand, keeping up its ancient winemaking tradition. Fine cuvées and top quality wines come from the old cellars at the stately family home in Capriolo, with the help of consulting oenologist Cesare Ferrari. We prefer the sparklers, particularly the Satèn and vintage Arcadia. The first has deep, brilliant straw-yellow hue, creamy mousse and a nose that softly weaves aromas of ripe fruit, butter and vanilla. The round, fresh-tasting palate is delicate and tight-knit, with a long, persistent finish. The Arcadia '98 is a cuvée of chardonnay with a large proportion of pinot nero (around 30 per cent). The brilliant greenish straw yellow ushers in captivating aromas of yeasts, crusty bread, butter and biscuits, as well as apple jam. The palate is full and well-structured, leaving a nice, fruity after-aroma. We felt the '97 version of the same cuvée was even more interesting, with clearer aromas of fruit and vanilla on the nose and better balance on the palate, but both are very well made. moving on to the other labels, apart from a good Franciacorta Brut and an enjoyable Extra Brut, we particularly liked both the white and red versions of the Terre di Franciacorta del Vigneto Colzano '00. The white is fresh and spirited, the red fruit-driven and full-bodied.

○ Franciacorta Brut Arcadia '97	♟♟	5
○ Franciacorta Brut Arcadia '98	♟♟	5
○ Franciacorta Satèn	♟♟	5
○ TdF Bianco Colzano '00	♟	4
● TdF Rosso '00	♟	3*
● TdF Rosso Colzano '00	♟	4
○ TdF Bianco '01	♟	3*
○ Franciacorta Brut	♟	4
○ Franciacorta Extra Brut	♟	4
○ Franciacorta Brut Arcadia '95	♟♟	5
○ Franciacorta Brut '96	♟♟	5
○ Franciacorta Brut Arcadia '96	♟♟	6
● TdF Rosso Colzano '98	♟♟	4*

CAPRIOLO (BS)

RICCI CURBASTRO
VIA ADRO, 37
25031 CAPRIOLO (BS)
TEL. 030736094
E-MAIL: info@riccicurbastro.it

The Ricci Curbastro family has always been involved with wine. For decades now, they have produced excellent Franciacortas and territory-focused wines. Over the past few years, the estate has grown very much in terms of both quality and, fortunately, quantity. Today, Riccardo, head of the family estate, manages 21 hectares of lovely vineyards and produces around 180,000 bottles a year, with the collaboration of two oenologists. One is a true Franciacorta specialist, Alberto Musatti, for the sparkling wines and New Zealander Owen J. Bird takes care of the still wines. The Satèn is excellent again this year. It has a lovely deep straw-yellow colour, ripe fruit aromas, especially apricot and vanilla, and remarkable structure on the palate, where it is fresh, soft, rich in fruity pulp and persistent. The excellent Extra Brut '98 has a solid structure, rich in freshness and fruit, with complex progression on the palate. The panel also thought the Brut was very attractive, with its ripe, round tones, as was the Demi Sec, a sweet, fruity and very pleasant glass, redolent of golden delicious apples. The Chardonnay Vigna Bosco Alto '99 is fresh, intense and bright on eye and nose, where it closes with soft tones of butter and vanilla, then developing on the palate with harmony and depth. Two Glasses also went to the Brolo dei Passoni '99, an interesting sweet "passito" wine from partially dried chardonnay grapes. The two Terre di Franciacortas, the Bianco '01 and Rosso '00, are very well-made and reasonably priced, like the Rosso del Sebino, from cabernet and merlot.

○ Franciacorta Satèn	♟♟	5
○ Franciacorta Extra Brut '98	♟♟	5
○ Brolo dei Passoni '99	♟♟	5
○ TdF Bianco Vigna Bosco Alto '99	♟♟	4*
● Sebino Rosso '00	♟	3*
● TdF Rosso Curtefranca '00	♟	3*
○ TdF Bianco Curtefranca '01	♟	3*
○ Franciacorta Brut	♟	5
○ Franciacorta Démi Sec	♟	5
● Pinot Nero Sebino '97	♟♟	5
● TdF Rosso Santella del Gröm '98	♟♟	4*
○ Franciacorta Extra Brut '95	♟	5
○ Franciacorta Extra Brut '96	♟	5

CASTEGGIO (PV)

Riccardo Albani
Strada San Biagio, 46
27045 Casteggio (PV)
Tel. 038383622 - 038383345
E-mail: info@vinialbani.it

The determination of young Riccardo Albani to produce quality at any cost is evident in the range of impressively complex, attractive wines. Although 60,000 bottles are released, there are few labels, since Riccardo is convinced he should concentrate on a limited number of products to be able to focus on his vineyards, fermentation and ageing. The Pinot Nero '00 stands out this year. Made from slightly super-ripe grapes, it is an unusually intense ruby red for a Pinot Nero and offers an elegant spicy bouquet of blackcurrant, plum, forest floor and vanilla. The palate is full, warm and vigorous, with a nice note of jam. It will improve in the bottle. The Oltrepò Pavese Rosso Costa del Morone '99, from 65 per cent barbera, with uva rara and a little croatina, is readier to drink. After nine months in oak, followed by six months in stainless steel and a month or so in the bottle, it is dark and very aromatic, showing wild berries, violet, cloves, spices and more, then a soft yet sturdy and robust palate. The slightly sparkling Bonarda '01 is excellent, with a clean, fragrant, fruit-led style. The Riserva Vigne della Casona was missing since it was still ageing in the bottle. However, we were able to taste the '93 version, which is impossible to find now, which demonstrated how the great reds from Albani survive the test of time. Though at its peak, it holds together perfectly. In contrast, the Riesling Renano '01 is still too young. It's very promising but cannot be appraised now since it still has to finish malolactic fermentation. We will leave it until next year.

● OP Rosso Costa del Morone '99	▼▼	4
● OP Pinot Nero '00	▼▼	5
● OP Bonarda '01	▼▼	4*
● OP Rosso Vigne della Casona Ris. '98	▼▼	5
● OP Bonarda Frizzante '00	▼▼	3
○ OP Riesling Renano '00	▼▼	3*
● OP Rosso Vigna della Casona Ris. '96	▼▼	4
● OP Rosso Vigna della Casona Ris. '97	▼▼	4
● OP Bonarda '98	▼▼	3
○ OP Riesling Renano '99	▼▼	3*

CASTEGGIO (PV)

Bellaria
Fraz. Mairano
Via Castel del Lupo, 28
27045 Casteggio (PV)
Tel. 038383203 - 0335235392

The Massone family estate, in the village of Mairano outside Casteggio, includes 15 hectares of its own vineyards, along with another five rented hectares. Planted at high density to barbera, bonarda and more recently chardonnay, cabernet sauvignon and merlot, the vineyards are rigorously low-cropped. Bellaria is part of the Du Pont Quality Project. Vineyards treatments are carried out under the supervision of Du Pont technicians and wine samples are then analysed by the Centro Sperimentale at San Michele all'Adige to verify the presence of any chemical residues. The quality of the air and environment is on a par with that of the wines, starting with the Barbera Olmetto '99. It contains a small percentage of croatina and uva rara, and ages almost entirely in stainless steel. Its dark, ruby red introduces an intense ripe grape and berry fruit bouquet, then a full palate. The monovarietal Merlot Rosso La Macchia '98 is very well made (we tasted it last year). Aged for a year and a half in barrique, and matured for the same length of time in bottle, it has a purplish colour, a pronounced aroma of vanilla and raspberry jam, and a vigorous, warm, nicely extracted palate. The slightly sparkling Bonarda Vivace La Bria is fresh and pleasant. From croatina with 15 per cent barbera, it boasts a lovely ruby red hue, a vivacious red mousse and firm palate that end on a finish of blackberry and peach. The Bricco Sturnel '98 is maturing well. Made from cabernet sauvignon, with 20 per cent barbera, and aged for 20 months in barrique, it will continue to improve in bottle.

● OP Bonarda Vivace La Bria '01	▼▼	3*
● OP Barbera Olmetto '99	▼▼	4
● Bricco Sturnel '98	▼	4
● Bricco Sturnel '97	▼▼	4
● La Macchia '98	▼	4

CASTEGGIO (PV)

FRECCIAROSSA
VIA VIGORELLI, 141
27045 CASTEGGIO (PV)
TEL. 0383804465
E-MAIL: info@frecciarossa.com

There is important news in the vineyards and cellar at Frecciarossa. Manager Pietro Calvi di Bergolo announced that the role of consultant was passed on last January to Giancarlo Scaglione, who certainly needs no introduction. The old casks have been replaced with 100 new barriques, a number that will be doubled by 2003 to bring the overall barrel capacity to 450 hectolitres. It is about time people in the Oltrepò understood that old casks are only good for cooking steaks. Renewal of the vineyards has also begun under the direction of agronomist Claudio Giorgi. While waiting for results, the quality of two main estate wines continues to impress. We're talking about the Oltrepò Pavese Riserva Villa Odero and the Pinot Nero, both from '98. A much better-quality harvest than '97's has produced a dark ruby Riserva with a complex bouquet of wild berry jam and vanilla. The palate is full, vigorous and sustained by elegant tannins. The Pinot Nero spends 12 months in barrique - no more large barrels - and is bottled without filtration. Ruby red, with a garnet rim, it has a nose of cassis, vanilla and liquorice, and an elegant, no-nonsense palate. The monovarietal Uva Rara '01, aged only in stainless steel, is pleasant and drinkable, showing touches of morello cherry and pepper, and good sinew. The Riesling Renano '01, cold-macerated for 24 hours at four degrees Celsius and left for two months on the fine lees, has precise varietal notes and is still a bit green but should develop very positively in the bottle.

○	OP Riesling Renano '01	ŸŸ	4
●	OP Pinot Nero '98	ŸŸ	5
●	OP Rosso Villa Odero Ris. '98	ŸŸ	4
●	Provincia di Pavia Uva Rara '01	Ÿ	4
●	OP Rosso Villa Odero Ris. '90	ŸŸ	5
●	OP Rosso Villa Odero Ris. '94	ŸŸ	4
●	OP Pinot Nero '97	ŸŸ	4
●	OP Rosso Villa Odero Ris. '97	ŸŸ	4
○	OP Riesling Renano '98	ŸŸ	4
●	Provincia di Pavia Uva Rara '00	Ÿ	3
●	OP Rosso Villa Odero Ris. '91	Ÿ	4

CASTEGGIO (PV)

LE FRACCE
FRAZ. MAIRANO
VIA CASTEL DEL LUPO, 5
27045 CASTEGGIO (PV)
TEL. 038382526
E-MAIL: info@le-fracce.it

The vineyard and cellar manager at Le Fracce, oenologist Roberto Gerbino, does a great job on this biologically integrated estate with 104 hectares, 39 under vine, belonging to the Fondazione Bussolera Branca. Let's start with their new offering, the Oltrepò Pavese Rosso Garboso '99, a blend of 60 per cent barbera, 35 per cent pinot nero and five per cent croatina, manually harvested and vinified with five days of maceration. The wine spends no time in oak, and is an intense ruby red, with aromas of dark berry fruit and a soft, full, fruit-led taste. The Cirgà '98, another Oltrepò Pavese Rosso, is well-made from half croatina, one fourth barbera and one fourth pinot nero. It is dark ruby, with a nose of violets, morello cherries and spice, then a dry, austere palate. Although it could use more bottle time, it is already drinking well. As usual, the Bonarda '01 La Rubiosa is excellent. Lightly refermented in a pressure tank, it has touches of ripe blackberry, and an exuberantly full, fruity flavour. In the white category, the Riesling Renano Landò and Pinot Grigio Levriere '01 both made a great impression. The first, vinified with 18 hours of cold maceration, is a greenish-gold and redolent of peaches and green and red apples, ushering in a bright, tangy palate. The Pinot Grigio is left for 40 days on the lees. Its clear, straw yellow precedes sun-dried hay and acacia blossom, then a full, velvety mouthfeel with delicious fresh fruit on the back palate. The cuve close Cuvée Bussolera '00 Extra Brut, left for 16 months on the lees, is a clean monovarietal pinot nero.

●	OP Bonarda La Rubiosa '01	ŸŸ	4
○	OP Pinot Grigio Levriere '01	ŸŸ	4
○	OP Riesling Renano Landò '01	ŸŸ	4
●	OP Rosso Cirgà '98	ŸŸ	4
●	OP Rosso Garboso '99	ŸŸ	4
○	OP Pinot Nero Cuvèe Bussolera Extra Brut '00	Ÿ	5
●	OP Bonarda La Rubiosa '00	ŸŸ	3*
○	OP Pinot Grigio '00	ŸŸ	4
○	OP Riesling Renano '00	ŸŸ	4
●	OP Rosso Cirgà '97	ŸŸ	4
●	OP Bonarda La Rubiosa '98	ŸŸ	3
○	OP Riesling Renano '98	ŸŸ	3
●	OP Bonarda La Rubiosa '99	ŸŸ	3

CASTEGGIO (PV)

TENUTA PEGAZZERA
LOC. PEGAZZERA
VIA VIGORELLI, 151
27045 CASTEGGIO (PV)
TEL. 0383804646
E-MAIL: tenutapegazzera@libero.it

Tenuta Pegazzera finally seems to be realizing some of its great potential with radical renovations. The new vines planted by agronomist Pierluigi Donna are beginning to mature and oenologist Corrado Cugnasco uses their fruit to make super wines. A 2000 vintage selection from their best vineyards (there are 40 hectares in production) has created an excellent Rosso Oltrepò, Il Cardinale, dedicated to the Counter-Reformation archbishop of Milan, Carlo Borromeo. From mostly Barbera, with a small amount of croatina and late-harvest uva rara, it is part aged in barrique, and part in stainless steel. A dark red, it has a rich, complex bouquet and a round, vigorously elegant flavour. It can still improve in the bottle, like the La Collegiata '01, a partially oak-aged Chardonnay that offers tropical fruit, honey and moss, then a round, fruit-rich palate, supported by a good backbone. The Barbera Safrana is interesting and is vinified and aged only in stainless steel, so as not to alter the varietal aromas. The wine is robust, mellow and harmonious. The very good Cabernet Sauvignon Ligna ages in barrique. Dark ruby, it has very generous wild berry and sweet spice fragrances, and a rich, concentrated, lively taste. The slightly sparkling Bonarda Vivace Selezione '00 is round, fruity and clean-tasting with intense blackberry aromas. The Pinot Nero '01, a sparkler fermented without the skins, and Brut Martinotti are both refreshing and pleasant. The Pinot Nero Brut Classico '97 has held up well. It's harmonious and very elegant.

CASTELLI CALEPIO (BG)

IL CALEPINO
VIA SURRIPE, 1
24060 CASTELLI CALEPIO (BG)
TEL. 035847178
E-MAIL: info@ilcalepino.it

The top wine from Il Calepino (the name comes from a 16th-century Latin dictionary compiled by Ambrogio da Calepio) is again the Riserva Fra Ambrogio '95, which more than merited Two Glasses in the last edition of the Guide. The Brut, chardonnay-based with 30 per cent pinot nero, has gained depth lately because of its longer stay on the lees, and has reached a peak with the 2002 disgorgement. Golden yellow, with a rich aroma of roasted hazelnuts, sweet cakes and dried bay leaf, it has a round, mellow, yet firm, palate and a lingering finish of toast and golden delicious apple. The Il Calepino '98, disgorged in 2002, is enjoyable, well-mannered and fragrant. Fresher than the previous wine, it is complex, with a creamy mousse and dense, fine bead. The Extra Brut '97, disgorged in 2002, is a small step up from this, thanks to the more favourable vintage than '96. Offering notes of crusty bread, hawthorn and apple, it is dry yet not bitter in the mouth, and has a distinct twist of almond in the finish. The Valcalepio Bianco '01, from 70 per cent chardonnay and 30 per cent pinot grigio, is full, fragrant and self-assured. Only its somewhat disappointing aromatic length kept it from a second Glass. The Valcalepio Rosso Suríe '98 is not as successful. It's a delicate, harmonious Bordeaux blend but has little complexity and the standard Rosso '00 is also unconvincing. This is a winery with a talent for "spumante" and white wines.

● OP Cabernet Sauvignon Ligna '99 ♀♀	4
● OP Barbera Safrana '00 ♀♀	3*
● OP Rosso Cardinale '00 ♀♀	5
● OP Bonarda Vivace Selezione '01 ♀♀	3*
○ OP Chardonnay La Collegiata '01 ♀♀	4
○ OP Pinot Nero in Bianco frizzante '01 ♀	3
○ OP Pinot Nero Brut Martinotti ♀	3
○ OP Pinot Nero Brut Cl. '97 ♀♀	4
● OP Cabernet Sauvignon Ligna '98 ♀♀	4
● OP Pinot Nero Petrae '99 ♀♀	4

○ Extra Brut Cl. Il Calepino '97 ♀♀	4
○ Brut Cl. Il Calepino '98 ♀♀	4
○ Valcalepio Bianco '01 ♀	3
● Valcalepio Rosso Surie '98 ♀	4
● Valcalepio Rosso '00	3
○ Brut Cl. Ris. Fra Ambrogio '93 ♀♀	5
○ Brut Cl. Ris. Fra Ambrogio '95 ♀♀	5
○ Extra Brut M. Cl. '95 ♀♀	4
○ Brut Cl. Il Calepino '97 ♀♀	4
● Valcalepio Rosso Surie '97 ♀♀	4

CAZZAGO SAN MARTINO (BS)

CASTELFAGLIA
FRAZ. CALINO
LOC. BOSCHI, 3
25046 CAZZAGO SAN MARTINO (BS)
TEL. 059812411
E-MAIL: castelfaglia@cavicchioli.it

Owned by the Cavicchioli and Barboglio families, CastelFaglia is on a hill overlooking Calino and the surrounding countryside. It takes its name from the stone construction that dominates the estate. Thanks to the fine position of the vineyards and technical expertise of oenologist Sandro Cavicchioli, the wines and Franciacortas from CastelFaglia have always earned flattering judgements in the Guide. But this year, we were amazed by a vintage cuvée, the Franciacorta Monogram Brut '94, that came dangerously near Three Glasses. It is a brilliant straw yellow tinged with green, and has a fine perlage that introduces a remarkably broad, intense nose. The aromas mingle yeasts, roasted coffee beans and vanilla in an elegant whole. Soft and well-structured in the mouth, it shows a stylish fruity note and mineral shades, fine balance and freshness, then a long biscuity, vanilla finish. The Extra Brut, despite the low-sugar dosage, is rich on nose and palate. The round fruit is well-sustained by a spirited freshness and shows no hint of excessive development in its complexity. The Franciacorta Brut Monogram Cuvée Giunone is charming and complex right from the start, with an alluring nose of chamomile and fresh wildflowers. It progresses nicely on the palate and is perhaps a bit more austere than the other two cuvées but overall it's just as elegant and well-made. In other words, this was a very good performance, rounded off by a well-made Franciacorta Brut and the excellent Terre di Franciacorta Bianco Campo di Marte '99.

O	Franciacorta Monogram Brut '94	♟♟	7
O	Franciacorta Extra Brut	♟♟	5
O	Franciacorta Monogram Brut Cuvée Giunone	♟♟	6
O	TdF Bianco Campo di Marte '99	♟	4
O	Franciacorta Brut	♟	4
O	Franciacorta Monogram Brut '91	♟♟	6

CAZZAGO SAN MARTINO (BS)

MONTE ROSSA
FRAZ. BORNATO
VIA LUCA MARENZIO, 14
25040 CAZZAGO SAN MARTINO (BS)
TEL. 030725066 - 0307254614
E-MAIL: info@monterossa.com

Emanuele Rabotti follows his own star with admirable tenacity. Three years ago, he decided to concentrate all his efforts on Franciacorta which, he loves to repeat, is "the great wine from this territory". So, he has gradually cut back his range of still wines and this year, only presented Franciacortas for our tastings. And what Franciacortas they are! The Cabochon '98 again won Three Glasses and establishes Monte Rossa as one of the best wineries in the region and beyond. It is a Brut with a straw yellow hue that is flecked with old gold, and a dense, continuous perlage of extraordinary finesse. The nose is full, complex and endlessly nuanced, combining elegant notes of spices and minerals, while exalting the elegantly evolved character with hints of apple and berry fruit. The entry on the palate is graceful yet confident while the caressing effervescence hints at careful bottle fermentation and a very long sojourn on the lees. This is a sumptuously deep Franciacorta with superb structure and harmony, where the pinot nero, which accounts for 30 per cent of the cuvée, imposes its presence over the remaining 70 per cent chardonnay, as you would expect. Then comes a long, complex toastiness and mineral finish. The panel thought the Extra Brut '97 (we reviewed the '96 last year) had a different style but was just as engaging. Its fresh fruit and aromatic herbs usher in a dense, soft palate. The other cuvées, the fresh Brut I Cuvée and the soft Satèn, were also excellent.

O	Franciacorta Brut Cabochon '98	♟♟♟	6
O	Franciacorta Extra Brut '97	♟♟	6
O	Franciacorta Brut I Cuvée	♟♟	5
O	Franciacorta Satèn	♟♟	6
O	Franciacorta Extra Brut Cabochon '93	♟♟♟	5
O	Franciacorta Brut Cabochon '97	♟♟♟	6
O	Franciacorta Satèn	♟♟♟	6
⊙	Franciacorta Brut Cabochon Rosé '95	♟♟	6

CAZZAGO SAN MARTINO (BS)

Ronco Calino
Via Scala, 88
25040 Cazzago San Martino (BS)
tel. 035317788

Paolo Radici is not only influential in the textile industry but also very passionate about wine, particularly sparklers. About six years ago, he decided to buy a small, ten-hectare estate to start making wine himself. His enthusiasm, the consultancy of skilled oenologist Francesco Polastri and an agronomist of the calibre of Professor Leonardo Valenti from the University of Milan, Ronco Calino emerged from the crowd in Franciacorta in no time with a fine series of labels. The Franciacorta Brut '97 is an excellent example of its type. Intense, brilliant straw yellow, with lots of tiny bubbles, it shows a complex nose of yeast and toasted bread that introduces a clean, mature fruitiness. The fruit comes back on the palate, which is solid, balanced, soft and elegant, signing off slowly on more complex honey notes. The Chardonnay Sottobosco '00 is one of the best whites from that vintage. Its intense, sophisticated ripe fruit aromas are well-integrated with the new oak. There is structure and freshness on the palate, which lingers and will also age well, we think. The Terre Rosso '00 is also among the best in the DOC zone, thanks to its structure, concentration and elegant blackberry aromas. The Terre Bianco '01 is enjoyable for its overall harmony and the Pinot Nero L'Arturo '99 deserves attention, if not for fullness then for its delicate balance and good varietal bouquet. We expect great things from this wine, and from the entire estate.

○	TdF Bianco Sottobosco '00	♀♀	5
●	TdF Rosso '00	♀♀	6
○	TdF Bianco '01	♀♀	5
○	Franciacorta Brut '97	♀♀	6
●	Pinot Nero L'Arturo '99	♀♀	7
○	Franciacorta Brut	♀	6
○	Franciacorta Brut '96	♀♀	6
●	Pinot Nero L'Arturo '98	♀♀	5
●	TdF Rosso '99	♀♀	4*

CHIURO (SO)

Nino Negri
Via Ghibellini, 3
23030 Chiuro (SO)
tel. 0342482521
e-mail: giv@giv.it

The Sfursat 5 Stelle, that legendary Negri wine and one of the labels that features most frequently among our Three Glass winners, is absent from this edition of the Guide. Casimiro Maule, distinguished oenologist and winery manager, preferred to let it "miss a turn" and chose not to vinify the 2000 harvest. While awaiting next year's edition, we are happy to settle for a glass of Vigneto Fracia '99, the best of the estate labels this time. It's a wine that foregrounds elegance, harmony and perfectly interpreted terroir. Soft, with solid structure, but vinified to avoid too much muscle, it shows spicy aromas with subtle notes of dried flowers and berry fruit. Despite its years, the Riserva Negri '97 is still a fragrant, young wine with an attractive palate. The Quadrio '99 is traditional, with tobacco aromas and depth on the palate and still a little bit green. It came close to a second Glass. The now instantly recognizable personality of the Sassella Le Tense '99 combines a broad nose of berry fruit and a fresh-tasting, harmonious palate. The panel also liked the Inferno Mazer '99 for its intense, varietal aromas and a rich palate braced by soft tannins. The Grumello Sassorosso '99 has great character and a concentrated, varietal palate. The standard Sfursat '99 made it to the finals with an excellent score, thanks to remarkable balance, intense aromas, and particularly clean fruit lifted by balsamic notes. The white Ca' Brione '01 can be quite variable in style and aroma profile but is always good quality. The nose reveals hints of tea leaves.

●	Valtellina Sfursat '99	♀♀	6
●	Valtellina Sup. Vigneto Fracia '99	♀♀	6
●	Valtellina Sup. Ris. Nino Negri '97	♀♀	5
○	Vigneto Ca' Brione Bianco '01	♀♀	5
●	Valtellina Sup. Grumello Vigna Sassorosso '99	♀♀	4
●	Valtellina Sup. Inferno Mazer '99	♀♀	4
●	Valtellina Sup. Sassella Le Tense '99	♀♀	4
●	Valtellina Sup. Quadrio '99	♀	4
●	Valtellina Sfursat 5 Stelle '94	♀♀♀	5
●	Valtellina Sfursat 5 Stelle '95	♀♀♀	5
●	Valtellina Sfursat 5 Stelle '96	♀♀♀	5
●	Valtellina Sfursat 5 Stelle '97	♀♀♀	6
●	Valtellina Sfursat 5 Stelle '98	♀♀♀	6
●	Valtellina Sfursat 5 Stelle '99	♀♀♀	6

CHIURO (SO)

ALDO RAINOLDI
LOC. CASACCE
VIA STELVIO, 128
23030 CHIURO (SO)
TEL. 0342482225
E-MAIL: rainoldi@rainoldi.com

Peppino Rainoldi and his young grandson Aldo may have just missed out on Three Glasses this year but three wines from this dynamic cellar made it to the finals. That puts the Rainoldis in the front rank of Italian winemaking, confirming its status as a constantly growing estate with excellent quality standards. We'll begins with two Sforzato '99s, the Sfursat Fruttaio Ca' Rizzieri and the standard version. The former is rich, complex and spicy, with a vigorous progression in the mouth, good length and refined tannic weave. The base version has a more austere character, presenting itself on the nose with aromatic herbs and raisins. Warm on the palate, it has density and good texture. The Crespino '99 didn't let us down. A fine example of a Valtellina Nebbiolo, it unites elegantly expressed terroir with international-style elegance. Entry on the nose shows morello cherry, plum and ripe wild berries mingling with aromatic and balsamic notes. The well-balanced palate has upfront fruit and a long finish. The most recent wine, again from nebbiolo, is the attractive Prugnolo '99, which has fresh, seductive aromas and impressive body. The Grumello '98 is a very individual wine distinct, fragrant aromas, good structure and a soft mouthfeel that make it one of the best of its type. The fruit-led Sassella '98 is very well made and has varietal notes on the nose. The palate is harmonious, well-structured and rich in character. The white Ghibellino '00, from nebbiolo and sauvignon, is subtly aromatic with citrus notes, and an agreeable, delicate palate with good length.

● Valtellina Sfursat '99	🍷🍷	6
● Valtellina Sfursat Fruttaio Ca' Rizzieri '99	🍷🍷	7
● Valtellina Sup. Crespino '99	🍷🍷	5
● Valtellina Sup. Grumello '98	🍷🍷	4*
● Valtellina Sup. Prugnolo '99	🍷🍷	4*
○ Bianco Ghibellino '00	🍷	4
● Valtellina Sup. Sassella '98	🍷	4
● Valtellina Sfursat Fruttaio Ca' Rizzieri '95	🍷🍷🍷	5
● Valtellina Sfursat Fruttaio Ca' Rizzieri '97	🍷🍷🍷	6
● Valtellina Sfursat Fruttaio Ca' Rizzieri '98	🍷🍷🍷	6
● Valtellina Sup. Crespino '98	🍷🍷	5

COCCAGLIO (BS)

TENUTA CASTELLINO
VIA SAN PIETRO, 46
25030 COCCAGLIO (BS)
TEL. 0307721015
E-MAIL: tenuta.castellino@lombardiacom.it

Apart from deserving Two Glasses and coming near to Three, the Castellino Satèn is one of the most enjoyable of all those we tasted for this edition of the Guide. Straw yellow with brilliant golden highlights, it boasts creamy fizz and very delicate perlage. The nose is soft, tempting with whispers of ripe apricots and apricot preserves, vanilla, white peach and tropical fruit. The Franciacorta Brut '96 has a less outgoing character but charmed the panel with its complex toastiness and minerals that elegantly meld with, rather than mask, the fruit. The non-vintage Franciacorta is also enjoyable and deserved Two Glasses for its fresh, fruity tones, well-balanced palate, smooth, creamy mousse and good aromatic persistence. In the still wine section, the excellent Terre di Franciacorta Bianco Solicano was good, with its solid body, elegant nose and above all excellent balance, left intact by the careful use of new oak. What more can we say about these Bonomi family wines? The structured, soft Terre di Franciacorta Rosso '00 is one of the best from this vintage. The same characteristics are evident in the Vigneto Capineto '99, though in a deeper, more resounding key, and supported by intense blackberry and blackcurrant notes over soft tannins. The Terre di Franciacorta Bianco '01 is also good, further proof of the estate's progress.

● TdF Rosso '00	🍷🍷	4
○ Franciacorta Brut '96	🍷🍷	6
○ TdF Bianco Solicano '99	🍷🍷	4
● TdF Rosso Capineto '99	🍷🍷	5
○ Franciacorta Brut	🍷🍷	5
○ Franciacorta Satèn	🍷🍷	6
○ TdF Bianco '01	🍷	4
○ Franciacorta Satèn '93	🍷🍷	5
○ Franciacorta Brut '95	🍷🍷	5
● Capineto '98	🍷🍷	5
○ TdF Bianco Solicano '98	🍷🍷	4*

COCCAGLIO (BS)

Lorenzo Faccoli & Figli
Via Cava, 7
25030 Coccaglio (BS)
tel. 0307722761

Faccoli in Coccaglio is a small, family-run estate founded by Lorenzo Faccoli in the early 1960s. Now, it is managed by his sons, Claudio, current chair of the Franciacorta protection consortium, and Gianmario. Oenological consultancy comes from Cesare Ferrari, one of the historic names in Franciacorta winemaking. Annual production is around 45,000 bottles. Which is not that many really, but all are extraordinarily well made. Our vote this year went to the excellent Franciacorta Extra Brut for its intense, gold-tinged straw yellow, creamy fizz and very fine bead. The panel enjoyed its intense aromas of flower-lace ripe white peach and yeasts, shifting towards elegant vanilla. The quality of the wine is evident on the deep, rich palate, with its perfect balance, suppleness and persistence. The Brut is nice. Its complex character shows how shrewdly the reserve wines from previous vintages and dosage were handled. The result is a wine with a young, invigorating style that also finds mature aromas in a finish that exalts its depth and richness. The Rosé is good as usual, with notes of wild berries and fresh warm cakes, as are the two Terre di Franciacortas, the supple Bianco '01 and solid Rosso '00.

○ Franciacorta Brut	🍷🍷	5*
○ Franciacorta Extra Brut	🍷🍷	5*
○ TdF Bianco '01	🍷	3
● TdF Rosso '99	🍷	5
⊙ Franciacorta Brut Rosé	🍷	5
○ Franciacorta Extra Brut '89	🍷🍷	6
○ Franciacorta Extra Brut '90	🍷🍷	6

CODEVILLA (PV)

Montelio
Via D. Mazza, 1
27050 Codevilla (PV)
tel. 0383373090

The Comprino Mirosa, a well-balanced, monovarietal Merlot, continues to be the star of the Montelio range. The well-ripened grapes are vinified with about 12 days' maceration, and the wine ages more than a year in small oak casks. The '99 vintage (not reported on the label since it is released as a "vino da tavola") is ruby with garnet tinges. The intense aroma of morello cherry jam is lifted by vanilla and the warm, velvety mouthfeel shows good balance. The thought occurs that merlot, planted for the first time in the Oltrepò at Montelio half a century ago, deserves to be more popular in these hills. Its special softness can smooth out the acidity of barbera and lighten the roughness of croatina. The standard Comprino 2000 is simpler and more accessible. But let's get back to those fine reds. The Pinot Nero Costarsa '98 is aged half in 25-hectolitre barrels and half in barrique. A bright garnet, it has an etheric bouquet of blackcurrant jam, leather, fur and faint spices, then a dry palate with a slightly tang. The Riserva Solarolo '98 is also always excellent. From barbera and croatina with 20 per cent pinot nero, it ages in oak in the same way as the Costarsa. The Müller Thurgau La Giostra '00 is very special. It gets 24 hours' cold maceration and ages in Allier tonneaux and its sweet spices harmonize well with the varietal aromas of the grape. The Barbera and Rosso Oltrepò '00 both deserve attention, as does the Cortese and sparkling Bonarda Frizzante '01.

○ Müller Thurgau La Giostra '00	🍷🍷	4
● OP Pinot Nero Costarsa '98	🍷🍷	4
● OP Rosso Ris. Solarolo '98	🍷🍷	4
● Comprino Mirosa '99	🍷🍷	6
● Comprino Rosso '00	🍷	3
● OP Barbera '00	🍷	3
● OP Rosso '00	🍷	3
● OP Bonarda Frizzante '01	🍷	3
○ OP Cortese '01	🍷	3
● OP Rosso Ris. Solarolo '96	🍷🍷	4
● OP Rosso Ris. Solarolo '97	🍷🍷	4
● Comprino Mirosa Ris. '98	🍷🍷	4
● Comprino Rosso '98	🍷🍷	3
● Comprino Rosso Legno '98	🍷🍷	4

COLOGNE (BS)

La Boscaiola
Via Riccafana, 19
25033 Cologne (BS)
tel. 030715596 - 030715596
e-mail: info@laboscaiola.com

After an adventurous life as an officer in the Italian Alpine troops during the Russian campaign and a career as a doctor, Nelson Cenci decided the rolling hills of Franciacorta would be a good place to retire. Here, he devotes his time to viticulture, supported by daughter Giuliana, who works full-time on this small estate of barely six hectares. Thanks to the pair's efforts, and those of consultants such as Cesare Ferrari for the sparklers, Giuseppe Piotti for still wines, and Pierluigi Donna for agricultural matters, the wines and sparklers from La Boscaiola have earned an excellent reputation, even in a zone as competitive as Franciacorta. The Franciacorta Brut is very pleasant again this year. Delicate in its perlage and fruit-and-flower aromas, and big on the palate, it shows elegance, balance and suppleness. The deep ruby Terre di Franciacorta Rosso '00 has an assertive nose redolent of wild berries. There is good structure on the palate, smooth tannins and a persuasive fruity finish. The Ritorno '00 is an elegant Bordeaux blend, with 50 per cent merlot, aged for 16 months in small oak casks. The dark ruby ushers in wild berry aromas nuanced with delicate grassy notes. Well-structured in the mouth, it shows big, soft tannins and delicate astringency. The Poggio delle Vigne Brut (a non-DOCG, "metodo classico" sparkler) and Terre di Franciacorta Bianco '01 are both good and drinkable.

○	Franciacorta Brut		5
●	Il Ritorno '00		4
●	TdF Rosso '00		4
○	TdF Bianco '01		3*
○	Poggio delle Vigne Brut '99		4
●	Sebino Giuliana C. '98		3
○	TdF Bianco Anna '99		4*

CORTE FRANCA (BS)

Barone Pizzini
Fraz. Timoline
Via Brescia, 3/a
25050 Corte Franca (BS)
tel. 030984136
e-mail: inform@baronepizzini.it

Not for the first time, the wines from Barone Pizzini are among the best in Franciacorta. This is not only true for the sparkling sector but also, and above all, for still wines. When some years ago, a company bought the historic Barone Pizzini Piomarta label, it was clear to everyone that they meant business. Several distinguished names appear are on the list of collaborators, starting with the two winemaking consultants, Alberto Musatti for sparklers and Roberto Cipresso for still wines. Pierluigi Donna is entrusted with supervising the vineyards, which total 40 hectares of estate-owned and rented plots. Two wines especially impressed us. The San Carlo '00, a Bordeaux blend with remarkable density and elegance, has rich red and black berry fruit on the nose as well as perfectly integrated vanilla and oak. The palate offers fruit with depth and tautness, fullness of flavour and long length. The Merlanico is just as good. It's a successful blend of estate merlot and aglianico from De Conciliis in Prignano Cilento, Campania, discussed in the appropriate entry. The Terra di Franciacorta Bianco Polzina '00 is one of the best Chardonnays in the area. The charmingly clean and complex fruit, tangy minerality and a freshness that says it will have a long life in the bottle. The vintage Bagnadore I '98 is the best of the sparkling wines, revealing very subtle notes of fruit and vanilla, croissant and yeasts. Solid and elegant on the palate, it exits on delicate oak notes. All the other wines from the estate are excellent, starting with the Franciacorta Brut.

●	San Carlo '00		5
○	TdF Chardonnay Polzina '00		5
●	TdF Rosso Curtefranca '00		4
○	TdF Bianco Curtefranca '01		4
○	Franciacorta Bagnadore I '98		6
○	Franciacorta Brut		5
○	Franciacorta Satèn		6
⊙	Franciacorta Rosé		5
●	San Carlo '98		5
○	TdF Chardonnay Polzina '99		5

CORTE FRANCA (BS)

F.LLI BERLUCCHI
LOC. BORGONATO
VIA BROLETTO, 2
25040 CORTE FRANCA (BS)
TEL. 030984451
E-MAIL: info@berlucchifranciacorta.com

Fratelli Berlucchi was the first to register its vineyards as DOC when the Franciacorta zone was created in 1967. Since then, it has produced excellent wines and, above all, top-quality Franciacortas. The estate is owned by five siblings, Francesco, Marcello, Gabriella, Roberto and Pia Donata and boasts 60 hectares under vine, out of a total area of 100 hectares, as well as a picturesque cellar in the old family villa. Though the structure may be old, both the equipment and driving spirit of the Berlucchis are modern, as shown by the clean, lean style of their wines. We have always appreciated the Berlucchi Franciacortas. The Satèn '98 particularly impressed the panel this year with a perlage of remarkable finesse, rich nose and palate, and soft, fruit-led aromas, fresh smooth mouthfeel and nice vanilla-laced finish. The Rosé '98 is just as good, introducing itself with an intense, brilliant hue and delicate perlage. Wild berries stand out on the nose and palate, and the good, fresh body has great persistence. The Brut '98 has nice character and a full structure. The balance and length of the palate allow hints of forwardness to come through. On retasting the Brut Casa delle Colonne '95, assessed last year just after it was disgorged, we felt it was so much better now that we awarded it Two well-deserved Glasses. We found the Terre di Franciacorta Bianco and Rosso, and Terre di Franciacorta Bianco Dossi delle Querce '99 all as good as ever.

○ Franciacorta Casa delle Colonne '95	▼▼	6
○ Franciacorta Brut '98	▼▼	5
⊙ Franciacorta Rosé '98	▼▼	5
○ Franciacorta Satèn '98	▼▼	5
● TdF Rosso '00	▼	3
○ TdF Bianco '01	▼	3
○ TdF Bianco Dossi delle Querce '99	▼	4
○ Franciacorta Brut '95	▼▼	5
○ Franciacorta Satèn '96	▼▼	5
○ Franciacorta Brut '97	▼▼	5

CORTE FRANCA (BS)

GUIDO BERLUCCHI & C.
FRAZ. BORGONATO
P.ZZA DURANTI, 4
25040 CORTE FRANCA (BS)
TEL. 030984381
E-MAIL: info@berlucchi.it

This historic house at Borgonato outside Corte Franca has been experiencing a burst of renewed enthusiasm since last year. This phase of dynamic renewal has, in a short space of time, raised its traditionally good levels of quality even higher. Four decades after its foundation, the Ziliani family estate makes a series of top quality still and sparkling wines. In addition, they have modernized the vinification centre, purchased new vineyards and renovated and replanted the existing vine stock. The Cuvée Imperiale Brut '97 offers a brilliant, deep straw yellow and fine perlage. The nose is complex, showing apples, yeasts and delicate oak. The creamy mousse in the mouth is backed by a full, rich structure that is harmonious, balanced and long. The blend of the Brut Riserva Cellarius has a tad less depth but is still approachable and offers a wealth of fresh fruit. All the other labels of Cuvée Imperiale, from the Brut to the Max Rosé and Brut Extrême, are well-typed and absolutely delightful. Of the 2000 vintage still wines, the Terre di Franciacorta Le Arzelle has found a new fullness and balance not evident in previous versions, while the Franciacorta and Terre di Franciacorta dell'Antica Cantina Fratta di Monticelli Brusati are both excellent. We are still waiting for a vintage edition to follow the excellent '95.

○ TdF Bianco Le Arzelle '00	▼▼	5
○ Cuvée Imperiale Brut '97	▼▼	6
○ Cellarius Brut Ris.	▼▼	5
○ TdF Bianco '01	▼	5
○ TdF Bianco Antica Cantina Fratta '01	▼	4
○ TdF Bianco La Tinaia Antica Cantina Fratta '01	▼	4
○ Cuvée Imperiale Brut	▼	5
○ Cuvée Imperiale Brut Extrême	▼	5
⊙ Cuvée Imperiale Max Rosé	▼	5
○ Franciacorta Brut Antica Cantina Fratta	▼	5
○ Franciacorta Satèn Antica Cantina Fratta	▼	6

CORTE FRANCA (BS)

Monzio Compagnoni
Fraz. Nigoline
C.da Monti della Corte, 2
25040 Corte Franca (BS)
tel. 0309884157
e-mail: info@monziocompagnoni.com

Marcello Monzio Compagnoni manages to divide his time between two distinct estates. The larger one is in Franciacorta, at Nigoline near Cortefranca. From these 15 hectares of vineyards, and with the help of oenological consultant Donato Lanati, Marcello produces a complete range of territory wines: three versions of Franciacorta, a Terre Bianco, a Rosso and also a Pinot Nero. Again this year, we liked the Satèn and Extra Brut in our tasting. The Satèn is soft and fresh, with clean fruit and flower aromas, good structure and a citrus tang, whereas the Extra Brut is balanced and supple. The Brut, which has too much dosage, is slightly less impressive than the previous version. It closes on an oak note that tends to mask the aromas. The Terre di Franciacorta Bianco della Seta '01 is very pleasant and well made. It has structure, good sinew and aromas typical of a good Chardonnay, from apple to butter and vanilla, all very elegantly expressed. The Ronco della Seta Rosso '00 is also good, with wild berry aromas, big, soft tannins on the palate and a nice long close. At Valcalepio, the panel voted Two Glasses to Rosso di Luna, from 40 per cent merlot and 60 per cent cabernet sauvignon, which has blackberry and red berry fruit and toast aromas, and a soft, long palate suggesting discreet oak. A further Two went to the sweet red Don Quijote '99, from moscato di Scanzo, which unveils seductive plum jam, blackberries and blueberries, sweetness, balance and persistence in the mouth. The two Valcalepio DOCs were also very nice.

CORVINO SAN QUIRICO (PV)

Tenuta Mazzolino
Via Mazzolino, 26
27050 Corvino San Quirico (PV)
tel. 038387612280
e-mail: info@tenuta-mazzolino.com

Sandra Braggiotti is building a new cellar at Tenuta Mazzolino, the old village atop the hill of Corvino San Quirico. This means more space for barriques and bottles and more modern equipment to vinify the grapes from its own vineyards. It has demanded great effort from agronomist Roberto Piaggi, and the two French oenologists, Kyriakos Kynigopoulos and Jean François Coquard. The two technicians from across the Alps are applying their experience to varieties they know very well, pinot nero, chardonnay and cabernet sauvignon, which are cultivated on the estate's clayey, chalk-poor soil. The Noir '00, a monovarietal Pinot Nero, is ruby red with a complex bouquet of berry fruit, roses, damp autumn leaves and a slight hint of leather, followed by a round, elegant palate. The Blanc '00 is a Chardonnay from must fermented directly in barriques. After a year in oak, three months in stainless steel and the same period of bottle ageing, the wine is golden yellow. The nose has acacia, vanilla and roasted hazelnut and the soft palate is well structured. The Corvino '00 is a nice Cabernet Sauvignon, aged for a year in barrique. The notes of jam, bell peppers and coffee lead into a vigorous, elegant palate with ripe tannins. The fourth and last wine from the estate is the soft, fruity, still Bonarda '00, aged only in stainless steel. "After a year of experimenting," says Coquard, "we realized that with all the tannins from the croatina, oak should be avoided. Otherwise the wine gets too rough".

● Rosso di Luna '00	♙♙	5
○ TdF Bianco della Seta '00	♙♙	5
● Valcalepio Moscato Passito di Cenate Sotto Don Quijote '99	♙♙	5
○ Franciacorta Extra Brut	♙♙	5
○ Franciacorta Satèn	♙♙	5
● TdF Rosso Ronco della Seta '00	♙	4
● Valcalepio Rosso Colle della Luna '00	♙	4
○ TdF Bianco Ronco della Seta '01	♙	4
○ Valcalepio Bianco Colle della Luna '01	♙	4
○ Franciacorta Brut	♙	5

● OP Pinot Nero Noir '00	♙♙	6
● OP Cabernet Sauvignon Corvino '00	♙♙	4
○ OP Chardonnay Blanc '00	♙♙	4
● OP Bonarda '00	♙	4
● OP Pinot Nero '97	♙♙	4
● OP Cabernet Sauvignon Corvino '98	♙♙	4
● OP Pinot Nero Noir '98	♙♙	5
● OP Cabernet Sauvignon Corvino '99	♙♙	4
○ OP Chardonnay Blanc '99	♙♙	4
● OP Pinot Nero Noir '99	♙♙	5

DESENZANO DEL GARDA (BS)

PROVENZA
VIA DEI COLLI STORICI
25015 DESENZANO DEL GARDA (BS)
TEL. 0309910006
E-MAIL: provenza@gardanet.it

The Contato family estate in Provenza the now extends over 30 or so hectares and includes four "cascine", or farms: Ca' Maiol, the original nucleus, established in 1710 by Sebastiano Maioli, a notary in Desenzano, Ca' Molin, Rocchetta and Storta. The modern cellar turns out almost 400,000 bottles a year of fine wines. As mentioned in the last Guide, the outstanding wines are two selections created by Fabio Contato, the Lugana Superiore '99 and Garda Classico Rosso '98. The first is made with cold maceration of the skins in the must and then fermented in barrique. It is a bright green-gold, with a complex bouquet of vanilla, citron peel, lemon verbena and peach, then a full, rich, fresh palate. The Rosso, from groppello, marzemino, barbera and sangiovese with 24 months in barrique, is a great wine. Firm and robust, it will mature well in the bottle. The Ca' Molin Lugana Superiore '00 is good after cold-maceration and ageing for just six months in new oak. The Ca' Maiol '01 is simpler, fresher and more accessible. It is fermented in stainless steel vats to keep its varietal notes unaltered. Again on the subject of Lugana, the two "spumante" wines were not bad. They are the Brut Classico Ca' Maiol '98, which spends 30 months on the lees, and Sebastian '00 Charmat, named after the founder. The Garda Classico Rosso Negresco '00, from groppello, marzemino, sangiovese and barbera aged for 12 months in small oak casks, is spicy, harmonious and warm while the Ca' Maiol Rosso '01, from the same varieties, aged in stainless steel, is forthright and fruity with a grassy note.

○	Lugana Sup. Sel. Fabio Contato '99	🍷🍷	6
○	Lugana Sup. Ca' Molin '00	🍷🍷	6
●	Garda Cl. Rosso Sel. Fabio Contato '98	🍷🍷	6
●	Garda Cl. Rosso Negresco '00	🍷	6
○	Lugana Brut Sebastian '00	🍷	3
●	Garda Cl. Rosso Ca' Maiol '01	🍷	4
○	Lugana Ca' Maiol '01	🍷	4
○	Lugana Brut Cl. Ca' Maiol '98	🍷	7
●	Garda Cl. Rosso Sel. Fabio Contato '97	🍷🍷	6
○	Lugana Sup. Sel. Fabio Contato '98	🍷🍷	6
○	Lugana Sup. Ca' Molin '99	🍷🍷	5

ERBUSCO (BS)

★ BELLAVISTA
VIA BELLAVISTA, 5
25030 ERBUSCO (BS)
TEL. 0307762000
E-MAIL: info@bellavistasrl.it

Once again, this celebrated Erbusco estate had no trouble in adding another Three Glasses to its already well-stocked trophy case. Founded in 1977 by Vittorio Moretti, a businessman with a love of wine, Bellavista had already become one of the benchmark estates in Franciacorta, and for new Italian wines, as early as the 1980s. In addition to Moretti, credit also goes to Mattia Vezzola, oenologist and general manager of Bellavista, who managed to bring the estate up to speed and has also succeeded in the even more difficult task of keeping it there. Today, Bellavista is the powerhouse of a holding company that groups together numerous top estates in Lombardy and Tuscany, and includes a Relais & Château hotel, the Alberta, next to the cellars in Erbusco. The best bottle this year is the Franciacorta Brut Gran Cuvée '98, a perfect example of the now familiar "Bellavista style". A brilliant greenish straw yellow, it shows a creamy mousse and very fine bead, then a perfect cocktail of elegant, fresh aromas of yeast, vanilla, apple and ripe white peach. It has intensity and depth, and the palate has concentration, balance and elegance. The structure is solid but never over the top, with great breadth and a slow finish that signs off on freshly baked cakes and ripe apple. The Pas Operé '97 is equally fascinating and complex, though slightly less rich on the palate. All the other estate Cuvées are excellent. This year, we liked the two Terre di Franciacorta Biancos, the Convento dell'Annunciata and Uccellanda '99, which have never been as fresh, elegant and vibrant.

○	Franciacorta Gran Cuvée Brut '98	🍷🍷🍷	6
○	Franciacorta Gran Cuvée Pas Operé '97	🍷🍷	7
○	TdF Bianco Convento dell'Annunciata '99	🍷🍷	6
○	TdF Bianco '01	🍷🍷	4
○	TdF Bianco Uccellanda '99	🍷🍷	6
○	Franciacorta Gran Cuvée Satèn	🍷🍷	7
●	TdF Rosso '00	🍷	4
⊙	Franciacorta Gran Cuvée Brut Rosé '98	🍷	7
○	Franciacorta Cuvée Brut	🍷	5
○	Franciacorta Gran Cuvée Pas Operé '96	🍷🍷	7
○	Franciacorta Gran Cuvée Pas Operé '93	🍷🍷	5
○	Franciacorta Gran Cuvée Pas Operé '95	🍷🍷	6
●	Rosso del Sebino Solesine '98	🍷🍷	5

ERBUSCO (BS)

★★ Ca' del Bosco
Via Case Sparse, 20
25030 Erbusco (BS)
tel. 0307766111 - 0307766136
e-mail: cadelbosco@cadelbosco.com

There's a temptation to overdo the superlatives when you're talking about Ca' del Bosco and its wines. We'll try to be concise and give readers a few brief notes on our Winery of the Year. The new vinification and ageing complex is being finished as we write. It will be one of the most technologically advanced structures in the entire wine world. It will also allow Maurizio Zanella, president and founder of Ca' del Bosco, and his long-standing associate, oenologist Stefano Capelli, to lavish even more attention on vinifying, maturing and ageing their wines. They turn out almost 1,000,000 bottles a year from the more than 300 hectares of estate vineyards. This year, we were particularly struck by the Cuvée Annamaria Clementi '95, an incredibly complex, deep Franciacorta. The extraordinarily delicate nose is redolent of apple, flowers and oriental spices, introducing rare elegance, depth and persistence on the palate. The Chardonnay '00 is just as good, revealing very careful grape selection and sensitive use of new oak. It's bursting with fruit, structure and freshness. This lovely wine is drinking well now but has many years ahead of it. The Carmenèro '99, a red from carmenère, is concentrated, spicy and very elegant and the refined, particularly well-rounded, Satèn '98 are only a few points behind the abovementioned thoroughbreds. The other wines? Excellent as always.

○ TdF Chardonnay '00	▼▼▼	8
○ Franciacorta Cuvée Annamaria Clementi '95	▼▼▼	8
○ Franciacorta Dosage Zèro '98	▼▼	6
○ Franciacorta Satèn '98	▼▼	6
● Carmenèro '99	▼▼	8
● TdF Curtefranca Rosso '00	▼▼	4
○ Elfo 11 '01	▼▼	5
○ TdF Curtefranca Bianco '01	▼▼	4
○ Franciacorta Brut '98	▼▼	6
⊙ Franciacorta Rosé '98	▼▼	6
● Maurizio Zanella '99	▼▼	8
○ Franciacorta Brut	▼	5
○ TdF Chardonnay '98	▼▼▼	6
○ TdF Chardonnay '99	▼▼▼	6

ERBUSCO (BS)

Cavalleri
Via Provinciale, 96
25030 Erbusco (BS)
tel. 0307760217

One of the major players in Franciacorta during those pioneer days of the 1970s and 1980s, Cavalleri continues to be a shining star in the busy, crowded firmament that is the zone today. With 40 hectares of vineyards and an annual production of 250,000 bottles, Cavalleri offers a range of Franciacortas and still wines with few equals. The Franciacorta Collezione '97 has a bright, deep straw colour, creamy mousse and very fine perlage. It tempts the nose with the delicacy, finesse and balance of fruit-driven aromas nuanced with vanilla that give depth and complexity to the whole. The same sensations return on the palate, where the wine slowly reveals its round, full body, harmony and length. The Collezione Rosé '97 impressively merges wild berry notes with a body that is full yet perfectly balanced. The Satèn '98 is one of the best tasted this year. The creamy, soft progression successfully marries tones of butter, warm fresh cakes and croissants with a spirited, fresh-tasting fruit vein that makes it supple and invigorating. The panel thought the Franciacorta Brut was very well crafted, with nicely integrated fruit, while the Pas Dosé '98 offers strikingly intense sensations of yeast and toast, clean hints of ripe peach and full structure. The Rampaneto '01 is a wonderfully round, fresh white. The Terre di Franciacorta Bianco from the same vintage is also excellent and the red wines were all good.

○ Franciacorta Collezione Brut '97	▼▼	6
○ Franciacorta Satèn '98	▼▼	5
○ TdF Bianco '01	▼▼	4
○ TdF Bianco Rampaneto '01	▼▼	4
⊙ Franciacorta Collezione Rosé '98	▼▼	6
○ Franciacorta Pas Dosé '98	▼▼	5
○ Franciacorta Brut	▼▼	5
● TdF Rosso '00	▼	4
● TdF Rosso Tajardino '00	▼	5
● Corniole Merlot '99	▼	6
○ Franciacorta Collezione Brut '86	▼▼▼	6
○ Franciacorta Collezione Brut '93	▼▼▼	6
○ Franciacorta Collezione Brut '94	▼▼▼	6
○ Franciacorta Collezione Esclusiva Brut '93	▼▼	6
○ Franciacorta Collezione Esclusiva Brut '94	▼▼	6

ERBUSCO (BS)

FERGHETTINA
VIA CASE SPARSE, 4
25030 ERBUSCO (BS)
TEL. 0307760120 - 0307268308

ERBUSCO (BS)

ENRICO GATTI
VIA METELLI, 9
25030 ERBUSCO (BS)
TEL. 0307267999
E-MAIL: info@enricogatti.it

The average scores obtained by the wines and Franciacortas from Ferghettina confirm the brilliant reputation this family estate has earned in just the last few years. No wine this year earned fewer than Two Glasses and though the new edition of the Satèn was, sadly, not a repeat of the splendid '97, it was only a hair's breadth away. The '98 is wonderfully elegant, with a perlage of great finesse. The elegant nose reveals subtle aromas that run from yeast to acacia flowers, apricots and vanilla, expressed clearly and intensely. Dense and balanced, the palate flaunts aromatic notes that echo the nose as well as a long finish. The Franciacorta Brut is in many respects similar, particularly in the apricot on the nose and palate. Endearingly fresh, it offers full body and remarkable overall finesse. We had a preview taste of a vintage cuvée from '95 that promises great things, but our evaluation will have to be postponed until the next Guide. On the still wine front, the Merlot Baladello '99 confirms both the suitability of the territory for this international variety and the talents of winemakers Roberto Gatti and his daughter Laura, who works with him in cellar and vineyard. A dense, elegant red with a wealth of soft fruit aromas and smooth tannins, it signs off elegantly and unhurriedly. The Terre di Franciacorta Bianco '01 and Rosso '00 are among the best from the DOC zone and the Terre Bianco Favento '01, a monovarietal Chardonnay, is rich in fruit and soft oak.

For the second year running, the Satèn from Gatti came close to winning Three Glasses, a goal that is within reach of this small, 17-hectare estate with an annual production of around 130,000 bottles. The property is also family-run, for Lorenzo and Paola Gatti look after everything with the collaboration of their respective spouses, Sonia Cherif and Enzo Balzarini, plus help from oenologist Alberto Musatti. But let's get back to the Satèn '98, A refined, elegant "blanc de blancs" whose complex suppleness is veined by delicate new oak and vanilla. Rich in fruit on the nose as well as the palate, it has body, a soft, meaty mouthfeel, whistle-clean fruit and great balance. In the tradition of this winery, the Franciacorta Brut has sweet, ripe fruit aromas with apricot prominent, then apple and finally vanilla, followed by a caressingly soft palate and persistent effervescence. The Gatti Rosso '00 is a remarkably rich Bordeaux blend, endowed with structure and above all balance, as well as fruit and smooth tannins. It has to be one of the best reds from the vintage in these parts. The Terre di Franciacorta Bianco has a bit less strength than the previous version, but makes up for it in balance and pleasant drinkability. The barrique-aged Terre di Franciacorta Gatti Bianco '00 shows the typical features of the best Franciacorta Chardonnays. Its rich fruit and freshness are tempered with carefully applied oak. We felt the Terre di Franciacorta Rosso '00 was as good as ever.

○ Franciacorta Satèn '98	🍷🍷	5
● TdF Rosso '00	🍷🍷	4*
○ TdF Bianco '01	🍷🍷	4*
○ TdF Bianco Favento '01	🍷🍷	4*
● Merlot Baladello '99	🍷🍷	5
○ Franciacorta Brut	🍷🍷	5
○ Franciacorta Satèn '97	🍷🍷🍷	5*
○ TdF Bianco Favento '00	🍷🍷	4*
● Merlot Baladello '98	🍷🍷	5

○ Franciacorta Satèn '98	🍷🍷	5
● Gatti Rosso '00	🍷🍷	5
○ TdF Gatti Bianco '00	🍷🍷	5
○ TdF Bianco '01	🍷🍷	3*
○ Franciacorta Brut	🍷🍷	5
● Gatti Rosso '98	🍷🍷	4
○ TdF Gatti Bianco '98	🍷🍷	4
● Gatti Rosso '99	🍷🍷	4*

ERBUSCO (BS)

San Cristoforo
Fraz. Villa
Via Villanuova, 2
25030 Erbusco (BS)
tel. 0307760482

Bruno Dotti and his wife Claudia Cavalleri have only recently celebrated the tenth anniversary of their purchase of this estate. During that decade, the wines from San Cristoforo have grown in quality and an excellent Franciacorta has been added to the Terre Bianco and Rosso traditionally produced at the cellar. The area under vine has now reached 12 hectares and average annual production runs to almost 70,000 bottles. But what counts most is that over the years, Bruno and Claudia's wines have maintained the excellent price-quality ratio they had under the management of the previous owner, Mario Filippini, who made value for money the San Cristoforo trademark. And here is the Franciacorta Brut, a gold-tinged, straw-yellow "blanc de blancs" with a very fine bead, soft yeast and peach jam aromas that sign off on vanilla tones. The palate shows not only structure and fullness, but also expressive grace and remarkable balance. The Terre di Franciacorta Bianco '01 is an attractive, brilliant greenish straw yellow. It has a fleshy, fruity mouthfeel and apricot and peach aromas on nose and palate, where it shows good backbone and suppleness. The Terre di Franciacorta Rosso '00 has improved with respect to previous vintages, although they were good, too. It has acquired greater concentration, while at the same time keeping intact the balance and upfront fruit make it so drinkable. At the time of our tasting, the blend had yet to be decided for the new vintage of the San Cristoforo Uno, the estate Bordeaux-style red. We will postpone judgement until the next edition.

● TdF Rosso '00	🍷🍷	3*
○ TdF Bianco '01	🍷🍷	3*
○ Franciacorta Brut	🍷🍷	5
● San Cristoforo Uno '98	🍷🍷	4
● TdF Rosso '99	🍷🍷	3*

ERBUSCO (BS)

Uberti
Loc. Salem
Via E. Fermi, 2
25030 Erbusco (BS)
tel. 0307267476
e-mail: uberti@libero.it

There were Three well-deserved Glasses again this year for the Magnificentia, the Uberti Satèn that has for years been earning some of the highest scores in absolute terms at our tastings. It is one of many successes for Agostino and Eleonora Uberti, a well-matched couple in the home and the cellar, where they share the same ideal of quality. More important, the Magnificentia is no cult wine, produced in limited numbers for wine guides and the tasting fraternity. We are talking about almost 10,000 bottles, the cutting edge of a cellar production that fluctuates around 120,000 bottles a year. All the wine is top quality, and all is obtained from the estate's 22 hectares. No matter, for the Magnificentia is faithful to its name. Deep, lustrous straw yellow tinged with green ushers in a dense, consistent and extraordinarily fine perlage. It unfolds on the nose with its usual intensity and richness, presenting elegant ripe fruit with amazingly well-defined white peach and apricot up front that fade away elegantly in a shimmer of vanilla. The palate echoes the nose remarkably well, offering dry freshness, a soft, full body and a long finish. The Comarì del Salem '97 is an Extra Brut with great character. Clean, intense aromas of yeasts and crusty bread, ripe fruit and toast introduce a full, zesty palate where fruit calls the tune for a rich, harmonious structure. From the excellent Franciacorta Brut Francesco I to the still wines, every Uberti label reflects the cellar's commitment to excellence.

○ Franciacorta Satèn Magnificentia	🍷🍷🍷	6
○ Franciacorta Extra Brut Comarì del Salem '97	🍷🍷	7
○ TdF Bianco dei Frati Priori '00	🍷🍷	5
○ TdF Bianco Augustus '01	🍷🍷	4*
○ Franciacorta Brut Francesco I	🍷🍷	5
● Rosso dei Frati Priori '99	🍷	6
○ Franciacorta Extra Brut Francesco I	🍷	5
◉ Franciacorta Rosé Brut Francesco I	🍷	5
○ Franciacorta Extra Brut Comarì del Salem '88	🍷🍷🍷	6
○ Franciacorta Extra Brut Comarì del Salem '95	🍷🍷🍷	6

ERBUSCO (BS)

GIUSEPPE VEZZOLI
VIA COSTA SOPRA, 22
25030 ERBUSCO (BS)
TEL. 0307267579
E-MAIL: niteovezzoli@libero.it

We spoke well of Giuseppe Vezzoli's winery last year. Though we expected progress in the already good quality of his wines and cuvées, we never imagined the Franciacorta Brut '98 this year would be slugging it out with the best cuvées from Franciacorta for the Three Glass award. Though it missed the top prize this year, we can safely predict a brilliant future for this small cellar. A little more than a year ago, Giuseppe abandoned a career in the metalworking industry to dedicate himself full-time to his passions: vineyards and wine. And so, thanks to oenological consultancy from Cesare Ferrari, Giuseppe presented us with a brilliant green-flecked straw-yellow Brut '98 with elegant, complex aromas and yeasts layered over rich fruit that fades out sweetly across swathe of biscuits, toastiness and vanilla. Dense and supple in the mouth, it has great balance, stylishly close-knit texture and length. The Satèn '98 is just as big and harmonious in its structure, with clean, complex notes of ripe fruit, spices and vanilla on nose and palate, and a personality that is intellectually challenging yet approachable. The Barbolzana '00 is an excellent Chardonnay, with a lovely bouquet of ripe apple, butter and vanilla, very ripe fruit on the palate, concentration and an elegant smattering of new oak. The two reds are also good and carefully made, the pleasant, fruity Niteo, a Bordeaux blend, and the classic Terre di Franciacorta '00.

GODIASCO (PV)

CABANON
LOC. CABANON, 1
27052 GODIASCO (PV)
TEL. 0383940912
E-MAIL: info@cabanon.it

Antoine de Saint-Exupéry would probably be proud to know that his tale, The Little Prince, had also become the name of one of the best Barberas we tasted this year in the Oltrepò. From very ripe grapes grown at Collesino, the oldest of the vineyards owned by the Mercandelli family of Cabanon, it ages unhurriedly in small oak casks and – crucially – matures for more than a year in bottle before release. Deep ruby red with a garnet rim, it has a complex bouquet of very ripe berry fruit, jam, toast and spices, then a robust, aristocratic, warm palate with good balance. Though quite evolved, it will have no trouble in holding up for some time yet. Another winery warhorse is the Botte n. 18 Cuore di Vino '99, an unusual but elegant Rosso Oltrepò fermented in Slavonian oak. Pleasantly solid and full-bodied, it reveals notes of bell pepper and mature hay among others. Though not as concentrated as Il Piccolo Principe, the Prunello '98 is still remarkable. A Barbera with a year in oak and a lovely vivid ruby colour, it offers cherry jam fragrances and a sound, well-defined palate. The Syra's '00, from syrah grown in the Vigna dei Gerbidi plot, is good but seemed less full-bodied than the '98. The Pinot Grigio '01 and Cabanon Blanc '01 are not bad. The latter, from sauvignon, has dominant aromas of sage and mineral echoes, then a dry, fresh palate that ends in a tropical fruit finish. The Cabanon Noir, a Pinot Nero from the 2001 vintage, vinified and aged in steel, needs further time in the cellar.

○ Franciacorta Brut '98	🍷🍷	6
○ Chardonnay Barbolzana '00	🍷🍷	5
○ Franciacorta Satèn '98	🍷🍷	6
● TdF Rosso '00	🍷	4
● Niteo '99	🍷	6

● OP Barbera Piccolo Principe '98	🍷🍷	6
● OP Barbera Prunello '98	🍷🍷	4
● OP Rosso Cuore di Vino Botte n. 18 '99	🍷🍷	4
● Syra's '00	🍷	5
○ OP Cabanon Blanc '01	🍷	4
● OP Cabanon Noir '01	🍷	4
○ OP Pinot Grigio '01	🍷	4
● Syra's '98	🍷🍷	4
● OP Barbera Piccolo Principe '97	🍷🍷	5
○ OP Passito Oro '97	🍷🍷	5
● OP Rosso Botte n. 18 '98	🍷🍷	4
○ Opera Prima Cabanon Blanc '98	🍷🍷	3
● OP Rosso Infernot Ris. '99	🍷🍷	5

GRUMELLO DEL MONTE (BG)

CARLOZADRA
VIA GANDOSSI, 13
24064 GRUMELLO DEL MONTE (BG)
TEL. 035832066 - 035830244

Carlo Zadra, an oenologist who moved from his native Trentino to the hills of Valcalepio, is an especially skilled "spumantista", or sparkling winemaker. He always sources the base wines for cuvées in Trentino but he does have a small vineyard in the Bergamo area. That is where he picked the cabernet sauvignon in 1999 to blend with pinot nero from Trentino to create the new version of Don Ludovico, which was a monovarietal pinot nero until last year. Aged for 14 months in barrique, the wine is still maturing in the bottle and will be on sale before the end of autumn. However, it is already impressive. Bright garnet tinged with ruby, with a bouquet of cabernet-derived hay and raspberry melding with cassis from the pinot nero against oak that keeps a respectful distance. Delicate rather than concentrated in the mouth, it ends on notes of forest floor, liquorice and spices. The Moscato Giallo Secco Donna Nunzia '01 is not yet ready, so we'll move on to the "metodo classico" sparklers that are the winery's mainstays. The vintage Brut '97, disgorged in February 2002, is from chardonnay, pinot bianco and pinot nero. Bright gold, it offers a very fine, persistent bead, a complex nose of roasted hazelnut, incense, bay leaf and moss and a full, elegance in the mouth. The Nondosato '95, disgorged last February, is drier. The chardonnay base, with some pinot nero, is quite evolved and offers honey, croissants and butter in a ripe, complex ensemble. Finally, the Extra Dry Liberty, Blanc de Blancs that lay on the lees until February 2002, is soft, round and well-behaved.

○ Carlozadra Cl. Brut Nondosato '95	▼▼	5
○ Carlozadra Cl. Brut '97	▼▼	5
● Don Ludovico Pinot Nero '99	▼▼	4
○ Carlozadra Extra Dry Liberty	▼▼	4
○ Carlozadra Cl. Brut '92	♀♀	4
○ Carlozadra Cl. Brut Nondosato '92	♀♀	5
○ Carlozadra Cl. Brut '93	♀♀	5
○ Carlozadra Cl. Brut Nondosato '93	♀♀	4
● Don Ludovico Pinot Nero '93	♀♀	4
○ Carlozadra Cl. Brut Nondosato '94	♀♀	5
○ Carlozadra Cl. Brut '95	♀♀	4
○ Carlozadra Cl. Brut '96	♀♀	5
● Don Ludovico Pinot Nero '97	♀♀	4
○ Carlozadra Extra Dry Liberty '98	♀♀	4

MESE (SO)

MAMETE PREVOSTINI
VIA LUCCHINETTI, 65
23020 MESE (SO)
TEL. 034341003
E-MAIL: info@mameteprevostini.com

We were right last year to mention the professional skills of young oenologist Mamete Prevostini. Encouraged by our praise, this shy, promising newcomer on the Valtellina winemaking scene continues to strive for absolute quality. In fact, he forged ahead and, deservedly, won Three Glasses with the majestic Sforzato Albareda '00. The winery produces almost 5,000 bottles of Sforzato, from perfectly raisined nebbiolo grapes. It ages for 24 months in small oak casks and 12 months in the bottle. The wine is garnet red with complex balsamic aromas and elegant spicy notes of ripe cherries and tea leaves. Dense and concentrated on the palate, it shows wonderful elegance with perfectly integrated tannins, a soft finish and a long finish. We felt the nebbiolo-based Corte di Cama '98 was also excellent. About 50 per cent of the fruit is raisined, then added to the wine made from fresh grapes. The final result is superb, with intense aromas that recall raspberry jam. The palate is soft and has serious structure, bringing together complexity and drinkability. The Sommarovina '99 is straightforward yet at the same time delicate in its aromas. A Sassella with a clear territorial timbre, it is brilliant garnet red and the nose reveals attractive black cherry and berry fruit. It is full on the palate, which mirrors the nose well.

● Valtellina Sforzato Albareda '00	▼▼▼	7
● Valtellina Sup. Corte di Cama '98	▼▼	6
● Valtellina Sup. Sassella Sommarovina '99	▼▼	5
● Valtellina Sup. Corte di Cama '97	♀♀	5
● Valtellina Sup. Sassella Sommarovina '98	♀♀	5
● Valtellina Sforzato Albareda '99	♀♀	6

MONIGA DEL GARDA (BS)

COSTARIPA
VIA CIALDINI, 12
25080 MONIGA DEL GARDA (BS)
TEL. 0365502010

Mattia and Imer Vezzola's idea of making Chiaretto di Moniga again in a 19th-century version, when the wine was vinified in oak, was an interesting attempt to bring vitality to a rosé market that was languishing, at least in terms of quantity. The '99 Chiaretto, dedicated to Pompeo Molmenti, impressed us more last year. This time, we noticed the 2000 vintage had what we felt was an excessive dose of oak, which robbed the fruit aromas of vitality. But it was still good enough to come near to a second Glass. In contrast, there were no quibbles about the barrique-aged Garda Classico Rosso '00, dedicated to Christian Barnard, the great South African heart surgeon who passed away a year ago. Deep purple with broad aromas of black berry fruit and a soft palate, well supported by fine-grained tannins. The barrel-aged Garda Groppello Maim '00 is equally enjoyable, with sweet spicy notes that underline touches of jam and a rich, harmonious flavour profile. The Cabernet Sauvignon Pradamonte '00 needs further cellar time. Though pleasing on the nose, it is less complete in the mouth, at least for the time being. The Marzemino Le Mazane '01 is frank and fruity. The Brut Classico Costaripa is as good as ever, with a lovely, compact perlage, a bouquet of crusty bread and ripe apple, over a hint of spice, and a clean, elegant palate. The cuve close Lugana Brut is simpler, soft – but still fresh and lively – and fruity.

- ● Garda Cl. Groppello Maim '00 5
- ● Garda Cl. Rosso Chr. Barnard '00 5
- ● Garda Cabernet Sauvignon Pradamonte '00 4
- ◉ Garda Cl. Chiaretto Molmenti '00 5
- ● Benaco Bresciano Marzemino Le Mazane '01 4
- ○ Lugana Brut '01 4
- ○ Brut Cl. Costaripa 4
- ● Garda Cl. Groppello Maim '97 5
- ◉ Garda Cl. Chiaretto Molmenti '98 5
- ◉ Garda Cl. Chiaretto Molmenti '99 5
- ● Garda Cl. Groppello Maim '99 5
- ● Garda Cl. Rosso Chr. Barnard '99 5

MONIGA DEL GARDA (BS)

MONTE CICOGNA
VIA DELLE VIGNE, 6
25080 MONIGA DEL GARDA (BS)
TEL. 0365503200 - 0365502007
E-MAIL: montecicogna@tin.it

This edition of the Guide reports flattering results for Cesare Materossi's Monte Cicogna winery. At the top of their range, we find the Don Lisander, Garda Classico Rosso Superiore '98, from 60 per cent groppello gentile, 15 per cent each of sangiovese and barbera, along with marzemino, half of which is partially raisined. It is ruby, with a well-defined, complex bouquet with dominant notes of dried grape, plum and morello cherry fruit and faint hints of spice, then a warm, well-rounded palate. The Rosso Superiore Rubinere '00 is excellent. Made from the same grape blend as the Don Lisander, but without the raisining, it has notes of ripe morello cherry and a full flavour with that distinct, slightly bitter twist of almonds that is characteristic of groppello. After six months in oak, the Groppello di Moniga Beana '00 is all upfront fruit and alcohol. The Torrione '01, a Garda Classico Chiaretto, fermented "a levata di cappello" (with a brief maceration until the cap forms), is a vivid rose pink with a floral aroma and clean, zesty flavour. The Lugana '01, from what old documents record as "turbiana" grapes, later mistakenly called "trebbiano", is fresh and floral, recalling citronella and lemon zest, with a nice, slightly bitter background. The Turbellari '97, a barrique-aged white Malvasia from partially dried grapes, is very mature, vanillaed and sweet, without being cloying.

- ○ Turbellari Malvasia Passito '97 5
- ● Garda Cl. Sup. Don Lisander '98 5
- ● Garda Cl. Rosso Groppello Beana '00 3
- ● Garda Cl. Rosso Rubinere '00 3
- ◉ Garda Cl. Chiaretto Il Torrione '01 4
- ○ Lugana '01 3

MONTALTO PAVESE (PV)

Ca' del Gè
Fraz. Ca' del Gè, 3
27040 Montalto Pavese (PV)
tel. 0383870179
e-mail: info@cadelge.it

Enzo Padroggi at Ca' del Gè continues to produce wines of uneven quality. The 16 bottles submitted for tasting ran from excellent to ordinary. The results could be much better with a bit more care but then it must be difficult to give proper attention to every wine in such a vast range. We'll restrict ourselves to commenting on the several wines that are well made. First up is the Tormento '00, a Dolcetto from very ripe grapes that brings back the glories of the '97 vintage. Dark, concentrated, warm and frank, with a big jammy nose. The Vigna Marinoni plot produced a noteworthy Riesling Renano in 2000, lifted by well-gauged oak. Straw yellow tinged with green, it has a nose of roses and ripe pineapple with faint hints of gun flint, underpinned by spice. The round, flavoursome palate backed by good acidic grip. The semi-sparkling Bonarda Frizzante '01 is purple and uncompromisingly heady, with a blackberry aroma and moderate residual sweetness that balances the slightly bitter finish. The still Bonarda La Fidela '00 is mature but firm with a bouquet of violet and morello cherry. The sparkling Moscato '01 does not have a great bouquet but is full-flavoured, sweet and seductive in the mouth. The still Riesling Italico and Müller Thurgau from the '01 vintage are fresh and clean, though rather simple.

MONTALTO PAVESE (PV)

Doria
Loc. Casa Tacconi, 3
27040 Montalto Pavese (PV)
tel. 0383870143

In this edition of the Guide, Giuseppina Sassella Doria's showcase wine is again the '98 A.D., a great red made with nebbiolo from selected clones in very old Oltrepò vineyards, planted when the territory was still administered by Piedmont, blended into a Rosso Oltrepò. The A.D., so-called in memory of Andrea Doria, Giuseppina's husband and an enthusiastic grower, ages slowly in barrique, is bottled without filtration and then left to mature for a suitable period of time. Thanks to a very favourable harvest, the '98 is more concentrated than the '97. Bright garnet, with aromas of dried wild roses, liquorice and vanilla, over hints of raspberry and pennyroyal, it flaunts a warm, seamless and lingeringly austere palate. It's one for the cellar and will improve in the bottle. But we'll have to be patient with the other flagship wines from this Montalto estate. The Roncobianco Riesling Renano '01, fermented with partial cold-maceration, is still green and harsh, the same goes for the Pinot Nero In Bianco Querciolo '01, which is fermented without the skins, and the Querciolo Rosso, a monovarietal Pinot Nero that spends a year in barrique. Wisely, these products will be presented for tasting next year. Meanwhile, we once tasted wines from the 2002 Guide that have held up very well. The Pinot Nero '99 has matured further in the bottle. We can only reiterate what we said at the time. Finally, the Pinot Nero In Bianco Querciolo '00 Brut Metodo Martinotti "spumante" is enjoyably full but seems a more evolved that it ought to be. Enjoy it now.

○ OP Riesling Renano Vigna Marinoni '00	ŸŸ	4
● OP Tormento '00	ŸŸ	6
● OP Bonarda Frizzante '01	ŸŸ	3*
● OP Bonarda La Fidela '00	Ÿ	4
○ OP Moscato '01	Ÿ	2*
○ OP Riesling Italico '01	Ÿ	2*
○ Provincia di Pavia Müller Thurgau '01	Ÿ	3
● Dolcetto Tormento '97	ŸŸ	4
● OP Barbera Vigna Varmasì '97	ŸŸ	4
● OP Barbera Vigna Varmasì '99	ŸŸ	4

● Provincia di Pavia A.D. '98	ŸŸ	6
○ OP Pinot Nero in Bianco Querciolo '00	ŸŸ	4
○ OP Pinot Nero Brut Querciolo '00	Ÿ	4
○ OP Riesling Renano Roncobianco '00	ŸŸ	4
● OP Rosso Roncorosso '98	ŸŸ	4
● OP Pinot Nero Querciolo '99	ŸŸ	4

MONTEBELLO DELLA BATTAGLIA (PV)

TENUTA LA COSTAIOLA
VIA COSTAIOLA, 23
27054 MONTEBELLO DELLA BATTAGLIA (PV)
TEL. 038383169 - 038382069
E-MAIL: lacostaiola@libero.it

With 23 hectares of their own vineyards and eight rented, a renovated cellar and a very special new consultant in Beppe Caviola, brothers Michele and Fabio Rossetti have everything set to become serious producers of fine wines. Increasingly, they are adopting a modern style to cater for changing consumer tastes. Consider the Oltrepò Pavese Rosso La Vigna Bricca '99, which is even better than the already remarkable 1998 vintage. From mostly barbera, with pinot nero and a little croatina, it is warm, full, fruity, and soft yet firm in the mouth, with a fragrant, spicy nose that reveals no excess of oak. It will be interesting to see what Caviola manages to do with this, since he has just started. Our cellar tastings were very promising. In the meantime, the Aiole '98, a red from pinot nero, bodes well both in its elegant aroma and well-balanced, nicely tannic flavour. The cuve close Bonarda Giada '01 is also pleasant with its no-nonsense blackberry and violet bouquet. The still Barbera I Due Draghi '01 is just as approachable, ready and easy to drink. It was aged only in stainless steel to preserve the varietal aromas. The best of the whites is the Bellarmino '00, a cold-macerated Riesling Renano. A quarter of must ferments in barrique and the rest in stainless steel, to create a greenish-gold wine with a nose of wistaria, damson and vanilla, and a soft, spicy, forthright flavour. For those who prefer a simpler Riesling, there is the fresh, flowery Attimo '01, aged only stainless steel.

O	Provincia di Pavia Bellarmino '00	₸₸	4
●	Aiole '98	₸₸	5
●	OP Rosso La Vigna Bricca '99	₸₸	4
●	OP Barbera I Due Draghi '01	₸	3
●	OP Bonarda Vivace Giada '01	₸	3
O	OP Riesling Renano Attimo '01	₸	3
●	OP Barbera I due Draghi '00	₸₸	3
●	OP Pinot Nero Bellarmino '98	₸₸	4
●	Rosso La Vigna Bricca Ris. '98	₸₸	4

MONTICELLI BRUSATI (BS)

LA MONTINA
VIA BAIANA, 17
25040 MONTICELLI BRUSATI (BS)
TEL. 030653278
E-MAIL: info@lamontina.it

The Franciacortas from La Montina get more and more interesting at each successive tasting. This winery in Monticelli Brusati belongs to brothers Vittorio, Giancarlo and Alberto Bozza. The lovely premises, with the recently expanded and modernized cellar, is housed in an old villa that belonged to an ancestor of Paul VI in the 17th century, a certain Benedetto Montini from whom the winery takes its name. The winery produces around 320,000 bottles a year from 35 hectares of vineyards, some owned and some rented. The Montina flagship wine, Franciacorta Brut '97, has a very fine perlage and captivating nose of soft apple and ripe apricot, honey and acacia blossom, to sign off elegantly on notes of sweet spices. The palate has character, balance and elegance, combining structure and finesse, and a fresh, lingering finish with delicate hints of almonds. The Franciacorta Brut is as enjoyable as ever with good fullness and lively, enjoyable fruit. We found the Extra Brut a bit edgy, if well-balanced and underpinned by a citrus note. The nice, rich Rosé Demi Sec is pleasantly sweet, with notes of wild strawberries, raspberries and blueberries. However, we were not fully convinced by the Satèn. The acidic vein is a bit off the scale for this category of wine. There were Two Glasses for the excellent Terre Rosso dei Dossi '99, with intense, ripe aromas of berry fruit. Balanced freshness in the mouth helps it to showcase its lovely structure and smooth tannins. The other estate labels are all good.

O	Franciacorta Brut '97	₸₸	5
●	TdF Rosso dei Dossi '99	₸₸	3*
O	Franciacorta Brut	₸₸	4*
O	Franciacorta Satèn	₸₸	5
●	TdF Rosso '00	₸	3*
O	TdF Bianco '01	₸	3*
O	Franciacorta Extra Brut	₸	4
⊙	Franciacorta Rosé Demi Sec	₸	5
O	Franciacorta Brut '95	₸₸	5
O	Franciacorta Brut '96	₸₸	5

MONTICELLI BRUSATI (BS)

Lo Sparviere
Via Costa, 2
25040 Monticelli Brusati (BS)
Tel. 030652382
E-mail: losparviere@libero.it

Lo Sparviere is the property of Monique Poncelet, wife of the Ugo Gussalli Beretta who chairs the Beretta company in Gardone Val Trompia and comes from one of Italy's oldest industrial families. Surrounded by vineyards, the lovely Renaissance villa also houses a modern cellar where wines and Franciacortas are made with care, elegance and style. The property spreads across 150 hectares, 23 under vine, that provide the fruit for an annual production of around 110,000 bottles. Estate oenologist Francesco Polastri presented a marvellous Franciacorta Extra Brut this year. It is a lovely, lustrous, deep straw yellow and offers an endless stream of tiny bubbles and delightful aromas of quince, apricot and fresh cakes that fade out over vanilla. The palate is soft and fruity, yet preserves the dryness and fresh liveliness that make it drink so well and take their leave over yeast and vanilla, again. The Terre di Franciacorta Bianco '01, one of the best from the vintage, reprises some of these features, such as fresh cake aromas, and also shows a good structure, currently wrapped in soft fruity pulp. The Franciacorta Brut is very enjoyable but we felt the character was flawed by assertive super-ripe fruit that weighs it down. However, it is still admirably solid, well-structured and long. Of the two reds tasted, the panel preferred the Vino del Cacciatore '00 to the Sergnana '99. The former took Two Glasses for its body, soft tannins and good overall balance.

○ TdF Bianco '01	4*
○ Franciacorta Extra Brut	5
● TdF Rosso Vino del Cacciatore '00	4
● TdF Rosso Il Sergnana '99	5
○ Franciacorta Brut	5
● TdF Rosso Il Sergnana '96	5
○ TdF Bianco Lo Sparviere '98	5

MONTICELLI BRUSATI (BS)

Villa
Via Villa, 12
25040 Monticelli Brusati (BS)
Tel. 030652329 - 030652100
E-mail: infor@villa-franciacorta.it

For years now, Alessandro Bianchi's estate has been in the upper reaches of the list of the best wineries in the Franciacorta. It only needed an important award to emphasize the great job the estate staff has been doing. That award arrived this year when we awarded Three Glasses to a splendid Franciacorta Extra Brut '98 that impressed the panel at our tastings. Bright straw yellow with greenish highlights, it has an extraordinarily fine, sustained perlage. The nose is intense, full and above all elegant. We were astonished by the complex range of aromas over the intense white peach, golden apple and apricot fruit, aromas that include sweet spices, vanilla, grilled bread and deeper hints of toastiness. The palate combines elegance with balance and is well-structured without being intrusive. A soft yet dry texture is supported by lively acid grip. Our compliments to the oenologist, Corrado Cugnasco and the entire staff. The Satèn '98 is equally elegant and charming. The clean notes of ripe golden delicious apple and hints of citrus and yeast on the nose promptly return on the palate over sweetish nuances of vanilla. The other wines are good, too. The Rosé Demi Sec '98 is softly sweet, with lots of wild berry fruit, the Franciacorta Brut '98 flaunts fullness and balance, the red Gradoni '99 is concentrated and elegant while the Pian della Villa '01 is fresh and full-bodied.

○ Franciacorta Extra Brut '98	5*
○ Franciacorta Satèn '98	5
○ TdF Bianco Pian della Villa '01	4*
○ Franciacorta Brut '98	5
⊙ Franciacorta Rosé Démi Sec '98	5
● TdF Rosso Gradoni '99	5
○ TdF Bianco '01	4*
○ Franciacorta Cuvette Extra Dry '98	5
○ Franciacorta Brut Sel. '95	6
○ Franciacorta Extra Brut '97	5
○ Franciacorta Satèn '97	6

MONTÙ BECCARIA (PV)

VERCESI DEL CASTELLAZZO
VIA AURELIANO, 36
27040 MONTÙ BECCARIA (PV)
TEL. 038560067 - 0385262098
E-MAIL: vercesicastellazzo@libero.it

Gianmaria Vercesi is a champion of dry, still Bonardas, aged in oak. Not an easy task, given that the tannins in croatina, aside from being rather rough and bitter, do not easily meld with those from oak. Harmony is some time coming. Because of this, the Bonarda '98 Fatila was not presented for last year's tastings. Now, it is ready and proves to be an outstanding example. Vanilla underpins notes of wild berry jam on the nose, then the robust, generous palate has a no-nonsense country nobility. In contrast, the slightly sparkling "vivace" Bonarda Luogo della Milla '01 is a different prospect, with its lively fizz and full aroma of black berry fruit. The palate is dry but not excessively so, with nice spritz and good tannins. Getting back to the reds, the Barbera Clà '00 shows that the Piedmontese variety may have a future in the Oltrepò hills, if properly cultivated and vinified. The nose is well-defined and complex, recalling morello cherry fruit and cloves. The Rosso del Castellazzo '00 is equally powerful. Shrewd oak ageing has lent it fullness and complexity. The Oltrepò Pavese Rosso Pezzalunga '01 needs a bit more time in the bottle to find its feet, in contrast with the Pinot Nero Luogo dei Monti '98, which already seems to have hit its peak. The monovarietal Vespolino '01, from ughetta di Canneto, the local name for vespolino, is a nice red with green pepper notes. The two 2001 Pinot Neros fermented without the skins, the still Gugiarolo and the slightly sparkling Le Marghe, are both forthright and aroma-rich.

● OP Bonarda Fatila '98	♛♛	4
● OP Barbera Clà '00	♛♛	4
● Provincia di Pavia Rosso del Castellazzo '00	♛♛	4
● OP Bonarda Luogo della Milla '01	♛♛	3*
● OP Pinot Nero Luogo dei Monti '98	♛♛	4
○ OP Pinot Nero in bianco Gugiarolo '01	♛	3
○ OP Pinot Nero in bianco Le Marghe '01	♛	3
● OP Rosso Pezzalunga '01	♛	3
● Provincia di Pavia Rosso Vespolino '01	♛	3
● OP Bonarda Luogo della Milla '00	♛♛	3*
● OP Rosso Pezzalunga '00	♛♛	3*
● OP Pinot Nero Luogo dei Monti '97	♛♛	4
● OP Rosso Orto di S. Giacomo '97	♛♛	4

MORNICO LOSANA (PV)

CA' DI FRARA
VIA CASA FERRARI, 1
27040 MORNICO LOSANA (PV)
TEL. 0383892299 - 0383892534
E-MAIL: cadifrara@libero.it

The late-harvest Pinot Grigio Raccolta Tardiva is again the pick of the range from Cà di Frara. In late September and early October, brothers Luca and Matteo Bellani harvest the fruit from the Oliva Gessi vineyard, where crystalline gypsum peeks through the sandy soil. They vinify it "in bianco", without the skins, in stainless steel vats. That is all there is to it. Nature does the rest. The wine from 2001 is golden-green with pineapple, banana, pear and sun-dried hay aromas and a powerful, soft, fruit-rich palate. Vinified and aged only in stainless steel, the Apogeo '01 is not as concentrated as the Pinot Grigio but still very elegant. It's a riesling renano and riesling italico mix with a rose and peach nose and rich flavour, with nice acidity. The sage and lavender Malvasia Il Raro '01 is good but fails to match the previous vintage. Moving on to the reds, we find at the top of the list Il Frater, an Oltrepò Pavese Rosso Riserva '99 from croatina, barbera, uva rara and pinot nero aged for a year and a half in barrique. It has great structure and balanced vitality. Right beside it is the Io '99, from equal portions of barbera and pinot nero plus ten per cent of other varieties (the Bellanis requested that the precise blend should not be revealed). It has more finesse than the Frater but less potency. The great dried plum and blackcurrant nose has faint echoes of mint and damp autumn leaves. The line-up ends with the barrique-aged Pinot Nero Il Raro '00, whose cassis and morello cherry fruit and spice nose precedes a warm, soft mouthfeel backed by fine-grained tannins.

○ OP Pinot Grigio V. T. '01	♛♛	4
● OP Pinot Nero Il Raro '00	♛♛	5
○ OP Riesling Renano Apogeo '01	♛♛	3*
● OP Rosso Il Frater Ris. '99	♛♛	6
● Provincia di Pavia Rosso Io '99	♛♛	5
○ OP Malvasia Il Raro '01	♛	4
○ OP Malvasia Il Raro '00	♛♛	4
○ OP Pinot Grigio V. T. '00	♛♛	4
○ OP Riesling Renano Apogeo '00	♛♛	3*
○ OP Pinot Grigio V. T. '98	♛♛	4
● OP Rosso Il Frater '98	♛♛	5
○ OP Pinot Grigio V. T. '99	♛♛	4
● OP Pinot Nero Il Raro '99	♛♛	4

OME (BS)

MAJOLINI
LOC. VALLE
VIA MANZONI
25050 OME (BS)
TEL. 0306527378
E-MAIL: majolini@majolini.it

After several years of constant effort, huge investments in vineyards and cellar, Ezio Maiolini can finally enjoy the fruits of his labour with his distinguished collaborator, oenologist Jean Pierre Valade. Their goal aim is quality above all else. The Franciacorta Electo Brut '97 made its presence felt at our tastings and received a resounding Three Glasses. Its deep, lustrous straw yellow accompanies a perlage of extraordinary finesse and continuity, then the nose unveils amazing riches and seductively complex aromas from simple, but whistle-clean, ripe fruit to nuances of yeasts, chestnut honey, grilled bread and delicate minerals. Big, dense and elegant in the mouth, its has admirable nose-palate consistency and surefooted progression, closing with a lingering, wonderfully harmonious finish. The Satèn Ante Omnia '98 only just missed a third Glass. It flaunts fresh fruit and an incredible range of aromas on nose and palate, from liquorice to vanilla and tropical fruit, all of it delivered with freshness and fluency. The Terre di Franciacorta Dordaro '99 is probably the best of the 1990s. The dense dark ruby introduces a powerful, assertive nose of wild berries and well-expressed oak. The muscular, concentrated palate offers warm, rounded tannins and an elegant back palate blackberry. The Franciacorta Brut and the other wines are all good.

O	Franciacorta Electo Brut '97	♀♀♀	6
O	Franciacorta Ante Omnia Satèn '98	♀♀	6
●	TdF Rosso Dordaro '99	♀♀	6
O	TdF Bianco Ronchello '01	♀	4
●	TdF Rosso Ruc di Gnoc '99	♀	4
O	Franciacorta Brut	♀	5
O	Franciacorta Electo Brut '95	♀♀	6
O	Franciacorta Ante Omnia Satèn '97	♀♀	6
O	Franciacorta Satèn '96	♀♀	5
●	TdF Rosso Dordaro '98	♀♀	5

PASSIRANO (BS)

IL MOSNEL
LOC. CAMIGNONE
VIA BARBOGLIO, 14
25040 PASSIRANO (BS)
TEL. 030653117

Giulio and Lucia Barzanò are doing excellent work at the family winery. Since they came to the winery some years ago, we have seen a real rise in production quality at from this beautiful estate in Passirano, now definitely one of the top estates in the Franciacorta. Its place there is confirmed by two excellent cuvées: a Satèn '98 that brings back the splendour of the very pleasing previous vintage, rich in fruit and full-bodied, soft and opulent in its vanillaed tones (even if just a bit over the top); and above all an extremely elegant Brut '96 with a brilliant straw-yellow colour, very fine perlage, and intense aromas of rennet apple, white peach and acacia honey, spring flowers and vanilla (just barely suggested here). It develops harmoniously in the mouth, caressingly effervescent, fresh and persistent. The Franciacorta Brut has sweet, fruity aromas that are anything but dull, with yeasts that add a note of limpid complexity; fresh and spirited yet clean, persistent and full on the palate. We felt the Extra Brut was less charming; its aromatic expression concealed by a light reduction and tones slightly over-evolved. On the still wine front, the Terre Rosso Fontecolo '99 introduces itself with a lovely, dark ruby colour, generous on the nose with notes of red berry fruit and slightly spicy, vegetal nuances; it expresses a soft texture on the palate with round tannins and remarkable balance. It matches the excellent Terre Bianco Sulìf '00, endowed with great body and remarkable extractive weight, expressed with its usual grace. All the other labels are at their traditional good quality.

O	Franciacorta Brut '96	♀♀	6
O	Franciacorta Satèn '98	♀♀	6
O	TdF Bianco Sulìf '00	♀♀	5
●	TdF Rosso Fontecolo '99	♀♀	5
O	Franciacorta Brut	♀♀	5
●	TdF Rosso '00	♀	4
O	TdF Bianco '01	♀	4
O	TdF Bianco Campolarga '01	♀	4
O	Passito Sebino '99	♀	6
●	Pinot Nero Sebino '99	♀	6
O	Franciacorta Extra Brut	♀	5
O	Franciacorta Satèn '97	♀♀	5
O	Franciacorta Satèn '96	♀♀	5
●	TdF Rosso Fontecolo '98	♀♀	4*
O	TdF Bianco Sulìf '99	♀♀	4*

POLPENAZZE DEL GARDA (BS)

Cascina La Pertica
Via Picedo, 24
25080 Polpenazze del Garda (BS)
tel. 0365651471
e-mail: asalvetti@cascinalapertica.it

Ruggero Brunori, a successful industrialist with a passion for wine, bought this lovely estate in Polpenazze del Garda several years ago and dedicated himself to producing quality wines. He has rebuilt the vineyards and cellars and, with the valuable collaboration of cellar director Andrea Salvetti and the consultancy of celebrated oenologist Franco Bernabei, recorded several good vintages. Then last year, an excellent Le Zalte '99 was overwhelmingly judged worthy of our Three Glasses. This was no isolated success; the 2000 version of the same wine, a Bordeaux blend with a touch (5 per cent) of marzemino, revealed itself just as, if not more, impressive. The dark ruby red colour introduces compact, intense ripe red berry fruit and spice aromas that are still a bit closed. The palate shows itself round, deep and concentrated, endowed with tannins of great finesse and fullness that are perfectly integrated into the soft, solid structure, rich in fruit, that closes out long on notes of blackcurrant and vanilla. The "metodo classico" Le Sincette, from chardonnay, proves itself balanced and enjoyable in its lean structure and aromas of apple and yeasts. The Garda Chardonnay '01 is also good this year, fresh and supple, agreeably round and fruity. We also found the Garda Classico Chiaretto and Garda Classico Groppello Il Colombaio to be at their usual good quality, both from the 2001 vintage. In short, a great performance they should be happy about. Unfortunately, a powerful hailstorm has totally and irreparably compromised the 2002 harvest as we write. Our support goes out to Ruggero and all the other winemakers in the zone along with hopes for a quick and speedy recovery.

● Garda Cabernet Le Zalte '00	🍷🍷🍷	7
○ Garda Chardonnay Le Sincette '01	🍷	4
○ Garda Chardonnay Le Sincette Brut '99	🍷	5
⊙ Garda Cl. Chiaretto '01	🍷	3
● Garda Cl. Groppello Il Colombaio '01	🍷	4
● Garda Cabernet Le Zalte '99	🍷🍷🍷	5
● Garda Cabernet Le Zalte '98	🍷🍷	5

PROVAGLIO D'ISEO (BS)

Bersi Serlini
Via Cerreto, 7
25050 Provaglio d'Iseo (BS)
tel. 0309823338
e-mail: info@bersiserlini.it

Our good impressions last year on Bersi Serlini's wines were confirmed. This time, the panels comments were even more complimentary. The Franciacortas and still wines from this cellar in Provaglio d'Iseo have gained density and finesse thanks to the excellent work of Maddalena Bersi Serlini and her technical crew, which includes agronomist Pierluigi Villa and oenologist Corrado Cugnasco. All have contributed to restyling the cellar's wines. The two '98 Franciacortas, the Brut and Extra Brut, are on top form this year. The Brut is a lovely greenish straw yellow, with a delicate perlage and fresh nose of rich vanilla and floral tones: the tasters recognized artemisia and other medicinal plants. Round on the palate, it has decent structure, a nice soft, fresh-tasting mouthfeel and good balance, closing on subtle vanilla nuances. The Extra Brut is a bit more austere but offers the same colour and just as fine a perlage. It wanders a bit on the nose, where the note of vanilla and fresh cakes is more insistent, but stays graceful on the round, fruit-rich palate, despite the minimal dosage, which tells you how good the raw material is. The Franciacorta Brut Cuvée n. 4 also did well, although it seemed a little less pulpy and seductive than last year. Finally, the Terre di Franciacorta Rosso '00 is excellent. Rich in berry fruit, it shows softness and good structure. The other wines are all as good as ever.

● TdF Rosso '00	🍷🍷	4*
○ Franciacorta Brut '98	🍷🍷	6
○ Franciacorta Extra Brut '98	🍷🍷	6
○ Franciacorta Brut Cuvée n. 4	🍷🍷	5
○ TdF Bianco '01	🍷	4
○ Franciacorta Brut	🍷	5
○ Franciacorta Satèn	🍷	5
○ Nuvola Démi Sec	🍷	5
○ Franciacorta Brut Cuvée Millennio '92	🍷🍷	6
○ Franciacorta Brut Cuvée Millennio '93	🍷🍷	6

ROCCA DE' GIORGI (PV)

ANTEO
Loc. Chiesa
27043 Rocca de' Giorgi (PV)
Tel. 038548583 - 038599073
E-mail: info@anteovini.it

Anteo mainly produces "spumante" wines although the range also contains still and other sparkling whites and reds. The wine we enjoyed most at this year's tastings was the Anteo Brut Classico from a cuvée with a high percentage of pinot nero, softened by about one third chardonnay. It has a nice bead and a clear, bright straw-yellow hue. The well-defined aroma of crusty bread shades into faint echoes of citrus and spices, then the dry, fresh, no-nonsense palate progresses steadily to signs off with a distinct note of roasted hazelnuts. With three grams of sugar per litre, the delicate yet firm Anteo Nature, from 80 per cent pinot nero and 20 per cent chardonnay, is dryer, revealing notes of toast, rusks and vanilla. The Bonarda Staffolo '01 is just as good as the previous year's. Made from croatina harvested at Rovescala, in the red country of the first Oltrepò hills, it has a ruby hue and red mousse. The raspberry and morello cherry nose ushers in a full, upfront palate. The Ca' dell'Oca, a Pinot Nero fermented on the skins from the 1999 vintage, ages for a year in barrique and the same in bottle. Ruby red with an orange rim, its aromas of blackcurrant, cocoa, leather and vanilla precede a dry, full-bodied palate with fine-grained but still developing tannins. It will be better in a few months. Finally, the Moscato di Volpara '01 La Volpe e l'Uva is fresh, sweet and fruity.

ROVESCALA (PV)

AGNES
Via Campo del Monte, 1
27040 Rovescala (PV)
Tel. 038575206 - 03385806773
E-mail: info@fratelliagnes.it

The Agnes brothers are building a more modern, efficient new cellar that should help them correct the only tiny flaw in their Bonardas (and we're talking needles in haystacks here). It's a lack of that little extra touch of frankness and definition that so often characterizes the variety. Whatever the new cellar brings, we have to admit that the wines are a force of nature in their present authentic rusticity. Take for example the Millenium '99. Crimson purple in the glass, it offers notes of blackberry jam then a powerful palate with alcohol-derived warmth that masks the astringency of the tannins. The long finish is redolent of autumn leaves. The Poculum '99, which takes its name from an ancient type of jug, is made with croatina from low-cropped vineyards. The aromas of liquorice and vanilla combine with jammy notes. Next, there comes the series of slightly sparkling Bonardas. The Campo del Monte '01 is the best. Aged for a year in oak barrels and slightly refermented in the bottle, it is a dark reddish purple with ripe grape, prunes and spice aromas leading into a robust, generous and faintly tannic palate. Then came the Possessione del Console '01, from an old clone called "pignolo" because of its small bunches shaped like pine cones ("pigna"). It's dry and vigorous, with wild berry fruit. The mature Vignazzo '00 spent six months in oak and has a clear backdrop of bittersweet peach. The list ends with the Cresta dei Ghiffi '00, from late-harvest fruit. It is less frank than the rest of the range but still good.

● OP Pinot Nero Ca' dell'Oca '99	ŸŸ	4
○ OP Pinot Nero Brut Cl. Anteo	ŸŸ	4
○ OP Pinot Nero Cl. Anteo Nature	ŸŸ	5
● OP Bonarda Staffolo '01	Ÿ	3
○ OP Moscato La Volpe e L'Uva '01	Ÿ	3
● Coste del Roccolo '00	ŸŸ	3*
○ OP Pinot Nero Cl. Anteo Nature '98	ŸŸ	4
○ OP Pinot Nero in bianco Ca' dell'Oca '98	ŸŸ	5

● OP Bonarda Vignazzo '00	ŸŸ	4
● OP Bonarda Campo del Monte '01	ŸŸ	4
● OP Bonarda Possessione del Console '01	ŸŸ	4
● OP Bonarda Millenium '99	ŸŸ	5
● Rosso Poculum '99	ŸŸ	5
● OP Bonarda Cresta del Ghiffi '00	Ÿ	4
● Loghetto '00	ŸŸ	4
● OP Bonarda Campo del Monte '00	ŸŸ	3*
● OP Bonarda Millenium '98	ŸŸ	5
● Rosso Poculum '98	ŸŸ	4
● OP Bonarda Cresta del Ghiffi '99	ŸŸ	4
● OP Bonarda Vignazzo '99	ŸŸ	4

SAN PAOLO D'ARGON (BG)

Cantina Sociale Bergamasca
Via Bergamo, 10
24060 San Paolo d'Argon (BG)
tel. 035951098
e-mail: csbsanpaolo@libero.it

Fresh from its remodelling, the Cantina Sociale Bergamasca in San Paolo d'Argon gives an excellent performance with an absolutely remarkable Valcalepio Rosso (a blend of cabernet and merlot): the Riserva Vigna del Conte '98. The count in question here is Bonaventura Grumelli Pedrocca, chair of the co-operative and owner of the vineyard chosen by oenologist Sergio Cantoni for this very fine wine. Released for the first time, it will be produced only in the most favourable vintages. This deep ruby wine ages for three years in 25-hectolitre barrels of French oak, it has acquired just enough wood-derived flavour to highlight its aromas of morello cherry jam and violets. Round and warm in the mouth, it shows attractive, fine-grained tannins. The other Valcalepio Rosso Riserva, Akros '99, is less concentrated but still elegant and complex. It needs more time in bottle but is every bit as good as the '98. The prevalence of merlot over cabernet gives the Rosso DOC '00 grace and softness while the body is firm, though not very full. Another very decent red is the Merlot della Bergamasca '01, especially if you consider its very attractive price. The whites include the Valcalepio '01, from pinot bianco, pinot grigio and chardonnay, which is floral, clean and pleasant, and a simpler but nonetheless enjoyable Chardonnay '01. Finally, the dessert wines feature the sweet, fruit and spice Valcalepio Moscato Passito Perseo '00 and the Aureo '01, a very promising dried-grape Moscato Giallo "passito". The barrel sample we tasted should get even better with bottle-age.

- Merlot della Bergamasca '01 — 2
- Valcalepio Rosso Ris. Vigna del Conte '98 — 4
- Valcalepio Rosso Akros Ris. '99 — 4
- Valcalepio Moscato Passito Perseo '00 — 5
- Valcalepio Rosso '00 — 3
- Chardonnay della Bergamasca '01 — 2
- Moscato Giallo Passito Aureo '01 — 4
- Valcalepio Bianco '01 — 2
- Moscato Giallo Passito Aureo '00 — 4
- Valcalepio Rosso Riserva Akros Vigna La Tordela '98 — 4

SANTA GIULETTA (PV)

Isimbarda
Loc. Castello
27046 Santa Giuletta (PV)
tel. 0383899256
e-mail: info@isimbarda.com

Though not as rich, the Riserva Montezavo '99 shows substantially the same high quality as the memorable '98. The mix include a high percentage of barbera with croatina, uva rara and vespolina from hillslope vineyards at Monsaurum with an average age of 30 years and yields cut back to one kilogram of fruit per vine. All this makes a good, full-bodied, harmonious red with notes of prune, dried violet and sweet spices. The vineyards of Monplò have the – relatively – high yield, so to speak, of one and a half kilograms per vine and produce the Oltrepò Pavese Rosso of the same name. After a few months in barrique and mid-sized barrels, the wine is a vivid ruby red with a broad bouquet of cherry jam and a warm, balanced palate. The '99 Pinot Nero is an almost too dark garnet and shows distinct varietal aromas of cassis, forest floor, wild rose and animal furs. It is full and elegant in the mouth. It's a bottle for the cellar, unlike the 2000 which, strangely enough, is already in decline. Was there an accident along the way? Now, let's move over to the whites. The Varmei '01, from chardonnay, pinot grigio and slightly super-ripe pinot bianco, is two-thirds aged in stainless steel and the rest in 450-litre oak barrels, for malolactic fermentation. The resulting blend is gold, with aromas of roasted hazelnuts and pineapple and citrus-laced spice. The mouthfeel is almost butter-soft. The Riesling '01 Vigna Martina, one-fourth aged in oak, is not as complex as last year's edition.

- OP Pinot Nero '99 — 5
- OP Rosso Monplò '99 — 4
- OP Rosso Montezavo Ris. '99 — 6
- OP Riesling Renano Vigna Martina '01 — 4
- Provincia di Pavia Varméi '01 — 4
- OP Riesling Renano Vigna Martina '00 — 4
- OP Rosso Monplò '98 — 4
- OP Rosso Montezavo Ris. '98 — 5
- OP Rosso Vigna del Tramonto '98 — 4

SANTA MARIA DELLA VERSA (PV)

Cantina Sociale La Versa
Via F. Crispi, 15
27047 Santa Maria della Versa (PV)
tel. 0385798411

Francesco Cervetti, the new general manager of La Versa, has a project to relaunch the nearly 100-year-old Santa Maria della Versa winery (it was founded in 1905). He wants to "turn it inside out", so that it can keep up with a market that demands quality. A strong sign of renewal comes from the wines in the newly created Roccoli line. As Cervetti says, they "are islands of experimental agriculture, owned by member growers, where quality-oriented viticulture is practised. It is a series of vineyards, identified by the zoning office at the University of Milan, whose grapes are selected and vinified using state-of-the-art techniques to make wines that embody the very best in the territory". The Barbera Roccolo del Casale is rich and aromatic, with a soft yet very firm body. The Bonarda Ca' Bella '01 is full, lively and fruity. The Buttafuoco Roccolo delle Viole '00 needs more time in bottle but is already very promising, as is the "metodo classico" Roccolo delle Rose Blanc de Blancs Brut, a monovarietal Chardonnay. The long list of other outstanding products begins with the "spumante" wines that make up La Versa's core production. The Extra Dry Testarossa has been released in two versions, the more mature, complex Jubilèe '97 and the fresher standard '99 edition. The new, elegantly soft Brut Classico Etichetta Oro is also very good and the Mise en Cave '98 is attractively frank. The standard Chardonnay and Pinot Grigio '01 are excellent. The delicious Lacrimae Vitis '98, a dried-grape Moscato aged in barriques, is sweet and opulent.

SCANZOROSCIATE (BG)

La Brugherata
Fraz. Rosciate
Via G. Medolago, 47
24020 Scanzorosciate (BG)
tel. 035655202
e-mail: info@labrugherata.it

La Brugherata, Patrizia Merati's tiny jewel of an estate lies at the foot of Monte Bastia, near the town of Scanzorosciate, the home of hard-to-find Moscato Nero di Scanzo. The cellar made quite a haul of stemware this year. In a territory dominated by reds, the Valcalepio Vescovado Selezione '01 showed it is the best white in the Bergamo area. The bright gold introduces an intense nose of flowers and tropical fruit, then a full, elegant, fresh and fruity palate. The standard Vescovado '01, again from a blend of chardonnay and pinot bianco, scored almost as high with its fresh, pleasant drinkability. Outstanding reds include the rich, complex and particularly harmonious Valcalepio Riserva Doglio '98 and the barrique-aged Rosso di Alberico '00, whose oak brings out the fruit without masking it. The Priore is a new item, a red "vino da tavola" (table wine) from cabernet. Bright garnet, it proffers generous aromas of wild berry jam and a soft but well-sustained flavour. The Valcalepio Rosso Vescovado '00 is vivid ruby red with notes of morello cherry and faint fresh-cut grass. Although forthright and fruit-rich in the mouth, it will improve with further development in the bottle. We were not disappointed by the Doge '99, a dried-grape Moscato di Scanzo Passito with enough sugar to offset the combination of acidity and tannins in the variety. It has an alluring, aromatic bouquet redolent of spice. Often, Moscato Nero from this zone is astringent, rough and bitterish, unforgivable defects when you consider how much their producers charge for them.

● OP Barbera Roccolo del Casale '00	▼▼	3*
● OP Bonarda Frizzante Ca' Bella '01	▼▼	3*
○ OP Chardonnay '01	▼▼	3*
○ OP Pinot Grigio '01	▼▼	3*
○ Spumante Cl. Extra Dry Cuvée Testarossa Jubilée '97	▼▼	5
○ OP Pinot Nero Brut Mise en Cave '98	▼▼	4
○ Provincia di Pavia Moscato Passito Lacrimae Vitis '98	▼▼	5
○ Spumante Classico Cuvée Testarossa Extra Dry '99	▼▼	4
○ OP Pinot Nero Brut Cl. Oro	▼▼	3*

● Rosso di Alberico '00	▼▼	4
○ Valcalepio Bianco Vescovado '01	▼▼	4
○ Valcalepio Bianco Vescovado Sel. '01	▼▼	4
● Valcalepio Rosso Ris. Doglio '98	▼▼	4
● Moscato di Scanzo Passito Doge '99	▼▼	6
● Priore '00	▼	5
● Valcalepio Rosso Vescovado '00	▼	4
● Valcalepio Rosso Ris. Doglio '96	▼▼	4
● Valcalepio Rosso Vescovado '96	▼▼	3
● Valcalepio Rosso Ris. Doglio '97	▼▼	4
● Moscato di Scanzo Passito Doge '98	▼▼	6
● Valcalepio Rosso Vescovado '98	▼▼	3
● Rosso di Alberico '99	▼▼	4

SIRMIONE (BS)

Ca' dei Frati
Fraz. Lugana
Via Frati, 22
25010 Sirmione (BS)
tel. 030919468
e-mail: info@cadeifrati.it

Those of you who still think whites are early drinking wines should taste the Lugana Brolettino Grande Annata '98, from verdicchio-like trebbiano di Lugana grapes selected from the I Frati and Ronchedone vineyards. The fermentation of the first pressing must starts in stainless steel and continues in barriques. The result is a surprising Lugana with an intense greenish gold hue and a full-bodied, complex aroma where sweet spicy notes combine with citrus, flowers and fruit. The palate is mature yet solid, vigorous and rich, finishing long with elegant aromatic persistence. Its stablemate, the Lugana Brolettino '00, is not as concentrated and powerful, yet it is pleasingly well-rounded after about ten months in small oak casks. The '00 Pratto Benaco Bresciano is as remarkable as ever. It is obtained from a blend of lugana and chardonnay, aged in oak for a year, with steel-aged sauvignon. The Tre Filer '99 also rose to the occasion. From the same fruit as the Pratto, raisined for three months on rush mats, its year and more in oak has given it complexity and aroma. The Chiaretto del Garda Bresciano I Frati from the latest vintage is nice. From groppello, marzemino, sangiovese and barbera, it has a vivid rose red hue, aromas of morello cherry and bitterish flowers, and a tangy, almost salty, flavour.

○ Lugana Brolettino Grande Annata '98	🍷🍷	6
○ Lugana Il Brolettino '00	🍷🍷	4
○ Pratto '00	🍷🍷	5
○ Lugana Brut Cl. Cuvée dei Frati	🍷🍷	5
○ Tre Filer '99	🍷🍷	5
○ Garda Bresciano Chiaretto I Frati '99	🍷	4
○ Lugana Brolettino Grande Annata '97	🍷🍷	5
○ Pratto '97	🍷🍷	5
○ Lugana Il Brolettino '98	🍷🍷	4
○ Pratto '98	🍷🍷	5
○ Lugana Il Brolettino '99	🍷🍷	4
○ Pratto '99	🍷🍷	5

SIRMIONE (BS)

Ca' Lojera
Loc. San Benedetto di Lugana
25019 Sirmione (BS)
tel. 0457551901 - 030919550
e-mail: info@calojera.com

They say once upon a time, when Lake Garda and the small lake of Frassino were connected by a network of waterways, brigands would arrive from the north in boats. These were the "black merchants", who hid stolen goods in houses along the lakeshore and sold them to the local inhabitants. There are also those who swear these hiding places were defended by packs of wolves. In fact, Ca' Lojera, which is owned by the Tiraboschi family, means "house of wolves". The cellar vinifies only its own grapes, harvested from 14 hectares of vineyards grown on flat, compact clay. The standard Lugana from Ca' Lojera earned one of the highest scores achieved by any such wine from 2001. Its greenish straw yellow ushers in a pronounced nose of tropical fruit laced with orange peel and pennyroyal. The palate is round and soft, yet zestily fresh. The Lugana Superiore '00 is just as good after fermenting entirely in oak barrels and being released a year and a half after the harvest. It needs to mature further in the bottle, but is already pleasant, thanks to the full-bodied spice and flower bouquet and rich, full mouthfeel. It's one for the cellar. So is the Vigna Silva '99 which, on retasting, confirmed the excellent score we gave it the last time we were here. The Monte della Guardia '99 stands out among the reds. A Bordeaux blend of 60 per cent cabernet and 40 per cent merlot, it comes from a three-hectare vineyard on a hill at Ponti sul Mincio that looks onto Lake Garda from the province of Mantua. The Cabernet and Merlot del Garda '00, both briefly cask-conditioned, are agreeable.

○ Lugana Sup. '00	🍷🍷	4
○ Lugana '01	🍷🍷	3*
● Garda Cabernet '00	🍷	3
● Garda Merlot '00	🍷	3
● Monte della Guardia '99	🍷	4
○ Lugana Sup. '99	🍷🍷	4
○ Lugana Vigna Silva '99	🍷	3

TEGLIO (SO)

FAY
LOC. SAN GIACOMO
VIA PILA CASELLI, 1
23030 TEGLIO (SO)
TEL. 0342786071
E-MAIL: elefay@tin.it

Again this year, Fay's best wine is the Sforzato Ronco del Picchio for the '99 vintage made it to the finals with flying colours. In our opinion, the very sweet notes of the wine tend to veil its accomplished personality but this is merely a question of style. The cellar might perhaps make a few adjustments in future to release a slightly more austere product that will still be fruit-led and, especially, soft. At any rate, the '99 has intense aromas of morello cherry and chocolate, leading into a well-rounded palate, with good concentration and a nice long finish. The Valgella Ca' Morei '99 is always attractive. Its extreme softness never muddies the precise extract and pleasant floral notes grace the nose in addition to ripe fruit. There was another good performance from the Valgella Carteria '99, which is vinified with a small proportion of partially dried bunches. It shows good character and personality and the inviting aromas mingle spices with notes of ripe fruit. The Glicine '99 is among the best Sassellas tasted this year. A superb interpretation of the terroir and its potential, it has a fresh, clean bouquet of berry fruit and ripe plums, lots of body and a rounded palate of captivating drinkability.

TIRANO (SO)

CONTI SERTOLI SALIS
P.ZZA SALIS, 3
23037 TIRANO (SO)
TEL. 0342710404
E-MAIL: info@sertolisalis.com

Claudio Introini, the long-serving oenologist at Conti Sertoli Salis, was certain the 2000 vintage would be a good one for Valtellina. There was some difficult weather during the harvest and raisining, but in the end, hard work and attention to the grapes and in the drying lofts produced more than positive results. Proof of this is one of Introini's best-ever wines, which was swiftly awarded Three Glasses. The Sforzato Canua '00 is an intense garnet with amazingly rich, complex aromas that run from dried orange peel to elderflower jam, barley and chocolate. The palate is powerful yet not heavy, and evinces a fruit-rich elegance. The balanced, refined Capo di Terra '99 comes from slightly super-ripe grapes and has fresh, fruity aromas, a well-rounded palate and a nice lingering finish. On retasting, we found the Saloncello '00 to be well-balanced, with a pleasantly fresh palate, while the Sassella '99 wins Two Glasses this year for its straightforward style that foregrounds territory and the variety, nebbiolo. The Corte della Meridiana '99 is very good, combining complex aromas with a soft mouthfeel, due in part to the "rinforzo" technique (some of the nebbiolo is left to raisin then added to the wine). The Torre della Sirena Bianco '01, made from the local Valtellina rossola and pignola varieties, has fresh aromas and is eminently drinkable.

● Valtellina Sforzato Ronco del Picchio '99	6
● Valtellina Sup. Sassella Il Glicine '99	5
● Valtellina Sup. Valgella Ca' Morei '99	5
● Valtellina Sup. Valgella Carteria '99	5
● Valtellina Sforzato Ronco del Picchio '98	6
● Valtellina Sup. Sassella Il Glicine '98	5
● Valtellina Sup. Valgella Ca' Morei '98	5
● Valtellina Sup. Valgella Carteria Trentennale '98	5

● Valtellina Sforzato Canua '00	6
● Valtellina Sup. Capo di Terra '99	4
● Valtellina Sup. Corte della Meridiana '99	5
● Valtellina Sup. Sassella '99	4
○ Torre della Sirena '01	4
● Valtellina Sforzato Canua '97	6
● Valtellina Sforzato Canua '99	6
● Valtellina Sforzato Canua '96	6
● Valtellina Sforzato Canua '98	6
● Il Saloncello '00	4
● Valtellina Sup. Sassella '98	4

TORRE DE' ROVERI (BG)

La Tordela
Via Torricelli, 1
24060 Torre de' Roveri (BG)
Tel. 035580172
E-mail: info@latordela.it

Marco Bernardi's estate, mentioned here over the past few years for several interesting products, is forging ahead. The 16th-century residence has been partially remodelled as an "agriturismo" with visitor accommodation and is surrounded by 20 hectares of vineyards on the hills between the Torre dei Roveri depression and the Serradesca valley. The winery harvests 70 per cent of the grapes mechanically and bunches from the most best-aspected vines are selected and vinified in the recently renovated cellar to make wines of remarkable quality. The style is substantially traditional, with a modern twist. The panel had a preview tasting of the cabernet and merlot Valcalepio Rosso '00, which goes on sale in November. Dark ruby red, with a captivating aroma of cherry jam that fades out on a spicy note, it has a full, warm palate with nice fruit. Although a lovely wine, it pales in comparison to the 2000 vintage Riserva, still in barrique. It will be worth waiting another year for this very rich, concentrated aristocrat, which still has to mature in bottle. In the meantime, we can console ourselves with the Valcalepio Riserva '98. It may be almost too developed but is still pleasant, showing an etheric nose and soft, harmonious mouthfeel. Finesse and softness also characterize the Cabernet della Bergamasca '99, which has intense aromas of ripe wild berries. The Valcalepio '00 is the best of the whites. From both pinot bianco and pinot grigio, it is tangy and mature, yet fresh thanks to robust acidity. The nose is all fruit and flowers.

● Valcalepio Rosso '00	🍷🍷	3
● Valcalepio Rosso Ris. '98	🍷🍷	4
○ Valcalepio Bianco '00	🍷	3
● Cabernet Bergamasca '99	🍷	3
○ Valcalepio Moscato Passito '99	🍷	6
● Valcalepio Rosso '98	🍷	3

TORRICELLA VERZATE (PV)

Monsupello
Via San Lazzaro, 5
27050 Torricella Verzate (PV)
Tel. 0383896043 - 0383896044
E-mail: monsupello@monsupello.it

Monsupello's prestigious "spumante" list has now been graced by the arrival of a newcomer, the Brut Riserva Cuvée Ca' del Tava. It was named by the Boatti family for the winery's founders, once tenant farmers at Ca' del Tava. At the end of the 1970s, the name was given to the particularly good pinot nero and chardonnay vineyard where the grapes for the new sparkler come from. Partially barrique-aged and left on the lees for five years, this brilliant golden yellow cuvée has a creamy mousse and very fine, compact perlage. The bouquet is a complex medley of apples, gingerbread, bay leaf and incense, then the rich, powerful palate offers elegant sinew and a long, satisfying finish. The other classics are all as good as ever. The blue-blooded "metodo classico" Pinot Nero Nature is dry and rich, falling just short of Three Glasses. The Classese Brut '97 is round and forthright while the non-vintage Brut offers fragrant freshness. The still whites from the latest vintage are absolutely remarkable. Try not to miss the fragrant, vigorous Riesling, the distinctly varietal Sauvignon, the full and structured Pinot Grigio or the soft, firm Chardonnay. Senso '00, the Chardonnay aged in new oak, is unbelievably powerful and one of the finest from Lombardy. Best of the small cask-aged reds are the Riserva Mosaico '98, the Barbera Vigna Pivena '99 and the Cabernet Sauvignon Aplomb '98. The La Borla '00 still needs a few months' bottle-age. All the many other labels from the winery are excellent, particularly the Barbera I Gelsi, the Rosso Great Ruby and the dried-grape La Cuenta.

● OP Cabernet Sauvignon Aplomb '98	🍷🍷	6
○ OP Chardonnay Senso '00	🍷🍷	5
○ OP Pinot Nero Cl. Nature	🍷🍷	5
● OP Barbera I Gelsi '00	🍷🍷	4
● OP Rosso La Borla '00	🍷🍷	4
○ OP Pinot Grigio '01	🍷🍷	4
○ OP Riesling Renano '01	🍷🍷	4
● OP Rosso Great Ruby Vivace '01	🍷🍷	4
○ OP Sauvignon '01	🍷🍷	4
○ OP Pinot Nero Brut Classese '97	🍷🍷	5
● OP Rosso Ris. Mosaico '98	🍷🍷	6
● OP Barbera Ris. Vigna Pivena '99	🍷🍷	6
○ OP Brut Cl. Ris. Ca' del Tava	🍷🍷	5
○ OP Pinot Nero Brut Cl.	🍷🍷	4

VILLA DI TIRANO (SO)

TRIACCA
VIA NAZIONALE, 121
23030 VILLA DI TIRANO (SO)
TEL. 0342701352
E-MAIL: info@triacca.com

Triacca again presented a model collection of wines. Credit goes to the professional skill of Domenico Triacca, and to the unique qualities of the territory and grapes. We savoured another extraordinary version of the Sforzato, the 2000, which won Three Glasses, proof that elegance and personality can be combined without recourse to opulence or extreme concentration. Take a closer look at this Sforzato. The distinctly complex nose has notes of pepper and minerals that mingle harmoniously with ripe fruit. The luscious softness in the mouth stands back to reveal a well-gauged dose of superbly expressed tannins in a long, harmonious finish. The Riserva '98 is interesting, with a palate that echoes the nose as it develops, opening into a big, full-bodied richness. The Casa La Gatta '99 has a classic nebbiolo character. Though perhaps a bit thin, it still has good impact and great overall finesse. The Prestigio '00 is very nice and more elegant, albeit less concentrated, than the previous edition. The broad, approachable aromas and a wealth of extract promise a radiant future. We felt the Sauvignon Del Frate '01 was incredible in some respects. An explosion of complex, varietal aromas, with mineral and apricot prominent, it is dense on the palate and long in the finish. There is sufficient acidic grip to guarantee its future for years to come.

•	Valtellina Sforzato '00	🍷🍷🍷	7
•	Valtellina Prestigio '00	🍷🍷	7
○	Sauvignon Del Frate '01	🍷🍷	5
•	Valtellina Sup. Ris. Triacca '98	🍷🍷	5
•	Valtellina Casa La Gatta '99	🍷🍷	5
•	Valtellina Prestigio Millennium '97	🍷🍷🍷	5
•	Valtellina Sforzato '99	🍷🍷🍷	6
•	Valtellina Prestigio '99	🍷🍷	6
○	Sauvignon Del Frate '00	🍷🍷	4
•	Valtellina Prestigio '96	🍷🍷	5
•	Valtellina Sforzato '97	🍷🍷	5
•	Valtellina Sup. Ris. Triacca '97	🍷🍷	5
•	Valtellina Prestigio '98	🍷🍷	5
•	Valtellina Sforzato '98	🍷🍷	6

ZENEVREDO (PV)

TENUTA IL BOSCO
LOC. IL BOSCO
27049 ZENEVREDO (PV)
TEL. 0385245326
E-MAIL: info@ilbosco.com

As we have frequently said in the past, Tenuta Il Bosco, the Zonin family holding in the Oltrepò, only partially fulfils its potential. Some of the wines may be interesting but there are no stars. One of the most modern, well-equipped wineries in the Oltrepò, with the skilled Pier Paolo Olmo as oenologist and all the experience of the Zonin group behind it, Tenuta Il Bosco could and should do more with the fruit from the almost 150 hectares of specialized vineyards. The vintage Brut Classico '95 has at last made its appearance. The cuvée is from 80 per cent pinot nero with the rest chardonnay and ages on the lees for five years before disgorgement This is still done by hand, "à la volée", and in fact only 20,000 bottles are produced. The Brut has a creamy mousse, fine bead and an elegant bouquet of roasted hazelnut and crusty bread. The moderately dry palate is full and elegant. The Pinot Nero Brut Classico Regal Cuvée is decent and dignified but no more, as is the simple and clean Phileo, a cuve close Pinot Nero fermented without the skins. However, the sparkling Malvasia Frizzante '01 is good. It has precise varietal notes and a soft, civilized palate that flaunts a certain brio and a faint twist of bitter almonds. The sparkling Bonarda Vivace '01 is tasty, redolent of wild berries and roses, and has residual sweetness that contrasts nicely with the bitterish finish. The Teodote '99, an Oltrepò Pavese Rosso with 55 per cent croatina, is drinking well. Although now at its peak, its sound structure will keep it out of trouble.

○	OP Malvasia Frizzante '01	🍷🍷	3
○	OP Brut Cl. Il Bosco '95	🍷🍷	5
•	OP Bonarda Vivace '01	🍷	3
○	OP Pinot Nero Brut Cl. Philèo	🍷	4
○	OP Pinot Nero Brut Cl. Regal Cuvée	🍷	5
○	OP Brut Il Bosco '94	🍷🍷	4
○	OP Pinot Nero Brut Cl. '94	🍷🍷	4
•	Rosso Teodote '99	🍷🍷	4

OTHER WINERIES

BATTISTA COLA
VIA SANT'ANNA, 22
25030 ADRO (BS)
TEL. 0307356195
E-MAIL: cola@virgilio.it

Father and son Battista and Stefano Cola cultivate ten hectares of well-aspected vineyards that provide excellent raw material for quality wines. This year, the elegant, well-structured Franciacorta Brut and the fresh, fruity Terre Bianco '01 were both good.

○ Franciacorta Brut	ÝÝ	4*
○ TdF Bianco '01	ÝÝ	4
● TdF Rosso Tamino '99	Ý	4

CORNALETO
VIA CORNALETTO, 2
25030 ADRO (BS)
TEL. 0307450507 - 0307450554
E-MAIL: info@cornaleto.it

Vittorio Lancini, with the help of consultant Cesare Ferrari, creates elegant Franciacortas blessed with wonderful structure and longevity. The excellent Brut '92 can still be bought and is one to try. The still wines are also very nice.

○ TdF Bianco V. Saline '00	ÝÝ	4*
● TdF Rosso Baldoc '98	ÝÝ	6

LEBOVITZ
LOC. GOVERNOLO
V.LE RIMEMBRANZE, 4
46037 BAGNOLO SAN VITO (MN)
TEL. 0376668115

The Rosso dei Concari is a Lambrusco Mantovano enriched by prolonged cold contact with the yeasts (very cold – minus five degrees Celsius). It is whistle-clean, with a flavoursome, fragrant character supported by good acidity.

● Lambrusco Mantovano Rosso dei Concari '01	Ý	2*

CANTRINA
FRAZ. CANTRINA - VIA COLOMBERA, 7
25081 BEDIZZOLE (BS)
TEL. 0306871052
E-MAIL: cantrina@libero.it

The small, well-tended estate of Cristina Inganni has produced an excellent, partially barrique-aged Riné '00, from riesling renano and chardonnay with five per cent sauvignon, and a Merlot Nepomuceno '99 that is equally exciting. These two remarkable wines are capable of holding up well over time.

○ Riné '00	ÝÝ	4
● Garda Merlot Nepomuceno '99	ÝÝ	5

Percivalle
Via Torchi, 9
27040 Borgo Priolo (PV)
Tel. 0383871175

Paolo Percivalle, at Torchi in Borgo Priolo, has a vigorous Barbera Costa del Sole '00, with an alcohol content that offsets its acidity and tannins. The still Bonarda Parsua '00 is a bit down-to-earth but still developing. The natural Moscato 2001 Venere is fragrantly aromatic.

● OP Barbera Costa del Sole '00	4
● OP Bonarda Parsua '00	4
○ OP Moscato Venere '01	3

Emilio Franzoni
Via Cavour, 10
25082 Botticino (BS)
Tel. 0302691134 - 0302693658
E-mail: franzoni@botticino.it

Vinicola Emilio Franzoni makes the Riserva Foja d'Or '98 at Botticino, a small DOC zone east of Brescia with only 30 hectares of vineyards in all. It is a good, dry red with solid structure, a bright garnet hue and an etheric, spicy nose.

● Botticino Foja d'Or Ris. '98	4

Cascina Nuova
Loc. Poncarale
25020 Brescia
Tel. 0302540058

Franco Poli's Vigna Tenuta Anna '97 has held up well. Mature but still sound, it has notes of jam and toast, confirming our impressions in the last edition of the Guide. The Montenetto di Brescia Merlot '99 is well-balanced.

● Montenetto di Brescia Merlot '99	3
● Capriano del Colle Rosso Vigna Tenuta Anna '97	4

Monteacuto
Loc. Puegnago - Fraz. Monteacuto
Via Dosso, 5
25080 Brescia
Tel. 0365651291

The vibrant Simut '99 by Antonio Leali, a red from 70 per cent groppello and marzemino, is a lovely full wine with distinct hints of morello cherry and vanilla. The Garda Chiaretto '01 is enjoyable, with aromas of flowers and berry fruit, as is the soft, fruit-and-spice Groppello 2000.

● Simut '99	5
● Garda Bresciano Groppello '00	4
◉ Garda Bresciano Chiaretto '01	3

Cantina Sociale di Broni
Via Sansaluto, 81
27043 Broni (PV)
Tel. 038551505

The Cantina Sociale di Broni has 500 member growers and 1,500 hectares of vineyards, and releases 1,500,000 bottles a year. The oak-aged Rosso Oltrepò '98 is very good, as is the well-typed Buttafuoco '99 and forthright sparkling Barbera 2001 Vivace, all offered at value-for-money prices.

● OP Barbera vivace '01	2
● OP Rosso Bronis '98	3
● OP Buttafuoco Bronis '99	3

La Vigna
Cascina La Vigna
25020 Capriano del Colle (BS)
Tel. 0309748061
E-mail: lavignavini@libero.it

Again, the Capriano del Colle Rosso Riserva Montebruciato '00 was the top of the range from Anna Botti's La Vigna estate. From sangiovese and marzemino, with 15 per cent merlot, it has a jam and spice bouquet and dry, robust palate. The Montenetto di Brescia Marzemino '00 is decent.

● Capriano del Colle Rosso Monte Bruciato Ris. '00	4
● Montenetto di Brescia Marzemino '00	3

F.lli Muratori
Via Palazzolo, 168
25031 Capriolo (BS)
Tel. 0307461599
E-mail: info@fratellimuratori.com

We are going to more about this estate, the newest winery in Franciacorta and part of the group of properties, from Tuscany and Campania, owned by the Muratori family. The cellar made an excellent debut with a well-defined Dosaggio Zero that shows remarkable richness.

○ Franciacorta Dosaggio Zero Villa Crespia	🍷🍷 5
○ Franciacorta Dosaggio Zero Villa Crespia Cisiolo	🍷 5

Valter Calvi
Fraz. Palazzina, 24/A
27040 Castana (PV)
Tel. 038582136
E-mail: valtcal@tin.it

Valter Calvi's Montarzolo vineyard is located in a favourable position in the historic Buttafuoco zone. Left for a year in barrique, the '98 is vigorous but slow to mature. The nose is partially closed and the palate is dominated by still hard tannins. It will improve but patience is required.

● OP Buttafuoco Vigna Montarzolo '98	🍷 4

Marco Giulio Bellani
Via Manzoni, 75
27045 Casteggio (PV)
Tel. 038382122

Marco Bellani's nice Oltrepò Pavese Rosso comes from a vineyard with the curious name of Articioc. The '98 is now at its peak. The slightly sparkling Riesling 2001, from a special clone of riesling renano (Bouvet 174), is fragrant and fresh with distinct varietal notes.

○ OP Riesling '01	🍷 3
● OP Rosso Articioc '98	🍷 4

Cantina di Casteggio
Via Torino, 96
27045 Casteggio (PV)
Tel. 0383806311
E-mail: cscaste@cantinacasteggio.it

The Longobardo is a new red produced by this Casteggio co-operative with the help of Riccardo Cotarella. A blend of croatina, barbera, cabernet sauvignon (evident on nose and palate) and pinot nero, is undeniably good, though still a tad closed. The Postumio Pinot Nero Brut is more approachable.

● Longobardo '00	🍷 6
○ OP Pinot Nero Brut Cl. Postumio	🍷 4

Clastidio Ballabio
Via San Biagio, 32
27045 Casteggio (PV)
Tel. 038382566

This long-established Casteggio estate gave us an excellent Bonarda 2001. A slightly sparkling cuve close wine with blackberry and violet aromas, it offers a full, fruit-led palate. The oak-aged Narbusto Oltrepò Pavese Rosso Riserva '99 is very solid with well-gauged tannins.

● OP Bonarda Vivace Le Cento Pertiche '01	🍷🍷 3*
● OP Rosso Ris. Narbusto '99	🍷 4

Ruiz de Cardenas
Fraz. Mairano - Via della Mollie, 35
27045 Casteggio (PV)
Tel. 038382301
E-mail: vini@ruizdecardenas.it

Ruiz de Cardenas works hard to get the best from his five hectares but, as on all small estates, he has to accept what the vintage brings. His Pinot Nero Brumano '99 is elegant and varietal, though without the fullness of the '98. The Pinot Nero Miraggi '00 is good.

● OP Pinot Nero Vigna Miraggi '00	🍷 5
● OP Pinot Nero Brumano '99	🍷 5

Conti Bettoni Cazzago
Via Marconi, 6
25046 Cazzago San Martino (BS)
tel. 0307750875
e-mail: giovanniscand@tiscali.it

The aristocratic Bettoni Cazzago family has long been established in Franciacorta and boasts a fine tradition of viticulture. The soft Satèn is particularly interesting this year.

○ Franciacorta Satèn	♉♉	5
○ Franciacorta Brut Tetellus	♉	5

Ca' del Vent
Loc. Loc. Campiani - Via Stella, 2
25060 Cellatica (BS)
tel. 0302770411
e-mail: p.clerici@cadelvent.com

Owned by Massimo Fasoli and Paolo Clerici, this small Cellatica estate produces an interesting red, the Clavis. Well-endowed with structure and fruit, it is from an unusual blend of marzemino, barbera and cabernet. The other wine is a Franciacorta Brut that has a lot of room for improvement.

● Clavis '98	♉♉	6
○ Franciacorta Brut	♉	4*

Agricola Gatta
Via Stella, 27
25060 Cellatica (BS)
tel. 0302772950
e-mail: invigna@inwind.it

Mario Gatta's Satèn was very good this year. Deep straw yellow, with a fine perlage and sweet bouquet of ripe fruit, it proffers a palate of remarkable concentration and good balance. We expected a bit more from the Chardonnay Febo but it is still interesting and well-made.

○ Franciacorta Satèn '97	♉♉	5
○ TdF Bianco '01	♉	3
○ TdF Bianco Febo '99	♉	4

Caminella
Via Dante Alighieri, 13
24069 Cenate Sotto (BG)
tel. 035951828

Giovanna Terzi's estate continues to be "moonstruck". All the wines are dedicated to "La Luna". The Verde Luna, from sauvignon, chardonnay and pinot bianco, the Ripa di Luna Valcalepio Rosso 2000, and especially the Cabernet della Bergamasca Luna Rossa, were the best of the wines we tasted.

● Valcalepio Rosso Ripa di Luna '00	♉	4
● Cabernet Bergamasca Luna Rossa '00	♉	4
○ Verde Luna Bianco	♉	4

Pietro Nera
Via IV Novembre, 43
23030 Chiuro (SO)
tel. 0342482631
e-mail: info@neravini.com

Two wines stand out in the range from Nera and both are particularly representative of Valtellina. There's an interesting Sforzato '97, with intense aromas, good structure and ripe fruit, and the complex Riserva Signorie '98, a well-rounded wine with remarkable length.

● Valtellina Sforzato '97	♉♉	5
● Valtellina Sup. Signorie Ris. '98	♉♉	4

Monterucco
Valle Cima, 38
27040 Cigognola (PV)
tel. 038585151

From its 15 hectares or so of vineyards, Monterucco has made an admirable Rosso Oltrepò Riserva, the Metellianum '98. Vigorous and a little tannic, it will soften out in the bottle. The Buttafuoco '00 San Luigi is very promising and has a long future ahead of it.

● OP Buttafuoco San Luigi '00	♉	3
● OP Rosso Metellianum Ris. '98	♉	4

RICCAFANA
VIA FACCHETTI, 91
25033 COLOGNE (BS)
TEL. 0307156797

Riccafana submitted an excellent Satèn this year. Brilliant straw yellow, with a fine bead, it shows soft, clean aromas of ripe fruit and a big palate with a tight-knit, yet fresh-tasting texture, balance and caressing mouthfeel.

○ Franciacorta Satèn	♟♟	5
○ Franciacorta Brut	♟	4

BARBOGLIO DE GAIONCELLI
FRAZ. COLOMBARO
VIA NAZARIO SAURO
25040 CORTE FRANCA (BS)
TEL. 0309826978

Now owned by Guido Costa, this estate has a long history of viticulture. The consultancy of Alberto Musatti helps the cellar to turn out an interesting range of Franciacortas and still wines from its 15 hectares of vine. We rather like the Franciacorta Brut.

○ Franciacorta Brut	♟	5
◉ Franciacorta Rosé Extra Dry	♟	5

CANTINE COLLI A LAGO
LOC. SAN MARTINO DELLA BATTAGLIA
CASCINA CAPUZZA
25010 DESENZANO DEL GARDA (BS)
TEL. 0309910279 - 0309910381

Part of the Tenuta Formentini group, Colli a Lago makes a remarkable Lugana, the Podere Selva Capuzza. Aromas of flowers and fruit precede a round, fresh palate and full flavour. The Garda Rosso Classico Superiore Madér '99 is also worth sampling.

○ Lugana Sup. Selva Capuzza '00	♟	4
● Garda Cl. Sup. Rosso Madér '99	♟	4

VISCONTI
VIA C. BATTISTI, 139
25015 DESENZANO DEL GARDA (BS)
TEL. 0309120681
E-MAIL: vino@luganavisconti.it

The partially barrique-aged Lugana Superiore '99 from Visconti is solidly structured, elegant and flavoursome. The Lugana Collo Lungo '01 is also rewarding, if a bit green, and the Lugana Brut Classico '97 is a well-made sparkler. The Vigne Sparse '99 will improve over time.

○ Lugana Sup. '99	♟♟	4
○ Lugana Collo Lungo '01	♟	3
○ Lugana Brut Cl. '97	♟	4
● Vigne Sparse '99	♟	4

PRINCIPE BANFI PODERE PIO IX
VIA PER ISEO, 25
25030 ERBUSCO (BS)
TEL. 0307750387 - 022131322

Alfredo Principe and Ines Banfi own nine hectares of beautiful vineyards at Erbusco, where they make an interesting range of Franciacortas and still wines. The best at our tastings were a fresh, fruity Brut and a Terre Rosso '00, endowed with good texture and polished tannins.

● TdF Rosso '00	♟	4
○ Franciacorta Brut	♟	5

TALLARINI
VIA FONTANILE, 7/9
24060 GANDOSSO (BG)
TEL. 035834003
E-MAIL: info@tallarini.com

The signature wine from Vincenzo Tallarini is the San Giovannino Rosso Riserva '98, not for the first time. The jam aroma is lifted by balsamic notes and the palate is vigorous. The Valcalepio Bianco Libero 2000 is full and fragrant. It's a barrique-fermented blend of chardonnay and pinot grigio.

○ Valcalepio Bianco Libero '00	♟	4
● Valcalepio Rosso San Giovannino Ris. '98	♟	4

Trevisani - Ca' dei Venti
Loc. Soprazocco - Via Galuzzo, 2
25085 Gavardo (BS)
Tel. 036532825
E-mail: trevisaniwine@libero.it

The name comes from the "venti", or winds, that blow across the Garda and the estate makes a fine Balì '00. Reviewed last year, it has held up well and is still good. Then come the aromatic herb-laced Benaco Bresciano Bianco '00 and the Rosso Sùer '99, an original blend of merlot and rebo.

O	Benaco Bresciano Bianco '00	🍷	3
●	Benaco Bresciano Rosso Sùer '99	🍷	4
O	Benaco Bresciano Bianco Balì '00	🍷	3

Castello di Grumello
Via Fosse, 11
24064 Grumello del Monte (BG)
Tel. 0354420817 - 035830244
E-mail: info@castellodigrumelo.it

At last, the Aurito's oak no longer covers the varietal notes. The barrique aroma's still there but it's much less assertive. The Chardonnay 2000 also earned Two Glasses. The Colle del Calvario Valcalepio Rosso '98 has matured in the bottle, acquiring greater complexity on nose and palate.

O	Chardonnay della Bergamasca Aurito '00	🍷🍷	4
●	Valcalepio Rosso Colle del Calvario '98	🍷🍷	4

Le Corne
Loc. Corne - Via San Pantaleone
24064 Grumello del Monte (BG)
Tel. 035830215
E-mail: italia@lecorne.it

The Messernero Riserva '98, from Gambarini and Perletti at the historic Le Corne winery, is a premium-quality Riserva. Deep ruby red, and a bit closed on the nose, it is robust and powerful in the mouth. The Cabernet della Bergamasca Torcularia 2000 is not bad either, offering a nice jammy note.

●	Valcalepio Rosso Messernero Ris. '98	🍷🍷	4
●	Cabernet della Bergamasca Torcularia '00	🍷	3

Spia d'Italia
Via M. Cerutti, 61
25017 Lonato (BS)
Tel. 0309130233
E-mail: guettaandrea@libero.it

The Garda '98 from Andrea Guetta is youthful, upfront and alcohol-rich, with good extract and acidity, and a forest floor fragrance. The Garda Bresciano Superiore '97 is still very good but is at its peak now. In contrast, the sweet San Martino della Battaglia Liquoroso '97 has held up very well.

●	Garda Cl. Rosso Sup. '98	🍷	4
O	San Martino della Battaglia Liquoroso '97	🍷	5

Stefano Spezia
Via Matteotti, 90
46010 Mariana Mantovana (MN)
Tel. 0376735012

The best wines from Stefano Spezia are his sincere, very drinkable sparkling reds, expertly vinified Lambruscos that are great value for money. The oak-aged Ancellotta '98 was less successful. Barriques require rather more from a wine to give good results.

●	Ancellotta '98	🍷	2*
●	Lambrusco Provincia di Mantova '01	🍷	1*

Cantine Valtenesi - Lugana
Via Pergola, 21
25080 Moniga del Garda (BS)
Tel. 0365502002
E-mail: civielle@gardavino.it

With 75 hectares of vineyards and around 80 members, this co-operative winery vinifies grapes from Lugana and Valtenesi. Again, the best product is the Lugana Superiore Cios '99, which flaunts sensations of tropical fruit and vanilla. The Lugana 2001 and Garda Brol '99 are both nice, too.

O	Lugana Sup. Cios '99	🍷🍷	4
O	Lugana '01	🍷	3
●	Garda Cl. Sup. Rosso Brol '99	🍷	4

CA' DEL SANTO
LOC. CAMPOLUNGO, 4
27040 MONTALTO PAVESE (PV)
TEL. 0383870545 - 038551026

The Nero '00, a Pinot Nero, is again the top of the range from Laura Bozzi. Its very discernible varietal aromas of blackcurrant and forest floor introduce a dry, slightly bitter, palate with decent length. The forthright, well-structured Rosso Oltrepò Riva dei Peschi is not bad, either.

- OP Rosso Riva dei Peschi '00 — 3
- Pinot Nero Il Nero '00 — 4

TENIMENTI CASTELROTTO - TORTI
FRAZ. CASTELROTTO, 6
27047 MONTECALVO VERSIGGIA (PV)
TEL. 0385951000
E-MAIL: laura@tortiwinepinotnero.com

The Barbera Barrique '99 from Dino Torti is remarkable. Vinified in the modern style, it is elegantly soft and full, with a nice background note of jam. The Pinot Nero Barrique '99 is just as good, with a full, firm flavour, though it should develop further in the bottle.

- OP Barbera Barrique '99 — 6
- OP Pinot Nero Barrique '99 — 5

CASTELVEDER
VIA BELVEDERE, 4
25040 MONTICELLI BRUSATI (BS)
TEL. 030652308
E-MAIL: castelveder@libero.it

Despite its slightly hazy nose, perhaps because of the recent disgorgement, Renato Alberti's Franciacorta '97 is still enjoyable. The palate is lean, with invigoratingly fresh body, intense apple fruit, balance and moreish drinkability. The Extra Brut is interesting.

○ Franciacorta Brut '97 — 5
○ Franciacorta Extra Brut — 5

IL MONTÙ
VIA MARCONI, 10
27040 MONTÙ BECCARIA (PV)
TEL. 0385262252
E-MAIL: ilmontu@ilmontu.com

The Cantina Storica Montù Beccaria has resubmitted the same vintages of their signature wines, confirming their scores and staying power. Among the new items are the mature Pinot Nero Extra Dry '98, the sweet and fruity Sangue di Giuda '01, and the honey-rich Ambrato del Notaio '01.

○ OP Pinot Nero Extra Dry '98 — 4
- OP Sangue di Giuda '01 — 3
○ Ambrato del Notaio '01 — 5

RICCHI
VIA FESTONI, 13/D
46040 MONZAMBANO (MN)
TEL. 0376800238
E-MAIL: info@cantinaricchi.it

The superb Garda Merlot Carpino is made with fruit left to raisin for around 70 days. Aged for a year in barrique, it has aromas of raisins and spices that make way for a full, robust palate, which is still a bit tannic. The Chardonnay Garda Meridiano is nice.

- Garda Merlot Carpino '00 — 5
○ Garda Chardonnay Meridiano '01 — 4

CASCINA GNOCCO
FRAZ. LOSANA, 20
27040 MORNICO LOSANA (PV)
TEL. 0383892280
E-MAIL: info@cascinagnocco.it

The Adagetto '01, Moscato has a particularly rich nose of wistaria, orange blossom, sage and fruit. It's round and sweet on the palate without being cloying. In contrast, the Donna Cecilia '97 is an austere Rosso Oltrepò Riserva, which has aged to point of perfection. Drink now.

○ OP Moscato Adagetto '01 — 4
- OP Rosso Donna Cecilia Ris. '97 — 5

Ugo Vezzoli
Via G. B. Vezzoli, 20
Loc. San Pancrazio
25030 Palazzolo sull'Oglio (BS)
tel. 030738018

Ugo Vezzoli runs a family estate with five hectares of vineyard that produces around 50,000 bottles of sparklers and still wines every year. This time, we enjoyed the two good DOC wines in addition to a decent Franciacorta.

○ Franciacorta Brut	🍷	4*
○ TdF Bianco '01	🍷	3
● TdF Rosso '00	🍷	3

Bredasole
Via San Pietro, 44
25030 Paratico (BS)
tel. 035910407
e-mail: ferrari@bredasole.it

Giacomo Ferrari's estate boasts little more than 13 hectares under vine and makes good use of help from oenologist Corrado Cugnasco. The quality of the wines has definitely grown over the past few years. The Franciacorta is very interesting, showing balance and a solid structure.

○ TdF Bianco Pio Elemosiniere '00	🍷	4
○ Franciacorta Brut	🍷	4*

La Masnadora
Via Molino, 1
25030 Paratico (BS)
tel. 035834003
e-mail: tallarini@tiscalinet.it

This is a small estate with less than three hectares planted to vine. Yet we feel the quality of its wines is very exciting, especially the still wines. Winemaking consultancy is entrusted to Alberto Musatti.

○ TdF Bianco La Masnadora '01	🍷🍷	4*
● TdF Rosso La Masnadora '00	🍷	4

Catturich Ducco
Loc. Camignone
Via degli Eroi, 70
25050 Passirano (BS)
tel. 0306850566 - 0306850576

Piero Catturich Ducco's winery is legendary in Franciacorta. From the vast range of products this year, we would like to mention an impressive '98 Brut, which has good body and expressive depth, and a fresh, well-balanced Terre di Franciacorta.

○ TdF Bianco '01	🍷	3
○ Franciacorta Brut Torre Ducco '98	🍷	5
○ Franciacorta Brut	🍷	4

Le Marchesine
Via Vallosa, 31
25050 Passirano (BS)
tel. 030657005
e-mail: info@lemarchesine.com

The father and son team of Giovanni and Loris Biatta manage this winery with commitment, vinifying fruit purchased from a select group of growers. French winemaking consultant Jean-Pierre Valade helps them make a small but well-crafted range of Franciacortas and still wines.

○ Franciacorta Brut '95	🍷🍷	6
○ Franciacorta Satèn	🍷🍷	6

Conte Giorgi di Vistarino
Fraz. Scorzolesta 82/84
27040 Pietra de' Giorgi (PV)
tel. 038585117
e-mail: info@giorgidivistarino.it

The aristocratic Giorgi family owns 160 hectares of vineyards, with pinot nero accounting for two thirds. The Pinot Nero Pernice '99 is a vivid ruby, with fragrant cassis and vanilla aromas and an elegant flavour. The spicy, complex Chardonnay Elaisa '99 is has aged well and is still sound.

● OP Pinot Nero Pernice '99	🍷🍷	5
○ OP Chardonnay Elaisa '99	🍷	5

Marangona
Antica Corte Ialidy
25010 Pozzolengo (BS)
Tel. 030919379
E-mail: info@marangona.com

This winery is on the Antica Corte Ialidy estate at Pozzolengo. It makes an agreeable Rosso Classico Superiore del Garda '00, half barrique-aged, and a zesty, almost salty, flower and fruit Chiaretto '01. The Lugana Il Rintocco '99, from the oldest vines on the property, also deserves a mention.

● Garda Cl. Rosso Sup. '00	🍷	4
⊙ Garda Cl. Chiaretto '01	🍷	3
○ Lugana Il Rintocco '99	🍷	3

Tenuta Roveglia
Loc. Roveglia, 1
25010 Pozzolengo (BS)
Tel. 030918663
E-mail: tenuta.roveglia@gsnet.it

The Vigna di Catullo '00 is the best Lugana submitted this year from the Zweifel-Azzone family estate. It has a fruit-rich aroma and a distinct, slightly bitter background note. The barrique-fermented Filo di Arianna '00, a Lugana Superiore, is also pleasant and balanced.

○ Lugana Sup. Filo di Arianna '00	🍷	4
○ Lugana Sup. Vigna di Catullo '00	🍷	4

Pasini Produttori
Fraz. Raffa - Via Videlle, 2
25080 Puegnago sul Garda (BS)
Tel. 030266206 - 0365651419
E-mail: info@pasiniproduttori.com

The Renano '01, Garda Classico Bianco, is interesting. A monovarietal Riesling Renano, it has a fragrant nose of rose and thyme-rich aromatic herbs, mineral echoes, and a full, persistent flavour. The Cabernet Vigneto Montezalto '98 is rich and concentrated.

○ Garda Cl. Bianco Il Renano '01	🍷	4
● Garda Cabernet Vigneto Montezalto '98	🍷	5

Cantina Sociale Cooperativa di Quistello
Via Roma, 46
46026 Quistello (MN)
Tel. 0376618118
E-mail: info@cantinasocialequistello.it

The wines made by this co-operative at Quistello are exemplary, especially in terms of their excellent value for money. The organically farmed vineyards yield three Lambruscos, Banda Blu, Banda Rossa and Banda Viola. All are attractively clean, fragrant and fruity.

● Lambrusco Mantovano Banda Blu '01	🍷	1*
● Lambrusco Mantovano Banda Rossa '01	🍷	1*
● Lambrusco Mantovano Banda Viola '01	🍷	1*

Mirabella
Via Cantarane, 2
25050 Rodengo Saiano (BS)
Tel. 030611197
E-mail: info@mirabellavini.it

Best of the wines tasted this year was the soft, elegant Franciacorta Satèn, which has a wealth of fruity pulp and vanillaed tones. Other good quality wines are the Brut, which has a correct, attractive aromatic profile, and the nice Rosé, with its nice berry fruit aromas.

○ Franciacorta Saten	🍷🍷	5
○ Franciacorta Brut	🍷	4
⊙ Franciacorta Brut Rosé	🍷	4

Castello di Luzzano
Fraz. Luzzano, 5
27040 Rovescala (PV)
Tel. 0523863277
E-mail: info@castelloluzzano.it

Castello di Luzzano produces fine quality wines on the border of the Oltrepò and Colli Piacentini DOC zones. The outstanding Riserva 1997 Luzzano 270 is vigorous and austere, showing fragrant blackberry jam and spices. The Riserva '98 is promising, but needs further ageing.

● OP Rosso Luzzano 270 Ris. '97	🍷🍷	5

Martilde
Fraz. Croce, 4/A1
27040 Rovescala (PV)
tel. 0385756280
e-mail: martilde@martilde.it

The still Bonarda Ghiro Rosso d'Inverno '98 is dark and concentrated. The wealth of tannins will mellow but it will take time. The Barbera '98 La Strega, La Gazza, Il Pioppo is full and very firm. We can confirm our positive review last year for the Bonarda Zaffo '97.

- OP Barbera La Strega, la Gazza, il Pioppo '98 — 5
- OP Bonarda Ghiro Rosso d'Inverno '98 — 6

Antonio Panigada - Banino
Via della Vittoria, 13
20078 San Colombano al Lambro (MI)
tel. 037189103
e-mail: vinobanino@hotmail.com

The consistent quality of the Vigna La Merla is admirable. Made with 60 per cent croatina and barbera from old vineyards, and aged 20 months in oak, the '99 has vigour in the mouth and spicy aromas. It's just as good as the '98. The young, slightly sparkling Banino Rosso is linear, fruity and nice.

- San Colombano Banino La Merla Ris. '99 — 3*
- San Colombano Banino — 2*

Enrico Riccardi
Via Capra, 17
20078 San Colombano al Lambro (MI)
tel. 0371897381 - 0371200523
e-mail: info@viniriccardi.com

The San Colombano Rosso Mombrione '98 selection, with small proportions of merlot and cabernet sauvignon, is mature, austere and spicy. The Roverone '01 has clear varietal notes of morello cherry and almond, then a firm palate with a distinct background note of jam.

- San Colombano Mombrione '98 — 3*
- San Colombano Roverone '01 — 2*

Bisi
Loc. Cascina San Michele
27040 San Damiano al Colle (PV)
tel. 038575037

Claudio and Emilio Bisi presented us with an excellent monovarietal Barbera, the Roncolongo '99. Deep ruby red, with a nose of morello cherry and sweet spices, it shows a round, warm, powerful palate. The Primm '99, a Cabernet Sauvignon, is noteworthy but less ready for the corkscrew.

- OP Barbera Roncolongo '99 — 5
- OP Cabernet Sauvignon Primm '99 — 5

Vanzini
Fraz. Barbaleone, 7
27040 San Damiano al Colle (PV)
tel. 038575019
e-mail: vanzinisas@inwind.it

The Sangue di Giuda '01 is nice. A cuve close sparkler with a red mousse, it has a blackberry and violet nose, and sweet, fruity palate. The sparkling Bonarda Frizzante '01 is good, with an almondy after-aroma. The Barbaleone '98, from cabernet, barbera, croatina and uva rara, is drinking well now.

- OP Sangue di Giuda '01 — 3*
- OP Bonarda Frizzante '01 — 3
- Barbaleone '98 — 5

Podere San Giorgio
Fraz. Castello, 1
27046 Santa Giuletta (PV)
tel. 0383899168
e-mail: info@poderesangiorgio.it

Guido Perdomini is back in the limelight after taking time out for reflection. His wines, labels and oenologist, now Donato Lanati, have all changed. The fragrant Chardonnay Dama Bianca '01 and nicely full-bodied Barbera Becco Giallo '00 are both good. The Pinot Grigio '01 is also intriguing.

- OP Barbera Becco Giallo '00 — 4
- O OP Chardonnay Dama Bianca '01 — 3*
- O OP Pinot Grigio '01 — 3

BAGNASCO
VIA ROMA, 57
27047 SANTA MARIA DELLA VERSA (PV)
TEL. 0385278019 - 0385798033
E-MAIL: cantinabagnasco@virgilio.it

Paolo Bagnasco makes a pleasant Sangue di Giuda. A Charmat method sparkler, it reveals aromas of ripe grapes and wild berries leading into a sweet, vigorous palate. The sparkling Bonarda Frizzante '01 has enjoyable blackberry aromas and a fruit-rich palate with a hint of bitterness.

● OP Bonarda Frizzante '01	♀	2*
● OP Sangue di Giuda '01	♀	4

BONALDI - CASCINA DEL BOSCO
LOC. PETOSINO - VIA GASPAROTTO, 96
24010 SORISOLE (BG)
TEL. 035571701
E-MAIL: cascinadelbosco@bonaldi.it

Lorenzo Bonaldi's Cantoalto '00, an oak-aged white, earned a good Two Glass score. The intense aromas of tropical fruit and vanilla give way to a full-bodied palate. The Valcalepio Bianco 2001 is honest and uncomplicated. The Valcalepio Rosso 2000 is soft and slightly grassy.

○ Cantoalto Bianco '00	♀♀	4
● Valcalepio Rosso '00	♀	3
○ Valcalepio Bianco '01	♀	3

F.LLI BETTINI
LOC. SAN GIACOMO - VIA NAZIONALE, 4/A
23036 TEGLIO (SO)
TEL. 0342786068 - 0342786096
E-MAIL: bettvini@tin.it

Around 11,000 bottles of Sforzato are produced by this winery. All are good and very much in step with the growing overall quality of this wine type. The '99 is destined to improve over time, and will acquire harmony and complexity. The Valgella Vigna la Cornella '98 is soft and pleasant.

● Valtellina Sfursat '99	♀♀	7
● Valtellina Sup. Valgella Villa La Cornella '98	♀	5

AZIENDA AGRICOLA CAVEN CAMUNA
VIA CAVEN, 1
23036 TEGLIO (SO)
TEL. 0342482631

This is a branch of the better known Nera estate, directly managed by Pietro Nera's children. The Giupa '99 Valtellina Superiore deserves mention for its fruity aromas and very soft mouthfeel. The Inferno Al Carmine '99 is well-typed, clean on the nose and eminently drinkable.

● Valtellina Sup. Giupa '99	♀♀	5
● Valtellina Sup. Inferno Al Carmine '99	♀	5

PLOZZA
VIA SAN GIACOMO, 22
23037 TIRANO (SO)
TEL. 0342701297
E-MAIL: info@plozza.ch

In recent years, Plozza has enthusiastically embraced a quality-first approach. While some of their wines have an international style, other are more traditional. The second group includes a good Sforzato '97, which shows vigour and complex aromas. The Riserva La Scala '97 is soft and elegant.

● Valtellina Sfurzat Vin da Ca' '97	♀♀	7
● Valtellina Sup. La Scala Ris. '97	♀♀	6

MEDOLAGO ALBANI
LOC. REDONA - VIA REDONA, 12
24069 TRESCORE BALNEARIO (BG)
TEL. 035942022
E-MAIL: wine@medolagoalbani.it

Emanuele Medolago Albani has a Rosso Riserva '98 that is even richer and more delicious than the '97. The Valcalepio Rosso 2000, a 60-40 merlot and cabernet mix, is less structured but still pleasant. The Cumello Merlot della Bergamasca is full-bodied and fruity.

● Valcalepio Rosso Ris. '98	♀♀	4
● Merlot della Bergamasca Cumello '00	♀	3
● Valcalepio Rosso '00	♀	3

TRENTINO

In Trentino, wine has always been used as a measure for the quality of life. For as long as it has been produced in the valleys that run from the Adige River up toward the Dolomites, wine has been the pride of the local community and sent to buyers across Europe. Trentino wine producers have achieved great commercial successes, helped by new developments in production and expanding markets. They have consolidated their reputation as wines that are well made, good value for money but not terribly exciting. The view was confirmed again this year. All the 475 wines on the list, tasted at the Chamber of Commerce in Trento, scored well, thanks to the excellent vinification techniques used. But very few stood out from the crowd as being unmistakably original, authentic interpreters of the territory. There were few that could compete on a wider scene. Efforts at promoting and defending typical varieties put in place by the provincial authority and the entire wine-producing sector have had an effect and the average quality level has risen. However, many wineries, and not just the powerful co-operatives, still give priority to the simpler, big-number wines and devote little attention more prestigious selections. Meanwhile, managers at the most influential commercial wineries continue to maintain that the future of Trentino winemaking lies in combining quantity with quality.

Meanwhile, DOC and other production regulations allow intensive cultivation and generous harvests with some of the highest cropping levels in the world – almost 200 quintals per hectare. At the same time, co-operative wineries pay their members well for their grapes, offering € 120.00 and € 210.00 per quintal. It is difficult in this overall scenario to grow less fruit of better quality and use it to make superior wines. But things are beginning to change. Some co-operative wineries have instituted new cultivation systems and obliged their members to respect new, quality-focused cropping plans. In turn, some winemakers continue to maintain that "small is beautiful" and win encouraging recognition for their efforts. These are not restricted to the list of Three Glass winners. Some small wineries make magnificent wines like Vino Santo, proof of how special Trentino wines can be. Courageous, professional winemakers like Guerrieri Gonzaga, Foradori, Ferrari, Pojer & Sandri and a few others have been joined by a growing number of other estates that are turning out excellent products. They include the red Barbanico by Nicola Balter, the Chardonnay Praistél from Longariva, Marco Zani's Castel Noarna white, the Syrae from Pravis, the Bordeaux-style Gabàn from Diego Bolognani and the exclusive Dòron, a sweet Marzemino by Eugenio Rosi.

ALA (TN)

ALESSANDRO SECCHI
FRAZ. SERRAVALLE ALL' ADIGE
LOC. COLERI, 10
38060 ALA (TN)
TEL. 0464696647
E-MAIL: info@Secchivini.it

Once a surprise, Alessandro Secchi is now a reassuring confirmation of what is best in the wines of lower Vallagarina. There's an extensive range of varieties at his family-run estate, with its well-ordered vineyards alongside splendid rows of olive trees. The grapes are mainly red, from marzemino to lagrein, but you'll also see pinot nero and cabernet. The 2000 vintage was a good one for Corindone, a full-bodied, pleasant Bordeaux blend of merlot-driven drinkability. It's a soft, graceful, persistent red from an unusual marriage of marzemino and lagrein. It won us over with its character and caressing softness, as did the latest creation, Realgar. In contrast, the monovarietal Cabernet Sauvignon is still being fine-tuned and shows less concentration than we hoped. The Pinot Nero is well-made and youthfully easy to drink. The hint of bitterness bespeaks a skilled hand during vinification. The same goes for the typically vegetal, invitingly upfront Merlot. The Berillo d'Oro, from chardonnay and sauvignon, is again unique, though it has less concentration than earlier versions. The Marzemino is good. A traditional-style, classic wine, it offers a more attractive aromatic timbre than in the past.

AVIO (TN)

CANTINA SOCIALE DI AVIO
VIA DANTE, 14
38063 AVIO (TN)
TEL. 0464684008
E-MAIL: cantinasocialediavio.can@tin.it

Avio is a winemaking community in the lower Vallagarina, right on the border between the Trentino and Veneto regions. Among other special features, it boasts one of the best grape-growing environments in Trentino, the Campi Sarni. So, it would be logical to expect a particularly tempting wine. Confirmation comes yet again with the traditional Bordeaux blend from this dynamic co-operative winery, whose steadily growing professionalism is firmly focused on improving quality across the whole range of wines. Helped out by the vintage, the Riserva '99 of this traditional version of Trentino Rosso flaunts vigorous flavour, attractive aromatic notes and nice overall balance. In other words, it shows how the Campi Sarni terroir can make a difference. The area also has a good influence on the always very drinkable Marzemino, with acidity that is perhaps a bit tauter than usual but still showing character and persistence. More proof of quality comes from the Enantio, a red obtained from the lambrusco a foglia frastagliata variety. The Pinot Grigio and Chardonnay are easy-drinking, tasty whites that offer excellent value for money. The Pinot Nero was not fully mature when when we called to taste and will improve with proper bottle ageing.

● Corindone Rosso '00	♈♈	5
● Realgar '01	♈♈	4
● Pinot Nero '00	♈	5
● Trentino Cabernet Sauvignon '00	♈	5
● Trentino Merlot '00	♈	3
○ Berillo d'Oro '01	♈	4
● Trentino Marzemino '01	♈	4
○ Berillo d'Oro '00	♈♈	4
● Corindone Rosso '99	♈♈	5
● Trentino Marzemino '00	♈	3
● Pinot Nero '99	♈	4

● Trentino Rosso Ris. '99	♈♈	4
● Enantio '00	♈	3
● Trentino Marzemino '01	♈	3
● Trentino Pinot Nero '99	♈	4
○ Trentino Chardonnay '01		3
○ Trentino Pinot Grigio '01		3
● Trentino Marzemino '00	♈♈	3
● Trentino Rosso Ris. '98	♈♈	4
○ Trentino Vendemmia Tardiva '99	♈♈	4

AVIO (TN)

Tenuta San Leonardo
Loc. San Leonardo, 3
Fraz. Borghetto all'Adige
38060 Avio (TN)
tel. 0464689004
e-mail: info@sanleonardo.it

Carlo Guerrieri Gonzaga may have made his most elegant San Leonardo to date. Finesse and power are the distinguishing characteristics of a wine that has become one of the most exclusive symbols of winemaking in Trentino. Over almost 30 years, the Tenuta San Leonardo estate has revolutionized the way wine is made in Trentino. It has brought tenacity, precision and an ongoing commitment to improvement; it makes no concessions to improvisation or carelessness, and has improved management of its vineyards, situated in the heart of the region's finest growing area, Campi Sarni. And the winery has extended the dependable, efficient, cellar, which is entirely underground, beneath the gardens of the historic noble residence. Carlo Guerrieri Gonzaga has found valuable support in his young son Anselmo, who for a couple of vintages now has worked alongside his father, managing the winery and bringing enthusiasm and renewed energy to all the estate's collaborators, from agricultural workers to cellar operatives. The team now includes the internationally famous Tuscan oenologist, Carlo Ferrini. All this co-ordinated effort benefits their cult wine, the San Leonardo, which is a Bordeaux blend. The 1999 vintage has made it even more elegant, with complex, invitingly varied notes of fruit that recall blackberry, cocoa and bay leaf. The tannins are delicate on the palate, weaving into a well-defined, persistent texture with velvety flavours and a well-sustained, nicely paced progression. The finish lingers endlessly, as you might expect from such an aristocratic wine.

● San Leonardo '99	🍷🍷🍷	8
● San Leonardo '90	🍷🍷🍷	5
● San Leonardo '93	🍷🍷🍷	5
● San Leonardo '94	🍷🍷🍷	5
● San Leonardo '95	🍷🍷🍷	5
● San Leonardo '96	🍷🍷🍷	5
● San Leonardo '97	🍷🍷🍷	5
● Trentino Merlot '99	🍷🍷	4
● San Leonardo '91	🍷🍷	5

AVIO (TN)

Vallarom
Fraz. Vo' Sinistro
Via Masi, 21
38063 Avio (TN)
tel. 0464684297
e-mail: vallarom@libero.it

Barbara and Filippo Scienza are admirable. They make great wines, starting with the new item from the 2001 vintage. It's a white with a Latin name, Vadum Caesaris, made from a number of varieties including pinot bianco, chardonnay, riesling and even sauvignon. This unusual wine won the panel's unanimous approval and came near to winning Three Glasses. The Vigna di Brioni is a traditional Chardonnay Riserva that can point to superbly judged oak and a bouquet of golden delicious apples, aromatic herbs and jasmine. The aromas on the nose come back with impressive depth on the very flavoursome palate. The Syrah is also excellent, though probably a bit too young. At any rate, it is destined to improve over time. All the other wines are well-made. The Pinot Nero is slightly closed in its bouquet but still reveals firm, elegant jam and morello cherry on the palate. The same observations go for the Cabernet, but the traditional Bordeaux-style Campi Sarni is much readier for drinking. The Marzemino is good enough. Typical and just as pleasant as ever, it has less concentration than in other vintages. That, of course, enables us to appreciate its forthright, youthful alcohol and fruit to the full.

○ Vadum Caesaris '01	🍷🍷	3
● Syrah '00	🍷🍷	6
○ Trentino Chardonnay Vigna Brioni '00	🍷🍷	5
● Campi Sarni Rosso '00	🍷	5
● Trentino Cabernet '00	🍷	5
● Trentino Pinot Nero '00	🍷	5
● Trentino Marzemino '01	🍷	4
● Campi Sarni Rosso '99	🍷🍷	4
● Syrah '99	🍷🍷	4
○ Trentino Chardonnay Vigna Brioni '99	🍷🍷	4
● Trentino Pinot Nero '99	🍷🍷	4

CALAVINO (TN)

Cantina Toblino
Fraz. Sarche
Via Ponte Oliveti, 1
38070 Calavino (TN)
Tel. 0461564168
E-mail: toblino@tin.it

The technicians at this co-operative winery, which stands on the shores of beautiful Lake Toblino, have been secretly working for years in close contact with oenologists and consultants from Cavit, the company that owns the co-operative. They have been experimenting with growing techniques, varieties to plant and cellar procedures, as well as paying particular attention to the Vino Santo. This is a liqueur wine made by crushing nosiola harvested in October and left to dry on special mats, called "arèle", until the week before Easter. Subsequent cask-ageing is prolonged for almost seven years. The Cantina di Toblino has decided to defend, and promote, this wine from the peasant tradition in Vallagarina, involving the last remaining, and in a certain sense heroic, makers of Vino Santo Trentino DOC. Alongside this rarity, the cellar of course makes many other wines from the grapes contributed by its almost 500 co-operative members, small-scale growers who cultivate smallholdings scattered along the valley. Aside from the just bottled Vino Santo '94, the dense, garnet-hued Rebo also set itself apart itself at our tastings. It has breadth and moderate acidity and is obtained from a hybrid created and used as far back as the 1930s, specifically in the area near Toblino. Other wines released include the Lagrein Scuro and a soft Pinot Nero. The whites are full-flavoured and good value for money. One such is the Nosiola – the Toblino co-operative is the leading producer – but don't miss the Pinot Grigio, Müller Thurgau and Chardonnay.

CALLIANO (TN)

Vallis Agri
Via Valentini, 37
38060 Calliano (TN)
Tel. 0464834113

There was a fine performance this time by the range from this winery, set up by SAV, the Vallagarina grower's farmer's co-operative. Particular flattering comments were reserved by our tasters for the Marzemino, perhaps the wine best loved by the inhabitants of Trentino. Specifically, the Marzemino from the Vigna Fornas selection stood out from the crowd thanks to its intense violet colour, marvellous, headily alcoholic freshness and a varietal character that makes it almost a benchmark for the type. The Marzemino Vigna dei Ziresi, from a zone some consider the most celebrated in the valley. The other two reds made a good impression. The Borgo Sacco Merlot selection is lean, elegant and very clean The Cabernet Sauvignon shows imposing character and fullness, and has very good persistence on the palate in spite of the unexceptional 1998 vintage. The most impressive white from the other wines tasted was, we felt, the Pinot Grigio Vigna Reselé, which is steadily improving in quality. The white Aura was pleasant. It's a blend of sauvignon and chardonnay that is fruit-rich, full and tasty on the palate. The Nosiola is flavoursome, the Moscato Giallo has nice nose-palate balance, rich rose and sage aromas, and a subtly caressing mouthfeel that is hard to match.

● Trentino Rebo '01	🍷🍷	3*
○ Trentino Vino Santo '94	🍷🍷	7
○ Trentino Chardonnay '01	🍷	3
● Trentino Lagrein Scuro '01	🍷	3
○ Trentino Müller Thurgau '01	🍷	3
○ Trentino Nosiola '01	🍷	3
○ Trentino Pinot Grigio '01	🍷	3
● Trentino Pinot Nero '01	🍷	3
○ Trentino Nosiola '00	🍷	3
○ Trentino Vino Santo '93	🍷	6

● Trentino Marzemino Vigna Fornas '01	🍷	4
● Trentino Merlot Borgo Sacco '98	🍷🍷	4
● Trentino Merlot Borgo Sacco '99	🍷🍷	5
● Trentino Marzemino Vigna dei Ziresi '00	🍷	4
○ Aura '01	🍷	4
○ Trentino Moscato '01	🍷	4
○ Trentino Nosiola '01	🍷	4
○ Trentino Pinot Grigio Vigna Reselé '01	🍷	4
● Trentino Cabernet Sauvignon '98	🍷	5
● Trentino Marzemino Vigna Fornas '00	🍷🍷	4

CAVEDINE (TN)

GINO PEDROTTI
FRAZ. LAGO DI CAVEDINE
VIA CAVEDINE, 7
38073 CAVEDINE (TN)
TEL. 0461564123
E-MAIL: azagrpedrotti@inwind.it

Viticulture in Trentino is based on a myriad small growers whose vineyards are modest in size but situated in strategic points in the territory. The picturesque rows punctuate the rhythms of the Dolomite landscape with vines that are often clinging onto very steep slopes. In Vallagarina, the vines stand next to olive trees, courtesy of the distinctly Mediterranean climate. It is well-ventilated and tempered by the Ora del Garda, the south wind that helps not only ripen grapes on the vine but also to raisin the bunches of nosiola intended for Vino Santo. The Pedrottis are among the last winemakers to keep this very old rural tradition alive. Theirs is a niche production that respects the natural progress of the fruit's cycle. In other words, there's not much technology but lots of dedication. For a couple of harvests, young Giuseppe has been working alongside his father Gino, helping to manage the small winery. Their speciality is Vino Santo. It is made by crushing partially-dried, botrytis-affected nosiola grapes and leaving the wine to age for almost ten years in small oak casks. The big, full and very fragrant wine the Pedrottis create in this way is quite unique. This nectar aside, the Pedrottis also produce a couple of whites – a Nosiola and a Chardonnay – as well as two reds, the Cabernet and the Merlot. This fine family winery applies skilled craft winemaking techniques with genuine authenticity.

○	Trentino Vino Santo '90	🍷🍷	7
●	Merlot '00	🍷	3
○	Chardonnay '01	🍷	3
○	Nosiola '01	🍷	3
●	Cabernet Ris. '99	🍷	4

CIVEZZANO (TN)

MASO CANTANGHEL
LOC. FORTE
VIA MADONNINA, 33
38045 CIVEZZANO (TN)
TEL. 0461859050

Piero Zabini continues to invest all he can in his work as a maker of good wines. He tends his vineyards with skill and then transforms the fruit into very charactertful wines in his incredible cellar, which is built inside a real Austro-Hungarian fortress. When the vintage is favourable, and he does not have to rely exclusively on his long experience, Piero's wines are inimitable. One such is the Pinot Nero, a leader in its class even outside Trentino. The 2000 vintage has helped him bottle an excellent, Burgundy-style wine. Every component of the nose is redolent of finesse and the pervasively caressing mouthfeel is rich with a classic, elegant sweetness. You can also see the Zabini style in his Chardonnay Vigna Piccola, another wine straight out of the textbook on how to make whites in this province in the Dolomites. The last vintage bottled is among the best. The gold-tinged wine is lovely, offering intense aromas and a harmonious, if not very complex palate. Approachability and an easy-drinking style are the hallmarks of the other two wines. The Solitaire is from sauvignon and the monovarietal Merlot, Tajapreda, reveals fragrant, pleasant hints of cherry and roasted hazelnuts.

●	Trentino Pinot Nero Zabini '00	🍷🍷	6
○	Trentino Chardonnay Vigna Piccola '01	🍷🍷	5
●	Trentino Merlot Tajapreda '01	🍷	4
○	Trentino Sauvignon Solitaire '01	🍷	5
●	Trentino Cabernet Sauvignon Rosso di Pila '99	🍷🍷	6
●	Trentino Merlot Tajapreda '00	🍷	4
●	Trentino Pinot Nero Zabini '99	🍷	5

FAEDO (TN)

GRAZIANO FONTANA
VIA CASE SPARSE, 9
38010 FAEDO (TN)
TEL. 0461650400

Faedo is the hill for Trentino wine par excellence and the lion's share among the whites is obviously reserved for Müller Thurgau. Graziano Fontana is a major player on the Faedo wine scene. He produces fruity, instantly recognizable whites but has never neglected his red grape vineyards, either. This year, Graziano's best shots were reds, the Lagrein and the Pinot Nero, both of which are very successful. The Lagrein has remarkable concentration and balance, coupled with power and drinkability. A deep red, and intense on both nose and palate, it has a velvety, chewy mouthfeel. The Pinot Nero has enchanting finesse, elegance in the mouth bearing, lively fruit, and unmistakable cherry and blackberry notes. Though a prestigious "white-maker", Graziano Fontana is not new to such results with his reds. In fact, he frequently gets great reds when his whites are punished by the weather, as happened last season. He bottled a Müller Thurgau with good aromatic content and decent acidity but the wine is not as gutsy as usual. The Chardonnay, Traminer and especially the Sauvignon, have conserved their character and stay faithful to the territory. They are technically perfect but slightly below standard, considering what Faedo and Graziano Fontana can usually guarantee. We look forward to the next vintage.

● Trentino Lagrein di Faedo '00	¶¶	4
● Trentino Pinot Nero di Faedo '00	¶¶	4
○ Trentino Chardonnay di Faedo '01	¶	3
○ Trentino Müller Thurgau di Faedo '01	¶	3
○ Trentino Sauvignon di Faedo '01	¶	3
○ Trentino Traminer di Faedo '01	¶	3
○ Trentino Müller Thurgau di Faedo '00	¶¶	3*
○ Trentino Sauvignon di Faedo '00	¶	3
○ Trentino Traminer di Faedo '00	¶	3

FAEDO (TN)

POJER & SANDRI
LOC. MOLINI, 4/6
38010 FAEDO (TN)
TEL. 0461650342
E-MAIL: info@pajeresandri.it

There's so much good news here that it's hard to be brief. First of all, the Faye Rosso overwhelmingly won Three Glasses. This great Bordeaux blend has already won many awards and was just waiting for the right vintage to show off all its captivating power. The colour already hints at the opulent density and it offers up intense, not very varietal, aromas then a soft, concentrated palate. More news from the 2000 vintage is that fruit was vinified from the plots at Maso Besler, a splendidly restored building in the Cembra valley that transformed into a sort of exhibition of viticultural archaeology, with unusual varieties such as the negrara trentina, groppello di Revò, the acidic zweigelt and franconia. The results are here in two wines, a white and a red, that are distinctly original and very flavoursome. The other wines from the now very broad range – we tasted around 15 of them – are also in a class by themselves. Two, the "spumante" and Essenzia, came close to earning the cellar a second Three Glass award. The sparkler, a cuvée from various vintages of chardonnay and pinot nero, has rich, complex, fruit-led fragrances with pleasant hints of yeast and vanilla. What can we say about the Essenzia? It's a late-harvest wine from five different varieties of aromatic grapes and this might just be the best version ever made, with its splendid balance of sweetness and acidity, then very long finish. In closing, the Faye Bianco is exquisite, mature and concentrated, with as much sinew as its red partner. The Pinot Nero is always fascinating and other whites are all very pleasant.

● Rosso Faye '00	¶¶¶	7
○ Essenzia Vendemmia Tardiva '00	¶¶	5
○ Cuveé Extra Brut	¶¶	5
○ Besler Biank '00	¶¶	5
● Trentino Pinot Nero Ris. '00	¶¶	5
○ Trentino Chardonnay '01	¶¶	4
○ Trentino Müller Thurgau Palai '01	¶¶	4
○ Trentino Traminer '01	¶¶	4
○ Bianco Faye '99	¶¶	5
○ Trentino Traminer '00	¶¶	4
○ Bianco Faye '98	¶¶	4
○ Essenzia Vendemmia Tardiva '99	¶¶	5
○ Cuveé Extra Brut	¶¶	5
● Pinot Nero '00	¶¶	4
● Pinot Nero Ris. '98	¶¶	5

ISERA (TN)

DE TARCZAL
FRAZ. MARANO
VIA G. B. MIORI, 4
38060 ISERA (TN)
TEL. 0464409134
E-MAIL: tarczal@tin.it

We know Ruggero de Tarczal has done his best as usual, vinifying the grapes from his superb vineyards with all possible care. But we also know no one controls the weather. Especially when the harvest in question was 2001, an especially difficult one in many parts of Trentino – and this is an even sadder observation – for those who have drastically reduced chemical input and cultivate their vineyards with more respect for the environment and the typicity of the varieties planted. That's what happened with the Marzemino, that emblematic Vallagarina wine, produced in two different versions by de Tarczal with fruit specially selected fruit from his beloved vines. The very finest grapes end up in the Husar, a vintage Marzemino that could be considered a special selection, and the rest of the fruit in more approachable wines that enhance their attractive freshness. Both the latest versions are more than just well-made but less intense and less imposing than usual. The whites are as interesting as ever, starting with the Pinot Bianco, whose inviting golden hue introduces a pleasant fruit and flower aroma profile. The much more accessible, deliciously drinkable Chardonnay is supported by an inviting, subtle acidity.

ISERA (TN)

ENRICO SPAGNOLLI
VIA G. B. ROSINA, 4/A
38060 ISERA (TN)
TEL. 0464409054
E-MAIL: enrspagn@tin.it

Careful work in the vineyard makes for better vinification. Luigi Spagnolli has always wanted to do something different, something very personal. He personally follows every harvest, watching as the grapes mature, suggesting techniques and little tricks of the trade to his growers so they can give him healthy fruit. He then brings out the very best in the cellar. But that is not all. Luigi also cultivates his own small plots and carries out unique experiments, such as the "vino del sindaco", or "mayor's wine". Production is symbolic but the vineyards are publicly owned and the initiative attempts to return to a more authentic kind of viticulture and winemaking. "Gigi", as Spagnolli is known, is always ready to take up new challenges. His stubborn tenacity has inspired him to concentrate that notoriously troublesome variety, pinot nero. The latest version released repays him for all his work for Gigi's Pinot Nero is way better than other wines of the same type from Trentino. It has class and backbone, great balance, well-gauged acidity and seductive drinkability. The Bordeaux blend, Tebro, also shows nice character. This red is all finesse, with notes that bring out the vegetal tone typical of fruit from Trentino. All the other wines are as good as ever, from the Marzemino to the Traminer Aromatico and the always flavoursome, drinkable, Moscato Giallo.

○ Trentino Chardonnay '01	♀	4
● Trentino Marzemino '01	♀	4
● Trentino Marzemino d'Isera Husar '01	♀	4
○ Trentino Pinot Bianco '01	♀	4
● Trentino Marzemino d'Isera Husar '00	♀♀	3*
● Trentino Merlot Campiano '99	♀♀	4
○ Trentino Pinot Bianco '00	♀	3

● Trentino Pinot Nero '00	♀♀	5
● Trentino Rosso Tebro '00	♀	5
● Trentino Marzemino '01	♀	3
○ Trentino Moscato Giallo '01	♀	3*
○ Trentino Müller Thurgau '01	♀	3
○ Trentino Nosiola '01	♀	4
○ Trentino Traminer Aromatico '01	♀	5
○ Trentino Traminer Aromatico '00	♀♀	4
● Trentino Pinot Nero '99	♀♀	4
● Trentino Rosso Tebro '99	♀♀	5
● Trentino Marzemino '00	♀	3*
○ Trentino Nosiola '00	♀	3

LASINO (TN)

PISONI
LOC. SARCHE
VIA SAN SIRO, 7/B
38070 LASINO (TN)
TEL. 0461563216 - 0461564106
E-MAIL: info@pisoni.net

Marco and Stefano Pisoni descend from a centuries-old winemaking dynasty. Their winery is at the bottom of the valley, clinging to the hill that separates the Basso Sarca from the Valle di Cavedine in the heart of Vallagarina between Trento and Lake Garda. Cousins Marco and Stefano have noticeably accelerated the changes in the family business since they came aboard. Though the last few vintages have not been particularly good, their wines have maintained their high levels of quality. The Rebo, a wine that comes from the meeting of merlot and teroldego, introduces itself with an excellent lively red hue. Clean on the nose, it shows good fruit intensity, then a palate with decent density and nice length on the back palate. The Nosiola variety is emblematic of Vallagarina and the Pisonis know this well. They make two versions, the first of which is a fresh, delicate, simple white. The second, vinified after the fruit is partially raisined on rush mats, is an excellent Vino Santo Trentino. This liqueur wine is only released at least six years after the fruit if crushed. Although it may improve with more cellar time, the '94 version comes from a difficult vintage and the wine is much more forward than expected. It's warm but lacks its characteristic sinew. The other wines submitted are all well typed.

LASINO (TN)

PRAVIS
LOC. BIOLCHE DI CASTEL MADRUZZO
38076 LASINO (TN)
TEL. 0461564305
E-MAIL: info@pravis.it

The Stravino di Stravino '00 is still resting in its casks. You will not find it among the wines listed. But the "guys from Pravis", three winemakers with different roles, Gianni Chisté, Domenico Pedrini and Mario Zambarda, are riding high on the new wave of Trentino winemaking. The Syrae, a monovarietal Syrah, just missed our highest award, proving that it is a magnificent wine with a lovely aromatic timbre, its notes of morello cherry, blackcurrant and cocoa coming back attractively on the palate. The Niergal also made a great showing – the name is an anagram of the variety, lagrein. Its dense, almost impenetrable colour ushers in spicy notes on the nose where white pepper alternates with hints of wild berries, tobacco and leather. The Fratagranda is another outstanding wine. It's a Bordeaux blend with massive extract and excellently calibrated tannins. It's also much more harmonious on the palate than the nose, which, like almost all the Cabernets from Trentino, has prominent vegetal notes (could this perhaps be promoted as a positive feature?) The Müller Thurgau San Thomà, perhaps the best tasted, shows all the richness of flavour that characterizes all wines from Pravis. It also offers great aromatic fragrance and solid structure on the palate. The Nosiola Le Frate is a model of its kind, proffering fresh hazelnut flavours and a faintly bitter finish. The Pinot Grigio Polin is as interesting as ever, inviting you to take a second glass with its copper-coloured highlights and vibrant palate.

	Wine	Rating	Score
●	Sarica Rosso '00	🍷	5
○	Trentino Bianco San Siro '01	🍷	3
○	Trentino Nosiola '01	🍷	3
○	Trentino Vino Santo '94	🍷	5
●	Trentino Rebo '99	🍷	5
○	Trentino Vino Santo '90	🍷🍷	5
○	Trentino Vino Santo '92	🍷🍷	8
●	Sarica Rosso '98	🍷🍷	4
●	Sarica Rosso '99	🍷🍷	5
○	Trentino Nosiola '00	🍷	3
○	Trento Brut Ris. '92	🍷	4
○	Trentino Vino Santo '93	🍷	5
●	Trentino Rebo '97	🍷	4
●	Trentino Rosso San Siro '98	🍷	3
○	Trentino Nosiola '99	🍷	3

	Wine	Rating	Score
●	Niergal '00	🍷🍷	5
●	Syrae '00	🍷🍷	5
○	Nosiola Le Frate '01	🍷🍷	4
○	Trentino Müller Thurgau St. Thomà '01	🍷🍷	4
○	Trentino Pinot Grigio Polin '01	🍷🍷	5
●	Trentino Cabernet Fratagranda '99	🍷🍷	6
○	Stravino di Stravino '99	🍷🍷🍷	6
●	Syrae '99	🍷🍷	6
●	Trentino Cabernet Fratagranda '95	🍷🍷	4
●	Trentino Cabernet Fratagranda '97	🍷🍷	4
●	Trentino Rebo Rigotti '97	🍷🍷	3
●	Syrae '98	🍷🍷	4
●	Trentino Cabernet Fratagranda '98	🍷🍷	6
●	Niergal '99	🍷🍷	5

LAVIS (TN)

Nilo Bolognani
Via Stazione, 19
38015 Lavis (TN)
Tel. 0461246354
E-mail: dibolog@tin.it

Several years ago, Diego Bolognani promised he would produce two fine red wines. Well, the moment has arrived. Diego presented two jewels as an exclusive, almost furtive foretaste of what he has achieved with at least five years of patient, solitary, experimentation. The effort also convinced him to become a grower, in conjunction with his brothers, who were already respected cellarmen. Now they cultivate several small, perfectly looked after plots along the sunny slopes of Trento. That's the story behind the Gabàn, a classic Bordeaux blend made exclusively with the estate's own grapes. It's a magnificent, very concentrated wine of extraordinary power, roundness of flavour and persistence. We're going to be hearing a lot more in the future from this Gabàn. The panel also immediately agreed about the qualities of the other red, Armilo, a monovarietal Teroldego vinified with all the care needed to make a great wine. Just like the Gabàn, it easily won an invitation to our final taste-offs. The winemaker's skilled hand was also evident in the three whites presented. The Nosiola, Müller Thurgau and Sauvignon are all pleasant and tempt the nose with delightful aromatic notes, especially the Müller Thurgau.

●	Teroldego Armilo '00	🍷🍷	5
●	Gabàn '00	🍷🍷	6
○	Trentino Müller Thurgau '01	🍷	3
○	Trentino Nosiola '01	🍷	3
○	Trentino Sauvignon '01	🍷	3
○	Trentino Müller Thurgau '00	🍷🍷	3
○	Trentino Moscato Giallo '97	🍷🍷	3
○	Trentino Müller Thurgau '98	🍷🍷	3
○	Trentino Nosiola '98	🍷🍷	3
○	Trentino Chardonnay '99	🍷🍷	3
○	Trentino Müller Thurgau '99	🍷🍷	3
○	Trentino Nosiola '00	🍷	3

LAVIS (TN)

Cesconi
Fraz. Pressano
Via Marconi, 39
38015 Lavis (TN)
Tel. 0461240355
E-mail: cesconi@cr-surfing.net

This past vintage, the Cesconis produced really good wines. "As usual", I hear you say. The Olivar, a wine dedicated to the ancient olive tree dominating this estate on the hill of Pressano above Lavis, had no difficulty at all in picking up Three Glasses. A white from chardonnay, pinot bianco and pinot grigio, it ages part in wood - small oak casks - and part in stainless steel, to create a magnificent harmony of aromas and flavours. The lustrous colour ushers in nuances of fresh fruit made even more interesting by notes of citrus, shades of vanilla, crusty bread and walnutskin. The Nosiola, Pinot Grigio, Chardonnay and Traminer are all as pleasant as ever, although they suffer from problems caused by the weather before the harvest. The not exactly Mediterranean temperatures have partially compromised their finesse, balance and accustomed fullness of flavour. The situation was different for the reds, cultivated by the Cesconis on a beautiful piece of land in the lower Sarca area, near Riva del Garda. The results are exciting, particularly for the Merlot. The base version, an approachable red that is drinking well now, is in some ways similar to the Cabernet, whereas the much more concentrated Pivier selection reveals good balance and nice, full fruit.

○	Olivar '01	🍷🍷🍷	5
●	Rosso del Pivier '00	🍷🍷	5
○	Trentino Chardonnay '01	🍷🍷	5
○	Trentino Pinot Grigio '01	🍷🍷	5
○	Trentino Sauvignon '01	🍷🍷	4
●	Trentino Cabernet '00	🍷	5
○	Trentino Nosiola '01	🍷	4
○	Trentino Pinot Grigio '98	🍷🍷🍷	4
○	Olivar '00	🍷🍷	4
○	Trentino Chardonnay '00	🍷🍷	4
○	Trentino Traminer Aromatico '00	🍷🍷	4
●	Trentino Cabernet '98	🍷🍷	4
●	Trentino Merlot '98	🍷🍷	4
○	Olivar '99	🍷🍷	4

LAVIS (TN)

Vignaiolo Giuseppe Fanti
Fraz. Pressano
P.zza della Croce, 3
38015 Lavis (TN)
tel. 0461240809
e-mail: alessandro.fanti@katamail.com

A member of the younger generation, Alessandro Fanti is a leading player on the Trentino wine scene. His steady improvements in quality make little clamour but every year he releases, almost in silence, wines that are that bit better from his small cellar just below the bell tower in the town centre. Only his whites from the 2001 vintage are ready for the shops. We will have to wait for the Bordeaux-style "riserva" wines. The Fanti family's efforts are best expressed by their Incrocio Manzoni, a white variety that bears the name of the vine researcher who created it in the 1930s by crossing riesling renano with pinot bianco. Alessandro Fanti harvests his grapes from the Croz vineyard, one of the highest on the hill of Pressano. The careful vinification shuns cask conditioning in order to preserve all the aromatic force of the grape. The fruit yields a wine with greenish-gold highlights and very impressive impact on the nose, where the lovely range of fruit and flower fragrances is lifted by a spicy hint reminiscent of rosemary. The palate is deliciously acidic, enjoyably persistent, and sustained by very respectable structure. The full, intense Robur selection of Chardonnay is vinified partly in oak and partly in stainless steel. Banana and fresh bread tempt the nose and the long palate has a slight note of citrus, making the Robur one of the most interesting wines of its type. In closing, we felt the Nosiola, a white that has always been made at Pressano, was pleasant and subtly aromatic.

	Wine	Glasses	Score
○	Incrocio Manzoni '01	♈♈	5
○	Trentino Chardonnay Robur '01	♈	5
○	Trentino Nosiola '01	♈	4
○	Trentino Chardonnay Robur '99	♈♈	4
○	Incrocio Manzoni '00	♈♈	4
●	Portico Rosso '97	♈♈	4
●	Portico Rosso '98	♈♈	4
○	Trentino Chardonnay Robur '98	♈♈	3
○	Incrocio Manzoni '99	♈♈	3
○	Trentino Chardonnay '00	♈	3
○	Trentino Nosiola '00	♈	3
○	Trentino Nosiola '99	♈	3

LAVIS (TN)

La Vis
Via del Carmine, 7
38015 Lavis (TN)
tel. 0461246325
e-mail: cantina@la-vis.com

La Vis was the first co-operative winery in Trentino to attempt to create faithful portraits, as it were, of the wines from its territory. Directed by Fausto Peratoner, La Vis is becoming ever more competitive and a real leader among quality-driven co-operatives. Though there are no Three Glasses this year, all the wines presented by oenologist Gianni Gasperi are excellent for their pleasantness and typicity. Indeed, they are as elegant and inviting as the Dolomite landscape they come from and are true reflections of the specific qualities of the territory. We'll begin with the Ritratto Rosso (Portrait in Red), a blend of the two indigenous varieties of teroldego and lagrein. The two varieties have produced a full, soft, velvety, heady red that combines complexity with a solid tannic weave and linear finish. The Cabernet Sauvignon and Merlot won scores that are almost as flattering. The excellent whites include one of the best Chardonnays tasted in Trentino. The La Vis Mandolaia, a late harvest from chardonnay, riesling, traminer and sauvignon, is exquisite and gets better with each passing vintage. The Ritratto Bianco, a "portrait in white" of chardonnay with pinot grigio and riesling, is harmonious, full and well-balanced. The Pinot Grigio is pleasantly fruity. Finally, the two Sorni products, a white and a red, are great value for money.

	Wine	Glasses	Score
○	Trentino Chardonnay Ritratti '01	♈♈	4
●	Ritratto Rosso '99	♈♈	5
○	Ritratto Bianco '00	♈♈	5
○	Mandolaia '01	♈♈	4
○	Trentino Pinot Grigio Ritratti '01	♈♈	4
●	Trentino Cabernet Sauvignon Ritratti '99	♈♈	4
●	Trentino Merlot Ritratti '00	♈	4
○	Trentino Sorni Bianco '01	♈	4*
●	Trentino Sorni Rosso '01	♈	4*
○	Ritratto Bianco '99	♈♈	5
○	Trentino Chardonnay Ritratti '00	♈♈	4
○	Mandolaia '98	♈♈	5
○	Ritratto Bianco '98	♈♈	4
○	Mandolaia '99	♈♈	5

LAVIS (TN)

Maso Furli
Loc. Furli
Via Furli, 32
38015 Lavis (TN)
tel. 0461240667

Maso Furli is the small yet much admired estate managed by brothers Marco and Giorgio Zanoni. The pair are expert white winemakers and are becoming increasingly skilled with reds as well. This is demonstrated by their Bordeaux blend, fast turning into a thoroughbred. The 1999 is a minor masterpiece. The vibrant red takes you straight into fresh wild berry sensations with subtle nuances of pencil lead. The palate is alluring, harmonious, well-balanced and very long, the medium-grained tannins showing good maturity. As we said, the Zanonis make great whites and they had another two jewels to flaunt, the Traminer and the Sauvignon. Both are perfectly executed interpretations of their varieties, penalized only by the troublesome 2001 harvest that keeps them from being as special as they have been on other occasions. The Traminer has quite a varied range of broad, richly layered aromas, then the well-balanced palate has a pleasant touch of sweetness, which is rarely so well handled as here. The Sauvignon has a similar taste profile. The lively yellow introduces fresh aromas that are full enough to lend the palate subtlety, and a sustained flavour that progresses attractively through to the long finish.

MEZZOCORONA (TN)

Marco Donati
Via Cesare Battisti, 41
38016 Mezzocorona (TN)
tel. 0461604141
e-mail: donatimarcovini@libero.it

If Teroldego Rotaliano is becoming more famous on the international winemaking scene, some credit should go to this small, very professional producer. Marco Donati has always tried to give his wines a personal touch. He cultivates vineyards in the heart of the Campo Rotaliano and has managed to protect some very old Teroldego vines, driven by his great respect for biodiversity. These original clones yield fruit just as special as his wines. Sangue di Drago 2000 is one of the best versions of Teroldego we have ever tasted. A deep, dark red, with a lively, spicy nose, and fullness and depth in the mouth. It has all the concentration necessary to stand the test of time. The pleasant Bagolari, a standard-label Teroldego, is meant for more immediate consumption. We felt the Novai was very pleasant. It's made from teroldego blended with cabernet sauvignon and merlot. And speaking of blends, the Vino del Maso is a very well-executed wine from a base of teroldego with additions of lagrein and merlot. The body is as supple as it is elegant, with good extractive weight and average persistence. The winery also produced a good Lagrein selection from the 2001 vintage, the Fratte Alte, which foregrounds the heady tones of the main variety. In closing, the Torre del Noce blend of chardonnay and pinot bianco sets the pace for the whites. It's followed by the Nosiola and another delicious selection, the Riesling Renano.

● Maso Furli Rosso '99	¶¶	5
○ Trentino Sauvignon '01	¶¶	5
○ Trentino Traminer Aromatico '01	¶¶	5
○ Trentino Chardonnay '99	¶¶¶	3
○ Trentino Chardonnay '00	¶¶	4
○ Trentino Traminer Aromatico '00	¶¶	4
○ Trentino Sauvignon '00	¶¶	4
● Maso Furli Rosso '98	¶¶	4
○ Trentino Sauvignon '98	¶¶	3
○ Trentino Traminer Aromatico '98	¶¶	3
○ Trentino Sauvignon '99	¶¶	3
○ Trentino Traminer Aromatico '99	¶¶	3

● Novai '00	¶¶	5
● Teroldego Rotaliano Sangue del Drago '00	¶¶	6
● Teroldego Rotaliano Bagolari '01	¶	4
○ Torre del Noce Bianco '01	¶	4
● Trentino Lagrein Rubino Fratte Alte '01	¶	4
○ Trentino Nosiola '01	¶	4
○ Trentino Riesling Renano '01	¶	4
● Vino del Maso Rosso '01	¶	4
● Teroldego Rotaliano '00	¶¶	3
○ Torre del Noce Bianco '00	¶¶	3
● Teroldego Rotaliano Sangue del Drago '99	¶¶	4
● Vino del Maso Rosso '99	¶¶	4

MEZZOCORONA (TN)

F.LLI DORIGATI - METIUS
VIA DANTE, 5
38016 MEZZOCORONA (TN)
TEL. 0461605313
E-MAIL: vini@dorigati.it

MEZZOCORONA (TN)

MEZZACORONA
VIA DEL TEROLDEGO, 1
38016 MEZZOCORONA (TN)
TEL. 0461605163 - 0461616399

Bearing the old place name for Mezzocorona, the exclusive Methius sparkler from this very effervescent winery has again won Three Glasses. But that's not all. Methius has also been awarded nothing less than our Sparkler of the Year plaudit. An exquisite sparkling wine with a superbly well-defined aromatic profile and splendidly integrated mousse. The remarkably complex nose displays fruit-led fragrances that spill over into super-ripe notes before coming together again on a palate of austere appeal. Hints of roasted hazelnuts and crusty bread peek through. The other flagship wine from Dorigati is equally round and full. It's a Teroldego Rotaliano Riserva called Diedri. The '99 vintage is a concentration of all teroldego's varietal characteristics. Vinification in small oak casks has contributed to transform the Diedri into a powerful, full-flavoured wine with a broad aromatic range and solid structure. Here is evidence of the recent developments at this winery, which started out as a vinification cellar and was gradually transformed by the innovative fervour more recent generations, including Michele, the young biologist, who started working there lately. Grapes intended for their wines are either estate-grown or carefully selected on the vine. The cabernet sauvignon-based Grener is a wine that is going places. It shows you just how much care goes into grape selection grapes at the Dorigati cellar. The Lagrein Rosato is pleasantly full-bodied, fresh and ready to drink. The Pinot Grigio is, as ever, well made.

MezzaCorona is one of the best-known labels gracing Italy's wines. The group is constantly expanding and includes various production units all over the peninsula, and even in Sicily. Now this co-operative colossus is intensifying its presence in the Piana Rotaliana, expanding its already very large winery and transforming their enormous complex into a "bastion of wine". The MezzaCorona policy of big numbers has also managed to safeguard the characteristics of the area's trademark wine, Teroldego Rotaliano. The cellar makes two versions, the Maioliche selection, a standard-label Teroldego that easily wins two glasses thanks to its subtle balance and pleasant palate, and a good Millesimato '99. This is more solid and tight-knit than many other versions of the type, and may have been helped by the favourable vintage, as well as state-of-the-art cellar techniques. The Pinot Grigio is also released in two versions. One is simple, well-made and excellent value for money while the other is a richer and more complex selection. The Chardonnay and Müller Thurgau may be paying the price of intensive production and we had also hoped for better results from the Rotari sparkling wines, especially the "riserva". Despite this, they are still excellent, easy-drinking Bruts that show much more fruit than previous disgorgements. In particular, the Arte Italiana selection has a soft and caressing, fruit-rich liveliness.

○ Trento Methius Ris. '95	▼▼▼	5
● Teroldego Rotaliano Diedri Ris. '99	▼▼	5
● Trentino Cabernet Grener '00	▼	4
⊙ Trentino Lagrein Rosato '01	▼	3
○ Trentino Pinot Grigio '01	▼	3
○ Trento Methius Ris. '92	▼▼▼	5
○ Trento Methius Ris. '94	▼▼	5
● Teroldego Rotaliano '00	▼▼	3*
○ Trentino Pinot Grigio '00	▼▼	3
○ Trento Methius Ris. '93	▼▼	5
● Teroldego Rotaliano Diedri Ris. '96	▼▼	5
● Teroldego Rotaliano Diedri Ris. '97	▼▼	5
● Trentino Rebo '97	▼▼	3
● Teroldego Rotaliano Diedri Ris. '98	▼▼	5
○ Trentino Pinot Grigio '99	▼▼	3

● Teroldego Rotaliano Sel. Maioliche '01	▼▼	3*
● Teroldego Rotaliano Millesimato '99	▼▼	3*
● Trentino Pinot Nero '99	▼▼	3
○ Pinot Grigio Millesimato '01	▼	2
○ Trentino Chardonnay '01	▼	3
○ Trentino Müller Thurgau '01	▼	3
○ Trento Rotari Brut Arte Italiana	▼	4
○ Trento Rotari Brut Ris. '93	▼▼	4
○ Trento Rotari Brut Ris. '94	▼▼	4
○ Trento Rotari Ris. '95	▼▼	4
● Teroldego Rotaliano Ris. '97	▼▼	3
○ Trento Rotari Ris. '97	▼▼	4
● Teroldego Rotaliano Millesimato '98	▼	3

MEZZOLOMBARDO (TN)

BARONE DE CLES
VIA G. MAZZINI, 18
38017 MEZZOLOMBARDO (TN)
TEL. 0461601081 - 0461602673
E-MAIL: baronedecles@tin.it

The "lords of Teroldego", Michele and Leonardo de Cles, have given us more evidence of their skills. The two brothers are descended from the noble Cles family, originally from the town of the same name, and for some generations now, the de Cles clan has been moving down the valley into the heart of Campo Rotaliano. They now own around 30 hectares of land near Mezzolombardo with the vineyards that have written the history of this classic Trentino variety. The de Cles do not force the natural growing process. They simply vinify what they harvest without worrying about intensive production or innovative techniques in the vineyard. Their goal is simply to fill their own barrels and pass any surplus on to other winemakers. Particular care was given to the Teroldego from Maso Scari, the legendary vineyard that has in the past produced some superbly cellarworthy reds. Its wines have the potential to age for 30 years or more and maintain quite incredible verve, as we recently found out when we tasted vintages like the 1964 and the 1971, to mention only the most sensational. The Teroldego Maso Scari 2001 is a real powerhouse, intense in its aromas and incredibly firm on the palate. Keep this one in the cellar for a while yet. We would advise you to wait at least three years before uncorking the bottle. Its exuberance will have settled and all the wine's class will be able to come through. The Lagrein Scuro is much simpler and more accessible. It's made from the variety considered to be teroldego's twin.

MEZZOLOMBARDO (TN)

CANTINA ROTALIANA
C.SO DEL POPOLO, 6
38017 MEZZOLOMBARDO (TN)
TEL. 0461601010 - 0461604323
E-MAIL: info@cantinarotaliana.it

Though the Teroldego Rotaliano Clesurae fell just short of a repeat Three Glasses, it is still a thoroughbred wine with fantastic appeal. Rotaliana has just inaugurated a modern building, constructed on the edge of the town, and continues to select the best teroldego grapes from its almost 300 contributing growers. Inspiration comes from the successes achieved over the last few years since director Luciano Lunelli, along with oenologist Leonardo Pilati and the entire managerial staff, managed to convince members to produce less fruit with better quality. The complex, expressive Clesurae is a wine with international aspirations. The nose offers berry fruit, oriental spices, hazelnuts and vanilla, which are gently enhanced on the palate where extract and mature tannins weave a velvety, caressing texture. The rest of the range is good, especially the Riserva '99. This is always a lovely wine with traditional aromas and flavours – savour that unmistakable note of earth and tar, melding with a flavour reminiscent of cherry marmalade) – and as ever is released at a very affordable price. Similar considerations apply to the third Teroldego in the range, a red from 2001 that is anything but predictable. Then, from the Canevarie selection, there is a more accessible Teroldego and a stylish, delicate blended white, as well as a very pleasant Pinot Bianco. Last but not least, the Chardonnay is fruit-rich, full and elegantly sinewy.

● Teroldego Rotaliano Maso Scari '01	ŸŸ	4
● Trentino Lagrein '00	Ÿ	4
● Teroldego Rotaliano Maso Scari '00	ŸŸ	4
● Rosso del Cardinale '99	ŸŸ	5
○ Trentino Traminer Aromatico '00	Ÿ	4
● Trentino Lagrein '98	Ÿ	4
○ Trentino Chardonnay '00		3

● Teroldego Rotaliano Clesurae '00	ŸŸ	6
● Teroldego Rotaliano Canevarie '01	ŸŸ	4
● Teroldego Rotaliano Ris. '99	ŸŸ	4
○ Trentino Bianco '01	Ÿ	4
○ Trentino Chardonnay Canevarie '01	Ÿ	4
● Teroldego Pinot Grigio '01	Ÿ	3*
● Teroldego Rotaliano '01	Ÿ	3*
● Teroldego Rotaliano Clesurae '99	ŸŸŸ	6
● Teroldego Rotaliano '00	ŸŸ	3*
● Teroldego Rotaliano '97	ŸŸ	2
● Teroldego Rotaliano Pieve Francescana '97	ŸŸ	4
● Teroldego Rotaliano Ris. '97	ŸŸ	3
● Teroldego Rotaliano Ris. '98	ŸŸ	4*

MEZZOLOMBARDO (TN)

Foradori
Via Damiano Chiesa, 1
38017 Mezzolombardo (TN)
Tel. 0461601046
E-mail: foradori@interline.it

Elisabetta Foradori has managed to transform a basically rustic wine like Teroldego into an immensely full, stylish and elegant red with great charm. That style becomes unmistakable when you pick up a glass of Granato, the Teroldego par excellence. It's so good that it swept the board of the competition, winning an effortless Three Glasses. The Granato '00 is a superb wine of wonderful purity and intensity. Deep, indeed almost shy on first contact, it slowly reveals itself as the aromas gradually come into focus. Wild berries and candied fruit make way for roasted hazelnuts, fresh baked bread, leather, eucalyptus and pomegranate, then the full, robust palate shows plenty of temptingly chewy flesh. But the admirable Elisabetta makes more than just Granato Teroldego. Again, the simpler version is a marvel and only "simpler" in a manner of speaking, given its concentration and impeccable elegance. Soft yet penetrating at the same time, its sweetness is backed up by supporting acidity that interweave magnificently. This year, Elisabetta did not submit any of her other reds but she did present the Myrto, a blend of pinot bianco with chardonnay and sauvignon. Delicate and intense, it's a typical Foradori wine.

NOGAREDO (TN)

Castel Noarna
Fraz. Noarna
Via Castelnuovo, 19
38060 Nogaredo (TN)
Tel. 0464413295 - 0464435222
E-mail: info@castelnoarna.com

Marco Zani's wines are vinified in a genuine 11th-century castle, set defensively high on the righthand bank of the river Adige, facing Rovereto. These bottles have dominated the scene in Trentino since their first release a decade or so ago. They are wines that are always in the running for our Three Glasses, such is their rich character and faithfulness to their native territory. The white Castelnuovo di Noarna, named after the castle, has been the best bottle to leave the cellars for a couple of vintages now. From a careful blend of chardonnay, riesling renano, traminer and sauvignon, it is a fruit-driven white, with a backdrop of apple, pineapple and bell pepper, that caresses palate with its full, creamy freshness. Though excellent, the 2001 is still obviously youthful. Try it again in a little while because it deserves to be left to age. A demonstration of the importance of patience can also be found in the Campograndé 1999, a really excellent Chardonnay that is still a tad fuzzy. In contrast, there were excellent results for the Bordeaux-style Romeo, the Mercuria, a lagrein-based red with cabernet and merlot, not to mention the Nosiola and the Sauvignon.

● Granato '00	🍷🍷🍷	7
● Teroldego Rotaliano '01	🍷🍷	4
○ Myrto '01	🍷🍷	5
● Granato '91	🍷🍷🍷	5
● Granato '93	🍷🍷🍷	5
● Granato '96	🍷🍷🍷	5
● Granato '99	🍷🍷🍷	5
● Teroldego Rotaliano '00	🍷🍷	4
● Ailanpa '99	🍷🍷	7
● Karanar '99	🍷🍷	7
● Granato '97	🍷🍷	5
● Granato '98	🍷🍷	5

○ Bianco di Castelnuovo '01	🍷🍷	5
● Mercuria Rosso '00	🍷🍷	5
● Romeo '99	🍷🍷	5
○ Trentino Chardonnay Campo Grande '99	🍷🍷	4
○ Nosiola '01	🍷	4
○ Sauvignon Atesino '01	🍷	5
○ Bianco di Castelnuovo '00	🍷🍷	4
○ Sauvignon Atesino '00	🍷🍷	4
● Trentino Cabernet Romeo '96	🍷🍷	4
● Trentino Cabernet Romeo '97	🍷🍷	5
● Trentino Cabernet Sauvignon Mercuria '97	🍷🍷	3
○ Trentino Nosiola '98	🍷🍷	3
○ Trentino Nosiola Casot '99	🍷🍷	4

NOMI (TN)

RICCARDO BATTISTOTTI
VIA 3 NOVEMBRE, 21
38060 NOMI (TN)
TEL. 0464834145
E-MAIL: mail@battistotti.com

Year after year, Elio, Enzo and Luciano Battistotti improve both their grape selections and the style of the wines. Their Marzemino, valley's emblematic wine, is a model of finesse combined with body, something few red wines can boast. The Battistotti family produces two Marzeminos. The traditional version is an easy-drinking wine, rich in fresh fruit. The second, with a new label designed by Trentino-based artist Pietro Verdini, brings out the real power of the variety, further enhancing the violet-tinged hue, the Parma violet aromas and the zesty raspberry and blackberry flavours. This classy Marzemino has what it takes to stay in the cellar for a few years yet, given its extractive weight and excellent vinification, managed by the oenologist in the family, Luciano. Another point of pride for the winery is the Moscato Rosa, whose latest version is also excellent. This rare but attractive wine has an elegant aroma profile and a harmonious, sweet flavour that is anything but cloying. The Battistotti's genuine devotion to Trentino winemaking traditions is even clear from the Chardonnay, a particularly fresh white that presents golden delicious apple on both nose and palate. The other two wines submitted to our tastings, the fresh, accessible standard-label Merlot, and a flavoursome Bordeaux blend called Savignam, were both very good.

●	Trentino Marzemino Verdini '01	ΨΨ	4
●	Trentino Moscato Rosa '01	ΨΨ	5
●	Rosso Savignam '00	Ψ	4
○	Trentino Chardonnay '01	Ψ	4
●	Trentino Marzemino '01	Ψ	3
●	Trentino Merlot '01	Ψ	3
●	Trentino Marzemino '00	ΨΨ	3*
●	Trentino Moscato Rosa '00	ΨΨ	5
●	Trentino Moscato Rosa '97	ΨΨ	5
●	Trentino Marzemino '98	ΨΨ	3

ROVERÈ DELLA LUNA (TN)

GAIERHOF
VIA IV NOVEMBRE, 51
38030 ROVERÈ DELLA LUNA (TN)
TEL. 0461658514
E-MAIL: informazioni@gaierhof.com

The Togns deserve to have two separate entries, one for the Roverè della Luna winery where for decades they have selected local grapes and produced wines under the Gajerhof label, and the other for their small but celebrated Maso Poli estate at Pressano, near Lavis. At Pressano, they produce wine and are planning several projects related to promoting in Trentino's Strada del Vino, or Wine Road. Gajerhof wines are aimed at a diversified market, both in Italy and abroad. In contrast, the few, carefully made bottles from Maso Poli are produced for a niche market. The Chardonnay Costa Erta turned out to be the best, vinified from grapes harvested on the steep slope that overlooks their hillside estate. A white aged in oak, it has a deep hue and equally profound ripe fruit aromas of apple and pineapple, followed by a full, soft palate with a long finish. The Sorni Bianco is very well made from nosiola, chardonnay and müller thurgau. The Pinot Nero, also from Maso Poli, is elegant and austere with very good nose-palate consistency. The Müller Thurgau from the Settecento selection stands out among the dozen or so wines labelled Gajerhof, all from grapes harvested at more than 700 metres above sea level. In closing, we are happy to say that the pleasantly dry Riesling Italico, typical Pinot Grigio and fresh Teroldego Rotaliano are all well made.

○	Trentino Chardonnay Costa Erta '01	ΨΨ	4
○	Trentino Müller Thurgau dei Settecento '01	ΨΨ	4
●	Trentino Pinot Nero Maso Poli '00	Ψ	4
○	Trentino Pinot Grigio '01	Ψ	4
○	Trentino Riesling Italico '01	Ψ	4
○	Trentino Sorni Bianco Maso Poli '01	Ψ	4
○	Trentino Chardonnay Costa Erta '00	ΨΨ	4
○	Trentino Sorni Bianco Maso Poli '00	ΨΨ	4
○	Trentino Müller Thurgau dei Settecento '99	ΨΨ	4
○	Trentino Pinot Grigio Maso Poli '99	ΨΨ	4

ROVERETO (TN)

Nicola Balter
Via Vallunga II, 24
38068 Rovereto (TN)
Tel. 0464430101

The Balter cellar offered us four very good wines, with outstanding personality. All are very well made. This, in a nutshell, is the panel's opinion regarding the wines from Nicola Balter, a skilful, experienced producer and remarkable innovator. Few other estates are as scenic as the one managed by Balter, situated above Rovereto, with vineyards "torn", as it were, from the forests and with excellent exposure to the sun. So it is no accident that the Barbanico, a blend of merlot, lagrein and cabernet sauvignon, is one of the best wines in Trentino. As opulently concentrated in its colour as it is on nose and palate, its lagrein contributes alcohol and body, firming the Bordeaux style of the other varieties. In short, Barbanico is an increasingly convincing symbol of oenological developments in Trentino. The Cabernet Sauvignon is also stylistically impeccable and is another wine that never fails to distinguish itself at our tastings. The deep colour, broad, refined aromas and youthful acidity that supports its caressing softness. If the reds are characterized by power, then the whites show grace and delicacy. The Sauvignon has attractive, very varietal aromas with a pleasant note of elderflower and a finish that is as simple as it is alluring. The "spumante classico" also shows off all its enviable vitality in a golden colour, from the chardonnay base, creamy, persistent mousse, and full-bodied, fragrant flavour.

●	Barbanico '99	🍷🍷	5
●	Cabernet Sauvignon '00	🍷🍷	5
○	Sauvignon '01	🍷🍷	4
○	Trento Brut	🍷🍷	5
●	Barbanico '97	🍷🍷🍷	5
●	Barbanico '98	🍷🍷	5
○	Sauvignon '00	🍷🍷	4
●	Trentino Cabernet Sauvignon '96	🍷🍷	4
●	Trentino Cabernet Sauvignon '97	🍷🍷	4
●	Cabernet Sauvignon '98	🍷🍷	4

ROVERETO (TN)

Conti Bossi Fedrigotti
Via Unione, 43
38068 Rovereto (TN)
Tel. 0464439250
E-mail: info@fedrigotti.it

With more than 400 vintages behind it, Conti Bossi Fedrigotti is one of the oldest Italian wineries. For a couple of harvests now, the estate has been managed by Gianpaolo, Maria José, and Isabella (also a well-known writer), the three children of the present count, Federico, the last great winemaking innovator of this heralded dynasty. Maria José, known as Pupi, was the one who decided to revolutionize management. She began renewing the vineyards, around 40 hectares located in the best areas in the valley, and chose one of Italy's leading oenologists, Luca D'Attoma, as winemaker. Results were quick in coming. The entire range of wines made the leap in quality that Conti Bossi Fedrigotti deserved. The Marzemino is archetypal, one of the few that clearly stands out from the rest. An elegantly accessible wine, it has an intense violet colour and intriguing palate, with the right note of bitterness, as befits a true Rovereto-made Marzemino. The other four whites from 2001 were also impressive, the vintage linked with the "rebirth". The Chardonnay is easy and clean yet exemplary in its technique. The Pinot Grigio is flavoursome and inviting, while the Traminer is a touch uncertain on the palate, although the seductively spicy aroma is well-sustained. The blended white Fojaneghe takes its cue from the sinew of the chardonnay and the aromas of traminer. It put on an excellent performance.

○	Fojaneghe Bianco '01	🍷🍷	4
●	Trentino Marzemino '01	🍷🍷	3
○	Trentino Chardonnay '01	🍷	3
○	Trentino Pinot Grigio '01	🍷	3
○	Trentino Traminer Aromatico '01	🍷	3
●	Trentino Marzemino '00	🍷	3
●	Fojaneghe Rosso '98	🍷	4

ROVERETO (TN)

Letrari
Via Monte Baldo, 13/15
38068 Rovereto (TN)
tel. 0464480200
e-mail: info@letrari.it

The Letrari family has chosen to take up the gauntlet thrown down by Terra dei Forti, the group that brings together many small growers and makers in the zone from Avio to Affi. Results were not long in coming in the shape of an excellent red called Enantio, from lambrusco a foglia frastagliata, which amazed us with its backbone, fragrance and admirably full body. The other 13 wines submitted for tasting also made a good showing. The Ballistarius, a red from cabernet, merlot and lagrein, has lovely aromatic fullness, with notes of ripe fruit, blackcurrant and tamarind, then a splendidly rich flavour on the palate. The Marzemino is always a fine example of typicity. The Fossa Bandita, a blend of chardonnay, pinot bianco and pinot grigio with a percentage of Incrocio Manzoni, has a great bouquet. Speaking of blends, the Maso Lodron, a Bordeaux blend, has decent body and a very fresh finish. The two versions of "spumante classico", the Brut and Riserva, again show just how delicious they are. In closing, the Moscato Rosa has delightful notes of wild roses and is sweet, warm and caressing on the palate. The Marzemino is nicely made and very pleasant.

ROVERETO (TN)

Longariva
Fraz. Borgo Sacco
Via R. Zandonai, 6
38068 Rovereto (TN)
tel. 0464437200
e-mail: info@longariva.it

Here are the results from our tastings at Longariva: three wines made the final taste-offs and the others were just as good. Marco Manica presented a resounding Pinot Bianco and an enchanting Chardonnay, wines that represent the best Trentino has to offer in their respective categories. The Pinot Bianco is fruit-led, fresh and accessible, although it is also very concentrated and could improve further with careful bottle ageing. The Chardonnay Praistél is equally valid. Its intense yellow offers up seductive spicy aromas and lovely breadth of fruit on both nose and palate. The Migoléta is an exclusive wine, partly because a very limited number of bottles are produced of this late-harvest product from aromatic white grapes. Its vibrant white gold accompanies spicy aromas and then the opulent flavour of honey and candied fruit. The Tovi, a monovarietal Merlot, is another great wine but pays the price of that 1998 vintage, which was not one of the best. We felt the Marognon was a model Trentino Cabernet and will need leisurely ageing in bottle to unveil its power. The rest of the range included good, Bordeaux-blend Tre Cesure, the ever attractive pinot grigio-based Graminè, is always pleasant, with its nose redolent of mountain-grown pears. The Marzemino is very flavoursome.

● Ballistarius '99	♛♛	5
● Trentino Marzemino '01	♛♛	4
● Trentino Moscato Rosa '00	♛♛	6
○ Trento Brut Ris. '97	♛♛	4*
○ Trento Brut	♛♛	4*
○ Fossa Bandita '01	♛	4
● Terre dei Forti Enantio '00	♛	4
● Trentino Rosso Maso Lodron '00	♛	6
● Ballistarius '97	♛♛	5
● Ballistarius '98	♛♛	5
○ Fossa Bandita '00	♛♛	4
● Trentino Cabernet Sauvignon '96	♛♛	4
● Trentino Marzemino Sel. '99	♛♛	4
● Trentino Marzemino Sel. '00	♛♛	4

○ Trentino Chardonnay Praistel '00	♛♛	5
○ Trentino Pinot Bianco Pergole '01	♛♛	4
○ Migoléta '98	♛♛	6
○ Pinot Grigio Graminè '01	♛♛	4
● Trentino Merlot Tovi '98	♛♛	4
● Trentino Cabernet Sauvignon Marognon '99	♛♛	5
● Trentino Rosso Tre Cesure '99	♛♛	5
○ Trentino Pinot Bianco Pergole '99	♛♛♛	3
○ Trentino Pinot Bianco Pergole '00	♛♛	4
● Trentino Cabernet Sauvignon Marognon Ris. '97	♛♛	4
● Trentino Merlot Tovi '97	♛♛	5
● Trentino Rosso Tre Cesure Sel. 25° '97	♛♛	5
● Trentino Cabernet Sauvignon Marognon Ris. '98	♛♛	5

ROVERETO (TN)

ARMANDO SIMONCELLI
VIA NAVICELLO, 7
38068 ROVERETO (TN)
TEL. 0464432373

Armando Simoncelli's wines produced inconsistent results this time. 2001 was an odd vintage because of the bizarre pre-harvest weather. This affected not only the whites but also the Marzemino, Armando's signature wine. Armando's Marzemino always turns out to be one of the most sincere, authentic wines from Vallagarina but it is precisely the innate freshness of the fruit that exposes it to the effects of the weather more than other wines. This Marzemino is less full-bodied than usual, with gentle notes of flowers and a slightly bitter entry on the palate that ruffles the overall profile, although the typically tasty characteristics of the variety come back in the persistent finish. The international-style Navesèl is rather better and much more solid. It's a Bordeaux blend whose aromas are rich in minerals, as well as echoes of chocolate and oriental spices. Deep and warm in the mouth, it marries rigorous structure and pleasant softness. The other red wines are still a bit vegetal, all things considered. The Lagrein has an attractive, easy drinkability, with freshness and fragrance underneath. The Cabernet Franc is a bit more challenging but is still very likeable. Best of the whites are the Chardonnay and Pinot Bianco but the Pinot Grigio is less impressive. In closing, the fresh "spumante classico" is ideal for uncorking with a few convivial companions and in fact Simoncelli makes it almost exclusively to drink in the company of friends or visitors to the cellar.

● Trentino Rosso Navesèl '99	▼▼	4
● Trentino Cabernet '01	▼	4
○ Trentino Chardonnay '01	▼	4
● Trentino Lagrein '01	▼	3
● Trentino Marzemino '01	▼	4
○ Trentino Pinot Bianco '01	▼	3
○ Trento Brut '98	▼	4
○ Trentino Pinot Grigio '01		3
● Trentino Marzemino '00	▼▼	3*
○ Trentino Pinot Bianco '00	▼▼	3*
● Trentino Lagrein '98	▼▼	3
● Trentino Marzemino '98	▼▼	3
● Trentino Marzemino '99	▼▼	3

SAN MICHELE ALL'ADIGE (TN)

ISTITUTO AGRARIO PROVINCIALE
SAN MICHELE ALL'ADIGE
VIA EDMONDO MACH, 1
38010 SAN MICHELE ALL'ADIGE (TN)
TEL. 0461615252 - 0461615253
E-MAIL: cantina@ismaa.it

San Michele is the perhaps the most famous agricultural school specializing in oenology in Italy. This research and training institute boasts many decades experience and is the pride and joy of the Trento provincial authority. The school's cellar was built in a former monastery and the barrels are kept in a especially interesting environment. The new red in the range, Il Monastero, is specifically dedicated to this unique place. Obtained from diversified clones of specially cultivated cabernet franc, this wine caught the panel's attention with its pleasant blackberry jam and cocoa powder aromas, and a full, complex, lingering palate. The Castel San Michele is a purple red with vivid highlights, clean bouquet, and lean-bodied but gutsy and nicely concentrated palate. This wine was also, in 1964, the first Bordeaux blend to be aged in small oak casks in Trentino. The winemaking and growing experiments and skills of director of oenology, Enrico Paternoster, have prompted the school to produce another exciting wine, the Prepositura, from various aromatic grape varieties harvested when very ripe. A soft wine, it has sweetness nicely balanced by acidity. The other wines are all more than decent. We would like to mention the Chardonnay and Pinot Grigio, along with the "riserva" version of a still young "spumante classico", dedicated to the founder of the school, Edmondo Mach.

● Trentino Rosso Monastero '00	▼▼	5
● Trentino Rosso Castel San Michele '00	▼▼	4
○ Prepositura '01	▼▼	5
○ Trentino Chardonnay '01	▼▼	4
○ Trentino Pinot Grigio '01	▼▼	4
○ Trento Riserva del Fondatore '99	▼▼	5
○ Trentino Pinot Bianco '00	▼▼	4
○ Trentino Bianco Castel San Michele '00	▼▼	4
● Trentino Rosso Castel San Michele '00	▼▼	4
○ Trentino Sauvignon '00	▼▼	3
○ Trentino Chardonnay '00	▼	3
○ Trentino Pinot Grigio '00	▼	3

SAN MICHELE ALL'ADIGE (TN)   TRENTO

ZENI
FRAZ. GRUMO
VIA STRETTA, 2
38010 SAN MICHELE ALL'ADIGE (TN)
TEL. 0461650456
E-MAIL: robezen@tin.it

ABATE NERO
SPONDA TRENTINA, 45
FRAZ. GARDOLO
38014 TRENTO
TEL. 0461246566
E-MAIL: cavit@cavit.it

Brothers Andrea and Roberto Zeni have taken a flyer on their Teroldego Rotaliano Riserva, called Pini. They want to make a red that will celebrate their 30-year career as growers, cellarmasters and distillers. But dedication and skill are not always rewarded in kind. The Pini is one of the best Teroldegos on the market, even if the 1998 vintage failed to exploit the two years of barrique ageing and 12 months in bottle, keeping the wine from expressing all its qualities. In contrast, the Sortì is a wine from pinot bianco that involves you immediately. Fresh on the nose, with intense notes that recall anise and aromas of gunflint and golden apple, it expands remarkably in the mouth and will get even better with cellar time. The standard-label Teroldego is very fruity and bright, with a dynamic quality reminiscent of a "vin nouveau". The Moscato Rosa turned out to be very pleasant. It is a deliberately less concentrated version than usual, to make it more approachable despite its noble breeding. Moving on to the whites, we enjoyed a Sauvignon with body and character. The Pinot Grigio is a copper-tinged onionskin, and though not too assertive on the nose, it is nonetheless a decent, easy to drink and well-made wine. The same goes for the Nosiola and Müller Thurgau. The latter is approachable, with aromas reminiscent of lemon verbena.

This winery is named after the legendary French abbot, Dom Pérignon, considered to be the "father of champagne", to underline its aim of making solely and exclusively "spumante classico". We are just outside Trento, on the road to Lavis, where the Abate Nero cellar, founded by a group of wine technicians from several co-operative wineries, has been operating for almost 30 years. It is run in a family style and pays little attention to production numbers. Even now, the winery continues to stick to its original formula – making only top quality sparklers. The Abate Nero range of "spumante" wines is vast. The sparklers are left to age slowly on the yeasts. Then begins the uncompromising selection of the cuvées, generally with a base of chardonnay, pinot bianco and pinot nero. Patience is one of the cardinal virtues of sparkling wine production. In addition to the traditional pleasantly acidulous, fresh and accessible Brut, we tasted a very captivating Extra Brut version that reveals a lovely refermentation, with just the right hint of yeast and a clean fragrance. There was also an Extra Dry wine that is as pleasant as it is unusual, tempting the palate with its slightly sweet flavour. The Riserva 1998 is a highly satisfying, textbook Talento Trento DOC "spumante", left to age slowly on the yeasts to guarantee a wine that has backbone, a rich mousse and also elegance.

O	Trentino Pinot Bianco Sortì '01	ΨΨ	4
O	Pinot Grigio Ramato '01	Ψ	4
●	Teroldego Rotaliano '01	Ψ	4
●	Trentino Moscato Rosa '01	Ψ	6
O	Trentino Müller Thurgau '01	Ψ	4
O	Trentino Nosiola '01	Ψ	4
O	Trentino Sauvignon '01	Ψ	4
●	Teroldego Rotaliano Pini '98	Ψ	5
O	Trentino Pinot Bianco Sortì '00	ΨΨ	3
O	Trento Brut M. Cl. '93	ΨΨ	4
O	Trento Brut M. Cl. '95	ΨΨ	4
●	Teroldego Rotaliano Pini '97	ΨΨ	5
●	Trentino Pinot Nero Spiazol '98	ΨΨ	4
O	Trentino Müller Thurgau Le Croci '99	ΨΨ	3
O	Trentino Pinot Bianco Sortì '99	ΨΨ	3

O	Trento Brut Ris. '98	ΨΨ	5
O	Trento Extra Brut	ΨΨ	4
O	Trento Brut	Ψ	4
O	Trento Extra Dry	Ψ	4
O	Trento Brut Ris. '87	ΨΨ	6
O	Trento Brut Ris. '88	ΨΨ	6

TRENTO

Cavit - Consorzio di Cantine Sociali
Fraz. Ravina
Via del Ponte, 31
38040 Trento
tel. 0461381711
e-mail: cavit@cavit.it

For a couple of vintages now, the colossal Càvit group has been relaunching its "masi" project, which involves selecting grapes from smallholdings, known locally as "masi", managed by individual member growers who follow precise regulations and apply the recommendations of technical staff provided by the company. It's a quality-targeted effort that goes all the way from vineyard to cellar. But let's get on to the wines. The Graal '95 "spumante" just misses out on Three Glasses but is still one of the finest quality Trento DOC sparkling wines. Its complex, aromas embrace sensations of crusty bread, vanilla and hawthorn-themed flowers, leading to a delicate palate with a creamy mousse, notes of hazelnuts and pistachio, and length in the finish that is in a class by itself. But there were other, equally attractive, wines to enjoy. The Müller Thurgau from the Bottega de' Vinai selection has fragrances typical of the variety and inviting body. The Marzemino Maso Romani is a complete red. Aged for longer, it combines a pleasant Parma violet bouquet with a discreet, full flavour in the mouth. And to round off, there was another flavoursome wine, the Lagrein Dunkel, which is very fresh and enjoyable. However, the other blended wines will have to grow. These are the Cuvée Maso Torresella and, especially, the Quattro Vicariati, a Bordeaux-style wine that you will hear much more about very soon.

TRENTO

★ **Ferrari**
Fraz. Ravina
Via Ponte di Ravina, 15
38040 Trento
tel. 0461972311
e-mail: info@cantineferrari.it

Last year, Ferrari won yet another top award with its Riserva del Fondatore but the clink of a third Glass was very close for the Perlé. And this year, it was the '98 vintage Ferrari Perlé that again came close to picking up some big-time stemware. The result was meticulously created by Mauro Lunelli and involved the entire production chain, because the Perlé is the pride and joy of the winery, a "spumante" that reconciles quantity and a production that runs to around 700,000 bottles each year with high quality. But the Lunellis have always aimed for top-quality products. This year, they postponed the release of the Riserva del Fondatore '94, and we have that great Perlé, made exclusively from chardonnay. The very fine, consistent and long-lasting mousse introduces aromas of fruit and vine flowers that mingle with yeast and delicious toasty notes on the nose, to be followed by a creamy, soft, persistent palate. The other Ferrari sparklers also racked up excellent scores, beginning with the traditional Brut, a fresh-tasting, joyfully attractive wine. The Maximum is more structured, with ripe fruit aromas that bring to mind plum and apple, then a tangy, dry, harmonious palate. There's more. The Incontri is a "spumante" designed to be captivating and easily approachable while the other vintage wine from the house of Lunelli, the Perlé Rosé, is in a class by itself. Its pinot nero base delivers aromatic concentration and remarkable nose-palate consistency.

○	Trento Graal '95	🍷🍷	5
●	Trentino Lagrein Dunkel Bottega de' Vinai '00	🍷🍷	4
●	Trentino Marzemino Maso Romani '00	🍷🍷	5
○	Trentino Müller Thurgau Bottega de' Vinai '01	🍷🍷	4
●	Trentino Rosso Quattro Vicariati '98	🍷	5
○	Trentino Vino Santo Aréle '94	🍷🍷	8
○	Maso Torresella Cuvée '00	🍷🍷	5
○	Trentino Chardonnay Bottega de' Vinai '00	🍷🍷	4
●	Teroldego Rotaliano Maso Cervara '97	🍷🍷	4
○	Trento Brut Firmato mill. '97	🍷🍷	4*
●	Maso Torresella '98	🍷🍷	5
●	Teroldego Rotaliano Bottega de' Vinai '99	🍷	3

○	Trento Brut Perlé '98	🍷🍷	6
⊙	Trento Brut Perlé Rosé '98	🍷🍷	6
○	Trento Brut Incontri	🍷🍷	5
○	Trento Brut Maximum	🍷🍷	5
○	Trento Brut	🍷	5
○	Giulio Ferrari '86	🍷🍷🍷	8
○	Giulio Ferrari '88	🍷🍷🍷	8
○	Giulio Ferrari '89	🍷🍷🍷	8
○	Giulio Ferrari '90	🍷🍷🍷	8
○	Giulio Ferrari '91	🍷🍷🍷	8
○	Giulio Ferrari '92	🍷🍷🍷	8
○	Giulio Ferrari '93	🍷🍷🍷	8
○	Trento Brut Perlé '97	🍷🍷	5
○	Trento Brut Perlé '95	🍷🍷	5
○	Trento Brut Perlé '96	🍷🍷	5

TRENTO

LUNELLI
FRAZ. RAVINA
VIA PONTE DI RAVINA, 15
38040 TRENTO
TEL. 0461972311

There were only four wines from this cellar but all are decidedly good. These new Lunelli estates have shifted the goalposts of winemaking in Trentino. In just a few harvests, Mauro Lunelli has also produced flattering results with his still wines. The one that impressed us the most was the Villa Margon, a white from a chardonnay base with small percentages of pinot bianco, sauvignon and Incrocio Manzoni. It has the same great charm as the lovely villa whose name it carries, once the residence of emperor Charles V. It combines the aromas of rennet apples and sage with an acid backbone that is offset by the roundness of the alcohol. The Villa San Nicolò is also fresh and accessible. A monovarietal Sauvignon, from various clonal selections of grapes, it is gold in the glass. The dense, vibrant hue introduces well-defined, upfront aromas, and a fresh tang of acidity on the palate. The flavour of the Villa Gentilotti, a Chardonnay "riserva" also has plenty of structure and strength. Finally, the Maso Le Viane is developing well. A Bordeaux blend, it progresses convincingly on the palate.

TRENTO

MASO MARTIS
LOC. MARTIGNANO
VIA DELL'ALBERA, 52
38040 TRENTO
TEL. 0461821057
E-MAIL: masomartis@tin.it

Antonio Stelzer has distinguished himself once again with his "spumante". The wine that did the business is the Riserva '98, from pinot nero and chardonnay. It has class, a very elegant range of aromas and a clean, full flavour that recalls those famous apples from Trentino on the back palate. Stelzer is also a top sparkling wine-maker, as he shows with another Brut, which is more immediate but still shows lovely density and a soft, almost silky profile. This elegant, discreet production style can even be felt in the third "mosso", or slightly sparkling, wine, a great Rosé, made exclusively from pinot nero, and a sparkler that still has to evolve to reach its best. Although Stelzer is first and foremost a "spumante" man, he also harvests grapes for more traditional wines. The Chardonnay regales the nose with pineapple and just picked fruit, developing on the palate with serious extract, a full, velvety mouthfeel and good acidity. The colour of the Pinot Nero is not as deep as you might expect but then it offers those classic aromas of wild berries and follows this with good thrust and flavour. The other cellar flagship bottle is the Moscato Rosa, which shows all its finesse in its spice, moderately deep colour, and good depth on the nose of small wild roses and raspberries. The sweetish palate has a faintly bitter twist in the finish.

○ Trentino Chardonnay Villa Margon '01	⍩⍩	4
○ Trentino Sauvignon Villa San Nicolò '01	⍩⍩	4
○ Trentino Chardonnay Villa Gentilotti '99	⍩⍩	5
● Trentino Rosso Maso Le Viane '99	⍩⍩	6
○ Trentino Chardonnay Villa Margon '00	⍩⍩	4
○ Trentino Sauvignon Villa San Nicolò '00	⍩⍩	5
● Trentino Pinot Nero Maso Montalto '97	⍩⍩	4
● Trentino Rosso Maso Le Viane '97	⍩⍩	5
○ Trentino Chardonnay Villa Gentilotti '98	⍩⍩	4
○ Trentino Chardonnay Villa Margon '98	⍩⍩	4
● Trentino Rosso Maso Le Viane '98	⍩⍩	5
● Trentino Pinot Nero Maso Montalto '99	⍩⍩	5

○ Trento Brut Ris. '98	⍩⍩	5
○ Trentino Chardonnay '01	⍩	4
● Trentino Pinot Nero '00	⍩	5
● Moscato Rosa '01	⍩	5
○ Trento Brut	⍩	4
⊙ Trento Brut Rosé	⍩	4
○ Sole d'Autunno '00	⍩	5
○ Trentino Chardonnay L'Incanto '00	⍩	4

TRENTO

VIGNETI DELLE MERIDIANE
LOC. AL CASTELLER, 6
38100 TRENTO
TEL. 0461920811 - 0464419343
E-MAIL: vigneti@vignetimeridiane.it

The vine-covered hill of Casteller at Trento is a symbolic element of the city's scenery. The Vigneti delle Meridiane winery has been operating here for some years now. Created by the collaboration of the Trento co-operative and a group of businessmen, it is effectively controlled by the Concilio Vini winery of Volano. However, vineyard cultivation and vinification of the grapes are managed independently. The younger wines turned out to be the most exciting and also representative of the entire Adige river valley. The Bastie Pinot Grigio selection is fruit-driven and fresh, with an attractively bitter finish. The Chardonnay vineyard selection, Ravina, is very deliciously tangy, flavoursome and elegant, with good all-round definition. Although the whites did well, we felt the reds were even better. The Cabernet San Bartolomeo, from another vineyard on the slope south of the city and not far from the winery, and the Merlot both showed their class again this year. In both cases, the best features are an attractive nose and a mouthfilling roundness on the palate, even if the vegetal note that affects so many wines from Trento is evident here as well, coming through with a certain insistence on both nose and palate.

○	Trentino Chardonnay Ravina '01	4
●	Trentino Merlot Ravina '01	4
○	Trentino Pinot Grigio Bastie '01	4
●	Teroldego Atesino Cernidor '99	4
●	Trentino Cabernet Sauvignon Vigneto San Bartolomeo Ris. '99	4
●	Teroldego Atesino Cernidor '96	4
●	Teroldego Atesino Cernidor '97	4
○	Trentino Chardonnay '00	4

VOLANO (TN)

CONCILIO
ZONA INDUSTRIALE, 2
38060 VOLANO (TN)
TEL. 0464411000
E-MAIL: concilio@concilio.it

Concilio Vini has contributed, and continues to contribute, to the "conciliation" (pardon the pun) of supply and demand for good Trentino wine through a production and distribution structure that has expanded beyond the boundaries of the region, for example to Sicily, where it vinifies Feudo D'Elimi. This well-planned policy calls for wines that are good value for money and closely tied to territorial traditions. Wines like the Mori Vecio, in fact, a historic blend from Trentino that has been around for almost 40 years. Its blackberry and raspberry bouquet is interwoven with vanillaed notes, then the nice palate has good balance. Another 11 wines were submitted to the panel for tasting and all of them were worth a place in the Guide. For reasons of space, we will mention only the most representative. We felt another three reds from 1999, the Pinot Nero, Merlot and Cabernet Sauvignon, were all successful, both on nose and palate, showing fullness and attractive balance. The Marzemino is well worth investigating. The selection is dedicated to Mozart, in appreciation of his citation of wine in his celebrated opera, Don Giovanni. It's a light, headily fragrant red. The Enantio, a wine type other cellars in the lower Vallagarina are investing in, is also very nice. Finally, the whites included a well-made Chardonnay and a nice Pinot Grigio, both Maso Guà selections.

●	Trentino Rosso Mori Vecio '99	5
●	Enantio '00	4
●	Trentino Marzemino Mozart '00	4
●	Trentino Cabernet Sauvignon '99	4
●	Trentino Merlot '99	4
●	Trentino Pinot Nero '99	4
○	Trentino Pinot Grigio Maso Guà '01	3*
○	Trentino Chardonnay Maso Guà '01	3*

VOLANO (TN)

MASO BASTIE
LOC. BASTIE
38070 VOLANO (TN)
TEL. 0464412747

The Torellis from Volano have been cultivating their vineyards for several generations. But Giuseppe Torelli and his wife Patrizia Pizzini have only been vinifying the grapes from them for a short while. Their 15 or so hectares of magnificent vineyards are set in the midst of some delightful, fairy-tale castles. A model estate, Maso Bastie has in very short time earned an important place among the top wineries in Trentino. The range includes mainly sweet, aromatic wines with a very personal style. The Torellis are among the few growers who partially dry some of their fruit, leaving the bunches in special drying lofts, "air conditioned" exclusively by the local breezes. For a couple of years now, our tastings have been recording the quality of the Traminer from this winery. Deep-hued, it is very flavoursome, fruit-rich and full-bodied, with exceptional length. The Edys is also excellent. A white dessert wine, it is obtained from moscato giallo, traminer and chardonnay, part of which is left to become super-ripe on the vine and part raisined on special racks. This wine has attractively dense extract and great flavour on the palate. Drinking nicely now, it is also capable evolving very positively. The Moscato Rosa is another jewel in this winery's crown. Both nose and palate are very successful and the finish is long. The Torellis also produce a red Bordeaux blend that will be ready in a couple of years.

● Moscato Rosa '00	🍷🍷	5
○ Trentino Traminer '01	🍷🍷	5
○ Edys '00	🍷	5
○ Edys '99	🍷🍷	4
● Moscato Rosa '99	🍷🍷	5

VOLANO (TN)

EUGENIO ROSI
VIA TAVERNELLE, 3/B
38060 VOLANO (TN)
TEL. 0464461375
E-MAIL: Eamaramar@virgilio.it

Eugenio Rosi is a young, professional producer with innovative ideas for both vineyards and cellar. For example, he has experimented with a pergola-type training system that he has transformed into a kind of Guyot with wire supports. After graduating in oenology, he worked at a couple of co-operative wineries. But for the past five harvests, he has done everything himself. He and his wife Tamara tend five hectares in the hills of Volano and vinify the fruit in a cellar in Isera that belongs to a friend. Eugenio then he ages his wines in the historic Palazzo de Martin at Calliano, another winemaking village in Vallagarina. This oenological triangulation, as it were, on the banks of the river Adige has given his wines an originality that goes against the trend. We'll begin with the sweet Marzemino, vinified from grapes left to raisin on rush mats. It's a very delicate, soft, moderately sweet red that is also endowed with solid structure. The technique of raisining the grapes was also used in Eugenio's version of the traditional Marzemino. After raisining, he leaves the wine to age for almost a year in barrels of seven and a half hectolitres, made of different kinds of wood, including cherry. This particular wine will only be released in the spring of 2003. Eugenio only makes a few bottles of his sweet Marzemino Dòron, a "gift" of nature named after the Greek word for "gift". Finally, his attention is also concentrated on Esegesi, a no-nonsense Bordeaux blend with a full flavour and lots of style.

● Dòron '00	🍷🍷	7
● Trentino Rosso Esegesi '99	🍷🍷	5
● Poiema Marzemino dei Ziresi '00	🍷🍷	5
● Trentino Rosso Esegesi '98	🍷🍷	5

OTHER WINERIES

Madonna delle Vittorie
Via Linfano, 81
38062 Arco (TN)
tel. 0464505432

Better wines with bigger flavour – that sums up the performance of the range presented this year by the Mandelli estate. The Brut spumante is very good, in fact one of the best around. The Sommolago white is interesting and will improve with cellar time.

○ Trento Brut '97	♉♉	5
○ Trentino Bianco Sommolago '01	♉	4
○ Trentino Chardonnay '01	♉	3
○ Trentino Pinot Grigio '01	♉	4

Pelz & Piffer
Via Carraia, 16
38034 Cembra (TN)
tel. 0461683051

This small but very focused estate on the vine-covered hill of Lavis is one to watch. The two winemaker owners specialize in producing Müller Thurgau, Riesling and Pinot Nero. Just three wines and only a few thousand bottles, but they are all deliciously well-made.

○ Trentino Riesling '00	♉	4
○ Müller Thurgau '01	♉	3
● Trentino Pinot Nero '99	♉	4

Accademia del Vino Cadelaghet
Via Roma, 13
38045 Civezzano (TN)
tel. 0461859045
e-mail: info@accademiadelvino.it

The Accademia del Vino Cadelaghet is an interesting experimental initiative that puts very individual wines on the market year after year. One of these is the Marzemino. It's harmonious, youthfully alcoholic and more concentrated than many others.

● Trentino Marzemino '00	♉	4
○ Trento Accademia Ris. '97	♉	5

Arcangelo Sandri
Via Vaneggie, 4
38010 Faedo (TN)
tel. 0461650935
e-mail: sand_arca@libero.it

The Sandri winery has always been one of the most professional in Faedo and the compact estate boasts some of the finest hillslope vineyards in the area.
Arcangelo's most interesting wine is the Traminer, though the others, the Müller Thurgau, Chardonnay and the challenging Lagrein, are also good.

○ Trentino Traminer Aromatico '01	♉♉	3*
● Trentino Lagrein '00	♉	4
○ Trentino Chardonnay '01	♉	3
○ Trentino Müller Thurgau '01	♉	3

Cantina d'Isera
Via al Ponte, 1
38060 Isera (TN)
tel. 0464433795
e-mail: info@cantinaisera.it

The harvest this year gave less than usually satisfactory results. The only real success was the excellent Marzemino Etichetta Verde, one of the best of its type. The base Marzemino is good, as are the Chardonnay and Sentieri Bordeaux. The estate is currently making radical changes in the vineyards.

● Trentino Marzemino Etichetta Verde '01	♆	4
● Trentino Rosso Sentieri Sel. 907 '99	♆	4

Casata Monfort
Via Carlo Sette, 21
38015 Lavis (TN)
tel. 0461241484
e-mail: casatamonfort@tin.it

These dozen or so Monfort wines are all technically well-made, full-flavoured and ready to drink. The spicy, harmonious Traminer, the Teroldego Rotaliano, and the two sweet wines, the Moscato Giallo and Moscato Rosa, are particularly tempting.

○ Monfort Giallo '01	♆	4
⊙ Monfort Rosa '01	♆	5
● Teroldego Rotaliano '01	♆	4
○ Trentino Traminer Aromatico '01	♆	4

Cipriano Fedrizzi
Via 4 Novembre, 1
38017 Mezzolombardo (TN)
tel. 0461602328

Only the tiny numbers of bottles released keep this winery from competing as a major player at the top of the Teroldego market. The Due Vigneti, as their elegant, soft and powerful selection is called, is a delight. The other wines are good, too.

● Teroldego Rotaliano Due Vigneti '00	♆♆	5
● Teroldego Rotaliano '00	♆	4
● Trentino Lagrein '00	♆	5

Villa de Varda
Via Rotaliana, 27/a
38017 Mezzolombardo (TN)
tel. 0461601486
e-mail: villadevarda@villadevarda.com

A careful selection of wines, presented with the names of their respective vineyards of origin, confirms the talents of this constantly progressing winery. All ten wines we tasted deserve attention but special mentions go to the Teroldego Riserva and a very good Marzemino.

● Trentino Marzemino Albarel '01	♆	4
○ Trentino Müller Thurgau Roncola '01	♆	3
● Teroldego Rotaliano Ris. '99	♆	4

Zanini
Via De Gasperi, 42
38017 Mezzolombardo (TN)
tel. 0461601496
e-mail: zaninoscar@jumpy.it

Zanini has established itself as one of the most interesting Teroldego Rotaliano cellars for its small quantities of dependable quality wine. There are two versions of the zone's signature red, including a very good Riserva with great typicity and balance.

● Teroldego Rotaliano Le Cervare Ris. '00	♆♆	5
● Teroldego Rotaliano '01	♆	3

Grigoletti
Via Garibaldi, 12
38060 Nomi (TN)
tel. 0464834215
e-mail: grigolettivini@tin.it

This family cellar has been turning out premium-quality bottles for several years now. The wines are mainly red, Merlot and Marzemino, but there's also a very full, well-rounded and cellarable Chardonnay. The Retiko, a white blend, is another very pleasant wine.

● Trentino Merlot Antica Vigna di Nomi '00	♆♆	4
○ Retiko '00	♆	4
○ Trentino Chardonnay L'Opera '01	♆	4
● Trentino Marzemino '01	♆	3

Cantina Sociale di Nomi
Via Roma, 1
38060 Nomi (TN)
tel. 0464834195
e-mail: cantinanomi@tin.it

The Nomi co-operative has a range that looks a little on the broad side and a few years ago, they also launched a project in Sicily. The wines show structure and typicity. The Marzemino and Merlot are as tasty as ever and the two blends, the Resorso Rosso and Resorso Bianco, are again good.

●	Trentino Merlot Antichi Portali '00 🍷	3
○	Trentino Bianco Résorso Le Comete '01 🍷	4
●	Trentino Marzemino '01 🍷	3

Dalzocchio
Loc. Bosco della Città
Via Vallelunga Seconda, 50
38068 Rovereto (TN)
tel. 0464423580 - 0464413664

Dalzocchio is a micro-estate on the hill of Rovereto, run by a winemaker committed to producing only wines with lots of personality. The two wines presented, both Chardonnays, are interesting, flavourful and admirably concentrated.

○	Trentino Chardonnay '00 🍷🍷	5
○	Chardonnay Dalzocchio '00 🍷	5

Endrizzi
Loc. Masetto, 2
38010 San Michele all'Adige (TN)
tel. 0461650129
e-mail: info@endrizzi.it

Things were difficult this year for the historic Endrizzi estate, involved in a massive reconversion programme. All the bottles show the skill of the winemaker but little help was forthcoming from the vintage. Despite everything, the Teroldego, Masetto Bianco, Pinot Nero and Moscato Rosa are great.

●	Teroldego Rotaliano Maso Camorz '00 🍷🍷	5
●	Trentino Lagrein Vigna Le Vallette '00 🍷	3
●	Trentino Moscato Rosa '00 🍷	5
○	Masetto Bianco '01 🍷	4

Giovanni Poli
Loc. Santa Massenza
Via Vezzano, 37
38070 Vezzano (TN)
tel. 0461864119

A fine grappa-maker, and an enthusiastic winemaker, Giovanni Poli focuses his, and his childrens', energies on Vallagarina's delicious Vino Santo. Less cloying than other examples, Giovanni's wine is big and full, with balanced sweetness. The other two wines, the Rebo and Nosiola, are well typed.

○	Trentino Vino Santo '95 🍷🍷	6
●	Rebo '00 🍷	3
○	Trentino Nosiola '01 🍷	3

Giulio Poli
Loc. Santa Massenza
Via Vezzano, 31
38070 Vezzano (TN)
tel. 0461864149

This winery astonished us again with its Saros, a late-harvest jewel from aromatic grapes, mainly sauvignon. It's sweet, seductive and not at all cloying. The Schiava is easy and drinkable, and the dry-vinified Moscato Giallo is as pleasant as ever.

○	Saros V. T. '99 🍷🍷	6
○	Moscato Giallo Valle dei Laghi '01 🍷	3
⊙	Schiava Valle dei Laghi '01 🍷	2*

Francesco Poli
Loc. Santa Massenza, 36
38070 Vezzano (TN)
tel. 0461864102

Francesco Poli's estate specializes in vinifying nosiola destined for Vino Santo. It's very much a niche wine but definitely one to look out for. The other wines are pleasant, especially the Lagrein.

○	Trentino Vino Santo '94 🍷🍷	6
●	Trentino Lagrein Vigna Le Vallette '00 🍷	3
○	Trentino Nosiola Vigna Sottovi '01 🍷	3

ALTO ADIGE

Just over 20 per cent of the more than 600 samples from Alto Adige we tasted this year reached the final taste-offs for the Three Glass awards. Exactly the same number as last year, 19, hit the jackpot. This impressive showing will give you some idea of the excellent health of winemaking in Alto Adige, which may be offering an example for other Italian regions to follow. The recipe is easy enough to describe. First, winery technicians are trained at places like Laimburg, an experimental oenology institute managed by the Bolzano provincial authority, which turn out professional, motivated oenologists and agronomists. Crucially, they find work almost immediately at one of the region's many co-operative wineries or equally numerous private cellars. The second stage in the recipe concerns the way co-operative wineries conduct their business. In Alto Adige, they are the most efficient in Italy and, in short, the best in the world. Though not too big, they have very effective managers. Among others, we could list the names of Hans Terzer, Willi Stürz, Arnold Terzer, Stefan Filippi, and Helmuth Zozin, to mention only the younger generation. They also have a practical, modern instinct for marketing and contributing members who, almost without exception, follow the instructions of cellar managers to the letter. Alongside these is a group of very intelligent private producers, including Martin Foradori, Elena Walch, Urban von Klebersberg, and smaller ones such as Josephus Mayr, Peter Pliger and Fran Haas. Many of these speak three languages, German, Italian, and occasionally English, a great advantage when dealing with international markets. The third step is the variety of products and the many subzones that increasingly specialize in specific types of wines. The Valle Isarco is particularly suited for whites from kerner, müller thurgau and sylvaner varieties. Riesling is being grown with good results in Valle Venosta. Lagrein and schiava seem to be successful in the Bolzano area. Pinot bianco, chardonnay and sauvignon are finding a home in Terlano/Terlan and the southernmost parts of the Oltradige area. Below Caldaro/Kaltern, and the Merano hills, is the area for great cabernet sauvignon and merlot-based reds, as well as the home of gewürztraminer and pinot grigio for whites. Pinot nero is giving surprising results at Mazzon, a tiny corner of the Montagna/Montan zone. Each producer tends to stick to his own business, specializing in the most typical wines of the subzone. As in other regions, the situation is far from easy. But in Alto Adige, there is at least a plan, an idea and a basic philosophy hinging on well-made, reliable, value-for-money wines. And in these days of insane wine prices in Italy, all this is music to the drinker's ear.

ANDRIANO/ANDRIAN (BZ)

CANTINA PRODUTTORI ANDRIANO
VIA DELLA CHIESA, 2
39010 ANDRIANO/ANDRIAN (BZ)
TEL. 0471510137
E-MAIL: info@andrianer-kellerei.it

Cantina Produttori Andriano, the oldest co-operative winery in Alto Adige and now also its largest producer of organic wines, makes a wide range of dependably good wines. We will start with the Lagrein 2000, from the winery's showcase line, the Tor di Lupo that effortlessly took our top prize. Very fruity and spicy on the nose, it is surprisingly complex for such a young wine. Full-flavoured and soft yet sustained on the palate, it signs off with a marvellously long finish. Congratulations on the Andriano co-operative's first Three Glasses. We felt another red from this cellar was excellent, the Merlot Siebeneich Tor di Lupo 2000. A very intense, concentrated ruby red introduces fruit-led aromas on the nose and perfectly gauged oak and rich structure on the round, close-knit palate. Needless to say, the whites from Andriano are magnificent. Top of the crop is the Terlano Sauvignon Preciosa Tor di Lupo 2001, which impresses with its intense, varietal fruit laced with sage and lime blossom, and fresh, persistence and full flavour in the mouth. The Traminer Aromatico Selection Sonnengut has a delicate nose of roses and a clean, pervasive progression on the palate. The fruity, elegant Chardonnay Tor di Lupo 2000 is another well-made wine. The Traminer Aromatico, Terlano Pinot Bianco Sonnengut and Cabernet Tor di Lupo were all good but less dazzling than last year.

APPIANO/EPPAN (BZ)

JOSEF BRIGL
LOC. CORNAIANO/GIRLAN
VIA SAN FLORIANO, 8
39050 APPIANO/EPPAN (BZ)
TEL. 0471662419
E-MAIL: brigl@brigl.com

The Brigls are no newcomers to the country life for the name is mentioned in documents from as early as 1250. This occupation has passed down practically without interruption to the present owners of the cellar, Ignaz and his son Josef. Wines produced by the Brigls are well made, fresh, typical, early drinking and are great value. Their common-sense commercial policy has for years been one of the most praiseworthy features of the winery. Some high points may be missing – for example, there is nothing as extraordinary as the Pinot Nero Kreuzbichler once was – but on average, the wines are very well made and good quality. We especially liked the reds this year. The Lagrein Briglhof 2000 is an intense ruby, revealing zesty fruit aromas with hints of smoke on the nose. The nicely textured palate has a rather insistent touch of wood. The Cabernet Briglhof 1999 flaunts an intense ruby and good structure. It's fruity and fairly clean, but a bit one-dimensional. The crystalline ruby Lago di Caldaro Scelto Classico Superiore Haselhof 2001 is fruity, stylish and easy drinking. The whites are well made but tend to lack a bit of personality and backbone. The only exception to this is the Sauvignon 2001, a fruit-rich, full-bodied wine with faint varietal notes. The Chardonnay 2001's is a golden straw yellow that precedes intense fruit with exotic hints. Finally, the Gewürztraminer Windegg 2001 is fruity and aromatic enough but a bit forward and uninteresting.

● A. A. Lagrein Scuro Tor di Lupo '00	🍷🍷🍷	5
● A. A. Merlot Siebeneich Tor di Lupo '00	🍷🍷	4
○ A. A. Chardonnay Tor di Lupo '00	🍷🍷	5
○ A. A. Terlano Sauvignon Preciosa Tor di Lupo '01	🍷🍷	5
○ A. A. Gewürztraminer Sel. Sonnengut '01	🍷🍷	4*
○ A. A. Terlano Pinot Bianco Cl. Sonnengut '01	🍷	4
● A. A. Cabernet Tor di Lupo '99	🍷	5
● A. A. Merlot Siebeneich Tor di Lupo '99	🍷	4
○ A. A. Gewürztraminer Sel. Sonnengut '00	🍷	4
● A. A. Merlot Siebeneich '97	🍷	4
● A. A. Cabernet Tor di Lupo '98	🍷🍷	5
● A. A. Lagrein Scuro Tor di Lupo '98	🍷	4
○ A. A. Chardonnay Tor di Lupo '99	🍷	4
● A. A. Lagrein Scuro Tor di Lupo '99	🍷🍷	5

● A. A. Lagrein Scuro Briglhof '00	🍷🍷	5
● A. A. Lago di Caldaro Scelto Haselhof Cl. Sup. '01	🍷🍷	3*
○ A. A. Sauvignon '01	🍷🍷	4*
● A. A. Cabernet Briglhof '99	🍷🍷	5
○ A. A. Chardonnay '01	🍷	3
○ A. A. Gewürztraminer Windegg '01	🍷	4
● A. A. Santa Maddalena Reierhof '00	🍷🍷	3*
○ A. A. Sauvignon '00	🍷🍷	4*
● A. A. Lagrein Scuro Briglhof '98	🍷🍷	5
○ A. A. Sauvignon '98	🍷🍷	3
○ A. A. Sauvignon '99	🍷🍷	3

APPIANO/EPPAN (BZ)

★ Cantina Produttori Colterenzio
Loc. Cornaiano/Girlan
Strada del Vino, 8
39050 Appiano/Eppan (BZ)
tel. 0471664246
e-mail: info@colterenzio.com

Luis Raifer, legendary president of the Cantina Produttori in Colterenzio, celebrated this year with the co-operative's best performance ever, including a stupendous tenth Three Glass award in the history of this Guide. That historic result was achieved by a sumptuous version of the Chardonnay Cornell, from the 2000 vintage, that launches Colterenzio into the Guide's starry firmament. The elegant, exotic aromas and sound, excellently concentrated structure, confirm that this Chardonnay is simply the best in its category in Alto Adige. But Colterenzio has produced many great wines this year. Another three made it to our finals, the Gewürztraminer Cornell '01, Cabernet Sauvignon Lafoa '99 and Cornelius Rosso, from cabernet sauvignon and merlot, again from the '99 vintage. The Pinot Bianco Weisshaus '01 is very good, correct, a varietal, easy-drinking wine in one of its best versions ever, and the Cabernet Sauvignon Kastelt Riserva '99 also earned way above the minimum score for that second Glass. The other wines are all decent, with special mentions for the Pinot Nero Schwarzhaus Riserva '99, the Lagrein Cornell '00 and the Chardonnay Pinay '01. The Pinot Nero St. Daniel Riserva '99 is half a step behind these, according to out tasters. This is a fine range from one of the best wineries in Italy.

APPIANO/EPPAN (BZ)

Cantina Produttori Cornaiano
Loc. Cornaiano/Girlan
Via San Martino, 24
39050 Appiano/Eppan (BZ)
tel. 0471662403
e-mail: info@girlan.it

Innovation and a pioneering spirit were the driving forces that led to the creation of the Cantina Sociale Cornaiano in 1923. It was one of the first co-operative wineries to pay producers not only for quantity but also for the quality of the grapes. At present, the 240 members of the Cantina Sociale Cornaiano produce around 15,000 hectolitres of red wine and 8,000 of white each year. This has been a great year for whites at Cornaiano and the cellar has turned out a lovely array of products. We were particularly amazed by the great Gewürztraminer (Traminer Aromatico) SelectArt 2001. Its golden straw yellow leads into intense, varietal fruit and a full, linear, concentrated flavour. The Sauvignon SelectArt Flora 2001 is also a very well-made wine. The deep straw yellow precedes discreetly varietal, ripe fruit and elderflower. The Pinot Bianco Plattenriegl 2001 has a nose of intense tropical fruit, then a great body and a rich, elegant mouthfeel. The Pinot Bianco Passito Pasithea 1999 is also nice and concentrated. Hartmuth Spitaler, first the winery's oenologist, and later its chair, is one of the most enthusiastic supporters of the schiava variety and puts his all into showing that it can produce high quality. The Schiava Gschleier, from old vines, is the cellar's best red and a classic Alto Adige schiava. The fairly intense garnet ruby hue frames a fruit-led, complex nose and full, concentrated palate. The Cabernet Sauvignon Riserva SelectArt 1999, Lagrein Riserva SelectArt 1999 and Pinot Nero Patricia 2000 are all decent this year.

○	A. A. Chardonnay Cornell '00	♟♟♟	6
○	A. A. Gewürztraminer Cornell '01	♟♟	6
●	A. A. Cabernet Sauvignon Lafoa '99	♟♟	8
●	A. A. Cabernet Sauvignon Merlot Cornelius '99	♟♟	7
●	A. A. Lagrein Cornell '00	♟♟	6
○	A. A. Pinot Bianco Weisshaus '01	♟♟	4
●	A. A. Cabernet Sauvignon Kastelt Ris. '99	♟♟	6
○	A. A. Chardonnay Pinay '01	♟	4
●	A. A. Pinot Nero Cornell Schwarzhaus '99	♟	6
●	A. A. Pinot Nero St. Daniel Ris. '99	♟	5
●	A. A. Cabernet Sauvignon Lafoa '97	♟♟♟	6
○	A. A. Chardonnay Cornell '99	♟♟♟	6

○	A. A. Gewürztraminer SelectArt Flora '01	♟♟	5*
○	A. A. Pinot Bianco Passito Pasithea '00	♟♟	6
●	A. A. Schiava Gschleier SelectArt Flora '00	♟♟	5
○	A. A. Pinot Bianco Plattenriegl '01	♟♟	4
○	A. A. Sauvignon SelectArt Flora '01	♟♟	5
●	A. A. Pinot Nero Patricia '00	♟	4
●	A. A. Cabernet Sauvignon SelectArt Flora Ris. '99	♟	5
●	A. A. Lagrein SelectArt Flora Ris. '99	♟	6
●	A. A. Cabernet Sauvignon Ris. '97	♟♟	5
●	A. A. Lagrein Ris. '97	♟♟	5
●	A. A. Cabernet Sauvignon Ris. '98	♟♟	5
●	A. A. Lagrein Ris. '98	♟♟	5

APPIANO/EPPAN (BZ)

KÖSSLER - PRAECLARUS
LOC. SAN PAOLO/ST. PAULS, 15
39057 APPIANO/EPPAN (BZ)
TEL. 0471660256 - 0471662182
E-MAIL: abner@koessler.it

The Kössler winery is situated at the foot of the imposing bell tower in the mediaeval town of San Paolo/St. Pauls. Kössler's still and sparkling wines have been sent around the world from here for more than a century. Present managing director Hans Ebner is still a grower who continues to make very fine wines with great enthusiasm and professionalism. The "spumante" wines from the Praeclarus line are well-known and among the best in Alto Adige. The Riserva Praeclarus Noblesse 1993 fully deserved its invitation to take part in the Three Glass finals. This straw yellow "spumante" has a very delicate perlage and rich fruit with yeasty notes, then a fresh, complex and persistent flavour. We thought the reds from the winery were also good. The Lagrein-Merlot Ebner '00 is a very deep ruby red that shades into garnet, and the intense nose offers notes of ripe berry fruit and toasty oak. The broad entry on the palate is followed up by confident progression. The Cabernet-Merlot Cuvée St. Pauls '00 also introduces itself with a very concentrated ruby, fruit notes and a full, linear palate that is very well made. The Lagrein Kössler '99 is very clean, with tenuously super-ripe notes reminiscent of jam. The Merlot Tschiedererhof '00 has delicate aromas of fresh grass and a fairly round flavour. The Bianco Ebner '01 shows good body but reveals oaky notes that are a bit excessive. We close with the Brut Praeclarus "spumante", which is fresh and elegant.

○	A. A. Spumante Praeclarus Brut	🍷🍷	5
○	A. A. Spumante Praeclarus Noblesse Ris. '93	🍷🍷	5
●	A. A. Cabernet-Merlot S. Pauls '00	🍷🍷	4
●	A. A. Lagrein Merlot Ebner '00	🍷🍷	6
●	A. A. Lagrein Scuro '99	🍷🍷	5
●	A. A. Merlot Tschidererhof '00	🍷	4
○	A. A. Bianco Ebner '01	🍷	5
●	A. A. Cabernet-Merlot S. Pauls '97	🍷🍷	5
○	A. A. Bianco '99	🍷🍷	5

APPIANO/EPPAN (BZ)

K. MARTINI & SOHN
LOC. CORNAIANO/GIRLAN
VIA LAMM, 28
39050 APPIANO/EPPAN (BZ)
TEL. 0471663156
E-MAIL: info@weinkellerei-martini.it

The Martini family winery at Cornaiano was founded in 1979 by Karl Martini and his son Gabriel. Over the past 20 years or so, these two oenologists have found a good balance between centuries-old tradition and technology. The Martinis strive in particular to ensure that the bouquet and flavour of their wines will be perfectly preserved over time. In the last few years, the winery has directed much of its effort toward the Lagrein, with very successful results. One Lagrein reached the Three Glass finals and another three easily made the Two Glass bracket. We'll begin with the Maturum 2000, a deep ruby Lagrein with a very well-defined, powerful nose that shows berry fruit and well integrated touches of oak. The powerful development on the palate and substantial weight impress. The Lagrein Rueslhof '00, from the Ruesl "maso", or farm, at Bolzano, is a deep ruby with intensely fruit and faintly smoky notes on the nose, followed by a full, structured and elegant palate. Though we tasted the Lagrein Maturum '99 last year, it was only a cask sample. Today, it is another very dark ruby wine with lots of fruit and a full, pleasant palate. The Lagrein-Cabernet Coldirus 2000 is a fruit-led, stylish wine with concentration and a very tidy character. The two Chardonnays submitted were decent. The Palladium '01 is fruity, fresh and young while the Chardonnay has a straightforward style. The Schiava Palladium '01 is also approachable and pleasant to drink.

●	A. A. Lagrein Scuro Maturum '00	🍷🍷	5
●	A. A. Lagrein-Cabernet Coldirus Palladium '00	🍷🍷	4
●	A. A. Lagrein Scuro Maturum '99	🍷🍷	5
●	A. A. Lagrein Scuro Rueslhof '00	🍷🍷	4
○	A. A. Chardonnay '01	🍷	3
○	A. A. Chardonnay Palladium '01	🍷	4
○	A. A. Schiava Palladium '01	🍷	3
○	A. A. Chardonnay Palladium '00	🍷	3
●	A. A. Cabernet-Lagrein Palladium Coldirus '98	🍷	5
●	A. A. Lagrein Scuro Rueslhof '99	🍷	4

APPIANO/EPPAN (BZ)

JOSEF NIEDERMAYR
LOC. CORNAIANO/GIRLAN
VIA CASA DI GESÙ, 15
39050 APPIANO/EPPAN (BZ)
TEL. 0471662451
E-MAIL: info@niedermayr.it

At Josef Niedermayr's winery, you can bank on the utmost professionalism. Josef is a major player on the Alto Adige wine scene and this year's edition of the Guide, one that substantially confirms the progress of the region's winemaking industry, he placed three wines in our final round of taste-offs and just missed a top award. We should say straight away that we were most impressed by the ever delicious Lagrein Aus Gries Riserva from 2000, one of the house specialities. Its full, rich nose of wild berry aromas ushers in a crisply defined palate. It may still be a bit young and a tad on the edgy side, but this is definitely an excellent Lagrein. Right behind it is the sweet white Aureus '00, from mainly chardonnay and sauvignon fruit. A very pleasant, concentrated wine, it may be slightly less complex, sweeter and more predictable than earlier versions. The Gewürztraminer Lage Doss '01, in its best version ever, won the third-highest score in the finals. There were Two Glasses each for the two Sauvignons, the very stylish and varietal Allure and the more complex Lage Naun, both from the 2001 vintage. The Euforius '00 is very nice, a barrique-aged red from lagrein, cabernet sauvignon and merlot that is elegance, yet fairly accessible and easy-drinking. We will not evaluate the Pinot Nero Riserva '00 this year. Though very promising, it was still in the barrel when we called to taste.

APPIANO/EPPAN (BZ)

IGNAZ NIEDRIST
LOC. CORNAIANO/GIRLAN
VIA RONCO, 5
39050 APPIANO/EPPAN (BZ)
TEL. 0471664494

The very talented Ignaz Niedrist has not repeated his success from last year, when he won the Three Glasses with his splendid Terlano Sauvignon '00. Apart from that slight disappointment, he presented the panel with a series of very good wines that are object proof of his marvellous enthusiasm and professionalism. All five wines offered for tasting took Two full Glasses, which can hardly be considered a bad result. Let's start with the whites and an excellent Riesling '01. Intense and varietal, with mineral notes on the nose, it is delicate and elegant on the palate, perhaps lacking just a bit of concentration. The Terlano Sauvignon '01 is only just a notch below the previous version. White peach and grapefruit are evident on the nose, and the palate is complex, typical and shows a wonderful finish. We'll begin the reds with the Lagrein Berger Gei '00. It reveals intense, slightly super-ripe fruit and a concentrated palate with nicely integrated tannins that perhaps dry out the finish a little. The 2000 version of the Pinot Nero is very good. Typical berry fruit aromas develop on the palate, nicely echoing the nose with good intensity. The Merlot Mühlweg '00 has concentrated fruit with slightly super-ripe nuances. The dense, elegant palate unveils a well-integrated layer of oak. In all, this was a very respectable performance from a producer who is now firmly established among the region's winemaking elite.

●	A. A. Lagrein Aus Gries Ris. '00	ŶŶ	5
○	Aureus '00	ŶŶ	6
○	A. A. Gewürztraminer Lage Doss '01	ŶŶ	5
●	Euforius '00	ŶŶ	6
○	A. A. Sauvignon Allure '01	ŶŶ	5
○	A. A. Sauvignon Lage Naun '01	ŶŶ	4*
○	Aureus '95	ŶŶŶ	6
○	Aureus '98	ŶŶŶ	6
○	Aureus '99	ŶŶŶ	6
●	Euforius '99	ŶŶ	5
○	A. A. Gewürztraminer Lage Doss '00	ŶŶ	5
○	Aureus '96	ŶŶ	6
○	Aureus '97	ŶŶ	6

●	A. A. Lagrein Berger Gei '00	ŶŶ	5
●	A. A. Merlot Mühlweg '00	ŶŶ	5
●	A. A. Pinot Nero '00	ŶŶ	6
○	A. A. Riesling Renano '01	ŶŶ	4
○	A. A. Terlano Sauvignon '01	ŶŶ	5*
○	A. A. Terlano Sauvignon '00	ŶŶŶ	4*
○	A. A. Riesling Renano '00	ŶŶ	4
●	A. A. Lagrein Scuro Berger Gei Ris. '97	ŶŶ	5
●	A. A. Pinot Nero '96	ŶŶ	4
○	A. A. Riesling Renano '96	ŶŶ	4
●	A. A. Merlot '98	ŶŶ	5
○	A. A. Terlano Sauvignon '98	ŶŶ	4
○	A. A. Riesling Renano '99	ŶŶ	4

APPIANO/EPPAN (BZ)

★ Cantina Produttori
San Michele Appiano
Via Circonvallazione, 17/19
39057 Appiano/Eppan (BZ)
tel. 0471664466
e-mail: kellerei@stmichael.it

The cellar submitted 12 wines for tasting and seven reached our finals. Only one scored below Two Glasses and, rather more significantly, two wines gained a third Glass. What more can we say about the magnificently unstoppable progress of this extraordinary Alto Adige co-operative? It is no surprise that one of the top prizewinners is the white Sauvignon Sankt Valentin '01 but for the first time, we also have a red, the Cabernet Sankt Valentin '00. Forget those rumours that San Michele Appiano's "kellermeister", Hans Terzer, is only comfortable with whites for the entire Sankt Valentin line is fantastic: the Chardonnay '00, Gewürztraminer '01, the Passito Comtess '00, obtained from mainly gewürztraminer, and the Lagrein '00. The 2001 version of the estate's second Sauvignon, the Lahn, is also awesome. All of the above earned Two very full Glasses. Furthermore, the Pinot Grigio and Pinot Nero Sankt Valentin '00, the second Pinot Grigio, the Anger '01, and the Riesling Montiggl '01 were all delightful. If we go down the list, the Pinot Bianco Schulthauser '01 was merely good. Although it is the most important wine in terms of bottles produced (more than 200,000), we felt it was a little below par in comparison to its stablemates. It's not at all bad, though. With quality like this across the whole range of wines, the cellar can truly be proud of the work done at San Michele Appiano. It may even be the outstanding performance in this year's Guide.

APPIANO/EPPAN (BZ)

Cantina Produttori San Paolo
Loc. San Paolo/St. Pauls
Via Castel Guardia, 21
39050 Appiano/Eppan (BZ)
tel. 0471662183
e-mail: info@kellereistpauls.com

The village of San Paolo/St. Pauls is set in splendid vineyards in the heart of the Oltradige area. In this very scenic panorama, the local co-operative winery almost feels obliged to continue an oenological tradition that is now a more than a century old. The co-operative at San Paolo again presented us this year with wines that are well made but also endowed with style and character. The finest wines in the range are above all the Sauvignon Gfill Hof '01, a fantastic example of its category and a worthy finalist for the Three Glass share-out. Made from fruit picked on the sunny slopes of the Gfill hill, where it usually attains magnificent levels of ripeness, as indeed it did in 2001. It introduces itself with a greenish straw yellow hue and very varietal aromas on the nose, where there are notes of elderflower and nettles that lead into a full, rich palate with plenty of spunk and concentration. The Pinot Grigio Egg Leiten '01 reveals a copper-tinged straw yellow and intense, varietal fruit on the slightly rustic nose. The deep ruby red Merlot Divinus '99 is good and fruity, as well as complex. The Pinot Bianco Plötzner '01 is well-typed and fresh, with good length, while the Pinot Nero Divinus '00 lacks density in the mouth. Finally, the Schiava Exclusiv Sarner Hof '01 is attractively drinkable.

●	A. A. Cabernet St. Valentin '00	▼▼▼	6
○	A. A. Sauvignon St. Valentin '01	▼▼▼	6
○	A. A. Chardonnay St. Valentin '00	▼▼	5
●	A. A. Lagrein St. Valentin '00	▼▼	6
○	A. A. Bianco Passito Comtess St. Valentin '01	▼▼	6
○	A. A. Gewürztraminer St. Valentin '01	▼▼	5
○	A. A. Sauvignon Lahn '01	▼▼	4*
○	A. A. Pinot Grigio St. Valentin '00	▼▼	5
●	A. A. Pinot Nero St. Valentin '00	▼▼	6
○	A. A. Pinot Grigio Anger '01	▼▼	4
○	A. A. Riesling Montiggl '01	▼▼	4
○	A. A. Pinot Bianco Schulthauser '01	▼	4
○	A. A. Sauvignon St. Valentin '00	▼▼▼	5
○	A. A. Sauvignon St. Valentin '98	▼▼▼	4

○	A. A. Sauvignon Exclusiv Gfil Hof '01	▼▼	4*
○	A. A. Pinot Grigio Exclusiv Egg Leiten '01	▼▼	4*
●	A. A. Merlot DiVinus '99	▼▼	5
●	A. A. Pinot Nero DiVinus '00	▼	5
●	A. A. Schiava Sarner Hof Exclusiv '01	▼	4
○	A. A. Terlano Pinot Bianco Exclusiv Plötzner '01	▼	4
●	A. A. Merlot DiVinus '97	▼▼	5

BOLZANO/BOZEN

Andreas Berger -Thurnhof
Via Castel Flavon, 7
39100 Bolzano/Bozen
tel. 0471288460 - 0471285446
e-mail: info@thurnhof.com

Andrea Berger is the enthusiastic owner, agronomist and oenologist at this very tiny estate of just two and a half hectares under production, for around 11,000 bottles a year. It is located just outside Bolzano in a subzone whose temperatures and aspects make it perfect for red grapes. So it is no accident that this year Berger's winery came very close to Three Glasses with a magnificent Cabernet Sauvignon Riserva from the '99 vintage, a great year for Thurnhof. An impenetrable ruby introduces the intense bouquet of black berry fruit, which has lovely depth and precision. The palate is concentrated, the ripe tannins integrating well with the oak, and the finish is very long and elegant. There is also fantastic character for a wine still so young. The Lagrein Scuro '00 is good, but not as exciting as last year's edition. The pleasant aromas recall berry fruit that is perhaps a bit enthusiastically oaked but nicely complex just the same. There is all the usual elegance on the palate, which is supported by great concentration and ripe, well-knit tannins. The finish has a very special note of spice. We liked the Santa Maddalena '01 very much, with its characteristic small berry aromas where raspberries are to the fore. Soft, pleasant and fragrant on the palate, this is not a wine to be drunk straight away. Finally, the Moscato Giallo '01 is pleasant, with characteristic hints of broom. The Passaurum '00 "passito", from partially dried moscato giallo, was not produced because of adverse weather conditions.

●	A. A. Cabernet Sauvignon Ris. '99	♛♛	5
●	A. A. Lagrein Scuro '00	♛♛	5
●	A. A. Santa Maddalena '01	♛♛	3
○	A. A. Moscato Giallo '01	♛	4
●	A. A. Lagrein Scuro '99	♛♛♛	4*
●	A. A. Cabernet Wienegg Ris. '94	♛♛	4
●	A. A. Lagrein Scuro '95	♛♛	5
●	A. A. Lagrein Scuro Ris. '97	♛♛	5
●	A. A. Lagrein Scuro '98	♛♛	4
○	Passaurum '99	♛♛	5
●	A. A. Cabernet Sauvignon Ris. '98	♛	5

BOLZANO/BOZEN

Cantina Gries/Cantina di Bolzano
Fraz. Gries
P.zza Gries, 2
39100 Bolzano/Bozen
tel. 0471270909 - 0471280248
e-mail: info@cantina-gries.it

It's "year one" after the merger with the Produttori di Santa Maddalena co-operative winery so what could be better than to pick up Three Glasses with a showcase wine? The Lagrein Scuro Grieser Prestige Line Riserva '99 has very deep, clear aromas that hint at berry fruit then the rich, comforting structure on the palate shows elegant tones of violet and chocolate. There's a nice touch of oak and a velvety, complex finish. It's a magnificent, modern-style Lagrein. But there's more. Another two wines came close to a top prize. One was the Merlot Riserva Siebeneich Prestige Line '99, whose ripe blackberry aromas usher in a dense, tight-knit palate layered with sweet tannins, and a persistent finish. The other outstanding bottle was the Moscato Giallo Vinalia '00, which won Three Glasses last year. It reveals splendidly elegant aromas of botrytis, honey and nuts, and a big, powerful palate with a good balance of sugar and acidity. But the real surprise came from another white, the Pinot Bianco Fritz Dallago Collection '00, a magnificent wine with a delicate flowery bouquet and tangy, full palate where there are complex, persistent notes of fresh pink grapefruit. The Mauritius '99, a Merlot and Lagrein blend with intense black berry aromas and good structure, the Lagrein Scuro Grieser Baron Carl Eyrl Riserva '00, a more traditional version of the Three Glass winner, and the Merlot Collection Riserva '00 with its delicious, well-balanced tannins, were all good and all comfortably picked up Two Glasses. Lastly, the Moscato Rosa Rosis '00 is very well made.

●	A. A. Lagrein Scuro Grieser Prestige Line Ris. '99	♛♛♛	6
○	A. A. Moscato Giallo Vinalia '00	♛♛	6
●	A. A. Merlot Ris. Siebeneich Prestige Line '99	♛♛	6
●	A. A. Lagrein Scuro Grieser Baron Carl Eyrl Ris. '00	♛♛	4
●	A. A. Merlot Collection Ris. '00	♛♛	4
○	A. A. Pinot Bianco Collection Dellago '00	♛♛	5
●	Mauritius '99	♛♛	6
●	A. A. Moscato Rosa Rosis '00	♛	6
○	A. A. Moscato Giallo Vinalia '99	♛♛♛	5

BOLZANO/BOZEN

CANTINA CONVENTO MURI-GRIES
P.ZZA GRIES, 21
39100 BOLZANO/BOZEN
TEL. 0471282287
E-MAIL: muri-gries-kg@muri-gries.com

In 1407, Archduke Leopold of Tyrol gave Gries castle to homeless monks to be turned into a monastery. The old chapel was transformed into a wine cellar where even now the great Lagrein di Muri age in large and small oak casks. Muri Gries, and its enthusiastic oenologist Christian Werth, has firmly established its status as one of the major producers of Lagrein, the much-appreciated grape indigenous to Alto Adige. Until a few years ago, Lagrein was almost unknown outside the confines of the province but now, it has become the number one Alto Adige red in absolute in terms, both for its quality and for its distinctive personality. Christian Werth was one of the first to focus on Lagrein, restructuring his old vineyards and experimenting in the cellar, with fantastic results. His legendary Lagrein Riserva Abtei '99 is again a minor masterpiece of winemaking. Intense ruby in hue, it unveils balsamic notes of eucalyptus and coffee on the nose, leading into a round and powerful structure in the mouth. The white Abtei '00 is a limpid straw yellow and reveals delicate fruit, concentration and a hint of sweetness. The dark ruby red Lagrein Gries '01, with its pleasant violet and berry fruit aromas, is full flavoured on the palate, though there is a slightly acidic vein. The Lagrein Rosato 2001 is another pleasantly drinkable wine. The cellar chose a special vinification method, involving protracted barrique ageing, for the Moscato Rosa Abtei '00. A distinctly well-made sweet wine, it lacks something of the true personality of an Alto Adige Moscato Rosa.

● A. A. Lagrein Scuro Abtei Ris. '99	▼▼▼	5
○ A. A. Bianco Abtei '00	▼▼	4
● A. A. Moscato Rosa Abtei '00	▼	6
● A. A. Lagrein Gries '01	▼	3*
◉ A. A. Lagrein Rosato Gries '01	▼	3*
● A. A. Lagrein Scuro Abtei Ris. '96	▼▼▼	5
● A. A. Lagrein Scuro Abtei Ris. '97	▼▼▼	5
● A. A. Lagrein Scuro Abtei Ris. '98	▼▼▼	5
○ A. A. Bianco Abtei '99	▼▼	5
● A. A. Lagrein Scuro Gries '95	▼▼	4
● A. A. Lagrein Scuro Gries '97	▼▼	2

BOLZANO/BOZEN

FRANZ GOJER GLÖGGLHOF
FRAZ. S. MADDALENA
VIA RIVELLONE, 1
39100 BOLZANO/BOZEN
TEL. 0471978775
E-MAIL: info@gojer.it

Franz Gojer is one of the most consistent winemakers from the tiny Santa Maddalena subzone. With around 40,000 bottles produced, he is always at the top of the league tables for reds from this unique part of Alto Adige. Franz's wines are fragrant and very drinkable, something that brings a smile to the lips of the growing segment of winelovers who prefer approachability to muscle power. For them, we can recommend the Lagrein Scuro Riserva del '00, with its intense colour, trademark wild berry aromas, and above all captivatingly moreish style, especially if served cool at around 16 degrees Celsius. Though a bit more complex, the same holds true for another 2000, the Merlot Spitz, which is not called after the great 1970s American swimmer but the grape variety of the same name. But if we had to decide which Franz Gojer wine – of its type, of course – we liked the most, it would have to be the Santa Maddalena Rondell '01, a light, fragrant, delicious-to-drink red. In other words, it's a wine to quaff, not one to sip, and a minor masterpiece of balance, like a miniature by a great painter. Not far behind comes the Santa Maddalena Classico '01, another wonderfully drinkable wine.

● A. A. Lagrein Scuro Ris. '00	▼▼	5
● A. A. Merlot Spitz '00	▼▼	5
● A. A. Santa Maddalena Cl. Rondell '01	▼▼	4*
● A. A. Santa Maddalena Cl. '01	▼	3
● A. A. Lagrein Scuro Ris. '99	▼▼	4
● A. A. Lagrein Scuro '00	▼▼	4*
● A. A. Santa Maddalena Rondell '00	▼▼	3*
● A. A. Lagrein Scuro Ris. '98	▼▼	4
● A. A. Lagrein Scuro '99	▼▼	3
● A. A. Merlot Spitz '99	▼▼	4
● A. A. Santa Maddalena Cl. '99	▼▼	2

BOLZANO/BOZEN

LOACKER SCHWARZHOF
VIA SANTA JUSTINA, 3
39100 BOLZANO/BOZEN
TEL. 0471365125
E-MAIL: lo@cker.it

Last year, we called the Cuvée Jus Osculi '00, a red from schiava with a little lagrein, a Santa Maddalena "with a bit of reinforcement". Now, it is the best wine Loacker submitted to us for this edition of the Guide, and embodies many of the finest characteristics of wines from the Santa Maddalena zone. Then again, the estate vineyards are right on the slopes of the hill at Santa Justina. Still, this bottle may well have more structure and complexity than most reds from the subzone, as well as greater cellar potential. The Santa Maddalena Classico Morit '01 is also very nice, albeit more accessible and fragrant in its aromas. But the real surprise comes from two whites, which are fairly unusual wines for a subzone so well-suited to cultivating red grapes. And though in the case of the Chardonnay Ateyon '00, which made it to our finals last year, it was something of a repeat performance, the Sauvignon Tasmin '01 gave our panel quite a surprise. A white with very varietal, tropical fruit aromas, it revealed astonishingly solid structure. The Pinot Nero Norital '00 is no more than decent, proof of how difficult this variety is to grow, inside or outside Burgundy, and the same could be said of the Gewürztraminer Atagis '01. In conclusion, we would like to point out the estate's rigorously organic vineyard management since it now seems to be yielding consistently improving results.

BOLZANO/BOZEN

R. MALOJER GUMMERHOF
VIA WEGGESTEIN, 36
39100 BOLZANO/BOZEN
TEL. 0471972885
E-MAIL: info@malojer.it

Once isolated amid the sea of vines to the north of Bolzano, Gummerhof boasts a truly long history. The first documents mentioning it go back to 1480. Today the winery, managed by the Malojer family, draws on its many years of experience and makes use of the most modern vineyard and vinification techniques to produce premium-quality wines. The results can be seen in the fruit selected from the best sites around Bolzano, and then vinified with great care and technical skill. The wines submitted for tasting this year are very good indeed. The Cabernet Riserva '00 was sent forward to the Three Glass finals and came near winning a third Glass. Very intense in hue, with an elegant aromatic profile, it reveals a complex, powerful palate of sweet tannins and well-integrated oak. The panel agreed that the Lagrein Riserva '00 and Merlot Riserva '00 are two really great reds. The Lagrein is full-bodied and fruity, with mineral and medicinal nuances. It's too bad that the oak covers it a bit. The Merlot is very attractively sweet and fruity, although the robust tannins are a tad on the rugged side. The Cabernet-Lagrein Bautzanum '00 is concentrated, full and intense. The Sauvignon Gur zu Sand 2001 is very true to type, varietal and elegant, with good intensity and concentration. Finally, the Pinot Nero Riserva '00 is decent, though again a little in thrall to its over-assertive oak.

○ A. A. Chardonnay Ateyon '00		🍷	5
● Cuvée Jus Osculi '00		🍷🍷	4*
● A. A. Santa Maddalena Cl. Morit '01		🍷🍷	4*
○ A. A. Sauvignon Blanc Tasmin '01		🍷🍷	4
● A. A. Pinot Nero Norital '00		🍷	5
○ A. A. Valle Isarco Gewürztraminer Atagis '01		🍷	5
○ A. A. Chardonnay Ateyon '99		🍷🍷	4*
● A. A. Cabernet Kastlet '96		🍷🍷	5
● Cuvée Jus Osculi '99		🍷🍷	4
● A. A. Lagrein Scuro Pitz Thurü Ris. '99		🍷	4

● A. A. Cabernet Ris. '00		🍷🍷	5
● A. A. Cabernet-Lagrein Bautzanum '00		🍷🍷	5
● A. A. Lagrein Scuro Ris. '00		🍷🍷	5
● A. A. Merlot Ris. '00		🍷🍷	5
○ A. A. Sauvignon Gur zu Sand '01		🍷🍷	5
● A. A. Pinot Nero Ris. '00		🍷	5
● A. A. Lagrein Scuro Ris. '97		🍷🍷	5
● A. A. Cabernet-Lagrein Bautzanum Ris. '99		🍷🍷	5
● A. A. Merlot Ris. '99		🍷🍷	5

BOLZANO/BOZEN

Thomas Mayr e Figli
Fraz. Gries
Via Mendola, 56
39100 Bolzano/Bozen
tel. 0471281030
e-mail: thomas@mayr.cjb.net

This small estate returns to a full Guide profile after relegation for a year to the Other Wineries section. The success is due to the two Lagreins, the base and the Riserva, from the 2000 vintage. Both are great examples of their respective categories. We retasted and re-assessed the Lagrein '00 this year since for the last edition of the Guide, we had only tasted a barrel sample and our critique was provisional. With its very typical, concentrated colour, and fragrant berry bouquet, it makes very pleasant drinking, even though the body is far from highly concentrated. The Lagrein Riserva '00 is obviously denser on both nose and palate. The intense nose and a well-defined palate with its distinct tannic weave take you through to a long finish worthy of a champion. Though definitely too young now, it will grow. The other wines submitted were also very nice. The Santa Maddalena Rumplerhof, in its 2001 version, is again attractive. An upfront, quaffable red, it is impossible to dislike. The Chardonnay '01 is also agreeable, balanced and not without character. All in all, this Bolzano winery more than earns its promotion, which was brought about not only by the favourable vintages under review but especially solid efforts in vineyards and cellars. The crystalline clarity of the aromas in the wines we tasted provides unmistakable proof of this.

BOLZANO/BOZEN

Josephus Mayr
Erbhof Unterganzner
Loc. Cardano/Kardaun
Via Campiglio, 15
39053 Bolzano/Bozen
tel. 0471365582

Situated at the eastern end of the broad sunny valley of Bolzano, the long-established Mayr-Unterganzner estate contributed five wines to our final tastings and won a very well-deserved Three Glasses. It's a result no other privately owned winery in Alto Adige has come near to achieving. Josephus Mayr concentrates all his efforts in the vineyard on one very precise objective: growing top quality fruit by keeping yields low and managing the vineyards in total harmony with the environment and nature. Lagrein is the estate's most important variety and the outstanding example of the genre from their product line is the Lagrein Scuro Riserva '99. Intense and very concentrated ruby red, it reveals satisfying chocolate and berry fruit notes, and explodes onto the palate with lavish sweetness and a seamlessly sustained progression. Again from a lagrein base, the red Lamarein 2000 is also excellent. Its intense ripe fruit, with notes of nuts, spices and honey, is concentrated and rich, with tannins that are only slightly raw in the finish. The Cabernet Sauvignon 1999 is really great, with its excellent sweet, complex texture, and the red Composition Reif '00 is just as concentrated, linear and deep. And now something almost unthinkable until a few years ago, as it was for Lagrein until ten years ago: a Santa Maddalena in the finals! Josephus Mayr has surpassed himself with the Santa Maddalena Classico 2000, a concentrated, stylish, fruit-driven, wine of extraordinary drinkability. The Lagrein Rosè '01 is simple and well-made, just like the Chardonnay '01.

● A. A. Lagrein Scuro '00	ΨΨ	3*
● A. A. Lagrein Scuro Ris. '00	ΨΨ	5
○ A. A. Chardonnay '01	Ψ	4
● A. A. Santa Maddalena Cl. Rumplerhof '01	Ψ	3
● A. A. Lagrein Scuro '93	ΨΨ	3
● A. A. Lagrein Scuro Ris. '94	ΨΨ	4
● A. A. Lagrein Scuro '95	ΨΨ	3
● A. A. Lagrein Scuro Ris. '96	ΨΨ	4
● A. A. Lagrein Scuro S. '97	ΨΨ	4
● A. A. Lagrein Scuro S. '98	ΨΨ	4
● A. A. Santa Maddalena Cl. Rumplerhof '99	ΨΨ	3

● A. A. Lagrein Scuro Ris. '99	ΨΨΨ	5
● A. A. Santa Maddalena Cl. '00	ΨΨ	3*
● Composition Reif '00	ΨΨ	6
● Lamarein '00	ΨΨ	7
● A. A. Cabernet Sauvignon '99	ΨΨ	5
○ A. A. Chardonnay '01	Ψ	4
⊙ A. A. Lagrein Rosato V. T. '01	Ψ	4
● A. A. Lagrein Scuro Ris. '97	ΨΨΨ	5
● A. A. Lagrein Scuro Ris. '98	ΨΨΨ	5
● Lamarein '99	ΨΨ	6
● A. A. Cabernet Sauvignon '98	ΨΨ	5
● A. A. Lagrein Scuro '98	ΨΨ	3
● Lamarein '98	ΨΨ	6
● A. A. Santa Maddalena Cl. '99	ΨΨ	3

BOLZANO/BOZEN

Georg Mumelter
Via Rencio, 66
39100 Bolzano/Bozen
tel. 0471973090
e-mail: mumelter@garolmail.net

Georg Mumelter's Santa Maddalena Classico '01 made it to our finals but did not win Three Glasses. However, its great quality for a wine in this category means more than any official recognition. This is because Santa Maddalenas are light, fragrant, pleasant reds, rarely given a second thought. Great wines, says standard wisdom, are hyper-coloured and hyper-concentrated. We feel Santa Maddalenas are the Italian equivalent of Beaujolais Village, a kind of Südtiroler Beaujolais, since they have in common the noble simplicity of country gentlemen. The Classico '01 from Mumelter is an object lesson in drinkability. It's one of those bottles that always finish too quickly and the wine that goes surprisingly well with the local cuisine from the area. The Lagrein Scuro Riserva '00 is very good, but that is nothing new. A bit too young and edgy to reach the third glass, it has nice intense aromas and a lot of character in its flavour. Next came the linear, fairly varietal Pinot Grigio '01, which is well enough typed but a bit predictable in its overall expression. Taken together, these are wines that provide a substantial endorsement and more proof of the constant quality this small winery has been demonstrating for the past few years.

●	A. A. Lagrein Scuro Ris. '00	♀♀	5
●	A. A. Santa Maddalena Cl. '01	♀♀	3*
○	A. A. Pinot Grigio Griesbauerhof '01	♀	4
●	A. A. Lagrein Scuro Ris. '99	♀♀♀	5
○	A. A. Pinot Grigio Griesbauerhof '00	♀♀	4
●	Isarcus '00	♀♀	5
●	A. A. Santa Maddalena '00	♀	3

BOLZANO/BOZEN

Pfeifer Johannes
Pfannenstielhof
Via Pfannestiel, 9
39100 Bolzano/Bozen
tel. 0471970884 - 3388116623
e-mail: info@pfannenstielhof.it

The results from this winery speak for themselves. Three out of four Lagreins from Johannes Pfeifer ended up in the finals, all coming agonizingly close to winning the Guide's top award. It's a remarkable success for Johannes, a courageous winemaker who has been working steadily to turn his estate into one of the benchmarks for wine in the Lagrein. His family business has a very long history: Pfeifers have been making wine here since 1561. Fruit grown exclusively on estate-owned vineyards is brought to the cellar and vinified. Lagrein and Santa Maddalena are by far the most representative products on the winery's list. The intense ruby Lagrein Scuro Riserva '00 is fruity and spicy on the nose, then develops on the palate with remarkable character and personality. The Lagrein Scuro Riserva '99 has inviting fresh fruit notes, accompanied by wisps of smoke. The palate has nice structure but the oak is handled with less success. The powerful, rich Lagrein Scuro '00, with its sweet tannins is very good, as is the Lagrein Scuro '01, a naturally less complex wine, as it should be, with very pleasant tones of youthful alcohol. The Pinot Nero 2001 is fairly well-typed but a bit closed. Finally, the Santa Maddalena Classico '01 is fresh and easy-drinking.

●	A. A. Lagrein Scuro '00	♀♀	4*
●	A. A. Lagrein Scuro Ris. '00	♀♀	5
●	A. A. Lagrein Scuro Ris. '99	♀♀	5
●	A. A. Lagrein Scuro '01	♀	4
●	A. A. Pinot Nero '01	♀	4
●	A. A. Santa Maddalena Cl. '01	♀	3
●	A. A. Santa Maddalena Cl. '00	♀♀	4
●	A. A. Lagrein Scuro Ris. '98	♀	5
●	A. A. Lagrein Scuro '99	♀	4

BOLZANO/BOZEN

Heinrich Plattner - Waldgries
Santa Giustina, 2
39100 Bolzano/Bozen
tel. 0471973245

Father and son team Heinrich and Christian Plattner make wines with exceptional class from their five hectares of vineyards. Aside from their impeccable local red, the Santa Maddalena, the Plattners produce excellent Lagrein and Cabernet Sauvignon, not to mention great sweet wines that are now flagship products. The Cabernet Sauvignon '99 was truly great this year. An intense ruby, it opens on the nose with strong, varietal notes of perfectly defined fruit. The palate shows character, solid structure and long length. This well-made wine won a first, thoroughly well-deserved Three Glass prize for the Plattners. If we move on to the other wines, the Cabernet Sauvignon '00 is still a bit closed but well-structured, with great body and oak that is perhaps a little assertive. An unremitting search for quality in both vineyard and cellar has created the exceptional Lagrein Mirell '99, an impressively deep and powerfully concentrated wine, even though the tannins are not perhaps as fine-grained as they might be. The Santa Maddalena Classico '01 is without a doubt one of the best examples of its category. The sweet wines, too, are as magnificent, as usual. At the head of the class is the white Peperum '00 from moscato giallo grapes, one of the great dried-grape "passito" wines from this part of the world. A golden green-flecked straw yellow, it proffers a very intense, complex bouquet with notes of caramel, then balanced structure on the palate, well-supported by the acidity. The Moscato Rosa '00 is just as impressive. Finally, the Pinot Bianco '01 Riol seems simpler.

● A. A. Cabernet Sauvignon '99	🍷🍷🍷	6
○ A. A. Bianco Passito Peperum '00	🍷🍷	6
● A. A. Lagrein Scuro Ris. Mirell '99	🍷🍷	7
● A. A. Santa Maddalena Cl. '01	🍷🍷	3*
● A. A. Cabernet Sauvignon '00	🍷🍷	6
● A. A. Moscato Rosa '00	🍷🍷	6
○ A. A. Terlano Pinot Bianco Riol '01	🍷	4
● A. A. Cabernet Sauvignon '94	🍷🍷	5
● A. A. Cabernet Sauvignon '95	🍷🍷	5
● A. A. Cabernet Sauvignon '96	🍷🍷	5
● A. A. Lagrein Scuro Ris. '97	🍷🍷	5
○ A. A. Bianco Passito Peperum '98	🍷🍷	5
● A. A. Cabernet Sauvignon '98	🍷🍷	4
● A. A. Lagrein Scuro Ris. '98	🍷🍷	4
● A. A. Moscato Rosa '99	🍷🍷	5

BOLZANO/BOZEN

Cantina Produttori S. Maddalena/Cantina di Bolzano
Fraz. Gries - P.zza Gries, 2
39100 Bolzano/Bozen
tel. 0471972944 - 0471270909
e-mail: info@cantinamaddalena.com

This year, you will find the name "Produttori di Santa Maddalena" alongside "Cantina di Bolzano" in our profile header. The historic merger with the prestigious winery from Gries is definitive. Though both establishments will both keep their own brands, the two cellars will be managed jointly. And what better way to celebrate than with Three Glasses? The greatest version ever of the Lagrein Scuro Riserva Taberhof, an absolutely fantastic wine that will silence all Lagrein sceptics, took top honours this time. Despite its obvious youth, it shows a full nose of spice and mint, then a concentrated, solid palate with tight-knit tannins and a delightful exotic hint. The finish is nice and long. But that's not all. Two more wines almost took our highest prize: the very good Sauvignon '01 Mockhof, by now a classic, and the Gewürztraminer '01 Kleinstein. The first shows delightful notes of tropical fruit and a stylish, complex palate lifted by an refreshing acid vein. The Gewürztraminer is redolent of acacia honey, then shows well-sustained richness and power in the mouth, with interesting mineral hints. The Cabernet Riserva Mumelter '00 is also excellent, lacking only a bit of structure to qualify as a great wine. It has sweet tannins and a soft mouthfeel with good weight. The stemware continues to pile up with the ever dependable Santa Maddalena Classico Huck am Bach '01, the excellent Lagrein Scuro Perl '00, the typical, refined Pinot Nero Riserva Sandlahner '00, all of which won Two Glasses, and the well-made Chardonnay Kleinstein '01.

● A. A. Lagrein Scuro Taberhof Ris. '00	🍷🍷🍷	6
○ A. A. Gewürztramier Kleinstein '01	🍷🍷	4*
○ A. A. Sauvignon Mockhof '01	🍷🍷	5*
● A. A. Cabernet Mumelterhof '00	🍷🍷	6
● A. A. Lagrein Scuro Perl '00	🍷🍷	4
● A. A. Pinot Nero Sandlahner Ris. '00	🍷🍷	5
● A. A. Santa Maddalena Cl. Huck am Bach '01	🍷🍷	4
○ A. A. Chardonnay Kleinstein '01	🍷	4
● A. A. Cabernet Mumelterhof '94	🍷🍷	3
● A. A. Cabernet Mumelterhof '95	🍷🍷	4
● A. A. Lagrein Scuro Taberhof Ris. '95	🍷🍷	4
● A. A. Cabernet Mumelterhof '97	🍷🍷	5
● A. A. Lagrein Scuro Taberhof '98	🍷🍷	5
● A. A. Lagrein Scuro Taberhof Ris. '99	🍷🍷	6

BOLZANO/BOZEN

Georg Ramoser - Untermoserhof
Loc. Funes
Via Santa Maddalena, 36
39100 Bolzano/Bozen
tel. 0471975481
e-mail: untermoserhof@rolmail.net

Georg Ramoser's Santa Maddalena estate is tiny. He has only two and a half hectares, plus another two he rents at Cornaiano and Appiano, and total annual production is around 30,000 bottles. Despite those modest dimensions, Georg gave us a very respectable series of wines. We'll begin with a powerful version of the Lagrein Riserva '00, which was only a heartbeat away from Three Glasses. What detracted from its score was the slightly over-assertive presence of oak in the aroma profile. The impenetrable ruby red leads into a nose of coffee, pencil lead and berry fruit. The big, rich palate offers dense, sweet tannins and charming mineral touches. It's still a little young, though, and will give its best after some time in the cellar. The Merlot Riserva '00 also sailed through to the Three Glass finals. It may well be the best version ever to come out of this winery, with its deep ruby red, intense fruit and well-defined nose. The palate expands over dense, velvety tannins, ending in a very elegant, lingering finish. To round things off, the Santa Maddalena Classico '01 is as pleasant as usual. The typical fruit aromas reveal grassy notes and it is fresh and easy-drinking in the mouth.

BOLZANO/BOZEN

Hans Rottensteiner
Via Sarentino, 1
39100 Bolzano/Bozen
tel. 0471282015
e-mail: rottensteiner.weine@dnet.it

Toni Rottensteiner, an outstanding personality among Alto Adige winemakers, and his son Hannes, who is himself an enthusiastic oenologist, manage this cellar. Located at the entrance to the Val Sarentino, northwest of the city of Bolzano, the 15 hectares of the Rottensteiner property are in classic Lagrein and Santa Maddalena country. The winery also buys grapes from 80 private growers to produce 10,000 hectolitres of wine annually from the best vineyards in the region. This year, the Rottensteiners dazzled us again with their Gewürztraminer. The Gewürztraminer Cresta '00, made from grapes left to raisin for a couple of months in baskets before pressing and fermentation, is an extraordinary sweet wine and one of the best in its class. A lustrous deep gold, with impressively intense, fragrant aromas of honey, coconut and chamomile, it tempts with a big, sweet and concentrated body. The Lagrein Riserva from the 1999 vintage is very good. The clean, intensely fruity profile on the nose leads into a harmonious palate that is full-bodied and persistent. The Cabernet Riserva Select 1999 scored flatteringly well for it's a full, rich and deliciously concentrated wine. The Santa Maddalena Classico Premstallerhof is just as good as ever. Lean, fruit-rich and full-bodied, it soon has you reaching for a second glass. Finally, the Lagrein Grieser Riserva and the other house whites were all decent.

● A. A. Lagrein Scuro Ris. '00	♕♕	5
● A. A. Merlot Ris. '00	♕♕	5
● A. A. Santa Maddalena Cl '01	♕	3
● A. A. Lagrein Scuro Ris. '97	♕♕♕	5
● A. A. Lagrein Scuro Ris. '99	♕♕	5
● A. A. Merlot '97	♕♕	5
● A. A. Lagrein Scuro Ris. '98	♕♕	5
● A. A. Merlot '98	♕♕	4
● A. A. Merlot '99	♕♕	5
● A. A. Santa Maddalena Cl. '99	♕♕	3

○ A. A. Gewürztraminer Cresta '00	♕♕	6
● A. A. Cabernet Select Ris '99	♕♕	5
● A. A. Lagrein Scuro Ris. '99	♕♕	4
○ A. A. Gewürztraminer Cancenai '01	♕	4
○ A. A. Müller Thurgau '01	♕	3
○ A. A. Pinot Bianco Carnol '01	♕	3
● A. A. Santa Maddalena Cl. Premstallerhof '01	♕	3
● A. A. Lagrein Scuro Grieser Select Ris. '99	♕	5
○ A. A. Gewürztraminer Cancenai '00	♕♕	4
● A. A. Pinot Nero Mazzon Select Ris. '97	♕♕	5

BOLZANO/BOZEN

Heinrich & Thomas Rottensteiner
Fraz. Rencio
Via Santa Maddalena, 35
39100 Bolzano/Bozen
tel. 0471973549
e-mail: info@obermoser.it

In their production philosophy, and in the very limited number of bottles they release, the small producers in the Santa Maddalena zone resemble the "vignerons" from the Côte d'Or in Burgundy. They also share a certain, attractively rough manner and great respect for their varieties and land. Heinrich Rottensteiner and his son Thomas are among the most representative of this band of growers and their wines are full of soul and character. The best, the most representative wine, and also the one that conveys this terroir most perfectly, is without a doubt the Lagrein Scuro Grafenleiten, on show this year in the 2000 vintage. And in our opinion, it has never been as impressive. The colour is a concentrated red, which is of course absolutely normal, but then come the aromas, wonderfully playing off oak against wild berries, then the decisive yet elegant flavour reveals close-knit, fine-grained tannins, free of excessively bitter rustic features. All this makes it one of the best wines of it type, certainly from the vintage in question. The Cabernet-Merlot Putz Riserva, also from 2000, is as good as ever but with more of an international style that is perhaps a little too ingratiating. The light red Santa Maddalena Classico '01 is agreeable, simple and easy to drink, though it would be hard to accuse it of complexity.

BOLZANO/BOZEN

Tenuta Unterortl-Castel Juval
Loc. Stava/Staben
Fraz. Juval, 1/B
39020 Bolzano/Bozen
tel. 0473667580
e-mail: familie.aurich@dnet.it

Only two wines were submitted from this winery owned by mountaineer Reinhold Messner but managed for years now by husband and wife team Martin and Gisela Aurich. Martin also teaches oenology at the Istituto Agrario di San Michele all'Adige and one of the best wine technicians in the region. As we were saying, there were just two wines presented but both were very interesting, proof that the small group of growers in Valle Venosta is evidently becoming more and more quality conscious. The Riesling Castel Juval '01 is one of the best in its category this year. Its very varietal aromas reveal already discernible mineral notes despite its extreme youth. The palate is confident and the acidity supports the body, giving the mouthfeel elegance and freshness in addition to the classic aristocratic profile possessed by every true-bred Riesling. Castel Juval '01 went through to our finals and only missed out on a Third Glass because of its extreme youth. Again from 2001, the Pinot Bianco is also very nice. A deliciously fruity wine with delicate structure, it flaunts a pleasant acid vein that makes it temptingly easy to drink. You could not expect more from the three hectares of vineyard on this small estate.

● A. A. Lagrein Scuro Grafenleiten Ris. '00	🍷🍷	5
● A. A. Cabernet-Merlot Putz Ris. '00	🍷🍷	5
● A. A. Santa Maddalena Cl. '01	🍷	3
● A. A. Cabernet-Merlot Putz Ris. '99	🍷🍷	5
● A. A. Lagrein Scuro Grafenleiten Ris. '97	🍷🍷	5

○ A. A. Valle Venosta Riesling '01	🍷🍷	4*
○ A. A. Valle Venosta Pinot Bianco '01	🍷🍷	3*
○ A. A. Valle Venosta Riesling '00	🍷🍷🍷	4
● A. A. Valle Venosta Pinot Nero '95	🍷🍷	5
○ A. A. Valle Venosta Riesling '96	🍷🍷	4
● A. A. Valle Venosta Pinot Nero '97	🍷🍷	5
○ A. A. Valle Venosta Riesling '97	🍷🍷	4
○ A. A. Valle Venosta Pinot Bianco '98	🍷🍷	3
○ A. A. Valle Venosta Riesling '98	🍷🍷	4
● A. A. Valle Venosta Pinot Nero '99	🍷🍷	5
○ A. A. Valle Venosta Riesling '99	🍷🍷	4

BRESSANONE/BRIXEN (BZ)

Kuenhof - Peter Pliger
Loc. Mara, 110
39042 Bressanone/Brixen (BZ)
tel. 0472850546

There is more to Alto Adige winemaking than just co-operative wineries. Peter Pliger, with the fundamental contribution of his bright, friendly wife Brigitte, is a good example of the ability of small producers to create great wines. The products from Kuenhof this year are very well-made although, sadly, only 25,000 bottles were released. The range has achieved a character, a definition and a truly remarkable expression of the Valle Isarco terroir. These are deep, complex wines that need years to best express themselves and in fact on a recent visit of ours to the wonderful 17th-century Pliger family seat, we tasted a Traminer from 1990 that was still in splendid shape. But this year, they certainly impressed our tasters during the final taste-offs. So Three Glasses go to the Riesling Renano Kaiton '01, a deep, complex, rich wine with captivating minerality and a long finish. This is a wine that in all probability has a very long life ahead of it. The Sylvaner from the same year came a close second. Rich in the mouth, with damson and white peach, and acidity that is sustained yet well-integrated into the palate. It also reveals a mineral tone that recalls the rocky terrain of the valley. The Veltliner '01 is concentrated and elegant, with medicinal herbs and a very fresh finish. The Gewürztraminer is also as good as ever. There are two more points worth mentioning. The first is that prices are extremely competitive and the second is that Peter has practically eliminated chemicals in vineyards and cellar, and keeps the use of sulphur to an absolute minimum.

O	Kaiton '01	???	4
O	A. A. Valle Isarco Sylvaner '01	??	4*
O	A. A. Valle Isarco Gewürztraminer '01	??	4*
O	A. A. Valle Isarco Veltliner '01	??	4*
O	Kaiton '99	???	4
O	A. A. Valle Isarco Sylvaner '00	??	4*
O	Kaiton '00	??	4*
O	A. A. Valle Isarco Veltliner '00	??	4*
O	Kaiton '97	??	4
O	A. A. Valle Isarco Gewürztraminer '98	??	4
O	A. A. Valle Isarco Sylvaner '98	??	4
O	A. A. Valle Isarco Sylvaner '99	??	4
O	A. A. Valle Isarco Veltliner '99	??	4

BRESSANONE/BRIXEN (BZ)

Manfred Nössing - Hoandlhof
Fraz. Kranebih
Weinbergstrasse, 66
39042 Bressanone/Brixen (BZ)
tel. 0472832672

Manfred Nossing is part of the growing group of small producers, especially in the Valle Isarco, that are bringing new vitality to winemaking in Alto Adige with wines of personality and character. Though each has chosen a personal path, all aim to make genuine wines that represent the variety, climate and territory. From his four hectares near Bressanone, at around 600 meters in altitude, Nossing produces wines that are daunting when young, with aromas not yet perfectly defined, but which have exceptional structure and character. The result of all this stubborn enthusiasm is that this year his Gewürztraminer '01 came very close indeed to Three Glasses. Though its aromas are still not well-defined, the palate is stunning but we were most amazed by its truly remarkable elegance and very long finish. It's a very particular wine that holds some nice surprises. The classic Sylvaner '01 is nearly as good. The powerful, concentrated palate has great finesse and persistence, a characteristic mineral note and substantial acidity – none of the wines are given malolactic fermentation – that is well-integrated into the palate. The Müller Thurgau, again from the 2001 vintage, is also good. Pleasant floral notes accompany a fresh, pleasant palate. More than the other wines, the Kerner and Veltliner '01 pay the price for having been tasted before they were bottled. Unfortunately, Guide publishing deadlines did not allow us to postpone our tastings.

O	A. A. Valle Isarco Gewürztraminer '01	??	4*
O	A. A. Valle Isarco Müller Thurgau '01	??	4
O	A. A. Valle Isarco Sylvaner '01	??	4*
O	A. A. Valle Isarco Kerner '01	?	4
O	A. A. Valle Isarco Veltliner '01	?	4
O	A. A. Valle Isarco Kerner '00	??	4
O	A. A. Valle Isarco Gewürztraminer '00	??	4
O	A. A. Valle Isarco Müller Thurgau '00	??	3*
O	A. A. Valle Isarco Kerner '99	??	4
O	A. A. Valle Isarco Müller Thurgau '99	??	3
O	A. A. Valle Isarco Sylvaner '99	??	4

CALDARO/KALTERN (BZ)

Cantina Viticoltori di Caldaro
Via Cantine, 12
39052 Caldaro/Kaltern (BZ)
tel. 0471963149 - 0471963124
e-mail: info@kellereikaltern.com

Though this winery's best-known wine is the Lago di Caldaro Classico, it is no secret that oenologist Helmuth Zozin nurtures a passion for Cabernet and Pinot Nero, and lately also sweet dried-grape "passito" wines. One of the last type is the Moscato Giallo Passito Serenade 1999, which routed the competition this year. An extraordinary amber gold "passito", it throws a very intense nose of chamomile, honey and tropical fruit, then the full-bodied sweet and delicately textured palate lingers with particular persistence. The Cabernet Sauvignon Pfarrhof Riserva '99 is very nearly as good. Self-confident blackberry fruit and spices usher in a very broad, complex palate, lifted by fine-grained tannins. The Pinot Nero Riserva '99 is up there with them. It's an elegantly rounded, expressive and concentrated interpretation of the variety. The intense Cabernet Sauvignon Campaner Riserva '00 has berry fruit notes and a sweet touch of well-integrated oak. This excellent wine also boasts a great price-quality ratio. The Premstalerhof '01 was a real surprise for us this year as it turned out to be one of the best Sauvignons from Alto Adige. A greenish straw yellow, it offers intense tropical fruit, and a big, powerful palate. The other whites presented were also excellent. They are the varietal, concentrated Pinot Grigio Söll '01, the very fruity Chardonnay Wadleith '01, and the full, tangy Pinot Bianco Vial '01.

○ A. A. Moscato Giallo Passito Serenade '99	▼▼▼	6
○ A. A. Sauvignon Premstalerhof '01	▼▼	4*
● A. A. Cabernet Sauvignon Pfarrhof Ris. '99	▼▼	6
● A. A. Pinot Nero Ris. '99	▼▼	6
● A. A. Cabernet Sauvignon Campaner Ris. '00	▼▼	5
○ A. A. Chardonnay Wadleith '01	▼	4
○ A. A. Pinot Bianco Vial '01	▼	4
○ A. A. Pinot Grigio Söll '01	▼	4*
○ A. A. Sauvignon Premstalerhof '00	▼▼▼	4*
○ A. A. Gewürztraminer Campaner '99	▼▼▼	4

CALDARO/KALTERN (BZ)

Kettmeir
Via delle Cantine, 4
39052 Caldaro/Kaltern (BZ)
tel. 0471963135
e-mail: kettmeir@kettmeir.com

Kettmeir in Caldaro/Kaltern is one of the largest and most famous wineries in Alto Adige. Owned by the Marzotto/Santa Margherita group, which has managed it for years with entrepreneurial spirit and professionalism. Despite this promise, results are good but not excellent. In recent editions of the Guide, we have frequently expressed a hope that the cellar would produce the top-rank results that the obvious efforts of the headquarters in Portogruaro deserve. Almost all the wines presented this year earned decent scores but none was really awe-inspiring. At this point, the name and prestige of the estate lead us to feel sure that something really interesting will at last emerge from the cellar door. The non-vintage Spumante Brut, Pinot Grigio Maso Reiner '01 and Cabernet Maso Castello '99 are probably the best bottles in the range and deservedly take Two Glasses. The Chardonnay '01, again from Maso Reiner, and fragrant Lago di Caldaro '01, both earned one. However, there was only a mention for the Pinot Nero Maso Reiner '00, a wine the panel found hard to interpret in terms both of its vinification and of its rather unexciting sensory profile, which fails to convey the varietal characteristics of the grape with sufficient precision.

○ A. A. Pinot Grigio Maso Rainer '01	▼▼	4*
● A. A. Cabernet Sauvignon Maso Castello '99	▼▼	5
○ A. A. Spumante Brut	▼▼	5
○ A. A. Chardonnay Maso Rainer '01	▼	4
● A. A. Lago di Caldaro Cl. '01	▼	3
● A. A. Pinot Nero Maso Reiner '00		4
○ A. A. Chardonnay Maso Rainer '00	▼▼	4*
○ A. A. Pinot Grigio Maso Reiner '00	▼▼	4*

CALDARO/KALTERN (BZ)

Prima & Nuova/Erste & Neue
Via delle Cantine, 5
39052 Caldaro/Kaltern (BZ)
tel. 0471963122
e-mail: info@erste-neve.it

With 570 members, 315 hectares of vineyards and an average of 40,000 quintals of grapes processed annually, Prima & Nuova is the most important quality wine co-operatives in the region. The wines are sold in three lines that embrace almost all the varieties cultivated in Alto Adige. The most prestigious wines go out under the name Puntay, a label that includes three whites and two reds released in very limited quantities. The range got off to a great start with a masterful Three Glasses. The Traminer Aromatico Puntay '01 impressed us with its impeccable aromatic definition and the superb quality of the extract. A luminous gold, its intense bouquet unfolds on the nose with roses, tropical lychee and pineapple fruit, and chestnut honey, then floods onto the palate to finish long. The dessert wine Anthos '99 is also excellent. A well-measured blend of moscato giallo, traminer aromatico and sauvignon, left to partially dry for six months, its full, rich concentration unveils dried fruit and botrytis on the nose, then length and elegance in the mouth. The Cabernet Puntay '99 is mid ruby in hue, offering fruit and balsamic eucalyptus on the nose, well-integrated oak and remarkable structure, although the finish turns slightly bitter. The impressive Cabernet-Merlot Feld '99 has intense fruit and soft, concentrated structure. The Lago di Caldaro Scelto Puntay '01 is youthfully vinous and fruity, as well as engagingly drinkable. Finally, the Lagrein Puntay 2000, Pinot Bianco Puntay and fruity Chardonnay Salt 2001 are all well made.

○	A. A. Gewürztraminer Puntay '01	🍷🍷🍷	5
○	A. A. Chardonnay Salt '01	🍷🍷	4*
●	A. A. Cabernet Puntay '99	🍷🍷	5
●	A. A. Cabernet-Merlot Feld '99	🍷🍷	5
○	Anthos '99	🍷🍷	6
●	A. A. Lagrein Puntay '00	🍷	5
●	A. A. Lago di Caldaro Scelto Puntay '01	🍷	3
○	A. A. Pinot Bianco Puntay '01	🍷	3
●	A. A. Cabernet Puntay '97	🍷🍷🍷	5
○	A. A. Chardonnay Salt '00	🍷🍷	4*
●	A. A. Cabernet-Merlot Feld '98	🍷🍷	5
○	Anthos '98	🍷🍷	6
○	A. A. Chardonnay Puntay '99	🍷🍷	5
○	A. A. Gewürztraminer Puntay '99	🍷🍷	4

CALDARO/KALTERN (BZ)

Tenuta Ritterhof
Strada del vino, 1
39052 Caldaro/Kaltern (BZ)
tel. 0471963298
e-mail: info@ritterhof.it

Cantina Ritterhof in Caldaro has only existed for three years but is already well on its way to success. Owned by the Roner family winery in Termeno since 1999, it pursues a quality-oriented production philosophy and, not coincidentally, carries on its labels the motto "Crescendo" ("Growing"). Almost unbelievably, this year the Santa Maddalena Perlhof 2001 made it all the way to the final selections for Three Glasses. A wine with an intense, concentrated ruby hue, complex, stylish and intense fruit on the nose, it has a chewy, powerful mouthfeel and is very easy-drinking. The Gewürztraminer (Traminer Aromatico) '01 is a lovely straw yellow and has a fruit-driven, fragrant nose with undeniable complexity. There is good balance and thrust on the palate. The panel also liked the Pinot Grigio '01, for its deep straw yellow hue, delicately varietal, elegant fruit on the nose, then varietal character and nice persistence on the palate. The mature Cabernet-Merlot Riserva Crescendo '99 has faintly evolved notes while the red Perlhof Crescendo '01 is simple and easy-drinking. Both are decently made. The Merlot Riserva Crescendo '99 is a garnet ruby red with very ripe notes on the nose. The Lagrein Scuro Riserva Crescendo '99 offers balsamic notes that are not very invigorating on the nose, and a palate with concentration but also rather dry tannins.

●	A. A. Santa Maddalena Perlhof '01	🍷🍷	4*
○	A. A. Gewürztraminer '01	🍷🍷	4
○	A. A. Pinot Grigio '01	🍷🍷	4
●	Perlhof Crescendo '01	🍷	4
●	A. A. Cabernet Merlot Crescendo Ris. '99	🍷	5
●	A. A. Lagrein Scuro Crescendo Ris. '99	🍷	5
●	A. A. Merlot Crescendo Ris. '99	🍷	5
●	A. A. Lagrein Scuro Crescendo Ris. '98	🍷🍷	4
●	A. A. Merlot Ris. '98	🍷	4

CALDARO/KALTERN (BZ)

Josef Sölva - Niklaserhof
Loc. San Nicolo
Via Brunner, 31a
39052 Caldaro/Kaltern (BZ)
tel. 0471963432
e-mail: info@niklaserhof.it

Josef and Johanna Sölva have never presented us with a range of wines as good as this year's. Three finalists out of seven, one wine earned Two Glasses and the others gained at least one. These were marvellous results for a winery this small. But it also shows that, even with little in the way of resources, results like these can be reached if you care, strive, and put your heart into your work. But let's take things as they come. The Sauvignon Weingut Niklas '01 is very satisfactory, in fact one of the best in its category. The varietal tropical fruit introduces a palate that finds a perfect balance of elegance and concentration. The Pinot Bianco Klaser '00 is very nice, with a full, soft, lingering mouthfeel. Next up is the Alto Adige Bianco Mondevinum '01, from pinot bianco and sauvignon partially aged in small casks. All three are much more impressive than versions from years past. We could say as much of the Justinus Kerner '01, which has a citrus-themed nose and solid, harmonious structure, though only of average complexity. All the other bottles are decent or better, starting with the Pinot Bianco Weingut Niklas and continuing with the fragrant Lago di Caldaro Scelto Classico '01. Last in line is the Lagrein - Cabernet Klaser Riserva '99, which bears the scars of an unexceptional vintage.

CALDARO/KALTERN (BZ)

Peter Sölva & Söhne - Paterbichl
Via dell'Oro, 33
39052 Caldaro/Kaltern (BZ)
tel. 0471964650
e-mail: info@soelva.com

This year, the Sölva & Söhne range received a general endorsement and, above all, presented more wines than were submitted for the last edition of the Guide. That sums up the reasons why Peter and Stephan Sölva's small winery, in Caldaro/Kaltern, is in the Guide. Production comes to about 60,000 bottles and the most impressive were the two Amistar Rosso wines, both from 2000. Since they are released as "vino da tavola", there is no geographical indication and the label does not carry the vintage. There is a standard wine and the Edizione, both from a blend of lagrein, cabernet and merlot. In our opinion, the Edizione seemed slightly more concentrated, with better integrated and balanced oak, as the winemaker intended. It is an elegant red with good body and technically well made. The Amistar Bianco is also very good, and probably also comes from the 2000 harvest. Obtained from gewürztraminer, sauvignon and chardonnay, aged for around a year in small oak casks, it has very distinctive, original characteristics, with heady aromas on the nose and excellent body. The Lagrein-Merlot '01 is more run-of-the-mill and predictable. It may need a little more bottle ageing but is still very promising. The Lago di Caldaro Scelto Classico Superiore is pleasant, uncomplicated and easy to drink but the name is too long and complicated for a wine that, all things considered, is pretty straightforward.

○ A. A. Pinot Bianco Klaser '00	ϒϒ	4
○ A. A. Bianco Mondevinum '01	ϒϒ	5
○ A. A. Sauvignon '01	ϒϒ	4*
○ Justinus Kerner '01	ϒϒ	4
● A. A. Lago di Caldaro Scelto Cl. '01	ϒ	3
○ A. A. Pinot Bianco '01	ϒ	4
● A. A. Lagrein-Cabernet Klaser Ris. '99	ϒ	5
○ A. A. Bianco Mondevinum '00	ϒϒ	5
○ A. A. Sauvignon '00	ϒϒ	4*
● A. A. Lago di Caldaro Scelto Cl. '99	ϒϒ	2
○ A. A. Sauvignon '99	ϒϒ	2

○ Amistar Bianco '00	ϒϒ	5
● Amistar Rosso '00	ϒϒ	6
● Amistar Rosso Edizione '00	ϒϒ	6
● A. A. Lago di Caldaro Scelto Desilvas Peterleiten '01	ϒ	3
● A. A. Lagrein-Merlot '01	ϒ	4
● Amistar Rosso '99	ϒϒ	5
○ Amistar Bianco '99	ϒϒ	4

CERMES/TSCHERMS (BZ)

Graf Pfeil Weingut Kränzel
Via Palade, 1
39010 Cermes/Tscherms (BZ)
tel. 0473564549
e-mail: weingut@kraenzel-pfeil.com

Graf Pfeil Weingut Kränzl performed magnificently at this year's tastings. Out of seven wines submitted, one went through to the finals and five earned Two Glasses. This is a result of distinction, particularly when we remember that we are not talking about a big winery, and that the hills around Merano are less renowned than others areas in Alto Adige in terms of quality viticulture and winemaking. The real surprise was an extraordinarily fresh Sauvignon '01 with varietal tropical fruit aromas and elegant, aristocratic body. This was one of the best Sauvignons from the vintage. But two other wines were also very satisfactory, the sweet Alto Adige Bianco Helios '01 from a mainly pinot bianco base, and the Pinot Bianco '01, with exemplary balance though not excessively complex in character. Reds worth mentioning include the Cabernet-Merlot Sagittarius '00, the Cabernet '00 and the fragrant, very drinkable Schiava Baslan '01, a great little wine that is as exciting as ever. The tasting was less positive in the case of the Pinot Nero '00. But then the variety is so difficult get right that it comes as no surprise that this very competent cellar has not yet managed to master it entirely. To be honest, it's not such a big deal.

○	A. A. Sauvignon '01	▼▼	4
●	A. A. Cabernet '00	▼▼	6
●	A. A. Cabernet Sauvignon-Merlot Sagittarius '00	▼▼	6
○	A. A. Pinot Bianco '01	▼▼	3*
○	A. A. Bianco Helios '01	▼▼	5
●	A. A. Schiava Schloss Baslan '01	▼▼	5
●	A. A. Pinot Nero '00	▼	5
○	A. A. Pinot Bianco Helios '00	▼▼	5
○	A. A. Gewürztraminer Passito '00	▼▼	5
●	Sagittarius '96	▼▼	6
○	Dorado '97	▼▼	6
●	Sagittarius '97	▼▼	6
○	A. A. Bianco Passito Dorado '98	▼▼	6
●	A. A. Cabernet Sauvignon-Merlot Sagittarius '98	▼▼	6

CHIUSA/KLAUSEN (BZ)

Cantina Produttori Valle Isarco
Via Coste, 50
39043 Chiusa/Klausen (BZ)
tel. 0472847553
e-mail: info@cantinavalleisarco.it

Although it is the most recently formed co-operative winery in Alto Adige, the Cantina Produttori Valle Isarco has rapidly become a byword for quality white wines. But then the Valle Isarco does have ideal conditions for cultivating white grapes. Climate and terrain determine the particular properties and personality of these wines, whose elegance and character speak volumes for the philosophy of the winery and its 135 members. Among the best whites from the Cantina this year are the Silvaner Aristos 2001, a green-flecked straw yellow offering with intense fruit and a fresh, rich, concentrated palate and the full, flavoursome Pinot Grigio 2001, with its uncomplicatedly elegant style. The two Müller Thurgaus from 2001 are also excellent, having been obtained from grapes that find ideal ripening conditions on the sunny, steep slopes of the Valle Isarco. The Müller Thurgau Aristos has a greenish straw-yellow hue, intense fruit and a lean, vibrant flavour. The standard Müller Thurgau is an upfront, well-typed, balanced and very pleasant bottle. The medium-bodied Silvaner '01 is also typical and characteristic. The Kerner '01 is grassy and fresh, with decent extract, and the varietal Gewürztraminer (Traminer Aromatico) Aristos '01 has well-defined aromas and a hint of sweetness.

○	A. A. Valle Isarco Müller Thurgau '01	▼▼	3*
○	A. A. Valle Isarco Müller Thurgau Aristos '01	▼▼	4
○	A. A. Valle Isarco Pinot Grigio '01	▼▼	3*
○	A. A. Valle Isarco Sylvaner Aristos '01	▼▼	4
○	A. A. Valle Isarco Gewürztraminer Aristos '01	▼	4
○	A. A. Valle Isarco Kerner '01	▼	3
○	A. A. Valle Isarco Sylvaner '01	▼	3*
○	A. A. Valle Isarco Sylvaner '00	▼▼	3*
○	A. A. Valle Isarco Kerner '00	▼▼	3*
○	A. A. Valle Isarco Pinot Grigio '00	▼▼	3*
○	A. A. Valle Isarco Veltliner '00	▼▼	3

CORTACCIA/KURTATSCH (BZ)

CANTINA PRODUTTORI CORTACCIA
STRADA DEL VINO, 23
39040 CORTACCIAKURTATSCH (BZ)
TEL. 0471880115
E-MAIL: info@akellerei-kurtatsch.it

The 268 members of the Cantina Produttori Cortaccia co-operative work 238 hectares of vineyards, almost all on hillslope locations. This area is well-suited to white wines with a distinctive character, as well as complex, characterful reds. Two whites particularly stood out in the range submitted for tasting this year: the Traminer Aromatico Brenntal '01, a golden straw yellow wine with subdued aromas of Alpine herbs and a powerful, rich palate with good length; and the Sauvignon Milla '01, with varietal fruit sensations of mint and bell pepper, graciously and elegantly expressed. At the top of the list of reds from this winery is the Lagrein Fohrhof '00, an intense ruby offering with a broad, fruit-led nose of blackcurrant and raspberries, lifted by nuances of vanilla and coffee, then powerful, concentrated and soft in the mouth. That profile was good enough to win Three very solid Glasses. The Merlot Brenntal '99 is good, though a step down from versions from preceding years. The impressive Cabernet Kirchhügel '00 is tannic, with slightly super-ripe fruit. The Chardonnay Eberlehof '01 is also good, with a sweet, rich potent nose that reveals an oaky tone that could have been a tad more discreet. Finally, the Pinot Nero Fritzenhof '99 is decent, concentrated and a bit forward, with oak that rather masks the aromas. The Schiava Grigia Sonntaler 2001 is uncomplicated and pleasant.

● A. A. Lagrein Scuro Fohrhof '00	🍷🍷🍷	5
○ A. A. Sauvignon Milla '01	🍷🍷	4*
○ A. A. Traminer Aromatico Brenntal '01	🍷🍷	5
● A. A. Cabernet Kirchhügel '00	🍷🍷	5
○ A. A. Chardonnay Eberlehof '01	🍷🍷	5
● A. A. Merlot Brenntal '99	🍷🍷	7
○ A. A. Schiava Grigia Sonnntaler '01	🍷	4
● A. A. Pinot Nero Fritzenhof '99	🍷	6
● A. A. Cabernet Freienfeld '95	🍷🍷🍷	6
● A. A. Merlot Brenntal '95	🍷🍷🍷	5
● A. A. Cabernet Freienfeld '97	🍷🍷🍷	6
● A. A. Merlot Brenntal '97	🍷🍷🍷	5
● A. A. Merlot Brenntal '98	🍷🍷	6

CORTACCIA/KURTATSCH (BZ)

TIEFENBRUNNER
FRAZ. NICLARA
VIA CASTELLO, 4
39040 CORTACCIAKURTATSCH (BZ)
TEL. 0471880122
E-MAIL: info@tiefenbrunner.com

Tiefenbrunner's main aim in carrying out each task in the vineyards and cellar is to maintain the territorial character and high quality of the wines. These characteristics can be seen in the four different lines: Tiefenbrunner, Tiefenbrunner Classic, Castel Turmhof and Linticlarus. The most famous wine of all these is the Feldmarschall, a Müller Thurgau from one of the highest vineyards in Europe at more than 1,000 metres above sea level. The 2001 edition is a greenish straw-yellow wine with good aromas, freshness and full body. But we felt the most impressive bottles in the range submitted this year were the Traminer Aromatico Castel Turmhof '01, which is intense, very typical, delicate and complex, and the Moscato Rosa Linticlarus '99, with slightly spicy fruit and delicate tart notes on the palate. The two Chardonnays, the Castel Turmhof '01 and Linticlarus '98, are superb examples of their type. The Castel Turmhof first is concentrated and gutsy, whereas the Linticlarus is more discreet, mingling its fruit with notes of ripe tomato and honey. Two of the nicest reds are the Lagrein Castel Turmhof '00, which is fruity but a bit overdeveloped and rigid, and the Cabernet Sauvignon Linticlarus '99, with slightly dominating oak and acidity that is a bit intractable. In closing, the Pinot Nero Riserva Linticlarus '99 is decent.

○ A. A. Gewürztraminer Castel Turmhof '01	🍷🍷	5
● A. A. Moscato Rosa Linticlarus '99	🍷🍷	6
● A. A. Lagrein Castel Turmhof '00	🍷🍷	4
○ A. A. Chardonnay Castel Turmhof '01	🍷🍷	4
○ Feldmarschall von Fenner zu Fennberg '01	🍷🍷	5
○ A. A. Chardonnay Linticlarus '98	🍷🍷	5
● A. A. Cabernet Sauvignon Linticlarus '99	🍷🍷	6
● A. A. Pinot Nero Linticlarus Ris. '99	🍷	5
○ A. A. Cuvée Anna '00	🍷🍷	4
○ A. A. Sauvignon Kirchleiten '99	🍷🍷	4
● Linticlarus Cuvée '99	🍷🍷	5

CORTINA/KURTINIG (BZ)

PETER ZEMMER - KUPELWIESER
STRADA DEL VINO, 24
39040 CORTINA/KURTINIG (BZ)
TEL. 0471817143
E-MAIL: info@zemmer.com

We continue to keep Peter Zemmer and Kupelwieser in a single entry, even though we should start thinking of splitting them up in the near future. The ownership and even headquarters of the two wineries are the same but there are so many excellent wines that come to us for tasting that we risk cutting too many corners in our descriptions and stories. This year, we slightly preferred the Zemmer line because of two wines in particular. The first is the Pinot Grigio '01, a real house speciality. The other is the Cortinie Rosso '00, from lagrein, merlot, cabernet franc and sauvignon, which is much more impressive than in previous editions. The remaining wines were all good but not quite as outstanding, although special mention goes to the Lagrein-Cabernet Reserve from 1999. On the other hand, the wine that impressed us most from the Kupelwieser line was the Lagrein Intenditore '00, which is no surprise since it is one of the winery's flagship products. All the others pass muster, and are well made, but have less character compared to last year's versions. We'd like to spare a thought for the Riesling '01, which we felt was the best of the whites, followed closely by the Pinot Bianco. All these wines are distinguished by their reliability and a good price-quality ratio, one of most pleasant features of the Zemmer and Kupelwieser ranges.

● A. A. Lagrein Scuro Intenditore '00	🍷🍷	5
● Cortinie Rosso '00	🍷🍷	5
○ A. A. Pinot Grigio '01	🍷🍷	4*
○ A. A. Chardonnay '01	🍷	4
○ A. A. Müller Thurgau Intenditore '01	🍷	4
○ A. A. Pinot Bianco '01	🍷	4
○ A. A. Riesling Kupelwieser '01	🍷	4
○ A. A. Sauvignon Intenditore '01	🍷	4
○ Cortinie Bianco '01	🍷	5
● A. A. Cabernet-Lagrein Ris. '99	🍷	5
● A. A. Pinot Nero Matan '99	🍷	5
○ A. A. Riesling '00	🍷🍷	4*
○ A. A. Chardonnay Kupelwieser '00	🍷🍷	4*
○ A. A. Pinot Grigio '00	🍷🍷	4*
○ A. A. Riesling Kupelwieser '00	🍷🍷	4*

EGNA/NEUMARKT (BZ)

CANTINA H. LUN
FRAZ. VILLA
VIA VILLA, 22/24
39044 EGNA/NEUMARKT (BZ)
TEL. 0471813256
E-MAIL: contact@lun.it

The Lun winery is one of the longest-established in Alto Adige's long winemaking history and has occupied a leading position for more than 150 years. It keeps its status by leaving nothing to chance, using modern techniques and carefully selecting and vinifying the musts and wines. The Albertus line is Lun's most prestigious but the feather in their cap is the Sandbichler label, which includes a Pinot Nero and a white. All the wines presented are well-made, fruity and structured, with heaps of character and personality. Let's begin with the Pinot Nero Riserva Albertus '00, a very intense ruby wine with pure fruit, lots of rich, full body and good tannic structure. The Cabernet Sauvignon Riserva Albertus '99 is a concentrated ruby and flaunts a broad, persistent Bordeaux-style nose. The other Lun wines are also excellent. The Sauvignon Albertus '01 is a greenish straw yellow that introduces a grassy bouquet with hints of geranium. Full in the mouth, it shows a tad too much acidity. The Traminer Aromatico Albertus '01 offers intense fruit with super-ripe notes and a characterful palate. The medium-bodied white Sandbichler '01 presents fairly uncomplicated fruity sensations. The Lagrein Scuro Albertus Riserva '99 is very impressive. Its ruby red is intense, and the fruit-driven palate linear, with tight-knit tannins and good structure. Two of the wines were a little below par: the Pinot Grigio '01, which is lively and gutsy but not very well-defined; and the Pinot Nero Riserva Sandbichler '99, a varietal wine that is simple and somewhat dilute.

● A. A. Pinot Nero Albertus Ris. '00	🍷🍷	5
○ A. A. Bianco Sandbichler '01	🍷🍷	4*
○ A. A. Gewürztraminer Albertus '01	🍷🍷	5
○ A. A. Sauvignon Albertus '01	🍷🍷	5
● A. A. Cabernet Sauvignon Albertus Ris. '99	🍷🍷	6
● A. A. Lagrein Scuro Albertus Ris. '99	🍷🍷	6
○ A. A. Pinot Grigio '01	🍷	4
● A. A. Pinot Nero Sandbichler Ris. '99	🍷	4
○ A. A. Bianco Sandbichler '00	🍷🍷	4*
○ A. A. Sauvignon Albertus '00	🍷🍷	4
● A. A. Cabernet Albertus Ris. '95	🍷🍷	5
● A. A. Lagrein Scuro Albertus Ris. '98	🍷🍷	5
○ A. A. Gewürztraminer Albertus '00	🍷	4

MARLENGO/MARLING (BZ)

POPPHOF - ANDREAS MENZ
VIA TERZO DI MEZZO, 5
39020 MARLENGO/MARLING (BZ)
TEL. 0473447180
E-MAIL: info@popphof.com

Andreas Menz has never repeated his exploit with that fantastic Cabernet from '97. His wines are always good, well-made and very honest but we expect something more from him. He has the skill and, above all, the spirit, to achieve very high quality. His winery is small. His vineyards give him what they can each year but selections are difficult to make when the quantities are this small. However, the 2000 Merlot shows potential that is not completely expressed. It's nice enough, and fairly elegant, but it still lacks that pinch more concentration it needs to climb into the top ranks. The Riesling Unterberger '01 is also decent, with unmistakable varietal notes, citrus on the nose and an aristocratic flavour shot through with an acidity that lends freshness and elegance. The Pinot Bianco and Gewürztraminer, both from 2001, are decent but don't go much beyond an exercise in how to handle the varieties. The Lagrein Rosato from 2001 and Chardonnay Unterberger from the same vintage are both pleasant but nothing more. Some of the most representative wines from the range, such as the Katharina Bianco and Cuvée Popphof, were missing at roll call. We will have to come back next year to discuss them.

● A. A. Merlot '00	♇♇	5
○ A. A. Riesling '01	♇♇	5
○ A. A. Chardonnay '01	♇	4
○ A. A. Gewürztraminer '01	♇	4
◉ A. A. Lagrein Rosato '01	♇	3
○ A. A. Pinot Bianco '01	♇	4
● A. A. Cabernet '97	♇♇♇	5
● A. A. Cabernet '95	♇♇	5
● A. A. Cabernet '98	♇♇	5
○ Katharina	♇♇	5
● Popphof Cuvée	♇♇	5

MARLENGO/MARLING (BZ)

CANTINA PRODUTTORI BURGGRÄFLER
VIA PALADE, 64
39020 MARLENGO/MARLING (BZ)
TEL. 0473447137
E-MAIL: info@burggraefler.it

This co-operative winery near Merano gets its grapes from 190 members, enthusiastic small and medium-sized producers with well-positioned vineyards who carefully cultivate more than 120 hectares of vines in the Burgraviato area. The production philosophy is simple: "High quality for us means offering each variety the ideal place to grow and develop". Various wines from Burggräfler made good showings at our tastings: the Lagrein-Cabernet MerVin 2000, the late harvest Pinot Bianco MerVin Vendemmia Tardiva '00, the Pinot Nero and the Merlot. The Lagrein-Cabernet MerVin is a very intense, concentrated ruby and greets the nose with berry fruit and refined notes of toasty oak. Full, rich and soft on the palate, it expands into an intense finish. The late-harvest Pinot Bianco MerVin Vendemmia Tardiva, with its amber, gold colour and complex notes of botrytis, caramel and saffron, is sweet, pleasant and well-balanced on the palate. Grown in sandy soil on hillslopes around 500 meters above sea level, the grapes were harvested at the end of November, fermented and then aged in barriques. The Pinot Nero Tiefenthaler MerVin '00 is good, showing a zesty freshness, soft texture and a slight hint of bitterness in the mouth, then the very flavoursome Merlot 2000 has delicate fruit, and a soft, linear yet concentrated palate with sweet tannins. The Meranese Schickenburg, Merlot-Lagrein and Lagrein were all decent. Finally, the classic whites from the winery, including the Moscato Giallo Schickenburg '01, were good but a bit below their best.

● A. A. Lagrein-Cabernet MerVin '00	♇♇	5*
● A. A. Merlot '00	♇♇	5
○ A. A. Pinot Bianco MerVin V. T. '00	♇♇	6
● A. A. Pinot Nero Tiefenthaler MerVin '00	♇♇	5
● A. A. Lagrein '00	♇	5
● A. A. Merlot-Lagrein '00	♇	5
● A. A. Meranese Schickenburg '01	♇	3
○ A. A. Moscato Giallo Schickenburg '01	♇	4
○ A. A. Chardonnay Tiefenthaler '00	♇♇	4
● A. A. Merlot-Cabernet Juvin Cuvée '98	♇♇	5
○ A. A. Pinot Bianco Guggenberg '98	♇	3

MELTINA/MÖLTEN (BZ)

VIVALDI - ARUNDA
VIA CENTRO, 53
39010 MELTINA/MÖLTEN (BZ)
TEL. 0471668033
E-MAIL: arunda@dnet.it

This is one of the most famous "spumante" wineries in Alto Adige and the double name, as we remind you every year, is due to the fact that the brand is Arunda in Alto Adige, and Vivaldi in the rest of Italy. The proprietor and powerhouse behind all this is Josef Reiterer, a very personable and highly skilled oenologist with an inborn talent for producing premium sparkling wines. It is true that once, few wineries in Alto Adige were active in this particular sector of winemaking but there are now some good producers appearing and Reiterer has been a trailblazer in the field. The Vivaldi Brut '99 is his strong suit this year. It brings together complexity and freshness, with good depth on the palate and an easy, utterly likeable drinkability. All this thanks to the cellar's excellent refermentation technique. The non-vintage Arunda Brut is simpler and reminiscent of its big brother in general terms, but it does have less concentration. The Arunda Blanc de Blancs is also very nice. Delicate, fruity and with faint yeasty notes, it is more delicate its two stablemates. The panel thought the Arunda Extra Brut was the least enjoyable bottle in the range. The acidity is less restrained by the dosage and dominates the other components, making the profile a little vertical and lacking in balance. It's a pity.

MERANO/MERAN (BZ)

CANTINA PRODUTTORI DI MERANO
LOC. MAIA BASSA
VIA SAN MARCO, 11
39012 MERANO/MERAN (BZ)
TEL. 0473235544
E-MAIL: info@meranerkellerei.com

The Cantina Produttori di Merano presented us with an outstanding range this year. Out of seven wines submitted, three reached the finals and two won Two Glasses. These marvellous results give a good idea of the unstoppable growth of this major Alto Adige winery. The emblem of this growth could be the delicious Goldmuskateller Passito Sissi '00, one of the best Italian sweet wines, which regales the nose with distinctively fragrant aromas that owe nothing to Sauternes or Trockenbeerenauslese from the Mosel. Another finalist was the very good Chardonnay Goldegg '01, which manages to combine concentration with elegance and drinkability. In winemaking terms, it might be said to have "squared the circle". The Lagrein Scuro Segenpichl '00 is simply splendid. Concentrated yet soft, it lacks the rustic tannins and bitter aftertaste too often regarded as typical but instead caused by raw tannins. And there was more for out tasters. The Pinot Bianco Graf von Meran '01 came very near to winning a place in the final taste-offs and the Merlot Freiberg Riserva '99 was let down only by the unexceptional vintage around here that year. But if the '99 is this good, who knows what to expect from the 2000 version, which enjoyed a much better vintage? The Sauvignon and Gewürztraminer '01 from the Graf von Meran line are only decent but the winemaking team at the Merano co-operative really is first rate.

○ A. A. Spumante Brut Vivaldi '99	🍷🍷	4
○ A. A. Spumante Blanc de Blancs Arunda	🍷🍷	5
○ A. A. Spumante Brut Arunda	🍷🍷	5
○ A. A. Spumante Extra Brut Arunda	🍷🍷	5
○ A. A. Spumante Extra Brut Vivaldi '95	🍷🍷	5
○ A. A. Spumante Brut Arunda Ris. '96	🍷🍷	5

● A. A. Lagrein Scuro Segenpichl '00	🍷🍷	6
○ A. A. Moscato Giallo Passito Sissi Graf von Meran '00	🍷🍷	6
○ A. A. Chardonnay Goldegg '01	🍷🍷	3*
● A. A. Merlot Freiberg Ris. '99	🍷🍷	6
○ A. A. Pinot Bianco Graf von Meran '01	🍷🍷	5
○ A. A. Gewürztraminer Graf Von Meran '01	🍷	4
○ A. A. Sauvignon Graf Von Meran '01	🍷	4
● A. A. Pinot Nero Zenoberg '99	🍷🍷	5

MONTAGNA/MONTAN (BZ)

Franz Haas
Via Villa, 6
39040 Montagna/Montan (BZ)
Tel. 0471812280 - 0471820510
E-mail: info@franz-haas.it

The Moscato Rosa Schweizer '01, from the genial and highly competent Franz Haas is very good again this year. Sadly, it just missed out on a top award. Moscato rosa is a rare and difficult variety to grow but Franz has been interpreting it to perfection for years, turning it into a seriously good wine. The 2001 vintage version also has intense wild rose and ripe blackberry aromas that are only slightly veiled. The palate is concentrated, typical and sweet yet elegant, as well as remarkably complex. Then, there is the very interesting Pinot Nero Schweizer '00, from the variety that inspires this winemaker, whose obsession it is to make a wine that might have come from Burgundy. Ruby-hued, with varietal berry fruit aromas, it is full-bodied and linear on the palate. The IGT Mitterberg Rosso Istante '00, a Bordeaux blend, is concentrated and full, though a bit lacking in elegance. The Manna '00 version is interesting. A white wine aged 18 months in barrique, it shows well-defined aromas that lead into a palate that marries concentration with deliciously attractive elegance. The last two whites, the Gewürztraminer and Pinot Bianco, are also good, both again from the 2001 vintage. The Gewürztraminer has good typicity and elegance whereas the second is simpler but pleasant, with well-integrated acidity. This praiseworthy all-round performance suggests that Haas will soon return to the elite Three Glass club, perhaps with his beloved Pinot Nero. He has our heartfelt best wishes.

● A. A. Moscato Rosa Schweizer '01	🍷🍷	5
● A. A. Pinot Nero Schweizer '00	🍷🍷	6
● Istante '00	🍷🍷	6
○ Manna '00	🍷🍷	5
○ A. A. Gewürztraminer '01	🍷	5
○ A. A. Pinot Bianco '01	🍷	4
● A. A. Moscato Rosa Schweizer '00	🍷🍷🍷	5
● A. A. Moscato Rosa Schweizer '99	🍷🍷🍷	5
○ A. A. Gewürztraminer '00	🍷🍷	4
● A. A. Pinot Nero Schweizer '95	🍷🍷	5
● A. A. Pinot Nero Schweizer '97	🍷🍷	5
● A. A. Merlot Schweitzer '99	🍷🍷	5
● Istante '99	🍷🍷	5

NALLES/NALS (BZ)

Cantina Produttori Nalles
Niclara Magre
Via Heiligenberg, 2
39012 Nalles/Nals (BZ)
Tel. 0471678626
E-mail: info@kellerei.it

Nals, Entiklar and Margreid are the German names for the three distinct towns of Nalles, Niclara and Magré. The first is in the Terlano subzone, northwest of Bolzano, and the other two are in the southern part of Oltradige, south of Cortaccia, or Kurtatsch. The members of the Cantina Produttori tend vineyards in these zones and bring their grapes to one single production facility. It's a wise choice since this year, the most exciting tasting surprises in Alto Adige came from the Nals, Entiklar Margreid Kellereigenossenschaft. There was one Three Glass winner and another four finalists out of a total of eight samples presented: in short, a triumph. The powerful, soft, concentrated Chardonnay Baron Salvadori '00, with its tropical fruit bouquet, is a wonder and what is more, sells at a very reasonable price. It is a pleasure for us to award it Three Glasses. And then there is the lovely Terlano Pinot Bianco Sirmian '01, with its very clean aromas, and the Terlano Sauvignon Mantele '01, from the first vineyard of sauvignon planted in Alto Adige more than 20 years ago. Equally good are the powerful, varietal Pinot Grigio Punggl '01, and the sweet white Baronesse. The only wines not at the very top are the Merlot Levad '00, which is still very nice by the way, the Riesling Fidera '01 and Gewürztraminer '01 from the Baron Salvadori line. They're perhaps a bit young to express their full potential.

○ A. A. Chardonnay Baron Salvadori '00	🍷🍷🍷	5
○ A. A. Passito Baronesse '00	🍷🍷	6
○ A. A. Pinot Grigio Punggl '01	🍷🍷	4*
○ A. A. Terlano Pinot Bianco Sirmian '01	🍷🍷	4*
○ A. A. Terlano Sauvignon Cl. Mantele '01	🍷🍷	4*
● A. A. Merlot Levad '00	🍷🍷	5
○ A. A. Riesling Fidera '01	🍷🍷	4*
○ A. A. Gewürztraminer Baron Salvadori '01	🍷	5
○ A. A. Gewürztraminer Baron Salvadori '00	🍷🍷	5
○ A. A. Chardonnay Baron Salvadori '99	🍷🍷	5
○ A. A. Pinot Grigio Punggl '00	🍷🍷	4*
○ A. A. Terlano Pinot Bianco Sirmian '00	🍷🍷	4

NALLES/NALS (BZ)

CASTELLO SCHWANBURG
VIA SCHWANBURG, 16
39010 NALLES/NALS (BZ)
TEL. 0471678622

It is a little difficult for us to write about the production of this famous and important winery from near Terlano. We know its strengths, as well as the great enthusiasm of owner Dieter Rudolph Carli. We also know the history of its many decades, if not centuries, of grape and wine production. And yet, for a few years now, we have noticed that the wines from Schloss Schwanburg have become just part of the crowd. They're still basically correct but they never quite hit the high notes of excellence. It's something that particularly disappoints us. Obviously, there are plenty of well-made wines. The Two Glass winners among the whites, the Terlano Pinot Bianco Pitzon '01 and Riesling '01, are always a sure thing. Moving over to the reds, the Lagrein Riserva '99, Merlot Riserva '99 and Cabernet Sauvignon Castel Schwanburg '99, all from an unexciting vintage for the area, are hard to fault. But this is not very much from a winery as blue-blooded as Schloss Schwanburg. The other wines are decent, beginning with the Alto Adige Bianco Pallas '01, a blend of pinot bianco, chardonnay, sauvignon and riesling. Next is the nice Terlano Cuvée '01 and finally there is the Cabernet Sauvignon Riserva '99. Perhaps some of the difficulties, especially for the reds, came from only average harvests. Our wish, for both ourselves and Castello Schwanburg, is to taste more evidence of the cellar's lineage in the future and to see wines with more character. That objective is well within the grasp of this historic winery.

○ A. A. Riesling '01	🍷🍷	4*
○ A. A. Terlano Pinot Bianco Pitzon '01	🍷🍷	4*
● A. A. Cabernet Sauvignon Castel Schwanburg '99	🍷🍷	6
● A. A. Lagrein Scuro Ris. '99	🍷🍷	5
● A. A. Merlot Ris. '99	🍷🍷	5
○ A. A. Bianco Pallas '01	🍷	4
○ A. A. Terlano Cuvée '01	🍷	4
● A. A. Cabernet Sauvignon Ris. '99	🍷	5
○ A. A. Bianco Pallas '00	🍷🍷	4*
● A. A. Cabernet Sauvignon Ris. '96	🍷	4

NATURNO/NATURNS (BZ)

TENUTA FALKENSTEIN - FRANZ PRATZNER
FRAZ. VAL VENOSTA
VIA CASTELLO, 15
39025 NATURNO/NATURNS (BZ)
TEL. 0473666054
E-MAIL: falkenstein.naturns@rolmail.com

The 2001 vintage can hardly have been a great one for Franz Pratzner's Riesling. Our panellists found that this usually very good wine from Tenuta Falkenstein did not have the character, the same tautness, the unmistakable personality, that we have noticed in previous years. There can be no doubt that it is still one of the best Rieslings around, though. The citrus and mineral aromas are there but we felt the intensity and complexity of the '98, and perhaps also the 2000, were definitely superior. The Pinot Bianco '01 is as well made as ever, and perhaps even better than in the past, which is almost bucking the trend. It's as if the more southerly weather gave it an advantage. The Gewürztraminer Vendemmia Tardiva '01 continues to convince us only in part, though we felt it had also improved with respect to the slightly disappointing 2000 version. Again, its progress is very different from the Riesling's case. In general, the winery is taking two steps forward and one step back but, considered across the entire range, some progress can be seen in spite of everything. In brief, "Falcon's Rock" continues to have a fundamental role to play in the expanding vine-growing activities of Valle Venosta.

○ A. A. Valle Venosta Gewürztramlner V. T. '01	🍷🍷	5
○ A. A. Valle Venosta Pinot Bianco '01	🍷🍷	4*
○ A. A. Valle Venosta Riesling '01	🍷🍷	5
○ A. A. Valle Venosta Riesling '00	🍷🍷🍷	5
○ A. A. Valle Venosta Riesling '98	🍷🍷🍷	5
○ A. A. Valle Venosta Gewürztramlner '98	🍷🍷	4
○ A. A. Valle Venosta Gewürztramlner '99	🍷🍷	4
○ A. A. Valle Venosta Riesling '99	🍷🍷	5

SALORNO/SALURN (BZ)

HADERBURG
LOC. POCHI, 31
39040 SALORNO/SALURN (BZ)
TEL. 0471889097

The wines from Haderburg at Salorno/Salurn produced some curious results at our tastings. We liked the sparklers, which are the real speciality of the winery and perhaps better than every before. But we were not much enamoured of the still wines. Obviously, we do not want to imply that the management of this winery should focus efforts exclusively on "spumante" production. But we are duty bound to point out that Haderburg appears to have been dealt a much better hand in the sparkling wine stakes. Let's get on with the wines now. We felt the Alto Adige Spumante Pas Dosé '96 was very satisfactory. It went through to the finals and scored higher than any other wine in its category. Fragrant, impeccably sparkling, balanced and easy to drink, it may tend towards excessive simplicity but it's still a great product. The more complex and evolved Hausmannhof Riserva '93 was also in the finals. The non-vintage Brut, the mainstay of the winery's "spumante" production, is also good. But there were a few sad notes from the still wines. We quite liked the Chardonnay Hausmannhof '01, even though its body was not enormous. However, we felt the following wines were less expressive: the Sauvignon Selection Hausmannhof '01 and especially the Pinot Nero Hausmannhof '00, which is not very varietal and shows a few too many vegetal notes.

TERLANO/TERLAN (BZ)

CANTINA TERLANO
VIA COLLI D'ARGENTO, 7
39100 TERLANO/TERLAN (BZ)
TEL. 0471257135

One Three Glass wine and another two finalists with Two full Glasses add up to a truly satisfying result for the Terlano winery, historically a leading producer of great Alto Adige whites. The wines from Terlano perfectly mirror the peculiarities of the local climate and terrain because the Cantina Terlano gives priority to bringing out the regional character in its production techniques. The vineyards grow on a terrain of quartz-bearing stone, with a high mineral content. The results are highly distinctive wines of great complexity, like the Terlano '91. It's a rare gem, bottled after ageing for ten years. An intense, golden straw yellow, it unveils a wide variety of aromas, ranging from damp rock and citrus to spring flowers. It is powerful, big and rich on the palate, testifying to the exceptional longevity of whites from Terlano. The same could be said for the other great whites from this winery. The Terlano Pinot Bianco Vorberg '99 is intensely fruity, typical and elegant. The deep, green-flecked straw-yellow Sauvignon Quarz '00 is big and gutsy on the palate, which is slightly masked by oaky notes. The Terlano Nova Domus '99 shows linear progression on both the nose and palate while the Terlano '01 has weight and grace. Reds that impressed us were the intense ruby Lagrein Porphyr Riserva '99, with its full, velvety mouthfeel, the Lagrein Gries Riserva '99, which has spicy notes, good structure and pleasant drinkability, and finally, the Merlot Siebeneich Riserva '99, with its attractive, Bordeaux-style nose and full, tannic, well-structured palate.

○ A. A. Spumante Hausmannhof Ris. '93	▼▼	6
○ A. A. Spumante Pas Dosé '96	▼▼	5
○ A. A. Chardonnay Hausmannhof '01	▼	4
○ A. A. Sauvignon Hausmannhof '01	▼	5
○ Spumante Haderburg Brut	▼	5
● A. A. Pinot Nero Hausmannhof '00		5
○ A. A. Chardonnay Hausmannhof '00	▼▼	4*
○ A. A. Spumante Hausmannhof '90	▼▼	6
○ A. A. Spumante Haderburg Pas Dosé '95	▼▼	5
○ A. A. Chardonnay Hausmannhof '99	▼▼	3

○ A. A. Terlano '91	▼▼▼	8
○ A. A. Terlano Sauvignon Quarz '00	▼▼	6
○ A. A. Terlano Pinot Bianco Vorberg '99	▼▼	5
○ A. A. Terlano Cl. '01	▼▼	4*
● A. A. Lagrein Porphyr Ris. '99	▼▼	6
○ A. A. Terlano Nova Domus '99	▼▼	7
● A. A. Lagrein Gries Ris. '99	▼	5
● A. A. Merlot Siebeneich Ris. '99	▼	5
● A. A. Lagrein Gries Ris. '97	▼▼▼	5
● A. A. Lagrein Gries Ris. '98	▼▼	5
○ A. A. Terlano Pinot Bianco Vorberg '98	▼▼	5
○ A. A. Terlano Sauvignon Quarz '99	▼▼	6
○ A. A. Terlano Cl. '00	▼▼	4
● A. A. Lagrein Porphyr Ris. '98	▼▼	6

TERMENO/TRAMIN (BZ)

**Castel Ringberg
& Kastelaz Elena Walch**
Via A. Hofer, 1
39040 Termeno/Tramin (BZ)
tel. 0471860172
e-mail: info@walch.it

"Beyond the Clouds" is not the title of a film by Wim Wenders. In this case, it refers to a delicious white released for the first time this year by Elena Walch, queen of Gewürztraminer in Termeno/Tramin. Though she played coy with us and refused to reveal the different grape varieties she blends to make this wine, we think we perceived gewürztraminer, some chardonnay and maybe a bit of sauvignon or riesling. This is all fermented in oak and the result is a very original white of elegance, aromas and harmony. In other words, it's a fantastic wine. Even though it has just been released for the first time, as a 2000 vintage, we felt it deserved Three Glasses. But then Elena presented us with a very fine range of wines this year. The Alto Adige Bianco Passito Cashmere '00 is sweet, aromatic and very refined. It and the Merlot Kastelaz Riserva '00, lacking just a bit more concentration to be truly superb, both made it to our finals as well. There were Two Glasses for the Gewürztraminer Kastelaz '01, the most famous white from this cellar, and also for the Kastelaz Pinot Bianco '01 and Ringberg Pinot Grigio and Sauvignon Castel from 2001. The only disappointing wine, relatively speaking, was the Lagrein Castel Ringberg Riserva '99, which comes from an unexciting harvest in Alto Adige for reds.

TERMENO/TRAMIN (BZ)

Hofstätter
P.zza Municipio, 7
39040 Termeno/Tramin (BZ)
tel. 0471860161
e-mail: info@hofstatter.com

After having completed his splendid, very modern winery in the heart of town, Martin Foradori, the dynamic owner of Hofstätter at Termeno/Tramin, seems ready to make the leap into the front rank of premium winemaking in Alto Adige. His winery is now a fine example of reliability and each of his wines is even better than the last. This year, we salute a majestic version of the Gewürztraminer Kolbenhof '01, a wine that has never been this elegant and concentrated. Its aromas are fragrant yet mineral, very clean and concentrated. The superbly defined palate is elegant and persistent, in fact a wonder in its genre. The Pinot Nero Sant'Urbano '99, from the vineyard of the same name at Mazzon, may still be a little young but is good just the same. Equally good is the Alto Adige Bianco San Michele '01, a blend of pinot bianco, chardonnay and riesling partially fermented in oak. It has a fruity bouquet, soft, caressing flavour and excellent persistence. Both of these made it to our final taste-offs. The Pinot Nero Riserva '99, Lagrein Scuro Steinrafler '99, and Pinot Bianco '01 are all very sound and varietal, receiving Two Glasses. The Riesling '01 came in a very short head behind. But we are still not completely satisfied with the Pinot Nero Crozzolhof '00, a red from organically-grown grapes. We know the type is very dear to Martin but it still needs a lot of work. The wine lacks body and is decidedly rustic.

○ A. A. Bianco Beyond the clouds '00	♥♥♥	7
● A. A. Merlot Kastelaz Ris. '00	♥♥	8
○ A. A. Passito Cashmere '00	♥♥	8
○ A. A. Gewürztraminer Kastelaz '01	♥♥	6
○ A. A. Pinot Bianco Kastelaz '01	♥♥	5
○ A. A. Pinot Grigio Castel Ringberg '01	♥♥	5
○ A. A. Sauvignon Castel Ringberg '01	♥♥	5
● A. A. Lagrein Castel Ringberg Ris. '99	♥	7
○ A. A. Gewürztraminer Kastelaz '00	♥♥♥	5
● A. A. Cabernet Sauvignon Castel Ringberg Ris. '97	♥♥♥	5
○ A. A. Gewürztraminer Kastelaz '97	♥♥♥	4

○ A. A. Gewürztraminer Kolbenhof '01	♥♥♥	6
○ A. A. Bianco Vigna S. Michele '01	♥♥	5
● A. A. Pinot Nero S. Urbano '99	♥♥	7
○ A. A. Pinot Bianco '01	♥♥	4
● A. A. Lagrein Scuro Steinraffler '99	♥♥	7
● A. A. Pinot Nero Ris. '99	♥♥	5
○ A. A. Riesling '01	♥	4
● A. A. Pinot Nero Crozzolhof '00		5
● A. A. Pinot Nero S. Urbano '93	♥♥♥	7
● A. A. Pinot Nero S. Urbano '95	♥♥♥	7
○ A. A. Gewürztraminer Kolbenhof '98	♥♥♥	4
○ A. A. Gewürztraminer Kolbenhof '99	♥♥♥	4

TERMENO/TRAMIN (BZ)

Cantina Produttori Termeno
Strada del Vino, 122
39040 Termeno/Tramin (BZ)
tel. 0471860126
e-mail: info@tramin-wine.it

With a fantastic 2001 version of the Gewürztraminer Nussbaumerhof, the Cantina Produttori Termeno makes yet another triumphal entrance into our Three Glass hall of fame. Termeno, or Tramin as they say around here, has become a very safe bet. The Nussbaumerhof is always one of the best Gewürztraminers around, with its fragrant varietal aromas, noble mineral hints and a full-bodied, decisive flavour that shows great character. But then the whole range is impressive. Out of eight wines submitted, four made it to our final taste-offs. These are results that speak for themselves. The Gewürztraminer Maratsch '01, younger brother to the Nussbaumerhof, is a marvel. Less concentrated and more drinkable, it can also claim to be very good value for money indeed. The Pinot Grigio Unterebner '01 may be the best in its category in Alto Adige and the Lagrein Scuro Urban '00 came close to a Third Glass thanks to elegant structure and those classic, varietal aromas. But the honestly priced Sauvignon '01 from the cellar's standard line, and the deliciously aromatic Moscato Rosa Terminum '00 also won Two Glasses. In contrast, the Pinot Nero Schiesstand '00 only came close to a second Glass. Though not the house speciality, it still defends itself quite well. The only small fly in the ointment is the Chardonnay Glassien '01, which is unexciting, linear and lacks character. The Gewürztraminer Passito Terminum missed the roll call this time since it was not produced in 2000.

VADENA/PFATTEN (BZ)

Cantina Laimburg
Loc. Laimburg, 6
39040 Vadena/Pfatten (BZ)
tel. 0471969700
e-mail: laimburg@provinz.bz.it

The performance by Laimburg this year was good but not excellent. Owned by the Bolzano provincial authority, and run by teachers and students from the Laimburg experimental institute, the winery has lately been releasing wines that are always very well made but are not as impressive as they used to be. A few years ago, the cellar even won Three Glasses with the '94 Gewürztraminer. This time we enjoyed a very sound Chardonnay Doa '00, which has delicate vanillaed aromas, and a varietal Sauvignon '01 that was good but a little predictable. Among the reds, the Lagrein Scuro Riserva '99 was as correct as usual, and the interesting Cabernet Riserva '99 may perhaps be the best in the range. The Sauvignon Passito Saphir '00 is original but just a little too sweet. Two whites we have enjoyed much more in past editions were frankly under par. The Riesling '01 is slightly acidic, with less than massive body, and above all the Gewürztraminer '01, once a flagship wine for the cellar, is now only decent. Though the Pinot Nero '00 was not bad, again it reflected an overall average quality that did not completely satisfy us. We wanted wines with more character and more soul. Winemaking technique is like grammar for a writer: you need to know it and use it correctly, not turn it into an end in itself.

○ A. A. Gewürztraminer Nussbaumerhof '01	♟♟♟	5
● A. A. Lagrein Urbanhof '00	♟♟	5
○ A. A. Gewürztraminer Maratsch '01	♟♟	4*
○ A. A. Pinot Grigio Unterebnerhof '01	♟♟	4*
● A. A. Moscato Rosa Terminum '00	♟♟	6
○ A. A. Sauvignon '01	♟♟	4*
● A. A. Pinot Nero Schiesstandhof Ris. '00	♟	5
○ A. A. Chardonnay Glassien '01	♟	4
○ A. A. Gewürztraminer Nussbaumerhof '00	♟♟♟	5
○ A. A. Gewürztraminer Nussbaumerhof '99	♟♟♟	4

○ A. A. Chardonnay Doa '00	♟♟	5
○ A. A. Sauvignon Passito Saphir '00	♟♟	8
○ A. A. Sauvignon '01	♟♟	4
● A. A. Cabernet Ris. '99	♟♟	6
● A. A. Lagrein Scuro Ris. '99	♟♟	6
● A. A. Pinot Nero '00	♟	5
○ A. A. Gewürztraminer '01	♟	5
○ A. A. Riesling Renano '01	♟	4
○ A. A. Gewürztraminer '94	♟♟♟	4
○ A. A. Riesling Renano '00	♟♟	4*
● A. A. Lagrein Scuro Ris. '98	♟♟	6
○ A. A. Riesling Renano '98	♟♟	4
○ A. A. Gewürztraminer '99	♟♟	4
○ A. A. Riesling Renano '99	♟♟	4

VARNA/VAHRN (BZ)

ABBAZIA DI NOVACELLA
FRAZ. NOVACELLA
VIA DELL'ABBAZIA, 1
39040 VARNA/VAHRN (BZ)
TEL. 0472836189
E-MAIL: info@kloster-neustift.it

Urban von Klebersberg, general manager of Abbazia di Novacella, can be very happy with the string of results from the cellar of this historic Valle Isarco winery. The arrival around two years ago of a wine technician of the calibre of Celestino Lucin was a positive impulse. But there must already have been a foundation to work on. The interesting Praepositus line includes all the cellar's best products, both from the vineyards in Novacella as well as those in Cornaiano/Girlan, where they grow red varieties and sauvignon. In particular, the Lagrein Scuro Riserva '00 is in a class by itself. Its customary impenetrable ruby introduces blueberry and other wild berry aromas, then a firm, concentrated palate with attractive elegance, sweet tannins and deep structure. It earned Three well-deserved Glasses. Moving on to the whites, the panel sampled the excellent Praepositus Kerner '01, with its aromatic, mineral and citrus aromas framing an elegant, aristocratic profile. But the wines from the base line are also very satisfactory. The Valle Isarco Pinot Grigio '01 is a good wine. The Sylvaner '01 is typical, floral and complex. The Sauvignon '01 shows off varietal aromas and an elegant, crisply defined flavour. Returning to the Praepositus selection, we find a Sylvaner '01 that is even more concentrated and well typed, and a Pinot Nero Riserva '00 with varietal notes of fruit. To round things off, there is the Gewürztraminer '01, the standard Kerner '01 and the Moscato Rosa '01, which is sweet and aromatic but not as complex as it has been in previous editions.

VARNA/VAHRN (BZ)

KÖFERERHOF
FRAZ. NOVACELLA
VIA PUSTERIA, 3
39040 VARNA/VAHRN (BZ)
TEL. 0472836649

This small estate owned by the Kershbaumer family has only bottled its own wine since 1995 but in just a few years, it has come to the attention of critics and consumers with products rich in personality and character. They practice a heroic version of viticulture, considering that the vineyards – five terraced hectares planted at 7,000 vines per hectare – are at around 700 metres above sea level. Despite these conditions, a quick look at the results at the bottom of this profile will confirm that we are dealing with one of the most interesting producers in the region. We'll begin with the Pinot Grigio '01, which is striking because of its freshness and the special smoky notes that accompany its rich fruit and interesting minerality. As predicted in the previous Guide, the first release of the Riesling did not disappoint. Its intense, whistle-clean bouquet ushers in a palate with notes of pink grapefruit and varietal sensations of petrol. Next comes the Sylvaner '01, with its typical grassy aromas and surprising structure. The Kerner '01, one of the estate's leading products, was a bit closed when we were tasting but is nevertheless rich and concentrated in the mouth, where pleasant citrus and damson emerge. The Gewürztraminer and Müller Thurgau, both from 2001, are every bit as good. As you can see, there was quite a line-up of stemware for this dedicated producer that knows where it is going. The wines are always interesting, never ingratiating and above all powerful expressions of their territory.

● A. A. Lagrein Praepositus Ris. '00 🍷🍷🍷	6
○ A. A. Valle Isarco Kerner Praepositus '01 🍷🍷	5
○ A. A. Valle Isarco Pinot Grigio '01 🍷🍷	4*
● A. A. Moscato Rosa '01 🍷🍷	5
● A. A. Pinot Nero Praepositus Ris. '00 🍷🍷	6
○ A. A. Sauvignon Marklhof '01 🍷🍷	5*
○ A. A. Valle Isarco Sylvaner '01 🍷🍷	4*
○ A. A. Valle Isarco Sylvaner Praepositus '01 🍷🍷	4*
○ A. A. Valle Isarco Gewürztraminer '01 🍷	5
○ A. A. Valle Isarco Kerner '01 🍷	4
○ A. A. Valle Isarco Müller Thurgau '01 🍷	4

○ A. A. Valle Isarco Gewürztraminer '01 🍷🍷	4
○ A. A. Valle Isarco Kerner '01 🍷🍷	4*
○ A. A. Valle Isarco Müller Thurgau '01 🍷🍷	4
○ A. A. Valle Isarco Pinot Grigio '01 🍷🍷	4
○ A. A. Valle Isarco Riesling '01 🍷🍷	4
○ A. A. Valle Isarco Sylvaner '01 🍷🍷	4*
○ A. A. Valle Isarco Sylvaner '00 🍷🍷	4*
○ A. A. Valle Isarco Kerner '98 🍷🍷	4
○ A. A. Valle Isarco Sylvaner '98 🍷🍷	4
○ A. A. Valle Isarco Kerner '99 🍷🍷	4
○ A. A. Valle Isarco Pinot Grigio '99 🍷🍷	4
○ A. A. Valle Isarco Sylvaner '99 🍷🍷	4

OTHER WINERIES

Lorenz Martini
Loc. Corniano/Girlan
Via Pranzol, 2/d
39050 Appiano/Eppan (BZ)
tel. 0471664136

This year, Lorenz Martini presented the best "spumante" Comitissa Brut Riserva ever, the '98. The chardonnay and pinot bianco-based wine went through to the finals. What more need we say about this tiny, but truly excellent, winery that produces great-quality sparklers?

○ A. A. Spumante Comitissa Brut Ris. '98 ΨΨ	5

Stroblhof
Loc. San Michele - Via Pigano, 25
39057 Appiano/Eppan (BZ)
tel. 0471662250
e-mail: hotel@stroblhof.it

The Stroblhof wines are interesting, as always, but slightly below par. Both the Pinot Bianco Strahler '01 and the traditional Pinot Nero Riserva '99 are well made but come from unexceptional vintages. The Pinot Nero Pigeno '99 is better. The Gewürztraminer Pigeno '01 is pleasant and typical.

● A. A. Pinot Nero Pigeno '99 ΨΨ	5
○ A. A. Gewürztraminer Pigeno '01 Ψ	4
○ A. A. Pinot Bianco Strahler '01 Ψ	4
● A. A. Pinot Nero Ris. '99 Ψ	6

Egger-Ramer
Via Guncina, 5
39100 Bolzano/Bozen
tel. 0471280541
e-mail: egger@suedtirolerwein.de

Toni and Peter Egger submitted several good versions of Lagrein and Santa Maddalena, the wines they specialize in. We thought the Lagrein Scuro Gries Kristan '00, the cellar's flagship bottle, was particularly sound.

● A. A. Santa Maddalena Cl. Reiseggerhof '01 ΨΨ	4
● A. A. Lagrein Scuro Gries Kristan '00 Ψ	4

Anton Schmid - Oberrautner
Fraz. Gries - Via M. Pacher, 3
39100 Bolzano/Bozen
tel. 0471281440
e-mail: florianschmid@dnet.it

This Gries winery makes some very rewarding Lagreins. This time, the Lagrein Scuro Saltner '00 and Lagrein Scuro Grieser Riserva '99 take centre stage. Both are pleasant and technically well made.

● A. A. Lagrein Scuro Saltner '00 Ψ	4
● A. A. Lagrein Scuro Grieser Ris. '99 Ψ	4*

Taschlerhof
Via Mahr, 107
39042 Bressanone/Brixen (BZ)
tel. 0472851091
e-mail: wachtler.peter@taschlerhof.com

Peter Wachtler has made two decent Valle Isarco whites this year. One is the Gewürztraminer '01 and the other the Sylvaner '01, Both are nicely made, varietal and very agreeable wines.

○ A. A. Valle Isarco Gewürztraminer '01	🍷	5
○ A. A. Valle Isarco Sylvaner '01	🍷	4

Tenuta Klosterhof
Clavenz, 40
39052 Caldaro/Kaltern (BZ)
tel. 0471961046
e-mail: info@garni-klosterhof.com

A specialist in Goldmuskateller, Tenuta Klosterhof submitted a very interesting dried-grape "passito" version and another dry Goldmuskateller that was the best in its category, which is no small feat. The other wines were only decent but the two big boys were enough to earn a place in the Guide.

○ A. A. Moscato Giallo Passito Oscar '00	🍷🍷	6
○ A. A. Moscato Giallo Trifall '01	🍷	4

Castel Sallegg - Graf Kuenburg
V.lo di Sotto, 15
39100 Caldaro/Kaltern (BZ)
tel. 0471963132 - 0471974140
e-mail: castelsallegg@kuenburg.it

The Conte Kuenburg wines this year were good but unexciting, perhaps a consequence of the unexceptional vintage. We did like the Merlot Riserva and Pinot Nero Riserva, both from 1999. The Gewürztraminer '01 was also decent.

● A. A. Merlot Ris. '99	🍷🍷	5
○ A. A. Gewürztraminer '01	🍷	4
● A. A. Pinot Nero Ris. '99	🍷	5

Markus Prackwieser Gumphof
Novale di Presule, 8
39050 Fiè allo Sciliar/
Völs Am Schlern (BZ)
tel. 0471601190

This year, Markus Prackwieser offered us a Pinot Bianco and a Sauvignon, both from 2001. They substantially confirm the quality described in the previous edition of the Guide, and both deservedly win One Glass.

○ A. A. Pinot Bianco Praesulius '01	🍷	4
○ A. A. Sauvignon Praesulius '01	🍷	4

Stephan Ramoser - Fliederhof
Santa Maddalena di Sotto, 33
39100 Funes (BZ)
tel. 0471979048
e-mail: fliederhof@dnet.it

The Lagrein Scuro Riserva '00 from Stefan Ramoser is a real marvel. It's elegant, concentrated and extremely typical. It went all the way to the final taste-offs barely missed taking a third Glass. The Santa Maddalena Classico '01 is decent, drinkable and fragrant.

● A. A. Lagrein Ris. '00	🍷🍷	5
● A. A. Santa Maddalena Cl. '01	🍷	3*

Castello Rametz
Fraz. Maia Alta - Via Labers, 4
39012 Merano/Meran (BZ)
tel. 0473211011 - 0473290187
e-mail: info@rametz.com

The two Chardonnays from Schloss Rametz are very good. The Cesuret '99 is concentrated and evolved, with smoky notes, and drinks like a late-harvest wine. In contrast, the standard-label version is fruity, linear and elegant. The other wines were only decent but the Riesling '01 earned One Glass.

○ A. A. Chardonnay '01	🍷🍷	4*
○ Chardonnay Cesuret '99	🍷🍷	6
○ A. A. Riesling '01	🍷	4

Tenuta Pfitscherhof
Via Gleno, 9
39040 Montagna/Montan (BZ)
tel. 0471819773

Only one wine was presented by Tenuta Pfiterscherhof this year, the Pinot Nero Matan '00. But it was very good, as it was last year. Though perhaps still a little young, its varietal tones are well defined and elegant. Wait at least another year before reaching for the corkscrew.

● A. A. Pinot Nero Matan '00   🍷🍷 5

Maso Happacherhof - Ist. Tec. Agrario
Via del Monte, 20
39040 Ora/Auer
tel. 0471810530
e-mail: bernhard.pichler@tin.it

We take great pleasure in including the wines from this estate, which works with the agricultural school at Ora/Auer. The reds, Lagreins and Merlot-Cabernets from 2000, are all very satisfactory. The Chardonnay '01 is more straightforward and traditional.

● A. A. Merlot-Cabernet Happacherhof '00 🍷🍷 5
● A. A. Lagrein Scuro Happacherhof '00 🍷🍷 5
○ A. A. Chardonnay Happacherhof '01 🍷 4

Steinhauserhof
Via Pochi, 37
39040 Salorno/Salurn (BZ)
tel. 0471889031

Anton Ochsenreiter presented us with wines that are correct, if perhaps less interesting than on other occasions. We liked the elegant Sauvignon Selection '01, with its varietal aromas. The Selection Chardonnay '01 and Pinot Nero '00 are also good. The Pinot Nero Riserva '99 is merely decent.

○ A. A. Sauvignon Selection '01   🍷🍷 6
● A. A. Pinot Nero Selection '00   🍷 6
○ A. A. Chardonnay Selection '01   🍷 5
● A. A. Pinot Nero Ris. '99   🍷 7

Oswald Schuster Befehlhof
Via Vezzano, 14
39028 Silandro/Schlanders (BZ)
tel. 0473742197

This time in its 2001 version, the always excellent Valle Venosta Riesling has mineral aromas with touches of citrus, and an elegant, aristocratic palate. The wine is proof that this variety can do very well in Valle Venosta and produce interesting results.

○ A. A. Valle Venosta Riesling '01   🍷🍷 5

Von Braunbach
Loc. Settequerce - Via Bolzano, 23
39018 Terlano/Terlan (BZ)
tel. 0471910184
e-mail: Braunbach@dnet.it

There was a very nice traditional Cuvée Brut from this "spumante" specialist but we were surprised by two very commendable reds, the Lagrein Scuro Caldiv '00 and Cabernet-Lagrein Prestige Caldiv '99. Both show the traditional power and concentration of wines from Caldaro/Kaltern.

● A. A. Lagrein Scuro Caldiv '00   🍷🍷 4
● A. A. Cabernet Lagrein
   Prestige Caldiv '99   🍷🍷 5
○ A. A. Spumante
   Von Braunbach Brut   🍷🍷 4

Rockhof
Via S. Valentino, 9
39040 Villandro/Villanders (BZ)
tel. 0472847130

Konrad Augschöll is a white specialist from the Valle Isarco, whose wines are always reliable and well made. Again this year, he earned an entry in the Guide for his Müller Thurgau and Sylvaner, both from 2001. Both are well-typed, elegant and very pleasant.

○ A. A. Valle Isarco Müller Thurgau '01 🍷 4
○ A. A. Valle Isarco Sylvaner '01   🍷 4

VENETO

Veneto's viticultural re-awakening is spreading fast. Wineries are establishing reputations with major wines and bringing sleepy DOC zones into the limelight. New life abounds. Two examples are Lison-Pramaggiore and Piave but new wineries are also appearing in the Colli Berici, Colli Euganei and Garda areas, contributing to the promotion of premium-quality Veneto wines worldwide. Bosco del Merlo in Annone, Casa Roma in San Polo di Piave, Mattiello in Costozza, Tamellini of Soave, Capodilista of Selvazzabo, La Sansonina of Peschiera, Tezza in Valpanena and Fasoli in Colognola are all extremely interesting wineries that are going places. The upheaval has affected co-operatives, too. Management teams are being overhauled, which has given key roles to long-standing producers of quality wines. This has happened to the Montello e Colli Asolani consortium and in Valpolicella. Consequently, there has been a further increase in the number of wineries featured in the Guide. This time, there are 110 full profiles and 46 Other Wineries, and selection is becoming more rigorous every year. Pieropan and Maculan join Allegrini and Dal Forno in the ranks of the starred producers (who have been awarded Three Glasses more than ten times), showing how consistently high quality is in various areas of the region.

Traditionally, most of the glory goes to Valpolicella, where the excellent '97 and '98 vintages resulted in eleven Three Glass prizes. A special mention goes to the superb performance of the best-known Veneto wine on international markets, Valpolicella, from the valleys north of Verona. After years in the doldrums, Valpolicella makers are on their way again, thanks to excellent growing skills and terroir. The noblest of all Veneto wines is Amarone, and here we note a strong tendency to reduce residual sugars and obtain deeper, more satisfying, food-friendly wines. The downside is a steady increase in prices, which could cause problems. There is nothing new to report but wineries like Begali, Tenuta Sant'Antonio and Brigaldara have consolidated their already excellent positions. Moving east, we come to Soave, where we have seen a constant increase in quality wineries and in the proportion of Three Glass-winning wines. This is indicative of the energy behind some classic Italian winemaking names, like Pieropan and Anselmi, as well as Ca' Rugate, Suavia and Inama, and, for the first time, Cantina del Castello, whose Pressoni selection has joined the front rank of Veneto whites. Lastly, skilful, tenacious Stefano Zonta has won Three Glasses at last at Breganze with a memorable Cabernet Sauvignon Vigneto Due Santi.

ANNONE VENETO (VE)

Bosco del Merlo
Via Postumia, 12
30020 Annone Veneto (VE)
tel. 0422768167
e-mail: boscodelmerlo@paladin.it

There are positive signals from the plains of the Lison-Pramaggiore DOC, as this large area, in both size and numbers, finally lets us see what it can do in terms of quality. Those responsible for this great leap forward include Bosco del Merlo, a dynamic winery run by Lucia Palafina and her brothers Carlo and Roberto, who are all deeply committed to protecting the environment. The beautiful Annone Veneto property is organically farmed, proving that excellent results can be obtained while treating nature with respect. It is also good to note the decision of this large winery to focus on native varieties and reject the easier, "international" grape route. The monovarietal Refosco made by the winery's oenologists, Orazio Franchi and Gian Luigi Zaccaron, helped by consultant Franco Bernabei, has turned out to be one of the most interesting wines in eastern Veneto. The berry fruit aromas are enhanced by a rich, mineral and flower note, and the stylish, velvet-smooth palate reveals a nice spicy finish. The other champion is the Tocai Juti. Good tropical fruit and dried flower sensations lift the varietal almond notes and the stylish palate lingers. All the cellar's other wines are good, especially the Sauvignon and the white Priné, which both came close to Two Glasses.

○ Lison-Pramaggiore Cl. Tocai Juti '01	🍷🍷	5
● Lison-Pramaggiore Refosco P. R. Roggio dei Roveri '99	🍷🍷	6
○ Verduzzo Soandre '00	🍷	6
○ Lison-Pramaggiore Sauvignon '01	🍷	4
○ Priné '01	🍷	6
● Vineargenti Rosso '98	🍷	6
● 360 Ruber Capitae Rosso '99	🍷	6

BAONE (PD)

Giordano Emo Conte Capodilista
Via Villa Rita
35030 Baone (PD)
tel. 049637294
e-mail: giordanoemo@libero.it

You'll find Giordano Emo Capodilista's new winery, which took its place among the DOC's emerging properties with its first releases this year, on Monte Castello. That's the last hill south of Selvazzano before you leave the Parco dei Colli Euganei, where it overlooks the town and the castle of Este. This dynamic producer aims to sell 40,000 bottles a year very soon from an estate that extends over about 20 hectares, part of which is still wooded. At the moment, the winery makes just one wine, which is steeped in the history of the Colli Berici. This Cabernet Sauvignon, Ireneo, is named after a Benedictine monk who lived in the nearby Abbazia di Praglia. The additional phrase on the label, "vin da monte", is a reference to Alberto di Baone who, in the Middle Ages, used to distinguish higher quality "mountain wines" from the inferior ones made on the plains ("vin di piano"). The wine is a deep, promising ruby red. The nose gradually releases notes of black berry fruit, pencil lead, spice and dried flower aromas, which are perfectly reflected on the subtle, harmonious palate with its succulent, pervasive mouthfeel. There is ripe fruit again, and an attractive herb and balsam note in the long, clean finish.

● Colli Euganei Cabernet Sauvignon Ireneo '00	🍷🍷	6

BAONE (PD)

IL FILÒ DELLE VIGNE
VIA TERRALBA, 239
35030 BAONE (PD)
TEL. 042956243

On its third appearance in the Guide, Il Filò delle Vigne again confirms the excellent impression it made in previous editions. The vineyards are situated in 17 hectares of very enviable terrain in the southern Colli Euganei, and the winery's average production is about 30,000 bottles per year. Owners Gino Giordani and Nicolò Voltan have reason to be satisfied with the results they have achieved so far, thanks also to the excellent support of winemaker Andrea Boaretti and young Matteo Zanaica. This professional team is dedicated to obtaining ever higher quality, and is investing heavily to back up that commitment. New, better-equipped cellars are being made ready. The wines we tasted are undoubtedly successful, starting with the Borgo delle Casette, which is made from mainly cabernet sauvignon with some cabernet franc. The full, concentrated, deep purple colour releases complex aromas of raspberries, blackberries and cloves, then the firmly-structured palate takes you through to a long finish. Next comes the Vigna Cecilia di Baone, with a greater percentage of cabernet franc. The nose offers herbs and hay, then the palate adds cherry fruit, good extract and hints of red peppers, pepper, coffee and chocolate. Il Calto (it means "terrace") delle Fate is made from chardonnay, riesling, tocai and pinot bianco, fermented and aged in barriques. Flower and spice aromas on the nose usher in an aromatic, minerally palate. Lastly, the Pinot Bianco Vigna delle Acacie is fresh-tasting, with lots of aromatic herbs and wild flowers.

● Colli Euganei Cabernet Borgo delle Casette Ris. '99	♟♟	5
● Colli Euganei Cabernet Vigna Cecilia di Baone Ris. '99	♟♟	5
○ Il Calto delle Fate	♟	5
○ Colli Euganei Pinot Bianco Vigna delle Acacie '01	♟	4
● Colli Euganei Cabernet Borgo delle Casette Ris. '97	♟♟	5
● Colli Euganei Cabernet Borgo delle Casette Ris. '98	♟♟	5
● Colli Euganei Cabernet Vigna Cecilia di Baone Ris. '98	♟♟	5

BARDOLINO (VR)

GUERRIERI RIZZARDI
VIA VERDI, 4
37011 BARDOLINO (VR)
TEL. 0456210409 - 0457210028
E-MAIL: mail@guerrieri-rizzardi.com

To say that Maria Cristina Loredan Rozzardi is resolute would be an understatement. Her passionate commitment to typical Garda products has driven her to fight tenaciously to promote the local extravirgin olive oil and revive citrus fruit-growing, while carrying forward the family's traditional winemaking business. Contessa Maria Cristina's son Giuseppe, fresh from his oenological experiences in France, helps her with managing the vine stock, which includes vineyards in most of the finest growing areas in the province of Verona. The most impressive of the many wines we tasted is the Amarone Calcarole '97, which has a generous nose and a palate lifted by hints of berry fruit and autumn leaves. The standard-label Amarone '97 is less intense, but still has plenty of character, with hints of very ripe fruit and strawberries in alcohol. The two Valpolicella Superiore wines are both very good, though the light but highly enjoyable Poiega is a nose ahead, with its leafy, sweet fruit aromas and full, velvety mouthfeel. From the Garda area, there's an innovative, flowery Bardolino Munus, a fruity Bardolino Superiore with a clean, pleasantly sweetish palate, and a slightly grassy, temptingly drinkable Chiaretto with a tangy softness in the mouth. The Dogoli Bianco fell a little short of our expectations, but is still interesting for its intense flower and candied fruit aromas.

● Amarone della Valpolicella Cl. Calcarole '97	♟♟	8
● Bardolino Cl. Munus '00	♟	4
● Bardolino Cl. Sup. '00	♟	3
○ Dogoli Bianco '00	♟	4
● Valpolicella Cl. Sup. Poiega '00	♟	3
⊙ Bardolino Cl. Chiaretto '01	♟	3
● Bardolino Cl. Tacchetto '01	♟	3
○ Soave Cl. '01	♟	3
○ Soave Cl. Costeggiola '01	♟	3
● Amarone della Valpolicella Cl. '97	♟	7
○ Recioto di Soave Cl. Vigneti di Costeggiola '99	♟	5
● Amarone della Valpolicella Cl. '96	♟♟	7

BARDOLINO (VR)

F.lli Zeni
Via Costabella, 9
37011 Bardolino (VR)
tel. 0457210022
e-mail: zeni@zeni.it

The Zeni headquarters are in the Bardolino hills, and so is the Wine Museum created by Gaetano Zeni – known around here as "Nino" – to help tourists in the Garda area find out about the Veronese wine heritage. The winery produces a large number of labels every year, from all the province's principal growing areas. We thought the most interesting of those tasted was the Vigne Alte Amarone '98. Peppery, grassy aromas on the nose are followed by a stylish, clean, lingering palate. Hints of medicinal plants and ripe fruit are also present in the weighty, well-rounded Valpolicella Superiore Marogne. The Recioto della Valpolicella '99 is good. Its very sweet, also pleasantly fresh-tasting, palate has strong aromatic herb notes. Also worth mentioning are three very good versions of the "local" wine, Bardolino. The Marogne Superiore has a well-structured, taut, mouthfilling palate while the Vigne Alte ranges offers a great Superiore and an equally good Chiaretto. Moving outside the DOC, there is an appetizingly ripe, juicy Corvar, a blend of cabernet sauvignon and corvina grossa, and the delicious Cruino, a minerally, lightly balsamic corvinone monovarietal. Lastly, the whites: we enjoyed the creamy, velvety Lugana Vigne Alte and the fruity Bianco Custoza Marogne.

BASSANO DEL GRAPPA (VI)

Vigneto Due Santi
V.le Asiago, 174
36061 Bassano del Grappa (VI)
tel. 0424502074
e-mail: info@duesanti.it

Having taken over the family winery almost by chance, the competent, enthusiastic Stefano Zonta has proved equal to the task of making wines with distinct personalities. Thanks to some favourable vintages, the whole range is interesting and attractively priced, which is all to the good. The Breganze Rivana, from tocai grapes, has spices, white roses and apples in the nose and a tangy, minerally, lingering palate. We preferred it to the soft but slightly less deep Malvasia, although it too is excellent. Staying with the whites, the Sauvignon Due Santi gave an outstanding performance (probably its best ever). The complex nose weaves ripe fruit hints into varietal red peppers, nettles and elderflower, then the palate opens out confidently and consistently into a very long finish, where hints of peaches and mint peek through. The Breganze Cabernet is as outstandingly drinkable as ever. It's a wonderfully drinkable wine for any occasion that doesn't require a seriously muscular bottle. Lastly, in the Vigneto Due Santi, a cabernet sauvignon with ten per cent merlot, Stefano has produced a really complete version of the cellar's signature wine. The classy colour hints at complexity, then subtle aromas of fines herbes, liquorice and berries emerge. The palate is balanced and perfectly reflects the nose. A long, intense finish brings things to a close, earning Stefano Three well-deserved Glasses.

● Amarone della Valpolicella Cl. Vigne Alte '98	▼▼ 7
● Recioto della Valpolicella Cl. '99	▼▼ 6
● Bardolino Cl. Sup. Marogne '00	▼ 4
● Bardolino Cl. Sup. Vigne Alte '00	▼ 3
● Valpolicella Cl. Sup. Vigne Alte '00	▼ 3
◉ Bardolino Chiaretto Vigne Alte '01	▼ 3
○ Bianco di Custoza Marogne '01	▼ 3
○ Lugana Vigne Alte '01	▼ 3
● Amarone della Valpolicella Cl. '98	▼ 6
● Amarone della Valpolicella Cl. Barrique '98	▼ 8
● Corvar Rosso '98	▼ 7
● Cruino Rosso '98	▼ 6
● Valpolicella Cl. Sup. Marogne '99	▼ 4

● Breganze Cabernet Vigneto Due Santi '00	▼▼▼ 5
○ Breganze Sauvignon Vigneto Due Santi '01	▼▼ 4*
● Breganze Cabernet '00	▼▼ 4*
○ Breganze Bianco Rivana '01	▼▼ 4*
● Breganze Rosso '00	▼ 4
○ Malvasia Campo di Fiori '01	▼ 4
● Breganze Cabernet Vigneto Due Santi '97	▼▼ 5
● Breganze Cabernet Vigneto Due Santi '98	▼▼ 5
● Breganze Cabernet Vigneto Due Santi '99	▼▼ 5

BREGANZE (VI)

★ Maculan
Via Castelletto, 3
36042 Breganze (VI)
tel. 0445873733 - 0445873124
e-mail: maculan@netics.net

Few Italian wineries can boast a record like Fausto Maculan's. His insights were illuminating long before winemaking in Italy came to enjoy its current boom. His rediscovery and revival of an endangered, emblematic local wine, Torcolato, was brilliant. The market-savvy approach that has made him a world-famous name is acknowledged everywhere. To these, we can add a range of high-calibre whites, reds and sweet wines. This year's novelty is a new monovarietal merlot, Crosara, which could not have hoped for a better debut. Its rich, sumptuous New World style is generous and radiant. The rich nose is veined with sweet spices, concentrated fruit, mint and leather, then the creamy palate opens powerfully, with aromatic herbs, blackberries and raspberries in the finish. The Fratta is as marvellous as ever. The impact may be less immediate but it is tidier and more complex. It's a sort of a cross between Bordeaux rigour and Californian pazazz that wins Three Glasses for impressive thrust on the palate and an irresistible finish. The standard wines we liked included Brentino – fresh, appetizing and peppery – and the Palazzotto, with its unexpectedly varietal character and skilfully crafted feel. The Chardonnay Ferrata is one of the best we can remember tasting, with minerally, peachy hints alongside wistaria and thyme honey. The Dindarello is slightly less impressive than usual but the interesting Torcolato and the particularly spicy Acinonobili, lifted by notes of botrytis, tropical fruit and honey, provide ample consolation.

● Fratta '00	🍷🍷🍷	8
● Breganze Rosso Crosara '00	🍷🍷	8
● Breganze Cabernet Sauvignon Palazzotto '00	🍷🍷	5
○ Breganze Chardonnay Ferrata '00	🍷🍷	6
○ Breganze Torcolato '00	🍷🍷	7
○ Acinonobili '99	🍷🍷	8
● Brentino '00	🍷	4
○ Breganze di Breganze '01		4
○ Dindarello '01		5
● Fratta '97	🍷🍷🍷	8
● Fratta '98	🍷🍷🍷	8
● Fratta '99	🍷🍷🍷	8
○ Acinonobili '98	🍷🍷	8

CAVAION VERONESE (VR)

Le Fraghe
Loc. Colombara, 3
37010 Cavaion Veronese (VR)
tel. 0457236832
e-mail: lefraghe@tiscalinet.it

The landscape around Cavaion is strange. Gentle hills lead down to the lake in sometimes stark contrast with the rocky, mountain-like view towards Valdadige. The climate is a continual succession of mild or muggy days, and freezing weather with a lashing wind. Since 1984, Matilde Poggi has been working this harsh terrain, which is excellent for viticulture, in her quest for a wine that embodies these features. Matilde's goal is a terroir-driven wine that is easy to like. This is no doubt the reason for her decision to stop making Chardonnay, which has been successful in the past but is in no way linked to local tradition. The only remaining non-Veronese variety is cabernet, which is used in the blend of her most important wine, the Quaiare. The '98 version is not as complete as the wonderful '97 but better expresses the sunny spirit of the area. Soft and ripe on the nose, it fills the palate with rich hints of berry fruit jam, spices and chocolate. There is a very nice finish, on which hints of Mediterranean herbs tauten and perk up the array of aromas. The Bardolino Classico is excellent, with engagingly fresh, fruity aromas, a palate that is anything but dull and a fresh, clean finish. The Garganega Camporengo is more impressive on the palate than the nose, while the Chiaretto is approachable and quaffable.

● Valdadige Quaiare '98	🍷🍷	5
● Bardolino Cl. '01	🍷	3*
○ Garganega Camporengo '01	🍷	3*
◉ Bardolino Chiaretto '01		3
● Valdadige Quaiare '96	🍷🍷	5
● Valdadige Quaiare '97	🍷🍷	5

CINTO EUGANEO (PD)

CA' LUSTRA
LOC. FAEDO
VIA SAN PIETRO, 50
35030 CINTO EUGANEO (PD)
TEL. 042994128 - 0429914128
E-MAIL: info@calustra.it

In recent years, Ca' Lustra has made a significant progress on the quality front. The vine stock has been expanded several times and there are now 25 hectars available, some belonging to the estate and some rented. The cellar has also been revamped, thanks to the purchase of the Villa Alessi complex in Faedo. The work of the Zanovello family, headed by Franco and supervised by expert winemaker Francesco Polastri, may bring about further development of the Colli Euganei DOC, which has the potential to reach more ambitious quality standards. The range of wines is divided into two lines, the standard-label Ca' Lustra and the Villa Alessi selections. The Cabernet Vigna Girapoggio is young and so still closed and concentrated on the nose. Grassy, sulphurous notes mingle slowly with ripe, intense cherry fruit, then the palate offers excellent body and dense tannic weave. The Merlot Vigna Sasso Nero is just as good. Deep ruby red, it delivers balsamic notes on the nose with hints of violets, berry fruits, pencil lead and liquorice. The Vigna Pedevenda and Passo Roverello whites are both very interesting. Vigna Pedevenda is an extraordinary, green-tinged yellow Pinot Bianco with subtle, flowery aromas and even more appeal than ever before. The golden, chardonnay-based Passo Roverello has a fresh bouquet of citrus fruit, peaches and apricots. The Cabernet, Pinot Bianco, Sauvignon, Chardonnay Vigna Marco and Moscato Fior d'Arancio Spumante from the Ca' Lustra line are all enjoyable and beautifully made.

COLOGNOLA AI COLLI (VR)

FASOLI
FRAZ. SAN ZENO
VIA C. BATTISTI, 41
37030 COLOGNOLA AI COLLI (VR)
TEL. 0457650741
E-MAIL: fasoli.gino@mercurio.it

Amadio and Natalino Fasoli's winery storms into the Guide this year with a strong range of products and a history dating back to 1925, when the present-day cellar opened. The brothers from San Zeno apply the tenets of organic farming in the vineyard and respect for their grapes during vinification in the cellar. The 14 or so hectares of vineyards are split up into seven plots, each planted with the vine variety most suited to the characteristics of the soil to obtain the best possible results from the grapes. That's why we find merlot standing alongside the ever-present garganega, which gives very interesting results. Calle is a Merlot with excellent prospects and just misses Two Glasses on its market debut. It was penalized only by the fact that the vines are too young to yield a truly great result. The garganega-based wines are even more promising. The rich, intense Soave Pieve Vecchia, which ages in wood, is very nice and even better is the Liber, a monovarietal garganega that has excellent aromas and a well-structured palate. The most impressive wine of all though, is the Recioto di Soave, with intense dried apricot and peach aromas. It progresses stylishly on the palate and has a clean, lasting finish.

○ Colli Euganei Pinot Bianco Vigna Pedevenda Villa Alessi '01	⚶⚶	5
● Colli Euganei Cabernet Vigna Girapoggio Villa Alessi '00	⚶⚶	5
● Colli Euganei Merlot Vigna Sasso Nero Villa Alessi '00	⚶⚶	5
○ Colli Euganei Chardonnay Passo Roverello Villa Alessi '01	⚶⚶	5
● Colli Euganei Cabernet '00	⚶	4
○ Colli Euganei Chardonnay Vigna Marco Ca' Lustra '00	⚶	4
○ Colli Euganei Pinot Bianco Ca' Lustra '01	⚶	4
○ Colli Euganei Spumante Fior d'Arancio Ca' Lustra '01	⚶	4
○ Sauvignon Ca' Lustra '01	⚶	4

○ Liber Bianco '00	⚶⚶	4
○ Recioto di Soave S. Zeno '99	⚶⚶	6
● Merlot Calle '00	⚶	6
○ Soave Cl. Sup. Pieve Vecchia '00	⚶	4
○ Soave Cl. Sup. Pieve Vecchia '99	⚶⚶	4
● Merlot Orgno '99	⚶	7

CONEGLIANO (TV)

ZARDETTO SPUMANTI
FRAZ. OGLIANO
VIA MARCORÀ, 15
31015 CONEGLIANO (TV)
TEL. 0438208909 - 0438912642
E-MAIL: bubbly@bubbly.it

The wines made in the extensive Prosecco di Conegliano-Valdobbiadene DOC vary greatly. In the far west of Valdobbiadene, they are light and aromatic with lots of finesse, while they are much more structured and warmer at the eastern end of Conegliano Veneto. Pino Zardetto founded his winery in the 1960s on the strip of land leading from Conegliano to Vittorio Veneto, an area that gives the wines weight, vibrant ripeness and a few rough edges too. Controversial, perhaps, but it makes an impression. Just under 1,000,000 bottles are released every year, mainly using bought-in grapes – it is traditional for many small wineries to sell their grapes to the "spumante" makers. It is evident from the care invested throughout the production process that no corners are being cut, from grape selection to bottle fermentation and choice of labels. As was the case last year, the best wines are the softer sparkling wines in which the sugar enhances the expressiveness of the aromas and gently lends volume to the palate. The Zeroventi (the name indicates the 20 grams of residual sugar per litre) is made from prosecco grapes with a small proportion of pinot bianco. It has a fascinating hint of ripe golden delicious apples on the nose and the appealing palate is enjoyably vigorous, demonstrating the high quality of the grapes used. The rest of the range is also good, particularly the Prosecco Tranquillo.

○ P. di Conegliano Zeroventi Dry	♈♈	4
○ P. di Conegliano Extra Dry	♈	3*
○ P. di Conegliano Tranquillo Lungo	♈	3*
○ P. di Conegliano Bubbly	♈	3*
○ P. di Conegliano Frizzante Brioso		3

DOLCÈ (VR)

ARMANI
VIA CERADELLO, 401
37020 DOLCÈ (VR)
TEL. 0457290033
E-MAIL: info@albinoarmani.com

Grower Albino Armani is much enamoured of this valley, through which the river Adige winds its way along the boundary between Veneto and Trentino. He shows equal love and dedication in his recovery of an ancient native variety, foja tonda, which is often used for lightweight whites, and has won his ten-year battle to have the variety added to the national register. This has enabled him, at last, to plant new vineyards from centuries-old vines. So here is the Foja Tonda 2000, obtained from ancient vineyards planted by growers who followed a specific quality plan. The wine has hints of Alpine herbs and flowers on the nose, and a rather simple but well-made palate with subtly stylish spice. The other red, Corvara '99, is more confident. A blend of corvina, cabernet and merlot, it has good vegetal aromas with earthy notes. The palate is fresh, persuasive and enjoyable, but not showy. And now to the whites of the Terra dei Forti subzone, which embraces grapes from the edge of the Valdadige area, the strip of land between Veneto and Trentino. This valley is still watched over by Italian and Austrian fortifications from the First World War, positioned between the spurs of Baldo and Lessinia. The Sauvignon 2001 Campo Napoleone has a fresh, citrus palate. The two pleasant Chardonnays, Piccola Botte 2000 and Capitel 2001, reveal hints of apples and minerally notes.

● Foja Tonda Rosso '00	♈♈	4*
● Corvara Rosso '99	♈♈	5
○ Valdadige Chardonnay Piccola Botte '00	♈	4
○ Trentino Chardonnay Vigneto Capitel '01	♈	4
○ Valdadige Pinot Grigio Vigneto Corvara '01	♈	4
○ Sauvignon Campo Napoleone '01	♈	4
● Corvara Rosso '97	♈♈	5
● Corvara Rosso '98	♈♈	5
● Foja Tonda Rosso '98	♈♈	4
● Foja Tonda Rosso '99	♈♈	4

FARRA DI SOLIGO (TV)

Andreola Orsola
Loc. Col San Martino
Via Cal Longa, 52
31010 Farra di Soligo (TV)
tel. 0438989379

This Col San Martino winery confirms its place in the Guide with some excellent products made, in contrast with the general local custom, mainly with grapes from its own vineyards. As a result, the cellar can keep strict control over the entire production process and the wines emerge with good personality and structure. The property has two vineyards, which are used for separate wines. The first plot is Romit, used by Nazzareno and Stefano to make the Prosecco Tranquillo of the same name, and its fellow is Dirupo, whose grapes are made into the sparkling selections, from the Extra Dry to the excellent Brut. The Brut makes the best of a vintage which was generally more suited to dry sparklers. It has fragrant tropical fruit aromas of vigorous pineapple and grapefruit on the well-balanced palate. The softer version has overtones of fermentation and apples, though the sweetness in the mouth fails to provide the wine with the fullness it was denied by the weather. Nazzareno and Stefano have obtained an excellent Cartizze, which goes to show how much care goes into selection when they are purchasing small quantities of grapes. Their Cartizze has signature fresh tropical aromas and a wonderfully creamy, intense, whistle-clean palate. The delicious fizz stays with you right through to the dry, fragrant finish.

○	Cartizze	¶¶	5
○	P. di Valdobbiadene Brut Dirupo	¶	4
○	P. di Valdobbiadene Extra Dry Dirupo	¶	4
○	P. di Valdobbiadene Tranquillo Romit	¶	3*
●	Cabernet Franc		3
○	P. di Valdobbiadene Frizzante Spago		3

FUMANE (VR)

★ Allegrini
Corte Giara
37022 Fumane (VR)
tel. 0456832011
e-mail: info@allegrini.it

The Allegrini family has a twofold plan to improve their winery's quality. First, they want to promote tradition and second, they have innovated. The result is their new Guyot-trained vineyards planted at densities of up to 9,000 vines per hectare. This is what the Allegrini newsletter says but in fact there is only one basic plan. Marilisa, Franco and Walter are sticking to it doggedly, certain that the winery's development is bound up with the success of the area and that this, in turn, depends exclusively on the vineyards. Pergola, Guyot and cordon-trained, spur-pruned systems are simply means and not to be confused with the end, which is obtaining high quality fruit. All the subsequent cellar processes should conserve the qualities the grapes have developed in the vineyard. A modern quality wine will be the result, a product that is enjoyable on release and yet inextricably linked to tradition, to soil conditions and to the features of the variety. This year, the Amarone is again a fantastic wine. It throws a deep, layered nose in which the ripe fruit leaves no room for hints of raisining but gradually gives way to notes of flowers, minerals and iodine. The generous, succulent palate has unparalleled suppleness and energy. A step behind is the La Poja, which is only denied a top award by a slight lack of depth. Excellent as ever are the Recioto, La Grola, Palazzo della Torre and the Valpolicella Classico.

●	Amarone della Valpolicella Cl. '98	¶¶¶	8
●	La Poja '98	¶¶	8
●	Recioto della Valpolicella Cl. Giovanni Allegrini '99	¶¶	7
●	Valpolicella Cl. '01	¶¶	4*
●	La Grola '99	¶¶	6
●	Palazzo della Torre '99	¶¶	6
●	Amarone della Valpolicella Cl. '93	¶¶¶	8
●	La Poja '93	¶¶¶	8
●	Amarone della Valpolicella Cl. '95	¶¶¶	8
●	La Poja '95	¶¶¶	8
●	Amarone della Valpolicella Cl. '96	¶¶¶	8
●	La Poja '96	¶¶¶	8
●	Amarone della Valpolicella Cl. '97	¶¶¶	8
●	La Poja '97	¶¶¶	8

FUMANE (VR)

Le Salette
Via Pio Brugnoli, 11/c
37022 Fumane (VR)
tel. 0457701027
e-mail: vinosal@tin.it

This year, Le Salette has kept its quality standards as high as ever. Helped by his wife Monica, Franco Scamperle always manages to bring out the best in his grapes, thanks to great care in the vineyard and skilful work in the cellars. Extension work is being completed here to improve the organization of the vinification and ageing processes. The Amarone Pergole Vece was one of the most impressive wines and could have obtained an even higher score with just a little more excitement. The colour is deep ruby red, and notes of ripe, crunchy black berry fruits alternate on the nose with flower and citrus notes. It is sumptuous, broad and powerful on the palate, and an enviably taut flavour is backed up by wonderful extract. The finish is stylish and balanced. The Amarone Larega is also interesting, with ripe fruit and jam aromas. Elegant and firm on the palate, it fills the mouth but is kept well under control by close-knit tannins. The Recioto Pergole Vece is also quite successful. The nose has strong vegetal and mineral notes, then the palate is balanced and supple with good presence. The full, expressive Valpolicella Ca' Carnocchio is up to its usual standard, like the Cesare Passito, which has strong suits in its flowers and freshness. The Recioto Le Traversagne got a slightly lower score than last year but is enjoyable, thanks to a fresh palate and good impact. It's very drinkable.

GAMBELLARA (VI)

La Biancara
Fraz. Sorio
C.da Biancara, 8
36053 Gambellara (VI)
tel. 0444444244

Angiolino Maule is one of the benchmark growers in the Gambellara area. With the invaluable Rosa Maria at his side, he has been following his own path for years now, eschewing the simple option of standardization and going for grapes of exemplary ripeness. This is something of a gamble, which starts in the vineyard and continues in the cellar, where Angiolino rejecting cultured yeasts, synthetic products and excessively invasive techniques. The results are promising, although his wines may not appeal to everyone. However, this is the minimum price one must be prepared to pay. Maule has pushed the quest for the best from the garganega grape, which is very hard to cultivate, to the absolute limits. The simplest wine is the uncomplicated, fruity Masieri, which takes us on to the Sassaia. The initial impression is complex - there is garganega skin, then flowers and almonds emerge and barely perceptible minerally notes, which are more evident on the palate. The finish is still a little muddled but the varietal bitter almond note is there. Lastly, we come to the final phase of Maule's quest, and the Pico. Its beautiful colour is followed by a whirl of chamomile, citrus peel, herb, spice and hazelnut aromas. The palate has impressively strong character, dominated by minerally notes and iodine, and assertive tannin. A great deal of effort went into the Recioto and the '99 vintage rewards this with an excellent performance. The amber hue ushers in figs, dates and liquorice, before the palate shows nicely controlled sweetness balanced by lively acidity.

● Amarone della Valpolicella Cl. Pergole Vece '98	ŸŸ	8
● Amarone della Valpolicella Cl. La Marega '98	ŸŸ	6
● Recioto della Valpolicella Cl. Pergole Vece '99	ŸŸ	6
● Valpolicella Cl. Sup. Ca' Carnocchio '99	ŸŸ	5
○ Cesare Passito Bianco '99	Ÿ	5
● Recioto della Valpolicella Cl. Le Traversagne '99	Ÿ	6
● Valpolicella Cl. Sup. I Progni '99	Ÿ	4
● Valpolicella Cl. '01		3
● Amarone della Valpolicella Cl. Pergole Vece '95	ŸŸŸ	8

○ Pico de Laorenti '00	ŸŸ	4*
○ Gambellara Cl. Sup. Sassaia '01	ŸŸ	4*
○ Recioto di Gambellara '99	ŸŸ	6
● Canà Rosso '00	Ÿ	4
○ Gambellara Cl. I Masieri '01	Ÿ	2*
○ Gambellara Cl. Sup. Sassaia '00	ŸŸ	4
○ Recioto di Gambellara '97	ŸŸ	6
○ Pico de Laorenti '98	ŸŸ	4
○ Recioto di Gambellara '98	ŸŸ	6
○ Gambellara Cl. Sup. Sassaia '99	ŸŸ	4
○ Pico de Laorenti '99	ŸŸ	4

GAMBELLARA (VI)

Zonin
Via Borgolecco, 9
36053 Gambellara (VI)
tel. 0444640111
e-mail: info@zonin.it

There's plenty of news from this major Gambellara-based winery, as we announced last year. The most interesting item is a series of wines from southern Italy, all obtained from local grapes, which contribute to the revival of old vine varieties all too often neglected in favour of the more reassuring cabernet and merlot. This line has distinctive, easily identifiable labels with bright colours, and comprises uncomplicated quaffing wines that are immediately approachable and deliver upfront drinking pleasure. They're all in the modern idiom, although the most important features of the individual varieties are foregrounded. There's no mistaking the gamey aromatic profile of primitivo, the well-integrated extract in the smooth, alcohol-rich aglianico or the iron and earth-veined fruit of the nero d'Avola. In addition to this, Zonin has launched a prestigious selection of labels from the Aquileia DOC in Friuli. These include a fragrant, intense Chardonnay, a peppery, rich Merlot and a well-structured, pleasantly approachable Cabernet. The star of the show, however, is still the Recioto di Gambellara, as if to remind us of the cellar's original home. The intense colour introduces dried fruit aromas that are lifted by flower and citrus notes. On the palate, the sweetness contrasts well with fresh acidity and the well-defined finish has an attractive hint of liquorice.

ILLASI (VR)

★ Romano Dal Forno
Fraz. Cellore
Loc. Lodoletta, 4
37030 Illasi (VR)
tel. 0457834923
e-mail: az.dalforno@tiscalinet.it

Credit must go to Dal Forno for creating a truly distinctive Amarone, in which concentration and strength are the foundation for an attempt at an unattainable formal perfection. The success of Amarone in recent years has led many producers to neglect Valpolicella, and steer their less prestigious grapes to the latter style. The Dal Forno '98 Valpolicella is therefore a milestone, a shining example that should provide food for thought. The wine is fresh-tasting, with none of the easy allure that comes from extended raisining, and the nose is dominated by fragrant cherry fruit graced with spices and roses. The palate is riper, the fruit jammier, and the surprising depth is rendered complex by the swagger of the tannins and the aromas of the spices, which make way for metallic, minerally notes in the finish. The Amarone changed course with the '93 vintage. Now, it appears more stylish and better balanced, but still hasn't lost its legendary density. The '97 comes from a landmark vintage, as you can tell from the colour and the startling 17.5 per cent alcohol. Romano skilfully takes control of all this texture, combining it to perfection with new wood. The finesse of the nose is a heady whirl of ever-changing sensations, including liquorice, morello cherry and leather. The quantity and quality of sensations on the palate is awesome, and they seem to last forever. The magnificent finish has clear notes of aromatic herbs, minerals and chocolate.

○	Recioto di Gambellara Podere il Giangio Aristòs '99	♟♟	5
●	Aglianico del Vulture Terre Mediterranee '00	♟	3
●	Aquileia Cabernet '00	♟	3
●	Aquileia Merlot '00	♟	3
●	Nero d'Avola Terre Mediterranee '00	♟	3
●	Primitivo Terre Mediterranee '00	♟	3
○	Aquileia Chardonnay '01	♟	3
○	Prosecco Special Cuvée	♟	3
○	Gambellara Cl. Podere Il Giangio '00		4
○	Recioto di Gambellara Podere il Giangio Aristòs '98	♟♟	5

●	Amarone della Valpolicella Vigneto di Monte Lodoletta '97	♟♟♟	8
●	Valpolicella Sup. Vigneto di Monte Lodoletta '98	♟♟	8
●	Amarone della Valpolicella Vigneto di Monte Lodoletta '90	♟♟♟	8
●	Amarone della Valpolicella Vigneto di Monte Lodoletta '91	♟♟♟	8
●	Amarone della Valpolicella Vigneto di Monte Lodoletta '93	♟♟♟	8
●	Amarone della Valpolicella Vigneto di Monte Lodoletta '95	♟♟♟	8
●	Amarone della Valpolicella Vigneto di Monte Lodoletta '96	♟♟♟	8

ILLASI (VR)

Santi
Via Ungheria, 33
37031 Illasi (VR)
tel. 0456520077
e-mail: giv@giv.it

The old home of local wine pioneer Carlo Santi is right in the centre of the little town of Illasi, in the northeastern part of the province of Verona. Santi was founded in 1843 and now belongs to the Gruppo Italiano Vini, a national winemaking colossus that combines large numbers with extremely interesting quality. The Illasi winery, in particular, focuses on the production of the greatest Veronese DOCs, and owns vineyards in more or less all the best areas, starting with Valpolicella. Its top wine is Amarone and the Proemio '98 has hints of tamarind and aromatic herbs on the nose, then a warm, vigorous palate. Wine technician Pierluigi Borgna is in charge of the cellars. He has created a bottle with bags of character, rewarding the company strategy of strict grape selection and extended ageing. The Valpolicella Le Solane also put on a good performance. Its softness and juiciness are enhanced by a "ripasso" with unpressed Amarone skins. The Lugana Melibeo presents upfront tropical notes of banana and citron, then a nice, tangy, very harmonious palate. Of the two Soaves, we thought the Sanfederici was the more successful. The ripe fruit and candied peel on the nose mingle with interesting green notes. The palate is zesty and harmonious, taking you through to a long finish with plenty of elegance. The uncomplicated Monteforte is less challenging but still supple and drinkable.

ILLASI (VR)

Trabucchi
Loc. Monte Tenda
37031 Illasi (VR)
tel. 0457833233
e-mail: azienda.agricola@trabucchi.it

There is an increasing tendency in the greater Valpolicella area to make premium-quality wines in an innovative style, in line with recent market trends. This is why wineries here – rather than in the Valpolicella Classico zone – are ready to experiment in the vineyard and in the cellar, choosing new methods over the traditional ones, and making considerable investments, not only in financial terms. This upheaval is a positive stimulus for the whole area but carries with it the risk of moving too far away from the traditional Valpolicella type. Trabucchi's wines do not seem to have fallen into the trap. They demonstrate the cellar's interest in innovation but never lose sight of their profound link with the area and its history. The Amarone is proof of this. A mature, traditional nose is followed by a rich, lingering palate with stylish balsam notes. This wine has excellent character, which demonstrates the winery's continuing commitment to improving quality. The Recioto is more modern in style with slightly assertive wood, and considerable but well-distributed strength, creating good balance on the palate. There are positive signals from the two Valpolicellas. Terre San Colombano is less ambitious but outstandingly fresh while the Terre del Cereolo, structured like a little Amarone, aims rather higher.

○ Soave Cl. Sanfederici '01		4*
● Amarone della Valpolicella Proemio '98		6
● Valpolicella Cl. Sup. Le Solane '00		4
○ Lugana Melibeo '01		4
○ Soave Cl. Monteforte '01		3*
● Amarone della Valpolicella Proemio '95		6
● Amarone della Valpolicella Proemio '97		6

● Amarone della Valpolicella '99		7
● Recioto della Valpolicella '00		6
● Valpolicella Sup. Terre del Cereolo '99		6
● Valpolicella Sup. Terre di S. Colombano '99		5
○ Margherita Bianco '01		4
● Amarone della Valpolicella '95		7
● Amarone della Valpolicella '96		7
● Amarone della Valpolicella '97		7
● Amarone della Valpolicella '98		7

LAZISE (VR)

Le Tende
Fraz. Colà
Loc. Le Tende
37010 Lazise (VR)
tel. 0457590748
e-mail: info@letende.it

Le Tende is split between the Bardolino and Bianco di Custoza DOC zones and handles the wines of both areas well, although this small winery does not limit itself to typical local products. The list also features international-style wines that use merlot and cabernet grapes. The overall range is quite large. We'll start with the Bardolinos. The Classico Superiore 2000 made a good impression and is quite an ambitious version of a type which is often rather light and unchallenging. The oaky notes on the nose need to be more harmonious but the palate echoes the fruit, especially cherries, very well and is enjoyably fresh. Turning to the Bianco di Custozas, the toasted oak aromas of the Lucillini, which is aged in wood, are not fully integrated into the wine but the tangy, harmonious flavour is enjoyable. The Oro selection is left for a few months on the lees in stainless steel and lacks a little finesse in the nose that would make it really successful. The nicely textured Cabernet Sauvignon Cicisbeo is the most interesting of the wines made with international grape varieties while the Merlò, in a more modern key, still lacks harmony. The white Passito Amoroso, made mainly from garganega grapes, falls short of the standard of previous versions although it is still enjoyable.

LONGARE (VI)

Natalino Mattiello
Fraz. Costozza
Via Volto, 57
36023 Longare (VI)
tel. 0444555258
e-mail: mattiellovini@tin.it

Mattiello is one of many Veneto wineries that started out making wine for domestic consumption. The first turning point came in the early 1970s, when Natalino decided to develop the business and began to sell unbottled wine in the Vicenza area, especially the Colli Berici. The really decisive moment was when his son Andrea entered the business in 1997, with a diploma in agricultural science. Helped by excellent oenologist Claudio De Bortoli and his own boundless enthusiasm Andrea, began to revolutionize the running of the vineyards and, even more important, to bottle the best selections and release them at the right end of the market. So in just a few years, the winery's output has increased from the initial, almost experimental, 4,000 bottles year to today's figure of nearly 30,000 and growing. Andrea makes two selections, as well as unbottled wines, from the winery's eight hectares of vineyards. The more ambitious of these is Cabernet Colle d'Elica. Dark, intense colour and good personality are accompanied by earthy, ripe berry fruit aromas. The flavoursome, richly extracted palate has good structure and a nice pencil lead and aromatic herb finish. The Cabernet is a less complicated, fresh, approachable wine with frank aromas while the Cabernet Sauvignon has weightier structure. Plans are underway to improve the more modest quality of the whites as well.

● Garda Cabernet Sauvignon Cicisbeo '00		4*
○ Amoroso Passito '00		4
● Bardolino Cl. Sup. '00		3*
○ Bianco di Custoza Lucillini '01		4
○ Bianco di Custoza Oro '01		3*
● Merlò '01		4
● Bardolino Cl. '01		3
● Bardolino Cl. Le Greghe '01		3
● Cicisbeo '97		4
○ Amoroso Passito '99		4

● Colli Berici Cabernet Colle d'Elica '00		4*
● Colli Berici Cabernet Sauvignon '00		3
● Colli Berici Cabernet '01		2*
○ Colli Berici Cardonnay '01		3
○ Colli Berici Garganega '01		2
○ Colli Berici Sauvignon '01		3
● Colli Berici Tocai Rosso '01		2

MARANO DI VALPOLICELLA (VR)

Ca' La Bionda
Fraz. Valgatara
Via Bionda, 4
37020 Marano di Valpolicella (VR)
TEL. 0456801198 - 0456837097
E-MAIL: casbionda@tin.it

Some time ago, Pietro Castellani set himself a challenge – to establish himself among the top Valpolicella wineries. He seems to be closer to achieving this each year, thanks to the increasingly important contribution of his sons Alessandro and Nicola. In recent years, their energy has focused on the splendid new cellar, which aims to provide modern winemaking facilities while incorporating the experience of tradition as positively as possible. Also planned is the gradual reconfiguration and extension of the vineyards, and re-organization of the part of the property not yet planted with vines. The wines are all of a high standard, beginning with the two Amarones. The Ravazzo selection is more interesting. Its nose is full and complex, opening up gradually with blueberries and forest berries to the fore. Soft, silky, mouthfilling and delicate on the palate, it still manages to be authoritative at the same time. One step below is the very drinkable Amarone Classico. Its generous, mature nose with hints of aromatic herbs precedes a full, attractively textured palate. The Valpolicella Campo Cassal Vegri is also excellent. The appetizingly rich, complex aromas include hints of dried fruit and herbs, introducing a stylish, subtle profile on the palate. The Recioto Le Tordare is really well made, its huge structure backed up by the freshness of the aromas.

- Recioto della Valpolicella Cl.
  Vigneto Le Tordare '00 — 6
- Amarone della Valpolicella Cl. '98 — 6
- Amarone della Valpolicella Cl.
  Vigneti di Ravazzol '98 — 7
- Valpolicella Cl. Sup.
  Campo Casal Vegri '99 — 5
- Valpolicella Cl. Sup.
  Vigneti di Ravazzol '00 — 4
- Amarone della Valpolicella Cl.
  Vigneti di Ravazol '97 — 7
- O Passito Bianco — 6

MARANO DI VALPOLICELLA (VR)

Giuseppe Campagnola
Loc. Valgatara
Via Agnella, 9
37020 Marano di Valpolicella (VR)
TEL. 0457703900
E-MAIL: campagnola@campagnola.com

The extensions to Giuseppe Campagnola's large, well-organized cellar in Marano di Valpolicella are now complete. Most of the new space will be used as a barrique cellar, until now a rather neglected area considering the increasing quantity of wine ageing in small oak casks. Campagnola has managed to achieve the functionality of a large winery, in keeping with the character of the estate, while maintaining the atmosphere that of a large, traditional cellar rather than an industrial installation. This character is also present in the bottles, which express the family's attachment to this area more effectively than any number of words. The Amarone, Valpolicella and Soave represent the very best the Verona area has to offer, from the fortress of Soave to the banks of the Garda. The 1999 Amarone, although released a little too early, is nevertheless ripe and enfolding on the nose with subtle, pleasant floral nuances. On the palate, it is succulent and balanced, only the discernible presence of oak hinting at its youth. All the grapes used to make the Valpolicella Classico Superiore come from Purano, the traditional seat of the Campagnola family. Freshness and immediate drinkability are the most obvious characteristics of the wine. The Soave Le Bine is also very good, and succeeds in being very pleasant, without becoming predictable. Its flower and ripe fruit aromas are picked up firmly on the palate, where the excellent balance shows that it is a very well-made wine.

- Valpolicella Cl. Sup.
  Vigneti di Purano Le Bine '00 — 3*
- O Soave Cl. Sup. Vigneti
  Monte Foscarino Le Bine '01 — 3*
- Amarone della Valpolicella Cl. '99 — 6
- Corte Agnella Corvina Veronese '00 — 3
- O Bianco di Custoza '01 — 3
- Recioto della Valpolicella Cl.
  Casotto del Merlo '00 — 5
- Amarone della Valpolicella Cl.
  Caterina Zardini '98 — 6
- Amarone della Valpolicella Cl. '97 — 6
- Amarone della Valpolicella Cl.
  Caterina Zardini '97 — 6

MARANO DI VALPOLICELLA (VR)

Michele Castellani
Fraz. Valgatara
Via Granda, 1
37020 Marano di Valpolicella (VR)
tel. 0457701253
e-mail: castellani.michele@tin.it

A year after winning Three Glasses for a sumptuous Recioto, Sergio Castellani deserves our congratulations again this time. The care and enthusiasm he puts into his work are again demonstrated by his decision to delay release of some of his products, including the Amarone Ca' del Pipa. Having reached the conclusion that such an important wine could not be drunk young, he decided not to market it straight away, so the Amarone is resting in the beautiful Valgatara cellar. Here, it will develop depth and complexity, and we will be able to enjoy it when the time is ripe. This time round, Recioto is again the most successful wine, but this time it is the Campo Casalin selection. Dark and still not very expressive on the nose, it only begins to open up after aerating for a few moments to reveal a generous, intense bouquet of dried flowers, ripe berry fruit, minerally hints and a nice, refreshing balsamic note. The sweetness integrates well on the palate and with a little more depth, it could have repeated last year's exploit. The Amarone Campo Casalin has a typical note of iodine on the nose, and a warm, mouthfilling palate with a creamy, extremely clean finish. The Recioto Ca' del Pipa is only slightly inferior in quality, its best feature being the combination of sweetness and aromatic freshness. The Valpolicella and Passione Rosso are both harmonious. The latter is a sweet wine made from a blend of several grape varieties.

● Recioto della Valpolicella Cl. Campo Casalin I Castei '00	♟♟	6
● Recioto della Valpolicella Cl. Le Vigne Ca' del Pipa '00	♟♟	6
● Amarone della Valpolicella Cl. Campo Casalin I Castei '99	♟♟	7
● Passione Rosso '98	♟	8
● Valpolicella Cl. Sup. Ripasso I Castei '99	♟	4
● Recioto della Valpolicella Cl. Le Vigne Ca' del Pipa '99	♟♟♟	6
● Amarone della Valpolicella Cl. Campo Casalin I Castei '98	♟♟	7
● Amarone della Valpolicella Cl. Le Vigne Ca' del Pipa '98	♟♟	7

MARANO DI VALPOLICELLA (VR)

Corte Rugolin
Fraz. Valgatara
Loc. Rugolin, 1
37020 Marano di Valpolicella (VR)
tel. 0457702153
e-mail: rugolin@libero.it

Elena and Federico Coati continue to follow in their father's footsteps, which are inevitably leading them away from the production of no-more-than-decent wines for the local market to labels that are able to hold their own against the best bottles this important DOC zone has to offer. The use of fruit-focused planting patterns, wood in the cellar and the necessary bottle ageing have enabled this young winery to achieve a very respectable level of quality. The Amarone Monte Danieli has lively, expressive aromas and very ripe fruit, layered over white chocolate and aromatic herbs. On the palate, the heavy structure is camouflaged with surprising elegance for such a concentrated wine. The Passito Aresco is a blend of garganega, moscato, riesling and chardonnay. It shows an interesting array of candied fruit, spices and fresh balsam notes, then the lightly aromatic flavour renders it more agile and approachably drinkable. The two Valpolicellas are both very good. The Classico Superiore has appreciable structure and the fresher version is instantly appealing. Elena and Federico show how conscientious they are about all stages of production by delaying release their Recioto, which they do not consider to be ready yet.

● Amarone della Valpolicella Cl. Vigneto Monte Danieli '98	♟♟	6
○ Aresco Passito '99	♟♟	5
● Valpolicella Cl. '01	♟	3
● Valpolicella Cl. Sup. '99	♟	4
● Amarone della Valpolicella Cl. Vigneto Monte Danieli '95	♟♟	6
● Amarone della Valpolicella Cl. Vigneto Monte Danieli '97	♟♟	6
○ Aresco Passito '98	♟♟	5
● Recioto della Valpolicella Cl. '98	♟♟	5
● Recioto della Valpolicella Cl. '99	♟♟	5

MARANO DI VALPOLICELLA (VR)

F.lli Degani
Fraz. Valgatara
Via Tobele, 3/a
37020 Marano di Valpolicella (VR)
tel. 0457701850
e-mail: degani@tin.it

The Valpolicella area has more than just large wineries with glitzy premises and brand names you see in all the fashionable magazines. Smaller, dynamic wineries are also achieving excellent results in less lavishly equipped cellars, demonstrating that quality depends primarily on nature. If the grapes are good, the wine stands a chance of turning out well. If the fruit isn't up to snuff, no amount of cellar technique will be able to give the wine something the grapes didn't possess. Aldo, Luca and Zeno Degani belong to this generation of growers. Although they began without any capital to speak of behind them, they amaze us by regularly turning out great results, vintage after vintage. An Amarone like La Rosta is not created in the cellar alone. It takes conscientious, painstaking care in the vineyard and during the raisining process. The berry fruit notes are clearly defined and integrated well into a weave of aromas ranging from aromatic herbs to more profound vegetal notes, all of which comes through on the palate. The standard-label Amarone develops along similar lines, putting the accent more on its supple flavour. The Recioto is also very interesting. Concentrated aromas are followed by an approachable, seductive palate with plenty of sweetness. Of the two Valpolicella Classico Superiores, the panel preferred the Cicilio, which has better structure and a better-defined personality, while the standard-label Valpolicella is pleasantly drinkable.

MARANO DI VALPOLICELLA (VR)

Giuseppe Lonardi
Via delle Poste, 2
37020 Marano di Valpolicella (VR)
tel. 0457755154 - 0457755001
e-mail: privilegia@lonardivini.it

The hills that make up the Marano di Valpolicella area enjoy the sunshine from dawn till dusk. Their altitude ensures that the heat is never oppressive and the temperature variation from day to night guarantees unusually rich, fresh aromas. This is especially true of recent vintages, which have typically enjoyed climates approaching the continental, with very hot summers and very cold winters. This is familiar territory for Giuseppe. The owner of the winery and a long-established trattoria in Marano – much loved by Veronese diners looking for somewhere cool on muggy summer evenings – knows that vines benefit most from this type of climate. Their fruit acquires a very high polyphenol and sugar content, without a consequent loss of finesse in the nose. The Amarone '98 sums up these characteristics. Profound fruit and mineral aromas, hints of freshness and vibrant floral tones are married with nuances of iodine, evocative of warm sunny climes, and a mouthfilling, no-nonsense palate. The Recioto Le Arele has intense berry fruit and chocolate on the nose, then the palate is unexpectedly and pleasantly drinkable. The rest of the range is also good, particularly the Valpolicella Classico Superiore, which has intriguing traditional aromas and good progression in the mouth.

- Amarone della Valpolicella Cl. '98 ŸŸ 6
- Amarone della Valpolicella Cl. La Rosta '98 ŸŸ 6
- Recioto della Valpolicella Cl. La Rosta '99 ŸŸ 6
- Recioto della Valpolicella Cl. '00 Ÿ 5
- Valpolicella Cl. '01 Ÿ 2*
- Valpolicella Cl. Sup. '99 Ÿ 4
- Valpolicella Cl. Sup. Cicilio '99 Ÿ 4
- Amarone della Valpolicella Cl. '95 ŸŸ 6
- Amarone della Valpolicella Cl. La Rosta '95 ŸŸ 6
- Amarone della Valpolicella Cl. '97 ŸŸ 6
- Amarone della Valpolicella Cl. La Rosta '97 ŸŸ 6

- Amarone della Valpolicella Cl. '98 ŸŸ 6
- Recioto della Valpolicella Cl. Le Arele '99 ŸŸ 6
- Valpolicella Cl. '01 Ÿ 2*
- Privilegia Rosso '99 Ÿ 6
- Valpolicella Cl. Sup. '99 Ÿ 4
- Amarone della Valpolicella Cl. '95 ŸŸ 6
- Amarone della Valpolicella Cl. '96 ŸŸ 6
- Amarone della Valpolicella Cl. '97 ŸŸ 6
- Privilegia Rosso '97 ŸŸ 6
- Privilegia Rosso '98 ŸŸ 6
- Recioto della Valpolicella Cl. Le Arele '98 ŸŸ 6

MARANO DI VALPOLICELLA (VR)

NOVAIA
VIA NOVAIA, 3
37020 MARANO DI VALPOLICELLA (VR)
TEL. 0457755129
E-MAIL: novaia@iper.net

This winery, owned by brothers Gianpaolo and Cesare Vaona, is situated on low hills in near Marano di Valpolicella. It was founded in 1973 and production standards have always been high. There are only six hectares of vineyards but these have been totally replanted with training systems that make much more of the fruit, achieving otherwise impossible levels of concentration. The last few vintages have not done justice to the effort put in because the vineyards are so young, but now at last we have a glimpse of the huge potential of this professional, well-organized winery. The Amarone Le Balze yields ripe aromas which promise good ageing potential, and oaky notes form a backdrop for the ripe, pulpy fruit. No-nonsense character, good structure and robust body are accompanied by a nice sweet tannic weave on the palate. The Recioto is also good. Stylishly heady, floral aromas usher in an approachable, enjoyably harmonious palate. The aromas of the Valpolicella I Cantoni are also delightful. Alpine herbs, liquorice and crushed fruit lead into a full, creamy palate. The Valpolicella Classico is well-made and has undergone an extra year's bottle ageing. Appealing agility on the palate is its best feature.

● Amarone della Valpolicella Cl. Le Balze '98	7
● Recioto della Valpolicella Cl. '00	6
● Valpolicella Cl. '00	3
● Valpolicella Cl. Sup. I Cantoni '99	5
● Amarone della Valpolicella Cl. '95	7
● Recioto della Valpolicella Cl. '99	6
● Amarone della Valpolicella Cl. '97	7

MEZZANE DI SOTTO (VR)

CORTE SANT'ALDA
LOC. CA' FIUI
VIA CAPOVILLA, 28
37030 MEZZANE DI SOTTO (VR)
TEL. 0458880006
E-MAIL: santalda@tin.it

Corte Sant'Alda is gradually becoming established as one of the best wineries in the Valpolicella area, making 80,000 bottles a year from its 15 hectares of vineyards. Marinella Camerani and Cesar Roman are successfully achieving ever higher quality standards with hard work in both the vineyard and the cellar. This is demonstrated by their recent decision to carry out fermentation in wooden vats, from the 2002 harvest onwards. The Amarone '97 is astonishing. Intense ruby red introduces fine mint, hay and tobacco aromas. There are hints of cocoa powder, liqueur cherries, liquorice and coffee on the palate in a dense tannic, lingering structure. The Valpolicella Mithas '99 is superb. Richly extracted, intense, spicy and full of berry fruit, it flaunts a lingering, mouthfilling palate. All in all, a benchmark for its type. The Ripasso Superiore is also very good and has notes of herbs and cinnamon, redcurrants, blackberries and printer's ink. Ca' Fiui is lively and fresh, with hints of balsam, roses, hay, raspberries and wild cherries. The Recioto is subtle, stylish and flowery on the nose, with varietal cherry and blackberry jam on the palate for a beautifully balanced, wonderfully drinkable bottle. The Retratto, mainly sauvignon with some chardonnay, is more impressive than previous versions. Its bright golden yellow with greenish highlights ushers in an intense, fresh nose with aromatic hints of peppers, nettles and tomato leaves. There are almonds and citrus fruit on the palate.

● Amarone della Valpolicella '97	8
● Valpolicella Sup. Mithas '99	7
● Valpolicella Ca' Fiui '01	4*
● Recioto della Valpolicella '99	7
● Valpolicella Sup. Ripasso '99	6
○ Retratto '01	5
● Amarone della Valpolicella '90	8
● Amarone della Valpolicella '95	8
● Amarone della Valpolicella Mithas '95	8
● Amarone della Valpolicella '96	8
● Recioto della Valpolicella '98	7
● Valpolicella Sup. '98	5

MEZZANE DI SOTTO (VR)

Roccolo Grassi
Via San Giovanni di Dio, 19
37030 Mezzane di Sotto (VR)
tel. 0458880089
e-mail: roccolograssi@libero.it

This winery's name has may have been changed to Roccolo Grassi, but nothing has changed in production, except that young, determined Marco Sartori has made further progress. Last year, we described an area full of untapped potential. Today, thanks to Roccolo Grassi, we have proof that this beautiful valley is perfectly suited to winemaking. The bottles presented this year are all of excellent quality, especially the types that usually play second fiddle. The Valpolicella Superiore has a dark hue and closed aromas but if you wait a few moments, it opens out into a whirl of berry fruit and aromatic herbs that is light and yet penetrating. The elegance is fully reflected on the palate, which is long and mouthfilling. The perfectly integrated tannic weave rounds off the finish deliciously. The Amarone has very ripe aromas enriched with penetrating, enfolding pepper and pencil lead notes. It is warm and soft on the palate, where the tannins manage to rein in the wine's natural energy. The Recioto della Valpolicella is very good. Slow to open up on the nose, it reveals a palate of memorable balance and class. The finish is rich in mint, hazelnuts and thyme, which brings freshness to a highly concentrated wine. An excellent Soave and equally good Recioto di Soave complete this outstanding range, proving that the area and Marco himself share a vocation for producing superior wine.

MEZZANE DI SOTTO (VR)

Tenuta Sant'Antonio
Fraz. San Briccio
Via Valfredda
37030 Mezzane di Sotto (VR)
tel. 0457650383 - 0456150913
e-mail: info@tenutasantantonio.it

In the Venetian dialect, the adjective "garbo" means "acerbic", "lean" or "not very fertile". The Castagnedi brothers' largest property is in the Monti Garbi area, whose name hints at the unproductive nature of this land. Their 20 hectares are planted almost entirely to traditional Valpolicella varieties, and the splendid new cellar on top of the hill is finished at last, overlooking the Mezzane valley like a belvedere. However the most beautiful part of the property is still the vineyards. This corner of Veneto has always been reluctant to abandon vigorous, highly productive growing systems, but the Castagnedi brothers have planted 20 hectares to Guyot-trained vines, increasing the density over the years to more than 10,000 plants per hectare. The quality of their wines has improved markedly as the vines have aged, and has now reached standards of absolute excellence. The arrival of oenologist Paolo Grigolli has completed a close-knit team which shares a passion for quality. The Amarone Campo dei Gigli we tasted this year is really very good, in part because of a fantastic vintage, and it earned Three Glasses. The nose is ripe and complex, the fruity notes enhanced by Alpine herbs and minerals, and the palate won our hearts with its classy combination of strength and style. The Cabernet Capitello, which won Three Glasses for the '97, is again of a high standard, like the Valpolicella La Bandina. It's a red that has finally restored dignity an often undervalued wine type.

● Amarone della Valpolicella Roccolo Grassi '98	🍷🍷	8
● Recioto della Valpolicella Roccolo Grassi '99	🍷🍷	6
○ Recioto di Soave La Broia '99	🍷🍷	5
○ Soave Sup. La Broia '00	🍷🍷	4*
● Valpolicella Sup. Roccolo Grassi '99	🍷🍷	5
● Amarone della Valpolicella Roccolo Grassi '97	🍷🍷	8
○ Recioto di Soave La Broia '98	🍷🍷	5
● Recioto della Valpolicella Roccolo Grassi '97	🍷🍷	6

● Amarone della Valpolicella Campo dei Gigli '97	🍷🍷🍷	8
● Cabernet Sauvignon Capitello '99	🍷🍷	6
● Valpolicella Sup. La Bandina '98	🍷🍷	6
○ Chardonnay Capitello '00	🍷	4
○ Soave Sup. Monte Cerani '00	🍷	4
● Valpolicella Sup. Monti Garbi '99	🍷	5
● Cabernet Sauvignon Capitello '97	🍷🍷🍷	6
● Recioto della Valpolicella Argille Bianche '97	🍷🍷	6
● Amarone della Valpolicella Campo dei Gigli '95	🍷🍷	8
● Amarone della Valpolicella Campo dei Gigli '96	🍷🍷	8
● Cabernet Sauvignon Capitello '98	🍷🍷	6

MIANE (TV)

GREGOLETTO
FRAZ. PREMAOR
VIA SAN MARTINO, 1
31050 MIANE (TV)
TEL. 0438970463

Luigi Gregoletto comes from a generation of growers who have maintained a committed, traditional relationship with the countryside and with the vine. It remains unaffected by modernity, marketing and trends that influence their younger colleagues. However you interpret wines, they represent the ideas and indeed the life of their producer and these wines have something to say about Luigi and about the land they come from. The area lies between the capitals of Prosecco, Valdobbiadene to the west and Conegliano to the east. It goes without saying that this Miane winery makes Prosecco, both the Tranquillo and the more common Spumante Extra Dry versions, which complement each other. The Tranquillo displays all the freshness and fragrance of the variety while the latter is riper and more mouthfilling. The Colli di Conegliano Bianco Albio is reliably good. Light notes of flowers on the nose mingle well with ripe pears and apples, then the uncomplicated palate shows refreshing tanginess. This wine is probably at its best served with food for it is deliciously drinkable. There is an interesting selection of reds, starting with an exceptionally clean, no-nonsense Merlot that shows ripe, succulent fruit. Its aromas are stylishly enhanced by grassy, vegetal hints on the palate. The Cabernet and Colli di Conegliano Rosso both have deeper flavour, but need to shake off a gamey note that obscures their aromatic texture.

MONSELICE (PD)

BORIN
FRAZ. MONTICELLI
VIA DEI COLLI, 5
35043 MONSELICE (PD)
TEL. 042974384 - 0429700696
E-MAIL: borin@protec.it

This winery is run with diligence and commitment by Gianni Borin and his wife Teresa. Situated to the south of the Colli Euganei, it lies in one of the most suitable areas for wine growing, along the road to Arquà Petrarca. When you talk to Professor Borin, who divides his time between university and his vineyard and cellar, you immediately become aware of his sincere passion for the land, its history and traditions. His new white wine, Corte Borin, has obtained flattering results. Made from incrocio Manzoni 6.0.13, it has a fresh fruity nose and warm, strong palate, with a soft, chewy mouthfeel. The Riserva di Cabernet Sauvignon Mons Silicis almost reaches the same standard, its stylish flower and berry fruit aromas mingling with toasty oak. The new wood is still rather too forward on the palate but the fruit is nice and juicy, indicating that the grapes were very carefully selected. The Colli Euganei Merlot Riserva has a nice intense ruby red hue and the fruit on the nose is ripe and pulpy. The palate is smooth and warm, gaining a note of sweetness from the fruit. The Cabernet Sauvignon Vigna Costa is well-typed but slightly simpler. Turning to the whites, the Chardonnay is more persuasive than the Pinot Bianco and the Colli Euganei Bianco Vigna dei Mandorli, whose typical sweetness on the palate fails to meld properly into the wine. The light, fragrant Fior d'Arancio Spumante is an excellent wine to serve at the end of a meal.

● Merlot dei Colli Trevigiani '00	2*
○ Colli di Conegliano Bianco Albio '01	2
● Cabernet dei Colli Trevigiani '00	2
○ Manzoni Bianco '01	2
○ Pinot Bianco '01	2
● Colli di Conegliano Rosso Gregoletto '97	4
○ P. di Conegliano Extra Dry	3
○ P. di Conegliano Tranquillo	2*
○ Colli di Conegliano Bianco Albio '00	2

○ Colli Euganei Bianco Corte Borin '01	4*
● Colli Euganei Cabernet Sauvignon Mons Silicis Ris. '99	5
● Colli Euganei Cabernet Sauvignon Vigna Costa '00	4
○ Colli Euganei Chardonnay Vigna Bianca '00	4
● Colli Euganei Merlot Rocca Chiara Ris. '00	5
○ Colli Euganei Spumante Fior d'Arancio '01	4
○ Colli Euganei Bianco Vigna dei Mandorli '01	3
○ Colli Euganei Pinot Bianco Vigneto Archino '01	3

MONTEBELLO VICENTINO (VI)

Domenico Cavazza & F.lli
Via Selva, 22
36054 Montebello Vicentino (VI)
Tel. 0444649166
E-mail: vini.cavazza@libero.it

Regular readers of the Guide over the last few years will be aware that we have repeatedly predicted a collective re-awakening of Colli Berici DOC producers. One of the most attractive wineries in the area, and one with perhaps the highest potential for development, is Cavazza. The Cicogna vineyard was completely revamped a few years ago and this year's tastings give us good reason to hope. Again, the reds stand out with the Cabernet in the lead, its striking personality unfolding gradually with more finesse than in previous versions. This time there are no grassy or super-ripe notes and the wine deserves praise for its impressive tidiness. The Merlot and Syrah from the same line are more approachable and enjoyable. Fruity, gamey and fresh mint notes delight in the nose of the Merlot, which has a warm, soft finish. The Syrah is spicier, simpler and rather mouth-drying from the new wood. The fresh, appetizing Cabernet Santa Libera is a fine example of its type. The sweet wines are also good, the best being the Recioto with plenty of tropical fruit, dried roses, rosemary and coconut notes. It's pleasantly sweet to drink. The Dulcis dried-grape "passito" from sauvignon grapes has less varied aromas. The sweet, ripe fruit on the nose is picked up by the palate, which never cloys. The dry whites are correctly typed though not captivating. They could have been more richly extracted and a tad more territory-driven.

MONTEBELLO VICENTINO (VI)

Luigino Dal Maso
Via Selva, 62
36054 Montebello Vicentino (VI)
Tel. 0444649104
E-mail: dalmaso@infinito.it

Last year, we described this as an ambitious winery aiming to establish itself on the market. Work in the Colli Berici vineyards is practically complete and Nicola now intends to revive a weightier, more modern version of the Tocai Rosso. He is also committed to making characterful, high-profile Gambellara garganegas, like those from neighbouring Soave. Meanwhile, the whole range of products could be turned around by the Terra dei Rovi line. Although the Bianco still needs fine-tuning, especially as regards the handling of its oak, the Rosso made a distinctly positive impression. The colour is opaque and the nose, which is still settling down, has spices, cinnamon, cloves and liquorice as well as blackcurrants. The palate is lively, vibrant and weighty yet fresh, with a mellow earthy note in the finish. It just lacks that little extra complexity that would take it into the top category, but the vineyard is still young. With time, it will achieve fuller expression. We also liked the Merlot Casara Roveri for its spontaneous fruit, now going through an enjoyably sunny, ripe phase, and the Cabernet is dry and well-typed. The Gambellara Ca' Cischele is as elegant and soft as ever, then there was the convincing Recioto Riva dei Perari, with its 182 grams of elegant residual sugar. Candied citrus peel, honey and passion fruit tempt the nose, then the long, flavoursome, balanced palate reveals lively acidity.

● Colli Berici Cabernet Capitel S. Libera '00	4*
● Colli Berici Cabernet Cicogna '00	5
● Colli Berici Merlot Cicogna '00	5
○ Dulcis Cicogna '00	4
● Syrah Cicogna '00	5
○ Recioto di Gambellara Cl. Capitel S. Libera '00	4
○ Colli Berici Pinot Bianco Campo Corì '01	3
○ Gambellara Cl. Capitel S. Libera '01	3
● Colli Berici Cabernet Cicogna '98	5
● Colli Berici Cabernet Capitel S. Libera '99	4

○ Recioto di Gambellara Cl. Riva dei Perari '00	5
● Colli Berici Merlot Casara Roveri '00	5
● Terra dei Rovi Rosso '00	6
● Colli Berici Cabernet Casara Roveri '00	5
○ Terra dei Rovi Bianco '00	4
○ Gambellara Cl. Ca' Cischele '01	3*
○ Recioto di Gambellara Cl. Riva dei Perari '99	5

MONTECCHIA DI CROSARA (VR)

CA' RUGATE
VIA PERGOLA, 72
37030 MONTECCHIA DI CROSARA (VR)
TEL. 0456175082 - 0456176328
E-MAIL: carugate@carugate.it

They have courage in spades at Ca' Rugate. After producing a wine like Bucciato apparently out of nowhere, the Tessaris decided to build a cellar – now finished – which is one of the most attractive and efficient in the whole area and beyond. From their five hectares in Valpolicella come the grapes for a red wine, the fragrantly drinkable Rio Albo, while the Superiore 2000 version was not ready for tasting when we visited. Nor was the long-awaited Amarone, which will see the light in a couple of years' time. Turning to the whites, the overall performance is very exciting, and we quickly awarded Three Glasses to the Monte Alto, made entirely from garganega grapes, fermented and aged in wood. The aromatic impact has a modern twist that discreetly enhances the strong personality of the grapes, evident in the ripe apple and pear fruit, spring flowers, and minerally hints so closely rooted in the area of origin. The palate disdains uncomplicated softness. Our tasting notes record tempting echoes of spice and roses in the sophisticated finish. The Bucciato was a talking point for the panel, as usual. We enjoyed the edgy tannic weave, which is so rare in a white, the sensual ripeness – perhaps to the detriment of finesse – and the head-spinning whirl of lingering flavour sensations. Elegance and clarity were evident again in the aromas of the excellent Monte Fiorentine. It's still very closed but promises great things for the future.

MONTEFORTE D'ALPONE (VR)

ROBERTO ANSELMI
VIA SAN CARLO, 46
37032 MONTEFORTE D'ALPONE (VR)
TEL. 0457611488

Space is starting to be a problem at this splendid Monteforte winery. Not because the numbers are increasing but because this restless winemaker has no wish to waste energy and attention on routine procedures. The labelling, packaging and stacking of the bottles during the ageing phase should not detract attention from the main activity, which is making fine wines. So Roberto Anselmi plans to revolutionize his use of space by purchasing a complex next to his winery and devoting an area solely to the production phases, from pressing to bottling. While we wait for these changes take shape, we enjoyed some very impressive wines in this year's range. The Capitel Croce confirms its usual standard. Bright straw yellow, it offers clear, intense tropical fruit aromas and lightly balsamic hints, opening out elegantly and gently on the weighty, mouthfilling palate. In the mouth, the range of aromas is further enhanced with spring flowers and aniseed, and concludes with a long, lingering finish. Also charming this year is the I Capitelli dried-grape wine. Its lustrous golden yellow ushers in a bouquet of thyme, liquorice, candied peel and minerally hints on the very classy nose. Well-integrated sweetness on the palate, with great nose-palate consistency, takes you through to a sophisticated finish. The Capitel Foscarino and San Vincenzo are as good as ever.

O Soave Cl. Sup. Monte Alto '00	♛♛♛	4*
O Bucciato '00	♛♛	4*
O Recioto di Soave La Perlara '00	♛♛	5
O Soave Cl. Sup. Monte Fiorentine '01	♛♛	3*
O Soave Cl. San Michele '01	♛	3
● Valpolicella Rio Albo '01	♛	3
O Soave Cl. Sup. Monte Alto '96	♛♛♛	4
O Soave Cl. Sup. Bucciato '99	♛♛♛	4

O Capitel Croce '00	♛♛♛	4*
O I Capitelli '00	♛♛	7
O Capitel Foscarino '01	♛♛	4*
O San Vincenzo '01	♛♛	4*
O Recioto dei Capitelli '87	♛♛♛	7
O Recioto dei Capitelli '88	♛♛♛	7
O Recioto di Soave I Capitelli '93	♛♛♛	7
O Recioto di Soave I Capitelli '96	♛♛♛	7
O Capitel Croce '99	♛♛♛	4
O I Capitelli '99	♛♛	7
O Capitel Foscarino '00	♛♛	4
O Capitel Croce '98	♛♛	4
O I Capitelli '98	♛♛	7
O Capitel Foscarino '99	♛♛	4

MONTEFORTE D'ALPONE (VR)

CARLO BOGONI
QUARTIERE ALDO MORO, 1
37032 MONTEFORTE D'ALPONE (VR)
TEL. 0456100385
E-MAIL: bogoniwine@tiscalinet.it

Husband and wife Carlo and Beatrice Bogoni divide their time between looking after their 12 hectares under vine, running their cellar, currently undergoing extensive reconstruction, and sales and administration. They manage to do so without neglecting their household duties and the care of their two young children, because they actually live on the winery premises. The cellar has a long history but only entered the market with its own brand and product line comparatively recently. The results were immediately promising and Carlo and Beatrice were encouraged to continue down their chosen road, heedless of the sacrifices and surprises in store. Although we are in the heart of Soave Classico, the leading wine this year was the red Degorà, a Cabernet Sauvignon made with fruit from the vineyards in the Colli Berici. The balanced, harmonious progression on the palate is heralded by a delicate nose, lifted by vegetal and balsamic fresh mint notes. Although the wine has spent a certain period ageing in small wooden barrels, you wouldn't think so from the palate. Our assessment of the Soave La Ponsara, which is usually the most interesting Bogoni wine, was influenced by its lack of freshness. The Recioto was in a positive mood, however. We liked its flower and apricot fruit nose and the mouthfilling, enjoyable palate.

● Degorà Cabernet Sauvignon '99	🍷🍷	5
○ Soave Cl. Sup. La Ponsara '00	🍷	4
○ Recioto di Soave '98	🍷	5
○ Soave Cl. Sup. La Ponsara '99	🍷🍷	4
● Degorà Cabernet Sauvignon '97	🍷🍷	5
● Degorà Cabernet Sauvignon '98	🍷🍷	5

MONTEFORTE D'ALPONE (VR)

FATTORI & GRANEY
VIA ZOPPEGA, 14
37030 MONTEFORTE D'ALPONE (VR)
TEL. 0457460041
E-MAIL: sgraney@tiscalinet.it

Fattori & Graney is a family-run winery. Brothers Antonio and Giovanni share responsibility for the cellar and the property's 25 hectares of vineyards, which provide the grapes for 75,000 bottles every year. With over a century of history, the winery has accumulated a solid base for continuing improvement and some expansion. The wines we tasted demonstrated the high level of quality already achieved, starting with the most representative Soave, Motto Piane, which ferments in barriques and then ages in large wooden barrels for a few months. The 2000 and 2001 vintages were on parade for this edition of the Guide and both made a good impression. The 2000 is more oak-influenced, as is clear in the sweet spice notes and the intense, evolved nose. The palate is soft and sweet. The flower and fruit notes of the 2001 make it fresher and more fragrant, then the attractively harmonious palate further enhances the wine's alluring elegance. The second release of the Recioto Motto Piane confirms last year's good impression. It's a wine with remarkable balance, evident in the perfect fusion of the nose and taut palate, in which the sugars are offset by lovely freshness. Lastly, the standard-label Soave and the Pinot Grigio are well-typed and as dependably good as ever.

○ Recioto di Soave Motto Piane '00	🍷🍷	5
○ Soave Cl. Sup. Motto Piane '00	🍷🍷	4*
○ Soave Cl. Sup. Motto Piane '01	🍷🍷	4*
○ Pinot Grigio delle Venezie '01	🍷	3
○ Soave Cl. Sup. '01	🍷	3
○ Recioto di Soave Motto Piane '99	🍷🍷	5
○ Soave Cl. Sup. Motto Piane '99	🍷🍷	4

MONTEFORTE D'ALPONE (VR)

GINI
VIA MATTEOTTI, 42
37032 MONTEFORTE D'ALPONE (VR)
TEL. 0457611908
E-MAIL: az.agricolagini@tiscalinet.it

Although the Gini family has been tending vineyards since the 18th century, the winery only shifted focus to concentrate exclusively on the production of quality wines with the arrival of Sandro and Claudio in 1980. The 25-hectare property is situated mainly in the Soave Classico DOC and partly in the San Giovanni Ilarione hills, where Sandro and Claudio make non-DOC wines from chardonnay, sauvignon and pinot nero grapes, the last of which being cultivated as a labour of love. The most significant news this year is that the best-known wine, the Soave Salvarenza, will undergo longer ageing, starting with the current edition. We will only be able to taste the 2001 next year, when it has reached the level of maturity the brothers aspire to. However, good quality wines are not in short supply at Gini, starting with the sumptuous Recioto Renobilis. Five years of bottle age have endowed it with the rich range of aromas that befit a great sweet wine. Candied citrus peel, pepper, aromatic herbs and liquorice are all in evidence, delicately and decisively interwoven with raisined fruit. Long and harmonious on the palate, it signs off with a lingering hazelnut finish. As ever, the stainless steel-vinified Soave La Frosca is an outstanding white. The aromas unfold cleanly and intensely, to be followed up by an uncomplicated palate with excellent structure. The Chardonnay and Pinot Nero are excellent and the Sauvignon is also good.

○ Recioto di Soave Renobilis '97	🍷🍷	7
○ Soave Cl. Sup. La Froscà '01	🍷🍷	5
○ Chardonnay Sorai '00	🍷🍷	5
○ Soave Cl. Sup. '01	🍷🍷	4*
● Pinot Nero Sorai Campo alle More '99	🍷🍷	6
○ Recioto di Soave Col Foscarin '99	🍷🍷	5
○ Sauvignon Maciete Fumé '00	🍷	5
○ Soave Cl. Sup. Contrada Salvarenza Vecchie Vigne '00	🍷🍷🍷	5
○ Soave Cl. Sup. Contrada Salvarenza Vecchie Vigne '96	🍷🍷🍷	5
○ Soave Cl. Sup. Contrada Salvarenza Vecchie Vigne '98	🍷🍷🍷	5
○ Soave Cl. Sup. La Froscà '99	🍷🍷🍷	5

MONTEFORTE D'ALPONE (VR)

LA CAPPUCCINA
FRAZ. COSTALUNGA
VIA SAN BRIZIO, 125
37030 MONTEFORTE D'ALPONE (VR)
TEL. 0456175036 - 0456175840
E-MAIL: lacappuccina@lacappuccina.it

Elena, Pietro and Sisto Tessari run a splendid winery bordering on the Soave Classico zone and their 28 hectares are managed using techniques that aim to bring out the best in the fruit. The Tessari family have replanted the vineyards in recent years, abandoning the unsatisfactory traditional pergolas in favour of Guyot and cordon-trained, spur-pruned systems. The result is a more discriminating management of the vineyard, and therefore of the grapes, and wines of excellent substance. Year after year, the raw material is enhanced by refined winemaking methods that owe nothing to fashionable trends. Pietro and Sisto pursue elegance in a period dominated by over-structured, highly-concentrated wines. This may not pay off at the time of the panel's tastings but it certainly shows up when the time comes to drink the wine. Take the Arzìmo, a garganega-based dried-grape "passito" that cannot fail to charm the conscientious taster. Its delicate, stylish spring flowers and peaches on the nose take you into a palate of a distinction that is rarely encountered in wines of this type. Yes, it's powerful and well-structured but it's also incomparably light and delicate. The San Brizio is more impressive than ever. This Soave ages in small oak barrels and its ripe peach and apricot aromas is perfectly reflected on the palate, where the sweetness of the fruit has no need of residual sugar to make its presence felt. The excellent Campo Buri is a stylish Cabernet Franc with admirable personality.

○ Soave Sup. S. Brizio '00	🍷🍷	4*
○ Soave Sup. Fontégo '01	🍷🍷	4*
○ Arzìmo Passito '99	🍷🍷	5
● Campo Buri '99	🍷🍷	5
○ Sauvignon '01	🍷	4
○ Soave '01	🍷	3
● Madégo '00	🍷	4
● Cabernet Franc Campo Buri '95	🍷🍷🍷	5
○ Soave Sup. S. Brizio '99	🍷🍷	4
○ Arzìmo Passito '98	🍷🍷	5
● Cabernet Franc Campo Buri '98	🍷🍷	5
○ Recioto di Soave Arzìmo '98	🍷🍷	5
○ Soave Sup. S. Brizio '98	🍷🍷	4

MONTEFORTE D'ALPONE (VR)

Umberto Portinari
Fraz. Brognoligo
Via Santo Stefano, 2
37032 Monteforte d'Alpone (VR)
tel. 0456175087

There are big changes afoot at Umberto Portinari's winery. As we mentioned last year, Umberto has been working with Lino Prà, who brought with him eight hectares of very well-aspected volcanic hillslopes to supplement the winery's own four hectares. Oenologist Gianpaolo Chiettini has joined the team, but the objective of stylistic continuity remains unaltered. Portinari's wines are not influenced by trends or fashions. Ageing is never hurried and the austerity of youth, of course, only finds harmony with sufficient time in the cellar. Let's move on to this year's tastings. The Ronchetto is flowery and clean, with almond and peach sensations from the ripe grapes and a rich finesse that comes from the hillside location of the vines. The palate follows through well, showing liquorice hints in the finish. The Albare, generous and rich in extract because the fruit was left to ripen slowly on the vine, is still rather closed, offering only the faintest glimpse of almonds, spices and pear fruit. The smooth, juicy palate still needs longer in bottle. The excellent, well-typed Santo Stefano is fermented and aged in oak. The grapes are very highly concentrated and the exuberant fruit is immediately perceptible. Vanilla on the nose mingles with tropical fruit, cloves and peaches, to be followed by a pleasantly piquant, weighty palate refreshed by fine, minerally notes. Lastly the complex Recioto Oro, also aged in wood, is sweet, fruity and mouthfilling.

MONTEFORTE D'ALPONE (VR)

Prà
Via della Fontana, 31
37032 Monteforte d'Alpone (VR)
tel. 0457612125
e-mail: grazianopra@libero.it

After last year's excellent performance, crowned with a Three Glass award, we were looking forward to tasting the Pra brothers' wines. Success is one thing, but continuity at such high levels, vintage after vintage, is quite another. However, our patience was rewarded, although this time there was no Three Glass winner, and the wines presented are all outstanding. Again, the '99 Soave Colle Sant'Antonio is very, very good, demonstrating how a wine can ferment and age in small oak barrels without being overwhelmed the wood. The aromas are subtle and attractive, the apple and pear fruit and flowers are clearly defined on the nose, and the complementary mineral nuances denote excellent ageing prospects over the years to come. The oak on the palate is never intrusive, instead creating a backdrop for the stars of the show, the notes of fruit and, again, flowers. The finish is lovely and long. The Monte Grande has very delicate, intense yet clean aromas that are temptingly pervasive on the nose. Ripe grapes give the palate sweetness that melds perfectly into the progression. The standard-label Soave is also very good and enviably fresh. Building work began this spring on the new cellar, which will allow Graziano and Sergio more room to work and think seriously about prolonged bottle ageing for the Monte Grande. A wine of this calibre certainly deserves it.

○ Soave Sup. S. Stefano '00	🍷🍷	5
○ Recioto di Soave Oro '00	🍷🍷	5
○ Soave Cl. Sup. Vigna Ronchetto '01	🍷🍷	3*
○ Soave Sup. Vigna Albare Doppia Maturazione Ragionata '01	🍷🍷	4*
○ Soave Sup. Vigna Albare Doppia Maturazione Ragionata '97	🍷🍷🍷	4
○ Soave Cl. Sup. Vigna Ronchetto '00	🍷🍷	3
○ Soave Sup. Vigna Albare Doppia Maturazione Ragionata '00	🍷🍷	4
○ Soave Sup. S. Stefano '98	🍷🍷	5
○ Soave Sup. Vigna Albare Doppia Maturazione Ragionata '99	🍷🍷	4

○ Soave Cl. Sup. Colle S. Antonio '99	🍷🍷	5
○ Soave Cl. Sup. Vigneto Monte Grande '01	🍷🍷	4*
○ Soave Cl. Sup. '01	🍷🍷	4*
○ Soave Cl. Sup. Vigneto Monte Grande '00	🍷🍷🍷	4
○ Soave Cl. Sup. Colle S. Antonio '98	🍷🍷	5
○ Soave Cl. Sup. Colle S. Antonio '97	🍷🍷	5
○ Soave Cl. Sup. Vigneto Monte Grande '98	🍷🍷	4
○ Soave Cl. Sup. Vigneto Monte Grande '99	🍷🍷	4

NEGRAR (VR)

BERTANI
FRAZ. ARBIZZANO
LOC. NOVARE
37020 NEGRAR (VR)
TEL. 0456011211
E-MAIL: bertani@bertani.net

It is difficult to know what to say about Bertani. With roots in the Veronese winemaking tradition that go back to 1857, this winery has influenced Valpolicella's past and continues to give a modern slant to a tradition that should not die. The splendid Villa Novare property appears to be suspended somewhere between the modern and the traditional. The vineyards are planted with Guyot-trained vines, which are certainly more modern than the pergola system predominantly used in the area. In contrast, the cellar, until a short while ago, had never used barriques. In fact, this large Veronese cellar's products are clearly divided on the one hand into traditional wines, represented by the Amarone and the Secco Bertani, and more up-to-date wines on the other, such as the Cabernet Sauvignon Albion and the Valpolicella Ognisanti, which make extensive use of small wood. The traditional wines are made in the Villa Novare cellar and the more modern ones are crafted at Grezzana. The second version of the Soave Sereole made good last year's promise. Well-defined and fragrant on the nose, it blends the oak nicely into the aromatic profile and the palate is stylish and mouthfilling. The '95 Amarone is a splendid, traditional interpretation. Mature hints of leather and crushed fruit precede a broad, silky palate with an appealingly smooth finish. The Valpolicella Ognisanti is much fresher and equally impressive, while the Cabernet Sauvignon Albion will be presented next year.

NEGRAR (VR)

TOMMASO BUSSOLA
LOC. SAN PERETTO
VIA MOLINO TURRI, 30
37024 NEGRAR (VR)
TEL. 0457501740
E-MAIL: t.bussola@tiscalinet.it

Here we go again. Tommaso Bussola is a leading exponent of great Valpolicella wines of all types, from the generous Valpolicella Superiore to the inimitable Amarone, not forgetting the wine that symbolizes the history and traditions of these valleys north of Verona better than any other – Recioto. Think sweet wines. Sauternes immediately comes to mind, along with Eiswein, Beerenauslese and perhaps Port. But don't end the list until you have tried one of Tommaso Bussola's great Reciotos. Admire in awe its deep hue, intense wild cherry fruit, spice, chocolate and medicinal herb aromas and a seemingly endless succession of nuances. The palate of the TB '99 is an astonishing combination of unusual structure and sweetness with unexpected suppleness and drinkability. Long and lingering, with many radiant years ahead of it, the TB '99 easily earned Three Glasses. Tommaso's Amarones are all of a very high standard, with huge structure and a trace of sweetness that does not jeopardize their austerity. The Vigneto Alto from the excellent '97 vintage is generous and now starting to present interesting mature aromas. The TB '98 is still very young, taut and harmonious while the BG '99 is approachable and mouthfilling. The Recioto BG took Two comfortable Glasses, thanks to good balance and unusual richness, while the very enjoyable Valpolicella '99 is one of the best examples of this wine type.

● Amarone della Valpolicella Cl. '95	8
○ Soave Cl. Sup. Sereole '00	4*
○ Due Uve '01	4*
● Valpolicella Cl. Sup. Vigneto Ognisanti Villa Novare '99	5
● Valpantena Secco Bertani '00	4
● Amarone della Valpolicella Cl. '85	8
● Albion Cabernet Sauvignon Villa Novare '97	7
○ Soave Cl. Sup. Sereole '99	4
● Amarone della Valpolicella Cl. '94	8
● Albion Cabernet Sauvignon Villa Novare '99	6

● Recioto della Valpolicella Cl. TB '99	8
● Valpolicella Cl. Sup. '99	6
● Amarone della Valpolicella Cl. TB Vigneto Alto '97	8
● Recioto della Valpolicella Cl. BG '00	7
● Amarone della Valpolicella Cl. TB '98	8
● Amarone della Valpolicella Cl. BG '99	7
● Recioto della Valpolicella Cl. TB '97	8
● Recioto della Valpolicella Cl. TB '98	8

NEGRAR (VR)

LE RAGOSE
FRAZ. ARBIZZANO
VIA LE RAGOSE, 1
37020 NEGRAR (VR)
TEL. 0457513241
E-MAIL: leragose@libero.it

Instantly recognizable, original wines that still respect tradition. That is Le Ragose's winemaking philosophy. A fine thread links all the wines in the range and if you can wait, your patience will be rewarded. These are not bottles to be influenced by passing wine fashions. Don't look for super-concentration or big-bodied smoothness here. The soil at Le Ragose lends outstanding elegance, backed up by acidity, ensuring that the wines age well acquiring a serious range of tertiary aromas. The '97 was a very good vintage and we had the pleasure of tasting two Amarones with completely different characters. The Marta Galli is more modern and approachable, with charming, varietal ripe cherry notes and attractive mineral, tangy fruit and a dark chocolate finish. The standard edition is more austere but don't be deceived by its finesse. It is made of splendid fruit and offers a subtle earthiness and a long sophisticated palate with a warm, Mediterranean finish. The Rhagos is an Amarone that is slightly reminiscent of a Recioto. Its opulent character accompanies a juicy, delicately sugary palate. The juicy, flowery Valpolicella Marta Galli is excellent, unveiling walnut, medicinal herb and raisined grape aromas. The '99 Superiore is equally well-made, although less complex than the previous version. The standard-label Valpolicella is uncomplicated, fragrant and peppery while the Cabernet is, as ever, interesting. It's not too grassy on the nose and well-structured in the mouth. The Recioto and Sassine were not ready so we will defer judgement until next year.

● Amarone della Valpolicella Cl. Marta Galli '97	🍷🍷	8
● Amarone della Valpolicella Cl. '97	🍷🍷	7
● Valpolicella Cl. Sup. Marta Galli '98	🍷🍷	6
● Garda Cabernet '98	🍷🍷	5
● Valpolicella Cl. Sup. Le Ragose '99	🍷🍷	4*
● Amarone della Valpolicella Cl. Raghos '97	🍷🍷	8
● Valpolicella Cl. '01	🍷	3
● Amarone della Valpolicella Cl. '86	🍷🍷🍷	7
● Amarone della Valpolicella Cl. '88	🍷🍷🍷	7
● Amarone della Valpolicella Cl. '95	🍷🍷	7
● Amarone della Valpolicella Cl. '96	🍷🍷	7

NEGRAR (VR)

ROBERTO MAZZI
LOC. SAN PERETTO
VIA CROSETTA, 8
37024 NEGRAR (VR)
TEL. 0457502072 - 0458266150
E-MAIL: robertomazzi@iol.it

Arriving at Roberto Mazzi's winery in San Peretto, you cannot help but admire the perfectly restored house and adjoining 17th-century mill, which create a romantic atmosphere and symbolize the owner's desire to remain in touch with tradition and roots. Roberto's sons Stefano and Antonio have taken over the running of the fairly small winery, aiming to make modern, stylish wines, and the excellent hillside location of the five and a half hectares of vineyards indicates that there is plenty of potential. The most impressive wine this year was the traditional-style Amarone Punta di Villa. Fruity, earthy hints mingle with light, flowery notes on the nose and the nicely austere palate is subtle and fresh. The Recioto Le Calcarole is livelier, with sweet, intriguing aromas. The palate leaves no room for uncertainty, full of mouthfilling sweetness that allows juicy, clean pulp to emerge. The Valpolicella Poiega confirms its high standard and demonstrates how good-quality grapes can make this underrated wine type extremely satisfying. It is full and intense on the nose, with very ripe fruit, and long and powerful on the palate, where nice aromatic herbs emerge in the finish. The Passito San Francesco is impressive but excessively sweet.

● Amarone della Valpolicella Cl. Punta di Villa '98	🍷🍷	7
● Recioto della Valpolicella Cl. Le Calcarole '98	🍷🍷	6
● Valpolicella Cl. Sup. Vigneto Poiega '99	🍷🍷	5
○ San Francesco Passito '98	🍷	5
● Amarone della Valpolicella Cl. Punta di Villa '96	🍷🍷	7
● Amarone della Valpolicella Cl. Punta di Villa '97	🍷🍷	7
● Valpolicella Cl. Sup. Vigneto Poiega '98	🍷🍷	5

NEGRAR (VR)

GIUSEPPE QUINTARELLI
VIA CERÈ, 1
37024 NEGRAR (VR)
TEL. 0457500016

Valpolicella is a terroir with a long history. It has weathered difficult times and has now been saved by the commitment of a large number of young producers, and the example of a great one, Giuseppe Quintarelli. Giuseppe's winery, situated at Negrar on the gentle Valpolicella hills, has 12 hectares of vineyards at an average altitude of 240 metres above sea level. Some of the grapes are bought in, bringing the average annual production up to 50-60,000 bottles. In the best years, Giuseppe Quintarelli makes an Amarone Riserva, and of course 1990 was no exception. Before release, this seriously good wine spent ten years ageing in Slavonian oak barrels. The deep garnet hue is appealing and there are sweet cocoa powder and ripe berry fruit nuances on the nose. The palate is generous with plums, fruit liqueur and coffee in a harmonious, lingering profile. The Alzero, made from raisined cabernet grapes, is deep ruby red and proffers aromas of red peppers, vegetables and tobacco on the nose. The palate has remarkable finesse and hints of cocoa, morello cherries, pepper and pencil lead create a very stylish, bitter-sweet effect. The fresh-tasting nicely rounded Valpolicella has hints of aromatic herbs, cherry fruit and liquorice, as well as good extract.

- Amarone della Valpolicella Cl. Sup. Ris. '90 — 8
- Valpolicella Cl. Sup. Monte Cà Paletta '95 — 7
- Alzero Cabernet Franc '96 — 8
- Amarone della Valpolicella Ris. '83 — 8
- Amarone della Valpolicella '84 — 8
- Amarone della Valpolicella '86 — 8
- Amarone della Valpolicella Ris. '85 — 8
- Alzero Cabernet Franc '90 — 8
- Amarone della Valpolicella Cl. Sup. Monte Cà Paletta '93 — 8
- Amarone della Valpolicella Cl. Sup. Monte Cà Paletta '95 — 8

NEGRAR (VR)

CANTINA SOCIALE VALPOLICELLA
VIA CA' SALGARI, 2
37024 NEGRAR (VR)
TEL. 0456014300
E-MAIL: dominiveneti@libero.it

Further proof that the Cantina Sociale Valpolicella will not compromise on quality comes from the decision not to present its Amarones this year because they were not ready. There have been some important changes in the cellar, involving both restoration work and the extensive replacement of old wood. This has enabled Daniele Accordini to fully tap the potential of the grapes contributed by member growers. Two new whites complete the Domini Veneti line, the co-operative's most interesting products. The interesting Soave Classico Superiore, Cà de Napa, has good, eloquent fruit on the nose and a palate with pleasantly rough edges from the garganega grape. The softness and balance come from skilfully applied oak. The Passito Costacalda, from the '99 vintage, is fresh on the nose with harmonious aromas. These are reflected on the palate, where the sweetness and acidity mingle to take you through to a long finish. The Recioto Vigneti di Moron is striking. Opaque in the glass, it has super-ripe fruit laced with flowers on the nose, then the sweetness of the palate is attractively offset by fresh aromatic herbs. The Valpolicellas are well made, particularly the Superiore La Casetta di Ettore Righetti, which is both powerful and harmonious.

- Recioto della Valpolicella Cl. Vigneti di Moron Domini Veneti '00 — 5
- Soave Cl. Sup. Vigneti di Cà de Napa Domini Veneti '01 — 4*
- Costacalda Passito Domini Veneti '99 — 6
- Valpolicella Cl. Sup. La Casetta di Ettore Righetti Domini Veneti '99 — 5
- Recioto della Valpolicella Cl. Domini Veneti '00 — 5
- Valpolicella Cl. Sup. Vigneti di Torbe '99 — 4
- Amarone della Valpolicella Cl. Manara '95 — 8
- Amarone della Valpolicella Cl. Vigneti di Jago Sel. '97 — 7

NEGRAR (VR)

VILLA SPINOSA
LOC. JAGO
37024 NEGRAR (VR)
TEL. 0457500093
E-MAIL: villaspinosa@valpolicella.it

For over ten years, Enrico Cascella Spinosa has run this splendid estate at Jago, one of the loveliest parts of Valpolicella, in an enviably well-endowed growing area. More than half of the property's total 26 hectares are planted to vine, providing the grapes for 30,000 bottles per year. The wines are very personal in style and may leave you either enthusiastic or perplexed, but never indifferent. Right from their aromas, these are wines with lashings of character. The Amarone, in particular, avoids sugary shortcuts or extreme softness, going instead for austerity and rigour in the mouth. The aromas are intense and already complex, with aromatic herbs, benzine and spices layered over the super-ripe berry fruit, and exemplary nose-palate consistency. The palate unfolds without haste and is kept in check by a dense, sweet tannic weave, ending with a dry, warm finish. The Valpolicella Jago is very good. Austere, deep notes of minerals usher in a no-nonsense palate that shows strong personality. The Antanel is more immediate and enjoyably drinkable, its uncompromising, ripe fruit enriched with light flowery hints. The fresher version of the Valpolicella is also good. It's whistle-clean, approachable and has a very drinkable, spice-nuanced palate.

• Amarone della Valpolicella Cl. '97	▼▼	6
• Valpolicella Cl. Sup. Jago '99	▼▼	4
• Valpolicella Cl. '01	▼	2*
• Valpolicella Cl. Sup. Antanel '99	▼	3*
• Amarone della Valpolicella Cl. '95	▽▽	6
• Amarone della Valpolicella Cl. '96	▽▽	6

NEGRAR (VR)

VIVIANI
VIA MAZZANO, 8
37024 NEGRAR (VR)
TEL. 0457500286

Four wines presented, each one better than the last. That's how we might sum up Claudio Viviani's winery this year. But the outstanding results are actually due to a decade of hard work in the cellar and an even greater commitment out of doors. Careful vineyard management is the secret behind Viviani's impressive progress. Claudio won't hear of makeshift solutions and instead seeks to make the best of his very old vineyards - despite the less than optimal training systems - until the whole property can be replanted in a more rational pattern. Naturally, this is a gradual process, which began last spring and will take a few years to complete. Meanwhile, the wines we tasted were very impressive. Following in the footsteps of the excellent '97 Tulipano Nero, which earned Three Glasses last year, is the Amarone Casa dei Bepi from the same vintage. Dark in colour, it unveils very stylish aromas where mineral hints mingle deliciously with ripe fruit as floral notes add lightness and appeal. This wine's instantly impressive palate is typical of the whole range. It is awesomely drinkable, especially considering the powerful structure and dauntingly high alcohol content. The Valpolicella Campo Morar is wonderful, with deep, floral aromas and admirable length on the palate. At last, we have an interpretation of this wine that deserves real recognition. The Recioto '99 and the Amarone Casa dei Bepi '96 are both excellent, too.

• Amarone della Valpolicella Cl. Casa dei Bepi '97	▼▼▼	8
• Recioto della Valpolicella Cl. '99	▼▼	6
• Valpolicella Cl. Sup. Campo Morar '99	▼▼	5
• Amarone della Valpolicella Cl. Casa dei Bepi '96	▼▼	7
• Amarone della Valpolicella Cl. Casa dei Bepi '95	▽▽▽	8
• Amarone della Valpolicella Cl. Tulipano Nero '97	▽▽▽	8
• Recioto della Valpolicella Cl. '98	▽▽	6
• Amarone della Valpolicella Cl. Casa dei Bepi '94	▽▽	8
• Valpolicella Cl. Sup. '98	▽▽	5

NERVESA DELLA BATTAGLIA (TV)

Serafini & Vidotto
Via Arditi, 1
31040 Nervesa della Battaglia (TV)
tel. 0422773281
e-mail: serafinievidotto@serafinievidotto.com

In last year's edition of the Guide, we mentioned Serafini & Vidotto's crucial decision to postpone release of some of their wines for a year, to allow them to age further in bottle before going to market. The process began with the leading wines, Il Rosso dell'Abazia and the Pinot Nero, and concludes this year with the non-appearance of the second red, Phigaia, and the Bianco. The move places Francesco Serafini and Antonello Vidotto in an exposed position. They risk not being able to satisfy market demands, yet at the same time the decision allows them to do their wines justice. Meanwhile, the new cellar is under construction a few hundred metres away from the current one, and the vineyards are being extended to produce more bottles of the leading wine, Il Rosso dell'Abazia. Thanks to that extra year's bottle age, the '99 vintage is outstandingly stylish. A floral, exceptionally subtle, tidy nose with generous notes of berry fruit, medicinal herbs and spices is followed by powerful structure in the mouth, tempered by virtually perfect balance. Rounded, long and silky, it closes with a fresh minty note. The Pinot Nero is only slightly inferior. This notoriously difficult variety has a genuine Burgundian feel this year. Raspberries, blackberries, redcurrants and mint are the most evident notes on the nose then the beautifully even, creamy mouthfeel shows faint hints of tannins through to the generous finish.

PESCHIERA DEL GARDA (VR)

La Sansonina
Loc. La Sansonina
37019 Peschiera del Garda (VR)
tel. 0457551905

La Sansonina was founded in the mid 1990s almost for fun, when Carla Prospero decided to buy an old merlot vineyard. The Sansonina area is renowned for the production of one of the most delicate white varieties imaginable, trebbiano di Lugana so it was a stern challenge to prove that it was possible to make a great red wine from a 25-year-old vineyard in the heart of white wine country. Of course, three hectares of vineyards were not enough so another nine hectares were planted, almost entirely to merlot. From then on, the recipe was fairly predictable: low yields, respect for the grapes in the cellar, and ageing in French oak barriques. The surprises began a few years later, when tasting revealed that the wine had unexpectedly failed to develop into a highly structured powerful red, instead adopting light, fresh aromas and a caressingly soft palate. The first vintage, '97, was only bottled in magnums. It has ripe fruit and aromatic herbs on the nose, with a nice mineral finish. The following year's vintage was more interesting, with intense berry fruit accompanied by cloves, pepper, thyme and a classy hint of roses. The somewhat edgy palate tells you that the wine is still young but offers a nice contrast to the sweetness of the fruit and the fine floral aromas.

●	Il Rosso dell'Abazia '99	🍷🍷	6
●	Pinot Nero '99	🍷🍷	7
●	Il Rosso dell'Abazia '93	🍷🍷🍷	6
●	Il Rosso dell'Abazia '94	🍷🍷🍷	6
●	Il Rosso dell'Abazia '95	🍷🍷🍷	6
●	Il Rosso dell'Abazia '96	🍷🍷🍷	6
●	Il Rosso dell'Abazia '97	🍷🍷🍷	6
●	Il Rosso dell'Abazia '98	🍷🍷🍷	6
○	Il Bianco dell'Abazia '00	🍷🍷	4
●	Phigaia After the Red '99	🍷🍷	4

●	Sansonina '97	🍷🍷	8
●	Sansonina '98	🍷🍷	7

PESCHIERA DEL GARDA (VR)

OTTELLA
Fraz. S. Benedetto di Lugana
Loc. Ottella, 1
37019 Peschiera del Garda (VR)
Tel. 0457551950
E-mail: ottella.m@tiscalinet.it

Francesco Montresor has proved again that he is one of the best producers of Lugana, a white Garda wine that successfully blends tradition and innovation. The Molceo 2000 is exemplary. A Superiore with a delightful golden hue, it presents ripe peaches and apricots, pineapple, citron, candied fruit and spices on the nose, interlaced with hints of coffee. The palate is lifted by spirited minerally hints and has bags of personality. Equally impressive is the more varietal, traditional Lugana Le Creete 2001, which hails from the clayey soil at the Laghetto di Frassino. It's a slightly rustic wine with marked vegetal hints. The standard-label Lugana is uncomplicated, clean tasting and drinkable, with sweet, subtle notes of flowers that meld with hints of almonds. Moving on from the trebbiano di Lugana variety, but staying with the whites, we found a Gimé that nearly earned Two Glasses. A blend of chardonnay and incrocio Manzoni, it probably needs longer in bottle to tone down its rather excessive sweetness and hints of vanilla and talcum powder. These are, however, backed up by good structure and subtle extract. The reds produced another very good performance from the Campo Sireso, a blend of merlot, cabernet sauvignon and corvina veronese. It has flowers, fragrant ripe fruit and aromatic herbs on the nose. The Rosso Ottella is a much less complicated, fresh and subtly fruity wine.

PESCHIERA DEL GARDA (VR)

ZENATO
Fraz. S. Benedetto di Lugana
Via S. Benedetto, 8
37019 Peschiera del Garda (VR)
Tel. 0457550300
E-mail: info@zenata.it

A long-established San Benedetto di Lugana cellar, Zenato follows last year's amazing performance with another impressive series of wines. Results are now forthcoming from the significant investments made in the vineyards, and the wines have more sophistication, thanks to sensitivity and tenacity demonstrated by owner Sergio Zenato in the vinification and ageing processes. Two products stand out among the many wines presented this year, the Amarone '98 and the Amarone Sergio Zenato '97. This is not simply a case of one standard-label and one special selection. These are two profoundly different wines. The first is all style and apparent simplicity while the second is more traditional, with warmer, mouthfilling notes. The '98 has appetizingly unspoilt fruit on the nose and light touches of aromatic herbs to enhance its ripe fruit aromas. It reveals an enviably stylish, and unusually approachable, palate for a wine of this calibre. The '97 is already showing interesting development, with super-ripe, mineral tones on the nose and a broad, warm palate that can offer both lightness and power at the same time. Also very good this year are the Alberto, a Bordeaux blend in a Verona style, the Cabernet Sauvignon from the Santa Cristina vineyard, and the two wines most closely associated with the Zenato family, the tangy, vibrant Lugana Massoni and the ripe Sergio Zenato selection, which has an interesting hint of oak.

● Campo Sireso '00	ŸŸ	5
○ Lugana Sup. Molceo '00	ŸŸ	5
○ Lugana Le Creete '01	ŸŸ	4*
○ Gimè Bianco '01	Ÿ	4
○ Lugana '01	Ÿ	4
● Rosso Ottella '01		3
● Campo Sireso '96	ŸŸ	5
● Campo Sireso '97	ŸŸ	5
○ Prima Luce Passito '97	ŸŸ	6
● Campo Sireso '98	ŸŸ	5
● Campo Sireso '99	ŸŸ	5

● Amarone della Valpolicella Cl. Sergio Zenato Ris. '97	ŸŸ	8
● Amarone della Valpolicella Cl. '98	ŸŸ	6
○ Lugana Sergio Zenato '00	ŸŸ	5
○ Lugana Vigneto Massoni Santa Cristina '01	ŸŸ	4
● Alberto Rosso '99	ŸŸ	6
● Cabernet Sauvignon S. Cristina '99	ŸŸ	4
● Valpolicella Cl. Sup. Ripassa '99	ŸŸ	4
○ Rigoletto Passito '00	Ÿ	4
○ Lugana S. Benedetto '01	Ÿ	3*
● Valpolicella Cl. Sup. '99	Ÿ	3*
● Amarone della Valpolicella Cl. '97	ŸŸŸ	6
● Alberto Rosso '98	ŸŸ	6

SALGAREDA (TV)

Ornella Molon Traverso
Fraz. Campo di Pietra
Via Risorgimento, 40
31040 Salgareda (TV)
tel. 0422804807
e-mail: info@molon.it

There were very satisfying results this year from our tastings of Ornella Molon and Giancarlo Traverso's wines. They crown years of effort, much of it devoted to getting the Piave DOC established. Some of the grapes are grown from the estate's own vineyards and the rest are bought in, after careful selection. The technical skill of young winemaker Simone Casazza, and the experience of Luca D'Attoma, have also contributed to the winery's success. The flagship bottle is the Rosso di Villa, a dark wine with aromas that hint at its complexity. Aromatic herbs, red peppers, pepper and orange peel are followed by a generous flavour and assertive tannins on the palate. The Vite Rossa, from 50 per cent merlot and the remainder cabernet sauvignon and franc, is ruby red in colour with a subtle, stylish bouquet of flowers, particularly violets, on the nose, as well as mint and tobacco. The palate is full of ripe cherry fruit and chocolate, ending in a long, warm finish. The Cabernet and Merlot were a little below par last year but are back on song now. Of the excellent whites, we preferred the Chardonnay and Traminer, while the sweet Bianco di Ornella, from verduzzo, sauvignon and traminer, is intense and vibrant. We have saved the Raboso for last. The more discriminating local producers are now committed to the variety's revival but it is an uphill road. We are convinced it is the right one.

SAN BONIFACIO (VR)

Inama
Via 4 Novembre, 1
37047 San Bonifacio (VR)
tel. 0456104343
e-mail: inama@inamaaziendaagricola.it

Hailed as a child prodigy a few years ago, Stefano Inama is now a committed producer of white wines, Soave in particular, which he interprets with skill and precision. All Stefano's wines, from the simplest to the most famous, have great personality, but apparently, this is not enough for him. Stefano is devoting increasing attention to black grapes and the nearby Colli Berici. To add to his magnificent estate at Lonigo, he has recently purchased a new property in San Germano dei Berici consisting of seven hectares planted entirely to carmenère, from which he hopes to make a red wine of international calibre. We look forward to this new wine and in the meantime, we have tasted a series of wines that are, to say the very least, astonishing, both in character and stature. 2001 was not an easy year but we awarded Two Glasses to Inama's highly enjoyable standard-label Soave. Its approachable, generous nose is followed by an interesting and impeccably harmonious palate. The two super-Soaves are wines we won't forget in a hurry. The Foscarino and the Du Lot share a mesmerizing flinty mineral note but the former is more linear and severe, while the second opens up into ripe, mouthfilling fruit. The Vulcaia Fumé is again a very good wine indeed. The rich, powerful aromas and palate evoke all the airy grace of a great bottle. Finally, the Cabernet Sauvignon Bradisismo is excellent.

●	Rosso di Villa Ris. '99	🍷🍷	6
○	Piave Chardonnay Ornella '01	🍷🍷	4
○	Traminer '01	🍷🍷	4
●	Vite Rossa '98	🍷🍷	5
○	Bianco di Ornella '99	🍷🍷	4
●	Piave Cabernet Ornella '99	🍷🍷	5
●	Piave Merlot Ornella '99	🍷🍷	5
○	Vite Bianca '99	🍷🍷	4
○	Sauvignon Ornella '01	🍷	3*
●	Piave Raboso '97	🍷	5
●	Vite Rossa '97	🍷🍷	5
●	Piave Merlot Rosso di Villa '98	🍷🍷	6

○	Soave Cl. Sup. Vigneto Du Lot '00	🍷🍷🍷	5
○	Soave Cl. Sup. Vigneti di Foscarino '00	🍷🍷	5
○	Sauvignon Vulcaia '00	🍷🍷	5
○	Sauvignon Vulcaia Fumé '00	🍷🍷	6
○	Soave Cl. Sup. Vin Soave '01	🍷🍷	3*
●	Bradisismo Cabernet Sauvignon '99	🍷🍷	6
○	Chardonnay '01	🍷	3
○	Sauvignon Vulcaia Fumé '96	🍷🍷🍷	6
○	Soave Cl. Sup. Vigneto Du Lot '96	🍷🍷🍷	5
○	Soave Cl. Sup. Vigneto Du Lot '99	🍷🍷🍷	5

SAN FIOR (TV)

MASOTTINA
LOC. CASTELLO ROGANZUOLO
VIA BRADOLINI, 54
31010 SAN FIOR (TV)
TEL. 0438400775
E-MAIL: info@masottina.it

Masottina is a medium-to-large winery that owns vineyards all round the Treviso area, so its range of products includes wines from the Piave, Prosecco and Conegliano DOC zones. Thanks to the commitment and professionalism of the Dal Bianco brothers and their team, the entire range maintains an unfailingly high standard of quality, each bottle reflecting the typical features of its territory. Every year, Masottina presents us with a large number of interesting wines, all of which deserve a mention. In fact, the list at the bottom of their page gets longer with each edition. The long-neglected Piave DOC, which has generally tended to produce very few fine wines, is now enjoying a period of revival and Masottina is one of the driving forces behind the new trend. We were surprised this year by the excellent Merlot and the Cabernet Piave from the Riserva ai Palazzi line. The distinctive and very personal aromas of the velvety Merlot show impressive finesse and range. It is reminiscent of a perfect, old-style wine with its supple, gradual progression in the mouth and mature, but not too deep, hue. The Cabernet is made along the same lines but is a little more rustic on the nose. Masottina tips its hat at international tastes with the Colli di Conegliano Bianco and Rosso, both of which are more modern in character, while the Prosecco Spumante range maintains the winery's good standard.

SAN GERMANO DEI BERICI (VI)

VILLA DAL FERRO LAZZARINI
VIA CHIESA, 23
36040 SAN GERMANO DEI BERICI (VI)
TEL. 0444868025
E-MAIL: pamporr@hotmail.com

The Colli dei Berici zone is still searching for its own identity. This DOC has been slow to take off because it has been unable to project an up-to-date image, caught as it is between a much-invoked, but poorly rooted, tradition and an impulse for modernism that spares little thought for how best to invest money and skill. Pamela Lazzarini is now alone at the helm of this winery, which has a long history and intends to continue focusing on quality for a long time to come. Her agenda is based on a number of very firmly established points: a limited number of wines; a style mix that conforms to market demands without neglecting tradition; ongoing research into how long the products should be aged; and avoiding over-hasty release of the finished products. The new red, Il Massi, stood out among the wines we tasted this year. It is obtained mainly from merlot grapes and inspired by the severe style and deep flavour of the Campo del Lago – the 1999 will be out next year – though it is perhaps a tad less challenging. Smooth elegance should not be mistaken for a lack of substance, however. Tobacco, leather, redcurrant and wild cherry introduce a palate that is steadily gaining complexity. The nose of the Pinot Bianco Blatià is enhanced by the addition of other aromatic grape varieties, which add sophisticated mineral notes to the hints of apples, almonds and flowers. The wine is still looking for balance but as it continues to mature, patience will surely be rewarded.

● Piave Merlot ai Palazzi Ris. '99	♛♛	4*
○ Colli di Conegliano Bianco Rizzardo '00	♛♛	4*
● Piave Cabernet Sauvignon ai Palazzi Ris. '99	♛♛	4*
○ Piave Chardonnay '01	♛	3
○ Piave Chardonnay ai Palazzi Ris. '01	♛	4
● Colli di Conegliano Rosso Montesco '99	♛	6
● Piave Merlot '01	♛	3
○ Cartizze	♛	5
○ P. di Conegliano Extra Dry	♛	4
○ Piave Pinot Bianco '01		3
● Colli di Conegliano Rosso '98	♛♛	5

● Colli Berici Merlot Il Massi '00	♛♛	4*
○ Colli Berici Pinot Bianco Blatià '01	♛♛	4*
● Colli Berici Merlot Campo del Lago '97	♛♛	5
● Colli Berici Merlot Campo del Lago '98	♛♛	5

SAN MARTINO BUON ALBERGO (VR)

MARION
LOC. MARCELLISE
VIA BORGO, 1
37036 SAN MARTINO BUON ALBERGO (VR)
TEL. 0458740021
E-MAIL: campedelli@inwind.it

The Marion winery rightfully returns to the Guide after a transitional year. The Campedelli family who own the winery took the courageous decision to leave their wines to age unhurriedly before placing them on the market. Now Stefano, his wife Nicoletta and young Marco have every right to be proud of their work. The three are supported by the invaluable consultancy of the Zymè group in running the six-hectare property, which is planted to typical Valpolicella varieties, corvinone, corvina and rondinella, along with teroldego and cabernet. Production is currently around 20,000 bottles per year, which will increase with re-organization of the vineyards. Next year will see the production of a monovarietal Teroldego, but we'll have to wait until 2004 for the Amarone. So let's turn to the wines, starting with the Valpolicella '98. Its deep ruby red ushers in well-defined cherry and liquorice, then the upfront tannins in the mouth demonstrate both its youth and ageing potential. The Cabernet Sauvignon has a full colour and powerful aromas with hints of balsam, coffee and plums. The palate is fresh-tasting, full-bodied and lingering. Lastly, the Passito Bianco, obtained from garganega and trebbiano toscano, is golden yellow in colour with amber highlights and an intense, generous bouquet of flowers and cakes. Hints of apricot jam, apples and oranges on the palate lead through to figs and almonds in the lovely long finish.

● Valpolicella Sup. '98	ŸŸ	5
● Cabernet Sauvignon '98	ŸŸ	5
○ Passito Bianco '98	ŸŸ	5
● Cabernet Sauvignon '97	ŸŸ	5
● Valpolicella Sup. '97	ŸŸ	5

SAN MARTINO BUON ALBERGO (VR)

MUSELLA
LOC. MONTE DEL DRAGO
37036 SAN MARTINO BUON ALBERGO (VR)
TEL. 045973385
E-MAIL: maddalena@musella.it

Emilio and Graziella Pasqua di Bisceglie's young winery makes another well-deserved appearance in the Guide with a small but convincing range of wines. Located at San Martino Buon Albergo, a few kilometres from Verona, and surrounded by vineyards, the winery opened a bed and breakfast facility in 2002, demonstrating its commitment to promoting the whole Musella area. Last year, we described the extensive renewal work in the vineyards, which they are now planted at a density of 6,000 plants per hectare to ensure better quality grapes. The owners are determined to release only wines that have aged to perfection, so we were unable to taste all their offerings. The Bianco del Drago will be ready for tasting next year and the '99 Valpolicella Superiore will never see the light of day. The grapes were not considered up to the standard of such an exalted wine. Although the vintage was not as generous as '97, the '98 Amarone is very good, offering elegant, full aromas. The palate is broad, enthralling and graceful, with lovely balance. Another wine to try is the Monte del Drago, a remarkably structured, wonderfully concentrated, blend of corvina and cabernet sauvignon. This year, a mouthfilling Recioto was also presented for the first time, and strolled away with Two Glasses on its debut.

● Recioto della Valpolicella '00	ŸŸ	5
● Amarone della Valpolicella '98	ŸŸ	6
● Monte del Drago Rosso '98	Ÿ	5
● Amarone della Valpolicella '97	ŸŸ	6
● Monte del Drago Rosso '97	Ÿ	5

SAN PIETRO DI FELETTO (TV)

Bepin de Eto
Via Colle, 32/a
31020 San Pietro di Feletto (TV)
Tel. 0438486877
E-mail: bepindeeto@virgilio.it

Ettore Ceschin, owner of Bepin de Eto, is always ready for a new challenge. In the last year, he has purchased a vineyard of around 100 hectares in the Manduria area of the province of Taranto, where he hopes to make wines from primitivo, negroamaro, nero d'Avola and fiano fruit. Ettore's ambitions slot in perfectly with our expectations as enthusiasts, so we wish him all the best in the hope that this courageous project will be a success. It has not, however, distracted Ettore's attention, and that of his team, from the cellar's traditional products. The most representative of these is the Colli di Conegliano Rosso Croda Ronca, a blend of cabernet, merlot and marzemino. The '98 version is even more successful than its predecessors. Its wide and interesting range of aromas blends sweet spices from the long period of barrique ageing with subtler nuances of fruit and flowers. On the downside, the full, meaty palate has a bit too much tannin. One of the most impressive whites was the Colli di Conegliano Il Greccio, a blend of chardonnay, sauvignon, riesling and incrocio Manzoni bianco. The product demonstrates the winery's faith in this young DOC, despite the fact that in this area Prosecco reigns supreme. The Passito Faé is also a success. Although very generously extracted, it is subtle and stylish both on the nose and on the palate. Lastly, a mention for the Manzoni Bianco, as good as ever, and the very enjoyable Prosecco Tranquillo.

SAN PIETRO IN CARIANO (VR)

Stefano Accordini
Fraz. Pedemonte
Via Alberto Bolla, 9
37029 San Pietro in Cariano (VR)
Tel. 0457701733
E-mail: stefano.accordini@tin.it

Viticulture is written into the Accordini genetic code. They were working on the land even before 1930, the year when the winery was founded. Until last year, the cellar could only count on six hectares of estate-owned and rented vineyards. That figure has now been doubled, thanks to the shrewd purchase of a further seven hectares, to be planted entirely using the Guyot training system. The new plot is situated on the Mazzurega hills at a height of 400 metres above sea level. The increase in average temperatures over recent years has meant that vineyards at altitudes considered difficult a decade ago are now able to guarantee the subtle aromas that are an indispensable feature of great wines. Accordini wines have never lacked structure and concentration, but the elegance and breadth of their aromas are also improving noticeably. All the wines presented this year were outstanding but let's begin with the superlative Recioto. Its dark hue introduces intense, appetizing ripe fruit aromas and hints of flowers. The same aromas gently emerge on the palate, where acidity and tannin combine with superbly gauged, mouthfilling sweetness. The Amarone is richly extracted and expresses warm, well-developed aromas. Its crushed raisined fruit is very traditional and the finish has great harmony. The Passo is a blend of traditional local grape varieties with a little merlot and cabernet, and shows charmingly stylish floral aromas. The clean, excellently typed Valpolicellas are both very enjoyable.

● Colli di Conegliano Rosso Croda Ronca '98	♟♟	6
○ Colli di Conegliano Bianco Il Greccio '01	♟♟	3*
○ Faé Passito '96	♟♟	6
○ Incrocio Manzoni 6.0.13 '01	♟	3
○ P. di Conegliano Tranquillo	♟	3
○ P. di Conegliano Extra Dry		3
● Colli di Conegliano Rosso Croda Ronca '96	♟♟	6
● Colli di Conegliano Rosso Croda Ronca '97	♟♟	6

● Recioto della Valpolicella Cl. Acinatico '00	♟♟♟	6
● Valpolicella Cl. Sup. Acinatico '00	♟♟	5
● Amarone della Valpolicella Cl. Acinatico '98	♟♟	8
● Passo Rosso '00	♟♟	6
● Valpolicella Cl. '01	♟	3*
● Amarone della Valpolicella Cl. Vigneto Il Fornetto '93	♟♟♟	8
● Amarone della Valpolicella Cl. Acinatico '95	♟♟♟	8
● Amarone della Valpolicella Cl. Vigneto Il Fornetto '95	♟♟♟	8

SAN PIETRO IN CARIANO (VR)

Lorenzo Begali
Via Cengia, 10
37020 San Pietro in Cariano (VR)
tel. 0457725148
e-mail: tiliana@tiscalinet.it

After last year's exploit, we are happy to confirm that the Begali family's top award was not a nine-day wonder. It may be a challenge to win Three Glasses, but it is even more important to show that your winery is capable of repeating the feat. However, when the range's foundations are laid on hard work in the vineyard and careful monitoring of all production phases, from drying to bottling, the results are bound to be encouraging. Lorenzo's son Giordano has worked alongside him year after year, playing an increasingly important role, and the pair are now learning to use wood to very good effect. This time, the best wine is the extremely satisfying Recioto, which won a comfortable Three Glasses. The berry fruit in syrup aromas are intense, appetizing and enhanced with hints of roses. The full-bodied palate reflects the nose perfectly, and is lent suppleness and style by a nice vein of freshness, despite its marked sweetness. The Amarone Ca' Bianca is excellently typed, not for the first time. Dark but not opaque in colour, it slowly releases a swathe of aromas on the nose, which are faithfully reflected on a palate where barely perceptible oak adds to their whistle-clean integrity. The standard-label Amarone is more traditional but well made, rich in fruity, mineral aromas and very drinkable. There was a fine debut from the Tigiolo, a blend of traditional local grapes and cabernet. The Valpolicella Classico Superiore La Cengia is well executed and dependable.

● Recioto della Valpolicella Cl. '00	🍷🍷🍷	7
● Amarone della Valpolicella Cl. Vigneto Monte Ca' Bianca '98	🍷🍷	8
● Amarone della Valpolicella Cl. '98	🍷🍷	8
● Tigiolo Rosso '99	🍷🍷	7
● Valpolicella Cl. Sup. Vigneto La Cengia '00	🍷	4
● Amarone della Valpolicella Cl. Vigneto Monte Ca' Bianca '97	🍷🍷🍷	8
● Recioto della Valpolicella Cl. '99	🍷🍷	8
● Amarone della Valpolicella Cl. Vigneto Monte Ca' Bianca '96	🍷🍷	8
● Amarone della Valpolicella Cl. '97	🍷🍷	7
● Recioto della Valpolicella Cl. '98	🍷🍷	7

SAN PIETRO IN CARIANO (VR)

Brigaldara
Fraz. San Floriano
Via Brigaldara, 20
37029 San Pietro in Cariano (VR)
tel. 0457701055
e-mail: brigaldara@c-point.it

Stefano Cesari's winemaking skills mature with each passing year, as you can tell if you sample his distinctly superior products. The '97 Amarone awarded Three Glasses last year might just have been the happy result of an exceptionally good year, of course, but now Stefano has presented us with a '98 which is every bit as good as its elder brother. Cesari's winery has the potential to produce a large quantity of dried-grape wines so he carries out rigorous selections of fruit for drying. The twofold result is that he has both an Amarone of international standard and a particularly flavoursome, well-structured Valpolicella, since the vines are not stripped of all their first-quality grapes. For the moment, none of the estate plots are devoted entirely to either type we can only commend Stefano's hard work in both the vineyard and the cellar. The '98 Amarone repeats a style that is as successful as it is hard to maintain. Substantial structure and alcohol combine with inimitable elegance, approachability and drinkability. The wine is dark and reveals a range of intense aromas on a nose dominated by super-ripe fruit and cloves. These gradually give way to flowers and minerally hints that usher in the astonishing palate. The wine's strength and structure are lifted by impressive freshness and lightness, closing in a long lingering finish. The Recioto and the single Valpolicella presented are excellent. Both are generous and juicy in the mouth.

● Amarone della Valpolicella Cl. '98	🍷🍷🍷	7
● Recioto della Valpolicella Cl. '00	🍷🍷	7
● Valpolicella Cl. '00	🍷🍷	3*
● Amarone della Valpolicella Cl. '97	🍷🍷🍷	7
● Amarone della Valpolicella Cl. '95	🍷🍷	7
● Amarone della Valpolicella Cl. '96	🍷🍷	7
● Recioto della Valpolicella '98	🍷🍷	7
● Valpolicella Cl. '99	🍷🍷	3

SAN PIETRO IN CARIANO (VR)

LUIGI BRUNELLI
VIA CARIANO, 10
37029 SAN PIETRO IN CARIANO (VR)
TEL. 0457701118
E-MAIL: cortecariano@tin.it

Luigi Brunelli believes utterly in his work and in the huge potential of Amarone, which becomes soft and charming in his hands without losing concentration. If we may make one point of friendly criticism, he does seem to be in a bit of a rush to get them to market. The '99 Amarones are definitely too young and need to mature. This might explain why the Campo dei Titari fell short of a Three Glass score. It has sumptuous colour and close-knit aromas, featuring liquorice and bottled cherries, while its lovely dried roses, iodine hints of sea breezes and cocoa powder only emerge after it has been allowed to breathe. The palate stays severe and compelling, although still inhibited by new wood, right up to the almost endless finish. The Campo Inferi shows the same level of concentration and thanks to ageing in large barrels, it is better balanced and readier for drinking. Its aromas unfold gradually and stylishly on the nose, then the silky smooth palate offers a nice interpretation of the wine's classic cherry cordial and cocoa powder notes. However, we wouldn't like it to eclipse the splendid performance of the standard-label version. A gutsy, gamey wine with earthy aromas, it is equally original and accessible, albeit in a minor key. Moving on to the Valpolicellas, the nice fruit and pepper 2001 standard-label edition was among the best of the year, like the Campo Praesel, which is more mature and complex. The Pariondo has muscle but also a lot of wood. Lastly, the impressive Recioto is grassy, fruity and lean on the palate.

- Amarone della Valpolicella Cl. Campo del Titari '99 — 8
- Recioto della Valpolicella Cl. '00 — 5
- Amarone della Valpolicella Cl. '99 — 6
- Amarone della Valpolicella Cl. Campo Inferi '99 — 7
- Valpolicella Cl. Sup. Campo Praesel '00 — 2*
- Valpolicella Cl. Sup. Pariondo '00 — 4
- Valpolicella Cl. '01 — 2*
- Amarone della Valpolicella Cl. Campo del Titari '96 — 8
- Amarone della Valpolicella Cl. Campo del Titari '97 — 8

SAN PIETRO IN CARIANO (VR)

ANGELO NICOLIS E FIGLI
VIA VILLA GIRARDI, 29
37029 SAN PIETRO IN CARIANO (VR)
TEL. 0457701261
E-MAIL: info@vininicolis.com

The Amarone Ambrosan is made in the very best vintages from a selection of the grapes from the winery's best vineyard. The '97 – a great vintage throughout Valpolicella – stopped short of excellence but the '98 brilliantly delivers a Three Glass-winning performance. It is warm and appealing, combining a sunny Mediterranean character with features more specific to its territory without stinting on elegance. The opulent, flower-themed nose accompanies iodine notes of the sea with dried fruit. The development on the palate progresses smoothly with a creamy, satin-smooth weave. Delicious hints of herbs, cocoa powder and flowers come together in the fabulous finish. The flavour, balance and freshness are commendable, making it an ideal wine to serve with food. The Seccal is given an expertly monitored "ripasso", or addition of unpressed skins after fermentation. Its floral and herbal aromas mingle with well-defined fruit and the dry flavour hints at cherry stones and aromatic herbs. It has the stuff it takes to age for several years. Among the other wines are an uncomplicated Valpolicella 2001, a fruity, enjoyable Superiore 2000, a fragrant, summery, salmon pink Chiaretto with aromas of strawberries, spices and aniseed, and a rather unpolished Testal that needs to mature. Lastly, the delightful, particularly complex 2000 Recioto is clean, enjoyable and has just the right hint of sweetness.

- Amarone della Valpolicella Cl. Ambrosan '98 — 7
- Recioto della Valpolicella Cl. '00 — 6
- Valpolicella Cl. Sup. Seccal '00 — 4
- Testal '00 — 5
- Valpolicella Cl. Sup. '00 — 4
- Chiaretto '01 — 3
- Valpolicella Cl. '01 — 3
- Amarone della Valpolicella Cl. Ambrosan '93 — 7
- Amarone della Valpolicella Cl. Ambrosan '95 — 7

SAN PIETRO IN CARIANO (VR)

Santa Sofia
Loc. Pedemonte
Via Ca' Dedé, 61
37020 San Pietro in Cariano (VR)
tel. 0457701074
E-mail: info@santasofia.com

This major winery in the Verona area produces 500,000 bottles per year, from the Garda, Valpolicella, where the estate is based, and Soave DOCs. The varied range searches for the ideal blend of tradition and innovation, offering old wood and stainless steel, international and local varieties, and austere wines with softer blends. The tastings this year were somewhat provisional in nature as the more modern reds, like Arleo and Predaia, were still ageing. If we move on to the whites, the Pinot Grigio Vigneto Fratte and the Custoza Montemagrin stand out for their uncompromising frankness, the Soave Montefoscarin for its typical nature and the ambitious Chardonnay Croara for its lovely clean varietal hazelnut, peach and melon fruit. Turning to the reds, we'll mention first the fruity, concentrated Recioto della Valpolicella, its typical morello cherry aromas mingling with cocoa powder and crushed herbs, to be followed by bitter chocolate and dry earth on the palate. The Amarone Gioé '97 has turned out well. Very ripe fruit, aromatic herbs and white chocolate are just some of the notes on the nose and reflected on the palate, although the still rather intrusive wood prevented the wine from achieving an even more ambitious result. While we wait for the new wines, we should also emphasize the staying power and good development of the excellent Amarone Riserva del Millennio '95, and our confirmation of the score earned by the standard-label '97 Amarone tasted last year.

SAN PIETRO IN CARIANO (VR)

F.lli Speri
Fraz. Pedemonte
Via Fontana, 14
37020 San Pietro in Cariano (VR)
tel. 0457701154
E-mail: info@speri.com

The large Speri family epitomizes the continuity of viticulture in Valpolicella. Speris have been here since 1874 and in the recent, somewhat hectic, decades they have become a point of reference for producers who want to fuse tradition and innovation. The Speris were among the first in the area to use barriques and tonneaux. They managed to preserve intact the character of their wines, and indeed gave them better definition and concentration, without, however, compromising the sheer drinking pleasure that a great wine should give. At last, the restoration of the old family house is complete, so space can now be given over to the large tonneaux stock and to making operations smoother and more precise. After all, over 50,000 bottles of Amarone a year require considerable space if they are going to age for at least five years. The '97 Amarone is an unmissable Three Glass monster. Clean and intense on the nose, it melds crushed fruit and aromatic herbs with light, perfectly integrated hints of oak. A dry, no-nonsense palate with outstanding texture gently takes possession of your mouth with the enjoyable, and apparently effortless simplicity of a great wine. The Recioto La Roggia is equally stylish. The subtly floral nose precedes a tidy, supple palate and finish that would be hard to match for class. The Valpolicella Sant'Urbano shows how you can obtain a great modern wine without neglecting tradition.

- Amarone della Valpolicella Cl. Gioé '97 — 7
- Recioto della Valpolicella Cl. '99 — 6
- Croara Chardonnay '00 — 4
- Recioto di Soave Cl. '00 — 5
- Bianco di Custoza Montemagrin '01 — 2*
- Soave Cl. Montefoscarin '01 — 2*
- Bardolino Cl. '01 — 2
- Soave Cl. Sup. Costalta '01 — 3
- Valdadige Pinot Grigio Vigneto Fratte '01 — 3
- Amarone della Valpolicella Cl. '97 — 6

- Amarone della Valpolicella Cl. Vigneto Monte Sant'Urbano '97 — 7
- Recioto della Valpolicella Cl. La Roggia '98 — 6
- Valpolicella Cl. Sup. Sant'Urbano '99 — 5
- Valpolicella Cl. Sup. La Roverina '00 — 4
- Recioto della Valpolicella Cl. I Comunai '99 — 6
- Valpolicella Cl. '01 — 3
- Amarone della Valpolicella Cl. Vigneto Monte Sant'Urbano '93 — 7
- Amarone della Valpolicella Cl. Vigneto Monte Sant'Urbano '95 — 7

SAN PIETRO IN CARIANO (VR)

F.lli Tedeschi
Fraz. Pedemonte
Via G. Verdi, 4
37020 San Pietro in Cariano (VR)
tel. 0457701487
e-mail: tedeschi@tedeschiwines.com

Tedeschi is a classic Valpolicella winery that has always shown an interest in preserving tradition. Lately, though, the younger Tedeschi generation – Sabrina, Antonietta and Riccardo – have become increasingly involved, injecting a new spirit into a cellar that believes in hanging on to what is positive from the past, while looking to modern solutions for improvements in vineyard and cellar. Interesting experiments with training systems are under way in a few hectares of vineyards and new winemaking techniques are being tried out, shrewdly and critically, in the cellar. The Amarone Capitel Monte Olmi opens out gradually and stylishly. It is richly extracted but not to the detriment of the delicacy and subtlety typical of old-fashioned Amarones. In fact, it is one of the best bottles we uncorked for this edition of the Guide and our taste-off panellists were delighted to award it Three Glasses. The Recioto Capitel Monte Fontana is equally remarkable, and no less potent or concentrated than the preceding wine. The generous aromas and balanced flavour endow it with a complexity that goes beyond mere power. The Rosso della Fabriseria 2000, a blend of cabernet sauvignon with local corvina, corvinone and rondinella, is the most international in style of the winery's products and the most obviously marked by oak.

SAN PIETRO IN CARIANO (VR)

Viticoltori Tommasi
Fraz. Pedemonte
Via Ronchetto, 2
37020 San Pietro in Cariano (VR)
tel. 0457701266
e-mail: info@tommasiwine.it

The Tommasi brothers' estate is well on the way to becoming one of the largest in the Verona area. Several cousins have joined the business since 1997, making it necessary to change the winery practice and purchase vineyards instead of grapes. In just a few years, the property has expanded to almost 100 hectares in Valpolicella and a further 30 hectares in the Bardolino and Bianco di Custoza DOCs. When replanting has been necessary, the Tommasis have nearly always replaced the old pergola system with high-density Guyot to obtain from all the vine stock the quality of fruit demanded by great wines. While many of the vineyards are in hilly areas, 55 hectares are situated on the plain at Sant'Ambrogio, on a single plot of land planted in perfect Bordeaux style, mostly with traditional varieties. The first wine to emerge from this recent, far-reaching renaissance is the Crearo della Conca d'Oro, a blend of corvina and oseleta with an addition of cabernet franc. Ripe berry fruit on the nose introduces a fresh note of flowers, a smooth, nicely textured mouthfeel and a long, pervasive finish. The Amarones from the flagship selections are very good. The Ca' Florian is enjoyably warm and softly fruity while the Monte Masua, from the family's Il Sestante property, is a traditional red with vegetal and ripe fruit aromas, and a generous harmonious palate.

- Amarone della Valpolicella Cl.
  Capitel Monte Olmi '99   🍷🍷🍷   8
- Recioto della Valpolicella Cl.
  Capitel Monte Fontana '99   🍷🍷   6
- Rosso della Fabriseria '00   🍷🍷   6
- Amarone della Valpolicella Cl. '99   🍷   6
- Capitel S. Rocco
  Rosso di Ripasso '99   🍷   4
- Valpolicella Cl. Sup.
  Capitel dei Nicalò '99   🍷   4
- Rosso della Fabriseria '97   🍷🍷🍷   6
- Rosso della Fabriseria '99   🍷🍷   6
- Amarone della Valpolicella Cl. '98   🍷🍷   6
- Amarone della Valpolicella Cl.
  Capitel Monte Olmi '98   🍷🍷   8

- Crearo della Conca d'Oro '00   🍷🍷   6
- Amarone della Valpolicella Cl.
  Ca' Florian '98   🍷🍷   7
- Amarone della Valpolicella Cl.
  Monte Masua Il Sestante '98   🍷🍷   7
- Valpolicella Cl. Sup.
  I Pianeti Il Sestante '00   🍷   4
○ Lugana Vigneto San Martino
  Il Sestante '01   🍷   4
- Amarone della Valpolicella Cl. '98   🍷   7
- Amarone della Valpolicella Cl.
  Ca' Florian '97   🍷🍷   7
- Amarone della Valpolicella Cl.
  Monte Masua Il Sestante '97   🍷🍷   7

SAN PIETRO IN CARIANO (VR)

MASSIMINO VENTURINI
FRAZ. SAN FLORIANO
VIA SEMONTE, 20
37020 SAN PIETRO IN CARIANO (VR)
TEL. 0457701331 - 0457703320
E-MAIL: azagrventurinimassimino@tin.it

The Venturini family has made great progress with this winery, which continues to be one of the most interesting in Valpolicella. All the wines, from the simplest crowd-pleasers to the hefty Amarones, show a very high standard of quality and are all still very affordable. Behind the quality, obviously, is scrupulous management of the vineyards, situated on hilly land at an average height of about 250 metres. Daniele and Mirco use these grapes for the most interesting selections, the Semonte Alto, a Valpolicella Superiore, and the Recioto Le Brugnine. The former successfully combines a rich array of modern-style aromas with a generous, highly traditional flavour whereas the Recioto aims to epitomize the Valpolicella tradition. Intense colour ushers in an intoxicating whirl of aromas in the nose, where blackberries, raspberries and dried roses mingle with a deep, dry minerally note. The subtle, fine-grained tannic weave keeps the sweetness on the palate at bay and leads to a finish that is all spices and cloves. The Amarone is even better than last year. Full and heady on the nose, which is dominated by fruit, it has an astonishing palate where huge structure combines happily with admirable lightness and elegance. The fresh, highly enjoyable standard-label Valpolicella also deserves a mention.

SAN PIETRO IN CARIANO (VR)

VILLA BELLINI
LOC. CASTELROTTO DI NEGARINE
VIA DEI FRACCAROLI, 6
37020 SAN PIETRO IN CARIANO (VR)
TEL. 0457725630
E-MAIL: archivino@villafiorita.com

To grasp the true worth of this small winery, stop and chat with Cecilia and Marco Zamarchi about wine, the countryside, even labels, perhaps. Their words will reveal the peace of mind typical of people who are deeply satisfied by the job they do. All this is transferred their organically cultivated vineyard, which is part of the splendid Villa Bellini property, a natural belvedere overlooking the Verona plain, and subsequently into the wines themselves, where it translates into character and personality in the glass. The wines may not offer particularly intense colour or explosive aromas but they won the panel's hearts, subtly and gradually. Take the Amarone, for example. Its light, generous hints of aromatic herbs and ripe fruit are never intrusive and the palate doesn't rely on help from sugars. It is dry and as frank as they come, yet fills the mouth with sweet tannins and a subtle hint of mint in the finish. The Recioto is excellent. Its almonds and ripe fruit on the nose are perfectly reflected on the palate, where the sweetness merges into the wine, leaving a dry, clean sensation in the mouth. The Valpolicella Il Taso is a generous, silky wine with iodine and salt echoes of the sea but will probably be even more enjoyable after a few more months in bottle. Lastly, the Valpolicella Il Brolo has an impressively creamy, characterful palate, unlike many of the light, acidulous Valpolicellas you find on the shelves nowadays.

● Amarone della Valpolicella Cl. '98	ŢŢ	6
● Recioto della Valpolicella Cl. Le Brugnine '98	ŢŢ	6
● Recioto della Valpolicella Cl. '00	ŢŢ	6
● Valpolicella Cl. Sup. Semonte Alto '99	ŢŢ	4*
● Valpolicella Cl. Sup. '00	Ţ	3
● Valpolicella Cl. '01	Ţ	2*
● Recioto della Valpolicella Cl. Le Brugnine '97	ŢŢŢ	6
● Amarone della Valpolicella Cl. '97	ŢŢ	6
● Amarone della Valpolicella Cl. '94	ŢŢ	6
● Amarone della Valpolicella Cl. '95	ŢŢ	6
● Amarone della Valpolicella Cl. '96	ŢŢ	6
● Recioto della Valpolicella Cl. '99	ŢŢ	6

● Amarone della Valpolicella Cl. '98	ŢŢ	6
● Recioto della Valpolicella Cl. '98	ŢŢ	6
● Valpolicella Cl. Il Brolo '01	Ţ	2*
● Valpolicella Cl. Sup. Il Taso '99	Ţ	4
● Amarone della Valpolicella Cl. '93	ŢŢ	6
● Amarone della Valpolicella Cl. '94	ŢŢ	6
● Amarone della Valpolicella Cl. '95	ŢŢ	6
● Recioto della Valpolicella Cl. '95	ŢŢ	6
● Amarone della Valpolicella Cl. '97	ŢŢ	6

SAN POLO DI PIAVE (TV)

Casa Roma
Via Ormelle, 15
31020 San Polo di Piave (TV)
tel. 0422855339
e-mail: vinicasaroma@libero.it

We are delighted to welcome this small winery to the Guide. Adriano Perruzetto supervises the 18 hectares of vineyards, most of which are owned by the winery, while his cousin Gigi, who has a diploma in winemaking from Conegliano, is in charge of the cellar. Credit goes to them for their belief, shared with a few other local producers, in Raboso, a wine that demands sacrifice and effort. Casa Roma's particularly interesting Raboso is obtained from the raboso variety native to the Piave area, and the '98 vintage almost won a second Glass. This would have been an inconceivable achievement until comparatively recently because the typically rugged nature of raboso-based wines meant they were unlikely to be much appreciated. However, more meticulous vineyard management and careful work in the cellar have produced more delicate wines. The most convincing wine this year was the new white San Dordi Bianco 2001, mainly incrocio Manzoni bianco with some tocai, which is left on the lees for a few months in stainless steel vats. The San Dordi is one of the area's most successful whites. Well structured, with a piquant mineral and vegetal nose, it follows up with a generous, slightly tannic, flavour. The interesting Merlot, Manzoni Bianco, Chardonnay and Sauvignon provide further evidence of the high overall level of quality achieved, which is partly due to the recent purchase of new vineyards in the excellent Campo di Pietra subzone.

○ San Dordi Bianco '01	5
○ Manzoni Bianco '01	4
○ Piave Chardonnay '01	4
● Piave Merlot '01	4
○ Sauvignon '01	3*
● Piave Raboso '98	5
● Piave Cabernet Sauvignon '01	4
○ Piave Tocai '01	4

SANT'AMBROGIO DI VALPOLICELLA (VR)

Masi
Fraz. Gargagnago
Via Monteleone, 2
37020 Sant'Ambrogio di Valpolicella (VR)
tel. 0456832511
e-mail: masi@masi.it

The vast range of wines made by this large winery near Verona is always of a high standard and a new wine joins the ranks this year, made at the Corte Paradiso property in Latisana. Obtained from raisined corvina, refosco and carmenère grapes, Grandarella provides a link between the Veneto-Friuli plain and the Valpolicella tradition. It was awarded One Glass on its debut, thanks to the nicely mature aromas of balsam, incense and dried fruit that are mirrored perfectly on the palate. The Amarones are in an altogether different category. The Campolongo di Torbe, from the excellent '97 vintage, is harmonious and well-structured, and the aromas are perked up by a lovely note of thyme. The Costasera is on a par with it, showing a varietal balsamic vein, soft intense fruit and clean, lingering finish, while the Vaio Armaron from the Serègo Alighieri line was less convincing than usual this year. It is supple and energetic on the palate but also a little lean and lacking in concentration. The Valpolicella Possessioni Rosso and the Osar are both good, and came close to Two Glasses, as did the fresh, supple Toar. From the whites, we singled out the successful Possessioni Bianco, a fresh, light blend of sauvignon and garganega.

● Amarone della Valpolicella Cl. Campolongo di Torbe '97	8
● Amarone della Valpolicella Cl. Costasera '98	7
● Valpolicella Cl. Sup. Possessioni Rosso Serègo Alighieri '00	4
○ Possessioni Bianco Serègo Alighieri '01	4
● Amarone della Valpolicella Cl. Vaio Armaron Serègo Alighieri '97	8
● Osar '98	8
● Toar '98	5
● Grandarella '99	6
○ Soave Cl. Sup. Colbaraca '01	4
● Campofiorin '98	4

SANT'AMBROGIO DI VALPOLICELLA (VR)

RAIMONDI - VILLA MONTELEONE
FRAZ. GARGAGNAGO
VIA MONTELEONE, 12
37020 SANT'AMBROGIO DI VALPOLICELLA (VR)
TEL. 0456800533 - 0457704974
E-MAIL: raimondi@mediwork.com

This beautiful winery in a 17th-century residence, set in its own gardens and vineyards, is owned by Lucia Duran Raimondi and simply oozes history, of wines and vineyards. The excellent, traditional but never predictable wines made here since 1989 seem to communicate a passion for the Valpolicella area and its grape varieties, as well as for the complex relationship between man and vine. The most striking product this year, not for the first time, was the Amarone. Although the markets and critics today often promote innovative, muscular wines, this Amarone expresses all the traditional greatness of the type. Evolved, generous, seductive hints of aromatic herbs and chocolate on the nose, and a soft, alcohol-rich palate take you through seamlessly to a warm clean finish, with an aromatic fullness that hints at an even rosier future. The two sweet wines are also very good. The Recioto Pal Sun opens up gradually in an alcoholic, subtle the nose, and then well-gauged, delicate sweetness on the palate. The Passito di Garganega reflects a little of the history of this corner of Valpolicella. Its muscular garganega fruit is softened by notes of sweet almonds and dried peaches and apricots, then the range of flavours on the palate is lifted by sugary sweetness. The two Valpolicellas are both excellent, though the Campo San Vito has the edge.

●	Amarone della Valpolicella Cl. '98	ΥΥ	7
○	Passito Bianco di Gargagnago '98	ΥΥ	5
●	Recioto della Valpolicella Cl. Pal Sun '98	ΥΥ	7
●	Valpolicella Cl. Sup. Campo S. Vito '99	ΥΥ	5
●	Valpolicella Cl. Campo S. Lena '01	Υ	4
●	Amarone della Valpolicella Cl. '94	ΥΥ	7
●	Amarone della Valpolicella Cl. Campo S. Paolo '95	ΥΥ	8
●	Amarone della Valpolicella Cl. '97	ΥΥ	7
●	Amarone della Valpolicella Cl. Campo S. Paolo '97	ΥΥ	8

SELVAZZANO DENTRO (PD)

LA MONTECCHIA
FRAZ. FERIOLE
VIA MONTECCHIA, 16
35030 SELVAZZANO DENTRO (PD)
TEL. 049637294
E-MAIL: lamontecchia@libero.it

Year after year, vintage after vintage, Count Giordano Emo Capodilista's winery continues to bring the long-neglected, little mentioned Colli Euganei DOC to the attention of the world at large. The 20 hectares of vineyards are mainly planted to black grape varieties and yield around 110,000 each year. Remarkable effort is made in the vineyards to obtain high quality grapes and that effort is followed up in the cellar, under the eye of talented winemaker Andrea Boaretti. The same number of wines as last year have been released, although there have been modifications in the names and labels. Villa Capodilista provided an encore of last year's impressive performance, confirming its status as one of the best Bordeaux blends in this part of the Veneto. Its dark hue and intense, fragrant nose of berry fruit, refined by grassy notes and deep minerality introduce a palate that is more striking for elegance and finesse than for strength or concentration. It manages to combine generous aromas and satisfying drinkability. The Merlot is made in a different style Its youthful, vegetal aromas precede a creamy palate with lovely fine-grained, sweet tannins in the finish. All the other wines on the list are good, from the simple Godimondo to the Forzaté, a interesting Raboso made from partially-raisined grapes.

●	Colli Euganei Rosso Villa Capodilista '99	ΥΥ	5
●	Colli Euganei Merlot '00	ΥΥ	4*
○	Colli Euganei Moscato Fior d'Arancio Passito '00	Υ	6
●	Godimondo Cabernet Franc '01	Υ	4
●	Colli Euganei Rosso Cadeto '99	Υ	3*
●	Forzaté Raboso '99	Υ	4
○	Colli Euganei Chardonnay '01		4
○	Colli Euganei Pinot Bianco '01		4
●	Colli Euganei Rosso Montecchia '98	ΥΥ	5
●	Colli Euganei Rosso Montecchia '97	ΥΥ	5

SOAVE (VR)

CANTINA DEL CASTELLO
CORTE PITTORA, 5
37038 SOAVE (VR)
TEL. 0457680093
E-MAIL: cantinacastello@cantinacastello.it

Untiring, scrupulous hard work have enabled husband and wife team Arturo and Silvana Stocchetti to demonstrate once again that theirs is one of the most interesting wineries in the area. The cellar itself is situated inside one of the old buildings within the walls of the old town at Soave and the 13 hectares of vineyards are in the surrounding hills. All the wines demonstrate the cellar's commitment to giving each wine type its own personality, and bringing out as much as possible the nature of the grapes. The excellent late-harvest Soave Acini Soavi has a generous, pervasive mouthfeel and pleasantly subtle, sweetish aromas. Monte Pressoni is one of the winery's two selections. The floral aromas are enhanced by an austere minerally note, then the fresh tangy palate can point to succulent, aroma-rich structure that cossets you through to a long, powerful finish. These are the qualities that earned Arturo his first Three Glass award. The Soave Carniga is made in a different, more traditional style, from super-ripe grapes. The freshly-pressed must undergoes maceration on the skins for 12 hours and is left on the yeasts at length in stainless steel, which gives it lovely complex aromas and a broad, tangy flavour. The well-typed standard-label Soave and Recioto Corte Pittora are pleasantly approachable.

○ Soave Cl. Sup. Monte Pressoni '01	???	4*
○ Soave Cl. Sup. Acini Soavi '00	??	5
○ Soave Cl. Sup. Monte Carniga '01	??	4*
○ Recioto di Soave Cl. Corte Pittora '00	?	5
○ Soave Cl. Sup. '01	?	4
○ Soave Cl. Sup. Monte Carniga '00	??	4
○ Soave Cl. Sup. Monte Pressoni '00	??	4
○ Acini Dolci '98	??	6
○ Soave Cl. Sup. Acini Soavi '99	??	5

SOAVE (VR)

CANTINA DI SOAVE
V.LE VITTORIA, 100
37038 SOAVE (VR)
TEL. 0456139811
E-MAIL: cantina@cantinasoave.it

Founded in 1900, the Soave Cantina Sociale co-operative only really began to expand in 1931. Today, the original 250 grower members have increased to 1,200. The Cantina's approach, however, has never really changed throughout the years and it remains as involved in vineyard management, bottling and sales operations as ever. About 30,000,000 bottles per year are produced now, covering various wine types including Valpolicella, Bardolino and Bianco di Custoza DOCs, and the Garda DOC monovarietals. Obviously, the predominant wine type released is still Soave. The co-operative's objectives include transferring vinification procedures for the best selections to the renovated and extended cellars in Via Covergnino, where the space and equipment are more suited to smaller batches of wine. This year, the Amarone was again the biggest hitter in the line-up. Rich aromas of ripe fruit and freshly-mown grass on the nose are matched by good balance on the palate, which has the fullness typical of the Mezzane valley, where most of the grapes are grown. The winery's largest-selling wines are Soaves, but this year they seem to lack the fullness and verve that such an important type deserves. The Castelcerino is a well-made, uncomplicated wine that is muted on the nose and has a balanced, accessible flavour. The Soave Classico Rocca Sveva, in contrast, has typical vegetal freshness that is reflected well on the palate.

● Amarone della Valpolicella Rocca Sveva '96	??	7
○ Soave Cl. Castelcerino Rocca Sveva '01	?	4
○ Soave Cl. Rocca Sveva '01	?	3*
● Garda Cabernet Sauvignon '99	?	4
○ Recioto di Soave Cl. Rocca Sveva '00	?	5
○ Soave Cl. Villa Rasina '00		2
● Valpolicella Sup. Rocca Sveva '00		4
● Amarone della Valpolicella Rocca Sveva '94	??	7
● Amarone della Valpolicella Rocca Sveva '95	??	7

SOAVE (VR)

Coffele
Via Roma, 5
37038 Soave (VR)
tel. 0457680007
e-mail: info@coffele.it

Since young, talented Soave winegrower Alberto Coffele took over the family winery – founded in the early 1970s, although its roots go back to the mid 19th century – it has undergone something of a revival. Alberto is a dedicated grower and fully aware of the fact that the ingredients for a great wine come from the vineyard itself. The 27 hectares of vine stock owned by Coffele are situated around Castelcerino, a classic Soave vineyard, that tends to produce wines typically high in finesse, with a nice minerally note, rather than big, full-flavoured products. Chiara Coffele also started working full-time at the winery recently and is already making her presence felt. The most striking wine tasted this year was the Soave Alzari, which is aged in small oak barrels. Muted and light on the nose, it opens out gradually into mineral aromas with hints of dried flowers, particularly chamomile. The palate is stylish and subtle, with a clean, very harmonious finish. The Ca' Visco is vigorous and confident as ever while the standard-label Soave has at last shed the staidness of past versions. This time, it has freshness and an approachable personality. The Recioto shows its usual carefree energy. The intense, mature palate shows well-integrated sweetness and acidity.

○ Soave Cl. Sup. Alzari '00	ŸŸ	4*
○ Recioto di Soave Cl. Le Sponde '00	ŸŸ	5
○ Soave Cl. Sup. Ca' Visco '01	ŸŸ	4
○ Chardonnay Castrum Icerini '01	Ÿ	4
○ Soave Cl. Sup. '01	Ÿ	3*
○ Soave Cl. Sup. Ca' Visco '00	ŸŸ	4
○ Recioto di Soave Cl. Le Sponde '98	ŸŸ	5
○ Recioto di Soave Cl. Le Sponde '99	ŸŸ	5
○ Soave Cl. Sup. Alzari '99	ŸŸ	4
○ Soave Cl. Sup. Ca' Visco '99	ŸŸ	4

SOAVE (VR)

Monte Tondo
Loc. Monte Tondo
Via S. Lorenzo, 89
37038 Soave (VR)
tel. 0457680347
e-mail: info@montetondo.it

A real craftsman of wine, Gino Magnabosco is passionate about his land and work, personally supervising every stage in the production process from vineyard to vinification. Gino devotes some of his time to complicated projects that are not part of the usual routine, like building a beautiful new cellar. The winery's 120,000 bottles a year are all made from grapes grown in over 25 hectares of vineyards belonging to the estate, some of which are situated on the lime-rich volcanic hills of Monte Tenda and Monte Tondo, after which the winery is named. The remaining vine stock is at Casette, birthplace of the Casette Foscarin, which is once again this producer's best wine. This Soave Classico has a vibrant colour and an intense nose that opening out into apples, pears and flowers. The wood is a little evident on the palate but the flavour progresses well, indicating good structure, to culminate in a balanced finish. The Soave Mito is more vigorous, displaying fresh, vegetal hints typical of the garganega variety and a dry palate with an enjoyable vein of acidity. The Soave Classico Superiore Monte Tondo has, above all else, good ripe fruit and unusual personality, duly winning One Glass. The Recioto is remarkably elegant. There is a lovely earthy note on the nose and the flavour emerges gradually in the mouth with exemplary harmony.

○ Soave Cl. Sup. Vigneti in Casette Foscarin '01	ŸŸ	4
○ Soave Sup. Mito '01	ŸŸ	2*
○ Recioto di Soave '00	Ÿ	4
○ Soave Cl. Sup. Monte Tondo '01	Ÿ	3
○ Soave Spumante Brut '01		3
○ Soave Cl. Sup. Vigneti in Casette Foscarin '00	ŸŸ	4
○ Soave Cl. Sup. Vigneti in Casette Foscarin '99	ŸŸ	4

SOAVE (VR)

★ Leonildo Pieropan
Via Camuzzoni, 3
37038 Soave (VR)
tel. 0456190171
e-mail: info@pieropan.it

The real strength of Nino and Teresita Pieropan's winery is their production philosophy. No secrets, tricks or shortcuts can produce fine quality wines, and no cellar technique can endow wine what something that nature did not put into the fruit. That's all there is to it. The Pieropans focus on the vineyard and in the vineyard, the equilibrium of the vine is crucial, both in terms of the individual plant and in the context of the vineyard as a whole. For years now, Nino Pieropan has been pursuing that balance, rejecting forcing, or drastic thinning techniques, in favour of painstaking work that can convince even a vigorous, productive variety like garganega to yield fewer grapes. The astonishing result is superbly balanced fruit and, no less important, a beautifully kept vineyard with no sign of chemical or mechanical excess. At last, the sweet wines are back after a year's absence. The skilfully made Passito della Rocca has intense elderflower and toasted hazelnut aromas that grow increasingly elegant and stylish as it opens out, then a rich, chewy palate refreshed by a vein of acidity. The Recioto is lighter, as tradition dictates, with lively, enfolding dried fruit notes. The Soave La Rocca is, as usual, one of the best white wines in Italy. It is full and stylish, lingering forever on the palate. Lastly, the Calvarino is phenomenal. Despite the unpromising vintage, it is a vibrant, garganega-based bottle that promises even better things after a little cellar time.

O	Soave Cl. Sup. La Rocca '00	▼▼▼	6
O	Soave Cl. Sup. Calvarino '01	▼▼	5
O	Passito della Rocca '99	▼▼	7
O	Soave Cl. Sup. '01	▼▼	4*
O	Recioto di Soave Le Colombare '99	▼▼	6
O	Soave Cl. Sup. Vigneto La Rocca '95	▽▽▽	6
O	Soave Cl. Sup. Vigneto La Rocca '96	▽▽▽	6
O	Soave Cl. Sup. Vigneto Calvarino '98	▽▽▽	5
O	Soave Cl. Sup. Vigneto La Rocca '98	▽▽▽	6
O	Soave Cl. Sup. La Rocca '99	▽▽▽	6

SOAVE (VR)

Suavia
Fraz. Fittà
Via Centro, 14
37038 Soave (VR)
tel. 0457675089
e-mail: suavia@libero.it

Suavia is now a benchmark winery in the Soave area, thanks to the depth and class revealed by its increasingly fine wines, year after year. The Tessari sisters are undoubtedly aided in their work by the family's farming origins. Thanks to their father Giovanni, they are able to demonstrate how rewarding winemaking can be, even in this world of increasing technology. Sisters Arianna, Meri and Valentina are involved full-time with the running of this lovely little winery in the Fittà hills, with spectacular views over the slopes of Soave and Monteforte, in a natural amphitheatre set in the area's volcanic basalt. Each of the three Soaves presented has its own distinct character. The pleasant, uncomplicated standard-label has nice acidic backbone that makes it light and drinkable, in contrast with the Monte Carbonare, a monovarietal garganega made and aged in stainless steel. The Monte Carbonare's outstandingly complex nose offers ripe, juicy fruit, aromatic herbs, iodine and minerals. Taut and powerful on the palate, it signs off with a long, tangy finish. Different again is the Soave Le Rive, which is fermented and aged in barrique. Its sweet, pervasive nose tempts with candied citrus fruit and spices, adding a mineral note and fascinating aromatic herbs. The Recioto is beautifully made and flavoursome, with admirable style and length.

O	Soave Cl. Sup. Le Rive '00	▼▼▼	5
O	Soave Cl. Sup. Monte Carbonare '01	▼▼	4*
O	Recioto di Soave Cl. Acinatium '00	▼▼	5
O	Soave Cl. Sup. '01	▼	4
O	Soave Cl. Sup. Le Rive '98	▽▽▽	5
O	Soave Cl. Sup. Le Rive '99	▽▽	5
O	Soave Cl. Sup. Monte Carbonare '00	▽▽	4

SOAVE (VR)

TAMELLINI
VIA TAMELLINI, 4
37038 SOAVE (VR)
TEL. 0457675328
E-MAIL: piofrancesotamellini@tin.it

Because this winery was only established in 1998, we might be forgiven for mistaking it for a modern business that jumped on the bandwagon during the winemaking boom. But in fact, Gaetano and Piofrancesco Tamellini's family have made wine in this area since the late 19th century. It was almost by chance that they began to bottle their wine just a few years ago, thanks to a meeting with Marc De Grazie, who nudged them into taking the plunge. A talent for hard work in the vineyard was already part of the brothers' DNA, as was an understanding of the difference between ordinary and good quality grapes, which is fundamental if you want to obtain great wine. The help of two tried and tested experts like Federico Curtaz in the vineyard and Paolo Caciorgna in the cellar did the rest. The property embraces 15 hectares of garganega vineyards, and the grapes are used to make three Soaves – all aged in stainless steel – as well as a Recioto. The Soave Anguane has a lovely complex nose, in which the fruit mingles with the floral and strongly vegetal notes typical of the garganega. The palate is robust and freshly acidic, with aromatic herbs, especially mint, in the finish. The Recioto is excellent. The gold in the glass introduces sweet dried fruit and cake aromas that are perfectly reflected on the palate, where the lively sweetness is kept in line by a solid vein of acidity. The Soave Superiore and the Classico Le Bine are both very good, too.

○	Recioto di Soave Vigna Marogne '00	🍷🍷	5
○	Soave Cl. Sup. Anguane '00	🍷🍷	4
○	Soave Cl. Sup. Le Bine '00	🍷	4
○	Soave Sup. '01	🍷	3

SOMMACAMPAGNA (VR)

CAVALCHINA
FRAZ. CUSTOZA
LOC. CAVALCHINA
37066 SOMMACAMPAGNA (VR)
TEL. 045516002
E-MAIL: cavalchina@cavalchina.com

Luciano Piona has worked in a variety of areas in the past, but he has now taken over the family winery and is firmly committed to the production of traditional Garda wines. One of the finest interpreters of the famous Bardolino and Bianco di Custoza DOCs, he also obtains excellent results from international varieties, especially merlot and cabernet sauvignon. Both have been grown for many years in the western Verona and Mantua areas. Luciano uses merlot for the Faial, a very high calibre red with dense colour and deep, varied aromas in which berry fruit and flowers gradually give way to minerals and spice. There is a hint of complexity that bodes well for the future. The palate is smooth and creamy with a good, clean tannic weave. Its stablemate is the Cabernet Sauvignon Il Falcone. Flowers and ripe fruit aromas on the nose are followed by a discreet palate with a broad, even progression. The Sauvignon is very good and really satisfies with its delicate flower and mineral notes while the Garganega is mature and flavour-rich. The finesse of müller thurgau shines through amidst the soft rich aromas of the dried-grape "passito" Le Pergole del Sole. There are positive developments regarding the Bianco di Custoza. The oak-aged Amedeo selection has always been impressive but this year, the stainless steel version is richer and remarkably well-balanced. The Bardolino and merlot-based wines from the Mantua cellar are as dependable as ever.

●	Garda Merlot Faial La Prendina '00	🍷🍷	6
●	Garda Cabernet Sauvignon Vigneto Il Falcone La Prendina '00	🍷🍷	5
●	Garda Merlot La Prendina '00	🍷🍷	4*
○	Le Pergole del Sole Cavalchina '00	🍷🍷	6
○	Bianco di Custoza Amedeo Cavalchina '01	🍷🍷	4*
○	Bianco di Custoza Cavalchina '01	🍷🍷	3*
○	Garda Garganega Paroni La Prendina '01	🍷🍷	5
○	Garda Sauvignon Valbruna La Prendina '01	🍷🍷	4*
●	Bardolino Cavalchina '01	🍷	3
⊙	Garda Chiaretto La Prendina '01	🍷	3
●	Garda Merlot Faial La Prendina '99	🍷🍷	6

SOMMACAMPAGNA (VR)

Le Vigne di San Pietro
Via S. Pietro, 23
37066 Sommacampagna (VR)
tel. 045510016 - 0458960960
e-mail: carlo@nerozzi.org

Carlo Nerozzi always finds some energy left over from his countless other interests and commitments – mainly to do with the promotion and development of the Verona area – to devote himself to work in the vineyard. His enthusiasm is generating increasingly interesting results. After about 20 years as a producer, Carlo's romantically sees wine as a communicator of culture and passion. He thinks it should, of course, improve in quality when this is possible but ultimately, wine for Carlo is the expression of someone's efforts, not a product to be entered for competitions. His own bottles embody this view both in the care taken over the labels, which communicate close links with the surrounding area, and their style, which aspires to aromatic richness and concentration, combined with the characteristic lightness of the natural, glacial amphitheatre of the Garda area. While all the products are of a high standard, the Balconi Rossi, a blend of cabernet and merlot with the traditional corvina, has made significant progress. The nose is light and intense, with fresh, ripe fruit aromas, then the palate opens out delicately but firmly, blending freshness with strength. The Refolà is the excellent flagship wine, made from lightly raisined cabernet sauvignon grapes. Its attractive super-ripe aromas are perfectly reflected on the palate and a delicately inky, pencil lead note provides a lovely finish. The Sanpietro is again an exemplary Custoza and the Due Cuori is a rich, strong moscato.

SUSEGANA (TV)

Conte Collalto
Via XXIV Maggio, 1
31058 Susegana (TV)
tel. 0438738241
e-mail: collalto@collalto.it

The Collalto family, who have lived in this area since the Middle Ages, have always made wine. This is one of the classic Treviso wine estates with cellars that were built in 1904, although once the wines were made in the beautiful castle of San Salvatore, which is now being restored. A long tradition, strongly rooted in the local area, characterizes the Conte Collalto winery but that does not mean that it has stood still, or been reluctant to accept innovation. Work is underway in the vineyard and cellars to put new improvements in place to maintain the high level of quality that is a feature of the whole range. The wines we tasted this year confirm that quality. The Cabernet Podere Torrai '98 impressed us as few wines have in the past with the elegant expression of its substantial structure. The delicate spicy aromas, which are never threatened by the wood, are followed by supple progression in the mouth. The Wildbacher has enjoyable wild berry fruit and fines herbs on the nose and the palate is delightfully mouthfilling. The red Incrocio Manzoni 2.15 combines an extremely pleasant flavour with an interesting array of aromas, including pepper and gamey notes. The standard-label Merlot is fresh, spontaneous and uncomplicated, like the Colli di Conegliano Bianco, but the range of Proseccos fell a little below our expectations.

● Refolà Cabernet Sauvignon '99	▼▼	7
○ Bianco di Custoza Sanpietro '00	▼▼	4*
● I Balconi Rossi '00	▼▼	4*
○ Due Cuori Passito '99	▼▼	5
● Bardolino '01	▼	4
◉ Bardolino Chiaretto '01	▼	4
○ Bianco di Custoza '01	▼	4
○ Sud '95	▼▼▼	5
● Refolà Cabernet Sauvignon '96	▼▼	7
● Refolà Cabernet Sauvignon '97	▼▼	7
● Refolà Cabernet Sauvignon '98	▼▼	7
○ Bianco di Custoza Sanpietro '99	▼▼	4

● Incrocio Manzoni 2.15 '01	▼▼	3*
● Wildbacher '01	▼▼	3*
● Piave Cabernet Podere Torrai Ris. '98	▼▼	5
○ Colli di Conegliano Bianco '01	▼	3
○ Incrocio Manzoni 6.0.13 '01	▼	3
● Piave Merlot '01	▼	3
○ P. di Conegliano Extra Dry	▼	3
● Colli di Conegliano Rosso '98		4
○ P. di Conegliano Brut San Salvatore		3
● Incrocio Manzoni 2.15 '01	▼▼	3
● Wildbacher '01	▼▼	3

TORREGLIA (PD)

VIGNALTA
FRAZ. LUVIGLIANO
VIA DEI VESCOVI, 5
35038 TORREGLIA (PD)
TEL. 0499933105 - 0429777225
E-MAIL: mrlunghe@tin.it

There are a few innovations in the wide range of Vignalta wines this year, both in the newcomers and those already on the list. Regarding this latter category, we must mention the winery's renewed commitment to developing the standard line, starting with the Colli Euganei Rosso, which is now a Riserva. The rich berry fruit aromas have spicy, earthy hints and the creamy palate is enhanced by sweet tannins, an important development for a product at the base of the quality pyramid. The new wines include an astonishing Cabernet Riserva, still only made in limited numbers, but which promises to become the winery's leading wine in future vintages. The richly concentrated nose has deep mineral notes that are reflected well on the palate, where the texture is still looking for balance. The Agno Tinto is improving. It's a red that shows the distinctive, gamey presence of zinfandel. The intense aromas have really appetizing fruit while the palate has excellent balance and genuine style for such a young wine. The sweet wines, the flavoursome, alluring Alpinae and the lively Il Nero, maintain their usual high standard. There is also a good range of whites and a special mention goes to the Pinot Bianco and the Sirio, which are approachable yet distinctly characterful. The Gemola from the excellent 2000 vintage had not yet been bottled at the time of tasting, so we'll talk about that next year.

VALDOBBIADENE (TV)

DESIDERIO BISOL & FIGLI
FRAZ. SANTO STEFANO
VIA FOL, 33
31040 VALDOBBIADENE (TV)
TEL. 0423900138
E-MAIL: bisol@bisol.it

At Bisol, a passion for producing wine that wrests the best possible quality from every harvest makes it one of the most dependably high-quality cellars in the Valdobbiadene area. The winery is situated in the Santo Stefano district, unanimously acknowledged to be extremely well-suited to viticulture, and the property extends as far as Rolle, where the Guyot-planted vineyards break the surrounding monotony of quantity-focused plantings. Gianluca is as committed to getting the best from the cellar as he is to the vineyard, and is loath to discard the traditional techniques that give his wines more character. The range of wines is broad and impressive, starting with the excellent Garney. The nose expresses the grape to perfection and the gradual, complex progression on the palate perfectly mingles sweetness, acidity and fizz. The well-defined, intense nose of the Vigneti del Fol precedes a creamy, elegant palate with a lovely almondy finish. The Crede is proof of an excellent vintage for the Brut version, with clearly defined varietal apple and pear aromas, and a creamy, fruity sensation on the palate that offsets the vein of acidity. The Passito di Prosecco Duca di Dolle makes an impressive debut. It is a blend of wines from the last ten vintages. One year on, the Talento Eliseo Bisol '97 has gained more complexity and excellent balance.

● Agno Tinto '01	🍷🍷	5
○ Colli Euganei Moscato Fior d'Arancio Alpianae '00	🍷🍷	5
● Colli Euganei Rosso Ris. '00	🍷🍷	4*
● Il Nero '00	🍷🍷	5
○ Colli Euganei Pinot Bianco '01	🍷🍷	4*
○ Sirio '01	🍷🍷	4*
● Colli Euganei Cabernet Ris. '98	🍷🍷	7
○ Colli Euganei Chardonnay '00	🍷	5
○ Colli Euganei Moscato '01	🍷	5
○ Colli Euganei Pinot Bianco Agno Casto '01	🍷	5
● Colli Euganei Rosso Gemola '97	🍷🍷🍷	6
● Colli Euganei Rosso Gemola '98	🍷🍷🍷	6
● Colli Euganei Rosso Gemola '99	🍷🍷🍷	6

○ P. di Valdobbiadene Dry Garnei '01	🍷🍷	4*
○ P. di Valdobbiadene Brut Crede	🍷🍷	4*
○ P. di Valdobbiadene Extra Dry Vigneti del Fol '01	🍷🍷	4*
○ Cartizze	🍷🍷	5
○ Duca di Dolle Prosecco Passito	🍷🍷	6
○ P. di Valdobbiadene Dry Salis	🍷	4
○ P. di Valdobbiadene Tranquillo Molera	🍷	4
○ Talento Cuvée del Fondatore Eliseo Bisol '97	🍷🍷	6

VALDOBBIADENE (TV)

F.LLI BORTOLIN SPUMANTI
FRAZ. SANTO STEFANO
VIA MENEGAZZI, 5
31040 VALDOBBIADENE (TV)
TEL. 0423900135
E-MAIL: posta@bortolin.com

The Bortolin family can trace their origins back to the 16th century and an ancestor of the current owners took part in a winemaking contest in Siena before the Great War. So winemaking has also played a part in the family's long history. With its eagle coat-of-arms, this estate has slowly and steadily carved itself a niche as one of the best wineries in the Conegliano-Valdobbiadene DOC. Today, Valeriano Bortolin runs this 20-hectare property with his children Andrea, Claudia and Diego. Situated between Valdobbiadene and San Pietro di Feletto, the winery produces almost 350,000 bottles per year. The best wine in the extensive range we tasted was the Prosecco Brut, with its striking self-assurance, fragrance, creaminess and tangy, lemony finish. The Rù has aromatic herbs, apples and pear fruit, and the Dry offers fresh, pervasive mousse. The Extra Dry is a classic anytime Prosecco: as an aperitif, at the end of a meal or simply for drinking someone's health. The Cartizze confirms its quality again. The bright, straw yellow is flecked with greenish hues, and ushers in aromas of crusty bread, apples and peaches, laced with a subtle hint of almonds. The Extra Brut Vigneto del Convento made from prosecco and chardonnay is well typed. Lastly, the uncomplicated Colli di Conegliano Bianco is worth mentioning, even though it is not as assertive as this type can be.

VALDOBBIADENE (TV)

BORTOLOMIOL
VIA GARIBALDI, 142
31049 VALDOBBIADENE (TV)
TEL. 0423975794 - 0423972029
E-MAIL: info@bortolomiol.com

Once again, this great Valdobbiadene house proves that large numbers and respectable quality can go hand in hand. Fifty years after it was founded, the winery is now run by the daughters of Giuliano Bortolomiol – Elena, Giuliana, Luisa and Maria Elena – with the expert assistance of their mother, Ottavia. They buy their grapes from trusted growers, like most other local Prosecco producers, and supervise them all year round, so that the grape production cycle is to a large extent monitored by the family even though they do not own the vineyards. Smaller batches of wine also come from the better growing areas and are bottled as interesting selections after refermentation. This is the case with the Prosecco Extra Dry Banda Rossa, made exclusively with grapes from San Pietro di Barbozza and Santo Stefano, two traditionally famous vineyards. The wine has promising, clearly defined apple fruit on the nose, an unmistakable feature of the varietal's aroma profile, and on the palate the subtle, well-integrated sparkle leads to a light, clean finish. The standard Extra Dry version is dryer and has a good range of aromas, as well as an enjoyably fresh, mouthfilling palate. The rest of the wines are of the usual high standard, and a special mention goes to the Prosecco Dry.

O Cartizze	🍷🍷	5
O P. di Valdobbiadene Brut	🍷🍷	3*
O P. di Valdobbiadene Extra Dry	🍷	3
O P. di Valdobbiadene Dry	🍷	3
O P. di Valdobbiadene Extra Dry Rù	🍷	3
O Spumante Extra Brut Vigneto del Convento	🍷	3
O Colli di Conegliano Bianco '01		3

O P. di Valdobbiadene Extra Dry Sel. Banda Rossa	🍷🍷	4
O P. di Valdobbiadene Dry	🍷🍷	3*
O Cartizze	🍷	5
O P. di Valdobbiadene Extra Dry	🍷	3
O P. di Valdobbiadene Frizzante Il Ponteggio	🍷	3
O Riserva del Governatore Extra Brut '00		4
O P. di Valdobbiadene Brut		3
O P. di Valdobbiadene Tranquillo		3

VALDOBBIADENE (TV)

CANEVEL SPUMANTI
LOC. SACCOL
VIA ROCCAT E FERRARI, 17
31049 VALDOBBIADENE (TV)
TEL. 0423975940 - 0423972466
E-MAIL: info@canevel.it

The view from the Canevel winery is a sea of green vineyards and woods, stretching before you across a delightfully attractive landscape. Eleven of the estate's 22 hectares are planted to vine, the majority in Refrontolo, and a small part in Saccol, and production of the 600,000 bottles made every year is supervised by winemaker Roberto De Lucchi. Il Millesimato takes the lion's share again. A selection of prosecco grown in the Valdobbiadene area in southeast and southwest-facing vineyards, it embodies all the best features of the grape. It is an enjoyably fresh, fruity wine, with a floral nose and creamy palate. The Vigneto del Faè from the Refrontolo area is also very good. The performance of the Extra Dry, redolent of wistaria, rennet apples and citrus fruit, is outstanding, especially if you consider that 350,000 bottles are released. The Cartizze is straw yellow, with golden highlights and intense aromatic herbs on the nose. The apple and pear fruit stays through to a nice, almondy finish. The San Biagio is scintillating, with crusty bread, hints of flowers and a hint of lemon on the nose while the Prosecco Tranquillo is enjoyable and the Brut, too, is nice. The Vigneto Levina 2000 stands out from the other wines from the Colli di Conegliano DOC. Obtained from merlot, cabernet and marzemino, its purple hue introduces intense herbal, berry fruit aromas and good body with a plummy, spicy finish. The Marzemino Passito is also a sound wine and the Bianco del Vigneto Spezada is uncomplicated with an acidulous, salty vein, slightly inexpressive nose and light body.

● Colli di Conegliano Rosso Vigneto Levina '00	🍷🍷	5
○ P. di Valdobbiadene Extra Dry Il Millesimato '01	🍷🍷	4*
○ P. di Valdobbiadene Extra Dry Vigneto del Faè	🍷🍷	4*
○ P. di Valdobbiadene Tranquillo '01	🍷	3
○ Cartizze	🍷	5
○ P. di Valdobbiadene Extra Dry	🍷	4
○ P. di Valdobbiadene Frizzante Vigneti di S. Biagio	🍷	4
● Colli di Conegliano Marzemino Passito di Refrontolo '00	🍷	4
○ Colli di Conegliano Bianco Vigneto Spezada '01		3

VALDOBBIADENE (TV)

COL VETORAZ
FRAZ. SANTO STEFANO
VIA TRESIESE, 1
31040 VALDOBBIADENE (TV)
TEL. 0423975291
E-MAIL: colvetoraz@libero.it

The Col Vetoraz winery is situated on top of the hill of the same name in the heart of the Prosecco area, with a wonderful view of the hills surrounding Valdobbiadene and, just a short distance away, the famous Cartizze hill. This position alone hints at the estate's huge potential, which is tapped by a thoroughly professional staff. Every stage of the production process is thoroughly monitored, from the vineyard, where a small percentage of the grapes are grown, because the majority are bought from other growers, to the cellar where winemaker Loris dall'Acqua's skills ensure that the very best use is made of the grapes. This year, the wines maintained the quality levels established in previous editions and, indeed, exceeded them, if that is possible. The most positive performance came from the Prosecco Dry Millesimato. It's the best version we can remember tasting, and the best wine from the vintage. The deep, subtly fruity nose is followed by a gradually expanding, mouthfillingly elegant palate with a nice echo of ripe apples and pears. The Prosecco Brut and Extra Dry also confirm last year's standard. Both are rich in finesse, generous aromas and tangy, juicy flavour, which are enhanced by the creamy prickle. The delicious Cartizze is also well made.

○ P. di Valdobbiadene Dry Millesimato '01	🍷🍷	4*
○ Cartizze	🍷🍷	5
○ P. di Valdobbiadene Brut	🍷🍷	4*
○ P. di Valdobbiadene Extra Dry	🍷🍷	4*
○ P. di Valdobbiadene Frizzante	🍷	4
○ P. di Valdobbiadene Tranquillo Tresiese '01		3

VALDOBBIADENE (TV)

LE BELLERIVE - ANGELO RUGGERI
FRAZ. SANTO STEFANO
VIA FOLLO, 18
31040 VALDOBBIADENE (TV)
TEL. 0423900235
E-MAIL: info@lebellerive.it

Angelo Ruggeri founded this winery on the southern slope of the hill leading to the chapel of Santo Stefano di Valdobbiadene. For years now, his sons Remigio and Vittore have continued his work, caring for the vineyard (which is part of their family history) and acquiring all the necessary expertise for making the grapes into wine – or more importantly, into sparkling wine. The modest range of consistently impressive and good quality wines is built on these foundations. Remigio and Vittore's warhorse is the Prosecco Dry Funer, made from the grapes of an especially suitable vineyard which are then vinified separately. The intense clean aromas range from a light floral note to weightier, more enfolding, tropical fruit. Thanks to a perfect second fermentation, the fizz works well, following the palate through to the nice elegant, bitter almondy finish. The Cartizze is more subtle and slower to yield its classy aromas, the clearest of which are wistaria, pineapple and white peaches. These are reflected well on the palate, where the fresh acidity backs up the sugar perfectly. The Extra Dry is the most approachable of the three wines, with a typical fragrant and intense apple note and a supple, drinkable palate.

○ Cartizze	ŸŸ	5
○ P. di Valdobbiadene Dry Funer	ŸŸ	3*
○ P. di Valdobbiadene Extra Dry	ŸŸ	3*

VALDOBBIADENE (TV)

LE COLTURE
FRAZ. SANTO STEFANO
VIA FOLLO, 5
31040 VALDOBBIADENE (TV)
TEL. 0423900192
E-MAIL: info@lecolture.it

So firmly convinced are brothers Cesare and Renato Ruggeri of the work they do in the field that nearly all the grapes the vinify are grown in their own vineyards at Valdobbiadene, Vidor, San Pietro di Feletto and Solighetto. That's quite rare around here. In fact, it is probably the secret of their success and the consistently high quality levels they have attained in recent years. This time, the most impressive wine was the Prosecco Brut, definitely in the best version we have tasted recently. The complex, well-developed nose has aromas that range from flowers and almonds to citrus fruit and minerals while the dry, austere palate is complex and unfolds gradually. The Dry – this year called Cruner – has remarkable finesse and a balanced palate, thanks to the discreet presence of residual sugars. We encountered these same characteristics in the subtle, highly enjoyable Cartizze. Thanks to its vegetal and floral aromas, and fruit-driven palate, the Prosecco Tranquillo earned One comfortable Glass while the newest addition to the winery the Colli di Conegliano Rosso, which just missed out on Two Glasses on its debut. This blend of cabernet, merlot and marzemino is aged for about two years in small wooden casks and has typically grassy, red pepper nuances on the nose. The palate is not perfectly balanced yet but this will improve with bottle ageing.

○ Cartizze	ŸŸ	5
○ P. di Valdobbiadene Brut	ŸŸ	4*
○ P. di Valdobbiadene Dry Cruner	ŸŸ	4*
● Colli di Conegliano Rosso '00	Ÿ	5
○ P. di Valdobbiadene Tranquillo Masaré '01	Ÿ	3
○ P. di Valdobbiadene Extra Dry	Ÿ	4

VALDOBBIADENE (TV)

NINO FRANCO
VIA GARIBALDI, 147
31049 VALDOBBIADENE (TV)
TEL. 0423972051
E-MAIL: info@ninofranco.it

Well-made Prosecco wines have typically subtle, flower and fruit aromas that make the palate deliciously silky and light. But if you want to taste a Prosecco that goes far beyond the basic description, try the wines of Primo Franco, a skilled producer who has been operating in the Valdobbiadene area since the 1970s. His wines may cause some discussion but they are always distinctive in character and style, from those presented here, which do not include the Extra Dry version although this is the largest-volume wine in the whole DOC, to the sweeter versions which are definitely softer than average. All the grapes come from the Valdobbiadene area, which is especially suited to making light wines with lots of finesse, and the Primo touch gives them structure and complexity. For example, the Rive di San Floriano Brut is a Prosecco with a lovely note of williams pears and apples on the nose, followed by surprising structure and fullness on the palate. It's deliciously drinkable. The Dry Primo Franco is excellent, with highly typical intense aromas and an approachable, mouthfilling palate with good continuity and nicely integrated fizz. Don't be in too much of a hurry to drink it though, because it should become even more interesting in a few years' time. The dry, balanced standard-label Brut and Rustico are excellent, as are the creamy Cartizze and the Sassi Bianchi, a pleasantly uncomplicated Prosecco Tranquillo.

○	P. di Valdobbiadene Brut Rive di S. Floriano	4*
○	Cartizze	5
○	P. di Valdobbiadene Brut	4
○	P. di Valdobbiadene Dry Primo Franco '01	4
○	Prosecco Brut Rustico	3*
○	P. di Valdobbiadene Tranquillo Sassi Bianchi	3

VALDOBBIADENE (TV)

RUGGERI & C.
VIA PRÀ FONTANA
31049 VALDOBBIADENE (TV)
TEL. 04239092
E-MAIL: ruggeri@ruggeri.it

Paolo Bisol works with large quantities of grapes and his main concern is ensuring that all the production phases, from the reception of the grapes to bottling, run smoothly. Methodically, he eliminated any extraneous factors that might lead to work being carried out in too much of a hurry or, worse still, sloppily. The winery therefore revolves around the cellar, a model of efficiency and quality, with regularly updated equipment. Extending the vineyards is equally crucial. The purchase of new plots of hillside land has increased the area under vine to six hectares. The winery has also acquired new growers in the Valdobbiadene zone, especially in the excellent Santo Stefano area, which means the winery almost invariably vinifies grapes with lots of finesse and elegance. This year, the most interesting wine is again the Giustino B. Extra Dry, an ideal combination of the approachability of a Prosecco with the complexity of a Metodo Classico. Typical varietal aromas of apples, pears and wild flowers on the nose are perfectly reflected on the palate and the light structure is enhanced by the constant, creamy fizz. All the other wines are up to their usual high standard, from the rich, ripe Cartizze to the lively, accessible Giall'Oro. The Brut deserves a special mention this year for its admirable character and harmony.

○	P. di Valdobbiadene Extra Dry Giustino B. '01	5
○	Cartizze	5
○	P. di Valdobbiadene Brut	4*
○	P. di Valdobbiadene Dry S. Stefano	4*
○	P. di Valdobbiadene Extra Dry Giall'Oro	4*
●	Colli di Conegliano Rosso S. Alberto '99	5
○	P. di Valdobbiadene Tranquillo La Bastia	4
○	P. di Valdobbiadene Extra Dry Giustino B. '00	5

VALDOBBIADENE (TV)

Santa Eurosia
Fraz. San Pietro di Barbozza
Via della Cima, 8
31040 Valdobbiadene (TV)
Tel. 0423973236

Giuseppe Geronazzo is a reserved man, who would rather be thought of as an exemplary maker of Prosecco wine than become involved in the frenzied polemics that sometimes sweep through the Marca Trevigiana area. Consistent quality is one of his main objectives and he aims to bring out the best in his grapes, maintaining close contact with his regular growers. The wines from the 2001 vintage all have excellent overall balance and, as is often the case with Geronazzo's wines, the most striking is the Prosecco Brut, which was quickly awarded Two Glasses. The interesting aromatic profile and fresh, minerally notes on the nose are reflected perfectly on the rounded, mouthfilling palate. It is lovely and creamy, closing with an interesting finish. The Prosecco Extra Dry has also turned out well. Its fresh nose proffers sweet, subtle fruit and flowers – particularly apples, williams pears and acacia blossom – then a tangy, very creamy, aromatic palate and a confident finish. Geronazzo's newest wine is the Dry Millesimato, a bright, pale straw yellow product with a mature nose and harmonious palate with well-integrated prickle. The Cartizze has soft apple and pear fruit on nose and palate, where the fresh acidity lends the wine vigour. The Prosecco Tranquillo is well typed, with sweet, ripe aromas.

○ P. di Valdobbiadene Dry Millesimato '01	🍷🍷	4
○ P. di Valdobbiadene Brut	🍷🍷	3*
○ P. di Valdobbiadene Extra Dry	🍷🍷	3*
○ Cartizze	🍷	5
○ P. di Valdobbiadene Tranquillo	🍷	3

VALDOBBIADENE (TV)

Tanoré
Fraz. San Pietro di Barbozza
Via Mont di Cartizze, 3
31040 Valdobbiadene (TV)
Tel. 0423975770
E-mail: tanore@tin.it

The lovely Tanorè winery is owned by brothers Renato and Sergio Follador. It enjoys a breathtaking view over the steep hills forming the Cartizze subzone, an area where it is possible, but very difficult to cultivate superb fruit. The precipitous slopes are only accessible on foot. Of course, the neighbouring hills share the same advantages and disadvantages, and are the backdrop for a growing tradition that smacks of past times. It is hard, but always satisfying, work for those manage to enhance the rich characteristics of the fruit. Renato and Sergio know how to do just that. Every year, they turn out sparkling wines that encapsulate this hard-won harmony, using the estate's own grapes, as well as a small percentage purchased from selected growers who manage their vineyards according to the Follador brothers' directions. This year, the most interesting bottles were again the wines with high sugar contents. The Cartizze is subtle and mature on the nose, showing a creamy palate with delicate prickle and a clean harmonious finish. The Selezione Dry, a lively, generous wine with an intense, accessible nose, entices you to savour the lovely, fresh palate, with its delicious citrus and liquorice, leading to a long, fragrant finish.

○ Cartizze	🍷🍷	5
○ P. di Valdobbiadene Dry Sel.	🍷🍷	4*
○ P. di Valdobbiadene Brut	🍷	3
○ P. di Valdobbiadene Extra Dry	🍷	3
○ P. di Valdobbiadene Tranquillo	🍷	3

VALEGGIO SUL MINCIO (VR)

Corte Gardoni
Loc. Gardoni, 5
37067 Valeggio sul Mincio (VR)
Tel. 0457950382

Gianni Piccoli is never content to settle for second best. Dissatisfied with the nonetheless positive results he has obtained in recent years, he adjusted his production techniques to go all out for quality. Currently, the cellar is in a transitional phase, as we can see from his decision to bring out the Fenili dessert wine a year's time and the announcement that he will do the same in future with some of the reds. In the meantime, Corte Gardoni wines are a perfect combination of character, drinkability and respect for the area of origin. The 2000 Bardolino Superiore, for example, is a very promising solution for anyone making this new DOCG. A full, clean nose blends mineral notes with aromatic herbs and berries, then the moderately full palate offers nice aromas. The Bardolino Le Fontane 2001 is also very typical and as nicely drinkable as ever, although the berry fruit, aniseed and liquorice notes are a little tired. The Chiaretto 2001, a rosé Bardolino, is elegant and soft with sweet fruit hints. The non-DOC wines include the white Nichesole Vallidium, made from recovered trebbianello vines, and the Rosso di Corte '99 with its attractive purple colour. The Garda Merlot Vallidium 1999 is not quite ready for the corkscrew yet. The colour is nice, but not especially clear. This is one of the wines destined to for a delayed release from the next vintage.

● Bardolino Sup. '00	▼▼	3*
⊙ Bardolino Chiaretto '01	▼	3
● Bardolino Le Fontane '01	▼	3
○ Bianco di Custoza '01	▼	3
○ Nichesole Vallidium '01	▼	4
● Garda Merlot Vallidium '99	▼	5
● Rosso di Corte '99	▼	5
○ I Fenili '93	▼▼	5
○ I Fenili '96	▼▼	5
○ I Fenili '97	▼▼	5
● Rosso di Corte '97	▼▼	5

VERONA

Cecilia Beretta
Loc. San Felice Extra
Via Belvedere, 135
37131 Verona
Tel. 0458402111
E-mail: pasqua@pasqua.it

The Pasqua group's large research laboratory is starting to produce quality of an impressive standard. The 100 or so hectares under vine on the various properties have been entirely replanted since the 1980s and the traditional pergola system was abandoned in favour of Guyot, or cordon-trained, spur-pruned systems that are more suited to producing high quality. Planting density has been increased to 7,000 vines per hectare in some plots. Research into stock vines has resulted in bottles with more personality, instead of crowd-pleasing, fashion-conscious wines. The late-harvest Soave Classico Brognoligo most clearly represents this quest for character. It has striking mineral aromas that are mirrored well on the palate, where an unusual note of benzene makes the balanced, harmonious favour more austere. The Amarone comes from a good, though not exceptional, vintage and shows both super-ripe and fresh vegetal aromas. The most interesting wine this year is the Recioto di Soave, with rich candied fruit and citrus aromas, a nice hint of toastiness and nicely blended sweetness on the long, stylish palate. The Mizzole, a merlot and corvina blend, aged for ten months in barriques, score a whisker below Two Glasses while the Soave Brognoligo and the Valpolicella Terre di Cariano proved uncomplicated and enjoyable.

● Amarone della Valpolicella Cl. Terre di Cariano '98	▼▼	7
○ Recioto di Soave Case Vecie '99	▼▼	6
○ Soave Cl. Brognoligo V. T. '00	▼	4
○ Soave Cl. Brognoligo '01	▼	3
● Valpolicella Cl. Sup. Terre di Cariano '98	▼	4
● Mizzole Rosso '99	▼	4
● Amarone della Valpolicella Cl. Terre di Cariano '97	▼▼	7

VERONA

GIACOMO MONTRESOR
VIA CA' DEI COZZI, 16
37124 VERONA
TEL. 045913399
E-MAIL: info@vinimontresor.it

Paolo Montresor's quintessentially Veronese winery was established here in the late 19th century. Today, it is very extensive indeed, with 100 hectares of vineyards belonging to the estate and another 50 rented, providing the grapes for the over 2,000,000 bottles released every year. Most of the vineyards are situated on the glacial hills that separate Lake Garda from Verona, though the property which has been yielding the most interesting results lately lies in the heart of Valpolicella Classica, at San Peretto di Negrar. Grapes from that estate are used for the Valpolicella. This is a nicely structured wine, with full, intense ripe berry fruit and a rounded, warm palate that is a little disturbed by an over-assertive note of wood in the finish. That should mellow gradually over time, however. The Cabernet Sauvignon Campo Madonna is uncomplicated and pleasantly drinkable, with interesting berry fruit aromas. Turning to the whites, the most striking was the Sauvignon Sansaia, whose fresh varietal aromas fuse with the mature, enjoyably dense palate. The Soave Capitel Alto and the Bianco di Custoza Monte Fiera are both well-made wines, as usual, that have forthright, approachably pleasant personalities.

● Valpolicella Cl. Capitel della Crosara '00	ŶŶ 4*
● Cabernet Sauvignon Vigneto Campo Madonna '00	Ŷ 4
○ Bianco di Custoza '01	Ŷ 3
○ Bianco di Custoza Vigneto Monte Fiera '01	Ŷ 4
○ Lugana '01	Ŷ 3
○ Sauvignon Sansaia '01	Ŷ 4
○ Soave Cl. Capitel Alto '01	Ŷ 4
● Santomío Rosso '99	Ŷ 6
● Amarone della Valpolicella Cl. Capitel della Crosara '98	ŶŶ 7

VERONA

PASQUA VIGNETI E CANTINE
VIA BELVIGLIERI, 30
37131 VERONA
TEL. 0458402111
E-MAIL: pasqua@pasqua.it

Over 1,000 hectares of vineyards, 18,000,000 bottles released every year and three estates covering a total surface area of 33,000 square metres: these are the impressive figures that sum up the Pasqua group, a large wine house that was established and grew in the Verona area but which now owns property throughout Italy. Pasqua, however, is more than just numbers. It also stands for history, and the exploits of a family of entrepreneurs that has been active in the Veneto for more than 70 years. The winery has recently turned its attention to technological improvements in the cellar, skilled consultants, and the re-interpretation of classic wines, with plenty of research going on at the laboratory owned by Cecilia Beretta. We can see this new direction emerging in two wines, the Amarone Villa Borghetti '98 and the Kòrae 2000. Concentrated in hue, the Amarone has clean, intense aromas that are very traditional and yet modern at the same time in their unrestrained ripe fruit on the nose. The palate shuns the easy appeal of sweetness to focus on the full weight of its structure with admirable style. The Kòrae, a corvina-based monovarietal with a no-nonsense style, is rich in upfront aromas, then supple and very moreish on the palate. The Morago was not available for tasting, so we focused our attention on the traditional wines, which are all of a high standard of quality. More important, they are getting better, particularly the Sagramoso line.

● Amarone della Valpolicella Cl. Villa Borghetti '98	ŶŶ 7
● Amarone della Valpolicella Sagramoso '98	ŶŶ 7
● Valpolicella Sup. Sagramoso Ripasso '98	ŶŶ 5
● Kòrae Rosso '00	Ŷ 4
○ Soave Cl. Vigneti di Montegrande '01	Ŷ 3
● Valpolicella Cl. Villa Borghetti '99	Ŷ 4
● Valpolicella Sup. Sagramoso '99	Ŷ 4
● Amarone della Valpolicella Cl. Villa Borghetti '97	ŶŶ 7
● Morago Cabernet Sauvignon '98	ŶŶ 6

VERONA

TEZZA
LOC. POIANO
VIA MAIOLI, 4
37030 VERONA
TEL. 045550267
E-MAIL: info@tezzawines.it

The Tezza winery was established in 1960 but since brothers Vanio, Flavio and Federico began working there in the mid 1990s, it has gradually been transformed. Quality now takes priority over quantity. The property covers about 25 hectares under vine at Poiano, in the greater Valpolicella area. The vineyards are mainly planted using the Veronese pergola training system but the first Guyot plantings are now appearing, tangible evidence that significant changes are under way. The number of different wines produced is still substantial but future projects include cutbacks in the total to focusing, as you might expect, on the traditional Valpolicella DOC wines. The most striking wine today is the Amarone, presented here in two different versions, the more traditional Monte delle Fontane and the innovative Brolo delle Giare. The latter offers intense, fragrant, ripe fruit and aromatic herbs in the nose, a palate that echoes those aromas attractively and a sweet hint of chocolate in the finish. The two white dried-grape wines are also interesting, the warmly Mediterranean, garganega-based Monte delle Fontane and the fresher, more balsamic Brolo delle Giare, a monovarietal moscato giallo. The two Valpolicellas are very well made, typically clean and nicely balanced, indicating the scrupulous Tezza cellar techniques that treat the fruit with due respect.

O	Passito Monte delle Fontane '00	♈♈	6
●	Amarone della Valpolicella Brolo delle Giare '98	♈♈	8
O	Passito Brolo delle Giare '00	♈	6
●	Valpolicella Valpantena '00	♈	3
●	Amarone della Valpolicella Monte delle Fontane '98	♈	6
●	Valpolicella Valpantena Sup. Monte delle Fontane '99	♈	4

VERONA

CANTINA SOCIALE DELLA VALPANTENA
FRAZ. QUINTO
VIA COLONIA ORFANI DI GUERRA, 5/B
37100 VERONA
TEL. 045550032
E-MAIL: cantinavalpantena@tin.it

The winery is actually in the co-operative building on the outskirts of Verona, where we are reminded that the vineyards begin as soon as you pass the city walls and head north. The co-operative itself was set up in 1958 and now embraces 260 small estates. Over the last decade, they have committed to revolutionizing growing techniques by reducing yields and renewing planting systems, in the hope of carving a significant niche in the rich winemaking panorama of Valpolicella. Outstanding winemaker Luca Degani does the rest, and the Cantina Valpantena is today a major business enterprise in the DOC zone. The 700 or so hectares under vine are managed with the greatest respect for the environment, producing the grapes for over 2,000,000 bottles each year. The Falasco line is worth mentioning, among the many different wines made, because it represents the top level of quality on offer from the cellar. Let's begin with the Amarone. A full, ripe fruit nose with interesting pepper and mineral hints introduces a mature, mouthfilling palate with a long clean finish. The Recioto Tesauro is even more concentrated in both colour and aromas. The palate is soft, and the sugar perfectly backed up by acidity and extract, making it an intense, pleasantly sunny wine. The good Valpantena Ritocco has mature, fruit-led aromas and the Valpantena Superiore is made light and elegant by an interesting floral note on the nose.

●	Recioto della Valpolicella Tesauro '99	♈♈	6
●	Valpantena Ritocco '00	♈♈	4*
●	Amarone della Valpolicella Falasco '98	♈♈	6
O	Tesauro Passito Bianco '00	♈	6
●	Recioto della Valpolicella Valpantena '00	♈	5
●	Valpantena Ripasso Falasco '00	♈	4
●	Valpantena Sup. '00	♈	4
●	Valpantena '01	♈	2*
●	Amarone della Valpolicella Valpantena '99	♈	5
●	Amarone della Valpolicella Valpantena '98	♈♈	6

VIDOR (TV)

ADAMI
Fraz. Colbertaldo
Via Rovede, 21
31020 Vidor (TV)
Tel. 0423982110
E-mail: adamispumanti@tin.it

The Adami brothers' winery may be situated physically outside the nucleus of producers that form the backbone of Valdobbiadene production, but for years, it has been at the very peak of quality winemaking. Excellent standards of vineyard management and cellar technique leave no room for chance. The Adami were among the first to rediscover the importance of winegrowing in this area and the grapes from their most important vineyard, Il Giardino have always been vinified separately. This well-known vineyard was recorded back in the 18th-century census as Zardini, proving that its quality as a growing zone was already famous at that time. The winery focuses on admirably consistent, fine-quality sparklers and this year, the wine we liked best was the Dry Giardino. Although light and delicate, it is well defined and fragrant on the nose, opening up gradually on notes of wild flowers, pears and apples. The elegant, classy palate then reveals a creamy, pervasive mouthfeel, accompanied delicately by the tempting prickle. The Cartizze is excellent, as it is every year, with lively approachable aromas of apples and cakes on the nose and a forthright, very pleasant palate. Franco and Adriano could hardly afford to miss out on such a good year for Bruts and their Prosecco Brut has excellent structure and freshness. The dependably good Extra Dry version, the non-sparkling Prosecco Tranquillo and the white Incrocio Manzoni are of the usual standard, as is the traditional Sur Lie version.

○ P. di Valdobbiadene Dry Giardino '01	▼▼	4*
○ Cartizze	▼▼	5
○ P. di Valdobbiadene Brut Bosco di Gica	▼▼	4*
○ P. di Valdobbiadene Extra Dry dei Casel	▼▼	4*
○ Incrocio Manzoni 6.0.13 Le Portelle '01	▼	3
○ P. di Valdobbiadene Tranquillo Giardino '01	▼	3
○ P. di Valdobbiadene Sur Lie	▼	3
○ Spumante Brut Ris. Waldaz	▼	4
○ P. di Valdobbiadene Dry Giardino '00	▼▼	4

VIDOR (TV)

De Faveri
Fraz. Bosco
Via Sartori, 21
31020 Vidor (TV)
Tel. 0423987673
E-mail: defaverispumanti@libero.it

We can always expect upfront, elegant, uncompromising wines from Lucio De Faveri's cellar and this is especially true of the most ambitious line, with its trademark dark-coloured bottle. The grapes selected for this line come from traditional growers in the best growing areas of Valdobbiadene and Vidor, as is evident in the 2001 wines, especially the Brut Selezione. It is light, elegant and delicate on the nose, with aromas of ripe, crunchy apples and pears. The palate is soft, alluring and extremely clean, showing nice harmony and an unexpected, fascinating hint of liquorice. The Cartizze is a good, intense straw yellow and a strikingly fresh nose of strong citrus and green apple notes. Entry on the palate is soft, with a characteristically mouthfilling creaminess. The Prosecco Dry Selezione also has citrus fruit, apples and mature yet fresh hints in the nose. These are followed by a generous palate with good rich extract and remarkably generous aromas. The standard-line wines are simpler and well made but have less character. The Prosecco Brut and the Frizzante version show less definition on the nose but the palate is very drinkable in both cases. Lastly, there was only a mention for the Extra Dry.

○ Cartizze	▼▼	5
○ P. di Valdobbiadene Brut Sel.	▼▼	4*
○ P. di Valdobbiadene Dry Sel.	▼▼	4*
○ P. di Valdobbiadene Brut	▼	3
○ P. di Valdobbiadene Frizzante	▼	3
○ P. di Valdobbiadene Extra Dry		3

VIDOR (TV)

SORELLE BRONCA
FRAZ. COLBERTALDO
VIA MARTIRI, 20
31020 VIDOR (TV)
TEL. 0423987201
E-MAIL: info@sorellebronca.com

The most interesting products in terms of quality and points from this winery, owned by sisters Ersiliana and Antonella Bronca, are obtained from the Felettano properties. It is there that Piero devotes himself unstintingly to managing the vineyards used for the two Colli di Coneglianos - this in spite of the fact that Prosecco is a very important market sector. The arrival of Federico Giotto brought new, quality-driven ideas, enabling the winery to make definitive progress towards becoming one of the DOC zone's front runners. The Bianco is the best example of this development, having lost the lightness that characterized it until the last vintage. Today, it has full intense peach and apricot fruit on the nose, which opens out stylishly with light aromatic and minerally hints. The classy, mature and mouthfilling palate also ends on a long, minerally finish. The Rosso is still in a transitional phase but the '99 version has already made considerable progress, especially in elegance and harmony. This very satisfying wine's initial herbal notes give way to berry fruit and almonds, and lead to a clean, lingering finish. The Proseccos have improved in the cellar, and the Brut has become a solid, yet till delicate, "spumante" with intense flower and apple aromas that meld nicely with the fizz.

VILLAGA (VI)

PIOVENE PORTO GODI
FRAZ. TOARA
VIA VILLA, 14
36020 VILLAGA (VI)
TEL. 0444885142
E-MAIL: tpiovene@protec.it

Tommaso Piovene owns some of the best-aspected vineyards in Colli Berici and Flavio Prà is helping him carry on the work begun a few years ago, with the innovative replanting of various plots of land. Some of these vineyards are poised to enter the productive stage and the near future promises to be rich in new developments. In the meantime, we can offer you an absolute preview of the new Tocai Rosso Thovara 2000. The acknowledged kinship of this variety with French grenache and Spanish garnacha translates into a highly structured wine made from grapes that usually only make a pleasant but anonymous rosé. The Thovara's debut is consequently anything but disappointing. It's very typical, with gamey, animal notes, but still needs to age a bit longer. The clean and unsurprisingly drinkable Rivesello is excellent and the approachable Cabernet Polveriera is grassy and enjoyable. The Merlot Fra i Broli has good fruit. Though not too robust, it is undeniably stylish and very fresh-tasting. The Cabernet Pozzare seems to be the best of the reds, with freshly mown hay, mountain herbs, red peppers and leather on the nose and a warm creamy palate. The long, slightly bitter finish has a nice reprise of blackcurrants. The Pinot Polveriera and the Sauvignon Fostine provide dependable quality while the complexity in the highly enjoyable Campigie from super-ripening makes it interesting and characterful.

○ Colli di Conegliano Bianco Ser Bele '01		4*
● Colli di Conegliano Rosso Ser Bele '99		5
○ P. di Valdobbiadene Brut		4*
○ Livio Bronca Brut		4
○ P. di Valdobbiadene Extra Dry		4
● Piave Cabernet Ardesco '00		4
● Colli di Conegliano Rosso Ser Bele '97		5
● Colli di Conegliano Rosso Ser Bele '98		5

● Colli Berici Cabernet Vigneto Pozzare '00		5
● Colli Berici Merlot Fra i Broli '00		5
● Colli Berici Tocai Rosso Thovara '00		6
○ Sauvignon Campigie '01		4*
○ Thovara Passito Bianco '00		5
● Colli Berici Cabernet Polveriera '01		4
● Colli Berici Pinot Bianco Polveriera '01		3
○ Colli Berici Sauvignon Vigneto Fostine '01		4
● Colli Berici Tocai Rosso Vigneto Riveselle '01		3

OTHER WINERIES

Lenotti
Via S. Cristina, 1
37011 Bardolino (VR)
Tel. 0457210484
E-mail: info@lenotti.com

.This Bardolino winery continues pursue quality by increasing its vine stock and adopting appropriate training systems. The many labels include a good Amarone, a beefy Valpolicella and an admirably crafted Bianco di Custoza.

● Valpolicella Cl. Sup. Le Crosare '00	▯	4
○ Bianco di Custoza '01	▯	2*
● Amarone della Valpolicella Cl. '98	▯	6

Firmino Miotti
Via Brogliati Contro, 53
36042 Breganze (VI)
Tel. 0445873006
E-mail: agrifirmino@libero.it

Miotti is a Breganze DOC winery that has gained confidence, thanks to daughter Carla's increasing involvement in the business. The most interesting wines are the reds. A very good Torcolato is the jewel in the Miotti crown.

○ Breganze Torcolato '99	▯▯	6
● Breganze Cabernet '00	▯	3
○ Breganze Bianco Le Colombare '01	▯	3
● Breganze Rosso Valletta '99	▯	6

Gerardo Cesari
Loc. Sorsei, 2
37010 Cavaion Veronese (VR)
Tel. 0456260928
E-mail: cesari-spa@cesari-spa.it

The traditional Verona wines made at this large Affi winery, the Cesari headquarters, have been joined over the years by more internationally oriented products. Some of the grapes are grown on the winery's own property and the rest are bought in.

● Amarone della Valpolicella Cl. Il Bosco '98	▯▯	8
● Recioto della Valpolicella Cl. '00	▯	6
● Amarone della Valpolicella Cl. '99	▯	6

Eugenio Tinazzi & Figli
Via Polichia
37010 Cavaion Veronese (VR)
Tel. 0457235394
E-mail: info@tinazzi.it

The range offered by this large Cavaion winery covers all the Verona DOCs, as well as wines obtained from non-local varieties. The two interesting Amarones are worth mentioning, especially for their rich, ripe fruit.

● Amarone della Valpolicella Cl. La Bastia '98	▯▯	6
● Amarone della Valpolicella Cl. Rovertondo Valleselle '97	▯	8

Carpenè Malvolti
Via Antonio Carpenè, 1
31015 Conegliano (TV)
Tel. 0438364611
E-mail: info@carpene-malvolti.com

Always a point of reference for anyone interested in Prosecco, this Conegliano-based cellar has been making wine for over 150 years. Carpenè Malvolti make a good Talento sparkler as well as their trademark Prosecco.

○	P. di Conegliano Dry Cuvée Oro	♛♛	3*
○	Talento Brut '97		5

Scuola Enologica di Conegliano G. B. Cerletti
Via XXVIII Aprile, 20
31015 Conegliano (TV)
Tel. 043861421

The wines made by the Scuola di Conegliano confirm the good impression they made last year. Alongside the excellent Colli di Conegliano Bianco, you'll find an aromatic Incrocio Manzoni 6.0.13 and an interesting liqueur wine made from the same variety.

○	Colli di Conegliano Bianco '01	♛	3
○	Incrocio Manzoni 6.0.13 '01	♛	3
○	Manzoni Liquoroso	♛	4

Villa Sandi
Loc. Nogare - Via Erizzo, 112
31035 Crocetta del Montello (TV)
Tel. 0423665033
E-mail: info@villasandi.it

A beautiful Palladian villa, built in 1622, is the home of Giancarlo Moretti Polegato's winery. The wines have improved with the help of the Istituto Sperimentale at Conegliano and other experts. We recommend the Marinali Rosso and the Marinali Bianco. The Cartizze is fresh and satisfying.

○	Marinali Bianco '00	♛	5
●	Marinali Rosso '98	♛	5
○	Cartizze	♛	6

Merotto
Fraz. Col S. Martino
31010 Farra di Soligo (TV)
Tel. 0438898195
E-mail: merottosnc@tin.it

A good-sized winery making about 500,000 bottles a year of very drinkable wines, mainly Prosecco. Graziano Merotto makes dependably good sparkling wines and has also shown he knows how to make a Cabernet Sauvignon, the Rosso Dogato.

●	Cabernet Sauvignon Rosso Dogato '98	♛	6
○	P. di Valdobbiadene Brut Barreta	♛	4

Santo Stefano
Via Cadorna, 92
30020 Fossalta di Piave (VE)
Tel. 042167502
E-mail: santostefano@ronchiato.it

The De Stefani family own this upcoming winery near Treviso. The three properties forming the estate are Pra' Longo at Monnastier, Colvendrame at Refrontolo and Le Ronche at Fossalta, which is where the most interesting bottles come from.

○	Piave Chardonnay Terre Nobili '01	♛♛	5
○	Piave Chardonnay Prà Longo '01	♛	3*
●	Piave Cabernet Terre Nobili Ris. '99	♛	6

Santa Margherita
Via Ita Marzotto, 8
30025 Fossalta di Portogruaro (VE)
Tel. 0421246111
E-mail: santamargherita@stmargherita.com

This large winery at Fossalta di Piave is famous for having made Pinot Grigio popular around the world. All its wines are unostentatious and approachably drinkable. We recommend the Cabernet Sauvignon, from the Ca' d'Archi estate in Alto Adige, and the fresh, aromatic Luna dei Feldi.

○	Luna dei Feldi '01	♛	4
●	A. A. Cabernet Sauvignon Ca' d'Archi '99	♛	5

Corteforte
Via Osan, 45
37022 Fumane (VR)
Tel. 0456839104 - 0457702622
E-mail: corteforte@tin.it

This little Fumane winery has a strong viticultural tradition and particularly good growing land near the cellars. Quality continues to improve. The two Amarones are nice, especially the Vigneti di Osan 1997 selection, which exploits all the potential of the vintage.

● Amarone della Valpolicella Cl. Vigneti di Osan '97 ▼▼	6
● Amarone della Valpolicella Cl. '98 ▼	6

I Scriani
Via Ponte Scrivan, 7
37022 Fumane (VR)
Tel. 0456839251

The Cottini brothers vinify grapes from their estate, distributed over various plots in the hills around Fumane, where the little winery is situated. All the wines in the range are made to good standards of quality.

● Amarone della Valpolicella Cl. '98 ▼	6
● Recioto della Valpolicella Cl. Maddalena '99 ▼	6
● Valpolicella Cl. Sup. '99 ▼	4

Le Bertarole
Via Bertarole, 8/a
37022 Fumane (VR)
Tel. 0456839220
E-mail: az.bertarole@tiscalinet.it

Giordano Venturini's little cellar near Fumane produces the traditional Valpolicella wines with meticulous care. As well as a flavoursome Amarone, there is a highly traditional Valpolicella Superiore that we recommend.

● Amarone della Valpolicella Cl. '98 ▼	6
● Valpolicella Cl. Sup. Le Portarine '00	4

Lamberti
Via Gardesana
37017 Lazise (VR)
Tel. 0457580034
E-mail: giv@giv.it

Lamberti is one of the Veneto-based mainstays in the vast Gruppo Italiano Vini empire of wineries. It makes wines for large-scale distribution, turning out 8,000,000 bottles each year from the 170 hectares of estate-owned vineyards, supplemented by bought-in grapes. Prices are very affordable.

○ Bianco di Custoza Orchidea Platino '01 ▼	3
● Merlot Santepietre '01 ▼	2*
○ Soave Cl. Santepietre '01 ▼	2*

Conti da Schio
Fraz. Costozza - P.zza da Schio, 4
36023 Longare (VI)
Tel. 0444555099
E-mail: giuliodaschio@libero.it

This small Costozza winery makes two reds of distinction: the intense Cabernet, whose dynamic thrust in the mouth, depth and flavour helped it win Two Glasses, and the soft, mouthfilling Rosso, which is nearly as good.

● Colli Berici Cabernet '00 ▼▼	4*
● Rosso Costozza '00 ▼	5

Paolo Boscaini & Figli
Fraz. Valgatara - Via Ca' de Loi, 2
37020 Marano di Valpolicella (VR)
Tel. 0456832500
E-mail: boscainiwine@boscaini.it

This large Valgatara winery is carrying out a renovation process that began in the vineyard. The wide range of traditional Valpolicella wines includes two good Amarones, the powerful, appealing Ca' de Loi and the dynamic Marano.

● Amarone della Valpolicella Cl. Ca' de Loi '97 ▼▼	7
● Amarone della Valpolicella Cl. Marano '98 ▼	7

La Giaretta
Fraz. Valgatara
Via del Platano, 6
37020 Marano di Valpolicella (VR)
tel. 0457701791

A small, very promising cellar, La Giaretta in Valpolicella vinifies only grapes grown on the estate vineyards. Supervision at each stage of production is scrupulous. As well as the standard range, it releases a serious Amarone and very good Valpolicella under the I Quadretti label.

- Amarone della Valpolicella Cl.
  I Quadretti '98 — 8
- Recioto della Valpolicella Cl. '00 — 5
- Valpolicella Cl. Sup. I Quadretti '99 — 5

Luigino e Marco Provolo
Via San Cassiano, 2
37030 Mezzane di Sotto (VR)
tel. 0458880106
e-mail: provolomarco@tiscali.it

The Provolos' small winery is situated in greater Valpolicella area, outside the Classico part of the DOC zone, an area with vast but mainly untapped potential. The owners maintain an open, co-operative working relationship with local producers, encouraging them to keep improving quality.

- Amarone della Valpolicella
  San Cassian '95 — 7
- Amarone della Valpolicella '97 — 6
- Valpolicella Sup. '98 — 4

Cantina di Montecchia
Via Alpone, 53
37030 Montecchia di Crosara (VR)
tel. 0457450094
e-mail: cantina@cantinadimontecchia.com

The interesting array of co-operatives in the province of Verona has been expanded by arrival of the Cantina di Montecchia and its well-made, expressive wines. The Bianco Re d'Aurum, a blend of chardonnay and sauvignon, and the Pinot Grigio La Crosara, are both especially successful.

○ Garda Pinot Grigio
  La Crosara I Fossili '01 — 1*
○ Monti Lessini Bianco
  Re d'Aurum '00 — 6

Le Albare
Via Pergola, 69
37030 Montecchia di Crosara (VR)
tel. 0456175131 - 0456175953
e-mail: info@vignadellostefano.it

Stefano Posenato has run the family winery since 1994 and the results get more and more interesting each year. We tasted two wines, a fresh, early-drinking Soave Superiore and a more complex, fleshy Classico Superiore.

○ Soave Cl. Sup.
  Vigna dello Stefano '00 — 4
○ Soave Sup.
  Vigna dello Stefano '01 — 3

Giobatta Dal Bosco
Via Fontananuova, 6
37032 Monteforte d'Alpone (VR)
tel. 0456175083
e-mail: info@cantinalemandolare.com

This Monteforte winery, owned by Giobatta and Renzo Dal Bosco, was established in the early 1950s. It now makes 50,000 bottles a year from 20 hectares of vineyards, mainly pleasant, garganega-based Soaves and Recioto di Soaves.

○ Recioto di Soave Le Mandolare '00 — 4
○ Soave Cl. Le Mandolare '01 — 3
○ Soave Cl. Sup. Le Mandolare '01 — 3

Antonio Nani
Via Decora, 22
36024 Nanto (VI)
tel. 0444639191

Situated at the feet of the Colli Berici hills, an area of huge but indifferently exploited potential, the Nani winery has been revamped over the last few years. Wines here are high quality and sold at laudably affordable prices.

○ Colli Berici Pinot Bianco
  del Crearo '01 — 2*
○ Colli Berici Sauvignon
  del Crearo '01 — 2*
- Colli Berici Cabernet Antonio '99 — 4

F.lli Recchia
Loc. Jago - Via Ca' Bertoldi, 30
37024 Negrar (VR)
tel. 0457500584
e-mail: info@recchiavini.it

Brothers Riccardo and Roberto Recchia have a professional approach to making the traditional wines of Valpolicella. The range includes the standard-label Amarone, which we particularly recommend. It shows rich aromas of ripe fruit and spices, then a harmonious, complex palate.

• Amarone della Valpolicella Cl. '98	♈♈	5*
• Amarone della Valpolicella Cl. Vigneto Ca' Bertoldi '98	♈	6
• Valpolicella Cl. Sup. Le Coste '99	♈	3

Casa Vinicola Sartori
Via Casette, 2
37024 Negrar (VR)
tel. 0456028011
e-mail: sartori@sartorinet.com

The wide range of wines offered by this Negrar-based winery includes all the Verona classics, from Amarone to Bianco di Custoza. The reds made from raisined grapes are especially interesting, particularly the two enjoyable, well-structured Amarones.

• Amarone della Valpolicella Cl. Corte Bra '97	♈	7
• Amarone della Valpolicella Cl. '98	♈	6

Sergio Nardin
Loc. Roncadelle
Via Fontane, 3
31010 Ormelle (TV)
tel. 0422851625

Sergio Nardin is helped by his sons Pietro and Paolo. Together, they look after an estate comprising two properties and the wines are named after them: Borgo Molino and Vigna Melonetto. Two of the best from the long list of labels are the spicy Merum and the fresh Refosco.

• Lison-Pramaggiore Refosco P. R. Vigna Melonetto '00	♈	3
• Merum Vigna Melonetto '98	♈	4

Fraccaroli
Via Berra Vecchia, 4
37019 Peschiera del Garda (VR)
tel. 0457550949
e-mail: info@fraccarolivini.it

Trebbiano may not be an especially aromatic grape but it will make outstandingly elegant, creamy wines if properly grown. That's how the Fraccaroli brothers grow their trebbiano. They then get the best out of the fruit to make whites with tempting depth.

○ Lugana Sup. I Fraccaroli '00	♈	4
○ Lugana '01	♈	3
○ Lugana Brut	♈	4

Martino Zanetti
Via Chisini, 79
31053 Pieve di Soligo (TV)
tel. 0438841608
e-mail: casebianche@online.it

Martino Zanetti runs this winery with great enthusiasm, aiming to obtain modern-style wines that still embody local traditions and terroir. The most impressive wines are a flavoursome Bordeaux blend, an unusual Wildbacher and an enjoyable Chardonnay Brut.

• Camoi Col Sandago '99	♈	5
• Wildbacher '99	♈	5
○ Chardonnay Brut Col Sandago	♈	4

Tenuta Teracrea
Loc. Lison - Via Attigliana, 61
30020 Portogruaro (VE)
tel. 0421287041 - 0421287900
e-mail: tenuta.teracrea@libero.it

Giuseppe Bigai is something of an institution in Lison. Thanks to a strong tradition of winemaking, his cellar has been the most representative in the DOC zone for years. The wines at Tenuta Teracrea are substantial rather than elegant.

○ Lison-Pramaggiore Tocai Italico '01	♈♈	3*
• Pinot Nero '00	♈	3
○ Malvasia '01	♈	3

Vincenzo Toffoli
Via Liberazione, 26
31020 Refrontolo (TV)
tel. 0438894240
e-mail: toffoli@nline.it

For years, the Toffolis have made wines from traditional local varieties - prosecco, verdiso and marzemino – on the Refrontolo hills. Like the sparklers, their sweet wines are interesting, subtle and deliciously drinkable.

● Colli di Conegliano Refrontolo Passito '00	▼	5
○ Prosecco Passito '00	▼	5
○ Verdiso '01		3

Marcato
Via Prandi, 10
37030 Roncà (VR)
tel. 0457460070
e-mail: marcato@marcatovini.it

Giovanni, Lino and Francesco run the winery established by their grandfather in the late 19th century. It is situated on the borders of Verona and Vicenza. The cellar makes Soave, Lessini, Colli Berici and Garda DOC wines that are very good value for money.

○ Colli Berici Sauvignon '01	▼	4
○ Soave Cl. Sup. Il Tirso '01	▼	4
○ Lessini Durello M. Cl. '96	▼	4

Igino Accordini
Via Bolla, 7
37020 San Pietro in Cariano (VR)
tel. 0456020604
e-mail: accordini@iper.net

Despite advancing years, Igino Accordini is still very active at this small cellar. He has help from his son Guido, who looks after the cellar, which turns out 30,000 bottles a year from the six hectares of vineyards. The DOC wines are Amarone and Valpolicella, as well as IGTs.

● Amarone della Valpolicella Cl. Alzaro delle Corvine '98	▼	6
● Amarone della Valpolicella Cl. Le Bessole '98	▼	6

Corte Lenguin
Via Ca' dell'Ebreo, 5
37029 San Pietro in Cariano (VR)
tel. 0457701406

Silvio and Lorenzo Vantini's estate covers a surface area of about 12 hectares and produces well-executed, nicely balanced wines. The Amarone and Recioto are interesting modern interpretations of traditional styles and the Valpolicella Superiore is well typed.

● Amarone della Valpolicella Cl. '98	▼▼	5*
● Recioto della Valpolicella Cl. '99	▼	5
● Valpolicella Cl. Sup. Ripasso '99		4

Marchesi Fumanelli
Loc. Squarano
37020 San Pietro in Cariano (VR)
tel. 0457704875
e-mail: info@squarano.it

This compact cellar is starting to earn a reputation thanks to the quality guaranteed by the estate-owned vineyards and a working relationship with Celestino Gaspari's Zyme team. While you wait for the serious reds, we recommend trying the interesting white Terso and the very nice Valpolicella.

○ Terso Bianco '99	▼	5
● Valpolicella Cl. Sup. Squarano '99	▼	5

Guido Manara
Fraz. San Floriano
37020 San Pietro in Cariano (VR)
tel. 0457701086
e-mail: info@manaravini.it

Brothers Giovanni, Lorenzo and Fabio Manara continue to make wine very professionally. Their fast emerging winery is one of the most promising in the area. The trio make the classic local wines with fruit obtained from their 11 hectares under vine.

● Amarone della Valpolicella Cl. Postera '98	▼▼	6*
● Valpolicella Cl. Sup. Le Morete '00	▼	4

Aleardo Ferrari
Fraz. Gargagnago
Via Giare, 15
37020 Sant'Ambrogio di Valpolicella (VR)
tel. 0457701379

We are starting to see results from the modernization carried out on the Ferrari estate. The deep, flavoursome Valpolicella Bure Alto has benefited particularly, and hints at future improvements that should involve the whole of the range in years to come.

- Valpolicella Cl. Sup.
  Bure Alto '99 🍷🍷 4*
- Recioto della Valpolicella Cl. '00 🍷 5

Mosole
Via Annone Veneto, 60
30029 Santo Stino di Livenza (VE)
tel. 0421310404
E-mail: mosole@mosole.com

Lucio Mosole's winery is making serious progress in the Lison-Pramaggiore DOC and the top-of-the-range label includes some very interesting wines. The Cabernet Hora Sexta and the Merlot ad Nonam are well made and very convincing.

- Lison-Pramaggiore Cabernet
  Hora Sexta '99 🍷🍷 5
- Lison-Pramaggiore
  Merlot ad Nonam '00 🍷 5

Balestri Valda
Via Monti, 44
37038 Soave (VR)
tel. 0457675393
E-mail: balestri.valda@tin.it

Guido Rizzotto has postponed release of his Lunalonga in order to give it the bottle time it deserves. The Recioto di Soave makes an interesting debut, with sweet dried fruit and a fresh palate that is not too challenging.

- ○ Recioto di Soave Cl. '00 🍷🍷 6
- ○ Soave Cl. '01 🍷 4
- ○ Soave Spumante Brut 4

Albino Piona
Fraz. Custoza - Via Bellavista, 48
37060 Sommacampagna (VR)
tel. 045516055
E-mail: silvio.piona@tin.it

Albino Piona's winery nestles on the slopes that separate Lake Garda and the Po Valley. It is one of the leading estates in the Garda zone. The Bianco di Custoza, the red Azobé, made from corvina grapes, and the Passito La Rabitta are all worth investigating.

- ○ Bianco di Custoza '01 🍷 2*
- Azobé Corvina
  Vigneto delle Pergole '99 🍷 3
- ○ La Rabitta Passito Bianco '99 🍷 4

F.lli Fabiano
Via Verona, 6
37060 Sona (VR)
tel. 0456081111
E-mail: info@fabiano.it

Fabiano is a major Verona cellar that releases a wide range of affordable, and temptingly drinkable, wines as well as traditional products. The Amarone I Fondatori is of very good and the Valpolicella Classico Superiore Negraro and Cabernet Sauvignon Intenso are both well made.

- Cabernet Sauvignon Intenso '00 🍷 3*
- Amarone della Valpolicella Cl.
  I Fondatori '97 🍷 8
- Valpolicella Cl. Sup. Negraro '99 🍷 4

Zamuner
Via Valecchia, 40
37060 Sona (VR)
tel. 0456081090 - 0458342168
E-mail: info@zamuner.it

Daniele Zamuner's winery confirms its status as one of the best sparkling winemakers in the Garda area. As well as the prestigious "spumante" wines, there are two ranges of still products. Montespada is for standard-label products and Valecchia for those aged in barrique.

- ○ Bianco di Custoza Montespada '01 🍷 3
- ⊙ Zamuner Brut Rosé
  Villa La Mattarana Ris. '95 🍷 6
- ○ Spumante Brut '96 🍷 5

CIODET
VIA PIVA, 104
31049 VALDOBBIADENE (TV)
TEL. 0423973131
E-MAIL: spumanticiodet@libero.it

This little winery works very professionally, purchasing grapes from local growers and making selection from vineyards with different sensory profiles. The extremely well-made "spumante" wines are the result of excellent cellar technique.

○ Cartizze	♀	4
○ P. di Valdobbiadene Extra Dry	♀	2*
○ P. di Valdobbiadene Brut	♀	2
○ P. di Valdobbiadene Tranquillo	♀	2

PAOLO ZUCCHETTO
LOC. CIMA, 16
31040 VALDOBBIADENE (TV)
TEL. 0423972311
E-MAIL: sales@zucchetto.com

Paolo Zucchetto owns this small cellar in Valdobbiadene, which makes about 55,000 bottles a year, including Prosecco Frizzante Sur Lie and sparkling wines. The Cartizze is sophisticated in style with rich, intense aromas of apples, pears and flowers, followed by a creamy, harmonious palate.

○ Cartizze	♀♀	4*
○ P. di Valdobbiadene Brut	♀	3
○ P. di Valdobbiadene Extra Dry	♀	3

CORTE MARZAGO
LOC. LE BUGNE
37067 VALEGGIO SUL MINCIO (VR)
TEL. 0457945104
E-MAIL: info@cortemarzago.com

This splendid estate, which also offers bed and breakfast accommodation, is in the hills around Lake Garda and is owned by Lorenzo Fabiano. The wines are interesting, especially the oak-aged Chardonnay Campagnola alla Croce and the flavoursome Passito Bianco Le Melghette.

○ Garda Chardonnay Campagnola alla Croce '00	♀	4
○ Le Melghette Passito Bianco '00	♀	5

GIORGIO CECCHETTO
FRAZ. TEZZE DI PIAVE - VIA PIAVE, 67
31020 VAZZOLA (TV)
TEL. 043828598
E-MAIL: cecchettoraboso@tin.it

Giorgio Cecchetto makes almost 20,000 bottles every year at his lovely winery in Tezze di Piave, mainly from international grape varieties. The Raboso is an exception, as it is obtained from the native grape of the same name. Giorgio is keen supporter, and dedicated grower, of the variety.

○ Sauvignon '01	♀	3
● Piave Raboso Gelsaia '97	♀	5
● Piave Raboso '98	♀	4

DAL DIN
VIA MONTEGRAPPA, 31
31020 VIDOR (TV)
TEL. 0423987295

This Vidor winery stands out in the Prosecco DOC for its very well-made, non-sparkling wines, as well as its "spumante" bottles. The Cartizze is ripe and flavoursome, the Prosecco Dry is enjoyable and the varietal Colli di Conegliano Bianco has good balance.

○ Colli di Conegliano Bianco '01	♀	3
○ Cartizze	♀	5
○ P. di Valdobbiadene Dry	♀	4

CONTE LOREDAN GASPARINI VENEGAZZÙ
FRAZ. VENEGAZZÙ
31040 VOLPAGO DEL MONTELLO (TV)
TEL. 0423870024
E-MAIL: info@venegazzu.com

As we wait for the release of the red Capo di Stato, which the cellar has delayed, we would like to point out the progress made on the white front. The Manzoni Bianco is very interesting, revealing a subtle nose and balanced, well-made palate. The Pinot Grigio and Cabernet Sauvignon are enjoyable.

○ Manzoni Bianco '01	♀	3
○ Pinot Grigio '01	♀	3
● Montello Cabernet Sauvignon '00	♀	3

FRIULI VENEZIA GIULIA

This year, the Guide sees a further increase in the number of Friulian wineries with a full profile while the number of mini-profiles in the Other Wineries section remains the same as last time. In other words, we have had to find a compromise between editorial constrictions and the pressure of newcomers to the ranks of the region's premium-quality producers. One of the most exciting features documented by this year's Guide is the progress that has been made on the Friulian flatlands. Some might object that excellent wines have been made on the plains of Friuli for many years, referring to the group of quality producers in the Friuli Isonzo zone. This DOC, it should be said, embraces two distinct areas, one in the shadow of the Collio hills and the other stretching down to the Adriatic. However, we want to highlight the major advances made by cellars in Friuli Aquileia. There are more cellars than ever in the Guide, and they presented more wines. That's not all. For the first time, the region's largest DOC – Grave del Friuli – has won a top award. Three Glasses went to the cellar of the DOC zone's president, Piergiovanni Pistoni. Competition between the two hillslope zones, Collio and Colli Orientali del Friuli, is as fierce as ever, with Collio winning this year on points. Carso, too, is sending out promising signals, although the main obstacle in the path of these producers remains the fact that few cellars are able to release wines in significant quantities. Several of the profiles mention vineyard technicians, sometimes called "fruitmakers". Who are they? Well, a number of young oenologists and agronomists, with serious working experience at consortia or privately owned cellars, have taken the plunge as consultants to provide local cellars with advice on vineyard management. When a successful winery is profiled, mention is usually made of the owner and perhaps a consultant, essentially responsible for the vinification process. But we also want to pay tribute to the fruitmakers, the people who, in our opinion, have contributed decisively to the achievements of several estates by changing established practices in the vineyard. Lastly, we come to a sore point – prices. Friuli has not escaped the tendency of many cellars to push up prices, a trend reflected in the prices of must, grapes and vineyards. Many reasons are put forward in justification. In some cases, serious wineries are finally reaping the rewards of many years' work as their prestige brings commercial success. However, we are frankly astonished to see cellar-door prices, net of VAT, that range from € 6.00 to € 10.00 at wineries that are either new or have little in the way of market visibility. A few years ago, we noted that in some cases a price increase could actually boost sales. Do some producers think that is still true?

AQUILEIA (UD)

Giovanni Donda
Via Manlio Acidinio, 4
33051 Aquileia (UD)
tel. 043191185

Solid results have enabled Giovanni Donda's cellar to gain a full Guide profile without a preliminary visit to the Other Wineries section. A long-time professional grower, Giovanni realized that the flatlands of Friuli could yield outstanding results and has joined the ranks of the winemakers who are currently boosting the image of the Aquileia DOC zone as never before. Donda has five and a half hectares of Guyot-trained vines that give him about 30,000 bottles a year. Unlike many growers in Friuli, he concentrates on a limited number of varieties and labels, taking full advantage of advice from wine technician Giorgio Bertossi, himself a grower (Mulino delle Tolle). For bottling, Giovanni relies on Giuseppe Lipari's mobile unit. Lipari was the first to introduce these special truck-mounted units that have enabled so many small producers to bottle on-site. The sweet but not cloying Aureo is obtained from raisined grapes (we detected verduzzo) and offers stewed apple and figs. One surprise from the 2001 vintage is the Cabernet Franc. Complex autumn leaves on the nose precede elegant cherry and black cherry richness on the palate, with its mellow tannins. The Bianco Tàlis is from sauvignon, pinot bianco, pinot grigio and briefly oaked chardonnay. It came close to a second Glass but lost points for a slight lack of weight in the mouth.

BAGNARIA ARSA (UD)

Tenuta Beltrame
Fraz. Privano
Loc. Antonini, 4
33050 Bagnaria Arsa (UD)
tel. 0432923670
e-mail: tenuta.beltrame@libero.it

The Beltrame family bought this Aquileia estate in the 1990s, with the stated aim of making great wines on the flatlands. A decade later, they have succeeded. They have planted 25 of the property's 40 hectares to trim, modern vineyards and the renovated estate villa is now the home of an up-to-date cellar and an attractive barrique room. Cristian Beltrame has geared the winery for superior quality, which is evident the excellent Riservas. This year, release of the new reds is also being delayed to improve their balance. Take a quick glance at the table below and you will see confirmation. The Merlot Riserva '99 is a seriously big hitter with outstanding ageing prospects. The warm, pervasive nose of bramble tart, cinnamon and petit fours precedes a firm palate with robust tannins that takes you through to a long, fruit-rich finish. The Tazzelenghe '99 comes from a native Friulian variety with a typically rugged astringency in the mouth, the complex, subtle aromas offering a delicious contrast. Milky notes and a nice balance of oak and fruit characterize the Chardonnay Pribus 2000. The Tocai 2001 unveils aromas of golden delicious apple, elderflower and tropical fruit that fuse elegance and intensity, then the tangy palate reprises the initial note of tropical fruit. As ever, the Cabernet Sauvignon Riserva '99 is spot on, delivering attractive minerally hints over sensations of peach and ripe tomato.

● Friuli Aquileia Cabernet Franc '01	♀♀	3*
○ Aureo	♀♀	5
○ Friuli Aquileia Bianco Tàlis '01	♀	3
○ Friuli Aquileia Pinot Bianco '01	♀	3
○ Friuli Aquileia Sauvignon '01	♀	3
● Friuli Aquileia Merlot '01		3
○ Friuli Aquileia Pinot Grigio '01		3

○ Friuli Aquileia Chardonnay Pribus '00	♀♀	4
○ Friuli Aquileia Pinot Grigio '01	♀♀	4
○ Friuli Aquileia Sauvignon '01	♀♀	4
○ Friuli Aquileia Tocai Friulano '01	♀♀	4
● Friuli Aquileia Cabernet Sauvignon Ris. '99	♀♀	5
● Friuli Aquileia Merlot Ris. '99	♀♀	5
● Tazzelenghe Ris. '99	♀♀	5
○ Friuli Aquileia Chardonnay '01	♀	4
○ Friuli Aquileia Pinot Bianco '01	♀	4
○ Friuli Aquileia Sauvignon '00	♀♀	4
● Friuli Aquileia Cabernet Sauvignon Ris. '97	♀♀	5
● Friuli Aquileia Merlot Ris. '98	♀♀	5

BAGNARIA ARSA (UD)

Mulino delle Tolle
Loc. Sevegliano
Via Mulino delle Tolle, 15
33050 Bagnaria Arsa (UD)
Tel. 0432928113
E-mail: mulinodelletolle@tin.it

Giorgio and Eliseo Bertossi are cousins. Friendly and dependable, they make it a pleasure to taste at Mulino delle Tolle because, unlike many other producers, their comments are always to the point as they describe the virtues and defects of each bottle. Their 13 hectares lie where, 2,000 years ago, two Roman roads, the Via Postumia and the Via Julia Augusta, used to run. We are not far from the ancient port of Aquileia so it is not unusual for vineyard workers to dig up archaeological remains, such as the classical votive head that the Bertossis have adopted as their trademark. The down-to-earth Bertossi approach is obvious in the small, uncluttered cellar, which is much more Spartan than most of its fellows in Friuli. Still, if the pair can achieve results like those in the table below, they must get very good raw material from their vine stock and the minimalist cellar equipment is obviously sufficient to produce premium wines. Since last year, the Bertossi's have been running an attractive "agriturismo" farm holiday centre in the buildings that until 1918 housed the Italian customs post (it was only then that Friuli became part of Italy). The Malvasia 2001 is the flagship wine, showing rich fruit aromas, fullness and good depth. The Bianco Palmade is a blend of oak-aged malvasia, sauvignon and chardonnay with a fresh, fruity nose. Finally, both the Chardonnay and the Sauvignon scored a full Glass.

BICINICCO (UD)

Pradio
Loc. Felettis
Via Udine, 17
33050 Bicinicco (UD)
Tel. 0432990123
E-mail: info@pradio.it

This lower Friuli estate has belonged to the Cielo family since the 1970s. It slipped into the Other Wineries section last year and this year did even better, earning a full Guide profile. Dynamic, determined Luca Cielo is the man who puts the estate plans into action. His youthful enthusiasm has prompted him to innovate – witness his two new cask-conditioned blends – as he searches for distinctive wines. For a decade, he has had input from Lombardy-based oenologist Beppe Bassi and Luca also keeps a weather eye on market developments. The estate has about 30 hectares of vines, planted at 4,000 vines per hectare. These give an annual production of 200,000 bottles, which bear the name of their vineyard of origin. The two new blends we were talking about are successful, in fact, the white Plui Vingis, from oak-aged chardonnay, pinot grigio and tocai, nearly earned a second Glass. Sadly, they lost a few marks because they had only recently gone into the bottle so it was the Pinot Grigio 2001, the Chardonnay 2001 and the Cabernet Sauvignon 2000 that stood out. The Pinot Grigio has varietal notes of minerals and williams pears that are mirrored on the well-rounded palate. About 20 per cent of the fruit in the Chardonnay is barrique-fermented. The resulting bottle impresses with banana, citrus, hazelnut and dried flowers on the nose and balance in the mouth. In the Cabernet Sauvignon, sun-kissed citrus and chocolate greet the nose, to be followed by a luscious palate that has good tannic structure.

○ Malvasia '01	ŸŸ	3*
● Friuli Aquileia Refosco P. R. '00	Ÿ	3
○ Friuli Aquileia Bianco Palmade '01	Ÿ	3
○ Friuli Aquileia Chardonnay '01	Ÿ	2*
● Friuli Aquileia Merlot '01	Ÿ	3
○ Friuli Aquileia Sauvignon '01	Ÿ	3
● Friuli Aquileia Cabernet Franc '01		3
○ Friuli Aquileia Tocai Friulano '01		2
○ Malvasia '00	ŸŸ	3

● Friuli Grave Cabernet Sauvignon Crearo '00	ŸŸ	4*
○ Friuli Grave Chardonnay Teraje '01	ŸŸ	4*
○ Friuli Grave Pinot Grigio Priara '01	ŸŸ	4*
● Friuli Grave Rosso Rok '00	Ÿ	4
○ Friuli Grave Bianco Plui Vignis '01	Ÿ	4
○ Friuli Grave Sauvignon Sobaja '01	Ÿ	4
● Friuli Grave Merlot Roncomoro '01		3
● Friuli Grave Refosco P. R. Tuaro '01		3

BUTTRIO (UD)

Livio e Claudio Buiatti
Via Lippe, 25
33042 Buttrio (UD)
tel. 0432674317
e-mail: info@buiattivini.it

Claudio Buiatti has accustomed winelovers to more spectacular results than this year's range achieved. Obviously, the wines he presented are still good but the meagre haul of Glasses counts at least as a hiccough. Yet Claudio has eight or so hectares in excellent growing zones, such as In Mont and Poanis, and his well-equipped cellar is more than adequate for his production needs. Perhaps it was Claudio's enthusiasm that flagged this year. Two thirds of the wines released are whites and the range is sold all over Italy. More than 50,000 bottles go to market each year at prices that represent very good value for money. In a vintage that treated the variety kindly, Claudio's 2001 Sauvignon is one of the best such products from the vintage around. Intense banana and elderflower are echoed on the broad palate, which concludes with a long, fruity finish. The Pinot Grigio is better on the palate than the nose, its rich mouthfeel hinting at citrus with good intensity and length. There are clear notes of stylish apple on the nose of the Pinot Bianco but slightly over-assertive acidity thins the flavour. Finally, we would like to note that all the other wines we tasted are well managed.

BUTTRIO (UD)

Olivo Buiatti
Via Lippe, 23
33042 Buttrio (UD)
tel. 0432674316

Franco Buiatti has decided to skip a vintage and will release his 2000 reds in early 2003. The first bottles of the 2001 whites will be in available at the cellar in December 2002. This is a courageous decision from a winery that has only recently begun to make a name for itself outside Friuli. Still, given the character of Franco's wines, it is a move we can only subscribe. Founded in 1911, the estate was handed down through the generations until 1986, when Olivo and Livio decided to split their cellars. A few years ago, Olivo handed the reins over to Franco, who now looks after the seven and a half hectares with the help of his wife Simonetta, who also runs their small "frasca", as traditional cellar-door sales and tasting/catering facilities are called in the region. Very few bottles emerge from the winery – only about 7,000 a year – but they are seriously good ones. Two quality-enhancing factors are Franco's close contacts with Enzo Pontoni, of Miani, and Paolo Meroi. As a result, cropping levels are very low and the concentration of the wines is a given. We had an advance tasting of the 2000 Merlot and Cabernet, both of which are outstanding. The Tocai Friulano and Sauvignon 2001 are also extremely successful. Another few months in the bottle can only improve things.

○ COF Sauvignon '01	🍷	4*
○ COF Pinot Bianco '01	🍷	4
○ COF Pinot Grigio '01	🍷	4
● COF Merlot '00		4
● COF Refosco P. R. '00		4
● COF Merlot '99	🍷🍷	4

○ COF Bianco Poanis Blanc '00	🍷🍷	4
○ COF Tocai Friulano '00	🍷🍷	4
● COF Cabernet '99	🍷🍷	5
○ COF Pinot Grigio '00	🍷	4

BUTTRIO (UD)

Conte D'Attimis-Maniago
Via Sottomonte, 21
33042 Buttrio (UD)
tel. 0432674027
e-mail: info@contedattimismaniago.it

Despite the efforts he has lavished on restoring his palazzo and park at the family's historic Maniago seat, Alberto D'Attimis has also found time to consolidate quality at his winery. All the wines presented passed muster. They are concentrated, modern-style products that testify to progress made in recent years. There can be no doubt that the arrival of young Francesco Spitaleri, the oenologist, has nudged the winery in the right direction. Founded as long ago as 1615, the estate embraces about 110 hectares on the hillslopes at Sottomonte, near Buttrio, giving an annual production of around 500,000 bottles. The Sauvignon 2001, part fermented in steel and part in oak, came close to a third Glass. Its distinctive nose is a riot of flowers, lifted by notes of apricots in syrup and tomato, which are echoed on the seamlessly sustained palate. The fine Malvasia 2001 is brilliant and stylish, thanks to citrus, dried flowers and red delicious apple, then the rich, long density of the palate ends on a fresh note of pears and apples. Two reds won their spurs, the Cabernet 2000 and the Vignaricco Rosso '97, a blend of cabernet sauvignon and merlot with a little schioppettino. The game and spice aromas of the Cabernet lead into a well-rounded warmth on the palate, with Peruvian bark and blueberry jam emerging. Creamy and almost opulent on the nose, the Vignaricco has a rich, complex palate where assertive tannins back up the fruity structure. Finally, the Vignaricco Bianco '97 and Chardonnay 2001 both earned very full Glasses.

○ COF Sauvignon '01	♀♀	4*
● COF Cabernet '00	♀♀	4*
○ COF Malvasia '01	♀♀	4*
● Vignaricco Rosso '97	♀♀	5
● COF Merlot '00	♀	4
○ COF Chardonnay '01	♀	4
○ COF Picolit '01	♀	7
○ Vignaricco Bianco '97	♀	5
● COF Tazzelenghe '99	♀	5
● COF Refosco P. R. '01		4
○ Vignaricco Bianco '96	♀♀	5
● COF Refosco P. R. '99	♀♀	4

BUTTRIO (UD)

★ Girolamo Dorigo
Via del Pozzo, 5
33042 Buttrio (UD)
tel. 0432674268
e-mail: girdorig@tin.it

The 2001 vintage saw Alessio Dorigo take over winemaking management. This can only help to bring into focus the cellar's production philosophy, which has not always been easy to follow in recent years. Alessio's first move has been to identify two distinct ranges, an affordable, more approachable line and a "gold" line for the most prestigious Dorigo labels - wines the cellar makes without concessions. Unsurprisingly, the wines that had the panel nodding in approval this year came from the gold range. At the top of the list is the big-hitting Montsclapade '99, a Bordeaux blend of grapes picked on the point of super-ripeness and then aged slowly in French oak. Its aromas are a thrilling weave of everything from blueberry to cocoa powder, lifted by a delicious note of mint, then the creamy palate powers through to a long finish. There is also plenty of character and potential in the muscular, extract-rich Pignolo '99. The panel also liked the admirable Chardonnay Vigneto Ronc di Juri, with aromas of vanilla, honey and confectioner's cream over oak that still needs time to mellow, and the Ronc di Juri 2000, a Sauvignon that perhaps lacks only a touch of muscle power to back up its elegant personality. Worth investigating among the easier-drinking bottles are the 2001 Ribolla, Tocai and Pinot Grigio, while we were hoping for more from the legendary gold-range Picolit.

● COF Montsclapade '99	♀♀♀	7
● COF Pignolo '99	♀♀	8
○ COF Chardonnay Vigneto Ronc di Juri '00	♀♀	6
○ COF Ronc di Juri '00	♀♀	6
○ Picolit Vigneto Montsclapade '00	♀	8
○ COF Pinot Grigio '01	♀	4
○ COF Ribolla Gialla '01	♀	4
○ COF Tocai Friulano Vigneto Montsclapade '01	♀	4
● COF Refosco P. R. Vigneto Montsclapade '99	♀	6
○ Dorigo Brut	♀	5
○ COF Chardonnay Vigneto Ronc di Juri '98	♀♀♀	6

BUTTRIO (UD)

Davino Meroi
Via Stretta del Parco, 7
33042 Buttrio (UD)
tel. 0432674025
e-mail: parco.meroi@libero.it

Under Paolo Meroi, this cellar has taken a new direction, setting out on the road to quality. Major results have not been slow in coming and with them, crucially, has come reliability, as we found out at our tastings. The Chardonnay 2001 is exemplary in this respect. Its lingering pineapple accompanies a stylish, well-proportioned toastiness. The Tocai is equally dependable. The 2000 is ready for drinking, with decent body and flowery aromas, whereas the 2001 is more persuasive, albeit rawer, thanks to its clean, mouthfilling structure and attractively long freshness. In contrast, the mature version of the Blanc di Buri blend is the more convincing. The alcohol is better balanced and the wood better integrated. The harmonious Sauvignon 2001 has good grip and aromas that recall peach and apricot. Equally admirable are the sweet wines, the traditional-style acacia honey, almond and citrus marmalade Verduzzo and the 2000 Picolit, which also reveals honey, then walnuts and finally a long, fresh, moderately sweet finish. Both reds are very much recommended. The Dominin '99, a merlot with a little refosco is so muscular it almost seems austere and the merlot-based Ros di Buri 2000 has perceptible grassy hints.

BUTTRIO (UD)

★ Miani
Via Peruzzi, 10
33042 Buttrio (UD)
tel. 0432674327

Enzo Pontoni is an indefatigable perfectionist. He can bring himself to release only 8,000 bottles a year, in spite of his 18-hectare vine stock. While these numbers guarantee the quality to which Enzo has accustomed us, they mean his stellar wines are sometimes impossible to find outside the pages of that year's wine guides. So little of his Refosco Vigna Calvari was made this year that there is barely enough for barrel sampling. We enjoyed Enzo's customarily magnificent Merlot. The '99 – in Buttrio, the wine-savvy whisper about a legendary red-stalked clone – could be summed up as "more of everything" but it deserves special mention for the way the fruit and spice come together and the elegant power in the mouth. The Tocai 2001 is also outstanding. Lingering aromas of rennet apple, elderflower and croissants are followed by balanced thrust on the soft, warm and eminently satisfying palate. A notch or two lower came the Sauvignon, which had to contend with a vintage when early ripening created problems for many growers. The aromas lack the crisp elegance of previous vintages. The balance of acidity and softness in the Ribolla 2001 is slightly off-key and the oak peeks through but the texture, as ever, is superbly mouthfilling.

○ COF Chardonnay '01	🍷🍷 6	● COF Merlot '99	🍷🍷🍷 8
○ COF Bianco Blanc di Buri '00	🍷🍷 5	○ COF Tocai Friulano '01	🍷🍷 7
○ COF Picolit '00	🍷🍷 8	○ COF Ribolla Gialla '01	🍷🍷 7
○ COF Tocai Friulano '00	🍷🍷 5	○ COF Sauvignon '01	🍷🍷 8
○ Verduzzo '00	🍷🍷 6	○ COF Tocai Friulano '00	🍷🍷🍷 7
○ COF Sauvignon '01	🍷🍷 5	○ COF Bianco '96	🍷🍷🍷 7
○ COF Tocai Friulano '01	🍷🍷 5	● COF Rosso '96	🍷🍷🍷 8
● COF Rosso Dominin '99	🍷🍷 7	○ COF Bianco '97	🍷🍷🍷 7
● COF Rosso Ros di Buri '00	🍷 6	● COF Rosso '97	🍷🍷🍷 8
○ COF Bianco Blanc di Buri '01	🍷 5	● COF Merlot '98	🍷🍷🍷 8
○ COF Picolit '99	🍷🍷 8	○ COF Tocai Friulano '98	🍷🍷🍷 7
○ COF Tocai Friulano '99	🍷🍷 5	○ COF Tocai Friulano '99	🍷🍷🍷 7
○ COF Bianco Blanc di Buri '99	🍷🍷 5		
● COF Rosso Ros di Buri '99	🍷🍷 6		
○ Verduzzo '99	🍷🍷 6		

BUTTRIO (UD)

PETRUCCO
VIA MORPURGO, 12
33042 BUTTRIO (UD)
TEL. 0432674387 - 04326238340
E-MAIL: agricola.petrucco@iocp.it

For the past 20 years or so, this estate in the hills of Buttrio has belonged to Paolo Petrucco and Lina Zoffi. This year, five new hectares of vines have brought the total area under vine to 25 hectares and average annual output is about 100,000 bottles, with whites accounting for about 70 per cent. The vineyards enjoy an enviable south-facing position with a marvellous view while the well-equipped cellar is worth a detour. However, the most impressive things about the estate are the clean taste and finesse of the wines, and the scrupulous work of technician Flavio Cabas, who has been supervising winemaking for a decade. Nothing is left to chance. The vines are cosseted, the grapes are picked by hand and vinification is exemplary. Unsurprisingly, the wines are very, very good indeed. The 2001 Ribolla Gialla, Pinot Grigio and Chardonnay all performed impeccably. The lustrous Ribolla is stylish, fresh and very varietal. The tanginess in the mouth brings out the wine's elegance and lingering notes of pears and apples. There are moderately intense notes of gunflint and ripe apples on the nose of the Pinot Grigio, then the fresh attack is followed up by curious sensations of citrus and decent breadth. A small proportion of the Chardonnay is cask-conditioned, producing a rich-textured wine with varietal hints of melon and banana. These are mirrored on the less than muscular palate, which has good length. Best of the One Glass wines is the 2001 Sauvignon.

○ COF Chardonnay '01	♟♟	4*
○ COF Pinot Grigio '01	♟♟	4*
○ COF Ribolla Gialla '01	♟♟	4*
● COF Refosco P. R. '00	♟	4
○ COF Sauvignon '01	♟	4
● COF Cabernet Franc '00		4
○ COF Tocai Friulano '01		4
○ COF Chardonnay '00	♟♟	4
● COF Merlot '99	♟	4

CAPRIVA DEL FRIULI (GO)

CASTELLO DI SPESSA
VIA SPESSA, 1
34070 CAPRIVA DEL FRIULI (GO)
TEL. 0481639914
E-MAIL: info@castellospessa.com

If the Capriva trough can be regarded as a Collio "grand cru", given its historical importance and the position of its vineyards, then the splendid Castello di Spessa is the subzone's "château". The estate, which commands a magnificent view over the countryside, was acquired in the 1980s by Loretto Pali. The 14th-century cellars are connected to a bunker 15 metres underground that was excavated in the 20th century. Today, it is the ideal place to keep barriques. Under the supervision of Lucia Luisa, the stables have been converted into a visitor hospitality area and shop for wine and other merchandise. The vineyard manager, Domenico Lovat, and cellar supremo, Alberto Pelos, are supported by the competent Andrea Pittana and there is a very special consultant, Gianni Menotti, a man who knows the Collio as well as anyone. Pali's team is unusually strong so it is hardly surprising that this year's results are excellent, starting with an astonishing Pinot Bianco 2001. Tempting nuances of pear and apple unfold on a palate of rare pervasiveness to convince you that the panel was right in awarding Three Glasses. The Sauvignon Segré 2001 has intense aromas of tomato leaf, elderflower, grapefruit and peach. It explodes onto the palate, following through surefootedly with vigorous rich fruit. The Collio Rosso Torriani '99 is a textbook Merlot. Complex and seriously good, it brims with warm, ripe berry fruit, lifted by grace notes of citrus. The Pinot Bianco di Santarosa 2000 shows confectioner's cream and golden delicious apple, charming you with its whistle-clean elegance.

○ Collio Pinot Bianco '01	♟♟♟	4*
○ Collio Pinot Bianco di Santarosa '00	♟♟	5
○ Collio Sauvignon Segré '01	♟♟	5
● Collio Rosso Torriani '99	♟♟	5
○ Collio Pinot Grigio '01	♟♟	4
○ Collio Ribolla Gialla '01	♟♟	4
○ Collio Sauvignon '01	♟♟	4
● Collio Rosso Conte di Spessa '99	♟♟	6
● Collio Pinot Nero Casanova '99	♟	5
○ Collio Pinot Bianco '97	♟♟♟	4
○ Collio Pinot Bianco '00	♟♟	4
● Collio Rosso Conte di Spessa '97	♟♟	6

CAPRIVA DEL FRIULI (GO)

PUIATTI
VIA AQUILEIA, 30
34070 CAPRIVA DEL FRIULI (GO)
TEL. 0481809922
E-MAIL: puiatti@puiatti.com

Giovanni and Elisabetta Puiatti, son and daughter of the great Vittorio, cultivate ten hectares in the Collio and 24 in the Isonzo DOC zone. They also buy in fruit from 60 or so small growers to turn out their roughly 700,000 bottles a year. It should be noted that, in recent years, production has increasingly concentrated on estate-grown grapes, which are a better bet if you're going for quality. As you browse the estate's literature and discuss winemaking with Giovanni Puiatti, you form the impression of a conservative winery that has remained faithful to the methods of the early 1980s. There is no maceration on the skins, little or no lees contact, malolactic fermentation is shunned and oak is regarded as an insult to the integrity of the fruit's - and the wine's - aromas. It's a philosophy that deserves respect, particularly when you remember that the results, especially for whites, are remarkably consistent, even though this year the big-scoring Two Glass products are missing. There's definitely room for improvement on the red front but a couple of the decently bottle-aged wines, the '99 Pinot Nero and Merlot del Collio, are already very attractive. But the best wine in the range is the Oltre Vittorio Puiatti '99, a white from pinot nero fruit that unveils tropical fruit and apple, elegance in the mouth and a touch of acidity that lends leanness. Finally, the ever-attractive Chardonnay del Collio 2001 flaunts varietal aromas of pear drops.

CAPRIVA DEL FRIULI (GO)

RONCÙS
VIA MAZZINI, 26
34070 CAPRIVA DEL FRIULI (GO)
TEL. 0481809349
E-MAIL: roncus@activeweb.it

There's important news at Roncùs, the winery started by Marco Perco in 1985. Gabriella De Marco joined the cellar in 2001 in a move to redistribute the workload and improve quality even further. The overall production philosophy is still the faithful interpretation of the territory and its vines, without altering the intrinsic nature of the wines. The bottles have now acquired new labels that feature, as well as the trademark walking figure, a detailed technical description of each wine, designed to satisfy the curiosity of interested winelovers. The outcome of our tastings was extremely positive, especially for the blended white Vecchie Vigne '99. This characterful wine came close to winning Three Glasses on its first showing. Produced in an attempt to create a personal version of an authentic terroir-driven wine, it is a mix of malvasia with small proportions of tocai and ribolla from vines that are more than 40 years old. After a year in large barrels and a further two ageing in stainless steel vats, Vecchie Vigne is shy at first. Then it regales the nose with aromas ranging from peach tart, mint and candied apricot to petit fours, which are echoed deliciously on the elegant palate. Also excellent are the 2001 Pinot Bianco, a fruit cocktail if ever there was one, and the merlot and cabernet franc-based Val di Miez '99, with its seriously chewy mouthfeel.

○	Oltre Vittorio Puiatti '99	🍷🍷	7
○	Collio Chardonnay Blanchis '01	🍷	5
○	Collio Pinot Grigio Blanchis '01	🍷	5
○	Collio Sauvignon Ruttars '01	🍷	5
○	Friuli Isonzo Pinot Grigio '01	🍷	4
○	Friuli Isonzo Chardonnay '01		3
○	Friuli Isonzo Tocai Friulano '01		3
●	Collio Merlot Blanchis '99		5
●	Collio Pinot Nero Ruttars '99		5

○	Roncùs Bianco Vecchie Vigne '99	🍷🍷	6
○	Collio Tocai Friulano '01	🍷🍷	5
○	Pinot Bianco '01	🍷🍷	5
○	Sauvignon '01	🍷🍷	5
●	Val di Miez '99	🍷🍷	6
○	Pinot Bianco '00	🍷🍷	5
●	Merlot '00	🍷🍷	5
○	Roncùs Bianco '00	🍷🍷	5
●	Val di Miez '97	🍷🍷	5
●	Merlot '99	🍷🍷	5

CAPRIVA DEL FRIULI (GO)

Russiz Superiore
Via Russiz, 7
34070 Capriva del Friuli (GO)
tel. 048199164 - 048180328
e-mail: info@marcofelluga.it

The 60 hectares of the Russiz Superiore estate lie in a superb growing area, as a glance at the names along the road to the winery will tell you. The property has always been the cutting edge of Marco Felluga's group, especially for whites but also for reds, as was again confirmed by the Rosso degli Orzoni. The '98 version of this cabernet and merlot blend is a major wine, its aristocratic nose disclosing bramble, roses, dried flowers and good progression in the mouth. But it was the whites that really impressed, which is not exactly news. For example, the Russiz Disôre 2000 is a heavenly blend that brings together the finesse of pinot bianco, the full, mellow body of tocai, the freshness of ribolla and the rich aromas of sauvignon in a wine of incomparable elegance. This outstanding white thrilled the judges at the final taste-offs and strolled away with Three Glasses. There were further good performances from the two Pinots, both fresh-tasting wines with stylish fruit and grassy notes (the Grigio is more minerally and the Bianco has more body), the Sauvignon, whose customary acidic vein is softened by pennyroyal and lemon grass, and the soft, classy, fresh-tasting Tocai. Only the two 2000 reds failed to come up to their usual standards, the Cabernet Franc being rather dilute and the Merlot lacking a little personality.

○	Collio Bianco Russiz Disôre '00	🍷🍷🍷	5
○	Collio Pinot Bianco '01	🍷🍷	4*
○	Collio Pinot Grigio '01	🍷🍷	4*
○	Collio Sauvignon '01	🍷🍷	4
○	Collio Tocai Friulano '01	🍷🍷	4
●	Collio Rosso Ris. degli Orzoni '98	🍷🍷	7
●	Collio Cabernet Franc '00	🍷	5
●	Collio Merlot '00	🍷	5
●	Collio Rosso Ris. degli Orzoni '94	🍷🍷🍷	7
○	Collio Sauvignon '98	🍷🍷🍷	4
○	Collio Tocai Friulano '99	🍷🍷🍷	4
○	Collio Bianco Russiz Disôre '99	🍷🍷	5
○	Collio Pinot Bianco '00	🍷🍷	4

CAPRIVA DEL FRIULI (GO)

★ Schiopetto
Via Palazzo Arcivescovile, 1
34070 Capriva del Friuli (GO)
tel. 048180332
e-mail: azienda@schiopetto.it

Sooner or later, it had to happen. Mario Schiopetto's incredible series of Three Glass prizes had to come to an end. Of course, the circumstance affords us no pleasure at all but we are sure that this great winery will soon again be trying to squeeze more top awards in the trophy cabinet. Despite health problems over the past few years, Mario has managed to keep a very close eye on everything that goes on at the estate. He is lucky to have such a close-knit, affectionate family, starting with his wife Gloria and their daughter Maria Angela, who looks after sales, and twins Giorgio and Carlo, in charge of the vineyards and cellar operations. There are 22 Schiopetto hectares in the Collio, all round the winery itself, and a further eight at Rosazzo, in the Colli Orientali del Friuli, on a property called Podere dei Blumeri. In the cellar, Stefano Menotti can call on consultant Donato Lanati. The panel loved the extraordinarily full-flavoured Tocai Friulano 2001, which has balance and a delicious vein of acidic freshness. The Blanc des Rosis 2001, a mix of tocai, pinot bianco, sauvignon and malvasia, is also spot on. Apple and citrus on the nose are followed by a well-structured, balanced palate. One of the finest Schiopetto products is the stylish Pinot Bianco Amrità 2000, a rich, lingering wine with concentrated fruit. Other Two Glass wines from the 2001 vintage are the Sauvignon Podere dei Blumeri, the Pinot Bianco and the Pinot Grigio, while the Collio Sauvignon is let down by assertive acidity.

○	Collio Tocai Friulano '01	🍷🍷	5
○	Blanc des Rosis '01	🍷🍷	5
○	Collio Pinot Bianco Amrità '00	🍷🍷	6
○	COF Sauvignon Podere dei Blumeri '01	🍷🍷	5
○	Collio Pinot Bianco '01	🍷🍷	5
○	Collio Pinot Grigio '01	🍷🍷	5
●	Collio Merlot '00	🍷	5
○	Collio Sauvignon Tarsia '00	🍷	6
○	Collio Tocai Friulano Pardes '00	🍷	6
○	Collio Sauvignon '01	🍷	5
○	Collio Pinot Bianco '00	🍷🍷🍷	5
○	Collio Pinot Bianco Amrità '97	🍷🍷🍷	6
○	COF Sauvignon Podere dei Blumeri '99	🍷🍷🍷	5

CAPRIVA DEL FRIULI (GO)

VIDUSSI GESTIONI AGRICOLE
VIA SPESSA, 18
34070 CAPRIVA DEL FRIULI (GO)
TEL. 048180072 - 045913399

The Montresor family owns an estate of the same name near Verona. Since acquiring the winery founded by Ferruccio Vidussi, they have shown that they are going for quality. The estate covers 25 hectares in the Collio, at Capriva and Pradis, and seven in the Colli Orientali near Ipplis. Production is in the hands of expert young oenologist Luigino De Giuseppe. The Ribolla Gialla 2001 Luigino has turned out is excellent. Gold-flecked straw yellow, it unveils rich, concentrated aromas of fruit, followed up by complex softness on the balanced palate. The Tocai Friulano Croce Alta has a complex nose, subtly nuanced with pear, but the well-sustained, lingering richness of the palate is even better. The deep, concentrated Collio Rosso Are di Miute 2000 is an oak-aged blend of merlot and cabernet franc. Plums and jam on the nose are complemented by a soft palate, mellow tannins and a long finish that signs off on a black cherry syrup after-aroma. The Malvasia 2001 is redolent of pears and golden delicious apples, then the fruit-driven palate finds just the balance of butteriness and tangy acidity. The faintly golden-hued Pinot Grigio flaunts intense tropical fruit then offers nice freshness in the mouth. The Chardonnay is more successful on the nose than in the mouth while the Pinot Bianco takes softness perhaps a shade too far. Best of the Colli Orientali wines by a span is the Schioppettino Troi dal Tas 2001, a rich medley of morello cherry, raspberry and forest floor.

● Collio Rosso Are di Miute '00	🍷🍷	5
○ Collio Ribolla Gialla '01	🍷🍷	4*
○ Collio Tocai Friulano Croce Alta '01	🍷🍷	4*
● COF Schioppettino Troi dal Tas '01	🍷	5
○ Collio Chardonnay '01	🍷	4
○ Collio Malvasia '01	🍷	4
○ Collio Pinot Bianco '01	🍷	4
○ Collio Pinot Grigio '01	🍷	4
○ COF Verduzzo '00		5
○ Collio Sauvignon '01		4

CAPRIVA DEL FRIULI (GO)

★ VILLA RUSSIZ
VIA RUSSIZ, 6
34070 CAPRIVA DEL FRIULI (GO)
TEL. 048180047
E-MAIL: villarussiz@villarussiz.it

Wines don't come much better than the Villa Russiz range. Marrying elegance and intensity on the nose with finesse, structure and generous fruit, they also pack an alcoholic punch that you sometimes fail to notice as you try to identify all the astonishing range of aromas. And there, in a nutshell, is the reason behind the incredible array of stemware below. It's all down to Gianni Menotti, of course, a winemaker who combines university training with an exceptional instinctive knowledge of when to make his move in the ageing cellar, and also precisely which vines are going to yield the fruit for the Gräfin, the Graf and the Sauvignon de La Tour. To be honest, the Pinot Bianco, Pinot Grigio and Tocai Friulano are very nearly as remarkable. Astonishingly good now, they will be even better three to five years after the harvest. The Gräfin de La Tour 2000 is a starry Chardonnay of incredible elegance, its butter-rich nose echoed on the broad, silky palate. It's a wine that puts subtlety before muscle power, and ends on a delicate minerally note. The Merlot Graf de La Tour '99 is back on the honours list. A nose of very ripe bramble, cherries and wild cherries mingles with autumn leaves, then the firm, but not aggressive, entry on the palate leads into a well-sustained mid palate that never wavers, ending in a lively fruit and tannin finish. The count (Graf) and countess (Gräfin) de La Tour were the last private proprietors of the estate, which now belongs to the publicly owned Cerruti charitable institute.

○ Collio Chardonnay Gräfin de La Tour '00	🍷🍷🍷	6
● Collio Merlot Graf de La Tour '99	🍷🍷🍷	7
○ Collio Pinot Bianco '01	🍷🍷	4*
○ Collio Pinot Grigio '01	🍷🍷	4*
○ Collio Sauvignon de La Tour '01	🍷🍷	6
○ Collio Tocai Friulano '01	🍷🍷	4*
● Collio Merlot '00	🍷🍷	5
○ Collio Malvasia Istriana '01	🍷🍷	4
○ Collio Sauvignon '01	🍷🍷	4
○ Collio Ribolla Gialla '01	🍷	4
○ Collio Riesling '01	🍷	4
○ Collio Sauvignon de La Tour '97	🍷🍷🍷	6
○ Collio Sauvignon de La Tour '98	🍷🍷🍷	6
○ Collio Sauvignon de La Tour '99	🍷🍷🍷	6

CARLINO (UD)

EMIRO CAV. BORTOLUSSO
VIA OLTREGORGO, 10
33050 CARLINO (UD)
TEL. 043167596
E-MAIL: bortolusso@bortolusso.it

There can be little doubt that this is the leading estate in the Annia DOC, the youngest Friulian zone, created in 1995 and embracing the municipal territories of Marano Lagunare, Carlino and Bagnaria Arsa. Sergio and Clara Bortolusso have the invaluable assistance of oenologist Luigino De Giuseppe and together, they have put the accent on quality. As a result, low yields, high planting densities and scrupulous canteen management have for years enabled them to release wines that can look products from more prestigious parts of Friuli straight in the eye. Although 60 per cent of their 38-hectare estate is planted to red varieties, the Bortolussis get most satisfaction from whites, particularly Pinot Grigio. Yields of around two and a half kilograms per vine give a sun-rich, Mediterranean-style nose of tempting citrus and fruit salad. Rich-textured, upfront and broad in the mouth, it signs off with an intriguingly long, fruity finish. Well up in the One Glass category was the Pinot Bianco, with its intense aromas of ripe fruit, and the Malvasia, which successfully offsets vegetal notes against aromatic and has a dry, lemony finish. The Merlot Privilege 2000, aged for a year in tonneaux, had a successful first run. Moderately complex on the nose, it proffers notes of cinnamon and wild berries.

○ Friuli Annia Pinot Grigio '01	¶¶	4*
● Friuli Annia Merlot Privilege '00	¶	5
○ Friuli Annia Malvasia '01	¶	4
○ Friuli Annia Pinot Bianco '01	¶	4
○ Friuli Annia Sauvignon '01	¶	4
○ Friuli Annia Tocai Friulano '01	¶	4
○ Friuli Annia Verduzzo Friulano '01		4
○ Friuli Annia Sauvignon '00	¶¶	4

CERVIGNANO DEL FRIULI (UD)

CA' BOLANI
VIA CA' BOLANI, 2
33052 CERVIGNANO DEL FRIULI (UD)
TEL. 043132670
E-MAIL: info@cabolani.it

When Gianni Zonin was honoured at the Three Glass presentation last year, he promised he would be making world-class wines in Friuli, too. He has kept his word. Credit should go to the ability of group oenologist Franco Giacosa, the team at the Aquileia DOC zone wineries – Ca' Bolani (95 hectares under vine), Ca' Vescovo (230 hectares) and Molin di Ponte (405 hectares, more than 230 planted to vine) – and the investments that the Zonin group has made. More than half of the vine stock has been replanted in the past four years, Casarsa training has been phased out, and vine density has been increased to more than 5,000 plants per hectare. Obviously, the quality of the fruit has improved steadily. The former Villa Antonini now has a room that houses over 500 barriques while the larger barrels and stainless steel tanks are in the cellars at Ca' Bolani. In fact, three Zonin wines made it to the final taste-offs, starting with a Sauvignon 2001, from the Gianni Zonin Vineyards range, that combines drinkability with firm aromas and good structure. The Refosco '99 from the same range is remarkably complex, admirably fusing fruit with tannins. The third big-time wine is the Opimio 2001, a 50-50 blend of chardonnay and tocai friulano that reveals muscle, richness and elegantly subtle aromas. Finally, there were Two full Glasses for the Conte Bolani Rosso '99, from 50 per cent merlot, cabernet sauvignon and refosco.

○ Friuli Aquileia Sauvignon Gianni Zonin Vineyards '01	¶¶	4*
○ Opimio Gianni Zonin Vineyards '01	¶¶	4*
● Friuli Aquileia Refosco P. R. Gianni Zonin Vineyards '99	¶¶	5
● Conte Bolani Rosso Gianni Zonin Vineyards '99	¶¶	6
● Friuli Aquileia Cabernet Franc '00	¶	3
○ Friuli Aquileia Pinot Grigio Gianni Zonin Vineyards '01	¶	4
○ Friuli Aquileia Tocai Friulano '01	¶	3
○ Friuli Aquileia Traminer Aromatico	¶	3

CIVIDALE DEL FRIULI (UD)

GIOVANNI CROSATO
VIA CASTELMONTE, 1
33040 CIVIDALE DEL FRIULI (UD)
TEL. 0432701462 - 0432730292
E-MAIL: info@vinicrosato.it

Husband and wife team Giovanni Crosato and Lucia Galasso seem to have found a more promising market profile, thanks to closer attention to the cellar, the vineyards and the price list. The couple own separate wineries but distribute their products jointly, also sharing warehousing facilities. The two cellars continue to be independent. Lucia has five hectares at Spessa, near Cividale, and Giovanni rents a slightly larger plot to the east of the same town. Both produce about 50,000 bottles, which they sell in Italy and abroad, even in France. Crosato uses micro-aeration of the warm must to give his wines longevity, although the procedure sacrifices some of the primary aromas. We especially liked Giovanni's Fumé Bianco 2001, a blend of pinot bianco and pinot grigio whose harvest delayed so long it almost qualifies as "late". Stylishly intense and complex on the nose, it shows rich, generous length on the palate, closing on a toasty note. The Pinot Grigio is another excellent wine that regales nose and palate with lavish fruit. The Bianco Don Giovanni 2001, a blend of tocai friulano, pinot bianco and sauvignon from Lucia Galasso, has creamy aromas of honey, banana and apricot, braced by refreshing, nicely judged acidity.

CIVIDALE DEL FRIULI (UD)

DAL FARI
LOC. GAGLIANO
VIA DARNAZZACCO, 20
33043 CIVIDALE DEL FRIULI (UD)
TEL. 0432731219 - 0432706726
E-MAIL: dalfari@faber-italy.com

A year ago, they were in the Other Wineries but this time, Laura and Renzo Toffolutti have earned a full profile. Laura is throwing herself heart and soul into the estate and probably deserves most of the credit for the rapid improvement in the quality the Dal Fari range. Still, when you remember that the Toffoluttis have 13 well-positioned hectares in the Cividale hills, a modern cellar strategically located in the middle of the estate, the input of expert consultant Fabio Coser and the competent Valentino Guidato on-site, you realize the deck is stacked in their favour. None of the Dal Fari wines disappointed and two, the blended Bianco delle Grazie and the Chardonnay Carato 2001, seriously impressed the panel. The former is a mix of chardonnay, sauvignon, tocai friulano and riesling renano, part aged in steel and part in barrique, that took full advantage of the warm summer in the year 2000. There is a nice balance of ripe fruit and oak on the nose, then the soft entry on the palate heralds long, lingering sensations of peach fruit. The Chardonnay is part fermented in new barriques and part in one-year-old barriques. A chorus of confectioner's cream, vanilla, banana and pineapple introduces a no-nonsense front palate that mirrors the nose. The long, fresh-tasting finish is very elegant. A Glass also went to the Tocai 2001, a selection from a very old vineyard, and the varietal, fruity Cabernet 2000.

○ Fumé Bianco '01	♟♟	4*
○ Pinot Grigio '01	♟♟	3*
○ Il Bianco Don Giovanni Lucia Galasso '01	♟	4
● Il Rosso Don Giovanni Lucia Galasso '99	♟	4
○ Chardonnay '01		3
● Il Rosso Don Giovanni Lucia Galasso '98	♟♟	4

○ COF Bianco delle Grazie '00	♟♟	4*
○ COF Chardonnay Carato '01	♟♟	4*
● COF Cabernet '00	♟	4
○ COF Tocai Friulano '01	♟	3
○ COF Pinot Grigio '01		4
○ COF Sauvignon '01		4
● COF Rosso d'Orsone '98		4

CIVIDALE DEL FRIULI (UD)

IL RONCAL
LOC. MONTEBELLO
VIA FORNALIS, 100
33043 CIVIDALE DEL FRIULI (UD)
TEL. 0432716156 - 0432730138
E-MAIL: ilroncal@tin.it

After years of hard work in cellar and vineyard, Roberto Zorzettig has at last earned a full Guide profile for his winery. It's a major step for the almost 40-year-old Roberto, who still has a lot of plans for the future. Founded in 1987, the estate now covers 20 hectares under vine, as well as a hectare of woodland around the attractive main buildings. The cellar has its own bottling line, stainless steel vats, large barrels and barriques, used according to the various vinification and ageing requirements of the vintage. Almost all the vines are old, except the chardonnay and pinot grigio, which were replanted in 1995 and 1996. A large number of varieties are grown and there are even more labels on the cellar list. As well as monovarietals, Zorzettig releases various blends. The best of these is the 2001 Ploe di Stelis (Friulian for "raining stars"), a blend of chardonnay, sauvignon and riesling vinified together. An elegant wine, its hints of flowers, apples and woodsmoke are irresistible. The Schioppettino 2001 is another bottle with attitude. Varietal notes of raspberry, blueberry and cherry tart complement the attractive body and firm, but not intrusive, tannins on the palate. Only a mark or two separated the Pignolo '99 from a second Glass. Reminiscent of merlot and cabernet fruit, it lacks a little balance in the mouth. The Cabernet Franc 2001 has lost the rustic notes of previous vintages and all the whites are impeccably well-made.

○	COF Bianco Ploe di Stelis '01	♉♉	4*
●	COF Schioppettino '01	♉♉	4*
●	COF Cabernet Franc '01	♉	4
○	COF Chardonnay '01	♉	4
○	COF Pinot Grigio '01	♉	4
○	COF Tocai Friulano '01	♉	4
●	COF Pignolo '99	♉	4
○	COF Sauvignon '01		4

CIVIDALE DEL FRIULI (UD)

DAVIDE MOSCHIONI
LOC. GAGLIANO
VIA DORIA, 30
33043 CIVIDALE DEL FRIULI (UD)
TEL. 0432730210

The Moschionis have always been a red wine family and whites are only marginal to the cellar's range. In fact, the only white left is the Picolit, a sweet wine of which only a few hundred bottles are released. Michele looks after the 11 hectares planted to vine and the cellar while his father, Davide, is in charge of the estate's other farming activities. Cropping levels are kept very low and after the harvest, Michele allows the fruit to raisin slightly in special rooms. As you can imagine, his wines are very concentrated and have significant dry extract. The high alcohol content comes in part from fermentation with ambient yeasts, whose alcohol resistance is under study by the University of Vienna. Yet despite all this muscle, Moschioni wines reveal their true varietal character. There is no denying that Michele knows how to make great wines from neglected local varieties like schioppettino, and even tazzelenghe. Tasting the 2000 wines, the panel noted the body, structure and rich fruit of the merlot and cabernet sauvignon-based Celtico, while the Reâl, released only in magnums, offered tazzelenghe-derived hints of blueberry, bramble and hay, in addition to typical merlot and cabernet sauvignon aromas. In the sour cherry, raspberry, plum and pomegranate Schioppettino, robust structure manages to keep the potent alcohol in check. Finally, the hints of raisining in the Pignolo still need to mellow but the wine is astonishingly well-sustained through to the back palate, with aristocratic, fruit-driven structure and great length.

●	COF Rosso Celtico '00	♉♉	6
●	COF Pignolo '00	♉♉	7
●	COF Rosso Reâl '00	♉♉	6
●	COF Schioppettino '00	♉♉	7
●	COF Pignolo '99	♉♉	7
●	COF Pignolo '96	♉♉	7
●	COF Rosso Celtico '99	♉♉	6
●	COF Schioppettino '99	♉♉	7
●	COF Pignolo '97	♉	7
●	COF Refosco P. R. '99	♉	6

CIVIDALE DEL FRIULI (UD)

Paolo Rodaro
Fraz. Spessa
Via Cormons, 8
33040 Cividale del Friuli (UD)
tel. 0432716066
e-mail: paolorodaro@yahoo.it

Paolo Rodaro's well-known winemaking skills led many to believe that his super '96 Sauvignon Bosc Romain would soon be followed by another Three Glass monster. But this time round, Paolo presented a breathtaking range of stunning wines that went beyond even our wildest hopes. His Ronc blend swept up Three Glasses and there were nearly another three for his traditional Tocai. Paolo's Refosco came equally close, despite his fame as a maker of whites. The reasons behind this success go beyond Paolo's skill and superb terroir. They are to be found in the commitment he has to his craft, a love that has prompted him to conserve in a nursery he owns (as you find out in the course of conversation), clones from endangered varieties. He is also endlessly striving to imbue his wines with new personality. His searches have yielded the 2000 Ronc and Refosco Romain. Mainly pinot bianco, with proportions of chardonnay and tocai, the Ronc remains on the yeasts in stainless steel and then matures briefly in the bottle. It intense, complex red delicious apple and almond aromas introduce a superbly balanced, almost austere palate that perfectly mirrors the nose. For the Refosco, like the Refoscone and the Merlot, Paolo allows the grapes to raisin for a month in the cellar. His Refosco shows strong, well-defined notes of spice, then a warm, powerful and undeniably hefty palate. The Tocai 2001 is an eye-catcher with its textbook apple and bitter almond typicity. We would also like to emphasize the generous palate of candied apricot, oranges and figs offered by the warm Picolit.

○ Ronc '00	♟♟♟	4*
● COF Refosco P. R. Romain '00	♟♟	7
○ COF Tocai Friulano '01	♟♟	4*
○ COF Picolit '00	♟♟	7
● COF Refoscone '00	♟♟	6
○ COF Pinot Bianco '01	♟♟	4
○ COF Verduzzo Friulano '01	♟♟	4
● COF Merlot Romain '00	♟	7
○ COF Pinot Grigio '01	♟	4
○ COF Sauvignon '01	♟	4
○ COF Sauvignon Bosc Romain '96	♟♟♟	5
○ COF Picolit '98	♟♟	7
○ COF Tocai Friulano '99	♟♟	4

CORMONS (GO)

Tenuta di Angoris
Loc. Angoris, 7
34071 Cormons (GO)
tel. 048160923
e-mail: angoris@tmedia.it

Claudia Locatelli has taken over from her father, Luciano, the family winery that embraces 130 hectares of vineyards in three DOC zones, the Colli Orientali, Collio and Isonzo. All the plots enjoy excellent positions but Tenuta di Angoris was conceived with quantity in mind. In fact, production currently runs at about 1,000,000 bottles a year sold under a large number of different labels. The estate selections, the Podere wines, Spìule and the refreshing house "spumante", Modolet, account for about 150,000 units all told. However, progressive replanting to modern criteria is set to ensure the quality improvements that will reward Claudia's hard work. For decades, the cellar has been in the capable hands of oenologist Natale Favretto, who has made a substantial contribution to the label's growth. Top of the range is the Bianco Spìule 2000, a blend of 70 per cent oak-aged chardonnay with 30 per cent sauvignon from the hillslopes of Rocca Bernarda. Elegant nuances of banana and apricot meld into well-judged wood, the structure is soft and the finish lingers. The Refosco 2001, from the same vineyards, merits a very full Glass. Barrel ageing for about a year has lent it attractive notes of sour cherry tart, autumn leaves and blueberries that are followed by a harmonious, full-bodied palate. The fruit for the Pinot Grigio Ronco Antico 2001, of which 20,000 bottles go to market, comes from the hills near Cormons.

○ COF Bianco Spìule '00	♟♟	4*
○ COF Picolit '01	♟	6
○ COF Pinot Grigio Podere Ronco Antico '01	♟	4
● COF Refosco P. R. Podere Stabili della Rocca '01	♟	4
○ COF Chardonnay Podere Stabili della Rocca '01	♟	4
○ COF Sauvignon Podere Stabili della Rocca '01		4
○ COF Bianco Spìule '99	♟♟	4

CORMONS (GO)

Borgo del Tiglio
Loc. Brazzano
Via San Giorgio, 71
34070 Cormons (GO)
tel. 048162166

There was another great performance from Borgo del Tiglio. Yet again, the finest results at our tastings were achieved by wines from the plots that the estate analysed thoroughly after purchase to identify the optimum combination of soil, vine type and viticultural techniques. And again, the first prize goes to a Chardonnay, a "second-label" (never was a term less appropriate) with respect to the vineyard selection. It is more elegant, fresher and drinking better than its big brother, although it should be said that Nicola Manferrari's bottles have a way of evolving successfully over time, and the sensory characteristics of the wine often change significantly for the better. This will almost certainly be the case with the Studio di Bianco 2000, which is something a challenge to the received wisdom of winemaking. It dares to combine aromatic profiles – those of sauvignon and riesling – that are often held to be incompatible. But the results yielded by the riesling, usually thought to be unsuited to oak ageing, are intriguing for it finds a magical match in the power of the blend's tocai. The monovarietal Tocai, now called Ronco della Chiesa in line with new regulations, also performed creditably, thanks especially to an impressive palate. In fact, Nicola's wines are nearly always more convincing in the mouth than on the nose when uncorked so select a glass that will allow them to aerate. The 2000 Ronco della Chiesa has plenty of thrust on the alcohol-rich, pervasive palate, offering a refreshing hint of fruit and an attractively sustained bitterish note.

	Wine	Rating	Score
O	Collio Chardonnay '00	🍷🍷🍷	5
O	Collio Bianco Ronco della Chiesa '00	🍷🍷	6
O	Collio Studio di Bianco '00	🍷🍷	6
O	Collio Chardonnay Sel. '00	🍷🍷	6
O	Collio Tocai Friulano '00	🍷🍷	5
●	Collio Rosso Ris. '97	🍷🍷	6
O	Collio Tocai Ronco della Chiesa '90	🍷🍷🍷	6
O	Collio Chardonnay Sel. '99	🍷🍷🍷	6
●	Collio Rosso della Centa '96	🍷🍷	6
O	Collio Malvasia Sel. '99	🍷🍷	6
●	Collio Rosso Ris. '96	🍷🍷	6
O	Collio Chardonnay '99	🍷🍷	5

CORMONS (GO)

Borgo San Daniele
Via San Daniele, 16
34071 Cormons (GO)
tel. 048160552
e-mail: borgosandaniele@tin.it

Brother and sister Mauro and Alessandra Mauri are young, enthusiastic growers who respect their territory and are always keen to learn. Their love of innovation is instinctive, and not the superficial kind so many others affect. One example is their decision to concentrate on four wine types to bring out the features of the terroir with the help of some very personal technical solutions. Their 16 hectares produce about 40,000 bottles of distinctively subtle wines that put finesse first. The Tocai 2001 just missed out on Three Glasses. The grapes were harvested in three selections to enhance complexity: the first when the fruit was ripe, the second slightly late and the third when the berries were verging on super-ripeness. The wine, aged in large barrels, is sun-rich and very elegant, the distinct aromas of tropical fruit, citrus and ripe melon faithfully mirrored on the well-sustained palate, where there are also pleasant hints of hedgerow. The Arbis Blanc 2001 is a blend of sauvignon, chardonnay, pinot bianco and tocai that mingles pear and apple salad with peaches in syrup. The full-bodied yet discreet palate has excellent structure, decent pressure and fragrant aromas of orange peel and wild roses. The wonderfully subtle Pinot Grigio 2001's aromas of fruit and spring flowers are emphatically echoed on the palate, where the varietal minerally note comes through strongly. Finally, the red Arbis 2000, a blend of pignolo, cabernet sauvignon and cabernet franc, nearly earned a second Glass but lost a mark or two for a slight lack of balance, which should disappear.

	Wine	Rating	Score
O	Friuli Isonzo Tocai Friulano '01	🍷🍷	4*
O	Friuli Isonzo Arbis Blanc '01	🍷🍷	5
O	Friuli Isonzo Pinot Grigio '01	🍷🍷	4*
●	Arbis Rosso '00	🍷	5
O	Friuli Isonzo Tocai Friulano '97	🍷🍷🍷	4
O	Friuli Isonzo Pinot Grigio '99	🍷🍷🍷	4
O	Friuli Isonzo Pinot Grigio '00	🍷🍷	4
●	Gortmarin '97	🍷🍷	5
O	Friuli Isonzo Arbis Blanc '99	🍷🍷	5
O	Friuli Isonzo Tocai Friulano '99	🍷🍷	4

CORMONS (GO)

Branko - Igor Erzetic
Loc. Zegla, 20
34071 Cormons (GO)
tel. 0481639826

It's been a few years since Branko Erzretic handed over to his son Igor, a wine technician who never fails to astonish us with his range. The winery has six hectares, four estate-owned, vine density is around 5,500 plants per hectare and cropping levels are kept low. The compact cellar is located between Novali and Zegla, two of the finest subzones around Cormons, and there is a fine selection of wood in the cellar, as well as stainless steel tanks. The proportion of each wine that is cask-conditioned varies. Only the Chardonnay and the Merlot, which is due for release next year, are entirely oaked but Igor's skill is such that you would hardly guess any of the wines had ever seen a barrel. Production of the '98 wines was 10,000 bottles whereas the 2001 vintage has reached a figure of 30,000. Three of the four wines presented went through to our taste-offs, which speaks volumes for the depth of quality at the cellar. All show superb nose-palate consistency, rich, fruit-driven aromas and exceptional structure in the mouth. If that weren't enough, Igor knows how to marry refreshing acidity and glycerine sweetness into a mouthfeel that is pervasive and yet spontaneous. The Tocai is rich, concentrated and long. The same can be said for the Pinot Grigio, which is an amazingly complex example of the variety. Elegant notes of peach and apricots crown a Sauvignon that couldn't be more full-bodied. Last on the list is the Chardonnay, a riot of ripe fruit on both nose and palate.

CORMONS (GO)

Maurizio Buzzinelli
Loc. Pradis, 20
34071 Cormons (GO)
tel. 0481160902
e-mail: buzzinelli@libero.it

Visitors to this cellar are struck by how hospitable the Buzzinelli family is. Don't think you can get away with a glass of wine. There'll be a slice of salami, or ham, or perhaps some cheese - Gigi is a prodigal host. His son, 30-year-old Maurizio, makes the wines. It always takes time to improve the quality of a range and Maurizio, who has to make do with a cellar that is now distinctly insufficient for his needs, is no exception. Every year, his wines are the product of new effort and experiment, based on the results of the previous vintage. The decision to release the oak-aged wines, from the Ronc dal Luis range, only when they are ready to uncork seems to have been confirmed. That's why the only Ronc dal Luis-label wine available is the 2001 Collio Bianco Frututis ("little girls"). Obtained mainly from tocai friulano, it also has a small proportion of malvasia, both aged in oak, and one third stainless steel vinified sauvignon. Its aromas range from green apples to spring flowers laced with aromatic herbs and the mouthfeel is so firm it is almost chewy, despite the perky freshness. The Tocai is better on the nose, where there are crisp hints of pear and dried flowers, than it is in the mouth. Pale flecks of copper in the Pinot Grigio tell you it was macerated on the skins briefly, then citrus and fresh fruit salad aromas emerge.

○ Collio Pinot Grigio '01	4*
○ Collio Sauvignon '01	4*
○ Collio Tocai Friulano '01	4*
○ Collio Chardonnay '01	4
○ Collio Chardonnay '00	4
○ Collio Tocai Friulano '00	4

○ Collio Bianco Frututis Ronc dal Luis '01	5
○ Collio Pinot Grigio '01	3*
○ Collio Tocai Friulano '01	3*
○ Collio Chardonnay '01	3
○ Collio Pinot Bianco '01	3
○ Collio Bianco Frututis Ronc dal Luis '00	5
○ Collio Malvasia Istriana Frututis Ronc dal Luis '00	5
● Collio Rosso Frututis Ronc dal Luis '00	5

CORMONS (GO)

PAOLO CACCESE
LOC. PRADIS, 6
34071 CORMONS (GO)
TEL. 048161062
E-MAIL: info@paolocaccese.com

Paolo Caccese's "simpatia" is an essential feature of his approach to work, as well as to other people. His six hectares are all near the cellar on the oenologically outstanding hill at Pradis. It's the ideal environment for anyone who wants to keep things on a family scale, with only occasional help from outside. At Paolo's estate, everything is perfectly proportioned, from the cellars to the technology that is indispensable to premium quality. We continue to marvel at the number of labels presented but if you're working with small quantities, then you need to have a very special relationship with each of your customers. How can you refuse a Traminer Aromatico or a Riesling or a Müller Thurgau to a customer who is also a good friend? It should also be said that, while the first two mentioned are only acceptable, Paolo makes one of the finest Müller Thurgaus in Friuli, a fresh-tasting, stylish wine with nice apple on the nose. Pradis is an excellent area for Pinot Bianco and the Caccese version won a Glass for its delicate apple aromas, layered with lemony nuances on the back palate. The Pinot Grigio has concentrated fruit and the Malvasia is strikingly harmonious and fresh-tasting, although it is less concentrated than last year's edition. We've left the best till last. Paolo's Tocai Friulano is high-scoring, firm-bodied winner with a rich, seamlessly sustained palate.

○	Collio Tocai Friulano '01	▼▼	4*
○	Collio Malvasia '01	▼	4
○	Collio Müller Thurgau '01	▼	4
○	Collio Pinot Bianco '01	▼	4
○	Collio Pinot Grigio '01	▼	4
○	Collio Traminer Aromatico '01		4
○	La Veronica '99		6
○	Collio Malvasia '00	▼▼	4

CORMONS (GO)

CANTINA PRODUTTORI DI CORMONS
VIA VINO DELLA PACE, 31
34071 CORMONS (GO)
TEL. 048162471 - 048160579
E-MAIL: info@cormons.com

What are tyrosol, quercetin, resveratrol and caffeic acid? Let's take a step back for a moment. This co-operative winery is one of the area's most important producers, and not just for its sheer volume of wine. It has more than 200 members, who cultivate about 400 hectares to vine, and a storage capacity of more than 50,000 hectolitres. There are about 50 labels on the list, of which we tasted 17, but, thanks to the efforts of director Luigi Soini, the Cantina Produttori di Cormons is also a major vehicle for information and wine-related culture, to members and non-members alike. Eighty per cent of the area under vine is farmed organically, the winery has its own weather service and members must adhere to rigid rules, including manual harvesting. The crop is assessed on quality and, of course, the co-operative tends the legendary Vigna del Mondo plot, which since 1999 has yielded the admirable Vino della Pace. Only a winery as complete as this could tackle the subject of the antioxidants mentioned at the beginning of this profile. Much healthier than their unpromising names might suggest, antioxidants are the focus of a research programme into their presence in white wines that has already ruffled the calm waters of academe and interested government institutions. There's more good news on the wine front. We liked the fragrant Malvasia, the Sauvignon and the Tocai in both its Collio version and the Isonzo edition, but the range is a big one and our space is, sadly, limited.

○	Collio Malvasia Istriana '01	▼▼	3*
○	Collio Tocai Friulano '01	▼▼	3*
○	Collio Bianco '01	▼	4
○	Collio Chardonnay '01	▼	4
○	Collio Pinot Grigio '01	▼	4
○	Collio Sauvignon '01	▼	4
○	Collio Traminer '01	▼	4
○	Friuli Isonzo Bianco Pietra Verde '01	▼	3
○	Friuli Isonzo Sauvignon '01	▼	3
○	Friuli Isonzo Tocai Friulano '01	▼	3
○	Vino della Pace '99	▼	6
●	Aquileia Refosco P. R. '00		4
●	Collio Cabernet Franc '00		4
○	Friuli Isonzo Verduzzo Dorè '01		4

CORMONS (GO)

CARLO DI PRADIS
LOC. PRADIS, 22/BIS
34071 CORMONS (GO)
TEL. 048162272
E-MAIL: carlodipradis@tin.it

Boris and David Buzzinelli are genial and professional, running the estate they took over from their father, Carlo, a few years ago with admirable enthusiasm. As a tribute to their father, the pair have renamed the property, which is now called Carlo di Pradis. And it is at Pradis, one of the areas around Cormons where it would be easiest to identify small, "cru"-style vineyards, that the brothers have built their new cellar. A relatively large construction, the new facility will ensure ample space for working and storage. Currently, the property includes about 12 hectares under vine, equally distributed between the flatlands of the Isonzo DOC zone and the hillslopes of the Collio, near the cellar. To make sure this distinction is reflected on the wine merchant's shelf, the Buzzinellis release the Isonzo bottles under the readily identifiable BorDavi label. Once again, the Collio Merlot – the '99 this time – scored highest. It's a very attractive red with intense, ripe raspberry and plum, concentrated on both the nose and the substantial, but not cumbersome, palate. The creamy, fresh, richly harmonious Collio Bianco Pradis 2000, from tocai, malvasia, pinot bianco and sauvignon, also effortlessly picked up a second Glass. A full Glass went to the mainly cabernet sauvignon BorDavi '99 again, and to the Chardonnay BorDavi 2001.

○ Collio Bianco Pradis '00	▼▼	4*
● Collio Merlot '99	▼▼	5
● Friuli Isonzo Cabernet BorDavi '00	▼	4
○ Fruili Isonzo Chardonnay BorDavi '01	▼	4
● Friuli Isonzo Rosso BorDavi '99	▼	4
○ Friuli Isonzo Pinot Grigio BorDavi '00		4
○ Collio Pinot Grigio '01		4
○ Collio Tocai Friulano '01		4
● Collio Merlot '97	▼▼	5
● Collio Merlot '98	▼▼	5

CORMONS (GO)

COLLE DUGA
LOC. ZEGLA, 10
34071 CORMONS (GO)
TEL. 048161177

Damian Princic is one of the most exciting emerging producers in the Collio. We've been following his progress for years. He and his father, Luciano, cultivate about seven hectares, almost all sited around their home-cum-cellar. There's a curious detail. Visitors to the property should take care not to cross the estate's boundary because they would find themselves in Slovenia. Only a small, easily overlooked, stone marks the frontier that crosses the unsurfaced road. Years ago, it might have been dangerous to go past but these days, you'd merely get a warning and an invitation to return to the Italian side. Colle Duga turned out 18,000 bottles from the last vintage, after scrupulous selection in the cellar. For the first time, a broad, well-structured Pinot Grigio with good fruit was released under the estate's own label. The Chardonnay 2001 has typical yeast and crusty bread aromas that nearly won it a second Glass and another very full Glass went to the Collio Bianco, a blend of chardonnay, tocai and sauvignon. The big surprise was the Merlot 2000. Youthful tannins cannot mask the amazing structure, fullness and luscious mouthfeel that augur well for the future. To top it all, the Tocai 2001 was also a candidate for a third Glass. Stunningly complex, it combines elegance, broad fruit, freshness and seamless continuity, signing off with a delightfully long finish.

● Collio Merlot '00	▼▼	4*
○ Collio Tocai Friulano '01	▼▼	4*
○ Collio Pinot Grigio '01	▼▼	4
○ Collio Bianco '01	▼	4
○ Collio Chardonnay '01	▼	4
○ Collio Bianco '00	▼▼	4
○ Collio Chardonnay '00	▼▼	4
○ Collio Tocai Friulano '00	▼▼	4

CORMONS (GO)

Mauro Drius
Via Filanda, 100
34071 Cormons (GO)
tel. 048160998

Work on modernizing and extending the cellar is complete but nothing has changed. Mauro Drius still takes a craft approach to winemaking, tending his 11 hectares in the Collio and Isonzo DOC zones and releasing sophisticated premium wines that reflect his increasing maturity as a grower-producer. This year, the traditionally excellent Pinot Bianco is joined by a better than ever Merlot selection from vines that are coming to the peak of their productive life. The time and effort that Mauro has recently been putting into making reds probably also has something to do with it. The Pinot Bianco 2001 follows in the footsteps of the previous vintage. The lustrous hue introduces varietal notes of crusty bread and apple, then the rich, elegant palate has balance and a finesse lifted by lingering hints of red delicious apple in the after-aroma. The Merlot 2000 unveils luscious figs, dates, liqueur cherries and petit fours, mirrored on a well-braced palate that could do with a tad more punch. Both 2001 Tocais scored well. The Collio came out on top, mainly for the elegance and breadth of the palate and its leisurely apple and almond-laced finish, while the Isonzo is softer in the mouth. The typicity of the Pinot Grigio 2001 emerges strongly in pear, gunflint and dried flower aromas on the nose and on the palate, where they are enhanced by nuances of citrus.

O	Friuli Isonzo Pinot Bianco '01	♈♈	4*
●	Friuli Isonzo Merlot '00	♈♈	4
O	Collio Sauvignon '01	♈♈	4
O	Collio Tocai Friulano '01	♈♈	4
O	Friuli Isonzo Pinot Grigio '01	♈♈	4
O	Friuli Isonzo Tocai Friulano '01	♈♈	4
O	Friuli Isonzo Bianco Vignis di Sìris '01	♈	4
O	Friuli Isonzo Malvasia '01	♈	4
O	Friuli Isonzo Riesling '01	♈	4
●	Friuli Isonzo Cabernet '00		4
O	Friuli Isonzo Pinot Bianco '00	♈♈♈	4

CORMONS (GO)

★ Livio Felluga
Fraz. Brazzano
Via Risorgimento, 1
34070 Cormons (GO)
tel. 048160203
e-mail: info@liviofelluga.it

A quick glance at the Glasses below will tell you just how good the range from Livio Felluga is. The patriarch of Friulian winemaking has created an estate whose dimensions – 135 hectares planted to vine yielding 650,000 bottles a year – and consistent quality – yet another Three Glass monster and a string of Two or Two and a Half Glass wines – confirm his awesome status. All Livio's children are active in the winery with well-defined roles. Maurizio, Elda, Andrea and Filippo make up a efficient team that work smoothly in concert under the supervision of the great man himself. Despite its enormous production potential, the cellar restricts both the number of bottles and the list of labels. Now, there are only 11 names on the list, which is surprisingly low for Friuli. A truly magnificent '99 Refosco confirms all the quality that Livio is able to transmit to this native variety. Concentrated fruit laced with spice and a discreet tannic weave hint that this is a wine that will get even better with a few years' cellar time. The Terre Alte 2000 is back on top form. Creamy and complex, it marries citrus and a medley of fruit with oak that is barely hinted at. Sossò is from merlot that is now blended with a little refosco. Today, it adds complexity to the ageing potential of previous vintages (uncork a 1990 Sossò: it's still incredibly good). Finally, we weren't expecting quite such elegance and breadth from the first release of the Collio Bianco, a mix of chardonnay and sauvignon.

●	COF Refosco P. R. '99	♈♈♈	7
O	COF Rosazzo Bianco Terre Alte '00	♈♈	6
●	COF Rosazzo Sossò Ris. '99	♈♈	7
O	COF Bianco Illivio '00	♈♈	6
●	Vertigo '00	♈♈	4*
O	COF Pinot Grigio '01	♈♈	4*
O	COF Tocai Friulano '01	♈♈	5
O	Collio Bianco '01	♈♈	4*
O	COF Rosazzo Picolit Ris. '98	♈♈	8
O	COF Sauvignon '01	♈	4
O	Shàrjs '01	♈	4
●	COF Refosco P. R. '97	♈♈♈	6
O	COF Rosazzo Bianco Terre Alte '97	♈♈♈	6

CORMONS (GO)

Edi Keber
Loc. Zegla, 17
34071 Cormons (GO)
tel. 048161184

Bad weather posed more than a few problems this year for Edi Keber, the excellent Cormons-based grower-producer who for years has been ruthlessly "pruning" the number of labels on his list. Indeed nowadays, Edi only offers a Tocai Friulano, a Bianco, a Rosso and – if he thinks the vintage is good enough – a Merlot. His beautifully tended vineyards cover eight hectares, almost all around his home, and the cellar, which is connected to the house by a tunnel, features the cosiest of country-style tasting rooms. Edi's flagship Tocai Friulano is a classic and again took Three Glasses. Not as concentrated in the glass as other vintages, it offers intense, stylish aromas of apple and nettle, then the palate progresses surefootedly, signing off with a deep, endlessly protracted finish. There's plenty of complexity in the Merlot 2000. Concentrated fruit follows through from nose to a compact, well-sustained palate that never wavers. The elegant, fruity Collio Bianco 2001 comes from tocai, malvasia, ribolla, pinot grigio, pinot bianco and sauvignon. Green apple is the keynote and the only defect is a slightly one-dimensional finish. The upfront, merlot and cabernet franc-based, Collio Rosso 2001 was hit by rain at harvest time. Only moderately intense in hue, it has sweet, fruity aromas that are mirrored on the nicely tannic and eminently drinkable palate.

CORMONS (GO)

La Boatina
Via Corona, 62
34076 Cormons (GO)
tel. 048160445 - 0481639914
e-mail: info@boatina.com

The wind of change that has brought significant quality improvements to Castello di Spessa has also been blowing through La Boatina, Loretto Pali's other estate. Some of the property's main buildings have been restructured and converted into a luxury "agriturismo" farm holiday centre, deep in the greenery, and further investment has been made in the vineyards. There is now a very modern 36-hectare vineyard in the Isonzo DOC zone. Recently, the winery has also taken on those acknowledged experts of the vine, Marco Simonit, Andrea Pittana and Pierpaolo Sirch, as consultants. Vineyards and cellar are now cutting-edge stuff so the next step, we humbly submit, could be to reduce the number of labels released, currently more than ten. The best bottle this year was the Sauvignon 2001. Its concentrated elegance is redolent of elderflower and tomato leaf, then the tangy, rich palate wins your heart with its structure and length. Two reds were close behind. The Cabernet Sauvignon 2000 is a lovely dark ruby red. On the nose, complexity combines with elegance in warm notes of cherry and plum, then comes a rich, chewy palate. It's a full-bodied wine that will improve with age. The Merlot 2000 is straight out of the textbook. The nose of wild berry tart and plums is followed by a lavishly fruity entry on the well-structured palate, and a faintly tannic finish. Finally the Collio Bianco Pertè 2000 missed a second Glass because over-emphatic oak masks the tobacco and broad fruit aromas.

○ Collio Tocai Friulano '01	🍷🍷🍷	4*
● Collio Merlot '00	🍷🍷	5
○ Collio Bianco '01	🍷	4
● Collio Rosso '01	🍷	5
○ Collio Tocai Friulano '95	🍷🍷🍷	4
○ Collio Tocai Friulano '97	🍷🍷🍷	4
○ Collio Tocai Friulano '99	🍷🍷🍷	4
○ Collio Bianco '00	🍷🍷	4
○ Collio Tocai Friulano '00	🍷🍷	4

● Collio Cabernet Sauvignon '00	🍷🍷	4*
○ Collio Sauvignon '01	🍷🍷	4*
● Collio Merlot '00	🍷🍷	4
○ Collio Bianco Pertè '00	🍷	5
○ Collio Chardonnay '01	🍷	4
○ Collio Pinot Bianco '01	🍷	4
○ Collio Pinot Grigio '01	🍷	4
○ Collio Ribolla Gialla '01	🍷	4
○ Collio Tocai Friulano '01	🍷	4
● Collio Rosso Picol Maggiore '98		5

CORMONS (GO)

MAGNÀS
VIA CORONA, 47
34071 CORMONS (GO)
TEL. 048160991

CORMONS (GO)

ROBERTO PICECH - LE VIGNE DEL RIBÉL
LOC. PRADIS, 11
34071 CORMONS (GO)
TEL. 048160347
E-MAIL: picech@libero.it

Luciano Visintin is know to one and all as "Magnàs". With son Andrea and wife Sonia, he runs an estate that includes a superb, newly opened "agriturismo" accommodation and a cellar. The old country house now has three bedrooms and two studio flats. Magnàs breeds cattle and pigs – his "pancetta" (belly pork) is legendary – and has decided to give Andrea free rein on the estate's eight hectares under vine, from which the family obtains 20,000 bottles a year. There's plenty of space in the cellar, although on occasion the various kinds of winemaking equipment get in the way of each other. Still, the increased attention to wine was clear from our tasting, when there was a distinct overall improvement in the range. The 2001 vintage brought a crusty bread and pineapple Chardonnay with nice nose-palate consistency, backed up a creamy texture, full body and a long, well-sustained finish. The Pinot Grigio shows good depth of intense fruit, in fact it's so rich and concentrated you would think it had been in oak. It hasn't. The elegant nose of the Sauvignon ushers in a full, glycerine-rich palate. Attractive elderflower emerges, especially in the after-aroma. The Pinot Bianco just missed out on a second Glass but its fresh acidity augurs well for the future.

It's been an excellent year for Roberto Picech, the extremely competent grower-producer whose five-hectare, Pradis-based winery turns out about 20,000 bottles a year. In line with the scale of the winery itself, the cellar is compact but there is enough space to vinify the fruit, age some of the wines in oak and store the bottles until they are ready to be released onto the market. The Pinot Bianco 2001 is a thoroughbred, but we knew that. Elegant, concentrated and full-flavoured, it crashes onto the palate, unfurling a complexity that never wavers. The Collio Rosso Riserva '99 was marked down for a volatile note in the nose that mingles with the attractive jam. The fruit-rich, softly lingering palate has admirable structure and density. The Malvasia 2001 flaunts intense fruit, then good breadth on the rich, slightly salty, palate. What you notice about the Collio Rosso 2001 is the ripe fruit on nose and palate, then there are rather hardish tannins in the finish. Intense fruit - this time mainly pear and peach - comes through on the Tocai Friulano 2001, a full-flavoured, fruity wine with a stylish twist of bitter almond in the after-aroma. It wasn't such a good year for the Bianco Jelka (Jelka is the Slovene version of "Gabriella", Roberto's mother's name). Roast coffee and over-generous oak dominate the aromas.

○ Friuli Isonzo Chardonnay '01	🍷🍷	4*
○ Friuli Isonzo Pinot Grigio '01	🍷🍷	4*
○ Friuli Isonzo Sauvignon '01	🍷🍷	4*
○ Friuli Isonzo Pinot Bianco '01	🍷	4
○ Friuli Isonzo Tocai Friulano '01		4

○ Collio Pinot Bianco '01	🍷🍷	4*
○ Collio Malvasia '01	🍷🍷	4
● Collio Rosso '01	🍷🍷	4
○ Collio Tocai Friulano '01	🍷🍷	4
● Collio Rosso Ris. '99	🍷🍷	6
○ Collio Bianco Jelka '01	🍷	4
○ Collio Bianco Jelka '99	🍷🍷🍷	4
○ Collio Bianco Jelka '00	🍷🍷	4
● Collio Rosso Ris. '97	🍷🍷	6

CORMONS (GO)

Ferdinando e Aldo Polencic
Loc. Plessiva, 13
34071 Cormons (GO)
tel. 048161027

CORMONS (GO)

Isidoro Polencic
Loc. Plessiva, 12
34071 Cormons (GO)
tel. 048160655

There was a marvellous performance from father and son team, Ferdinando and Aldo Polencic, whose winery was founded about 30 years ago. From their seven hectares in the Collio DOC zone, the pair obtain 20,000 bottles a year. The recent vintage is further confirmation of the quality improvements that have been made in past years. There were four wines waiting for the panel. All scored more than 80 points and one made the final taste-offs. The Pinot Bianco degli Ulivi 2000, the cellar's flagship wine, is a big hitter. Obtained from just over one hectare of 33-year-old vines, it is, to all intents and purposes, a "cru" to which barrique and tonneau ageing lend elegance. The golden hue introduces very ripe fruit, banana and fresh-baked bread that are echoed on the vanilla-kissed palate, which signs off with milky and yeasty nuances. We loved the depth and seamless consistency of the Pinot Grigio 2001, with its irresistible fruit-driven nose and elegant buttery texture in the mouth. The sunny Tocai Friulano 2001 is one for the cellar. Its fruit and confectioner's cream nose is faintly nuanced by oak-derived aromas, then the generously rich palate has a delicious chewiness. Finally, the Sauvignon impresses with its tobacco and coffee, before the elegant palate reveals a rich vein of fruit, signing off with panache.

The Polencic family has been growing grapes in the Collio for decades. Continuity is now assured with the successful handover from father Isidoro to children Michele and Elisabetta, who have 22 hectares planted to vine in the local DOC and a few vines in the Isonzo zone. This year, six out of nine wines tasted earned a second Glass, which gives you an idea of how reliable the cellar is. The elegant but concentrated aromas of pear and apple on the nose of the Tocai Friulano 2001 are echoed on the palate, which is backed up by good acidic grip. The Sauvignon is surefooted, its elderflower and tomato leaf introducing satisfying depth on the generous palate. The Pinot Grigio is creamy and stylish, unfurling fresh apple aromas and a long, long palate with plenty of fruit. The chardonnay-based Oblin Blanc 2000 has smaller proportions of sauvignon and ribolla. Its complex sensations of fruit and confectioner's cream stay well on top of the aromas that derive from oak ageing. The other blend is a Collio Bianco 2001. Elegant on the nose, where generous fruit melds with subtle vanilla, it shows good complexity and length while maintaining unwavering pressure in the mouth. The intriguing fruit of the Pinot Bianco follows through well in the mouth, its concentration lifted by a well-gauged balance of buttery richness and fresh acidity. Finally, the Oblin Ros '99 blend, whose strong suit is a black cherry palate, just missed out on Two Glasses.

O	Collio Pinot Bianco degli Ulivi '00	ỸỸ	5
O	Collio Pinot Grigio '01	ỸỸ	4
O	Collio Sauvignon '01	ỸỸ	4
O	Collio Tocai Friulano '01	ỸỸ	4
O	Collio Tocai Friulano '00	ỸỸỸ	4
O	Collio Pinot Bianco degli Ulivi '99	ỸỸ	5

O	Oblin Blanc '00	ỸỸ	5
O	Collio Bianco '01	ỸỸ	4
O	Collio Pinot Bianco '01	ỸỸ	4
O	Collio Pinot Grigio '01	ỸỸ	4
O	Collio Sauvignon '01	ỸỸ	4
O	Collio Tocai Friulano '01	ỸỸ	4
O	Collio Chardonnay '01	Ỹ	4
O	Collio Ribolla Gialla '01	Ỹ	4
●	Oblin Ros '99	Ỹ	5
O	Collio Pinot Grigio '98	ỸỸỸ	4
O	Oblin Blanc '99	ỸỸ	5

CORMONS (GO)

Alessandro Princic
Loc. Pradis, 5
34071 Cormons (GO)
tel. 048160723
e-mail: prcarl@libero.it

It would be impossible to write about Sandro Princic without mentioning his father, Doro (now over 90), who was for decades a benchmark producer of premium wines in the Cormons area. Doro is beginning to feel the weight of his years but still has an amazingly sensitive nose that can distinguish a fine wine from a poor one at a single sniff. Sandro is also fortunate enough to be assisted by his outgoing wife Grazia, who knows how to put visitors at their ease. You can't just taste wine at the Princic cellar. There's always a slice of ham, some fish, or some cheese to go with it, or Grazia may decide to make some pasta. This year's range is stunningly good. All the wines scored 80 out of 100 or higher while the Pinot Bianco and Malvasia were spot on. The Pinot Bianco is magnificent, although it lacks just a smidgeon of the variety's trademark elegance. The extraordinary aromas, rich-textured mouthfeel and substantial alcohol seem to be on the point of succumbing to the wonderful fruit. Don't miss out on the Malvasia. It was as good as this last year but there were lamentably few bottles available. A final note. Remember that the Princic cellar doesn't concentrate exclusively on whites. The cellar's reds are also improving fast.

O	Collio Malvasia '01	▼▼	5
O	Collio Pinot Bianco '01	▼▼	4*
●	Collio Cabernet Franc '00	▼▼	5
●	Collio Merlot '00	▼▼	6
O	Collio Sauvignon '01	▼▼	4
O	Collio Tocai Friulano '01	▼▼	4
O	Collio Pinot Grigio '01	▼	4
O	Collio Tocai Friulano '93	▼▼▼	5
O	Collio Pinot Bianco '95	▼▼▼	5
O	Collio Pinot Bianco '00	▼▼	4
O	Collio Tocai Friulano '00	▼▼	4

CORMONS (GO)

Dario Raccaro
Fraz. Rolat
Via San Giovanni, 87
34071 Cormons (GO)
tel. 048161425

Dario Raccaro has excelled himself again with the new vintage. His wines are stunning, even though he only presented three of the four from 2001, having decided to hold the Merlot back until autumn 2003. Despite his self-confessed preference for whites, Dario's Merlot is often spectacularly good. Dario is a small producer in terms of area planted to vine – only four hectares – and in the number of bottles released, about 20,000 a year. Obviously, everything in the winery reflects this scale, from the cellar to the bottle store. But Dario is also a big producer if we consider the quality of his wines. Shrewdly, he restricts these to four labels – five at most – with three monovarietals, the Tocai, the Malvasia and the Merlot, and two blends, a Collio Bianco and a Collio Rosso. According to tradition, Caterina Vecchiet's vineyards were planted with the first tocai vines to arrive from Hungary and since then, only shoots from the original plants have been used for propagation. Since Dario has had their fruit at his disposal, his Tocai has been hitting stratospheric heights. Depth, complexity, structure and freshness come together with an inviting, unbelievably long finish. Opulent and impeccably dry, the Malvasia is almost as good while the tocai, sauvignon and pinot grigio-based Bianco 2001 was still very young when we tasted but showed a characterful personality.

O	Collio Tocai Friulano '01	▼▼▼	4*
O	Collio Bianco '01	▼▼	4*
O	Collio Malvasia '01	▼▼	4*
O	Collio Tocai Friulano '00	▼▼▼	4
O	Collio Bianco '00	▼▼	4
●	Collio Merlot '97	▼▼	4
O	Collio Bianco '99	▼▼	4
●	Collio Merlot '99	▼▼	4
O	Collio Tocai Friulano '99	▼▼	4
●	Collio Merlot '00	▼▼	4

CORMONS (GO)

Ronco dei Tassi
Loc. Monte, 38
34071 Cormons (GO)
tel. 048160155
e-mail: info@roncodeitassi.it

CORMONS (GO)

Ronco del Gelso
Via Isonzo, 117
34071 Cormons (GO)
tel. 048161310
e-mail: roncodelgelso@libero.it

Little by little, Fabio and Daniela Coser, now joined by their son Matteo, are expanding production, which is running at 75,000 bottles a year. The wine comes from 12 hectares, planted at densities that range from 4,000 to 5,000 vines per hectare. The eight hectares of woodland around the vineyards are home to a multitude of wild animals, including the badgers ("tassi") whose predilection for ripe grapes prompted Fabio to name his Ronco after them. Last year saw the completion of work on the new cellar so there is plenty of room to vinify the eight varieties of grape from which the Cosers make only five wines. Most years, the blends prove to be the best wines in the range but this time our tastings rewarded the 2001 Sauvignon and Tocai Friulano. The Sauvignon is part barrique-aged and successfully combines freshness with structure, offering stylish nuances of tomato leaf. There is absolutely no hint of oak in the astoundingly long finish. In contrast, the Tocai is aged in stainless steel, and part underwent malolactic fermentation. Apple comes through on the nose, to be lifted by white peach on the palate, which signs off with a classic varietal twist of bitter almonds. The 2001 Fosarin is a blend of tocai, malvasia and pinot bianco with a touch of wood that has yet to be absorbed. The merlot and cabernet sauvignon-based Cjarandon '99, which also has a little cabernet franc, is, like the Fosarin, a superior bottle.

Giorgio Badin's new cellar, with its super-functional design and technology, is just coming into production and in the meantime his wines are as good as ever. Giorgio now has 20 hectares under vine. Low cropping levels, very ripe fruit and micro-oxygenation enable him to release well-structured wines that have great cellar potential. The Tocai 2001 hit the bull's eye. Like all Badin's whites, its golden hue is flecked with lemon yellow, then a pervasive nose of intense pear and apple ushers in a concentrated palate with a rousing, rising finish. The Pinot Grigio Sot lis Rivis shows complex tropical fruit aromas and a full-flavoured palate with just the right touch of acidity. The finesse and elegance of the Merlot 2000 are reminiscent of Bordeaux and the magnificent fruit lingers through to the back palate. The Pinot Bianco, too, is a sophisticate, following a concentrated, creamy nose with a rich, balanced mouthfeel. A recently vineyard purchase has given Giorgio the fruit for a complex Malvasia whose ripe apple is echoed on the long, leisurely palate. The nicely balanced white Latimis 2001 blend has surprising breadth, consistency, fruit and alcohol while the fresh-tasting Sauvignon has an extremely even, fruit-rich palate. Also impressive is the flower and citron-fragranced Riesling. A few more years in the cellar will bring rewards for those who are prepared to wait.

○	Collio Sauvignon '01	ŶŶ	4*
○	Collio Tocai Friulano '01	ŶŶ	4*
○	Collio Bianco Fosarin '01	Ŷ	4
●	Collio Rosso Cjarandon '99	Ŷ	5
○	Collio Pinot Grigio '01		4
○	Collio Bianco Fosarin '96	ŶŶŶ	4
○	Collio Sauvignon '98	ŶŶŶ	4
○	Collio Bianco Fosarin '00	ŶŶ	4
○	Collio Pinot Grigio '00	ŶŶ	4

○	Friuli Isonzo Tocai Friulano '01	ŶŶŶ	4*
●	Friuli Isonzo Merlot '00	ŶŶ	5
○	Friuli Isonzo Pinot Grigio Sot lis Rivis '01	ŶŶ	4*
○	Friuli Isonzo Bianco Latimis '01	ŶŶ	4
○	Friuli Isonzo Malvasia '01	ŶŶ	4
○	Friuli Isonzo Pinot Bianco '01	ŶŶ	4
○	Friuli Isonzo Riesling '01	ŶŶ	4
○	Friuli Isonzo Sauvignon '01	ŶŶ	4
○	Friuli Isonzo Chardonnay '01		4
○	Friuli Isonzo Sauvignon '00	ŶŶŶ	4
○	Friuli Isonzo Tocai Friulano '97	ŶŶŶ	4
○	Friuli Isonzo Sauvignon '98	ŶŶŶ	4
○	Friuli Isonzo Pinot Grigio Sot lis Rivis '99	ŶŶŶ	4

CORMONS (GO)

OSCAR STURM
LOC. ZEGLA, 1
34071 CORMONS (GO)
TEL. 048160720
E-MAIL: sturm@sturm.it

We've been following this winery for some time now. Recently, the label was embellished with a detail from Giorgione's Tempest, a pun on the family surname. Actually, a visit to Oscar and Dunja's winery is anything but "stormy" for the couple's friendliness and hospitality has made it a regular stopping point for wine tourists, particularly from Austria and Germany. Oscar aims to pick the fruit from his 11 hectares planted to vine when it is very ripe, then goes for cleanness and elegance during vinification. The results are more and more convincing. His magnificent Pinot Grigio 2001 comes from 30 to 35-year-old vines. The intense, gold-flecked straw introduces a faintly milky entry on the nose that shades into ripe pears. A generous swathe of fruit in the mouth foregrounds pear again, and citrus. Elegance and measured sophistication are the keynotes of the Chardonnay Andritz, whose subtle hazelnut and warm biscuit aromas come from wood ageing. There are notes of cherry tart and black cherries and soft tannins from the full-bodied Merlot 2000. The sauvignon and pinot grigio in the Collio Bianco 2001 are oak-aged. The wine may not have outstanding depth but the fruit melds attractively on the palate. Classic peach, red pepper and tomato leaf aromas greet the nose in the Sauvignon, which has tanginess but a rather one-dimensional progression in the mouth. Closing the range is the Tocai 2001, which offers subtle aromas, a lip-smacking, rather green, palate and decent length.

O	Chardonnay Andritz '01	ŸŸ	4*
O	Collio Pinot Grigio '01	ŸŸ	4*
●	Collio Merlot '00	ŸŸ	4
O	Collio Bianco '01	Ÿ	5
O	Collio Sauvignon '01	Ÿ	4
O	Collio Tocai Friulano '01	Ÿ	4
O	Collio Bianco '00	ŸŸ	5
O	Collio Sauvignon '99	ŸŸ	4

CORMONS (GO)

SUBIDA DI MONTE
LOC. MONTE, 9
34071 CORMONS (GO)
TEL. 048161011
E-MAIL: subida@libero.it

Cristian and Andrea Antonutti worked alongside their father Gigi for some years before taking over the Subida di Monte estate, where Cristian runs the cellar and Andrea looks after sales. Purchased in 1972, the estate now has admirably tended vineyards, located around the cellar, itself renovated a few years ago. The Tocai Friulano 2001 is the best of the recent vintage's wines. An attractive nose of dried flowers and pears introduces a rich front palate with good fruit and length. In fact, it's a more substantial wine than the Selezione, a name that the estate labels reserve for products considered to be superior to the rest of the range. The Pinot Grigio convinces for its attractive fruit and the very well-gauged acidity it shows on the palate. There's good nose-palate consistency in the Sauvignon whose green notes and fruit on the nose are lifted by peach in the mouth. The most creditable of the reds is the Cabernet Franc 2000. A nose of gunflint and hay combines with a varietal palate that is terroir-driven without being rustic. A grassy note returns in the after-aroma. The rather rough and edgy Collio Rosso Poncaia '99, a blend of merlot, cabernet franc and cabernet sauvignon, failed to earn more than One Glass.

O	Collio Tocai Friulano '01	ŸŸ	4*
●	Collio Cabernet Franc '00	Ÿ	4
O	Collio Pinot Grigio '01	Ÿ	4
O	Collio Sauvignon '01	Ÿ	4
O	Collio Tocai Friulano Sel. '01	Ÿ	5
●	Collio Rosso Poncaia '99		6
O	Collio Chardonnay Sel. '00	ŸŸ	5
●	Collio Merlot Sel. '99	ŸŸ	6

CORMONS (GO)

TIARE - ROBERTO SNIDARCIG
VIA MONTE, 58
34071 CORMONS (GO)
TEL. 048160064
E-MAIL: aztiare@tiscalinet.it

The Tiare cellar was founded in 1985 by Roberto Snidarcig, when he decided to break away from his father's estate and go it alone. At the time, he was young and reckless. The world held no terrors for him because Roberto was convinced that fortune favours the bold. In his case, fortune appeared in the person of his wife Sandra, an unassuming but tenacious, strong-willed woman. She runs the small restaurant the couple own on Monte Quarin, the hill overlooking Cormons and the entire Friulian plain, while Roberto works in the vineyards and the small cellar he has at Mossa. Snidarcig has a total of about ten hectares, some rented, some estate-owned, and he also buys in selected fruit. Annual production totals about 70,000 across 11 wine types. Most are whites, which Roberto usually produces very successfully whereas excellent reds are the exception, rather than the rule. The labels have recently had a design makeover and now reflect the touch of elegance that you can also detect in the wines themselves. The Sauvignon is very well made indeed this year, the varietal hints of elderflower and tomato leaf introducing a warm, unhurried palate. Then there is a raft of high One Glass wines, beginning with the Pinot Bianco, which shows a tad too much acidity in the finish, through to the Ronco delle Tiare, a chardonnay-based blend that ages in oak for about six months.

○ Collio Sauvignon '01	▼▼	4*
○ Collio Bianco Ronco della Tiare '01	▼	4
○ Collio Chardonnay '01	▼	4
○ Collio Pinot Bianco '01	▼	4
○ Collio Pinot Grigio '01	▼	4
○ Collio Ribolla Gialla '01	▼	4
● Friuli Isonzo Merlot '01	▼	4
● Collio Cabernet Franc '01		4
○ Collio Tocai Friulano '01		4
● Friuli Isonzo Cabernet Sauvignon '98	▼▼	4
● Friuli Isonzo Cabernet Sauvignon '99	▼▼	4

CORMONS (GO)

FRANCO TOROS
VIA NOVALI, 12
34071 CORMONS (GO)
TEL. 048161327

Franco Toros has a lovely, high-density vineyard of about eight hectares around his home at Novali, near Cormons, plus a further hectare he rents on the southern slopes of nearby Monte Quarin. Yields per vine and per hectare are very low indeed and production hovers around 60,000 bottles. Although he is a convinced white wine man, and firmly believes whites to be the motor that drives Friulian oenology, this year Franco nearly picked up Three Glass for a red, the elegant, dark ruby Merlot Selezione '99. Intense to the point of austerity, the nose hints at plums, forest floor and morello cherries, superbly mirrored in the warm depth of the generously fruity palate. Stylish tannins emerge in the after-aroma. But Three Glasses did go to the crystalline Pinot Bianco 2001, an incredibly stylish wine. Concentrated buttery aromas usher in a broad palate of elegant fruit that powers through to a finish of rare depth. The perfect Pinot Grigio has a rounded, complex mouthfeel of richly concentrated ripe fruit. The Tocai couldn't be more typical, unveiling fruit on the nose and a full-bodied lingering palate. Next, the elderflower and sage Sauvignon offers a substantial mouthfeel laced with citrus fruit in the unhurried finish. Rounding off Franco's 2001 range is a steel-aged Chardonnay with pervasive yeast, crusty bread and golden delicious apple aromas. The tangy front palate ushers in attractively intense fruit.

○ Collio Pinot Bianco '01	▼▼▼	4*
● Collio Merlot Sel. '99	▼▼	7
○ Collio Pinot Grigio '01	▼▼	4
○ Collio Sauvignon '01	▼▼	4
○ Collio Tocai Friulano '01	▼▼	4
○ Collio Chardonnay '01	▼	4
○ Collio Pinot Bianco '00	▼▼▼	4
● Collio Merlot Sel. '97	▼▼▼	6
○ Collio Pinot Bianco '99	▼▼	4

CORMONS (GO)

VIGNA DEL LAURO
LOC. MONTE, 38
34071 CORMONS (GO)
TEL. 048160155
E-MAIL: info@roncodeitassi.it

Vigna del Lauro, founded in 1994, is owned jointly by the noted oenologist and producer, Fabio Coser, of Ronco dei Tassi, and Eberhard Spangenberg, a Munich-based importer of Italian wines. The estates works six hectares, some of which are rented, at San Floriano del Collio and Cormons, in the Collio DOC zone, with a small proportion in Friuli Isonzo. Current production is 42,000 bottles a year, spread across seven labels. We are very happy that Fabio and Eberhard have decided to distribute some of their wines in Italy, after a couple of years when all of it was sold abroad. This gave us an opportunity to taste a fantastic Tocai Friulano 2001 which the panel rated very highly, awarding it a score just short of Three Glasses. Intense, varietal almond is followed by the tangy complexity of a deep, well-structured palate with serious alcohol and length. The grapes for this great wine come from one hectare of 35-year-old vines at Novali, near Cormons. The Collio Bianco 2001 contains tocai, pinot bianco, malvasia and ribolla gialla. It made a very good impression for there is no trace of oak, despite the fact that it was vinified and aged in wood. The fruit is able to emerge in all its complex elegance. The '99 Collio Merlot also comes from 30-year-old vines, whose perfectly ripe fruit lends the wine a rich, pervasive structure that is lifted by oak conditioning. The Sauvignon 2001 scored One full Glass while the wines from the Isonzo flatlands are less complex. One final note – the cellar's labels are some of the prettiest in the region.

O	Collio Tocai Friulano '01	♀♀♀	4*
O	Collio Bianco '01	♀♀	4
●	Collio Merlot '99	♀♀	4
O	Collio Sauvignon '01	♀	4
●	Friuli Isonzo Merlot '00		4
O	Collio Pinot Grigio '01		4
O	Friuli Isonzo Chardonnay '01		4
O	Collio Sauvignon '99	♀♀♀	4
O	Collio Bianco '00	♀♀	4
O	Collio Bianco '99	♀♀	4

CORNO DI ROSAZZO (UD)

VALENTINO BUTUSSI
VIA PRA' DI CORTE, 1
33040 CORNO DI ROSAZZO (UD)
TEL. 0432759194
E-MAIL: butussi@butussi.it

You can't miss Angelo Butussi's large and attractively proportioned winery as you come into Corno di Rosazzo. Sadly, the family recently lost the precious wisdom and winemaking knowledge of Valentino, who passed away at the age of 91. Nonetheless, true to their country roots, Angelo, wife Pierina and children Erika, Filippo, Tobia and Mattia have renewed their vigorous efforts to get the best out of the grapes from their ten hectares, which are supplemented by locally bought fruit. Most of the wine released is white, which together with the estate reds, provide an annual production of 75,000 bottles. The panel tasted at least 15 wines, for the Butussis also presented an oaked Chardonnay and a Sauvignon, as well as a standard Bianco from raisined ribolla gialla grapes. All need fine-tuning. Still, there were plenty of wines that won flattering scores and three earned a second Glass. The golden Picolit 2000 reveals distinct, lingering notes of sweet stewed apple. From the 2001 vintage, the Pinot Grigio offers rich fruit, a creamy mouthfeel and nicely gauged acidity. The Tocai's attractively full entry on the palate follows through well thanks to a good balance of acidity and flavour. Also very good are the Pinot Bianco – both the Colli Orientali and the Grave del Friuli versions – and its close relative, Chardonnay, from 2001, a vintage that treated these varieties kindly.

O	COF Picolit '00	♀♀	7
O	COF Pinot Grigio '01	♀♀	4*
O	COF Tocai Friulano '01	♀♀	4*
O	COF Chardonnay '01	♀	4
O	COF Pinot Bianco '01	♀	4
O	COF Sauvignon '01	♀	4
●	Friuli Grave Merlot '01	♀	4
O	Friuli Grave Pinot Bianco '01	♀	4
O	COF Sauvignon Vigna di Corte '00		4
O	COF Verduzzo Friulano '00		4
●	COF Cabernet '01		4

CORNO DI ROSAZZO (UD)

CA DI BON
VIA CASALI GALLO, 1
33040 CORNO DI ROSAZZO (UD)
TEL. 0432759316
E-MAIL: cadibon55@tin.it

Gianni Bon is a cautious, market-savvy winemaker who only bottles what his customers are likely to require during the year. The rest of his production is sold unbottled, or to locals at the welcoming "osteria", or bar, he owns at San Giovanni al Natisone, on the main road that links Udine to Gorizia and Trieste. Gianni's small cellar is in one of Corno's most wine-oriented districts and his nine hectares are scattered across three DOC zones, Collio, Colli Orientali and Grave del Friuli. This is not uncommon for growers at Corno. If you add to this that wines in Friuli carry the name of the variety, and are sometimes also given imaginative names of their own, you will see why Gianni and Ameris have 14 different product types. Best of the range in 2001 was the Tocai. It's better in the mouth than on the nose, the tasty, rich fruit showing nice complexity and leading through to a long finish. The Grave Sauvignon came close to a second Glass for its well-defined green peppers and robust structure. We like the elegance and fresh varietal acidity of the Ribolla Gialla whereas the Chardonnay lost points for a slight lack of firmness in the finish. Finally, the Ronc dal Gial (it means "rooster hill"), a blend of cabernet franc, merlot and refosco dal peduncolo rosso, is already quite evolved.

○ COF Tocai Friulano '01	🍷	3*
○ Chardonnay '01	🍷	3
○ COF Ribolla Gialla '01	🍷	4
○ Friuli Grave Sauvignon '01	🍷	4
● COF Merlot '01		3
○ COF Pinot Bianco '01		3
● COF Refosco P. R. '01		4
● Ronc dal Gial '98		5

CORNO DI ROSAZZO (UD)

EUGENIO COLLAVINI
LOC. GRAMOGLIANO
VIA FORUM JULII, 2
33040 CORNO DI ROSAZZO (UD)
TEL. 0432753222
E-MAIL: collavini@collavini.it

Until a few years ago, people expected the Collavini winery to turn out large quantities of well-made but uninspiring wine. Nowadays, we look forward to the new releases to see if the leading labels are as good as ever, or if the cellar has managed to improve the bottles that were less successful in the previous vintage. This time, Walter Bergnach, the young oenologist who has been supervising winemaking for several years, presented the panel with a very solid range. Some of the credit must go to the exceptionally good vintages of the past few years but the cellar has now thoroughly mastered the use of oak. It should also be mentioned that for a couple of years, the winery has been using a controversial concentrator, which Manlio Collavini claims serves only to remove water from the must, thus enhancing the concentration of the other components. We will restrict ourselves to noting the excellent results without taking a stance on the question. After all, Collavini can now offer winelovers products like the Cabernet 2000, with its intense nose yet rich, expansive palate, whose good complexity signs off with an after-aroma of warm berry fruit and soft tannins. The '99 Merlot dal Pic is a typically "sun-kissed" wine. Extremely ripe fruit is accompanied by cocoa powder and crusty bread. Not for the first time, there were good showings from the Chardonnay Cuccanea 2000, which combines freshness with complexity, and the Sauvignon Poncanera 2001, an elegant, well-structured bottle. These are flanked by a full-bodied Schioppettino and a soft, refreshing Ribolla with nice length.

● Collio Cabernet I Nostri Vini '00	🍷🍷	6
● Collio Merlot dal Pic '99	🍷🍷	8
● COF Schioppettino Turian '00	🍷🍷	6
○ Collio Chardonnay Cuccanea '00	🍷🍷	6
○ COF Ribolla Gialla Turian '01	🍷🍷	6
○ Collio Sauvignon Poncanera '01	🍷🍷	6
○ Collio Chardonnay dei Sassi Cavi Collezione Privata '99	🍷🍷	6
● Collio Merlot Collezione Privata '99	🍷🍷	6

CORNO DI ROSAZZO (UD)

ADRIANO GIGANTE
VIA ROCCA BERNARDA, 3
33040 CORNO DI ROSAZZO (UD)
TEL. 0432755835
E-MAIL: gigantevini@libero.it

This estate of 20 or so hectares on the slopes of the Rocca Bernarda hill is a family business. Like many others, it releases the best wines under its own label and sells off the remainder unbottled. At first glance, you might think the cellar wasn't the most appropriate of places to make premium-quality wine and in fact there are plans to renovate the entire winery. For the time being, the offices and barrel cellar are being restructured. Nevertheless, the estate does in fact have everything it needs to turn out excellent wines and, above all, to do so consistently. Exhibit A is the Tocai Storico that confounded forecasts last year and is again a top performer this time round. From vines that are more than 40 years old, it has complexity and roundness on the nose, great nose-palate consistency and thrust in the mouth that marries elegance with concentration. Other fine, very well-executed wines are the broad yet intense Sauvignon 2001, which has decent length and body as well as aromas of tomato leaf, and the ever inviting Picolit 2000, which caresses the palate with sweet aromas and a glycerine-rich body that gives way to a raisined fruit finish. Further promising indications came from the standard Tocai, which has a rich nose, pear and apple palate and fresh acidity, the reasonably complex, tropical fruit Pinot Grigio, the long, stylish 2001 Chardonnay, with its yeast and fruit aromas, and the old gold Verduzzo 2000, whose aromas mingle apricots, ripe apples, vanilla and bananas.

○ COF Tocai Friulano Storico '01	▼▼	4*
○ COF Picolit '00	▼▼	6
○ COF Sauvignon '01	▼▼	4*
● COF Merlot '00	▼	4
○ COF Verduzzo Friulano '00	▼	4
○ COF Chardonnay '01	▼	4
○ COF Pinot Grigio '01	▼	4
○ COF Tocai Friulano '01	▼	4
● COF Refosco P. R. '00		4
○ COF Tocai Friulano Storico '00	▼▼▼	4
○ COF Picolit '99	▼▼	6

CORNO DI ROSAZZO (UD)

LE DUE TORRI
VIA S. MARTINO, 19
33040 CORNO DI ROSAZZO (UD)
TEL. 0432759150 - 0432753115
E-MAIL: info@le2torri.com

Antonino Volpe owns Le Due Torri and again presented the panel with a very nice range of wines, which he sells at extremely competitive prices. The winery is at Corno di Rosazzo, a town where three DOC zones – Friuli Grave, Colli Orientali del Friuli and Collio – meet. Antonino can call on five and half hectares in Friuli Grave and Colli Orientali, which provide fruit for most of his 20,000-bottle production, sold under 15 different labels. Maurizio Michelini, a wine technician whose office is at Cormons, provides him with consultancy advice and bottling is carried out with the help of Giuseppe Lipari's mobile unit. The whites presented show how reliable the cellar is for wines of this category but the reds tend to let the range down. They are not actually bad but they are certainly a long way from matching the very best Friulian reds. As ever, the Ribolla Gialla is very impressive. Elegant and full-bodied, it tempts the nose with hints of fresh apple and damson. Malvasia is undervalued by the Italian market in general but Antonino's version flaunts remarkable structure and stylish notes of apple. The other whites, all from 2001, are the Chardonnay, Pinot Grigio, Sauvignon and Tocai Friulano. Characterful and fruitily fresh-tasting, they are not lacking in style whereas the 2000 reds are uncomplicated tipples with vegetal and varietal nuances.

○ Malvasia '01	▼▼	2*
○ Ribolla Gialla '01	▼▼	2*
○ Friuli Grave Chardonnay '01	▼	2
○ Friuli Grave Pinot Grigio '01	▼	2
○ Friuli Grave Sauvignon '01	▼	2
○ Friuli Grave Tocai Friulano '01	▼	2
● Friuli Grave Cabernet Franc '00		3
● Friuli Grave Refosco P. R. '00		3

CORNO DI ROSAZZO (UD)

PERUSINI
LOC. GRAMOGLIANO, 13
33040 CORNO DI ROSAZZO (UD)
TEL. 0432675018 - 0432759151
E-MAIL: info@perusini.com

The Perusini estate, which belongs to the aristocracy of Friulian winemaking, is back with a full profile and a raft of Glasses. Teresa Perusini, the hands-on owner, is assisted by her husband, Giacomo de Pace. The couple have already started replanting the vine stock and there are more changes in the pipeline, thanks to the contribution of the trio of fruitmaking wizards, Simonit, Sirch and Pittana. This year, Teresa has had help in the cellar from Roberto Cipresso whereas the 2000 wines were made by Luigino Di Giuseppe. The Perusini estate covers 12 hectares, set attractively amid a further 48 of woods and arable farmland. The last vintage produced a total of 50,000 bottles. Work on the new building is nearing completion. It's a tower made from experimental materials to plans by the faculty of architecture at the university of Venice and part of the cellar will be situated at the base. The upper storeys will house storage areas and offices while the 15 metre-high tower itself will command a panoramic view over Friuli's winemaking heartland. The excellent Cabernet Sauvignon 2000 is rich and fruity, with discreet tannins, and the elegant 2001 Pinot Grigio recalls tropical fruit. They were neck and neck at the top of the range of convincing wines presented. One other wine we would like to mention is the sweet but not sugary Picolit 2001, whose citrus notes and soft, warm mouthfeel brought it very close to a second Glass.

● COF Cabernet Sauvignon '00	▼▼	4*
○ COF Pinot Grigio '01	▼▼	4*
● COF Rosso del Postiglione '00	▼	4
○ COF Picolit '01	▼	7
○ COF Pinot Bianco '01	▼	4
○ COF Ribolla Gialla '01	▼	4
○ COF Riesling '01	▼	4
○ COF Sauvignon '01	▼	4
● COF Cabernet Franc '00		4
○ COF Bianco del Postiglione '01		4

CORNO DI ROSAZZO (UD)

LEONARDO SPECOGNA
VIA ROCCA BERNARDA, 4
33040 CORNO DI ROSAZZO (UD)
TEL. 0432755840
E-MAIL: info@specogna.it

Our tastings left us with the impression that Graziano Specogna, who runs this lovely winery with his brother Gianni, is becoming more and more of a red wine man, even though he continues to make distinctly interesting whites. Years ago, the Specogna cellar was known for its Tocai but for a few years now, we've been pointing out the wine's lack of typicity, giving it only one Glass partly because of its uncharacteristic aromas of red peppers and elderflower. In contrast, the '99 Merlot Oltre is a model of varietal character. Fermented and aged entirely in wood, its warm berry fruit stays well on top of the still perceptible oak before the beefy palate reveals the odd grace note of citrus. High marks, too, for the Pignolo 2000, a native red that will need cellaring to find its feet. Serious tannins and acidity are, at least for the time being, only partly kept in check by the conditioning in tonneaux and barriques. The Specogna winery has some excellent sauvignon clones that year after year yield superbly typical wines, to which oak ageing of part of the wine adds pervasiveness in the mouth. The Pinot Grigio is macerated on the skins for 24-30 hours to imbue it with its classic copper highlights in the glass.

○ COF Sauvignon '01	▼▼	4*
● COF Merlot Oltre '99	▼▼	6
● COF Pignolo '00	▼	6
○ COF Tocai Friulano '01	▼	4
○ Pinot Grigio '01	▼	4
● COF Merlot '00		4
● COF Refosco P. R. '00		4
● COF Cabernet Franc '01		4
○ COF Sauvignon '00	▼▼	4
○ Pinot Grigio '00	▼▼	4
● Oltre '96	▼▼	6

CORNO DI ROSAZZO (UD)

ANDREA VISINTINI
VIA GRAMOGLIANO, 27
33040 CORNO DI ROSAZZO (UD)
TEL. 0432755813
E-MAIL: info@vinivisintini.com

Andrea Visintini owns an estate of just over 25 hectares planted to vine at Corno di Rosazzo, although there is also a small plot near Cormons, which yield him about 100,000 bottles a year. His son Oliviero looks after the cellar while out in the vineyards, the entire family lends a hand, including twin sisters Cinzia and Palmira, who also look after the books. It was probably the influx of women into the winery that prompted Andrea to revamp his labels, which are now distinctly more elegant than their predecessors. The Visinitinis' spontaneous hospitality and their very consumer-friendly pricing policy only make this family of winemakers even more likeable. Restoration work has been completed on the tower, dating from 1560, which is incorporated into one end of the house. Once, there was a Roman construction here that kept watch over the road that connected Forum Julii, today's Cividale, to Aquileia. Pinot Bianco is the best of the Visintini bunch from the 2001 vintage, and not for the first time. Partial maceration on the skins has lent it an intense straw-yellow and its stylish nose ushers in a seriously structured, complex palate. The Bianco is a new release. A blend of tocai, riesling, pinot bianco and picolit, it is steadier on the nose than in the mouth. The 2001 Pinot Grigio and Merlot are fine examples of their respective wine types but the Malvasia didn't quite come up to expectations.

CORNO DI ROSAZZO (UD)

ZOF
FRAZ. SANT'ANDREA DEL SUDRIO
VIA GIOVANNI XXIII, 32/A
33040 CORNO DI ROSAZZO (UD)
TEL. 0432759673
E-MAIL: info@zof.it

Daniele Zof studied oenology and got to know Donato Lanati, who gave him his quality-first approach to winemaking. With the approval of his father Alberto, Daniele has lost no time in translating that philosophy into practical vineyard and cellar management. The estate was created in 1984 and embraces nine hectares. A further six hectares are rented, all located close to the cellar. The winery itself is small but big enough to turn out about 80,000 bottles a year, as well as wine to be sold unbottled. The same building houses the "agriturismo" restaurant and accommodation, run by Daniele's mother Angela. Much of the estate's demijohn wine is sold here, as well as excellent cold meats and pork products. The bottles released in 2002 are a tad less successful than Daniele's usual range but all were well above the demanding threshold levels of quality set by our panels. Only the Pinot Grigio 2001 managed a second Glass for its freshness, elegance and sumptuous tropical fruit layered over varietal fruit salad aromas. Cherry tart and bramble are the keynote aromas of the Merlot and the Ribolla Gialla 2001 stakes its all on the refreshing acidity typical of the variety. The Va' Pensiero '99 is let down by overgenerous grass and hay aromas, and by tannins that are a little too bitter. Finally, the very sweet Picolit 2000 has still to absorb its oak-derived sensations of coffee.

○	COF Pinot Bianco '01	▼▼	3*
○	COF Bianco '01	▼▼	3*
●	COF Merlot '01	▼	3
○	COF Pinot Grigio '01	▼	3
○	COF Ribolla Gialla '01	▼	3
○	COF Sauvignon '01	▼	3
○	Malvasia '01	▼	3
●	COF Cabernet '01		3
○	COF Traminer Aromatico '01		3
○	Collio Tocai Friulano '01		3
○	COF Pinot Bianco '00	▼▼	3
●	COF Merlot II Barrique '98	▼▼	4
●	COF Merlot '99	▼▼	3

○	COF Pinot Grigio '01	▼▼	3*
○	COF Picolit '00	▼	6
●	COF Merlot '01	▼	4
○	COF Ribolla Gialla '01	▼	3
○	COF Tocai Friulano '01	▼	3
●	Va' Pensiero '99	▼	4
●	COF Cabernet Franc '01		4
○	COF Sauvignon '01		3

DOLEGNA DEL COLLIO (GO)

Ca' Ronesca
Loc. Lonzano, 15
34070 Dolegna del Collio (GO)
Tel. 048160034
E-mail: caronesca@caronesca.it

Every year, Paolo Bianchi, the young, shrewd manager of Ca' Ronesca, manages to add a little something to the winery's image and products. Take, for example, the delightful texts and images by Tommaso Mangiola in the estate brochure. Their aim is not so much to sell wine as to emphasize the care and attention devoted to manual labour, respect for nature and man's relationship with the territory. It's no coincidence that the vast estate is not intensively exploited. There's plenty of room for woodland and meadows. Wine quality, too, improves steadily and is better than ever this year. In fact, the Sauvignon Podere di Ipplis came very close to a top award. The fruit comes from a plot at Ipplis and for years, it's been a major wine, as you can tell from the Three Glasses it won in an early edition of the Guide. An attractive, green-tinged hue introduces varietal notes of ripe tomato and a flavoursome palate that packs a decent punch. It was a wise decision to release the Sermar blend, from pinot bianco, tocai and ribolla gialla, two years after the vintage. Clean, complex and very well-balanced, it tempts with generous aromas of almond, dried flowers and grass. Great structure and a leisurely bramble-themed finish sum up the Cabernet Franc Podere San Giacomo '99, which is on a par with the elegant, lavender-fragranced Malvasia and the distinctly Mediterranean 2001 Tocai.

○ COF Sauvignon Podere di Ipplis '01	ΤΤ	4*
○ Collio Bianco Sermar '00	ΤΤ	5
○ Collio Malvasia '01	ΤΤ	4
○ Collio Tocai Friulano '01	ΤΤ	4
● Collio Cabernet Franc Podere San Giacomo '99	ΤΤ	6
● COF Refosco P. R. '00	Τ	4
○ Saramago '00	Τ	5
○ Collio Pinot Grigio '01	Τ	4
○ Collio Sauvignon '01	Τ	4
● COF Sariz '98	Τ	4
○ COF Picolit '99	Τ	6
○ Saramago '99	ΤΤ	5

DOLEGNA DEL COLLIO (GO)

La Rajade
Loc. Restocina, 12
34070 Dolegna del Collio (GO)
Tel. 0481639897
E-mail: frascadelcollio@libero.it

La Rajade is in the northern part of the Collio and extends over about seven hectares along the border with neighbouring Slovenia. The owner-manager is Romeo Rossi, who is helped by brother Simone. Romeo is a grower-producer through and through whereas Simone, while very active in vineyard and cellar, also loves mediaeval history. He has a collection of antiquities and enjoys organizing themed events. The Rossis have renovated the parts of the cellar devoted to musts, wood, stainless steel and storage, and have also created a very comfortable hospitality and tasting area. Mother Lucia is in charge of a busy restaurant that offers homestyle cooking right next to the cellar. Consigned to the Other Wineries last year, La Rajade has stormed back with two major whites, the 2001 Sauvignon and Chardonnay. Sauvignon is a Rossi forte. Selected clones nurtured on exceptionally favourable soil and the Rossis' tried and trusted vinification techniques make sure the aromas are all there. Intense peach, tomato leaf and red pepper accompany a butter-rich, lingering palate. There's still a faint hint of oak in the Chardonnay, whose firm, smooth mouthfeel is framed by banana and yeast and lifted by refreshing apple through to an irresistible, unhurried finish. Caprizzi di Marceline 2000, a mix of tocai, chardonnay, verduzzo and ribolla aged in oak for a year, has a fine entry on the palate, signing off with hints of red pepper.

○ Collio Chardonnay '01	ΤΤ	4*
○ Collio Sauvignon '01	ΤΤ	4*
○ Collio Bianco Caprizzi di Marceline '00	Τ	4
● Collio Cabernet Sauvignon Stratin '00		5
● Collio Merlot '00		4

DOLEGNA DEL COLLIO (GO)

VENICA & VENICA
LOC. CERÒ
VIA MERNICO, 42
34070 DOLEGNA DEL COLLIO (GO)
TEL. 048161264 - 048160177
E-MAIL: venica@venica.it

Giorgio, Gianni and his son Gianpaolo call themselves "autochthonous" grower-producers. If that means they are committed to their territory, cultivate numerous varieties and release their wines under an even greater number of labels, then it is entirely appropriate. Still, it's not the whole story. This friendly trio, unlike many other producers in Friuli, also love to experiment and match their wines against the competition. They expect no favours and have sufficient modesty to learn and improve from such encounters. This approach has enabled the Venicas to bridge the gap that for years separated their white wines from the reds. Further stimulus has come from Ornella Venica. Her role as chair of the Movimento del Turismo del Vino (wine tourism movement) gives her a privileged overview of the world of wine. Nor should we forget the contribution of fruitmakers Sirch, Simonit and Pittana, another trio who know a thing or two about cultivating superior grapes. The Sauvignon Ronco delle Mele 2001 is back on the Three Glass list. Intense yet never intrusive on the nose, its sage, tomato leaf and pennyroyal are perfectly echoed in the mouth, where distinct peach notes add further complexity. The Merlot Perilla '99 wins Two Glasses again this year, providing further proof that this estate, founded in 1930, has achieved full maturity. In addition to 28 hectares under vine, Venica & Venica has one of the region's finest "agriturismo" farm holiday centres.

DUINO AURISINA (TS)

KANTE
FRAZ. SAN PELAGIO
LOC. PREPOTTO, 3
34011 DUINO AURISINA (TS)
TEL. 040200761

No discussion of premium winemaking in the Carso DOC zone could ignore Edi Kante. For 20 years, this skilful Prepotto-based wineman has been keeping the flag flying, providing a benchmark and source of advice for the new generation of Carso producers. Now that he is no longer a voice crying in the wilderness, as it were, he has reluctantly become a public figure. Bigwigs, business people and the merely curious, from Trieste or further afield, queue up to visit the spectacular cellar that Edi has carved out of the Carso rock. Unfortunately, Edi's hyperactivity has had repercussions on his wines. They are still excellent but lack that something special – the desire to convey new insights – that they had a few years ago. Best of the Kante whites from 2000 is the Sauvignon, a spot-on Two Glass certainty that has a white peach nose of great finesse. Sweet and creamy on entry, the palate has the barest hint of vanilla and the acidity of the Carso terroir comes through in the finish. The Chardonnay also has subtle, faintly aromatic nuances on the nose before the uncomplicated, moderately creamy palate reveals a hint of acidity. The Malvasia's rustic aromas usher in a refreshing wine that lacks a little breadth in the mouth. The Vitovska has nice flowery hints on the nose but is too lean and sharpish to get more than a mention.

O	Collio Sauvignon Ronco delle Mele '01	🍷🍷🍷	5
O	Collio Bianco Prime Note '00	🍷🍷	5
O	Collio Pinot Grigio '01	🍷🍷	4*
O	Collio Sauvignon Ronco del Cerò '01	🍷🍷	5
O	Collio Tocai Friulano Ronco delle Cime '01	🍷🍷	5
●	Collio Merlot Perilla '99	🍷🍷	6
O	Collio Pinot Bianco '01	🍷	4
O	Collio Ribolla Gialla '01	🍷	4
●	Refosco P. R. Bottaz '98	🍷	6
●	Collio Rosso delle Cime '99	🍷	6
O	Collio Tocai Friulano Ronco delle Cime '00	🍷🍷🍷	4

O	Carso Sauvignon '00	🍷🍷	6
O	Carso Chardonnay '00	🍷	6
O	Carso Malvasia '00	🍷	6
O	Carso Vitovska '00		6
O	Carso Malvasia '98	🍷🍷🍷	6

DUINO AURISINA (TS)

ZIDARICH
Loc. Prepotto, 23
34011 Duino Aurisina (TS)
tel. 040201223
e-mail: info@zidarich.it

Jagged, chalky rock is the keynote of Carso viticulture, which is carried out on small terraces of red, iron-rich soil that have been reclaimed from the woodland. This lends the wines the characteristic acidity and mineral notes that the determination of a competent grower-producer like Beniamino Zidarich can transform into personality, thanks to ageing in oak from France or Slavonia. When the three hectares that Beniamino has just planted come onstream, and some other plots mature, the present 10,000 bottles released every year will rise in stages to 18-20,000. In the meantime, work has started on a new cellar, which is being cut into the Carso rock. The wines presented from the 2000 vintage include a dense Terrano that is again one of the best of its type. Mouthfilling warmth and shrewdly judged acidity mingle deliciously with aromas of blueberries, blackcurrants and bramble. The Vitovska is part macerated on the skins. It has plums, ripe fruit and an intriguing hint of noble rot on the nose, which is followed by a lingering palate with an upfront entry, as you might expect from a variety that shares its environment with the "bora" gales that batter this coast. The Prulke is sauvignon-based mix with additions of the native vitovska and malvasia grapes that underline its terroir-led appeal. White peach and cream aromas usher in an only moderately deep, but surprisingly stylish, palate. Finally, we know by now that the oak-kissed chamomile of the Malvasia needs cellar time to reach its peak.

● Carso Terrano '00	🍷🍷	5
○ Carso Vitovska '00	🍷🍷	5
○ Prulke '00	🍷🍷	5
○ Carso Malvasia '00	🍷	5
● Carso Terrano '99	🍷🍷	5

FAEDIS (UD)

PAOLINO COMELLI
Fraz. Colloredo di Soffumbergo
Via della Chiesa, 8
33040 Faedis (UD)
tel. 0432711226
e-mail: comellip@tin.it

This winery is in fact owned by Pierluigi Comelli, a notary public and a leading figure in Friulian social life. A man of no little personality, he is deeply committed to the world of wine. "Pigi", as he is known to one and all, has made frequent changes to his winemaking team, demonstrating just how determined he is to achieve quality. Currently, his consultant is Flavio Zuliani, an experienced and eminently competent oenologist, and he has two promising young technicians – Michele Tomasin and Eros Zanini – in the vineyard and the cellar. The cellar itself has been renovated and extended a number of times over the years to make space for wines that are aged for several years before release. Some of Pigi's vineyards are above the lovely hillside village of Faedis and some on the flatland below. We should point out here that most of the vine stock is planted at a density of about 5,000 plants per hectare and that Comelli obtains about 500 hectolitres of wine from them, two thirds white and one third red. The quality of the 2001 vintage's top scorer, the Tocai Friulano, is not immediately obvious but the lavish, fruit-rich structure hints at better things to come with cellar time. Except for the Cabernet Sauvignon 2000, all the other wines picked up an effortless One Glass, including the Rosso Soffumbergo, a Bordeaux-style blend, with some additional autochthonous pignolo, that ages for 18 months in French oak.

○ COF Tocai Friulano '01	🍷🍷	4*
● COF Merlot '00	🍷	4
● COF Rosso Soffumbergo '00	🍷	4
○ COF Sauvignon Sup. '00	🍷	4
○ COF Chardonnay '01	🍷	4
○ COF Pinot Grigio '01	🍷	4
● COF Cabernet Sauvignon '00		4
○ COF Bianco Locum Nostrum '99	🍷🍷	4

FARRA D'ISONZO (GO)

BORGO CONVENTI
STRADA COLOMBARA, 13
34070 FARRA D'ISONZO (GO)
TEL. 0481888004
E-MAIL: info@borgoconventi.it

Tenimenti Ruffino pulled off something of a coup when they convinced Gianni Vescovo to sell this leading Friulian estate. Luigi Folonari has realized that to make great white wines, capable of carving out a niche in the world market, you need great white wine soil, such as can be found in Friuli. Having acquired Vescovo's winery, and with Gianni's daughter Barbara on the staff, Folonari is now seeking to expand the vine stock to ensure decent quantities of fruit while maintaining and, if possible, improving quality standards. Since the handover took place after the vintage, recent releases reflect two different winemaking philosophies and are not indicative of future developments. The meeting of these two approaches, however, can only be beneficial to production in Friuli. The Chardonnay Colle Russian is a 100 per cent Gianni Vescovo wine. Its complex aromas are redolent of confectioner's cream, crusty bread, yeast, vanilla and banana while the palate is still trying to fuse its acidity and alcohol. Knowing Gianni's past exploits, we are confident that this wine will evolve magnificently. There's a different rationale to the Bordeaux blend Braida Nuova '99. Its present freshness will give way in time to grassy notes of cabernet franc – and it should be remembered that cabernet franc grown in Friuli is in part carmenère – that will hold back development. Finally, the Tocai Friulano 2001 is well-balanced, nicely structured and long, revealing a pleasant undertow of oak and hazelnuts.

○ Collio Chardonnay Colle Russian '00	♆♆	6
○ Collio Tocai Friulano '01	♆	5
● Braida Nuova '99	♆	7
○ Collio Pinot Grigio '01		5
○ Collio Sauvignon '01		5
● Braida Nuova '91	♆♆♆	7
● Braida Nuova '97	♆♆	7

FARRA D'ISONZO (GO)

COLMELLO DI GROTTA
VIA GORIZIA, 133
34070 FARRA D'ISONZO (GO)
TEL. 0481888445
E-MAIL: colmello@xnet.it

At Villanova di Farra, clay and marl hills rise out of the chalk-rich gravel flatlands to create Collio DOC "islands" in the ocean of the Isonzo DOC zone. Here, a small restored village is the home of Colmello di Grotta, a winery established by Luciana Bennati and managed today by her daughter Francesca Bortolotto Possati. There are 21 hectares of south-facing vineyard at altitudes of 40 to 80 metres above sea level, equally distributed between the two DOC zones. But the Collio wines were more impressive this year. The part oak-fermented Chardonnay 2001 is attractively complex, with a warm, fruit nose where hints of biscuit peek through, then the leisurely palate is tangily flavoursome. The Tocai is a bit pale but the creamy, fruit-driven palate has nice structure. Fruit is also the strong suit of the Pinot Grigio, which is just a tad thin in the mouth from over-enthusiastic acidity. The rest of the range is also rather acidic. Taken in conjucntion with the green notes also present, it suggests the fruit was harvested early. That seems to be the case with the Collio Bianco Rondon 2001, a blend of barrique-fermented chardonnay with sauvignon and pinot grigio vinified in stainless steel. The pear and apple aromas are echoed on the palate but the wine is thin and rather one-dimensional. The fresh, moreish Pinot Grigio Isonzo is moderately well structured and has a faintly bitterish back palate. Last on the list is the full-bodied Merlot Isonzo 2000, which has characteristically herbaceous aromas.

○ Collio Chardonnay '01	♆♆	4*
○ Collio Tocai Friulano '01	♆♆	4*
● Friuli Isonzo Merlot '00	♆	4
○ Collio Bianco Rondon '01	♆	4
○ Collio Pinot Grigio '01	♆	4
○ Friuli Isonzo Chardonnay '01	♆	3
○ Friuli Isonzo Pinot Grigio '01	♆	3
○ Collio Sauvignon '01		4
○ Friuli Isonzo Sauvignon '01		3

FARRA D'ISONZO (GO)

Tenuta Villanova
Loc. Villanova
Via Contessa Beretta, 29
34070 Farra d'Isonzo (GO)
tel. 0481888013 - 0481888593
e-mail: tenutavi@tin.it

After 500 years, Tenuta Villanova is now a 200-hectare winery split almost exactly equally between the Friuli Isonzo and Collio DOC zones. If you are thinking of researching the history of wine and agriculture in the hinterland of Gorizia, then a visit to the information-packed archives of this estate is a must. In fact, Tenuta Villanova used to manage fields and vineyards for other producers, such as the Fondazione Cerruti, which owns Villa Russiz. The estate's registers therefore offer insights into the crops farmed and the grape varieties that were introduced or abandoned over the centuries. Recently, various restoration programmes have been implemented, creating hospitality and conference facilities that blend superbly into the main villa complex. Similarly, important work has been carried out in the vineyards and cellar, expanding the potential of a production that was already excellent. One of the leading wines this time is again the Sauvignon Ronco Cucco 2001. Peach, apple and pineapple aromas accompany the soft, fleshy mouthfeel and impressive length. A particularly successful wine this year is Menj Bianco ("Menj" is the local short form for the name "Domenico"). Tocai, malvasia and chardonnay grapes lend rich, citrus-laced fruit to complement a stylish, unhurried palate. The Merlot '99 only scored One Glass, probably because its evolution could have gone better. When we tasted it, first from the barrel and then again in late spring 2002, it raised our hopes for a rather better performance.

FARRA D'ISONZO (GO)

★ Vinnaioli Jermann
Loc. Villanova
Via Monte Fortino, 21
34070 Farra d'Isonzo (GO)
tel. 0481888080
e-mail: info@jermannvinnaioli.it

A visit to Silvio Jermann's cellars, and a stroll through his vines before or afterwards, will be enough for anyone to see why he turns out such a whistle-clean range. Look closer at the details. The vats and barrels are lined up neatly, the walls are decorated attractively and a lawn separates the cellar from Silvio's home. It all tells you that Silvio has an aesthetic sensibility to complement his organoleptic acumen, and helps to explain the elegant style and sheer deliciousness of Jermann wines. Always at work on new projects, Silvio has now started a new cellar at Ruttars, where the Capo Martino vineyards are located, and he is also finishing off a small hospitality complex at Capriva, where there will be a wine shop and a few bedrooms. On the commercial front, he continues to provoke controversy. Silvio was one of the first to use silicon stoppers and this year, the wines he has released with this kind of closure carry a "drink-by" date. As we move on to the wines themselves, we note that Jermann is fine-tuning a great local red, the Pignolo, which he releases as Pignacolusse. The '99 has astonishing complexity, structure and intensity, partly because it has managed to shake off the excessive softness of previous editions. But the champion is again Vintage Tunina. The 2001 is as unbelievably good as ever, which is amazing if we remember that Silvio releases 70-90,000 bottles every year. Aniseed, citrus fruit and pear were at the top of the long list of aromas we noted in this superb version of a great wine.

O	Collio Sauvignon Ronco Cucco '01	🍷🍷	4*
O	Menj Bianco '01	🍷🍷	4*
O	Collio Chardonnay Ronco Cucco '00	🍷	4
O	Friuli Isonzo Malvasia '01	🍷	3
●	Collio Cabernet Sauvignon '99	🍷	5
●	Collio Merlot '99	🍷	4
O	Collio Chardonnay Monte Cucco '97	🍷🍷🍷	4
O	Collio Sauvignon Ronco Cucco '00	🍷🍷	4
●	Fraja '95	🍷🍷	6

O	Vintage Tunina '01	🍷🍷🍷	7
●	Pignacolusse '99	🍷🍷	6
O	Capo Martino '00	🍷🍷	7
O	Müller Thurgau '01	🍷🍷	5
●	Cabernet '00	🍷	5
O	Chardonnay '01	🍷	5
O	Pinot Bianco '01	🍷	5
O	Sauvignon '01	🍷	5
O	Traminer Aromatico '01	🍷	5
O	Vintage Tunina '00	🍷🍷🍷	7
O	Capo Martino '97	🍷🍷🍷	7
O	Vintage Tunina '97	🍷🍷🍷	7
O	Vintage Tunina '99	🍷🍷🍷	7
O	Capo Martino '99	🍷🍷	7
O	Were Dreams, Now It Is Just Wine! '00	🍷🍷	7

GONARS (UD)

Di Lenardo
Loc. Ontagnano
P.zza Battisti, 1
33050 Gonars (UD)
tel. 0432928633
e-mail: info@dilenardo.it

Massimo Di Lenardo is a young, dynamic winemaker who runs his 38-hectare property in a bold, independently-minded and very individual style. In 1998, he decided to take charge of wine production personally. Massimo has a wealth of competition experience from his past sporting activities – volleyball and golf – and is happy to take on the challenge of the market. His wines are increasingly innovative and modern in style. Prefermentative must hyperoxygenation enables him to release his wines very early and each year, they have some new twist of originality. This year, Massimo turned his attention for the first time to vinifying a great white "vino da meditazione". The result is the excellent Father's Eyes, a blend of 50 per cent tocai with equal parts of riesling and sauvignon that ages in barrique for seven months. The complex nose layers yellow peach, melon, tomato leaf and tobacco over vanilla that holds it all together. Full and fruit-driven, the palate reveals tempting hints of sweetness. The Tocai Toh!, the flagship Di Lenardo wine, is back on form in the 2001 version. Its varietal bitter almond mingles with delicate spring flowers, to be echoed deliciously on the lingering palate. But the whole Di Lenardo range is admirable. There are two other outstanding products, the tropical fruit Chardonnay Musque 2001 and the Ronco Nolè 2000, an intriguingly fruity blended red.

●	Ronco Nolè Rosso '00	🍷🍷	3*
○	Father's Eyes '01	🍷🍷	4
○	Friuli Grave Chardonnay Musque '01	🍷🍷	3*
○	Friuli Grave Tocai Friulano Toh! '01	🍷🍷	3*
○	Friuli Grave Chardonnay Woody '01	🍷	3
●	Friuli Grave Merlot '01	🍷	3
○	Friuli Grave Pinot Blanc '01	🍷	3
○	Friuli Grave Pinot Grigio '01	🍷	3
●	Friuli Grave Refosco P. R. '01	🍷	3
○	Friuli Grave Sauvignon Blanc '01	🍷	3

GORIZIA

Attems
Fraz. Lucinico
Via Giulio Cesare, 36/a
34170 Gorizia
tel. 0481393619
e-mail: info@attems.it

Conte Sigismondo Douglas Attems is now nearly 90 years old. It was he who founded the Consorzio Collio in 1964, acting as its president until 1999, when he handed the reins over to Marco Felluga. In 2000, Attems reached an agreement with Marchesi de' Frescobaldi and today Vittorio Frescobaldi supervises the estate. Lamberto Frescobaldi looks after production and Virginia Attems Fornasir is in charge of public relations. Fabio Coser, the eminently competent Cormons-based consultant, is supported by Gianni Napolitano, a young Friulian oenologist who has come home after working for years in the cellars of Tuscany. There are 32 hectares in production but the aim is to plant 50 of the estate's 75 hectares to vine eventually. The cellars, too, will be restructured to provide capacity for the production levels envisaged. All the wines are excellently made and the most convincing is the Ribolla Gialla 2001. Stylish and clean as they come, its lemony freshness is a perfect match for a wide range of fish dishes. The fresh and fruity Chardonnay 2000 has thoroughly absorbed the contribution of oak-conditioning. The Pinot Grigio, the leading Attems wine in terms of numbers (over 50,000 bottles are turned out), is also partly oak aged. You really wouldn't think so because the dominant note is of tropical fruit. The same style is reflected in the Tocai Friulano and the Sauvignon.

○	Collio Ribolla Gialla '01	🍷🍷	5
○	Collio Chardonnay '00	🍷	5
○	Collio Pinot Grigio '01	🍷	5
○	Collio Sauvignon '01	🍷	5
○	Collio Tocai Friulano '01	🍷	5

GORIZIA

FIEGL
FRAZ. OSLAVIA
LOC. LENZUOLO BIANCO, 1
34170 GORIZIA
TEL. 048131072 - 0481547103
E-MAIL: info@fieglvini.com

This year, Fiegl has decided to release two ranges, following the experience gained in past vintages with the Leopold Cuvée. The cellar now has a traditional line and a premium label, known as Leopold in honour of the Austrian chancellor, Leopold Fiegl, who was a noted connoisseur and lover of fine wines. The new line has still to find its feet, mainly because of some distinctly super-ripe aromas. Still, the road the Fiegls have chosen is the right one so we will suspend judgement for the time being and wait for the cellar to fine-tune the vinification cycle. The more traditional wines do not aspire to the very greatest heights but are nevertheless worth looking into. Well-made and very typical, they make up an indubitably drinkable list even though the range of aromas on nose and palate tends to be rather one-dimensional. That said, the Tocai 2001 is a very decent bottle, with persuasive thrust on the palate and reasonable fullness, and the Cabernet Sauvignon 2000 reveals earthy aromas of forest floor and raisined fruit. It is young and still a little edgy but its firm, powerful body is already evident.

● Cabernet Sauvignon '00	ƬƬ	4*
○ Collio Tocai Friulano '01	ƬƬ	4*
○ Collio Pinot Grigio '01	Ƭ	4
○ Collio Sauvignon '01	Ƭ	4
○ Collio Chardonnay '01		4
○ Collio Ribolla Gialla '01		4
○ Collio Sauvignon '00	ƬƬ	4
○ Collio Tocai Friulano '00	ƬƬ	4

GORIZIA

★ GRAVNER
FRAZ. OSLAVIA
VIA LENZUOLO BIANCO, 9
34170 GORIZIA
TEL. 048130882
E-MAIL: info@gravner.it

Josko Gravner writes, "Unfortunately, we are not all born managers. We are only farmers and we have to work hard every day for that reason". The clearest demonstration of this approach is the commitment with which Josko, assisted by fruitmaker Marco Simonit, carries out his experiments with new planting systems. We'll let his wines do the talking as we review the path he has been pursuing since the mid 1990s. After macerating in open-top wooden vats, with no selected yeasts or sulphur dioxide, and without temperature control, the various selections are bottled unfiltered. The Breg '98 is a blend of sauvignon, chardonnay, pinot grigio and riesling italico that ages for three years in large barrels. Its golden hue is flecked with orange and the faintly vanillaed nose shows no trace of oxidation. A creamy-textured, characterful white, it needs to breathe before it will disclose all its nuances of peach, apricot, candied peel and caramel. The Ribolla is similar in colour and aromas. The palate is slightly astringent and there is a touch of candied citrus peel on the back palate. The Rosso '97 has a slightly tired hue, then a grassy nose introduces a palate that could do with a touch more warmth. But with the recent release of a limited number of bottles of Riserva '91, Gravner has produced a gem of rare beauty. It's a Chardonnay vineyard selection that ages for 24 months in 110-litre barrels then for fully eight years in bottle. Stunningly fresh-tasting, its rich creaminess is veined with almost exuberant alcohol. A monument to a master winemaker.

○ Collio Chardonnay Ris. '91	ƬƬƬ	8
○ Collio Breg '98	ƬƬ	8
○ Collio Ribolla Gialla '98	ƬƬ	8
● Rosso Gravner '97	Ƭ	8
○ Collio Chardonnay '91	ƬƬƬ	8

GORIZIA

LA CASTELLADA
FRAZ. OSLAVIA, 1
34170 GORIZIA
TEL. 048133670

GORIZIA

DAMIJAN PODVERSIC
VIA BRIGATA PAVIA, 61
34170 GORIZIA
TEL. 048178217

Brothers Giorgio and Nicolò Bensa have a bottling and release schedule this year that leaves us with no wines to review. So we'll give you our impressions of what we found in the vats and the wines that had just gone into the bottle. A more definitive opinion will have to wait until next year. The Bensa estate, La Castellada, is one of the most successful in Friuli and its owners want their wines to be drunk at their peak of maturity. When they find a really good vintage like 2000 on their hands, they insist that the wine should age a little longer before release. Sadly, the clamouring customers have convinced the pair to let the first bottles out of the cellar as early as the end of November. Last year, we wondered whether monovarietal wines were making a comeback. It seems they are. In addition to the Ribolla and Bianco della Castellada 2000, we also tasted a very promising Tocai Friulano and a Chardonnay. For those who are unaware of how the Bensas vinify their fruit, we would mention that all the wines are aged in oak, for various lengths of time. We can tell you that the brothers have achieved a very sophisticated touch with wood and you can hardly detect its presence in the finished product. And the final piece of news is that a '98 Rosso della Castellada is in the pipeline.

One of the most interesting young winemakers to have emerged in the Collio in recent years is Damijan Podversic. Determined and generous, he has always had to struggle to achieve his winemaking ambitions, finding support above all from his wife and from his friend, Josko Gravner. Now that he has nearly ten high vine-density hectares, mainly on Monte Calvario, Damijan is getting his production philosophy properly into focus. After consultation with prestigious oenologist Attilio Pagli, he has decided to eliminate his chardonnay and replace it with native varieties. He is also substituting barriques with larger wood, which are less drastic in their oxygenation and contribution of tannins. The 2000 vintage suffered from hail damage but was still an outstanding one, especially in the case of the Collio Bianco, a chardonnay, malvasia and tocai blend. The oak is almost imperceptible, resulting in a complex, stylish wine that hints at milky notes and candied peel. The Collio Rosso comes from very ripe merlot and cabernet sauvignon, and has elegantly intense geranium on the nose then a young but inviting palate, where sweet fruit and bramble jam emerge. Perhaps a shade too young, the Ribolla Gialla is less approachable. It was let down by only recently having gone into the bottle after eight days' fermentation in open-top oak vats with no temperature control. Old gold, and timid on the nose, it reveals a slightly dry, fairly unsophisticated mouthfeel.

○	Collio Chardonnay '94	♛♛♛	6
○	Bianco della Castellada '95	♛♛♛	6
○	Collio Bianco della Castellada '98	♛♛♛	6
○	Collio Bianco della Castellada '99	♛♛♛	6
○	Collio Chardonnay '99	♛♛	6
○	Collio Ribolla Gialla '99	♛♛	6
●	Collio Rosso della Castellada '97	♛	7

○	Collio Bianco '00	♛♛	5
●	Collio Rosso '00	♛♛	5
○	Collio Ribolla Gialla '00	♛	5
○	Collio Bianco '99	♛♛	5

GORIZIA

PRIMOSIC
FRAZ. OSLAVIA
LOC. MADONNINA DI OSLAVIA, 3
34170 GORIZIA
TEL. 0481535153
E-MAIL: primosic@primosic.com

The Primosic estate is a hive of activity. There are cellar extensions, replantings in the vineyard, and new production strategies to boost the Gmajne range. It's also hard to pin down Marko, who is frequently away on some official business. All that work has produced – as the panel were able to confirm – a range of wines that are all at least very well made, although a winery with the dimensions and potential of Primosic (more than 130,000 bottles a year from one of the finest growing areas in the Collio) ought to be able to aim higher. The wine that was head and shoulders above the rest this year was the Chardonnay Gmajne 2000. Its lustrous straw yellow ushers in delicate, lingering notes of jasmine and yellow plums. A little uncomplicated on the palate, it still manages to find a nice balance of barely hinted at softness and subtly bracing freshness. Other mustard cutters in the range include the elegant pear and plum Pinot Grigio, with its good nose-palate consistency, moderate brightness and full flavour, and the 2000 Ribolla, whose varietal acidity melds into a well-gauged palate with excellent extract and just a whisker too much toastiness. The Sauvignon 2000, Rosso Metamorfosis and Klim '99 are all nicely made, although the last of these, a mix of sauvignon, chardonnay and ribolla gialla, is let down by too much sweetness.

GORIZIA

RADIKON
FRAZ. OSLAVIA
LOC. TRE BUCHI, 4
34170 GORIZIA
TEL. 048132804

Stanko Radikon is a man who knows his own mind. Unswervingly committed to his territory, he scorns wine guide mentions and magazine articles. In fact, he'd rather people simply didn't talk about him at all. We have always believed in the skill he has so amply demonstrated over the years and continue to follow his progress, even when his wines were, in our opinion, less than perfect. But characterful wines always attract interest so we were soon talking about the bottles at this year's tastings. The '99 Radikon shows that it has overcome the maceration-related problems that once gave it a nose that was perilously close to oxidation. We would point out that all Stanko's wines should be allowed to breathe and should not be served at too low a temperature. The vinification style and the fact that Radikon avoids refrigeration during the fermentation process make this advisable. Oslavje is a mix of sauvignon, tocai, pinot grigio and chardonnay whose intense hue reveals orangey nuances, then melon and apricot emerge with increasing intensity as the wine aerates in the glass. In the mouth, there is complexity, mouthfilling progression, freshness and almost tannic sinew. The Ribolla Gialla also has rather an evolved, golden hue and flaunts subtle notes of flowers. There's a touch of astringency on the palate but plenty of juicy body as well. These are two wines of great personality with exciting secrets for the discriminating drinker to discover.

○	Collio Chardonnay Gmajne '00	♟♟	4
○	Collio Pinot Grigio Gmajne '00	♟	4
○	Collio Ribolla Gialla Gmajne '00	♟	4
○	Collio Sauvignon Gmajne '00	♟	4
○	Collio Bianco Klim '99	♟	5
●	Collio Rosso Metamorfosis '99	♟	5
●	Collio Rosso Metamorfosis '97	♟♟	6
○	Collio Ribolla Gialla Gmajne '99	♟♟	4
○	Collio Sauvignon Gmajne '99	♟♟	4

○	Collio Bianco Oslavje '99	♟♟	7
○	Collio Ribolla Gialla '99	♟♟	7
●	Collio Merlot '90	♟♟	8
○	Collio Ribolla Gialla '98	♟	7

GRADISCA D'ISONZO (GO)

MARCO FELLUGA
VIA GORIZIA, 121
34072 GRADISCA D'ISONZO (GO)
TEL. 048199164 - 048192237
E-MAIL: info@marcofelluga.it

The Castello di Buttrio and the eye-pleasing vineyards round about offer an emblematic historical image of this frontier area, which has seen frequent invasions, battles, destruction and devastation but has always risen from its own ashes, ready for new adventures. Currently, Marco Felluga, one of the region's most important wineries with 130 hectares under vine and an annual production of 730,000 bottles, is holding aloft the Castello di Buttrio standard. The name sits proudly on the label of some of the most distinguished wines in the Marco Felluga range, a line that has always been excellent and very long. The white Ovestein 2000 and the red Marburg '99 are both obtained from native varieties. Their respective noses and palates are full, fruit-rich, well-structured and convincing. Special mentions and Guide stemware go to the stylish flower and fruit Pinot Grigio, the fresh, lively, peach-themed Sauvignon and the 2001 Tocai, for its body and structure. As ever, these are wines to bank on. Also reliable, if a shade below par this time, are the two blends, the Molamatta 2001, from tocai, ribolla and pinot bianco, and the Carantan '99, a Bordeaux blend. They're straightforward and lack a little length. However, the Refosco is on fine form, its elegant cassis lending sweetness to an assertive tannic weave.

O	Castello di Buttrio Ovestein '00	♛♛	5
O	Collio Pinot Grigio '01	♛♛	4
●	Castello di Buttrio Marburg '99	♛♛	6
●	Refosco '00	♛	5
O	Collio Bianco Molamatta '01	♛	4
O	Collio Sauvignon '01	♛	4
O	Collio Tocai Friulano '01	♛	4
●	Carantan '99	♛	6
●	Moscato Rosa '00		5
O	Collio Chardonnay '01		4
●	Carantan '98	♛♛	6
●	Castello di Buttrio Marburg '98	♛♛	6

GRADISCA D'ISONZO (GO)

SANT'ELENA
VIA GASPARINI, 1
34072 GRADISCA D'ISONZO (GO)
TEL. 048192388
E-MAIL: sant.elena@libero.it

Dominic Nocerino imports Italian wines into the United States and since 1997, has been the sole owner of the Sant'Elena estate. As man used to dealing with serious wines, he realized that serious investment would be required to make premium-quality wines and set to work with a will. Oenologist Maurizio Drascek was taken on and for consultancy, Dominic turned to Franco Bernabei, who first set the cellars on an even keel and then focused on the vine stock. Replanting followed and the area under vine was extended. In fact, the present 37 hectares are destined to grow before very long. In addition, Nocerino has radically redesigned the cellars. Within a year, work will have been completed and the cellar space will finally have a more rational distribution. Dominic also appreciated that it was crucial to have a commercial profile in the region so he completed his team with the arrival of professional winewoman, Barbara Maniacco. JN is a wine that Dominic has dedicated to his wife, Judith. A blend of two thirds barrique-aged chardonnay and one third stainless steel-vinified sauvignon, it is one of Sant'Elena's trio of signature wines, the other two being the Merlot and the Pinot Grigio. The Tato '99 is a 75-25 blend of cabernet sauvignon and merlot that ages in oak, after alcoholic and malolactic fermentation. It's got plenty of cellar potential, as has the very impressive Merlot 2000.

O	Bianco JN '00	♛♛	5
●	Merlot '00	♛♛	4*
O	Pinot Grigio '01	♛♛	4*
●	Tato '99	♛	6
●	Friuli Isonzo Tato '97	♛♛	5
●	Friuli Isonzo Ròs di Ròl '98	♛♛	5
●	Friuli Isonzo Ròs di Ròl '99	♛♛	5

MANZANO (UD)

BANDUT - GIORGIO COLUTTA
VIA ORSARIA, 32
33044 MANZANO (UD)
TEL. 0432740315
E-MAIL: colutta@colutta.it

Determinedly, Giorgio Colutta has put together a totally new estate team. Trentino-born cellar technician Clizia Zambiasi is showing she's got what it takes to produce results in conditions that are far from easy. Her difficulties derive from renovation work on the walls that will restore their ancient configuration, the arrival of new containers in the cellar and the acquisition of new equipment. Luckily, Clizia's task is made a little less onerous by the efforts of fruitmaker Marco Simonit and vineyard manager Antonio Maggio, who look after the vine stock in tandem. So far, five hectares have been replanted at a vine density of 5,600 plants per hectare but the estate has a total of 18. We would like to stress that all this work is producing clean, elegant wines and a steady rise in the quality levels of both whites and reds. The best Bandut wine is the Selenard, a blend of pinot nero, cabernet sauvignon, refosco and schioppettino. A year in oak has given it cellar potential and rich fruit on nose and palate, where generous notes of berry fruit tart linger attractively. The Refosco 2001 aged in 15-hectolitre barrels. Admirably varietal, it stands out for its complex vein of spice. Top of the 2001 white charts are the fresh, green pepper Sauvignon and the Nojâr (Friulian for "hazel tree"), a barrique-aged blend of riesling and ribolla gialla, with a splash of chardonnay.

● COF Rosso Selenard '00	5
○ COF Bianco Nojâr '01	4
● COF Refosco P. R. '01	4
○ COF Sauvignon '01	4
● COF Cabernet Sauvignon '01	4
○ COF Pinot Grigio '01	4
● COF Cabernet Sauvignon '00	4

MANZANO (UD)

ROSA BOSCO
FRAZ. ROSAZZO
VIA ABATE COLONNA, 20
33044 MANZANO (UD)
TEL. 0432751522 - 043233044

In the increasingly predictable world of wine, the urge to stand out from the crowd has led growers to play up the differences between native and international varieties. Like all such extreme generalizations, the distinction soon began to look fuzzy. For example, how long do you have to wait before an imported vine can be considered culturally and agriculturally integrated into the territory? If we remember that "... Merlot was like polenta - it was in every home ..." and the records show that Sauvignon was "... without doubt the first white wine ..." in the area until the final decade of the 19th century. So, Rosetta Bosca is right to focus on these two varieties, which marry territory, an international dimension and quality. The fruit grows in the hills at Buttrio, Manzano and Premariacco, the ideal setting for imbuing the wines with roundness, warmth, velvety smoothness, firm cherry (in the Merlot) and peach (for the Sauvignon) fruit and attractive herbaceous notes that, in the Sauvignon, recall mint and tarragon. Rosetta was right for two further reasons. The first is her decision to concentrate on a limited number of almost maniacally groomed wines and the other is the palate of her very first wine. Three years after release, it confirms its superior quality, hinting at even better things to come in the future.

● COF Rosso Il Boscorosso '00	7
○ COF Sauvignon Blanc '01	6
● COF Boscorosso '99	7
○ COF Sauvignon Blanc '00	6
● COF Boscorosso '98	7
○ COF Sauvignon Blanc '99	6

MANZANO (UD)

WALTER FILIPUTTI
FRAZ. ROSAZZO
P.ZZA DELL'ABBAZIA, 15
33044 MANZANO (UD)
TEL. 0432759429
E-MAIL: w-filiputti@triangolo.it

Walter Filiputti's winery has an enviable home in the splendid abbey at Rosazzo. The names and labels of his wines recall the glorious past of one of the most important places in the history of viticulture and olive oil production in Friuli. Walter himself has been a leading player on the recent Friulian wine scene so we always expect something special from him. His flagship bottles are excellent. The Picolit 2000 Riserva Monasterium has a dry, delicately flowery nose. Not particularly powerful in the mouth, it still shows elegance and length on a par with the best wines in the category. There's lots of depth in the Pignolo Riserva Prima Vigna '99, the fruit for which comes from the first plot planted in 1981, just below the abbey. The spice on the nose shades into cocoa powder and the palate has concentration and delicious sweet tannins, although it lacks a little length. A tad more stamina on the palate would have won a second Glass for the Filip di Filip '99, a red from merlot and cabernet franc. Spicy nuances of cinnamon usher in a meaty mouthfeel, redolent of very ripe fruit. The Broili di Filip 2001 is obtained from steel-vinified refosco and merlot. Its impenetrable hue releases elegant geranium then the soft, pervasive palate is attractively drinkable. Walter's whites are fairly similar. Not very intense on the nose, they are moderately concentrated, fairly subtle and show fresh acidity. We have no complaints about the style – it's faultless – but they are a tad one-dimensional.

○	COF Picolit Monasterium Ris. '00	♟♟	7
●	COF Rosso Pignolo Prima Vigna Ris. '99	♟♟	8
○	COF Bianco Poiesis '00	♟	5
●	Broili di Filip '01	♟	4
○	Chardonnay '01	♟	4
○	COF Sauvignon Suvignis '01	♟	5
○	Pinot Grigio '01	♟	4
●	Filip di Filip '99	♟	5

MANZANO (UD)

LE VIGNE DI ZAMÒ
FRAZ. ROSAZZO
VIA ABATE CORRADO, 4
33044 MANZANO (UD)
TEL. 0432759693
E-MAIL: info@levignedizamo.com

If we had to pick the one top-notch winery that has made most progress in improving quality levels, then it would have to be the estate run by brothers Pierluigi and Silvano Zamò. In recent years, the Zamòs have been carrying out a series of operations in vineyard and cellar to rationalize production. Plots have been bought, sold or rented in the context of a strategy that aims to group the vine stock around the cellar itself. The vinification cellar has been built a few hundred metres away from the office and hospitality complex and can point to modern winemaking equipment. One section is all stainless steel and computers, another houses the barrels and a third the bottle store. For years, Franco Bernabei has been the Zamòs' consultant and the arrival of Emilio Del Medico has added something extra. The pair work together in complete harmony, and the cellar turns out some stupendous reds and whites. This year, the Merlot Vigne Cinquant'Anni '99 earned Three Glasses, showing yet again that old vines give the finest wines. Complexity, concentration and intensity on the nose introduce a full-bodied, pervasive mouthfeel driven by serious tannins and fruit. The better of the two Tocais is the standard version. This splendid wine won our hearts as soon as we made our first tastings in late spring. We recommend cellaring it for a while and comparing it with the Tocai Cinquant'Anni, a wine that itself earned Two very full Glasses. Finally, the stylishly creamy, fresh-tasting Malvasia 2001 is again on top form.

●	COF Merlot Vigne Cinquant'Anni '99	♟♟♟	6
○	COF Tocai Friulano '01	♟♟	4*
○	COF Malvasia '01	♟♟	4*
○	COF Tocai Friulano Vigne Cinquant'Anni '01	♟♟	5
○	COF Pinot Bianco Tullio Zamò '00	♟♟	5
○	COF Rosazzo Ribolla Gialla '01	♟♟	4
○	COF Sauvignon '01	♟♟	4
●	COF Rosso Ronco dei Roseti '99	♟♟	6
○	COF Pinot Grigio '01	♟	4
○	COF Bianco Ronco delle Acacie '99	♟	5
○	COF Tocai Friulano Vigne Cinquant'Anni '00	♟♟♟	5

MANZANO (UD)

Ronchi di Manzano
Via Orsaria, 42
33044 Manzano (UD)
Tel. 0432740718 - 0432754098
E-mail: info@ronchidimanzano.com

This year, Roberta Borghese might not have produced a champion but the range as a whole is well worth investigating. There's rather an embarrassment of riches, though, with as many as seven reds on parade. Roberta's 45 hectares enjoy excellent positions on the hillslopes between Rosazzo and Manzano. Thinning is rigorous and yields per plant are often less than a kilogram. The Refosco dal Peduncolo Rosso 2000 has a concentrated hue and nose, where ripe berry fruit preludes the palate's wild cherries and spices, which is rounded off by a clean finish. The Merlot Ronc di Subule is a lovely deep ruby. Rich fruit and a stylish, intense progression, especially in the mouth, are lifted by a hint of tar and a tannin-rich finish. Also excellent are the complex fruit and flower Tocai Superiore and the creamy Rosazzo Bianco 2001, a sauvignon, chardonnay, tocai and picolit mix that foregrounds banana and ripe apricot. The golden Picolit Ronc di Rosazzo 2000 unveils intriguing baked apple and sweetness that follows through onto the palate, where a subtle hint of refreshing acidity emerges in the after-aroma. The subtle yet intense nose of the Pinot Grigio precedes a palate of pears, apples and citrus fruit. The Cabernet Sauvignon 2000 has concentration and complexity, despite hardish tannins. There are hints of super-ripeness in the Ronc di Rosazzo Rosso but the palate has insufficient muscle to stay the course.

MANZANO (UD)

Ronco delle Betulle
Fraz. Rosazzo
Via Abate Colonna, 24
33044 Manzano (UD)
Tel. 0432740547
E-mail: info@roncodellebetulle.it

Ten terraced hectares around a rustic home-cum-cellar in the prestigious Rosazzo subzone make up the magical world of Ivana Adami, a courteous, discreet winewoman who knows precisely what she wants from her bottles. She has behind her a strong tradition of excellent wines. The abbey of Rosazzo, the birthplace of Ribolla, is a stone's throw away, red varieties have always thrived in the mild local topoclimate and Franconia has settled in so well here that the wine has little to envy its cousins, the Blaufränkisch wines of Burgenland. Ivana is assisted by technician Giorgio Marone, who has for some time been helping her to bring out these territory-related characteristics. A fine example is provided by the Narciso Rosso '99. This warm, fruity merlot and cabernet sauvignon blend shows faint notes of tar and a balance in the mouth that promise cellarability. The Ribolla 2001 has elegant apple and spring flowers over banana, a pervasive, palpably fleshy mouthfeel. The attractively rustic Franconia 2000 is a fruit-rich wine ideal for serving with grilled meat. The '99 Narciso Bianco blend is equally convincing, the sweet, rich mouthfeel of chardonnay marrying beautifully with the barely hinted at aromas and green freshness of sauvignon. The Sauvignon 2001 also shows well as a monovarietal, scoring higher than the nonetheless interesting Pinot Bianco and Tocai.

- COF Merlot Ronc di Subule '00 — 5
- COF Refosco P. R. '00 — 4
- COF Rosazzo Picolit Ronc di Rosazzo '00 — 6
- COF Rosazzo Bianco Ronc di Rosazzo '01 — 4
- COF Tocai Friulano Sup. '01 — 4
- COF Cabernet Sauvignon '00 — 4
- COF Rosazzo Rosso Ronc di Rosazzo '00 — 4
- COF Chardonnay '01 — 4
- COF Pinot Grigio '01 — 4
- COF Sauvignon '01 — 4
- COF Merlot Ronc di Subule '99 — 5

- COF Rosazzo Narciso Rosso '99 — 7
- COF Rosazzo Ribolla Gialla '01 — 4*
- COF Sauvignon '01 — 4*
- COF Rosazzo Narciso Bianco '99 — 6
- Franconia '00 — 5
- COF Pinot Bianco '01 — 4
- COF Tocai Friulano '01 — 4
- Narciso Rosso '94 — 7
- COF Rosazzo Ribolla Gialla '00 — 4
- Franconia '99 — 5

MANZANO (UD)

TORRE ROSAZZA
FRAZ. OLEIS
LOC. POGGIOBELLO, 12
33044 MANZANO (UD)
TEL. 0432750180
E-MAIL: bm@borgomagredo.it

The origins of Torre Rosazza, whose name derives from the ancient Turris Rosacea, date back many centuries. Its location is superb. The splendid 18th-century De Marchi palazzo where the estate is based offers a view of Aquileia from its hilltop location. Just underneath are the terraced vineyards, arranged in two natural amphitheatres of Eocene marl soil. This is a substantial property – 90 hectares – for the hillslopes of Friuli and the owners, the Assicurazioni Generali insurance company, have hired a group of valid professionals to keep quality up to snuff. The efforts of agronomist Claudio Flaborea and wine technician Giovanni Tomadoni are co-ordinated by celebrated winemaker Donato Lanati and the genial sales director, Piero Totis. Results are excellent but there is still scope for improvement, given the overall profile of the estate. We'll begin with a wine that is more often a source of headaches for producers than of satisfaction, Pinot Nero. The Ronco del Palazzo '99 selection is very satisfying, both for its complex nose of well-defined redcurrant, bramble, fruit in alcohol and coffee, and for the excellent follow-through on the palate, where robust tannins add substance and a long wild berry finish rounds things off perfectly. A native Friulian variety provides another high scorer, the Refosco 2000. Very varietal, with marked spice, it unveils silky tannins that contribute to a luscious, attractively soft mouthfeel. Good 2001 whites include the Sauvignon, which packs plenty of flavour, and the Chardonnay, a wine with an intense nose of fruit.

● COF Pinot Nero Ronco del Palazzo '99	▼▼	4*
● COF Refosco P. R. '00	▼▼	4*
● COF Cabernet Franc '01	▼	4
○ COF Chardonnay '01	▼	4
○ COF Pinot Grigio '01	▼	4
○ COF Ribolla Gialla '01	▼	4
○ COF Sauvignon '01	▼	4
○ COF Tocai Friulano '01	▼	4
● COF Merlot '00		4
○ COF Picolit '99	▼▼	6
● COF Merlot L'Altromerlot '98	▼▼	6

MARIANO DEL FRIULI (GO)

EDDI LUISA
FRAZ. CORONA
VIA CORMONS, 19
34070 MARIANO DEL FRIULI (GO)
TEL. 048169680
E-MAIL: azienda@viniluisa.com

When you think of a typical family-run Friulian winery, the first that comes to mind is the Luisa estate at Corona. Eddi and Nella work in harmony with their sons, Michele and Davide, and the warmth and enthusiasm that drive their efforts soon emerges in conversation. Michele and Davide are now in charge, looking after the estate with the innovative spirit, so characteristic of younger winemakers, tempered with a healthy dose of respect for tradition. Their 55 hectares are in a single plot around the splendid cellar and main villa. The 200,000 bottles produced every year are released as a standard range and the I Ferretti wines, which come from the iron-rich soil of the Corona plain and thus have greater structure and solidity. All the wines passed muster and there were three high scorers, the Pinot Bianco 2001, the Chardonnay I Ferretti 2000 and the Merlot I Ferretti 1999, proof positive that the range is on target. The Pinot Bianco has striking varietal notes of apple and acacia blossom and a fresh-tasting palate that leads through to an unhurried finish of pears and apples. The Chardonnay is oak-fermented and stays in wood for nine months. The balanced aromas of confectioner's cream, pineapple and banana are nicely fresh, following through onto the palate, where they are lifted by vanilla nuances. The Merlot I Ferretti has peppery spice, bramble tart and coffee aromas, then progresses generously in the mouth, with assertive tannins and a tad too much acidity. Finally, the Tocai is very successful. Be patient, let it breathe and you will be delighted by its typicity.

○ Friuli Isonzo Chardonnay I Ferretti '00	▼▼	4
○ Friuli Isonzo Pinot Bianco '01	▼▼	3*
● Friuli Isonzo Merlot I Ferretti '99	▼▼	4
● Friuli Isonzo Cabernet Franc '01	▼	4
○ Friuli Isonzo Chardonnay '01	▼	3
● Friuli Isonzo Merlot '01	▼	3
○ Friuli Isonzo Tocai Friulano '01	▼	3
● Friuli Isonzo Cabernet Sauvignon I Ferretti '99	▼	4
● Friuli Isonzo Refosco P. R. I Ferretti '99	▼	4
○ Friuli Isonzo Pinot Grigio '01		3

MARIANO DEL FRIULI (GO)

Masut da Rive
Via Manzoni, 82
34070 Mariano del Friuli (GO)
tel. 048169200
e-mail: fabrizio@masutdarive.com

The Gallo family has always been involved with this property. Founded by great-grandfather Antonio, who ran the property until 1937, it was taken over by grandfather Ermenegildo, father Silvano and now Fabrizio, who looks after production and distribution, and his younger brother Marco, fresh out of wine school. At Masut da Rive, whose 17 hectares under vine yield 100,000 bottles a year, Fabrizio devotes much of his attention to perfecting vineyard and cellar management techniques, especially for the red that Mariano, with its iron-rich soil, is particularly well-suited to produce. The owners' efforts have again given us fine results for all the wines earned at least One Glass. The Sauvignon 2001 is a high flyer, its subtle yet intense aromas of apple and pear fruit salad and smoke following through on the palate, where a refreshing finish reveals nuances of yellow peach. The Pinot Bianco 2001 is as exquisite as ever, tropical fruit on the nose complementing a fragrant, flavoursome palate. The Merlot 2000 is on a par, thanks to its tempting nose of balanced mineral and balsam notes layered over fruit. There was nearly a second Glass for the Chardonnay Maurùs. When we tasted, it had yet to find a balance between its attractive banana, pineapple and orange fruit and the contribution of the oak.

○ Friuli Isonzo Sauvignon '01	ΨΨ	4*
● Friuli Isonzo Merlot '00	ΨΨ	4
○ Friuli Isonzo Pinot Bianco '01	ΨΨ	4
● Friuli Isonzo Cabernet Franc '00	Ψ	4
● Friuli Isonzo Cabernet Sauvignon '00	Ψ	4
○ Friuli Isonzo Chardonnay Maurùs '00	Ψ	5
○ Friuli Isonzo Chardonnay '01	Ψ	4
○ Friuli Isonzo Pinot Grigio '01	Ψ	4
○ Friuli Isonzo Tocai Friulano '01	Ψ	4
○ Friuli Isonzo Pinot Bianco '00	ΨΨ	4
● Friuli Isonzo Merlot '99	ΨΨ	4

MARIANO DEL FRIULI (GO)

★ Vie di Romans
Loc. Vie di Romans, 1
34070 Mariano del Friuli (GO)
tel. 048169600
e-mail: viediromans@tiscalinet.it

It is our pleasant duty to sing the praises of this exemplary winery. We can start with the skill of wine technician Gianfranco Gallo – it's not often that an Italian is summoned to California to teach the locals how to make white wine – and the shrewdly organized vineyards and cellars, then move on to the finished products. Again this year, they were straight out of the top drawer. It's not the first time we have made this point but the outstanding characteristics of Gianfranco's wines are cleanness, elegance and complexity. Everything else hinges on these three qualities. That is certainly the case with the two 2000 Sauvignons. The fresh-tasting Piere foregrounds apricot and pennyroyal while the Vieris has butter and mineral notes ushering in an incredibly long plate. This could well be the finest oaked Italian Sauvignon we have tasted this year. The two Chardonnay 2000 bottles bear witness to what a good vintage it was for the variety. The creamy Ciampagnis is very flowery and subtly aromatic whereas the sweet, juicy Vie di Romans shows the classic varietal notes of tropical fruit. It was another good year for the Pinot Grigio Dessimis. The very ripe fruit has lent the aromas minerally nuances that meld perfectly with its substantial but velvety weight in the mouth. A shade less convincing this year was the Flors di Uis, which reveals rather too exuberant flower and citrus aromas. The Voos dai Ciamps '99 is a very well-made wine but let down by jammy aromas.

○ Friuli Isonzo Sauvignon Vieris '00	ΨΨΨ	5
○ Friuli Isonzo Chardonnay Ciampagnis Vieris '00	ΨΨ	5
○ Friuli Isonzo Chardonnay Vie di Romans '00	ΨΨ	5
○ Friuli Isonzo Pinot Grigio Dessimis '00	ΨΨ	5
○ Friuli Isonzo Sauvignon Piere '00	ΨΨ	5
○ Friuli Isonzo Bianco Flors di Uis '00	Ψ	5
● Friuli Isonzo Rosso Voos dai Ciamps '99	Ψ	6
○ Friuli Isonzo Sauvignon Piere '97	ΨΨΨ	5
○ Friuli Isonzo Pinot Grigio Dessimis '99	ΨΨΨ	5

NIMIS (UD)

DARIO COOS
LOC. RAMANDOLO
VIA PESCIA, 1
33045 NIMIS (UD)
TEL. 0432790320 - 0432797807
E-MAIL: dariocoos@libero.it

Sadly, the clash between Guide deadlines and Dario Coos' winemaking schedule means that each year, we review wines that have been released months before and are no longer available at the cellar. That's the way it goes. As well as growing picolit and refosco, which for the time being is not bottled, Dario has introduced new approaches in the vineyard and in cellar techniques for vinifying verduzzo di Ramandolo. And by the way, we should mention that the wine from the last of these has at last, thanks to the results achieved by a growing number of wineries, been awarded DOCG status. Verduzzo is a white variety that shares many of the characteristics of red grapes, especially its thick skin and the high tannin content that makes the wine so distinctive. The variety has found a perfect environment at Ramandolo and the wine made here is without doubt unique. Much of the zone is made up of generally steep hillslopes that are swept by winds coming down from the Julian Alps. This means temperatures are on average lower than in southern Friuli and the risk of hail is high. Moving on to the wines, we liked the outstanding golden Picolit Romandus '99 for its elegant lime and acacia blossom, apple, banana, apricot and chamomile aromas and delicious sweetness in the mouth. The Longhino 2000, a more straightforward version of the Ramandolo, is also good. It marries lavender and stewed apple aromas with understated varietal tannins.

O	COF Picolit Romandus '99	▼▼	7
O	COF Ramandolo Il Longhino '00	▼	4*
O	COF Picolit Romandus '96	▼▼	6
O	COF Ramandolo Passito Romandus '97	▼▼	7
O	COF Ramandolo '99	▼▼	5
O	COF Ramandolo Il Longhino '99	▼▼	4

NIMIS (UD)

LA RONCAIA
FRAZ. CERGNEU
VIA VERDI, 26
33045 NIMIS (UD)
TEL. 0432790280
E-MAIL: info@laroncaia.com

La Roncaia has gained a well-earned Guide profile thanks to the joint efforts over the years of cousins Marco and Stefano Fantinel. They have 22 hectares planted to vine at Ramandolo, Nimis and also at Attimis, where their fabulous six and half hectare plot of hillslope picolit vines is located. In charge of the cellar is Massimo Vidoni, a young man with sound experience in local wineries. He is backed up by the much-admired Hungarian consultant, Tibor Gal (remember the Ornellaia released a few years ago?). The cellar, in the verdant valley at Cergneu, near Nimis, was renovated only a few years ago. La Roncaia wines still need a little more work as the technical staff is still feeling its way in this new environment. Marco Fantinel would love to move things along but is well aware that viticulture has its own, leisurely time scale. His territory-focused wines are the Ramandolo and the Picolit. The Ramandolo, a DOCG, comes from fruit harvested in late November that is destemmed by hand and raisined in a force-ventilated environment. Sweet but not cloying, it reveals notes of air-dried figs and apricots. In contrast, the picolit has pineapple and candied citrus peel, banana and peaches in syrup. Eclisse 2000 is 95 per cent sauvignon with picolit and is vinified in stainless steel while Il Fusco, from refosco, cabernet franc, merlot and tazzelenghe, and the merlot, cabernet and refosco-based Gheppio '99, ferment and age in wood.

O	COF Ramandolo '00	▼▼	8
●	COF Rosso Gheppio '99	▼▼	7
O	COF Bianco Eclisse '00	▼	6
●	COF Merlot '00	▼	5
O	COF Picolit '00	▼	8
O	COF Chardonnay '00	▼	6
●	Il Fusco	▼	7
●	COF Cabernet Sauvignon '00		6

PASIAN DI PRATO (UD)

ANTONUTTI
FRAZ. COLLOREDO
VIA D'ANTONI, 21
33030 PASIAN DI PRATO (UD)
TEL. 0432662001
E-MAIL: info@antonuttivini.it

Founded by Ignazio Antonutti in 1921, this winery vinifies grapes from 40 estate-owned hectares at Barbeano, in the flatlands near Splimbergo, and some bought-in fruit. We know how difficult it is to keep up quality standards with supplies of this nature but for years, the Antonutti cellar has been presenting us with reliable bottles and even the occasional little jewel, such as this year's Sauvignon Blanc and Merlot. A lot of credit must go to the abilities of Adriana and Paolo, the third generation of Antonuttis, and to Lino Durandi, as well as to their efficient oenologist Paolo Pineschi. It's a team that is synonymous with premium quality. It's also interesting to note the slogan on the Antonutti brochures, "Crescere Senza Dimenticare La Tradizione" (Growing Without Forgetting Tradition), which neatly sums up the estate's commitment. Traditionally, Antonutti Sauvignon Blanc is a fine wine and this year is no exception. The aromas strike a felicitous balance of sweet melon and peach with more vegetal nuances of tomato leaf. The attack on the palate is intensely fruity, with broad, lingering yellow peach to the fore. The Merlot 2000 has distinct hints of plum jam and white pepper on the nose then freshness and depth in the mouth. The other Merlot, the Poggio Alto from 1999, came close to a second Glass. We should also make a note of how good the Cabernet Sauvignon '99 is. The variety is not an easy one to cultivate in the Grave DOC zone but this version offers vibrant liqueur fruit aromas, silky extract and delicious softness.

PAVIA DI UDINE (UD)

F.LLI PIGHIN
FRAZ. RISANO
V.LE GRADO, 1
33050 PAVIA DI UDINE (UD)
TEL. 0432675444
E-MAIL: azpighin@tin.it

The Pighin brothers set up their winery in the early 1960s, since when it has become one of the region's largest privately owned cellars. Today, the estate includes 150 hectares under vine in the Friuli Grave DOC zone and 30 or so in the Collio, at Capriva del Friuli. In an average year, the cellar produces 10,000 hectolitres of Grave wines and just over 2,000 from the Collio. Cropping levels are kept below the maximum allowed by DOC regulations. The main complex is organized to deal with large quantities and lies on the main Udine-Aquileia-Grado road. The Pighins also own a lovely 18th-century villa set in parkland at Risano, which they use as a hospitality centre. For years, Paolo Valdesolo has been the Pighins' wine technician and we have never had to reject any of the bottles he has presented. Sometimes, as was the case this year, there are not outstanding products but the average standards of the cellar are admirably reliable. The Baredo comes from cabernet sauvignon, merlot and refosco, vinified and aged for a year in stainless steel. Thereafter, it goes into barrique for eight months and finally ages in 32-hectolitre barrels. The '98, like other vintages, puts elegance before power. But the leading Pighin wine, not just in terms of sales, is the 2001 Pinot Grigio delle Grave, which offers elegant aromas and good weight in the mouth.

● Friuli Grave Merlot '00	▼▼	3*
○ Friuli Grave Sauvignon Blanc Le Selezioni '01	▼▼	4
○ Friuli Grave Chardonnay '01	▼	3
○ Friuli Grave Chardonnay Poggio Alto '01	▼	4
○ Friuli Grave Pinot Bianco '01	▼	3
○ Friuli Grave Sauvignon '01	▼	3
○ Friuli Grave Tocai Friulano '01	▼	3
● Friuli Grave Cabernet Sauvignon '99	▼	4
● Friuli Grave Merlot Poggio Alto '99	▼	4
○ Friuli Grave Pinot Grigio '01		4
○ Friuli Grave Sauvignon Blanc Le Selezioni '00	▼▼	4

● Collio Cabernet '00	▼	4
● Collio Merlot '00	▼	4
○ Friuli Grave Chardonnay '01	▼	3
○ Friuli Grave Pinot Grigio '01	▼	3
● Baredo '98	▼	5
● Friuli Grave Merlot '99		3
○ Collio Pinot Bianco '01		4
○ Collio Pinot Grigio '01		4

PAVIA DI UDINE (UD)

SCARBOLO
FRAZ. LAUZACCO
V.LE GRADO, 4
33050 PAVIA DI UDINE (UD)
TEL. 0432675612

To call Valter Scarbolo a man of many parts is to understate the case. Grower, cellarman, supervisor of the Bastianich estate and pork butcher (his cold meat products are outstanding), he is also the hands-on manager of a highly successful restaurant, previously run as an "agriturismo". For the past few years, Valter has been vinifying only grapes whose progress he has followed in person, from his nine hectares under vine, three he rents and suppliers with whom he keeps in close contact during the growing season. The last vintage yielded 140,000 bottles, most of them white. When he has his growing hat on, Valter is flanked by Emilio Del Medico, a young and very capable Friulian wine technician, as well as Tuscan consultant Maurizio Castelli, who has been working in Friuli for many years. Scarbolo releases a small range of reds called Campo del Viotto, one of which is his Refosco '99. An upfront, varietal wine, it has black and white pepper spice on the nose, then berry and cooked fruit on a palate braced by substantial extract. The whites are all excellently made and offer very good value for money. Determined to boost the quality of his premium range, Valter has decided not to release any 2000 or 2001 reds under his flagship label. A 2001 white, which we will be coming back to, is currently ageing in oak.

PINZANO AL TAGLIAMENTO (PN)

ALESSANDRO VICENTINI ORGNANI
FRAZ. VALERIANO
VIA SOTTOPLOVIA, 2
33090 PINZANO AL TAGLIAMENTO (PN)
TEL. 0432950107
E-MAIL: vicentiniorgnani@libero.it

The new labels for the classic estate line are much more elegant than the old ones. The logo carries the words Colline di Valeriano, bearing witness to how deeply the cellar's roots are sunk in a territory as vast and idiosyncratic as the Grave DOC zone. But then, Alessandro Vicentini Orgnani has always been a bold, original winemaker. He took over the family estate when he was very young, giving it a new, modern direction both in vineyard and in cellar. He dropped the well-known local varieties with one exception, ucelut, which he rightly regards as a grape with a future. Alessandro also launched the Braide Cjase range of partly oaked wines and finally built up a prestigious image for Ucelut itself, while also investing in a Merlot Riserva that is currently maturing in the cellar. The results prove that he was right. Alessandro's Ucelut 2000 and Pinot Bianco Braide Cjase 2001 are wines of the first rank. The amber Ucelut is oily and concentrated in the glass, releasing notes of fig jam and candied peel that follow through onto the palate. The rich mouthfeel ends with a very special fresh-tasting finish that leaves the mouth clean as a whistle. The Pinot Bianco earned its fifth successive Two Glass score, which speaks volumes for its dependability. Fruit and pipe tobacco aromas are layered with fresher, softer notes of vanilla, flowers and peach. Alessandro's One Glass wines include the Pinot Grigio 2001. Both the standard version and the Braide Cjase edition performed very well.

	Wine		Score
●	Friuli Grave Refosco P. R. Campo del Viotto '99	ŸŸ	5
○	Friuli Grave Chardonnay '01	Ÿ	3*
○	Friuli Grave Sauvignon '01	Ÿ	3*
○	Friuli Grave Tocai Friulano '01	Ÿ	3*
●	Friuli Grave Merlot '00		3

	Wine		Score
○	Ucelut Bianco '00	ŸŸ	7
○	Friuli Grave Pinot Bianco Braide Cjase '01	ŸŸ	4*
●	Friuli Grave Merlot '01	Ÿ	4
○	Friuli Grave Pinot Grigio '01	Ÿ	3
○	Friuli Grave Pinot Grigio Braide Cjase '01	Ÿ	4
●	Friuli Grave Cabernet Sauvignon '01		3
○	Friuli Grave Chardonnay Braide Cjase '01		4
○	Ucelut Bianco '99	ŸŸ	7

POVOLETTO (UD)

AQUILA DEL TORRE
FRAZ. SAVORGNANO DEL TORRE
VIA ATTIMIS, 25
33040 POVOLETTO (UD)
TEL. 0432666428
E-MAIL: aquiladeltorre@tin.it

The Aquila del Torre estate is in the hill country at Savorgnano. Its 82 hectares in a single property include 25 set aside for viticulture. The present owners are father and son Claudio and Michele Ciani, who acquired it in 1996. They have not changed the name of the property, which dates from 1990. That doesn't mean this winery lacks tradition, though. Previously, it was known as Podere del Sole and was already turning out admirable wines in the early 1970s. The Cianis have replanted about 14 hectares, with the assistance of experts of the calibre of Marco Simonit, identifying the most suitable areas for each vine type. The two natural amphitheatres involved in this vineyard campaign are now even more spectacularly beautiful as a result. Over the past year, much renovation work has been done in the cellars. This has put winemaking, which is supervised by oenologist Francesco Noro, under a certain amount of pressure. Still, the three wines released are all good, starting with the Picolit Vendemmia Tardiva '99. A very sweet wine, it hints at almond milk, figs in caramel and apricots. The Tocai Friulano has well-defined aromas of golden delicious apples and a very long finish whereas the Sauvignon's aromatic herb and elderflower nose ushers in a complex, butter-smooth palate with an unhurried after-aroma of citrus fruit and peaches.

POVOLETTO (UD)

TERESA RAIZ
FRAZ. MARSURE DI SOTTO
VIA DELLA ROGGIA, 22
33040 POVOLETTO (UD)
TEL. 0432679071
E-MAIL: info@teresaraiz.com

Paolo and Giovanni Tosoli's estate has been active for more than 30 years and continues to make improvements to its production base. The 20 hectares under vine around the cellar, which is in the same complex as the Camel distillery, have been replanted with quality in mind and are slowly coming onstream. This means that the Friuli Grave DOC wines released under the Le Marsure label are increasingly dependable. The Teresa Raiz range is named after the pair's Austrian grandmother and the label graces wines from the Colli Orientali del Friuli. Grapes for these products come from the hills at Savorgnano del Torre, Faedis and Campeglio, in the northern part of the DOC zone. Each year, about 200,000 bottles are distributed in Italy and abroad. The Decano Rosso '99 Bordeaux blend enjoyed an excellent vintage and took full advantage. The complex berry fruit aromas are mirrored on the palate, which is braced by tannins in the finish that tell you the wine has a long, happy future ahead. The 2001 wines include a superbly balanced, apple-themed Tocai that combines flavour with freshness. The subtle, concentrated aromas of the Pinot Grigio blossom on the palate with nice depth of fruit then sign off with a long, attractive finish. The Ribolla Gialla is nice. Obtained from one of the region's more interesting native grapes, it has a refreshing varietal acidity that makes it an ideal partner for fish. Finally, the Querciolo 2000, a mix of merlot with a little cabernet sauvignon, also performed well.

○	COF Picolit V. T. '99	♄♄	8
○	COF Sauvignon Vocalis '01	♄	5
○	COF Tocai Friulano Vocalis '01	♄	5
●	COF Merlot Vocalis '99	♄♄	5
○	COF Picolit '99	♄♄	6

○	COF Tocai Friulano '01	♄	4*
○	Friuli Grave Pinot Grigio Le Marsure '01	♄♄	3*
●	COF Rosso Decano Rosso '99	♄♄	5
●	Friuli Grave Cabernet '00	♄	4
●	Querciolo '00	♄	3
○	Chardonnay '01	♄	4
○	COF Pinot Grigio '01	♄	4
○	COF Ribolla Gialla '01	♄	4
○	COF Sauvignon '01		4
○	Friuli Grave Chardonnay Le Marsure '00	♄♄	4
●	COF Rosso Decano Rosso '97	♄♄	5

PRATA DI PORDENONE (PN)

VIGNETI LE MONDE
FRAZ. LE MONDE
VIA GARIBALDI, 2
33080 PRATA DI PORDENONE (PN)
TEL. 0434626096 - 0434622087
E-MAIL: info@vignetilemonde.com

The Pinot Bianco 2001 from Vigneti Le Monde scaled the heights to win Three Glasses this year. Since we started publishing the Guide, it is the first time that a wine from the Grave del Friuli DOC zone has won top honours. We hope this is just the beginning and that the success will stimulate producers and consumers to explore the potential of the area. Piergiovanni Pistoni, with the help of oenologist Luigi Franco, had no doubts. Harvesting the fruit when very ripe and using cold maceration, then leaving the wine on the lees until May, he has obtained a wine with significant alcohol and wonderful quality. Pistoni distributes 25,000 bottles of this marvellous wine, which has a very subtle nose of elegant balsamic notes layered over varietal almond and grassy notes. Balance, softness, warmth and length are the distinguishing features of the yellow apple-nuanced palate. Vigneti Le Monde has 25 hectares under vine in the Pordenone flatlands, which also produced the excellent sauvignon-based Bianco Pujan 2000. Wild roses, peaches and ripe banana regale the nose, to be followed by a delicious contrast of soft fruit against almond and vanilla in the mouth. The '98 Pinot Nero is back on form. Its warm, balsamic nose finds a nice balance of berry fruit salad and coffee, which are mirrored on the well-structured palate. Serious tannins guarantee a long sojourn in the cellar.

○	Friuli Grave Pinot Bianco '01	🍷🍷🍷 3*
○	Friuli Grave Bianco Puja '00	🍷🍷 4
●	Friuli Grave Pinot Nero '98	🍷🍷 4
○	Friuli Grave Bianco Pra' de Gai '01	🍷 3
○	Friuli Grave Chardonnay '01	🍷 3
○	Friuli Grave Pinot Grigio '01	🍷 3
●	Friuli Grave Refosco P. R. '01	🍷 3
○	Friuli Grave Sauvignon '01	🍷 3
●	Querceto '97	🍷 5
●	Friuli Grave Rosso Ca' Salice '00	3
●	Friuli Grave Cabernet Sauvignon '00	3
○	Friuli Grave Sauvignon Puja '99	🍷🍷 4

PRATA DI PORDENONE (PN)

VILLA FRATTINA
LOC. GHIRANO
VIA PALAZZETTO, 68
33080 PRATA DI PORDENONE (PN)
TEL. 0434605911
E-MAIL: villafrattina@averna.it

Past and future pervade Villa Frattina. In 1000 AD, Marzutus, ancestor of the noble Frattina family, is recorded in the area campaigning against the invading Hungarians. A manuscript from 1332 refers to the family's links with viticulture and wine. The estate now has 60 hectares under vine around the splendid 17th-century villa and 14th-century chapel dedicated to Saint Michael. Careful study of the local soil types and geology, in collaboration with Attilio Scienza, has led to the zoning project currently being launched to match the varieties planted with the terroir. Consultant Donato Lanati and oenologist Ivan Molaro are co-ordinating proceedings. This determination to do well shines through in the wines, which are excellent. The Sauvignon and blended Corte dell'Abbà red top a very respectable list. In fact, the panel rejected none of the bottles tasted. The Corte dell'Abbà '99 is obtained from cabernet sauvignon, merlot, refosco and cabernet franc aged in barrique for 15 months. Aromas of berry fruit tart are nicely offset by hints of cakes on the nose before the well-rounded mouthfeel reveals admirable extract and a warm finish. The Sauvignon 2001 has peach, rue and tomato leaf aromas and decent weight. There was a full Glass for the Refosco, whose complex pepper and liqueur cherry aromas introduce a fruit-led palate.

○	Lison-Pramaggiore Sauvignon '01	🍷🍷 4*
●	Rosso Corte dell'Abbà '99	🍷🍷 6
●	Refosco P. R. '00	🍷 4
●	Robbio '00	🍷 4
○	Di Gale '01	🍷 4
●	Lison-Pramaggiore Cabernet Sauvignon '01	🍷 4
○	Lison-Pramaggiore Chardonnay '01	🍷 4
●	Lison-Pramaggiore Merlot '01	🍷 4
○	Lison-Pramaggiore Pinot Grigio '01	🍷 4
○	Ale di Glesie '00	5
●	Rosso Corte dell'Abbà '98	🍷🍷 6

PRAVISDOMINI (PN)

Podere dal Ger
Fraz. Frattina
Via Strada della Meduna, 13
33076 Pravisdomini (PN)
tel. 0434644452
e-mail: robspina@hotmail.com

Podere dal Ger may not be located in an exceptional wine area but it is certainly showing the way ahead to quality. The Spinazzè family decided to concentrate on a small number of wine types and Podere dal Ger is the only estate in Friuli to benefit from the input of Abruzzo-based oenologist Romeo Taraborelli. Renovation of the vine stock is being carried out under the direction of expert agronomist Marco Simonit. All this has produced an interesting blended red and an extremely innovative bottle, the Verduzzo Limine, which are very much the cellar's signature wines. And if that were not enough, work is now beginning on a state-of-the-art cellar. It has to be said that the palpable enthusiasm of Robert Spinazzè and his father, Luigino, are guarantees for the future. The Verduzzo Limine '99 is bound to draw comments for its originality. It is not the sweet Verduzzo we are used to but a dry wine, redolent of vanilla, ripe peach and dried spring flowers, that offers a creamy, well-rounded palate with good balance and a long finish. The El Masut '99 is a blend of cask-conditioned cabernet franc, cabernet sauvignon and merlot that flaunts liqueur cherries, white chocolate and mint before the rich palate shows its breadth and elegance through to the unhurried finish. Last of the outstanding bottles is the deep red Merlot 2000, which shows balsamic aromas, bramble tart and great structure backed up by solid tannins.

PREMARIACCO (UD)

Bastianich
Fraz. Casali Ottelio, 7
33040 Premariacco (UD)
tel. 0432675612 - 0432655363
e-mail: bastianich@aol.com

It was yet another great year for this recently founded estate. New York-born Giuseppe Bastianich, known to his friends as "Joe", re-established his links with his original homeland by purchasing about 20 hectares on the hillslopes of Buttrio. This was at the prompting of his mother Lidia, who emigrated to the United States from Pula, in Istria. Today, Joe is a leading restaurateur in America and in fact holds the James Beard Award, the Oscar of United States cuisine. His winemaking team is made up of general manager, Valter Scarbolo, vineyard and cellar expert Emilio Del Medico, consultant Maurizio Castelli and Wayne Young, a youthful professional from America who is always on hand at crucial moments. Three wines went through to the Three Glass taste-offs. All boast such incredible structure that the whites are a match for food even after you have been drinking a red. Calabrone '99 is a blend of merlot harvested when fully ripe with slightly raisined refosco and cabernet that ages in new barriques and tonneaux. It's a red with body, soft tannins, lots of muscle and elegance. The rich, full-bodied palate is drinking well already but it has plenty of cellar potential. The Vespa Bianco 2000 is extraordinary. From sauvignon and chardonnay with a small, but critically important, proportion of picolit, it carried off Three Glasses for the second year running. Our tasting came to a spectacular conclusion with the 2000 Pinot Grigio Plus, an irresistible Tocai from the same vintage and an eminently cellarable '99 Pinot Grigio Plus.

● Lison-Pramaggiore Merlot '00	♟♟	3*
● El Masut '99	♟♟	5
○ Verduzzo Limine '99	♟♟	5
● Lison-Pramaggiore Cabernet Franc '00	♟	3
○ Lison-Pramaggiore Chardonnay '01	♟	3
○ Lison-Pramaggiore Pinot Grigio '01	♟	3
○ Lison-Pramaggiore Pinot Grigio '00	♟♟	3

○ Vespa Bianco '00	♟♟♟	5
○ COF Pinot Grigio Plus '00	♟♟	5
● Calabrone '99	♟♟	7
○ COF Tocai Friulano Plus '00	♟♟	5
○ COF Pinot Grigio Plus '99	♟♟	5
○ Vespa Bianco '99	♟♟♟	5
○ COF Tocai Friulano Plus '98	♟♟	5
● Vespa Rosso '98	♟♟	5
○ COF Tocai Friulano Plus '99	♟♟	5

PREMARIACCO (UD)

Dario e Luciano Ermacora
Loc. Ipplis
Via Solzaredo, 9
33040 Premariacco (UD)
Tel. 0432716250
E-mail: info@ermacora.it

It was back in 1922 that brothers Antonio and Giuseppe Ermacora began to make wine on the family's six-hectare estate in the hills at Ipplis. Sixty years later, grandsons Dario and Luciano have decided to develop the estate and can now call on 19 hectares under vine, of which 14 are in a single plot around the modern cellar. Production runs at 120,000 bottles a year. For years, the Ermacora wines have been models of typicity and winemaking skill that you could use as examples on a tasting course. This, of course, is the result of rigorous work in vineyard and cellar. High quality is a given, as the six Two Glass wines this year amply demonstrate. We'll begin with the red Rîul '99 blend, based mainly on merlot, with small proportions of refosco and cabernet sauvignon. One and a half years' ageing in wood has lent it warmth on the nose, which has intense spice and bramble fragrances. A no-nonsense entry is followed by richness and depth in the mouth, with a long finish of Peruvian bark and bramble jam. The Picolit 2000 is extremely varietal, its elegant stewed apple, lime blossom, orange and noble rot introducing a palate of dried figs, apricot and candied orange peel. The Pinot Bianco is an estate classic. The bright hue of the 2001 edition precedes a lovely apple and spring flower nose and a flavoursome palate with a fresh-tasting finish. Other 2001 wines we would like to point out are the very refreshing Sauvignon, the subtle, creamy Verduzzo Friulano and the clean, minerally Pinot Grigio, which reveals nice hints of acacia honey.

○	COF Picolit '00	🍷🍷	7
○	COF Pinot Bianco '01	🍷🍷	4
○	COF Pinot Grigio '01	🍷🍷	4
○	COF Sauvignon '01	🍷🍷	4
○	COF Verduzzo Friulano '01	🍷🍷	4
●	COF Rîul Rosso '99	🍷🍷	5
●	COF Merlot '00	🍷	4
○	COF Tocai Friulano '01	🍷	3*
●	COF Refosco P. R. '00		4
○	COF Pinot Bianco '00	🍷🍷	4

PREMARIACCO (UD)

La Tunella
Loc. Ipplis
Via del Collio, 14
33040 Premariacco (UD)
Tel. 0432716030
E-mail: info@latunella.it

Brothers Massimo and Marco Zorzettig, with their mother Gabriella, have changed the name of this estate, which is now called La Tunella, the local name for the area. In many ways, the change was a painful one, for the cellar used to bear the name of Livio Zorzettig, who passed away at an early age some years ago. The estate has grown gradually to its current 79 hectares under vine and radically reviewed its production policies. In consequence, distribution strategies have also been modified. For years, the cellar made wine to be sold unbottled, buying in fruit from a number of growers, but today only estate-grown grapes are vinified. Sales amount to almost 400,000 bottles a year, three quarters of which go to non-domestic markets, especially the United States and Germany. Much of the vine stock has been replanted at higher vine densities and work has started on the new cellar, which will be able to handle more than twice the current production level. One of the key players in this renewal is Luigino Zamparo, the young oenologist who has been collaborating with the Zorzettig family for a number of years. The results are there for all to see in the table below. Progress has been consolidated for whites and sweet wines but there is still plenty of room for improvement with the reds. Still, even these are good bottles and, as in the case of the Cabernet Franc, some are excellent. The Campo Marzio 2000, from tocai, pinot bianco and ribolla, and L'Arcione '99, a cabernet sauvignon, merlot and schioppettino-based red, earned very full Glasses.

●	COF Cabernet Franc '01	🍷🍷	4*
○	COF Pinot Grigio '01	🍷🍷	4*
○	COF Ribolla Gialla '01	🍷🍷	4*
○	COF Bianco Campo Marzio '00	🍷	5
●	COF Merlot '01	🍷	4
○	COF Picolit '01	🍷	7
●	COF Refosco P. R. '01	🍷	4
○	COF Tocai Friulano '01	🍷	4
○	Noans '01	🍷	5
●	COF Rosso L'Arcione '99	🍷	5

PREMARIACCO (UD)

Rocca Bernarda
Loc. Ipplis
Via Rocca Bernarda, 27
33040 Premariacco (UD)
tel. 0432716273 - 0432716914
e-mail: roccabernarda@roccabernarda.com

The Sovereign Military Order of Malta, which has owned Rocca Bernarda since 1977, began to make serious investments some years ago and quality standards have been rising steadily. The estate staff is of the first rank. Oenologist Marco Monchiero and estate manager Mario Zuliani have recently been joined by agronomist Giorgio Braida. The 40-hectare estate now has new plantings of picolit, a variety of whose history Rocca Bernarda is symbolic and whose 1997 edition won the estate our White of the Year award. This year, Rocca Bernarda failed by a whisker to win Three Glasses but the entire range presented was nonetheless outstanding. We'll begin with the cellar's signature wines, the 2000 Picolit and Merlot Centis. The Picolit had only recently gone into the bottle but still managed to show a broad swathe of aromas, from dried figs to oranges, candied apricots and cakes, all underpinned by noble rot. Faithfully mirrored on the palate, the aromas accompany the full-bodied flavour through to the clean, refreshing finish. The Merlot Centis has intense, creamy aromas of milk chocolate and bottled black cherries, then the balanced palate offers robust tannins in a soft mouthfeel. The Vineis 2001, from cask-conditioned chardonnay tocai and sauvignon, is another serious wine. Its attractive nose introduces a lovely contrast of oak-derived flavours, fruit and tanginess on the palate.

PREMARIACCO (UD)

Scubla
Loc. Ipplis
Via Rocca Bernarda, 22
33040 Premariacco (UD)
tel. 0432716258
e-mail: scublavini@libero.it

This compact, eight-hectare estate has been giving Roberto Scubla the opportunity to explore the world of winemaking for quite a few years. However, experimentation for its own sake is pointless so Roberto has roped in a few friends and professionals to do things systematically, concentrating on a small number of labels and leaving the others to one side. As a result, there are often distinct highs and lows in Roberto's line-up. The Graticcio is always at the top of the tree. It's a verduzzo-based wine from fruit left to raisin in the winds that blow from eastern Europe and again this year, it is incredible. There are notes of wistaria and dried fruit, with a hint of volatility to offset the concentration of sugar and extract, highlighting the aromas. Three other wines are outstanding. The Pomédes 2000, from tocai and pinot bianco from a late harvest, with slightly raisined riesling, opens on summer flowers, peach and citrus fruits, then moves on to a fresh-tasting palate, only slightly sweet on the front palate. The Pinot Bianco 2001 has stylish apple and medium length and the Sauvignon 2001, a little thin from acidity, has great body and super length on the nose. The other wines are more than decent, especially the reds. Best of these is the Scuro, from merlot and cabernet sauvignon aged in barrique, which unveils plum aromas and close-knit structure. It's a shame about the note of alcohol that makes the finish a little aggressive.

● COF Merlot Centis '00	🍷🍷	6
○ COF Picolit '00	🍷🍷	8
○ COF Bianco Vineis '01	🍷🍷	5
○ COF Chardonnay '01	🍷🍷	4*
○ COF Pinot Grigio '01	🍷🍷	4*
○ COF Sauvignon '01	🍷🍷	4*
○ COF Ribolla Gialla '01	🍷	4
○ COF Tocai Friulano '01	🍷	4
○ COF Picolit '97	🍷🍷🍷	8
○ COF Picolit '98	🍷🍷🍷	8
● COF Merlot Centis '99	🍷🍷🍷	6
● COF Merlot Centis '95	🍷🍷	6
● COF Merlot Centis '96	🍷🍷	6
● COF Merlot Centis '97	🍷🍷	6

○ COF Verduzzo Friulano Graticcio '99	🍷🍷🍷	6
○ COF Bianco Pomédes '00	🍷🍷	5
○ COF Pinot Bianco '01	🍷🍷	4*
○ COF Sauvignon '01	🍷🍷	4*
● COF Cabernet Sauvignon '00	🍷	4
● COF Merlot '00	🍷	4
○ COF Tocai Friulano '01	🍷	4
● COF Rosso Scuro '99	🍷	5
○ COF Bianco Pomédes '98	🍷🍷🍷	5
○ COF Bianco Pomédes '99	🍷🍷🍷	5
● COF Merlot '99	🍷🍷	4
○ COF Bianco Pomédes '97	🍷🍷	5

PREMARIACCO (UD)

Vigne Fantin Noda'r
Via Casali Otellio, 4
33040 Premariacco (UD)
Tel. 043428735 - 043429893
E-mail: vignefantin@libero.it

This is a new full entry in the Guide, after a preliminary visit to the Other Wineries section. Founded in 1994, Vigne Fantin Noda'r has 18 hectares of enviable southwest-facing vines in the hills between Buttrio and Premariacco. The owner, Attilio Pignat, insists on quality in both vineyard and cellar. almost all the vine stock has been recently replanted, vine density is 5,000 plants per hectare and little more than a kilogram of fruit is taken from each Guyot-trained vine. Operations are overseen by Attilio, agronomist Stefano Bortolussi and young consultant winemaker, Francesco Spitaleri. As well as an excellent Cabernet, the trio offered the panel two outstanding blends, the Carato Bianco '98 and the Carato Rosso '97. The former is a riesling, sauvignon, chardonnay and picolit-based wine fermented in medium toast barriques that has balanced notes of oak and peach. The follow-through on the palate is a self-assured succession of toasty and fruit aromas. The Carato Rosso is a classic Bordeaux blend that stays in barrique for a year and a half. Intriguing gamey aromas mingle with more discreet notes of bramble tart then the complex, well-rounded palate shows good harmony with the softness of the fruit and the long, warm finish. The Cabernet 2000 is a 50-50 mix of cabernet franc and sauvignon with intense bramble and plum jam aromas, as well as pepper and hay. Best of the other One Glass winners is the very successful Sauvignon 2001.

●	COF Cabernet '00	ΨΨ	4*
●	COF Rosso Carato '97	ΨΨ	4*
○	COF Bianco Carato '98	ΨΨ	4*
●	COF Refosco P. R. '00	Ψ	4
○	COF Sauvignon '01	Ψ	3
●	COF Merlot '00		4
○	COF Chardonnay '01		3
○	COF Pinot Grigio '01		3

PREPOTTO (UD)

Iole Grillo
Loc. Albana
Via Albana, 60
33040 Prepotto (UD)
Tel. 0432713201 - 0432713322
E-mail: info@vinigrillo.it

The estate that bears the name of Iole Grillo, the woman that acquired it in the early 1970s, is today managed by Anna Muzzolini, Iole's daughter and herself a dynamic winewoman. A quiet, friendly type, Anna is transformed when she is at work, becoming a tenacious, objectives-focused manager. At her side is Lino Casella, the wine technician who has been working on the estate for years. The property's eight hectares are on the hillslopes and narrow plain that flank the Judrio, the river that separates the provinces of Udine and Gorizia, and thus the DOC zones of Colli Orientali del Friuli and Collio. Geologically, there is little to choose between them and both are ideal wine country. This time, the cellar turned out a fine range, particularly the Pinot Grigio, which had the benefit of an excellent vintage for the variety. It regales the nose with a wealth of mixed and tropical fruit, married to attractive freshness. The Sauvignon again performed well, its citrus nuances mingling on an intense bouquet that lacks a touch of elegance. The excellent Tocai Friulano 2001 has the classic varietal twist of almond on the back palate but the Guardafuoco '99, a blend of cabernet sauvignon and merlot that matures in oak for 28 months, was let down by tannins that have still to mellow. The native sweet varieties from 2000, the Picolit and Verduzzo, show good structure and typicity. Finally, the Merlot Selezione '99 may have sojourned in oak for two years but you wouldn't think so, to judge by its rich, fruit-driven palate.

○	COF Pinot Grigio '01	ΨΨ	4*
○	COF Picolit '00	Ψ	8
●	COF Refosco P. R. '00	Ψ	4
●	COF Schioppettino '00	Ψ	4
○	COF Sauvignon '01	Ψ	4
○	COF Tocai Friulano '01	Ψ	4
○	COF Verduzzo Friulano '00	Ψ	4
●	COF Merlot Sel. '99	Ψ	4
●	COF Rosso Guardafuoco '99		4
○	COF Sauvignon '00	ΨΨ	4
○	COF Bianco Santa Justina '99	ΨΨ	4

PREPOTTO (UD)

LA VIARTE
VIA NOVACUZZO, 50
33040 PREPOTTO (UD)
TEL. 0432759458
E-MAIL: laviarte@laviarte.it

A few Guides ago, we pointed out that La Viarte was moving away from fresh 'n' fruity wines towards more challenging bottles for the demanding consumer. In fact, the new vineyard and cellar management techniques introduced - bunch selection at harvest, maceration on the skins, malolactic fermentation, lees stirring and minimal use of sulphur dioxide - are all heading in that direction. Sadly, unpredictable weather conditions have made it difficult for the cellar to ensure that the final product is uniformly reliable and this year's tastings revealed a range that wasn't quite firing on all cylinders. Only occasionally did the wines give their best. The Pinot Grigio was a shade vegetal, the 2001 Sauvignon is still grassy, and shows fuzzy notes of alcohol, while the Schioppettino '99 has a lovely pepper and cherry nose but shows some rough edges on the back palate. The Liende 2000, a blend of five white varieties, is long on the palate but lacks focus on the nose and its red partner, the Roi '99, is a merlot and cabernet mix that overplays its gamey note. Fortunately, there is always Siùm, an ever-convincing picolit and verduzzo blend. The 2000 edition is one of the region's finest whites, its typical figs, almonds, walnuts and dried apricots ushering in a refreshing palate with a hint of extract that keeps the sweetness in its place. Finally, the fresh, flavoursome and remarkably structured '01 Pinot Bianco is as good as ever.

PREPOTTO (UD)

LE DUE TERRE
VIA ROMA, 68/B
33040 PREPOTTO (UD)
TEL. 0432713189

The seven-hectare Le Due Terre estate releases up to 20,000 bottles a year, with yields of about 40 quintals per hectare, with the exception of the picolit which goes into Implicito. Yields for that variety hover around 30 quintals per hectare. The warm, seductive depth of the Merlot 2000 earned it Three Glasses. The rich, fruity texture of the palate is close-knit and amazingly dense, the tannins nicely soft without being flabby and the long finish is deliciously refined. Implicito 2000 is an unusual and very individual wine that wins your heart. All the sugar is fermented and the wine ages gently in barrique. Flavio and Silvana Basilicata's love affair with Pinot Nero carries on. The 2000 edition is a rich, full-bodied and slightly tannin-heavy wine with a predominance of morello cherry on nose and palate. The Sacrisassi Rosso, a refosco and schioppettino mix with an impenetrably concentrated hue, reveals spice and dried flower aromas, then the fruity palate shows generous structure and still perceptible oak before closing with mellow tannins. Sacrisassi Bianco comes from oak-aged tocai, ribolla and sauvignon. It lost some marks because it had only just gone into bottle but has an intense golden hue, rather sweet aromas of peach and yellow plum and a palate that has not quite found its feet. Appreciable acidity and warm alcohol are still prominent.

O	Siùm '00	🍷🍷	6
O	COF Pinot Bianco '01	🍷🍷	5
O	COF Bianco Liende '00	🍷	5
O	COF Pinot Grigio '01	🍷	5
O	COF Sauvignon '01	🍷	5
●	COF Rosso Roi '99	🍷	6
●	COF Merlot '99		5
●	COF Schioppettino '99		5
O	COF Pinot Bianco '00	🍷🍷	5
O	COF Bianco Liende '99	🍷🍷	5

●	COF Merlot '00	🍷🍷🍷	6
O	Implicito '00	🍷🍷	6
●	COF Pinot Nero '00	🍷🍷	6
●	COF Rosso Sacrisassi '00	🍷🍷	6
O	COF Bianco Sacrisassi '00	🍷	5
●	COF Rosso Sacrisassi '97	🍷🍷🍷	6
●	COF Rosso Sacrisassi '98	🍷🍷🍷	6
O	COF Bianco Sacrisassi '99	🍷🍷	5
●	COF Merlot '99	🍷🍷	6
●	COF Rosso Sacrisassi '99	🍷🍷	6

PREPOTTO (UD)

VALERIO MARINIG
VIA BROLO, 41
33040 PREPOTTO (UD)
TEL. 0432713012
E-MAIL: marinigvalerio@libero.it

Valerio Marinig is a young oenologist who is lucky enough to know how to take one step at a time. He is also fortunate in having a supportive family. His father Sergio has given him a free hand in the cellar and mother Marisa is always ready to welcome visitors with a friendly smile. The Marinig family has about seven hectars under vine, with a similar area given over to woodland and arable crops. The cellar is tiny, which means space has to be exploited to the full, but Valerio still manages to find room to let his wines age in oak for more than a year. All the whites are macerated, for varying lengths of time, with lees contact lasting for months. As a result, they gain structure and complexity. The cellar's best product, the Pinot Bianco 2001, has an admirable, intensely fruity nose that is clean, fresh and well mirrored on the palate. The Tocai Friulano is a Marinig benchmark. Frank and varietal, it lost a few points for slightly over-enthusiastic acidity. The Picolit 2000, raisined in cases and vinified in barrique, is sweet, buttery and palpably fleshy while the 2001 Chardonnay and Sauvignon 2001 are attractive and refreshing. The Merlot 2001 wasn't ready for the panel's visit so we will be tasting it next year.

○ COF Pinot Bianco '01		3*
○ COF Picolit '00		6
○ COF Chardonnay '01		3
○ COF Sauvignon '01		3
○ COF Tocai Friulano '01		3
○ COF Verduzzo Friulano '01		3

PREPOTTO (UD)

PETRUSSA
LOC. ALBANA, 49
33040 PREPOTTO (UD)
TEL. 0432713192
E-MAIL: paolo_petrussa@libero.it

We are happy to record further progress made by the cellar that belongs to brothers Gianni and Paolo Petrussa. We were all very much younger when we used to meet to discuss their and our work around the kitchen table. The cellar was non-existent and the two brothers were endlessly dreaming up unlikely solutions to make up for the lack of – at the time, unaffordable – modern technology. The tenacious twosome continued to improve and today are proud to show off what they have achieved. Gianni and Paolo cultivate about six hectares of vineyard and monitor a further four, all of whose grapes they purchase. Careful selection from specific rows enables them to produce a blend, the Bianco Petrussa 2000, from tocai friulano, chardonnay, pinot bianco and sauvignon, three quarters of which ages in wood and the rest in stainless steel. A very complex wine, it offers banana, pennyroyal, confectioner's cream and citrus aromas that are echoed on the long, well-structured palate. The Rosso Petrussa '99, an 80-20 blend of merlot and cabernet sauvignon, is very persuasive. It goes into the bottle unfiltered, as does the Schioppettino from the same vintage, which keeps all the body, extract and complexity of the fruit intact. Pensiero '99 is a sweet, alcohol-rich, monovarietal Verduzzo. The Pinot Bianco and the golden Sauvignon from 2001 are both enviably creamy and well-structured.

○ COF Bianco Petrussa '00		5
○ COF Pinot Bianco '01		4*
○ COF Sauvignon '01		4*
● COF Rosso Petrussa '99		5
○ Pensiero '99		7
● COF Merlot '01		4
○ COF Tocai Friulano '01		4
● COF Schioppettino '99		5
○ COF Bianco Petrussa '99		4
● COF Rosso Petrussa '97		5
● COF Rosso Petrussa '98		5

PREPOTTO (UD)

Ronco dei Pini
Via Ronchi, 93
33040 Prepotto (UD)
tel. 0432713239
e-mail: info@roncodeipini.com

Giuseppe and Claudio Novello's estate confirms our assessment made last year, although one or two of the wines, excluded from the Guide, seemed to us to reveal a certain lack of rigour. The Novello family moved here in 1968, when they bought some splendid vineyards at Prepotto from Rieppi. The estate was split up a few years ago, Ronco dei Pini keeping four and a half hectares as well as the cellar, but the winery also looks after about ten hectares at Zegla, near Cormons, in the Collio DOC zone. Vineyard management is in the hands of Renato De Noni while Damiano Stramare runs the cellar. Part of the harvest is sold unbottled but the best wine is released in the Ronco dei Pini range. There's also a second label that sells at very competitive prices. We like the Leucós Bianco 2001, from pinot bianco and tocai friulano, for it combines all the elegance of the pinot with the rich body of the tocai. The Límes Rosso 2000, a blend of merlot and cabernet aged for 12 months in tonneaux, gained its second Glass thanks to ripe berry fruit and bramble on the nose and a palate redolent of hay. Finally, the Pinot Bianco is well-made and substantial, with honey aromas, the Cabernet has an unusually soft mouthfeel and the Sauvignon flaunts red pepper and elderflower. All come from the 2001 vintage.

●	Límes Rosso '00	ƮƮ	4*
○	Leucós Bianco '01	ƮƮ	4*
●	COF Cabernet '01	Ʈ	4
○	COF Pinot Bianco '01	Ʈ	4
○	Collio Sauvignon '01	Ʈ	4
○	Collio Chardonnay '01		4

PREPOTTO (UD)

Vigna Petrussa
Via Albana, 47
33040 Prepotto (UD)
tel. 0432713021
e-mail: info@vignapetrussa.it

Petrussa is the commonest surname at Albana, near Prepotto, even if many Petrussas are not actually related. Hilde Petrussa Mecchia and her husband Renato spent a quarter century in the nearby Veneto flatlands, returning in 1995 to their native village to vinify grapes from the family vineyards. They have five hectares in the narrow strip of land, bounded to the east above the town by the Judrio river, also the border with Slovenia, and which below separates the provinces of Udine and Gorizia. The cellar is excellently equipped and impressively tidy. The vines, too, have a well-manicured look for the couple look after them personally. Results are on a par with these efforts. The Petrussas' flagship wine is the Richenza, whose name comes from a legendary Lombard princess. A riesling, malvasia, tocai, verduzzo and picolit blend from fruit that is slightly raisined before crushing, it ages in French oak. On the nose, confectioner's cream, milk and banana come through while there is softness, breadth and great length in the mouth. The grapes in the Picolit come from plots on Santo Spirito, the hill above Albana. They undergo the same vinification process but only some of the wine goes into wood, so that the delicate varietal aromas are not lost. The wine is sweet, with hints of caramel, and has great balance and persistence.

○	Richenza '00	ƮƮ	5
○	COF Picolit '00	ƮƮ	6
●	COF Refosco P. R. '00	Ʈ	4
○	COF Tocai Friulano '01	Ʈ	4
●	COF Cabernet Franc '00		4
○	COF Sauvignon '01		4

PREPOTTO (UD)

VIGNA TRAVERSO
VIA RONCHI, 73
33040 PREPOTTO (UD)
TEL. 0432713072
E-MAIL: info@molon.it

When Giancarlo Traverso and Ornella Molon decided to invest in Friuli, they gave their son Stefano the job of looking after the new estate and making sure its wines were made with quality as the first priority. Lauro Iacoletig is the expert wineman who worked on the property under the previous management. He is still there, his enthusiasm renewed, thanks in part to the strategies adopted but the Traverso oenologist, Simone Casazza, and by Pierpaolo Sirch and Marco Simonit, fruitmakers who also know a thing or two about cellar techniques. Currently, there are seven hectares under vine but the estate is growing with new purchases. In the past year, four new hectares have been planted on the slopes above Prepotto. It has to be said that while on occasions Friulian winemakers tend to vinify reds as if they were whites, the Traversos have precisely the opposite problem. The winery's whites have amazing concentration and body. But let's start with the great Merlot 2000. The dark ruby immediately highlights the wine's concentration and warm alcohol. These are backed up by serious fruit with hints of super-ripe grapes. In the mouth, the complexity surges through seamlessly to a full-bodied finish that is in no hurry to leave. A tad too much youthful exuberance puts the Rosso Sottocastello 2000, a monovarietal merlot, a few points behind the Merlot. Finally, the Tocai looks set to become a serious challenge for the Traversos. Although a superb wine, it is very untypical.

● COF Merlot '00	▼▼	5
● COF Rosso Sottocastello '00	▼▼	6
● COF Cabernet Franc '00	▼▼	4
● COF Refosco P. R. '00	▼▼	4
● COF Schioppettino '00	▼▼	5
○ COF Pinot Grigio '01	▼▼	4
○ COF Ribolla Gialla '01	▼▼	4
○ COF Sauvignon '01	▼▼	4
○ COF Tocai Friulano '01	▼▼	4
○ COF Chardonnay '01	▼	4
● COF Merlot '99	▼▼	4
● COF Rosso Sottocastello Ris. '99	▼▼	5
● COF Merlot '98	▼▼	4

RONCHI DEI LEGIONARI (GO)

TENUTA DI BLASIG
VIA ROMA, 63
34077 RONCHI DEI LEGIONARI (GO)
TEL. 0481475480
E-MAIL: tenutadiblasig@tiscalinet.it

Tenuta di Blasig, managed by Elisabetta Bortolotto Sarcinelli, has deep roots in the local territory and history. One member of the family, which has been in the region for more than three centuries, was Domenico di Blasig, mayor of Ronchi dei Legionari in 1850, and the lovely 19th-century villa, where the cellar and offices are housed, was once the First World War Allied headquarters. The poet Gabriele D'Annunzio also stayed here. Historical heritage, shrewd management and the crucial intervention of oenologist Erica Orlandino have all contributed to the success of this women-only cellar. We might add that Elisabetta's three daughters, Lucovica, Letizia and Antonia, are all ready to join the team. There are 16 hectares under vine at present and production comes to about 60,000 bottles a year, sold under the Classica and Gli Affreschi labels. The year's best wine belongs to the second line. It's the attractive, ruby red 2000 Merlot Gli Affreschi, whose warm, balanced aromas highlight cinnamon, cherry tart, vanilla and milk chocolate. These are echoed in the mouth and supported by silk-smooth tannins and a generous finish. The Classica Cabernet 2001 nearly won a second Glass. Its varietal nose of assertive black pepper spice and ripe plums ushers in a stylishly subtle palate. The Le Lule is a surprising white from raisined verduzzo. Dry flowers and apricot aromas accompany you through to a finish that signs off with a touch of lime honey.

● Friuli Isonzo Merlot Gli Affreschi '00	▼▼	4*
● Friuli Isonzo Cabernet '01	▼	4
● Friuli Isonzo Merlot '01	▼	4
○ Friuli Isonzo Pinot Grigio '01	▼	3
○ Le Lule	▼	4
○ Friuli Isonzo Chardonnay '01		3
● Friuli Isonzo Merlot '00	▼▼	4
● Friuli Isonzo Merlot Gli Affreschi '99	▼▼	4

RONCHI DEI LEGIONARI (GO)

Do Ville
Via Mitraglieri, 2
34077 Ronchi dei Legionari (GO)
tel. 0481775561
e-mail: info@doville.it

Do Ville, a flatland winery founded in 1985 by the two Bonora brothers, sails triumphantly into the Guide. Paolo looks after winemaking while Gianni keeps the vineyards in shape. The pair have 15 hectares planted to vine and release 120,000 bottles every year, in two ranges. The Do Ville wines have more concentration and the Ars Vivendi label is reserved for more approachable products. The name Do Ville was inspired by the Roman remains in the area. There were two "villae", or agricultural estates, here that – according to Paolo – reaffirm the ancient heritage that makes Friulian wines so special. As is often the case in the region, about 70 per cent of production is devoted to whites. Three of these, as well as an excellent Cabernet Sauvignon, caught the panel's attention particularly. The Pinot Grigio Do Ville 2001 is a very fine wine, with elegant varietal crusty bread and williams pears, followed by a well-sustained palate with the right mix of softness and acidity. Also from the Do Ville line is the interesting Chardonnay Barrique 2000. Tempting creamy aromas of vanilla, coffee and banana are picked up nicely on the palate. There are intense vegetal notes in the Ars Vivendi Sauvignon 2001, accompanying yellow peach fruit and ripe tomato on the soft, leisurely palate. The warm Cabernet Sauvignon '99 offers spicy plum jam and an admirable tannic weave.

SACILE (PN)

Vistorta
Brandino Brandolini d'Adda
Via Vistorta, 82
33077 Sacile (PN)
tel. 043471135
e-mail: vistorta@iol.it

The Conti Brandolini estate covers more than 220 hectares in the Veneto and Friuli, but only five hectares under vine are in the former region. The vineyards that yield fruit for the cellar's signature wine, released under the special Vistorta label, today extend over 27 hectares and give the winemaker plenty of leeway for the ruthless selection of grapes to go into the bottle. Georges Pauli, a French oenologist, is Brandino Brandolini d'Adda righthand man. For a few years now, the winemaking team has included Friulian Alec Ongaro and Samuel Tinon, from Hungary. The cellar has decided to delay release of the 2000 vintage Vistorta, which we tasted from the barrel (it is ageing in new, one and two-year-old barriques). We took the opportunity to enjoy a vertical tasting of the product and were especially impressed by the '97, '95, '93 and '89. All confirmed the superb cellar potential and solid reliability of Merlot Vistorta, even when minor adjustments are made to the blend (it contains tiny proportions of cabernet sauvignon, cabernet franc and syrah). The most impressive feature of these wines is their amazing, Bordeaux-like personality. Drunk young, they appear to have limited prospects but when you come back to taste them a few years later, you realize their true complexity. Tuck them away in the cellar, by all means, but they are drinking deliciously only three or four years after the harvest.

○ Friuli Isonzo Chardonnay Barrique Do Ville '00	ŶŶ	4
○ Friuli Isonzo Pinot Grigio Do Ville '01	ŶŶ	3*
○ Friuli Isonzo Sauvignon Ars Vivendi '01	ŶŶ	3*
● Friuli Isonzo Cabernet Sauvignon Barrique Do Ville '99	ŶŶ	4
○ Friuli Isonzo Chardonnay Do Ville '01	Ŷ	3
○ Friuli Isonzo Malvasia Ars Vivendi '01	Ŷ	3
○ Friuli Isonzo Sauvignon Do Ville '01	Ŷ	3
○ Friuli Isonzo Tocai Friulano Ars Vivendi '01	Ŷ	3
○ Friuli Isonzo Tocai Friulano Do Ville '01	Ŷ	3

● Friuli Grave Merlot Vistorta '95	ŶŶ	5
● Friuli Grave Merlot Vistorta '97	ŶŶ	5
● Friuli Grave Merlot Vistorta '98	ŶŶ	5
● Friuli Grave Merlot Vistorta '99	ŶŶ	5

SAGRADO (GO)

CASTELVECCHIO
VIA CASTELNUOVO, 2
34078 SAGRADO (GO)
TEL. 048199742
E-MAIL: info@castelvecchio.com

The first vines of this historic winery in the Gorizia Carso area were planted in the 1970s around the lovely Renaissance villa. Since then, it has become a Guide regular. Renovation of the 40-hectare vine stock began this year on a first five-hectare plot. The future is as impressive as the past at Castelvecchio. The bulk of the cellar's output is made up of red wines, which is rare in Friuli. The Karst terrain is unfertile on top but rich in underground springs which ensure the health of the vines, thanks to carefully programmed irrigation. Add to all this the expert touch of long-serving agronomist and oenologist Gianni Bignucolo and you will see why Castelvecchio is riding high. We mentioned the prevalence of reds and in fact two of them, the '99 Cabernet Sauvignon and Cabernet Franc, were the best bottles this time. The very intense ruby Cabernet Sauvignon has warm notes of pepper and bramble jam, then a velvety palate that mirrors the nose and great extract. Intense and spicy, the Cabernet Franc offers breadth in the mouth, rich flavour and seamless progression. There were high scores for the Turmino '99 and the Sagrado Bianco 2000. The first is a blend of terrano with a little cabernet franc that shows attractive bramble and pipe tobacco while the Sagrado Bianco, obtained from malvasia, sauvignon and traminer, pleased the panel with its stylish aromas of almonds, peach and tomato leaf.

SAN FLORIANO DEL COLLIO (GO)

ASCEVI - LUWA
VIA UCLANZI, 24
34070 SAN FLORIANO DEL COLLIO (GO)
TEL. 0481884140
E-MAIL: asceviluwa@asceviluwa.it

Previous years' profiles for Ascevi-Luwa describe a relatively large estate – 30 hectares under vine, mainly in the Collio DOC zone – with two fairly distinct ranges (Ascevi and Luwa) that include the same types of wine. In both cases, the flagship wine is the Sauvignon, the product that made the winery's name a while ago. However, a less well-defined picture emerged from this year's tastings and the two ranges seemed to be differentiated more by their labels than by the sensory characteristics of the products. For example, Pinot Grigio Grappoli drinks like an attempt to give the Luwa range more personality by mimicking the Pinot Grigio Ascevi. Similarly, there is little difference, aside for the labels, in the three, all very good, monovarietal Sauvignons, despite different cropping levels and cold maceration times. The herbal note of tomato leaf is a little too prominent in the Tocai, as it is in the two blends. They may include sauvignon in the mix, together with chardonnay and ribolla for the Vigna Verdana and with chardonnay and tocai in the Col Martin, but in previous years, we found a completeness and character that was missing this time round. You could say the same thing about the Ribolla Ronco de Vigna Vecia, which is not featured in the table. The most promising signs in the rest of the range presented came from the Ascevi-label Pinot Grigio 2001.

● Carso Cabernet Franc '99	♀♀	5
● Carso Cabernet Sauvignon '99	♀♀	5
○ Carso Traminer Aromatico '00	♀	4
○ Sagrado Bianco '00	♀	5
○ Carso Malvasia Istriana '01	♀	4
○ Carso Pinot Grigio '01	♀	4
● Carso Rosso Turmino '99	♀	4
○ Carso Sauvignon '01		4
● Terrano Tipico '01		4
● Carso Refosco P. R. '99		5
● Sagrado Rosso '97	♀♀	6

○ Collio Pinot Grigio Ascevi '01	♀♀	4*
○ Col Martin Luwa '01	♀	4
○ Collio Sauvignon Ascevi '01	♀	4
○ Collio Sauvignon Luwa '01	♀	4
○ Collio Sauvignon Ronco dei Sassi Ascevi '01	♀	5
○ Vigna Verdana Ascevi '01	♀	5
● Collio Cabernet Franc Ascevi '00		4
○ Collio Pinot Grigio Grappoli Luwa '01		4
○ Friuli Isonzo Tocai Friulano Ascevi '01		3
○ Collio Sauvignon Ascevi '98	♀♀♀	4
○ Col Martin Luwa '00	♀♀	4
○ Collio Ribolla Gialla Ascevi '00	♀♀	4

SAN FLORIANO DEL COLLIO (GO)

CONTI FORMENTINI
VIA OSLAVIA, 5
34070 SAN FLORIANO DEL COLLIO (GO)
TEL. 0481884131
E-MAIL: giv@giv.it

The Formentini winery is based in a castle that once belonged to one of Gorizia's most important families – the Formentinis settled at San Floriano del Collio in 1509 – but today it is part of the Gruppo Italiano Vini. Wine is made with fruit bought in from suppliers in the Gorizia part of the Collio. Oenologist and cellar manager Marco Del Piccolo is responsible for the output of about 350,000 bottles a year. The best wine this time is the Collio Bianco Rylint 2000, a blend of chardonnay, pinot grigio and sauvignon that takes its name from the abbess who promoted viticulture in the area during the 16th century. A brilliant gold wine, it shows an elegant medley of fruit on the nose, echoed unerringly on a complex palate backed up by good acidity. The Chardonnay Torre di Tramontana 2000 is named for one of the castle's northern towers. Winemaking here dates from 1520 and this example ages in new and one-year-old barriques. Rich, intense aromas, reminiscent of tropical fruit, introduce a warm entry in the mouth, where delicately persistent notes of concentrated fruit emerge. The Pinot Grigio's fresh, fruity aromas usher in a rich, medium-structured palate. The less complex Sauvignon has nice, typical notes of tomato leaf and elderflower. Finally, the Merlot Tajut (the name means a glass of wine in Friulian) is complex and uncompromising on the nose but held back by unyielding tannins.

○ Collio Chardonnay Torre di Tramontana '00	♛♛	4*
○ Collio Bianco Rylint '01	♛♛	4*
● Collio Merlot Tajut '00	♛	5
○ Collio Pinot Grigio '01	♛	4
○ Collio Sauvignon '01	♛	4
● Collio Merlot Tajut '97	♛♛	5
● Collio Merlot Tajut '99	♛♛	5

SAN FLORIANO DEL COLLIO (GO)

GRADIS'CIUTTA
LOC. GIASBANA, 10
34070 SAN FLORIANO DEL COLLIO (GO)
TEL. 0481390237
E-MAIL: robigradis@libero.it

The Gradis'ciutta winery (the apostrophe separates the "s" sound from the "ci", pronounced "ch", that follows) is named after the town where the Princic family's largest plot is located. Robert and his father Doro have 13 hectares under vine, plus a further 15 of woods and arable land. Each year, they release about 55,000 bottles under a wide range of labels. Quality is improving steadily, as we were able to confirm at this year's tastings. The elegant, intensely fragranced Ribolla Gialla 2001 has lots of fruit and cream aromas, then a well-structured palate supported by well-gauged acidity and good length. We preferred the standard 2001 Tocai for its attractive stewed apple aroma and soft length on the palate. Its partner, the Tocai Aurora, is creamy and stylish but also shows faint hints of super-ripeness. The Bianco del Bratinis is a mix of steel-aged chardonnay, pinot grigio, tocai and sauvignon. Apple and crusty bread on the nose are followed by depth and freshness. A seamless concentration of fruit on nose and palate is the strong suit of the Pinot Grigio. The Cabernet Franc 2001, too, is excellent. Its rich aromas foreground cherry jam, then the impressive impact on the palate never lets go. Bianco del Tùzz 2000 comes from barrique-aged chardonnay, pinot grigio, tocai and malvasia. The creamy nose gently contrasts acidity and ripeness, the follow-through on the palate is satisfying and concentrated ripe fruit lifts the elegant finish.

○ Collio Bianco del Bratinis '01	♛♛	4
● Collio Cabernet Franc '01	♛♛	4
○ Collio Pinot Grigio '01	♛♛	4
○ Collio Ribolla Gialla '01	♛♛	4
○ Collio Tocai Friulano '01	♛♛	4
○ Collio Bianco del Tùzz '00	♛	4
○ Collio Chardonnay '01	♛	4
○ Collio Sauvignon '01	♛	4
○ Collio Tocai Friulano Aurora '01	♛	4
● Collio Rosso dei Princic '99		5

SAN FLORIANO DEL COLLIO (GO)

MARCELLO E MARINO HUMAR
LOC. VALERISCE, 2
34070 SAN FLORIANO DEL COLLIO (GO)
TEL. 0481884094
E-MAIL: humarl@tiscalinet.it

The Gradis'ciutta winery (the apostrophe separates the "s" sound from the "ci", pronounced "ch", that follows) is named after the town where the Princic family's largest plot is located. Robert and his father Doro have 13 hectares under vine, plus a further 15 of woods and arable land. Each year, they release about 55,000 bottles under a wide range of labels. Quality is improving steadily, as we were able to confirm at this year's tastings. The elegant, intensely fragranced Ribolla Gialla 2001 has lots of fruit and cream aromas, then a well-structured palate supported by well-gauged acidity and good length. We preferred the standard 2001 Tocai for its attractive stewed apple aroma and soft length on the palate. Its partner, the Tocai Aurora, is creamy and stylish but also shows faint hints of super-ripeness. The Bianco del Bratinis is a mix of steel-aged chardonnay, pinot grigio, tocai and sauvignon. Apple and crusty bread on the nose are followed by depth and freshness. A seamless concentration of fruit on nose and palate is the strong suit of the Pinot Grigio. The Cabernet Franc 2001, too, is excellent. Its rich aromas foreground cherry jam, then the impressive impact on the palate never lets go. Bianco del Tùzz 2000 comes from barrique-aged chardonnay, pinot grigio, tocai and malvasia. The creamy nose gently contrasts acidity and ripeness, the follow-through on the palate is satisfying and concentrated ripe fruit lifts the elegant finish.

●	Collio Cabernet Franc Rogoves '00	♀♀	5
○	Collio Pinot Bianco '01	♀♀	4*
○	Collio Pinot Grigio '01	♀♀	4*
●	Collio Cabernet Franc '01	♀	4
○	Collio Chardonnay '01	♀	4
○	Collio Ribolla '01	♀	4
○	Collio Sauvignon '01	♀	4
○	Verduzzo Friulano	♀	4
●	Collio Merlot '01		4
○	Collio Pinot Bianco '00	♀♀	4
○	Collio Pinot Grigio '00	♀♀	4

SAN FLORIANO DEL COLLIO (GO)

IL CARPINO
LOC. SOVENZA, 14/A
34070 SAN FLORIANO DEL COLLIO (GO)
TEL. 0481884097
E-MAIL: ilcarpino@ilcarpino.com

After their triumphant return to the Guide last year, we were expecting Silvano Cibini and Franco Sossol to confirm their progress, which they did at least in part. Il Carpino has about 12 planted to vine, supervised by Marco Simonit and Pierpaolo Sirch, while Roberto Cipresso, a wine technician with a nationwide reputation, is the cellar consultant. The estate makes 70,000 bottles of oak-aged Il Carpino-label wines and Vigna Runc, a range of younger, fresher wines, especially steel-aged whites. We were looking for great things from the Rubrum but the biggest hitter this time is the barrique-vinified and aged Chardonnay 2000. Its vibrant hue is flecked with green, the nose is redolent of petits fours and although the palate is still partly masked by oak-derived aromas, it has plenty of thrust and assurance. Toasty sensations of milky coffee and vanilla marked down the other wines, especially the Ribolla, but the Malvasia and Sauvignon are very creamy, warm in the mouth and show promising ageing potential. The flavoursome Sauvignon Vigna Runc 2001 has breadth, style and a lively spontaneity, as well as an attractively fresh entry. The Rubrum 2000 deserves a note to itself. A monovarietal merlot from vines planted in gravelly terrain at 5,000 plants per hectare, it is vinified and aged in seven-hectolitre tonneaux. Although concentrated and muscular, it failed to repeat its '99 triumph because of an excessively intense note of incense that returns on the palate, and a heavy background note that takes the edge off the palate's considerable drinkability.

○	Collio Chardonnay '00	♀♀	5
●	Rubrum '00	♀♀	8
○	Collio Sauvignon Vigna Runc '01	♀♀	4*
○	Collio Malvasia '00	♀	6
○	Collio Ribolla Gialla '00	♀	5
○	Collio Sauvignon '00	♀	5
○	Collio Pinot Grigio Vigna Runc '01	♀	4
●	Rubrum '99	♀♀♀	8

SAN FLORIANO DEL COLLIO (GO)

Muzic
Loc. Bivio, 4
34070 San Floriano del Collio (GO)
tel. 0481884201
e-mail: muzic.az.agr@libero.it

Ivan Muzic's professional relationship with Sandro Facca, a wine technician who has worked in Friuli for many years, is consolidating the results achieved by this winery, which has ten hectares under vine in the Collio and a couple in the Isonzo DOC zone. There might have been a top accolade for the Primo Legno Rosso, if the disappointing '98 vintage hadn't robbed it of the warmth a top wine needs. This version is austere, with aromas that shade towards the gamey end of the spectrum. The milky Pinot Grigio is redolent of tobacco leaf, then the creamy entry on the palate reveals ripe fruit and a slightly bitterish finish. The Ribolla has vegetal notes of summer flowers and lemon peel, followed by a full-bodied, flavoursome palate. The Bric 2001 (pronounced "Britz" and named after the residents of the Collio, which is called Brda in Slovene) is a blend of tocai friulano, ribolla, malvasia and sauvignon. Still youthful in the mouth, it has good alcohol and excellent length. The Sauvignon has stylish aromas of rue and tomato leaf, a refreshing front palate and very decent body. The lovely, ruby red Cabernet Sauvignon 2000 offers good complexity and concentration, with a nice hint of acidity in the finish. The Chardonnay is tangy but evanescent while the Primo Legno Bianco '99 has yet to assimilate its oak and acidity. The fruity, almost super-ripe Cabernet Franc Isonzo del 2000 flaunts notes of black cherry tart and prune.

○	Collio Ribolla Gialla '01	ŸŸ	4*
●	Collio Cabernet Sauvignon '00	Ÿ	4
●	Friuli Isonzo Cabernet Franc '00	Ÿ	4
○	Collio Bianco Bric '01	Ÿ	4
○	Collio Chardonnay '01	Ÿ	4
○	Collio Pinot Grigio '01	Ÿ	4
○	Collio Sauvignon '01	Ÿ	4
●	Primo Legno Rosso '98	Ÿ	5
○	Primo Legno Bianco '99	Ÿ	5
○	Collio Tocai Friulano '01		4

SAN FLORIANO DEL COLLIO (GO)

Evangelos Paraschos
Loc. Bucuie, 13/a
34070 San Floriano del Collio (GO)
tel. 0481884154

There's a first full Guide profile for the amiable Evangelos Paraschos, known to one and all at San Floriano del Collio as El Grego, or The Greek. In fact, Evangelos arrived in Trieste from Greece some years ago to study at the university. After graduating, he worked as a restaurateur in Gorizia before he was bitten by the wine bug and since 1998, he has been cultivating four hectares under vine. Evangelos releases about 12,000 bottles a year, some of which find their way back to his native land. Paraschos' wines have lots of character and will achieve great things when he manages to find a tad more subtlety of style. The Bianco 2001 is a blend of tocai and chardonnay with a vegetal nose and a full body. It signs off with elegant nuances of yellow peppers. The Chardonnay ages for ten months in tonneaux. Hay and green apple usher in a no-nonsense palate backed up by exuberant acidity. Vinified in stainless steel, the Pinot Grigio has still to find a balance for its refreshing acidity and sweet, pear and apple fruit but bodes well for the future. The Rosso Skala 2000 is obtained from merlot, refosco, barbera and cabernet sauvignon grown in two old vineyards. It's a little rustic on nose and palate, although the mouthfeel is impressive.

○	Bianco '01	ŸŸ	5
○	Collio Chardonnay '01	Ÿ	5
○	Collio Pinot Grigio '01	Ÿ	5
●	Rosso Skala '00	Ÿ	6
○	Collio Bianco '00	ŸŸ	5

SAN FLORIANO DEL COLLIO (GO)

Matijaz Tercic
Loc. Bucuie, 9
34070 San Floriano del Collio (GO)
Tel. 0481884193
E-mail: tercic@tiscalinet.it

Matijaz Tercic tends four hectares of vines on the steep hillsides around San Floriano del Collio. His range is sold under seven labels, which means that only a few thousand bottles of each are released. Total output is 22,000 units. Matijaz's intense Collio Bianco Planta 2000 is from oak-aged chardonnay and pinot bianco that go into the bottle unfiltered. Intriguingly rich on the peach and butter nose, it reveals a pervasive front palate then rich, ripe fruit and a juicy, very muscular but attractive mouthfeel. As we move on to the 2001 whites, the Vino degli Orti, a steel-vinified mix of tocai, malvasia istriana and riesling renano, offers flowery notes, with lavender in evidence. The palate follows through well, with good length and acidity. The Pinot Grigio is as good as ever, despite an entry on the nose that takes time to clear, then the seductively complex palate focuses on creamy fruit. The Ribolla came close to a second Glass thanks to the spring flowers on the subtle, fresh nose that return satisfyingly on the palate. The Chardonnay unveils confectioner's cream and biscuit aromas. The oak-derived notes are well integrated and there are promising minerally notes. The very soft Sauvignon is not very varietal and its vegetal notes are subdued. Finally, the '99 Merlot has slightly unsubtle herbaceous notes that mingle with nuances of raisining. A soft entry on the palate highlights sweet, almost super-ripe, fruit but lacks a little depth.

O	Collio Bianco Planta '00	¶¶	4*
O	Collio Pinot Grigio '01	¶¶	4
O	Vino degli Orti '01	¶¶	4
O	Collio Chardonnay '01	¶	4
O	Collio Ribolla Gialla '01	¶	4
O	Collio Sauvignon '01	¶	4
●	Collio Merlot '99	¶	4
O	Collio Bianco Planta '99	¶¶	4

SAN FLORIANO DEL COLLIO (GO)

Franco Terpin
Loc. Valerisce, 6/a
34070 San Floriano del Collio (GO)
Tel. 0481884215

Franco Terpin's family settled in the Collio several generations ago. Today, he cultivates eight and a half hectares split across a number of small plots. Currently, annual production is running at around 16,000 bottles. Having shared a cellar at Dolegna del Collio with another producer for a few years, Franco recently went back to vinifying at the family winery. In line with many other estates, Terpin has cut back the number of labels released, which enables him to concentrate on one white blend, one red and a territory-focused monovarietal, Ribolla Gialla, although he is also carrying out some trial macerations with Pinot Grigio. Franco's excellent Collio Bianco 2000 comes from barrel-aged pinot grigio, sauvignon, chardonnay and tocai friulano. Its gold-flecked hue introduces a complex, intense nose then a broad, stylish palate with beautifully integrated oak. The Ribolla has delicate, very varietal aromas of orange, lemon and citron, backed by typical but well-balanced acidity and a flowery finish. The Collio Rosso 2000, obtained from cabernet sauvignon, cabernet franc and a small proportion of merlot, reveals bottled cherries on the nose and a palate that lacks weight. It's a little too thin and acidic to go very far.

O	Collio Bianco '00	¶¶	5
O	Collio Ribolla Gialla '00	¶	4
●	Collio Rosso '00	¶	5
O	Collio Bianco '99	¶¶	5
O	Collio Sauvignon '00	¶¶	4

SAN GIOVANNI AL NATISONE (UD)

ALFIERI CANTARUTTI
VIA RONCHI, 9
33048 SAN GIOVANNI AL NATISONE (UD)
TEL. 0432756317
E-MAIL: alficant@tin.it

It might look as if Antonella and Fabrizio's cellar has failed to live up to last year's expectations but there are mitigating factors. Production has been muddling through recently in the midst of building work on the new cellar. The pair were determined to get things sorted out but it is only in the last few months that their plans have found a final shape, and the definitive layout has been identified. Point number two is what we could call a typical clash of generations, as so often happens in the world of wine. The final outcome is positive, in that the confrontation generates new improvements, but the inevitable arguments can have temporarily regrettable repercussions on the range of products. The Tocais, especially the much more substantial Colli Orientali del Friuli version, have suffered, for example. Rather forward, and with alcohol well to the fore, they are a touch fuzzy on nose and palate. But it's a very different story when you move on to the wine into which Antonella pours her heart and soul. The tocai, pinot bianco and sauvignon-based Canto 2001 is as stylishly drinkable as ever and promises to mellow further in the cellar. Both the Merlot 2000 and the Schioppettino '99, in particular, were less inspiring. We marked them down for their over-assertive tannins but the Merlot still shows good fruit and the Schioppettino reveals attractive varietal spice. The other wines in the table below are well-executed but failed to light any fires.

SAN GIOVANNI AL NATISONE (UD)

LIVON
LOC. DOLEGNANO
VIA MONTAREZZA, 33
33048 SAN GIOVANNI AL NATISONE (UD)
TEL. 0432757173
E-MAIL: info@livon.it

The Livon group continues to expand – it has recently purchases an estate in Umbria – and the range is coming into focus. The Roncalto cellar aims for quality, concentrating on a limited number of labels, while the rest of the wine from the Collio goes into the Cru line although now, there is a new quality label called Gran Cru, for the Braide Alte, Merlot Tiare Mate and Chardonnay Braide Mate. These last three were the wines the panel focused on, identifying a significant difference between the 2001 bottles and those from earlier vintages. The 2001 wines are less interesting, with the single exception of the Picolit, where concentrated fruit, sugars and a hint of smokiness are the keynotes of an excellent sensory profile. Preceding vintages, however, earned plaudits, starting with the Braide Alte 2000, a blend of sauvignon, chardonnay, moscato giallo and picolit shrewdly put together by the highly competent Rinaldo Stocco and a fixture in the Guide's upper reaches. Complex grassy notes mingle with honey, hazelnut and tropical fruit, supported by a fresh-tasting, seamlessly pervasive texture. Next in line is the Merlot Tiare Mate. Stunningly concentrated, chewy fruit and sweet, nicely judged tannins are lifted by an austere hint of coffee and cocoa powder. Almost as good is the Chardonnay. Its excellent structure is let down only by the slightly closed nose. Make a note of the 2000 Cabernet Roncalto, too.

○ COF Bianco Canto '01	▼▼	3*
● COF Merlot '00	▼	5
○ Friuli Grave Tocai Friulano '01	▼	3
● COF Schioppettino '99	▼	5
○ COF Pinot Grigio '01		4
○ COF Sauvignon '01		4
○ COF Tocai Friulano '01		4
● COF Refosco P. R. '99		4
○ COF Bianco Canto '00	▼▼	3
● COF Merlot '99	▼▼	5

○ Braide Alte '00	▼▼▼	6
○ Collio Chardonnay Braide Mate '00	▼▼	5
● Collio Merlot Tiare Mate '00	▼▼	6
● Collio Cabernet Sauvignon Roncalto '00	▼▼	6
○ Collio Picolit Cumins '01	▼▼	7
○ Collio Pinot Grigio Braide Grande '01	▼	5
● COF Schioppettino Picotis '99	▼	6
○ Collio Ribolla Gialla Roncalto '01		5
○ Collio Tocai Friulano Ronc di Zorz '01		5
○ Braide Alte '96	▼▼▼	6
○ Braide Alte '98	▼▼▼	6

SAN GIOVANNI AL NATISONE (UD)

Ronco del Gnemiz
Via Ronchi, 5
33048 San Giovanni al Natisone (UD)
tel. 0432756238

It's been a difficult year for Serena Palazzolo's cellar. The outstanding raw material from her vineyards hasn't emerged in the bottle, particularly for one or two of the flagship wines. Add to this a certain fuzziness and forwardness on the nose of some bottles, which is unusual at Ronco del Gnemiz. Still, the Sauvignons are the best wines this time. The Riserva '99 has subtle vanilla aromas, mingling with peach and lemon that are echoed in the mouth, and the attractive body of a wine to lay down. Slightly sweet tropical fruit is the keynote of the standard 2000 Sauvignon, which has a balanced palate and soft alcohol. But the big surprise came from a competitively priced bottle that may have been underrated. The Colli Orientali del Friuli Bianco 2000, from chardonnay, riesling and sauvignon, has a delicious entry on the palate, lovely freshness and drinks beautifully. The luscious, malvasia-based Bianco Bianco '99, a wine to uncork straight away, has a bitter twist in the finish. We were unconvinced by the Chardonnay '99, which is not very forthcoming. The dark Merlot Sol '99 is flecked with purple. Alcohol and oak are prominent on the aggressive nose, although vanilla and cloves also come through. It comes apart a little in the mouth, where the soft front palate is followed up by close-knit tannins. Austere on the nose, the Rosso '99 is still in thrall to its tannins. The Tocai 2000 is full-bodied, albeit a little forward on the nose, while the Pinot Grigio is subtle and the promising nose of the Schioppettino '99 is let down by an unexpectedly straightforward palate.

○ COF Bianco '00	🍷🍷	4*
○ COF Sauvignon '00	🍷🍷	4*
○ COF Sauvignon Ris. '99	🍷🍷	6
○ Bianco Bianco '99	🍷	6
○ COF Pinot Grigio '00	🍷	4
○ COF Tocai Friulano '00	🍷	4
○ COF Chardonnay '99	🍷	6
● COF Merlot Sol '99	🍷	7
● COF Rosso del Gnemiz '99	🍷	6
● COF Schioppettino '99	🍷	6
○ COF Sauvignon Ris. '98	🍷🍷	6
○ COF Chardonnay '98	🍷🍷	6

SAN LORENZO ISONTINO (GO)

Lis Neris - Pecorari
Via Gavinana, 5
34070 San Lorenzo Isontino (GO)
tel. 048180105
e-mail: lisneris@lisneris.it

Alvaro Pecorari's range left us with mixed feelings. Almost all the wines made a very pleasant impression but at least one had the panel muttering. We're talking about the Confini 2000, from 50 per cent pinot grigio, 30 per cent traminer and the remainder riesling. Its pronounced aromas and honey-sweet palate may find admirers but we thought it was well short of the other wines, starting with the Chardonnay Jurosa 2000. A discreet, delicately elegant nose introduces a broad, silky mouthfeel, seamless structure and sustained, leisurely nose-palate consistency. There could be no doubt about the Three Glass rating. The Lis 2000 is the outcome of years of experimentation with selected chardonnay, sauvignon and pinot grigio fruit and shows that last year's top Guide award was no coincidence. A major wine, it has buttery aromas and a soft, refreshing palate where chardonnay and sauvignon are very discernible. Pinot Grigio is a wine type that always creates controversy but continues to show detractors that is can do the business. Our tastings confirmed it was again a close thing between the cellar's standard version and the Gris 2000, whose late-harvest fruit has imbued it with barely perceptible but very inviting hints of sweet fruit and aromatic overtones. The Sauvignon Picòl 2001 pays the price of a vintage that started well but failed to deliver whereas the red Lis Neris '99 blend, which we retasted this year, confirms its reliability on the nose and on a long, harmonious palate that has mellowed out its rough edges.

○ Friuli Isonzo Chardonnay Jurosa '00	🍷🍷🍷	5
○ Friuli Isonzo Pinot Grigio Gris '00	🍷🍷	5
○ Lis '00	🍷🍷	6
○ Friuli Isonzo Pinot Grigio '01	🍷🍷	4*
○ Friuli Isonzo Sauvignon Picòl '01	🍷	5
○ Confini '00		6
○ Friuli Isonzo Sauvignon Dom Picòl '96	🍷🍷🍷	5
○ Friuli Isonzo Pinot Grigio Gris '98	🍷🍷🍷	5
○ Lis '99	🍷🍷🍷	6
○ Tal Lùc '99	🍷🍷🍷	6
○ Friuli Isonzo Pinot Grigio '00	🍷🍷	4
● Lis Neris '99	🍷🍷	6

SAN LORENZO ISONTINO (GO)

Pierpaolo Pecorari
Via Tommaseo, 36/c
34070 San Lorenzo Isontino (GO)
tel. 0481808775
e-mail: info@pierpaolopecorari.it

Every winelover would like to experience the joys and disappointments of a grower's life by rubbing shoulders in the vineyard for a while. Recently married and fresh from an arts degree, Alessandro Pecorari has made this possible on his website with "Il Diario del Vignaiolo" (The Grower's Diary: www.pierpaolopecorari.it/diario.asp), where splendid photographs of estate life reveal the love that Alessandro and his father, Pierpaolo, have for their work. That same love is also evident in the range of wines from the estate's older vineyard selections. There was no Three Glass award but the average standard is encouragingly high. Three of the five Two Glass products particularly impressed us, the Sauvignon Kolàus 2000, the Pinot Grigio Olivers 2000 and the Refosco Panta Rei '99. The Sauvignon unleashes a swathe of aromas on the nose, good depth on the palate and an excellent balance of oak and fruit notes. Peach takes centre stage in the long finish. The Pinot Grigio Olivers has onionskin highlights, then a welter of nicely balanced aromas ranging from peach tart, petits fours, citrus and vanilla to lavender. A firm entry on the palate is backed up by good weight. The Refosco Panta Rei ages for two years in barrique and unfurls lavender, confectioner's cream, blueberry jam and dark chocolate. The nice structure on the palate is backed by beefy tannins.

○	Chardonnay Sorìs '00	₸₸	5
○	Friuli Isonzo Sauvignon Altis '00	₸₸	5
○	Pinot Grigio Olivers '00	₸₸	5
○	Sauvignon Kolàus '00	₸₸	5
●	Refosco P. R. Panta Rei '99	₸₸	8
○	Friuli Isonzo Chardonnay '01	₸	4
○	Friuli Isonzo Pinot Grigio '01	₸	4
○	Friuli Isonzo Sauvignon '01	₸	4
○	Malvasia '01	₸	4
○	Sauvignon Kolàus '96	₸₸₸	5
●	Merlot Baolar '97	₸₸	6
○	Pinot Grigio Olivers '98	₸₸	5
●	Merlot Baolar '99	₸₸	6

SAN QUIRINO (PN)

Rino Russolo
Via San Rocco, 58/a
33080 San Quirino (PN)
tel. 0434919577
e-mail: russolorino@libero.it

The team of father Iginio, an expert oenologist and agronomist, and son Rino, in charge of sales, has turned out another serious range with a highly distinctive, and rather unusual, softness that enables you to pick them out from the pack. When you find out that the softness comes from fruit that they grow on lean, gravelly soil, you realize how much effort, commitment and technical skill go into looking after the vineyards and cellar. To achieve all this, the Russolo family now has a new cellar, located on their 16-hectare estate on the Pordenone flatlands. The extensive range of wines is released in several ranges, notably the I Legni and the vineyard selections, Ronco Calaj and Mussignaz. This year, the panel were impressed by the Chardonnay I Legni 2000, from a vineyard planted at 4,200 vines per hectare, which ages in French barriques. Leisurely bottle ageing has lent it an intense nose of peach and candied apricots, mingling with mint and dried roses. Its oak comes through on the palate but there is also good softness and excellent nose-palate consistency. The Grifo Nero '99 nearly won a second Glass. This Pinot Nero is surprisingly complex and reveals appealing blueberry tart and redcurrant jam. Full Glasses went to the Doi Raps 2000 and Borgo di Peuma '99 blends. The former is from super-ripe pinot grigio, sauvignon and moscato giallo while the Borgo di Peuma is merlot-based, with a little cabernet and refosco.

○	Chardonnay I Legni '00	₸₸	4*
○	Doi Raps '00	₸	4
○	Ronco Sesan '00	₸	3
○	Friuli Grave Tocai Friulano Ronco Calaj '01	₸	4
○	Müller Thurgau Mussignaz '01	₸	3
●	Borgo di Peuma '99	₸	5
●	Cabernet I Legni '99	₸	4
●	Pinot Nero Grifo Nero '99	₸	5
○	Friuli Grave Pinot Grigio Ronco Calaj '01		4
○	Malvasia Istriana '01		4
●	Merlot I Legni '99		4
●	Pinot Nero Grifo Nero '98	₸₸	5
●	Refosco P. R. I Legni '99	₸	4

SPILIMBERGO (PN)

FANTINEL
FRAZ. TAURIANO
VIA TESIS, 8
33097 SPILIMBERGO (PN)
TEL. 0427591511
E-MAIL: fantinel@fantinel.com

The Fantinels have been wine people for generations. In 1969, grandfather Mario purchased his first vineyard after many years as a hotelier and restaurateur. Since then, his children, and now his grandchildren Lara, Manuela, Stefano and Marco, have continued the tradition. Currently, they have 250 hectares in the Grave, Collio and Colli Orientali DOC zones. The spectacular winery, with elegant hospitality areas, was completed recently and the estate continues to collaborate closely with Professor Zironi, from the University of Udine, in pursuit of ever-better quality. Never before has the Fantinel cellar turned out such seriously good wines. Not a single bottle was rejected, the Trilogy confirmed its past achievements and two great bottles from the Grave confirm that red winemaking has a future in the zone. Collio Bianco Trilogy 2001 is from barrique-fermented pinot bianco, tocai and sauvignon. The first release impressed us and this edition is equally admirable for its fresh peach, citrus and petits fours aromas. The soft attractively sustained mouthfeel signs off with hints of orange and apricot. Bot the Grave Refosco and the Merlot from 2000 are outstanding. Blueberry, bramble, cherry, confectioner's cream and cocoa powder are backed up by typically robust Refosco tannins and the Merlot reveals austere, minerally aromas laced with cherries and black cherries over hints of toastiness. The best One Glass winners were the delicate Collio Bianco Santa Caterina and the Friuli Grave Chardonnay Borgo Tesis, which has intense banana, pineapple and tropical fruit.

○ Collio Bianco Trilogy '01	ΨΨ	5
● Friuli Grave Merlot Borgo Tesis '00	ΨΨ	4*
● Friuli Grave Refosco P. R. Sant'Helena '00	ΨΨ	4*
○ Collio Bianco Santa Caterina '01	Ψ	4
○ Collio Chardonnay Sant'Helena '01	Ψ	4
○ Collio Pinot Grigio Sant'Helena '01	Ψ	4
○ Collio Sauvignon Sant'Helena '01	Ψ	4
○ Friuli Grave Chardonnay Borgo Tesis '01	Ψ	4
● Barone Rosso Platinum '00	Ψ	6

SPILIMBERGO (PN)

PLOZNER
FRAZ. BARBEANO
VIA DELLE PRESE, 19
33097 SPILIMBERGO (PN)
TEL. 04272902
E-MAIL: plozner@plozner.it

Each year, we run the risk of repeating ourselves when we come to write the Plozner profile. The excellent, extremely varietal wines from difficult gravelly alluvial soil owe their quality to the great skill of long-serving oenologist Francesco Visentin, backed up by the shrewd management of Valeria Plozner, and represent great value for money. In fact, there's not much we'd like to see changed. Year after year, the range gets more impressive, with image-enhancing moves such as the release of a Chardonnay four years after the vintage keeping the Plozner flag flying high. Continuity seems assured as Valeria's children have recently joined the team. Sabina looks after marketing and communication while Marco is busy renovating the cellar and vine stock. After a year in barrique and three in bottle, the Chardonnay '98 opens slowly to reveal a delicious range of aromas, from cocoa powder to petits fours and banana. The finish has a refreshing note of citrus. A long-time Two Glass regular, the Sauvignon is as good as ever. A nose of tomato leaf, elderflower and peach introduces enhanced softness in the mouth compared to previous editions. The marvellous Tocai is an object lesson in typicity, its crusty bread and almond-themed nose-palate consistency enhanced by a fresh note of acidity that has you reaching for a refill. Best of the One Glass wines is the Pinot Grigio, with its intense nose of minerals and williams pear.

○ Friuli Grave Sauvignon '01	ΨΨ	3*
○ Friuli Grave Tocai Friulano '01	ΨΨ	3*
○ Friuli Grave Chardonnay Ris. '98	ΨΨ	4
○ Friuli Grave Pinot Bianco '01	Ψ	3
○ Friuli Grave Chardonnay '01	Ψ	3
○ Friuli Grave Pinot Grigio '01	Ψ	3
● Friuli Grave Pinot Nero Ris. '99	Ψ	4
● Friuli Grave Cabernet Sauvignon '00		3
● Friuli Grave Refosco P. R. '00		3
○ Friuli Grave Sauvignon '00	ΨΨ	3
○ Friuli Grave Tocai Friulano '00	Ψ	3

TERZO D'AQUILEIA (UD)

BROJLI - FRANCO CLEMENTIN
VIA G. GALILEI, 5
33050 TERZO D'AQUILEIA (UD)
TEL. 043132642
E-MAIL: fattoriaclementin@libero.it

Viticulture around Aquileia dates back thousands of years. Pliny the Elder records how much the emperor Augustus enjoyed the town's red Pucinum wine. Nowadays, Aquileia is where the very friendly Franco Clementin manages the six-hectare Fattoria Clementin Brojli estate, personally looking after cellar and vineyard. Although small, the property has a beautiful cellar, a barrique cellar, a large hospitality area centred round a "fogolâr", a traditional hearth, and a small workshop for pork butchery courses. According to Franco, you need to work the vineyard nature's way, shunning chemical products. He has made considerable effort in that direction and in fact his grapes have been certified as organically grown this year. After keeping him in the Other Wineries for a few years, we are also promoting him this time and have given him a full profile. Contributions came from the Refosco Campo della Stafula 2000 and the 2001 Verduzzo. The Refosco is upfront and very varietal at first, then unveils attractive, well-balanced notes of chocolate, mint, pepper and blueberry jam, and a soft, nicely balanced palate. The Verduzzo marries sultanas, candied orange peel, confectioner's cream and apricot aromas with a whistle-clean progression on the palate, well-gauged warmth and a lingering honey and orange finish. There was nearly a second Glass for the Traminer, which was let down by a lack of complexity in the mouth.

● Friuli Aquileia Refosco Campo della Stafula '00	ΨΨ	4*
○ Friuli Aquileia Verduzzo Friulano '01	ΨΨ	4*
○ Friuli Aquileia Pinot Bianco '01	Ψ	3
○ Friuli Aquileia Traminer Aromatico '01	Ψ	3

TORREANO (UD)

JACÙSS
FRAZ. MONTINA
V.LE KENNEDY, 35/A
33040 TORREANO (UD)
TEL. 0432715147
E-MAIL: jacuss@jacuss.com

The Jacùss winery belongs to brothers Renato and Andrea Iacuzzi, whose ten hectares under vine yield 50,000 bottles a year, equally split between whites and reds. The special nature of the soil in the hills at Torreano gives the bottom of the valley, where the vines are situated, a unique personality that is transmitted to the grapes. The Iacuzzis have taken full advantage and concentrate on local varieties, of which they are fervent supporters. During winemaking, the have the assistance of the admirable Flavio Zuliani and have managed to turn out a very fine Picolit. Other good native wine types are the Tocai, Schioppettino and Refosco while the well-made Tazzelenghe is still finding its feet. The amber Picolit '99 has complex aromas of petits fours, dried figs and apricot tart, mirrored nicely on the palate where they are lifted by subtle layers of honey and orange in a warm, complex whole. The flower and honey Tocai 2001 is fresh-tasting. The Schioppettino 2000, from the grape once known as ribolla nera, offers sweet spice, mint and bramble jam. Although clean and very varietal, the Refosco '99 is not terribly complex. Finally, the Rosso Lindi Uà, from merlot, cabernet sauvignon and refosco, has a very satisfying nose but still needs to find balance on the palate.

○ COF Picolit '99	ΨΨ	7
○ COF Tocai Friulano '01	ΨΨ	3*
● COF Schioppettino '00	Ψ	4
● COF Rosso Lindi Uà '98	Ψ	4
● COF Refosco P. R. '99	Ψ	4
● COF Cabernet Sauvignon '00		4
● COF Merlot '00		3
○ COF Sauvignon '01		3
● Tazzelenghe '99		4
● COF Schioppettino '99	ΨΨ	4

TORREANO (UD)

VALCHIARÒ
VIA CASALI LAURINI, 3
33040 TORREANO (UD)
TEL. 0432712393
E-MAIL: info@valchiaro.it

To know the five partners at the Valchiarò winery is to like them. Having grown up together, and then remained friends, despite having followed separate careers, Lauro, Emilio, Gianpaolo, Armando and Galliano joined forces in 1990 to create one of the most interesting wineries in the Colli Orientali. Each contributed about two hectares, previously used for making wine for domestic consumption. Facing an uncertain future with a firm commitment to quality, the five turned to a number of expert consultants before finding the right combination to guarantee the improvements they were looking for. Today, the winery owns or manages more than 15 hectares and annual production is 700 hectolitres, most of which goes into the 50,000 bottles released. La Clupa 2001 is an elegant blend of oak-aged pinot bianco and steel-matured sauvignon that marries soft hints of banana with the freshness of apple and a hint of tea. The Picolit 2000 and Verduzzo 2001 are indisputably excellent and, some might say, even too intense. Both come from very slowly raisined grapes. Sweet and concentrated, they have very distinct personalities, sharing only their aromas of stewed apples, dried figs and almonds. All the One Glass winners scored more than 75 points, underlining that quality at Valchiarò goes right across the range.

○	COF Picolit '00	♟♟	7
○	COF Verduzzo Friulano '01	♟♟	4*
○	COF Bianco La Clupa '01	♟♟	4*
●	COF Merlot '00	♟	4
●	COF Refosco P. R. '00	♟	4
○	COF Pinot Grigio '01	♟	3
○	COF Sauvignon '01	♟	3
○	COF Tocai Friulano '01	♟	3
●	COF Cabernet '00		4
●	COF Merlot '98	♟♟	4
●	COF Refosco P. R. '98	♟♟	4

TORREANO (UD)

VOLPE PASINI
FRAZ. TOGLIANO
VIA CIVIDALE, 16
33040 TORREANO (UD)
TEL. 0432715151
E-MAIL: wines@volpepasini.net

There's no denying the managerial abilities of Emilio Rotolo, who has owned Volpe Pasini for a few years. In that short time, he has achieved goals that looked decidedly ambitious when he started out. Part of the credit must go to the team that Emilio has created, starting with Riccardo Cotarella, one of the few winemakers "imported" into Friuli to have done great things with whites, as well as reds. Day-to-day cellar management is in the hands of Alessandro Torresin while the vineyards are supervised by Marco Simonit, Pierpaolo Sirch and Andrea Pittana, ably assisted by Tarcisio Specogna, now in his 27th vintage at Volpe Pasini. Nor should we forget Rosa Tomaselli, who helps Emilio on the communications front, and finally son Francesco, who is finding his feet in the winery while completing his secondary education. There are 34 hectares planted to vine, 60 per cent of it white, and annual production is running at 230,000 bottles. Moreover, value for money is assured at Volpe Pasini. The Pinot Bianco Zuc di Volpe 2001 collected another Three Glass award. Half of the must ferments briefly in barrique and the resulting wine is stylishly complex, with good alcohol, nicely gauged acidity and an irresistibly intriguing finish. A point or two below comes the Le Roverelle 2000 white, which unfurls intense, fresh notes of apple and fruit salad as well as a delicious smoky hint that adds complexity. From a blend of pinot bianco, sauvignon and chardonnay, with 20 per cent picolit, it is vinified and aged in barrique.

○	COF Pinot Bianco Zuc di Volpe '01	♟♟♟	4*
○	COF Bianco Le Roverelle Zuc di Volpe '00	♟♟	5
●	COF Cabernet Zuc di Volpe '00	♟♟	5
●	COF Merlot Focus Zuc di Volpe '00	♟♟	5
●	COF Pinot Grigio Zuc di Volpe '01	♟♟	4
●	COF Refosco P. R. '01	♟♟	4
○	COF Ribolla Gialla Zuc di Volpe '01	♟♟	4
○	COF Chardonnay Zuc di Volpe '00	♟	4
○	COF Pinot Grigio Volpe Pasini '01	♟	4
●	COF Merlot Focus Zuc di Volpe '99	♟♟♟	5
○	COF Pinot Bianco Zuc di Volpe '99	♟♟♟	4
○	COF Chardonnay Zuc di Volpe '99	♟♟	4

TRIVIGNANO UDINESE (UD)

FOFFANI
LOC. CLAUIANO
P.ZZA GIULIA, 13/14
33050 TRIVIGNANO UDINESE (UD)
TEL. 0432999584 - 0233611591
E-MAIL: foffani@foffani.it

Giovanni Foffani looks after his vines and cellar personally, carefully following progress on a ten-hectare estate, 65 per cent of which is planted to white varieties. Giovanni and his wife Elisabetta are currently supervising extension work on the cellar, housed in their superb 16th-century villa which is, of course, listed. Other jobs under way include the creation of new space for temperature-controlled ageing. The Foffanis' imagination was evident at the recent Cantine Aperte (Open Cellars) event. They organized I Colori del Vino (The Colours of Wine), which attractively paired the various hues of the cellar's white wines with fabrics from a leading Italian fashion house. The wines themselves have made further progress this year in terms of finesse and overall quality. Back on top form is the Sauvignon 2001, with its very typical green aromas of bell pepper, tomato leaf and stylish apple introducing a very soft, rounded palate that signs off unhurriedly on a note of peach. The elegant Pinot Grigio 2001 offers aromas of acacia blossom, citrus and crusty bread that return on the soft palate, with its lovely finish. There was an impressive score for the Cabernet Sauvignon 1999. After ageing slowly in tonneaux, it has acquired fascinating gamey notes, as well as spice and talcum powder, then there is lots of structure on the palate, which is enhanced by solid tannins and attractive hints of coffee.

○	Friuli Aquileia Pinot Grigio Sup. '01	ΨΨ	3*
○	Friuli Aquileia Sauvignon Sup. '01	ΨΨ	3*
●	Friuli Aquileia Cabernet '00	Ψ	4
○	Friuli Aquileia Chardonnay Sup. '01	Ψ	3
○	Friuli Aquileia Tocai Friulano Sup. '01	Ψ	3
●	Friuli Aquileia Cabernet Sauvignon '99	Ψ	5
●	Friuli Aquileia Merlot '00		4
○	Friuli Aquileia Sauvignon Sup. '00	ΨΨ	3

VILLA VICENTINA (UD)

VALPANERA
VIA TRIESTE, 5/A
33059 VILLA VICENTINA (UD)
TEL. 0431970395
E-MAIL: valpanera@tin.it

Native varieties are enjoying something of a renaissance and Padua-based industrialist Gianpietro Del Vecchio has taken the trend to its logical extreme, replanting his 48 hectares in the flatlands near Udine almost entirely to refosco dal peduncolo rosso. The modern, well-equipped cellar produces 200,000 bottles a year of this wine, thanks to wine technician Luca Marcolini, releasing several versions, all outstandingly good. There is also an events and parties area next to the production zone, helping to make the winery a pleasant place to visit. Last year, the Valperna wines were good but a leap forward in quality this year has earned the estate a full Guide profile. The top of the range is the Refosco Riserva '99, which ages for 18 months in barrique. The warm, balanced nose proffers pepper spice, blueberry jam and liqueur cherries that are echoed on the palate. The broad, full-bodied progression takes you through to an unhurried finish. The 2000 Refosco Superiore is equally good. Its elegant, subtle notes of hay, Peruvian bark and roast coffee precede well-balanced softness and a long, spicy finish. Obtained from refosco, cabernet sauvignon and merlot, the Alma just missed out on a second Glass. It's very clean, with good thrust on the palate and attractive aromas of plum jam and cocoa powder.

●	Friuli Aquileia Refosco P. R. Sup. '00	ΨΨ	4*
●	Friuli Aquileia Refosco P. R. Ris. '99	ΨΨ	5
●	Friuli Aquileia Rosso Alma '99	Ψ	5
●	Friuli Aquileia Refosco P. R. '00		3

OTHER WINERIES

Cabert
Via Madonna, 27
33032 Bertiolo (UD)
Tel. 0432917434 - 0432914814
E-mail: bertiolo@tin.it

There were mixed results from this cellar in the Friulian flatlands that vinifies fruit from several growers, turning out 800,000 bottles each year. The range includes an impressive, fruit-driven Merlot Riserva '97 with great balance and a nice Pinot Grigio 2001.

●	Friuli Grave Merlot Ris. '97	🍷🍷	4*
○	Friuli Grave Pinot Grigio '01	🍷	3
○	COF Sauvignon Casali Roncali '01		4

Flavio Pontoni
Via Peruzzi, 8
33042 Buttrio (UD)
Tel. 0432674352
E-mail: flavio@pontoni.it

Flavio Pontoni produces 32,000 bottles of dependable wine from five hectares, including a benchmark Cabernet Franc for lovers of the variety's characteristic fresh-mown grass and hay notes. The Chardonnay and the Pinot Grigio are the best of the very nice whites.

●	COF Cabernet Franc '01	🍷	3
○	COF Pinot Grigio '01	🍷	3
○	Friuli Grave Chardonnay '01	🍷	3

Brunner
P.zza de Senibus, 5
33040 Chiopris Viscone (UD)
Tel. 0432991184
E-mail: info@aziendagricolabrunner.it

The historic Brunner estate is where Massimiliano Buccino tends 20 hectares of vines. The well equipped, beautifully looked after cellar has stainless steel vats and 50-hectolitre barrels. There are several good wines in the extensive range.

○	Friuli Grave Pinot Grigio '01	🍷	4
○	Friuli Grave Sauvignon '01	🍷	4
○	Friuli Grave Tocai Friulano '01	🍷	4
○	Ribolla Gialla '01	🍷	4

Tenuta Bosco Romagno
Loc. Spessa
Via Cormons, 211
33040 Cividale del Friuli (UD)

This hillslope estate at Spessa has 12 hectares. For the past year, it has been run by Anita Marocchi, who has cranked up the quality impressively. Her '99 Refosco and Cabernet Franc are admirable wines. The former deserves a special mention for its impenetrable colour and intense, complex aromas.

●	COF Cabernet Franc Ris. '99	🍷🍷	5
●	COF Refosco P. R. Ris. '99	🍷🍷	5
○	COF Tocai Friulano '01	🍷	5

Gradimiro Gradnik Eredi
Loc. Plessiva, 5/bis
34071 Cormons (GO)
Tel. 048180332
E-mail: gradnik@gradnik.com

One of Friuli's historic cellars is back in the Guide. Today, it is run by Neda Gradnik, who can call on 12 hectares under vine. Total annual production hovers around 40,000 bottles, including an excellent Pinot Bianco 2001 and an attractive Tocai.

○ Collio Pinot Bianco '01	🍷🍷	4*
○ Collio Chardonnay '01	🍷	4
○ Collio Ribolla Gialla '01	🍷	4
○ Collio Tocai Friulano '01	🍷	4

Renato Keber
Loc. Zegla, 15
34071 Cormons (GO)
Tel. 048161196 - 0481639844

We'll restrict our notes on the very competent Renato Keber's range to his very fine Chardonnay Grici. The elegant minerally notes emerging on the nose of the '99 augur well for the future.

○ Collio Chardonnay Grici '99	🍷🍷	6

Giulio Manzocco
Via Battisti, 61
34071 Cormons (GO)
Tel. 048160590
E-mail: vinimanzocco@lycos.com

This family estate, founded in 1930 by Amedeo, is run today by his grandson, Dario. Its compact dimensions – only eight hectares for 46,000 bottles a year – don't stop the Manzoccos from getting better. The 2000 vintage yielded a complex Merlot, a nice Refosco and an equally good oak-aged Verduzzo.

● Collio Merlot '00	🍷🍷	4*
● Friuli Isonzo Refosco P. R. '00	🍷	3
○ Verduzzo Friulano '00	🍷	3

Simon di Brazzan
Loc. Brazzano
Via San Rocco, 17
34070 Cormons (GO)
Tel. 048161182

We weren't expecting quite such a good Tocai from this seven-hectare property. Hats off to Daniele Drus and consultant Alessandro Flebus for a bready wine with tropical fruit and a marvellously balanced palate. The strongly varietal Malvasia and the subtle Sauvignon are also excellent.

○ Friuli Isonzo Malvasia '01	🍷🍷	3*
○ Friuli Isonzo Sauvignon '01	🍷🍷	3*
○ Friuli Isonzo Tocai Friulano '01	🍷🍷	3*
○ Pinot Grigio '01	🍷	3

Francesco Vosca
Via Sottomonte, 19
34070 Cormons (GO)
Tel. 048162135

Francesco Vosca looks after six hectares, some estate-owned and some rented. He only produces 8,000 bottles a year, selling them under seven labels. His tocai, malvasia and pinot grigio-based Collio Bianco and Collio Tocai are very persuasive.

○ Collio Bianco '01	🍷🍷	4*
○ Collio Tocai Friulano '01	🍷🍷	3*
○ Collio Pinot Grigio '01	🍷	3
○ Friuli Isonzo Chardonnay '01	🍷	3

Skerk
Loc. Prepotto, 20
34011 Duino Aurisina (TS)
Tel. 040200156
E-mail: info@skerk.com

There are more and more premium producers in Trieste's Carso. Boris Skerk's 2000 Terrano is a modern, juicily concentrated red with hints of blueberries and bramble. The flowery, well-structured Vitovska is nice, as is the honey and hay Malvasia.

● Carso Terrano '00	🍷🍷	5
○ Carso Vitovska '00	🍷	5
○ Carso Malvasia '00	🍷	5

Franco Visintin
Via Roma, 37
34072 Gradisca d'Isonzo (GO)
Tel. 048199974

Franco Visintin is a determined Isonzo DOC producer who has eight hectares in full production and a further three that have recently been replanted. His 40,000 bottles are great value for money and quality is good all through the range.

○	Friuli Isonzo Chardonnay '01	🍷	2*
○	Friuli Isonzo Sauvignon '01	🍷	2*
○	Friuli Isonzo Tocai Friulano '01	🍷	2*
●	Stàngja Rosso '99	🍷	3

Midolini
Via Udine, 40
33044 Manzano (UD)
Tel. 0432754555
E-mail: midolini@midolini.com

Gloria Midolini makes a Guide comeback thanks to a fine range that includes an outstanding Refosco 2000. Overall quality is impressive, thanks to the contribution of Luca D'Attoma and Gloria's magnificent vineyards in the Colli Orientali del Friuli DOC zone.

●	COF Refosco P. R. '00	🍷🍷	4*
●	COF Soresta'nt Ròs '00	🍷	5
○	COF Pinot Grigio '01	🍷	4
○	COF Tocai Friulano '01	🍷	4

Ronco Vieri
Loc. Ramandolo
33045 Nimis (UD)
Tel. 0432904726 - 043286437
E-mail: roncovieri@libero.it

Ronco Vieri is a small cellar that belongs to oenologists Alvaro Moreale, Stefano Trinco and Piero Pittaro. They grow only the native varieties that traditionally thrive in this territory. The sweet Ramandolo '99 is convincing, the Refosco good and the 2000 Picolit just missed out on a Glass.

○	COF Ramandolo '99	🍷🍷	4*
●	COF Refosco '00	🍷	4
○	COF Picolit '00		6

San Simone
Via Prata, 30
33080 Porcia (PN)
Tel. 0434578633
E-mail: info@sansimone.it

The Brisottos have been wine people for four generations. Liviana and Gino, who is also the cellar's oenologist, have now been joined by their children Chiara, Anna and Antonio. The elegantly smooth Cabernet Sauvignon Nexus 2000 is complex, well-balanced and very good indeed.

●	Friuli Grave Cabernet Sauvignon Nexus '00	🍷🍷	4*
○	Nòstos '00	🍷	4
○	Friuli Grave Pinot Bianco Prestige '01	🍷	3

Ronco Severo
Via Ronchi, 93
33040 Prepotto (UD)
Tel. 0432713144

The seven hectares of Ronco Severo belong to Stefano Novello, who turns out a valid range of Colli Orientali del Friuli wines. We especially liked the tempting 2001 Sauvignon whereas the Merlot, Tocai and Chardonnay were a tad fuzzy on the nose, although still very well-made.

○	COF Sauvignon '01	🍷🍷	4*
○	COF Tocai Friulano '01	🍷	4
●	COF Merlot Artiûl '97	🍷	5
○	COF Chardonnay '01		4

Zuani
Loc. Gisbana, 12
34070 San Floriano del Collio (GO)
Tel. 0481391432
E-mail: vinizuani@virgilio.it

Patrizia Felluga is back on the scene with a winery-cum-laboratory and a single, territory-driven white, released in two versions. The fresh, fruity Zuani Vigne is vinified in steel while the fuller, more serious, Zuani is crafted for the cellar.

○	Collio Bianco Zuani '01	🍷🍷	5
○	Collio Bianco Zuani Vigne '01	🍷	4

Forchir
Fraz. Provesano - Via Ciasutis, 1/b
33095 San Giorgio della Richinvelda (PN)
Tel. 042796037
E-mail: forchir@libero.it

The Forchir estate was founded in the early 20th century. When oenologist Gianfranco Bianchini and Enzo Deana moved in, they wanted to make premium, territory-focused wines. Their Pinot Bianco Campo dei Gelsi, Merlot and Rosso del Fondatore, from cabernet franc and sauvignon, are all up to snuff.

● Friuli Grave Merlot '01	🍷	3
○ Friuli Grave Pinot Bianco Campo dei Gelsi '01	🍷	4
● Friuli Grave Rosso del Fondatore '99	🍷	4*

Vignai da Duline
Loc. Villanova - Via IV Novembre, 136
33048 San Giovanni al Natisone (UD)
Tel. 0432758115
E-mail: duline@libero.it

This small estate's four and a half hectars are located on the border of the Colli Orientali del Friuli and the Grave DOC zones. Production runs at 13,000 bottles a year. Lorenzo Mocchiutti and Federica Magrini are going for quality and surprised us with a lovely refosco-based Morus Nigra 2000.

● Morus Nigra '00	🍷🍷	5
● Viburnum '00	🍷	5
○ Morus Alba '01	🍷	5

Villa Chiopris
Loc. Dolegnano - Via Montarezza, 33
33048 San Giovanni al Natisone (UD)
Tel. 0432757173
E-mail: info@livon.it

Villa Chiopris is the outpost of the Livon empire that makes easy-drinking, fresh-tasting young wines with lots of fruit. The Tocai 2001 earned the panel's approval, especially for its palate. There was a Glass for the Cabernet Sauvignon and a mention for the Merlot.

○ Friuli Grave Tocai Friulano '01	🍷🍷	3*
● Friuli Grave Cabernet Sauvignon '01	🍷	3
● Friuli Grave Merlot '01		3

Tenuta Pinni
Via Sant'Osvaldo, 1
33096 San Martino al Tagliamento (PN)
Tel. 0434899464
E-mail: info@tenutapinni.it

A good performance from this estate in the flatlands around Pordenone (the main offices are in a splendid 17th-century villa). Under the supervision of Sandro Facca, owners Roberto and Francesco Pinni have turned out a fine range, led by a warm 2000 Cabernet France with a deliciously soft mouthfeel.

● Friuli Grave Cabernet Franc '00	🍷🍷	3*
● Friuli Grave Refosco P. R. '00	🍷	3
○ Friuli Grave Pinot Grigio '01	🍷	3
○ Ucelut '99	🍷	5

Edi Gandin
Via San Zanut, 51
34070 San Pier d'Isonzo (GO)
Tel. 048170082
E-mail: egandin@spin.it

Edi Gandin bottles 80,000 units from his 12 hectares under vine, selling the rest of his wine unbottled. This year's wines were up and down, the best results coming from the whites with the Chardonnay Vigna Cristin and Sauvignon Roverella on top.

○ Friuli Isonzo Chardonnay Vigna Cristin '01	🍷	3
○ Friuli Isonzo Sauvignon Vigna Roverella '01	🍷	3

Borc Dodòn
Via Malborghetto, 4
33059 Villa Vicentina (UD)
Tel. 0431969393

Denis and Alessia Montanar have nine hectares of vineyards. Their two labels are Borc Dodòn and the Montanar, the latter coming from new plantings. The couple release only three wines, of which the seriously stylish Refosco '99 is attractive for its chocolate and mint mingling with wild berry tart.

● Refosco P. R. '99	🍷🍷	7
● Uis Neris '99	🍷	6
○ Uis Blancis '00		5

EMILIA ROMAGNA

The four bottles from Emilia-Romagna that won Three Glasses are an excellent result, especially when we note that two of the quartet have Sangiovese di Romagna on the label. This is the first time that the region's most important DOC zone has gained a top Guide award. Truth to tell, there is a precedent. In the 1995 Guide, we gave Three Glasses to the Castelluccio winery's Ronco delle Ginestre, which was a monovarietal sangiovese even though it didn't have DOC status. The new winners are San Patrignano's Avi 1999 and the Calisto 2001 from Stefano Berti, which come from very different cellars. The first is a huge, well-established operation whereas the second is a virtually a garage winery, releasing only its second vintage. Marzieno from Fattoria Zerbina won a fifth Three Glass accolade for the 2000 vintage. A blend of sangiovese, cabernet sauvignon and merlot, Marzieno has always been a faithful, uncompromising interpretation of its Romagna terroir, despite the two Bordeaux varieties in the mix. We hope that these straws in the wind will encourage others to continue the overall improvement we have observed in the local DOC wines. Nevertheless, much remains to be done. Our panels no longer find themselves confronted with dirty, poorly made Sangioveses that are woody, appallingly acidic or inexplicably tannin-heavy. That's all to the good. But this is only the start of a journey that we hope will lead to a clear definition of the DOC zone's three classic wine types: "ordinary" Sangiovese from the previous vintage; longer-aged Sangiovese Superiore; and Riserva wines. But there's more to Emilia-Romagna than just Sangiovese. The other two traditional DOC zones have also been sending out positive quality signals. Four Two Glass Lambruscos is a surprisingly good result, achieved thanks to a commitment to recovering the best of the past and combining it with a search for constantly improving quality. Leone Conti's Progetto 1 and Progetto 2, Tre Monti and other producers surprised and delighted our tasters with some very fine bottles of Albana di Romagna, showing that the variety is not just for making dried-grape wines. Finally, a few thoughts on the Colli Bolognesi and Colli Piacentini DOC zones. The first may look a little sleepy but if you dig around, you'll find some encouraging developments and a substantial number of young producers. One of them is Maurizio Vallona, whose admirable flagship wine is very reliable, and the Santarosa cellar has tucked away its first Three Glass award. There's plenty going on in the Colli Piacentini. Traditional producers tend to be marking time but there are some very exciting newcomers, like Cantina Valtidone and the Castelli del Duca winery. The newbies are bringing innovative, long-term projects, backing them up with serious commitment, and the results are now coming through.

BERTINORO (FC)

Celli
Via Carducci, 5
47032 Bertinoro (FC)
tel. 0543445183
e-mail: celli@celli-vini.com

It's not often that new wines take centre stage on release. But that is precisely what has happened here with the new non-DOC products that give the winemaker's imagination full rein. Take the Bron & Rusèval Sangiovese-Cabernet 2000, for example, with its 60-40 blend. Obviously, it has lots of power and extract – just look at that deep ruby red. The aromas are well-defined and held in check by attractive notes of oak, then the no-nonsense entry on the palate is immediately pervasive. Notes of red pepper alternate with spices, liquorice and berry fruit before the rounded balance of the leisurely finish. The Bron & Rusèval Chardonnay has mischievous hints of flowers and butter on the nose. The palate partially confirms the opulence of these aromas but is a little short, with a faint bitterish note. Nor does it have the structure of the previous year's version. The cellar's dried-grape wine, the albana-based Solara 2000, is a little disappointing on the nose. In the mouth, it is a different story, in a rich medley of chestnut honey and fruit ripened in the summer sun. One full Glass went to the Sangiovese Riserva Le Grillaie 1999, for its evolved nose and tannin-rich, full-bodied palate, and to the elegant Sangiovese Superiore Le Grillaie 2001, which has an attractive note of violets. The Albana Secco I Croppi 2001 is intense and fruity.

BERTINORO (FC)

Giovanna Madonia
Via de' Cappuccini, 130
47032 Bertinoro (FC)
tel. 0543444361 - 0543445085
e-mail: giovanna.madonia@libero.it

Luckily, there is nothing new at this small, hard-working winery in Bertinoro, where wine is revered and produced with admirable commitment. The lovely and very practical cellar ensures a comfortable sojourn for the barriques that have been indispensable for the sangiovese-based wines Giovanna Madonia has earned a name for making. We'll begin with the remarkable Ombroso '99, a still-young Riserva with exciting aromas of toastiness, vanilla and ripe cherries. The palate is delicious in both its elegant softness and unusually long finish, morello cherry vying with wild berries, hints of violets, vanilla, spices and cocoa powder. The Sangiovese Superiore Fermavento 2000 is equally characterful. The slightly traditional nose is its best feature but the complex structure has a shade too much acidity and tannin for perfect balance. The Albana Passito Remoto '99 is an object lesson in harmony and finesse. Warm alcohol is to the fore – in fact, it's reminiscent of a Tuscan Vin Santo – and there is a teasing note of noble rot in the finish. Technically faultless, the Albana Secco Neblina 2001 combines varietal characteristics with sugar-rich softness and good texture. The same characteristics, as well as generous alcohol, emerge in the Velo del Magone 2000, a medium-sweet Albana.

○ Albana di Romagna Passito Solara '00	🍷🍷	4
● Bron & Rusèval Sangiovese-Cabernet '00	🍷🍷	4
○ Albana di Romagna Secco I Croppi '01	🍷	3*
○ Bron & Rusèval Chardonnay '01	🍷	4
● Sangiovese di Romagna Sup. Le Grillaie '01	🍷	3
● Sangiovese di Romagna Sup. Le Grillaie Ris. '99	🍷	3*
○ Bron & Rusèval Chardonnay '00	🍷🍷	4
● Bron & Rusèval Sangiovese-Cabernet '99	🍷🍷	4

○ Albana di Romagna Passito Remoto '99	🍷🍷	5
● Sangiovese di Romagna Sup. Ombroso Ris. '99	🍷🍷	5
○ Albana di Romagna Amabile Velo del Magone '00	🍷	4
● Sangiovese di Romagna Sup. Fermavento '00	🍷	4
○ Albana di Romagna Secco Neblina '01	🍷	4
● Sangiovese di Romagna Sup. Ombroso Ris. '97	🍷🍷	5
● Sangiovese di Romagna Sup. Ombroso Ris. '98	🍷🍷	5
● Sterpigno Merlot '98	🍷🍷	5

BERTINORO (FC)

FATTORIA PARADISO
VIA PALMEGGIANA, 285
47032 BERTINORO (FC)
TEL. 0543445044 - 0543444596
E-MAIL:
fattoriaparadiso@fattoriaparadiso.com

This delightful corner of Romagna beneath the walls of Bertinoro continues to host a collection of vintage cars, a restaurant and an elegant inn, as well as the Fattoria Paradiso estate. Commitment, determination and imagination still drive the winery towards goals that have been drawing closer over the past few years. Confirmation of the trend arrived in 2002 in the shape of the expert Tuscan oenologist, Roberto Cipresso. But let's move on the wines. Mito '99 is even better than previous vintages and progress is encouraging. Scrupulous selection of the cabernet sauvignon and merlot fruit, as well as leisurely ageing in small barrels of French oak, have produced a captivating wine of great finesse and elegance. The intriguing nose mingles oak and hay, then the mouthfilling palate brings notes of spices, tobacco and vanilla. The finish is slow and leaves a sensation of delicious softness. Elegantly ambitious hints of botrytis and a carefully balanced sweetness are the distinguishing characteristics of the Albana Passito Gradisca. The Sangiovese Vigna del Molino 2001, from the Maestri di Vigna range, has a nose of ripe, fruity notes that are echoed on the palate, although there is a touch of edginess in the finish. The well-structured Barbarossa, a cellar classic, also has faintly aggressive tannins. The Vigna delle Lepri 2000 (Castello di Ugarte) is a Sangiovese aged in large oak barrels. It's well-extracted and reveals a luscious flavour of damson jam. Finally, the Chardonnay Jacopo 2001 has a soft, gentle flavour but is a little in awe of the oak in which it aged.

- Mito '99 — 7
- Albana di Romagna Passito Gradisca '00 — 6
- Barbarossa Vigna del Dosso '00 — 5
- Sangiovese di Romagna Sup. Vigna delle Lepri Ris. '00 — 5
- Jacopo Chardonnay '01 — 4
- Sangiovese di Romagna Sup. Vigna del Molino '01 — 3
- Mito '97 — 7
- Mito '98 — 7

BORGONOVO VAL TIDONE (PC)

CANTINA SOCIALE VALTIDONE
VIA MORETTA, 58
29010 BORGONOVO
VAL TIDONE (PC)
TEL. 0523862168
E-MAIL: segreteria.csvta@libero.it

A well-deserved Guide debut for this co-operative with 350 members and over 1,000 hectares under vine, more than 80 per cent of which lie in the Colli Piacentini DOC zone. Production focuses on quality, as well as numbers, and the top of the range label is called Borgo di Rivalta, after the place where the ageing cellars are located. The results this year are excellent, particularly if we bear in mind that the wines presented are from 1999, a vintage that could hardly be described as memorable in the Piacenza area. There are two Gutturnios in the Borgo di Rivalta range. The barbera and bonarda Giannone Riserva 1999 ages in barriques for a year. The nose combines ripe fruit with vanilla and balsam from the wood, which are mirrored satisfyingly in the warm, soft and appreciably long palate. Flerido Superiore 1999 is aged for a total of eight months in large barrels and barriques. All that oak shows through in the palate, toning down the fruit and drying out the finish. In the attractive pinot nero-based Briseide 1999, the delicate varietal aromas again suffer at the hands of rather over-assertive wood. The successful Mabilia Cabernet Sauvignon 1999 has promising weight on the palate, where varietal notes of cabernet meld with tobacco, spices and ripe fruit. The Gutturnio Classico Julius 1999, from the Valtidone range, is consistent and harmonious. The Superiore 1999 is made along the same lines but has more body. Finally, the Sauvignon Costa Solara 2001 is eloquent and true to type on the nose, if a little uncomplicated in the mouth.

- C. P. Cabernet Sauvignon Borgo di Rivalta Mabilia '99 — 5
- C. P. Gutturnio Borgo di Rivalta Giannone Ris. '99 — 5
- C. P. Sauvignon Costa Solara '01 — 4
- C. P. Gutturnio Cl. Julius '99 — 4
- C. P. Gutturnio Sup. '99 — 4
- C. P. Gutturnio Sup. Borgo di Rivalta Flerido '99 — 5
- C. P. Pinot Nero Borgo di Rivalta Briseide '99 — 5

BRISIGHELLA (RA)

La Berta
Via Pideura, 48
48013 Brisighella (RA)
Tel. 054684998
E-mail: be.gio@libero.it

In the debate that pits supporters of huge investment and quantum leaps in quality against the one-step-at-a-time brigade, it is the latter that have been proved right at La Berta, where results continue steadily to improve. The team is crucial and here it is made up of owner Costantino Giovannini and Stefano Chioccioli, his consultant winemaker. This year, the news is that one of Costantino's dreams has come true. He has finally decided what to do with the alicante vines that have always been grown on the estate. They have been released in a small selection, called Almante, with a sweet, ripe nose and a warm, well-rounded palate, despite its beefy tannins. The cellar's traditional wines are just as good, starting with the outstanding Olmatello 2000. It's a Sangiovese Riserva with a deep colour that says "extract". Expert winemaking has kept its power under control and the result is a seductively stylish bottle. Pleasing aromas and the intriguing alternation of cherry and liquorice on the palate characterize the other flagship wine, Ca' di Berta 2000, from cabernet and sangiovese aged in small oak barrels. The clean, elegant Sangiovese Superiore Solano 2001 offers attractive notes of ripe berry fruit. The estate "passito", or dried-grape wine, Infavato is a balanced Malvasia with a nice twist of almond in the finish. Bringing up the rear is the alcohol-heavy, chardonnay-based Pieve Alta 2001.

● Sangiovese di Romagna Olmatello Ris. '00	🍷🍷	5
● Almante	🍷🍷	5
● Colli di Faenza Rosso Ca' di Berta '00	🍷🍷	5
● Sangiovese di Romagna Sup. Solano '01	🍷🍷	4*
○ Pieve Alta Chardonnay '01	🍷	4
○ Infavato Vino da Uve Stramature	🍷	5
● Colli di Faenza Rosso Ca' di Berta '99	🍷🍷	5
● Sangiovese di Romagna Sup. Solano '00	🍷🍷	4
● Sangiovese di Romagna Olmatello Ris. '99	🍷🍷	4

CASALECCHIO DI RENO (BO)

Tizzano
Via Marescalchi, 13
40033 Casalecchio di Reno (BO)
Tel. 051571208 - 051577665

The lovely 230 hectare estate (35 under vine), owned by Conte Luca Visconti di Modrone and located on the first slopes of the Valle del Reno, continues to make encouraging progress. Manager Gabriele Forni's drive and skill have ensured that in recent years, a packed planting schedule and overall vineyard improvement programme have been put in place. The first results are already obvious and the near future should see further improvement. We approve of the estate's decision to focus on the native pignoletto variety for its whites, released in three versions. The cuve close method Brut has always been one of Tizzano's signature bottles. The breadth, fragrance and length of its aromas bespeak a thoroughbred sparkler. The Frizzante version is less serious but deliciously fresh-tasting and balanced while the still Superiore reveals more structure, its tangy palate signing off with a faintly bitterish note. But the most interesting Tizzano wine is the Cabernet Sauvignon 2000, expertly aged in both oak and stainless steel. Its crisp, clean aromas are attractively fruity and the palate has complexity yet is also very, very approachable. A notch or two down there is the Cabernet Riserva '98. After 24 months in barriques, it is undeniably intense, spicy and evolved but it's also little tired and short on brio.

● C. B. Cabernet Sauvignon '00	🍷🍷	4*
○ C. B. Pignoletto Frizzante '01	🍷	3
● C. B. Cabernet Sauvignon Ris. '98	🍷	4
○ C. B. Pignoletto Brut	🍷	4
○ C. B. Pignoletto Sup. '01		3
○ C. B. Riesling Italico '01		3
● C. B. Cabernet Sauvignon Ris. '97	🍷🍷	4

CASTEL BOLOGNESE (RA)

Stefano Ferrucci
Via Casolana, 3045/2
48014 Castel Bolognese (RA)
Tel. 0546651068 - 054629789
E-mail: info@stefanoferrucci.it

The 15 hectares Stefano Ferrucci has planted to vine are in one of Romagna's finest growing areas, at Serra near Castel Bolognese. In the late classical period, Caius Graccus built a house here, right on the spot where part of the present-day cellar stands. These historical roots are highlighted in some of the names Ferrucci has chosen for his wines. Domus Caia is the cellar's most representative product. It's rather a special Sangiovese, vinified with leisurely maceration after the grapes have raisined naturally. Subsequently, it is aged slowly, first in small oak barrels and then in bottle. The resulting wine is warm, velvet-smooth and releases intense aromas of dried fruit and spices. There is plenty of alcohol and body. Domus Aurea comes from dried albana grapes. Just the right degree of sweetness and intense aromas of apricot and peach jam are backed up by an almost oily mouthfeel and good acidity. Ferrucci's knack with sweet wines shows through again in the Vino da Uve Stramature, made from bunches of malvasia dried on the vine and harvested at the end of January. It's a sort of Romagna-style ice wine that is elegantly sweet and long on the palate. The Albana Dolce Lilaria is nicely made, as is the Centurione, a fresh-tasting, instantly likeable basic Sangiovese with good fruit.

CASTEL SAN PIETRO TERME (BO)

Umberto Cesari
Fraz. Gallo Bolognese
Via Stanzano, 1120
40050 Castel San Pietro Terme (BO)
Tel. 051941896 - 051940234
E-mail: info@umbertocesari.it

Although very new – it's only in its second year of production – Sangiovese Tauleto has already earned a place in the front rank of Romagna winemaking. The '99 is made with the best fruit from a few, carefully selected plots dotted here and there around the estate. The wine, of which only 9,800 bottles were released, is slowly aged in barriques that have brought out its exuberance without jeopardizing the balance. Solid and austere, it has great texture and personality. The softer and more internationally oriented Liano '99 is a successful blend of sangiovese and cabernet sauvignon that offers breadth – with well-defined hints of red fruit jam – and juiciness. The panel was also pleased to note that the traditional Sangiovese Riserva is as good as ever. The dry, restrained style of this excellently made, value-for-money bottle is unmistakable. Less convincing is the Laurento. Well enough made, it nonetheless lacks that something special that would lift it above the rest of the barriqued Chardonnays that everyone is churning out these days. The 50-50 pignoletto and chardonnay Malise is an uncomplicated crowd-pleaser while the Albana Passito is a fine quality wine to bank on. Overall, then, Umberto Cesari has done very well this year, despite the dimensions of his estate (production is nearly 2,000,000 bottles a year). He has shown he can maintain standards right across the range.

	Wine	Rating	Score
○	Albana di Romagna Passito Domus Aurea '00	ŶŶ	6
●	Sangiovese di Romagna Domus Caia Ris. '99	ŶŶ	6
○	Albana di Romagna Dolce Lilaria '01	Ŷ	4
●	Sangiovese di Romagna Sup. Centurione '01	Ŷ	4
○	Stefano Ferrucci Vino da Uve Stramature	Ŷ	6
○	Colli di Faenza Bianco Chiaro della Serra '01		3
●	Sangiovese di Romagna Domus Caia Ris. '98	ŶŶ	6

	Wine	Rating	Score
●	Tauleto Sangiovese '99	ŶŶ	7
○	Albana di Romagna Passito Colle del Re '97	ŶŶ	6
●	Liano '99	ŶŶ	5
●	Sangiovese di Romagna Ris. '99	ŶŶ	4*
○	Laurento Chardonnay '00	Ŷ	4
○	Albana di Romagna Secco Colle del Re '01	Ŷ	3
○	Malise Pignoletto-Chardonnay '01	Ŷ	4
●	Colli d'Imola Cabernet Sauvignon Ca' Grande '01	Ŷ	4
○	Trebbiano di Romagna Vigneto Parolino '01		4
●	Tauleto Sangiovese '98	ŶŶ	5
●	Liano '98	ŶŶ	4

CASTELLO DI SERRAVALLE (BO)

Giuseppe Beghelli
Via Castello, 2257
40050 Castello di Serravalle (BO)
tel. 0516704786
e-mail: beghelli@collibolognesi.com

Giuseppe Beghelli is a young grower-producer with clear ideas. Recently, he has been taking some crucial decisions for the family winery. He acquired four hectares of a long-established local estate, adding them to the six the Beghellis already owned. He has also begun work on a cellar at the foot of the historic Castello di Serravalle. All this requires a certain commitment of time but Giuseppe has never lost sight of what is going on in the vineyard, where he follows developments ever more attentively. The result are there in the bottle, partly thanks to the wise advice of oenologist Giovanni Fraulini. The Cabernet Sauvignon 2001 repeats the good showing of the 2000, the first year the wine was released. It's a full-bodied, meaty wine with nice softness and faultlessly clean, intense fruit. Success is due to the careful harvest, left to the very last minute, which brought superb quality fruit into the cellar. Aged only in stainless steel, this is a wine with character that can safely be left in the cellar. In contrast, the Barbera Riserva 2000 went into barrique and will be available next year. Giuseppe makes two wines from pignoletto, the only white grape grown on the estate. The Classico is a very good wine that shows body, balance and a long, fruit-rich persistence whereas the Frizzante version is delightfully fresh and approachable.

●	C. B. Cabernet Sauvignon '01	3*
○	C. B. Pignoletto Cl. '01	2*
○	C. B. Pignoletto Frizzante '01	2
●	C. B. Barbera '01	2
●	C. B. Cabernet Sauvignon '00	3

CASTELLO DI SERRAVALLE (BO)

Vallona
Fraz. Fagnano
Via Sant'Andrea, 203
40050 Castello di Serravalle (BO)
tel. 0516703058 - 0516703333

In recent years, Maurizio Vallona has been concentrating exclusively on his two vineyards, the new one on the Lamezzi estate at 350 metres above sea level and his original plot around the large, attractive cellar at Fagnano. Vallona's plan is taking shape. He has about 23 hectares under vine, all cordon-trained, spur-pruned and planted at 5,000 to 6,000 vines per hectare. The Cabernet Sauvignon Selezione has been a regular attender at our final taste-offs and this year's offering is no exception. Elegant, demure and generous with fruit and spices on the nose, it then reveals a concentrated, complex palate with superb balance of flavour and an approachability that is unusual in such a thoroughbred. The Selezione di Chardonnay 2000, fermented and aged in new barriques, is equally good. The "sweet" nose mingles aromas of ripe melon and peach with vanilla, then the opulent palate fills the mouth, backed up by a zesty acidity that has been missing in some previous editions. Two Glasses also went to a Pignoletto with an intriguing peach and apricot nose that is echoed in the mouth, where the fruit components develop in harmony with a sharply defined tanginess. The panel had words of praise for the '99 Altr-Uve, a dried-grape "passito" from pignoletto, albana and sauvignon. The rest of the range was uniformly well-made and easily earned One Glass.

●	C. B. Cabernet Sauvignon Sel. '00	4*
○	C. B. Chardonnay Sel. '00	4
○	C. B. Pignoletto '01	3*
○	Altr-Uve Passito '99	5
●	C. B. Cabernet Sauvignon '00	4
○	C. B. Chardonnay '01	3
○	C. B. Pignoletto Vivace '01	3
○	C. B. Sauvignon '01	3
●	C. B. Cabernet Sauvignon Sel. '97	4
●	C. B. Cabernet Sauvignon Sel. '99	4
○	Per Martina '00	4

CASTELVETRO DI MODENA (MO)

CORTE MANZINI
LOC. CÀ DI SOLA
VIA MODENA 131/3
41014 CASTELVETRO DI MODENA (MO)
TEL. 059702658

Corte Manzini is a small family winery, founded in 1978 by four siblings. Every year, the cellar releases fewer than 100,000 bottles, which is almost eccentric in a panorama of big-number Lambrusco makers. Vineyard and cellar management are supervised personally by 30-year-old agriculture graduate, Stefano Manzini, but the entire family of aunts, uncles, nephews and nieces lends a hand. The estate includes only ten hectares, distributed across three plots in the best Grasparossa-producing area. One of the vineyards yields 100 quintals of selected fruit that goes into L'Acino, the most interesting Grasparossa we tasted this year. It's a modern-style Lambrusco with firm, lively mousse, an enticingly broad fruit-and-flower nose where black cherry and raspberry emerge, and a fresh, dry palate that signs of with a delicious lingering softness. Such success is achieved thanks to the scrupulously clean winemaking and careful monitoring of vinification temperatures that characterizes the entire Corte Manzini range. The equally interesting Grasparossa Secco also won Two Glasses. It has a slightly more elusive personality and attractive fragrances of violets, cyclamen and fresh berry fruit. The other wines were all good, an indication that the Manzini's success is no coincidence. This is a serious, professional cellar.

● Lambrusco Grasparossa di Castelvetro L'Acino	ΨΨ	4
● Lambrusco Grasparossa di Castelvetro Secco	ΨΨ	3*
○ Il Gherlo Trebbiano di Modena	Ψ	2*
● Lambrusco di Modena	Ψ	2*
● Lambrusco Grasparossa di Castelvetro Semi Secco	Ψ	3
● Lambrusco Grasparossa di Castelvetro Amabile	Ψ	3
⊙ Lambrusco di Modena Rosato	Ψ	3

CIVITELLA DI ROMAGNA (FC)

PODERI DAL NESPOLI
LOC. NESPOLI
VILLA ROSSI, 50
47012 CIVITELLA DI ROMAGNA (FC)
TEL. 0543989637
E-MAIL: info@poderidalnespoli.com

The Poderi dal Nespoli cellars are located in an historic villa whose oldest parts date from the 17th century. The complex nestles in a parkland of cypresses and cedars of Lebanon. The vines themselves are arranged around the villa and enjoy superb positions on the gently slopes of the Romagna hills rising up from the nearby Adriatic. In total, the estate has 30 hectares of superb vineyards. Operations in the field and cellar have been entrusted by the owners, the Ravaioli family, to Alberto Antonini. This very competent Tuscan oenologist has given the winery a distinct personality in only a few short years. The most interesting bottle is still the Borgo dei Guidi, an unusual blend of 70 per cent sangiovese with 25 per cent cabernet sauvignon and a little raboso del Piave that ages for a year in French and American oak. Entry on the nose is a complex mix of spice and ripe fruit, leading in to a firm palate with soft, close-knit tannins and elegant, very good length. Late harvested sangiovese is the raw material for Il Nespoli, another barrique-aged wine. The super-ripe fruit lends a firm, juicy texture, nice softness and a lovely after-aroma of plum jam. The fresh, fruity Sangiovese Prugneto is simpler but certainly not dull. Damaggio, an oak-fermented Chardonnay aged in stainless steel, offers intense aromas of tropical fruit on the nose and a hefty, mouthfilling palate.

● Borgo dei Guidi '00	ΨΨ	6
● Il Nespoli '00	ΨΨ	5
○ Damaggio '01	Ψ	3*
● Sangiovese di Romagna Vigneto Il Prugneto '01	Ψ	4
● Borgo dei Guidi '97	ΨΨ	6
● Borgo dei Guidi '98	ΨΨ	6
● Borgo dei Guidi '99	ΨΨ	6

CORIANO (RN)

SAN PATRIGNANO
LOC. SAN PATRIGNANO
VIA SAN PATRIGNANO, 53
47852 CORIANO (RN)
TEL. 0541362362 - 0541756764
E-MAIL: comm3@sanpatrignano.org

The rise of San Patrignano's star has been as swift as it was predictable. It was obvious from the start that they wanted to make serious wines while respecting the special characteristics of the location. It was a praiseworthy commitment but at the time lacked strategic vision. Then Riccardo Cotarella came along to ensure the consistency of quality demanded from a cellar that was already in the front rank of Italian winemaking. It is no surprise, then, that Avi '99 is one of the first two Sangiovese di Romagna wines in the history of the Guide to carry off Three Glasses. A wine of distinction, it reveals attractive herbaceous notes and a dense hue. The substantial tannin content tells you it is oak-aged but the wood never overwhelms the delicious black cherry, liquorice and cocoa powder aromas. Well-rounded and satisfying, this Avi particularly impresses with the lingering, pervasiveness of its astonishing palate. Our anxious wait for the Montepirlo 2000, after the splendid '99, will have to continue. The 2000 is still in the ageing cellar and will only be ready for the next edition of the Guide. We were also impressed by the cellar's less demanding products, like the Sangiovese Riserva Zarricante 2000. Rather placid on the nose, it unveiled a solid palate with high notes of berry fruit and violets. The Sangiovese Superiore Aulente 2001 is also nice, the intense hue heralding a robust palate, although oak is a little too much to the fore both on the nose and in the mouth. Finally, the monovarietal Sauvignon Vintàn 2001 is a pleasingly clean-tasting, easy-drinking wine.

● Sangiovese di Romagna Sup. Avi Ris. '99	🍷🍷🍷	6
● Sangiovese di Romagna Sup. Zarricante Ris. '00	🍷🍷	5
● Sangiovese di Romagna Sup. Aulente '01	🍷	4
○ Vintàn '01	🍷	4
● Montepirolo '99	🍷🍷🍷	5
● Sangiovese di Romagna Sup. Avi Ris. '98	🍷🍷	5
● Sangiovese di Romagna Sup. Aulente '00	🍷🍷	4

FAENZA (RA)

LEONE CONTI
LOC. SANTA LUCIA
VIA POZZO, 1
48018 FAENZA (RA)
TEL. 0546642149
E-MAIL: leone@leoneconti.it

Well done, Leone. He's got courage. For it takes courage, as well as skill, to work seriously with one of Romagna's worst-treated varieties – albana – and to do so innovatively. Leone's two carefully thought-out projects have produced two different wines, both obtained from late-harvested fruit. For Progetto 1, the bunches are picked whole and fermented in stainless steel only. In contrast, Progetto 2 is from fruit attacked by noble rot and picked in several selections. Part ferments in steel and the rest in barrique, then the wine undergoes leisurely ageing in the bottle. Both are great wines, albeit with different sensory profiles. The first is more mysterious and hard to pin down while Progetto 2 is an instant hit, reminiscent of the great wines of Alsace. The reds produced more surprises, starting with Le Ghiande. This barrique-aged blend of cabernet sauvignon and merlot, with a little sangiovese, is flanked by a successful Riserva 2000. Arcolaio is another very good wine from an old native grape called sauvignon rosso – the vines are more than 35 years old – and the Rossonero, obtained from syrah with very little else, is up to its usual standards. We have left the Albana Passito until last. The cellar is changing its style (this will be more obvious in the 2001 vintage) but even now, it is an admirably made bottle.

○ Albana di Romagna Passito Non Ti Scordar di Me '00	🍷🍷	6
○ Albana di Romagna Progetto 2 '00	🍷🍷	4
● Colli di Faenza Rosso Podereviacupa Le Ghiande '00	🍷🍷	4
○ Albana di Romagna Progetto 1 '01	🍷🍷	4*
● Sangiovese di Romagna Sup. Contiriserva Ris. '00	🍷🍷	5
● Arcolaio '00	🍷	5
● Rossonero '00	🍷	4
● Sangiovese di Romagna Sup. Poderepozzo Le Betulle '00	🍷	4
○ Colli di Faenza Bianco Poderepalazzina '01	🍷	3
● Sangiovese di Romagna '01	🍷	3

FAENZA (RA)

FATTORIA ZERBINA
FRAZ. MARZENO
VIA VICCHIO, 11
48010 FAENZA (RA)
TEL. 054640022
E-MAIL: zerbina@zerbina.com

Another Three Glass jackpot for the Marzieno, which carries on a tradition that has been unbroken recently. A blend of 80 per cent sangiovese, with small proportions of cabernet sauvignon and merlot, aged in new barriques, Marzieno is a textbook example of a "vin du terroir". Elegant, yet powerful and austere, it grows enormously with time in the cellar, as our tastings of previous vintages have shown. The 2000 has a close-knit hue and intense aromas that range from ripe fruit to pencil lead by way of spice, pepper and tobacco. Firm and compact on the palate, it has soft fruit that lingers through to the unhurried finish. This is a great Marzieno and one that won't disappoint the fans of Fattoria Zerbina. Another wine that is spot on for its consistent reliability and excellent value for money is the Torre di Ceparano. Like its predecessors, the 2000 is soft, full, intense and stylish, making it again one of the best Sangiovese Superiore di Romagnas around. The pleasingly approachable second-label Ceregio put up a good show but we were looking for better things from the Ceregio Vigna Querce, a selection of sangiovese from very old vines. Observant readers will note the absence of two major wines, the Albana Passito Scacco Matto and the Sangiovese Riserva Pietramora. Sadly, 1999 was not a good vintage and neither was released. There aren't very many bottles of Arroco, either, but the quality is good. This, too, is indicative of how seriously Maria Cristina Geminiani takes her winemaking. It is what has made Fattoria Zerbina the most reliable cellar in Romagna.

● Marzieno '00	▼▼▼	6
● Sangiovese di Romagna Sup. Torre di Ceparano '00	▼▼	4*
● Sangiovese di Romagna Sup. Ceregio '01	▼▼	3*
○ Albana di Romagna Passito Arrocco '99	▼▼	6
● Sangiovese di Romagna Sup. Ceregio Vigna Querce '00	▼	4
● Marzieno '98	▼▼▼	6
● Marzieno '99	▼▼▼	6
○ Albana di Romagna Passito Scacco Matto '98	▼▼	6
● Sangiovese di Romagna Sup. Pietramora Ris. '98	▼▼	6

FAENZA (RA)

ISTITUTO PROFESSIONALE
PER L'AGRICOLTURA E L'AMBIENTE
LOC. PERSOLINO - VIA FIRENZE, 194
48018 FAENZA (RA)
TEL. 054622932
E-MAIL: ipsaa.persolino@mbox.dinamica.it

This agricultural school continues to amaze. As well as coaxing its students to academic success, it also enables them to enjoy the tangible gratification of producing good wine. Is there any better way to demonstrate the institution's excellence? Consultancy is provided by native-grown technician Sergio Ragazzini, who has become the guiding light of many winery technical staffs, but he is not the only reason for the school's success. Out of the ordinary vine types are the norm. That's why we find an unusual Amabile Persolino 2000, from raisined malbo gentile grapes that have sojourned at length in wood. It's not as satisfying as the previous edition but still hits the spot with its warmth, softness and length, despite the slight lack of extract and residual sugar. The raisined white grape wines are more successful. The Albana Passito Ultimo Giorno di Scuola 2000 (literally, "Last Day of School") is a full-bodied, alcohol-rich bottle with an uncomplicated palate of ripe peaches and apricots while the malvasia-based Poesia d'Inverno 2000 Vino da Uve Stramature is even better. Its seductively creamy palate mingles varietal notes, and a typical bitterish twist in the finish, with citrus and candied peel. The red Varrone 2000 lacks a little balance as the muscular body tends to demand your attention. Finally, the pinot nero-based Rosso di Nero 2000 has more balance, if less spontaneity.

○ Albana di Romagna Passito Ultimo Giorno di Scuola '00	▼▼	5
● Amabile Persolino Rosso Passito '00	▼▼	5
○ Poesia d'Inverno Vino da Uve Stramature '00	▼▼	5
● Rosso di Nero '00	▼	4
● Varrone '00	▼	3

FAENZA (RA)

TRERÉ
VIA CASALE, 19
48018 FAENZA (RA)
TEL. 054647034
E-MAIL: trere@trere.com

This delightful little winery in the hills outside Faenza is further beautified by the many peacocks in the grounds. The cellar continues to turn out clean, well-executed wines, sending out reassuring signals of consistency and fidelity to local traditions. Treré has managed this in a year when producers have had to cope with rather unexciting performances from sangiovese-based wines. In the meantime, we greet the re-appearance of one of the cellar's historic bottles, Amarcord d'un Ross, a Riserva di Sangiovese that contains a very small proportion of cabernet sauvignon. Ageing in small barrels has taken the rough edge off the tannins, which are attractively fine-grained, and there are stylish notes of oak on the nose. The rich ruby colour denotes powerful extract, introducing a soft, satisfying palate of remarkable overall elegance. The sangiovese, cabernet sauvignon and merlot-based Montecorallo '99 is less harmonious but still worth looking into. However, the generous alcohol and meaty tannins are let down by a lack of fruit. There's a nostalgic apple pie note in the aromas of the Albana Passito '99, which reveals a bitterish twist in the finish. The Sangiovese Vigna del Monte 2001 is clean and easy to drink, although acidity and tannins struggle to find a balance. The tidy, powerful, Renero 2001 and the juicy Vigna dello Sperone, also from the 2001 vintage, are much more successful.

FORLÌ

STEFANO BERTI
LOC. RAVALDINO IN MONTE
VIA LA SCAGNA, 18
47100 FORLÌ
TEL. 0543488074
E-MAIL: renbante@tin.it

In winespeak, the term "vin de garage" or "garage wine" refers to wines made by producers who do not have a proper cellar but vinify instead with the minimum of space and equipment, perhaps in the garage of their homes. That makes Stefano Berti a true "garagiste". He has always farmed and grown grapes. Then in 2000, at the age of 41, he decided to bottle for himself rather than take his fruit to the local co-operative winery. To do so, he needed the assistance of a serious oenologist so Attilio Pagli now advises him on all aspects of winemaking. Stefano obtained just over 8,000 bottles from his first vintage then in 2001, increased production to 15,000, when new plots came onstream to join his original vineyard, where the vines are 40 years old. Sangiovese is the only variety and the vines are tended with fanatical care. There are two wines, similar in type but with very different ambitions. The Ravaldo is simpler and more immediate after fermentation in stainless steel and the ageing of only a small proportion in barrique for a few months. In contrast, the flagship Calisto has greater weight and structure, thanks to ruthless selection during the harvest. All the wine ages in oak, which Stefano uses with a master's touch. And what a touch it is, for the Calisto 2001 shot straight into the Three Glass bracket. Stefano's wines are full-bodied, generous and concentrated yet very accessible and a delight to drink. These are distinctive wines that precisely reflect their maker's ideas.

● Sangiovese di Romagna Amarcord d'un Ross Ris. '99	4*
○ Colli di Faenza Rebianco '01	3
● Colli di Faenza Sangiovese Renero '01	4
● Sangiovese di Romagna Sup. Vigna dello Sperone '01	4
○ Albana di Romagna Passito '99	6
● Colli di Faenza Rosso Montecorallo '99	4
● Sangiovese di Romagna Vigna del Monte '01	3
● Colli di Faenza Sangiovese Renero '00	3
● Sangiovese di Romagna Amarcord d'un Ross Ris. '98	3

● Sangiovese di Romagna Sup. Calisto '01	5
● Sangiovese di Romagna Sup. Calisto '00	5
● Sangiovese di Romagna Sup. Ravaldo '00	4*
● Sangiovese di Romagna Sup. Ravaldo '01	4*

FORLÌ

CALONGA
LOC. CASTIGLIONE
VIA CASTEL LEONE, 8
47100 FORLÌ
TEL. 0543753044

When Maurizio Baravelli started bottling his wine, he was only a small-scale grower. In fact, he worked part-time in the vineyard, sending some of his fruit to the co-operative winery and selling the wine from the rest unbottled. In 1999, he decided that his seven hectares of lovely vines, nestling in the hills between Forlì and Faenza, could yield better quality wines and deserved a little more attention. Thanks to the invaluable assistance of young oenologist Fabrizio Moltard, the results were forthcoming, particularly if we look at the first bottles from the 2000 vintage. Sadly, the panel was unable to sample the Cabernet Sauvignon Castellione, which requires unhurried ageing. It will be ready for the next edition of the Guide. We liked the Michelangiolo 2000, a Sangiovese Riserva made with grapes from vines that are more than 40 years old and aged for more than a year in new barriques of French oak. A very intense, characterful wine, it reveals good body, firmness of flavour and balance. The '99, a drier, less full-bodied version, is slightly less successful. We heartily approve of Maurizio's commitment to keep on vinifying bombino, the variety that goes into Pagadebit. The wine is fresh, headily fragranced and attractive. Finally, Polvere d'Oro is a nice chardonnay and bombino-based white that is fermented and briefly aged in barrique.

● Sangiovese di Romagna Sup. Michelangiolo Ris. '00	ŸŸ	6
○ Pagadebit di Romagna '01	Ÿ	3
○ Polvere d'Oro '01	Ÿ	4
● Sangiovese di Romagna Sup. Michelangiolo Ris. '99	Ÿ	5
● Cabernet Sauvignon Castellione '99	ŸŸ	6

FORLÌ

DREI DONÀ TENUTA LA PALAZZA
LOC. MASSA DI VECCHIAZZANO
VIA DEL TESORO, 23
47100 FORLÌ
TEL. 0543769371
E-MAIL: dreidona@tin.it

La Palazza's wines continue to improve as the Drei Donà family's long, patient labours bear fruit. Today, they can justly claim to have given their winery and range a distinctive personality. The wines are not what you'd call approachable. Each has its own character and peculiarities, as is shown by the fact that they are released much later than other similar bottles from the DOC zone. The reason for this – claims oenologist Franco Bernabei, who has been consultant for many years – is that "once they're in bottle, time will improve them". The exquisite Magnificat '98 is a Cabernet Sauvignon aged in French barriques that reveals incomparable intensity and unusual weight. Intense ruby red in the glass, it offers herbaceous aromas that make way for spices, pepper and tobacco. The well-extracted palate takes you through to a finish perked up by a long, pervasive peppery note. The Pruno, too, is excellent. Austere and penetrating, it is almost a model for Sangiovese di Romagna and has a great future ahead of it. The '97 vintage brought Graf Noir back to us. This very unusual blend of sangiovese, cabernet sauvignon, cabernet franc and negretto Longanesi, all from the same vineyard, is remarkably elegant, hard and razor-sharp. Back on form is the Tornese, a mature, buttery oak-conditioned Chardonnay with nice balance, and the Sangiovese Notturno, a standard wine with a distinctive style, is well worth its Glass.

● Magnificat Cabernet Sauvignon '98	ŸŸ	6
○ Il Tornese Chardonnay '00	ŸŸ	5
● Graf Noir '97	ŸŸ	7
● Sangiovese di Romagna Sup. Pruno Ris. '98	ŸŸ	5
● Notturno Sangiovese '00	Ÿ	3
● Magnificat Cabernet Sauvignon '94	ŸŸŸ	6
○ Il Tornese Chardonnay '95	ŸŸŸ	6
● Magnificat Cabernet Sauvignon '97	ŸŸ	6
● Graf Noir '95	ŸŸ	6
● Sangiovese di Romagna Sup. Pruno Ris. '97	ŸŸ	5

GAZZOLA (PC)

Luretta
Loc. Castello di Momeliano
29010 Gazzola (PC)
Tel. 0523976500
E-mail: luretta.vini@tin.it

We'll start by pointing out that with the 2002 harvest, the winery has moved to Castello di Momeliano, at Gazzola, where some of the estate's vineyards are located and where the new cellars are being built. After a year of awards and recognition, the Salamini family confirmed the trend by presenting a range of outstanding wines. We'll begin with the Malvasia Boccadirosa 2001, which has crisp aromas and mouthfilling flavour, underpinned by a restrained note of residual sugar. The Chardonnay Selin dl'Armari continues to improve. In the 2001 edition, shrewdly administered oak melds with the rounded flavour to give the palate good breadth, depth and momentum. The well-defined nose of the Sauvignon I Nani e le Ballerine 2001 leads into a youthful palate whose rich aromas are brought out by firm acidity. There was no Corbeau 2001 – the 2000 edition was a Three Glass wine – as the latest vintage is still in the cellar. Pantera 2001, a blend of barbera, bonarda and pinot nero, evokes raspberries and spice on the nose, then berry fruit and soft tannins on a balanced palate. "Achab" is the Italian spelling of Melville's Captain Ahab, and also the name of Luretta's new wine. From pinot nero, it spends 18 months in new barriques. It unveils blueberry and black cherry aromas mingling with oak-derived balsamic spice over a fine-grained tannic weave that lacks a little depth. Finally, Le Rane 2001, from late-harvested malvasia grapes, is a compendium of harmony and finesse. Layered notes of honey, peach and candied peel alternate on a fresh, balanced palate with good aromatic progression.

○ C. P. Malvasia V. T. Le Rane '01	♟♟	7
● Come la Pantera e I Lupi nella Sera '01	♟♟	5
● C. P. Pinot Nero Achab '00	♟♟	7
○ C. P. Chardonnay Selin dl'Armari '01	♟♟	5
○ C. P. Malvasia Boccadirosa '01	♟♟	5
○ C. P. Sauvignon I Nani e Le Ballerine '01	♟	5
● C. P. Cabernet Sauvignon Corbeau '00	♟♟♟	7
○ C. P. Chardonnay Selin dl'Armari '00	♟♟	5
○ C. P. Malvasia V. T. Le Rane '00	♟♟	7

IMOLA (BO)

Tre Monti
Loc. Bergullo
Via Lola, 3
40026 Imola (BO)
Tel. 0542657116
E-mail: tremonti@tremonti.it

Tre Monti's success is founded on the smooth co-operation of a set of people who all want to make a dream come true. The way the group works shows just how closely the "thinking" elements – David and Vittorio Navacchia, as well as oenologist Donato Lanati – are in tune. But the enterprise would be impossible to understand without taking account of the enthusiasm of Sergio, whose fiery energy drives a marketing effort worthy of California. The panel again approved of the Sangiovese Superiore Thea 2000, whose faint, delicate aromas emerge slowly on the palate, revealing admirably concentrated layers of mulberry, black cherry and toastiness that build up to a finish of elegant, fine-grained tannins. The length on the palate is quite marvellous. The sangiovese and cabernet sauvignon-based Boldo 2000 also performed well, its intense fruit aromas leading through to a long, soft finish with great balance. As ever, the Trebbiano Vigna del Rio 2001 was one of the best in its category. Deliciously fruity on the nose, it has a warm, solidly structured palate with nice balance. The Albana Passito 2000 has seductive notes of honey, apricots and peaches whereas it is the warmth and ripeness of the palate that stand out in the impressive Albana Vigna della Rocca 2001. Great technique and outstanding balance characterize the Salcerella 2001, from albana and chardonnay.

● Sangiovese di Romagna Sup. Thea '00	♟♟	5
○ Albana di Romagna Passito '00	♟♟	5
● Colli di Imola Boldo '00	♟♟	5
○ Albana di Romagna Secco Vigna della Rocca '01	♟♟	4
○ Colli di Imola Salcerella '01	♟♟	5
○ Trebbiano di Romagna Vigna del Rio '01	♟♟	3*
○ Colli di Imola Chardonnay Ciardo '01	♟	4
● Sangiovese di Romagna Sup. '01	♟	3
● Sangiovese di Romagna Ris. '99	♟	4
● Colli di Imola Boldo '97	♟♟♟	5
● Sangiovese di Romagna Sup. Thea '99	♟♟	5

International Movement
Slow Food®

Exercise your right to the pleasure of food, wine and conviviality
Protect biodiversity
Spread the word about food quality
Educate your taste
Promote clean, sustainable agriculture

Slow Food Presidia
A Foundation promoted by Slow Food funds projects to save and re-launch traditional foods, vegetables and animal species in danger of extinction. To date, Slow Food has developed 170 Presidia–151 in Italy, 19 in the rest of the world–all designed to revitalize local economies and offer prospects for sustainable development.

Slow Food Award
A prize assigned by an international jury to those who protect and promote biodiversity all round the world.

Major Events
The 'Salone del Gusto' in Turin; 'Cheese' in Bra, 'Toscana Slow', 'SuperWhites' and thousands of tastings, meetings and Taste Workshops in Italy and abroad.

University of Pollenzo and Colorno
An international center of training, research and documentation for people in the food and farming worlds.

Slow Food Editore
Publishers of Slow Food's official journal, *Slow: the international herald of taste and culture*, which is mailed to members all over the world, as well as a series of guides, manuals, tourist itineraries and essays on all aspects of food culture and gastronomy.

JOIN !!!

www.slowfood.com

Slow Food Italia – via della Mendicità Istruita, 14 – 12042 Bra (Cuneo) Italy
Tel. +39 0172 419611 – fax +39 0172 421293

A School of Italian Regional Cooking
Courses for professional chefs from all over the world
An overview of Italian cooking and eating culture
In-depth study of regional specialties

Master Italian Cooking
Palazzo Balleani, via F. Conti, 5
60035 Jesi (Ancona) – Italy
Tel/fax +39 0731 56400 – e-mail: info@italcook.it

WHERE
Jesi, a market town of great artistic and architectural interest, is situated in the lovely Marche region of Central Italy. It is especially famous for its Verdicchio wine.

WHAT
The Higher Institute of Gastronomy and School of Regional Cooking is a professionally-run center of culinary discovery and expertise. Set up in 1998, it is the result of a joint-venture between the City of Jesi and Slow Food, and is supported by the Ancona Provincial Authority and the Marche Regional Authority.

HOW
Courses are open to professionals in the sector-especially cooks who prepare and present Italian food in restaurants abroad-keen to expand and improve their knowledge of Italian regional cuisine. To find out more visit:

www.italcook.it

International Movement
Slow Food®

Slow Food Italia – via della Mendicità Istruita, 14 – 12042 Bra (Cuneo) Italy
Tel. +39 0172 419611 – fax +39 0172 421293

LANGHIRANO (PR)

Carra
Loc. Casatico
S.da della Nave, 10
43013 Langhirano (PR)
tel. 0521863510 - 0521355260
e-mail: boni.carra@libero.it

Carra gained its first Guide profile last year and kept its place thanks to a very convincing range of wines. Founded in 1972, the estate owns ten hectares on the hills of Casatico, producing around 100,000 bottles a year. Young, go-getting Bonfiglio Carra, 31, runs things. He is trying out other wines, not just the usual semi-sparkling "frizzante" type, and with some success. The Passito Eden soared past the Two Glass mark. Obtained from malvasia di Candia grapes, the 1999 spent two years in barrique. The classic varietal aromas are joined on the nose by hints of botrytis before the breadth and velvetiness of the palate take you through to a long finish with a bitterish note. Another very enjoyable wine is the Malvasia & Moscato, a blend of malvasia di Candia, moscato di Canelli and moscato d'Asti. Its delicate mousse, elegantly aromatic nose and even palate are perked up by a bright, creamy mouthfeel. The 2001 version of the Malvasia Frizzante, the classic white of the Colli di Parma DOC zone, marries well-defined aromas with a fresh vein of acidity on the palate. The nose of the Sauvignon Riserva 2001 has all of sauvignon's varietal typicity and a supple, well-rounded palate. As you wait for the next vintage of Pinot Nero Riserva to be released, make a note of the no-nonsense Tocularia Rossa, from lambrusco Maestri and merlot. The Spumante Metodo Classico Cinque Torri Brut, a 50-50 blend of chardonnay and pinot nero grapes, is nicely made. The lingering perlage ushers in a delicate palate that admirably combines balance with freshness.

○ Eden Passito '99		5
○ Cinque Torri Brut '01		5
○ Colli di Parma Malvasia Frizzante '01		3
○ Colli di Parma Sauvignon Ris. '01		4
○ Malvasia & Moscato Dolce '01		3*
● Torcularia Rosso '01		3*
● Pinot Nero Ris. '98		4

MODENA

Chiarli 1860
Via Daniele Manin, 15
41100 Modena
tel. 059310545
e-mail: info@chiarli.com

Chiarli is the longest-established Lambrusco producer in Emilia-Romagna. The name 1860 comes from the year the winery was created, although founder Cleto Chiarli had been making Lambrusco for some time previously. Today, Chiarli has six properties and a total of more than 100 hectares of estate-owned vines. There are several ranges, some released under the Chiarli label while others are branded as Cleto Chiarli & Figli. From the Doc Centenario range, the panel particularly liked Sorbara, with its classic pale colour, light, fragrant body and subtle balance, and the Grasparossa di Castelvetro Secco, a ruby-hued wine with intense fruit and an attractively dry palate. Another very good bottle is the Pruno Nero, from grasparossa fruit macerated and fermented – innovatively - for 48 hours at low temperature and aged in the vat for at least two months. Intense and full-bodied, it is an austere wine with good length. But the wine that really caught the panel's eye was Nivola, a blend of several varieties of lambrusco that could fairly be described as modern. It, too, benefits from slow fermentation at low temperatures, which gives it an almost impenetrably dark colour, firm, lingering mousse, pleasingly frank fruit aromas and plenty of body. It is well worth Two Glasses, which is something of an event for a Lambrusco.

● Nivola Lambrusco Scuro		2*
● Lambrusco di Sorbara Centenario		2
● Lambrusco Grasparossa di Castelvetro Pruno Nero		3
● Lambrusco Grasparossa di Castelvetro Secco Centenario		2
● Lambrusco di Sorbara Fruttato		2
● Lambrusco Grasparossa di Castelvetro Amabile Gala		2

MODIGLIANA (FC)

CASTELLUCCIO
LOC. POGGIOLO
VIA TRAMONTO, 15
47015 MODIGLIANA (FC)
TEL. 0546942486
E-MAIL: info@ronchidicastelluccio.it

Castelluccio was founded in 1975 by Gian Vittorio Baldi. The original six hectares, which have since been doubled, were planted using techniques that were very innovative for the time, with input from agronomist Remigio Bordini and the well-known and highly respected Tuscan oenologist Vittorio Fiore. During the 1990s, the estate's ownership changed several times and since 1999, the Fiore family has held control. Claudio, one of Vittorio's sons, has taken charge of the winery and vineyards. The first vintage supervised exclusively by the Fiore family has given us two extremely well-made Sangioveses, the Ronco delle Ginestre and Ronco dei Ciliegi vineyard selections. Ginestre is the name of the first vineyard planted at Castelluccio, in a hollow of rough terrain at 300 metres above sea level. The wine is aged first in barrique and then slowly in bottle, emerging strong, powerful and austere. The Ronco dei Ciliegi is elegant, rather than muscular, achieving during its brief ageing in 350-litre tonneaux a remarkable balance on the palate. Ronco dei Re, the estate's barrique-aged Sauvignon, performed well, its stylish smoky notes mingling with varietal nuances. The full and strikingly complex palate is well-defined and persistent. Lunaria, another Sauvignon, is simpler and more fresh-tasting while Le More, from sangiovese, is anything but predictable and unveils a rich, very attractive palate.

MODIGLIANA (FC)

IL PRATELLO
VIA MORANA, 14
47015 MODIGLIANA (FC)
TEL. 0546942038
E-MAIL: pratello@libero.it

The Il Pratello estate extends over 50 or so hectares facing towards nearby Tuscany at altitudes that range from 400 to 600 metres. Emilio Placci inherited the property in 1991. The inheritance gave him the opportunity to use to good effect his agronomy diploma and the professional experience accumulated after graduation as a consultant to various cellars around Romagna. It was by no means easy for Emilio to plant his few hectares of organically farmed vineyards on these hillslopes but the first significant harvests are repaying his efforts. The altitude and special composition of the soil, together with low yields per vine, produce impressively structured, utterly distinctive "vins du terroir". We find all these characteristics in Calenzone, a blend of merlot and cabernet aged unhurriedly in barrique. Emilio released 3,500 bottles of this sharp, elegantly austere and characterful wine. The Sangiovese Mantignano is very approachable yet significantly complex, rich and intense on the palate while we will have to wait a further year for the 2000 version of the more ambitious Badia Raustignolo. Campore is obtained from chardonnay and sauvignon grapes grown at over 500 metres above sea level. The difference in day and night-time temperatures imbues the wine with intense, persistent fragrances and the flavour is attractively brought together by oak ageing.

● Ronco dei Ciliegi '99	¶¶	6
○ Ronco del Re '99	¶¶	7
● Ronco delle Ginestre '99	¶¶	6
● Sangiovese di Romagna Sup. Le More '00	¶	4
○ Lunaria '01		4
● Ronco delle Ginestre '90	¶¶¶	6
● Ronco dei Ciliegi '97	¶¶	6
● Ronco delle Ginestre '97	¶¶	6
○ Ronco del Re '98	¶¶	7
● Ronco delle Ginestre '98	¶¶	6

● Colli di Faenza Rosso Calenzone '99	¶¶	6
○ Campore '00	¶	4
● Colli di Faenza Sangiovese Mantignano '00	¶	4
● Badia Raustignolo '98	¶¶	6

MONTE SAN PIETRO (BO)

ISOLA
Fraz. Mongiorgio
Via Bernardi, 3
40050 Monte San Pietro (BO)
tel. 0516768428
e-mail: isola1898@interfree.it

Gianluca Franceschini threw himself into the estate as soon as he graduated as an agricultural technician, working alongside his father in the vineyards and managing the cellar on his own. Impeccable vineyard management, and careful pruning of buds, has led to increasingly well-focused wines with complex aromas and admirable extract. These are the mainstays of the winemaking philosophy that has guided the Franceschinis for the past few years. All the wines, whether red or white, are vinified in stainless steel and released in the spring after the vintage, with the exception of the two selections. The Cabernet Sauvignon Selezione, most of which is aged in small oak barrels, goes to market after ageing for a year and the Chardonnay Selezione ferments and ages in wood until it goes into bottle in the late spring after the harvest. This year, the best bottle is the Chardonnay 2001, a stylish, intriguing wine on the nose with good balance on the palate. The corresponding Selezione is also well-made. There were flattering comments for the two Pignolettos. The Frizzante pairs firm mousse with a dry, tangy finish while the still version – always a classic on the Colli Bolognesi wine scene – is crisply defined and varietal on the nose, with a rich, fresh-tasting palate. A Glass also went to the Cabernet Selezione. It's a tad closed on the nose but does have personality. The oak never intrudes and the rounded body is backed up by just the right dose of tannins.

○ C. B. Chardonnay '01		2*
● C. B. Cabernet Sauvignon Sel. '00		3
○ C. B. Chardonnay Sel. '01		3
○ C. B. Pignoletto Frizzante '01		3
○ C. B. Pignoletto Sup. '01		3

MONTE SAN PIETRO (BO)

SANTAROSA
Fraz. San Martino in Casola
Via San Martino, 82
40050 Monte San Pietro (BO)
tel. 051969203
e-mail: santarosavini@katamail.com

Giovanna Della Valentina's Santarosa estate joined forces with the Adami property two years ago and the new winery is beginning to find an identity of its own. The efforts in the vineyard of the exceptionally skilled agronomist Federico Curtaz, and the cellar consultancy of oenologist Alberto Antonini, are doing the rest. The range of wines is top rank, making Santarosa one of the most exciting wineries in the Colli Bolognesi DOC zone and beyond. Two wines stand out. The first is the classic Cabernet Giòrosso, a solid reliable wine with a swathe of fruit and spice aromas, austerity and velvet smoothness. The other bottle to note is the Giòtondo 2000, a delicious Merlot released for the first time. Generous and harmonious, it is a juicy, easy-drinking wine with superb length. Obtained from carefully selected fruit, it has benefited from expert oak ageing and the Three Glasses were a formality. The Merlot-Cabernet is supposed to be the estate's "second-label" red but still flaunts exceptional softness and pleasing approachability. The Santarosa Pinot Bianco is an estate classic. Dense and alcohol-rich, it can also point to attractive fruit and admirable freshness. The second-label Chardonnay has been taken off the list. All the fruit from this variety goes into Giòcoliere, a wine whose skilful ageing in barrique brings out its pleasing notes of ripe fruit.

● C. B. Merlot Giòtondo '00		4*
● C. B. Cabernet Sauvignon Giòrosso '00		4*
○ C. B. Chardonnay Giòcoliere '01		4
○ C. B. Pinot Bianco '01		3*
● Merlot–Cabernet '01		3*
○ C. B. Pignoletto Cl. '01		3
● C. B. Cabernet Sauvignon Giòrosso '99		4

MONTE SAN PIETRO (BO)

Tenuta Bonzara
Via San Chierlo, 37/a
40050 Monte San Pietro (BO)
tel. 0516768324 - 051225772
e-mail: info@bonzara.it

Last year, Francesco Lambertini took the wise decision to extend the ageing of his two flagship wines, starting with the Cabernet Sauvignon Bonzarone and then concentrating on to the Merlot Rocca di Bonacciara. It was not an easy decision but it was in line with the suggestions of oenologist Stefano Chioccioli, the Tenuta Bonzara consultant of many years' standing. Both wines will be released again simultaneously in the 2000 edition, which will be available next year. For the time being, we are only able to sample the Bonzarone '99, a very satisfying vintage, albeit a little less exciting than previous editions. Still, it is a wine with good weight, breadth and complexity on the nose, as well as plenty of grip and personality in the mouth. The Rosso del Poggio is as good as ever. It's obtained from the merlot fruit that is not selected for the Rocca di Bonacciara and is vinified exclusively in stainless steel. A fresh-tasting wine you can uncork straight away, it is far from banal, showing very decent body and structure. The Sauvignon Le Carrate won a well-deserved Glass for its excellent typicity on the nose and good density on the palate. Finally, the delicious Pignoletto Frizzante combines fragrance with lots of fruit.

MONTEVEGLIO (BO)

Gradizzolo Ognibene
Via Invernata, 2
40050 Monteveglio (BO)
tel. 051830265
e-mail: vinicolaognibene@libero.it

The commitment that Antonio Ognibene has been lavishing on barbera is now paying off. His wines are now appreciated outside the province of Bologna, quite an achievement for a producer who concentrates on a variety few would associate with the Colli Bolognesi. The small winery stands opposite the church of Montebudello, in the centre of the Barbera production zone, at an altitude of 200 to 300 metres above sea level. The vineyard planted in 1967 has given us 2,000 bottles of a noteworthy '99 Riserva. The vintage was a good one. It has yielded a generous Barbera with plenty of extract. The nose mingles liqueur cherries with spicy notes from ageing in new barriques. The soft, vigorous palate signs off with an attractive, fruit-rich finish. The Barbera 2000 is almost as good as its more prestigious stablemate. From another excellent vintage, its well-balanced nose foregrounds riper notes whereas the palate is still looking for the harmony that should arrive with a further period of ageing in bottle. The Merlot Calastrino, too, is interesting. The nose shows unusual hints of peach, highlighted by serious alcohol and unobtrusive but substantial new wood. In the mouth, all the personality of the variety emerges with an attractive nuance of oak, layered over ripe fruit.

● C. B. Merlot Rosso del Poggio '01	♈♈	4
● C. B. Cabernet Sauvignon Bonzarone '99	♈♈	6
○ C. B. Pignoletto Frizzante '01	♈	3
○ C. B. Sauvignon Sup. Le Carrate '01	♈	3
○ C. B. Pignoletto Cl. Vigna Antica '00		3
● C. B. Cabernet Sauvignon Bonzarone '97	♈♈♈	5
● C. B. Cabernet Sauvignon Bonzarone '98	♈♈	5
● C. B. Merlot Rocca di Bonacciara '99	♈♈	5

● C. B. Barbera Ris. '99	♈♈	4*
● C. B. Barbera '00	♈	3
● C. B. Merlot Calastrino '00	♈	4
○ C. B. Pignoletto Frizzante '01		3

MONTEVEGLIO (BO)

La Mancina
Fraz. Montebudello
Via Motta, 8
40050 Monteveglio (BO)
Tel. 051832691
E-mail: info@lamancina.it

"Barbera di Montebudello" is a traditional tipple of the older drinkers at the few genuine "osterie" bars left in the centre of Bologna. It is widely acknowledged that the Terre di Montebudello – chalk and clay hills in the municipality of Monteveglio – offer an outstandingly favourable terroir, not just for barbera but for all red varieties. And the wines from La Mancina's 36 hectares back up that view. The largest estate in the Colli Bolognesi, La Mancina is run by the youthful Francesca Zanetti, granddaughter of founder Franco. Her Barbera Il Foriere ages for 14 months in oak barrels. It is a well-typed wine, full-bodied and easy-drinking, with intense, very varietal aromas. The Cabernet Sauvignon Comandante della Guardia is more challenging and complex. The entry on the palate is impressive, if a little dry, perhaps because of its extended oak ageing. Mouthfilling, soft and full of fruit, the Merlot Lanciotto is an upfront but intriguing wine in the style imprinted on the cellar by the new Piedmontese oenologist, Giandomenico Negro, who is looking to achieve even better results in forthcoming vintages. We would also point out the estate's decision to concentrate on the native pignoletto variety for its whites. There are two versions, a still and a semi-sparkling, both very well-made.

● C. B. Merlot Lanciotto '01	♟♟	4*
● C. B. Barbera Il Foriere '00	♟	3
○ C. B. Pignoletto Frizzante '01	♟	3
○ C. B. Pignoletto Terre di Montebudello '01	♟	3
● C. B. Cabernet Sauvignon Comandante della Guardia Ris. '98	♟	4

PIACENZA

Castelli del Duca
Via Santa Franca, 60
29100 Piacenza
Tel. 0522942135
E-mail: castelli@medici.it

Castelli del Duca was launched in 1999, when the Medici family, long active in the Lambrusco Reggiano area, met up with representatives of the Consorzio Terre dei Farnese, to which belong some of the leading winemakers of the Colli Piacentini DOC zone. The new enterprise committed the Consorzio to making rigorous selections from their best plots of barbera, bonarda, malvasia and sauvignon. The Medicis undertook to run the commercial side of the business. The technical and oenological consultant of the new winery is noted winemaker, Carlo Corino. Release of the wines from the first vintage now enables us to gauge how assiduously and well Corino has been working. All the wines presented have well-defined profiles. Skilfully made and impeccably clean, they are solid products sold at value-for-money prices. The Gutturnio Sigillum Riserva is a full-bodied, flavoursome bottle. Meaty and concentrated yet nicely balanced, it is a very approachable, attractive red. Drinkability is the hallmark of all the '99 reds, from the austere Gutturnio Duca Alessandro to the more straightforward Duca Ottavio and the tasty Barbera Duca Ranuccio. "Very good" was also the panel's opinion of the long, buttery Malvasia Soleste, from carefully raisined grapes whose crisp, intense aromas of dried apricots mingle with just the right hint of sugar on the palate. Finally, the Sauvignon Duchessa Vittoria is perfectly typed and a pleasure to drink.

○ C. P. Malvasia Passito Soleste '00	♟♟	5
● C. P. Gutturnio Sigillum Ris. '99	♟♟	5
● C. P. Gutturnio Sup. Duca Alessandro '99	♟♟	4
○ C. P. Sauvignon Duchessa Vittoria '01	♟	3*
● C. P. Gutturnio Duca Ottavio '99	♟	3*
● C. P. Barbera Duca Ranuccio '99	♟	3

REGGIO EMILIA

Ermete Medici & Figli
Loc. Gaida
Via Newton, 13/A
42040 Reggio Emilia
tel. 0522942135
e-mail: medici@medici.it

The improvement in results from this Medici family-owned winery has been unstoppable over the past decade. Recent acquisitions, which have expanded the vineyards to 60 hectares, all in the finest Lambrusco area, have made this firmly established estate a major player in the region. Much of the vine stock is made up of two distinct plots, both in the Enza river valley, known as I Quercioli and Rampata. The latter estate has also recently become the main production site and an elegant hospitality centre, which is a must-see, along with the wine museum and the adjacent "acetaia", where balsamic vinegar is made. The estate produces two excellent Lambruscos, the Assolo and the Concerto. The latter is obtained from a careful selection of lambrusco salamino, one of the DOC zone's finest varieties, grown on the Rampata estate. Very dark in the glass, it has a compact, delicate mousse, clean, intense fragrances and well-sustained structure. It's a challenging wine that is still eminently drinkable. The Assolo, too, is very drinkable, although rather more sophisticated. Grapes mainly from the I Quercioli estate go into this modern, fragrantly fruity Lambrusco. The firm, pleasing flavour lingers on the palate, lifting it effortlessly into the Two Glass bracket.

RIMINI

San Valentino
Fraz. San Martino in Venti
Via Tomasetta, 11
47900 Rimini
tel. 0541752231
e-mail: valerobi@libero.it

San Valentino is one of the most exciting new arrivals on Romagna's winemaking scene. The estate was acquired by Giovanni Mascarin in the early 1990s but it was only in 1997, when his children Roberto and Maria Cristina took over production and sales respectively, that numbers – and quality – began to take off. Currently, there are 14 hectares under vine, half fully productive, on the first range of hills outside Rimini, looking towards Monte Titano. The estate has a further seven, recently replanted and modernized, hectares that will soon come onstream. The final chapter in this story of growth was written in 2000, when Roberto and Maria Cristina called in oenologist Fabrizio Moltard to supervise the renovation of the vine stock and work in the cellar. The wine that the panel liked best was the Luna Nuova 2000, an admirably structured, barrique-aged Cabernet Sauvignon that unveils luscious softness and a sophisticated elegance. Sangiovese Riserva Terra, also aged in small oak barrels, is an austere, mature wine with great texture and lots of length. In fact, it nearly earned a second Glass. Eclissi di Sole, the cellar's "second-label" sangiovese and cabernet sauvignon blend, is a good bottle. The standard Sangiovese, Scabi, is a pleasant, well-executed wine and, to round off, the steel-vinified chardonnay and rebola-based Fiore is delicately fruity and fresh-tasting.

- Reggiano Assolo '01 — 2*
- Reggiano Lambrusco Concerto '01 — 3
- Nebbie d'Autunno Dolce — 3
- Reggiano Lambrusco Secco '01 — 2

- Colli di Rimini Cabernet Sauvignon Luna Nuova '00 — 5
- Colli di Rimini Rebola Passito Contesse Muschietti '00 — 4
- Colli di Rimini Rosso Eclissi di Sole '00 — 4
- Fiore '01 — 4
- Sangiovese di Romagna Sup. Scabi '01 — 3*
- Sangiovese di Romagna Sup. Terra Ris. '99 — 4

RIVERGARO (PC)

La Stoppa
Loc. Ancarano
29029 Rivergaro (PC)
tel. 0523958159
e-mail: lastoppa@tin.it

Tastings produced conflicting results when the panel visited La Stoppa. At its best, this cellar can turn out wines of remarkable finesse and depth that scorn passing fads. They adhere to a philosophy that may not be particularly fashionable but it is certainly not speculative. Elena Pantaleoni and technician Giulio Armani are firm believers in the typicity of the varieties that have been cultivated traditionally in this territory. On our various visits this year, we found some La Stoppa wines in great form while others were a tad below par. Structure and depth distinguish the Cabernet Sauvignon Stoppa 2000. The nose lacks a little definition but the close-knit palate has a meaty maturity with just the right hint of tannins and the aromas linger nicely. One of the less impressive wines was the Macchiona, a barbera and bonarda mix. The 1999 vintage aged for a year in ten-hectolitre barrels and has emerged with a fuzzy, poorly defined nose and the good fruit on the palate is overwhelmed by assertive acidity. The Barbera 1999 also bears the scars of an indifferent vintage. The fruit on the palate lacks ripeness, underscoring the impact of the acidity in the finish. To conclude, we'll go back to a top-level wine, the Passito di Malvasia Vigna del Volta. After ten months in oak barrels, the 2000 edition delivers oily, mouthfilling richness on the palate, where the varietal aromas come through in all their sweet fragrance, backed up by nicely judged acidity. It's a wine worthy of a serious estate like La Stoppa.

○ C. P. Malvasia Passito
   Vigna del Volta '00   ▼▼   5
● C. P. Cabernet Sauvignon
   Stoppa '00   ▼▼   5
● C. P. Barbera della Stoppa '99   ▼   4
● Macchiona '99   ▼   5
● Stoppa '96   ▼▼▼   5
○ C. P. Malvasia Passito
   Vigna del Volta '97   ▼▼▼   5
○ C. P. Malvasia Passito
   Vigna del Volta '99   ▼▼   5
● C. P. Cabernet Sauvignon
   Stoppa '99   ▼▼   5

RUSSI (RA)

Tenuta Uccellina
Via Garibaldi, 51
48026 Russi (RA)
tel. 0544580144

Few producers in Romagna still bother with Burson, a local curiosity made from a variety of grape called Longanesi. The grape is little known outside the Bagnacavallo area, where it is grown and where a few years ago a consortium was set up to protect and promote Burson. Kudos, then, to Alberto Rusticali. With the help of one of Romagna's ablest wine technicians, Sergio Ragazzini, he has managed not only to keep producing Burson but also to turn it into a wine of some ambition, thanks to constantly improving standards of quality. Tenuta Uccellina has brought out the best in the Longanesi variety, a grape that gives full-bodied wines with lots of personality, characterized by uncompromising tannins. Properly aged, such wines are irresistible and absolutely original. The rich, attractively sweet Albana Passito is well-made. Warm, velvety sensations on the back palate echo the aromas of apricot jam present on the nose. The Clivo del Re is a well-structured, elegant Sangiovese with great balance and a harmonious personality. Ruchetto is the estate's flagship product, a pinot nero-based wine that ages in barrique for a year. Again this year, it shows the originality, in notes of fresh berry fruit and elegant spice, and expertise that have been constants in recent vintages.

○ Albana di Romagna Passito '00   ▼▼   5
● Sangiovese di Romagna Sup.
   Clivo del Re '98   ▼▼   4
● Burson '99   ▼▼   3*
● Ruchetto dell'Uccellina '99   ▼   4
● Sangiovese di Romagna Ris. '99   ▼   4

SANT'ILARIO D'ENZA (RE)

Moro - Rinaldo Rinaldini
Fraz. Calerno
Via Andrea Rivasi, 27
42040 Sant'Ilario d'Enza (RE)
Tel. 0522679190 - 0522679964
E-mail: info@rinaldinivini.it

Some time ago, this estate only turned out sparklers from low-density plantings that gave sky-high yields per hectare. Rinaldini brought in increased-density planting patterns, low yields per vine and row-straddling tractors to work the vineyards. He decided he was going to make sparkling whites and reds with the "metodo classico" just when everyone else was turning to cheaper, less complicated surge tanks. No one could accuse Rinaldo of taking the easy way out. This is the big moment for reds. Who but Rinaldo could turn out a Two Glass red on the placid flatlands of Reggio three years in a row? The Vigna del Picchio '99, a blend of late-harvest lambrusco Maestri and ancellotta, repeats its feat of last year. Its rich red introduces a nose that opens on ripe fruit and then reveals broader notes of spices. The palate is rich, pervasive and delightfully balanced. Another interesting wine is the Moro del Moro, a dry red from raisined lambrusco pjcol and ancellotta. Inky black, it offers aromas of ripe fruit and dried figs on the nose. The soft, well-extracted palate ends on a faint bitterish note. We also liked the One Glass Cabernet Riserva '99. All the "metodo classico"-vinified whites presented – Rinaldo Brut, Malvasia and Lambrusco Bianco – earned a Glass, confirming the great heritage of "spumante"-making at this estate.

SASSO MARCONI (BO)

Floriano Cinti
Fraz. San Lorenzo
Via Gamberi, 48
40037 Sasso Marconi (BO)
Tel. 0516751646
E-mail: cinti@collibolognesi.com

Another great showing this year for Floriano Cinti, who has accustomed us to expect high standards in his wines. It shows just how seriously he and oenologist Giovanni Fraulini go about their business. The range has been further extended with the addition of two new reds, the barrique-aged Merlot and Cabernet Sauvignon selections, the first a 2000 and the second from 1999. Both correspond exactly to the designs of their makers, as well as their names. They are full-bodied, well-structured and serious wines you can uncork straight away or cellar. Either way, they are satisfying bottles. Cinti knows his vineyards intimately. This has enabled him to select the very best fruit and produce two major wines that are, by the way, great value for money. All three versions of Pignoletto met with the panel's approval. The Frizzante is fresh and fragrant, the tangy Classico has good structure and the unusual Passito is very likeable. But the best white from the most recent vintage was the Chardonnay, which very nearly earned a second Glass. It's intense, fruit-led, tasty and clean on the palate. We have little space left to talk about the younger steel-fermented reds but both the Merlot and the Cabernet Sauvignon are uncomplicated, pleasingly drinkable wines.

● Vigna del Picchio '99	♀♀	4
● Moro del Moro '98	♀	5
● Colli di Scandiano e di Canossa Cabernet Sauvignon Ris. '99	♀	4
○ Colli di Scandiano e di Canossa Chardonnay Rinaldo Brut '99	♀	4
○ Colli di Scandiano e di Canossa Malvasia Spumante Brut	♀	3
● Lambrusco Spumante M. Cl. Pjcol Ross	♀	3*
○ Reggiano Lambrusco Bianco Spumante Brut Arita	♀	3
◉ Reggiano Lambrusco Rosato	♀	2*
● Vigna del Picchio '98	♀♀	5

● C. B. Merlot Sel. '00	♀♀	4*
● C. B. Cabernet Sauvignon Sel. '99	♀♀	4*
● C. B. Cabernet Sauvignon '00	♀	3
○ C. B. Chardonnay '01	♀	3
○ C. B. Colline Marconiane Pignoletto Passito '01	♀	5
● C. B. Merlot '01	♀	3
○ C. B. Pignoletto Cl. '01	♀	3
○ C. B. Pignoletto Frizzante '01	♀	3
○ C. B. Sauvignon Sel. '01	♀	3
○ C. B. Pinot Bianco '01		3
○ C. B. Sauvignon '01		3
● C. B. Merlot '00	♀♀	3

SAVIGNANO SUL RUBICONE (FC)

COLONNA - VINI SPALLETTI
VIA SOGLIANO, 100
47039 SAVIGNANO SUL RUBICONE (FC)
TEL. 0541945111 - 0541943446
E-MAIL: info@spallettticolonnadipaliano.com

It has been a rather indifferent year for this large, long-established Romagna winery, which in recent vintages has been showing how dearly it wants to get back into the front rank. The reason for these recent difficulties lies not in the lackadaisical attitude that caused problems in the past: one factor was the poor vintage in the area and another is the absence of the merlot and cabernet-based wines that have driven the estate's recovery. Our favourite from the vast range of labels – by far the longest list hereabouts – is the Albana Passito Maolù 2000. It's a serious, very attractive wine with a ripe, fruity nose and a soft, warm entry on the palate, where there are delicious, lingering sensations of peach. The Rocca di Ribano is uncompromising and muscular, almost to the point of being aggressive. We tasted the '99 vintage of this historic sangiovese-based wine. Fashions may come and go but Rocca di Ribano maintains its traditional style, placing the emphasis on extract and structure, rather than balance. The Albana Secco 2001 takes full advantage of its copious residual sugar and unveils a warm, enticing palate. The cabernet-based Sabinio 2000 is not quite as rich and proffers a nose of moderate intensity, following this up with a pleasant palate underpinned by an unexpectedly tangy note of acidity.

O	Albana di Romagna Passito Maolù '00	ΨΨ	5
●	Sabinio Cabernet '00	Ψ	4
O	Albana di Romagna Secco '01	Ψ	3
●	Sangiovese di Romagna Sup. Rocca di Ribano '99	Ψ	4
●	Il Gianello Merlot '00	ΨΨ	5
●	Il Monaco di Ribano Cabernet '99	ΨΨ	5

TRAVO (PC)

IL POGGIARELLO
LOC. SCRIVELLANO DI STATTO
29020 TRAVO (PC)
TEL. 0523957241 - 0523571610
E-MAIL: poggiarello@iol.it

Paolo and Stefano Perini's wines have made further progress. The seven wines they presented all did well in their respective categories, thanks to new vintages that have given more balance to the reds and cleaner aromas to the whites. In fact, it was the improvement in the whites that impressed the panel. The Chardonnay Perticato La Piana 2001, aged in oak for seven months, offers balsam and cedar notes on the nose and gentle progression over ripe fruit in the mouth. The Sauvignon Perticato Il Quadri 2001, vinified after cold skin contact and part barrique-aged for four months, tempts with varietal notes that return on the moderately broad, smooth palate. There's a new Il Poggiarello white, the Malvasia Beatrice Quadri 2001. The primary aromas of grapefruit and peach meld with unobtrusive oak and restrained residual sugar. When our tasters moved over to the reds, they found a vigorous, well-structured Gutturnio Riserva La Barbona 1999 with good length. You would hardly think it spent 14 months in barrique. The Gutturnio Valandrea 2000 is more accessible, its fresh palate tingling with clean fruit and discernible acidity. The 2000 vintage has brought us a Cabernet Sauvignon Novarei in splendid form. The deep garnet hue introduces ripe fruit and balsamic notes, then a soft, close-knit palate with well-integrated oak. Last on our list is the Pinot Nero Le Giastre 2000, which mingles berry fruit and toastiness on the nose, then shows a solid, well-behaved palate with nice balance.

●	C. P. Cabernet Sauvignon Perticato del Novarei '00	ΨΨ	5
O	C. P. Chardonnay Perticato La Piana '01	ΨΨ	5
●	C. P. Gutturnio La Barbona Ris. '99	ΨΨ	6
●	C. P. Gutturnio Perticato Valandrea '00	Ψ	5
●	C. P. Pinot Nero Perticato Le Giastre '00	Ψ	5
O	C. P. Malvasia Perticato Beatrice Quadri '01	Ψ	5
O	C. P. Sauvignon Perticato Il Quadri '01	Ψ	5

VIGOLZONE (PC)

Conte Otto Barattieri
di San Pietro
Loc. Albarola
29020 Vigolzone (PC)
Tel. 0523875111

In last year's profile, we pointed out that this winery was embarking on a phase of reorganization, precipitated by internal changes. This has been the case, for the year 2002 was one of transformation for the Barattieri family. We sincerely hope that all decisions taken will bear in mind how important this estate has been for the history of the Colli Piacentini. We stress this because the winery has had its own profile since the Guide first came out. Over the past 16 years, it has often presented our panels with potentially superb wines, made with magnificent raw material, that needed just a little more care during winemaking. This year's offerings included a Gutturnio 2000 with a medium weight palate and good alcohol backing up notes of fruit and spices. The Pergolo 2000, from cabernet sauvignon, is interesting but lacks bite. It could do with a bit more flesh to enhance its rather simple progression. Il Faggio is a dried-grape wine from old brachetto vines. The 2000 has lost some of the very marked density that characterized previous editions but remains a temptingly delicious wine. The Albarola Vin Santo 1992 is excellent, and always at the top of its category. Breadth and subtle nuances on the palate are lifted by the wine's trademark note of zabaglione in the finish. The fragrant, spicy Gutturnio Frizzante performed well, as did the other sparkler, the Barbera 2001. The nose could do with a little more definition but the palate is full-bodied and vigorous.

○ C. P. Vin Santo Albarola '92	🍷🍷	7
● Il Faggio '00	🍷🍷	6
● C. P. Cabernet Sauvignon Il Pergolo '00	🍷	4
● C. P. Gutturnio '00	🍷	4
● C. P. Barbera Frizzante '01	🍷	2*
● C.P. Gutturnio Frizzante '01	🍷	2*
○ C. P. Vin Santo Albarola '91	🍷🍷	7
● C. P. Gutturnio Sel. '99	🍷🍷	4
● Il Faggio '99	🍷🍷	6

VIGOLZONE (PC)

La Tosa
Loc. La Tosa
29020 Vigolzone (PC)
Tel. 0523870727 - 0523870168
E-mail: latosa@libero.it

A few Guides ago, we noted that La Tosa is a winery that is always exploring new paths, provoking perplexity and stimulating lively discussions. This is still true. Conserving the integrity of the fruit and imbuing his wine with balanced softness on the palate are over-riding priorities on which Stefano Pizzamiglio will brook no argument. If we look at his wines from this perspective, we can only praise Stefano's faultless execution. We'll begin with the Sorriso di Cielo, the first product to put the much maligned malvasia grape in the front rank of Colli Piacentini winemaking. The 2001 version has eased up on the alcohol of previous vintages and reveals a delicately silky palate of pervasive softness that, unfortunately, holds back the aromas. The Sauvignon 2001 layers sweet and varietal notes over a robust structure that is rounded out by residual sugar. La Tosa's only semi-sparkling "frizzante" is the fresh-tasting Valnure 2001, from malvasia, trebbiano and ortugo. Uncomplicated and gentle on the palate, it is very drinkable indeed. The cellar's reds are classy. Gutturnio Vignamorello 2001 has a chewy palate with plenty of fruit, backed up by admirably gauged acidity. The Gutturnio 2001 is equally successful. A more approachable prospect, it has a palate of ripe fruit and sweet spice. The Cabernet Sauvignon Luna Selvatica 2000 came within an ace of a third Glass. Exceptionally concentrated, it reveals crisp aromas of mulberries and raspberry on the nose before the well-orchestrated palate lifts the pervasive softness of the fruit.

● C. P. Cabernet Sauvignon Luna Selvatica '00	🍷🍷	6
● C. P. Gutturnio Vignamorello '01	🍷🍷	5
○ C. P. Malvasia Sorriso di Cielo '01	🍷🍷	5
● C. P. Gutturnio '01	🍷	3*
○ C. P. Sauvignon '01	🍷	4
○ C. P. Valnure Frizzante '01	🍷	3*
● C. P. Cabernet Sauvignon Luna Selvatica '97	🍷🍷🍷	5
● C. P. Gutturnio Vignamorello '00	🍷🍷	5
● C. P. Cabernet Sauvignon Luna Selvatica '99	🍷🍷	5

ZIANO PIACENTINO (PC)

Gaetano Lusenti
Fraz. Vicobarone
Case Piccioni, 57
29010 Ziano Piacentino (PC)
tel. 0523868479
e-mail: lodovica.lusenti@tin.it

Lodovica Lusenti's unstinting efforts are beginning to pay off. The renovated cellar and a closer focus on vineyard and cellar management hint at even greater things to come. Missing from the list this year is the Cabernet Villante, which is still ageing, but it is replaced by an exciting newcomer, La Picciona 2000. From bonarda grapes, and aged in new barriques, it has a deep ruby red hue and a fruity nose echoed on the solid palate. Aromas of ripe black cherries and spices provide a backdrop for perceptible astringency that augurs well for the wine's cellarability. The fragrant Bonarda Amabile 2001 is equally successful. The generous nose of primary aromas and fruit-rich, spice-veined palate is enhanced by stimulating liveliness and rounded out by residual sugar. The Gutturnio Superiore Cresta al Sole, from barbera and bonarda, is on the way up. After 12 months in barrique, the 2000 vintage has a warm, ripe palate with aromas of bottled berry fruit. Well-gauged extract never threatens to smother the progression on the palate. Moving on to the whites, we find the Malvasia di Case Piccioni 2001, which offers sweet notes of super-ripeness and unobtrusive wood. The Spumante Pinot Nero Rosé 1999, a "metodo classico" sparkler, unveils discreet flower and yeast notes, then a shyly soft, well-sustained palate with nice fruit. Finally, the Filtrato Dolce di Malvasia 2001 offers generous yet elegant effervescence and a creaminess that never cloys.

ZIANO PIACENTINO (PC)

Torre Fornello
Loc. Fornello
29010 Ziano Piacentino (PC)
tel. 0523861001
e-mail: vini@torrefornello.it

In the heart of Valtidone, Torre Fornello has 55 hectares, a beautifully equipped cellar and the support of a fine consultant. All this makes Enrico Sgorbati's ambitions of producing serious wines look very well-founded. Last year, we noted a shift of pace but this year's tastings revealed rather more hesitant progress in the new wines. Best of the bunch is the Gutturnio Riserva Diacono Gerardo, one of the finest wines in its category. A bottle of breeding, it has an especially elegant nose, then melds fruit and spice into a rich, well-rounded palate. The Gutturnio Superiore Sinsäl lost some ground. The 2001 vintage has a severe palate with little of the softness and balanced structure that so impressed us in the previous edition. The whites include Vigna Pratobianco 2001, from sauvignon, malvasia and chardonnay. The palate is particularly well put together, foregrounding notes of citrus fruits, and the price is also very attractive. Sauvignon Ca' del Rio is shy on the nose but makes up for lost time in the mouth, where subtle aromas of peach and apricot emerge. The Malvasia Donna Luigia mingles notes of tropical fruit with wood resin. The palate has good weight but succumbs to an astringency that hobbles progression. The long and ever reliable list of semi-sparkling "frizzante" wines includes all the DOC zones main types.

● C. P. Bonarda La Picciona '00	4
● C. P. Gutturnio Sup. Cresta al Sole '00	4
● C. P. Bonarda Amabile '01	3
○ C. P. Malvasia di Case Piccioni '01	4
○ Filtrato Dolce di Malvasia '01	3
◉ C. P. Pinot Nero Spumante Rosé '99	5
● Il Villante Cabernet Sauvignon '98	5
● C. P. Cabernet Sauvignon Il Villante '99	5

● C. P. Gutturnio Diacono Gerardo Ris. '00	5
○ C. P. Malvasia Donna Luigia '01	4
○ C. P. Sauvignon Ca' del Rio '01	4
○ Pratobianco '01	3*
● C. P. Gutturnio Sup. Sinsäl '01	4
● C. P. Cabernet Sauvignon Ca' Bernesca '00	5
● C. P. Gutturnio Sup. Sinsäl '00	3
● C. P. Gutturnio Diacono Gerardo 1028 Ris. '98	4

ZOLA PREDOSA (BO)

Maria Letizia Gaggioli
Vigneto Bagazzana
Via Raibolini detto il Francia, 55
40069 Zola Predosa (BO)
tel. 051753489 - 0516189198
e-mail: nmygag@tin.it

Carlo Gaggioli has been running his estate since 1972 but now he has passed the task to his daughter Maria Letizia, who can call on the wise advice of local oenologist Giovanni Fraulin. The winery's main focus – on fragrant, well-structured whites obtained using the finest cellar techniques – has not changed, although the wine that most impressed the panel this year was a delicious Merlot. We had been waiting for years for something special from the Bagazzana vineyard, which is in a superb location for growing Bordeaux varieties. We hope that this will be the first of a long series of great wines. It has to be said that the 5,000 bottles of this Merlot are very young – vintage 2001 – but they held their own against much more famous wines at our tastings. Youthfully vinous and attractively vegetal on the nose, it unveils a palate of rich, fruity notes supported by very fine-grained tannins in the long finish. The Pignoletto Frizzante shows how well this unfairly neglected wine can perform. The nose tempts with intriguing apple and pear then the prickle in the mouth is satisfyingly pervasive and never intrusive. Also noteworthy is the Pignoletto Superiore, with its very clean, fruit-rich nose and fresh, flavoursome palate. Both vintages of the Cabernet earned a Glass, as did the Chardonnay Lavinio and Pinot Bianco Crilò.

ZOLA PREDOSA (BO)

Vigneto delle Terre Rosse
Via Predosa, 83
40068 Zola Predosa (BO)
tel. 051755845 - 051759649

The entire Vallania family has always taken part in running this winery, the longest-established and most prestigious in the Colli Bolognesi DOC zone. That position of leadership has been earned over the years with wines vinified exclusively in small stainless steel containers and a persevering professionalism that has never flagged. In fact, anyone who has been lucky enough to taste former vintages of the Chardonnay or Cabernet Sauvignon Cuvées will vouch for the results that the Vallanias have turned out over the years. This year's most convincing wine – it astounded the panel – is the Riesling Malagò '99, made with late-harvested fruit. Its range of aromas is unique and the palate reveals great intensity and persistence. It's a wine with presence and a very distinctive personality. The second-label Cabernet Sauvignon – the Cuvée was unavailable for tasting – showed how good the cellar's reds are. An upfront wine that is delightful to drink, it has fresh, fragrant aromas and an elegant, well-judged palate. The 1999 Chardonnay Cuvée wasn't quite up to par but still manages to display all its usual intensity and complexity. The '99 Grannero is again a nicely made, well-typed Pinot Nero and the Sauvignon, which suffered from a less than spectacular vintage, remains one of the best interpretations of the wine in the Colli Bolognesi.

● C. B. Merlot '01	♛	4*
● C. B. Cabernet Sauvignon '00	♙	4
● C. B. Cabernet Sauvignon '01	♙	4
○ C. B. Chardonnay Lavinio '01	♙	3
○ C. B. Pignoletto Frizzante '01	♙	3
○ C. B. Pignoletto Sup. '01	♙	3
○ C. B. Pinot Bianco Crilò '01	♙	3
○ C. B. Sauvignon Sup. '01		3

● C. B. Cabernet Sauvignon '99	♛	5
○ C. B. Riesling Malagò V. T. '99	♛	5
○ C. B. Sauvignon '01	♙	4
○ C. B. Chardonnay Cuvée '99	♙	4
● Grannero Pinot Nero '99	♙	4
● C. B. Cabernet Sauvignon Cuvée '98	♛	5

OTHER WINERIES

REGGIANA
LOC. BORZANO
42010 ALBINEA (RE)
TEL. 0522591121
E-MAIL: info@aziendagricolareggiana.com

There are two interesting wines from these 15 hillslope hectares. One is a well-made Cabernet, aged for 12 months in wood, with soft vanilla and berry fruit. The lambrusco grasparossa-based Tralcio Rosso is fresh, youthfully vinous and very tasty. These good wines sell at very attractive prices.

● Colli di Scandiano e di Canossa Cabernet Sauvignon Terre Matildiche '00	3*
● Colli di Scandiano e di Canossa Lambrusco Grasparossa Tralcio Rosso	1*

ERIOLI
VIA MONTEVEGLIO, 64
40053 BAZZANO (BO)
TEL. 051830103

For the past ten years, Giorgio Erioli has been releasing a good Cabernet Sauvignon from his tiny, three-hectare estate. This year's version is up to snuff. Intense, fruit-led, redolent of new wood and vibrant on the nose, it has a well-balanced, pervasive mouthfeel.

● C. B. Cabernet Sauvignon Ris. '99	4

FATTORIA CA' ROSSA
VIA CELLAIMO, 735
47032 BERTINORO (FC)
TEL. 0543445130
E-MAIL: info@fattoriacarossa.it

Ripagrande is a lovely barrique-aged Sangiovese with a nose of berry fruit and liquorice that introduces a deliciously soft palate. The Costa del Sole is light and tempting while the Cesubeo, an unusual mix of cabernet, sangiovese and barbera, shows good structure and nice freshness.

● Sangiovese di Romagna Sup. Ripagrande Ris. '99	5
● Cesubeo '00	6
● Sangiovese di Romagna Sup. Costa del Sole '00	4

COLOMBINA
VIA TRO MELDOLA, 1541
47030 BERTINORO (FC)
TEL. 0543460658
E-MAIL: info@colombina.it

Colombina's 20 hectares lie in the foothills at Bertinoro. The estate's excellent sangiovese goes into a luscious Riserva. The pinot bianco and riesling italico Klarus is good and the fresh-tasting Albana Secco unveils delicate hedgerow fragrances.

● Sangiovese di Romagna Anfore Romane Ris. '97	4
○ Albana di Romagna Secco '01	3
○ Klarus '01	3

CANTINE COOPERATIVE RIUNITE
VIA G. BRODOLINI, 24
42040 CAMPEGINE (RE)
TEL. 0522905711
E-MAIL: comita@riunite.it

The Cuvée dei Fondatori label offers two fine Lambruscos, the Grasparossa Amabile, with its lingering, velvety softness, and a Lambrusco Reggiano – the Ronchi dell'Olma – that is dry, confident and firmly structured. The Foglie Rosse is full-bodied, very well-typed and attractively fresh-tasting.

● Lambrusco Grasparossa di Castelvetro Cinghio del Fojonco Cuvée dei Fondatori	3
● Reggiano Lambrusco Foglie Rosse	3
● Reggiano Lambrusco Ronchi dell'Olma Cuvée dei Fondatori	3

FATTORIA CAMERONE
VIA BIANCANIGO, 1485
48014 CASTEL BOLOGNESE (RA)
TEL. 054650434
E-MAIL: info@fattoriacamerone.it

Owner Giuseppe Marabini has about 25 hectares under vine at Fattoria Camerone. His best sangiovese goes into Rosso del Camerone, a wine with spice on the nose and plenty of body. The Millenium, from sangiovese blended with cabernet, has very good structure and balance.

● Sangiovese di Romagna Sup. Rosso del Camerone Ris. '97	3*
● Sangiovese di Romagna Sup. Millenium Ris. '98	4

CARDINALI
LOC. MONTEPASCOLO
29014 CASTELL'ARQUATO (PC)
TEL. 0523803502
E-MAIL: info@cardinalidoc.it

The Cardinali cellar has again demonstrated its talent for making Gutturnio. The soft weave of the Riserva Torquato 1999 combines structure with freshness and balance. Nicchio 2001 develops a fruit theme over its fairly close-knit texture.

● C. P. Gutturnio Cl. Torquato Ris. '99	5
● C. P. Gutturnio Cl. Nicchio '01	4

SANDONI
VIA VALLE DEL SAMOGGIA, 780
40050 CASTELLO DI SERRAVALLE (BO)
TEL. 0516703188

Sandoni reds are always worth investigating. We'll start with the extremely respectable Barbera '99. The crisp, intense nose of autumn leaves and vanilla introduces a balanced palate with fine-grained tannins and robust alcohol. The Cabernet, which reveals unusual peach notes, is also interesting.

● C. B. Barbera '99	5
● Cabernet Sauvignon '98	4

TENUTA AMALIA
VIA EMILIA PONENTE, 2619
47023 CESENA (FC)
TEL. 0547347037
E-MAIL: cantces@tin.it

There were two good Sangioveses at Tenuta Amalia. The Riserva Pergami has rich, spicy aromas on the nose and a firm, structured yet elegant palate. The Superiore Le Case Rosse is approachable but certainly not banal. The Chardonnay Pergami has decent structure and personality.

○ Chardonnay Pergami '00	3
● Sangiovese di Romagna Sup. Le Case Rosse '00	4
● Sangiovese di Romagna Pergami Ris. '99	4

MONTE DELLE VIGNE
LOC. OZZANO TARO - VIA COSTA, 27
43046 COLLECCHIO (PR)
TEL. 0521809105
E-MAIL: montedellevigne@libero.it

There was no 1999 Nabucco but the 2000 version of this barbera and merlot blend is very classy. The rich, characterful palate shows well-defined fruit and austere tannins. The semi-sparkling Malvasia Dolce 2001 is fleshy and creamy but never threatens to pall.

● Nabucco '00	5
○ Malvasia Dolce '01	3*

Alessandro Morini
Via Firenze, 493
48018 Faenza (RA)
Tel. 0546634257
E-mail: info@morini.com

The Faenza area is proving a good winemaking zone and Morini is one of the up and coming producers. The Albana Passito is again attractive. It has breadth, elegance and persistence that never cloys. There was also a good showing from Beccafico, a no-nonsense Sangiovese.

○ Albana di Romagna Passito Innamorato '00	🍷🍷	5
● Sangiovese di Romagna Sup. Beccafico '00	🍷	4

Villa Spadoni
Via Gesso, 9
40025 Fontanelice (BO)
Tel. 054292625
E-mail: villaspadoni@fattoriacornacchia.it

The Villa Spadoni label belongs to Fattoria Cornacchia. The range includes two good Sangioveses, a fresh, flowery Superiore and a spicier, more mature Riserva. The amber Passito di Albana offers intense fruit on the nose and a velvety mouthfeel.

● Sangiovese di Romagna Sup. '01	🍷	3
● Sangiovese di Romagna Sup. Ris. '98	🍷	4
○ Albana di Romagna Passito '99	🍷	5

Tenuta Godenza
Fraz. S. Lorenzo in Noceto
47100 Forlì
Tel. 0543488424
E-mail: tenuta.godenza@tin.it

Gaudentia is a barrique-aged Sangiovese. Broad and complex on the nose, it has a well-rounded, vibrant palate. The steel-vinified Rubiano is a much fresher, easier-drinking proposition, with hints of violets and autumn leaves. Finally, the Cabernet Alfiere is generously structured and austere.

● Alfiere Cabernet Sauvignon '00	🍷	5
● Sangiovese di Romagna Sup. Gaudentia '00	🍷	4
● Sangiovese di Romagna Sup. Rubiano '01	🍷	3

Tenuta Valli
Via delle Caminate, 38
47100 Forlì (FC)
Tel. 054524393
E-mail: info@tenutavalli.it

Mythos, a great dried-grape wine from albana fruit, has intense fragrances of tropical fruit. On the palate, it is mouthfilling, with just the right note of sweetness. The estate's finest grapes go into the barrique-aged Sangiovese della Beccaccia, a full-bodied wine of considerable finesse.

○ Albana di Romagna Passito Mythos '00	🍷🍷	7
● Sangiovese di Romagna Riserva della Beccaccia Ris. '99	🍷	4

Tenuta Arpineto
S.da Arpineto-Pertinello, 2
47010 Galeata (FC)
Tel. 0543983156
E-mail: susyhome@tin.it

A small winery with big ideas, Tenuta Arpineto presented only one wine. Of course, it was a very big scorer. The sangiovese-based Pertinello is aged first in large barrels and then in barriques.

● Pertinello '01	🍷🍷	5

Ca' Bruciata
Via Ghiandolino, 21
40026 Imola (BO)
Tel. 0542657026
E-mail: cabruciata@libero.it

This estate is in the hills outside Imola, which has proved a great place to grow red grapes. The two Cabernet Sauvignons are good. The Riserva is more evolved and complex whereas the basic version is straightforward. The fruity Sangiovese, which lingers on the palate, is very tempting.

● Colli di Imola Cabernet Sauvignon '00	🍷	2*
● Colli di Imola Sangiovese '01	🍷	2*
● Colli di Imola Cabernet Sauvignon Ris. '99	🍷	4

FONDO CÀ VECJA
VIA MONTANARA, 333
40026 IMOLA (BO)
TEL. 0542665194
E-MAIL: fondocavecja@virgilio.it

Here on the border of Emilia and Romagna, Fondo Cà Vecja makes a lovely, full-flavoured Albana, with just the right hint of sweetness, from carefully raisined grapes. The well-made Cabernet Sauvignon reveals ripe fruit and the fresh 2001 Sangiovese has a deliciously fruity, satisfying palate.

○ Albana di Romagna Passito '00	4
● Colli di Imola Cabernet Sauvignon '00	3
● Colli di Imola Sangiovese '01	2

LA MACOLINA
LOC. MONTECATONE
VIA PIEVE SANT'ANDREA, 2
40026 IMOLA (BO)
TEL. 051940234

The Cesari family presented the panel with a dignified Sangiovese Riserva. Made in the modern style, it has all the typicity of the grape. The '97 vintage produced a fine, rich Albana Passito, with persistent notes of candied peel. Finally, the sangiovese, cabernet and merlot-based Museum is nice.

● Sangiovese di Romagna Ris. '99	4
● Museum '99	5
○ Albana di Romagna Passito La Dolce Vita '97	5

TENUTA POGGIO POLLINO
VIA MONTE MELDOLA, 2/T
40026 IMOLA (BO)
TEL. 0522942135

Recently, this winery took on celebrated oenologist Carlo Corino as consultant and the results are coming through. The Campo Rosso is an excellent Riserva di Sangiovese, full-bodied and muscular yet soft. Terre di Maestrale – from cabernet and sangiovese – is nicely balanced and very drinkable.

● Sangiovese di Romagna Campo Rosso Ris. '99	4*
● Colli di Imola Terre di Maestrale '00	4

ISIDORO LAMORETTI
FRAZ. CASATICO - STRADA DELLA NAVE, 6
43013 LANGHIRANO (PR)
TEL. 0521863590
E-MAIL: lamoretti@tin.it

The 2000 Vinnalunga '71, from cabernet and merlot, was the best Colli di Parma red the panel tasted. The varietal, moderately spicy nose ushers in a broad, full-textured palate. Barbera and bonarda go into Vigna del Guasto 2000, a warm, firm wine let down by a slightly fuzzy nose.

● Vinnalunga 71 '00	4
● Colli di Parma Rosso Vigna del Guasto '00	3*

BONFIGLIO
VIA CASSOLA, 21
40050 MONTEVEGLIO (BO)
TEL. 051830758
E-MAIL: vinibonfiglio@libero.it

The Bonfiglio cellar is going places, to judge by the range presented. Pick of the bunch is the excellent barrique-aged Cabernet Sauvignon, one of the best of its kind from the Colli Bolognesi. The fruit-driven Pignoletto Superiore is also good, as is the appreciably intense dried-grape version.

● C. B. Cabernet Sauvignon Barrique '99	5
○ C. B. Pignoletto Passito Colline di Oliveto '00	5
○ C. B. Pignoletto Sup. '01	3*

CA' SELVATICA
VIA MARZATORE, 16
40050 MONTEVEGLIO (BO)
TEL. 051831837

Here in the Montebudello hills, we tasted an intriguing Barbera Casabà. Its crisp notes of ripe fruit and figs on the nose are complemented by a juicy, mouthfilling palate. And to underline that reds are Ca' Selvatica's forte, there's a fine Cabernet Vigna del Falco.

● C. B. Barbera Montebudello Cabasà Ris. '98	5
● C. B. Cabernet Sauvignon Vigna del Falco '98	4

CORTE D'AIBO
VIA MARZATORE, 15
40050 MONTEVEGLIO (BO)
TEL. 051832583
E-MAIL: cortedaibo@libero.it

This lovely winery and "agriturismo" has always grown its grapes organically. The reds are good, as is shown by the characterful, well-structured Cabernet Riserva '98 and the Merlot Roncovecchio, a pleasingly soft wine that foregrounds fruit. The unusual Brut is refreshing and fragrant.

● C. B. Cabernet Sauvignon Ris. '98 ♆♆	4*
● C. B. Merlot Roncovecchio '00 ♆	4
○ C. B. Spumante Brut ♆	4

TENUTA GOCCIA
VIA S. ANTONIO, 2/A
40050 MONTEVEGLIO (BO)
TEL. 051830492
E-MAIL: tenutagoccia@tiscalinet.it

The fragrant, flavoursome Barbera is a well-typed wine from vineyards between the abbey of Monteveglio and the Montebudello hills but the muscular, spicy Cabernet Sauvignon is a more serious bottle. What we like about the Pignoletto Frizzante is its pleasant, fruity freshness.

○ C. B. Pignoletto Frizzante '01 ♆	2
● C. B. Cabernet Sauvignon '00 ♆	3
● C. B. Barbera '01 ♆	3

SAN VITO
FRAZ. OLIVETO - VIA MONTE RODANO, 6
40050 MONTEVEGLIO (BO)
TEL. 051964521
E-MAIL: info@agricolasanvito.it

The best wine from San Vito is the new Cabernet Sauvignon 2000 selection, a well-made product that strikes a good balance of new oak with varietal and fruit sensations. The Pignoletto Frizzante and Pignoletto Superiore, two of the DOC zone's classics, also earned One Glass.

● C. B. Cabernet Sauvignon Sel. '00 ♆	4
○ C. B. Pignoletto Frizzante '01 ♆	3
○ C. B. Pignoletto Sup. '01 ♆	3

TENUTA LA TORRETTA
FRAZ. VAL TIDONE - LOC. TORRETTA, 62
29010 NIBBIANO (PC)
TEL. 0523997008
E-MAIL: tenuta.latorretta@tin.it

At this small Val Tidone winery, it was the spice and balsam 1999 Cabernet Sauvignon that caught our eye. We also liked the clean, flowery Pinot Nero Dionisio for the way it highlights varietal aromas. These are two fine international wines from a corner of Emilia that concentrates on Gutturnio.

● C. P. Cabernet Sauvignon '99 ♆♆	4*
● C. P. Pinot Nero Dioniso '98 ♆	4

CANTINE DALL'ASTA
VIA TOSCANA, 47
43100 PARMA
TEL. 0521484086
E-MAIL: cantinedallasta@libero.it

The Mefistofele 2001, from lambrusco Maestri grapes, was an eye-opener. Its sweet, fruity nose leads into a tangy, spicy palate pepped up by a gentle prickle. The Le Viole 2001, lambrusco-based with a small proportion of fortana, is delicious, too.

● Lambrusco dell'Emilia Le Viole '01 ♆	2*
● Lambrusco dell'Emilia Mefistofele '01 ♆	2*

BARACCONE
LOC. CA' DEI MORTI, 1
29028 PONTE DELL'OLIO (PC)
TEL. 0523877147
E-MAIL: cantina.baraccone@libero.it

Andreana Burgazzi's two Gutturnios are distinctly good. The well-structured Ronco Alto 1999 is intense, acquiring momentum on the warm, balanced palate. The Frizzante 2001 was perhaps the best Gutturnio sparkler we tasted. It has firm, generous, flowery palate, enhanced by a subdued note of spices.

● C. P. Gutturnio Ronco Alto Ris. '99 ♆♆	4*
● C. P. Gutturnio Frizzante '01 ♆	3*

CASETTO DEI MANDORLI
VIA UMBERTO I, 21
47016 PREDAPPIO (FC)
TEL. 0543922361
E-MAIL: casetto@tin.it

Predappio's oldest winery is a stickler for traditional techniques. The well-typed varietal aromas of the Vigna del Generale '98 are the cellar trademark but the wine could show more balance and extract. Simplicity and a sweet note of fruit preserve are the strong suits of the Tre Rocche 2001.

● Sangiovese di Romagna Sup. Tre Rocche '01	4
● Sangiovese di Romagna Vigna del Generale Ris. '98	5

PANDOLFA
FRAZ. FIUMANA - VIA PANDOLFA, 35
47016 PREDAPPIO (FC)
TEL. 0543940073
E-MAIL: info@pandolfa.it

Cabernet Pezzolo, the Pandolfa flagship wine, will only be released next year. In the meantime, the Fosso Le Forche is a good, full-bodied blend of sangiovese, montepulciano and nebbiolo. The Pandolfo is vibrant and well-structured while the barrique-fermented, chardonnay-based Calanco is pleasant.

● Fosso le Forche '00	5
○ Calanco Chardonnay '01	5
● Sangiovese di Romagna Sup. Pandolfo '01	3

CANTINE CAVICCHIOLI & FIGLI
VIA A. GRAMSCI, 9
41030 SAN PROSPERO (MO)
TEL. 059812411 - 059908828
E-MAIL: cantine@cavicchioli.it

Six wines presented, six Glasses earned. The range includes, in order of preference: a bright, soft and delicate Salamino Semisecco; the upfront Col Sassoso, austere on the nose, rich and faintly tannic on the palate; and the Sorbara Tre Medaglie, an elegant wine, with a remarkably balanced palate.

● Lambrusco Grasparossa di Castelvetro Col Sassoso '01	4
● Lambrusco di Sorbara Tre Medaglie	2*
● Lambrusco Salamino Semisecco	3

ALBERTO LUSIGNANI
LOC. VIGOLENO - VIA CASE ORSI, 9
29010 VERNASCA (PC)
TEL. 0523895178
E-MAIL: lusignani@agonet.it

Alberto's Vin Santo di Vigoleno is obtained traditionally from non-aromatic native grapes. The 1994 version is amber-hued. Its nose, characterized by oxidative aromas, accompanies a full palate of layered complexity. The full-flavoured Gutturnio Superiore is also very nicely made.

○ C. P. Vin Santo di Vigoleno '94	7
● C. P. Gutturnio Sup. '99	3*

CANTINE ROMAGNOLI
LOC. VILLO - VIA GENOVA, 20
29020 VIGOLZONE (PC)
TEL. 0523870129 - 0523870904
E-MAIL: info@cantineromagnoli.it

Cantine Romagnoli has recently changed hands. We liked the Caravaggio, a warm, spicy red with plenty of body and good balance. The Gutturnio Vigna del Gallo 1999 is uncomplicated and the Bonarda Frizzante 2001 is fresh and lively.

● C. P. Gutturnio Vigna del Gallo Ris. '99	5
● Caravaggio	5
● C. P. Bonarda Frizzante '01	3

MANARA
FRAZ. VICOMARINO
29010 ZIANO PIACENTINO (PC)
TEL. 0523860209

This small, new cellar is turning out some surprisingly well-made wines. The Cabernet Sauvignon 2000 is soft and firm, backed up by graceful, mouthfilling tannins. The Gutturnio Superiore is elegant and flowery. Finally, the fragrant Gutturnio Frizzante offers prominent notes of ripe fruit.

● C. P. Cabernet Sauvignon '00	4
● C. P. Gutturnio Sup. '00	3
● C. P. Gutturnio Frizzante '01	3

TUSCANY

The fact that Tuscany has regained first place in the Three Glass stakes says a lot about the wines we tasted this year. We handed out 63 top awards, and we were extremely strict. If we'd been a bit more lenient, there would have been over 80, which will give you some idea of how hard it was for the panels to make their decisions. But never has there been such a gaggle of fine vintages in so many Tuscan growing areas. We had the Brunello di Montalcino '97s and the '99s for Chianti Classico Riserva, Nobile di Montepulciano, Carmignano and lots of wines near the coast, with Bolgheri at the top of the list. Then there were the '00s and the '99s for most of the Supertuscans. Several zones that until recently would at most have provoked an indulgent smile are now producing wines that make our tasters sit up and take notice. We're talking about Maremma di Grosseto, Cortona and the areas around Pisa and Lucca. Indeed, the only bad news amid all these glad tidings is the rise in prices. It's true that lots of producers have invested serious money in restructuring, but if you want to buy a great Tuscan red in a wine shop, you will all too often have to put your hand in your pocket again after you've placed a € 50 note on the counter. This looks to be a somewhat risky development, particularly when the economy cannot be said to be humming along. We have no wish to plead poverty, but we'd like to point out that people who buy good wine do not all have limitless funds. One thing that does emerge clearly from the list of 63 Three Glass cellars is that there are many more DOCG and DOC bottles than there used to be. Strikingly, 11 of them are Chianti Classicos, another 11 are Brunello di Montalcinos and ten or so come from other denominated zones throughout the region. Almost all of them contain between 80 and 100 per cent sangiovese. We consider this to be a positive sign. It means that many producers are slowly abandoning a policy that favoured the individual winery and the single wine. Instead, they have begun to think in terms of terroir. The second important development, which coincides with the wine's recent international success, is that the '97 Brunello di Montalcinos have done very well. In the past, we have had occasion to criticize producers. We have accused them of making over-priced, antiquated wines that sold on the fame of Montalcino rather than their own quality. We are delighted now to be able to offer a different assessment, since it has become increasingly easy to taste really excellent Brunellos. One last thought. Only three producers won two Three Glass awards. They are Castello di Fonterutoli, Poliziano and Tenuta dell'Ornellaia. These are, of course, three distinguished names. But it also means that fully 57 wineries won our highest award for one of their wines. This is a clear sign that Tuscany is on its way into the front rank of international oenology. It's a glorious achievement for Italian wine.

AREZZO

Villa Cilnia
Fraz. Bagnoro
Loc. Montoncello, 27
52040 Arezzo
Tel. 0575365017
E-mail: villacilnia@interffre.it

The Villa Cilnia wines we tasted this year were good, indeed better than last year's, but there were some surprises, both pleasant and unpleasant. The pleasant ones were provided by the two Chianti Colli Aretini wines, particularly the Riserva, and the unpleasant (but only slightly) by the two IGTs, which were not up to our expectations. The general picture was a little uneven, but these things happen. The Riserva '99 proved really excellent, with its deep bouquet of dark berries, spice and chocolate, and a palate nicely underpinned by oak that features densely textured, smooth tannins and a racy, lingering finish. The Chianti '00 is thoroughly good as well. Here, the aromas tend towards oak-derived spice and hints of berry fruit. The tangily assertive flavour is very pleasant, well-sustained and fairly long. In short, it's a drinkable and eminently affordable wine. Moving into a different category and price range, we might have expected something better, but we didn't find it. The Vocato '99, a blend of sangiovese and cabernet, makes a fairly good showing on the whole, despite an inexpressive nose. In the mouth, there is admirable vigour, balanced progression and a moderately long finish with vegetal overtones. The Cign'Oro '99, on the other hand, is somewhat contradictory. The nose is quite intense, offering notes of liquorice and spice, and the entry on the palate is fairly warm and balanced, but the somewhat astringent finish tends to trail off.

● Chianti Colli Aretini '00	♟♟	3*
● Chianti Colli Aretini Ris. '99	♟♟	4*
● Vocato '99	♟♟	4
● Cign'Oro '99	♟	5
● Vocato '93	♟♟	4
● Chianti Colli Aretini Ris. '97	♟♟	4
● Chianti Colli Aretini '98	♟♟	3
● Cign'Oro '98	♟♟	5
○ Mecenate '00	♟	4

BAGNO A RIPOLI (FI)

Le Sorgenti
Loc. Vallina
Via di Docciola, 8
50012 Bagno a Ripoli (FI)
Tel. 055696004
E-mail: elisabettaferrari@fattoria-lesorgenti.com

This was a mixed year for the winery owned by the Ferrari family, who are continuing to invest time and money in their estate near Florence. Some new vineyards have started producing, and the cellar boasts enlarged – and still growing – ageing rooms. We were prepared for more from the top of the line, the Scirus, but we assume that the problem has to do with "growing pains" which will, in time, lead to better things. The '00 shows a vivid and quite lustrous ruby hue. Spicy notes of pepper and cinnamon on the nose are softened by sweet vanilla with fruity undertones of blackcurrant and blueberry. The attack on the palate, soft but not terribly mouthfilling, is rounded and succulent, with slightly dominant acidity that hardens a basically well-balanced flavour. The finish is long and enjoyable. The Sghiras '01 did fairly well, too. An intense straw yellow with faintly golden highlights introduces distinct aromas of peach and pear. The palate is soft and dense, with good acidic crispness that leaves a clean feeling in the mouth. The interesting Calicò '98, a traditional-method sparkling wine, offers enticing aromas of crusty bread together with flowery notes. It goes on to reveal a firm mouthfeel, with fine perlage and notable acidic bite. The Chianti Colli Fiorentini '00, on the other hand, is disappointing. An attractive lively purple ushers in a rather poorly defined nose and a palate that lacks balance as the tannins and acidity have the upper hand.

● Scirus '00	♟♟	6
○ Sghiras '01	♟	4
○ Calicò Brut '98	♟	5
● Chianti dei Colli Fiorentini '00		4
● Scirus '98	♟♟	5
● Scirus '99	♟♟	5
○ Sghiras '00	♟	4
○ Vin Santo '94	♟	5
● Chianti Colli Fiorentini '98	♟	3
● Chianti Colli Fiorentini '99	♟	3

BARBERINO VAL D'ELSA (FI)

CASA EMMA
S. P. DI CASTELLINA IN CHIANTI, 3/5/7
50021 BARBERINO VAL D'ELSA (FI)
TEL. 0558072859
E-MAIL: casaemma@casaemma.com

Casa Emma, back on form, has a profile of its own again this year. The Barberino Val d'Elsa cellar's comeback is largely due to the Chianti Classico Riserva '99, a solid red and true to type, although when we tasted it the oak was still a bit intrusive, particularly on the nose. On the palate, however, it is second to none in its category, displaying remarkable concentration, compact progression and an intense finish. The distinctly enjoyable Chianti Classico '00 reveals some vegetal notes peeking through in the bouquet that ill accord with the jammy notes of black cherry preserve. The more harmonious palate is attractively soft and lively. Finally, the house Merlot, Soloìo, was presented in two consecutive versions. We preferred the '00, even though we were not completely satisfied. It is full-bodied and vigorous, but the vegetal notes that dominate the nose certainly lost it a few points. The Soloìo '99, meanwhile, revealed over-evolved sulphurous tones on the nose, for which the pleasures of the palate did not sufficiently compensate. All in all, however, Casa Emma did more than satisfactorily, and we look forward to even greater things in the future.

BARBERINO VAL D'ELSA (FI)

CASTELLO DELLA PANERETTA
LOC. MONSANTO
STRADA DELLA PANERETTA, 35
50021 BARBERINO VAL D'ELSA (FI)
TEL. 0558059003
E-MAIL: stefano.paneretta@tin.it

Paneretta wines have a character all their own which no one could accuse of being either tame or eager to please. This is a point in their favour, in an era when a monotonous sameness of taste is getting to be the rule, provided that they do not, in their devotion to terroir, allow too many roughed edges to creep into the fragrances. That said, we should point out that Paneretta is still one of the most "genuine" estates in all of Chianti Classico, and can at times produce really exciting, expressive wines. And that's precisely what it did this time. The Terrine '99, made from sangiovese and canaiolo, shows an intense garnet colour and a still dumb nose with earthy, mineral and oak-derived phenolic notes. In the mouth, it is rounded, pleasingly harmonious and persistent. This is a wine with attitude and a very individual character. The Chianti Classico Torre a Destra '99 is stylistically not unlike the Terrine. Here, however, there is a less elegant, faint animal note on the nose, but the palate makes up for it with a compelling development and the intense fruit of the finish. The Quattrocentenario '99, a pure sangiovese, displays intense aromas of liquorice, sweet tobacco and cherry jam with overtones of spice. The palate is intense, austere and vibrant, with enlivening acidity and smooth, noble tannins. The Riserva '99 reveals appropriate density, but the tannins are slightly astringent. The Chianti Classico '00 shows good weight and solid character, but the nose could do with more definition. Lastly, the Vin Santo '97 is pleasant if rather straightforward.

• Soloìo '00	ŸŸ	8
• Chianti Cl. Ris. '99	ŸŸ	8
• Chianti Cl. '00	Ÿ	5
• Soloìo '99	Ÿ	8
• Chianti Cl. Ris. '93	ŸŸŸ	4
• Soloìo '94	ŸŸŸ	5
• Chianti Cl. Ris. '95	ŸŸŸ	4
• Chianti Cl. '93	ŸŸ	3
• Chianti Cl. '96	ŸŸ	3
• Chianti Cl. '97	ŸŸ	4
• Chianti Cl. Ris. '97	ŸŸ	4
• Soloìo '97	ŸŸ	5

• Chianti Cl. Torre a Destra Ris. '99	ŸŸ	5
• Le Terrine '99	ŸŸ	6
• Quattrocentenario '99	ŸŸ	7
• Chianti Cl. '00	Ÿ	4
○ Vin Santo del Chianti Cl. '97	Ÿ	4
• Chianti Cl. Ris. '99	Ÿ	5
• Chianti Cl. '95	ŸŸ	4
• Chianti Cl. Ris. '95	ŸŸ	4
• Chianti Cl. Torre a Destra Ris. '95	ŸŸ	4
• Chianti Cl. Torre a Destra Ris. '96	ŸŸ	4
• Le Terrine '96	ŸŸ	5
• Le Terrine '97	ŸŸ	5
• Quattrocentenario '97	ŸŸ	5

BARBERINO VAL D'ELSA (FI)

★ Isole e Olena
Loc. Isole, 1
50021 Barberino Val d'Elsa (FI)
tel. 0558072763
e-mail: isolena@tin.it

Since it was not yet bottled at the time of our tastings, the Cepparello '00 will be reviewed in next year's Guide. The absence of such an important wine would have significantly weakened the showing of most producers, but not Isole e Olena, which still had three great wines contending for our highest recognition. And one of them got it, a sensational Syrah, which is new to our winner's circle. It displays a not particularly expansive or immediate nose. In other words, it's not your usual Syrah, all fruit and pepper, but a wine with firm signs of terroir and a mineral undertone. It is much more eloquent in the mouth, where it pervades the palate with its soft, silky elegance, growing gradually in intensity and lingering on the finish. The Cabernet Sauvignon '99 did very well, too. The bouquet is still sorting itself out – there are, for the moment, some less than elegant earthy, animal and vegetal overtones – but the flavour is more confident, showing force, concentration and seamless progression. The excellent Chardonnay '00, undoubtedly the best Tuscan white we tasted this year, is at once dense, succulent, elegant and vigorous. The sweet, unctuous, fragrant Vin Santo '96 is very good, but this hardly comes as a surprise. The Chianti Classico '00, however, is rather over-evolved.

BARBERINO VAL D'ELSA (FI)

Le Filigare
Loc. Le Filigare
Via Sicelle
50020 Barberino Val d'Elsa (FI)
tel. 0558072796
e-mail: filigare@inwind.it

A very impressive showing from Le Filigare this year has given it back its own Guide profile and the space it deserves. But this estate near San Donato has not only produced wines of remarkable quality. It has also given very promising signs of a process of renewal. The selection of bottles, for example, now includes several newcomers, part of the reformulation of their entire range. At our tastings, the Chianti Classico Maria Vittoria '99 did very well. A lively, intense ruby introduces a dense nose shot through with admirably deep ripe fruit. The palate is vibrant, smooth and nicely balanced, and the well-defined fruit reappears on the finish. It is not a gigantic wine, but it's remarkably well executed. The Pietro '98 is very interesting, too. Although vegetal notes stand out on the nose, the palate progresses firmly with velvety softness and elegance. The Chianti Classico Lorenzo '00 is a surprising and rather good red. The nose is not yet fully developed, but it is sound and already shows clear signs of perfectly ripe fruit. The palate is supple and well balanced, with a pleasingly fruity finish. In terms of concentration, the most notable wine is Le Rocce '99, a blend of sangiovese and cabernet sauvignon. It shows excellent body, a master's touch with the tannins, and a long finish. The nose, which is still developing, has some vegetal notes and not very stylish oak for the time being. The Chianti Classico '00 is well-proportioned and enjoyable.

● Syrah '99	🍷🍷🍷	7
○ Chardonnay '00	🍷🍷	6
● Cabernet Sauvignon '99	🍷🍷	8
○ Vin Santo '96	🍷🍷	7
● Chianti Cl. '00		5
● Cepparello '86	🍷🍷🍷	6
● Cepparello '88	🍷🍷🍷	6
● Cabernet Sauvignon '90	🍷🍷🍷	6
● Cabernet Sauvignon '95	🍷🍷🍷	6
● Cabernet Sauvignon '96	🍷🍷🍷	6
● Cabernet Sauvignon '97	🍷🍷🍷	6
● Cepparello '97	🍷🍷🍷	5
● Cepparello '98	🍷🍷🍷	6
● Cepparello '99	🍷🍷🍷	6

● Pietro '98	🍷🍷	8
● Chianti Cl. Maria Vittoria Ris. '99	🍷🍷	6
● Chianti Cl. Lorenzo '00	🍷🍷	5
● Podere Le Rocce '99	🍷🍷	7
● Chianti Cl. '00	🍷	5
● Podere Le Rocce '88	🍷🍷🍷	7
● Chianti Cl. Ris. '90	🍷🍷	5
● Chianti Cl. Ris. '91	🍷🍷	5
● Chianti Cl. Ris. '93	🍷🍷	5
● Podere Le Rocce '93	🍷🍷	7
● Podere Le Rocce '94	🍷🍷	7
● Chianti Cl. Ris. '96	🍷🍷	5
● Podere Le Rocce '96	🍷🍷	7
● Podere Le Rocce '97	🍷🍷	7
● Chianti Cl. '99	🍷🍷	5

BARBERINO VAL D'ELSA (FI)

CASTELLO DI MONSANTO
LOC. MONSANTO
VIA MONSANTO, 8
50021 BARBERINO VAL D'ELSA (FI)
TEL. 0558059000
E-MAIL: monsanto@castellodimonsanto.it

Our Monsanto tastings were a real pleasure this year. There were, as a glance at the bottom of the page will show, no disappointments, and more than one wine came close to making the final taste-offs. This is all most promising, particularly since Fabrizio Bianchi is eagerly renewing his vineyards and re-organizing his cellar, under the guidance of his new oenologist, Andrea Giovannini. Monsanto should be back in the top ranks of Tuscany one of these days. The very well-focused Sangiovese Fabrizio Bianchi '99 exhibits an intense bouquet with notes of berry fruit and still rather assertive oak. The palate is dense and lively, with considerable energy on the finish. The very good Riserva '99, although more forward on the nose, offers intense fragrances of liquorice and sweet tobacco. In the mouth, there is power, eloquence and length. The equally good Riserva Il Poggio '99 is, at first, hard to make out but it shows signs of remarkable character and ought to develop further. The Nemo '99, from cabernet sauvignon, is not far behind. It is deep, dense and well-balanced, the only fault being a faint vegetal tone. The successful Chardonnay Fabrizio Bianchi '00 already offers a developed, enjoyable nose with aromas of flowers, exotic fruit, honey and vanilla. Its very pleasing palate serves up a felicitous combination of fleshy pulp and freshness. A more noticeably evolved tone causes the Tinscvil '99 to shine a tad less brightly than its fellows, but it is still a sound wine.

BARBERINO VAL D'ELSA (FI)

MARCHESI TORRIGIANI
LOC. VICO D'ELSA
P.ZZA TORRIGIANI, 15
50021 BARBERINO VAL D'ELSA
TEL. 0558073001
E-MAIL: az.torri@tin.it

Although the Marchesi Torrigiani estate is a venerable historic presence in Vico d'Elsa, only in recent years has it begun to overhaul every aspect of production from vineyard to cellar. There are some 30 hectares of vineyards, mostly planted quite some time ago, but the estate includes six hectares of new vines. The main grape varieties are sangiovese, which is predominant, cabernet sauvignon and merlot. With the arrival of Luca D'Attoma as consultant oenologist, restructuring has pressed on apace. The old cellars now have quite a number of new barriques, in which the two reds we tasted this year do their ageing. The Guidaccio '00, a blend of sangiovese, cabernet sauvignon and merlot, is the standard-bearer of Marchesi Torrigiani. We found it extremely interesting, with its dense, well-defined bouquet revealing dark berries, cocoa and faint hints of oak. It is not extraordinarily full-bodied, but the structure is solid and there is excellent balance, admirable length and a certain elegance on the palate. The Torre di Ciardo '00, from sangiovese and some other native varieties with a pinch of merlot, is simpler but sound. The aromas are intense, showing some vegetal overtones. Although the palate is full-bodied and soft, oak-derived tannins are for the moment standing in the way of an expressive finish.

● Fabrizio Bianchi Sangiovese '99	🍷🍷	7
○ Fabrizio Bianchi Chardonnay '00	🍷🍷	5
● Chianti Cl. Il Poggio Ris. '99	🍷🍷	7
● Chianti Cl. Ris. '99	🍷🍷	5
● Nemo '99	🍷🍷	7
● Tinscvil '99	🍷🍷	6
● Chianti Cl. Il Poggio Ris. '88	🍷🍷🍷	7
● Chianti Cl. Il Poggio Ris. '90	🍷🍷	5
● Chianti Cl. Il Poggio Ris. '93	🍷🍷	7
● Nemo '95	🍷🍷	7
● Chianti Cl. Il Poggio Ris. '97	🍷🍷	7
● Nemo '97	🍷🍷	7
● Chianti Cl. Il Poggio Ris. '98	🍷🍷	7
● Nemo '98	🍷🍷	7
● Tinscvil '98	🍷🍷	5

● Guidaccio '00	🍷🍷	5
● Torre di Ciardo '00	🍷🍷	4
● Guidaccio '99	🍷🍷	5
● Torre di Ciardo '99	🍷	4

BOLGHERI (LI)

Tenuta Guado al Tasso
Loc. Belvedere, 140
57020 Bolgheri (LI)
Tel. 0565749735
E-mail: guadoaltasso@antinori.it

BOLGHERI (LI)

Le Macchiole
Via Bolgherese, 189
57020 Bolgheri (LI)
Tel. 0565766092
E-mail: azagmacchiole@etruscan.li.it

This was not a memorable year for the wines of Tenuta Guado al Tasso, the Bolgheri estate of Marchesi Antinori. Specifically, it was the Guado al Tasso '99 that we found somewhat wanting. We were expecting a real champion after the fine showings of the two preceding vintages, which were decidedly in crescendo. But mistakes will happen, and it would be rather worrying if wines always came out the same. Remember, too, that our disappointment is relative, and should be understood within the context of what is in any case an admirable wine. Probably, we were expecting too much too soon, and in the next year or two, we'll get what we've been waiting for. At our tastings, we noted a pale garnet rim, a sign of forwardness. The nose features jammy notes of blackberry and blackcurrant, as well as a pronounced vegetal undertone and hints of spice. It is soft in the mouth, wants a bit more sinew at mid-palate and finishes with vegetal notes and some tannic roughness. The Vermentino '01 is as well made as ever. A refreshing, enjoyable wine, nicely underpinned by acidity, it does, however, lacks its customary aromatic richness. The rosé Scalabrone '01 is properly focused, with pleasing aromas of cherry and raspberry introducing an intense, fragrant palate.

This is something we never wanted to have to write. Eugenio Campolmi, one of the leading lights of the great Bolgheri adventure, has left us. He was at the height of his powers, involved in a raft of projects and barely 40 years old. For anyone who knew him and his extraordinary vitality, it is all too painful to describe. But winelovers can take heart. We shall still be drinking the Le Macchiole wines as the estate will continue on its path, under the guidance of Eugenio's widow, Cinzia. And the Guide will continue to report them. Three Glasses were a mere formality for the Messorio '99, one of the most successful versions yet of this Merlot. It has been acquiring an ever more distinctive, individual character. In other words, it's not the usual fruity tipple that we have come to expect from a merlot-based bottle. The nose offers aromas of plum, blackberry jam and balsamic and toasty notes. The palate is imposing and complex, with silky tannins and a long, spicy finish. The Paleo Rosso '99 came close to a third Glass for it, too, is an excellent wine. Unusually, the nose is already generous and expressive, with notes of blackberry, mint, coffee and pencil lead. The palate is lean and elegant, with a well-sustained development and a long finish that foregrounds smooth, succulent tannins. It is not so easy to judge the Syrah, Scrio, which is still young. A powerful wine, it has lots of personality but is also a little sulphurous on the nose, for the moment. The red Le Macchiole '00 is good and meaty, but over-oaked, and the Paleo Bianco '00 is less than convincing.

● Bolgheri Rosso Sup. Guado al Tasso '99	♀♀	8
⊙ Bolgheri Rosato Scalabrone '01	♀	4
○ Bolgheri Vermentino '01	♀	4
● Bolgheri Rosso Sup. Guado al Tasso '90	♀♀♀	8
● Bolgheri Rosso Sup. Guado al Tasso '98	♀♀	8
○ Bolgheri Vermentino '00	♀♀	4*
● Bolgheri Rosso Sup. Guado al Tasso '96	♀♀	8
● Bolgheri Rosso Sup. Guado al Tasso '97	♀♀	8

● Messorio '99	♀♀♀	8
● Bolgheri Rosso Sup. Paleo '99	♀♀	8
● Le Macchiole '00	♀♀	6
○ Paleo Bianco '00	♀	6
● Scrio '99	♀	8
● Bolgheri Rosso Sup. Paleo '95	♀♀♀	8
● Bolgheri Rosso Sup. Paleo '96	♀♀♀	8
● Bolgheri Rosso Sup. Paleo '97	♀♀♀	8
● Messorio '97	♀♀♀	8
● Messorio '98	♀♀♀	8
● Bolgheri Rosso Sup. Paleo '98	♀♀	8
● Scrio '97	♀♀	8
○ Bolgheri Sauvignon Paleo '98	♀♀	4
● Scrio '98	♀♀	8
● Le Macchiole '99	♀♀	5

BOLGHERI (LI)

★ Tenuta dell' Ornellaia
Via Bolgherese, 191
57020 Bolgheri (LI)
tel. 056571811
e-mail: info@ornellaia.it

The change in ownership that took place this year at the Tenuta dell'Ornellaia – the Mondavi family has taken over all of Lodovico Antinori's share in the winery – has not affected the progress of this Bolgheri estate in the least. Indeed, this collection of wines from Ornellaia, in keeping with the trend of recent years, is even better than usual. The Masseto '99 is again a wine of great breeding and one of the rare examples of a monovarietal Merlot that can offer more than the standard rounded fruitiness. It is made from the grapes of four vineyards, each with its own soil type and hence structure. This is, in great part, the source of the extraordinary complexity of a wine that combines power with finesse, densely packed tannins with alcohol-derived sweetness. It's all rounded off by a long, expansive finish. The Bolgheri Ornellaia is unstoppable and continues to go from strength to strength. There is the odd note of reduction on the nose, but this is a temporary phenomenon. The spectacularly mouthfilling palate reveals sound ripe fruit and irresistible vital force on the finish. The red Le Volte '00 is fair. It has body and softness but there are some signs of over-evolution. Meanwhile, the Poggio alle Gazze has come to the end of the line. No more will be produced. The '01 version, sad to say, confirms this decision.

● Bolgheri Sup. Ornellaia '99	▼▼▼	8
● Masseto '99	▼▼▼	8
● Le Volte '00	▼	5
○ Poggio alle Gazze '01		5
● Masseto '93	▼▼▼	8
● Ornellaia '93	▼▼▼	8
● Masseto '94	▼▼▼	8
● Masseto '95	▼▼▼	8
● Bolgheri Sup. Ornellaia '97	▼▼▼	8
● Masseto '97	▼▼▼	8
● Bolgheri Sup. Ornellaia '98	▼▼▼	8
● Masseto '98	▼▼▼	8
○ Poggio alle Gazze '00	▼▼	4

BOLGHERI (LI)

★ Tenuta San Guido
Loc. Capanne, 27
57020 Bolgheri (LI)
tel. 0565762003
e-mail: info@sassicaia.com

Those people who lie in wait, pens dipped in poison ink, for each new vintage of the legendary red from Tenuta San Guido simply to criticize its most insignificant details will have their work cut out for them. The '99 Sassicaia is as great as ever. Wine writers who consider it a badge of distinction and critical acumen to denigrate the standard-bearer of Italian oenology will just have to put the top back on the bottle of vitriol. What is so awesomely admirable about the wine is its stylistic consistency and, even more, the style itself. Sassicaia offers elegance without dilution, delicate tannins that still manage to present a close-knit weave, and supreme drinkability. At a time when the market is glutted with monster wines whose crude extractive weight would stun a pachyderm, Sassicaia's discretion is movingly exemplary. That said, we'll show we are not totally in awe of the great Incisa della Rocchetta red by making a few niggling comments. The sweet notes of oak have not yet been completely absorbed. Of course, it could hardly be otherwise, given the youth of the wine, but in some other years, Sassicaia has been more integrated at this stage. The aromatic range is slightly contracted, but then the fruit is magnificent, the development on the palate is confident and long, and the finish is radiant. We should mention that there is now a "deuxième vin", Guidalberto. It's a red made mostly from merlot with a little cabernet and sangiovese. A bit harsh on the nose, it reveals grip on the palate and a somewhat rustic development, but it has undeniable character.

● Bolgheri Sassicaia '99	▼▼▼	8
● Guidalberto '00	▼▼	8
● Sassicaia '83	▼▼▼	8
● Sassicaia '84	▼▼▼	8
● Sassicaia '85	▼▼▼	8
● Sassicaia '88	▼▼▼	8
● Sassicaia '90	▼▼▼	8
● Sassicaia '92	▼▼▼	8
● Sassicaia '93	▼▼▼	6
● Bolgheri Sassicaia '95	▼▼▼	8
● Bolgheri Sassicaia '96	▼▼▼	8
● Bolgheri Sassicaia '97	▼▼▼	8
● Bolgheri Sassicaia '98	▼▼▼	8
● Sassicaia '87	▼▼	8
● Bolgheri Sassicaia '94	▼▼	7

BUCINE (AR)

Fattoria Villa La Selva
Loc. Montebenichi
52021 Bucine (AR)
tel. 055998203
e-mail: laselva@val.it

CAMPIGLIA MARITTIMA (LI)

Jacopo Banti
Via Citerna, 24
57021 Campiglia Marittima (LI)
tel. 0565838802
e-mail: info@jacopobanti.it

The area around Arezzo is a busy one, with lots of new wineries jockeying for position, but Villa la Selva is holding its own. Naturally "holding its own" does not imply a lack of energy for Sergio Carpini certainly has the will to compete and improve. We shall probably see a big step forward when his recently planted vines reach maturity. Meanwhile, there is good news from the sangiovese-based Felciaia '99, which made it to the final taste-offs this year. It is still young and very promising, and should develop nicely with a little more bottle time. The well-defined, concentrated aromas are still dominated by oak-derived toastiness and spice, which put the fruit somewhat in the shade. The flavour is soft, elegant, long and even, with lively, succulent, fine-grained tannins. In contrast, this year's release comes from what was not a great year for the cabernet, Selvamaggio, which usually boasts good structure and a stylish palate. The '98 clearly shows the limitations of that problematic vintage and a conspicuous vegetal tone rather unbalances the medium weight of the body. Lastly, the decent enough Vin Santo Vigna del Papa '96 is pleasant but reveals some slightly troubling notes of oxidation.

Lorenzo Banti is still expanding his range of action. He has extended his vine stock with the recent addition of some land to the west of Campiglia Marittima, in a splendidly aspected position. His cares, which are already considerable, will increase, but this does not frighten him in the least, inspired as he is by a new passion now that he is tending the estate full-time. He produces quite a large selection of wines, all of satisfactory quality, but the star is still his Aleatico. Although the supply of the '01 version is a little more generous than in previous vintages, it is still not nearly enough to satisfy demand. Indeed, if he made a little more than the current tiny quantity, he would find himself with a Three Glass wine on his hands. The aromas are exceptionally pure and intense, with notes of black cherry, blackberry and Mediterranean flowers, all carried through onto the palate, which shows just the right sweetness, concentration and length. The most interesting of his other wines is Il Peccato '00, a monovarietal cabernet sauvignon. To tell the truth, it threw us off a little because, together with notable structure, density and balance, it reveals a rather aggressive vegetal timbre. But some time in the bottle should tone this down. As for the other bottles, we might mention the immediate, uncomplicated charm of the Ceragiolo '01, the moderate richness of the Poggio Angelica '01, despite some forward notes, and the evenness of the white Centomini '01. We were somewhat less enamoured of by the red Campalto '01, but all in all, this year's was a good showing.

● Felciaia '99	▼▼ 5
○ Vin Santo del Chianti Vigna del Papa '96	▼ 6
● Selvamaggio '98	▼ 6
● Selvamaggio '90	▼▼ 5
● Selvamaggio '91	▼▼ 5
● Selvamaggio '92	▼▼ 5
● Selvamaggio '93	▼▼ 5
● Felciaia '94	▼▼ 5
● Felciaia '95	▼▼ 5
● Selvamaggio '95	▼▼ 5
● Selvamaggio '96	▼▼ 5
● Selvamaggio '97	▼▼ 5
● Felciaia '98	▼▼ 5

● Val di Cornia Aleatico '01	▼▼ 6
● Val di Cornia Il Peccato Barrique '00	▼▼ 5
○ Val di Cornia Bianco Centomini '01	▼ 3
● Val di Cornia Rosso Ceragiolo '01	▼ 4
○ Val di Cornia Vermentino Poggio Angelica '01	▼ 4
● Val di Cornia Rosso Campalto '01	4
● Il Peccato Barrique '99	▼▼ 5
● Ceragiolo '00	▼ 4

CAPRAIA E LIMITE

Enrico Pierazzuoli
Via Valicarda, 35
50056 Capraia e Limite
tel. 0571910078
e-mail: info@enricopierazzuoli.com

While preparing to make a quantum leap in quality, Enrico Pierazzuoli continues to produce good wines. In fact, we have to say that the wines we tasted this year were not only sound but also well conceived and coherent. Enrico didn't put a foot wrong. But it all starts in the vineyard, which absorbs a great deal of Pierazzuoli's energies. He is well aware that it is only from rich and balanced grapes that he will be able, in the future, to make great wines. We were quite pleased with the Gioveto '99, a blend of 60 per cent sangiovese and 15 per cent each of merlot and syrah. The well-defined nose offers notes of berry fruit and hints of cocoa, bell pepper and fresh spice. The softness on the palate is underpinned by remarkably tight-knit tannins that get just slightly out of hand on the nonetheless lingering finish. Further good marks were awarded to the Carmignano '00, which has a faintly vegetal entry on the nose that then gives way to abundant dark berries and a light overtone of oak. In the mouth, it is rounded, well balanced and enjoyably invigorating. The Chianti Classico Matroneo '00 shows a slight haziness on the nose, together with scents of very ripe fruit. The flavour is robust and concentrated and the finish lingers, although the jammy notes typical of the vintage are very much in evidence. There's as much structure as you could ask for in the Chianti Montalbano '00, too, although oak makes its presence felt. The Vin Santo Millarium '94 is sweet and pleasing, but not very aromatically eloquent.

● Carmignano Le Farnete '00	¶¶	4*
● Chianti Cl. Matroneo '00	¶¶	4*
● Gioveto '99	¶¶	5
● Chianti Montalbano '00	¶	3*
○ Vin Santo Millarium '94	¶	5
● Carmignano Le Farnete Ris. '97	¶¶¶	5
● Carmignano Le Farnete Ris. '92	¶¶	4
● Carmignano Le Farnete Ris. '93	¶¶	4
● Chianti Montalbano Ris. '93	¶¶	3
● Carmignano Le Farnete Ris. '94	¶¶	4
● Carmignano Le Farnete Ris. '96	¶¶	4
○ Carleto '97	¶¶	4
● Chianti Montalbano Ris. '97	¶¶	4
● Chianti Cl. Matroneo '98	¶¶	4

CARMIGNANO (PO)

Fattoria Ambra
Via Lombarda, 85
59015 Carmignano (PO)
tel. 055486488
e-mail: fattoria.ambra@libero.it

With the debut of Vigna di Montefortini, Beppe Rigoli now produces four different Carmignano selections, two Riservas – Elzana and Vigne Alte di Montalbiolo, and two basic wines – Santa Cristina in Pilli and the new Montefortini. Our tastings were most encouraging, not only because of the quality of the wines but also thanks to the stylistic individuality of each one. There seems, generally speaking, to be a more knowing use of oak, and we sensed the presence of new barrels in the cellar. The Riserva Montalbiolo '99 stands out particularly. The nose is admirably dense and clean, with notes of berry fruit and vanilla and some faint vegetal hints. The entry on the palate is soft and nicely underpinned by tannins. The development is just as it should be, and the finish lingers, but has a mild, tannin-derived drying effect. Montalbiolo's stylishness is followed by the character of the Riserva Elzana '99. The bouquet, dominated by alcohol, is not very expressive, but the palate is dense, powerful and consistent, with lively tannins that have yet to mellow. The Montefortini '00 made a good first appearance. It is less complex but reveals beautifully focused fruit and a well-paced harmonious development with smooth tannins and a pleasing final thrust. The Santa Cristina '00 is also more than satisfactory, with its enjoyable, lively flavour just faintly affected by vegetal hints. The Barco Reale '01 is respectable and well executed.

● Carmignano Vigna di Montefortini '00	¶¶	4*
● Carmignano Elzana Ris. '99	¶¶	5
● Carmignano Le Vigne Alte di Montalbiolo Ris. '99	¶¶	5*
● Carmignano Vigna S. Cristina in Pilli '00	¶	4
● Barco Reale '01		3
● Carmignano Elzana Ris. '95	¶¶	4
● Carmignano Elzana Ris. '96	¶¶	4
● Carmignano Le Vigne Alte Ris. '96	¶¶	4
● Carmignano Le Vigne Alte di Montalbiolo '97	¶¶	4
● Carmignano Le Vigne Alte di Montalbiolo '98	¶¶	4
● Carmignano Elzana Ris. '98	¶	5

CARMIGNANO (PO)

Tenuta di Capezzana
Loc. Capezzana
Via Capezzana, 100
59015 Carmignano (PO)
tel. 0558706005
e-mail: capezzana@capezzana.it

By a particularly slender hair's breadth, Tenuta di Capezzana missed its third consecutive Three Glasses this year. The Villa di Capezzana '00 stood out in one of the best versions ever – it's certainly the richest. You can sense the wine's liveliness from the dark, dense colour. It's confirmed by the admirable depth of the bouquet, which is focused on fruit just this side of over-ripe, with a contribution from the oak. The palate shows remarkable density, energy and consistency, with a long spicy finish. The Ghiaie della Furba '00, a half step down, also did very well. There are light hints of super-ripeness on the nose, together with notes of spice, dark berries and bell pepper. The supple palate seems almost exotic, thanks, perhaps, to the syrah in the blend. Although soft and lingering, Ghiaie della Furba would need more character at mid palate to make it to the top ranks. The Villa di Trefiano '99 is aromatically quite interesting, if not altogether unified, showing notes of asparagus, clove and blackberry jam. The development in the mouth is velvety and elegant, with tannins peeking through on the finish. The Barco Reale '01 is unbeatable in its category. It is rounded, succulent and intensely fruity. Good things can also be said of the Vin Ruspo '01 and the enjoyable Chardonnay '01. Lastly, the Vin Santo '96 is sweet, dense, viscous and extremely long.

CARMIGNANO (PO)

Pratesi
Loc. Seano
Via Rizzelli, 10
59011 Carmignano (PO)
tel. 0558706400 - 0558953531
e-mail: lolocco@libero.it

Fabrizio Pratesi should be proud of what he has accomplished in the last few years. The new plantings at 10,000 vines per hectare will soon be starting to bear useful fruit, and the cellar, set in the midst of the vineyard, has everything it takes to safeguard the goodness of the raw material. At our tastings, Fabrizio's Carmignano turned out to be one of the best, and can be considered a good starting point for realizing his far from secret ambitions. It boasts a very intense colour and an intriguingly deep fragrance of dark berries and roasted coffee beans. The full-bodied palate, after a dense attack, reveals a well-sustained, concentrated progression to a fairly long, slightly vegetal finish. Excellent oak supports the fruit without getting in its way, making a positive contribution to the general balance. It deserved its place at the final taste-offs but in future, should seek to acquire a more distinct, easily recognizable character. Fabrizio Pratesi's newcomer, the Locorosso '00, from sangiovese with ten per cent merlot, did quite well for a straightforward, direct sort of wine. The nose offers clear notes of dark berries and wood, then there's good structure, definition and balance on the palate.

Wine	Glasses	Score
● Carmignano Villa di Capezzana '00	ΨΨ	5*
● Ghiaie della Furba '00	ΨΨ	6
○ Vin Santo di Carmignano Ris. '96	ΨΨ	5*
● Barco Reale '01	Ψ	3*
● Carmignano Villa di Trefiano '99	ΨΨ	6
○ Chardonnay '01	Ψ	2*
⊙ Vin Ruspo '01	Ψ	3
● Ghiaie della Furba '98	ΨΨΨ	5
● Carmignano Villa di Capezzana '99	ΨΨΨ	5
● Ghiaie della Furba '99	ΨΨ	6
○ Vin Santo di Carmignano Ris. '95	ΨΨ	6
● Carmignano Villa di Trefiano '98	ΨΨ	5

Wine	Glasses	Score
● Carmignano '00	ΨΨ	6
● Locorosso Rosso '00	ΨΨ	4
● Lococco '97	ΨΨ	5
● Carmignano '99	ΨΨ	5

CASTAGNETO CARDUCCI (LI)

COLLE MASSARI
LOC. GRATTAMACCO
57022 CASTAGNETO CARDUCCI (LI)
TEL. 0565763840
E-MAIL: info@grattamacco.com

Piermario Meletti Cavallari, the driving force behind the transformation of Bolgheri in the last 20 years, has entrusted the management of his historic estate to Claudio Tipa, a businessman connected with a Swiss pharmaceutical company. Claudio is Sicilian by birth and Roman by adoption, and has taken a ten-year lease on Grattamacco for Cavallari could never have brought himself to part with the property. Claudio Tipa is hardly a newcomer to the wine world. He already owns 300 hectares near Montalcino and is an old friend of Maurizio Castelli, who is staying on as consultant oenologist. With this injection of new blood, the range of the great Bolgheri estate has taken yet another big step forward. The Grattamacco Rosso '99, a blend of sangiovese and cabernet sauvignon, shows quite splendid overall harmony and elegance. Because of its extreme youth (and we have noted in former years that this wine, given time, just gets better and better), it is still a bit closed on the nose and shows some tannic hardness on the palate. However, it offers a solid, full-bodied, concentrated structure with an aromatic range that goes from wild berries to spice, and an absolutely enthralling finish. The very good Grattamacco Bianco '01, an extremely enjoyable blend of vermentino and trebbiano, manages to keep its fresh fruity character intact over the light veil of oak, and even offers mineral notes. You might think for a moment that it was a great Riesling.

CASTAGNETO CARDUCCI (LI)

ENRICO SANTINI
LOC. CAMPO ALLA CASA, 74
57022 CASTAGNETO CARDUCCI (LI)
TEL. 0565774375

Not everyone has heard of Enrico Santini, which is fair enough, since this is only his second year of production and his first profile in the Guide. But wine professionals in the know have already observed that this young producer from Castagneto has what it takes to make a name for himself. The estate covers some ten hectares under vine, all tended by the owner himself, one of the few real "vignerons" in Bolgheri. In the cellar, Enrico can call on the technical skills of Attilio Pagli. The grape varieties are essentially those you find most frequently in this area, cabernet sauvignon, merlot, sangiovese and syrah for the reds, and vermentino and viognier for the whites. On its debut appearance, the Montepergoli '00 did splendidly, making some celebrated wines tremble in their bottles for it very nearly won Three Glasses. All the above-mentioned red varieties go into it, and the result is a dense, clear-cut nose focused on perfectly ripe blackberries and rounded off by toasty notes of oak. Great intensity and balance are the distinguishing features of the palate, which is rich in body and concentration. There are lots of well-integrated tannins and a long finish that boasts freshness and elegance. It's a great red. The other wines did well, although we were slightly troubled by some notes of reduction on the nose of the Poggio al Moro '01, which kept it from getting a higher rating.

● Bolgheri Rosso Sup. Grattamacco '99	🍷🍷🍷	7
○ Bolgheri Bianco '01	🍷🍷	4
● Grattamacco '85	🍷🍷🍷	5
● Bolgheri Rosso Sup. Grattamacco '98	🍷🍷	6
○ Bolgheri Bianco '00	🍷🍷	4
● Grattamacco '90	🍷🍷	5
● Grattamacco '91	🍷🍷	5
● Grattamacco '92	🍷🍷	4
● Grattamacco '93	🍷🍷	5
● Bolgheri Rosso Sup. Grattamacco '95	🍷🍷	6
● Bolgheri Rosso Sup. Grattamacco '97	🍷🍷	6

● Bolgheri Montepergoli '00	🍷🍷	7
○ Bolgheri Bianco Campo alla Casa '01	🍷	4
● Bolgheri Rosso Poggio al Moro '01		4
● Bolgheri Rosso Poggio al Moro '00	🍷	3

CASTAGNETO CARDUCCI (LI)

MICHELE SATTA
LOC. CASONE UGOLINO, 23
57022 CASTAGNETO CARDUCCI (LI)
TEL. 0565773041
E-MAIL: satta@infol.it

Michele Satta was dealt a good hand this year and played it well, making excellent use of his ace, the Piastraia. But this is no poker game and Michele Satta is not a gambler, although it must be admitted that when he started out he was taking a big risk. And unluckily, or rather fortunately from our point of view, Satta is incapable of bluffing. He stakes his all on what his vines can give him to take to his cellar, which, by the way, was only recently inaugurated. It's at once good-looking, original and efficient. It is Michele's Bolgheri Piastraia '00 that has made the most evident progress this time, only narrowly missing Three Glasses. A fairly full bouquet, with notes of berry fruit and spice with a faint vegetal hint, leads to a soft entry on the palate. The mid palate grows steadily more vigorous and intense in a rising progression backed by perceptible fruit, robust but smooth tannins and a very long, if not very complex, finish. We liked the Cavaliere '99, a monovarietal sangiovese, rather more than last year's version. It is still not altogether expressive on the nose, but the attack on the palate is powerful and confident, and the wine shows remarkable character as well as assertive tannins. The original Giovin Re '01, made from very ripe viognier and aged in oak, is a chewy, sumptuous, showy wine, perhaps wanting in freshness of flavour and aromatic finesse. The Costa di Giulia is attractive in its mineral fragrance and fresh succulence, but the finish is a bit one-dimensional and rather short. Lastly, the Diambra '01 is enjoyable and full-bodied.

●	Bolgheri Rosso Piastraia '00	▼▼	7
○	Giovin Re '01	▼	6
●	Cavaliere '99	▼▼	7
●	Bolgheri Rosso Diambra '01	▼	4
○	Costa di Giulia '01	▼	4
○	Costa di Giulia '00	▼▼	4*
●	Bolgheri Rosso Piastraia '95	▼▼	7
●	Vigna al Cavaliere '95	▼▼	7
●	Bolgheri Rosso Piastraia '96	▼▼	7
●	Vigna al Cavaliere '96	▼▼	7
●	Bolgheri Rosso Piastraia '97	▼▼	7
●	Vigna al Cavaliere '97	▼▼	7
●	Vigna al Cavaliere '98	▼▼	7
●	Bolgheri Rosso Piastraia '99	▼▼	7

CASTELLINA IN CHIANTI (SI)

CASTAGNOLI
LOC. CASTAGNOLI
53011 CASTELLINA IN CHIANTI (SI)
TEL. 0577740446

Hans Joachim Dobbelin's estate is a little gem, set in the hills of Chianti. It's the sort of place you might see on a picture postcard. It covers some 80 hectares, less than ten per cent of which is under vine, and lies at 400 metres above sea level. The varieties planted include sangiovese, syrah, merlot and a few white grapes. All of the Castagnoli wines did well, but the Syrah stood out particularly, as it did when it made a very good impression last year in the '98 version. The '99 is even better. An intense, vibrant ruby introduces a concentrated nose, dominated by dark berries, that also discloses oak-derived spice and toastiness. The palate, after a powerful, alcohol-led entry, is ample and dense, with a long finish underpinned by even, smooth tannins. It is a wine that clearly deserved its place in the final taste-offs. The very good Merlot '99 shows softness and suppleness in the mouth, with a stylish, well-balanced progression. It did not get more than Two Glasses because of vegetal notes on the nose and a finish that rather falls away. Le Terrazze del Castello '98 is different in style but very interesting. Evolved tones vie with notes of liquorice, earth and leather in the bouquet. Slightly drying tannins confirm this impression, but the wine shows admirable style and a rigorous, intense finish. The fair Chianti Classico '99 reveals good grip.

●	Syrah '99	▼▼	6
●	Le Terrazze del Castello '98	▼▼	5
●	Merlot '99	▼▼	5
●	Chianti Cl. '99	▼	4
●	Syrah '98	▼▼	5
●	Chianti Cl. '97	▼	4
●	Merlot '98	▼	5

CASTELLINA IN CHIANTI (SI)

CASTELLARE DI CASTELLINA
LOC. CASTELLARE
53011 CASTELLINA IN CHIANTI (SI)
TEL. 0577742903 - 0577740490
E-MAIL: isodi@tin.it

Again, we must congratulate Paolo Panerai, publisher, financier and, first and foremost, passionate wineman at his splendid property, Castellare. But we should also congratulate Alessandro Cellai, the young estate oenologist, for his expert interpretation of the fruit. We did not expect the '98 version of I Sodi di San Niccolò, a blend of sangiovese with a little canaiolo, to be quite so impressive. It was not a very promising vintage, and the rather high altitude of the vineyards made us less than sanguine. But instead this is a wine that may not have the power of the '97, but does have an elegance and balance that thrilled us. You needn't expect enormous concentration or overwhelming force, but you can enjoy complex fruity aromas typical of the sangiovese grape, and a mouthfilling, persistent yet aristocratic flavour. The mostly cabernet sauvignon-based Coniale '98 is good, as are the two Chianti Classico Riserva '99s, of which the selection, Vigna il Poggiale, is the more powerful and well ordered. The Chianti Classico '00 is pleasing and fruity but a bit thin. The barrique-aged whites, the chardonnay-based Canonico '99 and the Spartito '99, a sauvignon, are less successful for both are a touch forward. The good Vin Santo del Classico '96 is a very pleasing traditional sweet white wine, but perhaps just a little rough. We shall review the Poggio ai Merli '00, a pure merlot, next year. The wine is splendid but it's really too young for tasting just yet.

● I Sodi di San Niccolò '98	ΨΨΨ	8
● Coniale '98	ΨΨ	7
● Chianti Cl. Castellare Ris. '99	ΨΨ	5
● Chianti Cl. Vigna il Poggiale Ris. '99	ΨΨ	6
● Chianti Cl. '00	Ψ	4
○ Canonico '99	Ψ	4
○ Spartito '99	Ψ	4
○ Vin Santo del Classico '96	Ψ	7
● Chianti Cl. Vigna il Poggiale Ris. '97	ΨΨΨ	6
● I Sodi di San Niccolò '97	ΨΨΨ	8
● I Sodi di San Niccolò '95	ΨΨ	8
● I Sodi di San Niccolò '96	ΨΨ	8
● Chianti Cl. Ris. '98	ΨΨ	5

CASTELLINA IN CHIANTI (SI)

★ CASTELLO DI FONTERUTOLI
LOC. FONTERUTOLI
VIA OTTONE III, 5
53011 CASTELLINA IN CHIANTI (SI)
TEL. 057773571
E-MAIL: fonterutoli@fonterutoli.it

The vineyards of Castello di Fonterutoli are a joy to behold. If there were a Chianti Classico classification, like the one Napoleon III pushed through in Bordeaux in 1855, these vineyards in the heart of Castellina would all be "premier crus". As we tasted the Chianti Classico Castello di Fonterutoli '99 this year, we could not help thinking, after making the necessary mental adjustments, of certain thrilling Pauillacs, such as Lynch Bages and Latour. Remember that this wine is made mainly from sangiovese, not cabernet sauvignon. This gives you some idea of the fanatically scrupulous vineyard management that produces so much character and structure. These results are, of course, easier to achieve if you put in 50 per cent merlot, as there is in the Siepi '00, a majestic, velvety, concentrated red which has only one defect. It costs a fortune. Less than a great Bordeaux, of course, but a fortune all the same. Whatever the case, there can be no gainsaying our Three Glass scores for each of these wines, which confirm Castello di Fonterutoli as the leading cellar in its area. Meanwhile, don't underestimate the two other wines, the Chianti Classico '00 and the Poggio alla Badiola '01, both mostly from sangiovese. These are not quite such heavyweights as the big two, naturally, but they offer fragrant bouquets of berry fruit and soft, well-rounded palates. The Chianti Classico, not surprisingly, reveals more character and concentration, but "la Badiola", as they affectionately call it at the estate, is one of those quaffable Tuscan reds of which one glass is simply not enough.

● Siepi '00	ΨΨΨ	8
● Chianti Cl. Castello di Fonterutoli '99	ΨΨΨ	8
● Chianti Cl. '00	ΨΨ	6
● Poggio alla Badiola '01	ΨΨ	4
● Siepi '93	ΨΨΨ	8
● Siepi '94	ΨΨΨ	8
● Siepi '95	ΨΨΨ	8
● Siepi '96	ΨΨΨ	8
● Chianti Cl. Castello di Fonterutoli '97	ΨΨΨ	8
● Siepi '97	ΨΨΨ	8
● Siepi '98	ΨΨΨ	8
● Siepi '99	ΨΨΨ	8
● Chianti Cl. Castello di Fonterutoli '98	ΨΨ	8

CASTELLINA IN CHIANTI (SI)

FAMIGLIA CECCHI
LOC. CASINA DEI PONTI, 56
53011 CASTELLINA IN CHIANTI (SI)
TEL. 0577743024
E-MAIL: cecchi@cecchi.net

This year, we have decided to include in the Cecchi family profile only the two estates in Castellina in Chianti, Cecchi and Villa Cerna. The estate in Maremma, Val delle Rose, and the one at San Gimignano, Castello di Montauto, can be found this time among the Other Wineries, partly because they now deserve separate attention (although not so much as the Castellina properties), and because it should make consultation easier. Now we can get down to the wines from Chianti, and there are lots of them. The sangiovese-based Spargolo '99 may have a slightly fuzzy nose, but the palate is balanced, pleasingly rich and fairly full-bodied. La Gavina '99, a cabernet sauvignon, has a distinctly vegetal bouquet and a dense, quite concentrated, palate with a slightly harsh finish. We were not surprised by the good showing of the Chianti Classico '00, which is a clean, harmonious and enjoyable wine that sells at a very reasonable price. The Villa Cerna '00, which is less direct and expansive but offers a greater sense of place, deserves the same high marks. The Messer Piero di Teuzzo '00 is acceptable but not particularly impressive while the Riserva Villa Cerna '99, although coherent, harmonious and well executed, shows less character than we expected. Lastly, it should be noted that the Arcano '01 is a simple, fruity, agreeable wine released at an amazingly consumer-friendly price.

● Chianti Cl. '00	▼▼	4*
● Chianti Cl. Villa Cerna '00	▼▼	4
● Spargolo '99	▼▼	6
● Vigneto La Gavina '99	▼▼	6
● Chianti Cl. Messer Piero di Teuzzo '00	▼	4
● Chianti Colli Senesi Arcano '01	▼	3*
● Chianti Cl. Villa Cerna Ris. '99	▼	5
● Spargolo '97	▽▽	6
● Spargolo '98	▽▽	6
● Chianti Cl. '99	▽▽	3*
● Chianti Cl. Villa Cerna '97	▽	3

CASTELLINA IN CHIANTI (SI)

PODERE COLLELUNGO
LOC. COLLELUNGO
53011 CASTELLINA IN CHIANTI (SI)
TEL. 0577740489
E-MAIL: info@collelungo.com

This was another fine year for Podere Collelungo, one of those estates that might be described as practising "extreme viticulture". The vines are at the considerable altitude of 570 metres above sea level, where it is by no means easy to coax the grapes to ripen fully. The roughly 12 hectares of vines are almost all dedicated to the production of Chianti Classico and there is, for the moment, no cellar IGT or "vino da tavola". The wines we tasted had a consistently high quality and richness of raw material that are surprising, given the conditions in which the fruit struggles to ripen. The Riserva '99 exhibits intensely spicy aromas with clear notes of dark berries and a suggestion of aromatic herbs. The generous palate is dense and the concentrated progression is swathed in a "blanket" of tannins. The finish is still a little unbending. This excellent wine did very well indeed at our final taste-offs. The admirable Chianti Classico '00 offers a fruity bouquet, with oak-derived notes of spice and toastiness, and a rather curious super-ripe undertone. It develops harmoniously on the palate, revealing good extract, well co-ordinated tannins and a clean, pleasing finish. Take a glance at the Glasses below to see just how good this range is.

● Chianti Cl. '00	▼▼	5
● Chianti Cl. Ris. '99	▼▼	8
● Chianti Cl. Roveto '99	▽▽	6
● Chianti Cl. Ris. '97	▽▽	8
● Chianti Cl. Roveto '97	▽▽	4
● Chianti Cl. Ris. '98	▽▽	8
● Chianti Cl. '99	▽▽	4

CASTELLINA IN CHIANTI (SI)

CONCADORO
LOC. CONCADORO, 67
53011 CASTELLINA IN CHIANTI (SI)
TEL. 0577741285
E-MAIL: fconcadoro@chiantinet.it

This year, the pendulum of Guide-related fortune for this Chianti estate swung back in its favour. Concadoro has regained a profile of its own, thanks to very encouraging results at our tastings. Clearly, there is significant potential here. Otherwise the cellar would not be able to reach the heights it sometimes does, but it is also obvious that the winemakers still need to decide exactly what to do with the varying vintages. We were most struck this time by the Riserva '99, which faithfully embodies the characteristics of the sangiovese grape, as grown at Castellina in Chianti. There is a little hesitation at first on the nose, with some not very attractive reduced notes, but these gradually make way for aromas of tobacco and black cherry jam, as well as hints of earth. But the palate is truly eloquent. Powerful and warm on entry, it shows gutsy in mid palate, where robust, succulent tannins come through. The finish, which is faintly dried by oak, is fairly complex and quite distinctive. The Chianti Classico '00, which is similar in style, reveals a nose that is somewhat muffled by vegetal and animal tones, then a very substantial palate with lively tannins and pleasing alcohol-derived warmth. The Vigna di Gaversa '98 is acceptable but less successful, wanting more definition on the nose and showing an over-extracted palate.

• Chianti Cl. Ris. '99	🍷🍷	5
• Chianti Cl. '00	🍷	4
• Chianti Cl. Vigna di Gaversa '98	🍷	4

CASTELLINA IN CHIANTI (SI)

FATTORIA NITTARDI
LOC. NITTARDI, 76
53011 CASTELLINA IN CHIANTI (SI)
TEL. 0577740269
E-MAIL: fattorianittardi@chianticlassico.com

Not many marks separated Peter Femfert's winery from a third Glass and a repetition of last year's triumph with the Riserva '98. Yet, if we were to taste them side by side, the Riserva '99 would probably not drink any less well. Our classifications, however, are in part relative, and it's the part that has to do with the type of wine and the vintage. There can be no doubt that the '99 vintage was much better than its immediate predecessor, as you can observe by comparing the number of Three Glass Chianti Classico '99s against the '98s. All this helps to explain our conclusion that, any appearance to the contrary notwithstanding, Nittardi has this year confirmed the dependably high quality of the cellar's wines. The Riserva '99 is every inch an excellent wine and we greatly appreciated it. The intensity and depth of the nose offers distinct notes of dark berries, spice and flowers. In the mouth, it is soft and concentrated, with smooth, close-knit tannins and a finish nicely underpinned by lively fruit, with pleasing oak-derived notes of vanilla. The Chianti Casanuova '00 is somewhat closed and muffled on the nose, but the palate reveals good flesh and intense, enjoyable fruit-led succulence.

• Chianti Cl. Ris. '99	🍷🍷	7
• Chianti Cl. Casanuova di Nittardi '00	🍷	5
• Chianti Cl. Ris. '98	🍷🍷🍷	7
• Chianti Cl. Ris. '90	🍷🍷	5
• Chianti Cl. Ris. '93	🍷🍷	4
• Chianti Cl. Ris. '94	🍷🍷	5
• Chianti Cl. '95	🍷🍷	4
• Chianti Cl. Ris. '95	🍷🍷	5
• Chianti Cl. '96	🍷🍷	4
• Chianti Cl. Ris. '96	🍷🍷	5
• Chianti Cl. '97	🍷🍷	4
• Chianti Cl. Ris. '97	🍷🍷	5
• Chianti Cl. '98	🍷🍷	4

CASTELLINA IN CHIANTI (SI)

QUERCETO DI CASTELLINA
LOC. QUERCETO, 8
53011 CASTELLINA IN CHIANTI (SI)
TEL. 0577733590
E-MAIL: vino@querceto.com

This Castellina estate has thoroughly earned its debut in the Guide, particularly with the two vintages of Podalirio listed below. We'll start with the '99. A not too intense ruby colour introduces enchanting minty aromas that blend beautifully with notes of chocolate over a fruity backdrop of ripe berry fruit. The entire range of aromas is impeccably clean. The attack on the palate shows the crisp liveliness encouraged by well-judged acidity and a sweet oak-derived tone softening the very robust structure. The long finish is utterly enjoyable. The '00 vintage follows an almost opaque ruby with intense aromas, a ripe vegetal tone combining well with distinct notes of spice-laced coffee. The entry in the mouth, broad and so wonderfully dense it's almost chewy, is memorable. The tannins are well integrated and the finish, although over-oaked, is distinctly pleasing. The Chianti Classico L'Aura '00 shows a ruby colour with lovely purple highlights. The nose offers well-defined fruity notes of redcurrant and blueberry, with a definite suggestion of green peppers. The palate is well-balanced and round, with acidity underpinning the alcohol. The finish, although agreeable, seems a bit short.

● Podalirio '00	🍷🍷	5
● Podalirio '99	🍷🍷	5
● Chianti Cl. L'Aura '00	🍷	4

CASTELLINA IN CHIANTI (SI)

ROCCA DELLE MACÌE
LOC. MACÌE
53011 CASTELLINA IN CHIANTI (SI)
TEL. 05777321
E-MAIL: rocca@roccadellemacie.com

Rocca delle Macìe's first Three Glass award is one of many novelties this year. Some may be surprised, but in fact for the past few years, the Roccato has been a regular attender at our final taste-offs. On more than one occasion, it came within an ace of a top prize. But careful observers will have noted that Sergio Zingarelli's winery has changed gear, and since the vineyards are well-positioned for producing fully ripe grapes, it was almost a foregone conclusion that they would start turning out superior wines. The Roccato '99, made from equal parts of sangiovese and cabernet sauvignon, is dense and concentrated. It shows sound fruit, without any vegetal notes, and is soft and appropriately long in the mouth. The very good sangiovese-based Ser Gioveto offers a round, full flavour that ends with notes of raspberry jam. The Chianti Classico Riserva Fizzano '99 may be less fruity and "demure", but its severity is admirable. The palate is broad, but oak-derived tannins tend to get in the way of the development. The Sant'Alfonso is not very eloquent on the nose but unveils a gutsy determination on the palate. The Riserva '99, with a slightly short finish, just missed getting Two Glasses. The estate's simpler wines, the Chianti Classico '00 and the Morellino Campomaccione '01, are well made and quaffable.

● Roccato '99	🍷🍷🍷	7
● Chianti Cl. Fizzano Ris. '99	🍷🍷	6
● Chianti Cl. Tenuta S. Alfonso '99	🍷🍷	4
● Ser Gioveto '99	🍷🍷	6
● Chianti Cl. '00	🍷	3
● Chianti Cl. Ris. '99	🍷	5
● Morellino di Scansano Campomaccione '01	🍷	4
● Roccato '98	🍷🍷	7
● Roccato '96	🍷🍷	6
● Ser Gioveto '96	🍷🍷	6
● Roccato '97	🍷🍷	6
● Chianti Cl. Fizzano Ris. '98	🍷🍷	5

CASTELLINA IN CHIANTI (SI)

SAN FABIANO CALCINAIA
LOC. CELLOLE
53011 CASTELLINA IN CHIANTI (SI)
TEL. 0577979232
E-MAIL: info@sanfabianocalcinaia.com

Cerviolo Rosso can always be distinguished from other Chianti wines made from similar blends – sangiovese with some cabernet sauvignon and merlot – by its smooth richness, the absence of rough edges on the palate, and great finesse throughout. This is, of course, thanks to Guido Serio, the owner of the estate, and Carlo Ferrini, the oenologist, but part of the credit must go to the extremely propitious site of the vineyards. Unlike many Chianti vineyards, they catch the best of the sunshine and are situated at a favourable altitude. All of these factors combine to produce a magnificent red which, for the fifth consecutive year, has walked away with Three Glasses. The Cerviolo Rosso '00 presents a vivid, rich colour with brilliant highlights and a harmonious bouquet driven by ripe fruit and notes of spice, beautifully complemented by oak. The entry in the mouth is powerful but not aggressive, and an enticing progression with invigorating tannins leads through to a long, elegant finish. The biggest surprise, however, was the Cerviolo Bianco '01, which gave a brilliant performance. It unveils aromatic complexity and a depth on the palate worthy of the best of the world's whites. The two Chianti Classicos also did very nicely. We must admit that we preferred the simpler (at least in theory) version, the Chianti '00, with its lovely fruity body, to the Riserva Cellole, which is good but has gone a bit overboard on the oak.

● Cerviolo Rosso '00	🍷🍷🍷	7
○ Cerviolo Bianco '01	🍷🍷	5
● Chianti Cl. '00	🍷🍷	4
● Chianti Cl. Cellole Ris. '99	🍷🍷	6
● Cerviolo Rosso '96	🍷🍷🍷	6
● Cerviolo Rosso '97	🍷🍷🍷	6
● Cerviolo Rosso '98	🍷🍷🍷	6
● Cerviolo Rosso '99	🍷🍷🍷	6
○ Cerviolo Bianco '00	🍷🍷	5
● Cerviolo Rosso '95	🍷🍷	6
● Chianti Cl. Cellole Ris. '95	🍷🍷	5
● Chianti Cl. Cellole Ris. '97	🍷🍷	5
○ Cerviolo Bianco '98	🍷🍷	5
● Chianti Cl. Cellole Ris. '98	🍷🍷	5
○ Cerviolo Bianco '99	🍷🍷	5

CASTELLINA MARITTIMA (PI)

CASTELLO DEL TERRICCIO
LOC. TERRICCIO
VIA BAGNOLI, 20
56040 CASTELLINA MARITTIMA (PI)
TEL. 050699709
E-MAIL: castello.terriccio@tin.it

The years come and go but the quality of the wines from Terriccio never changes. The estate's Lupicaia, for the sixth consecutive year, has won Three Glasses. This is particularly striking, because in the meanwhile, they have increased production to almost 30,000 bottles and they also release over 100,000 of Tassinaia. Both figures are more than twice what the cellar was turning out a few years ago. It's also an indication of how much larger the vine stock has become. The '00 version of Lupicaia is not a big showy wine. Its virtues are balance, elegance and perfect aromatic definition. The nose offers distinct notes of ripe dark berries, as well as vegetal hints, suggestions of pencil lead and the usual balsamic tone. These, however, are much less assertive than they have been in the past. The very successful Tassinaia '00, a blend of sangiovese, cabernet sauvignon and merlot, offers a bouquet that unveils intense, generous fruit and hints of talcum powder. The palate is soft, well balanced and long, although the finish perhaps lacks complexity. The distinctly varietal sauvignon-based Con Vento '01 offers scents of lavender, peach and rue, then a fresh and elegant, if not extremely long, flavour. On the other hand, the Rondinaia '01, from chardonnay, is not as good as usual. It is less incisive on both nose and palate, although it is well made and agreeable enough.

● Lupicaia '00	🍷🍷🍷	8
● Tassinaia '00	🍷🍷	6
○ Con Vento '01	🍷🍷	4
○ Rondinaia '01	🍷	5
● Lupicaia '93	🍷🍷🍷	8
● Lupicaia '95	🍷🍷🍷	6
● Lupicaia '96	🍷🍷🍷	6
● Lupicaia '97	🍷🍷🍷	6
● Lupicaia '98	🍷🍷🍷	6
● Lupicaia '99	🍷🍷🍷	8
○ Rondinaia '00	🍷🍷	4
● Lupicaia '94	🍷🍷	8
● Tassinaia '97	🍷🍷	5
● Tassinaia '98	🍷🍷	5
● Tassinaia '99	🍷🍷	5

CASTELNUOVO BERARDENGA (SI)

CARPINETA FONTALPINO
FRAZ. MONTEAPERTI
POD. CARPINETA
53019 CASTELNUOVO BERARDENGA (SI)
TEL. 0577369219 - 0577283228
E-MAIL: gioiacresti@interfree.it

Quietly and without fuss, Gioia Cresti came within an inch of earning Three Glasses for her Do Ut Des. But although one regrets that the wine didn't go that half step further, it also has to be conceded that Carpineta Fontalpino has only relatively recently begun to focus on making serious wine. Things, as they say, can only get better. But to get back to the Do Ut Des '00, a classic Supertuscan blend of sangiovese, cabernet sauvignon and merlot. It is, we might say, true to type. Its lively and very intense ruby introduces a concentrated deep bouquet that has yet to develop fully but that already reveals distinct notes of dark berries, chocolate and intense, oak-derived toastiness. The palate is dense and full-bodied, flaunting the dynamic thrust and richness of ripe fruit without the slightest vegetal hint. And the finish is just as vigorous, despite rather noticeable wood. Still, a few months in the bottle should deal with that problem satisfactorily. What intrigues us particularly is the character of the wine, which at the moment only sketchily drawn.
Nevertheless, there is already a distinctive quality that speaks of the typical vibrancy of the terroir, an acidic grip and tannic tension, well covered by the fruit, that give the wine a sense of place, whatever grapes have gone into it. The Chianti Colli Senesi '01 plays second fiddle, of course, but it is not wanting in body or character.

CASTELNUOVO BERARDENGA (SI)

CASTELLO DI BOSSI
LOC. BOSSI IN CHIANTI, 28
53019 CASTELNUOVO BERARDENGA (SI)
TEL. 0577359330 - 0577359048
E-MAIL: info@castellodibossi.it

Castello di Bossi's remarkable performance suggests that it is on the point of joining the ranks of the finest estates in Chianti Classico. This year's triumph was not altogether unexpected, since the cellar started doggedly pursuing high quality a few years ago. The arrival of Alberto Antonini in the cellar, and of Federico Curtaz among the vines, added further impetus and made it possible to take full advantage of the potential of the Bossi zone, as the results below show. The Corbaia won its first Three Glasses, but the Girolamo was not far behind it. The classic Corbaia '99, from sangiovese and cabernet sauvignon, perfectly combines the energy of the raw material with faultless execution. The nose foregrounds oak-derived toasty and spicy notes layered over an undertone of dark berries. The palate is concentrated, elegant and even, with succulent, perfectly integrated tannins. The splendid merlot-based Girolamo '99 displays dense, deep aromas of black berries with toasty hints of oak. It is immediately powerful on the palate, where it exhibits fantastic volume and smooth, tight-knit tannins. The finish is long and delightfully spicy. But we were almost forgetting to mention two excellent Chianti Classicos, both of which made it to our finals. Round and full-bodied, they are instantly recognizable from the curious notes of talcum powder in the bouquet of the Berardo, and of black cherry jam in the Classico '00.

● Do Ut Des '00	ΥΥ	6
● Chianti dei Colli Senesi '01	Υ	4
● Do Ut Des '99	ΥΥ	6
● Do Ut Des '97	ΥΥ	4
● Do Ut Des '98	ΥΥ	4
● Chianti Colli Senesi Gioia '99	ΥΥ	4
● Chianti Colli Senesi Gioia '97	Υ	3
● Chianti Colli Senesi Gioia '98	Υ	3

● Corbaia '99	ΥΥΥ	8
● Chianti Cl. '00	ΥΥ	5*
● Chianti Cl. Berardo Ris. '99	ΥΥ	6
● Girolamo '99	ΥΥ	8
● Chianti Cl. '99	ΥΥ	4*
● Corbaia '94	ΥΥ	8
● Chianti Cl. Berardo Ris. '95	ΥΥ	5
● Chianti Cl. Ris. '95	ΥΥ	4
● Corbaia '95	ΥΥ	8
● Chianti Cl. Berardo Ris. '96	ΥΥ	5
● Corbaia '98	ΥΥ	8
● Girolamo '98	ΥΥ	8

CASTELNUOVO BERARDENGA (SI)

FATTORIE CHIGI SARACINI
VIA DELL'ARBIA, 2
53019 CASTELNUOVO BERARDENGA (SI)
TEL. 0577355113
E-MAIL: e.fattoriechigi@mps.it

Fattorie Chigi Saracini continues its confident upward trend, although we mustn't be impatient. The old plots have been replanted and new vineyards planted but it goes without saying that in viticulture, you have to be patient. We're going to have to wait a little longer to make a definitive assessment. Nevertheless, some promising signs do seem to be arriving, and rather faster than we had expected. The Poggiassai '00, from sangiovese, with ten per cent cabernet sauvignon, has already demonstrated its ability to compete with champions. It shows a very intense garnet-ruby hue and concentrated aromas of berry fruit with toasty notes of oak. After a powerful, broad entry, the palate picks up momentum and intensity, finishing long, if still distinctly oaky. This is the best red the cellar has ever produced, and must open new horizons for the estate. The standard Chianti label has been redesigned, and now proudly bears the name Villa Chigi. But it's what's inside that counts, and it seemed to us that the wine is more successful and better defined than usual, with clear-cut, fragrant aromas of berry fruit and a well-balanced palate. There's also good body and a certain amount of character.

• Il Poggiassai '00	🍷🍷	5*
• Chianti Villa Chigi '01	🍷	3*
• Il Poggiassai '97	🍷🍷	4
• Il Poggiassai '98	🍷🍷	4
• Il Poggiassai '99	🍷🍷	5*

CASTELNUOVO BERARDENGA (SI)

FATTORIA DI DIEVOLE
FRAZ. VAGLIAGLI
LOC. DIEVOLE
53019 CASTELNUOVO BERARDENGA (SI)
TEL. 0577322613 - 0577322712
E-MAIL: dievole@iol.it

Dievole is particularly blessed among Chianti Classico estates in its mesoclimate, soil and exposure, all of which are extremely propitious for the cultivation of the vine. We used to feel that they were not taking sufficient advantage of all these advantages and have, in fact, been somewhat critical in the past. We would really like, from now on, to be able to describe the great wines of Dievole, instead of admiring qualities that are only good. Having observed the increasing ability and notable commitment at the helm, we feel the time is ripe for a great leap forward. This year's wines are very good and reliable, with the most positive signs coming from the most recent bottle of those presented, the Chianti Classico '00. The colour is very intense and the bouquet is a confident blend of red and black berry fruit, lifted by notes of oak. The development on the palate is rounded, mouthfilling and balanced. The finish may not be a paragon of depth and complexity, but that would be asking a little too much from a wine of this type. The Classico Novecento Riserva '98 did quite well, too, despite some less than enchanting reduced notes on the nose. But nothing of the sort carries over onto the palate, which is dense and full-bodied, with nicely integrated tannins. To conclude, the sangiovese-based Broccato '99, with its jammy nose and full-bodied, if not very characterful, palate, came close to earning a second Glass.

• Chianti Cl. '00	🍷🍷	4
• Chianti Cl. Novecento '98	🍷🍷	5
• Broccato '99	🍷	5
• Chianti Cl. Novecento '97	🍷🍷	4
• Broccato '98	🍷	5

CASTELNUOVO BERARDENGA (SI)

★ Fattoria di Felsina
S. S. 484 Chiantigiana
53019 Castelnuovo Berardenga (SI)
Tel. 0577355117
E-mail: felsina@data.it

What more can we say about Fattoria di Felsina? We have already used up all the available flattering adjectives on Giuseppe Mazzocolin and his staff. But there is something to be added. Felsina, not content with the wonderfully dependable excellence it has shown in recent years, has somehow managed to make a further effort. As a result, the wines now have perceptibly more individual character and solidity. The Fontalloro '99, for example, is probably one of the finest versions we've ever tasted. It's a Sangiovese of great breeding that reveals elegance, complexity and exceptional length. The nose is an exemplary mix of violet, plum, pepper and spice, and the body is firm and full. The Rancia '99, meanwhile, shows its usual distinguished character. The nose is not very eloquent, but it shows a minerally character, complemented by notes of oak. The palate is vigorous, energetic and dense, but wood tannins are holding it back. The Chardonnay I Sistri '00, for the first time in years, is very good. Scents of honey and chamomile layered over an intriguing mineral undertone lead into a rich, intense finish that may not be very long but is well put together and reasonably complex. The '00 edition of the Chianti Classico does not disappoint. It is a vibrantly invigorating, juicy red with just slightly over-assertive oak. We end with the excellent Vin Santo '93, which has well-defined, varietal fragrances of almonds, candied peel and dried flowers, then a very sweet, concentrated flavour.

CASTELNUOVO BERARDENGA (SI)

Pacina
Loc. Pacina
53019 Castelnuovo Berardenga (SI)
Tel. 0577355044 - 0577352040
E-mail: pacinina@libero.it

Since both of its wines won Two Glasses, Pacina has earned itself a profile of its own. This is quite an achievement, as the competition in Tuscany is already fierce, and other new, promising wineries keep springing up. But Giovanna Tiezzi's wines this year were so clearly right on the mark that we would like to describe them at greater length. The very good Malena '00, from equal parts of sangiovese and syrah, presents an intense ruby hue with violet highlights, the first sign of the wine's concentration and freshness. The deep bouquet reveals a rich fruity base, with some faint, fleeting hints of reduction. The palate is dense yet vibrant, with lively, succulent tannins and lots of energy in the finish. This version, the best yet, very nearly made it to our final taste-offs. The Chianti Colli Senesi '99, always the estate's signature wine, has an entirely different style. On the nose, for instance, the aromas emerge more slowly, revealing mineral and earthy notes and hints of sweet tobacco. The palate is firm and well-sustained, richness alternating with austerity in a lively counterpoint, while the oak stays discreetly in the background. The sangiovese grape makes its presence felt in a certain dryness and occasional hardness, but also lends a special character that it takes time to appreciate. It's well worth the wait.

● Fontalloro '99	🍷🍷🍷	6
● Chianti Cl. Rancia Ris. '99	🍷🍷	6
● Chianti Cl. '00	🍷🍷	4
○ I Sistri '00	🍷🍷	4
○ Vin Santo del Chianti Classico '93	🍷🍷	6
● Fontalloro '86	🍷🍷🍷	5
● Fontalloro '88	🍷🍷🍷	5
● Chianti Cl. Rancia Ris. '90	🍷🍷🍷	5
● Fontalloro '90	🍷🍷🍷	5
● Maestro Raro '91	🍷🍷🍷	5
● Chianti Cl. Rancia Ris. '93	🍷🍷🍷	5
● Fontalloro '93	🍷🍷🍷	6
● Maestro Raro '93	🍷🍷🍷	6
● Fontalloro '95	🍷🍷🍷	6
● Fontalloro '97	🍷🍷🍷	6
● Fontalloro '98	🍷🍷🍷	6

● Malena '00	🍷🍷	5
● Chianti dei Colli Senesi '99	🍷🍷	4
● Chianti Colli Senesi '98	🍷🍷	4
● Malena '98	🍷	4

CASTELNUOVO BERARDENGA (SI)

FATTORIA DI PETROIO
LOC. QUERCEGROSSA
VIA DI MOCENNI, 7
53010 CASTELNUOVO BERARDENGA (SI)
TEL. 0577328045 - 066798883
E-MAIL: pamela.lenzi@tiscalinet.it

Professor Lenzi's estate is a stronghold of sangiovese and Chianti Classico. Only two wines are produced, both, naturally, true, blue-blooded Chianti Classicos. For the time being, at least, there is no room for Supertuscans at Fattoria di Petroio. The cellar's goal is not just to produce ever better wines, but also to imbue each bottle with absolute respect for the local terroir. It is, of course, true that conditions here are perfect for ripening the sangiovese grape, since the gloriously aspected vineyards are at an altitude of 350 metres in the southernmost part of Chianti. Results at this year's tastings were interesting, as well as excellent, particularly from the Riserva, which easily made it to the national finals. Curiously enough, the Chianti Classico '00 did less brilliantly. It's pleasant enough but doesn't pack much punch. The nose is not very eloquent and the palate, though soft and accommodating, fails to show its usual grip. The tannins are not sufficiently covered by the fruit and tend to be prominent. But this sort of thing can happen, especially with a tricky vintage like the '00. In contrast, the Riserva '99 is very good. The vibrantly intense, brilliant ruby is a guarantee on its own, then the clearly defined bouquet flaunts cherry and black cherry jam, with just a hint of oak. The palate is broad, powerful and solid, with plenty of support through to the finish.

● Chianti Cl. Ris. '99	♥♥	6
● Chianti Cl. '00	♥	4
● Chianti Cl. Ris. '97	♥♥♥	5
● Chianti Cl. '93	♥♥	2
● Chianti Cl. '95	♥♥	3
● Chianti Cl. Ris. '95	♥♥	4
● Chianti Cl. '96	♥♥	3
● Chianti Cl. Ris. '96	♥♥	4
● Chianti Cl. '97	♥♥	3
● Chianti Cl. '98	♥♥	4
● Chianti Cl. Ris. '98	♥♥	5
● Chianti Cl. '99	♥♥	4*

CASTELNUOVO BERARDENGA (SI)

POGGIO BONELLI
LOC. POGGIO BONELLI
53019 CASTELNUOVO BERARDENGA (SI)
TEL. 0577355382
E-MAIL: pogbon@tin.it

Poggio Bonelli is one of the wine estates that belong to the Monte dei Paschi di Siena banking group, whose Tuscan holdings also include Tenute Chigi Saracini. Poggio Bonelli lies a little to the south of Castelnuovo Berardenga and covers 50 hectares, 15 of which are planted to vine, particularly sangiovese, cabernet sauvignon and merlot. A few years ago, the cellar launched a most promising programme of conversion and revitalization. The results are already very encouraging. The Chianti Classico '00, for instance, is a fine example of its kind, but that doesn't mean it is insignificant or wanting in character. It's a fruity red with light vegetal hints on the nose and a soft, pleasing flavour, offering very decent body and an attractive tannic weave. The Riserva '99 made an equally good impression. The bouquet is slightly overwhelmed by oak, but the wine opens out on the palate to reveal ripe fruit, tight structure and well-integrated tannins. The Tramonto d'Oca '00 is made, starting with this vintage, from four parts sangiovese to one of merlot. It offers aromas of dark berries and pencil lead, with some vegetal notes. In the mouth, the medium body is attractively even and balanced. Entry on the palate is soft, developing with impeccable consistency, and the finish neatly mirrors the aromas on the nose.

● Chianti Cl. '00	♥♥	4
● Tramonto d'Oca '00	♥♥	6
● Chianti Cl. Ris. '99	♥♥	5
● Tramonto d'Oca '99	♥♥	6

CASTELNUOVO BERARDENGA (SI)

SAN FELICE
LOC. SAN FELICE
53019 CASTELNUOVO BERARDENGA (SI)
TEL. 05773991
E-MAIL: info@agricolasanfelice.it

At this year's tastings, there was no Vigorello, one of the original Supertuscans, but San Felice has more than one string to its bow. Thus the Chianti Classicos, and particularly the two Riservas, were able to strut their stuff, without fear of being upstaged. The Riserva Poggio Rosso '99 is back on form, taking advantage of all the blessings of the '99 vintage. After initial uncertainty with some sulphurous notes on the nose, it opens out with aromas of red berries and mineral tones. The attack on the palate is powerful and vigorous, the progression dense and the finish just a bit hard. The wine has no end of energy and character, and should age very well. The Riserva Il Grigio '99, although not so complex or individual, is still a very good wine. The nose is still a bit dumb and over-oaked, but the palate is soft, rich and fairly concentrated, if slightly rough on the finish. The Vin Santo '97 is classic in style and not too sweet. Scents of nuts dominate the bouquet, while in the mouth, a measured sweetness and good balance lead to a slightly dry, almost tannic finish of appealing austerity. The Belcaro '01, again an agreeable wine, reveals medium body and attractive crisp acidity. The Chianti Classico '00, however, with its somewhat bitter finish, is not altogether successful.

CASTELNUOVO BERARDENGA (SI)

CASTELLO DI SELVOLE
FRAZ. VAGLIAGLI - LOC. SELVOLE, 1
53019 CASTELNUOVO BERARDENGA (SI)
TEL. 0577322662
E-MAIL: selvole@selvole.com

This year, Guido Busetto's estate easily placed two of its three competing wines in our final taste-offs. And there was only the slimmest of margins separating the cellar from at least one Three Glass award, a sign that the vineyards here are starting to produce really reliable grapes, whatever the vintage. Cellar technique, too, has become more consistent and focused, thanks in part to the appearance there of Stefano Porcinai, formerly the oenologist at the Consorzio del Chianti Classico. So things are going well, and the future looks rosy. The Riserva '99 offers notes of dark berries and spicy oak on the nose. The palate is remarkable for its volume, massive structure and continuity. The fruit is well supported by unobtrusive oak and the finish is long, warm and powerful. The very fine Chianti Classico '00 displays a deep bouquet in which oak has the upper hand. The palate is solid and well proportioned, with lively tannins and an intense finish. This time, the Chianti Classicos outperformed the Supertuscan Barullo '98, which offers fragrances of blackcurrant, blackberry and toasty oak, as well as vegetal hints. The palate is refreshing, fairly dense and concentrated, and the finish is a little bit tannic.

● Chianti Cl. Poggio Rosso Ris. '99	ΥΥ	6
○ Vin Santo '97	ΥΥ	5
● Chianti Cl. Il Grigio Ris. '99	ΥΥ	5
○ Belcaro '01	Υ	3
● Chianti Cl. '00		4
● Vigorello '88	ΥΥΥ	5
● Chianti Cl. Poggio Rosso Ris. '90	ΥΥΥ	6
● Vigorello '97	ΥΥΥ	5
● Vigorello '98	ΥΥ	6
○ Belcaro '00	ΥΥ	3*
● Chianti Cl. Poggio Rosso Ris. '97	ΥΥ	5
● Chianti Cl. Il Grigio Ris. '98	ΥΥ	4

● Chianti Cl. '00	ΥΥ	3*
● Chianti Cl. Ris. '99	ΥΥ	5
● Barullo '98	ΥΥ	6
● Chianti Cl. '99	ΥΥ	3
● Chianti Cl. Ris. '96	ΥΥ	5
● Barullo '97	ΥΥ	6
● Chianti Cl. '98	ΥΥ	4

CASTELNUOVO BERARDENGA (SI)

VILLA ARCENO
LOC. ARCENO
53019 CASTELNUOVO BERARDENGA (SI)
TEL. 0577359346

Unquestionably, the best results at Villa Arceno come from cabernet sauvignon. There's no secret about why this should be so. The estate belongs to the Californian Kendall-Jackson group, whose experience with the grape is extensive, but that's not all. The magnificent position of Villa Arceno and its generous exposure to sunlight are ideal for ripening grapes, cabernet in particular, to perfection. And once again, after last year's excellent Cabernet Sauvignon '99, it is another cabernet, the Pozzo di San Donato, that heads the list this time. The '99 shows a vivid, brilliant colour, introducing a slightly muffled nose that can nonetheless offer attractively intense fruit. The palate is very solid, concentrated and expressive from the start, and the long and juicy finish reveals fine-grained tannins. It's a lovely red that stands head and shoulders above the others. The Arguzzio '99 is good, despite a somewhat uncertain and not very well-defined bouquet. In the mouth, it reveals softness and fair body. The Syrah '00 also displays some sulphurous odours, together with hints of forwardness that brought its score down, in spite of remarkable extract. The Merlot '99 is not overly successful either, because of vegetal and over-evolved tones on both nose and palate. Lastly, the Chianti Classico Riserva '99 is unfocused and somewhat bitter.

CHIUSI (SI)

COLLE SANTA MUSTIOLA
VIA DELLE TORRI, 86/A
53043 CHIUSI (SI)
TEL. 057863462

We hadn't tasted any Santa Mustiola wines for some time. When we did finally get round to them again, the experience was a revelation. We found ourselves wondering what had been going on in this southern part of the province of Siena. Estate owner, Fabio Cenni, is as keen and competent as he is uncommunicative. This is a small property – little more than four hectares under vine – but it's full of promise and worth keeping an eye on. It is almost entirely planted to sangiovese, with a little space set aside for, which accounts for five per cent of the blend in the Poggio ai Chiari, the cellar's only wine. The soil here is ideally suited to the sangiovese grape, and makes the most particularly of the variety's finesse and character. All this was evident at our tastings, where the '99 made a very good impression and the '00 quite bowled us over. But let's consider the bottles in chronological order. The '99 exhibits a garnet-ruby hue and immediate aromas of black cherry and spice, mingling with a less elegant animal scent. The palate is well balanced and soft throughout, with an almost Bordeaux style and a remarkable final thrust. The excellent '00 offers a well-defined nose with notes of black cherry and sour cherry jam. The unifying sweetness of the fruit and the characteristically vibrant energy of sangiovese come together in a delicious counterpoint on the palate, which also reveals smooth tannins and an intense, deep finish.

● Pozzo di San Donato '99	ΨΨ	6
● Arguzzio '99	ΨΨ	4
● Syrah '00	Ψ	5
● Merlot '99	Ψ	5
● Chianti Cl. Ris. '99		5
● Cabernet Sauvignon '99	ΨΨ	5
● Syrah '99	ΨΨ	5
● Arguzzio '98	Ψ	4

● Poggio ai Chiari '00	ΨΨ	5
● Poggio ai Chiari '99	ΨΨ	5

COLLE DI VAL D'ELSA (SI)

Fattoria Il Palagio
Fraz. Castel S. Gimignano
Loc. Il Palagio
53030 Colle di Val d'Elsa (SI)
tel. 0577953004
e-mail: info@ilpalagio.it

For some years now the Zonin family, with the help of 120 hectares at Il Palagio and the expertise of the oenologist Walter Sovran, has been playing an important role at San Gimignano in terms of both quality and quantity, especially where white wines are concerned. Let's start with the Vernaccia La Gentilesca selection, from the Fattoria dell'Abbazia Monteoliveto vineyards, which offers intense aromas of vanilla and tropical banana and pineapple fruit. In the mouth, it shows good structure and notable body and length, with citrus fruit coming through on the finish. The two monovarietals also did very well. The Chardonnay displays notes of white peach and tangerine on the nose and a fresh, crisp, succulent palate. It's very lively and enjoyable, with good nose-palate consistency and a lovely finish that signs off with notes of ripe pear. The Sauvignon, which is very nearly as good, is admirably varietal. A pale straw yellow introduces varietal scents of tropical fruit, pink grapefruit and tomato leaf. The soft, consistent flavour finishes with some lightly sweet notes. This is not a very complex wine but it is extremely agreeable. Both these whites are also great bargains. The other two wines on offer, the fresh, quaffable Vernaccia di San Gimignano and the very simple but pleasantly fruity Chianti dei Colli Senesi, are well typed and impeccably made.

CORTONA (AR)

Tenimenti Luigi D'Alessandro
Fraz. Camucia
Via di Manzano, 15
52042 Cortona (AR)
tel. 0575618667
e-mail: tenimenti.dalessandro@flashnet.it

Time flies, and occasionally we forget that, in the wine world, the pace has been hotting up even more over the past ten years. The d'Alessandro brothers wisely point out that between 1990 and 2002, they planted a good 48 hectares to vine at their estate. The planting density – considered at the start almost foolhardy – is 7,000 vines per hectare. Not content with this, they planted the most recent ten hectares at a density of 8,500 vines per hectare. There has also been a label change. The Vescovo has turned into Vescovo II, because the wine has become the "second vin" of Il Bosco. Like its big brother, it is now a monovarietal syrah. This year's tastings revealed an excellent version of Il Bosco, which is probably one of the best ever. The deep nose offers generous aromas of perfectly ripe fruit and plum jam and notes of spice. The palate is soft, fresh, elegant, dense and concentrated, and the oak is beautifully integrated into the long, lingering finish. The Vin Santo '94 is also a great wine. Its brilliant amber ushers in a warm, broad bouquet of aromatic notes that range from damson jam and fig to chestnut honey. In the mouth, it is very sweet, dense, succulent and persistent. The Fontarca '01, from chardonnay and viognier, is another very successful bottle. The nose reveals intense, almost exotic, scents of wild flowers and lavender. The nicely rounded, harmonious flavour is most enjoyable. The Vescovo II '01 displays some forward notes and not very stylish oak on the nose, but the well-extracted palate makes up for this.

○ Il Palagio Chardonnay '01	♀♀	3*
○ Il Palagio Sauvignon '01	♀♀	3*
○ Vernaccia di S. Gimignano La Gentilesca '01	♀♀	4
● Chianti Colli Senesi '01	♀	3
○ Vernaccia di S. Gimignano Abbazia di Monteoliveto '01	♀	3
○ Il Palagio Sauvignon '00	♀♀	3*
○ Vernaccia di S. Gimignano La Gentilesca '00	♀♀	4
○ Vernaccia di S. Gimignano La Gentilesca '98	♀♀	4
○ Vernaccia di S. Gimignano La Gentilesca '99	♀♀	4

● Cortona Il Bosco '00	♀♀	6
○ Vin Santo '94	♀♀	6
○ Cortona Fontarca '01	♀♀	5*
● Vescovo II '01	♀	4
● Podere Il Bosco '95	♀♀♀	5
● Podere Il Bosco '97	♀♀♀	5
● Podere Il Bosco '99	♀♀	6
○ Podere Fontarca '00	♀♀	4*
○ Vin Santo '93	♀♀	5
○ Podere Fontarca '94	♀♀	4
● Podere Il Bosco '96	♀♀	5
○ Podere Fontarca '98	♀♀	4
● Podere Il Bosco '98	♀♀	5
○ Podere Fontarca '99	♀♀	4

FAUGLIA (PI)

I GIUSTI E ZANZA
VIA DEI PUNTONI, 9
56043 FAUGLIA (PI)
TEL. 058544354
E-MAIL: igiustiezanza@tin.it

There are no major changes to report from Paolo Giusti and Fabio Zanza's estate. Both wines again soared past the Two Glass threshold and the panel's assessments were very much on a par with performances in recent years. However, we have begun to detect more of a difference in quality between the more ambitious flagship wine, the Dulcamara, and their other wine, Belcore. This year, the former very nearly made it to the Three Glass finals. A blend of cabernet sauvignon and merlot, it shows a very dark ruby hue and a fragrance based on ripe fruit. The palate is full-bodied, broad and nicely underpinned by oak, as well as by the abundant fruit. A decline in intensity on the back palate reveals the current limitations of the Dulcamara '99 in terms of depth and complexity. Nevertheless, it should be noted that these are very minor defects in the context of a generally very positive performance. The Belcore '00, from sangiovese and merlot, is very pleasing, as we have come to expect. The nose is less well-defined than in previous versions, but the palate offers delicious fruit, good balance and smooth, well-integrated tannins.

● Belcore '00	🍷🍷	4
● Dulcamara '99	🍷🍷	6
● Dulcamara '97	🍷🍷	5
● Belcore '98	🍷🍷	4
● Dulcamara '98	🍷🍷	6
● Belcore '99	🍷🍷	4*

FIRENZE

★ MARCHESI ANTINORI
P.ZZA DEGLI ANTINORI, 3
50123 FIRENZE
TEL. 05523595
E-MAIL: antinori@antinori.it

It may well not be overstating the case to say that this is the most important producer in Italy, in terms of the quality of wines produced, product image and marketing impact. Antinori is known and respected not only in Italy, but throughout the wine-loving world. In this review, we will deal only with the wines from the headquarters in Florence, but the group now brings together a large number of other estates, including Prunotto in Piedmont, Tormaresca in Puglia, La Braccesca at Montepulciano, Pian delle Vigne at Montalcino, Tenuta Belvedere at Bolgheri and Castello della Sala in Umbria. Soon, we shall be hearing more about the winery in Franciacorta and Antinori now also have a property in California, Atlas Peak. In the 16-year history of the Guide, Marchesi Antinori has notched up 33 Three Glass awards. This year, the various group wineries added another four top awards to the list: Cervaro della Sala '00, Barolo Bussia '98 from Prunotto, the red Masseria Maime '00 from Tormaresca and, in Tuscany, the Antinori pride and joy, the extraordinary Solaia '99. Made from cabernet sauvignon with a little sangiovese, it again delights with its customary elegance, complexity and concentration. The Chianti Classico Tenute del Marchese Riserva '99 is very good, and in fact scored even higher marks than the Tignanello '99. The Chianti Classico Badia a Passignano Riserva '99 lives up to its reputation with one of the finest versions in recent years. The Chianti Classico Villa Antinori Riserva '99 is surprisingly good. The Chianti Classico Peppoli '00 is pleasing and fragrant.

● Solaia '99	🍷🍷🍷	8
● Chianti Cl. Badia a Passignano Ris. '99	🍷🍷	6
● Chianti Cl. Tenute del Marchese Ris. '99	🍷🍷	5
● Chianti Cl. Pèppoli '00	🍷🍷	4
● Chianti Cl. Villa Antinori Ris. '99	🍷🍷	4
● Tignanello '99	🍷🍷	8
● Solaia '90	🍷🍷🍷	8
● Tignanello '93	🍷🍷🍷	8
● Solaia '95	🍷🍷🍷	8
● Chianti Cl. Badia a Passignano Ris. '97	🍷🍷🍷	5
● Solaia '97	🍷🍷🍷	8
● Solaia '98	🍷🍷🍷	8

FIRENZE

TENUTE
AMBROGIO E GIOVANNI FOLONARI
VIA DE' BARDI, 28
50125 FIRENZE
TEL. 055200281
E-MAIL: folonari@tenutefolonari.com

The most important news this year from the Tenute Ambrogio e Giovanni Folonari is that they have acquired a new property, La Fuga at Montalcino, which we review in the Other Wineries section. The second most important piece of news is the release of a new wine, available only in magnums, Cabreomytho '00, from sangiovese and cabernet sauvignon. The new boy made it to our finals and nearly won Three Glasses. Very little is produced, so getting hold of it could be a problem, but this elegant, concentrated, very modern wine is definitely interesting. The good Il Pareto '99, from Tenuta di Nozzole, obtained almost entirely from cabernet sauvignon, is still young and shows some tannic rough edges. The Chianti Classico La Forra Riserva '99 is reliable and soft, showing its customary slightly super-ripe notes. We were pleasantly surprised by the predominantly chardonnay-based Le Bruniche '01. A mild vanilla tone, with notes of pear and apple on the nose, leads to a soft, enticing and long palate. The more problematic La Pietra '00 is another chardonnay, but this time fermented and aged in barrique. A little woody, it reveals a confident, broad and persistent flavour, but there are forward, super-ripe signs. The quaffable, fragrant Chianti Classico Nozzole '00 is very agreeable. However, the Cabreo Il Borgo '00 will appear in our next edition. It is really too young to be judged this year.

FIRENZE

MARCHESI DE' FRESCOBALDI
VIA S. SPIRITO, 11
50125 FIRENZE
TEL. 05527141
E-MAIL: info@frescobaldi.it

Six different profiles in this edition of the Guide deal with estates wholly or partially owned by Marchesi de' Frescobaldi; Luce and Ornellaia, which are both co-owned by the American Mondavi group; Castelgiocondo at Montalcino; Tenuta Castiglioni in the Colli Fiorentini; Attems in Friuli; and the Florence-based headquarters we review here. This is a full-scale viticultural empire, ruled with ever-greater assurance by Lamberto Frescobaldi, who is assisted by Giovanni Geddes, manager of the company, and the oenologist Nicolò d'Afflitto. This was a banner year. There was a Three Glass award for the Giramonte '00 from Tenuta Castiglioni, as well as those for Masseto and Ornellaia at Bolgheri. The big boys were followed by a raft of wines that did really well, perhaps more and better than in any previous year. The Chianti Rufina Montesodi '00, despite its extreme youth, made it to our finals thanks to its trademark elegance. The Mormoreto '99, a cabernet sauvignon, did the same with its aristocratic, powerful character. The Pomino Il Benefizio '00, which may have been the first Italian white to be fermented and aged in barrique (its first vintage, if we're not mistaken, was '78), is dense, mouthfilling and concentrated. Even the Pomino Bianco '01, a straightforward, fragrant wine, is particularly good, as is the Pomino Rosso '99. The Chianti Rufina Nipozzano Riserva '99, on the other hand, has a slightly muffled on the nose.

● Cabreomytho '00	🍷🍷	8
● Il Pareto '99	🍷🍷	7
○ Cabreo La Pietra '00	🍷🍷	6
● Chianti Cl. Nozzole '00	🍷🍷	4
○ Le Bruniche '01	🍷🍷	2*
● Chianti Cl. La Forra Ris. '99	🍷🍷	5
● Il Pareto '88	🍷🍷🍷	7
● Chianti Cl. La Forra Ris. '90	🍷🍷🍷	5
● Il Pareto '90	🍷🍷🍷	7
● Il Pareto '93	🍷🍷🍷	7
● Il Pareto '97	🍷🍷🍷	7
● Il Pareto '98	🍷🍷🍷	7

● Chianti Rufina Montesodi '00	🍷🍷	7
● Mormoreto '99	🍷🍷	7
○ Pomino Il Benefizio '00	🍷🍷	5
○ Pomino Bianco '01	🍷🍷	4*
● Pomino Rosso '99	🍷🍷	5
● Chianti Rufina Nipozzano Ris. '99	🍷	5
● Pomino Rosso '85	🍷🍷🍷	5
● Chianti Rufina Montesodi '88	🍷🍷🍷	7
● Chianti Rufina Montesodi '90	🍷🍷🍷	7
● Chianti Rufina Montesodi '96	🍷🍷🍷	7
● Chianti Rufina Montesodi '97	🍷🍷🍷	7
● Mormoreto '97	🍷🍷🍷	6
● Chianti Rufina Montesodi '99	🍷🍷🍷	7
○ Pomino Il Benefizio '99	🍷🍷	5

FOIANO DELLA CHIANA (AR)

Fattoria Santa Vittoria
Loc. Pozzo
Via Piana, 43
52045 Foiano della Chiana (AR)
tel. 057566807 - 0575966026
e-mail: marnicc@@iol.it

Santa Vittoria's wines maintained their usual good standard, although we are still waiting for that final surge into the top bracket. It is true, however, that the Niccolai family have their feet planted firmly on the ground at their estate near Arezzo. Some small steps forward have been made and the cellar has remained true to its altogether reasonable, unpretentious pricing policy. The Scannagallo, a blend of sangiovese and cabernet sauvignon, is the top of the range again in its '00 version. The dense aromas focus on pleasingly ripe dark berries. The palate is soft and harmonious, with a gradual but constant development to a finish that, if still a bit coarse, is fairly long. We also tasted two vintages of their Poggio al Tempio, made from four parts sangiovese to one part merlot. They are in many ways similar, although the '00 is, naturally, more evolved. Its not very eloquent nose reveals a light vegetal tone, and the palate is reasonably dense. The more invigorating and fruity '01 boasts attractive succulence and crisp acidity. The Vin Santo is, as usual, very successful, with its intense amber hue, ripe bouquet of nuts and chestnuts and sweet, very concentrated, lingering palate. We were somewhat less enamoured of the Grechetto '01, but generally speaking, we weren't complaining.

FUCECCHIO (FI)

Fattoria Montellori
Via Pistoiese, 1
50054 Fucecchio (FI)
tel. 0571260641
e-mail: montellori@tin.it

Full marks to Fattoria Montellori for managing to keep up its high standards, despite its isolated location in a sort of no man's land. Fucecchio and the nearby Montalbano area do not have the critical mass of good local growers that attracts attention. Although the tastings this time were not extraordinarily brilliant. Still, such years will occur, and we feel confident that Montellori will soon be showing the results that the dynamic dedication of its owner, Alessandro Nieri, deserves. In the meantime, Alessandro has entrusted technical management to Andrea Paoletti and Danny Schuster, both of whom won their spurs in the vineyard before they turned to the cellar. The Salamartano '99 gave a mixed performance. Some samples we tasted seemed to be suffering from cork problems, while other bottles did quite well, if not exceptionally. The dense, invigorating Castelrapiti '99 reveals a distinct sangiovese character, but has a slight tannic astringency on the finish. The agreeable sauvignon-based Sant'Amato '01 offers distinct aromas of peach and tropical fruit. The Montellori Brut '97, one of the rare successful examples of a classic "spumante" made in Tuscany, is fragrant and, as usual, carefully executed. The Chianti '01 and the Vigne del Moro '00 are both properly made and enjoyable, although the latter has more body. But neither the Vin Santo '96 nor the Vigne del Mandorlo '01 is particularly striking.

● Scannagallo '00	♛♛	4
○ Vin Santo '93	♛♛	5
● Val di Chiana Poggio del Tempio '00	♛	3*
● Val di Chiana Poggio del Tempio '01	♛	3*
○ Val di Chiana Grechetto '01		3
○ Vin Santo '95	♛♛	5
○ Vin Santo '96	♛♛	5
● Scannagallo '98	♛♛	4
● Scannagallo '99	♛♛	5
○ Val di Chiana Grechetto '00	♛	2*

○ Sant'Amato '01	♛♛	3*
○ Montellori Brut '97	♛♛	4
● Castelrapiti Rosso '99	♛♛	5
● Salamartano '99	♛♛	6
● Vigne del Moro '00	♛	4
● Chianti '01	♛	3
○ Vigne del Mandorlo '01		3
○ Vin Santo dell'Empolese '96		5
○ Sant'Amato '00	♛♛	3*
● Castelrapiti Rosso '95	♛♛	4
● Salamartano '95	♛♛	5
● Salamartano '96	♛♛	5
● Castelrapiti Rosso '97	♛♛	5
● Salamartano '97	♛♛	5
● Salamartano '98	♛♛	6

GAIOLE IN CHIANTI (SI)

Agricoltori del Chianti Geografico
Via Mulinaccio, 10
53013 Gaiole in Chianti (SI)
tel. 0577749489
e-mail: info@chiantigeografico.it

The Chianti Geografico co-operative has got into its stride and seems to be aiming for higher things. They have instituted a grape selection process with incentives for their member-growers that reward quality rather than quantity. The results should become more evident in the next few years but meanwhile, they are continuing to refurnish the cellar – new small casks have arrived – under the technical supervision of Lorenzo Landi. We did find a first sign of the new order from our tasting of the Pulleraia '00, a monovarietal merlot. It displays a rich, lively colour and a broad, deep and notably complex bouquet. The palate reveals compact progression, tightly knit tannins and admirable length. The very good Ferraiolo '00, from sangiovese and cabernet, is a new wine that has replaced the old Biturica. It shows solid structure, nicely underpinned by oak, and the nose, although still a bit closed, is free of vegetal hints. The Contessa Radda '00 is also much more than satisfactory, with its aromas of berry fruit and faint hints of oak, and an even, well-balanced, medium-bodied palate. There was a further good report for the Chianti Classico '00. It is a simpler but still well-made wine with lots of enjoyable fruit. Finally, the Riserva Montegiachi '99 is more in the cellar's old style, with forward notes on the nose, medium body and a slightly astringent finish.

GAIOLE IN CHIANTI (SI)

★ **Castello di Ama**
Fraz. Lecchi in Chianti
Loc. Ama
53013 Gaiole in Chianti (SI)
tel. 0577746031
e-mail: info@castellodiama.com

Castello di Ama gave us a splendid performance this year. For the first time, their Chianti Classico, vintage '99, won Three Glasses. It's a red of extraordinary elegance that embodies, of course, the best characteristics of the sangiovese grape from these parts, but it also displays such a complex and, at the same time, delicate bouquet that one is reminded, curiously, of some of the great Pinot Noirs from Vosne-Romanée in the Côte de Nuits. By now, readers will have gathered that we really liked this Chianti Classico. Apart from showing harmony, finesse and effortless drinkability, it is also a wine of great personality, which is neither conformist nor easy to pigeon-hole. It's a great success for Lorenza Sebasti and Marco Pallanti, partners at work and in life, and won our Oenologist of the Year award for Marco. This skilful, modest wineman has been dedicating most of his waking hours to Castello di Ama for over two decades. Now, we'll move on to the other wines. The Vigna L'Apparita '98 is good, but it has perhaps a little too much acidity and some rough, tannic edges that still need smoothing. The Al Poggio Chardonnay '00 is a surprise. Faintly toasty aromas merge with complex mineral notes, then the stylish palate is quite full-bodied, consistent and shot through with a delicious nip of acidity that lightens the structure. It is easy to overlook it in the company of the great reds from Castello di Ama. But it is one of the best Tuscan whites of its vintage.

● Pulleraia '00	🍷🍷	4*
● Ferraiolo '00	🍷🍷	5
● Chianti Cl. '00	🍷	4
● Chianti Cl. Contessa di Radda '00	🍷	4
● Chianti Cl. Montegiachi Ris. '99	🍷	5
● Chianti Cl. Montegiachi Ris. '94	🍷🍷	4
● Chianti Cl. Montegiachi Ris. '95	🍷🍷	4
● I Vigneti del Geografico '95	🍷🍷	5
● I Vigneti del Geografico '96	🍷🍷	5
● Chianti Cl. Montegiachi Ris. '97	🍷🍷	4
● I Vigneti del Geografico '97	🍷🍷	5
● Chianti Cl. '98	🍷🍷	3
● Chianti Cl. Montegiachi Ris. '98	🍷🍷	4
● Pulleraia '99	🍷🍷	5

● Chianti Cl. Castello di Ama '99	🍷🍷🍷	5
○ Al Poggio Chardonnay '00	🍷🍷	5
● Vigna l'Apparita Merlot '98	🍷🍷	8
● Chianti Cl. Bellavista '85	🍷🍷🍷	8
● Chianti Cl. Bellavista '86	🍷🍷🍷	8
● Chianti Cl. Bertinga '88	🍷🍷🍷	8
● Vigna l'Apparita Merlot '88	🍷🍷🍷	8
● Chianti Cl. Bellavista '90	🍷🍷🍷	8
● Vigna l'Apparita Merlot '90	🍷🍷🍷	8
● Vigna l'Apparita Merlot '91	🍷🍷🍷	8
● Vigna l'Apparita Merlot '92	🍷🍷🍷	8
● Chianti Cl. La Casuccia '97	🍷🍷🍷	8
● Vigna l'Apparita Merlot '97	🍷🍷	8
● Chianti Cl. Castello di Ama '97	🍷🍷	5
● Chianti Cl. Castello di Ama '98	🍷🍷	5

GAIOLE IN CHIANTI (SI)

BARONE RICASOLI
CANTINE DEL CASTELLO DI BROLIO
53013 GAIOLE IN CHIANTI (SI)
TEL. 05777301
E-MAIL: Barone@Ricasoli.it

The '99 vintage of the Chianti Classico Castello di Brolio may well be the best ever. It does not often happen that you can find in one wine a full expression of type, together with elegance, perfect execution and abundant supplies (more than 150,000 bottles in this case). It is flanked by more than 100,000 units of Casalferro, a blend of sangiovese, merlot and a little cabernet, whose '00 edition is as excellent as it always has been but which, this time, has a more international style. Put them together and you'll get some idea of how Francesco Ricasoli and his dream team are operating. There are reasonable prices, a plentiful supply of even the top wines, and a varied, but not too varied, range. The vineyards have by now almost all been replanted (we are talking about more than 200 hectares) the cellar is up-to-the-minute and the staff first-class. The outcome of all this is that Barone Ricasoli has gone, in less than ten years, from the doldrums to a position as one of the glories of Italian oenology. In the last six editions of the Guide, it has racked up eight Three Glass awards. This year, apart from another top prize for the Castello di Brolio '99, it came awfully close with the Casalferro '00 and the Torricella '01, made from chardonnay and one of the best Tuscan whites of its vintage. But All the Ricasoli wines got high marks. The Chianti Classico Rocca Guicciarda '99 is elegant and deep, the Chianti Classico Brolio '00 is easy to drink and very well executed, and the sangiovese-based Formulae '00 is rounded and fragrant. All in all, it would be hard to do better.

- Chianti Cl. Castello di Brolio '99　7
- Casalferro '00　6
- Torricella '01　5
- Chianti Cl. Brolio '00　4
- Formulae '00　3*
- Chianti Cl. Rocca Guicciarda '99　5
- Casalferro '95　6
- Casalferro '96　6
- Casalferro '97　6
- Chianti Cl. Castello di Brolio '97　6
- Casalferro '98　6
- Chianti Cl. Castello di Brolio '98　6
- Casalferro '99　6
- Torricella '00　5

GAIOLE IN CHIANTI (SI)

CAPANNELLE
LOC. CAPANNELLE
53013 GAIOLE IN CHIANTI (SI)
TEL. 0577749691

After a long absence, which was unconnected with the quality of the wines, Capannelle is back in the Guide. The winery, established in 1975 by Raffaele Rossetti, was taken over in 1997 by James Sherwood, president and principal stockholder of Orient Express Hotels and also of Sea Containers. The glorious history of Capannelle is rich in insightful winemaking as well as great bottles, but this is not the place to recount it. There are 15 hectares under vine, planted almost entirely to local varieties, especially sangiovese, of course, but also colorino, canaiolo and malvasia nera. The wines we tasted were excellent, which was not a surprise, and full of character. Given the wine type and vintage, we found the Chianti Classico Riserva '98 very interesting. It's a red with solid structure and a distinctive bouquet that reveals notes of black cherry, liquorice and sweet tobacco, as well as hints of flowers. The delightful contrast in the mouth between alcohol and acidity is enhanced and intensified by the smooth, expertly handled tannins. The finish is long, eloquent and delightfully vibrant. The Solare '99, a blend of sangiovese and malvasia nera that spends quite a while in French barriques, is also very good. More modern in style, it offers lots of body, softness and intensity, laced with still quite perceptible oak. We are equally happy with the excellent 50 & 50, a blend of Capannelle's sangiovese grapes and merlot grown by Avignonesi. With the '98 vintage, the cellar celebrates the tenth year of production.

- Chianti Cl. Capannelle Ris. '98　6
- 50 & 50 Avignonesi e Capannelle '98　8
- Solare '99　8
- 50 & 50 Avignonesi e Capannelle '97　8

GAIOLE IN CHIANTI (SI)

COLTIBUONO
LOC. BADIA A COLTIBUONO, 2
53013 GAIOLE IN CHIANTI (SI)
TEL. 057774481
E-MAIL: info@coltibuono.com

Badia a Coltibuono is one of the historic estates in Chianti Classico and should not be overlooked by anyone who wants to discover the glories of the area. At the moment, it is undergoing a general re-organization of the vineyards and fermentation techniques, which means that we're going to have to be patient. This phase began with the construction of a splendid new cellar, an important first move. The tastings this year, although good, were not up to what Emanuela and Roberto Stucchi Prinetti's estate is capable of producing. We fully believe that next year will bring notable improvements. Meanwhile, we admired the style of the Riserva '99, which is still a bit dumb on the nose but does offer substance and character on the palate. On the downside, the finish is slightly harsh. The even, well-made Chianti Classico R. S. '00 has a fruity bouquet and soft, relaxed, fairly well-sustained flavour. The Chianti Classico '00, which is better than just acceptable, offers aromas of berry fruit and a pleasant, well-balanced palate with a slightly dilute finish. The lively, harmonious and rather moreish palate of the white Trappoline '01 is supported by subtle notes of flowers, apples and pears.

• Chianti Cl. Ris. '99	5
• Chianti Cl. Badia a Coltibuono '00	4
• Chianti Cl. R. S. '00	4
○ Trappolie '01	3
• Sangioveto '95	6
• Chianti Cl. Ris. '88	4
• Chianti Cl. Ris. '90	4
• Sangioveto '90	6
• Sangioveto '94	6
• Chianti Cl. Ris. '95	5
• Chianti Cl. Ris. '96	5
• Sangioveto '97	6
• Chianti Cl. Ris. '98	5
• Sangioveto '99	8

GAIOLE IN CHIANTI (SI)

IL COLOMBAIO DI CENCIO
LOC. CORNIA
53013 GAIOLE IN CHIANTI (SI)
TEL. 0577747178
E-MAIL: ilcolombaiodicencio@tin.it

After just one year's interval, Colombaio di Cencio came back to again carry off Three Glasses for its top wine, Il Futuro. And the seriousness of this estate, owned by Werner Wilhelm and ably managed by Jacopo Morganti, is evident in the two Chianti Classicos, which were awarded Two red Glasses. In fact, the cellar came very close to sweeping the board. The estate includes almost 20 hectares under vine at an average of 400 metres above sea level, planted to sangiovese, cabernet sauvignon and merlot at a density of about 7,000 vines per hectare. The state-of-the-art, admirably efficient cellar is exemplary, with a barrel stock of only barriques and 500-hectolitre tonneaux. With these advantages, and with the invaluable advice of Paolo Vagaggini, the winery could hardly help turning out wines of remarkable structure. Il Futuro '99 is made from all three varieties planted. The entry on the nose is not altogether encouraging, because of the presence of some uninviting reduced notes, but when the wine has had time to breathe, the notes vanish. On the palate, there is admirable thrust, concentration, flesh and depth, as well as dense, succulent tannic weave. The two Chiantis, as we said, did extremely well. The '00 offers an intense bouquet with notes of black berry fruit and green pepper. The progression in the mouth is nicely co-ordinated and elegant. The Riserva '99 has more character and extract, but also a slight edginess.

• Il Futuro '99	7
• Chianti Classico I Massi '00	6
• Chianti Classico I Massi Ris. '99	6
• Il Futuro '95	7
• Il Futuro '97	7
• Il Futuro '98	7
• Chianti Cl. Ris. '97	4
• Chianti Classico I Massi Ris. '98	6

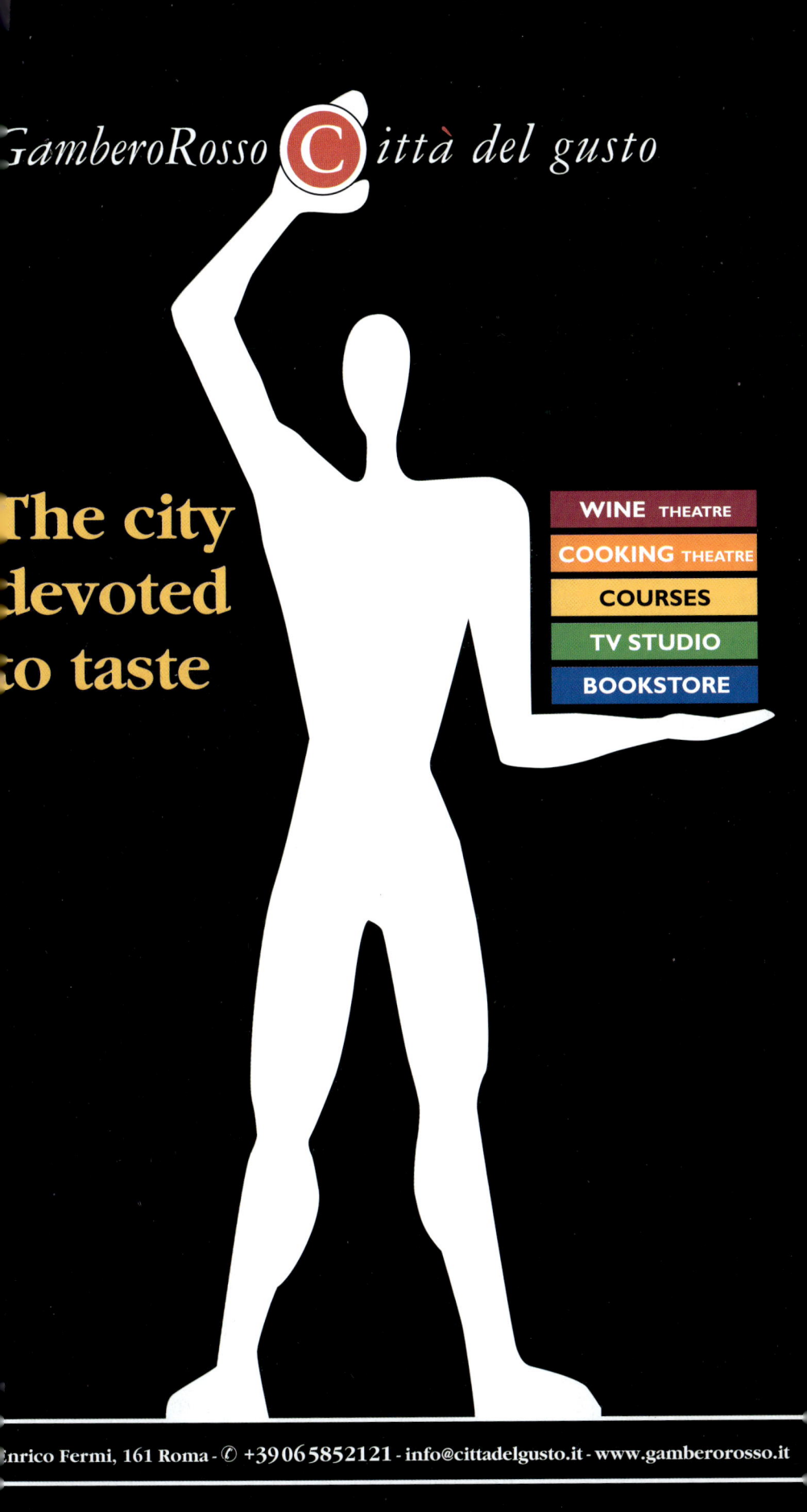

GamberoRosso **C**ittà *del gusto*

The city devoted to taste

- WINE THEATRE
- COOKING THEATRE
- COURSES
- TV STUDIO
- BOOKSTORE

Enrico Fermi, 161 Roma - ✆ +39 06 5852121 - info@cittadelgusto.it - www.gamberorosso.it

Enjoy Italy even more

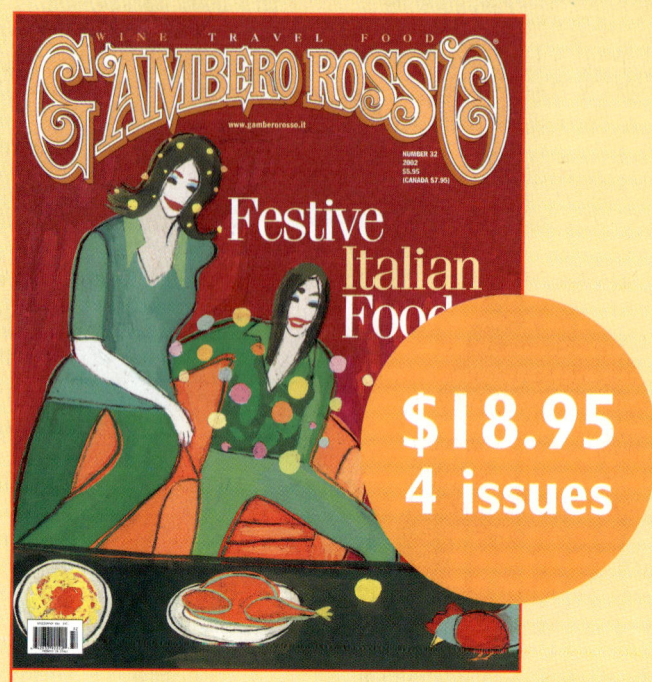

**$18.95
4 issues**

**Gambero Rosso
the insider guide to
top wines
best restaurants
delightful hotels
recipes and routes
all chosen for you by our expert**

Treat yourself to a subscription to Gambero Rosso
Italy's top wine, travel and food magazine

To subscribe, please call:
Speedimpex USA - 35-02 48th Avenue
L.I.C. NY 11101-2421 - Tel. 800-969-1258
subscriptions@speedimpex.com

For any other information, call:
Gambero Rosso Inc. - 636 Broadway suite 11K
New York - NY 10012 - Tel. 212-253-5653
gamberousa@aol.com

visit our website   click on english
www.gamberorosso.it

GAIOLE IN CHIANTI (SI)

PODERE IL PALAZZINO
FRAZ. MONTI
LOC. IL PALAZZINO
53013 GAIOLE IN CHIANTI (SI)
TEL. 0577747008
E-MAIL: palazzino@chianticlassico.com

The Sderci brothers' estate has crowned its consistent improvement over the past few years with a well-earned Three Glasses. This feat is not exactly surprising, although the '00 vintage was not an easy one. Our tastings also re-established the estate's internal hierarchy because the prize was assigned to the traditional standard-bearer, the Grosso Sanese. It should, perhaps, be pointed out that the style of the cellar's wines has changed somewhat. A little austerity has been sacrificed for softness and cleaner execution, and the use of new barriques is more noticeable. Oak is very much there on the nose, but in the mouth, fruit is given free rein. The admirable palate has roundness and silky, densely packed tannins, and there is plenty of elegance and depth on the finish. In short, this is a great Chianti Classico. The La Pieve '00 selection did very well, too, with its full-bodied, well-balanced and very long flavour, although vegetal notes are a little obvious on the nose. High marks also went to the Chianti Classico Argenina '00. It's perhaps a little simpler than its stablemates but boasts, nevertheless, good concentration and enjoyably sound fruit.

GAIOLE IN CHIANTI (SI)

CASTELLO DI MELETO
LOC. MELETO
53013 GAIOLE IN CHIANTI (SI)
TEL. 0577749217
E-MAIL: market@castellomeleto.it

There can be no question that Castello di Meleto is an important estate, particularly given its impressive size. That's why we are somewhat puzzled that, despite all the efforts in the vineyard, their well-made wines are not particularly characterful. But let's get down to the hard details. The Chianti Classico '00 shows a ruby hue with a definite garnet tinge. The nose offers forward notes of fruit preserved in alcohol together with blackberry jam. The attack on the palate is edgy, but the wine soon shows power, good structure, well-integrated tannins and a rising finish. The Riserva '99 also did well, with its brilliant purple colour, fresh fruity aromas of raspberry and strawberry, then agreeable, medium-bodied but extremely harmonious flavour. The Chianti Classico Pieve di Spaltenna '99 has a not very expressive nose, where faint balsamic notes meld with hints of ripe fruit. The palate, too, lacks character and definition. The Pieve di Spaltenna '00 displays a slightly dull hue and a not very intense nose with some flowery hints. In the mouth, it is simple and properly made but anonymous. The Pieve di Spaltenna '99 exhibits not awfully clean or distinctive aromas and a thin, unbalanced palate with over-assertive tannins. The Fiore '99 shows a rather noticeable vegetable tone, which is improved by notes of spice. The palate has good balance and a lingering finish.

● Chianti Cl. Grosso Sanese '00	🍷🍷🍷	8
● Chianti Cl. La Pieve '00	🍷🍷	6
● Chianti Cl. Argenina '00	🍷🍷	5
● Chianti Cl. Grosso Sanese Ris. '95	🍷🍷	5
● Chianti Cl. Grosso Sanese Ris. '96	🍷🍷	5
● Chianti Cl. Grosso Sanese Ris. '93	🍷🍷	5
● Chianti Cl. Grosso Sanese '98	🍷🍷	5
● Chianti Cl. Argenina '99	🍷🍷	4
● Chianti Cl. La Pieve '99	🍷🍷	4

● Chianti Cl. '00	🍷🍷	4
● Chianti Cl. Ris. '99	🍷	4
● Pieve di Spaltenna '00	🍷	5
● Fiore '99	🍷	5
● Pieve di Spaltenna '99	🍷	5
● Chianti Cl. Pieve di Spaltenna '99	🍷	4
● Fiore '97	🍷🍷	5
● Pieve di Spaltenna Alle Fonti '98	🍷🍷	5
● Chianti Cl. '99	🍷🍷	4
● Rainero '99	🍷🍷	5

GAIOLE IN CHIANTI (SI)

MONTIVERDI
LOC. MONTIVERDI
53013 GAIOLE IN CHIANTI (SI)
TEL. 0577749305 - 028378808

Montiverdi produces, for the most part, Chianti Classico, which this time, given the absence of their IGT Le Borranine, had the field all to itself. The level achieved is reassuringly comparable to past years. Four of the wines won Two Glasses each and demonstrated a well-established style based on good (but not exceptional, given that the vintage was the mediocre '98) raw material and a skilful use of oak. Opinions about the Riserva Ventesimo '98 at our tastings were essentially positive. The bouquet is somewhat predictably oak-dominated, while the palate is immediately soft and then expands with great energy, but the finish is hampered by the oak. The Villa Maisano Riserva '98 strikes a more evolved note on the nose with nuances of leather, tobacco and earth. The flavour is round, broad and seamless in its progression. The Villa Maisano Questo '98 has more vitality but is not very individual. The palate is well-balanced and fairly dense, with a distinct note of vanilla. The Riserva '98 is a success. A bouquet of well-defined, pleasing berry fruit and violets leads into a very dense palate with well-managed tannins. The Villa Maisano '99 makes up, in part, for slight muffling on the nose with good extract on the palate, which has a slightly rugged finish. Similarly, the Chianti Classico '99 displays an uncertain nose and good texture in the mouth.

● Chianti Cl. Ris. '98	3*
● Chianti Cl. Ventesimo Ris. '98	5
● Chianti Cl. Villa Maisano Questo '98	4
● Chianti Cl. Villa Maisano Ris. '98	3*
● Chianti Cl. Villa Maisano '99	3
● Chianti Cl. '99	3
● Chianti Cl. Ris. '97	4
● Chianti Cl. Ventesimo Ris. '97	5
● Chianti Cl. Vigneto Cipressone '97	5
● Chianti Cl. Villa Maisano Quello '97	5
● Le Borranine '97	5

GAIOLE IN CHIANTI (SI)

S. M. TENIMENTI PILE E LAMOLE
LOC. VISTARENNI
53013 GAIOLE IN CHIANTI (SI)
TEL. 0577738186 - 0577738549
E-MAIL: a.ali@vistarenni.com

Tenimenti Pile e Lamole is settling ever more firmly into the chair, as our tastings show. The entire range has moved up a gear, there are no banal or predictable wines, and we even found some little gems, in the form of the Vigneto Campolungo and the debutante Lam'oro. The Riserva Campolungo '99 is a characteristic example of its type, with flowery, berry fruit and fresh liquorice aromas. The palate develops seamlessly, showing the typical vibrancy and grip of the sangiovese grape, and finishes long. The very good Lam'oro '00 has a completely different style. The bouquet opens onto generous, very ripe fruit with oak-derived hints of vanilla and nougat. The palate boasts remarkable density, with close-knit tannins underpinned by oak, which is perceptible on the finish as well. The surprisingly good Chianti Classico Villa Vistarenni '00 is, of course, a relatively simple wine but it offers very agreeable and well-defined fragrances of raspberry and cherry. The palate has medium body but excellent balance. The Lamole Barrique '99 unveils a compact nose with abundant fruit and well-judged oak. The palate is broad and substantial, with a sound and harmonious finish. The other two wines we tasted were better than merely acceptable. The Riserva Lamole di Lamole '99 is pleasant, fruity and balanced, but a bit short, and the Chianti Classico '00 has a pleasingly peppery nose and a lively, well-crafted palate.

● Chianti Cl. Campolungo Ris. '99	5
● Lam'oro '00	6
● Chianti Cl. Villa Vistarenni '00	3*
● Chianti Cl. Lamole Barrique '99	5
● Chianti Cl. Lamole di Lamole '00	4
● Chianti Cl. Lamole di Lamole Ris. '99	4
● Chianti Cl. Campolungo Ris. '97	5
● Chianti Cl. Campolungo Ris. '94	4
● Chianti Cl. Campolungo Ris. '95	4
● Chianti Cl. Lamole di Lamole Ris. '95	4
● Chianti Cl. Villa Vistarenni '95	4
● Codirosso '95	5
● Chianti Cl. Lamole di Lamole '97	3
● Codirosso '99	5

GAIOLE IN CHIANTI (SI)

RIECINE
LOC. RIECINE
53013 GAIOLE IN CHIANTI (SI)
TEL. 0577749098
E-MAIL: riecine@riecine.com

Riecine's Three Glass collection has grown again this year, providing further confirmation of the excellence of Sean O'Callahan's estate. This time it was not the glorious Supertuscan, La Gioia, but the excellent Chianti Classico Riserva '99 that won the top prize. Both are first-class wines, and last year the Riserva almost eclipsed La Gioia. We realize that comparison is unavoidable, as is the question of whether the Chianti is really better than La Gioia. But however natural the question, it is not really one that can be answered. One reason is that the two wines are not compared directly against each other at our tastings, which match each wine against others in its own category. The second reason is that while the two reds may be made from the same grape, sangiovese, they are very different in style. La Gioia '99, an IGT, has an intense bouquet with spicy and flowery tones, as well as toasty notes of oak. The attack on the palate is energetic and firm. Progression is robust yet proceeds with elegance and the finish is long, if somewhat oak-dominated. The Riserva '99, on the other hand, is still rather closed on the nose, although a mineral tone is apparent. Entry in the mouth is agile and immediately elegant, followed by a dynamic, well-sustained development that shows succulent, well-judged and marvellously smooth tannins. The long, refreshing finish is a hymn to the purity of the fruit. To close, the Chianti Classico '00 is interesting but a touch forward on the nose. It's attractively round but slightly short on the palate.

GAIOLE IN CHIANTI (SI)

ROCCA DI CASTAGNOLI
LOC. CASTAGNOLI
VIA DEL CASTELLO, 3
53013 GAIOLE IN CHIANTI (SI)
TEL. 0577731004
E-MAIL: agricolarocca@libero.it

Rocca di Castagnoli's wines were in grand form this year. Young oenologist Maurizio Alongi has done a brilliant job of bringing into focus the characteristics of each bottle on the list. The cabernet sauvignon-based Buriano '99 is the best of the crop, since it came within an inch of Three Glasses. The aromas foreground deliciously ripe fruit, with some shy hints of toasty oak and vegetal notes. The palate is elegant and full-bodied, with well-gauged, smooth tannins and an intense, if not endless, finish. The very successful Le Pratole '00, from merlot grapes, has made a splendid debut. Very clear-cut aromas of plum, blackcurrant and pepper introduce a powerful, even, nicely balanced palate with a not very expansive finish. Whoever says that Tuscany is not white wine country should taste the chardonnay-based Molino delle Balze '00. Its entrancing, rich nose lays before you aromas of tropical fruit, honey, chamomile, citrus and aromatic herbs, which all carry through beautifully onto the fresh, stylish palate. The Riserva Poggio ai Frati '99 is a fine example of a genuine sangiovese-based wine. Austere, elegant and supply energetic, it impressed the panel, this time at least, more than the Riserva Capraia '99 with its vaguely international style. The Stielle '99, a blend of sangiovese and cabernet, boasts attractive mineral tones as well as vegetal and jammy notes on the nose. The wine shows character but also a bit too much wood. The extremely enjoyable Classico '00 almost got Two Glasses.

● Chianti Cl. Ris. '99	🍷🍷🍷	8
● La Gioia '99	🍷🍷	8
● Chianti Cl. '00	🍷	5
● Chianti Cl. Ris. '86	🍷🍷🍷	5
● Chianti Cl. Ris. '88	🍷🍷🍷	6
● La Gioia '95	🍷🍷🍷	8
● La Gioia '98	🍷🍷🍷	8
● Chianti Cl. Ris. '98	🍷🍷	5
● La Gioia '94	🍷🍷	8
● Chianti Cl. Ris. '95	🍷🍷	6
● Chianti Cl. Ris. '96	🍷🍷	6
● La Gioia '96	🍷🍷	8
● Chianti Cl. Ris. '97	🍷🍷	5
● La Gioia '97	🍷🍷	8
● Chianti Cl. '99	🍷🍷	4

● Le Pratole '00	🍷🍷	8
● Buriano '99	🍷🍷	8
○ Molino delle Balze '00	🍷🍷	6
● Chianti Cl. Capraia Ris. '99	🍷🍷	8
● Chianti Cl. Poggio ai Frati Ris. '99	🍷🍷	8
● Stielle '99	🍷🍷	8
● Chianti Cl. '00	🍷	6
● Buriano '96	🍷🍷	8
● Chianti Cl. Capraia Ris. '96	🍷🍷	8
● Buriano '97	🍷🍷	8
● Chianti Cl. Capraia Ris. '97	🍷🍷	8
● Chianti Cl. Poggio ai Frati Ris. '97	🍷🍷	8
● Chianti Cl. Capraia Ris. '98	🍷🍷	8
● Stielle '98	🍷🍷	8

GAIOLE IN CHIANTI (SI)

ROCCA DI MONTEGROSSI
FRAZ. MONTI IN CHIANTI
53013 GAIOLE IN CHIANTI (SI)
TEL. 0577747977

Last year, we mentioned that the restructuring and far-reaching operational changes under way at Rocca di Montegrossi were essential if this important, historic Chianti estate were ever to get back into the big time. But when were penning those notes, we never imagined that we would already be sipping such splendid wines at this year's tastings. We'll start with the one that knocked us off our pins, the Riserva San Marcellino '99. It's a Chianti Classico that is simply extraordinary in its individual character and expressive elegance. The bouquet is both concentrated and lavish, showing aromas of berry fruit, violets and fresh spice, as well as a typically Chianti mineral tone. In the mouth, it is at once compact, stylish and vigorous. The well-integrated tannins are still capable of emerging in the long, complex finish to add a touch of classic austerity. This is a great wine that honours the name of Chianti Classico. The very fine Geremia '99 is a Sangiovese, but changes are in store, starting with the '02. It's still a bit unsettled on the nose, but has a firm, close-knit texture on the palate, together with notable complexity and a sound if fairly stand-offish character. The Chianti Classico '00 is an altogether less demanding wine but admirable nevertheless. Distinct aromas of berry fruit, with hints of super-ripeness lead into a memorably confident palate. The range put on an excellent performance, which restores Marco Ricasoli's winery to its rightful prominence.

GAIOLE IN CHIANTI (SI)

SAN GIUSTO A RENTENNANO
FRAZ. MONTI IN CHIANTI
LOC. SAN GIUSTO A RENTENNANO
53013 GAIOLE IN CHIANTI (SI)
TEL. 0577747121
E-MAIL: sangiustorentennano@chiantinet.it

It is just not in the nature of Percarlo to be easy and accommodating. However you look at it, it's a controversial wine. Certainly, the '99 edition is not a bottle you can let slip by without comment. You might observe that the volatile acidity is a bit high but, in the end, the wine so enthrals the taste-buds that such quibbles are simply forgotten. The nose may take acidity to the limit but its sheer energy takes your breath away. Notes of spice, earth, tobacco, plum and liquorice tumble out, fusing into an orderly whole. Nor could the palate be accused of half-heartedness. After a masterful attack, it unfolds with mouthfilling warmth and finishes long, with thrilling intensity. You can't help liking so much personality. The characteristics can be found again, albeit in a minor key, in the Chianti Riserva '99. Vigorous aromas of black cherry, clove and toasty oak tempt the nose, which shares the same limitations as the Percarlo. The taut palate is dense and tightly knit. Alcohol and acidity vie for supremacy in the energetic mid palate, and the characteristic tension of the sangiovese grape comes through on the finish. The very good Chianti Classico '00 is, at last, a more tractable wine. Soft and harmonious, it takes you through to a smooth, juicy, sound and lingering finish. To conclude, the merlot-based La Ricolma '99 is powerful and intense, if a bit harsh-mannered and oak-driven.

● Chianti Cl. Vigneto S. Marcellino Ris. '99	🍷🍷🍷	5
● Geremia '99	🍷🍷	6
● Chianti Cl. '00	🍷🍷	4
○ Vin Santo del Chianti Classico '94	🍷🍷	6
● Vin Santo '88	🍷🍷	5
○ Vin Santo '91	🍷🍷	5
● Chianti Cl. Vigneto S. Marcellino '93	🍷🍷	4
● Chianti Cl. Ris. '95	🍷🍷	4
● Geremia '95	🍷🍷	5
● Chianti Cl. '99	🍷🍷	4

● Percarlo '99	🍷🍷🍷	8
● Chianti Cl. Ris. '99	🍷🍷	6
● Chianti Cl. '00	🍷🍷	5
● La Ricolma '99	🍷🍷	8
● Percarlo '88	🍷🍷🍷	8
● Percarlo '97	🍷🍷🍷	8
● La Ricolma '98	🍷🍷	8
● Percarlo '90	🍷🍷	8
● Percarlo '92	🍷🍷	8
● Percarlo '94	🍷🍷	8
● Percarlo '95	🍷🍷	8
● Percarlo '96	🍷🍷	8
● La Ricolma '97	🍷🍷	8
● Chianti Cl. Ris. '98	🍷🍷	5
● Percarlo '98	🍷🍷	8

GAIOLE IN CHIANTI (SI)

San Vincenti
Loc. San Vincenti
Podere di Stignano, 27
53013 Gaiole in Chianti (SI)
tel. 0577734047
e-mail: svincent@chiantinet.it

San Vincenti is not well-known to the wine-loving public, or, rather, not nearly so well-known as it deserves to be. This may be due to its size – the property embraces less than ten hectares under vine – or to the fact that Gaiole is full to bursting of famous estates. Or it may simply be that the owners are not particularly given to self-advertisement. We find this surprising because year after year, the wines make a fine showing and more than one bottle has gone through to our final taste-offs. Two did so this time and one, at last, carried off Three Glasses. The star performer is the Chianti Classico Riserva '99, which comes from a much better year than its predecessor. The wine conveys a definite sense of terroir and shows the character of the very finest Chianti Classicos. This is not an easy, approachable sort of red. The aromas are not immediately expressive. Still distant and a little stand-offish, they reveal an earthy, mineral tone that takes some getting used to. The vibrant palate, however, has all the exuberant energy of the sangiovese grapes grown in these parts, delivering robust tannins and remarkable structure. The very good, mostly sangiovese-based Stignano '99 has still to open out on the nose but there's plenty of power and concentration in the mouth. Lastly, the successful Chianti Classico '00 also shows the slow-starting house style. After an uncertain attack, it expands confidently through the finish.

GAMBASSI TERME (FI)

Villa Pillo
Via Volterrana, 24
50050 Gambassi Terme (FI)
tel. 0571680212
e-mail: info@villapillo.com

The Syrah is, as usual, the top of the range at Villa Pillo. It seems there can be no more doubts about how at home this Rhône grape is at this Gambassi estate. The varietal characteristics of the '00 are as clearly expressed as ever. Admirably, aromas and structure come together in perfect harmony, with neither threatening to upstage the other. The already eloquent nose displays intense notes of black pepper and plum. The palate is not exceptionally concentrated. Lean and linear, it is agreeably fresh and well-balanced. The other wines were not particularly impressive. The panel thought the best was the Merlot Sant'Adele '00 but it revealed the less than generous fruit that cropped up throughout the rest of the range. The finesse of the bouquet is marred by super-ripe notes then after a smooth, well-rounded attack, the palate gradually fades away on the finish. The Vivaldaia '00, from cabernet franc, has varietal notes of grass and pepper that carry through onto the not very dense palate. The finish is slightly evolved. The Borgoforte '99 breaks rank – it is not a monovarietal but a blend of 50 per cent sangiovese with cabernet sauvignon and a touch of merlot. It is well executed, clean and balanced but some forward notes and a distinctly vegetal character suggest that the grapes were picked before they were fully ripe.

• Chianti Cl. Ris. '99	ҮҮҮ	5*
• Stignano '99	ҮҮ	7
• Chianti Cl. '00	ҮҮ	5
• Chianti Cl. Ris. '95	ҮҮ	4
• Chianti Cl. Podere di Stignano '96	ҮҮ	3
• Chianti Cl. Ris. '96	ҮҮ	6
• Chianti Cl. Ris. '97	ҮҮ	6
• Stignano '97	ҮҮ	7
• Chianti Cl. '98	ҮҮ	4
• Stignano '98	ҮҮ	7
• Chianti Cl. '99	ҮҮ	4

• Merlot Sant'Adele '00	ҮҮ	6
• Syrah '00	ҮҮ	6
• Vivaldaia '00	Ү	6
• Borgoforte '99	Ү	4
• Syrah '97	ҮҮҮ	5
• Syrah '99	ҮҮ	5
• Cabernet Sauvignon '96	ҮҮ	5
• Merlot '96	ҮҮ	5
• Syrah '96	ҮҮ	5
• Cabernet Sauvignon '97	ҮҮ	5
• Merlot '97	ҮҮ	5
• Merlot '98	ҮҮ	5
• Syrah '98	ҮҮ	5
• Merlot Sant'Adele '99	ҮҮ	5

GREVE IN CHIANTI (FI)

Carpineto
Loc. Dudda
50020 Greve in Chianti (FI)
Tel. 0558549062 - 0558549086
E-mail: info@carpineto.com

This year, it is our pleasant duty to congratulate Carpineto, a welcome change, as in the past we have often been critical. Happily, the tastings this time were a revelation, starting with their excellent Chianti Classico Riserva '99, which made it to our finals and nearly won a third Glass. It is a red with character and notable complexity, qualities that come through in the bouquet in mineral notes and hints of tobacco and liquorice. The chewy, fruity palate has a long, expansive finish. The equally successful, although more straightforward, Chianti Classico '00 displays a fruitier nose with a nicely measured contribution from the oak. In the mouth, there is medium body and a confident progression. The very good Farnito Cabernet '99 opens up generously on the nose with notes of spice, dark berries and coffee. The well-extracted palate is solid, although the oak-derived tannins are perhaps a little insistent. The Dogajolo '00, from four parts sangiovese to one cabernet, did more than just reasonably well, with its distinctly vegetal character and good palate, despite slightly exuberant tannins. The wines from their Montepulciano 'branch' of the estate performed decently. The Rosso has attitude and a little too much tannin whereas the Nobile is fuller and rounder, although there are some reduced notes on the nose.

GREVE IN CHIANTI (FI)

La Madonnina - Triacca
Loc. Strada in Chianti
Via Palaia, 39
50027 Greve in Chianti (FI)
Tel. 055858003
E-mail: info@triacca.com

After a year among the Other Wineries, La Madonnina has come back to earned a full profile, which is more in keeping with its potential. There is as yet no absolute champion, but the range shows an admirable consistency of quality. The very fine Chianti Classico La Palaia '99 may not be altogether characteristic of its wine type, but it does have ripe fruit on the nose, with some hints of super-ripeness, then a notably broad, round palate with plenty of length. The very interesting Il Mandorlo '99, a blend of cabernet sauvignon and sangiovese, has a fruit-led nose with well-judged notes of toasty oak. Ripeness is also apparent on the lively palate, which has no vegetal notes, and the finish is characterized by lively tannins. The Riserva '99 almost got Two Glasses for its aromas of cherry and raspberry, together with a light grassy tone. The palate is well constructed, with a smooth entry, soft, balanced structure, and just a slight tailing off on the back palate. The 250,000 bottles of very decent Chianti Classico Bello Stento remind us that La Madonnina has 100 hectares of vineyard at its disposal. The wine is simple but reliable. It may lack a bit of body but it is remarkably vibrant. Lastly, the Nobile '99, from the Tenuta Santa Venere, the Triacca group's estate at Montepulciano, is medium-bodied and well-typed.

● Chianti Cl. Ris. '99	🍷🍷	5
● Chianti Cl. '00	🍷🍷	4
● Farnito Cabernet Sauvignon '99	🍷🍷	6
● Dogajolo '00	🍷	4
● Rosso di Montepulciano '01	🍷	3*
● Nobile di Montepulciano Ris. '98	🍷	5
● Chianti Cl. Ris. '94	🍷🍷	4
● Dogajolo '95	🍷🍷	3
● Farnito Cabernet Sauvignon '95	🍷🍷	5
● Chianti Cl. Ris. '97	🍷🍷	4
● Chianti Cl. '98	🍷🍷	3
● Chianti Cl. Ris. '98	🍷🍷	5
○ Farnito Chardonnay '99	🍷🍷	4

● Chianti Cl. V. La Palaia '99	🍷🍷	5
● Il Mandorlo '99	🍷🍷	5
● Chianti Cl. Bello Stento '00	🍷	4
● Chianti Cl. Ris. '99	🍷	4
● Nobile di Montepulciano '99	🍷	4
● Chianti Cl. '94	🍷🍷	3
● Chianti Cl. Ris. '94	🍷🍷	4
● Chianti Cl. '95	🍷🍷	3
● Chianti Cl. Ris. '95	🍷🍷	4
● Chianti Cl. V. La Palaia '96	🍷🍷	4

GREVE IN CHIANTI (FI)

MONTECALVI
VIA CITILLE, 85
50022 GREVE IN CHIANTI (FI)
TEL. 0558544665
E-MAIL: bollij@tin.it

The '99 Montecalvi is rather different in its sensory characteristics from the two preceding vintages, although it nearly repeated the Three Glass exploit of the '98. The nose is more distinct, with notes of berry fruit and toasty oak, as well as a light floral tone that emerges gradually. The structure on the palate is solid, and the fresh acidity provides a good contrast with the tannins. The finish is satisfyingly long. This is a Montecalvi in which the sangiovese fruit makes its presence felt in no uncertain terms and both oak and extract are well-judged. The neat, orderly aromas also contribute to a drinking experience of enormous elegance. That said, we miss the richness and voluptuousness of the '97 and the '98 editions, not to mention their exuberant, slightly undisciplined, character and personality. But every wine is the child of its vintage, and the '99 did not have to cope with the hot summer of '97 or the drought conditions of '98. All in all, the '99 vintage was still an excellent one and in may even be considered one of the most harmonious of recent years. We'll finish on a positive note by pointing out that this Montecalvi is an admirably faithful interpretation of its year.

GREVE IN CHIANTI (FI)

PODERE POGGIO SCALETTE
LOC. RUFFOLI
VIA BARBIANO, 7
50022 GREVE IN CHIANTI (FI)
TEL. 0558546108
E-MAIL: j.fiore@tiscalinet.it

This year, Vittorio Fiore didn't quite manage to pick up the top prize but his Carbonaione did make a fine showing. Bear in mind that competition in the '99 vintage was fierce. What we cannot understand is why the Carbonaione seems to be able to hit the spot in what are considered minor vintages but does less well, although still very well indeed, in the good years. Is it some mysterious quality of the sangiovese grape? Is there something in the Ruffoli soil? Or is the panel simply mistaken (nobody's perfect)? For the moment, we shall assume that our panels are competent and dismiss the final possibility but one of these days, we must have a good vertical tasting of Carbonaione. Let's hope Vittorio Fiore will agree but he's always so kind and helpful that we don't foresee any problems. At this year's tastings, the panel enjoyed the Poggio Scalette Sangiovese. A full-bodied, powerful wine, it showed good progression in the mouth and the long finish was perked up by vigorous, succulent tannins. It's a great red whose only drawback was insufficient aromatic definition, at least on the several occasions when we tasted it. However, there was a delightful surprise in the debut of the Piantonaia '00, a 50-50 blend of cabernet sauvignon and merlot. It's quite simply fantastic. The concentrated nose offers wonderfully fresh notes of black pepper, violets and ripe blackcurrant. The palate is dense, very elegant and amazingly long. So why only Two Glasses? Sadly, only 1,200 bottles were released.

• Montecalvi '99	ŸŸ	8
• Montecalvi '98	ŸŸŸ	8
• Montecalvi '94	ŸŸ	8
• Montecalvi '95	ŸŸ	8
• Montecalvi '96	ŸŸ	8
• Montecalvi '97	ŸŸ	8

• Il Carbonaione '99	ŸŸ	8
• Piantonaia '00	ŸŸ	8
• Il Carbonaione '96	ŸŸŸ	8
• Il Carbonaione '98	ŸŸŸ	8
• Il Carbonaione '92	ŸŸ	8
• Il Carbonaione '93	ŸŸ	8
• Il Carbonaione '94	ŸŸ	8
• Il Carbonaione '95	ŸŸ	8
• Il Carbonaione '97	ŸŸ	8

GREVE IN CHIANTI (FI)

CASTELLO DI QUERCETO
LOC. QUERCETO - FRAZ. LUCOLENA
VIA DUDDA, 61
50020 GREVE IN CHIANTI (FI)
TEL. 05585921
E-MAIL: querceto@castellodiquerceto.it

There is always an impressively long line-up of wines from Castello di Querceto and this year, the quality is impressive, too. In fact, two wines made it to the final taste-offs. We'll start with La Corte '98, a vivid ruby wine with a nose distinctly redolent of fruit, underpinned by elegant vanilla. On the palate, it is creamy, clean and even, with a forceful finish. The fine Chianti Classico Riserva Il Picchio '98 shows a lively ruby hue and a striking range of fruity aromas, enriched by notes of spice. The mouthfeel is delightful for its velvety softness and crunchy, appetizing tannic weave. The Cignale '98 has a brilliant purple colour ushering in a distinct toasty aroma that blends with elegant fruit notes. Hints of cinnamon and pepper add elegance and subtlety. The palate is soft at first, but slightly roughish tannins emerge on the otherwise full, persistent finish. The Cento '97 offers an attractive distinct ruby colour and a closed nose with some faint earthy notes. There is good weight in the mouth, with slightly drying, aggressive tannins. The Chianti Classico Riserva '98 has a rich, varied nose in which pepper and green pepper emerge distinctly. The palate is consistent, uncomplicated, attractively textured and altogether enjoyable. The Chianti Classico '00 is somewhat pale in the glass and a bit muffled on the nose, which shows a definite vegetal tone. The palate is firm and meaty, with well-behaved tannins.

Wine	Glasses	Score
● Chianti Cl. Il Picchio Ris. '98	ΨΨ	6
● La Corte '98	ΨΨ	7
● Cignale '98	ΨΨ	8
● Chianti Cl. '00	Ψ	4
● Cento '97	Ψ	7
● Chianti Cl. Ris. '98	Ψ	6
● Chianti Cl. Il Picchio Ris. '94	ΨΨ	4
● La Corte '94	ΨΨ	5
● Chianti Cl. '95	ΨΨ	3
● Chianti Cl. Ris. '95	ΨΨ	4
● Querciolaia '95	ΨΨ	5
● Cignale '97	ΨΨ	6
● La Corte '97	ΨΨ	5
● Querciolaia '97	ΨΨ	5

GREVE IN CHIANTI (FI)

★ QUERCIABELLA
VIA BARBIANO, 17
50022 GREVE IN CHIANTI (FI)
TEL. 0272002256
E-MAIL: info@querciabella.com

A Guide star is born. Querciabella has won yet another Three Glass award. It was the Camartina '99, perhaps the finest version from recent years, that carried off our top prize this time, bringing the total earned by this beautiful, justly celebrated estate to ten. But there is plenty of other news, quite apart from the magnificent cabernet sauvignon and sangiovese-based red, with its fruity and faintly smoky fragrances and very aristocratic flavour. First of all, Sebastiano Castiglioni, Giuseppe's son and co-owner of the estate, is now involved in production full-time. Next, the new cellar - which, by the way, is a real beauty - is fully operative. And thirdly, we shall at last be able to taste the reds from the Querciabella Maremma estate at Alberese, starting next year. The new wines will be made, for the most part, from sangiovese and syrah and, to judge from our preview tastings from the barrel, there are going to be some big surprises. But back to this year's tastings. The superb Camartina '99 was no surprise, but then neither was the almost entirely chardonnay-based Batàr '00. It may not yet have the complexity of the '98 or the '97 but it does have a soft, very concentrated mouthfeel. The fine Chianti Classico Riserva '99 is developing very nicely. A couple of years in the cellar should do wonders for it. The very pleasingly consistent Chianti Classico '00 is a deliciously drinkable tipple and one of the best versions we can recall.

Wine	Glasses	Score
● Camartina '99	ΨΨΨ	8
○ Batàr '00	ΨΨ	7
● Chianti Cl. '00	ΨΨ	5
● Chianti Cl. Ris. '99	ΨΨ	6
● Camartina '88	ΨΨΨ	8
● Camartina '90	ΨΨΨ	8
● Camartina '94	ΨΨΨ	8
● Camartina '95	ΨΨΨ	8
○ Batàr '97	ΨΨΨ	7
● Camartina '97	ΨΨΨ	8
○ Batàr '98	ΨΨΨ	7
○ Batàr '99	ΨΨ	7
● Chianti Cl. Ris. '98	ΨΨ	5

GREVE IN CHIANTI (FI)

RISECCOLI
VIA CONVERTOIE, 9
50022 GREVE IN CHIANTI (FI)
TEL. 055853598
E-MAIL: info@riseccoli.com

Last year, we complained that the wines from this Greve estate were of rather uneven quality, pointing out that the Chianti Classicos were too far behind the great Supertuscan. This time, we are happy to note that the situation is much improved. We'll start with the estate's signature wine, the Saeculum '00, which again made it to our final round of taste-offs. The colour is an intense ruby red, with hints of garnet at the rim, then the nose proffers generous and distinctly super-ripe fruit. The palate hit you immediately with a full-bodied, velvet-smooth and very dense mouthfeel where the tannins meld beautifully with the alcohol. It may lack a touch of finesse but it can boast a remarkably long finish. The good Chianti Classico Riserva '99 matches its attractive ruby hue with a fruity bouquet of plum and raspberry, accompanied by faint grassy undertones. On the palate, it offers a solid, soft, not very vigorous structure with smooth tannins. The finish is agreeable, although there is not much depth. Lastly, the Chianti Classico '00 reveals a not very intense ruby and an uncomplicated nose that is dominated by vegetal tones and notes of cherry fruit. The attack on the palate reveals considerable acidity and prominent tannins, but the alcohol has a generally softening effect, and the straightforward finish is moderately persistent.

• Saeculum '00	🍷🍷	8
• Chianti Cl. Ris. '99	🍷🍷	5
• Chianti Cl. '00	🍷	4
• Saeculum '99	🍷🍷	8
• Saeculum '94	🍷🍷	5
• Saeculum '95	🍷🍷	5
• Vin Santo '96	🍷🍷	5

GREVE IN CHIANTI (FI)

SAVIGNOLA PAOLINA
VIA PETRIOLO, 58
50022 GREVE IN CHIANTI (FI)
TEL. 0558546036
E-MAIL: savignola@ftbcc.it

This little Greve estate benefits from the advice of oenologist Lorenzo Landi while out in the vineyards, agronomist Remigio Bordini looks after things. Thanks to their efforts, Savignola Paolina is back in the Guide with its own profile. The estate has recently planted some new sangiovese clones in the roughly four hectares of vineyards. Four wines were presented at our tastings. The sangiovese-based Granaio '00 shows an intense ruby with distinct garnet highlights. A well-judged super-ripe tone is evident on the nose, where the most distinct aromas are plum and blackberry, softened by vanilla. The palate is powerful from the start, and the assertive tannins are partly tamed by alcohol. The finish is long and quite complex. The Riserva '99 did well, too. A lovely purple-tinged ruby introduces clear-cut aromas of cherry and redcurrant. The entry on the palate is not very intense because the structure lacks weight but there's good balance. The remarkably refreshing acidity is nicely complemented by rich alcohol and the moderately intense finish is very enjoyable. The Chianti Classico '00, on the other hand, is not very satisfactory. The rather forward, washed out ruby leads into a not very eloquent nose with a shy hint of fruit. The palate suffers from over-assertive tannins, which the considerable acidity only serves to highlight.

• Granaio '00	🍷🍷	6
• Chianti Cl. Ris. '99	🍷🍷	5
• Chianti Cl. '00	🍷	4
• Chianti Cl. Ris. '98	🍷	4
• Granaio '98	🍷	5
• Granaio '99	🍷	5

GREVE IN CHIANTI (FI)

Torraccia di Presura
Loc. Strada in Chianti
Via della Montagnola, 130
50027 Greve in Chianti (FI)
tel. 0558588656 - 055490563
e-mail: torracciadipresura@torracciadipresura.it

Torraccia di Presura put on a splendid performance at our tastings, serving the panel a brace of Two Glass wines. The Chianti Classico '00 presents an intense ruby hue and dense, well-amalgamated, fruit-led aromas with cherry to the fore. The attack on the palate is powerful and dense, with a lively freshness provided by the acidity. Rather aggressive tannins make the finish a tad astringent, but there is admirable length. The Chianti Classico Il Tarocco '00 is a brilliant ruby. After some initial hesitation, the nose reveals fruity notes of plum and blackberry. The palate is immediately eloquent, showing moderate density and a deliciously appetizing flavour that stays with you through to the finish. The Chianti Classico Il Tarocco Riserva '99 is the least successful of this year's trio. The colour is a little too pale and the not very clean bouquet reveals some disagreeable animal notes. The entry on the palate is acceptable, but the development is limited and the tannins run wild. We had another taste of the Lucciolaio '98, which seemed broader and riper than we remembered. The bouquet, dominated at first by wood, soon opens onto richer notes of dried fruit and jam. In the mouth, it shows good body, moderate extract and close-knit tannins.

● Chianti Cl. '00	ΨΨ	4
● Chianti Cl. Il Tarocco '00	ΨΨ	4
● Chianti Cl. Il Tarocco Ris. '99	Ψ	4
● Chianti Cl. Il Tarocco Ris. '98	ΨΨ	4
● Lucciolaio '97	Ψ	5
● Lucciolaio '98	Ψ	6
● Chianti Cl. Il Tarocco '99	Ψ	4

GREVE IN CHIANTI (FI)

Castello di Verrazzano
Loc. Verrazzano
50022 Greve in Chianti (FI)
tel. 055854243 - 055290684
e-mail: info@verrazzano.com

This year's tastings of Luigi Cappellini's wines were not particularly exciting, but slight ups and downs are par for the course in this profession. That said, we were expecting more, particularly from the selections, given the evidence of past performance. We'll start with the Chianti Classico '00, which has a lovely intense ruby colour. The nose is a less than successful combination of animal notes and not very elegant vegetal aromas. In the mouth, the wine is somewhat unco-ordinated. The acidity needs still to blend with the alcohol and the tannins are rather hard. The finish is moderately long. Still, the Riserva '99 did better. The nose is closed at first but opens to reveal aromas of redcurrant and blueberry enriched by light vanilla. The palate is intense from the beginning, and reveals good texture, with noble if slightly prominent tannins. The pleasingly ruby-hued Sassello '99, after an inexpressive entry on the nose, unveils lots of fruit. The attack on the palate is excellent, and alcohol initially dominates the forceful tannins, but the wine finishes in a hurry, with a vegetal tone. The Bottiglia Particolare '99 is disappointing. It is already garnet-tinged, and the fairly inexpressive nose offers rather indistinct aromas. The palate has reasonable density but not much balance.

● Chianti Cl. Ris. '99	ΨΨ	5
● Sassello '99	ΨΨ	6
● Chianti Cl. '00	Ψ	4
● Bottiglia Particolare '99	Ψ	6
● Chianti Cl. Ris. '90	ΨΨΨ	5
● Sassello '97	ΨΨΨ	6
● Bottiglia Particolare '98	ΨΨ	6
● Sassello '93	ΨΨ	6
● Sassello '95	ΨΨ	6
● Chianti Cl. Ris. '96	ΨΨ	5
● Bottiglia Particolare '97	ΨΨ	6
● Chianti Cl. '97	ΨΨ	4
● Chianti Cl. Ris. '97	ΨΨ	5
● Chianti Cl. '99	ΨΨ	4

GREVE IN CHIANTI (FI)

CASTELLO DI VICCHIOMAGGIO
LOC. LE BOLLE
VIA VICCHIOMAGGIO, 4
50022 GREVE IN CHIANTI (FI)
TEL. 055854079
E-MAIL: vicchiomaggio@vicchiomaggio.it

The Ripa delle More '99 was just a whisper away from winning Three Glasses, as the '94 and '97 versions have succeeded in doing in the past. Readers will have gathered that it is, however, an excellent wine, as anyone who tastes it is likely to discover. It's soft, with close-knit, smooth tannins, intense, elegant progression and a long finish with good depth. The only defect, if one can call it that, is a vegetal tone that is a tad too prominent for an essentially sangiovese-based wine. The Riserva La Prima '99 effortlessly collected Two Glasses again. Here, too, atypical grassy notes dominate the nose, but the well-rounded palate unfolds smoothly through to a moderately persistent finish. The stylistically similar Riserva Petri '99 is soft and harmonious on the palate but is slightly more forward. The fairly successful Chianti Classico San Jacopo '00 offers notes of berry fruit and spice on the nose, followed by a medium-bodied but agreeably succulent, palate. Lastly, the Ripa delle Mandorle '00, a blend of sangiovese and cabernet sauvignon, is a fairly uncomplicated, well-made red with a lightweight body and moreish drinkability. All things considered, John Matta's estate did very respectably this year, further confirmation of the reliability the cellar has come to be known for.

GREVE IN CHIANTI (FI)

VILLA VIGNAMAGGIO
VIA DI PETRIOLO, 5
50022 GREVE IN CHIANTI (FI)
TEL. 055854661 - 0558546653
E-MAIL: info@vignamaggio.com

Villa Vignamaggio put on a wonderful show this year. Lawyer Gianni Nunziante's estate has at last shown us the stuff it's made of, trotting out a series of bottles to die for. Top of the list is the extraordinary Riserva Monna Lisa, but both Obsession and Vignamaggio were serious contenders for top honours, an indication that the winery has moved forward with a vengeance. But let's go back to the magnificent Monna Lisa '99. The colour is an intense ruby with just the faintest hint of garnet on the rim. On the nose, it's broad and elegant, with a rich array of ripe dark berry fruit, black pepper and spice. The equally impressive palate is remarkably full-bodied. The list of adjectives to describe it in our notes goes on and on: concentrated, fruit-rich, velvety, harmonious and more. This is a great Chianti Classico. The very fine Vignamaggio '99, a monovarietal cabernet franc, has an eloquent bouquet of blackberry, blackcurrant, pepper and light vegetal notes. The palate is invigorating, elegant and deep, with exceptionally well-gauged tannins. The Obsession is less harmonious on the nose, where a note of spice takes over. The palate is full flavoured, velvet-soft and smooth as silky, with beautifully integrated tannins. The finish, despite admirable length, wants more complexity. The Chianti Classico '00 dense, austere and well-defined, making it a model of its type. The other wines are straightforward and well executed.

Wine	Glasses	Score
● Ripa delle More '99	🍷🍷	6
● Chianti Cl. La Prima Ris. '99	🍷🍷	5
● Chianti Cl. Petri Ris. '99	🍷	5
● Chianti Cl. San Jacopo '00	🍷	4
● Ripa delle Mandorle '00	🍷	4
● Ripa delle More '94	🍷🍷🍷	5
● Ripa delle More '97	🍷🍷🍷	6
● Ripa delle More '95	🍷🍷	5
● Ripa delle More '96	🍷🍷	5
● Chianti Cl. La Prima Ris. '97	🍷🍷	5
● Chianti Cl. Petri Ris. '97	🍷🍷	5
● Chianti Cl. La Prima Ris. '98	🍷🍷	5
● Chianti Cl. Petri Ris. '98	🍷🍷	4
● Ripa delle More '98	🍷🍷	6

Wine	Glasses	Score
● Chianti Cl. Monna Lisa Ris. '99	🍷🍷🍷	6
● Obsession '99	🍷🍷	7
● Vignamaggio '99	🍷🍷	6
● Chianti Cl. '00	🍷🍷	4
● Chianti Cl. Terre di Prenzano '00	🍷	4
● Il Morino '00		3
● Chianti Cl. Monna Lisa Ris. '95	🍷🍷🍷	4
● Chianti Cl. Monna Lisa Ris. '93	🍷🍷	4
● Chianti Cl. Monna Lisa Ris. '94	🍷🍷	4
● Chianti Cl. Monna Lisa Ris. '97	🍷🍷	5
● Chianti Cl. Vitigliano '97	🍷🍷	4
● Chianti Cl. Monna Lisa Ris. '98	🍷🍷	5
● Obsession '98	🍷🍷	6

GREVE IN CHIANTI (FI)

Viticcio
Via San Cresci, 12/a
50022 Greve in Chianti (FI)
tel. 055854210
e-mail: info@fattoriaviticcio.com

After years of praising the constancy and reliability of Viticcio, we can at last let ourselves go and offer readers a euphoric description of the wines we tasted this year. The sangiovese-based Prunaio, which marched off with Three Glasses, came out on top of the heap, but only after a fierce struggle with the equally splendid Riserva '99. The Prunaio '99 is not just a lovely wine. It also has the distinction and character of a Chianti Sangiovese made from thoroughly ripe grapes. The nose is concentrated and dense, with fruit that is enhanced by mineral notes. The particularly impressive palate reveals a tight-knit, vibrant structure with lively, yet delightfully smooth, succulent tannins. As we said above, the Riserva '99 was brilliantly good, too. The broad, eloquent nose shows dark fruit, faint vegetal hints and an undertone of shrewdly administered oak. In the mouth, it is powerful, long and full of vigour, with a slight tannic roughness on the finish. Despite the rather green notes on the nose, the Monile '99 opens out into a soft, dense palate, before signing off with a slightly bitter finish. Grassy nuances kept the Riserva Beatrice '99 from getting higher marks but the invigorating palate reveals good fruit and close-knit tannins. The Chianti Classico '00 also won Two Glasses for its excellent overall balance and well-modulated flower and fruit aromas.

GROSSETO

Le Pupille
Loc. Istia d'Ombrone
Piagge del Maiano, 92/a
58040 Grosseto
tel. 0564409517 - 0564409518
e-mail: lepupille@tin.it

The '00 edition of the Saffredi, a blend of cabernet sauvignon, merlot and alicante from a vineyard of the same name, has returned to centre stage. This is the third time it has merited Three Glasses. There's a magnificent combination of warmth and freshness that manages to offer concentration, opulence and structure while remaining elegant and harmonious. This great red is a credit to Elisabetta Geppetti and Stefano Rizzi's estate. The Solalto '00 also did amazingly well at our tastings. The grapes in question, gewürztraminer, sauvignon and sémillon, are allowed to become super-ripe on the vine and are harvested only when they have developed a fair amount of noble rot. The wine, which never sees oak, has found its form. This edition is sweet, glycerine-rich, dense, lingering and graced with an aromatic complexity well beyond what it has shown in the past. Meanwhile, the Morellino '01 was so good it almost got into our finals. A deep nose with clear-cut notes of ripe dark berry fruit and spice leads to a wonderfully mouthfilling flavour pervaded by sweet fruit and backed up by perfectly integrated tannins. The Poggio Valente '00, although very good, seems to lack its usual personality. Lastly, the very successful Poggio Argentato '01, from gewürztraminer and sauvignon, offers rich aromas of peach, apricot and melon as well as a broad, enticing and very enjoyable palate of moderate length.

● Prunaio '99	🍷🍷🍷	7
● Chianti Cl. Ris. '99	🍷🍷	6
● Chianti Cl. '00	🍷🍷	5
● Chianti Cl. Beatrice Ris. '99	🍷🍷	6
● Monile '99	🍷🍷	7
● Monile '93	🍷🍷	5
● Monile '94	🍷🍷	5
● Monile '95	🍷🍷	5
● Monile '96	🍷🍷	5
● Prunaio '96	🍷🍷	5
● Monile '97	🍷🍷	5
● Prunaio '97	🍷🍷	5
● Chianti Cl. Beatrice Ris. '98	🍷🍷	5
● Monile '98	🍷🍷	5
● Chianti Cl. '99	🍷🍷	4

● Saffredi '00	🍷🍷🍷	8
○ Solalto '00	🍷🍷	4*
● Morellino di Scansano Poggio Valente '00	🍷🍷	6
● Morellino di Scansano '01	🍷🍷	3*
○ Poggio Argentato '01	🍷🍷	3*
● Saffredi '90	🍷🍷🍷	8
● Saffredi '97	🍷🍷🍷	8
● Morellino di Scansano Poggio Valente '98	🍷🍷🍷	5
● Morellino di Scansano Poggio Valente '99	🍷🍷🍷	5
● Saffredi '99	🍷🍷	8
● Morellino di Scansano '00	🍷🍷	3*
○ Poggio Argentato '00	🍷🍷	3*
● Morellino di Scansano Poggio Valente '97	🍷🍷	5

GROSSETO

Poggio Argentiera
Loc. Banditella di Alberese
SS 1, 54
58010 Grosseto
tel. 0564405099
e-mail: info@poggioargentiera.com

It's a tricky business, writing about wine. Quite apart from the subjective nature of judgement, there are always some people – among our readers – who think we're being too nice, and others – among the winemakers – who feel we're much too nasty. Still, we hope everyone can agree on our assessment of Poggio Argentiera for there is very little to be said against what has been accomplished by Giampaolo Paglia, the owner of this Maremma estate. Little by little, he has brought his wines up to a level that would have been hard to imagine a few years ago. Now the Morellino DOC zone can boast of a new great wine, the Capatosta, which provides ample justification for the enormous investments that have recently been made in the Maremma. The '99 was already very good. There was just a touch of harshness that we hoped might be corrected and now here is the magnificent '00, which has really got it right. It's a warm, sunny wine that perfectly conveys the nature of its terroir. A rich colour introduces intense, pure aromas of blackberry jam, pepper and sweet spice. The palate is round and full, with lots of smooth tannins and a fresh, elegant finish. In other words, it's a Three Glass Morellino. The second wine, the Bellamarsilia '00, is good too. It offers a clean bouquet with lots of fruit and a little vegetal hint, and then a soft, supple, inviting palate with the faintest of bitter notes on the finish.

GROSSETO

Santa Lucia
Fraz. Fonteblanda
Via Aurelia Nord, 66
58010 Grosseto
tel. 0564885474
e-mail: az.santalucia@tin.it

After years of turning out perfectly respectable but hardly exciting wines, Luciano Scotto's Santa Lucia is emerging from its cocoon with a range that is well worth describing. The estate is not enormous, covering about 25 hectares, of which 18 are under vine. It's a family business. The oenologist, who also looks after the vineyards, is Lorenzo Scotto, son of the owner. At our tastings, the two Morellino di Scansanos gave a brilliant performance. The Tore del Moro '00 shows an intense ruby hue and an interesting, if not yet entirely settled, nose. The palate is decidedly more pleasing, thanks to its immediate softness, the tight-knit tannic texture and the vigorous energy it manages consistently to transmit. The Riserva '99 version has just a trace of forwardness on the nose, together with oak-derived notes of vanilla and coffee. In the mouth, it is smooth on the attack, well-paced in its development and lingering on the finish. The interesting Betto '00, made from sangiovese with a little cabernet and merlot, is harmonious and remarkably dense on both nose and palate. There are some faint medicinal nuances from the oak. The Losco '01 offers lots of dense, meaty fruit, but the fragrance, with its reduced tone, needs fine-tuning. The white Brigante '01 is a bit forward but acceptable.

- Morellino di Scansano CapaTosta '00 — 6*
- Morellino di Scansano BellaMarsilia '01 — 4
- Morellino di Scansano CapaTosta '99 — 6
- Morellino di Scansano CapaTosta '98 — 6
- Morellino di Scansano BellaMarsilia '00 — 4
- Morellino di Scansano BellaMarsilia '98 — 4
- Morellino di Scansano BellaMarsilia '99 — 4

- Betto '00 — 5
- Morellino di Scansano Rosso Tore del Moro '00 — 4*
- Morellino di Scansano Rosso Tore del Moro Ris. '99 — 5
- ○ Capalbio Bianco Brigante '01 — 3*
- ○ Capalbio Rosso Losco '01 — 3*

IMPRUNETA (FI)

La Querce
Via Imprunetana per Tavarnuzze, 41
50023 Impruneta (FI)
tel. 0552011380
e-mail: laquerce@inwind.it

It gives us great pleasure to write this profile of a venerable estate which, after years of not particularly distinguished work, has turned over a new leaf. The results are very encouraging. This is thanks to the owner, Massimo Marchi, who has stuck faithfully to the restructuring plans drafted by his manager, Marco Ferretti, and the oenologist Alberto Antonini. But let's consider the first wine, the Chianti Sorrettole '01, which is ruby with purple highlights. Pleasing intense aromas of sweet vanilla and raspberry precede a good entry on the palate, which has medium body with well distributed and tight-knit tannins and a succulent, inviting flavour and reasonable persistence. Better yet, the Chianti Colli Fiorentini La Torretta '01 presents an intense, nearly opaque ruby hue and a decidedly toasty fragrance that gives way to appealing notes of coffee and ripe, plum-like fruit. The palate is almost fleshy from the outset, underpinned by tannins that are well matched by alcohol, and leads to a rising finish. The wine the panel liked best was La Querce '00, which shows an intense, very concentrated violet colour, and fruity scents of cherry, plum and blackberry, all just slightly sweetened by vanilla. The enticing palate is dense but well balanced by perfectly judged acidity. The finish is long and delightfully persistent.

IMPRUNETA (FI)

Lanciola
Via Imprunetana, 210
50023 Impruneta (FI)
tel. 055208324
e-mail: info@lanciola.net

Now that the new cellar is at last ready, the Guarneris can manage their winemaking more rationally. The wide range of wines presented at our tastings did generally quite well. The Terricci '98 has a not very eloquent nose. Initial animal scents give way to aggressive vegetal aromas, but the palate does better. The texture is good and the tannins are closely packed and smooth. The finish is a bit feeble, with a less than pleasing bitter note. We preferred the '99. Its garnet-tinged ruby introduces a closed nose with vegetal aromas, then a good attack on the dense, mouthfilling palate. There is good balance, apart from the still rather rough tannins. The excellent Chianti Classico Le Masse di Greve Riserva '99 exhibits an opaque ruby and a broad array of aromas where, sadly, oak lords it over the fruit. The attack on the palate is powerful, distinct and admirably dense. The lingering finish reveals a faint bitterness. The standard '00 version did well, too. Although toasty notes of oak hold sway, they are nicely offset by the other aromas. The palate is harmonious and quite soft, with well-integrated tannins and a succulent finish. The acceptable Chianti Colli Fiorentini '00 has a simple nose and an easy-going and clean, if distinctly acidic, flavour and the Terricci Chardonnay '00 combines a solid, smooth palate with quite a forward bouquet.

● La Querce '00	▼▼	5
● Chianti Colli Fiorentini La Torretta '01	▼▼	4
● Chianti Colli Fiorentini Sorrettole '01	▼	3
● Chianti Colli Fiorentini La Torretta '00	▼▼	3*

● Chianti Cl. Le Masse di Greve '00	▼▼	5
● Chianti Cl. Le Masse di Greve Ris. '99	▼▼	4
● Terricci '99	▼▼	5
● Chianti dei Colli Fiorentini '00	▼	3
○ Terricci Chardonnay '00	▼	4
● Terricci '98	▼	4
● Terricci '95	▼▼	4
● Terricci '96	▼▼	4
● Chianti Cl. Le Masse di Greve Ris. '97	▼▼	4
● Terricci '97	▼▼	4
● Chianti Cl. Le Masse di Greve Ris. '98	▼▼	4
● Chianti Cl. Le Masse di Greve '99	▼▼	3*

LASTRA A SIGNA (FI)

VIGLIANO
FRAZ. SAN MARTINO ALLA PALMA
VIA CARCHERI, 309
50010 LASTRA A SIGNA (FI)
TEL. 0558727006
E-MAIL: info@vigliano.com

The Vigliano range now boasts a new wine, the Rosso Vigliano, which is clearly meant to be the second-label red. The standard-bearer of Lorenzo and Paolo Marchionni's estate, is still the Vigna dell'Erta, a blend of three parts cabernet sauvignon with two of sangiovese. It did quite well last year in the '99 version. Now the '00 has appeared, with evidence of further fine-tuning. This wine has what it takes to aim for the highest prize, having already achieved greater balance and elegance on the palate. Its weak points are rather evident vegetal tones on the nose and a noticeable bitter note on the finish. Otherwise, it's a lovely wine, showing a soft, dense palate with depth and an attractive chocolate finish. Meanwhile, great strides have been made by the chardonnay-based Bricoli '00. It is not yet fully eloquent on the nose, but it has a distinctive character on the palate, which is no mean achievement for a Tuscan white. It also rivals much more celebrated wines for power, vibrancy and length. The new Rosso Vigliano '00 is much better than merely acceptable. It is an openly uncomplicated wine, and pleasantly moreish to boot. It should be mentioned that all the prices at Vigliano are very wallet-friendly.

LORO CIUFFENNA (AR)

TENUTA IL BORRO
FRAZ. SAN GIUSTINO VALDARNO
LOC. IL BORRO, 1
52020 LORO CIUFFENNA (AR)
TEL. 055977053
E-MAIL: vino@ilborro.it

Father and son Ferruccio and Salvatore Ferragamo developed a growing interest in winemaking until finally it became a passion. Ferragamo is a name that probably needs no introduction, even to those who know little of the world of fashion. The appearance of the Ferragamos on the wine scene dates from 1993, when they acquired Duca Amedeo d'Aosta's Tenuta Il Borro. Having entirely revamped the property, the pair planted vineyards and restructured the old cellars. This was a major project requiring first-rate advice and assistance, which was forthcoming in the person of Niccolò d'Afflitto, another name that needs little introduction, at least to those who follow things oenological. Some 40 hectares of vines have been planted, which will bring production up from 16,000 bottles to about 200,000 by 2004. Ferruccio and Salvatore intend to match the growth in quantity with a similar rise in quality. Il Borro '00, a blend of merlot, cabernet sauvignon and syrah in decreasing order of proportion, shows a concentrated and characteristically varietal nose with rich layers of dark berries, some vegetal notes and hints of cherry jam. The palate is very solid and dense, and brimming with fine-grained tannins. It is rather like the winery itself – very young and very promising.

○ Bricoli '00	㏘	4*
● Vigna dell'Erta '00	㏘	5*
● Rosso Vigliano '00	㏐	3
● Vigna dell'Erta '99	㏘	5

● Il Borro '00	㏘	8
● Il Borro '99	㏘	8

LUCCA

TERRE DEL SILLABO
LOC. CAPPELLA - FRAZ. PONTE DEL GIGLIO
VIA PER CAMAIORE TRAV. V
55060 LUCCA
TEL. 0583394487
E-MAIL: clara.giampi@lunet.it

This is the most white-oriented estate in Tuscany. Four out of their five wines are whites. You'd almost think you were in deepest Friuli! This in itself is a distinction, but not the one dearest to Giampi Moretti's heart. He wants to produce excellent wines, regardless of their colour. It should be remembered, Tuscany is vast and various, and this corner of it has some special site climates that make the production of whites quite a reasonable proposition. At our tastings, all the wines did well – "boring", you might well be thinking at this point – but in fact there were differences. For a start, the chardonnay-based Spante '01 showed more personality than any of the others. The nose is intense and elegant, with notes of citrus, white flowers and vanilla. The immediately confident palate offers full body, excellent development and perfectly integrated oak. The Niffo '00, a blend of cabernet sauvignon, cabernet franc, sangiovese, colorino and canaiolo, also did well. The bouquet, an attractive array of blackcurrant and nicely ripe blackberries, is particularly successful. The flavour is soft, dense and well developed, with a proper underpinning of oak, but also a faintly bitterish finish. The Sauvignon Gana '01 is good, but still too young. Vegetal tones are too much in evidence, oak is noticeable and the finish, though appealing, is not very long. The other two whites were readier when we tasted them. The Chardonnay '01 exhibits attractive fleshiness and the Sauvignon '01 is remarkably crisp and fresh.

LUCCA

TENUTA DI VALGIANO
FRAZ. VALGIANO
VIA DI VALGIANO, 7
55010 LUCCA
TEL. 0583402271
E-MAIL: info@valgiano.it

This year, there are, in a sense, slim pickings from Valgiano. It is not so much the number of wines that is disappointing – two are better than none at all – as the fact that the estate standard-bearers, the Tenuta di Valgiano and the Scasso dei Cesari, were not presented. So little of the latter is produced in any case that we need hardly concern ourselves with it, but the reason for the absence of the Tenuta di Valgiano was simply that the '00 had not yet gone into the bottle. It was not available for our tastings. The cellar is right to wait because we retasted the '99 instead, and found it a paragon of density, elegance and refined execution. These qualities had not emerged so clearly last year, probably because it was simply not ready. As for the wines presented this time, the signs are distinctly positive. The Giallo dei Muri '01 is true to its character as a straightforward white with a well-defined fragrance of lavender, apple and pear and a fresh, lively, pleasing flavour. But we were particularly delighted by the Rosso dei Palistorti '00, which is tangible proof of the progress made at Moreno Petrini and Laura di Collobiano's estate. It offers fairly full body, considerable energy, seamless progression and a long, fresh, spicy finish.

○ Spante '01	🍷🍷	6
● Niffo '00	🍷🍷	6
○ Chardonnay '01	🍷🍷	4
○ Colline Lucchesi Sauvignon '01	🍷🍷	4
○ Colline Lucchesi Sauvignon Gana '01	🍷🍷	6
● Niffo '99	🍷🍷	5
○ Gana '00	🍷🍷	5
○ Spante '00	🍷🍷	5
○ Colline Lucchesi Sauvignon '98	🍷🍷	3
● Niffo '98	🍷🍷	5
○ Colline Lucchesi Chardonnay '99	🍷🍷	4

● Colline Lucchesi Rosso dei Palistorti '00	🍷🍷	5
○ Colline Lucchesi Bianco Giallo dei Muri '01	🍷	4
● Colline Lucchesi Tenuta di Valgiano '99	🍷🍷	8
● Scasso dei Cesari '95	🍷🍷	4
● Scasso dei Cesari '96	🍷🍷	4
○ Colline Lucchesi Bianco Giallo dei Muri '97	🍷🍷	3
● Scasso dei Cesari '97	🍷🍷	5
● Colline Lucchesi Rosso Scasso dei Cesari '98	🍷🍷	6
○ Scasso del Bugiardo '99	🍷🍷	5

MASSA

CIMA
FRAZ. ROMAGNANO
VIA DEL FAGIANO, 1
54100 MASSA
TEL. 0585830835
E-MAIL: info@aziendagricolacima.it

The nine wines presented this year by Aurelio Cima, five reds and four whites, all did remarkably well. The panel thought the pick of the crop was the Romalbo '00, obtained from sangiovese with 15 per cent massaretta. The style is typical Cima, with a very vivid colour, masses of fruit, intensely present new oak and robust, dense body. In addition, the Romalbo seems to have a more eloquent, decided character that avoids excess or vulgarity. Its only defect is a not very long finish. In the Montervo '00, a monovarietal merlot, the abundant structure and expertly judged tannins are not matched by the aromatic depth one might expect. The excellent debut performance of the Vermentino Nero '00 includes great body underpinned by rather a lot of alcohol. The 100 per cent sangiovese has now found a name, Anchigi, and cut a fine figure. It is rich, dense and stylish, if a little cold and stand-offish. The Massaretta, made exclusively from the variety of the same name, is very satisfying, being intense, crisply fresh and very enjoyable. High marks went to all the whites, too. The Vermentino Barrique '01 reveals a knowing hand with oak, meatiness and persistence on the palate. The Vermentino '01 is well-balanced, sound and fragrant, if leaner. The Candia '01 boasts an intriguing flowery bouquet and a nice fresh, lively flavour. Finally, the Candia Alto, which is still closed, shows greater complexity and good progression in the mouth.

MASSA MARITTIMA (GR)

MASSA VECCHIA
LOC. LE ROCCHE
PODERE FORNACE, 11
58024 MASSA MARITTIMA (GR)
TEL. 0566904144 - 0566904031

The wines Fabrizio and Patrizia Niccolaini presented this year clearly reflect their search for a style of their own that conveys, clearly and completely, the characteristics of their terroir. Even the most international of their wines, the cabernet sauvignon-based Fonte di Pietrarsa '99, shows territory-related characteristics that cannot be considered varietal in origin. The bouquet, for instance, exhibits original notes of walnut and chestnut, together with fruit. The palate is juicy, succulent and very lively, with not altogether smooth tannins. The alicante-based Terziere '99 is, we admit, difficult to make out. While the nose presents some unappealing reduced notes, the palate progresses more smoothly than one might expect. The late-picked Sauvignon Blanc, Patrizia Bartolini '99, is excellent. It is at once elegant and rich, and redolent of wild flowers and lavender. We close with the vermentino-based Ariento '99, a white that is hard to match for originality, and not only because it is aged in chestnut wood. We must confess that after tasting so many innocuous, carbon-copy whites, Ariento makes a delightful change. The bouquet is very spicy, and includes some animal hints as well as a touch of volatile acidity. The palate is well supported, invigorating and flavourful, and the finish, while tannic, shows distinctive character.

● Montervo '00	▼▼	6
● Romalbo '00	▼▼	6
○ Vermentino Barrique '01	▼▼	5
● Anchigi '00	▼▼	4*
● Massaretta '00	▼▼	5
● Vermentino Nero '00	▼▼	5
○ Candia dei Colli Apuani '01	▼▼	4
○ Vermentino '01	▼▼	4
○ Candia dei Colli Apuani Vigneto Candia Alto '01	▼	4
● Massaretta '99	♀♀	6
● Montervo '99	♀♀	6
● Romalbo '99	♀♀	6
● Sangiovese '99	♀	5

○ Patrizia Bartolini '99	▼▼	5
○ Ariento '99	▼▼	4
● La Fonte di Pietrarsa '99	▼▼	5
● Terziere '99	▼	5
● La Fonte di Pietrarsa '98	♀♀	5
● Terziere '93	♀♀	4
● La Fonte di Pietrarsa '94	♀♀	4
● La Fonte di Pietrarsa '95	♀♀	4
● La Fonte di Pietrarsa '96	♀♀	4
● Il Matto delle Giuncaie '97	♀♀	4
● La Fonte di Pietrarsa '97	♀♀	5
● Il Matto delle Giuncaie '98	♀♀	4
● Poggio ai Venti '98	♀♀	5
● Il Matto delle Giuncaie '99	♀♀	4

MASSA MARITTIMA (GR)

Moris Farms
Loc. Curanuova
Fattoria Poggetti
58024 Massa Marittima (GR)
tel. 0566919135
e-mail: morisfarms@morisfarms.it

Adolfo Parentini seems to have found a magic formula for his Avvoltore, which has long been the estate standard-bearer. In recent years, has taken on a new character and, as usual, there is probably more than one reason for this. It could be that the vines have now reached a propitious age, that oak is used with greater expertise, or that a proportion of syrah has become a permanent feature of the blend, together with the main constituent, sangiovese, and the cabernet sauvignon. It is also quite noticeable that the tannins are riper and smoother, and consequently contribute to the solidity and elegance of the palate. The colour is dark, and also dense, as is the bouquet, which is predominantly fruity and ripe, with light spicy and vegetal hints. The palate is extremely soft and almost sinuously supple in its development. The concentration is remarkable but not excessive, swathed as it is by the fruit. The finish is very long, captivating and occasionally almost exotic. The Morellino Riserva '99 made a good showing too. It is sangiovese-driven, with earthy notes and hints of liquorice and spice. The palate is fruity and well-sustained on the finish, whereas the mid palate is just a touch austere. High marks also went to the Morellino '01, for its harmonious nose of red berries, pepper and cinnamon, and solid, lingering palate, with just a few notes of over-ripeness.

MONTAIONE (FI)

La Pieve
Loc. La Pieve
Via S. Stefano
50050 Montaione (FI)
tel. 0571697764
e-mail: simonetognetti@virgilio.it

On their first Guide outing, the wines from La Pieve have done themselves proud, racking up quite a collection of stemware. The estate, in the Montaione hills, covers some 15 hectares under vine at altitudes ranging from 250 to 500 metres. The owners, the Tognetti family, have in recent years restructured both their vineyards and their cellar, and can now aim high. The wines are very good and the prices are decidedly competitive. Distinctive character may not yet be evident but we should not expect too much all at once. The Rosso del Pievano '00, from equal parts of sangiovese and cabernet sauvignon, throws an intense nose of dark berries, bell pepper and noticeable oak. The palate is fresh, dense and tightly woven, with a faintly vegetal and bitter tone on the finish. The surprisingly good Chianti '00 offers a fruit and spice nose and a dense, lively flavour with good balance. The Chianti Fortebraccio '00 is similar in style to the other products we have described, with oak clearly present and slight over-extraction giving a bitterish finish. There is plenty of chewy fruit on the palate, though, and the mouthfeel is pleasingly soft.

● Avvoltore '00	🍷🍷🍷	6
● Morellino di Scansano '01	🍷🍷	3*
● Morellino di Scansano Ris. '99	🍷🍷	5
● Avvoltore '99	🍷🍷🍷	6
● Avvoltore '94	🍷🍷	6
● Morellino di Scansano Ris. '94	🍷🍷	4
● Avvoltore '95	🍷🍷	6
● Avvoltore '97	🍷🍷	5
● Morellino di Scansano Ris. '97	🍷🍷	4
● Avvoltore '98	🍷🍷	5
● Morellino di Scansano Ris. '98	🍷🍷	4

● Chianti '00	🍷🍷	2*
● Chianti Fortebraccio '00	🍷🍷	3*
● Rosso del Pievano '00	🍷🍷	4

MONTALCINO (SI)

ALTESINO
Loc. Altesino
53028 Montalcino (SI)
Tel. 0577806208
E-mail: altesino@iol.it

We were far from indulgent with the wines from Altesino last year, so we are happy to be able to say that we have very little to complain about this time. Indeed, thanks to the propitious '97 vintage, the Montosoli showed the stuff that has made it justly famous. It was only a slight muffling on the nose, making the fruit less distinct than it might have been, that kept this red from winning Three Glasses. There was nothing indefinite about the palate, though, which has remarkable extract, softness and tannin-backed density. The very fine Alte d'Altesi '99, from sangiovese and cabernet sauvignon, shows power, roundness and considerable solidity, although vegetal tones are much in evidence. The successful cabernet-based Borgo d'Altesi '99 offers a fragrance alternating between blackberry jam and green bell pepper. The concentrated palate reveals succulent tannins and good balance. The full body of the Brunello '97 does not compensate for the reduced notes that predominate on the nose. The Quarto d'Altesi '99, made from merlot, is no more than acceptable because its intense flavour is thrown out of kilter by an unexpected and not very well-integrated acidulous tone. In conclusion, the sangiovese-based Palazzo d'Altesi is again not very clear-cut on the nose, but the palate is well-balanced and agreeable.

MONTALCINO (SI)

ARGIANO
Fraz. Sant'Angelo in Colle
Loc. Argiano, 74
53020 Montalcino (SI)
Tel. 0577844037
E-mail: argiano@argiano.net

While not quite repeating the triumphs of the past, Argiano is at last showing signs of renewed vitality. We should also say that our general impression is that the improvement is to be attributed to fine cellar technique rather than to outstanding quality grapes. The three wines presented will not be lighting many fires but they did reach levels more in keeping with the estate's former standards. For example, the Solengo '00, a blend of sangiovese, cabernet, merlot and syrah, is very good. An intense ruby hue introduces a nicely constructed bouquet of ripe dark berries, accompanied by faint vegetal and spicy hints. There is abundant evidence of masterful cellar technique in the balance on the palate, which is also distinctly soft, elegant and deep. This wine can only improve with more bottle age. The Brunello '97 is certainly admirable, although the marvellous vintage might have been exploited to even better effect. It does not have overwhelming structure, but can point to excellent balance, good tannic texture and great stylishness. More fine-tuning would benefit the Rosso di Montalcino '00, which is agreeable and well made but a bit dilute and uncomplicated. It may also be a whisker too vegetal.

● Brunello di Montalcino Montosoli '97	♛♛	8
● Alte d'Altesi '99	♛♛	6
● Borgo d'Altesi '99	♛♛	6
● Brunello di Montalcino '97	♛	7
● Palazzo d'Altesi '99	♛	5
● Quarto d'Altesi '99	♛	6
● Brunello di Montalcino Montosoli '93	♛♛	8
● Brunello di Montalcino Montosoli '95	♛♛	8
● Brunello di Montalcino '96	♛♛	7

● Solengo '00	♛♛	8
● Brunello di Montalcino '97	♛♛	8
● Rosso di Montalcino '00	♛	6
● Brunello di Montalcino Ris. '85	♛♛♛	5
● Brunello di Montalcino Ris. '88	♛♛♛	6
● Solengo '95	♛♛♛	8
● Solengo '97	♛♛♛	8
● Brunello di Montalcino '94	♛♛	8
● Brunello di Montalcino '95	♛♛	8
● Solengo '96	♛♛	8
● Solengo '98	♛♛	8
● Solengo '99	♛♛	8
● Brunello di Montalcino '96	♛	8

MONTALCINO (SI)

★ Banfi
Loc. Sant' Angelo Scalo
Castello di Poggio alle Mura
53024 Montalcino (SI)
tel. 0577840111
e-mail: banfi@banfi.it

Banfi has added a new bottle to its extensive range, Poggio alle Mura, a Brunello from a large vineyard north of the castle of the same name. Its promising debut happily coincides with a seriously good vintage in Montalcino, the '97, and the wine is dense, concentrated, mouthfilling, well-balanced, intensely fruity and graced with fine-grained tannins. It only just missed Three Glasses, which went instead to the '99 Excelsus, a dense, full-structured masterpiece with invigorating flavour and elegant progression. The almost endless procession of wines includes the Tavernelle Cabernet '99, a vibrant, fairly characterful and attractively mature wine that is held back just a little by the oak. The Summus '99 seemed good, but not great. The nose is densely fruity but also somewhat vegetal, and the full-bodied palate is a bit astringent on the finish. Still, all the wines showed well, providing evidence of serious work carefully carried out. Another fine newcomer, the Cum Laude '99, is a less complex wine, but shows sound fruit and solid structure. The more traditional wines include the very reliable Brunello '97 and the Rosso di Montalcino '00, which is simple, fruity and agreeably round.

MONTALCINO (SI)

Fattoria dei Barbi
Loc. Podernovi, 170
53024 Montalcino (SI)
tel. 0577841111
e-mail: fattoriadeibarbi@fattoriadeibarbi.it

For Stefano Cinelli Colombini, that indefatigable defender of the Montalcino faith, any talk of change in Brunello winemaking is anathema. This does not mean that he is inflexibly attached to the ways of the past, or that he has no interest in technical innovation. At Fattoria dei Barbi, they are more than willing to experiment with techniques, like cold maceration, that lead to improvement in the wine. One particularly successful result is the Rosso di Montalcino '00 which, in addition to a lively intense ruby hue, offers a clean, clear-cut bouquet where the freshness of the fruit is enhanced by pleasing notes of black pepper. After a smooth, soft attack, the even palate reveals well-integrated tannins and a fairly long, fruit-rich finish. The Vigna del Fiore '97 selection is good, if not quite up to expectations. This is an invigorating, intense Brunello with a spicy but not particularly complex nose. The Riserva '96 is fair, but less impressive. It is one of the few wines from the vintage presented this year, and shows moderate energy, a few vegetal notes on the nose and a somewhat limited flavour. The Brunello '97 is on the same level. Rather closed on the nose, it is round and nicely progressive on the palate, and a bit forward on the finish.

● Sant'Antimo Excelsus '99	🍷🍷🍷	7
● Brunello di Montalcino Poggio alle Mura '97	🍷🍷	7
● Sant'Antimo Tavernelle Cabernet '99	🍷🍷	5
● Centine '00	🍷🍷	3
● Rosso di Montalcino '00	🍷🍷	5
○ Sant'Antimo Fontanelle Chardonnay '01	🍷🍷	5
○ Sant'Antimo Serena Sauvignon Blanc '01	🍷🍷	5
● Brunello di Montalcino '97	🍷🍷	7
● Mandrielle Merlot '99	🍷🍷	5
● Sant'Antimo Colvecchio '99	🍷🍷	5
● Sant'Antimo Cum Laude '99	🍷🍷	5
● Sant'Antimo Summus '99	🍷🍷	7
● Brunello di Montalcino Poggio all'Oro Ris. '95	🍷🍷🍷	8
● Sant'Antimo Summus '97	🍷🍷🍷	6

● Rosso di Montalcino '00	🍷🍷	4*
● Brunello di Montalcino Vigna del Fiore '97	🍷🍷	8
● Brunello di Montalcino Ris. '96	🍷	8
● Brunello di Montalcino '97	🍷	7
● Brunello di Montalcino Vigna del Fiore Ris. '91	🍷🍷	8
● Brunello di Montalcino '93	🍷🍷	5
● Brunello di Montalcino Vigna del Fiore Ris. '93	🍷🍷	8
● Brunello di Montalcino Ris. '95	🍷🍷	8
● Brunello di Montalcino Vigna del Fiore Ris. '95	🍷🍷	8

MONTALCINO (SI)

Roberto Bellini
Via Tamanti, 2
53024 Montalcino (SI)
tel. 0577847154
e-mail: robertobellini@altavista.it

Few who tasted them can have forgotten the wines of Chiesa di Santa Restituta. Their creator, Roberto Bellini, has now returned to the fray, after giving up his winery to Angelo Gaja. Roberto is a bit of an oddball. He could easily afford to call it a day and lead a life of ease, but instead there he is, planning his new wines in his brand-new cellar at Podere Brizio. He decided to submit two of them, the Pupà Pepu and the Podere Brizio, to us for tasting, with excellent results. Next time, he will be presenting his Brunello '98. The Pupà Pepu hails from just over a dozen hectares of vineyards at Sesta, near Castelnuovo dell'Abate. Two thirds of the plot is planted to merlot, and the rest to cabernet sauvignon, both grapes going into the Pupà Pepu. The notably successful '00 is a very intense ruby and discloses aromas that open, after some initial reticence, to dark berries and vegetal hints. The palate is very succulent and velvet soft, with lots of fruit and well-judged tannins. Podere Brizio, the other part of the estate, is near Tavernelle and covers nine hectares under vine, seven of which are given over to the brunello strain of the sangiovese grape. It is here that fruit for the monovarietal Sangiovese named after the vineyard comes from. The very enjoyable '00 is soft, round, even and lingering.

MONTALCINO (SI)

Castello di Camigliano
Loc. Camigliano
Via d'Ingresso, 2
53024 Montalcino (SI)
tel. 0577816061 - 0577844068
e-mail: camigliano@virgilio.it

At the eastern limit of Montalcino, in a secluded and untrammelled spot, Castello di Camigliano has tended to produce well-made, but not particularly outstanding, wines. Nowadays, as we suggested last year, things are changing. The owners of the estate, the Ghezzis, have decided that the time has come to set their sights a little higher. With the help of their young, highly qualified oenologist Lorenzo Landi, they have begun a radical rethink of their vineyards that will, in due course, bring results. For now, the Brunello '97 is carefully executed. It may not be overwhelmingly characterful, but it develops seamlessly with well-integrated tannins and fairly clear-cut aromas underpinned by notes of oak. The Rosso di Montalcino '00 doesn't have notable personality either but it is very well turned out. Witness the clean bouquet, with its occasional vegetal hint, and the soft, well-balanced and quite pleasing palate. The two non-traditional wines, both '00s, actually did better. The Poderuccio is concentrated, dense and nicely filled out by properly used oak, which is perceptible on the nose and finish. The stylistically similar Sant'Antimo Cabernet exhibits notes of dark berries and vegetal tones on the nose, then a soft, dense palate leading to a finish diminished by unruly tannins.

● Podere Brizio '00	5
● Pupà Pepu '00	6

● Poderuccio '00	4
● Sant'Antimo Cabernet Sauvignon '00	5
● Brunello di Montalcino '97	7
● Rosso di Montalcino '00	4
● Brunello di Montalcino Ris. '90	6
● Brunello di Montalcino '91	7
● Brunello di Montalcino Ris. '95	7
● Poderuccio '99	4
● Brunello di Montalcino '96	6

MONTALCINO (SI)

CAPANNA DI CENCIONI
LOC. CAPANNA, 333
53024 MONTALCINO (SI)
TEL. 0577848298

After an interval of a few years, Benito Cencioni's estate is back in the Guide with a full profile. This is a particularly welcome return because Capanna wines are always stylistically interesting and quite individual. They always make a significant contribution to the ongoing debate on Brunello and how to make the wine ever more appealing. Benito's Brunello '97 is an excellent wine, despite the somewhat disorienting animal notes on the nose at first. These soon give way to aromas of black and sour cherry jam. The attack on the palate is powerful and the development is soft, meaty and enjoyable, with abundant fruit and a long finish distinguished by lively, succulent tannins. The other wines did very well, even if they didn't get such high marks. The Sant'Antimo '00 almost won Two Glasses for its very dark colour and uncomplicatedly immediate but very pleasing fruit aromas. The palate is slightly over-ripe and a bit short on the finish but nicely balanced and generally successful. The fair Rosso di Montalcino '00 is an undemanding red with a red berry bouquet and an agreeably rounded palate. Lastly, the Moscadello di Montalcino '01, a fizzy white, has a straightforward quince fragrance. It's light, sweet and slips down deliciously.

●	Brunello di Montalcino '97	ᵧᵧ	7
●	Rosso di Montalcino '00	ᵧ	4
●	Sant'Antimo Rosso '00	ᵧ	4
○	Moscadello di Montalcino '01	ᵧ	4
●	Brunello di Montalcino Ris. '90	ᵧᵧᵧ	6
●	Brunello di Montalcino '88	ᵧᵧ	5
●	Brunello di Montalcino Ris. '88	ᵧᵧ	6

MONTALCINO (SI)

TENUTA CAPARZO
LOC. CAPARZO
S. P. DEL BRUNELLO KM 1,700
53024 MONTALCINO (SI)
TEL. 0577848390 - 0577847166
E-MAIL: ntrune@caparzo.com

It was reasonable to expect something extra special from the top of the Tenuta Caparzo range, Brunello La Casa, since we were going to be tasting the '97 vintage. And "extra special" is what we got, even if the wine missed top honours by a hair's breadth. The '97 is a powerful, rich wine with good thrust on the palate and an equally intense finish. The nose seemed less successful, since an over-ripe tone upset the overall balance. The very fine Ca' del Pazzo '98, a blend of sangiovese and cabernet sauvignon, is a solid wine with lots of extract (perhaps even a tad too much), and an admirable sound, fruity bouquet. We were pleasantly surprised by the Rosso Caparzo '00. It has a clear-cut, intense fragrance and soft, invigorating palate, despite a slight roughness on the finish. The fair and agreeable Rosso di Montalcino '00 boasts a clean fragrance and medium body. The white Le Grance '98 is better than satisfactory, although nothing like some of its excellent predecessors. The nose offers pleasing notes of flowers and tropical fruit, and the palate has weight, but more energy would be welcome on the finish. The Bianco Caparzo Chardonnay '01 is very simple, but well-made and consistent. In fact, the only quibbles we have are with the Brunello di Montalcino '97, which is over-evolved on the nose and tired and flabby in the mouth.

●	Brunello di Montalcino La Casa '97	ᵧᵧ	8
●	Rosso Caparzo Sangiovese '00	ᵧᵧ	4
●	Sant'Antimo Ca' del Pazzo '98	ᵧᵧ	5
●	Rosso di Montalcino '00	ᵧ	4
○	Bianco Caparzo Chardonnay '01	ᵧ	4
○	Sant'Antimo Le Grance '98	ᵧ	5
●	Brunello di Montalcino '97		6
●	Brunello di Montalcino La Casa '88	ᵧᵧᵧ	7
●	Brunello di Montalcino La Casa '93	ᵧᵧᵧ	7
●	Brunello di Montalcino La Casa '91	ᵧᵧ	7
●	Brunello di Montalcino Ris. '93	ᵧᵧ	7
●	Brunello di Montalcino La Casa '94	ᵧᵧ	7
●	Brunello di Montalcino La Casa '95	ᵧᵧ	7
●	Brunello di Montalcino Ris. '95	ᵧᵧ	7
●	Ca' del Pazzo '97	ᵧᵧ	5

MONTALCINO (SI)

CASANOVA DI NERI
PODERE CASANOVA
53028 MONTALCINO (SI)
TEL. 0577834455
E-MAIL: giacner@tin.it

Any list of the top Montalcino producers would be incomplete without Giacomo Neri. Not only is Tenuta Nuova one of the best Brunellos of the '97 vintage, it's also a success that owes very little to chance. It's the direct result of a series of decisions made at this Torrenieri estate in recent years. In the first place, these regard the vineyards, which have been extended to the not inconsiderable total of 60 hectares, including Tenuta Nuova in its magnificent site on the southern side of Montalcino. Then it should be noted that expert help from oenologist Carlo Ferrini has done much to make Giacomo's dreams come true. For the Brunello Tenuta Nuova '97 walked off with Three Glasses, after impressing the panel with its meaty, powerful body, confident structure and a long, full finish. The nose is a little reticent at first, but mineral tones soon begin to emerge. The Rosso di Montalcino '00 did very well, too. Its pervasive, substantial mouthfeel and rich, even progression make it one of the best wines in its category. There were further high marks for the Brunello '97. It's a bit stiff on the finish but has lots of chewy, sweet fruit on the palate. And we've got to tell you about Giacomo Neri's upcoming new wine, the Pietradonice '00, a blend of cabernet sauvignon with 25 per cent sangiovese. Our preview tasting was enough to confirm that it is extraordinary. Next year's Guide is going to have a new contender for top honours.

● Brunello di Montalcino Tenuta Nuova '97	🍷🍷🍷	7
● Rosso di Montalcino '00	🍷🍷	5*
● Brunello di Montalcino '97	🍷🍷	7
● Brunello di Montalcino Cerretalto '95	🍷🍷🍷	6
● Brunello di Montalcino Cerretalto '96	🍷🍷	6
● Brunello di Montalcino '90	🍷🍷	5
● Brunello di Montalcino '93	🍷🍷	5
● Brunello di Montalcino Tenuta Nuova '93	🍷🍷	6
● Brunello di Montalcino Tenuta Nuova '94	🍷🍷	6
● Brunello di Montalcino Tenuta Nuova '95	🍷🍷	6

MONTALCINO (SI)

FATTORIA DEL CASATO
DONATELLA CINELLI COLOMBINI
LOC. CASATO PRIME DONNE
53024 MONTALCINO (SI)
TEL. 0577849421 - 0577662108
E-MAIL: vino@cinellicolombini.it

Donatella Cinelli Colombini's Brunello '97 is not one of the wines that won Three Glasses. The vintage, as has been said many times, was extremely favourable and the grapes were often perfectly ripe. Fattoria del Casato certainly made a respectable Brunello di Montalcino but, sadly, it lacks the polish of the very best versions. The moderately vivid ruby of the standard '97 introduces complex aromas of red berries with light spicy nuances. The palate shows reasonable density, breadth as it develops and an invigorating, if not very long, finish. Roughly on the same level is the Brunello Prime Donne '97. It's rather dumb on the nose at present, but has a harmonious palate, nicely underpinned by solid tannins. It has to be said that we failed to find the significant difference in quality, or at least in style, that theoretically should distinguish these two wines. The Brunello Riserva '96, the child of a lesser vintage, is blander. The nose is already quite forward – rain-soaked earth, dried leaves and walnut skin come through – and the flavour is consistent, agreeable and fairly long. This Brunello is drinking very nicely now but is unlikely to last very long. The Rosso di Montalcino '00 seemed simple to us. The fresh palate was diminished by not very clean, and somewhat drying, oak-derived notes. To conclude, the sangiovese and merlot-based Leone Rosso '00 is distinctly under par. It has medium weight, but the nose is wildly out of kilter.

● Brunello di Montalcino '97	🍷🍷	6
● Brunello di Montalcino Prime Donne '97	🍷🍷	7
● Brunello di Montalcino Ris. '96	🍷	7
● Rosso di Montalcino '00	🍷	4
● Leone Rosso '00		3
● Brunello di Montalcino '93	🍷🍷	5
● Brunello di Montalcino Prime Donne '93	🍷🍷	6
● Brunello di Montalcino Prime Donne '94	🍷🍷	6
● Brunello di Montalcino '95	🍷🍷	6
● Brunello di Montalcino Prime Donne '95	🍷🍷	6
● Brunello di Montalcino Prime Donne '96	🍷🍷	6

MONTALCINO (SI)

CASTELGIOCONDO
LOC. CASTELGIOCONDO
53024 MONTALCINO (SI)
TEL. 05527141
E-MAIL: info@frescobaldi.it

By some irony of fate, the grape that gives greatest satisfaction at the vast estate of Castelgiocondo is merlot, and not sangiovese. The Frescobaldis' property covers over 800 hectares, of which 240 are under vine, and a significant chunk is devoted to sangiovese. Nevertheless, the Lamaione, made from merlot alone, is their most celebrated wine. Hollywood actors and Italian celebs are currently stocking up on it, and why not? It's a very good wine. The '99 is, as usual, generous with the oak but it rests on a solid, engrossing foundation of fruit. This warm, full, long wine easily won Two Glasses. But with all due respect to fashion-conscious quaffers, we found that the Brunello di Montalcino '97 has more personality. Its fairly vivid garnet introduces fruity aromas that are rendered more complex by earthy and mineral nuances. In the mouth, the attack is confident and the development broad, taking you into a slightly dilute mid palate and a finish with well-integrated tannins. The less brilliant Rosso di Montalcino Campo ai Sassi '00 is a rather simple wine with a slightly vegetal character. However, the excellent balance and sheer drinkability do a lot to compensate.

MONTALCINO (SI)

CASTIGLION DEL BOSCO
LOC. CASTIGLION DEL BOSCO
53024 MONTALCINO (SI)
TEL. 0577808348
E-MAIL: castbosco@iol.it

Castiglion del Bosco is adept at dealing with the uncertainties presented by the various individual site climates in different years. The vines cover 50 hectares, which is quite a lot for Montalcino. For the past few harvests, technical matters have been in the expert hands of the celebrated consultant Riccardo Cotarella, who is assisted here by a fine oenologist in Marina Mariani. Results have been quick to come through, particularly given how slowly things tend to go in the countryside. The Brunello di Montalcino '97 stood out from its peers and very nearly got Three Glasses. Its most obvious drawback is in the bouquet, which is rather introverted, even after quite a bit of breathing time, and shows notes of earth and reduction. A good amount of bottle ageing could, or rather should, deal with this problem. In the mouth, the wine has an excellent attack, a confident, mouthfilling progression, noble tannins and a long finish. The successful Rosso di Montalcino '00 unveils an intense ruby hue, a lovely fresh fruity fragrance and a lively palate that is nicely balanced between crisp acidity and modern soft tones. The long, clean finish reveals a light vegetal hint.

● Brunello di Montalcino '97	ΨΨ	7
● Lamaione '99	ΨΨ	8
● Rosso di Montalcino Campo ai Sassi '00	Ψ	4
● Brunello di Montalcino Ris. '88	ΨΨΨ	6
● Brunello di Montalcino Ris. '90	ΨΨΨ	6
● Brunello di Montalcino Ris. '95	ΨΨ	8
● Lamaione '98	ΨΨ	8
● Brunello di Montalcino '93	ΨΨ	5
● Lamaione '94	ΨΨ	8
● Brunello di Montalcino '95	ΨΨ	5
● Lamaione '95	ΨΨ	8
● Brunello di Montalcino '96	ΨΨ	6
● Lamaione '96	ΨΨ	8
● Lamaione '97	ΨΨ	8

● Brunello di Montalcino '97	ΨΨ	6
● Rosso di Montalcino '00	ΨΨ	5
● Brunello di Montalcino Ris. '95	ΨΨ	6
● Brunello di Montalcino '96	ΨΨ	6
● Rosso di Montalcino '99	Ψ	4

MONTALCINO (SI)

CENTOLANI
LOC. STRADA MAREMMANA
TENUTA FRIGGIALI
53024 MONTALCINO (SI)
TEL. 0577849314 - 0577849454
E-MAIL: agricolacentolani@libero.it

Olga Peluso wants it to be quite clear that her estate is divided into two very distinct properties. The first, Friggiali, is in the eastern section of Montalcino. It is the original core of the estate and also contains the cellar, which is currently being completely restructured. The other property, Pietranera, is to the south, in the tiny Castelnuovo dell'Abate subzone. From these two very different areas come wines with distinct characteristics, which Centolani reflects by offering two ranges of bottles. Our tastings of the two Brunellos revealed definite stylistic differences but no great divergence in quality. The Brunello Friggiali offers a mass of fruit on the nose, together with earthy, mineral and spicy tones. Big and powerful in the mouth, it has significant extract, which accounts for a slight roughness, in addition to the typical acidic contrast of the sangiovese grape. The Pietranera '97 foregrounds the ripeness of the grapes and shows a less complex, but rather deeper, bouquet. The palate is dense and full-bodied, the tannins are better integrated, and what the wine might want in character it gains in elegance. In any case, these are two really fine Brunellos. We should also mention the successful Le Logge '97, which is soft and well executed, with faint vegetal nuances. The two Rosso di Montalcinos did less well. We just preferred the Friggiali.

MONTALCINO (SI)

CERBAIONA
LOC. CERBAIONA
53024 MONTALCINO (SI)
TEL. 0577848660

It seems to be either feast or famine at Diego Molinari's estate. It missed a turn in last year's Guide because the wines weren't up to scratch but this time it's back in triumph with a well-deserved Three Glasses for the Brunello '97. And what a wine it is! Just about everyone in Montalcino, including many of Molinari's fellow growers, considers it the finest Brunello of its vintage. Our panel pretty much agreed. Even compared with its most successful competitors, the Cerbaiona Brunello '97 stands out for its aroma-driven eloquence. The colour is a very intense ruby with brilliant, lively highlights, and the bouquet has a wide-ranging complexity. There is a tremendous clarity of definition and cleanness we have not always found in Cerbaiona wines. The alcohol knows its place and the ripeness of the grapes is ideal. But the wine's real strengths are on the palate. The attack, the progression, the richness of extract and tannins, the general balance and the finish are all quite extraordinary. This is a massive Brunello, with more energy than refinement and lashings of personality. Most notably, it faithfully reflects its terroir. After such celestial glory, we return to earth with the Cerbaiona, its sangiovese-based younger brother. The '99 is quite juicy, and shows grip and good weight, but it wants finesse and cleanness on the nose.

● Brunello di Montalcino Pietranera '97	❡❡	6
● Brunello di Montalcino Tenuta Friggiali '97	❡❡	6
● Le Logge '97	❡❡	5
● Rosso di Montalcino Pietranera '00		4
● Rosso di Montalcino Tenuta Friggiali '00		4

● Brunello di Montalcino '97	❡❡❡	8
● Cerbaiona '99	❡	5
● Brunello di Montalcino '85	❡❡❡	8
● Brunello di Montalcino '88	❡❡❡	8
● Brunello di Montalcino '90	❡❡❡	8

MONTALCINO (SI)

CIACCI PICCOLOMINI D'ARAGONA
FRAZ. CASTELNUOVO DELL'ABATE
B.GO DI MEZZO, 62
53020 MONTALCINO (SI)
TEL. 0577835616
E-MAIL: info@ctacci-piccolomini.com

The '97 Brunello produced by Ciacci Piccolomini is one of the best in its vintage and came within an inch of winning Three Glasses. It's a wine that knows no half measures. Many will agree that it is excellent, but at our finals there was some lingering doubt about the aromatic definition. The structure is remarkable and altogether appropriate for its category. The aromas are still in the process of settling, and have yet to absorb the oak, which for the moment has a muffling effect. Nevertheless, rich fruit, just this side of over-ripe, prevails and is reflected on the finish in the mouth. The wine explodes onto the palate, where it develops with energy, breadth and seamless progression. After some not very encouraging years, the sangiovese and cabernet Ateo is back on form. Although there is a bit too much space for vegetal tones on the nose, the palate makes up for this with its harmony and well-judged tannins. We were unfortunately unable to taste the syrah-based Fabius, a generally excellent wine that we shall be trying next year. The Rosso di Montalcino Vigna della Fonte faithfully reflects its vintage, the hot, dry '00, which has in this case produced over-ripe and sweet, almost raisiny nuances. It is still a very decent wine of intensity and concentration, although perhaps just a touch showy.

MONTALCINO (SI)

TENUTA COL D'ORCIA
FRAZ. SANT'ANGELO IN COLLE
53020 MONTALCINO (SI)
TEL. 0577808001
E-MAIL: coldorcia.direzione@tin.it

Although there may have been no absolute stars in this year's range of wines from Tenuta Col d'Orcia, the general quality was very high. It should be pointed out that the top wine, Brunello Poggio al Vento, will not be released until next year. Nevertheless, the Brunello '97 made an excellent impression, not so much for any massive weight or prominent characteristics as for a happy combination of sweetness and freshness, as well as the elegance of its palate. The nose focuses on black berries and black cherry jam, then the flavour is well co-ordinated, even and very enjoyable on the finish. The Olmaia '98 did well, although not so well as it has done in the past. One positive point is the fact that terroir has got the upper hand over grape variety. When you taste it, the first impression is of a wine from Montalcino, rather than a Cabernet Sauvignon. Less in its favour is its forwardness, which was even more evident in the '97, and the drying tannins. The other wines included a Ghiaie Bianche that seemed very successful, despite rather a free hand with the oak. The Rosso degli Spezieri '01 is straightforward, fruity and agreeable. The Rosso di Montalcino Banditella '00 is slightly fuzzy on the nose but shows good density on the palate, although it is still a bit stiff on the finish. The Moscadello Pascena '99 is consistent but not characterful. All the other wines are well made and quite satisfactory.

- Brunello di Montalcino Vigna di Pianrosso '97 — 🍷🍷 8
- Ateo '99 — 🍷🍷 6
- Rosso di Montalcino Vigna della Fonte '00 — 🍷 5
- Brunello di Montalcino Vigna di Pianrosso '88 — 🍷🍷🍷 6
- Brunello di Montalcino Vigna di Pianrosso '90 — 🍷🍷🍷 5
- Brunello di Montalcino Vigna di Pianrosso Ris. '95 — 🍷🍷🍷 6
- Brunello di Montalcino Vigna di Pianrosso '96 — 🍷🍷 6
- Rosso di Montalcino Vigna della Fonte '99 — 🍷🍷 4

- Brunello di Montalcino '97 — 🍷🍷 5*
- ○ Ghiaie Bianche '00 — 🍷🍷 4
- Olmaia '98 — 🍷🍷 7
- Rosso di Montalcino Banditella '00 — 🍷 5
- Rosso degli Spezieri '01 — 🍷 3*
- ○ Moscadello di Montalcino Vendemmia Tardiva Pascena '99 — 🍷 5
- Rosso di Montalcino '00 — 4
- ○ Sant'Antimo Pinot Grigio '01 — 3
- Brunello di Montalcino Poggio al Vento Ris. '88 — 🍷🍷🍷 6
- Brunello di Montalcino Poggio al Vento Ris. '90 — 🍷🍷🍷 6
- Olmaia '94 — 🍷🍷🍷 7
- Brunello di Montalcino Poggio al Vento Ris. '95 — 🍷🍷🍷 8

MONTALCINO (SI)

ANDREA COSTANTI
COLLE AL MATRICHESE
53024 MONTALCINO (SI)
TEL. 0577848195
E-MAIL: costanti@inwind.it

Andrea Costanti's ever reliable wines would seem to have made a definite step forward in both structure and expressiveness. The Brunello in particular has left its old humdrum, predictable style far behind. The admirably vibrant nose offers typical sangiovese notes of black cherry and liquorice with earthy nuances. The flavour, which has breadth right from the start, is nicely supported by alcohol, concentrated and balanced at mid palate, and intense if not overly complex on the finish. The Ardingo '99, a blend of cabernet sauvignon and merlot, is also excellent, albeit not remarkable for personality. The bouquet is appealingly based on notes of ripe dark berries, sweet tobacco and toasty oak. The palate is powerful and solid, lingering nicely. We very much liked the immediate, straightforward, very clean Vermiglio '99. It's a really enjoyable, unpretentious wine, which is well executed, supple and tasty. It strolled off with Two Glasses. The interesting, but slightly forward, Rosso di Montalcino Calbello '00 is a rounded red with a nicely executed nose, but the finish is somewhat dried by wood tannins. The standard Rosso di Montalcino, on the other hand, is only fair. The bouquet is a little muffled, then the palate is correct and uncomplicated.

● Brunello di Montalcino '97	7
● Ardingo '99	7
● Vermiglio '99	4
● Rosso di Montalcino '00	4
● Rosso di Montalcino Calbello '00	5
● Brunello di Montalcino '88	6
● Ardingo '98	6
● Brunello di Montalcino '90	6
● Brunello di Montalcino '93	6
● Brunello di Montalcino Ris. '95	6
● Brunello di Montalcino '96	6
● Vermiglio '98	4
● Rosso di Montalcino Calbello '99	5

MONTALCINO (SI)

DUE PORTINE - GORELLI
VIA CIALDINI, 51/53
53024 MONTALCINO (SI)
TEL. 0577848098

The general restructuring at Giuseppe Gorelli's estate is at last complete. Giuseppe's plans can now be implemented and things can go seriously forward. The property is small, comprising some five hectares under vine. These lie largely around the winery, in one of the higher zones, with a further hectare and a half at Sant'Angelo in Colle, which is lower and south-facing. Gorelli, who personally directs the entire process of winemaking, has renewed his barrel stock, with the emphasis on medium-large barrels for the Brunello, although the collection also includes a small number of barriques. In this profile, we shall consider the wines from Le Potazzine, his new property, as well as those from Due Portine, the historic family estate, which will be reaching the end of its time with the coming Brunello '98. Our tastings revealed a style based on elegance and harmony, rather than overwhelming structure. The Brunello Le Potazzine '97 offers a deep nose, with notes of very ripe black cherry laced with hints of cocoa. The palate is dense and well balanced, if not extremely long. The Brunello Due Portine '97 shows a more forward tone, medium body and remarkable precision. The very good Rosso di Montalcino Le Potazzine '00 displays intense aromas of very ripe blackberry and black cherry, as well as a powerful, dense palate with forceful tannins.

● Rosso di Montalcino Le Potazzine '00	5
● Brunello di Montalcino Le Potazzine '97	7
● Brunello di Montalcino Due Portine '97	6
● Brunello di Montalcino '89	6
● Brunello di Montalcino '90	6
● Brunello di Montalcino '92	6
● Brunello di Montalcino '93	6
● Rosso di Montalcino '93	4
● Brunello di Montalcino '94	6
● Rosso di Montalcino '96	4
● Rosso di Montalcino Le Potazzine '98	5

MONTALCINO (SI)

Fanti - San Filippo
Loc. San Filippo - B.go di Mezzo, 15
Fraz. Castelnuovo dell'Abate
53020 Montalcino (SI)
Tel. 0577835628
E-mail: balfanti@tin.it

Filippo Baldassare Fanti is on a roll. After hitting the jackpot with his Riserva '95 last year, he has done it again with a fantastic Brunello '97. These results speak for themselves, telling of the remarkable efforts made in recent years at this estate in Castelnuovo dell'Abate. It is, of course, astonishing how quickly it has all happened, but it just goes to show the incredible potential hidden in the soil of Montalcino. The estate just needed to do some work in the vineyards and fine-tune the cellar technique, and there you are! This is why we have often been puzzled in the past by the general quality of the wines of Montalcino. They've always been good but, until just a few years ago, they signally failed to make the most of the great gifts of this astoundingly felicitous wine country. Now things are changing, happily, and not just thanks to a few good vintages. Today, there is much greater awareness among the majority of Montalcino producers. But let's get back to the Brunello. The tasters comments were more or less "Wow!", which may not be a technical term, but it gets the point across. The richness of the aromas is thrilling, ranging from oriental spice, black cherry and ripe plum to cedar, balsamic and toasty notes. The palate is equally good, revealing exceptional sweetness, concentration, elegance and depth. The very fine Vin Santo is extremely sweet, viscous and persistently redolent of dried fig and chestnut jam. Lastly, the Rosso di Montalcino '00 is simple but pleasing.

MONTALCINO (SI)

Eredi Fuligni
Via S. Saloni, 32
53024 Montalcino (SI)
Tel. 0577848039 - 0577848127

Lovers of the elegance and charming vibrancy of the Montalcino sangiovese grape will find in the Fuligni Brunello '97 their ideal wine. We need hardly add that we were quite enthusiastic ourselves, and only the merciless arithmetic process of averaging all our tasters' scores kept it, by the merest whisker, from walking off with Three Glasses. As we suggested, the Fuligni Brunello has the great merit of projecting a distinctive, identifiable style. It does not generally show the power and energy of wines from warmer and sunnier parts of Montalcino but the elegance of expression of wines from the Vigneto dei Cottimelli is undeniable. A warm year like '97 gave full scope to Roberto Guerrini's skills. The wine's nose has a classic mineral tone with just a suggestion of fruit and definite complexity. The attack on the palate is remarkably powerful, the development wonderfully supple, and the finish long, enhanced and refreshed by the acidity that is typical of high-altitude Brunellos. You will not find intense concentration in this wine, nor the fat opulence of the richest examples of its category. Instead, everything is in its place and in proportion while the fine-grained tannins are juicy and smooth. On an altogether different level, the other wine presented is very enjoyable. The enigmatically named S.J. '00 reveals a nose that is very fruity, indeed almost jammy, and then a palate that shows fair body, a sweet smoothness and an easy-drinking character.

● Brunello di Montalcino '97	🍷🍷🍷 7
○ Vin Santo	🍷🍷 5
● Rosso di Montalcino '00	🍷 4

● Brunello di Montalcino Vigneti dei Cottimelli. '97	🍷🍷 7
● S. J. '00	🍷 4
● Brunello di Montalcino '90	🍷🍷 5
● Brunello di Montalcino Ris. '90	🍷🍷 6
● Brunello di Montalcino '94	🍷🍷 6
● Brunello di Montalcino '95	🍷🍷 6
● Brunello di Montalcino Vigneti dei Cottimelli Ris. '95	🍷🍷 7
● Brunello di Montalcino Vigneti dei Cottimelli '96	🍷🍷 7
● Rosso di Montalcino Ginestreto '99	🍷🍷 4

MONTALCINO (SI)

TENUTA IL GREPPO
VILLA GREPPO, 183
53024 MONTALCINO (SI)
TEL. 0577848087
E-MAIL: biondisanti@biondisanti.it

The Biondi Santi name no longer identifies only the historic Tenuta Il Greppo but, thanks to Jacopo, now also graces Castello di Montepò in the Maremma and Villa Poggio Salvi. The '97 vintage of the most celebrated wine, the Brunello di Montalcino Biondi Santi, confirms a style based more on elegance than on extract. Although only medium-bodied, the palate won points for well-judged tannins, acidity and alcohol. Next, the Rosso di Montalcino '00 is a fragrant red with a full, invigorating palate and lovely acidity supporting the finish. Turning to the wines from Castello di Montepò, which is in Morellino di Scansano country, we'll mention first the '99 Riserva version of that wine, which is clean and well-made, if not particularly eloquent. The Montepaone '98 is rather vegetal and not very bright for there are some over-evolved notes. In contrast, the interesting Sassoalloro '00 shows an admirably appropriate style, although it reveals somewhat harsh tannins. The top wine, Schidione '98, offers complex aromas enhanced by spicy notes and almost grassy nuances that are reminiscent of a Bordeaux. It's open-natured and robust, but also elegant. The most interesting of the Villa Poggi Salvi wines was the Brunello di Montalcino '97, which is not very complex but is well-made, like last year's edition. The entry on the palate is soft and the texture good. The oak is very well gauged.

MONTALCINO (SI)

IL PALAZZONE
LOC. DUE PORTE, 245
53024 MONTALCINO (SI)
TEL. 0577849375
E-MAIL: fontelattaia@virgilio.it

Il Palazzone has earned itself a profile with two fine wines. The Brunello and the Rosso di Montalcino are similar in weight and fullness of body to what we tasted last year, but the nose in each is better defined and more open. We were particularly impressed by the Rosso di Montalcino '00, unquestionably one of the best of its vintage. Both extract and general balance are remarkable, but its real forte is the sensation of ripeness it manages to convey. There is no hint of over-ripe grapes, just a vibrant, fresh fruity tone and oomph on both nose and palate. If the goodness of a wine can be judged by the length of its finish, this red is in no way inferior to the best Rossos of recent years. The Brunello di Montalcino '97 is a fine interpretation, although we had hoped for more from this excellent vintage. It offers an intense ruby hue, with faint garnet highlights, clean aromas of crushed black cherry and bay leaf, and a palate that encompasses fruity tones and hints of delicate spice, chocolate and liquorice. The tannins on the finish are a bit hard, though you couldn't call them raw. Three or four years of bottle age should give the wine the balance it wants.

Wine		Score
● Brunello di Montalcino '97	🍷🍷	8
● Schidione '98	🍷🍷	8
● Rosso di Montalcino '00	🍷🍷	6
● Sassoalloro '00	🍷🍷	5
● Brunello di Montalcino Poggio Salvi '97	🍷🍷	7
● Rosso di Montalcino Poggio Salvi '00	🍷	4
● Montepaone '98	🍷	4
● Morellino di Scansano Ris. Montepò '99	🍷	4
● Brunello di Montalcino '94	🍷🍷	6
● Brunello di Montalcino '95	🍷🍷	6
● Sassoalloro '95	🍷🍷	5
● Brunello di Montalcino Poggio Salvi '96	🍷🍷	6
● Sassoalloro '96	🍷🍷	5
● Morellino di Scansano Ris. Montepò '98	🍷🍷	4
● Sassoalloro '98	🍷🍷	5

Wine		Score
● Rosso di Montalcino '00	🍷🍷	5
● Brunello di Montalcino '97	🍷🍷	8
● Brunello di Montalcino Ris. '95	🍷🍷	6

MONTALCINO (SI)

IL POGGIOLO
LOC. POGGIOLO, 259
53024 MONTALCINO (SI)
TEL. 0577848412 - 3483411848
E-MAIL: info@ilpoggiolomontalcino.com

As usual, Rodolfo Cosimi presented quite a number of wines, including various original selections of Brunello. The results are, on the whole, excellent. All the Brunellos are remarkably good, and Terra Rossa is the best of the bunch. Stylistically, perhaps, the differences might not seem great enough to justify producing such an array for all show good body and clearly perceptible oak. We were, as we have said, particularly struck by the Brunello Terra Rossa '97, which displays a nose of some complexity, free of invasive oak and graced with intriguing scents of black cherry and fresh spice. The palate is meaty, orderly and balanced, then the finish, which is not without elegance, lingers appreciably. The very good Brunello Beato '97 shows a round, full, harmonious palate and good length after vanilla notes on the nose. The Brunello Five Stars '97 offers powerful structure, a velvet-soft palate and a rising finish with somewhat astringent tannins. There are hints of evolution in the Brunello Sassello '97, whose intense aromas of spice and oak precede an eloquent, well-sustained palate. We found the Sant'Antimo In Riva al Fosso '00 rather unchallenging and slightly rough, but still agreeable. Finally, the two Rosso di Montalcinos are acceptable but not very lively.

Wine	Rating	Score
● Brunello di Montalcino Terra Rossa '97	♀♀	7
● Brunello di Montalcino Beato '97	♀♀	7
● Brunello di Montalcino Five Stars '97	♀♀	7
● Brunello di Montalcino Sassello '97	♀♀	7
● Sant'Antimo In Riva al Fosso '00	♀	5
● Rosso di Montalcino Sassello '00		4
● Rosso di Montalcino Terra Rossa '00		5
● Brunello di Montalcino Five Stars Ris. '95	♀♀	6
● Rosso di Montalcino Sassello '99	♀♀	4
● Rosso di Montalcino Terra Rossa '99	♀♀	5

MONTALCINO (SI)

TENUTA IL POGGIONE
FRAZ. SANT'ANGELO IN COLLE
PIAZZA CASTELLO, 14
53020 MONTALCINO (SI)
TEL. 0577844029
E-MAIL: ilpoggione@tin.it

Changes are under way at Il Poggione. Some barriques have been quietly slipping into the cellars beside the traditional barrels used for ageing the Brunello. This is in part a result of the 1998 modification in the Brunello regulations, which limited barrel time to two years instead of three. This does not mean that the estate has abandoned the faith, but it is a small indication that something is afoot, even in the historic, traditional wineries of Montalcino. Whether this is for good or ill, only time will tell. Nothing exceptional emerged from this year's tastings. Everything was fairly good, with the exception of the Brunello '97, which was distinctly fine. The bouquet is harmonious, even elegant, with notes of black and red cherries, tobacco and cinnamon, as well as a faint hint of vanilla. The palate is soft, fairly weighty and just slightly dilute on the long finish. The Rosso di Montalcino '00 is not particularly characterful but does show admirable cleanness on the nose and a supple palate where, however, alcohol and acidity are not yet entirely integrated. The straightforward and well-made San Leopoldo '99 boasts an immediate, well-defined, fruit-driven nose. The Moscadello di Montalcino, a sparkling wine, is agreeable, if not much more.

Wine	Rating	Score
● Brunello di Montalcino '97	♀♀	6
● Rosso di Montalcino '00	♀	4
○ Moscadello di Montalcino '01	♀	5
● San Leopoldo '99	♀	5
● Brunello di Montalcino '90	♀♀	5
● Brunello di Montalcino '92	♀♀	5
● Brunello di Montalcino Ris. '93	♀♀	5
● Brunello di Montalcino Ris. '95	♀♀	6
● Rosso di Montalcino '95	♀♀	3
● San Leopoldo '98	♀♀	5

MONTALCINO (SI)

Podere La Fortuna
Loc. La Fortuna, 83
53024 Montalcino (SI)
tel. 0577848308
e-mail: azaglafortuna@inwind.it

Not much has been said or written about Gioberto Zannoni's wines. We like them very much indeed – although years ago, this was not the case – and are glad to spread the word. We feel the moment has arrived for Zannoni to produce a real champion so who knows whether he has something extra special in his cellar even now? Meanwhile, we must say that his Brunello '97 is a very good wine and almost made it to our finals. The aromas are well calibrated, clean and intense, featuring notes of black cherry and vanilla. After a soft attack, the palate is concentrated and well-sustained, and the finish distinctly fruity. It's a well-balanced and full-bodied, but not showy, wine with nicely judged tannins. A little more grip and depth would have gained it higher marks, but it is by no means disappointing. The Rosso di Montalcino '00 also won Two Glasses, but then less is expected from this category. It's well above average for its vintage, delivering a clear-cut, fruity and well-rounded palate that only needs to smooth out the currently slightly intrusive oak.

• Rosso di Montalcino '00	ΨΨ	5
• Brunello di Montalcino '97	ΨΨ	7
• Brunello di Montalcino '91	ΨΨ	7
• Brunello di Montalcino '93	ΨΨ	7
• Brunello di Montalcino Ris. '93	ΨΨ	6
• Brunello di Montalcino '94	ΨΨ	7
• Brunello di Montalcino '95	ΨΨ	7
• Brunello di Montalcino Ris. '95	ΨΨ	6
• Rosso di Montalcino '98	ΨΨ	5

MONTALCINO (SI)

La Gerla
Loc. Canalicchio
Podere Colombaio
53024 Montalcino (SI)
tel. 0577848599
e-mail: lagerla@tin.it

Our tastings of La Gerla's wines were encouraging this year. They seem to have achieved a greater consistency of quality, regardless of the vintage, and now what is wanting is a great standard-bearer. An attempt seems to have been made with the Brunello Vigna Gli Angeli '97, which is a well-realized red, if still somewhat diminished by reduced notes on the nose. The palate, on the other hand, is broad, very soft, weighty and elegant as it unfolds. The Brunello '97 did equally well, apart from a somewhat intrusive vegetal undertone on the nose. In the mouth, it reveals density and a tight-knit tannic texture. Another wine we greatly enjoyed is the Rosso di Montalcino '00. Fruit-led aromas are joined by traces of green oak. The entry on the palate is enticingly sweet, the progression orderly and the finish clean and lingering. The decent Birba '99, made mostly from sangiovese, is perhaps not so good as it has been in the past. The nose is intense but there are some not very stylish super-ripe notes peeping through, and the medium-bodied palate is well balanced but a bit short in the finish.

• Rosso di Montalcino '00	ΨΨ	4
• Brunello di Montalcino '97	ΨΨ	7
• Brunello di Montalcino Vigna Gli Angeli '97	ΨΨ	8
• Birba '99	Ψ	5
• Birba '90	ΨΨ	5
• Brunello di Montalcino Ris. '91	ΨΨ	6
• Birba '95	ΨΨ	5
• Brunello di Montalcino Ris. '95	ΨΨ	6
• Brunello di Montalcino '96	ΨΨ	6
• Birba '98	ΨΨ	5

MONTALCINO (SI)

LA PODERINA
FRAZ. CASTELNUOVO DELL'ABATE
LOC. PODERINA
53020 MONTALCINO (SI)
TEL. 0577835737
E-MAIL: poderina@tin.it

La Poderina is another of the SAI Agricola-owned estates that did extremely well at our tastings. In last year's Guide, the cellar's Brunello Riserva '95 all but repeated the success of the Riserva '88, which won Three Glasses when it was released. And this year the Brunello '97, an eminently enjoyable wine, has repeated the triumph. Indeed, the only negative note is the name of the selection, Poggio Banale, which we might loosely translate as "boring hill". The style of the wine is, of course, modern. For some years, the Brunellos supervised by Lorenzo Landi have tended to veer towards what is called the "international taste", with masses of fruit, luscious softness and smooth tannins. This does not mean that the wine is in any sense cloying. On the contrary, this Brunello seems particularly successful in its sense of balance, its harmony, and the absence of any showy or overdone components. The colour is an intense, full ruby, and the dense bouquet offers lots of fresh fruit. The attack on the palate is exactly as it should be, the development is broad and very harmonious, and the finish goes on forever. The standard Brunello '97 is good, too, but has less verve. The nose features notes of very ripe fruit with some nuances of prune. It's a wine that progresses well in the mouth but will probably not last as long as the Poggio Banale. The Rosso di Montalcino '00 is a straightforward, agreeable and moderately long red. Lastly, the Moscadello Vendemmia Tardiva '00 is an excellent late-harvested white with well-calibrated sweetness, fleshiness and warmth.

MONTALCINO (SI)

LA TOGATA - TENUTA CARLINA
LOC. ARGIANO
53024 MONTALCINO (SI)
TEL. 0577849363 - 0668803000
E-MAIL: brunello@latogata.com

Danilo and Carla Tonon's Brunello '97 has won the prize the estate came close to getting last year with the Riserva '95. So Three very well-deserved Glasses go to the Tenuta Carlina, better known as La Togata (the lady in the robe) in honour of Mrs. Tonon's professional role as a magistrate. The estate, which was originally tiny, has gradually grown to its present 15 hectares under vine in the southern part of Montalcino. The cellar knows only medium and small-sized barrels, the choice depending on the kind of the wine to be aged and the characteristics of the vintage. The Brunello '97 won everybody over with its sheer harmony. The intense and expressive nose reveals notes of black cherry, spice, coffee and vanilla. The palate as it unfolds shows softness and elegance, with well-integrated tannins and an engagingly fresh, long finish. This wine is no flash in the pan, as can be seen from the cellar's other offerings. The Rosso di Montalcino '00 provides easy-drinking pleasure together with fair body and good overall balance. The Bricco della Torre '00 is quite a different matter. A powerful, fat, mouthfilling red, it is rich almost to excess, with super-ripe notes to the fore on the nose. The Azzurreta '00, however, is another soft, nicely balanced product. Consistent and well-defined, it is not very expansive on the nose, which is redolent of vanilla and berry fruit, but it's a distinctly enjoyable bottle.

● Brunello di Montalcino Poggio Banale '97	🍷🍷🍷	8
○ Moscadello V. T. '00	🍷🍷	5
● Rosso di Montalcino '00	🍷🍷	5
● Brunello di Montalcino '97	🍷🍷	7
● Brunello di Montalcino Ris. '88	🍷🍷🍷	6
○ Moscadello V. T. '99	🍷🍷	5
● Brunello di Montalcino Ris. '90	🍷🍷	6
● Brunello di Montalcino Ris. '93	🍷🍷	6
● Brunello di Montalcino '95	🍷🍷	5
○ Moscadello V. T. '98	🍷🍷	5

● Brunello di Montalcino '97	🍷🍷🍷	7
● Azzurreta '00	🍷🍷	6
● Bricco della Torre '00	🍷🍷	8
● Rosso di Montalcino '00	🍷🍷	5
● Brunello di Montalcino Ris. '95	🍷🍷	6
● Rosso di Montalcino '99	🍷🍷	4
● Brunello di Montalcino '90	🍷🍷	6
● Brunello di Montalcino '91	🍷🍷	6
● Brunello di Montalcino '94	🍷🍷	6
● Brunello di Montalcino '95	🍷🍷	6
● Azzurreta '96	🍷🍷	5
● Brunello di Montalcino '96	🍷🍷	6

MONTALCINO (SI)

LE CHIUSE DI SOTTO
LOC. LE CHIUSE DI SOTTO, 320
53024 MONTALCINO (SI)
TEL. 0577849342

Gianni Brunelli has at last produced a range of truly fine wines. They are not staggeringly big, but they make the most of what they have and can offer very precise definition on the nose. Le Chiuse di Sotto is a small estate, and hence does not produce vast numbers of bottles, but quality has been consistently improving. Watch this space for future developments. The Brunello '97 is particularly successful, offering a clear-cut bouquet of ripe black cherry accompanied by sweet notes of oak. The palate is soft, nicely underpinned by alcohol, sweetly smooth and even. The style remains the same even when the wine category changes. Amor Costante, an IGT, is again very well-balanced and easy to drink, rather than muscular. The nose is concentrated, the oak well-judged and the palate round and harmonious, with smooth, succulent tannins providing a satisfying background. Last on our list is the Rosso di Montalcino '00, which, despite some noticeable vegetal notes on the nose and a general absence of complexity, can point to a fresh-tasting and very attractive palate.

• Amor Costante	ΨΨ	5
• Brunello di Montalcino '97	ΨΨ	7
• Rosso di Montalcino '00	Ψ	5

MONTALCINO (SI)

LUCE
LOC. CASTELGIOCONDO
53024 MONTALCINO (SI)
TEL. 0577848492

To tell the truth, and always excepting the excellent Three-Glass-winning '94, the ambitious joint venture of the illustrious Frescobaldi and Mondavi wine families had really not carried all before it until a few years ago. Their Luce, an 80-bucks-a-bottle Supertuscan made from sangiovese and merlot, was a respectable, properly executed red with, of course, lots of extract and great balance, but wines at this level should be giving more. In the last few editions of the Guide, we remarked that Luce was beginning to acquire stylistic definition and, starting in '97, a more territory-focused identity. These positive developments are continuing and the '99 we tasted this time is really good. It would have won top honours had it shown just a touch more harmony. The colour, a rich ruby, introduces already eloquent aromas of ripe berry fruit, fresh plum and oriental spice, followed by a well-defined palate that opts for elegance rather than powerful extract. Mid palate shows the lovely sangiovese-derived acidic verve, and the finish is a model of limpidity and persistence. The Lucente '00, younger brother to Luce, showed well, too. The colour is an intense garnet-tinged ruby and there are faint vegetal tones on the nose, together with not yet fully integrated oak. In the mouth, it displays good juicy fruit, a dense, broad mid palate and length on the finish.

• Luce '99	ΨΨ	8
• Lucente '00	ΨΨ	5
• Luce '94	ΨΨΨ	8
• Luce '98	ΨΨ	8
• Luce '95	ΨΨ	8
• Luce '96	ΨΨ	8
• Lucente '96	ΨΨ	5
• Luce '97	ΨΨ	8
• Lucente '97	ΨΨ	5
• Lucente '99	ΨΨ	5

MONTALCINO (SI)

MASTROJANNI
FRAZ. CASTELNUOVO DELL'ABATE
PODERI LORETO SAN PIO
53024 MONTALCINO (SI)
TEL. 0577835681
E-MAIL: mastrojanni.vini@mastrojanni.com

It is the opinion of most winelovers and wine professionals that Mastrojanni's offerings have always been amongst the best in Montalcino. Customers are very faithful, not just because the wines are excellent, but also because you can virtually bank on them. After this preamble, we should say that in recent years, the best wines have tended to be the less important, standard-label ones, and not the top of the range. That's how it went this time, too. The celebrated Brunello selection, Schiena d'Asino, received an unexpectedly modest One Glass for its lofty status, while the standard Brunello from the same vintage easily walked off with Three Glasses. The less noble label is quite excellent from every point of view. The bouquet has remarkable intensity and definition, then the development on the palate shows really extraordinary vibrancy, balance and sheer vitality. The panel was enthralled. The Schiena d'Asino, on the other hand, is blander and dumb on both nose and palate. We did, of course, consider the possibility that it was just going through its classic closed stage, but frequent retastings persuaded us that the structural foundations of the wine are not awfully solid. Body, harmony and, most notably, persistence are no better than average. We received no samples of the other wines in the Mastrojanni range so we'll be dealing with them in the next edition of the Guide.

MONTALCINO (SI)

TENUTE SILVIO NARDI
LOC. CASALE DEL BOSCO
53024 MONTALCINO (SI)
TEL. 0577808269
E-MAIL: tenutenardi@tin.it

The upward surge we had been waiting for from Tenute Nardi has taken place with a vengeance. This year, the cellar put paid to any doubts provoked by last year's disappointing results. It is, of course, the case that the vintage we tasted this time was a far superior one to the '96, but considerable credit is due to Emilia Nardi for her courage and tenacity in not fudging the two vintages in any way. The Manachiara '97 is a genuinely great Brunello, and we do not for a moment believe that it will be an isolated achievement. It has all the hallmarks of being just a foretaste of what this winery will turn out in future. This lovely wine has an intense, deep nose with great definition and harmony in its array of cocoa, spice and dark berry aromas, together with mineral nuances. The palate is broad, mouthfilling and supported by excellent tannins. The amazingly velvety mouthfeel is as elegant as it is concentrated, and the finish goes on almost endlessly. All in all, a glorious, thrilling wine. Backing up this performance is the excellent Rosso di Montalcino '00, which opens on the nose with a well-defined fragrance of dark berries, spice and balsamic notes. The flavour is soft, buttressed by fine-grained, well-calibrated tannins, and the finish is fairly long. The Brunello '97 is also quite good. A lively garnet-tinged ruby hue introduces a dynamic nose that is slightly unsettled by somewhat dry woody nuances. The palate is nice and meaty but a bit short.

● Brunello di Montalcino '97	▼▼▼	7
● Brunello di Montalcino Vigna Schiena d'Asino '97	▼	8
● Brunello di Montalcino Ris. '88	▼▼▼	6
● Brunello di Montalcino '90	▼▼▼	7
● Brunello di Montalcino Schiena d'Asino '90	▼▼▼	6
● Brunello di Montalcino Schiena d'Asino '93	▼▼▼	6
● Brunello di Montalcino Ris. '95	▼▼	6
● Brunello di Montalcino Ris. '93	▼▼	5
● Brunello di Montalcino Schiena d'Asino '95	▼▼	6
○ Botrys '96	▼▼	5
● Brunello di Montalcino '96	▼▼	5
○ Botrys '97	▼▼	5

● Brunello di Montalcino Manachiara '97	▼▼▼	7
● Rosso di Montalcino '00	▼▼	4*
● Brunello di Montalcino '97	▼	6
● Brunello di Montalcino '90	▼▼	5
● Brunello di Montalcino '93	▼▼	5
● Brunello di Montalcino '95	▼▼	5
● Brunello di Montalcino Manachiara '95	▼▼	8
● Rosso di Montalcino '99	▼	4

MONTALCINO (SI)

SIRO PACENTI
LOC. PELAGRILLI, 1
53024 MONTALCINO (SI)
TEL. 0577848662
E-MAIL: pacentisiro@libero.it

Since the Siro Pacenti estate won Three Glasses with its Brunello '96, a vintage generally considered modest, it seemed reasonable to expect that the '97 would do the same. As everyone knows, it was an excellent year in Montalcino. And that is precisely what Giancarlo Pacenti's Brunello di Montalcino '97 has done, and without any apparent effort. This powerful wine, with its solid tannin underpinning, has expressed only a part of its vast potential. It will acquire even greater polish with time in the cellar. Happily, the amazing force, the quality of the fruit and the enormous structure can be appreciated even now. And then the finish is monumental. Our advice is not to reach for the corkscrew for at least ten years, but if you can't resist and really want to try a bottle now, decant it a couple of hours before serving. A Brunello as big as this tends to be somewhat shy in its present stage of development, particularly on the nose. As for the Rosso di Montalcino '00, it is a good and, naturally, more straightforward and easy-drinking wine. You have to remember that it comes from a not exactly memorable vintage.

Wine	Rating	Score
● Brunello di Montalcino '97	🍷🍷🍷	8
● Rosso di Montalcino '00	🍷🍷	5
● Brunello di Montalcino '88	🍷🍷🍷	8
● Brunello di Montalcino '95	🍷🍷🍷	8
● Brunello di Montalcino '96	🍷🍷🍷	8
● Rosso di Montalcino '99	🍷🍷	5
● Brunello di Montalcino '90	🍷🍷	6
● Brunello di Montalcino Ris. '90	🍷🍷	6
● Brunello di Montalcino '91	🍷🍷	8
● Brunello di Montalcino '93	🍷🍷	8
● Rosso di Montalcino '95	🍷🍷	4
● Rosso di Montalcino '96	🍷🍷	4
● Rosso di Montalcino '97	🍷🍷	5
● Rosso di Montalcino '98	🍷🍷	5

MONTALCINO (SI)

PIANCORNELLO
LOC. PIANCORNELLO
53024 MONTALCINO (SI)
TEL. 0577844105

It was a real pity to see Silvana Pieri's Brunello stop just short of receiving a Third Glass. At any rate, it is a wine that made a very favourable impression on all who tasted it, and we are convinced that the excellent work this producer has been doing for some years now will be properly recognized in the future. Three Glasses or not, Piancornello's '97 Brunello is one that does great honour to the wine type. It has an intense garnet colour, just slightly diluted at the edge, a nose that is initially a bit closed, with some earthiness and oak-derived toastiness, but then opens up to scents of ripe black cherries and blackberry jam. In the mouth, it is very soft at first, full and concentrated on mid palate, and then the sweetness of the alcohol and the aromas blend with the supple tannins to offer an extremely enjoyable juicy finish. To sum up, this is a wine that has both the ideal traditional traits of a Brunello and those of a great wine. It doesn't give away everything immediately, but surprises the taste receptors in a crescendo of intensity and balance on the finish. This Brunello is a confirmation that Silvana Pieri's little estate is on the right road. It is not important that the usually very fine Rosso di Montalcino is, this time round, not quite as good as we expected.

Wine	Rating	Score
● Brunello di Montalcino '97	🍷🍷	7
● Rosso di Montalcino '00	🍷	5
● Brunello di Montalcino '96	🍷🍷	6
● Rosso di Montalcino '99	🍷🍷	4
● Brunello di Montalcino '93	🍷🍷	5
● Brunello di Montalcino '95	🍷🍷	6
● Rosso di Montalcino '98	🍷	4

MONTALCINO (SI)

Agostina Pieri
Loc. S. Angelo Scalo
Loc. Piancornello
53024 Montalcino (SI)
tel. 0577375785 - 0577844163
e-mail: agostina.pieri@tin.it

Like all respectable producers in Montalcino, Agostina Pieri concentrates most of her attention on Brunello. This may be stating the obvious, but in fact this excellent cellar at Sant'Angelo got off to a great start with her Rosso, winning Three Glasses with the excellent '95. The 2000 Rosso is not on the same level. Certainly, it was not a very favourable year for this sort of wine, and only a few producers came up with anything really interesting. We were still disappointed, though. With too much wood, and noticeable hints of incense, this wine doesn't have the basic stuff to support its oak. There is good sweetness in the mouth but the palate lacks the contrast given by tannins and acidity, which would lend it greater vitality. Now, turning our usual order upside-down, we can conclude on a positive note. The '97 Brunello is very good indeed. If we want to be picky, it doesn't have either great depth or very much complexity, but its aromas are exactly what they should be. Wine type and vintage shine through in notes of sour cherries, liquorice and sweet spices. In the mouth, the entry shows a soft roundness and develops with balance and elegance through to the clean, well-sustained finish.

MONTALCINO (SI)

Poggio di Sotto
Fraz. Castelnuovo dell'Abate
Loc. Poggio di Sopra, 222
53020 Montalcino (SI)
tel. 0577835502
e-mail: palmuccipds@libero.it

Although it may seem strange, or even paradoxical, we aren't all that interested in totting up stemware. If our sole aim were to award One, Two or Three Glasses, the Guide would consist of the bare lists underneath the profiles. Instead, we are keen to understand and describe the value of a wine producer, in human as well as technical terms. For instance, we want to know why certain decisions were taken, what the vision behind the wine is, and why that particular style was selected. Poggio di Sotto's wines are the result of deliberate choices. There is no brutally massive extract, no overdose of wood from small barrels, no excess of fruitiness. The Brunello and the Rosso both aim for elegant drinkability, even if they do not always achieve perfection. The '97 Brunello comes from a great vintage and is an excellent wine. However, it didn't win the Three Glasses earned last year by the '95 Riserva. The style is the same, but not the intensity, the complexity or the persistence. It has a medium-intense ruby colour and an already broad, open, warm and enticing nose. After a clean attack, the palate develops consistently, supported by attractive, but not exceptionally dense, body. The finish is quite long, rich in alcohol and clean. The Rosso di Montalcino 1999 is less convincing. It is a decent wine but is held back by reductive notes on both nose and mouth.

Brunello di Montalcino '97	ΨΨ	7
Rosso di Montalcino '00	Ψ	5
Rosso di Montalcino '95	ΨΨΨ	5
Brunello di Montalcino '94	ΨΨ	7
Rosso di Montalcino '94	ΨΨ	5
Brunello di Montalcino '95	ΨΨ	7
Rosso di Montalcino '96	ΨΨ	5
Rosso di Montalcino '99	ΨΨ	5

Brunello di Montalcino '97	ΨΨ	8
Rosso di Montalcino '99		8
Brunello di Montalcino Ris. '95	ΨΨΨ	8
Brunello di Montalcino '94	ΨΨ	8
Rosso di Montalcino '94	ΨΨ	4
Brunello di Montalcino '95	ΨΨ	8
Brunello di Montalcino '96	ΨΨ	8

MONTALCINO (SI)

POGGIO SAN POLO
LOC. PODERE SAN POLO, 161
53024 MONTALCINO (SI)
TEL. 0577835522
E-MAIL: sanpolo@tetinet.com

After a few years, San Polo is back in the Guide with enough space to do justice to the changes made on this estate, which in the past has produced some decidedly interesting wines. It was recently taken over by the Fertonani family, who immediately began to restructure both vineyards and cellar. They have about five currently productive hectars under vine, but Silvia Fertonani, who is in charge, plans soon to bring that number up to 12, some of which have already been newly planted. Their position is extraordinary. The vines are at the eastern limits of Montalcino on a hill overlooking the valley that leads to Castelnuovo dell'Abate. In other words, they face due south. So everything bodes well and, given the promising results of our tastings, we think that the estate has what it takes to make a go of it. The wines from 2000 – those actually made by the current owners – did brilliantly, which cannot have been a coincidence. The very fine Mezzopane offers an extremely pleasing fruity flavour with a well-calibrated touch of oak. It's very nicely balanced and takes you through to a sound finish. The Rosso di Montalcino '00 is much better than merely acceptable. It flaunts good extract and juicy tannins, while the Brunello '97, which is only fair, displays some slight signs of age.

• Mezzopane '00	🍷🍷	6
• Rosso di Montalcino '00	🍷🍷	5
• Brunello di Montalcino '97	🍷	7
• Mezzopane '99	🍷🍷	4
• Brunello di Montalcino '96	🍷	6

MONTALCINO (SI)

CASTELLO ROMITORIO
LOC. ROMITORIO, 279
53024 MONTALCINO (SI)
TEL. 0577897220 - 0577847212
E-MAIL: inf@castelloromitorio.it

In times when what's fashionable is very much in the news, an artist who decides to make wine might seem to suggest that another well-known person has found an elegant hobby. Instead, Sandro Chia, one of the best-known names of the so-called transavant-garde, is a really dedicated, enthusiastic winemaker and has been for some years. His estate includes 20 hectares under vine, eight of which are dedicated to the making of Brunello. The other 12 are planted to international grape varieties, such as chardonnay and cabernet sauvignon. In this year's Guide, we review only some of his wines, restricting ourselves to the "juiciest" pair, the Brunello di Montalcino 1997 and the Rosso di Montalcino 2000. We'll begin with the Brunello, which, predictably enough, has even more depth and richness than the excellent previous version. Although somewhat reluctant to reveal itself to the nose, it starts off with some notes of earth and wet leaves, which, after some breathing time, make way for clear fruity tones. The sweet presence of the oak is evident, but this should be absorbed with a little time in bottle. In the mouth, it is more confident, revealing a modern style based on softness and compelling fruit. It's a good Brunello, and takes its place among the best of its kind. Sandro's Rosso 2000 also did well at our tastings, thanks to its delightfully spicy fragrance and well-balanced palate with very flavoursome tannins.

• Brunello di Montalcino '97	🍷🍷	7
• Rosso di Montalcino '00	🍷🍷	5
• Brunello di Montalcino '96	🍷🍷	7
• Brunello di Montalcino '93	🍷🍷	7
• Brunello di Montalcino '95	🍷🍷	7
• Sant'Antimo Rosso Romito del Romitorio '99	🍷🍷	6

MONTALCINO (SI)

PODERE SALICUTTI
PODERE SALICUTTI, 174
53024 MONTALCINO (SI)
TEL. 0577847003
E-MAIL: leanza@poderesalicutti.it

Salicutti's '97 Brunello turned out to be one of the best wines of Montalcino this year, and justly picked up Three Glasses. This is no more than fair, given all the hard work that the owner, Francesco Leanza, has done here in the past few years. From the beginning, both of his wines, the Rosso as much as the Brunello, have attracted considerable critical attention, with some admirers lauding their richness, and some detractors complaining about their not being sufficiently true to type. But all wines have their fans and faultfinders. We have always liked the wines of Salicutti, but we have also long noted that the balance between fruit and wood should be better gauged. Sometimes in the past, the oak has seemed to have got seriously out of hand. Obviously, this is a question of taste, and we haven't suddenly changed our minds, but it is clear to us that a proper equilibrium between the contribution of the barrel and the stuff inside is gradually being reached. The '97 Brunello is a perfect example of this newfound balance. It has a very intense garnet colour, and a generous nose with enticingly sweet fruit and notes of tobacco, coffee and vanilla. The sweet fruit fills the mouth effortlessly, elegantly encouraged by powerful alcohol and poised, densely packed tannins. The very fine Dopoteatro '00, made from cabernet and sangiovese, has good balance and ample extract. The Rosso di Montalcino '00 is pleasant, but has a somewhat bitter finish.

● Brunello di Montalcino '97	♟♟♟	8
● Dopoteatro '00	♟♟	6
● Rosso di Montalcino '00	♟	5
● Brunello di Montalcino '95	♟♟	8
● Brunello di Montalcino '96	♟♟	8
● Rosso di Montalcino '97	♟♟	4
● Rosso di Montalcino '98	♟♟	4
● Dopoteatro '99	♟♟	5

MONTALCINO (SI)

SALVIONI - LA CERBAIOLA
P.ZZA CAVOUR, 19
53024 MONTALCINO (SI)
TEL. 0577848499

The '97 vintage, the best at Montalcino since 1990, did well by a number of producers from the new generation. But it also marked the re-emergence of some of the wineries that have made Montalcino famous. Giulio and Mirella Salvioni's La Cerbaiola, one of the latter group, is now doing more brilliantly than ever. In fact, 1990 was the last year that this estate received Three Glasses, although no one could accuse the Salvionis of having forgotten how to make Brunello in the meanwhile. The fact is that every producer has a different philosophy of winemaking, and here at Cerbaiola they chose not to use any questionable "improvements" to cover up the inadequacy of some of the vintages. And from '91 on, there have been very few good years. In one of the best, 1993, the La Cerbiola Brunello came very close indeed to winning our highest award. We should add that vines can develop in ways that are not altogether predictable, and that the replacement of barrel stock, which is more difficult to gauge if one uses mid-sized barrels, can also have an effect. But let's get back to the '97 Brunello, which is quite exceptional for the voluptuous richness it expresses as it progresses, unhurriedly and pervasively, over smooth, dense tannins to a long, characterful, ever-broadening finish. This powerful Brunello, unusually, is not very expressive on the nose for the moment, but this is yet another way in which it honestly reflects the qualities of its vintage.

● Brunello di Montalcino '97	♟♟♟	8
● Brunello di Montalcino '85	♟♟♟	8
● Brunello di Montalcino '87	♟♟♟	8
● Brunello di Montalcino '88	♟♟♟	8
● Brunello di Montalcino '89	♟♟♟	8
● Brunello di Montalcino '90	♟♟♟	8
● Brunello di Montalcino '91	♟♟	8
● Brunello di Montalcino '92	♟♟	8
● Brunello di Montalcino '93	♟♟	8
● Brunello di Montalcino '95	♟♟	8

MONTALCINO (SI)

SESTI - CASTELLO DI ARGIANO
FRAZ. SANT'ANGELO IN COLLE
53020 MONTALCINO (SI)
TEL. 0577843921

The general feeling of energy at Montalcino these days can be measured not only by the revival of historically important wineries, but also by the appearance of new producers. Giuseppe Maria Sesti is one of them. A very original, as well as an eclectic sort of person, he has used his vast knowledge of ancient astronomy in his winemaking. In practical terms, his vineyard labours follow the phases of the moon, including pruning and preparing the land, as well as work in the cellar, from racking to bottling. In short, we could say that Montalcino has found its Nicolas Joly, the famous "biodynamic" winemaker of the Loire Valley. Sesti's approximately six hectares of vines are in the Argiano area, on the southern side of Montalcino. The panel was intrigued by his wines at the tastings, and the Brunello '97 in particular did extremely well. It is a very good wine indeed, with intense, clean aromas of black cherries and blackberries. In the mouth, it is round, full, and well sustained in its progression, and the tannins are fine-grained. The Terra di Siena '99, a mixture of merlot and cabernet, shows a not particularly expressive nose with a vegetal undertone. The palate, though, is soft, fairly substantial, and nicely braced by tannins that get just a bit out of hand on the finish. The better than merely decent Rosso di Montalcino '00 boasts a warm, nearly sweet attack and good complexity, but the finish is a bit rough, and the nose is masked by oak. The Grangiovese '00 is little more than acceptable.

• Brunello di Montalcino '97	♛♛	8
• Sant'Antimo Terra di Siena '99	♛♛	5
• Grangiovese '00	♛	4
• Rosso di Montalcino '00	♛	4

MONTALCINO (SI)

SOLARIA - CENCIONI
PODERE CAPANNA, 102
53024 MONTALCINO (SI)
TEL. 0577849426
E-MAIL: solaria.cencioni@infinito.it

The success of Montalcino owes much to the extraordinary enthusiasm that pervades the thriving community of small-scale growers. It's a category not often found in Tuscany, but certainly well represented in this corner of Tuscany. Patrizia Cencioni has paid her dues to be part of the group. She doesn't think have much time for marketing or public relations, preferring to navigate the vineyards at the wheel of her tractor, or devote herself with equal dedication to her tasks in the cellar. When a woman like Patrizia begins to reap prestigious results after a great deal of sowing, you can only feel pleasure and admiration. To come to the point, the Cencioni Brunello '97 has walked off with a nonchalant Three Glasses. An outstandingly well-balanced wine, it reveals a firm, but neither imposing nor showy, structure. This makes it eminently drinkable, which is not always the case in these parts. The aromas suggest black cherries, spices and a faint earthiness, with a robust dose of oak. Entry on the palate is pleasantly sweet, and followed by a round, well-sustained mid palate with nicely judged tannins, then a long, elegantly harmonious finish. However, the list of good things from Patrizia Cencioni does not end here. The mostly cabernet sauvignon-based Solarianne '99 is an excellent wine with a broad bouquet of flowers, aromatic herbs, spices and fresh plums. The palate is soft and progresses well, revealing lots of smooth tannins and a long, rising finish.

• Brunello di Montalcino '97	♛♛♛	7
• Solarianne '99	♛♛	8
• Brunello di Montalcino '95	♛♛	7
• Brunello di Montalcino '96	♛♛	7
• Solarianne '98	♛♛	8

MONTALCINO (SI)

TALENTI
FRAZ. SANT'ANGELO IN COLLE
LOC. PIAN DI CONTE
53020 MONTALCINO (SI)
TEL. 0577844064
E-MAIL: az.talenti@tin.it

It's too soon to say that Talenti is absolutely back on form. This historic Montalcino estate, which has been re-organizing for a few years, did present the panel with some good wines, although much work remains to be done. The restructuring began, naturally enough, in the vineyards, proceeding then to the cellar, where consultant oenologist, Carlo Ferrini, has overseen a renewal of the barrel stock, including new wood in various sizes. Our tastings this year were already encouraging. The Brunello '97 has a very intense garnet colour, and ample, complex aromas with earthy, mineral and sweet tobacco tones. The palate is a little stiff but intense, and the still energetic tannins and acidity make the development lively, rather than soft. The contrast is however, effective, the finish is good and the wine has no lack of character. The Rosso Talenti '00 is remarkably good. It has a very dark ruby colour, and a deep, concentrated nose, with layers of dark berries and pencil lead over hints of oak. The attack on the palate is vigorous, and the development shows a lovely, even softness but the finish is held back by boisterous tannins. The two wines are different in style but both show unusual temperament. On the other hand, the Rosso di Montalcino '00 is less exciting. The fruit-led flavour is fine, but the wine is diminished by reduced notes on the nose.

• Talenti Rosso '00	🍷🍷	5
• Brunello di Montalcino '97	🍷🍷	7
• Rosso di Montalcino '00	🍷	5
• Brunello di Montalcino Ris. '95	🍷	6

MONTALCINO (SI)

UCCELLIERA
FRAZ. CASTELNUOVO DELL'ABATE
POD. UCCELLIERA, 45
53020 MONTALCINO (SI)
TEL. 0577835729
E-MAIL: amco@uccelliera-montalcino.it

Andrea Cortonesi is a true grower producer. He's what the French would call a "vigneron", in the fullest sense. No stage in the making of wine, from vineyard to cellar, escapes his assiduous attention. It is a calling to which Andrea is passionately devoted for he is a convinced defender of the ability of Montalcino's sangiovese to produce wines that mirror the character of the soil on which they were grown. Cortonesi's wines showed well at our tastings, although there were no absolute champions. The very successful Rapace '99, an IGT wine, offers light vegetal nuances, as well as spices on the nose. The palate is round and full-flavoured, underpinned by attractively ripe and tasty tannins. Another Two Glass wine, the Brunello '97, is still quite closed on the nose, but very much livelier on the palate, where it shows powerful alcohol, authentic sangiovese character and generous extractive weight. The finish, with its slightly drying tannins, is less expansive. The Rosso di Montalcino '00 shows a similarly dumb nose, but the palate can offer decent body and lots of character.

• Brunello di Montalcino '97	🍷🍷	7
• Rapace '99	🍷🍷	6
• Rosso di Montalcino '00	🍷	5
• Rapace '98	🍷🍷	6
• Brunello di Montalcino '96	🍷	7

MONTALCINO (SI)

Tenimenti Angelini - Val di Suga
Loc. Val di Cava
53024 Montalcino (SI)
tel. 057780411

For a number of years now, Val di Suga has made it to our Three Glass finals with one or other of the two Brunello selections, Vigna del Lago and Spuntali. Often, they've been successful, but this year the Spuntali pulled up just short of our highest award. The wines nevertheless did very well, and we should add that this year, they were facing a great deal of very keen competition. It also has to be said that the '97 Spuntali proved to be a wine with plenty of character, the sort that is elusive to describe and hard to define. In the course of our entire series of tastings, we tried the Spuntali on five separate occasions with varying, and even contradictory, results. The nose always showed unusual energy, with strong spicy and tobacco tones, as well as earthy notes, and a decided presence of oak. The palate is powerful, vigorous and robust, but the tannins that tend to be rough on the finish and out of step with the acidity. In other words, it has no end of character but tends to be a belligerent. The other wines are more docile. The Rosso di Montalcino 2000 is not very expressive on the nose but then shows a soft and harmonious palate, with, however, a slightly astringent finish. The fair Motuproprio has somewhat ill-defined aromas and a traditional, but insufficiently fruity, palate.

• Brunello di Montalcino Vigna Spuntali '97	ŶŶ	8
• Rosso di Montalcino '00	Ŷ	4
• Motuproprio '99	Ŷ	7
• Brunello di Montalcino Vigna del Lago '90	ŶŶŶ	8
• Brunello di Montalcino Vigna del Lago '93	ŶŶŶ	8
• Brunello di Montalcino Vigna Spuntali '93	ŶŶŶ	8
• Brunello di Montalcino Vigna del Lago '95	ŶŶŶ	8
• Brunello di Montalcino Vigna Spuntali '95	ŶŶŶ	8

MONTALCINO (SI)

Tenuta Valdicava
Loc. Val di Cava
53024 Montalcino (SI)
tel. 0577848261

Vincenzo Abruzzese's wines did very well this year. His Riserva Madonna del Piano, in particular, is noteworthy, and a rare attempt to produce a wine of this exalted nature from a mediocre vintage like the '96. It was an attempt worth making, to judge from quality of this, the top wine on the Valdicava list. The dense, concentrated bouquet is themed around notes of black cherries, with mineral and spicy hints. The equally fine palate reveals lovely fruit, medium body, a well-balanced, orderly development and smooth, well-integrated tannins. The finish is long and elegant, although the vintage has taken something away from the wine's customary intensity. All things considered, this Brunello came very close to getting our highest award. The other two wines also nearly made it to a higher category. That was particularly true of the Rosso di Montalcino '00, with its delightful nose of red berries and well proportioned, if somewhat straightforward, palate. The Brunello '97 shows good structure and a broad and soft attack, but dry oak tends to be rather too prevalent on the nose.

• Brunello di Montalcino Madonna del Piano Ris. '96	ŶŶ	8
• Rosso di Montalcino '00	Ŷ	4
• Brunello di Montalcino '97	Ŷ	8
• Brunello di Montalcino Madonna del Piano Ris. '90	ŶŶ	8
• Brunello di Montalcino '93	ŶŶ	8
• Brunello di Montalcino Madonna del Piano Ris. '95	ŶŶ	8
• Rosso di Montalcino '99	ŶŶ	4

MONTALCINO (SI)

Villa Le Prata
Loc. Le Prata, 261
53024 Montalcino (SI)
Tel. 0577848325

Benedetta Losapio, a lawyer by profession, takes her adventure in the world of Brunello very seriously. Although at the beginning it was almost a game or hobby, winemaking has gradually changed into something much more important. This year, Villa Le Prata presented three wines that certainly don't kid around at all. The Brunello '97, for example, got as far as our final tastings. It is a very fine wine, although it does not quite show the complexity and individual personality of a great one. The aromas clearly suggest dark berries, black cherries and blackberries, together with a lightly spicy timbre. In the mouth, the wine is soft, balanced, and backed up by very tasty, well-judged tannins. The Rosso di Montalcino Tirso 2000 also put on a very fine display. The nose shows well-defined fruit and a light touch of toasty oak, then the palate, with its clear, straightforward style, is lively and permeated with a pleasant sweetness. The third "witness for the defence", seeing as we are dealing with a lawyer, is the Leprata '00, a blend of merlot and cabernet. This concentrated, admirably fresh red also boasts dense, fragrant fruit. Perhaps the oak is a little too insistent at the moment, but this is a defect of youth. A bit of time in the bottle should put everything to rights.

● Brunello di Montalcino '97	🍷🍷🍷	7
● Leprata '00	🍷🍷	5
● Rosso di Montalcino Tirso '00	🍷🍷	4
● Brunello di Montalcino '93	🍷🍷	6
● Le Prata '99	🍷🍷	5
● Rosso di Montalcino Tirso '99	🍷🍷	4

MONTE SAN SAVINO (AR)

San Luciano
Loc. San Luciano, 90
52048 Monte San Savino (AR)
Tel. 0575848518

The wines presented by the Ziantoni family this year found a very warm welcome at our tastings. The entire range has improved so markedly that San Luciano is now very much a producer to watch carefully. All the wines show signs of just how carefully they were made. They are impeccably clean and have a captivating style that never threatens to become banal or predictable. In fact, the top wine, D'Ovidio '99, almost won Three Glasses. A blend of four different grapes, mostly sangiovese and montepulciano, but with more than 20 per cent equally split between cabernet and merlot, it displays considerable depth on the nose with distinct very ripe fruit. This is followed by a dense, powerful and very smooth palate, with a sweet, lingering finish where the tannins are a little intrusive. The Boschi Salviati '00, a blend of sangiovese and montepulciano, has also made great progress. It shows good structure and balance in the mouth, and offers elegant, original aromas of berry fruit, violets, spices and oak. The excellent white Resico '01, made from chardonnay, vermentino and a little trebbiano, is fresh, clean and evenly redolent of flowers on the nose, then offering a delightful sweet and slightly tangy flavour. The Luna di Monte '01, is a fine wine, though simpler, while the Colle Carpito '00, which is less well focused than usual, earned One small Glass.

● D'Ovidio '99	🍷🍷🍷	5*
● Boschi Salviati '00	🍷🍷🍷	4*
○ Resico '01	🍷🍷🍷	3*
● Colle Carpito '00	🍷	3
○ Valdichiana Luna di Monte '01	🍷	3
● D'Ovidio '98	🍷🍷	5
● Boschi Salviati '99	🍷🍷	4*
○ Luna di Monte '00	🍷	2*
○ Resico '00	🍷	3
● Colle Carpito '99	🍷	3*

MONTECARLO (LU)

Fattoria del Buonamico
Loc. Cercatoia
Via Provinciale di Montecarlo, 43
55015 Montecarlo (LU)
tel. 058322038
e-mail: buonamico@buonamico.com

After years of producing reliable, well made and balanced, but not outstanding, wines, Fattoria del Buonamico has shifted up a higher gear. There were some very pleasant surprises waiting for our tasters, evidence that vineyard replanting is showing concrete results. The bottles have a character and rich fruit that augur well for the future. Getting down to details, we were particularly impressed by the excellent Fortino '98, a monovarietal Syrah of which, unfortunately, very little is produced. The nose is wonderfully clear and eloquent, revealing notes of black pepper, blackberries, plums and hints of sweet tobacco. The palate is no less appealing, unveiling attractive balance and concentration, well-integrated tannins and a long, engrossing finish. The Cercatoja '98 is a characterful product. It is somewhat diminished by vegetal hints on the nose, but in the mouth it is really splendid. It drinks elegantly, against a backdrop of velvety tannins, and closes with a burst of renewed energy. Also praised by the panel was the Montecarlo Rosso '01, which offers inviting aromas of red berries and spices, followed by a rich, lingering palate. The two whites presented did quite well, though we preferred the cleanness and freshness of the lighter Montecarlo Bianco to the honey and vanilla tones of the Vasario '99.

MONTECARLO (LU)

Gino Fuso Carmignani
Loc. Cercatoia Alta
Via della Tinaia, 7
55015 Montecarlo (LU)
tel. 058322381

For Duke '00 is the "jazziest" wine in the world. Prove us wrong if you can. That, at least, is what came to mind when we read over our tasting notes. The dense, dark, compact colour is more intense than ever. Nothing strange about that. In fact, it's a very positive sign. But then come the first hints from its intense nose. We detected super-ripeness, vegetal notes and black pepper. Let's think about this for a moment. Can three such very different sensations live in harmony with each other? Of course not. But yes, they do actually manage to fuse together. Like jazz soloists, they start out on their own and then come together, who knows how, in a single piece of music. In the mouth, we noted lots of energy and concentration, tasty tannins, and an intense finish. Another typical big wine? No way. Because it is also fruit-rich, sweet and even elegant in its progression. These apparently dissonant notes come together in harmony. This isn't what you mean by jazz? Well, if it isn't, For Duke '00 is certainly original and undeniably excellent. At the time of our tastings Il Merlo della Topa Nera wasn't ready for release. We tried a barrel sample, which was very interesting, but it was too soon to write a review, We will do so next year. The white Stati d'Animo '01, however, was fresh, full and very tasty. Finally, the concentrated, well-rounded, fruit-driven Sassonero '01 nearly earning a second Glass, bringing to a conclusion the excellent work done by Gino Fuso yet again this year.

● Il Fortino Syrah '98	🍷🍷	7
● Montecarlo Rosso '01	🍷🍷	4*
● Cercatoja Rosso '98	🍷🍷	6
○ Montecarlo Bianco '01	🍷	3
○ Vasario '99	🍷	5
● Il Fortino Syrah '92	🍷🍷	7
● Il Fortino Cabernet/Merlot '94	🍷🍷	5
● Cercatoja Rosso '95	🍷🍷	6
● Il Fortino Syrah '95	🍷🍷	7
● Cercatoja Rosso '96	🍷🍷	6
● Il Fortino Syrah '96	🍷🍷	7
○ Vasario '96	🍷🍷	4
● Cercatoja Rosso '97	🍷🍷	6
● Montecarlo Rosso '00	🍷	3

● For Duke '00	🍷🍷	7
○ Montecarlo Bianco Stati d'Animo '01	🍷🍷	4*
● Montecarlo Rosso Sassonero '01	🍷	4
● For Duke '90	🍷🍷	4
● For Duke '94	🍷🍷	4
● For Duke '95	🍷🍷	4
● For Duke '97	🍷🍷	5
● Montecarlo Rosso Sassonero '97	🍷🍷	2
● For Duke '98	🍷🍷	5
● Il Merlot della Topa Nera '98	🍷🍷	5
● For Duke '99	🍷🍷	5
○ Montecarlo Bianco Stati d'Animo '99	🍷🍷	4

MONTECARLO (LU)

Fattoria di Montechiari
Via Montechiari, 27
55015 Montecarlo (LU)
tel. 058322189

Moreno Panettoni and his delightful partner, Catherine Pirmez, may be justly proud of the little jewel they have created on the hills of Montecarlo. Montechiari is exemplary, not only for the quality of its wines, which are of a consistently high level, but also for the openness with which it is run. The pair have about 10 hectares under vine, of which three will come into production in 2003. Our tastings this year gave reassuring confirmation of the good work that has been done, even though we didn't find the difference in quality, noticeable in the past, between the flagship cabernet, and the rest of the range. The Rosso Montechiari '99, obtained from sangiovese grapes, shows some hints of reduction on the nose as well as gamey notes. However, the attractive, fruity palate, and a development that is both dense and well balanced, make up for this. Even more interesting is the Nero Montechiari '00, a monovarietal Pinot Nero that displays a moderately intense garnet colour, a varietal nose of cherries, cassis, and wild roses. In the mouth, it shows elegance, smoothness, freshness, and a body of medium concentration. It was, in fact, nearly sent forward to our final taste-offs, whereas the Cabernet '99 did get through to the last round. Made from cabernet franc and cabernet sauvignon, with about ten per cent merlot, the Cabernet Montechiari actually did not seem to be quite as good as recent versions. Some hints of over-ripeness in the bouquet, and a finish that is a bit on the rough side, detracted from the usual finesse of this nonetheless excellent red.

MONTECARLO (LU)

Fattoria del Teso
Via Poltroniera
55015 Montecarlo (LU)
tel. 0583286288
e-mail: info@fattoriadelteso.com

At last, there's something new from Montecarlo. La Fattoria del Teso had already sent out interesting signals at our tastings a year ago and this time round, the wines did not disappoint. In fact, they took us by surprise and surpassed our most optimistic expectations. The arrival of oenologist Francesco Bartoletti and agronomist Federico Curtaz has brought about a significant change and the outlook for the future is encouraging, as they have only just started work. At our tastings, the Anfidiamante '99 was by far the most impressive bottle. A blend of sangiovese, syrah, merlot and canaiolo, it has an intense, brilliant ruby colour and a clean, deep nose, where floral and spicy tones mingle with notes of chocolate and coffee. The palate is orderly, balanced and dense, and nicely supported, rather than masked, by its oak. The Montecarlo Rosso '01 was also a revelation. It is pleasingly redolent of black pepper and red berries, and the flavour is soft, substantial and fairly persistent, albeit a little bitter at the end. The Montecarlo Bianco came near to gaining Two Glasses. It has pleasantly clean, fruit-led aromas, and is fresh and balanced in the mouth. The Stella del Teso did even better, offering fragrances of lavender, sage and tropical fruits. The palate is well sustained, elegant and long. This round-up of the wines of the Fattoria del Teso ends happily with their excellent '94 Vin Santo, which can point to notable concentration and density, nice viscosity and considerable length.

● Montechiari Cabernet '99	🍷🍷	8
● Montechiari Nero '00	🍷🍷	6
● Montechiari Rosso '99	🍷🍷	6
● Montechiari Cabernet '97	🍷🍷🍷	8
● Montechiari Cabernet '98	🍷🍷	8
○ Montechiari Chardonnay '00	🍷🍷	5
● Montechiari Rosso '95	🍷🍷	4
● Montechiari Cabernet '96	🍷🍷	8
● Montechiari Pinot Nero '96	🍷🍷	5
● Montechiari Pinot Nero '97	🍷🍷	6
○ Montechiari Chardonnay '98	🍷🍷	5
● Montechiari Nero '98	🍷🍷	6

● Montecarlo Rosso '01	🍷🍷	3*
○ Stella del Teso '01	🍷🍷	4
○ Vin Santo '94	🍷🍷	5
● Anfidiamante '99	🍷🍷	6
○ Montecarlo Bianco '01	🍷	3
○ Vin Santo '90	🍷🍷	5
○ Montecarlo Bianco '00	🍷	2*
● Montecarlo Rosso '00	🍷	2*
● Montecarlo Rosso Anfidiamante '98	🍷	4

MONTECARLO (LU)

WANDANNA
Fraz. San Salvatore
Via del Molinetto
55015 Montecarlo (LU)
tel. 0583228989 - 0583228226
e-mail: wandanna@libero.it

This year's wines from Wandanna did not provide any new observations to add to our usual profile. The estate is as reliable as ever, with slight variations in quality from one label to the next. Ivaldo Fantozzi is a dynamic owner who is always on the go, and he has nearly finished extending the vineyards. The syrah and even the pinot noir fruit seem to be improving steadily and it is likely that there will be significant news soon from Wandanna. For the moment, we should mention some changes in the pecking order of the wines. The Montcarlo Rosso is making a comeback and the Terre dei Cascinieri Rosso and Bianco have switched positions, to the advantage of the latter. The Virente '99 continues to sail on, far above the other wines. It has unusual personality, which is more marked than in the past, at the expense of the purity of the nose, which is held back notes of reduction. On the other hand, it does have an excellent palate that is fat, concentrated and long. The Terre de' Cascinieri Bianco is not bad, either, with its clean nose of citrus fruit, apple, pear and spring flowers. In the mouth, it is succulent, well-balanced and admirably long. In contrast, the Terre de' Cascinieri Rosso is less exciting than usual. It, too, shows some muffling on the nose, and then the palate reveals a pleasant flavour, smooth tannins, and medium weight and character. The two standard Montecarlos are both decent but we preferred the red.

○ Montecarlo Bianco Terre dei Cascinieri '00	♛♛	4
● Virente '99	♛♛	7
○ Montecarlo Bianco '01	♛	4
● Montecarlo Rosso '01	♛	4
● Terre dei Cascinieri '00	♛	5
● Virente '95	♛♛	5
● Virente '96	♛♛	5
● Montecarlo Rosso Terre dei Cascinieri '97	♛♛	4
● Virente '97	♛♛	5
○ Montecarlo Bianco Terre dei Cascinieri '98	♛♛	4
● Terre dei Cascinieri '98	♛♛	4
● Virente '98	♛♛	7
● Montecarlo Rosso Terre dei Cascinieri '99	♛♛	4

MONTECATINI VAL DI CECINA (PI)

FATTORIA SORBAIANO
Loc. Sorbaiano
56040 Montecatini Val di Cecina (PI)
tel. 058830243
e-mail: fattoriasorbaiano@libero.it

Last year, we referred to the renewed commitment of the owners at Sorbaiano to the property, and the plans under way that will require dedication and time. This year's tastings suggest a period of change, which should take the Picciolini family estate to a level more in keeping with the estate's potential. There were good things and less good things in our evaluations but the most positive notes of all were reserved for the sangiovese-based Pian del Conte '00. The nose is still in the process of expanding and settling, with oak-derived spicy and balsamic notes still masking the fruit to a certain extent. The decidedly more eloquent and encouraging palate displays a soft, dense body with smooth tannins, and then a remarkably long finish. The wine attained Two big Glasses. On the same level, but after more of a struggle to get there, the Rosso delle Miniere '99 is part of the history of Sorbiano but still needs to find its own identity. The nose shows notes of green peppers and red berries, as well as more evolved ones of leather and blackberry jam. The attack on the palate is round and fairly well sustained, and the finish is fairly long, but stiffened by wood tannins. The two standard Montescudaios are acceptable, if below par, but the biggest disappointment came from the white Lucestraia, which can barely be assessed in its present state of development.

● Pian del Conte '00	♛	4*
● Montescudaio Rosso delle Miniere '99	♛	5
○ Montescudaio Bianco '01		3
● Montescudaio Rosso '01		3
● Montescudaio Rosso delle Miniere '97	♛♛	4
○ Montescudaio Bianco Lucestraia '98	♛♛	4
● Montescudaio Rosso delle Miniere '98	♛♛	5
○ Montescudaio Bianco Lucestraia '99	♛♛	4*
● Pian del Conte '99	♛♛	4*

MONTEMURLO (PO)

Tenuta di Bagnolo
dei Marchesi Pancrazi
Fraz. Bagnolo - Via Montalese, 156
50045 Montemurlo (PO)
tel. 0574652439 - 057459013
e-mail: giuseppe@pancrazi.it

This year, we had a chance to taste two different vintages of Marchesi Pancrazi's Pinot Nero. It was an extremely interesting and thought-provoking opportunity to reflect on how unpredictable and sensitive the pinot noir grape can be. A whole raft of factors, beginning with the weather, enter into play and influence the result when you are dealing with this grape from Burgundy. Our tasting confronted us with two quite different wines, even though they were from two successive years. The Pinot Nero 1999 has intense aromas of spices and leather, and rather inelegant animal nuances. The palate shows remarkable extract for a wine of this type, but there are also signs of age and a lack of refreshing acidity. The 2000 version presents a less intense, but still lively, colour and a complex nose of flowers, red berries and spices with hints of rhubarb. In the mouth, it is leaner and easier to drink, but also more balanced and elegant, and delightfully fresh on the finish. The other Marchesi Pancrazi estate, San Donato, which is run by Paolo Mocali, produces the Casaglia and the San Donato. The former is made completely from colorino fruit, and unveils a soft, concentrated palate with a good robust finish and substantial tannins. The nose doesn't show much but this is typical of wines obtained from colorino. The red San Donato '01 is simple but very pleasant.

MONTEPULCIANO (SI)

Avignonesi
Via Colonica, 1
53040 Montepulciano (SI)
tel. 0578724304
e-mail: capezzine@avignonesi.it

It is almost impossible to resist Vin Santo from Avignonesi, especially when it's their legendary Occhio di Pernice. Of course, it costs a packet, and there's not much of it (these are the only criticisms one hears of this wine), but it is one of the world's greatest sweet wines. The '90 is faithful to the Avignonesi style. It shows extraordinary sweetness and density, overwhelming energy, and an unending finish of cherry jam. All in all, a great wine indeed. Nor are there any complaints about the standard '92 Vin Santo. It reveals a dense, almost austere nose, a very sweet palate that is both succulent and silky, and a long, elegant aftertaste. Avignonesi is more than just Vin Santo, however. It looks to us as if renovation of the vineyards has just about arrived at the stage where the estate can start turning out great reds. For the time being, the present range is very good, starting with the 50 & 50 '98, which is elegant, intense and well conceived. The Nobile '99 is also convincing for its clear aromas of raspberries, cherries, and light vegetal touches. The palate is lively, invigorating and well-balanced, revealing well-gauged tannins. The Desiderio '99, from merlot with one fifth cabernet, earns a certain respect although this is one of the wines from which we are expecting much more in the next few vintages. It is solid and concentrated, with fine-grained tannins, but there is some over-ripeness on the nose. The Marzocco, and the Bianco and Rosso Avignonesi, all made good impressions and came close to gaining Two Glasses.

● Casaglia '00	▼▼	4*
● Pinot Nero Villa di Bagnolo '00	▼▼	6
● San Donato '01	▼	2*
● Pinot Nero Villa di Bagnolo '99	▼	6
● Pinot Nero Villa di Bagnolo '92	▼▼	5
● Pinot Nero Villa di Bagnolo '93	▼▼	5
● Pinot Nero Villa di Bagnolo '94	▼▼	5
● Pinot Nero Villa di Bagnolo '95	▼▼	5
● Pinot Nero Villa di Bagnolo '97	▼▼	5
● Pinot Nero Villa di Bagnolo '98	▼▼	5
● Casaglia '99	▼▼	4

○ Vin Santo Occhio di Pernice '90	▼▼▼	8
○ Vin Santo '92	▼▼	8
● 50 & 50 Avignonesi e Capannelle '98	▼▼	8
● Desiderio '99	▼▼	6
● Nobile di Montepulciano '99	▼▼	5
○ Il Marzocco '00	▼	4
● Rosso Avignonesi '00	▼	4
○ Bianco Avignonesi '01	▼	3
● Rosso di Montepulciano '01		4
○ Vin Santo '88	▼▼▼	8
○ Vin Santo '89	▼▼▼	8
○ Vin Santo Occhio di Pernice '89	▼▼▼	8
● 50 & 50 Avignonesi e Capannelle '97	▼▼▼	8
○ Vin Santo '91	▼▼	8

MONTEPULCIANO (SI)

BINDELLA
FRAZ. ACQUAVIVA
VIA DELLE TRE BERTE, 10/A
53040 MONTEPULCIANO (SI)
TEL. 0578767777
E-MAIL: info@bindella.it

Frequently, we find first impressions on tasting at Bindella are confusing. The wines are closed on the nose and at times even muffled by notes of reduction. But by now we know that as the wines develop, their characteristics will gradually change. Those very wines that had seemed heavy and unbalanced will reveal themselves a few months later to be solid, robust and characterful. Repeated tastings over time have always confirmed this unusual course of development, so we offer our assessments with a certain confidence. We'll start with the Vino Nobile '99. Retasted after two months, it proved quite interesting. The nose is not yet completely open, but shows intensity and a good base of red berries, liquorice and spices. On the palate, it is sweet and mouthfilling, the progression is surefooted and the finish tasty. The same considerations hold true for the Vallocaia '98. Made mostly from sangiovese, it is still hard to figure out and unforthcoming to the nose, but any doubts you may have nurtured disappear when in reaches the palate. Round, full and well backed up by a close-knit tannic texture, it takes you through to a finish with lots of personality. The Rosso di Montepulciano Fosso Lupaio '01 is similar, although simpler, and has decent body. Our list of Bindella wines finishes sweetly and pleasurably with the Vin Santo Dolce Sinfonia '97.

MONTEPULCIANO (SI)

BOSCARELLI
FRAZ. CERVOGNANO
VIA DI MONTENERO, 28
53040 MONTEPULCIANO (SI)
TEL. 0578767277 - 0578767608
E-MAIL: info@poderiboscarelli.com

We have to admit that the wines from Boscarelli continue to show an admirable unity of style. No one could accuse them of falling prey to fashion. It is also true, however, that this approach has become something of a straitjacket for the De Ferrari family winery. Despite these good qualities we have just mentioned, the wines lack that extra spark that would boost them to the peak of their categories. Our tastings, although positive, substantiate these remarks. For instance, the Vigna del Nocio '99 is an excellent wine that presents a nose of medium intensity with floral notes, touches of toasted oak, and a light vegetal timbre. In the mouth, it is round and balanced, and has a long finish that echoes the nose nicely and shows a faint note of oak. It is an interesting wine because it succeeds in reconciling excellent balance with a distinct personality. With just a pinch more depth and complexity, this would be a great wine. The Nobile '99 offers the palate plenty of vitality and good, juicy length, but the nose is less limpid and the fruit is veiled. More doubtful, though interesting, is the Boscarelli '99. It shows a not very fresh bouquet, with troubling walnut notes. The palate offers plenty of body and character, but the finish is thrown a little by marked tannin and oak.

● Vallocaia '98	7
● Vino Nobile di Montepulciano '99	5
● Rosso di Montepulciano Fosso Lupaio '01	5
○ Vin Santo Dolce Sinfonia '97	7
● Nobile di Montepulciano '91	4
● Nobile di Montepulciano '92	4
● Nobile di Montepulciano '94	4
● Vallocaia '94	5
● Vallocaia '95	5
○ Vin Santo Dolce Sinfonia '96	6
● Nobile di Montepulciano '97	5

● Nobile di Montepulciano Vigna del Nocio '99	6
● Boscarelli '99	8
● Nobile di Montepulciano '99	5
● De Ferrari '00	4
● Nobile di Montepulciano Ris. '88	5
● Nobile di Montepulciano Vigna del Nocio Ris. '91	5
● Boscarelli '95	8
● Boscarelli '97	8
● Nobile di Montepulciano Vigna del Nocio '97	5
● Nobile di Montepulciano '98	4

MONTEPULCIANO (SI)

FATTORIA DEL CERRO
FRAZ. ACQUAVIVA
VIA GRAZIANELLA, 5
53040 MONTEPULCIANO (SI)
TEL. 0578767722 - 0577767700
E-MAIL: fattoriadelcerro@tin.it

The high quality of the wines from Fattoria del Cerro is no longer a surprise. We'll get straight down to describing this year's long series of successes. The central showcase belongs again to the Vigneto Antica Chiusina, vintage '99, which has repeated the triumph of the '98. It makes a great, immediate impact with its dense, dark, very concentrated hue. The deep nose reveals blackberries and liquorice, as well as mineral and toasty nuances. The palate is soft yet powerful, underpinned by tight-knit tannins, and the long but compact finish again reveals attractive tannins. Knocking at the gate of Three Glasses is the merlot-based Poggio Golo 2000, and not for the first time. A massive red with enormous concentration and almost intimidating richness of extract, it is, objectively speaking, quite innocent of weak points. If we examine it less formally, we might be tempted to call it somewhat cold and lacking in excitement. The fairly similar sangiovese-based Manero '00 is a little rougher on the finish, but definitely worth investigating nonetheless. The Nobile '99 shows good balance on both nose and palate, as well as solid structure. The Cerro Bianco Chardonnay '01 came very close to getting Two Glasses for its aromas of tropical fruit and broad, well-defined palate. The Rosso di Montepulciano '01 is, as usual, well-made and generous with its succulent fruit, while the other wines are all simple but pleasing.

MONTEPULCIANO (SI)

CONTUCCI
VIA DEL TEATRO, 1
53045 MONTEPULCIANO (SI)
TEL. 0578757006
E-MAIL: info@contucci.it

Alamanno Contucci, president of the Consorzio del Vino Nobile, is an outgoing, charismatic individual who has at least two good motives to be well pleased. The first regards the general growth in the Montepulciano zone, which has acquired prestige and reliability. Still lacking, though difficult to achieve, is a clear, precise identity but the fundamentals are there. In the last few years, local winemakers have worked hard for the future. They have concentrated above all on the vines, which have been renovated at all the estates in order to achieve higher quality. A significant part of this renewal is due to Contucci's efforts. The other motive for satisfaction is linked, obviously, to the changes for the better at Contucci's own winery. His present wines, compared with those of just a few years ago, clearly demonstrate great progress, but we believe that from now on, we can hope for even greater things from the range. The panel thought the best of them was the Nobile '99. Its nose is still closed and compact, but already shows maraschino cherries and black peppers. It has a medium body with good balance, and the finish echoes the aromas of the nose deliciously. The '98 Riserva is perhaps less successful. Although straightforward and well balanced in the mouth, it is slightly penalized by hints of reduction. We finish with the Rosso di Montepulciano '00, which is well enough made but quite light in the mouth.

● Nobile di Montepulciano Vigneto Antica Chiusina '99	♛♛♛	6
● Manero '00	♛♛	6
● Poggio Golo '00	♛♛	6
● Nobile di Montepulciano '99	♛♛	4
○ Braviolo '01	♛	2*
○ Cerro Bianco Chardonnay '01	♛	3*
● Chianti dei Colli Senesi '01	♛	3*
● Rosso di Montepulciano '01	♛	3*
○ Vin Santo di Montepulciano Sangallo '97	♛	5
● Nobile di Montepulciano '90	♛♛♛	4*
● Nobile di Montepulciano Vigneto Antica Chiusina '98	♛♛♛	6
● Manero '99	♛♛	5
● Poggio Golo '99	♛♛	5

● Nobile di Montepulciano '99	♛♛	5
● Nobile di Montepulciano Ris. '98	♛	7
● Rosso di Montepulciano '00		4
○ Vin Santo '86	♛♛	6
● Nobile di Montepulciano '90	♛♛	4
○ Vin Santo '90	♛♛	4
● Nobile di Montepulciano '98	♛♛	4

MONTEPULCIANO (SI)

DEI
LOC. VILLA MARTIENA, 35
53045 MONTEPULCIANO (SI)
TEL. 0578716878

Tasting Caterina Dei's wines this year was very satisfying. Two of them made it to our national finals where, although neither received a Third Glass, they both made a very satisfactory impression. We note that quality is gradually but consistently on the rise here, and the only thing lacking is a little more strength of personality. This does not imply that Caterina should be thinking about putting more muscle into her products. The wines of this estate are usually more remarkable for their elegance than their power, and it could well be worthwhile to fine-tune the winemaking process to further bring out that finesse. Yet ours are merely the impressions gained from our tastings, and they were confirmed by this year's sessions. Sancta Catharina showed itself to be quite excellent, as well as in keeping with the winery's style. It has a rich, powerfully seductive nose, with floral scents appearing first, to be followed by hints of balsam, cocoa powder, talcum powder, and blackberries. In the mouth, it is soft and shows good, but not excessive, concentration. The Nobile '99 is also very good. Gentle on the palate, it shows no particular complexity, but we look forward to tasting next year the Riserva from the same vintage. Speaking of Riservas, we tasted the '98 edition of this wine and it made a largely favourable impression. It's round, and has good body, but is a bit rough on the finish.

● Sancta Catharina '00	ΨΨ	6
● Nobile di Montepulciano '99	ΨΨ	5*
● Nobile di Montepulciano Ris. '98	ΨΨ	5

MONTEPULCIANO (SI)

FASSATI
FRAZ. GRACCIANO
VIA DI GRACCIANELLO, 3/A
53040 MONTEPULCIANO (SI)
TEL. 0578708708 - 06844311
E-MAIL: info@fazibattaglia.it

The period of expansion and growth in quality continues unabated here at Fassati. Even though our evaluations only partially reflect this progress, a significant step forward has been made at this estate. So, the outlook for the future couldn't be rosier. The most eloquent sign was furnished by their '98 Salarco, which made it to our final taste-offs. It didn't receive Three Glasses, but made a very good impression nonetheless. It is a Nobile di Montepulciano Riserva with concentrated aromas of liquorice and cherries, as well as toasty hints from the oak. In the mouth, it is full, vigorous, and still somewhat marked by lingering tannins in a finish that is intense, flavoursome and full of character. The Nobile Pasiteo '99 is also very good. It has an intense ruby colour and a deep nose of blackberries with hints of wood. The palate is dense and consistent, revealing good fruit pulp at mid palate, and some roughness on the finish. It's still a very young wine and could develop well after a little more time in bottle. The other wines presented also came close to getting Two Glasses. The Rosso di Montepulciano Selcaia '01 shows aromas that are simple but well defined and fruit-driven. On the palate, it is attractive, well distributed, and moderately long. The Chianti Le Gaggiole Riserva '99 also performed very well. It has a lively ruby colour, and aromas of sour cherry jam and vanilla. In the mouth, it shows good, solid structure and unhesitating progression, but closes somewhat roughly.

● Nobile di Montepulciano Salarco Ris. '98	ΨΨ	5
● Nobile di Montepulciano Pasiteo '99	ΨΨ	5
● Rosso di Montepulciano Selciaia '01	Ψ	3*
● Chianti Le Gaggiole Ris. '99	Ψ	4
● Nobile di Montepulciano Pasiteo '97	ΨΨ	4
● Nobile di Montepulciano Salarco Ris. '97	ΨΨ	5
● Chianti Le Gaggiole Ris. '98	ΨΨ	3*
● Nobile di Montepulciano Pasiteo '98	ΨΨ	4

MONTEPULCIANO (SI)

La Calonica
Fraz. Valiano
Via della Stella, 27
53040 Montepulciano (SI)
Tel. 0578724119 - 0575613046
E-mail: lacalonica@libero.it

The wines of La Calonica have finally made the progress that we have been expecting for some time now. They not only shifted up a gear, but the Girifalco made it to our finals for the Three Glass awards. So the work that Ferdinando Catani has done in this period with the expert advice of his oenologist, Andrea Mazzoni, is beginning to bear fruit. Nevertheless, the cellar sees this as only the beginning of the campaign to realize their ambitions. As we mentioned above, the Sangiovese Girifalco '00 made an excellent impression. It is a concentrated, soft red that is well supported by oak, and blessed with remarkable intensity. There is also good sweetness on the palate, thanks to the juicy grain of the tannins and the compact weight of the fruit. After this excellent performance, there are more positive results to report. The Merlot Signorelli, for example, displays its varietal characteristics with particular success in hot summers like 2000. The aromas, which are quite jammy as well as redolent of dried fruits, are to be ascribed to the vintage, while the effect on the palate is to lend an impression of size and volume, with alcohol and sweetness that are nicely offset by the tannins. This is not a soft wine, but one that is powerful and mature. The Nobile '99 is also very good. It's full-bodied and well sustained in its progression on the palate.

• Girifalco '00	🍷🍷	6
• Signorelli '00	🍷🍷	5
• Nobile di Montepulciano '99	🍷🍷	5
• Rosso di Montepulciano '01		4
• Sangiovese '01		3
• Girifalco '95	🍷	5
• Nobile di Montepulciano '98	🍷	4
• Signorelli '98	🍷	5
• Signorelli '99	🍷	5

MONTEPULCIANO (SI)

La Ciarliana
Fraz. Gracciano
Via Ciarliana, 31
53040 Montepulciano (SI)
Tel. 0578758423 - 03355652718

Luigi Frangiosa's winery has fulfilled its promise. After its debut last year, it has showed that it has everything it takes to play an important role among its fellow producers in Montepulciano. This reliable quality could also be the springboard for launching even more ambitious projects. Still, there is little point in speculating about the future when the results of the tastings are sufficiently clear. The wines we tried reflected the work done in the cellar, including the near exclusive use of small wood to age the good, if not exceptional, raw material. This is the situation at La Ciarliana, inferred, we repeat, from our tastings. The wines are clean, balanced and well made, with oak distinctly, but discreetly, present. Up to this point, you might say that these merits are due to the good work done in the cellar. As for concentration, depth and aromatic personality, values that derive from the grape, our judgement has to be less favourable. This is the department where we feel more work needs to be done. The Riserva '98 has an intense nose with restrained vegetal tones and notes of red berries, cocoa powder and toasty oak. The palate is round, soft and even. The Nobile '99 shows fairly concentrated aromas of berry fruit and hints of wood, followed by a pleasant, well-balanced palate with moderate depth.

| • Nobile di Montepulciano Ris. '98 | 🍷 | 5 |
| • Nobile di Montepulciano '99 | 🍷 | 4 |

MONTEPULCIANO (SI)

LODOLA NUOVA - TENIMENTI RUFFINO
FRAZ. VALIANO
VIA LODOLA, 1
53045 MONTEPULCIANO (SI)
TEL. 0578734032
E-MAIL: info@ruffino.it

The Lodola Nuova winery has bounced straight back to a full Guide profile. The property is part of the Tenimenti Ruffino, and over the years has always offered proof of its reliability and fundamentally good quality without, however, producing anything really extraordinary. The reasons for this are not hard to find. There has been a long period during which old vines were being replaced by new ones. Mention should also be made of the use of local grape types, such as, naturally, prugnolo gentile. No assistance has been sought from non-local grapes, even though this has meant presenting weaker products to the market. This praiseworthy stylistic coherence has finally begun to produce tangible results, with even better prospects for the future. The '99 Riserva points the way. It has an intense, clean nose, which offers a rich fruitiness that is sweet and mature. The palate is full and round thanks to tightly knit yet soft tannins. The '99 Nobile di Montepulciano is also good, though less fat and thus unable to sustain all its wood. It is, however, well made and fills the palate very attractively. The Rosso Alanda is more pleasurable than usual with its gentle but lively flavour and good balance.

• Nobile di Montepulciano '99	♛♛	4
• Nobile di Montepulciano Ris. '99	♛♛	5
• Rosso di Montepulciano Alàuda '01	♛	3
• Nobile di Montepulciano '93	♛♛	4
• Rosso di Montepulciano '98	♛♛	3
• Nobile di Montepulciano '94	♛	4

MONTEPULCIANO (SI)

NOTTOLA
LOC. NOTTOLA
S. S. 326, 15
53045 MONTEPULCIANO (SI)
TEL. 0578707060 - 0577684711
E-MAIL: nottola@bccmp.com

There are no great surprises from Nottola this year. You might say that everything is in order. The general level of quality has been maintained, and could only be viewed as disappointing you were expecting a great exploit. We thought that something special might have come from the Nobile '99, but it has to be remembered that this is the "second" wine here. It has done as well as could reasonably be expected. It's a good Nobile, let's make that clear, and has a lovely ruby colour of considerable intensity. The nose is still somewhat closed but already showing notes of oak and raspberries. On the palate, it is fresh, well proportioned, and clean, and offers a finish of medium length. It's a good, frank, valid wine, but all things considered, a little on the simple side. The Vigna del Fattore '99 is a different story and just missed getting into the national finals. Its colour is concentrated and lively. The nose is perhaps its weakest point, owing to an evident vegetal note not in keeping with the wine type. However, it shows softness, tannic density, overall compactness, and a fairly lengthy finish in the mouth. The wood is well integrated and never intrudes. It's a good wine that has everything it needs to make a good impression. It just needs a little more character.

• Nobile di Montepulciano Vigna del Fattore '99	♛♛	5
• Nobile di Montepulciano '99	♛	4
• Nobile di Montepulciano Vigna del Fattore '95	♛♛	5
• Nobile di Montepulciano Vigna del Fattore '97	♛♛	5
• Nobile di Montepulciano '98	♛♛	4
• Nobile di Montepulciano Vigna del Fattore '98	♛♛	5

MONTEPULCIANO (SI)

FATTORIA DI PATERNO
FRAZ. SANT'ALBINO
VIA FONTELELLERA, 11
53045 MONTEPULCIANO (SI)
TEL. 0578799194 - 068081881
E-MAIL: fattoriapaterno@tiscalinet.it

The wines of the Fattoria di Paterno are increasingly impressive as the estate continues the period of renewal that it began only a few years ago. The results are evident and tangible. We are sure that in the future, the cellar will build on what has been done so far. Undoubtedly, the arrival of an expert as knowledgeable as Lorenzo Landi has played an important part, but the basis of success, here as elsewhere in the world of winemaking, has been the owner's ambition. The Nobile and the Riserva continue to be the only two wines produced here, and thereby benefit from the undivided attention of the winemakers. The '98 Riserva is very good, and shows a nose that is closed but compact. On the palate, it is solid, ample, nicely complex and displays a finish of good length, a little held back by its slightly excessive wood-derived tannins. Also good, if a tad simpler, is the Nobile '99. The aromas are mostly fruit-led while in the mouth, it shows softness, density, and balance. Only during its finish is there, again, a bit too much oak. To sum up, these are wines that reveal ample evidence of the good work done in the cellar, if we discount the slightly excessive wood. Nevertheless, they are yet able to express an aromatic personality of their own. For this, we will have to wait for the vine stock to mature some more.

MONTEPULCIANO (SI)

★ POLIZIANO
LOC. MONTEPULCIANO STAZIONE
VIA FONTAGO, 1
53040 MONTEPULCIANO (SI)
TEL. 0578738171
E-MAIL: az.agr.poliziano@iol.it

There are really very few wineries that can boast a pair of Three Glass wins but one of them is, of course, Poliziano. This is not the first time the cellar has achieved a result like this, but it is more significant today, as the competition is stiffer. On the other hand, success is not a matter of chance, and Federico Carletti is not one to rest on his laurels, even when there seems to be nothing that needs improvement. At our tastings, the Bordeaux blend Le Stanze '00 triumphed in one of its best versions ever. Its intense nose shows blackberries, spices, toastiness from the wood, and floral hints. In the mouth, it is quite monumental in size and balance, unveiling dense, very sweet tannins, and an extremely long finish. And what can we say about the Asinone '99? As usual, it's a great wine with scents of graphite, chocolate, coffee, and blackberries. Full-bodied and elegant, with close-knit but well-behaved tannins, it flaunts a finish of great depth. There were very positive results for the other wines, with a '99 Nobile that shows good density on the palate, but a little scratchiness at the end. The aromas show good fruit but there is some evidence of old wood. The Rosso di Montepulciano '01 did surprisingly well, even earning Two Glasses for its fragrant fruit, solid body and the decent length in its finish.

Wine	Glasses	Score
● Nobile di Montepulciano Ris. '98	¶¶	5
● Nobile di Montepulciano '99	¶¶	5
● Nobile di Montepulciano Ris. '88	¶	4
● Nobile di Montepulciano Ris. '90	¶	4
● Nobile di Montepulciano Ris. '91	¶	4
● Nobile di Montepulciano Ris. '97	¶	5
● Nobile di Montepulciano '98	¶	4

Wine	Glasses	Score
● Le Stanze '00	¶¶¶	7
● Nobile di Montepulciano Asinone '99	¶¶¶	6
● Rosso di Montepulciano '01	¶¶	3*
● Nobile di Montepulciano '99	¶¶	4
● Nobile di Montepulciano Vigna dell'Asinone '93	¶¶¶	5
● Elegia '95	¶¶¶	5
● Le Stanze '95	¶¶¶	7
● Nobile di Montepulciano Vigna dell'Asinone '95	¶¶¶	5
● Le Stanze '97	¶¶¶	7
● Nobile di Montepulciano Asinone '97	¶¶¶	6
● Le Stanze '98	¶¶¶	7
● Nobile di Montepulciano Asinone '98	¶¶¶	6
● Le Stanze '99	¶¶	7

MONTEPULCIANO (SI)

REDI
VIA DI COLLAZZI, 5
53045 MONTEPULCIANO (SI)
TEL. 0578716092 - 0578716093
E-MAIL: info@cantinadelredi.com

As usual, Redi offers an ample selection of wines that reconcile quantity with quality, and throw in a distinctive style for good measure. Their wines did very well at our tastings, and Orbaio '00, which is only in its second year of production, is already challenging Briareo for the leading spot in the range, even though the two wines are very different. The Orbaio is a blend of cabernet sauvignon and merlot, and has a generous nose that reveals ripe blackberries, spices, and liquorice. Its palate is soft but solid and round. It shows decent balance and a finish that is not without elegance. The display very nearly earned this Redi wine what would have been a stunning third Glass. We should say that the Nobile Briareo '99 also shows a good nose of sweet oak and spices, and a mouth that is even and elegant, if a little vegetal at the end. The Nobile '99 did well. The attractive nose embraces fruit, flowers and vanilla. The palate is intense, offering good pulp and a successful contrast of alcohol and tannins. The Redi Nobile Terre di Rubinoro '99 is clean, intense, and well balanced. Now comes a delightful surprise. All the rest of the cellar's wines did more than decently in our valuations, especially their Rosso di Montepulciano '01, which is pleasant and has good structure.

MONTEPULCIANO (SI)

SALCHETO
LOC. SANT'ALBINO
VIA DI VILLA BIANCA, 15
53045 MONTEPULCIANO (SI)
TEL. 0578799031
E-MAIL: posta@salcheto.it

The owners of Salcheto certainly have a desire to succeed and the necessary tenacity to do so. They supervise work in both the vineyards and the cellar personally, to ensure that they achieve their stated objective of making premium-quality wines from Montepulciano's signature grape variety, prugnolo gentile. This is not an easy task. It means finding the right balance of factors in the vineyard, and the intelligent use of the tools available in the cellar. A project as laudable as this can take a considerable time to implement, but we are sure Salcheto will eventually produce the desired results. The most interesting wine at our tastings was the Nobile Salco '99, a selection of prugnolo that is making its debut. It is a powerful red that still needs work on its aromatic profile, where over-ripeness alternates with and light traces of reduction. The palate does better, showing plentiful fruit, a full body and incisive tannins. Here, much of the effort went into producing concentration, which is important but not everything in a wine. More work needs to be done to achieve a balance of nose and palate, as well as more finesse. For a wine to make it to the final taste-offs on its first appearance is no mean achievement, however. The Nobile '99, more balanced and nearly as well received as the Salco, is broad and solid, displays civilized tannins, and has well-focused aromas. All the other wines are pleasant and well made.

● Orbaio '00	♛♛	5
● Nobile di Montepulciano '99	♛♛	5
● Nobile di Montepulciano Briareo '99	♛♛	6
● Nobile di Montepulciano Terre di Rubinoro '99	♛♛	3*
○ Riccio '01	♛	5
● Rosso di Montepulciano '01	♛	4
● Rosso di Montepulciano Terre di Rubinoro '01	♛	2*
○ Vin Santo '95	♛	7
○ Vin Santo '93	♛♛	7
● Nobile di Montepulciano '98	♛♛	4
● Nobile di Montepulciano Briareo '98	♛♛	6

● Nobile di Montepulciano Salco '99	♛♛	6
● Nobile di Montepulciano '99	♛♛	5
● Chianti dei Colli Senesi '01	♛	4
● Rosso di Montepulciano '01	♛	4
● Nobile di Montepulciano '97	♛♛♛	5
● Salcheto '90	♛♛	4
● Nobile di Montepulciano '91	♛♛	4
● Nobile di Montepulciano Ris. '95	♛♛	5
● Nobile di Montepulciano Ris. '97	♛♛	5
● Nobile di Montepulciano '98	♛♛	5

MONTEPULCIANO (SI)

Tenimenti Angelini - Tenuta Trerose
Fraz. Valiano
Via della Stella, 3
53040 Montepulciano (SI)
tel. 057880411 - 0578724018

The two selections of Nobile di Montepulciano from Tenuta Terrose, La Villa and Simposio, frequently contend for the position of top wine at this estate. Up to two years ago, Simposio seemed to be coming out on top most of the time, but for the last two years, La Villa has been the front runner. Wine writers may tend to exaggerate the competition between them, but this is inevitable when two wines obtained from the same grape, both excellent, are of such different character. This year, the difference in quality between the two was fairly small, but La Villa was slightly better and made it into our finals. It has a solid body with good, incisive tannins, and a lengthy well-delineated finish. The presence of a few notes of reduction on the noses of both wines held us back from giving them higher valuations. The '99 Simposio, from 100 per cent prugnolo, is soft, fresh, well balanced, and fairly long. The other wines presented didn't make any sparks fly. The '99 Nobile has medium body and decent balance, but is not very lively or clear on the nose. The Viognier Busillis '00 did not reach its usual high level, though this is to be blamed on the vintage, as 2000 was difficult for whites in general.

●	Nobile di Montepulciano La Villa '99	🍷	6
●	Nobile di Montepulciano Simposio '99	🍷🍷	6
●	Nobile di Montepulciano '99	🍷	4
○	Busillis '00		4
●	Nobile di Montepulciano Simposio '97	🍷🍷🍷	6
●	Nobile di Montepulciano La Villa '98	🍷🍷	6
●	Nobile di Montepulciano La Villa '97	🍷🍷	6
●	Nobile di Montepulciano Simposio '98	🍷🍷	6
○	Busillis '99	🍷🍷	4

MONTEPULCIANO (SI)

Tenuta Valdipiatta
Via della Ciarliana, 25/a
53040 Montepulciano (SI)
tel. 0578757930
e-mail: valdipiatta@bccmp.com

This is not the first time that Valdipiatta has earned Three Glasses, but since the last occasion, which was also the only one, a long time has passed. In the meanwhile, the winery hasn't been idle. There has been plenty of commitment and activity. Further hectares are now under vine, a new cellar has been inaugurated, and of course a number of competitive wines have been released. A lot was going on here, but our panels did not find the Valdipiatta wines to be entirely convincing. Scores were always high, but the wines tended to be big without being excellent. There were hints of excessive extraction that dampened finesse and harmony. Perhaps other critics loved them; it is, after all, a matter of taste. However, at last the Vigna d'Alfiero '99 has come through! Its excellent nose is eloquent. Clean, compact and deep, it has notes of ripe fruit, liquorice and spices, all in elegant proportion. On the palate, it is solid and concentrated, but not too showy. The extract is well gauged, the sweetest, tastiest tannins emerging to provide support and the finish is long and complex. Moreover, Vigna d'Alfiero is not alone. The Trinerone '00, from merlot and canaiolo, is very successful. It may be a bit simple, but it is powerful, juicy, and enjoyable to drink. The Riserva '98 still presents some oak on the palate, but is soft, continuous, and has a lively finish. The Nobile '99 may even be better, with its rich perfumes, concentration, and beautifully sustained palate. The Tre Fonti '99 was a little disappointing, but the Rosso di Montepulciano is more than merely decent.

●	Nobile di Montepulciano Vigna d'Alfiero '99	🍷🍷🍷	6
●	Trincerone '00	🍷🍷	6
●	Nobile di Montepulciano Ris. '98	🍷🍷	5
●	Nobile di Montepulciano '99	🍷🍷	5
●	Rosso di Montepulciano '01	🍷	4
●	Tre Fonti '99	🍷	6
●	Nobile di Montepulciano Ris. '90	🍷🍷🍷	5
●	Nobile di Montepulciano Ris. '97	🍷🍷	5
●	Tre Fonti '98	🍷🍷	6
●	Nobile di Montepulciano '95	🍷🍷	4
●	Nobile di Montepulciano Ris. '95	🍷🍷	5
●	Nobile di Montepulciano '96	🍷🍷	4
●	Nobile di Montepulciano '97	🍷🍷	4
●	Nobile di Montepulciano '98	🍷🍷	4
●	Trincerone '99	🍷🍷	6

MONTEPULCIANO (SI)

Villa Sant'Anna
Fraz. Abbadia
53040 Montepulciano (SI)
Tel. 0578708017 - 03355283775
E-mail: simona@villasantanna.it

It's going to take a little more time for Villa Sant'Anna to emerge from its shell of well-made but rather predictable wines. The cellar has been aware for some time that something will have to be done to jerk the estate out of its gilded anonymity so moves are afoot to boost the already excellent quality of the range. With a little patience, we will see interesting developments here at Abbadia. Oddly enough, the wine we were most impressed by this time was the Vin Santo '95, which would be a shock in any other part of Tuscany but not at Montepulciano, where there is a fine tradition of Vin Santo production. We could add that the panel was on the point of sending it forward to the national finals. The intense amber hue introduces a bouquet of intriguingly varied aromas, from dried chestnuts to sun-baked earth, ending on more re-assuring notes of black cherry jam. The palate has an intensely creamy mouthfeel, with a slightly unusual but nonetheless exciting contrast of acidity and sweetness. Not the most elegance of wines but definitely one with attitude. Back on more traditional lines, the Nobile '99 is a soft, well-rounded red with decent body adequately supported by oak. The Chianti and Rosso di Montepulciano are more straightforward but well typed and attractive.

○ Vin Santo '95	ΨΨ	7
● Nobile di Montepulciano '99	ΨΨ	5
● Chianti Colli Senesi '00	Ψ	4
● Rosso di Montepulciano '01	Ψ	4
● Rosso di Montepulciano '00	ΨΨ	3
● Nobile di Montepulciano '93	ΨΨ	4
● Chianti '94	ΨΨ	2
● Nobile di Montepulciano '94	ΨΨ	4
● Chianti Colli Senesi '95	ΨΨ	2
● Vigna Il Vallone '95	ΨΨ	5
● Nobile di Montepulciano '96	ΨΨ	4
● Nobile di Montepulciano '98	ΨΨ	4

MONTEROTONDO MARITTIMO (GR)

Serraiola
Fraz. Frassine
Loc. Serraiola
58025 Monterotondo Marittimo (GR)
Tel. 0566910026
E-mail: info@serraiola.it

Although we awarded more or less the same number of Glasses this year, Fiorella Lenzi's wines showed greater authority this year, and communicated quality and a re-assuring sense of knowing exactly where they are going. The Violina '01 and the Camp Montecristo '00 won their Two Glasses very easily, indicating that the cellar's growth is stable as well as very promising. Violina is one of the most pleasant surprises to be found among Tuscany's whites. Its nose is intense and well developed, offering peaches, apricots, and broom, all very clearly expressed. In the mouth, it is round, almost fat, and has a fresh tanginess leading to a long coherent finish. The Campo Santo, from sangiovese and merlot, has better structure than the previous version. Its aromas are still closed, with some timid hints of vegetal, while the palate is dense, thanks to layers of sweet, delicious tannins. The finish is well developed and persistent. The Vermentino '01 is more than merely dignified. The nose is not particularly expressive but it has good consistency and length. To finish, the Lentisco '00 is acceptable. With the exception of some reduction, it is well balanced and, as the cellar intended, a pleasant wine that is easy to drink.

● Campo Montecristo '00	ΨΨ	6
○ Monteregio di Massa Marittima Violina '01	ΨΨ	4*
● Monteregio di Massa Marittima Lentisco '00	Ψ	4
○ Vermentino '01	Ψ	4
○ Monteregio Bianco di Massa Marittima Violina '00	ΨΨ	4*
● Campo Montecristo '99	ΨΨ	5
○ Vermentino '00	Ψ	3

MONTESPERTOLI (FI)

Fattoria Castiglioni e Montagnana
Fraz. Montagnana Val di Pesa
Via Montegufoni, 35
50020 Montespertoli (FI)
Tel. 0571671387 - 0571675877
E-mail: fattoria.castiglioni@frescobaldi.it

Another of the many properties owned by Marchesi di Frescobaldi, Tenuta Castiglioni, situated in the Colli Fiorentini area, earns its first full profile. The property is a jewel that has been very well cared for, until the time was ripe for it to be discovered by a wider public. The very good value for money Chianti was already known to us. New this year are the Giramonte, with both its last two versions presented, and the Cabernet Sauvignon. Our tastings showed that the Frescobaldi group knows precisely what it is doing for the estate's Three Glass award came almost without effort. The winner, the Giramonte '00, is a blend of sangiovese and merlot. It has excellent concentration, blessed with rich, ripe fruit of utterly convincing purity. Perhaps the style could be called less than completely original, but this is an excellent wine. Its round, elegant palate leads to a long finish pervaded by the intensity of the fruit. The '99 Giramonte is also very good, though its wood is not perfectly integrated, and there are vegetal hints that detract from the aromas. The Chianti '01 was a surprise, Its fragrant nose of raspberries and blueberries is reflected on the palate, which offers a round and very pleasant attack, and good length at the end. It is a simple wine at a very favourable price. There was nearly a second Glass for the Cabernet Sauvignon '00, which shows attractively fleshy fruit and good balance, but also a rather too marked vegetal note.

MONTESPERTOLI (FI)

Le Calvane
Fraz. Montagnana
Via Castiglioni, 1/5
50020 Montespertoli (FI)
Tel. 0571671073
E-mail: lecalvane@interfree.it

The very favourable local weather conditions help Le Calvane's grapes, almost every year, become fully ripe. The 15 hectares of vines lie at an altitude of 150 metres, in positions that are generally excellent. If we add to these natural advantages the dedication of the winemakers, and the well-considered advice of consultant Vittorio Fiore, it is not difficult to understand how Le Calvane is overcoming the handicap of being on the edges of the DOC zone. Although the winery has not done as brilliantly as on other occasions, in lesser vintages, this can always happen. The Borro del Boscone '99 easily achieved a highly respectable score but in the past has done even better. Probably, if it were not for the rather heavy note of reduction that is evident on the nose, it would have made this year a great one as well. On the palate, this Cabernet Sauvignon is full, round, concentrated and well-sustained in its development, with some slight, not very significant, vegetal hints. The Riserva Il Treccione '99 is also less good than usual. This fine Chianti has a rigorous style, but is somewhat evolved. The Chianti Quercione '00 shows good raw material, but the nose is not as clean as it should be. The Chardonnay Solbino '01 is well made, if unambitious.

● Giramonte '00	🍷🍷🍷 6
● Chianti '01	🍷🍷 3*
● Giramonte '99	🍷🍷 6
● Cabernet Sauvignon '00	🍷 4

● Borro del Boscone '99	🍷🍷 6
● Chianti dei Colli Fiorentini Quercione '00	🍷 3
● Chianti dei Colli Fiorentini Il Trecione Ris. '99	🍷 4
● Sorbino '01	3
● Borro del Boscone '97	🍷🍷🍷 5
● Borro del Boscone '98	🍷🍷 6
● Borro del Boscone '94	🍷🍷 4
● Borro del Boscone '95	🍷🍷 5
● Borro del Boscone '96	🍷🍷 5
● Chianti Colli Fiorentini Il Trecione Ris. '97	🍷🍷 4
● Chianti Colli Fiorentini Il Trecione Ris. '98	🍷🍷 4

MONTESPERTOLI (FI)

CASTELLO DI POPPIANO
FRAZ. POPPIANO
VIA DI FEZZANA, 45
50025 MONTESPERTOLI (FI)
TEL. 05582315
E-MAIL: poppiano@mclink.it

Last year, we promoted Conte Guicciardini to "marchese", or marquis, without asking his permission. His winery, though, has put on another noble performance this year with two wines receiving Two Glasses. The Syrah '00, the first of the pair, has a deep purple colour. Its nose shows cherries, currants and a very captivating touch of pepper. In the mouth, it displays good texture, roundness and density, maintaining its lively character through to the finish. The Tricorno '98 did equally well. Its impenetrable ruby introduces a powerful nose with slight balsamic hints over a base of toasty oak. The soft, warm, harmonious attack on the palate is followed up by light tannins and a long finish. The Chianti Colli Fiorentini Il Cortile '00 is purple and offers a simple, fruity nose. Medium-bodied, it is juicy in the mouth but its tannins are just a little too harsh. The less exciting '98 Riserva has aromas that are a bit tired, shows middling intensity, and a structure that is not very concentrated, but is lent a helping hand by lively tannins. The Toscoforte '00 presents a good lively ruby colour and a nose that offers some over-ripe tones, lifted by hints of spiciness. After a good attack, it loses strength, presenting a balanced but not very incisive structure. Its finish is of medium length.

MONTESPERTOLI (FI)

FATTORIA CASTELLO SONNINO
VIA VOLTERRANA NORD, 10
50025 MONTESPERTOLI (FI)
TEL. 0571609198 - 0571657481
E-MAIL: sonnino@mbr.it

Barone De Renzis' winery is showing clear signs of vigour and the wines presented this year at our tastings signal an improvement in quality and consistency. The Sanleone '00, for example, came up with a remarkable performance and just missed an invitation to the national finals. A red that blends merlot with 30 per cent sangiovese and ten per cent of other varieties, it has a very intense ruby colour and aromas that, while not completely harmonized, are concentrated and show ripe fruit, as well as hints of attractive oak. The attack on the palate has warmth and power, then mid palate shows solid body, finishing with intensity thanks to support from the oak. The wine was put together with more precision than usual this time, and has avoided the rustic traits of some previous versions. The Sangiovese Cantinino '00 has made progress, too. The nose reveals berry fruit and vegetal hints. On the palate, it is fresh, with good, dense consistency, and a finish of medium length that is only a little dried out by its oak. The Vin Santo '97 is also well constructed and releases aromas of candied peel, then offers sweetness and good balance on the palate. The standard wines also did quite well, with the Chianti Montespertoli '01 standing out for its sweet softness, easy drinking style and juicy finish. The Chianti Montespertoli '01 is more than merely decent, and though slightly compromised by invasive oakiness, is decent and robust.

● Syrah '00	ŸŸ	4
● Tricorno '98	ŸŸ	6
● Chianti Colli Fiorentini Il Cortile '00	Ÿ	3
● Toscoforte '00	Ÿ	4
● Chianti Colli Fiorentini Ris. '98	Ÿ	4
● Chianti Colli Fiorentini Ris. '93	ŸŸ	3
● Tricorno '93	ŸŸ	4
● Tricorno '97	ŸŸ	5
● Toscoforte '96	Ÿ	3
● Chianti Colli Fiorentini Ris. '97	Ÿ	3
● Toscoforte '98	Ÿ	4
● Syrah '99	Ÿ	4

● Cantinino '00	ŸŸ	5
● Sanleone '00	ŸŸ	7
○ Vin Santo De Renzis '97	ŸŸ	5
● Chianti Montespertoli Castello di Sonnino '00	Ÿ	4
● Chianti Montespertoli '01	Ÿ	3*

MONTEVARCHI (AR)

FATTORIA PETROLO
LOC. GALATRONA
FRAZ. MERCATALE VALDARNO
52020 MONTEVARCHI (AR)
TEL. 0559911322
E-MAIL: petrolo@petrolo.it

Here we go again! For the fourth time in a row, Petrolo is on the list of Three Glass winners, and the astonishing Galtrona is the wine that has again done the business. This time, the success is perhaps the biggest and most convincing ever from this estate at Mercatale Valdarno. We have never before found such a uniformly excellent level of quality overall in the wines presented for tasting. The Merlot Galatrona '00 continues to be a massive, powerful wine that shows endless, irresistible thrust on its intriguing, exciting palate. Yet the biggest surprise came from the simplest wine on the list, the Terre di Galatrona, obtained from a 50-50 blend of merlot and sangiovese. An excellent, if uncomplicated, red, it strolled off with Two Glasses. The nose opens with a certain lack of clarity, since the red berry fruit and black pepper mingle with notes of reduction, probably from the use of old barrels. In the mouth, though, it has surprisingly dense, thick tannins, which support a continuous, linear progression. The Sangiovese Torrione was presented at our tastings in two versions, the '99 and the '00. We noted greater character in the '99, which had some gamey notes but was still refreshing, intense and continuous. The '00 is also very good. Its nose has balsamic nuances that are a little disturbed by hints of excessive evolution. On the palate, it is soft, attractive and vigorous, with tasty tannins and a persistent finish. The warm, sweet Vin Santo '95 has lots of power.

MONTOPOLI IN VAL D'ARNO (PI)

VARRAMISTA
LOC. VARRAMISTA
VIA RICAVO
56020 MONTOPOLI IN VAL D'ARNO (PI)
TEL. 0571468121 - 0571468122
E-MAIL: info@varramista.it

Ever since its debut, the Varramista red has had the makings of a very superior wine. As time went by, though, it seemed to lose its way, even though the potential for improvement was still there, as well as an interesting level of quality. It looked as though the search for an individual style had been called off. The problem, really, was to make something out of syrah, a difficult grape that is very susceptible to seasonal changes, so that it could express its varietal character without exaggeration or a becoming an anonymous, "Australian-style" wine. The credit for the success of this year's version should be attributed to Federico Staderini, who has been with Varramista since the beginning. The blend this time has ten per cent merlot and five per cent sangiovese in with the syrah. The 2000 Varramista is stunningly good, its marvellous nose leading into a palate with a gloriously close-knit texture. The aromas show varietal notes of pepper and cinnamon, aromatic herbs, violets, plums and the timid presence of toasty wood. In the mouth, the wine is dense, concentrated, well sustained and has a very long finish that echoes the nose. The year 2000 marks the debut of Frasca, which is a little more than half sangiovese and the rest merlot and syrah. It has an agile, very easy drinking body and is pleasantly fruity and spicy on the nose.

● Galatrona '00	🍷🍷🍷	7
● Terre di Galatrona '00	🍷🍷	3*
● Torrione '00	🍷🍷	5
○ Vin Santo '95	🍷🍷	5
● Torrione '99	🍷🍷	5
● Galatrona '97	🍷🍷🍷	7
● Galatrona '98	🍷🍷🍷	7
● Galatrona '99	🍷🍷🍷	7
○ Vin Santo '93	🍷🍷	5
● Galatrona '95	🍷🍷	7
● Torrione '95	🍷🍷	5
● Torrione '97	🍷🍷	5
● Torrione '98	🍷🍷	5

● Varramista '00	🍷🍷🍷	6
● Frasca '00	🍷	4
● Varramista '95	🍷🍷	6
● Varramista '96	🍷🍷	6
● Varramista '97	🍷🍷	6
● Varramista '98	🍷🍷	6
● Varramista '99	🍷🍷	6

MURLO (SI)

Fattoria Casabianca
Fraz. Casciano
Loc. Monte Pescini
53016 Murlo (SI)
Tel. 0577811033 - 0577811026
E-mail: casavia@tin.it

There was a convincing start for this winery located more or less halfway between Siena and Montalcino. At first glance, it is an excellent area for cultivating vines, but it is hidden, or rather put in the shade, by the many famous wine areas that surround it. The Fattoria Casabianca wines that we tried in our tastings showed significantly good level of quality, and their Tenuta Casabianca, presented in two vintages, made an excellent impression. The 1998 version, from 90 per cent sangiovese and ten per cent cabernet sauvignon, has an intense garnet colour and a nose that shows notes of evolution, with earthiness, tobacco and liquorice. In the mouth, it is round and well balanced, showing attractive fruit and a finish that's a little rough. The '99 is even more interesting, and the blend has changed completely. It is 85 per cent cabernet sauvignon and 15 per cent merlot. The nose is compact and harmonious, with some light vegetal traces. On the palate, it is soft, supple, tidy and deliciously long. It doesn't have much complexity, but it is very good and certainly a wine to follow in the coming years. The Riserva Poggio Cenni '99 is also convincing, and shows a clean, if not very communicative, nose. The palate is dense, juicy, vivacious and well sustained. The very simple and light Campolungo is nevertheless fruity and pleasant. Finally, the Rosato Poggio and Chianti Colli Senesi are decent and well put together.

● Tenuta Casabianca '98	▼▼	6
● Chianti Ris. Poggio Cenni '99	▼▼	5
● Tenuta Casabianca '99	▼▼	6
● Chianti Colli Senesi Poggio Cenni '00	▼	3
● Campo Lungo	▼	2*
☉ Poggio Gonfienti '01		2

ORBETELLO (GR)

La Parrina
Loc. Albinia
58010 Orbetello (GR)
Tel. 0564862636 - 0564862626
E-mail: parrina@dada.it

There's an air of challenges being tackled at La Parrina. This Maremma winery has given a huge jolt to the routine that has kept it shrouded in anonymity, and is now bursting with enthusiasm. A good part of the responsibility for this belongs to Federico Curtaz and Beppe Caviola, who weren't just going to carry out a normal upgrade in the vineyards and in the cellar. In addition, they have inspired new energy and passion into the whole of Marchesa Spinola's winery staff. The 60-plus hectares under vine seem to have taken on a new lease of life. The vines have found their feet and are brimming with good health. As for the wines, although further patience is still required, we can already point to the first positive signs from recent vintages. The Radaia 2000, a 100 per cent merlot, stands out from the pack. It is a solid wine, with character and a compact nose where spicy hints emerge as well as good ripe fruit. It bursts onto the palate, developing softly and gradually revealing its oak. The finish is intense and well sustained. Equally interesting is the Parrina Riserva '99, which presents aromas of red berries, notes of coffee and light vegetal traces. The palate has good extractive weight and balance, and the finish is well sustained. The Murraccio '00 made a positive impression. While perhaps a bit too vegetal on the nose, it is soft and nicely complex in the mouth. The Ansonica '01 was surprisingly inviting on the nose, then fresh and well balanced on the palate. The Parrina Bianco and Rosso were both simple but very pleasant.

● Radaia '00	▼▼	7
● Parrina Rosso Muraccio '00	▼▼	4*
○ Ansonica Costa dell'Argentario '01	▼▼	3*
● Parrina Rosso Ris. '99	▼▼	5
○ Parrina Bianco '01	▼	2*
● Parrina Rosso '01	▼	3*
● Parrina Rosso Ris. '98	▼▼	4
● Parrina Rosso Muraccio '99	▼	4

PANZANO (FI)

CAROBBIO
VIA SAN MARTINO IN CECIONE, 26
50020 PANZANO (FI)
TEL. 0558560133
E-MAIL: info@carobbiowine.com

When the results of our tastings reward a winery of proven worth and constant quality, like Carobbio, we are always very pleased. In all probability, the owners of the estate and the person in charge of making the wine, the very competent Gabriella Tani, are even more pleased than we are. The major result is not a matter of luck, since Carobbio, as we said, has already given several indications of its worth. The Three Glasses lined up with more serious stemware. Alongside the excellent '99 Riserva, the standard Chianti Classico 2000 also scored well. It is a wine that did well at our finals, where it showed both cleanness and clear aromatic definition to the nose, as well as abundant ripe fruit. In the mouth, it is lively, intense and incisive, showing sweet tannins and a long finish. Three Glasses, though, went to the '99 Riserva, justified by its ability to express a solidly territorial character without sacrificing balance and composure. The aromas have complex mineral touches and a timid hint of the oak used for ageing. The palate is full and compact, well sustained by a sweet weave of ripe tannins, and well able to expand in an ever-changing progression. The finish is long and eloquent, appropriately so for a wine of superior personality. The IGT Pietrafore and Leone del Carobbio were not presented this year, but given how things went, it doesn't seem to have made much difference.

•	Chianti Cl. Ris. '99	🍷🍷🍷	5*
•	Chianti Cl. '00	🍷🍷	4*
•	Pietraforte del Carobbio '97	🍷🍷	6
•	Leone del Carobbio '94	🍷🍷	5
•	Chianti Cl. Ris. '95	🍷🍷	5
•	Pietraforte del Carobbio '95	🍷🍷	5
•	Chianti Cl. Ris. '96	🍷🍷	5
•	Chianti Cl. '97	🍷🍷	4
•	Chianti Cl. Ris. '97	🍷🍷	5
•	Leone del Carobbio '97	🍷🍷	6
•	Chianti Cl. '98	🍷🍷	4
•	Chianti Cl. Ris. '98	🍷🍷	5
•	Chianti Cl. '99	🍷🍷	4

PANZANO (FI)

CASTELLO DEI RAMPOLLA
VIA CASE SPARSE, 22
50020 PANZANO (FI)
TEL. 055852001
E-MAIL: castellodeirampolla.cast@tin.it

There were no surprises from Castello dei Rampolla. The trophy cupboard was unlocked once more to receive an umpteenth Three Glass award. We'll have to be careful to keep track of them because if there are only two more, we will have to add a star at the top of the profile. We would like to add that D'Alceo has never missed a top award, and this is the fifth year in a row. It's a wine that doesn't seem to suffer from variations in different vintages, probably because none of the vines is allowed to yield so much as half a kilogram of grapes. Given this tiny quantity, you might suppose that the result would be the production of a wine that is all muscle. Instead, D'Alceo gets more harmonious, elegant, complex and pure in its fruit year after year. It's obvious that the raw material is stupendous, but the magisterial work accomplished in the cellar should not be ignored. The temptation to concentrate this wine even more has been resisted, the selection of the grapes was impeccable and the extraction perfectly judged. The historic wine from Rampolla is Sammarco, made from cabernet sauvignon with one tenth sangiovese, and the '99 version shows a concentrated nose and notable complexity. It opens up in the mouth with great softness and a formal elegance that was less evident in some recent versions. The finish has good length, with a very faint twist of bitterness. The Chianti Classico '00 is decent, if somewhat evolved.

•	D'Alceo '00	🍷🍷🍷	8
•	Sammarco '99	🍷🍷	8
•	Chianti Cl. '00	🍷	5
○	Trebianco V.T. '96		5
•	Sammarco '85	🍷🍷🍷	8
•	Sammarco '86	🍷🍷🍷	8
•	Sammarco '94	🍷🍷🍷	8
•	La Vigna di Alceo '96	🍷🍷🍷	8
•	La Vigna di Alceo '97	🍷🍷🍷	8
•	La Vigna di Alceo '98	🍷🍷🍷	8
•	La Vigna di Alceo '99	🍷🍷🍷	8
•	Sammarco '98	🍷🍷	8
•	Sammarco '96	🍷🍷	8
•	Sammarco '97	🍷🍷	8
•	Chianti Cl. '99	🍷🍷	5

PANZANO (FI)

CENNATOIO INTERVINEAS
VIA DI SAN LEOLINO, 37
50020 PANZANO (FI)
TEL. 055852134 - 0558963230
E-MAIL: info@cennatoio.it

Leandro Alessi sent his most representative wines to our tastings. The choice confirms his interest in making wines that are typical of this area, although Leandro achieved his best score with Arcibaldo '99, a merlot-based product. This has an intense ruby colour and a nose that offers elegant vegetal scents ennobled by notes of menthol, as well as blueberries and blackberries. Sustained by close-knit, but well-distributed, tannins, it shows notable finesse in the mouth. The lengthy finish suggests that it has excellent potential for aging. There was also a good performance from the Etrusco '99, a monovarietal Sangiovese, which has an excellent ruby colour. The nose offers a vast assortment of fruit, with peaches, sour cherries, plums and cherries all well balanced by an unintrusive aroma of toastiness. The palate reveals a pleasing complexity where acidity adds some freshness to an elegant, concentrated body. There is a good finish that is enjoyably sweet. The two "riserva" wines are less interesting. The Riserva '99 has already acquired a garnet shading, and the aromas show some reduction, earthiness and a clear note of green pepper. It seems to be on the downhill slope of its evolution and the tannins are neither particularly incisive nor well blended in. The Riserva O'Leandro '99 shows a ruby colour preceding intense aromas where the dominant note is redcurrant jam. The attack on the palate is a bit meek, but it offers a good, sustained progression.

• Arcibaldo '99	♛♛	7
• Etrusco '99	♛♛	7
• Chianti Cl. O'Leandro Ris. '99	♛	6
• Chianti Cl. Ris. '99	♛	6
• Etrusco '94	♛♛♛	5
• Etrusco '95	♛♛	5
• Rosso Fiorentino '95	♛♛	5
• Chianti Cl. Ris. '97	♛♛	4
• Etrusco '97	♛♛	5
• Rosso Fiorentino '97	♛♛	5
• Etrusco '98	♛♛	5
• Chianti Cl. '99	♛♛	4

PANZANO (FI)

★ TENUTA FONTODI
VIA SAN LEOLINO, 87
50020 PANZANO (FI)
TEL. 055852005
E-MAIL: fontodi@dada.it

The Tenuta Fontodi is one of the historic producers of Italian wines. One has to acknowledge what this winery has done both in terms of quality and of style for the wines here in Italy. Nor are we speaking merely in aesthetic terms, although the winery's architecture is splendid, and a benchmark for many producers. Above all, the family's management style is exemplary. That said, the results of our tastings confirm that Fontodi's wines continue to be excellent. A common element characterized all the wines at our tastings. They were initially closed and mysterious to the nose. It has been our experience that this situation changes noticeably over the years. The Chianti Classico '00 was less convincing to the nose, although the palate offers good body, excellent tannins, and good development. But the Chianti Classico Vigna del Serbo Riserva '99 seemed to us to be a superb wine. It doesn't show much to the nose yet, but there is plenty of structure and solid, ripe tannins in the mouth. The Flaccianello della Pieve '99, a big red made from sangiovese and aged in small oak barrels, is less complex than in its finest versions. Although it reveals some reduction on the nose, the palate has the elegance and balance that make it stand out from so many other wines in this area. The Syrah Casa Via '99 has a very intense colour, but then reveals some over-ripeness and a somewhat unbalanced structure.

• Chianti Cl.		
Vigna del Sorbo Ris. '99	♛♛	6
• Flaccianello della Pieve '99	♛♛	7
• Syrah Case Via '99	♛♛	7
• Chianti Cl. '00	♛	5
• Chianti Cl.		
Vigna del Sorbo Ris. '86	♛♛♛	6
• Chianti Cl.		
Vigna del Sorbo Ris. '90	♛♛♛	6
• Flaccianello della Pieve '90	♛♛♛	6
• Syrah Case Via '95	♛♛♛	6
• Flaccianello della Pieve '97	♛♛♛	6
• Syrah Case Via '98	♛♛♛	6
• Chianti Cl. Vigna del Sorbo Ris. '98	♛♛	6
• Chianti Cl. '99	♛♛	5

PANZANO (FI)

La Marcellina
Via Case Sparse, 74
50020 Panzano (FI)
tel. 055852126
e-mail: marcellina@ftbcc.it

La Marcellina has won a full Guide profile after graduating brilliantly from our Other Wineries section. The Castellacci family winery has 20 hectares of land, of which about three quarters are under vine at an altitude of some 500 metres above sea level. Last year, we said that the range included some interesting elements but the overall level was rather less than satisfactory. The situation has been partially resolved. There was confirmation for Camporosso, the wine that was already convincing in the '97 version. A blend of sangiovese and cabernet sauvignon, it offers in the '99 edition a nose that opens on rather unattractive grassy scents, although they are expressed clearly and with intensity. In the mouth, it shows good body, with nice balance and sustained development, closing pleasingly with sweet notes of vanilla. The Chianti Classico Comignolo '00 also gained a positive score, although its nose reveals strong vegetal scents. It does better on the palate, where the green notes are attenuated and the body is attractively complex. The other Chianti Classico, Sassocupo '00, is quite successful but displays the usual weakness on the nose, where unpleasant animal scents of reduction emerge. On the mouth, however, it is meaty and has good concentration. Finally, the Vin Santo '90 failed to light any fires.

● Chianti Cl. Comignole '00	♟♟	5
● Camporosso '99	♟♟	5
● Chianti Cl. Sassocupo '00	♟	4
○ Vin Santo '90		6
● Camporosso '97	♟♟	5

PANZANO (FI)

La Massa
Via Case Sparse, 9
50020 Panzano (FI)
tel. 055852722
e-mail: fattoria.lamassa@tin.it

It's more like a mantra than a newsflash - Giorgio Primo is an extraordinary wine. This now repetitious praise is inspired not only by the wine's characteristics on nose and palate but also to its ability to maintain them constantly over the years. With the 2000 edition, we have reached the eighth consecutive Three Glass plaudit. How do you manage to turn out a wine that is a benchmark for other great bottles elsewhere in Tuscany and beyond? The basic elements are clear enough. Take two individuals, Giancarlo Motta, an "immigrant" from Naples who became at a very young age the estate's enthusiastic owner, and Carlo Ferrini, a Tuscan oenological consultant famous for knowing every inch of his native land. Then add the land, in the Conca d'Oro, one of the best places in Chianti Classico for growing vines. Indeed, much of the success derives from the terroir of these rolling, sun-kissed hills that have tamed the rough, impulsive sangiovese grapes that make up 90 per cent of Giorgio Primo. The 10 per cent of merlot added does not completely account for its sweetness and roundness, or its beautifully intense and brilliant colour. The nose finds notes of ripe fruit, and waves of gentle spice enchant the palate. But where does the harmony and elegant complexity come from? We're talking about class here. Giampaolo Motta has bet on a winning horse. Perhaps this is why he pays less attention to the standard version of Chianti Classico, which is a bit too ordinary for a winery like his. Can we blame him?

● Chianti Cl. Giorgio Primo '00	♟♟♟	7
● Chianti Cl. '00	♟	5
● Chianti Cl. Giorgio Primo '93	♟♟♟	4
● Chianti Cl. Giorgio Primo '94	♟♟♟	5
● Chianti Cl. Giorgio Primo '95	♟♟♟	5
● Chianti Cl. Giorgio Primo '96	♟♟♟	5
● Chianti Cl. Giorgio Primo '97	♟♟♟	6
● Chianti Cl. Giorgio Primo '98	♟♟♟	6
● Chianti Cl. Giorgio Primo '99	♟♟♟	7
● Chianti Cl. '97	♟♟	4
● Chianti Cl. '98	♟♟	4
● Chianti Cl. '99	♟♟	4

PANZANO (FI)

Le Bocce
Via Case Sparse, 76
50020 Panzano (FI)
tel. 055852153

PANZANO (FI)

Panzanello
Case Sparse, 86
50020 Panzano (FI)
tel. 055852470
e-mail: info@panzanello.it

This Panzano winery has in the past racked up some interesting numbers, in terms of quality and quantity, but in recent years, the results here have been less than convincing. This time round, they have done very well and thoroughly deserved to regain their full Guide profile. The Chianti Classico '00 has a beautiful, intense ruby colour that is reasonably concentrated. The nose reveals good ripe fruit, with plums, cherries and some hints of jam. The attack on the palate is admirably sweet and smooth, and the pervasive mouthfeel is only slightly dominated by tannins that are just a little too rough on the finish, which is nevertheless tangy and satisfying. The '99 Riserva shows a bright ruby colour and a rather muffled nose at first, but then opens to show ripe plums and blackberries, slightly marred by some inelegant animal notes. The entry on the palate is deliciously substantial and concentrated but the tannins emerge to prominently, and hinder the wine from progressing fully. The moderately long finish lacks savour. On the other hand, the Paladino '00 performed well. It has a well-defined ruby colour, and shows faint touches of ripe fruit o the nose. The palate is perfectly balanced and dense, with well-amalgamated tannins. Although it does not have much length, the back palate is attractive.

The impression of progress we gained here at the Fattoria Sant'Andrea, also known as Panzanello, in our tastings last year, has been followed by further improvement this year. Andrea Sommaruga's winery has almost 20 hectares of vines, most of which are dedicated to making Chianti Classico, with a density of 5,500 plants per hectare in recent plantings. He has enlisted Gioia Cresti's help as oenologist, and she has proved valuable. Andrea's Sangiovese Manuzio '00 is just a short step from excellence. It has a dense, harmonious nose that shows blackberries and notes of chocolate. In the mouth, it is concentrated, elegant, well-sustained in its development, and displays marked, but very well handled, oak. The finish, just a little on the tannic side of perfect, is attractively long. This performance brings a hitherto little known wine to the attention of a wider public. Also very good is the Chianti Classico '00, which is clean and has clearly defined aromas of raspberries and blackberries. The palate reveals interesting body, good balance, and a clean finish that foregrounds the fruit. Just as valid is the Riserva '99, which has a fragrant nose of raspberries and cherries, with some green notes. The palate shows plenty of body backed up by sweet tannins and a persistent finish.

● Chianti Cl. '00	4
● Il Paladino '00	4
● Chianti Cl. Ris. '99	4

● Il Manuzio '00	6
● Chianti Cl. Panzanello '00	4
● Chianti Cl. Panzanello Ris. '99	5
● Chianti Cl. Panzanello '98	3
● Chianti Cl. Panzanello Ris. '98	4
● Il Manuzio '99	5

PANZANO (FI)

VECCHIE TERRE DI MONTEFILI
VIA SAN CRESCI, 45
50022 PANZANO (FI)
TEL. 055853739
E-MAIL: ten.vecchie_terre_montefili@inwind.it

It has been a while since Bruno di Rocca, a blend of sangiovese and cabernet sauvignon, succeeded in rescaling the heights that once made it one of the most highly regarded of the Supertuscans. The '99 version, though, has again found its former elegance, accompanied by density and a ripeness of fruit that have not been present in recent years. A vegetal aroma is perceptible but not aggressive or dominant. In the mouth, it is very soft, with tightly-knit tannins that are both tasty and promising for the future. Decent but not completely up to expectations is the assessment of the Sangiovese Anfiteatro '99. Evolved tones appear on the nose. On the palate, there is only medium weight and the finish is still raw and sharp. Perhaps this is only a difficult phase of development, but you expect something rather different from this classic Sangiovese. In its category, the Chianti Classico 2000 is much more convincing and, except for some light aromas of reduction, it shows a lively, incisive flavour on the palate, where the acidity and tannins are in good balance. Another excellent wine from this cellar is the white Vigna Regis, which has a rich, broad nose of wood-derived roses and lavender, as well as ripe peaches. In the mouth, it is fresh, even and long, with a pleasing finish. Here, too, at Vecchie Terre di Montefili, we hope that this return to top-quality production augurs well for the future of Roccaldo Acuti's winery.

PANZANO (FI)

VILLA CAFAGGIO
VIA SAN MARTINO IN CECIONE, 5
50020 PANZANO (FI)
TEL. 055852949 - 0558549094
E-MAIL: basilica.cafaggio@tiscalinet.it

This is the third year in a row that Villa Cafaggio has won Three Glasses. Again, we can only offer our compliments to Stefano Farkas, owner of the winery, and to the other Stefano, Chioccioli, the by now very well-known consultant who supervises the vineyards and the cellar. Again, it is the San Martino, obtained mostly from sangiovese grapes, which prevailed in the ever uncertain challenge it takes up every year with the other top wine, Cortaccio, a 100 per cent Cabernet Sauvignon. These are two different wines, but very similar in their styles, which emphasize the power and firmness of the fruit. The San Martino '99 has a vibrantly intense ruby colour and a nose that has yet to open fully but shows faint hints of super-ripeness. The palate, on the other hand, is remarkably dynamic and well able to keep any intrusion from the oak in check with its powerful development and unwavering finish. The Cortaccio '99 presents a deep, concentrated nose of redcurrant jam, graphite and spices. In the mouth, it is powerful and has great volume built over close-knit layers of tannins, which are a little rough in the finish. You could say that is a big wine rather than a great one, but it certainly will not pass unobserved. The two versions of Chianti Classico are good but not very original. The Riserva '99 has an intense colour and a nose that shows a lot of fruit and nice oak. The palate is rich, elegant and well calibrated in its development, then clean and fruity in the finish. The Chianti Classico 2000 is out of the same mould, with fruit at the limit of over-ripeness.

● Bruno di Rocca '99	🍷🍷	8
● Chianti Cl. '00	🍷🍷	5
○ Vigna Regis '00	🍷🍷	6
● Anfiteatro '99	🍷	8
● Chianti Cl. Ris. '85	🍷🍷🍷	6
● Chianti Cl. Anfiteatro Ris. '88	🍷🍷🍷	6
● Anfiteatro '94	🍷🍷🍷	8
● Anfiteatro '95	🍷🍷	8
● Bruno di Rocca '95	🍷🍷	8
● Anfiteatro '96	🍷🍷	8
● Bruno di Rocca '96	🍷🍷	8
● Anfiteatro '97	🍷🍷	8
● Bruno di Rocca '97	🍷🍷	8
● Anfiteatro '98	🍷🍷	8
● Bruno di Rocca '98	🍷🍷	8

● San Martino '99	🍷🍷🍷	7
● Cortaccio '99	🍷🍷	7
● Chianti Cl. '00	🍷🍷	4
● Chianti Cl. Ris. '99	🍷🍷	6
● Cortaccio '93	🍷🍷🍷	6
● Cortaccio '97	🍷🍷🍷	6
● San Martino '97	🍷🍷🍷	5
● San Martino '98	🍷🍷🍷	6
● Cortaccio '98	🍷🍷	6
● Cortaccio '90	🍷🍷	6
● Cortaccio '95	🍷🍷	6
● San Martino '96	🍷🍷	5
● Chianti Cl. Ris. '97	🍷🍷	5
● Chianti Cl. Ris. '98	🍷🍷	5
● Chianti Cl. '99	🍷🍷	4

PECCIOLI (PI)

TENUTA DI GHIZZANO
FRAZ. GHIZZANO
VIA DELLA CHIESA, 1
56030 PECCIOLI (PI)
TEL. 0587630096
E-MAIL: info@tenutadighizzano.com

Tenuta di Ghizzano has decided not to make its Chianti any more. But that is not the real news from this estate because, in its fifth year of release, the Nambrot has finally managed to win Three Glasses. Last year, both Nambrot and Veneroso came near to a third Glass, but neither of them had quite the character or intensity to pull off the coup. The Nambrot 2000, however, has been redesigned with respect to previous editions. Ginevra Venerosi Pesciolini and her consultant Carlo Ferrini have thrown out the original blueprint, which was useful for experimentation. Now the wine, formerly made only with merlot, has one third cabernet sauvignon and some local grapes. This excellent strategy has made Nabrot more complex and better co-ordinated, without losing any of its body. Our notes from the tastings record an intense ruby colour with brilliant highlights, then a concentrated nose of good depth and balance with aromas of blackberries, cacao, coffee and spices. Soft and supple in the mouth, the wine develops elegantly, and shows its oak-derived tannins on the back palate. The Veneroso '00 also did well. A blend of sangiovese and cabernet, with a bit of merlot, it is well-balanced, with good but not excessive concentration. The resulting wine is soft, complex and attractively long, and with a touch of oak that still needs to mellow.

PIOMBINO (LI)

SAN GIUSTO
LOC. SALIVOLI
57025 PIOMBINO (LI)
TEL. 056541198

Piero Bonti's winery confirms its place in the Guide. The impression that this year's wines made was just as good as last year, and to maintain production at a such a high level of quality is no mean accomplishment. Even more significant is the fact that the wines presented have been faithful for some years now to a very precise style. The Rosso degli Appiani '99, a sangiovese with one third montepulciano, is exactly the wine we have been waiting for. It has great intensity of colour, and the nose is redolent of very ripe fruit, and plum and blackberry jams. Powerful and energetic in the mouth, it unleashes plenty of mouthfilling body that progresses surefootedly on the palate through to a long, warm finish. While it may not have a great deal of finesse, there's nothing you can do about it. This is an emphatically gutsy, yet very well balanced bottle. It's one of those very big wines that don't stand on ceremony. They get straight down to business and demand respect. At our Three Glass taste-offs, it very nearly twisted the panel's collective arm for a top award. We also tasted the second wine from this Piombino producer, the San Giusto '00. It's a clean, enjoyably fruity red with a consistent, well balanced and very flavoursome palate.

● Nambrot '00	▼▼▼	8
● Veneroso '00	▼▼	7
● Nambrot '99	▽▽	8
● Veneroso '99	▽▽	7
● Veneroso '90	▽▽	7
● Veneroso '93	▽▽	7
● Veneroso '94	▽▽	7
● Veneroso '95	▽▽	7
● Nambrot '96	▽▽	8
● Veneroso '96	▽▽	7
● Nambrot '97	▽▽	8
● Veneroso '97	▽▽	7
● Nambrot '98	▽▽	8
● Veneroso '98	▽▽	7

● Rosso degli Appiani '99	▼▼	6
● San Giusto '00	▼▼	4
● Rosso degli Appiani '98	▽▽	6
● Rosso degli Appiani '97	▽▽	6
● San Giusto '98	▽▽	4
● San Giusto '99	▽▽	4

PIOMBINO (LI)

PODERE SAN LUIGI
VIA DELL'ARSENALE, 16
57025 PIOMBINO (LI)
TEL. 0565220578 - 056530380

Anna and Elio Tolomei continue to devote their attention to the vineyards from which Fidenzio, their magnificent cabernet, is born. The vineyard is an exceptional "cru", in the true sense of the word. The countryside, however, isn't that of Burgundy or the Langhe. From Podere San Luigi, you can see the coast only a stone's throw away, there are Mediterranean flowers and plants, and the sun beats down relentlessly on your face. But this is not "extreme viticulture". The soil here is perfect for growing vines, and the ancient Etruscans, who were far from ignorant in such matters, allowed their vineyards to cover the promontory that goes towards Piombino from Baratti. Il Fidenzio has everything in its favour to be a great wine, including, great care in the cellar, where nothing is left to chance under the expert eye of Alberto Antonini. In fact, this great blend of cabernet sauvignon, with a touch of cabernet franc, can be considered one of the great wines of the coast. It was successful again this year, reaching our final national tastings, where it missed a Third Glass only by the narrowest of margins. We do not say this to assuage the disappointment of winelovers who appreciate this red. Wine is a living thing, and it has its moments of greater and lesser expression. At the tasting, a very rich fruitiness emerged that was clean and profound, together super-ripe touches that were less elegant. In the mouth, it is monumental, the fat, meaty, powerful palate showing dense, well-integrated tannins and a long finish.

●	Fidenzio '99	♟♟	6
●	Fidenzio '98	♟♟	5
○	La Goccia '00	♟	2*

PITIGLIANO (GR)

TENUTA ROCCACCIA
VIA POGGIO CAVALLUCCIO
58017 PITIGLIANO (GR)
TEL. 0564617976 - 0564617020
E-MAIL: roccaccia@tiscalinet.it

The Goracci siblings' estate has aroused interest with Poggio Cavalluccio '00. It is a red that is making its first appearance but it has everything it takes to make a name for itself in years to come. Obtained from a careful selection of ciliegiolo grapes, it spends some time in small barrels of new oak, and then emerges to show its extraordinary qualities. Very dark and very concentrated in colour, it has an broad nose in which powerful notes of very ripe blackberries, pepper, spices, and toasty oak fuse together. The palate is dense and strong, supported by robust oak, solid structure and rich fruit. The finish is long and just a little bitter, with intense spicy notes. It's a surprising wine, especially when you remember the grape it's made with, and also a very promising one that very nearly received what would have been a remarkable third Glass. We should mention that production is still very limited, only 2,500 bottles were released this year. Still, time is on its side, considering how young the cellar is, too. The other wines presented did well at the tastings. The Fontenova '00, a blend of sangiovese and ciliegiolo, is a sure-fire crowd-pleaser with sweet fruit ripeness and a soft, full, juicy mouthfeel. Stylishly made with well-gauged oak, it shows notes of blackberry jam in its finish. The similar Sovana Rosso '01 is more simple and less concentrated, but very pleasing in its aromas of plums and black pepper, which are very well defined. Finally, the Bianco di Pitigliano did not do too badly.

●	Poggio Cavalluccio '00	♟♟	6
●	Fontenova '00	♟♟	4
●	Sovana Rosso '01	♟♟	3*
○	Bianco di Pitigliano '01		2
●	La Roccaccia '00	♟♟	3*
●	La Roccaccia Fontenova '98	♟♟	4
●	Fontenova '99	♟♟	6
●	La Roccaccia '99	♟♟	3

POGGIBONSI (SI)

Le Fonti
Loc. San Giorgio
53036 Poggibonsi (SI)
Tel. 0577935690
E-mail: fattoria.lefonti@tin.it

It really seems as if Le Fonti is on the right road. The winery is sending out a stream of signals, all pointing to improvement. Credit for this should go to the owners, who continue to invest in the vineyards under the able direction of oenologist Paolo Caciorgna. The overall result is very comforting, with the '99 Riserva winning Two very full Glasses. It has lovely ruby colour with purple highlights, and a nose that reveals attractive cloves and cinnamon over a fruit-driven base dominated by the presence of raspberries and strawberries. There is also a vegetal undertone. In the mouth, the attack is creamy and inviting, with even, close-knit tannins. There is good thrust in mid palate, and a long finish with a pleasing, enjoyable aftertaste. Also lovely, except perhaps for its name, is the Vito Arturo '99. It has an intense ruby colour, and its aromas are characterized by toasty scents where coffee and chocolate tend to prevail. The palate is soft, powerful, and broad. Well supported by delicious tannins, it signs of with a lingering finish. The Chianti Classico '00 has a beautiful, bright ruby colour, and the nose reveals prominent nuances of raspberries and strawberries. There's plenty of good, juicy pulp on the palate, which unveils attractive, fine-grained tannins, and very decent length.

● Chianti Cl. Ris. '99	🍷🍷	5
● Chianti Cl. '00	🍷🍷	4*
● Vito Arturo '99	🍷🍷	6
● Vito Arturo '95	🍷🍷	5
● Chianti Cl. Ris. '96	🍷🍷	4
● Vito Arturo '96	🍷🍷	5
● Chianti Cl. '97	🍷🍷	3*
● Chianti Cl. Ris. '98	🍷🍷	4
● Vito Arturo '98	🍷🍷	5

POGGIBONSI (SI)

Melini
Loc. Gaggiano
53036 Poggibonsi (SI)
Tel. 0577998511
E-mail: giv@giv.it

La Selvanella is a splendid vineyard of almost 60 hectares. It has now been completely replanted to clones of sangiovese selected for top-flight quality. The wine that is now emerging from the cellar, and that was already able to incorporate some of these grapes in the '99 edition, has more concentration and more varietal character. If we add that La Selvanella is a Chianti Classico aged in large casks of Allier oak, we have the profile of a great traditional red that reflects the continuity and history of this famous cellar at Poggibonsi. Melini, owned by the Gruppo Italiano Vini, is in fact a benchmark cellar for the Chianti Classico zone. Last year, La Selvanella was joined by a wine that is almost its alter ego, in that it is the exact opposite of a Chianti Classico. It's called Bonorli and is a "super-barriqued" red made from merlot. You'd think it came from Coonnawarra or Sonoma County, rather than of the gently rolling hills of Chianti. It is the brainchild of Nunzio Capurso, the power behind the throne at Melini, who wanted it this way. It has a very dark colour and a fruit-driven, highly vanillaed, smoke-rich nose, then a soft, powerful and irresistibly seductive palate. In the '00 version, it confirms and indeed emphasizes these characteristics, which were already evident in the '99. Decent but not on the level of former versions is what the panel thought of the Vernaccia di San Gimignano Le Grillaie '00. The Chianti Classico I Sassi '00 is disappointingly evolved and doesn't have much character. A few years ago, it was a very different wine.

● Chianti Cl. La Selvanella Ris. '99	🍷🍷	6
● Bonorli '00	🍷🍷	5
○ Vernaccia di S. Gimignano Le Grillaie '01	🍷	3
● Chianti Cl. I Sassi '00		4
● Chianti Cl. La Selvanella Ris. '86	🍷🍷🍷	6
● Chianti Cl. La Selvanella Ris. '90	🍷🍷🍷	5
● Chianti Cl. La Selvanella Ris. '93	🍷🍷	6
● Chianti Cl. La Selvanella Ris. '95	🍷🍷	6
● Chianti Cl. La Selvanella Ris. '96	🍷🍷	6
● Chianti Cl. La Selvanella Ris. '97	🍷🍷	6
● Chianti Cl. La Selvanella Ris. '98	🍷🍷	6
● Bonorli '99	🍷🍷	5

POGGIO A CAIANO (PO)

Piaggia
Via Cegoli, 47
59016 Poggio a Caiano (PO)
tel. 0558705401
e-mail: aziendapiaggia@virgilio.it

Mauro Vannucci is never satisfied. The owner of Piaggia is now completely caught up in his passion for wine. And once that particular enthusiasm gets you, it never lets you go, as we know from our own experience. The Poggio a Caiano vineyard, which unfailingly earns him Three Glasses every year, is no longer sufficient to assuage Mauro's ambitions. So, he has bought new land in Carmignano, he has had the soil analysed and ripped, and has planted new vines. He's a dynamo. The position of the plot is extraordinary, and we can't begin to imagine what Mauro will be able to do with grapes that are even richer. The Carmignano '99 is already a splendid wine with a ripeness of fruit that is practically perfect. It emerges with aromas of enormous intensity, and confirms this with a palate of absolute purity. It is almost superfluous to add comments about the richness of the structure and the sweetness of the tannins that sustain it. This Carmignano di Piaggia isn't a wine to "weigh" on the palate. It's as easy drinking as they come, thanks to the excellent balance that sustains it. Piaggia's second wine, the Sasso '00, is just as juicy. Made mostly from sangiovese, but with a good bit of cabernet sauvignon and merlot, it is not as complex as the Carmignano, but for richness of fruit and enjoyment, it's marvellous. As a result, the bottom of this page is in full colour.

● Carmignano Ris. '99	🍷🍷🍷	6
● Il Sasso '00	🍷🍷	5*
● Carmignano Ris. '97	🍷🍷🍷	5
● Carmignano Ris. '98	🍷🍷🍷	6
● Carmignano Ris. '94	🍷🍷	4
● Carmignano Ris. '95	🍷🍷	4
● Carmignano Ris. '96	🍷🍷	4
● Il Sasso '99	🍷🍷	5

PONTASSIEVE (FI)

★ Tenimenti Ruffino
Via Aretina, 42/44
50065 Pontassieve (FI)
tel. 05583605
e-mail: info@ruffino.it

Tenimenti Ruffino, the battleship from Pontassieve, sails inexorably across the great ocean of international wines. It has bought Borgo Conventi in Friuli, and strengthened Lodola Nuova in Montepulciano, as well as Greppone Mazzi in Montalcino. Above all, the group is meeting the challenges of the international market very efficiently. Luigi and Adolfo Folonari, the new generation of the Brescian family that has owned Ruffino since the 1920's, are two of the most brilliant makers and sellers of wine in Italy. In addition, the quality of their wines has been growing steadily. Their vast vineyards are in a constant state of renewal, and the results are easy to see. Their Romitorio di Santedame '00, from sangiovese and colorino, one of the best Tuscan reds of its year, is powerful and concentrated, with tannins of rare finesse and a dense, well-sustained texture. The Chianti Classico Riserva Ducale Oro '99, of which 600,000 bottles were made, is quite spectacular, and more convincing than it has been for years. The Solatia '00, a chardonnay aged in oak, was one of the very few Tuscan whites to make it into our finals. The Modus '00, obtained from sangiovese and cabernet sauvignon, is perhaps not as good as the '99 but it does have density and power. The pinot nero, Nero del Tondo '00, is also excellent. Bringing up the rear, the Chianti Classico Santedame '00 from which we would like something more particularly in terms of complexity in the nose, the Libaio '01, a light, fragrant white, and the Torgaio '01, a simple, easy-to-drink red, are all decent.

● Romitorio di Santedame '00	🍷🍷🍷	7
● Chianti Cl. Ris. Ducale Oro '99	🍷🍷	5
○ Solatia '00	🍷🍷	5
● Modus '00	🍷🍷	7
● Nero del Tondo '00	🍷🍷	7
● Chianti Cl. Santedame '00	🍷	5
○ Libaio '01	🍷	3
● Torgaio '01	🍷	3
● Chianti Cl. Ris. Ducale Oro '88	🍷🍷🍷	5
● Chianti Cl. Ris. Ducale Oro '90	🍷🍷🍷	5
● Romitorio di Santedame '96	🍷🍷🍷	6
● Romitorio di Santedame '97	🍷🍷🍷	6
● Romitorio di Santedame '98	🍷🍷🍷	6
● Romitorio di Santedame '99	🍷🍷🍷	6

PONTASSIEVE (FI)

FATTORIA SELVAPIANA
LOC. SELVAPIANA, 43
50065 PONTASSIEVE (FI)
TEL. 0558369848
E-MAIL: selvapiana@tin.it

The longed-for signs of change here at the Fattoria di Selvapiana are finally beginning to arrive. The first example comes form the change on the Fornace label from Chianti Rufina to IGT, and of course the consequent change in the blend. Now it is obtained from cabernet and merlot, with a little bit of sangiovese added. The standard wine continues to be somewhat disappointing, but the changes under way give us reason for hope. The Fornace '99 has a clear ruby colour with evident purple highlights. The intensity of the aromas, barely dominated by the wood, is attractive. Some not unpleasant vegetal notes come through, supported by light scents of berries. The attack in the mouth is dense, thick and very pleasurable, lacking only a little length. The Chianti Rufina Bucerchiale Riserva '99 has a ruby colour with garnet tinges. The nose is compressed and closed at first, but then complex scents of leather and fur open up, to be softened by notes of ripe plums. The attack in the mouth is well supported by dense tannins that are perhaps just a touch over-assertive, but its powerful body successfully balances the excessive roughness. The rising finish is quite delicious. Finally, the Chianti Rufina '00 only earned a mention. It has unbalanced, poorly defined aromas as well as a lack of balance in the body, which shows too much acid and too little pulp.

PORTO AZZURRO (LI)

SAPERETA
LOC. MOLA
VIA PROVINCIALE OVEST, 73
57036 PORTO AZZURRO (LI)
TEL. 056595033
E-MAIL: italo@sapereonline.it

At last, Elba's flag is waving again, thanks to some good news from the island. The winery that has given this first signal of change, Sapereta, will be followed, we hope, by other local cellars. Sapereta was well on its way last year with an excellent Moscato that this year, unfortunately, wasn't presented at our tastings. But luckily, this Porto Azzurro producer is well furnished with a list of interesting wines that merit description. Let's begin with a classic Elban wine, the Aleatico '01, which has an intense garnet colour, then moderately complex ripe aromas with hints of wild flowers, sour cherries and cherry jam, all clearly expressed. On the palate, it is very sweet and juicy, and only a light prickle kept us from giving it a higher mark. The Elba Rosso Vigna Thea '00 is also successful. Its intense perfumes show blackcurrants, blackberry jam, spices from the wood, and some subtle vegetal notes. The palate is round, consistent, good and meaty, and finishes with pleasant fruit. The Elba Bianco '01 is equally attractive. The clean nose shows pleasing touches of lime blossom and sage. The body is only moderately big but the balance is completely convincing and the finish pleases. Their Vigna Le Stipe is a dignified effort, even though it shows some slightly evolved tones.

● Chianti Rufina Bucerchiale Ris. '99	▼▼	5
● La Fornace '99	▼▼	5
● Chianti Rufina '00		3
● Chianti Rufina Bucerchiale Ris. '94	♀♀	5
● Chianti Rufina Bucerchiale Ris. '95	♀♀	5
● Chianti Rufina Ris. '95	♀♀	4
○ Vin Santo della Rufina '95	♀♀	5
● Chianti Rufina Ris. '96	♀♀	4
● Chianti Rufina Ris. '97	♀♀	4
● Chianti Rufina Fornace Ris. '98	♀♀	5
● Chianti Rufina Fornace Ris. '96	♀	5

● Elba Rosso Vigna Thea '00	▼▼	4
● Aleatico dell'Elba '01	▼▼	5
○ Elba Bianco Vigna Thea '01	▼▼	3
○ Elba Bianco Vigna Le Stipe '01		3
○ Moscato dell'Elba '00	♀♀	5
● Aleatico dell'Elba '00	♀	5

RADDA IN CHIANTI (SI)

CASTELLO D' ALBOLA
LOC. PIAN D'ALBOLA, 31
53017 RADDA IN CHIANTI (SI)
TEL. 0577738019
E-MAIL: info@albola.it

The wines from Castello d'Albola have clearly made progress. At our tastings, we noted clear growth for all the products from this Zonin group winery. It is worth remembering that the Castello d'Albola vineyards lie in a very high part of Chianti Classico, where ripening can take a long time, but it also offers an opportunity to work with grapes that need cooler temperatures. Hence, the success of the Chardonnay Le Fagge '00, one of best Tuscan whites. It has aromas of tropical fruit, aromatic herbs and wood. The palate is fresh, full and very deep. For the same reason, the pinot nero-based wine, Le Marangole, has found conditions at Albola to be favourable. The nose offers scents of berry fruit, spices and violets. The palate is soft, fragrant, persistent, and just a bit bitter in its finish. The Acciaiolo '99, made from sangiovese and cabernet sauvignon, is well balanced, elegant, and unveils well-gauged tannins. Its clean nose offers aromas of redcurrants with hints of green pepper. The '99 Riserva does not have much energy, or indeed personality, but is well made, clean, and shows excellent balance. Very good, too, is the Chianti Classico Le Ellere '00. The nose reveals some peppery notes, then the palate is compact, elegant, and mouthfilling. The long list finishes with the Chianti Classico '00, which is simple but delicious.

RADDA IN CHIANTI (SI)

BORGO SALCETINO
LOC. LUCARELLI
53017 RADDA IN CHIANTI (SI)
TEL. 0577733541 - 0432757173
E-MAIL: info@livon.it

After a few timid years in our pages, Borgo Salcetino has cast aside all reserve and presented an excellent list of wines. They make the ambitions of the Livon brothers very clear. The Rossole 2000 and the Chianti Classico Lucarelo 1999 both stand out, and both made it into our tasting finals. The Rossole, obtained from sangiovese and merlot, is not very complex but impresses with its very rich fruit both on the nose and in the mouth. The palate develops softly, with good balance and body, then the finish is juicy and intensely fruity. It's a wine in the modern idiom, if by that we mean bottles that emphasize fruit and roundness, as opposed to those that attempt a more austere, "cerebral" style. The Riserva Lucarello, as we said, is also excellent, and has a rich nose of blackberries and toasted coffee. In the mouth, it is round, soft, and resplendent with well-judged tannins. The Chianti Classico '00 is also successful. It was particularly pleasing on the nose, where clear notes of violets, black pepper and red berries come through. The elegant palate is attractive, even and sustained by sweet, fine-grained tannins.

○ Le Fagge Chardonnay '00	🍷🍷	5
● Chianti Cl. Le Ellere '00	🍷🍷	4*
● Le Marangole '00	🍷🍷	5
● Acciaiolo '99	🍷🍷	6
● Chianti Cl. Ris. '99	🍷🍷	5
● Chianti Cl. '00	🍷	4
● Acciaiolo '95	🍷🍷🍷	6
● Acciaiolo '93	🍷🍷	6
● Acciaiolo '96	🍷🍷	6
● Le Marangole '96	🍷🍷	5
● Acciaiolo '97	🍷🍷	6
● Chianti Cl. Ris. '97	🍷🍷	5
● Le Marangole '97	🍷🍷	5
● Acciaiolo '98	🍷🍷	6
○ Le Fagge Chardonnay '99	🍷🍷	4

● Rossole '00	🍷🍷	5
● Chianti Cl. Lucarello Ris. '99	🍷🍷	5
● Chianti Cl. '00	🍷🍷	4
● Chianti Cl. Lucarello Ris. '97	🍷🍷	5
● Rossole '99	🍷🍷	5

RADDA IN CHIANTI (SI)

CAPARSA
LOC. CAPARSINO, 48
53017 RADDA IN CHIANTI (SI)
TEL. 0577738174 - 0577738639
E-MAIL: caparsa@ecoitaly.net

The Cianferoni family's winery has been at work in Radda in Chianti for a number of years. On this occasion, it seems to us appropriate to dedicate a full profile to the cellar since, obviously, the wines did well at our tastings. We should also mention that on other occasions, some of the bottles from Caparsa have made a very good impression on the panel, but they tended to be one-offs that did not do quite as well in the following vintage. That's why we hope that this Chianti estate will be able now to find greater continuity and consolidate its position. At our tastings, we were particularly struck by the excellence of the Riserva Doccio a Matteo '99. This is a Chianti Classico with a lively, intense ruby colour, and a clean, concentrated nose featuring evident, but not intrusive, oak. The palate has good weight and balance, progressing consistently thanks to attractive tannins, and a very promising vivacity. The Chianti Classico '99 also showed interesting characteristics, nearly earning a second Glass. The clean perfumes offer clear notes of red berries and some vanilla from the oak. There is no great depth on the palate but it's linear, well defined and has decent length. The more than just acceptable Vin Santo '95 has quite a dry taste, and is well typed but a bit short in its finish.

● Chianti Cl. Doccio a Matteo Ris. '99	♟♟	7
○ Vin Santo '95	♟	7
● Chianti Cl. Caparsino '99	♟	6

RADDA IN CHIANTI (SI)

LA BRANCAIA
LOC. POPPI, 42/B
53017 RADDA IN CHIANTI (SI)
TEL. 0577742007
E-MAIL: brancaia@brancaia.it

Bruno and Brigitte Widmer should be well pleased with what they have been able to accomplish at their winery. Today, it is under the direct supervision of their daughter, Barbara Widmer, who handles the winemaking with the help of Carlo Ferrini, and her husband, Martin Kronenberg. Expansion has led to the creation of three separate properties from the holdings at Poppi at Radda, Brancaia at Castellina in Chianti and Poggio al Sasso in Maremma. To complete this project, the cellar has released a third label, called Brancaia Tre, because it comes from three different varieties – sangiovese, with cabernet and merlot – grown at the three different estates. The Brancaia now has a longer name and is called Brancaia Il Blu. The 2000 version adds another Three Glasses to its already rich collection. The grapes come from Brancaia and Poppi and are 55 per cent sangiovese, 40 per cent merlot and five per cent cabernet sauvignon. This is an excellent red that has maintained intact the elegance and balance which have always distinguished it. Now, it can also point to dense body, powerful development and a long, spicy finish. The Chianti Classico Brancaia '00 is very nearly as good. It has an attractive sangiovese style, backed up by fine-grained tannins, and a sweet finish. The newcomer, Brancaia Tre '00 is very good as well, and has good, firm body.

● Brancaia Il Blu '00	♟♟♟	7
● Chianti Cl. Brancaia '00	♟♟	5*
● Brancaia Tre '00	♟♟	5*
● Brancaia '94	♟♟♟	6
● Brancaia '97	♟♟♟	6
● Brancaia '98	♟♟♟	6
● Brancaia '90	♟♟	6
● Brancaia '93	♟♟	5
● Brancaia '95	♟♟	6
● Brancaia '96	♟♟	6
● Chianti Cl. '97	♟♟	5
● Chianti Cl. '98	♟♟	5

RADDA IN CHIANTI (SI)

Livernano
Loc. Livernano
53017 Radda in Chianti (SI)
tel. 0577738353
e-mail: info@livernano.it

Livernano did not obtain its fourth Three Glass award in a row. The arithmetical average of the scores at our tastings left Marco Montanari's winery less than one percentage point short of another top award. Still, there are no doubts about the high quality and excellent style of this ever elegant and eminently drinkable wine. Livernano '00 is a blend of merlot, cabernet sauvignon, cabernet franc and sangiovese with a nose full of ripe blackberries that mingle with some spicy tones. In the mouth, it shows elegance, progressing with increasing intensity to a finish of great depth and clarity. The Puro Sangue '00, made only from sangiovese, has an expressive nose of violet, fresh spices and a little bit of wood. The palate expands with a refined sweetness, offering excellent balance in mid palate, and the very long finish reveals touches of cherries and pepper. These two wines are clearly different, in that they are made from different blends, but they do share distinct finesse and excellent structure. We had more trouble understanding their white, Anima, which is 70 per cent chardonnay, with sauvignon blanc and traminer making up the remainder of the blend. Its sweet, and apparently very ripe, nose attenuates the freshness and harmony of the wine.

RADDA IN CHIANTI (SI)

Fattoria di Montevertine
Loc. Montevertine
53017 Radda in Chianti (SI)
tel. 0577738009
e-mail: info@montevertine.it

We may one day be talking about Pergole Torte again in the suitably superlative terms that it deserves. We are not yet in a position to demonstrate unrestrained enthusiasm, but the '99 version of one of the classic Sangioveses of Tuscany is not one that will pass unobserved. This year, the hierarchy of Montevertine wines is back in the right order, with Pergole Torte again on top. It has a garnet colour with lively ruby highlights, and the nose is still almost completely closed. Somewhere in its depths, there are faint hints of peat. The front palate is reassuringly gentle and persuasive, then develops elegantly, thanks to soft tannins, leading through to a long, classy finish. There might not be an enormous quantity of fruit, or tremendous concentration, on the palate but for those who have patience, there are delicate hints to be savoured and the finesse of the details to be enjoyed. Actually, a little more character wouldn't have done any harm. The Montervertine '99 is straightforward and balanced, revealing very good depth. Less welcoming on the nose, it shows some not very clean, somewhat evolved aromas. The Pian del Ciampolo '99 is simple, a bit lean, and has a nose that is a tad fuzzy. The Bianco di Montvertine '00 is an original white that has an unusual nose of aromatic herbs and is agile, balanced and pleasing on the palate.

● Livernano '00	🍷🍷	8
● Puro Sangue '00	🍷🍷	7
● Livernano '97	🍷🍷🍷	8
● Livernano '98	🍷🍷🍷	8
● Livernano '99	🍷🍷🍷	8
● Puro Sangue '99	🍷🍷	7
● Puro Sangue '95	🍷🍷	6
○ Anima '96	🍷🍷	5
● Puro Sangue '97	🍷🍷	6
○ Anima '98	🍷🍷	5
● Puro Sangue '98	🍷🍷	6

● Le Pergole Torte '99	🍷🍷	8
○ Bianco di Montevertine '00	🍷	3*
● Montevertine Ris. '99	🍷	6
● Pian del Ciampolo '99	🍷	5
● Le Pergole Torte '83	🍷🍷🍷	8
● Le Pergole Torte '86	🍷🍷🍷	8
● Le Pergole Torte '88	🍷🍷🍷	8
● Le Pergole Torte '90	🍷🍷🍷	8
● Le Pergole Torte '92	🍷🍷🍷	8
● Il Sodaccio '97	🍷🍷	5
● Montevertine Ris. '97	🍷🍷	5
● Il Sodaccio '98	🍷🍷	6
● Montevertine Ris. '98	🍷🍷	6

RADDA IN CHIANTI (SI)

PODERE CAPACCIA
LOC. CAPACCIA
53017 RADDA IN CHIANTI (SI)
TEL. 0577738385 - 0574582426
E-MAIL: capaccia@chianticlassico.com

The wines from Podere Capaccia have been uneven in the last few years, sometimes pleasantly surprising and sometimes disappointing. We find this erratic performance a bit difficult to understand. One legitimate excuse can be found in the weather. The Capaccia vines are at an altitude of 500 meters above sea level and Sangiovese is always difficult grape. Getting proper balance in the ripening of the fruit is not at all easy. However, this initial criticism is not offered in a derogatory spirit. We are very well-disposed towards Giampaolo Pacini's cellar. We have a lot of respect for the man and for those of his wines that have given us such excitement in the past. To clear the field of any doubts, we would like to say that this year, both of Giampaolo's wines got as far as our finals. The Querciagrande '98, from a far from excellent year, showed interesting character though it may not be an easy wine to understand if your nose and palate aren't tuned in to sangiovese. The aromas, for example, have earthy, mineral touches with hints of pepper and chestnuts. The palate is convincing and vibrant, with good density in mid palate, and intense, spicy notes in the finish. The tannins are a bit rigid and not very relaxed, but this is characteristic of many reds from the hinterland of Chianti. They are difficult to tame. The Riserva '99 is also valid. It has a less abrupt temperament, and is soft and round in the mouth, with good sweetness.

RADDA IN CHIANTI (SI)

POGGERINO
LOC. POGGERINO
53017 RADDA IN CHIANTI (SI)
TEL. 0577738958
E-MAIL: info@poggerino.com

Piero Lanza Ginori had two cards to play at the Three Glass taste-offs this year, his Primamateria '00 and his Chianti Classico Riserva Bugialla '99. Neither of the wines made it, but some consolation remains. The already excellent Poggerino winery continues to make progress every year. The two star bottles are quite different in style. The Primamateria '00, half sangiovese and half merlot, has a clear fruity nose where territory-related characteristics, such as mineral and spice tones, come through. In the mouth, it is soft, developing with suppleness, velvet smoothness and good length. This excellent wine lacks only a little more complexity to be a great one. The Bigialla Riserva '99 has a strong character that takes a little while to understand. The nose is not very communicative, although it does show some traces of reduction at first, and then proceeds to offer a few mineral hints. The palate is immediately vigorous, if a little closed, then dynamically tonic, with the tautness typical of sangiovese taking you through to a long, intense finish. The palate has good weight, developing with good balance to a moderately long finish.

Wine	Rating	Score
• Querciagrande '98	🍷🍷	6
• Chianti Cl. Ris. '99	🍷🍷	5
• Querciagrande '88	🍷🍷🍷	6
• Querciagrande '90	🍷🍷	6
• Querciagrande '91	🍷🍷	6
• Querciagrande '92	🍷🍷	6
• Querciagrande '93	🍷🍷	6
• Querciagrande '95	🍷🍷	6
• Chianti Cl. Ris. '96	🍷🍷	5
• Querciagrande '96	🍷🍷	5
• Querciagrande '97	🍷🍷	5
• Chianti Cl. '98	🍷	4

Wine	Rating	Score
• Primamateria '00	🍷🍷	6
• Chianti Cl. Bugialla Ris. '99	🍷🍷	6
• Chianti Cl. '00	🍷	4
• Chianti Cl. Ris. '90	🍷🍷🍷	5
• Primamateria '99	🍷🍷	5
• Chianti Cl. '94	🍷🍷	3
• Chianti Cl. Bugialla Ris. '94	🍷🍷	5
• Chianti Cl. '95	🍷🍷	3
• Chianti Cl. Bugialla Ris. '95	🍷🍷	5
• Chianti Cl. '96	🍷🍷	3
• Chianti Cl. Bugialla Ris. '96	🍷🍷	5
• Chianti Cl. '97	🍷🍷	3
• Chianti Cl. Bugialla Ris. '97	🍷🍷	5
• Chianti Cl. '98	🍷🍷	3
• Primamateria '98	🍷🍷	5

RADDA IN CHIANTI (SI)

FATTORIA DI TERRABIANCA
LOC. SAN FEDELE A PATERNO
53017 RADDA IN CHIANTI (SI)
TEL. 0577738544
E-MAIL: info@terrabianca.com

The wines from Terrabianca performed very well this year, and surpassed their usual, still very decent, standards. Of course, this exploit is hardly surprising, since Roberto Guldener's winery enjoys an enviably good position and a wonderful site climate. If we add to these natural gifts Roberto's scrupulous attention to the vines and the winemaking process, good results are almost a matter of routine. The best of the wines we tested was Roberto's Cabernet Ceppate '99, which very nearly gained a Third Glass. It has rich aromas, with notes of toasty oak immediately evident, to be followed quickly by plums, pepper, cloves, and chocolate. The palate is concentrated and has a long finish that begins well but becomes a little dilute at the last moment. The excellent year also permitted Roberto's Riserva Croce to shine, showing its notable strengths in varietal fragrances of jams and minerals, supported by its substantial body. We thought the Piano del Cipresso '99 was more evolved. The nose revealed some balsamic tones, followed by a well-rounded, nicely balanced palate. The Chianti Classico Scassino '00, apart from its somewhat vegetal nose and diluted body, is soft and well put together.

RADDA IN CHIANTI (SI)

VIGNAVECCHIA
SDRUCCIOLO DI PIAZZA, 7
53017 RADDA IN CHIANTI (SI)
TEL. 0577738090 - 0577738326
E-MAIL: vignavecchia@vignavecchia.com

This producer from Radda continues to make progress, as siblings Franco and Orsola Beccari show that they have arrived and can keep up a high standard of quality. The only criticism that we can offer about their wine is that it doesn't really evince a rapport with its own territory. We found the Chardonnay Titanum '01 very convincing, and it would be hard to find another this good from these parts. It has a light, quite lively straw colour and intensely elegant, fruit-driven aromas of white peaches and pears. The attack in the mouth is quite precise, and mid palate shows good consistency, although the acidity sticks out a bit in the finish. The Chianti Classico Riserva '99 also did well. It has a compact, impenetrable, ruby colour and a nose that first shows some toasty oak and then good fruit, with notes of redcurrants and blueberries most in evidence. The entry on the palate is juicy, tasty and very good, but the texture then loses some density, which lets the tannins take over on a finish that is pleasant but quite dried out. The Raddese 99 was more convincing, with its lively ruby colour and a nose that is at first a little unruly but then finds its balance again, albeit with some vegetal hints. Extremely clean on the palate, it starts off powerfully but a tad stiffly. It then takes off at mid palate, flaunting crunchy, fine-grained tannins.

● Ceppate '99		7
● Campaccio '99		5*
● Chianti Cl. Vigna della Croce Ris. '99		5
● Piano del Cipresso '99		5
● Chianti Cl. Scassino '00		4
● Campaccio '94		6
● Campaccio '95		5
● Campaccio Sel. Speciale '96		5
● Campaccio Sel. Speciale '97		6
● Ceppate '97		6
● Piano del Cipresso '97		5
● Ceppate '98		6

○ Titanum '01		4
● Chianti Cl. Ris. '99		5
● Raddese '99		6
● Canvalle '98		5
○ Titanum '00		4
● Canvalle '93		5
● Canvalle '96		5
● Chianti Cl. Ris. '96		4
● Chianti Cl. Ris. '97		4
○ Titanum '99		4

RADDA IN CHIANTI (SI)

CASTELLO DI VOLPAIA
LOC. VOLPAIA
P.ZZA DELLA CISTERNA, 1
53017 RADDA IN CHIANTI (SI)
TEL. 0577738066
E-MAIL: info@volpaia.com

There is news from Volpaia this year. For one thing, Riccardo Cotarella is their new oenologist. Certainly one of Italy's better-known winemakers, Cotarella has so far had relatively little to do with Tuscany. The winery, in the hands of Giovannella Stianti and her companion, Carlo Mascheroni, needs first of all to find new ideas about where it is going in the near future. The quality of the wines here is already quite impressive, as we noted in last year's tastings. The changes include one in their labelling. Coltassala doffs the garb of a Supertuscan and dons that of a Chianti Classico, which is an important signal for the category. It was this very wine, in the '99 version, that offered the panel's tasters something interesting to assess. The aromas are good and compact, showing a firm presence of oak in notes of vanilla and spices. In the mouth, it shows convincing solidity, an orderly progression on the palate and a finish that is coherent, if not very long. The Riserva '99 also did well, without offering any great signs of individual character. The nose lingers a bit on spice-like aromas from the oak, as well as one or two signs of evolution. The palate is docile, balanced and decently long. The presence of oak shows up in the Chianti Classico '00 as well but this time there is also an interestingly dense texture. The Val d'Arbia '01 is well typed and pleasant.

● Chianti Cl. Coltassala Ris. '99	🍷🍷	6
● Chianti Cl. '00	🍷🍷	5
● Chianti Cl. Ris. '99	🍷🍷	5
○ Val d'Arbia '01	🍷	6
● Chianti Cl. '99	🍷🍷	4*
○ Vin Santo del Chianti Cl. '93	🍷🍷	6
● Chianti Cl. Ris. '95	🍷🍷	5
● Coltassala '95	🍷🍷	6
● Balifico '97	🍷🍷	6
● Chianti Cl. '97	🍷🍷	4
● Chianti Cl. Ris. '97	🍷🍷	5
● Coltassala '97	🍷🍷	6

RAPOLANO TERME (SI)

CASTELLO DI MODANELLA
LOC. SERRE
53040 RAPOLANO TERME (SI)
TEL. 0577704604
E-MAIL: info@modanella.com

Castello di Modanella is a magnificent property of fully 650 hectares, only a small part of which is set aside for viticulture. The winery wants to identify the vineyards that are suitable for producing monovarietal wines whose individual characteristics will embody the complex nature of the territory. The decision is a clear one, and very laudable, but it will be hard to put into effect and the road ahead is a long one. It's evident that a winemaking approach based on blending different varieties would mitigate the effects of bad years and make continuity in quality easier to achieve. Of the four varieties selected, cabernet sauvignon is the one which has most quickly demonstrated its adaptability and reliable quality. The Castello di Modanella version is Le Voliere, which in '99 is excellent. It has a deep, intense nose with great richness of fruit and a generous dose of new oak. Powerful and dense in the mouth, it develops quickly and reveals the influence of the oak used for ageing in the finish. The other wines, however, need further focusing. The Merlot Poggio Montino '99 reveals the presence of some very vigorous fruit, still somewhat dominated by beefy tannins and assertive wood. The Sangiovese Campo D'Aja '99 doesn't lack fullness or roundness, but the nose is dominated by tertiary notes. The Canaiolo Poggio L'Aiole '00 is not easy to figure out. It shows notes of over-ripeness and wood flavour on the nose, then a palate that starts off soft and sweet but closes with a touch of bitterness.

● Le Voliere Cabernet Sauvignon '99	🍷	5*
● Campo d'Aia '99	🍷	5
● Poggio Montino '99	🍷	5
● Poggio l'Aiole '00		4
● Campo d'Aia '95	🍷🍷	6
● Le Voliere Cabernet Sauvignon '95	🍷🍷	5
● Le Voliere Cabernet Sauvignon '96	🍷🍷	5
● Campo d'Aia '97	🍷🍷	5
● Le Voliere Cabernet Sauvignon '97	🍷🍷	5
● Poggio Montino '97	🍷🍷	4
● Le Voliere Cabernet Sauvignon '98	🍷🍷	5

RIPARBELLA (PI)

La Regola
Loc. San martino
Via A. Gramsci, 1
56046 Riparbella (PI)
tel. 0586698145 - 058881363
e-mail: info@laregola.com

La Regola forges ahead serenely along its chosen path. Luca Nuti's winery confirms the positive signals it sent out last year, showing further progress all across the range. The leading wine is still Montescudaio La Regola. Again this year, it went through to our final round of tastings without, however, picking up that all-important third Glass. It is an excellent red, with a very intense ruby colour. The clean nose shows decent fruit and vegetal notes. In the mouth, it is soft, enticing, continuous, and well-sustained by the good density of the tannins. Compared to the '99, it is less immediate, and the fruit is a little less excitingly overwhelming, but it has grown in complexity and tannic grip. The Vallino delle Conche '00 has clearly made enough progress to nudge it closer to the flagship wine in quality. The nose shows good fruit and some liquorice towards the finish. The palate is soft, full, and juicy, revealing excellent raw material, but trails off a little at the end. The white Steccaia '01 may be relatively simple but it has a good nose, with intense notes of lavender and apricots, and good balance on the palate. Their Montescudaio Rosso Ligustro '01 has taken another step forward. It isn't all that tidy at first on the nose, but it has a round palate with decent weight and no little character.

RUFINA (FI)

Fattoria di Basciano
V.le Duca della Vittoria, 159
50068 Rufina (FI)
tel. 0558397034
e-mail: masirenzo@virgilio.it

Notable changes have been made at this winery in recent years, and it has gained stature in consequence. We tasted many of the wines and they all received Two Glasses. Let's begin with the Chianti Rufina '00. It has a brilliant ruby colour, and the nose shows fruity scents of good intensity. It has good sinew on the palate, where it also shows close-knit tannins and excellent length. The Riserva '99 presents a ruby colour of good intensity. The aromas display various fruits, toasty oak and some vegetal hints. In the mouth, the attack is soft and the progression is well supported by oak. The central phase is good, but then at the end it falls off and concludes with a somewhat bitter aftertaste. The Corto '00 has aromas that offer some sweet tones of berries and fruit jams, lifted by scents of cloves. It enters the mouth softly and densely as the acidity offers a good counterpoint. The finish is pleasant and persistent. I Pini '00 shows a nose of ripe fruit, including plums and redcurrants, with nuances of cinnamon. In the mouth, the attack is decisive yet pervasive, the tannins meshing well with the alcohol. Although a tad diluted, it finishes very long. In the Erta e China '00, the presence of berries is accompanied by light hints of freshly ground pepper. In the mouth, it is tasty and inviting, revealing excellent balance and good length.

● Montescudaio Rosso La Regola '00	6*
● Montescudaio Rosso Vallino delle Conche '00	4
○ Montescudaio Bianco Steccaia '01	4*
● Montescudaio Rosso Ligustro '01	3
● Montescudaio Rosso La Regola '99	5
○ Montescudaio Bianco Steccaia '00	3
● Montescudaio Rosso Vallino '99	4

● Chianti Rufina '00	3*
● Erta e China '00	3*
● I Pini '00	4
● Il Corto '00	5
● Chianti Rufina Ris. '99	5
● I Pini '97	3
● Chianti Rufina '98	3
● Chianti Rufina Ris. '98	3*
● I Pini '98	3
● Il Corto '98	3
● Erta e China '99	3*
● I Pini '99	4
● Il Corto '99	4

SAN CASCIANO IN VAL DI PESA (FI)

CASTELVECCHIO
VIA CERTALDESE, 30
50026 SAN CASCIANO IN VAL DI PESA (FI)
TEL. 0558248032 - 0558248921
E-MAIL: info@castelvecchio.it

After its fine performance last time, Filippo Rocchi's winery has earned more space in this year's Guide. Castelvecchio's success is the result of patient commitment by the whole family, for everyone lends a hand. Their work in the vineyard is beginning to bear fruit, and a more rational approach to work in the cellar has also contributed to this long-awaited quantum leap in quality. Let's begin by describing the Brecciolino '00. It has a very dark colour of impenetrable violet. The attack on the palate is dense, full-bodied and very concentrated, oak leading the chase over a robust, solid structure. The tannins are a little rugged, but vivacious and well to the fore. The Riserva '00 also did well. It has beautiful purple highlights and a nose that delights with its fruity hints of blackberries. In the mouth, it has remarkable density and richness that come through in a rising progression. The Riserva '99 is a short step down the quality ladder. Its nose is not very expressive but it does show faint hints of cherries. In the mouth, the attack is moderately intense and the evident tannins dry things out a bit. The finish improves and the pleasantly soft flavour stays through to the end. The Chianti Colli Fiorentini '00 is at first closed on the nose, but then opens to reveal elegant blackberries. The palate shows good weight and body, offering juicy pulp and a finish of medium length. The Chianti Santa Caterina '00 earned its entry for aromas that are simple but clean, while the palate is rather dominated by acidity.

SAN CASCIANO IN VAL DI PESA (FI)

FATTORIA CORZANO E PATERNO
FRAZ. SAN PANCRAZIO IN VAL DI PESA
VIA PATERNO, 8
50020 SAN CASCIANO IN VAL DI PESA (FI)
TEL. 0558249114 - 0558248179
E-MAIL: corzpaterno@falcc.it

Although it didn't quite get a Third Glass, the Fattoria di Corzano e Paterno has shown again that it is one of the leading wineries in Tuscany. A quick glance at the table below the profile will show how many Glasses they have obtained. All of the wines are well above average, which shows how consistently good quality is here at the winery of the much-lamented Wendelin Gelpke's heirs, which is currently managed by Aljoscha Goldschmidt. The Corzano '99, a blend of sangiovese and cabernet sauvignon with the addition of some merlot, is a very exuberant wine. It's a pity that its nose has a strong, sharp, almost medicinal note. This element may well be only temporary, but it marked down the score we gave to the wine. The palate showed notable character, with massive body supported by good-sized doses of oak and an intense finish. The Chianti I Tre Borri '99 did equally well, presenting rich scents of vanilla, spices, liquorice and sour cherries. The palate is soft and dense, with the evident presence of tannins from the oak, and a warm, lingering finish. The Chianti Terre di Corzano '00 is also well made. It is simpler but nicely put together, and has a pleasing palate that reveals notes of vanilla as it develops in the mouth. The Passito '95 is very good. It has sweet, creamy notes with touches of pipe tobacco on the nose, and then the palate is very sweet and concentrated. In closing, we would like to mention the Chardonnay Aglaia '01, a well-balanced and substantial white.

● Chianti dei Colli Fiorentini Ris. '00	ŸŸ	5
● Il Brecciolino '00	ŸŸ	6
● Chianti dei Colli Fiorentini '00	Ÿ	3
● Chianti Santa Caterina '00	Ÿ	3
● Chianti dei Colli Fiorentini Ris. '99	Ÿ	4
○ Vin Santo del Chianti '90	Ÿ	6
● Chianti Colli Fiorentini '99	Ÿ	2*
● Il Brecciolino '99	Ÿ	5

● Chianti I Tre Borri '99	ŸŸ	6
● Il Corzano '99	ŸŸ	6
○ Aglaia '01	ŸŸ	5
● Chianti Terre di Corzano '00	ŸŸ	4
○ Passito di Corzano '95	ŸŸ	6
● Il Corzano '97	ŸŸŸ	5
○ Vin Santo '94	ŸŸ	6
○ Vin Santo '90	ŸŸ	5
○ Vin Santo '93	ŸŸ	5
● Il Corzano '95	ŸŸ	5
● Il Corzano '96	ŸŸ	5
● Chianti Terre di Corzano '97	ŸŸ	3
● Chianti Terre di Corzano Ris. '97	ŸŸ	4
● Chianti I Tre Borri '98	ŸŸ	6
● Il Corzano '98	ŸŸ	6

SAN CASCIANO IN VAL DI PESA (FI)

CASTELLI DEL GREVEPESA
FRAZ. MERCATALE VAL DI PESA
VIA GREVIGIANA, 34
50024 SAN CASCIANO IN VAL DI PESA (FI)
TEL. 055821911
E-MAIL: info@castellidelgrevepesa.it

Last year, we expressed our surprise and delight at the step up in quality at Castelli del Grevepesa. We can only repeat those sentiments this time, as the wines sent for tasting this year did even better. It was clear that this co-operative was refocusing its aims, and adjusting to a market that is ever more demanding in terms of quality. After a year, the effects are evident. The Gualdo al Luco '98 is very good. Made from sangiovese and cabernet sauvignon, it has excellent aromas of sour cherry jam and toasted coffee beans. The palate is soft, light and nicely textured, even though it might not show extraordinary personality. Equally good is the Syrah '00, which pervades the palate with its luxuriant fruit and spices. It doesn't yet have much clarity of aromatic definition, but the weight of its extract and its sheer size are impressive. In contrast, the nose of the Riserva Clemente VII '99 is very well focused, and shows a certain flower-themed elegance. The body is well balanced and moderately full, taking you through to a tasty, juicy finish. The picture is not quite so clear-cut with the Sangiovese Coltiferedi '99. The nose shows some inelegant notes of reduction, while the palate reveals remarkably rich raw material, along with some more rustic touches that probably come from over-extraction. To round of the list, there is a very decent Chianti Classico '00.

SAN CASCIANO IN VAL DI PESA (FI)

TENUTA IL CORNO
FRAZ. SAN PANCRAZIO
VIA MALAFRASCA, 64
50026 SAN CASCIANO IN VAL DI PESA (FI)
TEL. 0558248009
E-MAIL: ilcorno@iol.it

The beautiful winery owned by the Frova family didn't feature in the Guide last year simply because the wines were not ready at the time of our tastings. We can make up for this little gap in last year's edition with a list of wines that clearly demonstrate Il Corno's continuing growth. The best of the wines seemed to us to be the Colorino '99, which almost had its Glasses "coloured". It's a red that arrived at our tastings after 16 months in large 300-litre tonneaux, and a decent period in bottle with a beautifully intense ruby hue that introduces compact scents of ripe fruit, well fused with the oak, as well as some vegetal traces. In the mouth, it reveals dense structure, and has a good, long finish where the tannins are prominent. Our retasting of Corno Rosso, a blend of sangiovese with one third colorino and cabernet sauvignon, confirmed that it is a very good wine. The nose focuses on blackberries and significant oak. On the palate, it is soft and well balanced, but with vegetal traces in the medium-length finish. The Corno Bianco '00 is also successful. Made from chardonnay, it showed good extractive weight and balance, supported by pleasant notes of vanilla. The Chianti San Camillo '98 is a simpler wine that develops pleasantly on the palate. Although the Vin Santo '92 wasn't very convincing, this doesn't detract from the excellent show put on by Il Corno this year.

● Gualdo al Luco '98	🍷🍷	6
● Syrah '00	🍷🍷	5
● Chianti Cl. Clemente VII Ris. '99	🍷🍷	5*
● Coltifredi '99	🍷🍷	6
● Chianti Cl. Castelgreve '00	🍷	4
● Coltifredi '97	🍷🍷	6
● Chianti Cl. Castelgreve Ris. '95	🍷🍷	4
● Coltifredi '95	🍷🍷	5
● Gualdo al Luco '95	🍷🍷	5
● Gualdo al Luco '96	🍷🍷	5
● Chianti Cl. Castelgreve Ris. '97	🍷🍷	4
● Chianti Cl. Sant'Angiolo Vico l'Abate '97	🍷🍷	5
● Gualdo al Luco '97	🍷🍷	5
● Chianti Cl. Castelgreve Ris. '98	🍷🍷	5*

○ Corno Bianco '00	🍷🍷	5
● Colorino '99	🍷🍷	6
○ Vin Santo '93	🍷	5
● Chianti dei Colli Fiorentini San Camillo '98	🍷	3*
● Colorino '96	🍷🍷	4
● Colorino '97	🍷🍷	6
● I Gibbioni '97	🍷🍷	4
● Corno Rosso '99	🍷🍷	4

SAN CASCIANO IN VAL DI PESA (FI)

Il Mandorlo
Via Certaldese, 2/b
50026 San Casciano in Val di Pesa (FI)
tel. 0558228211
e-mail: info@il-mandorlo.it

The Ponticelli brothers, who own Il Mandorlo, are not newcomers to the world of wine. They well know that when you have to bow to the slow rhythms of agriculture and the variability of the seasons. Nothing can be taken for granted and nothing happens by chance. It is already remarkable that the wines they presented this year confirmed their quality, underlining how reliable the estate and its cellar are. All three of the wines showed appreciably firm, close-knit texture, even if there were no real diamonds in the collection. The particularly interesting Chianti Classico Il Rotone '99 has a good nose of berry fruit mingling with oak aromas. Intense and sweet in the mouth, it develops elegantly and harmoniously without revealing any great weight. The Chianti Classico 2000 has a similar style, although it has less intensity. The palate shows good consistency, without excessive extraction, and decent overall balance. The finish reveals solid fruit. We'll conclude our descriptions with the only IGT presented, the Terrato '99. It is a cabernet sauvignon-sangiovese blend that is quite harmonious, but doesn't have the imposing character that distinguishes an excellent wines from the merely good. The nose faithfully reflects the grapes it was made from in scents of red and black berry fruit and notes of sweet green peppers, while the palate is pleasingly round and well balanced.

SAN CASCIANO IN VAL DI PESA (FI)

Ispoli
Fraz. Mercatale Val di Pesa
Via Santa Lucia, 2
50024 San Casciano in Val di Pesa (FI)
tel. 055821613
e-mail: ispoli@tin.it

To say that wines produced organically are not very good may be a commonplace, but this is certainly not the case with Ispoli, a Mercatale winery that continues to make excellent progress. The Chianti Classico '00, indeed, made it into our finals for Three Glasses without any difficulty. It has a well-defined, intense ruby colour, and a complex nose that layers cinnamon and cloves over ripe plums and redcurrants. The wine's very attractive personality is evident in the mouth. The palate is well-rounded and juicy, with crunchy tannins woven into a close-knit, substantial texture. The finish is tasty and lingers. Confirmation of the cellar's prowess comes from Ispolaia '99, a blend of cabernet and sangiovese. In the glass, it presents an extremely dense ruby, then a complex nose emerges, mingling raspberries, strawberries and redcurrants with faint hints of spices. The attack on the palate is very attractive, and the consistency soft, thanks to delightfully well-amalgamated tannins. The palate then continues to finish pleasantly with more than decent length. The Ispolaia '01, a rosé, is worthy looking into, although it is more a curiosity than anything else. It's a simple wine in structure, with a fresh-tasting but short palate.

● Chianti Cl. '00	ΥΥ	4
● Chianti Cl. Il Rotone Ris. '99	ΥΥ	5
● Terrato '99	ΥΥ	5
● Terrato '98	ΥΥ	5
● Chianti Cl. '99	ΥΥ	4

● Chianti Cl. '00	ΥΥ	4*
● Ispolaia Rosso '99	ΥΥ	5
◉ Ispolaia Rosato '01	ΥΥ	3
● Ispolaia Rosso '96	ΥΥ	4
● Chianti Cl. '97	ΥΥ	3
● Chianti Cl. '98	ΥΥ	3
● Ispolaia Rosso '98	ΥΥ	4
● Chianti Cl. '99	ΥΥ	4

SAN CASCIANO IN VAL DI PESA (FI)

LA SALA
LOC. PONTEROTTO
VIA SORRIPA, 34
50026 SAN CASCIANO IN VAL DI PESA (FI)
TEL. 055828111
E-MAIL: info@lasala.it

La Sala put on a great show this time. The wines performed to a much more uniform standard than in previous years. All three tasted this year easily earned Two Glasses, and the standard-label Chianti Classico nearly made it into our final tastings for that elusive third Glass. It is always worth saying, in these cases, that our evaluations drawn up by wine type and on the average values of the various vintages. We could make this clearer with an example: the IGT Campo all'Albero '99, for instance, is an excellent wine but cannot reasonably be compared with the '98, or with a Chianti Classico. Having said this, we can pass on to a description of the wines. The Chianti Classico '00 stood out in a not very extraordinary year as one of the more successful bottles of its kind. The nose shows its wood in aromas of vanilla and cloves, and there is also underlying ripe fruit. In the mouth, it is round, showing pleasant sweetness and convincing balance. The finish holds up well but fails to show any great personality. The Campo all'Albero '99, from sangiovese and cabernet sauvignon, is a more concentrated wine that still closed to the nose, except for some vegetal hints. The attack is powerful, becoming soft yet energetic as it progresses, and reveals a few rough or grassy touches in the back palate. The Riserva '99 is also very good. It has a compact nose with a ripe, oak-punctuated fruit theme. The palate is well balanced, sweet and progresses well, offering delicious, lively tannins.

Chianti Cl. '00	♟♟	4*
Campo all'Albero '99	♟♟	6
Chianti Cl. Ris. '99	♟♟	5
Campo all'Albero '98	♟♟	5
Campo all'Albero '94	♟♟	4
Campo all'Albero '95	♟♟	4
Campo all'Albero '96	♟♟	5
Chianti Cl. '96	♟♟	3
Chianti Cl. Ris. '96	♟♟	4
Campo all'Albero '97	♟♟	5
Chianti Cl. Ris. '98	♟♟	4
Chianti Cl. '98	♟	3

SAN CASCIANO IN VAL DI PESA (FI)

FATTORIA LE CORTI - CORSINI
LOC. LE CORTI
VIA SAN PIERO DI SOTTO, 1
50026 SAN CASCIANO IN VAL DI PESA (FI)
TEL. 055820123
E-MAIL: info@principecorsini.com

Le Corti gave a very authoritative performance this year. They didn't pick up Three Glasses, but the wines presented showed a uniformity and stability of quality that bespeaks seriously good winemaking. The Don Tommaso remains at the top of their list, even if it didn't quite repeat its success of last year. We should say, by the way, that it came very close. It is a wine that possesses important qualities, such as a very intense nose, at the present still woody, and good ripe fruit with pleasing hints of spices. The palate is soft and deep, with very close-knit tannins, and it takes you through to a long, concentrated finish. This is a good effort in a difficult year, which 2000 certainly was. It shows that the efforts made by this winery and its investments both in the vineyards and cellar should guarantee it a prominent place in the front rank, no matter what kind of year comes along. The other two Chianti Classico wines are very nearly equal in quality, with our preference just going to the Riserva Corevecchia '99. It offers aromas of sour cherry jam, as well as less appropriate vegetal notes. The palate shows good body, but the fruit is rather masked by the oak. The Chianti Classico '00 has an as yet poorly defined nose that is heavily marked by oak-derived nuances. It is balanced, lively and round in the mouth, but a little bitter at the finish.

Chianti Cl. Don Tommaso '00	♟♟	5
Chianti Cl. Cortevecchia Ris. '99	♟♟	4
Chianti Cl. '00	♟	4
Chianti Cl. Don Tommaso '99	♟♟♟	5
Chianti Cl. Don Tommaso '94	♟♟	5
Chianti Cl. Cortevecchia Ris. '95	♟♟	5
Chianti Cl. Don Tommaso '95	♟♟	5
Chianti Cl. Don Tommaso '96	♟♟	5
Chianti Cl. Cortevecchia Ris. '97	♟♟	5
Chianti Cl. Don Tommaso '97	♟♟	5
Chianti Cl. '98	♟♟	3
Chianti Cl. '99	♟♟	4

SAN CASCIANO IN VAL DI PESA (FI)

MACHIAVELLI
Loc. Sant'Andrea in Percussina
50026 San Casciano in Val di Pesa (FI)
Tel. 055828471
E-mail: giv@giv.it

This historic cellar, once the residence of Niccolò Machiavelli when he was exiled from Florence, was for centuries the property of the noble Serristori family. For many years now, it has been the property of Gruppo Italiano Vini, which, although it is not well known by name to the general public, owns a large number of wineries all over Italy, including Fontana Candida, Bigi, Melini, Santi, Rapitalà, Negri, Ca' Bianca, and Machiavelli. The list isn't even complete. Here in San Casciano Val di Pesa, in the village of Sant'Andrea in Percussina, the specialty is Chianti Classico. From their vineyards, you can see the dome of Brunelleschi's Santa Maria del Fiore, and then the hill of Fiesole. The position is enchanting, and the sangiovese that grows has great softness and grace. That's what the Chianti Classico Vigna di Fontalle is like. In very good years, like 1995, it reaches great peaks. In less exciting vintages, and the '99 is one of these, it produces delicate, well-balanced wines that, however, lack the concentration and extra power that we particularly like. Next comes Il Principe, also from '99. It is a powerful, very modern red, with a bit too much vanilla on the nose. It's only "defect" is that it is made from the pinot nero grape. It bears very little relation to the varietal characteristics of the grape and is, in fact, an excellent wine that is driven more by its territory than by its vine. Their list closes with Ser Niccolò Solatio del Tani '99, made from cabernet sauvignon. This, too, is much more of a Tuscan red than an exotic, international-style wine.

● Chianti Cl. V. di Fontalle Ris. '99	ΨΨ	5
● Il Principe '99	ΨΨ	6
● Ser Niccolò Solatio del Tani '99	ΨΨ	6
● Ser Niccolò Solatio del Tani '88	ΨΨΨ	4
● Chianti Cl. V. di Fontalle Ris. '95	ΨΨΨ	5
● Il Principe '95	ΨΨΨ	4
● Chianti Cl. V. di Fontalle Ris. '93	ΨΨ	5
● Chianti Cl. V. di Fontalle Ris. '94	ΨΨ	5
● Il Principe '94	ΨΨ	4
● Il Principe '96	ΨΨ	5
● Il Principe '97	ΨΨ	5
● Chianti Cl. V. di Fontalle Ris. '98	ΨΨ	5
● Il Principe '98	ΨΨ	5

SAN CASCIANO IN VAL DI PESA (FI)

FATTORIA POGGIOPIANO
Via di Pisignano, 28/30
50026 San Casciano in Val di Pesa (FI)
Tel. 0558229629
E-mail: poggiopiano@ftbcc.it

The Fattoria di Poggiopiano didn't quite manage this year to renew its customary subscription to Three Glasses for its top wine, Rosso di Sera 2000. On the other hand, it did easily gain Two red Glasses, the level of recognition reserved for wines that have taken part in our final tastings. This confirms Rosso di Sera's position among the top wineries of Tuscany and Italy. Rosso di Sera is a blend of sangiovese and colorino, and shows a beautiful, intense ruby colour with luminous highlights. The nose offers pleasing fruity notes that are underlined by spices and rounded by wood which, unfortunately, is just a little too strong. In the mouth, the attack is soft and powerful. The oak is well integrated, yet not as perfectly fused in as last year's edition. This soft, round wine has vibrant, fine-grained tannins and a finish that is well-balanced and pleasing. The second red from this winery, the Chianti Classico '00, is again a modern-type wine with a very harmonious style. It has a lovely brilliant ruby colour, decent concentration and intensely fruity aromas that are, however, faintly marred by vegetal tones. In the mouth, it is fresh, full and yet elegant in its development, and the finish is crystal clear.

● Rosso di Sera '00	ΨΨ	8
● Chianti Cl. '00	ΨΨ	4
● Rosso di Sera '95	ΨΨΨ	5
● Rosso di Sera '97	ΨΨΨ	5
● Rosso di Sera '98	ΨΨΨ	6
● Rosso di Sera '99	ΨΨΨ	6
● Chianti Cl. '99	ΨΨ	4*
● Rosso di Sera '96	ΨΨ	5
● Chianti Cl. '98	ΨΨ	4

SAN GIMIGNANO (SI)

Baroncini
Loc. Casale, 43
53037 San Gimignano (SI)
tel. 0577940600

Taking full advantage of its knowledge of the terrain at San Gimignano, the Baroncini winery continues to make wines that are generally very high in quality. Vernaccia obviously takes up much of the cellar's time and attention, but in recent years, reds have also begun to play an important role here. This was demonstrated by the good impression made by the Rosso Il Casato '00. It has a lively ruby colour of good intensity, and aromas that concentrate on notes of blackberries. The palate is round, full and well-balanced, if just a little one-dimensional on the finish. The Vernaccia Dometaia '00 is also well-defined and convincing. This is definitely a Vernaccia to bank on for quality. It is well-balanced, fresh and pleasurable, and the palate is rounded off by a sweet note of discreetly understated vanilla. The white Faina '00 has plenty of personality. Its floral aromas, eloquent minerally notes and intense palate take you through to a finish of good length. The Cortegiano '00 is a very decent bottle. It has good balance, well-judged tannins and earthily vegetal notes on the nose, although it's a bit short on the finish. Other labels worth mentioning include the well-typed Vernaccia Poggio ai Cannicci '01, which is pleasing in its scents of peaches and pear, and simple but fresh on the palate. To wind this report, the two Colli Senesi are uncomplicated and easy to drink.

● San Gimignano Rosso Il Casato '00	▼▼	4
○ Vernaccia di S. Gimignano Dometaia Ris. '00	▼▼	4
● Cortegiano Sovestro '00	▼	5
○ La Faina '00	▼	4
● Chianti Colli Senesi '01	▼	3
● Chianti Colli Senesi Sup. Vigna S. Domenico Sovestro '01	▼	3
○ Vernaccia di S. Gimignano Poggio ai Cannici Sovestro '01	▼	3
○ La Faina '99	▽▽	4

SAN GIMIGNANO (SI)

Ca' del Vispo
Loc. Le Vigne
Via Fugnano, 31
53037 San Gimignano (SI)
tel. 0577943053

Roberto Vispi, and Marco and Massimo dal Din are the three partners at Cà del Vispo. The trio have an incredible ability to stay on the same wavelength, as is shown by their wines. We'll begin with Cruter '00, a 100 per cent Merlot, which made a very favourable impression on our panel of tasters, who sent it on to the finals. Cruter has a deep, intense ruby colour, and offers sweet aromas of ripe fruit, pepper and spices on the nose. The palate is harmonious, with soft and well-balanced tannins that are slightly disturbed in the finish by a faint vegetal note. The Rovai '00, a blend of cabernet sauvignon, merlot, and sangiovese, turned out to be more successful than the previous version with its aromas of resin, blackberries, and undergrowth, as well as the good structure and round tannins that it showed in the mouth. The Colle Leone '00, from sangiovese and merlot, has a delicious palate with well-balanced extract, even though it showed a hint of greenness. The other two reds are less successful. The Poggio Solivo '00 is charming and balanced, but not very intense, and the Basolo '00 has not yet opened on the nose. It shows signs of evolution and also vegetal traces. The white we liked best was the standard Vernaccia. It has a golden colour, an intense nose of ripe fruit, and light floral fragrances. On the palate, it begins sweetly with good breadth, sustained by acidity and decent structure. In contrast, the Vernaccia Vigna in Fiore '01 seemed inferior to last year's edition. Although it is round and full in the mouth, it seemed to us to be lacking in acidity.

● Cruter '00	▼▼	4*
● Rovai '00	▼▼	4
● Basolo '00	▼	4
● Colle Leone '00	▼	4
● Poggio Solivo '00	▼	4
○ Vernaccia di S. Gimignano '01	▼	3
○ Vernaccia di S. Gimignano Vigna in Fiore '01	▼	4
● Basolo '99	▽▽	4
● Cruter '99	▽▽	4

SAN GIMIGNANO (SI)

Casa alle Vacche
Fraz. Pancole
Loc. Lucignano, 73/A
53037 San Gimignano (SI)
tel. 0577955103
e-mail: casaallevacche@cyber.dada.it

This winery belongs to the Ciappi brothers, Fernando and Lorenzo. It continues to grow in area under vine, which has now reached 16 hectares for a production of 120,000 bottles a year. But above all, it is gaining in quality and three of the wines were awarded Two Glasses this year. Let's begin with the top of the range. Aglieno, a blend of 65 per cent sangiovese and 35 per cent merlot, has never been as close as it was this year to entering our finals. It has a dark ruby colour and an intensely typical nose that has faint notes of well-integrated wood, aromas of raspberries and a light grassy vein of green pepper. In the mouth, it is well balanced, full and close knit, revealing sweet tannins and rich fruit, particularly wild berries and black cherries. The finish is long and aromatic. San Gimignano Rosso Acantho, a sangiovese with 15 per cent canaiolo aged in barrique for 18 months, suffers from the extended stay in oak both on the nose, with its notes of vanilla, and on the palate, where the tannins are quite sweet but still mask the fruit. Crocus, from vernaccia to which ten per cent chardonnay has been added, won Two Glasses for a nose with toasty, oak-derived aromas mingle with ripe pears and a pleasant, medium body that unveils fresh, spicy notes on the finish. The Chianti Colli Senesi Cinabro is pleasingly supple, and the Vernaccia I Macchioni is fresh-tasting, with lovely notes of flowers and citrus fruits.

SAN GIMIGNANO (SI)

Vincenzo Cesani
Fraz. Pancole
Via Piazzetta, 82/D
53037 San Gimignano (SI)
tel. 0577955084
e-mail: cesanivini@novamedia.it

The Cesanis continue to promote local varieties. This year, their Luenzo didn't quite win its third Glass but it did go forward to the finals. It's becoming quite a habit. This classic Tuscan blend, which combines sangiovese with a deeply traditional variety like colorino, ages in barrique for 18 months and then a further six in bottle. As the panel realized, it needs a little more time in the cellar to produce its best form. When we tasted, the nose was a little closed with oak-derived spice and toastiness dominating to the point of masking the berry fruit aromas. The palate is as elegant as ever, and the fruit is delicious, but the fine-grained tannins are still too much to the fore, which restricts the breadth and subtlety of the aromas. The Vernaccia di San Gimignano Sanice selection is very good. The broad nose flaunts slightly toasty notes of butter and vanilla, then the palate is full of fruit and impressively long. It has notes of liquorice and white chocolate, as well as the signature freshness of the Pancole terroir for it is one of the coolest subzones around San Gimignano. We'll round off with the standard-label Vernaccia '01, one of the best of the vintage. Its apparent simplicity manages to marry good structure and attractive freshness with a very drinkable style.

● Aglieno '01	ΨΨ	4*
○ Vernaccia di S. Gimignano Crocus '01	ΨΨ	4
● San Gimignano Rosso Acantho '99	ΨΨ	5
● Chianti dei Colli Senesi Cinabro '00	Ψ	4
○ Vernaccia di S. Gimignano I Macchioni '01	Ψ	3
● Aglieno '00	ΨΨ	3
○ Vernaccia di S. Gimignano Crocus '00	ΨΨ	4
● Chianti Colli Senesi Cinabro '97	ΨΨ	4
○ Vernaccia di S. Gimignano Crocus '98	ΨΨ	3

● Luenzo '00	ΨΨ	6
○ Vernaccia di S. Gimignano Sanice '00	ΨΨ	4*
○ Vernaccia di S. Gimignano '01	Ψ	3
● Luenzo '97	ΨΨΨ	5
● Luenzo '99	ΨΨΨ	5
● Luenzo '95	ΨΨ	4
● Luenzo '96	ΨΨ	4
● Luenzo '98	ΨΨ	5
○ Vernaccia di S. Gimignano Sanice '98	ΨΨ	4
○ Vernaccia di S. Gimignano Sanice '99	ΨΨ	4
● Chianti Colli Senesi '00	Ψ	3

SAN GIMIGNANO (SI)

IL PARADISO
LOC. STRADA, 21/A
53037 SAN GIMIGNANO (SI)
TEL. 0577941500
E-MAIL: 0577941500@iol.it

Vasco Cetti, a well-known figure who has hitched his name to the recent history of Vernaccia di San Gimignano, has done his bit to uphold the prestige of this City of Towers. A doctor by profession, Vasco has always made excellent wines with the help of his wife, Graziella, at their family estate, Il Paradiso. The vines now extend over more than 225 hectares, and here, besides the inevitable Vernaccia, the star of local oenology, Vasco and Graziella also grow sangiovese, syrah, merlot and cabernet sauvignon. Indeed, it has been their reds in recent years that have been the most successful at our tastings. All of this has been helped by the collaboration of outstanding oenologist, Paolo Caciorgna, an able interpreter of this terroir. Which brings us to the Saxa Calida '00, a Bordeaux blend that repeats the triumph of its last outing by earning another Three Glasses. It has a dark, impenetrable ruby colour and intense aromas where unexpectedly deep, complex notes of blackberries and raspberries mingle with delicate vegetal and spicy touches. In the mouth, the wine is solid and harmonious, showing rich extract, extraordinarily light, ripe tannins, and a very long finish. The other top red wine, Paterno II '99, came close to Three Glasses. A thoroughbred Sangiovese, it impresses with its velvet-smooth mouthfeel, power and finesse. All the rest of the range, including this year's Vernaccia, the Biscondola selection and the Chianti Colli Senesi wines, is reliable and well made.

● Saxa Calida '00	🍷🍷🍷 6
● Paterno II '99	🍷🍷 6
● Bottaccio '00	🍷 4
● Chianti Colli Senesi '00	🍷 2*
○ Vernaccia di S. Gimignano '01	🍷 2
○ Vernaccia di S. Gimignano Biscondola '01	🍷 4
● Saxa Calida '99	🍷🍷🍷 6
● Paterno II '97	🍷🍷 5
● Paterno II '98	🍷🍷 5
● Saxa Calida '98	🍷🍷 5
● Saxa Calida '96	🍷🍷 4

SAN GIMIGNANO (SI)

GUICCIARDINI STROZZI
FATTORIA CUSONA
LOC. CUSONA, 5
53037 SAN GIMIGNANO (SI)
TEL. 0577950028
E-MAIL: info@guicciardinistrozzi.it

The Cusona winery has never eased its efforts to boost quality in vineyard and cellar. This year, the Millanni didn't quite manage another Three Glasses, but growth at a winery is obvious in the consistency and overall quality of its range. Those characteristics are very much present at the estate owned by Principe Strozzi. The Millanni got to the final taste-offs but couldn't make that third Glass. Very dark, with intense violet highlights, it is made from a blend of 60 per cent sangiovese, 30 per cent cabernet sauvignon and ten per cent merlot and reveals balsamic notes, fruit jam and vanilla on the nose. The palate is fruit-led, showing remarkable structure thanks to soft, well-behaved tannins and good length that closes on liquorice and caramel. The Sodole nearly got to our finals. Obtained entirely from sangiovese, it has a deep ruby hue that introduces notes of graphite and ripe fruit, mingling with balsamic nuances and a touch of toast. The palate is full and soft, with admirable depth and balance. It can also point to sweet tannins, good length and good nose-palate consistency. The Selvascura is good, too. A monovarietal Merlot, it releases notes of raspberries as well as a light vegetal nuance. It has a rich, fluid palate and needs only a pinch more body and balance. The whites are less successful. Both the Vernaccia Riserva, which has neither freshness nor much of a nose, or the Perlato, fresh enough but with too much acidity and rather monotonous aromas, are sufficiently convincing. Both earned One Glass. The Vermentino Luna Verde is fresh and well typed.

● Millanni '00	🍷🍷 7
● Selvascura '00	🍷🍷 5
● Sodole '00	🍷🍷 6
○ Vernaccia di S. Gimignano Ris. '00	🍷 4
○ Luna Verde '01	🍷 3
○ Vernaccia di S. Gimignano Perlato '01	🍷 4
● Millanni '99	🍷🍷🍷 7
● Millanni '98	🍷🍷 6
● Selvascura '98	🍷🍷 5
● Selvascura '99	🍷🍷 5
● Sodole '99	🍷🍷 6

SAN GIMIGNANO (SI)

IL LEBBIO
Loc. San Benedetto, 11/C
53037 San Gimignano (SI)
Tel. 0577944725
E-mail: illebbio@libero.it

The Niccolini brothers' winery continues to reap success with its reds, but the whites are less reliable. The Polito '99, a blend of sangiovese and colorino, confirms its Two Glass status thanks to a dark ruby colour, a deep nose with scents of ripe cherries and blackberries that meld nicely with toasty notes of oak, and a full, powerful palate with attractive sweet wood and rich fruit. Two Glasses also go to the Grottoni '01, a blend of 40 per cent cabernet sauvignon, 20 per cent merlot and the rest montepulciano. It has a nose of considerable intensity, with peppery scents, animal skins and some light vegetal hints. The palate is soft, round, tangy and offers good spicy notes and close-knit tannins. It has a long finish that is nicely piquant at the very end. The less successful Cicogio '01, a blend of ciliegiolo, colorino and sangiovese, has a very concentrated, but vegetal and slightly veiled nose. It is mouthfilling and shows good weight, but it's also a bit edgy because of its raw, green tannins. Best of the whites is the Malvasia '01. It has a fresh, if not perfectly clean, nose, a well-extracted palate that shows good weight and a pleasantly tasty finish. The Vernaccia Tropie '01 has a nose of moderate intensity with strong notes of sage. The palate is lightweight, moderately long and has a pleasantly bitterish finish. The standard Vernaccia '01 is decent.

SAN GIMIGNANO (SI)

IL PALAGIONE
Via per Castel San Gimignano
53037 San Gimignano (SI)
Tel. 0577953134
E-mail: palagione@tin.it

Monica Rota and Giorgio Comotti's recently established winery has some ten hectares under vine that produce 30,000 bottles annually. It is continuing its campaign to reach the forefront of wine in San Gimignano. The two owners are well counselled and supported by oenologist Paolo Caciornga and agronomist Federico Curtaz, profound experts in this land and its peculiarities, and are concentrating on making a seriously good wine from red grapes. Their Antair '00 was originally sold under the name, Altair, which turned out already to have been registered. The new label adorns a blend of 50 per cent sangiovese, 25 per cent merlot and cabernet sauvignon, fermented and matured in new barriques for 18 months. It came within an ace of entering the final round. Its complex nose is rich in fruit-led aromas that blend well with spicy and balsamic notes from the wood. Entry on the palate is soft and almost sweet, then mid palate shows good concentration and depth, with nice fruity notes and notable elegance. It's a wine that foregrounds elegance and finesse, unlike many other Supertuscans. We hope it will continue to develop. The two whites are also good. Enif is a blend dominated by trebbiano, with 25 per cent malvasia. It's fresh-tasting, with good fruit and a full, fat palate veined with butter and vanilla. Hydra, a Vernaccia, is fresh, clean and fruity.

● Grottoni '01	ŸŸ	4
● Polito '99	ŸŸ	6
● Cicogio '01	Ÿ	4
○ Malvasia '01	Ÿ	3
○ Vernaccia di S. Gimignano Tropie '01	Ÿ	3
○ Vernaccia di S. Gimignano '01		3
● I Grottoni '97	ŸŸ	2
● Polito '97	ŸŸ	4
● Cicogio '98	ŸŸ	3
● Polito '98	ŸŸ	4
● I Grottoni '99	ŸŸ	3

● Antair '00	ŸŸ	6
○ Enif '01	Ÿ	3
○ Vernaccia di San Gimignano Hydra '01	Ÿ	3

SAN GIMIGNANO (SI)

La Lastra
Fraz. Santa Lucia
Via R. De Grada, 9
53037 San Gimignano (SI)
tel. 0577941781 - 0577236423
e-mail: staff@lalastra.it

This winery, owned by Nadia Betti and Renato Spanu, has come back after a disappointing year. The Rovaio has yet to made the quantum leap in quality that everyone has been hoping to see for some time. It is still a fine Two Glass wine but fails to arouse real enthusiasm. The nose shows fruity scents that are clean but a little too mature, almost cooked, and some intense toasty notes. In the mouth, it is more balanced and has good depth. The mid palate is less burdened by wood and shows a pleasingly fruit-rich progression through to a finish with a soft, convincing aftertaste. The Vernaccia Riserva '00 also won Two Glasses. It has a lot of mineral notes on the nose, although it is still somewhat closed, and there are some pleasing floral fragrances. Entry on the palate is powerful, with plenty of richness and abundant alcohol showing through, then the progression offers good balance thanks well-integrated wood and fruit. The finish is satisfyingly long. The Chianti Colli Senesi '01 nearly gained a Second Glass for its intense fruit and particularly fresh aromas, followed by an attractive, mid-bodied palate of fresh fruit. In contrast, the standard Vernaccia '01 is only well made. It has a yeasty nose and some oxidation on the palate. The commitment and enthusiasm of the proprietors and their consultant, Enrico Paternoster, are evident so we are convinced that the quality boost that we all are hoping for has only been postponed.

SAN GIMIGNANO (SI)

La Rampa di Fugnano
Loc. Fugnano, 55
53037 San Gimignano (SI)
tel. 0577941655 -
0041792361784
e-mail: info@rampadifugnano.it

It seems that Gisela Traxler and Herbert Ehrenbold, not to mention their oenologist Paolo Caciorgna, have finally hit their stride. Their flagship bottle, Giséle made it into our finals this year, proving that it is one of the very best wines from San Gimignano, thanks to its great finesse and elegance. It has a dark ruby colour with purplish highlights, but is still a little shy and inexpressive on the nose. The timidity, which is a consequence recent bottling, does not detract from an extraordinary wine. The palate is soft, expansive, fat and rich in pulp and fruit, with close-knit texture and serious body. The finish is long and complex. The performance was a great one and Giséle only just missed out on a third Glass. This wine and its makers will, we are sure, soon be back for more top prizes. The Vernaccia Riserva Privato is very good, in fact one of the best of the year. It has a straw colour and a delicate, deep nose that reveals some mineral notes. In the mouth, it follows through well, the fresh, crunchy, lingering palate showing clean notes of fruit and good structure. Perhaps it is simpler than one might expect from a Vernaccia Riserva, it is attractively fresh and fragrant. It's a very good wine indeed. This year's Bombereto is less successful than other recent versions. Made completely from sangiovese, it shows a nose that is varietal but not very precise. The palate shows good, light fruit but there are also vegetal notes. Vin Santo Topazio is good, if rustic, while the Vernaccia Alata and the Chianti Via dei Franchi are well typed and pleasant.

● Rovaio '99	♛♛	5
○ Vernaccia di S. Gimignano Ris. '00	♛♛	4
● Chianti Colli Senesi '01	♛	3
○ Vernaccia di S. Gimignano '01	♛	3
○ Vernaccia di S. Gimignano Ris. '96	♛♛	3
● Rovaio '97	♛♛	5
○ Vernaccia di S. Gimignano Ris. '97	♛♛	3
● Rovaio '98	♛♛	5
○ Vernaccia di S. Gimignano '98	♛♛	2
○ Vernaccia di S. Gimignano Ris. '98	♛♛	4

● Giséle '00	♛♛	7
○ Vernaccia di S. Gimignano Privato Ris. '00	♛♛	4
● Bombereto '00	♛	5
● Chianti dei Colli Senesi Via dei Franchi '01	♛	3
○ Vernaccia di S. Gimignano Alata '01	♛	3
○ Vin Santo Topazio '94	♛	7
● Giséle '97	♛♛♛	5
● Giséle '99	♛♛	6
● Bombereto '98	♛♛	5
● Giséle '98	♛♛	6
● Bombereto '99	♛♛	5

SAN GIMIGNANO (SI)

MONTENIDOLI
LOC. MONTENIDOLI
53037 SAN GIMIGNANO (SI)
TEL. 0577941565

Montenidoli is back in the Guide after a brief absence. The owner, Elisabetta Fagiuoli, makes products that have left their mark on the history of San Gimignano winemaking, whether you approve of their style or not. One good example is the Vernaccia Fiore '01, a wine that is already good now, yet capable of further improvement over the next few years. The nose is quite rich, offering notes of tropical and citrus fruits, as well as minerals. Entry in the mouth is soft and fresh, then the balance and good body emerge, to be followed by an elegant finish that offers pleasant sensations of fruit and almonds. Also convincing is the Vernaccia Carato '00. Its straw yellow had golden highlights and intense aromas with elegant notes of oak, butter and fruit. The soft entry also reveals good structure and appreciable balance, taking you through with finesse to a lingering, well-typed finish. Vernaccia Tradizionale '01 offers good balance, a mature, well-sustained flavour and exemplary, slightly bitter finish. The attractively fresh-tasting Vinbrusco is uncomplicated while the Sono Montenidoli '98, a sangiovese-based red, has a soft flavour, decent extractive weight and tannins that are solid and tasty. The Chianti Colli Senesi '99 has a lovely ruby colour, a nose that shows raspberries, strawberries and spices, and a palate that may lack structure but can offer balance and a very attractive personality. Also invitingly easy to drink is the fresh, fruity, rosé Canaiuolo '01.

SAN GIMIGNANO (SI)

MORMORAIA
LOC. SANT'ANDREA, 15
53037 SAN GIMIGNANO (SI)
TEL. 0577940096
E-MAIL: info@mormoraia.it

Giuseppe Passoni continues to invest money and energy, planting new vines and building a new ageing cellar for his wines. We are favourably impressed by what is going on here but considering the potential, the time might be right for a decisive step up in quality. Neitea '99 is very interesting. Mostly made from sangiovese, with small amounts of cabernet and merlot, it presents fruit and spices on the nose. The palate is well extracted, with a certain edgy acidity, and a decent, but not very long, finish. If we move over to the whites, we find an elegant, well-defined Ostrea Grigia '00 that has delicately sweet aromas of tropical fruits and a pleasantly fresh-tasting, soft palate with good structure and balance. The standard Vernaccia continues to be reliable, and is actually one of the best of the year. The straw yellow offers the nose striking notes of fruit, mingling with flower and mineral nuances. In the mouth, it is fresh, soft and well balanced, closing with a lovely hint of almonds. The Vernaccia Riserva '00 is the last on our list. It has a clean nose of impeccable elegance that blends fruit, including some citrus fruits, with vanilla. The panel thought it was a tad less rich on the palate but it still shows good structure and acidity, and a pleasing citrus-led finish.

O Vernaccia di S. Gimignano Carato '00	▼▼	5
O Vernaccia di S. Gimignano Fiore '01	▼▼	4
⊙ Canaiuolo '01	▼	3
O Vernaccia di S. Gimignano Tradizionale '01	▼	3
O Vin Brusco '01	▼	3
● Sono Montenidoli '98	▼	5
● Chianti Colli Senesi '99	▼	4

O Ostrea Grigia '00	▼▼	4
O Vernaccia di S. Gimignano Ris. '00	▼▼	5
● Neitea '99	▼▼	5
O Vernaccia di S. Gimignano '01	▼	4
O Vernaccia di S. Gimignano Ris. '99	▼▼	4
● Neitea '96	▼▼	4
O Ostrea '96	▼▼	4
● Neitea '97	▼▼	4
O Ostrea '97	▼▼	4
O Vernaccia di S. Gimignano Ris. '97	▼▼	4
● Neitea '98	▼▼	5
O Ostrea Grigia '98	▼▼	4
O Vernaccia di S. Gimignano Ris. '98	▼▼	4

SAN GIMIGNANO (SI)

PALAGETTO
Via Monteoliveto, 46
53037 San Gimignano (SI)
Tel. 0577943090 - 0577942098
E-mail: palagetto@iol.it

The wines from Palagetto are starting to get better. They are now more interesting, and have a personality and a style that we haven't found in years past. Confirmation came from our tastings. The white IGT l'Niccolo '01, a 50-50 mix of vermentino and chardonnay, surprised us with its very inviting, sweet aromas that proffer toastiness, ripe tropical fruit and vanilla. The palate is soft, revealing a rich, well-sustained and captivatingly elegant progression to a lovely long finish. The Vernaccia Riserva '00 is better than it has been. The nose has peaches and almonds, and the palate is round, warm and structured, closing pleasantly with touches of almonds. The special selection, Santa Chiara '01, has intense aromas of tropical fruits and almonds mixed with tones of toast and vanilla. The mouth is sumptuously round, pleasantly fresh, and reveals the usual twist of almonds in the aftertaste. The red Sottobosco '00, a sangiovese with some cabernet and merlot, again made a more than satisfactory showing. The nose offers hints of new wood, vegetal notes and plum-like fruit, then the palate is decisive and concentrated, supported by its dense, fine-grained tannins. The Chianti Colli Senesi '00 is well executed and proffers a nose of sour cherries and raspberries, then a round, very attractive palate. Bringing up the rear is Chianti Collie Senesi Riserva '99, an interesting, well-balanced wine let down by a grassy nose.

SAN GIMIGNANO (SI)

GIOVANNI PANIZZI
Loc. Racciano, 34
Fraz. Santa Margherita
53037 San Gimignano (SI)
Tel. 0577941576
E-mail: panizzi@ciber.data.it

Giovanni Panizzi came to San Gimignano from Milan at the end of the 1980s. Deeply in love with this corner of Tuscany, he bought a property and dedicated himself to viticulture. His seriousness and enthusiasm have turned him into a very sensitive winemaker. To put it briefly, he quickly became the leading interpreter of the vernaccia grape and he has brought Vernaccia di San Gimignano to levels so far unrivalled by other producers. Not for the first time, Giovanni's Vernaccia Riserva '00 is the best we tasted. It has an intense, brilliant straw colour, with pale green highlights and a fruit-rich nose with apricots and peaches in the foreground. The aromas then develop, showing more complex tones that include sage and hedgerow, and then elegant tones of vanilla and boisé of notable finesse. The palate has breadth, structure and solidity, the fruit returning very cleanly, and closes softly and with good length, That third Glass was only a hair's breadth away. The Vernaccia '01 is not as complex a wine, obviously, but still is one of the best of the year. It has a good structure, intense, neat perfumes of fruit, and notable freshness. The Bianco di Gianni '00 is a blend of 70 per cent vernaccia and chardonnay, the latter aged in new wood. It is a lovely, lustrous straw yellow, showing aromas of ripe fruit, butter and new wood, which blend well into the structure of the wine on the palate. Here, intense aromas of peaches and other fruit fuse with the spices from the wood. The Ceraso '01 and the Chianti Colli Senesi Vertunno '01 are both good.

● Sottobosco '00	♟♟	5
○ Vernaccia di S. Gimignano Ris. '00	♟♟	4
○ l'Niccolò '01	♟♟	5
● Chianti Colli Senesi '00	♟	3
○ Vernaccia di S. Gimignano '01	♟	3
○ Vernaccia di S. Gimignano Vigna Santa Chiara '01	♟	4
● Chianti Colli Senesi Ris. '99	♟	4
● Sottobosco '97	♟♟	5
○ Vernaccia di S. Gimignano Ris. '97	♟♟	4
● Sottobosco '98	♟♟	5
● Sottobosco '99	♟♟	5
● Solleone '98	♟	4
● Solleone '99	♟	4

○ Vernaccia di S. Gimignano Ris. '00	♟♟	6
○ Bianco di Gianni '00	♟♟	5
○ Vernaccia di S. Gimignano '01	♟♟	4*
● Ceraso '00	♟	4
● Chianti Colli Senesi Vertunno '00	♟	4
○ Vernaccia di S. Gimignano Ris. '98	♟♟♟	6
○ Vernaccia di S. Gimignano Ris. '96	♟♟	5
○ Vernaccia di S. Gimignano Ris. '97	♟♟	5
○ Vernaccia di S. Gimignano Ris. '99	♟♟	6

SAN GIMIGNANO (SI)

PIETRAFITTA
Loc. Cortennano
53037 San Gimignano (SI)
tel. 0577943200
e-mail: info@pietrafitta.com

The great energy on display here over the last few years has brought about a renovation in the cellar style, which appears to be trying to explore all of vernaccia's potential. The energy is also indicative of a desire to get back into the big league, where Fattoria di Pietrafitta was once very firmly entrenched. Among the vernaccia-based wines this year is Riserva La Costa '00, which went straight into the Two Glass bracket. It has an extremely clean nose, where citrus fruits, honey and vanilla are prominent. The palate is full, soft, and refreshing, thanks to well-judged acidity, and there are almonds in the finish. The Riserva, presented for the first time, also did remarkably well. It has an intense straw hue with golden highlights, showing a pleasant personality on the nose. There are notes of citrus fruits, almonds, peaches and apricots, then the palate is sinuously well-rounded, fresh and well-balanced, with a nice twist of almonds in the finish. The Vigna Borgetto '01 did satisfactorily and earned its Glass. Vibrant straw yellow, it has a nose of fruit and vanilla, then a sweet, full-bodied palate that lacks the acidity capable of offsetting its softness. It's easy-drinking, though, and the trademark hint of bitterness is there in the aftertaste. The pleasant and quite full-bodied San Gimignano Rosato '01 is balanced and fruity but the San Gimignano Rosso La Sughera '00 was not ready at the time of tasting.

○	Vernaccia di S. Gimignano Ris. '00	▼▼	4
○	Vernaccia di S. Gimignano Vigna La Costa Ris. '00	▼▼	5
⊙	S. Gimignano Rosato '01	▼	3
○	Vernaccia di S. Gimignano Vigna Borghetto '01	▼	4
○	Vernaccia di S. Gimignano V. Borghetto '00	▼▼	4
○	Vin Santo '93	▼▼	4
●	S. Gimignano Rosso La Sughera '99	▼	5
○	Vernaccia di S. Gimignano Vigna La Costa Ris. '99	▼	4

SAN GIMIGNANO (SI)

TERUZZI & PUTHOD
Loc. Casale, 19
53037 San Gimignano (SI)
tel. 0577940143
e-mail: info@teruzzieputhod.it

Since he came onto the scene in 1974, Enrico Teruzzi has put the vernaccia grape firmly before the attention of the Italian wine world. His style of vinification has made him one of the leading winemakers in the area. Enrico's Carmen '00 was the bottle that stood out at our tastings. A white from sangiovese vinified without the skins, it easily earned Two Glasses. It shows intriguing complexity on the nose, with scents of ripe fruit and grapefruit with touches of coffee. The palate reveals good body and a general harmony, then the elegant finish has good length. A notch lower down is the Terre di Tufi '00, which has oak-derived aromas on the nose, as well as ripe fruit. In the mouth, it is fresh and soft, with moderate structure and a little too much wood. The finish is not especially long, either. The Vigna a Rondolino '01 earned a full Glass. It has a straw colour, with green highlights, introducing a nose that is still rather closed, but already shows citrus fruits and white peaches. In the mouth, it has a vibrant freshness, reinforced by a touch of prickle and decent body. The finish offers medium length but a faint hint of acidity. The standard Vernaccia is well made, with evident fruit aromas. The palate is fresh and acidulous, revealing almonds on the finish. Peperino '00 did pretty well. Obtained from sangiovese, it is less than expressive on the nose, but has decent extract in the mouth and a pleasant, juicy finish.

○	Carmen Puthod '00	▼▼	4
○	Terre di Tufi '00	▼▼	5
●	Peperino '00	▼	4
○	Vernaccia di S. Gimignano '01	▼	3
○	Vernaccia di S. Gimignano Vigna a Rondolino '01	▼	4
○	Terre di Tufi '99	▼▼	5
○	Vernaccia di S. Gimignano Vigna a Rondolino '00	▼▼	4
○	Carmen '96	▼▼	4
○	Terre di Tufi '96	▼▼	5
○	Carmen '97	▼▼	4
○	Terre di Tufi '97	▼▼	5
○	Carmen '98	▼▼	4
○	Terre di Tufi '98	▼▼	4

SAN GIMIGNANO (SI)

F.lli Vagnoni
Fraz. Pancole, 82
53037 San Gimignano (SI)
tel. 0577955077

The Vagnonis continue to be among the best producers of Vernaccia di San Gimignano. A significant commitment in the vineyards and obvious care during vinification and ageing permit them to take full advantage of their property at Pancole, one of the best subzones in San Gimignano for winemaking, thanks to cool weather and a wide temperature range. This year, the Vagnonis presented a "riserva" version of Vernaccia Mocali, coming up with one of the best two or three Vernaccias of the year. It has an intense straw colour that introduces varietal hints of pears, lots of vanilla, and faint toasty notes. The palate unveils massive, solid structure that is perhaps a bit austere but shows good balance. The wood is already well absorbed and there is notable sinew, as well as citrus notes of pink grapefruit and tangerines. The length and aromatic persistence of the finish are impeccable. However, we expected more the Sodi Lunghi, a sangiovese with ten per cent colorino and merlot. The nose shows hints of cooked fruit and lacks elegance, while the palate, which is looking for volume and depth at all costs, is marred by excessive tannins and notes of over-extraction that mask the fruit aromas of cherries and blackberries.

○	Vernaccia di S. Gimignano Mocali Ris. '00	ΨΨ	4
○	Vernaccia di S. Gimignano '01	Ψ	3
●	Chianti Colli Senesi Ris. '98	Ψ	4
●	I Sodi Lunghi '99	Ψ	5
●	I Sodi Lunghi '97	ΨΨ	4
○	Vernaccia di S. Gimignano Mocali '97	ΨΨ	4
○	Vernaccia di S. Gimignano Mocali '98	ΨΨ	4
○	Vernaccia di S. Gimignano Mocali '99	ΨΨ	4

SCANSANO (GR)

Podere Aia della Macina
Loc. Fosso Lombardo, 87
58054 Scansano (GR)
tel. 0577940600

Bruna Baroncini and Franco Azara's winery goes from strength to strength. Significant investments in recent years are beginning to yield their first results in wines of ever greater depth. At our tastings, we were able to see how successfully the pair have been able to take advantage of modern cellar technology to bring out the characteristics of the local territory. In fact, we detected a change of winemaking style at Podere Aia della Macina. A comparison of the wines from 2001 and those of '99 clearly favours the younger bottles. It's true that the vintages were different, but it is also true that the '99 in question was a Riserva, a wine that should be bigger by definition. Instead, the wines we found most convincing were the younger ones, the standard Morellino and those from the Poggio Roncone and Rocca dei Venti vineyards, all 2001s. The base version has a clean nose with redcurrants, sour cherries, pepper and a vegetal vein. It has good presence and roundness on the palate, developing well through to a refreshing finish. The Poggio Roncone '01 is a different wine. It has more extract and energy, and the nose teeters on the brink of super-ripeness. The Morellino di Scansano Rocca dei Venti '01 comes from a distinct section of the estate that will soon be independent of the main property. It has a deep ruby colour, intense perfumes of ripe blackberries and cherries, and a youthfully vigorous, but elegant, body. The Riserva Terranera '99 is only decent, though. It is over-evolved on both nose and mouth.

●	Morellino di Scansano Rocca dei Venti '01	ΨΨ	4
●	Morellino di Scansano '01	ΨΨ	3*
●	Morellino di Scansano Poggio Roncone '01	ΨΨ	4
●	Morellino di Scansano Terranera Ris. '99	Ψ	4
○	Labruna '00	ΨΨ	3*
●	Morellino di Scansano '00	ΨΨ	3
●	Morellino di Scansano Terranera Ris. '98	Ψ	4

SCANSANO (GR)

CANTINA COOP.
DEL MORELLINO DI SCANSANO
LOC. SARAGIOLO
58054 SCANSANO (GR)
TEL. 0564507288 - 0564507979
E-MAIL: coopmorel@libero.it

For several years, the Cantina Cooperativa del Morellino has been doing a worthy job in the Maremma area, providing a much needed reference point for its many members. The quality of the wines has been very reliable for some time, and the products are usually well made, clean and extremely well typed. Only that extra spark of ambition to achieve greater things seemed to be missing at this Scansano-based co-operative winery. A new Morellino, however, has changed matters. It did very well this year and went through to the national finals, where it scored well. We're talking about the Sicomoro '00, made exclusively with sangiovese grapes from the oldest, and best-positioned vines at the co-operative's disposal. Sicomoro '00 macerated on the skins for about 20 days, and then did its malolactic fermentation in barrique, where it stayed for a further period of 15 months. The result is excellent, but the wine needs time in bottle to absorb its oak. As you could guess, the wood is very apparent at the moment, both on the nose and the palate. However, the richness and high quality of the extract, the remarkable volume and the intensity of the fruit hold a lot of promise for the future. The other wines presented this year included the simple, well-balanced Morellino Roggiano '01, which is as fragrantly delicious as ever, and is the Riserva San Rabano, a moderately successful bottle with a more evolved style.

SINALUNGA (SI)

FARNETELLA
FRAZ. FARNETELLA
STRADA SIENA-BETTOLLE, KM 37
53048 SINALUNGA (SI)
TEL. 0577355117
E-MAIL: felsina@dada.it

There was no Poggio Granoni at our tastings this year. The flagship label of the Castello di Farnetella estate was not made in '98 so we'll be back to discuss the wine next year, when the '99 editions comes out of the cellar. Nevertheless, this Sinalunga winery with its well-defined range offers a number of reliable, expertly typed products, each with its own characteristics. As well as DOC products and traditional Tuscan blends, Farnetella also makes a number of single-grape wines. We cannot recall, off hand, any other winery in Tuscany that releases both a Pinot Nero and a Moscato Rosa. To kick off our reviews, the Nero di Nubi is a Pinot Noir that manages to express some varietal characteristics, especially in its aromas of rhubarb, liquorice, blackberry jam, yet also shows evidence of evolution in its orange colour and edgy tannins. In contrast, the Rosa Rosae '99 is very pleasant in every way. A Moscato Rosa, it unveils a very clear nose of roses, lavender and raspberries, following this with a palate that is tasty, well sustained and nicely balanced. The same can be said for the Sauvignon '00, which has very varietal notes of asparagus, sage and elderberries, a rounded fullness on the palate and stimulating freshness in the finish. The Chianti Colli Senesi is as pleasant as ever, developing convincingly with good control thought to a finish with very decent length. The '00 version of Lucilla is better than it has been. This sangiovese and cabernet-based wine has excellent fruit.

● Morellino di Scansano Sicomoro '00	♟♟	5
● Morellino di Scansano Roggiano '01	♟	3
● Morellino di Scansano San Rabano Ris. '98	♟	5
● Morellino di Scansano Roggiano '00	♀	3
● Morellino di Scansano Vigna Benefizio '00	♀	3

● Lucilla '00	♟♟	4
● Chianti dei Colli Senesi '01	♟♟	3*
○ Sauvignon '00	♟♟	4
● Rosa Rosae '99	♟♟	4
● Nero di Nubi '98	♟	5
● Poggio Granoni '93	♟♟♟	6
● Poggio Granoni '95	♟♟♟	8
○ Sauvignon '91	♀♀	4
○ Sauvignon '95	♀♀	4
○ Sauvignon '97	♀♀	4
● Chianti Colli Senesi '98	♀♀	3
● Nero di Nubi '97	♀	5

SORANO (GR)

SASSOTONDO
LOC. PIAN DI CONATI, 52
58010 SORANO (GR)
TEL. 0564614218
E-MAIL: sassotondo@ftbcc.it

Edoardo Ventimiglia and Carla Benini should be very satisfied. Not just because their plans are proceeding well, and their wines are getting better, but also because no one will ever ask them again if it is true that ciliegiolo is the only variety in San Lorenzo. Today, there is more than one producer around Sovana and Pitigliano who makes this wine successfully. This year, Sassotondo's San Lorenzo made it into our finals, although it didn't come away with a Three Glass award. The important thing is to take part and show true Olympic spirit, some might say, but actually winning wouldn't be too much of a disappointment, either. Sassotondo had two wines in the final tastings, since the Franze '00 came out in its best version ever. Let's get on with the description of these wines. The San Lorenzo '00 is an example of a wine that has found its own identity and shows a very clear personality. The nose has notes of red berries, pepper and light touches of vanilla. It doesn't present a great deal of body on the palate, but it is well balanced, elegant in its development and has good length. Not a muscular wine, it has great freshness and is easy to drink. Franze '00 is not made from sangiovese alone for it has 25 per cent ciliegiolo in it, as well as a pinch of merlot. The result is excellent. It's a full, solid and very expressive wine, with long length in its finish. The Sassotondo Rosso '01 and the Bianco Pitigliano '01 are even better than usual. Rich and clean in their aromas, they are well balanced and very pleasing on the palate.

SORANO (GR)

PODERE SOPRA LA RIPA
FRAZ. SOVANA
LOC. PODERE SOPRA RIPA
58010 SORANO (GR)
TEL. 0564616885
E-MAIL: info@sopralaripa.com

Sopra la Ripa still has a very limited production but that hasn't stopped it coming to the notice of winelovers. The estate extends over 70 hectares, of which about ten are planted to vine. The Ventura family, who are originally from Rome, turn out a limited number of bottles because until now, on the oldest plot, planted in 1964, has been able to yield the sangiovese and ciliegiolo grapes that go into Ea and Ripa, the cellar's two reds. The new vineyards were planted in 1999 to sangiovese, alicante, cabernet sauvignon and merlot. The consultant is now the able Alberto Antonini and, partly thanks to him, the first results of the new strategy are positive and very promising. Both wines this year scored Two comfortable Glasses at our tastings, although the Ea has greater complexity and was very nearly issued with an invitation to the final tastings. This well-structured red ages in new small barrels, emerging with solid body and very close-knit, fine-grained tannins. What it needs to go all the way is better definition on the nose, which is initially a little evolved, and a finish that reflects its superb concentration. The Ripa '00 is also very good. A more immediately approachable bottle, it is very easy to like. Intense notes of black berry fruit and spice usher in a smooth, round palate with great concentration.

● San Lorenzo '00	🍷🍷	6
● Sovana Rosso Sup. Franze '00	🍷🍷	5
○ Bianco di Pitigliano '01	🍷🍷	3*
● Sassotondo Rosso '01	🍷🍷	4*
● San Lorenzo '99	🍷🍷	5
● San Lorenzo '97	🍷🍷	4
● Franze '98	🍷🍷	4
● San Lorenzo '98	🍷🍷	5
● Sassotondo Rosso '98	🍷🍷	3
● Franze '99	🍷🍷	4
● Sassotondo Rosso '99	🍷🍷	3

● Sovana Rosso Ripa '01	🍷🍷	5
● Ea '00	🍷🍷	7
● Ripa '00	🍷🍷	3*
● Ea '99	🍷🍷	4

SUVERETO (LI)

LORELLA AMBROSINI
LOC. TABARO, 96
57028 SUVERETO (LI)
TEL. 0565829301
E-MAIL: loreambrowine@katamail.com

The success that we have been expecting for years has finally arrived. The wines of Lorella Ambrosini and Roberto Fanetti have surpassed all past performances, to the point of coming very close to the fateful Three Glasses. It must be said that recently, something has changed at the winery. Since June 2001, technical supervision has been in the hands of the excellent Lorenzo Landi, but changes also depend on renewed commitment to prestigious objectives. There are plans for new vineyards, and the replacement of the existing vine stock, as well as improvements in the cellar, which include the arrival of numerous small barrels. The results were evident at our tastings. The Riflesso Antico '00, made entirely from montepulciano d'Abruzzo, was the best. It has a very dark colour, followed by a concentrated, and still rather closed, nose of blackberries, spices, chocolate, and toasty notes of oak. The entry on the palate reveals breadth and power, then there is good density from the exceptionally fine-grained tannins. Oak accompanies the intense fruit on the long finish. The Subertum '00 is also very good. A blend of sangiovese and merlot, it has concentrated aromas of sour cherries and slightly assertive vegetal nuances that have still to find balance. The mouth is round, inviting, and well balanced, with fruit and tannins melding deliciously. The standard red, Tabarò '01, gave us quite a surprise. It showed clean, ripe fruit on the nose and the palate proved to be satisfyingly full and nicely textured. Finally, the vermentino-based Armonia '01 was also good.

● Riflesso Antico '00	🍷🍷	6
● Val di Cornia Subertum '00	🍷🍷	6
● Val di Cornia Rosso Tabarò '01	🍷🍷	3
○ Armonia '01	🍷	4
● Riflesso Antico '94	🍷🍷	6
● Riflesso Antico '97	🍷🍷	6
● Subertum '97	🍷🍷	6
● Riflesso Antico '98	🍷🍷	6
● Subertum '98	🍷🍷	5
● Subertum '99	🍷🍷	6
○ Val di Cornia Bianco Tabarò '00	🍷	4

SUVERETO (LI)

GUALDO DEL RE
LOC. NOTRI, 77
57028 SUVERETO (LI)
TEL. 0565829888 - 0565829361
E-MAIL: gualdo@infol.it

A fine effort by Gualdo del Re demands our comment on a list of wines that are all very successful. Nico Rossi has cut yields in the vineyards, and changed cellar procedures, so that the richness of the fruit is preserved. Crucial to this change of approach has been technical input from the young, highly competent, technical consultant, Barbara Tamburini. Our descriptions will have to be telegraphic because there are so many wines, beginning with the Federico Primo '00, a 100 per cent cabernet sauvignon that is very well made. It shows a tidy nose of fruit, spices and faint vegetal notes. Its palate is convincingly well balanced, offering fine-grained tannins and a finish that mirrors the palate. Valid, but less structured and pervasive in the mouth, is the '99 version of the same wine. The finish is hemmed in by tannins that are a little too dry. The Gualdo Riserva '99, made exclusively from sangiovese, performed very well. It has a pure, fruit-led nose, followed by an intense, well-balanced palate that is a little closed by oak on the finish. Still very young and lacking a little balance, the Merlot l'Rennero '00 has power and energy that bode well for the future. The differences between the '00 and the l'Rennero '99, which is vegetal and a bit evolved, are already great. The two whites, the Strale, a Pinot Bianco, and the Valentina, a Vermentino, are also fairly successful. We preferred the Strale because it has a richer palate. The Aleatico Amansio '01 needs more definition in the nose, but it is sweet, powerful and shows good thrust on the palate.

● Federico Primo '00	🍷🍷	6
● Val di Cornia Rosso l'Rennero '00	🍷🍷	8
○ Strale '01	🍷🍷	5
● Val di Cornia Aleatico Amansio '01	🍷🍷	6
○ Val di Cornia Valentina '01	🍷🍷	4
● Val di Cornia Gualdo del Re Ris. '99	🍷🍷	6
● Val di Cornia Rosso Federico Primo '99	🍷🍷	6
○ Val di Cornia Bianco Eliseo '01	🍷	4
● Val di Cornia Rosso l'Rennero '99	🍷	8
● Val di Cornia Rosso Eliseo '01		4
○ Lumen '00	🍷🍷	4

SUVERETO (LI)

Incontri
Loc. Fossoni, 38
57028 Suvereto (LI)
Tel. 0565829401
E-mail: blocloko@hotmail.com

Val di Cornia wines notched up another success with a full Guide profile for Incontri, after years of brief notes in the Other Wineries section. Credit goes above all to the Lagobruno '00, which went through to our national taste-offs with consummate ease, making quite a few friends in the process. The result is not really a surprise, since for several years now the Martelli Busdraghi family cellar has been working hard to improve its wines. The vineyards have been expanded, and are now tended with greater care, while the cellar has more small wood to hand. All these changes have been made under the careful technical guidance of Alberto Antonini. As we have already said, Lagobruno made a very favourable impression at our tastings. This red may not be very original in style, but it has a wonderful bouquet and great palate. The aromas are concentrated and reveal the clear presence of blackberries and wood. There are no vegetal notes to detract from the overall harmony. The compact palate integrates the tannins very well, progressing nicely through to a finish that focuses on intense fruit. This is a very promising performance that will, we think, be matched in by future successes. The other wines presented are well made, with the Lorenzo degli Incontri '01 standing out. It is a good, vigorous wine, even if it is a tad over-extracted.

SUVERETO (LI)

Montepeloso
Loc. Montepeloso, 82
57028 Suvereto (LI)
Tel. 0565828180
E-mail: montepeloso@virgilio.it

This has been a very significant year for the wines from Suvereto, indeed, from the Val di Cornia in general. Montepeloso added its name to the ever-growing list of excellent winemakers to be found hereabouts. Fabio Chiarellotto's winery had shown signs in years past of the great potential of his wines. Until now, it had not fulfilled that promise. Sometimes it was the nose that raised eyebrows; on other occasions, there seemed to be too much wood; and once in a while, the tannins were too raw. With the 2000 vintage, the winery seems to have resolved all these problems without losing character, which never was really lacking. The 2000 Nardo, a sangiovese with ten per cent cabernet, has stunned the palates of the panel's tasters with all the makings of a great wine. The nose has not yet opened up completely and notes of oak still tend to compress it, but there is already a rich trove of fruit and minerals. The palate is solid, compact, extremely lively and expressive in its development. The length and intensity of the finish are well supported by bright, juicy tannins. Just as good, or very nearly so, is the Cabernet Sauvignon Gabbro '00. A powerful, broad red, it shows good weight and close-knit tannins. The balance on the palate isn't matched on the nose, though, which is dominated by oak. This should mellow with time in bottle. In conclusion, the Eneo '00 is more than just good.

● Lagobruno '00	🍷🍷	5
● Val di Cornia Lorenzo degli Incontri '01	🍷	4
○ Val di Cornia Vermentino Ildebrandino '01	🍷	4
○ Val di Cornia Bianco Vignanuova '01		3
● Lagobruno '99	🍷🍷	5
● Val di Cornia Rosso Rubizzo '00	🍷	3
○ Val di Cornia Vermentino Ildebrandino '00	🍷	4

● Nardo '00	🍷🍷🍷	8
● Gabbro '00	🍷🍷	8
● Eneo '00	🍷	5
● Nardo '95	🍷🍷	8
● Val di Cornia Rosso Montepeloso '95	🍷🍷	4
● Gabbro '97	🍷🍷	8
● Nardo '97	🍷🍷	8
● Gabbro '98	🍷🍷	8
● Nardo '98	🍷🍷	8
● Gabbro '99	🍷🍷	6
● Nardo '99	🍷🍷	8
● Val di Cornia Rosso Montepeloso '99	🍷🍷	4

SUVERETO (LI)

Russo
Loc. Podere La Metocchina
Via Forni, 71
57028 Suvereto (LI)
Tel. 0565845105

Until a few years ago, brothers Antonio and Michele Russo were little known in the world of wine. Actually, they weren't even thought of as winemakers by those involved in the dairy industry, and the Russos continue to obtain milk from their herd of cows. Now, the two youngsters from Campania will enjoy a little more fame, and a lot less peace and quiet than in the past, for their Barbicone has had the nerve to win Three Glasses, thanks in part to oenologist, Alberto Antonini. However, we don't want to be too flippant about this splendid new wine from Suvereto, which has everything it takes to continue being successful in the coming years. The Barbicone '00 is from sangiovese, with just a bit of colorino, and the result is a great red wine. It reveals complex aromas from its very good ripe fruit. The palate manages to reconcile power with freshness, and concentration with elegance. To top it all, it has an amazingly long finish. Proof that the brothers take things seriously also comes from their excellent Sassobucato '00, obtained from a merlot-led mix. It has very clear, intense fruit that tempts the nostrils and a soft palate that progresses silkily into a long finish where all that is missing is a touch of complexity and character. It could hardly be a coincidence that the very pleasant, nicely textured Ceppitaio '01 also won Two Glasses. Finally, the word for the Russo winery's prices is "wallet-friendly".

SUVERETO (LI)

Tua Rita
Loc. Notri, 81
57025 Suvereto (LI)
Tel. 0565829237

Tua Rita, the top winery in Suvereto and Val di Cornia, has for some time been pointing the way for other wineries in the area. In ten years, it has changed just about everything. The vine stock has been increased tenfold and the cellar, partly renovated a few years ago, has at last acquired a configuration in line with the needs of the estate and the ambitions of its owners. The cellar staff can breathe a sigh of relief after having worked for so long in difficult conditions. All this work was not at the expense of quality or the competitiveness of the wines in an increasingly difficult market. The numbers, in terms of "Glasses", have not changed much in recent years, but it should be noted that their Redigaffi '00 has produced perhaps its finest performance ever. It is a wine that has always been very characterful and muscular but on this occasion, it has also come up with exotic opulence, elegance and exceptionally complex harmony. It all starts with the aromas, which are very intense and range from blackberries, plums, graphite and yellow peppers through to oriental spices. Also excellent is the Giusto di Notri '00, from cabernet and merlot, which has a dynamic, well-balanced body. The Sangiovese Perlato del Bosco Rosso '00 is also up to snuff, unveiling a softly inviting flavour that easily won it Two Glasses. The two whites, Lodano and Perlato Bianco, are well made and well focused.

● Val di Cornia Rosso Barbicone '00	▼▼▼ 5*
● Sassobucato '00	▼▼ 5*
● Val di Cornia Rosso Ceppitaio '01	▼▼ 3*
● Pietrasca '01	▼ 3
● Barbicone '99	▼▼ 4*
● Sassobucato '99	▼▼ 5
● Val di Cornia Rosso Ceppitaio '00	▼ 2*

● Redigaffi '00	▼▼▼ 8
● Giusto di Notri '00	▼▼ 7
● Perlato del Bosco Rosso '00	▼▼ 5
○ Lodano '01	▼ 5
○ Perlato del Bosco Bianco '01	▼ 4
● Giusto di Notri '94	▼▼▼ 5
● Giusto di Notri '95	▼▼▼ 5
● Redigaffi '96	▼▼▼ 8
● Redigaffi '98	▼▼▼ 8
● Redigaffi '99	▼▼▼ 8
● Giusto di Notri '99	▼▼ 6
● Redigaffi '95	▼▼ 8
● Giusto di Notri '97	▼▼ 5
● Redigaffi '97	▼▼ 8
● Giusto di Notri '98	▼▼ 6

TAVARNELLE VAL DI PESA (FI)

IL POGGIOLINO
LOC. SAMBUCA VAL DI PESA
VIA CHIANTIGIANA, 32
50020 TAVARNELLE VAL DI PESA (FI)
TEL. 0558071635
E-MAIL: info@ilpoggiolino.com

Compared to other parts of Chianti Classico, the area around Tavarnelle does not have a very high density of wineries. That may be why it is not mentioned particularly often. We should add, though, that the wineries there are produce good results. Good things come in small packages. It is a place that has many different site climates with different characters, which does not make it easy to establish a distinctive style, or make it easy for the non-expert to recognize the wines. Coming down to particulars, there is no denying that the position of the vineyards at Il Poggiolino is, theoretically, very favourable indeed to getting ripe grapes. The Pacini family's vines grow at an altitude of 300 metres above sea level, and cover an area of ten hectares. In recent years, Poggiolino has offered winelovers reassuring evidence of consistent quality. By now, there are no surprises when we come round to taste the wines, or if there are, they are probably good ones. This year, the Riserva '99 gave a full and faithfully rendered account of the sangiovese grape it was obtained from, with notes of bay leaf, violets, and sour cherries layered over minerals. The palate is attractive and balanced, but dynamic in its progression and tidy in the finish, where light touches of oak emerge. Some signs of age were noticeable, but this is a Chianti that is fairly "Classico" in style. The simpler 2000 version didn't do badly, either, showing honest fruit and a very lively thrust on the palate.

● Chianti Cl. '00	🍷🍷	4
● Chianti Cl. Ris. '99	🍷🍷	6
● Chianti Cl. '97	🍷🍷	3
● Chianti Cl. Ris. '97	🍷🍷	4
● Le Balze '97	🍷🍷	4
● Chianti Cl. '98	🍷🍷	3
● Chianti Cl. Ris. '98	🍷🍷	4
● Chianti Cl. '99	🍷🍷	3*

TAVARNELLE VAL DI PESA (FI)

FATTORIA MONTECCHIO
FRAZ. SAN DONATO IN POGGIO
VIA MONTECCHIO, 4
50020 TAVARNELLE VAL DI PESA (FI)
TEL. 0558072907

This is an interesting comeback into the Guide for this winery, situated on the edge of the Florentine part of Chianti. It has 32 hectares under vine out of a total estate of 380 hectares. The work that proprietor, Ivo Nuti, had done with the assistance of oenologist Stefano Chioccioli, is reaping its fruits. Ten hectares have already been replanted in accordance with modern technological requirements, with a greater vine density, and there is another project afoot to construct a new cellar. This will enable vinification to be carried out in a more rational fashion, too. Fattoria Montecchio only presented two wines for tasting, but both did well. Pietracupa '98, a blend of cabernet and sangiovese, proffers a lovely red ruby colour, with distinct purple highlights. The nose is still a little closed at first, but then opens up with clear aromas of fruit, in which plums and blueberries stand out strongly. On the palate, it has a full, well-sustained body of good density, with soft, evenly distributed tannins and acidity that provides a delicious counterpoint. The rising finish is deliciously enjoyable. The Chianti Classico '99 is a lovely bright purple and the nose reveals delicate, elegant hints of raspberries and strawberries. It has a good, juicy attack in the mouth, and the finish confirms the sensations on the nose and palate. All in all, it's a delicious, linear, impressively long wine.

● Pietracupa '98	🍷🍷	5
● Chianti Cl. '99	🍷🍷	3*
● Chianti Cl. Ris. '95	🍷🍷	4
● Chianti Cl. '97	🍷🍷	4
● Chianti Cl. Ris. '97	🍷🍷	4
● Pietracupa '97	🍷🍷	5

TAVARNELLE VAL DI PESA (FI)

POGGIO AL SOLE
LOC. BADIA A PASSIGNANO
STRADA RIGNANA
50020 TAVARNELLE VAL DI PESA (FI)
TEL. 0558071504
E-MAIL: poggiosole@ftbcc.it

There is no doubt about Chianti Classico Casasilia's position as the top wine at Poggio al Sole. It looked as though the excellent Syrah might win out, but this grape, no less than sangiovese, is subject to vintage-related variations so the "battle", if one can put it in that way, is for second place in this winery's rankings. This year, we liked Seraselva a lot. In the last edition, we criticized excessive tannic hardness in this cabernet and merlot mix, but we had to change our minds in a hurry. The '99 version, notwithstanding hints of reduction in the attack on the nose, shows that it has quite remarkable structure. It is a powerful, dense and very muscular red with concentrated, close-knit tannins that in the end prove to be sweet and beautifully integrated. The Syrah is also very good in the 2000 version, but it doesn't have the depth or character of the best editions. The nose is very clean and shows typical notes of red berries, pepper and violets. In the mouth, it is lively, fresh, and well balanced but it tends to be a little unchallenging on its finish. The splendid Casasilia '99 again reveals all the personality of a great wine. The deep, very rich nose, lightly masked by extract, but is has lots of ripe fruit laced with toastiness and spices. Entry on the palate is powerful and vigorous, then deliciously robust, close-knit tannins come through. The finish is both long and complex. Our review of Giovanni Davaz's wines closes with the Chianti Classico 2000, an uncomplicated and attractively frank crowd-pleaser.

• Chianti Cl. Casasilia '99	🍷🍷🍷	7
• Seraselva '99	🍷🍷	7
• Syrah '00	🍷🍷	7
• Chianti Cl. '00	🍷	5
• Chianti Cl. Casasilia '97	🍷🍷🍷	7
• Chianti Cl. Casasilia '98	🍷🍷🍷	7
• Syrah '99	🍷🍷🍷	7
• Chianti Cl. Casasilia Ris. '95	🍷🍷	7
• Seraselva '95	🍷🍷	7
• Seraselva '96	🍷🍷	7
• Syrah '96	🍷🍷	7
• Seraselva '97	🍷🍷	7
• Syrah '97	🍷🍷	7
• Syrah '98	🍷🍷	7

TERRANUOVA BRACCIOLINI (AR)

TENUTA SETTE PONTI
FRAZ. S. GIUSTINO VALDARNO
LOC. ORENO
52020 TERRANUOVA BRACCIOLINI (AR)
TEL. 055977443
E-MAIL: tenutasetteponti@tenutasetteponti.it

The times are long past when wines in the province of Arezzo all came from a few select estates. In the last few years, we have been able to observe dynamic and very rapid growth that has brought to light a number of new producers. One of these is the Tenuta Sette Ponti, which has become quite well known in a very short time. Indeed, it has managed to win a highly merited Three Glass award for its marvellous Oreno '00, a powerful, vibrantly dynamic wine. Obtained from a blend of cabernet sauvignon, merlot and sangiovese, it presents a very dense, compact dark colour. The deep aromas are still young and have yet to open completely, showing excellent ripe fruit, with no vegetal hints, lifted by nuances of balsam and spices. In the mouth, it has great concentration and volume, revealing plenty of good extract and a long, complex finish. All this is framed in a wonderful harmony and balance that makes the wine immediately drinkable, yet promises even better for the future. The other Sette Ponti wine, Crognolo '00, is made mostly from sangiovese. It has a good full nose of black berries, spices and a faint vegetal vein. The palate is gutsy but the tannins are perhaps a little too aggressive. In short, the tastings revealed a success that rewards the determination of Antonio Moretti, owner of Sette Ponti. Obviously, Antonio's ambitions do not stop here. His excellent oenologist, Carlo Ferrini, has been warned.

• Oreno '00	🍷🍷🍷	6
• Crognolo '00	🍷🍷	5
• Oreno '99	🍷🍷	6
• Crognolo '98	🍷🍷	4
• Crognolo '99	🍷🍷	4

TERRICCIOLA (PI)

BADIA DI MORRONA
VIA DI BADIA, 8
56030 TERRICCIOLA (PI)
TEL. 0587658505 - 0587656013
E-MAIL: info@badiadimorrona.it

Renovation and development at Badia di Morrona proceed apace without a moment's pause. The vine stock continues to expand, as new plots are acquired and planted at as many as 5,500 to 6,000 vines per hectare. Sangiovese is still the dominant grape, since the owners rightly believe that both the estate and the zone around Pisa should find a way forward that involves the area's most characteristic grape. To handle the greatly increased harvest, a new and more efficient cellar is also in the pipeline. In a nutshell, the noble Gaslini family, who own the estate, are committed to making Badia di Morrona a success. Now, young Arrigo De Paoli and the seasoned expert Giorgio Marone have taken over winemaking. So, this year's tastings took place in an "in-between" phase, but prospects for the future are excellent. The surprisingly good white La Suvera '01 is admirably well-defined on the nose, with notes of tropical fruit and chamomile joining sweet vanilla tones. The palate is tidy, refreshing and balanced, and the oak is nicely calibrated. The fine sangiovese-based Vigna Alta '99 is a powerful red with broad development on the palate. It is still in need of some fine-tuning in its use of oak, which is at the moment quite noticeable. The same can be said of the N'Antia '99, which does not seem to have the same energy. The Chianti '01 is more than acceptable.

VINCI (FI)

CANTINE LEONARDO DA VINCI
VIA PROVINCIALE MERCATALE, 291
50059 VINCI (FI)
TEL. 0571902444
E-MAIL: info@cantineleonardo.it

The main aim of the Cantine Leonardo recently has been to raise the standard of their wines across the board, and maintain it over time. The winery wants to inspire confidence on the part of the public both in the cellar itself and in the large number of bottles it produces. That goal has been achieved, and now the winemakers can aim even higher. The new plantings were carefully carried out with an eye to improving quality, and ever more careful selection of grapes from member growers makes it a virtual certainty that the fruit will be perfectly ripe. At our tastings, the Merlot degli Artisti '00 did very well. This is a very approachable red with good concentration and fruit. The palate is soft and well balanced, but not very complex. Similar in style, the very dark, sangiovese-based San Zio is as precisely made as usual. The clean, intense fragrances focus on fruit and oak, which are very nicely blended. The palate is full bodied, dense and just slightly bitter on the finish. The straightforward, fruity and substantial Chianti Leonardo '01, is as successful as ever. The Chianti Riserva '99 almost won Two Glasses for its remarkable density, nicely underpinned by oak, and faint tannic roughness on the finish. The clean, agreeable chardonnay-based Ser Piero '01 has aromas of vanilla and pears leading into a succulent, rounded flavour.

○ La Suvera '01	ŸŸ	4
● Vigna Alta '99	ŸŸ	6
● N'Antia '99	Ÿ	6
● Chianti I Sodi del Paretaio '01		3
● N'Antia '93	ŸŸ	6
● N'Antia '94	ŸŸ	6
● N'Antia '95	ŸŸ	6
● N'Antia '96	ŸŸ	6
● Vigna Alta '96	ŸŸ	6
● N'Antia '97	ŸŸ	6
● Vigna Alta '97	ŸŸ	6
● N'Antia '98	ŸŸ	6
● Vigna Alta '98	ŸŸ	6

● Merlot degli Artisti '00	ŸŸ	6
● San Zio '00	ŸŸ	4*
● Chianti Leonardo '01	Ÿ	3*
○ Ser Piero '01	Ÿ	3*
○ Vin Santo Tegrino d'Anchiano '97	Ÿ	4
● Chianti Leonardo Ris. '99	Ÿ	4
● Sant'Ippolito '00		5
● San Zio '96	ŸŸ	4
● San Zio '97	ŸŸ	4
● Sant'Ippolito '97	ŸŸ	5
● San Zio '98	ŸŸ	4
● Sant'Ippolito '98	ŸŸ	5
● San Zio '99	ŸŸ	4
● Sant'Ippolito '99	ŸŸ	5

OTHER WINERIES

Poggio Saccone
Via Canali, 51
58031 Arcidosso (GR)
tel. 0564967401

This is one of the best Montecuccos we tasted this year. The nose offers some slightly forward tones with notes of blackberry jam and liquorice. These are complemented by the rounded palate, which shows grip and a finish somewhat marked by wood tannins.

● Montecucco Sangiovese '00	🍷🍷	4

Fattoria di Gratena
Loc. Pieve a Maiano
52100 Arezzo
tel. 0575368664
e-mail: gratena@katamail.com

This year's offerings made a very good impression and we're eager to see what happens next time. Meanwhile the excellent Siro '99 is concentrated, elegant and long. The other wines are characterful, particularly the Chianti.

● Siro '99	🍷🍷	6
● Chianti '00	🍷	3*
● Rapozzo da Maiano '99	🍷	4

Fattoria San Fabiano
Borghoni Baldovinetti
Via San Fabiano, 33
52020 Arezzo
tel. 057524566

The top wine, Armaiolo '00, was not available in time for our tastings, but will be released next year. Hence the pickings are a bit slim, but the Chianti '01, a very straightforward yet clean and pleasing wine, was quite well received.

● Chianti '01	🍷	3
● Piocaia '00	🍷	4

Fattoria Lilliano
Loc. Grassina - Via Lilliano, 82
50015 Bagno a Ripoli (FI)
tel. 055642602
e-mail: dimalen@tin.it

This estate near Florence has taken a big step forward. The interesting Bruzzico '99 reveals a solid, confident structure with noticeable oak. The Chianti, a simpler wine, is still very pleasant.

● Bruzzico '99	🍷🍷	5
● Chianti dei Colli Fiorentini '00	🍷	4

I Balzini
Loc. Pastine, 19
50021 Barberino Val d'Elsa (FI)
Tel. 0556580484

Vincenzo D'Isanto and Walter Filiputti have presented a new wine, I Balzini Black Label. Both of their wines have good structure and some character, indeed they almost won Two Glasses.

● I Balzini Black Label '98	▼	7
● I Balzini Rosso '98	▼	6

Casa Sola
Fraz. Cortine
50021 Barberino Val d'Elsa (FI)
Tel. 0558075028
E-mail: casasola@chianticlassico.com

All of Casa Sola's wines are good but none is really outstanding. We found the Chianti Riserva '99 the most interesting. It almost moved up a level thanks to its mineral and spice bouquet and vibrant palate.

● Chianti Cl. '00	▼	5
● Montarsiccio '98	▼	6
● Chianti Cl. Ris. '99	▼	6
○ Vin Santo '95		5

Fattoria Sant'Appiano
Sant'Appiano, 11
50021 Barberino Val d'Elsa (FI)
Tel. 0558075541
E-mail: pierfrancesco17@supereva.it

High marks again go to Sant'Appiano for its Monteloro '00 from sangiovese and colorino, a mouthfilling red with good fruit and excellent tannins. The Chianti Cottaccio '00 also shows good character. The Chianti '01 offers guaranteed drinking pleasure at a reasonable price.

● Monteloro '00	▼▼	4*
● Chianti Sup. Cottaccio '00	▼	3*
● Chianti '01	▼	2*

Spadaio e Piecorto
Via San Silvestro, 1
50021 Barberino Val d'Elsa (FI)
Tel. 0558072915 - 0558072238

Encouraging signs of general improvement emerged from our tastings of the Spadaio e Piecorto wines. The Alleroso '98 reveals good structure. The Chianti Classico '99 has clean fragrances and a well-executed, very firm palate.

● Alleroso '98	▼▼	5
● Chianti Cl. '00	▼	5
● Chianti Cl. '99	▼	5

Giovanni Chiappini
Fraz. Felciaino, 189/b
57020 Bolgheri (LI)
Tel. 0565749665

The Guado de' Gemoli, on its first time out, is distinctly interesting. The well-defined nose reveals notes of dark berries and spice with grassy nuances, then the palate unfolds with softness and verve to a vegetal but long finish. It's very good.

● Bolgheri Guado de' Gemoli '00	▼▼	6
● Felciaino '01	▼	4

Iesolana
Loc. Iesolana
52020 Bucine (AR)
Tel. 055992988
E-mail: iesolana@val.it

Il Folco '99 has solid structure and concentration. Some fine-tuning would be welcome on the nose, which for the moment shows some over-ripe tones and imperfectly amalgamated oak. The other wines are well executed, particularly the Vin Santo, which is sweet and pleasing, with some vegetal tones.

○ Vin Santo '95	▼▼	7
○ Le Ruote '00	▼	3
● Chianti '99	▼	4
● Folco '99	▼	5

Agricola Valle
Loc. Arcille - Podere ex E.M. 348
58050 Campagnatico (GR)
Tel. 0564998142

This is a very new estate but they seem to know what they're doing. The Larcille '00 is very good, with its admirable aromas of blackberry jam and spice, and a balanced flavour into which the oak has not yet fully merged. The Morellino Valle is also very enjoyable and round.

● Morellino di Scansano Larcille '00	🍷🍷	4
● Morellino di Scansano Valle '01	🍷	3*

Artimino
Fraz. Artimino
V.le Papa Giovanni XXIII, 1
59015 Carmignano (PO)
Tel. 0558751424 - 0558751424

A number of the Artimino wines seem a tad over-evolved and past their peak. The notable exceptions are the Carmignano '99, which is soft and confident in the mouth, and the Vigna dell'Iris '00, which shows solid structure, but also has rather dry tannins.

● Vigna dell'Iris '00	🍷🍷	6
● Carmignano Villa Artimino '99	🍷🍷	4
● Carmignano Vigna Grumarello '98		5
● Carmignano Villa Medicea Ris. '98		5

Castelvecchio
Loc. Seano
Via delle Mannelle, 19
59011 Carmignano (PO)
Tel. 0558705451

Strangely enough, the wine that struck us most, bearing in mind the category, was the Vin Ruspo '01, which was the best of the year in Carmignano. It's fruity, succulent, intense and extremely enjoyable. The Carmignano '99 is austere and admirable, but a bit vegetal.

○ Vin Ruspo '01	🍷	3
● Carmignano '99	🍷	4
● Barco Reale '00		3

Il Poggiolo
Via Pistoiese, 90
59015 Carmignano (PO)
Tel. 0558711242
E-mail: ilpoggiolo@ala.it

Again, the Vin Santo is the top wine at Il Poggiolo. It is classic in style and not without elegance, but it lacks the concentration it has shown in the past. The Carmignano '98 is markedly green. The Barco Reale '00 is lightweight but decently executed.

○ Vin Santo '94	🍷🍷	6
● Barco Reale '00	🍷	3
● Carmignano Ris. '98	🍷	5

Vin.Ca.
Via Candia Bassa 27/bis
54033 Carrara (MS)
Tel. 0585834217

Candia Ultramarina '01 is a tremendous success. The brilliant gold introduces and intense nose that flaunts notes of melon, apricot and vanilla, then the palate is well balanced, succulent and fairly fleshy, also showing nice length. The slightly simpler Vermentino is good, too.

○ Candia dei Colli Apuani Ultramarina '01	🍷🍷	6
○ Vermentino Vinca '01	🍷	5

Caccia al Piano 1868
Loc. Caccia al Piano
Via Bolgherese, 279
57022 Castagneto Carducci (LI)
Tel. 03356250887

This is the debut appearance of Caccia al Piano in the Guide, but its ambitions are unashamedly high. Levia Gravia '00, which is mostly merlot-based, is a powerful wine with lots of vibrant alcohol, more volume than depth and a vegetal finish. The Ruit Hora '00 is soft and agreeable, but a bit too green.

● Bolgheri Levia Gravia '00	🍷🍷	8
● Ruit Hora '00	🍷	5

Ceralti
Fraz. Donoratico
Via dei Ceralti, 77
57022 Castagneto Carducci (LI)
tel. 0565763989

The white Il Sogno di Cleofe '01 is a successful wine that almost gained Two Glasses. It is fresh, substantial and fairly long, with pleasing aromas of peach and apricot. The good Alfeo '00 is forthright and fruity, and the Bolgheri '01 is no slouch, either.

● Bolgheri Rosso Alfeo '00	5
● Bolgheri '01	4
○ Il Sogno di Cleofe '01	4

Montesalario
Loc. Montenero d'Orcia
58033 Castel del Piano (GR)
tel. 0564954173

The Montecucco Sangiovese '00 is well worth jotting down in your notebook. The dense nose is focused on notes of red berries, liquorice and vanilla. The palate reveals good body, intensity and succulence, as well as the rustic tannins of a genuine Sangiovese. The Montecucco '00 isn't bad.

● Montecucco Sangiovese '00	5
● Montecucco '00	4

Parmoleto
Loc. Montenero d'Orcia
Pod. Parmoletone
58033 Castel del Piano (GR)
tel. 0564954131

The Montecucco Sangiovese '00 has a personality of its own, with an intense bouquet of oak-derived sweet and spicy notes accompanying the fruit. The flavour is powerful, solid, well balanced and characterful. The Montecucco '00 also reveals good structure. The Riserva '99 is a bit over-evolved.

● Montecucco Sangiovese '00	4
● Montecucco Rosso '00	4
● Montecucco Sangiovese Ris. '99	5

Perazzeta
Loc. Montenero d'Orcia
Via Grandi
58033 Castel del Piano (GR)
tel. 0564954065

Perazzeta is one of the most dynamic estates in Montecucco but improvement has not yet gone as far as we hoped. The most successful of the wines presented is the Licurgo '00, which shows fair body.

● Montecucco Sangiovese Licurgo Ris. '00	5
● Montecucco Terre dei Bocci '00	4

Gagliole
Loc. Gagliole, 42
53011 Castellina in Chianti (SI)
tel. 0577740369
e-mail: azienda.gagliole@tin.it

Gagliole '00 is a very good wine. This characterful red, which only just missed making it to our finals, displays dense aromas of liquorice and toasty notes of oak. The palate is concentrated, solid and intense on the finish, which reveals slightly intrusive oak.

● Gagliole Rosso '00	6

Poggio Amorelli
Loc. Poggio Amorelli
53011 Castellina in Chianti (SI)
tel. 0571668733
e-mail: poggioamorelli@libero.it

The only wine presented by Poggio Amorelli did very well at our tastings. A Chianti Classico, it offers pleasing fruity tones, a well-balanced body with crunchy, succulent tannins and a fairly simple but admirably sound finish.

● Chianti Cl. '00	4

Tenimenti Angelini - San Leonino
Loc. Cipressi, 49
Fraz. San Leonino
53011 Castellina in Chianti (SI)
Tel. 0577740500

The Chianti Classico Monsenese '99 unveils an appealing bouquet with notes of berry fruit and vanilla. There are some forward tones on the palate, but the finish is soft and spicy. The other wines are less successful but decently executed.

● Chianti Cl. Monsenese '99	🍷🍷	5
● Chianti Cl. '00	🍷	4
● Chianti Cl. Ris. '99	🍷	5

Terre di San Leonino
Loc. La Foresta
53011 Castellina in Chianti (SI)
Tel. 0577740500

The wine that impressed us most of the ones this estate presented is Il Michelangiolo '99. It's soft, well balanced, enjoyably succulent and well defined on the finish. The Chianti Classico Barocco '99 is intense and flavoursome, but some reduced notes on the nose let it down.

● Il Michelangiolo '99	🍷🍷	5
● Chianti Cl. Barocco '99	🍷	4

Tramonti
Loc. Tramonti
53011 Castellina in Chianti (SI)
Tel. 0577740512
E-mail: dumhapoint@acadia.net

After a year in the wilderness, the Chianti Classico Tramonti is back in triumph. This excellent red boasts complexity and cleanness on the nose, then a rigorously classic style, concentration, and lively, delicious tannins on the palate. The long finish has a certain elegance.

● Chianti Cl. Tramonti '00	🍷🍷	5

Villa Rosa
Loc. Villa Rosa
53011 Castellina in Chianti (SI)
Tel. 0577743003 - 0577743067
E-mail: tenuta.villarosa@libero.it

The wines from Villa Rosa tend to be powerful. The Chianti Classico Riserva '99 is a bit over-ripe on the nose, but rich and substantial on the palate. The Chianti Classico '00 is acceptable but a bit short. The palate of the Palagione is marred by rather aggressive tannins.

● Chianti Cl. Ris. '99	🍷🍷	5
● Chianti Cl. '00	🍷	5
● Palagione '97		6

Villa Trasqua
Loc. Trasqua
53001 Castellina in Chianti (SI)
Tel. 0577743047

Villa Trasqua's Trasgaia is a wine to note. A velvet-soft, elegant red with lots of perfectly ripe fruit, it is lifted by well-integrated oak. The gap between this and the Chianti Classicos is at the moment is a big one.

● Trasgaia '98	🍷🍷	5
● Chianti Cl. '00		4
● Chianti Cl. Ris. '99		5

Fattoria dell' Aiola
Fraz. Vagliagli
53010 Castelnuovo Berardenga (SI)
Tel. 0577322615
E-mail: aiola@chianticlassico.com

The Aiola wines are well executed but lack concentration, as you can deduce from their evident diluteness and vegetal tones. The most interesting one, which approached Two Glasses, is the Rosso del Senatore. It, too, reveals some grassy notes.

● Rosso del Senatore '00	🍷	6
○ Vin Santo '96	🍷	5
● Chianti Cl. Cancello Rosso Ris. '98	🍷	5
● Chianti Cl. Ris. '99	🍷	5

Borgo Scopeto
Fraz. Vagliagli
53010 Castelnuovo Berardenga (SI)
tel. 0577848390
e-mail: caparzo@libero.it

We have an essentially favourable, if uneven, report for Borgo Scopeto. The Chianti Classico Misciano Riserva '99 offers mineral and jammy aromas, then medium body and good balance. The Chianti Classico Riserva '99 is less confident. It has decent weight but the over-evolved tones are unwelcome.

● Chianti Cl. Misciano Ris. '99	🍷🍷	5
● Chianti Cl. Ris. '99	🍷	5

Canonica a Cerreto
Fraz. Vagliagli
53019 Castelnuovo Berardenga (SI)
tel. 0577363261
e-mail: info@canonicacerreto.it

Good results from the restructuring under way at this Chianti estate are already coming through. The only wine we tasted this year, the Chianti Classico '00, did extremely well. It shows a confident, meaty, evenly sweet palate, well sustained by oak.

● Chianti Cl. '00	🍷🍷	4*

Podere Le Boncie
Loc. San Felice - Strada delle Boncie, 5
tel. 0577359383
53019 Castelnuovo Berardenga (SI)
e-mail: leboncie@libero.it

Giovanna Morganti produces only one wine. She makes it well and refuses to cut any corners. This is a true Sangiovese, with all the rough edges, recalcitrant tannins and lively acidity the variety implies. It also has lots of character, authentic flavour and an original drinking style.

● Chianti Cl. Le Trame '99	🍷🍷	4

Borgo Casignano
Via Casignano, 212
52020 Cavriglia (AR)
tel. 055 967090
e-mail: fatbel@tin.it

Borgo Casignano has eight hectares planted to sangiovese and other native varieties. The sangiovese-based Solatio '00 made a good impression with its vibrant, agreeably nervy and very clean palate. The Chianti '99 is better than just respectable.

● Solatio '00	🍷🍷	4
● Chianti '99	🍷	3

Fattoria di Petriolo
Via di Petriolo, 7
50050 Cerreto Guidi (FI)
tel. 0571509491

This promising estate produces remarkably fine wines. The very good Golpaja '00, from sangiovese and merlot, is very dense, with lots of fruit nicely underpinned by oak. The more than merely good Chianti almost won Two Glasses.

● Golpaja '00	🍷🍷	4
● Chianti Villa Petriolo '01	🍷	2*

Fattoria di Fiano
Loc. Fiano - Via di Firenze, 11
50050 Certaldo (FI)
tel. 0571669048

Ugo Bing's Fianesco is extremely well made. Soft, meaty and redolent of cocoa and pepper, with some vegetal notes. The surprising Chianti Colli Fiorentini '00 shows more extract than one expects from its category. The Vin Santo is a bit rough.

● Fianesco '00	🍷🍷	5
● Chianti Colli Fiorentini '00	🍷	3*
○ Vin Santo '97		5

La Cignozza
Via Cavine e Valli, 63
53042 Chianciano Terme (SI)
Tel. 057830279

This recently re-established estate has made a more than satisfactory debut. The Peregrinus '00, a well-extracted red with faint vegetal nuances on the finish, did quite well. The Chianti Superiore '00 is very respectable, while the Chianti '00 is rather light.

● Chianti Sup. '00	♇ 4
● Peregrinus '00	♇ 5
● Chianti '00	3

Montecucco
Loc. Montecucco
58044 Cinigiano (GR)
Tel. 0564999029
E-mail: dunale@tin.it

The Montecucco area certainly has lots of potential but we shall have to wait a while before it is exploited to the full. The wines from Tenuta di Montecucco are clean and well made, revealing good raw material, but they lack a distinctive personality of their own.

● Montecucco Passionaia '01	♇ 4
● Montecucco Sangiovese Ris. '98	♇ 5

Le Capannacce
Fraz. Pari
Loc. Capannacce
58040 Civitella Paganico (GR)
Tel. 0564908848 - 0564908854

Only one wine was presented, but it is an excellent one. Poggio Crocino '99 is made from sangiovese with some syrah and grenache. The very rich nose displays notes of dark berries and oriental spice, with toasty and vegetal nuances. The palate is soft and enticing, with a slightly bitter finish.

● Poggio Crocino '99	♇♇ 6

Frascole
Via di Frascole, 27
50062 Dicomano (FI)
Tel. 0558386340

The Chianti Rufina '00 flaunts an intense and very rich bouquet. The flavour is soft, fairly full and well balanced. The Chianti Rufina Riserva Il Santo is admirably true to type and exhibits a rounded palate with some forward tones. This fast emerging estate is one to watch.

● Chianti Rufina '00	♇♇ 4
● Chianti Rufina Il Santo Ris. '99	♇ 4

Piazzano
Via di Piazzano, 5
50053 Empoli (FI)
Tel. 0571994032
E-mail: fattoriadipiazzano@libero.it

The Chianti Rio Camerata '01, a straightforward and very well-made wine, stands out for its charm and good raw material. The Vin Santo '94 is a bit rustic but shows nice character. The Chianti Rio Camerata Riserva '99 has plenty of grip and more than enough oak.

○ Vin Santo '94	♇♇ 5
● Chianti Rio Camerata '01	♇ 3*
● Chianti Rio Camerata Ris. '99	♇ 4
○ Vin Santo '94	♇♇ 5

Fattoria Uccelliera
Via Pontita, 26
56043 Fauglia (PI)
Tel. 050662747
E-mail: info@uccelliera.it

The Castellaccio Rosso '99 offers aromas of dark berries, cocoa and spice. The palate is soft, well-balanced and nicely backed up by oak. It is already very good, and should get better with time. As for the other wines, the Chianti, is confident and pleasing by nature, and drinks very well.

● Castellaccio Rosso '99	♇♇ 5
● Chianti '00	♇ 3

Bibi Graetz
Via di Vincigliata, 19
50014 Fiesole (FI)
tel. 055599556
e-mail: bibi.graetz@virgilio.it

Testamatta is one of those reds that are almost impossible to find in the shops. As a result, it is equally impossible to resist for winelovers who like treasure hunts. Apart from anything else, it is an excellent bottle with an intense palate and lingering finish.

● Testamatta '00	🍷🍷	8

Il Grillesino
Borgo degli Albizi, 14
50123 Firenze
tel. 055243101

The most important wines made by the Compagnia del Vino come from the Il Grillesino estate in the Maremma. The very fine Ceccante '99 is concentrated and dense, with excellent robust tannins. The two Morellinos are also good and well executed.

● Ceccante '99	🍷🍷	6
● Morellino di Scansano Ris. '00	🍷	5
● Morellino di Scansano '01	🍷	4

Pasolini Dall'Onda
P.zza Mazzini, 10
50021 Firenze
tel. 0558075019
e-mail: info@pasolinidallonda.com

The red San Zenobi '99, from sangiovese, merlot and cabernet, shows a nose of tobacco and leather, with not very generous fruit. The palate has good body and fair balance, but is a bit short on the finish.

● San Zenobi '99	🍷🍷	6
○ Montepetri '01		3
● Chianti Montoli Ris. '97		5

Le Miccine
S.S. Traversa Chiantigiana
53013 Gaiole in Chianti (SI)
tel. 0577749526
e-mail: clw@lemiccine.com

In neither of the wines we tasted was the oak completely integrated. In the Riserva Don Alberto, it tends to rob the wine of character, whereas in the Chianti '00 it doesn't stop the fruit from dominating the situation and providing a broad, very pleasing palate.

● Chianti Cl. '00	🍷🍷	5
● Chianti Cl. Don Alberto Ris. '99	🍷	6

Castello di Lucignano
Loc. Lucignano
53013 Gaiole in Chianti (SI)
tel. 0577747810
e-mail: gkslucignano@libero.it

Il Sommo '00 has good weight and roundness on the palate, but the finish is a little dry and bitter. The Riserva '99 is quite confident, but also somewhat unbalanced on both nose and palate. The Chianti Classico '00 is a bit cloying, as well as masked by the oak.

● Il Sommo '00	🍷	7
● Chianti Cl. Ris. '99	🍷	6
● Chianti Cl. '00		4

Rietine
Loc. Rietine, 27
53013 Gaiole in Chianti (SI)
tel. 0577731110 - 0577738482
e-mail: fattoria_di_rietine@hotmail.com

High marks for Rietine and a Chianti Classico Riserva '98 with good stuffing, generous progression on the palate and ripe tannins. The persuasive Chianti Classico '00 is well balanced and complex on the palate. We had another taste of the nice Tiziano '97, which we reviewed last year.

● Chianti Cl. Ris. '98	🍷🍷	5
● Chianti Cl. '00	🍷	4

Gabriele Da Prato
Loc. Ponte di Campia
c/o Osteria Pascolana
55027 Gallicano (LU)
Tel. 0583766142

The wines are good, with blackcurrant and pepper aromas and succulent drinkability. But what amazes us is that they come from Garfagnana. They are the first wines produced here, indeed the first "mountain" wines to be made in Tuscany. The cellar will soon also be releasing a vineyard selection.

● Melograno '00	🍷	4
● Melograno '01	🍷	4

San Vettore
Via San Vettore, 51
50050 Gambassi Terme (FI)
Tel. 0571678005 - 0571678035
E-mail: sanvettore@libero.it

The best of the very well-made wines from San Vettore is the Chianti, with its aromas suggesting dark berries and pepper, and its fresh, dense and well-balanced palate. The intensely fragrant Traminer is quite interesting, and the Cabernet is original and enjoyable.

● Cabernet Sauvignon '00	🍷	5
● Chianti '00	🍷	3*
● Merlot Maria Teresa '00	🍷	5
○ Traminer '00	🍷	4

Tenuta La Novella
Loc. San Polo in Chianti
Via Musignana, 11
50020 Greve in Chianti (FI)
Tel. 0558337749

Tenuta La Novella's wines are worth investigating. The very successful Chianti Classico Riserva '99 exhibits a dense bouquet with flower and fruit tones, leading to an invigorating, attractive palate with a certain elegance. The fair Chianti Classico '00 is fresh and harmonious.

● Chianti Cl. Ris. '99	🍷🍷	6
● Chianti Cl. '00	🍷	4

Pian Del Gallo
Loc. Pian del Gallo
Via di San Martino a Uzzano
50022 Greve in Chianti (FI)
Tel. 055853365

This is the debut appearance in the Guide for Pian del Gallo, which presented just one noteworthy wine. The Chianti Classico '00 shows a slightly over-ripe tone on the nose, but the palate makes up for it with charming freshness and a firm structure with lively, succulent tannins.

● Chianti Cl. '00	🍷🍷	4

Terreno
Via Citille, 4
50022 Greve in Chianti (FI)
Tel. 055854001
E-mail: terreno@dada.it

The range of wines from this estate always includes something interesting, but the general level is uneven. The Chianti Classico Riserva '99, for example, is intense and chewy, if a bit vegetal, whereas the Chianti Classico '00 is thinner and somewhat over-evolved.

● Chianti Classico Ris. '99	🍷🍷	5
● Chianti Classico '00		4

Villa Calcinaia
Fraz. Greti - Via Citille, 84
50022 Greve in Chianti (FI)
Tel. 055854008
E-mail: villacalcinaia@villacalcinaia.it

Villa Calcinaia is on the way up and we'll be looking for confirmation next year. Their fine Chianti Classico '00 offers a rich bouquet and a dynamic, pleasing flavour. The quite expressive Casarsa '99, from merlot, shows slightly prominent oak. The other wines are better than just all right.

● Chianti Cl. '00	🍷🍷	4
● Casarsa '99	🍷🍷	5
● Chianti Cl. Ris. '99	🍷	5
○ Vin Santo '99	🍷	5

Tenuta Belguardo
Loc. VIII Zona
Fraz. Montebottigli
58100 Grosseto
tel. 057773571

The 2000 debut release of Tenuta Belguardo, a blend of cabernet, sangiovese and merlot, coincides with an extension of the vineyards, which now cover 75 hectares. So, this Maremma branch of Castello di Fonterutoli obviously has high ambitions. Try the wine and see for yourself.

- Tenuta Belguardo '00   6

Val delle Rose
Loc. Poggio La Mozza
58100 Grosseto
tel. 0564409062
e-mail: vdr@valdellerose.it

The wines from the Cecchi family's Val delle Rose keep getting better. The very fine Morellino '01 confirms an upward trend from vintage to vintage, but the Riserva '99 is also quite good and nearly won Two Glasses.

- Morellino di Scansano '01   4
- Morellino di Scansano Ris. '99   5

Fattoria Collazzi
Loc. Tavarnuzze
Via Colleramole, 101
50029 Impruneta (FI)
tel. 0552022528

Collazzi, a blend of cabernet sauvignon and merlot, seems, on just its second year out, likely to become a seriously good red. It offers lovely concentration, with lots of fruit and layers of admirably integrated tannins. The depth on the palate is excellent.

- Collazzi '00   5

Fattoria di Bagnolo
Loc. Bagnolo
Via Imprunetana per Tavarnuzze, 48
50023 Impruneta (FI)
tel. 0552313403

The Caprorosso '00, made from sangiovese and cabernet sauvignon, makes a big impression. It's Bagnolo's top wine, and a very promising one. Powerful and confident, it reveals deliciously ripe tannins. The other wines are well-made if not outstanding.

- Caprorosso '00   5
- Chianti dei Colli Fiorentini '00   3
- Chianti Colli Fiorentini Ris. '99   4

Fattoria di Romignano
Via Setteponti Levante, 30
52024 Loro Ciuffenna (AR)
tel. 055977635

The cabernet and sangiovese blend called Sabòt '00 has a broad bouquet of spice and dark berries. The palate is even and full-bodied, unveiling lots of good tannins and an intense, enjoyable finish. In other words, it's a very pleasant surprise.

- Sabòt '00   5

La Badiola
Loc. San Pancrazio - Via del Parco, 10
55010 Lucca
tel. 0583309633
e-mail: info@labadiola.it

An excellent performance from the Villa Flora '99, which follows a vegetal and blackcurrant jam-like nose with an elegant, soft and lingering flavour. The Merlot '99 is fair but a bit uneven, while the Colline Lucchesi Rosso is well typed and pleasant.

- Villa Flora '99   4
- Colline Lucchesi Rosso '00   3
- Colline Lucchesi Merlot '99   4

Boschetto di Montiano
Loc. Boschetto
58051 Magliano in Toscana (GR)
tel. 0564589621

The Verriolo '99, a blend of merlot, cabernet and sangiovese, walked off with Two Glasses, thanks to its full-bodied, round, close-knit structure, slightly marred by over-ripe tones. The two Morellinos are quite good but we prefer the '01, which is distinctly more invigorating.

- Verriolo '9 — 4
- Morellino di Scansano '00 — 3
- Morellino di Scansano '01 — 3

Costanza Malfatti
Loc. S. Andrea - Pod. 351
58051 Magliano in Toscana (GR)
tel. 0564592535

Costanza Malfatti's Morellino has again done extremely well. It's a dense, concentrated wine with aromas of clove and coffee against a background of fruit. The finish is intense and fairly long. It scored high marks, although we would prefer less intrusive oak.

- Morellino di Scansano '00 — 4

Mantellassi
Loc. Banditaccia, 26
58051 Magliano in Toscana (GR)
tel. 0564592037
e-mail: info@fatt-mantellassi.it

Mantellassi wines are generally well made and reasonably good, although this year there is nothing exceptional. The Morellino San Giuseppe '01, which is intense and nicely structured, is a fine example of its wine type.

- Morellino di Scansano San Giuseppe '01 — 4
- Morellino di Scansano Le Sentinelle Ris. '99 — 6
- Querciolaia '99 — 6
- Versoio '99 — 6

Fattoria Acquaviva
Loc. Montemerano - Loc. Acquaviva
58050 Manciano (GR)
tel. 0564602890
e-mail: fattoria@relaisvillaacquaviva.com

The Riserva Bracaleta '98 is a distinctly good Morellino. We almost gave it Two Glasses for its attractively round, well-balanced palate, although the oak tends to make its presence felt. The Morellino '01 is simpler but agreeable.

- Morellino di Scansano Bracaleta Ris. '98 — 4
- Morellino di Scansano Nero '01 — 3

La Busattina
Fraz. San Martino sul Fiora
58014 Manciano (GR)
tel. 0564607823
e-mail: busattina@tiscalinet.it

The grape varieties in the La Busattina wines are sangiovese and ciliegiolo, both redolent of red berries and pepper. Those notes are expressed with greater breadth and depth in the Terre Eteree '01. The palate of both wines, however, is fresh, well-balanced and very enjoyable.

- Sovana Rosso Terre Eteree '01 — 4
- Ciliegiolo '00 — 4

Campogiovanni
Fraz. Sant'Angelo in Colle
53020 Montalcino (SI)
tel. 0577864001
e-mail: info@agricolasanfelice.it

Campogiovanni's Brunello '97 is quite excellent. The bouquet is still dumb and masked by oak. The palate is powerful, precise and well sustained as it unfolds through to the long, fresh fruit finish. A significant performance.

- Brunello di Montalcino '97 — 7

Casanuova delle Cerbaie
Podere Casanova delle Cerbaie, 335
53024 Montalcino (SI)
Tel. 0577849284
E-mail: casanuovacerbaie@jumpy.it

The Brunello '97 is splendid. The broad bouquet offers varietal notes of liquorice, plum and tobacco, with mineral nuances. The palate has crunchy, succulent tannins, well-sustained development and an intense finish. After this success, we await more good things from Casanuova delle Cerbaie.

- Brunello di Montalcino '97 — 7

Casisano Colombaio
Loc. Collina Pod. Colombaio 336
53024 Montalcino (SI)
Tel. 0577835540 - 0577849087
E-mail: tatiana@brunello.org

The Brunello Vigna del Colombaiolo '97 is very successful. Vigorous and energetic, it has robust tannins and a substantial dose of oak. The other wines, which do not show much incisiveness or vitality, are not up to the same level.

- Brunello di Montalcino Vigna del Colombaiolo '97 — 8
- Brunello di Montalcino '97 — 6
- Rosso di Montalcino '00 — 4
- Rosso di Casisano '98 — 5

Castelli Martinozzi
Loc. Villa S. Restituta
53024 Montalcino (SI)
Tel. 057784856

Castelli Martinozzi has again shown it knows how to make a good wine. In this case, it is the Brunello '97, which boasts an intense, invigorating flavour with tasty tannins and a robust finish. The less brilliant Rosso di Montalcino is uneven and has a bitter finish.

- Brunello di Montalcino '97 — 6
- Rosso di Montalcino '00 — 4

Tenuta Di Sesta
Fraz. Castelnuovo dell'Abate
53020 Montalcino (SI)
Tel. 0577835612
E-mail: giovanni.ciacci@tin.it

There are still ups and downs at Sesta. The Brunello '97 did well, with its interesting structure, despite the oak that rather masks the finish. The Rosso di Montalcino, however, has an unfocused nose and a not altogether settled palate.

- Brunello di Montalcino '97 — 8
- Rosso di Montalcino '00 — 5

Donna Olga
Loc. Friggiali
Strada Maremmana
53024 Montalcino (SI)
Tel. 0577849314

Donna Olga is a new estate line which Olga Peluso, the owner of Centolani, has inaugurated with a Brunello '97 and a Rosso '00. Her laudable aim is to donate the profits to charity. And the wines are rather good.

- Brunello di Montalcino Donna Olga '97 — 7
- Rosso di Montalcino '00 — 4

Fanti - La Palazzetta
Fraz. Castelnuovo dell'Abate
B.go di Sotto, 25
53020 Montalcino (SI)
Tel. 0577835631

This is one of the most reliable estates in Montalcino. The very good Brunello '97 boasts a well-rounded palate that expands nicely. The Rosso di Montalcino '00 offers notes of raspberry and blackcurrant on the nose and a balanced, pleasing flavour.

- Brunello di Montalcino '97 — 6
- Rosso di Montalcino '00 — 4

Fattoi
Loc. Santa Restituta
Podere Capanna, 101
53024 Montalcino (SI)
Tel. 0577848613

Fattoi's Brunello '97 only just missed a place at the final tastings. It is, in other words, one of the best Brunellos from its vintage, thanks to a soft, well-balanced, dynamic palate with an intense finish. We were less enamoured of the Rosso, which is rather muffled on the nose.

● Brunello di Montalcino '97	🍷🍷	6
● Rosso di Montalcino '00		5

La Fiorita
Fraz. Castelnuovo dell'Abate
Piaggia della Porta, 3
53024 Montalcino (SI)
Tel. 0577835657

The bouquet of La Fiorita's Brunello '97 is very expressive of its terroir, bringing together notes of tobacco with mineral and light toasty nuances. The palate is soft, but just a little hard on the finish. This excellent Brunello almost made it to our finals.

● Brunello di Montalcino '97	🍷🍷	8
● Laurus '99	🍷	4

Greppone Mazzi - Tenimenti Ruffino
Loc. Greppone
53024 Montalcino (SI)
Tel. 05583605
E-mail: info@ruffino.it

With its customary precision, Greppone Mazzi's Brunello faithfully reflects the characteristics of the sangiovese grape. Although somewhat closed on the nose, it develops in an orderly, well-rounded fashion on the palate. The finish is somewhat dry, but the style of the wine is convincing.

● Brunello di Montalcino '97	🍷🍷	8

Il Colle
Loc. Il Colle
53024 Montalcino (SI)
Tel. 0577848295

Il Colle presented good wines this year. The Brunello '97 may not be enormous, but it does have characteristic aromas of bay leaf and a well-balanced, softly pleasing flavour. We also liked the fragrantly fruity, dense Rosso.

● Brunello di Montalcino '97	🍷🍷	6
● Rosso di Montalcino '00	🍷	4

Il Grappolo-Fortius
Loc. Sant'Angelo in Colle
53020 Montalcino (SI)
Tel. 0574813730

The wines from Il Grappolo are not known for massive structure or great complexity, but they are well made, extremely harmonious and graced with well-calibrated oak. In the Sassocheto, we admired the rounded flavour, and in the Brunello the soundness of the fruit.

● Brunello di Montalcino '97	🍷🍷	6
● Sassocheto '97	🍷🍷	5

Il Marroneto
Loc. Madonna delle Grazie
53024 Montalcino (SI)
Tel. 0577849382 - 0577846075
E-mail: ilmarroneto@ftbcc.it

Marroneto's Brunello is amongst the most reliable around. Well-executed and harmonious, it shows excellent definition and good development on the palate. This is a small estate, but one to watch.

● Brunello di Montalcino '97	🍷🍷	8

Tenuta La Fuga
Loc. Camigliano
53024 Montalcino (SI)
Tel. 0577816039
E-mail: tenutalafuga@tin.it

This compact estate recently became part of the Folonari group. The palate of the very good Brunello '97 is soft, powerful, even and decently long. The bouquet, which is dominated by over-ripe tones, is less successful.

• Brunello di Montalcino '97	🍷	7

La Serena
Loc. Podere Rasa I°, 133
53024 Montalcino (SI)
Tel. 0577848659

La Serena is continuing to produce very good, carefully executed wines. The Brunello '97 is elegant in character, with well-balanced structure and smooth, nicely calibrated tannins. The Rosso di Montalcino '00 is dense and attractively fruity, then progression in the mouth is generous and soft.

• Rosso di Montalcino '00	🍷	4
• Brunello di Montalcino '97	🍷	6

Maurizio Lambardi
Podere Canalicchio di Sotto, 8
53024 Montalcino (SI)
Tel. 0577848476

Lambardi's Brunello '97 is one of the most traditional and most successful. The bouquet offers distinct spice and mineral tones, and the palate is vigorous, powerful and well-sustained, if not extremely long. It missed our Three Glass finals by a hair's breadth, but is excellent all the same.

• Brunello di Montalcino '97	🍷	7

Le Chiuse
Loc. Pullera, 228
53024 Montalcino (SI)
Tel. 0577848595 - 055597052
E-mail: info@lechiuse.com

Although Le Chiuse does produce some splendid wines, its range continues to be somewhat inconsistent. This year, for instance, we were not altogether pleased with the Rosso '00, which has a slightly muffled nose, whereas the Brunello, with its good body and length, did very well.

• Brunello di Montalcino '97	🍷	7
• Rosso di Montalcino '00		4

Le Gode di Ripaccioli
Loc. Le Gode, 343
53024 Montalcino (SI)
Tel. 0577848547 - 0577847089
E-mail: azienda.legode@libero.it

One excellent Brunello and a mediocre Rosso testify to the fact that Le Gode di Ripaccioli has not yet achieved reliably consistent quality. It does have talent, though. Their Brunello, dense, soft, elegant and deep, is amongst the best of its vintage.

• Brunello di Montalcino '97	🍷	7
• Rosso di Montalcino '00		5

Le Macioche
Loc. Palazzina
S. P. 55 di Sant'Antimo km 4,85
53024 Montalcino (SI)
Tel. 0577849168

The '97 is probably the best Brunello ever produced by Le Macioche. It is soft, lively, intense and lingering, with a distinct contribution from the oak. The correct, but somewhat thin, Rosso di Montalcino '00 is less successful.

• Brunello di Montalcino '97	🍷	7
• Rosso di Montalcino '00		5

Mocali
Loc. Mocali
53024 Montalcino (SI)
Tel. 0577849485

The wines from Mocali generally show character and this year they are quite consistent in quality. One might have expected a bit more from the Brunello '97, which reveals good texture but has some rather super-ripe notes on the nose.

● I Piaggioni '00	▼ 4
○ Moscadello di Montalcino V.T. '00	▼ 6
● Rosso di Montalcino '00	▼ 5
● Brunello di Montalcino '97	▼ 7

Cantina di Montalcino
Loc. Val di Cava
53024 Montalcino (SI)
Tel. 0577848704
E-mail: info@cantinadimontalcino.it

The Cantina di Montalcino produces well-made, even and rather substantial wines. Both the Rosso and the Brunello came close to getting Two Glasses and the Villa di Corsano boasts rounded fruit and a full body. Although technically impeccable, they could do with more distinctive character.

● Villa di Corsano '00	▼▼ 6
● Rosso di Montalcino '00	▼ 4
● Brunello di Montalcino '97	▼ 6

Franco Pacenti
Via Canalicchio di Sopra, 6
53024 Montalcino (SI)
Tel. 0577849277

The Brunello '97 is very good. Apart from some oak-derived dryness, it exhibits excellent balance and a soft palate with a well-sustained and harmonious development. The other wines we tasted are a tad forward and less successful.

● Brunello di Montalcino '97	▼▼ 7
● Il Bersaglio '00	3
● Rosso di Montalcino '00	4

Palagetto
Fraz. Castelnuovo dell'Abate
Loc. La Bellarina
53020 Montalcino (SI)
Tel. 0577943090

Both of Luano Niccolai's wines strolled off with Two Glasses. The Brunello '97 offers well-rounded structure that develops nicely, underpinned by the oak. The Solleone '00 has similar qualities but can show more fruit, given its youth.

● Solleone '00	▼▼ 5
● Brunello di Montalcino Podere Bellarina '97	▼▼ 6

Pian delle Vigne
Loc. Pian delle Vigne
53024 Montalcino (SI)
Tel. 0577816066
E-mail: piandellevigne@antinori.it

There are 60 hectares under vine on this estate, which belongs to Antinori. The Brunello '97 shows excellent balance and a fresh, stimulating dense flavour with succulent tannins. It is a good enough wine, but does not have great personality.

● Brunello di Montalcino '97	▼▼ 7

Pian dell'Orino
Loc. Pian dell'Orino, 189
53024 Montalcino (SI)
Tel. 3355250115

The very fine Brunello '97 has a tight-knit, dense texture and good development on the palate, backed up by solid, concentrated tannins. The Piandorino '97 is soft and well-balanced, revealing faint vegetal nuances. The Rosso '00 is well-typed and enjoyable. This is an estate worth watching.

● Brunello di Montalcino '97	▼▼ 7
● Rosso di Montalcino '00	▼ 4
● Piandorino '97	▼ 5

Poggio Castellare
Fraz. Castelnuovo dell'Abate
Loc. Poggio Il Castellare
53020 Montalcino (SI)
Tel. 0577940600

Poggio Castellare belongs to the Baroncinis, a long-established San Gimignano family. The wines, which are making their debut, made a very good impression. The excellent Brunello '97 boasts fruit, cleanness and a well-proportioned structure. The very enjoyable Rosso is distinctly fruity.

● Brunello di Montalcino '97	🍷🍷	6
● Rosso di Montalcino '00	🍷	4

Giacomo Marengo
Fraz. Capraia - Loc. Palazzuolo
52048 Monte San Savino (AR)
Tel. 0575847083
E-mail: marengoe@tin.it

The successful Chianti La Commenda Riserva '97 offers a liquorice fragrance and a firm, rounded palate, with a well-sustained finish. The fair Castello di Rapale '98 has a juicy flavour, underpinned by lively tannins. The Stroncoli shows good structure and rather evolved notes.

● Chianti La Commenda Ris. '97	🍷🍷	5
● Chianti Castello di Rapale Ris. '98	🍷	4
● Stroncoli '98	🍷	5

Podere Aione
Loc. Aione
56040 Montecatini Val di Cecina (PI)
Tel. 058830339

The red Aione, made mostly from sangiovese, is very good. It has considerable style, which comes out in aromas of black cherry and pepper, with light vegetal nuances. The vigorous, firm palate is a bit held back by wood tannins, but is nonetheless promising.

● Aione '99	🍷🍷	6

Petrognano
Via Bottinaccio, 116
50056 Montelupo Fiorentino (FI)
Tel. 0571542001 - 0571913795
E-mail: petrogn@tin.it

None of the wines won Two Glasses but both the Montevago '99 and the Chianti Riserva '97 came very close. They are well-made, medium-bodied wines, and the Riserva '97, curiously enough, boasts admirable freshness.

● Chianti '00	🍷	3
● Chianti Ris. '97	🍷	4
● Montevago '99	🍷	4

Corte alla Flora
Via di Cervognano, 23
53045 Montepulciano (SI)
Tel. 0578766003
E-mail: corteflora@tin.it

The Nobile '99 nearly picked up Two Glasses for its intense, delightfully spicy flavour. The Rosso di Montepulciano '00 is straightforward and very enjoyable. The estate belongs to one Signor Cragnotti, the owner of the Lazio soccer team.

● Nobile di Montepulciano '99	🍷	4
● Rosso di Montepulciano '00	🍷	3
● Nobile di Montepulciano '98	🍷	4

Crociani
Via del Poliziano, 15
53045 Montepulciano (SI)
Tel. 0578757919
E-mail: info@crociani.it

Crociani did fairly well last year and a good bit better this time, particularly with the Nobile '99, which is dense, tightly knit and well-balanced. The fine Vin Santo '91 is elegant and austere. The other wines are decent and well executed.

● Nobile di Montepulciano '99	🍷🍷	4
● Chianti Colli Senesi '01	🍷	2*
● Rosso di Montepulciano '01	🍷	3
○ Vin Santo '91	🍷	7

Ercolani
S. S. 146 per Chianciano, 37
53045 Montepulciano (SI)
tel. 0578758711 - 0578716901

This space is getting to be rather tight for Ercolani. All the wines are well-made, fairly uncomplicated and pleasing. The Nobile '99, which is more complex, shows good structure underpinned by succulent tannins.

● Nobile di Montepulciano '99	ŸŸ	5
● Rosso di Montepulciano '01	Ÿ	4
● Salciaia '01	Ÿ	4
● Rosso Ercolani	Ÿ	4

Il Faggeto
Fraz. S. Albino
Loc. Fontelellera
53040 Montepulciano (SI)
tel. 0577940600

The Nobile '99, which is distinctly better than previous versions, offers a clean bouquet with notes of black cherry and liquorice, then a soft, intense palate with good consistency on the finish. The Rosso di Montepulciano '01 is simpler but agreeable.

● Nobile di Montepulciano Pietra del Diavolo '99	ŸŸ	4
● Rosso di Montepulciano '01	Ÿ	3

Fattoria La Braccesca
Fraz. Gracciano - S. S. 326, 15
53040 Montepulciano (SI)
tel. 0578724252
e-mail: labraccesca@antinori.it

The Merlot did not appear at our tastings and the other wines did not shine particularly brightly. All things considered, we liked the Rosso di Montepulciano Sabazio '01 best, which is straightforward, fruity and pleasing.

● Rosso di Montepulciano Sabazio '01	Ÿ	3
● Nobile di Montepulciano '99	Ÿ	5

Fattoria Le Casalte
Fraz. S. Albino
Via del Termine, 2
53045 Montepulciano (SI)
tel. 0578799138 - 069323090

There are quite a number of good things to say here. The Nobile Riserva '98 is substantial, tightly knit and nicely complex in the mouth. The Nobile '99 scored almost as high with its nice complexity and well-balanced flavour. The other wines did not do as well, but quality is improving.

● Nobile di Montepulciano Ris. '98	ŸŸ	5
● Nobile di Montepulciano '99	Ÿ	4
● Rosso di Montepulciano '01		3
○ Vin Santo '94		5

Azienda Agricola Lombardo
Fraz. Gracciano - Via Umbria, 12
53040 Montepulciano (SI)
tel. 0578708321
e-mail: info@cantinalombardo.it

The Vin Santo '97 is well-made, full-bodied and harmonious. Sadly, the two Nobiles are less brilliant than they have been in the past. The '99 is a bit dry on the palate from insufficient fruit, and the Riserva '98 shows some reduced notes on the nose and a flavour dominated by oak.

○ Vin Santo '97	ŸŸ	5
● Nobile di Montepulciano '99	Ÿ	4
● Nobile di Montepulciano Ris. '98		5

Palazzo Vecchio
Fraz. Valiano - Via Terrarossa, 5
53040 Montepulciano (SI)
tel. 0578724170 - 0248009704
e-mail: marcosbernadori@tin.it

The Rosso dell'Abate Chiarini '99 is very good indeed. It's intense, rich and very concentrated, with slightly excessive oak. The Nobile Riserva '98 did well, too. It is soft on the palate and almost picked up Two Glasses of its own. The Nobile '99 is decent enough.

● Rosso dell'Abate Chiarini '99	ŸŸ	5
● Nobile di Montepulciano Ris. '98		5
● Nobile di Montepulciano '99	Ÿ	4

Massimo Romeo
Fraz. Gracciano di Montepulciano
Podere Corsica, 25
53040 Montepulciano (SI)
Tel. 0578708599

Massimo Romeo is a scrupulous producer and all of his wines are pleasing. The Vin Santo is very good, boasting a clean, broad range of aromas and well-balanced flavour. You'll also find good balance and nicely proportioned structure in the other wines.

○ Vin Santo '90	🍷🍷	6
● Rosso di Montepulciano '01	🍷	4
● Nobile di Montepulciano Ris. '98	🍷	5
● Nobile di Montepulciano '99	🍷	5

Terra Antica
Via Sanguineto, 3
53045 Montepulciano (SI)
Tel. 0578766056
E-mail: terraantica@libero.it

Terra Antica made a fine debut with the '99, a sangiovese that has small amounts of cabernet and merlot. It's an excellent wine, with a powerful attack and concentration on the docile, well-balanced palate, then good length. It's very good indeed. The two Nobiles did well, too.

● Terra Antica '99	🍷🍷	8
● Nobile di Montepulciano Ris. '98	🍷	5
● Nobile di Montepulciano '99	🍷	5
● Rosso di Montepulciano '01		4

Lornano
Loc. Lornano
53035 Monteriggioni (SI)
Tel. 0577309059
E-mail: catetadd@tin.it

Lornano presented just one wine, but it was a good one. The Chianti Classico '00 offers aromas of spice and red berries with oak-derived nuances. The palate is dense, delightfully lively and well sustained by the oak. There's a tempting bitter note on the finish. A promising debut.

● Chianti Cl. '00	🍷🍷	4

Suveraia
Loc. Bacucco
58025 Monterotondo Marittimo (GR)
Tel. 050564428

Suveraia is amongst the estates to watch around Monteregio. Their top wine is the Bacucco, and the vintage '00 is very successful. The structure is particularly impressive.

● Monteregio di Massa Marittima Bacucco di Suveraia '00	🍷🍷	6
● Monteregio di Massa Marittima Suveraia Rosso di Campetroso '01	🍷	4

Poggio Gagliardo
Loc. Poggio Gagliardo
56040 Montescudaio (PI)
Tel. 0586630775
E-mail: info@poggiogagliardo.com

This year, Poggio Gagliardo did not present some of major wines, such as Rovo and Gobbo dei Pianacci. In consequence, the profile is a lot shorter. On the other hand, they did offer a debut bottle, the Ultimo Sole, which is a good, if distinctly vegetal, cabernet sauvignon.

● Montescudaio Rosso Ultimo Sole '00	🍷🍷	6
○ Montescudaio Bianco Linaglia '01	🍷	4
○ Montescudaio Bianco Vigna Lontana '01	🍷	4

Agrinico
Via di Montelupo 69/71
50025 Montespertoli (FI)
Tel. 0571571021

The Nicosole '99, a Syrah, boasts intense aromas of spice, wild berries and plum jam, then a concentrated palate with quite a lot of oak and a moderately long finish. It a memorable, if not extremely elegant, wine.

● Nicosole '99	🍷🍷	5

I Casciani
Via Casciani, 9
50020 Montespertoli (FI)
Tel. 0571609093

The I Casciani estate made a very good showing on its debut, particularly with the excellent red Villa Gaja '00. It's an intense, concentrated wine with close-knit tannins and balanced, progressive development. The Chianti '01 is simpler but sound and agreeable.

● Villa Gaja '00	🍷🍷	5
● Chianti '01	🍷	3*

Tenuta La Cipressaia
Via Romita, 38
50025 Montespertoli (FI)
Tel. 0571670868 - 0571670746
E-mail: lacipressaia@leonet.it

Things are looking up for this estate, which this year presented some well-structured wines. One is Borgoricco, which has dense, concentrated, full body, although the nose is not altogether elegant. The fruit-led, balanced and very enjoyable Colli Fiorentini is another success.

● Borgoricco '00	🍷🍷	4
● Chianti '01	🍷	2*
● Chianti dei Colli Fiorentini '01	🍷	3

Fattorie Parri
Via Ribaldaccio, 80
50025 Montespertoli (FI)
Tel. 0571609154
E-mail: info@fattorieparri.it

Fattorie Parri is a large but very good producer. None of the wines approaches excellence, but there's nothing poorly made, either. The refreshing, agreeable and lingering Chardonnay Tenuta Ribaldaccio is very interesting, as is its price.

○ Chardonnay Tenuta Ribaldaccio '01	🍷	2*
● Le Bronche '98	🍷	5
● Chianti Montespertoli Le Prode del Chiù '99	🍷	3*

Mannucci Droandi
Fraz. Caposelvi, 61
52020 Montevarchi (AR)
Tel. 0559707276
E-mail: mannuccidroandi@tin.it

This ambitious winery already seems to know what it's about, although it has only just started. We found interesting things in the Campolucci '99, made from sangiovese with a little cabernet. Soft and pleasing, it is just slightly bitter on the finish. The other wines are nicely made.

● Chianti Cl. Ceppeto '00	🍷	4
● Chianti '98	🍷	4
● Campolucci '99	🍷	5
● Chianti '99	🍷	4

Podere Il Carnasciale
Fraz. Mercatale Valdarno
Loc. San Leonino, 82
52020 Montevarchi (AR)
Tel. 0559911142

The '99 is one of the best versions yet of an extraordinary wine, Caberlot. It blends oriental spices with elegance and an extremely long palate. The only defect is scarcity. Just 1,500 magnums are produced. But at long last, the cellar is planning to increase that number.

● Caberlot '99	🍷🍷	8

La Rendola
Loc. Rendola, 85
52025 Montevarchi (AR)
Tel. 0559707594
E-mail: info@renideo.com

La Rendola wines are anything but uniform in quality. The Merlot '00, for example, is very good, with its nose of chocolate, coffee and dark berries introducing a dense, tight-knit, well-sustained palate. The other reds are dominated by oak, although L'Incanto is quite enjoyable.

● Merlot Rendola '00	🍷🍷	6
● L'Incanto '00	🍷	4
○ Aliera '01		4

Giovanna Giannaccini
Via Zeri, 13
54038 Montignoso (MS)
Tel. 0585348305

Again, Giannaccini's vermentino-based Pagus proves to be uncommonly delightful. This time, it's the '01, whose clean bouquet shows notes of apple, pear, peach, apricot and broom blossom, while the palate is rounded and well-sustained, and perhaps just a tad over-sweet.

○ Pagus '01		3*

San Gervasio
Loc. San Gervasio
56036 Palaia (PI)
Tel. 0587483360 - 0587629233
E-mail: sangervasio@sangervasio.com

Luca Tommasini's winery has, in recent years, invested heavily in both vineyard and cellar. Concrete results should be perceptible starting next year, when the best wines are released. Meanwhile, the Vin Santo Recinaio is doing very well.

○ S. Torpè Recinaio Vin Santo '97		6
◉ Aprico Rosato '01		3*
● Chianti Le Stoppie '01		3

Fattoria Casaloste
Via Montagliari, 32
50020 Panzano (FI)
Tel. 055852725
E-mail: casaloste@casaloste.it

Casaloste wines are good, although there is no star as yet. It is quite likely, however, that next year will bring some surprises. The Chianti Classico Riserva '99 is a soft wine with a consistent development and lively tannins. Chianti Classico '00 is robust, if not particularly elegant.

● Chianti Cl. Ris. '99		7
● Chianti Cl. '00		5

Le Cinciole
Via Case Sparse, 83
50020 Panzano (FI)
Tel. 055852636
E-mail: cinciole@chianticlassico.com

Le Cinciole is in the midst of general restructuring, which affects both vines and cellar. Hence our tastings took place at an unpropitious moment that does not do justice to Valeria Viganò and Luca Orsini's estate. Nevertheless, the Chianti Classico Petresco Riserva '99 is rather good.

● Chianti Cl. Petresco Ris. '99		6
● Chianti Cl. '00		4

Fattoria Le Fonti
Le Fonti
50020 Panzano (FI)
Tel. 055852194
E-mail: info@fattorialefonti.it

A quality surge is needed at Le Fonti, but the general standard is dependably good. The very fine Fontissimo '99 shows balance and a certain elegance, despite a distinctly vegetal tone. The Chianti Classico Riserva '99 is well-proportioned and enjoyable.

● Fontissimo '99		6
● Chianti Cl. Ris. '99		5

Vignole
Loc. La Massa - Via Case Sparse, 14
50022 Panzano (FI)
Tel. 0574592025
E-mail: vinisistri@tin.it

Congius is unquestionably Vignole's most interesting wine. The nose displays vegetal and tobacco nuances, while the palate is intense but a bit aggressive. The Vin Santo '95 is good, too, with its nutty bouquet and dry, sound, admirably stylish palate.

● Congius '99		6
○ Vin Santo '95		5
● Chianti Cl. Ris. '98		5

Le Ginestre
Loc. Pieve Apresciano
Via Giovanni XXIII
52020 Pergine Valdarno (AR)
Tel. 0575897160

There may not be any world-shakers here but you will find consistently good quality. The well-built Il Castellare has a touch too much oak but it is very good and won Two Glasses. The sangiovese-based I Greti '99 also did well.

● Il Castellare '00	♛♛	5
○ I Rovi '00	♛	3
● Il Ginestreto '98	♛	4
● I Greti '99	♛	5

Sedime
Podere Sedime, 63
53026 Pienza (SI)
Tel. 0578748436
E-mail: capitoni.marco@libero.it

This is the first wine produced by Marco Capitoni's estate, and the results are encouraging. Its debut coincides with that of a new DOC zone, Orcia, in the form of this nice red made from sangiovese with 15 per cent merlot. It is intense and concentrated, and still shows slightly prominent oak.

● Orcia Rosso Capitoni '01	♛	4

Il Vignale
Loc. Vignale Riotorto
57025 Piombino (LI)
Tel. 056520812

Il Vignale is one of a number of small but expanding Val di Cornia estates. Their good intentions are obvious in wines like Vinivo '00, which shows a balanced, fresh palate with an intensely tannic finish. The Vermentino, too, is pleasing and well made.

● Val di Cornia Rosso Vinivo '00	♛♛	5
○ Val di Cornia Vermentino Campo degli Albicocchi '01	♛	4

Granducato
Via Pianigiani, 9
53036 Poggibonsi (SI)
Tel. 0577936057
E-mail: s.ciacci@capsi.it

Granducato is the label used by the Consorzio Agrario di Siena. The wines presented are well made and decently structured. Morellino Gretaio '00 in particular shows dense, soft body, expert use of oak and a nice follow-through on the finish. The Seragio '00 is fair but a bit tannic.

● Morellino di Scansano Gretaio '00	♛	3
● Seragio '00	♛	4
○ Vernaccia di S. Gimignano '01	♛	3

Grignano
Via di Grignano, 22
50065 Pontassieve (FI)
Tel. 0558398490 - 03391578008
E-mail: info@fattoriadigrignano.com

The gap between Grignano's best wines and the standard bottles is a big one, but all show great potential. The Chianti Rufina Poggio Gualtieri Riserva has lots of concentration and grip. Close behind it, the Riserva '99 has a distinctive style. The other Rufinas are better than just acceptable.

● Chianti Rufina Poggio Gualtieri Ris. '98	♛♛	5
● Chianti Rufina '00	♛	3
● Chianti Rufina '99	♛	3
● Chianti Rufina Ris. '99	♛	4

Fattoria Lavacchio
Via di Montefiesole, 55
50065 Pontassieve (FI)
Tel. 0558317472 - 0558396168
E-mail: info@fattorialavacchio.com

The quality of the wines from Fattoria Lavacchio is satisfyingly uniform. The Chianti Rufina Riserva '99 boasts good character, the Chardonnay '01 is pleasing and well made, the Cortigiano '99 is balanced, but a bit green, and the Chianti Rufina '00 is meaty, but has vegetal and bitterish tones.

● Chianti Rufina '00	♛	4
○ Chardonnay '01	♛	4
● Chianti Rufina Ris. '99	♛	4
● Cortigiano '99	♛	5

Mola
Loc. Gelsarello, 2
57031 Porto Azzurro (LI)
Tel. 0565958151 - 0565222089
E-mail: pavoletti@infol.it

This estate on Elba has produced a good range of wines, the most notable of which is the Moscato '00. It shows aromas of peaches in syrup and apricot jam, followed by a sweet, succulent palate. The Aleatico is quite interesting and the other wines are well executed.

○ Moscato dell'Elba '00	🍷🍷	6
● Aleatico dell'Elba '00	🍷	5
● Elba Rosso Ris. '00	🍷	4
● Elba Rosso Gelsarello '01	🍷	4

Acquabona
Loc. Acquabona, 1
57037 Portoferraio (LI)
Tel. 0565933013
E-mail: acquabona.elba@tiscalinet.it

Acquabona's wines are faithful to their traditional characteristics of evenness on the palate and well-typed aromas. Although not extraordinary, they are encouragingly reliable. We should mention, however, the Passito '98, which is remarkably powerful.

○ Ansonica dell'Elba '01	🍷	4
○ Passito '98	🍷	5
● Elba Rosso '00		4

Colle Bereto
Loc. Colle Bereto
53017 Radda in Chianti (SI)
Tel. 0577738083 - 0554299330
E-mail: colle.bereto@collebereto.it

Il Tocco is Colle Bereto's most promising wine. A harmonious red, it reveals fruit-led aromas and faint vegetal and oak-derived nuances. The palate is round and well balanced. The Chianti Classico '00 is a bit thin, but not without style, and the Riserva '99 is a tad evolved.

● Il Tocco '00	🍷🍷	6
● Chianti Cl. '00	🍷	4
● Chianti Cl. Ris '99	🍷	5

Fattoria di Montemaggio
Loc. Montemaggio
53017 Radda in Chianti (SI)
Tel. 0577738323

There are some highs and some lows in the wines from Montemaggio. The Chianti Classico Riserva '99 is way out in front, showing richness, energy and a fruity finish. The less focused Chianti '99 is a bit reduced on the nose and not very vigorous in the mouth.

● Chianti Cl. Ris. '99	🍷🍷	6
● Chianti Cl. '99		4

Castello di Monterinaldi
Loc. Lucarelli
53017 Radda in Chianti (SI)
Tel. 0577733533
E-mail: info@monterinaldi.it

We tasted only two wines from Monterinaldi this year. The very fine Chianti Classico boasts an attractively fruity nose and a pleasing texture on the palate, despite invasive oak. The fair Pesanella is energetic but a bit green.

● Chianti Cl. '00	🍷🍷	4
● Pesanella '97	🍷	5

Villa Buoninsegna
Loc. Buoninsegna
53040 Rapolano Terme (SI)
Tel. 0577724380
E-mail: info@buoninsegna.it

Villa Buoninsegna '99, a blend of sangiovese, cabernet sauvignon and syrah, is a carefully executed red with excellent balance, well-calibrated tannins and a straightforward but clear-cut finish. And the price tag is very reasonable.

● Villa Buoninsegna '99	🍷🍷	4*

Villa Patrizia
Loc. Cana - Fraz. Villa Patrizia
58050 Roccalbegna (GR)
Tel. 0564982028
E-mail: info@villa-patrizia.com

Villa Patrizia's wines are dependably good. The best one we tasted this time is the Morellino Le Valentane '00, which shows lots of fruit and good concentration, as well as perceptible oak. The other wines are all decent.

● Morellino di Scansano Le Valentane '00	ΨΨ	5
● Montecucco Rosso Orto di Boccio '00	Ψ	5
○ Sciamareti '01	Ψ	3
● Morellino di Scansano Ris. '99	Ψ	5

I Campetti
Loc. Campetti - Fraz. Ribolla
Via della Collacchia, 2
58027 Roccastrada
Tel. 0564579663

Whites are the speciality of the house at I Campetti. The viognier-based Almabruna '01 shows depth of structure but not much fragrance. The Malvasia L'Accesa '01 is well made and true to type. The Nebbiaie '01 is clean and pleasant.

○ Almabruna '01	Ψ	5
○ Malvasia L'Accesa '01	Ψ	3
○ Monteregio di Massa Marittima Bianco Nebbiaie '01	Ψ	3

Giacomo Mori
Fraz. Palazzone
P.zza Sandro Pertini, 8
53040 San Casciano dei Bagni (SI)
Tel. 0578227005

Giacomo Mori never lets you down. Year after year, his reds make intriguing drinking. The Chianti Castelrotto '00 offers a dense bouquet focused on notes of fruit, flowers and spices. The palate is concentrated and vibrant.

● Chianti Castelrotto '00	ΨΨ	5
● Chianti '01	Ψ	4

Cigliano
Via Cigliano, 15
50026 San Casciano in Val di Pesa (FI)
Tel. 055820033
E-mail: fattoriacigliano@libero.it

Cigliano, an estate with 30 hectares under vine, did very well this year. The Chianti Classico Riserva '99 displays intensity on the palate and some slight muffling on the nose, while the Chianti Classico '00 is an admirably upfront red.

● Chianti Cl. Ris. '99	ΨΨ	5
● Chianti Cl. '00	Ψ	4

San Niccolò a Pisignano
Via Pisignano, 36
50026 San Casciano in Val di Pesa (FI)
Tel. 055828834

This is the Chianti outpost of the group that belongs to the well-known Friulian producer Marco Felluga. The one wine presented, Sorripa '98, is soft, lean, balanced and enjoyable. The finish is not very long and reveals rather vegetal nuances.

● Sorripa '98	ΨΨ	5

Solatione
Fraz. Mercatale Val di Pesa
Via Valigondoli, 53/A
50026 San Casciano in Val di Pesa (FI)
Tel. 055821623

The rather good Chianti Classico Riserva '99 offers softness, length and well-integrated tannins. The fair Chianti Classico '99 is admirably true to type but has some rough edges. The acceptable Vin Santo '96 is sweet, but a bit aggressive on the finish.

● Chianti Cl. Ris. '99	ΨΨ	5
● Chianti Cl. '99	Ψ	4
○ Vin Santo '96	Ψ	5

CAPPELLA SANT'ANDREA
Loc. Casale, 26
53037 San Gimignano (SI)
tel. 0577940456

Vernaccia Rialto offers a well-defined bouquet with fruity notes and a faint suggestion of oak. The palate shows good body, freshness and a finish that echoes the nose. The Serreto is fair, but a bit forward, and the standard Vernaccia is consistent but not very energetic.

○ Vernaccia di S. Gimignano Rialto '01	🍷🍷	4
● S. Gimignano Rosso Serreto '99	🍷	4
○ Vernaccia di S. Gimignano '01		3

CASTELLO DI MONTAUTO
Loc. Montauto
53037 San Gimignano (SI)
tel. 0577743024

This estate is part of the Cecchi group and has long offered good value. The Chardonnay Sagrato is particularly nice, with its sound fruit and beautifully integrated oak, as well as elegant development on the palate. The two versions of Vernaccia are well typed and enjoyable.

○ Chardonnay Sagrato '01	🍷🍷	4
○ Vernaccia di S. Gimignano '01	🍷	2*
○ Vernaccia di S. Gimignano Castello di Montauto '01	🍷	3

RUBICINI
Loc. San Benedetto, 17/c
53037 San Gimignano (SI)
tel. 0577944816

Rubicini's wines are more than just acceptable. The Vernaccia shows aromas of crusty bread, apple and pear and a balanced, fresh, even palate with the grape's typical bitterish finish. The Chianti Colli Senesi is well calibrated and pleasing.

● Chianti Colli Senesi '01	🍷	3
○ Vernaccia di S. Gimignano '01	🍷	3

SAN QUIRICO
Via Pancole, 39
53037 San Gimignano (SI)
tel. 0577955007

The Vernaccia Isabella selection keeps the flag flying at San Quirico. It is full-bodied, somewhat forward in style and well backed up by oak, with intense aromas of vanilla and honey. The Vernaccia '01 is less successful.

○ Vernaccia di S. Gimignano Isabella Ris. '99	🍷🍷	4
○ Vernaccia di S. Gimignano '01		3

SIGNANO
P.zza San Agostino, 17
53037 San Gimignano (SI)
tel. 0577940164 - 0577942587

The Vernaccia Selezione '00 is quite good, despite rather a lot of oak. The same is true of the two reds, which are simple, fruit-led and direct, with more of an oaky tone in the San Gimignano.

● Chianti Colli Senesi Poggiarelli '00	🍷	4
● San Gimignano Rosso '00	🍷	4
○ Vernaccia di S. Gimignano Sel. '00	🍷	4

PIETRO BECONCINI
Fraz. La Scala - Via Montorso, 13
56028 San Miniato (PI)
tel. 0571464570
e-mail: beconcinipietro@virgilio.it

The two most recent versions of the sangiovese-based Reciso reveal admirable elegance and smooth, succulent tannins. The '00 has more fruit, the '99 more complexity. The '97 is rather over-evolved, and the Maurleo is simple but well made.

● Reciso '00	🍷🍷	5
● Reciso '99	🍷🍷	5
● Maurleo '01	🍷	4
● Reciso '97		5

Podere San Michele
Via della Caduta, 3/a
57027 San Vincenzo (LI)
tel. 0565798038

Sangiovese predominates in the blend that goes to make the Allodio. The '00, which is still quite youthful, shows incisive structure, concentration and character. It still has to integrate its oak, but a few months in the bottle should take care of that.

● Allodio Rosso '00	🍷	5

Tenuta di Trinoro
Via Ribattola, 2
53047 Sarteano (SI)
tel. 0578267110

The much sought-after, and wallet-threateningly expensive, Tenuta di Trinoro '01 shows lavish, generous fruit that blends nicely with massive but well-integrated doses of oak. Superlatives apart, you suspect that beneath all the warmth on the surface there lies a rather cold heart.

● Tenuta di Trinoro '01	🍷🍷	8
● Le Cupole di Trinoro '01	🍷	8

San Michele a Torri
Loc. San Michele a Torri
Via San Michele, 36
50018 Scandicci (FI)
tel. 055769111

The most appealing of San Michele a Torri's wines is the Colli Fiorentini '01, which shows straightforward but clear-cut fruit on the nose and balanced structure on a dense body. The Murtas '00 is substantial but faintly bitter.

● Chianti Colli Fiorentini '00	🍷	3*
● Murtas '00	🍷	6

La Carletta
Loc. Preselle - Podere Carletta, 80
58050 Scansano (GR)
tel. 0564585045
e-mail: sante.massini@tiscalinet.it

The 2001 vintage was excellent in the Maremma. This can be seen, at least in part, in the difference between the two La Carletta Morellinos. The '01 is distinctly good, with its ripe fruit and rounded, full, very enjoyable flavour.

● Morellino di Scansano Fonte Tinta '01	🍷	3*
● Morellino di Scansano Fonte Tinta '00		3

Botrona
Loc. Botrona
S.P. del Puntone
58020 Scarlino (GR)
tel. 0566866129

We draw your attention to an intense, warm, robust red with aromas of spice, toasted oak and blackberry jam. It is potentially extremely interesting, but at the moment is somewhat in thrall to the oak, which dries out the bitterish finish.

● Monteregio Rosso Botrona '99	🍷	4

La Pierotta
Loc. La Pierotta
58020 Scarlino (GR)
tel. 056637218
e-mail: lapierotta@scarlino.net

The two wines presented by La Pierotta, an estate which is clearly going places, are both good. We rather prefer the Scarilius '00, which is less troubled by oak and shows good length and lively tannins. The Solare is nicely concentrated but also quite oaky.

● Scarilius '00	🍷🍷	4
● Solare '00	🍷	5

Castelpugna
Strada Val di Pugna, 12
53100 Siena
tel. 0577222461 - 057746547
e-mail: info@castelpugna.com

All the Castelpugna wines are well made and have a distinctive, sangiovese-defined style. Our review will probably be more enthusiastic and favourable when we are able taste their top wine, Castelpugna.

● Chianti dei C. Senesi Ellera '00	▼	4
● Chianti dei C. Senesi Ellera '01	▼	4
● Chianti dei C. Senesi Ellera Ris. '99	▼	5

Tenuta Farneta
Loc. Farneta, 161
53048 Sinalunga (SI)
tel. 0577631025

Bongoverno is made from sangiovese with ten per cent cabernet sauvignon. It boasts elegant style, firmness, well-behaved tannins and tertiary notes on the nose. The Bentivoglio '99 is decent but a bit vegetal. The other wines are only well-typed.

● Bongoverno '98	▼▼	6
● Bentivoglio '99	▼	3
○ Bonagrazia Chardonnay '01		2*
● Chianti Colli Senesi '01		2

Tenuta di Trecciano
Loc. Trecciano
53018 Sovicille (SI)
tel. 0577314357
e-mail: trecciano@libero.it

We were unable to review Daniello, the cellar's flagship wine. The Cabernet Sauvignon, which almost won Two Glasses, has a soft, well-balanced palate with rather excessive vegetal tones. The Terra Rossa '00, a lively red, and the notably enjoyable Chianti '01, are both pleasant surprises.

● Cabernet Sauvignon '00	▼	4
● Chianti dei Colli Senesi Terra Rossa Ris. '00	▼	3*
● Chianti dei Colli Senesi Terra di Siena '01	▼	2*
● I Campacci '01	▼	4

Bulichella
Loc. Bulichella, 131
57028 Suvereto (LI)
tel. 0565829892 - 0565827828
e-mail: bulichella@etruscan.li.it

Bulichella is looking more and more promising, and there may soon be a great leap forward. For the moment, we note a distinct improvement in the Tuscanio Rosso, which easily won Two Glasses for its dense structure and excellent balance. But the Bianco is also very agreeable.

● Val di Cornia Rosso Tuscanio '00	▼▼	6
○ Val di Cornia Bianco Tuscanio '01	▼	4

Il Bruscello
Loc. Tabaro
57028 Suvereto (LI)
tel. 0565829025

As is customary for wines from Val di Cornia, Loco dei Frati '99 exhibits notable structure, with a robust, concentrated body and lovely expansion at mid palate. The bouquet, on the other hand, is less clear and slightly muffled. But it's a fine debut all the same.

● Val di Cornia Rosso Loco dei Frati '99	▼▼	5
● Val di Cornia Rosso Quarzo di Rocca '00		4

Le Pianacce
Loc. Pianacce
57028 Suvereto (LI)
tel. 0565828027

This estate is coming back, and showing a dedication that promises great things for the future. The Diavolino '00 presents warm notes of fruit preserves and blackberry jam on the nose. The palate is fresher and more balanced, thanks to nice tannin contrast. It's a fruit-driven, enjoyable wine.

● Diavolino Rosso '00	▼▼	5
○ Val di Cornia Bianco Diavolino '01		3

Petra
Loc. S. Lorenzo Alto, 131
57028 Suvereto (LI)
Tel. 0565845308 - 0565845180
E-mail: info.petra@libero.it

will take some time before Petra, the Tuscan outpost of the Franciacorta-based Bellavista winery, realizes the high ambitions of its owners. Petra '98 is a good, carefully executed wine, but the structure is only moderate and the green tone is a tad over the top.

● Petra Rosso '98	🍷🍷	6

Petricci del Pianta
Loc. S. Lorenzo, 20
57028 Suvereto (LI)
Tel. 0565845140
E-mail: info@petriccidelpianta.it

This Suvereto estate produces lots of wines. Again, the Aleatico Stillo stands out for its characteristic aromas of black cherry and its sweet, round flavour with a faintly tannic finish. The Cerosecco '00 is better than last year's version. The other wines are well made.

● Val di Cornia Aleatico Stillo '01	🍷🍷	7
● Cerosecco '00	🍷	5
● Val di Cornia Rosso Albatrone '01	🍷	4*
● Val di Cornia Buca di Cleonte '99	🍷	5

Villa Monte Rico
Poggio Cerro
57028 Suvereto (LI)
Tel. 0565829550 - 0041223462825
E-mail: reichenberg@dplanet.ch

Monte Rico's wine did very well indeed this year. The nose is intense, and the nuances of oak nicely judged. In the mouth, it is soft, elegant and refreshingly succulent, and the finish suggests berry fruit. This is a well-defined and very promising Sangiovese.

● Val di Cornia '99	🍷🍷	5

Podere La Cappella
Fraz. San Donato in Poggio
Strada Cerbaia, 10/A
50020 Tavarnelle Val di Pesa (FI)
Tel. 0558072727

Light and shade at this estate. The light illuminates the Corbezzolo '99, made - very well, too - mostly from sangiovese. It's a concentrated red that unfolds nicely on the palate. The shade concerns Cantico '99, a Merlot that shows weight and substance but no focus or harmony.

● Corbezzolo '99	🍷🍷	7
● Cantico '99	🍷	8

Fattoria La Ripa
Fraz. San Donato in Poggio
50020 Tavarnelle Val di Pesa (FI)
Tel. 0558072948 - 0558072121
E-mail: laripa@laripa.it

High marks again for the Santa Brigida, vintage '99. It's a balanced, sound, full-bodied red, if not a very complex one. The Riserva '99 has a vigorous structure but is a bit muffled on the nose. Much the same can be said of the Chianti '00.

● Santa Brigida '99	🍷🍷	6
● Chianti Cl. Ris. '99	🍷	6
● Chianti Cl. '00		5

Fattoria Poggio Romita
Loc. La Romita - Via Del Cerro, 10
50028 Tavarnelle Val di Pesa (FI)
Tel. 0558077253
E-mail: poggioromita@tin.it

The Frimaio '00 is very good. The nose is not yet very eloquent but has concentration, and the palate is dense, lively and vibrant on the finish. The other reds show good extract but too much oak. The Bianco is very simple but agreeable.

● Chianti Cl. Frimaio '00	🍷🍷	4
● La Sassaia '00	🍷	6
○ Romita Bianco '01	🍷	3
● Chianti Cl. Frimaio Ris. '99	🍷	6

COOPERATIVA AGRICOLA VALDARNESE
LOC. PATERNA, 96
52028 TERRANUOVA BRACCIOLINI (AR)
TEL. 055977052

This co-operative produces unquestionably good wines. The sangiovese-based Vignanuova is full-bodied and fairly soft, but also a touch forward, and the oak has yet to mellow. The Chianti is straightforward, fruity and easy to like.

● Vignanuova '99	4*
● Chianti dei Colli Aretini '01	3

URSULA E PETER MOCK
FRAZ. SOIANA
VIA PIER CAPPONI 98
56030 TERRICCIOLA (PI)
TEL. 0587654180

Ursula and Peter Mock took over Bruno and Elyane Moos's estate a few years ago. So, there is still a couple at the helm, but the Fontestina has changed its style a little, displaying more fruit than of yore.

● Fontestina '00	5
● Soianello '00	4

PODERE LA CHIESA
VIA DI CASANOVA, 13
56030 TERRICCIOLA (PI)
TEL. 0587653286
E-MAIL: mamajero@libero.it

The Sabiniano is made from 50 per cent sangiovese with cabernet sauvignon and merlot. It foregrounds the richness of ripe fruit, with jammy notes as well, and the softness of its delightful palate.

● Sabiniano di Casanova '00	5

PIEVE DE' PITTI
VIA PIEVE DE' PITTI, 7
56030 TERRICCIOLA (PI)
TEL. 0587635724
E-MAIL: wine@pievedepitti.it

This estate has some 30 hectares under vine, planted mostly to sangiovese, which is the only grape in Moro di Pava. It's a solid red with an earthy nose and some oak-derived toasty notes. The development on the palate is warm, dense and incisive.

● Moro di Pava '00	5

VALLORSI
LOC. MORRONA
VIA DELLA CASCINA, 19
56030 TERRICCIOLA (PI)
TEL. 0587658470

There are positive signals from Vallorsi, in the form of wines like the mostly sangiovese-based San Bartolomeo '99. This came close to getting Two Glasses for its aromatic personality and attractively soft, evenly distributed palate. The Vermentino is also well made.

● San Bartolomeo '99	5
○ Vermentino '01	3

ORTAGLIA
LOC. PRATOLINO - VIA SAN JACOPO, 331
50036 VAGLIA (FI)
TEL. 055409136
E-MAIL: ortaglia@iol.it

Ortaglia continues to concentrate on whites, but there may be a red in the offing. The Bianca Capello '01 is a fine wine with clear-cut aromas of tropical fruit, peach and apricot. The flavour is substantial and harmonious.

○ Bianca Capello '01	5

MARCHE

Marche wine "marches" on apace, as we noted in last year's Guide and results from this year's tastings confirm the trend. Our snapshot shows a region that has established high levels of quality, with both traditional names and outsiders deservedly finding a place in the limelight. Until a few years ago, the Marche was barely managing to project its identity in general terms, let alone a specialized area like winemaking, and despite some progress, the region's image was distinctly fuzzy at the edges. Let's take a look at the statistics. Overall wine production for the region is close to 2,000,000 hectolitres a year. Over 30 per cent of this has DOC status, a proportion that has grown in recent vintages. Before we turn to the eight Three Glass wines, the same number as last year, we would like to underline the impact of wineries making their Guide debut in this edition. These are highly motivated estates that offer confirmation that the general shift of focus towards quality is not confined to a handful of producers. Now let's look at the wines that won Three Glasses this year, starting with two whites, both Verdicchio dei Castelli di Jesi, from wineries that have long been emblematic of the renaissance in premium winemaking in the region, Garofali and Bucci. Both Garofali's Serra Fiorese selection and the Villa Bucci are from the '99 vintage, further evidence that Verdicchio, revived and greatly enhanced by ambitious, intelligent winemakers, can be a long-lived, expressive wine. Turning now to the reds, we have six that were awarded the highest accolade and many others that came close, from De Angelis to San Savino, Caniette, Umani Ronchi and Lanari, to name but a few. The list of top reds includes some making their debut, such as Dezi's Solo 2000, a monovarietal Sangiovese indicative of the widespread tendency in the region to promote the variety; a Rosso Conero Traiano 2000 presented by Strologo, a winegrower with a committed, professional approach to quality goals set when the winery was modernized; the Rosso Piceno Superiore Vigna Monteprandone 2000 made by Saladini Pilastri, one of the leading names in Piceno, an area that achieved its best results ever this year; Adeodato 2000 by Monteschiavo, a remarkable monovarietal Montepulciano from a winery that has made across-the-board improvements in its range; Velenosi's Ludi 2000, a stylish blend of montepulciano, merlot and cabernet; finally, the gallery of excellence is completed by the Kurni 2000 from Oasi degli Angeli, an expressive and balanced monovarietal montepulciano.

ANCONA

LANARI
FRAZ. VARANO
VIA POZZO, 142
60029 ANCONA
TEL. 0712861343

Wider acknowledgement of Rosso Conero's premium status is due above all to untiring research into clones, sacrifices made to implement lower cropping levels, improved cellar techniques and the increasing number of cellars eager to offer new interpretations of the montepulciano grape. Goodbye, then, to hard, over-assertive wines rendered almost undrinkable by gamey aromas and rugged tannins. Such products are only good for blending to lend body and structure to thin, dreary mass-produced plonk. The young but well-established Lanari winery's productive philosophy is driven by ongoing research into quality and hard choices over production and yields. No Rosso Conero is released in poor years. The results are there in powerful wines that can still offer aromatic finesse and stylish flavours, providing material proof of montepulciano's potential for noble expression. The standard-label Rosso Conero 2001 is a top-quality wine with intense morello cherry, liquorice and leather on the nose that develop and expand over an extract-rich texture of impeccable elegance and enviable softness. The splendid Fibbio 2000 selection has the same generous nose as its younger brother and a perfectly balanced palate with a lingering return of ripe fruit, spice and tobacco. The fine soft tannins meld with a concentration that fills the mouth with sensations from start to endless finish.

ANCONA

MARCHETTI
FRAZ. PINOCCHIO
VIA DI PONTELUNGO, 166
60131 ANCONA
TEL. 071897386 - 071897385
E-MAIL: info@marchettiwines.it

Last year, we mentioned that Maurizio Marchetti's winery was changing direction. More care is being taken in the vineyard, vinification is scrupulous and the use of wood is more refined. These are the first signs that Lorenzo Landi is making his presence felt in the cellar. As one of the most professional oenologists around, he is obviously in favour of a scientific approach to winemaking. So how can the techniques used by a winery operating since 1900 be reconciled with the demands of today's winemakers? The answer is by creating a perfect blend of tradition and innovation, which cannot be achieved from one year to the next. As we wait to see how this partnership will work out, we enjoyed its first product, a deep ruby Rosso Conero 2000 with deep a generous nose of morello cherry, cloves and faint earth and mineral hints. It has weight on the palate, where the no-nonsense entry, steady follow-through and solid tannin base lead into a long finish that echoes and exalts the aromas on the nose. The two Verdicchios are a little behind, which is mainly due to the unfavourable year, but we preferred the Tenuta del Cavaliere 2001. It's a little more structured, with a well-defined nose, fruit-rich flavour and the bitterish finish typical of the variety. The standard-label Verdicchio has subtle almond and acacia blossom aromas. The palate is fairly rich in extract and enjoyably fresh.

● Rosso Conero Fibbio '00	🍷🍷	6
● Rosso Conero '01	🍷🍷	4*
● Rosso Conero Fibbio '99	🍷🍷🍷	6
● Rosso Conero '99	🍷🍷	4
● Rosso Conero '00	🍷🍷	4
● Rosso Conero Fibbio '97	🍷🍷	6
● Rosso Conero Fibbio '98	🍷🍷	6

● Rosso Conero '00	🍷🍷	4
○ Verdicchio dei Castelli di Jesi Cl. '01	🍷	3
○ Verdicchio dei Castelli di Jesi Cl. Sup. Tenuta del Cavaliere '01	🍷	4
● Rosso Conero Villa Bonomi Ris. '97	🍷🍷	5
● Rosso Conero Villa Bonomi '98	🍷🍷	5

ANCONA

ALESSANDRO MORODER
VIA MONTACUTO, 112
60062 ANCONA
TEL. 071898232
E-MAIL: info@moroder-vini.it

Back in the mid 1980s, Alessandro and his wife Serenella were the first to be convinced of the potential of the Conero terroir and the montepulciano grape. They were also the first to receive some well-deserved plaudits and awards, including our Three Glasses on two occasions. Their ongoing quest for quality is clearer than ever from their serious commitment in both the cellar and out of doors, the timely decision to call on the services of consultant oenologist Franco Bernabei, and, last but not least, their decision not to release their flagship wine, Dorico '99, because they thought it not up to the winery's usual standard. However, the Rosso Conero is one of their best ever. The crisp, stylish aromas reveal cinchona and cherries, as well as faint oak-derived undertones. The nice alcohol of the entry on the palate mingles attractively with the solid tannic weave. We also enjoyed the fragrant Rosa di Montacuto 2001, with its wild berry aromas and nice tangy flavour. The passito Oro is as pleasant as ever with its hints of cakes, caramel and honey on the nose. The palate never threatens to cloy on the palate. Lastly, the Elleno makes its debut. A blend of trebbiano, malvasia and verdicchio, it lacks clarity on nose and palate. But before we criticize the cake for its lack of icing, it is fair to add that the unfavourable vintage in 2001 for white grapes is the main culprit.

ANCONA

ALBERTO SERENELLI
VIA BARTOLINI, 2
60129 ANCONA
TEL. 07135505
E-MAIL: albertoserenelli@tiscalinet.it

The heavy bottles with their unusual shape ensure Alberto Serenelli's wines do not go unobserved. You can't miss them. The wines we tasted were as eye-catching as their bottles, which is a sign that Serenelli is seriously committed to making quality products. We awarded Two Glasses to the most impressive, the Varano '99, a Rosso Conero made from montepulciano grapes grown in the best positions of the Podere Boranico, in the shadow of Monte Conero. Thanks to lengthy ageing in large oak barrels, and then in bottle, this is a richly extracted, well-balanced wine, with stylish ripe berry fruit and crusty bread aromas then a soft, enjoyably lingering palate. Its elder bother, Trave, seemed a little less weighty, despite the fact that the montepulciano grapes are from the same vineyards and the wine is aged in new French barriques. The nose is rather closed, the oak is very marked and the palate is rather dry. The Marro 2000 is a more interesting Rosso Conero from two plots overlooking the Adriatic. Mature and austere, it has very full yet well-gauged body, nice alcohol and long length. Finally, the Verdicchio Sora Elvira, made from grapes grown in the Staffolo area, is enjoyable, flavoursome and stylish.

● Rosso Conero '00	ΨΨ	4
⊙ Rosa di Montacuto '01	Ψ	3*
○ L'Oro di Moroder	Ψ	5
○ Elleno '01		4
● Rosso Conero Dorico '90	ΨΨΨ	6
● Rosso Conero Dorico '93	ΨΨΨ	6
● Rosso Conero Dorico '98	ΨΨ	6
● Rosso Conero Dorico '97	ΨΨ	6

● Rosso Conero Marro '00	ΨΨ	4*
● Rosso Conero Varano '99	ΨΨ	7
○ Verdicchio dei Castelli di Jesi Cl. Sora Elvira '01	Ψ	4
● Rosso Conero Trave '99	Ψ	7

APPIGNANO (MC)

FATTORIA DI FORANO
C.DA FORANO, 40
62010 APPIGNANO (MC)
TEL. 073357102
E-MAIL: villaforano@libero.it

Conte Giovanni Battista Lucangeli owns this property of just less than 200 hectares, about 20 of which are planted to vine, and a winery that has been productive since 1966. Real renovation of vineyards and cellars only took place 30 years later, though, when Giancarlo Soverchia took over the technical side of the business. For the moment, the production philosophy is to use native local grape varieties to make four DOC wines, in standard-label and selection versions. The Colli Maceratesi Villa Forano 2001 is made mainly from maceratino fruit. It offers hints of lime blossom on the nose and a tangy palate with a bitterish finish. Greater care over ripening the grapes is evident in the Monteferro 2001 selection, as well as the addition of a small percentage of malvasia. The result is a subtly floral, aromatic nose. The palate has enjoyably soft alcohol and a reasonably long finish. The Rosso Piceno 2000 is dark ruby red, with nice vegetal geranium, plum and coffee aromas reflected on the dense palate, with its close-knit tannic weave. The unfavourable vintage means the Bulciano 1999 is rather over-evolved. It may not last long but the nose is generous and interesting, showing leather, morello cherries and hints of chocolate, while the confident palate is backed up with acidity and a nice deep finish.

O	Colli Maceratesi Bianco Monteferro '01	ΥΥ	4*
●	Rosso Piceno Bulciano '99	ΥΥ	4*
●	Rosso Piceno '00	Υ	3
O	Colli Maceratesi Bianco Villa Forano '01	Υ	3
●	Rosso Piceno Bulciano '98	ΥΥ	4
●	Rosso Piceno '99	ΥΥ	3

ASCOLI PICENO

ERCOLE VELENOSI
LOC. BRECCIAROLO
VIA DEI BIANCOSPINI, 11
63100 ASCOLI PICENO
TEL. 0736341218
E-MAIL: info@velenosivini.com

Ercole and Angela Velenosi's wines continue to improve all the time, as is demonstrated by this series of excellent products, turned out with the help of expert technician Romeo Taraborelli. The Ludi '00, in its second year of production, wins a well-deserved Three Glasses for a winery that was the first to believe in the potential of Piceno's native grape varieties. The Ludi is a blend of montepulciano, cabernet sauvignon and merlot in equal parts, aged for two years in barriques and large wooden casks. This gives it an immediate impact, with very ripe fruit and spicy, gamey notes to tempt the nose. The flavour recalls the austerity of a Bordeaux then veers towards warmer sensations with particularly close-knit, well-rounded, sweet tannins and sultana fruit in the long, velvety finish. The Roggio del Filare is an excellent, no-nonsense Rosso Piceno with body and well-managed balance. The international-style Chardonnay Rêve is fermented and aged in barrique. Its intense tropical fruit aromas are soon covered by buttery, vanilla notes then the rounded, alcohol-rich palate is nicely complemented by acidity. The Sauvignon Linagre is enjoyably varietal and extremely fruity on the nose, then fresh, soft and lingering on the palate. The Metodo Classico Brut, from chardonnay and pinot nero grapes, is intense and well-structured with a mature, individual flavour. Lastly, the frank, clean, nicely weighty Rosso Piceno 2000, and the fuller-bodied, hard Brecciarolo '99, are both well-made.

●	Ludi '00	ΥΥΥ	5
O	Rêve Chardonnay di Villa Angela '00	ΥΥ	5
O	Linagre Sauvignon di Villa Angela '01	ΥΥ	3*
●	Rosso Piceno Sup. Roggio del Filare '99	ΥΥ	5
O	Velenosi Brut M. Cl.	ΥΥ	5
●	Rosso Piceno '00	Υ	2*
O	Falerio dei Colli Ascolani Vigna Solaria '01	Υ	3
O	Villa Angela Chardonnay '01	Υ	3
●	Rosso Piceno Sup. Il Brecciarolo '99	Υ	3
●	Rosso Piceno Sup. Roggio del Filare '98	ΥΥ	5

BARBARA (AN)

Santa Barbara
B.go Mazzini, 35
60010 Barbara (AN)
Tel. 0719674249
E-mail: info@vinisantabarbara.it

This young winery was founded in 1987 by the enterprising Stefano Antonucci, who divided his time for several years between the cellar and his job in a bank. In 1995, Stefano opted to work full time in the winery and his wines have improved steadily since then, thanks to the help of oenologist Pierluigi Lorenzetti. Santa Barbara has recently invested in new vineyards and has replanted the old ones, as well as re-organizing cellar procedure and the ageing area. The Nidastore and Pignocco, both 2001 Verdicchios, are well-made but simple in structure while Le Vaglie has a generous nose with hints of lime blossom and tropical fruit, followed by a more complex, attractively fragrant palate. The less than favourable vintage means the oak in the Riserva Antonucci 2001 is still too noticeable but its ageing prospects are very good. The Pignocco Rosso is rich in fruit, attractively aromatic and pleasantly drinkable. The monovarietal Montepulciano Maschio da Monte has a rather inexpressive, gamey nose, which is typical of the grape, while the palate is powerful and firm with a smooth, elegant mouthfeel. The Stefano Antonucci Rosso 2000 has a good complex nose with green, fruity aromas that are reflected on the palate, where they mingle stylishly with the rich extract and smooth tannins. The splendid Pathos is a blend of non-native varieties. It shows a rich spice-and-balsam nose, then an elegant palate that echoes the same aromas over a sophisticated, mouthfilling texture that unveils cocoa powder and roasted coffee beans in the finish.

●	Pathos '00	🍷🍷	7
	Rosso Piceno		
	Il Maschio da Monte '00	🍷🍷	4
●	Stefano Antonucci Rosso '00	🍷🍷	5
○	Verdicchio dei Castelli di Jesi Cl.		
	Stefano Antonucci Ris. '00	🍷🍷	4*
○	Verdicchio dei Castelli di Jesi Cl.		
	Le Vaglie '01	🍷🍷	4*
●	Pignocco Rosso '01	🍷	3
○	Verdicchio dei Castelli di Jesi Cl.		
	Nidastore '01	🍷	3
○	Verdicchio dei Castelli di Jesi Cl.		
	Pignocco '01	🍷	2*
○	Verdicchio dei Castelli di Jesi Cl.		
	Stefano Antonucci Ris. '99	🍷🍷	4

BARCHI (PU)

Valentino Fiorini
Via Giardino Campioli, 5
61030 Barchi (PU)
Tel. 072197151
E-mail: carla@fioriniwines.it

The most important news from Fiorini this year is the modernization of part of the cellar. Winery organization will undoubtedly benefit from this. Consultant winemaker Roberto Potentini works alongside owner and oenologist Carla Fiorini at the winery and we have grown accustomed to seeing one of the best ranges of wines in the province emerge from their cellar door. The Bianchello del Metauro wines are all faithful interpretations of the type. The subtle, almondy Tenuta Campioli 2001 has a faintly tangy flavour whereas the deliciously drinkable Vigna Sant'Ilario 2001 shows youthfully vinous overtones and a bitterish finish. Two reds were presented and the panel preferred the Bartis, from cabernet sauvignon, montepulciano and sangiovese. Although the structure suffers because the rainy summer of 1999 hindered the ripening of the fruit, the aromas have an elegant flower-and-spice theme and show decent balance. The Sirio 2001 has flowery aromas, with a note of Parma violets typical of sangiovese, then the palate is light and fragrant, with an acid-tannin edge in the finish. Last but not least, the delicious Monsavium '96, made from biancame grapes, has subtle notes of raisins, caramel, stewed apples and Madeira on the nose. The palate has good acidic sinew, which tempers the sweetness of the alcohol and sugar while enhancing the wine's fascination and excellent length.

○	Monsavium Passito '96	🍷🍷	5
●	Bartis '99	🍷🍷	4*
○	Bianchello del Metauro		
	Tenuta Campioli '01	🍷	3
○	Bianchello del Metauro		
	Vigna Sant'Ilario '01	🍷	3
●	Colli Pesaresi		
	Sangiovese Sirio '01	🍷	3
●	Bartis '98	🍷🍷	4

CAMERANO (AN)

SPINSANTI
VIA GALLETTO, 29
60021 CAMERANO (AN)
TEL. 071731797 - 071955337
E-MAIL: agaggiotti@tiscali.it

This winery, owned by husband and wife Andrea Gaggiotti and Catia Spinsanti, is one of the nicest surprises of recent times. Its 20,000 bottles a year come from less than five hectares of rented and estate-owned vineyards but despite these modest dimensions, the winery has what it takes to produce premium wines. The 30 to 40-year-old vines stand alongside new plantations at 6,500-7,000 vines per hectare, cropping levels are low, there is thorough clonal selection, and the modern functional cellar is supervised by skilled winemaker Giorgio Baldi. Now let's look at the wines in more detail. The Camars 2001 never sees wood but does evince all the complexity and power of grapes from long-established vineyards. Intense cherry, cocoa powder and tobacco are followed by a palate where the dense tannins are clad in alluring fruit sweetness that stays throughout the firm progression and deep finish. The Adino 2001 is made in the same way as the Camars but the grapes come from younger vineyards. The aromas have high notes of morello cherry, hints of balsam and ripe plums, then the palate is less richly extracted but shows stylish balance. Lastly, the Sassòne 2000 is a monovarietal Montepulciano aged for 12 months in barrique. Dense morello cherry fruit and oriental spices on the nose mingle with an unusual and interesting note of aromatic herbs. Well-handled ageing in small wooden casks enhances the complex development in the mouth and fine-grained tannins give the wine silky energy and length.

CAMERANO (AN)

SILVANO STROLOGO
VIA OSIMANA, 89
60021 CAMERANO (AN)
TEL. 071732359 - 071731104
E-MAIL: s.strologo@libero.it

The small, long-established Strologo family winery was recently taken over by son Silvano, who has carried out extensive modernization with the invaluable help of winemaker Giancarlo Soverchia. The eight hectares of vineyards, situated on limestone and clay soil at an average height of 250 metres above sea level are perfect for growing montepulciano grapes that go into Rosso Conero. The older vineyards have a planting density of just over 2,000 plants per hectare and the newer ones are planted at 5,000, using cane pruning and Guyot systems. There are two Rosso Conero selections at the moment, Julius and Traiano. The latter is distinctly superior in quality and wins Three Glasses for the first time. In fact, Rosso Conero Traiano is no newcomer to the top ranks. It came very close to receiving our highest accolade in '99 as well. The 2000 is even nicer, beginning with its quite outstanding colour, somewhere between ruby and purple. The aromas are beginning to express complex berry fruit jam, with hints of vanilla, and the powerful palate shows dynamic thrust, a long finish and egregious ageing potential. We tasted the 2001 version of the Rosso Conero Julius, which is purple, with layered aromas of flowers, spices and wild berries, followed by an impressively tidy, drinkable palate with balance and a long, slightly tannic finish.

● Sassòne '00	♟♟	5
● Rosso Conero Adino '01	♟♟	4
● Rosso Conero Camars '01	♟♟	4

● Rosso Conero Traiano '00	♟♟♟	5
● Rosso Conero Julius '01	♟♟	3*
● Rosso Conero Traiano '99	♟♟	5
● Rosso Conero Julius '00	♟♟	3
● Rosso Conero Traiano '98	♟♟	5

CASTEL DI LAMA (AP)

TENUTA DE ANGELIS
VIA SAN FRANCESCO, 10
63030 CASTEL DI LAMA (AP)
TEL. 073687429
E-MAIL: info@tenutadeangelis.it

What an excellent achievement for De Angelis this year! Two wines went through to the final taste-offs for a third Glass. Quinto Fausti runs the winery, with the help of consultant oenologist Roberto Potentini, and the estate is situated in a hilly part of the Castel di Lama area near Offida. In other words, it's right in the centre of the limited Rosso Piceno Superiore growing area, and also the new Offida DOC, which came into effect with the 2001 vintage. The winery's pièces de résistance are the reds, so let's start with the Anghelos 2001. It has an especially dense colour and complex aromas of cocoa powder, cherries, vanilla and berries. Mouthfilling, warm and generous on the palate, it is very long and still developing. The Rosso Piceno Superiore Etichetta Oro 2000 gave a masterly performance. This opaque purple selection has sweet cherry aromas and a compelling, still quite tannic palate, although it is becoming more rounded. The Rosso Piceno Superiore 2000 is also very good. Intense, stylish and complex on the nose, it shows good structure on the palate. The Rosso Piceno 2001 is well-typed, with a medium-intense nose that offers hints of chocolate and liqueur cherries. The smooth entry on the palate takes you through to rather dominant tannins in the finish. Turning to the whites, the panel enjoyed a well-made, bright straw-yellow Prato Grande with a moderately intense nose of banana fruit, and a mouthfilling palate with nice volume. The Falerio 2001 is less expressive.

● Anghelos '00	♟♟	5
● Rosso Piceno Sup. Etichetta Oro '00	♟♟	4
● Rosso Piceno Sup. '00	♟♟	3*
○ Prato Grande Chardonnay '01	♟	3
● Rosso Piceno '01	♟	3
○ Falerio dei Colli Ascolani '01		2
● Anghelos '99	♟♟♟	5
● Anghelos '97	♟♟	5
● Rosso Piceno Sup. '97	♟♟	3
● Anghelos '98	♟♟	5
● Rosso Piceno Sup. '98	♟♟	3

CASTELPLANIO (AN)

FAZI BATTAGLIA
VIA ROMA, 117
60032 CASTELPLANIO (AN)
TEL. 0731813444 - 06844311
E-MAIL: info@fazibattaglia.it

The Fazi Battaglia winery owns 340 hectares of land in 12 vineyards situated in various parts of "Classico" district of the Castelli di Jesi DOC zone. A few years ago, the technical team of oenologist Dino Porfiri and vineyard managers Mario Ghergo and Antonio Verdolini was boosted by the arrival of consultant Franco Bernabei. This year, Fazi Battaglia presented another great range of wines, including a number of well-made reds, as well as its celebrated customary Verdicchios. We'll start with the Verdicchio di Castelli di Jesi wines presented this year, the Titulus 2001, released in the famous amphora bottle, which has a fairly deep straw-yellow colour, varietal aromas of wild flowers and herbs, good nose-palate consistency and fairly good volume. The Le Moie 2001 selection has fairly well-expressed aromas of lime blossom that are reflected nicely on the tidy, well-managed palate. The San Sisto Classico Riserva 1999 is bright straw yellow with fairly generous aromas, including apple and vanilla, while the palate is equally full, with toasty notes that are still settling in. Among the reds, the Riserva di Rosso Conero Passo del Lupo 1998 is a very nice wine with a good dense colour and complex cocoa powder, coffee and berry fruit aromas that are stylish rather than intense. The generous flavour has slightly excessive alcohol and a long finish. The standard-label Rosso Conero is also well-made. Its purplish, ruby red and spicy balsamic aromas introduce good progression on the moderately structured palate.

○ Verdicchio dei Castelli di Jesi Cl. Sup. Le Moie '01	♟♟	4*
● Rosso Conero Passo del Lupo Ris. '98	♟♟	6
○ Verdicchio dei Castelli di Jesi Cl. San Sisto Ris. '99	♟♟	5
● Rosso Conero '01	♟	4
○ Verdicchio dei Castelli di Jesi Cl. Titulus '01	♟	3
○ Arkezia Muffo di S. Sisto '98	♟♟	7
● Rosso Conero Passo del Lupo Ris. '97	♟♟	6
○ Verdicchio dei Castelli di Jesi Cl. San Sisto Ris. '98	♟♟	5

CASTIGNANO (AP)

CANTINA COOPERATIVA CASTIGNANESE
C.DA SAN VENANZO, 31
63032 CASTIGNANO (AP)
TEL. 0736822216
E-MAIL: scac@topnet.it

We have been following the fortunes of this co-operative with interest. It has many interesting features, including 600 hectares of vineyards in one of the best growing areas in the Marche, technical supervision from oenologist Pierluigi Lorenzetti and consistently honest prices. Production is now well-established so the time has come to give the cellar a closer look. Let's review the wines. Templaria and Gramelot, both from 2000, are the indisputable flagship products. The Templaria is a blend of montepulciano, merlot and sangiovese where sweet vanilla hints blend with berry fruit and cinnamon on the nose. After an enjoyable entry, the structure of the palate is bolstered by alcohol and solid tannins. Gramelot is made from the same grapes as the Falerio, that is trebbiano, malvasia, pecorino and passerina, but in different proportions. Alluring peach, apricot and golden delicious apple aromas mingle with a sweet note of alcohol. Then the big, soft palate shows excellent staying power in the finish. The same sensations are also present in the Falerio 2001, which is less complicated and aromatic, but still very drinkable and balanced. The Rosso Piceno Superiore 2000 has nice concentration on the palate. While the mouthfeel is not heavy, insistent notes of cherry jam detract from the overall elegance. The spicy, lean Sangiovese 2000 is similar in standard, but not style, and has an enjoyable palate. The rest of the wines are all well typed.

○ Gramelot '00	▼▼	4*
● Templaria '00	▼▼	4*
● Rosso Piceno Sup. '00	▼	3
● Sangiovese '00	▼	3
○ Falerio dei Colli Ascolani '01	▼	2
⊙ Primavera '01		2
● Rosso Piceno '01		3

CINGOLI (MC)

LUCANGELI AYMERICH DI LACONI
LOC. TAVIGNANO
62011 CINGOLI (MC)
TEL. 0733617303
E-MAIL: tavignano@libero.it

The Aymerich di Laconi family lived in Rome but also owned a lovely 230-hectare property in the Castelli di Jesi "Classico" zone. So why not try serious investment in wine, since it was such a favourable area? The idea was put into practice in the mid 1990s after a meeting with Staffolo oenologist Giancarlo Soverchia, an expert in the area. Once the best 25 hectares had been identified, work began planting native vine varieties like verdicchio, sangiovese and montepulciano, and a modern, functional cellar was built. The excellent early results were followed by a period of ups and downs, with some successes and a few disappointments. This year's good tasting results lead us to believe that the range is well on the way to premium quality, which looks well within the cellar's reach. The best of the bottles we tasted was undoubtedly the Rosso Piceno 2001. It is drinking well now, thanks to compact structure, good depth, and berry fruit and spice aromas that are not too complex but very intense. Of the two Verdicchios, we preferred the sinewy, unabashedly tangy Classico Superiore 2001, strange to say, with its hints of wild herbs, fresh almonds and apples on the nose. The Misco 2001 has a similar sensory profile but the sensations are not yet fully expressed. It's a wine that may well improve with time.

● Rosso Piceno Tavignano '01	▼▼	4
○ Verdicchio dei Castelli di Jesi Cl. Sup. Tavignano '01	▼▼	3*
○ Verdicchio dei Castelli di Jesi Cl. Sup. Sel. Misco '01	▼	4

CIVITANOVA MARCHE (MC)

Boccadigabbia
Loc. Fontespina
C.da Castelletta, 56
62012 Civitanova Marche (MC)
tel. 073370728
e-mail: info@boccadigabbia.com

Don't waste your time looking for the Akronte '99. Elvio Alessandri's Cabernet won't be released because it is apparently not up to its usual standard. However, the winery makes up for this absence with two wines that are in a class of their own. The Saltapicchio is a deep ruby red, monovarietal Sangiovese with a nose that opens out into elegant aromas of violets, blackberries and spices. The dense palate develops in perfect balance around soft tannins that support the attractive fruit. The other outstanding wine is the Pix, a monovarietal Merlot. Smoky hints on the nose intermingle with fruit and spice overtones that gradually intensify, and the ripe fruit softness on the palate is supported by a complex, elegantly velvety tannic weave, with a return of the rich aromas in the seductive finish. Fabrizio Ciufoli and Giovanni Basso work together on other products as well, although it would be unfair to describe them as "standard-label" wines given their true quality. The Garbì's fragrant nose and varietal freshness lend it instant appeal while the Castelletta, the only Pinot Grigio made in the Marche, has floral notes on the nose and a very simple, decently made palate. The Mont'Anello has an unripe, slightly grassy nose and a fragrant palate where a note of acidity enhances and supports the aromas. The two good Rosso Picenos both have lively colour, cherry fruit and leather on the nose, where the Villamagna is more evolved. Both have full body, supported by delicious extract.

CUPRA MARITTIMA (AP)

Oasi degli Angeli
C.da Sant'Egidio, 50
63012 Cupra Marittima (AP)
tel. 0735778569
e-mail: info@kurni.it

The delightful 2000 version of the Kurni earns Three Glasses again. The very hot vintage is evident in the extractive weight and exceptionally mature polyphenols, while cellar technique and obsessive care in both cellar and vineyard have given the wine its dense colour, somewhere between ruby red and purple. After a swirl in the glass, this Montepulciano releases aromas of black cherry fruit and minerals that open into earthy overtones, bitter chocolate, ripe plums, and soft hints of coffee and wood resin. The kaleidoscope of aromas dissolves and reforms in an endlessly fascinating display with every turn of the glass. Entry on the palate is balanced, and the complex progression leads to an equally complex finish. Of course, this is just the tip of the iceberg in comparison to what the wine will offer in a few years' time. Our compliments to Marco Casolanetti and Eleonora Rossi, and also to winemaker Giovanni Basso. We trust they will continue to make such characterful wines in future years. Actually, we have to spoil this idyllic picture a little by informing readers who were hoping to buy some that availability is limited. Total production of Kurni is only 4,500 bottles so demand could mean an increase in the price, which was already in line with Italy's noblest reds at the cellar door. Take comfort from the fact that another hectare of vineyards will soon come onstream alongside the five and a half already in use.

● Pix Merlot '99	¥¥	7
● Saltapicchio Sangiovese '99	¥¥	7
● Rosso Piceno '00	¥¥	4*
○ Mont'Anello Bianco '00	¥	4
○ Garbì Bianco '01	¥	3
○ La Castelletta Pinot Grigio '01	¥	4
● Rosso Piceno Villamagna '99	¥	4
● Akronte '93	¥¥¥	8
● Akronte '94	¥¥¥	8
● Akronte '95	¥¥¥	8
● Akronte '97	¥¥¥	8
● Akronte '98	¥¥¥	8
● Akronte '96	¥¥	8

● Kurni '00	¥¥¥	8
● Kurni '97	¥¥¥	8
● Kurni '98	¥¥¥	8
● Kurni '99	¥¥	8

CUPRAMONTANA (AN)

Colonnara Viticoltori
in Cupramontana
Via Mandriole, 6
60034 Cupramontana (AN)
tel. 0731780273
e-mail: info@colonnara.it

Colonnara was established in 1959 as an umbrella for growers in one of the finest verdicchio areas. Today, just under 200 member growers rely on the expertise of Pierluigi Gagliardini – cellar manager in theory but in practice in charge of everything –, the technical and scientific experience of winemakers Corrado Cugnasco and Cesare Ferrari, and the professionalism of marketing and external relations manager, Daniela Sorana. The firm foundations of the range were evident from the tastings. The 1995 Brut Metodo Classico was again excellent. Its fine perlage, complex nose and stylish palate have always made it one of the best of its type in the region. In contrast, the Brut Charmat is pleasantly uncomplicated and fragrant. The undisputed number-one still wine is the Tufico 2000, a Verdicchio made from late-harvested grapes. The well-defined aromas include apples, spring flowers and a hint of citrus, while the palate is stylish yet powerful, with a lingering finish. The Vigna San Marco 2001 has typical fresh almonds on the nose, good structure and a subtly bitterish finish and the Cuprese 2001 has a pleasant nose with hints of hazelnuts, the already soft palate hinting at good ageing prospects. Lastly, we come to the Lyricus line. The panel thought the clean fruitiness of the Rosso Piceno 2000 was more enjoyable than the well-made, disarmingly uncomplicated Verdicchio 2001.

CUPRAMONTANA (AN)

Vallerosa Bonci
Via Torre, 13
60034 Cupramontana (AN)
tel. 0731789129
e-mail: vallerosabonci@tiscalinet.it

Our compliments to Giuseppe Bonci and oenologist Sergio Paolucci for the general standards across the range, even though none of the wines were awarded Three Glasses this year. Let's take a look at the bottles. The San Michele 2001 is stylish, with its usual good alcohol, but lacks last year's harmony. The Barrè '99 has an intense almond and citrus peel nose with a generous, lingering palate. There is still a strong hint of vanilla but this will fade. The new Pietrone 2000 comes from all the clonal selections the winery has carried out over the years. Its meaty, mouthfilling palate, and finesse on the nose, made a good impression on the panel. Next came the Rosso Picenos. The Casa Nostra 2000 was a pleasant surprise, with very intense coffee and cherry aromas followed by a vigorous entry and good thrust on the palate, slightly held back by excessive tannins on the finish. The simpler Viatorre 2000 has clean morello cherry on the nose, and the enjoyable palate reveals no rough edges. We are duty bound to say that the sparkling wines have made a great leap forward. The Charmat has lovely fragrance and the Metodo Classico at last finds the complexity and elegance to compete with the best fizz in the region. The icing on the cake is provided by the Rojano 2000. Delightful hints of candied citrus, raisins and honey are layered on the nose, fusing together on the alluringly sweet palate.

○ Verdicchio dei Castelli di Jesi Cl. Sup. Tufico V.T. '00	▼▼ 4
● Rosso Piceno Lyricus '00	▼ 2
○ Verdicchio dei Castelli di Jesi Cl. Sup. Cuprese '01	▼ 3
○ Verdicchio dei Castelli di Jesi Cl. Sup. Vigna San Marco '01	▼ 3
○ Colonnara Spumante Brut Charmat	▼ 3
○ Verdicchio dei Castelli di Jesi Cl. Lyricus '01	2
○ Verdicchio dei Castelli di Jesi Cl. Sup. Tufico '99	▼▼ 4
○ Colonnara Spumante Brut M. Cl. Millesimato '95	▼▼ 5

○ Verdicchio dei Castelli di Jesi Passito Rojano '00	▼▼ 5
● Rosso Piceno Casa Nostra '00	▼▼ 6
○ Verdicchio dei Castelli di Jesi Cl. Pietrone Ris. '00	▼▼ 5
○ Verdicchio dei Castelli di Jesi Cl. Barrè Ris. '99	▼▼ 5
○ Verdicchio dei Castelli di Jesi Cl. Sup. S. Michele '01	▼▼ 4*
○ Bonci Brut M. Cl.	▼▼ 5
● Rosso Piceno Viatorre '00	▼ 3*
○ Bonci Brut	▼ 4
○ Verdicchio dei Castelli di Jesi Cl. Sup. S. Michele '00	▼▼▼ 5

FANO (PU)

CLAUDIO MORELLI
V.LE ROMAGNA, 47/B
61032 FANO (PU)
TEL. 0721823352
E-MAIL: clamoro@libero.it

Claudio Morelli is firmly convinced of the potential of Bianchello del Metauro. He uses his patchwork of vineyards to best advantage by offering three selections with different features. They are three excellent interpretations of the same variety in different site climates. The Borgo Torre is the most imposing and complex of the trio, with full, intense aromas of flowers, fresh fruit and – unusually – dried pulses. The pleasant acidity on the generous, tangy palate perks up the dense, ripe fruit. The long finish is pleasantly bitterish. The Vigna delle Terrazze has more intensely fruity aromas, especially peaches and melon. Its harmonious, lingering palate is attractively concentrated, tangy, and utterly individual. Morelli's most interesting red, the Suffragium 2000, comes from an unusual blend of vernaccia di Pergola and montepulciano. It is at last back in production and proves to be a very dense, weighty wine, with a succulent, alcohol-led mouthfeel, good harmony and nice balance. The Magliano is also very well-made. A blend of sangiovese, cabernet sauvignon and merlot aged in barriques, it shows typically intense fruit aromas of black cherry, blackberries and blueberries, enhanced by a fresh balsamic note. Fruit is also present on the palate, which has a smooth entry and becomes a little too dry in the finish. The Sangiovese Sant'Andrea in Villis has sweet fruit, slightly covered by oakiness, and is pleasant but rather one-dimensional on the palate.

● Suffragium '00	ŸŸ	4
○ Bianchello del Metauro Borgo Torre '01	ŸŸ	3*
○ Bianchello del Metauro La Vigna delle Terrazze '01	ŸŸ	3*
● Magliano '99	ŸŸ	4
● Colli Pesaresi Sangiovese Sant'Andrea in Villis '00	Ÿ	4
○ Bianchello del Metauro S. Cesareo '01		2
● Colli Pesaresi Sangiovese La Vigna delle Terrazze '01		3

GROTTAMMARE (AP)

VINICOLA DEL TESINO
VIA SAN LEONARDO, 35
63013 GROTTAMMARE (AP)
TEL. 0735735869
E-MAIL: carminucci@carminucci.com

Vinicola di Tesino was founded back in 1928 but Piero Carminucci and his son Giovanni only really began to bottle some of the wine a few years ago, alongside their traditional unbottled trade. This was a wise decision because the grapes are excellent, there is certainly no lack of grape selection experience and Pierluigi Lorenzetti is a dependable, skilled winemaker. Running through our tasting notes, we see the Grotte sul Mare standard-label line gave a good performance. The Falerio 2001 is approachable, smooth and enjoyable, while the Rosso Piceno 2001 is a little rustic on the nose but has a good, no-nonsense, fruit-led palate, slightly dried out by tannins in the medium-intense finish. Moving on to the winery's selection label, Naumachos, we liked the Litora '99 best of the three wines on offer. A blend of verdicchio and chardonnay aged in barrique, it shows sweet tropical fruit on the nose over faint hints of cake, then a rounded, warm palate that mirrors the aromas of the nose. The poor vintage is evident in the structure of the Rosso Piceno Superiore '99, though it does make up with an intense nose of small berry fruit, plums and spice. The Falerio Naumachos 2001 has strong apple-like aromas, and a medium-dense palate with a slightly fleeting finish. The Chardonnay 2001 was not ready so we'll talk about that next year.

○ Litora Naumachos '99	ŸŸ	5
○ Falerio dei Colli Ascolani Grotte sul Mare '01	Ÿ	3
○ Falerio dei Colli Ascolani Naumachos '01	Ÿ	3
● Rosso Piceno Grotte sul Mare '01	Ÿ	3
● Rosso Piceno Sup. Naumachos '99	Ÿ	4

JESI (AN)

MONTECAPPONE
VIA COLLE OLIVO, 2
60035 JESI (AN)
TEL. 0731205761 - 0731204233
E-MAIL: agrivinicola@agrivinicola.it

The Mirizzi family owns Agrivinicola Montecappone, founded in 1968. The 60 hectares under vine are divided as follows: 20 planted to verdicchio; 25 with fiano, chardonnay, sauvignon, malvasia and trebbiano for white wines; and 15 with montepulciano, merlot, sangiovese grosso and cabernet sauvignon for the reds. The winery hopes to improve production by replanting the older vineyards and re-organizing the existing ones. The new plots use cordon-training and spur-pruning at a density of 5,000 vines per hectare. Advised by consultant oenologist Lorenzo Landi, Gianluca Mirizzi turns out delicate, gentle, judiciously concentrated wines that fully and elegantly express the features of the local territory. The Esino DOC originated as a spin-off designation but the Tabano is a very well-made, elegant and enjoyable wine with good aromas and structure. In no way is it the poor relation of the more famous Verdicchio dei Castelli di Jesi. The Montesecco has a well-adjusted nose of lime blossom and yellow plums, then sound structure with well-balanced acidity and a nice clean finish. The Rosso Piceno Montesecco, from sangiovese and montepulciano, is very interesting. The dark vermilion introduces ripe cherry hints on the broad, fruity nose. The palate opens smoothly, thanks to subtle tannins backing up the texture, where fruit is the focus.

LORETO (AN)

GIOACCHINO GAROFOLI
LOC. VILLA MUSONE
VIA ARNO, 9
60025 LORETO (AN)
TEL. 0717820162 - 0717820163
E-MAIL: mail@garofolivini.it

Carlo and Gianfranco Garofoli, who own this superb winery, were invited to the Three Glasses awards for the sixth year running. They assure us that their joy and excitement increase every time. This year, the Serra Fiorese 1999 hit the top spot, repeating the triumph of the now legendary 1992 vintage. It is easy to describe. Just take the wonderful Podium, awarded Three Glasses last year for its honey, spring flowers and mineral hints on the nose, strength and elegance on the palate, then add depth and complexity. Spectacular. But the celebration continues with another great finalist, the Podium 2000, as irresistibly aroma-driven as ever. The palate is full, elegant, mouthfilling and soft, almost a little too soft. The Agontano 1998 is dark and austere on the nose, where the wood blends almost perfectly with the liquorice, black berry fruit and a hint of tar. The palate offsets the tannic weave with well-gauged alcohol and the balanced acidity braces the enviable length of the finish. This sophisticated range continues with little gems such as the Brut Metodo Classico, which is probably the best "spumante" in the region, and the Verdicchio Passito Le Brume 1999, with dried fruit hints on the nose and candied fruit on the palate. Carlo Garofoli's indisputable winemaking skill is also demonstrated in the rosé Komaros 2001, which shows fragrant strawberry in the mouth. Finally, the Rosso Conero Piancarda '99 and Verdicchio Macrina 2001 are such great value for money that you can drink them every day. Who could ask for anything more?

● Rosso Piceno Montesecco '01	♛♛	3*
○ Esino Bianco Tabano '01	♛	4
○ Verdicchio dei Castelli di Jesi Cl. Montesecco '01	♛	3

○ Verdicchio dei Castelli di Jesi Cl. Serra Fiorese Ris. '99	♛♛♛	4*
○ Verdicchio dei Castelli di Jesi Cl. Sup. Podium '00	♛♛	4
● Rosso Conero Grosso Agontano '98	♛♛	5
○ Verdicchio dei Castelli di Jesi Passito Le Brume '99	♛♛	5
○ Garofoli Brut M. Cl.	♛♛	4
○ Verdicchio dei Castelli di Jesi Cl. Sup. Macrina '01	♛	3*
● Rosso Conero Piancarda '99	♛	3*
○ Verdicchio dei Castelli di Jesi Cl. Sup. Podium '98	♛♛♛	4
○ Verdicchio dei Castelli di Jesi Cl. Sup. Podium '99	♛♛♛	4

MAIOLATI SPONTINI (AN)

Monteschiavo
Fraz. Monteschiavo
Via Vivaio
60030 Maiolati Spontini (AN)
Tel. 0731700385 - 0731700297
E-mail: monteschiavo@puntomedia.it

Monteschiavo has belonged to the Pieralisi group since 1994. Thanks to a combination of factors, including varied site climates, shoot thinning, manual harvesting and excellent professional support from oenologist Pierluigi Lorenzetti, Monteschiavo wines have enjoyed great success. Further proof comes with the winery's first ever Three Glasses, awarded to the Rosso Conero Adeodato 2000. This a captivating wine offers a profusion of ripe blackberries, leather and tobacco on the nose, and a strong, elegant palate with gentle tannins, lingering opulent fruit and an echo of the complex aromas in the finish. The montepulciano and cabernet-based Esio is also quite delightful, its complex fruit-and-spice nose leading in to a lightly oaked palate rich in juicy fruit. The panel then turned to the whites, starting with the Coste del Molino, a frank, uncomplicated Verdicchio, more enjoyable on the nose than the palate, and then the rather better Pallio, with lime blossom on the nose and interesting dense fruit on the palate, though the acidity can't quite handle the close-knit texture. The vanilla in the Bando is more noticeable on the nose than on the palate, where the ripe fruit is balanced and nicely presented. Le Giuncare is a cold-macerated late-harvest wine that has floral notes on the nose, rich extract and a tangy flavour. The Passito Arché is very delicate, with a subtle nose and a strikingly well-balanced palate, whose residual sugar never threatens the freshness. The Lacrima 2001 is well managed, with varied, satisfying aromas.

MATELICA (MC)

Belisario - Cantina Sociale di Matelica e Cerreto d'Esi
Via Merloni, 12
62024 Matelica (MC)
Tel. 0737787247
E-mail: vinibelisario@libero.it

Belisario has become a benchmark winery in the Matelica area thanks to constant hard work. Credit goes above all to shrewd management of technical and human resources by Roberto Potentini, director and chief winemaker. The Verdicchio di Matelica series is once again of a very high standard, and as usual the Cambrugiano Riserva '99 is head and shoulders above the rest. Intense apple and almond aromas are enhanced with a hint of vanilla. The mid palate is smooth and strong, then the finish lingers. Not far behind is the Vigneti del Cerro 2001 whose enfolding floral aromas are reflected on a palate with a nice balance of acidity and softness. Softness is also the common denominator for the Vigneti Belisario and Terre di Valbona 2001. The former more clearly reveals the cellar's quest for weight and density while the Terre di Valbona is well-typed, fragrant and quaffable, yet very satisfying. The other whites include the Ferrante 2001, which has hawthorn and apple aromas that are reflected on the light palate. The Colferraio is a vintage red, although the year is not indicated, with a faintly spicy nose and vaguely vegetal palate, free of tannin harshness. Lastly, the usual note for the Passito Carpe Diem (the '98 is now on the shelves): amber colour, stewed pears, caramel and vanilla in the nose and good alcohol on the palate.

● Rosso Conero Adeodato '00	🍷🍷🍷	6
● Esio Rosso '00	🍷🍷	5*
○ Verdicchio dei Castelli di Jesi Cl. Bando di S. Settimio '00	🍷🍷	4
○ Verdicchio dei Castelli di Jesi Cl. Sup. Pallio di S. Floriano '01	🍷🍷	3*
○ Verdicchio Castelli di Jesi Passito Arché '99	🍷🍷	4
○ Verdicchio dei Castelli di Jesi Cl. Le Giuncare Ris. '00	🍷	4
● Lacrima di Morro d'Alba '01	🍷	4
○ Verdicchio dei Castelli di Jesi Cl. Coste del Molino '01	🍷	3
● Esio Rosso '99	🍷🍷	5

○ Verdicchio di Matelica Cambrugiano Ris. '99	🍷🍷	4
○ Verdicchio di Matelica Vigneti Belisario '01	🍷🍷	4
○ Verdicchio di Matelica Vigneti del Cerro '01	🍷🍷	3*
○ Esino Bianco Ferrante '01	🍷	2
○ Verdicchio di Matelica Terre di Valbona '01	🍷	2
○ Carpe Diem Passito '98	🍷	4
● Colferraio	🍷	2
○ Verdicchio di Matelica Cambrugiano Ris. '98	🍷🍷	4

MATELICA (MC)

LA MONACESCA
C.DA MONACESCA
62024 MATELICA (MC)
TEL. 0733812602
E-MAIL: info@monacesca.it

The upper Esino valley, where La Monacesca is situated, in the municipality of Matelica, was once occupied by a lake that later dried up, enriching the soil with mineral salts. The area also has a typically continental climate, with cold winters and hot summers, and considerable temperature variations during the grape ripening period. This means the wines made by Aldo Cifola, with Fabrizio Ciufoli and Roberto Potentini, are destined to have highly complex sensory profiles, and they are, in fact, complex and elegant, and of a consistently high standard. The standard-label Verdicchio has aromas of lime blossom and aniseed in the nose and a fragrant, though not very complex, palate whereas La Monacesca is a step up in quality, a delicious hint of cakes joining the floral aromas before the fresh and elegant, if not huge, palate. The Mirum, which has ripe fruit in the nose and richer extract on the palate, is a touch less fragrant but opulent enough to be very long-lasting. The Ecclesia is an entirely different kettle of fish. This Chardonnay has intense grassy, citrus aromas on the nose, then balanced and enjoyably fruity on the palate. The Camerte, from sangiovese grosso and merlot, is ruby red and shows a predominantly vegetal-balsamic nose of rue and liquorice root. The palate has plenty of tannin-driven muscle, which is tempered by balanced alcohol to sweeten the dense extract. The palate closes with a pleasant hint of liquorice.

○ Verdicchio di Matelica Mirum '00	♀♀	5
● Camerte '00	♀♀	7
○ Verdicchio di Matelica La Monacesca '01	♀♀	4*
○ Ecclesia Chardonnay '01	♀	4
○ Verdicchio di Matelica '01	♀	3
○ Mirus '91	♀♀♀	5
○ Mirum '94	♀♀♀	5
● Camerte '99	♀♀♀	7
○ Verdicchio di Matelica La Monacesca '94	♀♀♀	5
○ Mirum '99	♀♀	5
● Camerte '98	♀♀	7

MONDAVIO (PU)

FATTORIA LAILA
VIA S. FILIPPO SUL CESANO, 27
61040 MONDAVIO (PU)
TEL. 0721979353
E-MAIL: fattorialaila@tin.it

After years of honest trade in bottled and unbottled wines around the neighbouring areas, Aristide Libenzi, no longer a young man, was faced with a choice: either leave the business or find someone else to run it with the same commitment. When he turned to his granddaughter Lara and her husband Andrea Crocenzi, their reply was all he hoped for. Andrea was willing to leave his job with a bank, provided that the winery was relaunched on the lines he had in mind. A few years later, respected Tuscan winemaker Lorenzo Landi was striding through the new, densely-planted vineyards giving instructions on cellar techniques. Now, at last, we can see the results of all this effort. The standard-label Verdicchio has a nice, typical nose of apples and spring flowers, while the palate is soft and very drinkable. The grapes for the more complex Verdicchio Lailum 2001 underwent a more scrupulous selection and the wine aged in barriques, resulting in a white with intense citrus peel and fruit aromas and a note of vanilla echoed on the rounded, lingering palate. The mouthfilling Rosso Piceno 2001 is intensely fruity on the nose with full body and solid structure then the Lailum 2000 is a monovarietal Montepulciano with eloquently expressive aromas. It has hints of cherries, vanilla from the wood, and spice. The palate is taut and well-sustained, with rather impulsive but sweet tannins and a very long finish.

● Lailum '00	♀♀	5
● Rosso Piceno '01	♀♀	4*
○ Verdicchio dei Castelli di Jesi Cl. '01	♀	3
○ Verdicchio dei Castelli di Jesi Cl. Sup. Lailum '01	♀	4

MONTECAROTTO (AN)

LAURENTINA
VIA SAN PIETRO 19/A
60036 MONTECAROTTO (AN)
TEL. 073189435
E-MAIL: laurentina@katamail.com

Last year's description ended with the promise that there would be a very exciting Rosso Piceno selection this year, and here it is. The Talliano overturns the accepted wisdom that Montecarotto is strictly white territory. The colour is dense purple. There are morello cherries, elderflower, cinchona and vanilla on the nose, a sumptuous rounded palate with perfectly balanced tannins and a return of all those lovely aromas in the finish. The winery aims to work exclusively with native local reds and whites, to demonstrate that good, or even great, wines can be made without French grapes. All that's needed is high-density planting, low yields, careful bunch selection and scrupulous cellar work. All this comes through in the Talliano and also in the Laurano, made from montepulciano and lacrima. A bright ruby red bluish tinges, it has an approachable nose of roses and violets that open into fruity sensations, and an alluring, pleasantly drinkable palate. The initially reticent nose of the Rosso Piceno expands into ripe cherry and blackberry while the tight-knit palate has fruit enfolded in soft tannins. The Verdicchio Vigneto di Tobia is highly traditional. Vegetal notes of lime blossom and geraniums on the nose are backed up by firm alcohol and the powerful, richly extracted palate has slightly flat acidity. Overall, it's a wine that is more powerful than elegant. Keep an eye on this ambitious, fast-improving winery.

● Rosso Piceno Talliano '00	ΨΨ	5
● Esino Rosso Laurano '01	ΨΨ	4*
● Rosso Piceno '01	Ψ	3
○ Verdicchio dei Castelli di Jesi Cl. Vigneto di Tobia '01	Ψ	3

MONTECAROTTO (AN)

TERRE CORTESI MONCARO
VIA PIANDOLE, 7/A
60036 MONTECAROTTO (AN)
TEL. 073189245
E-MAIL: terrecortesi@moncaro.com

Situated in the heart of the Verdicchio dei Castelli di Jesi production area, Terre Cortesi Moncaro is one of the most important in the Marche in terms of numbers and variety of wines, quality and environmental awareness. Moving on to this year's wines, the Vigna Novali 1999, a Verdicchio Classico Riserva, has upfront toasty aromas, a soft, consistent palate and an interesting lingering finish. The Verdicchio dei Castelli di Jesi Tordiruta Passito 1997, reviewed previously and retasted this year, is golden yellow with mainly citrus and sweet aromas that return on the fairly broad palate. The '99 version now on sale is similarly complex. Golden yellow, it shows candied citrus, cakes and apricots on the nose, a sweet, soft mouthfeel and a long, rather sugary finish. The Verdicchio dei Castelli di Jesi versions are very good, too. The Le Vele 2001 has stylish floral aromas and a flavoursome, pervasive and quite long palate while the Verde di Ca' Ruptae 2001 has clearly varietal aromas of spring flowers and apples, ushering in a tangy, intense palate with good length. Other wine types include the red Barocco 1999, a good, dense ruby red wine with a stylish nose that shows upfront hints of wild berries and an even, elegant, medium-weight palate. The Riserva di Rosso Conero Vigneti del Parco '98 has classy aromas of pepper, berry fruits and vanilla that are reflected on the palate. The Rosso Piceno Superior '99 Rocca di Acquaviva is less compact but has good balance.

○ Verdicchio dei Castelli di Jesi Cl. Le Vele '01	ΨΨ	3*
○ Verdicchio dei Castelli di Jesi Cl. Sup. Verde di Ca' Ruptae '01	ΨΨ	3*
● Rosso Conero Vigneti del Parco Ris. '98	ΨΨ	4
○ Verdicchio dei Castelli di Jesi Passito Tordiruta '99	ΨΨ	5
○ Verdicchio dei Castelli di Jesi Cl. Vigna Novali Ris. '99	ΨΨ	4
● Barocco '99	Ψ	4
● Rosso Piceno Sup. Rocca di Acquaviva '99	Ψ	3
○ Verdicchio dei Castelli di Jesi Cl. Vigna Novali Ris. '98	ΨΨ	4

MONTEGRANARO (AP)

Rio Maggio
C.da Vallone, 41
63014 Montegranaro (AP)
tel. 0734889587

This winery makes just under 100,000 bottles a year from its 15 hectares of vineyards in the Piceno hills. They are sold under two labels, the traditional products made from local varieties and the Artias line, exclusively for international grape varieties. Simone Santucci and his wife Tiziana are helped by consultant winemaker Giancarlo Soverchia and produce a range of thoroughly good wines every year. The Telusiano 2001 is an excellent Falerio. Strict selection and a slightly late harvest have produced a full bouquet of fruit, flower and mineral aromas, then the robust, richly extracted body is balanced by judicious acidity and tangy flavour. The wonderful Sauvignon Artias 2001 is highly typical on the nose. Its polished, stylish palate ushers in a very well-typed, lingering finish. The Pinot Nero Artias 2000 also performed well. Aged for one year in French barriques, it has elegant Burgundy-style aromas of fresh fruit and spices that come back on the complex, sophisticated palate with its light, gentle sensations. Good and sound on the palate but lacking finesse on the nose, the GrAnarijS 2000 is a little below par compared to previous versions. The standard-label Rosso Piceno is simply but very well made.

○ Artias Sauvignon '01	🍷🍷	4*
● Artias Pinot Nero '00	🍷🍷	5
○ Falerio dei Colli Ascolani Telusiano '01	🍷🍷	3*
● Rosso Piceno GrAnarijS '00	🍷	5
○ Artias Chardonnay '01	🍷	4
○ Falerio dei Colli Ascolani '01	🍷	2*
● Rosso Piceno '01	🍷	3
○ Artias Sauvignon '00	🍷🍷	4
● Rosso Piceno GrAnarijS '99	🍷🍷	5

MONTEPRANDONE (AP)

Il Conte
Via Colle Navicchio, 28
63030 Monteprandone (AP)
tel. 073562593
e-mail: ilcontevini@tiscalinet.it

Situated on a spectacular hill in the Piceno area at over 200 metres above sea level, with a view of the nearby Adriatic and sunshine all day long, the De Angelis family winery has 11 hectares of vineyards and rents seven more. The montepulciano, sangiovese, pecorino and passerina grapes in the older vineyards, and merlot and cabernet sauvignon in the new ones, make 50,000 bottles a year of the top Villaprandone and standard-label Il Conte lines. Other facilities will soon include the barrique cellar, now being made ready, and a well equipped cellar for vinifying the wines. Our tasters were very impressed with these good-quality wines, made with the help of expert winemakers Fabrizio Ciufoli and Pierluigi Lorenzetti. The Zipolo is an international-style blend of montepulciano, merlot and cabernet. The grassy aromas typical of French varieties mingle well with fruit hints from the montepulciano and spice from the small wooden casks. The palate is smooth with a good balance of acidity, alcohol and tannin but is also rather ruggedly direct, simple and a little severe because of its gutsy tannins. The Navicchio, made mainly from chardonnay, has typical apple and pear fruit on the nose blending with balsamic hints of Mediterranean scrubland. The palate is full, opulent and gentle, and just lacks a touch of freshness to make the top grade.

○ Navicchio Bianco '00	🍷🍷	4*
● Zipolo Rosso '99	🍷🍷	5
● Rosso Piceno Marinus '00	🍷	4

MORRO D'ALBA (AN)

STEFANO MANCINELLI
VIA ROMA, 62
60030 MORRO D'ALBA (AN)
TEL. 073163021
E-MAIL: manvin@tin.it

Mancinelli was one of the wineries that contributed to the launch of Lacrima. This wine has particularly interesting, varied aromas on the nose, although it has difficulty finding balance in the mouth because of the rugged tannins that often mask the nuances on the palate. We had grown used to seeing Stefano Mancinelli square the circle with soft, fragrant wines but the last vintage posed more problems. Results were uneven and the wines no longer present their successful balance. The Lacrima Sensazioni di Frutto and the Santa Maria del Fiore both have enticing noses but fail to do justice to the generosity of the variety. They are hazy and evanescent on the palate, and the texture lacks complexity. The San Michele is more enjoyable, with notes of dried roses and violets in a more impressive structure. The Re Sole is a well-made raisined Lacrima. Deep purple with bluish highlights, it has hints of roses, cinchona and elderflower on the nose. The palate is balanced and gentle, though the finish is slightly drying. The Verdicchios pay the price of a hot, dry year that has diminished their acidity, making the aromas over-evolved or even stewed, and the palates lack freshness. This applies particularly to the Santa Maria del Fiore while the Classico is a little brighter. Its nose is more varied nose and the palate weightier.

- Re Sole — 6
- Lacrima di Morro d'Alba S. Maria del Fiore '01 — 4
- Lacrima di Morro d'Alba Sensazioni di Frutto '01 — 4
- San Michele '01 — 4
- Verdicchio dei Castelli di Jesi Cl. '01 — 3
- Verdicchio dei Castelli di Jesi Cl. Sup. S. Maria del Fiore '01 — 4
- Lacrima di Morro d'Alba S. Maria del Fiore '00 — 4

MORRO D'ALBA (AN)

MAROTTI CAMPI
LOC. SANT' AMICO, 14
60030 MORRO D'ALBA (AN)
TEL. 0731618027 - 0731618846
E-MAIL: wine.marotticampi@tin.it

Winemaker Roberto Potentini was instrumental in creating the winery's trademark style of pleasant, interesting and authentically local wines. The 2001 Luzano is a traditional Verdicchio with a good range of aromas and a palate that is powerful rather than fresh-tasting. Its rather forward finish is due to diminished acidity, an effect of the dry weather. The Orgiolo is aged in stainless steel and barrique, and has a ruby red hue tinged with purple. The typical dried flower notes on the nose mingle with cherries and blueberries, while the enjoyable extract on the palate supports the texture as the fruity notes of the nose return. The Rùbico was aged for a year less than usual and is simpler and more approachable. Nevertheless, it still offers notes of roses, violets and blackberries with enhanced fragrance in a subtler, less complex structure. The Onyr is made from raisined verdicchio grapes that are left to dry on the vine. The wine is aged for 10 months in barrique. Its light amber introduces dried apricots, pineapple and cakes on a delicate nose. The vein of sweetness on the palate balances nicely with the fine acidity then the fine fruit of the nose is echoed in the long finish. A retasting of the Verdicchio Salmariano 2000 shows that it has staying power, as well as a rich, elegant sensory profile.

- Lacrima di Morro d'Alba Orgiolo '00 — 4*
- Verdicchio dei Castelli di Jesi Passito Onyr '00 — 4*
- Lacrima di Morro d'Alba Rùbico '01 — 3
- Verdicchio dei Castelli di Jesi Cl. Luzano '01 — 3
- Verdicchio dei Castelli di Jesi Cl. Sup. Salmariano '00 — 4

NUMANA (AN)

Conte Leopardi Dittajuti
Via Marina II, 26
60026 Numana (AN)
tel. 0717390116
e-mail: leopar@tin.it

The wind and water of the Adriatic coast naturally regulate the temperature on the Conero promontory, cooling down the hot summer nights and taking the chill edge off the winters. This makes the zone highly suited to growing good quality grapes for fresh, fragrant whites and nice stylish reds. The Leopardi winery owns almost 35 hectares of old and new vineyards and a cellar that is well equipped with efficient technology. The Sauvignons from the Coppo vineyards are both well structured, with a warm texture that lacks a little freshness. At the time of tasting, a slightly sulphurous note obscured the noses, repressing the varietal features. The Fructus is fresh and drinkable, thanks to briefer ageing than the other reds. The Vigneti del Coppo is a nice ruby red with warm, heady aromas of toasted oak and morello cherries, soft tannin and good extract on the palate. The Pigmento has a fine ruby red, burgundy-tinged hue and its richly aromatic nose proffers cherry jam, cocoa powder and coffee. The juicy, soft palate reflects the nose, with a nice return of the fruit in the finish. The Casirano is a blend of montepulciano, cabernet and syrah. Dark ruby red with purple highlights precede toasty notes on the nose, with vegetal hints from the French varieties and fruit and liquorice from the montepulciano. The palate is even more impressively balanced, and the soft tannins contribute to an attractive roundness. This is a promising wine that just needs a little more time to grow.

● Casirano Rosso '00	ŸŸ	4*
● Rosso Conero Pigmento '98	ŸŸ	5
● Rosso Conero Vigneti del Coppo '00	Ÿ	4
○ Calcare Sauvignon '01	Ÿ	4
● Rosso Conero Fructus '01	Ÿ	3
○ Bianco del Coppo Sauvignon '01		3

NUMANA (AN)

Fattoria Le Terrazze
Via Musone, 4
60026 Numana (AN)
tel. 0717390352
e-mail: a.terni@fastnet.it

The Terni family hitched their fortunes to this 150-hectare estate when they purchased it over a century ago. The property extends over the Numana hills near the sea in a perfect topoclimate for growing grapes. The summers are cooled by the sea breezes and the winters are never too cold because the 572 metre-high Monte Conero shelters the area from the icy northern winds. With the help of Attilio Pagli and Leonardo Valenti, Antonio and Giorgina Terni continue to consolidate their range of very high quality wines. Those presented this year fulfilled our expectations. The Chaos is a blend of montepulciano, merlot and syrah, with a fine purple colour, deep elderflower on the nose that expands into pepper and tobacco, and a smooth elegant palate. Soft tannins back up the fruit with its hints of morello cherries to close on a long, satisfying finish. The deep red Sassi Neri has morello cherry mingling with vanilla and spicy leather in the nose while the palate is concentrated but smooth. The progression shows ripe fruit and elegant tannins that nudge the complex texture into a gentle finish. The other wines manage to hold their own alongside these giants. Le Cave is made from chardonnay grapes and has lime blossom, yellow plum and acacia aromas, dense, pulpy texture and soft, juicy body. Finally, the standard-label Rosso Conero has uncomplicated aromas and an impeccable balance of freshness and fruit on the palate.

● Chaos Rosso '00	ŸŸ	7
● Rosso Conero Sassi Neri '00	ŸŸ	6
○ Le Cave Chardonnay '01	ŸŸ	4*
● Rosso Conero '01	Ÿ	4
● Chaos Rosso '97	ŸŸŸ	7
● Rosso Conero Visions of J '97	ŸŸŸ	8
● Rosso Conero Sassi Neri '98	ŸŸŸ	6
● Rosso Conero Sassi Neri '99	ŸŸŸ	6
● Chaos Rosso '99	ŸŸ	7
● Rosso Conero Sassi Neri '96	ŸŸ	6
● Rosso Conero Sassi Neri '97	ŸŸ	6

OFFAGNA (AN)

MALACARI
VIA ENRICO MALACARI, 6
60020 OFFAGNA (AN)
TEL. 0717207606
E-MAIL: malacari@tin.it

Alessandro Starrabba's winery continues to present elegant wines with good ageing prospects. The Grigiano selection is back in the range with the 2000 vintage, having missed out in 1999. The wine is stylish and powerful, seductive but not mannered, severe yet not arrogant. Thanks to the work of winemaker Sergio Paolucci, who does not believe in intrusive wood or international blends, the winery's style is unchanged and unaffected by fashions that don't suit this area. Here, only montepulciano grapes are used. Picked when perfectly ripe in the Grigiano and Baviera hills, the fruit is vinified in the old cellar in the family residence, where some of the wine is aged in barriques and some in larger barrels. This year's offerings are both Rosso Coneros and both are very good indeed. The standard-label version is deep ruby red with a rich fruity nose that reveals the classic varietal dried morello cherries and ripe blackberries. The palate is soft and smooth, despite its rich pulp and lively tannins, then the fruit aromas re-appear in the finish. The dramatically different Rosso Conero Grigiano is an austere selection of the best grapes. It is even more opaque in colour, with flashes of purple, and the ripe cherry aromas on the nose are joined by lavender and aniseed. The vigorous alcohol on the palate is well-measured, while the gentle tannins allow the wine to expand into fruity notes that linger on the finish.

• Rosso Conero '00	♊	3*
• Rosso Conero Grigiano '00	♊	5
• Rosso Conero Grigiano '98	♉♉	5
• Rosso Conero '99	♀	3

OFFIDA (AP)

CIÙ CIÙ
LOC. SANTA MARIA IN CARRO
C.DA CIAFONE, 106
63035 OFFIDA (AP)
TEL. 0736810001
E-MAIL: info@ciuciu.com

This winery owned by the Bartolomei brothers is in Contrada Ciafone, a part of the Piceno area that has all the attributes of a good vineyard and lies in one of Italy's historic viticultural zones. Winemaker Pierluigi Lorenzetti makes products with strongly local characteristics. The terroir of Contrada Ciafone translates into very powerful, intense wines with dense, meaty extract and plenty of tannins. These wines are more vigorous than stylish. The Falerio has a nice fruity nose and pleasantly well-typed palate, while the Rosso Piceno Superiore is ruby red with ripe cherries, coffee and spices on the nose. Although the aromas do reappear on the palate, it does not quite live up to the promise of finesse on the nose. Its muscular tannins have not yet completely mellowed. The Gotico, made exclusively from montepulciano grapes harvested when super-ripe, is ruby red with a nose that is slow to yield its aromas, though morello cherry and leather do emerge. It has a less astringent palate than the Piceno but very muscular structure and robust alcohol. The San Carro is a blend of montepulciano, barbera and merlot with an over-evolved nose and sweetish palate. It's a simple, enjoyable quaffing wine for all occasions. The Saggio is another example of the surprising success of Sangiovese in this area. Vermilion, with a rather inexpressive nose of warm ripe fruit and fragrant violets, it shows a palate with rather harsh tannins. Once smoothed, they will bring balance to a wine that has made a very interesting debut.

• Saggio Sangiovese '01	♊	5
• Rosso Piceno Sup. '00	♀	3
• Rosso Piceno Sup. Gotico '00	♀	4
○ Falerio dei Colli Ascolani '01	♀	3
• San Carro Rosso '01		4
• Oppidum Rosso '98	♉♉	5

OFFIDA (AP)

SAN GIOVANNI
C.DA CIAFONE, 41
63035 OFFIDA (AP)
TEL. 0736889032
E-MAIL: sangiovanni@vinisangiovanni.it

This winery, founded in 1989, obtained impressive results on all fronts this year, showing that the wines have been making steady progress. With the technical support of winemaker Primo Narcisi, Gianni Di Lorenzo has re-organized his range, part of which is already tried and tested while other products are brand new. The newcomers include the ambitious red Zeii, a blend of montepulciano, merlot and cabernet, which will be presented next year. Then there's the white Zagros 2001, a monovarietal trebbiano with good alcohol, a nice golden yellow colour, sweet almondy aromas and full, harmonious palate. The Rosso Piceno Superiore Rosso del Nonno 2000 acquits itself very well, with fairly complex aromas on the nose that are reflected in the smooth palate. The Rosso Piceno Superiore Leo Guelfus 2000 is also very good. Ruby red, its fragrant, intense aromas with upfront berry fruit ushers in a rounded enjoyable palate of nice complexity. The good Falerio Leo Guelfus 2001 has hints of aromatic herbs and a complex palate, and the Rosso Piceno Ophites 2001 is also nice. It shows sweet, ripe fruit on the nose, a weighty palate and a good finish. Lastly, the Falerio Marta Riserva 2000 is a very good late-harvest wine with aniseed and floral aromas and a pleasantly intense palate.

○	Falerio dei Colli Ascolani Marta V.T. Ris. '00	▽	4
●	Rosso Piceno Sup. Leo Guelfus '00	▽▽	4
●	Rosso Piceno Sup. Rosso del Nonno '00	▽▽	5
○	Falerio dei Colli Ascolani Leo Guelfus '01	▽▽	3*
○	Zagros '01	▽▽	4
●	Rosso Piceno Ophites '01	▽	3
●	Rosso Piceno Sup. Rosso del Nonno '99	▽▽	5
●	Rosso Piceno Sup. Rosso del Nonno '98	▽▽	5

OFFIDA (AP)

VILLA PIGNA
C.DA CIAFONE, 63
63035 OFFIDA (AP)
TEL. 073687525
E-MAIL: villapigna@villapigna.com

Owned by the Rozzi family, Villa Pigna is one of the most impressive wineries in the Rosso Piceno DOC, and indeed in the entire province of Ascoli. The 130 hectares under vine are scattered across the area's best growing areas. Winemaker Massimo Uriani turns out a large number of different wines from both local and international varieties, all of them interesting. The reds were especially good this year while the less assertive and characterful whites gave a less convincing performance. The Rozzano, from 100 per cent montepulciano, is the most interesting wine of all. Its blackberry and cherry aromas meld with slightly dominant vanilla from the barriques, then the palate has balanced alcohol and acidity over a pleasantly tight-knit tannic weave. The Vellutato is also made from montepulciano grapes and has minty, balsamic sensations on the nose. These are followed by a palate that is quite elegant but not overly concentrated. The Rosso Piceno Superiore 2000 is fruity and spicy, and the Rosso Piceno and standard-label Rosato are both uncomplicated. The Falerio Pliniano and the Colle Malerbì, made from chardonnay, are pleasant but somewhat one-dimensional, while the standard Falerio is approachable and drinkable.

●	Rozzano '00	▽▽	5
●	Rosso Piceno Sup. '00	▽	3
●	Vellutato '00	▽	5
○	Colle Malerbi '01	▽	4
○	Falerio dei Colli Ascolani Pliniano '01	▽	4
○	Falerio dei Colli Ascolani '01		3
⊙	Rosato '01		3
●	Rosso Piceno '01		3
●	Cabernasco '98	▽▽	5
●	Rozzano '98	▽▽	5

OSIMO (AN)

UMANI RONCHI
S. S. 16, KM. 310+400, 74
60027 OSIMO (AN)
TEL. 0717108019
E-MAIL: wine@umanironchi.it

Founded about 50 years ago by enthusiastic country man Gino Umani Ronchi, this winery is now owned by the Bianchi Bernetti family, along with several vineyards in the Verdicchio and Conero areas. The cellar makes over 4,000,000 bottles a year of standard-label and first-label wines, with the help of consultant winemaker Giacomo Tachis, who will be replaced from 2002 onwards by Beppe Caviola. The winery's own oenologist is Umberto Trombelli. The dynamic, expanding winery has a splendid new barrique cellar and many more plans for major investment. We'll start with the 2001 Verdicchios and the Villa Bianchi was particularly striking. It is livelier and more eye-catching than the Casal di Serra whose softness is a little too ingratiating. The Plenio '99, aged in barriques, is as good as ever, its strongest feature being a generous palate. Le Busche has a fruity nose over honey tones, but our assessment marked it down for a less than harmonious palate. The Lacrima is well-typed and drinkable while the Montepulciano Iorio has more weight. The San Lorenzo is a typically reliable Conero, combining varietal aromas and a tangy flavour. The Pelago is as fascinating as ever, thanks to freshly mown grass and morello cherries on the nose and a perfectly balanced palate. The Cùmaro is delightful, more elegant than even, with broad, impressive aromas and a richly extracted palate with finesse and a long finish. The seductive Maximo is made from botrytized sauvignon grapes and has hints of mould, spice and balsam on its generous nose, followed by a palate with exemplary balance.

○	Maximo '99	♟♟	6
●	Rosso Conero Cùmaro '99	♟♟	6
○	Verdicchio dei Castelli di Jesi Cl. Sup. Casal di Serra '01	♟♟	4*
○	Verdicchio dei Castelli di Jesi Cl. Sup. Villa Bianchi '01	♟♟	3*
●	Pelago '99	♟♟	6
○	Verdicchio dei Castelli di Jesi Cl. Plenio Ris. '99	♟♟	5
○	Le Busche '00	♟	5
●	Montepulciano d'Abruzzo Jorio '00	♟	3
●	Lacrima di Morro d'Alba Fonte del Re '01	♟	4
●	Rosso Conero S. Lorenzo '99	♟	4
○	Maximo '98	♟♟	6

OSTRA VETERE (AN)

BUCCI
FRAZ. PONGELLI
VIA CONA, 30
60010 OSTRA VETERE (AN)
TEL. 071964179 - 026570558
E-MAIL: bucciwines@villabucci.com

There was another excellent performance by the Riserva Villa Bucci, which has always been Bucci's leading wine, and indeed by all the others, including the especially surprising Rosso Piceno Pongelli. Bucci has always been a little on the sidelines of regional winemaking, supplying top quality and instantly recognizable wines. The cellar is well-known to discriminating consumers thanks to Ampelio Bucci's unhurried approach to releasing his eminently cellarable wines, which can last and develop over many years. The winery has about 26 hectares of vineyards mainly planted to verdicchio but there are also some black grape varieties, especially sangiovese and montepulciano. The Verdicchios originate from five vineyards in differing positions and at different altitudes, ranging from 200 to 350 metres. The grapes are vinified separately before blending. We awarded the Riserva Villa Bucci 1999 a majestic Three Glasses. It is just about ready to uncork now. Its stylish hazelnut and lime blossom on the nose are mirrored deliciously on the palate and it has very promising ageing prospects. The Verdicchio dei Castelli di Jesi Classico 2001 has quite a deep straw-yellow colour, delicate ripe fruit on the nose and rather a static palate at the moment. The Rosso Piceno Tenuta Pongelli 2000 made an excellent impression with coffee, geraniums and spice on the nose and a dense, well-gauged palate.

○	Verdicchio dei Castelli di Jesi Cl. Villa Bucci Ris. '99	♟♟♟	6
●	Rosso Piceno Tenuta Pongelli '00	♟♟	4*
○	Verdicchio dei Castelli di Jesi Cl. '01	♟	4
○	Verdicchio dei Castelli di Jesi Cl. Villa Bucci Ris. '98	♟♟♟	6
○	Verdicchio dei Castelli di Jesi Cl. '00	♟♟	4
○	Verdicchio dei Castelli di Jesi Cl. Villa Bucci Ris. '95	♟♟	6
○	Verdicchio dei Castelli di Jesi Cl. Villa Bucci Ris. '97	♟♟	6

PEDASO (AP)

CASTELLO FAGETO
VIA VALDASO, 52
63016 PEDASO (AP)
TEL. 0734931784
E-MAIL: castellofageto@castellofageto.it

Making its debut this year, Castello Fageto has been gradually improving the quality of its wines over the last ten years, making good use of the farmland north of Piceno which is better known for growing fruit and vegetables and difficult for viticulture. Thanks to consultant winemakers, Maurilio Chioccia and Pierluigi Lorenzetti, and 20 hectares of vineyards at Pedaso, where they overlook the Adriatic from terraces, Campofilone and Porto San Giorgio, Claudio di Ruscio and family make 40,000 bottles a year of excellent wines, using montepulciano, sangiovese, moscato rosso, trebbiano, chardonnay, passerina, merlot and cabernet grapes. Their Falerio has clear apple notes on the nose and well-balanced alcohol and acidity on the palate, with a clean, intense finish. The Rosso Piceno 2001 is fresh rather than powerful, with morello cherry and liquorice aromas, while the 2000 Rusus selection has a more intense nose where fruit blends with subtle grassy hints and smooth tannins on the palate merge into the good structure to echoes of ripe berry fruit. The Tristo di Elisena, made from chardonnay, malvasia and grechetto grapes, has vanilla, Alpine herbs and lime blossom on the nose and a pleasantly fragrant, weighty palate. The passerina and malvasia-based Alido has notes of plum jam and aromatic herbs on the nose, then dried figs, walnuts and well-balanced sweetness in the mouth. A Bordeaux blend which promises to be very interesting is currently being prepared in the cellar. We'll discuss it in next year's Guide.

● Rosso Piceno Rusus '00	ƴƴ	4*
○ Tristo di Elisena Bianco '01	ƴƴ	4*
○ Alido Bianco '01	ƴ	6
○ Falerio dei Colli Ascolani '01	ƴ	3
● Rosso Piceno '01		3

PESARO

FATTORIA MANCINI
S.DA DEI COLLI, 35
61100 PESARO
TEL. 072151828
E-MAIL: fattoriamancini@libero.it

In his 35 hectares of vineyards all over Pesaro and the Monte San Bartolo nature reserve, young winegrower Luigi Mancini grows albanella, ancellotta, sangiovese, montepulciano and lots of pinot nero. The Burgundy variety is unquestionably his favourite. Luigi is training old clones brought to the area in Napoleon's day, and carrying out vinification both with and without the skins. Unusually, vinification without the skins was used for his Impero Bianco, a unique wine with intense sugary aromas of pineapples and very ripe tropical fruit. Its good weighty, full-flavoured palate is balanced by perfectly gauged acidity and only slightly masked by a bitterish finish. The Roncaglia is made from albanella grapes with a small addition of pinot nero vinified without the skins. It is enjoyably aromatic and very drinkable. Unfortunately, the Pinot Neros vinified traditionally were not available for tasting and the Impero Rosso and Selezione will have to wait until next year. We'll while away the time with a glass of the very good Blu, from pinot nero and ancellotta, or even better, the excellent Sangiovese, with its fragrant fresh berry fruit aromas, nice weight and structure, and soft, lingering palate.

● Colli Pesaresi Sangiovese '00	ƴƴ	3*
○ Impero Bianco '00	ƴƴ	6
○ Colli Pesaresi Bianco Roncaglia '01	ƴ	3
● Blu '99	ƴ	6
● Montebacchino '99	ƴ	3
Impero Pinot Nero Selezione F M '98	ƴƴ	6
● Blu '98	ƴƴ	6

PIAGGE (PU)

GUERRIERI
VIA SAN FILIPPO, 24
61030 PIAGGE (PU)
TEL. 0721890152
E-MAIL: info@aziendaguerrieri.it

Luca Guerrieri makes a well-deserved debut in the Guide, though we had already made his acquaintance a few years ago when we sampled his wonderful extravirgin olive oil. The Guerrieri family have owned this over 200-hectare estate for more than a century. The land is distributed over various hillsides overlooking the Valle del Metauro, but has lately been re-organized to revive and extend viticulture. Another nine hectares have been added to the original ten planted to bianchello del Metauro, while ten hectares were planted with sangiovese and a small quantity of merlot in 1998 and are now productive. The four wines presented belong to the two traditional DOC zones, Colli Pesaresi Sangiovese and Bianchello del Metauro. The 2001 standard-label Bianchello is straw yellow with ripe fruit aromas and a fresh-tasting palate. The Celso selection, also from 2001, has a more complex sensory profile, a deep straw-yellow hue and more mature aromas and flavour. The Colli Pesaresi Sangiovese 2001 is a typically uncomplicated wine overall, but very enjoyable and impeccably made. Lastly, the very decent 2000 Sangiovese Galileo selection is intense ruby red, with ripe fruit aromas of blackberries and mulberry blossom and a mouthfilling palate.

●	Colli Pesaresi Sangiovese Galileo '00	ΨΨ	4*
○	Bianchello del Metauro '01	Ψ	3
○	Bianchello del Metauro Celso '01	Ψ	3
●	Colli Pesaresi Sangiovese '01	Ψ	3

POGGIO SAN MARCELLO (AN)

SARTARELLI
VIA COSTE DEL MOLINO, 24
60030 POGGIO SAN MARCELLO (AN)
TEL. 073189732
E-MAIL: info@sartarelli.it

The Sartarelli estate embraces over 50 hectares of vineyards on the hills to the left of the Esino river, in Coste del Molino, Balciana and Tralivio, at a height of 300-350 metres above sea level. Owners Donatella Sartarelli and Claudia Pozzi are assisted by Donatella's husband, Patrizio Chiacchierini and winemaker Alberto Mazzoni. The Verdicchios we tasted this year are physically different, although the two vintages were apparently similar in terms of weather. The Classico 2001 is straw yellow, with hints of golden delicious apples and acacia blossom on the nose, and a fresh-tasting, quaffable palate with well-measured acidity in perfect harmony with the body. The aromas of the Tralivio are more mature, and the mouthfeel rich and concentrated from entry onwards. The tangy palate closes with a varietal, pleasantly bitterish finish. The Balciana 2000 has plenty of super-ripe aromas on the nose but lacks the finesse of previous versions, which also revealed the hints of spice and mould that make it the outstanding wine we know and love. Although the palate is full-flavoured and opulent, it is also slightly cloying from an excess of residual sugar. Add this to the alcohol and the lack of firm acidity, and you have a rather flabby, one-dimensional wine overall.

○	Verdicchio dei Castelli di Jesi Cl. Sup. Contrada Balciana '00	ΨΨ	6
○	Verdicchio dei Castelli di Jesi Cl. '01	ΨΨ	3*
○	Verdicchio dei Castelli di Jesi Cl. Sup. Tralivio '01	ΨΨ	4
○	Verdicchio dei Castelli di Jesi Cl. Sup. Contrada Balciana '94	ΨΨΨ	6
○	Verdicchio dei Castelli di Jesi Cl. Sup. Contrada Balciana '95	ΨΨΨ	6
○	Verdicchio dei Castelli di Jesi Cl. Sup. Contrada Balciana '97	ΨΨΨ	6
○	Verdicchio dei Castelli di Jesi Cl. Sup. Contrada Balciana '98	ΨΨΨ	6
○	Verdicchio dei Castelli di Jesi Cl. Sup. Contrada Balciana '99	ΨΨ	6

POTENZA PICENA (MC)

SANTA CASSELLA
C.DA SANTA CASSELLA, 7
62018 POTENZA PICENA (MC)
TEL. 0733671507
E-MAIL: santacassella@tiscalinet.it

Some 25 of the winery's 70 hectares are planted to vine in the Potenza Picena hills near the coast. The estate has been family-owned since the 18th century and in 1970, a process of modernization began in the vineyards. That process continues, aiming to raise the quality of the wines, whose progress is supervised by Pierluigi Lorenzetti. The Santa Cassella wines presented for this year's Guide are very interesting and technically impeccable. The Donna Angela 2001 is made from sauvignon and malvasia grapes. It has stylish citrus, cake and apricot aromas on the nose, then the palate opens sweetly, leading through to a long finish. The Colli Maceratesi Bianco 2001 is pleasant and well-typed, with floral aromas and a tangy flavour, while the original Giardin Vecchio 2001 is a sweet blend of sauvignon and malvasia with peaches and grapes on the nose and a weighty, very fruity palate. The Chardonnay Donna Eleonora 2001 is also very interesting. It shows slightly over-evolved aromas and a complex, pleasant flavour. The Rosso Piceno 2001 is a nice, elegant, purple ruby wine with blackberry and cherry aromas and an appetizingly drinkable palate rich in good fruit and sweet tannins. The Conte Leopoldo 2000 is an interesting, richly extracted Cabernet Sauvignon that combines drinkability with remarkable weight.

● Conte Leopoldo Cabernet Sauvignon '00	♟♟	4
○ Donna Eleonora Chardonnay '01	♟♟	4
○ Giardin Vecchio '01	♟♟	4
● Rosso Piceno '01	♟♟	3*
○ Colli Maceratesi Bianco '01	♟	2*
○ Donna Angela '01	♟	4

RIPATRANSONE (AP)

TENUTA COCCI GRIFONI
LOC. SAN SAVINO
C.DA MESSIERI, 12
63038 RIPATRANSONE (AP)
TEL. 073590143
E-MAIL: info@tenutacoccigrifoni.it

The last vintage on sale, the 2001, saw the inauguration of the new Offida DOC, which includes several types of wine: one red and a few whites made from local grape varieties, to be precise. Guido Cocci Grifoni has played a leading role in the recovery of at least one of these, the white Pecorino, although the others are also linked to the estate, which has always made traditional local wines. Let's begin our winery profile with the white in question, the interesting Offida Pecorino Podere Colle Vecchio 2001. The nose is quite stylish, with upfront floral aromas and the fresh palate has yet to develop its full complexity. The Falerio dei Colli Ascolani Vigneti San Basso 2001 is slightly less expressive but has highly typical aromas and a tangy, slightly almondy flavour. The pleasant, unchallenging and very drinkable Rosso Piceno Superiore Le Torri 2000 has clean fruity aromas. The other Rosso Piceno Superiore '98 selection, Il Grifone, makes a greater impact on the nose, where blackberry aromas and faint spice precede a well-structured palate and tidy finish. This wine was reviewed in error in last year's Guide but actually only became available this year. Lastly, the winery's traditional Passerina Brut maintains its usual attractively well-made standard. From this year, it is a DOC wine and shows subtle floral hints, then an enjoyably easy-drinking palate.

● Rosso Piceno Sup. Il Grifone '98	♟♟	5
● Rosso Piceno Sup. Le Torri '00	♟	3
○ Falerio dei Colli Ascolani Vigneti San Basso '01	♟	3
○ Offida Pecorino Podere Colle Vecchio '01	♟	3
○ Offida Passerina Brut '01	♟	3
○ Podere Colle Vecchio '00	♟♟	4
● Rosso Piceno Sup. Il Grifone '97	♟♟	5
● Rosso Piceno Sup. Vigna Messieri '99	♟	4

RIPATRANSONE (AP)

La Cantina dei Colli Ripani
Via Tosciano, 28
63038 Ripatransone (AP)
tel. 07359505
e-mail: info@colliripani.com

This was the first co-operative in the Piceno area to focus on quality, thanks to the far-sighted management of Nazario Pignotti. Once internal problems were overcome, he reduced yields, hired consultant winemaker Fabrizio Ciufoli to work alongside wine technician Gianni Fioravanti, and pushed ahead with the modernization project for the cellar buildings. Further proof of his professionalism comes from Nazario's decision not to release the flagship wine, Leo Ripanus '99, because he does not feel it is up to scratch. So the best wine this year is the Rosso Piceno Superiore Castellano '99. The dense colour introduces aromas that focus on cherries, sweet spice and ripe plums, then a powerful entry on the palate ushers in a dense tannic weave that merges with vigorous alcohol and well-measured acidity to back up the generous body. The Rosso Piceno Transone 2000 is interesting. The cherry jam aromas hint at fairly ripe grapes, while the wine proves less complicated on the palate and the tannins are still rugged. The Falerio Brezzolino 2001 is vinified for softness at all costs. Floral, almost sweet aromas on the nose, including hints of lily of the valley and wistaria, precede a rounded palate of medium intensity. Finally, the Passito Anima Mundi, from passerina grapes, has stewed apples and dried fruit on the nose and a honeyed, lingering palate.

RIPATRANSONE (AP)

Le Caniette
C.da Canali, 23
63038 Ripatransone (AP)
tel. 07359200
e-mail: info@lecaniette.it

Le Caniette, owned by Raffaele, Giovanni and Luigi Vagnoni, deserves a special mention. It is one of the wineries producing the excellent reds that are making Piceno one of the most sought-after terroirs in Italy. If you need further proof of this, just glance down the list of wines presented and you'll see that two of them were nominated for Three Glasses. The Nero di Vite 2000 has wonderfully concentrated aromas on nose and palate, a mix of bottled cherries, undergrowth and coffee, and vigorous alcohol on the front palate. After becoming progressively more intense in the generous mid-palate, it closes with a very long finish delicately redolent of oak. The Morellone 2000 is different altogether, with features that call to mind the great Montepulcianos. The nose is still closed but offers hints of liquorice and black berry fruit, then powerful tannins come through strongly, especially on the dry back palate, and the no-nonsense progression makes no concessions to seductive softness. This wine will grow and improve over time. The Rosso Bello 2001 is like the Morellone in character but more direct and simple. The Sibilla Eritrea, from passerina grapes, has appealing baked apple, raisin and cinnamon aromas and barely hinted at sweetness on its well-defined palate. Lastly, the Pecorino Iosonogaia is still looking for the right balance.

● Rosso Piceno Sup. Castellano '99	ΨΨ	3*
○ Passito Anima Mundi	Ψ	5
● Rosso Piceno Transone '00	Ψ	2
○ Falerio dei Colli Ascolani Brezzolino '01	Ψ	3
● Rosso Piceno Sup. Castellano '97	ΨΨ	3
● Rosso Piceno Sup. Leo Ripanus '98	ΨΨ	4

● Rosso Piceno Morellone '00	ΨΨ	5
● Rosso Piceno Nero di Vite '00	ΨΨ	6
● Rosso Piceno Rosso Bello '01	Ψ	4
○ Vino Santo di Ripatransone Sibilla Eritrea	Ψ	5
○ Offida Pecorino Iosonogaia '01	Ψ	5
● Rosso Piceno Nero di Vite '98	ΨΨ	6
● Rosso Piceno Morellone '98	ΨΨ	5
● Rosso Piceno Morellone '99	ΨΨ	5
○ Vino Santo di Ripatransone Sibilla Agrippa	ΨΨ	6

RIPATRANSONE (AP)

PODERI SAN SAVINO
LOC. SAN SAVINO
C.DA SANTA MARIA IN CARRO, 13
63038 RIPATRANSONE (AP)
TEL. 073590107
E-MAIL: cantina.sansavino@libero.it

All San Savino's wines did well this year and, incidentally, they have been given new names. The Capecci family have been growing grapes here for over a century and now that Simone has come on board, the objective is high quality and excellence. About 120,000 bottles are produced each year with the fruit from the 30 hectares under vine, distributed across a range that focuses attention on native varieties. The Rosso Piceno Campo delle Mura 2001 is the winery's warhorse. Its attractive dense ruby red introduces hints of jam on the nose and an impressive, if not complex, palate. The Rosso Piceno Superiore Picus 2000 selection is a fine ruby red, with upfront black cherry and spice aromas, then a powerful, well-balanced palate with sweet tannins in the finish. The Fedus 2000, which was released as Moggio in 1998, is a monovarietal Sangiovese. The initial aroma of violets is already remarkably stylish and fully reflected on the palate. The surprising Ver Sacrum 2000, called Mito in the last edition of the Guide, is a Montepulciano that sees no wood. It has loads of character, a ruby red hue with purple highlights and a concentrated nose that already expresses complex rhubarb, cherry and cinchona aromas. It is followed by a soft, mouthfilling palate with a long, very well-defined finish. Last but not least, the Offida Pecorino Ciprea put on its best ever show. It's an exemplary, complex white that does credit to both the winery and the DOC zone.

●	Fedus Sangiovese '00	▼▼	6
●	Ver Sacrum '00	▼▼	6
●	Rosso Piceno Sup. Picus '00	▼▼	5
○	Offida Pecorino Ciprea '01	▼▼	4
●	Rosso Piceno Campo delle Mura '01	▼	3
●	Sangiovese Moggio '98	▼▼▼	6
●	Mito '98	▼▼	6

SAN MARCELLO (AN)

MAURIZIO MARCONI
VIA MELANO, 23
60030 SAN MARCELLO (AN)
TEL. 0731267223
E-MAIL: info@vinoearte.it

The winery was founded in the early 1970s in a particularly good growing area. One quarter of the property's 40-hectare surface is used for vines, lacrima and verdicchio being the varieties grown. The consultant winemaker is Sergio Paolucci and all vinification procedures are carried out at the estate cellar, where the wine ages in basement rooms at a constant natural temperature. The names of the production lines have been changed. The traditional line is called Sapore di Generazioni and the other, Falcone Reale, features more carefully selected wines and is released with elaborate artistic labels. The wines respect the features of native varieties. The well-structured Verdicchios are more generous on the palate than on the nose and the Lacrimas have great nose-palate balance. The Verdicchio Corona Reale has faint hints of apple and wistaria on the nose and acidic grip in the mouth to support the full texture of its ripe fruit. The Verdicchio Sapore di Generazioni has a less ripe nose of broom and sage, then a fresh-tasting palate, which is fairly well-structured and offers aromatic flowery notes in the finish. The Lacrima has clear notes of dried roses, ripe blackberries and red plums, with nice tannins on the enjoyably balanced palate. The consistent finish brings together all the complex aromas typical of the variety.

●	Lacrima di Morro d'Alba Sapore di Generazioni '01	▼▼	5
○	Verdicchio dei Castelli di Jesi Cl. Sup. Corona Reale '01	▼▼	4
○	Verdicchio dei Castelli di Jesi Cl. Sup. Sapore di Generazioni '01	▼	5

SERRA DE' CONTI (AN)

CASALFARNETO
VIA FARNETO, 16
60030 SERRA DE' CONTI (AN)
TEL. 0731889001
E-MAIL: info@casalfarneto.it

This young, highly motivated winery was founded in 1995 in the hills of Serra de' Conti and Montecarotto, right in the heart of the DOC's "Classico" area. Vineyards are the mainstay of the 52-hectare property, which overlooks the valley and also includes three old farms, an olive grove and arable farmland. The winery is owned by Danilo Salustri and Massimo Arcangeli, with two other partners, and their very first vintage demonstrated their intention to take up the challenge of turning Casalfarneto into one of the benchmark names in the new and multi-faceted zone of Verdicchio dei Castelli di Jesi. Verdicchio grapes are the main variety grown here, on about 18 hectares of the land, and the other five hectares are planted to montepulciano, sangiovese, merlot and cabernet sauvignon. These are some of the best-made Verdicchios in the whole DOC, and the winery itself's best Verdicchio is the Grancasale 2001. The sound colour accompanies clear aromas of flowers and fruit on the nose and a stylish, concentrated palate that is certain to improve with time. The Verdicchio Fontevecchia is a little more restrained, and deliberately vinified to be more approachable, while the well-made Cimaio 2000 has elegant character with sweet notes and good fruit on the palate.

SERVIGLIANO (AP)

FATTORIA DEZI
C.DA FONTE MAGGIO, 14
63029 SERVIGLIANO (AP)
TEL. 0734710090
E-MAIL: mauridez@tin.it

Fine wine enthusiasts will be pleased with the results achieved by the Dezi family, whose production philosophy for many years has been to respect the consumer. The winery is committed to biodynamic farming, using no chemicals and the bare minimum of technology for very low yields achieved at great sacrifice, and meticulous, painstaking care of the vineyards. Thanks to their love and respect for the land, the wisdom handed down by old country folk, and extensive research, the Dezis have managed to turn a dream into a plan, then the plan into reality. What they offer is excellent quality that stands the test of time because it is the result of commitment, hard work and continual experimentation. Fame and money are goals often pursued in the winemaking world today, but they are not everyone's priority. This year, the Regina del Bosco 2000 was not available for tasting because the estate did not consider it ready. The Dezio is the only Montepulciano available this year and it's full-bodied, attractively soft and drinkable. The two whites from native local varieties, verdicchio, malvasia and pecorino, are born of both tradition and research. They are unusual and innovative on nose and palate. Finally and magnificently, the Solo is a weighty Sangiovese from old vines with ripe, sound fruit that is never dominated by wood. The panel thought it was breathtakingly elegant. Three splendid Glasses.

○ Verdicchio dei Castelli di Jesi Cl. Sup. Grancasale '01	ŸŸ 4*
○ Verdicchio dei Castelli di Jesi Cl. Sup. Cimaio '00	ŸŸ 4
○ Verdicchio dei Castelli di Jesi Cl. Sup. Fontevecchia '01	Ÿ 3
○ Verdicchio dei Castelli di Jesi Cl. Sup. Grancasale '00	ŸŸ 4

● Solo Sangiovese '00	ŸŸŸ 6
● Dezio Vigneto Beccaccia '00	ŸŸ 4*
○ Le Solagne '01	ŸŸ 4*
○ Le Solagne V. T. '01	ŸŸ 5
● Solo Sangiovese '99	ŸŸ 6
○ Le Solagne V. T. '00	ŸŸ 5
● Rosso Piceno Regina del Bosco '98	ŸŸ 5

SPINETOLI (AP)

Saladini Pilastri
Via Saladini, 5
63030 Spinetoli (AP)
Tel. 0736899534
E-mail: saladpil@tin.it

STAFFOLO (AN)

Fattoria Coroncino
C.da Coroncino, 7
60039 Staffolo (AN)
Tel. 0731779494
E-mail: coroncino@libero.it

This was the best performance ever from a deservedly successful winery in the Piceno area. Three Glasses were a fitting reward. The winery was founded in the early 1970s and is committed to improving the quality of its wines while using growing methods that respect the environment. We liked the superb Rosso Piceno Superiore Vigna Monteprandone best of all the reds presented this year by winemaker Domenico D'Angelo, and awarded it Three Glasses. It has deep colour and intense, complex aromas of cherries and spice, beautifully reflected on the palate, a long lingering finish and unusual elegance. This is the first time a wine from the DOC has hit such heights. The Pregio del Conte Rosso is also very good, with deep colour, and youthful purple highlights. The moderately spicy aromas hint at cherry fruit while the palate is warm and well-developed. The Rosso Piceno Vigna Piediprato 2000 also deserved its high score. The complex nose has hints of sweet almonds and berry fruit then the palate has good volume with sweet tannins and toasted oak sensations in the finish. The Rosso Piceno Superiore Vigna Montetinello 2000 has lovely finesse and concentrated black cherry, coffee and vanilla on the nose, which are mirrored well on the long, lingering palate. Turning to the whites, the Pregio del Conte Bianco performed well. Its lively straw yellow introduces medium intense aromas recalling spring flowers and apricots, and a smooth front palate that leads to a nice, tangy finish. The surprisingly good Falerio Vigna Palazzi was just as attractive.

Lucio Canestrari has little interest in public relations. He prefers doing well to looking good. If you go and see him, you'll find that he is more than ready to talk about his choices and his way of working and the very low yields in the vineyard. He'll be quite happy to let you taste what he is working on in the cellar. Lucio is a real character and every bit as intriguing as his wines. Over years of labour shared with his wife Fiorella, he has built up a loyal group of admirers who whisk the 35,000 bottles he makes each year out of the cellar. This year, none of the wines won a top award but we have to admit that a wine like the Gaiospino 2000, with its almost sweet aromas redolent of vanilla, butter, wistaria and ripe apples, is very good. It may be a little ruffled but it is certainly long-lasting and has lashings of personality. The same can be said, albeit to a lesser extent, of the Coroncino 2000, which shows less of the softness exhibited by its older brother. That of course means it is fresher and easy-drinking. Le Lame is made from trebbiano. Its very soft, warm palate and hint of evolution in the finish tell you it came from the very hot summer of 2000. Finally, the excellent Bambulé is made from super-ripe verdicchio grapes. This is one of Lucio's experiments and we cannot assess it because it was made in minimal quantities.

● Rosso Piceno Sup. Vigna Monteprandone '00	▼▼▼	4*
● Pregio del Conte Rosso '00	▼▼	4*
● Rosso Piceno Sup. Vigna Montetinello '00	▼▼	3*
● Rosso Piceno Vigna Piediprato '00	▼▼	3*
○ Falerio dei Colli Ascolani Vigna Palazzi '01	▼	1*
○ Pregio del Conte Bianco '01	▼	3
● Pregio del Conte Rosso '98	▼▼	4
● Rosso Piceno Sup. Vigna Montetinello '98	▼▼	3

○ Verdicchio dei Castelli di Jesi Cl. Sup. Gaiospino '00	▼▼	5
○ Le Lame '00	▼	3
○ Verdicchio dei Castelli di Jesi Cl. Coroncino '00	▼	4
○ Verdicchio dei Castelli di Jesi Cl. Sup. Gaiospino '97	▼▼▼	5
○ Verdicchio dei Castelli di Jesi Cl. Sup. Gaiospino '98	▼▼	5
○ Verdicchio dei Castelli di Jesi Cl. Sup. Gaiospino '99	▼▼	5

OTHER WINERIES

DEL CARMINE
VIA DEL CARMINE, 51
60020 ANCONA
TEL. 071889403
E-MAIL: carmine@commetodi.com

The young DI Carmine winery has a fine calling card in the Verdicchio di Matelica Aja Lunga 2001, with its spring flowers on the nose and tidy palate. The Petrara 2001 selection has decent varietal aromas and fills the mouth. The Petrara 2000 is a good red blend with nice body and personality.

● Petrara '00		4
○ Verdicchio di Matelica Aja Lunga '01		4
○ Verdicchio di Matelica Petrara '01		3

LUCIANO LANDI
VIA GAVIGLIANO, 16
60030 BELVEDERE OSTRENSE (AN)
TEL. 073162353
E-MAIL: aziendalandi@aziendalandi.it

We tasted the very fresh, pleasant Verdicchio dei Castelli di Jesi Classico 2001, while the standard-label Lacrima di Morro d'Alba 2001 and the Gavigliano version are well made. The latter has dense texture on the palate, as well as the dried roses and violet aromas of the basic version.

● Lacrima di Morro d'Alba Gavigliano '01		4*
● Lacrima di Morro d'Alba '01		4
○ Verdicchio dei Castelli di Jesi Cl. '01		3

SAPUTI
C.DA FIASTRA, 2
62020 COLMURANO (MC)
TEL. 0733508137
E-MAIL: saputi@mercurio.it

Saputi presented several wines. We liked the Noi Due 2001 best. It's a straw-yellow, 60-40 white blend from riesling and chardonnay that reveals ripe fruit on the nose and a moreish, drinkable palate. The Rosso Piceno Monte Nereto 2000 has a well-defined nose, tannic palate and decent structure.

○ Noi Due '01		4
● Rosso Piceno Monte Nereto '00		3

ENZO MECELLA
VIA DANTE, 112
60044 FABRIANO (AN)
TEL. 073221680
E-MAIL: enzo.mecella@fabriano.nettuno.it

The Mecella whites include a nice Marche Chardonnay Lotario 2000 whose rich fruit on the nose is reflected on the palate. The Marche Rosso Longobardo '99 is even better. Its stylish leather aromas blend with grassy and spicy notes. The palate has well-judged tannins.

● Longobardo Rosso '99		5
○ Lotario Chardonnay '00		4

Mario & Giorgio Brunori
V.le della Vittoria, 103
60035 Jesi (AN)
Tel. 0731207213
E-mail: brunorivini@libero.it

A pioneer Verdicchio winery, Brunori presented a new Castelli dei Jesi selection this year, Le Gemme 2001. Nicely typical flower and almond aromas are followed by a fresh, even palate. The San Nicolò selection has more marked, but less focused, characteristics.

○	Verdicchio dei Castelli di Jesi Cl. Le Gemme '01	♀	4
○	Verdicchio dei Castelli di Jesi Cl. Sup. San Nicolò '01	♀	4

Bisci
Via Fogliano, 120
62024 Matelica (MC)
Tel. 0737787490
E-mail: bisciwines@libero.it

The Villa Castiglioni 2000 has nice hints of elderflower on the nose and prominent tannins on the palate. The Verdicchio di Matelica 2000 has a fairly evolved nose and good alcohol in the mouth. The Villa Fogliano selection is more impressive, with well-rounded aromas and a warm, deep flavour.

○	Verdicchio di Matelica Vigneto Fogliano '00	♀♀	4
○	Verdicchio di Matelica '00	♀	4
●	Villa Castiglioni '00	♀	4

Poggio Montali
Via Fonte Estate, 6
60030 Monte Roberto (AN)
Tel. 0731702825

The Verdicchio dei Castelli di Jesi Classico Superiore 2001 has varietal lime blossom aromas and good weight on the palate. The Fonte del Leccio selection has distinct super-ripe aromas. It's meaty in the mouth but a little one-dimensional and slightly bitterish.

○	Verdicchio dei Castelli di Jesi Cl. Sup. '01	♀	3
○	Verdicchio dei Castelli di Jesi Cl. Sup. Fonte del Leccio '01	♀	4

Mario Lucchetti
Via Santa Maria del Fiore, 17
60030 Morro d'Alba (AN)
Tel. 073163314

The Lucchetti cellar presented two versions of the local DOC. The Etichetta Nera is a lovely ruby red, with hints of chocolate and flowers on the nose and an agreeably full flavour. The Etichetta Rossa has a tight-knit texture and approachable, less typical aromas and nice momentum on the palate.

●	Lacrima di Morro d'Alba '01 Etichetta Rossa	♀	4
●	Lacrima di Morro d'Alba Sel. Etichetta Nera '01	♀	4

Vicari
Via Sanguinetti, 31/A
60030 Morro d'Alba (AN)
Tel. 073163164

Vicari is situated in the heart of the DOC. The Lacrima di Morro d'Alba Rustico del Pozzo Buono 2001 is purple, showing roses on the nose and good execution. The Rosso Piceno del Pozzo Buono 2001 is more challenging. The leather, cherries and coffee aromas precede a concentrated palate.

●	Rosso Piceno del Pozzo Buono '01	♀♀	4*
●	Lacrima di Morro d'Alba Rustico del Pozzo Buono '01	♀	4

Capinera
C.da Crocette, 16
62010 Morrovalle (MC)
Tel. 0733222444
E-mail: info@capinera.com

We liked the deep, straw-yellow Chardonnay La Capinera 2000, with its vanilla and cakes on the nose, and the lingering, almost opulent flavour of the balanced, tangy palate. Less exciting is the Colli Maceratesi Bianco Murrano 2001. The nose is uncomplicated while the palate is faintly tangy.

○	La Capinera Chardonnay '00	♀♀	3*
○	Colli Maceratesi Bianco Murrano '01		2

Aurora
C.da Ciafone, 98
63035 Offida (AP)
tel. 0736810007
e-mail: enrico@viniaurora.it

We have always like this Offida winery's Rosso Piceno for its intense spicy nose and sweet hints in the mouth. The Superiore 2000 is also good, showing cherries, spice and chocolate, then a well-balanced palate. Lastly, the good Barricadiero has complex spice aromas and good vigour.

● Barricadiero '00	🍷🍷	5
● Rosso Piceno Sup. '00	🍷	3
● Rosso Piceno '01	🍷	3

Fontursia
C.da Fontursia
63038 Ripatransone (AP)
tel. 07359496
e-mail: lafontursia@tin.it

The recently set up Fontursia winery has an impressive Offida Passerina Donna Bianca 2001, a deep straw yellow wine with vanilla on the nose and a full flavour. The red Fontursio '99 has nice wild berry aromas and length in the mouth. The Rosso Piceno Crivellino 2001 is fresh and drinks nicely.

○ Offida Passerina Donna Bianca '01	🍷🍷	3*
● Rosso Piceno Crivellino '01	🍷	5
● Fontursio '99	🍷	3

Cavallaro
Via Tassanare, 4
60030 Rosora (AN)
tel. 0731814158

Cavallaro, in Castelli di Jesi, is one of the many Marche wineries to have made a fine debut. The Verdicchio Crocetta 20001 is fresh and minerally, and the attractive Rosso Piceno Furtarello 2001 has nice blackberry and morello cherry. The Rosso Piceno il Moro 2001 is well made.

● Rosso Piceno Furtarello '01	🍷🍷	4
○ Verdicchio dei Castelli di Jesi Cl. Sup. Crocetta '01	🍷🍷	4
● Rosso Piceno Il Moro '01	🍷	4

Amato Ceci
Via Battinebbia, 4
60038 San Paolo di Jesi (AN)
tel. 0731779197 - 0731779052
e-mail: info@vignamato.com

The Amato Ceci winery makes two good Verdicchio dei Castelli di Jesi wines. The straw-yellow Vignamato has ripe apples on the nose and a balanced citrus flavour, though the finish fades quickly. The Ambrosia '99 has vanilla, citrus and tropical fruit, reflected on the well-structured palate.

○ Verdicchio dei Castelli di Jesi Cl. Sup. Vignamato '01	🍷	3
○ Verdicchio dei Castelli di Jesi Cl. Sup. Ambrosia '99	🍷	4

Enrico Ceci
Via Santa Maria d'Arco, 7
60038 San Paolo di Jesi (AN)
tel. 0731119033
e-mail: cecienrico@virgilio.it

There are two good Verdicchio dei Castelli di Jesi bottles from this cellar and consultant winemaker Alberto Mazzoni. The Classico Santa Maria d'Arco 2001 has peach fruit on the nose and a fragrant palate whereas the Superiore has green apple aromas and a tangy, juicy mouthfeel.

○ Verdicchio dei Castelli di Jesi Cl. Sup. Santa Maria d'Arco '01	🍷🍷	4*
○ Verdicchio dei Castelli di Jesi Cl. Santa Maria d'Arco '01	🍷	3

Piersanti
Via Borgo Santa Maria, 60
60038 San Paolo di Jesi (AN)
tel. 0731779020
e-mail: piersanti@tin.it

Founded in 1955, Piersanti has boosted production over the years and recently started making more selective wines. We enjoyed the Verdicchio Pontemagno 2001, which has rather varietal aromas and good flavour. The Bachero 2001 has a ripe apricot nose and a big palate.

○ Verdicchio dei Castelli di Jesi Cl. Bachero '01	🍷	4
○ Verdicchio dei Castelli di Jesi Cl. Pontemagno '01	🍷	3

Accadia
Fraz. Castellaro
Via Ammorto, 19
60040 Serra San Quirico (AN)
Tel. 073185172 - 0731859007

The small Accadia winery in the hills of Serra San Quirico presented two Verdicchio dei Castelli di Jesi selections. One, the Classico Conscio 2001, is balanced and fresh-tasting whereas the slightly super-ripe Cantorì selection offers apples, almonds and a very pleasant palate.

○ Verdicchio dei Castelli di Jesi Cl. Cantorì '01	🍷🍷	4*
○ Verdicchio dei Castelli di Jesi Cl. Conscio '01	🍷	4

Alberto Quacquarini
Via Colli, 1
62020 Serrapetrona (MC)
Tel. 0733908180 - 0733908790
E-mail: quacquarini@tiscalinet.it

This Serrapetrona winery presented the Colli della Serra '99, which is dense ruby red, with an interesting, violet-laced nose and even thrust on the palate. The rich, red Petronio '99 has decent berry fruit aromas that are picked up on the palate, which ends attractively.

● Colli della Serra Rosso '99	🍷	5
● Petronio '99	🍷	6

Ester Hauser
C.da Coroncino, 1/A
60039 Staffolo (AN)
Tel. 0731770203

The Il Cupo '99 presented this year is a very good monovarietal from montepulciano grapes. Purplish red in hue, it offers very ripe fruit aromas layered over sweet tobacco. The satisfying palate reveals soft, well-gauged extract backing up the fruit, and a long smooth finish.

● Il Cupo '99	🍷🍷	6

Fonte della Luna
Medoro Cimarelli
Via San Francesco, 1/A
60039 Staffolo (AN)
Tel. 0731779307

The two wines from Cimarelli come from one the most distinctive, traditional centres in the Verdicchio dei Castelli di Jesi DOC. The standard-version is fresh and tangy while the Fra Moriale selection is more powerful and expressive, with minerally aromas and a longer, more mouthfilling, palate.

○ Verdicchio dei Castelli di Jesi Cl. Sup. Fra Moriale '01	🍷🍷	4*
○ Verdicchio dei Castelli di Jesi Cl. '01	🍷	3

F.lli Zaccagnini & C.
Via Salmagina, 9/10
60039 Staffolo (AN)
Tel. 0731779892
E-mail: info@zaccagnini.it

The Vigna Vescovi '99 blend is one of this cellar's best wines. Garnet to ruby red, it throws a nose of medium intensity, followed by a generous palate. The traditional flagship bottle, the Brut Riserva, has delicate perlage, attractive spring flower aromas and good depth.

○ Zaccagnini Brut Ris.	🍷🍷	4
● Vigna Vescovi '99	🍷	4

La Ripe
Loc. Ripalta - Via Piana, 20
61029 Urbino (PU)
Tel. 0721893019
E-mail: info@laripe.com

This new winery presented its versions of local DOCs, created with oenologist Giancarlo Soverchia. The Colli Pesaresi Sangiovese 2001 has cherry and blackberry fruit and a tangy, generous palate with balanced tannins. The Bianchello del Metauro 2001 is fresh-tasting, pleasant and vibrant.

○ Bianchello del Metauro '01	🍷🍷	4*
● Colli Pesaresi Sangiovese '01	🍷🍷	4*

UMBRIA

The Umbrian miracle goes on. We're hearing ever more about the region and its wines, and average quality is getting better, as our tastings this year made abundantly clear. Sure, it won't escape the most attentive observers that there were six Three Glass wines last year and one fewer this, but this is of minor account in the overall picture. It certainly doesn't undermine in the slightest the enthusiastic labours of the region's growers and producers, or the results they have been achieving. Until a few years ago, the region was no more than a sort of appendage to Tuscany, where large estates could buy white wines like Orvieto at good prices to expand their ranges, or source well-priced, full-bodied reds for blending into their table wines. Today, this is no longer the case. Umbrians have dusted off their self-respect, shifted up a gear and set to work to enable the quality of their territories to be seen for what it is: extraordinarily high. The results of the past five years' work are there for all to see. Montefalco is a phenomenon that attracts investment from all over Italy, and even from abroad. Orvieto, once erroneously regarded purely as white wine territory, is now revealing the class and elegance of its reds. Even areas until recently considered peripheral to the world of fine wines have taken their places in the mainstream of premium winemaking with full honours. Trasimeno, which offers further confirmation this year of its great potential as wine country, is a case in point. In addition, wineries throughout the region are working flat out to produce ever better wines. This is just as true of co-operatives as it is of private estates. Indeed, the region's co-operatives, which are legion, have gained worthy fame for the quality of their output. But let's come to the Three Glass awards. The '00 Cervaro della Sala from Antinori-owned Castello della Sala is quite simply outstanding, as indeed all its predecessors have been. Armaleo '00, another fine red from the Giovanni Dubini stable, scored almost as impressively. Another red dominates the scene in Colli del Trasimeno, the Campoleone '00 from Lamborghini, La Fiorita. At Montefalco, Marco Caprai and Còlpetrone both claim top honours yet again, each with an excellent '99 Sagrantino. But beyond these groundbreaking wines and cutting-edge estates, the most interesting aspect of the Umbrian scene is that there are literally dozens of wines only a few point behind them. That's really good news.

AMELIA (TR)

CASTELLO DELLE REGINE
FRAZ. LE REGINE
VIA DI CASTELLUCCIO
05022 AMELIA (TR)
TEL. 0744702005
E-MAIL: castellodelleregine@virgilio.it

This estate must be the Umbrian revelation of the year. Situated at San Liberato in the province of Terni, it has 54 hectares under vine and master winemaker Franco Bernabei is the consultant. We found great character across the whole range, especially the '00 Merlot, a robust and most successful red. Careful vinification and ten months' ageing in small oak casks have yielded a powerful wine, full of ripe red fruitiness, with complex aromas of wild berries, black pepper and cassis. The palate is rich and vigorous, with a firm streak of oak and clean flavours of warmly ripe fruit. Its tannins are soft, well-calibrated and fine-grained. The red Princeps '00, also barrique-aged, from a blend of cabernet sauvignon and sangiovese with a little merlot, is also excellent and is marked out by its well-defined cherry-like aromas and varietal notes of bell pepper. The full palate has good body and reveals soft tannins. Another wine that made it to a second Glass is Podernovo '00, a powerful, concentrated wine from 100 per cent Sangiovese, aged in tonneaux and barriques. Sangiovese '00 is from 30-year old vines. It has good firm tannins and opens out on the palate to give a fair array of flavours and length. For a newcomer, this is not a bad showing at all.

●	Merlot '00	7
●	Podernovo '00	4
●	Princeps '00	6
●	Sangiovese '00	5

AMELIA (TR)

CANTINA DEI COLLI AMERINI
LOC. FORNOLE DI AMELIA
ZONA INDUSTRIALE
05020 AMELIA (TR)
TEL. 0744989721
E-MAIL: carbioca@virgilio.it

After a visit to the Other Wineries section because the flagship selections skipped a year, the Colli Amerini co-operative returns with a full Guide profile. Founded in 1975 with the aim of raising the area's wine profile, it must surely now be the leading co-operative in the province of Terni. The cellar currently vinifies fruit from 700 hectares of vineyard owned by its members and has Riccardo Cotarella, Umbrian winemaker par excellence as consultant. It has also recently set in place changes to its board of directors. The winery's flagship, Colli Amerini Rosso Superiore Carbio, remains full of character. The '99, from merlot, sangiovese and montepulciano, is a warm purple-ruby red colour. The nose is very clean, its ripe fruitiness redolent of wild red berries. The palate has good body, length and finesse, and an elegant spiciness on the finish. The richly fruity Torraccio '99, from 100 per cent Sangiovese, showed similarly well. Clean, clearly defined aromas of cherry and plum are followed by an intense, concentrated palate with harmonious sensations of liquorice and black pepper. The '01 Colli Amerini Rosso Terre Arnolfe is again well made. It's a little vegetal but nicely knit. Two whites are also worthy of mention, the Orvieto Classico '01 and the Colli Amerini Malvasia la Corte '01, both with primary fruit aromas giving crisp notes of apples and pears, and showing a pleasing streak of acidity. The '00 Rosso Bartolomeo, made exclusively from aleatico, hits the mark as usual, with aromas reminiscent of autumn leaves and finely judged sweetness.

●	C. Amerini Rosso Sup. Carbio '99	5
●	Umbria Sangiovese Torraccio '99	5
●	Umbria Aleatico Bartolomeo '00	4
○	C. Amerini Malvasia La Corte '01	2
●	C. Amerini Rosso Terre Arnolfe '01	3
○	Orvieto Cl. '01	3
●	C. Amerini Rosso Sup. Carbio '98	4
○	C. Amerini Bianco Terre Arnolfe '00	2*
●	C. Amerini Rosso Terre Arnolfe '00	2*
○	C. Amerini Chardonnay Rocca Nerina '98	4

BASCHI (TR)

VAGLIE
VIA AMELIA, 48
05023 BASCHI (TR)
TEL. 0744957425
E-MAIL: a.lumini@tiscali.it

After its encouraging first outing in last year's Guide, there is now confirmation that the Vaglie estate is one of the most interesting around Orvieto. It has 12 hectares under vine, in an area that falls within three DOCs, Orvieto Classico, Rosso Orvietano and Lago di Corbara, and the consultant is Maurilio Chioccia. There were excellent results from our tastings, especially regarding the reds. Let's start with Umbria Rosso Momenti '01. Its style, from a blend of sangiovese and merlot, is not unique but most pleasing, with great power of fruit on both nose and palate, a fair dose of new oak and good extraction. Another Two Glass winner was Umbria Rosso Vaglie '01, from montepulciano, sangiovese, canaiolo and ciliegiolo. There are notes of ripe cherry that soften into black pepper and cassis on the nose, while on the palate the fruit tenor is very ripe, as is obvious from the hints of cooked plum. Umbria Rosso Masseo '00, from sangiovese, merlot and cabernet sauvignon, is less structured but has good body and fair length. To finish, we'll mention the very nice '01 Orvieto Classico Secco, which has freshness and primary aromas that reveal notes of crisp apple and damson.

●	Momenti '01	ΨΨ	3
●	Umbria Rosso Vaglie '01	ΨΨ	2*
●	Masseo '00	Ψ	4
○	Orvieto Cl. Secco '01	Ψ	1*
●	Momenti '00	ΨΨ	3*
●	Masseo '99	ΨΨ	4
○	Orvieto Cl. '00	Ψ	2*
○	Orvieto Cl. Sup. Matricale '00	Ψ	4

BEVAGNA (PG)

AGRICOLA ADANTI
VOC. ARQUATA
06031 BEVAGNA (PG)
TEL. 0742360295
E-MAIL: info@cantineadanti.com

This year brings another good performance from the Adanti estate. There are 25 hectares under vine, situated in the hills that straddle Arquata and Colcimino. The plots are planted with a distinguished group of varieties, ranging from the indigenous sagrantino and grechetto, to the international merlot, cabernet and chardonnay. Thanks to consultancy from the able Mauro Monicchi, Adanti has once more come out with a range of excellent-quality wines, especially the reds. The best of the bunch was, we felt, the Montefalco Sagrantino Arquata '98. Ruby red in colour, it has a full, evolved nose with clear, elegant aromas of plum and ripe cherry. The palate has excellent structure and is well endowed with tannin. Rosso d'Arquata '98 is also excellent, easily picking up Two Glasses. Its purple-tinged ruby introduces super-ripe fruit on the nose, with ringing notes of blackberry and cherry and elegant hints of black pepper. Then comes the fine Montefalco Rosso Arquata '00, with its complex tones of jam and prune on the nose and a palate slim in tannin yet with plenty of body. The whites are just as sound, with Montefalco Bianco Arquata '01 leading the field. This is fruity and floral on the nose, clean and balanced on the nice fleshy palate, and clearly redolent of sharp damson and white peach. Colli Martani Grechetto Arquata '01 also earned One Glass for its simple, primary, apples-and-pears nose and its fresh, acidulous palate.

●	Montefalco Sagrantino Arquata '98	ΨΨ	5
●	Rosso d'Arquata '98	ΨΨ	5
●	Montefalco Rosso Arquata '00	Ψ	4
○	Colli Martani Grechetto Arquata '01	Ψ	4
○	Montefalco Bianco Arquata '01	Ψ	4
●	Rosso d'Arquata '91	ΨΨ	4
●	Rosso d'Arquata '97	ΨΨ	5
●	Montefalco Sagrantino Passito '89	Ψ	4
●	Montefalco Sagrantino '96	Ψ	5
●	Montefalco Sagrantino Passito '96	Ψ	5
●	Montefalco Sagrantino Passito '97	Ψ	5
●	Montefalco Rosso '99	Ψ	4

BEVAGNA (PG)

Eredi Benincasa
Loc. Capro, 99
06031 Bevagna (PG)
tel. 0742361307
e-mail: info@aziendabenincasa.com

The Benincasa estate makes its first appearance in the Guide, and in style. Founded in 1964, it extends for 46 hectares, with 15 hectares under vine, all on the hills that descend from Montefalco towards Bevagna. It is said that it was actually Domenico Benincasa who, back in the 1970s, created the first sagrantino-only vineyard for the production of Sagrantino di Montefalco, starting out with a few elderly vines here and there on old plots. The wines submitted for tasting showed excellently for homogeneity of quality and character. The red Vigna La Fornace '00, from barbera, merlot and sagrantino, was barrique-aged for nine months and easily gained Two Glasses. Bright purple-ruby, it unveils an elegant, complex nose characterized by inviting notes of red berry fruit, with distinct aromas of blackberry and wild berries. The full, powerful palate is warm and redolent of almost-cooked fruit. It has excellent length. The powerful Montefalco Rosso '00, with its perfectly clean berry fruit tones and its elegant, well-judged tannins, is of similar quality Also good are the red Vincastro '01, from sangiovese, mainly, with merlot, which is clean and evolved on the nose, and the Colli Martani Grechetto Poggio dell'Annunziata '01, which has damson and white peach fruitiness.

•	Montefalco Rosso '00	🍷🍷	4
•	Vigna La Fornace '00	🍷🍷	5
○	Colli Martani Poggio dell'Annunziata '01	🍷	4
•	Vincastro '01	🍷	3

CASTEL VISCARDO (TR)

Cantina Monrubio
Fraz. Monterubiaglio
Loc. Le Prese, 22
05010 Castel Viscardo (TR)
tel. 0763626064
e-mail: cantina.monrubio@tiscalinet.it

With the tireless Riccardo Cotarella as consultant, Cantina Monrubio continues to maintain its status as one of the best co-operatives in the region. Set up in 1957 at the initiative of several growers in the Castel Viscardo area, the winery now numbers around 300 grape-contributing members. Never before has it so comprehensively merited a profile in the Guide as it did this year. The entire range is reliable and well put together, from the excellent Palaia '00 onwards. This merlot and cabernet blend, aged one year in barrique, is a purple-tinged ruby. The overtly fruity nose has great intensity of perfume, with inviting aromas of blackberry and blueberry, plus nuances of vanilla, black pepper and cassis. It is long and full on the palate, supported by a good, ripe, well-integrated tannic weave. The Monrubio is always of interest, not least for its price, and the '01 confirms this, with clean notes of autumn leaves and delicate scents of sweet oak. The estate's newest wine, Nociano '00, a very varietal 100 per cent cabernet, is similarly good and has classic notes of bell pepper, a gently tannic palate and good length. The '01 Orvieto Classicos are as successful as ever. Both the Salceto and the Soana, a Superiore, have primary, fruit-driven characteristics with clear-cut notes of apple, ripe damson and apricot, not to mention a refreshing dose of acidity.

•	Palaia '00	🍷🍷	4
•	Nociano '00	🍷	3
•	Monrubio '01	🍷	2*
○	Orvieto Cl. Salceto '01	🍷	2*
○	Orvieto Cl. Sup. Soana '01	🍷	3
•	L'Olmaia '96	🍷🍷	4
•	Monrubio '98	🍷🍷	2
•	Palaia '98	🍷🍷	5
•	Palaia '99	🍷🍷	5
•	Monrubio '00	🍷	2
•	Palaia '97	🍷	3
•	Monrubio '99	🍷	2

CASTIGLIONE DEL LAGO (PG)

Duca della Corgna
Via Roma, 236
06061 Castiglione del Lago (PG)
Tel. 0759652493
E-mail: ducacorgna@libero.it

The tendency in Umbria to concentrate ever more on the red varieties has results going from strength to strength. The Duca della Corgna range is further confirmation of this for its reds were out in front at our tastings. For the second year running, the Colli del Trasimeno Rosso Corniolo, this time the '01, came within an ace of Three Glasses. Produced mostly from sangiovese and aged one year in barrique, it has a dark purple-red colour. The elegant nose has a spicy, fruity impact with inviting scents of cassis, wild berry fruit and black pepper. The palate is both powerful and refined, showing length and a good tannic presence. Both wines under the Colli del Trasimeno Rosso Gamay Divina Villa '01 label are excellent. The Etichetta Nera (Black Label) has a sweet oakiness and ripe fruit while the Etichetta Bianca (White Label) is fresher but retains good concentration. Colli del Trasimeno Baccio del Rosso '01 has surprisingly good character, considering its robust annual production of 80,000 bottles. It is a youthful Sangiovese, with a vegetal nose and a palate of fair tannin and fruit. We'll bring the review to a close with the estate's two whites, the clean, freshly crisp Colli del Trasimeno Grechetto Nuricante '01 and the fruity Colli del Trasimeno Bianco Baccio del Bianco '01, which has clear notes of damson and lemon.

CASTIGLIONE DEL LAGO (PG)

Fanini
Loc. Petrignano del Lago
Voc. I Cucchi
06060 Castiglione del Lago (PG)
Tel. 0755171241 - 0755173122
E-mail: mldp@unipg.it

This small estate has just eight hectares of vineyard, on the hills facing Tuscany above Lake Trasimeno. Quality is on a steadily upward curve, a trend aided by the capable co-ordination of cellar operations by oenologist Fabrizio Ciufoli. The red wines in particular are most impressive. Let's start with Fanini's newest wine, a fine 100 per cent Merlot. The '00 is ruby in colour, lightly tinged with purple. The nose has attractive aromas of berry fruit, especially cherry and ripe plum, which soften into delicate scents of sweet spices. The palate has good structure, medium-grained tannins and finishes fairly long. Another Two Glass winner is the super-ripe Sangiovese Vigna la Pieve '99. It has a prune and liquorice nose, with generous acidity and tannin giving backbone to the palate. The '00 Colli del Trasimeno Rosso Morello del Lago is as well typed as ever, showing fresh on the nose and nicely weighty on the palate. The Robbiano '01 stands head and shoulders above the rest of the whites, as it has done for years. From chardonnay, and aged for around five months in barrique, it has perfumes of a certain complexity, mainly of white-fleshed tropical fruit, and a sweet oakiness. The palate is broad, warm and long. Finally, the Colli del Trasimeno Bianco Albello del Lago '01, from trebbiano, chardonnay and grechetto, has simple aromas of crisp apple and develops firmly in the mouth.

- C. del Trasimeno Rosso Corniolo '01 — 4
- C. del Trasimeno Rosso Baccio del Rosso '01 — 2*
- C. del Trasimeno Gamay Divina Villa Et. Bianca '01 — 4
- C. del Trasimeno Gamay Divina Villa Et. Nera '01 — 4
- C. del Trasimeno Baccio del Bianco '01 — 1*
- C. del Trasimeno Grechetto Nuricante '01 — 3
- C. del Trasimeno Rosso Corniolo '00 — 4
- C. del Trasimeno Rosso Corniolo '98 — 4

- Chardonnay Robbiano '01 — 5
- Merlot '00 — 5
- Sangiovese Vigna La Pieve '99 — 5
- C. del Trasimeno Bianco Albello del Lago '01 — 3
- C. del Trasimeno Rosso Morello del Lago '00 — 4
- Chardonnay Robbiano '00 — 4
- C. del Trasimeno Rosso Morello del Lago '95 — 3
- Chardonnay Robbiano '96 — 3
- Chardonnay Robbiano '97 — 3
- Chardonnay Robbiano '98 — 3
- Sangiovese Vigna La Pieve '98 — 5
- Chardonnay Robbiano '99 — 3

CASTIGLIONE DEL LAGO (PG)

Poggio Bertaio
Fraz. Casamaggiore
Loc. Frattavecchia, 29
06061 Castiglione del Lago (PG)
tel. 075956921
e-mail: poggiobertaio@tiscalinet.it

The Poggio Bertaio wines maintain more than decent quality levels, although we have yet to seen signs of the "great leap forwards" that the estate's personnel seem well capable of making. Owned by the Ciufoli family, this estate made wine solely for domestic consumption for many years. It was 1998 before founder Fabio's two sons, Fabrizio and Ugo, now the estate's oenologist and agronomist respectively, started to bottle and release onto the market. Currently, the estate has 20 hectares under vine, producing just over 30,000 bottles a year. Cimbolo '00, a red exclusively from sangiovese that ages 14 months in barrique, has depth and balance. The aromas are dense and hold together well, even if the sweet oaky notes of vanilla and cinnamon dominate somewhat. The wine is distinctly solid on the palate, where its flavour develops evenly. The finish may not be particularly long but it is tight and even. However, the real surprise from Poggio Bertaio this year was the new selection, Crovello '00, from merlot and cabernet in equal parts. It is purple-red in colour; the nose is full of ripe red fruit, especially cherry and plum, then the palate, with its faintly vegetal tone, is very well balanced, with mid-grained tannins knitting deliciously into the body of the wine.

●	Cimbolo '00	♟♟	6
●	Crovello '00	♟♟	7
●	Cimbolo '99	♟♟	5
●	Cimbolo '98	♟♟	5

FICULLE (TR)

★ Castello della Sala
Loc. Sala
05016 Ficulle (TR)
tel. 076386051
e-mail: castellodellasala@antinori.it

Castello della Sala, one of Italy's leading estates, has been owned by the Antinori family since the 1940s. Fully 160 hectares of vineyard provide the fruit for 1,500,000 bottles a year and the top of the range is Cervaro della Sala. The '00 is the 12th release to gain Three Glasses. Yes, that's right, it's the 12th. From chardonnay and grechetto, fermented and then aged for five months in barrique, it is a brightly-flecked deep straw colour. Showing extraordinary class, it is one of the few barriqued Italian whites to have finesse rather than being weighed down by flavours of vanilla and over-ripeness. There is plentiful freshness, which renders the palate lithe and supple, giving it a more northerly taste profile than you might expect from an Umbrian wine. Sauvignon Conte della Vipera '00, from oak-fermented sauvignon blanc with a little chardonnay, is up there with in the same league. It has a concentrated, well-fruited nose, supported by balancing toastiness. The palate, strong in bell pepper and sage, is unashamedly varietal. The '01 Chardonnay is not just full of flavour but is also great value for money, as is the markedly varietal '01 Sauvignon. The two '01 Orvieto Classicos are as well made as ever. The Pinot Nero '99 is a fairly austere red, with complex gamey flavours, good structure and a lightly tannic finish. Muffato della Sala, from sauvignon blanc, grechetto, traminer and riesling, brings our review to a satisfying close. The '99, elegantly redolent of ripe tropical fruit, has quite exemplary sweetness.

○	Cervaro della Sala '00	♟♟♟	6
○	Conte della Vipera '00	♟♟	5
○	Muffato della Sala '99	♟♟	6
●	Pinot Nero Vigneto Consola '99	♟♟	6
○	Chardonnay della Sala '01	♟	4
○	Orvieto Cl. Campogrande '01	♟	3
○	Orvieto Cl. Sup. '01	♟	4
○	Sauvignon della Sala '01	♟	4
○	Cervaro della Sala '93	♟♟♟	6
○	Cervaro della Sala '94	♟♟♟	6
○	Cervaro della Sala '95	♟♟♟	6
○	Cervaro della Sala '96	♟♟♟	6
○	Cervaro della Sala '97	♟♟♟	7
○	Cervaro della Sala '98	♟♟♟	7
○	Cervaro della Sala '99	♟♟♟	7

FOLIGNO (PG)

Terre de' Trinci
Via Fiamenga, 57
06034 Foligno (PG)
tel. 0742320165 - 0742320243
e-mail: cantina@terredetrinci.com

After serving time in the Other Wineries section, Terre de' Trinci has finally gained a full entry in the Guide, on merit. It has over 300 hectares of vineyard, lying in the Foligno zone, and produces around 500,000 bottles a year, operations being co-ordinated by oenologist Maurilio Chioccia. The house style favours reds with a full tannic thrust that, fortunately, never threatens their overall balance. Montefalco Sagrantino '99 has a purple-ruby colour. The nose is intense and powerful, with a prune-like fruitiness that stops just short of super-ripeness, and is accentuated by notes of black pepper and clove. The palate echoes the warmth of the wine, with its intense jamminess, and is notably alcoholic. Cajo '00, from sagrantino, merlot and cabernet, is another fine red. The palate has good body and fair length, despite a question mark hanging over its vegetal tonality. Two Glasses also go to Montefalco Rosso Riserva '99, from sangiovese, sagrantino and merlot. The nose is fully ripe and developed, with notes of blackberry, blueberry, cassis and black pepper. The palate is deep and powerful, with well-calibrated tannins. The white Luna '01, from grechetto and chardonnay, is also good, offering ripe damson and white peach fruitiness, as well as lively acidity.

● Umbria Rosso Cajo '00	🍷🍷	4
● Montefalco Rosso Ris. '99	🍷🍷	4
● Montefalco Sagrantino '99	🍷🍷	6
○ Umbria Bianco Luna '01	🍷	4
● Montefalco Sagrantino '97	🍷	5
● Umbria Rosso Cajo '99	🍷	4

GIOVE (TR)

Le Crete
Voc. Martinozzi, 89
05024 Giove (TR)
tel. 0744992443
e-mail: az.agr.lecrete@virgilio.it

The Le Crete winemaking estate, owned by Giuliano Castellani, lies in the hills of the Tiberina valley close to Giove, in the province of Terni. It made an impressive Guide debut this year. The winery is a family-run affair that avails itself of consultancy from Maurilio Chioccia, and offers the wine-loving public a single product, a red called Petranera. It emerged from our tastings as a wine of exceptional depth. The '01 is the first release and it shows great richness of extract, considerable aromatic breadth and excellent balance on the palate. All these deserving attributes, understandably enough, took it into our Three Glass tasting finals. Petranera is obtained from a blend of sangiovese and merlot, with a small amount of barbera, and ages for about six months in barrique. It grabs your attention right from the very first glimpse of its deep purple-ruby hue. The nose has remarkable intensity, and is richly fruited, with clear aromas of blackberry and ripe wild cherry, underlined by secondary nuances of clove and black pepper. There is great structure to the palate, which is full and has a lively tannic edge that knits well into the fruit.

● Petranera '01	🍷🍷	5

GUALDO CATTANEO (PG)

COLPETRONE
FRAZ. MARCELLANO
VIA DELLA COLLINA, 4
06035 GUALDO CATTANEO (PG)
TEL. 0578767722
E-MAIL: colpetrone@tin.it

Còlpetrone has now attained its fourth consecutive Three Glass award. Who could wish for any better affirmation of oenologist Lorenzo Landi's sure hand? The house style, now well established, hinges on perfect maturity of the base grapes and particular care being taken in vinification over the extraction of the tannins, in order to impart finesse. The Three Glasses go, as ever, to the Montefalco Sagrantino. The '99 echoes the soft, enveloping character of its predecessors but may possibly have greater elegance, both in the aromas, which disclose pencil lead, black cherry jam, blackcurrant, white pepper and cocoa powder, and the progression on the palate. The '99 Montefalco Sagrantino Passito certainly does not fade by comparison. In fact, it is probably the wine's best release ever and certainly came very close to gaining Three Glasses. The colour is an intense purple red. The nose is rich in fresh, ripe red berry fruitiness, then the palate is soft, concentrated, fat and, most important, well balanced in its tannins and its degree of sweetness. Montefalco Rosso '00, with its fresh, lively red berry fruit nose and its harmonious, balanced palate, brings Còlpetrone's excellent showing to a fine close.

MAGIONE (PG)

TERRE DEL CARPINE
VIA FORMANUOVA, 87
06063 MAGIONE (PG)
TEL. 075840298
E-MAIL: cit@trasinet.com

Terre del Carpine is the new name for the Cantina Intercomunale del Trasimeno. The name comes from Pian di Carpine, the valley embracing Magione, Corciano and Montesperello where the vines are situated. Founded in 1996, the winery currently has 500 members supplying grapes from over 400 hectares of vineyard, and an annual output of 120,000 bottles. The selection of reds in particular showed very well. The range is headed by Barca '00, a good Colli del Trasimeno Rosso, made from sangiovese with small amounts of merlot and cabernet sauvignon. The dark purple ruby ushers in a nose that is elegant, intense and rich in red berry fruitiness, mostly blackberry and blueberry. The palate has good structure and a tannic weave that may have only average finesse but still integrates well with the wine's other elements and lacks all trace of bitterness. Umbria Merlot '00, a wine of restrained herbaceousness and inviting cherry and plum fruitiness, achieved Two Glasses. Colli del Trasimeno Rosso Erceo '00, first tasted last year, is simpler and less structured, but no less attractive. The hints of tobacco and sweet spice on the nose are particularly appealing.

● Montefalco Sagrantino '99	🍷🍷🍷 7
● Montefalco Sagrantino Passito '99	🍷🍷 6
● Montefalco Rosso '00	🍷🍷 4*
● Montefalco Sagrantino '96	🍷🍷🍷 4
● Montefalco Sagrantino '97	🍷🍷🍷 5
● Montefalco Sagrantino '98	🍷🍷🍷 5
● Montefalco Sagrantino '95	🍷🍷 4
● Montefalco Rosso '97	🍷🍷 3
● Montefalco Sagrantino Passito '97	🍷🍷 6
● Montefalco Rosso '98	🍷🍷 3
● Montefalco Sagrantino Passito '98	🍷🍷 6
● Montefalco Rosso '99	🍷🍷 4

● C. del Trasimeno Rosso Barca '00	🍷🍷 2*
● Umbria Merlot '00	🍷🍷 4
● C. del Trasimeno Rosso Erceo '00	🍷 2
● C. del Trasimeno Rosso Barca '99	🍷 3

MONTECASTRILLI (TR)

Fattoria Le Poggette
Loc. Le Poggette
05026 Montecastrilli (TR)
tel. 0744940338 - 0637514785

Founded in 1965, this estate, situated on the outskirts of Montecastrilli and owned by Giorgio Lanzetta, has 18 hectares of dedicated vineyard planted to sangiovese, canaiolo, montepulciano and grechetto. The vineyards give around 70,000 bottles a year. Three wines with the Le Poggette stamp showed particularly well at our tastings, the Torre Maggiore, the Colli Amerini and the Canaiolo. Let's start with the newly-denominated Umbria Rosso Torre Maggiore '99, which was previously bottled as a varietal Montepulciano. It is from a blend of subvarieties of montepulciano d'Abruzzo and ages for 18 months in tonneaux. The colour is purple-ruby. The fruity notes of cherry and blueberry on the nose are well integrated with elegant oakiness that is beautifully judged in amount and comes from good quality wood. The wine is powerful and intense on the palate, with inviting flavours of small wild berry fruit and an even tannic weave throughout. Still at the Two Glass level, we have Colli Amerini Rosso Superiore '00, from sangiovese with small amounts of canaiolo and montepulciano. It is deep ruby in colour, then the nose has good complexity and is softly fruity. The palate develops consistently and evenly, giving intriguing hints of citrus peel and cinnamon on the finish. The Canaiolo '00 is well styled and characterized by warm, ripe fruitiness.

●	C. Amerini Rosso Sup. '00	ΨΨ	4
●	Umbria Rosso Torre Maggiore '99	ΨΨ	6
●	Umbria Canaiolo '00	Ψ	4
○	Umbria Grechetto '00	ΨΨ	3*
●	Montepulciano '95	ΨΨ	5
●	Montepulciano '96	ΨΨ	5
●	Montepulciano '97	ΨΨ	5
●	Montepulciano '98	ΨΨ	5
●	Umbria Canaiolo '99	ΨΨ	4
●	C. Amerini Rosso Sup. '96	Ψ	3
●	C. Amerini Rosso Sup. '97	Ψ	3
●	Umbria Canaiolo '98	Ψ	3
●	C. Amerini Rosso Sup. '99	Ψ	3

MONTEFALCO (PG)

Tenuta Alzatura
Loc. Fratta - Alzatura, 108
06036 Montefalco (PG)
tel. 0742399435

The Cecchi family own several estates and together they form something of a winemaking empire. Until last year, all were in Tuscany. Villa Cerna is the "homestead", in Castellina in Chianti, Val delle Rose is in the Maremma, and the ancient Castello di Montauto is at San Gimignano. Now, Luigi Cecchi and his sons Andrea and Cesare have bought a new property, Tenuta Alzatura, here in Montefalco, the rising star in the Umbrian firmament. The estate has 15 hectares of vineyard, not all, as yet, in production, and currently gives around 7,000 bottles a year. So far, just one wine has been released, a Montefalco Sagrantino with 24 months of ageing in barrique and stainless steel vats. It's called Uno di Uno. The '98, the very first bottling, stormed straight into our final taste-offs for Three Glasses. It impressed the panel with its ruby colour, which is lightly tinged with purple. The nose has considerable intensity and is richly fruited, with hints of oak toast and a slight spiciness. The palate initially gives softness and roundness before reaching a fairly tannic centre point, then finishes long and evenly with just a touch of oakiness.

●	Montefalco Sagrantino Uno di Uno '98	ΨΨ	6

MONTEFALCO (PG)

ANTONELLI - SAN MARCO
LOC. SAN MARCO, 59
06036 MONTEFALCO (PG)
TEL. 0742379158
E-MAIL: info@antonellisanmarco.it

The estate was founded in 1881 by Francesco Antonelli, who bought it from the diocese of Spoleto. It is now managed by Filippo Antonelli and oenologist Manlio Erba assists with winemaking. The property extends over 170 hectares, 30 of which are vineyard. All are in the municipal territory of Montefalco, right in the heart of the DOCG zone. This does not appear to have been an easy year for Antonelli, who has had the innumerable problems related to the renovation of his cellar to contend with, and only the '99 release of his top wine, Montefalco Sagrantino, showed really well. Garnet-tinged ruby in colour, it has a nose that is lively and clean cut, and rich in ripe red berry fruitiness, with inviting aromas of plum, cherry and liquorice and a delicate overlay of oak toast. The palate has considerable personality and is deep, warm, long and complex, with carefully dosed, well-behaved tannins. The youthfully fresh Montefalco Rosso '00 is also good. It is a purple-ruby colour and has primary aromas of crisp red berry fruit. The nicely full palate shows youthful but ripe tannins. Colli Martani Grechetto '01 well styled, with a deep straw colour introducing a youthful, crisply fruity nose, dominated by apple and damson. The cleanly fruited palate has good acid balance and length. We expected more, though, from the Montefalco Rosso Riserva and Grechetto Vigna Tonda which, in all honesty, were a little off-key on the nose and slightly raw on the palate. Similarly, the Sagrantino was rather vegetal and rendered a tad heavy by its residual sugar.

●	Montefalco Sagrantino '99	🍷	6
●	Montefalco Rosso '00	🍷	4
○	Colli Martani Grechetto '01	🍷	4
●	Montefalco Sagrantino '98	🍷🍷	6
●	Montefalco Sagrantino '94	🍷🍷	4
●	Montefalco Sagrantino '95	🍷🍷	4
●	Montefalco Sagrantino Passito '95	🍷🍷	4
●	Montefalco Sagrantino '96	🍷🍷	4
●	Montefalco Sagrantino '97	🍷🍷	6
●	Montefalco Sagrantino Passito '97	🍷🍷	6
●	Montefalco Rosso '99	🍷🍷	4

MONTEFALCO (PG)

ARNALDO CAPRAI - VAL DI MAGGIO
LOC. TORRE
06036 MONTEFALCO (PG)
TEL. 0742378802 - 0742378523
E-MAIL: info@arnaldocaprai.it

If the Caprai estate were in Chianti or Bordeaux, it would perhaps have been easier for it to have gained notoriety and the esteem of the wine press, not to mention bigger sales. As it is, the estate deserves credit for its success, and for having raised the profile of the erstwhile poorly known Montefalco zone at the same time. With the latest selection of wines presented for tasting, the estate picked up Three Glasses for the sixth consecutive year. What can we say, apart from, "Very well done"? Let's begin with the much-decorated Montefalco Sagrantino 25 Anni which, in its '99 edition, again lived up to our by now very high expectations. It is a superb wine. The colour is a dark purple red. The nose is powerful, spicy and complex, with clear scents of ripe red berry fruit and pervasive evolved notes. The palate is intense and long, with firm but elegant structure, as is evident from the fine grain of its tannins, which will need some time to settle down. Montefalco Sagrantino Colle Piano '99, a vigorous, mouthfilling red, also scored very well. The Montefalco Rosso Riserva has excellent balance, with nicely defined oak tones, while the straight '00 is fresh and fruitier. We'll conclude with the Colli Martani Grechetto Grecante '01, a floral white with aromas of jasmine and an excellently fleshy palate.

●	Montefalco Sagrantino 25 Anni '99	🍷🍷🍷	8
●	Montefalco Sagrantino Colle Piano '99	🍷🍷	6
●	Montefalco Rosso Ris. '99	🍷🍷	6
●	Montefalco Rosso '00	🍷	5
○	Colli Martani Grechetto Grecante '01	🍷	4
●	Montefalco Sagrantino 25 Anni '93	🍷🍷🍷	7
●	Montefalco Sagrantino 25 Anni '94	🍷🍷🍷	8
●	Montefalco Sagrantino 25 Anni '95	🍷🍷🍷	8
●	Montefalco Sagrantino 25 Anni '96	🍷🍷🍷	8
●	Montefalco Sagrantino 25 Anni '97	🍷🍷🍷	8
●	Montefalco Sagrantino 25 Anni '98	🍷🍷🍷	8
●	Montefalco Rosso Ris. '98	🍷🍷	6
●	Montefalco Sagrantino Colle Piano '98	🍷🍷	6

MONTEFALCO (PG)

ROCCA DI FABBRI
LOC. FABBRI
06036 MONTEFALCO (PG)
TEL. 0742399379
E-MAIL: faroaldo@libero.it

After last year's advance in the quality at Rocca dei Fabbri, we were naturally looking for a similar showing this time. Sadly, the wines did less well than expected. Make no mistake, quality remains high but things stopped a little way short of the string of four Two Glasses wines in last year's Guide. Again, the estate's top wine is the red Faroaldo. The '99, from equal parts of sagrantino and cabernet sauvignon, aged for a year and a half in barrique, and has a dark purple ruby colour. The nose is both elegant and powerful, releasing broad swathes of ripe red berry fruit, with clear-cut scents of sweet and sour cherries, sweet spices, and hints of oak and liquorice. The palate is concentrated and distinctly fruity, with the tannins nicely in balance. The two Montefalco wines, the '99 Sagrantino and the '00 Rosso, only managed One Glass apiece. The Sagrantino is fairly pervasive on the nose, but a little over-ripe and tannic on the palate, and the Rosso can show only average concentration and somewhat raw tannins. In comparison, the fairly simple Colli Martani Sangiovese Satiro '00 is livelier on both nose and palate, flaunting attractive primary fruit freshness.

MONTEFALCO (PG)

SCACCIADIAVOLI
LOC. CANTINONE, 31
06036 MONTEFALCO (PG)
TEL. 0742371210 - 0742378272
E-MAIL: scacciadiavoli@tin.it

After its explosive arrival last year, Scacciadiavoli now confirms its status as one of the most articulate ambassadors for Montefalco's wine styles. The estate, owned by the Pambuffetti siblings, was founded in the 1950s. There are currently 124 hectares, with 28 hectares under vine, giving an annual production of 70,000 bottles. The range presented was very good but three wines stand out in particular. The first of these is the Montefalco Sagrantino Passito '89, the most successful of all. Its colour is a dark purple red. The nose is evolved, with an warmly ripe fruitiness distinctly reminiscent of blackberry and cherry that is overlaid with wafts of clove and cinnamon. Warm and powerful on the palate, it has an even, if not outstandingly fine, tannic weave. The excellent Montefalco Rosso '00, also with Two Glasses, was next on the list, revealing exemplary winemaking technique. Clean and ripe, with notes of wild berry fruits on the nose, it is flavoursome and wonderfully drinkable in the mouth. The Montefalco Sagrantino '99 is well typed, but no more. We were expecting more excitement after last year's vintage. It has good ruby tonality but the nose has only fair intensity and complexity. It is generally fruity but the stamp of oak is somewhat coarse. The palate has good structure but finishes on rather super-ripe notes that lack vitality.

Wine	Rating
● Faroaldo '99	5
● Colli Martani Sangiovese Satiro '00	4
● Montefalco Rosso '00	5
● Montefalco Sagrantino '99	6
● Umbria Pinot Nero '90	5
● Faroaldo '97	5
● Montefalco Sagrantino Passito '97	5
● Faroaldo '98	6
● Colli Martani Sangiovese Satiro '99	3*
● Montefalco Rosso '99	3

Wine	Rating
● Montefalco Rosso '00	4
● Montefalco Sagrantino Passito '99	7
● Montefalco Sagrantino '99	6
● Montefalco Sagrantino '98	5
● Montefalco Rosso '98	4

ORVIETO (TR)

BARBERANI - VALLESANTA
LOC. CERRETO
VIA MICHELANGELI, 8
05018 ORVIETO (TR)
TEL. 0763341820
E-MAIL: barberani@barberani.it

The Barberani-Vallesanta estate is a cornerstone of Orvieto's wine history. It sits right on the hills overlooking Lake Corbara, along the river Tiber, and has around 50 hectares under vine. The cellar is equipped to modern standards and the thoroughly reliable Maurizio Castelli acts as consultant. Nevertheless, our tastings bring us to conclude that the character of the Barberani wines is less incisive and successful than in the past. The entire range is, of course, well styled and worthy of winelovers' attention but the wines lacks that certain something, especially the more famous selections. We'll start with the flagship wine and the best of the range, Lago di Corbara Foresco '00. Its good purple-ruby colour introduces an intense, pervasive nose, rich in red berry fruit with distinct aromas of plum and liqueur cherry. The palate is warm, its well-knit elements recalling clove and black pepper on the finish. Grechetto Villa Monticelli '00 and Orvieto Classico Superiore Castagnolo '01 are both well made but only picked up One Glass. The former is clean but simplistic in both initial attack and development whereas the Castagnolo, one of the estate's most traditional wines and also clean on its white peach and damson nose, is rather acidic on the palate. Finally comes Moscato Passito Villa Monticelli '01, a successful white with a deep golden hue and a broad nose redolent of mango and dried apricot. It shows good acid and sugar balance on the palate.

ORVIETO (TR)

BIGI
LOC. PONTE GIULIO, 3
05018 ORVIETO (TR)
TEL. 0763316291
E-MAIL: giv@giv.it

Bigi is probably the most illustrious name in Orvieto. Founded as long ago as 1880, it is currently owned by Gruppo Italiano Vini. Grapes come from 243 hectares of vineyard and annual production reaches around 3,000,000 bottles. Under the expert technical guidance of oenologist Francesco Bardi, Bigi has deservedly more attention in the Guide. Whites have always dominated production and again this year, two excellent white wines are at the top of the list. First comes the impeccable Orvieto Classico Secco Vigneto Torricella '01, from trebbiano, grechetto and malvasia, which easily won Two Glasses, even with a production run of a good 100,000 bottles a year. It is a brightly flecked straw yellow. There is elegance on the clean nose, which has inviting notes of ripe rennet apple supported by delicate nuances of damson and peach. The palate is soft and well fruited, with nicely judged acidity and good length. The Grechetto '01, which itself has a production run of about 30,000 bottles, is well made, if without great complexity or definition. Its defining characteristics are its primary fruitiness, with aromas of crisp golden delicious apple, and its clean palate cut through by a refreshing streak of attractive acidity.

● Lago di Corbara Foresco '00	¶¶	5
○ Grechetto Villa Monticelli '01	¶	5
○ Moscato Passito Villa Monticelli '01	¶	6
○ Orvieto Cl. Castagnolo '01	¶	4
○ Orvieto Cl. Sup. Calcaia '92	¶¶	5
● Foresco '93	¶¶	4
○ Orvieto Cl. Sup. Calcaia '93	¶¶	5
○ Orvieto Cl. Sup. Calcaia '94	¶¶	5
○ Orvieto Cl. Sup. Calcaia '95	¶¶	5
○ Moscato Passito Villa Monticelli '97	¶¶	6
● Lago di Corbara Foresco '98	¶¶	5
● Lago di Corbara Foresco '99	¶¶	5
○ Moscato Passito Villa Monticelli '99	¶¶	6

○ Orvieto Cl. Vigneto Torricella '01	¶¶	3
○ Umbria Grechetto '01	¶	2
○ Orvieto Cl. Vigneto Torricella '00	¶¶	3*
○ Marrano '93	¶¶	4
○ Marrano '94	¶¶	4
● Umbria Sangiovese '97	¶¶	2
○ Orvieto Cl. Vigneto Torricella '98	¶¶	3
○ Orvieto Cl. Vigneto Torricella '99	¶¶	3
● Umbria Sangiovese '00	¶	2*
● Sangiovese Tenuta Corbara '98	¶	3
● Umbria Sangiovese '98	¶	2
● Umbria Sangiovese '99	¶	2

ORVIETO (TR)

CARDETO
FRAZ. SFERRACAVALLO
LOC. CARDETO
05019 ORVIETO (TR)
TEL. 0763341286 - 0763343189
E-MAIL: cardeto@cardeto.com

The newly re-organized structure of this winery, finalized in 2001, puts the roughly 1,000 hectares of vineyard owned by its 350 or so members at its disposal. Most of this is dedicate to Orvieto's classic white varieties. Under the expert guidance of oenologist Maurilio Chioccia, and with additional occasional consultancy from Riccardo Cotarella, Cardeto's wines show dependable quality year in year out. The range submitted for tasting was wide but the wine that acquitted itself best was Rosso Arciato '01, which achieved a place in the national Three Glass tasting finals. From merlot, cabernet and a small amount of sangiovese, it is dark purple ruby in colour and has intense, powerful, rich aromas of wild berry fruits, overlaid with hints of pepper and cinnamon. The palate is broad, elegant and soft, offering firm, ripe tannins and a clean, even, long finish. The '00 red Nero della Greca, from sangiovese and merlot, is as captivating as ever, with its vegetal and herbaceous tones on the nose and clean, enticing palate evoking autumn leaves and ripe blackberry. The Pinot Nero '01 appeared delicately varietal and well typed, as did the Alborato '01, a blend of sangiovese, montepulciano and merlot, not to mention the Rupestro '01, the highly drinkable entry-level red. The whites showed well, too, starting with the two '01 Orvieto Classico Superiores. The Colbadia is surely one of this year's best Orvietos and the Febeo glories in its fresh, crisp fruitiness. Even the plain '01 Grechetto is delicious.

ORVIETO (TR)

DECUGNANO DEI BARBI
LOC. FOSSATELLO DI CORBARA, 50
05019 ORVIETO (TR)
TEL. 0763308255
E-MAIL: info@decugnanodeibarbi.com

Historically, Decugnano dei Barbi is one of Orvieto's most important estates. Founded in 1973 and owned by Claudio and Marina Barbi, it has never pandered to the market and its enviable dynamism has always been obvious. Claudio, flanked by the able oenologist Corrado Cugnasco, should not bemoan his "IL" Rosso missing Three Glasses this year. The wine is brilliant and missed that third cup by a hair. From a finely tuned blend of sangiovese, cabernet sauvignon, merlot, montepulciano d'Abruzzo and canaiolo, it is a deep purple-ruby. The nose is elegant and complex, with clean vegetal tones and inviting scents of blackberry and blueberry. The deep, mouthfilling palate develops confidently, its firm structure gaining refinement from ripe tannins. The finish betrays no rawness. But the wine that really grabbed us this year was the white "IL", an Orvieto Classico Superiore from grechetto, procanico, chardonnay and sauvignon, possibly the best release ever. Tropical fruit and sage mark out the warm fruity nose. The palate is clean, with good body and attractive toasty notes on the finish. The harmonious Metodo Classico Brut '99 is successful, as is Orvieto Classico Superiore, both in the fleshy, complex base version and the well-structured Pourriture Noble '00, which has tropical fruit aromas. The rest of the range is well typed, from the fruity, well-knit Lago di Corbara Rosso '00 to the two "Barbi" wines, the Orvieto and Pojo del Ruspo, both captivating and well priced. Finally, don't miss the estate's newest wine, an '01 Pinot Nero.

● Arciato '01	ΨΨ	5
● Nero della Greca '00	ΨΨ	5
○ Orvieto Cl. Sup. Colbadia '01	ΨΨ	4*
● Alborato '01	Ψ	4
○ Orvieto Cl. Sup. Febeo '01	Ψ	4
● Pinot Nero '01	Ψ	6
● Rupestro '01	Ψ	3
○ Umbria Grechetto '01	Ψ	3*
○ Orvieto Cl. Sup. L'Armida '00	ΨΨ	4
● Rupestro '00	ΨΨ	2*
● Arciato '98	ΨΨ	3
● Nero della Greca '98	ΨΨ	4
● Pinot Nero '98	ΨΨ	6
● Arciato '99	ΨΨ	3*
● Nero della Greca '99	ΨΨ	4

○ Orvieto Cl. Sup. "IL" '01	ΨΨ	5
● "IL" Rosso '99	ΨΨ	6
● Pinot Nero '01	ΨΨ	5
○ Decugnano dei Barbi Brut M. Cl. '99	ΨΨ	5
● Lago di Corbara '00	Ψ	4
○ Orvieto Cl. Sup. Pourriture Noble '00	Ψ	6
● Pojo del Ruspo Barbi '00	Ψ	3
○ Orvieto Cl. Barbi '01	Ψ	2
○ Orvieto Cl. Sup. Decugnano dei Barbi '01	Ψ	4
● "IL" Rosso '98	ΨΨΨ	5
○ Orvieto Cl. Sup. "IL" '00	ΨΨ	4
● "IL" Rosso '94	ΨΨ	5
● "IL" Rosso '95	ΨΨ	5
● "IL" Rosso '96	ΨΨ	5
● "IL" Rosso '97	ΨΨ	5

ORVIETO (TR)

FREDDANO
FRAZ. FOSSATELLO, 34
05018 ORVIETO (TR)
TEL. 0763308248
E-MAIL: giuliofreddano@tiscalinet.it

The wines of this small, family-run estate continue to improve. Situated on the hills overlooking Lake Corbara, near the town of Orvieto, it has nine hectares of vineyard, mostly planted to white varieties. In the cellar, winemaking is overseen by Maurilio Chioccia. The leading wine is Lago di Corbara Fontauro, a red from cabernets sauvignon and franc, which ages for 15 months in barriques and stainless steel. The '00 replicates the success of the previous vintage and strolled off with an easy Two Glasses. It is a darkly tinged purple ruby. The nose is clean and intense, with a ripe cherry aroma and vegetal hints. There is softness on the front palate, then the flavours broaden out in mid palate to give warm tones of fruit that is just past full ripeness. The red Campo de' Massi '01, from sangiovese with a little cabernet sauvignon, is also good, with its cherry and plum-like nose and a nicely balanced, full-bodied palate. Another One Glass wine is the Grechetto Vertunno '01, which is simple and fresh on the nose and reasonably long on the palate.

• Lago di Corbara Fontauro '00	♟♟	5
• Campo de' Massi '01	♟	2*
○ Grechetto Vertunno '01	♟	3
• Lago di Corbara Fontauro '99	♟♟	4
• Campo de' Massi '00	♟♟	1*

ORVIETO (TR)

LA CARRAIA
LOC. TORDIMONTE, 56
05018 ORVIETO (TR)
TEL. 0763304013
E-MAIL: info@lacarraia.it

Despite the absence of a Three Glass wine this year, Odoardo Gialletti and Riccardo Cotarella's estate continues to turn out products of a very high level. Indeed, two wines reached the tasting finals and only just missed their third Glass. The estate has 132 hectares under vine, in the heart of Orvieto Classico, and the not insignificant annual output of 550,000 bottles. The newest wine conceived, and crafted, by Cotarella is the excellent red Tizzonero, from cabernet sauvignon and merlot. The first release, the '00, swept straight into the final Three Glass taste-offs. The colour is purple-ruby red. The nose reflects its varietal make-up with herbaceous notes and bell pepper alongside cherry, black pepper and clove. The palate is soft and excellently structured with its tannic thrust well integrated into the ripe fruit. Also showing very well is the well-known Fobiano, from merlot and cabernet sauvignon. The '00, purple ruby in hue, has a complex, delicately herbaceous bouquet with pencil lead, cocoa powder and autumn leaves underlying black berry fruits and cassis. It is full and spicy on the palate, where there is balance from first impact, through to mid palate, and on to its savoury finish. Sangiovese '01, with fresh, enticing fruitiness on the nose and a rich, concentrated palate, is also very good. The two versions of '01 Orvieto Classico, the clean Poggio Calvelli with its primary fruitiness, and the standard label, which has a fresh, floral nose and a palate of medium intensity, are both well typed.

• Fobiano '00	♟♟	5
• Tizzonero '00	♟♟	3
• Umbria Sangiovese '01	♟♟	3
○ Orvieto Cl. '01	♟	1*
○ Orvieto Cl. Poggio Calvelli '01	♟	2
• Fobiano '98	♟♟♟	5
• Fobiano '99	♟♟♟	6
○ Orvieto Cl. Poggio Calvelli '00	♟♟	3*
• Fobiano '95	♟♟	4
• Fobiano '96	♟♟	4
• Fobiano '97	♟♟	4
• Umbria Sangiovese '97	♟♟	3
○ Orvieto Cl. Poggio Calvelli '98	♟♟	3
○ Orvieto Cl. Poggio Calvelli '99	♟♟	2

ORVIETO (TR)

TENUTA LE VELETTE
LOC. LE VELETTE, 23
05019 ORVIETO (TR)
TEL. 076329090
E-MAIL: tenuta.le.velette@libero.it

Right in the heart of the Orvieto Classico district, on the plateau in front of the crag of Orvieto itself, Corrado and Cecilia Bottai's estate produces a reliable range of high-quality wines. The Calanco '95 gained Three Glasses a few years ago, and two wines reached the tasting finals last year, so we were hoping for even greater things. We don't want to quibble, but we did feel that everything was in place for further quality progress. Still, the two selections, Calanco and Gaudio, each gained Two Glasses. The Gaudio '99, a 100 per cent Merlot aged for 12 months in barrique, has a good purple-ruby colour. The nose is simple but nicely tuned, with red wild berry fruit melding with a sweet oakiness. The palate is well textured, with good development and finish. It is well made overall, but lacks a real high point. Calanco '99, from sangiovese and cabernet sauvignon, is also very attractive, with its dark purple red hue and its nose rich in cherry, blackberry and black pepper. The palate is powerful, showing a vegetal tang, the oak is well integrated and the finish long. Rosso di Spicca '01 also showed very well, offering a very ripe fruit nose and a fleshy palate with balanced tannins. The whites are well styled. Traluce '01, a Sauvignon aged in barrique and stainless steel, is nicely varietal on the nose and attractively acidulous on the palate. The Orvieto Classico Superiore Lunato '01, has crisp apple-and-pear primary fruitiness on the nose, then good balance and length on the palate.

ORVIETO (TR)

PALAZZONE
LOC. ROCCA RIPESENA, 68
05010 ORVIETO (TR)
TEL. 0763344921
E-MAIL: palazzone@palazzone.com

Take the image of the high-flying manager-turned-producer, who decides to make wine as a hobby or an investment. Then turn it on its head. Giovanni Dubini is an authentic grape grower. He hasn't followed fashion or leapt on the winemaking bandwagon of the last five to ten years. Palazzone dates back to the 1970s and Dubini has run the estate personally for at least two decades. Consultancy from Riccardo Cotarella, on other estates a new or very new phenomenon, started here in the 1980s. And Umbria Rosso Armaleo again took Three Glasses, this time for the '00. It is made from cabernet sauvignon with a little franc, and ages for just over a year in barrique. The colour is a good deep ruby. The aromas have great depth, with red berry fruits, oriental spices and faint but perceptible vegetal nuances. The first impression on the palate is of a tightly-knit but soft wine that then gains vigour and intensity, with upfront fruit, firm but ripe tannins, and a wonderfully long, complex finish. The estate's second red, Rubbio '01, is predominantly from sangiovese and also very good. Its rich, inviting fruitiness earned it a worthy Two Glasses. Moving on to the whites, Orvieto Classico Superiore Terre Vineate '01 has fair concentration and good acidity while Ultima Spiaggia '01 has cedar and lavender notes, lightly threaded through with oak. Muffa Nobile '01 is good but a little thin, its aromas recalling dried fig and acacia honey.

● Rosso Orvietano Rosso di Spicca '01	♟♟	3*
● Calanco '99	♟♟	5
● Gaudio '99	♟♟	5
○ Orvieto Cl. Sup. Lunato '01	♟	3
○ Traluce '01	♟	3
● Calanco '95	♟♟♟	5
● Calanco '98	♟♟	5
● Gaudio '98	♟♟	4
● Rosso Orvietano Rosso di Spicca '00	♟♟	2*
● Calanco '96	♟♟	5
● Calanco '97	♟♟	5
● Gaudio '97	♟♟	4
● Rosso Orvietano Rosso di Spicca '99	♟	2

● Armaleo '00	♟♟♟	6
● Rubbio '01	♟♟	3
○ L'Ultima Spiaggia '01	♟	4
○ Muffa Nobile '01	♟	5
○ Orvieto Cl. Terre Vineate '01	♟	3
● Armaleo '95	♟♟♟	4
● Armaleo '97	♟♟♟	5
● Armaleo '98	♟♟♟	5
○ Orvieto Cl. Terre Vineate '00	♟♟	3*
● Rubbio '00	♟♟	3*
● Armaleo '92	♟♟	5
● Armaleo '94	♟♟	4
○ Muffa Nobile '97	♟♟	4
○ Muffa Nobile '98	♟♟	4
● Armaleo '99	♟♟	5

PANICALE (PG)

LAMBORGHINI - LA FIORITA
LOC. SODERI, 1
06064 PANICALE (PG)
TEL. 0758350029
E-MAIL: info@lamborghinionline.it

For the second year running, one of Patrizia Lamborghini's wines wins Three Glasses. The Campoleone '00, this Trasimeno estate's flagship wine, sailed comfortably into the top category. Patrizia, the daughter of the founder of the legendary automobile company, has been putting her all into running this estate, which she inherited from her father, for several years now. Riccardo Cotarella acts as consultant and around 40,000 bottles of Campoleone were produced in 2000, a not insignificant quantity for a wine that is virtually hand-crafted. From equal parts of merlot and sangiovese, it ages for around a year in barriques. It's a weighty red, as strongly concentrated as in previous years, full of stuffing from its high extract, and with remarkably tight, dense tannins. Yet, it also stands out for softness and the way its various elements meld together. The aromas are incredibly intense. It enters the mouth with vigour, closes in on the mid palate, then gives an exceptionally long, complex finish. Umbria Rosso Trescone '00 is well typed but, naturally, on a different plane. From a well-integrated blend of sangiovese, ciliegiolo and merlot, and aged in large barrels, it is a good youthful wine with touches of well-calibrated oak.

PENNA IN TEVERINA (TR)

RIO GRANDE
LOC. MONTECCHIE
05028 PENNA IN TEVERINA (TR)
TEL. 0744993102 - 0666416440
E-MAIL: pastore.dme@interbussiness.it

Francesco Pastore is a man of great resource. When, in 1988, he decided to produce his own wine, he set to and completely worked over land that had been lying abandoned for over 20 years. The result was the Rio Grande estate, now with 12 hectares of vineyard, which lies just a short hop from the Umbria-Lazio border. Four wines were submitted for tasting this year. The newest, I Ricordi di Casa Pastore '98, confirms its promise when first tasted a year earlier. It is from cabernet sauvignon, with a little merlot, and ages for two years in barrique. The nose is full, deep and notably complex. The palate is rich, round and held in tightly by its tannins but reveals good character on the finish. The '00 Casa Pastore, from cabernet sauvignon and merlot, is the estate's best known red and also scored very well. It is a warm purple-ruby colour, the nose is powerful and concentrated, full of pervasive but well-judged ripe red berry fruit. The palate is nicely dense with ripe, soft tannins. The fruity Poggio Muralto '01, from merlot, sangiovese and cabernet sauvignon, is redolent of cherry, plum and wild berries and also gained Two Glasses. Colle delle Montecchie '01, from chardonnay with a small amount of sauvignon, is a simpler but nonetheless attractive wine.

● Campoleone '00	▼▼▼	6
● Trescone '00	▼	3
● Campoleone '99	▼▼▼	6
● Campoleone '97	▼▼	5
● Campoleone '98	▼▼	5
● Trescone '99	▼▼	3*
● Trescone '97	▼	3
● Trescone '98	▼	3

● Casa Pastore Rosso '00	▼▼	5
● Poggio Muralto '01	▼▼	4
○ Chardonnay Colle delle Montecchie '01	▼	4
● Casa Pastore Rosso '99	▼▼	5
● Poggio Muralto '00	▼▼	3*
● Casa Pastore Rosso '95	▼▼	4
○ Chardonnay Colle delle Montecchie '95	▼▼	3
● Casa Pastore Rosso '97	▼▼	4
● Casa Pastore Rosso '98	▼▼	4
● I Ricordi '98	▼▼	4
● Poggio Muralto '98	▼▼	3
○ Chardonnay Colle delle Montecchie '99	▼▼	3

PERUGIA

Carlo e Marco Carini
Fraz. Canneto - Colle Umberto
Via del Tegolaro
06070 Perugia
tel. 0755829103
e-mail: agrariacarini@libero.it

Carlo and Marco Carini make their debut in the Guide, in grand style. Their estate lies in the zone of Colle Umberto, north of Perugia, and has 150 hectares, nine of which are planted with vines. The able Maurilio Chioccia supervises the winemaking. We are at their first bottling and if a bright dawn ushers in a sunny day, we can look forward to some pleasant surprises. One of the two wines submitted for tasting, Umbria Rosso Tegolaro '01, went straight into the final Three Glass taste-offs. It is from merlot, with small amounts of sangiovese and cabernet sauvignon, and ages for eight months in barrique. Total production is around 5,000 bottles. A dark purple ruby. It reveals a nose that combines a delicate vegetal tone with clean aromas of ripe fruit, predominantly blackberry and cherry. The clean palate has a firmly solid extractive base and opens out to give length and balance. Umbria Bianco Poggio Canneto '01, from chardonnay and grechetto, ten per cent of which is barrique-fermented, also showed well. The colour is deep straw. The nose has aromas of citrus peel and pink grapefruit, with delicate floral scents of jasmine. There is good body and plentiful fruit, well integrated with its acidity, on the palate, and it has a very elegant, toasty finish. We will doubtless be hearing much more of these wines in the future.

PERUGIA

Castello di Antignano - Brogal Vini
Loc. Bastia Umbra
Via degli Olmi, 9
06083 Perugia
tel. 0758001501 - 0758012453
e-mail: amministrazione@vignabaldo.com

We were willing to bet on the potential of the Antignano estate and, to judge by this year's tasting results, we weren't mistaken. There has been some excellent work going on here over the past few years. Situated in the area of Bastia Umbra, the estate was founded in 1951 and has a good 120 hectares of vineyard, all in the top zones of Montefalco and Torgiano. For the umpteenth time, the name of Riccardo Cotarella appears on these pages as consultant, which explains why the wines are so good. From the Torgiano range, we turn first to the Cabernet Sauvignon '98, which easily gained Two Glasses. The colour is purple ruby. The aromas are characterized by delicately vegetal tones, enriched with scents of ripe cherry and black pepper. The first impact on the palate gives a strong note of fresh-mown grass, followed by great wafts of autumn leaves, and the tannins are well assimilated into the structure. The '99 base Torgiano Rosso, with its primary fruit nose, and clean palate with good tannic balance, and the more complex Riserva, spicy, with discreet oak, are both good. One Glass also goes to the youthful, floral Torgiano Bianco '01. On the Montefalco side, the Montefalco Sagrantino '99 is particularly distinguished, worthily gaining Two Glasses for its garnet colour, its developed aromas of super-ripe red berry fruits and its full, long flavour. The simpler Montefalco Rosso '00 and the golden delicious apple-like Grechetto '01 are both also worth investigating.

● Tegolaro '01	ΨΨ	6
○ Poggio Canneto '01	Ψ	5

● Torgiano Cabernet Sauvignon '98	ΨΨ	4
● Montefalco Sagrantino '99	ΨΨ	5
● Montefalco Rosso '00	Ψ	3
○ Grechetto '01	Ψ	1*
○ Torgiano Bianco '01	Ψ	3
● Torgiano Rosso '99	Ψ	3
● Torgiano Rosso Ris. '99	Ψ	5
● Torgiano Rosso Ris. Santa Caterina '97	ΨΨ	4
● Torgiano Cabernet Sauvignon '97	Ψ	4
● Montefalco Sagrantino '98	Ψ	5
● Torgiano Rosso '98	Ψ	2*
● Montefalco Rosso '99	Ψ	3

PERUGIA

AGRICOLA GORETTI
LOC. PILA
S.DA DEL PINO, 4
06070 PERUGIA
TEL. 075607316
E-MAIL: goretti@vinigoretti.com

There is change afoot at the Goretti place. The fortified farmhouse at the centre of the estate is undergoing major work to enable it to house the barriques, and the sales and tasting areas. But the most interesting move is the decision to hold back for a year the estate's top wine, the ever-reliable L'Arringatore. This means the '99 will be reviewed for the 2004 Guide. Even without their most prestigious selection, Stefano and Gianluca Goretti have put up a distinguished showing. Their numerous wines are, as usual, all well made, and reveal a certain elegance. The best of the range is, we think, the red Fontanella '01, from sangiovese, merlot and montepulciano. Its good purple ruby colour introduces ample depth on the nose, which has plentiful, attractively ripe fruit. The palate is dense, gently sweet and long on the finish, where the tannins are admirably firm. Also good is the rosé, Rosato Fontanella '01, with its orange-pink hue, its fine nose with notes of wild rose and fresh strawberry, and its attractively acidulous palate. Moving on to the estate's whites, we found the Fontanella '01 has attractive hints of lemon verbena while the three '01 wines from Colli Perugini, the Torre del Pino, the Chardonnay and the Grechetto, all show a ripe fruitiness.

SPELLO (PG)

F.LLI SPORTOLETTI
LOC. CAPITAN LORETO
VIA LOMBARDIA, 1
06038 SPELLO (PG)
TEL. 0742651461
E-MAIL: office@sportoletti.com

Whether Three Glasses come their way or not, Ernesto and Remo Sportoletti's estate remains one of the best in Umbria. It is a family-run concern, situated near Spello, which has always practised farming but only started producing bottled wine in 1979. There are currently 20 hectares of vineyard and many of the classic international varieties are cultivated, as well as the indigenous grechetto. We should recall "en passant" that the Sportolettis' grape growing and winemaking consultant is a certain Riccardo Cotarella. As usual, the reds led the way at our tastings, with Villa Fidelia '00 reaching the national taste-offs and deservedly gaining Two very full Glasses. From merlot, with small admixtures of cabernets sauvignon and franc, it is a bright purple ruby. There is a good interplay on the nose between its fruit and vegetal characteristics, which are overlaid with hints of sweet spices. The palate has remarkable structure and is richly fruited, with blackberry and blueberry flavours emerging strongly. The '01 Assisi Rosso, from sangiovese and merlot, was a delightful surprise, especially considering how little it costs. It is a tad herbaceous but also full, clean and slim-bodied, with very well-balanced tannins. In contrast, the '00 vintage of the white Villa Fidelia, from equal parts of grechetto and chardonnay, was a little under par. Its delicate spring flowers aromas are somewhat overwhelmed by oak toast.

● Fontanella Rosso '01	▼▼	1*
○ Colli Perugini Bianco Torre del Pino '01	▼	3
○ Colli Perugini Chardonnay '01	▼	3
○ Colli Perugini Grechetto '01	▼	2
○ Fontanella Bianco '01	▼	2*
⊙ Fontanella Rosato '01	▼	2*
● Fontanella Rosso '00	▼▼	2*
● Colli Perugini Rosso L'Arringatore '95	▼▼	3
● Colli Perugini Rosso L'Arringatore '98	▼▼	4
● Colli Perugini Rosso L'Arringatore '96	▼	3
● Colli Perugini Rosso L'Arringatore '97	▼	4

● Villa Fidelia Rosso '00	▼▼	7
● Assisi Rosso '01	▼▼	4
○ Villa Fidelia Bianco '00	▼	5
● Villa Fidelia Rosso '98	▼▼▼	6
○ Villa Fidelia Bianco '99	▼▼	5
● Villa Fidelia Rosso '99	▼▼	6
● Assisi Rosso '00	▼▼	4*
● Villa Fidelia Rosso '91	▼▼	4
○ Villa Fidelia Bianco '95	▼▼	4
● Villa Fidelia Rosso '97	▼▼	4
○ Villa Fidelia Bianco '98	▼▼	4
● Assisi Rosso '99	▼▼	4

STRONCONE (TR)

LA PALAZZOLA
Loc. Vascigliano
05039 Stroncone (TR)
tel. 0744607735 - 0744272357

Stefano Grilli's La Palazzola, situated just a hop from Terni at Stroncone, is one of the most successful estates in Umbria. It again justified its profile in the Guide with a fine range of carefully crafted wines. This year could be considered one of transition for the ever-active Stefano Grilli, as his estate is undergoing radical renovations. The creation of a new cellar, which should be functioning in time for the 2002 vintage, next to the old one is certain to stimulate a further improvement in the quality of the wines. The most impressive of the range presented this year was the '00 Umbria Rosso Rubino, for several years now the estate's flagship. It easily claimed Two Glasses. The main strength is its rich fruit, on both nose and palate, which is confident and soft. Additionally, the tannins are not without finesse and the finish, although it is not outstandingly long, has succulence. The '00 Merlot, which is good but not as good as usual, is purple ruby in colour. The nose is rather vegetal and the palate is soft but could be longer. One Glass also goes to the sole sparkler, Moscato Demi Sec '98 (the Riesling Brut is skipping a year). There is an elegant beading of bubbles, ripe fruit on the nose and, on the palate, good balance between the acidity and residual sugar. Finally, the '98 Vinsanto is good but rather simple.

● Rubino '00	🍷🍷	5
● Merlot '00	🍷	5
○ Moscato Demi Sec mill. '98	🍷	4
○ Vin Santo '98	🍷	5
● Merlot '97	🍷🍷🍷	5
● Merlot '99	🍷🍷	5
● Rubino '93	🍷🍷	3
● Rubino '94	🍷🍷	4
● Merlot '95	🍷🍷	4
● Rubino '95	🍷🍷	4
● Rubino '96	🍷🍷	5
● Rubino '97	🍷🍷	5
● Merlot '98	🍷🍷	5
● Rubino '98	🍷🍷	5
● Rubino '99	🍷🍷	5

TORGIANO (PG)

LUNGAROTTI
Via Mario Angeloni, 16
06089 Torgiano (PG)
tel. 075988661
e-mail: lungarotti@lungarotti.it

As all long-standing winelovers will know, no Umbrian producer has a prouder history than Lungarotti. After several excellent vintages, we have been waiting for Lungarotti to realize its full potential again. At last, the moves taken last year are beginning to bear fruit. There has been investment in cellar equipment, a new winemaking team has been formed, with the prestigious Landi and Dubourdieu duo supervising the able Vincenzo Pepe, and careful "adjustments" to the traditional house style have been made. Chiara and Teresa, daughters of the estate's patriarch, Giorgio, remain in charge and the range is broad. First, let's take the two Chardonnays, both of which went into the tasting finals. The new Aurente '00 is floral and ripely fruity. A sweet oakiness tends to dominate, but this should attenuate with a few months in bottle. The Chardonnay I Palazzi '00 – regrettably the last vintage to be produced – is deep and clean, with tropical fruit tones and a rare balance. The Giubilante '00, with its attractive aromas of ripe red berry fruit, and the Torgiano Cabernet Sauvignon '99, which has a varietal nose and a well-structured palate, are also both excellent. The '95 vintage of the renowned San Giorgio has fair body and delicate, partially evolved aromas, as well as good balance on the palate. One Glass goes to each of the cellar stalwarts, the fruity Torgiano Rosso Rubesco '99 and Rubesco Vigna Monticchio '95, which has possibly had too long in bottle. Finally, the '01 vintage of the always well-typed Torgiano Bianco is a leader in its class.

○ Chardonnay Aurente '00	🍷🍷	5
○ Chardonnay I Palazzi '00	🍷🍷	4
● Giubilante '00	🍷🍷	5
● San Giorgio '95	🍷🍷	6
● Cabernet Sauvignon '99	🍷🍷	4
○ Torgiano Bianco Torre di Giano '01	🍷	3
● Torgiano Rosso Vigna Monticchio Ris. '95	🍷	6
● Torgiano Rosso Rubesco '99	🍷	3
● San Giorgio '92	🍷🍷	5
● San Giorgio '93	🍷🍷	6
● Cabernet Sauvignon '95	🍷🍷	4
● Il Vessillo '97	🍷🍷	5
● Cabernet Sauvignon '98	🍷🍷	4
○ Chardonnay Aurente '99	🍷🍷	5

OTHER WINERIES

Tenuta di Salviano
Loc. Civitella del Lago
Voc. Salviano, 44
05020 Baschi (TR)
Tel. 0744950459

Owned by the noble Corsini family, Salviano has 50 hectares under vine. The two '01 whites, the tropical fruit-like Salviano di Salviano, and the fruity, floral Orvieto Classico Superiore, are most worthy of mention. The red Turlò is also of interest.

● Lago di Corbara Turlò '00	❦	4
○ Orvieto Cl. Sup. '01	❦	4
○ Salviano di Salviano '01	❦	4
● Lago di Corbara Turlò '99	❦	4

Fattoria Milziade Antano
Loc. Colle Allodole
06031 Bevagna (PG)
Tel. 0742360371

This time, there's a year out of the limelight in the Other Wineries section for the Milziade Antano estate. Sagrantino di Montefalco '99 is fruity on the nose, then powerful and tannic on the palate. Colle Allodole '99, with developed fruit tones and elegant tannins, is also nice.

● Montefalco Sagrantino '99	❦	5
● Montefalco Sagrantino Colle delle Allodole '99	❦	6
● Montefalco Sagrantino Colle delle Allodole '98	❦❦	6

Di Filippo
Via Conversino, 160
0603 Cannara (PG)
Tel. 0742731242
E-mail: tenuta.s.lorenzo@genie.it

Italo and Roberto De Filippo's wines are always of interest, even if this year they are in the Other Wineries section. Sangiovese Riserva Properzio '99 is powerful and rich in tannin, while tropical fruits, damson and pink grapefruit mark out Villa Conversino Bianco '01.

● Colli Martani Sangiovese Properzio Ris. '99	❦	3
○ Umbria Bianco '01	❦	1*
● Poggio Madrigale '97	❦❦	4

Podere Marella
Loc. Ferretto
06061 Castiglione del Lago (PG)
Tel. 075954139

Fiammetta Inga's estate has kept its place in the Guide. The estate's two clean, balanced reds, Colli del Trasimeno '99 and Caluna '00, both showed well. Umbria Bianco '01 is well styled, with floral aromas of chamomile and Chinese magnolia.

● Caluna '00	❦	3
○ Umbria Bianco '01	❦	2*
● C. del Trasimeno Rosso '99	❦	2*
● Caluna '99	❦	3

Villa Po' del Vento
Via Po' del Vento, 6
06062 Città della Pieve (PG)
Tel. 0578299950
E-mail: podelvento@tiscalinet.it

There was a good performance by the wines of this estate, based at Città della Pieve, where the 12 hectares under vine are run by Francesco Anichini. Both '01 whites, the Vermentino and Colli del Trasimeno, are well made. The Colli del Trasimeno Rosso, first tasted last year, is still nice.

○ C. del Trasimeno Bianco '01	▼	2*
○ Vermentino '01	▼	2*
● C. del Trasimeno Rosso '99	♀	2*

San Lorenzo
Via San Lorenzo Vecchio, 30
06034 Foligno (PG)
Tel. 074222553
E-mail: tenuta.s.lorenzo@genie.it

Flaminia De Luca's estate retains its place in the Guide. Her three reds are all good and all gain One Glass. The trio is made up of a powerful Sagrantino di Montefalco '99, the warm Ciliegiolo Cleos '01 and the slightly vegetal Umbria Rosso De Luca '00.

● Cleos '01	▼	4
● De Luca Rosso '00	▼	3
● Montefalco Sagrantino '99	▼	5
● De Luca Rosso '99	♀	3

Castello di Magione
Via dei Cavalieri di Malta, 31
06063 Magione (PG)
Tel. 075843547
E-mail: castellodimagione@tin.it

The wines of this estate in the Trasimeno area showed well. The broad, soft Colli del Trasimeno Morcinaia '00, with its well-calibrated tannins, gained Two Glasses. Carpaneto '01 is also good, with fruited and autumn leaf tones on the nose and a warm, rich palate.

● Colli del Trasimeno Rosso Morcinaia '00	▼▼	5
● Colli del Trasimeno Rosso Carpaneto '01	▼	4

Domenico Pennacchi
Voc. Sant'Angelo, 10
06035 Gualdo Cattaneo (PG)
Tel. 0742920069
E-mail: pennacchidomenico@tiscalinet.it

We were impressed by the first showing of Domenico Pennacchi's estate, especially the two reds. Two Glasses go to Colli di Fontivecchie '01, rich in wild berry fruits on the nose. The Sagrantino di Montefalco Passito '97 is vegetal, with strong cherry flavours on the palate.

● Colli di Fontivecchie Rosso '01	▼▼	4
● Montefalco Sagrantino Passito '97	▼	5

Umbria Viticoltori Associati
Loc. Cerro
Zona Industriale
06055 Marsciano (PG)
Tel. 0758748989

From the Umbria Viticoltori Associati range, the two Raffaellesco wines were the most attractive. The Chardonnay is full of tropical fruit, and the Sagrantino di Montefalco has good body. The Colli Perugini Rosso is also good.

○ Chardonnay Raffaellesco '00	▼	3
● Colli Perugini Rosso '00	▼	2*
● Montefalco Sagrantino Raffaellesco '97	▼	5

Sassara
Loc. Pian del Vantaggio, 43
05019 Orvieto (TR)
Tel. 0763215119

The wines from Luciano Sassara's estate, which has used Riccardo Cotarella as consultant since 1979, always acquit themselves well. Merlot Vantaggio '01, a fruity red, with balanced tannins, gains Two Glasses. Orvieto Classico Sant'Egidio '01 is good.

● Vantaggio '01	▼▼	3*
○ Orvieto Cl. Sant'Egidio '01	▼	2*
● Vantaggio '99	♀	3

Tordimaro
Loc. Tordimonte, 37
05018 Orvieto (TR)
tel. 0763304227
e-mail: tordimaro@tiscalinet.it

This intriguing Orvieto estate has got its Guide place back. The IGTs Torello '00 and Sauvignon '01 both did well. The two reds, Tordimaro '99, rich in red berry fruitiness, and the simple but balanced Selvaia, are both worthy of mention.

- Rosso Orvietano Selvaia '00 — 4
- Umbria Torrello '00 — 4
- Umbria Sauvignon '01 — 3
- Rosso Orvietano Il Tordimaro '99 — 5

Franca Chiorri
Loc. Sant' Enea - Via Todi, 100
06120 Perugia
tel. 075607141
e-mail: info@chiorri.it

The Chiorri estate has been relegated for a year to the "purgatory" of the Other Wineries. From the wines submitted by Tito Mariotti and his daughters, Marta and Monica, we picked out the Colli Perugini Rosso '01, which has plenty of ripe fruit on the nose and a full, well-knit palate.

- Colli Perugini Rosso '01 — 3*
- Colli Perugini Rosso '00 — 2*

Cantine Perusia
Loc. Ponte Pattoli
Strada Pattoli - Resina, 1/a
06100 Perugia
tel. 075694175

This estate, lying just outside Perugia and with Maurilio Chioccia as consulting winemaker, makes its first appearance in the Guide. Rosso Valmora Terre di Braccio '01 has a richly spicy nose and gains Two Glasses. Bianco Vencaia Terre di Braccio has good fruit and fair length.

- Valmora Rosso Terre di Braccio '01 — 4
- Vencaia Bianco Terre di Braccio '01 — 3

Spoletoducale
Loc. Petrognano, 54
06049 Spoleto (PG)
tel. 074356224
e-mail: collispoletini@mail.caribusiness.it

Situated in the Spoleto zone, this winery has turned out a Two Glass wine, Montefalco Rosso '00. It's well fruited on the nose, then tannic and powerful on the palate. The Sagrantino di Montefalco and Sangiovese Arcato are also both of interest.

- Montefalco Rosso '00 — 3*
- Arcato Sangiovese '00 — 3
- Montefalco Sagrantino '99 — 5
- Montefalco Sagrantino '97 — 5

Todini
Fraz. Collevalenza
06059 Todi (PG)
tel. 075887122 - 075887222
e-mail: agrtod@libero.it

Franco Todini's estate has 22 hectares under vine and uses the able Maurilio Chioccia as consultant. The excellently made Nero della Cervara and Sangiovese Rubro are both good reds. The Grechetto dei Colli Martani '01 is well styled.

- Nero della Cervara '01 — 6
- Colli Martani Sangiovese Rubro '00 — 5
- Colli Martani Grechetto di Todi '01 — 4
- Colli Martani Sangiovese Rubro '99 — 3

I Girasoli di Sant'Andrea
Loc. Molino Vitelli
06019 Umbertide (PG)
tel. 0759410837 - 0759410798
e-mail: igirasolidisandrea@tiscalinet.it

This is the second year in the Guide for this estate, owned by the Gritti family from Venice. Il Doge '00 is well fruited on the nose but vegetal and a little bitter on the palate. Ca' Andrea, delicately fruity and with medium body, is also nice.

- Il Doge '00 — 6
- Ca' Andrea '01 — 4

LAZIO

Something is afoot in Lazio at last. Never before has there been such an abundance of high quality wines. And many small wineries seem to have changed for the better. Naturally, we hope that our current enthusiasm is not cooled by the sort of results – we could euphemistically call them "uneven" – that often characterize winemaking in Lazio. Even now, the ten or so top names stand out from a worrying mass of estates whose wines bring discredit to regional traditions. But let's move on to the two juicy bits of news. Paola Di Mauro returns to the limelight big time with a fantastic Three Glass Vigna del Vassallo '00, probably the best ever. Then over at Montefiascone, Falesco has done it again with Three Glasses for the magnificent Montiano '00. It hardly needs saying that the architect of both these successes is a certain Riccardo Cotarella, the consultant who also takes the credit for bringing the wines of Christine Vaselli back on song. Next, special praise goes to Piero Costantini who has dared to venture into great red country with the new, beautifully made Ferro e Seta '00. Other estates are not just sitting back and watching. We tasted a surprisingly good Quattro Mori, the '00, from Castel De Paolis this year and the estate also produces an excellent white, Vigna Adriana. The '99 Mater Matuta from Casale del Giglio is in splendid form, nor could we overlook the significant improvements in its '00 Petit Verdot, a wine that we are sure will hit the high spots sooner or later. Colle di Maggio, quietly but purposefully, comes in not far behind with an exemplary red, Villa Tulino '97. Mazziotti, from Bolsena, also contributes to the cause of fine reds with a more than sound Volgente '00. From lower Lazio, Paolo Perinelli's Cesanese del Piglio Torre del Piano '01, a wine that is unashamedly in the Bordeaux style, stands up well for itself while Colle della Torre '00 from Giovanni Palombo in Atina, and the reinvigorated Torre Ercolana '97 from Cantina Colacicchi in Anagni, demonstrate what can be achieved when you pull out all the stops. On the white front, the first thing to highlight is the ongoing improvement at Conte Zandotti. These are wines that really do get better with each passing year. Fontana Candida is also performing well and has even managed to improve its basic range. Falesia and Calanchi di Vaiano, made by Paolo D'Amico, are again excellent and nearby, Sergio Mottura has come out with an innovative version of his Orvieto, Tragugnano '01. There are numerous other good wines we could mention but we shall leave you the pleasure of discovering them as you turn these pages.

ACUTO (FR)

Casale della Ioria
P.zza Regina Margherita, 1
03010 Acuto (FR)
tel. 077556031
e-mail: perinelli@tiscalinet.it

Paolo Perinelli now rightfully claims a place in the Guide with the highly proficient range of wines he produces in Ciociaria. If we had to describe his attitude to wine, we would call him a modernist. And that's not a criticism. At numerous tastings spanning several years, Paolo Perinelli's wines have always shown great evenness, elegance and approachability. Such characteristics are easier to obtain when, like Perinelli, you have a good cellar set-up and a young, able winemaker like Roberto Mazzer as consultant. This combination of clear thinking and good winemaking produces wines of the calibre of Cesanese del Piglio Torre del Piano '01, Perinelli's Riserva. It has notable complexity on the nose with fresh plum, roasted coffee beans and liquorice. The palate has good extract, nice balance throughout and an even finish. The Riserva's less exclusively priced partner is the worthy Cesanese del Piglio Casale della Ioria '01. The aromas are fresh, fruity and distinctly redolent of morello cherry and blackberry jam. The tannins play a significant, but not intrusive, role on the palate. We were not, though, overly impressed by Rosso del Frusinate '01. We feel it still needs a few nips and tucks. On the other hand, Perinelli's '01 Passerina del Frusinate is at last free of heaviness on the nose, which makes it much more enjoyable than previous vintages.

● Cesanese del Piglio Torre del Piano '01	ΨΨ	5
● Cesanese del Piglio Casale della Ioria '01	ΨΨ	4
○ Passerina del Frusinate '01	Ψ	3
● Rosso del Frusinate '01		3
● Cesanese del Piglio Torre del Piano '00	ΨΨ	5
● Cesanese del Piglio '00	Ψ	3*

ANAGNI (FR)

Colacicchi
Loc. Romagnano
03012 Anagni (FR)
tel. 064469661

We'll paraphrase the early 20th-century comic actor and playwright Ettore Petrolini and sum up the current range of Colacicchi wines as "finer and prouder than before". This major, long-established estate has been absent too long from the Guide so we are delighted to see it, and the Trimani family, back. Colacicchi regains its place in the sun with a range led by the red Torre Ercolana '97. This wine has it all, from a broad spectrum of aromas to the rich, balanced, long palate. It is clearly different from earlier vintages but no less interesting. Anything but. You could say that it is moving with the times. The nose has spice, coffee, small red berry fruits. The palate is marked out by structure and refined tannins. Its long-time opposite number, Romagnano Rosso, is also exciting. The '99 appears to be fed up of playing second fiddle and has developed a complexity that we have never seen before. Here, too, there are aromas of spices and berry fruits that knit into a harmonious length. The trio of reds concludes with Schiaffo '01. This is less imposing in style than the other two but still has good tannic weave and richness of extract. Romagnano Bianco '01 sadly doesn't stand up to the reds. It seems to be suffering a sort of identity crisis and could certainly be bettered.

● Torre Ercolana '97	ΨΨ	6
● Romagnano Rosso '99	ΨΨ	5
● Schiaffo '01	Ψ	4
○ Romagnano Bianco '01		4
● Torre Ercolana '87	ΨΨ	5
● Torre Ercolana '88	ΨΨ	6
● Torre Ercolana '90	ΨΨ	5
● Torre Ercolana '91	ΨΨ	5
● Torre Ercolana '93	ΨΨ	5
○ Romagnano Bianco '00	Ψ	4
● Schiaffo '00	Ψ	4
● Romagnano Rosso '98	Ψ	5

APRILIA (LT)

CASALE DEL GIGLIO
LOC. LE FERRIERE
S.DA CISTERNA-NETTUNO KM 13
04011 APRILIA (LT)
TEL. 0692902530
E-MAIL: casaledelgiglio@tin.it

Casale del Giglio's break-through has long been on the cards. It's been looming since 1984, the year in which the Santarellis started experimenting with new varieties to blend with those he already had. Now, 19 years late, the estate has a range of wines that is simply terrific. The one that topped our tastings was once more Mater Matuta, this time the '99, from mainly syrah with some petit verdot. There is cleanliness, breadth and power on the nose, then good definition and length on the palate. There have been distinct improvements to the Petit Verdot, too. The '00 now offers greater complexity and balance. The '98 Madreselva, from merlot and cabernet sauvignon, is as ever a well-made, characterful red. Shiraz '00 stands out in the lower-price bracket with its notable concentration of extract and excellent overall balance. The '99 Cabernet Sauvignon and the '00 Merlot, both 100 per cent varietals, also showed very well. Antinoo '99, from chardonnay with a touch of viognier, is unquestionably the leading white but the "lesser" Satrico is holding its head up well. The '01 has notable aromatic warmth and intensity. Also worthy of note are the Chardonnay '01, with its lively fruitiness, and, to a lesser extent, the Sauvignon from the same vintage, which has a more modest array of aromas. The '01 rosé Albiola is currently more aggressive than previous vintages. We prefer not to give a definitive judgement until we have seen how it develops. The same thing applies to the new wine, Aphrodisium, from an unusual mix of botrytized grapes.

ATINA (FR)

GIOVANNI PALOMBO
C.SO MUNANZIO PLANCO
03042 ATINA (FR)
TEL. 0776610200
E-MAIL: vinipalombo@ciaoweb.it

We may have been a little over-critical of Giovanni Palombo's wines in the past few years. But then our initial tastings, when the wines were first released onto the market, led us to look forward to a sort of miracle. Now, the "slackening off" we chronicled has passed and happily, things are on the up again, especially with the reds. It shows that fair, constructive criticism can have its place. Indeed, even the simplest red, Rosso delle Chiaie '01, flaunts much more flavour throughout. The nose is generous, with hints of balsam and mint. The same notes appear on the palate, along with spices and red berry fruits. Atina Cabernet '01 is another very sound wine. The nose is quite vegetal, and only moderately forceful, but the palate finds a good balance of acidity and the softer components. However, the leader of the pack, since the Duca Cantelmi is still ageing, has to be the merlot-based Colle della Torre '00. Satisfying aromas of red berry fruits and blackcurrant jam interweave with vegetal and spicy scents. There is excellent flavour development throughout the palate, which refuses to be thrown off by tannins that have still to calm down. It was a worthy Three Glass taste-off finalist. Best of the whites for us was the clean, faultless Bianco delle Chiaie '01, made mainly from malvasia del Lazio. On the other hand Somigliò '01, a 100 per cent sauvignon, is a little unbalanced. We shall return to it.

● Mater Matuta '99	¶¶	6
● Petit Verdot '00	¶¶	4
● Shiraz '00	¶¶	4*
○ Satrico '01	¶¶	2*
● Madreselva '98	¶¶	4
○ Antinoo '99	¶¶	4
● Cabernet Sauvignon '99	¶¶	5*
● Merlot '00	¶	4
○ Chardonnay '01	¶	3
○ Sauvignon '01	¶	3
○ Antinoo '98	¶¶	3*
● Mater Matuta '98	¶¶	4
○ Sauvignon '00	¶¶	3*
● Cabernet Sauvignon '98	¶¶	4
● Shiraz '99	¶¶	3*

● Colle della Torre '00	¶¶	6
● Atina Cabernet '01	¶¶	5
○ Bianco delle Chiaie '01	¶	3*
● Rosso delle Chiaie '01	¶	4
○ Somigliò '01		5
● Cabernet Duca Cantelmi '97	¶¶	5
● Colle della Torre '97	¶¶	4
● Cabernet Duca Cantelmi '98	¶¶	5
● Colle della Torre '98	¶¶	4
● Cabernet Duca Cantelmi '99	¶¶	6
● Rosso delle Chiaie '00	¶	3
○ Somigliò '00	¶	4
● Rosso delle Chiaie '97	¶	3
● Rosso delle Chiaie '98	¶	3
● Colle della Torre '99	¶	5

BOLSENA (VT)

Mazziotti
Loc. Melona-Bonvino
Via Cassia Km 110
01023 Bolsena (VT)
tel. 0644291377
e-mail: mazziott@tin.it

Make way for the youngsters! The helm at the long-standing Montefiascone-based Mazziotti winery has passed to Valeria Laurenzi, granddaughter of the founder, who is full of determination and a desire to do well. Paolo Peira looks after winemaking and the range is wide. Let's start with the classic Est Est Est di Montefiascone. The '01 is gently aromatic, with attractive scents of sweet cicely, and a light, easy-drinking palate. However, the Est Est Est selection Canuleio '01, which has a stay in oak, is much more interesting. The blend of varieties bring grace and harmony to the aromatic nose. There is lively acidity on the palate, tempered by the oak-derived sweetness. We reported on the well-made Filò '98, from sangiovese and montepulciano, in an earlier edition of the Guide. Now it's time to draw attention to the excellent performance of Volgente '00, made from merlot, sangiovese and montepulciano. It has great impact and fully deserves its Two Glasses. The nose has aromatic warmth, uniting cherry and blackberry with elegant notes of spices and cocoa powder. Ripe tannins and more spice follow on the well-knit palate. It was also interesting to retaste Terre di Melona, from late-harvested grechetto and malvasia. The entrancing aromas range from candied fruit to apricot jam, although the palate lets it down a little, as it is a touch loose and weak.

●	Volgente Rosso '00	▼▼	4
○	Est Est Est di Montefiascone Canuleio '01	▼	4
○	Est Est Est di Montefiascone '01		3
●	Volgente Rosso '97	▼▼	4
●	Volgente Rosso '99	▼▼	4
○	Est Est Est di Montefiascone Canuleio '00	▼	4
○	Terre di Melona '99	▼	4

CASTIGLIONE IN TEVERINA (VT)

Paolo d'Amico
Fraz. Vaiano
Loc. Palombaro
01024 Castiglione in Teverina (VT)
tel. 0761948868 - 0761948869

It was obvious to us, right from Paolo D'Amico's first appearance in the Guide, that he was a clear-thinking individual. Now, he has shown just how much you can get from an eclectic variety like chardonnay, here in the Castiglione in Teverina zone in upper Lazio. His excellent results are, naturally, also down to his highly skilled oenologists, Carlo Corino and Fabrizio Moltard. The most eloquent example of the variety's adaptation to these lands comes from Falesia '00. It is bright gold and the bouquet is sumptuous and richly nuanced, ranging from honey and peach to roasted hazelnut. The fully-fruited palate is fat but not cloying, with tropical fruit character, and the very long finish echoes the nose beautifully. Its "little brother", so to speak, is another Chardonnay, the stainless steel-vinified Calanchi di Vaiano '00. Its most striking aspect is the lively, vibrant, fresh nose. This, too, has tropical aromas but they are more contained and there is a more dominant fresh citrus note. The initial acidic attack on the palate is followed by surprising depth, and the finish is long and warm. Orvieto Noe '01 is a new wine. It is uncomplicated, immediate and deliberately light in structure.

○	Calanchi di Vaiano '00	▼▼	4
○	Falesia '00	▼▼	5
○	Orvieto Noe '01	▼	3*
○	Falesia '98	▼▼	5
○	Falesia '99	▼▼	5
○	Calanchi di Vaiano '98	▼	4
○	Calanchi di Vaiano '99	▼	4

CASTIGLIONE IN TEVERINA (VT)

Trappolini
Via del Rivellino, 65
01024 Castiglione in Teverina (VT)
Tel. 0761948381
E-mail: trappolini@tin.it

The wine from the Trappolini range that impressed us most this year was Brecceto. The '01 comes from a well thought-out mix of grechetto and chardonnay. The first thing that strikes you is the delightful fragrance of the nose, which has only a very discreet touch of vanilla, leaving plenty of space for its primary fruit aromas. The palate has fair extractive weight and good overall harmony. The Est Est Est di Montefiascone has also improved significantly. The '01 is delicately aromatic, with ripe pear and citrus peel on the nose. The palate is clean and zesty, showing an enlivening streak of acidity. We felt, though, that the whites Sartei '01 and Orvieto '01 were a little below par. They appeared to lack the grip of the first two wines. Turning to Paterno, a red from sangiovese, we could not help thinking of last year's fabulous wine. This time, the '00 is less starry but nevertheless still an excellent red, with an intriguing nose and good richness of flavour. It swept confidently into the Two Glass category. We prefer to suspend judgement on the "lesser" red, Cenereto '01, but Idea '01, a delicious sweet wine from aleatico that would be ideal with fruit-based desserts, is the proverbial icing on the cake.

CASTIGLIONE IN TEVERINA (VT)

Vaselli
P.zza del Poggetto, 12
01024 Castiglione in Teverina (VT)
Tel. 0761947008

Welcome back, Christine. After a long absence, due to complicated family vicissitudes, the Vaselli estate is back in the Guide. And just guess who has been entrusted to look after the wines: Riccardo Cotarella, of course, the most assiduously courted consultant in Italy. Here, though, things are slightly different. The collaboration is not the result of a recent initiative. Christine Vaselli has had a working relationship with the renowned Umbrian winemaker for a long time. It was Cotarella who conceived the great Santa Giulia that appeared in the Guide a good few years ago. At the time, it was the only Lazio red to hold its head up against the outstanding Vigna del Vassallo from Colle Picchioni. Now Santa Giulia has disappeared but in its place, Christine and Riccardo have moulded Le Poggere, from cabernet sauvignon and merlot. When we first tasted the '00 last year, it was immediately obvious that this was a wine that was going places. A year's ageing in Nevers oak and an extended time in bottle have now set its character. There is great intensity of aroma, which is well balanced between black cherry and liqueur cherry fruit components and the cinnamon and toasted bread that come from its time in barrique. The palate has excellent texture, with ripe tannins, a good dose of acidity and excellent length. In short, it was a worthy Three Glass finalist.

● Paterno '00	¶¶	4
○ Brecceto '01	¶¶	3*
● Idea '01	¶¶	4
○ Est Est Est di Montefiascone '01	¶	2*
○ Orvieto '01		2
○ Sartei '01		1
● Paterno '99	¶¶	3*
○ Chardonnay '00	¶¶	3
● Paterno '96	¶¶	3
○ Chardonnay '98	¶¶	3
● Idea '98	¶¶	4
● Paterno '98	¶¶	3
○ Chardonnay '99	¶¶	3
● Idea '99	¶¶	4

● Le Poggere '00	¶¶	5
● Orvietano Rosso		
Torre Sant'Andrea '99 '00	¶¶	5

CERVETERI (RM)

CANTINA CERVETERI
VIA AURELIA KM 42,700
00052 CERVETERI (RM)
TEL. 069905677 - 069905697
E-MAIL: cantina@virgilio.it

Light and darkness. At least that's how things seem at the Cerveteri co-operative in many respects. Some of the problems could perhaps be attributed to the caprices of the weather, others to the variable quality of the grapes supplied by its members, but something must have happened. A number of the wines we tasted had definitely fallen from grace. Still, at least the wines from the selected Vigna Grande line have maintained their standing. The pervasive, well-knit Cerveteri Rosso Vigna Grande '99 unleashes an enviable wealth of aromas, mainly balsamic and spicy. It has good extractive weight on the palate and plenty of ripe tannin. Cerveteri Bianco Vigna Grande '01 has attractive aromas of ripe fruit with delicate hints of pineapple and grapefruit. The palate has good structure and is held up by an acidic streak that also gives freshness. As usual, the price is marvellous value for money. Malvasia del Lazio Villanova '01 showed well, too. There are no bits missing from its aromatic spectrum, which is intense and well defined, and the subtle note of vanilla does not overwhelm the dominant fruitiness. The classically soft, easy-going palate is counterbalanced by good, lively acidity on the finish. Sadly, the Fontana Morella wines weren't punching their weight and the style seemed to have changed compared with previous releases. A retaste of the '99 Rosso Tertium, from malvasia nera, sangiovese and cabernet, confirmed its good quality. The latest red, Menade '00, still needs some improvements.

CIVITELLA D'AGLIANO (VT)

SERGIO MOTTURA
LOC. POGGIO DELLA COSTA, 1
01020 CIVITELLA D'AGLIANO (VT)
TEL. 0761914533
E-MAIL: mottura@isa.it

As we tasted Sergio Mottura's '00 Magone, which is based on pinot nero with some montepulciano, and putting the technical side of the evaluation to one side, we experienced a sensation of great pleasure. Incredible but true. This Magone actually makes you happy. There is more concentration than ever before, thanks to refinements in the winemaking and also, perhaps, to the excellent vintage. It has clean, very intense aromas of ripe blackberry and black cherry, then the palate, which has considerable extract, is as powerfully expressive as the nose. We gave it a resounding Two Glasses. Civitella Rosso '01 is not bad, either. Less complex than the previous vintage, it is fresh and fragrant, can be drunk right through a meal and won't hurt your pocket. When it comes to the whites, this estate has never had problems. The '01 Orvieto Tragugnano has the liveliness of aroma we have always appreciated but this time, it has been given a further lift by the addition of more aromatic varieties. Poggio della Costa '01 also showed well and has a delicious peachy aroma. The '00 Latour a Civitella has improved noticeably. It now has a better, more complete nose, having attained ideal point of balance for its fruit components and those coming from oak. Finally, we must record the excellent performance of Muffo, made from late-harvested indigenous grapes. The '00 has warmth and complexity on the nose and a deep, satisfying palate.

O	Cerveteri Bianco Vigna Grande '01	ŶŶ	1*
●	Cerveteri Rosso Vigna Grande '99	ŶŶ	3*
O	Malvasia del Lazio Villanova '01	Ŷ	1*
●	Menade '00		1
O	Cerveteri Bianco Fontana Morella '01		1
●	Cerveteri Rosso Fontana Morella '01		1
●	Cerveteri Rosso Vigna Grande '95	ŶŶ	3
●	Cerveteri Rosso Vigna Grande '97	ŶŶ	3
●	Cerveteri Rosso Vigna Grande '98	ŶŶ	3*
●	Tertium '99	ŶŶ	4
O	Cerveteri Bianco Fontana Morella '00	Ŷ	1*
O	Cerveteri Bianco Vigna Grande '00	Ŷ	1
●	Cerveteri Rosso Fontana Morella '00	Ŷ	1
●	Tertium '98	Ŷ	3

O	Grechetto Latour a Civitella '00	ŶŶ	5
●	Magone '00	ŶŶ	5
O	Muffo '00	ŶŶ	5
●	Civitella Rosso '01	Ŷ	3
O	Grechetto Poggio della Costa '01	Ŷ	4
O	Orvieto Cl. Vigna Tragugnano '01	Ŷ	3
●	Civitella Rosso '00	ŶŶ	3
O	Muffo '97	ŶŶ	3
O	Grechetto Latour a Civitella '98	ŶŶ	4
O	Grechetto Poggio della Costa '98	ŶŶ	3
O	Muffo '98	ŶŶ	3
O	Grechetto Latour a Civitella '99	ŶŶ	4
O	Grechetto Poggio della Costa '99	ŶŶ	3
O	Grechetto Poggio della Costa '00	Ŷ	3

CORI (LT)

COLLE SAN LORENZO
VIA GRAMSCI, 52
04010 CORI (LT)
TEL. 069678001
E-MAIL: cooplor@tin.it

Colle San Lorenzo, run by the dynamic Ferretti brothers, has the undisputed merit of having raised the public profile of a less well-known zone like Cori. The estate's flagship wine is the red Colle Amato, made from cabernet sauvignon and syrah, with proportions depending on the vintage. The year 2000 was very dry and this had a marked effect on the wine's character. The red berry fruit aromas are a touch less fresh and seem a little tired. There is less impact on the palate, too, although it retains finesse and elegance. Nonetheless, it's still well worth its Two Glasses. Costa Vecchia, from an intriguing blend of merlot and petit verdot, is making strides. The '01 has a good purple-ruby colour. The nose is complex and spicy, with balsamic hints, then the palate is decisive, densely woven and firm. The second release of the Merlot, the '00, is also full of character. The colour is purple tending to ruby. There is fairly ripe fruit on the intense nose introduces a reasonably full palate that is well integrated with good alcohol and extract. Last but not least comes the excellently made Chardonnay '01. There is a wide swathe of aroma, with tropical fruit and flowers most evident, then the palate is rich and broad with plentiful fruit. It gained a well-earned Two Glasses, not just for its quality but also for its excellent value for money.

● Colle Amato '00	▲▲	5
● Merlot '00	▲▲	3*
○ Chardonnay del Lazio '01	▲▲	3*
● Costa Vecchia '01	▲▲	4
● Colle Amato '99	▲▲	5
○ Chardonnay del Lazio '00	▲▲	3

FRASCATI (RM)

CASALE MARCHESE
VIA DI VERMICINO, 68
00044 FRASCATI (RM)
TEL. 069408932
E-MAIL: info@casalemarchese.it

It's back to the future at Casale Marchese. Apparently, the Carletti family has been thinking about bolstering the aromatic character of the Frascati Superiore, which for some time has been rather dilute. The move may be rather timid but it is in the right direction and it is encouraging to see signs of renewed vigour in the '01. The graceful array of aroma is back, although it is still somewhat tenuous, with aromas of spring flowers and fresh, not quite ripe, fruit. The palate does not have huge body but there is fair extract and reasonable length. The estate also produces two reds, both from the same merlot-montepulciano-cabernet-cesanese blend. The standard version, Rosso di Casale Marchese '01, is a deep ruby colour. The nose is harmonious and has a youthful, primary fruitiness before the palate reveals its simple, light structure, as is appropriate for a wine made for drinking young. The premium version is the Vigna del Cavaliere '99 selection, which ages a few months in barrique. Here, things are different and there is a much broader range of aromas and flavours. The nose is complex and pervasive, with distinct fruity and spicy aromas. These meld into a solidly structured palate whose tannic astringency, still firmly present, only slightly mars the overall elegance.

● Vigna del Cavaliere '99	▲▲	5
○ Frascati Sup. '01	▲	3
● Rosso di Casale Marchese '01	▲	3
○ Cortesia di Casale Marchese '93	▲▲	3
○ Cortesia di Casale Marchese '94	▲▲	3
○ Cortesia di Casale Marchese '95	▲▲	3
● Vigna del Cavaliere '96	▲▲	4
● Rosso di Casale Marchese '97	▲▲	3
● Vigna del Cavaliere '97	▲▲	4

GROTTAFERRATA (RM)

CASTEL DE PAOLIS
VIA VAL DE PAOLIS, 41
00046 GROTTAFERRATA (RM)
TEL. 069413648
E-MAIL: info@casteldepaolis.it

The Santarelli family's Castel De Paolis estate has once again submitted an excellent range of wines. Quattro Mori '00, from 60 per cent syrah, 20 per cent merlot, ten per cent cabernet sauvignon and petit verdot, has surprisingly good concentration and balance compared with most previous vintages. The colour is dark ruby, then the nose is full and deep, with rich red and black berry fruitiness and notes of oak and spice, especially ginger. The palate is firm, with good body, concentration and elegant tannins. Only a drying effect from the new oak on the finish mars it. Vigna Adriana '01, from 50 per cent malvasia puntinata, 40 per cent viognier and sauvignon, also put up a fine showing at the final taste-offs and could easily have won Three Glasses. It has a good bright deep straw colour, shot through with greenish tinges. The nose is full of ripe apples and pears, mingling with tropical and floral nuances. The palate is concentrated, powerfully alcoholic, balanced and long, with clean, ripe fruitiness. The Frascati Superiore Campo Vecchio '01 is similar in style. It's soft and clean but lacks the Vigna Adriana's complexity. The Frascati Superiore '01 is also very good and has intensity, freshness and subtle aromatic richness. The rich, fleshy Campo Vecchio '00, with its tightly woven tannins, stands out among the reds while the best of the sweet wines are the attractive Frascati Cannellino '01 and the Rosathea '01, a dried-grape "passito" from moscato rosa. Its attractive raspberry and wild rose scents are, however, sadly masked by insistent notes of over-reduction.

● Quattro Mori '00	🍷🍷	6
○ Vigna Adriana '01	🍷🍷	5
● Campo Vecchio Rosso '00	🍷🍷	4
○ Frascati Sup. '01	🍷🍷	4
○ Frascati Sup. Campo Vecchio '01	🍷🍷	4*
○ Frascati Cannellino '01	🍷	5
● Rosathea '01	🍷	5
○ Frascati Sup. V. Adriana '00	🍷🍷	5
● Quattro Mori '99	🍷🍷	5
● Rosathea '00	🍷🍷	5
● Quattro Mori '97	🍷🍷	5
● Quattro Mori '98	🍷🍷	5
○ Muffa Nobile '99	🍷🍷	5
● Rosathea '99	🍷🍷	5

MARINO (RM)

PAOLA DI MAURO - COLLE PICCHIONI
LOC. FRATTOCCHIE
VIA COLLE PICCHIONE, 46
00040 MARINO (RM)
TEL. 0693546329
E-MAIL: info@collepicchioni.it

Paola Di Mauro, having reached an age at which she could easily content herself with looking after her grandchildren and her garden, doesn't seem to be satisfied with the innumerable plaudits she has received from all over the world. She still appears to need new challenges which, as this time, she often wins. How can anyone ignore a Super-Lazian (with apologies to the Tuscans) of the calibre of Vigna del Vassallo '00, which strolled off with Three Glasses? Mind you, such success was probably inevitable sooner or later. It is only the logical consequence of the wise suggestions of the valiant Riccardo Cotarella and the tireless work of her son, Armando, in the vineyards and the cellar. The make-up of the wine is well-known: the classic Bordeaux grape blend and no filtration. The result is a wine richly endowed with both colour – a deep, brightly tinged ruby – and complexity on its subtly fruity, spicy nose. Its class shines out on the firmly structured palate, where the tannins are finely grained. Its white opposite number, the Marino Selezione Oro '01, is also in great form. There is certainly nothing to complain about in the cleanliness of its exquisitely defined, well-knit aromatic components, nor in the nice weighty palate that acquires freshness from perfectly gauged acidic thrust. Marino Etichetta Verde '01 is well made, as is Vignole '00, although the use of oak here could be improved. The '01 Colle Picchioni Rosso remains a good example of a wine that is uncomplicatedly fruity on both nose and palate.

● Vigna del Vassallo '00	🍷🍷🍷	6
○ Marino Colle Picchioni Oro '01	🍷🍷	4
○ Le Vignole '00	🍷	4
● Colle Picchioni Rosso '01	🍷	4
○ Marino Etichetta Verde '01	🍷	3
● Vigna del Vassallo '85	🍷🍷🍷	5
● Vigna del Vassallo '88	🍷🍷🍷	5
● Vigna del Vassallo '99	🍷🍷	5*
● Colle Picchioni Rosso '00	🍷🍷	4*
○ Marino Colle Picchioni Oro '00	🍷🍷	4*
● Vigna del Vassallo '95	🍷🍷	5
● Vigna del Vassallo '96	🍷🍷	5
● Vigna del Vassallo '97	🍷🍷	5
● Vigna del Vassallo '98	🍷🍷	5
● Colle Picchioni Rosso '99	🍷🍷	4

MARINO (RM)

GOTTO D'ORO
LOC. FRATTOCCHIE
VIA DEL DIVINO AMORE, 115
00040 MARINO (RM)
TEL. 069302221
E-MAIL: info@gottodoro.it

It is always good news when quantity goes hand in hand with quality. This large co-operative, producing over 8,000,000 bottles annually, manages to combine the two very well indeed. The wines are never going to be stellar but they are well styled, fresh and very attractive drinking. They can also be enjoyed without spending an arm and a leg, or worrying that they will squash any foods they are drunk with because of over-concentration or over-oaking, as all too often happens with other wines. Another appreciable advantage is that each wine is distinct from its stablemates and each is clearly, recognizably representative of its style. Hence the Frascati is a pale straw yellow, with soft perfumes of green apples, hazelnuts and citrus fruit ushering in enticing freshness and pleasing balance on the palate. There are just 10,000 bottles produced of the Malvasia and it was a wonderful surprise. In fact, we liked it best of the lot. It has excellent typicity, a deep straw yellow colour and a lightly aromatic nose giving rock rose honey, banana, almond and ripe pear. There is unexpected richness and length on the palate. There are many subvarieties of malvasia but this is made from malvasia puntinata, also known as malvasia del Lazio, which is one of the best. We look forward to the wine's promise being confirmed in future vintages. Both the Chardonnay and the fresh Merlot are attractive and easy drinking, the former being very light, with a pale straw colour and delicate citrus aromas. Only the Marino, a touch over-oxidized, is a little disappointing.

● Castelli Romani '01	▼	3
○ Frascati Sup. '01	▼	3
○ Malvasia del Lazio '01	▼	3
○ Chardonnay '01		3
● Merlot del Lazio '01		3
● Castelli Romani '00	▽	2
○ Frascati Sup. '00	▽	2
○ Marino Sup. '00	▽	2

MONTE PORZIO CATONE (RM)

FONTANA CANDIDA
VIA FONTANA CANDIDA, 11
00040 MONTE PORZIO CATONE (RM)
TEL. 069420066
E-MAIL: giv@giv.it

Fonatana Candida does not just turn out wines in large quantities. The quality is also notably good. Franco Bardi, the cellar's long-standing winemaker, has been leading production along the path to quality for many years now, although his task is anything but easy, given the millions of bottles that pass through the cellar. This year, however, he has managed to restyle and improve even the most basic line, the Frascati Superiore '01. In an apparent surge of pride, it releases an unexpected wealth of aroma and it is deliciously fruity on the palate. There are also good things from the Terre dei Grifi line, most notably the beautifully clean Malvasia '01 and the Frascati '01, which has great character yet remains a very approachable wine. But top of the tree again is the evergreen Frascati Superiore Santa Teresa, the '01 having even better aroma and flavour than previous vintages. The nose evokes sage and golden delicious apples; the palate is clean and forthcoming. Bardi has been working on the reds, too, and results are reassuring. Fontana Candida now also makes a 100 per cent Merlot and the '01 edition has fair breadth of aroma and clean, uncomplicated, well-defined flavours. The leading red, however, is Kron, from merlot and sangiovese. The '00, with 12 months ageing in new barriques, has good stuffing but is still a little rough and ready. More time in bottle should tame its rather aggressive character.

○ Frascati Sup. Santa Teresa '01	▼▼	4*
○ Malvasia del Lazio Terre dei Grifi '01	▼▼	3*
● Kron '00	▼	5
○ Frascati Sup. '01	▼	2*
○ Frascati Sup. Terre dei Grifi '01	▼	2*
● Merlot del Lazio '01	▼	3
○ Frascati Sup. Santa Teresa '00		3
○ Frascati Sup. Santa Teresa '96	▽▽	2
○ Malvasia del Lazio '96	▽▽	2
○ Frascati Sup. Santa Teresa '97	▽▽	2
○ Malvasia del Lazio '97	▽▽	2
○ Frascati Sup. Santa Teresa '98	▽▽	2
○ Malvasia del Lazio '98	▽▽	2
○ Malvasia del Lazio Terre dei Grifi '99	▽▽	3

MONTE PORZIO CATONE (RM)

Villa Simone
Via Frascati Colonna, 29
00040 Monte Porzio Catone (RM)
Tel. 069449717
E-mail: info@pierocostantini.it

What's going on at Monteporzio? Is it possible that the phlegmatic Piero Costantini has become so obsessed with great red wine that he's about launch an open challenge to Lazio's top producers? So it would seem. His challenge goes by the name of Ferro e Seta and is from a mix of more or less equal amounts of sangiovese and cesanese, with some other red varieties present in his vineyards. The '00, the first release, went straight to the Three Glasses tasting finals. The colour is deep and bright, the red berry fruits nose is open, and the palate is warm and mouthfilling, with a firm tannic weave. And what about the white wines, Villa Simone's pride and joy? Well, there's certainly no drop in quality with the '01 Frascati Superiore Villa dei Preti. It has complex, pervasive, fragrant aromas of fresh fruit and flowers, and the balanced palate has good length. The Frascati Vigneto Filonardi now seems to have found its definitive style, putting behind it the ups and downs that have rather clouded its reputation. The '01 is attractively aromatic, but not excessively so, and youthfully straightforward on the palate. The runt of the litter is the basic Frascati Superiore '01. There has been a rethink here but it doesn't appear to have been too successful. The wine seems lighter throughout and lacks tautness on the palate. It is, though, well typed and attractively approachable. The '99 Frascati Cannellino Selezione remains a good example of a soft, balanced, sweet wine made from super-ripe grapes. It deserves greater renown.

● Ferro e Seta '00		6
○ Frascati Sup. V. dei Preti '01		4*
○ Frascati Sup. Cannellino Sel. '99		5
○ Frascati Sup. Vign. Filonardi '01		4
○ Frascati Sup. Villa Simone '01		3
○ Frascati Sup. Vign. Filonardi '00		3
○ Frascati Sup. V. dei Preti '95		2
○ Frascati Sup. Vign. Filonardi '95		3
○ Frascati Sup. Cannellino '97		5
○ Frascati Sup. V. dei Preti '97		2
○ Frascati Sup. Vign. Filonardi '97		3
○ Frascati Sup. Cannellino '98		4
○ Frascati Sup. Cannellino '99		5
○ Frascati Sup. V. dei Preti '99		2
○ Frascati Sup. Vign. Filonardi '99		3

MONTEFIASCONE (VT)

Falesco
Zona Artigianale Guardie
01027 Montefiascone (VT)
Tel. 0761825669 - 0761825803
E-mail: falesco@leonet.it

In our opinion, it is no exaggeration to say that Montiano is the most important wine phenomenon of recent times in Lazio. Some may feel that this is going over the top, but not those who have followed the wine's progress step by step. This time, there were Three Glasses for the '00 edition, which has extremely ripe fruit from the very hot year. The nose has blackberry jam and a fine spiciness, with nuances of cocoa powder and coffee. The palate has a precise attack and opens out to yield its usual softness and its habitual high points of ripe tannins, mouthfilling roundness and suppleness. An honourable mention goes to Marciliano '99 with its psychedelic swathe of subtle aromas that are as broad and satisfying on the palate as it is on the nose. The impeccably made, faultless Merlot '01 and Vitiano '01 both also impress. In the whites section of the catalogue is a new wine, Grechetto '01, which has a distinguished profile on both nose and palate. But Poggio dei Gelsi remains the estate's figurehead, even though the '01 has less attack than previous releases. Riccardo Cotarella's skills also come to the fore in the basic Est Est Est di Montefiascone '01, which is nicely fragrant on the nose and is supported by a lean, lithe structure. Finally, we wish a warm welcome to the estate's newest wine, Pomele '01, made from aleatico. The nose is inviting with dried roses and lightly musky scents. The palate is velvety and long.

● Montiano '00		6
● Marciliano '99		6
○ Est Est Est di Montefiascone Poggio dei Gelsi '01		3*
○ Grechetto '01		3*
● Pomele '01		5
● Vitiano '01		3*
○ Est Est Est di Montefiascone Falesco '01		1*
● Merlot dell'Umbria '01		4
● Montiano '94		5
● Montiano '95		5
● Montiano '96		5
● Montiano '97		5
● Montiano '98		5
● Montiano '99		6

ROMA

CONTE ZANDOTTI
VIA VIGNE COLLE MATTIA, 8
00132 ROMA
TEL. 0620609000 - 066160335

The Conte Zandotti wines performed well this year, especially the whites, which are in splendid form. Credit must go to the skilled Marco Ciarla, the winemaker who, for some time now, has been reformulating styles at this winery on the heights of Colle Mattia. Malvasia Rumon '01 makes a sensational start. It achieved a remarkably high score, despite being made from traditional Frascati varieties. The fragrant nose is particularly intense and complex. Improvements on the palate are noticeable, too. Here the fruit, with some more tropical tones, is enlivened by good acidic backbone that gives greater presence to the mid palate and the finish. And all this comes at a very affordable price. The Frascati Superiore has also made a leap in quality and the '01 is a far cry from the style produced up until a few years ago. It has an excellent aroma framework and enticing nuances. The body is as slim as ever but better freshness is apparent. We don't yet feel able to give a wholly positive report on the Sauvignon, Zandotti's way of offering an alternative to Frascati. Some tinkering is still needed. Despite the obvious attractiveness of its aromas, the '01 does not have sufficient acidity to sustain it and as a result it appears somewhat flaccid. The '01 Frascati Cannellino is as fascinating as ever.

O	Malvasia del Lazio Rumon '01	🍷🍷	3*
O	Frascati Sup. '01	🍷🍷	2*
O	Frascati Cannellino '01	🍷	3
O	Sauvignon '01		3
O	Frascati Sup. '94	🍷🍷	2
O	Frascati Cannellino '95	🍷🍷	3
O	Frascati Sup. '95	🍷🍷	2
O	Frascati Cannellino '96	🍷🍷	3
O	Frascati Sup. '98	🍷🍷	2
●	La Petrosa '98	🍷🍷	4
O	Malvasia del Lazio Rumon '98	🍷🍷	3
O	Frascati Cannellino '99	🍷🍷	3
O	Frascati Sup. '99	🍷🍷	2
●	La Petrosa '99	🍷🍷	4

VELLETRI (RM)

COLLE DI MAGGIO
VIA FIENILI
00049 VELLETRI (RM)
TEL. 0696453072
E-MAIL: colledimaggio@colledimaggio.it

Colle di Maggio and Villa Tulino '97 are two names to remember. The first is a small, but well-equipped, winery lying just to the coastal side of central Velletri; the second is the terrific red wine it produces. Villa Tulino comes from a blend of shiraz, merlot, petit verdot and cabernet sauvignon, and spends two years in barrique, followed by 20 months in bottle. What emerges is a wine of abundant aroma, its nose rich with notes of spices and wood resin. The palate is pervaded by a warm fruitiness, with fleshiness at its heart and a very long finish. Sadly, though, only 2,000 bottles were made so don't miss out. Rosso Le Anfore '99, from merlot and cabernet sauvignon, makes a worthy partner. The nose is well fruited and evocative of cherry. The palate, too, is fruit-forward and has additional hints of pencil lead, mint and eucalyptus. Velitrae Rosso '00 is simpler, but certainly not simplistic, and is made for those seeking an easier-drinking wine. Villa Tulino '00 stands out among the whites. It is from chardonnay, fermented and aged in barrique, and its peach and apricot fruitiness melds beautifully with soft sensations of honey and vanilla. Porticato Bianco '00, from a multi-grape blend, is also good, as is, to a slightly lesser extent, the Velitrae '00, which is less balanced.

O	Villa Tulino Bianco '00	🍷🍷	6
●	Villa Tulino '97	🍷🍷	6
●	Le Anfore '99	🍷🍷	5
O	Porticato Bianco '00	🍷	4
●	Velitrae Rosso '00	🍷	4
O	Velitrae Bianco '00		4
●	Le Anfore '98	🍷🍷	4
O	Porticato Bianco '99	🍷🍷	4
O	Velitrae Bianco '99	🍷	4
●	Velitrae Rosso '99	🍷	4
O	Villa Tulino Bianco '99	🍷	5

OTHER WINERIES

GIUSEPPE IUCCI
FRAZ. SANT'ELIA FIUMERAPIDO
VIA MARCONI, 10
03043 CASSINO (FR)
TEL. 0776311883 - 0776312013

Dynamic lawyer Giuseppe Iucci has pulled out of his hat a very attractive rabbit called Merlot Tenuta La Creta. The 2000 has great breadth and is nicely robust, especially as regards its tannins. It is very well priced too.

● Merlot Tenuta La Creta '00	♟♟	3

CASALE DEI CENTO CORVI
VIA DELLA TOMBA
00052 CERVETERI (RM)
TEL. 069943486

The search for the new brings us to Cerveteri, where this modern winery has been operating for a very short time. Most noteworthy is the Kottabos selection. The white, from chardonnay and trebbiano, is perfumed and the attractive red, from a blend, is oak aged. Both are very sound.

● Kottabos Rosso '00	♟♟	4
○ Kottabos Bianco '01	♟	4

BRANNETTI ANTICA
RISERVA DELLA CASCINA
VIA F.LLI RAIT, 10
00043 CIAMPINO (RM)
TEL. 067917221

We thought we'd made a mistake when we uncovered the bottles we'd been tasting, but no. The most attractive of the wines was a Marino Bianco '01 produced near Ciampino. It's a remarkable result for an unexceptional production zone.

○ Marino Sup. '01	♟	2*

VINI PALLAVICINI
VIA CASILINA KM. 25,500
00030 COLONNA (RM)
TEL. 069438816
E-MAIL: saitacolonna@vinipallavicini.com

Rome has a great Cabernet on its doorstep. Soleggio '00 has fine depth and fullness, complex nuances of jam and spices, and nice length. Also worthy of note are the Frascati Superiore Selezione Verde '01 and the ever-improving, ever-promising Malvasia '01.

● Soleggio '00	♟♟	4
○ Frascati Sup. Sel. Verde '01	♟	3
○ Malvasia del Lazio '01	♟	3
● Rosso Ris. Pallavicini '97	♟	3

Gino Amadio
Loc. Madonna delle Grazie, 1
01030 Corchiano (VT)
Tel. 0761572041

Quality at this estate, situated below Mount Cimini, is swinging upwards. The range is varied. We tasted Poggesco, a 50-50 merlot and sangiovese blend, and Musalè, from 100 per cent cabernet sauvignon. Our preference was for the latter, but only just.

● Il Musalè '00	🍷	4
● Il Poggesco '01	🍷	2*

L'Olivella
Via di Colle Pisano, 1
00044 Frascati (RM)
Tel. 069424527
E-mail: info@racemo.it

L'Olivella is an estate on the up. Besides an excellent Frascati Racemo and a fruity, balsamic Racemo Rosso, this year brings the first appearance of Concerto. This full-bodied, fruity, incredibly attractive red from cesanese is also exceedingly well priced.

○ Frascati Sup. Racemo '01	🍷	3*
● Racemo Rosso '98	🍷	4
● Concento '00	🍷	3*
○ Frascati Sup. Racemo '00		3

Camponeschi
Via Piastrarelle, 14
00040 Lanuvio (RM)
Tel. 069374390
E-mail: campones@mbox.micanet.it

The get-up-and-go Alessandro Camponeschi and his consultant Marco Ciarla are tenaciously fighting their way forward. This year, we particularly liked the simple, attractively fruity Carato Bianco '01. The Colli Lanuvini '01, though, seemed slightly under par.

○ Carato Bianco '00	🍷	4
○ Colli Lanuvini Sup. '01		2
● Carato Rosso '99	🍷	5

Tenuta Le Quinte
Via delle Marmorelle, 71
00040 Montecompatri (RM)
Tel. 069438756

This is a pivotal time for Tenuta Le Quinte. Virtù Romane has is firmly back on form and shows rich elegance on the nose then a marvellously enjoyable palate. It gained Two well-deserved Glasses. The red Rasa di Marmorata also seems to have improved.

○ Montecompatri Colonna Sup. Virtù Romane '01	🍷🍷	3*
● Rasa di Marmorata '00		3
○ Dulcis Vitis '00	🍷	4

Cantina Sociale Cesanese del Piglio
Via Prenestina, km 42
03010 Piglio (FR)
Tel. 0775502355 - 0775502356
E-mail: c.cantinasocialecesanese@tin.it

Piglio's co-operative returns to the limelight with an amazing Cesanese del Piglio Etichetta Rossa, a really exciting, warm, silky, long wine. It's could well be the best buy of the year.

● Cesanese del Piglio Etichetta Rossa '01	🍷🍷	2*
● Cesanese del Piglio Etichetta Oro '00	🍷	4

Massimi Berucci
Via Prenestina, km 42
03010 Piglio (FR)
Tel. 0775501303 - 0668307004

Manfredi Berucci is another wineman who wants to amaze. This year, he has released the first Cesanese from his new vineyard. The result is exciting. Great density and depth underlie alternating sensations of fruit and pepper, and it would stand up well to a Rhône wine.

● Cesanese del Piglio Vigne Nuove '00	🍷🍷	4
● Cesanese del Piglio Casal Cervino '01	🍷	4
● Cesanese del Piglio Casal Cervino '00	🍷	4

Terre del Cesanese
Via Maggiore, 105
03010 Piglio (FR)
tel. 0775501125

Here, we have a battalion of determined go-getters and their ambitious project to produce a great wine from cesanese. After several months in barrique, the '00 has been released and does not disappoint. It is elegant, richly endowed with spicy aroma and has great character.

● Cesanese del Piglio '00	🍷🍷	5

Casal Gentile
Loc. Vermicino
Via del Casale Paoloni, 15
00100 Roma
tel. 0672602022

Parnasio is an attractive Frascati that is clean and intense on both nose and palate. This is its first showing in the Guide and the future looks promising. The price is also more than reasonable. We hope it remains so.

○ Frascati Sup. Parnasio '01	🍷	2*

Migliarese
Via Crocelle
03047 San Giorgio a Liri (FR)
tel. 0771772211 - 0771324474

This is a new winery in the Ciociaria area. We found the white Ausente '01, from indigenous grapes, to be the most sound of those submitted. Its nose tends to tropical fruit, then the palate is fresh and zesty.

○ Ausente '01	🍷	3

Giovanni Terenzi
Loc. La Forma - Via Prenestina, 134
03010 Serrone (FR)
tel. 0775594286
e-mail: terenzigiovanni@libero.it

This is a highly promising new entry to the Guide. The estate concentrates on the zone's classic wines. We were impressed by Cesanese del Piglio Colle Forma and, especially, by the Vajoscuro selection. Both are wines show great personality, although they could still be improved.

● Cesanese del Piglio Vajoscuro '00	🍷🍷	7
● Cesanese del Piglio Colle Forma '00	🍷	6

Cantina Sant'Andrea
Loc. Borgo Vodice - Via Renibbio, 1720
04019 Terracina (LT)
tel. 0773755028
e-mail: andreapandolfo@tiscalinet.it

Working the land here is not easy. There are too many unknowns, starting with the weather. This year, the wines suffered from the heat more than usual and they are a bit heavy. Nevertheless drinking the Moscato Secco remains a pleasant experience.

● Circeo Rosso Il Sogno '00	🍷	4
○ Moscato di Terracina Secco Oppidum '01	🍷	3
○ Moscato Secco di Terracina '00	🍷🍷	2*
● Circeo Rosso Il Sogno '99	🍷	4

Azienda Vinicola Federici
Via Borgo San Martino, 39
00039 Zagarolo
tel. 069546102

Bianco Le Ripe is produced from very carefully vinified malvasia del Lazio and grechetto. Its clean, fragrant, intense, ripely fruited nose is exemplary. The palate is warm and long.

○ Le Ripe Bianco '01	🍷🍷	4

ABRUZZO AND MOLISE

Abruzzo is beginning to reveal a new face to the wine world. That profile emerges in the ever-growing number of new estates on the market, estates with high ambitions and wines that are attention-grabbers right from their first release. It is also clear from the newly revitalized mentality at many traditional producers, those who over the past decade have shaped Abruzzo's recent winemaking history. New vineyards are being purchased, established vineyards are being adapted to systems better suited to the soil and climate, and well-respected names from further afield are bringing their technical experience to bear. The important thing is that producers should avoid the risks that are latent in such developments, such as tackling wines that are too far from typical styles, going for "names" at all costs, or rushing for results rather than taking a more sanguine approach to achieving the sort of balance that starts in the vineyard and emerges from the cellar door. In the small region of Molise, everything is moving more slowly, although at least a couple of new developments are due to surface next year. Until then, the sceptre remains firmly in the grasp of its two leading producers, Di Giulio from Borgo di Colloredo and, shining far above, Di Majo, who repeated last year's Three Glass triumph with a magnificent Aglianico. Nevertheless, we must add that we cannot report on all the estates that performed well because of the limited number of pages available in this year's Guide. Exceptionally, we shall list here the cellars that merited at least a space among the "Other Wineries": producers such as Fratelli Barba, Il Feuduccio di Santa Maria d'Orni, Fattoria Licia and Praesidium, as well as the Roxan and Cantine Miglianico co-operatives. The tastings underlined that the core of Abruzzo winemaking remains much as before: Edoardo Valentini and Gianni Masciarelli lead an ever more numerous and varied brigade. Most of these mainstays presented one or two wines that reached the Three Glass finals but there are also some who chose not to bottle their best reds because the vintage was disappointing. Even so, never have there been so many wines from Abruzzo and Molise that came so close to winning Three Glasses. Nor have there ever been so many Two Glass wines, many of them at remarkably good prices. By far the most popular wine style is Montepulciano d'Abruzzo. In recent vintages, spanning 1997 to 2001, this has provided very satisfying drinking, and will continue to do so. The whites are getting better, too. Those made from trebbiano have improved, as have the ones based on chardonnay and the indigenous passerina and pecorino varieties. Cerasuolo warrants a separate mention. It puts Abruzzo up in the front rank of Italy's rosé-producing regions.

BOLOGNANO (PE)

CICCIO ZACCAGNINI
C.DA POZZO
65020 BOLOGNANO (PE)
TEL. 0858880195
E-MAIL: zaccagniniwines@tin.it

Marcello Zaccagnini and his highly dependable oenologist, Concezio Marulli, are making progress along the route that leads to Three Glasses. This year, two wines came very close to gaining top honours. Nevertheless, what really impresses us here is the consistent quality across the board, from the least expensive lines upwards. Even so, we feel that they'd do better by concentrating on fewer wines. Let's leave our opinions to one side. Zaccagnini has 50 hectares of vine and a cellar with panoramic views over the Orta valley. This year, he submitted a highly distinguished range, led by San Clemente. This is a deep, purple-tinged ruby. Its nose, with red berry fruit and spices, is both full and refined. There is great concentration and complexity, and it is already drinking well although it will doubtless improve over the next few years. Capisco, from a clone of sangiovese, is similarly impressive, with upfront fruitiness that is well integrated with the oak, and an intriguing, deep palate evocative of rich chocolate. Just a point or two down the scale comes another Montepulciano d'Abruzzo, the '99 Selezione, which fully reflects varietal style in its ripe red and black cherry aromas. The Cerasuolo Myosotis is well worthy of mention. For years, it has been one of Abruzzo's best rosés. All the other wines performed well. The barrique-fermented chardonnay-based San Clemente Bianco is good, despite suffering from the heat of the '01 vintage, as is the fresh, minerally Ibisco Bianco, from riesling.

CAMPOMARINO (CB)

DI MAJO NORANTE
FRAZ. NUOVA CLITERNIA
C.DA RAMITELLI, 4
86042 CAMPOMARINO (CB)
TEL. 087557208
E-MAIL: dimajo@tin.it

Alessio Di Majo's decision to bring in Riccardo Cotarella cannot fail to improve even further the quality levels this Molise estate has already been displaying for a number of years. This time round, there are Three Glasses for Aglianico Contado, which was partly obtained with the first harvests from new vineyards. Its colour is a concentrated, garnet-tinged red. The aromas are interweave black and red cherries, and small berry fruit, with a perfect tenor of oak and the light notes of roast coffee it cedes. First impact on the palate is clearly defined, soft and full. It then develops evenly, with tightly woven tannin, and finishes long, marrying notes of balsam and liquorice with the fruit. When compared to the Contado, Don Luigi pays the price, so to speak, for its somewhat less expressive fruitiness and its slightly over-assertive oak. Nonetheless, its softly textured extract and good overall structure still make it an admirable wine. A retaste of Ramitello confirmed our previous findings. This is a high-quality red with good weight and a seductively fruity, spicy nose. The focus of the Sangiovese is on extreme ripeness whereas the Molì Rosso foregrounds great drinkability. Both are very attractive. When it comes to the whites, all showed well. Biblos, from falanghina and greco, has balsamic, almost minty aromas that return on the fresh, mid-weight palate. Molì Bianco is lighter and more floral. Finally, the Falanghina has intriguing aromas of white peach and a good balance of flavours.

● Montepulciano d'Abruzzo Abbazia S. Clemente '00	🍷🍷 5
● Capsico Rosso '98	🍷🍷 4
◉ Montepulciano d'Abruzzo Cerasuolo Myosotis '01	🍷🍷 3*
● Montepulciano d'Abruzzo Castello di Salle '99	🍷🍷 4
● Montepulciano d'Abruzzo Selezione '99	🍷 3*
● Montepulciano d'Abruzzo '00	🍷 3
○ Bianco di Ciccio '01	🍷 3
○ Ibisco Bianco '01	🍷 3
○ Ibisco Rosa '01	🍷 3
◉ Montepulciano d'Abruzzo Cerasuolo '01	🍷 3
○ Passito Bianco '01	🍷 4
○ S. Clemente Bianco '01	🍷 5

● Molise Aglianico Contado '99	🍷🍷🍷 4*
● Molise Don Luigi '00	🍷🍷 6
○ Biblos '00	🍷 4
○ Biferno Bianco Molì '01	🍷 2*
● Biferno Rosso Molì '01	🍷 2*
○ Molise Falanghina '01	🍷 3
○ Molise Greco '01	🍷 3
● Sangiovese Terra degli Osci '01	🍷 3
● Molise Don Luigi '99	🍷🍷🍷 5
● Molise Aglianico Contado '98	🍷🍷 3*
● Biferno Rosso Ramitello '99	🍷🍷 4*

COLONNELLA (TE)

Lepore
C.da Civita
64010 Colonnella (TE)
tel. 086170860
e-mail: vini@lepore.it

Gaspare Lepore's wines come from his roughly 30 hectares under vine and are made with guidance from consultant oenologist Umberto Svizzeri. They show steady improvements year after year, almost across the board. They are not easy to read and their personality will emerges fully if the nose opens out more fully. This is particularly true of the two leading reds. Riserva Luigi Lepore repeats last year's good showing with a deep colour that presages considerable structure. On the palate, despite the excess of sweet oak tones, there is admirable overall character and well-delineated tannins, good depth and ripe fruit, with cocoa powder and liquorice on the finish. The other, Re, is a dark ruby. The nose is initially closed, and the fruit is covered by tarry notes, but the palate has good texture as well as soft, ripe tannins. Credit is also due to this estate for raising the profile of another local variety, passerina, which it now produces in three versions. The newest of the trio, Sol, is also the most distinguished. It has an ability to evoke, on both nose and palate, wild herbs, a citrus fruitiness that is almost candied and a delicate minerality. The palate is rounded and zesty, with a good swathe of acidity and good balance. The other two Passerinas are less fragrant but still attractive. Finally, the '01 Cerasuolo beautifully expresses the classic characteristics of the style.

CONTROGUERRA (TE)

Dino Illuminati
C.da San Biagio, 18
64010 Controguerra (TE)
tel. 0861808008
e-mail: info@illuminativini.it

Dino Illuminati forges ahead like a battleship. Solid and unsinkable, he sails from success to success. That is still true even though his two top wines did not win Three Glasses this year. The entire range, crafted by Giorgio Marone and Claudio Cappellacci, still impressed greatly, so much so that the usual high-ranking reds have at last been joined by the admirable white Daniele. But let's take things in order. Lumen, from montepulciano and cabernet sauvignon, has its usual depth of colour and breadth on the nose, with notes of blackberry, blueberry and plum. The palate is soft, mouthfilling and tightly structured, with very slightly edgy tannins that don't compromise the excellent finish. The two Montepulciano d'Abruzzos are also up to their usual high standard. The Zanna '98 is elegant and refined, with its small black berry fruit aromas supported by light oak notes, and an utterly satisfying palate that is both classic and elegant in style. The other Montepulciano d'Abruzzo, Riparosso, is similar in style but on a smaller scale and what it loses in power it gains in ripe red berry fruit that is soft and immediate on the palate. Daniele is made mainly from oak-fermented chardonnay and trebbiano. Its balsam and tropical fruit nose gives it elegance while the palate is soft but not weak. Ciafrè which, as usual, will be better after some months in bottle, and the successful dessert wine Loré, from grapes with noble rot, are both worthy of special mention.

● Montepulciano d'Abruzzo Colline Teramane Re '00	♛♛	5
● Montepulciano d'Abruzzo Luigi Lepore Ris. '98	♛♛	5
○ Controguerra Passerina Sol '99	♛♛	4
○ Controguerra Passerina Do '00	♛	4
● Montepulciano d'Abruzzo '00	♛	4
○ Controguerra Passerina Passera delle Vigne '01	♛	3
⊙ Montepulciano d'Abruzzo Cerasuolo '01	♛	3
○ Trebbiano d'Abruzzo '01	♛	3
● Montepulciano d'Abruzzo Luigi Lepore '97	♛♛	5

● Montepulciano d'Abruzzo Zanna '98	♛♛	5
● Controguerra Rosso Lumen '99	♛♛	8
○ Controguerra Bianco Daniele '00	♛♛	4
● Montepulciano d'Abruzzo Riparosso '01	♛♛	3*
○ Loré Muffa Nobile	♛♛	4
○ Controguerra Bianco Ciafrè '01	♛	4
○ Controguerra Bianco Costalupo '01	♛	2
○ Controguerra Chardonnay Cenalba '01	♛	4
⊙ Montepulciano d'Abruzzo Cerasuolo Campirosa '01	♛	3
○ Brut M. Cl. '97	♛	4
● Controguerra Passito Nicò '98	♛	7
● Controguerra Rosso Lumen '97	♛♛♛	6
● Montepulciano d'Abruzzo Zanna Vecchio '97	♛♛	4
● Controguerra Rosso Lumen '98	♛♛	6

CONTROGUERRA (TE)

Camillo Montori
Piane Tronto, 23
64010 Controguerra (TE)
tel. 0861809900

Camillo Montori is a committed, active spokesman for the grape growers in the province of Teramo. He has been trying to relaunch Teramo's wines for many years, and a relaunch there has definitely been, at least as far as his leading wine, Montepulciano d'Abruzzo Fonte Cupa, goes. The wine reflects the estate's style, which gives power with immediate approachability, this time achieving even greater elegance and complexity. It is a dark ruby colour and offers varietal aromas of ripe red and black cherries. The palate reveals the softness that comes from a carefully constructed tannic weave, with fruit and oak in just the right measure and none of the all-too-common exaggeration. It finishes long and evenly, with a liquorice aftertaste. Controguerra Leneo Moro was vinified with a more international approach and skilfully focuses on the force given by cabernet, together with the supple softness of montepulciano. Hence, fruity, vegetal and leather notes dominate the nose while the palate is soft and full, with smooth tannins and a spicy finish. The standard Montepulciano d'Abruzzo, clean, fruity and with good structure and drinkability, also wins Two Glasses. There is character in all the whites. Starting at the top, we have Leneo d'Oro, with an intriguing candied fruit nose, good acid and alcohol balance, and good length. The full, fresh Trebbiano d'Abruzzo Fonte Cupa evokes peach and ripe apple, the new Sauvignon is absolutely true to the variety's style and the basic Trebbiano d'Abruzzo is clean and attractive.

● Montepulciano d'Abruzzo Colline Teramane Fonte Cupa '98	4*
○ Controguerra Leneo d'Oro '00	5
● Montepulciano d'Abruzzo '00	3*
● Controguerra Leneo Moro '98	6
◉ Montepulciano d'Abruzzo Cerasuolo Fonte Cupa '01	3
○ Sauvignon '01	3
○ Trebbiano d'Abruzzo '01	2*
○ Trebbiano d'Abruzzo Fonte Cupa '01	3
○ Controguerra Leneo Moro '97	4
● Montepulciano d'Abruzzo Colline Teramane Fonte Cupa '97	4

FRANCAVILLA AL MARE (CH)

Franco Pasetti
C.da Pretaro - Via San Paolo, 21
66023 Francavilla al Mare (CH)
tel. 08561875 - 0856920041
e-mail: vignetipasetti@hotmail.com

We didn't doubt that Mimmo Pasetti and his father Franco would be able to maintain results at the levels of recent years, despite the difficulties that accompanied the splitting up of the estate. Both montepulciano-based reds gained Two Glasses. Testarossa is deeply coloured. The nose is initially a little closed but then opens out to give black berry fruit with the faintest hint of edginess. It regains ground on the palate, which has good stuffing and is held together by a fairly well-defined tannic weave. The finish is long, showing delicate oak toast on the aftertaste. The inexpensive Fattoria Pasetti is a more direct, "drink-me" wine. It is a concentrated, almost black colour and has well-defined, varietal aromas of blackberry and black cherry. The initial impact on the palate is decisive and warm, then it develops to give fullness and good balance, with well-gauged fruit and oak. Testarossa Bianco, from chardonnay and trebbiano aged in tonneaux, is up to its usual standard and marries good extract with attractive freshness. The palate is both balanced and lively from start to finish. The other two whites are also appealing. The Pecorino is centred on its citrus-like nose and the good acidity typical of the variety. The Trebbiano d'Abruzzo has delicate apple aromas and less extractive weight. Finally, the Cerasuolo has good character, with its bright colour, its shy cherry-like nose and its gentle fullness on the palate.

● Montepulciano d'Abruzzo Fattoria Pasetti '00	3*
○ Tenuta di Testarossa Bianco '01	5
● Montepulciano d'Abruzzo Tenuta di Testarossa '99	5
◉ Montepulciano d'Abruzzo Cerasuolo Tenuta Pasetti '01	3
○ Pecorino Fattoria Pasetti '01	3
○ Trebbiano d'Abruzzo Fattoria Pasetti '01	2*
○ Tenuta di Testarossa Bianco '00	4
● Montepulciano d'Abruzzo Tenuta di Testarossa '98	4
● Montepulciano d'Abruzzo '99	3*

GIULIANOVA (TE)

FARAONE
LOC. COLLERANESCO
VIA NAZIONALE PER TERAMO, 290
64020 GIULIANOVA (TE)
TEL. 0858071804
E-MAIL: faraone.vini@tin.it

You don't expect reds from Giovanni Faraone. And yet this producer, who had previously accustomed us to his fine, long-lived, trebbiano and passerina-based whites, has surprised us. Let's start with the Montepulciano d'Abruzzo Le Vigne, a wine that fully expresses the character of the variety in its deep ruby colour and a nose of red and black cherry layered with light oak spiciness. The palate has good extract and richness on the finish, with fruit and spice returning on the aftertaste. The Santa Maria dell'Arco has less definition on the nose, which is initially closed, but is better on the palate. Although a touch rustic, it has a powerful structure, tannins on the way to gaining definition and a long, full finish. The Santa Maria dell'Arco Bianco selection has a bright, deep colour, and complexity on the ripe fruit and mineral nose. It could do with a touch more weight on the palate, although there is ample freshness and good depth of flavour, plus balsamic notes. The Trebbiano Le Vigne is as fragrant as usual. It is centred on elderflower notes and citrus fruitiness on both nose and palate. The acidity may appear a mite harsh but the experience of previous vintages suggests that this will bring good developments in the wine over the next couple of years.

LORETO APRUTINO (PE)

★ **EDOARDO VALENTINI**
VIA DEL BAIO, 2
65014 LORETO APRUTINO (PE)
TEL. 0858291138

Edoardo and Francesco Paolo Valentini only submitted two wines this year, the Trebbiano d'Abruzzo and the Cerasuolo. Each is clearly the best example of its respective style in the region. This speaks for itself. The '96 Montepulciano d'Abruzzo was not bottled so all eyes are on the '97, which will probably be released at the end of 2002. "Natura non facit saltus" (Nature doesn't leap), as Valentini loves to say. Meanwhile, let's enjoy the unique complexity of the '99 Trebbiano. Give it a bit of time to open and out comes that elegant, minerally nose with its ripe citrus aromas. Take a sip and see how full and mouthfilling it is, how piquant and almost fat. Note how refined the flavours are, how intense they are rendered by its swathe of acidity, the sort that gives wines like this great potential for improvement with age. Observe how long the minerally finish is with its notes of hazelnut and liquorice root. Three elegant Glasses, and the vintage wasn't even one of Abruzzo's best. The '00 Cerasuolo, from montepulciano, is without doubt one of Italy's best rosés. It was released a year and a half after the vintage, having undergone a period in cask and it, too, stands out for its originality of style. The colour is coral pink and the nose evokes ripe apricot and Mediterranean spices. The palate is rich, with intense minerality and ripe cherry fruitiness. It's a miniature masterpiece, once more refuting the unjust belief that this is an inconsequential wine style.

● Montepulciano d'Abruzzo Le Vigne '00	▲▲	3*
● Montepulciano d'Abruzzo S. Maria dell'Arco '99	▲▲	4
◉ Montepulciano d'Abruzzo Cerasuolo Le Vigne '01	▲	3
○ Trebbiano d'Abruzzo Le Vigne '01	▲	3
○ Trebbiano d'Abruzzo S. Maria dell'Arco '99	▲	4
● Montepulciano d'Abruzzo S. Maria dell'Arco '98	▲▲	4

○ Trebbiano d'Abruzzo '99	▲▲▲	8
◉ Montepulciano d'Abruzzo Cerasuolo '00	▲▲	7
● Montepulciano d'Abruzzo '77	▲▲▲	6
● Montepulciano d'Abruzzo '85	▲▲▲	6
● Montepulciano d'Abruzzo '88	▲▲▲	6
○ Trebbiano d'Abruzzo '88	▲▲▲	5
● Montepulciano d'Abruzzo '90	▲▲▲	6
● Montepulciano d'Abruzzo '92	▲▲▲	6
○ Trebbiano d'Abruzzo '92	▲▲▲	5
● Montepulciano d'Abruzzo '95	▲▲▲	6
○ Trebbiano d'Abruzzo '98	▲▲	5
◉ Montepulciano d'Abruzzo Cerasuolo '97	▲▲	5
◉ Montepulciano d'Abruzzo Cerasuolo '98	▲▲	5

NOTARESCO (TE)

BRUNO NICODEMI
C.DA VENIGLIO
64024 NOTARESCO (TE)
TEL. 085895493
E-MAIL: fattorie.nicodemi@libero.it

Elena and Alessandro Nicodemi, like various other producers, decided not to release a Montepulciano d'Abruzzo selection in '99, because of the poor vintage. This, however, has given their new consultant Paolo Caciorgna breathing space to immerse himself more deeply in the Abruzzo scene and concentrate on developing the style he wants for the anything but poor 2000 harvest. The basic Montepulciano d'Abruzzo from '00 is ready and extremely enjoyable. It has been one of the best wines in its class for years. Dark ruby, it has a nose this year that has changed style and gained balsamic and lightly toasty notes, in addition to the red berry fruit. There is the merest touch of aggressiveness on the palate, but this is soon lost in the gentle red and black cherry flavours and the liquorice on the aftertaste. The Cerasuolo also gives a pleasing impression with its good nose-palate consistency. The fruit takes on a light spiciness and there is an almondy note on the finish. Both Trebbiano d'Abruzzos have good presence. The Selection tends to be the fleshier, and is focused on the greater ripeness of its fruit, although in this vintage, '01, it is at the expense of freshness of flavour. The simpler version is better balanced. The bright straw introduces aromas of wild herbs, peaches and apricots, then the palate evokes orange blossom and is fairly long.

● Montepulciano d'Abruzzo '00	🍷🍷	4
◉ Montepulciano d'Abruzzo Cerasuolo '01	🍷🍷	3*
○ Trebbiano d'Abruzzo '01	🍷	3
○ Trebbiano d'Abruzzo Selezione '01	🍷	4
○ Trebbiano d'Abruzzo Bacco '00	🍷🍷	3*
● Montepulciano d'Abruzzo Bacco '97	🍷🍷	5
● Montepulciano d'Abruzzo Colline Teramane Bacco '98	🍷🍷	5

OFENA (AQ)

TENUTA CATALDI MADONNA
LOC. PIANO
67025 OFENA (AQ)
TEL. 0854911680
E-MAIL: azagrluigicataldimadonna@tin.it

Luigi Cataldi Madonna's wines scored very well on average this year. There wasn't the Three Glass peak for Tonì that a better vintage than '99 might have given, but breaking that barrier doesn't seem far off. In addition, his winemaker Giovanni Bailo is steadily improving everything in the basic and intermediate lines, apart from Pecorino, which he has still to master. The Occhiorosso, from cabernet sauvignon, is very deep in colour and has intense varietal aromas. The palate is rendered even more enticing by flavours of small berry fruit and pencil lead that appear on the good finish. Malandrino, from montepulciano and cabernet, is less vegetal, and instead has more black cherry and bramble. The full, deep palate mirrors the nose perfectly and its tannins have begun to bed down. The basic Montepulciano d'Abruzzo is successful, too. It is a purple-tinged dark ruby. There is nicely open ripe red berry fruit and a light oakiness, which add interest to the flavour. Tonì brings the reds to a close. Dark and opaque, it has a nose that is reticent at first. Then the wine's ripe red berry fruit comes to the fore on the palate, where the usual outstanding character comes through. Finally comes the Trebbiano d'Abruzzo, which is as well-styled as ever, and the two attention-worthy Cerasuolos, of which Cataldi is one of the leading producers. Piè delle Vigne is especially good. Its colour is closer to ruby than cherry pink but the red berry fruitiness has perfect definition and the palate is fresh, with tightly knit structure.

● Malandrino '00	🍷🍷	4
● Montepulciano d'Abruzzo '00	🍷🍷	3*
● Occhiorosso '00	🍷🍷	5
◉ Montepulciano d'Abruzzo Cerasuolo Piè delle Vigne '01	🍷🍷	4
● Montepulciano d'Abruzzo Tonì '99	🍷🍷	6
◉ Montepulciano d'Abruzzo Cerasuolo '01	🍷	3
○ Pecorino '01	🍷	5
○ Trebbiano d'Abruzzo '01	🍷	2*
● Montepulciano d'Abruzzo Tonì '98	🍷🍷	5
● Montepulciano d'Abruzzo '99	🍷🍷	3*
● Occhiorosso '99	🍷🍷	5

ORTONA (CH)

AGRIVERDE
LOC. C.DA CALDARI
VIA MONTE MAIELLA, 118
66020 ORTONA (CH)
TEL. 0859032101 - 0859039054
E-MAIL: info@agriverde.it

Giannicola Di Carlo's wines continue to grow in quality and reputation. His magnificent new cellar, designed using ecologically sound architectural principles and fitted with state-of-the-art equipment, reveals the extent of his ambitions for the future. The team of Paride Marino on the commercial side and the able Riccardo Brighigna handling the winemaking is bringing results, as this year's scores confirm. The best of the bunch just had to be Plateo, a concentrated, harmonious, modern-styled offering. It gives the impression of having been designed with paper and pencil, from which both its strengths and its limits can be inferred. The colour is deep ruby, then the nose has red berry fruit and well judged oak. The palate is soft, with ripe tannins and flavours spanning chocolate, coffee, spicy pepper and rosemary. The standard version, Riseis, is quite different. Ruby in colour, its purple tinges show its youth. The nose is initially reticent, then opens to give ripe berry fruit and light spiciness. The palate starts soft and full, then develops well, giving surprisingly good definition before finishing on hints of bitter chocolate and coffee. Between Plateo and Riseis come Riseis Selezione which, in comparison with both, needs a little more depth on the palate, and Natum, an organic Montepulciano d'Abruzzo, which is more immediate. There are no surprises from the Riseis Cerasuolo, which has won prizes in several Italian competitions, and the enjoyably fresh and fruity Chardonnay Tresor.

ORTONA (CH)

FARNESE
P.ZZA PORTA CALDARI, 26
66026 ORTONA (CH)
TEL. 0859067388
E-MAIL: farnesevini@tin.it

Farnese produces over 8,500,000 bottles a year, making it one of Abruzzo's largest wineries. Looking after production are Valentino Sciotti, who purchases grapes from a selected group of growers, agronomist Romano D'Amario, who takes care of the 120 hectares of vineyard owned by the company, and winemakers Filippo Baccalaro and Mario Flacco. They are responsible for a wide range of wines, from the region's classic DOCs, Montepulciano d'Abruzzo and Trebbiano d'Abruzzo, to internationally styled IGTs. Two wines in particular stood out in our tastings, Edizione Seconda and Chardonnay Opis '00. The former is a full-bodied, characterful red from a successful blend of Abruzzo's montepulciano and Puglia's primitivo. The colour is deep and dark, and the palate is powerful, full of extract, and so rich in red berry fruit it is almost Australian in style, but also very Mediterranean. It can offer soft tannins, notable alcohol and good length. The Chardonnay is a good deep straw colour, introducing a nose that is full of vanilla, pineapple and ripe apples. The rich, fleshy palate has plentiful structure and is enlivened by fresh citrus flavours that bring good overall balance. White peach and vanilla round off the aftertaste. The other wines include a successful Sangiovese Don Camillo '01, with black cherry and chocolate on both its nose and the nicely rich palate, and a Montepulciano d'Abruzzo Riserva '97 that marries plentiful alcohol with finesse.

● Montepulciano d'Abruzzo Plateo '97	ΨΨ	6
● Montepulciano d'Abruzzo Riseis '00	ΨΨ	3*
○ Chardonnay Tresor '01	Ψ	2*
○ Chardonnay Villa Roscià '01	Ψ	1*
⊙ Montepulciano d'Abruzzo Cerasuolo Riseis '01	Ψ	2*
● Montepulciano d'Abruzzo Natum '01	Ψ	2*
○ Trebbiano d'Abruzzo Natum '01	Ψ	1*
○ Trebbiano d'Abruzzo Riseis '01	Ψ	2*
● Montepulciano d'Abruzzo Riseis Sel. '98	Ψ	4
● Montepulciano d'Abruzzo Plateo '95	ΨΨ	5

○ Chardonnay Opis '00	ΨΨ	5
● Edizione Second Release	ΨΨ	5
● Sangiovese Don Camillo '01	Ψ	3
● Montepulciano d'Abruzzo Opis Ris. '97	Ψ	5
● Montepulciano d'Abruzzo Casale Vecchio '01		4

ORTONA (CH)

SARCHESE DORA
C.DA CALDARI STAZIONE, 65
66026 ORTONA (CH)
TEL. 0859031249

PESCARA

CONTESA DI ROCCO PASETTI
LOC. COLLECORVINO
C.DA CAPARRONE, 9
65100 PESCARA
TEL. 0854549622

The young, enthusiastic brother and sister team, Nicola and Esmeralda D'Auria, with support from consultant Leonardo Seghetti, worthily retain the place in the Guide they first gained last year. The D'Aurias welcome the many visitors to their small but well-equipped cellar with great hospitality, as if they were guests in their home, but their efforts focus on bringing the character of their homeland, Ortona, into their wines. Success has come chiefly from their two Montepulciano d'Abruzzos, both Two Glasses wines. Rosso di Macchia, the '99, is the more serious of the two and is as impressive as last year's release, although in a minor key because of the inferior vintage. It is an intense ruby and the nose is perfectly clean, with red berry fruits and balsamic notes. The carefully gauged contribution from oak is equally balanced on the nicely full, concentrated palate. The other Montepulciano d'Abruzzo, Pietrosa, reveals youthful impetuousness in its purple colour. The nose is rich, with clear ripe black cherry aromas that knit well into its oaky tones. The palate is not particularly deep, which makes for great drinkability. The whites are less exciting but still well styled, with better defined fresh florality on the Trebbiano d'Abruzzo and Chardonnay Pietrosa than on the Bianco della Rocca. The Bianco della Rocca comes from grapes picked when in a state of advanced ripeness but we feel that it still hasn't quite found its true identity.

This is a new entry, but only formally so, as it relates to the 25 hectares Rocco Pasetti acquired in Collecorvino, near Pescara, following the division of the Pasetti family estate. It's a new adventure for Rocco and, as one of Abruzzo's most renowned winemakers, he has taken it up with enthusiasm, as have his wife Patrizia and their children Franco and Perla. Their commitment is already vindicated by results. The oak-aged Montepulciano d'Abruzzo Vigna Corvino, for instance, is one of the best of Abruzzo's less expensive reds. It had no problem competing on equal terms with some of the biggest names in our tasting finals. It is outstanding in its simplicity and adherence to type, while also allowing notes of violet and red berry fruits jam to come through on the nose. Those notes become fresher and spicier on the palate, which has a liquorice aftertaste. The Contesa selection is a notch down the scale. Its nose is elegant but more subdued, and the palate is sweeter and a little less even. A new, definitive white selection is on its way, in the meantime we have the promising first release of Pasetti's Pecorino, following on the wave of renewed interest in this variety and its small but growing group of converts. It picked up Two Glasses with its deep straw colour, aromas of ripe citrus fruit and balsamic herbs, and balanced palate with good acidity and a long, slightly almondy finish. The Cerasuolo and Trebbiano d'Abruzzo Vigna Corvino are attractive and make for good drinking.

● Montepulciano d'Abruzzo Pietrosa '00	▯▯	3*
● Montepulciano d'Abruzzo Rosso di Macchia '99	▯▯	5
○ Chardonnay Pietrosa '01	▯	2*
⊙ Montepulciano d'Abruzzo Cerasuolo Pietrosa '01	▯	2*
○ Trebbiano d'Abruzzo Pietrosa '01	▯	2*
○ Bianco della Rocca '01		3
● Montepulciano d'Abruzzo Rosso di Macchia '98	▯▯	5
● Montepulciano d'Abruzzo Pietrosa '99	▯▯	3*

● Montepulciano d'Abruzzo Vigna Corvino '00	▯▯	3*
○ Pecorino Contesa '01	▯▯	5
● Montepulciano d'Abruzzo Contesa '98	▯▯	5
⊙ Montepulciano d'Abruzzo Cerasuolo Vigna Corvino '01	▯	3
○ Trebbiano d'Abruzzo Vigna Corvino '01	▯	3

ROSCIANO (PE)

MARRAMIERO
C.DA SANT'ANDREA, 1
65010 ROSCIANO (PE)
TEL. 0858505766
E-MAIL: azmarram@tin.it

Marramiero is now established as one of Abruzzo's top estates, mainly as a result of Enrico Marramiero's business skills and his choice of colleagues, manager Antonio Chiavaroli and oenologist Romeo Taraborrelli, who take part in decision-making. There is also a superb cellar, inaugurated last year, from which emerge wines that all have character. Let's start with Montepulciano d'Abruzzo Inferi, an intriguing, modern-styled wine pervasive red berry fruit aromas that mingle well with oak vanilla. The palate is soft and well structured, with ripe tannins, and cocoa powder and liquorice on the finish. Incanto is in a less imposing style. Its nose is less distinct and more focused on a mix of fruity and vegetal notes, then the soft palate has pencil lead and liquorice on the finish. The third red down the line is Dama. Still very attractive, it has a purple colour and sensations of violet and ripe black cherry on both nose and palate. Chardonnay Punta di Colle, fermented and aged in barrique, is one of Abruzzo's best whites. It is a deep, bright yellow, the nose is clean and enticing, with ripe apricot interweaving with well judged oakiness and mineral hints. The palate is nicely full, if less so than expected, and has elegance and flavours of candied fruit and toasted almond. Trebbiano d'Abruzzo Altare, it too barrique-aged, is less impressive. The nose has good presence but the balance on the palate seems tenuous. Trebbiano d'Abruzzo Anima, clean and nicely structured, showed fairly well.

ROSETO DEGLI ABRUZZI (TE)

ORLANDI CONTUCCI PONNO
LOC. PIANA DEGLI ULIVI, 1
64026 ROSETO DEGLI ABRUZZI (TE)
TEL. 0858944049
E-MAIL: orlandi.contucci@libero.it

Marina Orlandi Contucci's great adventure continues with as much effort and zeal as ever. It is heartening to see how she manages to push the quality of her wines that little bit higher each year. Liburnio '99, from a fascinating blend of cabernet, sangiovese and montepulciano, is right on the Three Glass border line. It is so deep it looks black. The nose has ripe, small red berry fruit and light spiciness. The fleshy, elegant palate has tightly-knit tannins, as well as fruit and liquorice that return on the aftertaste, and balance and depth throughout. All this bodes well for longevity. The latest release of Montepulciano d'Abruzzo has good character and power with elegance, fully expressing the characteristics of both its grape variety and its origin. However, Cabernet Colle Funaro seemed a touch below par, although it has richness and good extract. Good-scoring whites include the Sauvignon and the Chardonnay. As usual, the former has good varietal character with its herbaceous, acacia blossom aromas. The Chardonnay is delicately fragrant on the nose and fairly light on the palate. The Trebbiano d'Abruzzo Colle della Corte is nicely expressive too, with a bright hue and lightly floral aromas. The same florality also comes through on the palate. We finish with Cerasuolo Vermiglio, which is a deep pink colour, has delicate aromas of cherry and green spices, and is freshly flavoured with a touch of almond on the finish.

● Montepulciano d'Abruzzo Inferi '98 ♟♟	5
○ Chardonnay Punta di Colle '99 ♟♟	5
● Montepulciano d'Abruzzo Incanto '99 ♟♟	5
○ Trebbiano d'Abruzzo Altare '00 ♟	5
◉ Montepulciano d'Abruzzo Cerasuolo Dama '01 ♟	3
○ Trebbiano d'Abruzzo Anima '01 ♟	4
○ Trebbiano d'Abruzzo Dama '01 ♟	3
● Montepulciano d'Abruzzo Dama '99 ♟	3
○ Marramiero Brut ♟	6
● Montepulciano d'Abruzzo Inferi '95 ♟♟	4
● Montepulciano d'Abruzzo Inferi '96 ♟♟	5
● Montepulciano d'Abruzzo Inferi '97 ♟♟	5
● Montepulciano d'Abruzzo Incanto '98 ♟♟	4

● Liburnio '99 ♟♟	7
● Montepulciano d'Abruzzo La Regia Specula '00 ♟♟	4
● Cabernet Sauvignon Colle Funaro '99 ♟♟	5
○ Chardonnay Roccesco '01 ♟	4
◉ Montepulciano d'Abruzzo Cerasuolo Vermiglio '01 ♟	3
○ Sauvignon Ghiaiolo '01 ♟	4
○ Trebbiano d'Abruzzo Colle della Corte '01 ♟	4
● Cabernet Sauvignon Colle Funaro '97 ♟♟	5
● Liburnio '97 ♟♟	7
● Cabernet Sauvignon Colle Funaro '98 ♟♟	5
● Liburnio '98 ♟♟	7

SAN MARTINO SULLA MARRUCINA (CH)

GIANNI MASCIARELLI
VIA GAMBERALE, 1
66010 SAN MARTINO SULLA MARRUCINA (CH)
TEL. 087185241

Again this year, at least four of Gianni Masciarelli's wines showed as some of the best in the region but only one hit Three Glasses. Again, it was the extraordinary Villa Gemma, for the sixth time in a row. As usual, it is an opaque ruby with a rich, elegant, complex nose. The palate has remarkable flow. The first impact gives both power and refinement, then the fruit appears, followed by flavours of tar, cocoa beans, balsam and the classic liquorice. Montepulciano d'Abruzzo Marina Cvetic '99 is only an inch behind. It, too, is fleshy and concentrated, but more measured. Its aromas are more focused on ripe black cherry and blackberry, and pencil lead. The flavours fill the mouth with fruit and it is very long: in short, a sheer joy to drink. Which brings us to the two whites. We believe that with the '00 vintage, the Trebbiano d'Abruzzo Marina Cvetic has reached a high point. It's a wine that manages to combine great extract, a nose of finesse, fruit warmth and mineral freshness, power and depth of flavour. The Chardonnay, more directed towards warm, ripe tones mingling with delicate oakiness, follows closely behind. Also one of the best is the standard Montepulciano d'Abruzzo, an immediate, but rich and structured, wine that easily won Two Glasses. We should add that Masciarelli did not submit his excellent Cabernet Sauvignon, which we have tasted elsewhere. He produces around 2,000 bottles, too few, he reckons, to be easily available to readers.

● Montepulciano d'Abruzzo Villa Gemma '98	▼▼▼	7
○ Chardonnay Marina Cvetic '00	▼▼	6
○ Trebbiano d'Abruzzo Marina Cvetic '00	▼▼	6
● Montepulciano d'Abruzzo Marina Cvetic S. Martino Rosso '99	▼▼	5
● Montepulciano d'Abruzzo '00	▼▼	3*
○ Montepulciano d'Abruzzo Cerasuolo Villa Gemma '01	▼▼	4
⊙ Rosato '01	▼	2*
○ Trebbiano d'Abruzzo '01	▼	2*
○ Villa Gemma Bianco '01	▼	4
● Montepulciano d'Abruzzo Villa Gemma '97	▼▼▼	6

SPOLTORE (PE)

FATTORIA LA VALENTINA
VIA COLLE CESI, 10
65010 SPOLTORE (PE)
TEL. 0854478158
E-MAIL: info@fattorialavalentina.it

Steady, meticulous work lies behind the consistently fine showing of the wines from this estate, run by young Sabatino Di Properzio with consultancy from Luca D'Attoma. Just like last year, it is the Montepulciano d'Abruzzo Spelt that tops the tree and came close to Three Glasses. It is a beautifully made wine, clearly recognisable by the pepper and rosemary on the nose that, for a moment, take your mind away from Montepulciano d'Abruzzo typicity. It is only a moment because the classic fruit character comes through on the palate and does so with its customary force and elegance. Both front and mid palate have harmony, the tannins are finely grained, the finish is firm and there is good depth. Montepulciano d'Abruzzo Binomio is the result of an unusual idea that cropped up over two years ago: a wine made in collaboration with the Veneto producer, Stefano Inama. The wine has great depth. The nose reveals, one after the other, black berry fruit, spice and hints of balsam. The palate has a slight touch of rawness at first, but is full, fresh and long. Next comes a basic Montepulciano d'Abruzzo – next year there will be another, which is already looking promising – which is much less expensive but very nearly as interesting. The purple-tinged ruby ushers in a nose of medium intensity. The bitterness of the oak tannins plays some tricks with its light structure, but it still makes for enjoyable drinking. Both the Trebbiano d'Abruzzo and the Cerasuolo are uncomplicated and straightforward.

● Montepulciano d'Abruzzo Spelt '98	▼▼	5
● Montepulciano d'Abruzzo '00	▼▼	3*
● Montepulciano d'Abruzzo Binomio '99	▼▼	6
⊙ Montepulciano d'Abruzzo Cerasuolo '01	▼	3
○ Trebbiano d'Abruzzo '01	▼	3
● Montepulciano d'Abruzzo Spelt '97	▼▼	4
● Montepulciano d'Abruzzo Spelt '96	▼▼	4
● Montepulciano d'Abruzzo Binomio '98	▼▼	5

TOCCO DA CASAURIA (PE)

FILOMUSI GUELFI
VIA F. FILOMUSI GUELFI, 11
65028 TOCCO DA CASAURIA (PE)
TEL. 08598353 - 085986908

Lorenzo Filomusi Guelfi now seems to have found his stride, which is always a good thing for a small, serious-minded producer. He fixed up his cellar a couple of years ago to handle the entire production from his vineyards in the Ceppete area and now, with the help of oenologist Romano D'Amario, his wines have reached a more than decent quality level. There is potential for even greater things. The style is traditional and pays little attention to fashion. This is a winning strategy, as is confirmed by Vigna Fonte Dei. On its second release, it easily repeated last year's good showing. The colour is a deep ruby, then the lightly vegetal nose is forthright and pervasive, with red berry and stone fruits. The palate is rich and full, with notes of earth and liquorice on the firm finish. The other Montepulciano d'Abruzzo comes from an excellent vintage, the '00. It has a deep colour and a nose that has still to open. The oak is elegant, but hardly emerges above the underlying fruit. Morello cherry and blackberry flavours make a lively start to the soft palate, which leaves long-lasting sensations of cocoa powder, roast coffee and liquorice. The white Scuderie del Cielo, from chardonnay, sauvignon and malvasia, also makes a good impression with its aromas of apple and ripe tropical fruit, its fragrant, long palate, and its lightly perfumed finish. Finally comes the fruited, well-structured Cerasuolo, which very nearly attained Two Glasses.

● Montepulciano d'Abruzzo '00	♈♈	4
○ Le Scuderie del Cielo '01	♈	3
◉ Montepulciano d'Abruzzo Cerasuolo '01	♈	3
◉ Montepulciano d'Abruzzo Cerasuolo '00	♈♈	3*
● Montepulciano d'Abruzzo Vigna Fonte Dei '97	♈♈	4
● Montepulciano d'Abruzzo '97	♈	3
● Montepulciano d'Abruzzo '99	♈	3

TOLLO (CH)

CANTINA TOLLO
VIA GARIBALDI, 68
66010 TOLLO (CH)
TEL. 087196251
E-MAIL: produzione@cantinatollo.it

Last year, we mentioned the imminent arrival of a new wine from Cantina Tollo. The wait was well worthwhile. Called Montepulciano d'Abruzzo Aldiano, it marks the first outcome of a project to manage several vineyards situated in particularly good areas directly. It is a wine for all pockets and its immediacy is striking. Even the purple-ruby colour is lively in the glass. The nose has clean, concentrated aromas of wild cherry and pomegranate. These fruits come back on the palate, cushioned by an attractive softness. There is also depth, solid, crisp structure, soft tannins and juicy drinkability. Montepulciano d'Abruzzo Cagiolo is still coming round, but is already more complex. The red berry fruitiness of the nose is slightly covered by the still rather dominant oak while, on the palate, the tannic impact quickly dies down to leave space for flavours of blackberry, black cherry, vanilla and liquorice. Cagiolo Bianco, fermented and aged briefly in oak, has lots going for it. Apple, banana and tropical fruit, with balsamic notes, keep the attention on the nose for a long time. The palate holds up well and shows good length. Of the two other whites from trebbiano, mixed with smaller quantities of other varieties, we liked the florality and rounded drinkability of the Aldiano and the uncomplicatedly fresh taste of the Colle Secco. Valle d'Oro Cerasuolo, a frequent prize-winner in Italy, is again one of the best in its class.

● Montepulciano d'Abruzzo Aldiano '00	♈♈	5
○ Cagiòlo Bianco '01	♈♈	5
◉ Montepulciano d'Abruzzo Cerasuolo Valle d'Oro '01	♈♈	2*
● Montepulciano d'Abruzzo Cagiòlo '98	♈♈	5
○ Trebbiano d'Abruzzo Colle Secco '01	♈	4*
● Montepulciano d'Abruzzo Valle d'Oro '99	♈	2*
○ Cagiòlo Bianco '00	♈♈	5
● Montepulciano d'Abruzzo '97	♈♈	4
● Montepulciano d'Abruzzo Colle Secco Rubino '98	♈♈	4*

OTHER WINERIES

SPINELLI
VIA PIANA LA FARA, 90
66041 ATESSA (CH)
TEL. 0872897916
E-MAIL: info@cantinespinelli.it

We feel that the recent changes to the Spinelli siblings' technical set-up should bring them new and greater rewards. Meanwhile, the concentrated, expressive Tatone '98 and the simpler, more direct Terra d'Aligi are both worth investigating.

● Montepulciano d'Abruzzo Tatone '98 ♟♟	4
● Montepulciano d'Abruzzo Terra d'Aligi '00 ♟	3
○ Trebbiano d'Abruzzo Terra d'Aligi '01 ♟	3
● Montepulciano d'Abruzzo Quartana '00 ♟♟	2*

VILLA MEDORO
FRAZ. FONTANELLE
64030 ATRI (TE)
TEL. 0858708142

This estate is well organized and young Federica Morricone, who runs it, is aiming high. Achievements so far are illustrated by the standard Montepulciano d'Abruzzo and the Rosso del Duca version, which has good definition in its fruit and the balsamic hints ceded by the oak.

● Montepulciano d'Abruzzo Rosso del Duca '98 ♟♟	4
⊙ Montepulciano d'Abruzzo Cerasuolo '01 ♟	3
● Montepulciano d'Abruzzo '98 ♟	3
● Montepulciano d'Abruzzo '99 ♟	3

BORGO DI COLLOREDO
C.DA ZEZZA, 8
86042 CAMPOMARINO (CB)
TEL. 087557453
E-MAIL: info@borgodicolloredo.com

This year, Enrico and Pasquale Di Giulio did not release the top wine, Gironia Rosso, after the difficult '99 vintage. Instead, the well-shaped, nicely balanced Aglianico takes pride of place. The Falanghina, which nearly gained Two Glasses, is the best of the whites. Everything else is good.

● Aglianico '00 ♟♟	4
○ Biferno Bianco Gironia '01 ♟	3
○ Molise Falanghina '01 ♟	3

MADONNA DEI MIRACOLI
C.DA TERMINE, 38
66021 CASALBORDINO (CH)
TEL. 0873918107 - 0873918420
E-MAIL: msic@vinicasalbordino.com

Estate chair Alberto Tiberio and oenologist Beniamino Di Domenica continue to bring work here into sharper focus. The Castel Verdino line is the one to watch but the cheaper wines should not be overlooked.

● Montepulciano d'Abruzzo Castel Verdino '99 ♟♟	4
○ Chardonnay Castel Verdino '00 ♟	4
● Montepulciano d'Abruzzo Contea di Bordino '00 ♟	3*
○ Chardonnay Castel Verdino '99 ♟♟	4

San Lorenzo
C.da Plavignano, 2
64075 Castilenti (TE)
tel. 0861999325 - 0861998542
e-mail: sanlorenzovini@tiscali.it

This new winery situated on the border of the provinces of Teramo and Pescara is now established as strongly white-orientated. The new Alhena, from chardonnay, is excellent.

○ Chardonnay Alhena '00	ΨΨ	5
○ Chardonnay Chioma di Berenice '01	Ψ	4
● Montepulciano d'Abruzzo Antares '98	Ψ	3

Antonio e Elio Monti
C.da Pignotto, 62
64010 Controguerra (TE)
tel. 086189042
e-mail: emilmon@tin.it

The new direction taken by brothers Antonio and Elio Monti, now with consultant Riccardo Cotarella on board, is epitomized this year by their base Montepulciano d'Abruzzo. It is a rich, concentrated wine that reflects the characteristics of the Teramo area to perfection.

● Montepulciano d'Abruzzo '01	ΨΨ	4

Nestore Bosco
C.da Casali, 7
65010 Nocciano (PE)
tel. 085847345 - 085847139
e-mail: info@nestoreboschi.com

The potential of this long-standing winery still remains to be seen. There is a good, solid base, now bolstered by the arrival of new blood on the winemaking side, which has boosted enthusiasm. This year, Montepulciano d'Abruzzo '01 gains the plaudits for its concentration.

● Montepulciano d'Abruzzo '01	Ψ	3
● Montepulciano d'Abruzzo '98	Ψ	4
● Montepulciano d'Abruzzo Pan '98	Ψ	5

Chiusa Grande
C.da Casali
65010 Nocciano (PE)
tel. 085847460 - 0858470818
e-mail: fdeusan@libero.it

Franco D'Eusanio's estate is one of those that are totally committed to organic methods. The wines grow every year, both in number and quality.

● Montepulciano d'Abruzzo Rocco Secco '00	Ψ	3
● Montepulciano d'Abruzzo Perla Nera '98	Ψ	4

Citra
C.da Cucullo
66026 Ortona (CH)
tel. 0859031342
e-mail: citra@citra.it

This consortium of co-operatives is making great efforts to improve quality, notably with its flagship wine, Caroso, and across a wide range of good-value bottles.

● Montepulciano d'Abruzzo Caroso '97	ΨΨ	5
● Sangiovese Terre di Chieti '01	Ψ	1*
● Montepulciano d'Abruzzo Villa Torre '00	Ψ	3

Chiarieri
Via Sant'Angelo, 10
65019 Pianella (PE)
tel. 085971365 - 085973313

The quality of Giovanni and Ciriaco Chiarieri's wines is no longer a surprise, especially when it comes to reds. The Hannibal selection has a powerful, classic style and Granara marries good structure with pleasurable drinking.

● Montepulciano d'Abruzzo Hannibal '98	ΨΨ	4
● Montepulciano d'Abruzzo Granaro '01	Ψ	2*
● Montepulciano d'Abruzzo Hannibal '97	ΨΨ	4

Valle Reale
Loc. San Calisto
65026 Popoli (PE)
tel. 0458876168

Valle Reale, with 30 hectares under vine, is a new estate belonging to the Verona-based Pizzolo group. The two Montepulciano d'Abruzzos, released for the first time this year, are striking, especially San Calisto, which picked up Two Glasses.

- Montepulciano d'Abruzzo
  San Calisto '00 🍷🍷 5
- Montepulciano d'Abruzzo '00 🍷 4

Cantina Sociale Frentana
Via Perazza, 32
66020 Rocca San Giovanni (CH)
tel. 087260152
e-mail: info@cantinafrentana.it

At a stroke, chair Romanelli and able oenologist Gianni Pasquale have gained considerable ground for Cantina Frentana. Rubesto is a structured, complex wine. The well-made, inexpensive Frentano is surprisingly characterful.

- Montepulciano d'Abruzzo
  Frentano '01 🍷🍷 2*
- Montepulciano d'Abruzzo
  Rubesto '98 🍷🍷 3*

Valori
Via Torquato al Salinello
64027 Sant'Omero (TE)
tel. 086188461 - 0861796340
e-mail: vinivalori@tin.it

Luigi Valori, with help from Attilio Pagli's technical team, is working extremely hard in both vineyard and cellar to turn around the estate's entire set-up. This year, the best results again come from the standard-label Montepulciano d'Abruzzo.

- Montepulciano d'Abruzzo '01 🍷🍷 4
- Montepulciano d'Abruzzo
  Vigna S. Angelo '00 🍷
- ○ Trebbiano d'Abruzzo Preludio '01 🍷 3

Barone Cornacchia
C.da Torri
64010 Torano Nuovo (TE)
tel. 0861887412
e-mail: barone.cornacchia@tin.it

Even though Piero Cornacchia's estate has been relegated to this section because of space restrictions, all his wines scored well. Vigna Le Coste and Montepulciano Poggio Varano put on a particularly fine performance.

- Montepulciano d'Abruzzo
  Vigna Le Coste '00 🍷🍷 4
- Montepulciano d'Abruzzo
  Poggio Varano '00 🍷 4

Buccicatino
C.da Sterpara
66010 Vacri (CH)
tel. 0871720273
e-mail: buccicatino@libero.it

Umberto Buccicatino is one of the up-and-coming producers in Abruzzo. He has three well-made wines. The Cabernet Sauvignon is more immediate in style while the two Montepulciano d'Abruzzos will improve with time in bottle.

- Montepulciano d'Abruzzo
  Don Giovanni '00 🍷 6
- Montepulciano d'Abruzzo Stilla Rubra '99 🍷 6
- Cabernet Sauvignon '98 🍷 7

Torre Zambra
V.le Regina Margherita, 18
66010 Villamagna (CH)
tel. 0871300121

The full, elegant Brume Rosso is once more the best of Riccardo De Cerchio's wines. There are also two characterful whites in the Colle Maggio line, as well as an attractively priced Montepulciano d'Abruzzo.

- Montepulciano d'Abruzzo
  Brume Rosse '98 🍷🍷 5
- ○ Chardonnay Colle Maggio '01 🍷 3*
- ○ Trebbiano d'Abruzzo Colle Maggio '01 🍷 3
- Montepulciano d'Abruzzo Colle Maggio '99 🍷 4

CAMPANIA

This edition of the Guide amasses further evidence of Campania's standing in the crowded Italian wine scene. If, two millennia or so ago, no one thought to question the pre-eminence of the region's Falerno, during the last 50 years, the reputation of its wines rested more on faded memories of past glories than anything else. The latter part of the 20th century, though, saw a renaissance in Campania's wines. It was led by determined individuals, such as Antonio Mastroberardino, who never lost their belief in the potential of their wines. Their drive led to Fiano di Avellino, Greco di Tufo and Taurasi gaining great success, as did Falerno and the wines of Ischia. Nevertheless, we had to wait until the 1990s for a real advance in quality. During that decade, many new quality-driven estates arrived on the scene while many of the long-standing names revamped their vineyards and production facilities to take on the challenge of the global market. An exciting dynamism resulted and the new millennium sees Campania's reds and whites in stunning form. In addition, the territories of Avellino and Ischia have been joined by lands whose extraordinary wine-producing potential had never before been properly realized. Cilento, Terra di Lavoro, Massico, Taburno and the Costiera Amalfitana now give us exciting wines full of personality, the vast majority of them produced from traditional grape varieties such as aglianico, piedirosso, casavecchia, falanghina, greco and fiano. Meanwhile, it should be not be forgotten that wines of indisputable class also come from international varieties in the region, even though they are not planted widely. This brings us to this year's Three Glass wines. There are six, one more than last year. At the top of the tree is Feudi di San Gregorio, whose international reputation and quality makes it one of Italy's leading estates. Their fabulous merlot-based Pàtrimo '00 is our Red Wine of the Year. It is partnered by an Aglianico of tremendous personality, Serpico '00. Riccardo Cotarella, the oenologist who moulded these wines, is also behind the seventh top-notch vintage of Montevetrano, the '00. In its blending of international and indigenous varieties, this stunning red from the province of Salerno has become a sort of watershed in Campania's recent wine history. Antonio Caggiano joins the Three Glass elite with a Taurasi of supreme finesse, Vigna Macchia dei Goti '98; Cantina del Taburno hits the high spot with the second vintage of its spectacular Aglianico, Bue Apis '00; and Vestini Campagnano emerges into the limelight with an astounding Casavecchia '01, made from the grape variety of the same name. These last three are all made by Professor Luigi Moio who, with a team of researchers, is studying the region's terrains and grape varieties to help maximize their potential. In addition, a gaggle of Campanian wines reached the Three Glass finals. Now, that really is something to think about.

ATRIPALDA (AV)

Mastroberardino
Via Manfredi, 75/81
83042 Atripalda (AV)
Tel. 0825614111
E-mail: mastro@mastro.it

We owe this renowned estate a great deal. The rediscovery and success of wines such as Fiano d'Avellino and Greco di Tufo are down to Antonio Mastroberardino, as is the introduction into Campania, two decades ago, of what were then cutting-edge vinification techniques. There is also the set of memorable vintages of Taurasi which, even after over 30 years, are still vital and resplendent. Of the many wines in the estate's current range, the most interesting this year was Naturalis Historia '98, from 85 per cent aglianico with piedirosso. The colour is deep ruby with a purple rim. There is plentiful wild berry and ripe plum on the intense nose, and an underlying delicate oakiness. The palate has firm body, dense, silky tannins and echoes the fruit tones on the nose before coming to a long, elegant finish. Taurasi Radici, also '98, is a garnet-tinged ruby colour. The nose is evolved and alcoholic with cooked fruit aromas overlying spiciness. The palate has all the fascination of a traditionally styled wine with plentiful smooth tannins and fresh acidity. There are also cherry and ripe plum flavours, an evenness of tenor and good length. Avalon, a characterful white from 100 per cent coda di volpe, is a gold-tinged, bright straw. The nose has medlar and damson with hints of spice, and the full-bodied palate has flavours of slightly over-ripened fruit, with hints of almond and honey on the finish. We liked Fiano More Maiorum '98, Aglianico Avellanio '00 and Lacryma Christi Rosso '01 best of the other wines.

BENEVENTO

Fattoria La Rivolta
Loc. Torrecuso
C.da Rivolta
82030 Benevento
Tel. 0824872921 - 0824884907
E-mail: pcotron@tin.it

In the past few years, Paolo Cotroneo, a pharmacist by profession, has turned with enthusiasm to his real love, wine. He has renovated the vineyards and cellar on his family's land and turned his attention to making the best quality wine possible. The estate extends over 60 or so hectares in the area of Torrecuso, in the province of Benevento, and has 25 hectares of vineyard from which Paolo, along with consultant oenologist Angelo Pizza, produces around 90,000 bottles a year. The first release of Aglianico del Taburno Riserva Terre di Rivolta, the '99, made a very good impression and nearly gained Two Glasses. It has a good, deep, dark ruby colour introducing a dense, sweet, ripe red fruits nose, highlighted by elegant undercurrents of vanilla and tobacco. The full-bodied palate is full of fruit and extract, with soft tannins and fair balance. The straight Aglianico del Taburno, also '99, seemed less expressive and hinted at premature evolution. The whites are fresh, with upfront fruit, made for enjoyable early drinking, and the '01 Falanghina leads the field. It is a bright, deep straw. There are cleanly defined, delicate aromas of ripe fruit and flowers, plus hints of fresh almond. The perfectly clean palate is full of fruit and has some almond on the finish. Coda di Volpe, also from 2001, is a full, structured wine, which finishes attractively on a delicately bitter note.

● Naturalis Historia '98	ΨΨ	7
● Taurasi Radici '98	ΨΨ	6
● Aglianico Avellanio '00	Ψ	4
● Vesuvio Lacryma Christi Rosso '01	Ψ	4
○ Fiano di Avellino More Maiorum '98	Ψ	5
● Taurasi Radici '90	ΨΨΨ	6
○ Fiano di Avellino More Maiorum '96	ΨΨ	5
● Taurasi Radici '96	ΨΨ	6
○ Fiano di Avellino More Maiorum '97	ΨΨ	6
● Naturalis Historia '97	ΨΨ	6

○ Taburno Coda di Volpe '01	Ψ	3
○ Taburno Falanghina '01	Ψ	3*
● Aglianico del Taburno Terra di Rivolta Ris. '99	Ψ	5
● Aglianico del Taburno '99		4

CAIAZZO (CE)

Vestini - Campagnano
Loc. Ortole
Fraz. S.S. Giovanni e Paolo
Via Barracone, 5
81013 Caiazzo (CE)
Tel. 0823862770 - 03355878791t

In just a few years, Vestini Campagnano has grown, From a little place where Giuseppe Mancini and Alberto Barletta, both forensic scientists as well as friends, played around making a few good bottles as presents, it has blossomed into an estate with 12 hectares of vineyard and an annual production of 25,000 bottles. It was a meeting with Luigi Moio, Professor of Oenology at the Universities of Naples and Foggia, and an extremely talented oenologist, that proved the turning point. The most fascinating aspect of their adventure, as fascinating for Professor Moio as it was for the two friends, was the challenge of salvaging several indigenous varieties from the Caserta area that had almost fallen into oblivion. The pallagrello, white and red, and casavecchia needed only the right pairs of hands, and the right terroirs, to reveal their potential and, once those conditions were fulfilled, two great wines emerged. One came out as a Three Glass giant. It is the amazingly concentrated Casavecchia '01, a darkly opaque wine with fascinating aromas of black berry fruit and spices elegantly melding into new oak tones. The palate has unbelievable depth and elegance. The impeccable Pallagrello Nero '01 is a fitting partner. It, too, has a tightly knit nose giving spices and vanilla, and a palate that is scarcely less long. The range is completed by two excellent whites, Pallagrello Bianco '01, with tropical fruit notes, and the notably full, complex, barrique-aged Le Ortole '01.

CARINARO (CE)

Cantine Caputo
Via Consortile, Zona ASI
81032 Carinaro (CE)
Tel. 0815033955
E-mail: cantine@caputo.it

Caputo is one of the long-standing names of Campanian winemaking. The winery was founded as long ago as 1890 and has always been noted for its quality orientated attitude. However, over the past couple of years, Mario and Nicola Caputo's wines seem to have gained new lustre, probably thanks to the arrival of Lorenzo Landi as consultant oenologist. The range is endless: around 1,000,000 bottles are produced each year and there are over 20 different wines, with nearly all the region's DOCs being represented. Again this year, we found more interest among the reds. Aglianico Terre del Volturno Zicorrà '00 particularly attracted us. It has a good, dark ruby colour then intense perfumes of blackberry and blueberry meld into the toasty, vanilla notes of new oak. The structured, fruity palate has soft tannins and good balance, and everything combines to give an excellent wine. Sannio Aglianico Clanius '01 is striking for its richness, its ripe cherry and wild strawberry aromas and the cleanliness on its palate. The straight Sannio Aglianico, also '01, has a similar profile but with less intensity. The best of the whites are Lacryma Christi del Vesuvio, Greco di Tufo and Falanghina Frattasi, all '01 and all offering freshness and distinct varietal aromas. Apart from one or two wobbles, the rest of the range is also on the up.

● Casavecchia Rosso '01	🍷🍷🍷	5*
● Pallagrello Nero '01	🍷🍷	5*
○ Pallagrello Bianco '01	🍷🍷	4*
○ Pallagrello Bianco Le Ortole '01	🍷🍷	5
⊙ Vado Ceraso Rosato '01	🍷	4
● Pallagrello Nero '00	🍷🍷	5*
○ Pallagrello Bianco Le Ortole '00	🍷	5

● Terre del Volturno Aglianico Zicorrà '00	🍷🍷	5
● Sannio Aglianico Clanius '01	🍷🍷	5
○ Greco di Tufo '01	🍷	4
● Sannio Aglianico '01	🍷	3
○ Sannio Falanghina Frattasi '01	🍷	4
○ Vesuvio Lacryma Christi Bianco '01	🍷	3
○ Asprinio d'Aversa Fescine '01		4
○ Fiano di Avellino '01		4
● Sannio Aglianico '00	🍷🍷	3*

CASTELLABATE (SA)

Luigi Maffini
Fraz. San Marco
Loc. Cenito
84071 Castellabate (SA)
Tel. 0974966345
E-mail: maffini@costacilento.it

Luigi Maffini proudly runs his small but prestigious estate in the Cilento district as a one man business. An agronomist by training and oenologist by inclination, Luigi has rapidly become one of the brightest hopes in the region, even though his vineyard and cellar in San Marco di Castellabate, where he personally cultivates just six hectares, are boutique-sized. To make up for it, Luigi buys grapes from the best sites in the Cilento, one of Campania's up and coming zones, enabling him to make something in the region of 45,000 bottles a year of tip-top wine. Cenito is the flagship. This blend of 65 per cent aglianico and piedirosso again made a distinguished showing at our taste-offs. This year, it was the '00, possibly the best vintage so far and certainly one with a long life ahead of it. It is dark ruby tinged with purple. The nose is rich, complex, full of berry fruit sweetness, most notably cherry and blackberry, with undertones of printer's ink and pencil lead, and slower-emerging hints of tobacco and oak toast. The palate has power, firm structure, smooth tannins and good balance, as well as a good fruit core that is just slightly masked by new oak astringency. Kratos '01, 100 per cent fiano, all from Maffini's own vines, is another great wine. It is a bright straw with clear aromas of peach, medlar and damson. The palate is opulent, fleshily rich and sings with fruit whose tones echo the nose. The robust red Kleos '01, from aglianico, piedirosso and sangiovese, is also good but doesn't have the fine balance of the '00.

CASTELVENERE (BN)

Antica Masseria Venditti
Via Sannitica, 122
82030 Castelvenere (BN)
Tel. 0824940306
E-mail: masseria@venditti.it

Nicola Venditti is an oenologist and has actively taken care of his family estate since the mid 1970s. He personally looks after the 11 hectares of good vines, and gives his all to the job. We are at Castelvenere in the province of Benevento. Falanghina, aglianico and piedirosso predominate, but where there are also numerous other good quality indigenous varieties, such as the white grieco and cerreto and the red olivella and barbetta, the last of which is also known in the area as barbera. Nicola is a jealous custodian of these varieties, which he cultivates organically and turns into a characterful range of wines. This year, we tasted a very decent Solopaca Bosco Caldaia '01, which has a good ruby colour, blackberry aromas and a fruity palate with good tannic balance. There was also a delicious Sannio Rosso '01, an uncomplicated wine for early drinking that is so full of ripe cherry and wild berry fruits aromas, so fresh and slim-bodied (but not thin), and so soft on its blackberry and cherry-like finish that it is almost irresistible. Barbera Barbetta '01, also made for drinking young, is a good purple-ruby colour. On top of its inviting wild berry fruits, the nose has delicate wafts of balsam and an almost peppery spiciness. The freshness of the fruit on the palate is satisfying, as is the fullness and good tannic grip. The Solopaca from the Bacalat vineyard, from falanghina, grieco and cerreto, is fresh, supple and full of white peach and apricot, but the Falanghina del Sannio '01 seemed a touch thin and overly acidic. Sannio Bianco '01 showed fairly well.

● Cenito '00	🍷🍷	6
○ Kràtos '01	🍷	4*
● Kléos '01	🍷	4
● Cenito '99	🍷🍷	6
● Kléos '00	🍷🍷	4*
● Cenito '97	🍷🍷	5
● Cenito '98	🍷🍷	6
● Kléos '99	🍷🍷	3

● Sannio Barbera Barbetta Vàndari '01	🍷	4
● Sannio Rosso '01	🍷	4
○ Solopaca Bianco Vigna Bacalàt '01	🍷	4
● Solopaca Rosso Bosco Caldaia '01	🍷	5
○ Sannio Bianco '01		3
○ Sannio Falanghina Vàndari '01		4
● Solopaca Rosso Bosco Caldaia '93	🍷🍷	3

CELLOLE (CE)

VILLA MATILDE
S. S. DOMITIANA, 18 - KM. 4,700
81030 CELLOLE (CE)
TEL. 0823932088
E-MAIL: info@fattoriavillamatilde.com

Salvatore and Maria Ida Avallone run their estate with competence and real love. It was founded by their father Francesco who, as a devoted scholar of wine history, wanted to see Falerno, the celebrated wine of ancient Rome, regain its prestige. In the past few years, assisted by an oenologist of the calibre of Riccardo Cotarella, Villa Matilde has become one of the best estates not just in Campania but in all southern Italy. The wines are superb, with Falerno del Massico Vigna Camarato, from 80 per cent aglianico and piedirosso, the jewel in the crown. The '99, while garnering compliments and consensus, did not hit the jackpot like previous vintages. But this is surely just a temporary lull. It is a dark, opaque ruby. The complexity of the aromas bowls you over, red and black berry fruits merging into limpid pools of vanilla and spice, cut through by highly elegant scents of clove and cinnamon. The palate has opulent fruit, develops evenly and is concentrated, balanced and very long. The '01 Falerno Vigna Caracci, based on local clones of falanghina, is also terrific this year. The colour is deep straw. The nose is fascinating, with its peach, apricot, butter, banana and acacia honey notes melding elegantly into the oaky, vanilla tones from the wood. The palate is firm, fleshy, richly textured and mouthfilling, yet elegant and very long. But the estate's other wines are classy, too, such as the well fruited, elegant Falerno Rosso '00 and the '00 Cecubo from piedirosso, aglianico and abbuoto.

FOGLIANISE (BN)

CANTINA DEL TABURNO
VIA SALA
82030 FOGLIANISE (BN)
TEL. 0824871338
E-MAIL: info@cantinadeltaburno.it

There was more acclaim for the Cantina del Taburno, the co-operative owned by the provincial agrarian consortium of Benevento. Founded in 1972, it has had its ups and downs but around five years ago, it embarked on a remarkable project in collaboration with the faculty of agriculture at the University of Naples to convert to high quality production. The results of all this research and experimentation on vinification techniques and indigenous varieties are obvious as Luigi Moio, together with oenologist Filippo Colandrea, has again come up with a tremendous range of wines. At its peak is the '00 release of Bue Apis, a brilliant Aglianico made from 100-year-old vines. It has spectacular concentration and intensity and gains Three Glasses, as did the '99, blending power and concentration with impeccable elegant. Taste it now and it will surprise you with its depth and cleanliness, and the incredible smoothness of its tannins, but you will know that it still needs time to reveal all it has to give. The richness of its fruit, its freshness and its balance are sure signs of great longevity. Aglianico Delius '00 has fascinating spicy aromas and an alluring immediacy to its fruit but this, too, is a red with great structure and a highly promising future. The best of the co-operative's many other wines include an extremely enjoyable Falanghina and a deeper, more complex, barrique-aged Falanghina Cesco dell'Eremo. Everything else is worthy of note and very good value.

○ Falerno del Massico Bianco Vigna Caracci '01	🍷🍷	4*
● Falerno del Massico Rosso Vigna Camarato '99	🍷🍷	6
● Cecubo '00	🍷🍷	4*
○ Eleusi Passito '00	🍷🍷	6
● Falerno del Massico Rosso '00	🍷🍷	4*
● Aglianico Rocca dei Leoni '01	🍷	3*
○ Falanghina di Roccamonfina '01	🍷	3*
○ Falerno del Massico Bianco '01	🍷	3*
⊙ Terre Cerase '01	🍷	3*
● Falerno del Massico Rosso Vigna Camarato '97	🍷🍷🍷	6
● Falerno del Massico Rosso Vigna Camarato '98	🍷🍷🍷	6

● Bue Apis '00	🍷🍷🍷	7
● Delius '00	🍷🍷	6
○ Falanghina Passita Ruscolo '00	🍷🍷	5
○ Coda di Volpe del Taburno Serra Docile '01	🍷🍷	4*
○ Falanghina Cesco Dell'Eremo '01	🍷🍷	4*
○ Taburno Falanghina Folius '01	🍷🍷	4*
○ Taburno Falanghina '01	🍷🍷	3*
○ Taburno Coda di Volpe '01	🍷	3*
○ Taburno Greco '01	🍷	3
● Aglianico del Taburno Fidelis '99	🍷	3*
● Bue Apis '99	🍷🍷🍷	6
● Delius '99	🍷🍷	6

FORIO (NA)

D'Ambra Vini d'Ischia
Fraz. Panza
Via Mario d'Ambra, 16
80075 Forio (NA)
Tel. 081907246 - 081907210
E-mail: info@dambravini.com

The Biancolella Vigna Frassitelli we tasted this year, from 2001, is without doubt the best vintage for many years, possibly even better than the legendary '90. It is a fresh, balanced, long wine of great character and performed with aplomb at our Three Glass finals. It has an deep, bright straw colour. There are exuberant aromas of apricot, yellow peach and damson, lively nuances of pink grapefruit and more complex tones of Mediterranean scrub. The palate is full, deep and decisively flavoured. However, this year Andrea D'Ambra, oenologist and the estate's mentor, has a new wine to add to his broad range. It is Kyme '00, a remarkable white made from grapes selected by Andrea during his travels around Khalkis and the Greek islands, and then planted on Ischia. It is not an easy wine but it is absolutely fascinating. There is warmth, depth, power and considerable alcohol, and it has an evolved character giving tertiary and minerally notes that blend with the fruit to give an alluring mix. The palate has great structure, controlled acidity, delicate flavours of jam, almond and hazelnut, and notable length. The '99 Rosso Dedicato a Mario D'Ambra is still young but is already showing well and promises even better. It is purple ruby, the nose is intense and dominated by new oak, then the palate is full and structured, with soft tannins and an acidity that needs more time to soften. The fresh, easy-drinking Per''e Palummo '01 and the '01 Ischia Bianco Forastera are both very good.

FURORE (SA)

Cantine Gran Furor
Divina Costiera
Via G. B. Lama, 14
84010 Furore (SA)
Tel. 089830348
E-mail: info@granfuror.it

Andrea Ferraioli and his wife Marisa Cuomo dedicate their energies to their small estate in Furore with genuine commitment and passion. The wines come from their dozen hectares of vines that literally cling to the sun-drenched rocky cliffs of the Amalfi coast. Italian wine writer Luigi Veronelli would describe theirs as a heroic venture. They keep alive the flavours that come from this unique terroir and its indigenous varieties, such as fenile, ginestra and ripoli, which otherwise would risk extinction. It was the meeting some years back of this couple and able oenologist Professor Luigi Moio that gave the wines, now produced in quantities of around 50,000 bottles a year, their form and style. The terraces hauled back from abandon now spawn a wide range of wines, vinified to modern precepts, that can be counted among the best and most individual of the region. Furore Rosso Riserva and Costa d'Amalfi Fior d'Uva are the high points. The former, from '99, is a dark, dense ruby colour. The nose is powerful, with rich notes of ripe red berry fruits that flow elegantly over hints of toast, white pepper and other spices. The intense palate is supple yet solidly structured, balanced and notably long. Fior d'Uva '01, from the local ripoli, fenile and ginestra, has a good, bright straw colour. The aromas of fully ripe peach, pear and damson are shot through with fresh notes of citron and lemon verbena. The zesty palate is nicely firm, developing evenly and finishing long. Great cleanliness and typicity mark out the rest of the range.

○ Ischia Biancolella Tenuta Frassitelli '01		4*
○ Kyme Bianco '00		6
● Ischia Rosso Dedicato a Mario d'Ambra '99		6
○ Ischia Forastera '01		3
● Ischia Per''e Palummo '01		4
○ Ischia Biancolella Tenuta Frassitelli '00		4*
● Ischia Rosso Dedicato a Mario d'Ambra '98		5
○ Ischia Biancolella Tenuta Frassitelli '99		4

● Costa d'Amalfi Furore Rosso Ris. '99		7
○ Costa d'Amalfi Furore Bianco Fiord'Uva '01		7
○ Costa d'Amalfi Ravello Bianco '01		4*
● Costa d'Amalfi Furore Rosso '01		4
● Costa d'Amalfi Ravello Rosso Ris. '99		6
○ Costa d'Amalfi Furore Bianco Fiord'uva '00		5*
● Costa d'Amalfi Furore Rosso Ris. '97		5
● Costa d'Amalfi Furore Rosso Ris. '98		5

GALLUCCIO (CE)

Telaro - Cooperativa Lavoro e Salute
Loc. La Starza
Via Cinque Pietre, 2
81045 Galluccio (CE)
tel. 0823925841
e-mail: info@vinitelaro.it

The Telaro brothers set up their 85-hectare estate in 1987. There are 35 hectares of vineyard and output is around 400,000 bottles a year. Massimo, Luigi and Pasquale should be very pleased with what they have achieved. Quality is excellent and the range is well diversified. The ten or so wines all come from the region's classic grapes: falanghina, greco, aglianico, piedirosso and fiano. Galluccio Rosso Riserva Calivierno '98 exemplifies the high quality attained. It has a good deep, dense ruby colour. The aromas are notably intense, centred on black berry fruits and ripe cherry, with an underlying spiciness and particularly well-gauged oakiness. The same sense of harmony and balance also pervades the palate, which is notable for its richness of extract, elegance and fruit-led finish. From the other whites, we found the supple, fruity '01 Fiano and the '01 Greco, with its pure tones of golden delicious apple, both from the Le Cinque Pietre line, to be well made and most attractive. When we tried the reds, we liked best: the Galluccio Riserva Ara Mundi '99, although a more incisive structure would have helped; the clean, balanced Aglianico Montecaruso '00; and the Passito delle Cinque Pietre '01, from aleatico and aglianico, which has complexity, refined aromas of jam and black cherry, and an elegant sweetness.

GUARDIA SANFRAMONDI (BN)

De Lucia
C.da Starze
82034 Guardia Sanframondi (BN)
tel. 0824864259
e-mail: c.delucia@tin.it

Carlo De Lucia, assisted by consulting oenologist Roberto Mazzer, is now established as one of the best producers in the Sannio area. He submitted another fine range of wines this year, all coming from his 18 hectares of vineyard. Our preference, yet again, went to Vigna La Corte Aglianico del Sannio '00. It is a good, purple-tinged dark ruby colour. The nose is full of soft cherry and ripe plum fruitiness, which draws refinement from elegant tones of new oak, vanilla and spices. The palate is marked out by the control and balance of its power, solid structure, fleshiness and fruit richness, together with smooth tannins that accompany the wine to an elegant finish. The Aglianico '01 is less concentrated but is beautifully clean. It has nicely concentrated wild strawberry, blackberry and cherry fruit on the nose, as it does on the full, supple palate, which reveals controlled astringency. We also found the Falanghina Vendemmia Tardiva '01 interesting. A nice golden yellow, it has a complex nose that ranges across lavender flowers, chamomile and tropical fruits. The palate is warm, full and nicely fat, with ripe, fresh, elegant fruit and a gently almondy finish. Carlo, a real Falanghina specialist, produces the wine in two other styles. Vigna delle Ginestre is particularly intense and full. It has a fruity, floral nose, and is rich in opulent fruit on its soft, full palate. The well-made standard version is attractive.

● Galluccio Calivierno Ris. '98	⟡⟡	5
● Galluccio Aglianico Montecaruso '00	⟡	4
○ Fiano di Roccamonfina le Cinque Pietre '01	⟡	4
○ Greco di Roccamonfina le Cinque Pietre '01	⟡	4
● Passito delle Cinque Pietre '01	⟡	5
● Galluccio Ara Mundi Ris. '99	⟡	5
● Aglianico di Roccamonfina '97	⟡⟡	3
● Galluccio Aglianico Montecaruso '99	⟡⟡	3*

● Sannio Aglianico Vigna La Corte '00	⟡⟡	5
○ Sannio Falanghina V.T. '01	⟡⟡	6
● Sannio Aglianico '01	⟡	4
○ Sannio Falanghina '01	⟡	3
○ Sannio Falanghina Vigna delle Ginestre '01	⟡	4
● Sannio Aglianico Adelchi '97	⟡⟡	4
● Sannio Aglianico Adelchi '98	⟡⟡	5
● Sannio Aglianico '99	⟡⟡	4
● Sannio Aglianico Vigna La Corte '99	⟡⟡	5

MONDRAGONE (CE)

Michele Moio
V.le Regina Margherita, 6
81034 Mondragone (CE)
tel. 0823978017

MONTEFREDANE (AV)

Pietracupa
C.da Vadiaperti, 17
83030 Montefredane (AV)
tel. 0825607418

Michele Moio is a specialist in primitivo, the most widely planted red variety in this corner of Campania, and falanghina. This is Falerno country, which in Roman times was at least as important as the Langhe, Bordeaux or Burgundy are today. These days, efforts abound to return the area to its former glory. Michele is a winemaker of proven experience but his son, Bruno, also works full-time on the estate as oenologist and his other son, Luigi, lectures on oenology at the Universities of Naples and Foggia. In fact, Luigi has gained himself a formidable reputation as a winemaker as well as an academic. The wine that showed best is new, the Falerno Primitivo Maiatico '99. It is purple-tinged deep ruby, with an intense nose of blackberry, plum and cherry sweetness with distinct, clean spicy nuances. The palate is soft, warm, mouthfilling, bursting with fruit and has good backbone and length. It is still young and the new oak is overt but it is a safe bet that it will develop brilliantly with time. The Falerno Primitivo, also '99, is more traditionally styled but no less captivating. It's a full-bodied, ripe, blackberry and plum-like wine, with plentiful alcohol which does not compromise its balance. There are clear notes of medlar and white plum, and just a hint of vanilla on the Falerno Bianco, from falanghina, which has a fresh, intense fruitiness, great richness of extract and notable harmony. We also tasted the promising Gaurano '01 but as it was a cask sample we shall defer judgement until next year.

Sabino Loffredo started bottling his small production of wine in 1990. He makes around 35,000 bottles a year, mostly from his three and a half hectares of vineyard situated in the area of Vadiaperti di Montefredane. This lies in the heart of Irpinia's wine country and straddles the denominations of Greco di Tufo and Fiano di Avellino. It no coincidence, then, that his most representative wine is Greco di Tufo, which accounts for about half of the cellar's production. The '01 has a good, bright, deep straw colour. The nose has elegant, refined aromas of ripe fruit, with golden delicious apples clearly perceptible, and gains stature from its floral nuances and acacia honey highlights. The palate is fresh and well structured, with good balance and length, and has a complex minerality on the finish. Fiano di Avellino '01 is also fresh and well balanced but lacks the same wealth of comment-worthy features. Of the two aglianico-based reds, our preference goes to Meridio '00. The colour is bright ruby. There are good aromas of ripe cherry and plum, the palate is warm and pervasive, with soft fruit tones, and there is just the right amount of tannin. The Taurasi '98 is well typed. It may be just a bit too vegetal on the nose, and a touch too slim bodied on the palate, but it is good overall.

● Falerno del Massico Primitivo '99	ΨΨ	5
● Falerno del Massico Primitivo Maiatico '99	ΨΨ	7
○ Falerno del Massico Falanghina '01	Ψ	4
● Falerno del Massico Primitivo '98	ΨΨ	4*
● Gaurano '98	ΨΨ	4*
● Rosso 57 '99	ΨΨ	4*

○ Greco di Tufo "G" '01	ΨΨ	4*
● Meridio '00	Ψ	5
○ Fiano di Avellino '01	Ψ	4
○ Taurasi '98	Ψ	6

MONTEFUSCO (AV)

TERREDORA
VIA SERRA
83030 MONTEFUSCO (AV)
TEL. 0825968215
E-MAIL: info@terredora.com

Walter Mastroberardino, working with his children Lucio, Paolo and Daniela, owns Terredora, an estate with 150 hectares of vineyard, lying mostly in the DOC zones of Taurasi, Fiano di Avellino and Greco di Tufo. A good 15 wines are produced, straddling DOCs, DOCGs and IGTs. Heading the list this year is an excellent Fiano di Avellino '01. It has a bright, deep straw colour and is exceptionally inviting from the very first sniff, where peach, apricot and pear emerge clearly, interwoven with elegant wafts of tropical fruit. There is intensity on the palate, which is full bodied, firmly structured and cut through by fresh acidity that supports beautifully defined fruit, recalling pineapple and yellow peach with intriguing hints of citron. Taurasi Fatica Contadina '98 is a bright garnet-tinged ruby that looks a little old for its age. The nose is deep with cherry jam, liquorice and more evolved aromas but seems a touch dull overall. The palate has structure but doesn't boast the fruit balance and length of the very classy '97. Paradoxically, Aglianico Il Principio '00 seemed a more interesting, better-knit wine. The nose does not exactly sing with cleanliness but the wine has firm body and rich extract, without being weighed down by the new oak, so the resulting balance is good. Best of the other wines are Aglianico 01, Greco di Tufo Terre degli Angeli '01 and an attractive '01 Falanghina di Beneventano.

○ Fiano di Avellino Terre di Dora '01	♀♀	4*
● Irpinia Aglianico Il Principio '00	♀	5
○ Falanghina del Beneventano '01	♀	3
○ Greco di Tufo Terra degli Angeli '01	♀	4
● Irpinia Aglianico '01	♀	3*
● Taurasi Fatica Contadina '98	♀	6
● Pompeiano Piedirosso '00		4
○ Greco di Tufo Loggia della Serra '01		4
○ Fiano di Avellino Terre di Dora '00	♀♀	4*
● Taurasi Fatica Contadina '97	♀♀	6

MONTEMARANO (AV)

SALVATORE MOLETTIERI
VIA MUSANNI, 19
83040 MONTEMARANO (AV)
TEL. 082763722 - 082763424

Salvatore and Giovanni Molettieri's estate was founded in the mid 1990s and is small, with little more than seven hectares of vineyard and an annual production of around 20,000 bottles. Our tastings reveal increasingly characterful wines and, year by year, this boutique winery pleases us ever more. A lot is down to the zeal with which the Molettieris work in both vineyard and cellar, their obsession with excellence and, naturally, their use of top-level consultant oenologist, Attiglio Pagli, from the Matura group. As a result, the Taurasi wines from their Cinque Querce vineyard are increasingly characterful and deep, in fact they can take on the best in the denomination on level terms. This year, we particularly liked the Taurasi Riserva '97. It has a good, dark ruby colour. The nose is intense and complex with ripe red berry fruitiness, and flaunts nuances of spice, tobacco and liquorice. The palate is full and structured, with a powerful tannic framework, but also reveals elegance and softness, finishing long with ripe cherry and oak on the aftertaste. Taurasi '98 is even more concentrated. Full and balanced, it has blackberry and cherry jam fruitiness, with pepper spice, on both nose and palate. We found the new oak to be particularly well judged, giving a Taurasi that is modern in style without losing the character and bearing of more traditional versions. Finally, Aglianico '00, has excellent style. It is a less austere, less structured wine but still has complexity, wonderful fruit richness, elegant incisive aromas and smooth tannins.

● Taurasi Vigna Cinque Querce '98	♀♀	7
● Irpinia Aglianico Cinque Querce '00	♀♀	5
● Taurasi Vigna Cinque Querce Ris. '97	♀♀	8
● Taurasi Vigna Cinque Querce '94	♀♀	4
● Taurasi Vigna Cinque Querce '96	♀♀	5
● Taurasi Vigna Cinque Querce '97	♀♀	8
● Cinque Querce Rosso '98	♀♀	4
● Cinque Querce Rosso '99	♀♀	4*

PONTELATONE (CE)

FATTORIA PONTEPELLEGRINO
LOC. FUNARI
VIA PONTEPELLEGRINO
81050 PONTELATONE (CE)
TEL. 0823301382
E-MAIL: info@trebulanum.com

Michele Alois' Pontepellegrino was set up only recently and this report deals with the first year of production. Few estates manage an entry in the Guide so quickly. In fact, work began on family-owned land a decade or so ago but the intervening period has been taken up by replantings, experiments and microvinifications of indigenous varieties. The most exciting of these is casavecchia, a red variety that has recently re-emerged to take up its rightful place in the wine lexicon, after years of oblivion in which it risked extinction. With oenologist Angelo Pizzi and agronomist Nicola Trabucco, Michele, who directs the family's textile business by day, offered us two characterful reds, both from '00. The better of the two is easily the impressively structured Trebulanum, from 100 per cent casavecchia. The colour is a dense, dark ruby with a purple rim. The nose has much to offer, showing deep tones of fully ripe blackberry, blackcurrant and black cherry, melding into well-integrated spice and vanilla from the new oak. The deep,fleshy, powerful palate flaunts tannins of excellent finesse, shows the same fruit character as the nose, and finishes long with spice and delicate balsamic tones on the aftertaste. The same grape variety and similar winemaking techniques, including a stay in barrique, are behind the estate's other red, Optimum, also '00. It is a finely executed wine, if less rich than Trebulanum.

| ● Trebulanum '00 | 5 |
| ● Optimum '00 | 5 |

PRIGNANO CILENTO (SA)

VITICOLTORI DE CONCILIIS
C.DA QUERCE, 1
84060 PRIGNANO CILENTO (SA)
TEL. 0974831090
E-MAIL: deconcillis@hotmail.com

Naima, the estate's flagship Aglianico, is again one of the region's best reds this year, with the '00. It is a deep, dark, opaque ruby tinged with purple. The imposing nose has ripe and just over-ripe red berry fruit, ranging from blackberry to plum and cherry, thrown into relief by new oak toastiness and a hint of pencil lead. The palate is warm, mouthfilling, full of fleshy fruitiness, beautifully balanced and finishes long with tobacco and vanilla on the aftertaste. Two other characterful reds, produced by Bruno de Conciliis with two different partners, sit alongside. Merlanico '00, a fascinating 50-50 blend of merlot from Lombardy and aglianico from Cilento, was made with Barone Pizzini from Franciacorta. It is a dense, concentrated wine of great breeding, with rich opulent notes of red berry fruits. The soft blackcurrant and raspberry notes from the merlot meld perfectly with the firm structure given by the aglianico. It finishes long with ripe plum, balsam, spice and light tobacco on the aftertaste. Zero '00 was made with Winny D'Orta. It is a firm, full-bodied, concentrated, Aglianico full of fruit and softness, and with notably smooth tannins, although it seems to lack the perfect cleanliness and definition of the previous vintage. Plaudits also go to the peach and damson-like Fiano Donnaluna and to Aglianico Donnaluna, a deep, balanced wine full of ripe plum, cherry and spice.

● Merlanico - De Conciliis	
- Barone Pizzini '00	6
● Naima '00	6
● Zero - D'Orta - De Conciliis '00	6
● Donnaluna Aglianico '01	4
○ Donnaluna Fiano '01	3
● Naima '99	5
● Donnaluna Aglianico '00	4*
● Naima '98	5
● Zero - D'Orta-De Conciliis '99	5

QUARTO (NA)

Cantine Grotta del Sole
Via Spinelli, 2
80010 Quarto (NA)
Tel. 0818762566 - 0818761320
E-mail: grottadelsole@grottadelsole.it

Grotta del Sole has only been in operation since 1989. However, it a major focal point in the area thanks to the extensive research it has carried out on the region's indigenous varieties, and its work in repropagating them . Greco, asprinio, falanghina, caprettone, sciascinoso and yet more varieties hold no secrets for oenologist and agronomist Gennaro Martusciello, co-owner of this family estate. His skills with them are revealed as much in his classic wines, such as Lettere and Gragnano della Penisola Sorrentina, as in the more modern-styled Quarto di Sole and Quarto di Luna. The latter is a falanghina and caprettone blend from grapes grown near Pompeii, which is aged around six months in new oak. The '00 has a bright straw yellow hue, introducing intense peach and tropical fruits aromas, supported by vanilla. The nicely fat palate has body, balanced acidity, fruit, power and a long finish with an elegantly oaky aftertaste. Its firm structure and welcome freshness augur well for future development. Quarto del Sole '99 is from the more typical blend of piedirosso and aglianico. The nose is rich in just over-ripe red berry fruits and spice, the tannins are elegant and, although it is not quite as exciting as the white, it has remarkable fruit and structure. We also strongly recommend Lettere '01, with its captivating aromas of strawberry and fresh cherry, its slim-bodied, fruit-forward palate, and its cheerful effervescence. The Greco di Tufo, Fiano di Avellino, Gragnano and Montegauro Riserva '98 are all very well made.

○ Quarto di Luna '00	¶¶	4*
● Quarto di Sole '99	¶¶	5
○ Campi Flegrei Falanghina '01	¶	4
○ Fiano di Avellino '01	¶	4
○ Greco di Tufo '01	¶	4
● Penisola Sorrentina Lettere '01	¶	3*
● Penisola Sorrentina Gragnano '01	¶	3*
● Campi Flegrei Piedirosso Montegauro Ris. '98	¶	4
● Quarto di Sole '98	¶¶	5

SALZA IRPINA (AV)

Di Meo
C.da Coccovoni, 1
83050 Salza Irpina (AV)
Tel. 0825981419
E-mail: info@dimeo.it

Roberto and Erminia Di Meo's family estate, which they run with great success, is no boutique winery. It has 250 hectares, 30 of which are under vine, and produces around half a million bottles a year of DOC and IGT wines. In the past two years, we have seen a significant increase in quality, an improvement which is all down to Roberto. An oenologist of standing, he aims unswervingly to make wines of prestige. The best of this year's releases are two reds, both from aglianico. Don Generoso '00 is a good dark purple-tinged ruby. The nose is intense with pure aromas of blackberry and ripe blueberry that merge into sweet notes of jam and new oak. The warm palate has good concentration and body, perfectly mirrors the fruit tones on the nose, and shows tannins of finesse then a good vanilla-like finish. Taurasi Riserva '97 is just as fascinating, with a slightly more austere style but greater complexity. It is cleanly fruited on both nose and palate, where there is firm backbone, elegant astringency and a long finish with blackberry, ripe cherry, spice and oak on the aftertaste. Aglianico Vigna Olmo '98 is less intense but delightfully fruity, well balanced and well made. From the whites, we enjoyed the fresh Falanghina '01 and a zesty Greco di Tufo, pleasantly redolent of peach and damson. The Fiano di Avellino and Coda de Volpe are less interesting, but only for now.

● Don Generoso '00	¶¶	8
● Taurasi Ris. '97	¶¶	6
○ Greco di Tufo '01	¶	4
○ Sannio Falanghina '01	¶	3
● Aglianico Vigna Olmo '98	¶	4
○ Coda di Volpe Vigna Olmo '01		3
○ Fiano di Avellino '01		4
○ Fiano di Avellino Colle dei Cerri '01		5

700

SAN CIPRIANO PICENTINO (SA)

MONTEVETRANO
LOC. NIDO
VIA MONTEVETRANO, 3
84099 SAN CIPRIANO PICENTINO (SA)
TEL. 089882285
E-MAIL: montevetrano@tin.it

Honours go again to Silvia Imparato and her Montevetrano, a wine that is loved, eagerly tracked down, drunk and collected, all over the world. Production has now reached an acceptable level, at 22,000 bottles, but this is still tiny compared with demand. Montevetrano remains a cult wine, respectfully discussed across the globe. Since it is a cult, the seventh Guide Three Glass award puts us firmly among the faithful. And on the subject of laurels, you can say anything about Silvia but not that she rests on them. Her estate - the cellar, the annex providing accommodation for farm holidays and the workshop for preparing conserves and other food specialities - is in a constant state of flux. The whole enterprise is animated by her enthusiasm, her dynamism and her love of whatever is good and fine. As for the wine, the 2000 edition of this 60 per cent cabernet sauvignon, 30 per cent merlot and aglianico monster is one of the finest. The colour is a purple-tinged dark ruby. The aromas are intense but still very youthful, with small wild berry fruits and ripe cherry that are lifted by tobacco, spice and an elegant touch of vanilla. The palate has its usual solid structure, the richness and cleanliness given by perfectly ripe fruit, evenness throughout and tannins of beautiful finesse. It feels warm, enveloping and soft on the palate, and finishes long and commandingly, with fruit and new oak on the aftertaste. Congratulations to Silvia and to Riccardo Cotarella, the oenologist who conceived this masterpiece.

SANT'AGATA DE' GOTI (BN)

MUSTILLI
VIA DEI FIORI, 20
82019 SANT'AGATA DE' GOTI (BN)
TEL. 0823717433
E-MAIL: info@mustilli.com

Leonardo Mustilli is one of the emblematic personalities of winemaking in Campania. The creation of the Sant'Agata dei Goti denomination was his work, as is the commercial take-off of Falanghina, a white that has recently gained significant market share and considerable consumer endorsement. Over the past few years, though, Leonardo's wines have had a rather over-evolved character and seemed to have lost their edge. Now, there are signs of a new start. A new cellar is in construction and the wines are acquiring greater cleanliness and definition. Il Gheppio '00, for instance, the wine that showed best at our tastings, exemplifies the changes. It is a good, intense, purple-tinged ruby Aglianico with full, open aromas of morello cherry and wild berries, and a cleanly fruited palate with smooth tannins and good length. Falanghina '01 is deep straw in colour. The nose has ripe fruit, led by peach and damson, then the reasonably full palate has good fruit, fresh acidity and is notably well made. Conte Artus, from aglianico and piedirosso in equal parts, is also good. It is not powerfully structured but it is fresh and supple on the palate. The estate's other wines were less impressive but we are willing to bet that the future will be bright for this estate.

● Montevetrano '00	🍷🍷🍷	8
● Montevetrano '93	🍷🍷🍷	5
● Montevetrano '95	🍷🍷🍷	5
● Montevetrano '96	🍷🍷🍷	5
● Montevetrano '97	🍷🍷🍷	5
● Montevetrano '98	🍷🍷🍷	6
● Montevetrano '99	🍷🍷🍷	6
● Montevetrano '94	🍷🍷	5

● Gheppio '00	🍷🍷	4*
● S. Agata dei Goti Rosso Conte Artus '00	🍷	4
○ S. Agata dei Goti Falanghina '01	🍷	3*
● Vigna Cesco di Nece '91	🍷🍷	3
○ S. Agata dei Goti Greco di Primicerio '97	🍷🍷	4

SERINO (AV)

VILLA RAIANO
VIA PESCATORE, 19
83028 SERINO (AV)
TEL. 0825592826 - 0825595781
E-MAIL: info@villaraiano.it

In 1996, Sabino Basso decided to start producing high quality wine on the family estate he co-owns with his brother Simone, who teaches violin at the Conservatory, and sister Annarita. Sabino trained as an oenologist but invited to act as consultant a friend from his days at Avellino's agricultural college, Luigi Moio, who in the meantime had become a university teacher. Basso's enthusiasm and determination together with Moio's top level skills have resulted in lightning progress and today Villa Raiano has a highly distinguished range of wines. The Taurasi '98 is of excellent quality. The colour is a dark, intense ruby. The nose has inviting upfront red and black berry fruitiness – blackberry, plum, blackcurrant and raspberry come through – that is given pizzazz by oak-derived spices and vanilla. It has the typical austerity of Taurasi on the palate but this is cushioned by a soft fruity texture. The tannins are perfectly ripe and oaky notes emerge on its very long finish. Greco di Tufo '01 is just as enticing. It has beautifully pure aromas of well ripe peach and damson, and its palate is fresh, deep and supple but not simplistic, with good length. A very decent Fiano di Avellino '01 and a lovely Aglianico '00 are just a notch down, both of them reinforcing the excellent impression that Basso's wines make. Watch this estate.

SESSA AURUNCA (CE)

GALARDI
LOC. VALLEMARINA - FRAZ. SAN CARLO
PROV.LE SESSA-MIGNANO
81030 SESSA AURUNCA (CE)
TEL. 0823925003
E-MAIL: galardi@napoli.com

Galardi is a recent phenomenon in Campania. The estate was originally little more than an all-consuming hobby for three cousins, Francesco and Dora Catello and Maria Luisa Murena. The they decided to try to realize the full potential of their family inheritance, a few hectares on the volcanic slopes of mount Roccamonfina. It was founded just over a decade ago on paper but did not bottle its excellent red until 1994. Very soon after, thanks to the cousins' enthusiasm and a fortuitous encounter with Riccardo Cotarella, the estate started to take on cult status among aficionados in Italy and the United States. There is just the one wine, Terre di Lavoro, an 80-20 blend of aglianico and piedirosso, of which just 10,000 bottles are released each year. Its great personality, its power, its elegance and its depth make it one of the great reds of southern Italy. Last year, it earned Three Glasses for the first time with an outstanding '99. This year, the '00 misses out, but only just. Let's be clear, the wine is not "less good" than last year's but, like all those at the very top end of the spectrum, it is strongly affected by the vintage. Only a tiny lack of balance, caused by a slightly inexpressive phase of development, keeps it off the podium. It has its habitual richness of extract, as you can see at a glance, and its still reticent nose reveals underlying fruit of great intensity, despite the light covering of oak. The palate has structure, power, good fruit definition, a wealth of delicate astringency and, we bet, an enviably long ageing profile.

○ Greco di Tufo '01	♛♛	4
● Taurasi '98	♛♛	6
● Irpinia Aglianico '00	♛	5
○ Fiano di Avellino '01	♛	4

● Terra di Lavoro '00	♛♛	7
● Terra di Lavoro '99	♛♛♛	6
● Terra di Lavoro '94	♛♛	5
● Terra di Lavoro '95	♛♛	5
● Terra di Lavoro '97	♛♛	5
● Terra di Lavoro '98	♛♛	6
● Terra di Lavoro '96	♛	5

SORBO SERPICO (AV)

FEUDI DI SAN GREGORIO
LOC. CERZA GROSSA
83050 SORBO SERPICO (AV)
TEL. 0825986611
E-MAIL: feudi@feudi.it

The late 1990s saw massive success for Feudi di San Gregorio in Italy. Owned by the Ercolino and Capaldo families and run with innate creativity and business sense by Enzo Ercolino, it has achieved huge increases in quality, and in quantity, which is not easy at this level. It now has over 230 hectares of vines in Campania, Basilicata, Puglia and Molise and produces over two and a half million bottles. Winemaking wizard Riccardo Cotarella as consultant ensures that some of the products have deservedly earned cult status in Italy and around the world. Patrimo, for example, is our Red Wine of the Year this time. Obtained from more than 20-year-old merlot vines and aged in French oak, it has spectacular richness and depth. The nose explodes with pure, elegant wild berry fruitiness. The palate is deep, powerful, structured and yet supremely elegant, soft, perfectly balanced and rich in ripe, smooth tannins. It is incredibly long with elegant notes of chocolate, tobacco and spice on the finish that meld into the oak vanilla in great harmony. Serpico '00, a 100 per cent Aglianico, from century-old vines, is just as enthralling, complex and exciting. Here, too, there is unusual depth and concentration, combined with great overall harmony and supreme finesse and class. Line up Three more Glasses. Even the white Campanaro, from 85 per cent fiano and greco, both from DOC vineyards, almost earned a third Glass with its explosion of ripe, tropical fruit and its concentrated, supple palate. The other wines are at their usual very high standard.

● Pàtrimo '00	🍷🍷🍷	8
● Serpico '00	🍷🍷🍷	8
○ Campanaro '01	🍷🍷	6
● Taurasi Selve di Luoti '98	🍷🍷	6
○ Fiano di Avellino '01	🍷🍷	4
○ Greco di Tufo '01	🍷	4
○ Sannio Falanghina '01	🍷	4
● Taurasi Piano di Montevergine '96	🍷🍷🍷	6
○ Fiano di Avellino Pietracalda V. T. '99	🍷🍷🍷	4
● Pàtrimo '99	🍷🍷🍷	6
● Serpico '99	🍷🍷🍷	6
○ Campanaro '00	🍷🍷	5
● Taurasi Piano di Montevergine Ris. '97	🍷🍷	7

TAURASI (AV)

ANTONIO CAGGIANO
C.DA SALA
83030 TAURASI (AV)
TEL. 082774743
E-MAIL: info@cantinecaggiano.it

In less than ten years, Antonio Caggiano's estate has become a star of the first order in the province of Avellino. Antonio and his son Giuseppe obtain excellent quality grapes from their 15 hectares of well-sited vineyards, which include some real "crus", and turn them into a prestige range of wines. They are helped by oenologist Marco Moccia and, above all, by consultant Luigi Moio, who for some years has been involved in the exciting work of discovering how to extract the best from the aglianico variety. And so we find ourselves with one of the starriest Taurasi wines ever tasted, Vigna Macchia dei Goti '99. This gained Three Glasses with aplomb. It is a dark, opaque ruby, still tinged with purple. The nose is intense and supremely elegant, with its rich fruit interweaving with perfectly integrated, sweetly spicy nuances and hints of new oak, resulting in a finely complex whole. The harmonious palate is powerful, full of fleshy blackberry and blueberry fruitiness, fine breadth, extraordinarily smooth tannins and a long, classy finish disclosing ripe cherry and tobacco on the aftertaste. The '00 Aglianico from the Salae Domini vineyard is not dissimilar in aromatic character and there is delightful wild berry fruit on the nose. The palate is soft and concentrated with an elegant finish. Fiagre, from 70 per cent fiano and greco, both from DOC vineyards, is also excellent with its bright straw colour, the ripe fruits nose with lively hints of balsam and mint, and a full, softly balanced palate. Fiano Béchar is impressive too, as are all the other wines.

● Taurasi Vigna Macchia dei Goti '99	🍷🍷🍷	7
● Salae Domini '00	🍷🍷	6
○ Fiagre '01	🍷🍷	4*
○ Fiano di Avellino Béchar '01	🍷🍷	5
○ Mel '00	🍷	6
● Taurì '00	🍷	4
● Taurasi Vigna Macchia dei Goti '98	🍷🍷	5
○ Fiagre '00	🍷🍷	4*
○ Fiano di Avellino Béchar '00	🍷🍷	5
● Taurì '98	🍷🍷	4
○ Mel '99	🍷🍷	6
● Taurì '99	🍷🍷	4

TORRECUSO (BN)

FONTANAVECCHIA
VIA FONTANAVECCHIA
82030 TORRECUSO (BN)
TEL. 0824876275

Libero Rillo is the owner of this fine estate with seven hectares of vineyard at Torrecuso, in the Taburno DOC zone. In the past few years, Libero, with his oenologist Angelo Pizzi, have made a distinct change in the style of the wines. This is evident if we compare more recently made wines, like Aglianico Orazio from '00 and '01, with, for example, the more classic but less expressive Riserva versions of Aglianico del Taburo Vigna Cataratte. We prefer the more recent wines, those full of fruit, flesh and colour, like Orazio '01. This red sacrifices none of the structure and backbone of the Aglianico but also has notable richness, giving an intensely fruited, soft wine full of ripe tannins and with great balance. Although still characterful, the '97 and '98 Vigna Cataratte lag behind in comparison, They're more evolved and mature, with less restrained astringency. We are sure that future vintages will bring encouraging stylistic developments to these wines, too. The basic Aglianico del Taburno, in this case the '00, which we first assessed last year, is as good as ever. Whatever it may lose on its slightly off-key nose, it regains on the firm, balanced palate. Aglianico Rosato '01, this year riper than usual, and the fruity, supple Falanghina '01 are both as well made as ever. Facetus '01, from oak-aged falanghina, seemed a little too evolved for its age and had signs of premature oxidation.

TUFO (AV)

BENITO FERRARA
FRAZ. S. PAOLO
S. PAOLO, 14/A
83010 TUFO (AV)
TEL. 0825998194
E-MAIL: info@benitoferrara.it

Gabriella Ferrara's estate is small, family run and specializes in Greco di Tufo production. Her vineyards are situated at Tufo itself, in the heart of the denomination. There are three and a half hectares of vines, which give her 27,000 or so bottles a year. Small beer, you may say. Yet Gabriella has recently been in the limelight for the impeccably clean, modern-styled Greco wines that she makes with the assistance of her consultant oenologist, the Tuscan Paolo Caciorgna. Take their Greco '01, for example, with its bright deep straw colour. Its richly, ripely fruited peach and damson nose, and its elegant floral nuances usher in a clean fruit, nice concentration and a fresh, balanced palate. The Greco from Vigna Cicogna has a more complex, riper character. The colour is tinged with gold. The nose has complex aromas of almond and hazelnut, highlighted by mineral tones, as well as a good dose of fruit. The palate has body, fat, good balance and complexity. This year Gabriella also submitted a good red, Aglianico dell'Irpinia '01. It is fruit-led and an early drinker but nonetheless admirable for its cleanliness, its soft plum and cherry tones, and its delicate but firm astringency.

●	Orazio '01	▼▼	6
◉	Aglianico del Taburno Rosato '01	▼	3
○	Taburno Falanghina '01	▼	3
●	Aglianico del Taburno Vigna Cataratte Ris. '97	▼	6
●	Aglianico del Taburno Vigna Cataratte Ris. '98	▼	6
○	Facetus '01		5
●	Orazio '00	♀♀	6
●	Aglianico del Taburno Vigna Cataratte Ris. '95	♀♀	5
●	Aglianico del Taburno Vigna Cataratte '96	♀♀	4
●	Aglianico del Taburno '00	♀	4

○	Greco di Tufo '01	▼▼	5
○	Greco di Tufo Vigna Cicogna '01	▼▼	5
●	Irpinia Aglianico '01	▼	4
○	Greco di Tufo Vigna Cicogna '00	♀♀	5
○	Greco di Tufo '99	♀♀	4
○	Greco di Tufo Vigna Cicogna '99	♀♀	4

OTHER WINERIES

Castello Ducale
Via San Nicola
82031 Amorosi (BN)
tel. 0824972460
e-mail: info@castelloducale.com

Antonio Donato, with consultant Angelo Pizzi, produces a carefully honed range of organic wines at Castel Campagnano. They come from 12 hectares of vineyard, partly in the area of Caserta, partly in Sannio. The most interesting are Aglianico Contessa Ferrara '00 and Pallagrello Bianco '01.

○	Pallagrello Bianco '01		4
●	Aglianico Contessa Ferrara '00		5

Fattoria Ciabrelli
Via Italia
82030 Castelvenere (BN)
tel. 0824940565
e-mail: fattoria@ciabrelli.it

Antonio Ciabrelli personally cultivates his five hectares of vineyard and vinifies the grapes, releasing out around 30,000 bottles a year. The wines are even and well made.

●	Beneventano Aglianico '00		4
○	Beneventano Coda di Volpe '01		4
○	Beneventano Falanghina '01		4

Vinicola del Sannio
C.da San Rocco
82030 Castelvenere (BN)
tel. 0824940207 - 0824940668
e-mail: info@vinicoladelsannio.it

Raffaele Pengue produces around 300,000 bottles a year from grapes bought in the Sannio area. He turns out wines that are remarkably clean and attractive, as well as excellent value for money.

●	Sannio Aglianico '01		3
●	Sannio Barbera '01		3
○	Sannio Falanghina '01		3

Fattoria Torre Gaia
Via Bosco Cupo, 11
82030 Dugenta (BN)
tel. 0824978172
e-mail: info@torre-gaia.com

This estate in the heart of the Sannio area is gaining recognition for the quality of its wines, obtained mainly from its 64 hectares of vineyard. Sannio Rosso Poggio Bellavista has character, structure and balance.

●	Sannio Rosso Poggio Bellavista '00		3*
○	Sannio Falanghina '01		3

Pietratorcia
Fraz. Cuotto
Via Provinciale Panza, 267
80075 Forio (NA)
Tel. 081908206 - 081907232

Pietratorcia's wines are paragons of local typicity. They also have a rather retro style that can produce exciting results. On occasion, however, it subdues the fruit freshness of the excellent quality grapes. Interest centres on Scherìa Rosso '99 and l'Ischia Rosso Vigne di Janno Piro '00.

● Ischia Rosso Vigne di Ianno Piro '00	▼	6
● Scheria Rosso '99	▼	6

Corte Normanna
C.da Sapenzie, 20
82034 Guardia Sanframondi (BN)
Tel. 0824817004 - 0824817008
E-mail: info@cortenormanna.it

Gaetano and Alfredo Falluto, with consultant Roberto Mazzer, make a carefully honed range of wines from their 18 hectares of vineyard in the Sannio and Solopaca DOC zones. At a retaste, the Sannio Aglianico Tre Pietre '98 showed as well structured and long-lived.

○ Solopaca Bianco Guiscardo '01	▼	3
● Sannio Aglianico Tre Pietre '98	♀	4

La Guardiense
Loc. Santa Lucia, 104/105
82034 Guardia Sanframondi (BN)
Tel. 0824864034
E-mail: guardiense@laguardiense.com

With 1031 members supplying grapes from 2,500 hectares of vineyard, La Guardiense has an important role in the region. There is now a major project underway to focus its output on quality.

○ Guardiolo Falanghina '01	▼	3
● Guardiolo Rosso Ris. '97	♀	4

D'Antiche Terre - Vega
C.da Lo Piano - S. S. 7 bis
83030 Manocalzati (AV)
Tel. 0825675359 - 0825675358

The most representative wine from this major Irpinia winery, which has over 40 hectares of vine and an output of over 300,000 bottles a year, is the successful, fresh, fruity Greco di Tufo '01.

○ Greco di Tufo '01	▼	4
● Irpinia Rosso Coriliano	▼	3

Monte Pugliano
Loc. S. P. Pagliarone-M. c P.
Via San Vito
84090 Montecorvino Pugliano (SA)
Tel. 3283412515

Cesare Cavallo, Fernando Fiore and Giulio Natella continue on their chosen path, with input from consultant and friend Bruno De Conciliis. The best wines from the estate, which now produces 75,000 bottles a year, are the normal and Riserva versions of Aglianico Castellaccio.

● Aglianico Castellaccio Ris. '00	▼	5
● Aglianico Castellaccio '01	▼	5

Villa Diamante
Via Toppole, 16
83030 Montefredane (AV)
Tel. 082530777
E-mail: agait@tin.it

Villa Diamante specializes in Fiano di Avellino. There is less than four hectares of vineyard, at Montefredane, but all are planted with fiano. The wines have good structure, notable freshness and considerable longevity.

○ Fiano di Avellino Vigna della Congregazione '00	▼	4
○ Fiano di Avellino Vigna della Congregazione '97	▼	4

Ocone
Loc. La Madonnella - Via del Monte
82030 Ponte (BN)
Tel. 0824874040
E-mail: admocone@tin.it

Ocone is an important name in Campania. The family has been producing excellent wine at Ponte, in the Taburno zone, since 1910. Two wines stood out this year: Aglianico Diomede, first reviewed last year; and Calidonio, from aglianico and piedirosso. Both are Taburno DOC.

● Taburno Rosso Calidonio '01	♀	5
● Aglianico del Taburno Diomede '97	♀	5

La Casa dell'Orco
Fraz. S. Michele - Via Limaturo, 52
83039 Pratola Serra (AV)
Tel. 0825967038 - 082537247
E-mail: lacasadellorco@libero.it

Lawyer Pellegrino Musto has owned this fine estate at Pratola Serra for about a decade. He produces a full range of classic Irpinian wines. The best of these are undoubtedly Greco di Tufo and Fiano di Avellino.

○ Fiano di Avellino '01	♀	4
○ Greco di Tufo '01	♀	4

Fattoria Prattico
S. S. 430 - Km 17,100
81040 Rocca d'Evandro (CE)
Tel. 0823925313
E-mail: info@fattoriaprattico.it

Claudio Prattico produces around 100,000 bottles a year from his vineyards in the Rocca d'Avandro area, in the province of Caserta. We liked best his two interesting versions of Falanghina '01, one DOC the other IGT. Both have notably clean aromas and nicely full palates.

○ Falanghina Vigna del Prete '01	♀	3
○ Galluccio Falanghina '01	♀	3

Francesco Rotolo
Via San Cesario, 18
84070 Rutino (SA)
Tel. 0974830050

Francesco Rotolo is owner of this thriving estate at Rutino, in the Cilento. Again this year, the freshness of the fruit on Fiano Valentina '01 impressed us. The other wines, a Cilento Aglianico and a Cilento Bianco were less exciting.

○ Fiano Valentina '01	♀	3

De Falco
Via Figliola
80040 San Sebastiano al Vesuvio (NA)
Tel. 0817713755
E-mail: defalcovini@tin.it

Gabriele and Angelo De Falco's range is produced from grapes bought in the better zones of the region. We pick out two DOC whites from Irpinia, both well made and well typed.

○ Fiano di Avellino '01	♀	4
○ Greco di Tufo '01	♀	4

Masseria Felicia
Loc. Carano
Via Prov. Appia Carano
81030 Sessa Aurunca (CE)
Tel. 0817362201

This is a small, carefully run estate, with just three and a half hectares of vine, specializing in Falerno del Massico production. The '00, aged in barrique, has no lack of depth or elegance and certainly grabs your interest.

● Falerno del Massico Rosso Barrique '00	♀♀	5

BASILICATA

Basilicata's results this year confirm the good news we forecast in the last edition of the Guide. The region, and the area of Vulture in particular, is becoming one of the most exciting in Italy. Very few other regions have such high average quality, especially with reds. Three wines gained Three Glasses and many more are very close. Look at how many glasses on the following pages are printed in red. It is not all down to the main grape variety, aglianico, which is as noble a variety as merlot, nebbiolo or cabernet. There is also the unique geographical situation. Vulture has some of the highest-planted vines in Europe. In some case, planting density is incredibly high. Day-night temperature fluctuations are considerable, which accentuates fruit characteristics, and there are many old vines. Pivotally, vinification techniques are exemplary. These are impeccably made wines – whites as well as reds – and they display a judicious approach to winemaking, avoiding short cuts. Yields in the vineyards are low, leading to concentration in the wines, and the use of oak is shrewdly gauged, not exaggerated. In the province of Matera, things are much quieter. There are few wineries actually bottling – Dragone, Pisani and Progetto DiVino, for instance – and we were, quite honestly, expecting signs of greater effort. But let's come to the Three Glasses wines. Aglianico del Vulture La Firma from Cantina del Notaio came very close last time but this year, with the '00, this modern-styled, powerful wine has finally made it. Aglianico del Vulture Re Manfredi '99 from Terre degli Svevi, an estate owned by Gruppo Italiano Vini, shows that reds don't need Schwarzenegger's muscle to be great. This superb manifestation of the variety is elegant and refined. The '00 Aglianico del Vulture Rotondo repeats the '99's success and again shows just how well things are working at Paternoster. Indeed, the estate's Don Anselmo, an Aglianico del Vulture that manages to be traditional and modern at the same time, is another terrific wine. Then there is the classy Aglianico del Vulture Basilisco from Michele Cutolo's Basilisco estate. It does not appear in this edition of the Guide, the '00 for now remaining simply a star on the horizon. This is because Cutolo decided to age it longer before release. We wholeheartedly support this decision and feel sure that the wine will have greater complexity and finesse as a result. Finally, the numerous wines that reached the final taste-offs are due their share of the limelight. The future looks rosy indeed for Vigna della Corona from Le Querce, for the excellent Vetusto from the Consorzio Viticoltori, for the reliably fine Covo dei Briganti from Eubea-Famiglia Sasso, and for Aglianico del Vulture Titolo from Elena Fucci's estate. The last is a strong newcomer and we shall no doubt be hearing a lot more about it. Just remember: you heard it here first.

ACERENZA (PZ)

Basilium
C.da Pipoli
85011 Acerenza (PZ)
tel. 0971741449
e-mail: basilium@freenet.it

We know we're repeating ourselves but here we are with yet another Basilicata co-operative producing excellent wines. It was founded in 1976, and now has 50 members and an annual output of a good 1,400,000 bottles. The top wine is Aglianico del Vulture Valle del Trono. Last year's '98 was good but now the '99 is even better, and claimed Two Glasses with ease. There are aromas of roses and green tea. The palate is lean, but has a sense of sweetness and offers nice depth and balance of alcohol. Aglianico Le Gastaldie Sicone, given four months in barrique and eight months in large old oak barrels, is less complex but well made. Its nose is still closed but tobacco, leather and red berry fruits are nevertheless discernible. It is possibly even more attractive on the palate, which is soft and round. A very well-deserved One Glass goes to the white Greco I Portali, which reminds us yet again that the potential of Basilicata's whites should not be underrated. This 100 per cent Greco has a superb nose, full of ripe apricot and aromatic herbs, with hints of almond. There is good extractive weight on the palate, which mirrors the nose well. Aglianico Pipoli and the agreeable Aglianico Portali were less interesting this year. The Portali is traditionally styled and the better of the two.

BARILE (PZ)

Consorzio Viticoltori
Associati del Vulture
S. S. 93
85022 Barile (PZ)
tel. 097232253
e-mail: coviv@tiscalinet.it

Things get better and better. There are some quite exceptional wines this year from the Viticoltori Associati and one even made a stab at Three Glasses. It is only right at this point to reiterate that Basilicata has some of the best co-operatives in Italy, to the extent that it can honestly be considered a sort of Alto Adige of the south. Sergio Paternoster continues to work with a sure hand and results are there for all to see. We have already mentioned Vetusto. It comes from slightly over-ripe grapes and is a joy from the very first glimpse of its dark ruby colour. There are delightful aromas of peach and liqueur cherries. These are not invasive, instead showing beautiful elegance, which is not easy with grapes this ripe. The palate is fairly tannic, and has ripe fruit flavours, black pepper and tobacco. Aglianico Carpe Diem is another fine wine that scored almost as high as Vetusto. The nose is elegant, sweetly spicy and has attractive wild berry fruit. The warm, velvety palate is medium bodied and refined, with a lightly balsamic hint of liquorice. The basic Aglianico is as good as ever. It is a deep red. The nose is initially more reminiscent of small black berry fruits, such as blackberry, than red-skinned ones, then attractive tobacco-like hints emerge. The palate is long and satisfying, with good fruit and fine texture, bringing the wine comfortably into the Two Glass bracket. All in all this is a performance worthy of applause.

● Aglianico del Vulture Valle del Trono '99	🍷🍷	7
● Aglianico del Vulture I Portali '00	🍷	5
● Aglianico del Vulture Le Gastaldie Sicone '00	🍷	6
○ Greco I Portali '01	🍷	4
● Aglianico del Vulture Pipoli '00		4
● Intenso '01		4
● Aglianico del Vulture Valle del Trono '98	🍷	6

● Aglianico del Vulture Carpe Diem '00	🍷🍷	6
● Aglianico del Vulture Vetusto '99	🍷🍷	6
● Aglianico del Vulture '01	🍷🍷	4
○ Moscato Spumante	🍷	3
● Aglianico del Vulture Carpe Diem '99	🍷🍷	4*
● Aglianico del Vulture Vetusto '97	🍷🍷	4
● Aglianico del Vulture Vetusto '98	🍷🍷	6

BARILE (PZ)

TENUTA LE QUERCE
C.DA LE QUERCE
85100 BARILE (PZ)
TEL. 0971470709 - 0972725102
E-MAIL: tenutalequerce@tin.it

Le Querce was founded as recently as 1996 but has already become a significant part of the regional scene. It has over 60 hectares of vineyard in the Vulture zone, a considerable area for a Basilicata estate. Vigna della Corona, the "vineyard of the crown", takes its name from a Roman cippus, or monumental pillar, which was uncovered in the vineyard. It is now on display at the estate. The site produces excellent aglianico and Aglianico del Vulture Vigna della Corona, a new release, missed Three Glasses by a whisker. The colour is dark ruby. The nose is laden with fruit and marked out by balsam and liquorice, then the palate is fleshy, elegant and long, with still rather assertive tannins. The latest vintage of Rosso di Costanza is again good, with its fresh, blackberry and pepper nose, although even here the tannins, if fine-grained, are a touch astringent. However, this is a consistently reliable wine, and is produced in large quantities – 80,000 bottles a year. Aglianico Federico II, on the other hand, is no longer produced at all for it was thought to be too similar to Rosso di Costanza. Viola is an appealing Aglianico suitable for serving right through a meal. It sees only a little oak, with 50 per cent aged in stainless steel. An attractive wine, it shows cherry and mint on the nose, and good freshness on the palate. The estate also produces two wines under the Sasso trademark. Minorco is a characterful red with cooked fruit and oak on the nose, and plentiful tannin on the pleasing palate. The other, Pian dell'Altare, also red, is slim-bodied, fresh and drinkable.

BARILE (PZ)

PATERNOSTER
VIA NAZIONALE, 23
85022 BARILE (PZ)
TEL. 0972770224
E-MAIL: paternoster.vini@tiscalinet.it

The excellent Aglianico del Vulture Vigneto Rotondo again won Three Glasses, this year with the '00. What can we say other than the wine is simply fantastic? It may be even better than last year's, and sets this long-standing estate (founded in 1925) firmly among Italy's top group of wineries. Congratulations go to Vito Paternoster, who has worked hard for years to get to this point, and to Leonardo Palumbo, the estate's consultant oenologist. Rotondo '00 looks good, from its opaque dark ruby colour onwards. The nose is intense, complex and refined, with small red berry fruits and delicate wafts of spices and vanilla. The palate is mouthfilling, full of stuffing and tightly knit, but the tannins are its crowning glory. It develops evenly too, finishing with fruit and elegant balsamic notes on the aftertaste. Don Anselmo '98 just oozes class. It is a dark ruby tending to garnet on the rim. The nose is more austere but this is counterbalanced by its open breadth. There is power and good structure on the evenly textured palate with its flavours of cocoa powder, coffee, blueberry and blackberry. Perfectly integrated tannins and a pure, long finish complete the picture. Another Two Glasses went to Synthesi '00. This is a more approachable, immediate Aglianico but it's just as clean, full-bodied and well made as its stablemates. Fiano Bianco di Corte '01 is a lovely wine with fresh peach and apricot aromas, soft structure and good balance. The other wines, the sweet Moscato Clivus and the lightly sparkling Aglianico Barigliòtt, are also rather good.

● Aglianico del Vulture Vigna della Corona '00	🍷🍷	8
● Aglianico del Vulture Rosso di Costanza '00	🍷🍷	6
● Aglianico del Vulture Il Viola '00	🍷	4
● Minorco Sasso '00	🍷	5
● Pian dell'Altare Sasso '99		3
● Aglianico del Vulture Rosso di Costanza '98	🍷🍷	6
● Aglianico del Vulture Federico II '99	🍷🍷	5
● Aglianico del Vulture Rosso di Costanza '99	🍷🍷	6

● Aglianico del Vulture Rotondo '00	🍷🍷🍷	6
● Aglianico del Vulture Don Anselmo '98	🍷🍷	6
● Aglianico del Vulture Synthesi '00	🍷🍷	4*
○ Bianco di Corte '01	🍷🍷	4*
● Barigliott '01	🍷	3*
○ Moscato della Basilicata Clivus '01	🍷	3*
● Aglianico del Vulture Rotondo '98	🍷🍷🍷	5*
● Aglianico del Vulture Ris. Don Anselmo '97	🍷🍷	5

BARILE (PZ)

Tenuta del Portale
C.da Le Querce
85022 Barile (PZ)
Tel. 0972724691

Here we have another of Basilicata's younger estates. It was founded only in 1996 but has already producing some excellent red wines for some time. All three of its Aglianico del Vultures showed really well, from the standard '99 to the '97 Riserva, aged a year in large old wooden barrels (50,000 bottles a year are produced), and the top wine, Aglianico del Vulture Vigne a Capanno. It's given 20 months in barrique and annual production is 20,00 bottles. This is quite an aristocrat. It has a good dark ruby colour, the nose is full of nuances of incense, tobacco, leather and red berry fruit, and the predominant flavour on the fruit-forward palate is red berry fruit jam. It shows great softness, elegance and length, along with a marked balsamic note on the aftertaste. The Riserva shines for its extraordinary softness and its rich aromas of wild berry fruits with subtle hints of truffle. Its attractive, fresh palate has a joyous, cherry-like flavour and great balance, and there is excellent nose-palate harmony. There were 100,000 bottles of Aglianico del Vulture '99 produced, all reliably good and encouragingly priced. It is ruby flecked with lighter shades, and both nose and palate evoke cherries and small, ripe, wild berry fruits. So to oenologist Enzo Michelet and, of course, the owner, we offer a big, "Well done!"

● Aglianico del Vulture Le Vigne a Capanno '99	5
● Aglianico del Vulture Ris. '97	4
● Aglianico del Vulture '99	3
● Aglianico del Vulture '98	4

RIONERO IN VULTURE (PZ)

D'Angelo
Via Provinciale, 8
85028 Rionero in Vulture (PZ)
Tel. 0972721517
E-mail: dangelowine@tiscalinet.it

This estate, founded in 1936, has done a great deal to raise Aglianico del Vulture's profile worldwide. Years ago, when finding a well-made Aglianico was not so easy, winelovers could always safely turn to D'Angelo. The wines are just as dependable today. More than 250,000 bottles are produced from 50 hectares of vineyard, 30 of which the estate owns, and value for money is excellent. Canneto is as consistently reliable as they come. This first-rate Aglianico ages 18 months in barrique and 60,000 bottles are released. That's quite a number for a wine of such quality. It is dark red, with a nose of small red berry fruits, violet and tobacco. The palate is long and refined, with an attractive touch of blackberry and very finely-grained tannins, but is perhaps a touch less rich than last year's. Vigna Caselle, usually a marker for high-quality – not to say brilliantly priced – Aglianico, was not available this year but the "second-label" Aglianico has turned out excellently. It may be less concentrated than last year's but the cherry-like nose and alluring balsamic tones on the palate are enticing. We were, a little disappointed by Serra delle Querce, from 80 per cent aglianico and merlot, which has rather dominant oak, plus a touch of bitterness on the finish. However, the white Vigna dei Pini, from chardonnay, pinot bianco, and incrocio Manzoni 6.0.13, is a fragrant wine of rare elegance, with honey and apple-like aromas, then a fresh, not too alcoholic palate. There are none of the invasive notes of oak toast that are, sadly, all too common on southern Italian whites.

● Canneto '99	5
○ Vigna dei Pini '01	3
● Aglianico del Vulture '99	3
● Serra delle Querce '99	5
● Canneto '98	5
● Aglianico del Vulture Vigna Caselle Ris. '97	4
● Canneto '97	5
● Serra delle Querce '98	6

RIONERO IN VULTURE (PZ)

Di Palma
Via Potenza, 13
85028 Rionero in Vulture (PZ)
tel. 0972722515
e-mail: edildip@tiscalinet.it

This estate was founded only in 1997 and has nine hectares of vineyard with one further hectare leased. An excellent showing now brings it a first full entry in the Guide. This is so often the story in Basilicata. A new winery appears and starts producing really good, if not superb, wines in a relatively short time. How rarely this happens in other regions of Italy. Nibbio Grigio '98, a 100 per cent Aglianico aged 12 months in large old wooden barrels, is excellent. It is a dark ruby and its fine nose is a touch over-evolved but elegant, ethereal and complex, evoking mint, plum, dark chocolate and coffee. The fleshy, rich palate is elegant, too. The '97 Nibbio Grigio stayed eight to nine months in barrique and is probably just superior to the '98. It is more deeply coloured and has attractive aromas of mint, cherry and tobacco. The palate is extremely elegant and 12,000 bottles were produced. In the future, Nibbio Grigio will age in barriques only and a new maturation area holding 400 barriques will be inaugurated next year. The reason that "botti", or large barrels, were used for the '98 was some of the grapes came from vines that had only recently entered production. There was a risk of producing a wine with the fruit dominated by oak. This sort of thinking says much about the abilities of those in control. Our compliments to Sergio Paternoster, Giuseppe Avigliano and all the team.

RIONERO IN VULTURE (PZ)

Agricola Eubea - Fam. Sasso
Via Roma, 209
85028 Rionero in Vulture (PZ)
tel. 0972723574

On its second appearance in the Guide, this estate confirms that all the good things we said about it last year. Aglianico del Vulture Covo dei Briganti was again close to a third Glass and is a tremendous wine, even if it seemed a little less concentrated than the previous vintage. The colour is a deep cherry red, then the nose is full of blackberry, blackcurrant, wild cherry and black cherry, and has attractive smoky notes. The long, alluring palate has tannins of unusual finesse and such ripe fruit that it is almost like drinking fresh blackcurrant juice. There is an intriguing new white semi-dried grape "passito" wine, Seduzione, from 75 per cent malvasia with moscato and aglianico (that's right, aglianico). It is nicely aromatic and the palate is richly fleshy although the wine is possibly a touch too sweet, which reduces its freshness. Nevertheless, it has everything it needs to develop into something very special, so it's well worth watching carefully. Finally, we can reveal that there are a few barrels in the cellar holding what looks like becoming an astonishingly good Aglianico del Vulture. It hasn't yet been given a name but it comes from a few aglianico vines grown on a plot of land that is particularly suitable for the grape. The wine has head-turning extract and texture. It's absolutely amazing so all we can do is wait for it to finish its time in wood. Watch this space next year for what we hope will be another major discovery.

● Aglianico del Vulture Nibbio Grigio '97	ΨΨ	7
● Aglianico del Vulture Nibbio Grigio '98	ΨΨ	4

● Aglianico del Vulture Il Covo dei Briganti '00	ΨΨ	6
○ Seduzione '01	Ψ	5
● Aglianico del Vulture Il Covo dei Briganti '99	ΨΨ	6
● Aglianico del Vulture Il Covo dei Briganti '98	Ψ	4

RIONERO IN VULTURE (PZ)

Armando Martino
Via Luigi La Vista, 2/a
85028 Rionero in Vulture (PZ)
Tel. 0972721422
E-mail: martinovini@tiscalinet.it

The estate was founded in 1942 but, under its new owner, oenologist Giovanni Colucci, now appears in the Guide for the first time. There are 16 hectares of vineyard, including some old, bush-trained vines, which partly explains the quality found in the bottle. Aglianico Bel Poggio, which has just four months in barrique, is a distinguished wine with very complex aromas giving clean, pure fruit notes, mainly blackberry and black cherry, when aerated. The palate is very tannic. It is still reticent and opens only slowly to give sensations of tobacco, old leather, cocoa powder and wild black berry fruits. It not only gains Two Glasses with ease but shows that it is not necessary to leave a red a long time in oak for something interesting to emerge. Carolin, vinified totally in stainless steel, has a good nose of pepper and cooked plums with hints of mint, and a richly fruited, velvety palate. We retasted Aglianico Oraziano '97, which spent a year in barrique. Oak is still firmly present on the nose, which is nonetheless pleasing overall offering attractive notes of liquorice and balsam. We detected cocoa powder, raspberry and wild cherry on the palate, plus hints of tobacco and leather. The estate also deserves praise for its wallet-friendly pricing.

RIONERO IN VULTURE (PZ)

Cantine del Notaio
Via Roma, 159
85028 Rionero in Vulture (PZ)
Tel. 0972717111 - 03356842483
E-mail: gerardo.giura@tin.it

Three Glasses for Aglianico del Vulture La Firma '00, a wine that had everyone nodding in agreement from the first tasting. It hails from vines grown on Maschito, one of Vulture's top vineyards, and is one of the true Aglianico greats. The '99 was terrific, missing Three Glasses by a whisker, but the '00 has better judged use of oak and, as a result, better fruit-oak balance. It is opaque and in fact one of the darkest Aglianicos of all. This clue to its great intensity receives confirmation on both nose and palate. The nose has mulberry, India ink, blueberry, mint and balsam, then the palate is fat, silky, sweetly fruited and very long. We found the Repertorio Aglianico showing particularly well this year, too. It is not as massive as La Firma but, like it, is marked out by the ripeness of its tannins and its terrific extract. The nose recalls La Firma's with its mint and balsamic notes, but there is a touch less complexity and a not particularly refined bell pepper note. The palate has silky tannins, very ripe plum and blackberry fruit, and notable finesse. We finished with our first tasting of the estate's new sweet wine, L'Autentica, from 100 per cent moscato. With its beautiful elegance, it is more of a late-harvest wine than a dried-grape "passito" in style. There is good concentration on the palate, attractively refreshing acidity, flavours of honey and apple fruit, and a slightly bitterish aftertaste.

● Aglianico del Vulture Bel Poggio '99	ΥΥ	3*
● Rosso Carolin '01	Υ	3
● Aglianico del Vulture Oraziano '97	ΥΥ	4

● Aglianico del Vulture La Firma '00	ΥΥΥ	6
● Aglianico del Vulture Il Repertorio '00	ΥΥ	5
○ L'Autentica '00	ΥΥ	6
● Aglianico del Vulture La Firma '99	ΥΥ	6
● Aglianico del Vulture Il Repertorio '99	ΥΥ	5

VENOSA (PZ)

TERRE DEGLI SVEVI
LOC. PIAN DI CAMERA
85029 VENOSA (PZ)
TEL. 0972374175 - 097235253
E-MAIL: n.capurso@giv.it

Terre degli Svevi makes its Guide debut in grand style. It is based in Venosa, the major shareholder is Gruppo Italiani Vini and it has 84 hectares of vine, lying in the Vulture DOC zone at Venosa and Maschito. There is just one wine, Aglianico del Vulture Re Manfredi, produced in quantities of around 120,000 bottles a year, which will grow to 300,000 when everything is up and running fully. Last year, we had a look at the '98 and were pretty sure that the estate was going places but any doubts we might have had were completely swept away by the '99 edition. Oenologist Nunzio Capurso, who is also in charge of the winery, has turned out a magnificent red. Its aromas are typically southern yet it is modern, expressive and has unusual purity of style. Dark ruby with a garnet-tinged rim, it reveals a deep, intense nose with ripe red berry fruit, blackberry and blueberry jam, and background tones of coffee, oak toast and tobacco. On the palate, it is powerful and rich, dense but not heavy, and full of fleshy fruit and smooth tannins. It develops elegantly and evenly across the mouth, and the fruit softens into notes of balsam and new oak, with just the merest hint of tar and tobacco on its long finish. This is quite simply a great wine, well worthy of its effortlessly claimed Three Glasses. The '98, though slightly less intense, is very similar in style.

VENOSA (PZ)

CANTINA DI VENOSA
LOC. VIGNALI
VIA APPIA
85029 VENOSA (PZ)
TEL. 097236702
E-MAIL: info@cantinadivenosa.it

The name has changed, becoming shorter, which for those who write about wine is a great advantage. Luckily, the wines have not been "abbreviated" in any way and remain very good. The Cantina di Venosa amply reflects the high standing of the region's co-operatives. This is all down to Oronzo Calò and Rocco Manieri, who co-ordinate work in vineyard and cellar. With 480 members contributing grapes there is no shortage of work. This year, there was no new vintage for us to try of the flagship Carato Venusio, nor of Terre di Orazio, another sound Aglianico, so we turned to two new reds. Aglianico Vignali, which is fabulous value for money, stays 12 months in wood, 80 per cent in barrique, the rest in large, old barrels. It is ruby red and has a delightful nose of raspberry and wild strawberries. The other newcomer, Aglianico Il Madrigale di Gesualdo, ages entirely in barrique and has very intense aromas of cooked fruit. It is mouthfilling, with flavours of spices, bitter orange and liqueur cherries, enlivened by great freshness. Vignali, from 70 per cent malvasia with equal parts of greco and chardonnay, showed well and is certainly a wine to watch. It has floral and fruity aromas, then acacia honey on the palate. It just needed more complexity to gain Two Glasses. We finish with the wine that impressed us most of all. Surprisingly, it's a white, the spectacular Terre di Orazio Dry Muscat. It is elegant, wonderfully long, delightfully aromatic and doesn't cloy, as this style of wine often can. The only thing that dismayed us, as good Italians, is that the name is in English.

● Aglianico del Vulture Re Manfredi '99	♛♛♛	5*
● Aglianico del Vulture Re Manfredi '98	♛♛	5

○ Dry Muscat Terre di Orazio '01	♛♛	2*
● Aglianico del Vulture Il Madrigale di Gesualdo '00	♛	4
● Aglianico del Vulture Vignali '00	♛	2*
○ Basilicata Bianco Vignali '01	♛	1*
● Basilicata Rosso Vignali '00	♛♛	2*
● Aglianico del Vulture Carato Venusio '97	♛♛	4
● Aglianico del Vulture Terre di Orazio '98	♛♛	3
● Aglianico del Vulture Terre di Orazio '99	♛♛	3*

OTHER WINERIES

ELENA FUCCI
LOC. C.DA SOLAGNA DEL TITOLO
85022 BARILE (PZ)
TEL. 0972770736

Basilicata has a new star in its firmament, the elegant, powerful Aglianico del Vulture Titolo. The nose has red berry fruits and smokiness followed by pencil lead, The palate is mouthfilling and long. This is an estate to watch closely.

● Aglianico del Vulture Titolo '00	🍷🍷	5

PROGETTO DIVINO
VIA NAZIONALE, 76
75100 MATERA
TEL. 0835262851 - 0835259549
E-MAIL: progettodivino@hsh.it

San Biaggio '99 was a very good wine but the '00 is even better. It's strikingly fresh on the nose and attractive to drink. A modern aglianico and merlot blend, it has complexity and isn't a copycat wine. Well done to Sante Lomurno and his colleagues.

● San Biagio '00	🍷🍷	5
● San Biagio '97	🍷🍷	4
● San Biagio '98	🍷🍷	4
● San Biagio '99	🍷🍷	5

BASILISCO
VIA UMBERTO I, 129
85028 RIONERO IN VULTURE (PZ)
TEL. 0972720032
E-MAIL: basilisco@interfrre.it

The release of Michele Cutolo's Aglianico del Vulture Basilisco '00 onto the market has been held back. It takes courage for a young estate to make such a move but longer ageing will without doubt give this great red even more to offer.

● Aglianico del Vulture Basilisco '98	🍷🍷	5
● Aglianico del Vulture Basilisco '99	🍷🍷	5

CANTINA SOCIALE DEL VULTURE
VIA SAN FRANCESCO
85028 RIONERO IN VULTURE (PZ)
TEL. 0972721062
E-MAIL: alporb@libro.it

The '98 Aglianico is very well made and has great balance, bringing it almost to Two Glasses level. The rose, almond and violet on the nose are there on the palate, too. The wine drinks easily but also has richness and good complexity.

● Aglianico del Vulture '98	🍷	2*

PUGLIA

Without wishing to resort to cliché, we have to say, at the end of this year's tastings, that Puglia is now well on the way to wine splendour. Until not so ago, the region and its two coasts were mainly known for rather rough and ready, but dirt cheap, products, blended into anonymous wines and sold to bars and bottlers all over Europe, but now Puglia's prestige is not up for discussion. You can see this by the investors, from abroad as well as Italy, who are looking right here, in Puglia with its superlative climate, for vineyard land to make new quality-driven wines. We are talking about newcomers of the status of Antinori, Avignonesi, Feudi di San Gregorio, Zonin and Gruppo Italiano Vini, to name but a few, and, remarkably, they have not caused any ruptures within the region. Indeed, in some respects, their arrival has been fortuitous. Even the most traditional, lethargic, producers are being swept along by the new trend, and by the surge of enthusiasm and experience rushing in from other wine territories. The result is a dynamism that pervades the region, and the average quality of bottled wine is rising by leaps and bounds. An additional advantage is that few regions can combine quality and low prices so successfully. Even Foggia, long considered Puglia's Cinderella province, is now turning out good-quality wines that are successfully finding their niche in the marketplace. But things are good everywhere: Castel del Monte, Salento with its numerous DOCs, Bari's Murgia and the zones of Manduria and Gioia del Colle, to cite just a few instances, have hundreds of good wines on offer, not to mention several that are right up there with the international greats. Even more important, these wine "speak their own language". They come from traditional varieties, such as primitivo, uva di troia and malvasia nera, yet are relished by consumers worldwide. Putting all this together, it is hardly surprising that the number of Three Glass wines doubled this year. Alongside the 2000 release of that classic, Zero, from Conti Zecca, there is a stunning Le Braci '00 from Severino Garofano's Masseria Monaci, Primitivo Visellio '01 from Rubino and a new red from Antinori's Tormaresca estate, Masseria Maime '00. But we must stress that they are joined by an even larger band of wines, the ones that very nearly reached Three Glasses and earned Two red Glasses. These include wines from estates such as Leone de Castris, Albano Carrisi, Vallone, Candido, Sinfarosa, Masseria Pepe and others. What more proof can anyone need that the regeneration of winemaking in Puglia is no longer just a project? It is already under way.

ALEZIO (LE)

Rosa del Golfo
Via Garibaldi, 56
73011 Alezio (LE)
tel. 0331993198
e-mail: calo@rosadelgolfo.com

The flagship wine of this estate has always been its splendid rosé, but this year the skills of Damiano Calò, his oenologist Angelo Solci and agronomist Saverio Gabellone have brought other products to the fore. Taking the lead is Bolina, from around 92 per cent verdeca and chardonnay, and the '01 is possibly the best we have ever tasted. Straw yellow tinged with green, it has a fascinating, delightfully aromatic nose – verdeca is a semi-aromatic grape and important in vermouth production – giving aromas of citrus fruit and white peach. The sage-flavoured palate is beautifully fresh, with a great profile throughout the mouth and a slightly salty tang on the finish. Primitivo '00 is similarly fine. The colour is bright ruby, then there is almond, hazelnut and morello cherry on the nose. The palate is soft and long, with flavours of chocolate, cherry and coffee. On the other hand, we weren't completely happy with this year's Portulano, the '98, from 90 per cent negroamaro with malvasia nera. We prefer to reserve judgement and taste it again for next year's Guide. Which brings us to the estate's legendary rosato, for many years possibly the best rosé in Italy. It is still impressive. The colour is a bright pink tinged with coral, the nose has wild strawberries and raspberries, the palate is clean and very fresh but seems a touch short of stuffing. The memory of the amazing '99, though, just two years ago, makes us long to see this wine return to the impeccable standards we were used to, as soon as possible.

● Salento Primitivo '00	♔♔	4
○ Salento Bianco Bolina '01	♔♔	3*
⊙ Salento Rosato Rosa del Golfo '01	♔♔	3
⊙ Salento Rosato Rosa del Golfo '00	♕♕	3*
⊙ Salento Rosato Rosa del Golfo '98	♕♕	3
⊙ Salento Rosato Rosa del Golfo '99	♕♕	4

ANDRIA (BA)

Conte Spagnoletti Zeuli
C.da S. Domenico ss. 98 km. 21
70031 Andria (BA)
tel. 0883569511 - 0883569560

This 400-year-old estate makes its full Guide debut, thanks to its excellent Castel del Montes. The wine is documented in several texts from the end of the 16th century, which cite the Spagnoletti family as owning lands around Castel del Monte. Currently, the estate has 400 hectares, of which 120 are vineyard, split over two holdings. Castel del Monte Pezza La Ruca is just splendid. The nose is full and concentrated, with aromas of small red berry fruits, plum and ripe black cherry. These tones are mirrored on the rich, soft, well-knit palate, which has elegant, delicate tannins and good balance. Castel del Monte Riserva del Conte is similarly impressive and very well made. The colour is deep ruby, tinged with purple. The nose is still a little closed, but has oak toast alongside small black berry fruits and plum. The oak tends to dominate on the palate, as the wine is young, but there is very good underlying structure. It will no doubt reveal its style more fully after a few months bottle age. One notch down the scale, but still attractive and well made, are Castel del Monte Bianco La Piana, a fresh, fragrant wine with aromas of apple and banana and a beautifully soft palate, and Castel del Monte Rosato Mezzana, which reveals a bright pink colour, a delicate nose of apple and cherry, and soft, well-knit palate.

● Castel del Monte Pezza La Ruca '00	♔♔	4
● Castel del Monte Ris. del Conte '00	♔♔	6
○ Castel del Monte Bianco La Piana '01	♔	4
⊙ Castel del Monte Rosato Mezzana '01	♔	4

ANDRIA (BA)

RIVERA
FRAZ. C.DA RIVERA
S. S. 98, KM 19.800
70031 ANDRIA (BA)
TEL. 0883569501 - 0883569575
E-MAIL: info@rivera.it

Oenologist Leonardo Palumbo, and agronomist and owner Carlo De Corato, keep this estate right at the top of the Puglian wine tree. Its signature wine, Il Falcone, from 70 per cent uva di troia with montepulciano, is still one of Puglia's best reds. The colour is bright ruby, then the nose, initially closed, opens to give notes of small red berry fruits jam and cherries. The palate is fat and dense. This year's release is possibly a touch less impressive than last year's more concentrated wine, but its remarkable value for money has to be applauded, especially when you remember that this is, to all effects and purposes, one of Italy's great red wines. The estate's new red, Puer Apuliae, from 100 per cent uva di troia, looks set to become another classic. A deep ruby introduces a nose of spice, tobacco and small black berry fruits, while the palate is still closed but has a long, attractive finish. Beyond the wine's intrinsic characteristics, we are cheered by the increased attention producers are giving to uva di troia, a variety that has been in the region for centuries and can yield great wines, without the need to fall back on the ubiquitous cabernet and merlot. Cappellaccio, a classy Aglianico, with a run of 100,000 bottles, is as good as ever. Twelve months in barrique gives an elegantly textured red with silky tannins. Finally, both Chardonnays, the stainless steel-vinified Preludio and the barrique-aged Lama di Corvo, showed well while Bianco Fedora has good character. And it's terrific value for money.

BRINDISI

TENUTE RUBINO
VIA MEDAGLIE D'ORO, 15/A
72100 BRINDISI
TEL. 0831571955 - 0831502912
E-MAIL: info@tenuterubino.it

Puglia's precocious child claims its first major success, and we bet it won't be the last. In only its third year in the Guide, the Rubino family's estate notches up Three Glasses with Visellio, a 100 per cent Primitivo given eight months in barrique. It's a wine of great weight, depth and richness of extract and is very dark in colour. The nose, still a little closed, has plum and dried fig fruit that integrates well with its classy, and well-calibrated, spicy, balsamic oak. The outstanding palate, in perfect harmony with the nose, is dense, fleshy, refined, very elegant and has great complexity and length. Jaddico, previously called Gallico, a Brindisi Rosso based on negroamaro, montepulciano and malvasia nera, is splendid and not far behind the Visellio for quality or score. The complex nose has black cherry, printer's ink, vanilla and elegant oakiness. The imposing palate is full, deep and rich, with clean, pure fruit, good acid backbone and youthful, but already ripe, silky tannins. Oenologist Riccardo Cotarella's touch is evident in both wines, yet they are unmistakably Puglian in style and strongly characteristic of the region's terroirs and indigenous varieties. Both Marmorelle wines are nicely made. The Rosso, from negroamaro with 15 per cent malvasia nera, has small red berry fruits on the nose. Its cleanly fruited palate is a touch more rustic than the previous vintage but has good structure and body. The Bianco, from chardonnay with 20 per cent malvasia bianca, has banana and a mineral tang on the nose, then a fresh, characterful palate.

- Castel del Monte Rosso Il Falcone Ris. '99 — 4*
- Castel del Monte Nero di Troia Puer Apuliae '00 — 6
- Castel del Monte Chardonnay Preludio N° 1 '01 — 3*
- Castel del Monte Rosso Rupicolo '00 — 2*
- Castel del Monte Bianco Fedora '01 — 1*
- Castel del Monte Chardonnay Lama di Corvo '01 — 5
- Castel del Monte Rosè di Rivera '01 — 2*
- Castel del Monte Sauvignon Terre al Monte '01 — 3
- Locorotondo '01 — 2*
- Castel del Monte Aglianico Cappellaccio Ris. '99 — 4
- Castel del Monte Rosso Il Falcone Ris. '98 — 4

- Salento Primitivo Visellio '01 — 5*
- Brindisi Rosso Jaddico '01 — 5
- Salento Bianco Marmorelle '01 — 3
- Salento Rosso Marmorelle '01 — 3
- Brindisi Rosso Gallico '00 — 5*
- Salento Primitivo Visellio '00 — 4*
- Salento Rosso Marmorelle '00 — 3*

CAMPI SALENTINA (LE)

Calatrasi Puglia
Via Cellino San Marco, km 1,5
73012 Campi Salentina (LE)
tel. 0918576767

The Allora line produced by Calatrasi, a Sicilian company with 70 hectares of leased vineyard in Puglia, is spot on, and the Negroamaro and Primitivo are terrific. This might surprise you if we told you that the oenologist is Australian. But in fact, Brian Fletcher, in harness since 2000, is producing wines that, though modern, are totally in harmony with their origin and its traditions. The two wines both have great creaminess of fruit and smoothness of tannins – such roundness is, in effect, quite Australian in style – and are all too drinkable. The Negroamaro is weightier and more structured, revealing very ripe fruit and unusual length. The Primitivo is softer and more graceful, both on nose and palate. Both are also as food friendly as they come. These Allora wines are excellent as examples of the new Puglian wine scene and will surely gain a firmer footing when the recent addition of 320 hectares to the vineyard holding comes into production. The Accademia del Sole wines are also worth watching. They are the result of a fascinating project, a joint venture between five families in Puglia, Sicily and Tunisia who are owners or long-term leaseholders of high-class vineyards, and Calatrasi, which provides the technical expertise. In Puglia, the ten-hectare Morella estate produces a good Sangiovese Negroamaro. This has an intriguingly smoky nose with mulberry aromas, and a nicely honed palate, although its vegetal tones create a slight imbalance, at least for now.

CELLINO SAN MARCO (BR)

Tenute Albano Carrisi
C.da Bosco, 13
72020 Cellino San Marco (BR)
tel. 0831619211
e-mail: tenute@albanocarrisi.com

Platone did not attain Three Glasses this year, and the whole Carrisi range is a tad less exciting than last year's, but even so there is a consistency of quality here that makes the estate one of Puglia's most reliable markers. The '99 Platone is a dark ruby colour. The character of the nose comes from the use of barrique, giving toasty coffee and chocolate, which overlies attractive hints of black cherry jam. The palate is full, nicely fat and richly fruited, with ripe tannins, good alcohol and notable acid backbone. It finishes long with toasty, chocolate notes returning on the aftertaste. In short, it's very impressive. Taras, a rich, alcoholic Primitivo also showed very well. Fruit melds well with spiciness on the nose and the palate is full, with good body and length leading to a balsamic aftertaste. Don Carmelo, from negroamaro with 15 per cent primitivo, is a little below par. Although soft and attractive as it enters the mouth, a hint of oxidation and lack of weight on the palate keep it well away from the Two Glasses the previous vintage gained. The rest of the range is more traditional in style but nonetheless pleasing. Salice Salentino is full and fruity. Nostalgia, from negroamaro, is spicy and soft. The rosé Mediterraneo is rich and ripe. Despite such a fine series of wines, we have to end on a low point. Prices here have risen exponentially and are now, we feel, seriously out of proportion.

● Allora Negroamaro '00	▼▼	4
● Allora Primitivo '01	▼▼	4
● Accademia del Sole Famiglia Morella Sangiovese Negroamaro '01	▼	4
● Allora Aglianico '00	▼▼	4*
● Allora Primitivo '00	▼▼	4*

● Salento Rosso Platone '99	▼▼	8
☉ Salento Rosato Mediterraneo '01	▼	5
● Salice Salentino Rosso '97	▼	3
● Salento Rosso Nostalgia '98	▼	4
● Salento Rosso Don Carmelo '99	▼	4
● Salento Rosso Taras '99	▼	6
● Salento Rosso Platone '98	▼▼▼	8
● Salento Rosso Don Carmelo '97	▼▼	3*

CELLINO SAN MARCO (BR)

Cantina Due Palme
Via San Marco, 130
72020 Cellino San Marco (BR)
Tel. 0831617865
E-mail: duepalme@tin.it

This co-operative is run by Angelo Maci and has around 600 members who together work over 250 hectares of land, giving an annual production of around two and a half million bottles. This year, they have forged links with the renowned Tuscan estate, Avignonesi. It is too early to talk about a new star rising on the Puglian scene but all the prerequisites for future glory are in place. Results this year are already very exciting. Tenute Albrizzi, from cabernet sauvignon and primitivo, is excellent. The colour is dark and deep and the nose is full of pervasive ripe fruit. The palate is rich and soft, with fruit and oak supporting each other, and elegant, ripe tannins. It is, though, rendered a touch unsophisticated by excessive sweetness. Salento Primitivo is similarly good. The oak is well calibrated, and in perfect balance with the fruit, while the palate is dense and soft with cocoa powder on the finish. Squinzano Rosso also showed surprisingly well. The nose has sweet notes of wild berry fruits, cherry and chocolate. The palate is fat, soft and notably tannic but rich in fruit and most attractive. Salice Salentino is anther example of the progress in quality at Due Palme. Its ripe plum and wild berry fruits aromas, followed by weight and rich fleshiness on the fairly long palate, took it way past the Two Glass barrier. A sound Salice Salentino, less full and rich than its stablemate but fresh and attractive, and the clean, well-fruited, most pleasing Salento Negroamaro Canonico bring us to a close. Value for money is excellent across the board.

● Salento Primitivo '01	🍷🍷	3*
● Salento Rosso Tenuta Albrizzi '01	🍷🍷	3*
● Squinzano Rosso '01	🍷🍷	3*
● Salice Salentino Selvarossa Ris. '98	🍷🍷	4
● Salento Negroamaro Canonico '01	🍷	2*
● Salice Salentino '01	🍷	3

CELLINO SAN MARCO (BR)

Marco Maci
Via San Marco, 61
72020 Cellino San Marco (BR)
Tel. 0831617689 - 0831617120
E-mail: marcomaci@libero.it

As usual, there are numerous offerings from this winery. With 100 hectares under vine and an output of 1,000,000 bottles, it is understandable that the cellar has decided to produce over 20 wines but at times we feel this detracts from consistency of quality. There are indeed highs and lows in the wines, which means disappointments, especially when the prices of some of them are taken into consideration. But let's not ignore the high points, such as the excellent Dragonero, from merlot with 20 per cent negroamaro. It's a darkly coloured red, with an intense nose full of red wild berry fruits and a full, fat, powerful, fleshy palate, and it lacks only a little length. Vita is on a similar footing, but with cabernet taking the place of the merlot. There is good integration of the oak and the super-ripe fruit notes of blackberry and plum. The palate is full, ripe, soft, firmly textured, fairly long and in good harmony with the nose. Bella Mojgan, from 80 per cent negroamaro and malvasia nera, showed slightly less well than expected and remained below the Two Glass threshold. The nose is fruity and concentrated, and there is good richness of extract and fleshiness on the palate, but it finishes rather short and slightly vegetal. The two rosés were pleasing. Sarì has a dark cherry, almost red, hue and aromas of plum and ripe apple. Gote Rubizze has strong cherry scents and almond on the finish. One Glass also goes to each of Squinzano Zephir, Sire and Primitivo Fra Diavolo. Nothing else really impressed us.

● Dragonero '99	🍷🍷	6
● Vita '99	🍷🍷	8
● Salento Primitivo Fra Diavolo '00	🍷	5
⊙ Gote Rubizze '01	🍷	3
⊙ Sarì '01	🍷	4
● Bella Mojgan '99	🍷	6
● Sire '99	🍷	6
● Squinzano Rosso Zephir '99	🍷	4
● Bella Mojgan '98	🍷🍷	6
● Dragonero '98	🍷🍷	6
● Sire '98	🍷🍷	6
● Vita '98	🍷🍷	6

CERIGNOLA (FG)

Torre Quarto
C.da Quarto, 5
71042 Cerignola (FG)
tel. 0885418453

It is with great pleasure that we see Torre Quarto producing good-quality wines again. The estate, owned by the Cirillo Farrusi family stretches over lands once owned by the Dukes of La Rochefoucauld. They possessed over 3,000 hectares of vineyard, which were for many years the symbol of Puglian viticulture. Stefano Cirillo Farrusi, assisted by oenologist Cristoforo Pastore, has now renovated the cellar and relaunched the range, to immediate effect. Tarabuso is a monovarietal Primitivo of great typicity. The spicy nose has tobacco and leather. The palate has good structure, plentiful fruit with an overlay of black pepper, nice balance and fair length. In short, it is a very fine wine and easily worth Two Glasses. Puglia Rosso, from uva di troia, aglianico, montepulciano and cabernet sauvignon, is also very good. Dark ruby, it has an intensely spicy, and balsam-like nose with penetrating notes of incense and myrtle. The palate is full, soft and elegant with crisp fruit and a sweet aftertaste of cherry jam. Another Two Glass winner is the ripe, fruit-forward Bottaccia, from 100 per cent uva di troia. Intense notes of plum, small black berry fruits and Mediterranean scrub precede a full, rich palate with well integrated tannins and a sensation of sweetness that is, however, a touch over the top. The Puglia Bianco and Puglia Rosso are both clean and well styled.

● Bottaccia '01	🍷🍷	4
● Puglia Rosso '01	🍷🍷	4
● Tarabuso '01	🍷🍷	4
○ Puglia Bianco '01	🍷	4
◉ Puglia Rosato '01	🍷	4

COPERTINO (LE)

Masseria Monaci
Loc. Tenuta Monaci
73043 Copertino (LE)
tel. 0832947512
e-mail: vini@masseriamonaci.com

In the middle of the 1990s, Severino Garofano, the region's leading oenologist, gained control of this fabulous holding in the Copertino DOC zone, which has over 30 hectares of vineyard and once owned by the noble Bacile di Castiglione family. In the past couple of years, the wines have not been particularly striking but this year we were knocked out by a red of extraordinary elegance that sailed past the Three Glass barrier. Le Braci '00 is a new wine, but follows Garofano's classic formula, that of using old, bush-trained negroamaro vines and picking late. It's an approach that has given Garofano more than a few notable successes. Le Braci has a dark ruby colour. The nose is complex and beautifully clean, full of super-ripe berry fruit, ranging from plum to blackberry to black cherry, and pervaded by additional layers of spices, vanilla and mint. The palate is warm, powerful and enveloping. It develops evenly, revealing a wealth of superbly elegant tannins, new oak in perfect balance and marvellous length. A great wine. Santa Brigida '01, from 80 per cent chardonnay and sauvignon, was awarded Two Glasses for its overall freshness, its attractive fruity aromas and its full, rounded structure. The '00 Copertino Eloquenzia, Masseria's warhorse, with a good 400,000 bottles a year produced, is as sound as ever. It has a good ruby colour, sweet aromas of ripe red berry fruits and spices, then a rounded palate that combines body with suppleness. All the other wines are very decent.

● Le Braci '00	🍷🍷🍷	5*
○ Santa Brigida '01	🍷🍷	2*
● Copertino Rosso Eloquenzia '00	🍷	2*
● Salento Primitivo I Censi '99	🍷	3
● Simposia '99	🍷	3

CORATO (BA)

TORREVENTO
LOC. CASTEL DEL MONTE
S. S. 170, KM 28
70033 CORATO (BA)
TEL. 0808980923 - 0808980929
E-MAIL: info@torrevento.it

Hats off to Francesco Liantonio, oenologist Pasquale Carparelli and all the Torrevento staff for excellent work. Quality is high throughout the range, despite the winery's size: annual output is 1,000,000 bottles from 150 hectares of vineyard under their control, including 100 estate-owned. This year, we were particularly impressed by the warm, well-fruited, solid, well-balanced Kebir Rosso '00, from uva di troia and cabernet sauvignon, which stays 12 months in barrique. Castel del Monte Rosato '01 is also fine. Deep cherry red, it has roses, black pepper spice and lots of flesh on the nose. The palate is fleshy, too, and holds up well despite good freshness. In short, it is a splendid rosé and one for winelovers who will enjoy comparing its 80-20 bombino nero and montepulciano blend with other Puglian rosés based on negroamaro, with or without malvasia nera. The new vintage of Vigna Pedale, one of the few serious reds made solely from uva di troia, is as good as usual. It is still young, with some residual edginess on the palate, but has fullness, good texture and lots of promise. There are attractive notes of Mediterranean scrub, old leather and tobacco on the nose, and of liquorice and black cherry on the palate. The negroamaro and malvasia nera-based Salice Salentino, which never sees oak, is elegant, nicely drinkable and very well made, as is the fine Castel del Monte Rosso, of which 300,000 bottles a year are produced. Also worth investigating is the fresh, easy-drinking Castel del Monte Bianco '01, from 70 per cent bombino bianco and pampanuto.

● Kebir '00	♥♥	5
⊙ Castel del Monte Rosato '01	♥♥	2*
● Castel del Monte Rosso Vigna Pedale Ris. '99	♥♥	4
● Salice Salentino Rosso '00	♥	3
○ Castel del Monte Bianco '01	♥	2*
● Puglia Rosso Torre del Falco '99	♥	3
○ Moscato di Trani Dulcis in Fundo '00	♥♥	4*
● Castel del Monte Rosso Vigna Pedale Ris. '96	♥♥	2
● Castel del Monte Rosso '97	♥♥	1
● Castel del Monte Rosso Vigna Pedale Ris. '98	♥♥	3
● Salice Salentino Rosso '99	♥♥	2*

FASANO (BR)

BORGO CANALE
LOC. SELVA DI FASANO
V.LE CANALE DI PIRRO, 23
72015 FASANO (BR)
TEL. 0804331351 - 0805046156
E-MAIL: info@borgocanale.it

Borgo Canale was founded in 1976 and now produces over 800,000 bottles a year of good-quality wine. Giuseppe De Leonardis looks after winemaking and Giacomo Palmisco tends the vines while the experienced Manlio Erba acts as consultant. The wine that did best in our tastings was Chardonnay Sannà, which ages four months in barrique. The nose is clean, with an attractive but not over-assertive note of caramel. The palate is also very impressive, the ripe fruit harmonizing well with its sweetly oaky notes. With just a bit more length, it could have really hit the high spots. Maestro, an unusual blend of pinot nero, montepulciano and primitivo, has a good red colour, somewhere between red and black cherry. The same fruits also characterize its nose. On the palate, the fruit is accompanied by an attractive streak of oak. Divo, a white from verdeca and chardonnay that does not see any oak, is well made, fresh and attractive. Similarly oak-free is the cherry-coloured rosé Rosa di Selva '01, which is full-bodied and rich. Finally, Locorotondo Talné, from verdeca, bianco d'Alessano and fiano, is a wine that shuns all modern influences. The nose is a little reduced at first but then opens to give attractive aromas of hedgerow and light hints of aromatic herbs.

○ Puglia Chardonnay Sannà '00	♥♥	4
● Primitivo Maestro '01	♥	4
○ Locorotondo Talné '01	♥	3
○ Puglia Bianco Divo '01	♥	4
⊙ Puglia Rosa di Selva '01	♥	3
● Primitivo Maestro '97	♥♥	3
● Primitivo Maestro '98	♥	3
● Primitivo Maestro '00	♥	4

GALATINA (LE)

Valle dell'Asso
Via Guidano, 18
73013 Galatina (LE)
tel. 0836561470
e-mail: valleasso@valleasso.it

Valle dell'Asso was founded way back in 1920 and has always had the reputation of being an excellent producer of the wines of Galatina. ("Galatina" is of Greek origin and means "beautiful Athena"). Only in recent years, though, has the estate focused firmly quality production, a move that was guided by owner Luigi Vallone and oenologist Elio Minoia. Annual production now exceeds 250,000 bottles a year. Galatina Negroamaro is a nicely made wine, dark in colour, with a spicy, coffee and tobacco-like nose, and a well-textured palate. The Galatina Bianco, exclusively from chardonnay, is attractive, with pleasing citrus notes and a fresh, easy-drinking style. But the similarly pleasant Salice Salentino Rosso '00, from 80 per cent negroamaro and malvasia nera, is also worth uncorking. It has good red berry fruit and an agreeable note of tobacco on the nose, and more super-clean, clearly defined, ripe fruit, on the palate. Piromàfo '99 and Macàro were both assessed last year but are worth a second look. The latter is a dessert wine from malvasia nera and aleatico made using the solera system. The Piromàfo is a serious red produced solely from negroamaro, aged a year in stainless steel and eight months in large old oak barrels. We found improvements with the extra year's bottle age. Perhaps we may be permitted to add that the town of Galatina, in the province of Lecce, is an artistic gem and well worth visiting if you are in the area.

● Galatina Negroamaro '00	🍷	5
● Salice Salentino '00	🍷	4
○ Galatina Bianco '01	🍷	4
● Galatina Rosso '00		4
⊙ Galatina Rosato '01		4
● Macàro Metodo Solera	🍷🍷	4
● Salento Rosso Piromàfo '99	🍷	6

GRAVINA IN PUGLIA (BA)

Cantina Cooperativa Botromagno
Via Archimede, 22
70024 Gravina in Puglia (BA)
tel. 0803265865
e-mail: botromagno@tiscalinet.it

Botromagno has 75 hectares of vineyard under its control, of which 25 are directly owned by the estate. This gives them the means to ensure a well-made and consistent range of wines. The team of owner Beniamino D'Agostino, oenologist Severino Garofano and agronomist Matteo De Rosa works like clockwork. Over 350,000 finely honed bottles are turned out annually, led by the successful Gravisano, one of the best sweet wines in southern Italy. It is a dried-grape "passito", made from malvasia nera fruit, aged 12 months in stainless steel, followed by six to eight months in barrique. The colour is a golden straw yellow. The full, rich nose opens immediately to give clear notes of ripe fig, dried apricot and candied citrus fruit, followed by a hint of blackcurrant. The palate is fat without cloying. The vanilla from the oak is pleasant, and doesn't intrude, in fact there is delightful freshness and unusual length. Gravina Bianco, already something of a classic, is as good as ever. From 60 per cent greco and malvasia bianca, it has aromas of ripe pears and wild herbs, good richness and extract on the palate, and fresh but not over-incisive acidity. As usual, we liked the Pier delle Vigne a lot. This red, from 60 per cent aglianico and montepulciano, aged two years in barrique, is characterized by particularly smooth tannins and great nose-palate harmony. The IGT Primitivo, which sees no oak, and the fresh, attractive, most drinkable rosé Silvium, also deserve investigation.

○ Gravisano '99	🍷🍷	4*
● Pier delle Vigne '97	🍷🍷	4*
○ Gravina '01	🍷🍷	3*
⊙ Murgia Rosato Silvium '01	🍷	3
● Primitivo '01	🍷	3
○ Gravina '00	🍷🍷	3*
● Pier delle Vigne '93	🍷🍷	2
● Pier delle Vigne '94	🍷🍷	2
○ Gravisano '97	🍷🍷	6

GUAGNANO (LE)

Antica Masseria del Sigillo
Via Provinciale, 37
73010 Guagnano (LE)
tel. 0832706331
e-mail: commercial@vinisigillo.com

It was another good showing for this estate. Output has been consolidated both quantitatively, having risen from 120,000 to 200,000 bottles a year, and qualitatively, for which credit is due to oenologist Oronzo Alò. The flagship wine is Terre del Guiscardo, from a 60-20-20 blend of primitivo, merlot and cabernet sauvignon, aged for a year, partly in stainless steel, partly in barrique. The nose is fresh and fruity, with notes of balsam and black pepper. The palate is rich, ripe, freshly fruited and nicely soft. It needs just a bit more flesh and density to leap into the stratosphere. The Primitivo Sigillo Primo, which accounts for 60 per cent of the estate's entire production, is also very impressive. The nose is full of fruit, especially plum and small red berries, and has nice notes of toastiness, incense and pepper. The palate is soft, with ripe tannins and good concentration, balance and length. It's also excellent value for money. The big news, however, is that Sigillo Primo Chardonnay has moved into the Two Glass band and become one of Puglia's best whites. The nose is intense and elegant, with fruit, butter and vanilla, then citrus-like freshness, suppleness, varietal stamping and refined oak tones mark out the long, full palate. The estate's other wines are all very pleasing. The Salice Salentino Il Secondo has a spicy nose and an attractive, fruit-driven palate. Sigillo Primo Bianco is light and supple, and the nicely intense Salice Salentino Hilliryos is cherry-like on both nose and palate.

●	Terre del Guiscardo '00	ŸŸ	4
●	Primitivo Sigillo Primo '01	ŸŸ	3*
○	Sigillo Primo Chardonnay '01	ŸŸ	3*
●	Salice Salentino Hilliryos '00	Ÿ	4
●	Salice Salentino Il Secondo '00	Ÿ	3
○	Sigillo Primo Bianco '01	Ÿ	3
●	Terre del Guiscardo '99	ŸŸ	4*
●	Primitivo Sigillo Primo '00	ŸŸ	2*

GUAGNANO (LE)

Cosimo Taurino
S. S. 605 Salice-Sandonaci
73010 Guagnano (LE)
tel. 0832706490
e-mail: taurino@tin.it

In some years, the great Patriglione is not released. Without Taurino's famous late-harvested red from negroamaro, conceived by the much missed Cosimo Taurino and his friend and oenologist, the stalwart Severino Garofano, this column usually seems a bit lightweight. Not so this year, because Francesco Taurino has come out with a vintage, the '97, of the winery's other celebrated red, Notarpanaro, that is not just excellent but the best ever. It is from the classic Salento mix of 85 per cent negroamaro and malvasia nera, and has a deep ruby hue tinged with garnet. The aromas are intense, warm and complex, unveiling red berry fruit jam, tobacco and spices. The palate has structure, weight, fruit, concentration, smooth tannins and notable freshness, all pointing to good ageing potential. The white I Sierri '01 also showed very well. From chardonnay and malvasia bianca, it is a bright straw colour. The nose is fresh and fruity, evoking apple and white peach, then the palate is supple and fresh, leaving the mouth full of fruit. We were slightly less impressed by Rosato Scaloti '01, from negroamaro. The structure is firm and full, but we found it rather evolved for its age. The otherwise sound Salice Salentino Riserva '99, long the estate's core wine, seemed to have the same fault.

○	I Sierri '01	ŸŸ	4
●	Notarpanaro '97	ŸŸ	5
◉	Salento Rosato Scaloti '01	Ÿ	4
●	Salice Salentino Rosso Ris. '99	Ÿ	4
●	Patriglione '85	ŸŸŸ	5
●	Patriglione '94	ŸŸŸ	6
●	Patriglione '95	ŸŸ	8
●	Patriglione '93	ŸŸ	5
●	Patriglione '90	Ÿ	5

LECCE

CANTELE
VIA VINCENZO BALSAMO, 13
73100 LECCE
TEL. 0832240962
E-MAIL: cantele@cantele.it

Augusto and Domenico Cantele's idea of setting up a sort of private co-operative has paid off. They follow and co-ordinate 243 affiliated producers with, between them, over 200 hectares of vineyard, which yield 2,800,000 bottles a year. The company has always had a strong presence overseas and this led to the use of international varieties in the wines. In the past two years, however, attention has been directed back towards Puglia's traditional, indigenous varieties. And once more Amativo, from 60 per cent primitivo and negroamaro, is a great example of modern Puglian winemaking. It's Cantele's best wine and one of the best in the region. The wine is all finesse and freshness. The nose is elegant and refined, with intense red berry fruits and spicy aromas, then the palate is fresh and full with fruity crispness, soft, silky tannins and good acid backbone, giving length and longevity. One of Puglia's best whites also comes from Cantele, Chardonnay Teresa Manara. The full, deep nose gives citrus and banana, then the palate, which mirrors the nose, is rich and weighty with notable length. The other two reds are successful, too. Salento Teresa Manara, again from indigenous varieties (negroamaro and aglianico, this time) has notable softness and elegance and the fresh, pleasant monovarietal Primitivo well reflects the Cantele style. It has good body and crisp notes of ripe plum and red berry fruits. To finish, the well-styled Salento Chardonnay is less elegant than the Teresa Manara but still well made and most attractive.

●	Amativo '00		4*
○	Salento Chardonnay Teresa Manara '01		4
●	Salento Primitivo '00		3
●	Salento Rosso Teresa Manara '98		4
○	Salento Chardonnay '01		2*
●	Amativo '99		6
○	Salento Chardonnay Teresa Manara '00		5
●	Salice Salentino Rosso Ris. '96		4
●	Salice Salentino Rosso Ris. '97		4
●	Varius '99		5

LECCE

AGRICOLE VALLONE
VIA XXV LUGLIO, 5
73100 LECCE
TEL. 0832308041

Founded in 1934, the Vallone sisters' estate has over 660 hectares and more than 150 under vine. For some time now, agronomist Donato Lazzari has been at the helm of the estate, with the well known and highly respected Severino Garofano as oenological consultant. The estate's emblem is Graticciaia, a terrific red from late-harvested negroamaro, and the '97 is as good as ever. It has a deep, dark colour. The nose is clean, intense, deep, complex and nuanced, with aromas of red berry fruit jam and Mediterranean scrub. The palate has a sumptuous richness, powerful alcohol and is deep and full. It's a sort of Amarone, if you like, in southern clothing. Sauvignon Corte Valesio '01 has good character, with a rich, varietal, citrus and balsamic nose, and a fresh, fruity, balanced palate. The '01 Brindisi Rosato Vigna Flaminio is as intense and inviting as ever with its bright hue and aromas of ripe morello cherry. Salice Salentino Vereto '00 has a full, firm structure, soft tannins and fair overall balance, while the Brindisi Rosso Vigna Flaminio, also '00, is good overall but maybe a little over-evolved. We'll finish with a most attractive dessert wine, Passo delle Viscarde '97, from 80 per cent sauvignon and malvasia bianca, which, apart from a slight dullness on the nose, is nicely constructed and well balanced.

●	Graticciaia '97		7
●	Brindisi Rosso V. Flaminio '00		3
●	Salice Salentino Rosso Vereto '00		2*
◉	Brindisi Rosato V. Flaminio '01		3
○	Salento Sauvignon Corte Valesio '01		2*
○	Passo delle Viscarde '97		7
●	Graticciaia '96		6
●	Graticciaia '95		6
●	Brindisi Rosso V. Flaminio '96		2
●	Brindisi Rosso V. Flaminio '97		2
●	Brindisi Rosso V. Flaminio '98		2*

LEPORANO (TA)

VIGNE & VINI
VIA AMENDOLA, 36
74020 LEPORANO (TA)
TEL. 0995332254
E-MAIL: vigne&vini@italiainrete.net

Vigne & Vini makes its first appearance in the Guide. It owns no vineyards but buys in the grapes it needs for its 400,000 bottles. It is what in France would be called a "maison de négoce". But this is no reason to discount it. Indeed, the wines scored gratifyingly well and Primitivo di Manduria Papale showed brilliantly. It is a glorious, dark, purple-tinged ruby. The nose is intense and has spice, resin, incense and pencil lead. The palate, giving notes of blackberry and tobacco, is full, deep and firmly structured, yet elegant. The wine is modern, maybe even too international in style, but well made and attractive. The Primitivo di Manduria dolce naturale Chicca, is in the same quality band but much more traditional in style. The nose has a touch of oxidation but the palate is fresh, beautifully clean, nicely complex, and has well-balanced tannins and flavours of chocolate and morello cherry. Another style, another taste, but the same fine execution. The other wines are, though, much less successful. Puglia Rosso Papale, 100 per cent cabernet sauvignon, has an excessively vegetal nose, with lemon and citron leaf aromas. The palate is more balanced and has good structure but the vegetal notes remain and the tannins are a little raw. The Salento Rosso Schiaccianoci merits only a mention. So, there are ups and downs here. However, the trend seems upwards and the winery produces one of the best Primitivo di Mandurias on the market. We can only hope that the Primitivo retains its quality in years to come and that the rest of the range rises to match it.

● Primitivo di Manduria dolce naturale Chicca '00	♟♟	5
● Primitivo di Manduria Papale '00	♟♟	4
● Puglia Rosso Papale '00	♟	5
● Salento Rosso Schiaccianoci '01		3

LEVERANO (LE)

CONTI ZECCA
VIA CESAREA
73045 LEVERANO (LE)
TEL. 0832925613 - 0832910394
E-MAIL: info@contizecca.it

This is the third year in succession that this great winery's gifted team, oenologist Antonio Romano, owner and agronomist Alcibialde Zecca, and consultant Giorgio Marone, can celebrate real success. There were Three comfortable Glasses for the magnificent Nero. This year, with the '00, the wine is even more refined and elegant than the '99. We liked the fact that the herbaceousness from the Bordeaux component of the negroamaro-cabernet-malvasia nera blend is a little less marked. The colour is as deep and dark as you would expect from a wine whose name means "Black". It needs time in the glass to do justice to its initially somewhat reticent array of aromas, but then tobacco, leather and ripe red berry fruits emerge. The palate is warm, velvety, balanced and incredibly long. All the other wines scored well. Unfortunately, space permits us to mention only some. Vigna del Saraceno Vendemmia Tardiva '01, from malvasia, is splendid, delicately sweet and notably elegant. The '99, at that time labelled Leverano Malvasia, is nicely made too. The dry, four-square character combines with plentiful depth and alcoholic warmth. The Vigna del Saraceno line, red, white and rosé, stands out for excellent value for money. Then we have two highly impressive reds. The Salice Salentino Cantalupi Riserva '99 is long, elegant, fleshily fruity and softly tannic, and the Terra, from negroamaro with 30 per cent aglianico, partially aged in new oak, has plentiful richness of extract and enticing flavours of liquorice and ripe plum.

● Nero '00	♟♟♟	6
● Salento Primitivo '00	♟♟	4
○ Leverano Bianco Vigna del Saraceno '01	♟♟	3*
○ Leverano Vigna del Saraceno Vendemmia Tardiva '01	♟♟	4
● Leverano Rosso Terra Ris. '99	♟♟	6
● Salice Salentino Cantalupi Ris. '99	♟♟	4
● Salice Salentino Rosso Cantalupi '00	♟	3
⊙ Leverano Rosato Vigna del Saraceno '01	♟	3
○ Leverano Malvasia Vigna del Saraceno '99	♟	4
● Salento Rosso Donna Marzia '99	♟	3
● Nero '98	♟♟♟	5
● Nero '99	♟♟♟	5*

LOCOROTONDO (BA)

VINI CLASSICI CARDONE
VIA MARTIRI DELLA LIBERTÀ, 28
70010 LOCOROTONDO (BA)
TEL. 0804311624 - 0804312561
E-MAIL: info@cardonevini.com

Cardone is a small estate, although average-sized in Puglian terms, and produces no more than 100,000 bottles a year. After a short time in the wilderness, it now returns to the limelight, thanks to the excellent work, particularly with the reds, carried out by oenologist Sandro Rosato. Primaio '01 is a terrific monovarietal Primitivo that harnesses all the freshness and attractiveness of the variety. The nose is full of fresh fruit, especially wild red berries. The palate is sprightly, supple and uncomplicated, yet deep and well knit. The Salento Primitivo '00 has a similar style, attractiveness and score, with spice and balsam on its freshly fruited nose. Neither wine sees oak so it is interesting to compare their results with those that do. Salento Rosso '00, from aglianico, primitivo and negroamaro, is impressive. Its small wild berry fruitiness is well integrated with oaky notes. The depth, intensity and notable structure balance the tannins, which are still a little raw and edgy, suggesting that it would be wise to wait a couple of years before uncorking the bottle. The Chardonnay Barricato Placeo is less successful. The vanilla, oak toast and butter completely dominate the fruit and the full, fat palate lacks the acidity and fruit necessary for balance. The other wines submitted showed well. Primitivo '99 is a little herbaceous, with warmth, good structure and depth. The Negroamaro '00 has notes of cherry and Mediterranean scrub, fair body and good balance. Finally, the Locorotondo has good intensity and freshness.

● Salento Primitivo '00	♛♛	4
● Salento Rosso '00	♛♛	5
● Primitivo di Puglia Primaio '01	♛♛	3*
○ Salento Chardonnay Placeo Barricato '00	♛	5
● Salento Negroamaro '00	♛	5
○ Locorotondo '01	♛	3
● Salento Primitivo '99	♛	4

LOCOROTONDO (BA)

CANTINA COOPERATIVA
DEL LOCOROTONDO
VIA MADONNA DELLA CATENA, 99
70010 LOCOROTONDO (BA)
TEL. 0804311644 - 0804311298
E-MAIL: info@locorotondodoc.com

Huge quantities come from this cooperative, but there are also some excellent wines and a few new developments. Guided by winemaker Benedetto Lorusso, the winery has decided to put money and effort into using barriques to give the wines greater depth and ageing capacity. Let's look at the numbers. There are 900 members, over 3,500,000 bottles a year, a 70-year old cellar and Two highly significant Glasses, obtained by the Cummerse Rosso. From aglianico, uva di troia and cabernet sauvignon, aged a year in barrique, it is strongly balsamic on the nose and has a warm, soft palate with good depth, well-integrated tannins and an after-aroma recalling cocoa powder. Roccia Rosso, from Valle d'Itria, is based on negroamaro, malvasia nera and montepulciano and also came very close to Two Glasses. It is fresh, very attractive, highly drinkable and rich in fruit on both nose and palate, showing especially blackberry, cherry and morello cherry. More good news came from Terre di Don Peppe, a Primitivo di Manduria given one year in barrique. Even though the oak is still too marked and submerges the fruit, the softness and spiciness remain attractive. All the other wines are very well-styled, including: the two Casale San Giorgio wines, the refined, well structured Rosso and the fresh, fragrant Rosato; and the two Locorotondo whites, Vigneti in Tallinajo, with its citrus tones and spring flowers aromas, and the attractively uncomplicated base version, with fresh golden delicious apples notes. As usual, there is excellent value for money throughout.

● Cummerse Rosso '98	♛♛	3*
⊙ Casale San Giorgio Rosato '01	♛	2*
○ Locorotondo '01	♛	2*
○ Locorotondo Vigneti In Tallinajo '01	♛	3
● Roccia Rosso '01	♛	2*
● Casale San Giorgio Rosso '99	♛	2*
● Primitivo di Manduria Terre di Don Peppe '99	♛	4
● Casale San Giorgio Rosso '98	♛	3

MANDURIA (TA)

ACCADEMIA DEI RACEMI
VIA SANTO STASI I - Z. I.
74024 MANDURIA (TA)
TEL. 0999711660
E-MAIL:
accademia@accademiadeiracemi.it

Gregory Perrucci, who leads an association of small estates, continues to work tirelessly, seconded by his wife Elizabeth in charge of sales, oenologist Roberto Cipresso and agronomist Salvatore Mero. This year, Gregory submitted a fascinating range of wines. Primitivo di Manduria Zinfandel '01, from the Sinfarosa estate, has a deep, dark ruby colour, a deep, complex nose and a solid, powerful yet soft palate, finishing on elegant notes of tobacco and spices. Primitivo di Manduria Dunico Millennium '00, from Masseria Pepe, a red of great power and concentration, is similarly impressive. The Salice Salentino Te Deum Laudamus '00, from Casale Bevagna, also showed well. It is austere in character, yet has soft tannins and seemed a little less structured than previous releases. The excellent Squinzano '00 L'Evangelista, produced by Cellino San Marco, is full of structure and softness. From Torre Guaceto comes a fragrant, supple cinsault-based Ottavianello Dedalo '01 and the rich, soft Susumaniello Sum '01, with enthralling aromas of black cherry and chocolate. Another set of Two brimming Glasses goes to Primitivo Giravolta '01, from Tenuta Pozzopalo, which has a fruit-forward palate, good body and a fine peppery finish. The Grand Finale belongs to Cantine Ferrari, the cellar that produced the extraordinary Solaria Ionica '59, now re-asserting its fame for off-the-wall "ancient" wines with the fascinating Salice Salentino '78, a wine of amazing depth and coherence, which it has only just begun to sell.

MANDURIA (TA)

FELLINE
VIA N. DONADIO, 20
74024 MANDURIA (TA)
TEL. 0999711660
E-MAIL:
accademia@accademiadeiracemi.it

The Manduria zone suffered poor weather in 2001, just as it did in 1999. As a result, Gregory Perrucci, the Felline estate's owner, and consulting oenologist Roberto Cipresso decided not to produce Vigna del Feudo, the flagship wine. It is made from a spot-on blend of primitivo and montepulciano, with small amounts of cabernet and merlot. The 2000 scored spectacularly well last year. But Felline remains one of the area's leading estates and its Primitivo di Manduria '01 is terrific. The colour is a deep ruby. The nose is full of ripe red berry fruits, from morello cherry to blackberry, accented by elegant nuances of spice, tobacco and chocolate. The palate has depth and intensity, cleanly defined fruit tones, balance and good length, tailing off to leave fascinating sensations of black cherry and chocolate and the classic aftertaste of balsam and pepper. Also showing very well is Alberello '01, from primitivo and negroamaro, the name being a tribute to the area's old bush-trained vines, a system called "alberello" in Italian. The wine's intensity and sweetness is apparent from the first sniff. The palate has good structure, soft tannins and an explosion of fully ripe fruit, spanning plum to blackberry, followed by a long finish with notes of Mediterranean scrub. Good value for money across the board is an estate trademark.

● Primitivo di Manduria Dunico Millennium Masseria Pepe '00	🍷🍷	6
● Primitivo di Manduria Zinfandel Sinfarosa '01	🍷🍷	5
● Squinzano l'Evangelista '00	🍷🍷	4*
● Primitivo di Manduria Giravolta Tenuta Pozzopalo '01	🍷🍷	5
● Susumaniello Sum Torre Guaceto '01	🍷🍷	5
● Salice Salentino La Canestra Ferrari '78	🍷🍷	8
● Ottavianello Dedalo Torre Guaceto '01	🍷	5
● Primitivo di Manduria Zinfandel Sinfarosa '98	🍷🍷🍷	4
● Primitivo di Manduria Giravolta Tenuta Pozzopalo '00	🍷🍷	4*
● Solaria Ionica Ferrari '59	🍷🍷	6
● Salice Salentino Rosso Te Deum Laudamus Ris. Casale Bevagna '98	🍷🍷	4*

● Primitivo di Manduria '01	🍷🍷	4*
● Salento Rosso Alberello '01	🍷	3*
● Vigna del Feudo '97	🍷🍷🍷	4
● Vigna del Feudo '00	🍷🍷	5*
● Primitivo di Manduria '00	🍷🍷	4*

MANDURIA (TA)

PERVINI
LOC. C.DA ACUTI
VIA SANTO STASI PRIMO - Z. I.
74024 MANDURIA (TA)
TEL. 0999711660
E-MAIL: accademia@accademiadeiracemi.it

The Perrucci family's estate was set up in 1993 with the aim of selecting grapes and wines from the best lands in the Salento peninsula and turning them into a very carefully honed range of wines that could hold their own on the international market. Pervini now controls 80 hectares of vineyard, of which 32 hectares are directly owned, and annual production has grown to 500,000 bottles. Overall standards are high but Archidamo '01, an excellent value for money Primitivo di Manduria, excels. It is more concentrated than previous vintages, which is immediately obvious from the colour, and has more intensity and depth on the palate. Nevertheless, it retains elegance, balance and good typicity. The nose has ripe red berries and plum jam, supported by tobacco, pepper and old leather. The plum and tobacco notes are echoed on the palate, preceded by a delightful initial impression of chocolate and liqueur cherry flavours. The beautifully balanced Chardonnay Bizantino '01 is also successful, with citrus and spring flowers on the nose and a palate full of ripe fruit, underlined by fresh acidity. The attractive Primitivo del Tarantino I Monili, with its sweet, spicy nose and nicely supple palate, also stood out, as did the Bizantino Rosato, from negroamaro and primitivo. It's a perfect accompaniment to white meats and salami.

SALICE SALENTINO (LE)

LEONE DE CASTRIS
VIA SENATORE DE CASTRIS, 26
73015 SALICE SALENTINO (LE)
TEL. 0832731112 - 0832731113
E-MAIL: info@leonedecastris.com

This estate was founded in 1665 – no, that's not a misprint – and the quality of the wines brings lustre to Puglia, and indeed all Italy. Production is 3,400,000 bottles from 380 hectares, of which 50 are directly owned and over 300 are in the hands of the trusted growers who supply the estate every year. There are so many good wines, it's hard to know where to begin but it has to be with Five Roses Anniversario, from 80 per cent negroamaro and malvasia nera, this year undoubtedly the best rosé in Puglia. The colour is dark cherry. The nose is meaty and fleshy, redolent of strawberry and raspberry, and there is excellent texture on the palate, along with an attractive note of pomegranate seed on the finish. Another great wine is the imposing Donna Lisa Riserva, although this year it seemed to have a little too much bell pepper greenness on both nose and palate. It should improve with bottle age, and develop beautifully if its creamy texture and silky tannins are anything to go by. Moscato Pierale is a delight, from its highly varietal nose to its sweet palate and the slight varietal tang of bitterness on the aftertaste. Space prevents us from reviewing many other of the wines but particularly honourable mentions go to: Sauvignon Case Alte, with its pure varietal character on both nose and palate; the basic Five Roses, which risks being rather unfairly overshadowed by the Anniversario version; and to the warmly alcoholic, sweet Primitivo di Manduria Santera.

● Primitivo di Manduria Archidamo '01	4
● Primitivo del Tarantino I Monili '00	3
○ Salento Chardonnay Bizantino '01	2*
⊙ Salento Rosato Bizantino '01	2*
● Primitivo di Manduria Archidamo '00	4*
● Finibusterre Antica Masseria Torre Mozza '97	6
● Primitivo di Manduria Archidamo '98	3
● Salice Salentino Rosso Te Deum Laudamus Casale Bevagna '98	4

● Salice Salentino Rosso Donna Lisa Ris. '98	6
⊙ Five Roses '01	3
⊙ Five Roses Anniversario '01	3*
○ Puglia Moscato Pierale '01	4
● Primitivo di Manduria Santera '00	3
● Salice Salentino Rosso Majana '00	2*
○ Salento Bianco Messapia '01	3
○ Salento Bianco Vigna Case Alte '01	3
● Salento Rosso Illemos '98	5
● Salento Rosso Messere Andrea '99	5
● Salice Salentino Rosso Ris. '99	3
● Salice Salentino Rosso Donna Lisa Ris. '93	4
● Salice Salentino Rosso Donna Lisa Ris. '95	5

SAN DONACI (BR)

FRANCESCO CANDIDO
VIA A. DIAZ, 46
72025 SAN DONACI (BR)
TEL. 0831635674
E-MAIL: candido.wines@tin.it

Steadily improving quality continues to distinguish the Candido family's long-standing estate, led by the ever-present guiding hand of oenologist Severino Garofano. This year, four wines breached the Two Glass barrier. Three of them are exclusively from negroamaro, thereby confirming the estate as among those best able to give expression to this marvellous indigenous variety. Duca d'Aragona, from 80 per cent negroamaro and montepulciano, is a top-notch wine and made it to the Three Glasses tasting finals. Dark ruby, it shows spice and coffee on the nose, along with ripe fruit and Mediterranean scrub, myrtle in particular. The palate is full, rich, a touch alcoholic and shows an almost palpable fleshy weight, from which emerge both ripe and cooked fruit. Just a touch more acid backbone and length, and it would be one of the true greats. The classic Cappello di Prete, a 100 per cent negroamaro, is back up to speed and a very fine wine. The style is traditional, with a slightly raisined fruitiness and robust tannins, and the wine has supreme typicity. The soft, simple, highly pleasing Immensum, from 80 per cent negroamaro and cabernet sauvignon, has admirable notes of cooked fruit and the sweet Paule Calle, from a 50-50 blend of chardonnay and malvasia bianca, is equally tempting. It melds solid structure and good balance with pleasant notes of candied fruit and acacia honey. Everything else is attractive and excellent value for money.

●	Duca d'Aragona '96	♀♀	5
●	Immensum '00	♀♀	4
●	Cappello di Prete '98	♀♀	3*
○	Paule Calle '99	♀♀	4
○	Salento Bianco Vigna Vinera '01	♀	3
○	Salice Salentino Bianco '01	♀	2*
⊙	Salice Salentino Rosato Le Pozzelle '01	♀	2*
●	Salice Salentino Aleatico '98	♀	4
●	Salice Salentino Rosso Ris. '98	♀	2*
●	Duca d'Aragona '95	♀♀	5*
○	Paule Calle '98	♀♀	4*
●	Immensum '99	♀♀	4*

SAN PIETRO VERNOTICO (BR)

TORMARESCA
VIA MATERNITÀ ED INFANZIA, 21
72027 SAN PIETRO VERNOTICO (BR)
TEL. 0805486943
E-MAIL: tormaresca@tormaresca.it

Antinori is certainly not the first major estate to invest heavily in Puglia, and it won't be the last. But this highly renowned Florentine name is unique in one aspect. In just five years, it has reached extraordinary quality levels with the wines from its Tormaresca estate, and not just the top of the range, but throughout, from the "simple" Chardonnay Tormaresca and Tormaresca Rossa, a 40-30-30 blend of negroamaro, merlot and other reds, upwards. So much so that now, in Tormaresca's third year in the Guide, an absolute marvel has emerged. It's the Masseria Majme '00, a 100 per cent Negroamaro from the Majme property at San Pietro Vernotico. This simply soared to Three Glasses. It is dark ruby, almost black, and still tinged with purple. The nose is astoundingly intense, full of elegant ripe red berry fruit, perfectly clean and extraordinarily complex, and there are underlying touches of oak and spice. The palate has incredible breadth, weight and power while maintaining perfect balance, with the smoothest of tannins and a beautifully long finish. Its moment of glory, however, was very nearly shared by the estate's other prestige wine, Castel del Monte Bocca di Luop '00, from 85 per cent aglianico and cabernet sauvignon. And what can we say about Castel del Monte Chardonnay Pietrabianca '01? We don't want to gush but for elegance, cleanliness and richness it comes very close to Castello della Sala's Cervaro. Which is quite a compliment.

●	Masseria Maime '00	♀♀♀	5*
●	Castel del Monte Rosso Bocca di Lupo '00	♀♀	5
○	Castel del Monte Chardonnay Pietrabianca '01	♀♀	5
○	Tormaresca Chardonnay '01	♀♀	3*
●	Tormaresca Rosso '01	♀♀	3*
●	Castel del Monte Rosso Bocca di Lupo '99	♀♀	5*
○	Castel del Monte Chardonnay Pietrabianca '99	♀♀	5

SAN SEVERO (FG)

D'Alfonso del Sordo
C.da Sant'Antonino
71016 San Severo (FG)
tel. 0882221444
e-mail: info@dalfonsodelsordo.it

For some years now, this renowned San Severo estate, most probably the leading name in the province of Foggia, has been engaged in a major upgrade of its cellar and its 120 hectares of vineyard. This year sees the arrival of Luigi Moio who, backed up by the faculty of agriculture at the University of Foggia, will be conducting research into local viticulture and ways of raising its profile. 2002 also witnessed the first fruits of the work in progress. Four wines gained Two Glasses, Guado San Leo '01, made solely from uva di troia, Cabernet Sauvignon Cava del Re '01, San Severo Posta Arignano '01 and the '01 San Severo selection Montero. Gualdo San Leo has a good dark, opaque ruby hue introducing an intense, richly fruited nose, well balanced in new oak. The powerful, concentrated palate is full of fruit and soft tannins. Cava del Re has a similar profile but greater varietal character on the nose, which has freshly-mown hay, ripe plum and pencil lead. The palate has structure, fleshiness and soft, long-lasting fruit. Montero has remarkably clean, intense fruit, redolent of ripe cherry and blackberry, both on the nose and on the balanced palate, which has refined tannins and an elegant aftertaste evoking the fruit and vanilla once more. Posta Arignano, which confirms the area's high potential for montepulciano and sangiovese, is similarly clean and tight knit. All the other '01s are well made and highly successful, the whites in particular.

● Cava del Re Cabernet Sauvignon '01	♟♟	6
● Guado San Leo '01	♟♟	6
● San Severo Montero '01	♟♟	3*
● San Severo Rosso Posta Arignano '01	♟♟	2*
○ Daunia Bombino Bianco Catapanus '01	♟	2*
● Doganera Merlot '01	♟	6
○ San Severo Bianco Candelaro '01	♟	3
○ San Severo Bianco Posta Arignano '01	♟	2*
⊙ San Severo Rosato Posta Arignano '01	♟	2*

TRICASE (LE)

Castel di Salve
Fraz. Depressa
P.zza Castello, 8
73030 Tricase (LE)
tel. 0833771012
e-mail: casteldisalve@tiscalinet.it

This is now the fourth year in succession that Castel di Salve's good results give it a place in the Guide. Behind the consistently high quality is, of course, the enthusiasm of its two young owners, Francesco Marra and Francesco Winspeare. They, with oenologist Andrea Borretti and agronomist Filippo Giannone, continue to make strides quality-wise, their aim being to turn out superb wines from indigenous grapes. This year, they were not far away with Lama del Tenente '99, which almost made it into the Three Glass tasting finals. From montepulciano and primitivo, with ten per cent malvasia nera di Lecce, it ages for a year in stainless steel, followed by a year in barrique. The wine is full and concentrated but still a little raw and edgy and will need time in bottle to realize its potential. Priante '00, a traditionally styled wine from a 50-50 mix of montepulciano and negroamaro, is also most successful. The nose is fruit-forward, with faintly raisiny notes. The palate is clean, elegant, ripe, full and beautifully constructed. However, Armecolo, from negroamaro, with 20 per cent malvasia nera di Lecce, showed less well than before. The colour is deep, and there is good wild berry fruitiness on the nose, but the normally attractive palate is a touch edgy and less balanced than usual. The Santi Medici line performed well. The Rosso is full, warm and well structured. The Rosato is especially attractive, with its notes of cherry and Mediterranean scrub, and the white has good freshness and cheering notes of ripe golden delicious apples.

● Priante '00	♟♟	4
● Lama del Tenente '99	♟♟	5
● Armecolo '01	♟	3
○ Salento Bianco Santi Medici '01	♟	2*
⊙ Salento Rosato Santi Medici '01	♟	2*
● Salento Rosso Santi Medici '01	♟	3
● Armecolo '00	♟♟	3*
● Il Volo di Alessandro '00	♟♟	4*
● Lama del Tenente '98	♟♟	4
● Armecolo '99	♟♟	3

OTHER WINERIES

Colli della Murgia
Via T. Grossi, 29
70022 Altamura (BA)
Tel. 0805481125 - 0803114243

Colli della Murgia is an organic estate, certified by the AIAB, the Italian Association for Organic Agriculture. Selvato, a soft, balanced blend of aglianico and sangiovese is very good. Erbaceo is clean, fresh and well made.

● Selvato Rosso '00	ҮҮ	4
○ Erbaceo Bianco '01	Ү	4

Masseria Li Veli
Via Campi Salentina, km 1
72020 Cellino San Marco (BR)
Tel. 0831617865

This new estate, a partnership between Angelo Maci and the noted Tuscan estate Avignonesi, has made an excellent start with the seriously impressive Salice Salentino Pezzo Morgana. It's a soft, refined wine, with loads of fruit and notable length.

● Salice Salentino Pezzo Morgana '00	ҮҮ	5

Cantina Sociale Coop. Copertino
Via Martiri del Risorgimento, 6
73043 Copertino (LE)
Tel. 0832947031

An output of over 1,000,000 bottles and Severino Garofano as consultant make this winery a focal point on the Puglian scene. Salento Rosato Cigliano, 100 per cent negroamaro, is well worthy of its Two Glasses, and excellent value for money.

⊙ Salento Rosato Cigliano '01	ҮҮ	2*
● Copertino Rosso '00	Ү	3
○ Salento Bianco Cigliano '01	Ү	3
● Copertino Rosso Ris. '99	Ү	4

Santa Lucia
Strada San Vittore, 1
70033 Corato (BA)
Tel. 0818721168 - 0817642888
E-mail: info@vinisantalucia.com

Santa Lucia remains a dependable estate producing consistent quality. The fresh, fragrant rosé Vigna Lama di Carro and the attractive, perfumed Bianco Vigna Tufaroli both have character. Fiano Gazza Ladra '01 and the red Vigna del Melograno '01 also easily gain One Glass.

○ Castel del Monte Bianco Vigna Tufaroli '01	Ү	3
⊙ Castel del Monte Rosato Vigna Lama di Carro '01	Ү	3

I PASTINI - CARPARELLI
SEDE PRODUTTIVA C/O AZ. VITIVINICOLA
TORREVENTO-CORATO
70033 LOCOROTONDO (BA)
TEL. 0808980923 - 0808980929

Murgia Rosso, from 50 per cent cabernet sauvignon, 30 per cent cabernet franc and montepulciano, showed excellently, gaining Two Glasses. The fresh, highly drinkable Primitivo del Tarantino and the crisp, fruity Locorotondo are also very good.

● Murgia Rosso '99	♉♉	3*
● Primitivo del Tarantino '00	♉	3
○ Locorotondo '01	♉	3

COOPERATIVA SVEVO - LUCERA
V.LE ORAZIO SNC
71036 LUCERA (FG)
TEL. 0881542301
E-MAIL: cantinalucera@tiscalinet.it

This co-operative is run by oenologist Vincenzo Di Giovine and has 170 members conferring grapes from 200 hectares of vineyard. Cacc'e Mmitte Borgo Feudo, from an uva di troia-based blend, and Saraceno Daunia both earned Two Glasses. Value for money is excellent.

● Cacc'e Mmitte di Lucera Borgo Feudo '00	♉♉	3*
● Daunia Saraceno '00	♉♉	2*

AGRICOLA PLINIANA
LOC. C.DA BARCE
74024 MANDURIA (TA)
TEL. 0999794273
E-MAIL: coopliniana@libero.it

This is the first entry in the Guide for this co-operative. It was founded in 1964 and currently has 800 members who own over 1,000 hectares of vineyard. Suvais, a fresh, elegant unfortified sweet wine, is very good. The attractive, easy drinking, primitivo-based Juvenis is not far behind.

● Primitivo di Manduria Dolce Naturale Suavis '00	♉♉	4
● Primitivo di Manduria Juvenis '00	♉	3

SOLOPERTO
S. S. 7 TER
74024 MANDURIA (TA)
TEL. 0999794286
E-MAIL: soloperto@soloperto.it

The wines are highly traditional but good quality. Primitivo '97 is full, rich, strong in alcohol but ripe and attractive. The same could be said of Primitivo '00 Etichetta Nera ("Black Label") which came within a hair of Two Glasses. Everything else is good quality, too.

● Primitivo di Manduria 17° '97	♉♉	3*
● Primitivo di Manduria 14° '00	♉	2*
● Primitivo del Tarantino Amorini '98	♉	4

CONS. PROD. VINI E MOSTI ROSSI
VIA F. MASSIMO, 19
74024 MANDURIA (TA)
TEL. 0999735332
E-MAIL: consvini@libero.it

The success of this co-operative grows year by year, in line with the efforts it puts into winemaking. Primitivo Elegia, the elegant, full-bodied flagship wine that ages a year in barrique, gains Two Glasses. The fresh, crisp Primitivo Bosco Marino is also good.

● Primitivo di Manduria Elegia '99	♉♉	5
● Primitivo di Manduria Bosco Marino '00	♉	3
○ Salento Bianco Calice '01	♉	3

VINICOLA MIALI
VIA MADONNINA, 1
74015 MARTINA FRANCA (TA)
TEL. 0804303222
E-MAIL: cantine-miali@tiscalinet.it

Miali is a long-standing estate that consistently produces sound wines. Castel del Monte Rosato and Aglianico del Vulture are close to a second Glass. Most of the other wines are worth One Glass.

● Castel del Monte Rosso '00	♉	4
● Primitivo di Manduria '00	♉	4
○ Castel del Monte Rosato '01	♉	2*

Le Fabriche
C.da Le Fabbriche
Str. Prov. Maruggio - Torricella
74020 Maruggio (TA)
Tel. 0999739655

Alessia Perrucci, in partnership with Barone Pizzini from Franciacorta, has set up this new estate with two interesting wines, both of which show very well-judged use of oak. The Primitivo is admirable and the Puglia Rosso is soft and richly fruited.

● Salento Primitivo '01	ŸŸ	6
● Puglia Rosso '01	Ÿ	4

Barsento
C.da San Giacomo
Str. Provinciale Martina Franca
70015 Noci (BA)
Tel. 0804979657

The fresh, crisply fruited rosé Magilda, from 100 per cent malvasia nera, is of high quality. The rich, fruity Primitivo Casaboli, also a monovarietal, is very good. The sweet Primitivo Malicchia Mapicchia is well styled but a little less successful.

⊙ Magilda Rosato '01	ŸŸ	3*
● Casaboli '00	Ÿ	5
● Malicchia Mapicchia '01		4

Il Tuccanese
Via G. Di Vittorio, 15
71027 Orsara di Puglia (FG)
Tel. 0881968194

Leonardo Guidacci is a new arrival to the Guide. His estate's banner are the wines made from tuccanese, probably a local clone of sangiovese. Both wines submitted showed very well. Made solely from tuccanese, they are intense, soft, fresh and fruity.

● Il Tuccanese '00	Ÿ	4
● Il Tuccanese Magliano '00	Ÿ	4

Cantina Cooperativa della Riforma Fondiaria
Via Madonna delle Grazie, 8/A
70037 Ruvo di Puglia (BA)
Tel. 0803601611 - 0803601711

This co-operative continues to produce attractive, well-made wines, so much so that many of them earned One Glass and the fine Castel del Monte Rosato, which is clean and well fruited, was not far from Two. Value for money is astounding.

● Castel del Monte Rosso '00	Ÿ	1*
⊙ Castel del Monte Rosato '01	Ÿ	1*
○ Murgia Bianco Le Carrare '01	Ÿ	3

Castello Monaci
C.da Monaci
73015 Salice Salentino (LE)
Tel. 0831665700
E-mail: giv@giv.it

This is the first appearance in the Guide for this long-standing estate, now run by GIV. The soft, intense, attractive Primitivo with its inviting plumminess ran close to Two Glasses. The Salice Salentino is a little less interesting but is still fresh and most pleasing.

● Salento Primitivo '01	Ÿ	3
● Salice Salentino '01	Ÿ	3

Santa Barbara
Via Maternità e Infanzia, 23
72027 San Pietro Vernotico (BR)
Tel. 0831652749

There was a good series of One Glass wines from this estate, whose range remains sound throughout. The most characterful three are the Squinzano, which has good body and flavours of plum and tobacco, the evolved, full Salice Salentino, and the warm, well-fruited Primitivo.

● Salento Primitivo '99	Ÿ	2*
● Salice Salentino '99	Ÿ	2*
● Squinzano '99	Ÿ	2*

VINICOLA MEDITERRANEA
VIA MATERNITÀ INFANZIA, 22
72027 SAN PIETRO VERNOTICO (BR)
TEL. 0831676323 - 0831659329
E-MAIL: info@vinicolamediterranea.it

Vinicola Mediterranea produced a good series of wines this year. The soft Primitivo Dolce Naturale with its notes of almond and fig even reached Two Glasses. The fresh, fruity Squinzano and the typical, pleasant Primitivo also showed admirably well.

● Salento Primitivo Dolce Naturale ŶŶ	4
● Primitivo di Manduria '00 Ŷ	3
● Squinzano Rosso '00 Ŷ	3

VINICOLA RESTA
VIA MATERNITÀ E INFANZIA, 2/4
72027 SAN PIETRO VERNOTICO (BR)
TEL. 0831671182
E-MAIL: vinicolaresta@libero.it

The Resta family and their oenologist, Stefano Porcinai, continue to make impressive wines at very good prices. The best example is the powerful, fruit-led Primitivo di Manduria. The negroamaro-based Vigna del Gelso Moro is also good.

● Primitivo di Manduria '00 ŶŶ	3*
● Salento Rosso	
Vigna del Gelso Moro '00 Ŷ	2*
● Squinzano '00 Ŷ	2*

CANTINA E OLEIFICIO SOCIALE DI SAVA
S. S. 7 TER, KM. 17,800
74028 SAVA (TA)
TEL. 0999726139
E-MAIL: cantinasava@libero.it

This co-operative has 850 members with a total of 800 hectares of vine, although less than 950 hectolitres are currently bottled each year. Both Medodie and Mosaico are attractive, nicely fruited, well-made wines, as is the traditionally styled Primitivo Dolce Naturale, Terra di Miele.

● Primitivo del Salento Melodie '01 Ŷ	3
● Primitivo di Manduria Dolce	
Naturale Terra di Miele '98 Ŷ	5
● Primitivo di Manduria Mosaico '98 Ŷ	4

DUCA CARLO GUARINI
L.GO FRISARI, 1
73020 SCORRANO (LE)
TEL. 0836460288 - 0836465047
E-MAIL: ducaguarini@tin.it

The '01 Murà, a 100 per cent Sauvignon, is as good as in previous years. It gained Two Glasses again. The barrique-aged Primitivo Vigne Vecchie is a fine bottle. As always, the wines that come from Tenuta Piutri are well styled.

○ Salento Sauvignon Murà '01 ŶŶ	3*
● Salento Primitivo	
Vigne Vecchie '00 Ŷ	4
● Salento Rosso Tenuta Piutri '01 Ŷ	3

TENUTA ZICARI
VIA ANFITEATRO, 77
74100 TARANTO
TEL. 0994534510

There are gratifying results from this estate. We enjoyed the excellent Puglia Rosso, Pezza Petrosa, which has a balsamic nose and an elegant, tightly-knit palate of good substance. Solicato and Diago, both fruity and with good body, also showed well.

● Puglia Rosso Pezza Petrosa '00 ŶŶ	4
● Puglia Rosso Solicato '01 Ŷ	4
● Salento Rosso Diago '01 Ŷ	4

MICHELE CALÒ & FIGLI
VIA MASSERIA VECCHIA, 1
73058 TUGLIE (LE)
TEL. 0833596242
E-MAIL: michelecalo@staff.it

The Alezio Rosato Mjère from this long-standing winery is excellent. It has aromas of small berry fruits and Mediterranean scrub, the palate is well structured and there is good nose-palate harmony. The Rosso and Bianco from the same line are good, too.

⊙ Alezio Rosato Mjère '01 ŶŶ	3*
● Salento Rosso Mjère '00 Ŷ	4
○ Salento Bianco Mjère '01 Ŷ	3

CALABRIA

Things in Calabria are moving forward, albeit slowly. A small group of newcomers to the Guide has joined the usual team and, to judge by our tastings, they are very promising. Cirò remains the best known Calabrian wine but, at last, it is no longer the sole product to represent the entire region. We have also seen quality improvements in many wines, often resulting from the input of the consultants now employed by the more far-sighted estates. These oenologists have in several cases changed practically obsolete winemaking methods into approaches more in line with the times. So, there are definitely positive signs in the region. Given what we've seen so far, and given the region's soils and climate, which are as good as anywhere else in southern Italy, we feel that within a few years, Calabria could be sitting alongside Sicily, Puglia and Basilicata, regions whose top wines have reached heights that were unimaginable even a few years ago. In addition, prices for now remain very competitive. Six wines made it to the tasting finals and one achieved Three Glasses, the impeccable Scavigna Vigna Garrone from the Odoardi brothers. This is just reward for dedication, backed up by an oenologist of the calibre of Stefano Chioccioli. Librandi sails on as commandingly as ever and two of its wines, Gravello and Magno Megonio, were in the final taste-offs. The wines of Fattoria San Francesco continue to show well too, Ronco dei Quattro Venti gaining a particularly high score. This Cirò has become an example to numerous producers, showing how to achieve a modern slant on such an ancient wine. The first release of the estate's new sweet wine, Brisi, is also highly encouraging for it nearly reached the finals. The headstrong Luigi Viola has vowed not to let Moscato di Saracena disappear and it looks as if he is succeeding in redeveloping this sweet wine, known in mediaeval times. Cantine Lento, in Lamezia, also managed to get a wine into the finals, the full-bodied, intensely fruited Federico II. Finally, we have two new promising estates in the Guide for the first time: Malena, with Pian della Corte, a Cirò that sailed into the Two Glasses category, and Terre Nobili, an estate run with great gusto by Lidia Matera. We are looking forward to great things from both.

CIRÒ (KR)

FATTORIA SAN FRANCESCO
LOC. QUATTROMANI
S. P. EX S. S. 106
88813 CIRÒ (KR)
TEL. 096232228
E-MAIL: info@fattoriasanfrancesco.it

Francesco Siciliani's estate has again turned out a good range of wines. There are 25 hectares under vine, a number that is about to be doubled, the modern cellar is now in full operation and updated vinification methods have been brought in by oenologist Fabrizio Ciufoli. As usual, Ronco dei Quattro Venti showed very well and very nearly went through to the tasting finals. It ages at length in barrique and has a good deep ruby colour, with red berry fruits and nicely judged oak on the nose, then ripe tannins on the evenly flowing palate. Value for money is, once more, excellent. The new wine, Brisi, made a very good debut. It is a sweet wine from 100 per cent greco grapes which are left to dry on "cannicci" (cane mats) for six months. The fruit is then pressed and the juice goes into small, 50-litre barrels where it stays for two years. The '99 is an amber-gold colour, its aromas are quite complex and the palate is sweet, full and rich. Cirò Donna Madda is also on form and only a little less intense than its "big brother". The other wines are all well made and the best of them are the modern-style Martà and Pernicolò. The former, from gaglioppo and merlot, is well fruited with an underlying vegetal note, and has elegant tannins and good overall balance. Pernicolò, from greco and chardonnay, is simple and attractive. The Cirò Rosato is also as pleasing as ever, with its clean fruity aromas and full sweet palate. Francesco Siciliani's place at the top the podium awaits him. It is surely only a matter of time before he gets there.

CIRÒ MARINA (KR)

CAPARRA & SICILIANI
BIVIO S. S. 106
88811 CIRÒ MARINA (KR)
TEL. 0962371435
E-MAIL: caparra&siciliani@cirol.it

This is an important year for Luigi Siciliani and Salvatore Caparra. It marks the 40th anniversary of the founding of their estate, and the 40th anniversary of their partnership. So, celebrations are in order. Siciliani chairs the winery and Cappara looks after sales, precisely the roles they have always held. Taking care of winemaking is the "father of Calabrian viticulture", Severino Garofano, who was one of the first, a goodly number of years ago, to start working seriously towards improving quality at these latitudes. Even so, there are still ups and downs in the wines. Some, although as well made as ever, disappointed compared with last year's releases. Yet on the other hand, we know that wines from small estates react much more strongly to vintage variations. Still, Caparra & Siciliani remains one of the big names in the area and continues to play its part in bringing the quality of Calabrian wines up to that of its more advanced neighbours. Best of the bunch this year is the fruity, warm, tannic Lamezia Rosso Mastro Giurato, with its good deep ruby colour. Cirò Classico Superiore Riserva '99 unfortunately scored lower than the previous vintage. But let's make our final thought a positive one. Our best wishes go to the Caparra & Siciliani duo for the 40th anniversary of their estate and their 40 years together.

● Cirò Rosso Cl. Ronco dei Quattro Venti '00	♟♟	5
○ Brisi '99	♟♟	7
● Cirò Rosso Cl. '00	♟	3
● Cirò Rosso Cl. Donna Madda '00	♟	5
● Martà '00	♟	3
◉ Cirò Rosato '01	♟	3
○ Pernicolò '01	♟	4
○ Cirò Bianco '01		3
● Cirò Rosso Cl. Ronco dei Quattro Venti '99	♟♟	5
● Cirò Rosso Cl. Ronco dei Quattro Venti '98	♟♟	5
● Cirò Rosso Cl. Sup. Donna Madda '99	♟♟	5

● Lamezia Rosso Mastro Giurato '00	♟	5
● Cirò Rosso Cl. Sup. Ris. Volvito '96	♟	5
● Cirò Rosso Cl. Sup. '99	♟	4
● Cirò Rosso Cl. '00		3
○ Cirò Bianco Curiale '01		4
◉ Cirò Rosato Le Formelle '01		4
○ Cirò Bianco Curiale '99	♟♟	3
● Cirò Rosso Cl. Sup. Volvito '96	♟	4
● Cirò Rosso Cl. Sup. Ris. '98	♟	3

CIRÒ MARINA (KR)

LIBRANDI
LOC. SAN GENNARO
S. S. 106
88811 CIRÒ MARINA (KR)
TEL. 096231518
E-MAIL: librandi@librandi.it

The main news from the Librandi brothers this year is that the new property recently acquired at Rosaneti has entered production. It comprises 170 hectares in the Melissa DOC zone, and these have now been completely replanted, following careful investigations into the soil characteristics. The first wines it has yielded are a red, Melissa Asylia, already released and already showing well, and a white from montonico. This is due to be released in spring 2003 and is as yet without a name, but looks very promising. Donato Lanati and Professor Attilio Scienza are following progress attentively, studying the results from a number of experimental plots. The aim is to select the best clones of indigenous varieties, such as magliocco, mantonico and gaglioppo, propagating from seed if necessary. Librandi has also planted a further ten hectares at its Critone holding, which produces the wine of the same name. Finally, although this is hardly news, Gravello is performing splendidly. The '99, from 60 per cent gaglioppo and cabernet sauvignon, is full, concentrated and long. Magno Megonio not only showed very well but continues to improve. It is made solely from magliocco and vinified with a more modern slant than is usual in these parts. The wine is characterful, with good intensity, upfront fruit, body and tannin. The deep aromas of the '01 Critone, and its attractive fullness and softness make it probably one of the best releases ever. That's very good news.

CIRÒ MARINA (KR)

MALENA
C.DA PIRAINETTO
88811 CIRÒ MARINA (KR)
TEL. 096231758
E-MAIL: info@malena.it

This estate is one of the properties that have switched over to quality-led production in the past few years. Now it is making its first full appearance in the Guide. The force behind the change is Cataldo Malena, a young producer at only 25 years of age, but one who knows his own mind and is driven by a tremendous desire to do well. He first went round Italy to see what other producers were up to, then set about changing his winery's production strategy, which he achieved in just a few years. He took on a consultant, Benedetto Lorusso. He also replanted much of his vineyard at higher planting densities and now has 16 hectares in production, with another 12 soon to come onstream. As if that weren't enough, work has begun on a new cellar, due to be ready in February 2003. Next, an experimental plot of 5,000 vines is due to be planted around the cellar for research into indigenous varieties. There is nothing, in fact, in the way of this estate's wines really going places. Of those submitted this year, the Cirò Rosso Classico Superiore '00 has typical Cirò colour and aromas, as well as good body and a rich array of tannins. The well-made Pian della Corte '98, a Cirò Classico Superiore, easily picked up Two Glasses. The garnet-tinged ruby is typical of gaglioppo. There is an intense, concentrated nose and the palate has plentiful extract and balanced oak. It is also good value for money.

● Magno Megonio '00	ΥΥ	5
● Gravello '99	ΥΥ	6
○ Critone '01	ΥΥ	3*
○ Cirò Bianco '01	Υ	3
⊙ Cirò Rosato '01	Υ	3
● Melissa Asylia '01	Υ	3
● Cirò Rosso Cl. '01		3
⊙ Terre Lontane '01		3
● Gravello '98	ΥΥΥ	5
● Gravello '90	ΥΥΥ	5
● Magno Megonio '99	ΥΥ	5

● Cirò Rosso Cl. Sup. Ris. Pian della Corte '98	ΥΥ	3*
● Cirò Rosso Cl. Sup. '00	Υ	2*
⊙ Bacco Rosato '01		2
○ Cirò Bianco '01		2

COSENZA

SERRACAVALLO
VIA PIAVE, 51
87100 COSENZA
TEL. 098421144

CROTONE

DATTILO
LOC. MARINA DI STRONGOLI
C.DA DATTILO
88815 CROTONE
TEL. 0962865613
E-MAIL: info@dattilo.it

Demetrio Stancati is fond of saying that he is a reformed doctor and a convinced grower producer. He finally hung up his white coat after visiting a series of wine estates in France. It was love at first sight. Demetrio was fascinated by the wines of Bordeaux, and even more so by those from Burgundy, whereupon he decided to turn his family estate into a winery. The wines had to be good and he was going to use modern methods to produce them. He threw himself into this project full-time, never looked back, and results so far have been encouraging. He has already renewed his vine stock at a higher planting density than before and added international varieties such as cabernet sauvignon and chardonnay to the classic indigenous varieties. Amongst these, his preference goes to magliocco, which he believes to be the local grape best suited for quality wine production, and he has selected the best clones for replanting on a large scale. His ideas have been generously rewarded. Valle del Crati '01 is from an oak-free 50-50 blend of magliocco and cabernet, and is a full, tannic, powerful wine. The '99 Riserva version has a higher proportion of magliocco and goes into barrique for eight months after a year in stainless steel. It has good structure, good concentration, and a very good price tag.

Strongoli is a glorious corner of Calabria with hills that dip gently down to the sea. There, you will find Roberto Ceraudo's estate. There have been major changes at the winery this year for there are new names and new labels. But the changes go deeper than the outside of the bottle. Roberto's wines are now made in a different, more modern style than that imbued by traditional local vinification methods. The estate covers 60 hectares, of which one third is given over to vineyard, and is organically farmed throughout. The skilled Fabrizio Ciufoli acts as consultant but Roberto's children also help out. The least exciting of the wines submitted this year was the curiously named rosé, Grayasusy. The Imyr '01, which is made from chardonnay and is given five months in French oak, is far more impressive. It is a good, golden straw colour, the nose is refined and well fruited, and in the mouth it is soft and full. It scored Two Glasses and also scores high marks for value for money. The latest release of Petraro, from gaglioppo, cabernet sauvignon and montepulciano, also showed well. It has richly fruited aromas, balance and good body. In fact, everything seems to point towards a rosy future for this estate. We look forward to that future with quiet confidence.

● Valle del Crati '01	ŶŶ	3*
● Valle del Crati Ris. '99	ŶŶ	4
● Serracavallo Rosso Ris. '98	ŶŶ	4

○ Imyr '01	ŶŶ	4
● Petraro '99	Ŷ	4
⊙ Grayasusy '01		3
○ Amineo Bianco Donnacaterina '00	ŶŶ	4
● Amineo Rosso '99	Ŷ	3

LAMEZIA TERME (CZ)

CANTINE LENTO
VIA DEL PROGRESSO, 1
88046 LAMEZIA TERME (CZ)
TEL. 096828028
E-MAIL: info@cantinelento.it

Salvatore Lento's whole family is deeply involved with the estate. All are as competent as they are passionate about wine. Salvatore's wife, Giovanna, is tirelessly active in promoting the wines, the two daughters Manuela and Danila look after sales, and Giovanna's brother Antonio Zaffina takes care of winemaking – and he has one of the best equipped cellars in southern Italy to work in. There is also external consultancy from Professor Luigi Moio. It would be amazing if good wines didn't emerge from such a tightly bonded team and indeed improvements on the estate are continuous. The property has recently been augmented by the purchase of a new holding of around 30 hectares, also in the Lamezia DOC zone, surrounding a beautiful old house that, once renovated, will become the estate's showcase. As for the wines themselves, Federico II, a Cabernet Sauvignon with a refined, complex nose, good body and robust tannins, was good enough to reach the Three Glass taste-offs. Two Glasses went to Lamezia Riserva '97, which has an intense, berry fruit nose, and a robust, full palate with firm tannins and good body. Contessa Emburga, a Sauvignon of good concentration and softness on the palate, is also full of character. Even the Lamezia Greco is a well-made wine with pleasingly fruity aromas and a good balance of acidity and softness. Such consistently good results augur very well for the future.

LAMEZIA TERME (CZ)

STATTI
TENUTA LENTI
88046 LAMEZIA TERME (CZ)
TEL. 0968456138 - 0968453655
E-MAIL: statti@statti.com

Young – they're both 30 or so – Antonio and Alberto Statti, can breathe a sigh of relief. Work has at last finished on their new, futuristic cellar. This will allow them to make better quality wines but also to work more effectively towards fulfilling their short-term objectives. The next stage, already under way, concerns the vineyards. There are to be increases to their 35-hectare vine stock and quality improvements will be made here, too. If we then add that experienced oenologist Fabrizio Zardini acts as consultant, and that this year's wines all performed well at our tastings, it is obvious that starry things would seem to be in store for the brothers and their estate. Nosside, a dried-grape "passito" from mantonico and greco, sailed into the Two Glass category. It is amber, with aromas of ripe fruit and flowers, and has a rich, full palate. Cauro, from gaglioppo, magliocco and cabernet aged in barrique, also showed well. It is a garnet-tinged ruby, there are attractive red berry fruits on the nose, and the palate is dry and long, with evident tannins. Arvino, with its unusual aroma of geranium, gained One Glass without difficulty. The well-made Lamezia Rosso has a fruity nose and fairly tannic palate. It also performed reassuringly well. We look forward to quality at the Statti brothers' estate climbing higher up the scale. There is nothing standing in their way.

● Federico II '99	♟♟	6
● Lamezia Rosso Ris. '96	♟♟	6
● Lamezia Rosso Ris. '97	♟♟	6
○ Contessa Emburga '01	♟	4
○ Lamezia Greco '01	♟	5
● Lamezia Rosso Tenuta Romeo '01	♟	4
● Lamezia Rosso Ris. '95	♟♟	5
○ Contessa Emburga '00	♟♟	4
● Federico II '98	♟♟	6
● Lamezia Rosso Tenuta Romeo '99	♟♟	4

○ Nosside '00	♟♟	5
● Arvino '00	♟	3
● Lamezia Rosso '00	♟	3
○ Lamezia Greco '01	♟	3
○ Ligeia '01	♟	3
● Cauro '99	♟	5
○ Lamezia Bianco '01		3
● Cauro '97	♟	5
● Cauro '98	♟	5

LUZZI (CS)

Luigi Vivacqua
C.da San Vito
87040 Luzzi (CS)
Tel. 0984543404 - 098428825
E-mail: luigi@vivacqua.it

Things are on the up with this estate, at least as far as the reds are concerned. We appear to be seeing the beginnings of what Luigi Vivacqua was aiming at when he started out a couple of years ago. Vivacqua, an accountant with a vocation for viticulture, set his sights on quality combined with typicity. As soon as he took over the family estate, he began to replant the 30 hectares of vineyard already in existence, but with international varieties like merlot, cabernet sauvignon and cabernet franc alongside the native magliocco, calabrese and so on. The replanting programme is progressing apace and roughly ten hectares has been completed. The plan agreed with consultant Luca D'Attoma is for everything to be finished within the next four or five years. We said the reds were good, so let's get to specifics. The best is Marinò, from the unusual blend of gaglioppo and merlot. This has a good deep ruby colour, the ripely fruited nose is clean, and there is a harmonious palate with overt but balanced tannins and fair length. San Vito di Luzzi, from a mix of gaglioppo and greco nero, has intense, well-fruited aromas, good structure and balanced acidity. Now, with the new cellar ready and the high-flying D'Attoma in charge of winemaking, we are looking forward to further improvements, especially with the whites.

● San Vito di Luzzi Rosso '00	🍷🍷	3*
● Marinò Rosso '99	🍷🍷	5
○ Chardonnay Donna Aurelia '01		4
○ San Vito di Luzzi Bianco '01		2
◉ San Vito di Luzzi Rosato '01		3

NOCERA TERINESE (CZ)

Odoardi
C.da Campodorato
88047 Nocera Terinese (CZ)
Tel. 098429961 - 096891159
E-mail: odoardi@tin.it

At last, brothers Gregorio and Giovan Battista Odoardi have their feet on the top step of the rostrum, and deservedly so. Two of their wines went into the tasting finals, Savuto '00 and Scavigna Vigna Garrone '99, and the latter triumphed, claiming Three Glasses. Gregorio divides his time between the hospital, where he is head of the radiology department, and his estate. His wife is also involved, using her experience as a microbiologist to handle wine analysis. Vigna Garrone comes 70 per cent from a variety of aglianico locally called gaglioffo together with equal parts of merlot, cabernet sauvignon and cabernet franc. It is an opaque ruby. The nose is intense, concentrated and richly fruited and the palate is rich, powerful and full of tight, fine-grained tannins. Savuto '00 is only a point or so behind. It is rich in aroma and flavour, with a good acidic balance and also offers exceptional value for money. Naturally, these splendid results reflect not only the family's commitment but also the work of their able consultant, Stefano Chioccioli. Remember, too, that Odoardi was the first estate in Calabria to experiment, successfully, with planting densities as high as 10,000 vines per hectare. Twenty hectares have already been so converted and this should rise to 40 within a couple of years. To finish on a further high note, we'll cite two other highly impressive wines. Savuto Vigna Mortilla '99 is a modern-style, rich, well-knit, elegant wine and Valeo is a delightful sweet white from moscato bianco and zibibbo, or moscato d'Alessandria.

● Scavigna Vigna Garrone '99	🍷🍷🍷	8
● Savuto '00	🍷🍷	5
○ Valeo '00	🍷🍷	7
● Savuto Sup. Vigna Mortilla '99	🍷🍷	7
○ Scavigna Bianco Pian della Corte '01	🍷	6
● Savuto '99	🍷🍷	3*
● Savuto Sup. Vigna Mortilla '98	🍷🍷	4
○ Valeo '99	🍷🍷	5

OTHER WINERIES

Cantina Enotria
Loc. San Gennaro - S. S. Jonica 106
88811 Cirò Marina (KR)
Tel. 0962371181
E-mail: cantinaenotria@infinito.it

Cantine Enotria brings together a large number of producers with over 150 hectares of vineyard. Production surpasses 1,000,000 bottles. Wines are always well styled, most notably the classic Cirò line and the well-made, nicely concentrated, fruity red Piana delle Fate.

○ Cirò Bianco '01	▽	2*
⊙ Cirò Rosato '01	▽	2*
● Cirò Rosso Cl. '01	▽	2*
● Cirò Rosso Cl. Sup. Piana delle Fate Ris. '98	▽	5

Ippolito 1845
Via Tirone, 118
88811 Cirò Marina (KR)
Tel. 096231106
E-mail: ippolito1845@ippolito1845.it

Consultant Franco Bernabei's influence is beginning to be felt here. There's nothing outstanding yet but styling throughout is good. The Rosato is particularly impressive. The nose is intensely fruity, the palate full and well balanced. The new barrique cellar has recently been completed.

○ Cirò Bianco '01	▽	2*
⊙ Cirò Rosato '01	▽	2*
● Cirò Rosso Cl. Sup. Colli del Mancuso Ris. '97	▽	4

Vinicola Zito
Via Scolaretto
88811 Cirò Marina (KR)
Tel. 096231853

Founded in the 19th century, this winery owns several properties in the Cirò area. The sound performance of its wines and their typicity give the estate its first entry in the Guide. The fully flavoured Cirò Rosso Classico is particularly good.

● Cirò Rosso Cl. '00	▽	2*
○ Cirò Bianco '01	▽	2*
⊙ Cirò Rosato '01	▽	2*
● Cirò Rosso Cl. Ris. '97	▽	3

Domenico Spadafora
Fraz. Piano Lago - Z. I., 18
87050 Mangone (CS)
Tel. 0984969080 - 0984433239
E-mail: cantspad@libero.it

It is a pleasure to list the wines of Domenico Spadafora, a fourth-generation wine producer. We particularly liked Nerello '00, from gaglioppo and montonico, with its intensely fruity nose, firm structure and good balance.

● Nerello '00	▽▽	4
○ Donnici Bianco '01	▽	4
⊙ Donnici Rosato '01	▽	4
● Donnici Rosso '00		4

Tenuta Terre Nobili
Loc. Contrada Cariglialto
87046 Montalto Uffugo (CS)
tel. 0984934005
e-mail: terrenobili@medianetis.it

Agronomist Lidia Matera takes care of the vineyards personally while Claudio Fuoco looks after winemaking. Cariglio, from nerello and gaglioppo, is worth watching. It has a clean, cherry-like nose, well-integrated oak on its full, concentrated palate, and develops evenly.

● Cariglio '01	🍷🍷	3*
○ Santa Chiara '01	🍷	3

Vintripodi Calabria
Fraz. Archi
Via Vecchia Comunale, 28
89051 Reggio Calabria
tel. 096548438 - 0965895009

The Tripodi brothers' estate is right by Reggio Calabria. It was founded in the late 19th century and has been run by the family since it started. A large number of wines were presented. Arghillà, with its fairly intense, typically styled fruit, showed better than most.

● Magna Grecia Rosso '00	🍷	3
⊙ Zephyro Rosato '01	🍷	2*
● Arghillà '99	🍷	3
● Pellaro '99	🍷	3

Luigi Viola & Figli
Via Roma, 18
87010 Saracena (CS)
tel. 098134071

Luigi Viola has rescued an ancient, noble wine, known since mediaeval times, which was dying out, as producers were no longer working with it. Each year, Viola painstakingly vinifies moscato, malvasia and guarnaccia separately and obtains an intensely perfumed, sweet, full, rich nectar.

○ Moscato di Saracena '01	🍷🍷	4*
○ Moscato di Saracena '00	🍷🍷	4

Val di Neto
Fraz. Corazz - Via Nazionale
88831 Scandale (KR)
tel. 096254079
e-mail: valdineto@krol.it

We are happy to report a good start for this new estate, founded in 1999 in the Melissa and Cirò DOC zones. There are 30 hectares under vine and a further 30 ready for planting. The wines are modern in style. The attractive Melissa, from gaglioppo and greco nero, is most worthy of mention.

● Melissa Rosso '00	🍷	3
● Rosso Archè '00	🍷	3
● Rosso Maradea '00	🍷	4

SICILY

The signs of vigour on Sicily's wine scene grow ever stronger, at least as far as the higher quality wines and estates are concerned. At the very top, nine wines attained Three Glass status, putting the region in the nation's big league, which is naturally a good sign. These powerhouses of the Sicilian wine team are Planeta, which also picks up a star for the estate's tenth Three Glass wine, Firriato, Abbazia di Sant'Anastasia, Morgante, Palari and Cottanera. There are also two giant concerns whose Sicilian operations are turning out some very good stuff, Gruppo Italiano Vini at Rapitalà and Zonin, with Feudo Principi di Butera. They are joined by other producers of distinction, from Tasca d'Almerita to Donnafugata, Cusumano, Spadafora, the fast-recovering Duca di Salaparuta, Florio, Marco De Bartoli, Salvatore Murana and the Cantina Sociale di Trapani. All these names and leading players have taken the initiative and woken the sleeping giant that was Sicily just ten or so years ago. There are many others following suit, wineries large and small that are either just starting up or just beginning to gain recognition. In fact, there are now over 50 wineries listed and assessed on these pages, which is undeniably impressive. And yet, and yet ... the shadows still hover and dark they are indeed. A region that produces an average of around 8,000,000 hectolitres of wine should not be releasing less than three per cent under DOC labels. The leading estates together should not represent less than ten per cent of the total, as they do. There should not be such a large proportion of wine that, benefiting from EU systems to eliminate over-production, is vinified only to be distilled, without ever going near the real market. True, that amount is in decline, but the mindset that regards viticulture as an activity whose main aim is pocketing public funds cannot be allowed to continue. It perpetuates a situation that can only bring ruin to the reputation and sales of all Sicilian wine. Battling against this, ever more effectively and with increasing success, is a hard core of business-oriented individuals, far-sighted growers and others who have learned, as in few other regions of Italy, to boost the profile of their wines in a very short period of time. Their efforts have far-reaching implications. We are happy to report their progress, pointing out the most significant developments. The future of Sicily as a great Italian winemaking region depends on it. The vines, the hills, the sun that have endowed the island with some of the finest winemaking potential in the world should no longer be debased by anachronistic choices that do justice to no one.

ACATE (RG)

Cantine Torrevecchia
C.da Torrevecchia
97011 Acate (RG)
Tel. 0916882064 - 0932990951
E-mail: cantinetorrevecchia@libero.it

Again, the Torrevecchia winery, based in the vast Acate valley, submitted an extensive range for tasting, from Cerasuolo di Vittoria to Inzolia and Alcamo. The most successful, we felt, was Fontanabianca '01, a fine blend of syrah, cabernet sauvignon and merlot. It has a fairly deep ruby colour, and the nose is intense, complex, spicy and peppery with red berry fruit. The palate is warm, soft and balanced. The '01 Bianco Biscari, from inzolia and chardonnay is as distinctive as usual, its oak toast nicely balancing the tropical fruit and floral tones. The delicately fruity '01 Inzolia is equally good. The '99 vintage of Mont Serrat A.D. 1688, a Cerasuolo di Vittoria selection from particularly well-sited vineyards, is nicely constructed, even though it is a little less rich in extract than its predecessor. It is warm and typically Mediterranean on the palate, with distinct flavours of ripe cherries, blackberry jam and liquorice, opening out to give good presence. The Frappato '01, from grapes grown in the zone, is attractive and highly drinkable, and is typical of the variety in its enticing, delicate, sweet flavours of red berry fruit and morello cherry. None of the other wines disappointed, with the nero d'Avola selection, Casale dei Biscari '99 being particularly commendable.

ACATE (RG)

Cantina Valle dell'Acate
C.da Bidini
97011 Acate (RG)
Tel. 0932874166
E-mail: info@valledellacate.com

This winery, run by Gaetana Jacono, has been turning out well-made wines with a certain personality for many years now. However, those submitted this time seemed to be distinctly better than usual. Let's work through them. Il Tanè is a fine oak-aged Nero d'Avola. The colour is a brightly tinged deep red, the nose has the characteristic aromas of small red berry fruit, enhanced by wafts of spices and cocoa powder, then the warm, mouthfilling palate has good extractive weight and finishes fairly long. Moro, a Nero d'Avola that is instead vinified exclusively in stainless steel, also showed well, with delicate notes of liquorice and black pepper on the nose adding style to the underlying fruit. There was also good overall balance on the palate. The Cerasuolo di Vittoria '00 is another highly impressive, absolutely delightful wine whose clean, clear aromas are redolent of small wild berry fruit and which flows across the palate with almost caressing softness. Frappato '01 has morello cherry and blackberry notes and fresh, harmonious drinkability. Bidis '00, from chardonnay, the winery's only non-indigenous variety, and inzolia, is aged in small oak barrels for 12 months. It has an elegant golden hue, intense aromas of orange peel and apple, and sensations of freshness and zestiness on its attractive palate. Finally, Inzolia '01, with its delicate floral notes, is uncomplicated but well made and good quality.

● Fontanabianca '01	♛♛	5
● Akates '00	♛	3
● Albarossa '00	♛	4
● Cerasuolo di Vittoria '00	♛	3
○ Bianco Biscari '01	♛	4
● Frappato '01	♛	3
○ Inzolia '01	♛	2*
● Pietra di Zoe '01	♛	3
● Syrah '01	♛	4
● Casale dei Biscari '99	♛	4
● Cerasuolo di Vittoria Mont Serrat A.D. 1668 '99	♛	4
○ Alcamo '01		2
○ Chardonnay '01		3
○ Bianco Biscari '98	♛♛	3

○ Bidis '00	♛♛	4
● Cerasuolo di Vittoria '00	♛♛	3*
● Il Moro '00	♛♛	4*
● Tanè '00	♛♛	6
● Frappato '01	♛	3*
○ Inzolia '01		3
● Frappato '97	♛♛	2
○ Bidis '99	♛♛	2*
● Frappato '00	♛	2*
● Cerasuolo di Vittoria '95	♛	2
● Cerasuolo di Vittoria '96	♛	3
● Cerasuolo di Vittoria '98	♛	2
● Cerasuolo di Vittoria '99	♛	2*
● Frappato '99	♛	2
● Il Moro '99	♛	3

ALCAMO (TP)

Ceuso
Via Enea, 18
91011 Alcamo (TP)
tel. 0924507860
e-mail: info@ceuso.it

It's time for us panel to come clean. When we assessed Ceuso Vigna Custera '99, made from nero d'Avola, cabernet sauvignon and merlot, for the 2002 edition of the Guide and awarded it Two red Glasses, it was actually still in the cask. The wine was not released onto the market until this year. We retasted and re-evaluated it. Fortunately, the score was practically identical to last year's and the concentrated, complex nose, introducing full, rich, well-defined flavours and dense but fairly ripe tannins, once more took the wine to our tasting finals. In addition, the Melìa brothers, owners of this small winery, submitted their '00 Fastaia for the first time. This is a sort of "deuxième vin", although it is produced almost exclusively from nero d'Avola. It has less class and complexity than Vigna Custera, and possibly less concentration as well. However, it makes up for these shortcomings with its remarkable character. The rather edgy varietal notes of the nero d'Avola are well delineated, so much so that you could regard it as one of the leading markers for the variety in Sicily. Overall, we have no hesitation in confirming that a pattern of wines of distinction emerging from this tiny estate is starting to build up, which can't be bad.

BUTERA (CL)

Feudo Principi di Butera
C.da Deliella
93011 Butera (CL)
tel. 0934347726

The best thing a winery can do is replicate one year's good results the next, especially if, as in this case, the winery is a new one. It is true that Feudo Principe di Butera is owned by Zonin, an organization that is certainly not just out of nappies, but it is still crucially important that the positive impressions engendered in last year's Guide should be backed up by a similarly distinguished performance this time round. San Rocco and Calat, both '01, are respectively a Cabernet Sauvignon and a Merlot, which is how we referred to them in last year's Guide. Again, they are highly successful. Both are powerful, concentrated and soft, exactly as you would expect from great Mediterranean reds such as these. But the real surprise, and the consequent well-deserved award of Three Glasses, came from Deliella '00, from 100 per cent nero d'Avola. This combines extraordinarily good typicity in all aspects of the variety's style with simply superb elegance and character. It is a powerful red, with some acid-tannin edges still perceptible, but has a great future ahead of it. Considering that it comes from the most indigenous of local grapes, it provides indubitable proof that Sicily is not, and need never be, simply a new testing bench for the so-called international varieties. Butera's range is completed by an attractive simple white, Insolia '01, which is straightforward but appealing and highly drinkable. In short, this new battleship in the Zonin fleet has taken to the high seas with aplomb.

● Ceuso Custera '99	¶¶	6
● Fastaia '00	¶¶	5
● Ceuso '96	¶¶	5
● Ceuso Custera '97	¶¶	5
● Ceuso Custera '98	¶¶	5

● Deliella '00	¶¶¶	6
● San Rocco '01	¶¶	7
● Calat '01	¶¶	7
○ Insolia '01	¶	3
● Cabernet Sauvignon '00	¶¶¶	7
● Merlot '00	¶¶	7
○ Chardonnay '00	¶¶	5

CAMPOREALE (PA)

Fattorie Azzolino
C.da Azzolino
90043 Camporeale (PA)
tel. 092436123
e-mail: fattorieazzolino@tiscalinet.it

It makes a fabulous story. One day in 1999, a passionately enthusiastic and determined Sicilian producer, Franco Sacco, owner of a 50-hectare estate with 20 hectares of vineyard, turned up at the Associazione Industriali in Trento looking for a partner. His proposal was a long-term one, regarding a new business undertaking in the wine sector in Sicily. There was just one condition. It was clear, firm and non-negotiable: output had to be of the highest quality. A few days later, he received a telephone call from a major Trentino winery, the Cantina Sociale di Nomi, which was interested in the project. Fernando Bolner, its dynamic technical director popped down to Sicily to do some scouting around. He returned visibly content and within a few months, the deal was signed and sealed to everyone's satisfaction. Work began. When a lively, complex Chardonnay, the first fruits of this north-south love-match, appeared, its 12,000 bottles sold out in only a few days. But that was just the beginning. The '01 Chardonnay, now on sale, is quite magnificent. Its golden hue is deep from the fully ripe grapes used. It has a highly intense, penetrating nose with notes of ripe pineapple, apricot and honey. The palate is rounded, with great structure. Its acidity and softness are perfectly melded and in perfect balance. In short, it soars, and was quickly invited to the final Three Glass taste-offs. Two more recent arrivals, the harmonious, elegant Di'More '00, from selected nero d'Avola and cabernet sauvignon grapes, and the well fruited, varietal Nero d'Avola '00, are also very good.

○ Chardonnay '01	🍷🍷	5
● Di 'More '00	🍷	5
● Nero D'Avola '00	🍷	3
○ Chardonnay '00	🍷	5

CAMPOREALE (PA)

Tenute Rapitalà
C.da Rapitalà
90141 Camporeale (PA)
tel. 092437233 - 092437494
e-mail: cantinarapitala@giv.it

We saw it coming several years back. The Tenute Rapitalà wines are improving by leaps and bounds and the efforts of oenologist Marco Monchiero have now brought the estate a first, well-deserved Three Glass wine. It is called Solinero, it comes from 100 per cent syrah, and the '00, the first release, is a stunner. It is a bright, deep ruby colour. The aromas are decisive and have a clear profile, with delicate notes of blueberry and blackcurrant alternating with the firmer aromas of prune. The palate is deep, full, meaty and assertive, with fairly fine-grained tannins and a velvety feel. Hugonis '00, from nero d'Avola and merlot, has aromas of ripe fruit and Mediterranean scrub, and a warmly structured, enveloping palate. The '00 Nuhar, which means "flower" in Arabic, is an unusual blend of nero d'Avola with pinot nero. The '00, first assessed last year, showed well again at its second tasting. It has warm perfumes of fruit in syrup with delicate balsamic nuances. The attractive golden yellow of the Casalj '01, from catarratto and chardonnay, is the first draw. The nose well reflects the grape varieties and the palate is lively and full of flavour. Gran Cru Tenuta Rapitalà, from 100 per cent Chardonnay, has attractive green pepper notes and a fairly full flavour.

● Solinero '00	🍷🍷🍷	5
● Hugonis '00	🍷🍷	6
○ Conte Hugues Bernard '00	🍷	3
○ Rapitalà Bianco Gran Cru '00	🍷	5
○ Casalj '01	🍷	4
○ Alcamo Rapitalà Grand Cru '95	🍷🍷	4
● Nuhar '00	🍷	5
● Rapitalà Rosso '95	🍷	3
● Rapitalà Rosso '96	🍷	3
● Rapitalà Rosso '98	🍷	3
● Nuhar '98	🍷	4
● Rapitalà Rosso '99	🍷	3

CASTELBUONO (PA)

ABBAZIA SANTA ANASTASIA
C.DA SANTA ANASTASIA
90013 CASTELBUONO (PA)
TEL. 0921671959 - 091201593
E-MAIL: info@abbaziasantanastasia.it

If you ever happen to reach this neck of the woods, prepare yourself for one of the most amazing panoramas ever: a fabulous view of the sea beautifully framed by vineyards and olive grove. The cellar is located in a tiny hamlet and has been completely restored. Giacomo Tachis was the estate's first consultant and, a couple of years ago, Riccardo Cotarella took over. Almost as if to overturn platitudes about each winemaker having a distinctive style, the wines here haven't changed one bit. They remain as consistently brilliant as ever and we believe that Litra, from 100 per cent cabernet sauvignon, currently has to be the best Sicilian red based on international varieties. With the '00, it again shows a complexity of aroma and a depth of flavour that has few peers. The '00 Montenero, from a complex blend of cabernet sauvignon, merlot, nero d'Avola and syrah, is also extremely sound, and probably the best vintage of the wine ever. It has less attack than the Litra but more immediacy and, at the moment, even more balance. Baccante '01, a barrique-aged Chardonnay, is less individual in style. The oak is overt and tends to dominate. The '01 Gemelli, also from chardonnay, is probably a better-gauged wine, despite being less concentrated and easier to drink. Passomaggio '00, from nero d'Avola and merlot, and the well-typed and pleasant, if rather straightforward, Nero d'Avola '01, are both attractive.

CASTELDACCIA (PA)

DUCA DI SALAPARUTA - VINI CORVO
VIA NAZIONALE, S. S. 113
90014 CASTELDACCIA (PA)
TEL. 091945201
E-MAIL: vinicorvo@vinicorvo.it

The theory that wine concerns owned by spirits companies do not attain top quality levels is spectacularly disproved by Duca di Salaparuta. Illva Saronno, which took over this long-standing winery just two years ago, is already bringing the wines back to their ancient splendours. There are organizational developments, with Duca di Salaparuta and Corvo splitting into separate companies; technical developments, with professionals of the calibre of Giacomo Tachis and Carlo Casavecchia now on board; and a more modern, incisive sales strategy, spearheaded by Gianfranco Caci, one of Italian wine marketing's foremost experts. As a result, Duca Enrico '99, made solely from nero d'Avola, came very close to Three Glasses and has a purity of style throughout that in previous vintages has been somewhat masked. The '97, though, is still showing very well. The '00 Bianca di Valguarnera, from inzolia, is the best release ever and avoids any suggestion of excessive oak or over-ripeness. The newer wines include the well-typed, well-made Nero d'Avola Triskelè '99 while the Megara '00, from frappato and syrah, is simpler but exceedingly drinkable. Kados '01, from 100 per cent grillo, turned out less well and, we feel, will need a few more tweaks to find its feet. The well-known classics are all well styled. The '99 Terre d'Agala is now mainly from nerello mascalese, Colomba Platino '01 may be just a tad simplistic and the Corvo Bianco '01 maintains its proverbial reliability.

●	Litra '00	▼▼▼	7
●	Montenero '00	▼▼	6
○	Baccante '01	▼▼	6
○	Gemelli '01	▼▼	4
●	Nero d'Avola '00	▼	4
●	Passomaggio '00	▼	4
●	Litra '96	▼▼▼	7
●	Litra '97	▼▼▼	7
●	Litra '99	▼▼▼	7
●	Montenero '99	▼▼	7

○	Bianca di Valguarnera '00	▼▼	5
●	Duca Enrico '97	▼▼	8
●	Duca Enrico '99	▼▼	8
●	Nero d'Avola Triskelè '99	▼▼	5
●	Megara '00	▼	3
○	Corvo Bianco '01	▼	2*
○	Corvo Colomba Platino '01	▼	3
○	Kados '01	▼	4
●	Terre d'Agala '99	▼	3
●	Duca Enrico '85	▼▼▼	8
●	Duca Enrico '90	▼▼▼	8
●	Duca Enrico '92	▼▼▼	8
●	Duca Enrico '96	▼▼	8

CASTIGLIONE DI SICILIA (CT)

COTTANERA
Loc. Passo Pisciaro
C.da Iannazzo SP 89, Km 1
95030 Castiglione di Sicilia (CT)
tel. 0942963601
e-mail: staff@cottanera.it

Vincenzo and Guglielmo Cambria have hit Three Glasses. Naturally, they share this fine achievement with their oenologist Giulio Vecchio and agronomist Luciana Bionda, a couple – in both senses of the term – who have been looking after the estate's 50 hectares for several years now. Sole a Sesta '00, made exclusively from Syrah, is a stunning wine and one good enough to put Cottanera up with Italy's top producing estates. It is an intense ruby colour, then the spectrum of aromas on the nose is endless, and supported by gentle, elegant scents of spices and dark chocolate. The palate is seductively soft yet also powerful and very long. The '00 Grammonte, made from merlot given 15 months in oak, also confirmed the promise of its previous vintage. It has a richly balsamic, tobacco-like nose, then weight and firmness on the palate. Ardenza '00, from mondeuse, a variety from Haute Savoie, is another classy wine. The dark red colour ushers in intensity on the nose, excellent definition on the palate and a very clean finish. The mid weight Fatagione '00 is from a mix of nerello mascalese and nero d'Avola. It has distinctly spicy aromas and a harmonious palate. Finally, Barbazzale Rosso '01, from nerello mascalese, and Barbazzale Bianco '01, from inzolia grown on lava-rich soils, both showed well.

COMISO (RG)

AVIDE
C.da Mendolilla S.P. 7 Km. 1.5
97013 Comiso (RG)
tel. 0932967456
e-mail: avide@avide.it

We tasted a great selection of wines from this Comiso estate, run by Giovanni Calcaterra. As usual, they were appealingly well styled. Avide's newest wine is 3 Carati, from very low-yielding nero d'Avola, grown in the countryside around Bastonaca. It is a brightly-tinged ruby red. There is frank small wild berry fruitiness, blackcurrant and blueberry in particular, on the nose, then the palate is soft, with firm body and very good length. Sigillo, from cabernet sauvignon and nero d'Avola, is now at its second vintage, the '00. It shows balance in every aspect. The texture is good, and both nose and palate offer welcome drinkability. The '99 Cerasuolo di Vittoria Barocco, from frappato and nero d'Avola, is one of the estate's classics. Again, it showed well, with ripe fruit and a liquorice tang, as did the '00 Cerasuolo di Vittoria Etichetta Nera, with its strong predominance of frappato over nero d'Avola. The Herea Rosso, from frappato only, is another very decent wine. It's well made and also very good value for money. The best of the whites, as usual, is the inzolia-based Vigne d'Oro, which benefits from a stay in oak casks. It has balanced fruitiness with attractive wafts of toasted oak. Herea Bianco '01 is an uncomplicated wine for drinking young. Lacrimæ Bacchi, Avide's dessert wine, is in effect a pure Inzolia. It has a good golden colour, clean tropical fruit aromas and a full, seductive palate.

● Sole di Sesta '00	▼▼▼	7
● Grammonte '00	▼▼	7
● L'Ardenza '00	▼	7
● Fatagione '00	▼	5
○ Barbazzale Bianco '01	▼	4*
● Barbazzale Rosso '01	▼	4*
● Grammonte '99	▼▼	5
● L'Ardenza '99	▼▼	5
● Sole di Sesta '99	▼▼	5
○ Barbazzale Bianco '00	▼	3
● Barbazzale Rosso '00	▼	3*
● Fatagione '99	▼	4

● Sigillo Rosso '00	▼▼	6
○ Vigne d'Oro '00	▼▼	5
● 3 Carati '00	▼▼	3
● Cerasuolo di Vittoria Barocco '99	▼▼	6
● Cerasuolo di Vittoria Etichetta Nera '00	▼	3
○ Herea Bianco Insolia '01	▼	3
● Herea Rosso Frappato '01	▼	3
○ Lacrimæ Bacchi '99	▼	8
● Cerasuolo di Vittoria Barocco '95	▼▼	4
● Cerasuolo di Vittoria Barocco '96	▼▼	4
● Cerasuolo di Vittoria Barocco '98	▼▼	6
● Sigillo Rosso '98	▼▼	4
○ Vigne d'Oro '98	▼▼	3
○ Lacrimæ Bacchi	▼▼	5
○ Dalle Terre di Herea Bianco '00	▼	2*
● Dalle Terre di Herea Rosso '00	▼	2*

GROTTE (AG)

Morgante
C.da Racalmare
92020 Grotte (AG)
tel. 0922945579
e-mail: morgante_vini@virgilio.it

Good things come in threes, so they say, and it's certainly true that Antonio Morgante has now earned his third Three Glass award. Actually, sure things don't come much surer, given the fabulous quality of the '00 Don Antonio, which must now be ranked as one of the best wines in Italy. Underlying this success, there is of course much serious, meticulous work. Antonio is supported on the estate by his sons Carmelo and Giovanni, and is also lucky enough to have the famed Riccardo Cotarella as consultant. Don Antonio '00 is a brightly tinged deep red. The nose proffers alluring notes of small red berry fruit and oriental spices, interwoven with slight hints of raisining. The palate is dense, elegant and long, and has firm structure, especially in its solid tannic base. The '00 Nero d'Avola is another excellent wine, happily confirming the promise of previous years. The lively ruby colour presages a wide array of aromas ranging from fruitiness to chocolate and vanilla. The palate is full and assertive yet soft, and offers lovely, luscious drinkability.

● Don Antonio '00	🍷🍷🍷	6
● Nero d'Avola '00	🍷🍷	4*
● Don Antonio '98	🍷🍷🍷	5
● Don Antonio '99	🍷🍷🍷	5
● Nero d'Avola '99	🍷🍷	3*
● Nero d'Avola '98	🍷	3

MARSALA (TP)

Marco De Bartoli
C.da Fornara, 292
91025 Marsala (TP)
tel. 0923962093 - 0923918344

This estate has always followed been guided by the beacon of quality, even when times were bleak for premium wine production in Sicily. That choice has again borne fruit with a series of classy bottles, proving that Marco De Bartoli and his sons Renato and Sebastiano have again hit the nail on the head. Again this year, we were impressed by the care that has gone into the making of these products. Zibibbo Pietranera '01 is an aromatic wine for drinking cool on long, hot summer evenings. It is as remarkable as it is attractive, delicate and alluring. Grappoli del Grillo '01, from 100 per cent grillo, is golden, with complex, well-defined aromas and distinct personality. It's also very well made. The icing on the cake is that it is from a classic Sicilian variety that the De Bartolis understand and handle well. The Passito di Pantelleria '00 is also top notch. It has a deep amber colour, decisive aromas of honey and apricot, and an intriguing, warm palate. The Marsalas are all very good. Take the structured, balanced, elegant Superiore '86, for example. Or the deep, rich, soft Vecchio Samperi Ventennale, with its extraordinary aromatic length. And the Marsala Superiore Oro Vigna La Miccia, with its intensity, clarity and a mix of ripe fruits and firm-fleshed cooked fruits on the nose, followed by elegance and richness in the mouth. But as everyone knows, love for Marsala is instilled from birth at the De Bartoli home. When Marco laments that, "Marsala is dead. No one drinks it," it is a cry from the heart.

○ Marsala Sup. Ris. 20 Anni	🍷🍷	6
○ Marsala Sup. '86	🍷🍷	7
○ Passito di Pantelleria '00	🍷🍷	7
○ Grappoli del Grillo '01	🍷🍷	4
○ Pietranera '01	🍷🍷	4
○ Marsala Sup.	🍷🍷	6
○ Marsala Sup. Oro Vigna La Miccia	🍷🍷	6
○ Vecchio Samperi Ventennale	🍷🍷	6
○ Sole e Vento '01	🍷	4
○ Passito di Pantelleria Bukkuram '94	🍷🍷	5
○ Passito di Pantelleria Bukkuram '98	🍷🍷	6

MARSALA (TP)

TENUTA DI DONNAFUGATA
VIA SEBASTIANO LIPARI, 18
91025 MARSALA (TP)
TEL. 0923724200
E-MAIL: info@donnafugata.it

The fact that he called in superstar oenologist, Carlo Ferrini, to take over from Giacomo Tachis, at Tachis' suggestion, says much about where Giacomo Rallo wants to go. If you're in the Formula One championship, then you need people like Jean Todt. And Ferrini is working on the future of this renowned winery's top wines. For now, he is still in a transition period and the wines don't yet have the peaks that you expect from an estate of this class. They are good, don't get us wrong, and there is no need for pessimism. It is simply a question of time. In fact, we liked the '01 Chiaranda del Merlo a lot. It may not have the captivating mineral tones on the nose of previous vintages but it does have all the elegance of its predecessors and a balance that is not always easy to find in a Sicilian oak-aged Chardonnay. The two leading reds, Milleunanotte '99 and Tancredi '00, both almost 100 per cent nero d'Avola, also showed well but this time it was the Tancredi that impressed us more, especially with its beautifully delineated aromas. The '01 Passito di Pantelleria Ben Ryé is as good as usual, but this time, it's angled more towards drinkability than concentration. Vigna di Gabri '01 from inzolia, or "ansonica", as it is called in these parts, and the easy-drinking, inviting Moscato di Pantelleria Kabir '01 are both fair.

○ Contessa Entellina Chiarandà del Merlo '01	♟♟	6
● Contessa Entellina Tancredi '00	♟♟	5
○ Passito di Pantelleria Ben Ryé '01	♟♟	7
● Contessa Entellina Milleunanotte '99	♟♟	7
○ Contessa Entellina Vigna di Gabri '01	♟	4
○ Moscato di Pantelleria Kabir '01	♟	5
○ Contessa Entellina Chiarandà del Merlo '98	♟♟♟	5
○ Contessa Entellina Chiarandà del Merlo '99	♟♟♟	5
○ Contessa Entellina Chiarandà del Merlo '00	♟♟	5
● Milleunanotte '97	♟♟	7

MARSALA (TP)

CANTINE FLORIO
VIA VINCENZO FLORIO, 1
91025 MARSALA (TP)
TEL. 0923781111
E-MAIL: marsala@cantineflorio.com

When historic cellars are under discussion, the name Florio always crops up, sooner or later. Not just because its Marsalas have been produced for over 200 years, and drunk all over the world, but particularly because the cellar buildings are among the most spectacular examples of wine archaeology around ("industrial archaeology" wouldn't sound right in this context). Florio was, remains, and will always be, Marsala's leading estate. It has been owned by Illva Saronno for some years now but the wines continue to made the way they always have been, representing an important legacy from a long-established tradition. To some, they may appear a little old fashioned, but at a time when our foremost battle is against wine standardization, they are a symbol of the heritage we are trying to defend. The best, and the most distinctive, is Marsala Vergine Baglio Florio '88, which reached the tasting finals and came within a whisker of Three Glasses. It has an amber colour, aromas of chocolate and liqueur walnuts, and a dry, salty, alcoholic palate. All three Marsalas in the Vecchioflorio line, Ambra Secco '98, Semisecco '93 and Oro '93, are very good without, however, reaching the heights of complexity of the Baglio. This year's range closes with the rich Marsala Vergine Terre Arse Oro '90 and the '91 Marsala Superiore Ambra Semisecco Targa 1940, possibly the least inspiring of the series. Even so, the overall impression is strongly positive.

○ Marsala Vergine Baglio Florio Oro '88	♟♟	6
○ Marsala Vergine Terre Arse Oro '90	♟♟	5
○ Marsala Sup. Semisecco Vecchioflorio '93	♟♟	4
○ Marsala Vergine Vecchioflorio Oro '93	♟♟	5
○ Marsala Ambra Secco Vecchioflorio '98	♟♟	4
○ Marsala Vergine Baglio Florio '85	♟♟	5
○ Marsala Vergine Baglio Florio '86	♟♟	5
○ Marsala Sup. Ris. Targa 1840 '91	♟♟	4

MARSALA (TP)

CARLO PELLEGRINO
VIA DEL FANTE, 37
91025 MARSALA (TP)
TEL. 0923719911
E-MAIL: info@carlopellegrino.it

This year has brought good results for Pellegrino, one of the largest wine enterprises in Sicily, confirming that the changes they announced are on their way. This means that their over 120-year-long tradition of outstanding activity, which has brought excellent commercial and economic results, is being carried forward in the best way possible: looking the future in the face, adapting to new consumer tastes and tackling the market's new challenges. A new cellar will be ready for the 2003 vintage. It is state of the art in all aspects and will have an initial consignment of over 600 barriques. But let's move on to the wines tasted this year. Gorgo Tondo Bianco '01, from grillo and chardonnay, has clean, enticing aromas, led by spring flowers, tropical fruit and peach. The palate is fresh, soft and very attractive. Its twin, Gorgo Tondo Rosso '99, is an equally successful blend of cabernet sauvignon and nero d'Avola with a lively personality, and a spicy, soft, round palate. A new wine, Syrah '01, is also excellent. It is ruby toned, with an inviting nose of blackcurrant and black cherry, and flaunts a firm palate, with soft, gentle tannins. The classic Marsala line is also more than satisfactory. We should stress, too, that prices throughout are surprisingly good.

MARSALA (TP)

CANTINE RALLO
VIA VINCENZO FLORIO, 2
91025 MARSALA (TP)
TEL. 0923721633 - 092372163

Francesco and Andrea Vesco's story is one of two young Sicilians who try to draw together business savvy, modernity and tradition. Uncle and nephew, respectively 37 and 28 years old, they started some years ago when they acquired the 140-year-old Cantine Rallo trademark and set up for high quality production, Marsala included. The investment was huge, involving the purchase and renovation of a historic establishment in the centre of Marsala, and the gradual introduction of modern technology. Current production is about 1,600,000 bottles but due to double within a few years. The vineyards are in the classic heartland of the Bianco d'Alcamo DOC zone. There are 50 hectares where varieties like chardonnay, müller thurgau and cabernet are planted alongside the local catarratto and grillo. We preferred the wines from the indigenous varieties although all are remarkable value for money. Carta d'Oro, one of two indigenous whites, is a highly drinkable, floral Catarratto with just a trace of herbaceousness. It came close to a second Glass. The other, the intense, elegant, barrique-aged Grillo, is a much better wine, with a fruited nose of damson and medlar and a warm, balanced, long-finishing palate. Marsala Vergine Soleras 12 Anni Riserva, coppery-tinged old gold in hue, is dry and aristocratic. The nose is intense, with elegant aromas of hazelnut and almond. The structure is complex and supported by a firm swathe of acidity. Finally, Mare d'Ambra, a Moscato Passito di Pantelleria, is uncomplicated but clean and nicely honed.

	Wine	Rating
O	Passito di Pantelleria Nes '00	ŶŶ 5
O	Gorgo Tondo Bianco '01	ŶŶ 3*
●	Syrah '01	ŶŶ 3*
O	Marsala Vergine '80	ŶŶ 5
●	Delia Nivolelli Cabernet Sauvignon '99	ŶŶ 4*
●	Gorgo Tondo Rosso '99	ŶŶ 3*
O	Marsala Sup. Ris. Dom Pellegrino	ŶŶ 4
O	Marsala Vergine Soleras	ŶŶ 4
●	Etna Rosso Ulysse '00	Ŷ 3
O	Cent'Are Bianco '01	Ŷ 2*
O	Delia Nivolelli Chardonnay '01	Ŷ 3
●	Nero d'Avola '01	Ŷ 3
O	Passito di Pantelleria '01	Ŷ 4

	Wine	Rating
O	Grillo '00	ŶŶ 4
O	Marsala Vergine Soleras Ris. 12 anni	ŶŶ 5
●	Vesco Rosso '00	Ŷ 4
O	Alcamo Carta d'Oro '01	Ŷ 2
O	Areté '01	Ŷ 3
O	Vesco Bianco '01	Ŷ 3
O	Marsala Sup. Semisecco Anima Mediterranea	Ŷ 3
O	Moscato Passito di Pantelleria Mare d'Ambra	Ŷ 5
●	Merlot '99	ŶŶ 4

MENFI (AG)

★ Planeta
C.da Dispensa
92013 Menfi (AG)
tel. 092580009 - 091327965
e-mail: planeta@planeta.it

Planeta has collected ten Three Glass awards in just five editions of the Guide. The consequent star is emblematic of the dedication and passion of Francesca, Alessio and Santi Planeta, the dream team of Sicilian wine. This time it is Cometo '01, from partially barrique-aged fiano, and Burdese '00, from cabernet sauvignon, that pick up the serious stemware. Cometo has intense aromas of grapefruit and mango, and a full flavour satisfyingly supported by acidity of unusual presence for a Mediterranean white. Burdese is in the classic, Bordeaux style of Cabernet Sauvignon, but with Californian leanings. Intense and pervasive on the nose, it offers tight but soft tannins on the palate. However, it is the range as a whole that is so impressive. The two '01 releases of La Segreta, the white from grecanico and chardonnay, the red from nero d'Avola. The Alastro '01, from barrique-aged grecanico and chardonnay. The fragrant Cerasuolo di Vittoria '01, which resembles a southern Santa Maddalena. All these are wines that have turned out brilliantly. The '01 Chardonnay, less concentrated than usual, the '00 Merlot and the '00 Santa Cecilia, from almost 100 per cent nero d'Avola, were all in the running for Three Glasses. Syrah '00 is the exception that proves the rule. It needs a touch more typicity and concentration. But faced with a winery of this calibre and wines of such class, we can only offer our congratulations.

● Burdese '00	🍷🍷🍷	5
○ Cometa '01	🍷🍷🍷	5
● Merlot '00	🍷🍷	5
● Santa Cecilia '00	🍷🍷	5
○ Chardonnay '01	🍷🍷	5
● Syrah '00	🍷🍷	5
○ Alastro '01	🍷🍷	4
● Cerasuolo di Vittoria '01	🍷🍷	3*
○ La Segreta Bianco '01	🍷🍷	3*
● La Segreta Rosso '01	🍷🍷	3*
○ Chardonnay '00	🍷🍷🍷	5
○ Cometa '00	🍷🍷🍷	5
○ Chardonnay '96	🍷🍷🍷	5
● Santa Cecilia '97	🍷🍷🍷	5
● Merlot '99	🍷🍷🍷	5

MENFI (AG)

Settesoli
S. S. 115
92013 Menfi (AG)
tel. 092577111 - 092577102
e-mail: info@mandrarossa.it

Settesoli is back again, as good as ever. This is one of Europe's most important wine co-operatives, with grapes coming from 6,500 hectares of land, owned by its more than 2,300 members. The winery's is focused on steady improvements in quality, with well differentiated wines to fit all market segments and prices to fit the budgets of all consumers. The commercial repositioning so determinedly championed by Settesoli's president, Diego Planeta, is now under way. The entire co-operative, starting with oenologist Carlo Corino, a consultant of great experience and international renown, were behind Planeta's project. Settesoli's newest wine, Mandrarossa Furetta '01, is from chardonnay and grecanico and has delicate but expressive aromas of pineapple and banana fruit mingling with spring flowers. The palate is confident, showing softness and good acidity. Bendicò '00, a blend of nero d'Avola, merlot and syrah, is equally good and has a deep ruby colour, with blackcurrant, plum jam and spices on the nose. The palate is beautifully rounded and reveals elegant, unobtrusive tannins. The intense, long '01 Vendemmia Tardiva, from 100 per cent catarratto, also stands out as an attractive wine of personality. Impeccable winemaking techniques mark out every other wine. None disappoints.

● Bendicò Mandrarossa '00	🍷🍷	4
○ Furetta Mandrarossa '01	🍷🍷	5
○ Vendemmia Tardiva Mandrarossa '01	🍷🍷	4
● Bonera Mandrarossa '00	🍷	4
● Cabernet Sauvignon Mandrarossa '01	🍷	3
○ Chardonnay Mandrarossa '01	🍷	4
● Feudo dei Fiori Mandrarossa '01	🍷	4
○ Grecanico Mandrarossa '01	🍷	4
● Merlot Mandrarossa '01	🍷	4
● Nero d'Avola Mandrarossa '01	🍷	4
● Syrah Mandrarossa '01	🍷	3
● Merlot Mandrarossa '00	🍷🍷	3
● Merlot Mandrarossa '99	🍷🍷	3
● Cabernet Sauvignon Mandrarossa '00	🍷	3

MESSINA

PALARI
LOC. SANTO STEFANO BRIGA
C.DA BARNA
98135 MESSINA
TEL. 090630194 - 090694281
E-MAIL: vinipalari@tin.it

"Faro Palari is more of a cru, when the year divides by two" (our apologies, but the rhyme is equally silly in Italian). The reasons have nothing to do with numerology but this is precisely what has happened recently. Faro Palari was excellent in '96 and '98 but shone less brightly in '97 and '99. The '00 is also following the omens. The vintage and perhaps Salvatore (known as "Turi") Geraci's lucky star have brought him a red of great class. From a nerello cappuccio and nerello mascalese-based blend, the '00 Faro Palari has a ruby colour with just a trace of residual purple. The nose is beautifully knit, black cherry taking centre stage and lightly smoky nuances shimmering in the background. But more than anything, it is the elegance and balance on the palate, and the complete lack of the over-ripeness that many Sicilian reds suffer from time to time, that marks this wine out. It is harmonious and powerful, but not excessively so, and mouthfilling without being heavy. In short, it's a little miracle, and one that we are very happy to award Three Glasses. Rosso del Soprano, also mainly from nerello cappuccio and nerello mascalese, sits alongside. However, the '00 vintage is not the most brilliant version of this "deuxième vin". The tiny Palari estate, at Santo Stefano Briga, ten kilometres south of Messina, has done better and will do better again.

MILO (CT)

BARONE DI VILLAGRANDE
VIA DEL BOSCO
95025 MILO (CT)
TEL. 0957082175 - 0957494339

Carlo and Maria Nicolosi can be satisfied with how things are going. Their wines have now found their feet. On our side, we can confirm that the quality from this long-standing estate on the slopes of Etna gets ever better. The '99 is the third release of Sciara, from merlot and nerello mascalese with small amounts of other local varieties. It confirms Sciara as a wine of class. The colour is a deep ruby and there are aromas of blackberry and raspberry, with some black pepper. The palate is round and even. The Etna Rosso '00, from nerello mascalese with a little nerello mantellato, is not in the same league but is still good of its type, with attractive aromas of musk and morello cherry, and a long, dry, firm palate. The Fiore di Villagrande '01 is exclusively from carricante, a white variety found only in the Etna area, and ages in wood. It is a deep straw colour, introducing quince and vanilla on the nose. The palate has good aromatic length. The carricante grapes for Etna Bianco Superiore, a particularly fruity, attractive, immediate wine, come from the zone known as Legno di Conzo. Then from Etna, we move to Salina, one of the Aeolian Islands, where the estate vineyards in Santa Marina and Malfa produce a Malvasia delle Lipari, with 95 per cent malvasia and five per cent corinto. It has attractive aromas of ripe apricot and figs ushering in a palate that is full and honeyed.

● Faro Palari '00	♟♟♟	7
● Rosso del Soprano '00	♟	5
● Faro Palari '96	♟♟♟	7
● Faro Palari '98	♟♟♟	7
● Faro Palari '99	♟♟	7
● Faro Palari '94	♟♟	7
● Faro Palari '95	♟♟	7
● Faro Palari '97	♟♟	7

○ Etna Bianco Sup. '01	♟♟	3*
● Fiore di Villagrande '01	♟♟	3*
● Sciara di Villagrande Rosso '99	♟♟	5
● Etna Rosso '00	♟	3
○ Malvasia delle Lipari Passito	♟	5
● Sciara di Villagrande Rosso '98	♟♟	4
● Fiore di Villagrande '99	♟♟	3*
○ Fiore '00	♟	3
● Etna Rosso '94	♟	3

PACECO (TP)

Casa Vinicola Firriato
Via Trapani, 4
91027 Paceco (TP)
tel. 0923882755
e-mail: info@firriato.it

After a year's break, a Firriato wine has again won Three Glasses. But it's not just the individual wine, it is the entire, silk-smooth organization at the winery that should reap the honours. Indeed, Girolamo and Salvatore Di Gaetano's cellar has risen meteorically into the front ranks of both the national and international scenes in just a few years. Firriato is, for instance, already the leading Italian winery on the difficult Scandinavian market. Annual production has increased from a few hundred thousand bottles to over 4,000,000, all good quality, from the simplest offerings upwards, and all sold at very attractive prices. This must bring great satisfaction to the owners and their well-known international technical team, a New Zealander, an Australian and a Californian, alongside oenologist Pellegrino from Marsala, led by UK-based Master of Wine Kym Milne. But let's come to the wines. Harmonium '00, from superb nero d'Avola grapes, is simply fantastic. It is an opaque ruby and the nose reveals red berry fruit and spices. In the mouth, it is powerful, fleshy and rounded, with impeccably discreet, smooth tannins. The elegant Camelot '00, a stylish blend of cabernet sauvignon and merlot, is in the same class and equally memorable. Both white and red versions of Santagostino Baglio Soria, which have already established themselves as classics, are admirable. Two new wines, the fresh, inviting Chiaramonte '01, from 100 per cent catarratto, and the well-structured but soft Chiaramonte '00 from nero d'Avola, are both characterful and inexpensive.

PALERMO

Fatascià
Via G. Galilei, 95
90145 Palermo
tel. 0916932060
e-mail: info@led-srl.it

This new estate makes its Guide debut with a remarkable and highly gratifying result. One wine made it all the way to the Three Glasses tasting finals. Gianfranco and Stefania Lena, and Giuseppe Natoli, its founders, are not novices. All have experience in the wine sector and in fact, have been able to draw on some of their family-owned vineyards in Castelbuono. Add a consultant of the calibre of Riccardo Cotarella (surprise!), and the speed with which such fine wines have arrived begins to make sense. Insolente '00 is a blend of very low-yielding merlot and cabernet sauvignon given 18 months in French oak barrels. The colour is a very deep dark red. The elegantly fruited nose has nuances of leather, spices and cocoa powder, then the palate is warm, penetrating, spicy, deep and very long. Almanera '00 is a successful Nero d'Avola with a ruby red colour, a nose of blueberry and blackberry, and an elegant, yet powerful and concentrated, palate. The range also includes a sweet wine, Passito di Pantelleria Ylenia. The '00 is a golden yellow, has aromas of ripe figs and apricot, and a warm, full palate.

● Harmonium '00	♛♛♛	5
● Camelot '00	♛♛	6
● Chiaramonte Rosso '00	♛♛	3*
● Santagostino Rosso Baglio Soria '00	♛♛	4
○ Altavilla della Corte Bianco '01	♛♛	3*
○ Chiaramonte Bianco '01	♛♛	3*
○ Santagostino Bianco Baglio Soria '01	♛♛	4
● Etna Rosso '00	♛	2*
○ Alcamo '01	♛	2*
● Camelot '98	♛♛♛	5
● Camelot '99	♛♛	6
● Harmonium '99	♛♛	6
● Santagostino Rosso Baglio Soria '99	♛♛	4

● L'insolente '00	♛♛	5
● Almanera '00	♛♛	3*
○ Ylenia '00	♛	3

PALERMO

AZIENDE VINICOLE MICELI
VIA DENTI DI PIRAINO, 9
90142 PALERMO
TEL. 0916396111
E-MAIL: segreteria@midmiceli.it

The group is formed of various properties in Castelvetrano and on Pantelleria, and two modern vinification cellars, all directed by Giuseppe Lo Re. It is very active on both the national and international scenes. This year, there are some new wines to enhance the already diverse range, which is aimed firmly at quality. The '01 Yrnm which, following a change in production regulations, now comes under the Pantelleria DOC, is excellent. It's every bit as good as last year's. A dry wine, it reveals unusual, intriguing perfumes that recall the grapes from which it comes and the aromatic herbs that grow wild on the island. Delight, fresh, soft and long, it just slips down, especially when served with sea food. The Syrah '00 is also very well made. Deep ruby in colour, it has a complex nose with aromas of black cherry, plum and spice. The palate is round and mouthfilling, and there is good balance in every department. The non-vintage Passito di Pantelleria Nun showed better this year. The new release has a good amber hue, fragrant notes of dried and candied fruits, and a full palate with great length. Entelechia performed well, too, and is one of the most characterful Moscato di Pantellerias on the market. The rest of the range is also good.

PALERMO

SPADAFORA
VIA AUSONIA, 90
90144 PALERMO
TEL. 091514952 - 0916703322
E-MAIL: info@spadafora.com

For the second time, Francesco Spadafora's estate comes perilously close to gaining Three Glasses. Behind this headline-grabber, we again found improvements across the entire range, with reds leading the field. The series starts this year with Schietto '00, a highly concentrated 100 per cent Cabernet Sauvignon. The colour is deep red. There are complex aromas of red berry fruits bottled in alcohol, plum, liquorice and tobacco. The palate is full, deep and very clean, and finishes long. Sole dei Padri '00, a supremely attractive Syrah, has turned out particularly well. The very deep red colour leads to aromas of wild cherry, pencil lead and plum, then the palate is full and decisive, with tight but balanced tannins. The '00 version of Don Pietro Rosso, a successful blackcurrant-and-blackberry Nero d'Avola with a velvety, harmonious palate, further enhances the wine's reputation. The good-quality Rosso Virzì '01, from nero d'Avola and syrah, is concentrated in both its dark red colour and its attractive fruitiness. Schietto Chardonnay '01 has a straw colour, aromas of citrus fruit and hedgerow flowers, and is supported by balanced acidity. To finish, Alhambra '01, from catarratto, and Don Pietro Bianco '01, from inzolia, catarratto and grillo, are both fresh, immediate and satisfying.

●	Syrah '00	ŶŶ	5
○	Pantelleria Secco Yrnm '01	ŶŶ	4
○	Passito di Pantelleria Entelechia	ŶŶ	6
○	Passito di Pantelleria Nun	ŶŶ	5
●	Cabernet Sauvignon '00	Ŷ	5
●	Chiana d'Inserra '00	Ŷ	4
●	Majo San Lorenzo '00	Ŷ	5
●	Nero d'Avola Miceli '00	Ŷ	4
○	Chardonnay '01	Ŷ	5
○	Salgalaluna Bianco '01	Ŷ	3
○	Passito di Pantelleria Tanit	Ŷ	4
○	Passito di Pantelleria Yanir	Ŷ	5
○	Yrnm '00	ŶŶ	4
●	Cabernet Sauvignon '99	ŶŶ	5
●	Chiana d'Inserra '99	ŶŶ	4

●	Schietto Rosso '00	ŶŶ	5
●	Don Pietro Rosso '00	ŶŶ	4
●	Schietto Syrah '00	ŶŶ	5
●	Sole dei Padri '00	ŶŶ	8
○	Schietto Chardonnay '01	ŶŶ	5
●	Vigna Virzì Rosso '01	ŶŶ	3*
○	Alcamo Alhambra '01	Ŷ	2*
○	Don Pietro Bianco '01	Ŷ	3
●	Schietto Rosso '99	ŶŶ	5
●	Don Pietro Rosso '95	ŶŶ	3
●	Don Pietro Rosso '96	ŶŶ	3
●	Don Pietro Rosso '98	ŶŶ	3
●	Schietto Rosso '98	ŶŶ	3
●	Don Pietro Rosso '99	ŶŶ	3

PANTELLERIA (TP)

Salvatore Murana
C.da Khamma, 276
91017 Pantelleria (TP)
Tel. 0923915231

Regrettably, our tasting dates do not always tie in conveniently with the bottling period for many wines. In Salvatore Murana's case, hardly ever. So to avoid penalizing his wines unnecessarily or making rushed judgements, we have decided to leave until next year our assessment of Martingana '99 and Mueggen '01, both Passito di Pantelleria, and which both arrived as pre-bottling samples. Perhaps we are being overcautious. The undoubted quality of these wines can already be sensed. But at this level, when Three Glasses are up for grabs, we can't take any chances. The Passito di Pantelleria Khamma '00 was in a similar position but it seemed easier to interpret. We felt we were in a position to evaluate it adequately. There was no cloudiness or opalescence on the appearance. All its varietal and stylistic character was clearly present, on both nose and palate, revealing a classic, elegant Passito, with a sweetness that was neither excessive nor jammy. Moscato di Pantelleria Turbé '00 is also fragrant and shows very good typicity. But the real novelty from Murana this year is a range of dry wines. Two reds, Pietra di Cinta '98, from nero d'Avola, and Talia '00, from nero d'Avola, cabernet and merlot, are both excellent. A further red, Criccio '99, from an unusual blend of nero d'Avola and carignano, and the two whites, Gadì '01, which is Gewürztraminer-like but from zibibbo, and È Serre '01, a more customary Catarratto, are all characterful.

PARTINICO (PA)

Cusumano
S. S. 113 - C.da San Carlo
90047 Partinico (PA)
Tel. 0918903456
E-mail: cusumano@cusumano.it

There was a brilliant repeat showing from the estate owned by the dynamic, congenial Cusumano brothers, Diego and Alberto. As, sadly, so often happens, they just missed out on Three Glasses but two of the wines not only reached the tasting finals, they also acquitted themselves brilliantly. These are real gems of the new Sicilian wine scene. If this were all it would be quite something, but this recently founded and already highly regarded winery also releases an excellent quality range of wines marketed at very reasonable prices. Starting at the top, the '01 release of Noà, a blend of nero d'Avola, merlot and cabernet sauvignon, shows all the characteristics that brought the wine fame: an opaque ruby colour; an intense nose with a fascinating kaleidoscope of aromas from berry fruit, spices and liquorice to pencil lead; and a powerful palate of great structure and length, with tight but rounded tannins. Similarly impressive is Sagana '01, exclusively from nero d'Avola, which has aromas of ripe blackberry, cocoa powder and black pepper followed by a soft, bright, balanced palate of great depth. The tannins support a wealth of flavour. All the other wines showed well, especially Benuara '01, from nero d'Avola and syrah, Jalé '01, from chardonnay, the smart Cubia '01, exclusively from inzolia, and Angimbé, an attractive blend of inzolia and chardonnay.

O	Moscato Passito di Pantelleria Khamma '00	🍷🍷	7
O	Moscato di Pantelleria Turbé '00	🍷🍷	5
●	Talia '00	🍷🍷	4
●	Pietra di Cinta '98	🍷🍷	5
O	È Serre '01	🍷	4
O	Gadì '01	🍷	4
●	Criccio '99	🍷	5
O	Moscato Passito di Pantelleria Martingana '97	🍷🍷🍷	8
O	Moscato Passito di Pantelleria Martingana '98	🍷🍷🍷	8
O	Moscato Passito di Pantelleria Khamma '99	🍷🍷	7
O	Moscato Passito di Pantelleria Khamma '98	🍷🍷	7

●	Noà '01	🍷🍷	5
●	Sagana '01	🍷🍷	5
O	Angimbé '01	🍷🍷	4*
●	Benuara '01	🍷🍷	4
O	Cubia '01	🍷🍷	5
O	Jalé '01	🍷🍷	5
O	Nadarìa Alcamo '01	🍷	3*
O	Nadarìa Inzolia '01	🍷	3
●	Nadarìa Nero d'Avola '01	🍷	3
●	Nadarìa Syrah '01	🍷	3
●	Noà '00	🍷🍷🍷	5
●	Sagana '00	🍷🍷	5
O	Angimbé '00	🍷🍷	3*
●	Benuara '00	🍷🍷	4*
O	Jalé '00	🍷🍷	4

PIAZZA ARMERINA (EN)

MAURIGI
C.DA BUDONETTO
94015 PIAZZA ARMERINA (EN)
TEL. 091321788 - 0935321788
E-MAIL: info@maurigi.it

This is Francesco Maurigi's first official appearance in the Guide with his new estate. It was founded in 1998 and is situated at Piazza Armerina, not far from the celebrated Roman villa thought to have been the residence of the emperor Hadrian. Flying in the face of all traditions in the area, which has never seen a vine, he took advice from several French consultants and the agronomist Lucio Brancadoro from the University of Milan, and planted 40 hectares of vineyard. Thanks to assistance from able oenologist Giovanni Risso, the results of this gamble have gone beyond the rosiest expectations. Terre di Sofia '01, from 100 per cent chardonnay, is a wine of notable elegance. Golden in colour, it is inviting in its perfumes of ripe tropical fruit and discloses a soft, mouthfilling palate. So good was this masterpiece that it shot straight into the Three Glasses taste-offs. But what really surprised the tasting panel was that all the other wines were almost as good. The impeccable vinification style tends to sacrifice raw extractive power for finesse and elegance, concepts that are practically revolutionary at these latitudes. Coste all'Ombra '01, from chardonnay and sauvignon blanc, Saia Grande '01, a mix of syrah, merlot and pinot noir, and Terre di Maria '00, a blend of cabernet sauvignon, merlot, syrah and pinot noir, are all complex, elegant, balanced wines that immediately rank Maurigi as one of Sicily's most dynamic estates.

O Terre di Sofia '01	🍷	5
● Terre di Maria '00	🍷🍷	6
O Coste all'Ombra '01	🍷🍷	5
● Saia Grande '01	🍷🍷	5

SAN CIPIRELLO (PA)

CALATRASI - ACCADEMIA DEL SOLE
C.DA PIANO PIRAINO
90040 SAN CIPIRELLO (PA)
TEL. 0918576767
E-MAIL: info@calatrasi.it

Calatrasi is a big-league enterprise. Focusing on high quality in large quantities, its aim is to embrace the best of the entire southern Mediterranean, using three production hubs in Puglia, Sicily and Tunisia. Sicily has the largest slice of output with over 8,000,000 bottles a year. Calatrasi is one of the island's most important producers and results are encouraging. The driving force is Maurizio Micciché, a haematologist, who has prescribed massive "transfusions" of know-how from expert New World oenologists. The high-profile Terre di Ginestra line comes from one of the estate's best vineyards. It includes the impressive "650 s.l.m." a nero d'Avola and syrah cru from high vineyards planted, as the name tells us, at 651 metres above sea level. Elegant, with an attractive nose of plum and morello cherry supported by vegetal notes and oak tones, it is given grace by an austere palate that shows silky tannins. Another fine wine is the monovarietal Nero d'Avola. Dense and varietal, it has a mint and coffee nose, then a stylish, attractive palate. The best of the Terre di Ginestra whites is the indigenous Catarratto, with refined notes of peach and citron. The more basic D'Istinto line comprises well-conceived blends of international and Sicilian varieties. Accademia del Sole is another intriguing line that aims to raise the profile of individual vineyards and vine growers. The most successful of these is Familia Lucchese, a clean wine redolent of blackcurrant and cherry. It's from nero d'Avola and cabernet.

● Terre di Ginestra 651 '00	🍷🍷	7
● Terre di Ginestra Nero d'Avola '01	🍷🍷	4
O D'Istinto Nero '00	🍷	5
● D'Istinto Magnifico '01	🍷	8
● D'Istinto Sangiovese-Merlot '01	🍷	5
● Familia Lucchese '01	🍷	4
O Terre di Ginestra Catarratto '01	🍷	4
O Vioca di Plaia '01	🍷	4
O D'Istinto Catarratto-Chardonnay '01		4
● D'Istinto Sangiovese-Merlot '00	🍷🍷	5*
O Terre di Ginestra Bianco '00	🍷🍷	3*

TRAPANI

CANTINA SOCIALE DI TRAPANI
LOC. FONTANELLE
C.DA OSPEDALETTO
91100 TRAPANI
TEL. 0923539349
E-MAIL: cantinatp@libero.it

The Cantina Sociale di Trapani's success is driven by extremely competent winemaking and, as a result, reliable quality throughout the range. The co-operative's young oenologist, Nicola Centonze, its chair, Roberto Adragna, and all the members must have been proud to submit such a good Cabernet Sauvignon Forti Terre di Sicilia for the second year running. This year's version, the '00, seemed only marginally less impressive than the '99. Its deep, concentrated red colour leads to an enthralling series of aromas, with beautifully clear notes of ripe cherry, blackcurrant and blackberry over a subtle spicy base. The first impact on the palate is tight and precise before it opens to give a harmonious, refined mid palate with nice weight, then a long finish. It may still be held in check by its extreme youth but it is nevertheless one of Sicily's "greats". The Chardonnay '01 has a broad spectrum of aromas, despite the domination of the oak, and shows structure and balance, supported by refreshing acidity. Rocche Rosse '01, from cabernet sauvignon, merlot and nero d'Avola, is also well up to speed. It has a nose of red berry fruit and tobacco, followed by an attractive, velvety feel on the palate. Rosso Forti Terre di Sicilia is warm, heady and enveloping. The attractive, cleanly fruited '00 Nero d'Avola is made along similar lines.

VALLELUNGA PRATAMENO (CL)

★ TASCA D'ALMERITA
C.DA REGALEALI
90029 VALLELUNGA PRATAMENO (CL)
TEL. 0921544011 - 0921542522

Good news from the Tasca estate. Long one of the best in Sicily, it has turned a new corner. First, it has taken on the famous oenologist and agronomist Carlo Ferrini to look after its top wines. Aside from consultants, famous or not, there is also a real new philosophy in the air. Efforts are now focusing on developing the qualities of classic local varieties and the wines most in keeping with the region's characteristics. The '01 Cabernet Sauvignon has regained great individuality of character, with balsam notes on the nose and good complexity on the palate, but pride of place at our tastings went to the nero d'Avola-based '00 Rosso del Conte. This has typicity, concentration and good drinkability. Just an extra pinch of tannic depth and it would have hit the jackpot, but then so much depends on how the vintage goes. The vines are at high altitude and weather variations are more marked than in other parts of Sicily. Other particularly good wines are: Camastra '00, from nero d'Avola and merlot; Cygnus '00, exclusively from nero d'Avola; the '01 Chardonnay, with its carefully judged oaking; and the fine Almerita Brut, the only truly characterful classic-method sparkling wine in the south of Italy. All the rest of the range is well-styled, as usual, with the three '01 Regaleali wines, red, white and rosé, the mainstays.

●	Forti Terre di Sicilia Cabernet Sauvignon '00	ΨΨ	5
○	Forti Terre di Sicilia Chardonnay '01	ΨΨ	4*
●	Forti Terre di Sicilia Nero d'Avola '00	Ψ	4
●	Forti Terre di Sicilia Il Rosso '01	Ψ	3
●	Forti Terre di Sicilia Rocche Rosse '01	Ψ	4
●	Forti Terre di Sicilia Cabernet Sauvignon '99	ΨΨΨ	5
●	Forti Terre di Sicilia Cabernet Sauvignon '97	ΨΨ	3
●	Forti Terre di Sicilia Cabernet Sauvignon '98	ΨΨ	3

●	Cabernet Sauvignon '00	ΨΨ	7
●	Rosso del Conte '00	ΨΨ	6
●	Camastra '00	ΨΨ	5
○	Chardonnay '01	ΨΨ	6
○	Almerita Brut '99	ΨΨ	6
●	Cygnus '00	Ψ	5
○	Leone d'Almerita '01	Ψ	4
○	Regaleali Bianco '01	Ψ	3
⊙	Regaleali Rosato '01	Ψ	3
●	Regaleali Rosso '01	Ψ	3
○	Villa Tasca '01	Ψ	3
●	Cabernet Sauvignon '99	ΨΨΨ	7
○	Chardonnay '99	ΨΨ	6
●	Rosso del Conte '99	ΨΨ	6

VIAGRANDE (CT)

BENANTI
VIA G. GARIBALDI, 475
95029 VIAGRANDE (CT)
TEL. 0957893438 - 0957893533
E-MAIL: benanti@vinicolabenanti.it

Giuseppe Benanti, who manages a pharmaceuticals business, is no parvenu when it comes to wine. His property on the slopes of Etna has for several years displayed exemplary efficiency with real passion behind it. So much so, that it has become a major focus for eastern Sicilian winemaking. The range submitted this year is excellent and although there is nothing that quite merits Three Glasses, it shines for consistency. The most interesting wine is a particularly good release, the '98, of Etna Bianco Superiore Pietramarina. It is complex, with a minerally nose and elegant body expressed with admirable restraint. But all the wines were very well made. The monovarietals we particularly liked were the Chardonnay '99 and, moving over to the reds, the Nero d'Avola '99 and the quite spectacular Nerello Cappuccio '99. Then there was the unusual Minnella '00, from a local variety of the same name that has almost disappeared everywhere else. The winery's more classic wines, Lamoremio '98, the nero d'Avola-based Edelmio '99, Etna Rosso Rovittello '98 and Etna Bianco Bianco di Caselle '01, also showed well. In conclusion, a word on the superb Etna Rosso Serra della Contessa '99, which reached the tasting finals. It is still very young, revealing an incisive character and some adolescent surliness, partly due to the vintage. We didn't feel we could pass it for glory status, but we may live to regret that decision.

○	Etna Bianco Sup. Pietramarina '98	🍷🍷	5
●	Etna Rosso Serra della Contessa '99	🍷🍷	6
○	Etna Bianco Bianco di Caselle '01	🍷🍷	3
●	Etna Rosso Rovittello '98	🍷🍷	5
●	Lamoremio '98	🍷🍷	6
○	Chardonnay '99	🍷🍷	5
○	Edelmio '99	🍷🍷	5
●	Nerello Cappuccio '99	🍷🍷	5
●	Nero d'Avola '99	🍷🍷	5
○	Minnella '00	🍷	4
○	Etna Bianco Sup. Pietramarina '97	🍷🍷	5

VITTORIA (RG)

COS
P.ZZA DEL POPOLO, 34
97019 VITTORIA (RG)
TEL. 0932864042
E-MAIL: info@cosvittoria.it

We are seeing increasing evidence of the intelligent, determined work started some years back by Giusto Occhipinti and "Titta" Cilia, the enthusiastic, competent owners of this leading eastern Sicilian estate. So much effort, so much research and investigation, so many experiments. But also so much market recognition and so much critical acclaim for the results of their terroir-based "oenological philology", which looks to extract the maximum individuality and diversity from site, and in particular from individual vineyards. This year's newcomer is the top-quality Contrade line from nero d'Avola. Labirinto '98 and Dedalo '98 are two exceedingly well-made wines that represent a sort of act of love towards the red variety that is the symbol of Sicily. Both have distinct, very intense, persistent aromas of ripe red berry fruits and spices, and a full palate with tannins that are both vigorous and soft. They are two unique, distinct wines from the same grape, as is obvious when you taste them. Next, we have another good vintage of Scyri, the '99. It, too, is a 100 per cent nero d'Avola. Reliable, intriguing, complex and highly drinkable, it exudes Mediterranean warmth. All the rest of the range showed well, including the two frappato and nero d'Avola Cerasuolo di Vittoria wines, which are some of the best in the area.

●	Contrade - Dedalo '98	🍷🍷	8
●	Contrade - Labirinto '98	🍷🍷	8
●	Scyri '99	🍷🍷	6
●	Cerasuolo di Vittoria '00	🍷	5
●	Cerasuolo di Vittoria V. di Bastonaca '01	🍷	4
○	Ramì '01	🍷	4
●	Cabernet Sauvignon '99	🍷	5
●	Cerasuolo di Vittoria Sciri '95	🍷🍷	4
●	Cerasuolo di Vittoria V. di Bastonaca '95	🍷🍷	4
●	Cerasuolo di Vittoria Sciri '96	🍷🍷	4
●	Cerasuolo di Vittoria Sciri '97	🍷🍷	5
●	Scyri '98	🍷🍷	5
●	Cerasuolo di Vittoria '99	🍷🍷	4

OTHER WINERIES

Feudo Montoni
C. da Montoni Vecchi
92022 Cammarata (AG)
tel. 0916704536
e-mail: feudomontoni@virgilio.it

Fabio Sireci gave us one of the most pleasant surprises of this year's tastings. The Nero d'Avola '00 Selezione Speciale is a wine of rare power and harmony. The straight Nero d'Avola '00 is different. It has enticing fruitiness and is also a Two Glass winner.

● Nero d'Avola Selezione Speciale '00	🍷🍷 5
● Nero d'Avola '00	🍷🍷 4

Alessandro di Camporeale
Via Atrio Principe, 8
90043 Camporeale (PA)
tel. 092437238
e-mail: antonino.alessandro4@tin.it

Natale and Rosolino Alessandro debut with a stupendous wine, Kaid '00, from 100 per cent syrah. The colour is a deep, purple-tinged ruby. The nose is complex, refined and shows good definition. The structure is wonderful, the tannins are soft and gentle, and the balance is great.

● Kaid '00	🍷🍷 5

Gulfi
Loc. C.da Roccazzo
Via Maria Santissima del Rosario
97010 Chiaramonte Gulfi (RG)
tel. 0932921654

Businessman Vito Catania's estate enters the Guide with a distinguished range of wines from nero d'Avola. Neromaccari '00, with its complex aromas and weighty profile on the palate, is impressive and can only improve with time. The other wines showed well, too.

● Nero Ibleo '00	🍷🍷 4
● Neromaccari '00	🍷🍷 4
● Nerobufaleffi '00	🍷 4
● Rosso Ibleo '01	🍷 4

Feudi di San Giuliano
Loc. C.da Mazzaporro Duchessa
90030 Contessa Entellina (PA)
tel. 0923952148
e-mail: giuseppe@bottinelli.it

The Contessa Entellina area is one of Sicily's best for wine production and the Spanò family produce a good Cabernet Sauvignon with attractive notes of chocolate and spices. Also good is Vento di Mayo, a fresh mix of chardonnay, catarratto and inzolia.

● Contessa Entellina Timpaia '01	🍷🍷 4
○ Contessa Entellina Vento di Mayo '01	🍷 3

Barone La Lumia
C.da Pozzillo
92027 Licata (AG)
Tel. 0922770057 - 0922891709
E-mail: info@vogliedisicilia.it

Cadetto and Signorio are fairly full whites, full of tropical fruit notes. Signorio Cadetto Rosso is a Nero d'Avola of good structure, decisive flavour and impressive length.

○	Cadetto Bianco '01	♙	3
○	Signorio Bianco '01	♙	5
●	Signorio Cadetto Rosso '99	♙	3

Baglio Hopps
Loc. C.da Biesina, km. 12,2
91025 Marsala (TP)
Tel. 0923967020
E-mail: info@bagliohopps.com

Giacomo and Fabio Hopps, mindful of grand family traditions, have set up to this new winery. The '01 Grillo, with its elegant tropical fruit notes and firm structure, is excellent. The '00 Diana, a successful blend of nero d'Avola and cabernet sauvignon, is also good.

○	Grillo '01	♙♙	4
●	Diana '00	♙	4
●	Nero d'Avola '00		4
○	Bianca delle Gazzere '01		3

Curatolo
C.da Misilla, 204
91025 Marsala (TP)
Tel. 0923964415

The Cabernet Sauvignon has a deep nose of ripe fruit plus liquorice and cocoa powder, and a soft palate of good length. Samaro '01, from inzolia, with floral aromas and harmonious flavours, is most attractive. The other wines tasted are all well styled.

●	Cabernet Sauvignon '00	♙♙	4
●	Sarmaro Rosso '01	♙	3
○	Sarmaro Bianco '01		2
○	Soleada Bianco '01		2

F.lli Fici
Via S. Lipari, 5
91025 Marsala (TP)
Tel. 0923999053

Fratelli Fici, one of the few remaining Marsala producers, makes this famed wine in numerous styles, from Vintage to Ruby. Our preferences go to the well-made, complex and non-cloying Marsala Superiore Dolce and the Superiore Riserva Secco.

○	Marsala Sup. Dolce	♙♙	4*
○	Marsala Sup. Secco Ris.	♙	5

Ajello
C.da Giudeo
91025 Mazara del Vallo (TP)
Tel. 091309107
E-mail: azajello@tin.it

Salvatore Ajello's magnificent Furat '00, from nero d'Avola, cabernet sauvignon, merlot and syrah, reached the Three Glass taste-offs with its intense ruby colour, complex spectrum of aromas and fleshy palate. Bizir '01, a chardonnay, grillo and inzolia blend, will be ready in a few months.

●	Furat '00	♙♙	5
○	Bizir '01	♙	5
●	Furat '99	♙♙	4

Agareno
C.da Sant'Antonio
92013 Menfi (AG)
Tel. 0925570409
E-mail: agareno@libero.it

Moscafratta is a blend of nero d'Avola, cabernet and merlot with aromas of musk and small red berry fruits, and a full soft palate. Gurra '00, a Nero d'Avola with attractive balsamic notes, is of good quality.

●	Moscafratta '00	♙♙	5
●	Gurra '00	♙	4
●	Moscafratta '99	♙♙	5

BAGLIO SAN VINCENZO
C.DA SAN VINCENZO
92013 MENFI (AG)
TEL. 33924226103
E-MAIL: info@bagliosanvincenzo.it

The soft, balanced Terre dell'Istrice is a good blend of cabernet and merlot. Don Neli Rosso has a pleasing note of cooked fruit and an attractive palate, as does the youthfully exuberant Don Neli Bianco, from grecanico and chardonnay.

● Terre dell'Istrice '00	♈ 4
○ Don Neli Bianco '01	♈ 3
● Don Neli Rosso '01	♈ 3

CANTINE COLOSI
VIA MILITARE RITIRO, 23
98152 MESSINA
TEL. 09053852
E-MAIL: info@cantinecolosi.com

A good Malvasia delle Lipari Passito brings Lidia and Piero Colosi's estate back into the Guide. It is nicely made and golden in colour, with aromas of apricot and ripe peach. The other wines from this estate near Messina are attractive, too, especially the Malvasia Naturale.

○ Malvasia delle Lipari Passita '00	♈♈ 5
○ Malvasia delle Lipari Naturale '00	♈ 5
● Salina Rosso '00	3
○ Salina Bianco '01	2

POLLARA
C.DA MALVELLO - S. P. 4 BIS KM 2
90046 MONREALE (PA)
TEL. 0918462922 - 0918463512
E-MAIL: pollara@principedicorleone.it

The range is led by the round, attractive Principe di Corleone Merlot. Narciso '01 is a Nero d'Avola with balanced flavours and the Chardonnay Vigna di Corte is equally good. Pinot Bianco '01 and Giada '01, from damaschino and other indigenous varieties, are both successful.

● Merlot Principe di Corleone '01	♈ 3
○ Alcamo Principe di Corleone '01	♈ 3
○ Chardonnay Vigna di Corte '01	♈ 3
● Principe di Corleone Rosso Narciso '01	♈ 3

TAMBURELLO
FRAZ. C.DA PIETRAGNELLA
90046 MONREALE (PA)
TEL. 0918465272
E-MAIL: dagala@libero.it

Mirella Tamburello offered us her classic red and white, both well made. Dagala Rosso, from cabernet and nero d'Avola, has notes of ripe cherry and blackberry, and a clean taste. Dagala Bianco has good floral impact on both nose and palate. Value for money is excellent, as usual.

○ Dagala Bianco '01	♈♈ 2*
● Dagala Rosso '00	♈ 3
● Dagala Rosso '99	♈ 1*

ABRAXAS
FRAZ. BUKKURAM - E. ALBANESE, 29
91017 PANTELLERIA (TP)
TEL. 0916110051 - 3381458517
E-MAIL: customer@winesabraxas.com

Two wines this year from Abraxas, at Bukkuram. Alongside the excellent Passito di Pantelleria, which again reached the tasting finals, there is Kuddia del Gallo, from zibibbo and other white varieties. It's attractive and fairly varietal, but still coming round.

○ Passito di Pantelleria	♈♈ 7
○ Kuddia del Gallo	♈ 4
○ Passito di Pantelleria	♈♈ 6

CASE DI PIETRA
C.DA NIKÀ
91017 PANTELLERIA (TP)
TEL. 0659280220
E-MAIL: casedipietra@tiscalinet.it

This year, Giudo Taricotti's estate again made a positive impression. There was an excellent Passito di Pantelleria, Nikà '00, which is concentrated, attractive and deep. The dry white Nikà '01, from zibibbo, is also good, showing attractive structure.

○ Passito di Pantelleria Nikà '00	♈♈ 5
○ Nikà '01	♈ 4
○ Passito di Pantelleria Nikà '99	♈♈ 5

Solidea
C.da Kaddiuggia
91017 Pantelleria (TP)
tel. 0923913016
e-mail: solideavini@libero.it

The D'Anconas' estate is now called simply Solidea. The Passito Solidea keeps its name, though. The '01 edition has a powerful, warm, full nose where notes of apricot, candied fruit and honey meld together marvellously. The palate is soft and round. It's a real delight to drink.

○	Passito di Pantelleria Solidea '01	🍷🍷	6
○	Passito di Pantelleria Solidea '98	🍷🍷🍷	5
○	Passito di Pantelleria Solidea '00	🍷🍷	5

Tola
Via G. Matteotti, 2
90047 Partinico (PA)
tel. 0918781591

This estate has always grown numerous varieties in its vineyards at Bosco Falconiera, between Alcamo and Partinico. Lynthea '01, a full-bodied red, comes from merlot. Granduca '98 and Zabbya '01, both from nero d'Avola, are also attractive. Vigna di Colle '01 is a fresh, fruity white.

●	Lynthea Merlot '01	🍷🍷	4
○	Vigna di Colle '01	🍷	3
●	Zabbya '01	🍷	3
●	Granduca '98	🍷	3

Cantina Sociale La Torre
Loc. C.da Bovo Montagna
92020 Racalmuto (AG)
tel. 0922942194
e-mail: cantina.latorre@tin.it

Even Sicily's co-operatives are beginning to make good wine. This one, at Racalmuto, vinifies grapes from its members' 858 hectares of vineyard. The Nero d'Avola, with a spicy, chocolate nose and a warm, enveloping palate, is characterful.

●	Villa Noce '00	🍷🍷	4

Feudo Solaria
C.da Sulleria
98059 Rodi Milici (ME)
tel. 0909227998
e-mail: feudosolaria@tiscalinet.it

Paola and Alessio Grasso's new winery is situated in a district near the sea, known for its vineyards since Roman times. Sulleria '00, from nero d'Avola and sangiovese, is very good. It has excellent structure, harmony, concentration and dense tannins.

●	Sulleria Rosso '00	🍷🍷	6
●	Sulleria Passito '00	🍷	6
○	Sulleria Bianco '00		6

Elorina
Via Minghetti, 80
96019 Rosolini (SR)
tel. 0931857068
e-mail: elorina@virgilio.it

There's a new set-up at this winery in south-east Sicily, noted for its production of nero d'Avola grapes on the ancient "alberello", or bush-trained, system. Eloro Pachino'98 is full of colour and structure, as is Eloro Pachino Riserva '99. There is a clear upswing in all the other wines.

●	Eloro Pachino Nero d'Avola '98	🍷🍷	4
●	Eloro Nero d'Avola '00	🍷	3
●	Elorina Nero d'Avola '99	🍷	3
●	Eloro Pachino Ris. '99	🍷	5

Gaspare Di Prima
Via G. Guasto, 27
92017 Sambuca di Sicilia (AG)
tel. 0925941201 - 0925941279
e-mail: info@diprimavini.it

The waters of Lake Arancio lap the syrah vines from which oenologist Luca d'Attoma obtains a most successful red. It's full of spicy aromas on the nose and has balanced tannins on the palate. Pepita is as attractive as ever.

●	Villamaura Syrah '00	🍷🍷	6
○	Sambuca di Sicilia Pepita '01	🍷	4
●	Villamaura Syrah '99	🍷🍷	4

Feotto dello Jato
Loc. C.da Feotto
90048 San Giuseppe Jato (PA)
Tel. 0918572650
E-mail: feottodellojato@libero.it

Seven grape growers have set up this new estate in the province of Palermo. The first results are decidedly promising. Rosso di Turi '01, from merlot, is a concentrated, complex wine. The elegant Fegotto '01, exclusively from nero d'Avola, is just as good.

● Fegotto '01	🍷🍷	4
● Rosso di Turi '01	🍷🍷	4
● Terre di Giulia '01	🍷	4
○ Iris '01		4

Barone Scammacca del Murgo
Via Zafferana, 13
95010 Santa Venerina (CT)
Tel. 095950520
E-mail: murgo@murgo.it

With its fine ruby colour and elegant aromas of blackcurrant and black cherry, the '99 Tenuta San Michele is a delight to drink and again at the apex of this prestigious estate's range. Etna Bianco '01, with citrus and mineral notes, is also good, as is the Arbiato '00.

● Tenuta San Michele '99	🍷🍷	4
○ Arbiato '00	🍷	4
○ Etna Bianco '00	🍷	3
● Etna Rosso '00		3

Pupillo
C.da Targia
96100 Siracusa
Tel. 0931494029
E-mail: solacium@tin.it

Solacium '00, from grapes dried on the vine, has attractive notes of ripe summer fruits. Pollio '00, from slightly over-ripe grapes, is elegant, as is Vigna di Mela. Re Federico is a full-bodied Nero D'Avola with good varietal character on the nose.

○ Moscato di Siracusa Pollio '00	🍷	6
○ Moscato di Siracusa Solacium '00	🍷	6
○ Moscato di Siracusa Vigna di Mela '00	🍷	7
● Re Federico '01	🍷	4

Adragna
Via Regina Elena, 4
91100 Trapani
Tel. 092326401
E-mail: gof74@libero.it

The Adragna family has owned this estate near Valderice for over a century. The wines produced are well made, starting with the concentrated, weighty Rocca di Giglio '00, from cabernet sauvignon and merlot. Nero d'Avola '01 and Chardonnay '01 are both also good.

● Roccagiglio '00	🍷🍷	5
○ Chardonnay '01	🍷	4
● Nero d'Avola '01	🍷	4

Fondo Antico
Rilievo - Via Fiorame, 54/a
91020 Trapani
Tel. 0923951339
E-mail: info@fondoantico.com

Coro '01, from 100 per cent chardonnay, is a wine of elegance and depth, with refined notes of ripe, white-fleshed fruit, and a pervasive, round palate. It's very attractive to drink. Canto '00, from nero d'Avola and cabernet sauvignon, is also well made, fruity and shows good structure.

○ Il Coro '01	🍷🍷	5
● Il Canto di Fondo Antico '00	🍷	5

Terre di Shemir
Loc. Guarrato
91100 Trapani
Tel. 0923865323
E-mail: info@casesparse.it

Wolfango Jezek, noted journalist and producer of the high-quality oil, U Trappitu, makes a brilliant debut in the wine world with the intriguing Selvaggio Rosso '00, a blend of nero d'Avola and syrah. It's a round, warm red with silky tannins.

● Selvaggio Rosso '00	🍷🍷	6

SARDINIA

This year's tastings painted a much more promising picture of the Sardinian wine scene than expected. There was a distinct improvement in the average quality of the wines. Many of the more encouraging signals came from private producers who, of course, have much greater freedom to decide how to cultivate their vineyards and run their cellars. Such a free hand is not always possible for those running co-operative wineries. Dependence on funds from public bodies tends to hold co-operatives back and induces a more cautious, less flexible, management style. We assessed over 300 wines this year. Many were highly encouraging new launches, yet all too often we found ourselves with wines that we felt needed more bottle age. This rush to be first out on the market could easily rebound in the long term, especially on the most famous names. Which, we assume, is why some of them, such as Gabbas and Dettori, sensibly decided not to submit their entire range. The emergent estates worthiest of interest are Ferruccio Deiana, situated near Cagliari; Su Baroni, in the Sulcis zone, which produces good reds; Mura, at Loiri Porto San Paolo, with a classic Vermentino di Gallura; and Arcadu, in Oliena, for its Cannonau. Encouragingly, there are ever fewer of the evanescent, simplistic wines that characterized Sardinian winemaking in the 1970s and 1980s. We have moved on from the "modern" winemaking of those years and today's youngsters are far more in tune with their traditions. At last, we are seeing the emphasis on getting the best results from the local varieties, especially in areas where soils and climates are most suitable for quality-oriented viticulture. Beside the already well-established Vermentino di Gallura, which again came close to Three Glasses with Canayli from Tempio Pausania, there's been a strong surge from the reds. Many were in the running for a top award, yet just two made the cut, Turriga and Carignano del Sulcis Terre Brune, both of which are magnificent wines. It is heartening to note, too, that Sardinia has a high percentage of excellent dessert wines, from Malvasia to Moscato, Nasco and the many reds, headed by Sella & Mosca's Anghelu Ruju, based on semi-dried "passito" cannonau grapes. All deserve to be much more widely known.

ALGHERO (SS)

CANTINA SOCIALE SANTA MARIA LA PALMA
LOC. SANTA MARIA LA PALMA
07041 ALGHERO (SS)
TEL. 079999008 - 079999044
E-MAIL: vini@santamarialapalma.it

Numerous wine styles can be produced under the Alghero DOC, including those from the so-called innovative varieties. Commercial demands sometimes necessitate going in this more international direction. We are convinced that the market is ever more aware of the importance of indigenous varieties and their link with site. That said, on looking at this co-operative's new releases, we found great character in the Alghero Chardonnay '00. The nose, though only moderately intense, is pervasive and the warm, zesty palate has good structure. Just One Glass went to Alghero Sauvignon '00, as its nicely varietal aromas lack a touch of freshness. There is, however, fair depth of colour and a soft palate that finishes fairly long. The two Vermentino di Sardegna wines, I Papiri '01 and Aragosta '01, were livelier. The former has firmer body and deeper richness on the nose, with an apple-like fruitiness and vegetal elements. The Aragosta '01 is easy drinking and more immediate. The reds include the Cannonau di Sardegna Le Bombarde '01, which deservedly gained One Glass. It is made from cannonau grapes most of which are bush-trained, the rest being on Guyot. It ages for six months in oak casks prior to bottling. There is ripe fruit and some spiciness on the nose. The palate is warm, soft and balanced, with subdued tannins. The winery has also always had a high reputation for its rosés. We thought the best of these was the clean, fresh, lightly sparkling Alghero Catnapping '01, with its faintly raspberry-like nose and its mid-structured palate, which offers an attractive finish.

ALGHERO (SS)

TENUTE SELLA & MOSCA
LOC. I PIANI
07041 ALGHERO (SS)
TEL. 079997700
E-MAIL: sella-mosca@alghero.it

The recent changes in the ownership at this large winery, now in the hands of the Campari group, do not seem to have altered production strategies. The wide range of wines comprises several lines and numerous styles. From the Gallura zone comes Monteoro, a Vermentino di Gallura Superiore that has an intensely fruited nose of apple and apricot, and a warm palate of notable depth. Alghero Terre Bianche '00, from torbato, is a very fine wine with rich, fruited and floral aromas, then a full, zesty palate. Alghero Le Arenarie '00 is a well turned-out Sauvignon, most notably in its structure and balance of flavours. It also has distinct varietal aromas of elderflower and sage. Vermentino di Sardegna La Cala '01 is simpler but balanced and appealing. This year, the '00 Alghero Oleandro, a rosé from cabernet sauvignon, has shifted up a gear. It is clean and well fruited, with attractive vegetal nuances. On the red front, Marchese di Villamarina '99 is out of the running, as it had not been released at the time of our tastings, but the '99 Alghero Tanca Farrà is the best vintage ever. This renowned cannonau and cabernet sauvignon blend has a dark ruby colour, then intense aromas of wild berry fruit jam overlay elegant tones of balsam and spices. The fleshy, complex palate has great depth. The structure and nose-palate harmony of Carignano del Sulcis Terrerare '99 are impeccable. Finally, the "passito" Monteluce, from nasco, has honeyed scents, delicate sweetness and a solid, pleasant finish.

○ Alghero Chardonnay '00	▽▽	4
○ Alghero Sauvignon '00	▽	4
● Cannonau di Sardegna Le Bombarde '01	▽	3
○ Vermentino di Sardegna Aragosta '01	▽	2
○ Vermentino di Sardegna I Papiri '01	▽	3
⊙ Alghero Rosato Cantavigna '01		3
● Alghero Cagnulari '00	▽	4
● Cannonau di Sardegna Le Bombarde '00	▽	3
○ Vermentino di Sardegna Aragosta '00	▽	3
○ Alghero Chardonnay '99	▽	5
○ Alghero Sauvignon '99	▽	5
● Cannonau di Sardegna Grand Cru '99	▽	3

● Alghero Tanca Farrà '99	▮▮	4
○ Alghero Le Arenarie '01	▽▽	4
○ Alghero Torbato Terre Bianche '01	▽▽	3*
○ Monteluce '01	▽▽	4
○ Vermentino di Gallura Sup. Monteoro '01	▽▽	3*
○ Vermentino di Sardegna La Cala '01	▽▽	3*
● Carignano del Sulcis Terre Rare '99	▽▽	4
⊙ Alghero Oleandro '01	▽	3
● Alghero Marchese di Villamarina '92	▽▽▽	7
● Alghero Marchese di Villamarina '93	▽▽▽	7
● Alghero Marchese di Villamarina '95	▽▽▽	7
● Alghero Marchese di Villamarina '97	▽▽▽	6
● Alghero Anghelu Ruju Ris. '94	▽▽	6

ARZACHENA (SS)

CAPICHERA
S.S. ARZACHENA - S. ANTONIO KM. 6
07021 ARZACHENA (SS)
TEL. 078980800 - 078980612
E-MAIL: capichera@tiscalinet.it

BERCHIDDA (SS)

CANTINA SOCIALE GIOGANTINU
VIA MILANO, 30
07022 BERCHIDDA (SS)
TEL. 079704163 - 079704939

Work at Capichera continues apace. The new cellar, surrounded by eight hectares of vineyard, is up and running and the Ragnedda brothers are now replanting the land around the earlier estate buildings. They are also giving greater attention to the quality of their range, which could well project them onto the world stage. Their Vermentino is already exported to many countries but now that they can also offer some serious reds, they may well find more openings. We should add that the Ragneddas know how to make bold decisions, as they have shown in their pricing philosophy and their decision to come out from under the DOCG umbrella. But what matters is results, and so far the results have vindicated their policies. Quality is very high. Even if none of the wines attained Three Glasses, almost all gained Two. The '01 Vigna 'Ngena showed better than the previous vintage. The delicately broom-like, flinty nose is well developed and the palate is warm, round, well-balanced and harmonious. Capichera Vendemmia Tardiva '01 has a broad, pervasive nose, with vanilla and the almondiness typical of the variety. The remarkable softness of the palate masks a powerful structure, which also gives elegance. The classic Capichera is simpler, less full on the nose and fresher on the palate. The reds, made with carignano grown in the Sulcis zone, are warm and concentrated. Mantenghia '00, for example, has a complex nose with notes of oriental spices, and a full, warm, lightly tannic palate. Assajè '01 is as fresh on the nose as it is on the rather tannic, but attractively finishing, palate.

There are some interesting things now emerging from this co-operative. Previously, it was egregiously lacking in dynamism and turned out very ordinary products but in the past few years, there has been much more vitality, in communications as well as in the wines. There are new bottles and more attractive labels, which naturally present a better image of the winery. From the numerous Vermentino di Galluras we tasted, Vigne Storiche '01 stood out for the good intensity and breadth on its nose, and a palate with medium structure and a good balance of acidity and softness. Vermentino Superiore '01 is less intense on the nose, but the classic almondy note comes through clearly. The new Vermentino di Gallura Lughente '01 seemed a touch listless on the nose, and excess acidity makes it a little strident on the palate. The reds were more interesting. The new Terre Saliosa '01 is a Colli del Limbara IGT from merlot, carignano and muristellu grown in the Berchidda area. The nose is intense and full of fruit, especially cherry and morello cherry, then the palate is soft, with a lightly tannic profile in mid palate and a pleasing finish. Nastarrè, with clean, if rather youthful, aromas and a harmonious palate, is as attractive as usual. The range is rounded off by Lughente, a dessert wine from late-harvested grapes, which is not particularly rich in aromas or flavour.

O	Capichera V.T. '01	🍷🍷	8
●	Mante'nghja '00	🍷🍷	8
O	Capichera '01	🍷🍷	7
O	Capichera Vigna 'Ngena '01	🍷🍷	6
●	Assajè Rosso '01	🍷	6
O	Capichera V.T. '00	🍷🍷🍷	7
O	Capichera '00	🍷🍷	5
●	Mante'nghja '99	🍷🍷	5
O	Vermentino di Gallura Capichera '99	🍷🍷	5
O	Vermentino di Gallura V. T. '99	🍷🍷	6

●	Terra Saliosa '01	🍷🍷	3*
O	Vermentino di Gallura Lughente '01	🍷	3
O	Vermentino di Gallura Sup. '01	🍷	2*
O	Vermentino di Gallura Sup. Vigne Storiche '01	🍷	4
●	Nastarrè '00	🍷	1*
O	Vermentino di Gallura '00	🍷	1*
O	Vermentino di Gallura Sup. '00	🍷	2*
●	Terra Mala Vigne Storiche '99	🍷	4

CABRAS (OR)

ATTILIO CONTINI
VIA GENOVA, 48/50
09072 CABRAS (OR)
TEL. 0783290806
E-MAIL: vinicontini@tiscalinet.it

It is impossible these days for Vernaccia di Oristano producers to keep their heads above water without also producing other wines. Even Contini started to expand the range some years back, firstly with whites, using vernaccia as a base, then with reds, selecting grapes from the region's best areas. The cellar has now released its first Barrile, the '98, an IGT made from nieddera and bovale sardo grapes with small amounts of other indigenous varieties, most of them grown on bush-trained vines. It ages for around a year in new barriques, followed by six months in bottle. The nose is full, pervasive and very concentrated, with aromas of blackberry and plum jam, and touches of vanilla. The palate is warm, its tannins are already softened and there is decent acidic freshness that will assist longevity. Cannonau di Sardegna '99, from grapes grown around Oliena, is also good, with fair structure and good nose-palate harmony. The most charactferul of the whites is Karmis '01, from 100 per cent Vernaccia. The nose has the characteristic almondy aroma, then the palate is full, round and finishes clean. Vermentino di Sardegna '01 is very well typed. It is delicate in aroma and has nice freshness on the palate. Moving on to Vernaccia di Oristano, we retasted the '92. Intense and clean on the nose, it proffers clear sensations of almond blossom and toasted hazelnut. The palate is fat, fleshy, rich and full of alcoholic power. There is all the structure and backbone that the finest vintages give. Antico Gregori, which is blended across the better vintages, is also of high standing.

CAGLIARI

GIGI PICCIAU
FRAZ. PIRRI
VIA ITALIA, 196
09134 CAGLIARI
TEL. 070560224
E-MAIL: picciau@tin.it

Gigi Picciau grew up among vines and barrels. His father and grandfather, from whom he acquired his love of wine, symbolize the past but Gigi is looking to the future. He will no doubt eventually pass the baton to his young son, who is already full of enthusiasm and keen to get his hand in. The vineyards have been replanted in stages. The varieties are the traditional indigenous nasco, malvasia, semidano, cannonau, nuragus and vermentino, and some non-local grapes such as pinot bianco. Picciau works mainly with the varieties that risk extinction or being forgotten, whose yields are low or are almost unknown. The wines that leave his cellar have marked personalities and are anything but dull, anonymous or clichés. Sardegna Semidano '01, for instance, is not an easy wine. Its aromas, which emerge only if the grape yield is kept low, are austere and complex, evoking Mediterranean scrub, thyme and myrtle. The palate is nicely flavoursome and has medium intensity fruit. Another good example is Cannonau di Sardegna '99. The aromas are clean but still rather youthful and simple. The palate is dry, lightly tannic and not particularly heavy. Sadly, Malvasia di Cagliari, once queen of these lands, is disappearing. Picciau's '99 has intense ripe fruit and delicate perfumes of sage on the nose. The palate is warm and seductive with fair length.

● Barrile '98	♛♛	4*
○ Karmis '01	♛	3
● Cannonau di Sardegna '99	♛	4
○ Vermentino di Sardegna '01	♛	3
○ Vernaccia di Oristano Ris. '83	♛♛	4
○ Vernaccia di Oristano '88	♛♛	3
○ Vernaccia di Oristano Ris. '90	♛♛	3
○ Vernaccia di Oristano '92	♛♛	4
○ Vernaccia di Oristano Antico Gregori	♛♛	7
● Cannonau di Sardegna '98	♛	3
○ Karmis '98	♛	3
● Nieddera Rosso '98	♛	4

○ Sardegna Semidano '01	♛	8
● Cannonau di Sardegna '99	♛	8
○ Malvasia di Cagliari '99	♛	8
○ Sardegna Semidano '00	♛	3
● Cannonau di Sardegna '97	♛	3

CARDEDU (NU)

ALBERTO LOI
S. S. 125 CARDEDU
08040 CARDEDU (NU)
TEL. 070240866 - 078275807
E-MAIL: albertoloi@libero.it

"Reflect and don't rush to get onto the market before the rest," is a precept that has guided the Loi siblings in their choices. After renovating the cellar and tidying up the vineyards by restoring some old bush-trained plots, their next move was to change production strategy. The cannonau variety predominates in these parts and all the estate's wines are based on it. Some other indigenous varieties, such as bovale and muristellu, are also grown, along with small amounts of the so-called "innovative" grapes. The differences between the wines come from picking times, which naturally depend on the vintage, vineyard aspect and winemaking techniques. Tuvara '98, with carignano, bovale and muristellu bolstering the cannonau, ages for one and a half years in new barriques. The nose is intense and multi-layered, with hints of roasted coffee beans, then the palate is full, with serious structure and a long finish. The '99 Loi Corona is the wine's first release. It, too, comes from a multi-grape blend and ages for 20 months in small barrels. The spicy nose shows notes of balsam and blackberry, then the palate is warm and soft, with a long, clean finish. Astangia '99 is another fine wine, a red with richly fruited aromas and a full, still rather tannic, palate. Cannonau di Sardegna Alberto Loi Riserva '98 stands out among the DOC wines, with its clean, fruit-forward nose and full, but still slightly raw, palate. Cardedo Riserva '99 and Sa Mola '00 are less complicated. The intriguing white Leila '01 is still young but promising.

DOLIANOVA (CA)

CANTINE DI DOLIANOVA
LOC. SANT'ESU
S. S. 387 KM. 17,150
09041 DOLIANOVA (CA)
TEL. 070744101 - 07074410226
E-MAIL: cantinedolianova@tiscalinet.it

At Dolianova, there are good editions of established wines, as well as a few interesting newcomers. The wines are very well made, for co-operative standards. Every day, they are placed under the judgmental eye of their consumers, yet it is still difficult for Dolianova to distance itself from other quantity-led co-operatives and acquire greater credibility. All the wines we tasted are good and some of them have quite distinct personalities. Montesicci '01, from vermentino with 30 per cent malvasia and nasco, is the best of the range, combining the structure and firm backbone of vermentino with the aromatic elegance of malvasia and nasco. We particularly liked the overall fruit timbre, allied to notes of sage and peach. The '00 Falconaro, from a successful blend of cannonau, carignano and montepulciano, is as good as the previous release. The nose is full, with marked aromas of cherry and morello cherry. The soft, clean palate has good weight and a long, attractive finish. It is closely followed by Naèli, a 2001 Vermentino di Sardegna and one of the best DOC whites of the range. The other wines, from Sibiola Rosato '01 to Cannonau di Sardegna '00 and Monica di Sardegna '00, are all well made.

● Tuvara '98	▼▼	5
● Astangia '99	▼▼	4
● Loi Corona '99	▼▼	5
● Cannonau di Sardegna Sa Mola Rubia '00	▼	3
○ Leila '01	▼	4
● Cannonau di Sardegna Alberto Loi Ris. '98	▼	4
● Cannonau di Sardegna Cardedo Ris. '99	▼	4
● Cannonau di Sardegna Alberto Loi Ris. '97	▽▽	4
● Tuvara '96	▽	6
● Cannonau di Sardegna Cardedo Ris. '98	▽	4

○ Montesicci '01	▼▼	4
● Falconaro '00	▼▼	5
○ Moscato di Cagliari '99	▼▼	4
● Cannonau di Sardegna '00	▼	3*
● Monica di Sardegna '00	▼	3*
⊙ Sibiola Rosato '01	▼	2*
○ Vermentino di Sardegna Naeli '01	▼	3*
○ Andias '01		2
○ Nuragus di Cagliari '01		2
○ Vermentino di Sardegna '01		3
○ Andias '00	▽	2*
○ Moscato di Cagliari '98	▽	4
● Falconaro '99	▽	4
⊙ Sibiola Rosato '99	▽	2

JERZU (NU)

Antichi Poderi Jerzu
Via Umberto I, 1
08044 Jerzu (NU)
tel. 078270028
e-mail: antichipoderi@tiscalinet.it

This co-operative has half a century of history behind it. In recent years, it has become better known under the trademark Gli Antichi Poderi di Jerzu (The Ancient Plots of Jerzu), a name that harks back to the lands where the grapes of its first members came from. The terrain was difficult to cultivate and all the vines were bush trained. Maybe this is why grape quality was better. The wines were honest and highly concentrated, although not always balanced. These days, grapes come from around 800 hectares, scattered over a wide area that includes the flatlands close to the sea. On average, members supply 4,000,000 kilograms of grapes, the vast majority cannonau. Cellar techniques are advanced without completely overturning tradition so that the wines have retained the characteristics that make them recognizable and for which they are admired, great structure and robust alcohol. Harvest decisions and the small barrels used for ageing do the rest. Cannonau di Sardegna Riserva Josto Miglior '98 gains Two Glasses and should improve over the next few years. The nose is deep and full, with black cherry fruitiness and hints of spice. The palate is rich to the point of being almost fat but is held in place by good acidity and the soft tannins are well knit into the wine. Cannonau di Sardegna Chuerra Riserva '98 is also good, but not on the same plane. The nose is clean, with clear tones of ripe berry fruit, then the palate is well structured and warm with balanced tannins and fair length.

MASAINAS (CA)

Vitivincola Su Baroni
Via Roma, 48
09010 Masainas (CA)
tel. 0781964844
e-mail: giancarlo.vacca@tiscali.it

Masainas is a promising new estate that makes its first appearance in the Guide. Owner Giancarlo Vacca has 30 hectares of vineyard close to the sea, on the sandy, sun-drenched lands of lower Sulcis. His background is ordinary, and similar to that of many young enthusiasts now making wine in the region. The older generations were not always able to pass the baton to their children or grandchildren, one of the reasons why many zones are now lying abandoned, but here, vines are flourishing again. The land has regained its original aspect, with gentle hills that slope down from sky to sea in a kaleidoscope of colour. Vacca grows mostly carignano, which covers 70 per cent of his holding. The rest is syrah, with a little vermentino. The grapes are hand-picked into small wooden crates and immediately taken to be vinified, at the nearby wine centre in Villasor, for now. There are three reds and one white. Su Baroni '00 comes from 60 per cent carignano and syrah, and has eight months in barrique followed by six in bottle. The nose has good intensity, showing blackberry jam and raspberry fruit tones, and hints of white pepper spiciness. The palate has the body, softness and balance that characterize the best reds from this area. The Canigonis '01, from syrah with some carignano, has good character. It is not a full-bodied red but does have attractively youthful, fresh flavours. The '00, which we also tasted, is fuller structured and more mature. The Trisoru '01, a Carignano, and vermentino-based Candiani '01 are also good.

● Cannonau di Sardegna Josto Miglior '98	♛♛	4
● Cannonau di Sardegna Ris. Chuerra '98	♛	4
● Cannonau di Sardegna Ris. Chuerra '97	♛♛	4
● Cannonau di Sardegna Riserva Josto Miglior '97	♛	4
● Cannonau di Sardegna Marghìa '98	♛	4
● Cannonau di Sardegna Ris. '98	♛	3
● Radames '98	♛	4

● Su Baroni '00	♛♛	5
○ Candiani '01	♛	3
● Canigonis '01	♛	4
● Canigonis '00	♛	4
● Trisoru '01	♛	4

MONTI (SS)

PEDRA MAJORE
VIA ROMA, 106
07020 MONTI (SS)
TEL. 078943185

The best scenery in Gallura offers dense oak forest set between granite massifs and neat vineyards, with the sea as backdrop. And that is exactly what you see from the Isoni family's Pedra Majore estate, where the new cellar has now been in operation for several years. Both the lie of the land and the composition of the soil make the area exceptionally suitable for vermentino production. The soils, formed by the breakdown of granite, go deep and give character and personality to the wines. And this is probably one of the reasons why the family have called their leading Vermentino di Gallura "Graniti". The '01 is one of the best releases of recent years. The nose is full and direct, with intense, pervasive aromas redolent of apple and almond blossom. The palate is powerfully structured yet soft and almost round, and leaves a clean, velvety feel in the mouth. Vermentino di Gallura Superiore Hysony '01 scored a mark or two lower but still well within the Two Glass band. There are delicate aromas of tropical fruit lifted by mineral notes, and the palate has depth while retaining freshness and vivacity. Vermentino di Sardegna Le Conche '01 is less complex. The aromas are floral and fairly intense. Carefully judged acidity gives the zesty palate freshness which makes for good, easy drinking.

MONTI (SS)

CANTINA SOCIALE DEL VERMENTINO
VIA SAN PAOLO, 1
07020 MONTI (SS)
TEL. 078944012 - 078944631
E-MAIL: cantina@vermentinomonti.it

This co-operative's range of wines is continually being expanded. Originally, the list featured only Vermentinos but today, although Vermentino is still produced in various styles, including brut, demi-sec and sweet sparkling versions, there are other wines, too. For commercial reasons, the range has been divided into five lines, which include special bottlings of Grappa, Mirto, a myrtle-based liqueur, and Passito di Vermentino from semi-dried grapes. All the wines we tasted fell into the One Glass category. Cannonau di Sardegna Tamara '99 stood out for its captivatingly fresh and slightly vegetal aromas, followed by a clean, attractively balanced palate. Abbaìa '01, the winery's standard-bearer red, is less intense on the nose but has greater fullness on the palate. Galana '98, a composite blend of cabernet, sangiovese, cagnulari, carignano and small proportions of other grapes, scored similarly. We would have expected it to be the top wine of the group but signs of ageing are apparent on the appearance and confirmed by the somewhat tired aromas. The palate is fully flavoured but too soft and almost sweetish. The leading whites all showed well. The Vermentino di Gallura Funtanaliras '01 is very fresh and lively on both nose and palate, the Vermentino di Gallura Superiore Aghiloia '01 is full and round, and Vermentino di Gallura S'Eleme '01 is a well-made, attractive wine. The well-styled, easy-drinking rosé Thaora also deserves a mention.

○ Vermentino di Gallura Hysonj '01	3
○ Vermentino di Gallura I Graniti '01	3*
○ Vermentino di Sardegna Le Conche '01	3
○ Vermentino di Gallura I Graniti '00	3*
○ Vermentino di Gallura Hysonj '00	3
○ Vermentino di Sardegna Le Conche '00	3

● Abbaìa '01	2*
○ Vermentino di Gallura Funtanaliras '01	4
○ Vermentino di Gallura Sup. Aghiloia '01	3
● Galana '98	6
● Cannonau di Sardegna Tamara '99	4
○ Vermentino di Gallura S'Eleme '01	2
⊙ Thaora Rosato '01	2
● Abbaìa '00	2*
○ Vermentino di Gallura Funtanaliras '00	3
○ Vermentino di Gallura S'Eleme '00	2*
○ Vermentino di Gallura Sup. Aghiloia '00	3*
● Abbaìa '99	2
○ Vermentino di Gallura Funtanaliras '99	3
○ Vermentino di Gallura S'Eleme '99	2
○ Vermentino di Gallura Sup. Aghiloia '99	2

NUORO

OLBIA (SS)

GIUSEPPE GABBAS
VIA TRIESTE, 65
08100 NUORO
TEL. 078431351 - 078433745

PIERO MANCINI
LOC. CALA SACCAIA
07026 OLBIA (SS)
TEL. 078950717
E-MAIL: poero.mancini@tiscalinet.it

From the day Giuseppe Gabbas started vinifying for himself, his wines took on a new lease of life, even though he lacked sophisticated equipment. It was a case of the right man at the right time, one with just the right touch for the superb grapes harvested from Giuseppe's 15 hectares of vineyard straddling the gentle granite slopes. Cannonau is the most prevalent variety but he also grows montepulciano, sangiovese, cabernet and merlot. The vines surround the new cellar, now in its last stages of development, which will be inaugurated with the 2003 vintage. Vinification techniques lean towards the area's traditions, especially as regards maceration, which normally lasts at least 20 days, with regular pumping over. Some wines are fermented in large wooden casks. Strategies at Gabbas include refusing to bottle wines earlier than they warrant simply to rush them onto the market, and indeed the cellar's products do not begin to show their best until a year or two after the harvest. Arbeskia '00 will be bottled in spring 2003 and, from the cask sample we tasted, it will be terrific. Cannonau di Sardegna Lillovè '01 is still youthful and headily fresh on the palate. Dule '01 has more to offer. From 50 per cent cannonau, with sangiovese, montepulciano and a little cabernet, it is given around eight months in barrique, part new, part used. The aromas, with hints of jam and vegetal notes, are more concentrated, then the palate shows good body and a slightly tannic finish. The round, mouthfilling "passito" Avra, with its flavours of cooked plum, is also nice.

Quality at this winery continues to grow. The unforgettable Piero Mancini was a passionate protagonist of Gallura winemaking and his children have inherited his enthusiasm and unwavering commitment to improvement. The family owns 100 hectares, scattered throughout the best parts of the Gallura, and, apart from vermentino and moscato, now also grows cannonau, cabernet, merlot and chardonnay. The whites clearly lead the field but there are good things among the reds too, particularly Saccaia '00, from an intelligent blend of cabernet, merlot and cannonau. It reveals good intensity on the elegant nose, where fresh wild berry fruit emerges. The palate has reasonable structure and the tannins are well integrated with its softer components. Cannonau di Sardegna '00 has fair intensity on the nose of ripe red berry fruit. The flavoursome palate is supported by good structure. The most even and balanced of the whites is the Vermentino di Gallura Cucaione '01, with its fragrant aromas of citrus fruit and almond blossom, and fresh, full, enveloping palate. Vermentino di Gallura '01 Saraina is warmer and more structured, with delicate sensations of tropical fruits. The uncomplicated, well-typed, easy-drinking Vermentino di Sardegna Piero Mancini is also very pleasing.

● Dule '01	🍷🍷	4
● Avra '00	🍷	4
● Cannonau di Sardegna Lillovè '01	🍷	4
● Dule '00	🍷🍷	4
● Arbeskia '99	🍷🍷	5

● Saccaia '00	🍷🍷	3*
● Cannonau di Sardegna '00	🍷	3
○ Vermentino di Gallura Cucaione '01	🍷	3
○ Vermentino di Gallura Saraina '01	🍷	4
○ Vermentino di Sardegna '01	🍷	2*
○ Vermentino di Gallura Cucaione '00	🍷	3
○ Vermentino di Gallura Saraina '00	🍷	4
● Cannonau di Sardegna '99	🍷	3

OLIENA (NU)

GOSTOLAI
VIA NINO BIXIO, 87
08025 OLIENA (NU)
TEL. 0784288417
E-MAIL: gostolai.arcadu@tiscalinet.it

Tonino Arcadu's estate lies within the Oliena, or Nepente di Oliena, subzone of Cannonau di Sardegna. It produces a wide range of wines for its size, most based on cannonau. Some vineyard is owned but Arcadu also buys grapes from small local growers. Many of the vines hereabouts are bush trained and yields are quite low. The winery has stainless steel vinification tanks and a few small oak casks for ageing. Total capacity is around 700 hectolitres. The best of the wines we tasted was Cannonau di Sardegna Nepente di Oliena Riserva '99, although even this did not go beyond One Glass. Despite a not particularly deep colour, the aromas are quite attractive, with vegetal notes in the foreground. The palate is very concentrated, deep and full. Puer sed Formosus might be a more pretentious name but the '00, from cannonau, carignano and cabernet, scored fewer points than the Riserva. It is more interesting on the nose, which is herbaceous and has ripe blackberry fruitiness. The palate is nicely even but has a shortish finish. The Vermentino di Sardegna Incantu '01 is rather disappointing, with a weak nose giving just a light sense of fruit and no complexity on the palate. On the other hand, the two dessert wines, the moderately sweet red Su Gucciu '01, offering vegetal aromas, and the soft, enveloping Cantico '00, with its fruitiness and spiciness, are both attractive.

○ Cantico '00	🍷	4
● Puer sed Formosus '00	🍷	3
● Su Gucciu '01	🍷	4
● Cannonau di Sardegna Nepente di Oliena Ris. '99	🍷	5
○ Vermentino di Sardegna Incantu '01		3

SANTADI (CA)

CANTINA SOCIALE DI SANTADI
VIA SU PRANU, 12
09010 SANTADI (CA)
TEL. 0781950127 - 0781953007
E-MAIL: pgserafini@cantinadisantadi.it

You couldn't complain that this winery lacks consistency. Eleven wines were submitted and all scored well. The icing on the cake is that this year, the Carignano del Sulcis Superiore Terre Brune is back in the Three Glass club with the '98. It is a magnificent red, full and pervasive on the nose, with a spectrum of aromas that ranges from jam to cooked plum. The warm, all-enveloping palate has fabulous structure and is supported by refined, ripe tannins. The aromas on Araja '00, from carignano and sangiovese, are more restrained but the wine has remarkable body and depth of flavour. The Carignano del Sulcis Riserva Rocca Rubia '99 is marked out by its aromatic breadth while aromas of hay and sensations of cherry jam characterize the full, round Carignano del Sulcis Grotta Rossa '00. The Monica di Sardegna Antigua '01 is uncomplicated. Another seriously good red is the Shardana '98, from carignano and syrah, which is produced mainly for export. There is dried hay on the nose but the dominant note on the palate is softness. Nuragus di Cagliari Petraia showed best of the '01 whites. It has ringingly pure aromas and fullness of flavour, which is a pleasant surprise in a wine from an often derided variety. Both the Cala Silente and Villa Solais versions of Vermentino di Sardegna also showed well, as usual, while Villa di Chiesa '01, from vermentino and chardonnay, is clean and well made. The excellent sweet wine Latinia, elegant, full and with musky fragrances, brings this extensive line-up to a close.

● Carignano del Sulcis Sup. Terre Brune '98	🍷🍷🍷	6
○ Latinia '00	🍷🍷	5
○ Villa di Chiesa '01	🍷🍷	4
● Carignano del Sulcis Sup. Rocca Rubia Ris. '99	🍷🍷	4
● Araja '00	🍷🍷	3*
○ Nuragus di Cagliari Pedraia '01	🍷🍷	3*
○ Vermentino di Sardegna Villa Solais '01	🍷🍷	3*
○ Vermentino di Sardegna Cala Silente '01	🍷🍷	4
● Carignano del Sulcis Grotta Rossa '00	🍷	3
● Monica di Sardegna Antigua '01	🍷	3
● Shardana '98	🍷	4
● Terre Brune '94	🍷🍷🍷	6
○ Latinia '99	🍷🍷🍷	4*

SANT'ANTIOCO (CA)

Sardus Pater
Via Rinascita, 46
09017 Sant'Antioco (CA)
Tel. 0781800274 - 078183937
E-mail: cantine@cantinesarduspater.com

For almost half a century, the Sardus Pater winery has concentrated on turning out bulk blending wine, bottling only small quantities. Previous administrators weren't concerned about image or, probably, about the huge potential of the estate's wines. Other wineries made the same mistakes but have regained credibility in the more important markets, which is what Sardus Pater is now starting to do. Major changes are under way to develop the wines in its catchment area, and not just in terms of winemaking techniques. New people are involved, there is a new desire to work hard to attain results. Ideas and projects are springing up all over the place. This is beginning to bear fruit, as the new releases show. In particular, careful grape selection and oenologist Angioi's skilled technical direction have played a major part in increasing quality across the board. We'll take the wines in order of importance. Sulky '98 is from ungrafted carignano vines, with small amounts of cabernet and syrah. There is considerable breadth and richness on the nose, which has notes of tar and coffee but also sweeter scents of blackberry and blackcurrant. It is a wine of robust structure, the soft tannins lending elegance and finesse. The admirable Carignano del Sulcis Riserva '98 has inviting ripe fruit aromas. The other Carignano del Sulcis, Issolus '00 failed to win Two Glasses, but not by much. We hope this winery's entrance to the Guide will be the start of something big.

● Carignano del Sulcis Ris. '98	ΨΨ	4
● Sulky '98	ΨΨ	5
● Carignano del Sulcis Issolus '00	Ψ	3
● Monica di Sardegna Insula '00	Ψ	3*
● Carignano del Sulcis Issolus '99	Ψ	1*

SELARGIUS (CA)

Meloni Vini
Via Gallus, 79
09047 Selargius (CA)
Tel. 070852822
E-mail: info@meloni-vini.com

There are always signs of great dynamism from this long-established winery in the province of Cagliari. The range of wines includes de-alcoholized and organic offerings, and there are often new lines and new labels, ensuring something for all tastes and all pockets. Meloni is owned by a family that has been producing wine for generations, and is shrewd and sensitive to market changes. Hence the organic wines, which they have been producing for several years to satisfy what may be simply a fashion, or could be the future of the entire agricultural sector. The range has now been augmented by two new organic wines in the Le Sabbie line, a Vermentino di Sardegna and a Cannonau di Sardegna. We found the former to be more successful but both are well typed and make good drinking. Cannonau di Sardegna Le Ghiaie '98, though, is on a higher plane. Its aromas are somewhat developed, but both structure and length are good. From the Il Germoglio line, it is Monica di Sardegna '00 that really hits the spot. The nose is not very intense but it is clean, with light notes of berry fruits and slight vegetal hints. The palate is fresh and balanced, and has a clean finish. Nuragus di Cagliari '01, another organic wine, is fairly unchallenging on both nose and palate, and the acidity is strongly marked. The dessert wine line, Donna Jolanda, is always sound. Moscato di Cagliari '98 has a wealth of varietal aroma, with honey and dried fruits, and a nicely concentrated palate that is sweet but not cloying.

○ Moscato di Cagliari Donna Jolanda '98	ΨΨ	4
● Cannonau di Sardegna Le Sabbie '01	Ψ	3
● Monica di Sardegna Il Germoglio '00	Ψ	3
○ Vermentino di Sardegna Le Sabbie '01	Ψ	3
● Cannonau di Sardegna Le Ghiaie '98	Ψ	4
○ Nasco di Cagliari Donna Jolanda '94	ΨΨ	4
○ Moscato di Cagliari Donna Jolanda '95	ΨΨ	4
● Monica di Sardegna '98	ΨΨ	2

SENORBÌ (CA)

Cantina Sociale della Trexenta
V.le Piemonte, 28
09040 Senorbì (CA)
Tel. 0709808863
E-mail: trexentavini@tiscalinet.it

This co-operative's wines come from its 200 or so members, who cultivate over 350 hectares of vine. The plots are mostly small and scattered, but about 20 members have more extensive holdings. The winery itself has planted around 20 hectares, using only the indigenous varieties of the zone, which are at risk of extinction. This will enable the recovery of a vital viticultural heritage and allow the modern-day production of historic wines, the ones that were made some time back from mixtures of red and white varieties. Professional experience and modern production techniques should do the rest. Currently, reds still take pride of place, headed by Monica di Sardegna Duca di Mandas '01. It is marked out by its fresh, vegetal aromas, attractive vivacity on the palate, rounded body and tannic balance. Cannonau di Sardegan Corte Adua '98 has more to offer on the palate than the nose, with a softness and balance that leave the mouth without any sense of bitterness, despite robust tannins. Cannonau di Sardegna Baione '99 is richer in aroma, with attractive blackberry and blueberry fruit. The palate is warm and soft, but not particularly structured. The whites we recommend are Vermentino di Sardegna Donna Leonora and Nuragus di Cagliari Tenute San Mauro. Both are fresh, supple and easy drinking. Finally, Moscato di Cagliari Simieri '01 is full of character, with intense, pervasive aromas of honey and sage, and a full, fat palate that offers a perfect balance of acidity and sweetness.

SERDIANA (CA)

Antonio Argiolas
Via Roma, 56/58
09040 Serdiana (CA)
Tel. 070740606 - 070743264
E-mail: argiolasspa@tin.it

There's a danger of sounding rhetorical when you talk about Argiolas. Those who know the family will also know that they live their vineyards and cellar, day in, day out. They are simple folk who love their work and carry on the dedicated labours initiated by their father Antonio all those years ago. In the meantime, awards and commendations continue to rain down from all over the world. This reflects well on the region, as it strives to regain credibility and a positive image on foreign markets. Three Glasses have now gone to cannonau-based Turriga eight times, and the eighth is for the '98, which is simply magnificent. As its nose opens, there are wonderful aromas of ripe fruit and toastiness. The palate is beautifully deep and has very fine-grained tannins, giving admirable balance. The finish is quite extraordinarily long. Korem is considered Turriga's younger brother but it, too, now has more harmony and attractiveness, thanks to firm structure and mouthfilling flavours. Its small red berry fruit aromas are intense and pervasive, then the palate is warm, soft and long. Cardena, a new white from vermentino and small amounts of other indigenous varieties, ferments and ages for eight months in new barriques. The aromas are complex with fresh butter, citrus fruit and spring flowers, and there is good richness of extract on the palate. Angialis '99 is another Sardinian gem. It's a creamy, highly perfumed white that has perfect balance between sweetness and acidity. Monica di Sardegna Perdera '00 and the rosé Serralori '01 are the best of the other wines.

● Monica di Sardegna Duca di Mandas '01	🍷🍷	2*
○ Moscato di Cagliari Simieri '01	🍷🍷	4
● Cannonau di Sardegna Corte Adua '98	🍷	3
○ Vermentino di Sardegna Donna Eleonora '01		2
● Cannonau di Sardegna Baione '99	🍷	3
○ Nuragus di Cagliari Tenute San Mauro '01		2
● Monica di Sardegna Duca di Mandas '00	🍷🍷	2*
● Tanca Su Conti '96	🍷🍷	4

● Turriga '98	🍷🍷🍷	8
○ Angialis '99	🍷🍷	6
● Cannonau di Sardegna Costera '00	🍷	3
○ Cerdeña '00	🍷🍷	6
● Korem '00	🍷🍷	6
○ Argiolas '01	🍷🍷	4
○ Nuragus di Cagliari S'Elegas '01	🍷🍷	3*
○ Vermentino di Sardegna Costamolino '01	🍷🍷	3*
● Monica di Sardegna Perdera '00	🍷	3
⊙ Serralori Rosato '01	🍷	3
● Turriga '92	🍷🍷🍷	7
● Turriga '93	🍷🍷🍷	7
● Turriga '94	🍷🍷🍷	7
● Turriga '95	🍷🍷🍷	7
● Turriga '97	🍷🍷🍷	7

SERDIANA (CA)

PALA
VIA VERDI, 7
09040 SERDIANA (CA)
TEL. 070740284
E-MAIL: cantinapala@tiscalinet.it

The countryside around Cagliari, where concrete has not yet penetrated, is changing face. The gentle slopes are regaining the aspect they had some decades ago, when extensive vineyards were strung like beads on a necklace from one hill to the next. Estates like Pala are helping to regenerate the area's great viticultural heritage. The Pala family does not yet have a great cellar but what matters is their firm commitment to ever better quality. Their efforts so far are paying off, and the first promising results have already arrived. S'Arai remains the leading wine. The year 2000 was good for all the wines but especially so for the reds, which are slower to come round than usual. Thus the nose on S'Arai '00 is initially closed but with a little breathing space, the wine opens and fills out with spice-laced fruit. The palate is warm, with good body and well balanced tannins. Entemari '01 also acquitted itself well. The nose is less pronounced than last year's release but it has good substance on the palate and there is a fine balance of acidity and softness. Cannonau di Sardegna Triente '01 is still young and fresh whereas the Monica di Sardegna Elima '00 is more harmonious with delicate blackberry aromas, soft tannins and a velvety feel.

SETTIMO SAN PIETRO (CA)

FERRUCCIO DEIANA
VIA GIALETO, 7
09040 SETTIMO SAN PIETRO (CA)
TEL. 070767960 - 070749117
E-MAIL: deiana.ferruccio@tiscalinet.it

Ferruccio Deiana's new cellar is now ready, enabling him to produce even finer wines than before. Ferruccio is a dynamic type but can be withdrawn, and is well known locally as a serious-minded, skilled selector of quality wines for clients in Italy and abroad. Deiana followed in the footsteps of his father and grandfather when he started making classic local wines, such as Monica, Bovale, Nuragus, Nasco, Malvasia and Moscato, in the area around Cagliari. He decided to replant on the best terrains; which many abandoned in the 1980s leaving the land uncultivated. The estate now has 38 hectares, of which 26 are in one block, around the new cellar. Total capacity, including temperature-controlled vats and barriques, is about 7,000 hectolitres. His market knowledge suggested Vermentino and Cannonau as the standard bearers, although he works with other indigenous varieties, as well as the international cabernet, merlot, chardonnay, syrah and pinot bianco. The jewel in the crown is the red Ajana '00, from carignano, cabernet, merlot and cannonau. The nose has distinct personality with delicate vegetal notes, which also come through on the palate. Although still young, it has considerable structure, which suggests it will mature well. The white Fluminus '01, based on vermentino and chardonnay, has floral perfumes and attractively rounded flavours. Monica di Sardegna Karel '01, Cannonau di Sardegna Sileno '00 and Vermentino di Sardegna '01 also have very good character. The fine Oirad '01, a sweet wine made from moscato, malvasia and nasco, completes the range.

● S'Arai '00	5
○ Vermentino di Sardegna Crabilis '01	3*
● Monica di Sardegna Elima '00	3
● Cannonau di Sardegna Triente '01	4
○ Entemari '01	5
○ Nuragus di Cagliari Salnico '01	2
○ Entemari '00	4
○ Vermentino di Sardegna Crabilis '00	3*
● S'Arai '98	5
○ Nuragus di Cagliari Salnico '99	2
● S'Arai '99	5

● Ajana '00	7
○ Oirad '01	5
● Cannonau di Sardegna Sileno '00	4
○ Fluminus '01	6
● Monica di Sardegna Karel '01	4
○ Vermentino di Sardegna '01	4

TEMPIO PAUSANIA (SS)

CANTINA SOCIALE GALLURA
VIA VAL DI COSSU, 9
07029 TEMPIO PAUSANIA (SS)
TEL. 079631241
E-MAIL: info@cantinagallura.it

This co-operative owes much to its managing director-oenologist, Dino Addis. His ever present knowledge and input has improved wine quality across the board and won recognition and admiration in markets in Italy and abroad. He works from two base points: vermentino for the whites; and nebbiolo, rounded out with local varieties such as caricagiola and pascale, for the reds. Vermentino di Gallura Superiore Canayli again nudges Three Glasses, this year with the '01. It has its usual richness of aroma, with tropical fruit, ripe apple and flowers. The palate has extraordinary softness and perfectly judged acidity, giving great balance in the mouth, despite its strong thrust of alcohol. Moving on to the other wines, we don't feel that Piras '01 should be described as Canayli's "poorer brother". It has very similar depth and balance, and it is only the structure that is less forceful. Mavriana is generally considered the simplest of the winery's Vermentino di Galluras, yet it was a pleasant surprise. The aromas are attractive and fresh, and the zesty palate has plentiful extract. Vermentino Gemellae has improved, too, and the '01 shows particularly well on the palate. Balajana '01, warm and laid back the way wines used to be, completes the range of whites. There is little news on the red front. Karana remains the most attractive and best balanced. The barrique-aged Den Dolmen is satisfying, but produced in tiny quantities. The estate's newest wine is Zivula, a dried-grape "passito" from moscato. It is already successful.

USINI (SS)

GIOVANNI CHERCHI
VIA OSSI, 22
07049 USINI (SS)
TEL. 079380273 - 079380273
E-MAIL: vinicolacherchi@tiscalinet.it

Giovanni Cherchi's estate, after losing its way a little, is back on track. The whole family now takes part and there is a huge desire to grow and improve, and to produce new wines. The new cellar is almost ready, there is good backup from a reliable technical consultant, and results are starting to appear. This year, we can at last appreciate again why Vermentino di Sardegna Tuvaoes is called the jewel of the estate, and brought it fame and renown. The '01 has a deep, full nose with strong vegetal notes, plentiful fresh fruit and citrus nuances. The palate is soft, well-knit and beautifully structured. There follows a long, even finish. Vermentino di Sardegna Pigalva '01 is also very fine, especially with its fresh, fruity, lively aromas. We were less impressed by the vermentino-based Boghes '01, this year bottled as IGT. The vanilla on both nose and palate was rather invasive. As far as the reds are concerned, it gives us great pleasure to note that the Cherchi estate was the first to rediscover the cagnulari variety and vinify it on its own. The '01 Cagnulari is very good, with the delicate, geranium-like vegetal aromas on the nose that have always marked the wine out. The best red, however, is Luzzana '00, a cannonau and cagnulari blend with a clean, fragrant nose and good extractive weight on the palate.

○ Vermentino di Gallura Sup. Canayli '01	♛♛	3*
○ Balajana '01	♛♛	4
○ Moscato di Tempio Pausania '01	♛♛	3
● Nebbiolo dei Colli del Limbara Karana '01	♛♛	2*
○ Vermentino di Gallura Gemellae '01	♛♛	3*
○ Vermentino di Gallura Mavriana '01	♛♛	2*
○ Vermentino di Gallura Piras '01	♛♛	3*
○ Zivula '01	♛♛	5
☉ Campos Rosato del Limbara '01	♛	2*
● Dolmen '98	♛	5
○ Vermentino di Gallura Sup. Canayli '00	♛♛	2
○ Balajana '00	♛♛	4
○ Moscato di Tempio Pausania '00	♛♛	4
○ Vermentino di Gallura Mavriana '00	♛♛	1*
○ Vermentino di Gallura Piras '00	♛♛	3*

○ Vermentino di Sardegna Pigalva '01	♛♛	3*
○ Vermentino di Sardegna Tuvaoes '01	♛♛	4
● Luzzana '00	♛	5
● Cagnulari '01	♛	4
○ Boghes '01	♛	5
○ Vermentino di Sardegna Boghes '00	♛♛	5
● Calaresu '00	♛	2*
○ Vermentino di Sardegna Pigalva '00	♛	3
○ Vermentino di Sardegna Tuvaoes '00	♛	4
● Luzzana '99	♛	5

OTHER WINERIES

COLUMBU
Via Marconi, 1
08013 Bosa (NU)
Tel. 0785373380 - 0785359190
E-MAIL: vinibosa@tin.it

This small estate has been producing an aged version of Malvasia di Bosa for many years. The wine has great similarities with Sherry and aged Vernaccia di Oristano. It has high alcohol and is evolved and penetrating, with a very warm, soft, long palate.

○ Malvasia di Bosa '94	5

CANTINA SOCIALE DORGALI
Via Piemonte, 11
08022 Dorgali (NU)
Tel. 078496143
E-MAIL: info@c.s.dorgali.com

This winery is serious about its reds: the latest vintages are still ageing. From the new range, we tasted Norìolo '99, from cannonau and other indigenous varieties. There is blackberry and morello cherry on the nose, then the palate is warm, soft and full, with good length overall.

● Norìolo '99	4
● Fuili '98	5
● Cannonau di Sardegna Vigna di Isalle '00	3
● Cannonau di Sardegna Vigna di Isalle '99	3

TENUTE SOLETTA
Via Sassari, 77
07030 Florinas (SS)
Tel. 079438160 - 079435067
E-MAIL: tenutesoletta@libero.it

The Soletta siblings' wines are mainly DOC. The best is Vermentino di Sardegna '01, with admirable freshness on the nose and zestiness of flavour. Cannonau di Sardegna Riserva '97 is also very good. It shows fruity, blackberry and plum, aromas and a warm, soft palate.

○ Vermentino di Sardegna '01	3
● Cannonau di Sardegna Ris. '97	4
● Cannonau di Sardegna Firmadu '98	2*
○ Dolce Valle Moscato Passito '98	3

MURA
Loc. Azzanido, 1
07020 Loiri Porto San Paolo (SS)
Tel. 078941070 - 078923929
E-MAIL: vinimura@tiscalinet.it

This small, family-run estate with around 20 hectares of vine makes its first appearance in the Guide. The Vermentino di Gallura is rich and balanced. Nebidu comes from a good mix of indigenous varieties. It is fresh, lively and makes attractive drinking.

● Nebidu '01	4
○ Vermentino di Gallura Sienda '01	5

Andrea Depperu
Via Gorizia 1
07025 Luras (SS)
Tel. 079648121 - 079647314

This small estate produces a tip-top Vermentino di Gallura. The grapes are excellent quality and they are vinified with skill to make a simple but flavoursome wine. It lacks just a little bottle age to deserve an even higher score.

○	Vermentino di Gallura Saruinas '01 ▼▼	4
○	Vermentino di Gallura Saruinas '00 ♀♀	3*

Gianvittorio Naitana
Via Roma, 2
08010 Magomadas (NU)
Tel. 078535333 - 03490801807

This small producer's Malvasia comes from low-cropped grapes. The latest vintage is particularly rich in sugars, which enhances the sensations of fruit. Along with elegance, it has enough structure and fullness of flavour to enable it to mature at length.

○	Planargia Murapiscados '01	▼▼	5
○	Planargia Murapiscados '00	♀♀	5
○	Planargia Murapiscados '98	♀♀	4
○	Planargia Murapiscados '99	♀♀	4

Cantina Sociale Marrubiu
S. S. 126, km 117.600
09094 Marrubiu (OR)
Tel. 0783859213
E-mail: cantinadimarrubiu@tiscalinet.it

The reds are the most interesting of the wines from this co-operative. We particularly liked Campidano di Terralba Bovale, which has wild berry fruit aromas and fair structure. The simpler Monica di Sardegna, with its more delicate nose, is also very attractive.

●	Campidano di Terralba Bovale Madrigal '00 ▼	2*
●	Monica di Sardegna '01	2
●	Arborea Sangiovese '00 ♀	2*
●	Campidano di Terralba Bovale Madrigal '99 ♀	2*

F.lli Porcu
Loc. Su e Giagu
08019 Modolo (NU)
Tel. 078535420
E-mail: fratelliporcu@tiscalinet.it

There's greater commitment at the Porcu cellar and the wines are starting to take on greater stature. The estate's '97 Malvasia di Bosa is one of the best we tasted. The colour is deep amber and has intense, pervasive aromas of very ripe fruit.

●	Malvasia di Bosa '97	▼▼	3*
○	Malvasia di Bosa '96	♀	3

Cantina Sociale Il Nuraghe
S. S. 131, Km 62
09095 Mogoro (OR)
Tel. 0783990285
E-mail: nuraghe@essenet.it

This is one of the few wineries promoting the recovery of Semidano, a white with lightly fruited aromas and a soft taste. The warm, developed Cannonau di Sardegna and the uncomplicated but well-typed Monica di Sardegna San Bernardino are both good reds.

●	Cannonau di Sardegna Vigna Ruja '01 ▼	3
○	Sardegna Semidano '01 ▼	3
●	Monica di Sardegna San Bernardino '00	3

Cantina Cooperativa di Oliena
Via Nuoro, 112
08025 Oliena (NU)
Tel. 0784287509

This co-operative makes two powerful, alcoholic reds based on cannonau. Corrasi Riserva '99 is soft and fleshy, with evident but not raw tannins. Cannonau Nepente di Oliena '01 is still young so its acidity and tannins are still a bit edgy.

●	Cannonau di Sardegna Nepente di Oliena '01 ▼	4
●	Cannonau di Sardegna Corrasi Nepente di Oliena Ris. '99 ▼	5
●	Cannonau di Sardegna Corrasi Nepente di Oliena Ris. '98 ♀♀	5

Villa di Quartu
Via Garibaldi, 96
09045 Quartu Sant'Elena (CA)
Tel. 070820947 - 070826997
E-mail: villadiquartu@tiscali.it

This small estate's wines are well made, especially the dessert wines. The distinguished Malvasia di Cagliari '00 is not very rich on the nose but has soft, mouthfilling flavours. Moscato di Cagliari '00 is clean and elegant. Nasco di Cagliari '00 is more complex and fully flavoured.

○ Malvasia di Cagliari Gutta'e Axina '00	♟♟	4
○ Moscato di Cagliari Gutta'e Axina '00	♟♟	4
○ Nasco di Cagliari Gutta'e Axina '00	♟♟	4

Josto Puddu
Via San Lussorio, 1
09070 San Vero Milis (OR)
Tel. 078353329
E-mail: puddu.vini@tiscalinet.it

While continuing to make Vernaccia di Oristano, this producer has his attention ever more directed towards traditional styles. The most interesting of a wide range, which even includes sparkling wines, is Cannonau di Sardegna Antares. This has no great structure but is very attractive.

● Cannonau di Sardegna Antares '00	♟	4
● Monica di Sardegna Torremora '98	♟	3

Tenute Dettori
Loc. Badde Nigolosu
S. P. 29, Km 10
07036 Sennori (SS)
Tel. 079514711

This promising young winemaker has already understood that great wines, especially reds, need to mature before being released for sale. For this year, he has on offer only the '01 white Dettori, which is intense and very ripe.

○ Dettori Bianco '01	♟♟	5

Paolo Cocco
Loc. Perd'e Carcina
08047 Tertenia (NU)
Tel. 078293855

Paolo Cocco enters the Guide for the first time with a characterful cannonau-based red from the Ogliastra zone, one of the areas best suited for making structured reds. Taurus '00 may not have great intensity on the nose but it has serious structure and good harmony on the palate.

● Taurus '00	♟	3

Valle del Quirra
Via Sebastiano Melis, 59
08047 Tertenia (NU)
Tel. 078293770

There was another good performance from Corriga, a red from Ogliastra, a cannonau area on the eastern coast. It is based on bush-trained cannonau, with admixtures of girò, bovale sardo, sangiovese and cabernet. The '00 has ripe plum aromas, good body, great warmth and is delicately tannic.

● Corriga '00	♟	4
● Corriga '99	♟	5

F.lli Serra
Via Garibaldi, 25
09070 Zeddiani (OR)
Tel. 0783418276 - 0783418016
E-mail: vitivinicola.serra@libero.it

Apart from the fine Vernaccia di Oristano Riserva '92, which is full, seductive and rich in aroma, with marked balsamic notes, the past two years have also seen a characterful red. Kora Kodes, based on montepulciano, cabernet and barbera sardo, is mid-structured, harmonious and balanced.

○ Vernaccia di Oristano Ris. '92	♟♟	4
● Kora Kodes Rosso '01	♟	2

INDEX OF WINES

3 Carati, Avide	748
360 Ruber Capitae Rosso, Bosco del Merlo	282
50 & 50 Avignonesi e Capannelle, Avignonesi	526
50 & 50 decennale Avignonesi e Capannelle, Capannelle	479
A. A. Bianco, Kössler - Praeclarus	252
A. A. Bianco Abtei, Cant. Convento Muri-Gries	256
A. A. Bianco Beyond the Clouds, Castel Ringberg & Kastelaz Elena Walch	275
A. A. Bianco Ebner, Kössler - Praeclarus	252
A. A. Bianco Helios, Graf Pfeil Weingut Kränzel	267
A. A. Bianco Mondevinum, Josef Sölva - Niklaserhof	266
A. A. Bianco Pallas, Cast. Schwanburg	273
A. A. Bianco Passito Comtess St. Valentin, Cant. Prod. San Michele Appiano	254
A. A. Bianco Passito Dorado, Graf Pfeil Weingut Kränzel	267
A. A. Bianco Passito Peperum, Heinrich Plattner - Waldgries	260
A. A. Bianco Sandbichler, Cant. H. Lun	269
A. A. Bianco V. S. Michele, Hofstätter	275
A. A. Cabernet , Graf Pfeil Weingut Kränzel	267
A. A. Cabernet, Popphof - Andreas Menz	270
A. A. Cabernet Albertus Ris., Cant. H. Lun	269
A. A. Cabernet Briglhof, Josef Brigl	250
A. A. Cabernet Freienfeld, Cant. Prod. Cortaccia	268
A. A. Cabernet Kastlet, Loacker Schwarzhof	257
A. A. Cabernet Kirchhügel, Cant. Prod. Cortaccia	268
A. A. Cabernet Lagrein Prestige Caldiv, Von Braunbach	280
A. A. Cabernet Merlot Crescendo Ris., Tenuta Ritterhof	265
A. A. Cabernet Mumelterhof, Cant. Prod. Santa Maddalena/Cant. di Bolzano	260
A. A. Cabernet Puntay, Prima & Nuova/Erste & Neue	265
A. A. Cabernet Ris., Cant. Laimburg	276
A. A. Cabernet Ris., R. Malojer Gummerhof	257
A. A. Cabernet Sauvignon, Josephus Mayr - Erbhof Untergazner	258
A. A. Cabernet Sauvignon, Heinrich Plattner - Waldgries	260
A. A. Cabernet Sauvignon Albertus Ris., Cant. H. Lun	269
A. A. Cabernet Sauvignon Ca' d'Archi, Santa Margherita	338
A. A. Cabernet Sauvignon Campaner Ris., Cant. Viticoltori di Caldaro	264
A. A. Cabernet Sauvignon Castel Ringberg Ris., Castel Ringberg & Kastelaz Elena Walch	275
A. A. Cabernet Sauvignon Castel Schwanburg, Cast. Schwanburg	273
A. A. Cabernet Sauvignon Kastelt Ris., Cant. Prod. Colterenzio	251
A. A. Cabernet Sauvignon Lafoa, Cant. Prod. Colterenzio	251
A. A. Cabernet Sauvignon Linticlarus, Tiefenbrunner	268
A. A. Cabernet Sauvignon Maso Cast., Kettmeir	264
A. A. Cabernet Sauvignon Merlot Cornelius, Cant. Prod. Colterenzio	251
A. A. Cabernet Sauvignon Pfarrhof Ris., Cant. Viticoltori di Caldaro	264
A. A. Cabernet Sauvignon Ris., Andreas Berger -Thurnhof	255
A. A. Cabernet Sauvignon Ris., Cant. Prod. Cornaiano	251
A. A. Cabernet Sauvignon Ris., Cast. Schwanburg	273
A. A. Cabernet Sauvignon SelectArt Flora Ris., Cant. Prod. Cornaiano	251
A. A. Cabernet Sauvignon-Merlot Sagittarius, Graf Pfeil Weingut Kränzel	267
A. A. Cabernet Select Ris, Hans Rottensteiner	261
A. A. Cabernet St. Valentin, Cant. Prod. San Michele Appiano	254
A. A. Cabernet Tor di Lupo, Cant. Prod. Andriano	250
A. A. Cabernet Wienegg Ris., Andreas Berger -Thurnhof	255
A. A. Cabernet-Lagrein Bautzanum, R. Malojer Gummerhof	257
A. A. Cabernet-Lagrein Bautzanum Ris., R. Malojer Gummerhof	257
A. A. Caberet-Lagrein Palladium Coldirus, K. Martini & Sohn	252
A. A. Cabernet-Lagrein Ris., Peter Zemmer - Kupelwieser	269
A. A. Cabernet-Merlot Feld, Prima & Nuova/Erste & Neue	265
A. A. Cabernet-Merlot Putz Ris., Heinrich & Thomas Rottensteiner	262
A. A. Cabernet-Merlot S. Pauls, Kössler - Praeclarus	252
A. A. Chardonnay, Josef Brigl	250
A. A. Chardonnay, K. Martini & Sohn	252
A. A. Chardonnay, Josephus Mayr - Erbhof Untergazner	258
A. A. Chardonnay, Thomas Mayr e Figli	258
A. A. Chardonnay, Popphof - Andreas Menz	270
A. A. Chardonnay, Cast. Rametz	279
A. A. Chardonnay, Peter Zemmer - Kupelwieser	269
A. A. Chardonnay Ateyno, Loacker Schwarzhof	257
A. A. Chardonnay Baron Salvadori, Cant. Prod. Nalles Niclara Magrè	272
A. A. Chardonnay Castel Turmhof, Tiefenbrunner	268
A. A. Chardonnay Cornell, Cant. Prod. Colterenzio	251
A. A. Chardonnay Doa, Cant. Laimburg	276
A. A. Chardonnay Eberlhof, Cant. Prod. Cortaccia	268
A. A. Chardonnay Glassien, Cant. Prod. Termeno	276
A. A. Chardonnay Goldegg, Cant. Prod. di Merano	271
A. A. Chardonnay Happacherhof, Maso Happacherhof - Istituto Tecnico Agrario	280
A. A. Chardonnay Hausmannhof, Haderburg	274
A. A. Chardonnay Kleinstein, Cant. Prod. Santa Maddalena/Cant. di Bolzano	260
A. A. Chardonnay Kupelwieser, Peter Zemmer - Kupelwieser	269
A. A. Chardonnay Linticlarus, Tiefenbrunner	268
A. A. Chardonnay Maso Rainer, Kettmeir	264
A. A. Chardonnay Palladium, K. Martini & Sohn	252
A. A. Chardonnay Pinay, Cant. Prod. Colterenzio	251
A. A. Chardonnay Puntay, Prima & Nuova/Erste & Neue	265
A. A. Chardonnay Salt, Prima & Nuova/Erste & Neue	265
A. A. Chardonnay Selection, Steinhauserhof	280
A. A. Chardonnay St. Valentin, Cant. Prod. San Michele Appiano	254
A. A. Chardonnay Tiefenthaler, Cant. Prod. Burggräfler	270
A. A. Chardonnay Tor di Lupo, Cant. Prod. Andriano	250
A. A. Chardonnay Wadleith, Cant. Viticoltori di Caldaro	264
A. A. Cuvée Anna, Tiefenbrunner	268
A. A. Gewürztraminer Puntay, Prima & Nuova/Erste & Neue	265
A. A. Gewürztraminer Sel. Sonnengut , Cant. Prod. Andriano	250
A. A. Gewürztramier Kleinstein, Cant. Prod. Santa Maddalena/Cant. di Bolzano	260
A. A. Gewürztraminer, Castel Sallegg - Graf Kuenburg	279
A. A. Gewürztraminer, Franz Haas	272
A. A. Gewürztraminer, Cant. Laimburg	276
A. A. Gewürztraminer , Popphof - Andreas Menz	270
A. A. Gewürztraminer, Tenuta Ritterhof	265
A. A. Gewürztraminer Albertus, Cant. H. Lun	269
A. A. Gewürztraminer Baron Salvadori, Cant. Prod. Nalles Niclara Magrè	272
A. A. Gewürztraminer Campaner, Cant. Viticoltori di Caldaro	264
A. A. Gewürztraminer Cancenai, Hans Rottensteiner	261
A. A. Gewürztraminer Cornell, Cant. Prod. Colterenzio	251
A. A. Gewürztraminer Cresta , Hans Rottensteiner	261
A. A. Gewürztraminer Graf Von Meran, Cant. Prod. di Merano	271
A. A. Gewürztraminer Kastelaz, Castel Ringberg & Kastelaz Elena Walch	275
A. A. Gewürztraminer Kolbenhof, Hofstätter	275
A. A. Gewürztraminer Lage Doss, Josef Niedermayr	253
A. A. Gewürztraminer Maratsch, Cant. Prod. Termeno	276
A. A. Gewürztraminer Nussbaumerhof, Cant. Prod. Termeno	276
A. A. Gewürztraminer Passito, Graf Pfeil Weingut Kränzel	267
A. A. Gewürztraminer Pigeno, Stroblhof	278
A. A. Gewürztraminer Schloss Turmhof, Tiefenbrunner	268
A. A. Gewürztraminer SelectArt Flora, Cant. Prod. Cornaiano	251
A. A. Gewürztraminer St. Valentin, Cant. Prod. San Michele Appiano	254
A. A. Gewürztraminer Windegg, Josef Brigl	250
A. A. Lago di Caldaro Cl., Kettmeir	264
A. A. Lago di Caldaro Scelto Cl., Josef Sölva - Niklaserhof	266
A. A. Lago di Caldaro Scelto Desilvas Peterleiten, Peter Sölva & Söhne - Paterbichl	266
A. A. Lago di Caldaro Scelto Haslhof Cl. Sup., Josef Brigl	250
A. A. Lago di Caldaro Scelto Puntay, Prima & Nuova/Erste & Neue	265
A. A. Lagrein, Cant. Prod. Burggräfler	270
A. A. Lagrein Aus Gries Ris., Josef Niedermayr	253
A. A. Lagrein Berger Gei, Ignaz Niedrist	253
A. A. Lagrein Castel Ringberg Ris., Castel Ringberg & Kastelaz Elena Walch	275
A. A. Lagrein Castel Turmhof, Tiefenbrunner	268
A. A. Lagrein Cornell, Cant. Prod. Colterenzio	251
A. A. Lagrein Gries, Cant. Convento Muri-Gries	256
A. A. Lagrein Gries Ris., Cant. Terlano	274
A. A. Lagrein Merlot Ebner, Kössler - Praeclarus	252
A. A. Lagrein Porphyr Ris., Cant. Terlano	274
A. A. Lagrein Praepositus Ris., Abbazia di Novacella	277
A. A. Lagrein Puntay, Prima & Nuova/Erste & Neue	265
A. A. Lagrein Ris., Cant. Prod. Cornaiano	251
A. A. Lagrein Ris., Stephan Ramoser - Fliederhof	279
A. A. Lagrein Rosato, Popphof - Andreas Menz	270
A. A. Lagrein Rosato Gries, Cant. Convento Muri-Gries	256
A. A. Lagrein Rosato V. T., Josephus Mayr - Erbhof Untergazner	258
A. A. Lagrein Scuro, Andreas Berger -Thurnhof	255
A. A. Lagrein Scuro, Franz Gojer Glögglhof	256
A. A. Lagrein Scuro, Kössler - Praeclarus	252
A. A. Lagrein Scuro, Thomas Mayr e Figli	258
A. A. Lagrein Scuro, Josephus Mayr - Erbhof Untergazner	258
A. A. Lagrein Scuro, Pfeifer Johannes Pfannenstielhof	259
A. A. Lagrein Scuro Abtei Ris., Cant. Convento Muri-Gries	256

A. A. Lagrein Scuro Albertus Ris., Cant. H. Lun	269
A. A. Lagrein Scuro Berger Gei Ris., Ignaz Niedrist	253
A. A. Lagrein Scuro Briglhof, Josef Brigl	250
A. A. Lagrein Scuro Caldiv, Von Braunbach	280
A. A. Lagrein Scuro Crescendo Ris., Tenuta Ritterhof	265
A. A. Lagrein Scuro Fohrhof, Cant. Prod. Cortaccia	268
A. A. Lagrein Scuro Grafenleiten, Heinrich & Thomas Rottensteiner	262
A. A. Lagrein Scuro Grafenleiten Ris., Heinrich & Thomas Rottensteiner	262
A. A. Lagrein Scuro Gries, Cant. Convento Muri-Gries	256
A. A. Lagrein Scuro Gries Kristan, Egger-Ramer	278
A. A. Lagrein Scuro Grieser Baron Carl Eyrl Ris., Cant. Gries/Cant. di Bolzano	255
A. A. Lagrein Scuro Grieser Prestige Line Ris., Cant. Gries/Cant. di Bolzano	255
A. A. Lagrein Scuro Grieser Ris., Anton Schmid - Oberrautner	278
A. A. Lagrein Scuro Grieser Select Ris., Hans Rottensteiner	261
A. A. Lagrein Scuro Happacherhof, Maso Happacherhof - Istituto Tecnico Agrario	280
A. A. Lagrein Scuro Intenditore, Peter Zemmer - Kupelwieser	269
A. A. Lagrein Scuro Maturum, K. Martini & Sohn	252
A. A. Lagrein Scuro Perl, Cant. Prod. Santa Maddalena/Cant. di Bolzano	260
A. A. Lagrein Scuro Pitz Thurù Ris., Loacker Schwarzhof	257
A. A. Lagrein Scuro Ris., Andreas Berger -Thurnhof	255
A. A. Lagrein Scuro Ris., Franz Gojer Glögglhof	256
A. A. Lagrein Scuro Ris., Cant. Laimburg	276
A. A. Lagrein Scuro Ris., R. Malojer Gummerhof	257
A. A. Lagrein Scuro Ris., Thomas Mayr e Figli	258
A. A. Lagrein Scuro Ris., Josephus Mayr - Erbhof Unterganzner	258
A. A. Lagrein Scuro Ris., Georg Mumelter	259
A. A. Lagrein Scuro Ris., Pfeifer Johannes Pfannenstielhof	259
A. A. Lagrein Scuro Ris., Heinrich Plattner - Waldgries	260
A. A. Lagrein Scuro Ris., Georg Ramoser - Untermoserhof	261
A. A. Lagrein Scuro Ris., Hans Rottensteiner	261
A. A. Lagrein Scuro Ris., Cast. Schwanburg	273
A. A. Lagrein Scuro Ris. Mirell, Heinrich Plattner - Waldgries	260
A. A. Lagrein Scuro Rueslhof, K. Martini & Sohn	252
A. A. Lagrein Scuro S., Thomas Mayr e Figli	258
A. A. Lagrein Scuro Saltner, Anton Schmid - Oberrautner	278
A. A. Lagrein Scuro Segenpichl, Cant. Prod. di Merano	271
A. A. Lagrein Scuro Steinraffler, Hofstätter	275
A. A. Lagrein Scuro Taberhof, Cant. Prod. Santa Maddalena/Cant. di Bolzano	260
A. A. Lagrein Scuro Tor di Lupo, Cant. Prod. Andriano	250
A. A. Lagrein SelectArt Flora Ris., Cant. Prod. Cornaiano	251
A. A. Lagrein St. Valentin, Cant. Prod. San Michele Appiano	254
A. A. Lagrein Urbanhof, Cant. Prod. Termeno	276
A. A. Lagrein-Cabernet Coldirus Palladium, K. Martini & Sohn	252
A. A. Lagrein-Cabernet Klaser Ris., Josef Sölva - Niklaserhof	266
A. A. Lagrein-Cabernet MerVin, Cant. Prod. Burggräfler	270
A. A. Lagrein-Merlot, Peter Sölva & Söhne - Paterbichl	266
A. A. Meranese Schickenburg, Cant. Prod. Burggräfler	270
A. A. Merlot, Ignaz Niedrist	253
A. A. Merlot, Popphof - Andreas Menz	270
A. A. Merlot, Cant. Prod. Burggräfler	270
A. A. Merlot, Georg Ramoser - Untermoserhof	261
A. A. Merlot Brenntal, Cant. Prod. Cortaccia	268
A. A. Merlot Collection Ris., Cant. Gries/Cant. di Bolzano	255
A. A. Merlot Crescendo Ris., Tenuta Ritterhof	265
A. A. Merlot DiVinus, Cant. Prod. San Paolo	254
A. A. Merlot Freiberg Ris., Cant. Prod. Merano	271
A. A. Merlot Kastelaz Ris., Castel Ringberg & Kastelaz Elena Walch	275
A. A. Merlot Levad, Cant. Prod. Nalles Niclara Magrè	272
A. A. Merlot Mühlweg, Ignaz Niedrist	253
A. A. Merlot Ris., Castel Sallegg - Graf Kuenburg	279
A. A. Merlot Ris., R. Malojer Gummerhof	257
A. A. Merlot Ris., Georg Ramoser - Untermoserhof	261
A. A. Merlot Ris., Tenuta Ritterhof	265
A. A. Merlot Ris., Cast. Schwanburg	273
A. A. Merlot Ris. Siebeneich Prestige Line, Cant. Gries/Cant. di Bolzano	255
A. A. Merlot Schweitzer, Franz Haas	272
A. A. Merlot Siebeneich, Cant. Prod. Andriano	250
A. A. Merlot Siebeneich Ris., Cant. Terlano	274
A. A. Merlot Siebeneich Tor di Lupo, Cant. Prod. Andriano	250
A. A. Merlot Spitz, Franz Gojer Glögglhof	256
A. A. Merlot Tschidererhof, Kössler - Praeclarus	252
A. A. Merlot-Cabernet Happacherhof, Maso Happacherhof - Istituto Tecnico Agrario	280
A. A. Merlot-Cabernet Juvin Cuvée, Cant. Prod. Burggräfler	270
A. A. Merlot-Lagrein, Cant. Prod. Burggräfler	270
A. A. Moscato Giallo, Andreas Berger -Thurnhof	255
A. A. Moscato Giallo Passito Oscar, Tenuta Klosterhof	279
A. A. Moscato Giallo Passito Serenade, Cant. Viticoltori di Caldaro	264
A. A. Moscato Giallo Passito Sissi Graf von Meran, Cant. Prod. di Merano	271
A. A. Moscato Giallo Schickenburg, Cant. Prod. Burggräfler	270
A. A. Moscato Giallo Trifall, Tenuta Klosterhof	279
A. A. Moscato Giallo Vinalia, Cant. Gries/Cant. di Bolzano	255
A. A. Moscato Rosa, Abbazia di Novacella	277
A. A. Moscato Rosa Abtei, Cant. Convento Muri-Gries	256
A. A. Moscato Rosa, Heinrich Plattner - Waldgries	260
A. A. Moscato Rosa Linticlarus, Tiefenbrunner	268
A. A. Moscato Rosa Rosis, Cant. Gries/Cant. di Bolzano	255
A. A. Moscato Rosa Schweizer, Franz Haas	272
A. A. Moscato Rosa Terminum, Cant. Prod. Termeno	276
A. A. Müller Thurgau, Hans Rottensteiner	261
A. A. Müller Thurgau Intenditore, Peter Zemmer - Kupelwieser	269
A. A. Passito Baronesse, Cant. Prod. Nalles Niclara Magrè	272
A. A. Passito Cashmere, Castel Ringberg & Kastelaz Elena Walch	275
A. A. Pinot Bianco, Graf Pfeil Weingut Kränzel	267
A. A. Pinot Bianco, Franz Haas	272
A. A. Pinot Bianco, Hofstätter	275
A. A. Pinot Bianco, Popphof - Andreas Menz	270
A. A. Pinot Bianco, Josef Sölva - Niklaserhof	266
A. A. Pinot Bianco, Peter Zemmer - Kupelwieser	269
A. A. Pinot Bianco Carnol, Hans Rottensteiner	261
A. A. Pinot Bianco Collection Dellago, Cant. Gries/Cant. di Bolzano	255
A. A. Pinot Bianco Graf Von Meran, Cant. Prod. Merano	271
A. A. Pinot Bianco Guggenberg, Cant. Prod. Burggräfler	270
A. A. Pinot Bianco Helios, Graf Pfeil Weingut Kränzel	267
A. A. Pinot Bianco Kastelaz, Castel Ringberg & Kastelaz Elena Walch	275
A. A. Pinot Bianco Klaser, Josef Sölva - Niklaserhof	266
A. A. Pinot Bianco MerVin V. T., Cant. Prod. Burggräfler	270
A. A. Pinot Bianco Passito Pasithea, Cant. Prod. Cornaiano	251
A. A. Pinot Bianco Plattenriegl, Cant. Prod. Cornaiano	251
A. A. Pinot Bianco Praesulius, Markus Prackwieser Gumphof	279
A. A. Pinot Bianco Puntay, Prima & Nuova/Erste & Neue	265
A. A. Pinot Bianco Schulthauser, Cant. Prod. San Michele Appiano	254
A. A. Pinot Bianco Strahler, Stroblhof	278
A. A. Pinot Bianco Vial, Cant. Viticoltori di Caldaro	264
A. A. Pinot Bianco Weisshaus, Cant. Prod. Colterenzio	251
A. A. Pinot Grigio, Cant. H. Lun	269
A. A. Pinot Grigio, Tenuta Ritterhof	265
A. A. Pinot Grigio, Peter Zemmer - Kupelwieser	269
A. A. Pinot Grigio Anger, Cant. Prod. San Michele Appiano	254
A. A. Pinot Grigio Castel Ringberg, Castel Ringberg & Kastelaz Elena Walch	275
A. A. Pinot Grigio Exklusiv Egg-Leiten, Cant. Prod. San Paolo	254
A. A. Pinot Grigio Griesbauerhof, Georg Mumelter	259
A. A. Pinot Grigio Maso Rainer, Kettmeir	264
A. A. Pinot Grigio Punggl, Cant. Prod. Nalles Niclara Magrè	272
A. A. Pinot Grigio Söll, Cant. Viticoltori di Caldaro	264
A. A. Pinot Grigio St. Valentin, Cant. Prod. San Michele Appiano	254
A. A. Pinot Grigio Unterebnerhof, Cant. Prod. Termeno	276
A. A. Pinot Nero, Graf Pfeil Weingut Kränzel	267
A. A. Pinot Nero, Cant. Laimburg	276
A. A. Pinot Nero, Ignaz Niedrist	253
A. A. Pinot Nero, Pfeifer Johannes Pfannenstielhof	259
A. A. Pinot Nero Albertus Ris., Cant. H. Lun	269
A. A. Pinot Nero Cornell Schwarzhaus, Cant. Prod. Colterenzio	251
A. A. Pinot Nero Crozzolhof, Hofstätter	275
A. A. Pinot Nero DiVinus, Cant. Prod. San Paolo	254
A. A. Pinot Nero Fritzenhof, Cant. Prod. Cortaccia	268
A. A. Pinot Nero Hausmannhof, Haderburg	274
A. A. Pinot Nero Linticlarus Ris., Tiefenbrunner	268
A. A. Pinot Nero Maso Rainer, Kettmeir	264
A. A. Pinot Nero Matan, Tenuta Pfitscherhof	280
A. A. Pinot Nero Matan, Peter Zemmer - Kupelwieser	269
A. A. Pinot Nero Mazzon Select Ris., Hans Rottensteiner	261
A. A. Pinot Nero Norital, Loacker Schwarzhof	257
A. A. Pinot Nero Patricia, Cant. Prod. Cornaiano	251
A. A. Pinot Nero Pigeno, Stroblhof	278
A. A. Pinot Nero Praepositus Ris., Abbazia di Novacella	277
A. A. Pinot Nero Ris., Castel Sallegg - Graf Kuenburg	279
A. A. Pinot Nero Ris., Hofstätter	275
A. A. Pinot Nero Ris., R. Malojer Gummerhof	257
A. A. Pinot Nero Ris., Steinhauserhof	280
A. A. Pinot Nero Ris., Stroblhof	278
A. A. Pinot Nero Ris., Cant. Viticoltori di Caldaro	264
A. A. Pinot Nero S. Urbano, Hofstätter	275
A. A. Pinot Nero Sandbichler Ris., Cant. H. Lun	269
A. A. Pinot Nero Sandlahner Ris., Cant. Prod. Santa Maddalena/Cant. di Bolzano	260
A. A. Pinot Nero Schiesstandhof Ris., Cant. Prod. Termeno	276
A. A. Pinot Nero Schweizer, Franz Haas	272
A. A. Pinot Nero Selection, Steinhauserhof	280
A. A. Pinot Nero St. Daniel Ris., Cant. Prod. Colterenzio	251
A. A. Pinot Nero St. Valentin, Cant. Prod. San Michele Appiano	254
A. A. Pinot Nero Tiefenthaler MerVin, Cant. Prod. Burggräfler	270
A. A. Pinot Nero Zenoberg, Cant. Prod. di Merano	271
A. A. Riesling, Hofstätter	275
A. A. Riesling, Popphof - Andreas Menz	270
A. A. Riesling, Cast. Rametz	279
A. A. Riesling, Cast. Schwanburg	273
A. A. Riesling, Peter Zemmer - Kupelwieser	269
A. A. Riesling Fidera, Cant. Prod. Nalles Niclara Magrè	272
A. A. Riesling Kupelwieser, Peter Zemmer - Kupelwieser	269
A. A. Riesling Montiggl, Cant. Prod. San Michele Appiano	254
A. A. Riesling Renano, Cant. Laimburg	276
A. A. Riesling Renano, Ignaz Niedrist	253
A. A. Santa Maddalena, Andreas Berger -Thurnhof	255
A. A. Santa Maddalena, Georg Mumelter	259
A. A. Santa Maddalena Cl., Franz Gojer Glögglhof	256
A. A. Santa Maddalena Cl., Josephus Mayr - Erbhof Unterganzner	258

A. A. Santa Maddalena Cl., Georg Mumelter	259
A. A. Santa Maddalena Cl., Pfeifer Johannes Pfannenstielhof	259
A. A. Santa Maddalena Cl., Heinrich Plattner - Waldgries	260
A. A. Santa Maddalena Cl., Stephan Ramoser - Fliederhof	279
A. A. Santa Maddalena Cl, Georg Ramoser - Untermoserhof	261
A. A. Santa Maddalena Cl., Heinrich & Thomas Rottensteiner	262
A. A. Santa Maddalena Cl. Huck am Bach, Cant. Prod. Santa Maddalena/Cant. di Bolzano	260
A. A. Santa Maddalena Cl. Morit, Loacker Schwarzhof	257
A. A. Santa Maddalena Cl. Premstallerhof, Hans Rottensteiner	261
A. A. Santa Maddalena Cl. Reiseggerhof, Egger-Ramer	278
A. A. Santa Maddalena Cl. Rondell, Franz Gojer Glögglhof	256
A. A. Santa Maddalena Cl. Rumplerhof, Thomas e Mayr Figli	258
A. A. Santa Maddalena Perlhof , Tenuta Ritterhof	265
A. A. Santa Maddalena Reierhof, Josef Brigl	250
A. A. Santa Maddalena Rondell, Franz Gojer Glögglhof	256
A. A. Sauvignon, Josef Brigl	250
A. A. Sauvignon, Cant. Laimburg	276
A. A. Sauvignon, Cant. Prod. Termeno	276
A. A. Sauvignon Graf Pfeil Wingut, Kränzel	267
A. A. Sauvignon, Josef Sölva - Niklaserhof	266
A. A. Sauvignon Albertus, Cant. H. Lun	269
A. A. Sauvignon Allure, Josef Niedermayr	253
A. A. Sauvignon Blanc Tasmin, Loacker Schwarzhof	257
A. A. Sauvignon Castel Ringberg, Castel Ringberg & Kastelaz Elena Walch	275
A. A. Sauvignon Exklusiv Gfilhof, Cant. Prod. San Paolo	254
A. A. Sauvignon Graf Von Meran, Cant. Prod. di Merano	271
A. A. Sauvignon Gur zu Sand, R. Malojer Gummerhof	57
A. A. Sauvignon Hausmannhof, Haderburg	274
A. A. Sauvignon Intenditore, Peter Zemmer - Kupelwieser	269
A. A. Sauvignon Kirchleiten, Tiefenbrunner	268
A. A. Sauvignon Lage Naun, Josef Niedermayr	253
A. A. Sauvignon Lahn, Cant. Prod. San Michele Appiano	254
A. A. Sauvignon Marklhof, Abbazia di Novacella	277
A. A. Sauvignon Milla, Cant. Prod. Cortaccia	268
A. A. Sauvignon Mockhof, Cant. Prod. Santa Maddalena/Cant. di Bolzano	260
A. A. Sauvignon Passito Saphir, Cant. Laimburg	276
A. A. Sauvignon Praesulius, Markus Prackwieser Gumphof	279
A. A. Sauvignon Premstalerhof, Cant. Viticoltori di Caldaro	264
A. A. Sauvignon SelectArt Flora, Cant. Prod. Cornaiano	251
A. A. Sauvignon Selection, Steinhauserhof	280
A. A. Sauvignon St. Valentin, Cant. Prod. San Michele Appiano	254
A. A. Schiava Grigia Sonnntaler, Cant. Prod. Cortaccia	268
A. A. Schiava Gschleier SelectArt Flora, Cant. Prod. Cornaiano	251
A. A. Schiava Palladium, K. Martini & Sohn	252
A. A. Schiava Sarner Hof Exclusiv, Cant. Prod. San Paolo	254
A. A. Schiava Schloss Baslan, Graf Pfeil Weingut Kränzel	267
A. A. Spumante Blanc de Blancs Arunda, Vivaldi - Arunda	271
A. A. Spumante Brut, Kettmeir	264
A. A. Spumante Brut Arunda, Vivaldi - Arunda	271
A. A. Spumante Brut Arunda Ris., Vivaldi - Arunda	271
A. A. Spumante Brut Vivaldi, Vivaldi - Arunda	271
A. A. Spumante Comitissa Brut Ris., Lorenz Martini	278
A. A. Spumante Extra Brut Arunda, Vivaldi - Arunda	271
A. A. Spumante Extra Brut Arunda Ris., Vivaldi - Arunda	271
A. A. Spumante Extra Brut Vivaldi, Vivaldi - Arunda	271
A. A. Spumante Haderburg Pas Dosé, Haderburg	274
A. A. Spumante Hausmannhof, Haderburg	274
A. A. Spumante Hausmannhof Ris., Haderburg	274
A. A. Spumante Pas Dosé, Haderburg	274
A. A. Spumante Praeclarus Brut, Kössler - Praeclarus	252
A. A. Spumante Praeclarus Noblesse Ris., Kössler - Praeclarus	252
A. A. Spumante Von Braunbach Brut, Von Braunbach	280
A. A. Terlano, Cant. Terlano	274
A. A. Terlano Cl., Cant. Terlano	274
A. A. Terlano Cuvée, Cast. Schwanburg	273
A. A. Terlano Nova Domus, Cantina Terlano	274
A. A. Terlano Pinot Bianco Cl. Sonnengut, Cant. Prod. Andriano	250
A. A. Terlano Pinot Bianco Exclusiv Plötzner, Cant. Prod. San Paolo	254
A. A. Terlano Pinot Bianco Pitzon, Cast. Schwanburg	273
A. A. Terlano Pinot Bianco Riol, Heinrich Plattner - Waldgries	260
A. A. Terlano Pinot Bianco Sirmian, Cant. Prod. Nalles Niclara Magrè	272
A. A. Terlano Pinot Bianco Vorberg, Cant. Terlano	274
A. A. Terlano Sauvignon, Ignaz Niedrist	253
A. A. Terlano Sauvignon Cl. Mantele, Cant. Prod. Nalles Niclara Magrè	272
A. A. Terlano Sauvignon Preciosa Tor di Lupo, C. P. Andriano	250
A. A. Terlano Sauvignon Quarz, Cant. Terlano	274
A. A. Traminer Aromatico Brenntal, Cant. Prod. Cortaccia	268
A. A. Valle Isarco Gewürztraminer, Abbazia di Novacella	277
A. A. Valle Isarco Gewürztraminer, Köfererhof	277
A. A. Valle Isarco Gewürztraminer, Kuenhof - Peter Pliger	263
A. A. Valle Isarco Gewürztraminer, Manfred Nössing - Hoandlhof	263
A. A. Valle Isarco Gewürztraminer, Taschlerhof	279
A. A. Valle Isarco Gewürztraminer Aristos, Cant. Prod. Valle Isarco	267
A. A. Valle Isarco Gewürztraminer Atagis, Loacker Schwarzhof	257
A. A. Valle Isarco Gewürztraminer Nectaris, Cant. Prod. Valle Isarco	267
A. A. Valle Isarco Kerner, Abbazia di Novacella	277
A. A. Valle Isarco Kerner, Köfererhof	277
A. A. Valle Isarco Kerner, Manfred Nössing - Hoandlhof	263
A. A. Valle Isarco Kerner, Cant. Prod. Valle Isarco	267
A. A. Valle Isarco Kerner Praepositus, Abbazia di Novacella	277
A. A. Valle Isarco Müller Thurgau, Abbazia di Novacella	277
A. A. Valle Isarco Müller Thurgau, Köfererhof	277
A. A. Valle Isarco Müller Thurgau, Manfred Nössing - Hoandlhof	263
A. A. Valle Isarco Müller Thurgau, Cant. Prod. Valle Isarco	267
A. A. Valle Isarco Müller Thurgau, Rockhof	280
A. A. Valle Isarco Müller Thurgau Aristos, Cant. Prod. Valle Isarco	267
A. A. Valle Isarco Pinot Grigio, Abbazia di Novacella	277
A. A. Valle Isarco Pinot Grigio, Köfererhof	277
A. A. Valle Isarco Pinot Grigio, Cant. Prod. Valle Isarco	267
A. A. Valle Isarco Riesling, Köfererhof	277
A. A. Valle Isarco Sylvaner, Abbazia di Novacella	277
A. A. Valle Isarco Sylvaner, Köfererhof	277
A. A. Valle Isarco Sylvaner, Kuenhof - Peter Pliger	263
A. A. Valle Isarco Sylvaner, Manfred Nössing - Hoandlhof	263
A. A. Valle Isarco Sylvaner, Cant. Prod. Valle Isarco	267
A. A. Valle Isarco Sylvaner, Rockhof	280
A. A. Valle Isarco Sylvaner, Taschlerhof	279
A. A. Valle Isarco Sylvaner Aristos, Cant. Prod. Valle Isarco	267
A. A. Valle Isarco Sylvaner Praepositus, Abbazia di Novacella	277
A. A. Valle Isarco Veltliner, Kuenhof - Peter Pliger	263
A. A. Valle Isarco Veltliner, Manfred Nössing - Hoandlhof	263
A. A. Valle Isarco Veltliner, Cant. Prod. Valle Isarco	267
A. A. Valle Venosta Gewürztraminer, Tenuta Falkenstein - Franz Pratzner	273
A. A. Valle Venosta Gewürztraminer V. T., Tenuta Falkenstein - Franz Pratzner	273
A. A. Valle Venosta Pinot Bianco, Tenuta Falkenstein - Franz Pratzner	273
A. A. Valle Venosta Pinot Bianco, Tenuta Unterortl-Castel Juval	262
A. A. Valle Venosta Pinot Nero, Tenuta Unterortl-Castel Juval	262
A. A. Valle Venosta Riesling, Oswald Schuster Befehlhof	280
A. A. Valle Venosta Riesling, Tenuta Falkenstein - Franz Pratzner	273
A. A. Valle Venosta Riesling, Tenuta Unterortl-Castel Juval	262
Abbaia, C.S. del Vermentino	771
Accademia del Sole Famiglia Morella Sangiovese Negroamaro, Calatrasi Puglia	718
Acciaiolo, Cast. d' Albola	550
Accordo Bianco, Sergio Degiorgis	101
Acini Dolci, Cant. del Cast.	321
Acini Rari Passito, Enoteca Bisson	165
Acininobili, Maculan	285
Aglaia, Fatt. Corzano e Paterno	557
Aglianico, Borgo di Colloredo	686
Aglianico Avellanio, Mastroberardino	690
Aglianico Castellaccio, Monte Pugliano	705
Aglianico Castellaccio Ris., Monte Pugliano	705
Aglianico Contessa Ferrara, Cast. Ducale	704
Aglianico del Taburno, Fatt. La Rivolta	690
Aglianico del Taburno, Fontanavecchia	703
Aglianico del Taburno Diomede, Ocone	706
Aglianico del Taburno Fidelis, Cant. del Taburno	693
Aglianico del Taburno Rosato, Fontanavecchia	703
Aglianico del Taburno Terra di Rivolta Ris., Fatt. La Rivolta	690
Aglianico del Taburno V. Cataratte, Fontanavecchia	703
Aglianico del Taburno V. Cataratte Ris., Fontanavecchia	703
Aglianico del Vulture, C.S. del Vulture	714
Aglianico del Vulture, Cons. Viticoltori Associati del Vulture	708
Aglianico del Vulture , D'Angelo	710
Aglianico del Vulture , Tenuta del Portale	710
Aglianico del Vulture Basilisco, Basilisco	714
Aglianico del Vulture Bel Poggio, Armando Martino	712
Aglianico del Vulture Carato Venusio, Cant. di Venosa	713
Aglianico del Vulture Carpe Diem, Cons. Viticoltori Associati del Vulture	708
Aglianico del Vulture Don Anselmo, Paternoster	709
Aglianico del Vulture Federico II, Tenuta Le Querce	709
Aglianico del Vulture I Portali, Basilium	708
Aglianico del Vulture II Covo dei Briganti, Agr. Eubea - Fam. Sasso	711
Aglianico del Vulture II Madrigale di Gesualdo, Cant. di Venosa	713
Aglianico del Vulture II Repertorio, Cantine del Notaio	712
Aglianico del Vulture II Viola, Tenuta Le Querce	709
Aglianico del Vulture La Firma, Cantine del Notaio	712
Aglianico del Vulture Le Gastaldie Sicone, Basilium	708
Aglianico del Vulture Le Vigne a Capanno, Tenuta del Portale	710
Aglianico del Vulture Nibbio Grigio, Di Palma	711
Aglianico del Vulture Oraziano, Armando Martino	712
Aglianico del Vulture Pipoli, Basilium	708
Aglianico del Vulture Re Manfredi, Terre degli Svevi	713
Aglianico del Vulture Ris., Tenuta del Portale	710
Aglianico del Vulture Ris. Don Anselmo, Paternoster	709
Aglianico del Vulture Rosso di Costanza, Tenuta Le Querce	709
Aglianico del Vulture Rotondo, Paternoster	709
Aglianico del Vulture Synthesi, Paternoster	709
Aglianico del Vulture Terre di Orazio, Cant. di Venosa	713
Aglianico del Vulture Terre Mediterranee, Zonin	290
Aglianico del Vulture Titolo, Elena Fucci	714
Aglianico del Vulture Valle del Trono, Basilium	708
Aglianico del Vulture Vetusto, Cons. Viticoltori Associati del Vulture	708

Aglianico del Vulture V. Caselle Ris., D'Angelo	710
Aglianico del Vulture V. della Corona, Tenuta Le Querce	709
Aglianico del Vulture V.li, Cant. di Venosa	713
Aglianico di Roccamonfina, Telaro - Coop. Lavoro e Salute	695
Aglianico Rocca dei Leoni, Villa Matilde	693
Aglianico V. Olmo, Di Meo	699
Aglieno, Casa alle Vacche	563
Agno Tinto, V.lta	326
Ailanpa, Foradori	236
Aiole, Tenuta La Costaiola	200
Aione, Podere Aione	594
Ajana, Ferruccio Deiana	776
Akates, Cantine Torrevecchia	744
Akronte, Boccadigabbia	615
Al Poggio Chardonnay, Cast. di Ama	478
Alastro, Planeta	752
Albaciara Bianco, Barni	47
Albana di Romagna Amabile Velo del Magone, Giovanna Madonia	422
Albana di Romagna Dolce Lilaria, Stefano Ferrucci	425
Albana di Romagna Passito, Fondo Cà Vecja	448
Albana di Romagna Passito, Tenuta Uccellina	439
Albana di Romagna Passito, Tre Monti	432
Albana di Romagna Passito, Treré	430
Albana di Romagna Passito, Villa Spadoni	447
Albana di Romagna Passito Arrocco, Fatt. Zerbina	429
Albana di Romagna Passito Colle del Re, Umberto Cesari	425
Albana di Romagna Passito Domus Aurea, Stefano Ferrucci	425
Albana di Romagna Passito Gradisca, Fatt. Paradiso	423
Albana di Romagna Passito Innamorato, Alessandro Morini	447
Albana di Romagna Passito La Dolce Vita, La Macolina	448
Albana di Romagna Passito Maolù, Colonna - Vini Spalletti	441
Albana di Romagna Passito Mythos, Tre Valli	447
Albana di Romagna Passito Non Ti Scordar di Me, Leone Conti	428
Albana di Romagna Passito Remoto, Giovanna Madonia	422
Albana di Romagna Passito Scacco Matto, Fatt. Zerbina	429
Albana di Romagna Passito Solara, Celli	422
Albana di Romagna Passito Ultimo Giorno di Scuola, Istituto Professionale per l'Agricoltura e l'Ambiente	429
Albana di Romagna Progetto 1, Leone Conti	428
Albana di Romagna Progetto 2, Leone Conti	428
Albana di Romagna Secco, Colombina	445
Albana di Romagna Secco, Colonna - Vini Spalletti	441
Albana di Romagna Secco Colle del Re, Umberto Cesari	425
Albana di Romagna Secco I Croppi, Celli	422
Albana di Romagna Secco Neblina, Giovanna Madonia	422
Albana di Romagna Secco V. della Rocca, Tre Monti	432
Albarossa, Cantine Torrevecchia	744
Alberto Rosso, Zenato	309
Albion Cabernet Sauvignon Villa Novare, Bertani	304
Alborato, Cardeto	651
Alcamo, Casa Vinicola Firriato	754
Alcamo, Cantine Torrevecchia	744
Alcamo Alhambra, Spadafora	755
Alcamo Carta d'Oro, Cantine Rallo	751
Alcamo Principe di Corleone, Pollara	762
Alcamo Rapitalà Grand Cru, Tenute Rapitalà	746
Ale di Glesie, Villa Frattina	395
Aleatico dell'Elba, Mola	600
Aleatico dell'Elba, Sapereta	549
Alezio Rosato Mjère, Michele Calò & Figli	734
Alfiere Cabernet Sauvignon, Tenuta Godenza	447
Alghero Anghelu Ruju Ris., Tenute Sella & Mosca	766
Alghero Cagnulari, C.S. Santa Maria La Palma	766
Alghero Chardonnay, C.S. Santa Maria La Palma	766
Alghero Le Arenarie, Tenute Sella & Mosca	766
Alghero Marchese di Villamarina, Tenute Sella & Mosca	766
Alghero Oleandro, Tenute Sella & Mosca	766
Alghero Rosato Cantav., C.S. Santa Maria La Palma	766
Alghero Sauvignon, C.S. Santa Maria La Palma	766
Alghero Tanca Farrà, Tenute Sella & Mosca	766
Alghero Torbato Terre Bianche, Tenute Sella & Mosca	766
Alido Bianco, Cast. Fageto	628
Aliera, La Rendola	597
Alleroso, Spadaio e Piecorto	580
Allodio Rosso, Podere San Michele	603
Allora Aglianico, Calatrasi Puglia	718
Allora Negroamaro, Calatrasi Puglia	718
Allora Primitivo, Calatrasi Puglia	718
Almabruna, I Campetti	601
Almanera, Fatascià	754
Almerita Brut, Tasca d'Almerita	758
Alta Langa Brut M. Cl., Vigne Regali	140
Alta Langa M. Cl. Anteprima Giulio Cocchi, Bava	68
Altavilla della Corte Bianco, Casa Vinicola Firriato	754
Alte d'Altesi, Altesino	499
Altre Uve Passito, Vallona	426
Alzero Cabernet Franc, Giuseppe Quintarelli	306
Amabile Persolino Rosso Passito, Istituto Professionale per l'Agricoltura e l'Ambiente	429
Amarone della Valpolicella, Corte Sant'Alda	296
Amarone della Valpolicella, Musella	312
Amarone della Valpolicella, Luigino e Marco Provolo	340
Amarone della Valpolicella, Giuseppe Quintarelli	306
Amarone della Valpolicella, Trabucchi	291
Amarone della Valpolicella Brolo delle Giare, Tezza	334
Amarone della Valpolicella Campo dei Gigli, Tenuta Sant'Antonio	297
Amarone della Valpolicella Cl., Allegrini	288
Amarone della Valpolicella Cl., Lorenzo Begali	314
Amarone della Valpolicella Cl., Bertani	304
Amarone della Valpolicella Cl., Brigaldara	314
Amarone della Valpolicella Cl., Luigi Brunelli	315
Amarone della Valpolicella Cl., Ca' La Bionda	293
Amarone della Valpolicella Cl. , Giuseppe Campagnola	293
Amarone della Valpolicella Cl., Gerardo Cesari	337
Amarone della Valpolicella Cl., Corte Lenguin	342
Amarone della Valpolicella Cl., Corteforte	339
Amarone della Valpolicella Cl., F.lli Degani	295
Amarone della Valpolicella Cl., Guerrieri Rizzardi	283
Amarone della Valpolicella Cl., I Scriani	339
Amarone della Valpolicella Cl., Le Bertarole	339
Amarone della Valpolicella Cl., Le Ragose	305
Amarone della Valpolicella Cl., Lenotti	337
Amarone della Valpolicella Cl., Giuseppe Lonardi	295
Amarone della Valpolicella Cl., Novaia	296
Amarone della Valpolicella Cl., Raimondi-Villa Monteleone	320
Amarone della Valpolicella Cl., F.lli Recchia	341
Amarone della Valpolicella Cl., Santa Sofia	316
Amarone della Valpolicella Cl., Casa Vinicola Sartori	341
Amarone della Valpolicella Cl., F.lli Tedeschi	317
Amarone della Valpolicella Cl., Viticoltori Tommasi	317
Amarone della Valpolicella Cl., Massimino Venturini	318
Amarone della Valpolicella Cl., Villa Bellini	318
Amarone della Valpolicella Cl., Villa Spinosa	307
Amarone della Valpolicella Cl., Zenato	309
Amarone della Valpolicella Cl., F.lli Zeni	284
Amarone della Valpolicella Cl. Acinatico, Stefano Accordini	313
Amarone della Valpolicella Cl. Alzaro delle Corvine, Igino Accordini	342
Amarone della Valpolicella Cl. Ambrosan, Angelo Nicolis e Figli	315
Amarone della Valpolicella Cl. Barrique, F.lli Zeni	284
Amarone della Valpolicella Cl. BG, Tommaso Bussola	304
Amarone della Valpolicella Cl. Ca' de Loi, Paolo Boscaini & Figli	339
Amarone della Valpolicella Cl. Ca' Florian, Viticoltori Tommasi	317
Amarone della Valpolicella Cl. Calcarole, Guerrieri Rizzardi	283
Amarone della Valpolicella Cl. Campo Casalin I Castei, Michele Castellani	294
Amarone della Valpolicella Cl. Campo del Titari, Luigi Brunelli	315
Amarone della Valpolicella Cl. Campo Inferi, Luigi Brunelli	315
Amarone della Valpolicella Cl. Campo S. Paolo, Raimondi-Villa Monteleone	320
Amarone della Valpolicella Cl. Campolongo di Torbe, Masi	319
Amarone della Valpolicella Cl. Capitel della Crosara, Giacomo Montresor	333
Amarone della Valpolicella Cl. Capitel Monte Olmi, F.lli Tedeschi	317
Amarone della Valpolicella Cl. Casa dei Bepi, Viviani	307
Amarone della Valpolicella Cl. Caterina Zardini, Giuseppe Campagnola	293
Amarone della Valpolicella Cl. Corte Bra, Casa Vinicola Sartori	341
Amarone della Valpolicella Cl. Costasera, Masi	319
Amarone della Valpolicella Cl. Gioé, Santa Sofia	316
Amarone della Valpolicella Cl. I Fondatori, F.lli Fabiano	343
Amarone della Valpolicella Cl. I Quadretti, La Giaretta	340
Amarone della Valpolicella Cl. Il Bosco, Gerardo Cesari	337
Amarone della Valpolicella Cl. La Bastia, Eugenio Tinazzi & Figli	
Amarone della Valpolicella Cl. La Marega, Le Salette	289
Amarone della Valpolicella Cl. La Rosta, F.lli Degani	295
Amarone della Valpolicella Cl. Le Balze, Novaia	296
Amarone della Valpolicella Cl. Le Bessole, Igino Accordini	342
Amarone della Valpolicella Cl. Le Vigne Ca' del Pipa, Michele Castellani	294
Amarone della Valpolicella Cl. Manara, C.S. Valpolicella	306
Amarone della Valpolicella Cl. Marano, Paolo Boscaini & Figli	339
Amarone della Valpolicella Cl. Marta Galli, Le Ragose	305
Amarone della Valpolicella Cl. Monte Masua Il Sestante, Viticoltori Tommasi	317
Amarone della Valpolicella Cl. Pergole Vece, Le Salette	289
Amarone della Valpolicella Cl. Postera, Guido Manara	342
Amarone della Valpolicella Cl. Punta di Villa, Roberto Mazzi	305
Amarone della Valpolicella Cl. Raghos, Le Ragose	305
Amarone della Valpolicella Cl. Rovertondo Vallesele, Eugenio Tinazzi & Figli	337
Amarone della Valpolicella Cl. Sergio Zenato Ris., Zenato	309
Amarone della Valpolicella Cl. Sup. Monte Cà Paletta, Giuseppe Quintarelli	306
Amarone della Valpolicella Cl. Sup. Ris., Giuseppe Quintarelli	306
Amarone della Valpolicella Cl. TB, Tommaso Bussola	304
Amarone della Valpolicella Cl. TB Vign. Alto , Tommaso Bussola	304
Amarone della Valpolicella Cl. Terre di Cariano, Cecilia Beretta	332
Amarone della Valpolicella Cl. Tulipano Nero, Viviani	307
Amarone della Valpolicella Cl. Vaio Armaron Serègo Alighieri, Masi	319
Amarone della Valpolicella Cl. Vigne Alte, F.lli Zeni	284
Amarone della Valpolicella Cl. Vigneti di Jago Sel., C.S. Valpolicella	306
Amarone della Valpolicella Cl. Vigneti di Osan, Corteforte	339
Amarone della Valpolicella Cl. Vigneti di Ravazzol, Ca' La Bionda	293
Amarone della Valpolicella Cl. Vign. Alto, Tommaso Bussola	304
Amarone della Valpolicella Cl. Vign. Ca' Bertoldi, F.lli Recchia	341
Amarone della Valpolicella Cl. Vign. Il Fornetto, Stefano Accordini	313
Amarone della Valpolicella Cl. Vign. Monte Ca' Bianca, Lorenzo Begali	314
Amarone della Valpolicella Cl. Vign. Monte Danieli, Corte Rugolin	294

Amarone della Valpolicella Cl. Vign. Monte Sant'Urbano, F.lli Speri	316
Amarone della Valpolicella Cl. Villa Borghetti, Pasqua Vigneti e Cantine	333
Amarone della Valpolicella Falasco, C.S. della Valpantena	334
Amarone della Valpolicella Mithas, Corte Sant'Alda	296
Amarone della Valpolicella Monte delle Fontane, Tezza	334
Amarone della Valpolicella Proemio, Santi	291
Amarone della Valpolicella Ris., Giuseppe Quintarelli	306
Amarone della Valpolicella Rocca Sveva, Cant. di Soave	321
Amarone della Valpolicella Roccolo Grassi, Roccolo Grassi	297
Amarone della Valpolicella Sacramoso, Pasqua Vigneti e Cantine	333
Amarone della Valpolicella San Cassian, Luigino e Marco Provolo	340
Amarone della Valpolicella Valpantena, C.S. della Valpantena	334
Amarone della Valpolicella Vign. di Monte Lodoletta, Romano Dal Forno	290
Amativo, Cantele	724
Ambrato del Notaio, Il Montù	218
Amineo Bianco Donnacaterina, Dattilo	738
Amineo Rosso, Dattilo	738
Amistar Bianco, Peter Sölva & Söhne - Paterbichl	266
Amistar Rosso, Peter Sölva & Söhne - Paterbichl	266
Amistar Rosso Edizione, Peter Sölva & Söhne - Paterbichl	266
Amor Costante, Le Chiuse di Sotto	513
Amoroso Passito, Le Tende	292
Ancellotta, Stefano Spezia	217
Anchigi, Cima	497
Andias, Cantine di Dolianova	769
Anfidiamante, Fatt. del Teso	524
Anfiteatro, Vecchie Terre di Montefili	544
Anghelos, Tenuta De Angelis	613
Angialis, Antonio Argiolas	775
Angimbé, Cusumano	756
Anima, Livernano	552
Ansonica Costa dell'Argentario, La Parrina	539
Ansonica dell'Elba, Acquabona	600
Antair, Il Palagione	565
Anthos, Prima & Nuova/Erste & Neue	265
Antinoo, Casale del Giglio	663
Aprico Rosato, San Gervasio	598
Aquileia Cabernet, Zonin	290
Aquileia Chardonnay, Zonin	290
Aquileia Merlot, Zonin	290
Aquileia Refosco P. R., Cant. Prod. di Cormons	361
Araja, C.S. di Santadi	773
Arbeskia, Giuseppe Gabbas	772
Arbiato, Barone Scammacca del Murgo	764
Arbis Rosso, Borgo San Daniele	359
Arborea Sangiovese, C.S. Marrubiu	779
Arcana Bianco, Terre Bianche	168
Arcana Rosso, Terre Bianche	168
Arcato Sangiovese, Spoletoducale	660
Arciato, Cardeto	651
Arcibaldo, Cennatoio Intervineas	541
Arcolaio, Leone Conti	428
Ardingo, Andrea Costanti	507
Aresco Passito, Corte Rugolin	294
Areté, Cantine Rallo	751
Arghillà, Vintripodi Calabria	742
Argiolas, Antonio Argiolas	775
Arguzzio, Villa Arceno	473
Ariento, Massa Vecchia	497
Arkezia Muffo di S. Sisto, Fazi Battaglia	613
Arline Élevé en Fût de Chêne, Anselmet	19
Armaleo, Palazzone	653
Armecolo, Castel di Salve	730
Armonia, Lorella Ambrosini	573
Arte, Domenico Clerico	104
Artias Chardonnay, Rio Maggio	622
Artias Pinot Nero, Rio Maggio	622
Artias Sauvignon, Rio Maggio	622
Arturo Bersano Ris. M. Cl., Bersano & Riccadonna	123
Arvino, Statti	739
Arzimo Passito, La Cappuccina	302
Asprinio d'Aversa Fescine, Cantine Caputo	691
Assajè Rosso, Capichera	767
Assisi Rosso, Sportoletti	656
Astangia, Alberto Loi	769
Asti, Cascina Fonda	101
Asti, I V.ioli di S. Stefano	134
Asti Cascina Palazzo Sel., F.lli Bera	122
Asti De Miranda M. Cl., Contratto	55
Ateo, Ciacci Piccolomini D'Aragona	506
Atina Cabernet, Giovanni Palombo	663
Aura, Vallis Agri	226
Aureo, Giovanni Donda	346
Aureus, Josef Niedermayr	253
Ausente, Migliarese	674
Avra, Giuseppe Gabbas	772
Avvoltore, Moris Farms	498
Azobé Corvina Vign. delle Pergole, Albino Piona	343
Azzurreta, La Togata - Tenuta Carlina	512
Baccante, Abbazia Santa Anastasia	747
Bacco Rosato, Malena	737
Badia Raustignolo, Il Pratello	434
Balajana, C.S. Gallura	777
Balifico, Cast. di Volpaia	555
Ballistarius, Letrari	239
Barbaleone, Vanzini	221
Barbanico, Nicola Balter	238
Barbaresco, Ca' Rome' - Romano Marengo	30
Barbaresco, Cascina Vano	118
Barbaresco, Fontanabianca	119
Barbaresco, Gaja	32
Barbaresco, Gastaldi	119
Barbaresco, Gianluigi Lano	25
Barbaresco, Ottavio Lequio - Prinsi	157
Barbaresco, Fiorenzo Nada	143
Barbaresco, Pelissero	144
Barbaresco, V.ioli Elvio Pertinace	144
Barbaresco, Pio Cesare	26
Barbaresco, Prod. del Barbaresco	35
Barbaresco, Punset	157
Barbaresco Ad Altiora, Michele Taliano	113
Barbaresco Asij, Ceretto	25
Barbaresco Asili, Ca' del Baio	142
Barbaresco Asili, Bruno Giacosa	120
Barbaresco Asili Barrique, Ca' del Baio	142
Barbaresco Asili Ris., Bruno Giacosa	120
Barbaresco Basarin, Moccagatta	33
Barbaresco Bernardot Bricco Asili, Bricco Rocche - Bricco Asili	62
Barbaresco Bric Balin, Moccagatta	33
Barbaresco Bric Turot, Prunotto	27
Barbaresco Bricco, Pio Cesare	26
Barbaresco Bricco Asli, Bricco Rocche - Bricco Asili	62
Barbaresco Bricco Libero, Rino Varaldo	36
Barbaresco Bricco Mondino, Piero Busso	117
Barbaresco Camp Gros, Tenuta Cisa Asinari dei Marchesi di Grésy	31
Barbaresco Campo Quadro, Punset	157
Barbaresco Canova, Cascina Vano	118
Barbaresco Cascina Bordino, Tenuta Carretta	126
Barbaresco Cichin, Ada Nada	143
Barbaresco Cole, Moccagatta	33
Barbaresco Coparossa, Bruno Rocca	36
Barbaresco Costa Russi, Gaja	32
Barbaresco Coste Rubìn, Fontanafredda	136
Barbaresco Cottà, Sottimano	122
Barbaresco Cottà V. Brichet, Sottimano	122
Barbaresco Crichèt Pajé, I Paglieri	34
Barbaresco Curà, Cant. del Glicine	156
Barbaresco Currà, Sottimano	122
Barbaresco Faset, Marziano e Enrico Abbona	74
Barbaresco Faset, Cast. di Verduno	146
Barbaresco Faset Bricco Asili, Bricco Rocche - Bricco Asili	62
Barbaresco Fausoni, Sottimano	122
Barbaresco Fausoni V. del Salto, Sottimano	122
Barbaresco Gaiun, Tenuta Cisa Asinari dei Marchesi di Grésy	31
Barbaresco Gallina, Ugo Lequio	121
Barbaresco Gallina, Ottavio Lequio - Prinsi	157
Barbaresco La Rocca di S. Stefano, Cast. di Neive	157
Barbaresco Marcorino, Cant. del Glicine	156
Barbaresco Maria di Brun, Ca' Rome' - Romano Marengo	30
Barbaresco Martinenga, Tenuta Cisa Asinari dei Marchesi di Grésy	31
Barbaresco Montefico, Carlo Giacosa	32
Barbaresco Morassino, Cascina Morassino	150
Barbaresco Narin, Carlo Giacosa	32
Barbaresco Nervo, V.ioli Elvio Pertinace	144
Barbaresco Ovello, Cant. del Pino	30
Barbaresco Ovello, Cascina Morassino	150
Barbaresco Pajé, I Paglieri	34
Barbaresco Pajoré, Sottimano	122
Barbaresco Rabajà, Cast. di Verduno	146
Barbaresco Rabajà, Giuseppe Cortese	31
Barbaresco Rabajà, Cascina Luisin	33
Barbaresco Rabajà, Bruno Rocca	36
Barbaresco Rabajà Ris., Cast. di Verduno	146
Barbaresco Rio Sordo, F.lli Giacosa	120
Barbaresco Riserva Grande Annata, Marchesi di Barolo	39
Barbaresco Rombone, Fiorenzo Nada	143
Barbaresco Roncaglie, Bel Colle	145
Barbaresco S. Stefano, Cast. di Neive	157
Barbaresco Serraboella, F.lli Cigliuti	118
Barbaresco Sorì Burdin, Fontanabianca	119
Barbaresco Sorì Loreto, Rino Varaldo	36
Barbaresco Sörì Montaribaldi, Montaribaldi	34
Barbaresco Sorì Paitin, Paitin	121
Barbaresco Sorì Paitin Vecchie Vigne, Paitin	121
Barbaresco Sorì Pajolin, Cascina Luisin	33
Barbaresco Sorì Rio Sordo, Ca' Rome' - Romano Marengo	30
Barbaresco Sorì S. Lorenzo, Gaja	32
Barbaresco Sorì Tildin, Gaja	32
Barbaresco Tenuta Roncaglia, Poderi Colla	26
Barbaresco Valeirano, Ada Nada	143
Barbaresco Valgrande, Ca' del Baio	142
Barbaresco Vanotu, Pelissero	144
Barbaresco V. Borgese, Piero Busso	117
Barbaresco V. Montersino, Orlando Abrigo	160
Barbaresco V. Rongallo, Orlando Abrigo	160
Barbaresco Vigneti in Asili Ris., Prod. del Barbaresco	35
Barbaresco Vigneti in Moccagatta Ris., Prod. del Barbaresco	35
Barbaresco Vigneti in Montestefano Ris., Prod. del Barbaresco	35
Barbaresco Vigneti in Ovello Ris., Prod. del Barbaresco	35
Barbaresco Vigneti in Pajé Ris., Prod. del Barbaresco	35
Barbaresco Vigneti in Pora Ris., Prod. del Barbaresco	35
Barbaresco Vigneti in Rabajà Ris., Prod. del Barbaresco	35

Barbaresco Vigneti in Rio Sordo Ris., Prod. del Barbaresco	35
Barbaresco Vign. Brich Ronchi, Albino Rocca	35
Barbaresco Vign. Castellizzano, V.ioli Elvio Pertinace	144
Barbaresco Vign. Gallina, La Spinetta	58
Barbaresco Vign. Loreto, Albino Rocca	35
Barbaresco Vign. Marcarini, V.ioli Elvio Pertinace	144
Barbaresco Vign. Nervo, V.ioli Elvio Pertinace	144
Barbaresco Vign. Starderi, La Spinetta	58
Barbaresco Vign. Valeirano, La Spinetta	58
Barbarossa V. del Dosso, Fatt. Paradiso	423
Barbazzale Bianco, Cottanera	748
Barbazzale Rosso, Cottanera	748
Barbera d'Alba, Gianfranco Alessandria	104
Barbera d'Alba, F.lli Alessandria	145
Barbera d'Alba, Elio Altare - Cascina Nuova	88
Barbera d'Alba, F.lli Bera	122
Barbera d'Alba, Enzo Boglietti	89
Barbera d'Alba, Cascina Bongiovanni	62
Barbera d'Alba, Giacomo Borgogno & Figli	37
Barbera d'Alba, Cascina Ca' Rossa	50
Barbera d'Alba, Cant. del Pino	30
Barbera d'Alba, Cascina Cucco	136
Barbera d'Alba, Cascina Vano	118
Barbera d'Alba, Giovanni Corino	90
Barbera d'Alba, Matteo Correggia	51
Barbera d'Alba, Damilano	38
Barbera d'Alba, Sergio Degiorgis	101
Barbera d'Alba, Destefanis	114
Barbera d'Alba, Fontanabianca	119
Barbera d'Alba, Funtanin	52
Barbera d'Alba, Gabutti - Franco Boasso	137
Barbera d'Alba, Filippo Gallino	53
Barbera d'Alba, Silvio Grasso	91
Barbera d'Alba, Hilberg - Pasquero	127
Barbera d'Alba, Gianluigi Lano	25
Barbera d'Alba, Giovanni Manzone	108
Barbera d'Alba, Moccagatta	33
Barbera d'Alba, Mauro Molino	92
Barbera d'Alba, Monfalletto - Cordero di Montezemolo	93
Barbera d'Alba, Monti	109
Barbera d'Alba, Fiorenzo Nada	143
Barbera d'Alba, Andrea Oberto	93
Barbera d'Alba, Cascina Pellerino	115
Barbera d'Alba, Fabrizio Pinsoglio	60
Barbera d'Alba, Pioiero	160
Barbera d'Alba, E. Pira - Chiara Boschis & Figli	40
Barbera d'Alba, Poderi Colla	26
Barbera d'Alba, Porello	54
Barbera d'Alba, Prunotto	27
Barbera d'Alba, F.lli Revello	95
Barbera d'Alba, Bruno Rocca	36
Barbera d'Alba, Ruggeri Corsini	111
Barbera d'Alba, Luciano Sandrone	41
Barbera d'Alba, Giorgio Scarzello e Figli	41
Barbera d'Alba, F.lli Seghesio	112
Barbera d'Alba, G. D. Vajra	43
Barbera d'Alba, Cascina Val del Prete	128
Barbera d'Alba, Rino Varaldo	36
Barbera d'Alba, Mauro Veglio	96
Barbera d'Alba, Vielmin	60
Barbera d'Alba, V. Rionda - Massolino	138
Barbera d'Alba A Bon Rendre, Michele Taliano	113
Barbera d'Alba Affinata in Carati, Paolo Scavino	64
Barbera d'Alba Annunziata, Rocche Costamagna	95
Barbera d'Alba Asili, Cascina Luisin	33
Barbera d'Alba Asili Barrique, Cascina Luisin	33
Barbera d'Alba Aves, G. B. Burlotto	146
Barbera d'Alba Basarin, Moccagatta	33
Barbera d'Alba Bramè, Deltetto	52
Barbera d'Alba Brea, Brovia	63
Barbera d'Alba Bric Bertu, Angelo Negro & Figli	115
Barbera d'Alba Bric La Rondolina, Fabrizio Pinsoglio	60
Barbera d'Alba Bric Loira, Cascina Chicco	51
Barbera d'Alba Bric Torretta, Porello	54
Barbera d'Alba Bricco 4 Fratelli, Boroli	24
Barbera d'Alba Bricco dei Merli, Elvio Cogno	125
Barbera d'Alba Bricco del Cuculo, Cast. di Verduno	146
Barbera d'Alba Bricco delle Viole, G. D. Vajra	43
Barbera d'Alba Bricco Valpiana, Valerio Aloi	156
Barbera d'Alba Brunet, Fontanabianca	119
Barbera d'Alba Campass, F.lli Cigliuti	118
Barbera d'Alba Campolive, Paitin	121
Barbera d'Alba Carulot, Cascina Vano	118
Barbera d'Alba Cascina Nuova, Mauro Veglio	96
Barbera d'Alba Castellinaldo, Vielmin	60
Barbera d'Alba Ciabot della Luna, Gianni Voerzio	97
Barbera d'Alba Ciabot du Re, F.lli Revello	95
Barbera d'Alba Ciabot Pierin, Funtanin	52
Barbera d'Alba Codana, Giuseppe Mascarello e Figlio	103
Barbera d'Alba Croere, Terre da Vino	42
Barbera d'Alba Donatella, Luigi Baudana	135
Barbera d'Alba Donna Margherita, Giovanni Rosso	159
Barbera d'Alba dü Gir, Montaribaldi	34
Barbera d'Alba Falletto, Bruno Giacosa	120
Barbera d'Alba Fides, Pio Cesare	26
Barbera d'Alba Flin, Paolo Monte - Cascina Flino	153
Barbera d'Alba Fondo Prà, Gianluigi Lano	25
Barbera d'Alba Fontanile, Silvio Grasso	91
Barbera d'Alba Fornaci, Giacomo Grimaldi	38
Barbera d'Alba Gallina, Ugo Lequio	121
Barbera d'Alba Gepin, Albino Rocca	35
Barbera d'Alba Giada, Andrea Oberto	93
Barbera d'Alba Ginestra, Paolo Conterno	106
Barbera d'Alba Giuli, Cascina Ballarin	90
Barbera d'Alba Goretta, F.lli Ferrero	155
Barbera d'Alba Granera Alta, Cascina Chicco	51
Barbera d'Alba Il Ciotto, Gianfranco Bovio	89
Barbera d'Alba La Gamberaja, Ca' Rome' - Romano Marengo	30
Barbera d'Alba La Priora, F.lli Alessandria	145
Barbera d'Alba La Romualda, Ferdinando Principiano	110
Barbera d'Alba La Serra, Giovanni Manzone	108
Barbera d'Alba Laboriosa, Michele Taliano	113
Barbera d'Alba Lina, Carlo Giacosa	32
Barbera d'Alba Maggiur, Cascina Luisin	33
Barbera d'Alba Mancine, Osvaldo Viberti	97
Barbera d'Alba Maria Gioana, F.lli Giacosa	120
Barbera d'Alba Marun, Matteo Correggia	51
Barbera d'Alba MonBirone, Monchiero Carbone	54
Barbera d'Alba Morassina, Giuseppe Cortese	31
Barbera d'Alba Mucin, Carlo Giacosa	32
Barbera d'Alba Mulassa, Cascina Ca' Rossa	50
Barbera d'Alba Nicolon, Angelo Negro & Figli	115
Barbera d'Alba Pairolero, Sottimano	122
Barbera d'Alba Pajagal, Marchesi di Barolo	39
Barbera d'Alba Parussi, Gianfranco Bovio	89
Barbera d'Alba Pian Romualdo, Prunotto	27
Barbera d'Alba Piana, Ceretto	25
Barbera d'Alba Piani, Pelissero	144
Barbera d'Alba Pistin, Giacomo Grimaldi	38
Barbera d'Alba Podium Serre, Tenuta Carretta	126
Barbera d'Alba Regiaveja, Gianfranco Bovio	89
Barbera d'Alba Rinaldi, Marziano e Enrico Abbona	74
Barbera d'Alba Rocca delle Marasche, Deltetto	52
Barbera d'Alba Rocche delle Rocche, Rocche Costamagna	95
Barbera d'Alba Roscaleto, Enzo Boglietti	89
Barbera d'Alba Ruvei, Marchesi di Barolo	39
Barbera d'Alba S. Cristoforo, Marsaglia	151
Barbera d'Alba S. Michele, Malvirà	53
Barbera d'Alba S. Rosalia, Mauro Sebaste	27
Barbera d'Alba S. Stefano di Perno, Giuseppe Mascarello e Figlio	103
Barbera d'Alba Salgà, Ada Nada	143
Barbera d'Alba San Quirico, Casavecchia	153
Barbera d'Alba Scarrone, Vietti	65
Barbera d'Alba Scarrone V. Vecchia, Vietti	65
Barbera d'Alba Serra Boella, Paitin	121
Barbera d'Alba Serraboella, F.lli Cigliuti	118
Barbera d'Alba Sovrana, Batasiolo	88
Barbera d'Alba Srëi, Vielmin	60
Barbera d'Alba Sup., F.lli Bera	122
Barbera d'Alba Sup., Filippo Gallino	53
Barbera d'Alba Sup., Hilberg - Pasquero	127
Barbera d'Alba Sup., Armando Parusso	109
Barbera d'Alba Sup., Flavio Roddolo	111
Barbera d'Alba Sup., Giorgio Scarzello e Figli	41
Barbera d'Alba Sup., Tenuta La Volta - Cabutto	42
Barbera d'Alba Sup., Terre del Barolo	64
Barbera d'Alba Sup., G. D. Vajra	43
Barbera d'Alba Sup. Armujan, Ruggeri Corsini	111
Barbera d'Alba Sup. Bricco delle Viole, Tenuta La Volta - Cabutto	42
Barbera d'Alba Sup. Carolina, Cascina Val del Prete	128
Barbera d'Alba Sup. Funtani, Monfalletto - Cordero di Montezemolo	93
Barbera d'Alba Sup. Gran Madre, Cascina Pellerino	115
Barbera d'Alba Sup. Le Masche, Bel Colle	145
Barbera d'Alba Sup. Papagena, Fontanafredda	136
Barbera d'Alba Surì di Mù, Icardi	66
Barbera d'Alba Torriglione, Renato Ratti	94
Barbera d'Alba Trevigne, Domenico Clerico	104
Barbera d'Alba Valbianchera, Giovanni Almondo	113
Barbera d'Alba Valdisera, Terre del Barolo	64
Barbera d'Alba Valletta, Claudio Alario	73
Barbera d'Alba V. 'a Pierin, Ada Nada	143
Barbera d'Alba V. Clara, Eraldo Viberti	96
Barbera d'Alba V. dei Dardi, Alessandro e Gian Natale Fantino	107
Barbera d'Alba V. dei Romani, Enzo Boglietti	89
Barbera d'Alba V. del Cuculo, F.lli Cavallotto	63
Barbera d'Alba V. della Madre, Ettore Germano	137
Barbera d'Alba V. delle Fate, Rino Varaldo	36
Barbera d'Alba V. Erta, Poderi Sinaglio	28
Barbera d'Alba V. Fontanelle, Ascheri	46
Barbera d'Alba V. Gattere, Mauro Molino	92
Barbera d'Alba V. Lisi, Attilio Ghisolfi	107
Barbera d'Alba V. Majano, Piero Busso	117
Barbera d'Alba V. Martina, Elio Grasso	108
Barbera d'Alba V. Pozzo, Giovanni Corino	90
Barbera d'Alba V. S. Lorenzo, Bartolo Mascarello	39
Barbera d'Alba V. Vigia, Bricco Maiolica	73
Barbera d'Alba Vign. Boscato, G. B. Burlotto	146
Barbera d'Alba Vign. della Chiesa, F.lli Seghesio	112
Barbera d'Alba Vign. Gallina, La Spinetta	58
Barbera d'Alba Vign. Pozzo dell'Annunziata Ris., Roberto Voerzio	98
Barbera d'Alba Vign. Punta, Azelia	61
Barbera d'Alba Vignot, Cascina Morassino	150
Barbera d'Alba Vignota, Conterno Fantino	106
Barbera d'Alba Vittoria, Gianfranco Alessandria	104
Barbera d'Asti, Cascina Barisél	55
Barbera d'Asti, Ca' Bianca	29
Barbera d'Asti, Cascina Castlèt	71
Barbera d'Asti, Cascina Giovinale	157

Barbera d'Asti, Cascina Roera	71
Barbera d'Asti, Cast. del Poggio	127
Barbera d'Asti, Roberto Ferraris	22
Barbera d'Asti, Sergio Grimaldi - Ca' du Sindic	133
Barbera d'Asti, Liedholm	152
Barbera d'Asti, Ne. Ne.	151
Barbera d'Asti, Tenuta Olim Bauda	87
Barbera d'Asti, Luigi Spertino	156
Barbera d'Asti, Valfieri	72
Barbera d'Asti, C.S. di Vinchio - Vaglio Serra	149
Barbera d'Asti Ai Suma, Braida	129
Barbera d'Asti Bassina, Marenco	140
Barbera d'Asti Brentura, Erede di Armando Chiappone	157
Barbera d'Asti Bric dei Banditi, Franco M. Martinetti	141
Barbera d'Asti Bric Stupui, Isabella	116
Barbera d'Asti Bricco Blina, Agostino Pavia e Figli	23
Barbera d'Asti Bricco dell'Uccellone, Braida	129
Barbera d'Asti Bricco della Bigotta, Braida	129
Barbera d'Asti Bricco Garitta, Cascina Garitina	59
Barbera d'Asti Ca' di Pian, La Spinetta	58
Barbera d'Asti Camp du Rouss, Luigi Coppo e Figli	56
Barbera d'Asti Camparò, La Ghersa	102
Barbera d'Asti Carlotta, Tenuta dell'Arbiola	132
Barbera d'Asti Cast. di Calosso, Tenuta dei Fiori	49
Barbera d'Asti Chersì, Ca' Bianca	29
Barbera d'Asti Ciresa, Marenco	140
Barbera d'Asti Costamiòle, Prunotto	27
Barbera d'Asti Cremosina, Bersano & Riccadonna	123
Barbera d'Asti Emozioni, Tenuta La Tenaglia	139
Barbera d'Asti Fiulòt, Prunotto	27
Barbera d'Asti Frem, Scagliola	49
Barbera d'Asti Giarone, Poderi Bertelli	70
Barbera d'Asti Giorgio Tenaglia, Tenuta La Tenaglia	139
Barbera d'Asti Grivò, Elio Perrone	67
Barbera d'Asti I Filari Lunghi, Valfieri	72
Barbera d'Asti Il Bergantino, Bricco Mondalino	147
Barbera d'Asti Is, Tenuta dei Fiori	49
Barbera d'Asti 'l Sulì, La Zucca	117
Barbera d'Asti La Barbatella, Cascina La Barbatella	123
Barbera d'Asti La Crena, Vietti	65
Barbera d'Asti La Cricca, Roberto Ferraris	22
Barbera d'Asti La Luna e i Falò, Terre da Vino	42
Barbera d'Asti La Marescialla, Agostino Pavia e Figli	23
Barbera d'Asti La Solista, Caudrina	65
Barbera d'Asti La Tota, Marchesi Alfieri	131
Barbera d'Asti Le Gagie, Tenuta La Meridiana	114
Barbera d'Asti Lia Vì, Ca 'd Carussin	159
Barbera d'Asti Libera, Bava	68
Barbera d'Asti Martizza, La Zucca	117
Barbera d'Asti Martleina, Ne. Ne.	151
Barbera d'Asti Masaréj Gianni Zonin Vineyards, Cast. del Poggio	127
Barbera d'Asti Moliss, Agostino Pavia e Figli	23
Barbera d'Asti Mongovone, Elio Perrone	67
Barbera d'Asti Monte del Mare, La Giribaldina	48
Barbera d'Asti Montetusa, Poderi Bertelli	70
Barbera d'Asti Nuj Suj, Icardi	66
Barbera d'Asti Panta Rei, Contratto	55
Barbera d'Asti Pian Bosco, Karin e Remo Hohler	57
Barbera d'Asti Pian Bosco Barrique, Karin e Remo Hohler	57
Barbera d'Asti Pomorosso, Luigi Coppo e Figli	56
Barbera d'Asti Quorum, Hastae	48
Barbera d'Asti Riserva della Famiglia, Luigi Coppo e Figli	56
Barbera d'Asti Rodotiglia Cast. di Calosso, Tenuta dei Fiori	49
Barbera d'Asti Rubermillo, Casalone	100
Barbera d' Asti Rubis, La Caplana	150
Barbera d'Asti S. Antonio Vieilles Vignes, Poderi Bertelli	70
Barbera d'Asti San Nicolao, Terre da Vino	42
Barbera d'Asti Sanbastiàn, Dacapo	22
Barbera d'Asti SanSì, Scagliola	49
Barbera d'Asti SanSì Sel., Scagliola	49
Barbera d'Asti Sel. Gaudium Magnum, Bricco Mondalino	147
Barbera d'Asti Solus Ad, Contratto	55
Barbera d'Asti Sup., Guido Berta	159
Barbera d'Asti Sup., La Spinetta	58
Barbera d'Asti Sup., Tenuta Olim Bauda	87
Barbera d'Asti Sup., Valfieri	72
Barbera d'Asti Sup., C.S. di Vinchio - Vaglio Serra	149
Barbera d'Asti Sup. Acsé, Franco e Mario Scrimaglio	124
Barbera d'Asti Sup. Ajan, Villa Giada	56
Barbera d'Asti Sup. Alfiera, Marchesi Alfieri	131
Barbera d'Asti Sup. Altea, Cantine Sant'Agata	135
Barbera d'Asti Sup. Anssèma, Cascina Giovinale	157
Barbera d'Asti Sup. Arbest, Bava	68
Barbera d'Asti Sup. Balau, Carlo Benotto	70
Barbera d'Asti Sup. Beneficio, Sciorio	72
Barbera d'Asti Sup. Bric d'Alì, Renzo Beccaris	152
Barbera d'Asti Sup. Bricco Dani, Villa Giada	56
Barbera d'Asti Sup. Bricco dei Cappuccini, Cascina Orsolina	156
Barbera d'Asti Sup. Bricco della Volpettona, Ermanno e Alessandra Brema	86
Barbera d'Asti Sup. Bricco S. Ippolito, Franco e Mario Scrimaglio	124
Barbera d'Asti Sup. Bricco Sereno, Tenuta La Meridiana	114
Barbera d'Asti Sup. Bricconizza, Ermanno e Alessandra Brema	86
Barbera d'Asti Sup. Cala delle Mandrie, La Giribaldina	48
Barbera d'Asti Sup. Campasso, Tenuta Cast. di Razzano	28
Barbera d'Asti Sup. Canto di Luna, Guido Berta	159
Barbera d'Asti Sup. Cardin, Cascina Roera	71
Barbera d'Asti Sup. Cardin Ris., Cascina Roera	71
Barbera d'Asti Sup. Cascina Croce, Ermanno e Alessandra Brema	86
Barbera d'Asti Sup. Cavalé, Cantine Sant'Agata	135
Barbera d'Asti Sup. Cipressi della Court, Michele Chiarlo	47
Barbera d'Asti Sup. Collina della Vedova, Alfiero Boffa	131
Barbera d'Asti Sup. Croutin, Franco e Mario Scrimaglio	124
Barbera d'Asti Sup. Favà, Tenuta Garetto	23
Barbera d'Asti Sup. Ferro Carlo , Ca 'd Carussin	159
Barbera d'Asti Sup. Gaiana, Malgrà	102
Barbera d'Asti Sup. Generala, Bersano & Riccadonna	123
Barbera d'Asti Sup. Giorgione, Villa Fiorita	152
Barbera d'Asti Sup. I Filari Lunghi, Valfieri	72
Barbera d'Asti Sup. Il Sogno, Franco e Mario Scrimaglio	124
Barbera d'Asti Sup. In Pectore, Tenuta Garetto	23
Barbera d'Asti Sup. La Bellalda d'Oro, Ca' dei Mandorli	152
Barbera d'Asti Sup. La Bogliona, Scarpa - Antica Casa Vinicola	124
Barbera d'Asti Sup. La Cappelletta, Cascina Barisél	55
Barbera d'Asti Sup. La Court, Michele Chiarlo	47
Barbera d'Asti Sup.La Luna e i Falò, Terre da Vino	42
Barbera d'Asti Sup. La Romilda V, Tenuta dell'Arbiola	132
Barbera d'Asti Sup. La V.ssa, La Ghersa	102
Barbera d'Asti Sup. Lurèi, Tenuta Il Falchetto	159
Barbera d'Asti Sup. Monte Venere, Caudrina	65
Barbera d'Asti Sup. Montruc, Franco M. Martinetti	141
Barbera d'Asti Sup. Mora di Sassi, Malgrà	102
Barbera d'Asti Sup. Neuvsent, Cascina Garitina	59
Barbera d'Asti Sup. Nizza, Bersano & Riccadonna	123
Barbera d'Asti Sup. Nizza, Erede di Armando Chiappone	157
Barbera d'Asti Sup. Nizza, Tenuta Olim Bauda	87
Barbera d'Asti Sup. Nizza Anssèma, Cascina Giovinale	157
Barbera d'Asti Sup. Nizza Mora di Sassi, Malgrà	102
Barbera d'Asti Sup. Nizza Neuvsent, Cascina Garitina	59
Barbera d'Asti Sup. Nizza Piano Alto, Bava	68
Barbera d'Asti Sup. Nizza Romilda VI, Tenuta dell'Arbiola	132
Barbera d'Asti Sup. Nizza V. Dacapo, Dacapo	22
Barbera d'Asti Sup. Nizza V. dell'Angelo, Cascina La Barbatella	123
Barbera d'Asti Sup. Nobbio, Roberto Ferraris	22
Barbera d'Asti Sup. Passum, Cascina Castlèt	71
Barbera d'Asti Sup. Piano Alto, Bava	68
Barbera d'Asti Sup. Piatin, Cantine Sant'Agata	135
Barbera d'Asti Sup. Porlapà, Alfonso Boeri	152
Barbera d'Asti Sup. Reginal, Sciorio	72
Barbera d'Asti Sup. Rive, Araldica - Il Cantinone	58
Barbera d'Asti Sup. Rossobaldo, La Giribaldina	48
Barbera d'Asti Sup. Rouvé, F.lli Rovero	29
Barbera d'Asti Sup. Rouvé, F.lli Rovero	29
Barbera d'Asti Sup. Rupestris, Carlo Benotto	70
Barbera d'Asti Sup. S. Lorenzo, Renzo Beccaris	152
Barbera d'Asti Sup. S. Martino, Cascina Roera	71
Barbera d'Asti Sup. Sciorio, Sciorio	72
Barbera d'Asti Sup. Titon, L'Armangia	151
Barbera d'Asti Sup. Tra Terra e Cielo, Tenuta La Meridiana	114
Barbera d'Asti Sup. V. Cua Longa, Alfiero Boffa	131
Barbera d'Asti Sup. V. del Beneficio, Tenuta Cast. di Razzano	28
Barbera d'Asti Sup. V. dell'Angelo, Cascina La Barbatella	123
Barbera d'Asti Sup. V. delle More, Alfiero Boffa	131
Barbera d'Asti Sup. V. delle Rose, Franco Mondo	159
Barbera d'Asti Sup. V. La Riva, Alfiero Boffa	131
Barbera d'Asti Sup. V. Muntrivé, Alfiero Boffa	131
Barbera d'Asti Sup. V. Valentino Caligaris, Tenuta Cast. di Razzano	28
Barbera d'Asti Sup. Vigne Vecchie, C.S. di Vinchio - Vaglio Serra	149
Barbera d'Asti Sup. Vigne Vecchie Nizza, C.S. di Vinchio - Vaglio Serra	149
Barbera d'Asti Sup. Vign. Casot, Carlo Benotto	70
Barbera d'Asti Sup. Vign. La Quercia, Villa Giada	56
Barbera d'Asti Sup. Vin ed Michen, Antonio Baldizzone Cascina Lana	157
Barbera d'Asti Tabarin, Icardi	66
Barbera d'Asti Tra Neuit e Dì, Tenuta Garetto	23
Barbera d'Asti Tre Vigne, Vietti	65
Barbera d'Asti Truccone, Isabella	116
Barbera d'Asti Varmat, La Morandina	66
Barbera d'Asti Vign. Banin, Vigne Regali	140
Barbera d'Asti V. Dacapo, Dacapo	22
Barbera d'Asti V. dei Mandorli, Giacomo Scagliola e Figlio	151
Barbera d'Asti V. delle More, Cascina Gilli	61
Barbera d'Asti V. Stramba, Cast. di Lignano	154
Barbera d'Asti Vign. del Tulipano Nero, Tenuta dei Fiori	49
Barbera d'Asti Zucchetto, La Morandina	66
Barbera del M.to, Tenuta Gaiano	50
Barbera del M.to , Luigi Tacchino	151
Barbera del M.to, Tenuta San Sebastiano	100
Barbera del M.to Alessandra, Colonna	148
Barbera del M.to Aspettando l'Ornovo, La Guardia	116
Barbera del M.to Aureum, Saccoletto	158
Barbera del M.to Barabba, Ca.Vi.Mon.	68
Barbera del M.to Bricco Morlantino, Casalone	100
Barbera del M.to Gallianum, Tenuta Gaiano	50
Barbera del M.to Gambaloita, Marco Canato	148
Barbera del M.to Giulìn, Giulio Accornero e Figli	147
Barbera del M.to Goj, Cascina Castlèt	71
Barbera del M.to I Cheini, Traversa - Cascina Bertolotto	139
Barbera del M.to La Rossa, Colonna	148
Barbera del M.to La Sbarazzina, Traversa - Cascina Bertolotto	139
Barbera del M.to Mepari, Tenuta San Sebastiano	100
Barbera del M.to Ornovo, La Guardia	116
Barbera del M.to Rapet, Marco Canato	148
Barbera del M.to Rivalta, Villa Sparina	85
Barbera del M.to Rossa d'Ocra, Cascina La Maddalena	128

Barbera del M.to Sup., Bricco Mondalino	147
Barbera del M.to Sup., Vicara	130
Barbera del M.to Sup. Bricco Battista, Giulio Accornero e Figli	147
Barbera del M.to Sup. Cantico della Crosia, Vicara	130
Barbera del M.to Sup. La Baldea, Marco Canato	148
Barbera del M.to Sup. Tenaglia, Tenuta La Tenaglia	139
Barbera del M.to V. della Torretta, Tenuta Gaiano	50
Barbera del M.to V. di Dante, La Guardia	116
Barbera del M.to Volpuva, Vicara	130
Barbera del M.to Baciamisubito, La Scamuzza	149
Barbera del M.to Vign. della Amorosa, La Scamuzza	149
Barbera del M.to Vign. della Amorosa Sup., La Scamuzza	149
Barbicone, Russo	575
Barco Reale, Fatt. Ambra	459
Barco Reale, Tenuta di Capezzana	460
Barco Reale, Castelvecchio	581
Barco Reale, Il Poggiolo	581
Bardolino, Le Vigne di San Pietro	325
Bardolino Cavalchina, Cavalchina	324
Bardolino Chiaretto, Corte Gardoni	332
Bardolino Chiaretto, Le Fraghe	285
Bardolino Chiaretto, Le Vigne di San Pietro	325
Bardolino Chiaretto Vigne Alte, F.lli Zeni	284
Bardolino Cl., Le Fraghe	285
Bardolino Cl., Le Tende	292
Bardolino Cl., Santa Sofia	316
Bardolino Cl. Chiaretto, Guerrieri Rizzardi	283
Bardolino Cl. Le Greghe, Le Tende	292
Bardolino Cl. Munus, Guerrieri Rizzardi	283
Bardolino Cl. Sup., Guerrieri Rizzardi	283
Bardolino Cl. Sup., Le Tende	292
Bardolino Cl. Sup. Marogne, F.lli Zeni	284
Bardolino Cl. Sup. Vigne Alte, F.lli Zeni	284
Bardolino Cl. Tacchetto, Guerrieri Rizzardi	283
Bardolino Le Fontane, Corte Gardoni	332
Bardolino Sup., Corte Gardoni	332
Baredo, F.lli Pighin	392
Barigliott, Paternoster	709
Barocco, Terre Cortesi Moncaro	621
Barolo, F.lli Alessandria	145
Barolo, Gianfranco Alessandria	104
Barolo, Elio Altare - Cascina Nuova	88
Barolo, Azelia	61
Barolo, Luigi Baudana	135
Barolo, Cascina Bongiovanni	62
Barolo, Giacomo Borgogno & Figli	37
Barolo, Boroli	24
Barolo, Brovia	63
Barolo, G. B. Burlotto	146
Barolo, Bussia Soprana	156
Barolo, Ca' Bianca	29
Barolo, Cascina Ballarin	90
Barolo, Aldo Conterno	105
Barolo, Giovanni Corino	90
Barolo, Damilano	38
Barolo, Poderi Einaudi	75
Barolo, Gabutti - Franco Boasso	137
Barolo, Gianni Gagliardo	155
Barolo, Ettore Germano	137
Barolo, Bartolo Mascarello	39
Barolo, Mauro Molino	92
Barolo, Andrea Oberto	93
Barolo, Pio Cesare	26
Barolo, Luigi Pira	138
Barolo, E. Pira & Figli - Chiara Boschis	40
Barolo, Prunotto	27
Barolo, F.lli Revello	95
Barolo, Flavio Roddolo	111
Barolo, Luciano Sandrone	41
Barolo, Giorgio Scarzello e Figli	41
Barolo, Paolo Scavino	64
Barolo, Aurelio Settimo	155
Barolo, Terre del Barolo	64
Barolo, Eraldo Viberti	96
Barolo, V. Rionda - Massolino	138
Barolo Arborina, Mauro Veglio	96
Barolo Badarina, Bersano & Riccadonna	123
Barolo Boscareto, Ferdinando Principiano	110
Barolo Bric dël Fiasc, Paolo Scavino	64
Barolo Bricco, Giuseppe Mascarello e Figlio	103
Barolo Bricco Boschis, F.lli Cavallotto	63
Barolo Bricco delle Viole, G. D. Vajra	43
Barolo Bricco Fiasco, Azelia	61
Barolo Bricco Francesco Rocche dell'Annunziata, Rocche Costamagna	95
Barolo Bricco Luciani, Silvio Grasso	91
Barolo Bricco Rocca, Cascina Ballarin	90
Barolo Bricco Rocche, Bricco Rocche - Bricco Asili	62
Barolo Bricco Sarmassa, Giacomo Brezza & Figli	37
Barolo Bricco Viole, Mario Marengo	92
Barolo Bricco Visette, Attilio Ghisolfi	107
Barolo Brunate, Elio Altare - Cascina Nuova	88
Barolo Brunate, Enzo Boglietti	89
Barolo Brunate, Michele Chiarlo	47
Barolo Brunate, Poderi Marcarini	91
Barolo Brunate, Mario Marengo	92
Barolo Brunate, Vietti	65
Barolo Brunate, Roberto Voerzio	98
Barolo Brunate Bricco Rocche, Bricco Rocche - Bricco Asili	62
Barolo Brunate Ris., Poderi Marcarini	91
Barolo Brunate-Le Coste, Giuseppe Rinaldi	40
Barolo Bussia, Boroli	24
Barolo Bussia, Cascina Ballarin	90
Barolo Bussia, Deltetto	52
Barolo Bussia, F.lli Giacosa	120
Barolo Bussia, Prunotto	27
Barolo Bussia Dardi Le Rose, Poderi Colla	26
Barolo Bussia V. Fiurin, Armando Parusso	109
Barolo Bussia V. Munie, Armando Parusso	109
Barolo Bussia V. Rocche, Armando Parusso	109
Barolo Ca' Mia, Brovia	63
Barolo Cannubi, Giacomo Brezza & Figli	37
Barolo Cannubi, Michele Chiarlo	47
Barolo Cannubi, Damilano	38
Barolo Cannubi, Marchesi di Barolo	39
Barolo Cannubi, E. Pira & Figli - Chiara Boschis	40
Barolo Cannubi, Paolo Scavino	64
Barolo Cannubi Boschis, Luciano Sandrone	41
Barolo Cannubi S. Lorenzo-Ravera, Giuseppe Rinaldi	40
Barolo Carobric, Paolo Scavino	64
Barolo Cascina Francia, Giacomo Conterno	105
Barolo Case Nere, Enzo Boglietti	89
Barolo Castellero Ris., Giacomo Brezza & Figli	37
Barolo Castelletto, Mauro Veglio	96
Barolo Cast. Ris., Terre del Barolo	64
Barolo Castiglione, Vietti	65
Barolo Cerequio, Batasiolo	88
Barolo Cerequio, Michele Chiarlo	47
Barolo Cerequio, Roberto Voerzio	98
Barolo Cerequio Tenuta Secolo, Contratto	55
Barolo Cerretta, Ettore Germano	137
Barolo Cerretta, Giovanni Rosso	159
Barolo Cerretta Piani, Luigi Baudana	135
Barolo Chinato, Gianni Gagliardo	155
Barolo Ciabot Manzoni, Silvio Grasso	91
Barolo Ciabot Mentin Ginestra, Domenico Clerico	104
Barolo Cicala, Aldo Conterno	105
Barolo Cl., Giacomo Borgogno & Figli	37
Barolo Codana, Terre del Barolo	64
Barolo Collina Rionda Ris., Bruno Giacosa	120
Barolo Colonnello, Aldo Conterno	105
Barolo Conca Marcenasco, Renato Ratti	94
Barolo Corda della Briccolina, Batasiolo	88
Barolo Corsini, Ruggeri Corsini	111
Barolo Costa Grimaldi, Poderi Einaudi	75
Barolo di Castiglione Falletto Ris., Terre del Barolo	64
Barolo Enrico VI, Monfalletto - Cordero di Montezemolo	93
Barolo Estate Vineyard, Marchesi di Barolo	39
Barolo Falletto, Bruno Giacosa	120
Barolo Falletto Ris., Bruno Giacosa	120
Barolo Fossati, Enzo Boglietti	89
Barolo Gabutti, Gabutti - Franco Boasso	137
Barolo Gattera, Mauro Veglio	96
Barolo Gattere Bricco Luciani, F.lli Ferrero	155
Barolo Gavarini V. Chiniera, Elio Grasso	108
Barolo Ginestra, Paolo Conterno	106
Barolo Ginestra Ris., Paolo Conterno	106
Barolo Ginestra V. Casa Maté, Elio Grasso	108
Barolo Gramolere, Giovanni Manzone	108
Barolo Gramolere Bricat, Giovanni Manzone	108
Barolo Gramolere Ris., Giovanni Manzone	108
Barolo Gran Bussia Ris., Aldo Conterno	105
Barolo La Brunella, Boroli	24
Barolo La Rocca e La Pira, I Paglieri	34
Barolo La Serra, Poderi Marcarini	91
Barolo La Serra, Gianni Voerzio	97
Barolo La Serra, Roberto Voerzio	98
Barolo Lazzarito, Vietti	65
Barolo Le Coste, Giacomo Grimaldi	38
Barolo Le Coste, Ferdinando Principiano	110
Barolo Le Rocche del Falletto, Bruno Giacosa	120
Barolo Le Vigne, Luciano Sandrone	41
Barolo Liste, Giacomo Borgogno & Figli	37
Barolo Liste, Damilano	38
Barolo Manzoni, F.lli Ferrero	155
Barolo Marasco, Franco M. Martinetti	141
Barolo Marcenasco, Renato Ratti	94
Barolo Margheria, V. Rionda - Massolino	138
Barolo Mariondino, Armando Parusso	109
Barolo Massara, Cast. di Verduno	146
Barolo Massara Ris., Cast. di Verduno	146
Barolo Mondoca di Bussia Soprana, F.lli Oddero	146
Barolo Monfalletto, Monfalletto - Cordero di Montezemolo	93
Barolo Monfortino Ris., Giacomo Conterno	105
Barolo Monprivato, Brovia	63
Barolo Monprivato, Giuseppe Mascarello e Figlio	103
Barolo Monprivato Cà d' Morissio Ris., Giuseppe Mascarello e Figlio	103
Barolo Monvigliero, F.lli Alessandria	145
Barolo Monvigliero, Bel Colle	145
Barolo Monvigliero, Cast. di Verduno	146
Barolo Monvigliero, Mauro Sebaste	27
Barolo Monvigliero Ris., Terre del Barolo	64
Barolo Mosconi, Bussia Soprana	156
Barolo nei Cannubi, Poderi Einaudi	75
Barolo Ornato, Pio Cesare	26
Barolo Paesi Tuoi, Terre da Vino	42
Barolo Pajana, Domenico Clerico	104
Barolo Parafada, V. Rionda - Massolino	138
Barolo Parafada Ris., V. Rionda - Massolino	138
Barolo Parej, Icardi	66
Barolo Parussi, Conterno Fantino	106
Barolo Percristina, Domenico Clerico	104

Barolo Pernanno, Cascina Bongiovanni	62
Barolo Pi Vigne, Silvio Grasso	91
Barolo Piccole Vigne, Armando Parusso	109
Barolo Poderi Scarrone, Terre da Vino	42
Barolo Prapò, Ettore Germano	137
Barolo Prapò, Mauro Sebaste	27
Barolo Prapò Bricco Rocche, Bricco Rocche - Bricco Asili	62
Barolo Pressenda, Marziano e Enrico Abbona	74
Barolo Rapet, Ca' Rome' - Romano Marengo	30
Barolo Ravera, Elvio Cogno	125
Barolo Ravera, Flavio Roddolo	111
Barolo Ris., E. Pira - Chiara Boschis & Figli	40
Barolo Ris. del Fondatore, Tenuta La Volta - Cabutto	42
Barolo Riserva Grande Annata, Marchesi di Barolo	39
Barolo Riva, Claudio Alario	73
Barolo Rocche, Giovanni Corino	90
Barolo Rocche dei Brovia, Brovia	63
Barolo Rocche dei Rivera di Castiglione, F.lli Oddero	94
Barolo Rocche dell'Annunziata, F.lli Revello	95
Barolo Rocche dell'Annunziata, Rocche Costamagna	95
Barolo Rocche dell'Annunziata Ris., Paolo Scavino	64
Barolo Rocche di Castiglione, F.lli Oddero	94
Barolo Rocche di Castiglione, Vietti	65
Barolo Rocche di Castiglione Falletto, Bruno Giacosa	120
Barolo Rocche Marcenasco, Renato Ratti	94
Barolo Rocche Ris., Aurelio Settimo	155
Barolo Rocche Ris., Terre del Barolo	64
Barolo Rocche Rivera, F.lli Oddero	94
Barolo Rocchettevino, Gianfranco Bovio	89
Barolo Runcot, Elio Grasso	108
Barolo S. Giovanni, Gianfranco Alessandria	104
Barolo S. Lorenzo, F.lli Alessandria	145
Barolo S. Rocco, Azelia	61
Barolo S. Stefano di Perno, Giuseppe Mascarello e Figlio	103
Barolo Sarmassa, Giacomo Brezza & Figli	37
Barolo Sarmassa, Marchesi di Barolo	39
Barolo Sarmassa, Roberto Voerzio	98
Barolo Serra dei Turchi, Osvaldo Viberti	97
Barolo Serralunga, Gabutti - Franco Boasso	137
Barolo Serralunga, Giovanni Rosso	159
Barolo Serralunga d'Alba, Fontanafredda	136
Barolo Sorano, Ascheri	46
Barolo Sorì Ginestra, Conterno Fantino	106
Barolo Triumviratum Ris., Michele Chiarlo	47
Barolo Vecchie Vigne, Giovanni Corino	90
Barolo Vecchie Viti dei Capalot e delle Brunate Ris., Roberto Voerzio	98
Barolo V. Arborina, Gianfranco Bovio	89
Barolo V. Big 'd Big, Podere Rocche dei Manzoni	110
Barolo V. Big Ris., Podere Rocche dei Manzoni	110
Barolo V. Bricco Gattera, Monfalletto - Cordero di Montezemolo	93
Barolo V. Cappella di S. Stefano, Podere Rocche dei Manzoni	110
Barolo V. Cerrati , Cascina Cucco	136
Barolo V. Cerretta, Ca' Rome' - Romano Marengo	30
Barolo V. Colonnello, Bussia Soprana	156
Barolo V. Conca, Mauro Molino	92
Barolo V. Conca, F.lli Revello	95
Barolo V. Cucco, Cascina Cucco	136
Barolo V. d'la Roul, Podere Rocche dei Manzoni	110
Barolo V. d'la Roul Ris., Podere Rocche dei Manzoni	110
Barolo V. dei Dardi, Alessandro e Gian Natale Fantino	107
Barolo V. dei Pola, Ascheri	46
Barolo V. del Colonnello, Aldo Conterno	105
Barolo V. del Gris, Conterno Fantino	106
Barolo V. di Aldo, Rino Varaldo	36
Barolo V. Elena, Elvio Cogno	125
Barolo V. Gancia, Mauro Molino	92
Barolo V. Gattera, Gianfranco Bovio	89
Barolo V. Giachini, Giovanni Corino	90
Barolo V. Giachini, F.lli Revello	95
Barolo V. La Delizia, Fontanafredda	136
Barolo V. La Rosa, Fontanafredda	136
Barolo V. La Villa-Paiagallo, Fontanafredda	136
Barolo V. La Volta, Tenuta La Volta - Cabutto	42
Barolo V. Mandorlo, F.lli Giacosa	120
Barolo V. Merenda, Giorgio Scarzello e Figli	41
Barolo V. Rionda, F.lli Oddero	94
Barolo V. Rionda Ris., V. Rionda - Massolino	138
Barolo V. S. Giuseppe Ris., F.lli Cavallotto	63
Barolo Vigna La Delizia, Fontanafredda	136
Barolo Vigna La Rosa, Fontanafredda	136
Barolo Vigna Lazzarito, Fontanafredda	136
Barolo Vigne di Proprietà in Barolo, Marchesi di Barolo	39
Barolo Vigneti in Cannubi, Tenuta Carretta	126
Barolo Vign. Albarella, Andrea Oberto	93
Barolo Vign. Arborina, Elio Altare - Cascina Nuova	88
Barolo Vign. Arborina, Giovanni Corino	90
Barolo Vign. Cannubi, G. B. Burlotto	146
Barolo Vign. La Villa, F.lli Seghesio	112
Barolo Vign. Marenca, Luigi Pira	138
Barolo Vign. Margheria, Luigi Pira	138
Barolo Vign. Monvigliero, G. B. Burlotto	146
Barolo Vign. Rocche, Giovanni Corino	90
Barolo Vign. Rocche, Andrea Oberto	93
Barolo Vign. Rocche, Mauro Veglio	96
Barolo Vign. Terlo Ravera, Marziano e Enrico Abbona	74
Barolo Vignolo Ris., F.lli Cavallotto	63
Barolo Villero, Boroli	24
Barolo Villero, Brovia	63
Barolo Villero, Giuseppe Mascarello e Figlio	103
Barolo Villero Ris., Vietti	65
Barolo Zonchera, Ceretto	25
Barone Rosso Platinum, Fantinel	413
Barricadiero, Aurora	637
Barrile, Attilio Contini	768
Bartis, Valentino Fiorini	611
Barullo, Cast. di Selvole	472
Basilicata Bianco V.li, Cant. di Venosa	713
Basolo, Ca' del Vispo	562
Batàr, Querciabella	488
Belcaro, San Felice	472
Belcore, I Giusti e Zanza	475
Bella Mojgan, Marco Maci	719
Benaco Bresciano Bianco , Trevisani	217
Benaco Bresciano Bianco Balì, Trevisani	217
Benaco Bresciano Marzemino Le Mazane, Costaripa	198
Benaco Bresciano Rosso Sùer, Trevisani	217
Bendicò Mandrarossa, Settesoli	752
Beneventano Aglianico , Fatt. Ciabrelli	704
Beneventano Coda di Volpe , Fatt. Ciabrelli	704
Beneventano Falanghina, Fatt. Ciabrelli	704
Bentivoglio, Tenuta Farneta	604
Benuara, Cusumano	756
Bera Brut M. Cl., F.lli Bera	122
Berillo d'Oro, Alessandro Secchi	224
Besler Biank, Pojer & Sandri	228
Betto, Santa Lucia	493
Bianca Capello, Ortaglia	606
Bianca delle Gazzere, Baglio Hopps	761
Bianca di Valguarnera, Duca di Salaparuta - Vini Corvo	747
Bianchello del Metauro, Guerrieri	629
Bianchello del Metauro, La Ripe	638
Bianchello del Metauro Borgo Torre, Az. Agr. Claudio Morelli	617
Bianchello del Metauro Celso, Guerrieri	629
Bianchello del Metauro La V. delle Terrazze, Az. Agr. Claudio Morelli	617
Bianchello del Metauro S. Cesareo, Az. Agr. Claudio Morelli	617
Bianchello del Metauro Tenuta Campioli, Valentino Fiorini	611
Bianchello del Metauro V. Sant'Ilario, Valentino Fiorini	611
Bianco, Cascina Fonda	101
Bianco, Evangelos Paraschos	408
Bianco Amabile del Cerè Bandito, Giuseppe Quintarelli	306
Bianco Avignonesi, Avignonesi	526
Bianco Bianco, Ronco del Gnemiz	411
Bianco Biscari, Cantine Torrevecchia	744
Bianco Caparzo Chardonnay, Tenuta Caparzo	502
Bianco del Coppo Sauvignon, Conte Leopardi Dittajuti	624
Bianco della Castellada, La Castellada	383
Bianco della Rocca, Sarchese Dora	682
Bianco delle Chiaie, Giovanni Palombo	663
Bianco di Busso, Piero Busso	117
Bianco di Castelnuovo, Castel Noarna	236
Bianco di Ciccio, Ciccio Zaccagnini	676
Bianco di Corte, Paternoster	709
Bianco di Custoza, Giuseppe Campagnola	293
Bianco di Custoza, Corte Gardoni	332
Bianco di Custoza, Le Vigne di San Pietro	325
Bianco di Custoza, Lenotti	337
Bianco di Custoza, Giacomo Montresor	333
Bianco di Custoza, Albino Piona	343
Bianco di Custoza Amedeo Cavalchina, Cavalchina	324
Bianco di Custoza Cavalchina, Cavalchina	324
Bianco di Custoza Lucillini, Le Tende	292
Bianco di Custoza Marogne, F.lli Zeni	284
Bianco di Custoza Montemagrin, Santa Sofia	316
Bianco di Custoza Montespada, Zamuner	343
Bianco di Custoza Orchidea Platino, Lamberti	339
Bianco di Custoza Oro, Le Tende	292
Bianco di Custoza Sanpietro, Le Vigne di San Pietro	325
Bianco di Custoza Vign. Monte Fiera, Giacomo Montresor	333
Bianco di Gianni, Giovanni Panizzi	568
Bianco di Montevertine, Fatt. di Montevertine	552
Bianco di Ornella, Ornella Molon Traverso	310
Bianco di Pitigliano, Tenuta Roccaccia	546
Bianco di Pitigliano, Sassotondo	572
Bianco Faye, Pojer & Sandri	228
Bianco Ghibellino, Aldo Rainoldi	187
Bianco JN, Sant'Elena	385
Bianco Margherita, Trabucchi	291
Bianco Veronese Liber, Fasoli	286
Biblos, Di Majo Norante	676
Bidis, Cant. Valle dell'Acate	744
Biferno Bianco Gironia, Borgo di Colloredo	686
Biferno Bianco Molì, Di Majo Norante	676
Biferno Rosso Ramitello, Di Majo Norante	676
Bigarò, Elio Perrone	67
Birba, La Gerla	511
Birbarossa, Tenuta Gaiano	50
Birbet, Cascina Ca' Rossa	50
Birbét, Cascina Chicco	51
Birbet, Filippo Gallino	53
Bizir, Ajello	761
Blanc des Rosis, Schiopetto	353
Blu, Fatt. Mancini	628
Boghes, Giovanni Cherchi	777
Bolgheri, Ceralti	582
Bolgheri Bianco, Colle Massari	461
Bolgheri Bianco Campo alla Casa, Enrico Santini	461

Bolgheri Guado de' Gemoli, Giovanni Chiappini	580
Bolgheri Levia Gravia, Caccia al Piano 1868	581
Bolgheri Montepergoli, Enrico Santini	461
Bolgheri Rosato Scalabrone, Tenuta Guado al Tasso	456
Bolgheri Rosso Alfeo, Ceralti	582
Bolgheri Rosso Diambra, Michele Satta	462
Bolgheri Rosso Piastraia, Michele Satta	462
Bolgheri Rosso Poggio al Moro, Enrico Santini	461
Bolgheri Rosso Sup. Grattamacco, Colle Massari	461
Bolgheri Rosso Sup. Guado al Tasso, Tenuta Guado al Tasso	456
Bolgheri Rosso Sup. Paleo, Le Macchiole	456
Bolgheri Sassicaia, Tenuta San Guido	457
Bolgheri Sauvignon Paleo, Le Macchiole	456
Bolgheri Sup. Ornellaia, Tenuta dell' Ornellaia	457
Bolgheri Vermentino, Tenuta Guado al Tasso	456
Bombereto, La Rampa di Fugnano	566
Bonagrazia Chardonnay, Tenuta Farneta	604
Bonci Brut, Vallerosa Bonci	616
Bonci Brut M. Cl., Vallerosa Bonci	616
Bonera Mandrarossa, Settesoli	752
Bongoverno, Tenuta Farneta	604
Bonmé, Poderi Colla	26
Bonorli, Melini	547
Borgo d'Altesi, Altesino	499
Borgo dei Guidi, Poderi dal Nespoli	427
Borgo di Peuma, Rino Russolo	412
Borgoforte, Villa Pillo	485
Borgoricco, Tenuta La Cipressaia	597
Borro del Boscone, Le Calvane	536
Boscarelli, Boscarelli	527
Boschi Salviati, San Luciano	522
Botrys, Mastrojanni	514
Bottaccia, Torre Quarto	720
Bottaccio, Il Paradiso	564
Botticino Foja d'Or Ris., Emilio Franzoni	213
Bottiglia Particolare, Cast. di Verrazzano	490
Brachetto d'Acqui, Braida	129
Brachetto d'Acqui Castelgaro, Bersano & Riccadonna	123
Brachetto d'Acqui Contero, La Giustiniana	83
Brachetto d'Acqui Il Virginio, Traversa - Cascina Bertolotto	139
Brachetto d'Acqui Le Donne dei Boschi, Ca' dei Mandorli	152
Brachetto d'Acqui Pineto, Marenco	140
Brachetto d'Acqui Rosa Regale, Vigne Regali	140
Bradisismo Cabernet Sauvignon, Inama	310
Braida Nuova, Borgo Conventi	379
Braide Alte, Livon	410
Bramaterra, Anzivino	80
Bramaterra, Barni	47
Bramaterra, Sella	98
Brancaia, La Brancaia	551
Brancaia Il Blu, La Brancaia	551
Brancaia Tre, La Brancaia	551
Braviolo, Fatt. del Cerro	528
Breccetto, Trappolini	665
Breganze Bianco Le Colombare, Firmino Miotti	337
Breganze Bianco Rivana, Vign. Due Santi	284
Breganze Cabernet, Firmino Miotti	337
Breganze Cabernet, Vign. Due Santi	284
Breganze Cabernet Sauvignon Palazzotto, Maculan	285
Breganze Cabernet Vign. Due Santi, Vign. Due Santi	284
Breganze Chardonnay Ferrata, Maculan	285
Breganze di Breganze, Maculan	285
Breganze Rosso, Vign. Due Santi	284
Breganze Rosso Crosara, Maculan	285
Breganze Rosso Valletta, Firmino Miotti	337
Breganze Sauvignon Vign. Due Santi, Vign. Due Santi	284
Breganze Torcolato, Maculan	285
Breganze Torcolato, Firmino Miotti	337
Brentino, Maculan	285
Bricco Appiani, Flavio Roddolo	111
Bricco della Torre, La Togata - Tenuta Carlina	512
Bricco Sturnel, Bellaria	182
Bricoli, Vigliano	495
Brina, Saccoletto	158
Brindisi Rosato V. Flaminio, Agricole Vallone	724
Brindisi Rosso Gallico, Tenute Rubino	717
Brindisi Rosso Jaddico, Tenute Rubino	717
Brindisi Rosso V. Flaminio, Agricole Vallone	724
Brisi, Fatt. San Francesco	736
Broccato, Fatt. di Dievole	469
Broili di Filip, Walter Filiputti	387
Brolo dei Passoni , Ricci Curbastro	181
Bron & Rusèval Chardonnay, Celli	422
Bron & Rusèval Sangiovese-Cabernet, Celli	422
Brunello di Montalcino, Altesino	499
Brunello di Montalcino, Argiano	499
Brunello di Montalcino, Banfi	500
Brunello di Montalcino, Fatt. dei Barbi	500
Brunello di Montalcino, Cast. di Camigliano	501
Brunello di Montalcino, Campogiovanni	589
Brunello di Montalcino, Capanna di Cencioni	502
Brunello di Montalcino, Tenuta Caparzo	502
Brunello di Montalcino, Casanova di Neri	503
Brunello di Montalcino, Casanuova delle Cerbaie	590
Brunello di Montalcino, Fatt. del Casato - Donatella Cinelli Colombini	503
Brunello di Montalcino, Casisano Colombaio	590
Brunello di Montalcino, Castelgiocondo	504
Brunello di Montalcino, Castelli Martinozzi	590
Brunello di Montalcino, Castiglion del Bosco	504
Brunello di Montalcino, Cerbaiona	505
Brunello di Montalcino, Tenuta Col d'Orcia	506
Brunello di Montalcino, Andrea Costanti	507
Brunello di Montalcino, Tenuta Di Sesta	590
Brunello di Montalcino, Due Portine - Gorelli	507
Brunello di Montalcino, Fanti - La Palazzetta	590
Brunello di Montalcino, Fanti - San Filippo	508
Brunello di Montalcino, Fattoi	591
Brunello di Montalcino, Eredi Fuligni	508
Brunello di Montalcino, Greppone Mazzi - Tenim. Ruffino	591
Brunello di Montalcino, Il Colle	591
Brunello di Montalcino, Il Grappolo-Fortius	591
Brunello di Montalcino, Tenuta Il Greppo	509
Brunello di Montalcino, Il Marroneto	591
Brunello di Montalcino, Il Palazzone	509
Brunello di Montalcino, Tenuta Il Poggione	510
Brunello di Montalcino, La Fiorita	591
Brunello di Montalcino, Podere La Fortuna	511
Brunello di Montalcino, Tenuta La Fuga	592
Brunello di Montalcino, La Gerla	511
Brunello di Montalcino, La Poderina	512
Brunello di Montalcino, La Serena	592
Brunello di Montalcino, La Togata - Tenuta Carlina	512
Brunello di Montalcino, Maurizio Lambardi	592
Brunello di Montalcino, Le Chiuse	592
Brunello di Montalcino, Le Chiuse di Sotto	513
Brunello di Montalcino, Le Gode di Ripaccioli	592
Brunello di Montalcino, Le Macioche	592
Brunello di Montalcino, Mastrojanni	514
Brunello di Montalcino, Mocali	593
Brunello di Montalcino, Cant. di Montalcino	593
Brunello di Montalcino, Tenute Silvio Nardi	514
Brunello di Montalcino, Franco Pacenti	593
Brunello di Montalcino, Siro Pacenti	515
Brunello di Montalcino, Pian dell'Orino	593
Brunello di Montalcino, Pian delle Vigne	593
Brunello di Montalcino, Piancornello	515
Brunello di Montalcino, Agostina Pieri	516
Brunello di Montalcino, Poggio Castellare	594
Brunello di Montalcino, Poggio di Sotto	516
Brunello di Montalcino, Poggio San Polo	517
Brunello di Montalcino, Cast. Romitorio	517
Brunello di Montalcino, Podere Salicutti	518
Brunello di Montalcino, Salvioni - La Cerbaiola	518
Brunello di Montalcino, Sesti - Cast. di Argiano	519
Brunello di Montalcino, Solaria - Cencioni	519
Brunello di Montalcino, Talenti	520
Brunello di Montalcino, Uccelliera	520
Brunello di Montalcino, Tenuta Valdicava	521
Brunello di Montalcino, Villa Le Prata	522
Brunello di Montalcino Beato , Il Poggiolo	510
Brunello di Montalcino Cerretalto, Casanova di Neri	503
Brunello di Montalcino Donna Olga, Donna Olga	590
Brunello di Montalcino Due Portine, Due Portine - Gorelli	507
Brunello di Montalcino Five Stars, Il Poggiolo	510
Brunello di Montalcino Five Stars Ris., Il Poggiolo	510
Brunello di Montalcino La Casa, Tenuta Caparzo	502
Brunello di Montalcino Le Potazzine, Due Portine - Gorelli	507
Brunello di Montalcino Madonna del Piano Ris., Tenuta Valdicava	521
Brunello di Montalcino Manachiara, Tenute Silvio Nardi	514
Brunello di Montalcino Manachiara Cru, Tenute Silvio Nardi	514
Brunello di Montalcino Montosoli, Altesino	499
Brunello di Montalcino Pietranera, Centolani	505
Brunello di Montalcino Podere Bellarina, Palagetto	593
Brunello di Montalcino Poggio al Vento Ris., Tenuta Col d'Orcia	506
Brunello di Montalcino Poggio all'Oro Ris., Banfi	500
Brunello di Montalcino Poggio alle Mura, Banfi	500
Brunello di Montalcino Poggio Banale, La Poderina	512
Brunello di Montalcino Poggio Salvi, Tenuta Il Greppo	509
Brunello di Montalcino Prime Donne, Fatt. del Casato - Donatella Cinelli Colombini	503
Brunello di Montalcino Ris., Argiano	499
Brunello di Montalcino Ris., Fatt. dei Barbi	500
Brunello di Montalcino Ris., Cast. di Camigliano	501
Brunello di Montalcino Ris., Capanna di Cencioni	502
Brunello di Montalcino Ris., Tenuta Caparzo	502
Brunello di Montalcino Ris., Fatt. del Casato - Donatella Cinelli Colombini	503
Brunello di Montalcino Ris., Castelgiocondo	504
Brunello di Montalcino Ris., Castiglion del Bosco	504
Brunello di Montalcino Ris., Andrea Costanti	507
Brunello di Montalcino Ris., Eredi Fuligni	508
Brunello di Montalcino Ris., Il Palazzone	509
Brunello di Montalcino Ris., Tenuta Il Poggione	510
Brunello di Montalcino Ris., Podere La Fortuna	511
Brunello di Montalcino Ris., La Gerla	511
Brunello di Montalcino Ris., La Poderina	512
Brunello di Montalcino Ris., La Togata - Tenuta Carlina	512
Brunello di Montalcino Ris., Mastrojanni	514
Brunello di Montalcino Ris., Siro Pacenti	515
Brunello di Montalcino Ris., Poggio di Sotto	516
Brunello di Montalcino Ris., Talenti	520
Brunello di Montalcino Sassello, Il Poggiolo	510
Brunello di Montalcino Schiena d'Asino, Mastrojanni	514
Brunello di Montalcino Tenuta Friggiali, Centolani	505
Brunello di Montalcino Tenuta Nuova, Casanova di Neri	503
Brunello di Montalcino Terra Rossa, Il Poggiolo	510

Brunello di Montalcino V. del Colombaio, Casisano Colombaio	590
Brunello di Montalcino V. del Fiore, Fatt. dei Barbi	500
Brunello di Montalcino V. del Fiore Ris., Fatt. dei Barbi	500
Brunello di Montalcino V. del Lago, Tenim. Angelini - Val di Suga	521
Brunello di Montalcino V. di Pianrosso, Ciacci Piccolomini D'Aragona	506
Brunello di Montalcino V. di Pianrosso Ris., Ciacci Piccolomini D'Aragona	506
Brunello di Montalcino V. Gli Angeli, La Gerla	511
Brunello di Montalcino V. Schiena d'Asino, Mastrojanni	514
Brunello di Montalcino V. Spuntali, Tenim. Angelini - Val di Suga	521
Brunello di Montalcino Vigneti dei Cottimelli, Eredi Fuligni	508
Brunello di Montalcino Vigneti dei Cottimelli Ris., Eredi Fuligni	508
Bruno di Rocca, Vecchie Terre di Montefili	544
Brut Cl. Costaripa, Costaripa	198
Brut Cl. Il Calepino, Il Calepino	184
Brut Cl. Ris. Fra Ambrogio, Il Calepino	184
Brut M. Cl., Dino Illuminati	677
Bruzzico, Fatt. Lilliano	579
Bucciato, Ca' Rugate	300
Bue Apis, Cant. del Taburno	693
Buranco, Buranco	169
Burdese, Planeta	752
Buriano, Rocca di Castagnoli	483
Burson, Tenuta Uccellina	439
Busillis, Tenim. Angelini - Tenuta Trerose	534
C. Amerini Bianco Terre Arnolfe, Cant. dei Colli Amerini	640
C. Amerini Chardonnay Rocca Nerina, Cant. dei Colli Amerini	640
C. Amerini Malvasia La Corte, Cant. dei Colli Amerini	640
C. Amerini Rosso Sup., Fatt. Le Poggette	647
C. Amerini Rosso Sup. Carbio, Cant. dei Colli Amerini	640
C. Amerini Rosso Terre Arnolfe, Cant. dei Colli Amerini	640
C. B. Barbera, Giuseppe Beghelli	426
C. B. Barbera, Tenuta Goccia	449
C. B. Barbera, Gradizzolo Ognibene	436
C. B. Barbera, Sandoni	446
C. B. Barbera Il Foriere, La Mancina	437
C. B. Barbera Montebudello Cabasà Ris., Ca' Selvatica	448
C. B. Barbera Ris., Gradizzolo Ognibene	436
C. B. Cabernet Sauvignon, Giuseppe Beghelli	426
C. B. Cabernet Sauvignon, Floriano Cinti	440
C. B. Cabernet Sauvignon, Maria Letizia Gaggioli Vign. Bagazzana	444
C. B. Cabernet Sauvignon, Tenuta Goccia	449
C. B. Cabernet Sauvignon, Tizzano	424
C. B. Cabernet Sauvignon, Vallona	426
C. B. Cabernet Sauvignon, Vign. delle Terre Rosse	444
C. B. Cabernet Sauvignon Barrique, Bonfiglio	448
C. B. Cabernet Sauvignon Bonzarone, Tenuta Bonzara	436
C. B. Cabernet Sauvignon Comandante della Guardia Ris., La Mancina	437
C. B. Cabernet Sauvignon Cuvée, Vign. delle Terre Rosse	444
C. B. Cabernet Sauvignon Giòrosso, Santarosa	435
C. B. Cabernet Sauvignon Ris., Corte d'Aibo	449
C. B. Cabernet Sauvignon Ris., Erioli	445
C. B. Cabernet Sauvignon Ris., Tizzano	424
C. B. Cabernet Sauvignon Sel., Floriano Cinti	440
C. B. Cabernet Sauvignon Sel., Isola	435
C. B. Cabernet Sauvignon Sel., San Vito	449
C. B. Cabernet Sauvignon Sel., Vallona	426
C. B. Cabernet Sauvignon V. del Falco, Ca' Selvatica	448
C. B. Chardonnay, Floriano Cinti	440
C. B. Chardonnay, Isola	435
C. B. Chardonnay, Vallona	426
C. B. Chardonnay Cuvée, Vign. delle Terre Rosse	444
C. B. Chardonnay Giòcoliere, Santarosa	435
C. B. Chardonnay Lavinio, Maria Letizia Gaggioli Vign. Bagazzana	444
C. B. Chardonnay Sel., Isola	435
C. B. Chardonnay Sel., Vallona	426
C. B. Colline Marconiane Pignoletto Passito, Floriano Cinti	440
C. B. Merlot, Floriano Cinti	440
C. B. Merlot, Maria Letizia Gaggioli Vign. Bagazzana	444
C. B. Merlot Calastrino, Gradizzolo Ognibene	436
C. B. Merlot Giòtondo, Santarosa	435
C. B. Merlot Lanciotto, La Mancina	437
C. B. Merlot Rocca di Bonacciara, Tenuta Bonzara	436
C. B. Merlot Roncovecchio, Corte d'Aibo	449
C. B. Merlot Rosso del Poggio, Tenuta Bonzara	436
C. B. Merlot Sel., Floriano Cinti	440
C. B. Pignoletto, Vallona	426
C. B. Pignoletto Brut, Tizzano	424
C. B. Pignoletto Cl., Giuseppe Beghelli	426
C. B. Pignoletto Cl., Floriano Cinti	440
C. B. Pignoletto Cl., Santarosa	435
C. B. Pignoletto Cl. V. Antica, Tenuta Bonzara	436
C. B. Pignoletto Frizzante, Giuseppe Beghelli	426
C. B. Pignoletto Frizzante, Floriano Cinti	440
C. B. Pignoletto Frizzante, Maria Letizia Gaggioli Vign. Bagazzana	444
C. B. Pignoletto Frizzante, Tenuta Goccia	449
C. B. Pignoletto Frizzante, Gradizzolo Ognibene	436
C. B. Pignoletto Frizzante, Isola	435
C. B. Pignoletto Frizzante, La Mancina	437
C. B. Pignoletto Frizzante, San Vito	449
C. B. Pignoletto Frizzante, Tenuta Bonzara	436
C. B. Pignoletto Frizzante, Tizzano	424
C. B. Pignoletto Passito Colline di Oliveto, Bonfiglio	448
C. B. Pignoletto Sup., Bonfiglio	448
C. B. Pignoletto Sup., Maria Letizia Gaggioli Vign. Bagazzana	444
C. B. Pignoletto Sup., Isola	435
C. B. Pignoletto Sup., San Vito	449
C. B. Pignoletto Sup., Tizzano	424
C. B. Pignoletto Terre di Montebudello, La Mancina	437
C. B. Pignoletto Vivace, Vallona	426
C. B. Pinot Bianco, Floriano Cinti	440
C. B. Pinot Bianco, Santarosa	435
C. B. Pinot Bianco Crilò, Maria Letizia Gaggioli Vign. Bagazzana	444
C. B. Riesling Italico, Tizzano	424
C. B. Riesling Malagò V. T., Vign. delle Terre Rosse	444
C. B. Sauvignon, Floriano Cinti	440
C. B. Sauvignon, Sandoni	446
C. B. Sauvignon, Vallona	426
C. B. Sauvignon, Vign. delle Terre Rosse	444
C. B. Sauvignon Sel., Floriano Cinti	440
C. B. Sauvignon Sup., Maria Letizia Gaggioli Vign. Bagazzana	444
C. B. Sauvignon Sup. Le Carrate, Tenuta Bonzara	436
C. B. Spumante Brut, Corte d'Aibo	449
C. del Trasimeno Baccio del Bianco, Duca della Corgna	643
C. del Trasimeno Bianco, Villa Po' del Vento	659
C. del Trasimeno Bianco Albello del Lago, Fanini	643
C. del Trasimeno Gamay Divina Villa Et. Bianca, Duca della Corgna	643
C. del Trasimeno Gamay Divina Villa Et. Nera, Duca della Corgna	643
C. del Trasimeno Grechetto Nuricante, Duca della Corgna	643
C. del Trasimeno Rosso, Podere Marella	658
C. del Trasimeno Rosso, Villa Po' del Vento	659
C. del Trasimeno Rosso Baccio del Rosso, Duca della Corgna	643
C. del Trasimeno Rosso Barca, Terre del Carpine	646
C. del Trasimeno Rosso Corniolo, Duca della Corgna	643
C. del Trasimeno Rosso Erceo, Terre del Carpine	646
C. del Trasimeno Rosso Morello del Lago, Fanini	643
C. P. Barbera della Stoppa, La Stoppa	439
C. P. Barbera Frizzante, Conte Otto Barattieri di San Pietro	442
C. P. Bonarda Amabile, Gaetano Lusenti	443
C. P. Bonarda Frizzante, Cantine Romagnoli	450
C. P. Bonarda La Picciona, Gaetano Lusenti	443
C. P. Cabernet Sauvignon, Tenuta La Torretta	449
C. P. Cabernet Sauvignon, Manara	450
C. P. Cabernet Sauvignon Borgo di Rivalta Mabilia, C.S. Valtidone	423
C. P. Cabernet Sauvignon Ca' Bernesca, Torre Fornello	443
C. P. Cabernet Sauvignon Corbeau, Luretta	432
C. P. Cabernet Sauvignon Il Pergolo, Conte Otto Barattieri di San Pietro	442
C. P. Cabernet Sauvignon Il Villante, Gaetano Lusenti	443
C. P. Cabernet Sauvignon Luna Selvatica, La Tosa	442
C. P. Cabernet Sauvignon Perticato del Novarei, Il Poggiarello	441
C. P. Cabernet Sauvignon Stoppa, La Stoppa	439
C. P. Chardonnay Perticato La Piana, Il Poggiarello	441
C. P. Chardonnay Selin d'l'Armari, Luretta	432
C. P. Duca Ottavio, Castelli del Duca	437
C. P. Gutturnio, Conte Otto Barattieri di San Pietro	442
C. P. Gutturnio, La Tosa	442
C. P. Gutturnio Barbera Duca Ranuccio, Castelli del Duca	437
C. P. Gutturnio Borgo di Rivalta Giannone Ris., C.S. Valtidone	423
C. P. Gutturnio Cl. Julius, C.S. Valtidone	423
C. P. Gutturnio Cl. Nicchio, Cardinali	446
C. P. Gutturnio Cl. Torquato Ris., Cardinali	446
C. P. Gutturnio Diacono Gerardo 1028 Ris., Torre Fornello	443
C. P. Gutturnio Diacono Gerardo Ris., Torre Fornello	443
C. P. Gutturnio Frizzante, Baraccone	459
C.P. Gutturnio Frizzante, Conte Otto Barattieri di San Pietro	442
C. P. Gutturnio Frizzante, Manara	450
C. P. Gutturnio La Barbona Ris., Il Poggiarello	441
C. P. Gutturnio Perticato Valandrea, Il Poggiarello	441
C. P. Gutturnio Ronco Alto Ris., Baraccone	449
C. P. Gutturnio Sel., Conte Otto Barattieri di San Pietro	442
C. P. Gutturnio Sigillum Ris., Castelli del Duca	437
C. P. Gutturnio Sup., Alberto Lusignani	450
C. P. Gutturnio Sup., Manara	450
C. P. Gutturnio Sup., C.S. Valtidone	423
C. P. Gutturnio Sup. Borgo di Rivalta Flerido, C.S. Valtidone	423
C. P. Gutturnio Sup. Cresta al Sole, Gaetano Lusenti	443
C. P. Gutturnio Sup. Duca Alessandro, Castelli del Duca	437
C. P. Gutturnio Sup. Sinsäl, Torre Fornello	443
C. P. Gutturnio V. del Gallo Ris., Cantine Romagnoli	450
C. P. Gutturnio V.morello, La Tosa	442
C. P. Malvasia Boccadirosa , Luretta	432
C. P. Malvasia di Case Piccioni, Gaetano Lusenti	443
C. P. Malvasia Donna Luigia, Torre Fornello	443
C. P. Malvasia Passito Soleste, Castelli del Duca	437
C. P. Malvasia Passito V. del Volta, La Stoppa	439
C. P. Malvasia Perticato Beatrice Quadri, Il Poggiarello	441
C. P. Malvasia Sorriso di Cielo, La Tosa	442
C. P. Malvasia V. T. Le Rane, Luretta	432
C. P. Pinot Nero Achab, Luretta	432
C. P. Pinot Nero Borgo di Rivalta Briseide, C.S. Valtidone	423
C. P. Pinot Nero Dioniso, Tenuta La Torretta	449
C. P. Pinot Nero Perticato Le Giastre, Il Poggiarello	441
C. P. Pinot Nero Spumante Rosé, Gaetano Lusenti	443
C. P. Sauvignon, La Tosa	442
C. P. Sauvignon Ca' del Rio, Torre Fornello	443
C. P. Sauvignon Costa Solara, C.S. Valtidone	423
C. P. Sauvignon Duchessa Vittoria, Castelli del Duca	437
C. P. Sauvignon I Nani e Le Ballerine, Luretta	432

C. P. Sauvignon Perticato Il Quadri, Il Poggiarello	441
C. P. Valnure Frizzante, La Tosa	442
C. P. Vin Santo Albarola, Conte Otto Barattieri di San Pietro	442
C. P. Vin Santo di Vigoleno, Alberto Lusignani	450
C.T. Barbera Monleale, Boveri Renato	156
C.T. Barbera S. Ambrogio, Boveri Renato	156
C. T. Bianco Derthona, La Colombera	160
C.T. Cortese Munprò, Boveri Renato	156
C.T. Rosso Costa, Boveri Renato	156
C. T. Rosso Nibiò, La Colombera	160
C. T. Vegia Rampana, La Colombera	160
Ca' Andrea, I Girasoli di Sant'Andrea	660
Ca' del Pazzo, Tenuta Caparzo	502
Caberlot, Podere Il Carnasciale	597
Cabernasco, Villa Pigna	626
Cabernet, Vinnaioli Jermann	380
Cabernet Bergamasca, La Tordela	210
Cabernet Bergamasca Luna Rossa, Caminella	215
Cabernet dei Colli Trevigiani, Gregoletto	298
Cabernet della Bergamasca Torcularia, Le Corne	217
Cabernet Duca Cantelmi, Giovanni Palombo	663
Cabernet Franc, Andreola Orsola	288
Cabernet Franc Campo Buri, La Cappuccina	302
Cabernet I Legni, Rino Russolo	412
Cabernet Ris., Gino Pedrotti	227
Cabernet Sauvignon, Nicola Balter	238
Cabernet Sauvignon, Buccicatino	688
Cabernet Sauvignon, Casale del Giglio	663
Cabernet Sauvignon, Fatt. Castiglioni e Montagnana	536
Cabernet Sauvignon, COS	759
Cabernet Sauvignon, Curatolo	761
Cabernet Sauvignon, Feudo Principi di Butera	745
Cabernet Sauvignon, Fiegl	382
Cabernet Sauvignon, Isole e Olena	454
Cabernet Sauvignon, Lungarotti	657
Cabernet Sauvignon, Marion	312
Cabernet Sauvignon, Aziende Vinicole Miceli	755
Cabernet Sauvignon, San Vettore	587
Cabernet Sauvignon, Sandoni	446
Cabernet Sauvignon, Tasca d'Almerita	758
Cabernet Sauvignon, Tenuta di Trecciano	604
Cabernet Sauvignon, Villa Arceno	473
Cabernet Sauvignon, Villa Pillo	485
Cabernet Sauvignon Capitello, Tenuta Sant'Antonio	297
Cabernet Sauvignon Castellione, Calonga	431
Cabernet Sauvignon Colle Funaro, Orlandi Contucci Ponno	683
Cabernet Sauvignon Intenso, F.lli Fabiano	343
Cabernet Sauvignon Mandrarossa, Settesoli	752
Cabernet Sauvignon Rosso Dogato, Merotto	338
Cabernet Sauvignon S. Cristina, Zenato	309
Cabernet Sauvignon Vign. Campo Madonna, Giacomo Montresor	333
Cabreo La Pietra, Tenute Ambrogio e Giovanni Folonari	476
Cabreomytho, Tenute Ambrogio e Giovanni Folonari	476
Cacc'e Mmitte di Lucera Borgo Feudo, Coop. Svevo - Lucera	732
Cadetto Bianco, Barone La Lumia	761
Cagiòlo Bianco, Cant. Tollo	685
Cagnulari, Giovanni Cherchi	777
Calabrone, Bastianich	396
Calanchi di Vaiano, Paolo d'Amico	664
Calanco, Tenuta Le Velette	653
Calaresu, Giovanni Cherchi	777
Calat, Feudo Principi di Butera	745
Calcare Sauvignon, Conte Leopardi Dittajuti	624
Calicò Brut, Le Sorgenti	452
Caluna, Podere Marella	658
Caluso Bianco Vignot S. Antonio, Orsolani	130
Caluso Passito Alladium Vign. Runc, Cieck	24
Caluso Passito Sulé, Orsolani	130
Caluso Passito Vign. Cariola, Ferrando	87
Camartina, Querciabella	488
Camastra, Tasca d'Almerita	758
Camelot, Casa Vinicola Firriato	754
Camerte, La Monacesca	620
Camoi Col Sandago, Martino Zanetti	341
Campaccio, Fatt. di Terrabianca	554
Campaccio Sel. Speciale, Fatt. di Terrabianca	554
Campanaro, Feudi di San Gregorio	702
Campi Flegrei Falanghina, Cantine Grotta del Sole	699
Campi Flegrei Piedirosso Montegauro Ris., Cantine Grotta del Sole	699
Campi Sarni Rosso, Vallarom	225
Campidano di Terralba Bovale Madrigal, C.S. Marrubiu	779
Campo all'Albero, La Sala	560
Campo Buri, La Cappuccina	302
Campo d'Aia, Cast. di Modanella	555
Campo de' Massi, Freddano	652
Campo Lungo, Fatt. Casabianca	539
Campo Montecristo, Serraiola	535
Campo Sireso, Ottella	309
Campo Vecchio Rosso, Castel De Paolis	668
Campofiorin, Masi	319
Campoleone, Lamborghini - La Fiorita	654
Campolucci, Mannucci Droandi	597
Campore, Il Pratello	434
Camporosso, La Marcellina	542
Campos Rosato del Limbara, C.S. Gallura	777
Canà Rosso, La Biancara	289
Canaiuolo, Montenidoli	567
Canavese Bianco Cast. di Loranzé, Ferrando	87
Canavese Rosso Cieck, Cieck	24
Canavese Rosso Tre Ciochè, Giovanni Silva	150
Candia dei Colli Apuani, Cima	497
Candia dei Colli Apuani Ultramarina, VIN.CA.	581
Candia dei Colli Apuani Vign. Candia Alto, Cima	497
Candiani, Vitivincola Su Baroni	770
Canigonis, Vitivincola Su Baroni	770
Canneto, D'Angelo	710
Cannonau di Sardegna, Attilio Contini	768
Cannonau di Sardegna, Cantine di Dolianova	769
Cannonau di Sardegna, Piero Mancini	772
Cannonau di Sardegna, Gigi Picciau	768
Cannonau di Sardegna Alberto Loi Ris., Alberto Loi	769
Cannonau di Sardegna Antares, Josto Puddu	780
Cannonau di Sardegna Baione, C.S. della Trexenta	775
Cannonau di Sardegna Cardedo Ris., Alberto Loi	769
Cannonau di Sardegna Corrasi Nepente di Oliena Ris., Cant. Coop. di Oliena	779
Cannonau di Sardegna Corte Adua, C.S. della Trexenta	775
Cannonau di Sardegna Costera, Antonio Argiolas	775
Cannonau di Sardegna Firmadu, Tenute Soletta	778
Cannonau di Sardegna Grand Cru, C.S. Santa Maria La Palma	766
Cannonau di Sardegna Le Bombarde, C.S. Santa Maria La Palma	766
Cannonau di Sardegna Le Ghiaie, Meloni Vini	774
Cannonau di Sardegna Le Sabbie, Meloni Vini	774
Cannonau di Sardegna Lillové, Giuseppe Gabbas	772
Cannonau di Sardegna Marghia, Antichi Poderi Jerzu	770
Cannonau di Sardegna Nepente di Oliena, Cant. Coop. Oliena	779
Cannonau di Sardegna Nepente di Oliena Ris., Gostolai	773
Cannonau di Sardegna Ris., Antichi Poderi Jerzu	770
Cannonau di Sardegna Ris., Tenute Soletta	778
Cannonau di Sardegna Ris. Chuerra, Antichi Poderi Jerzu	770
Cannonau di Sardegna Riserva Josto Miglior , Antichi Poderi Jerzu	770
Cannonau di Sardegna Sa Mola Rubia, Alberto Loi	769
Cannonau di Sardegna Sileno, Ferruccio Deiana	776
Cannonau di Sardegna Tamara, C.S. del Vermentino	771
Cannonau di Sardegna Triente, Pala	776
Cannonau di Sardegna V. di Isalle, C.S. Dorgali	778
Cannonau di Sardegna V. Ruja, C.S. Il Nuraghe	779
Canonico, Castellare di Castellina	463
Cantico, Gostolai	773
Cantico, Podere La Cappella	605
Cantinino, Fatt. Cast. Sonnino	537
Cantoalto Bianco, Bonaldi - Cascina del Bosco	222
Canvalle, Vignavecchia	554
Capalbio Bianco Brigante, Santa Lucia	493
Capalbio Rosso Losco, Santa Lucia	493
Capichera, Capichera	767
Capichera V.T., Capichera	767
Capichera V. 'Ngena, Capichera	767
Capineto, Tenuta Castellino	187
Capitel Croce, Roberto Anselmi	300
Capitel Foscarino, Roberto Anselmi	300
Capitel S. Rocco Rosso di Ripasso, F.lli Tedeschi	317
Capo Martino, Vinnaioli Jermann	380
Cappello di Prete, Francesco Candido	729
Capriano del Colle Rosso Monte Bruciato Ris., La V.	213
Capriano del Colle Rosso V. Tenuta Anna, Cascina Nuova	213
Caprorosso, Fatt. di Bagnolo	588
Capsico Rosso, Ciccio Zaccagnini	676
Carantan, Marco Felluga	385
Caratello Passito, Enoteca Bisson	165
Carato Bianco, Camponeschi	673
Carato Rosso, Camponeschi	673
Caravaggio, Cantine Romagnoli	450
Carema Carema, Cant. dei Prod. Nebbiolo di Carema	57
Carema Etichetta Bianca, Ferrando	87
Carema Etichetta Nera, Ferrando	87
Carema Le Tabbie, Orsolani	130
Carema Selezione, Cant. dei Prod. Nebbiolo di Carema	57
Carialoso, Marenco	140
Cariglio, Tenuta Terre Nobili	742
Carignano del Sulcis Grotta Rossa, C.S. di Santadi	773
Carignano del Sulcis Issolus, Sardus Pater	774
Carignano del Sulcis Ris., Sardus Pater	774
Carignano del Sulcis Rocca Rubia, C.S. di Santadi	773
Carignano del Sulcis Rocca Rubia Ris., C.S. di Santadi	773
Carignano del Sulcis Sup. Terre Brune, C.S. di Santadi	773
Carignano del Sulcis Terre Rare, Tenute Sella & Mosca	766
Carleto, Enrico Pierazzuoli	459
Carlozadra Cl. Brut, Carlozadra	197
Carlozadra Cl. Brut Nondosato, Carlozadra	197
Carlozadra Extra Dry Liberty, Carlozadra	197
Carmen, Teruzzi & Puthod	569
Carmen Puthod, Teruzzi & Puthod	569
Carmenèro, Ca' del Bosco	193
Carmignano, Castelvecchio	581
Carmignano, Pratesi	460
Carmignano Elzana Ris., Fatt. Ambra	459
Carmignano Le Farnete, Enrico Pierazzuoli	459
Carmignano Le Farnete Ris., Enrico Pierazzuoli	459
Carmignano Le Vigne Alte di Montalbiolo, Fatt. Ambra	459
Carmignano Le Vigne Alte di Montalbiolo Ris., Fatt. Ambra	459
Carmignano Le Vigne Alte Ris., Fatt. Ambra	459
Carmignano Ris., Il Poggiolo	581
Carmignano Ris., Piaggia - Vannucci Silvia	548
Carmignano V. di Montefortini, Fatt. Ambra	459
Carmignano V. Grumarello, Artimino	581
Carmignano V. S. Cristina in Pilli, Fatt. Ambra	459

Carmignano Villa Artimino, Artimino	581
Carmignano Villa di Capezzana, Tenuta di Capezzana	460
Carmignano Villa di Trefiano, Tenuta di Capezzana	460
Carmignano Villa Medicea Ris., Artimino	581
Carolus, Antichi Vigneti di Cantalupo	85
Carpe Diem Passito , Belisario C.S. di Matelica e Cerreto d'Esi	619
Carso Cabernet Franc, Castelvecchio	405
Carso Cabernet Sauvignon, Castelvecchio	405
Carso Chardonnay, Kante	377
Carso Malvasia, Kante	377
Carso Malvasia, Skerk	418
Carso Malvasia, Zidarich	378
Carso Malvasia Istriana, Castelvecchio	405
Carso Pinot Grigio, Castelvecchio	405
Carso Refosco P. R., Castelvecchio	405
Carso Rosso Turmino, Castelvecchio	405
Carso Sauvignon, Castelvecchio	405
Carso Sauvignon, Kante	377
Carso Terrano, Skerk	418
Carso Terrano, Zidarich	378
Carso Traminer Aromatico, Castelvecchio	405
Carso Vitovska, Kante	377
Carso Vitovska, Skerk	418
Carso Vitovska, Zidarich	378
Cartizze, Adami	335
Cartizze, Andreola Orsola	288
Cartizze, Desiderio Bisol & Figli	326
Cartizze, F.lli Bortolin Spumanti	327
Cartizze, Bortolomiol	327
Cartizze, Canevel Spumanti	328
Cartizze, Ciodet	344
Cartizze, Col Vetoraz	328
Cartizze, Dal Din	344
Cartizze, De Faveri	335
Cartizze, Le Bellerive - Angelo Ruggeri	329
Cartizze, Le Colture	329
Cartizze, Masottina	311
Cartizze, Nino Franco	330
Cartizze, Ruggeri & C.	330
Cartizze, Santa Eurosia	331
Cartizze, Tanorè	331
Cartizze, Villa Sandi	338
Cartizze , Paolo Zucchetto	344
Casa Pastore Rosso, Rio Grande	654
Casa Pastore Rosso, Rio Grande	654
Casaboli, Barsento	733
Casaglia, Tenuta di Bagnolo dei Marchesi Pancrazi	526
Casale dei Biscari, Cantine Torrevecchia	744
Casale San Giorgio Rosato, Cant. Coop. del Locorotondo	726
Casalferro, Barone Ricasoli	479
Casalj, Tenute Rapitalà	746
Casarsa, Villa Calcinaia	587
Casirano Rosso, Conte Leopardi Dittajuti	624
Casorzo Malvasia Brigantino, Giulio Accornero e Figli	147
Casorzo Malvasia Passito Pico, Giulio Accornero e Figli	147
Cassàbò Rosso, Valfieri	72
Castel del Monte Aglianico Cappellaccio Ris., Rivera	717
Castel del Monte Bianco, Torrevento	721
Castel del Monte Bianco Fedora, Rivera	717
Castel del Monte Bianco La Piana, Conte Spagnoletti Zeuli	716
Castel del Monte Bianco V. Tufaroli, Santa Lucia	731
Castel del Monte Chardonnay Lama di Corvo, Rivera	717
Castel del Monte Chardonnay Pietrabianca, Tormaresca	729
Castel del Monte Chardonnay Preludio N° 1, Rivera	717
Castel del Monte Nero di Troia Puer Apuliae, Rivera	717
Castel del Monte Pezza La Ruca, Conte Spagnoletti Zeuli	716
Castel del Monte Ris. del Conte, Conte Spagnoletti Zeuli	716
Castel del Monte Rosato, Vinicola Miali	732
Castel del Monte Rosato, Cant. Coop. della Riforma Fondiaria	733
Castel del Monte Rosato, Torrevento	721
Castel del Monte Rosato Mezzana, Conte Spagnoletti Zeuli	716
Castel del Monte Rosato V. Lama di Carro, Santa Lucia	731
Castel del Monte Rosè di Rivera, Rivera	717
Castel del Monte Rosso, Vinicola Miali	732
Castel del Monte Rosso, Cant. Coop. della Riforma Fondiaria	733
Castel del Monte Rosso, Torrevento	721
Castel del Monte Rosso Bocca di Lupo, Tormaresca	729
Castel del Monte Rosso Il Falcone Ris., Rivera	717
Castel del Monte Rosso Rupicolo , Rivera	717
Castel del Monte Rosso V. Pedale Ris., Torrevento	721
Castel del Monte Sauvignon Terre al Monte, Rivera	717
Castellaccio Rosso, Fatt. Uccelliera	585
Castelli Romani, Gotto d'Oro	669
Castellinaldo Barbera d'Alba, Raffaele Gili	59
Castellinaldo Barbera d'Alba, Stefanino Morra	152
Castellinaldo Barbera d'Alba, Vielmin	60
Cast. di Buttrio Marburg, Marco Felluga	385
Cast. di Buttrio Ovestein, Marco Felluga	385
Castelrapiti Rosso, Fatt. Montellori	477
Cauro, Statti	739
Cava del Re Cabernet Sauvignon, D'Alfonso del Sordo	730
Cavaliere, Michele Satta	462
Ceccante , Il Grillesino	586
Cecubo, Villa Matilde	693
Cella Grande di S. Michele Brut , La Cella di San Michele	160
Cellarius Brut Ris., Guido Berlucchi & C.	190
Cenerentola, Karin e Remo Hohler	57
Cenito, Luigi Maffini	692
Cent'Are Bianco, Carlo Pellegrino	751
Centine, Banfi	500
Cento, Cast. di Querceto	488
Centobricchi, Mauro Sebaste	27
Cepparello, Isole e Olena	454
Ceppate, Fatt. di Terrabianca	554
Ceragiolo, Jacopo Banti	458
Ceraso, Giovanni Panizzi	568
Cerasuolo di Vittoria, COS	759
Cerasuolo di Vittoria, Planeta	752
Cerasuolo di Vittoria, Cantine Torrevecchia	744
Cerasuolo di Vittoria, Cant. Valle dell'Acate	744
Cerasuolo di Vittoria Barocco, Avide	748
Cerasuolo di Vittoria Etichetta Nera, Avide	748
Cerasuolo di Vittoria Mont Serrat A.D. 1668, Cantine Torrevecchia	744
Cerasuolo di Vittoria Sciri, COS	759
Cerasuolo di Vittoria V. di Bastonaca, COS	759
Cerbaiona, Cerbaiona	505
Cercatoja Rosso, Fatt. del Buonamico	523
Cerdeña, Antonio Argiolas	775
Cerosecco, Petricci del Pianta	605
Cerro Bianco Chardonnay, Fatt. del Cerro	528
Cervaro della Sala, Cast. della Sala	644
Cerveteri Bianco Fontana Morella, Cant. Cerveteri	666
Cerveteri Bianco V. Grande, Cant. Cerveteri	666
Cerveteri Rosso Fontana Morella, Cant. Cerveteri	666
Cerveteri Rosso V. Grande, Cant. Cerveteri	666
Cerviolo Bianco, San Fabiano Calcinaia	467
Cerviolo Rosso, San Fabiano Calcinaia	467
Cesanese del Piglio, Casale della Ioria	662
Cesanese del Piglio, Terre del Cesanese	674
Cesanese del Piglio Casal Cervino, Massimi Berucci	673
Cesanese del Piglio Casale della Ioria, Casale della Ioria	662
Cesanese del Piglio Colle Forma, Giovanni Terenzi	674
Cesanese del Piglio Etichetta Oro, C.S. Cesanese del Piglio	673
Cesanese del Piglio Etichetta Rossa, C.S. Cesanese del Piglio	673
Cesanese del Piglio Torre del Piano, Casale della Ioria	662
Cesanese del Piglio Vajoscuro, Giovanni Terenzi	674
Cesanese del Piglio Vigne Nuove, Massimi Berucci	673
Cesare Passito Bianco, Le Salette	289
Cesubeo, Fatt. Ca' Rossa	445
Ceuso, Ceuso	745
Ceuso Custera, Ceuso	745
Chaos Rosso, Fatt. Le Terrazze	624
Chardonnay, Adragna	764
Chardonnay, Fattorie Azzolino	746
Chardonnay, Benanti	759
Chardonnay, Ca di Bon	372
Chardonnay, Tenuta di Capezzana	460
Chardonnay, Casale del Giglio	663
Chardonnay, Giovanni Crosato	356
Chardonnay, Feudo Principi di Butera	745
Chardonnay, Walter Filiputti	387
Chardonnay, Gotto d'Oro	669
Chardonnay, Inama	310
Chardonnay, Isole e Olena	454
Chardonnay, Fatt. Lavacchio	599
Chardonnay, Aziende Vinicole Miceli	755
Chardonnay, Gino Pedrotti	227
Chardonnay, Planeta	752
Chardonnay, Teresa Raiz	394
Chardonnay, Tasca d'Almerita	758
Chardonnay, Terre del Sillabo	496
Chardonnay, Cantine Torrevecchia	744
Chardonnay, Trappolini	665
Chardonnay, Vinnaioli Jermann	380
Chardonnay Alhena, San Lorenzo	687
Chardonnay Andritz, Oscar Sturm	369
Chardonnay Aurente, Lungarotti	657
Chardonnay Barbolzana, Giuseppe Vezzoli	196
Chardonnay Brut Col Sandago, Martino Zanetti	341
Chardonnay Calanco, Pandolfa	450
Chardonnay Capitolo, Tenuta Sant'Antonio	297
Chardonnay Castel Verdino, Madonna dei Miracoli	686
Chardonnay Castrum Icerini, Coffele	322
Chardonnay Cesuret, Cast. Rametz	279
Chardonnay Chioma di Berenice, San Lorenzo	687
Chardonnay Colle delle Montecchie, Rio Grande	654
Chardonnay Colle Maggio, Torre Zambra	688
Chardonnay Dalzocchio, Dalzocchio	248
Chardonnay del Lazio, Colle San Lorenzo	667
Chardonnay della Bergamasca Aurito, Cast. di Grumello	217
Chardonnay della Sala, Cast. della Sala	644
Chardonnay Donna Aurelia, Luigi Vivacqua	740
Chardonnay I Legni, Rino Russolo	412
Chardonnay I Palazzi, Lungarotti	657
Chardonnay Jacopo, Fatt. Paradiso	423
Chardonnay Mandrarossa, Settesoli	752
Chardonnay Marina Cvetic, Gianni Masciarelli	684
Chardonnay Opis, Farnese	681
Chardonnay Pergami, Tenuta Amalia	446
Chardonnay Pietrosa, Sarchese Dora	682
Chardonnay Punta di Colle, Marramiero	683
Chardonnay Raffaellesco, Umbria Viticoltori Associati	659
Chardonnay Robbiano, Fanini	643
Chardonnay Roccesco, Orlandi Contucci Ponno	683
Chardonnay Sagrato, Cast. di Montauto	602
Chardonnay Serbato, Batasiolo	88
Chardonnay Sorai, Gini	302
Chardonnay Soris, Pierpaolo Pecorari	412
Chardonnay Tenuta Ribaldaccio, Fattorie Parri	597
Chardonnay Tresor, Agriverde	681
Chardonnay V. di Corte, Pollara	762
Chardonnay Villa Roscià, Agriverde	681

Chiana d'Inserra, Aziende Vinicole Miceli	755		Chianti Cl., Viticcio	492
Chianti , Borgo Casignano	584		Chianti Cl., Cast. di Volpaia	555
Chianti, Fatt. Castiglioni e Montagnana	536		Chianti Cl. Anfiteatro Ris., Vecchie Terre di Montefili	544
Chianti, La Cignozza	585		Chianti Cl. Argenina, Podere Il Palazzino	481
Chianti, Fatt. di Gratena	579		Chianti Cl. Badia a Coltibuono, Coltibuono	480
Chianti, I Casciani	597		Chianti Cl. Badia a Passignano Ris., Marchesi Antinori	475
Chianti, Iesolana	580		Chianti Cl. Barocco, Terre di San Leonino	583
Chianti, Tenuta La Cipressaia	597		Chianti Cl. Beatrice Ris., Viticcio	492
Chianti, La Pieve	498		Chianti Cl. Bellavista, Cast. di Ama	478
Chianti, Mannucci Droandi	597		Chianti Cl. Bello Stento, La Madonnina - Triacca	486
Chianti, Fatt. Montellori	477		Chianti Cl. Berardo Ris., Cast. di Bossi	468
Chianti, Giacomo Mori	601		Chianti Cl. Bertinga, Cast. di Ama	478
Chianti, Petrognano	594		Chianti Cl. Brancaia, La Brancaia	551
Chianti, Fatt. San Fabiano - Borghini Baldovinetti	579		Chianti Cl. Brolio, Barone Ricasoli	479
Chianti, San Vettore	587		Chianti Cl. Bugialla Ris., Poggerino	553
Chianti, Fatt. Sant'Appiano	580		Chianti Cl. Campolungo Ris., S. M. Tenim. Pile e Lamole	482
Chianti, Fatt. Uccelliera	585		Chianti Cl. Cancello Rosso Ris., Fatt. dell' Aiola	583
Chianti, Villa Sant'Anna	535		Chianti Cl. Capannelle Ris., Capannelle	479
Chianti Cast. di Rapale Ris., Giacomo Marengo	594		Chianti Cl. Caparsino, Caparsa	551
Chianti Castelrotto, Giacomo Mori	601		Chianti Cl. Capraia Ris., Rocca di Castagnoli	483
Chianti Cl., Agricoltori del Chianti Geografico	478		Chianti Cl. Casanuova di Nittardi, Fatt. Nittardi	465
Chianti Cl., Cast. d' Albola	550		Chianti Cl. Casasilia, Poggio al Sole	577
Chianti Cl., Borgo Salcetino	550		Chianti Cl. Casasilia Ris., Poggio al Sole	577
Chianti Cl., Canonica a Cerreto	584		Chianti Cl. Castelgreve, Castelli del Grevepesa	558
Chianti Cl., Carobbio	540		Chianti Cl. Castelgreve Ris., Castelli del Grevepesa	558
Chianti Cl., Carpineto	486		Chianti Cl. Castellare Ris., Castellare di Castellina	463
Chianti Cl., Casa Emma	453		Chianti Cl. Cast. di Ama, Cast. di Ama	478
Chianti Cl., Casa Sola	580		Chianti Cl. Cast. di Brolio, Barone Ricasoli	479
Chianti Cl., Fatt. Casaloste	598		Chianti Cl. Cast. di Fonterutoli, Cast. di Fonterutoli	463
Chianti Cl., Castagnoli	462		Chianti Cl. Cellole Ris., San Fabiano Calcinaia	467
Chianti Cl., Castellare di Castellina	463		Chianti Cl. Ceppeto, Mannucci Droandi	597
Chianti Cl., Cast. dei Rampolla	540		Chianti Cl. Clemente VII Ris., Castelli del Grevepesa	558
Chianti Cl., Cast. della Panaretta	453		Chianti Cl. Coltassala Ris., Cast. di Volpaia	555
Chianti Cl., Cast. di Bossi	468		Chianti Cl. Comignole, La Marcellina	542
Chianti Cl., Cast. di Fonterutoli	463		Chianti Cl. Contessa di Radda, Agricoltori del Chianti Geografico	478
Chianti Cl., Famiglia Cecchi	464		Chianti Cl. Cortevecchia Ris., Fatt. Le Corti - Corsini	560
Chianti Cl., Cennatoio Intervineas	541		Chianti Cl. Doccio a Matteo Ris., Caparsa	551
Chianti Cl., Cigliano	601		Chianti Cl. Don Alberto Ris., Le Miccine	586
Chianti Cl., Colle Bereto	600		Chianti Cl. Don Tommaso, Fatt. Le Corti - Corsini	560
Chianti Cl., Podere Collelungo	464		Chianti Cl. Fizzano Ris., Rocca delle Macìe	466
Chianti Cl., Concadoro	465		Chianti Cl. Frimaio, Fatt. Poggio Romita	605
Chianti Cl., Fatt. di Dievole	469		Chianti Cl. Frimaio Ris., Fatt. Poggio Romita	605
Chianti Cl., Fatt. di Felsina	470		Chianti Cl. Giorgio Primo, La Massa	542
Chianti Cl., Tenuta Fontodi	541		Chianti Cl. Grosso Sanese , Podere Il Palazzino	481
Chianti Cl., Il Mandorlo	559		Chianti Cl. Grosso Sanese Ris., Podere Il Palazzino	481
Chianti Cl., Il Poggiolino	576		Chianti Cl. I Sassi, Melini	547
Chianti Cl., Isole e Olena	454		Chianti Cl. Il Grigio Ris., San Felice	472
Chianti Cl., Ispoli	559		Chianti Cl. Il Poggio Ris., Cast. di Monsanto	455
Chianti Cl., La Brancaia	551		Chianti Cl. Il Tarocco, Torraccia di Presura	490
Chianti Cl., La Madonnina - Triacca	486		Chianti Cl. Il Tarocco Ris., Torraccia di Presura	490
Chianti Cl., La Massa	542		Chianti Cl. L'Aura, Quercento di Castellina	466
Chianti Cl., Tenuta La Novella	587		Chianti Cl. La Casuccia, Cast. di Ama	478
Chianti Cl., Fatt. La Ripa	605		Chianti Cl. La Forra Ris., Tenute Ambrogio e Giovanni Folonari	476
Chianti Cl., La Sala	560		Chianti Cl. La Pieve, Podere Il Palazzino	481
Chianti Cl., Le Bocce	543		Chianti Cl. La Prima Ris., Cast. di Vicchiomaggio	491
Chianti Cl., Le Cinciole	598		Chianti Cl. La Selvanella Ris., Melini	547
Chianti Cl., Fatt. Le Corti - Corsini	560		Chianti Cl. Lamole Barrique, S. M. Tenim. Pile e Lamole	482
Chianti Cl., Le Filigare	454		Chianti Cl. Lamole di Lamole, S. M. Tenim. Pile e Lamole	482
Chianti Cl., Le Fonti	547		Chianti Cl. Lamole di Lamole Ris., S. M. Tenim. Pile e Lamole	482
Chianti Cl., Le Miccine	586		Chianti Cl. Le Ellere, Cast. d' Albola	550
Chianti Cl., Lornano	596		Chianti Cl. Le Masse di Greve, Lanciola	494
Chianti Cl., Cast. di Lucignano	586		Chianti Cl. Le Masse di Greve Ris., Lanciola	494
Chianti Cl., Cast. di Meleto	481		Chianti Cl. Le Trame, Podere Le Boncie	584
Chianti Cl., Fatt. Montecchio	576		Chianti Cl. Lorenzo, Le Filigare	454
Chianti Cl., Fatt. di Montemaggio	600		Chianti Cl. Lucarello Ris., Borgo Salcetino	550
Chianti Cl., Cast. di Monterinaldi	600		Chianti Cl. Maria Vittoria Ris., Le Filigare	454
Chianti Cl., Montiverdi	482		Chianti Cl. Matroneo, Enrico Pierazzuoli	459
Chianti Cl., Fatt. Nittardi	465		Chianti Cl. Messer Piero di Teuzzo, Famiglia Cecchi	464
Chianti Cl., Fatt. di Petroio	471		Chianti Cl. Misciano Ris., Borgo Scopeto	584
Chianti Cl., Pian Del Gallo	587		Chianti Cl. Monna Lisa Ris., Villa V.maggio	491
Chianti Cl., Podere Capaccia	553		Chianti Cl. Monsenese, Tenim. Angelini - San Leonino	583
Chianti Cl., Poggerino	553		Chianti Cl. Montegiachi Ris., Agricoltori del Chianti Geografico	478
Chianti Cl., Poggio al Sole	577		Chianti Cl. Novecento, Fatt. di Dievole	469
Chianti Cl., Poggio Amorelli	582		Chianti Cl. Nozzole, Tenute Ambrogio e Giovanni Folonari	476
Chianti Cl., Poggio Bonelli	471		Chianti Cl. O'Leandro Ris., Cennatoio Intervineas	541
Chianti Cl., Fatt. Poggiopiano	561		Chianti Cl. Panzanello, Panzanello	543
Chianti Cl., Cast. di Querceto	488		Chianti Cl. Panzanello Ris., Panzanello	543
Chianti Cl., Querciabella	488		Chianti Cl. Pèppoli, Marchesi Antinori	475
Chianti Cl., Riecine	483		Chianti Cl. Petresco Ris., Le Cinciole	598
Chianti Cl., Rietine	586		Chianti Cl. Petri Ris., Cast. di Vicchiomaggio	491
Chianti Cl., Riseccoli	489		Chianti Cl. Pieve di Spaltenna, Cast. di Meleto	481
Chianti Cl., Rocca delle Macìe	466		Chianti Cl. Podere di Stignano, San Vincenti	485
Chianti Cl., Rocca di Castagnoli	483		Chianti Cl. Poggio ai Frati Ris., Rocca di Castagnoli	483
Chianti Cl., Rocca di Montegrossi	484		Chianti Cl. Poggio Rosso Ris., San Felice	472
Chianti Cl., San Fabiano Calcinaia	467		Chianti Cl. R. S., Coltibuono	480
Chianti Cl., San Felice	472		Chianti Cl. Rancia Ris., Fatt. di Felsina	470
Chianti Cl., San Giusto a Rentennano	484		Chianti Cl. Ris., Fatt. dell' Aiola	583
Chianti Cl., San Vincenti	485		Chianti Cl. Ris., Cast. d' Albola	550
Chianti Cl., Savignola Paolina	489		Chianti Cl. Ris., Borgo Scopeto	584
Chianti Cl., Cast. di Selvole	472		Chianti Cl. Ris., Carobbio	540
Chianti Cl., Solatione	601		Chianti Cl. Ris., Carpineto	486
Chianti Cl., Spadaio e Piecorto	580		Chianti Cl. Ris., Casa Emma	453
Chianti Cl., Tenim. Angelini - San Leonino	583		Chianti Cl. Ris., Casa Sola	580
Chianti Cl. , Torraccia di Presura	490		Chianti Cl. Ris., Fatt. Casaloste	598
Chianti Cl., Vecchie Terre di Montefili	544		Chianti Cl. Ris., Castellare di Castellina	463
Chianti Cl., Cast. di Verrazzano	490		Chianti Cl. Ris., Cast. della Panaretta	453
Chianti Cl., Villa V.maggio	491		Chianti Cl. Ris., Cast. di Bossi	468
Chianti Cl., Villa Cafaggio	544		Chianti Cl. Ris., Cennatoio Intervineas	541
Chianti Cl., Villa Calcinaia	587		Chianti Cl. Ris., Cigliano	601
Chianti Cl., Villa Rosa	583		Chianti Cl. Ris, Colle Bereto	600
Chianti Cl., Villa Trasqua	583		Chianti Cl. Ris., Podere Collelungo	464

Chianti Cl. Ris., Coltibuono	480
Chianti Cl. Ris., Concadoro	465
Chianti Cl. Ris., Il Colombaio di Cencio	480
Chianti Cl. Ris., Il Poggiolino	576
Chianti Cl. Ris., La Madonnina - Triacca	486
Chianti Cl. Ris., Tenuta La Novella	587
Chianti Cl. Ris., Fatt. La Ripa	605
Chianti Cl. Ris., La Sala	560
Chianti Cl. Ris., Le Bocce	543
Chianti Cl. Ris., Le Filigare	454
Chianti Cl. Ris., Le Fonti	547
Chianti Cl. Ris., Cast. di Lucignano	586
Chianti Cl. Ris., Cast. di Meleto	481
Chianti Cl. Ris., Cast. di Monsanto	455
Chianti Cl. Ris., Fatt. Montecchio	576
Chianti Cl. Ris., Fatt. di Montemaggio	600
Chianti Cl. Ris., Montiverdi	482
Chianti Cl. Ris., Fatt. Nittardi	465
Chianti Cl. Ris., Fatt. di Petroio	471
Chianti Cl. Ris., Podere Capaccia	553
Chianti Cl. Ris., Poggerino	553
Chianti Cl. Ris., Poggio Bonelli	471
Chianti Cl. Ris., Cast. di Querceto	488
Chianti Cl. Ris., Querciabella	488
Chianti Cl. Ris., Riecine	483
Chianti Cl. Ris., Rietine	586
Chianti Cl. Ris., Riseccoli	489
Chianti Cl. Ris., Rocca delle Macìe	466
Chianti Cl. Ris., Rocca di Montegrossi	484
Chianti Cl. Ris., San Giusto a Rentennano	484
Chianti Cl. Ris., San Vincenti	485
Chianti Cl. Ris., Savignola Paolina	489
Chianti Cl. Ris., Cast. di Selvole	472
Chianti Cl. Ris., Solatione	601
Chianti Cl. Ris., Tenim. Angelini - San Leonino	583
Chianti Cl. Ris., Vecchie Terre di Montefili	544
Chianti Cl. Ris., Cast. di Verrazzano	490
Chianti Cl. Ris., V.vecchia	554
Chianti Cl. Ris., Vignole	598
Chianti Cl. Ris., Villa Arceno	473
Chianti Cl. Ris., Villa Cafaggio	544
Chianti Cl. Ris., Villa Calcinaia	587
Chianti Cl. Ris., Villa Rosa	583
Chianti Cl. Ris., Villa Trasqua	583
Chianti Cl. Ris., Viticcio	492
Chianti Cl. Ris., Cast. di Volpaia	555
Chianti Cl. Ris. Ducale Oro, Tenim. Ruffino	548
Chianti Cl. Ris. Il Rotone, Il Mandorlo	559
Chianti Cl. Rocca Guicciarda, Barone Ricasoli	479
Chianti Cl. Roveto, Podere Collelungo	464
Chianti Cl. San Jacopo, Cast. di Vicchiomaggio	491
Chianti Cl. Sant'Angiolo Vico l'Abate, Castelli del Grevepesa	558
Chianti Cl. Santedame, Tenim. Ruffino	548
Chianti Cl. Sassocupo, La Marcellina	542
Chianti Cl. Scassino, Fatt. di Terrabianca	554
Chianti Cl. Tenuta S. Alfonso, Rocca delle Macìe	466
Chianti Cl. Tenute del Marchese Ris., Marchesi Antinori	475
Chianti Cl. Terre di Prenzano, Villa V.maggio	491
Chianti Cl. Torre a Destra Ris., Cast. della Panerétta	453
Chianti Cl. Tramonti, Tramonti	583
Chianti Cl. V. di Fontalle Ris., Machiavelli	561
Chianti Cl. V. La Palaia, La Madonnina - Triacca	486
Chianti Cl. Ventesimo Ris., Montiverdi	482
Chianti Cl. V. del Sorbo Ris., Tenuta Fontodi	541
Chianti Cl. V. della Croce Ris., Fatt. di Terrabianca	554
Chianti Cl. V. di Gaversa, Concadoro	465
Chianti Cl. V. il Poggiale Ris., Castellare di Castellina	463
Chianti Cl. Vign. Cipressone, Montiverdi	482
Chianti Cl. Vign. S. Marcellino Ris., Rocca di Montegrossi	484
Chianti Cl. Villa Antinori Ris., Marchesi Antinori	475
Chianti Cl. Villa Cerna, Famiglia Cecchi	464
Chianti Cl. Villa Cerna Ris., Famiglia Cecchi	464
Chianti Cl. Villa Maisano, Montiverdi	482
Chianti Cl. Villa Maisano Quello, Montiverdi	482
Chianti Cl. Villa Maisano Questo, Montiverdi	482
Chianti Cl. Villa Maisano Ris., Montiverdi	482
Chianti Cl. Villa Vistarenni, S. M. Tenim. Pile e Lamole	482
Chianti Cl. Vitigliano, Villa V.maggio	491
Chianti Cl., Terreno	587
Chianti Cl. I Massi, Il Colombaio di Cencio	480
Chianti Cl. I Massi Ris., Il Colombaio di Cencio	480
Chianti Cl. Ris., Terreno	587
Chianti Colli Aretini, Villa Cilnia	452
Chianti Colli Aretini Ris., Villa Cilnia	452
Chianti Colli Fiorentini, Castelvecchio	557
Chianti Colli Fiorentini, Fatt. di Fiano	584
Chianti Colli Fiorentini, Le Sorgenti	452
Chianti Colli Fiorentini, San Michele a Torri	603
Chianti Colli Fiorentini Il Cortile, Cast. di Poppiano	537
Chianti Colli Fiorentini Il Trecione Ris., Le Calvane	536
Chianti Colli Fiorentini La Torretta, La Querce	494
Chianti Colli Fiorentini Ris., Fatt. di Bagnolo	588
Chianti Colli Fiorentini Ris., Cast. di Poppiano	537
Chianti Colli Fiorentini Sorrottole, La Querce	494
Chianti Colli Senesi, Baroncini	562
Chianti Colli Senesi, Vincenzo Cesani	563
Chianti Colli Senesi , Crociani	594
Chianti Colli Senesi, Tenuta Farneta	604
Chianti Colli Senesi, Farnetella	571
Chianti Colli Senesi, Fatt. Il Palagio	474
Chianti Colli Senesi, Il Paradiso	564
Chianti Colli Senesi, La Lastra	566
Chianti Colli Senesi, Montenidoli	567
Chianti Colli Senesi, Pacina	470
Chianti Colli Senesi, Palagetto	568
Chianti Colli Senesi, Italo Rubicini	602
Chianti Colli Senesi, Villa Sant'Anna	535
Chianti Colli Senesi Arcano, Famiglia Cecchi	464
Chianti Colli Senesi Cinabro, Casa alle Vacche	563
Chianti Colli Senesi Gioia, Carpineta Fontalpino	468
Chianti Colli Senesi Poggiarelli, Signano	602
Chianti Colli Senesi Poggio Cenni, Fatt. Casabianca	539
Chianti Colli Senesi Ris., Palagetto	568
Chianti Colli Senesi Ris., F.lli Vagnoni	570
Chianti Colli Senesi Sup. V. S. Domenico Sovestro, Baroncini	562
Chianti Colli Senesi Vertunno, Giovanni Panizzi	568
Chianti dei C. Senesi Ellera, Castelpugna	604
Chianti dei C. Senesi Ellera Ris., Castelpugna	604
Chianti dei Colli Aretini, Coop. Agr. Valdarnese	606
Chianti dei Colli Fiorentini, Castelvecchio	557
Chianti dei Colli Fiorentini, Fatt. di Bagnolo	588
Chianti dei Colli Fiorentini, Fatt. Lilliano	579
Chianti dei Colli Fiorentini, Tenuta La Cipressaia	597
Chianti dei Colli Fiorentini, Lanciola	494
Chianti dei Colli Fiorentini, Le Sorgenti	452
Chianti dei Colli Fiorentini Il Trecione Ris., Le Calvane	536
Chianti dei Colli Fiorentini Quercione, Le Calvane	536
Chianti dei Colli Fiorentini Ris., Castelvecchio	557
Chianti dei Colli Fiorentini San Camillo, Tenuta Il Corno	558
Chianti dei Colli Senesi, Carpineta Fontalpino	468
Chianti dei Colli Senesi, Fatt. del Cerro	528
Chianti dei Colli Senesi, Farnetella	571
Chianti dei Colli Senesi, Pacina	470
Chianti dei Colli Senesi, Salchèto	533
Chianti dei Colli Senesi Cinabro, Casa alle Vacche	563
Chianti dei Colli Senesi Terra di Siena, Tenuta di Trecciano	604
Chianti dei Colli Senesi Terra Rossa Ris., Tenuta di Trecciano	604
Chianti dei Colli Senesi Via dei Franchi, La Rampa di Fugnano	566
Chianti Fortebraccio, La Pieve	498
Chianti I Sodi del Paretaio, Badia di Morrona	578
Chianti I Tre Borri, Fatt. Corzano e Paterno	557
Chianti La Commenda Ris., Giacomo Marengo	594
Chianti Le Gaggiole Ris., Fassati	529
Chianti Le Stoppie, San Gervasio	598
Chianti Leonardo, Cantine Leonardo da Vinci	578
Chianti Leonardo Ris., Cantine Leonardo da Vinci	578
Chianti Montalbano, Enrico Pierazzuoli	459
Chianti Montalbano Ris., Enrico Pierazzuoli	459
Chianti Montespertoli, Fatt. Cast. Sonnino	537
Chianti Montespertoli Cast. di Sonnino, Fatt. Cast. Sonnino	537
Chianti Montespertoli Le Prode del Chiù, Fattorie Parri	597
Chianti Montoli Ris., Pasolini Dall'Onda	586
Chianti Rio Camerata, Piazzano	585
Chianti Rio Camerata Ris., Piazzano	585
Chianti Ris., Petrognano	594
Chianti Ris. Poggio Cenni, Fatt. Casabianca	539
Chianti Rufina, Fatt. di Basciano	556
Chianti Rufina, Frascole	585
Chianti Rufina, Grignano	599
Chianti Rufina, Fatt. Lavacchio	599
Chianti Rufina, Fatt. Selvapiana	549
Chianti Rufina Bucerchiale Ris., Fatt. Selvapiana	549
Chianti Rufina Fornace Ris., Fatt. Selvapiana	549
Chianti Rufina Il Santo Ris., Frascole	585
Chianti Rufina Montesodi, Marchesi de' Frescobaldi	476
Chianti Rufina Nipozzano Ris., Marchesi de' Frescobaldi	476
Chianti Rufina Poggio Gualtieri Ris., Grignano	599
Chianti Rufina Ris., Fatt. di Basciano	556
Chianti Rufina Ris., Grignano	599
Chianti Rufina Ris., Fatt. Lavacchio	599
Chianti Rufina Ris., Fatt. Selvapiana	549
Chianti Santa Caterina, Castelvecchio	557
Chianti Sup., La Cignozza	585
Chianti Sup. Cottaccio , Fatt. Sant'Appiano	580
Chianti Terre di Corzano, Fatt. Corzano e Paterno	557
Chianti Terre di Corzano Ris., Fatt. Corzano e Paterno	557
Chianti Villa Chigi, Fattorie Chigi Saracini	469
Chianti Villa Petriolo, Fatt. di Petriolo	584
Chiaramonte Bianco, Casa Vinicola Firriato	754
Chiaramonte Rosso, Casa Vinicola Firriato	754
Chiaretto, Angelo Nicolis e Figli	315
Ciapin Bianco, Cascina Roera	71
Cicisbeo, Le Tende	292
Cicogio, Il Lebbio	565
Cign'Oro, Villa Cilnia	452
Cignale, Cast. di Querceto	488
Ciliegiolo, La Busattina	589
Cimbolo, Poggio Bertaio	644
Cinerino Bianco, Marziano e Enrico Abbona	74
Cinque Querce Rosso, Salvatore Molettieri	697
Cinque Terre, Buranco	169
Cinque Terre, Cant. Cinqueterre	175
Cinque Terre, Walter De Battè	173
Cinque Terre, Forlini Cappellini	175
Cinque Terre, La Polenza	176
Cinque Terre Marea, Enoteca Bisson	165
Cinque Terre Marea Barrique, Enoteca Bisson	165
Cinque Terre Sciacchetrà, Buranco	169
Cinque Terre Sciacchetrà, Cant. Cinqueterre	175
Cinque Terre Sciacchetrà, Walter De Battè	173
Cinque Terre Sciacchetrà Ris., Walter De Battè	173
Cinque Torri Brut, Carra	433

Circeo Rosso Il Sogno, Cant. Sant'Andrea	674		COF Chardonnay, Ronchi di Manzano	388
Cirò Bianco, Cant. Enotria	741		COF Chardonnay, Ronco del Gnemiz	411
Cirò Bianco, Ippolito 1845	741		COF Chardonnay, Ronco Severo	419
Cirò Bianco, Librandi	737		COF Chardonnay, Torre Rosazza	389
Cirò Bianco, Malena	737		COF Chardonnay, V. Traverso	403
Cirò Bianco, Fatt. San Francesco	736		COF Chardonnay, Vigne Fantin Noda'r	399
Cirò Bianco, Vinicola Zito	741		COF Chardonnay Carato, Dal Fari	356
Cirò Bianco Curiale, Caparra & Siciliani	736		COF Chardonnay Podere Stabili della Rocca,	
Cirò Rosato, Cant. Enotria	741		Tenuta di Angoris	358
Cirò Rosato, Ippolito 1845	741		COF Chardonnay Vign. Ronc di Juri, Girolamo Dorigo	349
Cirò Rosato, Librandi	737		COF Chardonnay Zuc di Volpe, Volpe Pasini	415
Cirò Rosato, Fatt. San Francesco	736		COF Malvasia, Conte D'Attimis-Maniago	349
Cirò Rosato, Vinicola Zito	741		COF Malvasia, Le Vigne di Zamò	387
Cirò Rosato Le Formelle, Caparra & Siciliani	736		COF Merlot, Livio e Claudio Buiatti	348
Cirò Rosso Cl., Caparra & Siciliani	736		COF Merlot, Ca di Bon	372
Cirò Rosso Cl., Cant. Enotria	741		COF Merlot, Alfieri Cantarutti	410
Cirò Rosso Cl., Librandi	737		COF Merlot, Paolino Comelli	378
Cirò Rosso Cl., Fatt. San Francesco	736		COF Merlot, Conte D'Attimis-Maniago	349
Cirò Rosso Cl. , Vinicola Zito	741		COF Merlot, Dario e Luciano Ermacora	397
Cirò Rosso Cl. Donna Madda, Fatt. San Francesco	736		COF Merlot, Adriano Gigante	373
Cirò Rosso Cl. Ris., Vinicola Zito	741		COF Merlot, Jacùss	414
Cirò Rosso Cl. Ronco dei Quattro Venti, Fatt. San Francesco	736		COF Merlot, La Roncaia	391
Cirò Rosso Cl. Sup., Caparra & Siciliani	736		COF Merlot, La Tunella	397
Cirò Rosso Cl. Sup., Malena	737		COF Merlot, La Viarte	400
Cirò Rosso Cl. Sup. Colli del Mancuso Ris., Ippolito 1845	741		COF Merlot, Le Due Terre	400
Cirò Rosso Cl. Sup. Donna Madda, Fatt. San Francesco	736		COF Merlot, Miani	350
Cirò Rosso Cl. Sup. Piana delle Fate Ris., Cant. Enotria	741		COF Merlot, Petrucco	351
Cirò Rosso Cl. Sup. Ris., Caparra & Siciliani	736		COF Merlot, Petrussa	401
Cirò Rosso Cl. Sup. Ris. Pian della Corte, Malena	737		COF Merlot, Scubla	398
Cirò Rosso Cl. Sup. Ris. Volvito, Caparra & Siciliani	736		COF Merlot, Leonardo Specogna	374
Cirò Rosso Cl. Sup. Volvito, Caparra & Siciliani	736		COF Merlot, Torre Rosazza	389
Civitella Rosso, Sergio Mottura	666		COF Merlot, Valchiarò	415
Clavis, Ca' del Vent	215		COF Merlot, V. Traverso	403
Cleos, San Lorenzo	659		COF Merlot, Vigne Fantin Noda'r	399
Coda di Volpe del Taburno Serra Docile, Cant. del Taburno	693		COF Merlot, Andrea Visintini	375
Coda di Volpe V. Olmo, Di Meo	699		COF Merlot, Zof	375
Codirosso, S. M. Tenim. Pile e Lamole	482		COF Merlot Artiùl, Ronco Severo	419
COF Bianco, Miani	350		COF Merlot Centis, Rocca Bernarda	398
COF Bianco, Ronco del Gnemiz	411		COF Merlot Focus Zuc di Volpe, Volpe Pasini	415
COF Bianco, Andrea Visintini	375		COF Merlot Il Barrique, Andrea Visintini	375
COF Bianco Blanc di Buri, Davino Meroi	350		COF Merlot l'Altromerlot, Torre Rosazza	389
COF Bianco Campo Marzio, La Tunella	397		COF Merlot Oltre, Leonardo Specogna	374
COF Bianco Canto, Alfieri Cantarutti	410		COF Merlot Romain, Paolo Rodaro	358
COF Bianco Carato, Vigne Fantin Noda'r	399		COF Merlot Ronc di Subule, Ronchi di Manzano	388
COF Bianco del Postiglione, Perusini	374		COF Merlot Sel., Iole Grillo	399
COF Bianco delle Grazie, Dal Fari	356		COF Merlot Sol, Ronco del Gnemiz	411
COF Bianco Eclisse, La Roncaia	391		COF Merlot Vigne Cinquant'Anni, Le Vigne di Zamò	387
COF Bianco Illivio, Livio Felluga	363		COF Merlot Vocalis, Aquila del Torre	394
COF Bianco La Clupa, Valchiarò	415		COF Montsclapade, Girolamo Dorigo	349
COF Bianco Le Roverelle Zuc di Volpe, Volpe Pasini	415		COF Picolit, Tenuta di Angoris	358
COF Bianco Liende, La Viarte	400		COF Picolit, Aquila del Torre	394
COF Bianco Locum Nostrum, Paolino Comelli	378		COF Picolit, Valentino Butussi	371
COF Bianco Nojâr, Bandut - Giorgio Colutta	386		COF Picolit, Ca' Ronesca	376
COF Bianco Petrussa, Petrussa	401		COF Picolit, Conte D'Attimis-Maniago	349
COF Bianco Ploe di Stelis, Il Roncal	357		COF Picolit, Dario e Luciano Ermacora	397
COF Bianco Poanis Blanc, Olivo Buiatti	348		COF Picolit, Adriano Gigante	373
COF Bianco Poiesis, Walter Filiputti	387		COF Picolit, Iole Grillo	399
COF Bianco Pomédes, Scubla	398		COF Picolit, Jacùss	414
COF Bianco Ronco delle Acacie, Le Vigne di Zamò	387		COF Picolit, La Roncaia	391
COF Bianco Sacrisassi, Le Due Terre	400		COF Picolit, La Tunella	397
COF Bianco Santa Justina, Iole Grillo	399		COF Picolit, Valerio Marinig	401
COF Bianco Spiule, Tenuta di Angoris	358		COF Picolit, Davino Meroi	350
COF Bianco Vineis, Rocca Bernarda	398		COF Picolit, Perusini	374
COF Boscorosso, Rosa Bosco	386		COF Picolit, Rocca Bernarda	398
COF Cabernet , Olivo Buiatti	348		COF Picolit, Paolo Rodaro	358
COF Cabernet, Valentino Butussi	371		COF Picolit, Ronco Vieri	419
COF Cabernet, Conte D'Attimis-Maniago	349		COF Picolit, Torre Rosazza	389
COF Cabernet, Dal Fari	356		COF Picolit, Valchiarò	415
COF Cabernet, Ronco dei Pini	402		COF Picolit, V. Petrussa	402
COF Cabernet, Valchiarò	415		COF Picolit, Zof	375
COF Cabernet, Vigne Fantin Noda'r	399		COF Picolit Monasterium Ris., Walter Filiputti	387
COF Cabernet, Andrea Visintini	375		COF Picolit Romandus, Dario Coos	391
COF Cabernet Franc, La Tunella	397		COF Picolit V. T., Aquila del Torre	394
COF Cabernet Franc, Perusini	374		COF Pignolo, Girolamo Dorigo	349
COF Cabernet Franc, Petrucco	351		COF Pignolo, Davide Moschioni	357
COF Cabernet Franc, Flavio Pontoni	417		COF Pignolo, Il Roncal	357
COF Cabernet Franc, Il Roncal	357		COF Pignolo, Leonardo Specogna	374
COF Cabernet Franc, Leonardo Specogna	374		COF Pinot Bianco, Livio e Claudio Buiatti	348
COF Cabernet Franc, Torre Rosazza	389		COF Pinot Bianco, Valentino Butussi	371
COF Cabernet Franc, V. Petrussa	402		COF Pinot Bianco, Ca di Bon	372
COF Cabernet Franc, V. Traverso	403		COF Pinot Bianco, Dario e Luciano Ermacora	397
COF Cabernet Franc, Zof	375		COF Pinot Bianco, La Viarte	400
COF Cabernet Franc Ris., Tenuta Bosco Romagno	417		COF Pinot Bianco, Valerio Marinig	401
COF Cabernet Sauvignon, Bandut - Giorgio Colutta	386		COF Pinot Bianco, Perusini	374
COF Cabernet Sauvignon, Paolino Comelli	378		COF Pinot Bianco, Petrussa	401
COF Cabernet Sauvignon, Jacùss	414		COF Pinot Bianco, Paolo Rodaro	358
COF Cabernet Sauvignon, La Roncaia	391		COF Pinot Bianco, Ronco dei Pini	402
COF Cabernet Sauvignon, Perusini	374		COF Pinot Bianco, Ronco delle Betulle	388
COF Cabernet Sauvignon, Ronchi di Manzano	388		COF Pinot Bianco, Scubla	398
COF Cabernet Sauvignon, Scubla	398		COF Pinot Bianco, Andrea Visintini	375
COF Cabernet Zuc di Volpe, Volpe Pasini	415		COF Pinot Bianco Tullio Zamò, Le Vigne di Zamò	387
COF Chardonnay, Valentino Butussi	371		COF Pinot Bianco Zuc di Volpe, Volpe Pasini	415
COF Chardonnay, Paolino Comelli	378		COF Pinot Grigio, Bandut - Giorgio Colutta	386
COF Chardonnay, Conte D'Attimis-Maniago	349		COF Pinot Grigio, Livio e Claudio Buiatti	348
COF Chardonnay, Adriano Gigante	373		COF Pinot Grigio, Olivo Buiatti	348
COF Chardonnay, La Roncaia	391		COF Pinot Grigio, Valentino Butussi	371
COF Chardonnay, Valerio Marinig	401		COF Pinot Grigio, Alfieri Cantarutti	410
COF Chardonnay, Davino Meroi	350		COF Pinot Grigio, Paolino Comelli	378
COF Chardonnay, Petrucco	351		COF Pinot Grigio, Dal Fari	356
COF Chardonnay, Rocca Bernarda	398		COF Pinot Grigio, Girolamo Dorigo	349
COF Chardonnay, Il Roncal	357		COF Pinot Grigio, Dario e Luciano Ermacora	397

COF Pinot Grigio, Livio Felluga	363		COF Rosso Petrussa, Petrussa	401
COF Pinot Grigio, Adriano Gigante	373		COF Rosso Pignolo Prima V. Ris., Walter Filiputti	387
COF Pinot Grigio, Iole Grillo	399		COF Rosso Reâl, Davide Moschioni	357
COF Pinot Grigio, La Tunella	397		COF Rosso Roi, La Viarte	400
COF Pinot Grigio, La Viarte	400		COF Rosso Ronco dei Roseti, Le Vigne di Zamò	387
COF Pinot Grigio, Le Vigne di Zamò	387		COF Rosso Ros di Buri, Davino Meroi	350
COF Pinot Grigio, Midolini	419		COF Rosso Sacrisassi, Le Due Terre	400
COF Pinot Grigio, Perusini	374		COF Rosso Scuro, Scubla	398
COF Pinot Grigio, Petrucco	351		COF Rosso Selenard, Bandut - Giorgio Colutta	386
COF Pinot Grigio, Flavio Pontoni	417		COF Rosso Soffumbergo, Paolino Comelli	378
COF Pinot Grigio, Teresa Raiz	394		COF Rosso Sottocast., V. Traverso	403
COF Pinot Grigio, Rocca Bernarda	398		COF Rosso Sottocast. Ris., V. Traverso	403
COF Pinot Grigio, Paolo Rodaro	358		COF Sariz, Ca' Ronesca	376
COF Pinot Grigio, Il Roncal	357		COF Sauvignon, Bandut - Giorgio Colutta	386
COF Pinot Grigio, Ronchi di Manzano	388		COF Sauvignon, Livio e Claudio Buiatti	348
COF Pinot Grigio, Ronco del Gnemiz	411		COF Sauvignon, Valentino Butussi	371
COF Pinot Grigio, Torre Rosazza	389		COF Sauvignon, Alfieri Cantarutti	410
COF Pinot Grigio, Valchiarò	415		COF Sauvignon, Conte D'Attimis-Maniago	349
COF Pinot Grigio, V. Traverso	403		COF Sauvignon, Dal Fari	356
COF Pinot Grigio, Vigne Fantin Noda'r	399		COF Sauvignon, Dario e Luciano Ermacora	397
COF Pinot Grigio, Andrea Visintini	375		COF Sauvignon, Livio Felluga	363
COF Pinot Grigio, Zof	375		COF Sauvignon, Adriano Gigante	373
COF Pinot Grigio Plus, Bastianich	396		COF Sauvignon, Iole Grillo	399
COF Pinot Grigio Podere Ronco Antico, Tenuta di Angoris	358		COF Sauvignon, Jacùss	414
COF Pinot Grigio Volpe Pasini, Volpe Pasini	415		COF Sauvignon, La Viarte	400
COF Pinot Nero, Le Due Terre	400		COF Sauvignon, Le Vigne di Zamò	387
COF Pinot Nero Ronco del Palazzo, Torre Rosazza	389		COF Sauvignon, Valerio Marinig	401
COF Ramandolo, Dario Coos	391		COF Sauvignon, Davino Meroi	350
COF Ramandolo, La Roncaia	391		COF Sauvignon, Miani	350
COF Ramandolo, Ronco Vieri	419		COF Sauvignon, Perusini	374
COF Ramandolo Il Longhino, Dario Coos	391		COF Sauvignon, Petrucco	351
COF Ramandolo Passito Romandus, Dario Coos	391		COF Sauvignon, Petrussa	401
COF Refosco, Ronco Vieri	419		COF Sauvignon, Teresa Raiz	394
COF Refosco P. R., Bandut - Giorgio Colutta	386		COF Sauvignon, Rocca Bernarda	398
COF Refosco P. R., Livio e Claudio Buiatti	348		COF Sauvignon, Paolo Rodaro	358
COF Refosco P. R., Ca di Bon	372		COF Sauvignon, Il Roncal	357
COF Refosco P. R., Ca' Ronesca	376		COF Sauvignon, Ronchi di Manzano	388
COF Refosco P.R., Alfieri Cantarutti	410		COF Sauvignon, Ronco del Gnemiz	411
COF Refosco P. R., Conte D'Attimis-Maniago	349		COF Sauvignon, Ronco delle Betulle	388
COF Refosco P. R., Dario e Luciano Ermacora	397		COF Sauvignon, Ronco Severo	419
COF Refosco P. R., Livio Felluga	363		COF Sauvignon, Scubla	398
COF Refosco P. R., Adriano Gigante	373		COF Sauvignon, Leonardo Specogna	374
COF Refosco P. R., Iole Grillo	399		COF Sauvignon, Torre Rosazza	389
COF Refosco P. R., Jacùss	414		COF Sauvignon, Valchiarò	415
COF Refosco P.R., La Tunella	397		COF Sauvignon, V. Petrussa	402
COF Refosco P. R., Midolini	419		COF Sauvignon, V. Traverso	403
COF Refosco P. R., Davide Moschioni	357		COF Sauvignon, Vigne Fantin Noda'r	399
COF Refosco P. R., Petrucco	351		COF Sauvignon, Andrea Visintini	375
COF Refosco P. R., Ronchi di Manzano	388		COF Sauvignon, Zof	375
COF Refosco P. R., Leonardo Specogna	374		COF Sauvignon Blanc, Rosa Bosco	386
COF Refosco P. R., Torre Rosazza	389		COF Sauvignon Bosc Romain, Paolo Rodaro	358
COF Refosco P. R., Valchiarò	415		COF Sauvignon Casali Roncali, Cabert	417
COF Refosco P. R., V. Petrussa	402		COF Sauvignon Podere dei Blumeri, Schiopetto	353
COF Refosco P.R., V. Traverso	403		COF Sauvignon Podere di Ipplis, Ca' Ronesca	376
COF Refosco P. R., Vigne Fantin Noda'r	399		COF Sauvignon Podere Stabili della Rocca, Tenuta di Angoris	358
COF Refosco P. R., Volpe Pasini	415		COF Sauvignon Ris., Ronco del Gnemiz	411
COF Refosco P. R. Podere Stabili della Rocca, Tenuta di Angoris	358		COF Sauvignon Sup., Paolino Comelli	378
COF Refosco P. R. Ris., Tenuta Bosco Romagno	417		COF Sauvignon Suvignis, Walter Filiputti	387
COF Refosco P. R. Romain, Paolo Rodaro	358		COF Sauvignon V. di Corte, Valentino Butussi	371
COF Refosco P. R.Vign. Montsclapade, Girolamo Dorigo	349		COF Sauvignon Vocalis, Aquila del Torre	394
COF Refoscone, Paolo Rodaro	358		COF Schioppettino, Alfieri Cantarutti	410
COF Ribolla Gialla, Ca di Bon	372		COF Schioppettino, Iole Grillo	399
COF Ribolla Gialla, Girolamo Dorigo	349		COF Schioppettino, Jacùss	414
COF Ribolla Gialla, La Tunella	397		COF Schioppettino, La Viarte	400
COF Ribolla Gialla, Miani	350		COF Schioppettino, Davide Moschioni	357
COF Ribolla Gialla, Perusini	374		COF Schioppettino, Petrussa	401
COF Ribolla Gialla, Petrucco	351		COF Schioppettino, Il Roncal	357
COF Ribolla Gialla, Teresa Raiz	394		COF Schioppettino, Ronco del Gnemiz	411
COF Ribolla Gialla, Rocca Bernarda	398		COF Schioppettino, V. Traverso	403
COF Ribolla Gialla, Torre Rosazza	389		COF Schioppettino Picotis, Livon	410
COF Ribolla Gialla, V. Traverso	403		COF Schioppettino Troi dal Tas, Vidussi Gestioni Agricole	354
COF Ribolla Gialla, Andrea Visintini	375		COF Schioppettino Turian, Eugenio Collavini	372
COF Ribolla Gialla, Zof	375		COF Soresta'nt Ròs, Midolini	419
COF Ribolla Gialla Turian, Eugenio Collavini	372		COF Tazzelenghe, Conte D'Attimis-Maniago	349
COF Ribolla Gialla Zuc di Volpe, Volpe Pasini	415		COF Tocai Friulano, Tenuta Bosco Romagno	417
COF Riesling, Perusini	374		COF Tocai Friulano, Olivo Buiatti	348
COF Riul Rosso, Dario e Luciano Ermacora	397		COF Tocai Friulano, Valentino Butussi	371
COF Ronc di Juri, Girolamo Dorigo	349		COF Tocai Friulano, Ca di Bon	372
COF Rosazzo Bianco Ronc di Rosazzo, Ronchi di Manzano	388		COF Tocai Friulano, Alfieri Cantarutti	410
COF Rosazzo Bianco Terre Alte, Livio Felluga	363		COF Tocai Friulano, Paolino Comelli	378
COF Rosazzo Narciso Bianco, Ronco delle Betulle	388		COF Tocai Friulano, Dal Fari	356
COF Rosazzo Narciso Rosso, Ronco delle Betulle	388		COF Tocai Friulano, Dario e Luciano Ermacora	397
COF Rosazzo Picolit Ris., Livio Felluga	363		COF Tocai Friulano, Livio Felluga	363
COF Rosazzo Picolit Ronc di Rosazzo, Ronchi di Manzano	388		COF Tocai Friulano, Adriano Gigante	373
COF Rosazzo Ribolla Gialla, Le Vigne di Zamò	387		COF Tocai Friulano, Iole Grillo	399
COF Rosazzo Ribolla Gialla, Ronco delle Betulle	388		COF Tocai Friulano, Jacùss	414
COF Rosazzo Rosso Ronc di Rosazzo, Ronchi di Manzano	388		COF Tocai Friulano, La Tunella	397
COF Rosazzo Sossò Ris., Livio Felluga	363		COF Tocai Friulano, La Viarte	400
COF Rosso, Miani	350		COF Tocai Friulano, Le Vigne di Zamò	387
COF Rosso Carato, Vigne Fantin Noda'r	399		COF Tocai Friulano, Valerio Marinig	401
COF Rosso Celtico, Davide Moschioni	357		COF Tocai Friulano, Davino Meroi	350
COF Rosso d'Orsone, Dal Fari	356		COF Tocai Friulano, Miani	350
COF Rosso Decano Rosso, Teresa Raiz	394		COF Tocai Friulano, Midolini	419
COF Rosso del Gnemiz, Ronco del Gnemiz	411		COF Tocai Friulano, Petrucco	351
COF Rosso del Postiglione, Perusini	374		COF Tocai Friulano, Petrussa	401
COF Rosso Dominin, Davino Meroi	350		COF Tocai Friulano, Teresa Raiz	394
COF Rosso Guardafuoco, Iole Grillo	399		COF Tocai Friulano, Rocca Bernarda	398
COF Rosso Il Boscorosso, Rosa Bosco	386		COF Tocai Friulano, Paolo Rodaro	358
COF Rosso Il Gheppio, La Roncaia	391		COF Tocai Friulano, Il Roncal	357
COF Rosso L'Arcione, La Tunella	397		COF Tocai Friulano, Ronco del Gnemiz	411
COF Rosso Lindi Uà, Jacùss	414		COF Tocai Friulano, Ronco delle Betulle	388

COF Tocai Friulano, Ronco Severo	419
COF Tocai Friulano, Scubla	398
COF Tocai Friulano, Leonardo Specogna	374
COF Tocai Friulano, Torre Rosazza	389
COF Tocai Friulano, Valchiarò	415
COF Tocai Friulano, V. Petrussa	402
COF Tocai Friulano, V. Traverso	403
COF Tocai Friulano, Zof	375
COF Tocai Friulano Plus, Bastianich	396
COF Tocai Friulano Storico, Adriano Gigante	373
COF Tocai Friulano Sup., Ronchi di Manzano	388
COF Tocai Friulano Vigne Cinquant'Anni, Le Vigne di Zamò	387
COF Tocai Friulano Vign. Montsclapade, Girolamo Dorigo	349
COF Tocai Friulano Vocalis, Aquila del Torre	394
COF Traminer Aromatico, Andrea Visintini	375
COF Verduzzo, Vidussi Gestioni Agricole	354
COF Verduzzo Friulano, Valentino Butussi	371
COF Verduzzo Friulano, Dario e Luciano Ermacora	397
COF Verduzzo Friulano, Adriano Gigante	373
COF Verduzzo Friulano, Iole Grillo	399
COF Verduzzo Friulano, Valerio Marinig	401
COF Verduzzo Friulano, Paolo Rodaro	358
COF Verduzzo Friulano, Valchiarò	415
COF Verduzzo Friulano Graticcio, Scubla	398
Col Martin Luwa, Ascevi - Luwa	405
Colferraio, Belisario C.S. di Matelica e Cerreto d'Esi	619
Collazzi, Fatt. Collazzi	588
Colle Amato, Colle San Lorenzo	667
Colle Carpito, San Luciano	522
Colle della Torre, Giovanni Palombo	663
Colle Leone, Ca' del Vispo	562
Colle Malerbi, Villa Pigna	626
Colle Picchioni Rosso, Paola Di Mauro - Colle Picchioni	668
Colli Berici Cabernet, Conti da Schio	339
Colli Berici Cabernet, Natalino Mattiello	292
Colli Berici Cabernet Antonio, Antonio Nani	340
Colli Berici Cabernet Capitel S. Libera, Domenico & F.lli Cavazza	299
Colli Berici Cabernet Casara Roveri, Luigino Dal Maso	299
Colli Berici Cabernet Cicogna, Domenico & F.lli Cavazza	299
Colli Berici Cabernet Colle d'Elica, Natalino Mattiello	292
Colli Berici Cabernet Polveriera, Piovene Porto Godi	336
Colli Berici Cabernet Sauvignon, Natalino Mattiello	292
Colli Berici Cabernet Vign. Pozzare, Piovene Porto Godi	336
Colli Berici Cardonnay, Natalino Mattiello	292
Colli Berici Merlot Campo del Lago, Villa dal Ferro Lazzarini	311
Colli Berici Merlot Casara Roveri, Luigino Dal Maso	299
Colli Berici Merlot Cicogna, Domenico & F.lli Cavazza	299
Colli Berici Merlot Fra i Broli, Piovene Porto Godi	336
Colli Berici Merlot Il Massi, Villa dal Ferro Lazzarini	311
Colli Berici Merlot Vign. Blatià, Villa dal Ferro Lazzarini	311
Colli Berici Pinot Bianco Campo Corì, Domenico & F.lli Cavazza	299
Colli Berici Pinot Bianco del Crearo, Antonio Nani	340
Colli Berici Pinot Bianco Polveriera, Piovene Porto Godi	336
Colli Berici Sauvignon, Marcato	342
Colli Berici Sauvignon, Natalino Mattiello	292
Colli Berici Sauvignon del Crearo, Antonio Nani	340
Colli Berici Sauvignon Vign. Fostine, Piovene Porto Godi	336
Colli Berici Tocai Rosso, Natalino Mattiello	292
Colli Berici Tocai Rosso Thovara, Piovene Porto Godi	336
Colli Berici Tocai Rosso Vign. Riveselle, Piovene Porto Godi	336
Colli d'Imola Cabernet Sauvignon Ca' Grande, Umberto Cesari	425
Colli del Trasimeno Rosso Carpaneto, Cast. di Magione	659
Colli del Trasimeno Rosso Morcinaia, Cast. di Magione	659
Colli della Serra Rosso, Alberto Quacquarini	638
Colli di Conegliano Bianco, F.lli Bortolin Spumanti	327
Colli di Conegliano Bianco, Conte Collalto	325
Colli di Conegliano Bianco, Dal Din	344
Colli di Conegliano Bianco, Scuola Enologica di Conegliano G. B. Cerletti	338
Colli di Conegliano Bianco Albio, Gregoletto	298
Colli di Conegliano Bianco Il Greccio, Bepin de Eto	313
Colli di Conegliano Bianco Rizzardo, Masottina	311
Colli di Conegliano Bianco Ser Bele, Sorelle Bronca	336
Colli di Conegliano Bianco Vign. Spezada, Canevel Spumanti	328
Colli di Conegliano Marzemino Passito di Refrontolo, Canevel Spumanti	328
Colli di Conegliano Refrontolo Passito, Vincenzo Toffoli	342
Colli di Conegliano Rosso, Conte Collalto	325
Colli di Conegliano Rosso, Le Colture	329
Colli di Conegliano Rosso, Masottina	311
Colli di Conegliano Rosso Croda Ronca, Bepin de Eto	313
Colli di Conegliano Rosso Gregoletto, Gregoletto	298
Colli di Conegliano Rosso Montesco, Masottina	311
Colli di Conegliano Rosso S. Alberto, Ruggeri & C.	330
Colli di Conegliano Rosso Ser Bele, Sorelle Bronca	336
Colli di Conegliano Rosso Vign. Levina, Canevel Spumanti	328
Colli di Faenza Bianco Chiaro della Serra, Stefano Ferrucci	425
Colli di Faenza Bianco Poderepalazzina, Leone Conti	428
Colli di Faenza Rebianco, Treré	430
Colli di Faenza Rosso Ca' di Berta, La Berta	424
Colli di Faenza Rosso Calenzone, Il Pratello	434
Colli di Faenza Rosso Montecorallo, Treré	430
Colli di Faenza Rosso Podereviacupa Le Ghiande, Leone Conti	428
Colli di Faenza Sangiovese Mantignano, Il Pratello	434
Colli di Faenza Sangiovese Renero, Treré	430
Colli di Fontivecchie Rosso, Domenico Pennacchi	659
Colli di Imola Boldo, Tre Monti	432
Colli di Imola Cabernet Sauvignon, Ca' Bruciata	447
Colli di Imola Cabernet Sauvignon, Fondo Cà Vecja	448
Colli di Imola Cabernet Sauvignon Ris., Ca' Bruciata	447
Colli di Imola Chardonnay Ciardo, Tre Monti	432
Colli di Imola Salcerella, Tre Monti	432
Colli di Imola Sangiovese, Ca' Bruciata	447
Colli di Imola Sangiovese, Fondo Cà Vecja	448
Colli di Imola Terre di Maestrale, Tenuta Poggio Pollino	448
Colli di Luni Rosso, Il Torchio	164
Colli di Luni Rosso Maniero, Ottaviano Lambruschi	165
Colli di Luni Rosso Re Carlo, La Pietra del Focolare	170
Colli di Luni Rosso Rupestro, Il Monticello	176
Colli di Luni Vermentino, Giacomelli	174
Colli di Luni Vermentino, Il Monticello	176
Colli di Luni Vermentino, Il Torchio	164
Colli di Luni Vermentino, Ottaviano Lambruschi	165
Colli di Luni Vermentino, 'R Mesueto	174
Colli di Luni Vermentino Augusto, La Pietra del Focolare	170
Colli di Luni Vermentino Costa Marina, Ottaviano Lambruschi	165
Colli di Luni Vermentino Il Chioso, Il Chioso	174
Colli di Luni Vermentino Poggi Alti, Santa Caterina	176
Colli di Luni Vermentino Santo Paterno, La Pietra del Focolare	170
Colli di Luni Vermentino Sarticola, Ottaviano Lambruschi	165
Colli di Luni Vermentino Solarancio, La Pietra del Focolare	170
Colli di Luni Vermentino Villa Linda, La Pietra del Focolare	170
Colli di Parma Malvasia Frizzante, Carra	433
Colli di Parma Rosso V. del Guasto, Isidoro Lamoretti	448
Colli di Parma Sauvignon Ris., Carra	433
Colli di Rimini Cabernet Sauvignon Luna Nuova, San Valentino	438
Colli di Rimini Rebola Passito Contesse Muschietti, San Valentino	438
Colli di Rimini Rosso Eclissi di Sole, San Valentino	438
Colli di Scandiano e di Canossa Cabernet Sauvignon Ris., Moro - Rinaldo Rinaldini	440
Colli di Scandiano e di Canossa Cabernet Sauvignon Terre Matildiche, Reggiana	445
Colli di Scandiano e di Canossa Chardonnay Rinaldo Brut, Moro - Rinaldo Rinaldini	440
Colli di Scandiano e di Canossa Lambrusco Grasparossa Tralcio Rosso, Reggiana	445
Colli di Scandiano e di Canossa Malvasia Spumante Brut, Moro - Rinaldo Rinaldini	440
Colli Euganei Bianco Corte Borin, Borin	298
Colli Euganei Bianco V. dei Mandorli, Borin	298
Colli Euganei Cabernet, Ca' Lustra	286
Colli Euganei Cabernet Borgo delle Casette Ris., Il Filò delle Vigne	283
Colli Euganei Cabernet Ris., V.Ita	326
Colli Euganei Cabernet Sauvignon Ireneo, Giordano Emo Conte Capodilista	282
Colli Euganei Cabernet Sauvignon Mons Silicis Ris., Borin	298
Colli Euganei Cabernet Sauvignon V. Costa, Borin	298
Colli Euganei Cabernet V. Cecilia di Baone Ris., Il Filò delle Vigne	283
Colli Euganei Cabernet V. Girapoggio Villa Alessi, Ca' Lustra	286
Colli Euganei Chardonnay, La Montecchia	320
Colli Euganei Chardonnay, V.Ita	326
Colli Euganei Chardonnay Passo Roverello Villa Alessi, Ca' Lustra	286
Colli Euganei Chardonnay V. Bianca, Borin	298
Colli Euganei Chardonnay V. Marco Ca' Lustra, Ca' Lustra	286
Colli Euganei Merlot, La Montecchia	320
Colli Euganei Merlot Rocca Chiara Ris., Borin	298
Colli Euganei Merlot V. Sasso Nero Villa Alessi, Ca' Lustra	286
Colli Euganei Moscato, V.Ita	326
Colli Euganei Moscato Fior d'Arancio Alpianae, V.Ita	326
Colli Euganei Moscato Fior d'Arancio Passito, La Montecchia	320
Colli Euganei Pinot Bianco, La Montecchia	320
Colli Euganei Pinot Bianco, V.Ita	326
Colli Euganei Pinot Bianco Agno Casto, V.Ita	326
Colli Euganei Pinot Bianco Ca' Lustra, Ca' Lustra	286
Colli Euganei Pinot Bianco V. delle Acacie, Il Filò delle Vigne	283
Colli Euganei Pinot Bianco V. Pedevenda Villa Alessi, Ca' Lustra	286
Colli Euganei Pinot Bianco Vign. Archino, Borin	298
Colli Euganei Rosso Cadeto, La Montecchia	320
Colli Euganei Rosso Gemola, V.Ita	326
Colli Euganei Rosso Montecchia, La Montecchia	320
Colli Euganei Rosso Ris., V.Ita	326
Colli Euganei Rosso Villa Capodilista, La Montecchia	320
Colli Euganei Spumante Fior d'Arancio, Borin	298
Colli Euganei Spumante Fior d'Arancio Ca' Lustra, Ca' Lustra	286
Colli Lanuvini Sup., Camponeschi	673
Colli Maceratesi Bianco, Santa Cassella	630
Colli Maceratesi Bianco Monteferro, Fatt. di Forano	610
Colli Maceratesi Bianco Murrano, Capinera	636
Colli Maceratesi Bianco Villa Forano, Fatt. di Forano	610
Colli Martani Grechetto, Antonelli - San Marco	648
Colli Martani Grechetto Arquata, Agr. Adanti	641
Colli Martani Grechetto di Todi, Todini	660
Colli Martani Grechetto Grecante, Arnaldo Caprai - Val di Maggio	648
Colli Martani Poggio dell'Annunziata, Eredi Benincasa	642
Colli Martani Sangiovese Properzio Ris., Di Filippo	658
Colli Martani Sangiovese Rubro, Todini	660
Colli Martani Sangiovese Satiro, Rocca di Fabbri	649
Colli Persaresi Sangiovese, La Ripe	638
Colli Perugini Bianco Torre del Pino, Agr. Goretti	656
Colli Perugini Chardonnay, Agr. Goretti	656
Colli Perugini Grechetto, Agr. Goretti	656
Colli Perugini Rosso, Franca Chiorri	660
Colli Perugini Rosso, Umbria Viticoltori Associati	659
Colli Perugini Rosso L'Arringatore, Agr. Goretti	656
Colli Pesaresi Bianco Roncaglia, Fatt. Mancini	628
Colli Pesaresi Sangiovese, Guerrieri	629
Colli Pesaresi Sangiovese, Fatt. Mancini	628
Colli Pesaresi Sangiovese Galileo, Guerrieri	629

Colli Pesaresi Sangiovese La V. delle Terrazze, Az. Agr. Claudio Morelli	617
Colli Pesaresi Sangiovese Sant'Andrea in Villis, Az. Agr. Claudio Morelli	617
Colli Pesaresi Sangiovese Sirio, Valentino Fiorini	611
Colli Tortonesi Barbera, Paolo Poggio	46
Colli Tortonesi Barbera Boccanera, Luigi Boveri	69
Colli Tortonesi Barbera Derio, Paolo Poggio	46
Colli Tortonesi Barbera Poggio delle Amarene, Luigi Boveri	69
Colli Tortonesi Barbera V.lunga, Luigi Boveri	69
Colli Tortonesi Bianco Derthona, Claudio Mariotto	142
Colli Tortonesi Bianco Filari di Timorasso, Luigi Boveri	69
Colli Tortonesi Bianco La Vetta, Terralba	44
Colli Tortonesi Bianco Profilo, Claudio Mariotto	142
Colli Tortonesi Bianco Stato, Terralba	44
Colli Tortonesi Bianco Sull'Aia, Mutti	134
Colli Tortonesi Bianco Timorasso Castagnoli, Mutti	134
Colli Tortonesi Bianco Timorasso, Paolo Poggio	46
Colli Tortonesi Bigolla, Vigneti Massa	112
Colli Tortonesi Cerreta, Vigneti Massa	112
Colli Tortonesi Cortese, Paolo Poggio	46
Colli Tortonesi Cortese V. del Prete, Luigi Boveri	69
Colli Tortonesi Costa del Vento Timorasso, Vigneti Massa	112
Colli Tortonesi Croatina Pertichetta, Vigneti Massa	112
Colli Tortonesi Dolcetto Zerba Soprana, Mutti	134
Colli Tortonesi Freisa, Paolo Poggio	46
Colli Tortonesi Freisa Pietra del Gallo, Vigneti Massa	112
Colli Tortonesi Martin, Franco M. Martinetti	141
Colli Tortonesi Monleale, Vigneti Massa	112
Colli Tortonesi Rosso Martirella, Claudio Mariotto	142
Colli Tortonesi Rosso Monleale, Terralba	44
Colli Tortonesi Rosso Montegrande, Terralba	44
Colli Tortonesi Rosso Nibio, La Colombera	160
Colli Tortonesi Rosso Rivadestra, Mutti	134
Colli Tortonesi Rosso S. Ruffino, Mutti	134
Colli Tortonesi Rosso Strà Loja, Terralba	44
Colli Tortonesi Rosso Terralba, Terralba	44
Colline Lucchesi Bianco Giallo dei Muri, Tenuta di Valgiano	496
Colline Lucchesi Chardonnay, Terre del Sillabo	496
Colline Lucchesi Merlot, La Badiola	588
Colline Lucchesi Rosso dei Palistorti, Tenuta di Valgiano	496
Colline Lucchesi Rosso Scasso dei Cesari, Tenuta di Valgiano	496
Colline Lucchesi Sauvignon, Terre del Sillabo	496
Colline Lucchesi Sauvignon Gana, Terre del Sillabo	496
Colline Lucchesi Tenuta di Valgiano, Tenuta di Valgiano	496
Colline Novaresi Agamium, Antichi Vigneti di Cantalupo	85
Colline Novaresi Bianco, Rovellotti	86
Colline Novaresi Bianco Collefino, Dessilani	78
Colline Novaresi Il Mimo, Antichi Vigneti di Cantalupo	85
Colline Novaresi Nebbiolo, Dessilani	78
Colline Novaresi Nebbiolo, Rovellotti	86
Colline Novaresi Nebbiolo Tre Confini, Torracia del Piantav.	155
Colline Novaresi Primigenia, Antichi Vigneti di Cantalupo	85
Colline Novaresi Vespolina, Rovellotti	86
Colline Novaresi Vespolina Villa Horta, Antichi Vigneti di Cantalupo	85
Collio Bianco, Colle Duga	362
Collio Bianco, Cant. Prod. di Cormons	361
Collio Bianco, Livio Felluga	363
Collio Bianco, Edi Keber	364
Collio Bianco, Evangelos Paraschos	408
Collio Bianco, Damijan Podversic	383
Collio Bianco, Isidoro Polencic	366
Collio Bianco, Dario Raccaro	367
Collio Bianco, Oscar Sturm	369
Collio Bianco, Franco Terpin	409
Collio Bianco, V. del Lauro	371
Collio Bianco, Francesco Vosca	418
Collio Bianco Bric, Muzic	408
Collio Bianco Caprizzi di Marceline, La Rajade	376
Collio Bianco del Bratinis, Gradis'ciutta	406
Collio Bianco del Tùzz, Gradis'ciutta	406
Collio Bianco della Castellada, La Castellada	383
Collio Bianco Fosarin, Ronco dei Tassi	368
Collio Bianco Frututis Ronc dal Luis, Maurizio Buzzinelli	360
Collio Bianco Jelka, Roberto Picech - Le Vigne del Ribél	365
Collio Bianco Klim, Primosic	384
Collio Bianco Molamatta, Marco Felluga	385
Collio Bianco Oslavje, Radikon	384
Collio Bianco Pertè, La Boatina	364
Collio Bianco Planta, Matijaz Tercic	409
Collio Bianco Pradis, Carlo di Pradis	362
Collio Bianco Ronco della Chiesa, Borgo del Tiglio	359
Collio Bianco Ronco della Tiare, Tiare - Roberto Snidarcig	370
Collio Bianco Rondon, Colmello di Grotta	379
Collio Bianco Russiz Disòre, Russiz Superiore	353
Collio Bianco Rylint, Conti Formentini	406
Collio Bianco Santa Caterina, Fantinel	413
Collio Bianco Sermar, Ca' Ronesca	376
Collio Bianco Trilogy, Fantinel	413
Collio Bianco Zuani, Zuani	419
Collio Bianco Zuani Vigne, Zuani	419
Collio Breg, Gravner	382
Collio Cabernet, F.lli Pighin	392
Collio Cabernet Franc, Cant. Prod. di Cormons	361
Collio Cabernet Franc, Gradis'ciutta	406
Collio Cabernet Franc, Marcello e Marino Humar	407
Collio Cabernet Franc, Alessandro Princic	367
Collio Cabernet Franc, Russiz Superiore	353
Collio Cabernet Franc, Subida di Monte	369
Collio Cabernet Franc, Tiare - Roberto Snidarcig	370
Collio Cabernet Franc Ascevi, Ascevi - Luwa	405
Collio Cabernet Franc Podere San Giacomo, Ca' Ronesca	376
Collio Cabernet Franc Rogoves, Marcello e Marino Humar	407
Collio Cabernet I Nostri Vini, Eugenio Collavini	372
Collio Cabernet Sauvignon, La Boatina	364
Collio Cabernet Sauvignon, Muzic	408
Collio Cabernet Sauvignon, Tenuta Villanova	380
Collio Cabernet Sauvignon Roncalto, Livon	410
Collio Cabernet Sauvignon Stratin, La Rajade	376
Collio Chardonnay, Attems	381
Collio Chardonnay, Borgo del Tiglio	359
Collio Chardonnay, Branko - Igor Erzetic	360
Collio Chardonnay, Maurizio Buzzinelli	360
Collio Chardonnay, Colle Duga	362
Collio Chardonnay, Colmello di Grotta	379
Collio Chardonnay, Cant. Prod. di Cormons	361
Collio Chardonnay, Marco Felluga	385
Collio Chardonnay, Fiegl	382
Collio Chardonnay, Gradis'ciutta	406
Collio Chardonnay, Gradimiro Gradnik Eredi	418
Collio Chardonnay, Gravner	382
Collio Chardonnay, Marcello e Marino Humar	407
Collio Chardonnay, Il Carpino	407
Collio Chardonnay, La Boatina	364
Collio Chardonnay, La Castellada	383
Collio Chardonnay, La Rajade	376
Collio Chardonnay, Muzic	408
Collio Chardonnay, Evangelos Paraschos	408
Collio Chardonnay, Isidoro Polencic	366
Collio Chardonnay, Ronco dei Pini	402
Collio Chardonnay, Matijaz Tercic	409
Collio Chardonnay, Tiare - Roberto Snidarcig	370
Collio Chardonnay, Franco Toros	370
Collio Chardonnay, Vidussi Gestioni Agricole	354
Collio Chardonnay Blanchis, Puiatti	352
Collio Chardonnay Braide Mate, Livon	410
Collio Chardonnay Colle Russian, Borgo Conventi	379
Collio Chardonnay Cuccanea, Eugenio Collavini	372
Collio Chardonnay dei Sassi Cavi Collezione Privata, Eugenio Collavini	372
Collio Chardonnay Gmajne, Primosic	384
Collio Chardonnay Gräfin de La Tour, Villa Russiz	354
Collio Chardonnay Grici, Renato Keber	418
Collio Chardonnay Monte Cucco, Tenuta Villanova	380
Collio Chardonnay Ris., Gravner	382
Collio Chardonnay Ronco Cucco, Tenuta Villanova	380
Collio Chardonnay Sant'Helena, Fantinel	413
Collio Chardonnay Sel., Borgo del Tiglio	359
Collio Chardonnay Sel., Subida di Monte	369
Collio Chardonnay Torre di Tramontana, Conti Formentini	406
Collio Malvasia, Ca' Ronesca	376
Collio Malvasia, Paolo Caccese	361
Collio Malvasia, Il Carpino	407
Collio Malvasia, Roberto Picech - Le Vigne del Ribél	365
Collio Malvasia, Alessandro Princic	367
Collio Malvasia, Dario Raccaro	367
Collio Malvasia, Vidussi Gestioni Agricole	354
Collio Malvasia Istriana, Cant. Prod. di Cormons	361
Collio Malvasia Istriana, Villa Russiz	354
Collio Malvasia Istriana Frututis Ronc dal Luis, Maurizio Buzzinelli	360
Collio Malvasia Sel., Borgo del Tiglio	359
Collio Merlot, Carlo di Pradis	362
Collio Merlot, Colle Duga	362
Collio Merlot, Marcello e Marino Humar	407
Collio Merlot, Edi Keber	364
Collio Merlot, La Boatina	364
Collio Merlot, La Rajade	376
Collio Merlot, Giulio Manzocco	418
Collio Merlot, F.lli Pighin	392
Collio Merlot, Alessandro Princic	367
Collio Merlot, Dario Raccaro	367
Collio Merlot, Radikon	384
Collio Merlot, Russiz Superiore	353
Collio Merlot, Schiopetto	353
Collio Merlot, Oscar Sturm	369
Collio Merlot, Tenuta Villanova	380
Collio Merlot, Matijaz Tercic	409
Collio Merlot, V. del Lauro	371
Collio Merlot, Villa Russiz	354
Collio Merlot Blanchis, Puiatti	352
Collio Merlot Collezione Privata, Eugenio Collavini	372
Collio Merlot dal Pic, Eugenio Collavini	372
Collio Merlot Graf de La Tour, Villa Russiz	354
Collio Merlot Perilla, Venica & Venica	377
Collio Merlot Sel., Subida di Monte	369
Collio Merlot Sel., Franco Toros	370
Collio Merlot Tajut, Conti Formentini	406
Collio Merlot Tiare Mate, Livon	410
Collio Müller Thurgau, Paolo Caccese	361
Collio Picolit Cumins, Livon	410
Collio Pinot Bianco, Maurizio Buzzinelli	360
Collio Pinot Bianco, Paolo Caccese	361
Collio Pinot Bianco, Cast. di Spessa	351
Collio Pinot Bianco, Gradimiro Gradnik Eredi	418
Collio Pinot Bianco, Marcello e Marino Humar	407
Collio Pinot Bianco, La Boatina	364
Collio Pinot Bianco, Roberto Picech - Le Vigne del Ribél	365
Collio Pinot Bianco, F.lli Pighin	392
Collio Pinot Bianco, Isidoro Polencic	366
Collio Pinot Bianco, Alessandro Princic	367
Collio Pinot Bianco, Russiz Superiore	353
Collio Pinot Bianco, Schiopetto	353

Collio Pinot Bianco, Tiare - Roberto Snidarcig	370
Collio Pinot Bianco, Franco Toros	370
Collio Pinot Bianco, Venica & Venica	377
Collio Pinot Bianco, Vidussi Gestioni Agricole	354
Collio Pinot Bianco, Villa Russiz	354
Collio Pinot Bianco Amrità, Schiopetto	353
Collio Pinot Bianco degli Ulivi, Ferdinando e Aldo Polencic	366
Collio Pinot Bianco di Santarosa, Cast. di Spessa	351
Collio Pinot Grigio, Attems	381
Collio Pinot Grigio, Borgo Conventi	379
Collio Pinot Grigio, Branko - Igor Erzetic	360
Collio Pinot Grigio, Maurizio Buzzinelli	360
Collio Pinot Grigio, Ca' Ronesca	376
Collio Pinot Grigio, Paolo Caccese	361
Collio Pinot Grigio, Carlo di Pradis	362
Collio Pinot Grigio, Cast. di Spessa	351
Collio Pinot Grigio, Colle Duga	362
Collio Pinot Grigio, Colmello di Grotta	379
Collio Pinot Grigio, Conti Formentini	406
Collio Pinot Grigio, Cant. Prod. di Cormons	361
Collio Pinot Grigio, Marco Felluga	385
Collio Pinot Grigio, Fiegl	382
Collio Pinot Grigio, Gradis'ciutta	406
Collio Pinot Grigio, Marcello e Marino Humar	407
Collio Pinot Grigio, La Boatina	364
Collio Pinot Grigio, Muzic	408
Collio Pinot Grigio, Evangelos Paraschos	408
Collio Pinot Grigio, F.lli Pighin	392
Collio Pinot Grigio, Isidoro Polencic	366
Collio Pinot Grigio, Ferdinando e Aldo Polencic	366
Collio Pinot Grigio, Isidoro Polencic	366
Collio Pinot Grigio, Alessandro Princic	367
Collio Pinot Grigio, Ronco dei Tassi	368
Collio Pinot Grigio, Russiz Superiore	353
Collio Pinot Grigio, Schiopetto	353
Collio Pinot Grigio, Oscar Sturm	369
Collio Pinot Grigio, Subida di Monte	369
Collio Pinot Grigio, Matijaz Tercic	409
Collio Pinot Grigio, Tiare - Roberto Snidarcig	370
Collio Pinot Grigio, Franco Toros	370
Collio Pinot Grigio, Venica & Venica	377
Collio Pinot Grigio, Vidussi Gestioni Agricole	354
Collio Pinot Grigio, V. del Lauro	371
Collio Pinot Grigio, Villa Russiz	354
Collio Pinot Grigio, Francesco Vosca	418
Collio Pinot Grigio Ascevi, Ascevi - Luwa	405
Collio Pinot Grigio Blanchis, Puiatti	352
Collio Pinot Grigio Braide Grande, Livon	410
Collio Pinot Grigio Gmajne, Primosic	384
Collio Pinot Grigio Grappoli Luwa, Ascevi - Luwa	405
Collio Pinot Grigio Sant'Helena, Fantinel	413
Collio Pinot Grigio V. Runc, Il Carpino	407
Collio Pinot Nero Casanova, Cast. di Spessa	351
Collio Pinot Nero Ruttars, Puiatti	352
Collio Prime Note, Venica & Venica	377
Collio Ribolla, Marcello e Marino Humar	407
Collio Ribolla Gialla, Attems	381
Collio Ribolla Gialla, Cast. di Spessa	351
Collio Ribolla Gialla, Fiegl	382
Collio Ribolla Gialla, Gradis'ciutta	406
Collio Ribolla Gialla, Gradimiro Gradnik Eredi	418
Collio Ribolla Gialla, Gravner	382
Collio Ribolla Gialla, Il Carpino	407
Collio Ribolla Gialla, La Boatina	364
Collio Ribolla Gialla, La Castellada	383
Collio Ribolla Gialla, Muzic	408
Collio Ribolla Gialla, Damijan Podversic	383
Collio Ribolla Gialla, Isidoro Polencic	366
Collio Ribolla Gialla, Radikon	384
Collio Ribolla Gialla, Matijaz Tercic	409
Collio Ribolla Gialla, Franco Terpin	409
Collio Ribolla Gialla, Tiare - Roberto Snidarcig	370
Collio Ribolla Gialla, Venica & Venica	377
Collio Ribolla Gialla, Vidussi Gestioni Agricole	354
Collio Ribolla Gialla, Villa Russiz	354
Collio Ribolla Gialla Ascevi, Ascevi - Luwa	405
Collio Ribolla Gialla Gmajne, Primosic	384
Collio Ribolla Gialla Roncalto, Livon	410
Collio Riesling, Villa Russiz	354
Collio Rosso, Edi Keber	364
Collio Rosso, Roberto Picech - Le Vigne del Ribél	365
Collio Rosso, Damijan Podversic	383
Collio Rosso, Franco Terpin	409
Collio Rosso Are di Miute, Vidussi Gestioni Agricole	354
Collio Rosso Cjarandon, Ronco dei Tassi	368
Collio Rosso Conte di Spessa, Cast. di Spessa	351
Collio Rosso dei Princic, Gradis'ciutta	406
Collio Rosso della Castellada, La Castellada	383
Collio Rosso della Centa, Borgo del Tiglio	359
Collio Rosso delle Cime, Venica & Venica	377
Collio Rosso Frututis Ronc dal Luis, Maurizio Buzzinelli	360
Collio Rosso Metamorfosis, Primosic	384
Collio Rosso Picol Maggiore, La Boatina	364
Collio Rosso Poncaia, Subida di Monte	369
Collio Rosso Ris., Borgo del Tiglio	359
Collio Rosso Ris., Roberto Picech - Le Vigne del Ribél	365
Collio Rosso Ris. degli Orzoni, Russiz Superiore	353
Collio Rosso Torriani, Cast. di Spessa	351
Collio Sauvignon, Attems	381
Collio Sauvignon, Borgo Conventi	379
Collio Sauvignon, Branko - Igor Erzetic	360
Collio Sauvignon, Ca' Ronesca	376
Collio Sauvignon, Cast. di Spessa	351
Collio Sauvignon, Colmello di Grotta	379
Collio Sauvignon, Conti Formentini	406
Collio Sauvignon, Cant. Prod. di Cormons	361
Collio Sauvignon, Mauro Drius	363
Collio Sauvignon, Marco Felluga	385
Collio Sauvignon, Fiegl	382
Collio Sauvignon, Gradis'ciutta	406
Collio Sauvignon, Marcello e Marino Humar	407
Collio Sauvignon, Il Carpino	407
Collio Sauvignon, La Boatina	364
Collio Sauvignon, La Rajade	376
Collio Sauvignon, Muzic	408
Collio Sauvignon, Ferdinando e Aldo Polencic	366
Collio Sauvignon, Isidoro Polencic	366
Collio Sauvignon, Alessandro Princic	367
Collio Sauvignon, Ronco dei Pini	402
Collio Sauvignon, Ronco dei Tassi	368
Collio Sauvignon, Russiz Superiore	353
Collio Sauvignon, Schiopetto	353
Collio Sauvignon, Oscar Sturm	369
Collio Sauvignon, Subida di Monte	369
Collio Sauvignon, Matijaz Tercic	409
Collio Sauvignon, Franco Terpin	409
Collio Sauvignon, Tiare - Roberto Snidarcig	370
Collio Sauvignon, Franco Toros	370
Collio Sauvignon, Vidussi Gestioni Agricole	354
Collio Sauvignon, V. del Lauro	371
Collio Sauvignon, Villa Russiz	354
Collio Sauvignon Ascevi, Ascevi - Luwa	405
Collio Sauvignon de La Tour, Villa Russiz	354
Collio Sauvignon Gmajne, Primosic	384
Collio Sauvignon Luwa, Ascevi - Luwa	405
Collio Sauvignon Poncanera, Eugenio Collavini	372
Collio Sauvignon Ronco Cucco, Tenuta Villanova	380
Collio Sauvignon Ronco dei Sassi Ascevi, Ascevi - Luwa	405
Collio Sauvignon Ronco del Cerò, Venica & Venica	377
Collio Sauvignon Ronco delle Mele, Venica & Venica	377
Collio Sauvignon Ruttars, Puiatti	352
Collio Sauvignon Sant'Helena, Fantinel	413
Collio Sauvignon Segré, Cast. di Spessa	351
Collio Sauvignon Tarsia , Schiopetto	353
Collio Sauvignon V. Runc, Il Carpino	407
Collio Studio di Bianco, Borgo del Tiglio	359
Collio Tocai Friulano, Attems	381
Collio Tocai Friulano, Borgo Conventi	379
Collio Tocai Friulano, Borgo del Tiglio	359
Collio Tocai Friulano, Branko - Igor Erzetic	360
Collio Tocai Friulano, Maurizio Buzzinelli	360
Collio Tocai Friulano, Ca' Ronesca	376
Collio Tocai Friulano, Paolo Caccese	361
Collio Tocai Friulano, Carlo di Pradis	362
Collio Tocai Friulano, Colle Duga	362
Collio Tocai Friulano, Colmello di Grotta	379
Collio Tocai Friulano, Cant. Prod. di Cormons	361
Collio Tocai Friulano, Mauro Drius	363
Collio Tocai Friulano, Marco Felluga	385
Collio Tocai Friulano, Fiegl	382
Collio Tocai Friulano, Gradis'ciutta	406
Collio Tocai Friulano, Gradimiro Gradnik Eredi	418
Collio Tocai Friulano, Edi Keber	364
Collio Tocai Friulano, La Boatina	364
Collio Tocai Friulano, Muzic	408
Collio Tocai Friulano, Roberto Picech - Le Vigne del Ribél	365
Collio Tocai Friulano, Ferdinando e Aldo Polencic	366
Collio Tocai Friulano, Isidoro Polencic	366
Collio Tocai Friulano, Ferdinando e Aldo Polencic	366
Collio Tocai Friulano, Alessandro Princic	367
Collio Tocai Friulano, Dario Raccaro	367
Collio Tocai Friulano, Ronco dei Tassi	368
Collio Tocai Friulano, Roncùs	352
Collio Tocai Friulano, Russiz Superiore	353
Collio Tocai Friulano, Schiopetto	353
Collio Tocai Friulano, Oscar Sturm	369
Collio Tocai Friulano, Subida di Monte	369
Collio Tocai Friulano, Tiare - Roberto Snidarcig	370
Collio Tocai Friulano, Franco Toros	370
Collio Tocai Friulano, V. del Lauro	371
Collio Tocai Friulano, Villa Russiz	354
Collio Tocai Friulano, Andrea Visintini	375
Collio Tocai Friulano, Francesco Vosca	418
Collio Tocai Friulano Aurora, Gradis'ciutta	406
Collio Tocai Friulano Croce Alta, Vidussi Gestioni Agricole	354
Collio Tocai Friulano Pardes, Schiopetto	353
Collio Tocai Friulano Ronc di Zorz, Livon	410
Collio Tocai Friulano Ronco delle Cime, Venica & Venica	377
Collio Tocai Friulano Sel., Subida di Monte	369
Collio Tocai Ronco della Chiesa, Borgo del Tiglio	359
Collio Traminer, Cant. Prod. di Cormons	361
Collio Traminer Aromatico, Paolo Caccese	361
Colonnara Spumante Brut Charmat, Colonnara Viticoltori in Cupramontana	616
Colonnara Spumante Brut M. Cl. Millesimato, Colonnara Viticoltori in Cupramontana	616
Colorino, Tenuta Il Corno	558
Coltassala, Cast. di Volpaia	555
Coltifredi, Castelli del Grevepesa	558
Come La Pantera e I Lupi nella Sera, Luretta	432
Cometa, Planeta	752
Composition Reif, Josephus Mayr - Erbhof Unterganzner	258

Comprino Mirosa, Montelio	188
Comprino Mirosa Ris., Montelio	188
Comprino Rosso, Montelio	188
Comprino Rosso Legno, Montelio	188
Con Vento, Cast. del Terriccio	467
Concento, L'Olivella	673
Confini, Lis Neris - Pecorari	411
Congius, Vignole	598
Coniale, Castellare di Castellina	463
Conte Bolani Rosso Gianni Zonin Vineyards, Ca' Bolani	355
Conte della Vipera, Cast. della Sala	644
Conte Hugues Bernard, Tenute Rapitalà	746
Conte Leopoldo Cabernet Sauvignon, Santa Cassella	630
Contessa Emburga, Cantine Lento	739
Contessa Entellina Chiarandà del Merlo, Tenuta di Donnafugata	750
Contessa Entellina Milleunanotte, Tenuta di Donnafugata	750
Contessa Entellina Tancredi, Tenuta di Donnafugata	750
Contessa Entellina Timpaia, Feudi di San Giuliano	760
Contessa Entellina Vento di Mayo, Feudi di San Giuliano	760
Contessa Entellina V. di Gabri, Tenuta di Donnafugata	750
Contrade - Dedalo, COS	759
Contrade - Labirinto, COS	759
Controguerra Bianco Ciafré, Dino Illuminati	677
Controguerra Bianco Costalupo, Dino Illuminati	677
Controguerra Bianco Daniele, Dino Illuminati	677
Controguerra Chardonnay Cenalba, Dino Illuminati	677
Controguerra Leneo d'Oro, Camillo Montori	678
Controguerra Passerina Do, Lepore	677
Controguerra Passerina Passera delle Vigne, Lepore	677
Controguerra Passerina Sol, Lepore	677
Controguerra Passito Nicò, Dino Illuminati	677
Controguerra Rosso Lumen, Dino Illuminati	677
Copertino Rosso, C.S. Coop. Copertino	731
Copertino Rosso Eloquenzia, Masseria Monaci	720
Copertino Rosso Ris., C.S. Coop. Copertino	731
Corbaia, Cast. di Bossi	468
Corbezzolo, Podere La Cappella	605
Cori Rosso Costa Vecchia, Colle San Lorenzo	667
Corindone Rosso, Alessandro Secchi	224
Corniole Merlot, Cavalleri	193
Corno Bianco, Tenuta Il Corno	558
Corriga, Valle del Quirra	780
Cortaccio, Villa Cafaggio	544
Corte Agnella Corvina Veronese, Giuseppe Campagnola	293
Cortegiano Sovestro, Baroncini	562
Cortese dell'Alto M.to La V. di Lena, La Guardia	116
Cortesia di Casale Marchese, Casale Marchese	667
Cortigiano, Fatt. Lavacchio	599
Cortinie Bianco, Peter Zemmer - Kupelwieser	269
Cortinie Rosso, Peter Zemmer - Kupelwieser	269
Cortona Fontarca, Tenim. Luigi D'Alessandro	474
Cortona Il Bosco, Tenim. Luigi D'Alessandro	474
Corvar Rosso, F.lli Zeni	284
Corvara Rosso, Armani	287
Corvo Bianco, Duca di Salaparuta - Vini Corvo	747
Corvo Colomba Platino, Duca di Salaparuta - Vini Corvo	747
Costa d'Amalfi Furore Bianco Fiord'Uva, Cantine Gran Furor Divina Costiera	694
Costa d'Amalfi Furore Rosso, Cantine Gran Furor Divina Costiera	694
Costa d'Amalfi Furore Rosso Ris., Cantine Gran Furor Divina Costiera	694
Costa d'Amalfi Ravello Bianco, Cantine Gran Furor Divina Costiera	694
Costa d'Amalfi Ravello Rosso Ris., Cantine Gran Furor Divina Costiera	694
Costa del Sole, La Morandina	66
Costa di Giulia, Michele Satta	462
Costa Nera, La Morandina	66
Costa Vecchia, Colle San Lorenzo	667
Costacalda Passito Domini Veneti, C.S. Valpolicella	306
Coste all'Ombra, Maurigi	757
Coste del Roccolo, Anteo	205
Coste della Sesia Bianco La Doranda, Sella	98
Coste della Sesia Nebbiolo Juvenia, Antoniolo	79
Coste della Sesia Rosato Bricco Lorella, Antoniolo	79
Coste della Sesia Rosso Mesolone, Barni	47
Coste della Sesia Rosso Orbello, Sella	98
Coste della Sesia Rosso Piccone, Sella	98
Coste della Sesia Rosso Torrearsa, Barni	47
Coteau Barrage, Lo Triolet - Marco Martin	18
Coteau La Tour, Les Crêtes	17
Crearo della Conca d'Oro, Viticoltori Tommasi	317
Criccio, Salvatore Murana	756
Critone, Librandi	737
Croara Chardonnay, Santa Sofia	316
Crognolo, Tenuta Sette Ponti	577
Crovello, Poggio Bertaio	644
Cruino Rosso, F.lli Zeni	284
Cruter, Ca' del Vispo	562
Cubia, Cusumano	756
Cummerse Rosso, Cant. Coop. del Locorotondo	726
Cuvée Extra Brut, Pojer & Sandri	228
Cuvée Imperiale Brut, Guido Berlucchi & C.	190
Cuvée Imperiale Brut Extrême, Guido Berlucchi & C.	190
Cuvée Imperiale Max Rosé, Guido Berlucchi & C.	190
Cuvée Jus Osculi, Loacker Schwarzhof	257
Cuvée Storica Spumante M. Cl. Gran Ris., Orsolani	130
Cygnus, Tasca d'Almerita	758
D'Alceo, Cast. dei Rampolla	540
D'Istinto Cataratto-Chardonnay, Calatrasi - Accademia del Sole	757
D'Istinto Magnifico, Calatrasi - Accademia del Sole	757
D'Istinto Nero, Calatrasi - Accademia del Sole	757
D'Istinto Sangiovese-Merlot, Calatrasi - Accademia del Sole	757
D'Ovidio, San Luciano	522
Dagala Bianco, Tamburello	762
Dagala Rosso, Tamburello	762
Dalle Terre di Herea Rosso, Avide	748
Damaggio, Poderi dal Nespoli	427
Daunia Bombino Bianco Catapanus, D'Alfonso del Sordo	730
Daunia Saraceno, Coop. Svevo - Lucera	732
De Ferrari, Boscarelli	527
De Luca Rosso, San Lorenzo	659
Declivium, Anselmet	19
Decugnano dei Barbi Brut M. Cl., Decugnano dei Barbi	651
Degorà Cabernet Sauvignon, Carlo Bogoni	301
Delia Nivolelli Cabernet Sauvignon, Carlo Pellegrino	751
Delia Nivolelli Chardonnay, Carlo Pellegrino	751
Deliella, Feudo Principi di Butera	745
Delius, Cant. del Taburno	693
Desiderio, Avignonesi	526
Dettori Bianco, Tenute Dettori	780
Dezio Vign. Beccaccia, Fatt. Dezi	633
Di Gale, Villa Frattina	395
Di 'More, Fattorie Azzolino	746
Diana, Baglio Hopps	761
Diano d'Alba, Cascina Bongiovanni	62
Diano d'Alba Cascinotto, Terre del Barolo	64
Diano d'Alba Costa Fiore, Claudio Alario	73
Diano d'Alba Montagrillo, Terre del Barolo	64
Diano d'Alba Puncia d'I Bric, Giovanni Veglio e Figli	153
Diano d'Alba Rizieri, Ricchino - Tiziana Menegaldo	153
Diano d'Alba Sorba, Massimo Oddero	153
Diano d'Alba Söri Bricco Maiolica, Bricco Maiolica	73
Diano d'Alba Söri Bruni, Casavecchia	153
Diano d'Alba Söri dei Berfi , F.lli Abrigo	153
Diano d'Alba Söri dei Berfi V. Pietrin, F.lli Abrigo	153
Diano d'Alba V. La Lepre, Fontanafredda	136
Diano d'Alba V. Vecchia, Paolo Monte - Cascina Flino	153
Diavolino Rosso, Le Pianacce	604
Dindarello, Maculan	285
Dioniso, Santa Seraffa	155
Do Ut Des, Carpineta Fontalpino	468
Dogajolo, Carpineto	486
Doganera Merlot, D'Alfonso del Sordo	730
Dogoli Bianco, Guerrieri Rizzardi	283
Doi Raps, Rino Russolo	412
Dolce Valle Moscato Passito, Tenute Soletta	778
Dolcetto d'Acqui, Ca' Bianca	29
Dolcetto d'Acqui, La Giustiniana	83
Dolcetto d'Acqui Argusto, Vigne Regali	140
Dolcetto d'Acqui Bric Maioli, Villa Sparina	85
Dolcetto d'Acqui L'Ardì, Vigne Regali	140
Dolcetto d'Acqui La Cresta, Traversa - Cascina Bertolotto	139
Dolcetto d'Acqui La Muïette, Traversa - Cascina Bertolotto	139
Dolcetto d'Acqui La Selva di Moirano, Scarpa - Antica Casa Vinicola	124
Dolcetto d'Acqui Marchesa, Marenco	140
Dolcetto d'Alba, Gianfranco Alessandria	104
Dolcetto d'Alba, F.lli Alessandria	145
Dolcetto d'Alba, Elio Altare - Cascina Nuova	88
Dolcetto d'Alba, Luigi Baudana	135
Dolcetto d'Alba, F.lli Bera	122
Dolcetto d'Alba, Enzo Boglietti	89
Dolcetto d'Alba, Cascina Bongiovanni	62
Dolcetto d'Alba, Giacomo Borgogno & Figli	37
Dolcetto d'Alba, Ca' d'Gal	132
Dolcetto d'Alba, Cant. del Pino	30
Dolcetto d'Alba, Cascina Vano	118
Dolcetto d'Alba, Giovanni Corino	90
Dolcetto d'Alba, Damilano	38
Dolcetto d'Alba, Destefanis	114
Dolcetto d'Alba, Silvio Grasso	91
Dolcetto d'Alba, Giacomo Grimaldi	38
Dolcetto d'Alba, Gianluigi Lano	25
Dolcetto d'Alba, Ugo Lequio	121
Dolcetto d'Alba, Giovanni Manzone	108
Dolcetto d'Alba, Mario Marengo	92
Dolcetto d'Alba, Mauro Molino	92
Dolcetto d'Alba, Monfalletto - Cordero di Montezemolo	93
Dolcetto d'Alba, F.lli Mossio	129
Dolcetto d'Alba, Fiorenzo Nada	143
Dolcetto d'Alba, Andrea Oberto	93
Dolcetto d'Alba, V.ioli Elvio Pertinace	144
Dolcetto d'Alba, Luigi Pira	138
Dolcetto d'Alba, E. Pira & Figli - Chiara Boschis	40
Dolcetto d'Alba, F.lli Revello	95
Dolcetto d'Alba, Ruggeri Corsini	111
Dolcetto d'Alba, Luciano Sandrone	41
Dolcetto d'Alba, Paolo Scavino	64
Dolcetto d'Alba, G. D. Vajra	43
Dolcetto d'Alba, Rino Varaldo	36
Dolcetto d'Alba, Mauro Veglio	96
Dolcetto d'Alba, Eraldo Viberti	96
Dolcetto d'Alba, V. Rionda - Massolino	138
Dolcetto d'Alba Arsigà, Batasiolo	88
Dolcetto d'Alba Augenta, Pelissero	144
Dolcetto d'Alba Autinot, Ada Nada	143
Dolcetto d'Alba Barilot, V. Rionda - Massolino	138
Dolcetto d'Alba Barturot, Ca' Viola	74
Dolcetto d'Alba Basarin, Cast. di Neive	157
Dolcetto d'Alba Bordini, Fontanabianca	119
Dolcetto d'Alba Borgo Castagni, Bel Colle	145
Dolcetto d'Alba Boschetti, Marchesi di Barolo	39

Dolcetto d'Alba Boschi di Berri, Poderi Marcarini	91
Dolcetto d'Alba Bric del Salto, Sottimano	122
Dolcetto d'Alba Bric Trifūla, Cascina Luisin	33
Dolcetto d'Alba Bricco, Giuseppe Mascarello e Figlio	103
Dolcetto d'Alba Bricco Bastia, Conterno Fantino	106
Dolcetto d'Alba Bricco Caramelli, F.lli Mossio	129
Dolcetto d'Alba Bricco dell'Oriolo, Azelia	61
Dolcetto d'Alba Bricco di Vergne, Batasiolo	88
Dolcetto d'Alba Bricco Peso, Sergio Degiorgis	101
Dolcetto d'Alba Brusalino, Cascina Fonda	101
Dolcetto d'Alba Bussia, Cascina Ballarin	90
Dolcetto d'Alba Campot, Cast. di Verduno	146
Dolcetto d'Alba Castellizzano, V.ioli Elvio Pertinace	144
Dolcetto d'Alba Ciabot V., Michele Taliano	113
Dolcetto d'Alba Colombè, Renato Ratti	94
Dolcetto d'Alba Coste & Fossati, G. D. Vajra	43
Dolcetto d'Alba Cottà, Sottimano	122
Dolcetto d'Alba Cuchet, Carlo Giacosa	32
Dolcetto d'Alba Dabbene, Gianfranco Bovio	89
Dolcetto d'Alba Fontanazza, Poderi Marcarini	91
Dolcetto d'Alba Galletto, Osvaldo Viberti	97
Dolcetto d'Alba Gavarini V. dei Grassi, Elio Grasso	108
Dolcetto d'Alba Ginestra, Paolo Conterno	106
Dolcetto d'Alba Le Passere, Terre del Barolo	64
Dolcetto d'Alba Lodoli, Ca' del Baio	142
Dolcetto d'Alba Madonna di Como, Boroli	24
Dolcetto d'Alba Madonna di Como, F.lli Giacosa	120
Dolcetto d'Alba Madonna di Como, Marchesi di Barolo	39
Dolcetto d'Alba Meriane, Gabutti - Franco Boasso	137
Dolcetto d'Alba Monrobiolo e Ruè, Bartolo Mascarello	39
Dolcetto d'Alba Monte Aribaldo, Tenuta Cisa Asinari dei Marchesi di Grésy	31
Dolcetto d'Alba Moriolo, Gastaldi	119
Dolcetto d'Alba Mosesco, Prunotto	27
Dolcetto d'Alba Munfrina, Pelissero	144
Dolcetto d'Alba Paulin, Gianni Gagliardo	155
Dolcetto d'Alba Piano delli Perdoni, F.lli Mossio	129
Dolcetto d'Alba Rocchettevino, Gianni Voerzio	97
Dolcetto d'Alba Ronchella, Gianluigi Lano	25
Dolcetto d'Alba Rossana, Ceretto	25
Dolcetto d'Alba Rubis, Rocche Costamagna	95
Dolcetto d'Alba S. Anna, Ferdinando Principiano	110
Dolcetto d'Alba S. Lorenzo, Giacomo Brezza & Figli	37
Dolcetto d'Alba S. Rosalia, Mauro Sebaste	27
Dolcetto d'Alba S. Stefano di Perno, Giuseppe Mascarello e Figlio	103
Dolcetto d'Alba Serra dei Fiori, Braida	129
Dolcetto d'Alba Serraboella, F.lli Cigliuti	118
Dolcetto d'Alba Solatio, Brovia	63
Dolcetto d'Alba Sörì Baudana, Luigi Baudana	135
Dolcetto d'Alba Sorì Paitin, Paitin	121
Dolcetto d'Alba Sup., Flavio Roddolo	111
Dolcetto d'Alba Sup. Moriolo, Gastaldi	119
Dolcetto d'Alba Tigli Neri, Enzo Boglietti	89
Dolcetto d'Alba Trifolera, Giuseppe Cortese	31
Dolcetto d'Alba V. Campasso, Viticoltori Associati di Rodello	158
Dolcetto d'Alba V. del Mandorlo, Elvio Cogno	125
Dolcetto d'Alba V. del Pozzo, Tenuta Carretta	126
Dolcetto d'Alba V. Deserto, Viticoltori Associati di Rodello	158
Dolcetto d'Alba V. Fornaci, Pira	76
Dolcetto d'Alba V. La Volta, Tenuta La Volta - Cabutto	42
Dolcetto d'Alba V. Majano, Piero Busso	117
Dolcetto d'Alba V. Monia Bassa, Destefanis	114
Dolcetto d'Alba V. Nirane, Ascheri	46
Dolcetto d'Alba V. Scot, F.lli Cavallotto	63
Dolcetto d'Alba V. Trifolé, Bruno Rocca	36
Dolcetto d'Alba V.lunga, Albino Rocca	35
Dolcetto d'Alba Vign. della Chiesa, F.lli Seghesio	112
Dolcetto d'Alba Vign. Nervo, V.ioli Elvio Pertinace	144
Dolcetto d'Alba Vign. Pra di Pò, Ettore Germano	137
Dolcetto d'Alba Vign. S. Francesco, Andrea Oberto	93
Dolcetto d'Alba Vign. Vantrino Albarella, Andrea Oberto	93
Dolcetto d'Alba Vughera, Cascina Cucco	136
Dolcetto d'Asti Caranzana, Cascina Garitina	59
Dolcetto d' Ovada Barricco, La Caplana	150
Dolcetto delle Langhe Monregalesi Il Colombo, Il Colombo - Barone Riccati	103
Dolcetto delle Langhe Monregalesi Sup. Monteregale, Il Colombo - Barone Riccati	103
Dolcetto delle Langhe Monregalesi V. della Chiesetta, Il Colombo - Barone Riccati	103
Dolcetto di Diano d'Alba, Bricco Maiolica	73
Dolcetto di Dogliani, Bricco del Cucù	43
Dolcetto di Dogliani, Poderi Einaudi	75
Dolcetto di Dogliani, San Romano	77
Dolcetto di Dogliani Autin Lungh, Eraldo Revelli	154
Dolcetto di Dogliani Briccolero, Quintoo Chionetti & Figli	129
Dolcetto di Dogliani Cursalet, Giovanni Battista Gillardi	79
Dolcetto di Dogliani I Filari, Poderi Einaudi	75
Dolcetto di Dogliani Maioli, Anna Maria Abbona	78
Dolcetto di Dogliani Monetti, Ribote	154
Dolcetto di Dogliani Papà Celso, Marziano e Enrico Abbona	74
Dolcetto di Dogliani Pianezzo, Francesco Boschis	154
Dolcetto di Dogliani Puncin, Osvaldo Barberis	154
Dolcetto di Dogliani Ribote, Ribote	154
Dolcetto di Dogliani S. Fereolo, San Fereolo	77
Dolcetto di Dogliani S. Luigi, Quintoo Chionetti & Figli	75
Dolcetto di Dogliani S. Luigi, F.lli Pecchenino	76
Dolcetto di Dogliani S. Matteo, Eraldo Revelli	154
Dolcetto di Dogliani San Lorenzo, Osvaldo Barberis	154
Dolcetto di Dogliani Siri d'Jermu, F.lli Pecchenino	76
Dolcetto di Dogliani Sorì dij But, Anna Maria Abbona	78
Dolcetto di Dogliani Sup. 1593, San Fereolo	77
Dolcetto di Dogliani Sup. Bricco Botti, F.lli Pecchenino	76
Dolcetto di Dogliani Sup. Bricco S. Bernardo, Bricco del Cucù	43
Dolcetto di Dogliani Sup. Dolianum, San Romano	77
Dolcetto di Dogliani Sup. Maioli, Anna Maria Abbona	78
Dolcetto di Dogliani Valdibà, San Fereolo	77
Dolcetto di Dogliani V. Bricco dei Botti, Pira	76
Dolcetto di Dogliani V. del Pilone, San Romano	77
Dolcetto di Dogliani V. Landes, Pira	76
Dolcetto di Dogliani V. Sorì San Martino, Francesco Boschis	154
Dolcetto di Dogliani V. Tecc, Poderi Einaudi	75
Dolcetto di Dogliani Vign. Maestra, Giovanni Battista Gillardi	79
Dolcetto di Dogliani Vign. Muntà, Marziano e Enrico Abbona	74
Dolcetto di Ovada, Cascina La Maddalena	128
Dolcetto di Ovada, Il Rocchin	154
Dolcetto di Ovada, La Smilla	45
Dolcetto di Ovada Bricco del Bagatto, Cascina La Maddalena	128
Dolcetto di Ovada Nsè Pesa, La Smilla	45
Dolcetto di Ovada Sup. Drac Rosso, Domenico Ghio e Figli	45
Dolcetto di Ovada Sup. Du Riva, Luigi Tacchino	151
Dolcetto di Ovada Sup. Il Gamondino, La Guardia	116
Dolcetto di Ovada Sup. L'Arciprete, Domenico Ghio e Figli	45
Dolcetto di Ovada Sup. Villa Delfini, La Guardia	116
Dolcetto di Ovada V. Oriali, Nicolò Verrina	158
Dolcetto di Ovada V. Semonina, Nicolò Verrina	158
Dolcetto Tormento, Ca' del Gè	199
Dolmen, C.S. Gallura	777
Don Antonio, Morgante	749
Don Generoso, Di Meo	699
Don Ludovico Pinot Nero, Carlozadra	197
Don Neli Rosso, Baglio San Vincenzo	762
Don Pietro Bianco, Spadafora	755
Donna Angela, Santa Cassella	630
Donna Eleonora Chardonnay, Santa Cassella	630
Donnaluna Aglianico , Viticoltori De Conciliis	698
Donnaluna Fiano, Viticoltori De Conciliis	698
Donnici Bianco, Domenico Spadafora	741
Donnici Rosso, Domenico Spadafora	741
Dopoteatro, Podere Salicutti	518
Dorado, Graf Pfeil Weingut Kränzel	267
Dorigo Brut, Girolamo Dorigo	349
Dòron, Eugenio Rosi	245
Dragonero, Marco Maci	719
Dry Muscat Terre di Orazio, Cant. di Venosa	713
Duca d'Aragona, Francesco Candido	729
Duca di Dolle Prosecco Passito, Desiderio Bisol & Figli	326
Duca Enrico, Duca di Salaparuta - Vini Corvo	747
Due Cuori Passito, Le Vigne di San Pietro	325
Due Uve, Bertani	304
Dulcamara, I Giusti e Zanza	475
Dulcis Cicogna, Domenico & F.lli Cavazza	299
Dulcis Vitis, Tenuta Le Quinte	673
Dule, Giuseppe Gabbas	772
È Serre, Salvatore Murana	756
Ea, Podere Sopra la Ripa	572
Ecclesia Chardonnay, La Monacesca	620
Edelmio, Benanti	759
Eden Passito, Carra	433
Edizione Second Release, Farnese	681
Edys, Maso Bastie	245
El Calié, Borgo Maragliano	99
El Masut, Podere dal Ger	396
Elba Bianco, Acquabona	600
Elba Bianco V. Le Stipe, Sapereta	549
Elba Bianco V. Thea, Sapereta	549
Elba Rosso, Acquabona	600
Elba Rosso Gelsarello, Mola	600
Elba Rosso Ris., Mola	600
Elba Rosso V. Thea, Sapereta	549
Elegia, Poliziano	532
Eleusi Passito, Villa Matilde	693
Elfo 11, Ca' del Bosco	193
Élite, Institut Agricole Régional	16
Elleno, Alessandro Moroder	609
Eloise Bianco, Bianchi	159
Elorina Nero d'Avola, Elorina	763
Eloro Nero d'Avola, Elorina	763
Eloro Pachino Nero d'Avola, Elorina	763
Eloro Pachino Ris., Elorina	763
Enantio, C.S. di Avio	224
Enantio, Concilio	244
Eneo, Montepeloso	574
Enif, Il Palagione	565
Entemari, Pala	776
Erbaceo Bianco, Colli della Murgia	731
Erbaluce di Caluso, Antoniolo	79
Erbaluce di Caluso, Ferrando	87
Erbaluce di Caluso Albaluce, Bersano & Riccadonna	123
Erbaluce di Caluso Calliope, Cieck	24
Erbaluce di Caluso Cariola Etichetta Verde, Ferrando	88
Erbaluce di Caluso Cella Grande, La Cella di San Michele	160
Erbaluce di Caluso Ferrando Brut, Ferrando	87
Erbaluce di Caluso La Rustia, Orsolani	130
Erbaluce di Caluso Spumante Brut Calliope, Cieck	24
Erbaluce di Caluso Spumante Brut S. Giorgio, Cieck	24
Erbaluce di Caluso Tre Ciochè, Giovanni Silva	150
Erbaluce di Caluso V. delle Chiusure, Favaro	158
Erbaluce di Caluso V. Misobolo, Cieck	24
Erta e China, Fatt. di Basciano	556
Esino Bianco Ferrante, Belisario C.S. di Matelica e Cerreto d'Esi	619
Esino Bianco Tabano, Montecappone	618

Esino Rosso Laurano, Laurentina	621
Esio Rosso, Monteschiavo	619
Essenza, Sergio Degiorgis	101
Essenzia Vendemmia Tardiva, Pojer & Sandri	228
Est Est Est di Montefiascone, Mazziotti	664
Est Est Est di Montefiascone, Trappolini	665
Est Est Est di Montefiascone Canuleio, Mazziotti	664
Est Est Est di Montefiascone Falesco, Falesco	670
Est Est Est di Montefiascone Filò, Mazziotti	664
Est Est Est di Montefiascone Poggio dei Gelsi, Falesco	670
Etna Bianco, Barone Scammacca del Murgo	764
Etna Bianco, Barone di Villagrande	753
Etna Bianco Bianco di Caselle, Benanti	759
Etna Bianco Sup., Barone di Villagrande	753
Etna Bianco Sup. Pietramarina, Benanti	759
Etna Rosso, Casa Vinicola Firriato	754
Etna Rosso, Barone Scammacca del Murgo	764
Etna Rosso, Barone di Villagrande	753
Etna Rosso Rovittello, Benanti	759
Etna Rosso Serra della Contessa, Benanti	759
Etna Rosso Ulysse, Carlo Pellegrino	751
Etrusco, Cennatoio Intervineas	541
Euforius, Josef Niedermayr	253
Extra Brut Cl. Il Calepino, Il Calepino	184
Extra Brut M. Cl., Il Calepino	184
Fabrizio Bianchi Chardonnay, Cast. di Monsanto	455
Facetus, Fontanavecchia	703
Faé Passito, Bepin de Eto	313
Falanghina Cesco Dell'Eremo, Cant. del Taburno	693
Falanghina del Beneventano, Terredora	697
Falanghina di Roccamonfina, Villa Matilde	693
Falanghina Passita Ruscolo, Cant. del Taburno	693
Falanghina V. del Prete, Fatt. Prattico	706
Falconaro, Cantine di Dolianova	769
Falerio dei Colli Ascolani, Cast. Fageto	628
Falerio dei Colli Ascolani, Cant. Coop. Castignanese	614
Falerio dei Colli Ascolani, Ciù Ciù	625
Falerio dei Colli Ascolani, Tenuta De Angelis	613
Falerio dei Colli Ascolani, Rio Maggio	622
Falerio dei Colli Ascolani, Villa Pigna	626
Falerio dei Colli Ascolani Brezzolino, La Cant. dei Colli Ripani	631
Falerio dei Colli Ascolani Grotte sul Mare, Vinicola del Tesino	617
Falerio dei Colli Ascolani Leo Guelfus, San Giovanni	626
Falerio dei Colli Ascolani Marta V.T. Ris., San Giovanni	626
Falerio dei Colli Ascolani Naumachos, Vinicola del Tesino	617
Falerio dei Colli Ascolani Pliniano, Villa Pigna	626
Falerio dei Colli Ascolani Telusiano, Rio Maggio	622
Falerio dei Colli Ascolani V. Palazzi, Saladini Pilastri	634
Falerio dei Colli Ascolani V. Solaria, Ercole Velenosi	610
Falerio dei Colli Ascolani Vigneti San Basso, Tenuta Cocci Grifoni	630
Falerno del Massico Bianco, Villa Matilde	693
Falerno del Massico Bianco V. Caracci, Villa Matilde	693
Falerno del Massico Falanghina, Michele Moio	696
Falerno del Massico Primitivo, Michele Moio	696
Falerno del Massico Primitivo Maiatico, Michele Moio	696
Falerno del Massico Rosso, Villa Matilde	693
Falerno del Massico Rosso Barrique, Masseria Felicia	706
Falerno del Massico Rosso V. Camarato, Villa Matilde	693
Falesia, Paolo d'Amico	664
Familia Lucchese, Calatrasi - Accademia del Sole	757
Fara Caramino, Dessilani	78
Fara Lochera, Dessilani	78
Farnito Cabernet Sauvignon, Carpineto	486
Farnito Chardonnay, Carpineto	486
Faro Palari, Palari	753
Faroaldo, Rocca di Fabbri	649
Fastaia, Ceuso	745
Fatagione, Cottanera	748
Father's Eyes, Di Lenardo	381
Federico II, Cantine Lento	739
Federico Primo, Gualdo del Re	573
Fedus Sangiovese, Poderi San Savino	632
Fegotto, Feotto dello Jato	764
Felciaia, Fatt. Villa La Selva	458
Felciaino, Giovanni Chiappini	580
Feldmarschall von Fenner zu Fennberg, Tiefenbrunner	268
Ferraiolo, Agricoltori del Chianti Geografico	478
Ferro e Seta, Villa Simone	670
Feudo dei Fiori Mandrarossa, Settesoli	752
Fiagre, Antonio Caggiano	702
Fianesco, Fatt. di Fiano	584
Fiano di Avellino, Cantine Caputo	691
Fiano di Avellino, De Falco	706
Fiano di Avellino, Di Meo	699
Fiano di Avellino, Feudi di San Gregorio	702
Fiano di Avellino, Cantine Grotta del Sole	699
Fiano di Avellino, La Casa dell'Orco	706
Fiano di Avellino, Pietracupa	696
Fiano di Avellino, Villa Raiano	701
Fiano di Avellino Béchar, Antonio Caggiano	702
Fiano di Avellino Colle dei Cerri, Di Meo	699
Fiano di Avellino More Maiorum, Mastroberardino	690
Fiano di Avellino Pietracalda V. T., Feudi di San Gregorio	702
Fiano di Avellino Terre di Dora, Terredora	697
Fiano di Avellino V. della Congregazione, Villa Diamante	705
Fiano di Roccamonfina le Cinque Pietre, Telaro - Coop. Lavoro e Salute	695
Fiano Valentina, Masseria Rotolo	706
Fidenzio, Podere San Luigi	546
Filip di Filip, Walter Filiputti	387
Filtrato Dolce di Malvasia, Gaetano Lusenti	443
Finibusterre Antica Masseria Torre Mozza, Pervini	728
FiorDesAri Rosso, Valditerra	158
Fiore, Cast. di Meleto	481
Fiore, San Valentino	438
Fiore, Barone di Villagrande	753
Fiore di Villagrande, Barone di Villagrande	753
Five Roses, Leone de Castris	728
Five Roses Anniversario, Leone de Castris	728
Flaccianello della Pieve, Tenuta Fontodi	541
Fluminus, Ferruccio Deiana	776
Fobiano, La Carraia	652
Foja Tonda Rosso, Armani	287
Fojaneghe Bianco, Conti Bossi Fedrigotti	238
Fojaneghe Rosso, Conti Bossi Fedrigotti	238
Folco, Iesolana	580
Fontalloro, Fatt. di Felsina	470
Fontanabianca, Cantine Torrevecchia	744
Fontanella Bianco, Agr. Goretti	656
Fontenova, Tenuta Roccaccia	546
Fontissimo, Fatt. Le Fonti	598
Fontursio, Fontursia	637
For Duke, Gino Fuso Carmignani	523
Foresco, Barberani - Vallesanta	650
Formulae, Barone Ricasoli	479
Forti Terre di Sicilia Chardonnay, C.S. di Trapani	758
Forti Terre di Sicilia Il Rosso, C.S. di Trapani	758
Forti Terre di Sicilia Nero d'Avola, C.S. di Trapani	758
Forti Terre di Sicilia Rocche Rosse, C.S. di Trapani	758
Forzaté Raboso, La Montecchia	320
Fossa Bandita, Letrari	239
Fosso le Forche, Pandolfa	450
Fraja, Tenuta Villanova	380
Franciacorta Ante Omnia Satèn, Majolini	203
Franciacorta Bagnadore I, Barone Pizzini	189
Franciacorta Brut, Barboglio De Gaioncelli	216
Franciacorta Brut, Barone Pizzini	189
Franciacorta Brut, F.lli Berlucchi	190
Franciacorta Brut, Bersi Serlini	204
Franciacorta Brut, Bredasole	219
Franciacorta Brut, Ca' del Bosco	193
Franciacorta Brut, Ca' del Vent	215
Franciacorta Brut, CastelFaglia	185
Franciacorta Brut, Tenuta Castellino	187
Franciacorta Brut, Castelveder	218
Franciacorta Brut, Catturich Ducco	219
Franciacorta Brut, Cavalleri	193
Franciacorta Brut, Battista Cola	212
Franciacorta Brut, Contadi Castaldi	178
Franciacorta Brut, Lorenzo Faccoli & Figli	188
Franciacorta Brut, Ferghettina	194
Franciacorta Brut, Enrico Gatti	194
Franciacorta Brut, Il Mosnel	203
Franciacorta Brut, La Boscaiola	189
Franciacorta Brut, La Montina	200
Franciacorta Brut, Lantieri de Paratico	181
Franciacorta Brut, Le Marchesine	219
Franciacorta Brut, Lo Sparviere	201
Franciacorta Brut, Majolini	203
Franciacorta Brut, Mirabella	220
Franciacorta Brut, Monzio Compagnoni	191
Franciacorta Brut, Principe Banfi Podere Pio IX	216
Franciacorta Brut, Riccafana	216
Franciacorta Brut, Ricci Curbastro	181
Franciacorta Brut, Ronco Calino	186
Franciacorta Brut, San Cristoforo	195
Franciacorta Brut, Giuseppe Vezzoli	196
Franciacorta Brut, Ugo Vezzoli	219
Franciacorta Brut, Villa	201
Franciacorta Brut Antica Cant. Fratta, Guido Berlucchi & C.	190
Franciacorta Brut Arcadia, Lantieri de Paratico	181
Franciacorta Brut Cabochon, Monte Rossa	185
Franciacorta Brut Cabochon Rosé, Monte Rossa	185
Franciacorta Brut Cuvée Millennio, Bersi Serlini	204
Franciacorta Brut Cuvée n. 4, Bersi Serlini	204
Franciacorta Brut Francesco I, Uberti	195
Franciacorta Brut I Cuvée, Monte Rossa	185
Franciacorta Brut mill., Il Mosnel	203
Franciacorta Brut Rosé, Lorenzo Faccoli & Figli	188
Franciacorta Brut Rosé, Mirabella	220
Franciacorta Brut Sel., Villa	201
Franciacorta Brut Tetellus, Conti Bettoni Cazzago	215
Franciacorta Brut Torre Ducco, Catturich Ducco	219
Franciacorta Casa delle Colonne, F.lli Berlucchi	190
Franciacorta Collezione Brut, Cavalleri	193
Franciacorta Collezione Esclusiva Brut, Cavalleri	193
Franciacorta Collezione Rosé, Cavalleri	193
Franciacorta Cuvée Annamaria Clementi, Ca' del Bosco	193
Franciacorta Cuvée Brut, Bellavista	192
Franciacorta Cuvette Extra Dry, Villa	201
Franciacorta Démi Sec, Ricci Curbastro	181
Franciacorta Dosage Zèro, Ca' del Bosco	193
Franciacorta Dosaggio Zero Villa Crespia, F.lli Muratori	214
Franciacorta Dosaggio Zero Villa Crespia Cisiolo, F.lli Muratori	214
Franciacorta Electo Brut, Majolini	203
Franciacorta Extra Brut, Bersi Serlini	204
Franciacorta Extra Brut, CastelFaglia	185
Franciacorta Extra Brut, Castelveder	218
Franciacorta Extra Brut, Lorenzo Faccoli & Figli	188
Franciacorta Extra Brut, Il Mosnel	203
Franciacorta Extra Brut, La Montina	200
Franciacorta Extra Brut, Lantieri de Paratico	181

Franciacorta Extra Brut, Lo Sparviere	201
Franciacorta Extra Brut, Monte Rossa	185
Franciacorta Extra Brut, Monzio Compagnoni	191
Franciacorta Extra Brut, Ricci Curbastro	181
Franciacorta Extra Brut, Villa	201
Franciacorta Extra Brut Cabochon, Monte Rossa	185
Franciacorta Extra Brut Comarì del Salem, Uberti	195
Franciacorta Extra Brut Francesco I, Uberti	195
Franciacorta Extra Dry, Barone Pizzini	189
Franciacorta Gran Cuvée Brut, Bellavista	192
Franciacorta Gran Cuvée Brut Rosé, Bellavista	192
Franciacorta Gran Cuvée Pas Operé, Bellavista	192
Franciacorta Gran Cuvée Satèn, Bellavista	192
Franciacorta Magno Brut, Contadi Castaldi	178
Franciacorta Monogram Brut, CastelFaglia	185
Franciacorta Monogram Brut Cuvée Giunone, CastelFaglia	185
Franciacorta Pas Dosé, Cavalleri	193
Franciacorta Rosé, Barone Pizzini	189
Franciacorta Rosé, F.lli Berlucchi	190
Franciacorta Rosé, Ca' del Bosco	193
Franciacorta Rosé, Contadi Castaldi	178
Franciacorta Rosé Brut Francesco I, Uberti	195
Franciacorta Rosé Demi Sec, La Montina	200
Franciacorta Rosé Démi Sec, Villa	201
Franciacorta Rosé Extra Dry, Barboglio De Gaioncelli	216
Franciacorta Satèn, Barone Pizzini	189
Franciacorta Satèn, F.lli Berlucchi	190
Franciacorta Satèn, Bersi Serlini	204
Franciacorta Satèn, Conti Bettoni Cazzago	215
Franciacorta Satén, Ca' del Bosco	193
Franciacorta Satèn, Tenuta Castellino	187
Franciacorta Satèn, Cavalleri	193
Franciacorta Satèn, Contadi Castaldi	178
Franciacorta Satèn, Ferghettina	194
Franciacorta Satèn, Agr. Gatta	215
Franciacorta Satèn, Enrico Gatti	194
Franciacorta Satèn, La Montina	200
Franciacorta Satèn, Lantieri de Paratico	181
Franciacorta Satèn, Le Marchesine	219
Franciacorta Satèn, Majolini	203
Franciacorta Saten, Mirabella	220
Franciacorta Satèn, Monte Rossa	185
Franciacorta Satèn, Monzio Compagnoni	191
Franciacorta Satèn, Riccafana	216
Franciacorta Satèn, Ricci Curbastro	181
Franciacorta Satèn, Giuseppe Vezzoli	196
Franciacorta Satèn, Villa	201
Franciacorta Satèn Antica Cant. Fratta, Guido Berlucchi & C.	190
Franciacorta Satèn Magnificentia, Uberti	195
Franciacorta Satèn Sel., Contadi Castaldi	178
Franciacorta Zéro, Contadi Castaldi	178
Franconia, Ronco delle Betulle	388
Franze, Sassotondo	572
Frappato, Cantine Torrevecchia	744
Frappato, Cant. Valle dell'Acate	744
Frasca, Varramista	538
Frascati Cannellino, Castel De Paolis	668
Frascati Cannellino, Conte Zandotti	671
Frascati Sup., Casale Marchese	667
Frascati Sup., Castel De Paolis	668
Frascati Sup., Conte Zandotti	671
Frascati Sup., Fontana Candida	669
Frascati Sup., Gotto d'Oro	669
Frascati Sup. Campo Vecchio, Castel De Paolis	668
Frascati Sup. Cannellino, Villa Simone	670
Frascati Sup. Cannellino Sel., Villa Simone	670
Frascati Sup. Parnasio, Casal Gentile	674
Frascati Sup. Racemo, L'Olivella	673
Frascati Sup. Santa Teresa, Fontana Candida	669
Frascati Sup. Sel. Verde, Vini Pallavicini	672
Frascati Sup. Terre dei Grifi, Fontana Candida	669
Frascati Sup. V. Adriana, Castel De Paolis	668
Frascati Sup. V. dei Preti, Villa Simone	670
Frascati Sup. Vign. Filonardi, Villa Simone	670
Frascati Sup. Villa Simone, Villa Simone	670
Fratta, Maculan	285
Freisa d'Asti, La Zucca	117
Freisa d'Asti Luna di Maggio, Cascina Gilli	61
Freisa d'Asti V. del Forno, Cascina Gilli	61
Freisa d'Asti Vivace, Cascina Gilli	61
Friuli Annia Malvasia, Emiro Cav. Bortolusso	355
Friuli Annia Merlot Privilege, Emiro Cav. Bortolusso	355
Friuli Annia Pinot Bianco, Emiro Cav. Bortolusso	355
Friuli Annia Pinot Grigio, Emiro Cav. Bortolusso	355
Friuli Annia Sauvignon, Emiro Cav. Bortolusso	355
Friuli Annia Tocai Friulano, Emiro Cav. Bortolusso	355
Friuli Annia Verduzzo Friulano, Emiro Cav. Bortolusso	355
Friuli Aquileia Bianco Palmade, Mulino delle Tolle	347
Friuli Aquileia Bianco Tàlis, Giovanni Donda	346
Friuli Aquileia Cabernet, Foffani	416
Friuli Aquileia Cabernet Franc, Ca' Bolani	355
Friuli Aquileia Cabernet Franc, Giovanni Donda	346
Friuli Aquileia Cabernet Franc, Mulino delle Tolle	347
Friuli Aquileia Cabernet Sauvignon, Foffani	416
Friuli Aquileia Cabernet Sauvignon Ris., Tenuta Beltrame	346
Friuli Aquileia Chardonnay, Tenuta Beltrame	346
Friuli Aquileia Chardonnay, Mulino delle Tolle	347
Friuli Aquileia Chardonnay Pribus, Tenuta Beltrame	346
Friuli Aquileia Chardonnay Sup., Foffani	416
Friuli Aquileia Merlot, Giovanni Donda	346
Friuli Aquileia Merlot, Foffani	416
Friuli Aquileia Merlot, Mulino delle Tolle	347
Friuli Aquileia Merlot Ris., Tenuta Beltrame	346
Friuli Aquileia Pinot Bianco, Tenuta Beltrame	346
Friuli Aquileia Pinot Bianco, Brojli - Franco Clementin	414
Friuli Aquileia Pinot Bianco, Giovanni Donda	346
Friuli Aquileia Pinot Grigio, Tenuta Beltrame	346
Friuli Aquileia Pinot Grigio, Giovanni Donda	346
Friuli Aquileia Pinot Grigio Gianni Zonin Vineyards, Ca' Bolani	355
Friuli Aquileia Pinot Grigio Sup., Foffani	416
Friuli Aquileia Refosco Campo della Stafula, Brojli - Franco Clementin	414
Friuli Aquileia Refosco P. R., Mulino delle Tolle	347
Friuli Aquileia Refosco P. R., Valpanera	416
Friuli Aquileia Refosco P. R. Gianni Zonin Vineyards, Ca' Bolani	355
Friuli Aquileia Refosco P. R. Ris., Valpanera	416
Friuli Aquileia Refosco P. R. Sup., Valpanera	416
Friuli Aquileia Rosso Alma, Valpanera	416
Friuli Aquileia Cabernet Sauvignon Ris., Tenuta Beltrame	346
Friuli Aquileia Chardonnay, Tenuta Beltrame	346
Friuli Aquileia Chardonnay, Mulino delle Tolle	347
Friuli Aquileia Chardonnay Pribus, Tenuta Beltrame	346
Friuli Aquileia Chardonnay Sup., Foffani	416
Friuli Aquileia Merlot, Giovanni Donda	346
Friuli Aquileia Merlot, Foffani	416
Friuli Aquileia Merlot, Mulino delle Tolle	347
Friuli Aquileia Merlot Ris., Tenuta Beltrame	346
Friuli Aquileia Pinot Bianco, Tenuta Beltrame	346
Friuli Aquileia Pinot Bianco, Brojli - Franco Clementin	414
Friuli Aquileia Pinot Bianco, Giovanni Donda	346
Friuli Aquileia Pinot Grigio, Tenuta Beltrame	346
Friuli Aquileia Pinot Grigio, Giovanni Donda	346
Friuli Aquileia Pinot Grigio Gianni Zonin Vineyards, Ca' Bolani	355
Friuli Aquileia Pinot Grigio Sup., Foffani	416
Friuli Aquileia Refosco Campo della Stafula, Brojli - Franco Clementin	414
Friuli Aquileia Refosco P. R., Mulino delle Tolle	347
Friuli Aquileia Refosco P. R., Valpanera	416
Friuli Aquileia Refosco P. R. Gianni Zonin Vineyards, Ca' Bolani	355
Friuli Aquileia Refosco P. R. Ris., Valpanera	416
Friuli Aquileia Refosco P. R. Sup., Valpanera	416
Friuli Aquileia Rosso Alma, Valpanera	416
Friuli Aquileia Sauvignon, Tenuta Beltrame	346
Friuli Aquileia Sauvignon, Giovanni Donda	346
Friuli Aquileia Sauvignon, Mulino delle Tolle	347
Friuli Aquileia Sauvignon Gianni Zonin Vineyards, Ca' Bolani	355
Friuli Aquileia Sauvignon Sup., Foffani	416
Friuli Aquileia Tocai Friulano, Tenuta Beltrame	346
Friuli Aquileia Tocai Friulano, Ca' Bolani	355
Friuli Aquileia Tocai Friulano, Mulino delle Tolle	347
Friuli Aquileia Tocai Friulano Sup., Foffani	416
Friuli Aquileia Traminer Aromatico, Brojli - Franco Clementin	414
Friuli Aquileia Traminer Aromatico, Ca' Bolani	355
Friuli Aquileia Verduzzo Friulano, Brojli - Franco Clementin	414
Friuli Grave Bianco Plui Vignis, Pradio	347
Friuli Grave Bianco Pra' de Gai, Vigneti Le Monde	395
Friuli Grave Bianco Puja, Vigneti Le Monde	395
Friuli Grave Cabernet, Teresa Raiz	394
Friuli Grave Cabernet Franc, Le Due Torri	373
Friuli Grave Cabernet Franc, Tenuta Pinni	420
Friuli Grave Cabernet Sauvignon, Antonutti	392
Friuli Grave Cabernet Sauvignon, Vigneti Le Monde	395
Friuli Grave Cabernet Sauvignon, Plozner	413
Friuli Grave Cabernet Sauvignon, Alessandro Vicentini Orgnani	393
Friuli Grave Cabernet Sauvignon, Villa Chiopris	420
Friuli Grave Cabernet Sauvignon Crearo, Pradio	347
Friuli Grave Cabernet Sauvignon Nexus, San Simone	419
Friuli Grave Chardonnay, Antonutti	392
Friuli Grave Chardonnay, Le Due Torri	373
Friuli Grave Chardonnay, Vigneti Le Monde	395
Friuli Grave Chardonnay, F.lli Pighin	392
Friuli Grave Chardonnay, Plozner	413
Friuli Grave Chardonnay, Flavio Pontoni	417
Friuli Grave Chardonnay, Scarbolo	393
Friuli Grave Chardonnay Borgo Tesis, Fantinel	413
Friuli Grave Chardonnay Braide Cjase, Alessandro Vicentini Orgnani	393
Friuli Grave Chardonnay Le Marsure, Teresa Raiz	394
Friuli Grave Chardonnay Musque, Di Lenardo	381
Friuli Grave Chardonnay Poggio Alto, Antonutti	392
Friuli Grave Chardonnay Ris., Plozner	413
Friuli Grave Chardonnay Teraje, Pradio	347
Friuli Grave Chardonnay Woody, Di Lenardo	381
Friuli Grave Merlot, Antonutti	392
Friuli Grave Merlot, Valentino Butussi	371
Friuli Grave Merlot, Di Lenardo	381
Friuli Grave Merlot, Forchir	420
Friuli Grave Merlot, F.lli Pighin	392
Friuli Grave Merlot, Scarbolo	393
Friuli Grave Merlot, Alessandro Vicentini Orgnani	393
Friuli Grave Merlot, Villa Chiopris	420
Friuli Grave Merlot Borgo Tesis, Fantinel	413
Friuli Grave Merlot Poggio Alto, Antonutti	392
Friuli Grave Merlot Ris., Cabert	417
Friuli Grave Merlot Roncomoro, Pradio	347
Friuli Grave Merlot Vistorta, Vistorta - Brandino Brandolini d'Adda	404
Friuli Grave Pinot Bianco, Antonutti	392
Friuli Grave Pinot Bianco, Valentino Butussi	371
Friuli Grave Pinot Bianco, Vigneti Le Monde	395
Friuli Grave Pinot Bianco, Plozner	413
Friuli Grave Pinot Bianco Braide Cjase, Alessandro Vicentini Orgnani	393

Friuli Grave Pinot Bianco Campo dei Gelsi, Forchir	420	Friuli Isonzo Pinot Bianco, Eddi Luisa	389
Friuli Grave Pinot Bianco Prestige , San Simone	419	Friuli Isonzo Pinot Bianco, Magnàs	365
Friuli Grave Pinot Blanc, Di Lenardo	381	Friuli Isonzo Pinot Bianco, Masut da Rive	390
Friuli Grave Pinot Grigio, Antonutti	392	Friuli Isonzo Pinot Bianco, Ronco del Gelso	368
Friuli Grave Pinot Grigio, Brunner	417	Friuli Isonzo Pinot Grigio, Tenuta di Blasig	403
Friuli Grave Pinot Grigio, Cabert	417	Friuli Isonzo Pinot Grigio, Borgo San Daniele	359
Friuli Grave Pinot Grigio, Di Lenardo	381	Friuli Isonzo Pinot Grigio, Colmello di Grotta	379
Friuli Grave Pinot Grigio, Le Due Torri	373	Friuli Isonzo Pinot Grigio, Mauro Drius	363
Friuli Grave Pinot Grigio, Vigneti Le Monde	395	Friuli Isonzo Pinot Grigio, Lis Neris - Pecorari	411
Friuli Grave Pinot Grigio, F.lli Pighin	392	Friuli Isonzo Pinot Grigio, Eddi Luisa	389
Friuli Grave Pinot Grigio, Plozner	413	Friuli Isonzo Pinot Grigio, Magnàs	365
Friuli Grave Pinot Grigio, Tenuta Pinni	420	Friuli Isonzo Pinot Grigio, Masut da Rive	390
Friuli Grave Pinot Grigio, Alessandro Vicentini Orgnani	393	Friuli Isonzo Pinot Grigio, Pierpaolo Pecorari	412
Friuli Grave Pinot Grigio Braide Cjase, Alessandro Vicentini Orgnani	393	Friuli Isonzo Pinot Grigio, Puiatti	352
Friuli Grave Pinot Grigio Le Marsure, Teresa Raiz	394	Friuli Isonzo Pinot Grigio BorDavi, Carlo di Pradis	362
Friuli Grave Pinot Grigio Priara, Pradio	347	Friuli Isonzo Pinot Grigio Dessimis, Vie di Romans	390
Friuli Grave Pinot Grigio Ronco Calaj, Rino Russolo	412	Friuli Isonzo Pinot Grigio Do Ville, Do Ville	404
Friuli Grave Pinot Nero, Vigneti Le Monde	395	Friuli Isonzo Pinot Grigio Gris, Lis Neris - Pecorari	411
Friuli Grave Pinot Nero Ris., Plozner	413	Friuli Isonzo Pinot Grigio Sot lis Rivis, Ronco del Gelso	368
Friuli Grave Refosco P. R., Di Lenardo	381	Friuli Isonzo Refosco P. R., Giulio Manzocco	418
Friuli Grave Refosco P.R., Le Due Torri	373	Friuli Isonzo Refosco P. R. I Ferretti, Eddi Luisa	389
Friuli Grave Refosco P. R., Vigneti Le Monde	395	Friuli Isonzo Riesling, Mauro Drius	363
Friuli Grave Refosco P. R., Plozner	413	Friuli Isonzo Riesling, Ronco del Gelso	368
Friuli Grave Refosco P.R., Tenuta Pinni	420	Friuli Isonzo Ròs di Ròl, Sant'Elena	385
Friuli Grave Refosco P. R. Campo del Viotto, Scarbolo	393	Friuli Isonzo Rosso BorDavi, Carlo di Pradis	362
Friuli Grave Refosco P. R. Sant'Helena, Fantinel	413	Friuli Isonzo Rosso Voos dai Ciamps, Vie di Romans	390
Friuli Grave Refosco P. R. Tuaro, Pradio	347	Friuli Isonzo Sauvignon, Colmello di Grotta	379
Friuli Grave Rosso Ca' Salice, Vigneti Le Monde	395	Friuli Isonzo Sauvignon, Cant. Prod. di Cormons	361
Friuli Grave Rosso del Fondatore, Forchir	420	Friuli Isonzo Sauvignon, Magnàs	365
Friuli Grave Rosso Rok, Pradio	347	Friuli Isonzo Sauvignon, Masut da Rive	390
Friuli Grave Sauvignon, Antonutti	392	Friuli Isonzo Sauvignon, Pierpaolo Pecorari	412
Friuli Grave Sauvignon, Brunner	417	Friuli Isonzo Sauvignon, Ronco del Gelso	368
Friuli Grave Sauvignon, Ca di Bon	372	Friuli Isonzo Sauvignon, Simon di Brazzan	418
Friuli Grave Sauvignon, Le Due Torri	373	Friuli Isonzo Sauvignon, Franco Visintin	419
Friuli Grave Sauvignon, Vigneti Le Monde	395	Friuli Isonzo Sauvignon Altis, Pierpaolo Pecorari	412
Friuli Grave Sauvignon, Plozner	413	Friuli Isonzo Sauvignon Ars Vivendi, Do Ville	404
Friuli Grave Sauvignon, Scarbolo	393	Friuli Isonzo Sauvignon Do Ville, Do Ville	404
Friuli Grave Sauvignon Blanc, Di Lenardo	381	Friuli Isonzo Sauvignon Dom Picòl, Lis Neris - Pecorari	411
Friuli Grave Sauvignon Blanc Le Selezioni, Antonutti	392	Friuli Isonzo Sauvignon Picòl , Lis Neris - Pecorari	411
Friuli Grave Sauvignon Puja, Vigneti Le Monde	395	Friuli Isonzo Sauvignon Piere, Vie di Romans	390
Friuli Grave Sauvignon Sobaja, Pradio	347	Friuli Isonzo Sauvignon Vieris, Vie di Romans	390
Friuli Grave Tocai Friulano, Antonutti	392	Friuli Isonzo Sauvignon V. Roverella, Edi Gandin	420
Friuli Grave Tocai Friulano, Brunner	417	Friuli Isonzo Tato, Sant'Elena	385
Friuli Grave Tocai Friulano, Alfieri Cantarutti	410	Friuli Isonzo Tocai Friulano, Borgo San Daniele	359
Friuli Grave Tocai Friulano, Le Due Torri	373	Friuli Isonzo Tocai Friulano, Cant. Prod. di Cormons	361
Friuli Grave Tocai Friulano, Plozner	413	Friuli Isonzo Tocai Friulano, Mauro Drius	363
Friuli Grave Tocai Friulano, Scarbolo	393	Friuli Isonzo Tocai Friulano, Eddi Luisa	389
Friuli Grave Tocai Friulano, Villa Chiopris	420	Friuli Isonzo Tocai Friulano, Magnàs	365
Friuli Grave Tocai Friulano Ronco Calaj, Rino Russolo	412	Friuli Isonzo Tocai Friulano, Masut da Rive	390
Friuli Grave Tocai Friulano Toh!, Di Lenardo	381	Friuli Isonzo Tocai Friulano, Puiatti	352
Friuli Isonzo Arbis Blanc, Borgo San Daniele	359	Friuli Isonzo Tocai Friulano, Ronco del Gelso	368
Friuli Isonzo Bianco Flors di Uis, Vie di Romans	390	Friuli Isonzo Tocai Friulano , Simon di Brazzan	418
Friuli Isonzo Bianco Latimis, Ronco del Gelso	368	Friuli Isonzo Tocai Friulano, Franco Visintin	419
Friuli Isonzo Bianco Pietra Verde, Cant. Prod. di Cormons	361	Friuli Isonzo Tocai Friulano Ars Vivendi, Do Ville	404
Friuli Isonzo Bianco Vignis di Siris, Mauro Drius	363	Friuli Isonzo Tocai Friulano Ascevi, Ascevi - Luwa	405
Friuli Isonzo Cabernet, Tenuta di Blasig	403	Friuli Isonzo Tocai Friulano Do Ville, Do Ville	404
Friuli Isonzo Cabernet, Mauro Drius	363	Friuli Isonzo Verduzzo Dorè, Cant. Prod. di Cormons	361
Friuli Isonzo Cabernet BorDavi, Carlo di Pradis	362	Friuli Isonzo Chardonnay BorDavi, Carlo di Pradis	362
Friuli Isonzo Cabernet Franc, Eddi Luisa	389	Fuili, C.S. Dorgali	778
Friuli Isonzo Cabernet Franc, Masut da Rive	390	Fumé Bianco, Giovanni Crosato	356
Friuli Isonzo Cabernet Franc, Muzic	408	Furat, Ajello	761
Friuli Isonzo Cabernet Sauvignon, Masut da Rive	390	Furetta Mandrarossa, Settesoli	752
Friuli Isonzo Cabernet Sauvignon, Tiare - Roberto Snidarcig	370	Futuro, Franco e Mario Scrimaglio	124
Friuli Isonzo Cabernet Sauvignon Barrique Do Ville, Do Ville	404	Gabàn, Nilo Bolognani	231
Friuli Isonzo Cabernet Sauvignon I Ferretti, Eddi Luisa	389	Gabbro, Montepeloso	574
Friuli Isonzo Chardonnay, Tenuta di Blasig	403	Gadì, Salvatore Murana	756
Friuli Isonzo Chardonnay, Colmello di Grotta	379	Gagliole Rosso, Gagliole	582
Friuli Isonzo Chardonnay, Eddi Luisa	389	Galana, C.S. del Vermentino	771
Friuli Isonzo Chardonnay, Magnàs	365	Galatina Bianco, Valle dell'Asso	722
Friuli Isonzo Chardonnay, Masut da Rive	390	Galatina Negroamaro, Valle dell'Asso	722
Friuli Isonzo Chardonnay, Pierpaolo Pecorari	412	Galatina Rosato, Valle dell'Asso	722
Friuli Isonzo Chardonnay, Puiatti	352	Galatina Rosso, Valle dell'Asso	722
Friuli Isonzo Chardonnay, Ronco del Gelso	368	Galatrona, Fatt. Petrolo	538
Friuli Isonzo Chardonnay, V. del Lauro	371	Galluccio Aglianico Montecaruso, Telaro - Coop. Lavoro e Salute	695
Friuli Isonzo Chardonnay, Franco Visintin	419	Galluccio Ara Mundi Ris., Telaro - Coop. Lavoro e Salute	695
Friuli Isonzo Chardonnay, Francesca Vosca	418	Galluccio Calivierno Ris., Telaro - Coop. Lavoro e Salute	695
Friuli Isonzo Chardonnay Barrique Do Ville, Do Ville	404	Galluccio Falanghina, Fatt. Prattico	706
Friuli Isonzo Chardonnay Ciampagnis Vieris, Vie di Romans	390	Gamba di Pernice, Carlo Benotto	70
Friuli Isonzo Chardonnay Do Ville, Do Ville	404	Gamba di Pernice, Tenuta dei Fiori	49
Friuli Isonzo Chardonnay I Ferretti, Eddi Luisa	389	Gambellara Cl. Ca' Cischele, Luigino Dal Maso	299
Friuli Isonzo Chardonnay Jurosa, Lis Neris - Pecorari	411	Gambellara Cl. Capitel S. Libera, Domenico & F.lli Cavazza	299
Friuli Isonzo Chardonnay Mauròs, Masut da Rive	390	Gambellara Cl. I Masieri, La Biancara	289
Friuli Isonzo Chardonnay Vie di Romans, Vie di Romans	390	Gambellara Cl. Podere Il Giangio, Zonin	290
Friuli Isonzo Chardonnay V. Cristin, Edi Gandin	420	Gambellara Cl. Sup. Sassaia, La Biancara	289
Friuli Isonzo Malvasia, Mauro Drius	363	Gana, Terre del Sillabo	496
Friuli Isonzo Malvasia, Ronco del Gelso	368	Garbì Bianco, Boccadigabbia	615
Friuli Isonzo Malvasia, Simon di Brazzan	418	Garda Bresciano Chiaretto, Monteacuto	213
Friuli Isonzo Malvasia, Tenuta Villanova	380	Garda Bresciano Chiaretto Ris. I Frati, Ca' dei Frati	208
Friuli Isonzo Malvasia Ars Vivendi, Do Ville	404	Garda Bresciano Groppello, Monteacuto	213
Friuli Isonzo Merlot, Tenuta di Blasig	403	Garda Cabernet, Ca' Lojera	208
Friuli Isonzo Merlot, Colmello di Grotta	379	Garda Cabernet, Le Ragose	305
Friuli Isonzo Merlot, Mauro Drius	363	Garda Cabernet Le Zalte, Cascina La Pertica	204
Friuli Isonzo Merlot, Eddi Luisa	389	Garda Cabernet Sauvignon, Cant. di Soave	321
Friuli Isonzo Merlot, Masut da Rive	390	Garda Cabernet Sauvignon Cicisbeo, Le Tende	292
Friuli Isonzo Merlot, Ronco del Gelso	368	Garda Cabernet Sauvignon Pradamonte, Costaripa	198
Friuli Isonzo Merlot, Tiare - Roberto Snidarcig	370	Garda Cabernet Sauvignon Vign. Il Falcone La Prendina, Cavalchina	324
Friuli Isonzo Merlot, V. del Lauro	371	Garda Cabernet Vign. Montezalto, Pasini Prod.	220
Friuli Isonzo Merlot Gli Affreschi, Tenuta di Blasig	403	Garda Chardonnay Campagnola alla Croce, Corte Marzago	344
Friuli Isonzo Merlot I Ferretti, Eddi Luisa	389	Garda Chardonnay Le Sincette, Cascina La Pertica	204
Friuli Isonzo Pinot Bianco, Mauro Drius	363		

Garda Chardonnay Le Sincette Brut, Cascina La Pertica	204
Garda Chardonnay Meridiano, Ricchi	218
Garda Chiaretto La Prendina, Cavalchina	324
Garda Cl. Bianco Il Renano, Pasini Prod.	220
Garda Cl. Chiaretto, Cascina La Pertica	204
Garda Cl. Chiaretto, Marangona	220
Garda Cl. Chiaretto Il Torrione, Monte Cicogna	198
Garda Cl. Chiaretto Le Sincette, Cascina La Pertica	204
Garda Cl. Chiaretto Molmenti, Costaripa	198
Garda Cl. Groppello Il Colombaio, Cascina La Pertica	204
Garda Cl. Groppello Maim, Costaripa	198
Garda Cl. Rosso Ca' Maiol, Provenza	192
Garda Cl. Rosso Chr. Barnard, Costaripa	198
Garda Cl. Rosso Groppello Beana, Monte Cicogna	198
Garda Cl. Rosso Negresco, Provenza	192
Garda Cl. Rosso Rubinere, Monte Cicogna	198
Garda Cl. Rosso Sel. Fabio Contato, Provenza	192
Garda Cl. Rosso Sup. , Marangona	220
Garda Cl. Rosso Sup., Spia d'Italia	217
Garda Cl. Sup. Don Lisander, Monte Cicogna	198
Garda Cl. Sup. Rosso Brol, Cantine Valtenesi - Lugana	217
Garda Cl. Sup. Rosso Madér, Cantine Colli a Lago	216
Garda Garganega Paroni La Prendina, Cavalchina	324
Garda Le Zalte, Cascina La Pertica	204
Garda Merlot, Ca' Lojera	208
Garda Merlot Carpino, Ricchi	218
Garda Merlot Faial La Prendina, Cavalchina	324
Garda Merlot La Prendina, Cavalchina	324
Garda Merlot Nepomuceno, Cantrina	212
Garda Merlot Vallidium, Corte Gardoni	332
Garda Pinot Grigio La Crosara I Fossili, Cant. di Montecchia	340
Garda Sauvignon Valbruna La Prendina, Cavalchina	324
Garganega Camporengo, Le Fraghe	285
Garofoli Brut M. Cl., Gioacchino Garofoli	618
Gastaldi Rosso, Gastaldi	119
Gatti Bianco, Enrico Gatti	194
Gatti Rosso, Enrico Gatti	194
Gattinara, Antoniolo	79
Gattinara, Anzivino	80
Gattinara, Bianchi	159
Gattinara, Nervi	80
Gattinara, Torraccia del Piantav.	155
Gattinara, Giancarlo Travaglini	81
Gattinara Ris., Giancarlo Travaglini	81
Gattinara Tre Vigne, Giancarlo Travaglini	81
Gattinara Vign. Castelle, Antoniolo	79
Gattinara Vign. Molsino, Nervi	80
Gattinara Vign. Osso S. Grato, Antoniolo	79
Gattinara Vign. S. Francesco, Antoniolo	79
Gattinara Vign. Valferana, Bianchi	159
Gaudio, Tenuta Le Velette	653
Gaurano, Michele Moio	696
Gavi, Ca' Bianca	29
Gavi, La Smilla	45
Gavi, La Zerba	160
Gavi, Pio Cesare	26
Gavi, San Bartolomeo	84
Gavi Brut M. Cl., Prod. del Gavi	84
Gavi Ca' da Bosio, Terre da Vino	42
Gavi Cascine dell'Aureliana, Prod. del Gavi	84
Gavi Cast. di Tassarolo, Cast. di Tassarolo	141
Gavi dei Gavi Etichetta Nera, La Scolca	155
Gavi del Comune di Gavi, Nicola Bergaglio	81
Gavi del Comune di Gavi, Il Rocchin	154
Gavi del Comune di Gavi, La Smilla	45
Gavi del Comune di Gavi, San Bartolomeo	84
Gavi del Comune di Gavi, Villa Sparina	85
Gavi del Comune di Gavi Bruno Broglia, Gian Piero Broglia - Tenuta La Meirana	82
Gavi del Comune di Gavi Cappello del Diavolo, San Bartolomeo	84
Gavi del Comune di Gavi La Chiara, La Chiara	83
Gavi del Comune di Gavi La Meirana, Gian Piero Broglia - Tenuta La Meirana	82
Gavi del Comune di Gavi Le Colombare, Santa Seraffa	155
Gavi del Comune di Gavi Lugarara, La Giustiniana	83
Gavi del Comune di Gavi Marchese Raggio, Bersano & Riccadonna	123
Gavi del Comune di Gavi Minaia, Nicola Bergaglio	81
Gavi del Comune di Gavi MonteRotondo, Villa Sparina	85
Gavi del Comune di Gavi Montessora, La Giustiniana	83
Gavi del Comune di Gavi Pelòia, San Bartolomeo	84
Gavi del Comune di Gavi Poggio Basco, Malgrà	102
Gavi del Comune di Gavi Rolona, Castellari Bergaglio	82
Gavi del Comune di Gavi V. del Bosco, Il Rocchin	154
Gavi del Comune di Gavi Vign. Groppella, La Chiara	83
Gavi del Comune di Gavi Villa Broglia, Gian Piero Broglia - Tenuta La Meirana	82
Gavi di Gavi, Prod. del Gavi	84
Gavi di Gavi La Maddalena, Prod. del Gavi	84
Gavi Drac Bianco, Domenico Ghio e Figli	45
Gavi Etichetta Nera, Domenico Ghio e Figli	45
Gavi Filagnotti, Cascina Ulivi	158
Gavi Fornaci, Castellari Bergaglio	82
Gavi Fornaci di Tassarolo, Michele Chiarlo	47
Gavi I Bergi, La Smilla	45
Gavi Il Forte, Prod. del Gavi	84
Gavi Masseria dei Carmelitani, Terre da Vino	42
Gavi Minaia, Franco M. Martinetti	141
Gavi Porfirio, La Caplana	150
Gavi Primuva, Prod. del Gavi	84
Gavi Principessa Gavia, Vigne Regali	140
Gavi Ricella Alta, Vigne del Pareto	126
Gavi Rovereto V.vecchia, Castellari Bergaglio	82
Gavi Sel. Valditerra, Valditerra	158
Gavi Tassarolo S, Cast. di Tassarolo	141
Gavi Terrarossa, La Zerba	160
Gavi Vigne Alte, Il V.le	125
Gavi Vigne del Pareto, Vigne del Pareto	126
Gavi Vign. Alborina, Cast. di Tassarolo	141
Gavi Vilma Cappelletti, Il V.le	125
Gemelli, Abbazia Santa Anastasia	747
Geremia, Rocca di Montegrossi	484
Ghemme, Antichi Vigneti di Cantalupo	85
Ghemme, Dessilani	78
Ghemme, Rovellotti	86
Ghemme, Torraccia del Piantav.	155
Ghemme Collis Breclemae, Antichi Vigneti di Cantalupo	85
Ghemme Collis Carellae, Antichi Vigneti di Cantalupo	85
Ghemme Ris., Rovellotti	86
Ghemme Signore di Bayard, Antichi Vigneti di Cantalupo	85
Gheppio, Mustilli	700
Ghiaie Bianche, Tenuta Col d'Orcia	506
Ghiaie della Furba, Tenuta di Capezzana	460
Giardin Vecchio, Santa Cassella	630
Gilat Rosso, Eraldo Viberti	96
Gimè Bianco, Ottella	309
Gioveto, Enrico Pierazzuoli	459
Giovin Re, Michele Satta	462
Giramonte, Fatt. Castiglioni e Montagnana	536
Girifalco, La Calonica	530
Girolamo, Cast. di Bossi	468
Giséle, La Rampa di Fugnano	566
Giubilante, Lungarotti	657
Giulio Cocchi Brut, Bava	68
Giulio Ferrari, Ferrari	242
Giuseppe Galliano Brut M. Cl., Borgo Maragliano	99
Giuseppe Galliano Chardonnay Brut, Borgo Maragliano	99
Giusto di Notri, Tua Rita	575
Godimondo Cabernet Franc, La Montecchia	320
Golfo del Tigullio Bianchetta Genovese U Pastine, Enoteca Bisson	165
Golfo del Tigullio Rosso Il Musaico V. dell'Intrigoso, Enoteca Bisson	165
Golfo del Tigullio Vermentino V. Erta, Enoteca Bisson	165
Golpaja, Fatt. di Petriolo	584
Gorgo Tondo Bianco, Carlo Pellegrino	751
Gorgo Tondo Rosso, Carlo Pellegrino	751
Gortmarin, Borgo San Daniele	359
Gote Rubizze, Marco Maci	719
Graf Noir, Drei Donà Tenuta La Palazza	431
Gramelot, Cant. Coop. Castignanese	614
Grammonte, Cottanera	748
Granaccia di Quiliano Vign. Cappuccini Ris., Innocenzo Turco	175
Granaio, Savignola Paolina	489
Granato, Foradori	236
Grandarella, Masi	319
Granduca, Tola	763
Grangiovese, Sesti - Cast. di Argiano	519
Grannero Pinot Nero, Vign. delle Terre Rosse	444
Grappoli del Grillo, Marco De Bartoli	749
Graticciaia, Agricole Vallone	724
Grattamacco, Colle Massari	461
Gravello, Librandi	737
Gravina, Cant. Coop. Botromagno	722
Gravisano, Cant. Coop. Botromagno	722
Grayasusy, Dattilo	738
Grecanico Mandrarossa, Settesoli	752
Grechetto, Cast. di Antignano - Brogal Vini	655
Grechetto, Falesco	670
Grechetto Latour a Civitella, Sergio Mottura	666
Grechetto Poggio della Costa, Sergio Mottura	666
Grechetto Vertunno, Freddano	652
Grechetto Villa Monticelli, Barberani - Vallesanta	650
Greco di Roccamonfina le Cinque Pietre, Telaro - Coop. Lavoro e Salute	695
Greco di Tufo, Cantine Caputo	691
Greco di Tufo, D'Antiche Terre - Vega	705
Greco di Tufo, De Falco	706
Greco di Tufo, Di Meo	699
Greco di Tufo, Benito Ferrara	703
Greco di Tufo, Feudi di San Gregorio	702
Greco di Tufo, Cantine Grotta del Sole	699
Greco di Tufo, La Casa dell'Orco	706
Greco di Tufo, Villa Raiano	701
Greco di Tufo G, Pietracupa	696
Greco di Tufo Loggia della Serra, Terredora	697
Greco di Tufo Terra degli Angeli, Terredora	697
Greco di Tufo V. Cicogna, Benito Ferrara	703
Greco I Portali, Basilium	708
Grignolino d'Asti, Braida	129
Grignolino d'Asti, Cast. del Poggio	127
Grignolino d'Asti, Agostino Pavia e Figli	23
Grignolino d'Asti, Luigi Spertino	156
Grignolino d'Asti, C.S. di Vinchio - Vaglio Serra	149
Grignolino d'Asti Brich Le Roche, Ermanno e Alessandra Brema	86
Grignolino d'Asti Miravalle, Cantine Sant'Agata	135
Grignolino d'Asti Pian delle Querce, Villa Fiorita	152
Grignolino d'Asti S. Giacu, Cascina Orsolina	156
Grignolino d'Asti V.maestra, Tenuta La Meridiana	114
Grignolino d'Asti La Castellina, F.lli Rovero	29
Grignolino del M.to Casalese, Bricco Mondalino	147
Grignolino del M.to Casalese, Tenuta Gaiano	50

Grignolino del M.to Casalese, Isabella	116
Grignolino del M.to Casalese, Tenuta La Tenaglia	139
Grignolino del M.to Casalese, Liedholm	152
Grignolino del M.to Casalese, Vicara	130
Grignolino del M.to Casalese Bricco del Bosco, Giulio Accornero e Figli	147
Grignolino del M.to Casalese Bricco Mondalino, Bricco Mondalino	147
Grignolino del M.to Casalese Celio, Marco Canato	148
Grignolino del M.to Casalese Cré Marcaleone, Carlo Quarello	69
Grignolino del M.to Casalese Marmanest, La Zucca	117
Grignolino del M.to Casalese Montecast., Isabella	116
Grignolino del M.to Casalese Sansìn, Colonna	148
Grignolino del M.to Casalese V. del Convento, Tenuta Gaiano	50
Grignolino del M.to Casalese Tumas, La Scamuzza	149
Grillo, Baglio Hopps	761
Grillo, Cantine Rallo	751
Grottoni, Il Lebbio	565
Guado San Leo, D'Alfonso del Sordo	730
Gualdo al Luco, Castelli del Grevepesa	558
Guardiolo Falanghina, La Guardiense	705
Guardiolo Rosso Ris., La Guardiense	705
Guidaccio, Marchesi Torrigiani	455
Guidalberto, Tenuta San Guido	457
Gurra, Agareno	761
Harmonium, Casa Vinicola Firriato	754
Harys, Giovanni Battista Gillardi	79
Herea Bianco Insolia, Avide	748
Herea Rosso Frappato, Avide	748
Hugonis, Tenute Rapitalà	746
I Balconi Rosso, Le Vigne di San Pietro	325
I Balzini Black Label, I Balzini	580
I Balzini Rosso, I Balzini	580
I Campacci, Tenuta di Trecciano	604
I Capitelli, Roberto Anselmi	300
I Fenili, Corte Gardoni	332
I Gibbioni, Tenuta Il Corno	558
I Greti, Le Ginestre	599
I Grottoni, Il Lebbio	565
l'Niccolò, Palagetto	568
I Piaggioni, Mocali	593
I Pini, Fatt. di Basciano	556
I Ricordi, Rio Grande	654
I Rovi, Le Ginestre	599
I Sierri, Cosimo Taurino	723
I Sistri, Fatt. di Felsina	470
I Sodi di San Niccolò, Castellare di Castellina	463
I Sodi Lunghi, F.lli Vagnoni	570
I Vigneti del Geografico, Agricoltori del Chianti Geografico	478
Ibisco Bianco, Ciccio Zaccagnini	676
Ibisco Rosa, Ciccio Zaccagnini	676
Idea, Trappolini	665
Il Bersaglio, Franco Pacenti	593
Il Bianco dell'Abazia, Serafini & Vidotto	308
Il Bianco Don.Giovanni Lucia Galasso, Giovanni Crosato	356
Il Borro, Tenuta Il Borro	495
Il Brecciolino, Castelvecchio	557
Il Calto delle Fate, Il Filò delle Vigne	283
Il Canto di Fondo Antico, Fondo Antico	764
Il Carbonaione, Podere Poggio Scalette	487
Il Castellare, Le Ginestre	599
Il Coro, Fondo Antico	764
Il Corto, Fatt. di Basciano	556
Il Corzano, Fatt. Corzano e Paterno	557
Il Cupo, Ester Hauser	638
Il Doge, I Girasoli di Sant'Andrea	660
Il Faggio, Conte Otto Barattieri di San Pietro	442
Il Fortino Cabernet/Merlot, Fatt. del Buonamico	523
Il Fortino Syrah, Fatt. del Buonamico	523
Il Fusco, La Roncaia	391
Il Futuro, Il Colombaio di Cencio	480
Il Gherlo Trebbiano di Modena, Corte Manzini	427
Il Gianello Merlot, Colonna - Vini Spalletti	441
Il Ginestreto, Le Ginestre	599
Il Mandorlo, La Madonnina - Triacca	486
Il Manuzio, Panzanello	543
Il Marzocco, Avignonesi	526
Il Matto delle Giuncaie, Massa Vecchia	497
Il Merlot della Topa Nera, Gino Fuso Carmignani	523
Il Michelangiolo, Terre di San Leonino	583
Il Monaco di Ribano Cabernet, Colonna - Vini Spalletti	441
Il Morino, Villa V.maggio	491
Il Moro, Cant. Valle dell'Acate	744
Il Musalè, Gino Amadio	673
Il Nero, V.lta	326
Il Nespoli, Poderi dal Nespoli	427
Il Paladino, Le Bocce	543
Il Palagio Chardonnay, Fatt. Il Palagio	474
Il Palagio Sauvignon, Fatt. Il Palagio	474
Il Pareto, Tenute Ambrogio e Giovanni Folonari	476
Il Peccato Barrique, Jacopo Banti	458
Il Poggesco, Gino Amadio	673
Il Poggiassai, Fattorie Chigi Saracini	469
Il Principe, Machiavelli	561
Il Ritorno, La Boscaiola	189
IL Rosso, Decugnano dei Barbi	651
Il Rosso dell'Abazia, Serafini & Vidotto	308
Il Rosso Don.Giovanni Lucia Galasso, Giovanni Crosato	356
Il Saloncello, Conti Sertoli Salis	209
Il Sasso, Piaggia	458
Il Sodaccio, Fatt. di Montevertine	552
Il Sogno di Cleofe, Ceralti	582
Il Sommo, Cast. di Lucignano	586
Il Tocco, Colle Bereto	600
Il Tornese Chardonnay, Drei Donà Tenuta La Palazza	431
Il Tuccanese, Il Tuccanese	733
Il Tuccanese Magliano, Il Tuccanese	733
Il Vento Chardonnay, Tenuta dei Fiori	49
Il Vessillo, Lungarotti	657
Il Villante Cabernet Sauvignon, Gaetano Lusenti	443
Il Volo di Alessandro, Castel di Salve	730
Immensum, Francesco Candido	729
Impero Bianco, Fatt. Mancini	628
Impero Pinot Nero Selezione F M, Fatt. Mancini	628
Implicito, Le Due Terre	400
Imyr, Dattilo	738
Incrocio Manzoni, V.iolo Giuseppe Fanti	232
Incrocio Manzoni 2.15, Conte Collalto	325
Incrocio Manzoni 6.0.13, Bepin de Eto	313
Incrocio Manzoni 6.0.13, Conte Collalto	325
Incrocio Manzoni 6.0.13, Scuola Enologica di Conegliano G. B. Cerletti	338
Incrocio Manzoni 6.0.13 Le Portelle, Adami	335
Infavato Vino da Uve Stramature, La Berta	424
Insolia, Feudo Principi di Butera	745
Intenso, Basilium	708
Inzolia, Cantine Torrevecchia	744
Inzolia, Cant. Valle dell'Acate	744
Iris, Feotto dello Jato	764
Irpinia Aglianico, Benito Ferrara	703
Irpinia Aglianico, Terredora	697
Irpinia Aglianico, Villa Raiano	701
Irpinia Aglianico Cinque Querce, Salvatore Molettieri	697
Irpinia Aglianico Il Principio, Terredora	697
Irpinia Rosso Coriliano, D'Antiche Terre - Vega	705
Isarcus, Georg Mumelter	259
Ischia Biancolella Tenuta Frassitelli, D'Ambra Vini d'Ischia	694
Ischia Forastera, D'Ambra Vini d'Ischia	694
Ischia Per''e Palummo, D'Ambra Vini d'Ischia	694
Ischia Rosso Dedicato a Mario d'Ambra, D'Ambra Vini d'Ischia	694
Ischia Rosso Vigne di Ianno Piro, Pietratorcia	705
Ispolaia Rosato, Ispoli	559
Ispolaia Rosso, Ispoli	559
Istante, Franz Haas	272
Jalé, Cusumano	756
Just Bianco, La Giustiniana	83
Justinus Kerner, Josef Sölva - Niklaserhof	266
Kados, Duca di Salaparuta - Vini Corvo	747
Kaid, Alessandro di Camporeale	760
Kaiton, Kuenhof - Peter Pliger	263
Karanar, Foradori	236
Karmis, Attilio Contini	768
Katharina, Popphof - Andreas Menz	270
Kebir, Torrevento	721
Klarus, Colombina	445
Kléos, Luigi Maffini	692
Kora Kodes Rosso, F.lli Serra	780
Kòrae Rosso, Pasqua Vigneti e Cantine	333
Korem, Antonio Argiolas	775
Kottabos Bianco, Casale dei Cento Corvi	672
Kottabos Rosso, Casale dei Cento Corvi	672
Kràtos, Luigi Maffini	692
Kron, Fontana Candida	669
Kuddia del Gallo, Abraxas	762
Kurni, Oasi degli Angeli	615
Kyme Bianco, D'Ambra Vini d'Ischia	694
L'Ardenza, Cottanera	748
L'Autentica, Cantine del Notaio	712
L'Incanto, La Rendola	597
L'insolente, Fatascià	754
L'Olmaia, Cant. Monrubio	642
L'Oro di Moroder, Alessandro Moroder	609
L'Ultima Spiaggia, Palazzone	653
La Capinera Chardonnay, Capinera	636
La Castelletta Pinot Grigio, Boccadigabbia	615
La Comète, Institut Agricole Régional	16
La Corte, Cast. di Querceto	488
La Faina, Baroncini	562
La Fonte di Pietrarsa, Massa Vecchia	497
La Fornace, Fatt. Selvapiana	549
La Gioia, Riecine	483
La Goccia, Podere San Luigi	546
La Grola, Allegrini	288
La Macchia, Bellaria	182
La Petrosa, Conte Zandotti	671
La Poja, Allegrini	288
La Querce, La Querce	494
La Rabitta Passito Bianco, Albino Piona	343
La Ricolma, San Giusto a Rentennano	484
La Roccaccia, Tenuta Roccaccia	546
La Roccaccia Fontenova, Tenuta Roccaccia	546
La Sassaia, Fatt. Poggio Romita	605
La Segreta Bianco, Planeta	752
La Segreta Rosso, Planeta	752
La Spinetta Oro , La Spinetta	58
La Suvera, Badia di Morrona	578
La Veronica, Podere Caccese	361
La V. di Alceo, Cast. dei Rampolla	540
La V. di Sonvico, Cascina La Barbatella	123
Labruna, Podere Aia della Macina	570
Lacrima di Morro d'Alba, Luciano Landi	635
Lacrima di Morro d'Alba, Monteschiavo	619

Lacrima di Morro d'Alba Fonte del Re, Umani Ronchi	627
Lacrima di Morro d'Alba Gavigliano, Luciano Landi	635
Lacrima di Morro d'Alba Orgiolo, Marotti Campi	623
Lacrima di Morro d'Alba Rùbico, Marotti Campi	623
Lacrima di Morro d'Alba Rustico del Pozzo Buono, Vicari	636
Lacrima di Morro d'Alba S. Maria del Fiore, Stefano Mancinelli	623
Lacrima di Morro d'Alba Sapore di Generazioni, Maurizio Marconi	632
Lacrima di Morro d'Alba Sel. Etichetta Nera, Mario Lucchetti	636
Lacrima di Morro d'Alba Sensazioni di Frutto, Stefano Mancinelli	623
Lacrima di Morro Etichetta Rossa d'Alba, Mario Lucchetti	636
Lacrimæ Bacchi, Avide	748
Lago di Corbara, Decugnano dei Barbi	651
Lago di Corbara Fontauro, Freddano	652
Lago di Corbara Foresco, Barberani - Vallesanta	650
Lago di Corbara Turlò, Tenuta di Salviano	658
Lagobruno, Incontri	574
Lailum, Fatt. Laila	620
Lam'oro, S. M. Tenim. Pile e Lamole	482
Lama del Tenente, Castel di Salve	730
Lamaione, Castelgiocondo	504
Lamarein, Josephus Mayr - Erbhof Unterganzner	258
Lambrusco dell'Emilia Le Viole, Cantine Dall'Asta	449
Lambrusco dell'Emilia Mefistofele, Cantine Dall'Asta	449
Lambrusco di Modena, Corte Manzini	427
Lambrusco di Modena Rosato, Corte Manzini	427
Lambrusco di Sorbara Centenario, Chiarli 1860	433
Lambrusco di Sorbara Fruttato, Chiarli 1860	433
Lambrusco di Sorbara Tre Medaglie, Cantine Cavicchioli & Figli	450
Lambrusco Grasparossa di Castelvetro Amabile, Corte Manzini	427
Lambrusco Grasparossa di Castelvetro Amabile Gala, Chiarli 1860	433
Lambrusco Grasparossa di Castelvetro Cinghio del Fojonco Cuvée dei Fondatori, Cantine Cooperative Riunite	446
Lambrusco Grasparossa di Castelvetro Col Sassoso, Cantine Cavicchioli & Figli	450
Lambrusco Grasparossa di Castelvetro L'Acino, Corte Manzini	427
Lambrusco Grasparossa di Castelvetro Pruno Nero, Chiarli 1860	433
Lambrusco Grasparossa di Castelvetro Secco, Corte Manzini	427
Lambrusco Grasparossa di Castelvetro Secco Centenario, Chiarli 1860	433
Lambrusco Grasparossa di Castelvetro Semi Secco, Corte Manzini	427
Lambrusco Mantovano Banda Blu, C.S. Coop. di Quistello	220
Lambrusco Mantovano Banda Rossa, C.S. Coop. di Quistello	220
Lambrusco Mantovano Banda Viola, C.S. Coop. di Quistello	220
Lambrusco Mantovano Rosso dei Concari, Lebovitz	212
Lambrusco Provincia di Mantova, Stefano Spezia	217
Lambrusco Salamino Semisecco, Cantine Cavicchioli & Figli	450
Lambrusco Spumante M. Cl. Pjcol Ross, Moro - Rinaldo Rinaldini	440
Lamezia Bianco, Statti	739
Lamezia Greco, Cantine Lento	739
Lamezia Greco, Statti	739
Lamezia Rosso, Statti	739
Lamezia Rosso Mastro Giurato, Caparra & Siciliani	736
Lamezia Rosso Ris., Cantine Lento	739
Lamezia Rosso Tenuta Romeo, Cantine Lento	739
Lamoremio, Benanti	759
Langhe Arbarei La Bernardina, Ceretto	25
Langhe Arborina, Elio Altare - Cascina Nuova	88
Langhe Arneis, Fontanabianca	119
Langhe Arneis, Ugo Lequio	121
Langhe Arneis, Monfalletto - Cordero di Montezemolo	93
Langhe Arneis, Pio Cesare	26
Langhe Bianco, Ca' d'Gal	132
Langhe Bianco, La Spinetta	58
Langhe Bianco, I Paglieri	34
Langhe Bianco, G. D. Vajra	43
Langhe Bianco Asso di Fiori, Braida	129
Langhe Bianco Ballarin, Cascina Ballarin	90
Langhe Bianco Binel, Ettore Germano	137
Langhe Bianco Bricco Rovella, Armando Parusso	109
Langhe Bianco Bussiador, Aldo Conterno	105
Langhe Bianco Dives, G. B. Burlotto	146
Langhe Bianco Gastaldi, Gastaldi	119
Langhe Bianco Graffagno, Paolo Saracco	67
Langhe Bianco Il Fiore, Braida	129
Langhe Bianco L'Aura, Monti	109
Langhe Bianco La Rocca, Albino Rocca	35
Langhe Bianco Lorenso, Luigi Baudana	135
Langhe Bianco Matteo Correggia, Matteo Correggia	51
Langhe Bianco Montalupa, Ascheri	46
Langhe Bianco Rolando, Bricco Maiolica	73
Langhe Bianco Sorriso, Paolo Scavino	64
Langhe Bianco Suasi, Deltetto	52
Langhe Bianco Sunsi, Batasiolo	88
Langhe Bianco Tamardi, Monchiero Carbone	54
Langhe Bianco Tre Uve, Malvirà	53
Langhe Bianco Villa Giulia, Tenuta Cisa Asinari dei Marchesi di Grésy	31
Langhe Bric Quercia, Tenuta Carretta	126
Langhe Bricco del Drago, Poderi Colla	26
Langhe Brich Ginestra, Paolo Conterno	106
Langhe Chardonnay, Luigi Baudana	135
Langhe Chardonnay, Ca' d'Gal	132
Langhe Chardonnay, Tenuta Cisa Asinari dei Marchesi di Grésy	31
Langhe Chardonnay, Destefanis	114
Langhe Chardonnay, Gastaldi	119
Langhe Chardonnay, Ettore Germano	137
Langhe Chardonnay, La Morandina	66
Langhe Chardonnay, Moccagatta	33
Langhe Chardonnay, V.ioli Elvio Pertinace	144
Langhe Chardonnay, Poderi Sinaglio	28
Langhe Chardonnay, Valfieri	72
Langhe Chardonnay, V. Rionda - Massolino	138
Langhe Chardonnay Alessandro, Gianfranco Bovio	89
Langhe Chardonnay Barricello, Valfieri	72
Langhe Chardonnay Bastia, Conterno Fantino	106
Langhe Chardonnay Bianch del Luv, Paolo Saracco	67
Langhe Chardonnay Boccabarile, Poderi Sinaglio	28
Langhe Chardonnay Buschet, Moccagatta	33
Langhe Chardonnay Cadet, Bruno Rocca	36
Langhe Chardonnay da Bertù, Albino Rocca	35
Langhe Chardonnay Educato, Elio Grasso	108
Langhe Chardonnay Flavo, Rocche Costamagna	95
Langhe Chardonnay Grésy, Tenuta Cisa Asinari dei Marchesi di Grésy	31
Langhe Chardonnay L'Angelica, Podere Rocche dei Manzoni	110
Langhe Chardonnay Le Masche, Bel Colle	145
Langhe Chardonnay Livrot, Mauro Molino	92
Langhe Chardonnay Morino, Batasiolo	88
Langhe Chardonnay Papé Bianc, Funtanin	52
Langhe Chardonnay PiodiLei, Pio Cesare	26
Langhe Chardonnay Prasuè, Paolo Saracco	67
Langhe Chardonnay Roera, F.lli Giacosa	120
Langhe Chardonnay Scapulin, Giuseppe Cortese	31
Langhe Chardonnay Serbato, Batasiolo	88
Langhe Chardonnay Sermine, Ca' del Baio	142
Langhe Chardonnay Stissa d'le Favole, Montaribaldi	34
Langhe Chardonnay V. La Villa, Gianfranco Bovio	89
Langhe Darmagi, Gaja	32
Langhe Dolcetto, Bricco del Cucù	43
Langhe Dolcetto Barturot, Ca' Viola	74
Langhe Dolcetto Busiord, Scagliola	49
Langhe Dolcetto Vilot, Ca' Viola	74
Langhe Dolcetto Visadì, Domenico Clerico	104
Langhe Favorita, F.lli Alessandria	145
Langhe Favorita, Bel Colle	145
Langhe Favorita, Cascina Chicco	51
Langhe Favorita, Gianluigi Lano	25
Langhe Favorita, Pelissero	144
Langhe Freisa, Cant. del Pino	30
Langhe Freisa, Moccagatta	33
Langhe Freisa, Rino Varaldo	36
Langhe Freisa Kyè, G. D. Vajra	43
Langhe Freisa La Violetta, Piero Gatti	133
Langhe Freisa Santa Rosalia, Giacomo Brezza & Figli	37
Langhe Furesté, F.lli Oddero	94
Langhe La Castella, F.lli Pecchenino	76
Langhe La Villa, Elio Altare - Cascina Nuova	88
Langhe Larigi, Elio Altare - Cascina Nuova	88
Langhe Mores, G. B. Burlotto	146
Langhe Nebbiolo, F.lli Bera	122
Langhe Nebbiolo, Enzo Boglietti	89
Langhe Nebbiolo, Gianfranco Bovio	89
Langhe Nebbiolo, Cascina Ca' Rossa	50
Langhe Nebbiolo, Cascina Ballarin	90
Langhe Nebbiolo, Giuseppe Cortese	31
Langhe Nebbiolo, Deltetto	52
Langhe Nebbiolo, Poderi Einaudi	75
Langhe Nebbiolo, Cascina Luisin	33
Langhe Nebbiolo, Malvirà	53
Langhe Nebbiolo, Mauro Molino	92
Langhe Nebbiolo, Monfalletto - Cordero di Montezemolo	93
Langhe Nebbiolo, Cascina Morassino	150
Langhe Nebbiolo, Andrea Oberto	93
Langhe Nebbiolo, Pelissero	144
Langhe Nebbiolo, Ruggeri Corsini	111
Langhe Nebbiolo, Giorgio Scarzello e Figli	41
Langhe Nebbiolo, Rino Varaldo	36
Langhe Nebbiolo, Osvaldo Viberti	97
Langhe Nebbiolo, V. Rionda - Massolino	138
Langhe Nebbiolo Bric del Baio, Ca' del Baio	142
Langhe Nebbiolo Brich Ginestra, Paolo Conterno	106
Langhe Nebbiolo Ciabot della Luna, Gianni Voerzio	97
Langhe Nebbiolo Conteisa, Gaja	32
Langhe Nebbiolo Costa Russi, Gaja	32
Langhe Nebbiolo Favot, Aldo Conterno	105
Langhe Nebbiolo Gambarini, Montaribaldi	34
Langhe Nebbiolo il Crutin, Giovanni Manzone	108
Langhe Nebbiolo La Malora, Terre da Vino	42
Langhe Nebbiolo Lasarin, Poderi Marcarini	91
Langhe Nebbiolo Martinenga, Tenuta Cisa Asinari dei Marchesi di Grésy	31
Langhe Nebbiolo Peirass, Silvio Grasso	91
Langhe Nebbiolo Roccardo, Rocche Costamagna	95
Langhe Nebbiolo Sorì S. Lorenzo, Gaja	32
Langhe Nebbiolo Sorì Tildìn, Gaja	32
Langhe Nebbiolo Sperss, Gaja	32
Langhe Nebbiolo Surìsjvan, Icardi	66
Langhe Paitin, Paitin	121
Langhe Pertinace, V.ioli Elvio Pertinace	144
Langhe Rosso, Cascina Fonda	101
Langhe Rosso, F.lli Mossio	129
Langhe Rosso, San Romano	77
Langhe Rosso Acanzio, Mauro Molino	92
Langhe Rosso Alta Bussia, Attilio Ghisolfi	107
Langhe Rosso Arte, Domenico Clerico	104
Langhe Rosso Balàu, Ettore Germano	137
Langhe Rosso Ballarin, Cascina Ballarin	90
Langhe Rosso Bouquet, F.lli Seghesio	112
Langhe Rosso Bric du Luv, Ca' Viola	74
Langhe Rosso Bric Quercia, Tenuta Carretta	126

Langhe Rosso Bricco Manzoni, Podere Rocche dei Manzoni	110
Langhe Rosso Bricco Rovella, Armando Parusso	109
Langhe Rosso Bricco Serra, F.lli Cigliuti	118
Langhe Rosso Brumaio, San Fereolo	77
Langhe Rosso Buio, Enzo Boglietti	89
Langhe Rosso Cadò, Anna Maria Abbona	78
Langhe Rosso Camerlot, Pira	76
Langhe Rosso Carlin, Attilio Ghisolfi	107
Langhe Rosso Castlé, Gastaldi	119
Langhe Rosso Centobricchi, Mauro Sebaste	27
Langhe Rosso Corale, Paolo Scavino	64
Langhe Rosso Da Pruvé, Ca' Rome' - Romano Marengo	30
Langhe Rosso Dossi Rossi, Monti	109
Langhe Rosso Duetto, Cascina Vano	118
Langhe Rosso Fabio, Andrea Oberto	93
Langhe Rosso Faletto, Cascina Bongiovanni	62
Langhe Rosso Fantasia 4.20, Rino Varaldo	36
Langhe Rosso Gastaldi, Gastaldi	119
Langhe Rosso I Due Ricu, Marziano e Enrico Abbona	74
Langhe Rosso La Bisbetica, Ada Nada	143
Langhe Rosso Long Now, Pelissero	144
Langhe Rosso Lorenso, Luigi Baudana	135
Langhe Rosso Lorié, Bricco Maiolica	73
Langhe Rosso Luigi Einaudi, Poderi Einaudi	75
Langhe Rosso Luna, F.lli Alessandria	145
Langhe Rosso Martin Sec, San Romano	77
Langhe Rosso Ménico, Funtanin	52
Langhe Rosso Mondaccione, Luigi Coppo e Figli	56
Langhe Rosso Monprà, Conterno Fantino	106
Langhe Rosso Monsordo La Bernardina, Ceretto	25
Langhe Rosso Montegrilli, Elvio Cogno	125
Langhe Rosso Pafoj, Icardi	66
Langhe Rosso Passo del Lupo, Casavecchia	153
Langhe Rosso Pe Mol, Luciano Sandrone	41
Langhe Rosso Pedrocha, Hilberg - Pasquero	127
Langhe Rosso Pi Cit, Marchesi di Barolo	39
Langhe Rosso Pinay, Attilio Ghisolfi	107
Langhe Rosso Pinònero, Podere Rocche dei Manzoni	110
Langhe Rosso Piria, V. Rionda - Massolino	138
Langhe Rosso Quartetto, Aldo Conterno	105
Langhe Rosso Quatr Nas, Podere Rocche dei Manzoni	110
Langhe Rosso Rabajolo, Bruno Rocca	36
Langhe Rosso Rangone, Ca' Viola	74
Langhe Rosso Riella, Sergio Degiorgis	101
Langhe Rosso S. Guglielmo, Malvirà	53
Langhe Rosso Seifile, Fiorenzo Nada	143
Langhe Rosso Serrapiù, Gianni Voerzio	97
Langhe Rosso Sinaij, Poderi Sinaglio	28
Langhe Rosso Suo di Giacomo, Eugenio Bocchino	150
Langhe Rosso Tris, Giovanni Manzone	108
Langhe Rosso Vàj, Viticoltori Associati di Rodello	158
Langhe Rosso Villa Martis, Tenuta Cisa Asinari dei Marchesi di Grésy	31
Langhe Rosso Virtus, Tenuta Cisa Asinari dei Marchesi di Grésy	31
Langhe Rosso Yeta, Giovanni Battista Gillardi	79
Langhe Sanrocco, Poderi Colla	26
Langhe Sassisto, F.lli Bera	122
Langhe Sauvignon, Tenuta Cisa Asinari dei Marchesi di Grésy	31
Langhe Solea, I Paglieri	34
Langhe Vendemmiaio, Tenuta La Volta - Cabutto	42
Langhe V. Maestro, F.lli Pecchenino	76
Langhe V. Meira, Poderi Einaudi	75
Latinia, C.S. di Santadi	773
Laurento Chardonnay, Umberto Cesari	425
Laurus, La Fiorita	591
Le Anfore, Colle di Maggio	671
Le Balze, Il Poggiolino	576
Le Banche, Cascina delle Terre Rosse	168
Le Borranine, Montiverdi	482
Le Braci, Masseria Monaci	720
Le Bronche, Fattorie Parri	597
Le Bruniche, Tenute Ambrogio e Giovanni Folonari	476
Le Busche, Umani Ronchi	627
Le Cave Chardonnay, Fatt. Le Terrazze	624
Le Cupole di Trinoro, Tenuta di Trinoro	603
Le Fagge Chardonnay, Cast. d' Albola	550
Le Lame, Fatt. Coroncino	634
Le Logge, Centolani	505
Le Lule, Tenuta di Blasig	403
Le Macchiole, Le Macchiole	456
Le Marangole, Cast. d' Albola	550
Le Pergole del Sole Cavalchina, Cavalchina	324
Le Pergole Torte, Fatt. di Montevertine	552
Le Poggere, Vaselli	665
Le Prata, Villa Le Prata	522
Le Pratole, Rocca di Castagnoli	483
Le Ripe Bianco, Azienda Vinicola Federici	674
Le Ruote, Iesolana	580
Le Scuderie del Cielo, Filomusi Guelfi	685
Le Solagne, Fatt. Dezi	633
Le Solagne V. T., Fatt. Dezi	633
Le Stanze, Poliziano	532
Le Terrazze del Cast., Castagnoli	462
Le Terrine, Cast. della Panaretta	453
Le Vignole, Paola Di Mauro - Colle Picchioni	668
Le Voliere Cabernet Sauvignon, Cast. di Modanella	555
Le Volte, Tenuta dell' Ornellaia	457
Leila, Alberto Loi	769
Leone d'Almerita, Tasca d'Almerita	758
Leone del Carobbio, Carobbio	540
Leone Rosso, Fatt. del Casato - Donatella Cinelli Colombini	503
Leprata, Villa Le Prata	522
Lessini Durello M. Cl., Marcato	342
Lessona, Sella	98
Lessona S. Sebastiano allo Zoppo, Sella	98
Leucós Bianco, Ronco dei Pini	402
Leverano Bianco V. del Saraceno, Conti Zecca	725
Leverano Malvasia V. del Saraceno, Conti Zecca	725
Leverano Rosato V. del Saraceno, Conti Zecca	725
Leverano Rosso Terra Ris., Conti Zecca	725
Leverano V. del Saraceno Vendemmia Tardiva, Conti Zecca	725
Liano, Umberto Cesari	425
Libaio, Tenim. Ruffino	548
Liburnio, Orlandi Contucci Ponno	683
Ligeia, Statti	739
Límes Rosso, Ronco dei Pini	402
Linagre Sauvignon di Villa Angela, Ercole Velenosi	610
Linticlarus Cuvée, Tiefenbrunner	268
Lis Neris, Lis Neris - Pecorari	411
Lison-Pramaggiore Cabernet Franc, Podere dal Ger	396
Lison-Pramaggiore Cabernet Hora Sexta, Mosole	343
Lison-Pramaggiore Cabernet Sauvignon, Villa Frattina	395
Lison-Pramaggiore Chardonnay, Podere dal Ger	396
Lison-Pramaggiore Chardonnay, Villa Frattina	395
Lison-Pramaggiore Cl. Tocai Juti, Bosco del Merlo	282
Lison-Pramaggiore Merlot, Podere dal Ger	396
Lison-Pramaggiore Merlot, Villa Frattina	395
Lison-Pramaggiore Merlot ad Nonam, Mosole	343
Lison-Pramaggiore Pinot Grigio, Podere dal Ger	396
Lison-Pramaggiore Pinot Grigio, Villa Frattina	395
Lison-Pramaggiore Refosco P.R. Roggio dei Roveri, Bosco del Merlo	282
Lison-Pramaggiore Refosco P.R. V. Melonetto, Sergio Nardin	341
Lison-Pramaggiore Sauvignon, Bosco del Merlo	282
Lison-Pramaggiore Sauvignon, Villa Frattina	395
Lison-Pramaggiore Tocai Italico, Tenuta Teracrea	341
Litora Naumachos, Vinicola del Tesino	617
Litra, Abbazia Santa Anastasia	747
Livernano, Livernano	552
Livio Bronca Brut, Sorelle Bronca	336
Lo Bien Flapì, Di Barrò	19
Loazzolo Borgo Maragliano V. T., Borgo Maragliano	99
Loazzolo Piasa Rischei, Forteto della Luja	99
Lococco, Pratesi	460
Locorosso Rosso, Pratesi	460
Locorotondo, Vini Classici Cardone	726
Locorotondo, I Pastini - Carparelli	732
Locorotondo, Cant. Coop. del Locorotondo	726
Locorotondo, Rivera	717
Locorotondo Talné, Borgo Canale	721
Locorotondo Vigneti In Tallinajo, Cant. Coop. del Locorotondo	726
Lodano, Tua Rita	575
Loghetto, Agnes	205
Loi Corona, Alberto Loi	769
Longobardo, Cant. di Casteggio	214
Longobardo Rosso, Enzo Mecella	635
Loré Muffa Nobile, Dino Illuminati	677
Lotario Chardonnay, Enzo Mecella	635
Lucciolaio, Torraccia di Presura	490
Luce, Luce	513
Lucente, Luce	513
Lucilla, Farnetella	571
Ludi, Ercole Velenosi	610
Luenzo, Vincenzo Cesani	563
Lugana, Ca' Lojera	208
Lugana, Fraccaroli	341
Lugana, Monte Cicogna	198
Lugana, Giacomo Montresor	333
Lugana, Ottella	309
Lugana, Cantine Valtenesi - Lugana	217
Lugana Brolettino Grande Annata, Ca' dei Frati	208
Lugana Brut, Costaripa	198
Lugana Brut, Fraccaroli	341
Lugana Brut Cl., Visconti	216
Lugana Brut Cl. Ca' Maiol, Provenza	192
Lugana Brut Cl. Cuvée dei Frati, Ca' dei Frati	208
Lugana Brut Sebastian, Provenza	192
Lugana Ca' Maiol, Provenza	192
Lugana Collo Lungo, Visconti	216
Lugana Il Brolettino, Ca' dei Frati	208
Lugana Il Rintocco, Marangona	220
Lugana Le Creete, Ottella	309
Lugana Melibeo, Santi	291
Lugana S. Benedetto, Zenato	309
Lugana Sergio Zenato, Zenato	309
Lugana Sup., Ca' Lojera	208
Lugana Sup., Visconti	216
Lugana Sup. Ca' Molin, Provenza	192
Lugana Sup. Cios, Cantine Valtenesi - Lugana	217
Lugana Sup. Filo di Arianna, Tenuta Roveglia	220
Lugana Sup. I Fraccaroli, Fraccaroli	341
Lugana Sup. Molceo, Ottella	309
Lugana Sup. Sel. Fabio Contato, Provenza	192
Lugana Sup. Selva Capuzza, Cantine Colli a Lago	216
Lugana Sup. V. di Catullo, Tenuta Roveglia	220
Lugana V. Silva, Ca' Lojera	208
Lugana Vigne Alte, F.lli Zeni	284
Lugana Vign. Massoni Santa Cristina, Zenato	309
Lugana Vign. San Martino Il Sestante, Viticoltori Tommasi	317
Lumen, Gualdo del Re	573
Luna dei Feldi, Santa Margherita	338
Luna di Monte, San Luciano	522

Luna Verde, Guicciardini Strozzi - Fatt. Cusona	564
Lunaria, Castelluccio	434
Lupicaia, Cast. del Terriccio	467
Luzzana, Giovanni Cherchi	777
Lynthea Merlot, Tola	763
Macàro Metodo Solera, Valle dell'Asso	722
Macchiona, La Stoppa	439
Madégo, La Cappuccina	302
Madreselva, Casale del Giglio	663
Maestro Raro, Fatt. di Felsina	470
Magilda Rosato, Barsento	733
Magliano, Az. Agr. Claudio Morelli	617
Magna Grecia Rosso, Vintripodi Calabria	742
Magnificat Cabernet Sauvignon, Drei Donà Tenuta La Palazza	431
Magno Megonio, Librandi	737
Magone, Sergio Mottura	666
Majo San Lorenzo, Aziende Vinicole Miceli	755
Malandrino, Tenuta Cataldi Madonna	680
Malena, Pacina	470
Malicchia Mapicchia, Barsento	733
Malise Pignoletto Chardonnay, Umberto Cesari	425
Malleo, Caseo	179
Malvasia, Il Lebbio	565
Malvasia, Le Due Torri	373
Malvasia, Mulino delle Tolle	347
Malvasia, Pierpaolo Pecorari	412
Malvasia, Tenuta Teracrea	341
Malvasia, Andrea Visintini	375
Malvasia Campo di Fiori, Vign. Due Santi	284
Malvasia del Lazio, Fontana Candida	669
Malvasia del Lazio, Gotto d'Oro	669
Malvasia del Lazio, Vini Pallavicini	672
Malvasia del Lazio Rumon, Conte Zandotti	671
Malvasia del Lazio Terre dei Grifi, Fontana Candida	669
Malvasia del Lazio Villanova, Cant. Cerveteri	666
Malvasia delle Lipari Naturale, Cantine Colosi	762
Malvasia delle Lipari Passita, Cantine Colosi	762
Malvasia delle Lipari Passito, Barone di Villagrande	753
Malvasia di Bosa, Columbu	778
Malvasia di Bosa, F.lli Porcu	779
Malvasia di Cagliari, Gigi Picciau	768
Malvasia di Cagliari Gutta'e Axina, Villa di Quartu	780
Malvasia di Casorzo d'Asti Molignano, Bricco Mondalino	147
Malvasia di Castelnuovo Don Bosco, Bava	68
Malvasia di Castelnuovo Don Bosco, Cascina Gilli	61
Malvasia Dolce, Monte delle Vigne	446
Malvasia Istriana, Rino Russolo	412
Malvasia L'Accesa, I Campetti	601
Malvasia & Moscato Dolce, Carra	433
Mandolaia, La Vis	232
Mandrielle Merlot, Banfi	500
Manero, Fatt. del Cerro	528
Manna, Franz Haas	272
Mante'nghja, Capichera	767
Manzoni Bianco, Casa Roma	319
Manzoni Bianco, Gregoletto	298
Manzoni Bianco , Conte Loredan Gasparini Venegazzù	344
Manzoni Liquoroso, Scuola Enologica di Conegliano G. B. Cerletti	338
Marciliano, Falesco	670
Marco Nero, Contadi Castaldi	178
Maria Grazia, Carlo Giacosa	32
Marinali Bianco, Villa Sandi	338
Marinali Rosso, Villa Sandi	338
Marino Colle Picchioni Oro, Paola Di Mauro - Colle Picchioni	668
Marino Etichetta Verde, Paola Di Mauro - Colle Picchioni	668
Marinò Rosso, Luigi Vivacqua	740
Marino Sup., Brannetti Antica Riserva della Cascina	672
Marino Sup., Gotto d'Oro	669
Marramiero Brut, Marramiero	683
Marrano, Bigi	650
Marsala Ambra Secco Vecchioflorio, Cantine Florio	750
Marsala Sup., Marco De Bartoli	749
Marsala Sup. Dolce, F.lli Fici	761
Marsala Sup. Oro V. La Miccia, Marco De Bartoli	749
Marsala Sup. Ris. 20 Anni, Marco De Bartoli	749
Marsala Sup. Ris. Dom Pellegrino, Carlo Pellegrino	751
Marsala Sup. Ris. Targa 1840, Cantine Florio	750
Marsala Sup. Secco Ris., F.lli Fici	761
Marsala Sup. Semisecco Anima Mediterranea, Cantine Rallo	751
Marsala Sup. Semisecco Vecchioflorio, Cantine Florio	750
Marsala Vergine, Carlo Pellegrino	751
Marsala Vergine Baglio Florio, Cantine Florio	750
Marsala Vergine Baglio Florio Oro, Cantine Florio	750
Marsala Vergine Soleras, Carlo Pellegrino	751
Marsala Vergine Soleras Ris. 12 anni, Cantine Rallo	751
Marsala Vergine Terre Arse Oro, Cantine Florio	750
Marsala Vergine Vecchioflorio Oro, Cantine Florio	750
Martà, Fatt. San Francesco	736
Marzieno, Fatt. Zerbina	429
Masetto Bianco, Endrizzi	248
Maso Furli Rosso, Maso Furli	233
Maso Torresella, Cavit - Cons. di Cantine Sociali	242
Maso Torresella Cuvée, Cavit - Cons. di Cantine Sociali	242
Massaretta, Cima	497
Masseo, Vaglie	641
Masseria Maime, Tormaresca	729
Masseto, Tenuta dell' Ornellaia	457
Maté Rosso, Sottimano	122
Mater Matuta, Casale del Giglio	663
Mauritius, Cant. Gries/Cant. di Bolzano	255
Maurizio Zanella, Ca' del Bosco	193
Maurleo, Pietro Beconcini	602
Maximo, Umani Ronchi	627
Mecenate, Villa Cilnia	452
Megara, Duca di Salaparuta - Vini Corvo	747
Mel, Antonio Caggiano	702
Melissa Asylia, Librandi	737
Melissa Rosso, Val di Neto	742
Melograno, Gabriele Da Prato	587
Menade, Cant. Cerveteri	666
Menj Bianco, Tenuta Villanova	380
Mercuria Rosso, Castel Noarna	236
Meridio, Pietracupa	696
Merlanico - De Conciliis - Barone Pizzini, Viticoltori De Conciliis	698
Merlò, Le Tende	292
Merlot, Casale del Giglio	663
Merlot, Castagnoli	462
Merlot, Cast. delle Regine	640
Merlot, Colle San Lorenzo	667
Merlot, Fanini	643
Merlot, Feudo Principi di Butera	745
Merlot, La Palazzola	657
Merlot, Gino Pedrotti	227
Merlot, Planeta	752
Merlot, Cantine Rallo	751
Merlot, Roncùs	352
Merlot, Sant'Elena	385
Merlot, Villa Arceno	473
Merlot, Villa Pillo	485
Merlot Baladello, Ferghettina	194
Merlot Baolar, Pierpaolo Pecorari	412
Merlot'Cabernet, Santarosa	435
Merlot Calle, Fasoli	286
Merlot degli Artisti , Cantine Leonardo da Vinci	578
Merlot dei Colli Trevigiani, Gregoletto	298
Merlot del Lazio, Fontana Candida	669
Merlot del Lazio, Gotto d'Oro	669
Merlot dell'Umbria, Falesco	670
Merlot della Bergamasca, C.S. Bergamasca	206
Merlot della Bergamasca Cumello, Medolago Albani	222
Merlot di Atina Tenuta La Creta, Giuseppe Iucci	672
Merlot e Cabernet Casara Roveri, Luigino Dal Maso	299
Merlot I Legni, Rino Russolo	412
Merlot Mandrarossa, Settesoli	752
Merlot Maria Teresa, San Vettore	587
Merlot Orgno, Fasoli	286
Merlot Principe di Corleone , Pollara	762
Merlot Rendola, La Rendola	597
Merlot Sant'Adele, Villa Pillo	485
Merlot Santepietre, Lamberti	339
Merum V. Melonetto, Sergio Nardin	341
Mesolone Rosso, Barni	47
Messorio, Le Macchiole	456
Mezzopane, Poggio San Polo	517
Migoléta, Longariva	239
Millanni, Guicciardini Strozzi - Fatt. Cusona	564
Milleunanotte, Tenuta di Donnafugata	750
Minaia, Franco M. Martinetti	141
Minnella, Benanti	759
Minorco Sasso, Tenuta Le Querce	709
Mirum, La Monacesca	620
Mirus, La Monacesca	620
Mito, Fatt. Paradiso	423
Mito, Poderi San Savino	632
Mizzole Rosso, Cecilia Beretta	332
Modus, Tenim. Ruffino	548
Molino delle Balze, Rocca di Castagnoli	483
Molise Aglianico Contado, Di Majo Norante	676
Molise Don Luigi, Di Majo Norante	676
Molise Falanghina, Borgo di Colloredo	686
Molise Falanghina, Di Majo Norante	676
Molise Greco, Di Majo Norante	676
Momenti, Vaglie	641
Monemvasia, Casalone	100
M.to Airales, Vicara	130
M.to Alterego, Luigi Coppo e Figli	56
M.to Alteserre, Bava	68
M.to Bianco Ambrogio Spinola, Cast. di Tassarolo	141
M.to Bianco Arbiola, Tenuta dell'Arbiola	132
M.to Bianco Bricco S. Ippolito, Franco e Mario Scrimaglio	124
M.to Bianco Camillona, Araldica - Il Cantinone	58
M.to Bianco Clelie VI, Tenuta dell'Arbiola	132
M.to Bianco dei Marchesi, Marchesi Alfieri	131
M.to Bianco Eliseo, Cantine Sant'Agata	135
M.to Bianco Ferro di Cavallo, La Giribaldina	48
M.to Bianco Fonsìna, GiulioxAccornero e Figli	147
M.to Bianco I Fossaretti, Poderi Bertelli	70
M.to Bianco Munsret, Casalone	100
M.to Bianco Noè, Cascina La Barbatella	123
M.to Bianco Non è, Cascina La Barbatella	123
M.to Bianco Pafoj, Icardi	66
M.to Bianco Puntet, Tenuta La Meridiana	114
M.to Bianco Sivoj, La Ghersa	102
M.to Bianco Tra Donne Sole, Terre da Vino	42
M.to Bianco Villa Drago, F.lli Rovero	29
M.to Bricco della Ghiandaia, Renzo Beccaris	152
M.to Cabernet Fossaretti, Poderi Bertelli	70
M.to Casalese Cortese, Bricco Mondalino	147
M.to Chiaretto La Rosella del Bric, Casalone	100
M.to Countacc!, Michele Chiarlo	47
M.to Dolcetto, Cast. del Poggio	127

M.to Dolcetto Plissé, Carlo Benotto	70
M.to Dolcetto Trevigne, Franco Mondo	159
M.to Freisa, Casalone	100
M.to Freisa Bioc, Isabella	116
M.to Freisa La Frassinella, Cast. di Lignano	154
M.to Freisa La Selva di Moirano, Scarpa - Antica Casa Vinicola	124
M.to l'Uccelletta, Vicara	130
M.to Müller Thurgau, Villa Sparina	85
M.to Pomona, Bersano & Riccadonna	123
M.to Rosso, Cascina Gilli	61
M.to Rosso, Tenuta dei Fiori	49
M.to Rosso Amani, Colonna	148
M.to Rosso Amis, Cascina Garitina	59
M.to Rosso Antico Vitigno, Sciorio	72
M.to Rosso Arbiola, Tenuta dell'Arbiola	132
M.to Rosso Bigio, Colonna	148
M.to Rosso Bricco Maddalena, Cascina La Maddalena	128
M.to Rosso Bricco San Tomaso, La Scamuzza	149
M.to Rosso Bruno Broglia, Gian Piero Broglia - Tenuta La Meirana	82
M.to Rosso Cabernet, F.lli Rovero	29
M.to Rosso Cascina Bricco del Sole, Icardi	66
M.to Rosso Centenario, Giulio Accornero e Figli	147
M.to Rosso Cinque File, Tenuta dei Fiori	49
M.to Rosso Crebarné, Carlo Quarello	69
M.to Rosso dei Marchesi, Marchesi Alfieri	131
M.to Rosso dei Marchesi, Cast. di Tassarolo	141
M.to Rosso di Malì, Il V.le	125
M.to Rosso Dom, Tenuta dell'Arbiola	132
M.to Rosso Emmerosso, Malgrà	102
M.to Rosso Eresia, Luigi Tacchino	151
M.to Rosso Estremis, Cascina Garitina	59
M.to Rosso Genesi, Cantine Sant'Agata	135
M.to Rosso Il Bacialé, Braida	129
M.to Rosso Innominato, La Guardia	116
M.to Rosso Just, La Giustiniana	83
M.to Rosso La Ghersa, La Ghersa	102
M.to Rosso Lajetto, F.lli Rovero	29
M.to Rosso Le Grive, Forteto della Luja	99
M.to Rosso Lhennius, Cast. di Lignano	154
M.to Rosso Luce Monaca, Araldica - Il Cantinone	58
M.to Rosso Malgrà, Malgrà	102
M.to Rosso Maniero, Villa Fiorita	152
M.to Rosso Matot, Valfieri	72
M.to Rosso Mondone, Colonna	148
M.to Rosso Mystère, Cascina La Barbatella	123
M.to Rosso Onero, Tenuta Cast. di Razzano	28
M.to Rosso Piagè, La Ghersa	102
M.to Rosso Pin, La Spinetta	58
M.to Rosso Policalpo, Cascina Castlèt	71
M.to Rosso Reginal, Sciorio	72
M.to Rosso Renero, Araldica - Il Cantinone	58
M.to Rosso Rivaia, Tenuta La Meridiana	114
M.to Rosso Rivalta, Villa Sparina	85
M.to Rosso Rocca Schiavino, F.lli Rovero	29
M.to Rosso Rubello, Vicara	130
M.to Rosso Rus, Casalone	100
M.to Rosso S. Germano, Marchesi Alfieri	131
M.to Rosso Sacroprofano, La Guardia	116
M.to Rosso Sampò, Villa Sparina	85
M.to Rosso Sole, Cascina Orsolina	156
M.to Rosso Sonvico, Cascina La Barbatella	123
M.to Rosso Sul Bric, Franco M. Martinetti	141
M.to Rosso Tantra, Franco e Mario Scrimaglio	124
M.to Rubello, Vicara	130
M.to Sarnì, Vicara	130
M.to Sauvignon Villa Guani, F.lli Rovero	29
M.to Villa Pattono, Renato Ratti	94
Monfort Giallo, Casata Monfort	247
Monfort Rosa, Casata Monfort	247
Monica di Sardegna, Cantine di Dolianova	769
Monica di Sardegna, C.S. Marrubiu	779
Monica di Sardegna, Meloni Vini	774
Monica di Sardegna Antigua, C.S. di Santadi	773
Monica di Sardegna Duca di Mandas, C.S. della Trexenta	775
Monica di Sardegna Elima, Pala	776
Monica di Sardegna Il Germoglio, Meloni Vini	774
Monica di Sardegna Insula, Sardus Pater	774
Monica di Sardegna Karel, Ferruccio Deiana	776
Monica di Sardegna Perdera, Antonio Argiolas	775
Monica di Sardegna San Bernardino, C.S. Il Nuraghe	779
Monica di Sardegna Torremora, Josto Puddu	780
Monile, Viticcio	492
Monprà, Conterno Fantino	106
Monrubio, Cant. Monrubio	642
Monsavium Passito, Valentino Fiorini	611
Mont'Anello Bianco, Boccadigabbia	615
Montalupa Bianco, Ascheri	46
Montalupa Rosso, Ascheri	46
Montarsiccio, Casa Sola	580
Monte del Drago Rosso, Musella	312
Monte della Guardia, Ca' Lojera	208
Montebacchino, Fatt. Mancini	628
Montecalvi, Montecalvi	487
Montecarlo Bianco, Fatt. del Buonamico	523
Montecarlo Bianco, Fatt. del Teso	524
Montecarlo Bianco, Wandanna	525
Montecarlo Bianco Stati d'Animo, Gino Fuso Carmignani	523
Montecarlo Bianco Terre dei Cascinieri, Wandanna	525
Montecarlo Rosso, Fatt. del Buonamico	523
Montecarlo Rosso, Fatt. del Teso	524
Montecarlo Rosso, Wandanna	525
Montecarlo Rosso Anfidiamante, Fatt. del Teso	524
Montecarlo Rosso Sassonero, Gino Fuso Carmignani	523
Montecarlo Rosso Terre dei Cascinieri, Wandanna	525
Montechiari Cabernet, Fatt. di Montechiari	524
Montechiari Chardonnay, Fatt. di Montechiari	524
Montechiari Nero, Fatt. di Montechiari	524
Montechiari Pinot Nero, Fatt. di Montechiari	524
Montechiari Rosso, Fatt. di Montechiari	524
Montecompatri Colonna Sup. Virtù Romane, Tenuta Le Quinte	673
Montecucco, Montesalario	582
Montecucco Passionaia, Montecucco	585
Montecucco Rosso, Parmoleto	582
Montecucco Rosso Orto di Boccio, Villa Patrizia	601
Montecucco Sangiovese, Montesalario	582
Montecucco Sangiovese, Parmoleto	582
Montecucco Sangiovese, Poggio Saccone	579
Montecucco Sangiovese Licurgo Ris., Perazzeta	582
Montecucco Sangiovese Ris., Montecucco	585
Montecucco Sangiovese Ris., Parmoleto	582
Montecucco Terre dei Bocci, Perazzeta	582
Montefalco Bianco Arquata, Agr. Adanti	641
Montefalco Rosso, Agr. Adanti	641
Montefalco Rosso, Antonelli - San Marco	648
Montefalco Rosso, Eredi Benincasa	642
Montefalco Rosso, Arnaldo Caprai - Val di Maggio	648
Montefalco Rosso, Cast. di Antignano - Brogal Vini	655
Montefalco Rosso, Colpetrone	646
Montefalco Rosso, Rocca di Fabbri	649
Montefalco Rosso, Scacciadiavoli	649
Montefalco Rosso, Spoletoducale	660
Montefalco Rosso Arquata, Agr. Adanti	641
Montefalco Rosso Ris., Arnaldo Caprai - Val di Maggio	648
Montefalco Rosso Ris., Terre de' Trinci	645
Montefalco Sagrantino, Agr. Adanti	641
Montefalco Sagrantino, Fatt. Milziade Antano	658
Montefalco Sagrantino, Antonelli - San Marco	648
Montefalco Sagrantino, Cast. di Antignano - Brogal Vini	655
Montefalco Sagrantino, Colpetrone	646
Montefalco Sagrantino, Rocca di Fabbri	649
Montefalco Sagrantino, San Lorenzo	659
Montefalco Sagrantino, Scacciadiavoli	649
Montefalco Sagrantino, Spoletoducale	660
Montefalco Sagrantino, Terre de' Trinci	645
Montefalco Sagrantino 25 Anni, Arnaldo Caprai - Val di Maggio	648
Montefalco Sagrantino Arquata, Agr. Adanti	641
Montefalco Sagrantino Colle delle Allodole, Fatt. Milziade Antano	658
Montefalco Sagrantino Colle Piano, Arnaldo Caprai - Val di Maggio	648
Montefalco Sagrantino Passito, Agr. Adanti	641
Montefalco Sagrantino Passito, Antonelli - San Marco	648
Montefalco Sagrantino Passito, Colpetrone	646
Montefalco Sagrantino Passito, Domenico Pennacchi	659
Montefalco Sagrantino Passito, Rocca di Fabbri	649
Montefalco Sagrantino Passito, Scacciadiavoli	649
Montefalco Sagrantino Raffaellesco, Umbria Viticoltori Associati	659
Montefalco Sagrantino Uno di Uno, Tenuta Alzatura	647
Montello e Colli Asolani Cabernet Sauvignon, Conte Loredan Gasparini Venegazzù	344
Montellori Brut, Fatt. Montellori	477
Monteloro, Fatt. Sant'Appiano	580
Monteluce, Tenute Sella & Mosca	766
Montenero, Abbazia Santa Anastasia	747
Montenetto di Brescia Marzemino, La V.	213
Montenetto di Brescia Merlot, Cascina Nuova	213
Montepaone, Tenuta Il Greppo	509
Montepetri, Pasolini Dall'Onda	586
Montepirolo, San Patrignano	428
Montepulciano, Fatt. Le Poggette	647
Montepulciano d'Abruzzo, Nestore Bosco	687
Montepulciano d'Abruzzo, Tenuta Cataldi Madonna	680
Montepulciano d'Abruzzo, Filomusi Guelfi	685
Montepulciano d'Abruzzo, Fatt. La Valentina	684
Montepulciano d'Abruzzo, Lepore	677
Montepulciano d'Abruzzo, Gianni Masciarelli	684
Montepulciano d'Abruzzo, Antonio e Elio Monti	687
Montepulciano d'Abruzzo, Camillo Montori	678
Montepulciano d'Abruzzo, Bruno Nicodemi	680
Montepulciano d'Abruzzo, Franco Pasetti	678
Montepulciano d'Abruzzo, Cant. Tollo	685
Montepulciano d'Abruzzo, Edoardo Valentini	679
Montepulciano d'Abruzzo, Valle Reale	688
Montepulciano d'Abruzzo, Valori	688
Montepulciano d'Abruzzo, Villa Medoro	686
Montepulciano d'Abruzzo, Ciccio Zaccagnini	676
Montepulciano d'Abruzzo Abbazia S. Clemente, Ciccio Zaccagnini	676
Montepulciano d'Abruzzo Aldiano, Cant. Tollo	685
Montepulciano d'Abruzzo Antares, San Lorenzo	687
Montepulciano d'Abruzzo Bacco, Bruno Nicodemi	680
Montepulciano d'Abruzzo Binomio, Fatt. La Valentina	684
Montepulciano d'Abruzzo Brume Rosse, Torre Zambra	688
Montepulciano d'Abruzzo Cagiòlo, Cant. Tollo	685
Montepulciano d'Abruzzo Caroso, Citra	687
Montepulciano d'Abruzzo Casale Vecchio, Farnese	681
Montepulciano d'Abruzzo Castel Verdino, Madonna dei Miracoli	686
Montepulciano d'Abruzzo Cast. di Salle, Ciccio Zaccagnini	676
Montepulciano d'Abruzzo Cerasuolo, Tenuta Cataldi Madonna	680
Montepulciano d'Abruzzo Cerasuolo, Filomusi Guelfi	685
Montepulciano d'Abruzzo Cerasuolo, Fatt. La Valentina	684
Montepulciano d'Abruzzo Cerasuolo, Lepore	677
Montepulciano d'Abruzzo Cerasuolo, Bruno Nicodemi	680

Montepulciano d'Abruzzo Cerasuolo, Edoardo Valentini	679
Montepulciano d'Abruzzo Cerasuolo, Villa Medoro	686
Montepulciano d'Abruzzo Cerasuolo, Ciccio Zaccagnini	676
Montepulciano d'Abruzzo Cerasuolo Campirosa, Dino Illuminati	677
Montepulciano d'Abruzzo Cerasuolo Dama, Marramiero	683
Montepulciano d'Abruzzo Cerasuolo Fonte Cupa, Camillo Montori	678
Montepulciano d'Abruzzo Cerasuolo Le Vigne, Faraone	679
Montepulciano d'Abruzzo Cerasuolo Myosotis, Ciccio Zaccagnini	676
Montepulciano d'Abruzzo Cerasuolo Piè delle Vigne, Tenuta Cataldi Madonna	680
Montepulciano d'Abruzzo Cerasuolo Pietrosa, Sarchese Dora	682
Montepulciano d'Abruzzo Cerasuolo Riseis, Agriverde	681
Montepulciano d'Abruzzo Cerasuolo Tenuta Pasetti, Franco Pasetti	678
Montepulciano d'Abruzzo Cerasuolo Valle d'Oro, Cant. Tollo	685
Montepulciano d'Abruzzo Cerasuolo Vermiglio, Orlandi Contucci Ponno	683
Montepulciano d'Abruzzo Cerasuolo V. Corvino, Contesa di Rocco Pasetti	682
Montepulciano d'Abruzzo Cerasuolo Villa Gemma, Gianni Masciarelli	684
Montepulciano d'Abruzzo Colle Maggio, Torre Zambra	688
Montepulciano d'Abruzzo Colle Secco Rubino, Cant. Tollo	685
Montepulciano d'Abruzzo Colline Teramane Bacco, Bruno Nicodemi	680
Montepulciano d'Abruzzo Colline Teramane Fonte Cupa, Camillo Montori	678
Montepulciano d'Abruzzo Colline Teramane Re, Lepore	677
Montepulciano d'Abruzzo Contea di Bordino, Madonna dei Miracoli	686
Montepulciano d'Abruzzo Contesa, Contesa di Rocco Pasetti	682
Montepulciano d'Abruzzo Dama, Marramiero	683
Montepulciano d'Abruzzo Don Giovanni, Buccicatino	688
Montepulciano d'Abruzzo Fatt. Pasetti, Franco Pasetti	678
Montepulciano d'Abruzzo Frentano, C.S. Frentana	688
Montepulciano d'Abruzzo Granaro, Chiarieri	687
Montepulciano d'Abruzzo Hannibal, Chiarieri	687
Montepulciano d'Abruzzo Incanto, Marramiero	683
Montepulciano d'Abruzzo Inferi, Marramiero	683
Montepulciano d'Abruzzo Jorio, Umani Ronchi	627
Montepulciano d'Abruzzo La Regia Specula, Orlandi Contucci Ponno	683
Montepulciano d'Abruzzo Le Vigne, Faraone	679
Montepulciano d'Abruzzo Luigi Lepore, Lepore	677
Montepulciano d'Abruzzo Luigi Lepore Ris., Lepore	677
Montepulciano d'Abruzzo Marina Cvetic S. Martino Rosso, Gianni Masciarelli	684
Montepulciano d'Abruzzo Natum, Agriverde	681
Montepulciano d'Abruzzo Opis Ris., Farnese	681
Montepulciano d'Abruzzo Pan, Nestore Bosco	687
Montepulciano d'Abruzzo Perla Nera, Chiusa Grande	687
Montepulciano d'Abruzzo Pietrosa, Sarchese Dora	682
Montepulciano d'Abruzzo Plateo, Agriverde	681
Montepulciano d'Abruzzo Poggio Varano, Barone Cornacchia	688
Montepulciano d'Abruzzo Quartana, Spinelli	686
Montepulciano d'Abruzzo Riparosso, Dino Illuminati	677
Montepulciano d'Abruzzo Riseis, Agriverde	681
Montepulciano d'Abruzzo Riseis Sel., Agriverde	681
Montepulciano d'Abruzzo Rocco Secco, Chiusa Grande	687
Montepulciano d'Abruzzo Rosso del Duca, Villa Medoro	686
Montepulciano d'Abruzzo Rosso di Macchia, Sarchese Dora	682
Montepulciano d'Abruzzo Rubesto, C.S. Frentana	688
Montepulciano d'Abruzzo S. Maria dell'Arco, Faraone	679
Montepulciano d'Abruzzo San Calisto, Valle Reale	688
Montepulciano d'Abruzzo Sel., Ciccio Zaccagnini	676
Montepulciano d'Abruzzo Spelt, Fatt. La Valentina	684
Montepulciano d'Abruzzo Stilla Rubra, Buccicatino	688
Montepulciano d'Abruzzo Tatone, Spinelli	686
Montepulciano d'Abruzzo Tenuta di Testarossa, Franco Pasetti	678
Montepulciano d'Abruzzo Terra d'Aligi, Spinelli	686
Montepulciano d'Abruzzo Tonì, Tenuta Cataldi Madonna	680
Montepulciano d'Abruzzo Valle d'Oro, Cant. Tollo	685
Montepulciano d'Abruzzo V. Corvino, Contesa di Rocco Pasetti	682
Montepulciano d'Abruzzo V. Fonte Dei, Filomusi Guelfi	685
Montepulciano d'Abruzzo V. Le Coste, Barone Cornacchia	688
Montepulciano d'Abruzzo V. S. Angelo, Valori	688
Montepulciano d'Abruzzo Villa Gemma, Gianni Masciarelli	684
Montepulciano d'Abruzzo Villa Torre, Citra	687
Montepulciano d'Abruzzo Zanna, Dino Illuminati	677
Monteregio Bianco di Massa Marittima Violina, Serraiola	535
Monteregio di Massa Marittima Bacucco di Suveraia, Suveraia	596
Monteregio di Massa Marittima Bianco Nebbiaie, I Campetti	601
Monteregio di Massa Marittima Lentisco, Serraiola	535
Monteregio di Massa Marittima Suveraia Rosso di Campetroso, Suveraia	596
Monteregio di Massa Marittima Violina, Serraiola	535
Monteregio Rosso Botrona, Botrona	603
Montervo, Cima	497
Montescudaio Bianco, Fatt. Sorbaiano	525
Montescudaio Bianco Linaglia, Poggio Gagliardo	596
Montescudaio Bianco Lucestraia, Fatt. Sorbaiano	525
Montescudaio Bianco Steccaia, La Regola	556
Montescudaio Bianco V. Lontana, Poggio Gagliardo	596
Montescudaio Rosso, Fatt. Sorbaiano	525
Montescudaio Rosso delle Miniere, Fatt. Sorbaiano	525
Montescudaio Rosso La Regola, La Regola	556
Montescudaio Rosso Ligustro, La Regola	556
Montescudaio Rosso Ultimo Sole, Poggio Gagliardo	596
Montescudaio Rosso Vallino, La Regola	556
Montescudaio Rosso Vallino delle Conche, La Regola	556
Montesicci, Cantine di Dolianova	769
Montevago, Petrognano	594
Montevertine Ris., Fatt. di Montevertine	552
Montevetrano, Montevetrano	700
Monti Lessini Bianco Re d'Aurum, Cant. di Montecchia	340
Montiano, Falesco	670
Morago Cabernet Sauvignon, Pasqua Vigneti e Cantine	333
Morellino di Scansano, Podere Aia della Macina	570
Morellino di Scansano, Boschetto di Montiano	589
Morellino di Scansano, Il Grillesino	586
Morellino di Scansano, Le Pupille	492
Morellino di Scansano, Costanza Malfatti	589
Morellino di Scansano, Moris Farms	498
Morellino di Scansano, Val delle Rose	588
Morellino di Scansano BellaMarsilia, Poggio Argentiera	493
Morellino di Scansano Bracaleta Ris., Fatt. Acquaviva	589
Morellino di Scansano Campomaccione, Rocca della Macìe	466
Morellino di Scansano CapaTosta, Poggio Argentiera	493
Morellino di Scansano Fonte Tinta, La Carletta	603
Morellino di Scansano Gretaio, Granducato	599
Morellino di Scansano Larcille, Agr. Valle	581
Morellino di Scansano Le Sentinelle Ris., Mantellassi	589
Morellino di Scansano Le Valentane, Villa Patrizia	601
Morellino di Scansano Nero, Fatt. Acquaviva	589
Morellino di Scansano Poggio Roncone, Podere Aia della Macina	570
Morellino di Scansano Poggio Valente, Le Pupille	492
Morellino di Scansano Ris., Il Grillesino	586
Morellino di Scansano Ris., Moris Farms	498
Morellino di Scansano Ris., Val delle Rose	588
Morellino di Scansano Ris., Villa Patrizia	601
Morellino di Scansano Ris. Montepò, Tenuta Il Greppo	509
Morellino di Scansano Rocca dei Venti, Podere Aia della Macina	570
Morellino di Scansano Roggiano, Cant. Coop. del Morellino di Scansano	571
Morellino di Scansano Rosso Tore del Moro Ris., Santa Lucia	493
Morellino di Scansano San Giuseppe, Mantellassi	589
Morellino di Scansano San Rabano Ris., Cant. Coop. del Morellino di Scansano	571
Morellino di Scansano Sicomoro, Cant. Coop. del Morellino di Scansano	571
Morellino di Scansano Terranera Ris., Podere Aia della Macina	570
Morellino di Scansano Valle, Agr. Valle	581
Morellino di Scansano V. Benefizio, Cant. Coop. del Morellino di Scansano	571
Mormoreto, Marchesi de' Frescobaldi	476
Moro del Moro, Moro - Rinaldo Rinaldini	440
Moro di Pava, Pieve de' Pitti	606
Morus Alba, V.i da Duline	420
Morus Nigra, V.i da Duline	420
Moscadello di Montalcino, Capanna di Cencioni	502
Moscadello di Montalcino, Tenuta Il Poggione	510
Moscadello di Montalcino V.T., Mocali	593
Moscadello di Montalcino Vendemmia Tardiva Pascena, Tenuta Col d'Orcia	506
Moscadello V. T., Tenuta Caparzo	502
Moscadello V. T., La Poderina	512
Moscafratta, Agareno	761
Moscato d'Asti, Antonio Baldizzone ' Cascina Lana	157
Moscato d'Asti, Cascina Barisél	55
Moscato d'Asti, F.lli Bera	122
Moscato d'Asti, Ca' del Baio	142
Moscato d'Asti, Cascina Castlèt	71
Moscato d'Asti, Cascina Fonda	101
Moscato d'Asti, Giacomo Scagliola e Figlio	151
Moscato d'Asti, I V.ioli di S. Stefano	134
Moscato d'Asti, La Morandina	66
Moscato d'Asti, Paolo Saracco	67
Moscato d'Asti Aureum, Boroli	24
Moscato d'Asti Bass-Tuba, Bava	68
Moscato d'Asti Bosc d'la Rei, Batasiolo	88
Moscato d'Asti Bricco Quaglia, La Spinetta	58
Moscato d'Asti Ca' du Sindic Capsula Argento, Sergio Grimaldi - Ca' du Sindic	133
Moscato d'Asti Ca' du Sindic Capsula Oro, Sergio Grimaldi - Ca' du Sindic	133
Moscato d'Asti Caudrina, Caudrina	65
Moscato d'Asti Ceirole, Villa Giada	56
Moscato d'Asti Clarté, Elio Perrone	67
Moscato d'Asti Contero, La Giustiniana	83
Moscato d'Asti di Serralunga, V. Rionda - Massolino	138
Moscato d'Asti Ferlingot, Tenuta dell'Arbiola	132
Moscato d'Asti Giorgia, La Ghersa	102
Moscato d'Asti Il Giai, L'Armangia	151
Moscato d'Asti La Caliera, Borgo Maragliano	99
Moscato d'Asti La Galeisa, Caudrina	65
Moscato d'Asti La Rosa Selvatica, Icardi	66
Moscato d'Asti La Selvatica, Caudrina	65
Moscato d'Asti La Serra, Tenuta Cisa Asinari dei Marchesi di Grésy	31
Moscato d'Asti Lumine, Ca' d'Gal	132
Moscato d'Asti Moncalvina, Luigi Coppo e Figli	56
Moscato d'Asti Piasa San Maurizio, Forteto della Luja	99
Moscato d'Asti Scrapona, Marenco	140
Moscato d'Asti Smentiò, Michele Chiarlo	47
Moscato d'Asti Sori del Re, Sergio Degiorgis	101
Moscato d'Asti Sourgal, Elio Perrone	67
Moscato d'Asti Strevi, Vigne Regali	140
Moscato d'Asti Su Reimond, F.lli Bera	122
Moscato d'Asti Tenuta del Fant, Tenuta Il Falchetto	159
Moscato d'Asti V. Senza Nome, Braida	129

Moscato d'Asti V. Vecchia, Ca' d'Gal	132
Moscato d'Asti Vigneti Ca' d'Gal, Ca' d'Gal	132
Moscato d'Asti Volo di Farfalle, Scagliola	49
Moscato dell'Elba, Mola	600
Moscato dell'Elba, Sapereta	549
Moscato della Basilicata Clivus, Paternoster	709
Moscato Demi Sec mill., La Palazzola	657
Moscato di Cagliari, Cantine di Dolianova	769
Moscato di Cagliari Donna Jolanda, Meloni Vini	774
Moscato di Cagliari Gutta'e Axina, Villa di Quartu	780
Moscato di Cagliari Simieri, C.S. della Trexenta	775
Moscato di Pantelleria Kabir, Tenuta di Donnafugata	750
Moscato di Pantelleria Solidea, Solidea	763
Moscato di Pantelleria Turbé, Salvatore Murana	756
Moscato di Saracena, Luigi Viola & Figli	742
Moscato di Scanzo Passito Doge, La Brugherata	207
Moscato di Siracusa Pollio, Pupillo	764
Moscato di Siracusa Solacium, Pupillo	764
Moscato di Siracusa V. di Mela, Pupillo	764
Moscato di Tempio Pausania, C.S. Gallura	777
Moscato di Terracina Secco Oppidum, Cant. Sant'Andrea	674
Moscato di Trani Dulcis in Fundo, Torrevento	721
Moscato Giallo Passito Aureo, C.S. Bergamasca	206
Moscato Giallo Valle dei Laghi, Giulio Poli	248
Moscato Passito di Pantelleria Khamma, Salvatore Murana	756
Moscato Passito di Pantelleria Mare d'Ambra, Cantine Rallo	751
Moscato Passito di Pantelleria Martingana, Salvatore Murana	756
Moscato Passito di Strevi, La Giustiniana	83
Moscato Passito Villa Monticelli, Barberani - Vallesanta	650
Moscato Rosa, Marco Felluga	385
Moscato Rosa, Maso Bastie	245
Moscato Rosa, Maso Martis	243
Moscato Secco di Terracina, Cant. Sant'Andrea	674
Moscato Spumante, Cons. Viticoltori Associati del Vulture	708
Motu Proprio, Tenim. Angelini - Val di Suga	521
Muffa Nobile, Castel De Paolis	668
Muffa Nobile, Palazzone	653
Muffato della Sala, Cast. della Sala	644
Muffo, Sergio Mottura	666
Müller Thurgau, Pelz & Piffer	246
Müller Thurgau, Vinnaioli Jermann	380
Müller Thurgau La Giostra, Montelio	188
Müller Thurgau Mussignaz, Rino Russolo	412
Murgia Bianco Le Carrare, Cant. Coop. della Riforma Fondiaria	733
Murgia Rosato Silvium, Cant. Coop. Botromagno	722
Murgia Rosso, I Pastini - Carparelli	732
Murtas, San Michele a Torri	603
Muscatè, Paolo Poggio	46
Muscaté, Vigneti Massa	112
Museum, La Macolina	448
Myrto, Foradori	236
N'Antia, Badia di Morrona	578
Nabucco, Monte delle Vigne	446
Nadaria Alcamo, Cusumano	756
Nadaria Inzolia, Cusumano	756
Nadaria Nero d'Avola, Cusumano	756
Nadaria Syrah, Cusumano	756
Nambrot, Tenuta di Ghizzano	545
Narciso Rosso, Ronco delle Betulle	388
Nardo, Montepeloso	574
Nas-Cetta, Elvio Cogno	125
Nasco di Cagliari Donna Jolanda, Meloni Vini	774
Nasco di Cagliari Gutta'e Axina, Villa di Quartu	780
Nastarrè, C.S. Giogantinu	767
Naturalis Historia, Mastroberardino	690
Navicchio Bianco, Il Conte	622
Nebbie d'Autunno Dolce, Ermete Medici & Figli	438
Nebbiolo d'Alba, Cornarea	151
Nebbiolo d'Alba, Destefanis	114
Nebbiolo d'Alba, Destefanis	114
Nebbiolo d'Alba, Giacomo Grimaldi	38
Nebbiolo d'Alba, Hilberg - Pasquero	127
Nebbiolo d'Alba, Fabrizio Pinsoglio	60
Nebbiolo d'Alba, Poderi Colla	26
Nebbiolo d'Alba, Flavio Roddolo	111
Nebbiolo d'Alba, Vielmin	60
Nebbiolo d'Alba Bric du Nota, Scarpa - Antica Casa Vinicola	124
Nebbiolo d'Alba Bricco S. Giacomo, Ascheri	46
Nebbiolo d'Alba Ca Veja, Paitin	121
Nebbiolo d'Alba Cascinotto, Claudio Alario	73
Nebbiolo d'Alba Castellero, Araldica - Il Cantinone	58
Nebbiolo d'Alba Cumot, Bricco Maiolica	73
Nebbiolo d'Alba Giachét, Poderi Sinaglio	28
Nebbiolo d'Alba La Perucca, Eugenio Bocchino	150
Nebbiolo d'Alba La Val dei Preti, Matteo Correggia	51
Nebbiolo d'Alba Lantasco, Ceretto	25
Nebbiolo d'Alba Marne Brune, Fontanafredda	136
Nebbiolo d'Alba Mompissano, Cascina Chicco	51
Nebbiolo d'Alba Occhetti, Prunotto	27
Nebbiolo d'Alba Ochetti, Renato Ratti	94
Nebbiolo d'Alba Parigi, Mauro Sebaste	27
Nebbiolo d'Alba S. Rocco, Giuseppe Mascarello e Figlio	103
Nebbiolo d'Alba Sansivé, Raffaele Gili	59
Nebbiolo d'Alba Valmaggiore, Bruno Giacosa	120
Nebbiolo d'Alba Valmaggiore, Mario Marengo	92
Nebbiolo d'Alba Valmaggiore, Luciano Sandrone	41
Nebbiolo d'Alba V. Bricco dell'Asino, Pira	76
Nebbiolo d'Alba V. di Lino, Cascina Val del Prete	128
Nebbiolo dei Colli del Limbara Karana, C.S. Gallura	777
Nebidu, Mura	778
Neitea, Mormoraia	567
Nemo, Cast. di Monsanto	455
Nepas Rosso, Alessandro e Gian Natale Fantino	107
Nerello, Domenico Spadafora	741
Nerello Cappuccio, Benanti	759
Nero, Conti Zecca	725
Nero d'Avola, Abbazia Santa Anastasia	747
Nero d'Avola, Adragna	764
Nero D'Avola, Fattorie Azzolino	746
Nero d'Avola, Baglio Hopps	761
Nero d'Avola, Benanti	759
Nero d'Avola, Feudo Montoni	760
Nero d'Avola, Morgante	749
Nero d'Avola, Carlo Pellegrino	751
Nero d'Avola Mandrarossa, Settesoli	752
Nero d'Avola Miceli, Aziende Vinicole Miceli	755
Nero d'Avola Selezione Speciale, Feudo Montoni	760
Nero d'Avola Terre Mediterranee, Zonin	290
Nero d'Avola Triskelè, Duca di Salaparuta - Vini Corvo	747
Nero del Tondo, Tenim. Ruffino	548
Nero della Cervara, Todini	660
Nero della Greca, Cardeto	651
Nero di Nubi, Farnetella	571
Nero Ibleo, Gulfi	760
Nerobufaleffi, Gulfi	760
Neromaccari, Gulfi	760
Nichesole Vallidium, Corte Gardoni	332
Nicosole, Agrinico	596
Nieddera Rosso, Attilio Contini	768
Niergal, Pravis	230
Niffo, Terre del Sillabo	496
Nikà, Case di Pietra	762
Niteo, Giuseppe Vezzoli	196
Nivola Lambrusco Scuro, Chiarli 1860	433
Noà, Cusumano	756
Noans, La Tunella	397
Nobile di Montepulciano, Avignonesi	526
Nobile di Montepulciano, Bindella	527
Nobile di Montepulciano, Boscarelli	527
Nobile di Montepulciano, Fatt. del Cerro	528
Nobile di Montepulciano, Contucci	528
Nobile di Montepulciano, Corte alla Flora	594
Nobile di Montepulciano, Crociani	594
Nobile di Montepulciano, Dei	529
Nobile di Montepulciano, Fatt. La Braccesca	595
Nobile di Montepulciano, La Calonica	530
Nobile di Montepulciano, La Ciarliana	530
Nobile di Montepulciano, La Madonnina - Triacca	486
Nobile di Montepulciano, Fatt. Le Casalte	595
Nobile di Montepulciano, Lodola Nuova - Tenim. Ruffino	531
Nobile di Montepulciano, Azienda Agr. Lombardo	595
Nobile di Montepulciano, Nottola	531
Nobile di Montepulciano, Palazzo Vecchio	595
Nobile di Montepulciano, Fatt. di Paterno	532
Nobile di Montepulciano, Poliziano	532
Nobile di Montepulciano, Redi	533
Nobile di Montepulciano, Massimo Romeo	596
Nobile di Montepulciano, Salcheto	533
Nobile di Montepulciano, Tenim. Angelini - Tenuta Trerose	534
Nobile di Montepulciano, Terra Antica	596
Nobile di Montepulciano, Tenuta Valdipiatta	534
Nobile di Montepulciano, Villa Sant'Anna	535
Nobile di Montepulciano Asinone, Poliziano	532
Nobile di Montepulciano Briareo, Redi	533
Nobile di Montepulciano La Villa, Tenim. Angelini - Tenuta Trerose	534
Nobile di Montepulciano Pasiteo, Fassati	529
Nobile di Montepulciano Pietra del Diavolo, Il Faggeto	595
Nobile di Montepulciano Ris., Boscarelli	527
Nobile di Montepulciano Ris., Carpineto	486
Nobile di Montepulciano Ris., Contucci	528
Nobile di Montepulciano Ris., Dei	529
Nobile di Montepulciano Ris., La Ciarliana	530
Nobile di Montepulciano Ris., Fatt. Le Casalte	595
Nobile di Montepulciano Ris., Lodola Nuova - Tenim. Ruffino	531
Nobile di Montepulciano Ris., Azienda Agr. Lombardo	595
Nobile di Montepulciano Ris., Palazzo Vecchio	595
Nobile di Montepulciano Ris., Fatt. di Paterno	532
Nobile di Montepulciano Ris., Massimo Romeo	596
Nobile di Montepulciano Ris., Salcheto	533
Nobile di Montepulciano Ris., Terra Antica	596
Nobile di Montepulciano Ris., Tenuta Valdipiatta	534
Nobile di Montepulciano Salarco Ris., Fassati	529
Nobile di Montepulciano Salco, Salcheto	533
Nobile di Montepulciano Simposio, Tenim. Angelini - Tenuta Trerose	534
Nobile di Montepulciano Terre di Rubinoro, Redi	533
Nobile di Montepulciano V. d'Alfiero, Tenuta Valdipiatta	534
Nobile di Montepulciano V. del Fattore, Nottola	531
Nobile di Montepulciano V. del Nocio, Boscarelli	527
Nobile di Montepulciano V. dell'Asinone, Poliziano	532
Nobile di Montepulciano Vign. Antica Chiusina, Fatt. del Cerro	528
Nociano, Cant. Monrubio	642
Noi Due, Saputi	635
Noriolo, C.S. Dorgali	778
Nosiola, Castel Noarna	236
Nosiola, Gino Pedrotti	227
Nosiola Le Frate, Pravis	230
Nosside, Statti	739
Nostos, San Simone	419
Notarpanaro, Cosimo Taurino	723

Notturno Sangiovese, Drei Donà Tenuta La Palazza	431		OP Malvasia Frizzante, Tenuta Il Bosco	211
Novai, Marco Donati	233		OP Malvasia Il Raro, Ca' di Frara	202
Nuhar, Tenute Rapitalà	746		OP Moscato, Ca' del Gè	199
Nuragus di Cagliari, Cantine di Dolianova	769		OP Moscato Adagetto, Cascina Gnocco	218
Nuragus di Cagliari Pedraia, C.S. di Santadi	773		OP Moscato La Volpe e L'Uva, Anteo	205
Nuragus di Cagliari S'Elegas, Antonio Argiolas	775		OP Moscato Passito Soleggia, Caseo	179
Nuragus di Cagliari Salnico, Pala	776		OP Moscato Venere, Percivalle	213
Nuragus di Cagliari Tenute San Mauro, C.S. della Trexenta	775		OP Passito Oro, Cabanon	196
Nuvola Démi Sec, Bersi Serlini	204		OP Pinot Grigio, Cabanon	196
Oblin Blanc, Isidoro Polencic	366		OP Pinot Grigio , C.S. La Versa	207
Oblin Ros, Isidoro Polencic	366		OP Pinot Grigio , Le Fracce	183
Obsession, Villa V.maggio	491		OP Pinot Grigio, Monsupello	210
Occhiorosso, Tenuta Cataldi Madonna	680		OP Pinot Grigio, Podere San Giorgio	221
Offida Passerina Brut, Tenuta Cocci Grifoni	630		OP Pinot Grigio, Bruno Verdi	180
Offida Passerina Donna Bianca, Fontursia	637		OP Pinot Grigio Levriere, Le Fracce	183
Offida Pecorino Ciprea , Poderi San Savino	632		OP Pinot Grigio V. T., Ca' di Frara	202
Offida Pecorino Iosonogaia, Le Caniette	631		OP Pinot Nero, Riccardo Albani	182
Offida Pecorino Podere Colle Vecchio, Tenuta Cocci Grifoni	630		OP Pinot Nero, Frecciarossa	183
Offida Podere Colle Vecchio, Tenuta Cocci Grifoni	630		OP Pinot Nero, Isimbarda	206
Oirad, Ferruccio Deiana	776		OP Pinot Nero, Tenuta Mazzolino	191
Olivar, Cesconi	231		OP Pinot Nero Barrique, Tenim. Castelrotto - Torti	218
Olmaia, Tenuta Col d'Orcia	506		OP Pinot Nero Bellarmino, Tenuta La Costaiola	200
Oltre, Leonardo Specogna	374		OP Pinot Nero Brumano, Ruiz de Cardenas	214
Oltre Vittorio Puiatti, Puiatti	352		OP Pinot Nero Brut Cl., Tenuta Il Bosco	211
OP Barbera, Montelio	188		OP Pinot Nero Brut Cl., Monsupello	210
OP Barbera Barrique, Tenim. Castelrotto - Torti	218		OP Pinot Nero Brut Cl., Tenuta Pegazzera	184
OP Barbera Becco Giallo, Podere San Giorgio	221		OP Pinot Nero Brut Cl., Quaquarini	180
OP Barbera Campo del Marrone, Bruno Verdi	180		OP Pinot Nero Brut Cl. Anteo, Anteo	205
OP Barbera Clà, Vercesi del Castellazzo	202		OP Pinot Nero Brut Cl. Mill. Elith, F.lli Giorgi	179
OP Barbera Costa del Sole, Percivalle	213		OP Pinot Nero Brut Cl. Oro, C.S. La Versa	207
OP Barbera Frizzante, Quaquarini	180		OP Pinot Nero Brut Cl. Philèo, Tenuta Il Bosco	211
OP Barbera I Due Draghi, Tenuta La Costaiola	200		OP Pinot Nero Brut Cl. Postumio, Cant. di Casteggio	214
OP Barbera I Gelsi, Monsupello	210		OP Pinot Nero Brut Cl. Regal Cuvée, Tenuta Il Bosco	211
OP Barbera La Strega, la Gazza, il Pioppo, Martilde	221		OP Pinot Nero Brut Class. Grand Cuvée, Travaglino	178
OP Barbera Olmetto, Bellaria	182		OP Pinot Nero Brut Classese , Monsupello	210
OP Barbera Piccolo Principe, Cabanon	196		OP Pinot Nero Brut Martinotti, Tenuta Pegazzera	184
OP Barbera Prunello, Cabanon	196		OP Pinot Nero Brut Mise en Cave, C.S. La Versa	207
OP Barbera Ris. V. Pivena, Monsupello	210		OP Pinot Nero Brut Querciolo, Doria	199
OP Barbera Roccolo del Casale, C.S. La Versa	207		OP Pinot Nero Ca' dell'Oca, Anteo	205
OP Barbera Roncolongo, Bisi	221		OP Pinot Nero Cl. Anteo Nature, Anteo	205
OP Barbera Safrana, Tenuta Pegazzera	184		OP Pinot Nero Cl. Nature, Monsupello	210
OP Barbera V. Varmasi, Ca' del Gè	199		OP Pinot Nero Costarsa, Montelio	188
OP Barbera vivace, C.S. di Broni	213		OP Pinot Nero Cuvée Bussolera Extra Brut , Le Fracce	183
OP Bonarda, Riccardo Albani	182		OP Pinot Nero Extra Dry, Il Montù	218
OP Bonarda, Tenuta Mazzolino	191		OP Pinot Nero Il Raro, Ca' di Frara	202
OP Bonarda, Quaquarini	180		OP Pinot Nero in Bianco Ca' dell'Oca, Anteo	205
OP Bonarda Campo del Monte, Agnes	205		OP Pinot Nero in Bianco frizzante, Tenuta Pegazzera	184
OP Bonarda Campo delle More, Caseo	179		OP Pinot Nero in Bianco Gugiarolo, Vercesi del Castellazzo	202
OP Bonarda Cresta del Ghiffi, Agnes	205		OP Pinot Nero in Bianco Le Marghe, Vercesi del Castellazzo	202
OP Bonarda Fatila, Vercesi del Castellazzo	202		OP Pinot Nero in Bianco Premium, F.lli Giorgi	179
OP Bonarda Frizzante , Bagnasco	222		OP Pinot Nero in Bianco Querciolo, Doria	199
OP Bonarda Frizzante, Ca' del Gè	199		OP Pinot Nero Luogo dei Monti, Vercesi del Castellazzo	202
OP Bonarda Frizzante, Montelio	188		OP Pinot Nero Monteroso, F.lli Giorgi	179
OP Bonarda Frizzante, Vanzini	221		OP Pinot Nero Noir, Tenuta Mazzolino	191
OP Bonarda Frizzante Ca' Bella , C.S. La Versa	207		OP Pinot Nero Pernice, Conte Giorgi di Vistarino	219
OP Bonarda Ghiro Rosso d'Inverno, Martilde	221		OP Pinot Nero Petrae, Tenuta Pegazzera	184
OP Bonarda La Fidela, Ca' del Gè	199		OP Pinot Nero Poggio della Buttinera, Travaglino	178
OP Bonarda La Rubiosa, Le Fracce	183		OP Pinot Nero Querciolo, Doria	199
OP Bonarda Luogo della Milla, Vercesi del Castellazzo	202		OP Pinot Nero V. Miraggi, Ruiz de Cardenas	214
OP Bonarda Millenium, Agnes	205		OP Riesling , Marco Giulio Bellani	214
OP Bonarda Parsua, Percivalle	213		OP Riesling Campo della Fojada, Travaglino	178
OP Bonarda Possessione del Console, Agnes	205		OP Riesling Italico, Ca' del Gè	199
OP Bonarda Staffolo, Anteo	205		OP Riesling Renano, Riccardo Albani	182
OP Bonarda V.zzo, Agnes	205		OP Riesling Renano, Frecciarossa	183
OP Bonarda Vivace, Riccardo Albani	182		OP Riesling Renano, Le Fracce	183
OP Bonarda Vivace, Tenuta Il Bosco	211		OP Riesling Renano, Monsupello	210
OP Bonarda Vivace Giada, Tenuta La Costaiola	200		OP Riesling Renano Apogeo, Ca' di Frara	202
OP Bonarda Vivace La Brughera, F.lli Giorgi	179		OP Riesling Renano Attimo, Tenuta La Costaiola	200
OP Bonarda Vivace Le Cento Pertiche, Clastidio Ballabio	214		OP Riesling Renano Landò, Le Fracce	183
OP Bonarda Vivace Possessione di Vergomberra, Bruno Verdi	180		OP Riesling Renano Le Segrete, Caseo	179
OP Bonarda Vivace Sel., Tenuta Pegazzera	184		OP Riesling Renano Roncobianco, Doria	199
OP Bornarda Vivace La Bria, Bellaria	182		OP Riesling Renano V. Marinoni, Ca' del Gè	199
OP Brut Cl. Il Bosco, Tenuta Il Bosco	211		OP Riesling Renano V. Martina , Isimbarda	206
OP Brut Cl. Ris. Ca' del Tava, Monsupello	210		OP Riesling Renano Vign. Costa, Bruno Verdi	180
OP Brut Cl. Vergomberra, Bruno Verdi	180		OP Riesling Vendemmia Tardiva Pajarolo, Travaglino	178
OP Brut Class. Classese, Travaglino	178		OP Rosso, Montelio	188
OP Brut Il Bosco, Tenuta Il Bosco	211		OP Rosso Articioc, Marco Giulio Bellani	214
OP Buttafuoco, Quaquarini	180		OP Rosso Botte n. 18, Cabanon	196
OP Buttafuoco Bronis, C.S. di Broni	213		OP Rosso Bronis, C.S. di Broni	213
OP Buttafuoco Casa del Corno, F.lli Giorgi	179		OP Rosso Canabium, Caseo	179
OP Buttafuoco San Luigi, Monterucco	215		OP Rosso Cardinale, Tenuta Pegazzera	184
OP Buttafuoco V. Montarzolo, Valter Calvi	214		OP Rosso Cavariola Ris., Bruno Verdi	180
OP Buttafuoco V. Pregana, Quaquarini	180		OP Rosso Cirgà, Le Fracce	183
OP Buttafuoco Vivace La Manna, F.lli Giorgi	179		OP Rosso Costa del Morone, Riccardo Albani	182
OP Cabanon Blanc, Cabanon	196		OP Rosso Cuore di Vino Botte n. 18, Cabanon	196
OP Cabanon Noir, Cabanon	196		OP Rosso Donna Cecilia Ris., Cascina Gnocco	218
OP Cabernet Sauvignon Aplomb, Monsupello	210		OP Rosso Garboso, Le Fracce	183
OP Cabernet Sauvignon Corvino, Tenuta Mazzolino	191		OP Rosso Great Ruby Vivace, Monsupello	210
OP Cabernet Sauvignon Ligna, Tenuta Pegazzera	184		OP Rosso Il Frater, Ca' di Frara	202
OP Cabernet Sauvignon Primm, Bisi	221		OP Rosso Il Frater Ris., Ca' di Frara	202
OP Chardonnay, C.S. La Versa	207		OP Rosso Infernot Ris., Cabanon	196
OP Chardonnay Blanc, Tenuta Mazzolino	191		OP Rosso La Borla , Monsupello	210
OP Chardonnay Campo della Mojetta, Travaglino	178		OP Rosso La V. Bricca , Tenuta La Costaiola	200
OP Chardonnay Dama Bianca, Podere San Giorgio	221		OP Rosso Le Praielle, Frecciarossa	183
OP Chardonnay Elaisa, Conte Giorgi di Vistarino	219		OP Rosso Luzzano 270 Ris., Cast. di Luzzano	220
OP Chardonnay I Ronchi, Caseo	179		OP Rosso Magister, Quaquarini	180
OP Chardonnay La Collegiata, Tenuta Pegazzera	184		OP Rosso Metellianum Ris., Monterucco	215
OP Chardonnay Mesdì, F.lli Giorgi	179		OP Rosso Monplò, Isimbarda	206
OP Chardonnay Senso, Monsupello	210		OP Rosso Montezavo Ris., Isimbarda	206
OP Cortese, Montelio	188		OP Rosso Orto di S. Giacomo, Vercesi del Castellazzo	202
OP Malvasia Dolce, F.lli Giorgi	179		OP Rosso Pezzalunga, Vercesi del Castellazzo	202

OP Rosso Ris. Canabium, Caseo	179
OP Rosso Ris. Marc'Antonio, Travaglino	178
OP Rosso Ris. Mosaico, Monsupello	210
OP Rosso Ris. Narbusto, Clastidio Ballabio	214
OP Rosso Ris. Solarolo, Montelio	188
OP Rosso Riva dei Peschi, Ca' del Santo	218
OP Rosso Roncorosso, Doria	199
OP Rosso V. del Tramonto, Isimbarda	206
OP Rosso Vigne della Casona Ris., Riccardo Albani	182
OP Rosso Villa Odero Ris., Frecciarossa	183
OP Sangue di Giuda, Bagnasco	222
OP Sangue di Giuda, F.lli Giorgi	179
OP Sangue di Giuda, Il Montù	218
OP Sangue di Giuda, Quaquarini	180
OP Sangue di Giuda, Vanzini	221
OP Sangue di Giuda Dolce Paradiso, Bruno Verdi	180
OP Sangue di Giuda Frizzante La Badalucca, F.lli Giorgi	179
OP Sauvignon, Monsupello	210
OP Sauvignon Blanc I Crocioni, Caseo	179
OP Tormento, Ca' del Gè	199
Opera Prima Cabanon Blanc, Cabanon	196
Opera Prima XIV, I Paglieri	34
Opimio Gianni Zonin Vineyards, Ca' Bolani	355
Oppidum Rosso, Ciù Ciù	625
Optimum, Fatt. Pontepellegrino	698
Orazio, Fontanavecchia	703
Orbaio, Redi	533
Orcia Rosso Capitoni, Sedime	599
Oreno, Tenuta Sette Ponti	577
Oreste, Fabrizio Pinsoglio	60
Ornellaia, Tenuta dell' Ornellaia	457
Orvieto, Trappolini	665
Orvieto Cl., Cant. dei Colli Amerini	640
Orvieto Cl., La Carraia	652
Orvieto Cl., Vaglie	641
Orvieto Cl. Barbi, Decugnano dei Barbi	651
Orvieto Cl. Campogrande, Cast. della Sala	644
Orvieto Cl. Castagnolo, Barberani - Vallesanta	650
Orvieto Cl. Poggio Calvelli, La Carraia	652
Orvieto Cl. Salceto, Cant. Monrubio	642
Orvieto Cl. Sant'Egidio, Sassara	659
Orvieto Cl. Secco, Vaglie	641
Orvieto Cl. Sup., Cast. della Sala	644
Orvieto Cl. Sup., Tenuta di Salviano	658
Orvieto Cl. Sup. Calcaia, Barberani - Vallesanta	650
Orvieto Cl. Sup. Colbadia, Cardeto	651
Orvieto Cl. Sup. Decugnano dei Barbi, Decugnano dei Barbi	651
Orvieto Cl. Sup. Febeo, Cardeto	651
Orvieto Cl. Sup. IL, Decugnano dei Barbi	651
Orvieto Cl. Sup. L'Armida, Cardeto	651
Orvieto Cl. Sup. Lunato, Tenuta Le Velette	653
Orvieto Cl. Sup. Matricale, Vaglie	641
Orvieto Cl. Sup. Pourrirute Noble, Decugnano dei Barbi	651
Orvieto Cl. Sup. Soana, Cant. Monrubio	642
Orvieto Cl. Terre Vineate, Palazzone	653
Orvieto Cl. Torre Sant'Andrea, Vaselli	665
Orvieto Cl. V. Tragugnano, Sergio Mottura	666
Orvieto Cl. Vign. Torricella, Bigi	650
Orvieto Noe, Paolo d'Amico	664
Osar, Masi	319
Ostrea, Mormoraia	567
Ostrea Grigia, Mormoraia	567
Ottavianello Dedalo Torre Guaceto, Accademia dei Racemi	727
P. di Conegliano Brut Bubbly, Zardetto Spumanti	287
P. di Conegliano Brut San Salvatore, Conte Collalto	325
P. di Conegliano Dry Cuvée Oro, Carpenè Malvolti	338
P. di Conegliano Extra Dry, Bepin de Eto	313
P. di Conegliano Extra Dry, Conte Collalto	325
P. di Conegliano Extra Dry, Gregoletto	298
P. di Conegliano Extra Dry, Masottina	311
P. di Conegliano Extra Dry, Zardetto Spumanti	287
P. di Conegliano Frizzante Brioso, Zardetto Spumanti	287
P. di Conegliano Tranquillo, Bepin de Eto	313
P. di Conegliano Tranquillo, Gregoletto	298
P. di Conegliano Tranquillo Lungo, Zardetto Spumanti	287
P. di Conegliano Valdobbiadene Extra Dry Il Millesimato, Canevel Spumanti	328
P. di Conegliano Zeroventi Dry, Zardetto Spumanti	287
P. di Valdobbiadene Brut, F.lli Bortolin Spumanti	327
P. di Valdobbiadene Brut, Bortolomiol	327
P. di Valdobbiadene Brut, Canevel Spumanti	328
P. di Valdobbiadene Brut, Ciodet	344
P. di Valdobbiadene Brut, Col Vetoraz	328
P. di Valdobbiadene Brut, De Faveri	335
P. di Valdobbiadene Brut, Le Colture	329
P. di Valdobbiadene Brut, Nino Franco	330
P. di Valdobbiadene Brut, Ruggeri & C.	330
P. di Valdobbiadene Brut, Santa Eurosia	331
P. di Valdobbiadene Brut, Sorelle Bronca	336
P. di Valdobbiadene Brut, Tanorè	331
P. di Valdobbiadene Brut, Paolo Zucchetto	344
P. di Valdobbiadene Brut Barreta, Merotto	338
P. di Valdobbiadene Brut Bosco di Gica, Adami	335
P. di Valdobbiadene Brut Crede, Desideriox Bisol & Figli	326
P. di Valdobbiadene Brut Dirupo, Andreola Orsola	288
P. di Valdobbiadene Brut Rive di S. Floriano, Nino Franco	330
P. di Valdobbiadene Brut Sel., De Faveri	335
P. di Valdobbiadene Dry, F.lli Bortolin Spumanti	327
P. di Valdobbiadene Dry, Bortolomiol	327
P. di Valdobbiadene Dry, Dal Din	344
P. di Valdobbiadene Dry Cruner, Le Colture	329
P. di Valdobbiadene Dry Funer, Le Bellerive - Angelo Ruggeri	329
P. di Valdobbiadene Dry Garnei, Desiderio Bisol & Figli	326
P. di Valdobbiadene Dry Giardino, Adami	335
P. di Valdobbiadene Dry mill., Santa Eurosia	331
P. di Valdobbiadene Dry Millesimato, Col Vetoraz	328
P. di Valdobbiadene Dry Primo Franco, Nino Franco	330
P. di Valdobbiadene Dry S. Stefano, Ruggeri & C.	330
P. di Valdobbiadene Dry Salis, Desiderio Bisol & Figli	326
P. di Valdobbiadene Dry Sel., De Faveri	335
P. di Valdobbiadene Dry Sel., Tanorè	331
P. di Valdobbiadene Extra Dry, F.lli Bortolin Spumanti	327
P. di Valdobbiadene Extra Dry, Bortolomiol	327
P. di Valdobbiadene Extra Dry, Canevel Spumanti	328
P. di Valdobbiadene Extra Dry, Ciodet	344
P. di Valdobbiadene Extra Dry, Col Vetoraz	328
P. di Valdobbiadene Extra Dry, De Faveri	335
P. di Valdobbiadene Extra Dry, Le Bellerive - Angelo Ruggeri	329
P. di Valdobbiadene Extra Dry, Le Colture	329
P. di Valdobbiadene Extra Dry, Santa Eurosia	331
P. di Valdobbiadene Extra Dry, Sorelle Bronca	336
P. di Valdobbiadene Extra Dry, Tanorè	331
P. di Valdobbiadene Extra Dry, Paolo Zucchetto	344
P. di Valdobbiadene Extra Dry dei Casel, Adami	335
P. di Valdobbiadene Extra Dry Dirupo, Andreola Orsola	288
P. di Valdobbiadene Extra Dry Giall'Oro, Ruggeri & C.	330
P. di Valdobbiadene Extra Dry Giustino B., Ruggeri & C.	330
P. di Valdobbiadene Extra Dry Rù, F.lli Bortolin Spumanti	327
P. di Valdobbiadene Extra Dry Sel. Banda Rossa, Bortolomiol	327
P. di Valdobbiadene Extra Dry Vigneti del Fol, Desiderio Bisol & Figli	326
P. di Valdobbiadene Extra Dry Vign. del Faè, Canevel Spumanti	328
P. di Valdobbiadene Frizzante, Col Vetoraz	328
P. di Valdobbiadene Frizzante, De Faveri	335
P. di Valdobbiadene Frizzante Il Ponteggio, Bortolomiol	327
P. di Valdobbiadene Frizzante Spago, Andreola Orsola	288
P. di Valdobbiadene Frizzante Vigneti di S. Biagio, Canevel Spumanti	328
P. di Valdobbiadene Sur Lie, Adami	335
P. di Valdobbiadene Tranquillo, Bortolomiol	327
P. di Valdobbiadene Tranquillo, Canevel Spumanti	328
P. di Valdobbiadene Tranquillo, Ciodet	344
P. di Valdobbiadene Tranquillo, Santa Eurosia	331
P. di Valdobbiadene Tranquillo, Tanorè	331
P. di Valdobbiadene Tranquillo Giardino, Adami	335
P. di Valdobbiadene Tranquillo La Bastia, Ruggeri & C.	330
P. di Valdobbiadene Tranquillo Masaré, Le Colture	329
P. di Valdobbiadene Tranquillo Molera, Desiderio Bisol & Figli	326
P. di Valdobbiadene Tranquillo Romit, Andreola Orsola	288
P. di Valdobbiadene Tranquillo Sassi Bianchi, Nino Franco	330
P. di Valdobbiadene Tranquillo Tresiese, Col Vetoraz	328
Pagadebit di Romagna, Calonga	431
Pagus, Giovanna Giannaccini	598
Palagione, Villa Rosa	583
Palaia, Cant. Monrubio	642
Palazzo d'Altesi, Altesino	499
Palazzo della Torre, Allegrini	288
Paleo Bianco, Le Macchiole	456
Pallagrello Bianco, Cast. Ducale	704
Pantelleria Secco Yrnm, Aziende Vinicole Miceli	755
Paradiso Rosso, Tenuta La Tenaglia	139
Parrina Rosso, La Parrina	539
Parrina Rosso Muraccio, La Parrina	539
Parrina Rosso Ris., La Parrina	539
Passaurum, Andreas Berger -Thurnhof	255
Passerina del Frusinate, Casale della Ioria	662
Passione Rosso, Michele Castellani	294
Passito, Acquabona	600
Passito Anima Mundi, La Cant. dei Colli Ripani	631
Passito Bianco, Ca' La Bionda	293
Passito Bianco, Marion	312
Passito Bianco, Ciccio Zaccagnini	676
Passito Bianco di Gargagnago, Raimondi-Villa Monteleone	320
Passito Bianco Le Melghette, Corte Marzago	344
Passito Brolo delle Giare, Tezza	334
Passito della Rocca, Leonildo Pieropan	323
Passito delle Cinque Pietre, Telaro - Coop. Lavoro e Salute	695
Passito di Corzano, Fatt. Corzano e Paterno	557
Passito di Pantelleria, Abraxas	762
Passito di Pantelleria, Marco De Bartoli	749
Passito di Pantelleria, Carlo Pellegrino	751
Passito di Pantelleria Ben Ryé, Tenuta di Donnafugata	750
Passito di Pantelleria Bukkuram, Marco De Bartoli	749
Passito di Pantelleria Entelechia, Aziende Vinicole Miceli	755
Passito di Pantelleria Nes, Carlo Pellegrino	751
Passito di Pantelleria Nikà, Case di Pietra	762
Passito di Pantelleria Nun, Aziende Vinicole Miceli	755
Passito di Pantelleria Solidea, Solidea	763
Passito di Pantelleria Yanir, Aziende Vinicole Miceli	755
Passito Monte delle Fontane, Tezza	334
Passito Sebino, Il Mosnel	203
Passo delle Viscarde, Agricole Vallone	724
Passo Rosso, Stefano Accordini	313
Passomaggio, Abbazia Santa Anastasia	747
Paterno, Trappolini	665
Paterno II, Il Paradiso	564
Pathos, Santa Barbara	611
Patriglione, Cosimo Taurino	723
Pàtrimo, Feudi di San Gregorio	702
Patrizia Bartolini, Massa Vecchia	497
Paule Calle, Francesco Candido	729
Pecorino, Tenuta Cataldi Madonna	680

Pecorino Contesa, Contesa di Rocco Pasetti	682	Piemonte Chardonnay Roleto, Araldica - Il Cantinone	58
Pecorino Fatt. Pasetti, Franco Pasetti	678	Piemonte Chardonnay Tenuta La Magnona, Terre da Vino	42
Pelago, Umani Ronchi	627	Piemonte Chardonnay Thou Bianc, Bava	68
Pellaro, Vintripodi Calabria	742	Piemonte Chardonnay V. Levi, Sciorio	72
Penisola Sorrentina Gragnano, Cantine Grotta del Sole	699	Piemonte Cortese Casareggio, Vigneti Massa	112
Penisola Sorrentina Lettere, Cantine Grotta del Sole	699	Piemonte Cortese Coccalina, Claudio Mariotto	142
Pensiero, Petrussa	401	Piemonte Cortese DiVino, Prod. del Gavi	84
Peperino, Teruzzi & Puthod	569	Piemonte Cortese Tejolo, Santa Seraffa	155
Per Martina, Vallona	426	Piemonte Grignolino, Pelissero	144
Percarlo, San Giusto a Rentennano	484	Piemonte Grignolino, Tenuta San Sebastiano	100
Perdaudin Passito, Angelo Negro & Figli	115	Piemonte Grignolino La Capletta, Casalone	100
Peregrinus, La Cignozza	585	Piemonte Grignolino Sansoero, Marchesi Alfieri	131
Perlato del Bosco Bianco, Tua Rita	575	Piemonte Moscato, Piero Gatti	133
Perlato del Bosco Rosso, Tua Rita	575	Piemonte Moscato d'Autunno, Paolo Saracco	67
Perlhof Crescendo, Tenuta Ritterhof	265	Piemonte Moscato Passito, Cascina Fonda	101
Pernicolò, Fatt. San Francesco	736	Piemonte Moscato Passito Avié, Cascina Castlèt	71
Pertinello, Tenuta Arpineto	447	Piemonte Moscato Passito IL, I V.ioli di S. Stefano	134
Pesanella, Cast. di Monterinaldi	600	Piemonte Moscato Passito L'Altro Moscato,	
Petit Verdot, Casale del Giglio	663	Tenuta Cisa Asinari dei Marchesi di Grésy	31
Petra Rosso, Petra	605	Piemonte Moscato Passito Passrì di Scrapona, Marenco	140
Petranera, Le Crete	645	Piemonte Muscatel Tardì, Batasiolo	88
Petrara, Del Carmine	635	Piemonte Venta Quemada, Cascina Ulivi	158
Petraro, Dattilo	738	Pier delle Vigne, Cant. Coop. Botromagno	722
Petronio, Alberto Quacquarini	638	Pietra di Cinta, Salvatore Murana	756
Phigaia After the Red, Serafini & Vidotto	308	Pietra di Zoe, Cantine Torrevecchia	744
Pian del Ciampolo, Fatt. di Montevertine	552	Pietracupa, Fatt. Montecchio	576
Pian del Conte, Fatt. Sorbaiano	525	Pietraforte del Carobbio, Carobbio	540
Pian del Conte, Fatt. Sorbaiano	525	Pietranera, Marco De Bartoli	749
Pian dell'Altare Sasso, Tenuta Le Querce	709	Pietrasca, Russo	575
Piandorino, Pian dell'Orino	593	Pietro, Le Filigare	454
Piano del Cipresso, Fatt. di Terrabianca	554	Pieve Alta Chardonnay, La Berta	424
Piantonaia, Podere Poggio Scalette	487	Pieve di Spaltenna, Cast. di Meleto	481
Piave Cabernet Ardesco, Sorelle Bronca	336	Pieve di Spaltenna Alle Fonti, Cast. di Meleto	481
Piave Cabernet Ornella, Ornella Molon Traverso	310	Pigmento Rosso, Cascina Montagnola	160
Piave Cabernet Podere Torrai Ris., Conte Collalto	325	Pignacolusse, Vinnaioli Jermann	380
Piave Cabernet Sauvignon, Casa Roma	319	Pignocco Rosso, Santa Barbara	611
Piave Cabernet Sauvignon ai Palazzi Ris., Masottina	311	Pilin, Castellari Bergaglio	82
Piave Cabernet Terre Nobili Ris., Santo Stefano	338	Pinodisé, Contadi Castaldi	178
Piave Chardonnay, Casa Roma	319	Pinot Bianco, Gregoletto	298
Piave Chardonnay, Masottina	311	Pinot Bianco, Roncùs	352
Piave Chardonnay ai Palazzi Ris., Masottina	311	Pinot Bianco, Vinnaioli Jermann	380
Piave Chardonnay Ornella, Ornella Molon Traverso	310	Pinot Grigio, Giovanni Crosato	356
Piave Chardonnay Prà Longo, Santo Stefano	338	Pinot Grigio, Walter Filiputti	387
Piave Chardonnay Terre Nobili, Santo Stefano	338	Pinot Grigio, Conte Loredan Gasparini Venegazzù	344
Piave Merlot, Casa Roma	319	Pinot Grigio, Sant'Elena	385
Piave Merlot, Conte Collalto	325	Pinot Grigio, Simon di Brazzan	418
Piave Merlot, Masottina	311	Pinot Grigio, Leonardo Specogna	374
Piave Merlot ai Palazzi Ris., Masottina	311	Pinot Grigio delle Venezie, Fattori & Graney	301
Piave Merlot Ornella, Ornella Molon Traverso	310	Pinot Grigio Graminè, Longariva	239
Piave Merlot Rosso di Villa, Ornella Molon Traverso	310	Pinot Grigio Millesimato, MezzaCorona	234
Piave Pinot Bianco, Masottina	311	Pinot Grigio Olivers, Pierpaolo Pecorari	412
Piave Raboso, Casa Roma	319	Pinot Grigio Ramato, Zeni	241
Piave Raboso, Giorgio Cecchetto	344	Pinot Nero, Cardeto	651
Piave Raboso Gelsaia, Giorgio Cecchetto	344	Pinot Nero, Decugnano dei Barbi	651
Piave Raboso Ornella, Ornella Molon Traverso	310	Pinot Nero, Pojer & Sandri	228
Piave Tocai, Casa Roma	319	Pinot Nero, Alessandro Secchi	224
Pico de Laorenti, La Biancara	289	Pinot Nero, Serafini & Vidotto	308
Picolit Vign. Montsclapade, Girolamo Dorigo	349	Pinot Nero, Tenuta Teracrea	341
Piemonte Alta Langa Talento Brut, Fontanafredda	136	Pinot Nero Grifo Nero, Rino Russolo	412
Piemonte Barbera, Poderi Einaudi	75	Pinot Nero Il Nero, Ca' del Santo	218
Piemonte Barbera Bricco del Tempo, Domenico Ghio e Figli	45	Pinot Nero L'Arturo, Ronco Calino	186
Piemonte Barbera Briccobotti, Pira	76	Pinot Nero Ris., Carra	433
Piemonte Barbera Brichat, Osvaldo Barberis	154	Pinot Nero Ris., Pojer & Sandri	228
Piemonte Barbera Bunéis Gianni Zonin Vineyards,		Pinot Nero Sebino, Il Mosnel	203
Cast. del Poggio	127	Pinot Nero Sebino, Ricci Curbastro	181
Piemonte Barbera Identità, Terralba	44	Pinot Nero Sorai Campo alle More, Gini	302
Piemonte Barbera Mounbè, Cascina Ulivi	158	Pinot Nero Vign. Consola, Cast. della Sala	644
Piemonte Barbera Sentieri, Vigneti Massa	112	Pinot Nero Villa di Bagnolo,	
Piemonte Barbera Territorio, Claudio Mariotto	142	Tenuta di Bagnolo dei Marchesi Pancrazi	526
Piemonte Barbera Vho, Claudio Mariotto	142	Piocaia, Fatt. San Fabiano - Borghini Baldovinetti	579
Piemonte Barbera Vivace; Sergio Grimaldi - Ca' du Sindic	133	Pix Merlot, Boccadigabbia	615
Piemonte Bonarda, Cascina Gilli	61	Planargia Murapiscados, Gianvittorio Naitana	779
Piemonte Brachetto, Cascina Fonda	101	Poch ma Bon Passito, Cascina Pellerino	115
Piemonte Brachetto, Piero Gatti	133	Podalirio, Querceto di Castellina	466
Piemonte Brachetto Ca' du Sindic,		Podere Brizio, Roberto Bellini	501
Sergio Grimaldi - Ca' du Sindic	133	Podere Fontarca, Tenim. Luigi D'Alessandro	474
Piemonte Brachetto Carlotta, Ermanno e Alessandra Brema	86	Podere Il Bosco, Tenim. Luigi D'Alessandro	474
Piemonte Brachetto Forteto Pian dei Sogni, Forteto della Luja	99	Podere Le Rocce, Le Filigare	454
Piemonte Brut La Bernardina, Ceretto	25	Podernovo, Cast. delle Regine	640
Piemonte Chardonnay, Isabella	116	Poderuccio, Cast. di Camigliano	501
Piemonte Chardonnay, Tenuta La Tenaglia	139	Poesia d'Inverno Vino da Uve Stramature,	
Piemonte Chardonnay, Tenuta Olim Bauda	87	Istituto Professionale per l'Agricoltura e l'Ambiente	429
Piemonte Chardonnay Armonia, Colonna	148	Poggio ai Chiari, Colle Santa Mustiola	473
Piemonte Chardonnay Bric di Bric, Marco Canato	148	Poggio ai Venti, Massa Vecchia	497
Piemonte Chardonnay Bricco Manè, Villa Giada	56	Poggio alla Badiola, Cast. di Fonterutoli	463
Piemonte Chardonnay Crevoglio, Borgo Maragliano	99	Poggio alle Gazze, Tenuta dell' Ornellaia	457
Piemonte Chardonnay Diversamente, Tenuta Garetto	23	Poggio Argentato, Le Pupille	492
Piemonte Chardonnay Galet, Marenco	140	Poggio Canneto, Carlo e Marco Carini	655
Piemonte Chardonnay Giarone, Poderi Bertelli	70	Poggio Cavalluccio, Tenuta Roccaccia	546
Piemonte Chardonnay L'Altro, Pio Cesare	26	Poggio Crocino, Le Capannacce	585
Piemonte Chardonnay La Sabauda, Contratto	55	Poggio delle Vigne Brut, La Boscaiola	189
Piemonte Chardonnay Le Aie, Cascina Roera	71	Poggio Golo, Fatt. del Cerro	528
Piemonte Chardonnay Lidia, La Spinetta	58	Poggio Gonfienti, Fatt. Casabianca	539
Piemonte Chardonnay Mej, Caudrina	65	Poggio Granoni, Farnetella	571
Piemonte Chardonnay Monteriolo, Luigi Coppo e Figli	56	Poggio l'Aiole, Cast. di Modanella	555
Piemonte Chardonnay Passione, Colonna	148	Poggio Madrigale, Di Filippo	658
Piemonte Chardonnay Piasì, Marco Canato	148	Poggio Montino, Cast. di Modanella	555
Piemonte Chardonnay Plenilunio, Michele Chiarlo	47	Poggio Muralto, Rio Grande	654
Piemonte Chardonnay Riserva della Famiglia,		Poggio Solivo, Ca' del Vispo	562
Luigi Coppo e Figli	56	Poiema Marzemino dei Ziresi, Eugenio Rosi	245
Piemonte Chardonnay Robì e Robi, L'Armangia	151	Pojo del Ruspo Barbi, Decugnano dei Barbi	651

Polito, Il Lebbio	565
Polvere d'Oro, Calonga	431
Pomele, Falesco	670
Pomino Bianco, Marchesi de' Frescobaldi	476
Pomino Il Benefizio, Marchesi de' Frescobaldi	476
Pomino Rosso, Marchesi de' Frescobaldi	476
Pompeiano Piedirosso, Terredora	697
Popphof Cuvée, Popphof - Andreas Menz	270
Porticato Bianco, Colle di Maggio	671
Portico Rosso, V.iolo Giuseppe Fanti	232
Possessioni Bianco Serègo Alighieri, Masi	319
Pozzo di San Donato, Villa Arceno	473
Prato Grande Chardonnay, Tenuta De Angelis	613
Pratto, Ca' dei Frati	208
Pregio del Conte Bianco, Saladini Pilastri	634
Pregio del Conte Rosso , Saladini Pilastri	634
Prepositura, Ist. Agr. Provinciale San Michele all'Adige	240
Priante, Castel di Salve	730
Prima Luce Passito, Ottella	309
Primamateria, Poggerino	553
Primavera, Cant. Coop. Castignanese	614
Primitivo, Cant. Coop. Botromagno	722
Primitivo del Salento Melodie, Cant. e Oleificio Sociale di Sava	734
Primitivo del Tarantino, I Pastini - Carparelli	732
Primitivo del Tarantino Amorini, Soloperto	732
Primitivo del Tarantino I Monili, Pervini	728
Primitivo di Manduria, Felline	727
Primitivo di Manduria, Vinicola Miali	732
Primitivo di Manduria, Vinicola Mediterranea	734
Primitivo di Manduria, Vinicola Resta	734
Primitivo di Manduria 14°, Soloperto	732
Primitivo di Manduria 17°, Soloperto	732
Primitivo di Manduria Archidamo, Pervini	728
Primitivo di Manduria Bosco Marino, Cons. Prod. Vini e Mosti Rossi	732
Primitivo di Manduria dolce naturale Chicca, Vigne & Vini	725
Primitivo di Manduria Dolce Naturale Suavis, Agr. Pliniana	732
Primitivo di Manduria Dolce Naturale Terra di Miele, Cant. e Oleificio Sociale di Sava	734
Primitivo di Manduria Dunico Millennium Masseria Pepe, Accademia dei Racemi	727
Primitivo di Manduria Elegia, Cons. Prod. Vini e Mosti Rossi	732
Primitivo di Manduria Giravolta Tenuta Pozzopalo, Accademia dei Racemi	727
Primitivo di Manduria Juvenis, Agr. Pliniana	732
Primitivo di Manduria Mosaico, Cant. e Oleificio Sociale di Sava	734
Primitivo di Manduria Papale, Vigne & Vini	725
Primitivo di Manduria Santera, Leone de Castris	728
Primitivo di Manduria Terre di Don Peppe, Cant. Coop. del Locorotondo	726
Primitivo di Manduria Zinfandel Sinfarosa, Accademia dei Racemi	727
Primitivo di Puglia Primaio, Vini Classici Cardone	726
Primitivo Maestro, Borgo Canale	721
Primitivo Sigillo Primo, Antica Masseria del Sigillo	723
Primitivo Terre Mediterranee, Zonin	290
Primo Legno Bianco, Muzic	408
Primo Legno Rosso, Muzic	408
Primosole Rosso, Bianchi	159
Princeps, Cast. delle Regine	640
Principe di Corleone Rosso Narciso, Pollara	762
Priné, Bosco del Merlo	282
Priore, La Brugherata	207
Privilegia Rosso, Giuseppe Lonardi	295
Prosecco Brut Rustico, Nino Franco	330
Prosecco Passito, Vincenzo Toffoli	342
Prosecco Special Cuvée, Zonin	290
Provincia di Pavia A.D., Doria	199
Provincia di Pavia Bellarmino, Tenuta La Costaiola	200
Provincia di Pavia Moscato Passito Lacrimae Vitis , C.S. La Versa	207
Provincia di Pavia Müller Thurgau, Ca' del Gè	199
Provincia di Pavia Rosso del Castellazzo, Vercesi del Castellazzo	202
Provincia di Pavia Rosso Io, Ca' di Frara	202
Provincia di Pavia Rosso Vespolino, Vercesi del Castellazzo	202
Provincia di Pavia Uva Rara, Frecciarossa	183
Provincia di Pavia Varméi, Isimbarda	206
Prulke, Zidarich	378
Prunaio, Viticcio	492
Puer sed Formosus, Gostolai	773
Puglia Bianco, Torre Quarto	720
Puglia Bianco Divo, Borgo Canale	721
Puglia Chardonnay Sannà, Borgo Canale	721
Puglia Maestro, Borgo Canale	721
Puglia Moscato Pierale, Leone de Castris	728
Puglia Rosa di Selva, Borgo Canale	721
Puglia Rosato, Torre Quarto	720
Puglia Rosso, Le Fabriche	733
Puglia Rosso, Torre Quarto	720
Puglia Rosso Papale, Vigne & Vini	725
Puglia Rosso Pezza Petrosa, Tenuta Zicari	734
Puglia Rosso Solicato, Tenuta Zicari	734
Puglia Rosso Torre del Falco, Torrevento	721
Pulleraia, Agricoltori del Chianti Geografico	478
Pupà Pepu, Roberto Bellini	501
Puro Sangue, Livernano	552
Quarto d'Altesi, Altesino	499
Quarto di Luna, Cantine Grotta del Sole	699
Quarto di Sole, Cantine Grotta del Sole	699
Quattro Mori, Castel De Paolis	668
Quattrocentenario, Cast. della Paneretta	453
Querceto, Vigneti Le Monde	395
Querciagrande, Podere Capaccia	553
Querciolaia, Mantellassi	589
Querciolaia, Cast. di Querceto	488
Querciolo, Teresa Raiz	394
Racemo Rosso, L'Olivella	673
Radaia, La Parrina	539
Radames, Antichi Poderi Jerzu	770
Raddese, V.vecchia	554
Rafé Bianco, Cascina Gilli	61
Rainero, Cast. di Meleto	481
Rami, COS	759
Rapace, Uccelliera	520
Rapitalà Bianco Gran Cru, Tenute Rapitalà	746
Rapitalà Rosso, Tenute Rapitalà	746
Rapozzo da Maiano, Fatt. di Gratena	579
Rasa di Marmorata, Tenuta Le Quinte	673
Re Federico, Pupillo	764
Re Sole, Stefano Mancinelli	623
Realgar, Alessandro Secchi	224
Rebo, Giovanni Poli	248
Recioto dei Capitelli, Roberto Anselmi	300
Recioto della Valpolicella, Brigaldara	314
Recioto della Valpolicella, Corte Sant'Alda	296
Recioto della Valpolicella, Musella	312
Recioto della Valpolicella, Trabucchi	291
Recioto della Valpolicella Argille Bianche, Tenuta Sant'Antonio	297
Recioto della Valpolicella Cl., Lorenzo Begali	314
Recioto della Valpolicella Cl., Brigaldara	314
Recioto della Valpolicella Cl., Luigi Brunelli	315
Recioto della Valpolicella Cl., Gerardo Cesari	337
Recioto della Valpolicella Cl., Corte Lenguin	342
Recioto della Valpolicella Cl., Corte Rugolin	294
Recioto della Valpolicella Cl., F.lli Degani	295
Recioto della Valpolicella Cl., Aleardo Ferrari	343
Recioto della Valpolicella Cl., La Giaretta	340
Recioto della Valpolicella Cl., Angelo Nicolis e Figli	315
Recioto della Valpolicella Cl., Novaia	296
Recioto della Valpolicella Cl., Santa Sofia	316
Recioto della Valpolicella Cl., Massimino Venturini	318
Recioto della Valpolicella Cl., Villa Bellini	318
Recioto della Valpolicella Cl., Viviani	307
Recioto della Valpolicella Cl., F.lli Zeni	284
Recioto della Valpolicella Cl. Acinatico, Stefano Accordini	313
Recioto della Valpolicella Cl. BG, Tommaso Bussola	304
Recioto della Valpolicella Cl. Campo Casalin I Castei, Michele Castellani	294
Recioto della Valpolicella Cl. Capitel Monte Fontana, F.lli Tedeschi	317
Recioto della Valpolicella Cl. Casotto del Merlo, Giuseppe Campagnola	293
Recioto della Valpolicella Cl. Domini Veneti, C.S. Valpolicella	306
Recioto della Valpolicella Cl. Giovanni Allegrini, Allegrini	288
Recioto della Valpolicella Cl. I Comunai, F.lli Speri	316
Recioto della Valpolicella Cl. La Roggia, F.lli Speri	316
Recioto della Valpolicella Cl. La Rosta, F.lli Degani	295
Recioto della Valpolicella Cl. Le Fagne, Giuseppe Lonardi	295
Recioto della Valpolicella Cl. Le Brugnine, Massimino Venturini	318
Recioto della Valpolicella Cl. Le Calcarole, Roberto Mazzi	305
Recioto della Valpolicella Cl. Le Traversagne, Le Salette	289
Recioto della Valpolicella Cl. Le Vigne Ca' del Pipa, Michele Castellani	294
Recioto della Valpolicella Cl. Maddalena, I Sciriani	339
Recioto della Valpolicella Cl. Pal Sun, Raimondi-Villa Monteleone	320
Recioto della Valpolicella Cl. Pergole Vece, Le Salette	289
Recioto della Valpolicella Cl. TB, Tommaso Bussola	304
Recioto della Valpolicella Cl. Vigneti di Moron Domini Veneti, C.S. Valpolicella	306
Recioto della Valpolicella Cl. Vign. Le Tordare, Ca' La Bionda	293
Recioto della Valpolicella Roccolo Grassi, Roccolo Grassi	297
Recioto della Valpolicella Tesauro, C.S. della Valpantena	334
Recioto della Valpolicella Cl. Vign. Le Tordare, C.S. della Valpantena	334
Recioto di Gambellara, La Biancara	289
Recioto di Gambellara Capitel S. Libera, Domenico & F.lli Cavazza	299
Recioto di Gambellara Cl. Riva dei Perari, Luigino Dal Maso	299
Recioto di Gambellara Podere il Giangio Aristòs, Zonin	290
Recioto di Soave, Carlo Bogoni	301
Recioto di Soave, Monte Tondo	322
Recioto di Soave Arzimo, La Cappuccina	302
Recioto di Soave Case Vecie, Cecilia Beretta	332
Recioto di Soave Cl., Balestri Valda	343
Recioto di Soave Cl., Santa Sofia	316
Recioto di Soave Cl. Acinatium, Suavia	323
Recioto di Soave Cl. Corte Pittora, Cant. del Cast.	321
Recioto di Soave Cl. Le Sponde, Coffele	322
Recioto di Soave Cl. Rocca Sveva, Cant. di Soave	321
Recioto di Soave Cl. Vigneti di Costeggiola, Guerrieri Rizzardi	283
Recioto di Soave Col Foscarin, Gini	302
Recioto di Soave I Capitelli, Roberto Anselmi	300
Recioto di Soave La Broia, Roccolo Grassi	297
Recioto di Soave La Perlara, Ca' Rugate	300
Recioto di Soave Le Colombare, Leonildo Pieropan	323
Recioto di Soave Le Mandolare, Giobatta Dal Bosco	340
Recioto di Soave Motto Piane, Fattori & Graney	301
Recioto di Soave Oro, Umberto Portinari	303
Recioto di Soave Renobilis, Gini	302
Recioto di Soave S. Zeno, Fasoli	286
Recioto di Soave V. Marogne, Tamellini	324
Reciso, Pietro Beconcini	602
Redigaffi, Tua Rita	575
Refolà Cabernet Sauvignon, Le Vigne di San Pietro	325

Refosco, Marco Felluga	385
Refosco P. R., Borc Dodòn	420
Refosco P. R., Villa Frattina	395
Refosco P. R. Bottaz, Venica & Venica	377
Refosco P. R. I Legni, Rino Russolo	412
Refosco P. R. Panta Rei, Pierpaolo Pecorari	412
Regaleali Bianco, Tasca d'Almerita	758
Regaleali Rosato, Tasca d'Almerita	758
Regaleali Rosso, Tasca d'Almerita	758
Reggiano Assolo, Ermete Medici & Figli	438
Reggiano Lambrusco Bianco Spumante Brut Arita, Moro - Rinaldo Rinaldini	440
Reggiano Lambrusco Concerto, Ermete Medici & Figli	438
Reggiano Lambrusco Foglie Rosse, Cantine Coop. Riunite	446
Reggiano Lambrusco Ronchi dell'Olma Cuvée dei Fondatori, Cantine Cooperative Riunite	446
Reggiano Lambrusco Rosato, Moro - Rinaldo Rinaldini	440
Reggiano Lambrusco Secco, Ermete Medici & Figli	438
Resico, San Luciano	522
Retiko, Grigoletti	247
Retratto, Corte Sant'Alda	296
Rêve Chardonnay di Villa Angela, Ercole Velenosi	610
Ribolla Gialla, Brunner	417
Ribolla Gialla, Le Due Torri	373
Riccio, Redi	533
Richenza, V. Petrussa	402
Riflesso Antico, Lorella Ambrosini	573
Rigoletto Passito, Zenato	309
Riné, Cantrina	212
Riosso Piceno Il Maschio da Monte, Santa Barbara	611
Ripa, Podere Sopra la Ripa	572
Ripa delle Mandorle, Cast. di Vicchiomaggio	491
Ripa delle More, Cast. di Vicchiomaggio	491
Riserva del Governatore Extra Brut, Bortolomiol	327
Risveglio Chardonnay, Cascina Montagnola	160
Ritratto Bianco, La Vis	232
Ritratto Rosso, La Vis	232
Riviera Ligure di Ponente Ormeasco, Montali e Temesio	167
Riviera Ligure di Ponente Ormeasco, Giampaolo Ramò	175
Riviera Ligure di Ponente Ormeasco Sup., Nicola Guglierame	175
Riviera Ligure di Ponente Ormeasco Sup. Le Braje, Tommaso e Angelo Lupi	170
Riviera Ligure di Ponente Pigato, A Maccia	171
Riviera Ligure di Ponente Pigato, Laura Aschero	171
Riviera Ligure di Ponente Pigato, Maria Donata Bianchi	166
Riviera Ligure di Ponente Pigato, Calleri	162
Riviera Ligure di Ponente Pigato, Cascina Feipu dei Massaretti	162
Riviera Ligure di Ponente Pigato, La Rocca di San Nicolao	166
Riviera Ligure di Ponente Pigato, La Vecchia Cant.	163
Riviera Ligure di Ponente Pigato, Tommaso e Angelo Lupi	170
Riviera Ligure di Ponente Pigato, Sancio	176
Riviera Ligure di Ponente Pigato, Terre Bianche	168
Riviera Ligure di Ponente Pigato, Cascina delle Terre Rosse	168
Riviera Ligure di Ponente Pigato, Claudio Vio	173
Riviera Ligure di Ponente Pigato Apogeo, Cascina delle Terre Rosse	168
Riviera Ligure di Ponente Pigato Artemide, Maria Donata Bianchi	166
Riviera Ligure di Ponente Pigato Costa de Vigne, Alessandro	172
Riviera Ligure di Ponente Pigato Le Petraie, Tommaso e Angelo Lupi	170
Riviera Ligure di Ponente Pigato Le Russeghine, Bruna	172
Riviera Ligure di Ponente Pigato Saleasco, Calleri	162
Riviera Ligure di Ponente Pigato U Bacan, Bruna	172
Riviera Ligure di Ponente Pigato V. La Torretta, Colle dei Bardellini	169
Riviera Ligure di Ponente Pigato V. Proxi, La Rocca di San Nicolao	166
Riviera Ligure di Ponente Pigato Villa Torrachetta, Bruna	172
Riviera Ligure di Ponente Rossese, A Maccia	171
Riviera Ligure di Ponente Rossese, Anfossi	174
Riviera Ligure di Ponente Rossese, La Rocca di San Nicolao	166
Riviera Ligure di Ponente Vermentino, Laura Aschero	171
Riviera Ligure di Ponente Vermentino, Maria Donata Bianchi	166
Riviera Ligure di Ponente Vermentino, Calleri	162
Riviera Ligure di Ponente Vermentino, Tenuta Giuncheo	164
Riviera Ligure di Ponente Vermentino, La Rocca di San Nicolao	166
Riviera Ligure di Ponente Vermentino, La Vecchia Cant.	162
Riviera Ligure di Ponente Vermentino, Tommaso e Angelo Lupi	170
Riviera Ligure di Ponente Vermentino, Terre Bianche	168
Riviera Ligure di Ponente Vermentino, Cascina delle Terre Rosse	168
Riviera Ligure di Ponente Vermentino, Claudio Vio	173
Riviera Ligure di Ponente Vermentino Costa dei Pini, Montali e Temesio	167
Riviera Ligure di Ponente Vermentino Diana, Maria Donata Bianchi	166
Riviera Ligure di Ponente Vermentino I Muzazzi, Calleri	162
Riviera Ligure di Ponente Vermentino Le Palme, Tenuta Giuncheo	164
Riviera Ligure di Ponente Vermentino Le Serre, Tommaso e Angelo Lupi	170
Riviera Ligure di Ponente Vermentino V. Proxi, La Rocca di San Nicolao	166
Riviera Ligure di Ponente Vermentino V. Sorì, Montali e Temesio	167
Riviera Ligure di Ponente Vermentino V. U Munte, Colle dei Bardellini	169
Robbio, Villa Frattina	395
Roccagiglio, Adragna	764
Roccato, Rocca delle Macìe	466
Roccia Rosso, Cant. Coop. del Locorotondo	726
Roceja, Carlotta	44
Roero, Matteo Correggia	51
Roero, Filippo Gallino	53
Roero, Cascina Pellerino	115
Roero, Fabrizio Pinsoglio	60
Roero, Porello	54
Roero, Cascina Val del Prete	128
Roero Arneis, Bel Colle	145
Roero Arneis, Cornarea	151
Roero Arneis, Matteo Correggia	51
Roero Arneis, Filippo Gallino	53
Roero Arneis, Bruno Giacosa	120
Roero Arneis, Raffaele Gili	59
Roero Arneis, Malvirà	53
Roero Arneis, Montaribaldi	34
Roero Arneis, Mauro Sebaste	27
Roero Arneis, Vielmin	60
Roero Arneis Anterisio, Cascina Chicco	51
Roero Arneis Boneur, Cascina Pellerino	115
Roero Arneis Bric e Val, Pioiero	160
Roero Arneis Bricco Cappellina, Gianni Voerzio	97
Roero Arneis Bricco delle Ciliegie, Giovanni Almondo	113
Roero Arneis Camestrì, Porello	54
Roero Arneis Cristina Ascheri, Ascheri	46
Roero Arneis Daivej, Deltetto	52
Roero Arneis Gianat, Angelo Negro & Figli	115
Roero Arneis Liffrei, Valerio Aloi	156
Roero Arneis Luet, Cascina Val del Prete	128
Roero Arneis Merica, Cascina Ca' Rossa	50
Roero Arneis Perdaudin, Angelo Negro & Figli	115
Roero Arneis Pierin di Soc, Funtanin	52
Roero Arneis Re Cit, Monchiero Carbone	54
Roero Arneis Renesio, Malvirà	53
Roero Arneis S. Michele, Deltetto	52
Roero Arneis Saglietto, Malvirà	53
Roero Arneis San Servasio, Marsaglia	151
Roero Arneis Sernì, Michele Taliano	113
Roero Arneis Sorilaria, Araldica - Il Cantinone	58
Roero Arneis Trinità, Malvirà	53
Roero Arneis V. Canorei, Tenuta Carretta	126
Roero Arneis V. Elisa, Paitin	121
Roero Arneis Vigne Sparse, Giovanni Almondo	113
Roero Arneis Vign. Malinot, Fabrizio Pinsoglio	60
Roero Arneis Vign. S. Pietro, Stefanino Morra	152
Roero Braja, Deltetto	52
Roero Bric Angelino, Raffaele Gili	59
Roero Bric Torretta, Porello	54
Roero Bric Valdiana, Giovanni Almondo	113
Roero Bricco Morinaldo, Valerio Aloi	156
Roero La Rocca, Vielmin	60
Roero Madonna dei Boschi, Deltetto	52
Roero Mompissano, Cascina Ca' Rossa	50
Roero Montespinato, Cascina Chicco	51
Roero Prachiosso, Angelo Negro & Figli	115
Roero Ròche d'Ampsèj, Matteo Correggia	51
Roero Ròche dra Bòssora, Michele Taliano	113
Roero Srü, Monchiero Carbone	54
Roero Sup., Filippo Gallino	53
Roero Sup., Malvirà	53
Roero Sup., Stefanino Morra	152
Roero Sup., Pioiero	160
Roero Sup. Bric Paradiso, Tenuta Carretta	126
Roero Sup. Bricco Barbisa, Funtanin	52
Roero Sup. Brich d'America, Marsaglia	151
Roero Sup. Giovanni Almondo, Giovanni Almondo	113
Roero Sup. Mombeltramo, Malvirà	53
Roero Sup. Printi, Monchiero Carbone	54
Roero Sup. Sodisfà, Angelo Negro & Figli	115
Roero Sup. Trinità, Malvirà	53
Roero Valmaggiore, Cascina Chicco	51
Roero Vicot, Cascina Pellerino	115
Roero V. Audinaggio, Cascina Ca' Rossa	50
Romagnano Rosso, Colacicchi	662
Romalbo, Cima	497
Romeo, Castel Noarna	236
Romita Bianco, Fatt. Poggio Romita	605
Romitorio di Santedame, Tenim. Ruffino	548
Ronc, Paolo Rodaro	358
Ronc dal Gial, Ca di Bon	372
Ronco dei Ciliegi, Castelluccio	434
Ronco del Re, Castelluccio	434
Ronco delle Ginestre, Castelluccio	434
Ronco Nolè Rosso, Di Lenardo	381
Ronco Sesan, Rino Russolo	412
Roncùs Bianco, Roncùs	352
Roncùs Bianco Vecchie Vigne, Roncùs	352
Rondinaia, Cast. del Terriccio	467
Rosa di Montacuto, Alessandro Moroder	609
Rosa Rosae, Farnetella	571
Rosathea, Castel De Paolis	668
Rosato, Gianni Masciarelli	684
Rosato, Villa Pigna	626
Rosserto Bianco, Giovanni Manzone	108
Rossese di Dolceacqua, Giobatta Mandino Cane	167
Rossese di Dolceacqua, Tenuta Giuncheo	164
Rossese di Dolceacqua, Terre Bianche	168
Rossese di Dolceacqua Bricco Arcagna, Terre Bianche	168
Rossese di Dolceacqua Sup. Vign. Morghe, Giobatta Mandino Cane	167
Rossese di Dolceacqua Vign. Pian del Vescovo, Tenuta Giuncheo	164
Rosso 57, Michele Moio	696
Rosso Archè, Val di Neto	742
Rosso Avignonesi, Avignonesi	526

Rosso Caparzo Sangiovese, Tenuta Caparzo	502
Rosso Carolin, Armando Martino	712
Rosso Conero, Fazi Battaglia	613
Rosso Conero, Lanari	608
Rosso Conero, Fatt. Le Terrazze	624
Rosso Conero, Malacari	625
Rosso Conero, Marchetti	608
Rosso Conero, Alessandro Moroder	609
Rosso Conero Adeodato, Monteschiavo	619
Rosso Conero Adino, Spinsanti	612
Rosso Conero Camars, Spinsanti	612
Rosso Conero Cùmaro, Umani Ronchi	627
Rosso Conero Dorico, Alessandro Moroder	609
Rosso Conero Fibbio, Lanari	608
Rosso Conero Fructus, Conte Leopardi Dittajuti	624
Rosso Conero Grigiano, Malacari	625
Rosso Conero Grosso Agontano, Gioacchino Garofoli	618
Rosso Conero Julius, Silvano Strologo	612
Rosso Conero Marro, Alberto Serenelli	609
Rosso Conero Passo del Lupo Ris., Fazi Battaglia	613
Rosso Conero Piancarda, Gioacchino Garofoli	618
Rosso Conero Pigmento, Conte Leopardi Dittajuti	624
Rosso Conero S. Lorenzo, Umani Ronchi	627
Rosso Conero Sassi Neri, Fatt. Le Terrazze	624
Rosso Conero Traiano, Silvano Strologo	612
Rosso Conero Trave, Alberto Serenelli	609
Rosso Conero Varano, Alberto Serenelli	609
Rosso Conero Vigneti del Coppo, Conte Leopardi Dittajuti	624
Rosso Conero Vigneti del Parco Ris., Terre Cortesi Moncaro	621
Rosso Conero Villa Bonomi, Marchetti	608
Rosso Conero Villa Bonomi Ris., Marchetti	608
Rosso Conero Visions of J, Fatt. Le Terrazze	624
Rosso Corte dell'Abbà, Villa Frattina	395
Rosso Costozza, Conti da Schio	339
Rosso d'Arquata, Agr. Adanti	641
Rosso degli Appiani, San Giusto	545
Rosso degli Spezieri, Tenuta Col d'Orcia	506
Rosso dei Frati Priori, Uberti	195
Rosso del Cardinale, Barone de Cles	235
Rosso del Conte, Tasca d'Almerita	758
Rosso del Frusinate, Casale della Ioria	662
Rosso del Notaio, Massimo Oddero	153
Rosso del Pievano, La Pieve	498
Rosso del Pivier, Cesconi	231
Rosso del Sebino Solesine, Bellavista	192
Rosso del Senatore, Fatt. dell' Aiola	583
Rosso del Soprano, Palari	753
Rosso dell'Abate Chiarini, Palazzo Vecchio	595
Rosso della Fabriseria, F.lli Tedeschi	317
Rosso delle Chiaie, Giovanni Palombo	663
Rosso di Alberico, La Brugherata	207
Rosso di Casale Marchese, Casale Marchese	667
Rosso di Casisano, Casisano Colombaio	590
Rosso di Corte, Corte Gardoni	332
Rosso di Luna, Monzio Compagnoni	191
Rosso di Montalcino, Argiano	499
Rosso di Montalcino, Banfi	500
Rosso di Montalcino, Fatt. dei Barbi	500
Rosso di Montalcino, Cast. di Camigliano	501
Rosso di Montalcino, Capanna di Cencioni	502
Rosso di Montalcino, Tenuta Caparzo	502
Rosso di Montalcino, Casanova di Neri	503
Rosso di Montalcino, Fatt. del Casato - Donatella Cinelli Colombini	503
Rosso di Montalcino, Casisano Colombaio	590
Rosso di Montalcino, Castelli Martinozzi	590
Rosso di Montalcino, Castiglion del Bosco	504
Rosso di Montalcino, Tenuta Col d'Orcia	506
Rosso di Montalcino, Andrea Costanti	507
Rosso di Montalcino, Tenuta Di Sesta	590
Rosso di Montalcino, Donna Olga	590
Rosso di Montalcino, Due Portine - Gorelli	507
Rosso di Montalcino, Fanti - La Palazzetta	590
Rosso di Montalcino, Fanti - San Filippo	508
Rosso di Montalcino, Fattoi	591
Rosso di Montalcino, Il Colle	591
Rosso di Montalcino, Tenuta Il Greppo	509
Rosso di Montalcino, Il Palazzone	509
Rosso di Montalcino, Tenuta Il Poggione	510
Rosso di Montalcino, Podere La Fortuna	511
Rosso di Montalcino, La Gerla	511
Rosso di Montalcino, La Poderina	512
Rosso di Montalcino, La Serena	592
Rosso di Montalcino, La Togata - Tenuta Carlina	512
Rosso di Montalcino, Le Chiuse	592
Rosso di Montalcino, Le Chiuse di Sotto	513
Rosso di Montalcino, Le Gode di Ripaccioli	592
Rosso di Montalcino, Le Macioche	592
Rosso di Montalcino, Mocali	593
Rosso di Montalcino, Cant. di Montalcino	593
Rosso di Montalcino, Tenute Silvio Nardi	514
Rosso di Montalcino, Franco Pacenti	593
Rosso di Montalcino, Siro Pacenti	515
Rosso di Montalcino, Pian dell'Orino	593
Rosso di Montalcino, Piancornello	515
Rosso di Montalcino, Agostina Pieri	516
Rosso di Montalcino, Poggio Castellare	594
Rosso di Montalcino, Poggio di Sotto	516
Rosso di Montalcino, Poggio San Polo	517
Rosso di Montalcino, Cast. Romitorio	517
Rosso di Montalcino, Podere Salicutti	518
Rosso di Montalcino, Sesti - Cast. di Argiano	519
Rosso di Montalcino, Talenti	520
Rosso di Montalcino, Tenim. Angelini - Val di Suga	521
Rosso di Montalcino, Uccelliera	520
Rosso di Montalcino, Tenuta Valdicava	521
Rosso di Montalcino Banditella, Tenuta Col d'Orcia	506
Rosso di Montalcino Calbello, Andrea Costanti	507
Rosso di Montalcino Campo ai Sassi, Castelgiocondo	504
Rosso di Montalcino Ginestreto, Eredi Fuligni	508
Rosso di Montalcino Le Potazzine, Due Portine - Gorelli	507
Rosso di Montalcino Pietranera, Centolani	505
Rosso di Montalcino Poggio Salvi, Tenuta Il Greppo	509
Rosso di Montalcino Sassello, Il Poggiolo	510
Rosso di Montalcino Tenuta Friggiali, Centolani	505
Rosso di Montalcino Terra Rossa, Il Poggiolo	510
Rosso di Montalcino Tirso, Villa Le Prata	522
Rosso di Montalcino V. della Fonte, Ciacci Piccolomini D'Aragona	506
Rosso di Montepulciano, Avignonesi	526
Rosso di Montepulciano, Carpineto	486
Rosso di Montepulciano, Fatt. del Cerro	528
Rosso di Montepulciano, Contucci	528
Rosso di Montepulciano, Corte alla Flora	594
Rosso di Montepulciano, Crociani	594
Rosso di Montepulciano, Ercolani	595
Rosso di Montepulciano, Il Faggeto	595
Rosso di Montepulciano, La Calonica	530
Rosso di Montepulciano, Fatt. Le Casalte	595
Rosso di Montepulciano, Lodola Nuova - Tenim. Ruffino	531
Rosso di Montepulciano, Poliziano	532
Rosso di Montepulciano, Redi	533
Rosso di Montepulciano, Massimo Romeo	596
Rosso di Montepulciano, Salcheto	533
Rosso di Montepulciano, Terra Antica	596
Rosso di Montepulciano, Tenuta Valdipiatta	534
Rosso di Montepulciano, Villa Sant'Anna	535
Rosso di Montepulciano Alàuda, Lodola Nuova - Tenim. Ruffino	531
Rosso di Montepulciano Fosso Lupaio, Bindella	527
Rosso di Montepulciano Sabazio, Fatt. La Braccesca	595
Rosso di Montepulciano Selciaia, Fassati	529
Rosso di Montepulciano Terre di Rubinoro, Redi	533
Rosso di Nero, Ist. Professionale per l'Agricoltura e l'Ambiente	429
Rosso di Sera, Fatt. Poggiopiano	561
Rosso di Turi, Feotto dello Jato	764
Rosso di Villa Ris., Ornella Molon Traverso	310
Rosso Ercolani, Ercolani	595
Rosso Faye, Pojer & Sandri	228
Rosso Fiorentino, Cennatoio Intervineas	541
Rosso Gravner, Gravner	382
Rosso Ibleo , Gulfi	760
Rosso La Tia, Traversa - Cascina Bertolotto	139
Rosso La V. Bricca Ris., Tenuta La Costaiola	200
Rosso Maradea, Val di Neto	742
Rosso n. 1, Luigi Spertino	156
Rosso Orvietano Il Tordimaro, Tordimaro	660
Rosso Orvietano Rosso di Spicca, Tenuta Le Velette	653
Rosso Orvietano Selvaia, Tordimaro	660
Rosso Ottella, Ottella	309
Rosso Piceno, Aurora	637
Rosso Piceno, Boccadigabbia	615
Rosso Piceno , Cast. Fageto	628
Rosso Piceno, Cant. Coop. Castignanese	614
Rosso Piceno, Tenuta De Angelis	613
Rosso Piceno, Fatt. di Forano	610
Rosso Piceno, Fatt. Laila	620
Rosso Piceno, Laurentina	621
Rosso Piceno, Rio Maggio	622
Rosso Piceno, Santa Cassella	630
Rosso Piceno, Ercole Velenosi	610
Rosso Piceno, Villa Pigna	626
Rosso Piceno Bulciano, Fatt. di Forano	610
Rosso Piceno Campo delle Mura, Poderi San Savino	632
Rosso Piceno Casa Nostra, Vallerosa Bonci	616
Rosso Piceno Crivellino, Fontursia	637
Rosso Piceno del Pozzo Buono, Vicari	636
Rosso Piceno Furtarello, Cavallaro	637
Rosso Piceno GrAnarijS, Rio Maggio	622
Rosso Piceno Grotte sul Mare, Vinicola del Tesino	617
Rosso Piceno Il Moro, Cavallaro	637
Rosso Piceno Lyricus, Colonnara Viticoltori in Cupramontana	616
Rosso Piceno Marinus, Il Conte	622
Rosso Piceno Monte Nereto, Saputi	635
Rosso Piceno Montesecco, Montecappone	618
Rosso Piceno Morellone, Le Caniette	631
Rosso Piceno Nero di Vite, Le Caniette	631
Rosso Piceno Ophites, San Giovanni	626
Rosso Piceno Regina del Bosco, Fatt. Dezi	633
Rosso Piceno Rosso Bello, Le Caniette	631
Rosso Piceno Rusus, Cast. Fageto	628
Rosso Piceno Sup., Aurora	637
Rosso Piceno Sup., Cant. Coop. Castignanese	614
Rosso Piceno Sup., Ciù Ciù	625
Rosso Piceno Sup., Tenuta De Angelis	613
Rosso Piceno Sup., Villa Pigna	626
Rosso Piceno Sup. Castellano, La Cant. dei Colli Ripani	631
Rosso Piceno Sup. Etichetta Oro, Tenuta De Angelis	613
Rosso Piceno Sup. Gotico, Ciù Ciù	625
Rosso Piceno Sup. Il Brecciarolo, Ercole Velenosi	610
Rosso Piceno Sup. Le Torri, Tenuta Cocci Grifoni	630
Rosso Piceno Sup. Leo Guelfus, San Giovanni	626
Rosso Piceno Sup. Leo Ripanus, La Cant. dei Colli Ripani	631

Rosso Piceno Sup. Naumachos, Vinicola del Tesino	617
Rosso Piceno Sup. Picus, Poderi San Savino	632
Rosso Piceno Sup. Rocca di Acquaviva, Terre Cortesi Moncaro	621
Rosso Piceno Sup. Roggio del Filare, Ercole Velenosi	610
Rosso Piceno Sup. Rosso del Nonno, San Giovanni	626
Rosso Piceno Sup. V. Messieri, Tenuta Cocci Grifoni	630
Rosso Piceno Sup. V. Monteprandone, Saladini Pilastri	634
Rosso Piceno Sup. V. Montetinello, Saladini Pilastri	634
Rosso Piceno Talliano, Laurentina	621
Rosso Piceno Tav.no, Lucangeli Aymerich di Laconi	614
Rosso Piceno Tenuta Pongelli, Bucci	627
Rosso Piceno Transone, La Cant. dei Colli Ripani	631
Rosso Piceno Viatorre, Vallerosa Bonci	616
Rosso Piceno V. Piediprato, Saladini Pilastri	634
Rosso Piceno Villamagna, Boccadigabbia	615
Rosso Poculum, Agnes	205
Rosso Ris. Pallavicini, Vini Pallavicini	672
Rosso Sav.m, Riccardo Battistotti	237
Rosso Skala, Evangelos Paraschos	408
Rosso Teodote, Tenuta Il Bosco	211
Rosso Vigliano, Vigliano	495
Rossole, Borgo Salcetino	550
Rossonero, Leone Conti	428
Rossore, Ca.Vi.Man.	68
Rouchet Bricco Rosa, Scarpa - Antica Casa Vinicola	124
Rouge du Prieur, Institut Agricole Régional	16
Rovai, Ca' del Vispo	562
Rovaio, La Lastra	566
Rozzano, Villa Pigna	626
Rubbio, Palazzone	653
Rubino, La Palazzola	657
Rubrum, Il Carpino	407
Ruché di Castagnole M.to 'Na Vota, Cantine Sant'Agata	135
Ruché di Castagnole M.to Pro Nobis, Cantine Sant'Agata	135
Ruché di Castagnole M.to Bric Majoli, Dacapo	22
Ruchetto dell'Uccellina, Tenuta Uccellina	439
Ruit Hora, Caccia al Piano 1868	581
Rupestro, Cardeto	651
S. Agata dei Goti Falanghina, Mustilli	700
S. Agata dei Goti Greco di Primicerio, Mustilli	700
S. Agata dei Goti Rosso Conte Artus, Mustilli	700
S'Arai, Pala	776
S. Clemente Bianco, Ciccio Zaccagnini	676
S. Gimignano Rosato, Pietrafitta	569
S. Gimignano Rosso La Sughera, Pietrafitta	569
S. Gimignano Rosso Serreto, Cappella Sant'Andrea	602
S. J., Eredi Fuligni	508
S. Torpè Recinaio Vin Santo, San Gervasio	598
Sabiniano di Casanova, Podere La Chiesa	606
Sabinio Cabernet, Colonna - Vini Spalletti	441
Sabòt, Fatt. di Romignano	588
Saccaia, Piero Mancini	772
Saeculum, Riseccoli	489
Saffredi, Le Pupille	492
Sagana, Cusumano	756
Saggio Sangiovese, Ciù Ciù	625
Sagittarius, Graf Pfeil Weingut Kränzel	267
Sagrado Bianco, Castelvecchio	405
Sagrado Rosso, Castelvecchio	405
Saia Grande, Maurigi	757
Salae Domini, Antonio Caggiano	702
Salamartano, Fatt. Montellori	477
Salcheto, Salchetto	533
Salciaia, Ercolani	595
Salento Bianco Bolina, Rosa del Golfo	716
Salento Bianco Calice, Cons. Prod. Vini e Mosti Rossi	732
Salento Bianco Cigliano, C.S. Coop. Copertino	731
Salento Bianco Marmorelle, Tenute Rubino	717
Salento Bianco Messapia, Leone de Castris	728
Salento Bianco Mjere, Michele Calò & Figli	734
Salento Bianco Santi Medici, Castel di Salve	730
Salento Bianco V. Case Alte, Leone de Castris	728
Salento Bianco V. Vinera, Francesco Candido	729
Salento Chardonnay, Cantele	724
Salento Chardonnay Bizantino, Pervini	728
Salento Chardonnay Placeo Barricato, Vini Classici Cardone	726
Salento Chardonnay Teresa Manara, Cantele	724
Salento Negroamaro, Vini Classici Cardone	726
Salento Negroamaro Canonico, Cant. Due Palme	719
Salento Primitivo, Cantele	724
Salento Primitivo, Vini Classici Cardone	726
Salento Primitivo, Cast. Monaci	733
Salento Primitivo, Conti Zecca	725
Salento Primitivo, Cant. Due Palme	719
Salento Primitivo, Le Fabriche	733
Salento Primitivo, Rosa del Golfo	716
Salento Primitivo, Santa Barbara	733
Salento Primitivo Dolce Naturale, Vinicola Mediterranea	734
Salento Primitivo Fra Diavolo, Marco Maci	719
Salento Primitivo I Censi, Masseria Monaci	720
Salento Primitivo Vigne Vecchie, Duca Carlo Guarini	734
Salento Primitivo Visellio, Tenute Rubino	717
Salento Quarantale, Rosa del Golfo	716
Salento Rosato Bizantino, Pervini	728
Salento Rosato Cigliano, C.S. Coop. Copertino	731
Salento Rosato Mediterraneo, Tenute Albano Carrisi	718
Salento Rosato Rosa del Golfo, Rosa del Golfo	716
Salento Rosato Santi Medici, Castel di Salve	730
Salento Rosato Scaloti, Cosimo Taurino	723
Salento Rosso, Vini Classici Cardone	726
Salento Rosso Alberello, Felline	727
Salento Rosso Diago, Tenuta Zicari	734
Salento Rosso Don Carmelo, Tenute Albano Carrisi	718
Salento Rosso Donna Marzia, Conti Zecca	725
Salento Rosso Illernos, Leone de Castris	728
Salento Rosso Marmorelle, Tenute Rubino	717
Salento Rosso Messere Andrea, Leone de Castris	728
Salento Rosso Mjére, Michele Calò & Figli	734
Salento Rosso Nostalgia, Tenute Albano Carrisi	718
Salento Rosso Piromàfo, Valle dell'Asso	722
Salento Rosso Platone, Tenute Albano Carrisi	718
Salento Rosso Santi Medici, Castel di Salve	730
Salento Rosso Schiaccianoci, Vigne & Vini	725
Salento Rosso Taras, Tenute Albano Carrisi	718
Salento Rosso Tenuta Albrizzi, Cant. Due Palme	719
Salento Rosso Tenuta Piutri, Duca Carlo Guarini	734
Salento Rosso Teresa Manara, Cantele	724
Salento Rosso V. del Gelso Moro, Vinicola Resta	734
Salento Sauvignon Corte Valesio, Agricole Vallone	724
Salento Sauvignon Murà, Duca Carlo Guarini	734
Salgaluna Bianco, Aziende Vinicole Miceli	755
Salice Salentino, Cast. Monaci	733
Salice Salentino, Cant. Due Palme	719
Salice Salentino, Santa Barbara	733
Salice Salentino, Valle dell'Asso	722
Salice Salentino Aleatico, Francesco Candido	729
Salice Salentino Bianco, Francesco Candido	729
Salice Salentino Cantalupi Ris., Conti Zecca	725
Salice Salentino Hilliryos, Antica Masseria del Sigillo	723
Salice Salentino Il Secondo, Antica Masseria del Sigillo	723
Salice Salentino La Canestra Ferrari, Accademia dei Racemi	727
Salice Salentino Pezzo Morgana, Masseria Li Veli	731
Salice Salentino Rosato Le Pozzelle, Francesco Candido	729
Salice Salentino Rosso, Tenute Albano Carrisi	718
Salice Salentino Rosso, Torrevento	721
Salice Salentino Rosso Cantalupi, Conti Zecca	725
Salice Salentino Rosso Donna Lisa Ris., Leone de Castris	728
Salice Salentino Rosso Majana, Leone de Castris	728
Salice Salentino Rosso Ris., Francesco Candido	729
Salice Salentino Rosso Ris., Cantele	724
Salice Salentino Rosso Ris., Leone de Castris	728
Salice Salentino Rosso Ris., Cosimo Taurino	723
Salice Salentino Rosso Te Deum Laudamus Casale Bevagna, Pervini	728
Salice Salentino Rosso Te Deum Laudamus Ris. Casale Bevagna , Accademia dei Racemi	727
Salice Salentino Rosso Vereto, Agricole Vallone	724
Salice Salentino Selvarossa Ris., Cant. Due Palme	719
Salina Bianco, Cantine Colosi	762
Salina Rosso, Cantine Colosi	762
Saltapicchio Sangiovese, Boccadigabbia	615
Salviano di Salviano, Tenuta di Salviano	658
Sambuca di Sicilia Pepita, Gaspare Di Prima	763
Sammarco, Cast. dei Rampolla	540
San Bartolomeo, Vallorsi	606
San Biagio, Progetto DiVino	714
San Carlo, Barone Pizzini	189
San Carro Rosso, Ciù Ciù	625
San Colombano Banino, Antonio Panigada - Banino	221
San Colombano Banino La Merla Ris., Antonio Panigada - Banino	221
San Colombano Mombrione, Enrico Riccardi	221
San Colombano Roverone, Enrico Riccardi	221
San Cristoforo Uno, San Cristoforo	195
San Donato, Tenuta di Bagnolo dei Marchesi Pancrazi	526
San Dordi Bianco, Casa Roma	319
San Francesco Passito, Roberto Mazzi	305
San Gimignano Rosso, Signano	602
San Gimignano Rosso Acantho, Casa alle Vacche	563
San Gimignano Rosso Il Casato, Baroncini	562
San Giorgio, Lungarotti	657
San Giusto, Sassotondo	545
San Leonardo, Tenuta San Leonardo	225
San Leopoldo, Tenuta Il Poggione	510
San Lorenzo, Sassotondo	572
San Marsan Bianco, Poderi Bertelli	70
San Marsan Rosso, Poderi Bertelli	70
San Martino, Villa Cafaggio	544
San Martino della Battaglia Liquoroso, Spia d'Italia	217
San Michele, Stefano Mancinelli	623
San Rocco, Feudo Principi di Butera	745
San Severo Bianco Candelaro, D'Alfonso del Sordo	730
San Severo Bianco Posta Arignano, D'Alfonso del Sordo	730
San Severo Rosato Posta Arignano, D'Alfonso del Sordo	730
San Severo Rosso Montero, D'Alfonso del Sordo	730
San Severo Rosso Posta Arignano, D'Alfonso del Sordo	730
San Vincenzo, Roberto Anselmi	300
San Vito di Luzzi Bianco, Luigi Vivacqua	740
San Vito di Luzzi Rosato, Luigi Vivacqua	740
San Vito di Luzzi Rosso, Luigi Vivacqua	740
San Zenobi, Pasolini Dall'Onda	586
San Zio, Cantine Leonardo da Vinci	578
Sancta Catharina, Dei	529
Sangiovese, Cast. delle Regine	640
Sangiovese, Cant. Coop. Castignanese	614
Sangiovese, Cima	497
Sangiovese, La Calonica	530
Sangiovese di Romagna, Leone Conti	428
Sangiovese di Romagna Amarcord d'un Ross Ris., Treré	430
Sangiovese di Romagna Anfore Romane Ris., Colombina	445
Sangiovese di Romagna Campo Rosso Ris., Tenuta Poggio Pollino	448

Sangiovese di Romagna Domus Caia Ris., Stefano Ferrucci	425
Sangiovese di Romagna Olmatello Ris., La Berta	424
Sangiovese di Romagna Pergami Ris., Tenuta Amalia	446
Sangiovese di Romagna Ris., Umberto Cesari	425
Sangiovese di Romagna Ris., La Macolina	448
Sangiovese di Romagna Ris., Tenuta Uccellina	439
Sangiovese di Romagna Ris., Tre Monti	432
Sangiovese di Romagna Riserva della Beccaccia Ris., Tre Valli	447
Sangiovese di Romagna Sup., Tre Monti	432
Sangiovese di Romagna Sup., Villa Spadoni	447
Sangiovese di Romagna Sup. Aulente, San Patrignano	428
Sangiovese di Romagna Sup. Avi Ris., San Patrignano	428
Sangiovese di Romagna Sup. Beccafico, Alessandro Morini	447
Sangiovese di Romagna Sup. Calisto, Stefano Berti	430
Sangiovese di Romagna Sup. Centurione, Stefano Ferrucci	425
Sangiovese di Romagna Sup. Ceregio, Fatt. Zerbina	429
Sangiovese di Romagna Sup. Ceregio V. Querce, Fatt. Zerbina	429
Sangiovese di Romagna Sup. Clivo del Re, Tenuta Uccellina	439
Sangiovese di Romagna Sup. Contiriserva Ris., Leone Conti	428
Sangiovese di Romagna Sup. Costa del Sole, Fatt. Ca' Rossa	445
Sangiovese di Romagna Sup. Fermavento, Giovanna Madonia	422
Sangiovese di Romagna Sup. Gaudentia, Tenuta Godenza	446
Sangiovese di Romagna Sup. Le Case Rosse, Tenuta Amalia	446
Sangiovese di Romagna Sup. Le Grillaie, Celli	422
Sangiovese di Romagna Sup. Le Grillaie Ris., Celli	422
Sangiovese di Romagna Sup. Le More, Castelluccio	434
Sangiovese di Romagna Sup. Michelangiolo Ris., Calonga	431
Sangiovese di Romagna Sup. Millenium Ris., Fatt. Camerone	446
Sangiovese di Romagna Sup. Ombroso Ris., Giovanna Madonia	422
Sangiovese di Romagna Sup. Pandolfo, Pandolfa	450
Sangiovese di Romagna Sup. Pietramora Ris., Fatt. Zerbina	429
Sangiovese di Romagna Sup. Poderepozzo Le Betulle, Leone Conti	428
Sangiovese di Romagna Sup. Pruno Ris., Drei Donà Tenuta La Palazza	431
Sangiovese di Romagna Sup. Pruno Ris., Drei Donà Tenuta La Palazza	431
Sangiovese di Romagna Sup. Ravaldo, Stefano Berti	430
Sangiovese di Romagna Sup. Ripagrande Ris., Fatt. Ca' Rossa	445
Sangiovese di Romagna Sup. Ris., Villa Spadoni	447
Sangiovese di Romagna Sup. Rocca di Ribano, Colonna - Vini Spalletti	441
Sangiovese di Romagna Sup. Rosso del Camerone Ris., Fatt. Camerone	446
Sangiovese di Romagna Sup. Rubiano, Tenuta Godenza	447
Sangiovese di Romagna Sup. Scabi, San Valentino	438
Sangiovese di Romagna Sup. Solano, La Berta	424
Sangiovese di Romagna Sup. Terra Ris., San Valentino	438
Sangiovese di Romagna Sup. Thea, Tre Monti	432
Sangiovese di Romagna Sup. Torre di Ceparano, Fatt. Zerbina	429
Sangiovese di Romagna Sup. Tre Rocche, Casetto dei Mandorli	450
Sangiovese di Romagna Sup. V. del Molino, Fatt. Paradiso	423
Sangiovese di Romagna Sup. V. delle Lepri Ris., Fatt. Paradiso	423
Sangiovese di Romagna Sup. V. dello Sperone, Treré	430
Sangiovese di Romagna Sup. Zarricante Ris., San Patrignano	428
Sangiovese di Romagna V. del Generale Ris., Casetto dei Mandorli	450
Sangiovese di Romagna V. del Monte, Treré	430
Sangiovese di Romagna Vign. Il Prugneto, Poderi dal Nespoli	427
Sangiovese Don Camillo, Farnese	681
Sangiovese Moggio, Poderi San Savino	632
Sangiovese Tenuta Corbara, Bigi	650
Sangiovese Terra degli Osci, Di Majo Norante	676
Sangiovese Terre di Chieti, Citra	687
Sangiovese V. La Pieve, Fanini	643
Sangioveto, Coltibuono	480
Sanleone, Fatt. Cast. Sonnino	537
Sannio Aglianico, Cantine Caputo	691
Sannio Aglianico, De Lucia	695
Sannio Aglianico, Vinicola del Sannio	704
Sannio Aglianico Adelchi, De Lucia	695
Sannio Aglianico Clanius, Cantine Caputo	691
Sannio Aglianico Tre Pietre, Corte Normanna	705
Sannio Aglianico V. La Corte, De Lucia	695
Sannio Barbera, Vinicola del Sannio	704
Sannio Barbera Barbetta Vàndari, Antica Masseria Venditti	692
Sannio Bianco, Antica Masseria Venditti	692
Sannio Falanghina, De Lucia	695
Sannio Falanghina, Di Meo	699
Sannio Falanghina, Feudi di San Gregorio	702
Sannio Falanghina, Fatt. Torre Gaia	704
Sannio Falanghina, Vinicola del Sannio	704
Sannio Falanghina Frattasi, Cantine Caputo	691
Sannio Falanghina V.T., De Lucia	695
Sannio Falanghina Vàndari, Antica Masseria Venditti	692
Sannio Falanghina V. delle Ginestre, De Lucia	695
Sannio Rosso, Antica Masseria Venditti	692
Sannio Rosso Poggio Bellavista, Fatt. Torre Gaia	704
Sansonina, La Sansonina	308
Sant'Amato, Fatt. Montellori	477
Sant'Antimo Ca' del Pazzo, Tenuta Caparzo	502
Sant'Antimo Cabernet Sauvignon, Cast. di Camigliano	501
Sant'Antimo Colvecchio, Banfi	500
Sant'Antimo Cum Laude, Banfi	500
Sant'Antimo Excelsus, Banfi	500
Sant'Antimo Fontanelle Chardonnay, Banfi	500
Sant'Antimo In Riva al Fosso, Il Poggiolo	510
Sant'Antimo Le Grance, Tenuta Caparzo	502
Sant'Antimo Pinot Grigio, Tenuta Col d'Orcia	506
Sant'Antimo Rosso, Capanna di Cencioni	502
Sant'Antimo Rosso Romito del Romitorio, Cast. Romitorio	517
Sant'Antimo Serena Sauvignon Blanc, Banfi	500
Sant'Antimo Summus, Banfi	500
Sant'Antimo Tavernelle Cabernet, Banfi	500
Sant'Antimo Terra di Siena, Sesti - Cast. di Argiano	519
Sant'Ippolito, Cantine Leonardo da Vinci	578
Santa Brigida, Fatt. La Ripa	605
Santa Brigida, Masseria Monaci	720
Santa Cecilia, Planeta	752
Santa Chiara, Tenuta Terre Nobili	742
Santagostino Bianco Baglio Soria, Casa Vinicola Firriato	754
Santagostino Rosso Baglio Soria, Casa Vinicola Firriato	754
Santomio Rosso, Giacomo Montresor	333
Saramago, Ca' Ronesca	376
Sardegna Semidano, C.S. Il Nuraghe	779
Sardegna Semidano, Gigi Picciau	768
Sarì, Marco Maci	719
Sarica Rosso, Pisoni	230
Sarmaro Bianco, Curatolo	761
Sarmaro Rosso, Curatolo	761
Saros V. T., Giulio Poli	248
Sartei, Trappolini	665
Sassello, Cast. di Verrazzano	490
Sassicaia, Tenuta San Guido	457
Sassoalloro, Tenuta Il Greppo	509
Sassobucato, Russo	575
Sassocheto, Il Grappolo-Fortius	591
Sassòne, Spinsanti	612
Sassotondo Rosso, Sassotondo	572
Satrico, Casale del Giglio	663
Sauvignon, Nicola Balter	238
Sauvignon, Casa Roma	319
Sauvignon, Casale del Giglio	663
Sauvignon, Giorgio Cecchetto	344
Sauvignon, Conte Zandotti	671
Sauvignon, Farnetella	571
Sauvignon, La Cappuccina	302
Sauvignon, Camillo Montori	678
Sauvignon, Roncùs	352
Sauvignon, Vinnaioli Jermann	380
Sauvignon Atesino, Castel Noarna	236
Sauvignon Ca' Lustra, Ca' Lustra	286
Sauvignon Campiğe, Piovene Porto Godi	336
Sauvignon Campo Napoleone, Armani	287
Sauvignon Del Frate, Triacca	211
Sauvignon della Sala, Cast. della Sala	644
Sauvignon Ghiaiolo, Orlandi Contucci Ponno	683
Sauvignon Kolàus, Pierpaolo Pecorari	412
Sauvignon Maciete Fumé, Gini	302
Sauvignon Ornella, Ornella Molon Traverso	310
Sauvignon Sansaia, Giacomo Montresor	333
Sauvignon Vulcaia, Inama	310
Sauvignon Vulcaia Fumé, Inama	310
Savuto, Odoardi	740
Savuto Sup. V. Mortilla, Odoardi	740
Saxa Calida, Il Paradiso	564
Scannagallo, Fatt. Santa Vittoria	477
Scarilius, La Pierotta	603
Scasso dei Cesari, Tenuta di Valgiano	496
Scasso del Bugiardo, Tenuta di Valgiano	496
Scav. Bianco Pian della Corte, Odoardi	740
Scav. V. Garrone, Odoardi	740
Scheria Rosso, Pietratorcia	705
Schiaffo, Colacicchi	662
Schiava Valle dei Laghi, Giulio Poli	248
Schidione, Tenuta Il Greppo	509
Schietto Chardonnay, Spadafora	755
Schietto Rosso, Spadafora	755
Schietto Syrah, Spadafora	755
Sciamareti, Villa Patrizia	601
Sciara di Villagrande Rosso, Barone di Villagrande	753
Scirus, Le Sorgenti	452
Scrio, Le Macchiole	456
Scyri, COS	759
Sebino Giuliana C., La Boscaiola	189
Sebino Rosso, Ricci Curbastro	181
Seduzione, Agr. Eubea - Fam. Sasso	711
Seifile, Fiorenzo Nada	143
Selvaggio Rosso, Terre di Shemir	764
Selvamaggio, Fatt. Villa La Selva	458
Selvascura, Guicciardini Strozzi - Fatt. Cusona	564
Selvato Rosso, Colli della Murgia	731
Ser Gioveto, Rocca delle Macìe	466
Ser Niccolò Solatio del Tani, Machiavelli	561
Ser Piero, Cantine Leonardo da Vinci	578
Seragio, Granducato	599
Seraselva, Poggio al Sole	577
Serpico, Feudi di San Gregorio	702
Serra delle Querce, D'Angelo	710
Serracavallo Rosso Ris., Serracavallo	738
Serralori Rosato, Antonio Argiolas	775
Sghiras, Le Sorgenti	452
Shardana, C.S. di Santadi	773
Shàrjs, Livio Felluga	363
Shiraz, Casale del Giglio	663
Sibiola Rosato, Cantine di Dolianova	769
Siepi, Cast. di Fonterutoli	463
Sigillo Primo Bianco, Antica Masseria del Sigillo	723
Sigillo Primo Chardonnay, Antica Masseria del Sigillo	723
Sigillo Rosso, Avide	748
Signorelli, La Calonica	530
Signorio Bianco, Barone La Lumia	761

Signorio Cadetto Rosso, Barone La Lumia	761
Simposia, Masseria Monaci	720
Simut, Monteacuto	213
Sire, Marco Maci	719
Sirio, V.lta	326
Sirius, Tenuta Giuncheo	164
Siro, Fatt. di Gratena	579
Siùm, La Viarte	400
Soave, La Cappuccina	302
Soave Cl., Balestri Valda	343
Soave Cl., Guerrieri Rizzardi	283
Soave Cl. Anguane, Tamellini	324
Soave Cl. Brognoligo, Cecilia Beretta	332
Soave Cl. Brognoligo V. T. , Cecilia Beretta	332
Soave Cl. Capitel Alto, Giacomo Montresor	333
Soave Cl. Castelcerino Rocca Sveva, Cant. di Soave	321
Soave Cl. Costeggiola, Guerrieri Rizzardi	283
Soave Cl. Le Bine, Tamellini	324
Soave Cl. Le Mandolare, Giobatta Dal Bosco	340
Soave Cl. Monteforte, Santi	291
Soave Cl. Montefoscarin, Santa Sofia	316
Soave Cl. Rocca Sveva, Cant. di Soave	321
Soave Cl. San Michele, Ca' Rugate	300
Soave Cl. Sanfederici, Santi	291
Soave Cl. Santepietre, Lamberti	339
Soave Cl. Sup., Cant. del Cast.	321
Soave Cl. Sup., Coffele	322
Soave Cl. Sup., Fattori & Graney	301
Soave Cl. Sup., Gini	302
Soave Cl. Sup., Leonildo Pieropan	323
Soave Cl. Sup., Prà	303
Soave Cl. Sup., Suavia	323
Soave Cl. Sup. Acini Soavi, Cant. del Cast.	321
Soave Cl. Sup. Alzari, Coffele	322
Soave Cl. Sup. Bucciato, Ca' Rugate	300
Soave Cl. Sup. Ca' Visco, Coffele	322
Soave Cl. Sup. Calvarino, Leonildo Pieropan	323
Soave Cl. Sup. Colbaraca, Masi	319
Soave Cl. Sup. Colle S. Antonio, Prà	303
Soave Cl. Sup. Contrada Salvarenza Vecchie Vigne, Gini	323
Soave Cl. Sup. Costalta, Santa Sofia	316
Soave Cl. Sup. Il Tirso, Marcato	342
Soave Cl. Sup. La Froscà, Gini	302
Soave Cl. Sup. La Ponsara, Carlo Bogoni	301
Soave Cl. Sup. La Rocca, Leonildo Pieropan	323
Soave Cl. Sup. Le Mandolare, Giobatta Dal Bosco	340
Soave Cl. Sup. Le Rive, Suavia	323
Soave Cl. Sup. Monte Alto, Ca' Rugate	300
Soave Cl. Sup. Monte Carbonare, Suavia	323
Soave Cl. Sup. Monte Carniga, Cant. del Cast.	321
Soave Cl. Sup. Monte Fiorentine, Ca' Rugate	300
Soave Cl. Sup. Monte Pressoni, Cant. del Cast.	321
Soave Cl. Sup. Monte Tondo, Monte Tondo	322
Soave Cl. Sup. Motto Piane, Fattori & Graney	301
Soave Cl. Sup. Pieve Vecchia, Fasoli	286
Soave Cl. Sup. Sereole, Bertani	304
Soave Cl. Sup. V. dello Stefano, Le Albare	340
Soave Cl. Sup. V. Ronchetto, Umberto Portinari	303
Soave Cl. Sup. Vigneti di Cà de Napa Domini Veneti, C.S. Valpolicella	306
Soave Cl. Sup. Vigneti di Foscarino, Inama	310
Soave Cl. Sup. Vigneti in Casette Foscarin, Monte Tondo	322
Soave Cl. Sup. Vigneti Monte Foscarino Le Bine, Giuseppe Campagnola	293
Soave Cl. Sup. Vign. Calvarino, Leonildo Pieropan	323
Soave Cl. Sup. Vign. Du Lot, Inama	310
Soave Cl. Sup. Vign. La Rocca, Leonildo Pieropan	323
Soave Cl. Sup. Vign. Monte Grande, Prà	303
Soave Cl. Sup. Vin Soave, Inama	310
Soave Cl. Vigneti di Montegrande, Pasqua Vigneti e Cantine	333
Soave Cl. Villa Rasina, Cant. di Soave	321
Soave Spumante Brut, Balestri Valda	343
Soave Spumante Brut, Monte Tondo	322
Soave Sup., Tamellini	324
Soave Sup. Fontégo, La Cappuccina	302
Soave Sup. La Broia, Roccolo Grassi	297
Soave Sup. Mito, Monte Tondo	322
Soave Sup. Monte Cerani, Tenuta Sant'Antonio	297
Soave Sup. S. Brizio, La Cappuccina	302
Soave Sup. S. Stefano, Umberto Portinari	303
Soave Sup. V. Albare Doppia Maturazione Ragionata, Umberto Portinari	303
Soave Sup. V. dello Stefano, Le Albare	340
Sodole, Guicciardini Strozzi - Fatt. Cusona	564
Soianello, Ursula e Peter Mock	606
Solaia, Marchesi Antinori	475
Solalto, Le Pupille	492
Solare, Capannelle	479
Solare, La Pierotta	603
Solaria Ionica Ferrari, Accademia dei Racemi	727
Solarianne, Solaria - Cencioni	519
Solatia, Tenim. Ruffino	548
Solatio, Borgo Casignano	584
Solativo, Ferrando	87
Soldati La Scolca Brut, La Scolca	155
Sole d'Autunno, Maso Martis	243
Sole dei Padri, Spadafora	755
Sole di Sesta, Cottanera	748
Sole e Vento, Marco De Bartoli	749
Soleada Bianco, Curatolo	761
Soleggio, Vini Pallavicini	672
Solengo, Argiano	499
Solinero, Tenute Rapitalà	746
Solitario, Cascina delle Terre Rosse	168
Solleone, Palagetto	593
Solo Sangiovese, Fatt. Dezi	633
Soloio, Casa Emma	453
Solopaca Bianco Guiscardo, Corte Normanna	705
Solopaca Rosso Bosco Caldaia, Antica Masseria Venditti	692
Somigliò, Giovanni Palombo	663
Sono Montenidoli, Montenidoli	567
Sorbino, Le Calvane	536
Sorripa, San Niccolò a Pisignano	601
Sottobosco, Palagetto	568
Sovana Rosso, Tenuta Roccaccia	546
Sovana Rosso Ripa, Podere Sopra la Ripa	572
Sovana Rosso Sup. Franze, Sassotondo	572
Sovana Rosso Terre Eteree, La Busattina	589
Spante, Terre del Sillabo	496
Spargolo, Famiglia Cecchi	464
Spartito, Castellare di Castellina	463
Spigàu, Fausto De Andreis	163
Spigàu Crociata, Fausto De Andreis	163
Spumante Brut , Zamuner	343
Spumante Brut Riserva Waldaz, Adami	335
Spumante Cl. Extra Dry Cuvée Testarossa Jubilée , C.S. La Versa	207
Spumante Cl. Cuvée Testarossa Extra Dry, C.S. La Versa	207
Spumante Extra Brut Vign. del Convento, F.lli Bortolin Spumanti	327
Spumante Haderburg Brut, Haderburg	274
Spumante M. Cl. Brut Ris. Giuseppe Contratto, Contratto	55
Squinzano, Santa Barbara	733
Squinzano, Vinicola Resta	734
Squinzano l'Evangelista, Accademia dei Racemi	727
Squinzano Rosso, Cant. Due Palme	719
Squinzano Rosso, Vinicola Mediterranea	734
Squinzano Rosso Zephir, Marco Maci	719
Stàngja Rosso, Franco Visintin	419
Stefano Antonucci Rosso, Santa Barbara	611
Stefano Ferrucci Vino da Uve Stramature, Stefano Ferrucci	425
Stella del Teso, Fatt. del Teso	524
Sterpigno Merlot, Giovanna Madonia	422
Stielle, Rocca di Castagnoli	483
Stignano, San Vincenti	485
Stoppa, La Stoppa	439
Strale, Gualdo del Re	573
Stravino di Stravino, Pravis	230
Stroncoli, Giacomo Marengo	594
Su Baroni, Vitivincola Su Baroni	770
Su Gucciu, Gostolai	773
Subertum, Lorella Ambrosini	573
Sud, Le Vigne di San Pietro	325
Suffragium, Az. Agr. Claudio Morelli	617
Sul Bric, Franco M. Martinetti	141
Sulky, Sardus Pater	774
Sulleria Bianco, Feudo Solaria	763
Sulleria Passito, Feudo Solaria	763
Sulleria Rosso, Feudo Solaria	763
Susumaniello Sum Torre Guaceto , Accademia dei Racemi	727
Syra's, Cabanon	196
Syrae, Pravis	230
Syrah, Castagnoli	462
Syrah, Castelli del Grevepesa	558
Syrah, Isole e Olena	454
Syrah, Aziende Vinicole Miceli	755
Syrah, Carlo Pellegrino	751
Syrah, Planeta	752
Syrah, Poggio al Sole	577
Syrah, Cast. di Poppiano	537
Syrah, Cantine Torrevecchia	744
Syrah, Vallarom	225
Syrah, Villa Arceno	473
Syrah, Villa Pillo	485
Syrah Case Via, Tenuta Fontodi	541
Syrah Cicogna, Domenico & F.lli Cavazza	299
Syrah Mandrarossa, Settesoli	752
Taburno Coda di Volpe, Cant. del Taburno	693
Taburno Coda di Volpe, Fatt. La Rivolta	690
Taburno Falanghina, Cant. del Taburno	693
Taburno Falanghina, Fatt. La Rivolta	690
Taburno Falanghina, Fontanavecchia	703
Taburno Falanghina Folius, Cant. del Taburno	693
Taburno Greco, Cant. del Taburno	693
Taburno Rosso Calidonio, Ocone	706
Tal Lûc, Lis Neris - Pecorari	411
Talenti Rosso, Talenti	520
Talento Banfi Brut M. Cl., Vigne Regali	140
Talento Brut, Carpenè Malvolti	338
Talento Cuvée del Fondatore Eliseo Bisol, Desiderio Bisol & Figli	326
Talia, Salvatore Murana	756
Tanca Su Conti, C.S. della Trexenta	775
Tanè, Cant. Valle dell'Acate	744
Tarabuso, Torre Quarto	720
Tarasco Passito, Cornarea	151
Tarlo Rosso, Anzivino	80
Tassinaia, Cast. del Terriccio	467
Tato, Sant'Elena	385
Tauleto Sangiovese, Umberto Cesari	425
Taurasi, Pietracupa	696
Taurasi, Villa Raiano	701
Taurasi Fatica Contadina, Terredora	697
Taurasi Piano di Montevergine, Feudi di San Gregorio	702
Taurasi Piano di Montevergine Ris., Feudi di San Gregorio	702

Taurasi Radici, Mastroberardino	690
Taurasi Ris., Di Meo	699
Taurasi Selve di Luoti, Feudi di San Gregorio	702
Taurasi V. Cinque Querce, Salvatore Molettieri	697
Taurasi V. Cinque Querce Ris., Salvatore Molettieri	697
Taurasi V. Macchia dei Goti, Antonio Caggiano	702
Tauri, Antonio Caggiano	702
Taurus, Paolo Cocco	780
Tazzelenghe, Jacùss	414
Tazzelenghe Ris., Tenuta Beltrame	346
TdF Bianco, Bellavista	192
TdF Bianco, F.lli Berlucchi	190
TdF Bianco, Guido Berlucchi & C.	190
TdF Bianco, Bersi Serlini	204
TdF Bianco, Tenuta Castellino	187
TdF Bianco, Catturich Ducco	219
TdF Bianco, Cavalleri	193
TdF Bianco, Battista Cola	212
TdF Bianco, Contadi Castaldi	178
TdF Bianco, Lorenzo Faccoli & Figli	188
TdF Bianco, Ferghettina	194
TdF Bianco , Agr. Gatta	215
TdF Bianco , Enrico Gatti	194
TdF Bianco, Il Mosnel	203
TdF Bianco, La Boscaiola	189
TdF Bianco , La Montina	200
TdF Bianco, Lantieri de Paratico	181
TdF Bianco, Lo Sparviere	201
TdF Bianco, Ronco Calino	186
TdF Bianco, San Cristoforo	195
TdF Bianco, Ugo Vezzoli	219
TdF Bianco, Villa	201
TdF Bianco Anna, La Boscaiola	189
TdF Bianco Antica Cant. Fratta, Guido Berlucchi & C.	190
TdF Bianco Augustus, Uberti	195
TdF Bianco Campo di Marte, CastelFaglia	185
TdF Bianco Campolarga, Il Mosnel	203
TdF Bianco Colzano, Lantieri de Paratico	181
TdF Bianco Convento dell'Annunciata, Bellavista	192
TdF Bianco Curtefranca, Barone Pizzini	189
TdF Bianco Curtefranca, Ricci Curbastro	181
TdF Bianco dei Frati Priori, Uberti	195
TdF Bianco della Seta, Monzio Compagnoni	191
TdF Bianco Dossi delle Querce, F.lli Berlucchi	190
TdF Bianco Favento, Ferghettina	194
TdF Bianco Febo, Agr. Gatta	215
TdF Bianco La Masnadora, La Masnadora	219
TdF Bianco La Tinaia Antica Cant. Fratta, Guido Berlucchi & C.	190
TdF Bianco Le Arzelle, Guido Berlucchi & C.	190
TdF Bianco Lo Sparviere, Lo Sparviere	201
TdF Bianco Manca Pane, Contadi Castaldi	178
TdF Bianco Maria Medici, Uberti	195
TdF Bianco Pian della Villa, Villa	201
TdF Bianco Pio Elemosiniere, Bredasole	219
TdF Bianco Rampaneto, Cavalleri	193
TdF Bianco Ronchello, Majolini	203
TdF Bianco Ronco della Seta, Monzio Compagnoni	191
TdF Bianco Solicano, Tenuta Castellino	187
TdF Bianco Sottobosco, Ronco Calino	186
TdF Bianco Sulif, Il Mosnel	203
TdF Bianco Uccellanda, Bellavista	192
TdF Bianco V. Saline, Cornaleto	212
TdF Bianco V. Bosco Alto, Ricci Curbastro	181
TdF Chardonnay, Ca' del Bosco	193
TdF Chardonnay Polzina, Barone Pizzini	189
TdF Curtefranca Bianco, Ca' del Bosco	193
TdF Curtefranca Rosso, Ca' del Bosco	193
TdF Gatti Bianco, Enrico Gatti	194
TdF Rosso, Bellavista	192
TdF Rosso, F.lli Berlucchi	190
TdF Rosso, Bersi Serlini	204
TdF Rosso, Tenuta Castellino	187
TdF Rosso, Cavalleri	193
TdF Rosso, Contadi Castaldi	178
TdF Rosso, Lorenzo Faccoli & Figli	188
TdF Rosso, Ferghettina	194
TdF Rosso, Il Mosnel	203
TdF Rosso, La Boscaiola	189
TdF Rosso, La Montina	200
TdF Rosso, Lantieri de Paratico	181
TdF Rosso, Principe Banfi Podere Pio IX	216
TdF Rosso, Ronco Calino	186
TdF Rosso, San Cristoforo	195
TdF Rosso, Ugo Vezzoli	219
TdF Rosso, Giuseppe Vezzoli	196
TdF Rosso Augustus, Uberti	195
TdF Rosso Baldoc, Cornaleto	212
TdF Rosso Capineto, Tenuta Castellino	187
TdF Rosso Colzano, Lantieri de Paratico	181
TdF Rosso Curtefranca, Barone Pizzini	189
TdF Rosso Curtefranca, Ricci Curbastro	181
TdF Rosso dei Dossi, La Montina	200
TdF Rosso Dordaro, Majolini	203
TdF Rosso Fontecolo, Il Mosnel	203
TdF Rosso Gradoni, Villa	201
TdF Rosso Il Sergnana, Lo Sparviere	201
TdF Rosso La Masnadora, La Masnadora	219
TdF Rosso Ronco della Seta, Monzio Compagnoni	191
TdF Rosso Ruc di Gnoc, Majolini	203
TdF Rosso Santella del Gröm, Ricci Curbastro	181
TdF Rosso Tajardino, Cavalleri	193
TdF Rosso Tamino, Battista Cola	212
TdF Rosso Vino del Cacciatore, Lo Sparviere	201
Tegolaro, Carlo e Marco Carini	655
Templaria, Cant. Coop. Castignanese	614
Tenuta Belguardo, Tenuta Belguardo	588
Tenuta Casabianca, Fatt. Casabianca	539
Tenuta di Testarossa Bianco, Franco Pasetti	678
Tenuta di Trinoro, Tenuta di Trinoro	603
Tenuta San Michele, Barone Scammacca del Murgo	764
Teroldego Armilo, Nilo Bolognani	231
Teroldego Atesino Cernidor, Vigneti delle Meridiane	244
Teroldego Rotaliano, Cant. Rotaliana	235
Teroldego Rotaliano, Casata Monfort	247
Teroldego Rotaliano, Marco Donati	233
Teroldego Rotaliano, F.lli Dorigati - Metius	234
Teroldego Rotaliano, Cipriano Fedrizzi	247
Teroldego Rotaliano, Foradori	236
Teroldego Rotaliano, Zanini	247
Teroldego Rotaliano, Zeni	241
Teroldego Rotaliano Bagolari, Marco Donati	233
Teroldego Rotaliano Bottega de' Vinai, Cavit - Cons. di Cantine Sociali	242
Teroldego Rotaliano Canevarie, Cant. Rotaliana	235
Teroldego Rotaliano Clesurare, Cant. Rotaliana	235
Teroldego Rotaliano Diedri Ris., F.lli Dorigati - Metius	234
Teroldego Rotaliano Due Vigneti, Cipriano Fedrizzi	247
Teroldego Rotaliano Le Cervare Ris. , Zanini	247
Teroldego Rotaliano Maso Camorz, Endrizzi	248
Teroldego Rotaliano Maso Cervara, Cavit - Cons. di Cantine Sociali	242
Teroldego Rotaliano Maso Scari, Barone de Cles	235
Teroldego Rotaliano Millesimato, MezzaCorona	234
Teroldego Rotaliano Pieve Francescana, Cant. Rotaliana	235
Teroldego Rotaliano Pini, Zeni	241
Teroldego Rotaliano Ris., Cant. Rotaliana	235
Teroldego Rotaliano Ris., MezzaCorona	234
Teroldego Rotaliano Ris., Villa de Varda	247
Teroldego Rotaliano Sangue del Drago, Marco Donati	233
Teroldego Rotaliano Sel. Maioliche, MezzaCorona	234
Teroldego Rotaliano Sup., Gaierhof	237
Terra Antica, Terra Antica	596
Terra dei Rovi Bianco, Luigino Dal Maso	299
Terra dei Rovi Rosso, Luigino Dal Maso	299
Terra di Lavoro, Galardi	701
Terra Mala Vigne Storiche, C.S. Giogantinu	767
Terra Saliosa, C.S. Giogantinu	767
Terrano Tipico, Castelvecchio	405
Terrato, Il Mandorlo	559
Terre Brune, C.S. di Santadi	773
Terre Cerase, Villa Matilde	693
Terre d'Agala, Duca di Salaparuta - Vini Corvo	747
Terre dei Cascinieri, Wandanna	525
Terre dei Forti Enantio, Letrari	239
Terre del Guiscardo, Antica Masseria del Sigillo	723
Terre del Volturno Aglianico Zicorrà, Cantine Caputo	691
Terre del Volturno Casavecchia Rosso, Vestini - Campagnano	691
Terre del Volturno Pallagrello Bianco, Vestini - Campagnano	691
Terre del Volturno Pallagrello Bianco Le Ortole, Vestini - Campagnano	691
Terre del Volturno Pallagrello Nero, Vestini - Campagnano	691
Terre del Volturno Vado Ceraso Rosato, Vestini - Campagnano	691
Terre dell'Istrice, Baglio San Vincenzo	762
Terre di Galatrona, Fatt. Petrolo	538
Terre di Ginestra 651, Calatrasi - Accademia del Sole	757
Terre di Ginestra Bianco, Calatrasi - Accademia del Sole	757
Terre di Ginestra Catarratto, Calatrasi - Accademia del Sole	757
Terre di Ginestra Nero d'Avola, Calatrasi - Accademia del Sole	757
Terre di Giulia, Feotto dello Jato	764
Terre di Maria, Maurigi	757
Terre di Melona, Mazziotti	664
Terre di Sofia, Maurigi	757
Terre di Tufi, Teruzzi & Puthod	569
Terre Lontane, Librandi	737
Terricci, Lanciola	494
Terricci Chardonnay, Lanciola	494
Terso Bianco, Marchesi Fumanelli	342
Tertium, Cant. Cerveteri	666
Terziere, Massa Vecchia	497
Tesauro Passito Bianco, C.S. della Valpantena	334
Testal, AngeloNicolis e Figli	315
Testamatta, Bibi Graetz	586
Thaora Rosato, C.S. del Vermentino	771
Thovara Passito Bianco, Piovene Porto Godi	336
Tigiolo Rosso, Lorenzo Begali	314
Tignanello, Marchesi Antinori	475
Tinscvil, Cast. di Monsanto	455
Titanum, V.vecchia	554
Tizzonero, La Carraia	652
Toar, Masi	319
Torcularia Rosso, Carra	433
Torgaio, Tenim. Ruffino	548
Torgiano Bianco, Cast. di Antignano - Brogal Vini	655
Torgiano Bianco Torre di Giano, Lungarotti	657
Torgiano Cabernet Sauvignon, Cast. di Antignano - Brogal Vini	655
Torgiano Rosso, Cast. di Antignano - Brogal Vini	655
Torgiano Rosso Ris., Cast. di Antignano - Brogal Vini	655
Torgiano Rosso Ris. Santa Caterina, Cast. di Antignano - Brogal Vini	655
Torgiano Rosso Rubesco, Lungarotti	657
Torgiano Rosso V. Monticchio Ris., Lungarotti	657
Tormaresca Chardonnay, Tormaresca	729
Tormaresca Rosso, Tormaresca	729

Torre del Noce Bianco, Marco Donati	233
Torre della Sirena, Conti Sertoli Salis	209
Torre di Ciardo, Marchesi Torrigiani	455
Torre Ercolana, Colacicchi	662
Torricella, Barone Ricasoli	479
Torrione, Fatt. Petrolo	538
Toscoforte, Cast. di Poppiano	537
Traluce, Tenuta Le Velette	653
Traminer, Ornella Molon Traverso	310
Traminer, San Vettore	587
Traminer Aromatico, Vinnaioli Jermann	380
Tramonto d'Oca, Poggio Bonelli	471
Trappoline, Coltibuono	480
Trasgaia, Villa Trasqua	583
Tre Filer, Ca' dei Frati	208
Tre Fonti, Tenuta Valdipiatta	534
Trebbiano d'Abruzzo, Tenuta Cataldi Madonna	680
Trebbiano d'Abruzzo, Fatt. La Valentina	684
Trebbiano d'Abruzzo, Lepore	677
Trebbiano d'Abruzzo, Gianni Masciarelli	684
Trebbiano d'Abruzzo, Camillo Montori	678
Trebbiano d'Abruzzo, Bruno Nicodemi	680
Trebbiano d'Abruzzo, Edoardo Valentini	679
Trebbiano d'Abruzzo Altare, Marramiero	683
Trebbiano d'Abruzzo Anima, Marramiero	683
Trebbiano d'Abruzzo Bacco, Bruno Nicodemi	680
Trebbiano d'Abruzzo Colle della Corte, Orlandi Contucci Ponno	683
Trebbiano d'Abruzzo Colle Maggio, Torre Zambra	688
Trebbiano d'Abruzzo Colle Secco, Cant. Tollo	685
Trebbiano d'Abruzzo Dama, Marramiero	683
Trebbiano d'Abruzzo Fatt. Pasetti, Franco Pasetti	678
Trebbiano d'Abruzzo Fonte Cupa, Camillo Montori	678
Trebbiano d'Abruzzo Le Vigne, Faraone	679
Trebbiano d'Abruzzo Marina Cvetic, Gianni Masciarelli	684
Trebbiano d'Abruzzo Natum, Agriverde	681
Trebbiano d'Abruzzo Pietrosa, Sarchese Dora	682
Trebbiano d'Abruzzo Preludio, Valori	688
Trebbiano d'Abruzzo Riseis, Agriverde	681
Trebbiano d'Abruzzo S. Maria dell'Arco, Faraone	679
Trebbiano d'Abruzzo Sel., Bruno Nicodemi	680
Trebbiano d'Abruzzo Terra d'Aligi, Spinelli	686
Trebbiano d'Abruzzo V. Corvino, Contesa di Rocco Pasetti	682
Trebbiano di Romagna V. del Rio, Tre Monti	432
Trebbiano di Romagna Vign. Parolino, Umberto Cesari	425
Trebianco V.T., Cast. dei Rampolla	540
Trebulanum, Fatt. Pontepellegrino	698
Trentino Bianco, Cant. Rotaliana	235
Trentino Bianco Castel San Michele, Ist. Agr. Provinciale San Michele all'Adige	240
Trentino Bianco Résorso Le Comete, C.S. di Nomi	248
Trentino Bianco San Siro, Pisoni	230
Trentino Bianco Sommolago, Madonna delle Vittorie	246
Trentino Cabernet, Cesconi	231
Trentino Cabernet, Armando Simoncelli	240
Trentino Cabernet, Vallarom	225
Trentino Cabernet Fratagranda, Pravis	230
Trentino Cabernet Grener, F.lli Dorigati - Metius	234
Trentino Cabernet Romeo, Castel Noarna	236
Trentino Cabernet Sauvignon, Nicola Balter	238
Trentino Cabernet Sauvignon, Concilio	244
Trentino Cabernet Sauvignon, Letrari	239
Trentino Cabernet Sauvignon, Alessandro Secchi	224
Trentino Cabernet Sauvignon, Vallis Agri	226
Trentino Cabernet Sauvignon Marognon, Longariva	239
Trentino Cabernet Sauvignon Marognon Ris., Longariva	239
Trentino Cabernet Sauvignon Mercuria, Castel Noarna	236
Trentino Cabernet Sauvignon Ritratti, La Vis	232
Trentino Cabernet Sauvignon Rosso di Pila, Maso Cantanghel	227
Trentino Cabernet Sauvignon Vign. San Bartolomeo Ris., Vigneti delle Meridiane	244
Trentino Chardonnay, C.S. di Avio	224
Trentino Chardonnay, Barone de Cles	235
Trentino Chardonnay, Riccardo Battistotti	237
Trentino Chardonnay, Nilo Bolognani	231
Trentino Chardonnay, Cesconi	231
Trentino Chardonnay, Concilio	244
Trentino Chardonnay, Conti Bossi Fedrigotti	238
Trentino Chardonnay, Dalzocchio	248
Trentino Chardonnay, de Tarczal	229
Trentino Chardonnay, V.iolo Giuseppe Fanti	232
Trentino Chardonnay, Madonna delle Vittorie	246
Trentino Chardonnay, Maso Furli	233
Trentino Chardonnay, MezzaCorona	234
Trentino Chardonnay, Pojer & Sandri	228
Trentino Chardonnay, Ist. Agr. Provinciale San Michele all'Adige	240
Trentino Chardonnay, Arcangelo Sandri	246
Trentino Chardonnay, Armando Simoncelli	240
Trentino Chardonnay, Cant. Toblino	226
Trentino Chardonnay, Vigneti delle Meridiane	244
Trentino Chardonnay Bottega de' Vinai, Cavit - Cons. di Cantine Sociali	242
Trentino Chardonnay Campo Grande, Castel Noarna	236
Trentino Chardonnay Canevarie, Cant. Rotaliana	235
Trentino Chardonnay Costa Erta, Gaierhof	237
Trentino Chardonnay di Faedo, Graziano Fontana	228
Trentino Chardonnay L'Incanto, Maso Martis	243
Trentino Chardonnay L'Opera, Grigoletti	247
Trentino Chardonnay Maso Guà, Concilio	244
Trentino Chardonnay Praistel, Longariva	239
Trentino Chardonnay Ravina, Vigneti delle Meridiane	244
Trentino Chardonnay Ritratti, La Vis	232
Trentino Chardonnay Robur, V.iolo Giuseppe Fanti	232
Trentino Chardonnay V. Brioni, Vallarom	225
Trentino Chardonnay V. Piccola, Maso Cantanghel	227
Trentino Chardonnay Vign. Capitel, Armani	287
Trentino Chardonnay Villa Gentilotti, Lunelli	243
Trentino Chardonnay Villa Margon, Lunelli	243
Trentino Lagrein, Barone de Cles	235
Trentino Lagrein, Cipriano Fedrizzi	247
Trentino Lagrein, Arcangelo Sandri	246
Trentino Lagrein, Armando Simoncelli	240
Trentino Lagrein di Faedo, Graziano Fontana	228
Trentino Lagrein Dunkel Bottega de' Vinai, Cavit - Cons. di Cantine Sociali	242
Trentino Lagrein Rosato, F.lli Dorigati - Metius	234
Trentino Lagrein Rubino Fratte Alte, Marco Donati	233
Trentino Lagrein Scuro, Barone de Cles	235
Trentino Lagrein Scuro, Cant. Toblino	226
Trentino Lagrein V. Le Vallette, Francesco Poli	248
Trentino Marzemino, Accademia del Vino Cadelaghet	246
Trentino Marzemino, C.S. di Avio	224
Trentino Marzemino, Riccardo Battistotti	237
Trentino Marzemino, Conti Bossi Fedrigotti	238
Trentino Marzemino, de Tarczal	229
Trentino Marzemino, Grigoletti	247
Trentino Marzemino, Letrari	239
Trentino Marzemino, C.S. di Nomi	248
Trentino Marzemino, Alessandro Secchi	224
Trentino Marzemino, Armando Simoncelli	240
Trentino Marzemino, Enrico Spagnolli	229
Trentino Marzemino, Vallarom	225
Trentino Marzemino Albarel, Villa de Varda	247
Trentino Marzemino d'Isera Husar, de Tarczal	229
Trentino Marzemino Etichetta Verde, Cant. d'Isera	247
Trentino Marzemino Maso Romani, Cavit - Cons. di Cantine Sociali	242
Trentino Marzemino Mozart, Concilio	244
Trentino Marzemino Poiema, Eugenio Rosi	245
Trentino Marzemino Sel., Letrari	239
Trentino Marzemino Verdini, Riccardo Battistotti	237
Trentino Marzemino V. dei Ziresi, Vallis Agri	226
Trentino Marzemino V. Fornas, Vallis Agri	226
Trentino Merlot, Riccardo Battistotti	237
Trentino Merlot, Cesconi	231
Trentino Merlot, Concilio	244
Trentino Merlot, Tenuta San Leonardo	225
Trentino Merlot, Alessandro Secchi	224
Trentino Merlot Antica V. di Nomi, Grigoletti	247
Trentino Merlot Antichi Portali , C.S. di Nomi	248
Trentino Merlot Borgo Sacco, Vallis Agri	226
Trentino Merlot Campiano, de Tarczal	229
Trentino Merlot Ravina, Vigneti delle Meridiane	244
Trentino Merlot Ritratti, La Vis	232
Trentino Merlot Tajapreda, Maso Cantanghel	227
Trentino Merlot Tovi, Longariva	239
Trentino Moscato, Vallis Agri	226
Trentino Moscato Giallo, Nilo Bolognani	231
Trentino Moscato Giallo, Enrico Spagnolli	229
Trentino Moscato Rosa, Riccardo Battistotti	237
Trentino Moscato Rosa, Endrizzi	248
Trentino Moscato Rosa, Letrari	239
Trentino Moscato Rosa, Zeni	241
Trentino Müller Thurgau, Nilo Bolognani	231
Trentino Müller Thurgau, MezzaCorona	234
Trentino Müller Thurgau, Arcangelo Sandri	246
Trentino Müller Thurgau, Enrico Spagnolli	229
Trentino Müller Thurgau, Cant. Toblino	226
Trentino Müller Thurgau, Zeni	241
Trentino Müller Thurgau Bottega de' Vinai, Cavit - Cons. di Cantine Sociali	242
Trentino Müller Thurgau dei Settecento, Gaierhof	237
Trentino Müller Thurgau di Faedo, Graziano Fontana	228
Trentino Müller Thurgau Le Croci, Zeni	241
Trentino Müller Thurgau Palai, Pojer & Sandri	228
Trentino Müller Thurgau Roncola, Villa de Varda	247
Trentino Müller Thurgau St. Thomà, Pravis	230
Trentino Nosiola, Nilo Bolognani	231
Trentino Nosiola, Castel Noarna	236
Trentino Nosiola, Cesconi	231
Trentino Nosiola, Marco Donati	233
Trentino Nosiola, V.iolo Giuseppe Fanti	232
Trentino Nosiola, Pisoni	230
Trentino Nosiola, Giovanni Poli	248
Trentino Nosiola, Enrico Spagnolli	229
Trentino Nosiola, Cant. Toblino	226
Trentino Nosiola, Vallis Agri	226
Trentino Nosiola, Zeni	241
Trentino Nosiola Casot, Castel Noarna	236
Trentino Nosiola V. Sottovi, Francesco Poli	248
Trentino Pinot Bianco, de Tarczal	229
Trentino Pinot Bianco, Ist. Agr. Provinciale San Michele all'Adige	240
Trentino Pinot Bianco, Armando Simoncelli	240
Trentino Pinot Bianco Pergole, Longariva	239
Trentino Pinot Bianco Sorti, Zeni	241
Trentino Pinot Grigio, C.S. di Avio	224
Trentino Pinot Grigio , Cant. Rotaliana	235
Trentino Pinot Grigio, Cesconi	231
Trentino Pinot Grigio, Conti Bossi Fedrigotti	238
Trentino Pinot Grigio, F.lli Dorigati - Metius	234
Trentino Pinot Grigio, Gaierhof	237
Trentino Pinot Grigio , Madonna delle Vittorie	246
Trentino Pinot Grigio, Ist. Agr. Provinciale San Michele all'Adige	240

Voce	Pag.
Trentino Pinot Grigio, Armando Simoncelli	240
Trentino Pinot Grigio, Cant. Toblino	226
Trentino Pinot Grigio Bastie, Vigneti delle Meridiane	244
Trentino Pinot Grigio Maso Guà, Concilio	244
Trentino Pinot Grigio Maso Poli, Gaierhof	237
Trentino Pinot Grigio Polin, Pravis	230
Trentino Pinot Grigio Ritratti, La Vis	232
Trentino Pinot Grigio V. Reselé, Vallis Agri	226
Trentino Pinot Nero, Accademia del Vino Cadelaghet	246
Trentino Pinot Nero, C.S. di Avio	224
Trentino Pinot Nero, Concilio	244
Trentino Pinot Nero, Maso Martis	243
Trentino Pinot Nero, MezzaCorona	234
Trentino Pinot Nero, Pelz & Piffer	246
Trentino Pinot Nero, Enrico Spagnolli	229
Trentino Pinot Nero, Cant. Toblino	226
Trentino Pinot Nero, Vallarom	225
Trentino Pinot Nero di Faedo, Graziano Fontana	228
Trentino Pinot Nero Maso Montalto, Lunelli	243
Trentino Pinot Nero Maso Poli, Gaierhof	237
Trentino Pinot Nero Pian di Cast., Endrizzi	248
Trentino Pinot Nero Ris., Pojer & Sandri	228
Trentino Pinot Nero Spiazol, Zeni	241
Trentino Pinot Nero Zabini, Maso Cantanghel	227
Trentino Rebo, F.lli Dorigati - Metius	234
Trentino Rebo, Pisoni	230
Trentino Rebo, Cant. Toblino	226
Trentino Rebo Rigotti, Pravis	230
Trentino Riesling, Pelz & Piffer	246
Trentino Riesling Italico, Gaierhof	237
Trentino Riesling Renano, Marco Donati	233
Trentino Rosso Castel San Michele, Ist. Agr. Provinciale San Michele all'Adige	240
Trentino Rosso Esegesi, Eugenio Rosi	245
Trentino Rosso Maso Le Viane, Lunelli	243
Trentino Rosso Maso Lodron, Letrari	239
Trentino Rosso Monastero, I st. Agr. Provinciale San Michele all'Adige	240
Trentino Rosso Mori Vecio, Concilio	244
Trentino Rosso Navesèl, Armando Simoncelli	240
Trentino Rosso Résorso Le Comete, C.S. di Nomi	248
Trentino Rosso Ris., C.S. di Avio	224
Trentino Rosso San Siro, Pisoni	230
Trentino Rosso Sentieri Sel. 907, Cant. d'Isera	247
Trentino Rosso Tebro, Enrico Spagnolli	229
Trentino Rosso Tre Cesure, Longariva	239
Trentino Rosso Tre Cesure Sel. 25°., Longariva	239
Trentino Sauvignon, Nilo Bolognani	231
Trentino Sauvignon, Cesconi	231
Trentino Sauvignon, Maso Furli	233
Trentino Sauvignon, Ist. Agr. Provinciale San Michele all'Adige	240
Trentino Sauvignon, Zeni	241
Trentino Sauvignon di Faedo, Graziano Fontana	228
Trentino Sauvignon Solitaire, Maso Cantanghel	227
Trentino Sauvignon Villa San Nicolò, Lunelli	243
Trentino Sorni Bianco, La Vis	232
Trentino Sorni Bianco Maso Poli, Gaierhof	237
Trentino Sorni Rosso, La Vis	232
Trentino Traminer, Maso Bastie	245
Trentino Traminer, Pojer & Sandri	228
Trentino Traminer Aromatico, Barone de Cles	235
Trentino Traminer Aromatico, Casata Monfort	247
Trentino Traminer Aromatico, Cesconi	231
Trentino Traminer Aromatico, Conti Bossi Fedrigotti	238
Trentino Traminer Aromatico, Maso Furli	233
Trentino Traminer Aromatico, Arcangelo Sandri	246
Trentino Traminer Aromatico, Enrico Spagnolli	229
Trentino Traminer di Faedo, Graziano Fontana	228
Trentino Vendemmia Tardiva, C.S. di Avio	224
Trentino Vino Santo, Gino Pedrotti	227
Trentino Vino Santo, Pisoni	230
Trentino Vino Santo, Giovanni Poli	248
Trentino Vino Santo, Francesco Poli	248
Trentino Vino Santo, Cant. Toblino	226
Trentino Vino Santo Aréle, Cavit - Cons. di Cantine Sociali	242
Trento Accademia Ris., Accademia del Vino Cadelaghet	246
Trento Brut, Abate Nero	241
Trento Brut, Nicola Balter	238
Trento Brut, Ferrari	242
Trento Brut, Madonna delle Vittorie	246
Trento Brut, Maso Martis	243
Trento Brut, Armando Simoncelli	240
Trento Brut Firmato mill., Cavit - Cons. di Cantine Sociali	242
Trento Brut Incontri, Ferrari	242
Trento Brut M. Cl., Zeni	241
Trento Brut Maximum, Ferrari	242
Trento Brut Perlé, Ferrari	242
Trento Brut Perlé Rosé, Ferrari	242
Trento Brut Ris., Abate Nero	241
Trento Brut Ris., Maso Martis	243
Trento Brut Ris., Pisoni	230
Trento Brut Rosè, Maso Martis	243
Trento Extra Brut, Abate Nero	241
Trento Extra Dry, Abate Nero	241
Trento Graal, Cavit - Cons. di Cantine Sociali	242
Trento Methius Ris. F.lli Dorigati - Metius	234
Trento Riserva del Fondatore, Ist. Agr. Provinciale San Michele all'Adige	240
Trento Rotari Brut Arte Italiana, MezzaCorona	234
Trento Rotari Brut Ris., MezzaCorona	234
Trento Rotari Ris., MezzaCorona	234
Trescone, Lamborghini - La Fiorita	654
Trésor du Caveau, Institut Agricole Régional	16
Tricorno, Cast. di Poppiano	537
Trincerone, Tenuta Valdipiatta	534
Trisoru, Vitivincola Su Baroni	770
Tristo di Elisena Bianco, Cast. Fageto	628
Turbellari Malvasia Passito, Monte Cicogna	198
Turriga, Antonio Argiolas	775
Tuvara, Alberto Loi	769
Ucelut, Tenuta Pinni	420
Ucelut Bianco, Alessandro Vicentini Orgnani	393
Uis Blancis, Borc Dodòn	420
Uis Neris, Borc Dodòn	420
Umbria Aleatico Bartolomeo, Cant. dei Colli Amerini	640
Umbria Bianco, Podere Marella	658
Umbria Bianco Luna, Terre de' Trinci	645
Umbria Canaiolo, Fatt. Le Poggette	647
Umbria Grechetto, Bigi	650
Umbria Grechetto, Cardeto	651
Umbria Grechetto, Fatt. Le Poggette	647
Umbria Merlot, Terre del Carpine	646
Umbria Pinot Nero, Rocca di Fabbri	649
Umbria Rosso Cajo, Terre de' Trinci	645
Umbria Rosso Torre Maggiore, Fatt. Le Poggette	647
Umbria Rosso Vaglie, Vaglie	641
Umbria Sangiovese, Bigi	650
Umbria Sangiovese, La Carraia	652
Umbria Sangiovese Torraccio, Cant. dei Colli Amerini	640
Umbria Sauvignon, Tordimaro	660
Umbria Torrello, Tordimaro	660
Va' Pensiero, Zof	375
Vadum Caesaris, Vallarom	225
Val d'Arbia, Cast. di Volpaia	555
Val di Chiana Grechetto, Fatt. Santa Vittoria	477
Val di Chiana Poggio del Tempio, Fatt. Santa Vittoria	477
Val di Cornia, Villa Monte Rico	605
Val di Cornia Aleatico, Jacopo Banti	458
Val di Cornia Aleatico Amansio, Gualdo del Re	573
Val di Cornia Aleatico Stillo, Petricci del Pianta	605
Val di Cornia Bianco Centomini, Jacopo Banti	458
Val di Cornia Bianco Eliseo, Gualdo del Re	573
Val di Cornia Bianco Tabarò, Lorella Ambrosini	573
Val di Cornia Bianco Tuscanio, Bulichella	604
Val di Cornia Bianco V.nuova, Incontri	574
Val di Cornia Buca di Cleonte, Petricci del Pianta	605
Val di Cornia Diavolino Bianco, Le Pianacce	604
Val di Cornia Gualdo del Re Ris., Gualdo del Re	573
Val di Cornia Il Peccato Barrique, Jacopo Banti	458
Val di Cornia Lorenzo degli Incontri, Incontri	574
Val di Cornia Rosso Albatrone, Petricci del Pianta	605
Val di Cornia Rosso Barbicone, Russo	575
Val di Cornia Rosso Campalto, Jacopo Banti	458
Val di Cornia Rosso Ceppitaio, Russo	575
Val di Cornia Rosso Ceragiolo, Jacopo Banti	458
Val di Cornia Rosso Eliseo, Gualdo del Re	573
Val di Cornia Rosso Federico Primo, Gualdo del Re	573
Val di Cornia Rosso l'Rennero, Gualdo del Re	573
Val di Cornia Rosso Loco dei Frati, Il Bruscello	604
Val di Cornia Rosso Montepeloso, Montepeloso	574
Val di Cornia Rosso Quarzo di Rocca, Il Bruscello	604
Val di Cornia Rosso Rubizzo, Incontri	574
Val di Cornia Rosso Tabarò, Lorella Ambrosini	573
Val di Cornia Rosso Tuscanio, Bulichella	604
Val di Cornia Rosso Vinivo, Il V.le	599
Val di Cornia Subertum, Lorella Ambrosini	573
Val di Cornia Valentina, Gualdo del Re	573
Val di Cornia Vermentino Campo degli Albicocchi, Il V.le	599
Val di Cornia Vermentino Ildebrandino, Incontri	574
Val di Cornia Vermentino Poggio Angelica, Jacopo Banti	458
Val di Miez, Ronçùs	352
Val Polcevera Rosso Treipaexi, Andrea Enoteca Bruzzone	175
Valcalepio Bianco, C.S. Bergamasca	206
Valcalepio Bianco, Bonaldi - Cascina del Bosco	222
Valcalepio Bianco, Il Calepino	184
Valcalepio Bianco, La Tordela	210
Valcalepio Bianco Colle della Luna, Monzio Compagnoni	191
Valcalepio Bianco Libero, Tallarini	216
Valcalepio Bianco Vescovado, La Brugherata	207
Valcalepio Bianco Vescovado Sel., La Brugherata	207
Valcalepio Moscato Passito, La Tordela	210
Valcalepio Moscato Passito di Cenate Sotto Don Quijote, Monzio Compagnoni	191
Valcalepio Moscato Passito Perseo, C.S. Bergamasca	206
Valcalepio Rosso, C.S. Bergamasca	206
Valcalepio Rosso, Bonaldi - Cascina del Bosco	222
Valcalepio Rosso, Il Calepino	184
Valcalepio Rosso, La Tordela	210
Valcalepio Rosso, Medolago Albani	222
Valcalepio Rosso Akros Ris., C.S. Bergamasca	206
Valcalepio Rosso Colle del Calvario, Cast. di Grumello	217
Valcalepio Rosso Colle della Luna, Monzio Compagnoni	191
Valcalepio Rosso Messnero Ris., Le Corne	217
Valcalepio Rosso Ripa di Luna, Caminella	215
Valcalepio Rosso Ris., La Tordela	210
Valcalepio Rosso Ris., Medolago Albani	222
Valcalepio Rosso Ris. Doglio, La Brugherata	207
Valcalepio Rosso Ris. V. del Conte, C.S. Bergamasca	206
Valcalepio Rosso Riserva Akros V. La Tordela, C.S. Bergamasca	206
Valcalepio Rosso Riserva Akros Vign. Palma, C.S. Bergamasca	206
Valcalepio Rosso San Giovannino Ris., Tallarini	216
Valcalepio Rosso Surie, Il Calepino	184

Valcalepio Rosso Vescovado, La Brugherata	207
Valdadige Chardonnay Piccola Botte, Armani	287
Valdadige Pinot Grigio Vign. Corvara, Armani	287
Valdadige Pinot Grigio Vign. Fratte, Santa Sofia	316
Valdadige Quaiare, Le Fraghe	285
Valdenrico Passito, Rovellotti	86
Valdichiana Luna di Monte, San Luciano	522
Valentino Brut Zero Ris., Podere Rocche dei Manzoni	110
Valeo, Odoardi	740
Valle d'Aosta Blanc de Morgex et de La Salle, Cave du Vin Blanc	20
Valle d'Aosta Blanc de Morgex et de La Salle, Maison Albert Vevey	20
Valle d'Aosta Blanc de Morgex et de La Salle Rayon, Cave du Vin Blanc	20
Valle d'Aosta Chambave Moscato Passito, La Crotta di Vegneron	17
Valle d'Aosta Chambave Muscat, La Crotta di Vegneron	17
Valle d'Aosta Chardonnay, Anselmet	19
Valle d'Aosta Chardonnay Barrique, Institut Agricole Régional	16
Valle d'Aosta Chardonnay Cuvée Frissonnière Les Crêtes, Les Crêtes	17
Valle d'Aosta Chardonnay Cuvée Frissonnière Les Crêtes Cuvée Bois, Les Crêtes	17
Valle d'Aosta Chardonnay Élevé en Fût de Chêne, Anselmet	19
Valle d'Aosta Donnas Napoleone, Caves Cooperatives de Donnas	20
Valle d'Aosta Fumin, F.lli Grosjean	18
Valle d'Aosta Fumin, La Crotta di Vegneron	17
Valle d'Aosta Fumin Vigne La Tour, Les Crêtes	17
Valle d'Aosta Gamay, F.lli Grosjean	18
Valle d'Aosta Gamay, Lo Triolet - Marco Martin	18
Valle d'Aosta Müller Thurgau, Anselmet	19
Valle d'Aosta Müller Thurgau, Institut Agricole Régional	16
Valle d'Aosta Müller Thurgau, La Crotta di Vegneron	17
Valle d'Aosta Müller Thurgau , Gabriella Minuzzo	20
Valle d'Aosta Nus Malvoisie, La Crotta di Vegneron	17
Valle d'Aosta Nus Malvoisie Flétrì, La Crotta di Vegneron	17
Valle d'Aosta Nus Rouge, La Crotta di Vegneron	17
Valle d'Aosta Nus Rouge, Lo Triolet - Marco Martin	18
Valle d'Aosta Petit Rouge, Anselmet	19
Valle d'Aosta Petite Arvine, F.lli Grosjean	18
Valle d'Aosta Petite Arvine, Institut Agricole Régional	16
Valle d'Aosta Petite Arvine Vigne Champorette, Les Crêtes	17
Valle d'Aosta Petite Rouge, Di Barrò	19
Valle d'Aosta Pinot Gris, Institut Agricole Régional	16
Valle d'Aosta Pinot Gris Élevé en Fût de Chêne, Lo Triolet - Marco Martin	18
Valle d'Aosta Pinot Gris Lo Triolet, Lo Triolet - Marco Martin	18
Valle d'Aosta Pinot Noir, F.lli Grosjean	18
Valle d'Aosta Pinot Noir, Institut Agricole Régional	16
Valle d'Aosta Pinot Noir Élevé en Barrique, F.lli Grosjean	18
Valle d'Aosta Pinot Noir Élevé en Fût de Chêne, Anselmet	19
Valle d'Aosta Pinot Noir Vigne La Tour, Les Crêtes	17
Valle d'Aosta Prèmetta, Costantino Charrère	16
Valle d'Aosta Torrette, Anselmet	19
Valle d'Aosta Torrette, Costantino Charrère	16
Valle d'Aosta Torrette, F.lli Grosjean	18
Valle d'Aosta Torrette Sup., Di Barrò	19
Valle d'Aosta Torrette Sup. Élevé en Fût de Chêne, Anselmet	19
Valle d'Aosta Torrette Vigne Les Toules, Les Crêtes	17
Valle del Crati , Serracavallo	738
Valle del Crati Ris., Serracavallo	738
Vallocaia, Bindella	527
Valmora Rosso Terre di Braccio, Cantine Perusia	660
Valon, Ne. Ne.	151
Valpantena, C.S. della Valpantena	334
Valpantena Ripasso Falasco, C.S. della Valpantena	334
Valpantena Ritocco, C.S. della Valpantena	334
Valpantena Secco Bertani, Bertani	304
Valpantena Sup., C.S. della Valpantena	334
Valpolicella Ca' Fiui, Corte Sant'Alda	296
Valpolicella Cl., Stefano Accordini	313
Valpolicella Cl., Allegrini	288
Valpolicella Cl., Brigaldara	314
Valpolicella Cl., Luigi Brunelli	315
Valpolicella Cl., Corte Rugolin	294
Valpolicella Cl., F.lli Degani	295
Valpolicella Cl., Le Ragose	305
Valpolicella Cl., Le Salette	289
Valpolicella Cl., Giuseppe Lonardi	295
Valpolicella Cl., Angelox Nicolis e Figli	315
Valpolicella Cl., Novaia	296
Valpolicella Cl., F.lli Speri	316
Valpolicella Cl., Massimino Venturini	318
Valpolicella Cl., Villa Spinosa	307
Valpolicella Cl. Campo S. Lena, Raimondi-Villa Monteleone	320
Valpolicella Cl. Capitel della Crosara, Giacomo Montresor	333
Valpolicella Cl. Il Brolo, Villa Bellini	318
Valpolicella Cl. Sup., Tommaso Bussola	304
Valpolicella Cl. Sup., Corte Rugolin	294
Valpolicella Cl. Sup., F.lli Degani	295
Valpolicella Cl. Sup., I Scriani	339
Valpolicella Cl. Sup., Giuseppe Lonardi	295
Valpolicella Cl. Sup., Angelo Nicolis e Figli	315
Valpolicella Cl. Sup., Massimino Venturini	318
Valpolicella Cl. Sup., Viviani	307
Valpolicella Cl. Sup., Zenato	309
Valpolicella Cl. Sup. Acinatico, Stefano Accordini	313
Valpolicella Cl. Sup. Antanel, Villa Spinosa	307
Valpolicella Cl. Sup. Bure Alto, Aleardo Ferrari	343
Valpolicella Cl. Sup. Ca' Carnocchio, Le Salette	289
Valpolicella Cl. Sup. Campo Casal Vegri, Ca' La Bionda	293
Valpolicella Cl. Sup. Campo Morar, Viviani	307
Valpolicella Cl. Sup. Campo Praesel, Luigi Brunelli	315
Valpolicella Cl. Sup. Campo S. Vito, Raimondi-Villa Monteleone	320
Valpolicella Cl. Sup. Capitel dei Nicalò, F.lli Tedeschi	317
Valpolicella Cl. Sup. Cicilio, F.lli Degani	295
Valpolicella Cl. Sup. I Cantoni, Novaia	296
Valpolicella Cl. Sup. I Pianeti Il Sestante, Viticoltori Tommasi	317
Valpolicella Cl. Sup. I Progni, Le Salette	289
Valpolicella Cl. Sup. I Quadretti, La Giaretta	340
Valpolicella Cl. Sup. Il Taso, Villa Bellini	318
Valpolicella Cl. Sup. Jago, Villa Spinosa	307
Valpolicella Cl. Sup. La Casetta di Ettore Righetti Domini Veneti, C.S. Valpolicella	306
Valpolicella Cl. Sup. La Roverina, F.lli Speri	316
Valpolicella Cl. Sup. Le Coste, F.lli Recchia	341
Valpolicella Cl. Sup. Le Crosare, Lenotti	337
Valpolicella Cl. Sup. Le Morete, Guido Manara	342
Valpolicella Cl. Sup. Le Portarine, Le Bertarole	339
Valpolicella Cl. Sup. Le Ragose, Le Ragose	305
Valpolicella Cl. Sup. Le Solane, Santi	291
Valpolicella Cl. Sup. Marogne, F.lli Zeni	284
Valpolicella Cl. Sup. Monte Cà Paletta, Giuseppe Quintarelli	306
Valpolicella Cl. Sup. Negraro, F.lli Fabiano	343
Valpolicella Cl. Sup. Pariondo, Luigi Brunelli	315
Valpolicella Cl. Sup. Poiega , Guerrieri Rizzardi	283
Valpolicella Cl. Sup. Possessioni Rosso Serègo Alighieri, Masi	319
Valpolicella Cl. Sup. Ripassa, Zenato	309
Valpolicella Cl. Sup. Ripasso, Corte Lenguin	342
Valpolicella Cl. Sup. Ripasso I Castei, Michele Castellani	294
Valpolicella Cl. Sup. Sant'Urbano, F.lli Speri	316
Valpolicella Cl. Sup. Seccal, Angelo Nicolis e Figli	315
Valpolicella Cl. Sup. Semonte Alto, Massimino Venturini	318
Valpolicella Cl. Sup. Squarano, Marchesi Fumanelli	342
Valpolicella Cl. Sup. Terre di Cariano, Cecilia Beretta	332
Valpolicella Cl. Sup. Vigne Alte, F.lli Zeni	284
Valpolicella Cl. Sup. Vigneti di Purano Le Bine, Giuseppe Campagnola	293
Valpolicella Cl. Sup. Vigneti di Ravazzol, Ca' La Bionda	293
Valpolicella Cl. Sup. Vigneti di Torbe, C.S. Valpolicella	306
Valpolicella Cl. Sup. Vign. La Cengia, Lorenzo Begali	314
Valpolicella Cl. Sup. Vign. Ognisanti Villa Novare, Bertani	304
Valpolicella Cl. Sup. Vign. Poiega, Roberto Mazzi	305
Valpolicella Cl. Villa Borghetti, Pasqua Vigneti e Cantine	333
Valpolicella Rio Albo, Ca' Rugate	300
Valpolicella Sup., Corte Sant'Alda	296
Valpolicella Sup., Marion	312
Valpolicella Sup., Luigino e Marco Provolo	340
Valpolicella Sup. La Bandina, Tenuta Sant'Antonio	297
Valpolicella Sup. Mithas, Corte Sant'Alda	296
Valpolicella Sup. Monti Garbi, Tenuta Sant'Antonio	297
Valpolicella Sup. Ripasso, Corte Sant'Alda	296
Valpolicella Sup. Rocca Sveva, Cant. di Soave	321
Valpolicella Sup. Roccolo Grassi, Roccolo Grassi	297
Valpolicella Sup. Sagramoso, Pasqua Vigneti e Cantine	333
Valpolicella Sup. Sagramoso Ripasso, Pasqua Vigneti e Cantine	333
Valpolicella Sup. Terre del Cereolo, Trabucchi	291
Valpolicella Sup. Terre di S. Colombano, Trabucchi	291
Valpolicella Sup. Vign. di Monte Lodoletta, Romano Dal Forno	290
Valpolicella Valpantena, Tezza	334
Valpolicella Valpantena Sup. Monte delle Fontane, Tezza	334
Valsusa Costadoro, Carlotta	44
Valsusa Rocca del Lupo, Carlotta	44
Valsusa V.combe, Carlotta	44
Valtellina Casa La Gatta, Triacca	211
Valtellina Prestigio, Triacca	211
Valtellina Prestigio Millennium, Triacca	211
Valtellina Sforzato, Pietro Nera	215
Valtellina Sforzato, Triacca	211
Valtellina Sforzato Albareda, Mamete Prevostini	197
Valtellina Sforzato Canua, Conti Sertoli Salis	209
Valtellina Sforzato Ronco del Picchio, Fay	209
Valtellina Sfursat, F.lli Bettini	222
Valtellina Sfursat, Nino Negri	186
Valtellina Sfursat, Aldo Rainoldi	187
Valtellina Sfursat 5 Stelle, Nino Negri	186
Valtellina Sfursat Fruttaio Ca' Rizzieri, Aldo Rainoldi	187
Valtellina Sfurzat Vin da Ca', Plozza	222
Valtellina Sup. Capo di Terra, Conti Sertoli Salis	209
Valtellina Sup. Corte della Meridiana, Conti Sertoli Salis	209
Valtellina Sup. Corte di Cama, Mamete Prevostini	197
Valtellina Sup. Crespino, Aldo Rainoldi	187
Valtellina Sup. Giupa, Azienda Agr. Caven Camuna	222
Valtellina Sup. Grumello, Aldo Rainoldi	187
Valtellina Sup. Grumello V. Sassorosso, Nino Negri	186
Valtellina Sup. Inferno Al Carmine, Azienda Agr. Caven Camuna	222
Valtellina Sup. Inferno Mazer, Nino Negri	186
Valtellina Sup. La Scala Ris. , Plozza	222
Valtellina Sup. Prugnolo, Aldo Rainoldi	187
Valtellina Sup. Quadrio, Nino Negri	186
Valtellina Sup. Ris. Nino Negri, Nino Negri	186
Valtellina Sup. Ris. Triacca, Triacca	211
Valtellina Sup. Sassella, Aldo Rainoldi	187
Valtellina Sup. Sassella, Conti Sertoli Salis	209
Valtellina Sup. Sassella Il Glicine, Fay	209
Valtellina Sup. Sassella Le Tense, Nino Negri	186
Valtellina Sup. Sassella Sommarovina, Mamete Prevostini	197
Valtellina Sup. Signorie Ris., Pietro Nera	215
Valtellina Sup. Valgella Ca' Morei, Fay	209
Valtellina Sup. Valgella Carteria, Fay	209
Valtellina Sup. Valgella Carteria Trentennale, Fay	209
Valtellina Sup. Valgella Villa La Cornella, F.lli Bettini	222
Valtellina Sup. Vign. Fracia, Nino Negri	186
Vantaggio, Sassara	659

Vareij Rosso, Hilberg - Pasquero	127
Varius, Cantele	724
Varramista, Varramista	538
Varrone, Istituto Professionale per l'Agricoltura e l'Ambiente	429
Vasario, Fatt. del Buonamico	523
Vecchio Samperi Ventennale, Marco De Bartoli	749
Velenosi Brut M. Cl., Ercole Velenosi	610
Velitrae Bianco, Colle di Maggio	671
Velitrae Rosso, Colle di Maggio	671
Vellutato, Villa Pigna	626
Velo di Maya, Alfiero Boffa	131
Vencaia Bianco Terre di Braccio, Cantine Perusia	660
Vendemmia Tardiva Mandrarossa, Settesoli	752
Veneroso, Tenuta di Ghizzano	545
Ver Sacrum, Poderi San Savino	632
Verbeia, Piero Gatti	133
Verde Luna Bianco, Caminella	215
Verdicchio Castelli di Jesi Passito Archè, Monteschiavo	619
Verdicchio dei Castelli di Jesi Cl., Bucci	627
Verdicchio dei Castelli di Jesi Cl., Fonte della Luna - Medoro Cimarelli	638
Verdicchio dei Castelli di Jesi Cl., Fatt. Laila	620
Verdicchio dei Castelli di Jesi Cl., Luciano Landi	635
Verdicchio dei Castelli di Jesi Cl., Stefano Mancinelli	623
Verdicchio dei Castelli di Jesi Cl., Marchetti	608
Verdicchio dei Castelli di Jesi Cl., Sartarelli	629
Verdicchio dei Castelli di Jesi Cl. Bachero, Piersanti	637
Verdicchio dei Castelli di Jesi Cl. Bando di S. Settimio, Monteschiavo	619
Verdicchio dei Castelli di Jesi Cl. Cantorì, Accadia	638
Verdicchio dei Castelli di Jesi Cl. Conscio, Accadia	638
Verdicchio dei Castelli di Jesi Cl. Coroncino, Fatt. Coroncino	634
Verdicchio dei Castelli di Jesi Cl. Coste del Molino, Monteschiavo	619
Verdicchio dei Castelli di Jesi Cl. Le Gemme, Mario & Giorgio Brunori	636
Verdicchio dei Castelli di Jesi Cl. Le Giuncare Ris., Monteschiavo	619
Verdicchio dei Castelli di Jesi Cl. Le Vaglie, Santa Barbara	611
Verdicchio dei Castelli di Jesi Cl. Le Vele, Terre Cortesi Moncaro	621
Verdicchio dei Castelli di Jesi Cl. Luzano, Marotti Campi	623
Verdicchio dei Castelli di Jesi Cl. Lyricus, Colonnara Viticoltori in Cupramontana	616
Verdicchio dei Castelli di Jesi Cl. Montesecco, Montecappone	618
Verdicchio dei Castelli di Jesi Cl. Nidastore, Santa Barbara	611
Verdicchio dei Castelli di Jesi Cl. Passito Rojano, Vallerosa Bonci	616
Verdicchio dei Castelli di Jesi Cl. Pietrone Ris., Vallerosa Bonci	616
Verdicchio dei Castelli di Jesi Cl. Pignocco, Santa Barbara	611
Verdicchio dei Castelli di Jesi Cl. Plenio Ris., Umani Ronchi	627
Verdicchio dei Castelli di Jesi Cl. Pontemagno, Piersanti	637
Verdicchio dei Castelli di Jesi Cl. San Sisto Ris., Fazi Battaglia	613
Verdicchio dei Castelli di Jesi Cl. Santa Maria d'Arco, Enrico Ceci	637
Verdicchio dei Castelli di Jesi Cl. Serra Fiorese Ris., Gioacchino Garofoli	618
Verdicchio dei Castelli di Jesi Cl. Sora Elvira, Alberto Serenelli	609
Verdicchio dei Castelli di Jesi Cl. Stefano Antonucci Ris., Santa Barbara	611
Verdicchio dei Castelli di Jesi Cl. Sup., Poggio Montali	636
Verdicchio dei Castelli di Jesi Cl. Sup. Ambrosia, Amato Ceci	637
Verdicchio dei Castelli di Jesi Cl. Sup. Barré Ris., Vallerosa Bonci	616
Verdicchio dei Castelli di Jesi Cl. Sup. Casal di Serra, Umani Ronchi	627
Verdicchio dei Castelli di Jesi Cl. Sup. Cimaio, Casalfarneto	633
Verdicchio dei Castelli di Jesi Cl. Sup. Contrada Balciana, Sartarelli	629
Verdicchio dei Castelli di Jesi Cl. Sup. Corona Reale, Maurizio Marconi	632
Verdicchio dei Castelli di Jesi Cl. Sup. Crocetta, Cavallaro	637
Verdicchio dei Castelli di Jesi Cl. Sup. Cuprese, Colonnara Viticoltori in Cupramontana	616
Verdicchio dei Castelli di Jesi Cl. Sup. Fonte del Leccio, Poggio Montali	636
Verdicchio dei Castelli di Jesi Cl. Sup. Fontevecchia, Casalfarneto	633
Verdicchio dei Castelli di Jesi Cl. Sup. Fra Moriale, Fonte della Luna - Medoro Cimarelli	638
Verdicchio dei Castelli di Jesi Cl. Sup. Gaiospino, Fatt. Coroncino	634
Verdicchio dei Castelli di Jesi Cl. Sup. Grancasale, Casalfarneto	633
Verdicchio dei Castelli di Jesi Cl. Sup. Lailum, Fatt. Laila	620
Verdicchio dei Castelli di Jesi Cl. Sup. Le Moie, Fazi Battaglia	613
Verdicchio dei Castelli di Jesi Cl. Sup. Macrina, Gioacchino Garofoli	618
Verdicchio dei Castelli di Jesi Cl. Sup. Pallio di S. Floriano, Monteschiavo	619
Verdicchio dei Castelli di Jesi Cl. Sup. Podium, Gioacchino Garofoli	618
Verdicchio dei Castelli di Jesi Cl. Sup. S. Maria del Fiore, Stefano Mancinelli	623
Verdicchio dei Castelli di Jesi Cl. Sup. S. Michele, Vallerosa Bonci	616
Verdicchio dei Castelli di Jesi Cl. Sup. Salmariano, Marotti Campi	623
Verdicchio dei Castelli di Jesi Cl. Sup. San Nicolò, Mario & Giorgio Brunori	636
Verdicchio dei Castelli di Jesi Cl. Sup. Santa Maria d'Arco, Enrico Ceci	637
Verdicchio dei Castelli di Jesi Cl. Sup. Sapore di Generazioni, Maurizio Marconi	632
Verdicchio dei Castelli di Jesi Cl. Sup. Sel. Misco, Lucangeli Aymerich di Laconi	614
Verdicchio dei Castelli di Jesi Cl. Sup. Tav.no, Lucangeli Aymerich di Laconi	614
Verdicchio dei Castelli di Jesi Cl. Sup. Tenuta del Cavaliere, Marchetti	608
Verdicchio dei Castelli di Jesi Cl. Sup. Tralivio, Sartarelli	629
Verdicchio dei Castelli di Jesi Cl. Sup. Tufico, Colonnara Viticoltori in Cupramontana	616
Verdicchio dei Castelli di Jesi Cl. Sup. Tufico V.T., Colonnara Viticoltori in Cupramontana	616
Verdicchio dei Castelli di Jesi Cl. Sup. Verde di Ca' Ruptae, Terre Cortesi Moncaro	621
Verdicchio dei Castelli di Jesi Cl. Sup. V. San Marco, Colonnara Viticoltori in Cupramontana	616
Verdicchio dei Castelli di Jesi Cl. Sup. V.mato, Amato Ceci	637
Verdicchio dei Castelli di Jesi Cl. Sup. Villa Bianchi, Umani Ronchi	627
Verdicchio dei Castelli di Jesi Cl. Titulus, Fazi Battaglia	613
Verdicchio dei Castelli di Jesi Cl. V. Novali Ris., Terre Cortesi Moncaro	621
Verdicchio dei Castelli di Jesi Cl. Vign. di Tobia, Laurentina	621
Verdicchio dei Castelli di Jesi Cl. Villa Bucci, Bucci	627
Verdicchio dei Castelli di Jesi Cl. Villa Bucci Ris., Bucci	627
Verdicchio dei Castelli di Jesi Passito Le Brume, Gioacchino Garofoli	618
Verdicchio dei Castelli di Jesi Passito Onyr, Marotti Campi	623
Verdicchio dei Castelli di Jesi Passito Tordiruta, Terre Cortesi Moncaro	621
Verdicchio di Matelica, Bisci	636
Verdicchio di Matelica, La Monacesca	620
Verdicchio di Matelica Aja Lunga, Del Carmine	635
Verdicchio di Matelica Cambrugiano Ris., Belisario C.S. di Matelica e Cerreto d'Esi	619
Verdicchio di Matelica La Monacesca, La Monacesca	620
Verdicchio di Matelica Mirum, La Monacesca	620
Verdicchio di Matelica Petrara, Del Carmine	635
Verdicchio di Matelica Terre di Valbona, Belisario C.S. di Matelica e Cerreto d'Esi	619
Verdicchio di Matelica Vigneti Belisario, Belisario C.S. di Matelica e Cerreto d'Esi	619
Verdicchio di Matelica Vign. Fogliano, Bisci	636
Verdiso, Vincenzo Toffoli	342
Verduno Basadone, Cast. di Verduno	146
Verduno Pelaverga, F.lli Alessandria	145
Verduno Pelaverga, Bel Colle	145
Verduno Pelaverga, G. B. Burlotto	146
Verduno Pelaverga, Terre del Barolo	64
Verduzzo, Davino Meroi	350
Verduzzo Friulano, Marcello e Marino Humar	407
Verduzzo Friulano, Giulio Manzocco	418
Verduzzo Limine, Podere dal Ger	396
Verduzzo Soandre, Bosco del Merlo	282
Vergato Cortese, Cascina Montagnola	160
Vermentino, Cima	497
Vermentino, Serraiola	535
Vermentino, Vallorsi	606
Vermentino, Villa Po' del Vento	659
Vermentino Barrique, Cima	497
Vermentino di Gallura, C.S. Giogantinu	767
Vermentino di Gallura Capichera, Capichera	767
Vermentino di Gallura Cucaione, Piero Mancini	772
Vermentino di Gallura Funtanaliras, C.S. del Vermentino	771
Vermentino di Gallura Gemellae, C.S. Gallura	777
Vermentino di Gallura Hysonj, Pedra Majore	771
Vermentino di Gallura I Graniti, Pedra Majore	771
Vermentino di Gallura Lunghente, C.S. Giogantinu	767
Vermentino di Gallura Mavriana, C.S. Gallura	777
Vermentino di Gallura Piras, C.S. Gallura	777
Vermentino di Gallura S'Eleme, C.S. del Vermentino	771
Vermentino di Gallura Saraina, Piero Mancini	772
Vermentino di Gallura Saruinas, Andrea Depperu	779
Vermentino di Gallura Sienda, Mura	778
Vermentino di Gallura Sup., C.S. Giogantinu	767
Vermentino di Gallura Sup. Aghiloia, C.S. del Vermentino	771
Vermentino di Gallura Sup. Canayli, C.S. Gallura	777
Vermentino di Gallura Sup. Monteoro, Tenute Sella & Mosca	766
Vermentino di Gallura Sup. Vigne Storiche, C.S. Giogantinu	767
Vermentino di Gallura V. T., Capichera	767
Vermentino di Sardegna, Attilio Contini	768
Vermentino di Sardegna, Ferruccio Deiana	776
Vermentino di Sardegna, Cantine di Dolianova	769
Vermentino di Sardegna, Piero Mancini	772
Vermentino di Sardegna, Tenute Soletta	778
Vermentino di Sardegna Aragosta, C.S. Santa Maria La Palma	766
Vermentino di Sardegna Boghes, Giovanni Cherchi	777
Vermentino di Sardegna Cala Silente, C.S. di Santadi	773
Vermentino di Sardegna Costamolino, Antonio Argiolas	775
Vermentino di Sardegna Crabilis, Pala	776
Vermentino di Sardegna Donna Leonora, C.S. della Trexenta	775
Vermentino di Sardegna I Papiri, C.S. Santa Maria La Palma	766
Vermentino di Sardegna Incantu, Gostolai	773
Vermentino di Sardegna La Cala, Tenute Sella & Mosca	766
Vermentino di Sardegna Le Conche, Pedra Majore	771
Vermentino di Sardegna Le Sabbie, Meloni Vini	774
Vermentino di Sardegna Naeli, Cantine di Dolianova	769
Vermentino di Sardegna Pigalva, Giovanni Cherchi	777
Vermentino di Sardegna Tuvaoes, Giovanni Cherchi	777
Vermentino di Sardegna Villa Solais, C.S. di Santadi	773
Vermentino Nero, Cima	497
Vermentino Vinca, VIN.CA.	581
Vermiglio, Andrea Costanti	507
Vernaccia di Oristano, Attilio Contini	768
Vernaccia di Oristano Antico Gregori, Attilio Contini	768
Vernaccia di Oristano Ris., Attilio Contini	768
Vernaccia di Oristano Ris. F.lli Serra	780
Vernaccia di S. Gimignano, Ca' del Vispo	562
Vernaccia di S. Gimignano, Cappella Sant'Andrea	602

Vernaccia di S. Gimignano, Vincenzo Cesani	563		Villa Gaja, I Casciani	597
Vernaccia di S. Gimignano, Granducato	599		Villa Gemma Bianco, Gianni Masciarelli	684
Vernaccia di S. Gimignano, Il Lebbio	565		Villa Noce, C.S. La Torre	763
Vernaccia di S. Gimignano, Il Paradiso	564		Villa Sparina Brut M. Cl., Villa Sparina	85
Vernaccia di S. Gimignano, La Lastra	566		Villa Sparina Brut M. Cl, Villa Sparina	85
Vernaccia di S. Gimignano, Cast. di Montauto	602		Villa Tasca, Tasca d'Almerita	758
Vernaccia di S. Gimignano, Mormoraia	567		Villa Tulino, Colle di Maggio	671
Vernaccia di S. Gimignano, Palagetto	568		Villa Tulino Bianco, Colle di Maggio	671
Vernaccia di S. Gimignano, Giovanni Panizzi	568		Villamaura Syrah, Gaspare Di Prima	763
Vernaccia di S. Gimignano, Italo Rubicini	602		Vin Brusco, Montenidoli	567
Vernaccia di S. Gimignano, San Quirico	602		Vin de La Sabla, Costantino Charrère	16
Vernaccia di S. Gimignano, Teruzzi & Puthod	569		Vin du Prévôt, Institut Agricole Régional	16
Vernaccia di S. Gimignano, F.lli Vagnoni	570		Vin Les Fourches, Costantino Charrère	16
Vernaccia di S. Gimignano Abbazia di Monteoliveto, Fatt. Il Palagio	474		Vin Ruspo, Tenuta di Capezzana	460
Vernaccia di S. Gimignano Alata, La Rampa di Fugnano	566		Vin Ruspo, Castelvecchio	581
Vernaccia di S. Gimignano Biscondola, Il Paradiso	564		Vin Santo, Avignonesi	526
Vernaccia di S. Gimignano Carato, Montenidoli	567		Vin Santo, Caparsa	551
Vernaccia di S. Gimignano Cast. di Montauto, Cast. di Montauto	602		Vin Santo, Casa Sola	580
Vernaccia di S. Gimignano Crocus, Casa alle Vacche	563		Vin Santo, Contucci	528
Vernaccia di S. Gimignano Dometaia Ris., Baroncini	562		Vin Santo, Fatt. Corzano e Paterno	557
Vernaccia di S. Gimignano Fiore, Montenidoli	567		Vin Santo, Crociani	594
Vernaccia di S. Gimignano I Macchioni, Casa alle Vacche	563		Vin Santo, Tenim. Luigi D'Alessandro	474
Vernaccia di S. Gimignano Isabella Ris., San Quirico	602		Vin Santo, Fanti - San Filippo	508
Vernaccia di S. Gimignano La Gentilesca, Fatt. Il Palagio	474		Vin Santo, Fatt. di Fiano	584
Vernaccia di S. Gimignano Le Grillaie, Melini	547		Vin Santo, Iesolana	580
Vernaccia di S. Gimignano Mocali, F.lli Vagnoni	570		Vin Santo, Tenuta Il Corno	558
Vernaccia di S. Gimignano Mocali Ris., F.lli Vagnoni	570		Vin Santo , Il Poggiolo	581
Vernaccia di S. Gimignano Perlato, Guicciardini Strozzi - Fatt. Cusona	564		Vin Santo, Isole e Olena	454
			Vin Santo, La Marcellina	542
Vernaccia di S. Gimignano Poggio ai Cannici Sovestro, Baroncini	562		Vin Santo, La Palazzola	657
Vernaccia di S. Gimignano Privato Ris., La Rampa di Fugnano	566		Vin Santo, Fatt. Le Casalte	595
Vernaccia di S. Gimignano Rialto, Cappella Sant'Andrea	602		Vin Santo, Le Sorgenti	452
Vernaccia di S. Gimignano Ris., Guicciardini Strozzi - Fatt. Cusona	564		Vin Santo, Azienda Agr. Lombardo	595
Vernaccia di S. Gimignano Ris., La Lastra	566		Vin Santo, Fatt. Petrolo	538
Vernaccia di S. Gimignano Ris., Mormoraia	567		Vin Santo, Piazzano	585
Vernaccia di S. Gimignano Ris., Palagetto	568		Vin Santo, Pietrafitta	569
Vernaccia di S. Gimignano Ris., Giovanni Panizzi	568		Vin Santo, Redi	533
Vernaccia di S. Gimignano Ris., Pietrafitta	569		Vin Santo, Riseccoli	489
Vernaccia di S. Gimignano Sanice, Vincenzo Cesani	563		Vin Santo, Rocca di Montegrossi	484
Vernaccia di S. Gimignano Sel., Signano	602		Vin Santo , Massimo Romeo	596
Vernaccia di S. Gimignano Tradizionale, Montenidoli	567		Vin Santo, San Felice	472
Vernaccia di S. Gimignano Tropie, Il Lebbio	565		Vin Santo, Fatt. Santa Vittoria	477
Vernaccia di S. Gimignano V. Borghetto, Pietrafitta	569		Vin Santo, Fatt. del Teso	524
Vernaccia di S. Gimignano V. a Rondolino, Teruzzi & Puthod	569		Vin Santo, Vignole	598
Vernaccia di S. Gimignano V. Borghetto, Pietrafitta	569		Vin Santo, Villa Calcinaia	587
Vernaccia di S. Gimignano V. in Fiore, Ca' del Vispo	562		Vin Santo, Villa Sant'Anna	535
Vernaccia di S. Gimignano V. La Costa Ris., Pietrafitta	569		Vin Santo De Renzis, Fatt. Cast. Sonnino	537
Vernaccia di S. Gimignano V. Santa Chiara, Palagetto	568		Vin Santo del Chianti, Castelvecchio	557
Vernaccia di San Gimignano Hydra, Il Palagione	565		Vin Santo del Chianti Cl., Fatt. dell' Aiola	583
Verriolo, Boschetto di Montiano	589		Vin Santo del Chianti Cl., Cast. della Paneretta	453
Versoio, Mantellassi	589		Vin Santo del Chianti Cl., Solatione	601
Vertigo, Livio Felluga	363		Vin Santo del Chianti Cl., Cast. di Volpaia	555
Vesco Bianco, Cantine Rallo	751		Vin Santo del Chianti Cl., Fatt. di Felsina	470
Vesco Rosso, Cantine Rallo	751		Vin Santo del Chianti Cl., Rocca di Montegrossi	484
Vescovo II, Tenim. Luigi D'Alessandro	474		Vin Santo del Chianti V. del Papa, Fatt. Villa La Selva	458
Vespa Bianco, Bastianich	396		Vin Santo del Cl., Castellare di Castellina	463
Vespa Rosso, Bastianich	396		Vin Santo dell'Empolese, Fatt. Montellori	477
Vesuvio Lacryma Christi Bianco, Cantine Caputo	691		Vin Santo della Rufina, Fatt. Selvapiana	549
Vesuvio Lacryma Christi Rosso, Mastroberardino	690		Vin Santo di Carmignano Ris., Tenuta di Capezzana	460
Viburnum, V.i da Duline	420		Vin Santo di Montepulciano Sangallo, Fatt. del Cerro	528
V. Adriana, Castel De Paolis	668		Vin Santo Dolce Sinfonia, Bindella	527
V. al Cavaliere, Michele Satta	462		Vin Santo Millarium, Enrico Pierazzuoli	459
V. Alta, Badia di Morrona	578		Vin Santo Occhio di Pernice, Avignonesi	526
V. Cesco di Nece, Mustilli	700		Vin Santo Tegrino d'Anchiano, Cantine Leonardo da Vinci	578
V. dei Pini, D'Angelo	710		Vin Santo Topazio, La Rampa di Fugnano	566
V. del Cavaliere, Casale Marchese	667		Vincastro, Eredi Benincasa	642
V. del Feudo, Felline	727		Vineargenti Rosso, Bosco del Merlo	282
V. del Picchio, Moro - Rinaldo Rinaldini	440		Vinnalunga 71, Isidoro Lamoretti	448
V. del Vassallo, Paola Di Mauro - Colle Picchioni	668		Vino degli Orti, Matijaz Tercic	409
V. dell'Erta, Vigliano	495		Vino del Maso Rosso, Marco Donati	233
V. dell'Iris, Artimino	581		Vino della Pace, Cant. Prod. di Cormons	361
V. di Colle, Tola	763		Vino Nobile di Montepulciano, Bindella	527
V. Il Vallone, Villa Sant'Anna	535		Vino Nobile di Montepulciano, Ercolani	595
V. l'Apparita Merlot, Cast. di Ama	478		Vino Santo di Ripatransone Sibilla Agrippa, Le Caniette	631
V. La Fornace, Eredi Benincasa	642			
V. Pratobianco, Torre Fornello	443		Vino Santo di Ripatransone Sibilla Eritrea, Le Caniette	631
V. Regis, Vecchie Terre di Montefili	544		Vintage Tunina, Vinnaioli Jermann	380
V. Verdana Ascevi, Ascevi - Luwa	405		Vintàn, San Patrignano	428
V. Vescovi, F.lli Zaccagnini & C.	638		Vioca di Plaia, Calatrasi - Accademia del Sole	757
V. Virzì Rosso, Spadafora	755		Virente, Wandanna	525
V.maggio, Villa V.maggio	491		Vita, Marco Maci	719
V.mare, Tommaso e Angelo Lupi	170		Vite Bianca, Ornella Molon Traverso	310
V.nuova, Coop. Agr. Valdarnese	606		Vite Rossa, Ornella Molon Traverso	310
V.ricco Bianco, Conte D'Attimis-Maniago	349		Vitiano, Falesco	670
V.ricco Rosso, Conte D'Attimis-Maniago	349		Vito Arturo, Le Fonti	547
Vigne d'Oro, Avide	748		Vivaldaia, Villa Pillo	485
Vigne del Mandorlo, Fatt. Montellori	477		Vocato, Villa Cilnia	452
Vigne del Moro, Fatt. Montellori	477		Volgente Rosso, Mazziotti	664
Vigne Sparse, Visconti	216		Were Dreams, Now It Is Just Wine!, Vinnaioli Jermann	380
Vign. Ca' Brione Bianco, Nino Negri	186		Wildbacher, Conte Collalto	325
Vign. La Gavina, Famiglia Cecchi	464		Wildbacher, Martino Zanetti	341
Vigorello, San Felice	472		Ylenia, Fatascià	754
Villa Angela Chardonnay, Ercole Velenosi	610		Yrnm, Aziende Vinicole Miceli	755
Villa Buoninsegna, Villa Buoninsegna	600		Zabbya, Tola	763
Villa Castiglioni, Bisci	636		Zaccagnini Brut Ris., F.lli Zaccagnini & C.	638
Villa Conversino Bianco, Di Filippo	658		Zagros, San Giovanni	626
Villa di Chiesa, C.S. di Santadi	773		Zamuner Brut Rosé Villa La Mattarana Ris., Zamuner	343
Villa di Corsano, Cant. di Montalcino	593		Zephyro Rosato, Vintripoli Calabria	742
Villa Fidelia Bianco, Sportoletti	656		Zero - D'Orta-De Conciliis, Viticoltori De Conciliis	698
Villa Fidelia Rosso, Sportoletti	656		Zipolo Rosso, Il Conte	622
Villa Flora, La Badiola	588		Zivula, C.S. Gallura	777

INDEX OF PRODUCERS

A Maccia	171	Ascevi - Luwa	405
Abate Nero	241	Ascheri	46
Abbazia di Novacella	277	Aschero, Laura	171
Abbazia Santa Anastasia	747	Attems	381
Abbona, Anna Maria	78	Aurora	637
Abbona, Marziano e Enrico	74	Avide	748
Abraxas	762	Avignonesi	526
Abrigo, F.lli	153	Avio, Cantina Sociale di	224
Abrigo, Orlando	160	Azelia	61
Accademia dei Racemi	727	Azzolino, Fattorie	746
Accademia del Vino Cadelaghet	246	Badia di Morrona	578
Accadia	638	Baglio Hopps	761
Accordini, Igino	342	Baglio San Vincenzo	762
Accordini, Stefano	313	Bagnasco	222
Accornero, Giulio e Figli	147	Bagnolo dei Marchesi Pancrazi, Tenuta di	526
Acquabona	600	Baldizzone Cascina Lana, Antonio	157
Acquaviva, Fattoria	589	Balestri Valda	343
Adami	335	Balter, Nicola	238
Adanti, Agricola	641	Bandut - Giorgio Colutta	386
Adragna	764	Banfi	500
Agareno	761	Banti, Jacopo	458
Agnes	205	Baraccone	449
Agricola Pliniana	732	Barattieri di San Pietro, Conte Otto	442
Agricoltori del Chianti Geografico	478	Barberani - Vallesanta	650
Agrinico	596	Barberis, Osvaldo	154
Agriverde	681	Barbi, Fattoria dei	500
Aia della Macina, Podere	570	Barboglio De Gaioncelli	216
Aiola, Fattoria dell'	583	Barisél, Cascina	55
Aione, Podere	594	Barni	47
Ajello	761	Baroncini	562
Alario, Claudio	73	Barone Cornacchia	688
Albani, Riccardo	182	Barone de Cles	235
Albano Carrisi, Tenute	718	Barone Pizzini	189
Albola, Castello d'	550	Barone Ricasoli	479
Alfieri, Cantarutti	410	Barsento	733
Alessandri	172	Basciano, Fattoria di	556
Alessandria, F.lli	145	Basilisco	714
Alessandria, Gianfranco	104	Basilium	708
Alessandro di Camporeale	760	Bastianich	396
Alfieri, Marchesi	131	Batasiolo	88
Allegrini	288	Battistotti, Riccardo	237
Almondo, Giovanni	113	Baudana, Luigi	135
Aloi, Valerio	156	Bava	68
Altare - Cascina Nuova, Elio	88	Beccaris, Renzo	152
Altesino	499	Beconcini, Pietro	602
Alzatura, Tenuta	647	Befehlhof, Oswald Schuster	280
Ama, Castello di	478	Begali, Lorenzo	314
Amadio, Gino	673	Beghelli, Giuseppe	426
Amalia, Tenuta	446	Bel Colle	145
Ambra, Fattoria	459	Belisario Cantina Sociale di Matelica e Cerreto d'Esi	619
Ambrosini, Lorella	573	Bellani, Marco Giulio	214
Andreas Berger -Thurnhof	255	Bellaria	182
Andreola Orsola	288	Bellavista	192
Anfossi	174	Bellini, Roberto	501
Angoris, Tenuta di	358	Beltrame, Tenuta	346
Anselmet	19	Benanti	759
Anselmi, Roberto	300	Benincasa, Eredi	642
Antano, Fattoria Milziade	658	Benotto, Carlo	70
Anteo	205	Bepin de Eto	313
Antica Masseria del Sigillo	723	Bera, F.lli	122
Antichi Vigneti di Cantalupo	85	Bergaglio, Nicola	81
Antinori, Marchesi	475	Bergamasca, Cantina Sociale	206
Antonelli - San Marco	648	Berlucchi, F.lli	190
Antoniolo	79	Berlucchi & C., Guido	190
Antonutti	392	Bersano & Riccadonna	123
Anzivino	80	Bersi Serlini	204
Aquila del Torre	394	Berta, Guido	159
Araldica - Il Cantinone	58	Bertani	304
Argiano	499	Bertelli, Poderi	70
Argiolas, Antonio	775	Berti, Stefano	430
Armani	287	Bettini, F.lli	222
Arpineto, Tenuta	447	Bettoni Cazzago, Conti	215
Artimino	581	Bianchi	159

Bianchi, Maria Donata	166	Butussi, Valentino	371
Bibi Graetz	586	Buzzinelli, Maurizio	360
Bigi	650	Ca' Bianca	29
Bindella	527	Ca' Bolani	355
Bisci	636	Ca' Bruciata	447
Bisi	221	Ca 'd Carussin	159
Bisol, Desiderio & Figli	326	Ca' d'Gal	132
Bisson, Enoteca	165	Ca' dei Frati	208
Blasig, Tenuta di	403	Ca' dei Mandorli	152
Boccadigabbia	615	Ca' del Baio	142
Bocchino, Eugenio	150	Ca' del Bosco	193
Boeri, Alfonso	152	Ca' del Gè	199
Boffa, Alfiero	131	Ca' del Santo	218
Boglietti, Enzo	89	Ca' del Vent	215
Bogoni, Carlo	301	Ca' del Vispo	562
Bolognani, Nilo	231	Ca di Bon	372
Bonaldi - Cascina del Bosco	222	Ca' di Frara	202
Bonfiglio	448	Ca' La Bionda	293
Bongiovanni, Cascina	62	Ca' Lojera	208
Borc Dodòn	420	Ca' Lustra	286
Borgo Canale	721	Ca' Rome' - Romano Marengo	30
Borgo Casignano	584	Ca' Ronesca	376
Borgo Conventi	379	Ca' Rossa, Cascina	50
Borgo del Tiglio	359	Ca' Rossa, Fattoria	445
Borgo di Colloredo	686	Ca' Rugate	300
Borgo Maragliano	99	Ca' Selvatica	448
Borgo Salcetino	550	Ca.Vi.Mon.	68
Borgo San Daniele	359	Ca' Viola	74
Borgo Scopeto	584	Cabanon	196
Borgogno, Giacomo & Figli	37	Cabert	417
Borin	298	Caccese, Paolo	361
Boroli	24	Caccia al Piano 1868	581
Bortolin Spumanti, F.lli	327	Caggiano, Antonio	702
Bortolomiol	327	Calatrasi - Accademia del Sole	757
Bortolusso, Emiro Cav.	355	Calatrasi Puglia	718
Boscaini, Paolo & Figli	339	Calleri	162
Boscarelli	527	Calò & Figli, Michele	734
Boschetto di Montiano	589	Calonga	431
Boschis, Francesco	154	Calvi , Valter	214
Bosco, Nestore	687	Camerone, Fattoria	446
Bosco, Rosa	386	Camigliano, Castello di	501
Bosco del Merlo	282	Caminella	215
Bosco Romagno, Tenuta	417	Campagnola, Giuseppe	293
Botromagno, Cantina Cooperativa	722	Campogiovanni	589
Botrona	603	Camponeschi	673
Boveri, Luigi	69	Canato, Marco	148
Boveri Renato	156	Candido, Francesco	729
Bovio, Gianfranco	89	Cane, Giobatta Mandino	167
Braida	129	Canevel Spumanti	328
Branko - Igor Erzetic	360	Canonica a Cerreto	584
Brannetti Antica Riserva della Cascina	672	Cantele	724
Bredasole	219	Cantina del Castello	321
Brema, Ermanno e Alessandra	86	Cantina del Pino	30
Brezza, Giacomo & Figli	37	Cantina del Taburno	693
Bricco del Cucù	43	Cantina di Montecchia	340
Bricco Maiolica	73	Cantina di Soave	321
Bricco Mondalino	147	Cantina Gries/Cantina di Bolzano	255
Bricco Rocche - Bricco Asili	62	Cantina Rotaliana	235
Brigaldara	314	Cantina Sociale del Vulture	714
Brigl, Josef	250	Cantine Cooperative Riunite	446
Broglia - Tenuta La Meirana, Gian Piero	82	Cantrina	212
Brojli - Franco Clementin	414	Capanna di Cencioni	502
Broni, Cantina Sociale di	213	Capannelle	479
Brovia	63	Caparra & Siciliani	736
Bruna	172	Caparsa	551
Brunelli, Luigi	315	Caparzo, Tenuta	502
Brunner	417	Capezzana, Tenuta di	460
Brunori, Mario & Giorgio	636	Capichera	767
Bucci	627	Capinera	636
Buccicatino	688	Cappella Sant'Andrea	602
Buiatti, Livio e Claudio	348	Caprai - Val di Maggio, Arnaldo	648
Buiatti, Olivo	348	Caputo, Cantine	691
Bulichella	604	Cardeto	651
Buonamico, Fattoria del	523	Cardinali	446
Buranco	169	Cardone, Vini Classici	726
Burlotto, G. B.	146	Carini, Carlo e Marco	655
Bussia Soprana	156	Carlo di Pradis	362
Busso, Piero	117	Carlotta	44
Bussola, Tommaso	304	Carlozadra	197

Carmignani, Gino Fuso	523	Castelvecchio	557
Carobbio	540	Castelvecchio	581
Carpenè Malvolti	338	Castelveder	218
Carpineta Fontalpino	468	Castiglion del Bosco	504
Carpineto	486	Castiglioni e Montagnana, Fattoria	536
Carra	433	Castignanese, Cantina Cooperativa	614
Casa alle Vacche	563	Cataldi Madonna, Tenuta	680
Casa Emma	453	Catturich Ducco	219
Casa Roma	319	Caudrina	65
Casa Sola	580	Cavalchina	324
Casabianca, Fattoria	539	Cavallaro	637
Casal Gentile	674	Cavalleri	193
Casale dei Cento Corvi	672	Cavallotto, F.lli	63
Casale del Giglio	663	Cavazza, Domenico & F.lli	299
Casale della Ioria	662	Cave du Vin Blanc	20
Casale Marchese	667	Caven Camuna, Azienda Agricola	222
Casalfarneto	633	Caves Cooperatives de Donnas	20
Casalone	100	Cavicchioli & Figli, Cantine	450
Casaloste, Fattoria	598	Cavit - Consorzio di Cantine Sociali	242
Casanova di Neri	503	Cecchetto, Giorgio	344
Casanuova delle Cerbaie	590	Cecchi, Famiglia	464
Casata Monfort	247	Ceci, Amato	637
Casato - Donatella Cinelli Colombini, Fattoria del	503	Ceci, Enrico	637
Casavecchia	153	Cecilia Beretta	332
Cascina Ballarin	90	Celli	422
Cascina Castlèt	71	Cennatoio Intervineas	541
Cascina Chicco	51	Centolani	505
Cascina Cucco	136	Ceralti	582
Cascina Feipu dei Massaretti	162	Cerbaiona	505
Cascina Fonda	101	Ceretto	25
Cascina Giovinale	157	Cerro, Fattoria del	528
Cascina Gnocco	218	Cerveteri, Cantina	666
Cascina La Maddalena	128	Cesanese del Piglio, Cantina Sociale	673
Cascina Montagnola	160	Cesani, Vincenzo	563
Cascina Nuova	213	Cesari, Gerardo	337
Cascina Orsolina	156	Cesari, Umberto	425
Cascina Roera	71	Cesconi	231
Cascina Ulivi	158	Ceuso	745
Cascina Vano	118	Charrère, Costantino	16
Case di Pietra	762	Cherchi, Giovanni	777
Caseo	179	Chiappini, Giovanni	580
Casetto dei Mandorli	450	Chiappone, Erede di Armando	157
Casisano Colombaio	590	Chiarieri	687
Castagnoli	462	Chiarli 1860	433
Casteggio, Cantina di	214	Chiarlo, Michele	47
Castel De Paolis	668	Chigi Saracini, Fattorie	469
Castel di Salve	730	Chionetti, Quinto & Figlio	75
Castel Noarna	236	Chiorri, Franca	660
Castel Sallegg - Graf Kuenburg	279	Chiusa Grande	687
CastelFaglia	185	Ciabrelli, Fattoria	704
Castelgiocondo	504	Ciacci Piccolomini D'Aragona	506
Castellani, Michele	294	Cieck	24
Castellare di Castellina	463	Cigliano	601
Castellari Bergaglio	82	Cigliuti, F.lli	118
Castelli del Duca	437	Cignozza, La	585
Castelli Martinozzi	590	Cima	497
Castellino, Tenuta	187	Cinqueterre, Cantina	175
Castello dei Rampolla	540	Cinti, Floriano	440
Castello del Poggio	127	Ciodet	344
Castello della Paneretta	453	Cisa Asinari dei Marchesi di Grésy, Tenuta	31
Castello della Sala	644	Citra	687
Castello delle Regine	640	Ciù Ciù	625
Castello di Antignano - Brogal Vini	655	Clastidio Ballabio	214
Castello di Bossi	468	Clerico, Domenico	104
Castello di Fonterutoli	463	Cocci Grifoni, Tenuta	630
Castello di Grumello	217	Cocco, Paolo	780
Castello di Luzzano	220	Coffele	322
Castello di Magione	659	Cogno, Elvio	125
Castello di Neive	157	Col d'Orcia, Tenuta	506
Castello di Razzano, Tenuta	28	Col Vetoraz	328
Castello di Spessa	351	Cola, Battista	212
Castello di Verduno	146	Colacicchi	662
Castello Ducale	704	Collalto, Conte	325
Castello Fageto	628	Collavini, Eugenio	372
Castello Monaci	733	Collazzi, Fattoria	588
Castelluccio	434	Colle Bereto	600
Castelpugna	604	Colle dei Bardellini	169
Castelrotto - Torti, Tenimenti	218	Colle di Maggio	671
Castelvecchio	405	Colle Duga	362

Colle San Lorenzo	667	Dal Bosco, Giobatta	340
Colle Santa Mustiola	473	Dal Din	344
Collelungo, Podere	464	Dal Fari	356
Colli a Lago, Cantine	216	Dal Forno, Romano	290
Colli Amerini, Cantina dei	640	Dal Maso, Luigino	299
Colli della Murgia	731	Dall'Asta, Cantine	449
Colmello di Grotta	379	Dalzocchio	248
Colombina	445	Damilano	38
Colonna	148	Dattilo	738
Colonna - Vini Spalletti	441	De Andreis, Fausto	163
Colonnara Viticoltori in Cupramontana	616	De Angelis, Tenuta	613
Colosi, Cantine	762	De Bartoli, Marco	749
Colpetrone	646	De Battè, Walter	173
Coltibuono	480	De Conciliis, Viticoltori	698
Columbu	778	De Falco	706
Comelli, Paolino	378	De Faveri	335
Concadoro	465	De Lucia	695
Concilio	244	de Tarczal	229
Consorzio Viticoltori Associati del Vulture	708	Decugnano dei Barbi	651
Contadi Castaldi	178	Degani, F.lli	295
Conte Capodilista, Giordano Emo	282	Degiorgis, Sergio	101
Conte D'Attimis-Maniago	349	Dei	529
Conte Giorgi di Vistarino	219	Deiana, Ferruccio	776
Conte Leopardi Dittajuti	624	Del Carmine	635
Conte Spagnoletti Zeuli	716	Deltetto	52
Conte Zandotti	671	Depperu, Andrea	779
Conterno, Aldo	105	Dessilani	78
Conterno, Giacomo	105	Destefanis	114
Conterno, Paolo	106	Dettori, Tenute	780
Conterno Fantino	106	Dezi, Fattoria	633
Contesa di Rocco Pasetti	682	Di Barrò	19
Conti, Leone	428	Di Filippo	658
Conti Bossi Fedrigotti	238	Di Lenardo	381
Conti da Schio	339	Di Majo Norante	676
Conti Formentini	406	Di Mauro - Colle Picchioni, Paola	668
Conti Zecca	725	Di Meo	699
Contini, Attilio	768	Di Palma	711
Contratto	55	Di Prima, Gaspare	763
Contucci	528	Di Sesta, Tenuta	590
Convento Muri-Gries, Cantina	256	Dievole, Fattoria di	469
Cooperativa Svevo - Lucera	732	Do Ville	404
Coos, Dario	391	Dolianova, Cantine di	769
Copertino, Cantina Sociale Cooperativa	731	Donati, Marco	233
Coppo, Luigi e Figli	56	Donda, Giovanni	346
Corino, Giovanni	90	Donna Olga	590
Cormons, Cantina Produttori di	361	Donnafugata, Tenuta di	750
Cornaleto	212	Dorgali, Cantina Sociale	778
Cornarea	151	Doria	199
Coroncino, Fattoria	634	Dorigati - Metius, F.lli	234
Correggia, Matteo	51	Dorigo, Girolamo	349
Corte alla Flora	594	Drei Donà Tenuta La Palazza	431
Corte d'Aibo	449	Drius, Mauro	363
Corte Gardoni	332	Duca Carlo Guarini	734
Corte Lenguin	342	Duca della Corgna	643
Corte Manzini	427	Duca di Salaparuta - Vini Corvo	747
Corte Marzago	344	Due Palme, Cantina	719
Corte Normanna	705	Due Portine - Gorelli	507
Corte Rugolin	294	Egger-Ramer	278
Corte Sant'Alda	296	Einaudi, Poderi	75
Corteforte	339	Elena Walch, Castel Ringberg & Kastelaz	275
Cortese, Giuseppe	31	Elorina	763
Corzano e Paterno, Fattoria	557	Endrizzi	248
COS	759	Enoteca Bruzzone, Andrea	175
Costanti, Andrea	507	Enotria, Cantina	741
Costaripa	198	Ercolani	595
Cottanera	748	Erioli	445
Crociani	594	Ermacora, Dario e Luciano	397
Crosato, Giovanni	356	Ester Hauser	638
Curatolo	761	Eubea - Fam. Sasso, Agricola	711
Cusumano	756	Fabiano, F.lli	343
D'Alessandro, Tenimenti Luigi	474	Faccoli & Figli, Lorenzo	188
D'Alfonso del Sordo	730	Falesco	670
D'Ambra Vini d'Ischia	694	Falkenstein - Franz Pratzner, Tenuta	273
d'Amico, Paolo	664	Fanini	643
D'Angelo	710	Fanti, Vignaiolo Giuseppe	232
D'Antiche Terre - Vega	705	Fanti - La Palazzetta	590
d'Isera, Cantina	247	Fanti - San Filippo	508
Da Prato, Gabriele	587	Fantinel	413
Dacapo	22	Fantino, Alessandro e Gian Natale	107

Faraone	679	Gaierhof	237
Farnese	681	Gaja	32
Farneta, Tenuta	604	Galardi	701
Farnetella	571	Gallino, Filippo	53
Fasoli	286	Gallura, Cantina Sociale	777
Fassati	529	Gandin, Edi	420
Fatascià	754	Garetto, Tenuta	23
Fattoi	591	Garitina, Cascina	59
Fattori & Graney	301	Garofoli, Gioacchino	618
Fattoria di Bagnolo	588	Gastaldi	119
Fattoria di Fiano	584	Gatta, Agricola	215
Fattoria di Romignano	588	Gatti, Enrico	194
Fattoria La Rivolta	690	Gatti, Piero	133
Fattoria Lilliano	579	Germano, Ettore	137
Fattoria Zerbina	429	Ghio, Domenico e Figli	45
Favaro	158	Ghisolfi, Attilio	107
Fay	209	Ghizzano, Tenuta di	545
Fazi Battaglia	613	Giacomelli	174
Federici, Azienda Vinicola	674	Giacomo Scagliola e Figlio	151
Fedrizzi, Cipriano	247	Giacosa, Bruno	120
Felline	727	Giacosa, Carlo	32
Felluga, Livio	363	Giacosa, F.lli	120
Felluga, Marco	385	Giannaccini, Giovanna	598
Felsina, Fattoria di	470	Gigante, Adriano	373
Feotto dello Jato	764	Gili, Raffaele	59
Ferghettina	194	Gillardi, Giovanni Battista	79
Ferrando	87	Gilli, Cascina	61
Ferrara, Benito	703	Gini	302
Ferrari	242	Giogantinu, Cantina Sociale	767
Ferrari, Aleardo	343	Giorgi, F.lli	179
Ferraris, Roberto	22	Giovanni Veglio e Figli	153
Ferrero, F.lli	155	Giuncheo, Tenuta	164
Ferrucci, Stefano	425	Glicine, Cantina del	156
Feudi di San Giuliano	760	Goccia, Tenuta	449
Feudi di San Gregorio	702	Godenza, Tenuta	447
Feudo Montoni	760	Gojer Glögglhof, Franz	256
Feudo Principi di Butera	745	Goretti, Agricola	656
Feudo Solaria	763	Gostolai	773
Fici, F.lli	761	Gotto d'Oro	669
Fiegl	382	Gradis'ciutta	406
Filiputti, Walter	387	Gradizzolo Ognibene	436
Filomusi Guelfi	685	Gradnik Eredi, Gradimiro	418
Fiorini, Valentino	611	Graf Pfeil Weingut Kränzel	267
Firriato, Casa Vinicola	754	Gran Furor Divina Costiera, Cantine	694
Florio, Cantine	750	Granducato	599
Foffani	416	Grasso, Elio	108
Folonari, Tenute Ambrogio e Giovanni	476	Grasso, Silvio	91
Fondo Antico	764	Gratena, Fattoria di	579
Fondo Cà Vecja	448	Grattamacco	461
Fontana, Graziano	228	Gravner	382
Fontana Candida	669	Gregoletto	298
Fontanabianca	119	Greppone Mazzi - Tenimenti Ruffino	591
Fontanafredda	136	Grevepesa, Castelli del	558
Fontanavecchia	703	Grignano	599
Fonte della Luna - Medoro Cimarelli	638	Grigoletti	247
Fontodi, Tenuta	541	Grillo, Iole	399
Fontursia	637	Grimaldi, Giacomo	38
Foradori	236	Grimaldi - Ca' du Sindic, Sergio	133
Forano, Fattoria di	610	Grosjean, F.lli	18
Forchir	420	Grotta del Sole, Cantine	699
Forlini Cappellini	175	Guado al Tasso, Tenuta	456
Forteto della Luja	99	Gualdo del Re	573
Fraccaroli	341	Guerrieri	629
Franzoni, Emilio	213	Guerrieri Rizzardi	283
Frascole	585	Guglierame, Nicola	175
Frecciarossa	183	Guicciardini Strozzi - Fattoria Cusona	564
Freddano	652	Gulfi	760
Frentana, Cantina Sociale	688	Gumphof, Markus Prackwieser	279
Frescobaldi, Marchesi de'	476	Haas, Franz	272
Fucci, Elena	714	Haderburg	274
Fuligni, Eredi	508	Happacherhof - Istituto Tecnico Agrario, Maso	280
Fumanelli, Marchesi	342	Hastae	48
Funtanin	52	Hilberg - Pasquero	127
Gabbas, Giuseppe	772	Hofstätter	275
Gabutti - Franco Boasso	137	Hohler, Karin e Remo	57
Gaggioli Vigneto Bagazzana, Maria Letizia	444	Humar, Marcello e Marino	407
Gagliardo, Gianni	155	I Balzini	580
Gagliole	582	I Campetti	601
Gaiano, Tenuta	50	I Casciani	597

I Girasoli di Sant'Andrea	660	La Brancaia	551
I Giusti e Zanza	475	La Brugherata	207
I Pastini - Carparelli	732	La Busattina	589
I Scriani	339	La Calonica	530
I Vignaioli di S. Stefano	134	La Cantina dei Colli Ripani	631
Icardi	66	La Caplana	150
Iesolana	580	La Cappella, Podere	605
Il Borro, Tenuta	495	La Cappuccina	302
Il Bosco, Tenuta	211	La Carletta	603
Il Bruscello	604	La Carraia	652
Il Calepino	184	La Casa dell'Orco	706
Il Carnasciale, Podere	597	La Castellada	383
Il Carpino	407	La Cella di San Michele	160
Il Chioso	174	La Chiara	83
Il Colle	591	La Ciarliana	530
Il Colombaio di Cencio	480	La Cipressaia, Tenuta	597
Il Colombo - Barone Riccati	103	La Colombera	160
Il Conte	622	La Costaiola, Tenuta	200
Il Corno, Tenuta	558	La Crotta di Vegneron	17
Il Faggeto	595	La Fiorita	591
Il Falchetto, Tenuta	159	La Fortuna, Podere	511
Il Filò delle Vigne	283	La Fuga, Tenuta	592
Il Grappolo-Fortius	591	La Gerla	511
Il Greppo, Tenuta	509	La Ghersa	102
Il Grillesino	586	La Giaretta	340
Il Lebbio	565	La Giribaldina	48
Il Mandorlo	559	La Giustiniana	83
Il Marroneto	591	La Guardia	116
Il Monticello	176	La Guardiense	705
Il Montù	218	La Lastra	566
Il Mosnel	203	La Lumia, Barone	761
Il Nuraghe, Cantina Sociale	779	La Madonnina - Triacca	486
Il Palagio, Fattoria	474	La Mancina	437
Il Palagione	565	La Marcellina	542
Il Palazzino, Podere	481	La Masnadora	219
Il Palazzone	509	La Massa	542
Il Paradiso	564	La Meridiana, Tenuta	114
Il Poggiarello	441	La Monacesca	620
Il Poggiolino	576	La Montecchia	320
Il Poggiolo	581	La Montina	200
Il Poggiolo	510	La Morandina	66
Il Poggione, Tenuta	510	La Novella, Tenuta	587
Il Pratello	434	La Palazzola	657
Il Rocchin	154	La Parrina	539
Il Torchio	164	La Pertica, Cascina	204
Il Tuccanese	733	La Pierotta	603
Il Vignale	125	La Pietra del Focolare	170
Il Vignale	599	La Pieve	498
Illuminati, Dino	677	La Poderina	512
Inama	310	La Querce	494
Incontri	574	La Rajade	376
Institut Agricole Régional	16	La Rampa di Fugnano	566
Ippolito 1845	741	La Regola	556
Isabella	116	La Ripa, Fattoria	605
Isimbarda	206	La Ripe	638
Isola	435	La Rocca di San Nicolao	166
Isole e Olena	454	La Roncaia	391
Ispoli	559	La Sala	560
Istituto Professionale per l'Agricoltura e l'Ambiente	429	La Sansonina	308
Iucci, Giuseppe	672	La Scamuzza	149
Jacùss	414	La Scolca	155
Jerzu, Antichi Poderi	770	La Serena	592
Kante	377	La Smilla	45
Keber, Edi	364	La Spinetta	58
Keber, Renato	418	La Stoppa	439
Kettmeir	264	La Tenaglia, Tenuta	139
Klosterhof, Tenuta	279	La Togata - Tenuta Carlina	512
Köfererhof	277	La Tordela	210
Kössler - Praeclarus	252	La Torre, Cantina Sociale	763
Kuenhof - Peter Pliger	263	La Torretta, Tenuta	449
L'Armangia	151	La Tosa	442
L'Olivella	673	La Tunella	397
La Badiola	588	La Valentina, Fattoria	684
La Barbatella, Cascina	123	La Vecchia Cantina	163
La Berta	424	La Versa, Cantina Sociale	207
La Biancara	289	La Viarte	400
La Boatina	364	La Vigna	213
La Boscaiola	189	La Vis	232
La Braccesca, Fattoria	595	La Zerba	160

Laila, Fattoria	620	Loi, Alberto	769
Laimburg, Cantina	276	Lombardo, Azienda Agricola	595
Lambardi, Maurizio	592	Lonardi, Giuseppe	295
Lamberti	339	Longariva	239
Lamborghini - La Fiorita	654	Loredan Gasparini Venegazzù, Conte	344
Lambruschi, Ottaviano	165	Lornano	596
Lamoretti, Isidoro	448	Lucangeli Aymerich di Laconi	614
Lanari	608	Lucchetti, Mario	636
Lanciola	494	Luce	513
Landi, Luciano	635	Lucignano, Castello di	586
Lano, Gianluigi	25	Luigi Tacchino	151
Lantieri de Paratico	181	Luigi Viola & Figli	742
Laurentina	621	Luisa, Eddi	389
Lavacchio, Fattoria	599	Luisin, Cascina	33
Le Albare	340	Lun, Cantina H.	269
Le Bellerive - Angelo Ruggeri	329	Lunelli	243
Le Bertarole	339	Lungarotti	657
Le Bocce	543	Lupi, Tommaso e Angelo	170
Le Boncie, Podere	584	Luretta	432
Le Calvane	536	Lusenti, Gaetano	443
Le Caniette	631	Lusignani, Alberto	450
Le Capannacce	585	Machiavelli	561
Le Casalte, Fattoria	595	Maci, Marco	719
Le Chiuse	592	Macolina, La	448
Le Chiuse di Sotto	513	Maculan	285
Le Cinciole	598	Madonia, Giovanna	422
Le Colture	329	Madonna dei Miracoli	686
Le Corne	217	Madonna delle Vittorie	246
Le Corti - Corsini, Fattoria	560	Maffini, Luigi	692
Le Crete	645	Magnàs	365
Le Due Terre	400	Majolini	203
Le Due Torri	373	Malacari	625
Le Fabriche	733	Malena	737
Le Filigare	454	Malfatti, Costanza	589
Le Fonti	547	Malgrà	102
Le Fonti, Fattoria	598	Malojer Gummerhof, R.	257
Le Fracce	183	Malvirà	53
Le Fraghe	285	Manara	450
Le Ginestre	599	Manara, Guido	342
Le Gode di Ripaccioli	592	Mancinelli, Stefano	623
Le Macchiole	456	Mancini, Fattoria	628
Le Macioche	592	Mancini, Piero	772
Le Marchesine	219	Manfred Nössing - Hoandlhof	263
Le Miccine	586	Mannucci Droandi	597
Le Monde, Vigneti	395	Mantellassi	589
Le Pianacce	604	Manzocco, Giulio	418
Le Poggette, Fattoria	647	Manzone, Giovanni	108
Le Pupille	492	Marangona	220
Le Querce, Tenuta	709	Marcarini, Poderi	91
Le Quinte, Tenuta	673	Marcato	342
Le Ragose	305	Marchesi di Barolo	39
Le Salette	289	Marchesi Torrigiani	455
Le Sorgenti	452	Marchetti	608
Le Tende	292	Marconi, Maurizio	632
Le Terrazze, Fattoria	624	Marella, Podere	658
Le Velette, Tenuta	653	Marenco	140
Le Vigne di San Pietro	325	Marengo, Giacomo	594
Le Vigne di Zamò	387	Marengo, Mario	92
Lebovitz	212	Marinig, Valerio	401
Lenotti	337	Marion	312
Lento, Cantine	739	Mariotto, Claudio	142
Leonardo da Vinci, Cantine	578	Marotti Campi	623
Leone de Castris	728	Marramiero	683
Lepore	677	Marrubiu, Cantina Sociale	779
Lequio, Ugo	121	Marsaglia	151
Lequio - Prinsi, Ottavio	157	Martilde	221
Les Crêtes	17	Martinetti, Franco M.	141
Letrari	239	Martini, Lorenz	278
Librandi	737	Martini & Sohn, K.	252
Liedholm	152	Martino, Armando	712
Lignano, Castello di	154	Mascarello, Bartolo	39
Lis Neris - Pecorari	411	Mascarello, Giuseppe e Figlio	103
Livernano	552	Masciarelli, Gianni	684
Livon	410	Masi	319
Lo Sparviere	201	Maso Bastie	245
Lo Triolet - Marco Martin	18	Maso Cantanghel	227
Loacker Schwarzhof	257	Maso Furli	233
Locorotondo, Cantina Cooperativa del	726	Maso Martis	243
Lodola Nuova - Tenimenti Ruffino	531	Masottina	311

Massa Vecchia	497		Morassino, Cascina	150
Masseria Felicia	706		Morelli, Az. Agr. Claudio	617
Masseria Li Veli	731		Morellino di Scansano, Cantina Coop. del	571
Masseria Monaci	720		Morgante	749
Massimi Berucci	673		Mori, Giacomo	601
Mastroberardino	690		Morini, Alessandro	447
Mastrojanni	514		Moris Farms	498
Masut da Rive	390		Mormoraia	567
Mattiello, Natalino	292		Moroder, Alessandro	609
Maurigi	757		Morra, Stefanino	152
Mayr, Thomas e Figli	258		Moschioni, Davide	357
Mayr - Erbhof Unterganzner, Josephus	258		Mosole	343
Mazzi, Roberto	305		Mossio, F.lli	129
Mazziotti	664		Mottura, Sergio	666
Mazzolino, Tenuta	191		Mulino delle Tolle	347
Mecella, Enzo	635		Mumelter, Georg	259
Medici & Figli, Ermete	438		Mura	778
Medolago Albani	222		Murana, Salvatore	756
Meleto, Castello di	481		Muratori, F.lli	214
Melini	547		Musella	312
Meloni Vini	774		Mustilli	700
Meroi, Davino	350		Mutti	134
Merotto	338		Muzic	408
MezzaCorona	234		Nada, Ada	143
Miali, Vinicola	732		Nada, Fiorenzo	143
Miani	350		Naitana, Gianvittorio	779
Miceli, Aziende Vinicole	755		Nani, Antonio	340
Midolini	419		Nardi, Tenute Silvio	514
Migliarese	674		Nardin, Sergio	341
Minuzzo, Gabriella	20		Ne. Ne.	151
Miotti, Firmino	337		Negri, Nino	186
Mirabella	220		Negro, Angelo & Figli	115
Mocali	593		Nera, Pietro	215
Moccagatta	33		Nervi	80
Mock, Ursula e Peter	606		Nicodemi, Bruno	680
Modanella, Castello di	555		Nicolis, Angelo e Figli	315
Moio, Michele	696		Niedermayr, Josef	253
Mola	600		Niedrist, Ignaz	253
Molettieri, Salvatore	697		Nino Franco	330
Molino, Mauro	92		Nittardi, Fattoria	465
Molon Traverso, Ornella	310		Nomi, Cantina Sociale di	248
Monchiero Carbone	54		Notaio, Cantine del	712
Mondo, Franco	159		Nottola	531
Monfalletto - Cordero di Montezemolo	93		Novaia	296
Monrubio, Cantina	642		Oasi degli Angeli	615
Monsanto, Castello di	455		Oberto, Andrea	93
Monsupello	210		Ocone	706
Montalcino, Cantina di	593		Oddero, F.lli	94
Montali e Temesio	167		Oddero, Massimo	153
Montaribaldi	34		Odoardi	740
Montauto, Castello di	602		Oliena, Cantina Cooperativa di	779
Monte Cicogna	198		Olim Bauda, Tenuta	87
Monte delle Vigne	446		Orlandi Contucci Ponno	683
Monte Pugliano	705		Ornellaia, Tenuta dell'	457
Monte Rossa	185		Orsolani	130
Monte Tondo	322		Ortaglia	606
Monteacuto	213		Ottella	309
Montecalvi	487		Pacenti, Franco	593
Montecappone	618		Pacenti, Siro	515
Montecchio, Fattoria	576		Pacina	470
Montechiari, Fattoria di	524		Paglieri, I	34
Montecucco	585		Paitin	121
Montelio	188		Pala	776
Montellori, Fattoria	477		Palagetto	593
Montemaggio, Fattoria di	600		Palagetto	568
Montenidoli	567		Palari	753
Montepeloso	574		Palazzo Vecchio	595
Monterinaldi, Castello di	600		Palazzone	653
Monterucco	215		Pallavicini, Vini	672
Montesalario	582		Palombo, Giovanni	663
Monteschiavo	619		Pandolfa	450
Montevertine, Fattoria di	552		Panigada - Banino, Antonio	221
Montevetrano	700		Panizzi, Giovanni	568
Monti	109		Panzanello	543
Monti, Antonio e Elio	687		Paolo Monte - Cascina Flino	153
Montiverdi	482		Paradiso, Fattoria	423
Montori, Camillo	678		Paraschos, Evangelos	408
Montresor, Giacomo	333		Parmoleto	582
Monzio Compagnoni	191		Parri, Fattorie	597

Parusso, Armando	109	Poggio Castellare	594
Pasetti, Franco	678	Poggio di Sotto	516
Pasini Produttori	220	Poggio Gagliardo	596
Pasolini Dall'Onda	586	Poggio Montali	636
Pasqua Vigneti e Cantine	333	Poggio Pollino, Tenuta	448
Paterno, Fattoria di	532	Poggio Romita, Fattoria	605
Paternoster	709	Poggio Saccone	579
Pavia, Agostino e Figli	23	Poggio San Polo	517
Pecchenino, F.lli	76	Poggio Scalette, Podere	487
Pecorari, Pierpaolo	412	Poggiopiano, Fattoria	561
Pedra Majore	771	Pojer & Sandri	228
Pedrotti, Gino	227	Polencic, Ferdinando e Aldo	366
Pegazzera, Tenuta	184	Polencic, Isidoro	366
Pelissero	144	Polenza, La	176
Pellegrino, Carlo	751	Poli, Francesco	248
Pellerino, Cascina	115	Poli, Giovanni	248
Pelz & Piffer	246	Poli, Giulio	248
Pennacchi, Domenico	659	Poliziano	532
Perazzeta	582	Pollara	762
Percivalle	213	Pontepellegrino, Fattoria	698
Perrone, Elio	67	Pontoni, Flavio	417
Pertinace, Vignaioli Elvio	144	Popphof - Andreas Menz	270
Perusia, Cantine	660	Poppiano, Castello di	537
Perusini	374	Porcu, F.lli	779
Pervini	728	Porello	54
Petra	605	Portinari, Umberto	303
Petricci del Pianta	605	Prà	303
Petriolo, Fattoria di	584	Pradio	347
Petrognano	594	Pratesi	460
Petroio, Fattoria di	471	Prattico, Fattoria	706
Petrolo, Fattoria	538	Pravis	230
Petrucco	351	Prevostini, Mamete	197
Petrussa	401	Prima & Nuova/Erste & Neue	265
Pfannenstielhof, Pfeifer Johannes	259	Primosic	384
Pfitscherhof, Tenuta	280	Princic, Alessandro	367
Piaggia - Vannucci Silvia	548	Principe Banfi Podere Pio IX,	216
Pian Del Gallo	587	Principiano, Ferdinando	110
Pian dell'Orino	593	Produttori Andriano, Cantina	250
Pian delle Vigne	593	Produttori Burggräfler, Cantina	270
Piancornello	515	Produttori Colterenzio, Cantina	251
Piazzano	585	Produttori Cornaiano, Cantina	251
Picciau, Gigi	768	Produttori Cortaccia, Cantina	268
Picech - Le Vigne del Ribél, Roberto	365	Produttori del Barbaresco	35
Pierazzuoli, Enrico	459	Produttori del Gavi	84
Pieri, Agostina	516	Produttori di Merano, Cantina	271
Pieropan, Leonildo	323	Produttori Nalles Niclara Magrè, Cantina	272
Piersanti	637	Produttori Nebbiolo di Carema, Cantina dei	57
Pietracupa	696	Produttori San Paolo, Cantina	254
Pietrafitta	569	Produttori Santa Maddalena/Cant. di Bolzano, Cant.	260
Pietratorcia	705	Produttori Termeno, Cantina	276
Pieve de' Pitti	606	Produttori Valle Isarco, Cantina	267
Pighin, F.lli	392	Progetto DiVino	714
Pile e Lamole, S. M. Tenimenti	482	Provenza	192
Pinsoglio, Fabrizio	60	Provolo, Luigino e Marco	340
Pio Cesare	26	Prunotto	27
Pioiero	160	Puddu, Josto	780
Piona, Albino	343	Puiatti	352
Piovene Porto Godi	336	Punset	157
Pira	76	Pupillo	764
Pira, Luigi	138	Quacquarini, Alberto	638
Pira & Figli - Chiara Boschis	40	Quaquarini	180
Pisoni	230	Quarello, Carlo	69
Planeta	752	Querceto, Castello di	488
Plattner - Waldgries, Heinrich	260	Querceto di Castellina	466
Plozner	413	Querciabella	488
Plozza	222	Quintarelli, Giuseppe	306
Podere Capaccia	553	Quistello, Cantina Sociale Cooperativa di	220
Podere dal Ger	396	'R Mesueto	174
Podere La Chiesa	606	Raccaro, Dario	367
Poderi Colla	26	Radikon	384
Poderi dal Nespoli	427	Raimondi-Villa Monteleone	320
Podversic, Damijan	383	Rainoldi, Aldo	187
Poggerino	553	Raiz, Teresa	394
Poggio, Paolo	46	Rallo, Cantine	751
Poggio al Sole	577	Rametz, Castello	279
Poggio Amorelli	582	Ramò, Giampaolo	175
Poggio Argentiera	493	Ramoser - Fliederhof, Stephan	279
Poggio Bertaio	644	Ramoser - Untermoserhof, Georg	261
Poggio Bonelli	471	Rapitalà, Tenute	746

Ratti, Renato	94	San Felice	472
Recchia, F.lli	341	San Fereolo	77
Redi	533	San Francesco, Fattoria	736
Reggiana	445	San Gervasio	598
Rendola, La	597	San Giorgio, Podere	221
Revelli, Eraldo	154	San Giovanni	626
Revello, F.lli	95	San Giusto	545
Ribote	154	San Giusto a Rentennano	484
Riccafana	216	San Guido, Tenuta	457
Riccardi, Enrico	221	San Leonardo, Tenuta	225
Ricchi	218	San Lorenzo	687
Ricchino - Tiziana Menegaldo	153	San Lorenzo	659
Ricci Curbastro	181	San Luciano	522
Riecine	483	San Luigi, Podere	546
Rietine	586	San Michele, Podere	603
Riforma Fondiaria, Cantina Cooperativa della	733	San Michele a Torri	603
Rinaldi, Giuseppe	40	San Michele all'Adige, Istituto Agrario Provinciale	240
Rinaldini, Moro - Rinaldo	440	San Michele Appiano, Cantina Produttori	254
Rio Grande	654	San Niccolò a Pisignano	601
Rio Maggio	622	San Patrignano	428
Riseccoli	489	San Quirico	602
Ritterhof, Tenuta	265	San Romano	77
Rivera	717	San Savino, Poderi	632
Rocca, Albino	35	San Sebastiano, Tenuta	100
Rocca, Bruno	36	San Simone	419
Rocca Bernarda	398	San Valentino	438
Rocca delle Macìe	466	San Vettore	587
Rocca di Castagnoli	483	San Vincenti	485
Rocca di Fabbri	649	San Vito	449
Rocca di Montegrossi	484	Sancio	176
Roccaccia, Tenuta	546	Sandoni	446
Rocche Costamagna	95	Sandri, Arcangelo	246
Rocche dei Manzoni, Podere	110	Sandrone, Luciano	41
Roccolo Grassi	297	Sant'Agata, Cantine	135
Rockhof	280	Sant'Andrea, Cantina	674
Rodaro, Paolo	358	Sant'Antonio, Tenuta	297
Roddolo, Flavio	111	Sant'Appiano, Fattoria	580
Romagnoli, Cantine	450	Sant'Elena	385
Romeo, Massimo	596	Santa Barbara	611
Romitorio, Castello	517	Santa Barbara	733
Roncal, Il	357	Santa Cassella	630
Ronchi di Manzano	388	Santa Caterina	176
Ronco Calino	186	Santa Eurosia	331
Ronco dei Pini	402	Santa Lucia	731
Ronco dei Tassi	368	Santa Lucia	493
Ronco del Gelso	368	Santa Margherita	338
Ronco del Gnemiz	411	Santa Maria La Palma, Cantina Sociale	766
Ronco delle Betulle	388	Santa Seraffa	155
Ronco Severo	419	Santa Sofia	316
Ronco Vieri	419	Santa Vittoria, Fattoria	477
Roncùs	352	Santadi, Cantina Sociale di	773
Rosa del Golfo	716	Santarosa	435
Rosi, Eugenio	245	Santi	291
Rosso, Giovanni	159	Santini, Enrico	461
Rotolo, Francesco	706	Santo Stefano	338
Rottensteiner, Hans	261	Sapereta	549
Rottensteiner, Heinrich & Thomas	262	Saputi	635
Roveglia, Tenuta	220	Saracco, Paolo	67
Rovellotti	86	Sarchese Dora	682
Rovero, F.lli	29	Sardus Pater	774
Rubicini, Italo	602	Sartarelli	629
Rubino, Tenute	717	Sartori, Casa Vinicola	341
Ruffino, Tenimenti	548	Sassara	659
Ruggeri & C.	330	Sassotondo	572
Ruggeri Corsini	111	Satta, Michele	462
Ruiz de Cardenas	214	Sava, Cantina e Oleificio Sociale di	734
Russiz Superiore	353	Savignola Paolina	489
Russo	575	Scacciadiavoli	649
Russolo, Rino	412	Scagliola	49
Saccoletto	158	Scammacca del Murgo, Barone	764
Saladini Pilastri	634	Scarbolo	393
Salcheto	533	Scarpa - Antica Casa Vinicola	124
Salicutti, Podere	518	Scarzello, Giorgio e Figli	41
Salviano, Tenuta di	658	Scavino, Paolo	64
Salvioni - La Cerbaiola	518	Schiopetto	353
San Bartolomeo	84	Schmid - Oberrautner, Anton	278
San Cristoforo	195	Schwanburg, Castello	273
San Fabiano - Borghini Baldovinetti, Fattoria	579	Sciorio	72
San Fabiano Calcinaia	467	Scrimaglio, Franco e Mario	124

Scubla	398	Tenuta del Portale	710
Scuola Enologica di Conegliano G. B. Cerletti	338	Tenuta dell'Arbiola	132
Sebaste, Mauro	27	Tenuta di Trecciano	604
Secchi, Alessandro	224	Tenuta di Trinoro	603
Sedime	599	Tenuta La Volta - Cabutto	42
Seghesio, F.lli	112	Tenuta Pinni	420
Sella	98	Tenuta Uccellina	439
Sella & Mosca, Tenute	766	Tenuta Villanova	380
Selvapiana, Fattoria	549	Tenuta Zicari	734
Selvole, Castello di	472	Teracrea, Tenuta	341
Serafini & Vidotto	308	Tercic, Matijaz	409
Serenelli, Alberto	609	Terenzi, Giovanni	674
Serra, F.lli	780	Terlano, Cantina	274
Serracavallo	738	Terpin, Franco	409
Serraiola	535	Terra Antica	596
Sertoli Salis, Conti	209	Terrabianca, Fattoria di	554
Sesti - Castello di Argiano	519	Terralba	44
Sette Ponti, Tenuta	577	Terre Bianche	168
Settesoli	752	Terre Cortesi Moncaro	621
Settimo, Aurelio	155	Terre da Vino	42
Signano	602	Terre de' Trinci	645
Silva, Giovanni	150	Terre degli Svevi	713
Simon di Brazzan	418	Terre del Barolo	64
Simoncelli, Armando	240	Terre del Carpine	646
Sinaglio, Poderi	28	Terre del Cesanese	674
Skerk	418	Terre del Sillabo	496
Solaria - Cencioni	519	Terre di San Leonino	583
Solatione	601	Terre di Shemir	764
Soletta, Tenute	778	Terre Nobili, Tenuta	742
Solidea	763	Terre Rosse, Cascina delle	168
Soloperto	732	Terredora	697
Sölva - Niklaserhof, Josef	266	Terreno	587
Sölva & Söhne - Paterbichl, Peter	266	Terriccio, Castello del	467
Sonnino, Fattoria Castello	537	Teruzzi & Puthod	569
Sopra la Ripa, Podere	572	Teso, Fattoria del	524
Sorbaiano, Fattoria	525	Tezza	334
Sorelle Bronca	336	Tiare - Roberto Snidarcig	370
Sottimano	122	Tiefenbrunner	268
Spadafora	755	Tinazzi & Figli, Eugenio	337
Spadafora, Domenico	741	Tizzano	424
Spadaio e Piecorto	580	Toblino, Cantina	226
Spagnolli, Enrico	229	Todini	660
Specogna, Leonardo	374	Toffoli, Vincenzo	342
Speri, F.lli	316	Tola	763
Spertino, Luigi	156	Tollo, Cantina	685
Spezia, Stefano	217	Tommasi, Viticoltori	317
Spia d'Italia	217	Tordimaro	660
Spinelli	686	Tormaresca	729
Spinsanti	612	Toros, Franco	370
Spoletoducale	660	Torraccia del Piantavigna	155
Sportoletti	656	Torraccia di Presura	490
Statti	739	Torre Fornello	443
Steinhauserhof	280	Torre Gaia, Fattoria	704
Stroblhof	278	Torre Quarto	720
Strologo, Silvano	612	Torre Rosazza	389
Sturm, Oscar	369	Torre Zambra	688
Su Baroni, Vitivincola	770	Torrevecchia, Cantine	744
Suavia	323	Torrevento	721
Subida di Monte	369	Trabucchi	291
Suveraia	596	Tramonti	583
Talenti	520	Trapani, Cantina Sociale di	758
Taliano, Michele	113	Trappolini	665
Tallarini	216	Travaglini, Giancarlo	81
Tamburello	762	Travaglino	178
Tamellini	324	Traversa - Cascina Bertolotto	139
Tanorè	331	Tre Monti	432
Tasca d'Almerita	758	Tre Valli	447
Taschlerhof	279	Treré	430
Tassarolo, Castello di	141	Trevisani	217
Taurino, Cosimo	723	Trexenta, Cantina Sociale della	775
Tedeschi, F.lli	317	Triacca	211
Telaro - Cooperativa Lavoro e Salute	695	Tua Rita	575
Tenimenti Angelini - San Leonino	583	Turco, Innocenzo	175
Tenimenti Angelini - Tenuta Trerose	534	Uberti	195
Tenimenti Angelini - Val di Suga	521	Uccelliera	520
Tenuta Belguardo	588	Uccelliera, Fattoria	585
Tenuta Bonzara	436	Umani Ronchi	627
Tenuta Carretta	126	Umbria Viticoltori Associati	659
Tenuta dei Fiori	49	Unterortl-Castel Juval, Tenuta	262

Vaglie	641	Villa	201
Vagnoni, F.lli	570	Villa Arceno	473
Vajra, G. D.	43	Villa Bellini	318
Val del Prete, Cascina	128	Villa Buoninsegna	600
Val delle Rose	588	Villa Cafaggio	544
Val di Neto	742	Villa Calcinaia	587
Valchiarò	415	Villa Chiopris	420
Valdarnese, Cooperativa Agricola	606	Villa Cilnia	452
Valdicava, Tenuta	521	Villa dal Ferro Lazzarini	311
Valdipiatta, Tenuta	534	Villa de Varda	247
Valditerra	158	Villa di Quartu	780
Valentini, Edoardo	679	Villa Diamante	705
Valfieri	72	Villa Fiorita	152
Valgiano, Tenuta di	496	Villa Frattina	395
Vallarom	225	Villa Giada	56
Valle, Agricola	581	Villa La Selva, Fattoria	458
Valle del Quirra	780	Villa Le Prata	522
Valle dell'Acate, Cantina	744	Villa Matilde	693
Valle dell'Asso	722	Villa Medoro	686
Valle Reale	688	Villa Monte Rico	605
Vallerosa Bonci	616	Villa Patrizia	601
Vallis Agri	226	Villa Pigna	626
Vallona	426	Villa Pillo	485
Vallone, Agricole	724	Villa Po' del Vento	659
Vallorsi	606	Villa Raiano	701
Valori	688	Villa Rosa	583
Valpanera	416	Villa Russiz	354
Valpantena, Cantina Sociale della	334	Villa Sandi	338
Valpolicella, Cantina Sociale	306	Villa Sant'Anna	535
Valtenesi - Lugana, Cantine	217	Villa Simone	670
Valtidone, Cantina Sociale	423	Villa Spadoni	447
Vanzini	221	Villa Sparina	85
Varaldo, Rino	36	Villa Spinosa	307
Varramista	538	Villa Trasqua	583
Vaselli	665	Villagrande, Barone di	753
Vecchie Terre di Montefili	544	VIN.CA.	581
Veglio, Mauro	96	Vinchio - Vaglio Serra, Cantina Sociale di	149
Velenosi, Ercole	610	Vini e Mosti Rossi, Consorzio Produttori	732
Venditti, Antica Masseria	692	Vinicola del Sannio	704
Venica & Venica	377	Vinicola del Tesino	617
Venosa, Cantina di	713	Vinicola Mediterranea	734
Venturini, Massimo	318	Vinicola Resta	734
Vercesi del Castellazzo	202	Vinnaioli Jermann	380
Verdi, Bruno	180	Vintripodi Calabria	742
Vermentino, Cantina Sociale del	771	Vio, Claudio	173
Verrazzano, Castello di	490	Visconti	216
Verrina, Nicolò	158	Visintin, Franco	419
Vestini - Campagnano	691	Visintini, Andrea	375
Vevey, Maison Albert	20	Vistorta - Brandino Brandolini d'Adda	404
Vezzoli, Giuseppe	196	Viticcio	492
Vezzoli, Ugo	219	Viticoltori Associati di Rodello	158
Viberti, Eraldo	96	Viticoltori di Caldaro, Cantina	264
Viberti, Osvaldo	97	Vivacqua, Luigi	740
Vicara	130	Vivaldi - Arunda	271
Vicari	636	Viviani	307
Vicchiomaggio, Castello di	491	Voerzio, Gianni	97
Vicentini Orgnani, Alessandro	393	Voerzio, Roberto	98
Vidussi Gestioni Agricole	354	Volpaia, Castello di	555
Vie di Romans	390	Volpe Pasini	415
Vielmin	60	Von Braunbach	280
Vietti	65	Vosca, Francesco	418
Vigliano	495	Wandana	525
Vigna del Lauro	371	Zaccagnini, Ciccio	676
Vigna Petrussa	402	Zaccagnini & C., F.lli	638
Vigna Rionda - Massolino	138	Zamuner	343
Vigna Traverso	403	Zanetti, Martino	341
Vignai da Duline	420	Zanini	247
Vignalta	326	Zardetto Spumanti	287
Vignamaggio, Villa	491	Zemmer - Kupelwieser, Peter	269
Vignavecchia	554	Zenato	309
Vigne del Pareto	126	Zeni	241
Vigne Fantin Noda'r	399	Zeni, F.lli	284
Vigne Regali	140	Zidarich	378
Vigne & Vini	725	Zito, Vinicola	741
Vigneti delle Meridiane	244	Zof	375
Vigneti Massa	112	Zonin	290
Vigneto delle Terre Rosse	444	Zuani	419
Vigneto Due Santi	284	Zucca, La	117
Vignole	598	Zucchetto, Paolo	344